THE OFFICIAL ENCYCLOPEDIA

DISNEY A to Z

THE OFFICIAL ENCYCLOPEDIA
SIXTH EDITION

Disney Legend **Dave Smith**
Steven Vagnini

DISNEY
EDITIONS
LOS ANGELES • NEW YORK

Editorial Director: Wendy Lefkon
Senior Editors: Jim Fanning and Jennifer Eastwood
Senior Designer: Lindsay Broderick
Managing Editor: Monica Vasquez
Production: Anne Peters and Marybeth Tregarthen

ISBN: 978-1-368-06191-9
FAC-067395-23215
Printed in the United States of America
1 3 5 7 9 10 8 6 4 2
Visit www.disneybooks.com

SUSTAINABLE FORESTRY INITIATIVE   Certified Sourcing

www.forests.org
SFI-01681

Logo Applies to Text Stock Only

"As the years pass, I am sure more and more scholars will be inquiring into the realm of Walt Disney's impact on not only American life but that of the entire world. Needless to say, I am a Walt Disney admirer, and I would like to do my part to see that he is remembered through the works that he has produced."

—David R. Smith, Disney Legend
Letter to Oliver B. Johnston, Vice President, Merchandising,
Walt Disney Productions, dated January 11, 1967

"From flying elephants to the world around us and on into wondrous realms beyond—distilling a century of magic into one single volume is itself a marvel! Yet here, between these covers, is everything Disney . . . from A to Z."

—Becky Cline
Director, Walt Disney Archives

Introduction

D isney A to Z: The Official Encyclopedia is the first of its kind, a unique reference book. Everything you might want to look up about Disney is available in this book, in an easy-to-use form. The encyclopedia attempts to list all Disney theatrical shorts and features; all Disney TV shows, series, and specials; all Disney educational and nontheatrical films; all Disney park attractions, along with the park resorts, restaurants, and shops; key Disney company personnel; primary actors in Disney films and TV productions; important songs; and many other elements that make up the world of Disney.

Under the film entries, one can learn when the title was released, who starred in it, who directed it, what its running time was, where it was filmed, what it is about, and some interesting facts about its production. The park entries tell you when a particular attraction or restaurant opened, along with its closing date (if it is no longer there). The actor and actress entries tell what Disney films the person starred in, and the role he or she played, along with any TV appearances. There are special lists of Disney Academy Awards and Emmy Awards, animated features, cartoons starring the major characters, Mouseketeers through the years, feature films in chronological order, the Disney Channel Original Movies, and TV series. The company is constantly evolving, necessitating updates to entries as more awards are won, TV series come to an end, park attractions make way for new ones, and executives move on to new positions.

The genesis of this encyclopedia project was in January 1994. The day after the 6.7-magnitude earthquake hit Los Angeles, I had a meeting scheduled at The Walt Disney Studios with Bob Miller of Hyperion Books (now Disney Editions) to discuss possible future Disney-themed books that they might publish. As the building housing the Walt Disney Archives received major structural damage in the earthquake, everything was in disarray and we had to have our meeting at an outdoor table at the nearby Studio Commissary. As we sat there talking, one book I mentioned was one I had always felt would be of great interest to readers everywhere—a Disney encyclopedia. While I knew the book would be useful, I also knew that it would take a tremendous amount of research and writing. While it was something I would be very interested in attempting, I explained that this might be a project that I would probably only be able to undertake after I retired.

As the months went on, however, I continued to think about the encyclopedia, and I realized that I did not want to wait for my retirement. The book would be of great help to those of us in the Walt Disney Archives because it would combine detailed information from any number of different files. Everything would be in one alphabet, easy to look up when someone called with a question on the telephone. So, in June 1994, I decided to begin the compilation of the encyclopedia. Since I had no extra time during my workday, it would have to be done on my own time, at home on my own computer. The research phase took over 380 hours of my time over the next six months, not to mention the additional hours put in by research assistants.

Two years later, the first edition of *Disney A to Z: The Official Encyclopedia* was completed. We published a revised edition in 1998, with a plan for a new one every two years, but it took eight years before we had the third edition. The fourth edition came in 2015, and a fifth edition followed in 2016.

Dave Smith (1940–2019)
Disney Legend and Founder,
Walt Disney Archives
The Walt Disney Company
2016

In your hands is a rich tapestry of knowledge that Dave Smith collected and preserved over his fifty-year association with The Walt Disney Company. In the nearly three decades that have passed since his first edition of *Disney A to Z* was published, this official encyclopedia has been celebrated—and cemented—as the ultimate informational resource for all things Disney, serving as an invaluable research tool for casual Disney fans, devoted aficionados, guests, and Cast Members alike. As The Walt Disney Company enters its second century, this book refracts the wide prism of Disney's ever-growing worlds, preserving a seemingly endless array of information for all readers to explore. The people, characters, places, stories, and magic of 100 years of Disney are all in here, waiting for you to discover.

When it was originally published in 1996, *Disney A to Z* featured over 5,200 entries. Now, the total number has surpassed 9,000, with primary coverage from the beginnings of the company in 1923 up through early March 2023. It has been seven years since the fifth edition was published in 2016, and during those years, Disney has premiered hundreds of new feature films, shorts, and documentaries; opened dozens of exciting park attractions, hotels, restaurants, and shops; unveiled a fifth cruise ship; produced new stage shows; and debuted a variety of new TV series. With the launch of Disney+ in 2019 come new entries for the major Disney series and movies released for streaming, and also added is information about the companies and brands included in Disney's acquisition of 21st Century Fox the same year. This substantial growth has resulted in more than 2,000 new entries, along with more than 6,000 changes to existing ones—offering more Disney facts than ever before.

Information, of course, is at the heart of any encyclopedia. So to offer the most informational material possible within a finite page count, some additional changes were needed for this sixth edition. This included presenting the images in a new collage at the start of each section. Meanwhile, the Selected Bibliography, which was previously included as an appendix, has moved to a new digital format online at D23.com/bibliography, where it will continue to be updated. There, you will also find an online version of *Disney A to Z*, featuring additional images and further updates that will be made periodically. Finally, we are offering our special thanks and acknowledgments at the end of this book.

But most significant to *Disney A to Z*—in an enormous loss to the Disney community, to archival institutions everywhere, and to so many of us personally—was the passing of Dave Smith in February 2019. Dave's dedication to safeguarding both Disney (the organization) and Walt Disney (the man) was unwavering. He first invented, then stewarded, a model archive as Disney evolved into the world's preeminent entertainment company. He was committed to treating Disney history as a living legacy and perpetually positioned the company's past as a vital prologue for its future, along the way collecting, preserving, and showcasing thousands of Disney's priceless treasures. And to Dave, the most valuable treasure of all was the *information* contained in the collections of the Archives. It was therefore Dave's hope that this reference work would continue to be updated as The Walt Disney Company continued to grow and expand, and with the support of Disney Editions and of you—the reader and researcher—that hope has been realized.

Disney A to Z had a special meaning to Dave, and it has a very special meaning to all who have contributed to this new edition. Beyond this book's role as an invaluable informational resource, we recognize it as a symbol of Dave's commitment to preserving the ongoing Disney legacy and the accuracy of its living history. We are similarly committed to ensuring this updated edition follows Dave's direction, standards, and criteria for entry selection and creation, for which he generously shared his guidance over the years as my mentor and dear friend. It is nothing short of an honor for all of us involved to bring *Disney A to Z* forward into the company's next hundred years and to dedicate ourselves to upholding one of Dave's greatest legacies.

It is with immense gratitude to both Dave and my fellow staff members at the Archives that we welcome you to the centennial edition of *Disney A to Z*.

Steven Vagnini
Walt Disney Archives
The Walt Disney Company
2023

Because encyclopedias such as this tend to become dated rapidly, our aim is to keep the information up-to-date. We always welcome suggestions of new entries, along with changes or revisions, which you are invited to send to steven.m.vagnini@disney.com.

Letter from the Editors

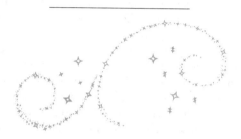

Wendy Lefkon, now editorial director of Disney Editions, had only recently started as the first "exclusively Disney" editor on the publishing staff of Hyperion books when Dave Smith and Bob Miller began talks about publishing an official Disney encyclopedia. The experience of editing that first edition with Dave would serve as her solid foundation in editing Disney-focused nonfiction for the next twenty-five years. Similarly, Jennifer Eastwood, now senior editor of Disney Editions, began using the second edition of *Disney A to Z* when she joined the staff of *Disney Magazine* as an editorial assistant and fact-checker. She first worked with Dave in that role and still remembers how special she felt when—*two years* prior to the third edition's publication—Dave e-mailed her a version of the unpublished updates to *Disney A to Z* that he kept as an always-living document of revised and new entries. Both of us have championed the existence of new editions of this encyclopedia ever since, and we are pleased and grateful to have Steven Vagnini carry forward this important work, and a special aspect of Dave's legacy, through this sixth edition.

Disney A to Z: The Official Encyclopedia is a book of facts meant to service the Disney fans, yes, but more so anyone who has a question about The Walt Disney Company and wants it precisely answered. This might be a journalist writing about the business aspects of the company or even someone preparing an opinion piece. And as we can attest firsthand, it is a fact-checker's go-to guide. (In Jennifer's space, the latest version of the encyclopedia rarely makes it back to the bookshelf, staying within arm's reach for quick daily reference.)

In truth, an encyclopedia is one of our favorite types of books. These fact-based record collections ask authors to treat their subject matter with comprehensive accuracy. Often arranged alphabetically, as is the case for *Disney A to Z*, compendiums of this nature offer a broad audience simple and clear access points to look up the many branches of a topic. The fundamental goal is to supply correct spellings, complete lists, and well-documented information—without passing judgment.

Assembling an encyclopedia illustrates the subtle difference between the acts of *curating* and *cataloging*. A curation exercise asks someone to first editorially choose, and then organize, pieces of information with the goal of telling a story. The choices of "what's in" and "what's out" of curated collections are fundamentally important to shape the picture and lead a reader through an intentional narrative. On the other hand, the exhaustive job of cataloging asks someone to classify *everything*. The goal of systematically organizing these pieces is to make this information manageable for someone without prior knowledge to navigate it easily. The ambitious aim is to leave nothing out, but there is no story goal. When constructed through earnest cataloging, encyclopedias are true reflections of a topic—and *Disney A to Z* very much is one.

We are fond of many Walt Disney quotes, but an especially grounded one is "I always like to look on the optimistic side of life, but I am realistic enough to know that life is a complex matter. With the laugh comes the tears, and in developing motion pictures or television shows, you must combine all the facts of life—drama, pathos, and humor." Just as The Walt Disney Company is a reflection of U.S. culture through the last hundred years, the entries of *Disney A to Z* echo that history, too. And, of course, it is a complicated history—one still being processed today.

Looking toward the future, The Walt Disney Company is committed to creating stories with inspirational and aspirational themes that reflect the rich diversity of the human experience around the globe. It's the reason the company has created teams such as Stories Matter, a group that is, for example, reviewing the vast Disney film library and adding advisories to content that includes negative depictions or mistreatment of people or cultures. As outlined at www.disney.com/StoriesMatter, their goal is to spark conversation and open dialogue about history that affects us all, acknowledging that some communities have been erased or forgotten altogether, and reiterating the company's commitment to giving voice to their stories as well.

In this context, we, as book editors, felt compelled to ask ourselves what the impact would be if *Disney A to Z* entries included *everything*, including subject matter that falls into the description above. The answer we came to is that *Disney A to Z* would keep its commitment to share accurate information about The Walt Disney Company. Each person reading an entry in *Disney A to Z* will pass their own judgment upon the facts presented and reach their own conclusions, and that is exactly the point. An encyclopedia, being a comprehensive cataloged collection, exists to provide access to the facts. To knowingly omit any historical points would be a disservice to our mission to inform and, in turn, be a disservice for those seeking to utilize vetted facts during their thoughtful conversations about the world.

Readers of *Disney A to Z* are invited to learn from the information provided here, feeling confident that each point has been verified to the best of our ability. That is the power of an encyclopedia and the responsibility of stewards of history. We are humbled and honored to be part of this commitment—through this edition and for all the ones to follow.

Wendy Lefkon
Editorial Director, Disney Editions
Disney Publishing
2023

Jennifer Eastwood
Senior Editor, Disney Editions
Disney Publishing
2023

1. Academy Awards 2. Adventure Thru Inner Space 3. Aircraft, Walt Disney's 4. *America on Parade*
5. Alice Comedies 6. *Adventures of Ichabod and Mr. Toad, The* (film) 7. *Alice's Wonderland Bakery* (TV)
8. Animation Building 9. Audio-Animatronics 10. *Adventures of the Gummi Bears, Disney's* (TV)

Aames, Willie Actor; appeared on TV in *Twister, Bull from the Sky* and *Runaway on the Rogue River*.

A&E Network With the acquisition of Capital Cities/ABC in 1996, Disney obtained a 37.5% ownership of the A&E Network, which is known for its *Biography* series and high-profile specials and original dramas. In 2012, Disney's ownership increased to 50%.

Aaron Stone (TV) Action-adventure series on Disney XD; aired Feb. 13, 2009–Jul. 30, 2010. Charlie Landers, a teenage boy who has mastered playing *Hero Rising*, an online game in which his avatar defends the world from members of the Omega Defiance, is enlisted by its creator, billionaire recluse T. Abner Hall, to become the real-life version of the legendary crime-fighting avatar, Aaron Stone. Hall informs Charlie that the Omega Defiance is real and out to destroy mankind, and he encourages the teen that he has what it takes to bring Aaron Stone to life. Stars Kelly Blatz (Charlie Landers/Aaron Stone), David Lambert (Jason Landers), J. P. Manoux (S.T.A.N.), Tania Gunadi (Emma), Jason Earles (Hunter). Filmed in Toronto.

Abbate, Nancy Mouseketeer from the 1950s *Mickey Mouse Club* TV show.

Abbott, Chuck Legendary attractions host and foreman at Disneyland for 36 years, beginning in 1955. He was named a Disney Legend in 2005.

ABC SEE AMERICAN BROADCASTING COMPANY.

ABC Commissary Art deco–style counter-service eatery in Disney's Hollywood Studios; opened Dec. 16, 1990, as the Disney-MGM Studios Commissary Restaurant. Also known as The Commissary. Patterned after a movie studio commissary, with awards on display. It became the ABC Commissary Jul. 1, 1997.

ABC Family After its acquisition of Fox Family Worldwide in Oct. 2001, Disney began operations of Fox Family Channel Nov. 12 and renamed it ABC Family. The cable network targeted adults aged 18–34, featuring original series, movies, and specials. On Jan. 12, 2016, the network was renamed Freeform, expanding its target market to ages 14–34. SEE ALSO FOX FAMILY WORLDWIDE.

ABC Kids The ABC-TV network's Saturday morning programming block for kids, airing Sep. 14, 2002–Aug. 27, 2011. It included programming also featured on Disney Channel, Toon Disney, and ABC Family.

ABC of Hand Tools, The (film) Training film showing the proper use and care of common hand tools, as well as the type of work performed by each tool; made for General Motors Corporation and delivered Feb. 5, 1946. Directed by Bill Roberts. General Motors continued to use the film and several editions of the accompanying booklet for many years as part of its training course.

ABC Signature Established in 2014, originally as a subsidiary of ABC Studios, to produce boutique, artist-driven programming for off-network and digital platforms, beginning with the series *Benched*. In 2020, ABC Signature merged with ABC Studios to form a single in-house production entity named ABC Signature, part of Disney Television Studios.

ABC Soap Opera Bistro Hollywood Pictures Backlot restaurant in Disney's California Adventure; open Feb. 8, 2001–Nov. 4, 2002, and succeeded by *Playhouse Disney—Live on Stage!*

ABC Sound Studio Sound effects demonstration attraction, titled One Saturday Morning, in Disney-MGM Studios; opened Jul. 1, 1997, replacing the Monster Sound Show. Seven guests picked added sound effects to a *101 Dalmatians: The Series* cartoon, and then the audience watched the humorous results. The show closed Feb. 20, 1999, and was succeeded in Apr. by Sounds Dangerous. The venue became Mickey Shorts Theater Mar. 4, 2020.

ABC Sound Studio: Sounds Dangerous Sound effects attraction in Disney's Hollywood Studios; ran Apr. 22, 1999–2012. Drew Carey starred as an actor playing gumshoe Charlie Foster, but when his hidden camera got damaged, the theater plunged into darkness, leaving the audience listening as the hilarious mystery unfolded. The theater was later used for *Star Wars* programs and films, including *Star Wars: Path of the Jedi*. SEE ALSO ABC SOUND STUDIO AND MONSTER SOUND SHOW.

ABC Studios In-house production company that developed and produced programming for network, cable, Web, VOD, mobile, and streaming platforms. Before Feb. 2007, it was known as Touchstone Television. In Aug. 2020, ABC Studios merged with the subsidiary ABC Signature to form a new single entity with the latter's name.

ABC SuperSign SEE TIMES SQUARE STUDIOS.

ABCD 2 (film) The story of an Indian dance troupe. A motley assortment of boys and girls who come from the backstreets of a Mumbai suburb and rise to fame, but suffer a sudden downfall, and then go to a world hip-hop dance competition in Las Vegas in a heroic attempt to seek vindication by regaining their lost glory and pride. A Hindi language film produced for Disney India by UTV Motion Pictures. Directed by Remo D'Souza. Released Jun. 19, 2015, in India and the U.S. Stars Varun Dhawan (Suresh), Shraddha Kapoor (Vinnie), Lauren Gottlieb (Olive), Prabhudheva (Vishnu Sir), Christine Vienna (Traveler). 154 min. A sequel to *ABCD: Any Body Can Dance* (2013).

ABC1 The first ABC-branded international TV channel; debuted in the U.K. in Sep. 2004, airing acquired programming as well as ABC shows from the U.S. Broadcasting ended in Sep. 2007.

Abner Country mouse in *The Country Cousin* (1936).

AbracadaBar Cocktail lounge next to Flying Fish on Disney's BoardWalk at Walt Disney World; opened Jul. 23, 2016. It is themed to the 1930s golden age of magic.

Abrams, J. J. Filmmaker; directed/wrote *Star Wars: The Force Awakens* and *The Rise of Skywalker*, and exec. produced *The Last Jedi*; wrote *Taking Care of Business, Gone Fishin'*, and *Armageddon*; and created the TV series *Felicity, Alias*, and *Lost*. He was exec. producer of *What About Brian* and composed the main title themes for *Felicity* and *Alias*.

Absent-Minded Inventors and the Search for Flubber (TV) Half-hour special; aired on ABC Nov. 21, 1997. A humorous look at strange inventions of the past and a promo for the release of *Flubber*. Hosted by Bill Nye.

Absent-Minded Professor, The (film) For the 3rd time, Professor Ned Brainard of Medfield College is so engrossed in a scientific experiment, he fails to show up for his wedding with Betsy Carlisle. But although he loses his girl to rival Professor Shelby Ashton, his absentmindedness pays off with the creation of Flubber, a rubbery substance with an antigravity agent. With his new invention, Brainard is able to make the puny Medfield basketball team victors over Rutland College, prevent a crook, Alonzo Hawk, from stealing Flubber, and win back Betsy, flying on a Flubberized Model T Ford to Washington, D.C., to give the powerful creation to a grateful government. Released Mar. 16, 1961. Directed by Robert Stevenson in black and white. 96 min. Stars Fred MacMurray (Ned Brainard), Nancy Olson (Betsy Carlisle), Keenan Wynn (Alonzo Hawk), Ed Wynn (Fire Chief),

Tommy Kirk (Biff Hawk), Leon Ames (Rufus Daggett), Edward Andrews (Defense Secretary), Elliott Reid (Shelby Ashton). Special effects were created by Robert A. Mattey and Eustace Lycett, who were nominated for an Academy Award, and included the sodium screen matte process, as well as miniatures and wire-supported mock-ups. The film's "Medfield Fight Song" was written by Richard M. and Robert B. Sherman—their first song for a Disney feature. The motion picture, made on a small budget, did fine business at the box office, led to a sequel, *Son of Flubber*, and had theatrical reissues in 1967 and 1974. First released on video in black and white in 1981, and in a colorized version in 1986, after an airing on The Disney Channel in March of that year. This was the first Disney film to be colorized, but the process was still in its infancy and the results were less than spectacular. In 1988–1989, 2 TV episodes based on the film were produced, starring Harry Anderson. SEE ALSO FLUBBER.

Absent-Minded Professor, The (TV) Henry Crawford, an absent-minded professor, programs his computer, named Albert in honor of Albert Einstein, to remind him of his girlfriend's poetry reading. But the computer was also programmed to analyze some old papers Henry found in his attic, and just before leaving for the poetry reading, he tests one formula. When an experiment goes awry, the result is a sort of flying rubber, called Flubber. His girlfriend, Ellen Whitley, does not share Henry's enthusiasm for his new substance, which he uses on some shoes and his Model T Ford. Albert is stolen by some teenagers, but Henry manages to get it back and patch things up with Ellen. Aired on Nov. 27, 1988. Directed by Robert Sheerer. Stars Harry Anderson (Henry Crawford), Mary Page Keller (Ellen Whitley), Cory Danziger (Gus), David Paymer (Oliphant), James Noble (Dr. Blount), Bibi Osterwald (Mrs. Nakamura), Stephen Dorff (Curtis), Jason Zalder (Greg). Roughly based on the 1961 feature film.

Absent-Minded Professor, The: Trading Places (TV) Henry Crawford is persuaded by ex-roommate Jack Brooker to switch places. Henry will go to work at the top secret Rhinebloom Labs, and Jack will teach Henry's classes. What Henry doesn't know is that Jack is worried that the lab may be involved in something illegal. When Henry tries to find out what is going on by using his computer, Albert, a virus is put into the computer. Henry and Jack learn the project is a weapons system, and, by using Flubber, they are able to sabotage a demonstration. Aired Feb. 26, 1989. Directed by Bob Sweeney. Stars Harry Anderson (Henry Crawford), Mary Page Keller (Ellen), Ed Begley Jr. (Jack Brooker), James Noble (Dean Blount), Richard Sanders (Dr. Dark), Ron Fassler (Hacker). A sequel to the 1988 TV episode, *The Absent-Minded Professor*.

Abu Aladdin's monkey friend; "voiced" by Frank Welker.

Abuela Alma Matriarch of the Madrigal family in *Encanto*; voiced by María Cecilia Botero.

Abu's Bazaar Shop in Arabian Coast in Tokyo DisneySea; opened Apr. 28, 2008. Guests can also try their skills at games inspired by *Aladdin*.

Academy Award Review of Walt Disney Cartoons (film) Compilation of 5 Oscar-winning cartoons (*Flowers and Trees*, *Three Little Pigs*, *The Tortoise and the Hare*, *Three Orphan Kittens*, and *The Country Cousin*) released May 19, 1937, partly to herald the forthcoming release of Walt's first feature-length animated film, *Snow White and the Seven Dwarfs*.

Academy Awards As of 2023, Disney has won a total of 132 Academy Awards, but the impressive number is that of these, 32 were won by Walt Disney personally. This is by far the record, and Walt Disney is listed in the *Guinness World Records* book for this distinction. (Second in line is Cedric Gibbons, the MGM art director, with 11 awards.) Most of Walt Disney's awards came to him as producer of a film. He also won the prestigious Irving Thalberg Award, given by the Academy of Motion Picture Arts and Sciences. Animated Disney characters have occasionally appeared on the Academy Awards show. While Minnie, Donald, and Daisy watched from the audience, Mickey Mouse interacted with Tom Selleck in 1988, an animated Belle and Beast appeared in 1992, Snow White was a guest in 1993, and Woody and Buzz Lightyear from *Toy Story* helped present an award in 1996. Mickey Mouse appeared again in 2003, as did Woody and Buzz in 2016. C-3PO, R2-D2, and BB-8 also appeared onstage in 2016. The use of a live Snow White in an uncomplimentary musical number with Rob Lowe in 1989 led to an immediate lawsuit by Disney, which was dropped after the Academy offered an apology.

The awards, listed by the year in which they were presented, are as follows:

*presented to Walt Disney

1.* 1932: *Flowers and Trees* (Cartoon Short Subject, 1931–1932)

2.* 1932: Special Award to Walt Disney for the creation of Mickey Mouse

3.* 1934: *Three Little Pigs* (Cartoon Short Subject, 1932–1933)

4.* 1935: *The Tortoise and the Hare* (Cartoon Production, 1934)

5.* 1936: *Three Orphan Kittens* (Cartoon Production, 1935)

6.* 1937: *The Country Cousin* (Cartoon Short Subject, 1936)

7.* 1938: *The Old Mill* (Cartoon Short Subject, 1937)

8.* 1938: Top Technical Award to Walt Disney Productions for the design and application to production of the multiplane camera, 1937

9.* 1939: *Ferdinand the Bull* (Cartoon Short Subject, 1938)

10.* 1939: Special Award to Walt Disney for *Snow White and the Seven Dwarfs*—recognized as a significant screen innovation, which has charmed millions and pioneered a great new entertainment field for the motion picture cartoon

11.* 1940: *The Ugly Duckling* (Cartoon Short Subject, 1939)

12. 1941: *Pinocchio* (Song, 1940: "When You Wish Upon a Star"; Leigh Harline and Ned Washington)

13. 1941: *Pinocchio* (Original Score, 1940: Leigh Harline, Paul J. Smith, and Ned Washington)

14.* 1942: Irving Thalberg Memorial Award to Walt Disney for "the most consistent high quality of production achievement by an individual producer." (This is not an Oscar but a special award in the form of a bust of Thalberg.)

15.* 1942: Special Technical Award for "outstanding contribution to the advancement of the use of sound in motion pictures through the production of *Fantasia*"

16.* 1942: *Lend a Paw* (Cartoon Short Subject, 1941)

17. 1942: Special Award to Leopold Stokowski and associates for their achievement "in the creation of a new form of visualized music" (*Fantasia*)

18. 1942: *Dumbo* (Original Score, 1941: Frank Churchill and Oliver Wallace)

19.* 1943: *Der Fuehrer's Face* (Best Cartoon Short Subject, 1942–1943)

20. 1947: Special Technical Award to Members of the Walt Disney Studio Sound Department, for a process of checking and locating noise in sound tracks

21. 1948: *Song of the South* (Song, 1947: "Zip-A-Dee-Doo-Dah"; music by Allie Wrubel, lyrics by Ray Gilbert)

22. 1948: *Song of the South* (Honorary Award to James Baskett, for his "able and heartwarming characterization of Uncle Remus, friend and storyteller to the children of the world")

23.* 1949: *Seal Island* (Two-Reel Short Subject, 1948)

24. 1950: Honorary Award to Bobby Driscoll, outstanding juvenile actor of 1949 (performances included *So Dear to My Heart*)

25.* 1951: *In Beaver Valley* (Two-Reel Short Subject, 1950)

26.* 1952: *Nature's Half Acre* (Two-Reel Short Subject, 1951)

27.* 1953: *Water Birds* (Two-Reel Short Subject, 1952)

28.* 1954: *The Living Desert* (Documentary Feature, 1953)

29.* 1954: *Bear Country* (Two-Reel Short Subject, 1953)

30.* 1954: *The Alaskan Eskimo* (Documentary Short Subject, 1953)

31.* 1954: *Toot, Whistle, Plunk and Boom* (Cartoon Short Subject, 1953)

32.* 1955: *The Vanishing Prairie* (Documentary Feature, 1954)

33.* 1955: *20,000 Leagues Under the Sea* (Achievement with Special Effects, 1954)

34. 1955: *20,000 Leagues Under the Sea* (Achievement in Art and Set Decoration, 1954: John Meehan and Emile Kuri)

35.* 1956: *Men Against the Arctic* (Documentary Short Subject, 1955)

36.* 1958: *The Wetback Hound* (Live-Action Short Subject, 1957: Walt Disney, exec. producer; Larry Lansburgh, producer)

37.* 1959: *White Wilderness* (Documentary Feature, 1958)

38.* 1959: *Grand Canyon* (Live-Action Short Subject, 1958)

39.* 1959: *Ama Girls* (Documentary Short Subject, 1958: Walt Disney, exec. producer; Ben Sharpsteen, producer)

40. 1960: Special Technical Award to Ub Iwerks

for the design of an improved optical printer for special effects and matte shots

41.* 1961: *The Horse with the Flying Tail* (Documentary Feature, 1960: Walt Disney, exec. producer; Larry Lansburgh, producer)

42. 1961: *Pollyanna* (Honorary Award to Hayley Mills for the most outstanding juvenile performance during 1960)

43. 1965: *Mary Poppins* (Actress, 1964: Julie Andrews)

44. 1965: *Mary Poppins* (Song, 1964: "Chim Chim Cher-ee"; Richard M. Sherman and Robert B. Sherman)

45. 1965: *Mary Poppins* (Musical Score, Original, 1964: Richard M. and Robert B. Sherman)

46. 1965: *Mary Poppins* (Film Editing, 1964: Cotton Warburton)

47. 1965: *Mary Poppins* (Special Visual Effects, 1964: Peter Ellenshaw, Hamilton S. Luske, and Eustace Lycett)

48. 1965: Special Technical Award to Petro Vlahos, Wadsworth Pohl, and Ub Iwerks for conception and perfection of techniques of color traveling matte composite cinematography [*Mary Poppins*]

49.* 1969: *Winnie the Pooh and the Blustery Day* (Cartoon Short Subject, 1968: Walt Disney, exec. producer)

50. 1970: *It's Tough to Be a Bird* (Cartoon Short Subject, 1969: Ward Kimball, producer)

51. 1972: *Bedknobs and Broomsticks* (Special Visual Effects, 1971: Danny Lee, Eustace Lycett, and Alan Maley)

52. 1986: Technical Achievement Award to David W. Spencer for the development of an animation photo transfer process (APT)

53. 1987: *The Color of Money* (Actor, 1986: Paul Newman)

54. 1989: *Who Framed Roger Rabbit* (Award for Special Achievement in Animation Direction to Richard Williams)

55. 1989: *Who Framed Roger Rabbit* (Film Editing, 1988: Arthur Schmidt)

56. 1989: *Who Framed Roger Rabbit* (Sound Effects Editing, 1988: Charles L. Campbell and Louis L. Edemann)

57. 1989: *Who Framed Roger Rabbit* (Visual Effects, 1988: Ken Ralston, Richard Williams, Edward Jones, George Gibbs)

58. 1990: *Dead Poets Society* (Original Screenplay, 1989: Tom Schulman)

59. 1990: *The Little Mermaid* (Original Score, 1989: Alan Menken)

60. 1990: *The Little Mermaid* (Best Song, 1989: "Under the Sea"; music by Alan Menken, lyrics by Howard Ashman)

61. 1991: *Dick Tracy* (Makeup, 1990: John Caglione, Jr. and Doug Drexler)

62. 1991: *Dick Tracy* (Art Direction/Set Decoration, 1990: Richard Sylbert [art]; Rick Simpson [set])

63. 1991: *Dick Tracy* (Best Song, 1990: "Sooner or Later [I Always Get My Man]"; music and lyrics by Stephen Sondheim)

64. 1992: Scientific/Technical Award to members of the Walt Disney feature animation department, for CAPS (Computer Animated Production System), showcased in *Beauty and the Beast*. The system enables the seamless combination of hand-drawn and computer animation. Disney employees receiving awards: Randy Cartwright, David B. Coons, Lem Davis, James Houston, Mark Kimball, Thomas Hahn, Peter Nye, Michael Shantzis, and David F. Wolf

65. 1992: Scientific/Technical Award to YCM Laboratories for the motion picture restoration process with liquid gate and registration correction on a contact printer, as used in the restoration of *Fantasia*

66. 1992: *Beauty and the Beast* (Original Score, 1991: Alan Menken)

67. 1992: *Beauty and the Beast* (Best Song, 1991: "Beauty and the Beast"; music by Alan Menken, lyrics by Howard Ashman)

68. 1993: *Aladdin* (Original Score, 1992: Alan Menken)

69. 1993: *Aladdin* (Best Song, 1992: "A Whole New World"; music by Alan Menken, lyrics by Tim Rice)

70. 1995: *Ed Wood* (Supporting Actor; 1994: Martin Landau)

71. 1995: *Ed Wood* (Makeup, 1994: Rick Baker, Ve Neill, and Yolanda Toussieng)

72. 1995: *The Lion King* (Original Score, 1994: Hans Zimmer)

73. 1995: *The Lion King* (Best Song, 1994: "Can You Feel the Love Tonight"; music by Elton John, lyrics by Tim Rice)

74. 1996: Special Achievement Oscar, 1995, to John Lasseter, director and co-writer of *Toy Story*, for "the development and inspired application of techniques that have made possible the first feature-length computer-animated film."

75. 1996: *Pocahontas* (Original Musical or Comedy Score, 1995: Alan Menken and Stephen Schwartz)

76. 1996: *Pocahontas* (Best Song, 1995: "Colors of the Wind"; music by Alan Menken, lyrics by Stephen Schwartz)

77. 1997: *Evita* (Best Song, 1996: "You Must Love Me"; music by Andrew Lloyd Webber, lyrics by Tim Rice)

78. 2000: *Tarzan* (Best Song, 1999: "You'll Be in My Heart"; music and lyrics by Phil Collins)

79. 2000: Scientific/Technical Award to Hoyt H. Yeatman Jr. of Dream Quest Images and John C. Brewer of Eastman Kodak for the identification and diagnosis leading to the elimination of the "red fringe" artifact in traveling matte composite photography.

80. 2002: *Monsters, Inc.* (Best Song, 2001: "If I Didn't Have You"; music and lyrics by Randy Newman)

81. 2002: *Pearl Harbor* (Best Sound Editing, 2001: George Watters II and Christopher Boyes)

82. 2003: Scientific/Technical Award to Eric Daniels, George Kanatics, Tasso Lappas, and Chris Springfield (Feature Animation) for the development of the Deep Canvas rendering software, which was used first in *Tarzan* and more extensively in *Treasure Planet*.

83. 2003: *Spirited Away* (Best Animated Feature, 2002: Hiyao Miyazaki, producer)

84. 2004: *Finding Nemo* (Best Animated Feature, 2003: Andrew Stanton, producer)

85. 2005: *The Incredibles* (Best Animated Feature, 2004: Brad Bird, writer and director)

86. 2005: *The Incredibles* (Best Sound Editing, 2004: Randy Thom and Michael Silvers)

87. 2006: *The Chronicles of Narnia: The Lion, the Witch, and the Wardrobe* (Best Makeup, 2005: Howard Berger and Tami Lane)

88. 2007: *Pirates of the Caribbean: Dead Man's Chest* (Best Visual Effects, 2006: John Knoll, Hal Hickel, Charles Gibson, Allen Hall)

89. 2008: *Ratatouille* (Best Animated Feature, 2007: Brad Bird, director)

90. 2009: *WALL•E* (Best Animated Feature, 2008: Andrew Stanton, director)

91. 2010: *Up* (Best Animated Feature, 2009: Pete Docter, director)

92. 2010: *Up* (Best Original Score, 2009: Michael Giacchino)

93. 2011: *Toy Story 3* (Best Animated Feature, 2010: Lee Unkrich, director)

94. 2011: *Toy Story 3* (Best Song, 2010: "We Belong Together"; music and lyrics by Randy Newman)

95. 2011: *Alice in Wonderland* (Best Art Direction, 2010: Robert Stromberg, production designer; Karen O'Hara, set decorator)

96. 2011: *Alice in Wonderland* (Best Costume Design, 2010: Colleen Attwood)

97. 2012: *The Help* (Best Supporting Actress, 2011: Octavia Spencer)

98. 2012: *The Muppets* (Best Original Song, 2011: "Man or Muppet"; music and lyrics by Bret McKenzie)

99. 2013: *Lincoln* (Best Actor, 2012: Daniel Day-Lewis)

100. 2013: *Lincoln* (Best Production Design, 2012: Rick Carter and Jim Erickson)

101. 2013: *Brave* (Best Animated Feature, 2012: Mark Andrews and Brenda Chapman, directors)

102. 2013: *Paperman* (Best Animated Short, 2012: John Kahrs, director)

103. 2014: *Frozen* (Best Animated Feature, 2013: Chris Buck and Jennifer Lee, directors; Peter Del Vecho, producer)

104. 2014: *Frozen* (Best Original Song, 2013: "Let It Go"; music and lyrics by Kristen Anderson-Lopez and Robert Lopez)

105. 2014: Scientific/Technical Award to Florian Kainz, Jeffery Yost, Philip Hubbard, and Jim Hourihan (ILM) for the architecture and development of the Zeno application framework.

106. 2014: Scientific/Technical Award to Oliver Maury, Ian Sachs, and Dan Piponi (ILM) for the creation of the ILM Plume system that simulates and renders fire, smoke, and explosions for motion picture visual effects.

107. 2015: *Big Hero 6* (Best Animated Feature, 2014: Don Hall and Chris Williams, directors; Roy Conli, producer)

108. 2015: *Feast* (Best Animated Short, 2014: Patrick Osborne, director; Kristina Reed, producer)

109. 2015: Scientific/Technical Award to Cary Phillips, Nicholas Popravka, Philip Peterson, and Colette Mullenhoff (ILM) for the architecture, development, and creation of the artist-driven interface of the ILM Shape Sculpting System.

110. 2015: Scientific/Technical Award to Brice Criswell and Ron Fedkiw (ILM) for the development of the ILM PhysBAM Destruction System.

111. 2016: *Bridge of Spies* (Best Supporting Actor, 2015: Mark Rylance)

112. 2016: *Inside Out* (Best Animated Feature, 2015: Pete Docter, director; Jonas Rivera, producer)

113. 2016: Scientific/Technical Award to Ronald Mallet and Christoph Bregler (ILM) for the design and engineering of the ILM Geometry Tracker, which facilitates convincing interaction of digital and live-action elements within a scene.
114. 2017: *O.J.: Made in America* (Best Documentary Feature, 2016: Ezra Edelman and Caroline Waterlow)
115. 2017: *The Jungle Book* (Best Visual Effects, 2016: Robert Legato, Adam Valdez, Andrew R. Jones, Dan Lemmon)
116. 2017: *Piper* (Best Animated Short, 2016: Alan Barillaro, director; Marc Sondheimer, producer)
117. 2017: *Zootopia* (Best Animated Feature, 2016: Byron Howard and Rich Moore, directors; Clark Spencer, producer)
118. 2017: Technical Achievement Award to Brian Whited for the design and development of the Meander drawing system at Walt Disney Animation Studios.
119. 2018: *Coco* (Best Animated Feature, 2017: Lee Unkrich, director; Darla K. Anderson, producer)
120. 2018: *Coco* (Best Original Song, 2017: "Remember Me"; music and lyrics by Kristen Anderson-Lopez and Robert Lopez)
121. 2018: Technical Achievement Award to Jason Smith and Jeff White for the original design and Rachel Rose and Mike Jutan for the architecture and engineering of the Block Party procedural rigging system at Industrial Light and Magic.
122. 2018: Technical Achievement Award to Rob Jensen for the foundational design and continued development; to Thomas Hahn for the animation toolset; and to George Elkoura, Adam Woodbury, and Dirk Van Gelder for the high-performance execution engine of the Presto Animation System at Pixar Animation Studios.
123. 2019: *Black Panther* (Best Costume Design, 2018: Ruth Carter)
124. 2019: *Black Panther* (Best Original Score, 2018: Ludwig Göransson)
125. 2019: *Black Panther* (Best Production Design, 2018: Hannah Beachler, production designer; Jay Hart, set decorator)
126. 2019: *Bao* (Best Animated Short, 2018: Domee Shi, director; Becky Neiman-Cobb, producer)
127. 2020: *Toy Story 4* (Best Animated Feature, 2019: Josh Cooley, director; Mark Nielsen and Jonas Rivera, producers)
128. 2021: *Soul* (Best Animated Feature, 2020: Pete Docter, director; Dana Murray, producer)
129. 2021: *Soul* (Best Original Score, 2020: Trent Reznor, Atticus Ross, Jon Batiste)
130. 2022: *Cruella* (Best Costume Design, 2021: Jenny Beavan)
131. 2022: *Encanto* (Best Animated Feature, 2021: Jared Bush and Byron Howard, directors; Yvett Merino and Clark Spencer, producers)
132. 2023: *Black Panther: Wakanda Forever* (Best Costume Design, 2022: Ruth E. Carter)

According to Jim (TV) Half-hour comedy series on ABC; aired Sep. 26, 2001–Jun. 9, 2009. Jim, a contractor in a design firm, is an all-American guy with a smart, sophisticated wife and 3 kids. He struggles with the issues of how to achieve the picket fence ideal life, yet keep a firm grip on his manhood. Stars Jim Belushi (Jim), Courtney Thorne-Smith (Cheryl), Kimberly Williams (Dana), Larry Joe Campbell (Andy), Taylor Atelian (Ruby), Billi Bruno (Gracie). From Touchstone Television in association with Brad Grey Television.

Ackerman, Josh Actor; appeared on the *Mickey Mouse Club* on The Disney Channel, beginning in 1989.

Acolyte, The (TV) Mystery-thriller *Star Wars* series planned for digital release on Disney+. A galaxy of shadowy secrets and emerging dark side powers is revealed in the final days of the High Republic era as a former Padawan reunites with her Jedi Master to investigate a series of crimes. But the forces they confront are more sinister than they ever anticipated. Stars Amandla Stenberg, Lee Jung-jae, Manny Jacinto, Dafne Keen, Jodie Turner-Smith, Rebecca Henderson, Charlie Barnett, Dean-Charles Chapman, Carrie-Anne Moss. From Lucasfilm.

Acorn Ball Crawl Attraction in Mickey's Toontown at Disneyland; open Jan. 24, 1993–Jan. 1998. Kids could plunge and burrow into a huge pile of red and yellow balls.

Acorns Gifts & Goods Apparel, souvenir, and sundry shop in Disney's Grand Californian Hotel & Spa; opened in 2001.

Acting Sheriff (TV) Unsold pilot (30 min.); aired on CBS Aug. 17, 1991. Small-time movie actor Brent McCord applies for the job of sheriff of a small Northern California town. Directed by Michael Lembeck. Stars Robert Goulet (Brent McCord), John Putch (Mike Swanson), Hillary Bailey Smith (Donna Singer).

Adams, Amy Actress; appeared in *Enchanted* (Giselle), *The Muppets* (Mary), and voiced Polly Purebred in *Underdog*. For Disney+, she produced and reprised her role as Giselle in *Disenchanted*.

Adès, Lucien (1920–1992) French music publisher who pioneered sing-along books in the 1950s. He was named a European Disney Legend in 1997.

Admiral Joe Fowler Riverboat Frontierland attraction in the Magic Kingdom at Walt Disney World; operated on the Rivers of America beginning Oct. 2, 1971, and retired in fall 1980. Its sister ship, the *Richard F. Irvine*, remained. Named after the retired admiral who led the construction of both Disneyland and Walt Disney World.

Adorable Snowman Frosted Treats *Monsters, Inc.*-inspired ice cream counter in Pixar Pier at Disney California Adventure; opened May 1, 2018, taking the place of the Paradise Pier Ice Cream Co.

Adrian, Iris (1913–1994) Character actress; appeared in *That Darn Cat!* (landlady), *The Love Bug* (carhop), *Scandalous John* (Mavis), *The Apple Dumpling Gang* (Poker Patty), *The Shaggy D.A.* (manageress), *Freaky Friday* (bus passenger), and *Herbie Goes Bananas* (loud American wife).

Adventure in Art, An (TV) Show aired Apr. 30, 1958. Directed by Wilfred Jackson and C. August Nichols. Using Robert Henri's book *The Art Spirit* as a reference, Walt explains how people see art in different ways, including the history of silhouettes. Later, he has 4 of his artists, each with a different style, paint 1 tree. That segment, featuring Marc Davis, Eyvind Earle, Joshua Meador, and Walt Peregoy, was later released as an educational film entitled *4 Artists Paint 1 Tree*. The show also emphasizes how music can be an inspiration to artists, as in Bach's "Toccata and Fugue in D Minor" from *Fantasia*.

Adventure in Color, An/Mathmagic Land (TV) The first episode of *Walt Disney's Wonderful World of Color*, when Disney's weekly TV series moved to NBC, changed its title from *Walt Disney Presents*, and began telecasting in color. Aired Sep. 24, 1961. Directed by Hamilton S. Luske. The show introduced the new character Professor Ludwig Von Drake, who gives a comic lesson about color. The kaleidoscopic opening, set to the new title song, "The Wonderful World of Color," by Richard M. and Robert B. Sherman, helped show off color TV sets, and make other viewers think, *Oh, how great this must look in color*, to the obvious glee of RCA, one of the sponsors. Veteran voice actor Paul Frees provided Von Drake's voice. The show concluded with *Donald in Mathmagic Land*.

Adventure in Dairyland (TV) Serial on the *Mickey Mouse Club* during the 1956–1957 season. Annette Funicello and Sammy Ogg visit a Wisconsin dairy farm. The first Disney appearance of Kevin Corcoran, here playing Moochie McCandless. Also stars Herb Newcombe, Fern Persons, Glen Graber, Mary Lu Delmonte. Directed by William Beaudine. 8 episodes.

Adventure in Satan's Canyon (TV) Show aired Nov. 3, 1974. Directed by William Beaudine Jr. A young man tries to master the kayak and becomes a hero in helping to save his coach, who is badly injured in an accident. To accomplish this feat, the young man has to navigate some very dangerous rapids in his kayak, giving himself confidence. The show was filmed in the wilds of the Pacific Northwest and along the Stanislaus River in California. Stars Richard Jaeckel, David Alan Bailey, Larry Pennell.

Adventure in the Magic Kingdom, An (TV) Show aired Apr. 9, 1958. Directed by Hamilton S. Luske. Tinker Bell leads a guided tour of Disneyland, which includes a live performance of the Mouseketeers in Holidayland and a sampling of fun and entertainment throughout the park. The show ends with the spectacular fireworks display in the sky above the castle. In 2013, the introduction to the show, featuring Walt Disney with Tinker Bell, was "re-created" for *Saving Mr. Banks*, with Tom Hanks appearing as Walt and Mark Henn providing the animation for Tinker Bell.

Adventure in Wildwood Heart (TV) Show aired Sep. 25, 1957. Directed by Hamilton S. Luske. Producer Winston Hibler explains how *Perri*, Disney's first and only True-Life Fantasy, was filmed. The film crew was so entranced by their setting in Utah that it became known among them as Wildwood Heart. It took almost 3 years to film the adventures of the squirrels.

Adventure Isle Area in Adventureland in Disneyland Paris; opened Apr. 12, 1992, with secret caves, grottoes, waterfalls, a floating bridge, suspension bridge, Skull Rock, and Pirate Galleon. Also a land in Shanghai Disneyland; opened Jun. 16, 2016, celebrating the ancient Arbori people's admiration for nature. Its attractions (Roaring Rapids, Camp Discovery, Soaring Over the Horizon) feature water, land, and sky. Its anchoring landmark, Roaring Mountain, is the highest "mountain" in Shanghai's Pudong New District.

Adventure Story, The (TV) Show aired Mar. 20, 1957. Directed by Wolfgang Reitherman. The story of the exploits of the Goofy family through the ages. New animation of fictional Goofy relatives was used to tie together 5 Goofy cartoons made 1945–1953. The alternate title is *The Goofy Adventure Story*.

Adventure Thru Inner Space Tomorrowland attraction in Disneyland; open Aug. 5, 1967–Sep. 2, 1985, and sponsored by Monsanto. Guests were transported by Atomobile through a mighty microscope to see what the inside of an atom might be like. It was the first attraction to use the Omnimover ride system. Superseded by Star Tours.

Adventure Thru the Walt Disney Archives (film) Hour-long documentary exploring the collections and 50-year history of the Walt Disney Archives. Hosted by Don Hahn. Directed by John Gleim. Premiered digitally Jun. 27, 2020, on D23.com, with a Nov. 19, 2021, release on Disney+.

Adventureland Land of mystery, romance, and adventure; opened in 1955 as one of the original lands of Disneyland, most noted for the Jungle Cruise, which takes up most of its space. The land was suggested by Walt's True-Life Adventure series and inspired by tropical and remote regions from around the world. Over the years, other attractions have been added, including the Swiss Family Treehouse (later Tarzan's Treehouse, then Adventureland Treehouse), Walt Disney's Enchanted Tiki Room, and Indiana Jones Adventure. Versions of Adventureland are also in the Magic Kingdom at Walt Disney World, Tokyo Disneyland, Disneyland Paris, and Hong Kong Disneyland. In Shanghai Disneyland, the area is known as Adventure Isle.

Adventureland Bazaar Adventureland shop in Disneyland; opened Jul. 17, 1955, selling leather, wood carvings, jewelry, ceramics, and other wares from around the world. A number of years later, designers renovating the shop had a very short construction schedule, so they dug around in the park's warehouses and found 2 of the former ticket booths that were once in front of Disneyland attractions, which they then disguised as sales counters. They were removed during a major remodeling in 1994. Also a shop in Tokyo Disneyland; opened Apr. 15, 1983.

Adventureland Steel Drum Band Ensemble in the Magic Kingdom at Walt Disney World; performed 1971–1999. Led by Edgar "Junior" Pouchet and his band, known as JP and the Silver Stars, from Trinidad. A steel drum band also performed in Disneyland and in Tokyo Disneyland.

Adventureland Treehouse Attraction in Disneyland; planned to open in 2023, taking the place of Tarzan's Treehouse. A tribute to the original Swiss Family Treehouse with new rooms, including the mother's music den, the young sons' nature room, and the teenage daughter's astronomer's loft.

Adventureland Veranda Restaurant in the Magic Kingdom at Walt Disney World; opened Oct. 1, 1971, serving fast food with a tropical flavor, such as hamburgers with teriyaki sauce and a pineapple ring. Sponsored by Kikkoman beginning Oct. 5, 1977. Closed in 1994; later utilized for special events and as a character-greeting spot. The restaurant reopened Dec. 16, 2015, as Jungle Navigation Co., Ltd. Skipper Canteen.

Adventurers Club Popular nightclub in Pleasure Island at Walt Disney World; open May 1, 1989–Sep. 27, 2008. Each evening guests were welcomed with the Kungaloosh, the club greeting, by notable members, such as aviator Hathaway Brown, club president Pamelia Perkins, and Colonel Critchlow Sunchbench. Live entertainment was performed in the Mask Room, Treasure Room, Library, and Main Salon, concluding with a farewell Hoopla. The club was adorned with unusual memorabilia supposedly from Merriweather Adam Pleasure's trips around the world, including some curios that interacted with guests. Replaced in 2018 by The Edison.

Adventurers Outpost See Beastly Bazaar.

Adventures by Disney Guided vacation travel program launched in May 2005, originally offering tours to Wyoming and Hawai'i. Other destinations were later added, with more than 50 global trips available by 2019. Planned as an immersive experience for a family, each tour for about 30 guests has 2 Disney tour guides, known as Adventure Guides. Activities in the weeklong vacation, or the shorter 2- to 5-day Escape trips, are planned around local cultures and storytelling. River cruise itineraries were introduced in 2016, with Expedition Cruising added in 2021. Bookings began for Private Adventures (up to 12 guests) Oct. 27, 2020. Private Jet Adventures were announced in 2022.

Adventures in Babysitting (film) Seventeen-year-old Chris Parker's babysitting assignment turns to bedlam when a frightened friend calls her from a bus station. Packing her charges into the family station wagon, they head for downtown Chicago to save the friend. They find themselves caught up in a comic nightmare in the urban jungle of the big city, a place very different from the suburbia which they know, tangling with car thieves and other unsavory characters. Released Jul. 1, 1987. Directed by Chris Columbus. A Touchstone film. 102 min. Stars Elisabeth Shue (Chris), Maia Brewton (Sara), Keith Coogan (Brad), Anthony Rapp (Daryl). Coogan, under the name Keith Mitchell, had voiced the young Tod in *The Fox and the Hound* in 1981. Filmed on location in Chicago and Toronto. Released in England as *A Night on the Town*.

Adventures in Babysitting (TV) Pilot for a series based on the 1987 Touchstone feature; aired on CBS on Jul. 7, 1989. 30 min. Directed by Joel Zwick. The babysitter takes her charges to a convenience store, which is then robbed. Stars Jennifer Guthrie (Chris), Joey Lawrence (Brad), Courtney Peldon (Sara), Brian Austin Green (Daryl).

Adventures in Babysitting (TV) A Disney Channel Original Movie; first aired Jun. 24, 2016. Jenny Parker and Lola Perez are 2 teen girls with distinctly different personalities. With accidently swapped phones, the dependable Jenny and audacious Lola are set to babysit 2 separate families on the same night. Lola's first attempt at babysitting takes an unforeseen turn when 1 of her charges sneaks out to go to a concert. Jenny, who has a reputation to protect, Lola, and the remaining kids head out and have the adventure of a lifetime during one magical night in the big city. Directed by John Schultz. Stars Sabrina Carpenter (Jenny), Sofia Carson (Lola), Nikki Hahn (Emily Cooper), Max Gecowets (Trey Anderson), Jet Jurgensmeyer (Bobby Anderson), Marison Horcher (AJ Anderson), Kevin Quinn (Zac Chase). Based on the 1987 film.

Adventures in Fantasy (TV) Show aired Nov. 6, 1957. Directed by Bill Justice. Tells how the inanimate can be brought to life through animation, with examples from the stories of *Johnny Fedora and Alice Bluebonnet*; *The Little House*; *Susie, the Little Blue Coupe*; and *Little Toot*.

Adventures in Music: Melody (film) Special cartoon released May 28, 1953. Directed by Charles Nichols and Ward Kimball. Professor Owl tries to teach his class about melody. Includes the song "The Bird and the Cricket and the Willow Tree." First cartoon ever filmed in 3-D. It was shown at the Fantasyland Theater in Disneyland as part of the *3-D Jamboree*. The 3-D process never really caught on at the time with theater audiences because of the need to wear the polarized glasses, but the show remained a novelty at Disneyland for several years. This film was the first in a proposed series of shorts where Professor Owl would teach musical principles to his class, but only 1 more, *Toot, Whistle, Plunk and Boom*, was made. See also 3-D.

Adventures in Wonderland See Disney's Adventures in Wonderland.

Adventures of Bullwhip Griffin, The (film) At the time of the California gold rush, Jack Flagg, a young boy from Boston, runs away to California to try and restore his family's fortune, pursued by the very proper family butler, Griffin. As the result of a lucky punch, Griffin becomes mistakenly renowned as a boxer. In a series of adventures, both boy and butler tangle with a crook, Judge Higgins, who uses many disguises. But they find their fortune, and the staid butler becomes his own man and marries Arabella, the boy's older sister. Released Mar. 3, 1967. Directed by James Neilson. 110 min. Stars Roddy McDowall (Bullwhip Griffin), Bryan Russell (Jack Flagg), Suzanne Pleshette (Arabella Flagg), Karl Malden (Judge Higgins), Harry

Guardino (Sam Trimble), Richard Haydn (Quentin Bartlett), Hermione Baddeley (Irene Chesney). Haydn had 16 years earlier voiced the Caterpillar in *Alice in Wonderland*. Based on the book *By the Great Horn Spoon*, by Sid Fleischman. Ward Kimball was credited with "titles and things," which included some inventive animation bits. Songs by Richard M. and Robert B. Sherman; the theme song is by Mel Leven and George Bruns.

Adventures of Chip 'n' Dale, The (TV) Show aired Feb. 27, 1959. Directed by Bill Justice. Chip and Dale as guest hosts present several cartoons in which they star. Re-titled for a 1978 rerun as *Mixed Nuts* and for later reruns as *The Misadventures of Chip 'n' Dale*.

Adventures of Clint and Mac, The (TV) Serial on the *Mickey Mouse Club* during the 1957–1958 season. Directed by Terrence Fisher. Two boys become involved with thieves in England who have stolen a famous manuscript from the British Museum. Stars Neil Wolfe, Jonathan Bailey, Sandra Michaels, John Warwick, Dorothy Smith, Bill Nagy, Mary Barclay. Narrated by Tim Considine. 15 episodes.

Adventures of Huck Finn, The (film) A carefree boy who hates his stifled existence under adoption to the Widow Douglas and Miss Watson fakes his own murder and sets off down the Mississippi with a runaway slave, Jim, as a companion. Jim dreams of traveling downriver to Cairo, Illinois, to buy his wife and children out of bondage. Along the way, Huck and Jim escape a deadly feud between 2 neighboring families and meet up with 2 crafty con men, the King and the Duke. When they attempt to steal the family fortune of the wealthy Wilks family, Huck cannot stand for it, and he tries to destroy their plot. His success brings him the gratitude of the Wilks sisters, who help Jim buy back his family. Based on the Mark Twain book. Released Apr. 2, 1993. Directed by Stephen Sommers. 108 min. Stars Elijah Wood (Huck), Courtney B. Vance (Jim), Robbie Coltrane (The Duke), and Jason Robards (The King). Primary filming took place in the vicinity of Natchez, Mississippi.

Adventures of Ichabod and Mr. Toad, The (film) The film begins in a library with actor Basil Rathbone telling the tale of *The Wind in the Willows* (from the book by Kenneth Grahame), about Mr. Toad, Squire of Toad Hall, whose love for transportation vehicles was insatiable. His friends Rat, Mole, and MacBadger try to help him when his mania leads to the loss of the deed to Toad Hall and a charge of car theft. Toad is thrown in jail, but upon escaping, he learns Winkie, the tavern keeper, and the weasels have taken over Toad Hall. But with his friends, Toad redeems his good name by recovering the deed to the estate and promises to reform, until he eyes a 1908 biplane. Back in the library, singer Bing Crosby picks up with *The Legend of Sleepy Hollow* (by Washington Irving), in which Ichabod Crane, a new schoolteacher, arrives in Sleepy Hollow and captures every lady's heart, except for Katrina Van Tassel, daughter of a wealthy farmer. Ichabod has his eye on the Van Tassel wealth, but his attempts to woo Katrina disturbs her bold suitor, Brom Bones, who tries to scare Ichabod away with the tale of the Headless Horseman. As Ichabod rides home that Halloween evening, he encounters the terrifying phantom and is mysteriously missing the next morning. While the townspeople spread rumors of Ichabod's whereabouts, Katrina weds Brom. Released Oct. 5, 1949. Directed by Jack Kinney, Clyde Geronimi, and James Algar. 68 min. Voices in the "Mr. Toad" segment included Eric Blore (Toad), J. Pat O'Malley (Cyril, Toad's horse), Claud Allister (Rat), Collin Campbell (Mole). Songs include "Ichabod," "Katrina," "The Headless Horseman," and "The Merrily Song." This was the last of several package pictures of the 1940s, during which the Walt Disney Studio had deep economic problems. Expenses were lowered by reusing animation cycles from *The Old Mill* (1937) and by patterning Katrina closely on Grace Martin from *The Martins and the Coys*. Henceforth, Walt Disney would be able to finance the production of regular, 1-story, animated features, beginning the next year with *Cinderella*. Its success ensured the continuation of animation at the Studio. The entire film of *The Adventures of Ichabod and Mr. Toad* was not initially released on videocassette, but the 2 parts were released separately. The complete feature was first released on laser disc in 1992 and on video in 1999.

Adventures of J. Thaddeus Toad, The (film) Educational title of the featurette released theatrically as *The Madcap Adventures of Mr. Toad* and *Wind in the Willows*, released in Sep. 1980. Originally part of *The Adventures of Ichabod and Mr. Toad*.

Adventures of Mickey Mouse (TV) Show aired Oct. 12, 1955. Directed by Jack Hannah and Bill Roberts. Walt discusses the career of Mickey Mouse, showing several cartoons, including *Mickey and the Beanstalk*. Re-titled for 1980 reruns as

Mickey's Greatest Adventures and edited for syn. as *Adventures with Mickey*.

Adventures of Mickey Mouse, The The very first hardback Disney book, published by David McKay in 1931. The story names a number of the barnyard animals, among them Donald Duck. The character of Donald Duck was not actually created until 3 years later. The book was preceded only by the slim, paper covered *Mickey Mouse Book*, published by Bibo-Lang in 1930.

Adventures of Pollyanna, The (TV) Show aired Apr. 10, 1982, based on the theatrical film *Pollyanna*. Pollyanna's Aunt Polly wants the girl to spend her time studying, but Pollyanna has other ideas. She joins a secret club with a group of orphans, and they spy on a mysterious new resident in town, only to learn that her standoffishness is because of her desire to shield a son with special needs. Pollyanna helps the town accept the boy and his mother. Directed by Robert Day. Stars Shirley Jones (Aunt Polly), Patsy Kensit (Pollyanna), Edward Winter (Dr. Chilton), Beverly Archer (Angelica), Lucille Benson (Mrs. Levelor), John Putch (Johnny). The town square set at the Studio became the town of Harrington; it had been built for *Something Wicked This Way Comes* and was later the last backlot set at the Studio to be torn down, in Jul. 1994.

Adventures of Spin and Marty, The (TV) Serial on the *Mickey Mouse Club* during the 1955–1956 season, starring David Stollery and Tim Considine, about a spoiled rich kid, Marty (Stollery), who goes to a summer boys' camp at the Triple-R Ranch. Spin (Considine), who was the most popular kid from the previous summer, is back, and they don't get along because Marty so obviously hates the camp. The summer climaxes with a big rodeo, and the boys eventually end their feud. Directed by William Beaudine Sr. Also stars Roy Barcroft, Harry Carey Jr., Lennie Geer, J. Pat O'Malley, B. G. Norman, Tim Hartnagel, Roger Broaddus, Sammy Ogg, Sammee Tong. 25 episodes. It was the first Disney production shot at the Golden Oak Ranch in Placerita Canyon; the Studio purchased the ranch 4 years later. Episodes of the serial were edited together and shown on The Disney Channel as *Spin and Marty: The Movie* in Oct. 1995. SEE ALSO FURTHER ADVENTURES OF SPIN AND MARTY, THE AND NEW ADVENTURES OF SPIN AND MARTY, THE.

Adventures of the Great Mouse Detective, The The 1992 reissue title of *The Great Mouse Detective*.

Adventures of the Gummi Bears, Disney's (TV) Animated series; aired on NBC Sep. 14, 1985–Sep. 2, 1989, and on ABC Sep. 9, 1989–Sep. 8, 1990. Syn. in 1990–1991. Gummi Bears are the mythical, medieval residents of Gummi Glen who fight ogres led by the evil Duke Igthorn to preserve their homes. Gummiberry juice can give them the ability to bounce out of danger. The Gummis are Zummi, Gruffi, Grammi, Tummi, Cubbi, and Sunni, who are aided by the Princess Calla and her humble page, Cavin. Voices include Paul Winchell (Zummi), June Foray (Grammi), Bill Scott (Gruffi/Toadwart), Noelle North (Cubbi/Calla), Katie Leigh (Sunni), Lorenzo Music (Tummi), Jason Marsden/R. J. Williams (Cavin), Michael Rye (Duke Igthorn). Corey Burton took over Bill Scott's roles after his passing in 1985, and Jim Cummings voiced Zummi after Paul Winchell departed the role. 65 episodes.

Adventures of Tom Thumb & Thumbelina, The (film) Direct-to-video release Aug. 6, 2002; animated feature produced by Hyperion Films. Thumbelina, a young teenage girl, is only 6 inches tall. She meets Tom Thumb, a teenager just a little shorter than herself, and they embark on a fantastic quest together, leading them to the comically villainous Mole King. Directed by Glenn Chaika. Voices include Jennifer Love Hewitt (Thumbelina), Elijah Wood (Tom Thumb), Peter Gallagher (Mole King), Bebe Neuwirth (Queen Mother), Michael Chiklis (Roman), Robert Guillaume (Ben).

Adventures with Mickey (TV) Syn., edited version of *The Adventures of Mickey Mouse*.

Advice on Lice (film) Educational film; released in Sep. 1985. Facts about the symptoms, transmission, treatment, and prevention of head lice.

Aerophile SEE CHARACTERS IN FLIGHT.

Aesop's Hare and the Tortoise (film) Educational film; released in Sep. 1986. 14 min. Walt Disney introduces an animated overview of Aesop's life, by way of footage from one of his TV lead-ins, followed by the popular fable. Re-titled in 1987 as *An Introduction to Aesop*.

Affleck, Ben Actor; appeared in *Armageddon* (A. J. Frost) and *Pearl Harbor* (Rafe McCawley), and on TV in *Almost Home* (Kevin Johnson). Also co-exec. producer, with Matt Damon, on *Push, Nevada*.

Africa Area in Disney's Animal Kingdom; opened Apr. 22, 1998. In the town of Harambe, visitors can dine at Tusker House Restaurant, shop at Mombasa Marketplace and Ziwani Traders, and tour a wildlife reserve on Kilimanjaro Safaris. A theater district opened in 2014, with *Festival of the Lion King* (relocated from the former Camp Minnie-Mickey), and the Harambe Market was added the following year. An Equatorial Africa pavilion had originally been announced for EPCOT but was never built; it was to have featured a film titled *Africa Rediscovered*, hosted by Alex Haley. SEE ALSO HARAMBE.

Africa Before Dark (film) Oswald the Lucky Rabbit cartoon; released Feb. 20, 1928. While trekking through the jungle, Oswald and an elephant have dangerous encounters with lions and a baby tiger. Oswald finally makes his escape with a flying machine.

African Cats (film) Disneynature documentary released in the U.S. Apr. 22, 2011, after an Apr. 21 release in Argentina. In one of the wildest places on Earth, we meet Mara, an endearing lion cub, who strives to grow up with her mother's strength, spirit, and wisdom; Sita, a fearless cheetah and mother of 5 mischievous newborns; and Fang, a proud leader of a lion pride who must defend his family from a rival lion and his sons. Directed by Keith Scholey and Alastair Fothergill. Narrated by Samuel L. Jackson. 89 min. The cinematographers, Owen Newman and Sophie Darlington, spent 2½ years filming in the 580-square-mile Masai Mara National Reserve in Kenya, one of the few remaining places in Africa where the big African cats—lions, cheetahs, and leopards—live in large numbers and in close proximity.

African Diary (film) Goofy cartoon. Goofy bungles his way on safari in Africa. The safari ends abruptly when a rhino chases Goofy and his safari all the way back to their ship on the Ivory Coast. Released Apr. 20, 1945; directed by Jack Kinney.

African Lion, The (film) True-Life Adventure feature released Sep. 14, 1955. Directed by James Algar, with a notable musical score by Paul Smith. The photography team of Alfred and Elma Milotte spent 3 years in Africa studying the realm of the king of beasts and came up with some fascinating footage of not only lions but giraffes, rhinoceroses, elephants, and baboons. The effects of a drought on the animals and the eventual tropical storms that end it round out the motion picture. The cost of film was not a major factor; the Milottes shot until they got the footage that would make an interesting film. Eventually, only about 6% of the film they shot was used in the final production. The movie's theme of the annual life cycle would years later be echoed in the "Circle of Life" in *The Lion King*. 72 min. SEE ALSO HIS MAJESTY, KING OF THE BEASTS (ABRIDGED 1958 TV AIRING) AND BEAVER VALLEY/CAMERAS IN AFRICA (BEHIND-THE-SCENES FOOTAGE).

African Lion and His Realm, The (film) Portion of *The African Lion*; released on 16 mm for schools in May 1969. A study of the lion reveals little-known facts about his domain and about other predators and grazers that live there.

After Market Shop Test Track gift shop in EPCOT as of Dec. 6, 2012. It was renamed Test Track SIMporium in Sep. 2017, offering toy cars, pit crew caps, and pins.

After You've Gone (film) A segment of *Make Mine Music*, with the Benny Goodman Quartet, using the song by Henry Creamer and Turner Leighton; a surreal episode with anthropomorphic musical instruments.

Age of Believing, The: The Disney Live Action Classics (TV) Documentary on Turner Classic Movies that follows the Studio's history as it ventured beyond its animation legacy to develop non-animated family fare, first airing Dec. 14, 2008. The story is told through film clips and interviews with actors and Disney historians. Directed by Peter Fitzgerald. 80 min. Narrated by Angela Lansbury.

Age of Not Believing, The Song from *Bedknobs and Broomsticks*; written by Richard M. and Robert B. Sherman. Nominated for an Academy Award.

Agrabah Fictional home of Aladdin.

Agrabah Bazaar Adventureland marketplace in the Magic Kingdom at Walt Disney World; opened Dec. 15, 2000. Originally, the location included 2 shops, The Magic Carpet and Oriental Imports, until ca. Apr. 1987, when they were replaced by The Elephant's Trunk (later called Elephant Tales).

Agrabah Marketplace Shop in Arabian Coast in Tokyo DisneySea; opened Sep. 4, 2001. Themed after Agrabah, it features the hut where Aladdin lived as a boy and Jasmine's palatial chamber.

Magic tricks and demonstrations of glass engraving are conducted here.

Agrati, Don (1944–2012) Mouseketeer from the 1950s *Mickey Mouse Club* TV show. He was later known as Don Grady on *My Three Sons* and other shows.

Aguilera, Christina Actress/singer; appeared on the *Mickey Mouse Club* on The Disney Channel beginning in 1993. She became a top-selling pop vocalist and performed "Reflection" for the end credits in *Mulan*. Also performed on TV in *Disney's American Teacher Awards*, *Walt Disney World Summer Jam Concert*, *The Disney Family Sing-along*, and *The Most Magical Story on Earth: 50 Years of Walt Disney World*. She was named a Disney Legend in 2019.

Agutter, Jenny Actress; appeared in *Amy* (Amy Medford) and *Marvel's The Avengers* and *Captain America: The Winter Soldier* (World Security Council member), and on TV years earlier as a child dancer in *Ballerina*.

Ahmanson, Caroline Leonetti (1918–2005) Member of the Disney Board of Directors 1975–1992.

Aida Stage musical version of the Aida story; opened as *Elaborate Lives: The Legend of Aida* at the Alliance Theater in Atlanta Oct. 7, 1998. This was the first cooperation between The Walt Disney Company and a nonprofit resident theater company. The title of the musical was shortened to *Aida* in 1999 when the CD album was released. The show played at Chicago's Palace Theatre Nov. 12, 1999–Jan. 9, 2000, and opened at the Palace Theatre on Broadway Mar. 23, 2000, after a month of pre-views, closing Sep. 5, 2004, after a successful run. The story of a love triangle among Aida, a Nubian princess forced into slavery; Amneris, an Egyptian princess; and Radames, the soldier they both love. Elton John and Tim Rice contributed 19 songs, including "Every Story Is a Love Story," "My Strongest Suit," and "Elaborate Lives." Original Broadway performers included Heather Headley (Aida), Adam Pascal (Radames), Sherie Rene Scott (Amneris). Winner of 4 Tony Awards, for Best Original Score (Elton John, Tim Rice), Best Orchestrations (Bob Crowley), Best Lighting Design (Natasha Katz), and Best Performance by a Leading Actress in a Musical (Heather Headley).

AIDS (film) Educational film; released in Sep. 1986. 18 min. Facts on the human immune system and the AIDS virus. The film was revised a year later with updated information.

AIDS: What Do We Tell Our Children? (film) Educational film; released in Aug. 1987. 20 min. The facts about AIDS presented to children.

AIDS: You've Got to Do Something (film) Educational film; released in Jun. 1992. 19 min. Narrated by Mayim Bialik. Provides teens with important facts about HIV and AIDS, with peer discussion and role-playing used to encourage them to become aware of individual and social responsibilities to help stop the spread of the disease.

Ainsley Harriott Show, The (TV) Britain's chef extraordinaire began a syn. run from Buena Vista Television Jan. 10, 2000, of an entertainment/talk/cooking show produced in New York City. The show ended Sep. 15, 2000.

Air Bud (film) An aspiring 12-year-old basketball player, Josh Framm, trying to deal with the death of his father, moves with his family to the sleepy town of Fernfield, Washington, where he has no friends and is too shy to try out for the school basketball team. One day he finds a runaway golden retriever while practicing on an abandoned court. The amazing thing about Buddy, the dog, is that he can accurately shoot hoops! Soon they make the school basketball team and astound the media. But there are problems when Buddy's bad-guy former owner, Norm Snively, discovers what is happening and comes up with a scheme to cash in on the dog's popularity. Josh and Buddy must keep one step ahead of Snively while rallying the town's school team as they aim for the state basketball finals. Directed by Charles Martin Smith. Released Aug. 1, 1997. Stars Kevin Zegers (Josh Framm), Michael Jeter (Norm Snively), Wendy Makkena (Jackie Framm), Eric Christmas (Judge Cranfield), Brendan Fletcher (Larry Willingham). 98 min. The dog, Buddy, was discovered by his trainer, Kevin DiCicco, when he crawled out of the woods near DiCicco's cabin in the mountains near Yosemite National Park in California. The abused year-old dog was dirty and hungry, and DiCicco worked many months to get him back into shape, eventually discovering his talents. Buddy was soon making regular appearances, including 2 on David Letterman's "Stupid Pet Tricks" segments. The town of Fernfield was created by the filmmakers in the environs of Vancouver. The film inspired a sequel,

Air Bud: Golden Receiver, and 3 further video sequels: *Air Bud: World Pup, Air Bud: Seventh Inning Fetch*, and *Air Bud Spikes Back*.

Air Bud: Golden Receiver (film) Sequel to 1997's *Air Bud*; released Aug. 14, 1998. The basketball playing dog, Buddy, helps out his best friend, Josh, by demonstrating that he also has amazing football skills that help Josh's team win the state championship. Directed by Richard Martin. Stars Kevin Zegers (Josh Framm), Cynthia Stevenson (Jackie), Gregory Harrison (Patrick). 90 min. From Keystone Pictures and Dimension Films; released on video labeled "Disney Presents" by Buena Vista Home Entertainment.

Air Bud: Seventh Inning Fetch (film) Direct-to-video release Jun. 18, 2002, by Walt Disney Home Entertainment; 4th film in the series, produced by Keystone Entertainment. Andrea Framm joins the junior high school baseball team to escape the tedium of her homelife. While she is not very good, her dog, Buddy, is a natural. But scientists interested in cloning kidnap the dog just before the big game. Directed by Robert Vince. Stars Caitlin Wachs (Andrea Framm), Richard Karn (Patrick), Cynthia Stevenson (Jackie), Kevin Zegers (Josh). 90 min.

Air Bud Spikes Back (film) Direct-to-video release Jun. 24, 2003, by Walt Disney Home Entertainment; 2nd film in the series, produced by Keystone Entertainment. Andrea Framm's best friend is moving out of town, so to make new friends, she and Buddy join the local beach volleyball team. Directed by Robert Vince. Stars Katija Pevec (Andrea), Jake D. Smith (Noah), Tyler Boissonnault (Connor), Cynthia Stevenson (Jackie), Edie McClurg (Grandma). 87 min.

Air Bud: World Pup (film) Direct-to-video release Dec. 12, 2000; sequel to *Air Bud* (1997) and *Air Bud Golden Receiver* (1998). Buddy's owner, Josh Framm, falls in love with his sister's new soccer coach, Emma, who also happens to be the only female on his high school's soccer team. Josh and Buddy join the soccer team, and Buddy himself falls in love with Emma's golden retriever, Molly. After some drama with kidnapped puppies, Buddy helps the team win the championship. Directed by Bill Bannerman. Stars Kevin Zegers (Josh Framm), Brittany Paige Bouck (Emma Putter), Caitlin Wachs (Andrea), Dale Midkiff (Patrick Framm). Several U.S. women's national soccer team players make cameo appearances.

Air Buddies (film) Direct-to-DVD release Dec. 12, 2006. The dogs, Buddy and Molly, are dognapped, and their puppies, B-Dawg, Budderball, Mudbud, Buddha, and Rosebud, collectively known as the Buddies, are off to save them. Along the way, the bumbling villains Denning and Grim constantly try to capture the puppies. And now, for the first time, the animals talk. Directed by Robert Vince. Voices include Skyler Gisondo (B-Dawg), Josh Flitter (Budderball), Spencer Fox (Mudbud), Dominic Scott Kay (Buddha), Abigail Breslin (Rosebud), Tom Everett Scott (Buddy), Molly Shannon (Molly), Paul Rae (Denning), Trevor Wright (Grim). It was the final film role for Patrick Cranshaw (Sheriff Bob) and Don Knotts (Deputy Sniffer). From Key Pix Productions and Buena Vista Home Entertainment. SEE ALSO SANTA BUDDIES, SNOW BUDDIES, SPACE BUDDIES, AND SPOOKY BUDDIES.

Air Up There, The (film) Assistant college basketball coach Jimmy Dolan is a competitive sportsman with a goal of taking over when his boss, Coach Ray Fox, retires. However, in order to be considered for the position, Jimmy needs to prove that he knows how to recruit star talent. Since all the best players are signing with competing schools, the chances for Jimmy's advancement look bleak until he gets the wild idea to scout for a wonder player in Africa. In Kenya he discovers a tall Winabi warrior, Saleh, who cannot be dazzled by fast-talking, recruiting techniques and promises of wonderful gifts and flashy cars. Jimmy's high-pressure techniques clash with the local customs, but he is finally able to prove himself when the tables are turned and he himself is recruited by the Winabi to help coach their misfit team so they can beat the team of a neighboring tribe, the Mingori, in a game with extremely high stakes—the Winabi's land, their cattle, and the future of the tribe. As a reward, Jimmy is able to draft the star player he needs. Directed by Paul M. Glaser. Released Jan. 7, 1994. A Hollywood Pictures film, in association with Interscope Communications. 107 min. Stars Kevin Bacon (Jimmy Dolan), Charles Gitonga Maina (Saleh), Yolanda Vazquez (Sister Susan), Winston Ntshona (Urudu). The filmmakers utilized the Samburu tribe of northern Kenya but transported them to the primary location in Hoedspruit, South Africa, for the filming. Other filming took place in Canada and Kenya.

Aircraft, Walt Disney's The company plane was a pride and joy of Walt Disney's. Throughout his career, the company used 3 planes, beginning with a Beechcraft Queen Air (1963–1965). The plane was traded in for a new tan and brown turboprop, the Beechcraft King Air (1965–1967), which was chosen for its fast and quiet features and used the N234MM tail number. The Disney pilots would make their initial air traffic call-ups, "Two, three, four, metro metro," but would also try, "Two, three, four, *Mickey Mouse*," an improper FAA communication. Soon, FAA en-route controllers began calling the Disney plane the "Mickey Mouse." Other corporate pilots became quite jealous of Disney's special treatment. A Grumman Gulfstream I was put in service in 1964 and used to survey the Walt Disney World property during the Florida land acquisition effort (along with other corporate purposes). It logged 277,282 miles traveling back and forth between Burbank and New York for preparations before and during the 1964–1965 New York World's Fair. Walt ordered a second Gulfstream, but it was canceled after his passing. The Gulfstream I was painted blue and white in 1985 and continued to be used for press events, goodwill tours, and community outreach. Upon being retired from service, the Gulfstream made its final landing on World Drive at Walt Disney World on Oct. 8, 1992, and was put on display at the former Studio Backlot Tour in Disney's Hollywood Studios. After the Tour closed in 2014, the plane was moved backstage and later repainted to its original color scheme, with updated wing edges and windows. In 2022, it was transported to Anaheim for display at the D23 Expo, where it was announced the Gulfstream would be exhibited at the Palm Springs Air Museum in California beginning Oct. 15. On Dec. 5, 2022, it was announced that the museum, in conjunction with Phoenix Air, will restore the plane's interior.

Ajax Title character in *Donald Duck and the Gorilla* (1944).

Akershus SEE RESTAURANT AKERSHUS.

Aladdin (film) Animated feature about a street-smart young thief in the mythical city of Agrabah who meets and falls in love with the Sultan's beautiful daughter, Jasmine, a young lady who seeks to escape her present lifestyle. Help comes when the evil vizier, Jafar, plots to get a magic lamp for his own rise to power, and decides he needs Aladdin, a true "diamond in the rough," to seek the lamp in the Cave of Wonders. Aladdin and his friend, the monkey Abu, gain the lamp and the wisecracking Genie inside for themselves. The Genie changes Aladdin into a prince so he can woo the princess, but the deception fails to impress Jasmine. As his true self, however, he uses his cunning and courage, with the help of the Genie, to defeat Jafar and his evil plans, in the end earning a princely title and the princess. Initial release on Nov. 11, 1992; general release on Nov. 25, 1992. Directed by John Musker and Ron Clements. 90 min. Aladdin has a speaking voice provided by Scott Weinger and a singing voice by Brad Kane. Other voices are Robin Williams (Genie), Jonathan Freeman (Jafar), Linda Larkin (Jasmine, speaking), Lea Salonga (Jasmine, singing), Gilbert Gottfried (Iago). The idea of adapting the Aladdin story as a Disney animated musical was first proposed by Howard Ashman in 1988 when he and Alan Menken were still working on *The Little Mermaid*. He wrote an initial treatment and collaborated on 6 songs with Menken, including "Arabian Nights," "Friend Like Me," and "Prince Ali." After Ashman's death in 1991, Tim Rice came on board to write some additional songs, notably "One Jump Ahead" and "A Whole New World." The art directors were influenced by Persian miniatures and Arabian calligraphy. Supervising animator Eric Goldberg was the first animator to work on the project; in creating the Genie, he was heavily influenced by the curved, fluid caricature style of artist Al Hirschfeld. Computer-generated imagery enabled the filmmakers to create the amazing magic carpet ride through the Cave of Wonders, the intricately patterned carpet itself, and the stunning tiger head cave. The film won Academy Awards for Best Song ("A Whole New World") and Best Original Score. The film became the highest-grossing animated film to date, earning over $200 million domestically. The video release in 1993 also set records. There were 2 made-for-video sequels: *The Return of Jafar* and *Aladdin and the King of Thieves*.

Aladdin (film) Live-action adaptation of Disney's animated classic. The streets of Agrabah are home to Aladdin, a charming street rat who is eager to leave his life of petty thievery behind, believing he is destined for greater things. Across town, the Sultan's daughter, Princess Jasmine, longs to experience life beyond the palace walls and use her title to better serve the people of Agrabah. After Aladdin accidentally conjures up the Genie, he and Jasmine embark on a dangerous and exciting adventure that will test their faith in themselves and their love for one another. Directed by Guy Ritchie. Released May 24, 2019 (also in 3-D and IMAX 3-D), after a May 22 international release. Stars Will Smith

(Genie/Mariner), Mena Massoud (Aladdin), Naomi Scott (Jasmine), Marwan Kenzari (Jafar), Navid Negahban (Sultan), Nasim Pedrad (Dalia), Billy Magnussen (Prince Anders), Numan Acar (Hakim). 128 min. Includes contemporized recordings of the songs from the 1992 animated feature, with 2 more added—"Speechless" and a new version of "Arabian Nights"—written by original *Aladdin* composer Alan Menken, with songwriters Benj Pasek and Justin Paul. Aladdin's sidekick, Abu, was entirely digital and based on a capuchin monkey. The biggest production number, "Prince Ali," features 250 dancers and 200 extras. Filmed in wide-screen format at Longcross Studios and Arborfield Studios in the U.K. and in the Hashemite Kingdom of Jordan. The desert vistas were shot in Jordan's Wadi Rum and Wadi Disi, where *Lawrence of Arabia* was filmed.

Aladdin (TV) Animated series based on the characters from the 1992 animated feature; premiered on Disney Channel Feb. 6, 1994; in syn. Sep. 5, 1994–Aug. 29, 1997; aired on CBS Sep. 17, 1994–Aug. 24, 1996. Follows the magical and often hilarious escapades of Aladdin, Jasmine, and the others within and beyond the land of Agrabah. Voices include Val Bettin (Sultan), Dan Castellaneta (Genie), Gilbert Gottfried (Iago), Scott Weinger (Aladdin), Linda Larkin (Jasmine), Jason Alexander (Abis Mal), Bebe Neuwirth (Mirage), Michael Jeter (Runtar), Julie Brown (Saleen). 86 episodes.

Aladdin A stage musical version of the animated film, helmed by Casey Nicholaw; opened at Seattle's 5th Avenue Theatre in Jul. 2011. It was intended for licensing to professional and regional theater groups. After that well-received pilot production, along with 2 others in Utah and Missouri, work began on an entirely new version for Broadway—with new script, reordered songs, and an original set design. This show opened in a pre-Broadway engagement at the Ed Mirvish Theatre in Toronto Nov. 13, 2013. The show, with Alan Menken resurrecting songs he had originally written with Howard Ashman for the film, began Broadway previews Feb. 26, 2014, at the New Amsterdam Theatre, and officially opened Mar. 20. The original Broadway cast included Adam Jacobs (Aladdin), James Monroe Iglehart (Genie), Courtney Reed (Jasmine), and Jonathan Freeman, reprising his film role of Jafar. Nominated for 5 Tony Awards, including Best Musical, and won for Best Performance by a Featured Actor in a Musical (Iglehart). In Feb. 2022, Disney Theatrical Pro-

ductions announced that a newly imagined North American tour would launch Oct. 2022, allowing the show to play in cities where the original tour had not played before.

Aladdin: A Musical Spectacular Elaborate, Broadway-caliber live musical stage show presented in the Hyperion Theater in Disney California Adventure, beginning in Dec. 2002, with an official debut Jan. 17, 2003. Generally, the show followed the plot of the movie, though Alan Menken composed 1 new song, "To Be Free," for Jasmine. The Genie usually stole the show with his contemporary pop-culture asides. A version of the show premiered on the *Disney Fantasy* cruise ship in 2012. The show at the Hyperion Theater closed Jan. 10, 2016, after nearly 14,000 performances, to be replaced by a new stage production, *Frozen—Live at the Hyperion*.

Aladdin and the King of Thieves (film) Animated motion picture; released exclusively on video Aug. 13, 1996. The wedding of the century turns into a great adventure, as the legendary Forty Thieves spoil the party in their search for the mysterious Hand of Midas—a magic treasure that turns all things to gold. Aladdin soon learns that his long-lost father is still alive, and the quest to find him leads directly to the secret den of the King of Thieves. This is the 2nd made-for-video sequel to *Aladdin*, following *The Return of Jafar*. A major new character is added to the story: Cassim, Aladdin's father. Directed by Tad Stones. Voices, many returning from the original cast, include Val Bettin, Jim Cummings, Gilbert Gottfried, Linda Larkin, Jerry Orbach (Sa'luk), John Rhys-Davies (Cassim), Scott Weinger, Frank Welker, Robin Williams.

Aladdin on Ice (TV) Special; aired on CBS on Nov. 17, 1995. Directed by Steve Binder. Videotaped on location in Cairo. Stars Kurt Browning (Aladdin) and Kristi Yamaguchi (Jasmine).

Aladdin's Oasis Taking the place of the Tahitian Terrace at Disneyland Jul. 2, 1993, and tied in with the release of *Aladdin*, this dinner theater presented an *Aladdin*-themed show and served "Americanized" Middle Eastern cuisine. The show was discontinued after a few years, but the restaurant opened during peak periods, and beginning in 1997, the venue was used for storytelling. Replaced by The Tropical Hideaway in 2018.

Aladdin's Royal Caravan Parade at Disneyland

ran Apr. 2, 1993–Jun. 1994, and in Disney-MGM Studios Dec. 21, 1992–Aug. 27, 1995, featuring the "Prince Ali" song. On 1 float, golden camels turned their heads from side to side and spit into the crowd lining the street; it was actually kind of refreshing on a summer day if you happened to be in a direct line for the expectorating creatures. The camels were later installed at The Magic Carpets of Aladdin in the Magic Kingdom.

Alameda Slim Yodeling cattle rustler in *Home on the Range*; voiced by Randy Quaid.

Alamo, The (film) An epic retelling of the 1836 battle in San Antonio de Bexar, where fewer than 200 men, led by James Bowie, Lt. Col. William B. Travis, and the legendary Davy Crockett, try to hold the small, ruined mission, the Alamo, against the much larger forces of Mexican general Antonio López de Santa Anna. The Texans and their deeds would pass into history as General Sam Houston's rallying cry for Texas independence and into legend for their symbolic significance. Released Apr. 9, 2004, after a Mar. 27 world premiere in San Antonio. Directed by John Lee Hancock. A Touchstone film. Stars Dennis Quaid (Sam Houston), Billy Bob Thornton (Davy Crockett), Jason Patric (Jim Bowie), Patrick Wilson (Col. William B. Travis), Jordi Mollá (Juan Seguín), Emilio Echevarria (Santa Anna). 137 min. Filmed in CinemaScope on location in Texas, with a 45-acre set of the Alamo and its courtyard built on a private ranch west of Austin. With 70 structures on 51 acres, it was the largest freestanding set ever built in North America.

Alamo Trading Post Wilderness supply shop at Disney Davy Crockett Ranch in Disneyland Paris; opened Apr. 12, 1992, offering apparel, housewares, and fresh produce.

Alan Smithee Film, An: Burn Hollywood Burn (film) This satirical story of the behind-the-scenes intrigue of a big-budget action/adventure Hollywood film reveals director Alan Smithee's bizarre odyssey through a series of interviews with real celebrities and fictional characters. The machinations and agendas of everyone and anyone in filmmaking—from the producer to the makeup artists—are revealed. Smithee makes his directorial debut on the biggest budget action film in Hollywood history, but when he becomes distraught over choices forced upon him by his producer, he takes the master negative hostage. A Hollywood Pictures film in association with Cinergi. Released

Feb. 27, 1998. Directed by Alan Smithee. Stars Ryan O'Neal (James Edmunds), Coolio (Dion Brothers), Chuck D. (Leon Brothers), Richard Jeni (Jerry Glover), Eric Idle (Alan Smithee), and special appearances by Sylvester Stallone, Whoopi Goldberg, Jackie Chan. Screenplay by Joe Eszterhas. "Alan Smithee" is a name that has historically been applied to Hollywood films when the director has asked to have his name removed. 86 min.

Alaska: Dances of the Caribou (TV) Highlights the caribou's annual trek to the magnificent North Slope of the Brooks Range and the pageant of life summertime brings to this breathtaking yet forbidden landscape. Aired in syn. beginning Feb. 14, 2000, as a New True-Life Adventure program. Produced by Bruce Reitherman. 45 min.

Alaska's Bush Pilot Heritage (film) A 16-mm release in Jun. 1973 of film from the TV show *A Salute to Alaska*. It's the story of the special breed of pilot who has challenged the perilous Alaskan landscape.

Alaskan Eskimo, The (film) People and Places featurette; released Feb. 18, 1953. Directed by James Algar. 27 min. Utilized footage shot in Alaska by the team of Alfred and Elma Milotte, depicting the everyday "homelife" of the families in a typical Eskimo village. The building and hunting activities of the summer, the winter activities underground when the blizzards come, and the celebration of spring with the "mask dance" are all shown. Walt Disney originally sent the Milottes to Alaska to film anything they found of interest, but when he selected their footage of the seals (for *Seal Island*) and wanted to present it with no indication of man's presence, there was no use for the rest of their film. So, some of the footage detailing the everyday homelife of Eskimos in a typical village was edited together to become this first People and Places featurette, the forerunner of a number of such travelogues. The project was as successful as *Seal Island* had been, for *The Alaskan Eskimo* also won an Academy Award.

Alaskan Gold Rush, The (film) A 16-mm release in Jun. 1973 of film from the TV show *A Salute to Alaska*. Historical photos in a family album tell the story of the hardy pioneers in the Alaskan gold rush.

Alaskan Sled Dog (film) Featurette released Jul. 3, 1957. Directed by Ben Sharpsteen. Filmed in

CinemaScope. 18 min. The story of an Eskimo father and son who train and groom a sled dog team. When the father is lost on an ice floe, the son takes the unproven team on the search and succeeds in finding his father.

Alberoni, Sherry SEE ALLEN, SHERRY.

Albert Curious monkey companion of Lord Henry Mystic in the Mystic Manor attraction at Hong Kong Disneyland.

Albert, Eddie (1906–2005) Actor; appeared in *Miracle of the White Stallions* (Rider Otto) and *Escape to Witch Mountain* (Jason), and on TV in *Beyond Witch Mountain* and *The Barefoot Executive* (Herbert Gower).

Alberto Scorfano Free-spirited teenage sea monster in *Luca*; voiced by Jack Dylan Grazer.

Albertson, Jack (1910–1981) Character actor; appeared in *The Shaggy Dog* (reporter), *Son of Flubber* (Mr. Barley), and *A Tiger Walks* (Sam Grant), and voiced Amos Slade in *The Fox and the Hound*.

Albright, Milt (1916–2014) Joined Disney in 1947 as a junior accountant and was promoted in 1954 to manager of accounting for Disneyland. He became the manager of Holidayland in 1957 and in 1958 founded the Magic Kingdom Club. He was instrumental in beginning the Grad Nites in 1961. He was named a Disney Legend in 2005.

Alcoholism: Who Gets Hurt? (film) Educational film using sequences from *Follow Me, Boys!* in the Questions!/Answers? series; released in Oct. 1975. Shows a youngster's dilemma in dealing with the problem of an alcohol-addicted parent.

Alda, Alan Actor/director; appeared in *Betsy's Wedding* (Eddie Hopper) and *Bridge of Spies* (Thomas Watters.)

Alden, Norman (1924–2012) Character actor; voiced Sir Kay in *The Sword in the Stone*, also appearing in *Ed Wood* (Cameraman Bill), and on TV in *Sunday Drive* (John Elliott).

Ale & Compass Restaurant New England comfort food and classic seafood dishes served in Disney's Yacht Club Resort at Walt Disney World; opened Nov. 26, 2017, taking the place of Captain's Grille.

Alec Baldwin Show, The (TV) Talk show; aired Oct. 14–Dec. 29, 2018, on ABC, after an initial Mar. 4 episode as *Sundays with Alec Baldwin*.

Aletter, Frank (1926–2009) Actor; appeared in *A Tiger Walks* (Joe Riley), *Now You See Him, Now You Don't* (TV Announcer), and *Run, Cougar, Run* (Sam Davis), and on TV in *The Golden Girls* in 1985 (Harry).

Alex, Inc. (TV) Comedy series on ABC; aired Mar. 28–May 16, 2018. Andy Schuman is a successful radio producer with a wife and 2 children. After years of making the kind of content that brings no creative fulfillment, Alex has an early midlife crisis, deciding to risk everything, including his savings, to start his own podcast business. He quickly realizes that it's going to be a lot harder than he thought. Stars Zach Braff (Alex Schuman), Michael Imperioli (Eddie), Tiya Sircar (Rooni Schuman), Hillary Anne Matthews (Deirdre), Elisha Henig (Ben Schuman), Audyssie James (Soraya Schuman). From Sony Pictures Television and ABC Studios.

Alexander, Jane Actress; appeared in *Night Crossing* (Doris Strelzyk), and on The Disney Channel in *A Friendship in Vienna* (Hannah Dornenwald).

Alexander, Jason Actor; appeared in *Pretty Woman* (Philip Stuckey), and on TV in *Rodgers & Hammerstein's Cinderella* (Lionel) and *Bob Patterson* (title role). He has also provided several voices, including Abis Mal in the *Aladdin* TV series and *The Return of Jafar*, Hugo in *The Hunchback of Notre Dame*, Lightning in *101 Dalmatians II: Patch's London Adventure*, Mr. Nibbles in *Fish Hooks*, and Coach Wallace in *Penn Zero: Part-Time Hero*.

Alexander, Stanley Voice of young Flower in *Bambi*.

Alexander and the Terrible, Horrible, No Good, Very Bad Day (film) Eleven-year-old Alexander experiences the most terrible and horrible day of his young life—a day that begins with gum stuck in his hair, followed by one calamity after another. But when Alexander tells his upbeat family about the misadventures of his disastrous day, he finds little sympathy and begins to wonder if bad things only happen to him. He soon learns that he is not alone when his mom, dad, brother, and sister all find themselves living through their own terrible, horrible, no good, very bad day. Directed by Miguel Arteta. Released Oct. 10, 2014, after an Oct. 6 premiere at the El Capitan Theatre. Stars Ed Oxenbould (Alexander), Jennifer Garner (Kelly), Steve Carell (Ben), Dylan Minette (Anthony), Kerris Dorsey (Emily). Dick Van Dyke makes a cameo. Based on the 1972 book by Judith Viorst. 81 min. Filmed in wide-screen format in the Los Angeles area.

Alford, Phillip Actor; appeared on TV in *Bristle Face* (Jace).

Alfredo's See L'Originale Alfredo di Roma Ristorante.

Algar, James (1912–1998) He joined Disney in 1934 as an animator and worked on *Snow White and the Seven Dwarfs*. Later became animation director on "The Sorcerer's Apprentice" segment of *Fantasia* and sequences of *Bambi* and *The Adventures of Ichabod and Mr. Toad*. Directed several of the True-Life Adventure films, produced *The Gnome-Mobile*, and wrote, produced, and narrated numerous TV shows. Also contributed to the Disney parks as writer/producer of shows, including Great Moments with Mr. Lincoln, The Hall of Presidents, and Circle-Vision 360. He retired in 1977 and was honored as a Disney Legend in 1998.

Alias (TV) One-hour action drama on ABC; aired Sep. 30, 2001–May 22, 2006. A 26-year-old graduate student, Sydney Bristow, discovers that her employer, SD-6, is not part of the government but instead is an enemy organization. She goes undercover at SD-6 as a double agent while actually working with the CIA. Her greatest ally is another fellow double agent: her father. Stars Jennifer Garner (Sydney Bristow), Victor Garber (Jack Bristow), Ron Rifkin (Arvin Sloane), Michael Vartan (Agent Vaughn), Carl Lumbly (Agent Dixon), Kevin Weisman (Marshall), Greg Grunberg (Eric Weiss), Mia Maestro (Nadia Santos). From Touchstone Television. The show earned 36 Emmy nominations, winning 4.

Alice and the Dog Catcher (film) Alice Comedy released Jul. 1, 1924.

Alice and the Three Bears (film) Alice Comedy released Dec. 1, 1924.

Alice at the Carnival (film) Alice Comedy released Feb. 7, 1927.

Alice at the Rodeo See Alice's Rodeo.

Alice Bluebonnet Girlfriend of Johnny Fedora in the segment about the romance between 2 hats in *Make Mine Music*.

Alice Cans the Cannibals (film) Alice Comedy released Jan. 1, 1925.

Alice Charms the Fish (film) Alice Comedy released Sep. 6, 1926.

Alice Chops the Suey (film) Alice Comedy released in 1925.

Alice Comedies Series of 56 silent cartoons made by Walt Disney between 1924–1927, with a live girl acting in Cartoonland. Walt first hired 4-year-old Virginia Davis and then Margie Gay, Dawn O'Day, and Lois Hardwick to be the little Alice romping in a cartoon world. Enthusiastically, he sent out the first unfinished pilot film, *Alice's Wonderland*, to cartoon distributors in New York City. One of them, Margaret Winkler, agreed to distribute the series, with payment beginning at $1,500 per reel. The pilot film had been made in Kansas City, and all 56 of the films in the series were made in Hollywood. Winkler married Charles Mintz, and he continued dealing with Walt Disney until 1927, when Disney tired of combining live action and animation and switched instead to the Oswald the Lucky Rabbit series. The signing of the contract to distribute the Alice Comedies, on Oct. 16, 1923, is considered the official start of the Disney company.

Alice Cuts the Ice (film) Alice Comedy released Nov. 1, 1926.

Alice Foils the Pirates (film) Alice Comedy released Jan. 24, 1927.

Alice Gets in Dutch (film) Alice Comedy released Nov. 1, 1924.

Alice Gets Stung (film) Alice Comedy released Feb. 1, 1925.

Alice Helps the Romance (film) Alice Comedy released Nov. 15, 1926.

Alice Hunting in Africa (film) Alice Comedy released Nov. 15, 1924.

Alice in the Alps (film) Alice Comedy released Mar. 21, 1927.

Alice in the Big League (film) Alice Comedy released Aug. 22, 1927.

Alice in the Jungle (film) Alice Comedy released Dec. 15, 1925.

Alice in the Klondike (film) Alice Comedy released Jun. 27, 1927.

Alice in the Wooly West (film) Alice Comedy released Oct. 4, 1926.

Alice in Wonderland (film) Animated version of Lewis Carroll's famous story of Alice and her adventures after falling down a rabbit hole. Following a White Rabbit, she meets such strange creatures as a talking doorknob, who helps her through a keyhole into Wonderland; Tweedledum and Tweedledee, who tell the story of "The Walrus and the Carpenter"; the Caterpillar; and the Mad Hatter and the March Hare celebrating an *unbirthday* at their tea party. Finally Alice has a showdown with the Queen of Hearts and her army of playing cards. The whole thing becomes such a nightmare that Alice awakens from her dream to the recitations of her sister and the purring of her cat, Dinah. Voices include Kathryn Beaumont (Alice), Verna Felton (Queen of Hearts), Bill Thompson (White Rabbit), Ed Wynn (Mad Hatter), Jerry Colonna (March Hare), Sterling Holloway (Cheshire Cat). Premiered in England Jul. 26, 1951, and released in the U.S. 2 days later. Directed by Clyde Geronimi, Hamilton S. Luske, Wilfred Jackson. Songs include "All in the Golden Afternoon" and "I'm Late," by Bob Hilliard and Sammy Fain, and "The Unbirthday Song," by Mack David, Al Hoffman, and Jerry Livingston. 75 min. Nominated for an Academy Award for Best Scoring of a Musical Picture. This animated feature had been on Walt Disney's mind since 1933, when he considered a live-action version starring Mary Pickford. He shelved the project after Paramount made a version but later had artist David Hall, a Hollywood artist and designer, create some concepts for an all-animated film. World War II intervened, and it was not until the late 1940s that work began again in earnest. One of Walt's big problems was that here he was dealing with a highly regarded classic, and what was charming and appropriately bizarre in book form seemed oddly out of place on the motion picture screen. Walt's feeling, expressed in later years, was that Alice had no "heart." An edited version aired on TV Nov. 3, 1954. The film was rediscovered by the psychedelic generation, when it was made available on 16 mm for schools, and it was rereleased in theaters in 1974 and 1981. First released on video in 1981.

Alice in Wonderland (film) Nineteen-year-old Alice, trying to escape from an unwanted marriage proposal, falls down a hole and returns to the whimsical world she first encountered as a young girl. She has no memory of her previous visit, and her childhood friends—the Mad Hatter, White Rabbit, Tweedledee and Tweedledum, March Hare, Dormouse, Caterpillar, and Cheshire Cat— wonder if she is the right Alice. She embarks on a fantastical journey through what she is told is really called Underland to find her true destiny, as predicted in a magical scroll, and end the Red Queen's reign of terror. Directed by Tim Burton. Released Mar. 5, 2010, in regular, 3-D, and IMAX versions, after a Feb. 25, 2010, Royal World Premiere in London. Stars Mia Wasikowska (Alice), Johnny Depp (Mad Hatter), Helena Bonham Carter (Iracebeth, the Red Queen), Anne Hathaway (White Queen), Crispin Glover (The Knave of Hearts), Matt Lucas (Tweedledee and Tweedledum), Leo Bill (Hamish); with the voices of Alan Rickman (Absolem, the Blue Caterpillar), Stephen Fry (Cheshire Cat), Michael Sheen (White Rabbit), Timothy Spall (Bayard), Christopher Lee (Jabberwocky), Paul Whitehouse (March Hare), Barbara Windsor (Dormouse). 109 min. Based on the books by Lewis Carroll. Tim Burton and Johnny Depp had earlier collaborated on *Ed Wood* for Disney. Danny Elfman composed the score. Nominated for 3 Academy Awards, winning for Art Direction (Robert Stromberg, Karen O'Hara) and Costume Design (Colleen Atwood).

Alice in Wonderland Fantasyland dark ride attraction in Disneyland, opened Jun. 14, 1958. Closed Sep. 6, 1982–Apr. 13, 1984, for a major remodeling. Kathryn Beaumont, who provided the voice for Alice in the 1951 motion picture, returned to record narration tracks for the attraction. New special effects and enhancements were introduced Jul. 4, 2014.

Alice in Wonderland: A Lesson in Appreciating Differences (film) Educational film; released in Sep. 1978. The film stresses appreciating others for their differences is an important quality in mature young people.

Alice in Wonderland Maze Fantasyland attraction in Shanghai Disneyland inspired by the live action *Alice in Wonderland*; opened Jun. 16, 2016. Guests choose their own path and wind through giant hedges and flowers on their way to the Mad Hatter's tea party, encountering characters along the way. FOR THE DISNEYLAND PARIS ATTRACTION, SEE ALICE'S CURIOUS LABYRINTH.

Alice Loses Out (film) Alice Comedy released in 1925.

Alice on the Farm (film) Alice Comedy released Jan. 1, 1926.

Alice Picks the Champ (film) Alice Comedy released in 1925.

Alice Plays Cupid (film) Alice Comedy released Oct. 15, 1925.

Alice Rattled by Rats (film) Alice Comedy released Nov. 15, 1925.

Alice Solves the Puzzle (film) Alice Comedy released Feb. 15, 1925.

Alice Stage Struck (film) Alice Comedy released in 1925.

Alice the Beach Nut (film) Alice Comedy released Aug. 8, 1927.

Alice the Collegiate (film) Alice Comedy released Mar. 7, 1927.

Alice the Fire Fighter (film) Alice Comedy released Oct. 18, 1926.

Alice the Golf Bug (film) Alice Comedy released Jan. 10, 1927.

Alice the Jail Bird (film) Alice Comedy released Sep. 15, 1925.

Alice the Lumber Jack (film) Alice Comedy released Dec. 27, 1926.

Alice the Peacemaker (film) Alice Comedy released Aug. 1, 1924.

Alice the Piper (film) Alice Comedy released Dec. 15, 1924.

Alice the Toreador (film) Alice Comedy released Jan. 15, 1925.

Alice the Whaler (film) Alice Comedy released Jul. 25, 1927.

Alice Through the Looking Glass (film) Alice has spent the past few years following in her father's footsteps and sailing the high seas. Upon her return to London, she comes across a magical looking glass and returns to the fantastical realm of Underland and her friends the White Rabbit, Absolem, the Cheshire Cat, and the Mad Hatter. The Hatter has lost his Muchness, so Mirana, the White Queen, sends Alice on a quest to borrow the Chronosphere, a metallic globe inside the chamber of the Grand Clock, which powers all time. Returning to the past, she comes across friends and enemies at different points in their lives and embarks on a perilous race to save the Hatter before time runs out. Directed by James Bobin and produced by Tim Burton. Released May 27, 2016, also in 3-D and IMAX, after a May 25 release in Italy. Stars Johnny Depp (Mad Hatter), Anne Hathaway (Mirana), Mia Wasikowska (Alice Kingsleigh), Rhys Ifans (Zanik Hightopp), Helena Bonham Carter (Red Queen); with the voices of Alan Rickman (Absolem, the Blue Caterpillar), Stephen Fry (Cheshire Cat), Michael Sheen (White Rabbit), Timothy Spall (Bayard). 113 min. Based on characters created by Lewis Carroll. A follow-up to the 2010 film *Alice in Wonderland*, directed by Tim Burton. Filmed in the U.K.

Alice Wins the Derby (film) Alice Comedy released in 1925.

Alice's Auto Race (film) Alice Comedy released Apr. 4, 1927.

Alice's Balloon Race (film) Alice Comedy released Jan. 15, 1926.

Alice's Brown Derby (film) Alice Comedy released Dec. 13, 1926.

Alice's Channel Swim (film) Alice Comedy released Jun. 13, 1927.

Alice's Circus Daze (film) Alice Comedy released Apr. 18, 1927.

Alice's Curious Labyrinth Maze attraction in Fantasyland at Disneyland Paris; opened Apr. 12, 1992. Guests try to find their way through the hedgerows to a castle, encountering various surprises along the way.

Alice's Day at Sea (film) First of the Alice Comedies; released Mar. 1, 1924. The first 6 Alice Comedies had extensive live-action beginnings, then went into the cartoon world. Beginning with the 7th cartoon, Walt Disney dispensed with the long live-action introductions. In this first film, Alice goes to the seashore with her dog and falls asleep in a rowboat. The cartoon segment features a shipwreck and battles with fish, birds, and an octopus.

Alice's Egg Plant (film) Alice Comedy released in 1925.

Alice's Fishy Story (film) Alice Comedy released Jun. 1, 1924.

Alice's Knaughty Knight (film) Alice Comedy released May 2, 1927.

Alice's Little Parade (film) Alice Comedy released Feb. 1, 1926.

Alice's Medicine Show (film) Alice Comedy released Jul. 11, 1927.

Alice's Monkey Business (film) Alice Comedy released Sep. 20, 1926.

Alice's Mysterious Mystery (film) Alice Comedy released Feb. 15, 1926.

Alice's Orphan (film) Alice Comedy released in 1926. An alternate title was *Alice's Ornery Orphan*.

Alice's Picnic (film) Alice Comedy released May 30, 1927.

Alice's Rodeo (film) Alice Comedy released Feb. 21, 1927. An alternate title was *Alice at the Rodeo*.

Alice's Spanish Guitar (film) Alice Comedy released Nov. 29, 1926.

Alice's Spooky Adventure (film) Alice Comedy released Apr. 1, 1924.

Alice's Tea Party Fantasyland attraction in Tokyo Disneyland; opened Mar. 8, 1986. Guests board a colorful teacup for a spin around a giant teapot. SEE ALSO MAD TEA PARTY (DISNEYLAND AND WALT DISNEY WORLD) AND MAD HATTER'S TEA CUPS (DISNEYLAND PARIS AND HONG KONG DISNEYLAND).

Alice's Three Bad Eggs (film) Alice Comedy released May 16, 1927.

Alice's Tin Pony (film) Alice Comedy released in 1925.

Alice's Wild West Show (film) Alice Comedy released May 1, 1924.

Alice's Wonderland (film) Pilot film for the Alice Comedy series made by Walt Disney in Kansas City in 1923. Alice visits an animation studio. Later she dreams that she goes to Cartoonland, dances for the animals, and is chased by lions that escape from the zoo. This film was never released as part of the series. Virginia Davis starred as Alice in this initial effort, and when Walt Disney moved to California and was able to sell a series based on this pilot film, he persuaded the Davis family to move west also, bringing young Virginia to continue in the role of Alice.

Alice's Wonderland Bakery (TV) Animated series; premiered Feb. 9, 2022, on Disney Channel, Disney Junior, and Disney+. Alice is a budding young baker at the enchanted Wonderland Bakery, where her magical treats help bring a new generation of friends and families together. Voices include Libby Rue (Alice), Abigail Estrella (Princess Rosa), CJ Uy (Hattie), Jack Stanton (Fergie, the White Rabbit), Secunda Wood (Cookie), Audrey Wasilewski (Dinah), Max Mittelman (Cheshire Cat). A new take on the 1951 animated film, with Alice as the great-granddaughter of the original heroine. From Disney Television Animation.

Alien Encounter SEE EXTRATERRORESTRIAL ALIEN ENCOUNTER, THE.

Alien Encounters from New Tomorrowland (TV) Syn. special aired Feb. 27, 1995. Directed by Andy Thomas. Robert Urich hosts a pseudo-documentary on the history of UFO sightings, which is used to introduce a brief look at The ExtraTERRORestrial Alien Encounter attraction and the newly remodeled New Tomorrowland in the Magic Kingdom at Walt Disney World. Produced by Walt Disney World.

Alien Pizza Planet SEE REDD ROCKETT'S PIZZA PORT.

Alien Swirling Saucers Toy Story Land attraction in Disney's Hollywood Studios; opened Jun. 30, 2018. In a giant Pizza Planet toy set, guests ride around in rockets that are pulled by flying saucers piloted by the Toy Story aliens.

Aliens of the Deep (film) Documentary; a team of young oceanographers and NASA scientists study, among other things, an ecosystem 2½ miles below the surface of the ocean that has hypothermal vents at its core. Directed by James Cameron. Released Jan. 28, 2005. A Walt Disney Pictures and Walden Media presentation of an Earthship production. For large-format/IMAX theaters, filmed in 70 mm. 47 min. Released on DVD in 2005.

Alive (film) In 1972, an airplane carrying a rugby team of Uruguayan college students crashed in the Andes en route to a game in Chile. Flying in poor visibility, the plane's wing clipped the side of a mountain, and the aircraft came to rest on the snow-covered Tinguiririca volcano at 11,500 feet. Several of the passengers and most of the crew died instantly, but the majority survived and waited to be rescued. On the 8th day, they learned via transistor radio that official search operations had been abandoned. Soon their food and drink were gone, and facing a certain future of starvation and death, they resorted to cannibalism. Finally, after 10 weeks, 2 men, Nando and Roberto, left camp and bravely traveled over the Andes, where they were able to find help. Directed by Frank Marshall. Released Jan. 15, 1993. A Touchstone film, co-produced with Paramount Pictures, with the latter handling international distribution. Based on the book by Piers Paul Read. 126 min. Stars Ethan Hawke (Nando Parrado), Vincent Spano (Antonio Balbi), Josh Hamilton (Roberto Canassa). The producers were able to obtain the usage of the exact type of aircraft involved in the crash—a Fairchild F-227 twin-engine turboprop. The plane crash was one of the most realistic ever filmed. Doubling for the actual location, the filmmakers used the Delphine glacier at an altitude of 9,500 feet in the Columbia Mountains near Panorama, British Columbia, Canada. The actual survivors of the crash were consulted to make the production as accurate as possible, and one of them, Nando Parrado, served

as technical adviser. A special video entitled *Alive: 20 Years Later* was also released in 1993.

All About Magic (TV) Show aired Jan. 30, 1957, with Walt using the Magic Mirror to act as emcee to explain about magic. Directed by Hamilton S. Luske. Stars Hans Conried as the Magic Mirror, from *Snow White and the Seven Dwarfs*, showing 2 magic-themed cartoons, as well as the "Bibbidi-Bobbidi-Boo" sequence from *Cinderella* and "The Sorcerer's Apprentice" segment from *Fantasia*.

All About the Washingtons (TV) Family sitcom on Netflix; digitally released Aug. 10, 2018. After Joey Washington decides to retire from a long career as a popular hip-hop artist, his wife, Justine, takes advantage of the opportunity to pursue a career of her own. Stars Joseph Simmons (Joey), Justine Simmons (Justine), Kiana Ledé (Veronica), Nathan Anderson (Wesley), Leah Rose Randall (Skyler), Maceo Smedley (Deavon). The show is autobiographical, with the principal actors playing fictionalized versions of themselves. From Amblin Television and ABC Signature.

All About Weightlessness (film) A 16-mm educational release of a portion of *Man in Space*; aired in Sep. 1964. Humans experience many unique problems as they venture into outer space.

All-American College Band Program begun at Disneyland in 1971 and Walt Disney World in 1972, welcoming talented college musicians from across the country to perform at one of the parks for the summer season. The name was changed to the Collegiate All-Star Band in 1998 but reverted to the original name in 2002. The next year marked Art Bartner's 25th year conducting the band at Disneyland. The Walt Disney World program was canceled after summer 2000, with the exception of a onetime group of 5 musicians in summer 2001.

All-American Girl (TV) Series on ABC; aired Sep. 14, 1994–Mar. 22, 1995. Explores the cultural and generational conflicts that arise between a free-spirited, completely assimilated Korean American college student Margaret Kim and her more conservative, traditional family. Stars Margaret Cho (Margaret Kim), Jodi Long (Mother), Clyde Kusatsu (Dad), Amy Hill (Grandma), Maddie Corman (Ruthie). From Touchstone Television.

All Because Man Wanted to Fly (film) Lighthearted look at early human efforts to fly, hosted by Orville, the albatross from *The Rescuers*, for the preshow of *American Journeys*, PSA's Circle-Vision 360 attraction in Disneyland. Premiered Jul. 4, 1984, and ran for 5 years. Includes footage from earlier Disney films, such as *It's Tough to Be a Bird*.

All in a Nutshell (film) Donald Duck cartoon. Donald steals Chip and Dale's nuts for his nut-butter shop, which is shaped like a giant walnut. Thinking the shop is a real nut, the chipmunks crack open the roof and steal the nut butter, with Donald chasing after them. When Donald runs into a tree and knocks himself silly, Chip and Dale load him into a log like a cannonball and drop a hornets nest into the log to "shoot" Donald into a nearby lake. Released Sep. 2, 1949; directed by Jack Hannah.

All in the Golden Afternoon Song from *Alice in Wonderland*; written by Bob Hilliard and Sammy Fain.

All New Adventure of Disney's Sport Goofy, An; Featuring Sport Goofy in Soccermania (TV) Special on NBC; aired May 27, 1987. 60 min. Directed by John Klawitter. Several Goofy and Mickey Mouse cartoons are shown, followed by *Sport Goofy in Soccermania*, a new Goofy cartoon, which debuted here. Uncle Scrooge agrees to sponsor the nephews' soccer team in order to get back a valuable trophy, which he mistakenly donated. The Beagle Boys are also after the trophy, and it is up to Sport Goofy to save the day. This cartoon was directed by Matt O'Callaghan.

All Star Cafe A 240-seat restaurant at Disney's Wide World of Sports at Walt Disney World; opened Feb. 26, 1998, also known as the Official All Star Cafe. Originally operated by Planet Hollywood International, but Disney took over the lease in Mar. 2000. Closed Sep. 30, 2007, reopening Nov. 21 as What's Next Café. It became ESPN Wide World of Sports Grill in 2010.

All-Star Resorts Moderate-priced group of hotels adorned with enormous, themed icons at Walt Disney World. Disney's All-Star Sports Resort premiered first, 1 unit at a time, beginning with the Apr. 29, 1994, opening of the Surf's Up rooms. Later units were Hoops Hotel (basketball), Touchdown (football), Home Run Hotel (baseball), and Center Court (tennis), which was the last to open (Aug. 11). Also includes the End Zone Food Court, Sport Goofy Gifts and Sundries, and the Surfboard Bay and Grand Slam Pools. Disney's

All-Star Music Resort followed in Nov. 1994, also opening in phases; the units are Calypso, Jazz, Rock Inn, Country Fair, and Broadway. Includes the Intermission Food Court, Maestro Mickey's shop, and the Calypso and Piano Pools. Disney's All-Star Movies Resort, added in 1999 (with the first rooms opening Jan. 15), includes units themed to *The Mighty Ducks*, *One Hundred and One Dalmatians*, *The Love Bug*, *Fantasia*, and *Toy Story*. Includes the World Premiere Food Court, Donald's Double Feature shop, and Fantasia Pool.

All the Cats Join In (film) Segment of *Make Mine Music* featuring Benny Goodman and his Orchestra, with an animated pencil drawing a group of lively teenagers having a jitterbug session at the local malt shop. The song is by Alec Wilder, Ray Gilbert, and Eddie Sauter.

All Together (film) Shows the advisability and necessity of purchasing Canadian war bonds. Made for the National Film Board of Canada and delivered Jan. 13, 1942. Mickey and the gang, including Pinocchio and Geppetto, lead a parade to help sell the war bonds.

All Wet (film) Oswald the Lucky Rabbit cartoon; released Oct. 31, 1927. Oswald takes the place of a lifeguard in an attempt to woo a dashing rabbit.

Allan-a-Dale Rooster narrator of *Robin Hood*; voiced by Roger Miller.

Allen, Barbara Jo (1906–1974) Actress; voiced Fauna in *Sleeping Beauty*, Goliath's mother in *Goliath II*, and the scullery maid in *The Sword in the Stone*.

Allen, Bob (1932–1987) He joined Disneyland in 1955 as a ride operator and later spent 2 years as the manager of the Celebrity Sports Center in Denver and as a project manager for the proposed Mineral King resort in California. He became director of General Services at Disneyland in 1968, 2 years later moving to Walt Disney World with the same title. In Florida, he became vice president of Resorts and, on Jan. 1, 1977, was promoted to vice president of Walt Disney World, a position he held until his untimely death in 1987. He was named a Disney Legend posthumously in 1996.

Allen, Rex (1920–1999) Actor/singer; with his distinctive homey western voice, he narrated such features and TV shows as *The Saga of Windwagon*

Smith, *The Legend of Lobo*; *The Incredible Journey*; *An Otter in the Family*; *Run, Appaloosa, Run*; *Cow Dog*; *Ringo, the Refugee Raccoon*; *Seems There Was This Moose*; *My Family Is a Menagerie*; and *Foods and Fun: A Nutrition Adventure*. He voiced the father in the Carousel of Progress (1964–1973) and the grandfather in the 1993 version. He was named a Disney Legend in 1996.

Allen, Sherry Mouseketeer from the 1950s *Mickey Mouse Club* TV show. Her real name is Sherry Alberoni.

Allen, Tim Actor/comedian; starred in *The Shaggy Dog* (Dave Douglas, 2006), *The Santa Clause* and its sequels (Scott Calvin), *Jungle 2 Jungle* (Michael Cromwell), *Big Trouble* (Eliot Arnold), and *Wild Hogs* (Doug Madden), and on TV in *Home Improvement* (Tim Taylor), *Disney's Great American Celebration*, and *The Dream Is Alive*. He voiced Buzz Lightyear in the Toy Story films and other appearances of the character, including *Ralph Breaks the Internet* and on TV in *Buzz Lightyear of Star Command*. Also narrated *Chimpanzee*. His book, *Don't Stand Too Close to a Naked Man*, was published in 1994 by Hyperion. For a time that year, he had the honor of starring in the No. 1 TV series, the No. 1 motion picture, and having the No. 1 book on the bestseller lists. For Disney+, he starred in and exec. produced *The Santa Clauses*. He was named a Disney Legend in 1999.

Allen, Woody Actor/director; appeared in *New York Stories* (Sheldon) and *Scenes from a Mall* (Nick).

Allers, Roger Story man/director; joined Disney in 1985 and was head of story for *Oliver & Company* and *Beauty and the Beast*. After working on the stories for other animated features, he made his feature film directing debut with Rob Minkoff on *The Lion King*. He later directed *The Little Matchgirl*.

Alley, Kirstie (1951–2022) Actress; appeared in *Shoot to Kill* (Sarah) and on TV in *Mickey's 60th Birthday*, *The Wonderful World of Disney: 40 Years of Television Magic* (host), and *Toothless* (Dr. Katherine Lewis).

Alley, Lindsey Actress; appeared in *Ernest Saves Christmas* (Patsy) and *Bedtime Stories* (Hokey Pokey Woman); on Disney Channel as a regular on the *Mickey Mouse Club* beginning in 1989, and as

Judy in *I Didn't Do It*; and as the stage mom in *Marvel's Jessica Jones*.

Alley Cats Strike! (TV) A Disney Channel Original Movie; first aired Mar. 18, 2000. Four hip teens are content with their nonconformist attitudes, retro styles of dress, and an interest in bowling and lounge music that have made them outcasts among their classmates at West Appleton Middle School. But when an annual interschool competition ends in a tie, the school has to turn to bowling to break it, and suddenly the teens are thrust into the spotlight, with the most popular and athletic kid in school, who has never bowled, added to their team. The teens must set aside their differences and learn to work together. Directed by Rod Daniel. Stars Kyle Schmid (Alex Thompson), Robert Ri'chard (Todd McLemore), Kaley Cuoco (Elisa), Mimi Paley (Delia), Joey Wilcots (Ken).

Allwine, Wayne (1947–2009) He took a job in the Disney Studio mail room in 1966, soon thereafter becoming a sound effects technician. He provided the voice of Mickey Mouse beginning in 1977, with his debut in *The New Mickey Mouse Club*, and continued as Mickey's official voice in films, theme parks, TV shows, records, video games, and consumer products. He learned his craft from veteran Disney sound effects wizard, and the previous voice of Mickey, Jimmy Macdonald. In 1991, he married Russi Taylor, the voice of Minnie Mouse and other characters. He was named a Disney Legend in 2008.

Almost Angels (film) The young Toni Fiala is a boy born to sing, and his greatest desire is to be accepted as one of the members of the Vienna Boys Choir. His father, a railroad engineer, wants his son to learn a trade, but his mother knows her son must be given a chance to sing. The mother makes the opportunity possible, and the boy wins his way into the choir. This story of the training, travel, and adventures of the boys within this famous institution is accompanied by the beautiful music of the choir. Toni's admiration for the oldest boy in the choir, Peter Schaefer, is tested when Peter's voice begins to change, and Toni convinces the other members of the choir to cover for him. When Peter is finally found out, he is able to obtain a position as assistant conductor. Released Sep. 26, 1962. Directed by Steve Previn. The international release title was *Born to Sing*. 93 min. Stars Peter Weck (Max Heller), Sean Scully (Peter Schaefer), Vincent Winter (Toni Fiala), Denis Gilmore (Friedel

Schmidt), Hans Holt (Elsinger), Fritz Eckhardt (Herr Fiala), Bruni Lobel (Frau Fiala), Gunther Philipp (radio commentator), the Vienna Boys Choir. Filmed on location in Austria.

Almost Home (TV) Series; aired on NBC Feb. 6–Jul. 3, 1993. Continued the story of *The Torkelsons*. Seattle businessman Brian Morgan has offered homespun Millicent Torkelson a job as the live-in nanny to his 2 rebellious teenagers, so the Torkelson clan packs up their small-town life in Pyramid Corners, Oklahoma, and heads for the big city. Blending the 2 families is as natural as mixing oil and water, but with her sunny approach to life, Millicent sets out to bridge the gap. Stars Connie Ray (Millicent Torkelson), Olivia Burnette (Dorothy Jane), Lee Norris (Chuckie Lee), Rachel Duncan (Mary Sue), Perry King (Brian Morgan), Brittany Murphy (Molly Morgan), Jason Marsden (Gregory Morgan). From Touchstone Television.

Almost There Song from *The Princess and the Frog*; written by Randy Newman. Nominated for an Academy Award.

Aloha Isle Refreshments Adventureland refreshment stand, serving Dole Whip, floats, and pineapple spears, in the Magic Kingdom at Walt Disney World; opened in 1982, presented by Dole. Formerly the Veranda Juice Bar. On Mar. 12, 2015, it switched locations with Sunshine Tree Terrace.

Alone Together (TV) Half-hour comedy on Freeform, Jan. 10–Aug 29, 2018. Misfits Esther and Benji are platonic best friends who want nothing more than to be accepted by the vain and status-obsessed culture of Los Angeles. Despite their at times contentious relationship, when push comes to shove, they've got each other's back—and they have nobody else to hang out with. Stars Esther Povitsky (Esther), Benji Aflalo (Benji), Chris D'Elia (Dean), Ginger Gonzaga (Alia), Edgar Blackmon (Jeff), Nikki Glaser (Annette). From The Lonely Island.

Along the Oregon Trail (TV) Show aired Nov. 14, 1956, as a behind-the-scenes look at the filming of *Westward Ho the Wagons!* Directed by William Beaudine. Walt Disney describes the Oregon Trail, then turns to Fess Parker, one of the stars of the film, to give a behind-the-scenes look at the production and, with Jeff York, to show how the pioneers lived and the hardships they faced. Iron Eyes

Cody and Sebastian Cabot, both also in the feature, tell how the Native Americans and the pioneers were suspicious of each other.

Alonzo Hawk Villain role played by actor Keenan Wynn in *The Absent-Minded Professor*, *Son of Flubber*, and *Herbie Rides Again*, all films written/produced by Bill Walsh.

Alpine Climbers (film) Mickey Mouse cartoon released Jul. 25, 1936. Directed by Dave Hand. In the mountains, Pluto and a friendly Saint Bernard imbibe from the big dog's keg of brandy after Pluto is rescued, and Mickey runs afoul of a mother eagle necessitating rescue by Donald Duck.

Alpine Gardens Quiet garden surrounding a pond between Tomorrowland and Fantasyland in Disneyland; once the site of the Monsanto House of the Future. It became Triton Gardens in Feb. 1996, Ariel's Grotto in 1997, and Pixie Hollow in Oct. 2008.

Alpine Haus Fantasyland sandwich stand in Tokyo Disneyland; open Mar. 20, 1985–Jan. 31, 1998, taking the place of Ice Cream Fantasy.

Al's Toy Barn Shop based on the toy store in *Toy Story 2*; opened Apr. 26, 2018, in Disney-Pixar Toy Story Land at Shanghai Disneyland. Also a character-greeting spot at Disney-MGM Studios, Jul. 27, 2000–2008.

Aluminum Hall of Fame SEE HALL OF ALUMINUM FAME.

Aly and AJ Pop-rock band featuring sisters Alyson and Amanda (AJ) Michalka, recording for Hollywood Records 2004–2010. In 2009 they changed their band's name to 78violet. Alyson appeared on Disney Channel in *Now You See It* (Allyson Miller) and *Phil of the Future* (Kelly Teslow); Amanda appeared in *Secretariat* (Kate Tweedy). They both starred in *Cow Belles* (Taylor and Courtney Callum).

Ama Girls (film) People and Places featurette released Jul. 9, 1958. Directed by Ben Sharpsteen. A typical day in the life of a family of fisherfolk of Japan. The elder daughter is an Ama, or diving girl, who collects "Heaven Grass," a variety of seaweed, as a crop. The girls' training is studied as well as the teamwork and stamina needed to harvest this marine crop. Filmed in CinemaScope. 29 min.

Academy Award winner. A 16 mm release as *Japan Harvests the Sea*.

'AMA'AMA – Contemporary Island Cooking Oceanfront restaurant at Aulani, A Disney Resort & Spa; opened Aug. 29, 2011, serving a melding of Hawaiian, Asian, and European specialties. Named after a type of mullet fish native to Hawai'i, it is themed as an 1890s beachside house that has expanded over the years.

Amazing Race, The (TV) Reality-adventure series pitting 11 teams against each other in a worldwide 30- to 40-day journey, with the first team to reach the final destination winning $1 million. Airing on CBS, it premiered Sep. 5, 2001. Hosted by Phil Keoghan. From Touchstone Television (later ABC Studios), in association with CBS Productions. The show won the Emmy Award for reality-competition program each year 2003–2009, 2011–2012, and in 2014.

Amazon Awakens, The (film) Educational film produced under the auspices of the Coordinator of Inter-American Affairs; travelogue on the history and geography of the Amazon basin, with information on the Ford Plantation at Fordlandia and the ambitious rubber program there. Delivered May 29, 1944.

Ambassador Beginning with Julie Reihm in 1965, Disneyland has selected a Cast Member to act as "Disneyland ambassador to the world." The ambassador serves as an emissary of goodwill—participating in community outreach, parades, TV and radio interviews, and other worldwide events—and hosts special visitors to Disneyland. Walt Disney World continued the tradition, beginning in 1971 with Debby Dane, as did Tokyo Disneyland in 1983 (Yaeko Terasaki); Disneyland Paris in 1991 (Sabine Marcon); Hong Kong Disneyland Resort in 2005 (Angela To); and Aulani, A Disney Resort & Spa (Janelle Sanqui) and Shanghai Disney Resort (Jennie Xu) in 2015. There is a detailed selection process among the Cast Members at each resort, with each judged on such qualities as poise and personality. For 1995, the program was changed at Disneyland and Walt Disney World to allow for a team of ambassadors, and males were included for the first time.

Ambition: What Price Fulfillment? (film) Educational film, using sequences from *Third Man on the Mountain*. In the Questions!/Answers? series; released in 1976. A boy's greatest ambition is to climb the mountain that took his father's life; should he give up that dream to save the life of a man he hates?

Ambrose Kitten star of *The Robber Kitten* (1935).

Ambush at Laredo (TV) Show, part 2 of *Texas John Slaughter*.

Ambush at Wagon Gap (TV) Title of part 1 of *Westward Ho the Wagons!*

Ameche, Don (1908–1993) Actor; appeared in *The Boatniks* (Commander Taylor), *Oscar* (Father Clemente), on TV in *Our Shining Moment*, and as the voice of Shadow in *Homeward Bound: The Incredible Journey*.

Amemiya, Hideo (1944–2001) He spent 30 years with Disney in the area of hotel management, starting out with the Polynesian Village at Walt Disney World in 1971, working on the Tokyo Disneyland project, and ending his career as senior vice president of Disneyland Resort Hotels. He was named a Disney Legend in 2005.

America Gardens Theatre Amphitheater in front of The American Adventure at EPCOT; opened Oct. 1, 1982. International groups often perform song and dance presentations tied to the countries of World Showcase. In 1993 the theater was partially enclosed and temporarily remodeled for *The Magical World of Barbie* show. Since 1994, the annual *Candlelight Processional* has been presented during the holidays, and concerts have been held here for the park's annual festival programs.

America on Parade Special American Bicentennial parade; ran at Walt Disney World Jun. 6, 1975–Sep. 6, 1976, and at Disneyland Jun. 12, 1975–Sep. 12, 1976. Disney designers, led by entertainment head Bob Jani, came up with elaborate floats—along with 150 larger-than-life, doll-like characters, called the "People of America"—that presented the story of America's history, culture, and achievements, from its pioneers to the present, all marching to a soundtrack of American popular songs recorded from a band organ, the Sadie Mae. The parade was led by Mickey Mouse, Donald Duck, and Goofy as the "Spirit of '76."

America on Parade (TV) Special for the American Bicentennial starring Red Skelton, featuring the

America on Parade pageant at Disneyland; aired Apr. 3, 1976. Directed by Clark Jones.

America Sings Tomorrowland attraction in the carousel theater at Disneyland; ran Jun. 29, 1974–Apr. 10, 1988, taking the place of the Carousel of Progress when that attraction moved to Walt Disney World. A total of 114 Audio-Animatronics animals presented a history of American popular music in 4 main acts, each representing a different musical era—the Early South, the Old West, the Gay Nineties, and Modern Times. The audience moved in turn to each of the scenes. The hosts were Sam the Eagle (voiced by Burl Ives) and his owl sidekick (Sam Edwards). When the attraction closed, most of the animal figures were moved to Critter Country to become part of Splash Mountain. America Sings is fondly remembered by many Disneyland guests.

America the Beautiful (film) Circarama (360°) film, which originally opened at the Brussels World's Fair in 1958 and was brought to Disneyland in 1960. A tour of the U.S. 16 min. The film was reshot in 1967 as a Circle-Vision 360 film for the park's new Tomorrowland in Disneyland. The new film opened Jun. 25, 1967, and ran 18 min. It was revised again in 1975 to include sequences of Philadelphia for the American Bicentennial. It closed Jan. 3, 1984, to be followed by *American Journeys*. The film was shot with 9 cameras, arranged on a circular stand. Shown in Tomorrowland in the Magic Kingdom at Walt Disney World Nov. 25, 1971–Mar. 15, 1974, and Mar. 15, 1975–Sep. 9, 1984; also followed by *American Journeys*. *America the Beautiful* was released on 16 mm film at normal screen size for educational use in 1980.

America Works . . . America Sings (film) Educational film; released in Sep. 1982. A glimpse of everyday people whose daily lives gave birth to the folk songs which have enriched our history.

American Adventure, The Host pavilion in World Showcase at EPCOT; opened Oct. 1, 1982, originally sponsored by Coca-Cola (until 1998) and American Express (until 2002). Audiences enter a 1,024-seat auditorium for the 29-min. show, in which hosts Benjamin Franklin and Mark Twain present the 350-year story of America. The production features some of Disney's most sophisticated Audio-Animatronics figures, including Will Rogers, who actually twirls his lasso, and Ben Franklin, who appears to climb several

steps. The score, composed by Buddy Baker, was recorded by the Philadelphia Orchestra. The closing film montage, *Golden Dream*, was updated in 1993, 2007, and 2018, each time incorporating new moments and icons of American history. The massive, 108,000-sq.-ft. pavilion takes the form of an English Georgian colonial mansion, using forced perspective to make the structure appear smaller than it really is. Also featured are The American Heritage Gallery, Regal Eagle Smokehouse (formerly Liberty Inn), The Art of Disney (formerly Heritage Manor Gifts), and the America Gardens Theatre. If you want to catch an architectural oversight, take a look at the columns in the rotunda; their capitals have been placed on sideways. SEE ALSO VOICES OF LIBERTY.

American Born Chinese (TV) Original series from 20th Television planned for digital release on Disney+ in spring 2023. Jin Wang is an average teenager juggling his high school social life with his homelife. When he meets a new foreign student on the first day of school, even more worlds collide as Jin is unwittingly entangled in a battle of Chinese mythological gods. Stars Michelle Yeoh (Guanyin), Ben Wang (Jin Wang), Yeo Yann Yann (Christine Wang), Chin Han (Simon Wang), Daniel Wu (Sun Wukong, the Monkey King), Ke Huy Quan (Freddy Wong), Jim Liu (Wei-Chen), Sydney Taylor (Amelia).

American Broadcasting Company In 1954, Walt Disney agreed to produce a regular TV series for the network, if they would help him out by investing in Disneyland. So, with a $500,000 investment and a guarantee of an additional $4.5 million in loans, ABC became a ⅓ owner of Disneyland. The TV series (also called *Disneyland*) began in the fall, and Walt Disney was able to use it to help promote the park he was building in Anaheim. For the park's invitational press preview, held Jul. 17, 1955, ABC produced the largest live-TV broadcast to date, with the grand opening of the park. Disney programs remained on ABC until 1961; a year earlier they had bought out the ABC investment in Disneyland for $7.5 million. Four decades later, on Jul. 31, 1995, Disney and Capital Cities/ABC announced a $19 billion merger of the 2 companies. After necessary government approvals, the merger was completed Feb. 9, 1996. With the deal, Disney acquired, among other enterprises, 9 VHF TV stations and 1 UHF TV station; 11 AM and 10 FM radio stations; a percentage of ESPN, The History Channel, A&E Network, and Lifetime Television;

and a publishing group that included 85 trade journals, 18 shopping guides, 2 consumer magazines, 21 weeklies, and 7 daily newspapers. Much of the publishing group was later sold. The ABC Radio stations were sold in 2006.

American Crime (TV) Drama series on ABC; aired Mar. 5, 2015–Apr. 30, 2017. Following the murder of war vet Matt Skokie and an assault on his wife, Gwen, 4 suspects are brought into custody. Their situations are far more complicated than anyone would have initially believed, and even the victim may have been far from an innocent bystander in his own murder. Stars Felicity Huffman (Barb Hanlon), Timothy Hutton (Russ Skokie), W. Earl Brown (Tom Carlin), Richard Cabral (Hector Tontz), Caitlin Gerard (Aubry Taylor), Regina King (Aliyah Shadeed). From ABC Studios. Regina King received an Emmy Award for Supporting Actress in a Limited Series or Movie in 2015 and 2016.

American Dragon: Jake Long (TV) Animated series on Disney Channel; premiered Jan. 21, 2005, and ended Sep. 1, 2007. Jake Long is a 13-year-old Chinese American kid in New York City who discovers he is descended from dragons. When he transforms into a fire-breather, it is his duty to protect the other groups of magical creatures living secretly among Gotham's famous landmarks. But the teen also has to confront the usual teenage conflicts, including a crush on Rose, the new girl in school. Voices include Dante Basco (Jake Long), Jeff Bennett (Jake's father), Amy Bruckner (Haley Long), Daveigh Chase (Rose Paxton), Lauren Tom (Jake's mother), Marlowe Gardiner-Heslin (David Long). From Disney Television Animation.

American Egg House Main Street, U.S.A. restaurant in Disneyland; open Jul. 14, 1978–Sep. 30, 1983, sponsored by the American Egg Board. Later Town Square Cafe. With alfresco and indoor dining, it was the first restaurant one encountered on entering the park, so it was popular for breakfast.

American Housewife (TV) Half-hour comedy series on ABC; aired Oct. 11, 2016–Mar. 31, 2021. Katie Otto is a confident, unapologetic wife and mother of 3, raising her flawed family in the wealthy town of Westport, Connecticut, that's filled with "perfect" mommies and their "perfect" children. Katie and her husband, Greg, work to ensure their offspring do not end up like everyone else. Despite her flaws and unconventional ways, Katie ultimately only wants the best for her kids

and will fight tooth and nail to instill some good old-fashioned values in them. Stars Katy Mixon (Katie Otto), Diedrich Bader (Greg Otto), Meg Donnelly (Taylor), Daniel DiMaggio (Oliver), Julia Butters (Anna-Kat), Carly Hughes (Angela), Ali Wong (Doris). From Kapital Entertainment and ABC Studios.

American Idol Experience, The Disney's Hollywood Studios attraction based on the popular TV series; presented in the SuperStar Television Theater Feb. 14, 2009–Aug. 30, 2014. Guests performed in hopes of becoming a star. The judges were all industry professionals who brought an expertise on music, showmanship, and what it takes to have that "star quality." Winners of each daytime show moved on to compete in the evening's grand finale, with the chance to win a "Dream Ticket" granting them front-of-line access to a future *American Idol* TV audition. Replaced by *For the First Time in Forever—A Frozen Sing-Along Celebration.*

American Journeys (film) Circle-Vision 360 presentation capturing the many facets and landscapes of America; played in Tomorrowland at Disneyland Jul. 4, 1984–Jul. 7, 1996, sponsored by PSA. In 1989, Delta took over the sponsorship. Also in the Magic Kingdom at Walt Disney World Sep. 15, 1984–Jan. 9, 1994, and in Tokyo Disneyland May 17, 1986–Aug. 31, 1992.

American Pottery SEE SHAW, EVAN K., CERAMICS.

American Teacher Awards, The Created by Disney as an annual salute to America's teachers; aired on The Disney Channel beginning Nov. 4, 1990. Top stars were on hand to pass out awards to teachers in a dozen categories, and then those winners themselves picked the Teacher of the Year. Short video pieces on each nominee showed them in their classrooms and creating a rapport with their students. The name changed to the DisneyHand Teacher Awards in 2003 and, later, the Disney Teacher Awards. The Outstanding Teacher honorees were: Sylvia Anne Washburn (1990); Edward M. Schroeder (1991); Rafe Esquith (1992); Patricia Ann Baltz and Leta Andrews (1993); Huong Tran Nguyen (1994); Richard Ruffalo (1995); Phoebe Irby (1996); Ray E. Chelewski (1998); Terri Lindner (1999); Ron Clark (2000); Ben Wentworth III (2001); John Passarini (2003); Jeffrey Thompson (2004); David Vixie (2005); and Amanda Mayeaux, Kathryn Pilcher, and Monique Wild (2006). The ceremony was held at the Pantages Theatre in

Hollywood (1990–92, 1996, 1998–99); The American Adventure in EPCOT (1993); Washington, D.C. (1994–95); the Dorothy Chandler Pavilion in Los Angeles (1998); the Shrine Auditorium in Los Angeles, airing on the Lifetime cable network (2000); CBS Television City, also on Lifetime (2001); the Disneyland Hotel, and announced on *The Wayne Brady Show* (2003); Disney's Grand Californian Hotel (2004); and the Disneyland Hotel (2005–06). There were no awards in 1997 or 2002. The show won an Emmy Award for Music Direction in 1991. The awards program evolved from a Disney Channel series entitled *The Disney Channel Salutes the American Teacher*, which began in 1989.

American Waterfront Port of call in Tokyo DisneySea; opened Sep. 4, 2001, re-creating 2 distinct harbors set in 1912. In New York, visitors may ride aboard an elevated train, watch a theatrical production in the Broadway district, and explore the luxury liner SS *Columbia*. The Hotel Hightower, the setting for the Tower of Terror, was added Sep. 4, 2006, and Toy Story Mania! followed Jul. 9, 2012. Nearby, the charming Cape Cod fishing community offers a general store, restaurant, and character show.

American Werewolf in Paris, An (film) Three young American college graduates, Andy, Brad, and Chris, traveling across Europe on a self-styled "Daredevil Tour," descend upon Paris seeking some serious fun and adventure. While planning a bungee jump from the Eiffel Tower, Andy sees the woman of his dreams, the beautiful and mysterious Serafine, who is intent on committing suicide. He makes the split-second decision to jump to save her, which he does; but he is injured and knocked unconscious, and she escapes. In searching for her later, he discovers that when the moon is full, she turns into a werewolf, and it is happening to him, too. A Hollywood Pictures release, in association with Cometstone Pictures and J & M Entertainment. Released Dec. 25, 1997. Directed by Anthony Waller. Stars Tom Everett Scott (Andy), Julie Delpy (Serafine), Vince Vieluf (Brad), Phil Buckman (Chris), Julie Bowen (Amy), Pierre Cossi (Claude), Tom Novembre (Inspector LeDuc), Thierry Lhermitte (Dr. Pigot). 98 min. Based on the characters created by John Landis in *An American Werewolf in London* (1981). Filmed on location in France, Luxembourg, and Holland.

Americana's Dutch Resort See Grosvenor Resort.

America's Cutest: Disney Side Howl-O-Ween (TV) One-hour special on Animal Planet; aired Oct. 18, 2014. Various dogs compete in 5 Disney-themed categories, with the winner to be honored as grand marshal of *Mickey's Boo-to-You Halloween Parade* at Walt Disney World. Narrated by John O'Hurley.

America's Heart & Soul (film) In this documentary, filmmaker Louis Schwartzberg emphasizes that it is the people that make America so special. Audiences meet ordinary Americans with extraordinary stories and learn their values, dreams, and passions. The unusual, captivating, inspiring, and emotional stories make us into something more than a collection of individuals. Released Jul. 2, 2004. Features the original song "The World Don't Bother Me None," by John Mellencamp. 88 min.

Ames, Leon (1903–1993) Actor; appeared as Medfield College president Rufus Daggett in *The Absent-Minded Professor* and *Son of Flubber*, and as the judge in *The Misadventures of Merlin Jones* and *The Monkey's Uncle*.

Among the Stars (TV) A 6-part docuseries; digitally premiered Oct. 6, 2021, on Disney+. Astronaut and former U.S. Navy captain Chris Cassidy makes 1 last mission—to fly to the International Space Station and help find the origins of the universe—but this quickly becomes a tale of the wider team at NASA, their roles on the mission, and their collective quest to succeed. Directed by Ben Turner. From Fulwell 73 Productions.

Amorette's Patisserie High-end bakery in the Disney Springs Town Center at Walt Disney World; opened May 15, 2016. Guests can watch pastry chefs decorate artful cakes in an onstage finishing kitchen.

Amos, John Actor; appeared in *The World's Greatest Athlete* (Coach Sam Archer).

Amos The "me" in *Ben and Me* (1953), a mouse who advises Ben Franklin and helps him come up with many of his great inventions; voiced by Sterling Holloway.

Amos Slade Farmer and hunter in *The Fox and the Hound*; voiced by Jack Albertson.

Amphibia (TV) Animated comedy series on Disney Channel; debuted Jun. 17, 2019. A 13-year-old,

Anne Boonchuy, is magically transported to the fantastical world of Amphibia, a rural marshland full of frog people. There, she meets an excitable young frog named Sprig Plantar; his unpredictable sister, Polly; and overprotective grandpa, Hop Pop. With Sprig's help, Anne will transform into a hero and discover the first true friendship of her life. Voices include Brenda Song (Anne Boonchuy), Justin Felbinger (Sprig Plantar), Amanda Leighton (Polly Plantar), Bill Farmer (Hop Pop Plantar). From Disney Television Animation.

Amsberry, Bob (Uncle Bob) (1928–1957) Adult Mouseketeer; he played a utility man on the 1950s *Mickey Mouse Club* TV show.

Amy (film) Amy is a young mother who has recently lost her cherished deaf son. She leaves her domineering and insensitive husband to go to a school to teach the deaf to speak in an era when sign language was considered the only feasible means of communication. In helping her students to overcome their physical challenges, she herself learns to be independent and self-reliant. Released Mar. 20, 1981. Directed by Vincent McEveety. 99 min. Stars Jenny Agutter (Amy), Barry Newman (Dr. Ben Corcoran), Kathleen Nolan (Helen), Chris Robinson (Elliott), Lou Fant (Lyle), Margaret O'Brien (Hazel), Nanette Fabray (Malvina). The characters of the deaf children were played by students from the California School for the Deaf. A shortened educational film version (31½ min.) was titled *Amy-on-the-Lips*, which was the working title of the feature.

Anaheim, California When Walt Disney was searching for a location for Disneyland, he hired the Stanford Research Institute to do the survey for him, and their preferred location turned out to be Anaheim. So, Walt's agents negotiated on the purchase of a 160-acre parcel of land where Harbor Boulevard intersects the Santa Ana Freeway (Interstate 5), and it was there that he built Disneyland in 1955. The success of Disneyland acted as a catalyst for the major growth of Anaheim that took place over the ensuing decades. In 1953, Disney Studio artists had designed a town mascot, Andy Anaheim, as well as floats for the annual Anaheim Halloween Parade, a relationship that would continue in the decades to follow. SEE ALSO CALIFORNIA ANGELS AND MIGHTY DUCKS, THE.

Anaheim Angels The California Angels baseball team changed its name to the Anaheim Angels in Nov. 1996, and unveiled new team colors and logos for the 1997 season. For the 1998 season, Anaheim Stadium, where the team plays its home games, was renamed Edison International Field of Anaheim. In Oct. 2002, the Angels won the World Series for the first time, beating the San Francisco Giants. Disney came to an agreement with businessman Arte Moreno in Apr. 2003 to sell the team for $185 million; the deal was finalized on May 22. SEE ALSO CALIFORNIA ANGELS.

Anaheim Sports, Inc. Disney operating entity that owned the Mighty Ducks and the Anaheim Angels. Formerly (before Dec. 1996) known as Disney Sports Enterprises.

Anastasia One of Cinderella's evil stepsisters in the 1951 animated film; voiced by Lucille Bliss.

Anderson, Anthony Actor; appeared on TV as Andre "Dre" Johnson in *black-ish*, *grown-ish*, and *mixed-ish*, also serving as exec. producer on all 3 series, and made guest appearances in *Samantha Who?* and *The Most Magical Story on Earth: 50 Years of Walt Disney World*. He voiced Stanley in *Doc McStuffins* and Ray Ray in *The Proud Family*. He was named a Disney Legend in 2022.

Anderson, Bill (1911–1997) Producer of TV programs (58 of the *Zorro* shows, *Texas John Slaughter*, *Daniel Boone*, *The Swamp Fox*) and motion pictures (*Third Man on the Mountain*, *Swiss Family Robinson*, *The Happiest Millionaire*, *Superdad*, *The Strongest Man in the World*, *The Shaggy D.A.*, and others). He began at Disney in 1943 in the production control department. He was promoted to production manager for the Studio in 1951 and vice president of Studio Operations in 1956. He was elected to the Board of Directors in 1960 and remained a member until 1984. He was named a Disney Legend posthumously in 2004.

Anderson, Ever Actress; appeared in *Black Widow* (Young Natasha) and as Wendy in *Peter Pan & Wendy* on Disney+.

Anderson, Harry (1952–2018) Actor; appeared on TV in *The Absent-Minded Professor* (Henry Crawford, 1988), *The Magical World of Disney*, and *The Disney-MGM Studios Theme Park Grand Opening*.

Anderson, John (1922–1992) Actor; appeared on

TV in *Shadow of Fear, For the Love of Willadean*, and *I-Man*. He voiced Mark Twain and Franklin Delano Roosevelt for The American Adventure at EPCOT.

Anderson, Ken (1909–1993) Artist; began his Disney career in 1934, contributing to many animated classics as art director beginning with *Snow White and the Seven Dwarfs*. Since he had an architectural background, he came up with innovative perspective on such Silly Symphony cartoons as *The Goddess of Spring* and *Three Orphan Kittens*. Specializing in character design in later years, he designed such characters as Shere Khan in *The Jungle Book* and Elliott in *Pete's Dragon*. He was production designer on such films as *Sleeping Beauty, One Hundred and One Dalmatians*, and *The Aristocats*. He also designed many parts of Disneyland, including major portions of Fantasyland and the Storybook Land Canal Boats. He retired in 1978 but continued to consult at WED Enterprises. He was honored with a Disney Legends Award in 1991.

Anderson, Michael, Jr. Actor; appeared in *In Search of the Castaways* (John Glenarven).

Anderson-Lopez, Kristen, and Lopez, Robert Songwriters; they first collaborated on the songs for *Finding Nemo—The Musical* at Disney's Animal Kingdom, then *Winnie the Pooh* (2011, for which Kristen also voiced Kanga), *Frozen* (winning the Academy Award for Best Song, "Let It Go"), *Coco* (also winning an Academy Award for "Remember Me"), and *Frozen 2*. Their song for *WandaVision*, "Agatha All Along," won them an Emmy for Best Original Music and Lyrics. Robert Lopez previously wrote songs for *Scrubs* and *Phineas and Ferb*.

Andi Mack (TV) Series on Disney Channel; aired Apr. 7, 2017–Jul. 24, 2019. On the eve of her 13th birthday, Andi learns that her older sister, Bex, is actually her mother. This revelation puts Andi on an unfamiliar path of self-discovery which she navigates with the help of her loving, albeit complicated, family; her 2 best friends, Cyrus and Buffy; and her middle school crush, Jonah Beck. Along the way, Andi learns that sometimes the unexpected is what makes life great. Stars Peyton Elizabeth Lee (Andi), Lilan Bowden (Bex), Lauren Tom (Celia Mack), Joshua Rush (Cyrus Goodman), Asher Angel (Jonah), Sofia Wylie (Buffy Driscoll). From Horizon Productions.

Andor (TV) *Star Wars* live-action series; digitally premiered Sep. 21, 2022, on Disney+. In an era filled with danger, deception, and intrigue, Cassian Andor embarks on a path that is destined to turn him into a rebel hero. Stars Diego Luna, Stellan Skarsgård, Adria Arjona, Fiona Shaw, Denise Gough, Kyle Soller, Genevieve O'Reilly. From Lucasfilm.

Andrews, Edward (1915–1985) Actor; appeared as the Secretary of Defense in *The Absent-Minded Professor* and *Son of Flubber*; also starred in *A Tiger Walks* (governor), *$1,000,000 Duck* (Morgan), *Now You See Him, Now You Don't* (Mr. Sampson), and *Charley and the Angel* (banker); and on TV in *The Whiz Kid and the Mystery at Riverton* (Mayor Massey) and *The Young Loner* (Bert Shannon).

Andrews, Julie Actress; appeared in the title role of *Mary Poppins*, for which she won the Academy Award for Best Actress; *The Princess Diaries* and *The Princess Diaries 2: Royal Engagement* (Queen Clarisse Renaldi); and *The Cat That Looked at a King*. She also narrated *Enchanted* and appeared on TV in *The Grand Opening of Walt Disney World* and in *Eloise at the Plaza* and *Eloise at Christmastime* (Nanny). She served as the official ambassador for Disneyland during its 50th anniversary in 2005, also narrating the park's fireworks spectacular, *Remember . . . Dreams Come True*, and the film *One Man's Dream: 100 Years of Magic* at Disney's Hollywood Studios. She was named a Disney Legend in 1991. Walt Disney discovered Andrews when she was starring as Queen Guinevere in *Camelot* on Broadway; after attending a performance, Walt made a beeline backstage to offer her the role of Mary Poppins.

Andrews' Raiders (TV) Two-part show; aired May 7 and 14, 1961; the TV version of *The Great Locomotive Chase*. The 2 episodes were titled *Secret Mission* and *Escape to Nowhere*.

Andy Young boy in the Toy Story films; voiced by John Morris.

Andy Burnett SEE SAGA OF ANDY BURNETT, THE.

Andy's Toy Box Toy Story Land shop in Hong Kong Disneyland; opened Feb. 6, 2013.

Angel, Heather (1909–1986) Actress; voiced the Sister in *Alice in Wonderland* and Mary Darling in *Peter Pan*.

Angelopoulos, Angel (1907–1990) He helped develop Disney merchandising in Greece, Yugoslavia, Turkey, and Egypt, and later helped Roy O. Disney raise funds for the California Institute of the Arts. Presented a European Disney Legends Award in 1997.

Angels in the Endzone (TV) A 2-hour movie on *The Wonderful World of Disney*; first aired Nov. 9, 1997. Al the angel visits a small town, altering the losing tradition of the Westfield High School Angels football team and changing the lives of 2 young brothers who are devastated by the sudden loss of their father. Directed by Gary Nadeau. Stars Christopher Lloyd (Al), Matthew Lawrence (Jesse Harper), David Gallagher (Kevin Harper), Paul Dooley (Coach Buck). Vancouver College (British Columbia, Canada) doubled for the fictional Westfield High, though their football field had to be re-marked for the movie; Canadian football is played on a 110-yard-long field, and American audiences would have been surprised by the presence of a 55 yard line.

Angels in the Infield (TV) A 2-hour movie on *The Wonderful World of Disney*; first aired Apr. 9, 2000. Big league pitcher Eddie Everett is on a losing streak, but his estranged young daughter, Laurel, wants to help restore his self-confidence. She prays for help, and along it comes in the guise of an angel, Bob Bugler, who still hasn't earned his wings; he's accompanied by a bunch of inept angel helpers. Directed by Robert King. Stars Patrick Warburton (Eddie Everett), Brittney Irvin (Laurel), Kurt Fuller (Simon), Rebecca Jenkins (Claire Everett), Duane Davis (Randy Fleck), David Alan Grier (Bob Bugler).

Angels in the Outfield (film) A foster child, Roger, is told with grim humor that there is about as much chance for his family getting back together as there is for the last-place Angels baseball team to win the pennant. But miracles do happen. When 11-year-old Roger prays for divine intervention, a band of real angels, including one named Al, answers the call. Although nobody except Roger can see or hear these heaven-sent guardians, it is not long before hot-tempered and skeptical team manager George Knox sees the extraordinary evidence of something magical helping his team out of the basement and into the playoffs. With the angels' presence being felt on and off the field, the players and young Roger discover the power of believing in dreams and finding the courage never to give up hope. Released Jul. 15, 1994. Directed by William Dear. Produced in association with Caravan Pictures. 103 min. Stars Danny Glover (George Knox), Tony Danza (Mel Clark), Brenda Fricker (Maggie Nelson), Ben Johnson (Hank Murphy), Jay O. Sanders (Wanch Wilder), Christopher Lloyd (Al), Joseph Gordon-Levitt (Roger). Many of the baseball stadium sequences were filmed at the Oakland Coliseum. The film was a remake of a 1951 MGM film starring Paul Douglas.

Anger Riley's hot-tempered emotion in *Inside Out*; voiced by Lewis Black.

Angie (film) Born and raised in the tightly knit neighborhood of Bensonhurst, Brooklyn, Angie has a growing need for personal fulfillment that expresses itself in ways her family and best friend, Tina, cannot understand. When Angie becomes pregnant by her longtime boyfriend, Vinnie, and begins an affair with Noel, a successful lawyer in Manhattan, everyone is aghast, increasingly so when Angie decides not to marry Vinnie but still have the baby. After the child is born and her affair with Noel ends, Angie embarks on a journey of self-discovery, facing her family's darkest secrets and learning to take responsibility for herself and her new baby. Released Mar. 4, 1994. Filmed in CinemaScope. Directed by Martha Coolidge. A Hollywood Pictures movie, in association with Caravan Pictures. Adapted from Avra Wing's novel *Angie, I Says*. 108 min. Stars Geena Davis (Angie), James Gandolfini (Vinnie), Aida Turturro (Tina), Philip Bosco (Frank), Stephen Rea (Noel). Location shooting took place in the Bensonhurst section of New York's borough of Brooklyn.

Angus MacBadger The accountant at Toad Hall in *The Adventures of Ichabod and Mr. Toad*; voiced by Campbell Grant.

Animagique Black light show based on the greatest moments from Disney classics in Walt Disney Studios Park at Disneyland Paris; open Mar. 16, 2002–Jan. 31, 2016, closing to make way for *Mickey and the Magician*.

Animal Kingdom, Disney's Disney's largest park, at 500 acres; opened Apr. 22, 1998, at Walt Disney World. Filled with dramatic animal encounters and thrilling attractions, the park entertains and educates visitors about creatures real, ancient, and imagined. Guests first enter through the lush Oasis, which leads to Discovery Island (formerly Safari Village). Here, the centerpiece is the enormous Tree of Life, intricately carved with more than 325 animal impressions. Below the tree is *It's Tough to Be a Bug!*, a special effects 3-D show about insects. Past the Discovery River, visitors enter Africa, where Kilimanjaro Safaris offers close-range views of a multitude of animals, including giraffes, zebras, antelopes, hippos, and elephants roaming a savanna larger than the entire Disneyland park. Lowland gorillas can be encountered on the Gorilla Falls Exploration Trail. In total, there are approx. 1,500 live animals throughout the park. The *Wildlife Express* train sends guests backstage to Rafiki's Planet Watch to learn about Disney's animal care and conservation efforts. Asia was added in 1999, with attractions including Maharajah Jungle Trek, Kali River Rapids, and Expedition Everest—Legend of the Forbidden Mountain (opened in 2006). Creatures of the past are explored in DinoLand U.S.A., with the thrilling DINOSAUR attraction. Animals of fantasy were originally the subject of Camp Minnie-Mickey, which was replaced in 2017 by Pandora – The World of Avatar. In 2022, initial plans to replace DinoLand U.S.A. with a new themed area were announced.

Animal Kingdom Lodge, Disney's Elegant 1,307-room resort hotel inspired by traditional African village communities; opened next to Disney's Animal Kingdom at Walt Disney World Apr. 16, 2001. Restaurants include Jiko – The Cooking Place, Boma – Flavors of Africa, and The Mara. The lodge's curved design provides views of 4 savannas that are home to more than 200 hoofed animals and birds that guests can observe from their room balconies. Disney Vacation Club accommodations (known as Disney's Animal Kingdom Villas—Jambo House) opened on the 5th and 6th floors Jul. 2, 2007. An adjacent Disney Vacation Club resort, Disney's Animal Kingdom Villas—Kidani Village, opened May 1, 2009.

Animals at Home in the Desert (film) Segment from *The Living Desert*; released on 16 mm for schools in Nov. 1974. Shows how desert animals have adapted to the region.

Animals of the South American Jungle (film) Segment from *Jungle Cat*; released on 16 mm for schools in Dec. 1974. Tells of such Amazon jungle animals as monkeys, marmosets, sloths, jaguars, and boa constrictors.

Animated Atlas of the World, The (film) Short animated film telling of the geological and meteorological aspects of the ocean; played in Seabase Alpha in The Living Seas at EPCOT, Jan. 15, 1986–2006. Directed by Mike West.

Animated features, classic The major full-length, hand-drawn animated features produced by Walt Disney Animation Studios (formerly Walt Disney Feature Animation) deemed Disney Classics. This list does not include direct-to-video features, theatrical features made by Disney Television Animation, stop-motion animated features (such as *Tim Burton's The Nightmare Before Christmas*), or computer-animated features (such as *Toy Story*). The films are as follows:

1. *Snow White and the Seven Dwarfs*, 1937
2. *Pinocchio*, 1940
3. *Fantasia*, 1940
4. *Dumbo*, 1941
5. *Bambi*, 1942
6. *Saludos Amigos*, 1943
7. *The Three Caballeros*, 1945
8. *Make Mine Music*, 1946
9. *Fun and Fancy Free*, 1947
10. *Melody Time*, 1948
11. *The Adventures of Ichabod and Mr. Toad*, 1949
12. *Cinderella*, 1950
13. *Alice in Wonderland*, 1951
14. *Peter Pan*, 1953
15. *Lady and the Tramp*, 1955
16. *Sleeping Beauty*, 1959
17. *One Hundred and One Dalmatians*, 1961
18. *The Sword in the Stone*, 1963
19. *The Jungle Book*, 1967
20. *The Aristocats*, 1970
21. *Robin Hood*, 1973
22. *The Many Adventures of Winnie the Pooh*, 1977
23. *The Rescuers*, 1977
24. *The Fox and the Hound*, 1981
25. *The Black Cauldron*, 1985
26. *The Great Mouse Detective*, 1986
27. *Oliver & Company*, 1988
28. *The Little Mermaid*, 1989
29. *The Rescuers Down Under*, 1990
30. *Beauty and the Beast*, 1991
31. *Aladdin*, 1992
32. *The Lion King*, 1994
33. *Pocahontas*, 1995
34. *The Hunchback of Notre Dame*, 1996
35. *Hercules*, 1997

36. *Mulan*, 1998
37. *Tarzan*, 1999
38. *Fantasia/2000*, 2000
39. *The Emperor's New Groove*, 2000
40. *Atlantis: The Lost Empire*, 2001
41. *Lilo & Stitch*, 2002
42. *Treasure Planet*, 2002
43. *Brother Bear*, 2003
44. *Home on the Range*, 2004
45. *The Princess and the Frog*, 2009
46. *Winnie the Pooh*, 2011

Animated features, computer The first film to extensively use computer technology was *Tron* in 1982, though it was primarily a live-action motion picture. Beginning with *The Black Cauldron*, digital elements found their way into the classic animated features, and computers soon simplified the inking and painting tasks. Eventually, most animated features were made primarily with computer imagery:

1. *Toy Story*, 1995 (Pixar)
2. *A Bug's Life*, 1998 (Pixar)
3. *Toy Story 2*, 1999 (Pixar)
4. *Dinosaur*, 2000
5. *Monsters, Inc.*, 2001 (Pixar)
6. *Finding Nemo*, 2003 (Pixar)
7. *The Incredibles*, 2004 (Pixar)
8. *Chicken Little*, 2005
9. *Cars*, 2006 (Pixar)
10. *Meet the Robinsons*, 2007
11. *Ratatouille*, 2007 (Pixar)
12. *WALL•E*, 2008 (Pixar)
13. *Bolt*, 2008
14. *Up*, 2009 (Pixar)
15. *Tangled*, 2010
16. *Toy Story 3*, 2010 (Pixar)
17. *Cars 2*, 2011 (Pixar)
18. *Brave*, 2012 (Pixar)
19. *Wreck-It Ralph*, 2012
20. *Monsters University*, 2013 (Pixar)
21. *Frozen*, 2013
22. *Big Hero 6*, 2014
23. *Inside Out*, 2015 (Pixar)
24. *The Good Dinosaur*, 2015 (Pixar)
25. *Zootopia*, 2016
26. *Finding Dory*, 2016 (Pixar)
27. *Moana*, 2016
28. *Cars 3*, 2017 (Pixar)
29. *Coco*, 2017 (Pixar)
30. *Incredibles 2*, 2018 (Pixar)
31. *Ralph Breaks the Internet*, 2018
32. *Toy Story 4*, 2019 (Pixar)
33. *Frozen 2*, 2019
34. *Onward*, 2020 (Pixar)
35. *Soul*, 2020 (Pixar)
36. *Raya and the Last Dragon*, 2021
37. *Luca*, 2021 (Pixar)
38. *Encanto*, 2021
39. *Turning Red*, 2022 (Pixar)
40. *Lightyear*, 2022 (Pixar)
41. *Strange World*, 2022

Animated features; live-action features with hand-drawn animated characters or segments

1. *The Reluctant Dragon*, 1941
2. *Victory Through Air Power*, 1943
3. *Song of the South*, 1946
4. *So Dear to My Heart*, 1949
5. *Mary Poppins*, 1964
6. *Bedknobs and Broomsticks*, 1971
7. *Pete's Dragon*, 1977
8. *Who Framed Roger Rabbit*, 1988
9. *The Lizzie McGuire Movie*, 2003
10. *Enchanted*, 2007
11. *Mary Poppins Returns*, 2018
12. *Chip 'n Dale: Rescue Rangers*, 2022
13. *Disenchanted*, 2022

Animated features, other Beginning in 1990, Disney had its Television Animation division (later DisneyToon Studios) produce a series of animated features, which debuted in movie theaters and then immediately made the transition to video or DVD:

1. *DuckTales: the Movie, Treasure of the Lost Lamp*, 1990 (released as a Disney Movietoon)
2. *A Goofy Movie*, 1995
3. *Doug's 1st Movie*, 1999
4. *The Tigger Movie*, 2000
5. *Recess: School's Out*, 2001
6. *Return to Never Land*, 2002
7. *The Jungle Book 2*, 2003 (from DisneyToon Studios)
8. *Piglet's Big Movie*, 2003
9. *Teacher's Pet*, 2004
10. *Pooh's Heffalump Movie*, 2005
11. *Tinker Bell*, 2008
12. *Tinker Bell and the Lost Treasure*, 2009
13. *Tinker Bell and the Great Fairy Rescue*, 2010
14. *Secret of the Wings*, 2012
15. *Planes*, 2013
16. *The Pirate Fairy*, 2014
17. *Planes: Fire & Rescue*, 2014
18. *Tinker Bell and the Legend of the Never-Beast*, 2015

SEE ALSO VIDEO FOR DIRECT-TO-VIDEO/DVD/
BLU-RAY ANIMATED FEATURES.

Animated features, stop-motion
1. *Tim Burton's The Nightmare Before Christmas*, 1993
2. *James and the Giant Peach*, 1996
3. *Frankenweenie*, 2012

Animation Academy Instructor-led Disney character drawing class in the DisneyQuest Create Zone at Walt Disney World; open Jun. 19, 1998–Jul. 3, 2017. Also in the Animation Station in L'Art de l'Animation Disney (later Animation Celebration) in Walt Disney Studios Park at Disneyland Paris beginning Mar. 16, 2002; in The Magic of Disney Animation at Disney's Hollywood Studios, Oct. 18, 2004–Jul. 12, 2015; in Disney Animation at Disney California Adventure beginning Oct. 10, 2005; and in Town Square at Hong Kong Disneyland beginning summer 2007. A similar class, The Animation Experience at Conservation Station, opened Jul. 11, 2019, in Disney's Animal Kingdom.

Animation Boutique Shop inside Animation Celebration in Walt Disney Studios Park at Disneyland Paris; opened in 2019, replacing The Disney Animation Gallery. Originally offering Frozen merchandise, it began offering Arribas France products in 2022.

Animation Building The major building at the Disney Studio in Burbank when it was built in 1939–1940, designed by industrial designer/architect Kem Weber. Divided into separate wings, the 3-story structure was earthquake resistant and provided space for the different animation units and the Studio's executive offices. It was one of the first major buildings to be air-conditioned in Southern California and was designed so that all of the offices had windows so the artists could work with natural outside light. Walt Disney's office was located on the 3rd floor. Over the years, as live-action production and other company activities encroached on animation, less and less of the building was used for its original purpose. Finally, in 1985, all the animation offices moved to buildings near Walt Disney Imagineering in Glendale. In late 1994, a newly constructed Animation Building opened at the Disney Studio, just across Riverside Drive, and the animators made a triumphant return to the lot. Designed by Robert A.M. Stern, the new building presented a free-flowing, loftlike environment to promote social interaction, with an 84-ft.-tall *Sorcerer's Apprentice* hat housing the office of Roy E. Disney. In 2010, the building was rededicated as the Roy E. Disney Animation Building. The original Animation Building has been featured in several live-action Disney films and TV shows, often doubling as a college building. SEE ALSO OFFICES, WALT DISNEY'S.

Animation Celebration SEE L'ART DE L'ANIMATION DISNEY.

Animation Courtyard Area in Disney's Hollywood Studios; home to attractions like *Voyage of the Little Mermaid* and *Disney Junior—Live on Stage!* Previously named Studio Courtyard, it once served as the entrance to the former Backstage Studio Tour and The Magic of Disney Animation experiences. Also a former area in Walt Disney Studios Park at Disneyland Paris, featuring a 60-ft.-high Sorcerer's hat; it later became part of Toon Studio.

Animation Gallery Shop in Disney-MGM Studios; open May 1, 1989–Aug. 23, 2015. Located at the end of the Animation Tour, it featured a selection of Disney cels and other artwork, along with books on animation. Superseded by Star Wars Launch Bay. SEE ALSO DISNEY ANIMATION GALLERY, THE (DISNEYLAND PARIS).

Animation photo transfer process A process known as APT, which was first used at the Disney Studio during the production of *The Black Cauldron*, whereby photography was used in the production of cels. David Spencer of the Studio's Still Camera Department won an Academy Award in 1986 for the development of the process. The computer, however, would soon render APT obsolete.

Animation Tour Attraction in Disney-MGM Studios; opened May 1, 1989. For the first time, guests could watch story personnel, animators, layout artists, background artists, and ink and paint technicians at work producing animated motion pictures. Large windows and explanatory TV monitors enabled guests walking through the department to see some of the intricate work that goes into the making of an animated film while not disturbing the artists. Guests found it fascinating. The animation staff in Florida contributed numerous scenes to the Disney animated features, and produced *John Henry, Off His Rockers, Trail Mix-Up,* and *Roller Coaster Rabbit* totally on their own. In the mid-1990s, they geared up to produce a complete animated feature, *Mulan*, by themselves, and it was primarily produced there. The Florida studio was also primarily responsible for the production of *Lilo & Stitch* and *Brother Bear*. It closed in 2004. SEE ALSO MAGIC OF DISNEY ANIMATION, THE.

Aniston, Jennifer Actress; appeared in *The Switch* (Kassie Larson), and on TV in *Herman's Head* (Suzie Brooks), *Dirt* (Tina Harrod), and *Cougar Town* (Glenn). She voiced Galatea in the *Hercules* TV series.

Anka, Paul Actor/singer; appeared in *Captain Ron* (Donaldson). He also had a brief show, *Anka*, on Disney Channel; aired Jan. 8, 1984, and ended, with repeats, Nov. 26, 1985.

Ann-Margret Actress; appeared in *Newsies* (Medda Larkson), *The Santa Clause 3: The Escape Clause* (Sylvia Newman), and *Old Dogs* (Martha), and on TV in *Army Wives* (Aunt Edie).

Anna SEE PRINCESS ANNA.

Anna (TV) Unsold pilot for a series; a feisty elderly woman and a struggling actor share an apartment in New York City. Aired on NBC on Aug. 25, 1990. 30 min. Directed by Noam Pitlik. Stars Maria Charles, Keith Diamond, Tom LaGrua, Dennis Lipscomb, Bill Macy, Herb Edelman.

Anna & Elsa's Boutique Shop in the Downtown Disney District at Disneyland Resort; opened Oct. 6, 2014, replacing Studio Disney 365. At a makeover parlor, Crystalizers (stylists) transformed kids into the style of their favorite *Frozen* characters. Closed Sep. 24, 2017, and became the Dream Boutique Oct. 7, no longer offering makeovers.

Annakin, Ken (1914–2009) For Disney, he directed *The Story of Robin Hood and His Merrie Men*, *The Sword and the Rose*, *Swiss Family Robinson*, and *Third Man on the Mountain*. He was named a Disney Legend in 2002.

Annapolis (film) After winning admission to the U.S. Naval Academy at Annapolis, Jake Huard wonders if a regular kid from a poor blue-collar family can fit into the academy's pressure cooker atmosphere. Barely making the grade as a plebe, Jake has one last shot at proving he has what it takes to become an officer—he decides to enter the notoriously fierce Navy boxing competition, known as the Brigade Championships, and face off against his archnemesis, midshipman Lt. Cole. Everything Jake has ever hoped for stands in the balance: the chance to make his father proud, validate his lieutenant's faith in him, stand up for his fellow plebes, and, most of all, forge a different future. A Touchstone film. Released Jan. 27, 2006. Directed by Justin Lin. Stars James Franco (Jake Huard), Tyrese Gibson (Cole), Jordana Brewster (Ali), Donnie Wahlberg (Burton), Chi McBride (McNally), Vicellous Reon Shannon (Twins), Wilmer Calderon (Estrada), Roger Fan (Loo), McCaleb Burnett (Whitaker). 104 min. Filmed in Pennsylvania, with Philadelphia's Girard College standing in for the Naval Academy in Annapolis, Maryland.

Anne Frank (TV) Four-hour miniseries; aired on ABC May 20–21, 2001. Based on Melissa Müller's book, *Anne Frank: A Biography*. Anne Frank, a Jewish girl living in Amsterdam during World War II, goes into hiding with her family to escape the Nazis. The miniseries encompasses her idyllic childhood before the war, her adolescence in Amsterdam, and her last months in captivity. Anne's diary, which she left behind, presents a moving narrative of Jews attempting to survive during the Holocaust. From Milk and Honey Productions, in association with Dorothy Pictures, Inc., for Touchstone Television. Directed by Robert Dornhelm. Stars Ben Kingsley (Otto Frank), Brenda Blethyn (Auguste Van Pels), Hannah Taylor Gordon (Anne Frank).

Anne of Avonlea: The Continuing Story of Anne of Green Gables (TV) Movie aired on The Disney Channel in 4 parts over 4 consecutive weeks. Directed by Kevin Sullivan. Premiered May 19, 1987. Anne is now a teacher in Avonlea, but she leaves town for another job because she feels she cannot marry Gilbert Blythe. When she returns on vacation, she eventually patches things up with Gilbert. 238 min. Stars Megan Follows, Colleen Dewhurst, Dame Wendy Hiller, Frank Converse, Jonathan Crombie, Patricia Hamilton. SEE ALSO AVONLEA.

Annette (TV) Serial on the *Mickey Mouse Club* during the 1957–1958 season. Directed by Charles Lamont. Country girl Annette goes to visit her town relatives and finds romance in the local school, though she is also accused of theft. Stars

Annette Funicello, Tim Considine, David Stollery, Judy Nugent, Richard Deacon, Sylvia Field, Mary Wickes, Roberta Shore, Doreen Tracy, Shelley Fabares, Sharon Baird, Tommy Cole. Based on *Margaret*, the book by Janette Sebring Lowrey. 20 episodes.

Annette's Diner A 1950s-style, all-American restaurant in Disney Village at Disneyland Paris; opened Apr. 12, 1992.

Annie (TV) A 2-hour movie on *The Wonderful World of Disney*; first aired Nov. 7, 1999. A new production of the classic musical about the little red-headed orphan who finds a permanent, loving home with the bighearted billionaire, Daddy Warbucks, much to the chagrin of her mean-spirited orphanage matron, Miss Hannigan. Directed by Rob Marshall. Stars Kathy Bates (Miss Hannigan), Alicia Morton (Annie), Alan Cumming (Rooster Hannigan), Audra McDonald (Grace Farrell), Kristin Chenoweth (Lily St. Regis), Victor Garber (Oliver Warbucks). Based on the Broadway musical written by Thomas Meehan, with music and lyrics by Charles Strouse and Martin Charnin. Andrea McArdle, who played Annie on Broadway 20 years previously, has a cameo role as "Star-to-Be." Filmed entirely on location in Los Angeles. The show won Emmys for choreography (Rob Marshall) and music direction (Paul Bogaev).

Anniversary Room China and giftware shop in the Lake Buena Vista Shopping Village at Walt Disney World; open Mar. 22, 1975–Sep. 24, 1977, and succeeded by Buena Vista Interiors.

Annual passports Special yearlong admission passes to the Disney parks, introduced at Walt Disney World Sep. 28, 1982, and at Disneyland Jun. 1983. Also available at Disneyland Paris, Tokyo Disney Resort, Hong Kong Disneyland (beginning Sep. 29, 2006), and Shanghai Disneyland (beginning Jan. 25, 2019). A Disney Premier Passport was first offered Mar. 11, 2010, providing entrance to all Disneyland Resort and Walt Disney World parks. Annual passports were suspended at Tokyo Disney Resort in 2020. The program ended at Disneyland Resort Aug. 15, 2021, and was succeeded by the Magic Key program Aug. 25.

Another Stakeout (film) In this sequel to *Stakeout*, Las Vegas police lose an important witness when their hideout is blown up by the criminals who want the witness dead. The search for the witness moves to Seattle where 2 police detectives are joined by a female assistant DA in staking out a couple on Bainbridge Island; the trio pose as father, mother, and son, and have as much trouble getting along with each other as they do with their surveillance. Released Jul. 23, 1993. Directed by John Badham. A Touchstone film. 109 min. Stars Richard Dreyfuss (Chris Lecce), Emilio Estevez (Bill Reimers), Rosie O'Donnell (Gina Garrett), Cathy Moriarty (Lu Delano), Dennis Farina (Brian O'Hara), Marcia Strassman (Pam O'Hara). Location filming took place in Las Vegas and in the vicinity of Vancouver.

Ansara, Michael (1922–2013) Actor; appeared in *The Bears and I* (Oliver Red Fern) and narrated *Shokee, the Everglades Panther*.

Anselmo, Tony Animator; joined Disney in 1980. The current voice of Donald Duck, he apprenticed with Clarence Nash for 3 years and then took over after Nash's death in 1985. He was named a Disney Legend in 2009.

A.N.T. Farm (TV) Comedy series on Disney Channel; debuted May 6, 2011, and ended Mar. 21, 2014. The show follows 12-year-old musical prodigy Chyna Parks and her gifted friends as they navigate high school as members of the prestigious A.N.T. (Advanced Natural Talents) program. Chyna's best friends are Olive Doyle, who has a photographic memory, and Fletcher Quimby, an artistic genius with a knack for using his creations for playful hijinks. Stars China Anne McClain (Chyna Parks), Sierra McCormick (Olive Doyle), Jake Short (Fletcher Quimby). From It's a Laugh Productions.

Ant-Man (film) Armed with astonishing ability to shrink in scale but increase in strength, master thief Scott Lang must embrace his inner-hero and help his mentor, Dr. Hank Pym, protect the secret behind his spectacular Ant-Man suit from a generation of towering threats. Against seemingly insurmountable obstacles, Pym and Lang must plan and pull off a heist that will save the world. Released Jul. 17, 2015, also in 3-D and 3-D IMAX. Directed by Peyton Reed. Stars Paul Rudd (Scott Lang/Ant-Man), Evangeline Lilly (Hope van Dyne), Corey Stoll (Darren Cross/Yellowjacket), Bobby Cannavale (Paxton), Michael Peña (Luis), Judy Greer (Maggie), Michael Douglas (Pym). 117 min. From Marvel Studios.

Ant-Man and the Wasp (film) In the aftermath of *Captain America: Civil War*, Scott Lang grapples with the consequences of his choices as both a superhero and a father. As he struggles to rebalance his homelife with his responsibilities as Ant-Man, he's confronted by Hope van Dyne and Dr. Hank Pym with an urgent new mission. Scott must once again put on the suit and learn to fight alongside the Wasp as the team works together to uncover secrets from their past. Released Jul. 6, 2018, also in 3-D and IMAX, after a Jul. 4 international release. Directed by Peyton Reed. Stars Paul Rudd (Scott Lang/Ant-Man), Evangeline Lilly (Hope van Dyne/The Wasp), Michael Douglas (Dr. Hank Pym), Laurence Fishburne (Dr. Bill Foster), Michelle Pfeiffer (Janet van Dyne), Walton Goggins (Sonny Burch), Abby Ryder Fortson (Cassie Lang). 118 min. Filmed in wide-screen format. From Marvel Studios.

Ant-Man and the Wasp: Nano Battle! Interactive attraction in Tomorrowland at Hong Kong Disneyland; opened Mar. 31, 2019, replacing Buzz Lightyear Astro Blasters. Guests board S.H.I.E.L.D.'s newest combat vehicle, D/AGR (Defense/Assault Ground Rover, aka "the Dagger"), shrink down to the size of an ant, and team up with Ant-Man and the Wasp to battle the evil Arnim Zola and his Swarmboat army.

Ant-Man and the Wasp: Quantumania (film) The third feature in the Ant-Man series. Scott Lang and Hope van Dyne continue to explore life as a couple who also happen to be Super Heroes. Their family—Hope's parents, Janet van Dyne and Hank Pym, and Scott's daughter, Cassie—are finally part of their day-to-day lives. Cassie, it turns out, shares her new family's passion for science and technology, specifically with regard to the Quantum Realm. But her curiosity leads to an unexpected, one-way trip for them all to the vast subatomic world, where they encounter strange new creatures, a stricken society, and a master of time whose menacing undertaking has only just begun. Released Feb. 17, 2023, also in 3-D, IMAX, and IMAX 3-D, following international releases beginning Feb. 15. Directed by Peyton Reed. 125 min. Stars Paul Rudd (Scott Lang/Ant-Man), Evangeline Lilly (Hope van Dyne/The Wasp), Jonathan Majors (Kang), Michael Douglas (Hank Pym), Michelle Pfeiffer (Janet van Dyne), Kathryn Newton (Cassie). From Marvel Studios. The first film in "Phase Five" of the Marvel Cinematic Universe. Filmed in wide-screen format.

Antarctica—Operation Deepfreeze (TV) Show aired Jun. 5, 1957, continuing the *Antarctica—Past and Present* theme from an earlier program (SEE NEXT ENTRY), with the efforts to explore Antarctica during the International Geophysical Year. Produced, directed, and narrated by Winston Hibler. The efforts to build bases at McMurdo Sound and Little America are chronicled.

Antarctica—Past and Present (TV) Show aired Sep. 12, 1956, beginning with a history of attempts to reach the South Pole, and continuing with the Operation Deepfreeze mission of the U.S. Navy. Directed and narrated by Winston Hibler. SEE ALSO To THE SOUTH POLE FOR SCIENCE for the THIRD PROGRAM IN THE ANTARCTICA TRILOGY.

Anwar, Gabrielle Actress; appeared in *Wild Hearts Can't Be Broken* (Sonora Webster) and *The Three Musketeers* (Queen Anne), and on TV in *Once Upon a Time* (Victoria Belfrey/Lady Tremaine).

Anything Can Happen Day Wednesday on the 1950s *Mickey Mouse Club*.

Apache Friendship (TV) Show, part 10 of *Texas John Slaughter*.

Apocalypto (film) The story is set in the times of the turbulent decline of the once great Mayan civilization. Jaguar Paw is a young father eking out a meager existence in the rain forest as a traditional hunter. His idyllic existence is brutally disrupted by a violent invading force, which captures him only after he manages to hide his pregnant wife and small son in a deep pit. Jaguar Paw is bound to a pole and taken on a perilous march through the forest to a great Mayan city, a city ruled by fear and oppression, where he is chosen to be sacrificed to the gods atop a mighty pyramid. Through a twist of fate and spurred by the power of his love for his family, he is able to make a desperate break for freedom, embarking on a long and harrowing foot chase, pursued by fierce warriors, to return home and attempt to save his way of life. A Touchstone film. Directed by Mel Gibson. Released Dec. 8, 2006. Stars Rudy Youngblood (Jaguar Paw), Dalia Hernandez (Seven), Jonathan Brewer (Blunted), Morris Birdyellowhead (Flint Sky), Carlos Emilio Baez (Turtles Run), Amilcar Ramirez (Curl Nose), Israel Contreras (Smoke Frog), Raoul Trujillo (Zero Wolf), Gerardo Terracena (Middle Eye). 138 min. Shot on location in Mexico's Catemaco rain forest and in Veracruz, with a cast made up entirely of indigenous peoples from the Americas. The dialogue is entirely in the Yucatec language, the primary Mayan dialect spoken in the Yucatan Peninsula today. Filmed in Super 35-Scope. Released on DVD in 2007.

Apollo God of the sun in "The Pastoral Symphony" segment of *Fantasia*. Also a character in *Hercules*; voiced by Keith David.

Appearances (TV) Unsold pilot for a series. Appearances are deceiving in the story of a "perfect" American family, at home and at work. Aired on NBC on Jun. 17, 1990. 120 min. Directed by Win Phelps. Stars Scott Paulin, Wendy Phillips, Casey Biggs, Matt McGrath, Ernest Borgnine, Robert Hooks.

Apple Dumpling Gang, The (film) In 1879, gambler Russel Donavan arrives in Quake City, California, always looking for a profitable poker game. But despite his frequent losses, he ends up with a shipment of valuables consigned to a local ne'er-do-well who has lit out for San Francisco. The "valuables"—the Bradley orphans (Bobby, 12, Clovis, 7, and Celia, 5)—arrive aboard a stagecoach driven by pretty "Dusty" Clydesdale. Desperate, Russel tries to unload the brood, who discover a huge gold nugget in a nearby mine, causing unwelcome interest by the bumbling Hash Knife Outfit. As Russel rewards the now-famous orphans with their favorite meal of apple dumplings, the numbskull desperadoes try to steal the gold but, as usual, are caught. However, the dangerous Stillwell gang also plans a bank heist but are undone when the children and the Hash Knife Outfit, aided by Russel and Dusty, break into the holdup. Russel and Dusty marry, uniting the happy, new family now known as "The Apple Dumpling Gang." Released Jul. 4, 1975. Directed by Norman Tokar. 100 min. Stars Bill Bixby (Russel Donavan), Tim Conway (Amos), Don Knotts (Theodore), Susan Clark (Magnolia), David Wayne (Col. T. T. Clydesdale), Slim Pickens (Frank Stillwell), Harry Morgan (Homer McCoy), John McGiver (Leonard Sharpe), Don Knight (John Wintle), Clay O'Brien (Bobby Bradley), Brad Savage (Clovis Bradley), Stacy Manning (Celia Bradley). The story was based on the book by Jack M. Bickham. The song "The Apple Dumpling Gang" was written by Shane Tatum and sung by Randy Sparks and The Back Porch Majority. While planning the sets for the film at the Disney Studio, the set designers decided that 3 versions of the bank had to be built. One was indoors on a soundstage (featuring exterior *and* interior sets), and 2 matching exteriors were built outdoors on the backlot (one of them roofless and with burned beams exposed, showing the aftermath of an explosion). Location filming took place at the Tropico gold mine in Rosamond, California, and in the Los Padres and Deschutes national forests in Oregon. The pairing of Tim Conway and Don Knotts worked so well that they were teamed in several later Disney films. The great popularity of the film spawned a sequel in 1979, *The Apple Dumpling Gang Rides Again*. SEE ALSO TALES OF THE APPLE DUMPLING GANG (TV REMAKE) AND GUN SHY (TV SERIES).

Apple Dumpling Gang Rides Again, The (film) Theodore and Amos, trying to quietly live down their checkered past as part of "The Apple Dumpling Gang," find themselves caught up in still another series of hilarious misadventures. Major Gaskill will lose his command of Fort Concho if he cannot stop the raids on his supply wagons, and it is up to Theodore and Amos to bungle their way to a triumphant finale, breaking up a dastardly smuggling ring. Released Jun. 27, 1979. Directed by Vincent McEveety. 89 min. Stars Tim Conway (Amos), Don Knotts (Theodore), Tim Matheson (Pvt. Jeff Reid), Kenneth Mars (Marshal), Elyssa Davalos (Millie), Jack Elam (Big Mac), Robert Pine (Lt. Jim Ravencroft), Harry Morgan (Major Gaskill), Ruth Buzzi (Tough Kate), Audrey Totter (Martha Osten). The film was shot on location in Sonora, California; Kanab, Utah; and at the Disney Studio in Burbank.

Appreciating Differences (film) Educational film in the Songs for Us series; released in Sep. 1989. 10 min. The film teaches children to value people of different ages, races, sexes, and those with disabilities.

April, May, and June Daisy had these 3 nieces (April, May, and June) in the comic books, making their first appearance in *Walt Disney's Comics and Stories* #149 in Feb. 1953. They didn't appear in animation until a cameo in *House of Mouse*. They took on a more regular role in *Legend of the Three Caballeros*.

Aquamania (film) Goofy cartoon released Dec. 20, 1961. Directed by Wolfgang Reitherman. Nominated for an Academy Award, this cartoon looks at how boatsman Goofy and his son spend a weekend. When Goofy demonstrates the art of waterskiing, his son is so impressed he quickly gets them into a championship race, where Goofy has all sorts of misadventures, including everything from an octopus to a roller coaster. Finally, Goofy manages to win the race and the cup.

Aquarela do Brasil (film) Segment of *Saludos Amigos* in which José Carioca teaches Donald Duck to dance the samba. Released as a short Jun. 24, 1955.

Aquatopia Attraction in Tokyo DisneySea; opened Sep. 4, 2001. Guests have a wild ride across the waters of Port Discovery on a hydroglider water vehicle, which spins and twirls across a shallow pool through a maze of fountains, rock formations, and whirlpools.

Arabian Coast Port of call in Tokyo DisneySea; opened Sep. 4, 2001. Visitors set sail on Sindbad's Storybook Voyage, ride upon a fanciful caravan, and explore areas inspired by the magic and mystery of *The One Thousand and One Nights*.

Arachnophobia (film) Fed up with the frustrations of big-city living, Dr. Ross Jennings moves his wife and 2 kids to the sleepy community of Canaima, California. They soon learn that they are not the only recent arrivals. Jennings discovers a deadly spider, accidentally imported from the Amazon jungles, that has mated and set thousands of offspring loose on the unsuspecting populace. Teamed up with exterminator Delbert McClintock, Jennings is forced to confront his past in the spine-tingling showdown. Released Jul. 18, 1990. Directed by Frank Marshall. The first film from Hollywood Pictures, in cooperation with Amblin Entertainment. 109 min. Stars Jeff Daniels (Ross Jennings), Harley Jane Kozak (Molly Jennings), John Goodman (Delbert McClintock), Julian Sands (Dr. James Atherton). The publicity for the film was highlighted by the phrase, "eight legs, two fangs, and an attitude." The lead spider was an Amazonian bird-eating tarantula, and the actors had to become accustomed, or at least less reticent, to working with the intimidating (and shockingly large) arachnids. Filming locations included Cambria, California, and a remote jungle region of Venezuela near Angel Falls. SEE ALSO THRILLS, CHILLS & SPIDERS: THE MAKING OF ARACHNOPHOBIA.

Aracuan Bird Zany character who bothers Donald Duck in *The Three Caballeros, Clown of the Jungle,* and *Melody Time.*

Aramaki, Hideo "Indian" (1915–2005) He began work at Disneyland as chef at the Tahitian Terrace in 1964 and 2 years later was promoted to executive chef over all the food facilities in Disneyland, a position which he held until his retirement in 1985. He was named a Disney Legend in 2005.

Arau, Alfonso Actor; appeared in *Scandalous John* (Paco) and *Run, Cougar, Run* (Etie), and voiced Papá Julio in *Coco.*

Arcata d'Antigiani Shop in Italy at EPCOT Center; open Oct. 1, 1982–Sep. 30, 1989, offering Italian handicrafts. Became Delizie Italiane.

Archimedes Merlin's wise, but cranky, owl friend in *The Sword in the Stone*; voiced by Junius C. Matthews.

Archinal, Harry (1928–2017) He began work for Disney in the New York City office of Buena Vista Distribution Co. in 1954. Later he became a sales supervisor for Latin America and eventually was named president of Buena Vista International in 1972. He retired in 1988 and was named a Disney Legend in 2009.

Archive Shop, The Mystic Point souvenir and collectibles shop in Hong Kong Disneyland; opened May 17, 2013.

Archiving the Archives: Forty Years of Preserving the Magic (film) Half-hour documentary produced on the occasion of the 40th anniversary of the Walt Disney Archives; premiered Jun. 25, 2010, at the Disney Studio, at a special D23 event honoring the Archives and its founder, Dave Smith. Directed by Rob Klein and Josh Turchetta.

Arctic Antics (film) Silly Symphony cartoon released Jun. 27, 1930. Directed by Ub Iwerks. Polar bears, seals, and penguins perform on cakes of ice and in the water.

Arctic Region and Its Polar Bears, The (film) Part of *White Wilderness*; released on 16 mm for schools in Sep. 1964. In the unmapped valleys, the annual thaw brings forth the walrus to confront his mortal enemy, the polar bear.

Arden, Eve (1912–1990) Actress; appeared in *The Strongest Man in the World* (Harriet).

ARDYs: A Radio Disney Music Celebration SEE RADIO DISNEY MUSIC AWARDS.

Arena at ESPN Wide World of Sports, The Opened Jan. 12, 2018, at Walt Disney World. The 300,000-sq.-ft. venue can be configured into 4 separate event spaces, accommodating performance and multi-competition events, like cheerleading, dance, martial arts, gymnastics, volleyball, and basketball.

Ariel Mermaid heroine of *The Little Mermaid*; voiced by Jodi Benson. Her sisters are Aquata, Andrina, Arista, Attina, Adella, and Alana.

Ariel's Nautical seafood restaurant in Disney's Beach Club Resort at Walt Disney World; open Nov. 19, 1990–May 3, 1997, later serving as a special events venue. Reopened briefly in 2017 while Captain's Grille was closed for refurbishment.

Ariel's Grotto Paradise Pier seafood restaurant in Disney California Adventure; opened Dec. 20, 2002, taking the place of Avalon Cove. Closed Jan. 7, 2018, to become Lamplight Lounge. Also a character-greeting spot in the Magic Kingdom at Walt Disney World (open in Fantasyland Oct. 1996–Apr. 11, 2010, then reopened in the Enchanted Forest in 2012); in Disneyland (at Triton Gardens, superseded by Pixie Hollow in 2008); and as Ariel's Greeting Grotto in Mermaid Lagoon at Tokyo DisneySea (opened Sep. 4, 2001).

Ariel's Playground Cavernous play area in Mermaid Lagoon at Tokyo DisneySea; opened Sep. 4, 2001. Families explore colorful settings inspired by *The Little Mermaid*, including Fishermen's Nets, Kelp Forest, Galleon Graveyard, Ariel's Grotto, Cave of Shadows, Sea Dragon, Ursula's Dungeon, Starfish Playpen, and Mermaid Sea Spray.

Aristocats, The (film) Animated feature in which a pedigreed mother cat, Duchess, and her 3 kittens—Toulouse, Berlioz, and Marie—are catnapped by a greedy butler named Edgar, who hopes to gain by getting the inheritance left to the family of cats by their owner, Madame Bonfamille. Things look hopeless for the cats until they are befriended by Thomas O'Malley, an easygoing alley cat. After the cats have many misadventures getting back to Paris, the villainous butler is frustrated when a gang of alley cats and a mouse named Roquefort join O'Malley to rescue Duchess and her kittens. Premiere in Los Angeles on Dec. 11, 1970; general release on Dec. 24, 1970. Directed by Wolfgang Reitherman. 78 min. Features the voices of Phil Harris (Thomas O'Malley), Eva Gabor (Duchess),

Sterling Holloway (Roquefort), Scatman Crothers (Scat Cat), Paul Winchell (Chinese Cat), Lord Tim Hudson (English Cat), Vito Scotti (Italian Cat), Thurl Ravenscroft (Russian Cat), Dean Clark (Berlioz), Liz English (Marie), Gary Dubin (Toulouse), Nancy Kulp (Frou-Frou), Charles Lane (Georges Hautecourt), Hermione Baddeley (Madame Adelaide Bonfamille), Roddy Maude-Roxby (Edgar), Bill Thompson (Uncle Waldo), George Lindsey (Lafayette), Pat Buttram (Napoleon), Monica Evans (Abigail Gabble), Carole Shelley (Amelia Gabble), Pete Renoudet (French Milkman), and Maurice Chevalier, who sang the title tune. This was the first feature-length animated cartoon completed without Walt Disney. The song "Ev'rybody Wants to Be a Cat" was written by Floyd Huddleston and Al Rinker. "Thomas O'Malley" was written by Terry Gilkyson, and Richard and Robert Sherman composed "The Aristocats," "Scales and Arpeggios," and "She Never Felt Alone" (which was cut from the film). For the background musical score, George Bruns featured the accordion-like musette for French flavor and, with his considerable background with jazz bands in the 1940s, provided a great deal of jazz music. The film was 4 years in the making, budgeted at over $4 million, and included more than 325,000 drawings made by 35 animators, with 20 main sequences to the film having 1,125 separate scenes using 900 painted backgrounds. The project employed some 250 people. The film was a box office success, earning reissues in 1980 and in 1987. First released on video in 1996.

AristoCats, The Fantasyland toy and souvenir shop in the Magic Kingdom at Walt Disney World; opened Nov. 1971. Closed Feb. 4, 1996, along with Mickey's Christmas Carol shop, to become Sir Mickey's. Also a toy and apparel shop in Tokyo Disneyland; opened Apr. 15, 1983, and succeeded by Kingdom Treasures in 2011.

Arizona Sheepdog (film) Featurette released May 25, 1955. Directed by Larry Lansburgh. 22 min. Nick and Rock are 2 sheepdogs, belonging to a herder in Arizona, who must help him get the sheep from the dry lands of the plains up to the lush mountain pastures. Along the way, they have to search for lost sheep and ford mountain streams, plus protect the herd from mountain lions. Later released on 16 mm as *Nicky and Rock—Working Sheep Dogs*.

Arjun: The Warrior Prince (film) An Indian animated film produced by UTV Motion Pictures and Walt Disney Pictures. Nine-year-old Arjun Pandava learns the art of warfare and grows into a mighty warrior, discovering what it takes to be a hero. Released in India and in a limited number of theaters in the U.S. May 25, 2012; released at the El Capitan Theatre in Hollywood Sep. 3, 2012, as the first Indian film to play there. Directed by Arnab Chaudhuri. Voices include Yuddvir Bakolia (Arjun), Anjan Srivastav (Lord Shiv), Sachin Khedekar (Lord Krishna), Ashok Banthia (Bheem), Ila Arun (Kunti), Vishnu Sharma (Bheeshma). Based on the ancient Indian epic *Mahabharata*. Shown in the U.S. in Hindi with English subtitles.

Arkin, Alan Actor; appeared in *The Rocketeer* (Peevy), *Indian Summer* (Unca Lou), *The Jerky Boys* (Ernie Lazarro), *Grosse Pointe Blank* (Dr. Oatman), *The Santa Clause 3: The Escape Clause* (Bud Newman), *Million Dollar Arm* (Ray Poitevint), *The Muppets* (tour guide), *Dumbo* (J. Griffin Remington, 2019), and in the title role on the TV series *Harry*.

Arledge, Roone (1931–2002) Longtime president of ABC Sports and ABC News. He was named a Disney Legend in 2007.

Arlen, Richard (1905–1976) Actor; appeared on TV in *The Sky's the Limit*.

Arlo Eager Apatosaurus in *The Good Dinosaur*; voiced by Raymond Ochoa and Jack McGraw.

Armageddon (film) An asteroid the size of Texas is heading directly toward Earth at 22,000 mph, with the potential to destroy the planet. NASA's executive director, Dan Truman, has only one option—to send up a crew to destroy it. He enlists the help of an unlikely hero, Harry S. Stamper, the world's foremost deep-core oil driller, and Stamper's roughneck team of drillers to land on the asteroid, drill 800 feet into its surface, and drop a nuclear device into the core. On this heroic journey, utilizing 2 space shuttles, *Freedom* and *Independence*, they face the most physically and emotionally challenging conditions ever encountered in order to save the world and prevent Armageddon. Directed by Michael Bay. A Touchstone film. Released Jul. 1, 1998, after a Jun. 29 World Premiere screening at the Kennedy Space Center. Stars Bruce Willis (Harry Stamper), Billy Bob Thornton (Dan Truman), Liv Tyler (Grace Stamper), Ben Affleck (A. J. Frost), Will Patton (Chick Chapple), Peter Stor-

mare (Lev Andropov), Keith David (General Kimsey), Owen Wilson (Oscar Choi), William Fichtner (Willie Sharp), Steve Buscemi (Rockhound). Filmed in CinemaScope. 151 min. NASA technical advisers helped give some scientific accuracy to the project, including former director of Advanced Programs Ivan Bekey and former astronaut Joseph Allen. In order to experience some of the astronaut training firsthand, Willis and Affleck, along with members of the crew, spent several days at the Johnson Space Center in Texas, where the 2 actors were the first civilians to be allowed in the lab's neutral-buoyancy tank, which astronauts train in to work in space suits. In order to construct the asteroid set on Stage 2 at the Disney Studios, one of the largest in Hollywood, craftsmen had to excavate up to 30 feet below the stage level, so there would be space for the tall set pieces. Exterior shots utilized vast terrain outside of Kadoka, South Dakota. NASA allowed the company to shoot actual shuttle launches at the Kennedy Space Center in Florida, and to film at the Johnson Space Center and Ellington Air Field in Texas (where they received a surprise visit from former president George H. W. Bush). *Armageddon* became Disney's highest-grossing film, until passed by *The Sixth Sense*. The original song "I Don't Want to Miss a Thing," written by Diane Warren and performed by Aerosmith, debuted No. 1 on the U.S. Billboard Hot 100 and earned the film 1 of its 4 Academy Award nominations.

Armageddon: Les Effets Speciaux Backlot attraction in Walt Disney Studios Park at Disneyland Paris; opened Mar. 16, 2002. Guests journeyed through the history of special effects before experiencing an up close demonstration on a set representing the 1998 film. Closed Mar. 31, 2019, to make way for Spider-Man W.E.B. Adventure.

Armstrong, Louis (1900–1971) Trumpet virtuoso; first performed in Disneyland for the 2nd Dixieland at Disneyland event Sep. 30, 1961, and then returned in 1962 and 1964–1967. He also appeared on the TV show *Disneyland After Dark*. In 1968, Buena Vista Records released an album: *Louis Armstrong—Disney Songs the Satchmo Way*.

Armstrong, Sam (1893–1976) Story man/background artist; worked at Disney 1934–1941.

Army Mascot, The (film) Pluto cartoon released May 22, 1942. Directed by Clyde Geronimi. Pluto yearns to be an army mascot because of the good food they get, and he outwits a goat mascot to earn the job. A World War II–era short.

Army Wives (TV) Series for Lifetime; aired Jun. 3, 2007–Jun. 9, 2013. Military life can exact a major toll on relationships, as shown in this drama series exploring the lives of wives, and 1 man, living on an active army post, who are constantly worried that their spouses will be called up to serve abroad. Stars Kim Delaney (Claudia Joy Holden), Sally Pressman (Roxy LeBlanc), Brigid Brannagh (Pamela Moran), Brian McNamara (Michael Holden), Roland Burton (Sterling K. Brown), Joan Burton (Wendy Davis), Drew Fuller (Trevor LeBlanc), Catherine Bell (Denise Sherwood). Adapted from the book *Under the Sabers: The Unwritten Code of Army Wives*, by Tanya Biank. The series eventually became the most successful in Lifetime's history. From Mark Gordon Co. and ABC Studios.

Arnold, Susan E. Member of the Disney Board of Directors May 1, 2007–2023. In 2018, she was named independent lead director and on Dec. 31, 2021, succeeded Bob Iger as chairman of the board.

Around the World in 80 Days (film) Eccentric London inventor Phileas Fogg has come up with the secrets of flight, electricity, and even Rollerblades, but the world has dismissed him as a crackpot. Desperate to be taken seriously, Fogg makes an outlandish bet with Lord Kelvin, the head of the Royal Academy of Science, to circumnavigate the globe in no more than 80 days. With his 2 sidekicks—Passepartout and femme fatale Monique—Fogg is headed on a frantic, heart-pounding, round-the-world race that takes our heroes to the world's most fascinating places by land, sea, and air, facing many adventures and obstacles along the way. Directed by Frank Coraci. A Walt Disney Pictures/Walden Media film. Released Jun. 16, 2004. Stars Steve Coogan (Phileas Fogg), Jackie Chan (Passepartout/Lau Xing), Cécile De France (Monique), Jim Broadbent (Lord Kelvin). Cameos include Kathy Bates (Queen Victoria), Owen and Luke Wilson (the Wright Brothers), Arnold Schwarzenegger (Prince Hapi). 120 min. Based on the novel by Jules Verne. A remake of Mike Todd's classic 1956 film for United Artists starring David Niven and Cantinflas. Filmed in Super 35-Scope.

Arquette, Rosanna Actress; appeared in *New York Stories* (Paulette) and *Gone Fishin'* (Rita).

Arribas Brothers Participant at Disney parks and resorts, first as glassblowers in Fantasyland in Disneyland beginning Jun. 15, 1967. The glassblowing and cutting work of Alfonso and Tomas Arribas had reportedly caught the attention of Walt Disney when the brothers represented Spain at the 1964–1965 New York World's Fair. After the success of their operations in Fantasyland (which ended in 1987), their brother, Manuel, joined them to begin operating Cristal d'Orleans, which had previously opened with another participant Jul. 24, 1966, in New Orleans Square. Items ranging from affordable small jewelry to large sculptures have been sold. In 1971, Alfonso and Tomas relocated to Walt Disney World to open Crystal Arts on Main Street, U.S.A. in the Magic Kingdom, and a similar shop opened Jun. 24, 1972, at Disneyland, where Manuel continued to work. At Walt Disney World, the brothers' work could additionally be seen in The King's Gallery inside Cinderella Castle (Dec. 1972–Jul. 5, 2007), as well as in La Princesa de Cristal in Caribbean Plaza (1974–1992). They continue to operate in the Marketplace at Disney Springs and at EPCOT, in Germany (Kunstarbeit in Kristall) and Mexico (also La Princesa de Cristal). In Oct. 1991, Arribas France was formed for the opening of Disneyland Paris, where product is sold in Merlin l'Enchanteur and Liberty Arcade, as well as in (as of Jun. 2022) Animation Boutique in Walt Disney Studios Park. There are additional locations in Tokyo Disneyland (The Glass Slipper and Agrabah Marketplace) and Shanghai Disneyland (Crystal Treasures). Their work is also sold on shopDisney.com. Tomas passed away in 2002, and Alfonso passed away in 2018 after retiring in Florida. Alfonso's son, Rudy, became president of the company. See also Eurospain.

Art Corner, The Disney animation art and supply shop in Tomorrowland at Disneyland; open Sep. 4, 1955–Sep. 5, 1966, with special displays, such as *The Art of Animation*, and appearances by sketch artists. Initially opened Jul. 1955 in a temporary spot on Main Street, U.S.A. until the Tomorrowland location was ready. In 1955, a cel from a recent Disney film cost $2 or $3; think what it would bring on the market today! Another Art Corner operated in Fantasyland for several years.

Art of Animation, The Tomorrowland display in Disneyland; ran May 28, 1960–Sep. 5, 1966, in The Art Corner. Walt Disney created this display after making *Sleeping Beauty*, showing the history and development of animation and utilizing elements from the 1959 feature to explain the actual animation process. Three traveling versions toured the U.S. beginning Dec. 1958; 1 continued to Europe, another to Japan, and a 3rd ended at Disneyland. Author Bob Thomas wrote a useful book, entitled *The Art of Animation*, explaining the animation process and also using *Sleeping Beauty* as a basis. There was really nothing to compare with the exhibit until the Animation Tour opened in Disney-MGM Studios at Walt Disney World in 1989, 23 years later. Also the name of an exhibit showing the stages of animation on Main Street, U.S.A. in Hong Kong Disneyland; opened Aug. 31, 2008, replacing The Disneyland Story—How Mickey Mouse Came to Hong Kong. SEE ALSO L'ART DE L'ANIMATION DISNEY/ART OF DISNEY ANIMATION.

Art of Animation Resort, Disney's Resort themed around the artistry of Disney animated films; opened at Walt Disney World in 4 stages, beginning May 31, 2012, ultimately with 1,120 family suites and 864 "value" category rooms. Units are themed to *The Lion King*, *Cars*, *The Little Mermaid*, and *Finding Nemo*. The *Nemo* unit was the first to open, with the 11,859-sq.-ft. Big Blue Pool (the largest at Walt Disney World). *The Little Mermaid* section was the last to open, in Sep. 2012. After checking in at Animation Hall, guests can dine at Landscape of Flavors, browse gifts in the Ink & Paint Shop, and play in the Pixel Play Arcade. The resort connects to Disney's Pop Century Resort around Hourglass Lake. Originally, the site for Art of Animation was intended to be the extension of Pop Century, with proposed units themed to American pop culture from the 1900s–1940s.

Art of Disney, The Shop selling Disney paintings, prints, and collectibles. The first location opened in the Disney Village Marketplace (now the Marketplace at Disney Springs) at Walt Disney World Aug. 28, 1994, taking the place of Country Address. Art of Disney merchandise was also sold in Centorium at EPCOT; it relocated to a dedicated shop in Innoventions West Oct. 1, 2000, and moved again to The American Adventure Dec. 16, 2019, taking the place of Heritage Manor Gifts. Another shop opened as the Main Street Gallery (previously Sun Bank) in Magic Kingdom, Sep. 6, 1997–Apr. 17, 2004; it moved into the King's Gallery in Cinderella Castle Apr. 20, 2004–Jul. 5, 2007, then to the Main Street Cinema in Nov. 2007. Art of Disney merchandise has also been sold in the former Animation Gallery at Disney's Hollywood Studios and Disney Outfitters (later Discovery Trading Company) at Disney's Animal Kingdom. SEE ALSO DISNEY GALLERY, THE (DISNEYLAND) AND WALT DISNEY GALLERY, THE.

Art of Self Defense, The (film) Goofy cartoon released Dec. 26, 1941. Directed by Jack Kinney. Goofy demonstrates, in his inimitable fashion, the arts of defense from the Stone Age to modern times, with the assistance of a narrator.

Art of Skiing, The (film) Goofy cartoon released Nov. 14, 1941. Directed by Jack Kinney. In his typical clumsy fashion, Goofy demonstrates various skiing techniques with the aid of offscreen narration. SEE ALSO MOUNT DISNEY.

Artemis Fowl (film) The spellbinding adventure that follows 12-year-old genius Artemis Fowl, a descendant of a long line of criminal masterminds, as he desperately tries to save his kidnapped father. In order to pay his ransom, Artemis must infiltrate an ancient, underground civilization—the advanced world of fairies—and bring the kidnapper the Aculos, the fairies' most powerful and coveted magical device. Cunning Artemis concocts a plan so dangerous that he finds himself in a perilous war of wits with the all-powerful fairies. Originally planned for theatrical release, it premiered digitally Jun. 12, 2020, on Disney+. Directed by Kenneth Branagh. Stars Ferdia Shaw (Artemis Fowl), Lara McDonnell (Holly Short), Josh Gad (Mulch Diggums), Tamara Smart (Juliet), Nonso Anozie (Domovoi Butler), Colin Farrell (Artemis Fowl Sr.), Judi Dench (Commander Root). 95 min. Based on the book series by Eoin Colfer. With more than 400 architectural drawings, the Fowl Manor was constructed as a fully functioning house, with central heating, a working kitchen, Wi-Fi, and a soundstage in the roof space. Filmed in wide-screen format in Northern Ireland and at Longcross Studios in England, with additional footage shot in Ho Chi Minh City, Vietnam; Thurso, Scotland; the Hill of Tara in The Republic of Ireland; and San Gimignano in Tuscany and Mount Vesuvius in Naples, Italy.

Artesanías Mexicanas Shop in Mexico at EPCOT; open Oct. 1, 1982–2009, and was succeeded by La Princesa de Cristal. Glass-blown items, crafts, and art objects from Mexico were sold. Presented by Arribas Brothers.

Artespana SEE EUROSPAIN.

Arthur Young servant who becomes king in *The Sword in the Stone*; voiced by Ricky Sorenson and Robert Reitherman. Also known as Wart.

Arthur, Bea (1922–2009) Actress; appeared on TV as Dorothy Zbornak in *The Golden Girls* (for which she won the Emmy Award as Outstanding Lead Actress in a Comedy Series in 1988) and in *Walt Disney World's 15th Birthday Celebration*. She was named a Disney Legend posthumously in 2009.

Artist Point Fine dining in Disney's Wilderness Lodge at Walt Disney World, decorated with dramatic landscape art; opened May 1994. A specialty was salmon, served sizzling on a cedar plank. It became Storybook Dining at Artist Point Dec. 17, 2018, with *Snow White and the Seven Dwarfs* entertainment.

Artist's Palette, The Counter-service restaurant and market in Disney's Saratoga Springs Resort & Spa at Walt Disney World; opened May 17, 2004.

Arts & Crafts Shop inside Sleeping Beauty Castle at Disneyland; opened in the 1950s. It was temporarily renamed the Clock Shop (ca. 1963) and later sold Arribas Bros. crystal products. Later named Castle Arts, which closed May 10, 1987, and became the Castle Christmas Shop. SEE ALSO GEPPETTO'S ARTS AND CRAFTS.

Arvida Corporation One of the biggest real estate and development companies in Florida, specializing in planned communities. It was purchased by Disney in May 1984 for $200 million in Disney stock, with the Bass Brothers ending up with 5.9% of the Disney stock as a result of the transaction. Part of the reason for the purchase was to dilute the value of the stock, which was at that time being bought up by a corporate raider, Saul Steinberg. While some thought the marriage of the 2 companies was ideal because of Disney's large land holdings in Florida, others were not so happy, and after Michael Eisner and Frank G. Wells took over the management of Disney, Arvida was sold in 1987 to JMB Realty Corporation for $404 million.

Assembling a Universe SEE MARVEL STUDIOS: ASSEMBLING A UNIVERSE.

Ashman, Howard (1951–1991) Lyricist; with composer Alan Menken, he wrote songs for *The Little Mermaid*, *Beauty and the Beast*, and *Alad-* *din*. He posthumously received an Oscar for the song "Beauty and the Beast," for he had died on Mar. 14, 1991, at the age of 40. He was named a Disney Legend in 2001. SEE ALSO HOWARD (DOCUMENTARY).

Ask Max (TV) Show aired Nov. 2, 1986. Directed by Vincent McEveety. A young scientific genius, Max, tries to impress a girl, but she ignores the overweight boy. By designing a special bicycle, which comes to the attention of a toy company, Max comes into great amounts of money, but he learns that money will not win him the girl. Instead, he becomes a hero by helping save an aircraft plant, which employs many locals, from closing. Stars Jeff B. Cohen, Ray Walston, Cassie Yates, Gino DeMauro.

Asner, Edward (1929–2021) Actor; appeared in *Gus* (Hank Cooper) and *Perfect Game* (Billy Hicks); on TV in *The Christmas Star* (Horace), *Thunder Alley* (Gil Jones), *Donald Duck's 50th Birthday*, and *Criminal Minds* (Roy Brooks); on The Disney Channel in *A Friendship in Vienna* (Opah Oskar); and on Disney+ in *Muppets Haunted Mansion* (Ghost of Claude). He provided several voices, including Carl Fredricksen in *Up*, Grumps in *Bonkers*, Evil Georgie in *Dinosaurs*, and Hudson and Burbank in *Gargoyles*.

Aspen Extreme (film) Two happy-go-lucky young men, Dexter and T. J., leave their humdrum jobs on the auto assembly lines of Detroit and head to Aspen to become ski instructors and win the famous Powder Eight competition. T. J. enjoys instant popularity, while Dexter finds Aspen life more difficult, and, after a disastrous rendezvous with the local drug ring, the 2 friends part. But their common dream of winning the Powder Eight reunites them until Dexter is accidentally killed during practice in a restricted zone. T. J. vows to win in memory of his partner, and, with an admiring pupil, he wins the race. Released Jan. 22, 1993. A Hollywood Pictures film. 118 min. Stars Paul Gross (T. J. Burke), Peter Berg (Dexter Rutecki), Finola Hughes (Bryce Kellogg), Teri Polo (Robin Hand). After opening shots in Detroit, the motion picture was filmed on location in Aspen, Colorado, with ski sequences in the Monashee range of the Canadian Rockies in British Columbia. The story was based on the real-life experiences of writer/director Patrick Hasburgh.

Associate, The (film) Laurel Ayers, a bright financial analyst, is disgusted when she is passed over for a well-deserved promotion, so she creates a perception that she has formed a partnership with a powerful financial whiz. Fabricating and donning the persona of "Robert S. Cutty," a strutting, ponytailed, bass-voiced man, Laurel maneuvers a number of successful financial deals until her underhanded rival, Frank, attempts to unmask Cutty and appropriate the disguise for his own personal gain. Laurel proves eventually that men do not have a monopoly on creative enterprise. Released Oct. 25, 1996. Directed by Donald Petrie. A Hollywood Pictures film. Stars Whoopi Goldberg (Laurel Ayers), Dianne Wiest (Sally), Tim Daly (Frank), Bebe Neuwirth (Camille), Lainie Kazan (Cindy Mason), Austin Pendleton (Aesop), George Martin (Walter Manchester), Eli Wallach (Fallon). 114 min. Based on the French film, *L'Associé*, which was adapted from the novel *El Socio* by Jenaro Prieto. Filmed entirely on location for 11 weeks in New York City. Special arrangements were required to accommodate a 130-person cast and crew team invading an active stock market trading floor (they shot on weekends). Academy Award–winning makeup artist Greg Cannom created the prosthetics to turn Goldberg into Cutty; it was a 3½-hour transformation process.

Astin, John Actor; appeared in 1977's *Freaky Friday* (Bill Andrews), and on TV in *Mr. Boogedy* (Neil Witherspoon). He hosted 2 episodes of *The Mouse Factory* and provided several voices for TV, including Sydney in *Disney's Aladdin*, Superintendent Skinner and Hank in *Recess*, and Santa Claus in *Higglytown Heroes*.

Astin, Mackenzie Actor; appeared in *Iron Will* (Will Stoneman), and on TV in *Selma, Lord, Selma* (Jonathan Daniels), *Lost* (Dr. Tom Brennan), *Grey's Anatomy* (Danny Wilson), *Criminal Minds* (Dylan Kohler), *Marvel's Agents of S.H.I.E.L.D.* (Tim Maguire), *Castle* (Phillip Bartlett), and as Noah Baker in *Scandal* and *How to Get Away with Murder*.

Astin, Sean Actor; appeared in *Encino Man* (Dave Morgan), and on TV in *The B.R.A.T. Patrol*. He voiced the title character in *Special Agent Oso*, Benngee in *Sofia the First*, Blaze in *Penn Zero: Part-Time Hero*, and Hercules in the *Kingdom Hearts* video game.

Astley, Amy She joined Touchstone Television in 1999 as a semi-senior secretary, later becoming a publicist for Buena Vista International Television and ABC. In 2012, she joined Walt Disney Animation Studios as director of Worldwide Communications and Publicity, expanding her role in 2021 to additionally oversee Creative Legacy, Brand Strategy, Unscripted Content, and the Animation Research Library as senior vice president. For Disney+, she exec. produced *Into the Unknown: Making Frozen 2*, *Zenimation*, and *Sketchbook*.

Astro-Jets Tomorrowland attraction in Disneyland, Mar. 24, 1956–Sep. 5, 1966. Also known as Tomorrowland Jets 1964–1966; later became Rocket Jets. By manipulating the handle, guests could make their jet rise and lower, giving themselves a bird's-eye view of Disneyland as the attraction rotated. At Walt Disney World, the attraction was first known as Star Jets and later as Astro Orbiter.

Astro Orbiter New name, in 1995, for the attraction formerly known as Star Jets in the Magic Kingdom at Walt Disney World. In Disneyland, the Astro Orbitor (with a new spelling) opened May 22, 1998, based on the Orbitron in Disneyland Paris.

Astronaut Wives Club, The (TV) Hour-long limited series on ABC; aired Jun. 18–Aug. 20, 2015. Based on the book by Lily Koppel, it tells the story of the women who were key players behind some of the biggest events in American history, as the wives of America's astronauts. Their husbands' work brought them publicity, and overnight these women were transformed from military spouses into American royalty. As their celebrity rose and tragedy began to touch their lives, they rallied together. Stars JoAnna Garcia Swisher (Betty Grissom), Yvonne Strahovski (Rene Carpenter), Dominique McElligott (Louise Shepard), Odette Annable (Trudy Cooper), Erin Cummings (Marge Slayton), Azure Parsons (Annie Glenn), Zoe Boyle (Jo Schirra), Desmond Harrington (Alan Shepard), Bret Harrison (Gordo Cooper). From ABC Studios.

Astuter Computer Revue EPCOT Computer Central show in Communicore, sponsored by Sperry; ran Oct. 1, 1982–Jan. 2, 1984. Superseded by Backstage Magic. Attempted to explain the workings of computers by utilizing animation and the actual computers used to operate many of the park attractions. The theme song, "The Computer Song," was written by Richard M. and Robert B. Sherman.

At Home with Donald Duck (TV) Show aired

Nov. 21, 1956. Directed by Jack Hannah. A compilation of cartoons for Donald's birthday. Includes a segment with Cubby O'Brien and the Firehouse Five Plus Two. A rerun in 1976 was titled *Happy Birthday Donald Duck* and substituted footage from the new *Mickey Mouse Club* for the latter segment.

At Home With Olaf Series of 21 brief animated shorts; digitally released Apr. 6–May 12, 2020, on Disney.com. Olaf finds moments of joy in everyday life around Arendelle. Directed by Hyrum Osmond. Features the voice of Josh Gad (Olaf). The final episode, "I Am With You," was directed by Dan Abraham and features a song of the same name by *Frozen* songwriters Kristen Anderson-Lopez and Robert Lopez. Produced at home by the Walt Disney Animation Studios staff during the 2020 COVID-19 pandemic.

At the Movies (TV) New title for *Ebert & Roeper and the Movies*. The motion picture review show changed to *At the Movies* with a new set and format beginning Sep. 6, 2008, starring Ben Lyons and Ben Mankiewicz. New critics took over on Sep. 5, 2009: A. O. (Tony) Scott of the *New York Times* and Michael Phillips of the *Chicago Tribune*. The show ended Aug. 15, 2010.

Atencio, Francis "X" (1919–2017) He joined Disney in 1938 as an inbetweener and became an assistant animator on *Fantasia*. He worked on the inventive *Noah's Ark*, *Jack and Old Mac*, and *A Symposium on Popular Songs*, using stop-motion animation in collaboration with Bill Justice. In 1965, he transferred to WED Enterprises, where he worked on the Primeval World, Pirates of the Caribbean, Adventure Thru Inner Space, and the Haunted Mansion. For the Disneyland attractions, he wrote the words for "Yo Ho (A Pirate's Life for Me)" and "Grim Grinning Ghosts." He later contributed designs for attractions at Walt Disney World and Tokyo Disneyland, also writing lyrics for Country Bear Jamboree, If You Had Wings, The American Adventure, and El Rio Del Tiempo. (The X stands for Xavier, but he was called X ever since high school pals gave him the nickname.) He retired in 1984 and was named a Disney Legend in 1996.

Atkinson, Rowan Actor; voiced Zazu in *The Lion King*.

Atlanta Braves Walt Disney World announced in Feb. 1996 that the Atlanta Braves would use

Disney's Wide World of Sports (now ESPN Wide World of Sports) for their spring training home beginning in 1998. However, they inaugurated the stadium at the sports complex with an exhibition game against the Cincinnati Reds Mar. 28, 1997. Their 22nd, and final, season at ESPN Wide World of Sports was conducted spring 2019.

Atlantic Dance Nightclub on Disney's BoardWalk at Walt Disney World; opened Jul. 1, 1996. The art deco–style dance hall has experimented with different styles, including Latin and swing. Also known as Atlantic Dance Hall.

Atlantic Wear & Wardrobe Emporium Seaside souvenirs sold in Disney's Beach Club Resort at Walt Disney World; open Nov. 19, 1990–Jan. 5, 2005, becoming Beach Club Marketplace (with grab 'n' go food service) Mar. 24.

Atlantis: Milo's Return (film) Direct-to-video release May 20, 2003; sequel to *Atlantis: The Lost Empire*. Milo, Kida, and their crew gear up for more action as the story begins just a few months after the original film's conclusion. While Kida—now Atlantean queen—and explorer Milo Thatch have set about rebuilding the city and restoring greatness to the Atlantean culture as a center of knowledge and learning, they are surprised by the return of Team Atlantis with billionaire Preston Whitmore in tow. The team must leave Atlantis to discover what mysterious powers are causing trouble in a new, fantastic location. Directed by Tad Stones, Toby Shelton, and Victor A. Cook. Voices include James Taylor (Milo), Cree Summer (Kida), Don Novello (Vinny Santorini), Stephen Barr (Cookie), Jacqueline Obradors (Audrey), John Mahoney (Preston B. Whitmore), Corey Burton (Mole), Florence Stanley (Mrs. Packard), Phil Morris (Dr. Sweet). 80 min. From Walt Disney Television Animation.

Atlantis: The Lost Empire (film) In 1914, an inexperienced young museum cartographer and linguistics expert, Milo Thatch, joins up with a group of daredevil explorers in an expedition funded by an eccentric billionaire, Preston B. Whitmore, to find the legendary lost empire of Atlantis. Milo is continuing a quest begun by his late grandfather. Utilizing a long-lost journal, which provides new clues to the location, they embark in a state-of-the-art submarine, the *Ulysses*, under fearless but cunning Commander Rourke. But what they find defies their expectations—crystal energy that has kept the

Atlantis inhabitants alive. Rourke steals the crystals and kidnaps the Atlantean princess, Kida. It is up to Milo to come to the rescue, save the princess, and protect the city from certain doom. Directed by Kirk Wise and Gary Trousdale. Released in Los Angeles and New York City on Jun. 8, and nationwide on Jun. 15, 2001. World premiere was at the El Capitan Theatre in Hollywood on Jun. 3. Voices include Michael J. Fox (Milo Thatch), James Garner (Commander Rourke), Cree Summer (Princess Kida), Leonard Nimoy (King of Atlantis), Phil Morris (Dr. Sweet), Jacqueline Obradors (Audrey Ramirez), Claudie Christian (Helga Sinclair), John Maloney (Preston B. Whitmore), Jim Varney (Cookie), David Ogden Stiers (Fenton Q. Harcourt), Don Novello (Vinny Santorini), Florence Stanley (Mrs. Packard). 96 min. James Newton Howard composed the film's epic score. The directors based the design on the style of cult comic book artist Mike Mignola, who served as an artistic consultant. For the Atlanteans, an original readable, speakable language was created by linguistics expert Marc Okrand. Filmed in CinemaScope. See Atlantis: Milo's Return for sequel.

Atom, The: A Closer Look (film) Updated educational version of *Our Friend the Atom*; released in Sep. 1980.

Atta Girl, Kelly! (TV) Three-part show aired Mar. 5, 12, and 19, 1967. The 3 episodes were titled *K for Kelly*, *Dog of Destiny*, and *The Seeing Eye*. Directed by James Sheldon. Story of a Seeing Eye dog, through its being raised as a puppy by a young boy who resists giving it up, to its rigorous training, and finally its placement with a blind attorney, who has lost a previous dog and finds it hard to trust the new one. Stars Billy Corcoran (Danny Richards), Beau Bridges (Matt Howell), Arthur Hill (Evan Clayton), J. D. Cannon, James Broderick, Jan Shepard.

Attmore, Billy "Pop" Actor; appeared in *Treasure of Matecumbe* (Thad), and as a Mouseketeer on the new *Mickey Mouse Club*. Billy was the only Mouseketeer to have earlier acted in a Disney movie.

Attwooll, Hugh (1914–1997) Production manager and associate producer for a number of Disney films made in Europe beginning with *Kidnapped*. He also worked on such films as *Greyfriars Bobby*, *The Moon-Spinners*, *Candleshoe*, *In Search of the Castaways*, *The Three Lives of Thomasina*, *The Littlest Horse Thieves*, and *Watcher in the Woods*. He was named a Disney Legend in 2002.

Atwater Ink & Paint Market house on Buena Vista Street in Disney California Adventure; opened Jun. 15, 2012. Coffee, tea, and treats are sold. The name refers to the Atwater Village district of Los Angeles, which was frequented by animators in the early days of the Disney Studio.

Atwell, Hayley Actress; appeared in *Cinderella* (Ella's Mother, 2015), *Christopher Robin* (Evelyn Robin), and as Peggy Carter in the Marvel Studios films, and on TV in *Conviction* (Hayes Morrison), *Marvel's Agent Carter*, and *Marvel's Agents of S.H.I.E.L.D.*

Atwell, Roy (1880–1962) He voiced Doc in *Snow White and the Seven Dwarfs*.

Au Chalet de la Marionnette Quick-service restaurant in Fantasyland in Disneyland Paris; opened Apr. 12, 1992. Within the walls of what looks like a small Alpine village, the chalet-style eatery features scenes from *Pinocchio*, with 1 section decorated as Geppetto's wrecked boat. See also Pinocchio Village Haus (Walt Disney World), Village Haus Restaurant (Disneyland), and Pinocchio Village Kitchen (Shanghai Disneyland).

Au Petit Café Restaurant in France at EPCOT Center; opened Oct. 1, 1982. Lighter fare than one would find at Les Chefs de France or Le Bistro de Paris, but still tasty French cuisine served in typical French sidewalk café style. It closed Jun. 9, 1997, to be incorporated into Les Chefs de France.

Auberge de Cendrillon Table-service restaurant in Fantasyland at Disneyland Paris; opened Apr. 12, 1992, sponsored by Vittel. Guests dine on fine French cuisine in a majestic medieval banquet hall.

Auberjonois, René (1940–2019) Actor; appeared in *Inspector Gadget* (Artemus Bradford), on TV in *The Christmas Star* (Mr. Summer) and *Geppetto* (Prof. Buonragazzo), and guest starred in *Grey's Anatomy* (Neil Sheridan) and *Criminal Minds* (Col. Ron Massey). He voiced Louis in *The Little Mermaid*, Nefir Hansenuf in *Disney's Aladdin*, and Concierge in *Planes: Fire & Rescue*.

Audio-Animatronics When Walt Disney found an antique mechanical singing bird in a shop while visiting New Orleans, he became intrigued. He reasoned that he and his staff had been doing animation on film for years, but it would be fun to try some 3-D animation. He had Wathel Rogers and other Studio technicians take the bird apart to see how it worked. Then work was started to come up with a prototype figure. Charles Cristadoro, a sculptor, modeled some human heads, utilizing actor Buddy Ebsen and staff members around the Studio as models, and experiments were made with cams, hydraulics, and other methods of enabling the figures to move realistically. One early concept was for a figure of Confucius who would interact with guests in a Chinese restaurant at Disneyland. The Chinese restaurant was never built, so the technicians turned instead to the nation's 16th president, Abraham Lincoln. When Robert Moses, head of the 1964–1965 New York World's Fair, saw the figure being tested at the Disney Studio, he knew that he had to have it for the fair. Walt agreed to speed up development of Lincoln, and the state of Illinois came forward to act as sponsor of Great Moments with Mr. Lincoln. The exhibit opened Apr. 1964 to great acclaim. But Audio-Animatronics figures had actually been used in a show that had opened at Disneyland the previous year. Less sophisticated figures of birds, flowers, and tiki gods populated the Enchanted Tiki Room. From then on, Audio-Animatronics figures would become a popular part of many of the attractions at the Disney parks, reaching high degrees of complexity in Pirates of the Caribbean, the Haunted Mansion, America Sings, Country Bear Jamboree, The Hall of Presidents, The American Adventure, The Great Movie Ride, Na'vi River Journey, and Enchanted Tale of Beauty and the Beast.

Audley, Eleanor (1905–1991) Actress; provided the voice of Lady Tremaine in *Cinderella* and Maleficent in *Sleeping Beauty*, appeared on TV in *The Swamp Fox* (Mrs. Videau), and made an uncredited appearance as the matron in *Never a Dull Moment*. At the Disney parks, she is the voice of the disembodied head of Madame Leota in the crystal ball in the Haunted Mansion.

Auguste Gusteau French culinary legend in *Ratatouille*; voiced by Brad Garrett.

Aulani, A Disney Resort & Spa Oceanfront resort on 21 acres in west Oahu's Ko Olina Resort & Marina; opened Aug. 29, 2011, with grand opening ceremonies held Sep. 23, 2011. The resort is inspired by Hawai'i's traditions and natural wonders so guests can gain a deeper understanding, appreciation, and enjoyment of the local culture. The 359 hotel rooms and 481 Disney Vacation Club villas are joined by a variety of idyllic restaurants, includ-

ing Makahiki – The Bounty of the Islands; shopping at Kālepa's Store; lounges and walk-up shacks, including The 'Ōlelo Room; a children's activity club (Aunty's Beach House); recreational activities; fireside entertainment; KA WA'A, a Lu'au at Aulani Resort; and Laniwai – A Disney Spa. Hidden throughout the resort are playful figures called Menehune, which, according to legend, are shy, mischievous people of the Hawaiian Islands. SEE ALSO WAIKOLOHE VALLEY (POOL AREA).

Aumont, Jean Pierre (1911–2001) Actor; appeared in *Jefferson in Paris* (D'Hancarville), and on TV in *The Horse Without a Head* (Inspector Sinet).

Aunt Jemima Pancake House Frontierland restaurant in Disneyland; open Aug. 9, 1955–Jan. 1962. Became Aunt Jemima's Kitchen (Jul. 17, 1962–1970), Magnolia Tree Terrace (1970–1971), and then River Belle Terrace. In the early days of Disneyland, Aunt Jemima herself would greet guests outside the restaurant. The restaurant was operated by Quaker Oats 1955–1967; Disneyland then took over the operation until 1970, though Quaker Oats remained as a sponsor for many years.

Aunt Peg's Village Store General store in American Waterfront at Tokyo DisneySea; opened Sep. 4, 2001. The red barn house–style building offers Duffy and ShellieMay merchandise and features a vegetable garden in the backyard.

Aunt Polly's Landing Counter-service restaurant serving lunches and ice cream on Tom Sawyer Island in the Magic Kingdom at Walt Disney World; opened in 1973. Also known as Aunt Polly's Restaurant and renamed Aunt Polly's Dockside Inn in 1995. There was also a refreshment stand on the original Tom Sawyer Island in Disneyland beginning Sep. 5, 1956, presented by Nesbitt's; it was later renamed Tom Sawyer Island Canteen.

Aunt Sarah Stern relative who comes to care for the baby in *Lady and the Tramp*; voiced by Verna Felton.

Auntie Edna (film) Animated short from Pixar; released digitally Oct. 23, 2018, and on the *Incredibles 2* Blu-ray Nov. 6. Edna Mode pulls an all-nighter designing a suit to harness baby Jack-Jack's seemingly limitless powers. Directed by Ted Mathot. Voices include Brad Bird (Edna Mode); Craig T. Nelson (Bob Parr); and Eli Fucile, Maeve

Andrews, Nick Bird, and Noelle Zuber (Jack-Jack). 5 min.

Auntie Gravity's Galactic Goodies Quick-service restaurant in Tomorrowland in the Magic Kingdom at Walt Disney World; opened Jun. 1994, serving soft-serve ice cream and other treats. It replaced The Lunching Pad.

Aurora Fine-dining restaurant in the Shanghai Disneyland Hotel; opened Jun. 16, 2016, with panoramic views of Shanghai Disneyland. The name pays homage to Princess Aurora from *Sleeping Beauty*.

Austin, Jake T. Actor; appeared on Disney Channel in *Johnny Kapahala: Back on Board* (Chris) and *Wizards of Waverly Place* (Max Russo), and on ABC Family in *The Fosters* (Jesus Foster).

Austin & Ally (TV) Series on Disney Channel; premiered Dec. 4, 2011. Teenagers Austin, an extroverted musician/singer, and Ally, a brilliant yet shy songwriter, become unlikely friends and combine their talents in an attempt to create a true musical tour de force. Stars Ross Lynch (Austin Moon), Laura Marano (Ally Dawson), Raini Rodriguez (Trish), Calum Worthy (Dez). From It's a Laugh Productions.

Authentic All Star Shop in Downtown Disney Marketplace at Walt Disney World; opened in 1996, replacing The City. Moved to the West Side, as All Star Gear, 1997–2000, with the original shop superseded by Pooh Corner. It was a retail counterpart to the All Star Cafe, which would open at Disney's Wide World of Sports in 1998.

Autograph Hound, The (film) Donald Duck cartoon released Sep. 1, 1939. Directed by Jack King. Despite a watchful security guard, Donald manages to sneak into a movie studio in his attempt to get autographs. But when the guard catches him and he gives his name, the stars, including Greta Garbo, Bette Davis, and Mickey Rooney, come to get *his* autograph. Includes caricatures of many movie stars.

Autopia Tomorrowland attraction in Disneyland; opened Jul. 17, 1955. Riders drive along winding, scenic roads. At its opening, the attraction captured America's fascination with the country's new freeway system. Sponsored by Richfield (1955–1970), Chevron (2000–2012), and Honda (beginning in 2016). Redesigned in 1959, 1964, and 1968, with another extensive remodeling Sep. 1999–Jun. 2000 for the Chevron sponsorship. A new story line was added Mar. 24, 2017, featuring Honda's ASIMO (Advanced Step in Innovative Mobility) humanoid robot and robotic friend, Bird, as they embark on a road trip. Also opened in Discoveryland at Disneyland Paris Apr. 12, 1992, and in Tomorrowland at Hong Kong Disneyland Jul. 13, 2006. Some guests who were youngsters in the 1950s still have their Richfield Autopia driver's license, on which they could place their thumbprint and biographical data necessary to make them a licensed Autopia driver. SEE ALSO FANTASYLAND AUTOPIA, JUNIOR AUTOPIA, MIDGET AUTOPIA, GRAND PRIX RACEWAY (WALT DISNEY WORLD), AND GRAND CIRCUIT RACEWAY (TOKYO DISNEYLAND).

Autry National Center Museum in Griffith Park in Los Angeles devoted to the people, culture, experiences, and history of the American West. It was established in 1988 by actor and businessman Gene Autry and was initially known as the Gene Autry Western Heritage Museum. The 6 permanent exhibition areas were designed by Walt Disney Imagineering. It was renamed the Autry Museum of the American West in 2015.

Autumn (film) Silly Symphony cartoon released Feb. 15, 1930. Directed by Ub Iwerks. The animals get ready for winter by foraging and preparing for hibernation.

Aux Epices Enchantées Restaurant in Adventureland in Disneyland Paris; opened Apr. 12, 1992. Sponsored by Maggi. Became Restaurant Hakuna Matata in May 1995.

Avalon Cove Gourmet restaurant on Paradise Pier in Disney California Adventure; opened Feb. 8, 2001. Guests dined on fish, steak, and other specialties while overlooking Paradise Bay. Upstairs, the Cove Bar offered cocktails and sushi. Operated by Wolfgang Puck until Sep. 30, 2001. It became Ariel's Grotto in 2002.

Avalon High (TV) A Disney Channel Original Movie; premiered Nov. 12, 2010. After transferring to Avalon High, Allie is shocked to discover that her new classmates are reincarnations of King Arthur and his court. The more Allie researches these interesting parallels between the past and present, the surer she is that her school is a contemporary Camelot, and it is up to her to solve the mystery before the notorious traitor Mordred wins again. Directed by Stuart Gillard. Stars Brittany Robertson (Allie), Molly C. Quinn (Jen), Gregg Sulkin (Will), Steve Valentine (Mr. Moore), Devon Graye (Marco), Joey Pollari (Miles), Christopher Tavarez (Lance). Based on the novel by Meg Cabot.

Avatar As part of its purchase of 21st Century Fox in 2019, Disney acquired James Cameron's 2009 sci-fi action adventure, *Avatar*, which became the world's highest-grossing film to date and would inspire Pandora – The World of Avatar at Disney's Animal Kingdom in 2017. A sequel, *Avatar: The Way of Water*, was in development for many years; it was released by 20th Century Studios Dec. 16, 2022, also in 3-D, IMAX, and IMAX 3-D, following international releases beginning Dec. 14. Set more than a decade after the events of the first film, it tells the story of the Sully family (Jake, Neytiri, and their kids), the trouble that follows them, the lengths they go to keep each other safe, the battles they fight to stay alive, and the tragedies they endure. Directed by James Cameron. 192 min. Stars Zoe Saldaña (Neytiri), Sam Worthington (Jake Sully), Sigourney Weaver (Kiri), Stephen Lang (Colonel Miles Quaritch), Cliff Curtis (Tonowari), Joel David Moore (Norm Spellman), CCH Pounder (Mo'at), Edie Falco (General Ardmore), Jemaine Clement (Dr. Ian Garvin), Kate Winslet (Ronal). A Lightstorm Entertainment Production. Academy Award winner for Best Visual Effects (Joe Letteri, Richard Baneham, Eric Saindon, Daniel Barrett), also nominated for Best Picture, Sound, and Production Design. Additional Avatar films are planned, and in Feb. 2023, it was announced an Avatar experience is in development for Disneyland Resort. SEE ALSO TOMORROWLAND PAVILION (AVATAR: EXPLORE PANDORA AT SHANGHAI DISNEYLAND).

Avatar Flight of Passage Attraction in Pandora – The World of Avatar at Disney's Animal Kingdom; opened May 27, 2017. Guests link to an avatar and climb atop a mountain banshee for a breathtaking 3-D flight over Pandora's landscape, discovering that bonding with a banshee is an important rite of passage for the Na'vi.

Ave Maria Composed by Franz Schubert, the sacred "Ave Maria," the concluding segment of *Fantasia*, was used in juxtaposition to the profane "Night on Bald Mountain" sequence in the film.

Avengers, Marvel's The (film) When an unexpected enemy, led by Loki, an exiled Norse god, emerges to threaten global safety and security, Nick Fury, director of the international peacekeeping agency known as S.H.I.E.L.D., finds himself in need of a team to pull the world back from the brink of disaster. Spanning the globe, a daring recruitment effort begins. The resulting superhero team of a lifetime, named the Avengers, consists of Iron Man, The Incredible Hulk, Thor, Captain America, and Black Widow. Released in 3-D and IMAX May 4, 2012, after an Apr. 25 international release. Directed by Joss Whedon. Stars Robert Downey Jr. (Tony Stark/Iron Man), Chris Evans (Steve Rogers/Captain America), Mark Ruffalo (Bruce Banner/The Hulk), Chris Hemsworth (Thor), Scarlett Johansson (Natasha Romanoff/Black Widow), Jeremy Renner (Clint Barton/Hawkeye), Tom Hiddleston (Loki), Samuel L. Jackson (Nick Fury), Gwyneth Paltrow (Pepper Potts). 143 min. Based on the Marvel comic book series *The Avengers*, first published in 1963. From Marvel Studios; distributed by Disney. Nominated for the Academy Award for Best Achievement in Visual Effects of 2012 (Janek Sirrs, Jeff White, Guy Williams, Daniel Sudick).

Avengers: Age of Ultron (film) Tony Stark tries to jump-start a dormant peacekeeping program, but things go awry and Earth's Mightiest Heroes, including Iron Man, Captain America, Thor, The Incredible Hulk, Black Widow, and Hawkeye, are put to the ultimate test as the fate of the planet hangs in the balance. As the villainous technological villain Ultron emerges, hell-bent on human extinction, it is up to the Avengers to stop him from enacting his terrible plans, and soon uneasy alliances and unexpected action pave the way for an epic and unique global adventure. Directed by Joss Whedon. Released in 3-D and IMAX May 1, 2015, following an Apr. 22 international release. Features most of the original *Avengers* cast; stars Robert Downey Jr., Chris Evans, Chris Hemsworth, Mark Ruffalo, Scarlett Johansson, Jeremy Renner, Samuel L. Jackson, Cobie Smulders (Agent Maria Hill), James Spader (Ultron). 141 min. Based on *The Avengers* comic book series. Filmed in widescreen. From Marvel Studios.

Avengers Assemble: Flight Force Roller coaster-style attraction in Avengers Campus in Walt Disney Studios Park at Disneyland Paris; opened Jul. 20, 2022, taking the place of Rock 'n' Roller Coaster avec Aerosmith. Boarding one of Stark Industries' hypersonic vehicles, guests team up with Captain Marvel and Iron Man to help save the world from an intergalactic threat.

Avengers Campus Marvel-themed area in Disney California Adventure; opened Jun. 4, 2021, taking the place of A Bug's Land. According to the story, Earth's mightiest champions have created this campus to discover, recruit, and train the next generation of heroes. Each attraction, shop, and dining area is hosted by a different Avenger, who shares their unique powers, technology, and knowledge with recruits. Attractions include WEB SLINGERS: A Spider-Man Adventure and Guardians of the Galaxy – Mission: BREAKOUT! A highlight is witnessing Spider-Man as he swings 65 feet over the area. In Sep. 2022, a future attraction was announced in which families will team up with Avengers and their allies to battle foes from the Multiverse, including a new villain, King Thanos. A second Avengers Campus opened in Walt Disney Studios Park at Disneyland Paris Jul. 20, 2022, following a preview period that began Jul. 16. Attractions there include Avengers Assemble: Flight Force and Spider-Man W.E.B. Adventure, with dining at Stark Factory and PYM Kitchen.

Avengers: Damage Control Multisensory virtual reality experience from ILMxLAB; ran Oct. 18, 2019–Mar. 2020, in The VOID in the Downtown Disney District at Disneyland Resort. After sinister forces intervened at a Wakandan Outreach Center, fans were recruited to fight side by side with the Avengers. SEE ALSO VOID, THE.

Avengers: Endgame (film) The Avengers have been soundly defeated by Thanos, who, after collecting the 6 Infinity Stones, imposed his will on all of humanity and randomly wiped out half of the world's population, including many of the Avengers. In the aftermath of the destruction, the remaining Avengers are faced with their biggest challenge yet: finding the resolve within themselves to get off the mat and find a way to defeat Thanos once and for all. Directed by Anthony Russo and Joe Russo. Released Apr. 26, 2019 (also in 3-D, IMAX, and IMAX 3-D), after an Apr. 22 premiere at the Los Angeles Convention Center and an Apr. 24 international release. Features most of the original *Avengers* cast; stars Robert Downey Jr., Chris Evans, Mark Ruffalo, Chris Hemsworth, Scarlett Johansson, Jeremy Renner, Don Cheadle (James Rhodes/War Machine), Paul Rudd (Scott Lang/Ant-Man),

Brie Larson (Carol Danvers/Captain Marvel), Karen Gillan (Nebula), Danai Gurira (Okoye), Josh Brolin (Thanos), and the voice of Bradley Cooper (Rocket). 181 min. From Marvel Studios. Filmed in wide-screen format. A follow-up to *Avengers: Infinity War*, it marked the conclusion to the first 22 films produced by Marvel Studios. The film became the first in history to surpass $1 billion in its opening weekend. Nominated for an Academy Award for Best Visual Effects (Dan DeLeeuw, Russell Earl, Matt Aitken, Dan Sudick).

Avengers: Infinity War (film) As the Avengers and their allies have continued to protect the world from threats too large for any one hero to handle, a new danger has emerged from the cosmic shadows: Thanos. A despot of intergalactic infamy, his goal is to collect all 6 Infinity Stones, artifacts of unimaginable power, and use them to inflict his twisted will on all of reality. Everything the Avengers have fought for has led up to this moment—with the fate of Earth and existence itself never more uncertain. Directed by Anthony Russo and Joe Russo. Released Apr. 27, 2018 (also in 3-D and IMAX), after an Apr. 25 international release. Its large-scale premiere on Apr. 23 took place in the El Capitan Theatre, the Dolby Theatre, and the TCL Chinese Theatre along Hollywood Boulevard, which was lined with an extensive display of film props, costumes, and vehicles. Features most of the original *Avengers* cast; stars Robert Downey Jr., Scarlett Johansson, Chris Evans, Chris Hemsworth, Tom Hiddleston, Tom Holland (Peter Parker/Spider-Man), Elizabeth Olsen (Wanda Maximoff/Scarlet Witch), Karen Gillan (Nebula), Josh Brolin (Thanos). 149 min. From Marvel Studios. Filmed in wide-screen format. It opened as the all-time highest-grossing film for its opening weekend. Nominated for an Academy Award for Best Visual Effects (Dan DeLeeuw, Kelly Port, Russell Earl, Dan Sudick).

Avenue M Arcade The largest store in Shanghai Disneyland; opened on Mickey Avenue Jun. 16, 2016. Mosaic panels depict residents as universal virtues: Mickey Mouse (hospitality), Minnie Mouse and Figaro (compassion), Donald Duck (worldly), Daisy Duck (friendliness), Goofy (optimism), Pluto and Fifi (generosity), and Chip and Dale (friendship). A portion of the store's exterior is inspired by the former Carthay Circle Theatre in Los Angeles.

Avigators Pleasure Island apparel shop at Walt Disney World; opened May 1, 1989, offering casual adult fashions with an aviator's flair. Closed Feb. 8, 2000, and superseded by Mouse House.

Avonlea (TV) Highly acclaimed weekly series on The Disney Channel; premiered Mar. 5, 1990, and aired its last new episode Dec. 8, 1996. Based on the stories by Lucy Maud Montgomery, who wrote *Anne of Green Gables*. Sara Stanley comes to Avonlea on Canada's Prince Edward Island to live with her relatives, and Avonlea is never the same again. She lives with her aunt, the spinster schoolteacher, Hetty King, and constantly bickers with her cousin, Felicity. Stars Sarah Polley (Sara Stanley), Jackie Burroughs (Hetty King), Mag Ruffman (Olivia), Cedric Smith (Alec King), Lally Cadeau (Janet King), Gema Zamprogna (Felicity), Zachary Bennett (Felix), R. H. Thomson (Jasper), Michael Mahonen (Gus). The show won the Emmy Award as Best Children's Program in 1993 and another Emmy for a guest appearance by Christopher Lloyd. SEE ALSO ANNE OF AVONLEA.

Award Wieners Food-service counter in Hollywood Land in Disney California Adventure; opened Feb. 8, 2001. Specialty hot dogs are offered in a retro trolley car. A seating area was added in Oct. 2008.

Awesome Planet (film) Film in The Land at EPCOT; opened Jan. 17, 2020, in the Harvest Theater, replacing *Circle of Life: An Environmental Fable*. A story about the beauty and diversity of Earth's biomes and the importance of caring for the planet. Musical score by Steven Price. Narrated by Ty Burrell. 10 min.

Awkwafina Actress; appeared in *Shang-Chi and the Legend of the Ten Rings* (Katy), and on Disney+ in *Marvel Studios: Assembled*. She voiced Sisu in *Raya and the Last Dragon* and Scuttle in *The Little Mermaid* (2023).

Aykroyd, Dan Actor; appeared in *Celtic Pride* (Jimmy Flaherty), *Grosse Pointe Blank* (Grocer), and *Pearl Harbor* (Capt. Thurmann), and on TV in *Soul Man* (Mike Weber).

Ayoade, Richard Actor; voiced Counselor Jerry in *Soul* and Q9-0 (Zero) in *The Mandalorian*.

Ayres, Lew (1908–1996) Actor; appeared in *The Biscuit Eater* (Mr. Ames).

Azaria, Hank Actor; appeared in *Pretty Woman* (detective), *Quiz Show* (Albert Freedman), *Grosse Pointe Blank* (Lardner), *Cradle Will Rock* (Marc Blitzstein), and *Mystery, Alaska* (Charles Danner), and on TV in *Herman's Head* (Jay Nichols), *Imagine That* (Josh Miller), and *If Not for You* (Craig).

1. *Bao* (film) 2. *Bedknobs and Broomsticks* (film) 3. *Baymax!* (TV) 4. Backlot 5. *Bambi* (film)
6. Books 7. Big Thunder Mountain Railroad 8. Blair, Mary 9. *Brave Little Tailor* (film)

B

B Resort Hotel in Lake Buena Vista at Walt Disney World, taking the place of the Royal Plaza in 2014. It opened with 394 guest rooms and suites.

Babbitt, Art (1907–1992) Animator; started at Disney in 1932 and is recognized with escalating Goofy to stardom by giving the character unique mannerisms and a rather clumsy walk in such films as *Mickey's Service Station* and *Moving Day*. He is known for his animation of the Evil Queen in *Snow White and the Seven Dwarfs*, Geppetto in *Pinocchio*, the stork in *Dumbo*, and the mushrooms in "The Nutcracker Suite" segment of *Fantasia*. He was instrumental in helping begin art classes for the animators. As an active proponent of unions, he left Disney in 1941 at the time of the bitter strike, returning only briefly in 1946–1947. He was named a Disney Legend in 2007.

Babe, the Blue Ox Co-star of Paul Bunyan in the 1958 animated featurette.

Babes in the Woods (film) Silly Symphony cartoon released Nov. 19, 1932. One of the first cartoons in color. Directed by Burt Gillett. Based on the Hansel and Gretel story. Two children wandering through a forest are lured into the house of a wicked witch, who lives with her collection of creatures. The boy is changed into a spider by a potion, and just as the girl is about to be changed into a rat, she is rescued by woodland dwarfs, and she finds a potion to transform her spider brother and the creatures back into the children they once were. The children help the dwarfs turn the witch into stone with her own cauldron.

Babes in Toyland (film) Just as Tom and Mary are to be married in Mother Goose Village, the villain, Barnaby, knowing Mary is to inherit a large sum of money when wed, has Tom kidnapped by his 2 henchmen who are to toss Tom into the sea. The henchmen then steal Mary's sheep, the sole support for her and the children she cares for. Just as it looks as if Mary will have to marry Barnaby, Tom, who has not really drowned at all, reappears, and takes off with Mary and the children to find the sheep. Traveling in the Forest of No Return, Tom's party ends up in Toyland, with Barnaby and his henchmen not far behind. There, Tom, Mary, and the kids help the Toymaker make toys for Christmas until the Toymaker's assistant, Grumio, invents a gun, which reduces everything to toy-size. Barnaby gets hold of the gun, reduces Tom and the Toymaker, and forces the latter to marry him to Mary. Before the ceremony is completed, Tom, who has mobilized the toy armies, attacks. In the furious battle, Mary reduces Barnaby, and Tom disposes of him in a duel. Grumio comes up with a restoring formula and all ends happily. Released Dec. 14, 1961. Directed by Jack Donohue. 106 min. Stars Ray Bolger (Barnaby), Tommy Sands (Tom Piper), Annette Funicello (Mary Contrary), Ed Wynn (Toymaker), Henry Calvin (Gonzorgo), Gene Sheldon (Roderigo), Tommy Kirk (Grumio), Kevin Corcoran (Boy Blue), Ann Jilliann (Bo Peep). This was the Studio's first live-action musical fantasy and featured numerous songs, including "I Can't Do the Sum," "Castle in Spain," "Just a Whisper Away," "Forest of No Return," and "Toyland," by George Bruns and

Mel Leven, based on the operetta by Victor Herbert and Glenn McDonough. For many, the special effects are the true highlight of the film, created by Eustace Lycett, Robert Mattey, Joshua Meador, Bill Justice, and X Atencio. Fabulous toys, from wooden soldiers to golden-haired dolls and guns that shoot to airships that fly, were specially designed for the exciting climax. Disney animation veteran Ward Kimball, himself a noted toy collector, headed the unit that created the mechanical toys. The film was promoted on the Disney TV series, and pieces from the set were reconstructed at the Disneyland Opera House where they remained as an attraction 1961–1963. SEE ALSO BACKSTAGE PARTY.

Babes in Toyland Exhibit Display of sets from the movie, shown in the Opera House on Main Street, U.S.A. in Disneyland Dec. 17, 1961–Sep. 30, 1963. Because *Babes in Toyland* contained some elaborate sets, Walt Disney thought they might be appealing on display in the park, though their popularity never matched that of the *20,000 Leagues Under the Sea* sets that were displayed in Tomorrowland.

Baby . . . Secret of the Lost Legend (film) A young scientist discovers the existence of a family of dinosaurs in the jungles of Africa. With her husband, she attempts to rescue them from an evil scientist who, with government support, is trying to capture the creatures. Soldiers kill the father and capture the mother, but the scientist manages to save the baby brontosaurus. After a series of hair-raising adventures, the couple defeats the evil scientist and reunites the infant with its mother. Released Mar. 22, 1985. Directed by B. W. L. Norton. A Touchstone film. 93 min. Stars William Katt (George Loomis), Sean Young (Susan Matthews-Loomis), Patrick McGoohan (Dr. Eric Kivist), Kyalo Mativo (Cephu). Central to the plot are the dinosaur characters designed and constructed by mechanical effects experts Ron Tantin and Isidoro Raponi. These characters, among the largest and most complex ever created for the screen, required almost 1 full year of planning. The dinosaur models range in size from a full-scale father (70 feet long and 25 feet high) to a miniature baby (30 inches long and 10 inches high). The dinosaurs were sculpted and molded in the U.S. and reconstructed at 2 "dino bases" in the Ivory Coast. After a global search, the filmmakers settled on the Ivory Coast because of its tropical rain forest and bush villages. The film crew, based in the country's capital,

Abidjan (population 1.5 million), utilized locations in the nearby Parc National du Banco for tropical jungle scenes. Several villages within a 70-kilometer radius and situated along the Comoe River were also primary sites. Filming was completed at the Disney Studio in Burbank.

Baby Center Opened Jul. 1957 on Main Street, U.S.A. at Disneyland in response to requests from mothers for a place they could change and care for their babies during a park visit. Disneyland nurses had an unexpected event happen Jul. 4, 1979, when the first baby was born in the park—Teresa Salcedo, who weighed in at 6 lbs. 10.5 oz. The happy but surprised parents were Rosa and Elias Salcedo of Los Angeles.

Baby Daddy (TV) Comedy series on Freeform (formerly ABC Family); aired Jun. 20, 2012–May 22, 2017. Bachelor Ben Wheeler, in his twenties, becomes a surprise dad to a baby girl when she is left on his doorstep by an ex-girlfriend. Ben decides to raise the baby with the help of his mother, his brother Danny, his best friend, and a close friend, Penny, who is harboring a secret crush on him. Stars Jean-Luc Bilodeau (Ben Wheeler), Melissa Peterman (Bonnie Wheeler), Derek Theler (Danny Wheeler), Tahj Mowry (Tucker Dobbs), and Chelsea Kane (Penny). From Don't Borrow Trouble/ABC Family.

Baby Einstein Company LLC, The Award-winning creator of the infant developmental media category specifically designed for babies and toddlers. Through unique combinations of real-world objects, music, art, language, science, poetry, and nature, Baby Einstein products expose little ones to the world around them in playful and enriching ways. Originally founded by a mom, the company's videos and products encourage parent-child interaction. It was a subsidiary of The Walt Disney Company from Nov. 2001 until Sep. 2013 upon being sold to Kids II.

Baby Herman Cigar-smoking "baby" in *Who Framed Roger Rabbit* and the Roger Rabbit cartoons; voiced by Lou Hirsch.

Baby Mine Song from *Dumbo*; written by Ned Washington and Frank Churchill. Nominated for an Academy Award.

Baby Mine Baby boutique in Fantasyland at Tokyo Disneyland; opened in 2001, taking the place of the

Tinker Bell Toy Shop. Later replaced by the Brave Little Tailor Shoppe.

Baby Weems (film) Segment of *The Reluctant Dragon*, with the story of a precocious baby genius who creates a big sensation but then fades into obscurity, told through story sketches with limited animation to demonstrate the story development process. Narrated by Alan Ladd.

Bacchus God of wine in "The Pastoral Symphony" segment of *Fantasia*.

Bacchus Lounge Opened at the Shanghai Disneyland Hotel Jun. 16, 2016, offering cocktails, wine, and high-end snack foods. Inspired by "The Pastoral Symphony" segment of *Fantasia*.

Back Home (TV) A Disney Channel Premiere Film; first aired Jun. 7, 1990. Directed by Piers Haggard. A mother eagerly awaits the return of her daughter from the U.S. in post-World War II England, but her daughter's new American sensibility creates conflicts with her family. Stars Hayley Mills (Peggy), Hayley Carr (Rusty), Adam Stevenson (Charlie). Based on the novel by Michelle Magorian. 103 min.

Back to Hannibal: The Return of Tom Sawyer and Huckleberry Finn (TV) A Disney Channel Premiere Film; first aired Oct. 21, 1990. Grown-up Tom and Huck return to Hannibal, Missouri, to save their friend Jim, accused of murdering Becky's husband. Directed by Paul Krasny. Stars Paul Winfield (Jim), Raphael Sbarge (Tom Sawyer), Mitchell Anderson (Huckleberry Finn), Ned Beatty (the Duke), Megan Follows (Becky Thatcher). 92 min.

Back to Neverland [sic] (film) Beginning of The Magic of Disney Animation tour in Disney-MGM Studios; ran May 1, 1989–Sep. 30, 2003. A "new" lost boy from *Peter Pan* gave guests a hilarious lesson in animation basics. Stars Walter Cronkite and Robin Williams. 9 min. Also played in Disney Animation at Disney's California Adventure in 2001; succeeded by *One Man's Dream: 100 Years of Magic*. (The correct spelling of the island in the Disney films is two words: Never Land.)

Back to School with the Mickey Mouse Club See Darkwing Duck Premiere.

Backlot Area at the Disney Studio in Burbank beyond the office buildings, shops, and sound-stages, where outdoor filming was done. Over the years, many different sets have occupied these various locations, which were hidden from the sight of passersby by large berms. The primary set areas were the *Zorro* set (featuring a town square, the fort, and Don Diego's home), the Western set (several streets with western-type saloons, blacksmith shops, etc., constructed for *Elfego Baca* and *Texas John Slaughter*), the residential street (with the look of a normal midwestern town, first used for *The Absent-Minded Professor*), and the business street (with shops and stores surrounding a town square, originally built for *The Ugly Dachshund* and *Follow Me, Boys!*, and completely reconstructed for *Something Wicked This Way Comes*). Other areas could be made to resemble whatever location was needed—a gold rush town with stream (for *The Adventures of Bullwhip Griffin*), a colonial-era estate (for *The Swamp Fox*), a Maine waterfront (for *Pete's Dragon*), a Viking settlement (for *The Island at the Top of the World*), an olive orchard (for *Monkeys, Go Home!*), or an English lane (for *Bedknobs and Broomsticks*). The backlot saw its primary usage from the late 1950s until the late 1970s. By then, backlots had lost some of their allure, as sophisticated audiences forced movie producers to seek out real, as opposed to the often fake-looking, sets. Besides, it became easier to go on location, with the availability of more portable equipment. Gradually, the seldom used backlot sets at the Disney Studio gave way to needed office buildings, warehouses, and parking garages. For TV production purposes, a short business street was built in 1997, remaining until 2014.

Backlot Express Quick-service restaurant in Disney's Hollywood Studios; opened May 1, 1989. Guests dine in a warehouse one would find at a movie studio, filled with paints, molding, hardware, and stunt gear. Also a restaurant in Walt Disney Studios Park at Disneyland Paris, Mar. 16, 2002–Aug. 2009; succeeded by the Disney Blockbuster Cafe.

Backson Imaginary creature presumed to be Christopher Robin's kidnapper in *Winnie the Pooh* (2011).

Backstage Magic EPCOT Computer Central show in Communicore sponsored by Sperry; ran Feb. 4, 1984–Oct. 1, 1993, replacing the Astuter Computer Revue. A host, Julie, and her electronic friend, I/O, showed how computers ran the park and its hundreds of Audio-Animatronics figures.

Backstage Party (TV) Show aired Dec. 17, 1961, as a tour of the Disney Studio and a party celebrating the completion of *Babes in Toyland*. Directed by Jack Donohue. Annette Funicello hosts the final segment by introducing various cast members who perform. A special award, a Mousecar (Disney equivalent of an Oscar) is presented to Ed Wynn. Also starred Ray Bolger, Tommy Sands, Tommy Kirk, Kevin Corcoran, Noah Beery.

Backstage Studio Tour Attraction in Disney-MGM Studios; opened May 1, 1989. One of the main reasons for building Disney-MGM Studios was to give guests an opportunity to discover what goes on behind the scenes during the making of movies and TV shows. This tour began with a tram ride through real production buildings, with windows showing costume and set construction areas. Then it continued on to the backlot, with a ride down a residential street before entering Catastrophe Canyon for a special effects demonstration. In the early days of the tour, the tram would drive guests around the New York Street backlot, but later visitors were welcome to stroll that area on their own. On exiting the tram, guests were encouraged to continue their tour to an area called Inside the Magic—Special Effects and Production Tour. Here were several special effects locations, followed by a walk along an enclosed catwalk above the soundstages, where filming was often in progress. One of the primary residents of 1 of the soundstages was The Disney Channel's *Mickey Mouse Club*. A highlight on the tour was the viewing of a short film called *The Lottery*, starring Bette Midler; then guests were directed through the sets of the film. In 1996, this last area was remodeled to show clips and sets from the live-action version of *101 Dalmatians*. The tour changed throughout the years, with the residential section removed for the construction of the *Lights, Motors, Action! Extreme Stunt Show*. It became Disney-MGM Studios Backlot Tour on Jun. 30, 1996, and in Jan. 2008 the Studio Backlot Tour. Pre-recorded narration took the place of a host in Mar. 2009, and the attraction closed Sep. 27, 2014. SEE ALSO RESIDENTIAL STREET.

Backstage with Disney on Broadway: Celebrating 20 Years (TV) One-hour special on ABC; aired Dec. 14, 2014, showcasing Disney's 8 Broadway musicals, hosted by Jesse Tyler Ferguson. Music from the Disney on Broadway catalog is featured, with performances by Elton John, Sam Palladio, Clare Bowen, Ashley Brown, and Adam Jacobs.

Backus, Jim (1913–1989) Actor; appeared in *Now You See Him, Now You Don't* (Timothy Forsythe) and *Pete's Dragon* (mayor), and on TV as a host of *The Mouse Factory*.

Bacon, Kevin Actor; appeared in *The Air Up There* (Jimmy Dolan).

Bad Company (film) An out-of-favor CIA agent is caught in a maze of deadly intrigue when he is sent to infiltrate an industrial espionage boutique and ends up being seduced by a master manipulator into taking over the operation. Their relationship erupts into uncontrollable passion with greed proving to be the underlying motivation in this tale of espionage and ruthless double-crossing. Released Jan. 20, 1995. Directed by Damian Harris. Filmed in CinemaScope. A Touchstone film. 108 min. Written by the Edgar Award–winning mystery writer Ross Thomas. Stars Ellen Barkin (Margaret Wells), Laurence Fishburne (Nelson Crowe), Frank Langella (Vic Grimes), Michael Beach (Tod Stapp), David Ogden Stiers (Judge Beach).

Bad Company (film) A different film from the one released in 1995 (SEE PRECEDING ENTRY) with the same title. Gaylord Oakes, a veteran CIA agent, must transform sarcastic, streetwise punk Jake Hayes into a sophisticated and savvy spy to replace his murdered identical twin brother. He has only 9 days to accomplish this mission before having to negotiate a sensitive nuclear weapons deal with terrorists. Directed by Joel Schumacher. A Touchstone film from Jerry Bruckheimer Films. Released Jun. 7, 2002. Stars Anthony Hopkins (Gaylord Oakes), Chris Rock (Jake Hayes), Matthew Marsh (Dragan Adjanic), Gabriel Macht (Seale), John Slattery (Roland Yates), Peter Stormare (Adrik Vas), Kerry Washington (Julie), Garcelle Beauvais-Nilon (Nicole). 117 min. Working title was *Black Sheep*. Filmed in Super 35 wide-screen format in New York City and Prague.

Bad Hair Day (TV) A Disney Channel Original Movie; premiered Feb. 13, 2015. Monica is a high school tech whiz who is bound and determined to be crowned prom queen. But on the big day, everything goes wrong, starting with her suddenly uncontrollable hair and a destroyed prom dress. She soon comes to rely on a cop who's in pursuit of a missing necklace that Monica unwittingly has in her possession. But they are also being pursued by a dogged jewel thief on a wild ride across the city. Directed by Erik Canuel. Stars Laura Marano

(Monica), Leigh-Allyn Baker (Liz), Christian Campbell (Pierce). From Muse Entertainment Enterprises. Filmed in Montreal.

Bad Sisters (TV) Ten-episode dark comedy/thriller series; digitally released on Apple TV+ Aug. 19–Oct. 14, 2022. The tight-knit Garvey sisters have always looked out for each other. When their brother-in-law winds up dead, his life insurers launch an investigation to prove malicious intent—and set their sights on the sisters, all of whom had ample reason to kill him. Stars Sharon Horgan (Eva Garvey), Anne-Marie Duff (Grace Williams), Eva Birthistle (Ursula Flynn), Sarah Greene (Bibi Garvey), Eve Hewson (Becka Garvey), Claes Bang (John Paul Williams), Brian Gleeson (Thomas Claffin), Daryl McCormack (Matthew Claffin). From Merman Television and ABC Signature.

Baddeley, Hermione (1906–1986) Character actress; appeared in *Mary Poppins* (Ellen), *The Adventures of Bullwhip Griffin* (Irene Chesny), and *The Happiest Millionaire* (Mrs. Worth), and voiced Madame Adelaide Bonfamille in *The Aristocats*.

Baer, Dale (1950–2021) He started at the Disney Studio in 1971, as the second artist hired into the inaugural animation training program, and went on to contribute to many animated shorts, theme park productions, and feature films, starting with *Robin Hood*. He served as supervising animator on *Who Framed Roger Rabbit*, *The Lion King* (adult Simba), *The Emperor's New Groove* (Yzma), *Home on the Range* (Alameda Slim), *Meet the Robinsons* (Wilbur), and *The Princess and the Frog* (frog hunters), and as a visual development artist on *Wreck-It Ralph*, *Frozen*, and *Zootopia*.

Baer, Parley (1914–2002) Actor; appeared in *Those Calloways* (Doane Shattuck), *The Ugly Dachshund* (Mel Chadwick), *Follow Me, Boys!* (Mayor Hi Plommer), and *The Adventures of Bullwhip Griffin* (chief executioner), and on TV in *The Boy Who Stole the Elephant*, *The Strange Monster of Strawberry Cove*, and *Bristle Face*.

Baggage Buster (film) Goofy cartoon released Mar. 28, 1941. Directed by Jack Kinney. In his efforts to load a magician's trunk, baggageman Goofy has a series of encounters with its contents, including rabbits, a bull, skeleton, and elephant.

Bagheera Sophisticated panther in *The Jungle Book*; voiced by Sebastian Cabot. Later voiced by Bob Joles in *The Jungle Book 2*.

Bagnall, George (1896–1978) Member of the Disney Board of Directors 1961–1974. His son, Michael, served for a time as the company's chief financial officer.

Baía (film) Segment of *The Three Caballeros* in which Donald Duck and José Carioca visit Baía, Brazil, and dance the samba.

Bailey, Halle Actress/singer/composer; starred in *The Little Mermaid* (Ariel, 2023). She appeared on TV in *grown-ish* (Sky Forster) and *The Most Magical Story on Earth: 50 Years of Walt Disney World*, and on Disney Channel in *Let It Shine* (choir girl), *Austin & Ally* (Halle), and the *Radio Disney Music Awards*. She wrote/performed "Warrior" for *A Wrinkle in Time* with her sister and *grown-ish* co-star, Chloe.

Bailey, Pearl (1918–1990) Singer/actress; voiced Big Mama in *The Fox and the Hound*.

Bailey (Turner), Grace (1904–1983) Began work at Disney in 1932 in the Ink & Paint Department and in 1954 became its head. She remained in that position until her retirement in 1972 and received a posthumous Disney Legends Award in 2000.

Bailey's Mistake (TV) A 2-hour movie on *The Wonderful World of Disney*; first aired Mar. 18, 2001. Liz Donovan, recently widowed, discovers that her late husband, Paul, had secretly spent their life savings to purchase property on Bailey's Mistake, a small island off the coast of Maine. She travels there with her 2 children, Dylan and Becca, determined to sell the property, but instead discovers a breathtakingly beautiful island with a touch of magic and mystery. Strange things happen, and there is a group of odd local residents. As Liz struggles with her dilemma, Dylan begins to display a magical gift for healing. The trip proves to be an emotional journey for the Donovans, as they come to terms with their loss and accept the gain of a "new" family. Directed by Michael M. Robin. Stars Linda Hamilton (Liz Donovan), Joan Plowright (Aunt Angie), Kyle Secor (Lowell Lenox), Jesse James (Dylan), Paz de la Huerta (Becca), Richard Burgi (Paul Donovan).

Baird, Sharon Mouseketeer from the 1950s *Mickey Mouse Club* TV show.

Bakalyan, Dick (1931–2015) Disney regular; appeared in *The Strongest Man in the World* (Cookie); *The Shaggy D.A.* (Freddie); *Return from Witch Mountain* (Eddie); *Follow Me, Boys!* (umpire); *Never a Dull Moment* (Bobby Macon); *The Computer Wore Tennis Shoes* (Chillie Walsh); *Now You See Him, Now You Don't* (Cookie); and *Charley and the Angel* (Buggs). Appeared on TV in *Way Down Cellar*, *The Whiz Kid and the Carnival Caper*, *The Young Runaways*, and *A Boy Called Nuthin'*. He narrated *It's Tough to Be a Bird* (M. C. Bird) and voiced Dinky in *The Fox and the Hound*.

Baker, Buddy (1918–2002) Composer; he joined the Disney Studio in 1955 to help George Bruns write music for *Davy Crockett* and would go on to score dozens of other TV shows and features, including the *Mickey Mouse Club*, *Zorro*, *Donald in Mathmagic Land*, *Toby Tyler*, *The Monkey's Uncle*, *The Gnome-Mobile*, the original Winnie the Pooh films, *The Apple Dumpling Gang*, and *The Fox and the Hound*. He specialized in the Disney attractions at the 1964–1965 New York World's Fair (including It's a Small World, Great Moments with Mr. Lincoln, and the Carousel of Progress), Disneyland (including the Haunted Mansion), Walt Disney World, and Tokyo Disneyland. He served as musical director for EPCOT Center, for which he composed scores for Universe of Energy, The American Adventure, World of Motion, *Wonders of China*, Kitchen Kabaret, Listen to the Land, and *Impressions de France*. He retired in 1983, the last staff composer at any major studio. He was honored as a Disney Legend in 1998.

Baker, Dee Bradley Voice actor; he has provided voices for films, including *G-Force* (Mooch), *Frankenweenie* (Persephone, 2012), *Shang-Chi and the Legend of the Ten Rings* (Morris), and *Night at the Museum: Kahmunrah Rises Again* (Dexter); and shows, including *Phineas and Ferb* (Perry the Platypus), *Monsters at Work* (Banana Bread), *The 7D* (Dopey), *Big Hero 6 The Series* (Mayoi), *Milo Murphy's Law* (Diogee), *W.I.T.C.H.* (Frost), *Vampirina* (Wolfie), *Handy Manny* (Turner), *Legend of the Three Caballeros* (Aracuan Bird), *T.O.T.S.* (Paulie), *Higglytown Heroes* (Pizza Guy), *Miles from Tomorrowland* (Merc), *Muppet Babies* (Animal, 2018), and *The Clone Wars* (Clone Troopers).

Baker, Diane Actress; appeared in *The Horse in the Gray Flannel Suit* (Suzie Clemens) and *The Joy Luck Club* (Mrs. Jordan).

Baker and the Beauty, The (TV) Hour-long romantic comedy series on ABC; aired Apr. 13–Jun. 1, 2020. Daniel Garcia is working in the family bakery and doing everything that his loving Cuban family expects him to do. But his life moves into the spotlight after he meets international superstar Noa Hamilton on a wild Miami night. Will this unlikely couple upend their lives to be together and pull their families into a culture clash? Stars Victor Rasuk (Daniel Garcia), Nathalie Kelley (Noa Hamilton), Carlos Gómez (Rafael Garcia), Dan Bucatinsky (Lewis), Lisa Vidal (Mari Garcia), David Del Rio (Mateo Garcia), Belissa Escobedo (Natalie), Michelle Veintimilla (Vanessa). From ABC Studios, Universal Television, and Keshet Studios.

Baker's Field Bakery Coffee shop inside the California Zephyr at Disney California Adventure; open Feb. 8, 2001–Aug. 1, 2011, in Sunshine Plaza. The name was a play on Bakersfield, the central California city.

Bakersfield P. D. (TV) Series on Fox; aired Sep. 14, 1993–Jan. 4, 1994. An African American, big-city detective tries to fit in with an all-white central California police department headed by a timid chief. Stars Giancarlo Esposito (Paul Gigante), Ron Eldard (Wade Preston), Brian Doyle-Murray (Phil Hampton), Chris Mulkey (Denny Boyer), Jack Hallett (Renny Stiles). From Touchstone Television and Rock Island Productions.

Bakery Tour, The SEE BOUDIN BAKERY, THE.

Baldwin, Alec Actor; appeared in *The Marrying Man* (Charley Pearl), *Pearl Harbor* (Jimmy Doolittle), and *The Last Shot* (Joe Devine); on TV in *The Alec Baldwin Show*; and narrated *The Royal Tenenbaums*.

Baldwin, Robert H. B. (1920–2016) Member of the Disney Board of Directors 1983–1985.

Baldwin, Stephen Actor; appeared in *Crossing the Bridge* (Danny Morgan) and *A Simple Twist of Fate* (Tanny Newland).

Bale, Christian Actor; appeared in *Newsies* (Jack Kelly), *Swing Kids* (Thomas), *Reign of Fire* (Quinn), *The Prestige* (Alfred Borden), and *Thor: Love and Thunder* (Gorr). He voiced Thomas in *Pocahontas* and the title character in *Howl's Moving Castle*.

Balk, Fairuza Actress; appeared in *Return to Oz* (Dorothy) and *The Waterboy* (Vicki Vallencourt).

Ballad of Davy Crockett, The Song from the *Davy Crockett* episodes of the *Disneyland* TV series. One of the most popular songs to come out of a Disney production, with 16 weeks at the top of the Hit Parade. It was written by George Bruns and Tom Blackburn, who dashed it off simply because the first episodes were running short, and something was needed to fill in the gaps.

Ballad of Hector the Stowaway Dog, The (TV) Two-part show; aired Jan. 5 and 12, 1964. Directed by Vincent McEveety. The 2 parts were titled *Where the Heck Is Hector?* and *Who the Heck Is Hector?* A trained Airedale is separated from his owner, who is the first mate on a freighter in Portugal. The sailor unwillingly gets mixed up in a jewel robbery, with the jewels sewn into Hector's collar. The dog manages to elude the thieves and aid the police in their capture, becoming a hero. Stars Guy Stockwell, Craig Hill, Eric Pohlmann. The 2 parts were edited together to become a feature entitled *The Million Dollar Collar* for release outside the U.S.

Ballad of Nessie, The (film) Short cartoon released with *Winnie the Pooh* Jul. 15, 2011. Nessie is really a very gentle sea monster, who is devastated when her home pond is taken over by a golf course developer named MacFroogle. With her only friend, a rubber duck named MacQuack, she goes on a quest to find a new home, but without luck she starts crying, and her tears create Loch Ness, which becomes her new home. Directed by Stevie Wermers-Skelton and Kevin Deters. Narrated by Billy Connolly. 6 min.

Ballad of Renegade Nell, The (TV) Original series planned for digital release on Disney+. When she's framed for murder, Nell Jackson is forced into a life of highway robbery, along with her 2 orphaned sisters, Roxanne and George. Aided by a plucky little spirit called Billy Blind, Nell realizes that fate has put her on the wrong side of the law for a reason—a reason much bigger than she could have ever imagined—that goes right up to Queen Anne and beyond, to the struggle for power raging across the battlefields of Europe. Stars Louisa Harland (Nell), Bo Bragason (Roxy), Florence Keen (George), Nick Mohammed (Billy Blind), Adrian Lester (Earl of Poynton), Alice Kremelberg (Sofia Wilmot), Frank Dillane (Charles Devereux), Craig Parkinson (Sam Trotter), Joely Richardson (Lady Eularia Moggerhanger), Pip Torrens (Lord Blancheford), Jake Dunn (Thomas), Enyi Okoronkwo (Rasselas). From Lookout Point. Among the first Disney-branded U.K. scripted programs for Disney+.

Ballard, Kaye (1925–2019) Actress; appeared in 1977's *Freaky Friday* (Coach Betsy).

Ballast Point Brewing Company Opened Jan. 16, 2019, in the Downtown Disney District at Disneyland Resort. Handcrafted drafts complement a menu of salads, small plates, and entrees. It took a space previously used by Build-A-Bear and Ridemakerz.

Ballerina (TV) Show aired in 2 parts Feb. 27–Mar. 6, 1966. Directed by Norman Campbell. Story of a young ballet student in Denmark who succeeds despite her mother's objections. Partly filmed at the Royal Theatre in Copenhagen. Stars Kirsten Simone, Astrid Villaume, Ole Wegener, Poul Reichardt, Jenny Agutter. This film introduced 11-year-old Jenny Agutter to American audiences; years later, she would appear in Disney's *Amy*.

Ballet Café Quick-service restaurant themed to "The Dance of the Hours" segment from *Fantasia* in the Shanghai Disneyland Hotel; opened Jun. 16, 2016

Balloon Farm (TV) A 2-hour movie on *The Wonderful World of Disney*; first aired Mar. 28, 1999. A peculiar farmer, Harvey H. Potter, arrives in the small town of Waterston, where the families are facing financial ruin because of a drought. Potter's crop turns out to be a field of brilliantly colored balloon plants. The townsfolk are entranced, seeing magical properties in the balloons, but only a little girl, Willow, stands by Potter when mistrust overtakes the town. Directed by William Dear. Stars Rip Torn (Harvey Potter), Mara Wilson (Willow), Roberts Blossom (Wheezle), Laurie Metcalf (Casey Johnson). Based on the book *Harvey Potter's Balloon Farm*, by Jerdine Nolen.

Baloo Happy-go-lucky bear who befriends Mowgli in *The Jungle Book*; voiced by Phil Harris. Also on TV in *TaleSpin* as a devil-may-care pilot for an air-courier service; voiced by Ed Gilbert. Later voiced by John Goodman in *The Jungle Book 2*.

Baloo's Dressing Room Special character-greeting attraction in Fantasyland at Disneyland; opened Mar. 15, 1991, as part of Disney Afternoon Avenue, and closed Sep. 8, 1991, displaced by the construction of Mickey's Toontown. The attraction was inspired by a similar area in Mickey's Birthdayland in the Magic Kingdom at Walt Disney World, where guests were able to visit Mickey Mouse in his dressing room. Eventually, Toontown would provide the experience of directly meeting Mickey.

Bambi (film) Animated life story of a fawn, Bambi, who grows up with friends Thumper, the rabbit, and Flower, the skunk, to be the Great Prince of the Forest. But in the meantime he suffers through the death of his mother at the hands of hunters, falls in love with Faline, and barely escapes a catastrophic forest fire. World premiere in London on Aug. 9, 1942; released in the U.S. on Aug. 13, 1942. Based on the book by Felix Salten. The supervising director was David Hand. Voices include Bobby Stewart/Donnie Dunagan/Hardy Albright/John Sutherland (Bambi), Paula Winslowe (Bambi's mother), Cammie King/Ann Gillis (Faline), Fred Shields (Bambi's father), Bill Wright (Friend Owl), Stanley Alexander/Sterling Holloway/Tim Davis (Flower), Peter Behn/Tim Davis (Thumper). Includes the songs "Love Is a Song" and "Little April Shower," written by Frank Churchill and Larry Morey. The film had been put into production as work on *Snow White and the Seven Dwarfs* was winding down. But the story of Bambi was different from anything else the Studio had ever attempted. It was more serious, and all the characters were animals. In striving for realism, the artists attended lectures from animal experts, made field trips to the Los Angeles Zoo, watched specially filmed nature footage shot in the forests of Maine, and even studied the movements of 2 fawns that were donated to the Studio. The meticulous work was time-consuming; even taking care to see that the spots on the fawn's back remained constant meant fewer drawings could be finished in a day. The overall look of the forest was established by artist Tyrus Wong. The film moved exceedingly slowly through the production process, but Walt was delighted with the results he was seeing. "Fellas, this stuff is pure gold," he told the animators. *Bambi* was released at a difficult time, with the U.S. deep in World War II, so its initial profits were low, but the story of the little deer coming of age has endured, and today *Bambi* is universally regarded as one of Walt Disney's most charming films. The film received Academy Award nominations for Best Sound, Best Song ("Love Is a Song"), and Best Scoring of a Dramatic or Comedy Picture. 70 min. It was rereleased in theaters in 1942, 1947, 1957, 1966, 1975, 1982, and 1988. First released on video in 1989.

Bambi: A Lesson in Perseverance (film) Educational film; released in Sep. 1978. When trying something new, like riding a bicycle, one is not always successful the first time, but the key is to not give up.

Bambi II (film) Direct-to-DVD release Feb. 7, 2006; animated sequel to *Bambi*. Following the tragic loss of his mother, the young fawn Bambi reunites with his father, The Great Prince, who must now teach him the ways of the forest. Their adventure together helps them overcome their initially awkward relationship and allows father and son to discover in each other something neither expected—family. Directed by Brian Pimental. Released theatrically abroad Jan. 26, 2006, beginning with Argentina. Voices include Patrick Stewart (The Great Prince of the Forest), Keith Ferguson (Friend Owl), Alexander Gould (Bambi), Brendon Baerg (Thumper), Nicky Jones (Flower). 73 min. From DisneyToon Studios.

BAMTech SEE DISNEY STREAMING SERVICES.

Bancroft, Tony He co-directed *Mulan* with Barry Cook, having joined Disney in 1989 as an animator, and among other contributions supervised the animation of Pumbaa in *The Lion King* and Kronk in *The Emperor's New Groove*. His twin brother, Tom, was also a Disney animator, supervising the animation of Mushu, the dragon, in *Mulan*.

Band Concert, The (film) Mickey Mouse cartoon, the first one in color; released Feb. 23, 1935. From then on, with the exception of *Mickey's Service Station* and *Mickey's Kangaroo*, all the Disney cartoons would be released in color. Directed by Wilfred Jackson. Mickey is a frustrated bandleader who must deal with obnoxious snack vendor and flute player Donald Duck (who tries to persuade the band to play "Turkey in the Straw"), and a cyclone before his concert of the "William Tell Overture" is completed. The cartoon was a major success, making Donald more popular than ever, and was later included in *Milestones for Mickey* (1974). Conductor Arturo Toscanini called this cartoon his favorite.

Banderas, Antonio Actor; appeared in *Two Much* (Art), *Evita* (Che), *Miami Rhapsody* (Antonio), *Play It to the Bone* (Caesar Dominguez), *The 13th Warrior* (Ahmed Ibn Fahdlan), and *Indiana Jones and the Dial of Destiny* (Renaldo).

Bank of America The bank operated a branch on Main Street, U.S.A. in Disneyland Jul. 17, 1955–Jul. 28, 1993. One of the longest-running participants in Disneyland, it was one of the only banks to have regular Sunday and holiday hours. It also sponsored the It's a Small World attraction 1966–1992. In the 1930s, Walt Disney depended on the Bank of America for funding, and it was Joe Rosenberg of the bank who was persuaded to come up with the money needed to finish *Snow White and the Seven Dwarfs*. SEE ALSO SUN BANK (WALT DISNEY WORLD).

Banker's Daughter, The (film) Oswald the Lucky Rabbit cartoon; released Nov. 28, 1927. As a bank robber makes off with the safe, Oswald follows in hot pursuit with the rabbit of his affection: the banker's daughter.

Banks, Steven Actor; appeared on TV in *The Steven Banks Show* and *Disney's Great American Celebration*.

Banks, Tyra Actress/producer; appeared in *Coyote Ugly* (Zoe), and on TV in *Life-Size* and *Life-Size 2: A Christmas Eve* (Eve), *Felicity* (Jane Scott), *Shake It Up* (Mrs. Burke), and *black-ish* (Gigi). She exec. produced *FABLife* and played the X-S Tech hostess in The ExtraTERRORestrial Alien Encounter at Walt Disney World.

Bannen, Ian (1928–1999) Actor; appeared in *The Watcher in the Woods* (John Keller) and *Night Crossing* (Josef Keller).

Banner in the Sky (TV) Series airing of *Third Man on the Mountain*, in 2 parts Mar. 17–24, 1963, with episode titles of *To Conquer the Mountain* and *The Killer Mountain*.

Bao (film) Short cartoon released with *Incredibles 2* on Jun. 15, 2018. In Toronto's Chinese community, an aging mom suffering from empty-nest syndrome gets another chance at motherhood when one of her dumplings springs to life as a lively, giggly dumpling boy. Mom excitedly welcomes this new bundle of joy into her life, but Dumpling starts growing up fast, and Mom must come to the bittersweet revelation that nothing stays cute and small forever. Directed by Domee Shi. 8 min. From Pixar. Academy Award winner for Best Animated Short of 2018.

Bar Girls (TV) Unsold pilot for a series; two mismatched women lawyers struggle to keep their law firm and the relationship afloat. Aired on CBS on Jul. 5, 1990. 60 min. Directed by Eric Laneuville. Stars Joanna Cassidy, Marcy Walker, John Terlesky, Tom O'Brien.

Barash, Olivia Actress; appeared on TV in *Child of Glass*.

Barbossa's Bounty Quick-service restaurant in Treasure Cove at Shanghai Disneyland; opened Jun. 16, 2016, with barbecue and seafood prepared in a live-show kitchen. Dining rooms are themed to its owner and namesake, Captain Hector Barbossa, as boats sail past into Pirates of the Caribbean—Battle for the Sunken Treasure.

Bardsley, Grant Actor; provided the voice of Taran in *The Black Cauldron*.

Bare Necessities, The Song from *The Jungle Book*; written by Terry Gilkyson. Nominated for an Academy Award.

Barefoot Executive, The (film) In the wacky world of TV, an ambitious mail room boy at the United Broadcasting Company, Steven Post, discovers that a chimpanzee being taken care of by his girlfriend, Jennifer, has an amazing talent—it can pick programs that will become hits. Steven secretly uses the chimp to catapult himself into a vice presidency and a lush life, but the secret is revealed by jealous rivals. Steven loses both the chimp and his girlfriend until he changes his ways and wins out. Released Mar. 17, 1971. Directed by Robert Butler. 96 min. Stars Kurt Russell (Steven Post), Joe Flynn (Wilbanks), Harry Morgan (Crampton), Wally Cox (Mertons), John Ritter (Roger), Heather North (Jennifer), Alan Hewitt (Farnsworth), Hayden Rorke (Clifford), Ruffles the Chimp. The film's song, "He's Gonna Make It," was written by Robert F. Brunner and Bruce Belland. The film was made with the cooperation of the National Academy of Television Arts and

Sciences. A week of location shooting was done in Long Beach, California, with the rest of the shooting schedule completed at the Disney Studios.

Barefoot Executive, The (TV) Two-hour movie; aired on ABC Nov. 11, 1995. A remake of the 1971 feature about the show business career of a young man who rises from mail boy to network vice president when he discovers a TV-loving chimpanzee with an unfailing knack for picking hit series. Directed by Susan Seidelman. Stars Jason London (Billy Murdock), Eddie Albert (Herbert Gower), Michael Marich (Wayne), Jay Mohr (Matt), Terri Ivens (Lisa), Yvonne De Carlo (Norma), Julia Sweeney (Thelma), Chris Elliott (Jase Wallenberg).

Barfi! (film) In this romantic comedy, 3 young people learn lessons about love and societal pressures. Barfi, speech and hearing impaired, falls in love with Shruti, but her parents pressure her to marry a "normal" man. Years later, Shruti runs into Barfi again; Barfi is now in love with Jhilmil, who is autistic. Shruti is still in love with Barfi, so she has to decide between her happiness and his. Released in India and the U.S. (limited) on Sep. 14, 2012, after a release the day before in Kuwait and New Zealand. Directed by Anurag Basu. Stars Ranbir Kapoor (Murphy/Barfi), Priyanka Chopra (Jhilmil Chatterjee), Ileana D'Cruz (Shruit Ghosh/Sengupta). 151 min. From UTV Motion Pictures and The Walt Disney Company India.

Barks, Carl (1901–2000) Barks went to work at the Disney Studio in 1935 as an inbetweener. He later joined the shorts story crew and was one of the artists instrumental in the creative evolution of Donald Duck. In 1942, he began doing comic books, starting with "Donald Duck Finds Pirate Gold," and continuing as artist-writer with the duck comics until his retirement in 1966. His most famous creation, perhaps, is Uncle Scrooge, who made his debut in a 1947 comic book story, "Christmas on Bear Mountain." Barks became the most famous of all of the Disney comic book artists, with a loyal following all over the world. During his retirement in the 1970s, Barks prepared a number of paintings featuring Donald and the other ducks. He was named a Disney Legend in 1991. At the age of 93 (in 1994), he made a lengthy trip to Europe to meet with fans.

Barley Lightfoot Burly and boisterous elf in *Onward*; voiced by Chris Pratt.

Barn Dance, The (film) The 4th Mickey Mouse cartoon; released in 1929. Directed by Walt Disney. When Mickey continually stomps on Minnie's feet during a dance, she spurns him for the better dancer, Pete. Mickey is left sitting on the floor, crying.

Barnes, Christopher Daniel Actor; appeared on TV in *Exile*, *Just Perfect*, and *Disney's All-Star Comedy Circus*. He voiced Prince Eric in *The Little Mermaid* and Prince Charming in *Cinderella II: Dreams Come True* and *Cinderella III: A Twist in Time*.

Barnstormer, The Family roller coaster attraction in Goofy's Wiseacres Farm in Mickey's Toontown Fair at Walt Disney World; opened Oct. 1, 1996. Guests boarded crop-dusting biplanes for a flight around—and into—Goofy's barn. It became The Barnstormer Featuring the Great Goofini as part of Storybook Circus on Feb. 12, 2012.

Barnyard Battle, The (film) Mickey Mouse cartoon; released in 1929. Directed by Walt Disney. Enduring a strenuous army physical, Mickey joins up to protect his home from enemy cats. At first he's one of many Mickey look-alike soldiers, as a machine gunner, using piano keys when he runs out of bullets. Mickey then fights alone against an army of cats, clobbering each with a hammer as they emerge from a tunnel. His fellow soldiers cheer for him and treat him as a hero.

Barnyard Broadcast, The (film) Mickey Mouse cartoon released Oct. 10, 1931. Directed by Burt Gillett. In this satire of radio broadcasting, Mickey runs the control room attempting to monitor the show and the audience. All goes well until howling cats spoil the broadcast and a chase ensues. In the pandemonium, the makeshift studio is destroyed, and Mickey signs off amid the debris.

Barnyard Concert, The (film) Mickey Mouse cartoon released Apr. 10, 1930. Directed by Walt Disney. Mickey attempts to conduct a farmyard concert even though the various members of the band tend to drift off.

Barnyard Olympics (film) Mickey Mouse cartoon released Apr. 15, 1932, to coincide with the Summer Olympics in Los Angeles. Directed by Wilfred Jackson. Despite Pete's continual cheating in a cross-country race, especially during the bicycle portion, Mickey ends up winning. A fun takeoff on Olympic events.

Barra, Mary T. Member of the Disney Board of Directors beginning in 2017.

Barrie, Barbara Actress; appeared on TV in *Child of Glass* (Emily) and *Army Wives* (Virginia), and voiced Alcmene in *Hercules*.

Barry of the Great St. Bernard (TV) Two-part show; aired Jan. 30 and Feb. 6, 1977. Directed by Frank Zuniga. An orphan at a hospice in the Alps trains a Saint Bernard pup to become a rescue dog. He proves his worth with a daring rescue after an avalanche. Stars Jean Claude Dauphin (Martin) and Pierre Tabard (Julius).

Barrymore, Drew Actress; appeared in *Mad Love* (Casey Roberts), on TV in *Disneyland's 30th Anniversary Celebration* and *EPCOT Center: The Opening Celebration*, and provided the voice of Chloe in *Beverly Hills Chihuahua*.

Barty, Billy (1924–2000) Actor; appeared in *Tough Guys* (Philly) and provided the voice of the Baitmouse in *The Rescuers Down Under* and Figment in Journey Into Imagination at EPCOT Center.

Baseball Fever (TV) Show, a group of baseball cartoons, aired Oct. 14, 1979. Directed by Jack Kinney and Jack Hannah.

BaseLine Tap House Corner pub specializing in California beer and wines on Grand Avenue at Disney's Hollywood Studios; opened Sep. 29, 2017. Took the space formerly occupied by The Writer's Stop.

Bashful One of the Seven Dwarfs; voiced by Scotty Mattraw.

Basic Communication Skills (film) Educational film in the Skills for the New Technology: What a Kid Needs to Know Today series; released in Sep. 1983. Focuses on how communication skills are as important as ever in the computer age.

Basil The Sherlock Holmes mouse character of Baker Street fame in *The Great Mouse Detective*; voiced by Barrie Ingham.

Basin Bath, body, and hair-care shop in the Downtown Disney District at Disneyland Resort; open Jan. 12, 2001–Dec. 2010, replaced by Sanuk. Also in the Marketplace at Disney Springs at Walt Disney World; opened Jan. 2003, taking the place of Generation BeneFITS. Another shop opened in Disney's Grand Floridian Resort & Spa Nov. 7, 2006, taking the place of Bally; it became Basin White Mar. 24, 2007.

Basinger, Kim Actress; appeared in *The Marrying Man* (Vicki Anderson).

Baskett, James (1904–1948) Actor; appeared in *Song of the South* as Uncle Remus and also voiced Brer Fox. He received a special Academy Award in 1948 for his portrayal of the kindly storyteller, therefore becoming the first actor in a Disney film to be recognized by the Academy of Motion Picture Arts and Sciences (the first such honor for an African American male actor).

Bassett, Angela Actress; appeared in *What's Love Got to Do with It?* (Tina Turner), *Mr. 3000* (Mo Simmons), and as Ramonda in *Black Panther* and later Marvel Studios films, and on TV in *Alias* (Hayden Chase). She voiced Groove in *Whispers: An Elephant's Tale*, Mildred in *Meet the Robinsons*, and Dorothea Williams in *Soul*. For Disney+, she narrated *The Imagineering Story*.

Bat en Rouge, Le SEE LE BAT EN ROUGE.

Bateman, Jason Actor; provided the voice of Nick Wilde in *Zootopia*. He appeared in *The Switch* (Wally Mars), and on TV in *The Thanksgiving Promise* (Steve Tilby), *Scrubs* (Mr. Sutton), *The Muppets*, and *Disneyland 60: The Wonderful World of Disney*.

Bates, Kathy Actress; appeared in *Dick Tracy* (Mrs. Green), *The War at Home* (Maureen Collier), *The Waterboy* (Mama Boucher), and *Around the World in 80 Days* (Queen Victoria), and on TV in *Annie* (Miss Hannigan).

Bath Day (film) Figaro cartoon released Oct. 11, 1946. Directed by Charles Nichols. To his displeasure, Figaro is bathed and perfumed by Minnie. An alley cat, Lucifer, and his gang chase Figaro for being so prissy. The gang is fooled into thinking that Figaro has beaten up Lucifer in an alley, hidden from their view. Figaro returns home victorious, but the victory is short-lived when Minnie decides he needs another unwanted bath.

Bath Parlour Shop in the Lake Buena Vista

Shopping Village at Walt Disney World; open Mar. 1975–Feb. 6, 1987, replaced by Mickey & Co.

Bathing Time for Baby (film) Educational film in which a stork teaches the proper method for baby bathing; made for Johnson & Johnson and delivered Mar. 19, 1946.

Bathroom of Tomorrow SEE CRANE COMPANY BATHROOM OF TOMORROW.

Battle for Survival (TV) Nature show on *Walt Disney Presents*; aired Apr. 9, 1961. Time-lapse and close-up photography captures some of nature's most closely guarded hiding places, as honeybees, grunion, and other insects, plants, and animals of land and sea must all battle for survival. Directed by James Algar.

Baucom, Bill (1910–1981) Actor; voiced Trusty in *Lady and the Tramp*.

Bauer, Cate Actress; provided the voice of Perdita in *One Hundred and One Dalmatians*.

Baxter, Tony Imagineer; he began his Disney career in 1965 scooping ice cream in Carnation Plaza Gardens at Disneyland. His persistence and some intriguing ideas landed him a job at WED Enterprises, where he worked up through the ranks to senior vice president of creative development. Some of his design projects include Big Thunder Mountain Railroad, Journey Into Imagination, the New Fantasyland at Disneyland, Star Tours, Splash Mountain, Indiana Jones Adventure, Finding Nemo Submarine Voyage, and Disneyland Paris, for which he served as executive producer. In 2013 Tony stepped down to become a creative adviser for Imagineering and the same year was named a Disney Legend.

Bay Area San Francisco-inspired district within the former Golden State section in Disney's California Adventure; opened Feb. 8, 2001, celebrating the people and cultures that have shaped California. Later incorporated into Paradise Gardens Park.

Bay Boutique Apparel and jewelry shop in Disney Newport Bay Club at Disneyland Paris; opened Apr. 12, 1992.

Bay Lake The largest body of water at Walt Disney World, at 450 acres; located east of Disney's Contemporary Resort. During construction, one of the first tasks was to clear the muck out of Bay Lake. Upon doing this, Walt Disney World executives were delighted to discover that beautiful white sand was actually covering the bottom. This sand was utilized to create attractive beaches. Discovery Island, a nature preserve which could be visited by guests 1974–1999, is located in Bay Lake. The lake is connected to the Seven Seas Lagoon in front of the Magic Kingdom by a unique water bridge over the main road to the Contemporary. Hotel guests can rent various types of watercraft for cruising. Disney's Fort Wilderness Resort & Campground and Disney's Wilderness Lodge are located along Bay Lake, as was the former River Country. Bay Lake is also the name of the municipality encompassing the 4 theme parks of Walt Disney World.

Bay Lake Tower Disney Vacation Club resort, connected by Sky Way Bridge to Disney's Contemporary Resort, at Walt Disney World; opened Aug. 4, 2009, with 16 stories and 295 villas. The resort has an urban boutique design, including several 2-story Grand Villas and the Top of the World Lounge providing views of the Magic Kingdom.

Baymax Healthcare robot built by Tadashi Hamada and friend of Hiro in *Big Hero 6*; voiced by Scott Adsit.

Baymax! (TV) Original animated series on Disney+; digitally premiered Jun. 29, 2022. In the fantastical city of San Fransokyo, the affable, inflatable healthcare companion sets out to accomplish what he was programmed to do—help others—in a series of healthcare capers, introducing characters who need Baymax's signature approach to healing in more ways than they realize. Voices include Scott Adsit (Baymax). From Walt Disney Animation Studios.

Baymax Dreams (TV) SEE BIG HERO 6 THE SERIES.

Bayou Boy (TV) Two-part show; aired Feb. 7 and 14, 1971. Directed by Gary Nelson. Two boys face danger, including a giant alligator, while searching for a lost silver church bell in Dead Man's Bayou. Stars John McIntire, Mitch Vogel, Mike Lookinland, Jeanette Nolan, Frank Silvera. A rerun of the show aired in 1979 as *The Boy from Deadman's Bayou*.

Bayside Takeout Port Discovery refreshment stand in Tokyo DisneySea; opened Jul. 2018.

Bayside Wharf Covered outdoor dining area in Arendelle Village; planned for World of Frozen in Hong Kong Disneyland in 2023.

Bayview Gifts Shop in Disney's Contemporary Resort at Walt Disney World offering premium Disney souvenirs. Also known as B.V.G. beginning in 2000.

BB-8 Skittish astromech droid introduced in *Star Wars: The Force Awakens*.

Be Our Chef (TV) Cooking competition series; premiered Mar. 27, 2020, on Disney+. Five food-loving families compete to have their Disney-inspired dish served at Walt Disney World. Hosted by Angela Kinsey. From INE Entertainment.

Be Our Guest Song from *Beauty and the Beast*; written by Howard Ashman and Alan Menken. Nominated for an Academy Award.

Be Our Guest Boutique *Beauty and the Beast*–themed shop in Fantasyland at Shanghai Disneyland; opened Jun. 16, 2016, offering home décor, collectibles, and souvenirs.

Be Our Guest Restaurant Opened Dec. 6, 2012, in the Beast's Castle, as part of the 2012 addition to Fantasyland in the Magic Kingdom at Walt Disney World. A sumptuously furnished, 550-seat restaurant themed to *Beauty and the Beast*, with a French–inspired menu. Guests can dine in the opulent ballroom, the foreboding West Wing, where an enchanted rose drops its petals, and the Rose Gallery, adorned with tapestries of characters from the story.

Be Prepared Song from *The Lion King*; written by Elton John and Tim Rice.

Beach, Adam Actor; starred in the title role in *Squanto: A Warrior's Tale* and appeared in *Mystery, Alaska* (Galin Winetka).

Beach Club Marketplace SEE ATLANTIC WEAR AND WARDROBE EMPORIUM.

Beach Club Resort, Disney's Resort along Crescent Lake in the EPCOT Resort Area at Walt Disney World; opened Nov. 19, 1990. Designed by Robert A.M. Stern, the hotel is connected to Disney's Yacht Club Resort and offers a short walk to an entrance to EPCOT, through the Inter-national Gateway next to the France pavilion. Architecture and décor are inspired by the charming summer cottages that sprang up along the New England seacoast during the Victorian era. Stormalong Bay, the 750,000-gallon, 3-acre swimming pool common to the 2 hotels, with its meandering waterways with whirlpools, lagoons, and slides, is one of the most unusual in the world. Guests can dine at Cape May Cafe, Beaches & Cream Soda Shop, Martha's Vineyard lounge, and grab a snack at the Beach Club Marketplace. Disney's Beach Club Villas, a Disney Vacation Club property, opened in 2002. SEE ALSO YACHT CLUB RESORT, DISNEY'S.

Beach Party, The (film) Mickey Mouse cartoon released Nov. 5, 1931. Directed by Burt Gillett. A beach party with Mickey and the gang is interrupted by a disgruntled octopus accidentally pulled ashore by Pluto. After a free-for-all, Mickey gets rid of the octopus by lassoing it with a rope with an anchor attached.

Beach Picnic (film) Donald Duck cartoon released Jun. 9, 1939. The first cartoon directed by Clyde ("Gerry") Geronimi. Donald, at the beach, teases Pluto with an inflatable rubber horse toy, but he gets a taste of his own medicine when an ant colony carries away his picnic food. Donald gets even angrier when he gets wrapped up in the flypaper he puts out to trap the ants.

Beaches (film) On a hot summer day in 1937, a remarkable and unlikely friendship begins on the beach in Atlantic City. Eleven-year-olds C. C. Bloom and Hilary Whitney are from different worlds; brash streetwise C. C. wants to be a famous singing star, while Hilary is a proper young lady from San Francisco. Although they go their separate ways, they vow to remain friends, and through letters they share each other's hopes, dreams, and frustrations. Years later their lives again entwine when Hilary, now a lawyer, moves in with rising actress C. C. Their friendship is strained when C. C.'s director, John—with whom she is in love—falls for Hilary. When Hilary returns to California to take care of her ailing father, John turns to C. C. Hilary marries another lawyer who eventually leaves her. The strength of Hilary and C. C.'s relationship sustains them through the successes and disappointments of their marriages and careers, through the birth of Hilary's daughter, and ultimately through a crisis that tests their love and teaches them the true meaning of friendship. Premiered in New York City Dec. 21, 1988; general release Jan. 13, 1989. Directed by Garry Marshall. A Touchstone film. 120 min. Stars Bette Midler (C. C. Bloom), Barbara Hershey (Hilary Whitney Essex), John Heard (John Pierce), Lainie Kazan (Leona Bloom), Spalding Gray (Dr. Richard Milstein), Mayim Bialik (C. C., age 11). Filmed at more than 42 locations in Los Angeles and New York City.

Beaches & Cream Soda Shop Old-style ice cream parlor adjacent to Stormalong Bay at Disney's Beach Club Resort at Walt Disney World; opened Nov. 19, 1990, serving burgers and ice cream specialties. For the ultimate experience, guests can order the Kitchen Sink—8 scoops of ice cream smothered in every topping. The dining room was expanded and redesigned with modern touches in 2019.

Beagle Boys Convict characters (who wear their prison numbers around their necks) from the comic books and, later, *DuckTales*. They were created by artist Carl Barks and debuted in *Walt Disney's Comics and Stories* no. 134 in Nov. 1951.

Beanblossom, Billie Jean Mouseketeer from the 1950s *Mickey Mouse Club* TV show.

Bear Country (film) True-Life Adventure featurette released Feb. 5, 1953. Directed by James Algar. Story of the American black bears from the time they are born and trained by their mothers, through the mating battles, and finally the mother's abandonment of her young. Academy Award winner. 33 min.

Bear Country The seventh "land" to open in Disneyland; the grand opening took place Mar. 25, 1972. Themed after rustic forests of the Northwest. The main attraction was the Country Bear Jamboree, with dining at the Mile Long Bar and Golden Bear Lodge (later Hungry Bear Restaurant). The area also included Teddi Barra's Swingin' Arcade, Ursus H. Bear's Wilderness Outpost, Indian Trading Post, Mike Fink Keel Boats, and Davy Crockett's Explorer Canoes. The land succeeded the Indian Village. Bear Country became Critter Country Dec. 10, 1988, during the construction of Splash Mountain.

Bear Family, The (film) Educational film made up from stock footage primarily from *Bear Country* and *White Wilderness*; released in Apr. 1970. Depicts the lifestyle of the bear, emphasizing the Kodiak black bear and the Arctic polar bear.

Bear in the Big Blue House (TV) Show on Disney Channel, debuting Oct. 20, 1997, and featuring the friendly and furry Bear, who welcomes kids into his Big Blue House for fun playtime with his friends Tutter, an industrious mouse; Pip & Pop, mischievous otters; Treelo, a highly excitable lemur; and Ojo, an imaginative little girl bear. Featured the talents of Noel MacNeal (Bear), Lynne Thigpen (Luna), Peter Linz (Tutter), Vicki Eibner (Ojo), Tyler Bunch (Treelo), Tara Mooney (Shadow). From Jim Henson Productions in association with Disney Channel. Winner of 3 Daytime Emmy Awards.

Bear in the Big Blue House—Live on Stage Attraction in Disney-MGM Studios, featuring Bear and other characters from his show; performed Jul. 4, 1999–Aug. 4, 2001. Replaced by *Playhouse Disney—Live on Stage!*

Bearly Asleep (film) Donald Duck cartoon released Aug. 19, 1955. Directed by Jack Hannah. When Humphrey the Bear is kicked out of his hibernation cave because of his snoring, he tries again and again to use Donald's house, ultimately disguising himself as an orphan bear to be taken back into the cave. Filmed in CinemaScope.

Bearly Country Frontierland shop in the Magic Kingdom at Walt Disney World; opened Jun. 6, 1985, selling plush bears, country crafts, and clothing. It replaced some of the queue space for Country Bear Jamboree. Closed Feb. 25, 1991, to become Prairie Outpost & Supply.

Bears (film) Disneynature documentary about a year in the life of a brown bear family in Alaska's coastal mountains and shores. Their journey begins as winter comes to an end and the bears emerge from hibernation to face the bitter cold. The world outside is exciting, but risky, as the cubs' playful descent down the mountain carries with it a looming threat of avalanches. As the season changes from spring to summer, the bears must find food, ultimately feasting at a plentiful salmon run, while staying safe from rival male bears and predators, including an ever-present wolf. Directed by Keith Scholey and Alastair Fothergill. Released Apr. 18, 2014, after an Apr. 17 release in Argentina. Narrated by John C. Reilly. 78 min.

Bears and I, The (film) Vietnam veteran Bob Leslie retreats into the wilderness, where he becomes a foster parent to 3 bear cubs and fights to preserve the dignity of the Bear Clan of the Taklute Indians. Red Fern believes the cubs would be better off dead than captive, although Bob explains he is only protecting them until they reach maturity. Later, Indian Sam wounds 1 bear and Bob promises to free him when he has recovered. Meanwhile Bob solves the problem of the Clan being reluctant to give up their land for a national park with his idea of making them all rangers—which is Bob's goal, too. Released Jul. 31, 1974. Directed by Bernard McEveety. 89 min. Stars Patrick Wayne (Bob), Chief Dan George (Chief Peter), Andrew Duggan (Commissioner Gaines), Michael Ansara (Oliver), Robert Pine (John), Val DeVargas (Sam Eagle Speaker), Hal Baylor (Foreman). John Denver composed and performed the song "Sweet Surrender" for this film. The movie was shot in the scenic grandeur of the central British Columbian wilderness on Chilko Lake. Members of a local Tŝilhqot'in community appeared in the film.

Bears and Bees, The (film) Silly Symphony cartoon released Jul. 9, 1932. Directed by Wilfred Jackson. When little cubs are chased away from a honey-filled beehive by a big bear, who greedily begins to eat the honey, the bees give chase. Meanwhile the cubs return and happily begin eating again.

Beast Enchanted prince in *Beauty and the Beast*; voiced by Robby Benson.

Beast, The (TV) One-hour series on ABC; aired Jun. 20–Jul. 18, 2001. Media mogul Jackson Burns builds a 24-hour broadcast news organization where the reporters not only cover the stories but are themselves covered as part of the story. Stars Frank Langella (Jackson Burns), Elizabeth Mitchell (Alice Allenby), Jason Gedrick (Reese McFadden), Peter Riegert (Ted Fisher). From Touchstone Television, with Imagine Entertainment.

Beastly Bazaar Shop on Discovery Island in Disney's Animal Kingdom; opened Apr. 22, 1998, selling hats, accessories, and souvenirs. Closed Aug. 2012, reopening in May 2013 as Adventurers Outpost, a character-greeting spot.

Beasts of Burden Family, The (film) Educational film; released in Jun. 1970. Details the use and usefulness of the working animals of the world that serve man, including huskies, elephants, burros, yaks, reindeer, and llamas.

Beatles, The: Get Back (TV) Three-part original docuseries on Disney+; released digitally Nov. 25–27, 2021. A look at The Beatles' Jan. 1969 recording sessions in which they attempt to write 14 new songs for their first live concert in over 2 years. Compiled from nearly 60 hours of footage and more than 150 hours of audio, most of which had been locked in a vault for more than half a century. Directed by Peter Jackson. Stars John Lennon, Paul McCartney, George Harrison, Ringo Starr. Presented by The Walt Disney Studios in association with Apple Corps Ltd. and WingNut Films Productions Ltd. Winner of 5 Emmy Awards in 2022, including Outstanding Documentary Series.

Beatles, The: Get Back – The Rooftop Concert (film) One-night event, held Jan. 30, 2022, in select IMAX theaters, followed by a global theatrical engagement Feb. 11–13. The Beatles' final performance, on the rooftop of Apple Corps' Savile Row headquarters Jan. 30, 1969. Directed by Peter Jackson. Stars John Lennon, Paul McCartney, George Harrison, Ringo Starr. 60 min. Presented by Disney in association with Apple Corps Ltd. and Wingnut Films.

Beatriz, Stephanie Actress; provided the voice of Mirabel in *Encanto*. On TV, she voiced Gosalyn Waddlemeyer in *DuckTales* (2017) and Ixlan in *Elena of Avalor*, and appeared in *Jessie* (Salma Espinoza) on Disney Channel and in *The Wonderful World of Disney: Magical Holiday Celebration* on ABC.

Beatty, Warren Actor; played the title role in *Dick Tracy*, and also directed the film.

Beaumont, Kathryn Actress; provided the voice of the title character in *Alice in Wonderland* and Wendy in *Peter Pan*, also serving as the live-action reference model for the characters. She appeared on TV in *One Hour in Wonderland* and *The Walt Disney Christmas Show*. She has returned to provide the voices since, including in 1984 for the Alice in Wonderland dark ride at Disneyland and in 1992 for *Fantasmic!*, for which she voiced Wendy. She was honored as a Disney Legend in 1998.

Beautiful Girl (TV) Two-hour movie; aired on ABC Family Oct. 19, 2003. A young elementary school music teacher, about to get married, becomes an unlikely beauty-pageant contestant in order to win a Hawaiian trip for a honeymoon. Even though she doesn't exactly emulate society's vision of stick-thin perfection, she has an incredible voice and stage presence, natural style, and undeniable spunk. Stars Marissa Jaret Winokur (Becca Wasserman), Mark Consuelos (Adam), Fran Drescher (Amanda Wasserman), Reagan Pasternak (Libby Leslie), Sarah Manninen (Rachel), Amanda Brugel (Connie), Joyce Gordon (Nana), Brooke D'Orsay (Eve). Filmed in Toronto. From Touchstone Television.

Beauty and the Beast (film) The beautiful Belle ignores her suitor, the vain Gaston, as she cares for her father, the eccentric Maurice. When Maurice stumbles upon a foreboding castle while lost in the woods, the servants, enchanted into household objects, try to make him welcome, but he is thrown into the dungeon by the Beast. Belle comes to rescue her father and agrees to remain in the castle as his substitute. In order to break the spell, Beast must learn to love another and to be loved in return. Belle seems a likely candidate, but it takes Beast a while to rein in his temper. Belle desperately misses her father, so Beast sadly allows her to leave. Gaston, realizing Beast is a rival for Belle's affection, leads the townsfolk to storm the castle. Belle rushes back in time to profess her love for Beast, and the spell is broken. Initial release in New York City on Nov. 13, 1991; general release on Nov. 22, 1991. Directed by Gary Trousdale and Kirk Wise. 84 min. Voices include Paige O'Hara (Belle), Robby Benson (Beast), Richard White (Gaston), Jerry Orbach (Lumiere), David Ogden Stiers (Cogsworth), Angela Lansbury (Mrs. Potts), Jo Ann Worley (Wardrobe). Academy Award nominee in 7 categories, including for the first time for an animated feature, that of Best Picture; it won for Best Song ("Beauty and the Beast" by Howard Ashman and Alan Menken) and Best Original Score. Angela Lansbury sang the title song in the story, and Celine Dion and Peabo Bryson sang another rendition over the film's end credits. Since lyricist Howard Ashman had passed away earlier in the year, the film was dedicated to him: TO OUR FRIEND, HOWARD, WHO GAVE A MERMAID HER VOICE AND A BEAST HIS SOUL, WE WILL BE FOREVER GRATEFUL. Production of the film took 3½ years and required the talents of nearly 600 animators, artists, and technicians. Portions of the film were animated at Disney's satellite facility in Disney-MGM Studios at Walt Disney World. Art directors working on the film traveled to the Loire Valley in France for inspiration and studied the great French romantic painters such as Jean-Honoré Fragonard and François Boucher. It was Ashman who came up with the idea of turning the enchanted objects into living creatures with unique personalities. Glen Keane, the supervising animator on the Beast, created his own hybrid beast by combining the mane of a lion, the beard and head structure of a buffalo, the tusks and nose bridge of a wild boar, the heavily muscled brow of a gorilla, the legs and tail of a wolf, and the big and bulky body of a bear. Computer-generated imagery was used in several parts of the film, most notably in the "Be Our Guest" sequence and in the creation of a striking 3-D ballroom background, allowing dramatic camera moves on the animated characters as they danced. It became the most successful animated feature in motion picture history up to that time, with domestic box office revenues in excess of $140 million. The film was reissued Jan. 1, 2002, in IMAX and other giant screen theaters and featured the song "Human Again" in a never-before-seen animated sequence (with a new running time of 90 min). A 3-D version premiered Jan. 13, 2012, on a program with the short *Tangled Ever After*.

Beauty and the Beast (film) A live-action telling of the classic story. A prince is turned into a hideous beast by a spell that can only be broken by true love. The beautiful Belle is trapped in his castle, discovering not only the Beast but also that the staff have been turned into household objects. The Beast realizes that this human girl, the first to visit the castle since it was enchanted, may be his last hope. Directed by Bill Condon. Released Mar. 17, 2017, after a Mar. 15 international release. Stars Emma Watson (Belle), Luke Evans (Gaston), Dan Stevens (Beast), Ewan McGregor (Lumière), Emma Thompson (Mrs. Potts), Josh Gad (LeFou), Ian McKellen (Cogsworth), Kevin Kline (Maurice), Audra McDonald (Garderobe), Stanley Tucci (Cadenza). 129 min. The Beast is almost all CG throughout the movie, a process which is also used with great effect in a spectacular "Be Our Guest" number. All of the songs have been retained from the 1991 animated feature, with three more added—"Evermore," "Days in the Sun," and "How Does a Moment Last Forever"—written by the original composer, Alan Menken, with lyrics by Sir Tim Rice. Filmed in wide-screen format at Shepperton Studios outside London. Received Academy Award nominations for Costume Design and Production Design.

Beauty and the Beast A stage version of the motion picture previewed in Houston and then played at the Palace Theatre on Broadway from Apr. 18, 1994–Sep. 5, 1999, when it moved to the Lunt-Fontanne Theatre, opening there Nov. 12, 1999. With a cast of 31, it includes 1 Ashman-Menken song written for but not used in the film ("Human Again") and several brand-new songs by Tim Rice and Alan Menken. The original Broadway cast starred Susan Egan (Belle), Terrence Mann (Beast), Tom Bosley (Maurice), Burke Moses (Gaston), Gary Beach (Lumiere), Heath Lamberts (Cogsworth). The show received 9 Tony nominations in 1994, which resulted in 1 award, to Ann Hould-Ward for the costumes. A new production of the show opened at the Shubert Theatre in Los Angeles Mar. 21, 1995, and there were later road show engagements in theaters throughout the world. The last performance on Broadway was Jul. 29, 2007, with a total of 5,464 performances and 46 previews. A Mandarin-language version of the show played in the Walt Disney Grand Theatre in Disneytown at Shanghai Disney Resort Jun. 14, 2018–Jan. 24, 2020. In Dec. 2021, Japan's Shiki Theater Company announced that a reimagined production, in association with Disney Theatrical Productions, would debut Oct. 2022 in the Maihama Amphitheater at Tokyo Disney Resort.

Beauty and the Beast (film) Educational production; released on videodisc in Mar. 1995. Meant as a companion to a study of the Disney film version, the disc features an interview with the screenwriter, along with segments on medieval castles, stained glass, and the stages of animation.

Beauty and the Beast: A 30th Celebration (TV) Two-hour special on *The Wonderful World of Disney*; aired Dec. 15, 2022, on ABC, followed by a digital release on Disney+ the next day. A musical adventure through the eyes of Belle using animation and live action in honor of the animated film's 30th anniversary. Taped in front of a live audience at The Walt Disney Studios in Burbank. Directed by Hamish Hamilton. Stars Rita Moreno (narrator), H.E.R. (Belle), Josh Groban (Beast), Joshua Henry (Gaston), Martin Short (Lumière), David Alan Grier (Cogsworth), Rizwan Manji (LeFou), Jon Jon Briones (Maurice), Shania Twain (Mrs. Potts), Leo Abelo Perry (Chip). From Done+Dusted, in association with Walt Disney Television Alternative and Electric Somewhere.

Beauty and the Beast: Belle's Magical World (film) SEE BELLE'S MAGICAL WORLD.

Beauty and the Beast—Live on Stage Musical show in Disney-MGM Studios (now Disney's Hollywood Studios); premiered in the Theater of the Stars Nov. 22, 1991, succeeding *Hollywood's Pretty Woman*. The show moved from Hollywood Boulevard to a new Theater of the Stars venue on Sunset Boulevard Jun. 15, 1994. The story of the film is presented onstage by Disney Cast Members using elaborate costumes and sets. The popularity of the show helped present an impetus for the creation of a *Beauty and the Beast* stage show for Broadway. Also ran in Videopolis in Disneyland Apr. 11, 1992–Apr. 30, 1995, and in Disneyland Paris Dec. 31, 1992–Jan. 1, 1997.

Beauty and the Beast Sing-Along (film) Film in the France pavilion at EPCOT; debuted Jan. 17, 2020, playing in rotation with *Impressions de France* in the Palais du Cinema. Audiences sing along to 4 songs from the 1991 film with new sequences revealing a twist to the story. Narrated by Angela Lansbury. Directed by Don Hahn. 14 min. Several artists from the original animated feature returned to contribute to the film.

Beauty and the Beast: The Enchanted Christmas (film) Direct-to-video animated feature; released Nov. 11, 1997. Belle attempts to cheer up Beast by planning an elaborate Christmas celebration, though the malevolent Forte, a pipe organ, plots to prevent Beast from falling in love with Belle. When Belle leaves the castle with her friends to search for the perfect Christmas tree, Forte convinces Beast that she has run away. After he captures and imprisons her, he finds a gift she had made for him and realizes that she must have true feelings for him, so he determines to give Belle the best Christmas celebration ever. Directed by Andy Knight. Besides the voices from the original 1991 motion picture of Paige O'Hara, Robby Benson, Jerry Orbach, David Ogden Stiers, and Angela Lansbury, there are the new characters of Angelique, voiced by Bernadette Peters, and Forte, voiced by Tim Curry. 80 min. Four new songs were composed by Rachel Portman and Don Black. This was the first made-for-video movie produced by Walt Disney Animation Canada, Inc., with studios in Toronto and Vancouver.

Beauty & the Briefcase (TV) An ABC Family Original Movie; premiered Apr. 18, 2010. Lane

Daniels, a bright, effervescent fashion journalist, has her career and love life intersect in a complicated way when she pitches the article "Switching Careers to Find Love" to *Cosmopolitan* magazine—her favorite magazine and ultimate career workplace aspiration. In order to pull the undercover story off, Lane lands a job at an investment bank filled with lots of eligible guys. But her perfect plan goes awry when she meets Liam, a gorgeous music producer who sweeps her off her feet outside the office. Since the rules for the story were that Lane could only date the businessmen where she worked, Liam is off-limits, and Lane is forced to choose between what she believes might be love and her *Cosmo* cover story. Directed by Gil Junger. Stars Hilary Duff (Lane Daniels), Matt Dallas (Seth), Michael McMillian (Tom), Chris Carmack (Liam), Jaime Pressly (Editor). Based on Daniella Brodsky's book, *Diary of a Working Girl*. Working title was *The Business of Falling in Love*. Filmed in New Orleans.

Beaver Brothers Explorer Canoes SEE DAVY CROCKETT'S EXPLORER CANOES.

Beaver Creek Tavern Rustic table-service restaurant in Disney Sequoia Lodge at Disneyland Paris; opened May 27, 1992.

Beaver Valley (film) True-Life Adventure featurette released Jul. 19, 1950. Directed by James Algar; photographed by Alfred Milotte; narrated by Winston Hibler; musical orchestrations by Paul Smith. 32 min. Portrays the beaver as the leading citizen of the pond area in which he lives, sharing space with moose, deer, crayfish, raccoons, otters, frogs, and all kinds of birds. Winner of the Academy Award for Best Two-Reel Short Subject. Also known as *In Beaver Valley*.

Beaver Valley/Cameras in Africa (TV) Show aired Dec. 29, 1954, featuring the True-Life Adventure featurette along with some behind-the-scenes footage of Alfred and Elma Milotte filming rhinos, cheetahs, and other animals for *The African Lion*. Directed by Winston Hibler and James Algar. Rerun entitled *Cameras in Africa/Beaver Valley*.

Bebop Hop, The A 1950s-style apparel and sports shop in World Bazaar at Tokyo Disneyland; opened Apr. 29, 1988, taking the place of the Southside Haberdashery. Closed May 2007 to become the Toy Station.

Because You Loved Me Song from *Up Close & Personal*; written by Diane Warren and performed by Celine Dion. Nominated for an Academy Award.

Beckett, Neil (1923–1994) Disney merchandise representative in New Zealand, 1964–1989. He was named a Disney Legend in 2003.

Becoming (TV) A Disney+ original docuseries; digitally released Sep. 18, 2020. Entertainers, musicians, and athletes revisit their hometown for an inspiring look into central moments in their life stories. Exec. produced by LeBron James and Maverick Carter. From ESPN Films, SpringHill Entertainment, Spoke Studios, and ITV America.

Becoming Cousteau (film) A National Geographic feature documentary; released Oct. 22, 2021, following an international festival run beginning Sep. 2. An inside look at Jacques-Yves Cousteau and his life, his iconic films and inventions, and the experiences that made him the 20th century's most unique and renowned environmental voice—and the man who inspired generations to protect the Earth. Directed by Liz Garbus. 94 min.

Bedard, Irene Actress; appeared in *Squanto: A Warrior's Tale* (Nakooma) and provided the speaking voice for the title character in *Pocahontas*. She later reprised the role in *Ralph Breaks the Internet* and voiced the Forest Ranger Hero in *Higglytown Heroes*.

Bedford, Brian (1935–2016) Actor; he voiced the title character in *Robin Hood*, and 2 decades later appeared in *Nixon* as Clyde Tolson. He appeared on TV in *Mr. St. Nick* (Jasper).

Bedknobs and Broomsticks (film) In Aug. 1940, an eccentric, ladylike spinster, Eglantine Price, becomes an apprentice witch, in hopes of finding a magic formula which will help England win the war against Nazi Germany. With the help of 3 London children, whom Miss Price takes in to save from the Blitz, she seeks out her amusing but bogus professor of witchcraft, Emelius Browne, and then ventures over to Portobello Road in search of the rare formula. Miss Price finally discovers that the words of the magical spell can be found on the legendary "Lost Isle of Naboombu," so she, Browne, and the children travel there, having adventures beneath the sea along the way.

They discover the lion king of Naboombu is wearing a medallion with the words to the spell on it, which they have to obtain. All of this magical travel is possible with the aid of a magical bedknob. Returning home, Miss Price uses the formula to raise a ghostly army of armor from the local museum that routs a band of invading Nazi commandos. Premiered in England Oct. 7, 1971; U.S. general release Dec. 13, 1971, after a Nov. 11 debut at New York's Radio City Music Hall. Directed by Robert Stevenson. 117 min. for the originally released version. Stars Angela Lansbury (Eglantine Price), David Tomlinson (Emelius Browne), Roddy McDowall (Mr. Jelk), Sam Jaffe (Bookman), John Ericson (Col. Heller), Bruce Forsyth (Swinburne), Tessie O'Shea (Mrs. Hobday), Reginald Owen (Gen. Teagler), Ian Weighill (Charlie), Roy Snart (Paul), Cindy O'Callaghan (Carrie). The creative talent behind *Mary Poppins* joined forces again for this film, including producer/writer Bill Walsh, director Robert Stevenson, songwriters Richard M. and Robert B. Sherman, music supervisor Irwin Kostal, art director Peter Ellenshaw, and special effects technician Eustace Lycett. Development had actually started in the early 1960s, and Walt Disney participated in story meetings and heard several of the songs for the film, which would ultimately include "The Old Home Guard," "The Age of Not Believing," "Eglantine," "Portobello Road," "The Beautiful Briny," and "Substitutiary Locomotion." The screenplay was based on Mary Norton's book, *Bed-Knob and Broomstick*, with additions by Bill Walsh, who came up with the German invasion sequence. The film was made entirely on the Disney Studio lot in Burbank, where outdoor sets included the town of Pepperinge Eye, and indoor sets featured a 3-block section of London's legendary Portobello Road. Up to 200 players jammed this set alone, which was filled with bric-a-brac and such oddments as a Sicilian sedan chair, Limoges china, and gas masks issued at the start of World War II. Among the performers and extras in the crowd were veterans of music halls, vaudeville, rep shows, radio, silent films, and early talkies. The ghostly medieval army's weapons and armor had originally been assembled in Spain for the film *El Cid*, and then were shipped to America to be used in the Warner Bros. musical *Camelot.* Ward Kimball was the director of the wonderful animation sequences on the Isle of Naboombu. Despite the effort, lavish budget, ingenuity, and special effects, the film was not a box office success, subsequently causing the Studio to edit the film down from its original length to 98 min. for a 1979 reissue. Academy Award winner for Best Special Visual Effects. The movie was also nominated for Best Art Direction/Set Direction, Best Song ("The Age of Not Believing"), Best Scoring, and Best Costume Design. It has remained a Disney favorite, with a video release in 1980. For the film's 25th anniversary, Disney Studio film preservationist Scott MacQueen attempted to find "lost" footage of musical numbers which had been cut from the film prior to its original 1971 release, including "A Step in the Right Direction," "With a Flair," and large segments of "Eglantine." The Studio ultimately uncovered 23 minutes of film, which were restored into a 140-min. special edition, screened Sep. 27, 1996, at the Academy of Motion Pictures Arts and Sciences; the special edition was later released on home video and DVD.

Bedknobs and Broomsticks Stage musical version of the 1971 Disney film; ran Aug. 14–21, 2021, at the Theatre Royal in Newcastle upon Tyne, England, followed by a tour throughout the U.K. and Ireland. Features songs from the film by Richard M. and Robert B. Sherman, with new music and lyrics by Neil Bartram.

Bedtime Stories (film) Skeeter Bronson, a hotel handyman, finds his life changed forever when the lavish bedtime stories he tells his niece and nephew start to mysteriously come true. The stories have settings ranging from the Old West and outer space to medieval times. When Skeeter tries to help his family by telling them one outlandish tale after another, featuring characters from real life, it is the kids' unexpected contributions that turn all of their lives upside down. Directed by Adam Shankman. Released Dec. 25, 2008, after a Dec. 24 release in Belgium, France, and Egypt. Stars Adam Sandler (Skeeter Bronson), Keri Russell (Jill), Russell Brand (Mickey), Teresa Palmer (Violet Nottingham), Richard Griffiths (Barry Nottingham), Lucy Lawless (Aspen), Courteney Cox (Wendy), Guy Pearce (Kendall), Jonathan Pryce (Marty Bronson), Aisha Tyler (Donna Hynde), Jonathan Morgan Heit (Patrick), Laura Ann Kesling (Bobbi). 99 min. Filmed in CinemaScope.

Bee at the Beach (film) Donald Duck cartoon released Oct. 13, 1950. Directed by Jack Hannah. When Donald accidentally upsets a bee through a series of mishaps (and some deliberate provocation), the conflict worsens until the bee gets the ultimate revenge by ruining Donald's rubber raft, leading to him being chased by sharks.

Bee on Guard (film) Donald Duck cartoon released Dec. 14, 1951. Directed by Jack Hannah. When Donald discovers bees taking honey from his flowers, he raids their beehive dressed as a giant bee, fooling the bee on guard. The bee is banished in disgrace but is welcomed back as a hero after he wins a ferocious battle with Donald.

Beebe, Lloyd (1916–2011) Nature photographer on the True-Life Adventure series and field producer for a number of Disney animal films, including *Charlie the Lonesome Cougar, King of the Grizzlies,* and *The Footloose Fox.*

Beezy Bear (film) Donald Duck cartoon released Sep. 2, 1955. Directed by Jack Hannah. Filmed in CinemaScope. Humphrey the Bear continually tries different ways to steal honey from Donald's beehives, resulting in conflicts between Donald and Ranger J. Audubon Woodlore when Donald wants the bears kept away.

Before and After (film) A respected, dedicated small-town pediatrician, Carolyn Ryan, finds her life thrown into turmoil when her teenage son, Jacob, disappears and is suspected of brutally murdering his girlfriend, whose body is found on an isolated snow-covered farm road. When Jacob returns home, Carolyn and her sculptor-husband, Ben, struggle to confront the tragedy and protect their son, even though the town and evidence is dead set against him. In doing so, they show how a family that is driven by love can survive such a catastrophe. A Hollywood Pictures film in association with Caravan Pictures. Directed by Barbet Schroeder. Released Feb. 23, 1996. Stars Meryl Streep (Carolyn Ryan), Liam Neeson (Ben Ryan), Edward Furlong (Jacob), Julia Weldon (Judith), Alfred Molina (Panos Demeris). 108 min. Filming took place primarily in the Berkshire County area of western Massachusetts, where an unseasonal lack of snow necessitated the bringing in of snow-making machines from a local ski resort.

Before It's Too Late: A Film on Teenage Suicide (film) Educational film; released in Sep. 1985. The film shows ways to spot suicidal behavior and help prevent teens from committing suicide.

Begley, Ed (1901–1970) Actor; appeared on TV in *The Secrets of the Pirate's Inn.*

Begley, Ed, Jr. Actor; appeared in *Now You See Him, Now You Don't* (Druffle), *Charley and the*

Angel (Derwood Moseby), and *Renaissance Man* (Jack Markin); on TV in *Tales of the Apple Dumpling Gang* (Amos), *The Absent-Minded Professor: Trading Places* (Jack Brooker), *The Shaggy Dog* (Mr. Daniels, 1994), *Murder She Purred: A Mrs. Murphy Mystery* (Fitz-Gilbert Hamilton), and *Bless This Mess* (Rudy); and on Disney Channel in *Hounded* (Ward Van Dusen), *The Suite Life on Deck* (Mayor Ragnar), and *Hannah Montana* (Woody).

Behind the Attraction (TV) Docuseries on Disney+; digitally premiered Jul. 21, 2021. Imagineers and historians reveal the origins and evolution of some of the Disney parks' most popular attractions, such as Jungle Cruise, Haunted Mansion, The Hall of Presidents, and Star Wars: Galaxy's Edge. Narrated by Paget Brewster. Directed by Brian Volk-Weiss. From Seven Bucks and The Nacelle Company.

Behind the Cameras in Lapland/Alaskan Eskimo (TV) Show aired Oct. 24, 1956, featuring the People and Places featurette about Alaska and the filming of one about the Laplanders. Directed by Winston Hibler and James Algar.

Behind the Magic: Snow White and the Seven Dwarfs (TV) Hour-long special on ABC aired Dec. 13, 2015. Animators, historians, composers, and archivists tell the story of Walt Disney's efforts to make an animated feature film in the 1930s. From seemingly insurmountable creative challenges to an expanding budget and looming deadlines, the production of *Snow White and the Seven Dwarfs* became a harrowing journey, but one which led to an unforgettable film. Directed by Jeremiah Crowell. Narrated by Ginnifer Goodwin. Interviewees include John Lasseter, Richard Sherman, Jennifer Lee, Chris Buck, Byron Howard, Alan Menken, J. B. Kaufman, Rebecca Cline, Eric Goldberg, Marge Champion.

Behind the Scenes of Walt Disney Studio (film) Robert Benchley leads a tour of the Disney Studio, as he tries to see Walt to sell him a story; originally released as part of *The Reluctant Dragon.* Released in 16 mm in Dec. 1952. 26 min.

Behind the Scenes with Fess Parker (TV) Show aired May 30, 1956. Directed by Francis D. Lyon. Walt Disney talks about trains and then introduces Fess Parker to narrate a behind-the-scenes look at the filming of *The Great Locomotive*

Chase. Actor Jeffrey Hunter and technical adviser Wilbur Kurtz join in, and Peter Ellenshaw is shown creating matte paintings. The actual filming of the chase is shown taking place near Clayton, Georgia, on the lines of the Tallulah Falls Railroad.

Behind the True-Life Cameras/Olympic Elk (TV) Show aired Sep. 21, 1955. Directed by Winston Hibler and James Algar. Cameramen are shown filming *Secrets of Life* in the desert and in the Everglades, and trailing after animals near Mount Kilimanjaro for *The African Lion*.

Behn, Peter Child actor; voice of the young Thumper in *Bambi*. In the 1980s, the Disney Studio tracked down Behn to help promote a reissue of *Bambi*; he was discovered working in the real estate business in Vermont.

Being Right: Can You Still Lose? (film) Educational film, using sequences from *Ride a Wild Pony*. In the Questions!/Answers? series; released in 1976. The dilemma of having a pony decide between 2 former owners is the focus of this film.

Beise, S. Clark (1898–1989) An executive with the Bank of America and a member of the Disney Board of Directors 1965–1975.

Bejewelled (TV) A Disney Channel Premiere Film; first aired Jan. 20, 1991. Four unlikely heroes tackle the mystery of a fortune in missing jewels, which disappeared while they were being transported to London for an exhibition. Directed by Terry Marcel. Stars Emma Samms (Stacey Orpington), Dirk Benedict (Gordon), Denis Lawson (Alistair Lord), Jade Magri (Eloise Dubois), Aeryk Egon (Marvin Birnbaum). 94 min.

Bekins Van Lines The company operated a locker area on Town Square in Disneyland 1955–1962, The locker area was later sponsored by Global Van Lines and National.

Belafsky, Marty Child actor; appeared in *Newsies* (Crutchy) and *Pearl Harbor* (Louie), and on TV in the series *Hull High*.

Believe . . . There's Magic in the Stars Fireworks spectacular created for Disneyland's 45th anniversary; debuted Feb. 18, 2000, taking the place of the long-running *Fantasy in the Sky*. A holiday version, *Believe . . . in Holiday Magic*, debuted

Nov. 3, 2000, and featured a simulated snowfall at various areas in the park. American Honda Motor Co. became the sponsor in Dec. 2004. For the 50th anniversary in 2005, the show changed to *Remember . . . Dreams Come True*.

Believe You Can . . . and You Can! (TV) Syn. special celebrating the opening of the New Fantasyland in Disneyland; aired Apr. 21, 1983. Directed by Lee Miller. Heather, a young girl, goes to Disneyland to find magic to prevent her family from moving to Minneapolis; instead she discovers the park's Fantasyland Problem Solver who shows her the New Fantasyland. Stars Heather O'Rourke, Morey Amsterdam, Lance Sloan, Mary Ann Seltzer.

Bell, Kristen Actress; provided the voice of Anna in the Frozen films and Priscilla in *Zootopia*. She appeared in *When in Rome* (Beth) and *You Again* (Marni), and on TV in *Lady Gaga & The Muppets' Holiday Spectacular* and *Mickey's 90th Spectacular*. For Disney+, she hosted and exec. produced *Encore!* She was named a Disney Legend in 2022.

Bell Telephone Science Series SEE RESTLESS SEA, THE. Two other films in the series narrated by Dr. Frank Baxter, *Our Mister Sun* and *Hemo the Magnificent*, were not made by Disney even though they contained animation.

Bella Minni Collections Mediterranean Harbor accessory shop in Tokyo DisneySea; opened Sep. 6, 2012, taking the place of Nicolo's Workshop. The Italian name translates to "pretty Minnie."

Bella Notte Song from *Lady and the Tramp*; written by Peggy Lee and Sonny Burke.

Bellamy, Ralph (1904–1991) Actor; appeared in *The Good Mother* (grandfather) and *Pretty Woman* (James Morse), and on The Disney Channel in *Love Leads the Way*.

BellaVista Lounge Lounge in the Tokyo DisneySea Hotel MiraCosta at Tokyo Disney Resort; opened Sep. 4, 2001. Visitors enjoy Italian dishes with views of Mediterranean Harbor.

Bellboy Donald (film) Donald Duck cartoon released Dec. 18, 1942. Directed by Jack King. Soon after the hotel manager warns bellboy Donald about being impolite to guests, Donald is taunted continually by Junior, Senator Pete's bratty son.

Eventually Donald ends up spanking Junior, after he has lost both his temper and his job.

Belle Heroine longing for adventure in *Beauty and the Beast*; voiced by Paige O'Hara. Also the title of a song by Howard Ashman and Alan Menken, nominated for an Academy Award.

Belle's Magical World (film) A direct-to-video release Jan. 13, 1998, featuring 3 animated films entitled *Perfect Word*, *Broken Wing*, and *Fifi's Folly*, with characters from the *Beauty and the Beast* feature film. Reissued in 2003 as *Beauty and the Beast: Belle's Magical World*, containing an extra segment, *Mrs. Potts' Party*.

Belle's Tales of Friendship (film) Direct-to-video release Aug. 17, 1999. A compilation of live-action and animated characters, classic Disney storytelling, and 5 new-to-video songs. Directed by Jimbo Marshall. With Lynsey McLeod (Belle).

Beloved (film) A decade after the Civil War, Sethe, a woman who had escaped from slavery at the Sweet Home plantation, continues to live in its shadow. She's living in a seemingly haunted house in rural Ohio at 124 Bluestone Road with her teenage daughter, Denver, when there's a surprise visit from Paul D., another Sweet Home survivor. Denver resents the presence of Paul D., but the 3 have even more problems when a mysterious stranger named Beloved appears in their midst. Beloved was the name of Sethe's child, who had died years before, and Sethe believes that this is the child, revived. A Touchstone film. Directed by Jonathan Demme. Released Oct. 16, 1998. Stars Oprah Winfrey (Sethe), Danny Glover (Paul D.), Thandie Newton (Beloved), Kimberly Elise (Denver), Beah Richards (Baby Suggs). 172 min. Oprah Winfrey was the guiding light behind the film, having optioned the rights to the novel in 1988 for her production company, Harpo Films. Based on the Pulitzer Prize–winning novel by Toni Morrison. Production took place in rural areas of Maryland and Pennsylvania near Philadelphia.

Belushi, James Actor; appeared in *Taking Care of Business* (Jimmy), *Mr. Destiny* (Larry Burrows), and *Underdog* (Dan), and on TV in *A Merry Mickey Celebration* and in the title role in *According to Jim*. He has also provided several voices, including Benny in *The Wild*, Phil Palmfeather in the *Mighty Ducks* TV series, Fang in *Gargoyles*, Demon in *Snow Dogs*, Glo-Bo in *Doc McStuffins*, and Coach Coachy in *The 7D*.

Ben Ali Gator Lead alligator dancer in "The Dance of the Hours" segment of *Fantasia*.

Ben and Me (film) Special cartoon featurette released Nov. 10, 1953. Directed by Hamilton S. Luske. Amos, a poor, little church mouse, comes to live with Ben Franklin, and through Amos's suggestions the Franklin stove and bifocals are invented, electricity is discovered, and the opening words of the Declaration of Independence are provided. Voices include Charlie Ruggles (Ben Franklin), Sterling Holloway (Amos), Hans Conried (Thomas Jefferson). Released by Buena Vista Distribution Company with *The Living Desert*. 21 min. First released on video in 1989.

Ben and Me/Peter and the Wolf (TV) Show aired Nov. 15, 1964. Directed by Hamilton S. Luske and Clyde Geronimi. The TV show aired both featurettes.

Ben Buzzard Crook who tries to sell Donald Duck a used airplane in *Flying Jalopy* (1943).

Benay-Albee Novelty Co. Company which introduced the Mickey Mouse ear hats for sale at Disneyland. The hats were patterned after those designed by Roy Williams and worn by the Mouseketeers on the *Mickey Mouse Club* TV show. During the 1950s, along with the Davy Crockett coonskin caps, these were the preferred item of headwear for kids throughout America.

Benched (TV) Series on USA Network; aired Oct. 28–Dec. 30, 2014. A high-powered corporate lawyer falls from grace into the rough-and-tumble world of public defenders. Stars Eliza Coupe (Nina Whitley), Jay Harrington (Phil), Oscar Nuñez (Carlos), Maria Bamford (Cheryl), Jolene Purdy (Micah), Carter MacIntyre (Trent). From ABC Signature.

Benchley, Robert (1889–1945) Humorist; appeared in *The Reluctant Dragon*, taking a tour of the Disney Studio.

Bengal Barbecue Quick-service food stand, featuring beef, chicken, and veggie skewers, in Adventureland at Disneyland; opened Jun. 4, 1990, replacing Sunkist "I Presume."

Benji the Hunted (film) Benji, the dog, becomes lost in the mountains after a fishing accident and is forced to become involved with animals that are normally a dog's mortal enemies, including a Kodiak bear, a black timber wolf, and a number of cougars. He aids some orphaned cougar cubs while trying to find his way back to civilization. Initial release in Dallas Jun. 5, 1987; general release on Jun. 19, 1987. Directed by Joe Camp. An Embark Production in association with Mulberry Square Productions. 89 min. Filmed in Oregon and Washington State. While there were other Benji motion pictures, this was the only one released by Disney.

Bennett, Rhona Actress; appeared on the *Mickey Mouse Club* on The Disney Channel beginning in 1991, and as Loquatia in *Homeboys in Outer Space*.

Bennett, Zachary Actor; appeared in *The Good Mother* (Young Bobby), on TV in *Designated Survivor* (Senator Feller), and on The Disney Channel in *Avonlea* (Felix King), *Back to Hannibal: The Return of Tom Sawyer* (Marcus), and *Looking for Miracles* (Sullivan Delaney).

Benny, Jack (1894–1974) Walt appeared on Jack Benny's TV hour on Nov. 3, 1965, in a skit where Jack asks Walt for 110 free passes to Disneyland for his crew.

Benny and the 'Roids (A Story About Steroid Abuse) (film) Educational film; released in Mar. 1988. 25 min. A high school football player learns the dangers of steroid abuse.

Benny the Cab The anthropomorphic taxi in *Who Framed Roger Rabbit*; voiced by Charles Fleischer.

Benson, Jodi Actress; she has provided several voices, including Ariel in *The Little Mermaid* and other appearances of the character; Barbie in *Toy Story 2*, *Toy Story 3*, and *Hawaiian Vacation*; Weebo in *Flubber*; Lady in *Lady and the Tramp II: Scamp's Adventure*; Anita in *101 Dalmatians II: Patch's London Adventure*; the Healing Fairy in *Secret of the Wings*; and Queen Emmaline in *Sofia the First*. She appeared in *Enchanted* (Sam), and on TV in *The Wonderful World of Disney presents The Little Mermaid Live!* She was named a Disney Legend in 2011.

Benson, Robby Actor; voiced the Beast in *Beauty*

and the Beast and other appearances of the character.

Bent-Tail Coyote character who appeared in 4 films, beginning with *The Legend of Coyote Rock* (1945); he was joined by his son, Bent-Tail Jr., in the next 3 films.

Berenger, Tom Actor; appeared in *Shoot to Kill* (Jonathan Knox), and on TV in *October Road* (The Commander).

Bergen, Edgar (1903–1978) Ventriloquist; appeared in *Fun and Fancy Free*, with his dummies Charlie McCarthy and Mortimer Snerd.

Berger, Richard (1939–2004) He served as the first president of the new company division called Walt Disney Pictures for 2 years beginning in 1982. He left the company when Jeffrey Katzenberg was brought in as chairman of Walt Disney Pictures.

Bergman, Alan He was named chairman, Disney Studios Content in Dec. 2020, then co-chairman, Disney Entertainment in Feb. 2023, overseeing the company's worldwide entertainment media and content businesses. Bergman joined The Walt Disney Company in 1996 as a director in the corporate controllership group and later became vice president of the operations planning group. In 2001, he was named senior vice president and chief financial officer of The Walt Disney Studios, then served as president 2005–2019 and as cochairman 2019–2020, playing a lead role in the Studios' integrations of Pixar, Marvel Studios, Lucasfilm, and the Fox film studios and its expansion into the production of content for the company's streaming services.

Berlin, Irving, Inc. The composer's music publishing company acquired the rights to publish and license the use of the earliest Disney songs, from the Mickey Mouse and Silly Symphony songs of the early 1930s ("Who's Afraid of the Big Bad Wolf?" was the most famous) up to those of *Snow White and the Seven Dwarfs* and *Pinocchio*. Many of the songs became classics and have been kept in print (and are now published by Bourne).

Berlinger, Warren Actor; appeared in *Small and Frye* and in the title role on the *Kilroy* miniseries on TV, and in the feature *The Shaggy D.A.* (Dip).

Berlioz Aspiring-musician kitten in *The Aristocats*; voiced by Dean Clark.

Bernard Shy and modest mouse lead in *The Rescuers* and *The Rescuers Down Under*; voiced by Bob Newhart.

Bernardi, Herschel (1923–1986) Actor; appeared in *No Deposit, No Return* and on TV in *I-Man*.

Berry, Halle Actress; appeared in *Father Hood* (Kathleen Mercer), *The Program* (Autumn), and *The Rich Man's Wife* (Josie Potenza), and on TV in *Oprah Winfrey Presents: Their Eyes Were Watching God* (Janie Crawford).

Berry, Ken (1933–2018) Actor; starred in *Herbie Rides Again* (Willoughby Whitfield) and *The Cat from Outer Space* (Frank), with TV appearances in *The Golden Girls* (Thor) and as a host on *The Mouse Factory*.

Bertha Mae Davy Crockett's keelboat in *Davy Crockett's Keelboat Race*; also one of the Mike Fink Keel Boats at Disneyland and in the Magic Kingdom at Walt Disney World.

Bertini, Antonio Joined Disney's Italian subsidiary in 1960 and headed it from 1963 until his retirement in 1990. He received a European Disney Legends Award in 1997.

Bertino, Al (1912–1996) Animator/story director; he joined the Disney Studio in 1939, animating on shorts and features such as *Pinocchio*, *Fantasia*, *Bambi*, *The Three Caballeros*, and *Cinderella*. He participated in Studio promotional tours as a sketch artist and in the 1950s served as a story director on shorts, also helping create the Humphrey the Bear and Ranger Woodlore cartoons. He also wrote for the *Disneyland* TV series before leaving the company in the late 1950s. A decade later, he joined WED Enterprises, where he was as a writer and storyboard artist for Walt Disney World and Disneyland attractions, including Country Bear Jamboree and America Sings, and he also contributed to the *Disney on Parade* touring show. He retired in 1977.

Best Doggoned Dog in the World, The (TV) Show aired Nov. 20, 1957. Walt shows how dogs and men have enjoyed a special relationship by showing scenes from *Old Yeller*, narrated by Dorothy McGuire, and the entire *Arizona Sheepdog* featurette. A 1961 rerun substituted *One Hundred and One Dalmatians* footage for *Old Yeller*.

Best Friends Whenever (TV) Series on Disney Channel; premiered Jun. 26, 2015. Best friends Shelby and Cyd gain the power to leap forward and backward in time whenever they want (and sometimes when they don't), when their aspiring scientist friend Barry's invention goes awry. They experience the twists and turns of friendship and must decide between fixing mistakes in the past or catching a glimpse of the future. While Barry and his assistant, Naldo, try to figure out how to replicate time travel for themselves, Cyd and Shelby use their newfound power to navigate high school life and Shelby's mischievous twin brothers, Bret and Chet. Stars Landry Bender (Cyd Ripley), Lauren Taylor (Shelby Marcus), Gus Kamp (Barry Eisenberg), Ricky Garcia (Naldo Montova), Benjamin Cole Royer (Bret Marcus), Matthew Lewis Royer (Chet Marcus). From It's a Laugh Productions, Inc.

Best in Snow (TV) Holiday special on Disney+; digitally released Nov. 18, 2022. Artistic teams from around the world gather in a magical snowy village, Snowdome, to compete for the title of Best in Snow, transforming 10-ft., 20-ton blocks of snow into beautiful creations inspired by Pixar, Marvel, Walt Disney Animation, Walt Disney Studios, and The Muppets Studio. Musical performances by host Tituss Burgess, along with Kermit the Frog and DCappella. From Six West Media and Milojo Productions.

Best of Country, The (TV) Special aired on CBS Jan. 27, 1995.

Best of Country '92: Countdown at the Neon Armadillo (TV) Special on ABC airing Dec. 10, 1992.

Best of Disney, The: 50 Years of Magic (TV) Two-hour special aired May 20, 1991, celebrating 50 years (actually 51) of the Disney Studio in Burbank. Directed by Don Mischer. With Harry Connick Jr., Dick Van Dyke, Shelley Long, Daryl Hannah, Neil Patrick Harris, Annette Funicello, Teri Garr, Barbara Walters, Bill Campbell. The stars are called upon to reminisce about their favorite moments in Disney films.

Best of Disney Music, The: A Legacy in Song (TV) Special on CBS aired Feb. 3, 1993. Part 2 aired May 21. 60 min. each. Angela Lansbury hosted the 1st part and Glenn Close the 2nd. Directed by Don Mischer.

Best of Friends Song from *The Fox and the Hound*; written by Stan Fidel and Richard Johnston.

Best of Walt Disney's True-Life Adventures, The (film) Compilation feature released Oct. 8, 1975. Directed by James Algar. 89 min. Narrated by Winston Hibler, the film opens with a salute to Walt Disney as a pioneer in the nature films genre. Animals of all kinds and many species of insects are captured in dramatic and fascinating moments from the Amazon to the Arctic. Hibler's conclusion aptly states an underlying truth noted making this True-Life Adventure collection ever popular: "As long as life goes on, nature and all her marvels will continue to fascinate mankind." Narration written by James Algar, Winston Hibler, and Ted Sears. This film, with segments originally fashioned by Ben Sharpsteen and James Algar, is also a tribute to photographers Alfred G. and Elma Milotte, N. Paul Kenworthy Jr., Robert H. Crandall, Hugh A. Wilmar, James R. Simon, Herb and Lois Crisler, Tom McHugh, Jack C. Couffer, John H. Storer, Stuart V. Jewell, Bert Harwell, Dick Borden, Alfred M. Bailey, Olin Sewall Pettingill Jr., Karl H. Maslowski, Lloyd Beebe, William Carrick, Cleveland P. Grant, Murl Deusing, and many others who roamed remote regions of the Earth to provide such memorable footage for the series. A variety of pieces of music scored for the series by Paul Smith, Oliver Wallace, and Buddy Baker is included.

Best Western Lake Buena Vista Resort Hotel Opened on Hotel Plaza Blvd. at Walt Disney World in 1999. The hotel was previously TraveLodge (which opened in 1972 and was temporarily renamed the Viscount 1984–1989). It was acquired by Drury Hotels in 2017 and closed Mar. 2020 to become the Drury Plaza Hotel Orlando.

BET Soundstage Club Opened Jun. 10, 1998, at Downtown Disney Pleasure Island as the only nightclub in the country carrying the Black Entertainment Television name. Fans of R&B, hip-hop, and rap could watch performances by their favorite artists while sampling drinks and Caribbean-style finger food. It took the place of the Neon Armadillo. It closed Sep. 27, 2008.

Betrayal (TV) One-hour drama series on ABC; aired Sep. 29, 2013–Jan. 19, 2014. Sara Hanley, a professional photographer, and Jack McAllister, a top attorney, meet and have an instant, undeniable attraction, realizing something is missing in their marriages. But soon an impossible situation arises—Sara's husband, Drew Stafford, and Jack find themselves on opposite sides of a high-profile murder investigation. Stars Hannah Ware (Sara Hanley), Chris Johnson (Drew Stafford), Stuart Townsend (Jack McAllister), James Cromwell (Thatcher Karsten), Henry Thomas (T. J. Karsten). From ABC Studios, Remainder Men, and Scripted World.

Betsy's Wedding (film) Eddie Hopper is determined to give his daughter Betsy a fantastic wedding with all the trimmings. Unfortunately Betsy doesn't want a big wedding. Overextended financially and emotionally, Eddie finds the 2 families battling, with everyone pushing for their own favorite traditions and in the way a sacred ceremony should be conducted. To make things worse, he gets into a questionable business deal with his unscrupulous brother-in-law. Everyone finds their lives changing as the pressures of the wedding mount. Released Jun. 22, 1990. Directed by Alan Alda. A Touchstone film. 94 min. Stars Alan Alda (Eddie Hopper), Joey Bishop (Eddie's father), Madeline Kahn (Lola Hopper), Molly Ringwald (Betsy Hopper), Catherine O'Hara (Gloria Henner), Joe Pesci (Oscar Henner), Ally Sheedy (Connie Hopper), Burt Young (Georgie). The film was a personal project of Alda's, who also wrote the screenplay; he came up with the idea from the wedding of his own youngest daughter. Filmed in New York City and in the beautiful old coastal town of Wilmington, North Carolina.

Better Nate Than Ever (film) Musical comedy. Thirteen-year-old Nate Foster has big Broadway dreams. There's only one problem: he can't even land a part in the school play. But when his parents leave town, Nate and his best friend, Libby, sneak off to the Big Apple for a once-in-a-lifetime opportunity to prove everyone wrong. A chance encounter with Nate's long-lost Aunt Heidi turns his journey upside down, and together they must learn that life's greatest adventures are only as big as your dreams. Digitally released Apr. 1, 2022, on Disney+, after a Mar. 15 premiere at the El Capitan Theatre in Hollywood. Directed by Tim Federle, who also wrote the film and the novel on which it is based. Stars Rueby Wood (Nate), Joshua Bassett (Anthony), Aria Brooks (Libby), Lisa Kudrow (Aunt Heidi). 92 min. The film also features some notable Broadway luminaries, including real-life married couple Michelle Federer and Norbert Leo Butz, who play Nate's parents, Sherrie and Rex, along with Brooks Ashmanskas (Casting Director), Priscilla Lopez (Serious Play Casting Director), Krystina Alabado (Assistant Casting Director), and Kayla Davion (Assistant Choreographer). Original songs by Lyndie Lane are "Big Time" and "No One Gets Left Behind." Filmed on location in New York.

Better Way to Go, A: An Introduction to Non-Manipulative Selling (film) Educational film from The Nick Price Story of Non-Manipulative Selling series; released in Feb. 1981. A salesman should be a skilled problem solver, not a persuader. By building trust, he can get repeat customers and increased sales.

Bettin, Val (1923–2021) Actor; he voiced several characters, including Dr. Dawson in *The Great Mouse Detective*, the Sultan in versions of the *Aladdin* story after the original feature film, King Tivius in the *Hercules* TV series, and Hebert Olsen in *W.I.T.C.H.*

Beverly Hills Chihuahua (film) A pampered Beverly Hills Chihuahua named Chloe finds herself accidentally lost on the "mean streets" of a Mexican city without a day spa or Rodeo Drive boutique anywhere in sight. Now alone for the first time in her spoiled life, she must rely on some unexpected friends, including a street-hardened German shepherd named Delgado and an amorous pup named Papi, to lend her a paw and help her find her inner strength on their incredible journey back home. Directed by Raja Gosnell. Released in the U.S. Oct. 3, 2008, after an Oct. 2 release in Australia. Stars Piper Perabo (Rachel Ashe), Jamie Lee Curtis (Aunt Viv), Manolo Cardona (Sam Cortez), and the voices of Drew Barrymore (Chloe), Andy Garcia (Delgado), George Lopez (Papi), Cheech Marin (Manuel), Paul Rodriguez (Chico), Plácido Domingo (Monte), Edward James Olmos (El Diablo). 91 min. Filming in Super 35 began in Mexico on Jul. 13, 2007. The working title had been *South of the Border*. Over 200 dogs were cast to appear in the picture, including almost 50 Chihuahuas. Chloe was played by a white deer head Chihuahua named Angel. The pack rat Manuel and the iguana Chico were fully computer-generated characters. Much of the film was shot on location in Mexico (Puerto Vallarta, Guadalajara, Mexico City, and near Hermosillo in the Sonoran Desert), with even several "Beverly Hills" locations (interior and exterior of Aunt Viv's mansion and an upscale lunch spot) being filmed in Puerto Vallarta.

Beverly Hills Chihuahua 2 (film) Direct-to-DVD sequel to 2008's *Beverly Hills Chihuahua*; released Feb. 1, 2011. The 5 rambunctious, mischievous puppies of Chihuahuas Papi and Chloe present one challenge after another. But when their human owners end up in trouble, the tiny pups will stop at nothing to save them, because in good times and hard times, the family always sticks together. Directed by Alex Zamm. Stars Marcus Coloma (Sam Cortez), Lupe Ontiveros (Mrs. Cortez), and the voices of George Lopez (Papi), Odette Yustman (Chloe), Ernie Hudson (Pedro), Bridgit Mendler (Appoline), Miguel Ferrer (Delgado), Emily Osment (Pep), Madison Pettis (Lala), Zachary Gordon (Papi Jr.). 83 min.

Beverly Hills Chihuahua 3: Viva la Fiesta! (film) Direct-to-DVD release Sep. 18, 2012. Papi and his 2- and 4-legged family move into the posh Langham Hotel in Beverly Hills, complete with a luxurious doggy spa. But there's trouble in puppy paradise when Rosa, the littlest member of the pack, feels smaller and less special than ever. Now it's up to Papi to help Rosa find, and celebrate, her inner strength, which turns out to be bigger than she ever dreamed. Directed by Lev L. Spiro. Stars Marcus Coloma (Sam) and Erin Cahill (Rachel Ashe), with the voices of George Lopez (Papi), Odette Annable (Chloe), Jake Busey (Oscar), Jon Curry (Gunther), Miguel Ferrer (Delgado), Ernie Hudson (Pedro), Kay Panabaker (Rosa), Emily Osment (Pep), Madison Pettis (Lala). 89 min. A sequel to *Beverly Hills Chihuahua* and *Beverly Hills Chihuahua 2*.

Beverly Hills Family Robinson (TV) Two-hour movie on ABC; premiered Jan. 25, 1997. Marsha Robinson, the star of a popular lifestyle TV program promoting her chic home décor and gourmet dinners, heads off on vacation to Hawai'i with her entire family, though they bristle at her presence. When modern-day pirates, however, take over their yacht, the family has to join forces to outwit them. They succeed, but find themselves shipwrecked on a tropical island, where the family builds a tree house for shelter that Marsha proceeds to transform into a showcase for castaway living. Daughter Jane falls for a handsome Windsurfer, Digger. Then the pirates return, leading to the family having to defend their unique home. Directed by Troy Miller. Stars Dyan Cannon (Marsha Robinson), Martin Mull (Dr. Doug Robinson),

Sarah Michelle Gellar (Jane), Ryan O'Donohue (Roger), Josh Picker (Digger), Kevin Weisman (Brinks), Michael Edwards-Stevens (Claude), Nique Needles (Melvin). The "island" scenes were filmed in Queensland, Australia.

Beverly Sunset Boutique Part of the Beverly Sunset Theater shop on Sunset Boulevard in Disney's Hollywood Studios; opened Jun. 29, 2018, replacing Sweet Spells.

Beymer, Richard Actor; appeared in *Johnny Tremain* (Rab Silsbee) and provided a voice for *Boys of the Western Sea* on the *Mickey Mouse Club*.

Beyoncé SEE KNOWLES-CARTER, BEYONCÉ.

Beyond (TV) Hour-long drama series on Freeform; debuted Jan. 2, 2017, and ended Mar. 22, 2018. When Holden wakes up from a coma after 12 years, he discovers he has mysterious new abilities, which land him in the middle of a dangerous conspiracy. Now that he's awake, Holden must figure out what happened to him during all those years and how to survive in a world that has changed significantly. But the biggest question of all may be, "Why did all of this happen to him?" Stars Burkely Duffield (Holden Matthews), Romy Rosemont (Diane Matthews), Michael McGrady (Tom Matthews), Jonathan Whitesell (Luke Matthews), Dilan Gwyn (Willa), Jeff Pierre (Jeff McArdle). From Imperative Entertainment and Automatik.

Beyond Witch Mountain (TV) Show aired Feb. 20, 1982. Directed by Robert Day. A pilot for a proposed series, based on the film *Escape to Witch Mountain*. Tony and Tia leave Witch Mountain to look for their Uncle Bene, and they all fall into the clutches of the evil Deranian. They have to use their special powers to outwit him. Stars Eddie Albert, Tracey Gould, Andrew K. Freeman, J. D. Cannon, Noah Beery, Efrem Zimbalist Jr. While Eddie Albert reprised his role as Jason O'Day from the motion picture, the rest of the cast was new.

BFG, The (film) Sophie, a precocious 10-year-old girl from London, arrives in Giant Country. Initially frightened by the mysterious giant who has brought her to his cave, she soon comes to realize that The BFG (as in Big Friendly Giant) is actually quite gentle and charming. The Giant stands 24-feet tall with enormous ears and a keen sense of smell but is endearingly dim-witted and keeps to himself for the most part. He introduces Sophie

to the wonders and perils of Giant Country and brings her to Dream Country, where he collects dreams and sends them to children, teaching her all about the magic and mystery of dreams. Having both been on their own in the world up until now, their affection for one another quickly grows. But Sophie's presence in Giant Country has attracted the unwanted attention of the other giants, including Bloodbottler and Fleshlumpeater, who have become increasingly bothersome. Sophie and the BFG travel to London to convince the Queen that giants do indeed exist, warn her of the precarious giant situation, and come up with a plan to get rid of the giants once and for all. Directed by Steven Spielberg. Released, also in 3-D, Jul. 1, 2016, after a Jun. 22 release in Sweden. Stars Mark Rylance (The BFG), Ruby Barnhill (Sophie), Penelope Wilton (Queen), Jemaine Clement (Fleshlumpeater), Rebecca Hall (Mary), Bill Hader (Bloodbottler). 118 min. Filmed in wide-screen format. Based on the book by Roald Dahl, which had earlier, in 1989, been made into an 87-minute animated TV feature by Cosgrove Hall Productions in the United Kingdom. From Walt Disney Pictures, Amblin Entertainment, and Reliance Entertainment in association with Walden Media.

Bialik, Mayim Actress; appeared in *Beaches* (C. C. Bloom at age 11), on TV in the title role in *Blossom* and as Dr. Bink in *The Secret Life of the American Teenager*, and guest starred in *Earth to Ned* on Disney+. She also narrated the educational film *AIDS: You've Got to Do Something* and voiced several characters for TV, including Kirsten Kurst in *Recess*, Cindy in *Lloyd in Space*, Willoughby in *Star vs. the Forces of Evil*, and Dr. Gem Jeodopolis in *Vampirina*.

Bianca Goldfish who appeared in *Mickey's Parrot* (1938) and *Lend a Paw* (1941).

Bianca Stylish and adventurous mouse lead in *The Rescuers* and *The Rescuers Down Under*; voiced by Eva Gabor.

Bibbidi-Bobbidi-Boo Song from *Cinderella*; written by Jerry Livingston, Mack David, and Al Hoffman. Nominated for an Academy Award.

Bibbidi Bobbidi Boutique Themed stores offering young guests the opportunity for a makeover to become a princess or knight. The first one opened in the World of Disney at Downtown Disney (now Disney Springs) at Walt Disney World Apr. 5,

2006; it moved to Once Upon a Toy Jun. 8, 2016. Additional locations opened in Cinderella Castle in the Magic Kingdom at Walt Disney World (Sep. 10, 2007, taking the place of The King's Gallery), the Tokyo Disneyland Hotel (Jul. 8, 2008), Fantasyland in Disneyland (Apr. 17, 2009, succeeding Once Upon a Time . . . The Disney Princess Shoppe), and, with the name My Little Princess, the Hong Kong Disneyland Hotel (May 23, 2009). They were later added to the Disney Cruise Line ships, beginning with the *Disney Fantasy* in 2012. On Nov. 25, 2013, a Bibbidi Bobbidi Boutique opened for the first time outside a Disney resort, at the world-famous Harrods department store in London. A version premiered inside Enchanted Storybook Castle in Shanghai Disneyland Jun. 16, 2016, followed by openings in World Bazaar at Tokyo Disneyland (Apr. 21, 2017, taking the place of The Disney Gallery and Disney Drawing Class), the Storybook Shoppe in Hong Kong Disneyland (Jul. 1, 2019), and at Disney's Grand Floridian Resort & Spa (Aug. 6, 2019, succeeding Ivy Trellis Salon).

Bibo-Lang, Inc. Publisher in 1930 of the very first *Mickey Mouse Book*, a thin, green-colored pamphlet which contained a story written by Mr. Bibo's 8-year-old daughter, Bobette. The first hardback book, *The Adventures of Mickey Mouse*, was published the following year by David McKay.

Bicentennial Man (film) Andrew Martin, an android programmed to perform menial tasks, displays uncharacteristically human emotions and is curious and creative. Over time, he recognizes that he has a unique destiny—to become human. Through 2 centuries and generations in the Martin family, Andrew discovers the intricacies of life and love, and what it truly means to be a human being. Released Dec. 17, 1999. Directed by Chris Columbus. Stars Robin Williams (Andrew Martin), Sam Neill (Sir), Embeth Davidtz (adult Little Miss/ Portia), Wendy Crewson (Ma'am), Oliver Platt (Rupert Burns), Hallie Kate Eisenberg (young Little Miss). 131 min. A co-production of Touchstone Pictures with Columbia Pictures, with Disney handling domestic distribution and Columbia handling international distribution. Based on the short story by Isaac Asimov and the novel *The Positronic Man* by Asimov and Robert Silverberg. The production's set designers had to modernize the look of San Francisco from the near future to 200 years hence. The film received an Academy Award nomination for Best Makeup.

Biehn, Michael Actor; appeared in *Tombstone* (Ringo) and *The Rock* (Charles Anderson), and on Disney+ in *The Mandalorian* (Lang).

Biergarten Restaurant Buffet dining in Germany at EPCOT; opened Oct. 1, 1982. Polka band entertainers yodel and play the 50-ft.-long alphorns at regular intervals during the day as diners enjoy their bratwurst, sauerkraut, and apple strudel in a festive Bavarian village. The restaurant's motto is "Jubel, Trubel, Heiterkeit," which roughly translates to "laughter and merriment."

Big Al Guitar-playing bear character who steals the show in Country Bear Jamboree at the Disney parks; his rendition of "Blood on the Saddle" was performed by Tex Ritter.

Big Bad Wolf, The Ferocious nemesis of the leads in the *Three Little Pigs* (1933), who went on to appear in 7 additional films. Billy Bletcher was the first to provide the voice of the character.

Big Bad Wolf, The (film) Silly Symphony cartoon released Apr. 14, 1934. Directed by Burt Gillett. Red Riding Hood is warned by the Three Little Pigs about the wolf, who is waiting for her at Grandmother's house. She is rescued in the nick of time by the Practical Pig, who gets rid of the wolf with hot coals and popcorn.

Big Bands at Disneyland (TV) Series on The Disney Channel consisting of 12 episodes; premiered Jun. 28, 1984, and continued, with repeats, until Aug. 29, 1985, with bands such as the Count Basie Orchestra, the Glenn Miller Orchestra, the Bob Crosby Orchestra, Les Brown and His Band of Renown, and the Tommy Dorsey Orchestra all performing in Carnation Plaza Gardens at Disneyland.

Big Brother Blues (film) Educational 16-mm film made in association with Metropolitan Life; released in 1992. A young teen is shocked to learn that his mother and stepfather are about to have a baby. He is not sure how he feels about losing his status as the only child, but eventually he finds himself excited by the prospect of becoming a big brother. 30 min.

Big Business (film) Two sets of twins, Rose and Sadie Shelton and Rose and Sadie Ratliff, are mixed up at birth. Years later the Sheltons are running a major corporation in New York City, with Rose not caring for the corporate life, and the Ratliffs are living in a poor West Virginia town that relies on a local furniture company for its survival, with Sadie longing for the joys of the big city. When the Sheltons' company tries to sell off the furniture company (and town), the Ratliffs go to New York City to protest. It is a major case of mistaken identities as all 4 ladies end up staying at the Plaza Hotel, pursued by their respective beaus. Released Jun. 10, 1988. Directed by Jim Abrahams. A Touchstone film. 98 min. Stars Bette Midler (Sadie Shelton/Sadie Ratliff), Lily Tomlin (Rose Shelton/Rose Ratliff), Fred Ward (Roone Dimmick), Edward Herrmann (Graham Sherbourne). The Plaza Hotel's lavish suites and distinctive lobby were re-created on a Disney soundstage, while exteriors and a scene in the Palm Court were filmed on location in New York City.

Big City Greens (TV) Animated comedy series on Disney Channel; premiered Jun. 18, 2018, following the offbeat adventures of 10-year-old Cricket Green, a mischievous and optimistic country boy who moves to the big city with his wildly out of place family—older sister, Tilly; father, Bill; and Gramma Alice. Cricket's natural curiosity and enthusiasm lead him and his family on epic journeys and into the hearts of his new neighbors. Voices include Chris Houghton (Cricket Green), Marieve Herington (Tilly Green), Bob Joles (Bill Green), Artemis Pebdani (Gramma Alice). From Disney Television Animation. A variety of spin-off, short-form series have included *Country Kids in the City* (2018), *Random Rings* (2019), *Big City Greens: Road Trip* (2019), and *Miss Tilly's Fun Time TV Minute!* (2020).

Big City Vehicles Attraction in American Waterfront at Tokyo DisneySea; opened Sep. 4, 2001, with a delivery truck, police wagon, tour bus, and town cars providing transportation.

Big Council, The (TV) Show; the 6th episode of *The Saga of Andy Burnett*.

Big Fib, The (TV) Comedy game show on Disney+; premiered May 22, 2020. Kid contestants determine who is an expert and who is a fibber. Hosted by Yvette Nicole Brown and her robot sidekick, C.L.I.V.E. (Computerized Library of Information & Virtual Expert), played by Rhys Darby. From Haymaker TV.

Big Fisherman, The (film) Not a Disney-produced film, but it was brought to the attention of Disney management in 1959, which decided to release it through its Buena Vista Distribution Company. Based on the novel by Lloyd C. Douglas. Directed by Frank Borzage. Howard Keel portrays Simon Peter, the rough and skeptical fisherman of Galilee who eventually becomes Christ's chief disciple and founder of his church. Also stars Susan Kohner, John Saxon, Martha Hyer, Herbert Lom. Filming locations included Lake Chatsworth and the Palm Springs area of Southern California. 180 min.

Big Game Safari Shooting Gallery See Safari Shooting Gallery.

Big Green, The (film) The arrival of British schoolteacher Anna Montgomery to the small town of Elma, Texas, and her determination to create a winning soccer team among the kids, creates many changes in the drab town. She is helped by sheriff Tom Palmer, who is anxious to best his rival, coach Jay Huffer from the big city. Directed by Holly Goldberg Sloan. A Walt Disney Picture, in association with Caravan Pictures. Released Sep. 29, 1995. Stars Steve Guttenberg (Tom Palmer), Olivia D'Abo (Anna Montgomery), Jay O. Sanders (Jay Huffer), John Terry (Edwin V. Douglas), Chauncey Leopardi (Evan Schiff), Patrick Renna (Larry Musgrove), Billy L. Sullivan (Jeffrey Luttrell). 100 min. Filmed on location around Austin, Texas, with the small town of Dale substituting for the fictional Elma. Since most of the child actors had no experience with soccer, the head coach of the University of Texas's varsity soccer team, Robert Parr, had to be called in to run an impromptu soccer camp.

Big Grizzly Mountain Runaway Mine Cars Runaway train attraction in Grizzly Gulch at Hong Kong Disneyland; opened Jul. 14, 2012. Passengers dash through mountain caves, trying to avoid mischievous resident grizzly bears, zip through the land backward, and end with a powerful and surprising high-speed launch that sends the mine train racing. Each train holds 24 guests.

Big Hero 6 (film) Action-comedy adventure from Walt Disney Animation Studios. Robotics prodigy Hiro Hamada finds himself in the grips of a criminal plot that threatens to destroy the fast-paced, high-tech city of San Fransokyo. With help from his closest companion, a healthcare robot named Baymax, Hiro joins forces with a reluctant team of first-time crime fighters on a mission to save their city. Inspired by the Marvel comics of the same name. Directed by Don Hall and Chris Williams. Released Nov. 7, 2014. Voices include Ryan Potter (Hiro Hamada), Scott Adsit (Baymax), Genesis Rodriguez (Honey Lemon), Jamie Chung (Go Go Tomago), T. J. Miller (Fred), Alan Tudyk (Alistair Krei), Damon Wayans, Jr. (Wasabi), Maya Rudolph (Aunt Cass), James Cromwell (Prof. Robert Callaghan), Daniel Henney (Tadashi Hamada). 102 min. It won the Academy Award for Best Animated Feature. San Fransokyo, a fictional mash-up of San Francisco and Tokyo, is so extensive and elaborate that it called for the development of a new rendering tool, called Hyperion, which allowed for more complex scenes with bigger crowds and greater detail. To develop Baymax, filmmakers met with robotics experts and researchers at several universities and tech labs, including Carnegie Mellon, where an inflatable vinyl arm helped inspire the character's soft personality.

Big Hero 6 The Series (TV) Animated series on Disney XD; premiered Nov. 20, 2017, and ended Feb. 15, 2021. The story picks up immediately following the events of the feature film, continuing the adventures and friendship of 14-year-old tech genius Hiro and his compassionate, cutting-edge robot, Baymax. Hiro faces daunting academic challenges and social trials as the new prodigy at San Fransokyo Institute of Technology. Along with their friends Wasabi, Honey Lemon, Go Go, and Fred, Hiro and Baymax form the legendary superhero team Big Hero 6 and embark on high-tech adventures as they protect their city from an array of scientifically enhanced villains. Voices include Ryan Potter (Hiro), Scott Adsit (Baymax), Jamie Chung (Go Go), Genesis Rodriguez (Honey Lemon), Khary Payton (Wasabi), Brooks Wheelan (Fred), Maya Rudolph (Aunt Cass). From Disney Television Animation. A spin-off short-form series digitally premiered Nov. 24, 2017, on Disney XD and its digital platforms. Another spin-off series, *Baymax Dreams*, premiered at the SIGGRAPH conference Aug. 14–16, 2018, with a Sep. 15 digital launch on DisneyNOW and Disney Channel YouTube; it was produced in collaboration with Unity Technologies, which earned a 2018 Technology & Engineering Emmy for the use of real-time 3-D gaming engines. Another spin-off, *Big Chibi 6: The Shorts*, digitally premiered Nov. 6, 2018, on Disney Channel YouTube, featuring the characters in Chibi form.

Big Mama Motherly owl in *The Fox and the Hound*; voiced by Pearl Bailey.

Big Pop, The Outer space–themed popcorn shop in Tomorrowland at Tokyo Disneyland; opened Sep. 28, 2020. Visitors can look into the kitchen, where popcorn is made in a variety of flavors.

Big Red (film) A boy's conviction that a handsome red setter can be handled and trained with love rather than harsh discipline brings him into conflict with Mr. Haggin, the owner of the kennel where he works. As an orphan hungering for love, he understands Big Red, who does not respond to Haggin's training methods. The boy's disobedience results in the dog being injured and the boy leaving. A series of adventures involving the dog, the boy, and Mr. Haggin brings about many valuable lessons to all. Released Jun. 6, 1962. The first Disney film directed by Norman Tokar, who went on to direct many other Disney features in the 1960s and 1970s. 89 min. Stars Walter Pidgeon (James Haggin), Gilles Payant (Rene Dumont), Emile Genest (Emile Fornet), Janette Bertrand (Therese Fornet). Besides interiors at the Disney Studio in Burbank, sequences were filmed on location near La Malbaie, Canada, along the shore of the St. Lawrence, and at Big Bear Lake in California. The songs "Mon Amour Perdu" and "Emile's Reel" were written by Richard M. and Robert B. Sherman.

Big Shot (TV) Original series on Disney+; digitally premiered Apr. 16, 2021, with the second and final season released Oct. 12, 2022. After getting ousted from the NCAA, a men's basketball coach is given a chance for redemption with a position at an elite private high school. He soon learns that the teenage players require empathy and are quite vulnerable—foreign concepts for the outwardly stoic coach, Marvyn Korn. By learning how to connect with his players, he starts to grow into the person he's always hoped to be. Stars John Stamos (Marvyn Korn), Jessalyn Gilsig (Holly Barrett), Richard Robichaux (George Pappas), Sophia Mitri Schloss (Emma Korn), Nell Verlaque (Louise Gruzinsky), Tiana Le (Destiny Winters), Monique Green (Olive Cooper), Tisha Custodio (Carolyn "Mouse" Smith), Cricket Wampler (Samantha "Giggles" Finkman), Yvette Nicole Brown (Sherilyn Thomas). From ABC Signature.

Big Swindle, The (TV) Show, the 2nd part of *The Further Adventures of Gallegher*.

Big Thunder Barbecue Outdoor restaurant in Big Thunder Ranch at Disneyland; opened Dec. 14, 1986. It was a unique eating area, with all the seating outdoors and the barbecued beef and chicken served from chuck wagons. Its name and theme changed Jun. 20, 1996, to the Festival of Foods, tying into the release of *The Hunchback of Notre Dame*. It reverted back to Big Thunder Barbecue May 30, 1997, and remained open until Jan. 20, 2001. It reopened in 2009 as Big Thunder Ranch Barbecue, featuring the Celebration Roundup and Barbecue. It closed Jan. 10, 2016, to make way for Star Wars: Galaxy's Edge.

Big Thunder Mountain Railroad Runaway mine train attraction in Frontierland at Disneyland; opened Sep. 2, 1979. Also a Frontierland attraction in the Magic Kingdom at Walt Disney World (opened Sep. 23, 1980) and Disneyland Paris (opened Apr. 12, 1992), and a Westernland attraction at Tokyo Disneyland (opened Jul. 4, 1987). It was originally designed in 1974 for Walt Disney World but approved for Disneyland first. Passengers embark on a harrowing journey through dark caverns and deep sandstone gorges, encountering swarming bats, crashing landslides, and rumbling earthquakes along the way. For the Disneyland attraction, Imagineer Tony Baxter was inspired by the charming scenery at Bryce Canyon National Park in Utah; the 3 other versions resemble scenery in Arizona's Monument Valley. The mountain itself is completely manufactured, with Disney Imagineers becoming experts on using cement and paint to create realistic rocks. To add to the gold rush era atmosphere of the Old West, the designers scoured the ghost towns of the western states and came up with ore carts, cogwheels, buckets, and other authentic mining equipment. The roller coaster-like ride might seem tame to thrill aficionados, but the addition of interesting, themed detail everywhere makes the experience unique. At Disneyland, Big Thunder Mountain replaced Mine Train Through Nature's Wonderland, with elements of that attraction retained. Uniquely at Disneyland Paris, the mountain rests on an island in the Rivers of the Far West. At Disneyland, the setting is the town of Rainbow Ridge; at Walt Disney World, the town is Tumbleweed; and at Disneyland Paris, it is Thunder Mesa. An interactive queue was added to the Walt Disney World attraction in 2013, and a new dynamite explosion scene replaced the earthquake sequence at Disneyland in 2014.

Big Thunder Ranch Frontierland area near Big Thunder Mountain at Disneyland, re-creating an 1880s working horse ranch; opened Jun. 27, 1986, including a petting area, ranch house, and stable. An outdoor restaurant, Big Thunder Ranch Barbecue, with cowboy-style grub in a rustic setting, opened Dec. 14, 1986. The Disneyland livestock had previously been kept in the Pony Farm behind the park, out of the sight of guests. Here, guests could now see and pet some of the horses, goats, and sheep, watch a blacksmith or harness maker at work, and visit the ranch house. For several years, Mickey Moo, a cow with a Mickey Mouse-shaped mark on her back, was a highlight. The ranch closed Feb. 1996 to make way for the Hunchback of Notre Dame Festival of Fools show, which closed Apr. 18, 1998. From 1998–2004, the area was used for corporate gatherings. On Apr. 2, 2004, it reopened as Little Patch of Heaven to promote *Home on the Range*, later returning to its original name. It closed Jan. 10, 2016, to make way for Star Wars: Galaxy's Edge.

Big Top Souvenirs Storybook Circus shop in the Magic Kingdom at Walt Disney World; opened Sep. 30, 2012. Offers snacks, treats, and souvenirs. Replaced Cornelius Coot's County Bounty in Mickey's Toontown Fair.

Big Top Toys Toy shop themed to *Dumbo* on Buena Vista Street in Disney California Adventure; opened Jun. 15, 2012.

Big Trouble (film) An ensemble comedy about a mysterious suitcase which brings together, and changes, the lives of a divorced dad, an unhappy housewife, 2 hit men, a pair of street thugs, 2 lovestruck teens, 2 FBI men, and a psychedelic toad. Directed by Barry Sonnenfeld. A Touchstone film. Released Apr. 5, 2002. Stars Tim Allen (Eliot Arnold), Omar Epps (Seitz), Dennis Farina (Henry), Janeane Garofalo (Monica Romero), Jason Lee (Puggy), Stanley Tucci (Arthur Herk), Ben Foster (Matt Arnold), Heavy D (Greer), Patrick Warburton (Walter Kramitz), Zooey Deschanel (Jenny Herk), Johnny Knoxville (Eddie), Rene Russo (Anna Herk), Tom Sizemore (Snake), Jack Kehler (Leonard). 85 min. Based on a novel by Dave Barry. Filmed at various sites in the Miami area. Since the film plot includes terrorists and a bomb secreted on an airplane, release of the film was delayed 6 months due to sensitivities arising from the Sep. 11, 2001, terrorist attacks in New York City; Washington, D.C.; and in Pennsylvania.

Big Wash, The (film) Goofy cartoon released Feb.

6, 1948. Directed by Clyde Geronimi. Goofy tries to give a circus elephant, Dolores, a bath, but she proves elusive and ends up blowing him into a mud puddle. Dolores was the name of Walt's secretary (Dolores Voght).

Bigfoot (TV) Two-hour show premiered Mar. 8, 1987. Directed by Danny Huston. A man and his intended bride take their respective children, who are not at all pleased with the impending marriage, camping, where they find a huge creature. The creature kidnaps the girl, and the others join a reclusive woman, Gladys, who has been studying the Sasquatch, in trying to rescue her. When the girl is rescued, she helps the others prevent the Sasquatch from being captured by a scientist. Stars Colleen Dewhurst, James Sloyan, Gracie Harrison, Joseph Maher, Adam Karl, Candace Cameron.

Bigle, Armand (1917–2007) He started a Disney magazine in Belgium in 1947, but soon relocated to Paris and headed the French and eventually all European merchandising operations for the company until his retirement in 1988. Received a European Disney Legends Award in 1997.

Bill Lizard in *Alice in Wonderland* who is asked to get a huge Alice out of the White Rabbit's house; voiced by Larry Grey.

Bill Nye, the Science Guy (TV) Series; syn. beginning Sep. 10, 1993. Nye demonstrates scientific principles and theories for kids, showing that science can be fun and exciting. It ended Oct. 3, 1997, with its 100th episode, though syn. episodes continued to air. Bill Nye has been featured in attractions at Walt Disney World, including Innoventions, Ellen's Energy Adventure, and DINOSAUR.

Billposters (film) Donald Duck cartoon released May 17, 1940. Directed by Clyde Geronimi. Donald and Goofy's plans to post bills fall apart when Goofy gets into trouble with a windmill and Donald meets his nemesis in an ornery goat.

Billy Bathgate (film) Young Billy, a streetwise kid from Bathgate Avenue in the Bronx, is convinced that success will come to him only if he is able to join mobster Dutch Schultz's gang. Starting out as a flunky for the crime ring, he soon graduates to trusted confidant only to find danger as his mentor's power and control wane. In an underworld populated by ruthless characters, it takes all of Billy's wits to survive and to save the life of Drew Preston, with whom he has his first love interest. Released Nov. 11, 1991. Directed by Robert Benton. A Touchstone film. Based on the acclaimed novel by E. L. Doctorow. 107 min. Stars Dustin Hoffman (Dutch Schultz), Nicole Kidman (Drew Preston), Loren Dean (Billy Bathgate), Bruce Willis (Bo Weinberg), Steven Hill (Otto Berman). The transformation of New York City locations into the 1930s milieu took a great deal of effort and extensive research. Shooting also took place at the Saratoga Race Track in upstate New York, the oldest track in America, and in Wilmington, Durham, and Hamlet, North Carolina; the last is an almost perfectly intact likeness of a 1930s eastern community.

Billy Bob's Country Western Saloon Bar in Disney Village at Disneyland Paris with concerts and dancing; opened Apr. 12, 1992. Upstairs, Le Grange offers all-you-can-eat Tex-Mex fare.

Billy Dilley's Super-Duper Subterranean Summer (TV) Animated series on Disney XD; premiered Jun. 3, 2017. During summer break, Billy Dilley, an eccentric science-obsessed 7th grader, and his lab partners, Zeke and Marsha, get stuck in a bizarre, magical world beneath the Earth's surface. Voices include Aaron Springer (Billy), Tom Kenny (Zeke), Catherine Wayne (Marsha). From Disney Television Animation.

Bing, Herman (1889–1947) Actor; voice of the Ringmaster in *Dumbo*.

Bing Bong Riley's imaginary friend in *Inside Out*; voiced by Richard Kind. He has the trunk of an elephant, the tail of a cat, and the body of cotton candy.

Bing Bong's Sweet Stuff Merchandise and confectionery shop in Pixar Pier at Disney California Adventure; opened Jul. 21, 2018, replacing Sideshow Shirts. Named after the imaginary character in *Inside Out*.

Birch, Thora Child actress; appeared in *Paradise* (Billie Pike) and *Hocus Pocus* (Dani).

Bird, Andy He joined Disney in Jan. 2004 as president of Walt Disney International and helped expand Disney's presence in more than 40 countries. He left the company in 2018.

Bird and the Robot Humorous robot and film presentation in the Transcenter in World of Motion at EPCOT Center; ran 1982–1996. An egocentric bird and a talented car manufacturing robot named Tiger demonstrated how robots are used on the automobile assembly line.

Bird Store, The (film) Silly Symphony cartoon released Jan. 16, 1932. Directed by Wilfred Jackson. When a crafty cat attempts to catch a baby canary, the other outraged birds force it into a large cage using a blowtorch. A spring in the cage sends the screaming cat through the roof and onto the flagpole of the local dog pound.

Birds, Baboons and Other Animals—Their Struggle for Survival (film) Portion of *The African Lion*; released on 16 mm for schools in May 1969. The telephoto lens helps one observe the habits of a veritable menagerie of strange and colorful creatures in the lion's domain.

Birds in the Spring (film) Silly Symphony cartoon released Mar. 11, 1933. Directed by Dave Hand. A baby bird, Otto, has many adventures when he runs away from home. He meets a hypnotic rattlesnake and runs into trouble with a hornet's nest. Rescued by his father and taken home, he is given a spanking.

Birds of a Feather (film) Silly Symphony cartoon released Feb. 3, 1931. Directed by Burt Gillett. The peaceful serenity of birds flying through the sky is broken by a hawk that steals a baby chick. By attacking in airplane formation, the birds rescue the baby and return it to its mother.

Birthday Party, The (film) Mickey Mouse cartoon released Jan. 7, 1931. Directed by Burt Gillett. The early Disney gang gives Mickey a surprise party, which includes the gift of a piano. Mickey shows his gratitude by entertaining them with an energetic musical number.

Biscuit Barrel, The Shop in the United Kingdom at EPCOT Center; open Oct. 1, 1982–Jan. 5, 1986, selling cookies, jellies, decorative tins, and potpourris. It later became Country Manor.

Biscuit Eater, The (film) In the backcountry of Tennessee, Lonnie McNeil, the son of a tenant farmer, tries to train a young hunting dog, Moreover, who is thought inferior because of a "bad streak" in him. With the help of his best friend,

Text, Lonnie maintains his faith in the dog. After overcoming serious obstacles, the dog proves that he has championship potential. Released Mar. 22, 1972. Directed by Vincent McEveety. 92 min. Stars Earl Holliman (Harve McNeil), Patricia Crowley (Mrs. McNeil), Lew Ayres (Mr. Ames), Johnny Whitaker (Lonnie), George Spell (Text Tomlin). Remake of a 1940 Paramount film. The dog that played Moreover was of a rare breed, a German wirehaired pointer. His real name was Rolph Von Wolfgang, and he was discovered playing with his master who was working as a tree trimmer at Disney's Golden Oak Ranch.

Bisontennial Ben Mascot with the features of an American buffalo and Benjamin Franklin; created by Disney in 1987 for the California Bicentennial Commission on the U.S. Constitution.

Bistro de Paris Upscale restaurant in France at EPCOT Center; opened Jun. 3, 1984. With the extreme popularity of Les Chefs de France, EPCOT executives decided more eating space was needed in the pavilion. An upstairs area above Les Chefs was unused, so they turned it into the new restaurant, also specializing in gourmet French cuisine. It closed Jul. 31, 2012, to become Monsieur Paul.

Bistrot Chez Rémy Parisian bistro in La Place de Rémy at Walt Disney Studios Park in Disneyland Paris; opened Jul. 10, 2014. Diners are shrunk down to the size of a rat, with oversized champagne corks and jar lids serving as seats and tables.

Bixby, Bill (1934–1993) Actor; appeared in *The Apple Dumpling Gang* (Russel Donavan).

Bizaardvark (TV) Series on Disney Channel; premiered Jun. 24, 2016. Paige and Frankie write funny songs and create music comedy videos for their online channel. Now with 10,000 subscribers, they are invited to produce their videos at the influential Vuuugle Studios. With the help of their longtime friend and agent, 12-year-old Bernie, plus fellow Vuuugle stars Dirk and Amelia, the best friends embark on comedic adventures in their quest to rule the blogosphere. Stars Olivia Rodrigo (Paige Olvera), Madison Hu (Frankie Wong), Jake Paul (Dirk Mann), DeVore Ledridge (Amelia Duckworth), Ethan Wacker (Bernie Schotz).

Black, Shirley Temple (1928–2014) Member of

the Disney Board of Directors 1974–1975. As a child, she presented the special Academy Award to Walt Disney in 1939 for *Snow White and the Seven Dwarfs*, and years later she helped dedicate the Sleeping Beauty Castle walk-through attraction in Disneyland. Also the subject of the TV movie *Child Star: The Shirley Temple Story*, for which she served as a consultant.

Black Arrow (TV) Movie on The Disney Channel; premiered Jan. 6, 1985. A wealthy lord in medieval England plans to murder 1 ward, marry another, and take over the property of both, but he is outwitted by the notorious Black Arrow. Directed by John Hough. Based on the Robert Louis Stevenson story. Stars Oliver Reed (Sir Daniel Brackley), Fernando Rey (Earl of Warwick), Benedict Taylor (Richard Shelton), Stephan Chase (Black Arrow), Georgia Slowe (Lady Joanna), Donald Pleasence (Oates). Filmed on location in Spain.

Black Beauty (film) A Disney+ original film from Constantin Film GmbH and JB Pictures. Black Beauty, a wild horse born free in the American West, is rounded up and taken away from her family. She is brought to Birtwick Stables, where she meets a spirited teenage girl, Jo Green. Beauty and Jo forge an unbreakable bond that carries Beauty through the different chapters, challenges, and adventures of her life. A contemporary reimagining of the book by Anna Sewell. Released digitally Nov. 27, 2020. Directed by Ashley Avis. Stars Mackenzie Foy (Jo Green), Iain Glen (John Manly), Calam Lynch (George Winthorp), Claire Forlani (Mrs. Winthorp), Fern Deacon (Georgina Winthorp), with the voice of Kate Winslet (Black Beauty). 108 min. Filmed in wide-screen format in and around Cape Town, South Africa.

Black Cauldron, The (film) Story of young Taran, a pig keeper, who attempts to rescue his clairvoyant pig, Hen Wen, from The Horned King's castle. The king tries to get Hen Wen to lead him to the mysterious Black Cauldron. Taran escapes with a young princess and a minstrel, and with the help of mischievous Gurgi, finds the Cauldron. Before they can destroy it, it is taken by The Horned King, who begins to unleash its awesome power of producing deathless warriors. Gurgi sacrifices himself to destroy the Cauldron's power and save his friends, but in the end, Taran defeats The Horned King and Gurgi is restored. Released Jul. 24, 1985. Directed by Ted Berman and Richard Rich. Filmed in 70 mm, stereo-surround Technirama. First Disney animated feature to receive a PG rating. Features the voices of John Hurt (The Horned King), Grant Bardsley (Taran), John Byner (Gurgi), Susan Sheridan (Eilonwy), Freddie Jones (Dallben), Nigel Hawthorne (Fflewddur Fflam), Phil Fondacaro (Creeper). 80 min. The production can be traced back to 1971, when the Disney Studio purchased the screen rights to Lloyd Alexander's *The Chronicles of Prydain*. The 5-volume mythological fantasy had been published in the mid-1960s to critical acclaim and commercial success. Adapting Alexander's books with their numerous story lines and cast of over 30 major characters proved to be a time-consuming task. Several important writer/animators worked on the development of a screenplay through the 1970s, until Joe Hale was named producer in 1980. He rewrote the script, capsulizing the sprawling story and making some changes. For instance, The Horned King was a minor character in the series, but since he had so many possibilities, Hale expanded his role, making the villain a composite of several characters from the books. Filmmakers took advantage of the latest technology, which became essential in the completion of the film. Video cameras gave animators and directors an immediate and inexpensive record of what their efforts might look like. Computers also made inroads in the manipulation of solid inanimate objects on-screen. The dimensions and volume of objects were fed into a computer, and then their shapes were perfectly maintained as their movement was generated by programming. Disney's venerable multiplane cameras were updated with computers to expedite and control aperture settings and time exposures. Another technological breakthrough was the development of the APT (animation photo transfer) process. The first major change in the Studio's method of transferring the artist's drawings to a cel since photocopying replaced hand inking 20 years earlier, the APT greatly improved the quality of the animator's art. In all, the animated film was 12 years in the making—5 years in actual production—at a cost of over $25 million. Over 1,165 different hues and colors were implemented and over 34 miles of film stock was utilized. This was the first animated Disney film made in cooperation with Silver Screen Partners II. The sheer lavishness of the production, however, did not guarantee huge grosses, and the film was a box office failure. David W. Spencer was presented with an Academy Award for his development of the APT process. First released on video in 1998.

Black Hole, The (film) The explorer craft USS

Palomino is returning to Earth after a fruitless 18-month search for extraterrestrial life when the crew comes upon a supposedly lost ship, the magnificent USS *Cygnus*, hovering near a black hole. The ship is controlled by Dr. Hans Reinhardt and his monstrous robot companion, Maximillian. But the initial wonderment and awe the *Palomino* crew have for the ship, and its resistance to the power of the black hole, turns to horror as they uncover Reinhardt's plans, which involve turning his former crew into robots and flying through the hole. As they try to escape, a meteorite shower damages the ship, and the survivors hang on as they are plunged into the most powerful force in the universe, heading toward the blinding light that holds whatever eternity awaits them. Premiered in London on Dec. 18, 1979; U.S. premiere on Dec. 20, 1979. Directed by Gary Nelson. First film made by the Disney Studio to receive a PG rating. 98 min. Stars Maximilian Schell (Dr. Hans Reinhardt), Anthony Perkins (Dr. Alex Durant), Robert Forster (Capt. Dan Holland), Ernest Borgnine (Harry Booth), Yvette Mimieux (Dr. Kate McCrae), Joseph Bottoms (Lt. Charles Pizer). The film was 5 years in development, 14 months in production, and cost $20 million. It failed to recoup its terrific cost but wowed audiences with the dazzling special effects created by ACES (Automatic Camera Effects Systems). All the soundstages at the Disney Studio were occupied by the production. Nearly 14 months of simultaneous and postproduction filming and processing were required by the Studio's photographic process laboratory and special effects departments. In some scenes, as many as 12 different photo processes were used simultaneously on the screen. Four Academy Award winners supervised the special effects: Peter Ellenshaw, production designer and director of special effects; Eustace Lycett and Art Cruickshank, special photographic effects; and Danny Lee, special visual effects. The film was nominated for Academy Awards for Cinematography (Frank Phillips) and Visual Effects. The film's original producer, Winston Hibler, died during production.

Black Holes: Monsters that Eat Space and Time (TV) Syn. special about the mysterious black holes with footage from *The Black Hole*; aired in Nov. 1979. Hosted by Durk Pearson. Directed by Chuck Staley.

Black Is King (film/TV) Visual album on Disney+; released digitally Jul. 31, 2020. Inspired by the 2019 album *The Lion King: The Gift*; lessons from the Disney film are reimagined for young kings and queens in search of their own crowns. Written, directed, and exec. produced by Beyoncé Knowles-Carter. Celebrity appearances include Jay-Z, Lupita Nyong'o, Naomi Campbell, Pharrell Williams. 85 min. From Parkwood Entertainment. Released by Walt Disney Studios Motion Pictures. Emmy winner for Outstanding Costumes for a Variety, Nonfiction, or Reality Program in 2021.

Black Panther (film) T'Challa, after the death of his father, the King of Wakanda, returns home to the isolated, technologically advanced African nation to succeed to the throne and take his rightful place as king. But when a powerful old enemy reappears, T'Challa's mettle as king—and Black Panther—is tested when he is drawn into a formidable conflict that puts the fate of Wakanda and the entire world at risk. Faced with treachery and danger, the young king must rally his allies and release the full power of Black Panther to defeat his foes and secure the safety of his people and their way of life. Directed by Ryan Coogler. Released Feb. 16, 2018 (also in IMAX and 3-D), after a Feb. 13 international release. Stars Chadwick Boseman (T'Challa/Black Panther), Michael B. Jordan (Erik Killmonger), Lupita Nyong'o (Nakia), Danai Gurira (Okoye), Martin Freeman (Everett K. Ross), Daniel Kaluuya (W'Kabi), Letitia Wright (Shuri), Winston Duke (M'Baku), Angela Bassett (Ramonda), Forest Whitaker (Zuri), Andy Serkis (Ulysses Klaue/ Klaw). 134 min. Filmed in wide-screen format. The Black Panther character made its first appearance in Marvel's *Fantastic Four* issue No. 2, published in 1966. The film was nominated for 7 Academy Awards for 2018, including Best Picture, winning 3: Best Costume Design (Ruth Carter), Best Original Score (Ludwig Göransson), and Best Production Design (Hannah Beachler and Jay Hart).

Black Panther: Wakanda Forever (film) Second feature in the Black Panther series. Queen Ramonda, Shuri, M'Baku, Okoye, and the Dora Milaje fight to protect their nation from intervening world powers in the wake of King T'Challa's death. As the Wakandans strive to embrace their next chapter, the heroes must band together with the help of War Dog Nakia and Everett Ross and forge a new path for the kingdom of Wakanda. Directed by Ryan Coogler. Released Nov. 11, 2022, also in 3-D, IMAX, and IMAX 3-D, after a Nov. 9 international release. Stars Letitia Wright (Shuri), Lupita Nyong'o (Nakia), Danai Gurira

(Okoye), Winston Duke (M'Baku), Florence Kasumba (Ayo), Dominique Thorne (Riri Williams), Michaela Coel (Aneka), Mabel Cadena (Namora), Alex Livinalli (Attuma), Tenoch Huerta (Namor), Martin Freeman (Everett Ross), Angela Bassett (Queen Ramonda). 161 min. When original *Black Panther* star Chadwick Boseman passed away in 2020, filmmakers considered what the next story could be; a new theme about coping with grief and overcoming loss became the driving force of the narrative. From Marvel Studios. Filmed in wide-screen format in and around Atlanta; on the MIT campus in Cambridge, Massachusetts; and in Puerto Rico. Academy Award winner for Best Costume Design (Ruth E. Carter), with additional nominations for Supporting Actress (Angela Bassett), Original Song ("Lift Me Up," by Tems, Ludwig Göransson, Rihanna, Ryan Coogler), Makeup and Hairstyling (Camille Friend, Joel Harlow), and Visual Effects (Geoffrey Baumann, Craig Hammack, R. Christopher White, Dan Sudick). A 3-episode documentary, *Voices Rising: The Music of Wakanda Forever*, digitally premiered Feb. 28, 2023, on Disney+.

Black Spire Outfitters Shop in Star Wars: Galaxy's Edge; opened May 31, 2019, in Disneyland and Aug. 29, 2019, in Disney's Hollywood Studios at Walt Disney World. Themed garments and gear are sold.

Black Widow (film) Natasha Romanoff (aka Black Widow) confronts the darker parts of her ledger when a dangerous conspiracy with ties to her past arises. Pursued by a force that will stop at nothing to bring her down, Natasha must deal with her history as a spy and the broken relationships left in her wake long before she became an Avenger. Released in theaters and on Disney+ Jul. 9, 2021, also in 3-D, IMAX, and IMAX 3-D, after a Jun. 27 screening in London and international premieres beginning Jun. 29. Directed by Cate Shortland. Stars Scarlett Johansson (Natasha/Black Widow), Ever Anderson (Young Natasha), Florence Pugh (Yelena), David Harbour (Alexei/The Red Guardian), Rachel Weisz (Melina), Ray Winstone (General Dreykov), O-T Fagbenle (Mason). 133 min. The first film in "Phase Four" of the Marvel Cinematic Universe, though it takes place on the heels of *Captain America: Civil War* and just before *Avengers: Infinity War*. Filmed in wide-screen format at Pinewood Studios in London (and elsewhere in the U.K.), Norway, Hungary, Morocco, and Atlanta, Georgia.

Blackbeard's Ghost (film) Upon his arrival in the tiny fishing town of Godolphin, where he will be track coach of the college team, Steve Walker inadvertently summons the ghost of the infamous Captain Blackbeard. The rascally old pirate causes him nothing but trouble, but, in the end, finally helps the coach win a track meet and a girlfriend, and outwit some gangsters, which earns the ghost his desired eternal rest. Released Feb. 8, 1968. Directed by Robert Stevenson. 107 min. Stars Peter Ustinov (Blackbeard), Dean Jones (Steve Walker), Suzanne Pleshette (Jo Anne Baker), Elsa Lanchester (Emily Stowecroft), Joby Baker (Silky Seymour). This supernatural comedy reteamed the popular Jones and Pleshette from *The Ugly Dachshund*, and with the spirited flamboyance of Ustinov as Blackbeard, made the film a box office winner, with a reissue in 1976. Based on the book by Ben Stahl, who presented his story to Walt Disney in 1965. Walt approved the film adaptation, assigning the screenplay to Bill Walsh and Don DaGradi, and supervised the casting. Shooting began in 1966, prior to Walt's passing. The incantation to summon Blackbeard's ghost is "Kree Kruh Vergo Gebba Kalto Kree," which brings to one's eyes and ears someone who is bound in limbo.

Blackbeard's Portrait Deck Pirate ship photo studio in Adventureland at Tokyo Disneyland; open Apr. 15, 1983–2007, and superseded by Pirate Treasure.

Blackberries in the Dark (film) Educational film about a grandmother and grandson learning to cope with a loved one's death. Released in Mar. 1988. 27 min.

black-ish (TV) Half-hour family comedy on ABC; aired Sep. 24, 2014–Apr. 19, 2022. Andre "Dre" Johnson and his physician wife, Rainbow, are living the American dream: great careers, 4 beautiful kids, and a colonial home in an upper-middle-class neighborhood. But has success brought too much assimilation for this family? With a little help from his dad, Dre sets out to establish a sense of cultural identity for his family that honors their past while embracing the future. Stars Anthony Anderson (Andre "Dre" Johnson), Tracee Ellis Ross (Rainbow Johnson), Yara Shahidi (Zoey), Marcus Scribner (Andre Jr. "Andy"), Miles Brown (Jack), Marsai Martin (Diane), Laurence Fishburne (Pops). From ABC Studios. Won an Emmy for Contemporary Hairstyling in 2020 ("Hair Day").

Blades, Rubén Actor; appeared in *Disorganized Crime* (Carlos Barrios), *Color of Night* (police lieutenant), and *Cradle Will Rock* (Diego Rivera), and on TV in *Gideon's Crossing* (Max Cabranes).

Blair, Janet (1921–2007) Actress; appeared in *The One and Only, Genuine, Original Family Band* (Katie Bower).

Blair, Mary (1911–1978) Artist; she started at the Disney Studio in 1940 as a color stylist and went on the 1941 Disney trip to Latin America with her husband, Lee Blair. Many of her unique color concepts are obvious in *Saludos Amigos* and *The Three Caballeros* and influenced the look of *Melody Time*, *Alice in Wonderland*, *Peter Pan*, and other animated films. She later contributed designs for the Disney parks, including It's a Small World, 2 elaborate tile murals for Tomorrowland in Disneyland (together titled *The Spirit of Creative Energies Among Children*), and another mural for the Grand Canyon Concourse in Disney's Contemporary Resort at Walt Disney World. Walt personally commissioned her to design a ceramic mural for the Jules Stein Eye Institute. She was named a Disney Legend posthumously in 1991.

Blame It on the Bellboy (film) A quirky bellboy in Venice, who has trouble with English homonyms, mixes up 3 guests in his hotel with similar-sounding names (Orton, Lawton, and Horton), causing chaos when each receives instructions meant for another. By the end of the film, everyone has realized the mistake and switches back—all the better for the experience. World premiere in London Jan. 24, 1992; U.S. release Mar. 6, 1992. Directed by Mark Herman. 78 min. Stars Dudley Moore (Melvyn Orton), Bryan Brown (Charlton Black), Bronson Pinchot (Bellboy), Patsy Kensit (Caroline Wright), Richard Griffiths (Maurice Horton), Andreas Katsulas (Scarpa), Alison Steadman (Rosemary Horton), Penelope Wilton (Patricia Fulford). A Hollywood Pictures film. Filmed on location in Venice, on the island of Murano, and at Lee International Studios near London.

Blame It on the Samba (film) Segment of *Melody Time* performed by the Dinning Sisters, with Ethel Smith at the organ. The Aracuan Bird uses the rhythm of the samba to cure Donald Duck and José Carioca of the blues. Released as a short Apr. 1, 1955.

Blanc, Mel (1908–1989) Voice artist and radio personality who supplied a hiccup for the non-speaking Gideon in *Pinocchio* and provided several voices of his famous Warner Bros. characters for *Who Framed Roger Rabbit*. He also provided the voice for Cousin Orville in the Carousel of Progress.

Blanche-Neige et les Sept Nains Snow White attraction in Fantasyland at Disneyland Paris; opened Apr. 12, 1992. Similar to the former Snow White's Scary Adventures at Disneyland and Walt Disney World.

Blanchett, Cate Actress; appeared in *Veronica Guerin* (Veronica Guerin), *The Life Aquatic with Steve Zissou* (Jane Winslett-Richardson), *Cinderella* (Lady Tremaine, 2015), and *Thor: Ragnarok* (Hela). She voiced Gran Mamare in *Ponyo*.

Blank: A Vinylmation Love Story (film) A stop-motion film. In search of lost soul mate Bow, an unpainted Vinylmation named Blank finds himself on a quest that alters the destiny of his entire world. Directed by Greg Shewchuk, Paul Foyder, Michael Ambs, Whitfield Scheidegger, and Regina Roy. Released Feb. 3, 2014, at the El Capitan Theatre in Hollywood and on Google Play's platforms Feb. 10, 2014. 38 min. From Disney Interactive Entertainment.

Blank Check (film) Eleven-year-old Preston Waters's rusty old bike is accidentally run over by a car driven by a crook named Quigley, who quickly dashes off a check to pay for the damages, but in his haste neglects to fill in the amount. Preston notices the oversight and boldly fills in an impressive amount—$1 million. Suddenly wealthy, Preston embarks on the wildest spending spree ever. He hires a personal chauffeur, buys a great house, and throws himself a spectacular 12th birthday bash. But the party's over when the FBI, along with Quigley and his thugs, descend and show up as uninvited guests. Preston discovers how hard it is to hold on to his newfound riches. Released Feb. 11, 1994. Directed by Rupert Wainwright. 93 min. Stars Brian Bonsall (Preston Waters), Karen Duffy (Shay Stanley), Miguel Ferrer (Quigley), James Rebhorn (Fred Waters), Tone Lōc (Juice), Jayne Atkinson (Sandra Waters), Michael Lerner (Biderman), Chris Demetral (Damian Waters). Filmed on location in Austin, Texas.

Blast to the Past Celebration and parade at Disneyland in the spring of 1988 and 1989. The young

Disneyland performers put on their (or perhaps their parents') attire from the 1950s and presented a rousing salute to the era. There was a daily parade, with period cars adding to the ambience, and a special show, the *Main Street Hop*, presented on Main Street, U.S.A. and featuring 5 huge jukeboxes, Hula-Hoops, Elvis, scooter riders, and confetti. Shows featured original entertainers from the 1950s and 1960s. As part of the event, Disneyland hosted the Super Hooper Duper event, smashing the world's record for the most persons hula-hooping at one time in one location—as 1,527 people gathered for the extravaganza in front of Sleeping Beauty Castle. SEE ALSO DISNEYLAND BLAST TO THE PAST (SYN. TV SPECIAL).

Blaze (film) Set against the colorful backdrop of 1959–1960 Louisiana, the scandalous liaison between Governor Earl K. Long and stripper Blaze Starr raised more than a few eyebrows. The governor's extramarital affair with the flamboyant redhead left Louisiana in a state of shock and rocked the very foundation of the Southern political machine. Released Dec. 13, 1989. Directed by Ron Shelton. A Touchstone film. 117 min. Stars Paul Newman (Earl Long), Lolita Davidovich (Blaze Starr), Jerry Hardin (Thibodeaux). Based on the book *Blaze Starr*, by Blaze Starr and Huey Perry. Filmed on location in Louisiana.

Bless This Mess (TV) Sitcom on ABC; aired Apr. 16, 2019–May 5, 2020. Newlyweds Rio and Mike drop everything, including their jobs and overbearing mother-in-law, to make the move from big-city New York to rural Nebraska in search of a simpler life. They soon realize that becoming farmers isn't as easy as they planned when they are faced with unexpected challenges. Stars Lake Bell (Rio), Dax Shepard (Mike), Ed Begley Jr. (Rudy), Pam Grier (Constance), and JT Neal (Jacob). From ABC Studios and 20th Century Fox Television.

Bletcher, Billy (1894–1979) Voice actor; voiced Pete, the Big Bad Wolf, and a host of other characters in the early cartoons.

Bleu, Corbin Actor; appeared in the High School Musical films (Chad Danforth), on Disney Channel in *Jump In!* (Izzy Daniels), and on TV in *Castle* (Hunter), *The Fosters* (Mercutio), and *The Disney Family Singalong*. He voiced the Magic Gourd in the U.S. DVD release of *The Secret of the Magic Gourd* and sang "Celebrate You," the anthem of the 2009 Disney parks "What Will You Celebrate?" campaign.

Bliss, Lucille (1916–2012) Voice of the stepsister Anastasia in *Cinderella*.

Blizzard Beach A 66-acre water park at Walt Disney World; opened Apr. 1, 1995. As the story goes, a freak snowstorm has hit Florida, prompting the opening of the region's first ski resort, with the paradox of being in the midst of a tropical lagoon. Mount Gushmore rises more than 120 feet high and features a variety of waterslides. There is Summit Plummet, Slush Gusher, Teamboat Springs, Toboggan Racer, Snow Stormers, Runoff Rapids, Melt-Away Bay, and Cross Country Creek. Food is available at Lottawatta Lodge, Avalunch, Cooling Hunt, Frostbite Freddy's Frozen Freshments, and I. C. Expeditions, and souvenirs are for sale at Beach Haus. Ice Gator is the water park's blue alligator mascot. On Nov. 13, 2022, new features from the Frozen films were introduced at the Tike's Peak children's play area.

Blood & Oil (TV) Hour-long drama series on ABC; aired Sep. 27–Dec. 13, 2015. An epic story of the American dream as seen through the lens of a speculative mania, riding up the boom and eventual bust of a major oil discovery in North Dakota. The series was filled with family rivalries, pure ambition, and characters that represent the authentic diversity of a boomtown. Key among the characters are working-class Billy and Cody Lefever, packing up and moving to North Dakota to try to cash in on the oil discovery, and wealthy Hap Briggs, the oil baron of the area, a great man willing to play a little dirty to get what he wants. Stars Don Johnson (Hap Briggs), Chace Crawford (Billy Lefever), Rebecca Rittenhouse (Cody), Amber Valletta (Carla), Scott Michael Foster (Wick Briggs), Adan Canto (A. J. Menendez), India de Beaufort (Jules Jackman), Delroy Lindo (Sheriff Tip Hamilton). From ABC Signature Studios.

Blood In, Blood Out: Bound by Honor Video release title of *Bound by Honor*.

Bloom, Orlando Actor; starred in several Pirates of the Caribbean films: *The Curse of the Black Pearl*, *Dead Man's Chest*, *At World's End*, and *Dead Men Tell No Tales*.

Blossom (TV) Series on NBC; aired Jan. 3, 1991–Jun. 5, 1995. A teenage girl, Blossom Russo, experiences life in a household with her father and 2 quirky brothers: one, Anthony, recovered from drug addiction and the other, Joey, not too bright and at an age when girls are becoming a big part of his life. Stars Mayim Bialik (Blossom), Ted Wass (Nick), Joey Lawrence (Joey), Michael Stoyanov (Anthony), Jenna Von Oy (Six), David Lascher (Vinnie).

Blu-ray See DVD.

Blue Bayou (film) Segment of *Make Mine Music*, originally meant for *Fantasia* with Debussy's "Clair de Lune." The Ken Darby Chorus performs the song, written by Bobby Worth and Ray Gilbert.

Blue Bayou (TV) Unsold pilot for a series; aired on NBC Jan. 15, 1990. A divorced real estate lawyer and her son face a new life in New Orleans, only to get involved in a murder case. 120 min. Directed by Karen Arthur. Stars Alfre Woodard, Mario Van Peebles, Ron Thinnes, Ashley Crow, Joseph Culp, Maxwell Caulfield, Elizabeth Ashley, Bibi Besch.

Blue Bayou Restaurant New Orleans Square restaurant in Disneyland; opened Mar. 18, 1967. One of the most attractive dining areas in Disneyland, it is located inside the building that houses Pirates of the Caribbean. As guests embark in their boat on their Pirates adventure, they can look to the right and see the diners enjoying their meals under strings of glowing balloon lanterns. The theming of a night sky, fireflies, and bayou sounds provide a welcome respite on a hot day. Cajun- and Creole-inspired dishes are served, with the guest-favorite Monte Cristo Sandwich. Also in Adventureland at Tokyo Disneyland; opened Apr. 15, 1983. The equivalent in Disneyland Paris is Captain Jack's – Restaurant des Pirates (previously the Blue Lagoon Restaurant).

Blue Bird Shoes for Children Children's footwear shop on Main Street, U.S.A. at Disneyland; open 1955–1956, and succeeded by Wonderland Music.

Blue Fairy Fairy who turns Pinocchio into a real boy in the 1940 animated feature; voiced by Evelyn Venable.

Blue Lagoon Restaurant Adventureland restaurant in Disneyland Paris; opened Apr. 12, 1992. The European equivalent of the Blue Bayou Res-

taurant in Disneyland, though the dining area is terraced to provide enhanced views of the boats floating by in Pirates of the Caribbean. It closed for refurbishment Jan. 8, 2017, reopening that July as Captain Jack's – Restaurant des Pirates.

Blue Men of Morocco, The (film) People and Places featurette; released Feb. 14, 1957. Directed by Ralph Wright. 31 min. The theme for this subject is going back in time. The action takes place in the Sahara desert, where the Blue Men of Morocco live in the 20th century as they did in biblical times. The film features their lifestyles, work, and journeys into Marrakech.

Blue Rhythm (film) Mickey Mouse cartoon released Aug. 18, 1931. Directed by Burt Gillett. Musical beginning with Mickey playing concert piano. Minnie sings the blues, Mickey joins her for a song and dance routine, then Mickey plays a clarinet solo imitating Ted Lewis. Finally, Mickey leads an orchestra of his gang, with the music getting so hot they eventually break through the floor.

Blue Ribbon Bakery Shop on Main Street, U.S.A. in Disneyland; opened Apr. 6, 1990, taking the place of the longtime Sunkist Citrus House. Moved into the Carnation Ice Cream Parlor Mar. 21, 1997. It closed Jan. 5, 2012, replaced by an expansion of Carnation Café.

Blue Sky Studios See 21st Century Fox.

Blue Umbrella, The (film) Short cartoon released Jun. 21, 2013, with *Monsters University*, after a debut at the Berlin International Film Festival Feb. 12, 2013. Falling for a red umbrella, a blue umbrella finds itself windblown and weather-beaten during a rainstorm. Directed by Saschka Unseld. 6 min. Rather than originating in the animation or story departments, this film began in Pixar's camera and staging department.

Blue Yonder, The (TV) Movie for The Disney Channel; aired Nov. 17, 1985. A young boy travels back in time to meet his grandfather, a pioneer aviator. Directed by Mark Rosman. Stars Peter Coyote (Max Knickerbocker), Huckleberry Fox (Jonathan), and Art Carney (Henry Coogan). Later shown on the Disney anthology series as *Time Flyer*.

Bluegrass Special, The (TV) Show aired May 22, 1977. Directed by Andrew V. McLaglen. The story of Woodhill, an unruly racehorse, who catches the eye of Penny, a girl who wants to be a jockey. Penny uses kindness rather than the whip to train Woodhill and eventually prove that she and her horse are worthy to race in the Bluegrass Special. Stars William Windom, Celeste Holm, Davy Jones, Devon Ericson, James Gleason.

Blumberg, Barry He was named president of Walt Disney Television Animation in Jan. 2003 after having served in positions of increasing responsibility in the division since 1994. He resigned in 2005.

Blunt, Emily Actress; appeared in *Dan in Real Life* (Ruthie Draper), *The Muppets* (receptionist), *Into the Woods* (Baker's Wife), *Jungle Cruise* (Lily Houghton), and as the title character in *Mary Poppins Returns*. She voiced Juliet in *Gnomeo & Juliet* and Nahoko Satomi in *The Wind Rises*.

Bluth, Don Animator/director; he joined Disney in 1955, working as an assistant animator on *Sleeping Beauty*. After being away for 14 years, he returned to animate on *Robin Hood* and *Winnie the Pooh and Tigger Too*. He served as a directing animator on *The Rescuers* and directed the animation for *Pete's Dragon* before leaving the Studio in 1979 to form his own company in partnership with Gary Goldman and John Pomeroy.

Bo Peep Free-spirited porcelain figure, once attached to Molly's bedside lamp, in the Toy Story films; voiced by Annie Potts.

Boag, Wally (1920–2011) Longtime comedian at the *Golden Horseshoe Revue* in Disneyland, which put him into the *Guinness World Records* book for the greatest number of performances of a show. He was best known for creating animal balloons as the show's traveling salesman and for spitting out a seemingly inexhaustible number of his "teeth" (beans) after being hit in the mouth as Pecos Bill. Boag opened the show at Disneyland in 1955, took time out to get the same show started at the Diamond Horseshoe in the Magic Kingdom at Walt Disney World in 1971, then returned to Disneyland for the remainder of his career. His last performance before his retirement was Jan. 28, 1982. Boag worked on scripts for various Disneyland projects, including Walt Disney's Enchanted Tiki Room, for which he provided the voice of José. He also had small roles in *The Absent-Minded Professor, Son of Flubber*, and *The Love Bug*. He was named a Disney Legend in 1995.

Board Stiff Surf and swimwear shop in the Disney Village Marketplace at Walt Disney World; opened Jun. 25, 1988, replacing the It's a Small World After All shop. Closed Apr. 15, 1992, superseded by The City.

BoardWalk, Disney's The "showplace of the shore" in the EPCOT Resort Area at Walt Disney World; opened Jul. 1, 1996. With the atmosphere of turn-of-the-century Atlantic City, the resort includes accommodations, entertainment, shopping, and dining (Trattoria al Forno, Flying Fish, Big River Grille & Brewing Works, AbracadaBar) along a quarter-mile boardwalk. There is Disney's BoardWalk Inn, with 378 rooms, and Disney's BoardWalk Villas with 532 rooms, along with a 20,000-sq.-ft. convention center. Entertainment includes Jellyrolls (a dueling piano bar) and Atlantic Dance. Visitors can ride surrey bikes or stroll along the promenade to Disney's Yacht & Beach Club Resorts and the International Gateway entrance to EPCOT. The carnival-themed Luna Park Pool, available to hotel guests, includes a 200-ft.-long Keister Coaster waterslide. Designed by Robert A.M. Stern.

BoardWalk Bakery On Disney's BoardWalk at Walt Disney World; opened Jul. 1, 1996, and closed Jul. 24, 2022, to become BoardWalk Deli. A new bakery, The Cake Bake Shop by Gwendolyn Rogers, is scheduled to open on the BoardWalk in 2023.

Boardwalk Bazaar Paradise Pier hat and souvenir shop in Disney California Adventure; opened Feb. 2012, taking the place of Man Hat 'n' Beach. Closed Jan. 2018.

Boardwalk Betty's Strips, Dips 'n' Chips Paradise Pier food counter in Disney's California Adventure; open Feb. 8, 2001–2006, and superseded by Toy Story Midway Mania!

Boardwalk Candy Palace Confectionery themed to 1892 Atlantic City on Main Street, U.S.A. in Disneyland Paris; opened Apr. 12, 1992, hosted by Nestlé.

BoardWalk Deli On Disney's BoardWalk at Walt Disney World; opened Aug. 15, 2022, taking the place of BoardWalk Bakery. Bagels, sandwiches, and desserts are served.

BoardWalk Ice Cream Shop on Disney's Board-Walk at Walt Disney World; opened May 20,

2021, taking the place of Ample Hills Creamery.

Boardwalk Pizza & Pasta Quick-service restaurant in Paradise Gardens Park at Disney California Adventure; opened Jul. 1, 2011, replacing Pizza Oom Mow Mow. Pasta, salads, and pizzas are served.

Boat Builders (film) Mickey Mouse cartoon released Feb. 25, 1938. Directed by Ben Sharpsteen. Mickey, Donald, and Goofy purchase a folding boat kit, but the boat is not as easy to put together as they hoped. After much trouble, Minnie christens the boat; it is launched and promptly collapses, throwing them all into the water. Rereleased in theaters in 2007 with *Meet the Robinsons*.

BOATHOUSE, The Nautically themed, 600-seat waterfront restaurant and raw bar in The Landing at Disney Springs at Walt Disney World; opened Apr. 13, 2015, serving steaks, chops, and fresh seafood in an upscale setting. On the lake, guests can ride around in restored amphibious vehicles, called Amphicars, or a 40-ft. Italian water taxi. Managed by Gibsons Restaurant Group.

Boatniks, The (film) Newly assigned to duty in the Coast Guard at Newport Beach, California, ensign Thomas Garland soon faces the problems caused by Sunday sailors, those amateur *boatniks* who go down to the sea in ships. But the ensign also finds himself involved in romantic complications with Kate Fairchild, as well as with jewel thieves, whose careers are ended with the cooperation of Thomas and Kate. Released Jul. 1, 1970. Directed by Norman Tokar. 100 min. Stars Robert Morse (Ensign Garland), Stefanie Powers (Kate), Phil Silvers (Harry Simmons), Norman Fell (Max), Mickey Shaughnessy (Charlie), Wally Cox (Jason), Don Ameche (Commander Taylor). The song, "The Boatniks," was written by Bruce Belland and Robert F. Brunner.

Boatwright's Dining Hall Full-service restaurant in Disney's Port Orleans Resort – Riverside at Walt Disney World; opened Feb. 2, 1992, serving southern Louisiana–inspired fare. The 200-seat eatery is patterned after a ship-making facility, with the hull of a lugger fishing boat as the centerpiece.

Bob Patterson (TV) Half-hour comedy series on ABC; aired Oct. 2–31, 2001. Bob Patterson is a successful yet insecure motivational speaker who tries to manage his career and family life. Stars Jason Alexander (Bob Patterson), Robert Klein (Landau), Jennifer Aspen (Janet), Chandra Wilson (Claudia), Phil Buckman (Vic), James Guidice (Jeffrey). A 20th Century Fox Television/Touchstone Television production.

Bobo Title character in *Mickey's Elephant* (1936).

Bodenheimer, George He was named co-chair of Disney Media Networks in 2004. He also served as president of ABC Sports (2003–2012) and president of ESPN, Inc. (1998–2012). He had originally joined ESPN in 1981. In 2012, he was named executive chairman, ESPN, Inc. He retired in 2014 and was named a Disney Legend the following year.

Body of Proof (TV) Drama series on ABC; aired Mar. 29, 2011–May 28, 2013. Dr. Megan Hunt was a brilliant neurosurgeon, but a devastating car accident ended her time in the operating room, and she became a medical examiner. As she, with her sharp instincts, puzzles who or what killed the victims, she also fudges the lines of where her job ends and where the police department begins. Stars Dana Delany (Megan Hunt), Jeri Ryan (Dr. Kate Murphy), Geoffrey Arend (Dr. Ethan Gross), John Caroll Lynch (Det. Bud Morris), Windell Middlebrooks (Dr. Curtis Brumfield), Nic Bishop (Peter Dunlap), Sonja Sohn (Det. Samantha Baker). The show premiered before its U.S. airing in Europe, with a world premiere in Italy Jan. 25, 2011, followed by airings in Spain, Poland, Hungary, and Bulgaria. From ABC Studios.

Body Wars Attraction in Wonders of Life at EPCOT; open Oct. 19, 1989–Jan. 1, 2007. At Miniaturized Exploration Technologies (MET), guests boarded a body probe, *Bravo 229*, and were shrunk down for a thrilling trip through the human body by way of the bloodstream. It used the same simulator technology that made Star Tours possible.

Boiler Room Barbecue Ship-shaped snack counter in Adventureland at Tokyo Disneyland; opened Jul. 21, 1992. It was renamed Boiler Room Bites in 2003.

Bolger, Ray (1904–1987) Actor; appeared in *Babes in Toyland* (Barnaby).

Bollenbach, Stephen F. (1942–2016) He joined The Walt Disney Company in 1995 as senior executive vice president and chief financial officer. He left the company in Feb. 1996.

Bolt (film) For super-dog Bolt, every day is filled with adventure, danger, and intrigue—at least until the cameras stop rolling. When the star of a hit TV show is accidentally shipped from his Hollywood soundstage to New York City, he begins his biggest adventure yet—a cross-country journey through the real world to get back to his owner and co-star, Penny. Armed only with the delusions that all his amazing feats and powers are real, and with the help of 2 unlikely traveling companions—a jaded, abandoned house cat named Mittens and a TV-obsessed hamster in a plastic ball named Rhino—Bolt discovers that he doesn't need superpowers to be a hero. Directed by Chris Williams and Byron Howard. The computer-generated animated feature from Walt Disney Animation Studios was released Nov. 21, 2008, in 2-D and Disney Digital 3-D. Voices include John Travolta (Bolt), Susie Essman (Mittens), Miley Cyrus (Penny), Mark Walton (Rhino), Malcolm McDowell (Dr. Calico), James Lipton (the director), Greg Germann (the agent). 96 min. Nominated for an Academy Award for Best Animated Feature. The film's working title was *American Dog*. A 6-min. *Bolt* featurette was released with *Beverly Hills Chihuahua* on Oct. 3, 2008. Bolt's design was loosely based on American white shepherds, with changes to the ears, nose, and overall body size. The film was Disney's first animated feature to be conceived and designed for 3-D. The DVD included the new short *Super Rhino*.

Boma – Flavors of Africa Buffet dining in Jambo House at Disney's Animal Kingdom Lodge at Walt Disney World; opened Apr. 16, 2001. Under thatched roofs resembling a village bazaar, guests can try flavors from more than 50 African countries.

Bon Voyage (film) Harry Willard finally makes good his promise to take his bride of 20 years on a long-delayed trip by ship to Europe. They are accompanied by their 19-year-old son, Elliott; 18-year-old daughter, Amy; and an active 11-year-old son named Skipper. From the time they arrive at the dock, there follows an unending series of comedy adventures and romantic encounters that keep the family constantly involved until, exhausted but happy, they start for home with memories which will benefit them all in the years to come. Released May 17, 1962. Directed by James Neilson. 132 min. Stars Fred MacMurray (Harry Willard), Jane Wyman (Katie Willard), Michael Callan (Nick O'Mara), Deborah Walley (Amy Willard), Tommy Kirk (Elliott Willard), Kevin Corcoran (Skipper Willard), Jessie Royce Landis (La Contessa). This Disney family film ran into some criticism for including a prostitute who flirts with Harry and young Elliott Willard. The film is based on the book of the same title by Marrijane and Joseph Hayes, and was shot on location in Europe. It was nominated for Academy Awards for Best Costume Design, by Bill Thomas, and Best Sound, by Robert O. Cook. The title song was written by Richard M. and Robert B. Sherman.

Bon Voyage Merchandise outlet at Maihama Station at Tokyo Disney Resort; opened Mar. 1, 2001. At 10,710 sq. feet, it is one of the largest Disney shops in Japan. Shaped like a giant suitcase and hatbox in the style of 1930s travel fashion.

Bonanza Outfitters Frontierland shop at Disneyland selling Western-themed clothing; opened Jun. 29, 1990, taking the place of the Pendleton Woolen Mills Dry Goods Store. Inside are 2 smaller shops: Crockett & Russel Hat Co. (formerly The Great American Buffalo Hat Company) and Silver Spur Supplies. SEE ALSO THUNDER MESA MERCANTILE BUILDING (DISNEYLAND PARIS).

Bondi, Beulah (1892–1981) Actress; appeared in *So Dear to My Heart* (Granny Kincaid).

Bone Bandit (film) Pluto cartoon released Apr. 30, 1948. Directed by Charles Nichols. Pluto's efforts to dig up a bone are frustrated by his allergy to goldenrod, and by a gopher who is using the bone to prop up his tunnel. Pluto and the gopher battle over the bone, ending up with the gopher also developing an allergy to goldenrod.

Bone Trouble (film) Pluto cartoon released Jun. 28, 1940. The first cartoon directed by Jack Kinney. Pluto steals Butch's bone and gets chased into a carnival hall of mirrors, where, though he is frightened by the distortions, he uses them to his advantage in his escape from the bulldog.

Bones and Muscles Get Rhythm, The (film) Educational film in the Wonders of Life series released Jan. 26, 1990. 11 min. How bones and muscles work together, illustrated through dance.

Boneyard, The Dinosaur dig play area in DinoLand U.S.A. at Disney's Animal Kingdom; opened Apr. 22, 1998. Young paleontologists (kids) can excavate fossils.

Bonfamille's Cafe Full-service restaurant in Disney's Port Orleans Resort at Walt Disney World; open May 17, 1991–Aug. 5, 2000, serving steaks, seafood, and specialty dishes.

Bongirno, Carl He first joined Disney as chief accountant and controller for Celebrity Sports Center in 1963, then moved to become treasurer of WED Enterprises. From 1972–1979, he was vice president of finance and treasurer of Walt Disney World; then, until his retirement in 1989, he served as president of Walt Disney Imagineering. He was named a Disney Legend in 2007.

Bongo (film) Segment of *Fun and Fancy Free*, narrated by Dinah Shore, with a young circus bear learning about romance. Released as a featurette Jan. 20, 1971. 32 min. First released on video in 1982.

Bongos Cuban Cafe Multilevel restaurant in Downtown Disney West Side at Walt Disney World; open Sep. 15, 1997–Aug. 18, 2019, succeeded by Summer House on the Lake. Created by Gloria and Emilio Estefan.

Bonham Carter, Helena Actress; appeared in *Alice in Wonderland* and *Alice Through the Looking Glass* (Red Queen), *The Lone Ranger* (Red Harrington), and *Cinderella* (Fairy Godmother).

Bonjour! Village Gifts Fantasyland shop in the Magic Kingdom at Walt Disney World; opened Dec. 6, 2012. *Beauty and the Beast* souvenirs are sold in a store resembling Belle's favorite bookshop from the animated film. SEE ALSO VILLAGE SHOPPES (TOKYO DISNEYLAND).

Bonkers (TV) Animated series on The Disney Channel; premiered Feb. 28, 1993, and syn. Sep. 6, 1993–Aug. 30, 1996. The show was introduced by a syn. 2-hour special, *Going Bonkers*. The character had been introduced in segments of *Raw Toonage* in fall 1992. Bonkers D. Bobcat becomes an off-the-wall, wildly enthusiastic recruit for the Hollywood Police Department—Toon Division. With his gruff, streetwise human partner, Detective Lucky Piquel, Bonkers tracks down cartoon criminals. Voices include Jim Cummings (Bonkers, Piquel), Nancy Cartwright (Fawn Deer), Frank Welker (Fall Apart Rabbit). 65 episodes.

Bonnet Creek Golf Club Opened at Walt Disney World Jan. 23, 1992. The course included the Eagle Pines (closed in 2007) and Osprey Ridge (closed in 2013 for incorporation into the Four Seasons resort development) courses. The club's name changed to the Eagle Pines & Osprey Ridge Golf Club Feb. 1, 2005.

Bono & The Edge: A Sort of Homecoming, with Dave Letterman (TV) Feature-length music docuspecial; scheduled for digital release Mar. 17, 2023, on Disney+. Filmmaker Morgan Neville captures Dave Letterman on his first visit to Dublin to hang out with Bono and The Edge in their hometown, experience Dublin, and join the two U2 musicians for a concert performance unlike any they've done before. From Imagine Documentaries, Neville's Tremolo Productions, and Worldwide Pants.

Bonsall, Brian Actor; appeared in *Father Hood* (Eddie Charles) and *Blank Check* (Preston Waters).

Boo Curious human girl in *Monsters, Inc.*; voiced by Mary Gibbs.

Book and Candle Shop SEE STORYBOOK STORE, THE.

Book of Boba Fett, The (TV) *Star Wars* series on Disney+; digitally premiered Dec. 29, 2021. Bounty hunter Boba Fett and mercenary Fennec Shand return to the sands of Tatooine to stake their claim on the territory once ruled by Jabba the Hutt and his crime syndicate. Stars Temuera Morrison (Boba Fett) and Ming-Na Wen (Fennec Shand). A spin-off of *The Mandalorian*. From Lucasfilm. In 2022, the series won the Emmy for Outstanding Special Visual Effects. *Under the Helmet: The Legacy of Boba Fett*, a 22-min. special about the origins and legacy of character, was digitally released Nov. 12, 2021.

Book of Masters, The (film) SEE KNIGA MASTEROV.

Book of Pooh, The (TV) Original series on Disney Channel beginning Jan. 22, 2001. The Pooh characters are presented in stories utilizing the 300-year-old art of Bunraku puppetry with computer-generated sets. Voices include Jim Cummings (Winnie the Pooh, Tigger), John Fiedler (Piglet), Ken Sansom (Rabbit), Peter Cullen (Eeyore), André Stojka (Owl), Stephanie D'Abruzzo (Kessie), Paul Tiesler (Christopher Robin). From Shadow Projects and Walt Disney Television.

Book of Pooh, The: Stories from the Heart (film) Direct-to-video release Jul. 17, 2001; features

Bunraku puppetry from the Disney Channel TV series. Pooh and his pals are in Christopher Robin's room awaiting his return when they discover his favorite storybook filled with endearing tales written about them. They flip through the pages and the stories magically come to life. Developed by Mitchell Kriegman. With the same voices as in the TV series *The Book of Pooh*.

Books The first Disney book was the *Mickey Mouse Book*, published by Bibo-Lang in 1930 and featuring a story written by Bobette Bibo, the young daughter of the publisher. It was followed in 1931 by *The Adventures of Mickey Mouse*, published in hardback and paperback by David McKay, the first of several Disney books from that publisher. Blue Ribbon Books published some Disney pop-up books in 1933, but it was a contract with Whitman Books that same year that began a virtual flood of Disney titles. Whitman, later known as Western Printing and Lithographing and Western Publishing, headquartered in Racine, Wisconsin, remained one of the major publishers of Disney books for many years. Disney Little Golden and Big Golden Books are fondly remembered by many; the books were kept in print many years after their original publication, and vintage and new titles have more recently been published by Penguin Random House. In 1972, Random House began Disney's Wonderful World of Reading book club, reaching millions of readers. Disney set up its own publishing arm in 1991, with the Hyperion, Hyperion Books for Children, Disney Press, and Mouse Works imprints. The Jump at the Sun imprint was added in 1998; it was the first children's book imprint devoted to celebrating the richness of African, African American, and Caribbean American culture. In 1999, the Hyperion imprint moved under the ABC group to focus on general interest publishing for adults as well as books tied to Disney/ABC, and Disney Book Group (DBG) created the Disney Editions imprint to continue releasing nonfiction Disney-themed adult titles, such as "art and making of" books and reference materials. Random House became a major publishing licensee in 2001 with a wide array of children's books tied to Disney animation and thus retired the need for Disney's Mouse Works imprint. In 2009, DBG began publishing e-book editions, and nearly all of the books published under Hyperion Books for Children transitioned to the new name Disney • Hyperion Books; similarly, Jump at the Sun became Disney • Jump at the Sun. DBG launched the Marvel Press imprint in 2011 tied to the Mar-

vel Studios release of *Thor*. In Jul. 2013, Hachette Book Group purchased the Hyperion imprint, with Disney retaining only the Disney/ABC titles. The following year, DBG formed the imprints Kingswell and Kingswell Teen and has since added the following imprints: Disney • Lucasfilm Press (2014), Rick Riordan Presents (2018), Hyperion Avenue (2022), and Andscape Books (2022). With Disney's purchase of 21st Century Fox in 2019, the company added National Geographic and National Geographic Kids to its in-house book publishing division—which changed its name to Buena Vista Books, Inc. in 2021.

Boomerang, Dog of Many Talents (TV) Two-part show; aired on Sep. 22 and 29, 1968. Directed by John Newland. A con man continually sells his dog, who then runs back to his owner. Then the con man himself is conned by a young widow into helping move a flock of 500 turkeys to market. Stars Darren McGavin, Patricia Crowley, and Darby Hinton.

Booth, Bob (1923–2009) He joined Disney in 1957 in the Studio Camera Service Department and in 1962 became supervisor of the Studio Machine Shop. In 1965, he was chosen to set up an innovative multi-craft research, development, and manufacturing subsidiary of the company, known as MAPO, where he worked for 20 years creating elements for the Disney parks. He retired in 1985 and was named a Disney Legend in 2008.

Booth, Nita Actress; appeared on the *Mickey Mouse Club* on The Disney Channel, beginning in 1991.

Boothe, Powers (1948–2017) Actor; appeared in *Tombstone* (Curly Bill), *Nixon* (Alexander Haig), *Con Air* (officer), and *Marvel's The Avengers* (World Security Council), with TV appearances in *Nashville* (Lamar Wyatt) and *Marvel's Agents of S.H.I.E.L.D.* (Gideon Malick).

Bootle Beetle (film) Donald Duck cartoon; released in Aug. 1947. Directed by Jack Hannah. An elderly beetle scolds a young one for running away by telling him of the hazards of meeting up with bug collector Donald. Donald, who's now elderly himself, is still searching for the beetle. The title character was voiced by Dink Trout.

Border Collie (TV) Serial on the *Mickey Mouse Club* during the 1955–1956 season, starring Bobby

Evans and Arthur N. Allen. Directed by Larry Lansburgh. Alvy Moore is the narrator. A boy trains his dog to be a sheepdog. 4 episodes.

Borgfeldt, George, & Co. Toy distributor who signed the first major contract to sell Disney character merchandise, in 1930. Borgfeldt was responsible for having the multitude of Disney bisque figurines, which were so popular in the 1930s, produced in Japan and imported into the U.S. for sale. They also handled games, wood figures, plush dolls, celluloid items, and many other types of novelties and toys.

Borgnine, Ernest (1917–2012) Actor; appeared in *The Black Hole* (Harry Booth), on TV in *Appearances*, and on The Disney Channel in *Love Leads the Way*.

Born in China (film) A Disneynature feature, filmed entirely in the wilds of China, following the adventures of 3 animal families—the panda, the golden monkey, and the snow leopard. The film navigates vast terrain, from the frigid mountains to the heart of the bamboo forest, on the wings of red-crowned cranes, tying the extraordinary tales together. Directed by Lu Chuan. Released in the U.S. Apr. 21, 2017, after an Aug. 5, 2016, release in China. Narrated by John Krasinski. 79 min.

Born to Run (TV) Two-part show; aired Mar. 25 and Apr. 1, 1979. Directed by Don Chaffey. An Australian youngster who shares a love for harness racing with his grandfather, a farmer who is going broke, finds a colt with wonderful promise. Despite some near-disastrous incidents along the way, the colt gets trained and goes on to win a big race that saves the farm. Released theatrically abroad in 1977. Stars Tom Farley (Matthew Boyd), Robert Bettles (Teddy Boyd), Andrew McFarlane (Doone Boyd).

Born Yesterday (film) Billie Dawn, a former Las Vegas showgirl and current mistress of millionaire Harry Brock, is forced into the political limelight of Washington, D.C. While Harry conducts "a little tax business," he finds Billie to be a social hindrance, so he hires savvy journalist Paul Verrall to make her over. In the process, Billie learns to think on her own and to understand the importance of her own individuality. When she falls in love with her handsome mentor, she decides to take matters into her own hands for the first time in her life and stand up to Harry. Learning that all of Harry's shady businesses are in her name, which gives her the real control, she turns the tables on him. Released Mar. 26, 1993. Directed by Luis Mandoki. A Hollywood Pictures film. 100 min. Stars Melanie Griffith (Billie Dawn), John Goodman (Harry Brock), Don Johnson (Paul Verrall), Edward Herrmann (Ed Devery). Based on the original Garson Kanin Broadway play from 1946, which starred Judy Holliday and Paul Douglas. Holliday repeated her performance in the 1950 screen version and won the Best Actress Academy Award. This remake was filmed partly on location at the Willard-Intercontinental Hotel in Washington, D.C., as well as at other local landmarks in our nation's capital such as the Navy Memorial, Georgetown University, and the Library of Congress.

Borrowers, The Children's book series by Mary Norton, made into an animated film by Studio Ghibli and released in the U.S. as *The Secret World of Arrietty*.

Bosché, Bill (1922–1990) Artist, writer, and producer at the Disney Studio for 30 years. He began as a layout artist on *Lady and the Tramp* and later transferred to the Story Department, where he wrote the landmark *Man in Space* TV show and contributed to other educational productions. He scripted several projects related to the Disney parks, including narration for *Project Florida* and *The Magic of Walt Disney World*. He also helped compile *The Walt Disney Story* film (for the park attraction of the same name) and was writer/producer/director of *O Canada!* for EPCOT Center.

Boseman, Chadwick (1976–2020) Actor; appeared as T'Challa/Black Panther in *Captain America: Civil War*, *Black Panther*, *Avengers: Infinity War*, and *Avengers: Endgame*. On TV, he appeared in *Castle* (Chuck Russell) and *Detroit 1-8-7* (Cameron James). In 2022, he was posthumously named a Disney Legend and also won the Emmy Award for Outstanding Character Voice-Over Performance (*What If . . . ?*).

Bosley, Tom (1927–2010) Actor; appeared in *Gus* (Spinner), on Broadway in *Beauty and the Beast* (Maurice), and voiced Santa Paws in *Santa Buddies*.

Boston Tea Party, The (film) A 16-mm release title of a portion of *Johnny Tremain*, released in May 1966. Dramatizes the significant role played by Johnny Tremain in Boston leading up to the American Revolution. Also the title of part 1, when the motion picture was shown on TV in 2 parts.

Bostwick, Barry Actor; appeared in *Spy Hard* (Norman Coleman), *Hannah Montana the Movie* (Mr. Bradley), and *Teen Beach Movie* (Big Poppa), with TV appearances in *Parent Trap III* and *Parent Trap Hawaiian Honeymoon* (Jeffrey Wyatt), *Ugly Betty* (Roger Adams), *Scandal* (Jerry Grant), *Cougar Town* (Roger), and *American Housewife* (Thomas). He has provided several voices, including Thunderbolt in *101 Dalmatians II: Patch's London Adventure*, Clyde Flynn in *Phineas and Ferb*, Doctor St. Croix in *Rapunzel's Tangled Adventure*, Mayor in *Incredibles 2*, and Clyde in *Milo Murphy's Law*.

Bottoms, Joseph Actor; appeared in *The Black Hole* (Lt. Charles Pizer), and on TV in the title role in *Major Effects*.

Bottoms, Timothy Actor; appeared on The Disney Channel in *Love Leads the Way* (Morris Frank) and on ABC in *Grey's Anatomy* (Carl Murphy).

Boudin Bakery, The Attraction in the Golden State area (later Pacific Wharf) in Disney California Adventure; opened Feb. 8, 2001, sponsored by Boudin Sourdough Bread Co. On The Bakery Tour, celebrity hosts Rosie O'Donnell and Colin Mochrie explain how sourdough bread is made as guests make their way through the bakery.

Boulangerie Pâtisserie Pastry shop in France in EPCOT; opened Oct. 1, 1982. It was not long after the opening of the park that lines were snaking throughout the courtyard; word had gotten around that the French pastries were wickedly delicious. Imagineers quickly redesigned the shop to enable greater capacity. It was moved and expanded in a new location Jan. 10, 2014, with a new name, Les Halles Boulangerie & Patisserie.

Boulder Ridge Villas SEE WILDERNESS LODGE, DISNEY'S.

Bound by Honor (film) Set against the background of East Los Angeles, the lives of 3 young men are traced during a 12-year span. When the half-Anglo, half-Chicano cousin, Miklo, of a barrio gang leader, Paco, arrives, he learns that the gang's motto is "Blood In, Blood Out," which means to join the gang, one must spill the blood of a rival gang member. Amid increasing gang

warfare, Miklo is arrested for killing an opposing gang leader and sent to prison, where he also finds gangs are powerful. Paco becomes an undercover cop, and while the lives of Miklo, Paco, and their cousin Cruz go in different directions, they eventually realize that they must look out for each other, for they are truly "blood brothers." Initial release Jan. 27, 1993, in Las Vegas; Tucson, Arizona; and Rochester, New York, under the title *Blood In, Blood Out*; general release Apr. 30, 1993. Directed by Taylor Hackford. A Hollywood Pictures film. 180 min. Video release in 1994 under the title *Blood In, Blood Out: Bound by Honor*. Stars Damian Chapa (Miklo), Jesse Borrego (Cruz), Benjamin Bratt (Paco), Enrique Castillo (Montana). Filmed on location in the barrio of East Los Angeles and in San Quentin State Prison in Northern California.

Boundin' (film) Animated short from Pixar Animation Studio; released with *The Incredibles* Nov. 5, 2004. A sheep in the American West is an elegant dancer until he is sheared, and then he loses his confidence. But a jackalope comes along and teaches the lamb about bounding instead of dancing, and his joy in life is restored. Directed by Bud Luckey, who also voiced all the characters. 5 min. Nominated for an Academy Award for Animated Short Film.

Bounds, Lillian Maiden name of Walt Disney's wife. They were married at the home of her brother in Lewiston, Idaho, on Jul. 13, 1925. SEE ALSO DISNEY, LILLIAN BOUNDS.

Bountiful Valley Farm District within the former Golden State area in Disney's California Adventure; opened Feb. 8, 2001, presented by Caterpillar. Agricultural exhibits, play areas, and a farmers' market paid tribute to California's heartland. Became part of A Bug's Land Oct. 7, 2002, and closed Sep. 7, 2010, to make way for Cars Land.

Bourguignon, Philippe He began as senior vice president of real estate for Euro Disney and was promoted to president of the French park in 1992. In Oct. 1996, he was given the additional title of exec. vice president for The Walt Disney Company Europe. He left the company in Feb. 1997.

BouTiki Shop in Disney's Polynesian Village Resort at Walt Disney World; opened May 2005. Tropical trinkets, Hawaiian shirts, surf wear, and other merchandise are sold.

Bouza, Barbara She joined Walt Disney Imagineering in Jun. 2020 as president, Business Operations, Design & Delivery. In Mar. 2021, she was named president, Business Management, Design & Development and in Dec. succeeded Bob Weis as president of Walt Disney Imagineering.

Bové, Lorelay After interning at Pixar, she joined Walt Disney Animation Studios in 2007 as a visual development artist and would contribute to the look of several films, including *The Princess and the Frog, Tangled, Wreck-It Ralph, Raya and the Last Dragon*, and *Encanto* (for which she served as associate production designer). She has also illustrated Disney picture books and Little Golden Books.

Bowers, Reveta Franklin Member of the Disney Board of Directors 1993–Mar. 19, 2003.

Bowler Hat Guy Lewis's spiteful nemesis in *Meet the Robinsons*; voiced by Stephen John Anderson.

Box Office Gifts Camera supply shop in the Town Square Theater on Main Street, U.S.A. in the Magic Kingdom at Walt Disney World; opened Apr. 1, 2011.

Boxleitner, Bruce Actor; appeared in *Tron* and *Tron: Legacy* (Alan Bradley/Tron), and later voiced the character in *Tron: Uprising*. Also appeared on The Disney Channel in *Down the Long Hills* (Scott Collins) and on Disney+ in *Prop Culture*.

Boy and the Bronc Buster, The (TV) Two-part show; aired Mar. 18 and 25, 1973. Directed by Bernard McEveety. An orphan boy joins a drifter on the rodeo circuit, where he learns to be a rodeo performer. But the drifter turns out to be wanted for murder, causing all sorts of complications. Stars Earl Holliman, Strother Martin, Vincent Van Patten, Jacqueline Scott, Lisa Gerritsen, Ken Swofford.

Boy Called Nuthin', A (TV) Two-part show; aired Dec. 10 and 17, 1967. Directed by Norman Tokar. A boy doesn't find the life he expects out West when he leaves Chicago to find his uncle. The West has changed—it is no longer "cowboys and Indians." He finds his uncle living in a shack, and in trying to be accepted and help out, the boy gets himself into all sorts of trouble, causing his uncle to refer to him as "Good for Nuthin'," a nickname that sticks. Eventually they see that they need each other. Stars Forrest Tucker, Ronny Howard, John

Carroll, Mary La Roche, Mickey Shaughnessy, Richard Bakalyan, Rafael Campos.

Boy from Deadman's Bayou, The SEE BAYOU BOY.

Boy Meets World (TV) Series aired on ABC Sep. 24, 1993–Sep. 8, 2000. A young junior high school student, Cory Matthews, is an average teenager, struggling with the complications of growing up and the mysteries of life. He tries to get by on his wits but also has the "misfortune" of being his teacher's (Mr. Feeny) next-door neighbor. During the 2nd season, Cory heads to John Adams High School, where Feeny is now principal. In the 6th season, Cory attends Pennbrook University, where Feeny is a college professor. Stars Ben Savage (Cory Matthews), William Daniels (Mr. Feeny), William Russ (Alan Matthews), Betsy Randle (Amy Matthews), Will Friedle (Eric Matthews), Rider Strong (Shawn), Tony Quinn (Jonathan Turner, 2nd season). Alex Désert joined the cast in the 1995–1996 season as teacher Eli Williams. Matthew Lawrence was added in 1997–1998 as Jack, Eric's roommate at college. Eventually, Cory marries his girlfriend, Topanga (Danielle Fishel). John Adams High School was named in reference to William Daniels's lead role in the original Broadway cast of *1776*. SEE ALSO GIRL MEETS WORLD.

Boy Who Flew with Condors, The (TV) Show aired Feb. 19, 1967, about a California teenager who yearns to pilot a glider. His studies of the condors helps him with his gliding lessons. Stars Christopher Jury, Margaret Birstner, Fred W. Harris.

Boy Who Stole the Elephant, The (TV) Two-part show; aired Sep. 20 and 27, 1970. A boy working in a small traveling circus steals an elephant, Queenie, on loan from another circus to save her from being sold and to return her to her rightful owner. Along the way, the elephant gets loose and causes havoc in a local town. Directed by Michael Caffey. Stars Mark Lester, David Wayne, June Havoc, Dabbs Greer, Parley Baer, Whitney Blake, Richard Kiel. Lester had recently received acclaim for starring in the title role in the Academy Award–winning motion picture *Oliver!*

Boy Who Talked to Badgers, The (TV) Two-part show; aired Sep. 14 and 21, 1975. Directed by Gary Nelson. A boy, Ben, seems to prefer animals to people and is even able to communicate with them, a trait that does not please his father. But when a badger helps save Ben's life after he falls in a creek and is carried away, the father comes to an understanding with his son. Stars Christian Juttner, Carl Betz, Salome Jens, Denver Pyle, Robert Donner, Stuart Lee.

Boyajian, Chuck (1917–2004) He was the first manager of custodial operations in Disneyland and contributed to the reputation for high standards in cleanliness that the park would receive. He helped establish custodial functions at Walt Disney World and Tokyo Disneyland until his retirement in 1981. He was named a Disney Legend in 2005.

Boyce, Cameron (1999–2019) Actor; appeared on Disney Channel in the Descendants movies (Carlos) and as Luke in *Jessie* and *Bunk'd*, with guest appearances in *Liv and Maddie*, *Shake It Up*, *Good Luck Charlie*, and the *Radio Disney Music Awards*. He was also one of the voices for Jake in *Jake and the Never Land Pirates*.

Boyd, Barton K. ("Bo") (1942–2011) He began with Disney in 1968 as an assistant supervisor in merchandise for Disneyland, then became a buyer and moved to Walt Disney World to help create the Merchandise Division there. He later returned to the corporate headquarters in California and eventually became chairman of Disney Consumer Products. He retired in 2001 and was named a Disney Legend in 2011.

Boyd, Carleton "Jack" (1916–1998) Effects animator at the Disney Studio 1939–1973, and again in 1981. He drew the Uncle Remus Sunday newspaper comic page 1963–1972, and, as 1 of his projects, helped compile *The Walt Disney Story* film for the park attraction of the same name.

Boyer, Charles (1934–2021) Artist; joined Disneyland in 1960 in the Marketing Art Department. He is noted for having created nearly 50 lithographs of Disneyland subjects, beginning in 1976. One of his more well-known efforts is a "Triple Self-Portrait" of Walt Disney. He retired in 1999 and was named a Disney Legend in 2005.

Boys (film) High school senior John Baker Jr. is nearing graduation at a private school for boys and dreading the future, where he is expected to follow in his father's footsteps. When he has a chance encounter with a sophisticated woman, Patty Vare, who has fallen from her horse, he aids her and surreptitiously shields her from the police and his fellow students in his dorm room. They find a mutual attraction turning to romance but are haunted by the unfolding story of a stolen car and a missing major league baseball pitcher. Directed by Stacy Cochran. A Touchstone film in association with Interscope Communications/PolyGram Filmed Entertainment. Released May 10, 1996. Stars Lukas Haas (John), Winona Ryder (Patty), John C. Reilly (Kellogg Curry), James Le Gros (Fenton Ray), Skeet Ulrich (Bud Valentine). 86 min. Based on the short story "Twenty Minutes" by James Salter. St. John's College in Annapolis, Maryland, doubled for the Sherwood School for Boys in the movie.

Boys, The: The Sherman Brothers' Story (film) Documentary about the careers of the songwriting team forged by brothers Richard M. and Robert B. Sherman. Directed by Jeffrey C. Sherman and Gregory V. Sherman. Produced by Crescendo/Traveling Light for Walt Disney Pictures. Premiered at the San Francisco International Film Festival Apr. 25, 2009, followed by a limited release May 22, 2009, in Los Angeles; San Francisco; New York City; and Palm Springs, California. 102 min. Released on DVD in 2010.

Boys of the Western Sea, The (TV) Serial on the *Mickey Mouse Club* during the 1956–1957 season. Life in a small fishing village in Norway, where the children have to help out. Some of the Mouseketeers joined other actors in dubbing the Norwegian voices into English. Stars Kjeld Bentzen, Anne Grete Hilding, Lars Henning-Jensen, Nette Hoj Hansen. Voices include Richard Beymer, Paul Frees, Billy Bletcher, Herb Vigran, Mary Lee Hobb, Tommy Kirk, Bobby Burgess, Lonnie Burr, Tommy Cole, Kevin Corcoran, David Stollery. 8 episodes.

Bracken, Eddie (1915–2002) Actor; appeared in *Oscar* (Five Spot Charlie), with a TV appearance in *The Golden Girls* (Buzz).

Bradley, Milton, Co. Manufacturer of games that had a license for Disney character games from 1931 to the present (off and on).

Bradley Time Company that took over the national license to manufacture Disney character watches in 1972 and produced hundreds of different varieties until 1987. They were a division of Elgin National Industries, Inc. SEE ALSO WATCHES.

Brady, Wayne Actor; appeared on TV in *The Wayne Brady Show*, as the Magician Lazardo in *Geppetto*, Mr. Wyatt in *Going to the Mat*, Chase in *Baby Daddy*, and Geoffrey in *mixed-ish*. He has provided several voices, including Eugene in *Milo Murphy's Law*, Clover in *Sofia the First*, and Stapler-Fist in *Phineas and Ferb The Movie: Candace Against the Universe*. He also composed songs for *The Weekenders* and performed the show's main title theme. At age 16, he was a Cast Member at Walt Disney World.

Braff, Zach Actor; appeared on TV in *Scrubs* (J. D. Dorian) and *Alex, Inc.* (Alex Schuman), and on Disney+ in *Cheaper by the Dozen* (Paul Baker). He voiced the title character in *Chicken Little* and Finley the winged monkey in *Oz The Great and Powerful*.

Brahe Pedersen, Poul (1910–1978) He oversaw Disney publications in Scandinavia for Gutenberghus 1955–1975 and was presented posthumously with a European Disney Legends Award in 1997.

Brain and the Nervous System Think Science, The (film) Educational film in the Wonders of Life series released Jan. 26, 1990. 11 min. How the brain and nervous system jointly control action and thought.

Brand New Life (TV) Limited series; aired in 1989–1990. After a pilot episode aired on NBC, Disney picked up 4 episodes to air on its anthology series. Stars Barbara Eden, Don Murray, Shawnee Smith, Jennie Garth, Byron Thomes, Alison Sweeney, David Tom. A divorced mother of 3 meets a wealthy widower, also with kids, and they soon marry. The series deals with the family's attempts to get along with each other.

Brand Spanking New Doug (TV) Animated series; premiered on ABC Sep. 7, 1996. Continuing the Nickelodeon series *Doug*, which premiered in 1991, this series shows Doug Funnie growing up. He is approaching his 12th birthday in this exaggerated portrayal of a child muddling through the misadventures of getting older. Voices include Thomas McHugh (Doug), Becca Lish (Theda Funnie, Judy Funnie, Connie Benge), Fred Newman (Skeeter Valentine, Ned Valentine, Mr. Dink), Chris Phillips (Roger Klotz), Alice Playten (Beebe Bluff), Connie Shulman (Patti Mayonnaise), Doug Preis (Chalky Studebaker, Bill Bluff, Phil Funnie, Lamar Bone). The series moved to syn. beginning Aug. 31, 1998, and changed its title to *Disney's Doug*, ending in 1999. A feature film based on the series was *Doug's 1st Movie* (1999). 65 episodes. From Jumbo Pictures, in association with Walt Disney Television.

Brandauer, Klaus Maria Actor; appeared in *White Fang* (Alex).

Brandis, Jonathan (1976–2003) Actor; appeared in *Our Shining Moment* (Michael "Scooter" McGuire), and on TV in *Blossom* (Stevie). He voiced Mozenrath in the *Aladdin* TV series.

Brandy Actress/singer; appeared on TV in the title role in *Rodgers & Hammerstein's Cinderella* and as Naomi in *Queens*, and on Disney Channel in *The Disney Channel Salutes the American Teacher*. She also voiced Latecia on *Jungle Cubs*.

Brandy & Mr. Whiskers (TV) Animated half-hour series on Disney Channel; aired Aug. 21, 2004–Aug. 25, 2006. Brandy, a pampered pooch, and Mr. Whiskers, an offbeat bunny, fall out of an airplane and are stranded in the lush Amazon rain forest. Joining them to become their jungle family are Lola Boa, a boa constrictor; Ed, a river otter; Cheryl & Meryl, sister toucans; Margo, a stick bug; and Gaspar LeGecko, the self-appointed king of the jungle. Voices include Kaley Cuoco (Brandy), Charlie Adler (Mr. Whiskers), Alanna Ubach (Lola Boa), Tom Kenny (Ed), Sherri Shepherd (Cheryl & Meryl), Jennifer Hale (Margo), Andre Sogliuzzo (Gaspar LeGecko). 21 episodes. From Disney Television Animation.

Brass Bazaar, The Shop in Morocco at EPCOT; opened Sep. 7, 1984, offering bowls, pitchers, and glassware.

Brass Boutique, The Shop offering decorative gifts and accessories in brass in New Orleans Square in Disneyland; opened Mar. 26, 1982, replacing La Boutique d'Or. Closed fall 1985 to make room for The Chocolate Collection.

B.R.A.T. Patrol, The (TV) Two-hour movie; aired on Oct. 26, 1986. Directed by Mollie Miller. An unofficial club of children living on a marine base constantly antagonize a group of Junior Marines. They name themselves the B.R.A.T. Patrol, which stands for "Born, Raised, and Trapped." In competing for the base's Youth Service Award, the 2 groups spar, but the outcasts discover a plot to steal military supplies and eventually are able to prove their suspicions to the authorities and win the award. Stars Sean Astin, Tim Thomerson, Jason Presson, Joe Wright, Brian Keith, Stephen Lee, Billy Jacoby. The movie was filmed at the El Toro (California) Marine Corps Air Station.

Braun, Nicholas Actor; appeared in *Sky High* (Zach) and *Prom* (Lloyd Taylor), on TV in *The Secret Life of the American Teenager* (Randy) and as a regular on *10 Things I Hate About You* (Cameron), and on Disney Channel in *Princess Protection Program* (Ed) and *Minutemen* (Zeke).

Brave (film) Animated feature from Pixar Animation Studios. In rugged and mythic Scotland, the impetuous, tangle-haired redhead Merida, though a daughter of royalty, would prefer to make her mark as a great archer. A clash of wills with her mother, who tries to arrange a marriage for her daughter, compels Merida to bolt off into the forest on her faithful horse. Merida is led by the will-o'-the-wisp to an enchanted place, where she makes a reckless choice, unleashing unintended peril on her father's kingdom and her mother's life. She has to struggle with the unpredictable forces of nature, magic, and a dark, ancient curse to set things right. Directed by Mark Andrews and Brenda Chapman. Released Jun. 22, 2012, also in 3-D, after a Jun. 10 screening at the Seattle International Film Festival, a Jun. 18 premiere in Hollywood, and international releases beginning Jun. 19. Voices include Kelly Macdonald (Princess Merida), Julie Walters (Witch), Billy Connolly (King Fergus), Emma Thompson (Queen Elinor), Kevin McKidd (Lord MacGuffin), Craig Ferguson (Lord MacIntosh), Robbie Coltrane (Lord Dingwall). 94 min. Working title was *The Bear and the Bow*. Songs include "Touch the Sky" and "Into the Open Air" (written by Alex Mandel and Mark Andrews) and "Learn Me Right" (written/performed by Birdy and Mumford & Sons). The filmmakers traveled to Scotland to get the details just right, returning with hundreds of drawings and reference photos; the film's Standing Stones were inspired by the Callanish Stones found in Outer Hebrides, Scotland. Won the 2012 Academy Award for Best Animated Feature.

Brave Engineer, The (film) Special cartoon released Mar. 3, 1950. Directed by Jack Kinney. Casey Jones is determined to get his train to the station on time, in spite of train robbers, a flood, and a head-on collision with another train. Although late, Casey finally arrives in the wrecked locomotive, with his watch reading, ON TIME . . . ALMOST.

Brave Little Tailor (film) Mickey Mouse cartoon released Sep. 23, 1938. Directed by Bill Roberts. In a medieval setting, Mickey, a tailor, gleefully exclaims that he's killed "seven with one blow." He's referring to flies that had been bothering him, but the townsfolk, who had been talking about giants, assume Mickey is a gallant giant-killer and take him to the king. The king orders Mickey to destroy a nearby giant, with the prize being a treasure of golden pazoozas and the hand of the fair Princess Minnie. Using his brain to outwit the giant's brawn, Mickey defeats the hulking figure and becomes a hero. This was one of the most elaborate, and expensive, Mickey Mouse cartoons ever made. And its extremely high cost forced Walt to take a closer look at budgets for later cartoons. Nominated for an Academy Award.

Brave Little Tailor Shoppe Fantasyland shop in Tokyo Disneyland; opened in 2018, replacing Baby Mine. Baby and toddler goods are sold. SEE ALSO SIR MICKEY'S (WALT DISNEY WORLD).

Brave Little Toaster, The (film) Not a Disney animated film, but it aired on The Disney Channel in 1988, on the Disney anthology series in 1991, and was released on Disney's home video label. A fantasy about 5 aging appliances who come to life and go in search of their missing master, from the novella by Thomas M. Disch. Directed by Jerry Rees. There were 2, again non-Disney, direct-to-video sequels: *The Brave Little Toaster to the Rescue* and *The Brave Little Toaster Goes to Mars*.

Brave Little Toaster Goes to Mars, The (film) Not made by Disney, but released by Walt Disney Home Video under the "Disney Presents" label May 19, 1998. The group of appliances from the original film are joined by others to take off on a trip to Mars to save the "Master's" new baby. Voices include Deanna Oliver (Toaster), Tim Stack (Lampy), Roger Kabler (Radio), Thurl Ravenscroft (Kirby), Eric Lloyd (Blanky), Farrah Fawcett (Faucet), Carol Channing (Fanny). The video for *The Brave Little Toaster to the Rescue* in 1999 did not include the "Disney Presents" label.

Brave New Girl (TV) An ABC Family Original Movie; debuted Apr. 25, 2004. Directed by Bobby

Roth. Holly has everything it takes to be a star—the voice, the dream, and the dedication—but she lacks the means to break away from her humble Texas upbringing. Then she gets the chance to attend a prestigious art and music school on the East Coast and her future suddenly looks bright, though she must compete for the star spot with the snobby Angela. Luckily Holly has the support of her mother and her roommate Ditz, who prove that being a star has nothing to do with fame and everything to do with faith, family, and friends. Stars Lindsey Haun (Holly), Virginia Madsen (Wanda), Jackie Rosenbaum (Ditz), Barbara Mamabolo (Angela). Based on the novel *A Mother's Gift* by Britney and Lynne Spears.

Braverman, Alan He joined The Walt Disney Company in 2003 as exec. vice president and general counsel, overseeing a team of attorneys responsible for the company's legal affairs, including public policy and government relations. Braverman had originally joined ABC in 1993 as a vice president, before being promoted to senior vice president and general counsel in 1996 and exec. vice president in 2000. He retired in Dec. 2021.

Braverman, Barry Imagineer; he began at WED Enterprises in 1977 and served as producer for several attractions, including the Image Works (Journey Into Imagination) and Wonders of Life, for a time heading the EPCOT design effort. Then he turned his attention to the West Coast, where he headed the Disneyland Resort Development team and led the design work on Disney California Adventure as executive producer. He left the company in 2006.

Brayton's Laguna Pottery This manufacturer of figurines made a number of Disney items 1938–1940 that are still popular with collectors. Some of their nicest items were characters from *Pinocchio* and *Ferdinand the Bull.*

Brazzle Dazzle Day Song from *Pete's Dragon*; written by Al Kasha and Joel Hirschhorn.

Breakfast of Champions (film) Dwayne Hoover, the leader of a vast financial empire which controls Midland City, is on the verge of a midlife crisis. As his identity as the most respected man in the city begins to unravel in his own mind, he meets an impoverished writer, Kilgore Trout, in town for a fine arts festival. Their worlds collide, and Midland City will never be the same. Directed by Alan Rudolph. Limited release Sep. 17, 1999, in New York City, Los Angeles, and Toronto. Stars Bruce Willis (Dwayne Hoover), Albert Finney (Kilgore Trout), Nick Nolte (Harry Le Sabre), Barbara Hershey (Celia Hoover), Glenne Headley (Francine Pefko), Omar Epps (Wayne Hoobler). 110 min. Based on the classic novel by Kurt Vonnegut Jr. The filmmakers picked Twin Falls, Idaho, as the ideal location to be Midland City.

Breakin' Through (film) Break-dancers and polished Broadway performers come together for a Broadway-bound musical, and the 2 groups have trouble adjusting to each other. An original video release in Sep. 1985. Directed by Peter Medak. 73 min. Stars Ben Vereen, Donna McKechnie, Reid Shelton. This film had originally been planned for a Disney Channel release, but the company opted for a video release instead.

Brennan, Eileen (1932–2013) Actress; appeared in *Stella* (Mrs. Wilkerson); on TV in *Freaky Friday* (Principal Handel, 1995), *Blossom* (Agnes), *Home Improvement* (Wanda), *Toothless* (board member), and *Kraft Salutes Walt Disney World's 10th Anniversary*; and on Disney Channel in *Lizzie McGuire* (Marge). She also voiced Lilith DuPrave in *Bonkers.*

Brennan, Walter (1894–1974) Actor; appeared in *Those Calloways* (Alf Simes), *The Gnome-Mobile* (D. J. Mulrooney, Knobby), and *The One and Only, Genuine, Original Family Band* (Grandpa Bower).

Brenner, Eve Actress; provided the voice of Queen Moustoria in *The Great Mouse Detective* and appeared on TV in *According to Jim* (Meier), *Grey's Anatomy* (Enid), and *The Rookie* (Ruth).

Brer Bar Refreshment area, serving soft drinks and snacks, in Critter Country at Disneyland; renamed from Mile Long Bar Jul. 17, 1989. Closed in 2002 and superseded by Pooh's Hunny Spot.

Brer Bear Burly character in *Song of the South*, remembered for his threat, "I'm gonna knock his head clean off." Voiced by Nicodemus Stewart.

Brer Fox Sly character always trying to get the best of Brer Rabbit in *Song of the South*; voiced by James Baskett (who also played Uncle Remus).

Brer Rabbit Happy-go-lucky character whose

cockiness seems to get him in and out of trouble in *Song of the South*; voiced by Johnny Lee.

Breslin, Spencer Actor; appeared in *Disney's The Kid* (Rusty Duritz), *The Santa Clause 2* and *The Santa Clause 3: The Escape Clause* (Curtis), *Raising Helen* (Henry Davis), *The Princess Diaries 2: Royal Engagement* (Prince Jacques), and *The Shaggy Dog* (Josh Douglas). Also on Disney Channel in *The Ultimate Christmas Present* (Joey Thompson) and *You Wish* (Stevie Lansing/Terrance Russell McCormack). He voiced Crandall in *Teamo Supremo* and Cubby in *Return to Never Land*.

Brian's Song (TV) Movie on *The Wonderful World of Disney*; first aired Dec. 2, 2001. A remake of the moving 1971 TV film about the life and death of Chicago Bears fullback Brian Piccolo and his friendship with Black player Gale Sayers. Directed by John Gray. Stars Sean Maher (Brian Piccolo), Mekhi Phifer (Gale Sayers), Ben Gazzara (George Halas), Paula Cale (Joy Piccolo), Elise Neal (Linda Sayers). Based on the book *I am Third*, by Gale Sayers and Al Silverman. From Storyline Entertainment, distributed by Columbia TriStar Television.

Briar Patch, The Shop in Critter Country in Disneyland; opened Dec. 1988, succeeding the Indian Trading Post. Inside, huge carrots appear to grow through the grass roof. In 2004, it became a hat shop. In 1986, a Brier Patch [sic] shop opened in Frontierland in the Magic Kingdom at Walt Disney World, offering wooden crafts and baskets; it closed after a more elaborate Briar Patch store opened at the exit of Splash Mountain Dec. 16, 1991. The Walt Disney World shop closed in 2020, and the Disneyland shop is set to follow.

Briar Rose Cottage Fantasyland shop in Disneyland; open May 29, 1987–Jul. 15, 1991, offering Disney figurines and collectible merchandise. Preceded by Mickey's Christmas Chalet and succeeded by Disney Villains.

Bride of Boogedy (TV) Two-hour movie; aired Apr. 12, 1987. Directed by Oz Scott. A sequel to *Mr. Boogedy*, it continues the story of the Davis family and the evil spirit that visits it. The ghost returns and puts the father under his spell. Stars Richard Masur, Mimi Kennedy, Tammy Lauren, David Faustino, Joshua Rudoy.

Bridge of Spies (film) James Donovan, a Brooklyn lawyer, finds himself thrust into the center of the Cold War when the CIA sends him on a near-impossible task to negotiate the release of a captured American U-2 pilot. Directed by Steven Spielberg. A DreamWorks film, released in the U.S. by Touchstone Oct. 16, 2015. Stars Tom Hanks (James Donovan), Mark Rylance (Rudolf Abel), Scott Shepherd (Hoffman), Amy Ryan (Mary), Sebastian Koch (Vogel), Alan Alda (Thomas Watters). 141 min. Filmed in wide-screen format. Received 6 Academy Award nominations, including for Best Picture and Original Screenplay, winning the Oscar for Best Supporting Actor (Mark Rylance).

Bridge to Terabithia (film) Jess Aarons is a young outsider on a quest to become the fastest kid in his school. But when the new girl in town, Leslie Burke, leaves Jess and everyone else in her dust, Jess's frustration with her ultimately leads to their becoming friends. At first it seems Jess and Leslie couldn't be more different—she's rich, he's poor; she's from the city, he's from the country—but when Leslie begins to open up the world of imagination to Jess, they find they have something amazing to share: the kingdom of Terabithia, a realm of giants, ogres, and other enchanted beings that can only be accessed by boldly swinging across a stream in the woods on a strand of rope. Here, Leslie and Jess rule as king and queen among the fantastical creatures they create, and not even the forces of evil can break their bond. Now, no matter what happens in the real world, in Terabithia Leslie gives Jess a magical place that will always be filled with amazing stories and dreams. Released Feb. 16, 2007. Directed by Gabor Csupo. From Walt Disney Pictures and Walden Media. Stars Joshua Ryan Hutcherson (Jess Aarons), AnnaSophia Robb (Leslie Burke), Zooey Deschanel (Miss Edmonds), Robert Patrick (Jack Aarons). 96 min. Based on the 1978 Newbery Medal–winning book by Katherine Paterson. The film was shot on location in the forests of New Zealand; visual effects were created by Weta Digital Ltd. of Wellington, New Zealand.

Bridges, Beau Actor; appeared in *Night Crossing* (Günter Wetzel) and *RocketMan* (Bud Nesbitt); on TV in *Atta Girl, Kelly* (Matt Howell), *A Fighting Choice* (Thad Taylor), *Desperate Housewives* (Eli), *Brothers & Sisters* (Nick Brody), *Code Black* (Pete Delaney), and *black-ish* (Paul); and on The Disney Channel in *Nightjohn* (Clel Waller). He voiced Sheriff Scaley Briggs in *Penn Zero: Part-Time Hero*. He also directed and appeared on TV in *The Thanksgiving Promise* (Hank), which starred his father, Lloyd, and son Jordan, along with his mother, Dorothy, and brother, Jeff.

Bridges, Jeff Actor; appeared in *Tron* and *Tron: Legacy* (Kevin Flynn/Clu) and *White Squall* (Sheldon), and on TV in *The Thanksgiving Promise* (uncredited).

Bridges, Lloyd (1913–1998) Actor; appeared in *Honey, I Blew Up the Kid* (Clifford Sterling) and *Jane Austen's Mafia!* (Vincenzo Cortini), and on TV in *The Thanksgiving Promise* and *In the Nick of Time*.

Bright, Randy (1938–1990) Starting as a ride operator at Disneyland in 1959, he moved in 1965 to the Disney University, working at both Disneyland and later Walt Disney World. In 1976, he moved to Walt Disney Imagineering in the field of concepts and show development, executive producing film projects for EPCOT Center and Tokyo Disneyland. He became vice president of concept development in 1983, responsible for all major shows and attractions for the Disney parks, and was named executive producer of the Disneyland and Walt Disney World theme parks in 1987. That year, he also wrote the first book on Disneyland history— *Disneyland: Inside Story*. He was named a Disney Legend in 2005.

Bright Lights (film) Oswald the Lucky Rabbit cartoon; released Mar. 19, 1928. Financially embarrassed, Oswald makes several attempts to sneak into a folly show. He is finally discovered but manages to disappear, leaving a wrecked show tent behind.

Brimley, Wilford (1934–2020) Actor; appeared in *Country* (Otis).

Brimstone, the Amish Horse (TV) Show aired Oct. 27, 1968. Directed by Larry Lansburgh. An Amish minister buys a crippled championship steeplechase horse and nurses him back to health. But the horse has not lost his yearning for the racetrack, a trait not appreciated in the strict Amish world. Stars Pamela Toll, Wallace Rooney, Phil Clark. Filmed on location in the Amish Country of Pennsylvania.

Bringing Down the House (film) Peter Sanderson still loves his ex-wife and cannot understand what he did wrong to make her leave him. He is doing his best to move on, becoming smitten with a brainy,

bombshell barrister he's been chatting with online. However, when she comes to the house for their first meeting, he quickly discovers she isn't refined, isn't Ivy League, and isn't even a lawyer. Instead, it's Charlene, a prison escapee, who proclaims her innocence and wants Peter to help clear her name. Charlene proceeds to turn Peter's perfectly ordered life upside down, jeopardizing his attempts to get back with his ex-wife and woo a billion-dollar client. A Touchstone film. Directed by Adam Shankman. Released Mar. 7, 2003. Stars Steve Martin (Peter Sanderson), Queen Latifah (Charlene Morton), Eugene Levy (Howie Rottman), Joan Plowright (Mrs. Arness), Jean Smart (Kate), Kimberly J. Brown (Sarah Sanderson), Angus T. Jones (Georgey Sanderson), Missi Pyle (Ashley), Michael Rosenbaum (Todd Gendler), Betty White (Mrs. Kline). 105 min. Filmed in Super 35-Scope in the Los Angeles area, with Peter's house located in Pasadena.

Bringing Out the Dead (film) A joint production from Touchstone and Paramount, this motion picture details the demanding job of a paramedic, showing how he comes into contact on a daily basis with the dead and dying. Frank Pierce, deeply troubled and becoming burned out with his job, is followed through a weekend of all-night duty. Directed by Martin Scorsese. Released Oct. 22, 1999. Stars Nicolas Cage (Frank Pierce), Patricia Arquette (Mary Burke), John Goodman (Larry), Ving Rhames (Marcus), Tom Sizemore (Tom Wolfe). 121 min. Disney handled the international distribution, with Paramount coordinating the domestic. Based on the novel by Joe Connelly.

Brink! (TV) A Disney Channel Original Movie; premiered Aug. 29, 1998. Andy Brinker ("Brink") is king of the "soul skaters" at the beach. He and his crew skate for the love of their sport, while their rivals, the X-Bladz, are sponsored and skate for the money. When Brink discovers he needs extra money to help with his family, he faces a major decision and decides to desert his friends for Team X-Bladz. When he finds out that the captain of his new team is resorting to sabotage, he rejoins his original team in a tournament against the X-Bladz. Directed by Greg Beeman. Stars Erik von Detten (Andy), Patrick Levis (Peter), Asher Gold (Jordan), Christina Vidal (Gabriella), Sam Horrigan (Val).

Bristle Face (TV) Two-part show; aired Jan. 26 and Feb. 2, 1964. Directed by Bob Sweeney. In the rolling, wooded hills of Tennessee in the 1920s, a 14-year-old orphan, Jace, comes to town with his hound dog, whom he tries to teach to hunt. Bristle Face is unskilled, but he shows remarkable ability in tracking down foxes. Jace stays with a kindly shopkeeper who defends the boy and Bristle Face against the sheriff whom they have angered. Stars Brian Keith, Philip Alford (Jace Landers), Jeff Donnell, Wallace Ford, Parley Baer, Slim Pickens, George Lindsey. Philip Alford had appeared as Jem Finch in the Academy Award–winning motion picture *To Kill a Mockingbird*, a film that Walt Disney was known to admire.

Broadway at the Top Show in the Top of the World at the Contemporary Resort at Walt Disney World; ran Jun. 29, 1981–Sep. 1993. Many guests found the medley of show tunes from some of the greatest Broadway shows of all time—sung by a quartet of talented performers—to be one of the highlights of their stay at Walt Disney World. The bar featured an absolutely marvelous view over the Seven Seas Lagoon toward the Magic Kingdom.

Broadway Hits at Royal Albert Hall, Disney's (TV) Filmed concert celebrating 2 decades of stage musicals from Disney Theatrical Productions; released digitally May 15, 2017, on BroadwayHD after a Dec. 21, 2016, TV premiere in the U.K. Hosted by John Barrowman. Performers include Ashley Brown, Merle Dandridge, Alton Fitzgerald White, Trevor Dion Nicholas, Scarlett Strallen, Josh Strickland, and Alan Menken, with the BBC Concert Orchestra. Directed by Jay Hatcher. 114 min. A collaboration between Disney Parks Live Entertainment and Disney Theatrical Productions, it earned two 2018 Daytime Emmy Awards (Outstanding Sound Mixing and Outstanding Directing—Special Class). The live performance was held Oct. 23, 2016, at Royal Albert Hall in London.

Broadway Music Theatre Theater in American Waterfront at Tokyo DisneySea; opened Sep. 4, 2001, with *Encore!*, a 30-min. theatrical journey that presented the best in song and dance from Broadway's most popular shows. *Encore!* ended Jul. 4, 2006, and was replaced Jul. 14 by *Big Band Beat*, a stylish revue with musicians and tap dancers.

Broadway Theater Formerly the Colony, this New York City theater hosted the premiere of

Fantasia on Nov. 13, 1940, 12 years after *Steamboat Willie* had opened there on Nov. 18, 1928. A plaque was installed in the lobby at the time of Mickey Mouse's 50th anniversary in 1978. The stage musical *Sister Act* opened there Apr. 20, 2011, after a Mar. 24 preview.

Broccoli & Co. Shop in The Land at EPCOT Center; open Dec. 1982–Oct. 25, 1993. A selection of merchandise was tied in with the Audio-Animatronics foodstuff characters performing in the nearby Kitchen Kabaret.

Broderick, James (1927–1982) Actor; appeared on TV in *Atta Girl, Kelly* (Cal Richards).

Broderick, Matthew Actor; voiced the adult Simba in *The Lion King*, portrayed the title character in *Inspector Gadget*, starred in *The Last Shot* (Steven Schats), and appeared on TV as Professor Harold Hill in *The Music Man*.

Broggie, Roger E. (1908–1991) He began at the Disney Studio in 1939 in the Studio Camera Service Department and later established the Studio Machine Shop. Being interested in trains, he helped Walt Disney with his train hobby and engineered the layout for the scale-model train in Walt's Holmby Hills backyard. He later headed MAPO (Manufacturing and Production Organization) and retired in 1975. One of the locomotives on the Walt Disney World Railroad is named after him. He was named a Disney Legend in 1990.

Broken Toys (film) Silly Symphony cartoon released Dec. 14, 1935. Directed by Ben Sharpsteen. Discarded toys at the city dump decide to repair themselves, including a sailor doll who restores the sight of a girl doll. The toys then march off to their new home, the local orphanage. Features caricatures of Hollywood stars as the toys.

Brom Bones Ichabod Crane's rival in *The Adventures of Ichabod and Mr. Toad*.

Brooks, Mel Actor; appeared in *Mickey's Audition* (movie director), and on TV in *Mickey's 50*. He created *The Nutt House*, and voiced Grandpa Mel in *Special Agent Oso* and Melephant Brooks in *Toy Story 4*.

Brooks, Mylin Actress; appeared on the *Mickey Mouse Club* on The Disney Channel, beginning in 1990.

Brophy, Ed (1895–1960) Actor; provided the voice of Timothy Mouse in *Dumbo*.

Brother Against Brother (TV) Show, the 2nd episode of *The Swamp Fox*.

Brother Bear (film) Set in the Pacific Northwest after the last Ice Age, this animated film tells the tale of 3 Native American brothers: Sitka, the eldest; Denahi; and Kenai, the youngest. After Sitka is accidentally killed by a bear, Kenai sets out on a quest of vengeance, only to be turned into a bear himself by the Great Spirits. As he discovers the world through the eyes of another, Kenai is befriended by a rambunctious bear cub named Koda and has a hilarious encounter with a pair of misguided moose, Tuke and Rutt. Kenai discovers that Denahi is attempting to avenge his death by trying to kill the bear that Kenai has become, believing that it is Kenai's killer. Before all is resolved, Kenai must decide whether he wants to change back into his human form or continue living as a bear. Released Nov. 1, 2003, after an Oct. 24 limited release in Los Angeles and New York City. Directed by Aaron Blaise and Robert Walker. Voices include Joaquin Phoenix (Kenai), Jeremy Suarez (Koda), Jason Raize (Denahi), Rick Moranis (Rutt), Dave Thomas (Tuke), D. B. Sweeney (Sitka), Michael Clarke Duncan (Tug), Joan Copeland (Tanana), Estelle Harris (Old Lady Bear), Bumper Robinson (Chipmunks). 85 min. Jason Raize had originated the role of Simba in the Broadway production of *The Lion King*. Includes 6 songs by Phil Collins, including "Look Through My Eyes," "Great Spirits," "On My Way," and "Welcome." Created at the Disney Feature Animation Studio in Florida. The last ²/₃ of the film, after Kenai is changed into a bear, are filmed in Cinema-Scope. The working title was *Bears*. It received an Academy Award nomination for Best Animated Feature.

Brother Bear 2 (film) Direct-to-DVD release Aug. 29, 2006, from DisneyToon Studios. Kenai emerges from his first hibernation eager to take his little brother, Koda, to Crowberry Ridge for the best spring berries. Their buddies Rutt and Tuke have come down with a severe case of spring fever, courting a pair of female moose with hilarious results. But Kenai and Koda are intent on following their plan until Kenai's childhood pal, Nita, shows up with a very human problem only Kenai can solve. It seems a simple carved amulet Kenai gave Nita long ago had a greater significance than either

of them realized. Now Nita cannot marry until she and Kenai burn the amulet together at Hokani Falls, their old stomping grounds. They set off on an arduous journey over icy mountains, raging rivers, and unforeseen obstacles. It is an adventure that renews their friendship, redefines who they are, and ultimately reveals that the Great Spirits have a surprising plan of their own. Directed by Benjamin Gluck. Stars Patrick Dempsey (Kenai), Jeremy Suarez (Koda), Rick Moranis (Rutt), Dave Thomas (Tuke), Mandy Moore (Nita), Wanda Sykes (Innoko), Andrea Martin (Anda), Catherine O'Hara (Kata), Kathy Najimy (Aunt Taggig), Wendie Malick (Aunt Sisinig), Michael Clarke Duncan (Tug). 73 min. The film features 3 original songs by Melissa Etheridge. Much of the work on the film was done by DisneyToon Studios Australia.

Brotherly Love (TV) Series on NBC debuting with a sneak preview Sep. 16, 1995, before starting its regular Sunday nighttime slot Sep. 24. The last show on NBC aired Apr. 1, 1996. The show began a new season on The WB Network Sep. 15, 1996. Life changes for the Roman family when Joe Roman trades his independent life on the road for the "stability" of a family he's never known. Coming to town to claim his share of a garage being run by his young, widowed stepmother, Joe becomes a father figure for his two half brothers. Stars real-life brothers Joey Lawrence (Joe Roman), Matthew Lawrence (Matt Roman), and Andrew Lawrence (Andy Roman), plus Michael McShane (Lloyd), Liz Vassey (Lou), Melinda Culea (Claire Roman).

Brothers & Sisters (TV) A 1-hour drama series on ABC; aired Sep. 24, 2006–May 8, 2011. As told through the insightful eyes of the family's most outspoken and public member, a group of siblings meet for a birthday celebration, only to find that underneath the idyllic family facade lie many secrets that threaten to tear the family apart or bring them closer together. Stars Calista Flockhart (Kitty Walker), Sally Field (Nora Walker), Ron Rifkin (Saul Holden), Balthazar Getty (Thomas Walker), Rachel Griffiths (Sarah Whedon), Dave Annable (Justin Walker), Matthew Rhys (Kevin Walker), Patricia Wettig (Holly Harper), John Pyper-Ferguson (Joe Whedon), Sarah Jane Morris (Julia Walker). From Touchstone Television.

Broughton, Bob (1917–2009) At the Disney Studio 1937–1982, he was a camera operator and camera-effects artist on both animated and live-action films, beginning with *Snow White and the Seven Dwarfs* and continuing to *The Black Hole*. He was named a Disney Legend in 2001.

Broughton, Bruce Composer; he has provided scores for Disney features, shorts, and direct-to-video films, including *The Rescuers Down Under*; *Trail Mix-Up*; *Roller Coaster Rabbit*; *Off His Rockers*; *Holy Matrimony*; *Tombstone*; *Honey, I Blew Up the Kid*; *Homeward Bound II: Lost in San Francisco*; *The Three Musketeers* (2004); and *Bambi II*. He was conductor and music supervisor for "Rhapsody in Blue" in *Fantasia/2000*. For TV, he wrote scores for *The Thanksgiving Promise* and *Dinosaurs*, and won Emmys for his work on *Eloise at the Plaza* and *Eloise at Christmastime*. Broughton has composed for films and attractions at the Disney parks, including *Mickey's Audition*; *The Making of Me*; *From Time to Time*; The Timekeeper; *Honey, I Shrunk the Audience*; Ellen's Energy Adventure; *It's Tough to Be a Bug!*; *Golden Dreams*; *Seasons of the Vine*; *One Man's Dream: 100 Years of Magic*; *CinéMagique*; *O Canada!*; Spaceship Earth; and Soarin' Around the World.

Brown, Ashley Actress; made her Broadway debut as Belle in *Beauty and the Beast* in 2005 and the following year originated the title role in *Mary Poppins* on Broadway. She previously performed in the national tour of *On the Record*. She appeared on TV in *Disney's Broadway Hits at Royal Albert Hall*, *Richard M. Sherman: Songs of a Lifetime*, and the *Walt Disney World Christmas Day Parade*. In 2015, she participated in the Disneyland Resort Diamond Celebration, recording "A Kiss Goodnight" for the *Disneyland Forever* fireworks show.

Brown, Brandy Actress; appeared on the *Mickey Mouse Club* on The Disney Channel 1989–1990.

Brown, Bryan Actor; appeared in *Cocktail* (Doug Coughlin) and *Blame It on the Bellboy* (Charlton Black).

Brown, Issac Ryan Actor; appeared on TV in *Devious Maids* (Deion), *How to Get Away with Murder* (Christophe), and *black-ish* (Young Dre), with a guest appearance in *The Rookie*, and on Disney Channel in *Raven's Home* (Booker Baxter), *Kim Possible* (Wade, 2019), *Disney's Magic Bake-Off* (host), *Bunk'd*, *Disney QUIZney*, and the *Radio Disney Music Awards*. He voiced Chai in *Whisker Haven Tales with the Palace Pets*, Bingo

in *Puppy Dog Pals*, Gus in *The Owl House*, and Haruna in *Miles from Tomorrowland*.

Brown, Yvette Nicole Actress; appeared in *Avengers: Endgame* (S.H.I.E.L.D. agent), on Disney+ in *Lady and the Tramp* (Aunt Sarah, 2019), *Disenchanted* (Rosaleen), *Big Shot* (Sherilyn Thomas), *Muppets Haunted Mansion* (Driver), *The Big Fib*, and *Earth to Ned*, and on TV in *That's So Raven* (Monica), *Shake It Up* (Madame Tiffany), *Melissa & Joey* (Calista), and *The Mayor* (Dina Rose). She has provided several voices for TV, including Ursula in *Once Upon a Time*, Luna in *Elena of Avalor*, Boat Maria in *Penn Zero: Part-Time Hero*, Daisy in *Puppy Dog Pals*, Chantel D'Avion in *The Rocketeer*, Captain Tully in *The Chicken Squad*, Mama Rabbit in *Alice's Wonderland Bakery*, and Chief Faye Fireson in *Firebuds*.

Brown Derby SEE HOLLYWOOD BROWN DERBY.

Browne, Roscoe Lee (1925–2007) Actor; he voiced Francis in *Oliver & Company*, Mr. Arrow in *Treasure Planet*, and Clarence in *The Proud Family*. He also appeared in *The World's Greatest Athlete* (Gazenga).

Bruce Great white shark leader of the Fish-Eaters Anonymous group in *Finding Nemo*; voiced by Barry Humphries.

Bruckheimer, Jerry Prolific producer of films released under the Touchstone and Disney banners. Titles have included *Con Air*, *Enemy of the State*, *Armageddon*, *Gone in 60 Seconds*, *Remember the Titans*, *Coyote Ugly*, *Pearl Harbor*, *Bad Company*, the Pirates of the Caribbean films, *Glory Road*, *Veronica Guerin*, *King Arthur*, the National Treasure films, *Confessions of a Shopaholic*, *G-Force*, *Prince of Persia: The Sands of Time*, *The Sorcerer's Apprentice*, and *The Lone Ranger*. Earlier, with Don Simpson, he produced *The Ref*, *Crimson Tide*, and *The Rock*. Bruckheimer's first-look production deal with Disney, which began in 1991, ended in 2014. He exec. produced *The Amazing Race* for CBS and *National Treasure: Edge of History* for Disney+.

Bruni Curious salamander and fire spirit in *Frozen 2*.

Brunner, Bob (1938–2009) Composer; hired by Disney in 1963, where for over 17 years he composed music for numerous TV shows and over a dozen features, including *That Darn Cat!*; *Monkeys, Go Home!*; *Blackbeard's Ghost*; *Never a Dull Moment*; *The Barefoot Executive*; and *The Castaway Cowboy*. As a kid he had been a Talent Roundup guest on the 1950s *Mickey Mouse Club*.

Bruno The lazy dog in Cinderella's household; voiced by Jim Macdonald.

Bruns, George (1914–1983) Composer/conductor; hired by Disney in 1953 to work on the music for *Sleeping Beauty*. He wrote "The Ballad of Davy Crockett," and besides *Sleeping Beauty*, received Academy Award nominations also for *Babes in Toyland* and *The Sword in the Stone*. He also wrote themes for such films as *The Love Bug*, *Zorro*, *The Absent-Minded Professor*, and *The Jungle Book*. Also composed music for Disney park attractions, including Pirates of the Caribbean and Country Bear Jamboree. He retired in 1975 and was named a Disney Legend posthumously in 2001.

Brutally Normal (TV) Half-hour comedy series on The WB Network; aired Jan. 24–Feb. 14, 2000. An introspective look at 4 teenage friends coming of age under the overwhelming pressures of high school. Stars Mike Damus (Robert "Pooh" Cutler), Lea Moreno (Anna Pricova), Eddie Kaye Thomas (Russell Wise), Tangie Ambrose (Dru Pope), Joanna Pacula (Gogi Pricova).

Bryan, Zachery Ty Actor; appeared in *First Kid* (Rob), and on TV in *Home Improvement* (Brad) and *Principal Takes a Holiday* (John Scaduto).

Bryson, John E. Became a member of the Disney Board of Directors Sep. 19, 2000. He was confirmed as U.S. secretary of commerce Oct. 20, 2011, and he subsequently resigned from the Disney board on Oct. 31.

Bubble Bee (film) Pluto cartoon released Jun. 24, 1949. Directed by Charles Nichols. After Pluto pounces on a "ball," which turns out to be a bubble gum machine, Pluto and a bee fight over the gumballs. After the bee stores the gumballs in its hive, Pluto destroys it, then uses the gum bubbles to keep the bee at bay until the bee wins by using the gum against Pluto.

Bubble Boy (film) Jimmy Livingston is a boy born without immunities and raised in a manufactured world provided by his well-intentioned, but mis-guided, mother. Jimmy is happy enough and has all the same experiences as other boys and girls growing up, except he lives in a bubble. When Jimmy realizes that he's in love with Chloe, the girl next door, he has no choice but to build a mobile "bubble suit" and set off across the country to stop Chloe's wedding. Directed by Blair Hayes. A Touchstone film. Released Aug. 24, 2001. Stars Jake Gyllenhaal (Jimmy Livingston), Swoosie Kurtz (Mrs. Livingston), Marley Shelton (Chloe), Danny Trejo (Slim), John Carroll Lynch (Mr. Livingston), Stephen Spinella (Chicken Man). 84 min. Filmed in CinemaScope.

Buchanan, Stuart (1893–1973) Disney animation staff member; he voiced the Huntsman in *Snow White and the Seven Dwarfs*.

Bücherwurm, Der SEE DER BÜCHERWURM.

Buck, Chris He joined the Disney Studio as an animator in 1978 and would contribute to *The Fox and the Hound*, *Who Framed Roger Rabbit*, *The Little Mermaid*, and *The Rescuers Down Under*. He served as a supervising animator on *Pocahontas* (Percy, Grandmother Willow, Wiggins) and *Home on the Range* (Maggie), and co-directed *Tarzan*, *Frozen* (accepting the Academy Award for Best Animated Feature), *Frozen 2*, and *Wish*.

Buck Horse character in *Home on the Range*; voiced by Cuba Gooding Jr.

Buckhoff, Michael He joined the staff of the Walt Disney Archives Photo Library in 2000, later serving as manager. He has maintained the company's expansive photography collection, written for company publications, and made appearances in company documentaries and at fan events.

Buddies (TV) Series on ABC; aired Mar. 5–Mar. 27, 1996, with 4 episodes. An interracial friendship, with its accompanying hijinks, between 2 young male filmmakers in Chicago. Stars Dave Chappelle (Dave Carlisle), Christopher Gartin (John Bailey), Paula Cale (Lorraine Bailey), Tanya Wright (Phyllis Brooks), Richard Roundtree (Henry Carlisle), Judith Ivey (Maureen). From Wind Dancer Productions and Touchstone Television.

Buena Vista Club Golf club in Lake Buena Vista, Nov. 22, 1974–Mar. 21, 1994. Also known as Lake Buena Vista Club. The restaurant in its country-club atmosphere featured the chef's specialty, a fantastic onion soup, with thick melted cheese overflowing the edges of the bowl. Renamed Disney Village Clubhouse in Sep. 1988. SEE ALSO LAKE BUENA VISTA GOLF COURSE AND POMPANO GRILL.

Buena Vista Concerts SEE DISNEY CONCERTS.

Buena Vista Distribution Company Founded by Disney in 1953 to distribute its films; its first release was *The Living Desert*. The headquarters were located in New York City until the 1970s, when they were moved to California. Irving Ludwig headed Buena Vista until his retirement, when Dick Cook took over. Later known as Buena Vista Pictures Distribution and Walt Disney Studios Motion Pictures. SEE ALSO LIVING DESERT, THE.

Buena Vista Games New parent in 2003 for Disney Interactive, the interactive games division of Disney Consumer Products. It created, marketed, and distributed a broad portfolio of PC and multi-platform video games worldwide, also licensing Disney properties to other game publishers. Its name changed to Disney Interactive Studios Feb. 8, 2007.

Buena Vista Interiors Decorating firm for the Lake Buena Vista community in Walt Disney World; established in the former Walt Disney World Preview Center building by Disney Studio head decorator Emile Kuri. The firm later moved to the Lake Buena Vista Shopping Village as a home furnishing gallery; opened Nov. 19, 1977, replacing Anniversary Room, and closed in 1980, superseded by the Christmas Chalet.

Buena Vista International Company incorporated in 1961 to handle the international distribution of Disney films. Occasionally, it will handle the international distribution of non-Disney films, such as *Die Hard with a Vengeance*, *Face/Off*, *Starship Troopers*, *Air Force One*, and *Bruce Almighty*. Its name changed to Walt Disney Studios Motion Pictures International in Jul. 2007.

Buena Vista Palace Hotel at Lake Buena Vista at Walt Disney World; opened Mar. 3, 1983. It became the Wyndham Palace Resort and Spa Nov. 1, 1998, then reverted to the Buena Vista Palace name in Aug. 2005. In Oct. 2016, it became the Hilton Orlando Buena Vista Palace.

Buena Vista Pictures Distribution SEE BUENA VISTA DISTRIBUTION COMPANY.

Buena Vista Records SEE WALT DISNEY RECORDS.

Buena Vista Street Located in Burbank, where the Walt Disney Studios are located (500 S. Buena Vista Street). At first, in the 1940s, the company used a 2400 W. Alameda address. The Studio lot is bordered on 4 sides by Buena Vista St., Alameda Ave., Keystone St., and the Los Angeles River. Riverside Drive runs through the south end of the property. It was from the name of Buena Vista Street that Disney chose the name for its distribution company and several other business arms, as well as for the city of Lake Buena Vista in Florida.

Buena Vista Street Area in Disney California Adventure; opened Jun. 15, 2012, replacing Sunshine Plaza. The street, with its own Red Car Trolley, unique shops, and eateries, is inspired by an idealized Los Angeles at the time Walt Disney started his studio in 1923. Included is Disney's version of the Carthay Circle Theatre, featuring the Carthay Circle Restaurant and Lounge, and the Fiddler, Fifer & Practical Café. Shops include Oswald's, Los Feliz Five & Dime, Big Top Toys, Elias & Co., and the Kingswell Shop.

Buffalo, The—Majestic Symbol of the Plains (film) Part of *The Vanishing Prairie*; released on 16 mm for schools in Sep. 1962. Describes the appearance, habitat, and food of the buffalo, plus efforts to prevent their extinction.

Buffalo Bill's Wild West Show Arena dinner show in Disney Village at Disneyland Paris; ran Apr. 12, 1992–Mar. 2020, reenacting fabled moments of the Old West with shoot-outs and sensational stunts, reminiscent of Buffalo Bill's foray into France many decades earlier.

Buffalo Dreams (TV) A Disney Channel Original Movie; premiered Mar. 11, 2005. Thomas Blackhorse, a Native American, rejects the customs of his Navajo tribe, much to his grandfather's chagrin. Josh Townsend, a Caucasian kid, newly relocated to New Mexico, takes a job on the buffalo preserve just so he can ride his mountain bike. Although Thomas is apprehensive, he allows Josh into his circle of friends, but soon feels betrayed when Josh makes the mistake of associating with local troublemakers who violate the restricted buffalo areas and desecrate sacred Navajo land. Directed by David Jackson. Stars Reiley McClendon (Josh Townsend), Simon R. Baker (Thomas Blackhorse), Graham Greene (John Blackhorse), George Newbern (Dr. Nick Townsend), Adrienne Bailon (Domino), Geraldine Keams (Abuela Rose), Christopher Robin Miller (Virgil), Seth Packard (Wylie), Jane Sibbett (Blaine Townsend), Tessa Vonn (Scout Blackhorse).

Buffalo Trading Co. Western shop in Disney Village at Disneyland Paris; open Apr. 12, 1992–2009, replaced by Starbucks.

Bug Juice (TV) Documentary series on Disney Channel about a group of kids, aged 12–15, that goes off to summer camp at Camp Waziyatah in Waterford, Maine. Premiered Mar. 1, 1998, after a preview the previous night. A new camp, Camp Highlander near Asheville, North Carolina, was featured in a 2nd series of 20 episodes and premiered Mar. 5, 2000. The 3rd season premiered Jun. 3, 2001, and utilized Brush Ranch Camps near Santa Fe, New Mexico. From Evolution Media.

Bug Juice: My Adventures at Camp (TV) A 16-part documentary series on Disney Channel; premiered Jul. 16, 2018, chronicling the team activities, new friendships, and the experience of being away from home for a new generation of kids at Camp Waziyatah in Waterford, Maine. A follow-up to the 1998 Disney Channel series. From Evolution Media.

Bugs in Love (film) Silly Symphony cartoon released Oct. 1, 1932. Directed by Burt Gillett. Nestled in a junk pile, a girl bug and boy bug are in love in their tiny village. When a crow captures the girl, the bugs sound the alarm and rescue her, imprisoning the crow in an old shoe.

Bug's Land, A Area based on *A Bug's Life* in Disney California Adventure; opened Oct. 7, 2002. Shrunk down to the size of a bug, guests could ride attractions at Flik's Fun Fair, including Flik's Flyers, Tuck & Roll's Drive 'em Buggies, Heimlich's Chew Chew Train, Francis's Ladybug Boogie, and Princess Dot Puddle Park. The area also encompassed the previously opened *It's Tough to Be a Bug!* and Bountiful Valley Farm. Closed Sep. 4, 2018, to make way for Avengers Campus.

Bug's Life, A (film) Animated feature from Pixar Animation Studios. A hungry hoard of grasshoppers, led by Hopper, annually extort food from a timid ant colony. A klutzy but inventive worker ant, Flik, tries to increase production with a harvesting contraption, but his plans go awry, and he finds himself instead sent out of the colony to find a way to stop the grasshoppers. Flik recruits a bunch of inept flea-circus performers to rally against Hopper's raid. Working together, they plan for a climactic confrontation with the grasshoppers. Directed by John Lasseter and Andrew Stanton. Released in Los Angeles Nov. 20, 1998, and nationwide on Nov. 25. Voices include Dave Foley (Flik), Kevin Spacey (Hopper), Julia Louis-Dreyfus (Princess Atta), Hayden Panettiere (Princess Dot), Phyllis Diller (The Queen), Richard Kind (Molt), David Hyde Pierce (Slim), Joe Ranft (Heimlich), Denis Leary (Francis), Jonathan Harris (Manny), Madeline Kahn (Gypsy), Bonnie Hunt (Rosie), Michael McShane (Tuck & Roll), John Ratzenberger (P. T. Flea), Brad Garrett (Dim), Roddy McDowall (Mr. Soil). 95 min. CinemaScope. Loosely based on Aesop's fable "The Ants and the Grasshopper," the film was a collaboration of Disney and Pixar as the 2nd fully computer-animated film using the animation style of *Toy Story*. There are 400 crowd scenes, featuring between 25 and 1,000 ants in each shot, with each character fully animated. Released on video in 1999 with consumers getting a choice of 5 package covers (featuring Flik, Francis, Heimlich, Dot, or Hopper). Nominated for an Academy Award for Original Musical Score by Randy Newman, who also wrote/performed the end-credits song, "The Time of Your Life."

Building a Building (film) Mickey Mouse cartoon released Jan. 7, 1933. Directed by Dave Hand. Mickey is a steam shovel operator at a construction site where Pete is the foreman; Minnie is selling box lunches. After Pete steals and eats Mickey's lunch, Minnie gives Mickey a box lunch. Pete attempts to kidnap Minnie, but Mickey and Minnie defeat him in a hot pursuit throughout the building. Mickey joins Minnie as co-operator of her box-lunch wagon, leaving Pete stuck in a cement mixer among fallen girders.

Building a Dream: The Magic Behind a Disney Castle Multimedia exhibition inside the Castle of Magical Dreams at Hong Kong Disneyland; opened Nov. 20, 2020. Visitors can learn how the original Sleeping Beauty Castle was transformed into the new park centerpiece and preview upcoming live entertainment.

Building of a Tire, The (film) Educational film made for the Firestone Tire and Rubber Co.; delivered Feb. 14, 1946. Directed by Lou Debney. The film shows the cross section of a tire and demonstrates the manufacturing of various parts, beginning at a rubber plantation and continuing to the finished tire.

Bujold, Geneviève Actress; appeared in *The Last Flight of Noah's Ark* (Bernadette Lafleur).

Bullock, Sandra Actress; appeared in *While You Were Sleeping* (Lucy) and *Gun Shy* (Judy Tipp). She also exec. produced and appeared in *The Proposal* (Margaret Tate).

Bullseye Woody's trusty horse introduced in *Toy Story 2*; voiced by Frank Welker (uncredited).

Bumble Boogie (film) Segment from *Melody Time*, featuring Freddy Martin and His Orchestra, with Jack Fina at the piano; the frenetic fantasy of a bee's musical nightmare.

Bunheads (TV) Drama series on ABC Family; premiered Jun. 11, 2012, and ended Feb. 25, 2013. A Las Vegas showgirl impulsively marries a man; moves to his sleepy coastal town of Paradise, California; and takes an uneasy role at her new mother-in-law's dance school. Stars Sutton Foster (Michelle Simms), Kaitlyn Jenkins (Boo), Julia Goldani Telles (Sasha), Bailey Buntain (Ginny), Emma Dumont (Melanie), Kelly Bishop (Fanny Flowers).

Bunk'd (TV) Series on Disney Channel; premiered Jul. 31, 2015. Emma, Ravi, and Zuri Ross have left their New York penthouse for a summer at Maine's rustic Camp Kikiwaka, where their parents met as teenagers. Now CITs (counselors in training), they must learn the ropes from the overly cheerful head counselor, Lou, and the camp heartthrob, Xander. Zuri makes new friends with 2 younger campers: the uptight Tiffany and compulsive fibber Jorge. The camp's owner, Gladys, is even scarier than the legendary creature that is rumored to stalk the grounds, and with the help of her sneaky niece Hazel, she's out to get the Ross kids because of her decades-old rivalry with their mom. Stars Peyton List (Emma Ross), Karan Brar (Ravi Ross), Skai Jackson (Zuri Ross), Miranda May (Lou), Kevin Quinn (Xander), Nina Lu (Tiffany), Nathan Arenas (Jorge). For its 6th season (beginning Jun. 10, 2022), the series was renamed *Bunk'd: Learning the Ropes*. From It's a Laugh Productions.

Bunnytown (TV) Puppet variety series produced in the U.K.; premiered Nov. 10, 2007, in the U.S. on Disney Channel. Set in the bustling world of Bunnytown, where laughter rules and carrots are a close 2nd, the bunnies create a humor-filled learning environment for preschool viewers and their families. Disney Channel's first full-scale international production, in association with Baker Coogan. Stars Ed Gaughan (Red), Andrew Buckley (Fred), and Polly Frame (Pinky Pinkerton). From Baker Coogan Productions and Spiffy Pictures, in association with Disney Channel.

Burbank, California Home of The Walt Disney Company, at 500 South Buena Vista Street, at the corner of Buena Vista and Alameda, since 1940.

Burger Invasion Paradise Pier food counter in Disney's California Adventure; opened Feb. 8, 2001. Guests could order McDonald's meals from a giant hamburger. Closed Sep. 2, 2008; replaced by Paradise Garden Grill.

Burgess, Bobby Mouseketeer from the 1950s *Mickey Mouse Club* TV show. Later went on to work with Lawrence Welk for many years.

Burke, Steve He joined Disney in 1985 as director of new business development and, in Dec. 1987, was promoted to vice president, The Disney Store, Inc. By 1990, he was executive vice president, specialty retailing, a post which he held until being selected as executive vice president, operations, for Euro Disney in late 1992. He was named president and chief operating officer of Euro Disney in Feb. 1995. He left Paris Mar. 1, 1996, to become executive vice president of Capital Cities/ABC, Inc. after its merger with The Walt Disney Company, and was promoted to president of broadcasting in Apr. 1997. He left the company in 1998.

Burley, Fulton (1923–2007) He took over the role of the silver-toned tenor in the *Golden Horseshoe Revue* at Disneyland in 1962. His humor and Irish-tenor voice made him an audience favorite at Disneyland and on publicity tours promoting upcoming movie releases. He voiced the Irish parrot, Michael, in Walt Disney's Enchanted Tiki Room. He was named a Disney Legend in 1995.

BURN•E (film) An unlucky welder robot named BURN•E, who's having problems trying to repair a light on the outside of the Axiom spaceship, is locked out when WALL•E and EVE rush in and the hatch slams shut. He has to attempt various methods to get back in. Directed by Angus MacLane. 8 min. From Pixar. Released Nov. 18, 2008, on the *WALL•E* DVD.

Burnett, Carol Actress; appeared in *Noises Off* (Dotty Otley), and on TV in *Carol & Co.* and *The Carol Burnett Show*, *Great Moments in Disney Animation*, *The Dream Is Alive*, and *Once Upon a Mattress* (Queen Aggravain). She provided the voice of Hara in *The Secret World of Arrietty* and Chairol Burnett in *Toy Story 4* and *Forky Asks a Question*.

Burns, Harriet (1928–2008) Imagineer; she joined the Disney Studio as a set and prop painter in 1955, contributing to the *Mickey Mouse Club*, and later was the first woman employed in a creative capacity by WED Enterprises, where she helped design and build prototypes for theme park attractions and then create elements of the attractions themselves. She retired in 1986 and was named a Disney Legend in 2000.

Burr, Lonnie Mouseketeer from the 1950s *Mickey Mouse Club* TV show. He went on to a career in writing and acting.

Burrell, Ty Actor; appeared in *National Treasure: Book of Secrets* (Connor) and *Muppets Most Wanted* (Jean Pierre Napoleon). He voiced Bailey in *Finding Dory*, Big Jack in *Doc McStuffins*, and at EPCOT narrated the Colortopia exhibit in Innoventions and *Awesome Planet* in The Land. He is perhaps best known for his role as Phil Dunphy in the 20th Century Fox–produced *Modern Family*.

Burrow (film) Animated short from Pixar; released digitally on Disney+ Dec. 25, 2020, with *Soul*. A young rabbit embarks on a journey to dig the burrow of her dreams, despite not having a clue about what she's doing. Rather than reveal to her neighbors her imperfections, she digs herself deeper and deeper into trouble. Directed by Madeline Sharafian. From the Pixar Animation Studios SparkShorts program. 6 min. Nominated for an Academy Award for Best Animated Short Film.

Bur-r-r Bank Ice Cream Shop inside the *California Zephyr* train in Sunshine Plaza at Disney California Adventure; open Feb. 8, 2001–Aug. 1, 2011. The name is a tribute to Burbank, where the Disney corporate headquarters is located.

Burstyn, Ellen Actress; appeared in *The Cemetery Club* (Esther Moskowitz), *When a Man Loves a Woman* (Emily), and *Roommates* (Judith), and on TV on *The Ellen Burstyn Show* and in *Flash* (Laura Strong).

Burton, Corey Voice actor; he has provided many voices for Disney since 1986. He voiced Gruffi Gummi in *Disney's Adventures of the Gummi Bears* (after the death of Bill Scott), as well as Gladstone Gander in *DuckTales*, Zipper and Dale in *Chip 'n' Dale Rescue Rangers*, Moliere in *Atlantis: The Lost Empire*, Onus in *Treasure Planet*, and Grumpy in *Ralph Breaks the Internet*. For TV, home video, and at the Disney parks, other roles have included Ludwig Von Drake, Mr. Smee, and Captain Hook. He provided the voice of General Knowledge in Cranium Command at EPCOT, the Ghost Host in Haunted Mansion Holiday at Disneyland, and the narration for the parking trams at Disneyland Resort and Walt Disney World, and for the Disney Resort Line at Tokyo Disney Resort.

Burton, Tim Filmmaker; he was hired by Disney as an artist in 1979, working on concepts for *The Black Cauldron*. During his 5 years at the Disney Studio, he prepared the inventive short films *Vincent* and *Frankenweenie*, but neither of them received broad releases. He left the company in 1984 to eventually direct such (non-Disney) hits as *Beetlejuice*, *Batman*, *Edward Scissorhands*, and *Batman Returns*. He returned to the Disney fold in the 1990s to produce *Tim Burton's The Nightmare Before Christmas*, *Cabin Boy*, and *James and the Giant Peach* and direct *Ed Wood*, and later returned to direct *Alice in Wonderland* (2010) and an updated *Frankenweenie* (2012). He later exec. produced *Alice Through the Looking Glass* and directed/exec. produced *Dumbo* (2019).

Buscemi, Steve Actor; appeared in *New York Stories* (Gregory Stark), *Billy Bathgate* (Irving), *Con Air* (Garland Greene), and *Armageddon* (Rockhound), and provided the voice of Randall Boggs in *Monsters, Inc.* and *Monsters University*, Wesley in *Home on the Range*, Bucky in *G-Force*, and Saloso in *Elena of Avalor*.

Bush, George H. W. On Sep. 30, 1991, President Bush presented medals to 575 persons being honored in The Daily Points of Light Celebration, which was televised live from the America Gardens amphitheater in EPCOT Center on The Disney Channel.

Bush, George W. As president, he spoke at private luncheons at Walt Disney World on Nov. 13, 2003 (Disney's Grand Floridian Resort & Spa) and Feb. 17, 2006 (Disney's Contemporary Resort).

Bush, Jared For Walt Disney Animation Studios, he helped develop *Frozen* and *Big Hero 6*; wrote the screenplay for *Moana*; wrote and co-directed *Zootopia* (also voicing Pronk Oryx-Antlerson); exec. produced *Raya and the Last Dragon*; and co-directed/co-wrote the screenplay for *Encanto*. For Disney XD, he co-created, exec. produced, and was writer for *Penn Zero: Part-Time Hero*.

Busy Beavers, The (film) Silly Symphony cartoon released Jun. 30, 1931. As beavers busily attempt to build a dam, a storm breaks. The colony is saved by a clever little beaver who uses his teeth to saw a large tree, which blocks the flood. Directed by Wilfred Jackson.

Butch Macho bulldog who had a constant rivalry with Pluto; appeared in 11 theatrical cartoons, beginning with *Bone Trouble* (1940).

Buttons, Red (1919–2006) Actor; appeared in *Pete's Dragon* (Hoagy).

Buttram, Pat (1915–1994) Actor; provided the voice of Napoleon (*The Aristocats*), the Sheriff of Nottingham (*Robin Hood*), Luke (*The Rescuers*), and Chief (*The Fox and the Hound*). He appeared on TV as a host of *The Mouse Factory*. His final role was the voice of the Possum Park emcee in *A Goofy Movie*.

Buy the Book Book and coffee shop on New York Street at Disney-MGM Studios; opened Oct. 2, 1996. Based on the store Ellen worked at on the ABC-TV series starring Ellen DeGeneres. Also known as Ellen's Buy the Book and Disney's Buy the Book. Formerly The Costume Shop. After the ABC series ended in 1998, it became The Writer's Stop (Jan. 1999–Apr. 2, 2016). Over the years, the shop was used for author and celebrity signings.

Buyer Be Wise (film) Educational film; released in Sep. 1982. Goofy makes common consumer errors, but Mickey Mouse and Donald Duck assist him in getting the best value for his money by setting priorities, comparing prices, and looking for sales.

Buzz Lightyear Smug space toy rival and, even-tually, best friend of Woody in the Toy Story films; voiced by Tim Allen.

Buzz Lightyear Astro Blasters Tomorrowland attraction in Disneyland and Tokyo Disneyland, taking the place of the Circle-Vision 360 film theaters. It was based upon its counterpart, Buzz Lightyear's Space Ranger Spin, in the Magic Kingdom at Walt Disney World. Opened in Tokyo Disneyland (known as Buzz Lightyear's Astro Blasters) Apr. 15, 2004, and in Disneyland May 5, 2005, after a soft opening in March. There was also a *Buzz Lightyear Astro Blasters Interactive Experience* where online users could team up with Disneyland guests by lighting up special targets that enabled them to obtain higher scores. Also in Hong Kong Disneyland, Sep. 12, 2005–Aug. 31, 2017; succeeded by Ant-Man and The Wasp: Nano Battle! Versions also opened in Disneyland Paris (Buzz Lightyear Laser Blast, Apr. 8, 2006) and Shanghai Disneyland (Buzz Lightyear Planet Rescue, Jun. 16, 2016), the latter featuring a new story line and interactive targeting system. The attractions are based on Disney • Pixar's *Toy Story 2*. An attraction with a similar name, Buzz Lightyear's AstroBlaster, was featured at the former DisneyQuest at Walt Disney World.

Buzz Lightyear of Star Command (TV) Traditionally animated (not CG-animated) series on ABC's *One Saturday Morning*; debuted Oct. 14, 2000 (and also on weekdays on UPN and syn., beginning Oct. 2, 2000). Follows Buzz Lightyear's adventures as he patrols the galaxy with his team of Space Rangers, battling evildoers "to infinity and beyond." Voices include Patrick Warburton (Buzz), Wayne Knight (Zurg), Adam Carolla (Nebula), Larry Miller (XR), Stephen Furst (Booster), Nicole Sullivan (Mira Nova). Based on the *Toy Story* character. 65 episodes.

Buzz Lightyear of Star Command: The Adventure Begins (film) Direct-to-video release Aug. 8, 2000. The Evil Emperor Zurg captures a group of aliens in order to uncover the secret of their Uni-mind, which lets them think as one. As Zurg attacks their planet to steal the Uni-mind, he zaps the entire galaxy with a device which puts almost everyone under his evil control. When he unleashes his most dastardly henchman, Agent Z, Buzz Lightyear, the greatest space hero ever, working with 3 intergalactic crime-fighting rookies (Mira Nova, Booster, and XR), attempts to save the day—and the entire galaxy. Directed by Tad Stones. Voices include Tim Allen (Buzz Lightyear), Nicole Sullivan (Princess Mira Nova), Larry Miller (XR), Stephen Furst (Booster), Wayne Knight (Zurg). 70 min. A joint project of Walt Disney Home Video, Walt Disney Television Animation, and Pixar Animation Studios. William Shatner performs "To Infinity and Beyond" with the Star Command chorus under the final credits.

Buzz Lightyear Planet Rescue Tomorrowland attraction in Shanghai Disneyland; opened Jun. 16, 2016. Using pulse blasters to fire at Power Source Zs, guests join Buzz Lightyear on an interactive adventure to infiltrate Emperor Zurg's secret lair and eliminate a dangerous crystal-powered Superblaster. SEE ALSO BUZZ LIGHTYEAR ASTRO BLASTERS.

Buzz Lightyear's Pizza Planet Restaurant Buffet service in Discoveryland at Disneyland Paris; opened Oct. 30, 1996, taking the place of Space Festival. Guests pass a robot guard and are served by assistant Space Rangers in fluorescent outfits. It later operated seasonally, closing permanently in 2016.

Buzz Lightyear's Space Ranger Spin Tomorrowland attraction in the Magic Kingdom at Walt Disney World; opened Oct. 7, 1998. Recruited by Buzz Lightyear to battle Emperor Zurg, guests board XP-37 space cruisers for an interactive adventure to the Gamma Quadrant and fire at "Z" targets by use of a laser cannon. Direct hits trigger animation, sound, and light effects, with scores tallied on the cruiser's dashboard. The attraction uses the same Omnimover ride system as its predecessors, beginning with If You Had Wings, but riders could now use a joystick to control the vehicle's direction—a full 360 degrees.

Based on Disney • Pixar's *Toy Story 2*. SEE ALSO BUZZ LIGHTYEAR ASTRO BLASTERS.

Buzz-Buzz Bee character in a number of Donald Duck cartoons, beginning with *Inferior Decorator* (1948); also known as Spike.

Buzz on Maggie, The (TV) Animated comedy on Disney Channel; debuted Jun. 17, 2005. In the metropolis of Stickyfeet, Maggie Pesky, an unusually creative and expressive tween-age fly, is fun-loving and highly energetic, but she causes problems with her inspired antics in the conventional world of flies, which lead to consequences she did not anticipate. When she is faced with one of the many routines of everyday life, she devises a way to make it fresh and exciting. Voices include Jessica DiCicco (Maggie Pesky), David Kaufman (Aldrin Pesky), Thom Adcox (Pupert Pesky), Cree Summer (Rayna), Brian Doyle-Murray and Susan Tolsky (Maggie's father and mother). Also aired on *ABC Kids* beginning Sep. 17, 2005.

Buzzi, Ruth Actress; appeared in *Freaky Friday* (opposing coach), *The North Avenue Irregulars* (Dr. Rheems), and *The Apple Dumpling Gang Rides Again* (Tough Kate). She provided voices in *It's Tough to Be a Bird*, *Chip 'n' Dale Rescue Rangers*, and *Darkwing Duck*.

B.V.G. SEE BAYVIEW GIFTS.

Bwana Bob's Adventureland merchandise and sundry kiosk in the Magic Kingdom at Walt Disney World; opened Dec. 1984.

By the Book Alternate title of *Renaissance Man* for a short test run in Seattle.

Byner, John Actor; voiced Gurgi and Doli in *The Black Cauldron* and appeared on TV as a host of *The Mouse Factory*.

1. Carousel of Progress 2. *Coco* (film) 3. Comic strips 4. *Cars on the Road* (TV) 5. Carthay Circle Restaurant
6. Castle of Magical Dreams 7. Carolwood Pacific Railroad 8. Country Bear Jamboree 9. Cheshire Cat

Caan, James (1940–2022) Actor; appeared in *Dick Tracy* (Spaldoni) and *The Program* (Coach Winters).

Cabane des Robinson, La SEE LA CABANE DES ROBINSON.

Cabin Boy (film) On his way to a luxury ocean cruise, Nathanial Mayweather, an insufferably spoiled rich kid, mistakenly boards *The Filthy Whore*, a dilapidated fishing trawler populated by a crew of scurrilous old salts who turn his life of leisure into misery as their menial cabin boy. The crew encounter a bunch of quirky mythical creatures in a mysterious Pacific Ocean area known as Hell's Bucket before finding an island where they plan to repair their boat and rid themselves of Mayweather. But after killing the 50-foot-tall giant shoe salesman, jealous husband of the 6-armed siren, Calli, Nathanial wins acceptance as well as the love of Trina, a long-distance swimmer. Reaching Hawaii, Nathanial discovers the pampered life no longer suits him, and he rejoins the crew. Released Jan. 7, 1994. A Touchstone film. Produced by Tim Burton and Denise DiNovi and directed by Adam Resnick. 80 min. Stars Chris Elliott (Nathanial Mayweather), Ritch Brinkley (Capt. Greybar), Brian Doyle-Murray (Skunk), James Gammon (Paps), Brion James (Big Teddy), Melora Walters (Trina). There is a cameo by David Letterman. Except for the fishing village, the movie was filmed almost entirely on soundstages in the Los Angeles area.

Cable Car Bake Shop Coffee and baked treat shop on Main Street, U.S.A. in Disneyland Paris; opened Apr. 12, 1992. Inspired by old-time San Francisco.

Cabot, Sebastian (1918–1977) Actor; provided the voice of Sir Ector in (and narrated) *The Sword in the Stone*, Bagheera in *The Jungle Book*, and narrated *The Many Adventures of Winnie the Pooh*. He appeared in *Westward Ho the Wagons!* (Bissonette) and *Johnny Tremain* (Jonathan Lyte), and on TV in *Along the Oregon Trail*.

Cactus Kid, The (film) Mickey Mouse cartoon released May 15, 1930. Directed by Walt Disney. After a series of song and dance routines by Mickey, Minnie, and Pedro (Pete), Pedro kidnaps Minnie, with Mickey chasing them on horseback across the desert. Mickey defeats Pedro and rescues Minnie. Pedro tumbles over a cliff and is flattened by a rock, but manages to walk away "accordion" style, while Mickey, Minnie, and their horse jeer at him.

Cadet Kelly (TV) A Disney Channel Original Movie; premiered Mar. 8, 2002. When the mom of carefree 14-year-old Kelly Collins marries the new commandant at a military academy, Kelly is forced to become the school's newest recruit. Her independent spirit clashes with the conformity of the school, but she takes up the challenge, and even becomes a member of the drill team. Directed by Larry Shaw. Stars Hilary Duff (Kelly Collins), Gary Cole (Sir), Christy Carlson Romano (Jennifer Stone), Shawn Ashmore (Brad Rigby), Andrea Lewis (Carla Hall), Aimee Garcia (Gloria Ramos),

Linda Kash (Samantha). 110 min. The film became the first Disney Channel movie to repeat on ABC's *Wonderful World of Disney*, Jul. 14, 2002.

Café de la Brousse Adventureland snack bar in Disneyland Paris; opened Apr. 12, 1992. Guests enjoy beverages and ice cream in shady huts along the water.

Café des Cascadeurs Art deco–style studio diner, seating 40 guests, in the Backlot at Walt Disney Studios Park in Disneyland Paris; opened Jun. 6, 2002. Guests dine in an Airstream travel trailer that was actually built in the 1940s and once served meals in the States and, later, Germany. The restaurant became Super Diner in 2022 when the area became Avengers Campus.

Café des Visionnaires Quick-service restaurant in Discoveryland at Disneyland Paris; opened Apr. 12, 1992. Closed Sep. 15, 1995, to be replaced by Arcade des Visionnaires in 1996.

Café Fantasia Piano lounge in the Disneyland Hotel at Disneyland Paris; opened Apr. 12, 1992.

Café Hyperion Discoveryland counter-service restaurant, part of Videopolis, in Disneyland Paris; opened Apr. 12, 1992. Inside a high-tech hangar, guests enjoy burgers and salads while watching a movie or live show. A highlight is a re-creation of the airship *Hyperion* from *The Island at the Top of the World*. Presented by Coca-Cola.

Café Mickey Italian-style restaurant overlooking Lake Disney in Disney Village at Disneyland Paris; opened winter 2001, taking the place of the Los Angeles Bar and Grill. A new restaurant, Rosalie, is planned to take its place in 2023.

Café Orléans Sidewalk café in New Orleans Square at Disneyland; opened in 1972. Formerly Creole Cafe. Guests dine on Cajun-Creole-style fare on a terrace overlooking the Rivers of America. A version opened in Adventureland at Tokyo Disneyland Apr. 15, 1983.

Cafe Portofino Rustic seaside Italian buffeteria in Mediterranean Harbor at Tokyo DisneySea; opened Sep. 4, 2001.

Caffe Villa Verde Casual-dining restaurant in the Disneyland Hotel at Disneyland Resort; open Jul. 1, 1983–1995, and superseded by Stromboli's

Ristorante. Over the years, Italian, American, and international specialties were served along the resort's "waterfront."

Cage Nightclub in Pleasure Island at Walt Disney World, featuring music videos showing on 170 monitors; open Apr. 7, 1990–Dec. 1992. Formerly Videopolis East, which later became 8TRAX.

Cage, Nicolas Actor; appeared in *Fire Birds* (Jake Preston), *The Rock* (Stanley Goodspeed), *Con Air* (Cameron Poe), *Snake Eyes* (Rick Santoro), *Bringing Out the Dead* (Frank Pierce), *Gone in 60 Seconds* (Memphis Raines), *The Sorcerer's Apprentice* (Balthazar), and *National Treasure* and *National Treasure 2* (Ben Gates). He voiced Speckles in *G-Force*.

Caine, Michael Actor; appeared in *Mr. Destiny* (Mike), *Noises Off* (Lloyd Fellowes), *The Muppet Christmas Carol* (Scrooge), and *The Prestige* (Cutter). He voiced Lord Redbrick in *Gnomeo & Juliet* and Finn McMissile in *Cars 2*.

Cake Bake Shop by Gwendolyn Rogers, The Table-service restaurant and bakery planned to open in 2023 on Disney's BoardWalk at Walt Disney World, taking the place of ESPN Club.

Calame, Niketa Actress; voiced the young Nala in *The Lion King*.

CalArts SEE CALIFORNIA INSTITUTE OF THE ARTS.

Calendar Girls (film) A group of ladies attend dull weekly meetings at the Women's Institute branch in fictitious Knapely, Yorkshire, but 2 regulars, Chris Harper and Annie Clark, feel the institute needs a shake-up. Their plan is for the group of mature women to pose nude for a calendar to raise money for a local hospital. As a result, they become international celebrities. A Touchstone film in association with Harbour Pictures for Buena Vista International. Limited U.S. release Dec. 19, 2003, after a world premiere Aug. 9 at the Locarno (Switzerland) Film Festival and a Sep. 5 United Kingdom release. Expanded release Jan. 1, 2004. Directed by Nigel Cole. Stars Helen Mirren (Chris Harper), Julie Walters (Annie Clark), John Alderton (John Clark), Linda Bassett (Cora), Annette Crosbie (Jessie), Philip Glenister (Lawrence), Ciaran Hinds (Rod), Celia Imrie (Celia), Geraldine James (Marie), Penelope Wilton (Ruth). 108 min. Filmed in Super 35-Scope on location in

England's Yorkshire (with the village of Kettlewell standing in for the fictional Knapely) and London.

California Adventure, Disney A 55-acre theme park at Disneyland Resort; opened as Disney's California Adventure Feb. 8, 2001, and built on the original parking lot of Disneyland. Guests initially entered the park through the Golden Gateway, a montage of state landmarks that created the image of a colorful California postcard. From there, Sunshine Plaza provided access to 3 main districts with attractions, restaurants, and shopping: Golden State, Hollywood Pictures Backlot, and Paradise Pier. Golden State celebrated California's cultural diversity and natural beauty with 6 themed districts: Condor Flats, Bountiful Valley Farm, Pacific Wharf, Bay Area, Grizzly Peak Recreation Area, and Golden Vine Winery. Grizzly Peak, a mountain shaped as the head of a grizzly bear, is home to Grizzly River Run, a whitewater rafting attraction, and also is an icon for the park. In Condor Flats, Soarin' Over California, a simulated hang gliding attraction, became an instant classic. Hollywood Pictures Backlot celebrated the glitz and glamour of the Hollywood moviemaking and TV mythos. Paradise Pier re-created the legendary California beach culture, styled after classic Pacific Coast amusement parks with high-tech rides and games of skill. The park premiered as part of a $1.4 billion expansion of the Disneyland Resort—which, in addition to the existing Disneyland Park, Disneyland Hotel, and Paradise Pier Hotel, also included Disney's Grand Californian Hotel, providing a second entrance into Disney's California Adventure; the Downtown Disney District, a themed retail, dining, and entertainment complex; and a new, 10,000-car parking structure, at the time the largest in the world. In 2002, Bountiful Valley Farm became part of a new district, A Bug's Land. The park's name was changed from Disney's California Adventure to Disney California Adventure in Jun. 2010. The park underwent a major transformation in 2012, with a grand reopening ceremony held Jun. 15. Buena Vista Street replaced the Golden Gateway and Sunshine Plaza, with the Carthay Circle Restaurant as the area's new focal point, and Cars Land was added, re-creating Radiator Springs from the Disney • Pixar film *Cars*. Hollywood Pictures Backlot was renamed Hollywood Land, and the Golden State name was retired, with its attractions and restaurants reorganized into Pacific Wharf, Grizzly Peak, and Condor Flats (which became Grizzly Peak Airfield in 2015). In 2018, Paradise Pier was divided into Paradise Gardens Park and Pixar Pier, and A Bug's Land closed to make way for Avengers Campus, which premiered in 2021. In Jun. 2022, a 3rd park entrance opened, providing direct access from Disney's Paradise Pier Hotel (later Pixar Place Hotel); and in summer 2023, Pacific Wharf is planned to be transformed into San Fransokyo Square.

California Angels On May 18, 1995, Disney announced it was purchasing 25% of the California Angels Major League Baseball team from owner Gene Autry; the remainder of the team would be acquired after Mr. Autry's death. The purchase took place May 15, 1996, when Disney Sports Enterprises became managing general partner for the team. A $100 million renovation of Anaheim Stadium was completed in 1998 by Walt Disney Imagineering, HOK Sport, and Robert Stern Architects. The team name was changed to the Anaheim Angels in Nov. 1996, with new team colors and logos. After Gene Autry's death, Disney completed its purchase of the team on Mar. 31, 1999. SEE ALSO ANAHEIM ANGELS.

California Grill Restaurant on the top floor of Disney's Contemporary Resort at Walt Disney World; opened May 15, 1995, taking the place of Top of the World. Flavors of the Pacific Coast are served from an onstage kitchen and sushi bar. Diners enjoy a spectacular view of the Magic Kingdom and Seven Seas Lagoon. Also a restaurant in the Disneyland Hotel at Disneyland Paris; opened Apr. 12, 1992, offering California-inspired fine dining in a Victorian setting.

California Institute of the Arts Art school founded in 1962, combining the Chouinard Art Institute and the Los Angeles Conservatory of Music. Walt Disney had been a longtime supporter of Chouinard because many of his artists had received training there, so he was an avid advocate for the new school. When he died in 1966, a large bequest from his estate helped finance the construction of the new campus for what's also known as CalArts, as the school would be known, on a 60-acre site in Valencia, and the U.S. Congress authorized the minting of a special commemorative medal, which could be sold to benefit the school's scholarship program. Eventually a character animation curriculum would be established at CalArts, and many of the students would be selected to become Disney animators.

California Screamin' Thrill attraction in Paradise Pier at Disney California Adventure; opened

Feb. 8, 2001, as the world's longest steel looping roller coaster, at 6,000 feet. It was designed to mirror the wooden look of coasters of yesteryear but with 21st-century technology. Riders in 24-passenger cars were catapulted past splashing waves, swooped in and out of the Paradise Pier boardwalk area, and experienced a 360-degree loop. Closed Jan. 7, 2018, to be redesigned as the Incredicoaster.

California Zephyr Train hosting Baker's Field Bakery, Bur-r-r Bank Ice Cream, and Engine-Ears Toys in Sunshine Plaza at Disney California Adventure, Feb. 8, 2001–Aug. 1, 2011. The cab once operated as a real locomotive. The train was donated to the Western Pacific Railroad Museum in Portola, California, Aug. 6, 2011.

Californy 'er Bust (film) Goofy cartoon released Jul. 13, 1945. Directed by Jack Kinney. A covered wagon train populated with Goofy look-alikes is attacked, but an opportune cyclone appears to carry them over the Rockies.

Call, Brandon Actor; appeared on TV in *The Richest Cat in the World* and voiced 1 of the Fairfolk in *The Black Cauldron*.

Call It Courage (TV) Show based on the book by Armstrong Sperry; aired Apr. 1, 1973. Directed by Roy Edward Disney. Filmed on Tahiti and Bora-Bora, the story of a Native boy, Mafatu, who, with his dog, tries to prove himself a man by setting sail in a small outrigger canoe. He is capsized in a storm and has to survive by his wits on an island inhabited by a fierce tribe. Stars Evan Temarii.

Call Your Mother (TV) Half-hour sitcom on ABC; aired Jan. 13–May 19, 2021. Jean, an empty nester mom, wonders how she ended up alone while her children live their best lives thousands of miles away. She decides her place is with her family, and as she reinserts herself into their lives, her kids realize they might actually need her more than they thought. Stars Kyra Sedgwick (Jean Raines), Rachel Sennott (Jackie Raines), Joey Bragg (Freddie Raines), Emma Caymares (Celia), Austin Crute (Lane), Patrick Brammall (Danny). From Sony Pictures Television and ABC Signature.

Callas, Charlie (1927–2011) Actor; voiced Elliott the dragon in *Pete's Dragon*.

Calling Dick Tracy Shop on Hollywood Boulevard

in Disney-MGM Studios; opened May 26, 1990. Guests could star in their own home video version of a Dick Tracy adventure. Closed Jan. 12, 1991, to become Legends of Hollywood.

Calvin, Henry (1918–1975) Actor; appeared in *Zorro* (Sgt. Garcia), *Toby Tyler* (Ben Cotter), and *Babes in Toyland* (Gonzorgo).

Calypso Trading Post Souvenir shop in Disney's Caribbean Beach Resort at Walt Disney World; opened Oct. 1, 1988. In 1994, it combined with the Calypso Straw Market to form a larger store.

Camarata, Salvador "Tutti" (1913–2005) A musical supervisor, arranger, and conductor who joined Disney in 1956 to help found Disneyland Records. Over a 5-year period, he supervised recordings of over 300 Disney record albums, featuring stars such as Annette Funicello, for whom he created a special "Annette sound" utilizing an echo. He was named a Disney Legend in 2003.

Cambridge, Godfrey (1933–1976) Actor; appeared in *The Biscuit Eater* (Willie Dorsey).

Cameo by Night (TV) Unsold pilot for a series; aired on NBC Jul. 12, 1987. A police department secretary by day, secret-identity crime fighter by night, solves a murder mystery. 60 min. Directed by Paul Lynch. Stars Sela Ward, Justin Deas, Thomas Ryan, Art LaFleur.

Camera Center Shop on Main Street, U.S.A. in Disneyland; opened Jul. 17, 1955. Moved into the former Carefree Corner Nov. 1994, becoming the Main Street Photo Supply Co. Presented over the years by Kodak, GAF, Polaroid, and Nikon. Closed Aug. 2021, and succeeded by Plaza Point. Also on Main Street, U.S.A. in the Magic Kingdom at Walt Disney World (opened Oct. 1, 1971) and in World Bazaar at Tokyo Disneyland (Apr. 15, 1983). The Magic Kingdom shop moved into the Exposition Hall Aug. 27, 1998, and closed in 2010, becoming Box Office Gifts Apr. 1, 2011. See also Town Square Photography (Disneyland Paris and Hong Kong Disneyland).

Cameras in Africa/Beaver Valley (TV) Rerun title of *Beaver Valley/Cameras in Africa*.

Cameras in Samoa/The Holland Story (TV) Show aired Nov. 7, 1956. Directed and narrated by Winston Hibler. The story of problems that occur when the dikes are breached in Holland, along with a visit behind the scenes with photographers Herbert and Trudi Knapp working on the People and Places film *Samoa*.

Cameron, Dove Actress; appeared on Disney Channel as the title characters in *Liv and Maddie*, Kayla in *Cloud 9*, and Mal in the Descendants movies, and on ABC in *Marvel's Agents of S.H.I.E.L.D.* (Ruby).

Cameron, Kirk Actor; appeared in the 1995 TV remake of *The Computer Wore Tennis Shoes* (Dexter Riley) and in bit parts in *Beyond Witch Mountain* and the *Herbie, the Love Bug* miniseries. Also appeared on Disney Channel in *You Lucky Dog* (Jack Morgan).

CAMP Shop/play hybrid experience that participated in the 2021 Disney Accelerator, a business development program designed to accelerate the growth of innovative companies. On May 28, 2022, CAMP launched its first Disney-themed experience, *Mickey & Friends x CAMP: An Extra Big Adventure*, at its Fifth Avenue flagship store in New York City, before it traveled on to other locations. Guests shrink down to the size of a crayon and help Mickey Mouse and friends get things back to normal in time for Mickey's big birthday party. It was followed on Oct. 8 by *Disney Encanto x CAMP*, a 6,000-sq.-ft. experience in which families can explore the Madrigal family's Casita, with secret passages, live music, and surprises behind magic doors.

Camp Davy Crockett See Davy Crockett Ranch.

Camp Discovery Attraction in Adventure Isle at Shanghai Disneyland; opened Jun. 16, 2016. Guests can discover tribal ruins in an elevated ropes course, join an archaeological dig, and trek past waterfalls and other wonders.

Camp Dog (film) Pluto cartoon released Sep. 22, 1950. Directed by Charles Nichols. While campers are away, Pluto must guard the campsite from 2 coyotes, Bent-Tail and his son, Junior. The coyotes try to steal food, with Junior complicating matters by "stealing" Pluto, whom he considers to be food. After a chase that destroys the camp, Pluto joins the coyotes in the hills rather than try to explain what's happened to the campers.

Camp Minnie-Mickey Area in Disney's Animal Kingdom at Walt Disney World; opened Apr. 22, 1998, resembling a rustic, Adirondack-style summer camp where Mickey Mouse and his pals have come to visit. Special productions were performed in the Lion King Theater (*Festival of the Lion King*) and Grandmother Willow's Grove (*Colors of the Wind, Friends from the Animal Forest*; later named *Pocahontas and Her Forest Friends*). Closed in 2014 to make way for Pandora – The World of Avatar, with *Festival of the Lion King* moving to a new theater in Africa.

Camp Nowhere (film) At the end of each school year, young Morris "Mud" Himmel and his friends are unceremoniously packed off by their wealthy parents to summer camps that specialize in computer programming, military training, or calorie counting. This summer, Morris and his clever cohorts have determined to create their own vacation haven. With help from out-of-work high school drama teacher Dennis Van Welker—who passes himself off to each of the kids' parents as the owner of a different phony theme camp—the kids fabricate an elaborate scheme to create their own camp filled with video games and junk food. But when Parents' Day approaches, the kids have to resort to even greater deceptions to try to fool the gullible parents. Released Aug. 26, 1994. Directed by Jonathan Prince. A Hollywood Pictures film. 96 min. Stars Christopher Lloyd (Dennis Van Welker), Jonathan Jackson (Morris "Mud" Himmel), Wendy Makkena (Dr. Celeste Dunbar), M. Emmet Walsh (T. R. Polk). Camp Nowhere was built on Disney's Golden Oak Ranch in Newhall, California.

Camp Rock (TV) A Disney Channel Original Movie; premiered Jun. 20, 2008. The film also aired on the ABC Network on Jun. 21 and ABC Family on Jun. 22. Members of a leading musical group, Connect 3, go to a camp for aspiring young music artists where 1 becomes a guest instructor in an effort to counter his bad boy rocker image. Among the campers is Mitchie Torres, a teen girl with an extraordinary voice and a driving ambition to be a pop singer. She can only spend her summer at the camp by helping her mom work in the mess hall between classes. When Shane overhears Mitchie singing from behind closed doors, he sets out to find the girl with the beautiful voice. Together, Mitchie and the boys learn to believe in themselves and to value the freedom to be who they want to be. Directed by Matthew Diamond. Stars Kevin Jonas

(Jason), Joseph Jonas (Shane Gray), Nick Jonas (Nate), Demi Lovato (Mitchie Torres), Alyson Stoner (Caitlyn Geller), Meaghan Jette Martin (Tess Tyler), Jasmine Richards (Peggy), Anna Maria Perez de Taglé (Ella), Maria Canals-Barrera (Connie Torres), Daniel Fathers (Brown), Roshon Fegan (Sander), Jordan Francis (Barron), Julie Brown (Dee La Duke).

Camp Rock 2: The Final Jam (TV) A Disney Channel Original Movie; premiered Sep. 3, 2010. The kids return to Camp Rock for another great summer of music and fun. However, they soon learn that a new state-of-the-art music/performance camp, Camp Star, has opened across the lake, and has lured away many of the Camp Rock instructors and campers, putting the future of Camp Rock in jeopardy. When Camp Star's hot-shot performer, Luke Williams, challenges Camp Rock to a musical showdown to see which camp has the stronger musical talent, everyone prepares for the ultimate battle of the bands. Meanwhile, Nate falls for Dana, the daughter of the owner of the rival camp. Directed by Paul Hoen. Stars Demi Lovato (Mitchie Torres), Kevin Jonas (Jason), Joe Jonas (Shane Gray), Nick Jonas (Nate), Matthew "Mdot" Finley (Luke Williams), Chloe Bridges (Dana Turner), Meaghan Martin (Tess Tyler), Alyson Stoner (Caitlyn Geller), Anna Maria Perez de Tagle (Ella), Roshon Fegan (Sander), Daniel Fathers (Brown), Maria Canals-Barrera (Connie Torres).

Camp Woodchuck Area in Westernland at Tokyo Disneyland; opened Nov. 22, 2016. Visitors explore the camp of the Junior Woodchucks organization, inspired by the Carl Barks comic books. At the Woodchuck Greeting Trail, guests can meet Donald Duck and Daisy Duck, and might even spot a rare bird—the Tri-crested Tittertwill (*Funnylookus Tittertwillus*)—nesting high up on a rock.

Camp Woodchuck Kitchen Quick-service mess hall in Camp Woodchuck at Tokyo Disneyland; opened Nov. 22, 2016, replacing Lucky Nugget Cafe. Visitors enjoy camping-style meals, like waffle sandwiches, inside the Junior Woodchucks' lodge or can dine on a terrace overlooking the Rivers of America.

Campbell, Bill Actor; appeared in *The Rocketeer* (Cliff Secord), and on TV in *The Best of Disney: 50 Years of Magic*, *Max Q: Emergency Landing* (Clay Jarvis), and the series *Once and Again* (Rick Sammler). He later voiced Dave Secord in *The Rocketeer* animated TV series.

Campbell, Collin (1926–2011) After 2 stints in the Traffic Department at the Disney Studio in the mid-1940s, he returned after art school to jobs in the Animation Department as inbetweener and layout artist for films, including *Lady and the Tramp* and *Sleeping Beauty*. He also designed sets for the *Mickey Mouse Club* and did costume sketches and matte work for live-action films. In 1961, Walt Disney reassigned him to WED Enterprises, where he helped develop the Enchanted Tiki Room, projects for the 1964–1965 New York World's Fair, Pirates of the Caribbean, and Club 33, before moving on to design much of the overall feel for Walt Disney World. He retired in 1990 after working on concept art for Disney-MGM Studios and Disneyland Paris and serving as art director for Typhoon Lagoon. He was named a Disney Legend posthumously in 2013.

Campbell, Rebecca She was named president of the ABC Owned Television Station Group in 2010 and, beginning in 2016, served as president of ABC Daytime. In 2018, she was appointed president, The Walt Disney Company – Europe, Middle East and Africa, and in 2019 became president of the Disneyland Resort. On May 18, 2020, she was promoted to chairman, International Operations & Direct-to-Consumer, part of Disney Media & Entertainment Distribution, and on Jan. 19, 2022, was named chairman, International Content and Operations, overseeing the company's international media teams and local and regional content production for Disney's streaming services. It was announced she will leave the company in 2023.

Camping Out (film) Mickey Mouse cartoon released Feb. 17, 1934. Directed by Dave Hand. When mosquitoes threaten Mickey, Minnie, Horace Horsecollar, and Clarabelle Cow's lazy summer day, Horace swats at them, which angers them and alerts more to form into an army formation. Mickey saves the day by catching the swarm in Clarabelle's bloomers.

Campos, Rafael (1936–1985) Actor; appeared in *The Light in the Forest* (Half Arrow), *Tonka* (Strong Bear), and *Savage Sam* (Young Warrior), and on TV in *A Boy Called Nuthin'* and *The Tenderfoot*.

Can of Worms (TV) A Disney Channel Original

Movie; premiered Apr. 10, 1999. Fourteen-year-old Mike Pillsbury is a great storyteller who spins elaborate tales about imaginary aliens who he believes left him on a doorstep to be raised by Earthlings. When a schoolmate humiliates him at a dance, he sends a plea into space begging for aliens to rescue him from Earth. Mike opens a can of worms when the aliens actually arrive, leaving him responsible for saving the world. Directed by Paul Schneider. Stars Michael Shulman (Mike Pillsbury), Marcus Turner (Scott), Erika Christensen (Katelyn), Adam Wylie (Nick), Andrew Ducote (Jay), Malcolm McDowell (voice of Barnabus). Filmed entirely on location in Vancouver.

Can You Feel the Love Tonight Song from *The Lion King*; written by Elton John and Tim Rice. Academy Award winner.

Canada World Showcase pavilion in EPCOT; opened Oct. 1, 1982. The Hôtel du Canada, patterned after the Château Laurier in Ottawa and Château Frontenac in Quebec, evokes a feeling of French Canada, while rocky cliffs, running streams, and waterfalls remind one of the western provinces. Inside the Moosehead Mine, guests will find the pavilion highlight: a Circle-Vision 360 film showcasing some of the country's spectacular scenery. There is a restaurant, Le Cellier (literally The Cellar). The Victoria Gardens are reminiscent of the Butchart Gardens in British Columbia. Shops include Northwest Mercantile and the Trading Post. In 1998, a large Raven totem pole was carved at the pavilion by Tsimshian artist David Boxley using a 700-year-old, 9,000-lb. tree trunk; he later carved Whale and Eagle totem poles, which were unveiled at the pavilion in Jan. 2017.

Canada Far and Wide in Circle-Vision 360 (film) An update to the *O Canada!* film at EPCOT; premiered Jan. 17, 2020. Musical score by Andrew Lockington. Narrated by Catherine O'Hara and Eugene Levy.

Canada '67 (film) Circle-Vision 360 film tour of Canada; prepared in 1967 for Expo 67 in Montreal. SEE O CANADA! FOR THE LATER CIRCLE-VISION FILM PRODUCED FOR EPCOT.

Canadian Bond Selling Shorts SEE THRIFTY PIG, THE; 7 WISE DWARFS; DONALD'S DECISION; AND ALL TOGETHER.

Canal Boats of the World Fantasyland attraction in

Disneyland; operated Jul. 17–Sep. 16, 1955, later becoming Storybook Land Canal Boats. The attraction became much more popular after the addition of the Storybook Land scenes.

Candido, Candy (1913–1999) Actor; he provided several voices, including the Indian Chief in *Peter Pan*, one of Maleficent's goons in *Sleeping Beauty*, the Crocodile in *Robin Hood*, and Fidget in *The Great Mouse Detective*.

Candle on the Water Song from *Pete's Dragon*; written by Al Kasha and Joel Hirschhorn. Nominated for an Academy Award.

Candlelight Procession A Christmastime tradition, beginning at Disneyland in 1958 with a concept developed by Dr. Charles C. Hirt of the University of Southern California School of Music. A guest narrator each year—with personalities including Dennis Morgan (in 1960, the first year with a celebrity narrator), Cary Grant, Gregory Peck, John Wayne, Rock Hudson, Dean Jones, Jimmy Stewart, Howard Keel, Elliott Gould, Olympia Dukakis, Marie Osmond, Dick Van Dyke, James Earl Jones, Lin-Manuel Miranda, and Sterling K. Brown—narrates the Christmas story as massed choirs holding candles process down Main Street, U.S.A. to fill the area in front of the train station. The centerpiece is a large Christmas tree made of risers on which gathers a choir decked out in bright green robes. A full orchestra provides the music for the inspiring presentation, usually presented on 2 separate nights. The Disneyland *Candlelight Procession and Ceremony* moved to a new home at the Fantasyland Theater in 1998, returning to Main Street, U.S.A. in 2003; and in 2012 it was presented 20 nights. With the opening of Magic Kingdom at Walt Disney World in 1971, a Florida version of the *Candlelight Procession* began a similar tradition. It moved to the America Gardens Theatre in EPCOT in 1994. Also known as the *Candlelight Processional and Ceremony*. There were no productions held in 2020 due to the COVID-19 pandemic.

Candleshoe (film) A street-tough tomboy from Los Angeles poses as the long-lost heiress to a stately English manor called Candleshoe in this tale of larceny, adventure, and comedy. A series of cryptic clues leads 14-year-old Casey Brown on a wild and dangerous search for a long-lost treasure. In a rousing finale, Casey and a group of lovable characters from Candleshoe outduel a greedy con man and his rowdies for the treasure and

Candleshoe as well. Initial release in Los Angeles Dec. 16, 1977, in order to qualify for Academy Award consideration (it did not receive any nominations); general release Feb. 10, 1978. Directed by Norman Tokar. 101 min. Stars David Niven (Priory), Helen Hayes (Lady St. Edmund), Jodie Foster (Casey), Leo McKern (Bundage), Veronica Quilligan (Cluny), Ian Sharrock (Peter), Sarah Tamakuni (Anna), David Samuels (Bobby), John Alderson (Jenkins), Mildred Shay (Mrs. McCress), Michael Balfour (Mr. McCress), Vivian Pickles (Grimsworthy). Based on the book *Christmas at Candleshoe*, by Michael Innes. Look for David Niven in 4 roles: the loyal butler, Priory; Scots gardener Gipping; Irish chauffeur John Henry; and retired cavalry officer Colonel Dennis. The Tudor mansion used in the film as Candleshoe is a stately house north of London, in Warwickshire, England, called Compton Wynyates, which has been in the Compton family since the 13th century and was often visited by King Henry VIII. Filming also took place in downtown Los Angeles, and several other locales in England: Kidderminster, on the Severn Valley Railway; Hambleden village, near Buckinghamshire; and Pinewood Studios in London, where all the interiors were filmed.

Candy, John (1950–1994) Actor/comedian; appeared in *Splash* (Freddie Bauer) and *Cool Runnings* (Irv), and voiced Wilbur in *The Rescuers Down Under*.

Candy Cauldron, Disney's Disney villain–inspired candy shop in the West Side at Disney Springs (formerly Downtown Disney); opened Sep. 15, 1997.

Candy Palace Shop on Main Street, U.S.A. in Disneyland; opened Jul. 22, 1955. Also known as Candyland. The large front window allows passersby to view, and perhaps lick their lips a bit, as the confectioners make fudge or dip strawberries in chocolate. SEE ALSO MAIN STREET CONFECTIONERY (WALT DISNEY WORLD), WORLD BAZAAR CONFECTIONERY (TOKYO DISNEYLAND), BOARDWALK CANDY PALACE (DISNEYLAND PARIS), MAIN STREET SWEETS (HONG KONG DISNEYLAND), AND SWEETHEARTS CONFECTIONERY (SHANGHAI DISNEYLAND).

Cane (TV) Series on CBS; aired Sep. 25–Dec. 18, 2007. The Duques are a large Cuban American family who own a rum and sugar empire in South Florida. Patriarch Pancho Duque has 2 sons, 1 of whom is adopted, whose approaches to business are as different as their approaches to life. The series is an epic drama about the family's external rivalries and internal power struggles. Stars Jimmy Smits (Alex Vega), Hector Elizondo (Pancho Duque), Nestor Carbonell (Frank Duque), Rita Moreno (Amalia Duque), Paola Turbay (Isabel Vega), Eddie Matos (Henry Duque), Michael Trevino (Jaime Vega), Lina Esco (Katie Vega), Samuel Carman (Artie Vega). From CBS Paramount Network Television, in association with ABC Studios.

Canine Caddy (film) Pluto cartoon released May 30, 1941. Directed by Clyde Geronimi. Pluto gets into trouble with a gopher while caddying for Mickey, and the tunnels they make during the chase wreck the golf course.

Canine Casanova (film) Pluto cartoon released Jul. 27, 1945. Directed by Charles Nichols. Pluto falls in love with a female dachshund whom he must rescue from the pound, only to find a family of puppies at her home.

Canine Patrol (film) Pluto cartoon released Dec. 7, 1945. Directed by Charles Nichols. While patrolling the beach, Pluto runs into a baby turtle who he will not allow to go into the water because of a "No Swimming" sign. But when Pluto inadvertently falls in quicksand, the turtle saves him, and they become friends.

Canna Fine-dining restaurant in the Tokyo Disneyland Hotel; opened Jul. 8, 2008. Stylish meals are served in a contemporary dining room inspired by the red canna flower.

Cannibal Capers (film) Silly Symphony cartoon released Mar. 20, 1930. Directed by Burt Gillett. A jungle tribe's riotous musical celebration is brought to an end by the inopportune appearance of a fierce lion.

Cannon, Dyan Actress; appeared in *That Darn Cat* (Mrs. Flint, 1997), and on TV in *Rock 'n' Roll Mom* (Annie Hackett) and *The Beverly Hills Family Robinson* (Marsha Robinson).

Can't Buy Me Love (film) High school senior Ronald Miller longs to be popular and comes up with a unique plan—he hires the most popular cheerleader in school, Cindy Mancini, to be his girlfriend. Ronald is transformed almost overnight from nerd to the most popular guy on campus, but he does not notice when Cindy develops real affection for him. Released Aug. 14, 1987. Directed by Steve Rash. A Touchstone film. 94 min. Stars Patrick Dempsey (Ronald Miller), Amanda Peterson (Cindy Mancini), Dennis Dugan (David Miller), Courtney Gains (Kenneth Wurman). Filmed entirely in Tucson, Arizona, with Tucson High School becoming the school in the movie. Hundreds of the students there got a chance to show off their acting talents as extras.

Canteen, The Snack and milkshake stand on Tom Sawyer Island in Tokyo Disneyland; open Apr. 15, 1983–May 6, 2019.

Cantina de San Angel, La See La Cantina de San Angel.

Canvas Back Duck (film) Donald Duck cartoon released Dec. 25, 1953. Directed by Jack Hannah. At a carnival, Donald shows his strength on the various "strength machines" in order to make his nephews proud. When a boy tells the nephews that his father can beat Donald, Donald doesn't hesitate to agree to fight, only to discover the father is the hulking Peewee Pete. They fight in the ring, and Donald manages to win.

Cape Cod Buffet restaurant, inspired by the New England seaside, in Disney Newport Bay Club at Disneyland Paris; opened Apr. 12, 1992. Mediterranean and international cuisine are served.

Cape Cod Confections American Waterfront sweets and beverage shop, themed as a fire station, in Tokyo DisneySea; opened Sep. 3, 2013. Hosted by Coca-Cola.

Cape Cod Cook-Off Counter-service restaurant in American Waterfront at Tokyo DisneySea; opened Sep. 4, 2001, serving burgers, chicken, and fish. Live shows are performed in the Town Hall, marked by its tall, white clock tower. See also Duffy and Friends.

Cape May Cafe Seafood buffet dining in Disney's Beach Club Resort at Walt Disney World; opened Nov. 19, 1990. The restaurant has been known for its evening clambake and character breakfast over the years.

Capelli, Gaudenzio He spent a 33-year career supervising Disney publications in Italy. He retired in 1994 and was honored with a European Disney Legends Award in 1997.

Capers, Virginia (1925–2004) Actress; appeared in

The World's Greatest Athlete, *The North Avenue Irregulars* (Cleo), and *What's Love Got to Do with It* (choir mistress).

Capital Cities/ABC See American Broadcasting Company.

CAPS The acronym for Computer Animation Production System, this Academy Award–winning (1992) technology, utilized during the production of Disney animated features, allows artists to assemble the animation, background, special effects, and computer-animated elements onto the final piece of film.

Captain America: Civil War (film) Steve Rogers leads a newly formed team of Avengers in their efforts to safeguard humanity. But after an incident involving the Avengers results in collateral damage, political pressure mounts to install a system of accountability, headed by a governing body to oversee and direct the team. The new status quo fractures the Avengers, resulting in 2 camps—1 led by Steve Rogers and his desire for the Avengers to remain free to defend humanity without government interference, and the other following Tony Stark's surprising decision to support governmental oversight and accountability. Directed by Anthony and Joe Russo. Released May 6, 2016, also in 3-D and IMAX, after an Apr. 27 international release. Features most of the original *Avengers* cast; stars Chris Evans, Robert Downey Jr., Scarlett Johansson, Jeremy Renner, Elizabeth Olsen (Wanda Maximoff/Scarlet Witch), Sebastian Stan (Bucky Barnes/Winter Soldier), Paul Rudd (Scott Lang/Ant-Man), Tom Holland (Peter Parker/Spider-Man), Emily VanCamp (Sharon Carter/Agent 13), Don Cheadle (James Rhodes/War Machine). 147 min. Filmed in wide-screen format. From Marvel Studios.

Captain America: The Winter Soldier (film) After the cataclysmic events in New York City with the Avengers, Steve Rogers, aka Captain America, is living quietly in Washington, D.C., and trying to adjust to the modern world. But when a S.H.I.E.L.D. colleague comes under attack, Steve becomes embroiled in a web of intrigue that threatens to put the world at risk. Joining forces with Natasha Romanoff (Black Widow), Captain America struggles to expose the ever-widening conspiracy while fighting off professional assassins sent to silence him at every turn. When the full scope of the villainous plot is revealed, Captain America and the Black Widow enlist the help of a new ally, the Falcon.

However, they soon find themselves up against an unexpected and formidable enemy: the Winter Soldier. Directed by Anthony and Joe Russo. Released Apr. 4, 2014, after a Mar. 26 international release. Stars Chris Evans (Captain America), Scarlett Johansson (The Black Widow), Sebastian Stan (James "Bucky" Barnes/The Winter Soldier), Cobie Smulders (Maria Hill), Frank Grillo (Brock Rumlow/Crossbones), Emily VanCamp (Sharon Carter/Agent 13), Hayley Atwell (Peggy Carter), Robert Redford (Alexander Pierce), Samuel L. Jackson (Nick Fury), Jenny Agutter (World Security Council member), Anthony Mackie (Sam Wilson/The Falcon). 136 min. Filmed in wide-screen format. From Marvel Studios. Received an Academy Award nomination for Visual Effects (Dan DeLeeuw, Russell Earl, Bryan Grill, Dan Sudick).

Captain Cook's Hideaway Small lounge with a mahogany-capped bar at Disney's Polynesian Village Resort; opened Oct. 1, 1971. In the early years, the Saltwater Express, later known as Stratton & Christopher, performed. In 1993, it became Captain Cook's Snack and Ice Cream Co., and in 2006 was remodeled into Capt. Cook's, offering sandwiches, salads, and flatbreads.

Captain EO (film) A 3-D musical science fiction adventure film; shown at the Journey Into Imagination pavilion in EPCOT Center Sep. 12, 1986–Jul. 6, 1994, and in Tomorrowland at Disneyland Sep. 18, 1986–Apr. 6, 1997. Captain EO and his crew of mythical space creatures—Hooter, Fuzzball, the Geex, Major Domo, Minor Domo—discover a colorless planet where they are confronted by the Supreme Leader and her forces of darkness. Using the power of music, dance, and light, EO and his crew are able to turn the black-and-white land into a magical world of color and happiness. 17 min. Also shown in Tomorrowland at Tokyo Disneyland Mar. 20, 1987–Sep. 1, 1996, and in *Ciné Magique* in Discoveryland at Disneyland Paris Apr. 12, 1992–Aug. 17, 1998. Stars Michael Jackson, Anjelica Huston, Dick Shawn. George Lucas was exec. producer and Francis Ford Coppola was director. To honor Michael Jackson after his death in 2009, the film ran again in Disneyland Feb. 23, 2010–Jun. 17, 2014; Disneyland Paris Jun. 12, 2010–Apr. 12, 2015; Tokyo Disneyland Jul. 1, 2010–Jun. 30, 2014; and EPCOT Jul. 2, 2010–Dec. 6, 2015.

Captain EO Backstage (TV) Show aired May 15, 1988. Directed by Muffett Kaufman. Behind the scenes of the making of the Michael Jackson film, edited from a Disney Channel special entitled *The Making of Captain EO* that aired with *Justin Case* in the Disney anthology time slot.

Captain Hook Menacing leader of the pirates in Never Land in *Peter Pan*; voiced by Hans Conried. The animators actually had a difficult time deciding how to handle the character's hook. James M. Barrie, the author of the original story, had the hook on the right arm, but the animators anticipated problems with that in animation. They wanted Hook to be able to make gestures, write, and perform other actions that are simpler to do with the right hand. So they made the decision to place the hook on the left.

Captain Hook's Galley Fantasyland quick-service restaurant in Disneyland, 1969–Aug. 29, 1982. Formerly the Chicken of the Sea Pirate Ship and Restaurant (1955–1969). Also opened in Fantasyland at Tokyo Disneyland, though not in a ship, Apr. 15, 1983. A version opened in Adventureland at Disneyland Paris Apr. 12, 1992; it closed in 2011, to remove the food-service facility, and reopened Mar. 2012 as the interactive Pirate Galleon.

Captain Jack's Oyster Bar Restaurant and lounge in the Lake Buena Vista Shopping Village (later Downtown Disney Marketplace) at Walt Disney World; opened Mar. 22, 1975. Located over the water of Village Lake, it was a popular spot to enjoy freshly shucked oysters, clams on the half shell, and the specialty frozen strawberry margarita. Named after Jack Olsen, who headed merchandise operations at Walt Disney World. It became Cap'n Jack's Restaurant Feb. 20, 2000, and closed Aug. 17, 2013.

Captain Jack's – Restaurant des Pirates Adventureland tavern in Disneyland Paris; opened Jul. 24, 2017, as an update to the Blue Lagoon Restaurant, with the staff now dressed as pirates. Seafood and creole dishes are served.

Captain John Smith Explorer who falls in love with Pocahontas; voiced by Mel Gibson.

Captain Marvel (film) Leaving her earthly life behind, Carol Danvers joins an intergalactic, elite Kree military team called Starforce, led by their enigmatic commander, Yon-Rogg. But after Danvers has trained and worked with the Starforce team, and become a valued member, she finds herself back on Earth with new questions about her past. While on Earth, she quickly lands on the radar of Nick Fury, and they must work together against a formidable enemy in the form of the Skrulls—the notorious Marvel bad guys made even more dangerous by their shape-shifting abilities—and their leader, Talos, who is spearheading a Skrull invasion of Earth. Released Mar. 8, 2019, also in 3-D and IMAX, after a Mar. 6 international release. Directed by Anna Boden and Ryan Fleck. Stars Brie Larson (Carol Danvers/Captain Marvel), Samuel L. Jackson (Nick Fury), Ben Mendelsohn (Talos), Annette Bening (Supreme Intelligence), Clark Gregg (Agent Coulson), Jude Law (Yon-Rogg). Based on the Marvel comic book series first published in 1967. The cat, Goose, was played primarily by a tabby named Reggie, who had 3 stand-ins (Archie, Gonzo, and Rizzo). 124 min. Filmed in wide-screen format.

Captain Ron (film) Floundering in a sea of stress, corporate executive Martin Harvey dreams of glamour, adventure, and nonstop cruises when he inherits his uncle's yacht. But when the family casts off, they soon discover the newly acquired craft is badly in need of an overhaul. Not knowing where to turn, the Harveys find their chances for a spontaneous adventure resurfacing when they encounter Captain Ron, a bedraggled and dreadlocked happy-go-lucky professional seafarer with dubious nautical skills. Even though the Harveys worry about Captain Ron setting a bad example for their children, a trip with him brings exciting adventures with guerrillas and pirates and a newfound respect for the bumbling sailor and his carefree nature. Released Sep. 18, 1992. Directed by Thom Eberhardt. A Touchstone film. 100 min. Stars Kurt Russell (Captain Ron), Martin Short (Martin Harvey), Mary Kay Place (Katherine Harvey). Much of the filming took place in and around Puerto Rico. Two identical 58-foot ketches from Florida became the before and after versions of *The Wanderer*.

Captain Sparky vs. The Flying Saucers (film) Stop-motion animated short; released Jan. 8, 2013, on the *Frankenweenie* Blu-ray. Victor plays a homemade sci-fi movie in which his faithful dog fends off an alien invasion in space. Directed by Mark Waring. Features the voice of Charlie Tahan (Victor Frankenstein). 3 min.

Captain's Galley SEE NEVER LAND POOL.

Captain's Grille Restaurant in Disney's Yacht Club Resort at Walt Disney World; opened Jan. 1, 2008, replacing the Yacht Club Galley. Closed May 24, 2017, temporarily moving into the nearby event space, Ariel's. On Nov. 4, 2017, the original location reopened as Ale & Compass Restaurant.

Captain's Tower Wooden landmark and pavilion at the center of the Lake Buena Vista Shopping Village (later Downtown Disney Marketplace); used for entertainment, seasonal merchandise displays, and special sales until Apr. 28, 2002. It became Disney's Pin Traders in Jul. 2002.

Captive Stallion, The (TV) Title of part 1 of *Comanche (Tonka)*.

Car Toon Spin SEE ROGER RABBIT'S CAR TOON SPIN.

Caravan Carousel Attraction in Arabian Coast at Tokyo DisneySea; opened Sep. 4, 2001. A 2-level carousel, featuring ebony horses, camels, elephants, griffins, and even the Genie himself.

Caravan Pictures Headed by Joe Roth and Roger Birnbaum, who signed an exclusive agreement with Disney in 1993 to produce at least 25 films to be distributed by Buena Vista Pictures Distribution. Their first pictures included *Angie, Angels in the Outfield, The Three Musketeers, I Love Trouble, A Low Down Dirty Shame, Houseguest, The Jerky Boys*, and *Heavyweights*. Caravan ceased to exist in 1999, and a new company, Spyglass Entertainment, headed by Birnbaum and Gary Barber, succeeded it.

Card Corner Shop, sponsored by Gibson, on Main Street, U.S.A. in Disneyland; open Jun. 14, 1985–Oct. 1988. Gibson earlier had a greeting card shop at another location Jul. 17, 1955–1959. SEE ALSO CAREFREE CORNER.

Careers in Math & Science: A Different View (film) Educational film; released in Sep. 1986. 19 min. Explores the importance of math and science classes to a student's future.

Carefree Corner Guest registration area on Main Street, U.S.A. in Disneyland, sponsored by INA (1956–1974); opened Aug. 22, 1956, taking the place of Plaza Apartments, and closed in 1985. Guests could sign their names in a book from their home state. It later became Card Corner, then returned to the Carefree Corner name in 1988. On Nov. 19, 1994, the area became Main Street Photo Supply. Also a photo souvenir and sundries shop on Mickey Avenue in Shanghai Disneyland; opened Jun. 16, 2016.

Careless Charlie Animated character in a number of the educational films made for the Coordinator of Inter-American Affairs unit during World War II. SEE SOUTH AMERICA.

Carell, Steve Actor; appeared in the title role in *Dan in Real Life* and as Ben in *Alexander and the Terrible, Horrible, No Good, Very Bad Day*. He voiced Mr. Delancey in *Disney's Fillmore*.

Carey, Harry, Jr. (1921–2012) Actor; appeared in *The Great Locomotive Chase* (William Bensinger), *Run, Cougar, Run* (Barney), and *Tombstone* (Marshal Fred White), and on TV in *Spin and Marty*, *Texas John Slaughter*, and *Ride a Northbound Horse*.

Carey, Mariah Singer/actress; she was named the godmother of the *Disney Fantasy* ship, which she christened in New York City. She recorded "Almost Home" for *Oz The Great and Powerful* and has performed on TV in the *Walt Disney World Christmas Day Parade*.

Caribbean Arcade The Walt Disney World counterpart to the Pirates Arcade in Disneyland; opened in Caribbean Plaza in the Magic Kingdom ca. 1974. Closed ca. 1980; succeeded by Lafitte's Portrait Deck. Also known as Caverna de los Piratas.

Caribbean Beach Resort, Disney's Resort hotel themed to the Caribbean islands; opened Oct. 1, 1988, as the first of Disney's moderate-priced hotels at Walt Disney World. At opening, it was one of the largest hotels anywhere in Florida. Guests stay in 1 of 5 island villages—Aruba, Barbados, Jamaica, Martinique, or Trinidad. Old Port Royale houses a food marketplace, restaurant, and merchandise facilities. A major refurbishment in 2018 added Sebastian's Bistro, a new front desk/concierge area in Old Port Royale, and moved the resort entryway from Buena Vista Drive to Victory Way. SEE OLD PORT ROYALE.

Caribbean Plaza Area in Adventureland in the Magic Kingdom at Walt Disney World; opened Dec. 1973, with Pirates of the Caribbean. Quaint shops and shaded courtyards evoke the romance of a tropical port city.

Carl Fredricksen Retired balloon salesman in *Up*; voiced by Ed Asner.

Carlo, the Sierra Coyote (TV) Show aired Feb. 3, 1974. Directed by James Algar. A coyote tries to escape the encroachment of man onto his territory and is befriended by the wife of a couple monitoring the environment for the government. The husband is suspicious of the coyote, but Carlo helps lead rescue dogs to him when he is lost. Stars Jana Milo, Steven S. Stewart, Hal Bokar, Dale Alexander.

Carlson, Joyce (1923–2008) After spending a decade and a half in the Disney Ink & Paint Department, she joined WED Enterprises as a show designer and was instrumental in designing and maintaining such attractions as It's a Small World and the Carousel of Progress. She retired in 2000 after 56 years at Disney and was named a Disney Legend the same year.

Carnation Café Table-service restaurant serving American comfort food on Main Street, U.S.A. in Disneyland; opened Mar. 21, 1997, on the patio of the former Carnation Ice Cream Parlor. It expanded Jun. 13, 2012, into the space vacated by Blue Ribbon Bakery. Diners enjoyed visiting with chef Oscar Martinez, who started at the Carnation Ice Cream Parlor in 1967; he retired Sep. 27, 2017, after 61 years at the park.

Carnation Ice Cream Parlor A mainstay on Main Street, U.S.A. in Disneyland; opened Jul. 17, 1955, where one could enjoy a meal or just an ice cream confection. An outdoor patio was added in 1977. On Mar. 21, 1997, the Blue Ribbon Bakery moved inside, while the patio became the Carnation Café.

Carnation Plaza Gardens Counter-service food and entertainment area in the Central Plaza at Disneyland; opened Aug. 18, 1956, and closed Apr. 2012 to become the Royal Theater at Fantasy Faire. Fondly remembered for live musical performances, special events, and swing dancing. Prior to its opening, it was the site of the Disneyland bandstand, which was moved to Magnolia Park in Frontierland.

Carney, Alan (1911–1973) Actor; appeared in *The Absent-Minded Professor* (First Referee), *Son of Flubber* (Referee), *Monkeys, Go Home!*

(Grocer), *The Adventures of Bullwhip Griffin* (Joe Turner), *Blackbeard's Ghost* (Bartender), and *Herbie Rides Again* (Judge).

Carney, Art (1918–2003) Actor; appeared on TV in *Christmas in Disneyland with Art Carney*, and on The Disney Channel in the movies *The Undergrads* and *The Blue Yonder*.

Carnival Time (TV) Show aired Mar. 4, 1962. Directed by Hamilton S. Luske. Ludwig Von Drake hosts a look at the major carnivals held in Rio de Janeiro and New Orleans, aided by José Carioca and Donald Duck, respectively, in the 2 cities.

Carol & Co. (TV) Series on NBC; aired Mar. 31, 1990–Aug. 19, 1991. Each week's show featured the ensemble cast playing different roles in comedic skits. Stars Carol Burnett, Meagen Fay, Terry Kiser, Richard Kind, Anita Barone, Peter Krause, Jeremy Piven. The show won Emmy Awards for Costume Design and for guest star Swoosie Kurtz. Continued on CBS as *The Carol Burnett Show*.

Carol Burnett Show, The (TV) Series on CBS; aired Nov. 1–Dec. 27, 1991. Continued *Carol & Co.* as a variety show, with Meagen Fay and Richard Kind being the only holdovers in the cast.

Carolwood Pacific Historical Society Michael Broggie (son of Roger Broggie, who helped Walt build his scale-model railroad) and his wife formed the society to perpetuate Walt's love of trains. After Lillian Disney died, the society arranged with the Los Angeles Live Steamers for Walt's barn, from which he operated his train, to be moved to Griffith Park in Los Angeles, where it opened in 1999. An exhibit was placed inside the barn, and later additions to the collection included Ollie Johnston's scale-model train station and the combine car from the original Santa Fe and Disneyland Railroad. It was later named The Carolwood Society.

Carolwood Pacific Railroad Walt Disney's love for trains led him to create this ⅛-scale-model railroad in his own backyard in LA's Holmby Hills in the early 1950s. It was named for the street on which the house was located. To keep things official, he even had his wife, Lillian, sign over to him a right-of-way through her flower gardens. The Carolwood Pacific later inspired Disney to include a railroad system in his plans for Disneyland.

Carolwood Records A sister country music imprint

to the Lyric Street Records label, part of the Disney Music Group; created Oct. 2, 2008, and located in Nashville, Tennessee. Their first album, in Sep. 2009, was *Love and Theft*. The label closed Nov. 2009.

Carolyn's Couture Designer apparel boutique in the Lake Buena Vista Shopping Village at Walt Disney World; opened Mar. 1975. Closed Sep. 30, 1978, to be incorporated into the Country Address shop.

Carousel Coffee Quick-service lobby café in Disney's BoardWalk Inn at Walt Disney World; opened Dec. 28, 2022, replacing Dundy's Sundries.

Carousel Inn & Suites Hotel across Harbor Boulevard from Disneyland; purchased by Disney Mar. 23, 2015, but operated by its existing management. The 5-story hotel featured 131 rooms. Closed Oct. 2016.

Carousel of Progress Attraction in the Progressland pavilion at the 1964–1965 New York World's Fair; opened Apr. 22, 1964, presented by General Electric. The show moved to Tomorrowland in Disneyland, where it ran Jul. 2, 1967–Sep. 9, 1973 (later replaced by America Sings), and then to the Magic Kingdom at Walt Disney World, opening Jan. 15, 1975. At the World's Fair and in Disneyland, the attraction introduced the popular theme song, "There's a Great Big Beautiful Tomorrow," written by Richard M. and Robert B. Sherman, which echoed General Electric's then-current philosophy. The show provides an entertaining glimpse at electrical progress in America, past and present. Guests are seated in a large auditorium that revolves around 6 stages, in which an Audio-Animatronics family presents the warm, sometimes humorous, story of life in "the good old days," in 4 main scenes, from the turn of the 20th century to the 1920s, 1940s, and, finally, into the near future. At Disneyland, audiences exited the theater by walking right onto the stage and taking a ramp up to the attraction's second level, where an enormous model, called Progress City, showcased many of the forward-thinking ideas that were being considered for Walt Disney's proposed community of tomorrow, EPCOT. The attraction was updated for its move to Walt Disney World, with the theme song changed to "The Best Time of Your Life," also written by the Sherman brothers, but reflecting General Electric's changed philosophy. General Electric ended sponsorship in 1985, and the show was completely rewritten in 1993, reopening in Nov. as Walt Disney's Carousel of Progress. For this latest incarnation, the attraction was repositioned as a tribute to Walt, and the original theme song returned. The scenes were also tied into 4 holidays as the story progressed. As the show was updated over the years, several different American actors provided the voice of Father: Rex Allen (1964–1973), Andrew Duggan (1975–1993), and Jean Shepherd (beginning in 1993); Rex Allen returned to voice the grandfather for the 1993 version. The idea for the Carousel of Progress originated in a proposed, but never-built, expansion of Disneyland called Edison Square. The show is widely considered to be representative of Walt Disney's personal philosophy, including his love of nostalgia and his "incurable optimism" for a brighter tomorrow.

Carpenter, Sabrina Actress; appeared on Disney Channel in *Girl Meets World* (Maya Hart), *Adventures in Babysitting* (Jenny), and the *Radio Disney Music Awards*; on Disney+ in *Clouds* (Sammy); and on ABC in the *Disney Parks Frozen Christmas Celebration, Disneyland 60: The Wonderful World of Disney*, and *The Disney Family Singalong: Volume II*. She voiced Princess Vivian in *Sofia the First*, Melissa Chase in *Milo Murphy's Law*, and Nina Glitter in *Mickey and the Roadster Racers*. In 2013, she became a recording artist for Hollywood Records.

Carpoolers (TV) Sitcom on ABC; aired Oct. 2, 2007–Mar. 4, 2008. The show follows the lives of 4 suburban husbands and dads who carpool to work together each day. Stars Fred Goss (Gracen), Jerry Minor (Aubrey), Jerry O'Connell (Laird), Tim Peper (Dougie). From ABC Studios, DreamWorks Television, and 3 Arts Entertainment.

Carradine, Robert Actor; appeared in *Max Keeble's Big Move* (Don) and *The Lizzie McGuire Movie* (Sam McGuire); on TV in *The Liberators, Disney's Totally Minnie* (Maxwell Dweeb), and *Mom's Got a Date with a Vampire* (Malachi Van Helsing); and on Disney Channel in *Lizzie McGuire* (Sam McGuire).

Carrey, Jim Actor; appeared in *Simon Birch* (adult Joe Wenteworth) and provided the voices of Ebenezer Scrooge and the ghosts in *Disney's A Christmas Carol*.

Carroll, Leo G. (1892–1972) Actor; appeared in *The Parent Trap* (Reverend Mosby).

Carroll, Lewis (1832–1898) Author of the book *Alice's Adventures in Wonderland*, published in 1865.

Carroll, Pat (1927–2022) Actress; she provided the voice of Ursula in *The Little Mermaid* and other appearances of the character, Morgana in *The Little Mermaid II: Return to the Sea*, and Old Lady Crowley in *Tangled: The Series*.

Carrousel de Lancelot, Le SEE LE CARROUSEL DE LANCELOT.

Cars (film) Animated feature from Pixar Animation Studios. Lightning McQueen, a hotshot rookie race car driven to succeed, discovers that life is about the journey, not the finish line, when he finds himself unexpectedly detoured in the sleepy Route 66 town of Radiator Springs. En route across the country to the big Piston Cup Championship in California to compete against 2 seasoned pros, Lightning gets to know the town's offbeat characters—including Sally (a snazzy 2002 Porsche), Doc Hudson (a 1951 Hudson Hornet with a mysterious past), and Mater (a rusty but trusty tow truck)—who help him realize that there are more important things than trophies, fame, and sponsorship. Released Jun. 9, 2006. A world premiere was held May 26, 2006, at Lowe's Motor Speedway in Charlotte, North Carolina. Directed by John Lasseter. Voices include Paul Newman (Doc Hudson), Richard Petty (The King), Owen Wilson (Lightning McQueen), Bonnie Hunt (Sally), Larry the Cable Guy (Mater) Cheech Marin (Ramone), George Carlin (Fillmore), Michael Keaton (Chick Hicks), Tony Shalhoub (Luigi), John Ratzenberger (Mack), Michael Wallis (Sheriff), Paul Dooley (Sarge), Jenifer Lewis (Flo), Katherine Helmond (Lizzie). 117 min. Computer-animated film. The idea for the film came from Lasseter's love of cars and a 2000 road trip with his family across the country. Randy Newman provided the score. The film is dedicated to longtime story man Joe Ranft, who passed away in 2005 after his work on the film was completed. Nominated for 2 Academy Awards: Best Original Song ("Our Town," by Randy Newman) and Best Animated Feature (John Lasseter).

Cars Land A 12-acre themed area in Disney California Adventure; opened Jun. 15, 2012. The town of Radiator Springs from Disney • Pixar's *Cars* is re-created in great detail, with attractions, including Luigi's Rollickin' Roadsters (formerly Luigi's Flying Tires), Mater's Junkyard Jamboree, and

Radiator Springs Racers. Dining is offered at the Cozy Cone Motel, Flo's V8 Cafe, and Fillmore's Taste-In, with shopping at Ramone's House of Body Art, Sarge's Surplus Hut, and Radiator Springs Curios. The Ornament Valley mountains serve as a majestic backdrop for the land; car buffs may notice the 6 mountain peaks look like tail fins of classic Cadillac models from 1957–1962. The land was originally proposed by Imagineer Kevin Rafferty as Carland, a celebration of California's car culture, before the Imagineers ever knew Pixar was working on a movie about cars.

Cars on the Road (TV) Original animated series on Disney+; digitally released Sep. 8, 2022. Lightning McQueen and Mater embark on a cross-country road trip to meet up with Mater's sister, encountering outrageous roadside attractions and colorful new characters along the way. Voices include Larry the Cable Guy (Mater), Owen Wilson (Lightning McQueen). Each episode is approx. 8 min. From Pixar Animation Studios.

Cars Quatre Roues Rallye Attraction in Worlds of Pixar (previously in Toon Studio) in Walt Disney Studios Park at Disneyland Paris; opened Jun. 9, 2007. Guests spin in cars in an attraction themed to a Radiator Springs service station from *Cars*.

Cars ROAD TRIP Worlds of Pixar attraction in Walt Disney Studios Park at Disneyland Paris; opened Jun. 17, 2021, following a Jun. 15 soft opening. Riders take an adventure along Route 66, glimpsing wacky roadside attractions, appearances by the *Cars* characters, and a flash flood car wash in Cars-tastrophe Canyon. Superseded the Studio Tram Tour.

Cars Toons (TV) Series of interstitial shorts in which the *Cars* characters are placed in comic situations; premiered Oct. 27, 2008, on Toon Disney and subsequently on Disney Channel and ABC Family. In the first 10 made-for-TV shorts, called *Mater's Tall Tales*, the rusty but trusty tow truck tells stories that may or may not be true: *Rescue Squad Mater, Mater the Greater, El Materdor, Unidentified Flying Mater, Monster Truck Mater, Heavy Metal Mater, Moon Mater, Mater Private Eye, Air Mater,* and *Time Travel Mater*. Mater's voice is provided by Larry the Cable Guy. Directed by John Lasseter and co-directed by Victor Navone and Rob Gibbs. 3 min. each. From Pixar Animation Studios. On Mar. 22, 2013, a series of 3 short *Cars Toons*, known as *Tales from Radiator Springs*, premiered on Disney Channel: *Hiccups, Bugged,* and *Spinning*. Directed by Jeremy Lasky and produced at Pixar Canada. SEE ALSO MATER AND THE GHOSTLIGHT; TOKYO MATER; AND RADIATOR SPRINGS 500½, THE.

Cars 2 (film) Animated feature from Pixar Animation Studios. Star race car Lightning McQueen and the tow truck Mater head overseas to compete in the first-ever World Grand Prix to determine the world's fastest car. Lightning faces his key competitor, the Italian Francesco Bernoulli. Mater gets caught up in an intriguing adventure of his own—international espionage, helping secret agent Finn McMissile and his associate, Holley Shiftwell, try to outwit the villains. Torn between assisting Lightning McQueen in the high-profile race and participating in a top secret spy mission, Mater undertakes a journey that leads him on an explosive chase through the streets of cities and towns in Japan, Italy, France, and Britain. Luckily, Mater's friends have come along and are able to help their old pal. Directed by John Lasseter and Brad Lewis. Released Jun. 24, 2011. Voices include Owen Wilson (Lightning McQueen), Larry the Cable Guy (Mater), John Turturro (Francesco Bernoulli), Michael Caine (Finn McMissile), Emily Mortimer (Holley Shiftwell), Eddie Izzard (Miles Axelrod), Vanessa Redgrave (The Queen/Mama Topolino), Bonnie Hunt (Sally), Tony Shalhoub (Luigi), Katherine Helmond (Lizzie), John Ratzenberger (Mack). Filmed in CinemaScope, with also Disney Digital 3-D and IMAX versions, and released with the short *Hawaiian Vacation*.

Cars 3 (film) Animated feature from Pixar Animation Studios. Blindsided by a new generation of blazing-fast racers, the legendary Lightning McQueen is suddenly pushed out of the sport he loves. To get back in the game, he will need the help of an eager, young race technician, Cruz Ramirez, with her own plan to win, plus inspiration from the late Fabulous Hudson Hornet and a few unexpected turns. Proving that #95 is not through yet will test the heart of a champion on Piston Cup Racing's biggest stage. Directed by Brian Fee. Released Jun. 16, 2017, also in 3-D, after Jun. 10 premiere festivities at the Anaheim Convention Center and Cars Land at Disney California Adventure and a Jun. 15 international release. Voices include Owen Wilson (Lightning McQueen), Cristela Alonzo (Cruz Ramirez), Larry the Cable Guy (Mater), Armie Hammer

(Jackson Storm), Nathan Fillion (Sterling), Cheech Marin (Ramone), Michael Wallis (Sheriff), Paul Dooley (Sarge), Kerry Washington (Natalie Certain), Bonnie Hunt (Sally Carrera), Tony Shalhoub (Luigi). 102 min. A new rendering system was used to make the film look more physically accurate than the previous Cars films, correctly modeling how light bounces off and interacts with materials and revealing such tiny details as concentric scratches and metallic flakes within car paint schemes. Filmed in wide-screen format. Released with the short *Lou*.

Carson, Blain Actor; appeared on the *Mickey Mouse Club* on The Disney Channel, 1991–1993.

Carson, Sofia Actress/singer; appeared in *Tini: El gran cambio de Violetta* (Melanie); on Disney Channel in the Descendants movies (Evie), *Austin & Ally* (Chelsea), *Adventures in Babysitting* (Lola), and the *Radio Disney Music Awards*; and on Disney+ in *Turning the Tables with Robin Roberts*. She voiced Maliga in *Elena of Avalor* and also made TV appearances in *Disneyland 60: The Wonderful World of Disney*, *Decorating Disney: Holiday Magic*, *Mickey's 90th Spectacular*, *The Disney Family Singalong*, *Disney Parks Unforgettable Christmas Celebration*, and *The Wonderful World of Disney: Magical Holiday Celebration*. She signed with Hollywood Records in 2016.

Carter, Charita Imagineer; she began at Walt Disney Imagineering in 1997 in accounting and finance, then joined the Scenic Illusions team as a creative producer, applying advanced visual effects to classic attractions. She has served as lead creative producer for Mickey & Minnie's Runaway Railway and Tiana's Bayou Adventure. In 2022, she was named executive creative producer of Relevancy Activations.

Carter, Jimmy As president, he addressed the 26th World Congress of the International Chamber of Commerce in the Magic Kingdom at Walt Disney World on Oct. 1, 1978. The former president jogged through Disneyland before it opened to guests one morning in May 1982. He has logged several visits to Walt Disney World over the years.

Carthay Circle Restaurant and Lounge Fine-dining restaurant at the end of Buena Vista Street in Disney California Adventure; opened Jun. 15, 2012. Signature dishes are served at the restaurant upstairs (200 indoor seats and 56 on the terrace), while downstairs is the 68-seat lounge. Fire Cracker Duck Wings have been a popular appetizer. The Spanish colonial–revival architecture was inspired by the former Carthay Circle Theatre in Los Angeles, where *Snow White and the Seven Dwarfs* premiered in 1937. Also in the building is a private lounge named 1901, exclusive to Club 33 members.

Carthay Circle Theatre Famed Hollywood theater that saw the premiere of *Snow White and the Seven Dwarfs* on Dec. 21, 1937. A road show engagement of *Fantasia*, with a Fantasound installation, played there for many months in 1941. The theater was demolished in 1969. It later inspired the Carthay Circle Restaurant in Disney California Adventure, as well as architecture on Sunset Boulevard in Disney-MGM Studios (now Disney's Hollywood Studios) and on Mickey Avenue in Shanghai Disneyland.

Cartoon All-Stars to the Rescue (TV) Special aired simultaneously throughout North America on most TV stations Apr. 21, 1990; released on video in association with McDonald's and the Academy of Television Arts and Sciences in Jun. 1990. TV's most popular cartoon characters (including Winnie the Pooh, Tigger, and Huey, Dewey, and Louie) help a young girl free her brother from the grip of drugs. Roy E. Disney was exec. producer.

Carvey, Dana Actor; appeared in *Tough Guys* (Richie Evans) and in Cranium Command in Wonders of Life at EPCOT (Right Ventricle).

Casa de Fritos Frontierland restaurant serving Mexican food at Disneyland; opened Aug. 11, 1955. A highlight for kids was dropping a coin into a slot, prompting the Frito Kid to deliver a small bag of Fritos by way of an elaborate mechanism. Became Casa Mexicana Oct. 1, 1982, and Rancho del Zocalo Feb. 6, 2001.

Casablanca Carpets Shop in Morocco at EPCOT; opened Sep. 7, 1984, offering decorative items.

Casanova (film) For the first time in his life, the legendary seducer, swashbuckler, master of disguise, and wit, Casanova, is about to meet his match with an alluring Venetian beauty, Francesca, who does the one thing he never thought possible: refuse him. Through a series of clever disguises and scheming ruses, he manages to get ever closer to Francesca. But he is playing the most dangerous game he has ever encountered—one that will risk not only his life and reputation, but his only chance at true passion. Limited release Dec. 25, 2005; general release Jan. 6, 2006. Directed by Lasse Hallström. A Touchstone film. Stars Heath Ledger (Giacomo Casanova), Sienna Miller (Francesca Bruni), Lena Olin (Andrea Bruni), Jeremy Irons (Bishop Pucci), Oliver Platt (Papprizzio). Began filming in Aug. 2004 in Venice, Italy, and was screened at the Venice Film Festival on Sep. 2, 2005. Filmed in Super 35-Scope.

Casbah Food Court Counter-service restaurant in Arabian Coast at Tokyo DisneySea; opened Sep. 4, 2001. Curry dishes are sold at food stalls.

Case of Murder, A (TV) Show; the first episode of *The Further Adventures of Gallegher.*

Case of the Missing Space, The (film) Educational film with Figment in the Language Arts Through Imagination series, where viewers solve a mystery message by deciphering scrambled words and symbols; released in Sep. 1989. 16 min.

Case of Treason, A (TV) Show; the 6th episode of *The Swamp Fox.*

Casebusters (TV) Show aired May 25, 1986. A brother and sister enjoy life in their suburban neighborhood—until a mysterious crime threatens their grandfather's small security business. Together they team up to solve the crime, conducting an investigation which leads them through some pretty hairy adventures. Directed by Wes Craven. Stars Noah Hathaway, Virginia Keehne, Pat Hingle, Gary Riley.

Casella, Max Actor; starred in *Newsies* (Racetrack) and *Ed Wood* (Paul Marco). He voiced Zini in *Dinosaur*, Tip in *The Little Mermaid II*, Tom Morrow 2.0 in Innoventions at EPCOT, and performed in the opening cast of *The Lion King* on Broadway (Timon).

Caselotti, Adriana (1916–1997) As a teenager, Caselotti provided the voice of Snow White. She was the first of 150 young girls tested for the role and was just 18 years old when Walt Disney selected her. The childlike quality of her voice appealed to Disney, who had been looking for someone younger to voice the princess. Caselotti reports, "I didn't tell anyone my age." She was named a Disney Legend in 1994.

Casey at the Bat (film) Segment of *Make Mine Music*, "A Musical Recitation" by Jerry Colonna, about the mighty but vain ballplayer who strikes out to end the game when his team had a chance to win it. Released as a short Jul. 16, 1954.

Casey Bats Again (film) Special cartoon released Jun. 18, 1954. Directed by Jack Kinney. Casey is dismayed while trying to have sons that can follow in their dad's footsteps. He instead has 9 daughters—just enough for a baseball team. He tries to regain his former glory with his all-daughter baseball team, which wins the championship despite Casey's interference.

Casey Jones Star of *The Brave Engineer* (1950).

Casey Jr. Determined little circus train in *Dumbo*; voiced by Margaret Wright. He first appeared in a segment of *The Reluctant Dragon* in which sound effects are showcased.

Casey Jr. Circus Train Fantasyland attraction in Disneyland; opened Jul. 31, 1955. Themed after the train in *Dumbo*. Before Storybook Land opened in 1956, this was simply a train ride, but the new attraction gave guests something to see as they rode around the small hills at the side of Fantasyland. Because of mechanical problems, the attraction was not ready for operation on opening day; it took 2 weeks to work the bugs out. SEE LE PETIT TRAIN DU CIRQUE (DISNEYLAND PARIS).

Casey's Corner Coca-Cola refreshment shop on Main Street, U.S.A. in Disneyland Paris; opened Apr. 12, 1992, serving hot dogs and soft drinks. Also the new name of the Coca-Cola Refreshment Corner in the Magic Kingdom at Walt Disney World, beginning May 27, 1995. Themed to the animated film *Casey at the Bat*.

Cassidy, Joanna Actress; appeared in *Who Framed Roger Rabbit* (Dolores) and *Where the Heart Is* (Jean), and on TV in *Bar Girls* (Claudia Reese), *Criminal Minds* (Mrs. Holden), *Desperate Housewives* (Melina Cominis), *Perception* (Ruby), and *Switched at Birth* (Lucille).

Cast Member Disney term for an employee. Disney theme park Cast Members are considered performers, as if they were onstage in a theater. They are putting on a show for the guests (never customers). Therefore, Cast Members wear costumes, not uniforms. When Disney Cast Members are in the park, they are onstage; when they return to their break areas, offices, or dressing rooms, they are backstage. They are known around the world for their exceptional service.

Castaway, The (film) Mickey Mouse cartoon released Apr. 6, 1931. Directed by Wilfred Jackson. Mickey is shipwrecked on an island after being adrift on a raft. Mickey plays a piano that has washed ashore, until a gorilla destroys it. Mickey manages to escape from the gorilla, plus a lion and an alligator. He then floats downstream on a turtle, which he stood on thinking it was a rock.

Castaway Cay Disney's 1,000-acre private island in The Bahamas, offering a daylong recreational stopover for Disney Cruise Line passengers beginning in 1998. The island was previously uninhabited, originally known as Gorda Cay, until shortly after the Disney purchase in Feb. 1996. Castaway Cay is fully themed, with Disney character greetings and activities for the whole family, including Castaway Family Beach; Serenity Bay, an adult-only beach with cabanas; Snorkeling Lagoon; the Pelican Plunge and Sprink-a-Leak water-play areas; kid's activities at Scuttle's Cove; the In Da Shade Game Pavilion; shopping at Buy the Seashore, Bahamian Retail, and She Sells Seashells . . . and Everything Else; and snorkel and watercraft rentals at Gil's Fins and Boats. All-you-can-eat lunch is served at Cookie's BBQ and Cookie's Too BBQ. Snorkelers might spot one of the *Nautilus* ride vehicles, from the former 20,000 Leagues Under the Sea attraction at Walt Disney World, submerged in the water. For several years, beginning in 2006, the 175-ft. *Flying Dutchman* ship, used in *Pirates of the Caribbean: Dead Man's Chest* and *Pirates of the Caribbean: At World's End*, was anchored offshore. The runDisney Castaway Cay 5K Challenge was introduced in 2014. "Cay" is pronounced "key."

Castaway Cowboy, The (film) On the island of Kauai, during the 1850s, a widow rancher, Henrietta MacAvoy, and her son, Booten, rescue Lincoln Costain from drowning. Lincoln is a Texas cowboy who had been stranded aboard a ship from which he elected to jump. Costain is persuaded to teach the local Hawaiian farmhands how to become cowboys so that they can profit from the wild cattle on Henrietta's land. After stopping a stampede, and eliminating his business/romantic competition, Costain remains on the island to guide his cadre of new cowboys. Released Aug. 7, 1974. Directed by Vincent McEveety. 91 min. Stars James Garner (Costain), Vera Miles (Henrietta), Robert Culp (Bryson), Eric Shea (Booton), Manu Tupou (Kimo), Gregory Sierra (Marrujo), Shug Fisher (Capt. Carey), Ralph Hanalei (Hopu), Kahana (Oka). The production was filmed on Kauai, with the waterslide scenes shot at Kilauea Falls. The main setting, the MacAvoy farm, was designed by production designer Robert Clatworthy and built on a bluff reachable only by private road. The waterfront set was built at Mahaulepu.

Castaway Creek Guests can ride inner tubes on the 2,100-ft.-long lazy river stream that meanders through Typhoon Lagoon at Walt Disney World; opened Jun. 1, 1989.

Castellaneta, Dan Actor; provided several voices in TV series, including *TaleSpin, Darkwing Duck, Goof Troop, Marsupilami, Aladdin, Hercules, Buzz Lightyear of Star Command, Lloyd in Space,* and *Kim Possible,* and also voiced the Genie in *The Return of Jafar.* He appeared on TV in *The Computer Wore Tennis Shoes* (Alan Winsdale, 1995), *Monk* (Tiny Werner), *Desperate Housewives* (Jeff Bicks), *Castle* (Judge Markway), and *Baby Daddy* (Peter Oliver).

Castle (TV) Comedy/drama series on ABC; aired Mar. 9, 2009–May 16, 2016. Famous mystery novelist Richard "Rick" Castle is bored with his own success, but when a real-world copycat murderer starts staging scenes from Castle's novels, he is teamed up with NYPD detective Kate Beckett to help solve the crimes. Castle's and Beckett's styles instantly clash and sparks begin to fly, leading both to danger and a hint of romance. Stars Nathan Fillion (Rick Castle), Stana Katic (Kate Beckett), Molly Quinn (Alexis), Susan Sullivan (Martha), Monet Mazur (Gina), Ruben Santiago-Hudson (Capt. Montgomery). From ABC Studios. To extend the fantasy into the real world, Hyperion Books and the showrunners created a series of real-life Nikki Heat crime novels, each with an author biography and photograph of the Castle character. The 1st, *Heat Wave* by Richard Castle, was released Sep. 29, 2009, hitting the *New York Times* bestseller list. The 8th, *High Heat,* released Oct. 25, 2016, continued the book series even after the show's finale. Similarly, a few Derrick Storm short stories and novels were released 2012–2014.

Castle Arts SEE ARTS & CRAFTS AND ARRIBAS BROTHERS.

Castle Camera Shop Fantasyland shop in the Magic Kingdom at Walt Disney World; open 1971–1983. It was succeeded by the Disneyana shop.

Castle Candy Shoppe Small shop inside Sleeping Beauty Castle in Disneyland; opened Sep. 20, 1957, originally as Castle Candy Kitchen. Operated by A.R.B. Corp. Closed Jun. 4, 1994; superseded by the Castle Heraldry Shoppe.

Castle Carrousel SEE CINDERELLA'S GOLDEN CARROUSEL.

Castle Christmas Shop Small shop inside Sleeping Beauty Castle in Disneyland; opened Jul. 3, 1987, taking the place of Castle Arts. Closed Jun. 9, 1996. It became Hugo's Secret Chamber Jun. 14–Dec. 9, 1996, offering *Hunchback of Notre Dame* merchandise, before becoming The Princess Boutique.

Castle Couture Fantasyland shop in the Magic Kingdom at Walt Disney World, featuring Disney Princess merchandise; opened Nov. 22, 2008, taking a section of Tinker Bell's Treasures. On May 20, 2019, it became the check-in area for Bibbidi Bobbidi Boutique.

Castle Heraldry Shoppe Shop inside Sleeping Beauty Castle in Disneyland; opened Jul. 11, 1994, taking the place of the Castle Candy Shoppe. Visitors could research their family history. The shop moved Jul. 2004, replacing the nearby Villains Lair shop. Closed Jan. 12, 2017, to become the Castle Holiday Shoppe.

Castle Holiday Shoppe Fantasyland shop in Disneyland; opened Apr. 20, 2017, taking the place of the Castle Heraldry Shoppe. Closed Oct. 2021, when a new holiday shop, Plaza Point, opened on Main Street, U.S.A. It became Merlin's Marvelous Miscellany in 2022.

Castle of Magical Dreams The 167-ft.-tall transformation of Sleeping Beauty Castle in Hong Kong Disneyland. After some 35 months of construction, the icon had its grand debut Nov. 21, 2020, at nearly double the size of the original castle. Design features are inspired by the stories of Disney princesses and heroines: Cinderella, Tiana, Aurora, Ariel, Mulan, Snow White, Moana, Merida, Belle, Rapunzel, Pocahontas, Jasmine, Anna, and Elsa. Inside are Enchanted Treasures (a jewelry shop), The Royal Reception Hall (character-greeting attraction), and an exhibition ("Building a Dream: The Magic Behind a Disney Castle").

Cat from Outer Space, The (film) An offbeat physicist, his girlfriend, and an odds-playing coworker try to help an extraterrestrial space cat, ZUNAR J5/90 DORIC FOURSEVEN, or, in Earth talk, Jake, fix his ship before the army or a power-hungry businessman cause a catastrophe by cat-napping the feline. The plot thickens when the alien falls for a lovely Persian Earth cat, Lucy Belle. Released Jun. 30, 1978. Directed by Norman Tokar. 103 min. Stars Ken Berry (Frank), Sandy Duncan (Liz), Harry Morgan (Gen. Stilton), Roddy McDowall (Stallwood), McLean Stevenson (Link), Jesse White (Earnest Ernie), Alan Young (Dr. Wenger), Hans Conried (Dr. Heffel), Ronnie Schell (Sgt. Duffy), William Prince (Mr. Olympus). The cat, Jake, was actually played by 2 Abyssinian cats—Rumple and his twin sister, Amber. The Abyssinian breed was selected by the producers because they thought it looked more "alien." Schell provided the voice for Jake. The movie was shot on the Disney Studio lot, in a soundstage and in the newly built Roy O. Disney Building; at a hangar at the Burbank airport; and on an army base built for the film on the Studio's 708-acre Golden Oak Ranch.

Cat Nap Pluto (film) Pluto cartoon released Aug. 13, 1948. Directed by Charles Nichols. Pluto, tired and sleepy from being out all night, tries to sleep despite Figaro's attempts to keep him awake. Pluto's sandman enlists the help of Figaro's sandman so both Pluto and Figaro can sleep.

Cat That Looked at a King, The (film) Julie Andrews and 2 kids leap into a chalk painting on the sidewalk and find themselves in the kingdom of King Cole. The king thinks he knows all the facts in the world but is bested by a cat who teaches him that he is not the cleverest man on Earth, but rather a merry old soul. From DisneyToon Studios. Directed by Dave Bossert (animation) and Peter Schneider (live action). Released Dec. 14, 2004, on the *Mary Poppins* DVD. Based on an original Mary Poppins story by P. L. Travers. Stars Julie Andrews, Dylan Cash, Olivia DeLaurentis. Voices are Sarah Ferguson (The Queen), Tracey Ullman (The Cat), David Ogden Stiers (King Cole/Prime Minister). 10 min.

Catal Restaurant and Uva Bar Catalan restaurant in the Downtown Disney District at Disneyland Resort; opened Jan. 12, 2001. Downstairs, an indoor/outdoor bar serves wine and tapas, with the dining room and alfresco terrace located upstairs. Managed by Patina Restaurant Group.

Catastrophe Canyon Action-packed special effects area on the Studio Backlot Tour in Disney-MGM Studios (later Disney's Hollywood Studios) at Walt Disney World; operated May 1, 1989–Sep. 27, 2014. Guests witnessed up close how flood, earthquake, and explosion effects are made. Also part of the Studio Tram Tour: Behind the Magic in Walt Disney Studios Park at Disneyland Paris; ran Mar. 16, 2002–Jan. 5, 2020, and became Cars-tastrophe Canyon on Cars ROAD TRIP.

Catch, The (TV) One-hour drama series on ABC; aired Mar. 24, 2016–May 11, 2017. Alice Vaughan is Los Angeles's top private investigator, but when her fiancé cons her out of millions and disappears, Alice goes on a private mission for payback. Alice will stop at nothing to get her man. Stars Mireille Enos (Alice Vaughan), Peter Krause (Kieran Booth), Alimi Ballard (Evan Derringer), Jay Hayden (James McGrath), Jacky Ido (Thomas Delgado), Sonya Walger (Zoe Taylor), Rose Rollins (Andie Derringer), Elvy Yost (Maria Dudek). From ABC Studios.

Catch a Flave Paradise Pier ice cream counter in Disney's California Adventure; opened Feb. 8, 2001. It became Paradise Pier Ice Cream Co. in 2010 and Adorable Snowman Frosted Treats in 2018.

Caterpillar Reclining on a toadstool and punctuating his speech with puffs of smoke, this *Alice in Wonderland* (1951) character was voiced by Richard Haydn.

Catlett, Walter (1889–1960) Voice of J. Worthington Foulfellow in *Pinocchio*.

Catmull, Ed Cofounder and president of Pixar Animation Studios, later named president of Walt Disney Animation Studios when Disney acquired Pixar in 2006. He received the Gordon E. Sawyer Oscar for technical contributions to the industry in 2009. Before Disney's acquisition, Catmull had received 4 scientific and technical Academy Awards. He retired in 2018.

Cat's Nightmare, The Copyright title of *The Cat's Out*.

Cat's Out, The (film) Silly Symphony cartoon released Jul. 28, 1931. Copyrighted as *The Cat's Nightmare*. Directed by Wilfred Jackson. After a cat is put out of the house, it is knocked out by a falling weather vane. The cat has a nightmare in which giant birds, bats, scarecrows, huge spiders, and monstrous trees scare it. The cat awakens from the nightmare and goes back into the house, only to be put outside again.

Catwalk Bar, The Cocktail bar overlooking the Soundstage Restaurant in Disney-MGM Studios; open May 1, 1989–1998.

Catz, Safra A. Member of the Disney Board of Directors beginning in 2018.

Cavalcade of Songs (TV) Show aired Feb. 16, 1955. Directed by Wilfred Jackson and Peter Godfrey. Walt Disney discusses the importance of music in the movies, reenacting with some of his current artists the story meeting which came up with "Who's Afraid of the Big Bad Wolf?" for *Three Little Pigs* and promoting the upcoming *Lady and the Tramp* by showing segments of the work in progress and looking in on the composers and singers at work on the score. Appearing are Ward Kimball, Frank Thomas, Pinto Colvig, Peggy Lee, Sonny Burke, Oliver Wallace, the Mello Men. With reissues of *Lady and the Tramp*, updated versions of the show aired Sep. 16, 1962, and Dec. 26, 1971; the latter incorporated songs from *Mary Poppins* and the newly released *Bedknobs and Broomsticks*.

Cavemen (TV) Half-hour comedy series on ABC; aired Oct. 2–Nov. 13, 2007. Three cavemen struggle with prejudice as they strive to live normal lives in 2007 Atlanta. Based on characters from a group of 7 popular GEICO Insurance TV commercials, which were introduced in 2004. Stars Bill English (Joel), Nick Kroll (Nick), Sam Huntington (Andy), Kaitlin Doubleday (Kate), Stephanie Lemelin (Thorne), Julie White (Leslie). From ABC Studios.

Caverna de los Piratas SEE CARIBBEAN ARCADE.

Cavin Courageous young page boy hero in the *Gummi Bears* TV series; voiced by Jason Marsden.

Cedric the Entertainer Actor/comedian; voiced Leadbottom in the Planes films, Uncle Bobby in

The Proud Family and *The Proud Family: Louder and Prouder*, and Trash Can in *Woke*. He was a host of *Who Wants to Be a Millionaire* (syn.) and had a guest role in *black-ish* (Smokey).

Cel The clear celluloid on which the characters were painted during the animation process. The painted celluloid, or cel, was placed over a background and photographed, becoming 1 frame of the animated film. There are 24 frames per second in an animated film, but most cels containing characters are often held for 2 frames. If there are several characters in a scene, each may be painted on a different cel. Since a typical animated short runs 6–8 min. in length, that equals 4,500–12,000 cels, or more, per cartoon. Cels up to 1940 were nitrate based and quite unstable. In fact, a pile of them could constitute a fire hazard. In 1940, Disney switched to cellulose acetate, a much safer medium. Disney cels were sold as works of art by the Courvoisier Galleries 1938–1946, and then at Disneyland beginning in 1955. The Disney Art Program, later known as Disney Art Editions and Disney Art Classics, began in the 1970s handling the sale of production cels, as well as creating special limited-edition cels, serigraphs, and other forms of collectible art. With *The Rescuers Down Under*, cels were no longer used in the production process, being replaced by the computer.

Celebrate the Magic See Magic, the Memories, and You!, The.

Celebrate the Spirit! Disney's All-Star 4th of July Spectacular (TV) Special on CBS; aired Jul. 4, 1992. Directed by Gary Halvorson. Entertainers perform at various locations at the Disney parks. Stars John Ritter, Kris Kross, Billy Ray Cyrus, Celine Dion. 120 min.

Celebration, Florida A 4,890-acre town built on the Walt Disney World property, in northwest Osceola County. Surrounded by a 4,600-acre greenbelt, the self-contained city includes residential villages, a school (kindergarten through middle school), a high school, a library, a hospital, a hotel, and rental apartments above downtown shops and restaurants. To develop a unique community for 20,000 residents, the Disney Development Co. created the Celebration Company, which outlined 5 foundational cornerstones for the community: Place, Community, Technology, Education, and Health. The master plan was developed by Cooper Robertson & Partners and Robert A.M.

Stern, who applied planning principles of New Urbanism. Additional architectural designs were done by Michael Graves, Charles Moore, César Pelli, and Philip Johnson, among others. Ground was broken in 1994, and the downtown area and first residential phase opened in 1996, with the first residents moving in Jun. 18. A fiber-optic information network linked all businesses and residences. In 2002, the golf course was sold to a private group, and the downtown area (shops, restaurants, offices, apartments) was sold to Lexin Capital Jan. 21, 2004.

Celebration Café Quick-service restaurant on the outskirts of Fantasyland in Shanghai Disneyland; opened Jun. 16, 2016, with rice and curry dishes, pizza, and other international dishes. Closed in 2017 to become part of Disney-Pixar Toy Story Land, as Toy Box Café.

Celebration of the Music from Coco, A (TV) Live-to-film concert special; digitally released Apr. 10, 2020, on Disney+. Songs from the Disney • Pixar film are performed, with appearances by Benjamin Bratt, Jaime Camil, Felipe Fernández del Paso, Alex Gonzalez, Sarah Hicks, Natalia Jiménez, Eva Longoria, Rudy Mancuso, Mariachi Divas, Luis Gerardo Méndez, Carlos Rivera, Alanna Ubach, and *Coco* director Lee Unkrich. 48 min. From Eventvision. The live event, *Disney • Pixar Coco – A Live-to-Film Concert Experience*, was performed Nov. 8–9, 2019, at the Hollywood Bowl in Los Angeles.

Celebration U.S.A. Parade Ran at Disneyland Jun. 21–Nov. 24, 1991. A tongue-in-cheek look at life in the U.S., celebrating the diversity of American lifestyles and America's patriotic pride.

Celebrity Celebration Aboard the Queen Mary (TV) Special on KCAL-TV in Los Angeles, celebrating "Voyage to 1939" at the *Queen Mary* and including information about the ship and its history; aired Apr. 15, 1990. 60 min. Directed by Rick Locke. Stars Wil Shriner, Melissa Manchester, Michael Feinstein.

Celebrity 5 & 10 Hollywood Boulevard shop at Disney-MGM Studios (later Disney's Hollywood Studios); opened May 1, 1989, offering jewelry, posters, and housewares. Inspired by the J. J. Newberry five-and-dime store chain.

Celebrity Gifts Shop in Disney's Hollywood

Hotel at Hong Kong Disneyland Resort; opened Sep. 12, 2005. Inspired by grand movie palaces from Hollywood's heyday.

Celebrity Sports Center Sports facility in Denver, built by a group of celebrity investors, including Walt Disney, radio and TV personality Art Linkletter, and actor John Payne; opened Sep. 17, 1960. Walt Disney Productions purchased the center in 1962 and used it as a training ground for Cast Members who would soon be operating resort facilities at Walt Disney World. The center was sold to a group of private investors on Mar. 29, 1979, and was eventually demolished in 1995.

Celeste in the City (TV) A 2-hour movie on ABC Family; aired Mar. 14, 2004. Celeste Blodgett, a small-town girl from Maine, moves to New York City, where she discovers her glamorous writing job is really only a fact-checker job, and her living quarters are dismal and rat-infested. Enter a helpful next-door neighbor, Kyle, and her gay cousin, Dana, who gives Celeste a makeover treatment and helps her gain the confidence needed to survive in the big city. Directed by Larry Shaw. Stars Majandra Delfino (Celeste), Nicholas Brendon (Dana), Ethan Embry (Kyle), Michael Boisvert (Mitch), Deborah Gibson (Monica), Sadie LeBlanc (Amanda). From Touchstone Television.

Celtic Pride (film) Jimmy Flaherty and Mike O'Hara are die-hard Boston Celtics fans who plan their lives around the basketball schedule and *SportsCenter*. While they are ecstatic that Boston is leading the NBA Championship Final series 3 games to 1, they also know that the Utah Jazz's flamboyant and obnoxious superstar, Lewis Scott, poses a big threat to the Celtics' date with destiny. Growing more desperate and depressed as the Jazz even up the series, they realize there is only one thing to do—kidnap Scott before the final game. When best-laid plans go awry, the threesome spend a wild night learning about the true spirit of competition and the joy of the game. Released Apr. 19, 1996. A Hollywood Pictures film in association with Caravan Pictures. Directed by Tom DeCerchio. Stars Dan Aykroyd (Jimmy Flaherty), Daniel Stern (Mike O'Hara), Damon Wayans (Lewis Scott), Gail O'Grady (Carol O'Hara). 90 min. Filmed on location in Boston, especially at the Boston Garden, then the home of the Celtics. The casting directors diligently worked to put together 2 teams of basketball players that could look like NBA-caliber players, and a training camp was set up for them at Brandeis University, just outside the city. Wayans himself had 4 months of intensive training.

Cemetery Club, The (film) Three lifelong friends—Esther, Doris, and Lucille—suddenly find themselves middle-aged widows and discover the transition to the singles scene both difficult and a challenge to their friendships. Lucille enjoys throwing herself into the over-50 singles circuit and brings her friends along. Doris will have none of it, preferring to remember her past and a loving marriage. Esther finds herself reluctantly falling in love again with a charming widower, Ben. Conflicts come to a climax at a wedding party for their oft-married friend Selma. Esther learns that Doris and Lucille interfered with her relationship with Ben, and she is bitterly angry. But she learns to forgive and discovers that she has the courage to live the single life and patch up her relationship with Ben. Initial release Feb. 3, 1993; general release Feb. 12, 1993. Directed by Bill Duke. A Touchstone film. 107 min. Stars Ellen Burstyn (Esther Moskowitz), Olympia Dukakis (Doris Silverman), Diane Ladd (Lucille Rubin), Danny Aiello (Ben Katz), Lainie Kazan (Selma), Christina Ricci (Jessica). Based on the stage play by Ivan Menchell. Filmed on location in the Jewish community in Pittsburgh.

Centennial Hall Disney merchandise shop on Main Street, U.S.A. in Hong Kong Disneyland; opened Sep. 12, 2005.

Center Street Boutique Shop on Main Street, U.S.A. in Hong Kong Disneyland; opened Jan. 2011, replacing a portion of the Crystal Arts shop. Jewelry, glassware, and apparel are sold.

Center Street Coffeehouse Art deco–style table-service restaurant in World Bazaar in Tokyo Disneyland; opened Apr. 15, 1983.

Centertown Market Fast-casual restaurant in Disney's Caribbean Beach Resort at Walt Disney World; opened Oct. 8, 2018, taking the place of the Old Port Royale Center Towne food court. Latin and Caribbean–inspired specialties are served.

CenTOONial Park Area at the entrance to Mickey's Toontown at Disneyland; planned to open March 19, 2023. An interactive fountain and a tree with large roots provide play experiences for kids.

Centorium Store in Communicore East (later

Innoventions East) in EPCOT Center; opened Oct. 1, 1982. The central, and largest, merchandising facility in Future World, where guests could buy items themed to all of the Future World pavilions, as well as generic EPCOT items. Art of Disney products were later offered on the 2nd floor. The Centorium was remodeled and became MouseGear in Sep. 1999.

Ceramic Mural, The (film) Educational film; giving a step-by-step account of the design and construction of a unique ceramic mural. Released in 16 mm in Sep. 1967.

Chaffey, Don (1917–1990) Director of *Pete's Dragon*, *The Three Lives of Thomasina*, *Ride a Wild Pony*, *Born to Run*, *Greyfriars Bobby*, *The Prince and the Pauper*, and *The Horse Without a Head*.

Chain Gang, The (film) Mickey Mouse cartoon released Sep. 5, 1930. The first appearance of a character who would become Pluto. Directed by Burt Gillett. Mickey is a convict who escapes and is tracked by guards using bloodhounds. After a wild horse ride, Mickey hits a post, is thrown off a cliff, crashes through the prison roof, and falls back into his cell.

Chalet Candle Shop SEE POTTERY CHALET.

Challenge of Survival, The: Chemicals (film) Educational film; released in Aug. 1984. The film illustrates the problems caused by chemicals used in pest control.

Challenge of Survival, The: Land (film) Educational film; released in Aug. 1984. The film shows how conservation tillage can minimize soil erosion.

Challenge of Survival, The: Water (film) Educational film; released in Aug. 1984. The film explains how improper irrigation can ruin soil, and drip irrigation is one method of reducing water runoff.

Challengers, The (TV) Syn. series, aired Sep. 3, 1990–Aug. 30, 1991. A game show featuring a question-and-answer format based on current events. Hosted by Dick Clark.

Champion, Marge (1919–2020) Actress; a veteran of the golden age of MGM musicals, she had, in the mid-1930s, as Marjorie Belcher, been the live-action model for Snow White. Later she also modeled for the Blue Fairy in *Pinocchio* and Hyacinth Hippo in *Fantasia*. She married Disney animator Art Babbitt, and later dancer Gower Champion, with whom she had a lengthy movie career. She was named a Disney Legend in 2007.

Chan, Jackie Actor; appeared in *An Alan Smithee Film: Burn Hollywood Burn*, *Shanghai Noon* and *Shanghai Knights* (Chon Wang), and *Around the World in 80 Days* (Passepartout/ Lau Xing).

Chandar, the Black Leopard of Ceylon (TV) Two-part show; aired Nov. 26 and Dec. 3, 1972. Friendship between a Ceylonese holy man and his disciple, and a leopard. The leopard had been saved by the holy man when young, and years later he returns the favor. Stars Frederick Steyne and Esram Jayasinghe.

Chandrila Collection, The Boutique aboard Star Wars: Galactic Starcruiser at Walt Disney World; opened Mar. 1, 2022, offering robes, tunics, and alien headwear, along with remote-control SK droids and commemorative items.

Chang, Amy L. Member of the Disney Board of Directors beginning in 2021.

Chang Can Dunk (film) A Disney+ original film; planned for digital release Mar. 10, 2023. Chang, a 16-year-old, Asian American high school student in the marching band, bets the school basketball star that he can dunk by homecoming. The bet leads the 5' 8" Chang on a quest to find the hops he needs to dunk in order to impress his crush, Kristy, and finally gain the attention and respect of his high school peers. But before he can rise up and truly throw one down, he'll have to reexamine everything he knows about himself, his friendships, and his family. Directed by Jingyi Shao. Stars Bloom Li (Chang), Ben Wang (Bo), Dexter Darden (Deandre), Chase Liefeld (Matt), Zoe Renee (Kristy). For authenticity, filmmakers brought on one of the foremost dunk experts, Connor Barth, to help train the actors. From Walt Disney Studios.

Changing Attitudes Women's fashion and accessory shop in Pleasure Island at Walt Disney World; open May 1, 1989–Apr. 1, 2006.

Chango, Guardian of the Mayan Treasure (TV) Show aired Mar. 19, 1972. Attendants at a Mayan ruin befriend a baby spider monkey, who helps them in their search for a fabled treasure. Stars Alonzo Fuentes, Juan Maldonado, Alex Tinne.

Chantons La Reine des Neiges SEE FOR THE FIRST TIME IN FOREVER: A FROZEN SING-ALONG CELEBRATION.

Chao, Wing T. Imagineer; he joined Disney in 1972 to master plan the community of Lake Buena Vista at Walt Disney World, later participating in the expansion of theme parks, resort hotels, and other entertainment venues at the Disney parks. He was a key member in government negotiations to build Euro Disney Resort (later Disneyland Paris), as well as the Hong Kong Disneyland and, later, Shanghai Disney Resorts, also overseeing master planning, architecture, and design. He also oversaw design of the first 4 Disney Cruise Line ships and the towns of Val d'Europe and Celebration. His titles have included vice chairman of Walt Disney Parks and Resorts for Asia Pacific Development and executive vice president of Walt Disney Imagineering. He retired in 2009 and was named a Disney Legend in 2019. On Disney+, he appeared in an episode of *The Mandalorian.*

Chaparral Theater, The Frontierland theater in Disneyland Paris; opened Jul. 18, 1993, as The Chaparral Stage. The venue was originally outdoors and later partially enclosed. Shows have included *Hillbilly Hoedown, Pocahontas le Spectacle, Mickey's Winter Wonderland, The Tarzan Encounter, Goofy's Summer Camp, Chantons La Reine des Neiges,* and *The Forest of Enchantment: A Disney Musical Adventure.* On Jun. 30, 2019, the theater, rebuilt as the Frontierland Theater, reopened with *The Lion King: Rhythms of the Pride Lands.*

Chapeau, The Hat shop on Main Street, U.S.A. in the Magic Kingdom at Walt Disney World; open Oct. 1, 1971–Mar. 28, 2021. In the 1990s, the shop's backstory was tied into the film *Summer Magic,* with a marquee inspired by the hatbox from *Lady and the Tramp,* linking to Tony's Town Square Restaurant next door. Replaced by an expanded Main Street Confectionery. SEE ALSO LE CHAPEAU (NEW ORLEANS SQUARE AT DISNEYLAND).

Chapek, Robert (Bob) He served as chief executive officer of The Walt Disney Company from Feb. 25, 2020, until Nov. 20, 2022. He was also a member of the company's Board of Directors beginning Apr. 15, 2020, and served as chairman of Disney Parks, Experiences and Products (beginning in 2018); chairman of Walt Disney Parks and Resorts (beginning in 2015); and president of Disney Consumer Products (beginning in 2011). His earlier titles included president of Walt Disney Studios Home Entertainment, president of the Digital Entertainment Group, and president of distribution for The Walt Disney Studios. He joined Disney in 1993.

Character Carnival, Disney's Shop on Disney's BoardWalk at Walt Disney World; opened Jul. 1, 1996, selling housewares and Disney souvenirs.

Character Corner Tomorrowland shop in Tokyo Disneyland; open Apr. 15, 1983–Oct. 13, 1996. Replaced by Planet M.

Character merchandise SEE MERCHANDISE.

Character Shop, The Shop in Tomorrowland in Disneyland; open 1967–Sep. 15, 1986. After the Emporium, it became the largest shop for buying Disney character souvenirs. Replaced by Star Traders.

Characters in Flight Tethered balloon operated by Aerophile S.A. in the Disney Springs West Side (formerly Downtown Disney) at Walt Disney World; debuted Apr. 2009. Guests ascend up to 400 ft. for views of the resort as far as 10 miles away. Renamed Aerophile – The World Leader in Balloon Flight in 2017. Aerophile has operated a similar balloon, PanoraMagique, in Disney Village at Disneyland Paris; opened Apr. 9, 2005, as the largest tethered balloon in the world, with a volume of 212,000 cubic ft. and a diameter of 248 feet.

Charles, Josh Actor; appeared in *Dead Poets Society* (Knox Overstreet) and *Crossing the Bridge* (Mort Golden), and on TV in *Sports Night* (Dan Rydell).

Charley and the Angel (film) A small-town businessman, during the Great Depression, has neglected his family for his business. His guardian angel, Roy Zerney, helps him to realize the error of his ways and he becomes a public hero, basking in the warmth of his family's love and admiration, through a series of hectic events involving bootleggers and the police. Released Mar. 23, 1973. Directed by Vincent McEveety. 93 min. Stars Fred MacMurray (Charley Appleby), Henry Morgan (Angel), Cloris Leachman (Nettie), Kurt Russell (Ray), Kathleen Cody (Leonora), Vincent Van Patten (Willie), Scott Kolden (Rupert). This was the last of MacMurray's 7 films for Disney. Buddy Baker, the film's musical composer and conductor, utilized many golden tunes from the 1930s for the score, including "Three Little Words" and "You're Driving Me Crazy," as well as an original song, "Livin' One Day at a Time," written by Shane Tatum and Ed Scott. To create a 1930s setting for the film, Disney art directors and set designers found the ideal location in Pasadena, California, on a quiet residential street lined with small-frame bungalows. The filmmakers hid the modern TV antennas, added a few stylish touring cars, dressed the cast in costume, and, presto, they had re-created the 1930s.

Charlie Crowfoot and the Coati Mundi (TV) Show aired Sep. 19, 1971. A Native American working on an archaeological dig finds an injured coatimundi, names him Cocoa, and nurses him back to health. The rancher, on whose land the man is digging, hates the coatis but changes his tune when Cocoa helps save his life. Stars Edward Colunga, Robert Keyworth.

Charlie the Lonesome Cougar (film) In the Cascade range of the Pacific Northwest, a tiny, orphaned cougar kitten is found and adopted by a young forester. He names the cougar Charlie, who grows up having many humorous and hair-raising adventures in the logging community. Finally, for his protection, Charlie is given his freedom in a wildlife sanctuary. Released Oct. 18, 1967, on a bill with *The Jungle Book*. Field producers Lloyd Beebe, Charles L. Draper, Ford Beebe. 75 min. Stars Brian Russell (Potlatch), Ron Brown (Jess Bradley), Linda Wallace (Jess's fiancée). Narrated by Rex Allen.

Chart Room Café Quick-service restaurant in Disney Explorers Lodge at Hong Kong Disneyland Resort; opened Apr. 30, 2017, offering salads, sandwiches, and specialty coffees.

Chase, Chevy Actor; appeared in *Man of the House* (Jack), on TV in *Brothers & Sisters* (Stan Harris), and in the Monster Sound Show at Disney-MGM Studios.

Chase, Daveigh Actress; voiced Lilo in *Lilo & Stitch* (and other appearances of the character), Chihiro in *Spirited Away*, and Rose in Disney Channel's *American Dragon: Jake Long*.

Chasez, J. C. Actor/singer; appeared on the *Mickey Mouse Club* on The Disney Channel, beginning

in 1991. He was later a member of the boy band *NSYNC, appearing on the *Walt Disney World Very Merry Christmas Parade*. Later appeared on *Club Mickey Mouse*.

Chasing Life (TV) Series on ABC Family; premiered Jun. 10, 2014, and ended Sep. 28, 2015. April is a smart and quick-witted aspiring journalist at a Boston newspaper who tries to balance her ambitious career with her family—her widowed mom, rebellious little sister, and grandmother—while fostering a romance with her coworker Dominic. Stars Italia Ricci (April), Mary Page Keller (Sara), Richard Brancatisano (Dominic), Haley Ramm (Brenna). From BV Family Productions, Lionsgate, and Televisa, in association with ABC Family. Based on a successful Televisa Spanish-language Mexican TV series.

Chasing Waves (TV) An 8-part docuseries on Disney+; digitally released Jan. 11, 2023. A spotlight on the people and places defining Japan's reach in global surf culture in the wake of surfing's debut at the 2020 Tokyo Olympics. From Boardwalk Pictures and Station 10 Media.

Château de la Belle au Bois Dormant, Le SEE LE CHÂTEAU DE LA BELLE AU BOIS DORMANT.

Chaykin, Maury (1949–2010) Character actor; appeared in *Where the Heart Is* (Harry); *Mr. Destiny* (Guzelman); *Money for Nothing* (Vicente Goldoni); *Unstrung Heroes* (Arthur Lidz); and *Mystery, Alaska* (Bailey Pruitt); and on Disney Channel in *Northern Lights* (Ben).

Cheadle, Don Actor; appeared in *Mission to Mars* (Luke Graham) and as War Machine/James Rhodes in the Marvel Studios films, and on TV in *The Golden Palace* (Roland Wilson) and *Sidekicks*. He provided voices for *DuckTales* (2017).

Cheaper by the Dozen (film) A Disney+ original film from 20th Century Studios, but released under the Disney banner; digitally premiered Mar. 18, 2022. The funny and heartwarming story of the raucous exploits of a blended family of 12, the Bakers, as they navigate a hectic homelife while simultaneously managing their family business. Directed by Gail Lerner. Stars Gabrielle Union (Zoey Baker), Zach Braff (Paul Baker), Erika Christensen (Kate), Timon Kyle Durrett (Dom Clayton), Journee Brown (Deja), Kylie Rogers (Ella), Andre Robinson (DJ), Caylee

Blosenski (Harley), Aryan Simhadri (Hare$h), Leo Abelo Perry (Luca), Mykal-Michelle Harris (Luna), Christian Cote (Bailey), Sebastian Cote (Bronx), Luke Prael (Seth). 108 min. A new take on the 2003 hit family comedy from 20th Century Fox.

Cheetah (film) Teenagers Ted and Susan join their parents at a Kenyan research station. After befriending a young Native boy, Morogo, they find a baby cheetah whose mother has been killed by poachers. They manage to convince their parents to let them raise the cheetah, named Duma, as a pet. When it's time for the kids to return home, Duma has to be returned to the wild. Before this can be accomplished, he is captured by a local merchant hoping to race the cat against greyhounds. Ted and Susan disobey their parents and set out to rescue Duma with Morogo's help. Released Aug. 18, 1989. Directed by Jeff Blyth. 83 min. Stars Keith Coogan (Ted Johnson), Lucy Deakins (Susan Johnson), Collin Mothupi (Morogo). Filmed on location in Kenya, with the cast and crew setting up a small compound consisting of 85 tents as their base of operations.

Cheetah Girls, The (TV) A Disney Channel Original Movie; premiered Aug. 15, 2003. Four multitalented New York City teens from dissimilar homes and economic backgrounds—a cultural melting pot of Black, Italian, Dominican, Puerto Rican, and Cuban heritages—have a dream to take the world by storm with their music group. All the while, they navigate "cheeta-licious" fashion and boys (including their musical archrival), family, and parents. Directed by Oz Scott. Stars Raven (Galleria Garibaldi), Lynn Whitfield (Dorothea Garibaldi), Adrienne Bailon (Chanel), Kiely Williams (Aqua), Sabrina Bryan (Dorinda Thomas), Kyle Schmid (Derek), Sandra Caldwell (Drinka Champagne), Vincent Corazza (Jackal Johnson). Based on the books by Deborah Gregory.

Cheetah Girls One World, The (TV) A Disney Channel Original Movie, the 3rd in the Cheetah Girls series; premiered Aug. 22, 2008. The Cheetah Girls travel from New York City to India to star in a film directed by an aspiring Bollywood movie director. Upon arriving, they are shocked to learn their movie's producer has a role for only 1 Cheetah Girl. Dreams and friendships are tested as they begin to compete against each other for the title role. Before long, the 3 girls start to question their commitment to the Cheetah Girls' dream, and each must weigh her own aspirations against the group's future. Directed by Paul Hoen. Stars Sabrina

Bryan (Dorinda), Adrienne Bailon (Chanel), Kiely Williams (Aqua), Roshan Seth (Uncle Kamal), Kunal Sharma (Amar), Rupak Ginn (Rahim), Deepti Daryanani (Gita), Michael Steger (Vikram Bhatia). Filmed in Udaipur, India.

Cheetah Girls 2, The (TV) A Disney Channel Original Movie; premiered Aug. 25, 2006. As the talented Cheetah Girls plan a summer rehearsing at home in New York City, they learn Chanel must instead accompany her mother to Spain to meet her wealthy beau Luc's family. So, the ever-resourceful Galleria enters the group in a Barcelona music festival, and the spirited foursome—Galleria, Chanel, Aquanetta, and Dorinda—embarks on a Catalan adventure of a lifetime. Once the teens arrive in Spain, they meet Marisol, a talented Spanish solo singer and her manager/mother, Lola, who unbeknownst to the Cheetahs, could cause their group to break up. Each girl has different and exciting experiences, until finally the Cheetahs' dream of becoming stars may be dashed forever when they are informed they have broken a festival rule. Directed and choreographed by Kenny Ortega. Stars Raven-Symoné (Galleria Garibaldi), Adrienne Bailon (Chanel), Sabrina Bryan (Dorinda Thomas), Kiely Williams (Aquanetta), Lynn Whitfield (Dorothea Garibaldi), Lori Alter (Juanita), Belinda Peregrin (Marisol), Kim Manning (Lola), Golan Yosef (Joaquin), Abel Folk (Luc), Peter V. Newey (Angel). Filmed entirely on location in Barcelona.

Chef Art Smith's Homecomin' Restaurant serving Southern-style cuisine, with a fried chicken specialty, in Disney Springs at Walt Disney World; opened Jul. 12, 2016. A patio bar, Shine Bar & Social, was added in 2020.

Chef Donald (film) Donald Duck cartoon released Dec. 5, 1941. Directed by Jack King. Donald is inspired by a radio program to make waffles but accidentally adds rubber cement to the batter resulting in so much havoc that he charges off to the radio station to give them a piece of his mind.

Chef Mickey's Restaurant in the Disney Village Marketplace at Walt Disney World; opened Jul. 1990, replacing The Village Restaurant. Closed Sep. 30, 1995, and after extensive remodeling, became Rainforest Cafe in 1996. Also a character dining buffet in Disney's Contemporary Resort; opened Dec. 22, 1995, taking the place of the Contemporary Café. A similarly named casual buffet, Chef Mickey, opened in the Disney Ambassador Hotel at Tokyo Disney Resort Jul. 7, 2000, and in Disney's Hollywood Hotel at Hong Kong Disneyland Resort Sep. 12, 2005.

Chefs de France, Les SEE LES CHEFS DE FRANCE.

Chemistry Matters (film) Educational film addressing the chemical properties of mixtures and solutions; released Sep. 1986. 17 min.

Chen, John S. Member of the Disney Board of Directors Jan. 23, 2004–2019.

Chenoweth, Kristin Actress; appeared in *You Again* (Georgia), on TV in *Annie* (Lily St. Regis), *Meredith Willson's The Music Man* (Marian Paroo), *GCB* (Carlene Cockburn), *The Muppets, Dreams Come True: A Celebration of Disney Animation*, and *The Disney Family Singalong*, and on Disney Channel in *Descendants* (Maleficent). She voiced Rosetta in the Tinker Bell films and Sugar Plum Fairy in *Strange Magic*.

Chernabog Monstrous demon figure on Bald Mountain in *Fantasia*; animated by Bill Tytla.

Cherokee Trail, The (TV) Show aired Nov. 28, 1981. Directed by Kieth Merrill. The pilot for a series, later reworked as *Five Mile Creek* on The Disney Channel. A plucky woman and her daughter run a way station on a stagecoach line, to the great displeasure of the former manager who plots to drive them off. From the story by Louis L'Amour. Stars Cindy Pickett, Mary Larkin, Timothy Scott, David Hayward, Victor French, Richard Farnsworth, Tommy Petersen.

Cheshire Café Fantasyland cottage kiosk serving treats and slushies near Mad Tea Party in the Magic Kingdom at Walt Disney World; opened Nov. 10, 2011, replacing Enchanted Grove. Hosted by Minute Maid.

Cheshire Cat Mad, grinning character in *Alice in Wonderland*; voiced by Sterling Holloway.

Chesney, Diana (1916–2004) Actress; voiced Mrs. Judson in *The Great Mouse Detective*.

Chester & Hester's Dinosaur-themed amusement area in DinoLand U.S.A. at Disney's Animal Kingdom; opened Apr. 22, 1998, originally with a gift shop, Chester & Hester's Dinosaur Treasures. Expanded into Chester & Hester's Dino-Rama! Nov. 18, 2001, with TriceraTop Spin and Fossil Fun Games. A spinning coaster, Primeval Whirl, operated Apr. 18, 2002–2020. The area recalls the kitschy attractions of roadside America.

Chester, Yesterday's Horse (TV) Show aired Mar. 4, 1973. Directed by Larry Lansburgh. A Belgian draft horse in Oregon is retired, but proves he still has value when he helps save a man trapped in a burning truck. Stars Bill Williams, Barbara Hale, Russ McGubbin.

Chevalier, Maurice (1888–1972) Actor; appeared in *In Search of the Castaways* (Professor Paganel) and *Monkeys, Go Home!* (Father Sylvain), and sang the title song in *The Aristocats*. He recorded the Disneyland Records album *A Musical Tour of France with Maurice Chevalier* (1966). He was named a Disney Legend posthumously in 2002.

Chew, The (TV) Daytime series on ABC; aired Sep. 26, 2011–Jun. 15, 2018. Experts in food, lifestyle, and entertaining explore life through food. Starred Mario Batali, Michael Symon, Carla Hall, Clinton Kelly, Daphne Oz.

Chez Marianne (Souvenirs de Paris) Art deco–style boutique in La Place de Rémy in Walt Disney Studios Park at Disneyland Paris; opened Nov. 28, 2014. *Ratatouille* memorabilia, artwork, and sweets are sold.

Chiba Traders – Arts & Crafts Adventureland shop in Tokyo Disneyland; opened Apr. 15, 1983, offering products from Chiba Prefecture craftsmen. Closed Mar. 2013, to be superseded by Pacific Export.

Chibi Tiny Tales (TV) Animated short-form series; digitally premiered Jun. 7, 2020, on Disney Channel YouTube. Chibi-style versions of Disney Channel characters embark on wild adventures together. From Disney Television Animation. A spin-off of the *Big Chibi 6: The Shorts* digital series. SEE ALSO BIG HERO 6 THE SERIES.

Chibiverse (TV) Animated series on Disney Channel; premiered Jul. 30, 2022. Disney TV characters, including Phineas and Ferb, Cricket Green, Anne Boonchuy, Molly McGee, and Penny Proud, showcase their wild *Chibi Tiny Tales* adventures.

Chicago City where Walt Disney was born, on Dec. 5, 1901, at 1249 Tripp Avenue, in a home that had been built by his father, Elias. (The houses on Tripp Avenue have been renumbered, and the Disney birthplace is now 2156 Tripp, at the corner of Palmer.) Elias started out as a carpenter in the city, having moved there to work on the World's Colombian Exposition of 1893, and eventually began building houses that were designed by his wife, Flora. He also built the St. Paul Congregational Church, which the family attended. The family moved to Missouri in 1906, but they returned in 1917. Walt attended McKinley High School for a year, enrolled in night classes at the Chicago Academy of Fine Arts, and worked after school at the O-Zell jelly and fruit juice company, where Elias had taken a job. In 1918, Walt took a job at the post office, delivering mail before joining the Red Cross during World War I.

Chicken in the Rough (film) Chip and Dale cartoon released Jan. 19, 1951. Directed by Jack Hannah. Chip and Dale, picking acorns, come across a nest with eggs. A baby chick hatches from 1 of the eggs and Dale, in trying to stuff the chick back into the egg, gets involved with the rooster and ends up trapped under the hen with the rooster pacing outside.

Chicken Little (film) Special cartoon released Dec. 17, 1943. Directed by Clyde Geronimi. Foxey Loxey cons the farmyard chickens and dim-witted Chicken Little into believing his cave is the only safe place when the sky is falling. Once they enter, the chickens are devoured. Originally this film was planned to have definite wartime connotations, but it was made generic so it would have more lasting appeal.

Chicken Little (film) Computer-animated feature that presents a new twist to the classic fable of a young chicken who causes widespread panic when he mistakes a falling acorn for a piece of the sky. Chicken Little is determined to restore his reputation, but just as things are starting to go his way, a real piece of the sky lands on his head. Chicken Little and his band of misfit friends—Abby Mallard (aka Ugly Duckling), Runt of the Litter, and Fish Out of Water—attempt to save the world without sending the town into a whole new panic. Released Nov. 4, 2005. Directed by Mark Dindal. Voices include Zach Braff (Chicken Little), Patrick Stewart (Mr. Woolensworth), Joan Cusack (Abby Mallard), Steve Zahn (Runt of the Litter), Amy Sedaris (Foxy Loxy), Don Knotts (Mayor Turkey Lurkey), Garry Marshall (Buck Cluck), Wallace Shawn (Principal Fetchit), Dan Molina (Fish Out of Water). 81 min. The film opened in 100 theaters in a new Disney Digital 3-D process. Released on DVD in 2006.

Chicken of the Sea Pirate Ship and Restaurant Quick-service eatery in Fantasyland at Disneyland; opened Aug. 29, 1955, offering tuna sandwiches, salads, and burgers. A seating cove, with waterfalls and Skull Rock, was added along the lagoon in the early 1960s. It became Captain Hook's Galley in 1969 and closed in 1982. Originally, the ship was made entirely of wood, which began to rot after sitting in water for so long. Over the years the wood was partially replaced by concrete, so when it was decided to remove the ship for the remodeling of Fantasyland, it was not possible to save it. The Imagineers tried to salvage elements of the ship by carefully prying elaborate plasterwork off the stern. But when the truck transporting the items hit a bump, the plasterwork fell over and broke to pieces. The ship and Skull Rock were later re-created in Disneyland Paris as Captain Hook's Galley (later the Pirate Galleon).

Chicken Plantation Restaurant Frontierland restaurant in Disneyland, sponsored by Swift; open Jul. 17, 1955–Jan. 8, 1962. Also known as the Plantation House. Guests enjoyed fried chicken dinners along the Rivers of America, until the space was needed for the expansion of Frontierland and building of New Orleans Square. In the early days of the park, many visitors considered a meal at the Chicken Plantation the best in the park.

Chicken Squad, The (TV) Animated comedy series on Disney Junior; premiered May 14, 2021. A trio of chicken siblings—Coop, Sweetie, and Little Boo—and Captain Tully, a retired search and rescue dog, team up on problem-solving adventures in their backyard to help their animal friends. Voices include Yvette Nicole Brown (Captain Tully), Ramone Hamilton (Coop), Gabriella Graves (Sweetie), Maxwell Simkins (Little Boo), Tony Hale (Frazz). Inspired by the book series by Doreen Cronin. From Wild Canary in association with Disney Junior.

Chico, the Misunderstood Coyote (TV) Show aired Oct. 15, 1961. Directed by Walter Perkins. A witness to his mother's death at the hands of a man, the coyote, Chico, has learned to hate and fear him. Taken into captivity and exhibited in a small desert roadside zoo, Chico learns much but never loses his bitterness toward his enemy: man. Chico makes his escape and bounds off for a life of adventure in the desert where he mates with Tula. He sees an eagle grab one of his pups and worries when his mate raids a chicken coop. Realizing the dangers man poses to them, Chico decides to take his family deeper into the desert to protect and help them all survive. Narrated by Winston Hibler.

Chief Amos Slade's dog in *The Fox and the Hound*; voiced by Pat Buttram.

Child Molestation: Breaking the Silence (film) Educational film; released in Aug. 1984. The film offers guidelines on how to identify symptoms of child abuse and how to respond and report it. It also shows how to teach children to protect themselves.

Child of Glass (TV) Two-hour movie aired May 14, 1978. Directed by John Erman. The Ainsworths have moved into a haunted house and son Alexander discovers a ghost of a young girl who needs a riddle regarding a glass china doll solved before she can rest in peace. Alexander and a neighbor try to solve the mystery, but are attacked by the estate's ex-caretaker, who's bent on revenge. They finally manage to find the glass doll and set the ghost free. Stars Barbara Barrie, Biff McGuire, Katy Kurtzman, Steve Shaw, Anthony Zerbe, Nina Foch, Olivia Barash, Irene Tedrow.

Child Star: The Shirley Temple Story (TV) A 2-hour movie on *The Wonderful World of Disney*; first aired May 13, 2001. At the height of America's Great Depression, the number one movie star was Shirley Temple, a 6-year-old with ringlet curls and dimples who tap-danced, sang, and captivated the entire nation. She exemplified the genuine Hollywood star, complete with bodyguard, dolls, and other merchandise in her image, and cemented handprints at Grauman's Chinese Theatre in Hollywood. Directed by Nadia Tass. Stars Ashley Rose Orr (Shirley Temple), Emily Anne Hart (teen Shirley), Connie Britton (Gertrude Temple), Colin Friels (George Temple), Hinton Battle (Bill "Bojangles" Robinson). Based on Shirley Temple Black's autobiography, *Child Star*; she served as a consultant on this film. Filmed on location in Port Melbourne, Australia.

Childcraft Mail-order company offering educational toys and children's school furniture;

acquired by Disney in 1988. Disney sold the company in 1997.

Children of Japan, The: Learning the New, Remembering the Old (film) Educational film; released in Sep. 1987. 21 min. A day in the life of Japan and its culture as seen through the letters of pen pals.

Children of Mexico, The (film) Educational film; in the EPCOT Educational Media Collection, released Apr. 20, 1989. 26 min. A Mexican girl describes her lifestyle to an American pen pal.

Children of the Soviet Union (film) Educational film; released in Sep. 1988. 22 min. Soviet history and culture as seen through the eyes of a Leningrad student.

Chim Chim Cher-ee Song from *Mary Poppins*; written by Richard M. and Robert B. Sherman. Academy Award winner.

Chimpanzee (film) Disneynature documentary; released Apr. 20, 2012, following an Apr. 13 premiere at Downtown Disney West Side at Walt Disney World. Deep in the forests of Africa, after a rival band of chimpanzees confronts his family, a young chimp named Oscar is left to fend for himself until a surprising ally steps in to adopt him and change his life forever. Directed by Alastair Fothergill and Mark Linfield. Narrated by Tim Allen. 78 min. Filmed in the tropical jungles of the Ivory Coast and Uganda.

China World Showcase pavilion in EPCOT; opened Oct. 1, 1982. Entering through the Gate of the Golden Sun (styled after Beijing's Yunhui Yuyu Archway), visitors approach the pavilion's focal point, a re-creation of the Hall of Prayer for Good Harvests. Inside, one can view some of China's unique scenery in a Circle-Vision 360 presentation (originally *Wonders of China*, updated to *Reflections of China* May 22, 2003). Many guests come out of the film with a deep desire to someday see the real things on a trip to China. Nearby, the House of the Whispering Willows is a gallery displaying authentic cultural artifacts. Silk robes, vases, jade jewelry, and other items are sold in Yong Feng Shangdian, a marketplace of several shops all under one roof. China was one of the few World Showcase pavilions that did not have its own restaurant on opening day, which was surprising because of the popularity of Chinese cuisine with Americans. In 1985, the quick-service Lotus Blossom Café and table-service Nine Dragons Restaurant finally opened, the latter winning several restaurant awards. The pavilion's Chinese Garden is particularly beautiful, with more than 20 varieties of trees and shrubs, including Chinese elm, willow, pine, cherry, and oak trees.

China Cabinet World Bazaar chinaware and glassware shop in Tokyo Disneyland; open Apr. 15, 1983–1998, and superseded by The Home Store.

China Plate, The (film) Silly Symphony cartoon released May 23, 1931. Directed by Wilfred Jackson. A painted scene on a plate comes to life with a boy fisherman saving a young girl from drowning when she tries to capture a butterfly. The boy, attempting to catch the butterfly himself, accidentally jumps on a sleeping man, and a wild chase ensues. After evading a dragon, the boy and girl return to the safety of his fishing boat and kiss, as the China plate again becomes just a plate.

China Shop, The (film) Silly Symphony cartoon released Jan. 13, 1934. Directed by Wilfred Jackson. As a shopkeeper closes his store for the night, his china pieces come alive; next 2 figures dance until a china satyr runs off with the girl. The boy figure manages to save her and destroy the satyr, but also damages most of the store's pieces. When the resourceful owner arrives next morning, he sees all the damaged items and changes his sign to read ANTIQUES.

China Voyager Restaurant Adventureland restaurant serving noodle dishes in Tokyo Disneyland; opened Jul. 21, 1992. According to the story, it is a converted boathouse run by the grandson of a pirate ship cook.

Chip Clever chipmunk with the black nose (think "chocolate chip") who, with his partner, Dale, made life difficult for Donald Duck. The chipmunks appeared in 24 theatrical films, 3 in their own series. They made their film debut, unnamed, in *Private Pluto* (1943), and later made dozens of TV and streaming appearances, including in their own series, *Chip 'n' Dale Rescue Rangers* and *Chip 'n' Dale: Park Life*.

Chip Enchanted young, cracked cup in *Beauty and the Beast*; voiced by Michael Pierce.

Chip an' Dale (film) Donald Duck cartoon released Nov. 28, 1947. Directed by Jack Hannah. When Donald attempts to chop some firewood, he destroys the home of the chipmunks, who try everything in their power to save it from being burned . . . and succeed. Nominated for an Academy Award.

Chip & Dale's Trading Post Adventure Isle shop in Shanghai Disneyland; opened May 11, 2020, taking the place of Laughing Monkey Traders. According to the story, the chipmunks have set up this base in their search for the legendary giant acorn.

Chip & Dale's Treehouse Treats Outdoor market on Mickey Avenue in Shanghai Disneyland; opened Jun. 16, 2016, offering fresh fruit, water, and snacks.

Chip 'n' Dale: Park Life (TV) Animated series on Disney+; digitally premiered Jul. 28, 2021. Chip and Dale try to live the good life in a big city park while having giant-sized, sky-high adventures. Voices include Matthew Géczy (Chip), Kaycie Chase (Dale), Bill Farmer (Pluto), Sylvain Caruso (Donald Duck), David Gasman (Butch), Cindy Lee Delong (Clarice). From Xilam Animation and Walt Disney EMEA Productions.

Chip 'n' Dale Rescue Rangers (TV) Animated series; aired on The Disney Channel Mar. 4–Jul. 15, 1989, and then syn. beginning Sep. 18, 1989. The chipmunks are leaders of a secret international organization devoted to tackling unsolved mysteries and mysterious oddball crimes. Other members of the Rangers are Monterey Jack, Gadget, and Zipper, and they battle Fat Cat and his cohorts. Voices include Corey Burton (Zipper, Dale), Peter Cullen (Maps, Kirby, Muldoon), Jim Cummings (Monterey Jack, Fat Cat), Tress MacNeille (Chip, Gadget). 65 episodes.

Chip 'n Dale: Rescue Rangers (film) A hybrid live-action/animated action-comedy. Chip and Dale are living among cartoons and humans in modern-day Los Angeles, but their lives are quite different now. It has been decades since their successful television series was canceled, and Chip has succumbed to a life of suburban domesticity as an insurance salesman. Dale, meanwhile, has had CGI surgery and works the nostalgia convention circuit, desperate to relive his glory days. When a former castmate mysteriously disappears, Chip and Dale must repair their broken friendship and take on their Rescue Rangers detective personas once again to save their friend's life. Digitally released May 20, 2022, on Disney+. Directed by Akiva Schaffer. Stars KiKi Layn (Ellie), with the voices of John Mulaney (Chip), Andy Samberg (Dale), Will Arnett (Sweet Pete), Eric Bana (Monterey Jack), Flula Borg (DJ Herzogenaurach), Dennis Haysbert (Zipper), Keegan-Michael Key (Frog Co-Worker/Bjornson the Cheesemonger), Tress MacNeille (High-Pitched Chip/Gadget), Tim Robinson (Ugly Sonic), Seth Rogen (Bob the Warrior Viking/Pumbaa/Mantis/B.O.B.), J.K. Simmons (Captain Putty). 97 min. Filmed on location throughout Los Angeles and Southern California. The film features a meta-narrative inspired in part by *Who Framed Roger Rabbit*, breaking several conventions. The filmmakers also employed a variety of animation styles and techniques, including hand drawn, black and white, Claymation, CG, motion capture, and puppets. Winner of the 2022 Emmy Award for Outstanding Television Movie.

Chip 'n' Dale Rescue Rangers to the Rescue (TV) Syn. special as a preview to the animated series; first aired Sep. 30, 1989. 120 min.

Chip 'n Dale Treehouse Attraction in Mickey's Toontown at Disneyland; opened Jan. 24, 1993. Guests climb up into a redwood tree for a view of Mickey's Toontown. Ladders and slides make it a popular attraction for children. There was also an Acorn Ball Crawl 1993–1998. A version opened in Tokyo Disneyland Apr. 15, 1996.

Chip 'n' Dale's Café Quick-service restaurant at the Lake Buena Vista Golf Course at Walt Disney World; deli sandwiches, wraps, and snacks are served. The version at Disney's Magnolia Golf Course is named Chip 'n' Dale's Deli.

Chip 'n' Dale's GADGETcoaster See Gadget's Go Coaster.

Chip 'n' Dale's Nutty Tales (TV) Animated short-form series; premiered Nov. 13, 2017, on Disney Junior, Disney Channel, and DisneyNOW. Chip and Dale can't seem to stay away from trouble as they set off on adventures around Hot Dog Hills. Voices include Tress MacNeille (Chip), Corey Burton (Dale), Bill Farmer (Goofy), Bret Iwan (Mickey Mouse), Russi Taylor (Minnie Mouse), Daniel Ross (Donald Duck). A spin-off of *Mickey and the Roadster Racers*.

Chips Ahoy (film) Donald Duck cartoon released Feb. 24, 1956. Directed by Jack Kinney. Chip and Dale must steal a model ship from Donald in order to gather a plentiful supply of acorns on an island far out in a river. Donald's attempts to interfere are thwarted, as always, by the clever chipmunks, who get their food, inadvertently with Donald's help. Filmed in CinemaScope.

Chips, the War Dog (TV) A Disney Channel Premiere Film; first aired Mar. 24, 1990. Directed by Ed Kaplan. A German shepherd goes to war in the K-9 Corps during World War II. A misfit dog paired with a misfit soldier, they become a real team and eventually heroes. Stars Brandon Douglas (Danny Stauffer), William Devane (Col. Charnley), Paxton Whitehead (Smythe), Ellie Cornell (Kathy Lloyd), Ned Vaughn (Mitch Wilson). 91 min.

Chirac, Jacques (1932–2019) French prime minister who signed the Euro Disney protocol with Michael Eisner on Mar. 24, 1987.

Chocolat Rue Royale See next entry.

Chocolate Collection, The Shop offering imported gourmet chocolates in New Orleans Square at Disneyland; opened Nov. 15, 1985. Later renamed Chocolat Rue Royale, which closed Mar. 7, 1988, to become Mascarades d'Arlequin.

Choices (A Story About Staying in School) (film) Educational film in the EPCOT Educational Media Collection; released in Aug. 1988. 27 min. Two very different high school students explore goal setting versus dropping out of school.

Choir (TV) A 6-episode unscripted docuseries planned for digital release on Disney+. Based on the motivational story behind *America's Got Talent* finalists, the Detroit Youth Choir, and its artistic director, Anthony White. From Blumhouse Television, Maniac Productions, and Campfire. A *Choir* scripted drama series was also announced for Disney+.

Choose Your Tomorrow (film) A film supervised by David Jones for use in Horizons at EPCOT Center. It related 3 return trips to Earth: "Space," "Undersea," or "Desert," among which guests could choose. The film was produced in an empty hangar at the Burbank airport.

Chouinard Art Institute SEE CALIFORNIA INSTITUTE OF THE ARTS.

Christmas Again (TV) A Disney Channel Original Movie; first aired Dec. 3, 2021. Rowena is a high-spirited teenager experiencing a lackluster Christmas. She wants her life back the way it was—her parents back together, her dad's new girlfriend and her son out of the picture, and their family traditions to remain the same. After making a wish to a neighborhood Santa for a do-over, Ro unexpectedly finds herself reliving Christmas Day over and over again. In order to break the strange magical loop, she must learn to appreciate her loving family as it is, as well as the true meaning of Christmas. Directed by Andy Fickman. Stars Scarlett Estevez (Rowena), Alexis Carra (Carolina), Daniel Sunjata (Mike), Beth Lacke (Diane), Ashlyn Jade Lopez (Gabby), Priscilla Lopez (Abuela Sofia), Tony Amendola (Abuelo Hector), Gary Anthony Williams (Santa), James McCracken (Louie), Gabriel Ruiz (Gerry), Sean Parris (Bruce).

Christmas at Walt Disney World (TV) Show aired Dec. 10, 1978. Directed by Steve Binder. Mimes Shields and Yarnell, as a robot couple, visit the Florida park. Other performers include the band Pablo Cruise, Andrea McArdle, Danielle Spencer, Avery Schreiber, Phyllis Diller.

Christmas Capers (film) A 16-mm release title of *Toy Tinkers*; released in Oct. 1961.

Christmas Carol, Disney's A (film) Ebenezer Scrooge begins the Christmas holiday with his usual miserly contempt, barking at his faithful clerk and cheery nephew. But when the ghosts of Christmas Past, Present, and Yet to Come take him on an eye-opening journey revealing truths Old Scrooge is reluctant to face, he must open his heart to undo years of ill will before it is too late. Released Nov. 6, 2009, in the U.S., after a Nov. 3 world premiere at London's Leicester Square. Directed by Robert Zemeckis. Stars Jim Carrey (Ebenezer Scrooge/Ghosts), Cary Elwes (Dick Wilkins), Gary Oldman (Bob Cratchit/Marley/Tiny Tim), Colin Firth (Fred), Bob Hoskins (Fezziwig/Old Joe), Robin Wright Penn (Belle/Fan), Fionnula Flanagan (Mrs. Dilber). 96 min. Many of the actors play multiple roles. Filmed in CinemaScope and Disney Digital 3-D, using the performance-capture technique whereby the performances of the actors are captured digitally with computerized cameras in a full 360°. A 16,000-mile whistle-stop train tour of 4 cars promoting the film left Los Angeles May 25, 2009, hitting 40 cities in 6 months.

Christmas Chalet SEE DISNEY'S DAYS OF CHRISTMAS AND MICKEY'S CHRISTMAS CHALET.

Christmas Cupid (TV) Original movie for ABC Family; aired Dec. 12, 2010. High-powered Hollywood publicist Sloane finds herself haunted by the ghost of her recently departed infamous client, Caitlin. With just days away from Christmas, Caitlin takes Sloane on a journey to meet the ghosts of her ex-boyfriends from the past, present, and future to try and guide her to love. A modern-day take on Charles Dickens's *Christmas Carol*. Directed by Gil Junger. Stars Chad Michael Murray (Patrick), Christina Milian (Sloane Spencer), Ashley Benson (Caitlin Quinn), Jackée Harry (Mom).

Christmas Fantasy, A Holiday parade in Disneyland; began in 1995, succeeding the *Very Merry Christmas Parade*.

Christmas Fantasy on Ice SEE DISNEY'S CHRISTMAS FANTASY ON ICE.

Christmas in Disneyland with Art Carney (TV) Special aired Dec. 6, 1976. Directed by Marty Pasetta. A grumpy grandfather is persuaded to stay at Disneyland by his grandkids, and they witness Christmas festivities and special entertainment. Also stars Sandy Duncan, Glen Campbell, Brad Savage, Terri Lynn Wood.

Christmas in Many Lands Christmas festival in Disneyland held 1958–1964. The highlight was the *Parade of All Nations*, which had premiered in 1957. Thousands of participants dressed in the holiday attire of more than 2 dozen nations, with song and dance groups, marching bands, and decorative floats. The *Parade of Toys* was added in 1960, featuring more than 100 giant performing toys. The parades were succeeded by the long-running *Fantasy on Parade*.

Christmas Jollities (film) Shorts program; released by RKO in 1953.

Christmas Star, The (TV) Two-hour movie; aired on ABC Dec. 14, 1986. Directed by Alan Shapiro. A boy, having a miserable holiday, comes upon an escaped convict who he thinks is Santa Claus. The convict is trying to save his robbery loot, which is hidden in an old department store planned for demolition, and he enlists the boy and his friends to help. Stars Edward Asner, René Auberjonois, Jim Metzler, Susan Tyrrell, Zachary Ansley, Nicholas Van Burek, Fred Gwynne, John Payne.

Christmas Tree, The (TV) Two-hour movie; aired on ABC Dec. 22, 1996. Richard Reilly, the head gardener for Rockefeller Center, in searching for the perfect Christmas tree for the Center, locates one at the Brush Creek convent. But he has a run-in with Sister Anthony, the convent's gardener, who has an unusual attachment to the tree and refuses to surrender it. The sister and Reilly eventually forge a friendship, and she gives up the tree, but Reilly has to make a special trip to persuade her to come to New York City for the unveiling. Directed by Sally Field, in her directorial debut. Stars Andrew McCarthy (Richard Reilly), Julie Harris (Sister Anthony), Trini Alvarado (Beth). Inspired by Julie Salamon's novel of the same name.

Christmas Visitor, The (TV) A Disney Channel Premiere Film; first aired Dec. 5, 1987. A family on a drought-stricken sheep ranch in the Australian outback of the 1890s discovers the true meaning of Christmas with the help of an old vagrant who is mistaken for Father Christmas. Directed by George Miller. 101 min. Stars Dee Wallace Stone (Elizabeth O'Day), John Waters (Patrick O'Day), Nadine Garner (Sarah), Andrew Ferguson (Ned). Released on video in 1987 as *Miracle Down Under*.

Christmas with Walt Disney (film) Documentary created for The Walt Disney Family Museum chronicling Walt's life as a husband, father, and filmmaker during one of his favorite times of year. Features home movies of the Disney family at holiday time, along with sequences from Disney Christmas films and TV shows. Narrated by Diane Disney Miller. Directed by Don Hahn. Shown seasonally at the museum in San Francisco beginning Nov. 27, 2009. 51 min.

Christopher Robin The boy character in the Winnie the Pooh films; voiced by a succession of actors: Bruce Reitherman, Jon Walmsley, Timothy Turner, Kim Christianson, Edan Gross, Jack Boulter.

Christopher Robin (film) The young boy who embarked on countless adventures in the Hundred Acre Wood with his band of spirited and lovable stuffed animals has grown up and lost his way. He has a family of his own, but his work has become his life, leaving little time for his wife and daughter, and he has all but forgotten his idyllic childhood spent with a simpleminded, honey-loving stuffed bear and his friends. But when he is reunited with Winnie the Pooh, now tattered and soiled from years of hugs and play, a spark is rekindled, and he is reminded of the endless days of make-believe that defined his youth. Following an unfortunate mishap with Christopher Robin's briefcase, Pooh and the rest of the gang step out of the forest and into London to return the crucial possessions, because best friends will always be there for you. Released in the U.S. Aug. 3, 2018, after numerous international releases Aug. 1–2. Directed by Marc Forster. Stars Ewan McGregor (Christopher Robin), Hayley Atwell (Evelyn), Bronte Carmichael (Madeline Robin); with the voices of Jim Cummings (Winnie the Pooh/Tigger), Brad Garrett (Eeyore), Peter Capaldi (Rabbit), Toby Jones (Owl), Sophie Okonedo (Kanga), Nick Mohammed (Piglet). 104 min. Inspired by A. A. Milne's classic children's tales. Winnie the Pooh and friends make their first appearance in a live-action film as three-dimensional characters, thanks to sophisticated computer animation technology. Shot with traditional handheld cameras to help the stuffed animals' motions look more believable. Original *Winnie the Pooh* songwriter Richard M. Sherman contributed 3 new songs, making a cameo in the end credits to perform 2 of them. Filmed in widescreen format at Shepperton Studios outside London and on location throughout the U.K. The scenes taking place in the Hundred Acre Wood were filmed in Ashdown Forest (the original inspiration for the enchanting setting of Milne's books) and Windsor Great Park. Nominated for an Academy Award for Best Visual Effects (Christopher Lawrence, Michael Eames, Theo Jones, Chris Corbould).

Chronicles of Narnia, The: Prince Caspian (film) The 2nd film in the Chronicles of Narnia series. A year after their previous visit, the Pevensie siblings are pulled back into the land of Narnia, where they discover that 1,300 years in Narnian time has passed since they left. During their absence, the Golden Age of Narnia has become extinct, Narnia has been conquered by the Telmarines, and it is now under the control of the evil King Miraz, who rules the land without mercy. The children meet Narnia's rightful heir to the throne, the young Prince Caspian, who has been forced into hiding as his uncle Miraz plots to kill him in order to place his own newborn son on the throne. The Pevensie kids once again are enlisted to join the colorful creatures of Narnia in combatting the usurping king. A production of Walt Disney Pictures/Walden Media. Directed by Andrew Adamson. Released May 16, 2008, after a May 15 release in Chile, Indonesia, Russia, South Korea, and the Ukraine. Stars Georgie Henley (Lucy), Skandar Keynes (Edmund), Anna Popplewell (Susan), William Moseley (Peter), Peter Dinklage (Trumpkin), Warwick Davis (Nikabrik), Ben Barnes (Prince Caspian), Vincent Grass (Doctor Cornelius), Liam Neeson (voice of Aslan), Pierfrancesco Favino (General Glozelle), Sergio Castellitto (Miraz), Eddie Izzard (voice of Reepicheep), Tilda Swinton (White Witch). Based on C. S. Lewis's 1951 book. Filmed on location in New Zealand, Czech Republic, Poland, and Slovenia. Filmed in Super 35.

Chronicles of Narnia, The: The Lion, the Witch and the Wardrobe (film) Four Pevensie siblings—Lucy, Edmund, Susan, and Peter—in World War II England enter the world of Narnia through a magical wardrobe while playing a game of hide-and-seek in the rural country home of an elderly professor. Once there, the children discover a charming, peaceful land inhabited by talking beasts, dwarfs, fauns, centaurs, and giants that has become a world cursed to eternal winter by the evil White Witch, Jadis. Under the guidance of a noble and mystical ruler, the lion Aslan, the children fight to overcome the White Witch's powerful hold over Narnia in a spectacular, climactic battle that will free Narnia from Jadis's icy spell forever. Directed by Andrew Adamson. Released Dec. 9, 2005, after a world premiere at Royal Albert Hall in London on Dec. 7. A production of Walt Disney Pictures/Walden Media. Stars Georgie Henley (Lucy), Skandar Keynes (Edmund), Anna Popplewell (Susan), William Moseley (Peter), Tilda Swinton (White Witch), James Cosmo (Father Christmas), Dawn French (voice of Mrs. Beaver), James McAvoy (Mr. Tumnus), Rupert Everett (voice of Mr. Fox). Skandar Keynes is the great, great, great grandson of naturalist Charles Darwin. 140 min. The film was nominated for 3 Academy Awards and won for Best Makeup (Howard Berger and Tami Lane). It became the highest-grossing live-action Disney film, though soon passed by *Pirates of the Caribbean: Dead Man's Chest*. From the novel by C. S. Lewis. Filmed in Super 35-Scope in New Zealand, the Czech Republic, and London.

Chronicles of Narnia, The: The Voyage of the

Dawn Treader (film) The 3rd film in the Chronicles of Narnia series; released Dec. 10, 2010, directed by Michael Apted. Cast includes Ben Barnes (King Caspian), Georgie Henley (Lucy), Skandar Keynes (Edmund), Will Poulter (Eustace Clarence Scrubb), Tilda Swinton (White Witch). In Dec. 2008, Disney decided not to exercise its option to co-finance the movie, and Walden Media instead partnered with 20th Century Fox.

Chuck Wagon Westernland snack bar in Tokyo Disneyland, serving smoked turkey legs; open Jul. 1997–Mar. 2019, and succeeded by Cowboy Cookhouse.

Chuck Wagon Café Buffet dining in Disney Hotel Cheyenne at Disneyland Paris; opened Apr. 12, 1992. Diners enjoy hearty fare inside a Wild West wagon station.

Churchill, Frank (1901–1942) Composer; joined the Disney staff in 1930 and wrote the music for many of the short cartoons, including *Three Little Pigs*. He also wrote the songs for *Snow White and the Seven Dwarfs* and *Bambi*. His work for Disney earned 5 Academy Award nominations, including a win for Best Original Score (*Dumbo*, 1941). He was named a Disney Legend posthumously in 2001.

Ciao Alberto (film) Animated short from Pixar; digitally released Nov. 12, 2021, on Disney+. With his best friend, Luca, away at school, Alberto is enjoying his new life in Portorosso, working alongside Massimo, the imposing, one-armed fisherman of few words. He wants more than anything to impress his mentor, but it's easier said than done. Directed by McKenna Harris. Voices include Jack Dylan Grazer (Alberto), Marco Barricelli (Massimo), Jacob Tremblay (Luca). 7 min.

Cinderella (film) Animated feature; the famous rags-to-riches tale of a beautiful girl reduced to being a servant by her jealous stepmother and stepsisters, Anastasia and Drizella. With the help of a bit of magic by her Fairy Godmother, Cinderella is given a beautiful dress and use of a magnificent coach, and is able to attend a royal ball and inadvertently fall in love with the prince. Fleeing the ball at midnight, the hour when the magic spell is due to end, she leaves behind a glass slipper that the prince and Grand Duke use to search her out. With the help of her little mice and bird friends, she is discovered and assured a happy future. Voices include Ilene Woods (Cinderella), Eleanor Audley (Lady Tremaine), Verna Felton (Fairy Godmother), William Phipps (speaking voice of Prince Charming), Mike Douglas (singing voice of Prince Charming, uncredited). Released Feb. 15, 1950. Directed by Wilfred Jackson, Hamilton Luske, and Clyde Geronimi. 74 min. Songs include "A Dream Is a Wish Your Heart Makes," "The Work Song," "So This Is Love," and "Bibbidi-Bobbidi-Boo," all by Mack David, Jerry Livingston, and Al Hoffman, with "Bibbidi-Bobbidi-Boo" nominated for the Academy Award for Best Song. The film also received a nomination for Best Scoring of Musical Picture. During its original release, the public made the film one of the highest-grossing films of the year and Disney's most successful release since *Bambi*. Because of wartime economic problems, the Disney Studio had to be satisfied with its "package films" such as *Make Mine Music* and *Melody Time* for several years, but by the end of the 1940s, Walt was able to put together the financing for another full feature telling a single story. It was a gamble for the Studio, and if it had been unsuccessful, it probably would have sounded the death knell for animation at Disney. But its resounding success ensured that animation would continue. It was the first Disney film to have its songs published by the company's newly created in-house music arm, the Walt Disney Music Company. *Cinderella* was rereleased in theaters in 1957, 1965, 1973, 1981, and 1987. First released on video in 1988.

Cinderella (film) Live-action retelling of the Cinderella story. Young Ella's merchant father remarries after the death of her mother. Eager to support her loving father, Ella welcomes her new stepmother and her daughters, Anastasia and Drisella, into the family home. But, when Ella's father unexpectedly dies, she finds herself at the mercy of a jealous and cruel new family. Finally relegated to the role of a servant girl covered in ashes, and spitefully named Cinderella, Ella could easily begin to lose hope. But Ella does not give in to despair and meets a dashing stranger in the woods. Unaware that he is really a prince, Ella finally feels she has met a kindred soul. It appears her fortunes may be about to change when the palace sends out an open invitation for all maidens to attend a ball. Alas her stepmother forbids her to attend. But help is at hand when a kindly beggar woman steps forward and, with a pumpkin and a few mice, changes Cinderella's life forever. Released in the U.S. Mar. 13, 2015, after numerous international releases Mar.

6, 11, and 12. Directed by Kenneth Branagh. Stars Lily James (Ella), Cate Blanchett (Stepmother), Holliday Grainger (Anastasia), Sophie McShera (Drisella), Richard Madden (Kit/Prince), Helena Bonham Carter (Fairy Godmother), Stellan Skarsgård (Grand Duke), Derek Jacobi (King). 105 min. The grand palace was inspired by the architecture of the Louvre, the Palais Opéra, and the Hôtel de Soubise; each is noted for its grand, long staircases. For the palace ball, the filmmakers sought to create the most spectacular ballroom imaginable; while most films would have created the hall with CG effects, this one was instead built across 3 floors, filling the soundstage at 50 yards long, 35 yards wide, and 30 feet high. Above, 17 enormous custom-made chandeliers were brought in from Italy, with close to 5,000 oil candles that had to be lit by hand. Cinderella's blue gown required months of preparation, cleverly engineered to allow for both dancing and running away down the massive staircase. A total of 9 different versions of the gown would be created, each with more than 270 yards of fabric, numerous petticoats, more than 10,000 Swarovski crystals, and more than 3 miles of hems. To create a classic, timeless effect, the production was shot entirely on film. Filmed in widescreen format in England's Pinewood Studios and in and around London. Nominated for an Academy Award for Costume Design (Sandy Powell).

Cinderella (film) Laugh-O-gram film made by Walt in Kansas City in 1922. Cinderella's only friend is a cat. When Cinderella hears of the prince's ball, the Fairy Godmother appears and turns a garbage can into a tin lizzie in which she goes to the ball driven by the cat.

Cinderella (TV) Movie on *The Wonderful World of Disney*; first aired Nov. 2, 1997. *Rodgers & Hammerstein's Cinderella* was produced many years before on TV in versions starring Julie Andrews and Lesley Ann Warren, but this new version stars Brandy (Cinderella), Whitney Houston (Fairy Godmother), Whoopi Goldberg (Queen Constantina), Victor Garber (King Maximilian), Bernadette Peters (Stepmother), Jason Alexander (Lionel), Paolo Montalban (Prince), Natalie Desselle (Minerva), Veanne Cox (Calliope). Directed by Robert Iscove. 120 min. Most of the film's scenes were shot on stages at Sony Pictures Studios (formerly MGM Studios) in Culver City, California. Coincidentally, the palace set for *Cinderella* was constructed on the same soundstage where Dorothy followed the yellow brick road to Oz in the famous

1939 MGM film *The Wizard of Oz*. Visual designers were inspired by the style of Austrian artist Gustav Klimt, whose curious style was a synthesis of symbolism and art nouveau. To enhance the original musical score, and with permission from The Rodgers and Hammerstein Organization, 3 songs were added to the musical: "The Sweetest Sounds," written by Richard Rodgers for the 1962 Broadway musical *No Strings*; "Falling in Love with Love," by Rodgers and Lorenz Hart for *The Boys from Syracuse*; and "There's Music in You," by Rodgers and Oscar Hammerstein for the 1953 MGM film *Main Street to Broadway*.

Cinderella: A Lesson in Compromise (film) Educational film; released in Sep. 1981. Trying to get more than you need or deserve only leads to trouble.

Cinderella Carousel SEE CINDERELLA'S GOLDEN CARROUSEL.

Cinderella Castle Fantasyland palace-fortress towering 189 feet in the Magic Kingdom at Walt Disney World. Teams of designers at WED Enterprises studied European palaces and castles, including Fontainebleau, Versailles, and the chateaus of Chenonceau, Chambord, and Chaumont. They also turned to the original designs for the 1950 *Cinderella* film prepared by the Disney animation staff. The castle's chief designer was Herb Ryman, who had also worked on Sleeping Beauty Castle at Disneyland. The structure is made of concrete, steel, cement, plaster, and fiberglass; no bricks were used during its 18-month construction. Inside, the Charles Perrault *Cinderella* story is told through five 15-by-10-ft. mosaics made of a million bits of Italian glass in 500 colors, real silver, and 14-karat gold; it was designed by Dorothea Redmond and later duplicated for Tokyo Disneyland. Nearby, The King's Gallery sold tapestries, suits of armor, and damascene items; it became the Bibbidi Bobbidi Boutique in 2007. Upstairs was King Stefan's Banquet Hall, which puzzled Disney purists since King Stefan was the father of Princess Aurora in *Sleeping Beauty*, not Cinderella; this was rectified in 1997 with the renaming of the restaurant to Cinderella's Royal Table. For the park's 25th anniversary celebration in 1996–1997, the castle was transformed into the Cinderella Castle Cake with over 400 gallons of pink paint, more than 120 pieces of giant candy, and 26 giant candles (one to grow on). In 2005–06, as part of The Happiest Celebration on Earth, it was decorated with golden character statues and spirals, as well as an enormous magic mirror showing stained glass-style castles from other Disney parks around the world. In 2007, the Cinderella Castle Suite opened upstairs as part of The Year of a Million Dreams, enabling a different family to be selected to stay in the park each night; the Fouch family from Michigan was the first to stay in the suite, selected Jan. 25. In 2021, special touches were added to the castle for the park's 50th anniversary, including a royal blue jewel, gold detailing, and shimmering pearls and draping. There is also a Cinderella Castle in Tokyo Disneyland, whose exterior matches the one at Walt Disney World, but the interior contained the Cinderella Castle Mystery Tour (later Cinderella's Fairy Tale Hall) rather than a restaurant.

Cinderella Castle Mystery Tour Fantasyland attraction in Tokyo Disneyland; open Jul. 11, 1986–Apr. 5, 2006. A tour guide led visitors through the rooms of, and underneath, Cinderella Castle, where Disney villains appeared. It culminated with an encounter with The Horned King from *The Black Cauldron*, which proved to be frightening for younger guests. Replaced by Cinderella's Fairy Tale Hall.

Cinderella II: Dreams Come True (film) Direct-to-video release Feb. 26, 2002. Cinderella is now married to Prince Charming and getting used to living in the Royal Palace. When the prince departs on a business trip, Cinderella has to try to follow the rules of Prudence, the King's strict household adviser. With the help of her mouse friends, Cinderella realizes she needs to bring her own style to the palace. Jaq yearns to be human, and his wish is granted by the Fairy Godmother, but he soon comes to the realization that being human has its drawbacks. Romance is in the air, with stepsister Anastasia falling for the town baker, and the mice trying to set Lucifer up with the pampered palace cat, Pom-Pom, so they will be too busy to chase mice. Directed by John Kafka. Voices include Jennifer Hale (Cinderella). Christopher Daniel Barnes (Prince), Tress MacNeille (Anastasia), Russi Taylor (Drizella, Fairy Godmother, Beatrice, Countess Le Grande, Daphne, Mary Mouse), Rob Paulsen (Jaq, Sir Hugh, Baker), Corey Burton (Gus), Andre Stojka (King), Susanne Blakeslee (Stepmother), Holland Taylor (Prudence). 73 min.

Cinderella III: A Twist in Time (film) Direct-to-DVD release Feb. 6, 2007. When the Fairy Godmother's magic wand falls into the wrong hands, the glass slipper no longer fits Cinderella! Instead, her evil stepsister Anastasia is slated to marry Prince Charming! But with her loyal mice friends Gus and Jaq by her side, Cinderella is determined to make things right again. Directed by Frank Nissen. Voices include Jennifer Hale (Cinderella), Rob Paulsen (Jaq, Grand Duke, Bishop), Corey Burton (Gus), Russi Taylor (Fairy Godmother, Drizella), Tress MacNeille (Anastasia), Holland Taylor (Prudence), Susan Blakeslee (Stepmother), Frank Welker (Lucifer), Christopher Daniel Barnes (Prince), Andre Stojka (King). 74 min.

Cinderella: The Reunion, A Special Edition of 20/20 (TV) One-hour special; aired on ABC Aug. 23, 2022, before a digital release on Hulu the following day. The original cast and production team members of *Rodgers & Hammerstein's Cinderella* reunite to celebrate the 25th anniversary of the made-for-TV musical and explore how it expanded society's view of the term "princess." From ABC News Studios.

Cinderellabration: Lights of Romance Show created for the 20th anniversary of Tokyo Disneyland; performed in front of Cinderella Castle Jan. 25, 2003–Mar. 14, 2008. Another version, simply called Cinderellabration, played in the Magic Kingdom at Walt Disney World Mar. 17, 2005–Sep. 16, 2006. With sparkling pageantry, Disney princesses joined the gala coronation ceremony in which Cinderella was at last crowned a princess.

Cinderella's Fairy Tale Hall Attraction inside Cinderella Castle in Tokyo Disneyland; opened Apr. 15, 2011, replacing the Cinderella Castle Mystery Tour. Guests explore the castle to view paintings, dioramas, and other artwork that illustrate the princess's story.

Cinderella's Golden Carrousel Fantasyland attraction in the Magic Kingdom at Walt Disney World; opened Oct. 1, 1971. The carousel was originally built by the Philadelphia Toboggan Co. in 1917 for the Detroit Palace Garden Park; it later moved to Maplewood Olympic Park in New Jersey, where the Disney designers discovered it. The carousel was completely renovated, with scenes from *Cinderella* painted in the panels above the horses. The horses themselves are a marvel of craftsmanship, each one unique. Also opened in Fantasyland in Tokyo Disneyland (as Castle Carrousel) Apr. 15, 1983, and in Hong Kong Disneyland (as Cinderella Carousel) Sep. 12, 2005. The name of the Walt

Disney World attraction changed to Prince Charming Regal Carrousel Jun. 1, 2010.

Cinderella's Royal Table New name of King Stefan's Banquet Hall in Cinderella Castle in the Magic Kingdom at Walt Disney World, beginning Apr. 28, 1997. Guests dine in a medieval setting as they enjoy views out to Fantasyland and visits with Disney princesses. There are more than 40 coats of arms on display, each representing someone who played a significant role in Disney history, such as Roy O. Disney, Card Walker, and John Hench.

CinéMagique Film and special effects attraction presented in the Studio Theatre in Walt Disney Studios Park at Disneyland Paris; played Mar. 16, 2002–Mar. 29, 2017. A moviegoer (played by Martin Short) appears to be drawn from the audience and transported right into the movie screen, where he journeys through 100 years of European and American cinema. Also stars Julie Delpy, Alan Cumming, Tchéky Karyo. Replaced by the *Marvel: Super Heroes United* show.

CinéMagique featuring Captain EO A 3-D film attraction in Discoveryland at Disneyland Paris; opened Apr. 12, 1992. Shown until Aug. 17, 1998, after which it was replaced by *Chérie, J'ai Rétréci le Public (Honey, I Shrunk the Audience)*. The film ran again Jun. 12, 2010–Apr. 12, 2015. SEE CAPTAIN EO.

CinemaScope The first short cartoon filmed in the wide-screen process was *Toot, Whistle, Plunk and Boom*; the first animated feature was *Lady and the Tramp*.

Cinergi Pictures Entertainment Inc. After a multi-year distribution deal with Cinergi was canceled in Apr. 1997, Disney acquired Cinergi's film library; most of their films had originally been distributed by Disney.

Circarama This 360° motion picture process debuted at Disneyland in 1955, and originally required 11 cameras, but later only 9 were needed. The name of the process was later changed to Circle-Vision 360 due to complaints from the owners of the similar-sounding Cinerama. SEE ALSO CIRCLE-VISION/CIRCARAMA FOR A LIST OF THE FILMS.

Circarama, U.S.A. Tomorrowland attraction in Disneyland showing a 360° motion picture filmed with a camera invented by Disney technicians; opened Jul. 17, 1955, and sponsored by American Motors. The first film was called *A Tour of the West*. It featured 11 16-mm projectors and ran for 12 min. In 1960 the motion picture *America the Beautiful* was substituted, with the process renamed Circle-Vision 360 in 1967, and World Premiere Circle-Vision debuted in 1984.

Circle D Corral The Disneyland stables, home to horses, cows, donkeys, turkeys, and goats; it was known as the Pony Farm until 1980. The stables were relocated in 2016 to make way for Star Wars: Galaxy's Edge.

Circle of Life Song from *The Lion King*; written by Elton John and Tim Rice. Nominated for an Academy Award.

Circle of Life: An Environmental Fable (film) Live-action and animated film shown in the Harvest Theater in The Land at EPCOT; debuted Jan. 21, 1995, replacing *Symbiosis*. Directed by Bruce Morrow and Paul Justman. Simba, king of the Pride Lands, counsels Timon and Pumbaa, who are clearing the savanna for a new development, on how to respect the environment. 13 min. Closed Feb. 3, 2018, and later succeeded by a new film, *Awesome Planet*.

Circle-Vision 360 Tomorrowland attraction in the Magic Kingdom at Walt Disney World, which played *America the Beautiful*, *Magic Carpet 'Round the World*, and *American Journeys*. It closed Jan. 9, 1994, to be rebuilt as The Timekeeper. SEE ALSO CIRCLE-VISION/CIRCARAMA AND WORLD PREMIERE CIRCLE-VISION.

Circle-Vision/Circarama Process of 360° photography that began in Disneyland in 1955. The various films have been:

1. *Circarama U.S.A. (A Tour of the West)*, Disneyland, 1955 (11 cameras, 16 mm)
2. *America the Beautiful*, Brussels World's Fair, 1958 (opened at Disneyland in 1960)
3. *Italia '61*, Turin, Italy (for Fiat), 1961 (9 cameras, 16 mm, blown up to 35 mm)
4. *Magic of the Rails*, Lucerne, Switzerland (for Swiss Federal Railways), 1965 (name changed to Circle-Vision 360, 9 cameras, 35 mm)
5. *America the Beautiful*, Disneyland, 1967 (reshot film)
6. *Canada '67*, Expo 67, Montreal, 1967
7. *Magic Carpet 'Round the World*, Magic Kingdom at Walt Disney World, 1974
8. *America the Beautiful*, Magic Kingdom at Walt Disney World, 1975 (revised version)
9. *O Canada!*, EPCOT Center, 1982
10. *Wonders of China*, EPCOT Center, 1982
11. *Magic Carpet 'Round the World*, Tokyo Disneyland, 1983 (revised version)
12. *American Journeys*, Disneyland, 1984
13. *Portraits of Canada*, Expo '86, Vancouver, (for Telecom Canada), 1986
14. *From Time to Time*, Disneyland Paris, 1992 (revised versions for Visionarium in Tokyo Disneyland in 1993 and for The Timekeeper in the Magic Kingdom at Walt Disney World in 1994)
15. *Reflections of China*, EPCOT, 2003
16. *O Canada!*, EPCOT, 2007 (revised version)
17. *Canada Far and Wide in Circle-Vision 360*, EPCOT, 2020

SEE ALSO CIRCARAMA.

Circus Day Thursday's segment on the 1950s *Mickey Mouse Club*.

Circus Fantasy Entertainment spectacular at Disneyland in spring 1986, 1987, and 1988. Disney executives thought it would be good to have a special event at Disneyland during the off-season, so Main Street, U.S.A. and the Central Plaza were turned into a circus. There was a circus parade, clowns, and wild animals, along with various acts of skill featuring real circus performers.

Circus of the Stars Goes to Disneyland (TV) Special; aired on CBS Dec. 16, 1994. Hosts Leslie Nielsen, Scott Baio, and Harry Anderson are ringmasters introducing circus acts by celebrities, including Shemar Moore, Shae Harrison, Kelly Packard, Jenna Von Oy, A. J. Langer, and Debbe Dunning.

Cirque du Soleil Custom-built theater in the West Side at Downtown Disney (later Disney Springs) at Walt Disney World; opened Dec. 23, 1998, with *La Nouba* (a name derived from the French phrase "*faire la nouba*," meaning, "to live it up"). More than 60 performers blended circus art and theatrics with an array of colorful costumes, lighting, and original sets and music. The show explored the interplay of nightmares and dreams when 2 groups interacted: the monochromatic Urbains and the fantastical, colorful Cirques. The final performance was held Dec. 31, 2017. A new show, *Drawn to*

Life, debuted Nov. 18, 2021, exploring the bond between a father and daughter as Disney drawings come to life from an animator's desk. Another show, *Zed*, played at Tokyo Disney Resort Oct. 1, 2008–Dec. 31, 2011, based on the larger-than-life character Zed, a representation of humanity in all its guises, who grew as he discovered the world on a journey of initiation.

Cítricos Restaurant in Disney's Grand Floridian Resort & Spa at Walt Disney World; opened Nov. 8, 1997, replacing Flagler's. A highlight is the exhibition kitchen, where Floridian and Mediterranean dishes are prepared. A refurbishment in 2021 introduced a new interior design inspired by *Mary Poppins Returns*.

Citrus House World Bazaar counter-service restaurant in Tokyo Disneyland; opened Apr. 15, 1983, serving orange juice and sandwiches. Closed Aug. 1992, superseded by The Rainbow Fruit Market. SEE ALSO SUNKIST CITRUS HOUSE (DISNEYLAND).

City, The Trendy apparel shop in the Disney Village Marketplace at Walt Disney World; opened Apr. 1992, taking the place of Board Stiff. Closed in 1996, to be replaced by Authentic All Star.

City Fox, The (TV) Show aired Feb. 20, 1972. A young fox unexpectedly finds himself in San Francisco, where, after many misadventures, he is befriended by a boy in the city's Chinatown neighborhood. The boy helps the Humane Society take the fox back to the wilds. Directed by James Algar. With Tom Chan and Jerry Jerish.

City Hall Information area on Town Square in Disneyland; opened Jul. 17, 1955. Originally home of the Disneyland Publicity Department, it now houses Guest Relations and Main Street, U.S.A. operations offices. There are also City Hall locations at the other Disney parks.

Civil Action, A (film) A small-time, self-possessed personal-injury attorney's greed entangles him in a case that threatens to destroy him. The Woburn, Massachusetts, case (Anderson v. W. R. Grace and Beatrice Foods), regarding alleged water contamination—which appears to be a straightforward one—instead evolves into a labyrinthine lawsuit of epic proportions where truth, if it can be found at all, resides not in the courtroom, but buried deep in a network of deceit and corruption. A Touch-

stone film. Directed by Steven Zaillian. Released Dec. 25, 1998, in Los Angeles and New York City, and nationwide Jan. 8, 1999. Stars John Travolta (Jan Schlichtmann), Robert Duvall (Jerome Facher), James Gandolfini (Al Love), Dan Hedaya (John Riley), Zeljko Ivanek (Bill Crowley), John Lithgow (Judge Walter J. Skinner), William H. Macy (James Gordon), Kathleen Quinlan (Anne Anderson), Tony Shalhoub (Kevin Conway). 115 min. Paramount split the costs on this production and handled international distribution. Based on the best-selling book by Jonathan Harr. Exteriors were filmed in Boston and other parts of New England, but the federal courtroom set was built on a soundstage at Universal Studios. Many of the real-life people who were depicted in the film visited the sets during production, and some even appeared in cameo roles.

Civil War Several Disney movie and TV films were set in the era of the U.S. Civil War, including *The Great Locomotive Chase*, *Willie and the Yank*, *Johnny Shiloh*, *Million Dollar Dixie Deliverance*, and *The High Flying Spy*.

Clair de Lune The Claude Debussy piece was originally planned to be a segment in *Fantasia*, and animation of flying cranes in an ethereal swamp was filmed. But when *Fantasia* proved too long, the segment was shelved. Years later, a place for "Clair de Lune" was found in *Make Mine Music*, but because that film featured more contemporary music, the animation was instead matched to a different song: "Blue Bayou." In the 1990s, "Claire de Lune" was restored as originally intended for *Fantasia* and released on *The Fantasia Anthology* DVD in 2000.

Clara Cleans Her Teeth (film) Dental training film, made by Walt Disney after he moved to Hollywood, for Dr. Thomas B. McCrum of Kansas City, in 1926. Clara has problems with her teeth and refuses to see a dentist until she has a bad nightmare. Soon her teeth are fine, and she can eat snacks at school without her teeth hurting.

Clara Cluck Operatic diva chicken character who made her debut in *Orphans' Benefit* in 1934 and had 8 additional theatrical appearances. Voiced by Florence Gill, who is seen voicing the character in *The Reluctant Dragon*. Clara Cluck more recently appeared on TV, in *House of Mouse*, the *Mickey Mouse* shorts (2013), and *Mickey and the Roadster Racers*.

Clarabelle Cow Bovine character; appeared mostly in Mickey Mouse cartoons of the 1930s, often paired with Horace Horsecollar. She made her debut in *The Plowboy* (1929). More recent animated appearances include *Mickey's Christmas Carol*, *The Prince and the Pauper*, *The Three Musketeers*, *Get a Horse!*, and on TV in *House of Mouse*, the *Mickey Mouse* shorts (2013), and *Mickey Mouse Mixed-Up Adventures*.

Clarabelle's Walk-up window serving frozen treats in Mickey's Toontown at Disneyland; opened Jan. 24, 1993.

Clarabelle's Hand-Scooped Ice Cream Soda fountain and ice cream shop on Buena Vista Street in Disney California Adventure; opened Jun. 15, 2012.

Clark, Carroll (1894–1968) Longtime art director on most Disney features and TV shows from *The Great Locomotive Chase* to *The Love Bug*. He was nominated for an Academy Award for *Mary Poppins* and won an Emmy for *The Mooncussers*.

Clark, Dean He voiced Berlioz in *The Aristocats*.

Clark, Dick (1929–2012) Best known for the many years of hosting *American Bandstand* on ABC, Dick starred as himself for Disney in *Mickey's 50* and on *Blossom*, and hosted the syn. TV series *The Challengers*. He was named a Disney Legend in 2013.

Clark, Les (1907–1979) Leading Disney animator; the first of Walt's "Nine Old Men" to join the company (1927). He specialized in animating Mickey Mouse, beginning with one scene in *Steamboat Willie*, eventually animating on and directing many shorts and features. In his later years, he directed dozens of educational films, such as *Donald in Mathmagic Land*. He retired in 1975 and was named a Disney Legend posthumously in 1989.

Clark, Steven B. Publicist with Walt Disney Feature Animation and Disney Channel 1997–2001, Steven coauthored *Disney: The First 100 Years* with Dave Smith and wrote several Disney trivia and other games for Mattel. He joined ABC in 2002 and later became a vice president of Corporate Communications for The Walt Disney Company, where he founded and served as head of D23. He left the company in 2013.

Clark, Susan Actress; appeared in *The Apple*

Dumpling Gang (Magnolia "Dusty" Clydesdale) and *The North Avenue Irregulars* (Anne), and on TV in *Mickey's 50*.

Cleanliness Brings Health (film) Educational film produced under the auspices of the Coordinator of Inter-American Affairs. Story of the difference between 2 families: the "clean" family that cares for their food and home and remain happy, and the "careless" family that lives in filth and are unhealthy. Delivered Jun. 30, 1945.

Clement, Jemaine Actor/comedian; appeared in *Muppets Most Wanted* (Prison King), and on TV in *Legion* (Oliver Bird). He voiced Tamatoa in *Moana*, Fleshlumpeater in *The BFG*, and Dr. Zone in *Milo Murphy's Law*.

Clements, Ron Animator/director; he joined Disney in the early 1970s and worked as an assistant and animator on *Winnie the Pooh and Tigger Too*, *The Rescuers*, *Pete's Dragon*, *The Fox and the Hound*, and *The Black Cauldron*. He directed, with John Musker, *The Little Mermaid*, *Aladdin*, *Hercules*, *Treasure Planet*, *The Princess and the Frog*, and *Moana*. He retired in 2019.

Clemmons, Larry (1906–1988) Writer/story man; hired by Disney in 1932 and, except for the 1941–1955 period when he left the Studio, continued to work on stories for the Disney animated films. His writing credits on the features began with *The Reluctant Dragon* in 1941. He retired in 1978.

Cleo Geppetto's pet goldfish in *Pinocchio*.

Clerks (TV) Miramax Television animated series produced by Walt Disney Television Animation; premiered on ABC May 31, 2000, and ended Jun. 7 after 2 episodes. Based on characters from Kevin Smith's 1994 movie, *Clerks*, about goldbricking employees at a quick-stop food mart and next-door video store. Voices include Brian O'Halloran (Dante Hicks), Jeff Anderson (Randall Graves), Jason Mewes (Jay), Kevin Smith (Silent Bob).

Climbing High (film) Educational release in 16 mm in Jan. 1991; 25 min. A teen is pressured by his peers to try marijuana, but, as a dedicated rock climber, he discovers that the high he gets climbing mountains is far greater than any high he could get from a drug.

Cline, Becky She began at Disney in 1989, joining

the Walt Disney Archives staff in 1993. After 17 years in the department, she became director on the retirement of Dave Smith in 2010. She has authored several books and written dozens of articles on Disney history, spoken at company events, and overseen Archives exhibitions around the world, including the restoration of Walt Disney's studio offices in 2015. She has also helped develop outreach programs for Disney fans, such as D23.

Clint and Mac SEE ADVENTURES OF CLINT AND MAC, THE.

Clock Cleaners (film) Mickey Mouse cartoon released Oct. 15, 1937. Directed by Ben Sharpsteen. Mickey, Donald, and Goofy attempt to clean a huge clock on a high tower. Goofy is mystified by whoever is striking the bell, and when he is accidentally struck on the head by the bell-ringing figure, he begins to stagger dazedly about, performing daring acrobatics while Mickey tries to rescue him. Meanwhile, Donald fights a losing battle against a cantankerous mainspring he is trying to clean, with Mickey and Goofy being flung by a flexible flagpole outside into the mainspring with Donald. All 3 end up bounced into 1 of the gears of the clock and onto the floor, where parts of their bodies continue to move in unison like a pendulum.

Clock of the World Icon at the entrance to the original Tomorrowland in Disneyland, 1955–1966, displaying the time in the 24 different time zones around the world.

Clock Store, The (film) Silly Symphony cartoon released Sep. 28, 1931. Copyrighted as *In a Clock Store*. Directed by Wilfred Jackson. As night descends on a clock store, all the clocks come to life. A wall clock hits 2 alarm clocks when they are not looking and referees the resulting fight. Figures from different clocks dance together. A grandfather clock dances with a grandmother clock. Two cuckoo clock birds bump heads as they both announce the time.

Clock Watcher, The (film) Donald Duck cartoon released Jan. 26, 1945. Directed by Jack King. Donald works as a department store gift wrapper, but his job is threatened because of his tardiness, laziness, and playing with the merchandise.

Clooney, George Actor; appeared in *O Brother, Where Art Thou?* (Ulysses Everett McGill) and *Tomorrowland* (Frank Walker), with a TV cameo in *The Golden Girls* (Bobby).

Clopin's Festival of Foods Quick-service food court in Fantasyland at Hong Kong Disneyland; opened Sep. 12, 2005. Under a medieval festival tent, food stations serve regional noodles, Guangdong barbecue, and wok favorites.

Close, Glenn Actress; appeared in *Guardians of the Galaxy* (Nova Prime) and the live-action *101 Dalmatians* and *102 Dalmatians* (Cruella De Vil), on TV in *South Pacific* (Ensign Forbush), and served as an exec. producer of *Cruella*. She voiced Kala in *Tarzan* and *Tarzan II*.

Close-up on the Planets (film) Educational film; released in Sep. 1982. Computer animation and footage from NASA space missions explain how our solar system evolved and the place Earth has within the system.

Cloud 9 (TV) A Disney Channel Original Movie; premiered Jan. 17, 2014. Kayla Morgan, a prima donna snowboarder is unceremoniously dropped from her team and forced to train with Will Cloud, a former snowboarding champion who is struggling after a career-ending wipeout. A video capturing it went viral, branding him an "epic fail" on the Internet. Now, as Kayla trains with Will to redeem her stature, Will creates a training regimen that tests whether she is really committed to rise to the challenge of professional competition. Meanwhile, Kayla must somehow maneuver to inspire Will to overcome his biggest obstacle: self-doubt. Directed by Paul Hoen. Stars Luke Benward (Will), Dove Cameron (Kayla), Kiersey Clemons (Skye Sailor), Mike C. Manning (Nick Swift), Dillon Lane (Burke), Carlon Jeffery (Dink). 97 min.

Clouds (film) A Disney+ original film from Wayfarer Studios, Warner Bros. Pictures, and Mad Chance/La Scala Films. Zach Sobiech is a 17-year-old, fun-loving student with raw musical talent living with osteosarcoma, a rare bone cancer. At the start of his senior year, he is ready to take on the world, but when he receives the news that the disease has spread, he and his best friend and songwriting partner, Sammy, decide to spend Zach's limited time following their dreams. With the help of Zach's mentor, Mr. Weaver, Zach and Sammy are given the chance of a lifetime and are offered a record deal. Along with the support of his parents and the love of his life, Amy, Zach embarks on an unforgettable journey about friendship, love, and the power of music. Based on a true story. Released digitally Oct. 16, 2020, on Disney+, in conjunction with a premiere at the Disney+ Drive-In Festival at the Barker Hangar in Santa Monica, California. Directed by Justin Baldoni. Stars Fin Argus (Zach Sobiech), Neve Campbell (Laura Sobiech), Sabrina Carpenter (Sammy), Madison Iseman (Amy), Tom Everett Scott (Rob Sobiech), Lil Rel Howery (Mr. Weaver), Dylan Everett (Sam), Vivien Endicott Douglas (Alli), Summer H. Howell (Grace). 121 min. A 30-min. live virtual concert, *Clouds: A Musical Celebration*, was presented on Facebook Oct. 24, 2020, with performances by the film's actors and special guests.

Clown of the Jungle (film) Donald Duck cartoon released Jun. 20, 1947. Directed by Jack Hannah. Photographer Donald is harassed and driven half-mad by a crazy Aracuan bird who keeps sabotaging his photography of the jungle and its animals. The bird starred earlier in *The Three Caballeros* and *Melody Time*.

Club Buzz—Lightyear's Above the Rest Tomorrowland restaurant in Disneyland, formerly known as Tomorrowland Terrace; opened Jun. 30, 2001, and reverted to the Tomorrowland Terrace name in 2006.

Club Cool Exhibit in World Celebration at EPCOT; guests can sample Coca-Cola products from around the world. Originally debuted in Innoventions West in Jul. 1998, as Ice Station Cool, becoming Club Cool Nov. 18, 2005. Closed Sep. 7, 2019, later reopening Sep. 15, 2021, in a new site in the former Innoventions East. Beverly, the beverage from Italy, has a bitter taste that many guests don't expect.

Club Disney A new concept in Disney-themed entertainment; opened Feb. 21, 1997, in Thousand Oaks, California, featuring a play experience for children ages 4–10 and their parents. The 4 themed areas were called Pal Around Playground, Curiosity Castle, Starring You Studio, and The Chat Hat. Food was available in The Club Cafe, and there was a unique retail store. Birthday parties could be planned, and there were workshops on changing topics. Club Disney was the first location-based entertainment complex from the new Disney Regional Entertainment subsidiary. After 5 Club Disney sites were established, the clubs were all closed Nov. 1, 1999, when it was decided the return on investment

was insufficient. FOR THE WALT DISNEY WORLD ATTRACTION, SEE SUNSET SHOWCASE.

Club House Grill Restaurant overlooking Golf Disneyland in Disneyland Paris; opened Apr. 12, 1992.

Club Lake Villas Accommodations at Lake Buena Vista; opened Aug. 1980. Its name changed to Club Suites in 1989. Originally aimed at conventioneers attending meetings at the Walt Disney World Conference Center, each villa had 2 queen-size beds and a sofa bed, with a sitting area separated from the bedroom area. Became part of The Disney Institute in 1996.

Club Mickey Mouse Digital series following a new class of Mouseketeers as they create music, choreography, and friendships. The first Mouseketeers to premiere in the series were Regan Aliyah, Jenna Alvarez, Ky Baldwin, Gabe De Guzman, Leanne Tessa Langston, Brianna Mazzola, Sean Oliu, Will Simmons. Debuted Sep. 8, 2017, on Instagram and Facebook.

Club Penguin Disney acquired the online virtual world for kids aged 6–14 on Aug. 1, 2007. The multiplayer game, founded by Lane Merrifield, Dave Krysko, and Lance Priebe at New Horizon Interactive in Kelowna, Canada, had originally launched in Oct. 2005, and by the time of the acquisition had grown to 700,000 paid subscribers and 12 million users. The game was discontinued Mar. 29, 2017, and replaced by *Club Penguin Island*, which ended Dec. 18, 2018.

Club Suites Accommodations at Lake Buena Vista, formerly known as Club Lake Villas. When they became part of The Disney Institute in Feb. 1996, they were known as Bungalows.

Club 33 Membership program and private restaurant upstairs in New Orleans Square at Disneyland; opened Jun. 15, 1967; originally meant for park operating participants, VIPs, and their guests. Walt became very involved in the club's early planning but never saw the final product, having passed away 6 months before its opening. He and his wife, Lillian, had traveled to New Orleans with Disney Studio set decorator Emile Kuri to select the antiques that would be displayed inside. Initially, members entered the club by taking a 19th-century-style French lift to the 2nd floor, where they were seated in the main dining room or a wood-paneled trophy room, which displayed Lillian's butterfly collection and a menagerie of mounted animals. Some of these creatures were actually Audio-Animatronics figures meant to converse with guests (with the aid of microphones hidden in the light fixtures), but the process was never used; the trophy room later displayed Disney memorabilia. In 2014, the club underwent a major renovation/expansion, reopening Jul. 18. Among the changes were a new main entrance in the Court des Anges (Court of Angels); art nouveau–inspired interiors; a jazz lounge, Le Salon Nouveau; and a refurbished main dining room, now named Le Grand Salon. Versions of Club 33 have opened in Tokyo Disneyland (Apr. 15, 1983, in World Bazaar); Shanghai Disneyland (2016, on Mickey Avenue); and Walt Disney World (beginning 2018, where there is a venue in each of the 4 theme parks themed to Walt and Lillian's world travels). The "33" refers solely to the original club's street address on Royal Street at Disneyland. See also 1901, 21 Royal Street, and Disneyland Dream Suite.

Coats, Claude (1913–1992) Artist/Imagineer; hired by Disney in 1935 as a background painter, he worked on such films as *Snow White and the Seven Dwarfs, Fantasia, Dumbo, Saludos Amigos, Make Mine Music, Lady and the Tramp, Cinderella,* and *Peter Pan.* In 1955, he transferred to WED Enterprises, where as a show designer, he helped develop a variety of attractions, including Snow White's Adventures, Submarine Voyage, the Magic Skyway, Carousel of Progress, It's a Small World, Pirates of the Caribbean, the Haunted Mansion, and the Grand Canyon and Primeval World dioramas. For Walt Disney World, he helped create the Mickey Mouse Revue, Universe of Energy, Horizons, World of Motion, and several World Showcase pavilions, later contributing to Tokyo Disneyland. He was one of the few WED employees to receive a 50-year service award. He retired in 1989 and was named a Disney Legend in 1991.

Cobb, Charles E., Jr. Member of the Disney Board of Directors 1984–1987.

Coburn, James (1928–2002) Actor; appeared in *Sister Act 2: Back in the Habit* (Mr. Crisp) and *Snow Dogs* (Thunder Jack), and on TV in *Elfego Baca.* He voiced Waternoose in *Monsters, Inc.*

Coca-Cola Refreshment Corner Counter-service restaurant on Main Street, U.S.A. in Disneyland; opened Jul. 17, 1955. Guests enjoy all-American classics like hot dogs and chili bowls as a ragtime piano player serenades on the patio. Also known as Coke Corner and Corner Cafe. Coca-Cola is one of the few remaining opening-day participants at Disneyland. Also opened in the Magic Kingdom at Walt Disney World Oct. 1, 1971, and in Tokyo Disneyland Apr. 15, 1983. In Disneyland Paris, it is Casey's Corner, a name that was applied to the Walt Disney World location May 27, 1995. See also Main Street Corner Cafe (Hong Kong Disneyland).

Cocina Cucamonga Mexican Grill Counter-service restaurant overlooking the waterfront in Pacific Wharf at Disney California Adventure; opened Feb. 8, 2001. It switched locations with the Lucky Fortune Cookery in 2009.

Cock o' the Walk (film) Silly Symphony cartoon released Nov. 30, 1935. Directed by Ben Sharpsteen. A farmyard battle ensues between a hick rooster and a city slicker over the love of a beautiful lady pullet, who discovers the city rooster is married. The hick avenges her, becomes the champ, and resumes his romance with her.

Cocktail (film) Returning from his military service, young Brian Flanagan finds his hopes dashed when he tries to find a career bringing him power, excitement, and quick personal profit. He ends up as a bartender, but under the tutelage of seasoned pro Doug Coughlin. His flashy expertise and killer smile make him a star on the club circuit. Soon, Flanagan is swept up in a seductive world of easy money in New York City and Jamaica. Eventually, a spirited romance with Jordan Mooney helps bring perspective to the cocksure bartender's life. Released Jul. 29, 1988. Directed by Roger Donaldson. A Touchstone film. 103 min. Stars Tom Cruise (Brian Flanagan), Bryan Brown (Doug Coughlin), Elisabeth Shue (Jordan Mooney). Cruise and Brown spent several weeks at a bartending school, and soon each was adept at the flashy tricks that were so impressive in the movie. Filmed on location in New York City, Jamaica, and Toronto.

Coco (film) Animated feature from Pixar Animation Studios. Despite his family's generations-old ban on music, 12-year-old Miguel dreams of becoming an accomplished musician like his idol, Ernesto de la Cruz. Desperate to prove his talent, Miguel finds himself in the stunning colorful

Land of the Dead following a mysterious chain of events. Along the way, he meets charming trickster Héctor, and together they set off on an extraordinary journey to unlock the real story behind Miguel's family history. Directed by Lee Unkrich and Adrian Molina. Released Nov. 22, 2017, also in 3-D, after an Oct. 27 release in Mexico. Voices include Anthony Gonzalez (Miguel), Benjamin Bratt (Ernesto de la Cruz), Gael García Bernal (Héctor), Edward James Olmos (Chicharrón), Gabriel Iglesias (head clerk), Cheech Marin (Corrections Officer), Alfonso Arau (Papá Julio), Sofía Espinosa (Mamá). 105 min. Filmmakers collaborated with a team of cultural consultants—including political cartoonist Lalo Alcaraz, playwright Octavio Solis, and author/producer Marcela Davison Avilés—who advised on everything from character wardrobe to set décor. Artists set out to create as much contrast between the Land of the Living and the Land of the Dead as possible; the former is largely flat with simple camera treatments, while the latter is more visually vibrant and colorful. Filmed in a wide-screen format. Accompanying the release was the featurette *Olaf's Frozen Adventure*. Won Academy Awards for Best Animated Feature and Best Song ("Remember Me"), with music and lyrics by Kristen Anderson-Lopez and Robert Lopez.

Code Black (TV) Hour-long medical drama on CBS; aired Sep. 30, 2015–Jul. 18, 2018. At the busiest, most notorious ER in the nation, a staggering influx of patients can outweigh the limited resources available to the extraordinary doctors and nurses whose job is to treat them all—creating a condition known as Code Black. Stars Marcia Gay Harden (Dr. Leanne Rorish), Bonnie Somerville (Christa Lorenson), Raza Jaffrey (Dr. Neal Hudson), Luis Guzmán (Jesse Sallander). From ABC Studios in association with CBS Television Studios.

Cody Young boy who tries to save the eagle in *The Rescuers Down Under*; voiced by Adam Ryen.

Cody, Iron Eyes (1904–1999) Native American actor; appeared in *Westward Ho the Wagons!* (Chief Many Stars) and *Ernest Goes to Camp* (Old Indian Chief), and on TV in *Along the Oregon Trail* and *The Saga of Andy Burnett*. He hosted *The First Americans* on the *Mickey Mouse Club*.

Cody, Kathleen Actress; appeared in *Snowball*

Express (Chris Baxter), *Charley and the Angel* (Leonora Appleby), and *Superdad* (Wendy McCready).

Coffee Grinder, The Main Street, U.S.A. coffee, ice cream, and cake shop in Disneyland Paris; opened Apr. 12, 1992.

Coffee House, The Courtyard coffee shop in the Disneyland Hotel at Disneyland Resort; opened Sep. 6, 1995. An earlier Coffee Shop operated Feb. 15, 1956–1986, and was succeeded by the Monorail Cafe.

Cogsworth Enchanted mantel clock and sturdy, but stressed, voice of reason in *Beauty and the Beast*; voiced by David Ogden Stiers.

Cold-Blooded Penguin, The (film) Segment of *The Three Caballeros* in which Pablo Penguin cannot stand the cold weather at the South Pole, so he sets off for warmer climes. A 16-mm version was released in Dec. 1971.

Cold Creek Manor (film) Cooper Tilson and his wife, Leah, tiring of the hustle and bustle of New York City, pack up their kids and move into a recently repossessed mansion in the sticks of New York State. Once grand and elegant, the manor at Cold Creek is now a shambles, but the family has plenty of time to renovate. Then a mysterious former resident returns and a series of terrifying incidents occur at the house, leading the Tilsons to wonder about the family that used to live in their new home and what dark secrets are hidden inside. A Touchstone film. Directed by Mike Figgis. Released Sep. 19, 2003. Stars Dennis Quaid (Cooper Tilson), Sharon Stone (Leah Tilson), Stephen Dorff (Dale Massie), Juliette Lewis (Ruby), Kristen Stewart (Kristen Tilson), Ryan Wilson (Jesse Tilson), Dana Eskelson (Sheriff Ferguson), Christopher Plummer (Mr. Massie). 119 min. Filmed in Ontario, Canada.

Cold Storage (film) Pluto cartoon released Feb. 9, 1951. Directed by Jack Kinney. Pluto and a stork battle in the dead of winter for possession of Pluto's house, which is confiscated by the stork, until spring arrives.

Cold Turkey (film) Pluto cartoon released Sep. 21, 1951. Directed by Charles Nichols. Pluto and Milton, the cat, are persuaded by a TV commercial for Lurkey Turkey to cook one of their own, but the situation quickly explodes into a fight for the bird.

Cold War (film) Goofy cartoon released Apr. 27, 1951. Directed by Jack Kinney. When Goofy gets a cold, he is tormented by a virus character until his wife comes home and puts him to bed. The virus goes away, only to return 2 weeks later when Goofy is back at work, sitting in a draft.

Cole, Tommy Mouseketeer from the 1950s *Mickey Mouse Club* TV show. Tommy became a makeup artist in later years.

Coleman, Dabney Actor; appeared in *Where the Heart Is* (Stewart McBain), *Inspector Gadget* (Chief Quimby), and *Moonlight Mile* (Mike Mulcahey), and on TV in *My Date with the President's Daughter* (President Richmond) and *Everything I Know About Men* (Jack). He voiced Principal Prickly in *Recess*.

Coleman, Zendaya Actress/singer; appeared on Disney Channel in the title role in *K. C. Undercover* (also co-producer) and in *Frenemies* (Halley), *Zapped* (Zoey Stevens), *Shake It Up* and *Good Luck Charlie* (Rocky Blue), *A.N.T. Farm* (Sequoia), and the *Radio Disney Music Awards*. On ABC, she appeared in *black-ish* (Resheida), *Disneyland 60: The Wonderful World of Disney*, and the *Disney Parks Christmas Day Parade*. She voiced Fern in *Disney Fairies: Pixie Hollow Games*.

Colglazier, Michael He joined Disney in 1989 as a strategic planning analyst and held several leadership positions across Disney Parks and Resorts over the years, including as vice president of Disney Photo Imaging, of Disney Parks and Resorts Global Development, and of Disney's Animal Kingdom. In 2013, he was named president of the Disneyland Resort and 5 years later became president and managing director of Walt Disney Parks and Resorts' Asia Pacific Operation. In 2019, he was named president and managing director of Disney Parks International. He left the company in 2020.

Collector, The (film) SEE MICKEY'S 50.

Collector's Warehouse Shop at Guardians of the Galaxy – Mission: BREAKOUT! in Disney California Adventure; opened May 25, 2017, replacing Tower Hotel Gifts. Guests conclude their tour of the Collector's Fortress browsing superhero souvenirs.

College Bowl '87 (TV) Dick Cavett hosted this game show for college teams on The Disney Channel; taped in EPCOT Center. It aired Sep. 13, 1987–Dec. 20, 1987.

College Program SEE DISNEY COLLEGE PROGRAM.

College Road Trip (film) High school student Melanie is eagerly looking forward to her first big step toward independence when she plans a "girls only" road trip to check out prospective universities. But when her overprotective police chief father insists on escorting her instead, she soon finds her dream trip has turned into a nightmare adventure full of comical misfortune and turmoil. Dad is trying to assure total security and safety for his precious daughter, while Melanie has a 17-year-old's need to become a grown woman and have her own sense of independence. Directed by Roger Kumble. Released Mar. 7, 2008. Stars Martin Lawrence (James Porter), Raven-Symoné (Melanie), Kym E. Whitley (Michelle), Eshaya Draper (Trey), Lucas Grabeel (Scooter), Brenda Song (Nancy), Arnetia Walker (Grandma Porter), Margo Harshman (Katie), Donny Osmond (Doug Greenhut), Molly Ephraim (Wendy). 83 min. Primarily filmed in Connecticut, utilizing private academies, prep schools, and colleges in that state, standing in for Northwestern University, the University of Pennsylvania, and Georgetown University. Filmed in Super 35.

Collegiate All-Star Band SEE ALL-AMERICAN COLLEGE BAND.

Collette, Toni Actress; appeared in *The Sixth Sense* (Lynn Sear), for which she received an Academy Award nomination as Best Supporting Actress, and *The Last Shot* (Emily French).

Collins, Paul Actor; appeared in *The Marrying Man* (Butler) and *Instinct* (Tom Hanley), and voiced John in *Peter Pan*.

Collins, Phil Composer/musician; wrote and performed the songs in *Tarzan*, receiving an Oscar for "You'll Be in My Heart," later contributing new songs for the stage adaptation. He provided the voice of Lucky in *The Jungle Book 2* and wrote 6 songs for *Brother Bear*. He was named a Disney Legend in 2002.

Colonel Hathi Pompous leader of the elephants in *The Jungle Book*; voiced by J. Pat O'Malley.

Colonel Hathi's Pizza Outpost Counter-service restaurant in Adventureland at Disneyland Paris; opened Apr. 1994, taking the place of the Explorer's Club.

Colonel Hathi's Safari Club Adventureland Bazaar shop in the Magic Kingdom at Walt Disney World; opened in 1972, replacing the Safari Club arcade. Closed Dec. 1990 and succeeded by Island Supply Company.

Colonel's Cotton Mill A 195-seat family dining hall in Disney's Dixie Landings Resort at Walt Disney World; open Feb. 2, 1992–2001, and succeeded by the Riverside Mill Food Court when the resort became Disney's Port Orleans Resort – Riverside.

Colonna, Jerry (1903–1986) Actor/comedian; he gave the musical recitation of *Casey at the Bat* and later was the voice of the March Hare in *Alice in Wonderland*.

Colony Theater *Steamboat Willie* was released at this New York City theater Nov. 18, 1928. It later became the Broadway Theater.

Color The first Disney cartoon made in color was *Flowers and Trees* (1932). Walt Disney had the foresight to sign an exclusive 2-year agreement with Technicolor for the use of their new 3-color process in cartoons, so he received a terrific head start over the other cartoon producers in Hollywood. Disney then made every Silly Symphony in color, but for a time held off switching to color for the Mickey Mouse cartoons. The first Mickey Mouse theatrical release in color was *The Band Concert* (1935), and soon all succeeding cartoons would be in color. Walt Disney made almost all of his TV programs in color, which enabled them to be rebroadcast in color when he switched to color broadcasting in 1962. The few features that were made in black and white—*The Shaggy Dog, The Absent-Minded Professor, Son of Flubber*—had actually been planned for TV, and the intricate special effects processes utilized were thought to be less obvious in black and white. *The Absent-Minded Professor* was the first black-and-white Disney feature to be colorized, in 1986.

Color Gallery Interactive display from Dutch Boy Paints in Tomorrowland at Disneyland; open 1955–1963.

Color of Friendship, The (TV) A Disney Channel Original Movie; first aired Feb. 5, 2000. In 1977, African American congressman Ron V. Dellums and his family welcome a South African exchange student. But, expecting a student of color, they are surprised when a white South African woman arrives. Their surprise is no more than the girl's, a product of the apartheid system who views Black people as second-class citizens. The situation challenges them all with valuable lessons about racism and tolerance. Directed by Kevin Hooks. Stars Carl Lumbly (Ron Dellums), Penny Johnson (Roscoe Dellums), Lindsey Haun (Mahree), Shadia Simmons (Piper Dellums), Ahmad Stoner (Daniel), Anthony Burnett (Brandy Dellums), Travis Davis (Erik Dellums). The real Erik Dellums plays the role of Oliver.

Color of Money, The (film) Former pool hustler Fast Eddie Felson sees promise in a cocky kid, Vincent. With the help of Vincent's girlfriend, Carmen, he takes the kid under his wing to prepare him for a major Atlantic City, New Jersey, tournament. After a falling out, Felson takes up his cue stick again, and they end up playing against each other. Released Oct. 17, 1986. Directed by Martin Scorsese. A Touchstone film. 120 min. Stars Paul Newman (Eddie), Tom Cruise (Vincent), Mary Elizabeth Mastrantonio (Carmen), Helen Shaver (Janelle), John Turturro (Julian). Academy Award winner for Best Actor for Paul Newman. The filming took place in Chicago and Atlantic City.

Color of Night (film) Haunted by the bizarre suicide of a patient, New York City psychologist Dr. Bill Capa abandons his successful practice and relocates to Los Angeles. He soon finds himself entangled in an explosive relationship with an enigmatic woman named Rose, and in the investigation of the brutal murder of a friend and colleague, Dr. Bob Moore. After he is persuaded by a police detective to take over his friend's counseling sessions, he is shocked to discover that the fanatic murderer, probably someone in the group, is now stalking him. Released Aug. 19, 1994. Directed by Richard Rush. A Hollywood Pictures film, in association with Cinergi Pictures. 123 min. Stars Bruce Willis (Bill Capa), Jane March (Rose), Rubén Blades (Martinez), Lesley Ann Warren (Sondra), Brad Dourif (Clark), Lance Henriksen (Buck), Kevin J. O'Connor (Casey). Filmed at a variety of locations in Los Angeles and at Ren Mar Studios in New York City. The director's cut was released on video in 1995.

Colors of the Wind Song from *Pocahontas*; written by Alan Menken and Stephen Schwartz. Academy Award winner.

Coltrin, Robert ("Rob't") He joined the Walt Disney Imagineering show set design group in 1990, later working in concept design and art direction before becoming executive creative director. He was a creative force behind such attractions as *Muppet*Vision 3D*, Roger Rabbit's Car Toon Spin, Radiator Springs Racers, *Mickey's PhilharMagic*, and Mickey & Minnie's Runaway Railway. He retired in 2019 and was named a Disney Legend the following year.

Columbia Distributor of the Disney cartoons 1930–1932. In 1932, Walt Disney switched to United Artists.

Columbia Harbour House Two-story counter-service restaurant in Liberty Square in the Magic Kingdom at Walt Disney World; opened Jun. 10, 1972, serving seafood, fried chicken, and sandwiches. The atmosphere is of an 18th-century seaport meeting place.

Columbia Sailing Ship Frontierland attraction in Disneyland; opened Jun. 14, 1958. The belowdecks exhibit, featuring re-created quarters of 18th-century American sailors, opened Feb. 22, 1964. The original *Columbia* was the first ship to circumnavigate the globe in 1787, with the Columbia River in Oregon named after it when it explored the mouth of the river. Disney designers, led by Admiral Joe Fowler, studied historical records to make their reproduction as accurate as possible. It found additional use by taking on the guise of Captain Hook's pirate ship (later the *Black Pearl*) as a part of *Fantasmic!* More commonly known as the Sailing Ship *Columbia*.

Colvig, Pinto (1892–1967) Story man at the Disney Studio in the 1930s and the original voice of Goofy. Also supplied the voices of the Grasshopper (in *The Grasshopper and the Ants*), the Practical Pig in *Three Little Pigs*, and Sleepy and Grumpy in *Snow White and the Seven Dwarfs*. He helped Frank Churchill compose "Who's Afraid of the Big Bad Wolf?" in 1933. He resigned in 1937 but continued recording the Goofy voice from time to time. He was named a Disney Legend in 1993.

Comanche (TV) Title of *Tonka* for its airing in 1962.

Come Fly with Disney (TV) Syn. show from 1986 about flying, featuring the cartoons *Pedro, Goofy's Glider, The Plastics Inventor, The Flying Gauchito*, and *Test Pilot Donald*, and segments from *The Rescuers* and *Dumbo*.

Come Up, The (TV) Unscripted series on Freeform; premiered Sep. 13, 2022. Six young disruptors emerge from downtown New York to pursue love and art on their own terms, providing a glimpse into vibrant moments that define coming-of-age in a post-pandemic New York. Stars Taofeek Abijako, Fernando Casablancas, Ben Hard, Claude Shwartz, Ebon Gore, Sophia Wilson. From Cousins Productions.

Comedy Warehouse Nightclub in Pleasure Island at Walt Disney World; open May 1, 1989–Sep. 27, 2008. Stand-up comedians performed improvisational acts, often poking fun at Disney, which entertained adult audiences after a day in the parks. In the Pleasure Island story, the building had once been a power station, that later became a storage warehouse; props from retired Disney shows and attractions lined the shelves and walls. For several years after the club closed, special holiday versions of the show were performed in Disney's Hollywood Studios. Replaced by STK in 2016.

Comet Cafe Quick-service restaurant in Tomorrowland at Hong Kong Disneyland; opened Sep. 12, 2005, serving wok, BBQ, and noodles.

Comets: Time Capsules of the Solar System (film) Educational film; released in Sep. 1981. The film discusses the role comets play in contemporary scientific research about the solar system's beginnings.

Comic books The *Mickey Mouse Magazine*, which began publication in 1935, was actually the forerunner of Disney comic books. Starting out in large format, the magazine was reduced in size in stages until finally in 1940 it had reached normal comic book size. The final issue of the *Mickey Mouse Magazine* of Sep. 1940 was succeeded the next month by the first issue of *Walt Disney's Comics and Stories*. The original cover price was 10¢. Even earlier than the *Comics and Stories*, however, there had been a few one-shot Donald Duck comics. Following these and later one-shots, Donald Duck comics began a regular monthly publication schedule in 1952, as did the Mickey Mouse comics. Artist Carl Barks began drawing the Duck comics in 1942, and soon his unique style was exciting comic readers. He later created the character of Uncle Scrooge, who began starring in his own comic series, also in 1952. The comic books were created by artists employed by Western Publishing, not the Disney Studio. Dell Publishing was the original imprint, followed by Gold Key, then Whitman. Often a Disney movie or TV show would be promoted by 1 or more of the special comic books. The comics reached a peak in Sep. 1952, when over 3 million copies of a single issue of *Walt Disney's Comics and Stories* were sold. The 1980s brought changes to Disney comic publishing as Gladstone took over their production from Western Publishing for 4 years beginning in 1986, to be followed by several years of the Disney Studio producing the comics themselves. Gladstone returned in 1993, with Marvel handling a few of the comic lines. Gemstone Publishing then began publishing the Disney comic books in 2003 and continued till 2008; Boom! Kids published them 2009–2011. See also Disney Kingdoms.

Comic strips The *Mickey Mouse* comic strip, distributed by King Features Syndicate, debuted Jan. 13, 1930. Original artist Ub Iwerks drew the strip for a month and then was followed for 3 months by Win Smith. When Smith left, Walt Disney asked Floyd Gottfredson to take over the strip for a few weeks until they could find a replacement. Gottfredson continued to draw the strip for 45 years, until the day he retired. The *Mickey Mouse* Sunday page began Jan. 10, 1932, and was drawn by Manuel Gonzales for over 30 years. A *Donald Duck* daily strip began Feb. 7, 1938, drawn by Al Taliaferro, and continued until his death in 1969. Taliaferro also did the *Donald Duck* Sunday page. Over the years, these artists were aided by various writers and inkers. There was a *Silly Symphonies* Sunday page, a Sunday page devoted to current Disney film releases entitled *Walt Disney's Treasury of Classic Tales*, an *Uncle Remus* Sunday page, *Merry Menagerie* and *True-Life Adventure* daily panels, an annual Christmas strip, and *Scamp* and *Winnie the Pooh* strips.

Coming On (TV) Variety series on The Disney Channel; first aired Sep. 3, 1983, and continued, with repeats, until Aug. 26, 1985. Hosted by Jimmy Aleck (24 episodes). Featured talent from different colleges performing the full spectrum of contemporary entertainment, from soft rock, rock, soul, and jazz to comedy, pantomime, and regional specialties. Interviews and video capsules of campus life were included.

Commander-in-Chief (TV) One-hour drama series on ABC; aired Sep. 27, 2005–Jun. 14, 2006. Vice President Mackenzie Allen has 3 children at home, an ambitious husband at the office, and she is set to become the first female president of the U.S. Even though the current and dying president has asked her to step down and let someone "more appropriate" fill his shoes in the Oval Office, Mackenzie is unwilling to be a mere footnote in history, so she decides to trust her instincts and accept the job. Stars Geena Davis (Mackenzie Allen), Donald Sutherland (Nathan Templeton), Harry J. Lennix (Jim Gardner), Ever Carradine (Kelly Ludlow), Kyle Secor (Rod Allen), Julie Ann Emery (Joan Greer), Matthew Lanter (Horace Allen), Caitlin Wachs (Rebecca Allen), Jasmine Anthony (Amy Allen). From Touchstone Television and Battle Plan Productions.

Commander Porter's Men's apparel shop in Disney's Grand Floridian Resort & Spa at Walt Disney World; open Jun. 28, 1988–Apr. 4, 2019, and superseded by the Enchanted Rose lounge.

Commando Duck (film) Donald Duck cartoon released Jun. 2, 1944. Directed by Jack King. With the aid of a rubber raft, Donald manages to carry out his instructions to wipe out an enemy airfield by causing a flood to wash it away. A World War II-era short.

Commissary Restaurant See ABC Commissary (Disney's Hollywood Studios).

Communicore Central pair of pavilions in EPCOT Center; opened Oct. 1, 1982. Inside 2 primary buildings (Communicore East and Communicore West), which radiated out from Spaceship Earth, cutting-edge and hands-on science, information, and technological exhibits explored the themes of Future World. Included a shop (Centorium) and dining at Stargate Restaurant and Sunrise Terrace. The name stood for "community core." In Jul. 1994, it became Innoventions.

CommuniCore Hall and Plaza Multiuse facility and outdoor event space planned for World Celebration in EPCOT. It is located on the site of the former Communicore West/Innoventions West pavilion.

Community Service Awards Annual program to honor local service organizations with cash awards. Began at Disneyland in Nov. 1957, with $9,000 being distributed; for the program's 25th anniversary in 1982, the total amount was up to $175,000; and in 2004, it was $440,000. Also at Walt Disney World, with the first award granted Apr. 19, 1972; the resort has since awarded more than $34 million through application-based and recurring grants for nonprofits. The giving program was renamed DisneyHand – Helping Kids Shine, from 2004–ca. 2013, and was thereafter known as Disney Grants.

Community Transportation Services Former subsidiary of Walt Disney Productions; established in 1974 to market transportation systems originally developed for Disneyland and Walt Disney World, such as the Monorail and WEDway PeopleMover. SEE ALSO HOUSTON.

Company D Cast Member store at Disneyland Resort; opened Dec. 2, 1988. At Walt Disney World, a Company D opened in the Team Disney Building Jun. 4, 1991 (closing Oct. 28, 2016), in EPCOT Apr. 1, 1992, and later in Disney University, Disney's Hollywood Studios, and other backstage areas, including Disney Reservation Centers. Special merchandise, such as watches, buttons, and T-shirts, is often created solely for sale to Cast Members through Company D. The Walt Disney World stores closed Mar. 2020.

Computer Software Division of The Walt Disney Company created to produce computer games and other software utilizing the Disney characters and films. Their first products were *Tron* games for Mattel Electronics' Intellivision and Atari in 1982. In 1988, the division became Disney Software, which in turn became Disney Interactive in 1994.

Computer Wore Tennis Shoes, The (film) Dexter Riley, a science student, accidentally acquires all of the knowledge stored up in a used computer recently obtained for Medfield College when he tries to replace a fuse. The information includes data about a bookie ring, and Dexter's life is threatened. But he saves the day by capturing the crooks and winning a cash contest on TV for dear old Medfield. Released Dec. 31, 1969. Directed by Robert Butler. 91 min. Stars Kurt Russell (Dexter), Cesar Romero (A. J. Arno), Joe Flynn (Dean Higgins), William Schallert (Prof. Quigley), Alan Hewitt (Dean Collingsgood), Richard Bakalyan (Chillie). The song "The Computer Wore Tennis Shoes" was written by Robert Brunner and Bruce Belland. Technical adviser Ko Suzuki, who was working on the Walt Disney World project at the time, was called upon to design and program some of the electronic equipment that was needed and create graphs showing the comparisons of the human mind and a computer for use in Prof. Quigley's classroom lecture scene.

Computer Wore Tennis Shoes, The (TV) Two-hour movie remake of the 1969 motion picture; aired on ABC Feb. 18, 1995. It's the adventures of Dexter Riley, a not-so-brilliant college student who suddenly becomes the talk of the campus when he is struck by lightning while trying to reconnect a computer terminal. He becomes the repository of an enormous body of knowledge, which he can call upon at will. Stars Kirk Cameron (Dexter), Larry Miller, (Dean Valentine), Jason Bernard (Prof. Quigley), Jeff Maynard (Gozin), Anne Marie Tremko (Sarah), Andrew Woodworth (Will), Dean Jones (Dean Carlson). Directed by Peyton Reed.

Computers Are People, Too! (TV) Syn. show about computers, featuring footage from *Tron*; debuted May 23, 1982. Directed by Denis Sanders. Stars Elaine Joyce, Joseph Campanella, and Michael Iceberg.

Computers: The Friendly Invasion (film) Educational film taken from *Computers Are People, Too!*; released in Sep. 1982. Students are introduced to computers and their promise for the future.

Computers: The Truth of the Matter (film) Educational film; released in Oct. 1983. A positive introduction to computers.

Computers: Where They Come From and How They Work (film) Educational film; released in Apr. 1989. 9 min. History of computers from sticks and stones through microchips.

Con Air (film) When a group of the most dangerous and notorious prisoners in the U.S. penal system are transferred to a new super-maximum–security facility, parolee Cameron Poe hitches a ride on their Con Air transport flight only to find himself embroiled in a meticulously planned mid-air hijacking masterminded by Cyrus "The Virus" Grissom. On the ground, U.S. Marshal Vince Larkin faces impossible odds as he tries to avert the takeover and, at the same time, keep his overzealous superiors from blowing up the aircraft and its passengers. Together, Poe and Larkin must stop Cyrus and his band of savage, hardened lifers from massacring everyone on board as the damaged plane careens toward disaster on the famed Las Vegas strip. A Touchstone film. Directed by Simon West. Released Jun. 6, 1997. Stars Nicolas Cage (Cameron Poe), John Cusack (Vince Larkin), John Malkovich (Cyrus Grissom), Steve Buscemi (Garland Greene), Ving Rhames (Nathan Jones), Colm Meaney (Duncan Malloy), Mykelti Williamson (Baby-O), Rachel Ticotin (Sally Bishop). 115 min. Cinema-Scope. Filming took place at airports in Utah—in Salt Lake City, Ogden, and Wendover—and on the Las Vegas Strip, where 14 cameras were utilized to film the blowing up of the front of the soon-to-be-demolished Sands Hotel. Interiors were filmed in Los Angeles. Received Academy Award nominations for Best Sound and Best Original Song ("How Do I Live," by Diane Warren).

Conch Flats General Store Souvenir and convenience shop at Disney's Old Key West Resort (formerly Disney Vacation Club Resort) at Walt Disney World; opened Dec. 20, 1991. Named after the resort's imaginary town setting.

Conched Out Tropical gift and seashell shop in Disney Village Marketplace at Walt Disney World; opened Jun. 25, 1988, replacing Toys Fantastique. Closed Sep. 1992 and succeeded by the Discover store.

Concho, the Coyote Who Wasn't (TV) Show aired Apr. 10, 1966. A coyote adopted by an old Navajo, Delgado, thinks he is a sheepdog, though he is not accepted by the other dogs of the area. Delgado stars as himself.

Concourse Grille Table-service restaurant on the 4th floor (Grand Canyon Concourse level) of Disney's Contemporary Resort at Walt Disney World; opened Sep. 29, 1989, replacing the Terrace Café, and closed Jul. 1994. Became Concourse Steakhouse Aug. 10, 1994–May 31, 2008, and Contempo Cafe Nov. 15, 2008.

Condor Flats Airfield-themed district within the former Golden State area in Disney's California Adventure; opened Feb. 8, 2001. A paean to California's aviation history anchored by Soarin' Over California. Renamed Grizzly Peak Airfield in 2015.

Condorman (film) Woody Wilkins, a comic book artist of "Condorman" stories, occasionally tests the character's comic gadgetry himself. Woody is asked by a CIA-agent friend to deliver diplomatic papers to a Russian agent with whom he falls in love, and when she offers to defect, he bumbles through a series of exciting and comic chases in trying to save her from the KGB. First released in England Jul. 2, 1981, with a U.S. release Aug. 7, 1981. Directed by Charles Jarrott. 90 min. Stars Michael Crawford (Woody Wilkins), Oliver Reed (Krokov), Barbara Carerra (Natalia), James Hampton (Harry), Jean-Pierre Kalfon (Morovich), Dana Elcar (Russ), Vernon Dobtcheff (Russian agent), Robert Arden (CIA chief). Suggested by *The Game of X* by Robert Sheckley. The movie was filmed at Pinewood Studios in England as well as on location in France, Monaco, the former Yugoslavia, Italy, and Switzerland. First- and 2nd-unit crews filmed simultaneously in separate locations. While the principals filmed scenes with dialogue, the 2nd-unit crew performed high-speed chases—in racing cars on stretches of road in southern France, and with boats in the Mediterranean off Saint-Tropez and Nice—rigged explosions and crashes, and performed aerial work on the tram cable at Switzerland's Matterhorn and off Paris's Eiffel Tower. Automobiles and boats used in the movie were a speed enthusiast's dream: 7 Porsche 935 Turbo Carreras comprised the deadly pursuit squadron of the Russian KGB; 2 Group 5 Lemans Porsches, competition racing cars, were used by the squadron leader, Morovitch; and the "Condor Car" was portrayed by 4 modified Sterling racers. Woody Wilkins's comic book inventions, which include a machine gun/walking stick, a laser cannon, self-propelling jet rods to ride the cable up the Matterhorn, and his semi-aeronautic Condorman wings, were built by Academy Award–winning special effects artist Colin Chilvers.

Conestoga Wagons Frontierland attraction in Disneyland; ran Aug. 1955–Sep. 1959. Guests were transported on the trails utilized also by the stagecoaches.

Confectionery SEE MAIN STREET CONFECTIONERY.

Confessions of a Shopaholic (film) Rebecca Bloomwood is a sweet and charming New York City girl who has a tiny problem that is rapidly turning into a big problem: she is hopelessly addicted to shopping and is drowning in a sea of debt. While Rebecca has dreams of working for a top fashion magazine, she cannot quite get her foot in the door—that is, until she snags a job as an advice columnist for a financial magazine published by the same company. Overnight, her column becomes hugely popular, turning her into a celebrity. But when her compulsive shopping and growing debt issues threaten to destroy her love life and derail her career, she struggles to keep it all from spiraling out of control and is ultimately forced to reevaluate what is really important in life. Directed by P. J. Hogan. Released Feb. 13, 2009, after a Feb. 12 release in Russia and Thailand. From Touchstone Pictures and Jerry Bruckheimer Films. Stars Isla Fisher (Rebecca Bloomwood), Hugh Dancy (Luke Brandon), Krysten Ritter (Suze), Joan Cusack (Jane Bloomwood), John Goodman (Graham Bloomwood), John Lithgow (Edgar West), Wendie Malick (Miss Korch), Kristin Scott Thomas (Alette Naylor), Fred Armisen (Ryan Koenig), Leslie Bibb (Alicia Billington), Lynn Redgrave (drunken lady at ball), Robert Stanton (Derek Smeath), Julie Hagerty (Hayley). 105 min. Based on the best-selling novels by Sophie Kinsella. Filmed in CinemaScope on location in New York City, Miami, and Connecticut.

Confessions of a Teenage Drama Queen (film) Teen Lola Cep finds her life turned upside down when her family moves from New York City to the "cultural wasteland" of suburban New Jersey. As she juggles making new friends at a new school, while standing up to a new rival, Lola finds it hard enough just to live her life, let alone remember how important it is to live her dream. Released Feb. 20, 2004. Directed by Sara Sugarman. Stars Lindsay Lohan (Lola), Alison Pill (Ella), Megan Fox (Carla), Glenne Headly (Karen), Carol Kane (Miss Baggoli), Eli Marienthal (Sam), Adam Garcia (Stu). 90 min.

Confessions of an Ugly Stepsister (TV) A 2-hour movie on *The Wonderful World of Disney*; first aired Mar. 10, 2002. A provocative and sumptuous retelling of the Cinderella story seen through the eyes of the ugly stepsister, Iris. Directed by Gavin Millar. Stars Stockard Channing (Margarethe), Azura Skye (Iris), Trudie Styler (Fortune Teller), Emma Poole (Ruth), Jenna Harrison (Clara), Jonathan Pryce (The Master). From Alliance Atlantis in Luxembourg. In Disney's 1950 animated feature, the stepsisters were named Anastasia and Drizella.

Confirmation (TV) A 2-hour movie; aired on HBO Apr. 16, 2016. In 1991, Anita Hill, during congressional hearings, accused Clarence Thomas, the Supreme Court nominee, of sexual harassment. Directed by Rick Famuyiwa. Stars Kerry Washington (Anita Hill), Wendell Pierce (Clarence Thomas), Alison Wright (Virginia Thomas), Zoe Lister-Jones (Carolyn Hart), Greg Kinnear (Joe Biden), Eric Stonestreet (Kenneth Duberstein), Treat Williams (Ted Kennedy). From ABC Signature Studios, Groundswell Prods., and HBO Films.

Connections Café and Eatery Quick-service restaurant in World Celebration at EPCOT; officially opened Apr. 27, 2022, taking the place of Electric Umbrella. Connections Eatery offers burgers, salads, pizzas, and desserts inspired by global cuisine, with Starbucks products served at Connections Café. A large mural depicts the relationship between food, people, and places around the world.

Connery, Sean (1930–2020) Actor; appeared in *Darby O'Gill and the Little People* (Michael McBride), *Medicine Man* (Dr. Robert Campbell), and *The Rock* (John Patrick Mason). Three years after his *Darby O'Gill* role, he rose to fame as the first James Bond in the famous motion picture series.

Connors, Chuck (1921–1992) Actor; appeared in *Old Yeller* (Burn Sanderson).

Conried, Hans (1917–1982) Actor; appeared in *Davy Crockett* (Thimblerig), *The Cat from Outer Space* (Dr. Heffel), and *The Shaggy D.A.* (Prof. Whatley). He was also the voice of Captain Hook and Mr. Darling in *Peter Pan* and Thomas Jefferson in *Ben and Me*. On TV, he played the Magic Mirror on several shows and appeared in *Mickey's 50*.

Consenting Adults (film) A happily married couple, Richard and Priscilla Parker, is tantalized by the lifestyle of their new neighbors, Eddy and Kay Otis. Richard is lured into an overnight wife-swapping arrangement with Eddy. The next morning, the police discover Kay, apparently brutally murdered, with Richard's fingerprints all over the murder weapon. With the help of a sympathetic detective, Richard discovers that Kay is still alive and must race against time in order to save the life of his own wife from the real killer. Released Oct. 16, 1992. Directed by Alan J. Pakula. A Hollywood Pictures film. 99 min. Stars Kevin Kline (Richard Parker), Mary Elizabeth Mastrantonio (Priscilla Parker), Kevin Spacey (Eddy Otis). Filmed in Atlanta, and its suburbs, and at sites near Charleston, South Carolina.

Conservation Station Area in Disney's Animal Kingdom; opened Apr. 22, 1998. Climbing aboard the *Wildlife Express* train, guests are transported to this site, where they are given a backstage look at the park's veterinary headquarters and center for conservation programs. They can meet animal experts, learn about the behind-the-scenes operations of the park, and discover more about Disney's global commitment to wildlife and how they can help the animals they have seen in the park. The area was renamed Rafiki's Planet Watch in Oct. 2000, though the Conservation Station name remains for the animal-care encounters and exhibits.

Consider the Alternatives (film) Educational release in Dec. 1992. 20 min. In a magazine format, the hosts interview real kids about the many different decisions and choices they must make and demonstrate the 5 steps to decision-making.

Considine, Tim (1940–2022) Actor; appeared in the *Mickey Mouse Club*, as Spin in *Spin and Marty* (though he had originally tested for the role of Marty), Frank in *The Hardy Boys*, and Steve in *Annette*. Also on TV in *The Swamp Fox* (Gabe Marion). He appeared in *The Shaggy Dog* (Buzz Miller), narrated *The Adventures of Clint and Mac*, and made a cameo in *The New Adventures of Spin and Marty: Suspect Behavior*. He was named a Disney Legend in 2006.

Constellations Outer space boutique in Discoveryland at Disneyland Paris; opened Apr. 12, 1992.

Constitution, The: A History of Our Future (film) Educational film; released in Sep. 1989. 21 min. The history and significance of the U.S. Constitution is examined.

Consumer Products SEE MERCHANDISE.

Contempo Cafe Quick-service market café in Disney's Contemporary Resort at Walt Disney World; opened Nov. 15, 2008, replacing Concourse Steakhouse.

Contemporary Resort, Disney's A 1,084-room deluxe resort at Walt Disney World; opened Oct. 1, 1971. Built in cooperation with U.S. Steel, the structure was architecturally interesting, as the A-frame tower was built like an egg crate. The individual rooms were constructed a few miles away, then transported to the site, where they were slid into the 184-ft.-high, 468-ft.-long framework by huge cranes. It marked the first major use of modular steel construction. Flanking the tower, North

and South Garden Wings were built by stacking 3 of the unitized guest rooms on top of each other. The Monorail was designed to glide through the A-frame, above its 4th-floor level, and the interior of the "A" is open from there to the top. This area, called the Grand Canyon Concourse, features 90-ft.-tall tile murals depicting children and animals in the American Southwest; designed by artist Mary Blair, the murals encompass 18,000 sq. ft. around the central elevator core. The theme continued in the concourse's original restaurants, including the Grand Canyon Terrace (which later became Terrace Buffeteria, then Contemporary Café, then Chef Mickey's) and Terrace Lounge (later Outer Rim). To keep up with demand, additional dining was added in 1972: El Pueblo and the Terrace Cafe (later Concourse Grille, then Concourse Steakhouse, then Contempo Cafe). Early shops included Plaza Gifts & Sundries, Fantasia Shop, Kingdom Jewelers, Contemporary Woman, and Contemporary Man; several of these later combined to create B.V.G. (Bayview Gifts). The original convention hotel at Walt Disney World, the 2nd floor debuted with the Ballroom of the Americas, the Grand Republic Ballroom, and the Gulf Coast Room restaurant (closed in 1988). This level also provided elevator access to the 15th floor, home to the popular Top of the World supper club (which became the California Grill in 1995). A large exhibit space on the ground floor eventually became the popular Fiesta Fun Center (later Food and Fun Center), where kids could spend their hours playing video games, watching Disney movies, or enjoying a hamburger; this area became The Wave restaurant in 2008 and Steakhouse 71 in 2021. A separate convention facility was added in 1991, anchored by the 42,000-sq.-ft. Fantasia Ballroom. The North Garden Wing was demolished in 2007 to make way for a Disney Vacation Club resort, Bay Lake Tower, which opened Aug. 4, 2009, with 295 villas, and connects to the original tower's 5th floor via the Skyway Bridge. During the resort's initial development in the late 1960s, "Contemporary" was simply a working name; the Imagineers proposed several options, including the favored "Tempo Bay," but Roy O. Disney liked the working name and insisted "Contemporary" be used. The resort was dedicated by Bob Hope Oct. 24, 1971, in a ceremony later aired on NBC's *The Grand Opening of Walt Disney World*.

Contraption (TV) Series on The Disney Channel, hosted by Ralph Harris, with kids competing to answer questions about Disney films using a life-size 3-D game board. Debuted Apr. 18, 1983, and aired, with repeats, until Jan. 9, 1988. 40 episodes.

Contrary Condor (film) Donald Duck cartoon released Apr. 21, 1944. Directed by Jack King. Donald, as an egg collector climbing in the Andes, is almost too successful when he pretends to be a baby condor when caught trying to steal an egg by the mother condor. Donald's attempts to escape with the egg are complicated by a baby condor and the mother's flying lessons. He loses in the end, still tucked under the mother's wing, along with the egg and the baby condor.

Contrasts in Rhythm (film) Special cartoon combining *Bumble Boogie* and *Trees* from *Melody Time*; released Mar. 11, 1955.

Conversation With . . . , A (TV) Series of specials taped in Disney-MGM Studios at Walt Disney World for The Disney Channel. Features discussions and audience questions for such stars as George Burns, Carol Burnett, Bob Hope, Betty White. First aired in 1989.

Conviction (TV) Hour-long drama series on ABC; aired Oct. 3, 2016–Jan. 29, 2017. Lawyer and former first daughter Hayes Morrison accepts a job offered from her nemesis, NY district attorney Conner Wallace, to avoid jail time for cocaine possession and avoid hurting her mother's U.S. Senate campaign. Working with his team at the new Conviction Integrity Unit will let her use her brilliant mind to investigate cases where there is credible suspicion of wrongful conviction and give her a chance to turn things around with her high-powered family. Stars Hayley Atwell (Hayes Morrison), Eddie Cahill (Conner Wallace), Shawn Ashmore (Sam Spencer), Merrin Dungey (Maxine), Emily Kinney (Tess Thompson), Daniel Franzese (Jackson Morrison). From The Mark Gordon Company and ABC Studios.

Conway, Russ (1913–2009) Actor; he played the father, Fenton Hardy, in the *Hardy Boys* serials on the *Mickey Mouse Club*. Also appeared in *Moochie of the Little League* and *Moochie of Pop Warner Football* (Monty Morgan), *Boomerang* and *Dog of Many Talents* (Rancher), and *The World's Greatest Athlete* (field judge).

Conway, Tim (1933–2019) Actor; appeared in *The World's Greatest Athlete* (Milo), *The Apple Dumpling Gang* and *The Apple Dumpling Gang Rides*

Again (Amos), *Gus* (Crankcase), and *The Shaggy D.A.* (Tim), and on TV in *Walt Disney World Celebrity Circus*. He was named a Disney Legend in 2004.

Coogan, Jackie (1914–1984) Actor; appeared on TV in *The Kids Who Knew Too Much*.

Coogan, Keith Young actor; appeared in *Adventures in Babysitting* (Brad), *Cheetah* (Ted), and *In the Army Now* (Stoner #1). As Keith Mitchell, he provided the voice of the young Tod in *The Fox and the Hound* and appeared on TV in *Gun Shy* and *Tales of the Apple Dumpling Gang*. On The Disney Channel, he was in *Spooner* (D. B. Reynolds). Coogan had changed his name in honor of his grandfather, actor Jackie Coogan.

Cook, Barry After joining Disney in 1981 as an effects animator on *Tron*, he continued working on effects for the animated features. He directed the shorts *Off His Rockers* and *Trail Mix-Up*, as well as the feature *Mulan*, with Tony Bancroft. He left the company in 2004.

Cook, Dick Longtime president of Buena Vista Pictures Distribution, taking over from Irving Ludwig on the latter's retirement. He started with the company as a young man driving the train and Monorail at Disneyland. In 1996, he was named chairman of the Walt Disney Motion Pictures Group, and in 2002 he became chairman of Walt Disney Studios. He left the company in Sep. 2009.

Cooke, John He took over as president of The Disney Channel in 1985, when the channel had 1.9 million subscribers, and oversaw the growth to over 8 million in less than a decade. In Sep. 1994, he was named to head the Disney's America project, and in Jan. 1995 he was named executive vice president, corporate affairs for The Walt Disney Company. He left the company in 1999.

Cookes of Dublin SEE RAGLAN ROAD IRISH PUB AND RESTAURANT.

Cookie Carnival, The (film) Silly Symphony cartoon released May 25, 1935. Directed by Ben Sharpsteen. As a beauty contest progresses, a poor girl cookie cannot attend because of her rags. But, with the help of an ingenious boy cookie and the careful placement of candies and whipped cream, she wins the title of Cookie Queen and selects the boy as the king of the carnival.

Cookie jars, Turnabout SEE LEEDS CHINA CO.

Cookie Kid, The (film) Educational film produced by the Glynn Group; released in Sep. 1981. The girl holding the world's record for selling Girl Scout cookies shows how effective sales techniques and setting of personal goals lead to success.

Cookie Kitchen Quick-service coffee and pastry window on Main Street, U.S.A. in Disneyland Paris; opened Apr. 12, 1992. Themed to old-time San Francisco.

CookieAnn SEE DUFFY AND FRIENDS.

CookieAnn Bakery Café Mickey Avenue treat and collectibles shop in Shanghai Disneyland; opened Nov. 25, 2021, taking the place of Remy's Patisserie.

Cool Runnings (film) When 3 determined Jamaican sprinters fail to make the Olympics, they enlist a has-been sledding expert to mold them into a bobsled team instead and add an expert go-cart driver to their group. Through many hardships, not the least being the fact that there is no snow in Jamaica, they make it to the Olympics and earn the admiration of the world. Released Oct. 1, 1993. Directed by Jon Turteltaub. 98 min. Stars Leon (Derice Bannock), Doug E. Doug (Sanka Coffie), Rawle D. Lewis (Junior Bevil), Malik Yoba (Yul Brenner), John Candy (Irv). Based on the true story of the 1988 Jamaican Olympic bobsled team. The filmmakers traveled to Jamaica for the primary filming, and shot the Winter Olympics scenes in Calgary, Alberta, Canada. The title is a local Jamaican phrase which filmmakers spotted on a T-shirt during a scouting trip; they learned "Cool Runnings" meant "peaceful journeys," which matched the film's theme: a peaceful journey to fulfill oneself.

Coop & Cami Ask the World (TV) Live-action comedy series; premiered on Disney Channel Oct. 12, 2018. Middle school siblings Coop and Cami Wrather co-host a popular online show, *Would You Wrather*, while balancing life, family, and friendship. They are aided by their little brother, Ollie, and Coop's best friend, Fred, in answering offbeat questions for the show's millions of followers and helping them solve problems both mundane and madcap. Stars Dakota Lotus (Coop), Ruby Rose Turner (Cami), Olivia Sanabia (Charlotte Wrather), Albert Tsai (Fred), Paxton Booth (Ollie), Rebecca Metz (Jenna). From It's a Laugh Productions, Inc.

Coordinator of Inter-American Affairs SEE SOUTH AMERICA.

Copper Obedient hound character in *The Fox and the Hound*; voiced by Corey Feldman (young) and Kurt Russell (older).

Copper Creek Villas & Cabins Disney Vacation Club development at Disney's Wilderness Lodge at Walt Disney World; opened Jul. 17, 2017. Inspired by the mining and railroad history of the Pacific Northwest, it features 184 modern, nature-inspired rooms and 26 waterfront cabins.

Cora, Jim (1937–2021) He joined Disneyland as an attraction host in 1957 and after college moved into positions of increasing responsibility in park management. In 1971, he assisted in the opening of Walt Disney World and in 1979 became managing director of operations for the Tokyo Disneyland project. He held several executive leadership roles for the international parks, including vice president, Walt Disney Productions Japan, Ltd., and executive vice president and chief operating officer, Euro Disneyland Corp. In 1995, he was promoted to president, Disneyland International, and became the division's chairman in 1999. He retired in 2001 after 43 years with Disney. He was named a Disney Legend in 2005, and his book, *Not Just a Walk in the Park: My Worldwide Disney Resorts Career*, was published in 2021.

Coral Isle Café Restaurant on the 2nd floor overlooking the lobby area in the Great Ceremonial House of the Polynesian Village Resort at Walt Disney World; opened Oct. 1, 1971. Closed Jul. 25, 1998, to reopen Nov. 23 as Kona Café.

Coral Reef Restaurant Seafood dining in The Living Seas (later The Seas with Nemo & Friends) in EPCOT; opened Jan. 15, 1986. Large picture windows give diners an underwater view of a living coral reef, and many of its 2,000 sea creature inhabitants, in the pavilion's huge tank. The restaurant has been popular since its opening.

Corcoran, Brian (1951–2014) Child actor; appeared in *Babes in Toyland* (Willie Winkie), and on TV in *Daniel Boone*, *Texas John Slaughter*, and *Elfego Baca*.

Corcoran, Kevin (1949–2015) Actor; appeared in *Swiss Family Robinson* (Franz), *Old Yeller* (Arliss Coates), *The Shaggy Dog* (Moochie Daniels), *Toby Tyler* (Toby), *Pollyanna* (Jimmy Bean), *Babes in Toyland* (Boy Blue), *Bon Voyage* (Skipper Willard), *Savage Sam* (Arliss), and *A Tiger Walks* (Tom Hadley), and on TV in *Adventure in Dairyland* (Moochie McCandless, the role which gave him the nickname of Moochie), *Johnny Shiloh*, *Moochie of Pop Warner Football*, *Moochie of the Little League*, *The Mooncussers*, *Daniel Boone*, *The Further Adventures of Spin and Marty*, and *The New Adventures of Spin and Marty*. He provided a voice for *Boys of the Western Sea* and voiced the title character in *Goliath II*. He later served as a production assistant at the Disney Studio and was named a Disney Legend in 2006.

Corey, Wendell (1914–1968) Actor; appeared in *The Light in the Forest* (Wilse Owens).

Corky and White Shadow (TV) Serial on the *Mickey Mouse Club* during the 1955–1956 season, starring Darlene Gillespie, Buddy Ebsen, Lloyd Corrigan, Buzz Henry, Richard Powers. Directed by William Beaudine Sr. A sheriff's daughter and her German shepherd, White Shadow, get involved with a bank robber. 18 episodes.

Corky Romano (film) Good-natured veterinarian, Corky Romano, receives a surprising call from his long-lost father, "Pops," an underworld crime lord who has just been indicted by the grand jury and will soon go to trial. Pops realizes that his son is the 1 person who could infiltrate the FBI and abscond with the evidence against him. A computer hacker, intimidated into helping, goes overboard and makes Corky appear to be a superagent, a reputation he must live up to. As Agent Pissant, he tries to fake his way through one tough assignment after another while hunting for the elusive incriminating proof of his father's illegal activities. Directed by Rob Pritts. A Touchstone film. Released Oct. 12, 2001. Stars Chris Kattan (Corky Romano), Peter Berg (Paulie), Chris Penn (Peter), Richard Roundtree (Howard Shuster), Vinessa Shaw (Kate Russo), Matthew Glave (Brick Davis), Fred Ward (Leo Corrigan), Peter Falk (Pops). 86 min.

Corn Chips (film) Donald Duck cartoon released Mar. 23, 1951. Directed by Jack Hannah. Donald tricks Chip and Dale into shoveling his sidewalk after they dump snow on his just-shoveled sidewalk. They retaliate by stealing Donald's bowl of popcorn. When Donald builds a fire to smoke them out of their tree, the chipmunks dump a box of kernels into the tree, resulting in popcorn exploding all over the yard. Donald is back to shoveling the popcorn as if it was snow.

Corn Dog Castle Medieval-themed boardwalk stand in Paradise Pier (later Paradise Gardens Park) at Disney California Adventure; opened Feb. 8, 2001, serving hand-dipped, deep-fried corn dogs.

Cornelius Coot's County Bounty Large emporium inside the Toontown Hall of Fame tent in Mickey's Toontown Fair in the Magic Kingdom at Walt Disney World; open Jun. 29, 1996–Feb. 11, 2011. Named after the founder of Duckburg in the comics by Carl Barks. SEE ALSO MICKEY'S BIRTHDAYLAND.

Coronado Springs Resort, Disney's Moderately priced convention hotel at Walt Disney World; opened Aug. 1, 1997, with more than 1,900 themed rooms and suites. Guests can stay in Casitas inspired by residential areas of Mexico, Ranchos representing the American Southwest, and Cabanas themed to coastal fishing villages, all encircling a 15-acre lake called Lago Dorado. A 5-story representation of a Mayan temple towers over the Dig Site, a recreation area that includes a feature pool, the Explorer's Playground, Siestas Cantina, and Iguana Arcade. Inside the "city center" (El Centro), dining options include Maya Grill, El Mercado de Coronado (previously the Pepper Market food court), Rix Sports Bar and Grill, Café Rix, and Las Ventanas. Other locations include Panchito's (a merchandise market) and La Vida Health Club. A 220,000-sq.-ft. convention center includes 2 ballrooms, including the largest at Walt Disney World, at 60,214 sq. ft.; an exhibit hall; and 45 breakout rooms. In 2019, the 15-story Gran Destino Tower was added, introducing the themes of Spanish art and architecture. SEE GRAN DESTINO TOWER AND THREE BRIDGES BAR & GRILL.

Corpse Had a Familiar Face, The (TV) Two-hour movie; aired on CBS Mar. 27, 1994. A tough crime reporter is forced to examine her own life as she investigates the disappearance of an 18-year-old girl. Suggested by the autobiographical novel by Edna Buchanan. Directed by Joyce Chopra. Stars Elizabeth Montgomery (Edna Buchanan), Dennis Farina (Harry Lindstrom), Yaphet Kotto (Martin

Talbot), Audra Lindley (Jean Hirsch), Lee Horsley (Ben Nicholson). SEE ALSO DEADLINE FOR MURDER: FROM THE FILES OF EDNA BUCHANAN.

Corti, Jesse Actor; appeared in *Gone in 60 Seconds* (Cop) and *Bringing Down the House* (Italian FBI Agent), and on TV in *Desperate Housewives* (social worker). He has provided several voices, including Le Fou in *Beauty and the Beast*, Cement Head in *Darkwing Duck*, the March Hare in *Bonkers*, Jade in *Gargoyles*, the Spanish Dignitary in *Frozen*, Itsy in *Goldie and Bear*, and Mr. Manchas in *Zootopia*.

Cory in the House (TV) Disney Channel series; aired Jan. 12, 2007–Sep. 12, 2008. Cory Baxter's father, Victor, has been named presidential chef to the newly elected president. Living with his father in the staff quarters of the White House and attending an exclusive private school with the kids of Washington's power elite is all new to Cory. With some schemes of his own, Cory must contend with the president's precocious 8-year-old daughter, Sophie. As his amazing life in Washington begins, Cory has new friends in Meena, an ambassador's daughter, and Newt, heir to a political dynasty, but a nemesis in Jason Stickler, son of the CIA chief. Stars Kyle Massey (Cory Baxter), Rondell Sheridan (Victor Baxter), Jason Dolley (Newt Livingston III), Madison Pettis (Sophie Martinez), Maiara Walsh (Meena Paroom), Jack Thomas (Jason Stickler), John D'Aquino (President Martinez), Lisa Arch (Samantha Stevens). From It's a Laugh Productions.

Cosby, Bill Actor; appeared in *The Devil and Max Devlin* (Barney Satin) and *Jack* (Lawrence Woodruff).

Cosmic Capers (film) International theatrical release edited from *Mars and Beyond*; first released in England in Dec. 1979. 18 min.

Cosmic Encounter Tomorrowland shop selling space-themed merchandise in Tokyo Disneyland; opened Jul. 1989.

Cosmic Ray's Starlight Cafe Counter-service restaurant in the Magic Kingdom at Walt Disney World; opened Dec. 9, 1994, taking the place of Tomorrowland Terrace. Guests order their meal from 1 of 3 serving bays and proceed downstairs, where entertainment is performed on a rising stage. Hosted by Coca-Cola. SEE ALSO SONNY ECLIPSE.

Cost (film) Educational film from The People on Market Street series, produced by Terry Kahn; released in Sep. 1977. The giving of a party is used to illustrate the economic concept of cost.

Costa, Mary Actress/singer; provided the voice of Princess Aurora in *Sleeping Beauty*. She was named a Disney Legend in 1999.

Costello (TV) Half-hour comedy series on Fox; aired Sep. 8–Oct. 13, 1998. Sue Murphy lives in the garage at her parents' home and works at The Bulldog, a neighborhood pub in blue-collar, Irish Catholic South Boston, dreaming of a better life beyond getting married like the other girls, living in the all-too-familiar neighborhood, and serving drinks at the pub. Stars Sue Costello (Sue Murphy), Dan Lauria (Spud Murphy), Jenny O'Hara (Lottie Murphy), Chuck Walczak (Jimmy Murphy), Kerry O'Malley (Trish Donnelly), Josie DiVincenzo (Mary McDonough). From Touchstone Television/Wind Dancer Productions.

Costner, Kevin Actor; appeared in *Play It to the Bone* (Ringside Fan [himself]), *Open Range* (Charley Waite), *The Guardian* (Ben Randall), *Swing Vote* (Bud Johnson), and *McFarland USA* (Jim White).

Costume Shop, The Boutique on New York Street in Disney-MGM Studios; open Apr. 1, 1991–1996, and superseded by Buy the Book. Costumes, masks, and gifts were themed to the Disney Villains.

Cotino, a Storyliving by Disney community SEE STORYLIVING BY DISNEY.

Cottonwood Creek Ranch Critter Corral Petting farm in Frontierland at Disneyland Paris; open Apr. 12, 1992–2007, and superseded by Woody's Roundup Village.

Cottrell, Bill (1906–1995) President of Retlaw Enterprises, the Walt Disney family corporation, from 1964 until his retirement in 1982. He joined Disney in 1929 as a cameraman, then worked as a cutter and animation director before moving into the story department. He was a sequence director on *Snow White and the Seven Dwarfs* and worked on story for *Pinocchio*, *Saludos Amigos*, *Victory Through Air Power*, *The Three Caballeros*, *Melody Time*, *Alice in Wonderland*, and *Peter Pan*. In 1952, he became vice president of WED Enterprises, where he helped develop the *Zorro* TV series and assisted Walt in the planning, construction, and story lines for Disneyland. A talented writer, he also helped shape how Imagineering referred to activities in the park; for example, Bill suggested using terms like "attractions" and "experiences" instead of "rides." He was the first person to receive a 50-year Disney service award and was named a Disney Legend in 1994. He was married to Lillian Disney's sister, Hazel Sewell.

Cougar Town (TV) Comedy series; aired Sep. 23, 2009–May 29, 2012, on ABC. The series moved to TBS for its 4th season, Jan. 8, 2013–Mar. 31, 2015. A recently divorced 40-something single mother finds that starting over with the dating game is not easy. Her son is embarrassed by everything she says and does, and her ex-husband is still hanging around, as are her 2 best friends trying to offer encouragement. She learns to deal with the realities of dating and aging in a youth-obsessed culture. Stars Courteney Cox (Jules Cobb), Christa Miller (Ellie), Busy Philipps (Laurie), Dan Byrd (Travis), Brian Van Holt (Bobby), Josh Hopkins (Grayson), Ian Gomez (Andy). From Doozer and Coquette Prods., in association with ABC Studios.

Count of Monte Cristo, The (film) Alexandre Dumas's classic story of an innocent man, Edmond Dantes, wrongly but deliberately imprisoned on the infamous island prison of Chateau D'If and his brilliant strategy for revenge against those who betrayed him. After 13 years, he escapes from prison and transforms himself into the mysterious and wealthy Count of Monte Cristo, cleverly insinuating himself into the French nobility and systematically destroying the men who manipulated and enslaved him. A Touchstone film from Spyglass Entertainment. Released Jan. 25, 2002. Directed by Kevin Reynolds. Stars Jim Caviezel (Edmond Dantes), Guy Pearce (Fernand), Richard Harris (Abbe Faria), Dagmara Dominczyk (Mercedes), Luis Guzman (Jacopo), James Frain (Villefort), Henry Cavill (Albert). 131 min. Filmed on location in Ireland and Malta.

Countdown at the Neon Armadillo (TV) Series; syn. aired Sep. 17–Dec. 12, 1993. Spotlighted country-and-western music. SEE ALSO BEST OF COUNTRY '92.

Countdown to Extinction Thill attraction in Dino-Land U.S.A. at Disney's Animal Kingdom; opened Apr. 22, 1998, and sponsored by McDonald's until 2008. At the Dino Institute, visitors board the experimental Time Rover to be transported 65 million years back in time to track down a 3.5-ton Iguanodon. Thanks to the reckless programming of the Institute's Dr. Grant Seeker, the time travelers find themselves face-to-face with a ferocious Carnotaurus and the cataclysmic events that ended the reign of the dinosaurs. The attraction was renamed DINOSAUR May 1, 2000, to tie into the animated feature released that month.

Country (film) A soft-spoken farmer's wife, Jewell Ivy, demonstrates surprising heroism when faced with the government's forced foreclosure of her family's farm. Her husband, Gil, is nearly destroyed by the tragic turn of events. Jewell manages to hold her family together while enlisting the aid of other farmers facing the same problems. Released Sep. 29, 1984, after a Sep. 28 premiere at the New York Film Festival. A Touchstone film. Directed by Richard Pearce. 110 min. Stars Jessica Lange (Jewell Ivy), Sam Shephard (Gil Ivy), Wilford Brimley (Otis), Matt Clark (Tom McMullen), Therese Graham (Marlene Ivy), Levi L. Knebel (Carlisle Ivy), Jim Haynie (Arlon Brewer), Sandra Seacat (Louise Brewer), Alex Harvey (Fordyce). The film was co-produced by Lange. Along with screenwriter/co-producer William D. Wittliff, Lange fleshed out the basic plot of *Country* and met with farmers in the Midwest whose livelihoods had been threatened by forced foreclosures. The start of production saw cast and crew in a race against the elements to film an Iowa corn harvest. Sam Shepard took the controls of a massive gleaner-combine, which harvested the crop. Next the company moved onto the key set some 20 miles northeast of Waterloo in the farmlands of Iowa. There, a turn-of-the-century farmstead, slated to be demolished by its owner who wanted additional acreage for growing feed corn, became the Ivy farm. For 3 months the company worked 12-hour days capturing the reality of farm living. A secondary location was the rural hamlet of Readlyn, Iowa, with its giant grain elevators and broad main street. Winter arrived sooner than expected, and during the climactic auction sequence in which 100 local townspeople appeared, the wind chill factor steadied at 25° below 0°. Director Pearce could only film in 5-min. segments before the Iowans had to break for the barn where red-hot butane heaters unsuccessfully attempted to warm the icy air. The harsh winter caused the production to move back to the Disney Studio in Burbank, where interiors and the tornado sequences were filmed. The affecting piano solos were provided by George Winston.

Nominated for an Academy Award for Best Actress (Jessica Lange).

Country Address Women's fashions in the Lake Buena Vista Shopping Village at Walt Disney World; opened Mar. 1975. It moved into the former Miss Merrily's Madness shop in 1986, and then into the former Village Gifts & Sundries shop Mar. 1987, before closing Jul. 23, 1994. Succeeded by The Art of Disney.

Country Bear Jamboree Musical Audio-Animatronics show in Frontierland in the Magic Kingdom at Walt Disney World; opened Oct. 1, 1971. Presented by Pepsi-Cola and Frito-Lay until Oct. 1, 1982. Inside Grizzly Hall, master of ceremonies Henry hosts a tuneful country-and-western revue performed by a cast of 18 humorous bruins, including the Five Bear Rugs; the Sun Bonnets trio of Bunny, Bubbles, and Beulah; swinging Teddi Barra; and Big Al, who steals the show with his rendition of "Blood on the Saddle." All the while, the bears are heckled by a trio of mounted animals—a moose, Melvin; a buffalo, Buff; and a stag, Max. The first major attraction to debut in Walt Disney World and then be re-created at other Disney parks, beginning in Disneyland Mar. 24, 1972, in the new Bear Country (later Critter Country); presented by Wonder Bread fall 1974–fall 1989; renamed Country Bear Playhouse Jul. 4, 1986, and closed Sep. 9, 2001, to make way for The Many Adventures of Winnie the Pooh. With the debut of the Country Bear Christmas Special in 1984—with festive songs, sets, and costumes—it also became the first Disney attraction to be totally reprogrammed. The Christmas show was presented seasonally (until 2006 at Walt Disney World). Another show, the Country Bear Vacation Hoedown, debuted in 1986, replacing the original show (until Nov. 19, 1991, in Walt Disney World). Also a Westernland attraction in Tokyo Disneyland, where it is housed inside the Country Bear Theater; opened Apr. 15, 1983, hosted by House Foods Corporation. In Japan, the Jingle Bell Jamboree was added Dec. 1991 and Vacation Jamboree followed Jul. 1994, with all 3 shows rotating throughout the year. The attraction had originally been conceived for the proposed Mineral King ski resort project, which Disney had planned on building in the 1960s.

Country Bears, The (film) Like other celebrated rock and roll groups, the members of the legendary group, The Country Bears, were torn apart by the perils of their own success—ego, jealousy, and a little too much honey. An eager young fan, Beary Barrington, tries to convince the bitter ex-members of the rock band—brothers Ted and Fred Bedderhead, Tennessee O'Neal, and Zeb Zoober—to put aside their differences and perform a benefit concert to save Country Bear Hall, the legendary venue where the band got its start. Directed by Peter Hastings. Released Jul. 26, 2002. Stars Christopher Walken (Reed Thimple), Stephen Tobolowsky (Norbert Barrington), Daryl "Chill" Miller (Officer Hamm), M. C. Gainey (Roadie), Diedrich Bader (Officer Cheets and voice of Ted), Alex Rocco (Rip Holland), with the voices of Candy Ford (Trixie), James Gammon (Big Al), Brad Garrett (Fred), Toby Huss (Tennessee), Kevin Michael Richardson (Henry), Stephen Root (Zeb), Haley Joel Osment (Beary). 88 min. Featured are musical performances or appearances by real-life rock and roll legends Don Henley, John Hiatt, Elton John, Queen Latifah, Willie Nelson, Bonnie Raitt, Brian Setzer. Inspired by the attraction at Walt Disney World. Ironically, the Country Bear Playhouse at Disneyland closed the previous year. A full-size Country Bear Hall for the movie was constructed at the Disney Golden Oak Ranch in Newhall, California. The animatronic bear suits were created by the Jim Henson Creature Shop.

Country Cousin, The (film) Silly Symphony cartoon released Oct. 31, 1936. Directed by Wilfred Jackson. Academy Award winner for Best Cartoon. Abner, a mouse from the rural town of Podunk, goes to visit his glamorous big-city cousin, Monty. But when he accidentally becomes inebriated, is chased by a cat, and meets other terrors of big-city life, he quickly heads for home.

Country Coyote Goes Hollywood, A (film) Featurette released Jan. 28, 1965. Directed by Winston Hibler. Chico the coyote manages to hitch a ride to Los Angeles and has all sorts of misadventures with the local residents. He is finally sent away to live in the wild, only to hitch another ride to New York City. The main title sequences are done as if imprinted in the cement of Grauman's Chinese Theatre in Hollywood. 37 min.

Country Estates (TV) One-hour pilot for a series; aired Jul. 10, 1993. The Reed family moves to a suburban dream home, and while they try to cope with the pain of one son's death, the other becomes entangled in the apparent murder of a neighbor. Directed by Donald Petrie. Stars Scott Bairstow, Tom Irwin, Michelle Kelly, Perry King, Tina Lifford,

Jason London, Patrick Y. Malone, Vinessa Shaw, Barbara Williams, Bruce A. Young.

Country Manor Shop in the United Kingdom at EPCOT; opened Jan. 5, 1986. Formerly Biscuit Barrel.

County Bounty SEE CORNELIUS COOT'S COUNTY BOUNTY.

Court, The (TV) Hour-long series on ABC; aired Mar. 26–Apr. 9, 2002. Kate Nolan is the newest appointed Supreme Court justice, who must prove herself in a deeply divided court. At the same time, an aggressive TV reporter, Harlan Brandt, covers the court in a manner often at cross-purposes to the sanctity of the institution. Stars Sally Field (Kate Nolan), Pat Hingle (Chief Justice Amos Townsend), Diahann Carroll (Angela DeSett), Nicole DeHuff (Alexis Cameron), Hill Harper (Christopher Bell), Christina Hendricks (Betsy Tyler), Josh Radnor (Dylan Hirsch), Miguel Sandoval (Roberto Martinez), Chris Sarandon (Lucas Voorhees), Craig Bierko (Harlan Brandt).

Courtesy Is Caring (film) Educational film; released in Sep. 1987. 6 min. The role of courtesy in friendship and daily life.

Courting Alex (TV) Half-hour comedy series on CBS; aired Jan. 23–Mar. 29, 2006. Alex Rose works alongside her lawyer father, Bill, at his law firm, and while he is proud of her, it pains him that she is not married yet. If Bill had his way, Alex would settle down with Stephen, a star lawyer at the firm who is smitten with her. Alex turns to her friends for advice, but finds she has unexpected feelings for Scott, an impulsive, renaissance man she met while trying to negotiate a deal involving his tavern. Stars Jenna Elfman (Alex Rose), Dabney Coleman (Bill Rose), Hugh Bonneville (Julian), Josh Randall (Scott Larson), Jillian Bach (Molly), Josh Stamberg (Steven). From Touchstone Television and Paramount Network Television.

Courtland, Jerome (1926–2012) Actor; appeared in *Tonka* (Lt. Henry Nowlan), and on TV in the title role in *The Saga of Andy Burnett*. He later served as a producer at the Disney Studio for such films as *Escape to Witch Mountain*, *Pete's Dragon*, and *The Devil and Max Devlin*.

Courtyard by Marriott Hotel at Lake Buena Vista at Walt Disney World; opened Jan. 20, 1995, tak-

ing the place of the Howard Johnson Resort Hotel, which was remodeled and renamed. Closed Dec. 30, 2003, to become a Holiday Inn.

Courvoisier Galleries Art dealer Guthrie Courvoisier had the foresight to see the value of Disney cels and other artwork, and through his gallery in San Francisco, he sold Disney art, including pieces from *Snow White and the Seven Dwarfs, Pinocchio, Fantasia, Dumbo,* and *Bambi,* 1938–1946. This artwork, which he priced from a few dollars up to perhaps $50 for the most elaborate pieces with original production backgrounds, is today often worth many thousands of dollars.

Cover Story Hollywood Boulevard shop in Disney's Hollywood Studios; opened May 1, 1989. Guests can picture themselves on the cover of a Hollywood magazine.

COVID-19 pandemic Out of an abundance of caution, all of the Disney parks around the world closed amid the global outbreak of COVID-19 in early 2020. These would quickly become the longest closures of the Disney parks to date. (The previous record was held at the Tokyo Disney Resort parks, which were closed for several weeks in 2011 due to problems getting reliable electrical power after the Tōhoku earthquake and tsunami on Mar. 11.) After implementing enhanced health and safety measures, and limiting capacities, all the parks reopened by summer 2020 (with the exception of the Disneyland Resort parks, which remained closed an unprecedented 13 months).

The parks were closed on the following dates (at the time this book went to press):

1. Shanghai Disneyland: 1/25/20–5/10/20, 10/31/21–11/2/21, 3/21/22–6/29/22, 10/31/22–11/24/22, 11/29/22–12/7/22
2. Hong Kong Disneyland: 1/26/20–6/17/20, 7/15/20–9/24/20, 12/2/20–2/18/21, 1/7/22–4/20/22
3. Tokyo Disneyland and Tokyo DisneySea: 2/29/20–6/30/20
4. Disneyland and Disney California Adventure: 3/14/20–4/29/21
5. Magic Kingdom and Disney's Animal Kingdom (Walt Disney World): 3/16/20–7/10/20
6. EPCOT and Disney's Hollywood Studios (Walt Disney World): 3/16/20–7/14/20
7. Disneyland and Walt Disney Studios Park (Disneyland Paris): 3/16/20–7/14/20, 10/30/20–6/16/21

Outside of the parks, Disney Store locations throughout North America closed temporarily on Mar. 17, 2020, with some stores remaining closed. Additionally, Disney Cruise Line suspended new departures beginning Mar. 14, 2020. Sailings resumed Jul. 15, 2021, with 2-, 3-, and 4-night "Disney Magic at Sea" cruises out of Liverpool for U.K. residents aboard the *Disney Magic*. Regular guest sailings resumed Aug. 9, 2021, out of Port Canaveral, Florida, aboard the *Disney Dream*. SEE ALSO NATIONAL BASKETBALL ASSOCIATION ("NBA BUBBLE").

Cow Belles (TV) A Disney Channel Original Movie; premiered Mar. 24, 2006. The father of 2 wealthy, freewheeling teens, who owns a major dairy operation, puts them to work to teach them the responsibility of running a business. But trouble brews when someone empties the company's bank accounts, and now the sisters must put aside their pampered existence to save the business and their father's reputation. Directed by Francine McDougall. Stars Alyson Michalka (Taylor Callum), Amanda Michalka (Courtney Callum), Michael Trevino (Jackson Meade), Christian Serratos (Heather Perez), Amanda Tilson (Jenny Bryant). From Just Singer Entertainment. 90 min.

Cow Dog (film) Featurette released Nov. 6, 1956. Directed by Larry Lansburgh. 22 min. Tells the story of a California ranch family that, in their devotion to the raising of purebred Hereford cattle, must capture an outlaw Brahman bull. A neighboring rancher brings his 3 Australian herding dogs, Stub, Queen, and Shorty, to help in the roundup to apprehend the bull. They are greeted with enthusiasm because of their ability, and they eventually manage to flush out the bull. Originally released with *Secrets of Life*. Nominated for an Academy Award.

Cowboy Cookhouse Westernland snack bar in Tokyo Disneyland serving smoked turkey legs; opened Mar. 2019, replacing the Chuck Wagon.

Cowboy Cookout Barbecue Frontierland restaurant in Cottonwood Creek Ranch in Disneyland Paris; opened Apr. 12, 1992. Guests dine inside a large barn, one of the largest eateries in the park.

Cowboy Needs a Horse, A (film) Special cartoon released Nov. 6, 1956. Directed by Bill Justice. In this short featuring limited animation, a little boy dreams of such western adventures as capturing a bandit and rescuing a damsel. Features the song "A Cowboy Needs a Horse," by Paul Mason Howard and Billy Mills.

Cox, Brian Actor; appeared in *Iron Will* (Angus McTeague), *Rushmore* (Dr. Guggenheim), *The Rookie* (Jim Morris, Sr.), and *25th Hour* (James Brogan).

Cox, Courteney Actress; appeared in *Mr. Destiny* (Jewel Jagger) and *Bedtime Stories* (Wendy), and on TV in *Dirt* (Lucy Spiller), *Cougar Town* (Jules), and *Scrubs* (Dr. Maddox).

Cox, Wally (1912–1973) Actor; appeared in *The One and Only, Genuine, Original Family Band* (Mr. Wampler); *The Boatniks* (Jason); and *The Barefoot Executive* (Mertons), and on TV in *The Wacky Zoo of Morgan City* and as a host of *The Mouse Factory*.

Coyote, Peter Actor; appeared in *Outrageous Fortune* (Michael), on TV in *Phenomenon II* (Dr. John Ringold) and *Perception* (James Alan Pierce), and on The Disney Channel in *The Blue Yonder* (Max).

Coyote Ugly (film) A talented 21-year-old singer, Violet Sanford, moves to Manhattan looking for her big career break in show business. Eventually she is discovered while performing in a popular western bar, the Coyote Ugly, in Greenwich Village, where enterprising young women tantalize customers and the media alike with their outrageous antics. Violet finds success, and a genuine fan and loves-truck admirer in a young chef named Kevin. Released Aug. 4, 2000. A Touchstone/Jerry Bruckheimer film. Directed by David McNally. Stars Piper Perabo (Violet Sanford), Adam Garcia (Kevin), Maria Bello (Lil), Melanie Lynskey (Gloria), Izabella Miko (Cammie), Bridget Moynahan (Rachel), Tyra Banks (Zoe), John Goodman (Bill Sanford). 101 min. Filmed in CinemaScope.

Coyote's Lament, The (TV) Show aired Mar. 5, 1961. Directed by C. August Nichols. A coyote tells about his problems with man and his dogs in this animated compilation of Disney cartoons, with songs sung by the Sons of the Pioneers. Released theatrically abroad in 1968.

Cozy Cone Motel Five giant traffic cones, inspired by yesteryear's "wigwam motels" along Route 66, offer cone-themed treats in Cars Land at Disney California Adventure; opened Jun. 15, 2012. A guest favorite is Chili Cone Queso.

Crack: The Big Lie (film) Educational film; released in Feb. 1987. Based on actual case studies, a lesson on saying, "No."

Cradle Will Rock (film) The art and theater world of 1930s New York City is in the midst of a burgeoning cultural revolution. Different stories are interwoven to show how individual courage stood in the face of censorship and artists risked their livelihoods by performing in shows and painting their canvasses. Nelson Rockefeller hires Mexican artist Diego Rivera to paint the lobby of Rockefeller Center, an Italian propagandist sells da Vincis to help fund the Mussolini war effort, and a paranoid ventriloquist tries to rid his vaudeville troupe of Communists. The title refers to an infamous stage production being staged by Orson Welles's Federal Theater group, closed down on the eve of opening by soldiers. Released Dec. 8, 1999, in Los Angeles and New York City, and beginning Dec. 25, 1999, elsewhere. Directed by Tim Robbins. A Touchstone film. Stars Hank Azaria (Marc Blitzstein), Rubén Blades (Diego Rivera), John Cusack (Nelson Rockefeller), Cary Elwes (John Houseman), Philip Baker Hall (Grey Mathers), Cherry Jones (Hallie Flanagan), Angus MacFadyen (Orson Welles), Bill Murray (Tommy Crickshaw), Vanessa Redgrave (Countess La Grange), Susan Sarandon (Margherita Sarfatti), John Turturro (Aldo Silvano). 134 min. Filmed in CinemaScope.

Craig, Scott (1964–2003) Mouseketeer on the new *Mickey Mouse Club*.

Cramer, Joey Child actor; appeared in *Flight of the Navigator* (David Freeman), and on TV in *I-Man* (Eric Wilder).

Crane, Bob (1928–1978) Actor; appeared in *Superdad* (Charlie McReady) and *Gus* (Pepper).

Crane Company Bathroom of Tomorrow Display in Tomorrowland at Disneyland; open Apr. 5, 1956–Aug. 31, 1960. While an unlikely subject for Disneyland, it was actually quite intriguing to guests, for it featured the latest ideas in bathroom design. In the forecourt area, guests could turn large wheels to adjust the height of columns of water in a fountain.

Cranium Command Show about stress management in Wonders of Life at EPCOT; ran Oct. 19, 1989–Jan. 1, 2007. Guests entered a theater that doubled as the control room for the brain of a 12-year-old boy, Bobby. The fearless leader, General Knowledge, has put a rookie, Buzzy, in charge of Bobby's brain. Looking through Bobby's eyes, the audience could watch as he faced the typical dilemmas encountered on the first day of school—and witness the havoc created among his body crew as they went on overdrive. Featured comedians/actors George Wendt (Stomach), Dana Carvey (Right Ventricle), Kevin Nealon (Left Ventricle), Charles Grodin (Left Brain), Jon Lovitz (Right Brain), Bobcat Goldthwait (Adrenal Gland), Jeff Doucette (Bladder). Development took several years, with the final show overseen by Jerry Rees, along with directors Kirk Wise and Gary Trousdale. Unbeknownst to audiences, much of the production team appeared in the animated preshow film, including a young animator, Pete Docter, who would later join Pixar.

Crash & Bernstein (TV) Series on Disney XD; aired Oct. 8, 2012–Aug. 11, 2014. Living in a house full of girls, Wyatt Bernstein desperately wishes for a brother with whom he can do fun-guy stuff and who can provide him much needed male reinforcement at home. Enter Crash, a puppet creation that comes to life fully equipped with ninja weapons, strong opinions, an attitude, and never-ending energy. Crash helps Wyatt come out of his shell and Wyatt introduces Crash to life as a kid. Stars Cole Jensen (Wyatt), Landry Bender (Cleo), McKenna Grace (Jasmine), Oana Gregory (Amanda), Aaron R. Landon (Pesto), Danny Woodburn (Mr. Poulos), and Tim Lagasse as the voice of Crash. From It's a Laugh Productions.

Cravalho, Auli'i Actress; provided the voice of the title character in *Moana*. On TV, she has voiced Veronica in *Elena of Avalor* and the title character in *Hailey's On It!*, plus appeared in *The Wonderful World of Disney presents The Little Mermaid Live!* (Ariel) and *The Disney Family Singalong*. On Disney Channel, she appeared in the *Radio Disney Music Awards*.

Crawford, Johnny (1946–2021) Mouseketeer from the 1950s *Mickey Mouse Club* TV show.

Crawford, Michael Actor; appeared as Woody Wilkins in *Condorman*.

Crazy Over Daisy (film) Donald Duck cartoon released Mar. 24, 1950. Directed by Jack Hannah. When Donald attempts to get revenge on the chipmunks for wrecking his bike on his trip to Daisy's house, she scolds him for his cruel conduct. The song "Daisy Mae," written by Oliver Wallace, was later adapted at Disneyland as "Meet Me Down on Main Street," with new lyrics by Tom Adair.

Crazy with the Heat (film) Donald Duck and Goofy cartoon released Aug. 1, 1947. Directed by Bob Carlson. Donald and Goofy, wandering helplessly in the desert after their car runs out of gas, begin to see mirages.

Crazy/Beautiful (film) Nicole Oakley, the troubled daughter of a wealthy congressman, attends public school in the upscale community of LA's Pacific Palisades. As an act of defiance, she makes a play for the attentions of Carlos Nuñez, a straight A student who rides the bus for 2 hours each morning from his East Los Angeles home, and the rebellious flirtation develops into true romance. However, Nicole's self-destructive tendencies threaten Carlos's ambitions, leading to an emotional and climactic confrontation. Directed by John Stockwell. A Touchstone film. Released Jul. 20, 2001. Stars Kirsten Dunst (Nicole Oakley), Jay Hernandez (Carlos Nuñez), Lucinda Jenney (Courtney), Taryn Manning (Maddy), Rolando Molina (Hector), Bruce Davison (Congressman Tom Oakley). 99 min. Filmed on location in Pacific Palisades, Santa Monica, and other parts of Los Angeles.

Creations Shop Flagship store in World Celebration at EPCOT; opened Sep. 15, 2021, taking the place of MouseGear. Mementoes, apparel, housewares, and toys are sold. Throughout the shop, Mickey Mouse is represented in various artistic interpretations.

Creative Film Adventures, #1 (film) Educational film; released in Jul. 1976, which used segments of *One Day on Beetle Rock*, *The Three Caballeros*, and *Mars and Beyond* to inspire students to express their own feelings or interpretations through writing.

Creative Film Adventures, #2 (film) Educational film; released in Jul. 1976, which used *Wynken, Blynken and Nod* and a sequence from *Perri*, along with the "Clair de Lune" sequence meant for *Fantasia*, to get children to use their imaginations.

Creature Comforts Clothing and toy shop in Safari Village (later Discovery Island) in Disney's Animal Kingdom; opened Apr. 22, 1998. Closed Jan. 4, 2015, to reopen Jun. 19 as an Africa–inspired Starbucks shop.

Creature Stall Shop in Star Wars: Galaxy's Edge; opened May 31, 2019, in Disneyland and Aug. 29, 2019, in Disney's Hollywood Studios at Walt Disney World. Guests can purchase curious creatures from across the galaxy, stocked by Bina, the stall's proprietor.

Creeper Reptilelike henchman of The Horned King in *The Black Cauldron*; voiced by Phil Fondacaro.

Creole Cafe Restaurant with a 19th-century coffeehouse atmosphere in New Orleans Square at Disneyland; open 1966–1972. Replaced by Café Orléans.

Crest Theatre Theater in Westwood Village near UCLA in Los Angeles that had a relationship to run Disney films 1987–2002. Pacific Theaters, which had bought the theater in 1985, partnered with Disney. Disney hired noted theater designer Joe Musil to create a design and work with Disney Imagineers to totally refurbish the theater. The first phase of the renovations consisted of adding a new marquee and upgrading the projection and sound system and screen, leading up to an opening of *Three Men and a Baby* in 1987. The 2nd phase gave the theater an art deco look, with a lobby, auditorium, and restroom rehab, new carpet, and re-covered seats. The renovations were completed in time for *Big Business* to open in 1988.

Crew, The (film) Four former wiseguys, Bobby Bartellemeo, Joey "Bats" Pistella, Mike "The Brick" Donatelli, and Tony "The Mouth" Donato, are now getting on in years and living at the ratty Raj Mahal senior citizen residence hotel in Miami's South Beach. Management's plans for renovations of the building to force higher rents and attract a classier clientele are squeezing the geezers out so they hatch a seemingly simple scheme to save their retirement residence. Their caper goes awry and inadvertently entangles a paranoid drug lord who is convinced that he is about to be rubbed out by a mysterious gangland rival. Released Aug. 25, 2000. Directed by Michael Dinner. A Touchstone film. Stars Richard Dreyfuss (Bobby Bartellemeo), Burt Reynolds (Joey Pistella), Dan Hedaya (Mike Donatelli), Seymour Cassell (Tony Donato), Carrie-Anne Moss (Olivia Neal), Jennifer Tilly (Ferris), Lainie Kazan (Pepper Lowenstein), Miguel Sandoval (Raul Ventana), Jeremy Piven (Det. Steve Menteer). 88 min.

Cri-Crí, El Grillito Cantor (film) Bill Justice and X Atencio prepared an animated sequence featuring the Three Little Pigs in this Mexican film produced by Carlos Amador, directed by Tito Davidson, and released in 1963. The English-language title is *Cri-Cri, the Little Singing Cricket*.

Crimes of Fashion (TV) An ABC Family Original Movie; premiered Jul. 25, 2004. Brooke, a shy yet creative student at the top fashion school in the country, has her world change when the family she never knew needs her. Mob boss Dominic dies and leaves her in charge of the family business, a bumbling crime syndicate that has been trying to go legit. At the same time, the handsome new student Brooke is falling for is actually an undercover FBI agent aiming to get dirt on her to bring down the family empire. Directed by Stuart Gillard. Stars Kaley Cuoco (Brooke), Dominic Chianese (George), Megan Fox (Candace), James Kall (Bartender), Serena Lee (Page), Chuck Shamata (Sal Hugo), David Sparrow (Bruno).

Criminal Minds (TV) One-hour drama series on CBS; aired Sep. 22, 2005–Feb. 19, 2020. An elite squad of FBI profilers analyzes the country's most twisted criminal minds, anticipating their next move before they strike again. Leading the team is Special Agent Jason Gideon, the FBI's top behavioral analyst. The experts on Gideon's team include Special Agent Dr. Reid, a classically misunderstood genius; Special Agent Aaron Hotchner, a family man who is able to gain people's trust and unlock their secrets; Special Agent Derek Morgan, an expert on obsessional crimes; and Elle Greenway, an agent with a background in sexual offenses. Stars Mandy Patinkin (Jason Gideon), Thomas Gibson (Aaron Hotchner), Shemar Moore (Derek Morgan), Lola Glaudini (Elle Greenaway), Matthew Gubler (Dr. Reid). Mandy Patinkin left the show in 2007 and was replaced by Joe Mantegna (David Rossi). From Touchstone Television (later ABC Studios) and Paramount Network Television.

Criminal Minds: Beyond Borders (TV) Hour-long drama series on CBS; aired Mar. 16, 2016–

May 17, 2017. The specialized International Division of the FBI is tasked with solving crimes and coming to the rescue of Americans who find themselves in danger while abroad. The International Response Unit chief is Jack Garrett, a seasoned 10-year veteran of the Bureau, who with his team of agents is dedicated to safely returning U.S. residents home by profiling and identifying criminals who are beyond our borders. Stars Gary Sinise (Jack Garrett), Daniel Henney (Matthew Simmons), Alana De La Garza (Clara Seger), Tyler James Williams (Russ "Monty" Montgomery), Annie Funke (Mae Jarvis). From ABC Studios, in association with CBS Television Studios and The Mark Gordon Company.

Criminal Minds: Evolution (TV) Crime-drama series; digitally premiered on Paramount+ Nov. 24, 2022. The FBI's elite team of criminal profilers comes up against their greatest threat yet: an UnSub (unknown subject) who has used the pandemic to build a network of other serial killers. As the world opens back up and the network goes operational, the team must hunt them down, one murder at a time. Stars Joe Mantegna (David Rossi), A.J. Cook (Jennifer Jareau), Kirsten Vangsness (Penelope Garcia), Aisha Tyler (Dr. Tara Lewis), Adam Rodriguez (Luke Alvez), Paget Brewster (Emily Prentiss), Zach Gilford (Elias Voit). From ABC Signature and CBS Studios.

Criminal Minds: Suspect Behavior (TV) Hour-long drama series on CBS; aired Feb. 16–May 25, 2011. An elite team of agents within the FBI's Behavioral Analysis Unit use unconventional methods of investigation and aggressive tactics to capture the nation's most nefarious criminals. Stars Forest Whitaker (Sam Cooper), Janeane Garofalo (Beth Griffin), Matt Ryan (Mick Rawson), Michael Kelly (John "Prophet" Sims), Beau Garrett (Gina LaSalle), Kirsten Vangsness (Penelope Garcia). From ABC Studios, in association with CBS Television Studios.

Crimson Tide (film) When an American emergency patrol on a nuclear submarine receives an urgent but unverified message to launch a strike against rebel Russian missile sites, confusion and chaos erupt on board between rival officers, bringing the world to the brink of nuclear disaster. Released May 12, 1995. Directed by Tony Scott. 116 min. A Hollywood Pictures film. Stars Denzel Washington (Hunter), Gene Hackman (Ramsey), George Dzundza (Cob), Viggo Mortensen (Weps), James

Gandolfini (Lt. Bobby Daugherty), Matt Craven (Zimmer). Filmed in CinemaScope. Sets for the interior of the USS *Alabama* were constructed at the Culver Studios, with the largest hydraulic gimbal ever constructed created to simulate the sub's movement. One scene about the flooding of the *Alabama*'s bilge bay was shot for 14 hours 1 night in the chilly waters of the Culver City Municipal Pool. A 44-sq.-ft. cargo container housing the sets and cast was slowly lowered into the pool while the cameras rolled. Filming took place over 15 weeks, aided by 2 technical advisers who were both former commanding officers of the real USS *Alabama*.

Crimson Wing, The: Mystery of the Flamingos (film) Disneynature documentary about flamingos on the shores of Lake Natron in northern Tanzania. Directed by Matthew Aeberhard and Leander Ward. First released in France Dec. 17, 2008; DVD release in the U.S. Oct. 19, 2010.

Crisler Story, The/Prowlers of the Everglades (TV) Show aired Feb. 27, 1957. Directed by James Algar. Behind the scenes of *White Wilderness* with the photographer team of Herb and Lois Crisler spending over a year trying to get the right footage of the annual migration of the caribou, and an airing of the True-Life Adventure featurette about the Florida Everglades. Narrated by Winston Hibler.

Crisp, Donald (1880–1974) Actor; appeared in *Pollyanna* (Mayor Carl Warren) and *Greyfriars Bobby* (James Brown).

Cristal d'Orleans Shop on Royal Street in New Orleans Square at Disneyland; opened Jul. 24, 1966, selling Arribas Brothers collectibles.

Cristobalito, the Calypso Colt (TV) Show aired Sep. 13, 1970. In Puerto Rico, a young stableboy, Chago, steals an injured Paso Fino colt to save him from death, and nurses him back to health with the help of friends and neighbors. Chago has to convince the horse's owner that Cristobalito is ready for the All Island Horse Championships. Stars Roberto Vigoreaux and Walter Buso.

Critter Country Land at Disneyland; opened Nov. 23, 1988. When Splash Mountain was under construction, it was decided to change the name of the area from Bear Country, when the Country Bear Jamboree had been its biggest draw, to Critter Country, which would encompass the bears as well as the new characters who inhabited Splash Mountain. The ambience of the land remained refreshing—tall, shady trees giving a cool forest feel to the area, with rustic buildings nestled among them. The area also includes the Hungry Bear Restaurant, Harbour Galley, Davy Crockett's Explorer Canoes, and The Many Adventures of Winnie the Pooh (which replaced the Country Bear Playhouse in 2003). In 2020, it was announced that Splash Mountain would be replaced by a new attraction (Tiana's Bayou Adventure). Also in Tokyo Disneyland; opened Oct. 1, 1992, with Splash Mountain, Beaver Brothers Explorer Canoes, Grandma Sara's Kitchen, and Rackety's Raccoon Saloon.

Crockett & Russel Hat Co. See Great American Buffalo Hat Company, The.

Crockett's Tavern Rustic bar and lounge at Disney's Fort Wilderness Resort & Campground in Walt Disney World; opened Aug. 18, 1986, replacing the Campfire Snack Bar. Also a woodland tavern with buffet service at Disney Davy Crockett Ranch in Disneyland Paris; opened Apr. 12, 1992.

Crocodile Mercantile Shop in Critter Country at Disneyland; renamed from Ursus H. Bear's Wilderness Outpost on Nov. 23, 1988. Closed in 1995 to become Pooh Corner.

Croc's Bits 'n Bites See Never Land Pool.

Cronkite, Walter (1916–2009) Broadcast journalist/newsman; he was the narrator of Spaceship Earth in EPCOT Center 1986–1994; appeared with Robin Williams in *Back to Neverland* [sic] in The Magic of Disney Animation tour at Disney-MGM Studios; and narrated the holiday finale of *IllumiNations* at EPCOT. On TV, he appeared in *Walt Disney—One Man's Dream* and *The Disney-MGM Studios Theme Park Grand Opening*.

Crosby, Bing (1903–1977) Actor/singer; narrated the Ichabod Crane segment of *The Adventures of Ichabod and Mr. Toad*.

Cross, Marcia Actress; appeared on TV in *Desperate Housewives* (Bree Van De Kamp) and *Quantico* (President Claire Haas).

CrossGen Enterprises In Nov. 2004, Disney announced that it had acquired the assets of CrossGen Enterprises, a Tampa, Florida-based publisher of fantasy and science fiction comic books. In 2010, Marvel announced it would relaunch the imprint; three of the titles, *Ruse*, *Sigil*, and *Mystic*, were each released as 4-issue miniseries in 2011.

Crossing, The (TV) Hour-long drama series on ABC; aired Apr. 2–Jun. 9, 2018. Jude Ellis is the sheriff of Port Canaan, a small fishing town, whose plans for a quiet life change instantly when refugees from the U.S. in the future wash up on the beach seeking asylum from a war that has not happened yet. The sheriff and the Feds set out to uncover the truth behind the mysterious migration. Stars Steve Zahn (Jude Ellis), Natalie Martinez (Reece), Sandrine Holt (Emma Ren), Georgina Haig (Dr. Sophie Forbin), Tommy Bastow (Marshall), Rob Campbell (Paul). From ABC Studios.

Crossing the Bridge (film) Three teenage buddies, tempted by the promise of a lot of cash, confront their values and ethics when a pal asks them to smuggle drugs across the U.S./Canada border bridge. When the boys discover the package contains heroin instead of the promised hashish, they come to realize that their actions, and the potential consequences, may well affect them for the rest of their lives. Released Sep. 11, 1992. Directed by Mike Bender. A Touchstone film. 103 min. Stars Josh Charles (Mort Golden), Jason Gedrick (Tim Reese), Stephen Baldwin (Danny Morgan), Jeffrey Tambor (Uncle Alby). The filmmakers did careful research to set the movie in the 1970s, with primary filming taking place in Minneapolis.

Crossover, The (TV) Drama series from 20th Television; scheduled to premiere Apr. 4, 2023, on Disney Channel, followed by a digital release on Disney+ the next day. The coming-of-age story of teen brothers Josh and JB Bell, widely considered basketball phenomenon. Through his lyrical poetry, Josh narrates what happens on and off the court, as their former professional basketball-player father adjusts to life after basketball, and as their mother finally gets to pursue her own dreams. Based on the novel by Kwame Alexander. Narrated by Daveed Diggs. Stars Jalyn Hall (Josh Bell), Amir O' Neil (JB Bell), Derek Luke (Chuck Bell), Sabrina Revelle (Crystal Bell), Skyla I'Lece (Alex), Deja Monique Cruz (Maya), Trevor Raine Bush (Vondie).

Crossroads A 36-acre shopping/dining area in Lake Buena Vista at Walt Disney World; opened Feb. 1989, and sold to GE Capital Realty Group in 2001. Located across the main highway from the Downtown Disney area (now Disney Springs), it included a supermarket, shops, miniature golf, and restaurants. In Feb. 2019, the state of Florida acquired the complex in order to build a new interchange for Interstate 4 over the site; closed permanently Aug. 31, 2021.

Crossroads of the World Souvenir and sundry shop at the entrance of Hollywood Boulevard in Disney's Hollywood Studios; opened May 1, 1989, featuring a tall tower topped by Mickey Mouse. Inspired by the real-world 1936 shopping center icon on Sunset Boulevard.

Cross-Utilization Program, known as Cross-U, initiated at Walt Disney World during the Thanksgiving weekend in 1972, where office, clerical, and management Cast Members were trained to work in food service and operations roles in the parks during peak holiday periods when high attendance was expected.

Crosswalk (film) Animated short; digitally released Aug. 4, 2021, on Disney+. A law-abiding citizen must find his inner strength to cross the street at a light that won't change. Directed by Ryan Green. 4 min. From the Walt Disney Animation Studios Short Circuit program.

Crothers, Scatman (1910–1986) Actor/musician; appeared in *The Journey of Natty Gann* (Sherman); on TV in *NBC Salutes the 25th Anniversary of the Wonderful World of Disney*; and voiced Scat Cat in *The Aristocats*.

Crowe, Russell Actor; appeared in *Mystery, Alaska* (John Biebe); *Thor: Love and Thunder* (Zeus); and *The Insider* (Jeffrey Wigand), receiving an Academy Award nomination for the latter.

Crowley, Patricia Actress; appeared in *The Biscuit Eater* (Mary Lee McNeil), and on TV in *Boomerang, Dog of Many Talents*; *Menace on the Mountain*; *Return of the Big Cat*; *The Sky Trap*; and *Elfego Baca*.

Crown & Crest, The SEE HIS LORDSHIP.

Crown Jewel Theater SEE FOR THE FIRST TIME IN FOREVER—A FROZEN SING-ALONG CELEBRATION.

Crown of Corellia Dining Room Supper club on

the *Halcyon* at Star Wars: Galactic Starcruiser at Walt Disney World; opened Mar. 1, 2022, with live musical entertainment. The Captain's Table offers additional courses in a prime location in the center of the room.

Crow's Nest, The Camera supply shop between Adventureland and Frontierland in the Magic Kingdom at Walt Disney World; open ca. 1988–ca. 2010. Presented by Kodak. Replaced by A Pirate's Adventure: Treasures of the Seven Seas.

Cruella (film) Live-action origin story about Cruella de Vil. Amid the punk rock revolution of 1970s London, a clever and creative young grifter named Estella is determined to make a name for herself with her designs. She befriends a pair of young thieves who appreciate her appetite for mischief, and together they are able to build a life for themselves on the London streets. One day, Estella's flair for fashion catches the eye of The Baroness von Hellman, a fashion legend. But their relationship sets in motion a course of events and revelations that will cause Estella to embrace her wicked side and become the raucous, fashionable, and revenge-bent Cruella. Released May 28, 2021, in U.S. theaters and digitally on Disney+, after a May 26 international release. A May 18 premiere at the El Capitan Theatre marked the first major Hollywood red-carpet event during the coronavirus pandemic era. Directed by Craig Gillespie. Stars Emma Stone (Estella/Cruella), Emma Thompson (The Baroness), Joel Fry (Jasper), Paul Walter Hauser (Horace), Emily Beecham (Catherine/Maid), Kirby Howell-Baptiste (Anita Darling), Mark Strong (John the Valet), Kayvan Novak (Roger), John McCrea (Artie). 134 min. The film was shot in 2 different formats—35 mm for Estella/Cruella's grittier world and 65 mm for the refined world of The Baroness. The costumes were a major undertaking; Emma Stone had 47 costume changes and Emma Thompson had 33. Based on the novel *The Hundred and One Dalmatians* by Dodie Smith. Filmed in wide-screen format at Shepperton Studios and on location in central London and across the U.K., including a variety of manor houses such as Knebworth House. Nominated for 2 Academy Awards, winning for Best Costume Design (Jenny Beavan). In the 1961 Disney animated feature and 1996 live-action adaptation, the character's name is spelled Cruella De Vil.

Cruella De Vil Eccentric villainess who wanted to make coats of Dalmatian puppy fur in *One Hundred and One Dalmatians*; voiced by Betty Lou Gerson. Cruella lived in Hell Hall. Also the title of a song, written by Mel Leven, and misspelled "Cruella de Ville."

Cruise, Tom Actor; appeared in *The Color of Money* (Vincent) and *Cocktail* (Brian Flanagan).

Cruise of the Eagle (film) People and Places featurette released Mar. 19, 1959. Produced by Ben Sharpsteen. A glimpse at the varied and important services of the U.S. Coast Guard, which warn ships of dangerous shoals, keep sea lanes open with icebreakers, face gale-force winds and hurricanes to accurately forecast the weather in remote areas of the Atlantic and Pacific, and perform rescue services to ships and downed aircraft. Also explores a training program for personnel of the Coast Guard and their many hardships. Filmed in CinemaScope. 18 min.

Crumbs (TV) Half-hour comedy series on ABC; aired Jan. 12–Feb. 7, 2006. Estranged brothers Mitch and Jody Crumb reunite to deal with their mother, a recent release from a psychiatric country club who has yet to discover that her ex-husband, Billy, is about to have a baby with his new girlfriend. Central to everything is the dynamic between the 2 brothers: Mitch, the prodigal son, is returning home after a failed Hollywood career; Jody, the older brother, stayed in the confines of their small New England town to run the family business. The family will need to stick by one another despite their combustible relationships. Stars Fred Savage (Mitch), Eddie McClintock (Jody), Maggie Lawson (Andrea), William Devane (Billy), Jean Curtin (Suzanne). From Tollin/Robbins Productions in association with Touchstone Television.

Crump, Rolly (1930–2023) Imagineer/animator; he joined the Disney Studio in 1952 originally as an inbetweener and assistant animator, contributing to such films as *Peter Pan*, *Lady and the Tramp*, and *Sleeping Beauty*. In 1959, he moved into show design at WED Enterprises and was a key designer on several attractions and shows, including Walt Disney's Enchanted Tiki Room, the Disney pavilions for the 1964–1965 New York World's Fair, and the Haunted Mansion, including a never-built concept, the Museum of the Weird. He left the company in 1970 but returned a few times as a project designer for EPCOT Center and later as exec. designer for the park's Innoventions and The Land pavilions. He retired in 1996 and was named a Disney Legend in 2004.

Crusaders, The (TV) One-hour investigative advocacy series; syn. Sep. 10, 1993–Jan. 21, 1995. A team of award-winning journalists with reporter hosts—Mark Hyman, William La Jeunesse, Howard Thompson, Carla Wohl—help uncover solutions to the problems reported.

Crusading Reporter (TV) Show; the 2nd episode of *Gallegher Goes West.*

Crush Sea turtle with a surfer-dude attitude in *Finding Nemo;* voiced by Andrew Stanton.

Crush's Coaster Attraction in Worlds of Pixar (previously in Toon Studio) in Walt Disney Studios Park at Disneyland Paris; opened Jun. 9, 2007. Crush, from *Finding Nemo,* sends off guests on a spinning roller coaster in turtle shells to Sydney Harbor, the Great Barrier Reef, and the spiraling East Australian Current.

Cruz, Penélope Actress; appeared in *Pirates of the Caribbean: On Stranger Tides* (Angelica) and voiced Juarez in *G-Force.*

Crystal, Billy Actor; provided the voice of Mike Wazowski in *Monsters, Inc.* (and other appearances of the character) and Calcifer in *Howl's Moving Castle.* He was named a Disney Legend in 2013.

Crystal Arts Shop on Main Street, U.S.A. in the Magic Kingdom at Walt Disney World; opened in 1971, presented by Arribas Brothers. In 2007, it moved into the space formerly occupied by the Market House. Also opened at Disneyland Jun. 24, 1972; Hong Kong Disneyland Sep. 12, 2005 (superseded by Main Street Jewelers in 2016); and as Cristal Arts in Adventureland at Tokyo Disneyland in Apr. 1986.

Crystal Lotus Signature table-service restaurant in the Hong Kong Disneyland Hotel; opened Sep. 12, 2005, serving classic Chinese dishes in a contemporary style. Modern décor is inspired by the 5 basic elements of wood, metal, earth, fire, and water.

Crystal Palace Restaurant Central Plaza restaurant in the Magic Kingdom at Walt Disney World; opened Oct. 1, 1971. Inspired by the Victorian conservatories of the late 1800s, such as the Conserva-

tory of Flowers in San Francisco, this cafeteria-style eatery is one of the more elegant structures in the park. In 1996, it became an all-you-care-to-eat buffet, with table-side visits by Winnie the Pooh and friends. Also opened in Tokyo Disneyland Apr. 15, 1983; hosted by Meiji Co., Ltd.

Cub's Den Supervised children's activity center in Disney's Wilderness Lodge at Walt Disney World; operated May 1994–2017.

Culkin, Kieran Actor; appeared in *Father of the Bride* and *Father of the Bride, Part II* (Matty Banks), and in *Go Fish* (Andy "Fish" Troutner).

Cullman, Joseph F., III (1912–2004) Member of the Disney Board of Directors 1984–1987.

Cumberbatch, Benedict Actor; appeared in *A Saintly Switch* (Clarke), *War Horse* (Major Stewart), and as Doctor Strange in the Marvel Studios films. On Disney+, he narrated *Super/Natural.*

Cummings, Bob (1908–1990) Actor; appeared as 1 of the emcees, with Ronald Reagan and Art Linkletter, in *Dateline Disneyland,* the live opening-day TV show for Disneyland, Jul. 17, 1955. He returned in 1990 to appear on *Disneyland's 35th Anniversary Celebration.*

Cummings, Jim Voice actor; he has provided dozens of voices for Disney TV shows, films, and theme park attractions since 1985. Notable roles have included Winnie the Pooh, Tigger, Pete, and Hondo Ohnaka (in the *Star Wars* animated series). Also voiced Ed in *The Lion King,* Nessus in *Hercules,* Thompkins in *Redux Riding Hood,* and Ray in *The Princess and the Frog,* as well as Razoul in the *Aladdin* sequels, Featherstone in *Gnomeo & Juliet,* and Bering and Chikoot in *Brother Bear 2.* On TV, he voiced Lionel (*Dumbo's Circus*), Zummi Gummi (*Disney's Adventures of the Gummi Bears*), Monterey Jack and Fat Cat (*Chip 'n' Dale Rescue Rangers*), Don Karnage (*TaleSpin*), and the title characters of *Darkwing Duck* and *Bonkers,* plus roles in *DuckTales, Gargoyles, Mighty Ducks, Pepper Ann, The Legend of Tarzan, House of Mouse, The Replacements, Mickey Mouse Clubhouse, Sofia the First, Amphibia,* and other shows.

Cuoco, Kaley Actress; appeared on TV in *8 Simple Rules* (Bridget), *Toothless* (Lori), *Crimes of Fashion* (Brooke), *Alley Cats Strike!* (Elisa), and *Star*

Wars: Galaxy's Edge—Adventure Awaits. She voiced Brandy in *Brandy & Mr. Whiskers.*

Cup'n Saucer, The Main Street, U.S.A. shop in the Magic Kingdom at Walt Disney World; opened Oct. 1, 1971, selling fine china and gifts. Closed in 1986 to be incorporated into Uptown Jewelers.

Cupid (TV) One-hour comedy/drama series on ABC; aired Mar. 31–Jun. 16, 2009. Trevor Pierce, a larger-than-life character, may or may not be the Roman god of love, Cupid, sent to Earth to bring couples together. As fate would have it, Trevor is under the care of famous psychologist and self-help author Dr. Claire Allen, who is also dedicated to helping lonely hearts find their soul mates. While she agrees with his cause, she questions whether he is crazy or really is Cupid. Stars Bobby Cannavale (Trevor), Sarah Paulson (Claire Allen), Rick Gomez (Felix), Camille Guaty (Lita). From ABC Studios.

Cured Duck (film) Donald Duck cartoon released Oct. 26, 1945. Directed by Jack King. Daisy, disgusted with Donald's temper, forces him to take a course to cure it with the aid of an "insult" machine. He is cured and returns to Daisy, but he laughs at her hat, which causes her to go into a rage.

Curiosity Shop, The Children's apparel and jewelry shop on Main Street, U.S.A. in Hong Kong Disneyland; opened Sep. 12, 2005.

Curiouser Clothiers Designer apparel shop in Disney's Grand Floridian Resort & Spa at Walt Disney World; opened in 2019, taking the place of Summer Lace.

Currie, Finlay (1878–1968) Actor; appeared in *Treasure Island* (Captain Bones), *Rob Roy* (Hamish McPherson), *Kidnapped* (Cluny MacPherson), and *The Three Lives of Thomasina* (Grandpa Stirling).

Curry, Tim Actor; appeared in *Oscar* (Dr. Poole), *Passed Away* (Boyd Pinter), *The Three Musketeers* (Cardinal Richelieu), and *Muppet Treasure Island* (Long John Silver), and on TV in *Criminal Minds* (Billy Flynn). He has provided voices for TV, including *Darkwing Duck* (Taurus Bulba), *The Little Mermaid* (the Evil Manta), *Gargoyles* (Dr. Anton Sevarius), *Mighty Ducks* (Lord Dagaunus), and *Phineas and Ferb* (Stubbings, Worthington

Dubois). He voiced Forte in *Beauty and the Beast: The Enchanted Christmas*, Gen. Von Talon in *Valiant*, S.I.R. in the Alien Encounter attraction at Walt Disney World, and characters in the *Dinosaurs* TV series.

Curtain Call Collectibles Town Square Theater shop in the Magic Kingdom at Walt Disney World; opened Mar. 30, 2011. Character plush, apparel, and toys are sold.

Curtis, Jamie Lee Actress; appeared in *Freaky Friday* (Tess Coleman, 2003), *Beverly Hills Chihuahua* (Aunt Viv), *You Again* (Gail), and *Haunted Mansion* (Madame Leota, 2023), and at EPCOT in Ellen's Energy Adventure (Dr. Judy Peterson).

Curtis, Ken (1916–1991) Actor; he provided the voice of Nutsy in *Robin Hood.*

Cusack, Joan Actress; appeared in *Two Much* (Gloria), *Mr. Wrong* (Inga), *Grosse Pointe Blank* (Marcella), *Cradle Will Rock* (Hazel Huffman), *High Fidelity* (Liz), *The Last Shot* (Fanny Nash, uncredited), *Raising Helen* (Jenny Portman), *Ice Princess* (Joan Carlyle), and *Confessions of a Shopaholic* (Jane Bloomwood). She voiced Jessie in the Toy Story films, Abby Mallard in *Chicken Little*, and played Mom in *Mars Needs Moms.*

Cusack, John Actor; appeared in *The Journey of Natty Gann* (Harry), *Money for Nothing* (Joey Coyle), *Grosse Pointe Blank* (Martin), *Con Air* (Vince Larkin), *Cradle Will Rock* (Nelson Rockefeller), and *High Fidelity* (Rob Gordon).

Cutters (TV) Series on CBS; aired Jun. 11–Jul. 9, 1993. The wall is removed between a barbershop and a beauty salon next door, leading to a merger that brings all sorts of trouble. Stars Robert Hayes (Joe), Margaret Whitton (Adrienne), Julia Campbell (Lynn), Ray Buktenica (Chad), Julius Cary (Troy), Robin Tunney (Deb), Dakin Matthews (Harry). 5 episodes.

Cycles (film) Experimental animated short; premiered Aug. 12, 2018, at the SIGGRAPH computer graphics conference, followed by a Jan. 24, 2020, release on Disney+. The story centers on the true meaning of creating a home and the life inside it. Directed by Jeff Gipson. 3 min. Part of the Short Circuit program, it was the first virtual reality short film from Walt Disney Animation Studios.

Cyril Proudbottom Mr. Toad's horse in *The Adventures of Ichabod and Mr. Toad*; voiced by J. Pat O'Malley.

Cyrus, Miley Actress/singer; appeared on Disney Channel in *Hannah Montana* (Miley Stewart/ Hannah Montana) and *High School Musical 2* (girl at pool). She voiced Penny in *Bolt*, Celebrity Starr in *The Replacements*, and Yatta in *The Emperor's New School*. In movie theaters she appeared in *Hannah Montana the Movie*, *Hannah Montana & Miley Cyrus: Best of Both Worlds Concert*, and *The Last Song* (Ronnie). For Disney+, she exec. produced and starred in *Miley Cyrus – Endless Summer Vacation (Backyard Sessions)*.

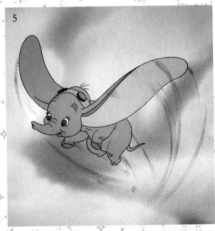

1. *Doc McStuffins* (TV) 2. Disney Emoji 3. Disney Legends 4. Disney Skyliner 5. *Dumbo* (film) 6. *Disney Wish*
7. Ducky and Bunny 8. Dream Is a Wish Your Heart Makes, A 9. Disney, Roy Oliver

D Sports Merchandise Shop SEE ESPN CLUB-HOUSE SHOP.

D Street Pop-culture shop offering unique apparel, novelties, and Vinylmation. First opened in the Downtown Disney District at Disneyland Resort Dec. 15, 2009, later specializing in *Star Wars* and Marvel merchandise. Closed Jan. 2, 2018, and succeeded by Disney Home. Also in Downtown Disney West Side at Walt Disney World; open Apr. 16, 2010–Dec. 2015, replaced by Star Wars Galactic Outpost.

D2: The Mighty Ducks (film) After an injury sidelines his career, the aggressive lawyer-turned-coach, Gordon Bombay, spends his days sharpening other people's skate blades at the local sports shop. However, when he is recruited to coach Team U.S.A. at the Junior Goodwill Games in Los Angeles, Gordon is reluctantly drawn back to the rink he has come to resent. He reunites his team of misfits to train in California, where the Ducks are quickly dazzled by the West Coast lifestyle, and the lure of earning big bucks with product endorsements. The players neglect their game, and the world championship seems an impossible goal unless Gordon can turn his once plucky players back into a dream team. Released Mar. 25, 1994. Directed by Sam Weisman. 107 min. Stars Emilio Estevez (Gordon Bombay), Michael Tucker (Tibbles), Jan Rubes (Jan), Kathryn Erbe (Michele), Joshua Jackson (Charlie). A sequel to *The Mighty Ducks*. The climactic championship face-off between Team U.S.A. and the Iceland team was filmed at the new Anaheim Arena, "The Arrowhead Pond," where the then Disney-owned Mighty Ducks NHL team plays. Among the 24,000 extras recruited to fill the stands were many local residents and Cast Members from nearby Disneyland. Parts of the movie were also filmed on location in Minneapolis.

D3: The Mighty Ducks (film) Gordon Bombay and the Ducks are back in Minneapolis fresh from their victories at the Goodwill Games. They have much to celebrate when they find out they've been given scholarships to the prestigious Eden Hall Academy. Once in the hallowed halls of Eden, however, the Ducks, led by team captain Charlie Conway, lose some of their focus. They become the junior varsity of the Eden Hall Warriors, resist an aggressive new coach, and suffer the indignities heaped upon them by the preppy varsity team that resents their coming to the school. Eventually the players bond with their coach and face a final test in an exciting showdown game against the varsity bullies. Even in the face of adversaries twice their size, the Duck spirit prevails. Released Oct. 4, 1996. Directed by Rob Lieberman. Stars Emilio Estevez (Gordon Bombay), Jeffrey Nordling (Orion), Joshua Jackson (Charlie), David Selby (Dean Buckley), Heidi Kling (Casey). 104 min. Doubling for the fictitious Eden Hall Academy was the College of St. Catherine, in St. Paul, Minnesota. For the film, the crew also completely refurbished the Columbia Ice Arena in Anoka County (Minnesota). Sequel to *The Mighty Ducks* and *D2: The Mighty Ducks*.

D23: The Official Disney Fan Club Announced Mar. 10, 2009, D23 represents the company's first major foray into providing an official organization for Disney fans. Membership includes a quarterly *Disney twenty-three* publication and special event opportunities such as Destination D23, Fanniversary, and D23 Expo, the largest Disney fan event, first held in Anaheim in Sep. 2009. The 23 refers to 1923, the year that the Disney company was founded.

D23 Expo Event first held Sep. 10–13, 2009, at the Anaheim Convention Center. All Disney divisions came together to create an incredible experience for Disney fans and enthusiasts, with announcements, screenings, seminars, displays, informational booths, and speakers, not to mention the availability of special merchandise to purchase. It returned to Anaheim in 2011 (Aug. 19–21), 2013 (Aug. 9–11), 2015 (Aug. 14–16), 2017 (Jul. 14–16), 2019 (Aug. 23–25), and 2022 (Sep. 9–11).

Da Vinci's Travel Photos Interactive photo studio in Mediterranean Harbor at Tokyo DisneySea; open Sep. 4, 2001–Feb. 2006. Replaced by the Biglietteria, where guests could enter a lottery for reserved seating at live shows.

Dad, Can I Borrow the Car? (film) Special cartoon featurette released Sep. 30, 1970. A young man humorously traces his involvement with "wheels" from his own birth, through childhood and teenage activities, including that important question, "Dad, can I borrow the car?" Then, an even more important topic comes up—love. But this only leads to a dune buggy wedding—and the wheels roll on. Directed by Ward Kimball. 22 min. Narrated by Kurt Russell.

Daddio (TV) Half-hour comedy series on NBC; aired Mar. 23–Oct. 13, 2000. Chris Woods has exchanged traditional domestic roles with his wife, Linda, who has a new career as a lawyer, to be their family's full-time caretaker. He gives a masculine approach to his new occupation, and receives advice, welcome and not, from his neighbors and friends. Stars Michael Chiklis (Chris Woods), Anita Barone (Linda Woods), Amy Wilson (Barb Krolak), Kevin Crowley (Rod Krolak), Suzy Nakamura (Holly Martin), Steve Ryan (Bobick), Cristina Kernan (Shannon), Martin Spanjers (Max), Mitch Holleman (Jake). From Big Fan and Touchstone Television.

Daddy Duck (film) Donald Duck cartoon released Apr. 16, 1948. Directed by Jack Hannah. When he adopts Joey, a young kangaroo, Donald finds out the hard way how difficult it is to be a parent. After a difficult bath time, Donald pretends that a bear rug has swallowed him. Joey rushes in and beats up the "bear" severely, so that by nap time, Donald needs a nap far worse than Joey does.

Dadnapped (TV) A Disney Channel Original Movie; first aired Feb. 16, 2009. Melissa is frustrated that her father, Neal, a best-selling author, is totally preoccupied with the hero of his spy novels, Tripp Zoome, and the fan activities surrounding the character. Tripp is cool, adventurous, and clever—basically everything Melissa thinks she's not. During a long-overdue father-daughter vacation, her dad goes missing, and now it is up to Melissa to muster the courage and know-how to find him . . . which suddenly puts her in the midst of her own adventurous plot. Directed by Paul Hoen. Stars Emily Osment (Melissa), Jason Earles (Merv), Moises Arias (Andre), David Henrie (Wheeze), George Newbern (Neal), Phill Lewis (Maurice), Denzel Whitaker (Sheldon).

Dafoe, Willem Actor; appeared in *The Life Aquatic with Steve Zissou* (Klaus Daimler), *John Carter* (Tars Tarkas), and *Togo* (Leonhard Seppala). He voiced Gill in *Finding Nemo*.

DaGradi, Don (1911–1991) Story man/writer; he joined the Disney Studio as a background painter and soon moved to the Story Department, where he was a writer for animated shorts. He contributed to animated features, including *Dumbo* (art direction); *The Three Caballeros* and *Make Mine Music* (layout); *Cinderella*, *Alice in Wonderland*, and *Peter Pan* (color and styling); *Lady and the Tramp* (story); and *Sleeping Beauty* (production design). He also worked briefly on Disneyland, helping to design the exteriors of some of the attractions and costumes for the park hosts and hostesses. In 1959, he broke into live-action film production, as a story-sketch and production artist, as well as sequence consultant. He later co-wrote, with Bill Walsh, the scripts for *Mary Poppins*; *Son of Flubber*; *Lt. Robin Crusoe, U.S.N.*; *Blackbeard's Ghost*; and *Bedknobs and Broomsticks*. He was named a Disney Legend posthumously in 1991.

Dailey, Dan (1913–1978) Actor; appeared on TV in *Michael O'Hara the Fourth*.

Dailey, Peter H. (1930–2018) Served as a member of the Disney Board of Directors in 1984.

Daily, Jody SEE KIDNEY, KEVIN, AND DAILY, JODY.

Daily Press vs. City Hall, The (TV) Show; the 3rd episode of *The Further Adventures of Gallegher*.

Dairy Bar Exhibit/food facility serving milk, ice cream, and milkshakes in Tomorrowland at Disneyland; open Jan. 21, 1956–Sep. 1, 1958, hosted by the American Dairy Association. An imaginative look at the future of dairy production was presented inside a barn-themed display. Succeeded by a Fun Fotos station.

Dairy Tale, A (film) Animated short released on the *Home on the Range* DVD Sep. 14, 2004. Mrs. Caloway attempts to tell the story of the three little pigs but is continually interrupted by her fellow Patch of Heaven denizens. Directed by Will Finn and John Sanford. Voices include Judi Dench (Mrs. Caloway), Roseanne Barr (Maggie), Joe Flaherty (Jeb), Jennifer Tilly (Grace). 3 min.

Daisy Duck Donald Duck's girlfriend made her debut as Donna Duck in *Don Donald* (1937), but was first known as Daisy in *Mr. Duck Steps Out* (1940). Originally, like Donald, she had a duck-like voice (provided by Clarence Nash), which changed to a more natural voice beginning in *Donald's Crime* (1945). As of the release of *Fantasia/2000* (1999), she has made 15 theatrical appearances. In the comic book stories, Daisy had 3 nieces—April, May, and June—who first appeared in *Walt Disney's Comics and Stories* no. 149 (Feb. 1953). On TV, she was given a more prominent role in shows like *Quack Pack*, *House of Mouse*, *Mickey Mouse Clubhouse*, and the *Mickey Mouse* shorts (2013). Over the decades, Daisy's voice has been supplied by several actors, including Gloria Blondell, Patricia Parris, Kath Soucie, and Diane Michelle, with Tress MacNeille serving as her main voice since the late 1990s.

Daisy's Diner Walk-up window in Mickey's Toontown, Disneyland; opened Jan. 24, 1993. Closed in 2020, reopening as Café Daisy in Mar. 2023.

Dale The scatterbrained chipmunk with the red nose, thatch of unruly hair, and buckteeth who, with his partner, Chip, makes life difficult for Donald Duck.

Dale, Jim Actor; appeared in *Pete's Dragon* (Doc Terminus), *Hot Lead and Cold Feet* (Eli, Wild Billy, Jasper Bloodshy), and *Unidentified Flying Oddball* (Sir Mordred).

Dalí, Salvador (1904–1989) The surrealist artist was invited to the Disney Studio in 1946 to work on a film project to be called *Destino*, based on a Mexican ballad. During many weeks at the Studio, he worked with Disney artists John Hench and Bob Cormack, and together they created Dalí-esque concepts and story sketches of ballerinas, baseball players, bicycles, and bugs for the proposed film. Unfortunately, it was not completed; only 18 sec. were filmed. The way-out style would have made its success problematical as a separate short cartoon, and Walt did not see how he could fit it into his production program for the 1940s package films. Then 57 years later, the Disney Studio finally completed a version of the film.

Dallas, Matt Actor; appeared on TV in the title role in *Kyle XY* (Kyle) and as Seth in *Beauty & the Briefcase*.

Dallben The wizard, and Taran's mentor, in *The Black Cauldron*; voiced by Freddie Jones.

Daly, Rad Actor; appeared in *Crimson Tide* (Lt. Comdr. Nelson) and *Shanghai Noon* (Saddle Rock Deputy), and on TV in *The Ghosts of Buxley Hall* (Jeremy Ross) and *The Kids Who Knew Too Much* (Bert Hale).

D'Amaro, Josh He joined the company in 1998 at Disneyland, where he held a number of leadership positions. He subsequently led teams at Adventures by Disney, sales and travel operations for Hong Kong Disneyland Resort, and finance for Disney Consumer Products licensing. At Walt Disney World, he served as vice president of Disney's Animal Kingdom, senior vice president of Resorts & Transportation Operations, and senior vice president of Commercial Strategy. He was named president of Disneyland Resort in 2018 and president of Walt Disney World Resort the following year. On May 18, 2020, he became chairman of Disney Parks, Experiences and Products.

Damon, Matt Actor; exec. produced *Push, Nevada*; voiced Koichi in *Ponyo*; and appeared in the *Thor* films (Actor Loki, uncredited).

Dan in Real Life (film) Dan Burns has a popular newspaper advice column, called "Dan in Real Life," but he has less success as a widower raising 3 daughters. When the family travels to his parents' house for a family reunion, Dan becomes infatuated with a woman, Marie, in a local bookstore, only to later discover that she is his brother's new girlfriend. Tensions rise as both Dan and Marie are staying in the same house but trying to keep the fact that they have met and been attracted to each other a secret. Released Oct. 26, 2007. A Touchstone film. Directed by Peter Hedges. Stars Steve Carell (Dan), Juliette Binoche (Marie), Dane Cook (Mitch), Dianne Wiest (Nana), John Mahoney (Poppy), Emily Blunt (Ruthie Draper), Amy Ryan (Eileen), Alison Pill (Jane), Brittany Robertson (Cara), Marlene Lawston (Lilly), Norbert Leo Butz (Clay), Jessica Hecht (Amy), Frank Wood (Howard). 98 min. Filmed in Rhode Island. Riven Rock, an all-wood beach house with a wraparound porch on Narragansett Bay in Jamestown, became the Burns family home.

Danbury Secret of Flexible Behavior, The (film) Educational film from The Nick Price Story of Non-Manipulative Selling series; released in Feb. 1981. The film shows how to use flexible behavior in dealing with a customer.

Dance of the Hours, The (film) Ballet segment in *Fantasia*, composed by Amilcare Ponchielli. To create realistic dance movements for the animals, animators studied performances by members of the Ballet Russe, including Irina Baranova (Mlle. Upanova), Tatiana Riabouchinska (Hyacinth Hippo), and Roman Jasinski (Elephanchine).

Dancy, Hugh Actor; appeared in *King Arthur* (Galahad) and *Confessions of a Shopaholic* (Luke Brandon).

Dane Browne, Debby She began at the Walt Disney World Preview Center in 1969 as 1 of the original 14 hostesses and was later named the first Walt Disney World Ambassador, serving 1970–1971. She later worked at the Contemporary Resort, assisted with the opening of EPCOT Center, and has remained active in the Disney Ambassador community.

Dangal (film) Real-life wrestler Mahavir Singh Phogat and his 2 wrestler daughters struggle to win at the Commonwealth Games despite social pressures. Directed by Nitesh Tiwari. Released Dec. 21, 2016, in the U.S. before a Dec. 23 release in India, in Hindi. Stars Aamir Khan (Mahavir Singh Phogat), Sakshi Tanwar (Daya Kaur), Fatima Sana Shaikh (Geeta Phogat), Sanya Malhotra (Babita Kumari), Aparshakti Khurana (Omkar). 161 min. From Disney India, produced by Aamir Khan Produc-

tions and Walt Disney Pictures. The film was tremendously successful, becoming Disney's 4th biggest worldwide hit and the top-grossing film in the history of Indian cinema.

Danger Bay (TV) Series on The Disney Channel; premiered Oct. 7, 1985. A curator-veterinarian at a Pacific Northwest aquarium lives with his family on a small island in Danger Bay. The children help their dad and also get into their own adventures. Stars Donnelly Rhodes (Grant Roberts), Susan Walden, Christopher Crabb, Ocean Hellman. Originally a Canadian TV series. 122 episodes.

Dangerous Minds (film) LouAnne Johnson teaches high school English to a group of tough, inner-city teenagers who have already accepted defeat. Her unconventional approach at instilling motivation and self-esteem in her students causes her many problems with a well-meaning but entrenched education establishment that tries to thwart her efforts at every turn. She shows that one person can make a difference. Released Aug. 11, 1995. A Hollywood Pictures film. Directed by John N. Smith. Stars Michelle Pfeiffer (LouAnne Johnson), George Dzundza (Hal Griffith), Robin Bartlett (Carla Nichols), Courtney Vance (George Grandey). 99 min. Based on the popular 1992 book detailing Johnson's real-life experiences, *My Posse Don't Do Homework*. The film was shot at various locations around the Los Angeles area, with more than 1/3 at the Washington Middle School in Pasadena. Some filming also took place at Burlingame High School in Northern California. Interiors were shot on a soundstage at the Warner-Hollywood Studios.

Dangerous Minds (TV) One-hour drama series on ABC; aired Sep. 30, 1996–Jul. 12, 1997. The story of LouAnne Johnson, an ex-Marine who comes to teach English to the bright but troubled students in a special high school program at Parkmont High School in Northern California. Totally committed to her students, Johnson is fiercely determined to support them, many of whom are confronted with seemingly insurmountable obstacles to their goals. Stars Annie Potts (LouAnne Johnson), Tamala Jones (Callie Timmons), Cedrick Terrell (James Revill), K. Todd Freeman (Jerome Griffin), Jenny Gago (Amanda Bardales), Greg Serano (Gusmaro Lopez), Maria Costa (Blanca Guerrero), LaToya Howlett (Alvina Edwards), Stanley Anderson (Bud Bartkus). Based on the 1995 feature film.

Daniel Boone: [I.] The Warrior's Path (TV) Show aired Dec. 4, 1960. Directed by Lewis R. Foster. In North Carolina, Daniel Boone hears amazing tales about Kentucky and decides to move his family there. But first he has to find the path that will lead him and earn enough money trapping to repay a loan. The Native community is not happy that settlers are coming and make life difficult for them. Stars Dewey Martin, Mala Powers, Richard Banke, Eddy Waller, Anthony Caruso. Many people erroneously remember the Fess Parker-starring *Daniel Boone* series as being a Disney show, since it starred the actor who had made Davy Crockett a household name for Disney. But it was not. Parker's series, made by 20th Century-Fox, aired on NBC 1964–1970.

Daniel Boone: [II.] And Chase the Buffalo (TV) Show aired Dec. 11, 1960. Directed by Lewis R. Foster. Boone yearns to return to Kentucky, to escape the tax collector, despite his wife's wishes. With his family remaining home, he leads a small group of farmers to Kentucky, only to be thrilled when his wife and children unexpectedly arrive to join him. Stars Dewey Martin, Mala Powers, Kevin Corcoran, Brian Corcoran, Kerry Corcoran, Whit Bissell.

Daniel Boone: [III.] The Wilderness Road (TV) Show aired Mar. 12, 1961. Directed by Lewis R. Foster. Daniel and his friends have troubles with Native warriors on their way to Kentucky. Stars Dewey Martin, Mala Powers, Diane Jergens, William Herrin, Slim Pickens, Kevin Corcoran, Anthony Caruso.

Daniel Boone: [IV.] The Promised Land (TV) Show aired Mar. 19, 1961. Directed by Lewis R. Foster. The wagon train on the way to Kentucky has to lighten the loads to get across the mountains and battle Native warriors. Stars Dewey Martin, Mala Powers, Diane Jergens, William Herrin, Kevin Corcoran.

Daniels, Jeff Actor; appeared in *Arachnophobia* (Ross Jennings), *101 Dalmatians* (Roger, 1996), and *My Favorite Martian* (Tim O'Hara), and on TV in *Walt Disney World's 25th Anniversary Party*.

Daniels, Lisa (1930–2010) Actress; she provided the voice of Perdita in *One Hundred and One Dalmatians*.

Daniels, William Actor; appeared on TV in *Boy Meets World* and *Girl Meets World* (Mr. Feeny), with guest appearances in *Scrubs* (Dr. Douglas) and

Grey's Anatomy (Dr. Craig Thomas). He voiced a robot pilot in *Kim Possible*.

Danner, Braden Actor; appeared on the *Mickey Mouse Club* on The Disney Channel in 1989.

Danner, Tasha Actor; appeared on the *Mickey Mouse Club* on The Disney Channel 1991–1993.

Danny Mischievous little black lamb in *So Dear to My Heart*. Named after the racehorse Dan Patch.

Danny (TV) Syn. talk show featuring Danny Bonaduce Sep. 11, 1995–Feb. 2, 1996.

Danny, the Champion of the World (TV) A Disney Channel Premiere Film; first aired Apr. 29, 1989. Directed by Gavin Millar. A widowed gas station attendant and his son, who live in a caravan behind the station, team up against a rich land baron to save their town. Based on the novel by Roald Dahl. Stars Jeremy Irons (William Smith), Sam Irons (Danny Smith), Cyril Cusack (Doc Spencer). 99 min. Not only is Jeremy Irons Sam's father, but Cyril Cusack is his grandfather (on his mother's side).

Dano, Hutch Actor; appeared on Disney Channel in *The Suite Life on Deck* (Moose), on Disney XD in *Zeke and Luther* (Zeke) and *Den Brother* (Alex Pearson), and voiced Gilbert Spookman in *Vampirina*. He is the grandson of actor Royal Dano.

Dano, Royal (1922–1994) Character actor; he provided the voice of Abraham Lincoln in Great Moments with Mr. Lincoln and The Hall of Presidents. Also appeared in *Savage Sam* (Pack Underwood), *Something Wicked This Way Comes* (Tom Fury), and *Spaced Invaders* (Wrenchmuller).

Danson, Ted Actor; appeared as Jack in *Three Men and a Baby* and *Three Men and a Little Lady*, and as Jeremy Brockett in *Mumford*.

Dante Miguel's loyal Xolo dog (short for Xoloitzcuintli) in *Coco*.

Danube, The (film) Final featurette in the People and Places series; released Apr. 27, 1960. Produced by Ben Sharpsteen. The people who live along the Danube are studied along with their traditions, in which they take great pride. Both old and new customs and festivals are shown. The film ends with a visit to the most famous of all the Danube cities: Vienna. Filmed in CinemaScope. 28 min.

Danza, Tony Actor; appeared in *Angels in the Outfield* (Mel Clark), and on TV in *Disney Goes to the Oscars*, *Disneyland's 35th Anniversary Celebration*, *The Walt Disney Company Presents the American Teacher Awards*, *The Garbage Picking Field Goal Kicking Philadelphia Phenomenon* (Barney Gorman), and *Noah* (Norman Waters). Also starred in the 2004 syn. *The Tony Danza Show*.

Dapper Dans, The Barbershop quartet that performs on Main Street, U.S.A. in Disneyland and the Magic Kingdom at Walt Disney World. Also performed for several years in Disneyland Paris (as the Main Street Quartet) and in Hong Kong Disneyland.

Dapper Dan's Hair Cuts Turn-of-the-century barbershop on Main Street, U.S.A. in Disneyland Paris; new name for the Harmony Barber Shop as of Sep. 21, 1993.

Darby O'Gill and the Little People (film) Darby O'Gill, who's used to spinning fairy tales instead of tending to his job as caretaker of Lord Fitzpatrick's estate in south Ireland, is about to be replaced by young Michael McBride of Dublin. Fearful of his daughter Katie's reaction and unwilling to give up his own standing in the community, he attempts to act as matchmaker to Michael and Katie to ensure their future. To help his plans, he captures his old friend King Brian of the leprechauns, who must grant Darby 3 wishes. King Brian is almost successful in furthering a romance when meddlesome Pony Sugrue, a jealous townsman, tells Katie of Michael's new job. In a rage, she renounces Michael and runs off after a runaway horse, only to fall and hit her head on some rocks. Near death, she is saved when Darby diverts the dreaded Costa Bower, the Death Coach, by making his 3rd wish—that he be taken instead of her. Inside the coach, King Brian then tricks Darby into making a 4th wish, which cancels out the previous wishes, and sends Darby back to Earth. Michael and Katie are married, and Darby is once again free to tell tales of his little friends, the leprechauns. World premiere in Dublin, Ireland, on Jun. 24, 1959; U.S. release on Jun. 26, 1959. Directed by Robert Stevenson. 90 min. Based on H. T. Kavanagh's Darby O'Gill stories. Stars Albert Sharpe (Darby O'Gill), Janet Munro (Katie O'Gill), Jimmy O'Dea (King Brian), Sean Connery (Michael McBride), Estelle Winwood (Sheelah), Kieron Moore (Pony Sugrue), Walter Fitzgerald (Lord Fitzpatrick). With this film, Janet Munro was signed to a Studio contract, but for Connery it would be 3 years before stardom would come with the James Bond series. The movie was director Stevenson's first major production, and on the strength of this assignment, he went on to direct many of the Studio's biggest hits in the 1960s. The film's production at the Studio began in the mid-1940s when Walt Disney discovered the stories, and in 1946 he sent artists to Ireland for background material, himself following soon afterward. He had a fondness for the country because his ancestors had come from there. The songs "The Wishing Song" and "Pretty Irish Girl" were written by Oliver Wallace and Lawrence E. Watkin. With the aid of lavish matte shots, the film was shot entirely in California. To film the forced perspective of the leprechauns' throne room, there was a need for huge sets, lit by many banks of lights, necessitating the building of an entire new soundstage at the Disney Studio. Special effects masters Peter Ellenshaw, Eustace Lycett, and Joshua Meador concocted the magic of the leprechauns, and their appeal was undeniable. Leprechaun means "little body" in Gaelic, and according to legend they are 21 inches tall, usually dressed in grass green, 5,000 years old, and immeasurably wealthy. Walt Disney dedicated the film, in the opening credits, to these very believable Little People: "My thanks to King Brian of Knocknasheega and his leprechauns, whose gracious cooperation made this picture possible." The movie features one of the scariest scenes ever to appear in a Disney movie—the wail of the hideous Banshee and the arrival of the dreaded Costa Bower. A TV show to promote the film, *I Captured the King of the Leprechauns*, starred Walt Disney and Pat O'Brien. The motion picture was reissued in 1969 and in 1977. First released on video in 1981.

D.A.R.E. to Be Aware: Angela's Story (film) Educational release in Jan. 1993. 10 min. A girl risks losing her boyfriend when she refuses to do drugs, but he respects her for her decision.

D.A.R.E. to Be Aware: Lauren's Story (film) Educational release in Dec. 1993. 14 min. A teen is angry with her parents, but her counselor suggests she try dealing differently with her anger than her usual retreat to her room to smoke a joint. She should listen to others' points of view and calmly state her own.

D.A.R.E. to Be Aware: Matt's Story (film) Educational release in Nov. 1992. 11 min. A teen is booked for drunk driving at the police station, and though he argues he was not drunk, the police officer tells him about the alcohol content of beer and explains the consequences of his actions—he hit a car, badly injuring a little boy.

D.A.R.E. to Be Aware: Michael's Story (film) Educational release in Nov. 1992. 12 min. Two boys are in trouble, owing $800 to a local drug dealer, so they turn to theft.

D.A.R.E. to Be Aware: Steve's Story (film) Educational release in Dec. 1993. 10 min. Rachel throws a party at her home, but her boyfriend, Steve, gets drunk on beer and becomes violent.

D.A.R.E. to Care: A Program for Parents (film) Educational release in 16 mm in Apr. 1991. 18 min. A video version at 27 min. was released in Oct. 1992. Narrated by Edward James Olmos. Today's parents face a very difficult challenge—finding a way to keep their kids safe from drugs.

D.A.R.E. to Say "No" (film) Educational film in the EPCOT Educational Media Collection; released in Sep. 1988. 16 min. Drug Abuse Resistance Education (D.A.R.E.) presents reasons why kids should resist peer pressure and refuse drugs.

Dark Water (film) Dahlia Williams is starting a new life; newly separated, with a new job and a new apartment on Roosevelt Island in New York City. She is determined to put her relationship with her estranged husband behind her and devote herself to raising her daughter, Ceci. As the strained separation disintegrates into a bitter custody battle, her situation takes a turn for the worse. Her new Apartment 9F—dilapidated, cramped, and worn—seems to take on a life of its own. Mysterious noises, persistent leaks of dark water, and strange happenings cause her imagination to run wild, sending her on a puzzling and mystifying pursuit to find out who is behind the endless mind games. As Dahlia frantically searches for the links between the riddles, the dark water seems to close around her. Directed by Walter Salles. A Touchstone film. Released Jul. 8, 2005. Stars Jennifer Connelly (Dahlia Williams), John C. Reilly (Mr. Murray), Pete Postlethwaite (Veeck), Dougray Scott (Kyle), Tim Roth (Jeff Platzer), Ariel Gade (Ceci), Camryn Manheim (Teacher), Perla Haney-Jardine (Young Dahlia). Shelley Duvall makes an uncredited appearance. 105 min. Filmed in CinemaScope. Based on the novel *Honogurai Mizuno Soko Kara*, by Koji Suzuki, and the Hideo Nakata film, *Dark Water*.

Darkroom, The Camera supply shop on Hollywood Boulevard in Disney's Hollywood Studios; opened May 1, 1989.

Darkwing Duck (TV) Animated series; premiered on The Disney Channel Apr. 6, 1991, then aired on ABC and in syn. beginning Sep. 7, 1991. The ABC run ended Sep. 11, 1993, and the syn. run stopped Sep. 1, 1995. It returned to syn. Sep. 2, 1996–Aug. 29, 1997. When average citizen Drake Mallard dons a mask, hat, and cape, he becomes the swashbuckling crime-buster, Darkwing Duck. With the help of his loyal (but often clueless) sidekick, Launchpad McQuack, he patrols the city of St. Canard. When he adopts his orphan niece, Gosalyn, who wants to help out with the crime-busting, his life changes drastically. Voices include Jim Cummings (Darkwing Duck/ Drake Mallard, Jim Muddlefoot, Negaduck), Christine Cavanaugh (Gosalyn Mallard), Terry McGovern (Launchpad), Katie Leigh (Honker Muddlefoot). 91 episodes. The show gained a loyal following, and some of the characters later appeared on *DuckTales* (2017).

Darkwing Duck Premiere, The; Back to School with the Mickey Mouse Club (TV) Syn. special; aired on Sep. 8, 1991. The new animated series and the return of the *Mickey Mouse Club* are both celebrated. The *Mickey Mouse Club* cast perform several skits and songs.

Darling The family name in *Peter Pan*, with George and Mary being the parents, and Wendy, John, and Michael the children. George and Mary are voiced by Hans Conried and Heather Angel. Also the name of the wife in *Lady and the Tramp*; voiced by Peggy Lee.

Darro, Frankie (1917–1976) Actor; the voice of Lampwick in *Pinocchio*.

Darrow, Henry (1933–2021) Actor; starred as Zorro in the TV series *Zorro and Son* and made a guest appearance in *The Golden Girls* (Fidel Santiago).

Darwell, Jane (1880–1967) Actress; she was 84 years old when she appeared as the Bird Woman in *Mary Poppins*. She had won an Oscar over 2 decades earlier for Best Supporting Actress in *The Grapes of Wrath*. She was living at the Motion Picture Country Home and Walt persuaded her to come out of retirement to play the role.

Das Kaufhaus Shop in Germany at EPCOT; replaced Der Bücherwurm in 1999. Steins, glassware, and hand-painted eggs are sold.

Dash A 10-year-old superhero with the power of superspeed in *The Incredibles* and *Incredibles 2*; voiced by Spencer Fox.

Date Nite Friday and Saturday evening summertime event at Disneyland beginning in 1957. Guests enjoyed live performers and dancing, along with the new *Fantasy in the Sky* fireworks.

Dateline Disneyland (TV) Opening day live-TV special for Disneyland; aired on ABC at 4:30 p.m. Pacific time on Sunday afternoon, Jul. 17, 1955, hosted by Art Linkletter, Bob Cummings, and Ronald Reagan. Directed by Stuart Phelps and John Rich. Because of the nationwide anticipation of the opening of Disneyland, fostered by Walt himself on his pre-opening reports on TV, this special had a huge audience, estimated at 90 million viewers. The show was the largest live production ever attempted, utilizing 24 cameras and a staff of hundreds, and it went off with relatively few miscues.

Davalos, Elyssa Actress; appeared in *The Apple Dumpling Gang Rides Again* (Millie Gaskill) and *Herbie Goes Bananas* (Melissa).

Dave the Barbarian (TV) Animated series on Disney Channel; premiered Jan. 23, 2004. In the Middle Ages, Dave and his offbeat family, including his primping older sister, Candy, and fierce younger sister, Fang, protect themselves and their kingdom from a world of odd foes. Complicating matters is brawny Dave's non-barbarian demeanor; he prefers the finer things in life, like origami, birdwatching, and gourmet cooking. With a combination of Dave's brute strength and his fine art skills, villains do not stand a chance. Voices include Danny Cooksey (Dave), Estelle Harris (Lula the magic sword), Tress MacNeille (Fang), Erica Luttrell (Candy), Kevin Michael Richardson (Uncle Oswidge), Frank Welker (Faffy), Jeff Bennett (narrator), Paul Rugg (The Dark Lord Chuckles, the Silly Piggy). 21 episodes.

Davidovich, Lolita Actress; appeared in *Adventures in Babysitting*, billed as Lolita David (Sue Ann), *Blaze* (Blaze Starr), *Jungle 2 Jungle* (Charlotte), *Play It to the Bone* (Grace Pasic), and *Mystery, Alaska* (Mary Jane Pitcher). Also on TV in *Blood & Oil* (Annie Briggs) and *How to Get Away with Murder* (Sandrine Castillo), with guest appearances in *Monk* (Natasha Lovara), *Criminal Minds* (Sandra Lombardini), and *Bunheads* (Mrs. Simms).

Davidson, John Actor; appeared in *The Happiest Millionaire* (Angie Duke) and *The One and Only, Genuine, Original Family Band* (Joe Carder), and on TV in *Sandy in Disneyland* and the *Walt Disney World Very Merry Christmas Parade*.

Davis, Alice (1929–2022) She joined Disney in 1959, designing a costume for Helene Stanley, the live-action reference model for Briar Rose in *Sleeping Beauty* (1959), and went on to design costumes for *Toby Tyler*. Her primary work was the research, design, and dressing of the Audio-Animatronics figures in the It's a Small World, Carousel of Progress, Pirates of the Caribbean, and Flight to the Moon attractions. She also established costuming procedures and developed quality control refurbishing techniques for WED Enterprises. She was the wife of Disney Legend Marc Davis (married in 1956) and was named a Disney Legend in 2004.

Davis, Bette (1908–1989) Actress; appeared in *The Watcher in the Woods* (Mrs. Aylwood) and *Return from Witch Mountain* (Letha).

Davis, Geena Actress; appeared in the title role in *Angie*, on TV in *The Geena Davis Show* (Teddie), *Commander-in-Chief* (Mackenzie Allen), and *Grey's Anatomy* (Dr. Nicole Herman), and voiced Princess Persephone in *Doc McStuffins*.

Davis, Lisa Actress; voiced Anita Radcliff in *One Hundred and One Dalmatians*.

Davis, Marc (1913–2000) Animator/designer; known as one of Walt's "Nine Old Men" of animation, he began at the Disney Studio in Dec. 1935 as an assistant animator on *Snow White and the Seven Dwarfs*. He developed such memorable characters as young Bambi and Thumper and gained a reputation for animating such distinctive female characters as Cinderella, Tinker Bell, Maleficent, and Cruella De Vil, among others. In 1962, he transferred to WED Enterprises, where his approach to three-dimensional storytelling added visual interest and humorous sight gags to attractions like the Mine Train Through Nature's Wonderland and Jungle Cruise. He contributed to all 4 of Disney's attractions at the 1964–1965 New York World's Fair and developed story and character concepts for several attractions, including Walt Disney's Enchanted Tiki Room, It's a Small World, Pirates of the Caribbean, the Haunted Mansion, Country Bear Jamboree, and America Sings. After his retirement in 1978, he consulted on attractions for EPCOT Center and Tokyo Disneyland. He was honored with the Disney Legends Award in 1989.

Davis, Marvin (1910–1998) Designer; joined WED Enterprises in 1953 to help in the conceptualization and architectural design of Disneyland, including the park's renowned hub-and-spoke layout. He was later an art director on such TV shows and films as *Zorro*, *The Swamp Fox*, *Moon Pilot*, *Babes in Toyland*, and *Big Red*, and in 1964 won an Emmy for art direction and scenic design for *Walt Disney's Wonderful World of Color*. In 1965, he returned to WED as a project designer on Walt's concept for EPCOT and the vast complex that would become Walt Disney World. In addition to the master plan for the overall resort property, he concentrated on the design of the hotels, including the Contemporary Resort and Polynesian Village. He retired in 1975 and was named a Disney Legend in 1994.

Davis, Ossie (1917–2005) Actor; appeared in *We'll Take Manhattan* (man in subway) and *The Ernest Green Story* (grandfather). He voiced Yar in *Dinosaur*.

Davis, Viola Actress; appeared in *The Help* (Aibileen Clark), and on TV as Annalise Keating in *Scandal* and *How to Get Away with Murder* (winning an Emmy for her performance in the latter series in 2015). Also made guest appearances in *Brothers & Sisters* (Ellen Snyder) and *Disneyland 60: The Wonderful World of Disney*, and voiced Helen Hanshaw in *Sofia the First*.

Davis, Virginia (1918–2009) Child actress whom Walt Disney brought from Kansas City to act as the title character in his Alice Comedies in 1923. She starred in the first 13 films in the series and was honored as a Disney Legend in 1998. SEE ALSO ALICE'S WONDERLAND.

Davy Crockett (TV) The most well known of all the Disney TV shows; aired on ABC between Dec.

15, 1954, and Dec. 14, 1955, winning an Emmy Award for Best Action or Adventure Series in 1956. Based on the true-life American folk legend who served as a militia scout and eventually as a member of the U.S. House of Representatives. Starred Fess Parker (Davy Crockett) and Buddy Ebsen (George Russel). The shows started a national craze and raised Parker to stardom. Because of the episodes' fame, many people erroneously believe that it was a lengthy series. In fact, there were only 3 shows the first season (1954–1955) of the Disney TV series: *Davy Crockett — Indian Fighter*, *Davy Crockett Goes to Congress*, and *Davy Crockett at the Alamo* (ending with Davy's death). By then, however, the series had become so popular that Walt Disney realized too late his mistake in killing off his hero at the end of the 3rd show. So he made 2 additional shows the next year based on the legends of Davy Crockett: *Davy Crockett's Keelboat Race* and *Davy Crockett and the River Pirates*. Thus, there were only 5 hour-long episodes starring Fess Parker. The shows were combined to make 2 theatrical features: *Davy Crockett, King of the Wild Frontier* (1955) and *Davy Crockett and the River Pirates* (1956). The Davy Crockett craze started a run on raccoon skins, both real and artificial, as kids across America yearned to dress like their frontier hero with the telltale cap. "The Ballad of Davy Crockett," written by Tom Blackburn and George Bruns, rushed to the top of the Hit Parade and remained there for 16 weeks. In all, the nationwide Crockett frenzy helped Disney licensees sell $300 million worth of merchandise. Fess Parker was never able to match the success of his Davy Crockett role, though he did don frontier garb again and star in a popular *Daniel Boone* TV series for NBC in the 1960s. Five more Davy Crockett episodes were made by Disney in 1988–1989, starring Tim Dunigan as Davy and Gary Grubbs as George Russel. These shows were entitled *Rainbow in the Thunder* (2 hours), *A Natural Man*, *Guardian Spirit*, *A Letter to Polly*, and *Warrior's Farewell*. The new series tried but failed to rekindle the enthusiasm of audiences that Parker's episodes had seen almost 4 decades earlier.

Davy Crockett: A Letter to Polly (TV) Episode 4 of the new series; aired Jun. 11, 1989. Directed by Harry Falk. Missing his family, Davy tries to take a letter to a peddler who can deliver it to them but on the way happens upon a cabin where the family has all been slaughtered during an attack by Native warriors, except for a boy, Aaron, who is so scared he can no longer speak. Davy takes Aaron with him and tries to calm his fears. Aaron finally speaks in order to save Davy. Stars Tim Dunigan (Davy), Aeryk Egan (Aaron), Garry Chalk (Major Benteen).

Davy Crockett: A Natural Man (TV) Episode 2 of the new series; aired Dec. 18, 1988. Directed by Charles Braverman. In searching the woods for a grizzly bear that has injured George, Davy finds his long-lost uncle, Jimmy Crockett. Jimmy has a son by a Creek maiden, Eyes Like Sky, who grew up to hate his father and all white men. Jimmy also harbors a secret about a rumored cache of gold. Stars Tim Dunigan (Davy), Barry Corbin (Jimmy), Rodger Gibson (Eyes Like Sky).

Davy Crockett and the River Pirates (TV) Episode 5, following the original trilogy; aired Dec. 14, 1955. Directed by Norman Foster. Some Native friends of Davy's have been falsely accused of raiding boat traffic on the Ohio River. With the help of George Russel and Mike Fink, Davy discovers a group of pirates masquerading as Indigenous Americans and manages to capture them. Stars Fess Parker (Davy Crockett), Buddy Ebsen (George Russel), Jeff York (Mike Fink), Kenneth Tobey (Jocko), Clem Bevans (Cap'n Cobb), Walter Catlett (Colonel Plug).

Davy Crockett and the River Pirates (film) Theatrical debut of Episodes 4 and 5 following the original trilogy; released Jul. 18, 1956. Directed by Norman Foster. 81 min. Stars Fess Parker (Davy Crockett), Buddy Ebsen (George Russel), Jeff York (Mike Fink), Kenneth Tobey (Jocko), Clem Bevans (Cap'n Cobb), Walter Catlett (Colonel Plug).

Davy Crockett Arcade SEE DAVY CROCKETT FRONTIER ARCADE.

Davy Crockett at the Alamo (TV) Episode 3 of the original trilogy; aired Feb. 23, 1955. Directed by Norman Foster. Davy heads west to Texas to help fight against the invading Mexican army, led by General Santa Anna, and has to fight his way into the Alamo, only to find that the situation there is hopeless. The stalwart defenders are eventually vanquished. Stars Fess Parker (Davy Crockett), Buddy Ebsen (George Russel), Hans Conried (Thimblerig), Kenneth Tobey (James Bowie), Don Megowan (Col. Billy Travis), Nick Cravat (Bustedluck).

Davy Crockett Frontier Arcade Frontierland shop in Disneyland; opened Jul. 17, 1955. Western-

themed products were sold. Also known as Davy Crockett Arcade. Became Davy Crockett's Pioneer Mercantile in 1987. SEE ALSO DAVY CROCKETT MUSEUM.

Davy Crockett Goes to Congress (TV) Episode 2 of the original trilogy; aired Jan. 26, 1955. Directed by Norman Foster. Davy tangles with Big Foot Mason when he tries to settle in Tennessee and, in winning the battle, is asked by the townsfolk to run for office. He declines until his wife's death changes matters, and he is soon elected to Congress. His homespun ways are refreshing on Capitol Hill, but Davy soon learns that he is not cut out for politics. Stars Fess Parker (Davy Crockett), Basil Ruysdael (Andrew Jackson), William Bakewell (Tobias Norton), Mike Mazurki (Bigfoot Mason), Helene Stanley (Polly Crockett).

Davy Crockett: Guardian Spirit (TV) Episode 3 of the new series; aired Jan. 13, 1989. Directed by Harry Falk. Davy and George are sent to find a Creek meeting place but happen upon a Native boy undertaking a coming-of-age ritual. In killing a wolf preparing to attack the boy, Davy unwittingly shames the boy with his tribe. In order to get the tribe to take the boy back, Davy feigns blindness. Stars Tim Dunigan (Davy), Garry Grubbs (George), Garry Chalk (Major Benteen), Evan Adams (boy).

Davy Crockett—Indian Fighter (TV) Episode 1 of the original trilogy; aired Dec. 15, 1954. Directed by Norman Foster. Davy is tired of the continuing war between the Native community and the settlers, so he helps the army in putting an end to it. In saving the life of a Native leader, he is shown to have compassion, and he helps push for the signing of a peace treaty. Stars Fess Parker, Buddy Ebsen, Basil Ruysdael, William Bakewell, Helene Stanley. This episode, along with the 2 that followed, were combined to become the theatrical feature *Davy Crockett, King of the Wild Frontier*.

Davy Crockett, King of the Wild Frontier (film) Feature film combining Episodes 1, 2, and 3 of the original trilogy; released May 25, 1955. 93 min. Stars Fess Parker and Buddy Ebsen.

Davy Crockett Museum For about a year after the park opened in 1955, Disneyland had a Davy Crockett Museum in the Davy Crockett Arcade in Frontierland. There was an Alamo exhibit, including life-size wax figures of Fess Parker and Buddy Ebsen, and a historical firearm display provided by the National Rifle Association. When the museum closed, the wax figures were moved to Fort Wilderness on Tom Sawyer Island, where they remained for several decades.

Davy Crockett: Rainbow in the Thunder (TV) Episode 1 of the new series aired as a 2-hour movie Nov. 20, 1988. Directed by Ian Thomas. Davy is a member of a band of Tennessee volunteers called upon to crush a Creek uprising. He sympathizes with the Native peoples but has to rescue a young settler, Ory Palmer, from them. He refuses to support an Indian Affairs bill, which President Jackson is proposing. Stars Tim Dunigan (Davy), Gary Grubbs (George), Samantha Eggar (Ory), David Hemmings (Jackson).

Davy Crockett Ranch, Disney Campground at Disneyland Paris; opened Apr. 12, 1992, as Camp Davy Crockett. The name changed to Davy Crockett Ranch in May 1993. Guests enjoy a peaceful stay in a fully equipped forest bungalow accommodating up to 6. Dining is available at Davy Crockett's Tavern (buffet service) and Crockett's Saloon (bar), with shopping at the Alamo Trading Post. Outdoor activities include mini-golf, tennis, and playground options.

Davy Crockett: Warrior's Farewell (TV) Episode 5 of the new series; aired Jun. 18, 1989. During the Creek uprising, the soldiers are intimidated by the appearance of a medicine man who seems to have caused an earthquake. A new civilian in camp, Callahan, wanting to test a powerful new rifle, attempts to kill the unarmed medicine man, but Davy saves him. This incident helps bring peace, and the Tennessee volunteers can head home to their families. Directed by James J. Quinn. Stars Tim Dunigan (Davy), Ken Swofford (Callahan), Clem Fox (medicine man).

Davy Crockett's Explorer Canoes Critter Country attraction in Disneyland; opened May 19, 1971. Formerly Indian War Canoes in Frontierland. The loading dock has moved several times as progress changed the layout along the Rivers of America. The only Disneyland attraction where guests have to work—their paddling is the only means of locomotion for the 35-ft.-long canoes, as they circle Tom Sawyer Island. Also in Frontierland in the Magic Kingdom at Walt Disney World; open

Oct. 1, 1971–1993, although the canoes continued to be used for Cast Member races. Also opened in Westernland in Tokyo Disneyland Apr. 15, 1983; it became Beaver Brothers Explorer Canoes in 1992. SEE ALSO INDIAN CANOES (DISNEYLAND PARIS).

Davy Crockett's Keelboat Race (TV) Episode 4 following the original trilogy; aired Nov. 16, 1955. Directed by Norman Foster. After a season of trapping, Davy and Georgie desire to take their furs downriver to New Orleans in their keelboat, the *Bertha Mae*, but are thwarted by Mike Fink. A challenge race pits the 2 against each other, with the furs the prize (against Fink eating his hat). Despite unfair maneuvers by Fink on the *Gullywhumper*, Davy wins. Stars Fess Parker, Buddy Ebsen, Jeff York, Kenneth Tobey, Clem Bevans. This show and *Davy Crockett and the River Pirates* were combined and released as the feature *Davy Crockett and the River Pirates*. The 2 keelboats ended up as a Frontierland attraction in Disneyland: Mike Fink Keel Boats.

Davy Crockett's Pioneer Mercantile Frontierland shop selling western merchandise in Disneyland; name change from Davy Crockett Frontier Arcade in 1987. It temporarily became The Spirit of Pocahontas Shop Aug. 25, 1995–Oct. 3, 1996, tied to the Fantasyland show. Reopened Oct. 4, 1996, as Pioneer Mercantile, offering apparel, headwear, leather jewelry, and old-fashioned souvenirs.

Dawa Bar SEE TUSKER HOUSE RESTAURANT.

Dawn of Better Living, The (film) Educational film about the development of home lighting from log cabin to present-day, and with each change a better lighting system; made for Westinghouse Electric Co., and delivered May 28, 1945.

Day, Dennis (1917–1988) Singer; narrated and performed the songs in *Johnny Appleseed*, also voicing several of the characters.

Day, Dennis (1942–2018) Mouseketeer from the 1950s *Mickey Mouse Club* TV show.

Day & Night (film) Animated short from Pixar Animation Studios; released Jun. 18, 2010, with *Toy Story 3*. When Day, a sunny fellow, encounters Night, a stranger of distinctly darker moods, sparks fly. They are suspicious of each other at first and quickly get off on the wrong foot. But as they discover each other's unique qualities—and come to realize that each of them offers a different window onto the same world—the friendship helps both to gain a new perspective. Directed by Teddy Newton. 6 min.

Day at Disneyland, A (film) Video souvenir of a visit to Disneyland; released in Jun. 1982. 27 min. An updated version was released in 1991; 31 min.

Day at EPCOT Center, A (film) Video souvenir of a visit to EPCOT Center; released in 1991. 29 min.

Day at the Disney Studios, A (film) Video souvenir of a visit to Disney-MGM Studios; released in 1995. 25 min.

Day at the Magic Kingdom, A (film) Video souvenir of a visit to the Magic Kingdom at Walt Disney World; released in 1991. 24 min.

Day Break (TV) One-hour drama series on ABC; aired Nov. 15–Dec. 13, 2006, with remaining episodes made available on ABC.com. Det. Brett Hopper is accused of killing Asst. DA Alberto Garza. Even though he has a solid alibi, no one believes him, and he realizes he has been framed. Not only he, but his loved ones, are in danger. He wakes up and relives the same day over and over. In order to break the cycle and move on, he will have to figure out who framed him and solve the complex mystery surrounding Garza's death. Also, he will have to heal the fractured relationships with those he loves, and only then will he be able to fix the problems and awaken to a brand-new day. Stars Taye Diggs (Brett Hopper), Meta Golding (Jennifer Mathis), Moon Bloodgood (Rita Shelten), Victoria Pratt (Andrea Battle), Ramon Rodriguez (Damien Ortiz), Adam Baldwin (Chad Shelten). From Touchstone Television.

Day in Nature's Community, A (TV) Educational film taken from the TV show *One Day on Beetle Rock*; released in Oct. 1975. A study of survival and ecological relationships among mountain animals in the Sierra Nevada.

Day in the Life of Donald Duck, A (TV) Show aired Feb. 1, 1956. Directed by Jack Hannah. Walt Disney and the Mouseketeers help tell about a typical day in Donald's life. The song, "Quack, Quack, Quack Donald Duck," was written and performed by Jimmie Dodd. Also stars Clarence Nash and Roy Williams.

Day-o (TV) A 2-hour movie on NBC; aired May 3, 1992. Directed by Michael Schultz. Grace has an imaginary friend, who only she can see, who helps her learn self-pride, both as a child and as an adult. Stars Delta Burke, Elijah Wood, Carlin Glynn, Charles Shaughnessy, Ashley Peldon. From Steve White Productions and Walt Disney Television.

DCappella Touring a cappella group performing reimagined Disney classics. Debuted on TV on *American Idol* Apr. 29, 2018. Co-created by musical director/arranger/producer Deke Sharon. Part of Disney Music Group.

Deacon, Richard (1923–1984) Actor; appeared in *That Darn Cat!* (drive-in manager), *The Gnome-Mobile* (Ralph Yarby), *Blackbeard's Ghost* (Dean Wheaton), and *The One and Only, Genuine, Original Family Band* (Charlie Wrenn), and on TV in the *Annette* serial on the *Mickey Mouse Club*.

Deacon Street Deer, The (TV) Show aired May 18, 1986. Directed by Jackie Cooper. A young deer is stranded in the big city, where he is helped by a boy who guards him against a neighborhood gang. A local street vendor helps the boy take the animal back to the forest. Stars Bumper Robinson, Eve Glazier, Mario Lopez, Sean De Veritch, Richard Mulligan.

Deacon, the High Noon Dog (TV) Show aired Mar. 16, 1975. Directed by Norman Wright. A mongrel dog goes searching for his young master, Jamie, and finds itself stranded in the desert. His adventures include the chasing of a cat into the O.K. Corral in Tombstone, Arizona, which inadvertently starts the famous battle. Eventually, Deacon is reunited with his master. Stars Frank Keith and Paul Szemenyei.

Dead of Summer (TV) Hour-long series on Freeform; premiered Jun. 28, 2016, and ended Aug. 30. In the late 1980s, with school out for the summer, counselors converge on Camp Stillwater, a seemingly idyllic midwestern summer camp. But Stillwater's dark, ancient mythology awakens, and what was supposed to be a summer of fun turns into one of unforgettable scares and evil at every turn. Stars Elizabeth Mitchell (Deborah Carpenter), Elizabeth Lail (Amy Hughes), Zelda Williams (Drew Reeves), Mark Indelicato (Blair Ramos), Alberto Frezza (Deputy Garrett Sykes). From ABC Signature Studios and Kitsis/Horowitz.

Dead Poets Society (film) John Keating, a dedicated English teacher, returns to his alma mater, a stuffy Eastern boys' prep school. The administration frowns upon his teaching methods, which encourage the students not to learn by rote, but to think and feel for themselves. He awakens such passion in one group of students that they revive the "Dead Poets Society," a secret club to which he once belonged. The "Dead Poets" meet at midnight in a cave to recite and even compose poetry. Ultimately, their quest for self-knowledge leads to tragedy, as 1 student, whose dreams of becoming an actor are smashed by his tyrannical father, chooses to die rather than continue to pretend he is something that he is not. Keating's career as a teacher is finished, but his spirit and his passion will live on in the students whose thoughts and minds he has helped to shape. Initial release on Jun. 2, 1989; general release on Jun. 9, 1989. Directed by Peter Weir. A Touchstone film. 129 min. Stars Robin Williams (John Keating), Robert Sean Leonard (Neil Perry), Ethan Hawke (Todd Anderson), Josh Charles (Knox Overstreet). Filmed at St. Andrew's School in Middletown, Delaware, primarily over the Thanksgiving and Christmas holidays so as not to disrupt the school's academic schedule. Nominated for 4 Academy Awards, winning for Best Screenplay (Tom Schulman).

Dead Presidents (film) Young African American buddies, who've returned from the war in Vietnam, find things changed at home. Their neighborhood is disintegrating, ravaged by drugs and chronic poverty. To try to save themselves, they turn to acquiring dead presidents—cold, hard cash—by any means necessary, even if they end up paying with their lives. General release on Oct. 6, 1995, with a limited release on Oct. 4. A Hollywood Pictures film. Directed by Albert and Allen Hughes. Filmed in CinemaScope. 121 min. Stars Larenz Tate (Anthony Curtis), Chris Tucker (Skip), Freddy Rodriguez (Jose), Bokeem Woodbine (Cleon), Keith David (Kirby), Rose Jackson (Juanita Benson), N'Bushe Wright (Delilah Benson). Filmed primarily in New York City.

Deadline for Murder: From the Files of Edna Buchanan (TV) Two-hour movie; aired on CBS May 9, 1995. A crime reporter for the *Miami Herald*, Edna Buchanan, is on the beat to find out who killed alleged mobster Johnny Cresta, who had been attempting to bring legalized gambling to town. Directed by Joyce Chopra. Stars Elizabeth Montgomery (Edna Buchanan), Dean Stockwell (Aaron Bliss), Yaphet Kotto (Marty Talbot), Audra

Lindley (Jean Buchanan). Montgomery reprised the role she had played in the previous season's TV movie, *The Corpse Had a Familiar Face*.

Dean, Loren Actor; appeared in the title role in *Billy Bathgate*, in *Enemy of the State* (Hicks), and *Mumford* (Dr. Mumford), and made a TV guest appearance in *Grey's Anatomy* (David).

Death: How Can You Live with It? (film) Educational film using sequences from *Napoleon and Samantha*. In the Questions!/Answers? series; released in 1976. A boy learns to accept the death of his grandfather.

Debt (TV) Half-hour series on Lifetime; aired Jun. 3, 1996–Jul. 3, 1998. A game show in which contestants had a chance to pay off their credit cards and other loans by answering questions. Hosted by Wink Martindale.

DeCarlo, Yvonne (1922–2007) Actress; appeared in *Oscar* (Aunt Rosa), and on TV in *The Barefoot Executive* (Norma, 1995).

Deceived (film) After 6 happily married years, Adrienne Saunders thinks she has it all. But after a bizarre tragedy in which her husband, Jack, is apparently killed, she is faced with a series of perplexing mysteries about the man she loved and thought she knew. She discovers a web of deceit along with some shocking truths. Evidence of murder, art forgery, and theft threaten her own life and that of her daughter. Released Sep. 27, 1991. Directed by Damian Harris. A Touchstone film. 108 min. Stars Goldie Hawn (Adrienne Saunders) and John Heard (Jack). Filmed primarily in Toronto, with some exterior locations in New York City.

Deceptive Detective, The (TV) Episode 2 of *Michael O'Hara the Fourth*.

Decimals: What's the Point? (film) Educational film; released in Sep. 1985. The look and sound of a music video are used to illustrate the basics of the decimal system.

Decision-Making: Critical Thought in Action (film) Educational film; released in Sep. 1983. A series of everyday situations are used to take students through the problem-solving process.

Decorating Disney: Halloween Magic (TV) Hour-long special on Freeform; aired Oct. 14, 2018.

Cierra Ramirez hosts a behind-the-scenes look at how Walt Disney World, Disneyland, and Disney Cruise Line prepare for Halloween. Produced by T Group for Freeform.

Decorating Disney: Holiday Magic (TV) Hour-long special on Freeform; aired Dec. 18, 2017. Hosts Whoopi Goldberg, Sofia Carson, and Jordan Fisher discover how Walt Disney World and Disneyland are transformed into the "merriest places on Earth." Produced by T Group for Freeform.

Dee, Nita Mouseketeer on the new *Mickey Mouse Club*. Her birth name was Benita Di Giampaolo.

Deep Rising (film) Somewhere in the South China Sea, horrific, lethal, and unstoppable creatures have emerged from the bottomless depths and attacked the world's most lavish luxury cruise ship, the *Argonautica*, on its maiden voyage. With indescribable strength and deadly precision, these inhuman forces have transformed the vessel into a horrific death trap. For the few remaining on the ship who have escaped, at least for the moment, plus the ill-fated smuggler John Finnegan and a bunch of mercenaries, who dock their crippled vessel, the *Saipan*, against the *Argonautica*, a living nightmare awaits. In the middle of nowhere, escape seems impossible. A Hollywood Pictures film in association with Cinergi Productions. Released Jan. 30, 1998. Directed by Stephen Sommers. 106 min. Stars Treat Williams (John Finnegan), Famke Janssen (Trillian), Anthony Heald (Canton), Kevin J. O'Connor (Pantucci), Wes Studi (Hanover), Derrick O'Connor (Capt. Atherton). Filmed in CinemaScope. Filming took place in and around Vancouver, with much of the production taking place at Versatile Shipyards, a historic ship-assembly plant there.

Deer Family, The (film) Educational film; released in Aug. 1968. Tells of the habits of the horned and antlered animals—deer, moose, antelope, caribou.

Defense Against Invasion (film) Educational film produced under the auspices of the Coordinator of Inter-American Affairs; shows the human body's ability to counteract germs through vaccination. The human body is compared to a city, and the film shows how the city (or body) would react should it be invaded by germs. The city (or body) could die if it does not avail itself of the protection that science can provide. Delivered Aug. 11, 1943. Directed by Jack King.

DeGeneres, Ellen Actress; appeared on TV in *Laurie Hill*, *These Friends of Mine*, and *Ellen*, on Disney Channel in the *Radio Disney Music Awards*, in the feature film *Mr. Wrong* (Martha), and in Ellen's Energy Adventure at EPCOT. She provided the voice of Dory in *Finding Nemo* and *Finding Dory*. In 1997 she made headlines when she came out as lesbian, followed by her character on the show, *Ellen*, doing the same on Apr. 30.

Deja, Andreas Animator; began at the Disney Studio in 1980 working on visual development and animation for *The Black Cauldron*. He helped animate dozens of characters, including the title character in *Who Framed Roger Rabbit* and Mickey Mouse in *The Prince and the Pauper*, *Runaway Brain*, and *Fantasia/2000*. Andreas was also supervising animator for Gaston (*Beauty and the Beast*), Jafar (*Aladdin*), Scar (*The Lion King*), Hercules (*Hercules*), Lilo (*Lilo & Stitch*), Slim (*Home on the Range*), Mama Odie and Juju (*The Princess and the Frog*), and Tigger (*Winnie the Pooh*, 2011). In 2015, he authored *The Nine Old Men: Lessons, Techniques, and Inspiration from Disney's Great Animators*. Appeared on Disney+ in *Prop Culture*. He was named a Disney Legend in 2015.

Déjà Vu (film) Called in to recover evidence after a bomb sets off a cataclysmic explosion on a New Orleans ferry, ATF agent Doug Carlin is about to discover that what most people believe is only in their heads is actually something far more powerful—and will lead him on a mind-bending race to save hundreds of innocent people. As Carlin's investigation deepens, it not only probes through the very fabric of space and time using top secret surveillance techniques that can look back in time, but it becomes an innovative love story that unfolds in reverse when Carlin discovers his puzzling emotional connection to a woman whose past holds the key to stopping a catastrophe that could destroy their future. There remains this question: Can he alter an event that has already happened? Directed by Tony Scott. A Touchstone/Jerry Bruckheimer film. Released Nov. 22, 2006. Stars Denzel Washington (Doug Carlin), Val Kilmer (Andrew Pryzwarra), Jim Caviezel (Carroll Oerstadt), Bruce Greenwood (Jack McCready), Paula Patton (Claire Kuchever), Adam Goldberg (Denny), Elden Henson (Gunnars), Erika Alexander (Shanti). 126 min. Filming took place in post-Hurricane Katrina New Orleans, and the credits include the statement, "This film is dedicated to the strength and enduring spirit of the people of New Orleans." The filming was set to begin in fall 2005, but Katrina hit in August, and the film had to be put on indefinite hold. By early 2006, the city had begun to rebuild its infrastructure, and the film company became the first to start shooting in New Orleans post-Katrina. The filmmakers leased the *Alvin Stumpf* ferry and filmed on it and on the Mississippi River for over a month, culminating with a huge simulated pyrotechnic explosion with flames reaching 350 feet high in the middle of the famed river under the Crescent City Connection bridge. Fifteen cameras filmed the explosion from different angles. In order to prevent undue alarm at the flaming spectacle, New Orleans media warned the public in advance. Filmed in Super 35-Scope.

Del Vecho, Peter Producer; he joined Walt Disney Feature Animation (now known as Walt Disney Animation Studios) in 1995 and served as production manager on *Hercules* and associate producer on *Treasure Planet* and *Chicken Little*. He went on to produce a number of films, including *The Princess and the Frog*, *Frozen*, *Winnie the Pooh* (2011), *Frozen 2*, *Raya and the Last Dragon*, and *Wish*.

Delaney, Tim Imagineer; he joined WED Enterprises in 1976 and would serve as a producer, field art director, and creative executive. He led the design of several areas at the Disney parks, including The Living Seas at EPCOT, Discoveryland at Disneyland Paris, Tomorrowland at Hong Kong Disneyland, and Paradise Pier at Disney California Adventure. He left the company in 2009.

Delaware The Walt Disney Company was reincorporated in Delaware Feb. 11, 1987.

de Leonardis, Roberto (1913–1984) He was involved with the translation and release of Disney films in Italy for 4 decades, later exec. producing the Circarama film *Italia '61*. He was honored posthumously with a European Disney Legends Award in 1997.

Delivery Boy, The (film) Mickey Mouse cartoon released Jun. 13, 1931. Mickey is delivering a wagon full of musical instruments when he stops to sing and dance with Minnie. Mickey accidentally hits a hornets' nest that lands on the mule pulling the wagon, upsetting it and causing the instruments to scatter everywhere. All the barnyard animals join in playing the instruments until Pluto chews on a stick of dynamite he has taken from a local demolition site. After the explosion, Mickey and Minnie continue to play on the damaged instruments. Directed by Burt Gillett.

Delivery Man (film) Affable underachiever David Wozniak finds his mundane life get twisted in a knot when he finds out that he fathered 533 children via sperm donations he made 20 years earlier. In debt to the mob and rejected by his pregnant girlfriend, things couldn't look worse for David when he's hit with a lawsuit from 142 of the 533 twentysomethings who want to know the identity of the donor. As David struggles to decide whether or not he should reveal his true identity, he embarks on a journey that leads him to discover not only his true self but the father he could become as well. Released Nov. 22, 2013, after a Nov. 21 release in Russia. Directed by Ken Scott. A DreamWorks film, released by Touchstone. Stars Vince Vaughn (David), Cobie Smulders (Emma), Chris Pratt (Brett), Britt Robertson (Kristen), Jack Reynor (Josh). 105 min.

Delizie Italiane Shop selling cookies, chocolates, and candies in Italy at EPCOT; opened Nov. 23, 1989; presented by Perugina. Took the place of Arcata d'Antigiani.

DeLoach, Nikki Actress; appeared on the *Mickey Mouse Club* on The Disney Channel beginning in 1993, and made guest appearances on TV in *Criminal Minds* (Audrey Hansen), *Castle* (Annie Klein), and *Grey's Anatomy* (Charlotte).

Delta Dreamflight Tomorrowland attraction in the Magic Kingdom at Walt Disney World; opened Jun. 26, 1989, replacing If You Could Fly. When Delta took over the sponsorship of the attraction from Eastern, they changed the name of If You Had Wings to If You Could Fly but continued to operate it until Delta Dreamflight could be designed and constructed to take its place. A lighthearted look at historic eras of aviation, from the first attempts at human flight to the transportation of the future. Delta discontinued sponsorship Jan. 1, 1996, and the attraction was renamed Take Flight. Closed Jan. 5, 1998, reopening Oct. 1998 as Buzz Lightyear's Space Ranger Spin.

DeLuise, Dom (1933–2009) Actor; he provided the voice of Fagin in *Oliver & Company*, hosted an episode of *The Mouse Factory*, and had a cameo in *Mickey's Audition*.

Demand (film) Educational film from The People on Market Street series, produced by Terry Kahn; released in Sep. 1977. Demand is demonstrated by use of pricing in a gas station.

Demarest, William (1892–1983) Actor; appeared in *Son of Flubber* (Mr. Hummel) and *That Darn Cat!* (Mr. MacDougal).

Demetral, Chris Actor; appeared in *Blank Check* (Damian Waters), and on TV in *Disneyland's 35th Anniversary Celebration* and as a guest star on *Blossom.*

Democracy—Equality or Privilege? (film) Educational film in the History Alive! series, produced by Turnley Walker; released in 1972. Covers the disagreements between Thomas Jefferson and Alexander Hamilton in the 1790s on how our new government should be conducted.

De Mornay, Rebecca Actress; appeared in *The Hand That Rocks the Cradle* (Peyton), *Guilty as Sin* (Jennifer Haines), and *The Three Musketeers* (Milady De Winter), and on Netflix in *Marvel's Jessica Jones* (Dorothy Walker).

Dempsey, Patrick Actor; appeared in *Can't Buy Me Love* (Ronald Miller), *Run* (Charlie Farrow), *Sweet Home Alabama* (Andrew), and *Enchanted* and *Disenchanted* (Robert), and on TV in *A Fighting Choice* (Kellin Taylor) and as Derek Shepherd in *Grey's Anatomy* and *Private Practice.* He voiced Kenai in *Brother Bear 2.* He was named a Disney Legend in 2022.

Dempster, Al (1911–2001) Background artist; he began at the Disney Studio in 1939 and created backgrounds for most animated features between *Fantasia* and *The Rescuers.* He was also noted for illustrations of more than a dozen Disney Golden Books. He retired in 1973 and was named a Disney Legend posthumously in 2006.

Den Brother (TV) A Disney Channel Original Movie; premiered Aug. 13, 2010. Alex, a teen hockey star, is suspended from his team after showboating during a game. He must swallow his pride and step in to be substitute leader of his little sister Emily's Bumble Bee troop. Alex, though, finds that he can get Emily and the girls to do his chores and make him snacks in exchange for merit badges; he also finds the opportunity to get closer to the beautiful Matisse Burrows, leader of another Bumble Bee troop. However, when his self-centered antics cost the scouts a spot at Camporee, Alex finally sees how he has affected those he cares about and must devise a plan that will get his troop into the camp. Directed by Mark L. Taylor. Stars Hutch Dano (Alex Pearson), G Hannelius (Emily Pearson), Vicki Lewis (Dina), Debra Mooney (Mrs. Jacklitz), Kelsey Chow (Matisse Burrows), David Lambert (Danny "Goose" Gustavo), Maurice Godin (Professor Pearson). Filmed in Salt Lake City.

Dench, Judi Actress; appeared in *Artemis Fowl* (Commander Root) and *Pirates of the Caribbean: On Stranger Tides* (Society Lady), voiced Mrs. Caloway in *Home on the Range* and *A Dairy Tale*, and became narrator of Spaceship Earth at EPCOT in 2007.

Dennehy, Brian (1938–2020) Actor; appeared in *Never Cry Wolf* (Rosie) and *Return to Snowy River* (Harrison), and voiced Django in *Ratatouille.*

Denver, John (1943–1997) Actor/singer; appeared on TV in *The Leftovers.* He composed his popular "Sweet Surrender" for *The Bears and I.*

Depardieu, Gérard French actor; appeared in *Green Card* (George), *My Father the Hero* (Andre), and *102 Dalmatians* (Jean Pierre Le Pelt), and in *From Time to Time* in Visionarium at Disneyland Paris.

Depp, Johnny Actor; starred in *Ed Wood* in the title role, and in the 5 Pirates of the Caribbean films (Captain Jack Sparrow). He portrayed the Mad Hatter in *Alice in Wonderland* and *Alice Through the Looking Glass*, Tonto in *The Lone Ranger,* and the wolf in *Into the Woods.* In 2011, he became the first actor to have starred in three $1 billion films: *Alice in Wonderland*, *Pirates of the Caribbean: Dead Man's Chest*, and *Pirates of the Caribbean: On Stranger Tides.* He was named a Disney Legend in 2015.

Der Bücherwurm Shop in Germany at EPCOT Center; open Oct. 1, 1982–1999. The building is based upon the Kaufhaus, a merchants' hall in the town of Freiburg, Germany. The shop sold prints and books about Germany. Replaced by a shop called Das Kaufhaus.

Der Fuehrer's Face (film) Donald Duck cartoon released Jan. 1, 1943. Directed by Jack Kinney. Donald has a nightmare that he is living in Nazi

Germany, envisioning bayonet discipline, starvation, hard work on the munitions assembly line, and "heiling Hitler." He awakens to find himself in the shadow of a Statue of Liberty and glad to be a U.S. citizen. Originally to be titled *Donald Duck in Nutziland*, but the success of the "Der Fuehrer's Face" song by Oliver Wallace caused it to be changed. One of the more famous renditions of the song was by Spike Jones. Academy Award winner for Best Cartoon. A World War II-era short.

Der Glöckner Von Notre Dame SEE HUNCHBACK OF NOTRE DAME, THE (MUSICAL).

Der Teddybär Shop in Germany at EPCOT; opened Oct. 1, 1982, offering a variety of stuffed bears, toys, and gifts.

Descendants (TV) A Disney Channel Original Movie; premiered Jul. 31, 2015. The story is set in the idyllic kingdom of Auradon where Ben, the benevolent teenaged son of the King and Queen (Beast and Belle from *Beauty and the Beast*), is poised to take the throne. His first proclamation: offer a chance at redemption to Mal, Evie, Carlos, and Jay, the troublemaking offspring of Maleficent, the Evil Queen, Cruella De Vil, and Jafar, who have been imprisoned on the forbidden Isle of the Lost for 20 years. These villainous descendants are allowed into Auradon for the first time to attend prep school alongside the teenage progeny of Fairy Godmother, Cinderella, Aurora, and Mulan. Only time will tell if these evil teens follow in the footsteps of their wicked parents. Directed by Kenny Ortega. Stars Dove Cameron (Mal), Cameron Boyce (Carlos), Booboo Stewart (Jay), Sofia Carson (Evie), Mitchell Hope (Ben), Melanie Paxson (Fairy Godmother), Brenna D'Amico (Jane), Kristin Chenoweth (Maleficent), Kathy Najimy (Evil Queen). A Bad Angels Production.

Descendants 2 (TV) A Disney Channel Original Movie; first aired on Disney Channel and other Disney platforms Jul. 21, 2017. The teenage sons and daughters of Disney's most famous villains continue their story in idyllic Auradon. Mal, daughter of Maleficent, under too much pressure to be royally perfect, returns to her rotten roots on the Isle of the Lost where her archenemy, Uma, daughter of Ursula, has taken her spot as self-proclaimed queen. Uma and her gang—including Harry, son of Captain Hook, and Gil, son of Gaston—try to break the barrier between the Isle of the Lost and Auradon and unleash all of the villains imprisoned on the isle. Stars Dove Cameron (Mal), Cameron Boyce (Carlos), Sofia Carson (Evie), Booboo Stewart (Jay), Mitchell Hope (Ben), China Anne McClain (Uma), Thomas Doherty (Harry), Dylan Playfair (Gil). A Bad Angels Production.

Descendants 3 (TV) A Disney Channel Original Movie; first aired Aug. 2, 2019. Mal, Evie, Carlos, and Jay return to the Isle of the Lost to recruit a new batch of villainous offspring to join them at Auradon Prep. But when a barrier breach jeopardizes the safety of Auradon during their departure off the Isle, Mal resolves to permanently close the barrier, fearing that nemeses Uma and Hades will wreak vengeance on the kingdom. Despite her decision, an unfathomable dark force threatens the people of Auradon, and it's up to Mal and the villain kids to save everyone in their most epic battle yet. Stars Dove Cameron (Mal), Cameron Boyce (Carlos), Sofia Carson (Evie), Booboo Stewart (Jay), Mitchell Hope (Ben), Sarah Jeffery (Audrey), Brenna D'Amico (Jane), Melanie Paxson (Fairy Godmother). A Bad Angels Production.

Descendants Wicked World (TV) Animated short-form series; premiered Sep. 18, 2015, on Disney Channel and its digital platforms. Set in Auradon and the Isle of the Lost, the story picks up after the final scene of the original *Descendants* movie. Voices include Dove Cameron (Mal), Sofia Carson (Evie), Cameron Boyce (Carlos), Booboo Stewart (Jay), Sarah Jeffery (Princess Audrey), Brenna D'Amico (Jane). From Bad Angels Productions and Disney Television Animation.

Deserter, The (TV) Episode 1 of *Willie and the Yank*.

de Seversky, Alexander (1894–1974) Author of *Victory Through Air Power*, which Walt Disney made into a film in 1943; de Seversky appeared as himself in the Disney film.

Designated Survivor (TV) Hour-long drama series on ABC; aired Sep. 21, 2016–May 16, 2018. Tom Kirkman is a lower-level cabinet member who is suddenly appointed president of the United States after a catastrophic attack on the U.S. Capitol during the State of the Union address. He struggles to keep the country and his own family from falling apart while navigating the highly volatile political arena and while leading the search to find who is responsible for the attack. Stars Kiefer Sutherland (Tom Kirkman), Natascha McElhone (Alex Kirkman),

Adan Canto (Aaron Stone), Italia Ricci (Emily Rhodes), LaMonica Garrett (Mike Ritter), Tanner Buchanan (Leo Kirkman), Kal Penn (Seth Wright), Maggie Q (Hannah Wells). From The Mark Gordon Company and ABC Studios. The series was picked up by Netflix in 2019.

deSouza, Francis A. Member of the Disney Board of Directors beginning in 2018.

Desperado from Tombstone (TV) Episode 9 of *Texas John Slaughter*.

Desperate Housewives (TV) Hour-long comedy/drama series on ABC; aired Oct. 3, 2004–May 13, 2012. After her death, Mary Alice Young was looking down into the lives of her family, friends, and neighbors. From her unique vantage point, Mary Alice saw more now than she ever did alive, and she commented on all the delicious and dark secrets that hid behind every neighbor's closed door in a seemingly perfect American suburb. Stars Brenda Strong (Mary Alice Young), Mark Moses (Paul Young), Cody Kasch (Zach Young), Teri Hatcher (Susan Mayer), Andrea Bowen (Jenna Mayer), Marcia Cross (Bree Van De Kamp), Stephen Culp (Rex Van De Kamp), Felicity Huffman (Lynette Scavo), Eva Longoria (Gabrielle Solis), Ricardo Chavira (Carlos Solis), James Denton (Mike Delfino), Kyle Searles (John), Nicolette Sheridan (Edie Britt), Jesse Metcalfe (John Rowland). Dana Delany was added to the cast as Katherine Mayfair in 2007, and Gale Harold was added as Jackson in 2008. From Touchstone Television. A Spanish-language version entitled *Amas de Casa Desesperadas* was produced for Latin America.

Destination: Careers (film) Educational film; released in Sep. 1984. Relates skills and interests to various job families and introduces job possibilities of the future.

Destination: Communications (film) Educational film; released in Sep. 1984. A history of the development of communication and a demonstration of how technology has broadened our ability to communicate.

Destination: Excellence (film) Educational film; released in Sep. 1984. Helps teachers motivate students to extend their talents and abilities to their highest potential, through examples of a variety of professionals who are tops in their fields.

Destination: Science (film) Educational film; released in Sep. 1984. An exploration of the world of science beyond the laboratory—how major discoveries came about as the result of scientific inquiry.

Destino (film) Walt Disney and Salvador Dalí collaborated on this surrealistic film in 1946 that for a number of reasons was not completed for years. Decades later, Roy E. Disney took up the cause, and the film was finally finished and released in 2003. It's a story about the search for true love between Chronos, a god personifying time, and a mortal woman, named Dahlia, who seek each other out across surreal landscapes. Premiered at the Annecy International Animation Film Festival in France Jun. 2, 2003, and theatrically in Los Angeles and New York City Dec. 19, 2003. 7 min. Directed by Dominique Monfery. The story is by Salvador Dalí and John Hench, and the film features the Mexican ballad "Destino," written by Armando Dominguez and performed by Dora Luz. Received an Academy Award nomination for Best Animated Short. SEE DALÍ, SALVADOR.

Destiny Bighearted, though clumsy, whale shark in *Finding Dory*; voiced by Kaitlin Olson.

Detroit 1-8-7 (TV) ABC drama series; aired Sep. 21, 2010–Mar. 20, 2011. The men and women of Detroit's police Homicide Unit are as smart and tough as they come. They have to be, working the neighborhoods of the once and future Motor City, a rebounding bastion of Middle America still saddled with the highest murder rate in the country. Stars Michael Imperioli (Det. Louis Fitch), Jon Michael Hill (Det. Damon Washington), James McDaniel (Sgt. Jesse Longford), Aisha Hinds (Lt. Maureen Mason), Natalie Martinez (Det. Ariana Sanchez), D. J. Cotrona (Det. John Stone), Shaun Majumder (Det. Vikram Mahajan), Erin Cummings (Dr. Abbey Ward). Filmed in Detroit. From ABC Studios.

Deuce Bigalow: Male Gigolo (film) Deuce is a naïve, down-on-his-luck guy who cleans fish tanks for a living. His life changes while fish-sitting for Antoine Laconte, a debonair, world-class male escort. He gets comfortable in Antoine's apartment, where his only rules are these: don't answer the phone and don't drive the Porsche. After a chain of events that virtually destroys the apartment and needing money to pay for the damages, Deuce mistakenly answers the business phone and becomes Deuce Bigalow: male gigolo, entering a world beyond his wildest dreams. Released Dec. 10, 1999. Directed by Mike Mitchell. A Touchstone film. Stars Rob Schneider (Deuce), Arija Bareikis (Kate), William Forsythe (Det. Fowler), Eddie Griffin (T. J. Hicks), Oded Fehr (Antoine). 88 min. Filmed on location in the Los Angeles area. Living Color designed the custom-made aquarium for Antoine's apartment; it was a 300-gallon octagon with exact replicas of coral reef sculptures, displaying a wide range of marine life from all over the world. A 2005 sequel, *Deuce Bigalow: European Gigolo*, was made by Columbia.

Devil and Max Devlin, The (film) To save his soul, minor-league sinner Max Devlin makes this deal with the devil's right-hand man, Barney: within 2 months he must convince 3 innocent people to sell their souls. Max makes his victims' dreams come true and tricks them into signing a "contract." At the last moment, Max learns that Barney lied, and he risks eternal damnation by burning the contracts and saving the others. Released Feb. 6, 1981. Directed by Steven Hilliard Stern. 95 min. Stars Elliott Gould (Max Devlin), Bill Cosby (Barney), Susan Anspach (Penny), Adam Rich (Toby), Julie Budd (Stella), Sonny Shroyer (Big Billy Hunniker), David Knell (Nerve Nordlinger). The film features the songs "Roses and Rainbows" by Marvin Hamlisch and Carole Bayer Sager and "Any Fool Could See" by Hamlisch and Allee Willis. Location shooting was done at Universal Studios, utilizing the Universal Studios Tour and Amphitheatre. In addition, several other places around the Los Angeles area were used, including the Troubadour club and the Music Center, the Pasadena Civic Auditorium, Indian Dunes, and Venice Beach . Disney makeup man Bob Schiffer was responsible for Bill Cosby's convincing devilish look. He provided Cosby with a red iridescent wig, with ears and horns sewn into the base, and a heavy mauve makeup coloring as a base for his face, on top of which he used a special red water-soluble makeup from Germany. The elaborate Hell set was constructed of huge plaster stalagmites and stalactites with menacing bursts of flame provided by 20 butane furnaces. When the smoke cleared after 4 days of filming in "Hell," the special effects department had consumed 150 gallons of butane fuel, not to mention the 36,000 lbs. of dry ice used to provide the eerie, low-lying smoke effect.

Devine, Adam Actor; appeared on Disney+ in *Magic Camp* (Andy) and *Becoming*. He voiced Galt in *Tron: Uprising*, Boone in *Penn Zero: Part-Time Hero*, and Poltergeist Pat in *Vampirina*.

Devine, Andy (1905–1997) Actor; appeared on TV in *Ride a Northbound Horse* and *Smoke*, and voiced Friar Tuck in *Robin Hood*.

Devious Maids (TV) Drama on Lifetime; aired Jun. 23, 2013–Aug. 8, 2016. A close-knit group of maids in Beverly Hills is bonded together by their jobs, life struggles, and the melodramatic universe that engulfs their wealthy and famous employers, including the shocking murder of a beloved housemaid. The staff is as clever, witty, outrageous, and downright devilish as their employers. Stars Ana Ortiz (Marisol), Dania Ramirez (Rosie), Roselyn Sánchez (Carmen), Edy Ganem (Valentine), Judy Reyes (Zolla). From ABC Studios.

DeVito, Danny Actor; appeared in *Ruthless People* (Sam Stone), *Tin Men* (Ernest Tilley), *Renaissance Man* (Bill Rago), *Dumbo* (Max Medici, 2019), and *Haunted Mansion* (2023), and provided the voice of Phil in *Hercules* and Bob in *The One and Only Ivan*.

Dewey One of Donald Duck's 3 nephews; originally voiced by Clarence Nash. Beginning with the *DuckTales* TV series, the nephews were voiced by Russi Taylor and given unique colors to wear (blue for Dewey). Voiced by Ben Schwartz in the new *DuckTales* (2017).

Dewhurst, Colleen (1926–1991) Actress; appeared on TV in *Bigfoot* (Gladys) and in *Lantern Hill* and *Anne of Avonlea* on The Disney Channel.

deWilde, Brandon (1942–1972) Actor; appeared in *Those Calloways* (Bucky), and on TV in *The Tenderfoot*.

Diamantopoulos, Chris Actor; he has provided several voices, including Mickey Mouse in the series of Disney Channel shorts (beginning in 2013), Frank Heffley in *Diary of a Wimpy Kid*, Storkules and Darkwing Duck in *DuckTales* (2017), and Brock Thunderstrike in *Tangled: The Series*. Also appeared in *Eli Stone* (Jake McCann).

Diamond, Eileen Mouseketeer from the 1950s *Mickey Mouse Club* TV show.

Diamond Celebration, Disneyland Resort In honor of the 60th anniversary of Disneyland, this celebration included sparkling diamond enhancements to Sleeping Beauty Castle and Carthay Circle Restaurant, as well as special entertainment: the *Disneyland Forever* fireworks spectacular and *Paint the Night* parade in Disneyland, and *World of Color – Celebrate! The Wonderful World of Walt Disney* and Diamond Mad T Party in Disney California Adventure. The celebration launched May 22, 2015 (with a 24-hour party beginning at 6 a.m.) and ended Sep. 5, 2016.

Diamond Horseshoe Revue Western variety show in the Magic Kingdom at Walt Disney World; opened Oct. 1, 1971. Based on the original *Golden Horseshoe Revue* in Disneyland, with musical performances, high-kicking cancan dancers, and a "Pecos Bill" finale, all hosted by Slue Foot Sue. Original Disneyland performer Wally Boag helped open the show at Walt Disney World. Changed to the *Diamond Horseshoe Jamboree* Oct. 1, 1986, with more audience participation and new characters: Ms. Lily, the saloon singer, and Sam the Bartender. It became the *Diamond Horseshoe Saloon Revue and Medicine Show* Apr. 7, 1995, with reservations no longer required; guests could walk in at any time during the show, purchase counter-service food, and watch variety acts by Wildcat Kate, Dr. Bill Yalater, or "Miss Lucille Lamour and her Lovely Ladies." The show ended Feb. 1, 2003, and *Goofy's Country Dancin' Jamboree*, starring Disney characters, ran Jul. 1, 2003–Sep. 2004. The saloon thereafter became a seasonal dining space, sometimes hosting character greetings. The *Diamond Horseshoe Revue* was also a show in Westernland at Tokyo Disneyland; opened Apr. 15, 1983, and succeeded by different entertainment over the years, including the *Hoop-Dee-Doo Musical Revue.*

Diamond Is a Boy's Best Friend, A (TV) Episode 1 of *Moochie of the Little League.*

Diamonds on Wheels (TV) Three-part show aired Mar. 10, 17, and 24, 1974. Directed by Jerome Courtland. Teenagers battle jewel thieves in England, when 1 of them acquires a car seat, in which the jewels had been hidden, from a junkyard to use in his racing car. The thieves follow the boys during the Hampshire Rally, an endurance race, but with the help of the police, are outwitted. Stars Patrick Allen, Peter Firth, George Sewell, Spencer Banks, Cynthia Lund. The director, Jerome Courtland, earlier starred as Andy Burnett for Disney. Originally released theatrically in England in Aug. 1973.

Diana Goddess of the moon in "The Pastoral Symphony" segment of *Fantasia.*

Diary of a Future President (TV) A Disney+ original series from CBS Studios; digitally premiered Jan. 17, 2020. The origin story of Cuban American and future leader Elena Cañero-Reed as she enters the 7th grade. Told using the narration of excerpts from Elena's diary, this family comedy follows Elena through the ups and downs of middle school, which set her on the path to becoming the president of the United States. Stars Tess Romero (Elena Cañero-Reed), Charlie Bushnell (Bobby Cañero-Reed), Selenis Leyva (Gabi Cañero-Reed), Michael Weaver (Sam Faber), Gina Rodriguez (Grown-Up Elena). Produced in association with I Can and I Will Productions.

Diary of a Wimpy Kid (film) A Disney+ original animated film from 20th Century Animation and Bardel Entertainment, released under the Disney banner. Greg Heffley is a scrawny but ambitious kid with an active imagination and big plans to be rich and famous—he just has to survive middle school first. To make matters worse, his best friend, Rowley, seems to coast through life and succeed at everything without even trying. As details of his attempts to fit in fill the pages of his journal, Greg learns to appreciate true friends and the satisfaction that comes from standing up for what is right. Digitally released Dec. 3, 2021. 56 min. Directed by Swinton Scott. Voices include Brady Noon (Greg Heffley), Ethan William Childress (Rowley Jefferson), Chris Diamantopoulos (Frank Heffley). Based on the first book in the series by Jeff Kinney.

Diary of a Wimpy Kid: Rodrick Rules (film) A Disney+ original animated film from 20th Century Studios and Bardel Entertainment, released under the Disney banner. The riotous antics of middle schooler Greg Heffley continue, focusing this time on his complicated relationship with older brother Rodrick, a lazy and undisciplined high schooler who spends too much time practicing with his rock band, Löded Diper. Digitally released Dec. 2, 2022. 74 min. Directed by Luke Cormican. Voices include Brady Noon (Greg), Ethan William Childress (Rowley), Ed Asner (Grandpa), Chris Diamantopoulos (Frank), Erica Cerra (Susan), Hunter Dillon (Rodrick). Based on the book by Jeff Kinney.

Dick Tracy (film) Legendary police detective Dick Tracy is the only man tough enough to take on gangster boss Big Boy Caprice and his band of menacing mobsters. Dedicated to his work but at the same time devoted to his loyal girlfriend, Tess Trueheart, Tracy finds himself torn between love and duty. His relentless crusade against crime becomes even more difficult when he gets saddled with an engaging orphan and meets seductive and sultry Breathless Mahoney, a torch singer determined to get the best of Tracy. A faceless character, the Blank, threatens both Tracy and Big Boy, and it takes all of Tracy's skills to save the city. Released Jun. 15, 1990. Directed by Warren Beatty. A Touchstone film. 105 min. Stars Warren Beatty (Dick Tracy), Charlie Korsmo (Kid), Madonna (Breathless Mahoney), Al Pacino (Big Boy Caprice), Glenne Headly (Tess Trueheart), Mandy Patinkin (88 Keys), Paul Sorvino (Lips Manlis), Dustin Hoffman (Mumbles), Dick Van Dyke (D.A. Fletcher), James Caan (Spaldoni). Based on the comic strip by Chester Gould. The unique and unusual faces for the gangster characters were created by makeup and prosthetics wizards John Caglione, Jr. and Doug Drexler. Some actors needed to endure up to 4 hours in the makeup room getting ready for the camera. *Dick Tracy*'s fantasy world was created on the backlot at the Warner Bros. Studio. The film won Academy Awards for Best Makeup (Caglione, Jr.; Drexler), Best Art Direction/Set Decoration (Richard Sylbert and Rick Simpson), and Best Song ("Sooner or Later [I Always Get My Man]" by Stephen Sondheim). The movie led to a shop, Dick Tracy, in Pleasure Island at Walt Disney World during part of 1990, and a stage show at Disney-MGM Studios, 1990–91.

Dick Tracy: Behind the Badge . . . Behind the Scenes (TV) Syn. special about the making of the Touchstone film; first aired on Jun. 13, 1990. 30 min. Directed by Gayle Hollenbaugh.

Dick Tracy Starring in Diamond Double-Cross Stage musical at the original Theater of the Stars in Disney-MGM Studios at Walt Disney World; ran May 21, 1990–Feb. 16, 1991, based on the Touchstone film. Also at Videopolis in Disneyland; ran Jun. 15–Dec. 31, 1990.

Die Weihnachts Ecke SEE PORZELLANHAUS.

Diesel, Vin Actor; appeared in *The Pacifier* (Shane Wolf) and provided the voice of Groot in *Guardians of the Galaxy* and other appearances of the character.

Diggs, Daveed Actor; appeared on TV in *black-ish* and *mixed-ish* (Johan), and *The Mayor* (Mac Etcetera), for which he also served as exec. producer. For *Soul*, he voiced Paul and served as a cultural and music consultant. He performed the song "Parlez-Vous Rap" in *Zootopia*, voiced Norath Kev in *Star Wars Resistance*, and narrated *The Crossover* for Disney+. It was announced that he will perform the role of Sebastian in *The Little Mermaid* (2023). He is known for originating the roles of Marquis de Lafayette and Thomas Jefferson in the Broadway musical *Hamilton*.

Diller, Phyllis (1917–2012) Actress; voiced the Queen in *A Bug's Life*. On TV, she hosted an episode of *The Mouse Factory* and made guest appearances in *Christmas at Walt Disney World*, *Circus of the Stars Goes to Disneyland*, *Boy Meets World* (Madame Ouspenskaya), *Blossom* (Mrs. Peterson), and on Disney Channel in *Even Stevens* (Coach Korns).

Dillon, Matt Actor; appeared in the title role in *Tex*, *Herbie: Fully Loaded* (Trip Murphy), and *Old Dogs* (Barry).

Dinah Seductive dachshund who captivated Pluto, appearing in 5 cartoons with him, beginning with *The Sleepwalker* (1942).

Dinah Alice's little kitten in *Alice in Wonderland*.

Dinky and Boomer Sparrow and woodpecker friends of Tod in *The Fox and the Hound*; voiced by Dick Bakalyan and Paul Winchell.

Dino Institute Shop Gift shop at the exit of DINOSAUR in Disney's Animal Kingdom; opened Apr. 22, 1998, selling souvenir ride photos and dinosaur items.

DinoLand U.S.A. Area in Disney's Animal Kingdom; opened Apr. 22, 1998, and presented by McDonald's until 2008. According to the story, this roadside destination had been built around an old fishing camp where dinosaur fossils were discovered in the 1940s. At the Dino Institute, visitors travel back to the late Cretaceous period and face extinction from a giant asteroid in DINOSAUR (from 1998–2000, it was named Countdown to Extinction). There is also the Cretaceous Trail, where guests can walk through the past amid a lush variety of cycads, palms, ferns, and other survivors from the age of the dinosaurs. At The Boneyard, kids can search for fossils in an open-air dig site playground. Nearby, 2 local entrepreneurs present a more whimsical perspective of dinosaurs at Chester & Hester's Dinosaur Treasures; their enterprise expanded in 2001–2002 with the Dino-Rama! roadside amusement area, featuring Primeval Whirl (closed in 2020), TriceraTop Spin, and Fossil Fun Games. Dining and snacks are available in Restaurantosaurus, Trilo-Bites (originally Petrifries), Dino-Bite Snacks, and Dino Diner (closed in 2022). There is also the Theater in the Wild, a 1,500-seat amphitheater, which was enclosed in 2007 to present *Finding Nemo—The Musical*. In 2022, initial plans to replace DinoLand U.S.A. with a new themed area were announced.

Dinosaur (film) During the Cretaceous period, 65 million years ago, a 3-ton iguanodon named Aladar is raised by a clan of lemurs and eventually reunited with his own kind. With flaming meteors devastating the landscape and water in diminishing supply, the dinosaurs find themselves in a race against time to reach the safety of their nesting grounds. When Aladar comes to the aid of a group of misfits unable to keep up with the breakneck pace of the herd, he makes an enemy of Kron, the stonehearted leader. Faced with such perils as treacherous rock slides and attacking Carnotaurus, Aladar and his friends must overcome tremendous obstacles before they can settle into a new life in a beautiful valley. Directed by Ralph Zondag and Eric Leighton. Released May 19, 2000. Voices include Ossie Davis (Yar), Della Reese (Eema), Joan Plowright (Baylene), D. B. Sweeney (Aladar), Alfre Woodard (Plio), Samuel E. Wright (Kron), Julianna Margulies (Neera), Hayden Panettiere (Suri), Peter Siragusa (Bruton), Max Casella (Zini). 82 min. Musical score by James Newton Howard. The film breaks new ground by combining state-of-the-art computer character animation with digitally enhanced live-action backgrounds. While previous features using computer animation (*Toy Story*, *Toy Story 2*, and *A Bug's Life*) were produced by Pixar in association with the Disney Studio, this film was the first to be produced in-house. The Countdown to Extinction attraction in Disney's Animal Kingdom was renamed DINOSAUR to tie in with the film.

DINOSAUR See Countdown to Extinction (Disney's Animal Kingdom).

Dinosaur Barbarian (film) Animated short; digitally released Aug. 4, 2021, on Disney+. Battling evil is all in a day's work for Dinosaur Barbarian, but what about taking out the trash? Sometimes even a superhero needs to clean up his act. Directed by Kim Hazel. 3 min. From the Walt Disney Animation Studios Short Circuit program.

Dinosaur Gertie's Ice Cream of Extinction Opened May 1, 1989, in Lakeside Circle in Disney-MGM Studios (later Echo Lake in Disney's Hollywood Studios). Gertie the Dinosaur was one of the first animated film characters, created by Winsor McCay in the early 20th century. The Disney Imagineers decided to honor McCay with this large dinosaur-shaped ice cream shop inspired by "California Crazy" architecture. Observant guests may even notice dinosaur-shaped footprints in the concrete walkway leading to it. The story of Gertie the Dinosaur is told in the *Disneyland* TV show *The Story of the Animated Drawing*.

Dinosaur Jack's Sunglass Shack Roadside-style shop inside a giant dinosaur; open Feb. 8, 2001–2009, on Paradise Pier in Disney's California Adventure.

Dinosaur . . . Secret of the Lost Legend (TV) Edited version of the feature *Baby*; aired Jan. 8, 1989.

Dinosaurs (TV) Comedy series; aired Apr. 26, 1991–Jul. 20, 1994, on ABC. Jim Henson Associates created the characters in this series covering the life of a highly evolved prehistoric family, the Sinclairs, living in the year 60,000,003 B.C. The bombastic Earl Sinclair, a middle-aged, blue-collar Megalosaurus, has worked as a tree pusher for 24 years. He stars with his even-tempered Allosaurus wife, Fran; 2 adolescent children, Robbie and Charlene; attention-grabbing Baby; and always critical mother-in-law, Grandma Ethyl. The family's relationships and antics provide a humorous look at our own society today. Voices include Stuart Pankin (Earl Sinclair), Jessica Walter (Fran Sinclair), Jason Willinger (Robbie), Sally Struthers (Charlene), John Kennedy (Baby), Sam McMurray (Roy Hess), Sherman Hemsley (B. P. Richfield), Florence Stanley (Ethyl). Amusingly, many of the characters share names with oil companies. From Michael Jacobs Productions and Jim Henson Productions, in association with Walt Disney Television. The show won an Emmy Award for Art Direction in 1991.

Dinosaurs Live! Small parade in Disney-MGM Studios at Walt Disney World; ran Sep. 26, 1991–Aug. 29, 1992. The Sinclair family, from the

Dinosaurs TV series, was named the park's family of the day.

Dino-Sue During a 1990 excavation trip in South Dakota, fossil hunter Sue Hendrickson discovered the largest and most complete T. rex skeleton found to date, which was named Sue in her honor. The bones were cleaned in the Fossil Preparation Lab at Disney's Animal Kingdom, and a replica was made for exhibition in the park, named Dino-Sue. The real Sue dinosaur is displayed in the Field Museum in Chicago.

Dinotopia (TV) A 6-hour miniseries from Hallmark Entertainment for *The Wonderful World of Disney*; aired May 12–14, 2002. Epic story of a lost continent where dinosaurs and humans live together in an almost-utopian world. Directed by Marco Brambilla. Stars David Thewlis (Cyrus Crabb), Katie Carr (Marion), Jim Carter (Mayor Waldo), Alice Krige (Rosemary), Tyron Leitso (Karl), Wentworth Miller (David). Based on the books by James Gurney. The largest production ever filmed at Pinewood Studios in London. A production of Hallmark Entertainment.

Dinotopia (TV) The miniseries continued as a weekly series on ABC; aired Nov. 28–Dec. 26, 2002. The new cast included Erik von Detten (Karl Scott), Shiloh Strong (David Scott), Michael Brandon (Frank Scott), Georgina Rylance (Marion), Jonathan Hyde (Mayor Waldo), Sophie Ward (Rosemary), Lisa Zane (Le Sage). Omid Djalili provides the voice of Zipeau. Strong is the older brother of Rider Strong, who played Shawn on *Boy Meets World*. The series was filmed in Budapest, Hungary.

Dion, Celine Singer; she performed, with Peabo Bryson, the title song "Beauty and the Beast" for the end credits of the 1991 animated film, later singing "How Does a Moment Last Forever" for the end credits of the 2017 live-action version. Also performed "Because You Loved Me" for *Up Close & Personal*. She made a cameo in *Muppets Most Wanted* (Piggy Fairy Godmother) and appeared on TV in *Celebrate the Spirit! Disney's All-Star 4th of July Spectacular*, *Disney's Countdown to Kid's Day*, *Disney's Pocahontas: The Musical Tradition Continues*, and the *Disney Parks Christmas Parade*.

Dirt (TV) Comedy series on FX Network; aired Jan. 2, 2007–Apr. 13, 2008. Lucy Spiller, a tabloid editor in chief of the magazines *Dirt* and *Now*, tries to make her way in the world of celebrity journalism, exposing the hidden truths behind celebrity lives. Lucy has a maniacal dedication to finding the truth, for reasons even she has yet to fully fathom, and is aided by a schizophrenic photographer with a genius for getting the money shot. Stars Courteney Cox (Lucy Spiller), Will McCormack (Leo), Ian Hart (Don Konkey), Josh Stewart (Holt McLaren), Laura Allen (Julia Mallory), Jeffrey Nordling (Brent Barrow). From Touchstone Television and Coquette Productions.

Dirty Sexy Money (TV) Drama series on ABC; aired Sep. 26, 2007–Aug. 8, 2009. An idealistic young lawyer gets to represent the rich, powerful, and ethically flexible Darling family after his father's unexpected death. Stars Peter Krause (Nick George), Donald Sutherland (Tripp Darling), William Baldwin (Sen. Patrick Darling), Jill Clayburgh (Letitia Darling). From ABC Studios.

Discover Magazine covering the world of science acquired by The Walt Disney Company on Sep. 13, 1991. Disney announced the sale of the magazine in Sep. 2005.

Discover Nature shop in the Disney Village Marketplace at Walt Disney World; opened in 1993, taking the place of Conched Out. Later moved into the original site of the Great Southern Craft Co., where it was replaced by the Christmas Chalet in 1996.

Discover Quest (film) Series of 3 educational productions, based on *Discover* magazine articles; released on laser disc in Dec. 1994. The titles are *Explorations in Earth Science*, *Explorations in Life Science*, and *Explorations in Physical Science*.

Discovery Arcade Exhibit area behind the Main Street, U.S.A. shops in Disneyland Paris, on the Discoveryland side of the street; opened Apr. 12, 1992. Imaginative gadgets and futuristic ideas from the 19th-century golden age of invention are showcased.

Discovery Bay Proposed expansion of Disneyland representing an 1850s–1880s age of discovery. Developed by Imagineer Tony Baxter in the late 1970s, the area would have included a ride on the airship *Hyperion* from *The Island at the Top of the World*, dining in Captain Nemo's *Nautilus*, and other adventures. The project was never built, though it would inspire areas and attractions in other Disney parks, including Journey

Into Imagination in EPCOT, Discoveryland in Disneyland Paris, and Mysterious Island in Tokyo DisneySea. The concept's Victorian-steampunk aesthetic is considered ahead of its time.

Discovery Day Thursday on the new *Mickey Mouse Club* (1977–1978).

Discovery Gifts Port Discovery shop in Tokyo DisneySea; opened Sep. 4, 2001. Originally complementing the StormRider attraction, it represented a kinetic power-generating, wind-harvesting machine. With the opening of Nemo & Friends SeaRider, it began offering aquatic merchandise.

Discovery Island Nature preserve at Walt Disney World; opened Apr. 8, 1974, as Treasure Island, and renamed Discovery Island in 1977. It closed Apr. 8, 1999. An 11½-acre island paradise in the center of Bay Lake home to more than 400 birds, 250 forms of plant life, and mammals, including miniature deer, giant rabbits, and marmosets. Among the 20+ display areas were Avian Way, one of the world's largest walk-through aviaries (later Aviary Outpost); bird shows at CooCoo Cabana (later the Parrot's Perch); Trumpeter Springs; Flamingo Lagoon; and Turtle Beach (later Tortoise Beach), home to large Galapagos tortoises. Snacks and shopping were available at the Thirsty Perch. Originally the island was themed to the Disney film *Treasure Island*, with locations like Smugglers' Roost, Doubloon Lagoon, the Gang Plank Walk, and a wrecked ship, *The Walrus*, along the shore. Since the area was a wildlife sanctuary, Disney curators helped the government try to save Florida dusky sparrows by beginning a breeding program, but the last pure dusky sparrow passed away of old age on the island. Prior to the development of the Walt Disney World property, it was known as Riles Island.

Discovery Island SEE SAFARI VILLAGE (DISNEY'S ANIMAL KINGDOM).

Discovery River Boats Short-lived attraction in Safari Village (now Discovery Island) at Disney's Animal Kingdom; open Apr. 22, 1998–Aug. 21, 1999. Guests boarded rusty-looking water taxis for one-way excursions around the Discovery River. It became the Radio Disney River Cruise as of Mar. 1999, with a soundtrack hosted by Radio Disney DJs.

Discovery Trading Company SEE DISNEY OUT-FITTERS (DISNEY'S ANIMAL KINGDOM).

Disenchanted (film) A sequel to *Enchanted*; digitally released on Disney+ Nov. 18, 2022. It has been 15 years since Giselle and Robert wed, but Giselle has grown disillusioned with life in the city. So, they move their growing family to the sleepy suburban community of Monroeville in search of a more fairy-tale life. Unfortunately, it isn't the quick fix she had hoped for. Suburbia has a whole new set of rules and a local queen bee, Malvina Monroe, who makes Giselle feel more out of place than ever. Frustrated that her happily ever after hasn't been so easy to find, she turns to the magic of Andalasia for help, accidentally transforming the entire town into a real-life fairy tale and placing her family's future happiness in jeopardy. Now, Giselle is in a race against time to reverse the spell and determine what happily ever after truly means to her and her family. Directed by Adam Shankman. Stars Amy Adams (Giselle), Patrick Dempsey (Robert Philip), Maya Rudolph (Malvina Monroe), Yvette Nicole Brown (Rosaleen), Jayma Mays (Ruby), Gabriella Baldacchino (Morgan Philip), Idina Menzel (Nancy Tremaine), James Marsden (Prince Edward). 118 min. Songs by Alan Menken and Stephen Schwartz. Looking for a quaint village that could represent both the New England–style Monroeville and fairy-tale Monrolasia, the production team ended up filming in Enniskerry, a village in County Wicklow, Ireland. Filmed in widescreen format.

Disney, Diane M. Older daughter of Walt and Lillian Disney; born on Dec. 18, 1933. With Pete Martin, she wrote a biography of her father in 1956. She married Ronald W. Miller, who later served as president of Walt Disney Productions, and they had 7 children. She inspired the CD-ROM *Walt Disney: An Intimate History of the Man and His Magic* and the documentary *Walt: The Man Behind the Myth*. She founded The Walt Disney Family Museum in San Francisco in 2009 and passed away on Nov. 19, 2013.

Disney, Edna Francis Wife of Roy O. Disney. She was born in 1890 and met Roy in Kansas City. They married in 1925 in Uncle Robert Disney's home on Kingswell Avenue in Los Angeles. The couple had 1 son, Roy E. Disney. Edna passed away in 1984 at age 94. She was named a Disney Legend posthumously in 2003.

Disney, Elias Father of Walt Disney, born Feb. 6, 1859, in Bluevale, Ontario, Canada, the son of Irish immigrants. While still in his teens, he moved with his family to the U.S., where they settled in Ellis, Kansas. In 1884, when a neighbor family named Call moved to Florida, Elias went with them and 4 years later married the daughter, Flora. Elias and Flora had bad luck growing oranges and running a hotel in Florida, so they moved to Chicago where Elias became a building contractor. After trying farming in Marceline, Missouri, running a newspaper delivery business in Kansas City, and working in a jelly factory in Chicago, Elias and Flora moved to Portland, Oregon, where their daughter was living. After the success of their sons, Walt and Roy, they moved to North Hollywood, California, to be near them in the late 1930s. Elias died on Sep. 13, 1941.

Disney, Flora Walt Disney's mother, born Flora Call in Steuben, Ohio, on Apr. 22, 1868. Her mother's family was of German ancestry. She was the 7th born in a family of 10 children. In 1879, the Calls sold their farm in Steuben and moved to Ellis, Kansas, where Flora caught the eye of a young neighbor named Elias Disney. Together, they had 5 children: Herbert Arthur, Raymond Arnold, Roy Oliver, Walter Elias, and Ruth Flora. She died Nov. 26, 1938.

Disney, Herbert A. Eldest brother of Walt Disney; born Dec. 8, 1888, in Florida and died Jan. 29, 1961. He was a mailman.

Disney, Lillian Bounds Wife of Walt Disney. She was born in Idaho in 1899 and came to work for Walt as a secretary shortly after he founded the Disney Brothers Cartoon Studio. They married in 1925 and had 2 children, Diane and Sharon. After Walt's death, she married John L. Truyens in 1969 but survived him on his death, in 1981. In 1987, she announced a $50 million gift to build a symphonic hall for the Los Angeles Philharmonic Orchestra, at the time perhaps the largest gift by an individual to a cultural organization. She died on Dec. 16, 1997, and was named a Disney Legend posthumously in 2003.

Disney, Ray One of Walt Disney's older brothers, born Dec. 30, 1890. He had been in the insurance business. He died on May 24, 1989, at the age of 98.

Disney, Roy Edward Son of Roy O. Disney and nephew of Walt Disney; born in 1930. Roy began working for the company in 1954 as an assistant film editor on the True-Life Adventure films. He helped write narration for animal-related TV shows (1957–1971) and also directed (1973–1978) and produced (1968–1977) many of the same types of shows. He was elected to the Board of Directors in 1967. He left the company for a few years but returned in 1984 as vice chairman of the board and head of the animation department. He was named a Disney Legend in 1998. He resigned on Nov. 30, 2003, but was later named director emeritus and a consultant, on Jul. 8, 2005. The Disney Studio's current Animation Building was dedicated to him in 2010. He passed away on Dec. 16, 2009.

Disney, Roy Oliver Older brother of Walt Disney, who founded the Disney company in partnership with Walt in 1923. Born Jun. 24, 1893; died Dec. 20, 1971. Served as president of Walt Disney Productions 1945–1968 and as chairman of the board 1964–1971. Roy was recuperating in Los Angeles from tuberculosis in 1923 when Walt persuaded him to join in the new venture making animated cartoons. Roy was the financial genius of the 2 brothers; Walt was the creative genius. Together, they made a great pair. Modest and unassuming, Roy generally stayed in the background, finding the money for Walt's projects. It was also Roy who managed the growth of licensing Disney consumer products. Roy was instrumental in deciding to break with outside motion picture distributors and form the Buena Vista Distribution Company in 1953. But it was only after Walt's death in 1966 that Roy took a major public leadership position in the company, postponing his retirement to supervise the building of Walt Disney World. Through his financial acumen, that $400 million project opened in 1971, with the company having no outstanding debt. Roy presided over the dedication of Walt Disney World in Oct. 1971, and died 2 months later. In 1976, a new office building at the Disney Studio in Burbank was named the Roy O. Disney Building in honor of the company's cofounder.

Disney, Ruth F. Walt Disney's sister, the youngest in the family, born in Chicago on Dec. 6, 1903. Ruth eventually moved to Portland, Oregon, where she married Theodore Beecher. Walt maintained a regular correspondence with her over the years. Ruth was a connoisseur of organ music, purchasing and outfitting an old theater organ at her home. She died on Apr. 7, 1995.

Disney, Sharon M. Second daughter of Walt and Lillian Disney; born on Dec. 31, 1936. She married Robert B. Brown, who died shortly after Walt, and later William Lund. She had 3 children.

She was one of the founders of Retlaw Enterprises. Sharon was elected to the Board of Directors of The Walt Disney Company in 1984 and passed away Feb. 16, 1993.

Disney, Walter Elias Founder of the Disney empire, Walt Disney was born on Dec. 5, 1901, in Chicago, son of Elias and Flora Call Disney. Elias decided a few years later to move his family to a farm in Marceline, Missouri, and it was there that the young Walt grew up and got his love for animals and the rural life, which would be so evident in his films. The family moved to Kansas City in 1911, and Walt delivered newspapers for his father, who had purchased a newspaper distribution business. Walt attended Benton School and occasionally surprised his teachers with his talent for drawing and acting. When the family moved back to Chicago, Walt attended one year of McKinley High School. The end of World War I saw Walt serving briefly in France as an ambulance driver, but then he returned to Kansas City and attempted to put his art talents to use. After a stint with the Kansas City Film Ad Company, he started his own company, Laugh-O-gram Films, and, with some of his talented friends, made his first animated cartoons. When that business failed, Walt moved to California, and there, with his brother Roy, he started the Disney Brothers Cartoon Studio in 1923. The company made a series of Alice Comedies, then a year's worth of Oswald the Lucky Rabbit cartoons. But in 1928 Walt made history by creating, with the help of his trusted colleague Ub Iwerks, the character of Mickey Mouse. The Mickey Mouse cartoons were immediately popular and ensured the success of the company. A series of Silly Symphony cartoons was added, and soon the Disney artists began work on their first animated feature film, *Snow White and the Seven Dwarfs*. That 1937 film was a huge success, becoming the highest-grossing film of all time, until it was surpassed by *Gone with the Wind*. Walt had never been able to make much money with the short cartoons, but the feature films were another story. With the profits from *Snow White*, he was able to build a new studio in Burbank. Other animated features followed, until World War II, which caused the Disney Studio to retrench. Much of the company's effort went into making training and propaganda films for the military. The end of the war brought peace, but prosperity took a while to arrive at Disney's doors. He bided his time with a group of package films, feature length, but containing a series of 2 or more short films loosely tied together. *Cinderella* and the move into live-action

films with *Treasure Island* in 1950 marked a return to financial success. A series of popular True-Life Adventure nature films and a move onto TV with a regular weekly program gained the Disney Studio added recognition. But it was the building of Disneyland, the first real theme park, in 1955 that finally made the Disney company financially secure. The added cash flow from the park, along with infusions of cash from merchandise licensing, enabled Walt Disney to attempt new projects. Just before his death on Dec. 15, 1966, Walt was busy planning his Experimental Prototype Community of Tomorrow (EPCOT), which he felt would help solve some of the country's urban problems. Walt Disney married Lillian Bounds in 1925, and they had 2 daughters, Diane and Sharon. Disney was a genius in knowing what the public wanted in the way of family entertainment, and he was willing to take chances to create that entertainment. He was an innovator, not a follower. When he heard of a new process or concept that interested him, he embraced it totally, often to the dismay of his financial advisers; but time and time again, Walt was proved right. He had his finger on the pulse of America, and a look at his "firsts" helps to show how successful he had been—the first synchronized sound cartoon, the first use of the storyboard, the first full-color cartoon, the first animated feature film, the first stereophonic theater installations with Fantasound, the first popular nature series, the first major movie producer to go on to TV, the first CinemaScope cartoon, the first 3-D cartoon, the first use of the Xerox process to facilitate the animation process, the first stereophonic TV broadcast, the first theme park. With each of these, Walt took a chance and proved that he knew what he was doing. All of these elements became standard in the entertainment industry. Walt Disney left a lasting legacy, one which The Walt Disney Company continues to expand upon today.

Disney • ABC Cable Networks Group Former entity that managed The Walt Disney Company's interest in global TV businesses, including multiple wholly owned international Disney Channels. In addition, the group managed Disney's equity interest in Lifetime, A&E, The History Channel, and E! Entertainment. In 2004, it became part of the new Disney•ABC Television Group.

Disney/ABC Studios at The Ranch SEE GOLDEN OAK RANCH.

Disney•ABC Television Group Former entity,

established in 2004 under Disney Media Networks, which encompassed The Walt Disney Company's worldwide media networks, including ABC Television Network, Disney Channels Worldwide, ABC Family (later Freeform), SOAPnet (later Disney Junior), Toon Disney (later Disney XD), and Jetix (formerly Fox Kids), as well as the TV production and syn. divisions Touchstone Television (later ABC Studios), Disney-ABC Domestic Television, Disney-ABC-ESPN Television, and Walt Disney Television Animation (later Disney Television Animation). It also managed the Radio Disney Network, general interest and nonfiction book imprint Hyperion, as well the company's equity interest in Lifetime Entertainment Services and A&E Television Networks. Disney Media Networks was restructured in 2019 with Disney's acquisition of 21st Century Fox.

Disney Adventures Colorfully illustrated, digest-sized, general interest magazine for kids 7–14; covered entertainment from both inside and outside the Disney company. Published 10 times annually Nov. 1990–Nov. 2007.

Disney Afternoon, The (TV) Two-hour package of animated series; premiered Sep. 10, 1990. The contents varied from year to year, as follows:

1. 1990–1991: *DuckTales, Disney's Adventures of the Gummi Bears, Chip 'n' Dale Rescue Rangers, TaleSpin*
2. 1991–1992: *DuckTales, Chip 'n' Dale Rescue Rangers, TaleSpin, Darkwing Duck*
3. 1992–1993: *Chip 'n' Dale Rescue Rangers, TaleSpin, Darkwing Duck, Goof Troop*
4. 1993–1994: *TaleSpin, Darkwing Duck, Goof Troop, Bonkers*
5. 1994–1995: *Darkwing Duck, Goof Troop, Bonkers, Aladdin*
6. 1995–1996: *Goof Troop, Bonkers, Aladdin, Gargoyles*
7. 1996–1997: *Darkwing Duck, Gargoyles, Aladdin, Quack Pack*
8. 1994–1995: additional programs played as part of *The Disney Afternoon* on selected days: *Gargoyles* and *The Shnookums & Meat Funny Cartoon Show.*
9. 1995–1996: *The Lion King's Timon & Pumbaa* was added.
10. 1996–1997: *Mighty Ducks* was added.

Disney Afternoon Avenue Special Fantasyland promotional overlay in Disneyland from Mar.

15–Nov. 10, 1991. The promenade in front of It's a Small World was decorated with building fronts modeled after those on the Disney animated TV shows, with areas to meet many of the characters. Nearby attractions were themed to *Disney Afternoon* shows, including Fantasyland Autopia (Rescue Rangers Raceway) and Motor Boat Cruise (Motor Boat Cruise to Gummi Glen). At Videopolis, the *Plane Crazy* show starred the characters from *TaleSpin.*

Disney Afternoon Live! at Disneyland (TV) Special on KCAL-TV, Los Angeles; aired Sep. 14, 1991. 60 min. Includes a look at Walt Disney Imagineering and how they design a new attraction, followed by the opening of Splash Mountain and a segment on some of the more unusual jobs at Disneyland (scuba diver, harness maker, pyrotechnician). Hosted by Carl Bell.

Disney Ambassador Hotel Elegant art deco–style hotel at Tokyo Disney Resort; opened Jul. 7, 2000. Themed to the golden age of Hollywood. Guests enjoy buffet dining at Chef Mickey, California–inspired cuisine at Empire Grill, and 1950s-style American fare at Tick Tock Diner. Shops include Festival Disney and Sunset Sundries.

Disney & Co. Main Street, U.S.A. toy and novelty shop in the Magic Kingdom at Walt Disney World; opened Mar. 1972. Replaced by a relocated Crystal Arts shop in 2007. Also in Disneyland Paris (opened Apr. 12, 1992), World Bazaar in Tokyo Disneyland (opened Jul. 8, 1983, taking the place of the Main Street Hat Market), and Disney's Hollywood Studios (opened May 1, 1989, within Mickey's of Hollywood).

Disney & Pixar Short Film Festival Debuted in the Magic Eye Theater at EPCOT Dec. 23, 2015, succeeding *Captain EO.* Three animated short films are presented in 3-D with special in-theater effects. The original films were *Get a Horse!, For the Birds,* and *La Luna.* At Disney California Adventure, a similar presentation, the Pixar Shorts Film Festival, debuted in the Sunset Showcase Theater for Pixar Fest in 2018, with additional shorts screened in the Tomorrowland Theater at Disneyland.

Disney Animation Hollywood Land attraction in Disney California Adventure; opened Feb. 8, 2001. Guests can meet Disney characters and explore hands-on exhibits that showcase the animation process: Animation Academy (previously

Drawn to Animation); Character Close-Up; Sorcerer's Workshop, with the Magic Mirror Realm, The Beast's Library, and Ursula's Grotto; and Turtle Talk with Crush (originally The Animation Screening Room, showing *Back to Neverland* [sic] until Dec. 2001, then *One Man's Dream: 100 Years of Magic* until 2005). The main lobby's Animation Courtyard gallery is a visual spectacular, with animation artwork and film clips projected on screens up to 40-ft. high. A similar attraction in Walt Disney Studios Park at Disneyland Paris, named L'Art de l'Animation Disney (Art of Disney Animation), opened Mar. 16, 2002; it was remodeled in 2019 and reopened as Animation Celebration. SEE ALSO MAGIC OF DISNEY ANIMATION, THE (DISNEY'S HOLLYWOOD STUDIOS).

Disney Animation Gallery, The Art and collectibles shop in the Art of Disney Animation (later Animation Celebration) in Walt Disney Studios Park at Disneyland Paris; opened Mar. 16, 2002. It became the Animation Boutique in 2019.

Disney Animation: Immersive Experience Special exhibit celebrating the 100th anniversary of The Walt Disney Studios. Guests head down a "rabbit hole" for a sonic and visual journey into an exhibit exploring the history of animation. Then, stepping into a vault, they become surrounded by a massive, 47-min. visual show immersing them into the worlds of Walt Disney Animation Studios films. Launched in Dec. 2022 in Toronto, before a U.S. tour began in Cleveland Jan. 2023. A collaboration between Walt Disney Animation Studios and Lighthouse Immersive.

Disney Animation: The Illusion of Life (TV) Show aired Apr. 26, 1981; tied to Frank Thomas and Ollie Johnston's book from which the show was titled. Directed by William Reid. Hayley Mills returns to the Disney Studio to discover how *The Fox and the Hound* is being made. She visits the Walt Disney Archives, learns how models are made for the animators, is shown the value of casting the right actors to provide the voices, and attends a recording session with Pearl Bailey.

Disney Art Editions SEE CEL.

Disney at Home Home décor and kitchenware shop in Downtown Disney Marketplace at Walt Disney World; opened Dec. 5, 1997, taking the place of the Christmas Chalet. It later moved into the former Resortwear Unlimited shop. Closed Jan. 2, 2005, to be replaced by an expanded Goofy's Candy Co.

Disney Baby Store The first Disney Baby Store, offering baby clothing, toys, and nursery décor, opened Sep. 8, 2012, in The Americana at Brand in Glendale, California. Closed in 2021.

Disney Blockbuster Cafe Backlot counter-service restaurant in Walt Disney Studios Park at Disneyland Paris; opened Aug. 2009, replacing Backlot Express. Dining areas featured décor from hit film series, including *Pirates of the Caribbean*, *High School Musical*, and *Iron Man*. Closed in 2019 to become Stark Factory when the area became Avengers Campus.

Disney Branded Television Division of Disney General Entertainment Content, as of 2020, that oversees Disney-branded television series, movies, and other programming spanning live-action, animated, and unscripted formats for the Disney+ streaming platform and the Disney Channel, Disney XD, and Disney Junior networks.

Disney Brothers Cartoon Studio Original name of the Disney company when it was formed as a partnership between Walt and Roy Disney in 1923.

Disney California Adventure SEE CALIFORNIA ADVENTURE, DISNEY.

Disney Catalog, The Mail-order catalog; began in 1984 as the *Disney Family Gift Catalog* and later titled simply *Disney*. Featured Disney merchandise exclusively. The printed catalog was discontinued in 2006, with shopping made available online.

Disney Channel, The Cable TV network; began broadcasting Apr. 18, 1983, with 18 hours of programming a day. It became a full 24-hour network Dec. 7, 1986. The channel became one of the fastest-growing pay-cable services, reaching over 35 million subscribers after a little over a decade on the air. It originated under the leadership of Jim Jimirro that was continued by John Cooke, Anne Sweeney, Rich Ross, and Gary Marsh. The channel features a mixture of Disney films, original programming, and family entertainment purchased from other producers. Many Disney films have had their world TV premieres on the channel. Until 1997, the channel published *The Disney Channel Magazine*, featuring articles, columns, and program notes. In

1993, it began a transition from premium to basic cable service, eventually expanding its reach to over 80 million homes. Gradually, starting in the mid-1990s, the channel instigated a new programming strategy that emphasizes 9- to 14-year-olds, the "tween" years, through original series and movies. Beginning in Mar. 1995 in Taiwan, a number of international channels were launched in such countries as Australia, Italy, Brazil, and the Philippines, totaling 24 of them by 2005. The Disney Channel officially dropped "The" from its name in 1997 to become Disney Channel. By 2020, there were 46 Disney Channels available in 33 languages worldwide.

Disney Channel Original Movies New designation for films previously known as Disney Channel Premiere Films. Chronologically, the film titles are:

1. *Northern Lights*, 8/23/97
2. *Under Wraps*, 10/25/97
3. *You Lucky Dog*, 6/27/98
4. *Brink!*, 8/29/98
5. *Halloweentown*, 10/17/98
6. *Zenon: Girl of the 21st Century*, 1/23/99
7. *Can of Worms*, 4/10/99
8. *The Thirteenth Year*, 5/15/99
9. *Smart House*, 6/26/99
10. *Johnny Tsunami*, 7/24/99
11. *Genius*, 8/21/99
12. *P.U.N.K.S.*, 9/4/99
13. *Don't Look Under the Bed*, 10/9/99
14. *Horse Sense*, 11/20/99
15. *Up, Up and Away*, 1/22/00
16. *The Color of Friendship*, 2/5/00
17. *Alley Cats Strike!*, 3/18/00
18. *Rip Girls*, 4/22/00
19. *Miracle in Lane 2*, 5/13/00
20. *Stepsister from Planet Weird*, 6/17/00
21. *Ready to Run*, 7/14/00
22. *Quints*, 8/18/00
23. *The Other Me*, 9/8/00
24. *Mom's Got a Date with a Vampire*, 10/13/00
25. *Phantom of the Megaplex*, 11/10/00
26. *The Ultimate Christmas Present*, 12/1/00
27. *Zenon: The Zequel*, 1/12/01
28. *Motocrossed*, 2/2/01
29. *The Luck of the Irish*, 3/9/01
30. *Hounded*, 4/13/01
31. *Jett Jackson: The Movie*, 6/8/01
32. *The Jennie Project*, 7/13/01
33. *Jumping Ship*, 8/17/01
34. *The Poof Point*, 9/14/01
35. *Halloweentown II: Kalabar's Revenge*, 10/12/01
36. *'Twas the Night*, 12/7/01
37. *Double Teamed*, 1/18/02
38. *Cadet Kelly*, 3/8/02
39. *Tru Confessions*, 4/5/02
40. *Get a Clue*, 6/28/02
41. *Gotta Kick It Up!*, 7/26/02
42. *A Ring of Endless Light*, 8/23/02
43. *The Scream Team*, 10/4/02
44. *You Wish!*, 1/10/03
45. *Right on Track*, 3/21/03
46. *The Even Stevens Movie*, 6/13/03
47. *Eddie's Million Dollar Cook/Off*, 7/18/03
48. *The Cheetah Girls*, 8/15/03
49. *Full-Court Miracle*, 11/21/03
50. *Pixel Perfect*, 1/16/04
51. *Going to the Mat*, 3/19/04
52. *Zenon: Z3*, 6/11/04
53. *Stuck in the Suburbs*, 7/16/04
54. *Tiger Cruise*, 8/6/04
55. *Halloweentown High*, 10/8/04
56. *Now You See It*, 1/14/05
57. *Buffalo Dreams*, 3/11/05
58. *Disney's Kim Possible Movie: So the Drama*, 4/8/05
59. *Go Figure*, 6/10/05
60. *Life Is Ruff*, 7/15/05
61. *The Proud Family Movie*, 8/19/05
62. *Twitches*, 10/14/05
63. *High School Musical*, 1/20/06
64. *Cow Belles*, 3/24/06
65. *Wendy Wu: Homecoming Warrior*, 6/16/06
66. *Read It and Weep*, 7/21/06
67. *The Cheetah Girls 2*, 8/21/06
68. *Return to Halloweentown*, 10/20/06
69. *Jump In!*, 1/12/07
70. *Johnny Kapahala: Back on Board*, 6/8/07
71. *High School Musical 2*, 8/17/07
72. *Twitches Too*, 10/12/07
73. *Minutemen*, 1/25/08
74. *Camp Rock*, 6/20/08
75. *Cheetah Girls One World*, 8/22/08
76. *Dadnapped*, 2/16/09
77. *Hatching Pete*, 4/24/09
78. *Princess Protection Program*, 6/26/09
79. *Wizards of Waverly Place: The Movie*, 8/28/09
80. *StarStruck*, 2/14/10
81. *Den Brother*, 8/13/10
82. *Camp Rock 2: The Final Jam*, 9/3/10
83. *Avalon High*, 11/12/10
84. *The Suite Life Movie*, 3/25/11
85. *Lemonade Mouth*, 4/15/11
86. *Phineas and Ferb the Movie: Across the 2nd Dimension*, 8/5/11

87. *Geek Charming*, 11/11/11
88. *Good Luck Charlie, It's Christmas*, 12/2/11
89. *Frenemies*, 1/13/12
90. *Radio Rebel*, 2/17/12
91. *Let It Shine*, 6/15/12
92. *Girl vs. Monster*, 10/12/12
93. *Teen Beach Movie*, 7/19/13
94. *Cloud 9*, 1/17/14
95. *Zapped*, 6/27/14
96. *How to Build a Better Boy*, 8/15/14
97. *Bad Hair Day*, 2/13/15
98. *Teen Beach 2*, 6/26/15
99. *Descendants*, 7/31/15
100. *Invisible Sister*, 10/9/15
101. *Adventures in Babysitting*, 6/24/16
102. *The Swap*, 10/7/16
103. *Tangled Before Ever After*, 3/10/17
104. *Descendants 2*, 7/21/17
105. *ZOMBIES*, 2/16/18
106. *Freaky Friday*, 8/10/18
107. *Kim Possible*, 2/15/19
108. *Descendants 3*, 8/2/19
109. *ZOMBIES 2*, 2/14/20
110. *Upside-Down Magic*, 7/31/20
111. *Spin*, 8/13/21
112. *Under Wraps*, 10/1/21
113. *Christmas Again*, 12/3/21
114. *ZOMBIES 3*, 8/12/22 (premiered 7/15/22 on Disney+)
115. *Under Wraps 2*, 9/25/22

Disney Channel Premiere Films Beginning in 1983, The Disney Channel commissioned a number of made-for-cable motion pictures for airing on the channel. In 1997, they ceased using the "Premiere Films" designation. Chronologically, the film titles are:

1. *Tiger Town*, 10/9/83
2. *Gone Are the Dayes*, 5/6/84
3. *Love Leads the Way*, 10/7/84
4. *Black Arrow*, 1/6/85
5. *Lots of Luck*, 2/3/85
6. *The Undergrads*, 5/5/85
7. *The Blue Yonder*, 11/17/85
8. *The Parent Trap II*, 7/26/86
9. *Spot Marks the X*, 10/18/86
10. *Down the Long Hills*, 11/15/86
11. *Strange Companions*, 2/28/87
12. *Anne of Avonlea: The Continuing Story of Anne of Green Gables*, 5/19/87
13. *Not Quite Human*, 6/19/87
14. *The Christmas Visitor*, 12/5/87
15. *Save the Dog*, 3/19/88

16. *Night Train to Kathmandu*, 6/5/88
17. *Ollie Hopnoodle's Haven of Bliss*, 8/6/88
18. *A Friendship in Vienna*, 8/27/88
19. *Good Old Boy*, 11/11/88
20. *Goodbye, Miss 4th of July*, 12/3/88
21. *Danny, the Champion of the World*, 4/29/89
22. *Looking for Miracles*, 6/3/89
23. *Great Expectations*, 7/9/89
24. *Not Quite Human II*, 9/23/89
25. *Spooner*, 12/2/89
26. *Lantern Hill*, 1/27/90
27. *Chips, the War Dog*, 3/24/90
28. *Mother Goose Rock 'n' Rhyme*, 5/19/90
29. *Back Home*, 6/7/90
30. *The Little Kidnappers*, 8/17/90
31. *Back to Hannibal: The Return of Tom Sawyer and Huckleberry Finn*, 10/21/90
32. *Bejewelled*, 1/20/91
33. *Perfect Harmony*, 3/31/91
34. *Mark Twain and Me*, 11/22/91
35. *Still Not Quite Human*, 5/31/92
36. *The Ernest Green Story*, 1/17/93
37. *Spies*, 3/7/93
38. *Heidi*, 7/18/93
39. *On Promised Land*, 4/17/94
40. *The Whipping Boy*, 7/31/94
41. *The Old Curiosity Shop*, 3/19/95
42. *The Four Diamonds*, 8/12/95
43. *The Little Riders*, 3/24/96
44. *Nightjohn*, 6/1/96

SEE ALSO DISNEY CHANNEL ORIGINAL MOVIES FOR LATER FILMS.

Disney Channel Presents the Radio Disney Music Awards (TV) SEE RADIO DISNEY MUSIC AWARDS.

Disney Channels Worldwide As of Jan. 2019, this global portfolio of kid-driven, family-inclusive entertainment channels and channel feeds was available in 164 countries/territories and 34 languages, reaching nearly 550 million viewers worldwide. The platform brands were Disney Channel, Disney XD, Disney Junior, Disney Cinemagic, Disney Cinema, Hungama, Dlife, and Radio Disney Networks. Became part of Disney Branded Television in 2020.

Disney Christmas Gift, A (TV) Special broadcast on CBS; aired Dec. 20, 1983 (different show than the series episode). A compilation of animated films.

Disney Christmas Gift, A (TV) Show premiered

Dec. 4, 1982. A holiday salute beginning and ending in Disneyland, with animated segments. Old Christmas cards and toys from the Walt Disney Archives are used as connecting footage.

Disney Classics Theater Finale of The Magic of Disney Animation tour in Disney-MGM Studios; open May 1, 1989–Sep. 30, 2003, presenting a film montage of classic moments in Disney animation. Also in the former Art of Disney Animation (L'Art de l'Animation Disney) in Walt Disney Studios Park at Disneyland Paris.

Disney Clothiers Main Street, U.S.A. shop; opened Feb. 24, 1985, in the Magic Kingdom at Walt Disney World and Mar. 23, 1985, in Disneyland, taking the place of the Hallmark card shop in both parks. Also in Disneyland Paris; opened Apr. 12, 1992.

Disney Club, The Membership club launched on Nov. 14, 2000, offering discounts on food and beverage, theme park tickets, guided tours, and merchandise. It replaced the Magic Kingdom Club. The club disbanded Dec. 31, 2003, in favor of a Disney-branded Visa card.

Disney Code: 9 (TV) A 6-episode series on Disney Channel; aired Jul. 26–Sep. 28, 2012. With elaborate, high-tech stunts, kids pull pranks on their parents. Hosted by Wes Dening.

Disney Collection, The World Bazaar shop in Tokyo Disneyland; opened Jul. 21, 1994, selling Disney cels, posters, and collectibles. Closed Aug. 2005, with the site later integrated into the World Bazaar Confectionery.

Disney College Program An internship program begun as the Magic Kingdom College Program, offering a work and learning experience, at Walt Disney World in 1980, with name changes to the Walt Disney World College Program in 1984, the Disney Theme Parks & Resorts College Program in 2005, and, later, the Disney College Program. Recruiters visit college campuses to inform prospective students about the program, answer questions, and even conduct on-the-spot interviews. The first students were housed at the Hidden Valley Trailer Park (later known as Snow White Village Campground). An international program, the World Showcase Fellowship Program, began with the opening of EPCOT in 1982. Disney professional internships, with focused learning and based on specific areas of study, began in 1992. Housing complexes for the students were added, beginning with Vista Way Apartments, in Apr. 1988; others followed: The Commons in Jan. 1998, Chatham Square in Jun. 2000, and Patterson Court in May 2008. College programs have also been operated at Disneyland (beginning in 1989), Disneyland Paris (beginning in 1992), and Walt Disney Imagineering. The learning component of the program changed through the years from business seminars to college-level courses that the American Council on Education has approved for college credit. The program paused in 2020 due to the COVID-19 pandemic, resuming at Walt Disney World in Jun. 2021 with a new centralized housing complex, Flamingo Crossings Village, which includes a resort-style pool, study areas, and fitness facilities.

Disney Concerts Division of Disney Music Group that produces concerts and tours, and licenses music to orchestras. Concerts have included *Pixar in Concert*, the *Star Wars Film Concert Series*, *Disney Princess – The Concert*, *Coco in Concert Live to Film*, *Encanto: The Sing-Along Film Concert*, and *Tim Burton's The Nightmare Before Christmas Live-to-Film Concert Experience*, which in 2019 accounted for over 900 performances. Previously known as Buena Vista Concerts, which launched in 2006 with *The Cheetah Girls: The Party's Just Begun Tour* and *High School Musical: The Concert*.

Disney Cruise Line After successful Disney cruises were licensed to other cruise operators, Disney decided to get into the cruise business itself. The first cruise ship, the *Disney Magic*, set out on its maiden voyage Jul. 30, 1998, from its home port, Port Canaveral, Florida. The 2nd ship, the *Disney Wonder*, had its maiden voyage Aug. 15, 1999. In Feb. 1996, Disney announced the purchase of Gorda Cay, 5 months later renamed Disney's Castaway Cay, a 1,000-acre uninhabited island in The Bahamas, which serves as a daylong stop for passengers on Bahamian and Caribbean cruises. The ships' design is inspired by the look of classic ocean liners from the golden age of transatlantic travel. Disney Cruise Line received special permission from the U.S. Coast Guard to paint the lifeboats Pantone #99 Yellow; together with red, white, and black (actually a deep shade of navy blue), these colors complete the color specifications of Mickey Mouse. In 2007, Disney Cruise Line announced plans for the building of 2 new, 130,000-ton cruise ships by the Meyer Werft shipyard in Papenburg, Germany; the new ships, the *Disney Dream* and the *Disney Fantasy*, embarked on their maiden voyages, respectively, Jan. 26, 2011, and Mar. 31, 2012. In 2016, plans were announced for the building of 2 additional, 135,000-ton cruise ships, and another ship was announced in 2017. The first of these 3 new ships, the *Disney Wish*, embarked on its maiden voyage Jul. 14, 2022, and the 2nd ship, the *Disney Treasure*, is scheduled for delivery in 2024. In 2019, Disney Cruise Line announced plans to create and manage a destination at Lighthouse Point on the island of Eleuthera in The Bahamas. Disney purchased 758 acres of the 919-acre site that year, with plans to develop less than 20% of the property. In 2022, Disney acquired the 208,000-gross-ton cruise ship previously known as the *Global Dream*, constructed by MV Werften in Wismar, Germany; in Nov. 2022, Disney Cruise Line announced the ship will be renamed with certain features reimagined by Walt Disney Imagineering and be based outside the U.S. The construction will be completed under the management of Meyer Werft.

Disney Development Co. Disney subsidiary, formed in Sep. 1984; responsible for master planning, development, and asset management of the company's non-theme park real estate assets, including resort hotels, company office buildings, and the town of Celebration. It merged with Walt Disney Imagineering in May 1996.

Disney Digital Books Announced in Sep. 2009, an ever-expanding library of over 500 new and classic Disney books was made available by subscription for use on any computer. The service ended in 2013.

Disney Digital Network On Mar. 24, 2014, Disney agreed to acquire Maker Studios, a supplier of online video content to YouTube. In 2017, Maker was integrated into the new Disney Digital Network, a creator/distributor of digital-first content for millennial and Generation Z audiences.

Disney Dollars Currency offered at the Disney parks beginning May 5, 1987, with equivalent value to U.S. currency. Mickey Mouse appeared on the $1 bill, and Goofy was on the $5 bill. A $10 bill featuring Minnie Mouse was added Nov. 20, 1989, and a $50 bill featuring Mickey Mouse was introduced Jul. 17, 2005, for the 50th anniversary of Disneyland. Disney Dollars were the first currency to be 4-color printed in the U.S. Limited-edition series featured different themes and characters, such as

Disney heroes and villains. Sales ended May 14, 2016.

Disney Dream The 3rd ship in the Disney Cruise Line fleet. Christened by Jennifer Hudson in Port Canaveral, Florida, Jan. 19, 2011, before setting sail on its Jan. 26 maiden voyage. At 130,000 tons, the ship is 40% larger than its predecessors, with 14 decks, a ship length of 1,115 feet, and a max. width of 125 feet. There are 1,250 staterooms, with a capacity of 4,000 passengers and 1,458 crew members. Innovations include Magical Portholes, which offer a real-time view of the world outside for inside cabin passengers, interactive floors in the children's club, and the AquaDuck, the first water coaster at sea, which allows riders to swoosh up, down, around, over the edge of the ship, and back before making a splash landing. Rotational dining includes Animator's Palate, Royal Palace, and Enchanted Garden, with signature dining at Palo and premium dining at a new restaurant, Remy, offering French–inspired cuisine. The interiors have an art deco look, with a bronze statue of Admiral Donald presiding over the lobby. The stern features a dreaming Sorcerer's Apprentice Mickey with the enchanted brooms. Construction on the ship began with a ceremony at the Meyer Werft shipyard in Papenburg, Germany, Mar. 2, 2009. Amid the COVID-19 global pandemic in early 2020, Disney Cruise Line suspended new departures beginning Mar. 14. The *Disney Dream* was the first ship in the fleet to resume regular guest sailings out of the U.S., with a 4-night cruise that departed Port Canaveral Aug. 9, 2021.

Disney Dreamers Academy Established in 2007, the Disney Dreamers Academy, with Steve Harvey and *Essence* magazine, is dedicated to providing youths, known as Dreamers, with experiences at Walt Disney World which allow them to explore possibilities that can turn their dreams into reality. In a 4-day program, the Dreamers engage in a variety of activities while working with community and industry leaders, Cast Members, and celebrities. The first career enrichment program was held in Jan. 2008, during The Year of a Million Dreams.

Disney Dress Shop, The Boutique selling vintage-inspired Disney dresses and accessories; opened in 2017 in the Marketplace at Disney Springs at Walt Disney World (as The Dress Shop on Cherry Tree Lane) and in the Downtown Disney District at Disneyland Resort. In 2018, the Disneyland shop moved into a larger venue, taking the place of the Dream Boutique. See also Marketplace Co-Op.

Disney Educational Productions Formerly the Walt Disney Educational Materials Co. and Walt Disney Educational Media Co., this is the unit involved in the production of educational films, videocassettes, videodiscs, DVDs, and other products for schools.

Disney Emoji Digital icons of Disney characters, introduced Feb. 27, 2015, in *Disney As Told by Emoji* (also known as *As Told by Disney Emoji*), a series of short animated retellings of Disney stories within the mechanics of a smartphone. Disney Emoji were later offered on mobile apps, via the *Disney Gif* (released Jun. 25, 2015) and *Disney Emoji Blitz* (released Jul. 14, 2016) apps, and sold as merchandise.

Disney Enchantment Fireworks spectacular in the Magic Kingdom at Walt Disney World; debuted Oct. 1, 2021, after a digital livestream premiere on Sep. 30. It superseded *Happily Ever After* as part of the Walt Disney World 50th anniversary celebration. For the first time, projection effects extended from Cinderella Castle down Main Street, U.S.A. It was announced the final performance will be held Apr. 2, 2023, to allow for the return of *Happily Ever After*.

Disney English The first Disney-operated learning center for teaching English as a 2nd language to children, using the Disney characters and stories; opened in Shanghai Oct. 2008, expanding to several other cities in China. The curriculum was developed in the U.S. and taught by North American tutors. The 26 learning centers closed in 2020.

Disney Explorers Lodge Resort hotel in Hong Kong Disneyland Resort; opened Apr. 30, 2017. Based on the mythology of 4 world explorers who built the lodge, adding artifacts gathered from their lifetime of travels. The 750 guest rooms are furnished according to the 4 tropical regions of Asia, Oceania, South America, and Africa, with each wing offering an outdoor garden with a corresponding theme: Hathi Jr. Garden (*The Jungle Book*), Little Squirt Garden (*Finding Nemo*), Kevin Garden (*Up*), and Rafiki Garden (*The Lion King*). Chinese and international cuisine are served at Dragon Wind and World of Color Restaurant, with shopping offered at The Trading Post. The lodge motto is *ad explorare et somniare* ("to explore and dream").

Disney Fair Live stage show, exhibits, games, and shops under a tent created to appear at state fairs nationwide; debuted at the Washington State Fair in Puyallup, Sep. 6–22, 1996, then later presented in Arizona. Instead of continuing with state fairs, the show was reworked as DisneyFest with plans for overseas productions. It began its first run in Singapore Oct. 30, 1997.

Disney Fairies Pixie Hollow Online virtual world launched in 2008 and closed Sep. 19, 2013. Users could create their own fairy, interact with other players, and explore the world of Tinker Bell and her friends.

Disney Fairies: Pixie Hollow Games (TV) Animated special on Disney Channel; premiered Nov. 19, 2011. Tinker Bell and her fairy friends gather to compete in the Pixie Hollow Games, a sports spectacle filled with pixie pageantry and fantastic fairy events. Directed by Bradley Raymond. Voices include Mae Whitman (Tinker Bell), Lucy Liu (Silvermist), Jason Dolley (Rumble), Anjelica Huston (Queen Clarion), Brenda Song (Chloe), Zendaya (Fern), Raven-Symoné (Iridessa), Megan Hilty (Rosetta). From Disneytoon Studios and Prana Studios.

Disney Fam Jam (TV) Family dance competition series; premiered Feb. 23, 2020, on Disney Channel and DisneyNOW. In each episode, 2 families hit the floor to win the most votes from the studio audience and each week's $10,000 prize. Stars choreographer Phil Wright and co-hosts Ariel Martin and Trevor Tordjman.

Disney Family Album (TV) A 20-episode series on The Disney Channel; aired Jun. 9, 1984–Jan. 1986. Each show highlighted people who have made Disney so successful, including the Disneyland Designers, Ward Kimball, Ollie Johnston, Annette Funicello, Jim Macdonald, Ken Anderson, Peter and Harrison Ellenshaw, Eric Larson, Richard M. and Robert B. Sherman, Clarence Nash, and Milt Kahl. Narrated by Buddy Ebsen.

Disney Family Singalong, The (TV) One-hour special on ABC; aired Apr. 16, 2020, during the COVID-19 pandemic, with celebrities and their families performing favorite Disney songs from home. Performers include Christina Aguilera, Michael Bublé, Kristin Chenoweth, Auli'i Cravalho, Elle Fanning, Jordan Fisher, Josh Gad, Alan Menken, Kenny Ortega, Donny Osmond. Hosted by Ryan Seacrest. A 2nd special, *The Disney Family Singalong: Volume II*, aired May 10, 2020, starring Julianne Hough, Donald Glover, Keke Palmer, Idina Menzel, Seth Rogen, Anika Noni Rose, Rebel Wilson, Shakira, and Disney on Broadway performers. And a third special, *The Disney Family Holiday Singalong*, aired Nov. 30, 2020, featured Andrea Bocelli, BTS, Michael Bublé, Chloe x Halle, Hayley Erbert, Adam Lambert, Leslie Odom Jr., Katy Perry, P!NK, Kerry Washington. For this special, Disney on Broadway made a return to the New Amsterdam Theatre for the first time since Mar. 2020, with a performance by the casts of *The Lion King* and *Aladdin*, as well as the North American touring companies of *Frozen*. From Done+Dusted.

Disney Family Sundays (TV) Series on Disney+; digitally premiered Nov. 12, 2019. Crafter Amber Kemp-Gerstel guides families through a step-by-step process of creating a Disney-inspired, "do-it-yourself" craft project. From Matador Content.

Disney Fantasy The 4th ship in the Disney Cruise Line fleet. Christened by Mariah Carey in New York City Mar. 1, 2012, before embarking on its maiden voyage Mar. 31. Like the *Disney Dream*, the *Fantasy* features 14 decks, a ship length of 1,115 feet, a max. width of 125 feet, and 1,250 staterooms, with a capacity of 4,000 passengers and 1,450 crew members. Similar to the other Disney ships, its early-20th-century aesthetic recalls the golden age of cruising, specially designed with families in mind, combining sleek style and convenient facilities with touches of Disney magic. A bronze statue of Mademoiselle Minnie Mouse is the atrium's centerpiece, and the stern features Dumbo and Timothy Mouse. While the interior of the *Dream* is presented in the art deco style, it is art nouveau on the *Fantasy*. Restaurants are Animator's Palate, Cabanas, Enchanted Garden, and Royal Court, with fine dining at Palo and Remy. Construction on the ship began with a keel laying ceremony at the Meyer Werft shipyard in Papenburg, Germany, Feb. 11, 2011.

Disney Fashion Disney Village shop in Disneyland Paris; opened in 2007, taking the place of Team Mickey. Disney clothing, jewelry, and vintage products are sold. Next door, Disney Fashion Junior, offering children's apparel, replaced World of Toys Sep. 30, 2009.

Disney Festival of Fantasy Parade Debuted in the Magic Kingdom at Walt Disney World Mar. 9, 2014. Whimsical floats, stilt performers, and a fire-breathing Maleficent dragon serve as a fanciful tribute to Fantasyland.

Disney Foundation Established in 1951 as a non-profit corporation dedicated exclusively to the support of charitable and educational activities. Contributions to the Disney Foundation come from The Walt Disney Company. In addition to the active support of numerous health, community, educational, and youth organizations in California, Florida, and New York, the foundation from time to time sponsors its own activities, such as a College Scholarship Program for the children of Disney employees.

Disney Gallery (TV) Documentary series about the making of Disney+ original series, featuring behind-the-scenes footage and conversations with filmmakers, cast, and crew. The 1st series, *Disney Gallery: The Mandalorian*, digitally premiered May 4, 2020, on Disney+. It was followed by *Disney Gallery: The Book of Boba Fett* on Jul. 27, 2022. Both series were exec. produced by Jon Favreau.

Disney Gallery, The Display of Disneyland-related artwork, designs, and models above Pirates of the Caribbean at Disneyland; opened Jul. 11, 1987, and closed Aug. 7, 2007. This area had originally been planned as an apartment for Walt and Roy Disney, and in fact, if you study the wrought iron railings on the balcony, you might spot the initials, WD and RD. After Walt's death, Roy decided not to build the apartment; instead, the area was later used as a VIP lounge by INA, one of the Disneyland participants, and as offices for those planning Tokyo Disneyland. When trying to decide how to help the traffic flow in front of Pirates of the Caribbean, Disney Imagineer Tony Baxter redesigned the queue area, but he also had the idea of building curved staircases up to the 2nd floor and opening the area up to guests. The Imagineers had long wanted a place where they could display some of their concept art for the park. The artwork in the Gallery was changed from time to time, and lithographs and other limited-edition pieces were sold there. Regular signings of books and prints helped draw guests to the Gallery. A new Disney Gallery opened in the former bank location on Main Street, U.S.A. on Oct. 2, 2009; in 2013 it moved to the lobby of the Opera House, as Disneyana took its place. A Disney Gallery also opened above World Bazaar in Tokyo Disneyland Apr. 15, 1993; it closed in 2016 to make way for the Bibbidi Bobbidi Boutique. Also the name of an art and collectibles shop in Disney Village at Disneyland Paris.

Disney General Entertainment Content Segment of The Walt Disney Company, as of 2020, that develops, produces, and markets programming for the company's streaming and linear platforms, including ABC Entertainment, ABC Studios, ABC News, the ABC Owned Television Stations Group, Freeform, 20th Television, FX Networks and FX Productions, the Disney Channel networks, and National Geographic Partners.

Disney Genie Digital service within the My Disney Experience app offering tailored recommendations and daily itineraries for Disney park guests; launched Oct. 19, 2021, in Walt Disney World and Dec. 8, 2021, at Disneyland Resort. Available separately for purchase, Disney Genie+ offers the ability to book Lightning Lane arrival windows for certain attractions, augmented reality digital photo filters, and audio tours.

Disney Goes to the Oscars (TV) Show aired Mar. 23, 1986. Directed by Andrew Solt. Covers some of the Disney Academy Award–winning films, with Tony Danza.

Disney Halloween, A (TV) Show aired Oct. 24, 1981. The Magic Mirror helps look at some of the legends surrounding Halloween, with segments from Disney cartoons and animated features.

Disney Home Shop in the Downtown Disney District at Disneyland Resort; opened Feb. 14, 2018, taking the place of D Street. Housewares, kitchen goods, and accessories are sold. Also a home goods store in Disneytown at Shanghai Disney Resort; opened Jul. 15, 2022, replacing Adidas.

Disney Imagination Campus Line of educational programs for visiting student groups at the Disney parks; debuted in 2022 at Walt Disney World and Disneyland Resort. Interactive workshops explore the arts, technology, science, leadership, and other subjects. The curriculum is developed in partnership with Kahoot!, a learning platform company. Disney Performing Arts and Grad Nite are also rolled into the program. Formerly known as Disney Youth Programs.

Disney Inn, The A 288-room golf hotel at Walt Disney World; new name for The Golf Resort as of Feb. 4, 1986. The country inn–style hotel was popular not only for golfers, but with other guests because of its more secluded location, not on the Monorail line, which made it seem quieter and more restful. The inn was loosely themed to *Snow White*, with Happy's Hollow (a recreation center), the Diamond Mine Snack Bar and Arcade, and Magic Mirror health club. Dining was offered at the Garden Gallery and Sand Trap. The resort was leased by the U.S. government in 1994 for military personnel and renamed Shades of Green.

Disney Insider (TV) Documentary series on Disney+; digitally premiered Mar. 20, 2020. Each episode consists of 3 unique stories that take viewers behind the scenes at The Walt Disney Company.

Disney Institute, The Participatory vacation experience; opened Feb. 9, 1996, at Walt Disney World. Guests chose from a wide selection of interactive programs (more than 60) in the areas of Entertainment Arts, Performing Arts, Story Arts, Design Arts, Culinary Arts, Lifestyles, Gardening & the Great Outdoors, and Sports and Fitness. The facilities were located at the Disney Village and included Seasons Dining Room, a store (Dabblers), studios for animation, design arts, culinary arts, radio and TV, a 400-seat cinema, a 225-seat amphitheater, and a large, 38,000-sq.-ft. sports and fitness center and spa. The former Village Resort accommodations became part of the Disney Institute—which featured Bungalows (formerly Club Suites), Townhouses (formerly Vacation Villas), Treehouse Villas, Fairway Villas, and Grand Vista Homes. In summer 2000 the institute no longer offered programs to individual tourists, but rather focused on programs that catered to groups and corporate retreats; the shift had begun in late 1996. The last guests stayed at The Disney Institute Feb. 11, 2002. In 2004, the institute was replaced by Disney's Saratoga Springs Resort & Spa, part of Disney Vacation Club. Even though it lost its home, Disney Institute has continued to teach professional development, reaching business audiences around the world to share strategies perfected through Disney's years of exceptional service and business excellence.

Disney Interactive Division formed in 1994 to develop, market, and distribute cartridge games and

CD-ROM software; it took the place of Disney Software. It expanded to deliver high-quality interactive entertainment experiences for guests across all current and emerging digital media platforms. Disney Interactive was merged with Disney Consumer Products in 2015.

Disney Internet Group Formed in 2000 as the umbrella organization for GO.com, ESPN.com, ABCNews.com, Disney.com, and similar businesses. On Aug. 7, 2000, a new ticker symbol, DIG, replaced the Go.com ticker on the New York Stock Exchange; the following year, on Mar. 20, 2001, the outstanding shares were converted into shares of Disney common stock. It combined with Disney Interactive Studios to become Disney Interactive Media Group in 2008. In 2012, the name was shortened to Disney Interactive. It merged with Disney Consumer Products in 2015.

Disney Junior Part of Disney Channels Worldwide, a multi-platform brand expressly for kids ages 2–7. Originally rolled out Feb. 14, 2011, as a programming block on Disney Channel in the U.S., taking the place of, and expanding, Playhouse Disney, and on 25 Playhouse Disney channels worldwide by Sep. 2011. Expanded into a 24-hr. cable channel for preschoolers, children, and their families Mar. 23, 2012, replacing SOAPnet. A new animated series, *Doc McStuffins*, debuted with the new channel.

Disney Junior Dance Party! See Playhouse Disney—Live on Stage!

Disney Junior Dance Party On Tour Traveling live concert experience for kids and their families, with songs from popular Disney Junior TV series, including *Mickey and the Roadster Racers*, *Doc McStuffins*, *Vampirina*, *Fancy Nancy*, and *Elena of Avalor*. Debuted Mar. 14, 2017, in Southern California.

Disney Junior Dream Factory Musical show in Production Courtyard in Walt Disney Studios Park at Disneyland Paris; opened Jul. 1, 2021, replacing Disney Junior—Live on Stage! Inside Studio D at Walt Disney Television Studios, audiences sing along with favorite Disney Junior characters in a show about believing in dreams.

Disney Junior Holiday Party! Touring stage production, beginning in Scranton, Pennsylvania, Nov. 1, 2019. Disney Junior stars, like Vampirina, the Puppy Dog Pals, and Elena of Avalor, perform holiday favorites.

Disney Junior—Live on Stage! See Playhouse Disney—Live on Stage!

Disney Junior Live On Tour: Costume Palooza Touring live concert experience; premiered Sep. 2, 2022, in Riverside, California. Mickey, Minnie, and friends are getting ready to throw a huge costume party, but mysterious green rain, wind, and smoke keep interrupting the fun. Featuring characters from *Doc McStuffins*, *Alice's Wonderland Bakery*, *Puppy Dog Pals*, and *Marvel's Spidey and his Amazing Friends*.

Disney Junior Live on Tour! Pirate & Princess Adventure Touring stage production, beginning in Savannah, Georgia, Jul. 26, 2013; featured characters from *Sofia the First* and *Jake and the Never Land Pirates*.

Disney Junior Play and Dance! See Playhouse Disney—Live on Stage!

Disney Kingdoms Publishing imprint for comic books from Marvel, inspired by theme parks. The initial series, beginning Jan. 15, 2014, was *Seekers of the Weird*, taken from Imagineer Rolly Crump's ideas for a never-realized Museum of the Weird attraction in Disneyland. Later series were *Figment*, *Big Thunder Mountain Railroad*, *Figment 2*, *The Haunted Mansion*, and *Enchanted Tiki Room*.

Disney KiteTails Live show in Asia at Disney's Animal Kingdom; debuted Oct. 1, 2021. Enormous three-dimensional kites and wind catchers of Disney characters took flight above the Discovery River Amphitheater to the beat of songs from *The Jungle Book* and *The Lion King*. The final performance was held Sep. 30, 2022. The venue previously hosted *Rivers of Light*.

Disney Launchpad: Shorts Incubator Program launched in 2020 for directors from underrepresented backgrounds to present diverse perspectives through original live-action shorts for proposed initial exhibition on Disney+. The inaugural series of 6 films, based on the "Discover" theme, were digitally released May 28, 2021: *American EID*, *Dinner Is Served*, *Growing Fangs*, *The Last of the Chupacabras*, *Let's Be Tigers*, and *The Little*

Prince(ss). For the 2nd season, planned for release in 2023, writers became eligible to apply in addition to directors; the 6 films are *Beautiful, FL*; *Black Belts*; *Maxine*; *Project CC*; *The Ghost*; and *The Roof*.

Disney Legends Since 1987, The Walt Disney Company has honored individuals who have made major contributions to the company over the years by placing bronze emblems in the sidewalk in front of the Studio theater and having the honorees put their signatures and handprints in the cement. Some individuals have been honored posthumously. There was no ceremony in 1988. Honorees are presented with the Disney Legends Award; created by Andrea Favilli, the bronze sculpture features 3 distinct elements: the Spiral (representing "imagination, the power of an idea"), the Hand (holding "the gifts of skill, discipline, and craftsmanship"), and the Wand and Star (representing "magic, the spark that is ignited when imagination and skill combine to create a new dream"). A new area, Disney Legends Plaza, was dedicated Oct. 16, 1998, in front of the Team Disney Building in commemoration of the company's 75th anniversary. Handprints and signatures were put on brass plaques on the pillars surrounding the Plaza, with the new ones being added after each ceremony. The Plaza also features a 2nd edition of a 14-ft. Disney Legends Award sculpture first unveiled at the 1997 ceremony in Disneyland Paris. Beginning in 2009, the Disney Legends were named biennially at the D23 Expo. The Disney Legends are:

1. 1987: Fred MacMurray.
2. 1989: Ub Iwerks, Les Clark, Marc Davis, Ollie Johnston, Milt Kahl, Ward Kimball, Eric Larson, John Lounsbery, Wolfgang Reitherman, Frank Thomas.
3. 1990: Roger Broggie, Joseph Fowler, John Hench, Richard Irvine, Herb Ryman, Richard M. Sherman, Robert B. Sherman.
4. 1991: Ken Anderson, Julie Andrews, Carl Barks, Mary Blair, Claude Coats, Don DaGradi, Sterling Holloway, Fess Parker, Bill Walsh.
5. 1992: Jimmie Dodd, Bill Evans, Annette Funicello, Joe Grant, Jack Hannah, Winston Hibler, Ken O'Connor, Roy Williams.
6. 1993: Pinto Colvig, Buddy Ebsen, Peter Ellenshaw, Blaine Gibson, Harper Goff, Irving Ludwig, Jimmy Macdonald, Clarence Nash, Donn Tatum, Card Walker.
7. 1994: Adriana Caselotti, Bill Cottrell, Marvin Davis, Van France, David Hand, Jack Lindquist, Bill Martin, Paul Smith, Frank Wells.
8. 1995: Wally Boag, Fulton Burley, Dean Jones, Angela Lansbury, Edward Meck, Fred Moore, Thurl Ravenscroft, Wathel Rogers, Betty Taylor.
9. 1996: Bob Allen, Rex Allen, X Atencio, Betty Lou Gerson, Bill Justice, Bob Matheison, Sam McKim, Bob Moore, Bill Peet, Joe Potter.
10. 1997: A special Disney Legends ceremony was held at Disneyland Paris to honor European Disney Legends (primarily individuals who had been instrumental in Disney film distribution and merchandise licensing in Europe through the years): Lucien Adès, Angel Angelopoulos, Antonio Bertini, Armand Bigle, Poul Brahe Pedersen, Gaudenzio Capelli, Roberto de Leonardis, Cyril Edgar, Wally Feignoux, Didier Fouret, Mario Gentilini, Cyril James, Horst Koblischek, Gunnar Mansson, Arnoldo Mondadori, Armand Palivoda, André Vanneste, Paul Winkler.
11. 1998: James Algar, Buddy Baker, Kathryn Beaumont, Virginia Davis, Roy E. Disney, Don Escen, Wilfred Jackson, Glynis Johns, Kay Kamen, Paul Kenworthy, Larry Lansburgh, Hayley Mills, Al and Elma Milotte, Norman "Stormy" Palmer, Lloyd Richardson, Kurt Russell, Ben Sharpsteen, Vladimir "Bill" Tytla, Dick Van Dyke. (A Legends ceremony in Japan in 1998 honored Masatomo Takahashi and Matsuo Yokoyama.)
12. 1999: Tim Allen, Mary Costa, Norman Ferguson, William Garity, Yale Gracey, Al Konetzni, Hamilton S. Luske, Dick Nunis, Charlie Ridgway.
13. 2000: Grace Bailey, Harriet Burns, Joyce Carlson, Ron Dominguez, Cliff Edwards, Becky Fallberg, Dick Jones, Dodie Roberts, Retta Scott, Ruthie Tompson.
14. 2001: (Ceremony held at Walt Disney World.) Howard Ashman, Bob Broughton, George Bruns, Frank Churchill, Leigh Harline, Fred Joerger, Alan Menken, Marty Sklar, Ned Washington, Tyrus Wong. Special commendation to Bob Thomas.
15. 2002: (Ceremony held in France.) Ken Annakin, Hugh Attwooll, Maurice Chevalier, Phil Collins, John Mills, Robert Newton, Sir Tim Rice, Robert Stevenson, Richard Todd, David Tomlinson.

16. 2003: Neil Beckett, Tutti Camarata, Edna Disney, Lillian Disney, Orlando Ferrante, Richard Fleischer, Floyd Gottfredson, Buddy Hackett, Harrison Price, Al Taliaferro, Ilene Woods.

17. 2004: Bill Anderson, Tim Conway, Rolly Crump, Alice Davis, Karen Dotrice, Matthew Garber, Leonard Goldenson, Bob Gurr, Ralph Kent, Irwin Kostal, Mel Shaw.

18. 2005: (Ceremony held at Disneyland.) Chuck Abbott, Milt Albright, Hideo Amemiya, Hideo "Indian" Aramaki, Charles "Chuck" Boyajian, Charles Boyer, Randy Bright, Jim Cora, Bob Jani, Mary Jones, Art Linkletter, Mary Anne Mang, Steve Martin, Tom Nabbe, Jack Olsen, Cicely Rigdon, Bill Sullivan, Jack Wagner, Vesey Walker.

19. 2006: Tim Considine, Kevin Corcoran, Al Dempster, Don Edgren, Paul Frees, Peter Jennings, Elton John, James A. Johnson, Tommy Kirk, Joe Ranft, David Stollery, Ginny Tyler.

20. 2007: Roone Arledge, Art Babbitt, Carl Bongirno, Marge Champion, Dick Huemer, Ron Logan, Lucille Martin, Tom Murphy, Randy Newman, Floyd Norman, Bob Schiffer, Dave Smith.

21. 2008: Wayne Allwine, Bob Booth, Neil Gallagher, Frank Gifford, Toshio Kagami, Burny Mattinson, Walt Peregoy, Dorothea Redmond, Russi Taylor, Oliver Wallace, Barbara Walters.

22. 2009: (Ceremony henceforth held at D23 Expo at Anaheim Convention Center.) Tony Anselmo, Harry Archinal, Bea Arthur, Bill Farmer, Estelle Getty, Don Iwerks, Rue McClanahan, Leota Toombs Thomas, Betty White, Robin Williams.

23. 2011: Jody Benson, Barton "Bo" Boyd, Jim Henson, Linda Larkin, Paige O'Hara, Regis Philbin, Anika Noni Rose, Lea Salonga, Ray Watson, Guy Williams, Bonita Wrather, Jack Wrather.

24. 2013: Tony Baxter, Collin Campbell, Dick Clark, Billy Crystal, John Goodman, Steve Jobs, Glen Keane, Ed Wynn.

25. 2015: George Bodenheimer, Julie Reihm Casaletto, Andreas Deja, Johnny Depp, Eyvind Earle, Danny Elfman, George Lucas, Susan Lucci, Carson Van Osten.

26. 2017: Carrie Fisher, Clyde Geronimi, Whoopi Goldberg, Manuel Gonzales, Mark Hamill, Wayne Jackson, Jack Kirby, Stan Lee, Garry Marshall, Julie Taymor, Oprah Winfrey.

27. 2019: Christina Aguilera, Wing T. Chao, Robert Downey Jr., Jon Favreau, James Earl Jones, Bette Midler, Kenny Ortega, Barnette Ricci, Robin Roberts, Diane Sawyer, Ming-Na Wen, Hans Zimmer.

28. 2022: Anthony Anderson, Kristen Bell, Chadwick Boseman, Rob't Coltrin (named in 2020), Patrick Dempsey, Robert Price "Bob" Foster (named in 2021), Josh Gad, Jonathan Groff, Don Hahn, Doris Hardoon, Idina Menzel, Chris Montan, Ellen Pompeo, Tracee Ellis Ross.

Disney Live! Mickey and Minnie's Doorway to Magic Touring stage production. Through a mysterious portal, Mickey, Minnie, and friends enter enchanted lands of more than 20 Disney characters. Premiered in Fortaleza, Brazil, Jun. 25, 2015, as *Disney Live! O Caminho Mágico de Mickey & Minnie*, with the U.S. debut Jan. 8, 2016, in Bakersfield, California.

Disney Live! Mickey's Magic Show The 2nd of the touring stage productions produced by Feld Entertainment. The theme of the show is discovering the magic within each of us. Premiered Apr. 21, 2006, in Columbia, South Carolina.

Disney Live! Mickey's Music Festival A lively concert featuring characters from *The Little Mermaid*, *Aladdin*, and *Toy Story*. Premiered Sep. 29, 2010, in Las Palmas, Canary Islands.

Disney Live! Rockin' Road Show Touring stage production. Mickey, Minnie, and the gang round up acts for a spontaneous talent show traveling the world on a "fantastical bus." Premiered Aug. 22, 2009, in Lakeland, Florida.

Disney Live! Three Classic Fairy Tales The first of the Disney Live! tours to debut in Asia; opened May 27, 2008, at the Shanghai Oriental Art Center. Aimed at introducing the Disney characters to Chinese audiences, the show featured Snow White, Cinderella, and Beauty and the Beast.

Disney Live! Winnie the Pooh First of a planned series of touring family stage productions featuring Disney characters and stories. The Hundred Acre Wood and its inhabitants are brought to the stage in an interactive production. Premiered Jun. 16, 2004, in Christchurch, New Zealand, with its U.S. premiere Jul. 29, 2005, in Fort Lauderdale, Florida. Produced by Feld Entertainment, Inc.

Disney Magazine Colorfully illustrated quarterly magazine with news and stories from all across the Disney company, sold on newsstands and by subscription summer 1996–summer 2005. The magazine evolved from *Disney News*, published by the Magic Kingdom Club starting in 1965, and contained articles about new films and park attractions, tips on culinary experiences, travel suggestions, question-and-answer columns, announcements of new Disney books, and other topics of interest to the Disney enthusiast.

Disney Magic First ship in the Disney Cruise Line fleet. Built in the Fincantieri shipyard in Marghera, Italy, the *Disney Magic* is 984 feet long and weighs 83,000 tons. Debuted with 875 staterooms, 4 restaurants (Parrot Cay, Animator's Palate, Lumiere's, Palo) and buffet dining (Topsider), the Walt Disney Theatre and Buena Vista Theatre, 3 swimming pools, and other amenities. The ship was christened by Patty Disney in a ceremony held Jul. 28, 1998, in Port Canaveral, Florida. The *Magic* embarked on its maiden voyage Jul. 30. As part of a dry dock refurbishment in 2013, Carioca's replaced Parrot Cay, Cabanas replaced Topsider, and the *Drawn to Magic* show was added to Animator's Palate. In Mar. 2018, Rapunzel's Royal Table, with live entertainment, replaced Carioca's. The ship's interiors feature a decorative art deco style evoking the elegance of a classic ocean liner, a design later complemented by its sister ship's (*Disney Wonder's*) art nouveau look. Goofy is seen painting the *Disney Magic* emblem on the stern, while the focal point of the atrium is a cast bronze statue of Helmsman Mickey. Sailings began with 3- and 4-day cruises to the Caribbean (including Disney's private island, Castaway Cay). The *Magic* switched to 7-day cruises (including stops at St. Maarten and St. Thomas/St. John) Aug. 12, 2000, and began alternate itineraries to Key West, Florida; Grand Cayman; and Cozumel, Mexico, May 11, 2002. From May 28–Aug. 20, 2005, the ship sailed out of Los Angeles to the Mexican ports of Puerto Vallarta, Mazatlán, and Cabo San Lucas. For summer 2007, 10- and 11-day cruises were offered through the Mediterranean out of Barcelona, Spain, and in summer 2008 it returned to the U.S. West Coast. For 2009, stops were added in the Caribbean at St. Croix or Tortola. The 2010 and 2011 Mediterranean cruises added Tunisia, Malta, and Corsica, and there were additionally four 2010 cruises to northern European ports out of Dover, England. In 2011, cruises were announced to Canada and the New England coast out of New York City and the western Caribbean out of Galveston, Texas. The ship returned to Europe in 2013, with 4-, 7-, and 12-night sailings. In 2014, Puerto Rico was added as a home port. In May 2017, a transatlantic crossing from Port Canaveral to Copenhagen included a stop in Amsterdam and Portland, England, with northern and western European, Norwegian, British Isles, and Mediterranean itineraries. In 2018, new ports of call included Genoa, Italy, and Cork, Ireland; plus Rome was added as a departure port. Disney cruises were suspended beginning Mar. 14, 2020, due to the COVID-19 pandemic; the *Disney Magic* was the first Disney Cruise Line ship to resume sailings, with 2-, 3-, and 4-night "Disney Magic at Sea" cruises for U.K. residents beginning Jul. 15, 2021, from Liverpool. The *Magic* resumed sailings from the U.S. Oct. 28, 2021, out of Miami.

Disney Magic Bake-Off (TV) Competitive series; debuted Aug. 13, 2021, on Disney Channel and DisneyNOW. Hosts Dara Reneé and Issac Ryan Brown, with judge Graciela Gomez, guide kid bakers through a series of challenges as they create Disney-inspired cakes. From Tastemade.

Disney MaxPass Digital tool offering Disney PhotoPass downloads and the convenience of mobile Disney FastPass through the Disneyland App; debuted Jul. 19, 2017, at the Disneyland Resort. The service was retired in 2021 and was succeeded by Disney Genie+.

Disney Mercantile Tokyo Disneyland Hotel souvenir shop at Tokyo Disney Resort; opened Jul. 8, 2008.

Disney-MGM Studios SEE DISNEY'S HOLLYWOOD STUDIOS.

Disney-MGM Studios Theme Park Grand Opening, The (TV) Two-hour show; aired Apr. 30, 1989, the evening before the public opening of the park. Directed by Jeff Margolis. With Harry Anderson, George Burns, Walter Cronkite, John Forsythe, Estelle Getty, Kate Jackson, Rue McClanahan, Ann Miller, Yves Montand, Willie Nelson, Tony Randall, John Ritter, Mickey Rooney, and many others. There are even cameos by Jane Fonda, Jimmy Stewart, Margaret Thatcher, Ronald Reagan, and Lech Walesa. The stars visit the various attractions at the park, ending with a spectacular "Hooray for Hollywood" production number. The show won an Emmy Award for choreographer Walter Painter.

Disney Mobile Cell phone service launched in Jun. 2006. Parents could monitor their children's phone usage and track their whereabouts with a global positioning system. The service was suspended Dec. 31, 2007.

Disney Movie Rewards Program in which points are earned for purchasing Disney DVDs, Blu-rays, digital movies, CDs, and movie tickets; began in 2006. Points can be redeemed for products, collectibles, Disney experiences, and travel opportunities. On Sep. 26, 2019, it became Disney Movie Insiders.

Disney Movies Anywhere Digital movie streaming service launched Feb. 25, 2014, whereby viewers could purchase and watch Disney, Pixar, and Marvel films. It was available for iPad, iPhone, iPod touch, and the Web, powered by iTunes. The service ended Feb. 28, 2018, and was replaced by Movies Anywhere, which additionally offered titles from 20th Century Fox, Sony, Universal, and Warner Bros.

Disney Music Group The music arm of The Walt Disney Company, home to Walt Disney Records, Hollywood Records, Disney Music Publishing, Buena Vista Records, and Disney Concerts. Also releases family music and film and television soundtracks. It was previously the Buena Vista Music Group. SEE ALSO MUSIC AND WALT DISNEY MUSIC COMPANY.

Disney My Music Story (TV) Original music documentary series; digitally released beginning Jan. 31, 2020, on Disney+ Japan and in the U.S. beginning Feb. 5, 2021. Each documentary features interviews and performances of famous Japanese artists who have collaborated with Disney, including Yoshiki, Perfume, and Sukima Switch.

Disney on Ice SEE WORLD ON ICE.

Disney on Parade Traveling arena show, which debuted in Chicago Dec. 25, 1969, after a Dec. 16 preview in Long Beach, California. Dozens of Disney characters put on lavish production numbers. There were 4 editions of the show, with some acts based on recently released films, such as *The Love Bug*, *The Aristocats*, and *Bedknobs and Broomsticks*. Ended in 1976 after an international run. The show was superseded by World on Ice.

Disney on Parade (TV) Show aired Dec. 19, 1971. Directed by Stan Harris. A videotaped version of the first tour of the arena show, taped in Adelaide, Australia.

Disney100 Cross-company global celebration commemorating 100 years of The Walt Disney Company; launched in 2023. Included are new park attractions and entertainment (including *Wondrous Journeys* and *World of Color – ONE* at Disneyland Resort); a global touring exhibition (SEE NEXT ENTRY); a European concert tour, *Disney100: The Concert*; and a Disney100–themed Destination D23 event at Walt Disney World.

Disney100: The Exhibition A 15,000-sq.-ft. touring exhibition; premiered Feb. 18, 2023, at The Franklin Institute in Philadelphia, with a 2nd, international unit debuting Apr. 18 in Munich. Visitors step through 10 immersive galleries showcasing how the philosophies of Walt Disney have guided Disney's past, present, and future, with interactive displays. More than 250 artifacts and works of art are featured. Additional planned stops include Chicago; Kansas City, Missouri; and London. From the Walt Disney Archives and Semmel Exhibitions.

Disney Online Business unit founded as a part of Disney Interactive in 1995 to develop The Walt Disney Company's presence in the online world. The first offering, Disney.com, a World Wide Web site, went online Feb. 21, 1996. Disney.com (www.disney.com) offers information and entertainment designed to showcase Disney's products and services, from movies and books to merchandise and theme parks. Entertainment subscription options for kids have also been available, starting with *Disney's Daily Blast* in 1997. Students and investors can find annual reports and financial information at www.disney.com/investors/.

Disney Outfitters Shop on Discovery Island (formerly Safari Village) in Disney's Animal Kingdom; opened Apr. 22, 1998. Renamed Wonders of the Wild 1999–2001, then reverted to Disney Outfitters. Inside, the rooms depict animals representing different directions, from underground to across the land and up into the constellations. Renamed Discovery Trading Company Mar. 15, 2016. An expansion, Riverside Depot, was added Dec. 8, 2015.

Disney Parks, Experiences and Products On Mar. 14, 2018, The Walt Disney Company announced a reorganization of its businesses, including the merging of Walt Disney Parks and Resorts with

Disney Consumer Products into a single segment named Disney Parks, Experiences and Consumer Products. In 2019, the name was shortened to Disney Parks, Experiences and Products.

Disney Performing Arts SEE MAGIC MUSIC DAYS AND DISNEY IMAGINATION CAMPUS.

Disney PhotoPass Service at the Disney parks; debuted Dec. 1, 2004, at Walt Disney World. Photographers using professional equipment take photos of guests throughout the parks. Guests receive a PhotoPass card, which they use each time they get a photo. Their vacation photos are then linked together into 1 online account for viewing and sharing. In 2014, PhotoPass was linked to MyMagic+. The service has also been offered at Disneyland Resort and at the former World of Disney store in New York City.

Disney-Pixar Toy Story Land The first major expansion of Shanghai Disneyland; opened Apr. 26, 2018. Guests feel as though they've been shrunk down to the size of a toy in a fully immersive land featuring 3 attractions—Slinky Dog Spin, Rex's Racer, and Woody's Roundup. Character greetings are offered at the Meeting Post, with shopping at Al's Toy Barn and dining at the Toy Box Café. SEE ALSO TOY STORY PLAYLAND (WALT DISNEY STUDIOS PARK) AND TOY STORY LAND (HONG KONG DISNEYLAND AND DISNEY'S HOLLYWOOD STUDIOS).

Disney+ Subscription-based video streaming service with Disney, Pixar, Marvel, *Star Wars*, and National Geographic programming. Original films, series, documentaries, and short-form content are available, along with access to select titles from Disney's library of films and TV shows. Launched Nov. 12, 2019, in the U.S., Canada, and the Netherlands, and in spring 2020 in other Western European countries. In Apr. 2020, paid subscribers of the Hotstar streaming service in India were converted to Disney+ Hotstar subscribers, and in Jun. 2020, subscribers of the Disney Deluxe service in Japan were converted to Disney+ subscribers. In Sep. 2020, Disney+ was launched in additional European countries, and Disney+ Hotstar was launched in Indonesia. In Nov. 2020, Disney+ was offered in Latin America, with additional launches in various Asia Pacific territories in 2021. As of 2021, programming included approximately 33,000 episodes and 1,850 movies from Disney's produced and acquired TV and film library, with approximately 75 original series and 40 original movies or specials. In early 2022, it was announced that Disney+ would launch in 42 additional countries and 11 territories in Europe, the Middle East, and Africa that summer. On Dec. 8, 2022, an ad-supported subscription was introduced in the U.S., with more than 100 advertisers at launch.

Disney Presents Goofy in How to Stay at Home SEE GOOFY IN HOW TO STAY AT HOME.

Disney Press Imprint created by Disney in 1991 for Disney-themed children's books. The first book, *101 Dalmatians: A Counting Book*, was published May 31, 1991.

Disney QUIZney (TV) A 7-min. live game show on Disney Channel; aired Jul. 16–27 and Sep. 17–28, 2018. Host Trinitee Stokes asks fast-paced questions about all things Disney, with audiences playing along on DisneyNOW to win cash prizes. A 10-min. version hosted by Disney Channel stars ran for 12 weeks beginning Apr. 29, 2019.

Disney Regional Entertainment Division of Disney formed in 1996 to create entertainment areas, such as sports complexes, interactive entertainment, and family play centers, for urban and suburban locations around the world. The first experiment was Club Disney (opened in Thousand Oaks, California, Feb. 1997), followed by Disney-Quest (the first of which opened Jun. 19, 1998) and ESPN Zone (which debuted in Baltimore Jul. 12, 1998).

Disney Research Inspired by Pixar's world-class research in computer graphics, Disney Research was launched in 2008 as a network of research labs that collaborate closely with academic institutions such as Carnegie Mellon University and the Swiss Federal Institute of Technology Zürich (ETH) to research novel technologies and deploy them on a global scale. Reporting to Walt Disney Imagineering, and originally headquartered in Pittsburgh, they are able to combine the best of academia and industry to engage with the global research community, working on a broad range of commercially important challenges.

Disney Showcase Main Street, U.S.A. souvenir shop in Disneyland; opened Oct. 27, 1989, succeeding Disneyland Presents a Preview of Coming Attractions in the space originally occupied by the Wurlitzer Music Hall.

Disney Signature Experiences Name, beginning in 2018, of Disney's umbrella of family travel and leisure businesses beyond theme parks. The businesses include Disney Cruise Line; Disney Vacation Club; Aulani, A Disney Resort & Spa; Adventures by Disney; National Geographic Expeditions; Disney Institute; and Storyliving by Disney. Previously known as New Vacation Operations.

Disney Skyliner Aerial transportation system at Walt Disney World; premiered Sep. 29, 2019, connecting EPCOT and Disney's Hollywood Studios to 4 resort hotels: Disney's Riviera Resort, Caribbean Beach Resort, Art of Animation Resort, and Pop Century Resort. Guests board cabins, some decorated with Disney characters, that offer bird's-eye views of the Walt Disney World property.

Disney Software SEE COMPUTER SOFTWARE.

Disney Sound Walt Disney Records imprint established in 2004 to create original music for the entire family. Its first release, on Feb. 15, 2005, was *Here Come the ABCs* from the alternative rock group They Might Be Giants, on DVD and CD.

Disney Springs Shopping, dining, and entertainment center at Walt Disney World, replacing Downtown Disney; the name change was made effective Sep. 29, 2015. The complex is inspired by Florida's waterfront towns, with a flowing spring and lakefront unifying 4 neighborhoods: Town Center (opened May 15, 2016), The Landing, Marketplace, and West Side. SEE ALSO DOWNTOWN DISNEY.

Disney Store, The The first Disney Store, selling Disney merchandise exclusively, opened Mar. 28, 1987, in the Glendale Galleria in California. With the exception of a store in the Orlando Airport operated by Walt Disney World, Disney had not tried retail outlets outside the parks. Michael Eisner and Frank Wells decided that Disney was missing a sure bet by not doing so. The Disney Store concept turned out to be highly successful and influenced other companies to pursue a similar strategy. All of the Disney Stores were owned and operated by The Walt Disney Company and hosted by Cast Members who were trained as rigorously as those in the theme parks to be friendly and helpful. As the number of stores grew, more and more merchandise was being designed and manufactured for their exclusive sale. By 1997, there were more than 600 stores in the U.S. and 10 other countries, with a peak in 1999 of 747 stores. The company then began closing less profitable stores, and the Japanese Disney Stores were sold to the Oriental Land Co., which owns Tokyo Disney Resort, in 2001. By Oct. 2003, the total was down to 481 stores. On Nov. 21, 2004, the 313 remaining North American Disney Stores were sold to Children's Place. Disney retained ownership of 105 European stores. On Apr. 30, 2008, Disney acquired 225 North American Disney Store outlets from Children's Place, and on Mar. 31, 2010, reacquired the Japanese Disney Stores from the Oriental Land Company. A major new store redesign was launched in Jun. 2010. By 2016, there were more than 200 Disney Stores in North America, plus over 100 in Europe and Japan. The world's largest Disney Store opened May 20, 2015, in Pudong, Shanghai, China. On Oct. 4, 2019, "Disney store at Target" launched in 25 Target stores nationwide, as a shop-in-shop concept offering Disney products, interactive displays, and photo spots. In Aug. 2021, it was announced the concept would extend to more than 160 Target locations. The same year, the company announced plans to focus on its e-commerce business and significantly reduced the number of Disney Store locations in North America and Europe. As of Oct. 2, 2021, Disney owns and operates approximately 40 Disney Stores in Japan, 20 stores in North America, 15 stores in Europe, and 2 stores in China.

Disney Storybook, A (TV) Two-part show; aired Nov. 14 and 21, 1981. Features *Mickey and the Beanstalk*, *Dumbo*, and *Working for Peanuts*.

Disney Streaming Services In 2016, Disney purchased a 33% stake in BAMTech—a video streaming and technology services company that had been created by Major League Baseball—to enable the company to launch new ESPN and Disney-branded streaming services. Disney increased its ownership to 75% in 2017. In 2018, BAMTech became a subsidiary of Disney Streaming Services, which houses all consumer-facing digital technology and products across the company, including the direct-to-consumer ESPN+ (launched Apr. 12, 2018) and Disney+ (launched Nov. 12, 2019). Disney increased its ownership of BAMTech to 85% in 2021 and acquired the remaining stake in 2022. BAMTech continues to operate Disney's direct-to-consumer sports business and provides streaming technology services to third parties.

Disney Studio SEE STUDIO.

Disney Studio 1 Guests entering this huge sound-stage in the Front Lot at Walt Disney Studios Park at Disneyland Paris find themselves on an elaborate Hollywood Boulevard set, complete with hundreds of movie props; opened Mar. 16, 2002. Visitors can dine at Restaurant en Coulisse, shop at Les Légendes d'Hollywood, and enjoy a snack at The Hep Cat Corner (added Jun. 2013).

Disney Studio Showcase (TV) Show on The Disney Channel, beginning Apr. 19, 1983, and ending Apr. 25, 1985, with such topics as behind-the-scenes looks at the Walt Disney Studios, award-winning commercials, a science fiction view of the future, a look at toy making, and a stylized version of *Hansel and Gretel*.

Disney Studio Store SEE STUDIO STORE, THE.

Disney Studios Australia As part of its purchase of 21st Century Fox in 2019, Disney acquired Fox Studios Australia, a 32-acre production facility in Moore Park in New South Wales. In Oct. 2022, the facility was renamed Disney Studios Australia. Since its opening in 1998, the studio has provided production services for TV shows and films, including *Moulin Rouge!, Star Wars: Attack of the Clones* and *Star Wars: Revenge of the Sith, Superman Returns, Shang-Chi and the Legend of the Ten Rings*, and *Thor: Love and Thunder*. There are 9 soundstages, plus construction workshops, backlots, scoring stages, and postproduction facilities.

Disney Sunday Movie, The (TV) Series on ABC; aired Feb. 2, 1986–Sep. 11, 1988.

Disney Tails Pet accessory shop in Downtown Disney Marketplace at Walt Disney World; opened Jul. 1, 2004, inside Pooh Corner. Closed in 2007, superseded by an expanded Mickey's Mart. Disney Tails became a brand of pet accessory products and, in 2018, a shop inside the Marketplace Co-Op at Disney Springs.

Disney Television Studios Umbrella of television studios formed after Disney's acquisition of 21st Century Fox in 2019. The production entities, as of Feb. 2021, are ABC Signature, 20th Television, 20th Television Animation, and Walt Disney Television Unscripted and Alternative. Part of Disney General Entertainment Content.

Disney Theatrical Group Disney's theatrical business, which produces and licenses Broadway productions around the world, including *Beauty and the Beast, The Lion King, Aida, Tarzan, Mary Poppins, The Little Mermaid, Peter and the Starcatcher, Newsies, Aladdin,* and *Frozen*. Other stage musicals have included the London hit *Shakespeare in Love*, stage productions of Disney's *High School Musical, Der Glöckner Von Notre Dame* in Berlin, and *King David* in concert. The group has collaborated with leading regional theaters to develop new stage titles, such as *The Jungle Book, The Hunchback of Notre Dame*, and *Freaky Friday*. Live shows are delivered globally through its license to Feld Entertainment, producer of *Disney on Ice* and *Marvel Universe Live!*, which have brought Disney stories and characters annually to over 12 million guests in nearly 50 countries. Musical titles are also licensed for local, school, and community theater productions through Music Theatre International, including arts education programs wherein accredited schools produce condensed, age-appropriate "Jr." and "kids" adaptations.

Disney Traders Shop in World Showcase Plaza in EPCOT; opened Apr. 9, 1987.

Disney Tsum Tsum The name, taken from a Japanese word which means "to stack," of an interactive game and line of cute plush Disney characters introduced in Japan in 2013. Because of its great popularity, it was brought to the U.S. in Jul. 2014, where it soon had a cult following. In the puzzle game app, Disney Tsum Tsums are collected, connected, and popped. The plush versions are meant to be stacked, forming a pyramid. Digital shorts featuring the Tsum Tsums have also aired on Disney Channel.

Disney University Company department created in 1962 at Disneyland to prepare new Cast Members for their roles by communicating a basic understanding of the Disney traditions and philosophies, to provide advanced training classes, and to handle cast communications and cast activities. The University evolved out of a training department, which had been established in spring 1955 by Van France, and a cast activities group known as the Disneyland Recreation Club started that same year. It was originally known as the University of Disneyland, but when Walt Disney World needed a similar department in 1971, the name Disney University was chosen. A 3rd Disney University was established at the Disney Studio in Burbank in 1977. Additional branches later opened in Tokyo Disneyland, Disneyland Paris, Hong Kong Disneyland, and Shanghai Disneyland.

Disney Vacation, A (TV) Show aired May 1, 1982. An animated look at vacations in Disney films.

Disney Vacation Club Vacation ownership program offering members stays at a Disney Vacation Club Resort and other options in destinations around the world. As of Dec. 2019, there were 14 Disney Vacation Club properties: Aulani, Disney Vacation Club Villas (Ko Olina, Hawai'i); Bay Lake Tower at Disney's Contemporary Resort; Disney's Animal Kingdom Villas—Jambo House/Disney's Animal Kingdom Villas—Kidani Village; Disney's Beach Club Villas; Disney's BoardWalk Villas; Disney's Hilton Head Island Resort; Disney's Old Key West Resort; Disney's Polynesian Villas & Bungalows; Disney's Saratoga Springs Resort & Spa; Disney's Vero Beach Resort; The Villas at Disney's Grand Californian Hotel & Spa; The Villas at Disney's Grand Floridian Resort & Spa; Boulder Ridge Villas and Copper Creek Villas & Cabins at Disney's Wilderness Lodge; and Disney's Riviera Resort. As of Feb. 2023, 2 additional properties have been announced: The Villas at Disneyland Hotel (scheduled to open Sep. 2023 at the Disneyland Resort) and a tower at Disney's Polynesian Village Resort (planned for Walt Disney World). The program debuted in 1991 with a flexible, vacation points-based system rather than the traditional fixed-week time-share model. SEE ALSO VACATION CLUB RESORT.

Disney Valentine, A (TV) Show aired Feb. 13, 1982. Clips from Disney cartoons take a look at romance.

Disney Vault Marketing term, used primarily in the 1990s and 2000s, for the practice of offering a limited retail period for Disney home videos and DVDs.

Disney Vault 28 Chic boutique in the Downtown Disney District at Disneyland Resort; opened Oct. 11, 2006, with a grand opening Nov. 12. Disney-themed designer-brand clothing and accessories were sold. Closed Sep. 24, 2017, and succeeded by Star Wars: Secrets of the Empire.

Disney Village New name, in 1996, for Festival Disney at Disneyland Paris. A phased transformation of the complex was announced Mar. 21, 2022, with plans for new dining, shopping, and enter-tainment, along with new façades, a lakeside park, boardwalk, enhanced pedestrian walkways, and terraces.

Disney Village Clubhouse New name, in Sep. 1988, of the Buena Vista Club, which was open 1974–1994. It was extensively remodeled and rebuilt to become the main building for the Disney Institute.

Disney Village Marketplace SEE DOWNTOWN DISNEY MARKETPLACE.

Disney Villains Fantasyland shop at Disneyland; opened Jul. 16, 1991. Formerly Merlin's Magic Shop (1955–1983), Mickey's Christmas Chalet (1983–1987), and Briar Rose Cottage (1987–1991). Closed May 30, 1996, to reopen Jun. 13 as The Sanctuary of Quasimodo, selling merchandise from *The Hunchback of Notre Dame*, until Feb. 9, 1997. For a year it was the Knights Shop, then reverted to a villains shop (Villain's Lair) Oct. 2, 1998. It became a new location for the Castle Heraldry Shoppe (2004–2017), then the Castle Holiday Shoppe (2017–2021) and Merlin's Marvelous Miscellany (opened 2022). Another villains shop opened on New York Street in Disney-MGM Studios (later Disney's Hollywood Studios) as The Costume Shop (1991–1996), followed by Villains in Vogue on Sunset Boulevard (1998–2015). It took merchandisers many years to appreciate the appeal of the Disney villains, but now there are several lines of specially produced items, and guests enjoy wearing T-shirts emblazoned with their favorite Disney foes.

Disney VoluntEARS In 1983, Disneyland Resort Cast Members formed the Disneyland Community Action Team to provide meaningful service to the community through volunteer work with non-profit organizations. The success of this organization led to a company-wide launch of the Disney VoluntEARS in 1992. Today, Disney VoluntEARS work on meaningful projects across the globe, with a primary focus on communities where Disney business units operate.

Disney Wilderness Preserve, The Disney agreed to purchase and preserve 8,500 acres of the Walker Ranch in south Osceola County, Florida, in 1992 in exchange for the right to develop up to 550 acres of wetlands on the Walt Disney World property, primarily including the town site of Celebration. Disney in turn donated the land to the Nature

Conservancy in 1993, and efforts began to return the drained ranchlands to their original habitat. Later in 1995, 3,000 additional acres were added to the preserve by the Orlando Aviation Authority to mitigate for airport expansion. The area opened to the public on Nov. 1, 1999, with a Conservation Learning Center and self-guided nature trails. In 2014, Disney purchased 3,000 additional acres of land west of the property to serve as a buffer for the preserve.

Disney Wildlife Conservation Fund Established by Walt Disney Attractions in 1995 to promote and enable global wildlife conservation through relationships with scientists, educators, and organizations committed to preserving the Earth's biodiversity. Annual grants are distributed to nonprofit organizations to protect and study endangered and threatened animals and their habitats. The name changed to the Disney Worldwide Conservation Fund in 2008 and to the Disney Conservation Fund in 2015.

Disney Wish The 5th ship in the Disney Cruise Line fleet. The christening ceremony took place Jun. 29, 2022, in Port Canaveral, Florida, prior to the Jul. 14 maiden voyage. Past, present, and future wish recipients of the Make-A-Wish program were honored as the ship's godchildren. At approx. 144,000 gross tons and 1,119 feet, the *Disney Wish* is slightly larger than the *Disney Dream* and *Disney Fantasy*, featuring 1,254 staterooms and a capacity of 4,000 passengers and 1,555 crew members. Like the other ships, the exterior aesthetic is inspired by classic ocean liners. Sculptures of Rapunzel and Pascal from *Tangled* adorn the stern. Inside, the overall design is based on the idea of enchantment—a motif introduced inside the fairy-tale-castle–inspired Grand Hall, where pixie dust appears to climb the 3-story columns and spill across the ceiling and chandelier. A bronze statue of Cinderella is the centerpiece. Rotational dining includes 1923, Arendelle: A Frozen Dining Adventure, and Worlds of Marvel, with upscale dining at Palo Steakhouse and Enchanté by Chef Arnaud Lallement. On the upper decks, the AquaMouse is a water attraction with show scenes based on the 2013 series of Mickey Mouse animated shorts. Also new to Disney Cruise Line are 4 extravagant royal suites inspired by *Sleeping Beauty*, as well as a 2-story, 1,966-sq.-ft. penthouse—the Wish Tower Suite—housed inside one of the ship's funnels above the upper decks. The traditional keel laying ceremony was held Apr. 8, 2021, at the Meyer Werft shipyard in Papenburg, Germany.

Disney Wonder The 2nd ship in the Disney Cruise Line fleet, constructed in the Fincantieri shipyard in Marghera, Italy. The *Disney Wonder* was christened Oct. 1, 1999, by a laser-projected Tinker Bell in Port Canaveral, Florida, and embarked on its maiden voyage Aug. 15. The *Wonder* is very similar to its sister ship, the *Disney Magic*, though its interior styling is more art nouveau than the *Magic*'s art deco. Triton's restaurant takes the place of Lumiere's, with a bronze statue of Ariel in the atrium. Donald Duck and nephew Huey are found on the stern with the ship's emblem. The Parrot Cay restaurant was replaced by Tiana's Place in 2016, and the Promenade Lounge became the French Quarter Lounge in 2019. The *Disney Wonder* and *Disney Magic* alternated on the short cruises to Castaway Cay and Nassau in The Bahamas until Aug. 2000, when the *Magic* switched to 7-day cruises and the *Wonder* added a stop at Freeport (in The Bahamas) to its 4-day cruises. Later, the *Wonder*'s itinerary reverted to Nassau and Castaway Cay, and occasionally Key West, Florida. Plans were made to base the ship in Los Angeles for Mexican Riviera tours beginning in 2011, with a summer base in Vancouver for 18 weeks of Alaska tours. In 2011, cruises were announced to the Hawaiian Islands, out of Los Angeles. In Dec. 2012, the *Wonder* began also using Miami as a home port, with sailings from New Orleans added in Feb. 2020. In 2022, sailings from Australia and New Zealand were announced for the following year.

Disney World Is Your World Show on the Tomorrowland Stage in the Magic Kingdom at Walt Disney World; performed Oct. 2, 1981–Sep. 17, 1994. The Kids of the Kingdom presented a musical salute to the park's themed lands.

Disney XD On Feb. 13, 2009, Toon Disney was rebranded as Disney XD, a basic cable channel with a mix of live-action and animated programming for kids ages 6–14, primarily targeting boys. Previously, Disney XD was also the name of a social networking community for kids on Disney.com (in this case short for Disney Xtreme Digital), launched in 2007.

Disneyana Term that refers to the collecting of Disney memorabilia. The first major auction featuring Disneyana was held at Sotheby's in Los Angeles on May 14, 1972. Cecil Munsey wrote his book, *Disneyana; Walt Disney Collectibles,* in 1974.

Disneyana Convention After witnessing the growth and popularity of Disneyana gatherings hosted by the Mouse Club and the NFFC, The Walt Disney Company through its Walt Disney Attractions Merchandise division decided to host its own. The first Disneyana Convention was held in the Contemporary Resort Convention Center at Walt Disney World Sep. 24–27, 1992, and featured sales of Disney memorabilia, convention logo merchandise, and special limited-edition collectibles, along with speakers, an auction, tours, meals, and gala entertainment events. The 750 conventioneers were thrilled by an event of the magnitude and scope that only Disney itself could produce. A 2nd Disneyana Convention, doubled in size, followed in 1993 at Disneyland Resort, with a return to Walt Disney World for the 3rd convention in 1994. The next year saw 2 Disneyana Conventions, 1 at each park. The 1996–2000 conventions were held at Walt Disney World, and the 2001 gathering was at Disneyland Resort. A final convention, in 2002, was in EPCOT.

Disneyana Fan Club The National Fantasy Fan Club (NFFC) voted to change its name to Disneyana Fan Club in 2009. SEE ALSO NATIONAL FANTASY FAN CLUB.

Disneyana Shop Opened Jan. 9, 1976, on Main Street, U.S.A. in Disneyland, switching locations with the Jewelry Shop across the street, May 30, 1986. For the first few years, the shop sold Disneyana merchandise, but it became too difficult to find this rare material to stock the shop, and it was feared that the extensive Disney purchases were creating their own artificial market prices for the material. Eventually, the shop turned instead to limited-editions and current collectible merchandise. Closed Apr. 14, 2013, to move and replace The Disney Gallery in the former Bank of Main Street building. Also opened Apr. 15, 1983, in Fantasyland in the Magic Kingdom at Walt Disney World, taking the place of the Castle Camera Shop. It moved to Main Street, U.S.A. Mar. 24, 1990, as Disneyana Collectibles, when an expanded Mad Hatter shop replaced the Fantasyland location. Closed Oct. 1, 1996, to make way for the Town Square Exposition Hall. Disneyana Collectibles also opened in Disneyland Paris Apr. 12, 1992.

DisneyFest SEE DISNEY FAIR.

DisneyHand Brand used from fall 2001–summer 2005 for the worldwide outreach of The Walt Disney Company, which is dedicated to making the dreams of families and children a reality through public service initiatives, community outreach, and volunteerism in areas of learning, compassion, the arts, and the environment.

DisneyHand Teacher Awards SEE AMERICAN TEACHER AWARDS.

Disneykins SEE MARX, LOUIS, AND CO.

Disneyland A new concept in family entertainment, the first Disney park, representing an investment of $17 million, opened in Anaheim to an invited audience Jul. 17, 1955, and to the public the next day. Walt Disney had enjoyed taking his 2 daughters to carnivals, zoos, and small amusement parks when they were young, but he found that he was sitting on the bench eating peanuts while they rode the merry-go-round and had all the fun. He wondered why a place could not be built where parents and children could go have fun together. Eventually he put some designers on his own personal payroll and began coming up with some concepts. He first thought was of building his park on a strip of land across Riverside Drive from the Disney Studio in Burbank, but when that space proved too small to hold all of his ideas, he hired the Stanford Research Institute (SRI) to survey the possibilities for a site. SRI identified the site in Anaheim, which was covered with orange groves and made up of parcels owned by 17 different people. By borrowing on his life insurance, selling his vacation home, and getting money from several companies, Walt was able to purchase an initial 160 acres and build Disneyland. It opened with an elaborate live-TV special, but people were already primed to see it. Walt had used episodes of the weekly evening TV show of the same name to present tantalizing glimpses of what the park would be like. After its opening, guests flocked to see what Walt had built. The first guests through the turnstiles were Christine Vess and her cousin Michael Schwartner, ages 5 and 7. The fame of Disneyland spread, and soon it was on the must-see lists for not only Americans, but also visitors from all over the world. Dedicated to "the ideals, the dreams, and the hard facts that have created America," the park was originally comprised of 5 themed lands surrounding a Central Plaza: Main Street, U.S.A.; Adventureland; Frontierland; Fantasyland; and Tomorrowland. Unlike his films,

Walt felt that Disneyland was something he could keep developing and adding to over time, saying at the opening, "Disneyland will never be completed. It will continue to grow as long as there is imagination left in the world." For nearly 7 decades now, Disneyland has continued to grow, with new lands added: New Orleans Square (1966), Bear Country (1972; became Critter Country in 1988), Mickey's Toontown (1993), and Star Wars: Galaxy's Edge (2019). New attractions have been added, as well, sometimes carving out new space and sometimes replacing ones that had become dated or inefficient. Parades, celebrity guests, celebrations, and other events provide additional incentives for the local populace to make return visits. As soon as Disneyland became a success, people throughout the world wanted Walt Disney to build a Disneyland in their town, but he bided his time until he had the park running smoothly. Only then did he start to listen to some of the entreaties, and his planning eventually led to his announcement of the Walt Disney World project in Florida shortly before his death. Disneyland was the first of its kind. Other companies have attempted to re-create the park since, but there will never be another like it. It is unique and continues to set the industry standard.

On opening day, these were the attractions:

1. King Arthur Carrousel
2. Peter Pan's Flight
3. Mad Tea Party
4. Mr. Toad's Wild Ride
5. Canal Boats of the World
6. Snow White's Adventures
7. Autopia
8. Space Station X-1
9. Santa Fe and Disneyland Railroad
10. Circarama
11. Horse-drawn Streetcars
12. Fire Wagon
13. Main Street Cinema
14. Surreys
15. Jungle Cruise
16. Stage Coach
17. Mule Pack
18. *Mark Twain* Riverboat
19. Penny Arcade
20. *Golden Horseshoe Revue*

Disneyland has welcomed millions of guests through the years, with the following record-breaking milestones:

1 millionth guest, 9/8/1955: Elsa Marquez
10 millionth guest, 12/31/1957: Leigh Woolfenden
25 millionth guest, 4/19/1961: Dr. Glenn C. Franklin
50 millionth guest, 8/12/1965: Mary Adams
100 millionth guest, 6/17/1971: Valerie Suldo
200 millionth guest, 1/8/1981: Gert Schelvis
250 millionth guest, 8/24/1985: Brooks Charles Arthur Burr
300 millionth guest, 9/1/1989: Claudine Masson
400 millionth guest, 7/5/1997: Minnie Pepito
450 millionth guest, 3/15/2001: Mark Ramirez
500 millionth guest, 1/8/2004: Bill Trow

The 2 billionth guest to visit a Disney park was 12-year-old Emmalee Mason of Colorado Springs, Colorado, who arrived at Disneyland on May 2, 2006.

Disneyland (TV) Anthology series on ABC hosted by Walt Disney; aired on Wednesday nights, Oct. 27, 1954–Sep. 3, 1958. It won the Emmy for Best Variety Series during its first season and another award the following year for Walt Disney as Best Producer of a Filmed Series. Each week's show was based on one of the themed realms of Disneyland, the park, which the series also served to promote. The weekly series continued with a new name, *Walt Disney Presents*, beginning Sep. 12, 1958. SEE ALSO TELEVISION.

Disneyland After Dark (TV) Show aired Apr. 15, 1962. Directed by Hamilton S. Luske and William Beaudine. Walt Disney takes the audience for a tour of Disneyland "when the lights go on." He presents a look at nighttime entertainment, with Louis Armstrong, Kid Ory, Johnny St. Cyr, Bobby Rydell, Annette Funicello, Bobby Burgess, Monette Moore, and the Osmond brothers (in their network TV premiere). A colorful fireworks display and audience participation songs at Plaza Gardens wind up the visit to the park at night. Released theatrically abroad.

Disneyland-Alweg Monorail System SEE MONORAIL.

Disneyland Around the Seasons (TV) Show aired Dec. 18, 1966. Directed by Hamilton S. Luske. The openings of the It's a Small World attraction and New Orleans Square are shown, with Walt providing information on the planning of Great Moments with Mr. Lincoln, Pirates of the Caribbean, and the Primeval World diorama, followed by a performance of the Christmas *Fantasy on Parade*. The show served as a tribute to Walt Disney, airing 3 days after his death.

Disneyland Band When Walt Disney wanted a band for opening day at the park, he asked British bandmaster Vesey Walker to assemble one. The band was hired only for a 2-week engagement, but it became so popular that it was held over and still performs at the park today. The band ranges from about 15–20 members and has been directed by Walker, James Christensen, Jim Barngrover, Stanford Freese, Dave Warble, Art Dragon, and Kurt Curtis. In Jul. 1982, the band celebrated its 50,000th performance. The band has performed in parades and concerts in various areas around the park, with a repertoire that includes marches, polkas, jazz, and waltzes, with perhaps the most-requested tune being the "Mickey Mouse Club March." The band has also performed in educational concerts for young people throughout Orange County, California. For Disneyland's 60th anniversary in 2015, the band was refreshed, playing with a new musical sound and high-energy choreography.

Disneyland Blast to the Past (TV) Syn. special; aired on KHJ-TV in Los Angeles on May 20, 1989. Directed by C. F. Bien and starring Jon "Bowzer" Bauman, Brian Beirne, and Little Anthony. 60 min. SEE ALSO BLAST TO THE PAST.

Disneyland Dream (film) Home movies of the Connecticut family of Robbins and Meg Barstow, along with their children Mary, David, and Daniel, from 1956, detailing a trip they won to Disneyland and other nearby sites through a contest sponsored by 3M Company. The films were edited and narration was added in 1995. 30 min. The home movie was selected for the 2009 Library of Congress National Film Registry, which stated, "Home movies have assumed a rapidly increasing importance in American cultural studies as they provide a priceless and authentic record of time and place."

Disneyland Dream Suite A 2,600-sq.-ft. suite above Pirates of the Caribbean in New Orleans Square in Disneyland; opened Jan. 31, 2008, as part of the Disney Dreams Giveaway during The Year of a Million Dreams. Later, the exclusive suite was awarded as a special prize for certain sweepstakes and events. Replacing The Disney Gallery, the space features a living room in French Provincial style, an open-air, Bayou-themed patio, and 2 master bedrooms—one representing the spirit of the American frontier and early 20th-century innovation, and the other evoking the flavor of jungle adventure stories as told in the Victorian era. Special décor pays tribute to the many inspirations for Disneyland, and special effects help bring the rooms to life. Art director Kim Irvine closely followed renderings designed by Dorothea Redmond when the space was originally conceived as a suite for Walt and Lillian Disney. SEE ALSO DISNEY GALLERY, THE.

Disneyland '59 (TV) Live 90-min. special sponsored by Kodak, introducing the Submarine Voyage, Matterhorn, Monorail, Motor Boat Cruise, and an enlarged Autopia. Aired on Jun. 15, 1959.

Disneyland—from the Pirates of the Caribbean to the World of Tomorrow (TV) Show aired Jan. 21, 1968. Directed by Hamilton S. Luske. The audience visits WED Enterprises and sees how Disneyland attractions are created, including Pirates and the new Tomorrowland. Hosted by Disneyland ambassador Marcia Miner.

Disneyland Goes to the World's Fair (TV) Show aired May 17, 1964. Directed by Hamilton S. Luske. A look at the history of world's fairs, followed by a preview of Disney attractions at the 1964–1965 New York World's Fair. Walt explains Audio-Animatronics technology, the new Disney process that helps bring characters to three-dimensional life.

Disneyland Hotel When Walt Disney built Disneyland in 1955, he did not have enough capital to build a hotel, too, but he reasoned that such a hotel would be very successful next to the park. So, he persuaded his friend Jack Wrather to build the hotel on Disney-owned land just across West Street from the park; the first rooms opened to guests Oct. 5, 1955. The Wrather Corporation expanded their hotel through the years, until it eventually had 3 towers (Bonita, Marina, and Sierra), but after Walt's death, the Disney company began making overtures to purchase the hotel. For one thing, it seemed unusual having the Disney name on a hotel that the Disney company did not own. In 1988, Disney purchased the entire Wrather Corporation, acquiring not only the Disneyland Hotel, but the lease to operate the *Queen Mary* in Long Beach, California. The hotel has the advantage of being attached to Disneyland by the Monorail; guests embarking at the hotel are whisked directly into the station in Tomorrowland inside the park. This Monorail line connecting the hotel to Disneyland was the first time a monorail had been built over a city street. The hotel has a large convention space (opened in 1972); outdoor activities, including 3 swimming pools; and a selection of restaurants from Goofy's Kitchen to the upscale Steakhouse 55. The 3 towers were renamed Magic, Dreams, and Wonder on Aug. 13, 2007. In 2009, the hotel began an extensive renovation, with a new theme paying tribute to the early days of the park; accordingly, the towers were renamed Adventure (2010), Frontier (2011), and Fantasy (2012), and the pool areas were replaced by the E-Ticket and D-Ticket Pools, incorporating nostalgic Disneyland iconography and waterslides in the shape of Mark I Monorail trains. In addition, 2011 also saw the opening of the Tangaroa Terrace restaurant and Trader Sam's Enchanted Tiki Bar. A fourth tower, The Villas at Disneyland Hotel, is scheduled to open Sep. 2023, adding 344 rooms to the resort's existing 973 guest rooms. This new, 12-story Disney Vacation Club property will feature designs and themes that blend Disney animated classics with contemporary aesthetics. SEE ALSO NEVER LAND POOL.

Disneyland Hotel Victorian-style hotel at Disneyland Paris; opened Apr. 12, 1992, as the first Disney resort integrated into a park entrance. The Imagineers originally envisioned the hotel as a traditional façade on Main Street, U.S.A., but Michael Eisner suggested making it a real, operating hotel. Dining is available at Inventions (buffet and character dining), California Grill (gourmet table service), and Café Fantasia (piano bar), with shopping at Galerie Mickey. There is also the Minnie Club playroom for children, the Celestial Spa, a pool, and fitness center. In Aug. 2021, a major refurbishment was announced to introduce a new royal theme, with reimagined public areas and guest rooms and suites inspired by Disney fairy-tale stories, including *Tangled, Beauty and the Beast, Cinderella,* and *Frozen*; the hotel is scheduled to reopen in 2024.

Disneyland Is Your Land Stage show at Disneyland beginning Mar. 23, 1985. The Kids of the Kingdom presented a musical salute to the park. An earlier version was performed during the 25th anniversary celebrations in 1980.

Disneyland Line Internal news publication for park Cast Members, 1969–2020; renamed the *Disneyland Resort Line* in 1999. It was preceded by the *Disneyland Recreation Club News* (1956) and *The Disneylander* (1957).

Disneyland Pacific Hotel The Walt Disney Company purchased this 502-room hotel located next door to the Disneyland Hotel—built in 1984 and formerly known as the Emerald and the Pan Pacific—from a Japanese company in Dec. 1995. Walkways and a park between the 2 hotels were finished on Mar. 22, 1996, completing the integration of the 2 facilities. Featured restaurants were Disney's PCH Grill (opened May 23, 1997, replacing Summertree) and Yamabuki, with shopping at The Disney Touch. It was renamed Disney's Paradise Pier Hotel in Oct. 2000, and another transformation, to the Pixar Place Hotel, was announced in 2022.

Disneyland Paris First Disney resort in Europe; opened with the original name of Euro Disney (the park itself was known as Euro Disneyland) Apr. 12, 1992. The Disneyland Paris name became official Oct. 1, 1994. Disney park planners had begun searching for a suitable European site for a park in the early 1980s. Eventually, 2 sites were selected as being ideal—one near Barcelona, Spain, and one near Paris. After years of studies and negotiations, the decision was made by Michael Eisner and Frank Wells to locate the park in France, at Marne-la-Vallée. After several years of construction, the park, Festival Disney (an area for shopping, dining, and nighttime entertainment, later renamed Disney Village), and a group of themed hotels opened. The original resort hotels were the Disneyland Hotel, Hotel Cheyenne, Hotel New York (later Disney Hotel New York – The Art of Marvel), Hotel Santa Fe, Newport Bay Club, Sequoia Lodge, and Camp Davy Crockett (later Davy Crockett Ranch). The resort also debuted with Golf Euro Disney (later known as Golf Disneyland Paris and Golf Disneyland) and Marne-la-Vallée–Chessy station. The park has a basic layout similar to Disneyland, with the major change being a substitution of Discoveryland for Tomorrowland. The Imagineers wanted to capture the intimacy and charm of Disneyland but provide the scale of Walt Disney World; exec. producer Tony Baxter coined a phrase that guided the design process—"a 40-foot path can be two 20-foot paths"—meaning, when the park is not crowded, there are two pleasant strolls rather than a giant wide space. Disneyland Paris is said by many to be the most beautiful of all the Disney parks, and it certainly introduced the latest technology in attractions and ideas in master planning and architecture. The park proceeded to attract almost 11 million visitors during its first year, making it the most popular tourist attraction in Europe. But because of unsatisfactory economic conditions, and the need to pay significant interest payments on the debt needed for construction, Disneyland Paris lost money in its first years. With a financial reorganization in 1994, the park's management hoped for an eventual turnaround, and they were confident that the park would eventually be a financial as well as a critical success. Profits were reported in 1995. A decade later, even though very popular with guests, the park still was having financial problems, necessitating concessions from banks holding its debt. With the addition of Walt Disney Studios Park in 2002, the resort name changed to Disneyland Resort Paris, then reverted back to Disneyland Paris May 2, 2009. In 2017, Disney bought out the resort's other investors to become the sole owner of Disneyland Paris. Val d'Europe, a town and shopping center, opened next to the resort Oct. 25, 2000, and Villages Nature Paris, an ecotourism complex, debuted Oct. 10, 2017, in the nearby commune of Bailly-Romainvilliers. The 100 millionth visitor (Stefan Seyffardt and family) was welcomed Jan. 10, 2001; Gérald Yernaux, with his family, became the 200 millionth visitor Aug. 12, 2008; and Beatrix Olivia, with her family, became the 250 millionth visitor in Nov. 2011.

Disneyland Presents a Preview of Coming Attractions Display on Main Street, U.S.A. in Disneyland; opened 1973, and renamed Disneyland Showcase in 1984. The location was originally home to the Wurlitzer shop. It took the place of Walt Disney—A Legacy for the Future when many of the awards in that exhibit were moved into The Walt Disney Story attractions at Disneyland and Magic Kingdom at Walt Disney World. Models, artists' renderings, and designs of attractions being planned were displayed. Closed Jul. 22, 1989, to become Disney Showcase, a merchandise shop.

Disneyland Presents Tales of Toontown (TV) A 60-min. syn. special; aired Jul. 10, 1993. In searching for a mischievous culprit who is mysteriously causing everything to go wacky in Toontown, Goofy enlists his human friend Spence Dempsey to discover the cause of all the crazy goings-on. Directed by Bruce Stuart Greenberg.

Disneyland Railroad Disneyland attraction that encircles the park; originally the Santa Fe and Disneyland Railroad (1955–1974), it changed to the new name Oct. 1, 1974. The original 2 locomotives, the *E. P. Ripley* and the *C. K. Holliday* were constructed at the Disney Studio and are named for pioneers of the Santa Fe Railroad. Because of the popularity of the trains, there was a need for more locomotives, so another was added in 1958, the *Fred G. Gurley*, which was named after the then-chairman of the railroad. Rather than build the new locomotive from scratch, the Disney designers found an old Baldwin locomotive built in 1894 which had been used to haul sugarcane in Louisiana. It was completely rebuilt for service at Disneyland. A 4th locomotive was located the following year and named for the Santa Fe Railway president, *Ernest S. Marsh*. It was a somewhat newer model, built in 1925 and used in New England at a lumber mill. All trains are now open air, to afford the best views of the Disneyland scenery and the 2 dioramas—the Grand Canyon (added Mar. 31, 1958) and Primeval World (added Jul. 1, 1966)—through which the trains pass. Originally, there was an enclosed passenger train, but the windows were too small to enable all guests to see the sights. The old passenger train was stored for many years in the back of the Disneyland roundhouse. There was also once a freight train on which guests rode like cattle in cattle cars; the novelty of that wore off quickly. Original stations were on Main Street, U.S.A. and in Frontierland. A Fantasyland station was added in 1956 and a Tomorrowland station opened in 1958. The Fantasyland station became the Videopolis station in 1988, and the Toontown station followed in 1992. A 5th locomotive, the *Ward Kimball*, was put into service Jun. 25, 2005, and dedicated Feb. 15, 2006, as part of the Disneyland 50th anniversary celebration; it was often operated by Kimball's grandson, Nate Lord, who was a steam train engineer at the park. Walt Disney was so fascinated with trains, he built a 1/8-scale-model railroad called the Carolwood Pacific Railroad in the backyard of his Holmby Hills home. He was adamant that a train be a major part of the Disneyland experience. Many guests use it to get an overall view of the park before they venture out to the other attractions. During the years that Disneyland used tickets for the attractions, the railroad ticket was a long strip with coupons to be punched by the conductor, similar to those used in real railroads of the period. SEE ALSO LILLY BELLE, EURO DISNEYLAND RAILROAD (DISNEYLAND PARIS), HONG KONG DISNEYLAND RAILROAD, WALT DISNEY WORLD RAILROAD, AND WESTERN RIVER RAILROAD (TOKYO DISNEYLAND).

Disneyland Resort General name for the Disney complex in Anaheim, including Disneyland, Disney California Adventure, the Disneyland Hotel, Disney's Grand Californian Hotel & Spa, Disney's Paradise Pier Hotel (to become the Pixar Place Hotel), and the Downtown Disney District.

Disneyland Resort Backlot Premiere Shop Shop inside Stage 17 at Disney California Adventure; opened Oct. 6, 2020, as part of the Downtown Disney District while the park was closed due to the COVD-19 pandemic. Became Super Store Featuring Avengers Campus Mar. 2022.

Disneyland Showcase SEE DISNEYLAND PRESENTS A PREVIEW OF COMING ATTRACTIONS.

Disneyland Showtime (TV) Show aired Mar. 22, 1970. Directed by Gordon Wiles. Performers visit Disneyland for the opening of the Haunted Mansion. When Donny Osmond gets lost, everyone goes searching, which offers the opportunity for a tour of the park. Kurt Russell narrates a look at the work that went into making the Haunted Mansion. Stars the Osmond brothers, Kurt Russell, and E. J. Peaker.

Disneyland 60: The Wonderful World of Disney (TV) A 2-hour special on ABC; aired Feb. 21, 2016, celebrating the 60th anniversary of Disneyland. Narrators speak of Walt Disney's inspiration for the park and the creativity and inventiveness that made it a success. Entertainment is provided by singers and the Los Angeles Philharmonic orchestra. Directed by Louis J. Horvitz. Stars include Idina Menzel, Derek Hough, Helen Mirren, Dick Van Dyke, Alfonso Ribeiro, Harrison Ford, Jason Bateman, Hilary Duff, John Stamos, Neil Patrick Harris, Viola Davis, Elton John. Recorded at Disneyland and at the Dolby Theatre in Hollywood.

Disneyland '61/Olympic Elk (TV) Show aired May 28, 1961. Directed by Hamilton S. Luske. Features an enlarged version of the theatrical featurette *Gala Day at Disneyland*, with Walt Disney showcasing the new Nature's Wonderland and an upcoming expansion of the Monorail. The show concludes with the True-Life Adventure featurette *The Olympic Elk*.

Disneyland Story, The (TV) Opening show of the *Disneyland* series; aired on ABC Oct. 27, 1954. Directed by Robert Florey. Walt Disney leads a tour of the Studio and uses artwork and models to introduce Disneyland park, then under construction. He then previews the shows that will run during the upcoming season, followed by a look at Mickey's career in *Tribute to Mickey Mouse*. Also known as *What Is Disneyland?*

Disneyland Story Presenting Great Moments with Mr. Lincoln, The Artwork and models chronicle the history of the park in The Disneyland Story, followed by an updated version of Great Moments with Mr. Lincoln; opened Dec. 18, 2009, replacing Disneyland: The First 50 Magical Years. The Disney Gallery was added in 2013. SEE GREAT MOMENTS WITH MR. LINCOLN.

Disneyland Tenth Anniversary Show, The (TV) Show aired Jan. 3, 1965. Directed by Hamilton S. Luske. The young lady who was to be the first of a long line of Disneyland ambassadors, Julie Reihm, then called "Miss Disneyland," joins Walt to look at some of the new attractions coming to the park, including Pirates of the Caribbean and the Haunted Mansion. Then there is a party at Disneyland for the Tencennial, followed by a look back over the park's development over the years, including a tour behind-the-scenes at Walt Disney's Enchanted Tiki Room. Celebrities at the park include Hayley Mills and John Mills, Louis Armstrong, and the Firehouse Five Plus Two.

Disneyland: The First 50 Magical Years Opera House exhibit on Main Street, U.S.A. in Disneyland; opened May 5, 2005, in celebration of the park's 50th anniversary. There were displays of concept artwork and models; ticket books and name tags; a large-scale model of Disneyland as it appeared on opening day; and a 17-min. humorous film look at the 50 years with Steve Martin (who as a young man worked at Disneyland in the Magic Shop) and Donald Duck. The attraction closed Mar. 15, 2009, to become The Disneyland Story Presenting Great Moments with Mr. Lincoln.

Disneyland the Park/Pecos Bill (TV) Show aired Apr. 3, 1957. Directed by Hamilton S. Luske and Clyde Geronimi. Walt Disney leads a tour by helicopter to Disneyland, with aerial views and visits to several of the attractions. The Mouseketeers are glimpsed on a visit there. The show concludes with *Pecos Bill* (a segment from *Melody Time*).

Disneyland, U.S.A. (film) People and Places featurette released Dec. 20, 1956. Directed by Hamilton S. Luske. Filmed in CinemaScope.

42 min. After an aerial view of Disneyland and a visit to the Disneyland Hotel, it is on through the entrance gates of the park for a tour of each of the 4 lands, as well as Main Street, U.S.A. and glimpses of annual parades and holiday festivities.

DisneylandForward On Mar. 25, 2021, the Disneyland Resort filed an application with the city of Anaheim to begin laying the groundwork for the resort's future development and expansion through this multi-year public planning effort.

Disneyland's All-Star Comedy Circus (TV) Show aired Dec. 11, 1988. Directed by Stan Harris. Several NBC series stars perform at Disneyland and introduce various circus acts. Stars Rue McClanahan, Christopher Daniel Barnes, Kim Fields, Danny Ponce.

Disneyland's Summer Vacation Party (TV) Two-hour NBC special featuring contemporary recording artists; aired May 23, 1986. Directed by Marty Pasetta. Stars Mindy Cohn, Kim Fields, Scott Valentine, and Malcolm-Jamal Warner, who host a long list of entertainers.

Disneyland's 30th Anniversary Celebration (TV) Two-hour special broadcast on NBC Feb. 18, 1985. Directed by Marty Pasetta. Stars John Forsythe, Drew Barrymore, and a host of entertainers.

Disneyland's 35th Anniversary Celebration (TV) Show aired Feb. 4, 1990. Directed by John Landis. Stars Tony Danza, Charles Fleischer, Jim Varney, the Muppets, Chris Demetral. Returning for the rededication are the 3 original TV hosts—Art Linkletter, Bob Cummings, and Ronald Reagan—and the first 2 kids to enter the park on opening day: Christine Vess and Michael Schwartner.

Disneyland's 25th Anniversary (TV) SEE KRAFT SALUTES: DISNEYLAND'S 25TH ANNIVERSARY.

DisneyLife Disney's first subscription-based international streaming service; launched Nov. 23, 2015, in the U.K. and later available in Ireland, the Philippines, and other countries. A selection of films, shows, soundtracks, and books were offered. The service was discontinued Apr. 23, 2020. A new streaming service, Disney+, launched in the U.K. Mar. 24, 2020, after its debut in the U.S. Nov. 12, 2019.

Disneynature A production banner announced Apr. 21, 2008, to produce nature documentaries for theatrical release. The unit was formed by Jean-Francois Camilleri and based in France. The first release, *The Crimson Wing: Mystery of the Flamingos*, debuted in France Dec. 17, 2008. In the U.S., the theatrical releases have included *Earth* (2009), *Oceans* (2010), *African Cats* (2011), *Chimpanzee* (2012), *Wings of Life* (2013), *Bears* (2014), *Monkey Kingdom* (2015), *Born in China* (2017), and *Penguins* (2019). *Dolphin Reef* and *Elephant* were released digitally in 2020 on Disney+, followed by *Polar Bear* in 2022. Behind-the-scenes documentaries chronicling the making of the films have also been released digitally, including *Growing Up Wild*, *Ghost of the Mountains*, *Expedition China*, *Penguins: Life on the Edge*, *Diving with Dolphins*, and *In the Footsteps of Elephant*. As a key pillar of Disneynature, the productions support the conservation of wildlife featured in the films. SEE ALSO TRUE-LIFE ADVENTURES.

DisneyNOW App providing access to TV shows, live streaming, and other content from Disney Channel, Disney XD, Disney Junior, and Radio Disney. Launched Sep. 28, 2017.

DisneyQuest High-tech indoor recreation site designed for families and children to spend 2–3 hours playing computer-based, virtual reality, and Internet games; opened Jun. 19, 1998, in Downtown Disney West Side at Walt Disney World. Inside the 100,000-sq.-ft. venue, 4 interactive areas were offered: the Explore Zone, Score Zone, Create Zone, and Replay Zone. Highlights included the Virtual Jungle Cruise, Mighty Ducks Pinball Slam, CyberSpace Mountain, and Buzz Lightyear's AstroBlaster. Dining was available at FoodQuest and the Wonderland Café (both presented by The Cheesecake Factory Express until May 2008). A 2nd DisneyQuest opened in Chicago Jun. 16, 1999, and closed Sep. 4, 2001. Plans for additional DisneyQuest facilities in such cities as Philadelphia and Toronto were then shelved. The Walt Disney World location closed Jul. 3, 2017, to make way for the NBA Experience.

Disney's The word *Disney's* is part of the official name of most of the Disney resort hotels. But in this book, the resorts are sometimes listed under their individual names. For example, it's Contemporary Resort, rather than Disney's Contemporary Resort. The word *Disney's* has also been omitted from some film titles.

Disney's Adventures in Wonderland (TV) Series on The Disney Channel; premiered Mar. 23, 1992, and in syn. beginning Sep. 6, 1993. It ended Sep. 10, 1995. The story builds on Lewis Carroll's literary richness and linguistic fun in a contemporary setting. Alice visits her wild and zany friends by stepping through her looking glass into a world of music, fantasy, and fun. Stars Elisabeth Harnois (Alice), John Robert Hoffman (Mad Hatter), Armelia McQueen (Red Queen), Reece Holland (March Hare). Originally produced at the Disney-MGM Studios at Walt Disney World, the show won an Emmy Award for Hairdressing in 1992, and 2 more for Writing and Makeup in 1994.

Disney's Adventures of the Gummi Bears (TV) See Adventures of the Gummi Bears, Disney's.

Disney's Aladdin See Aladdin (TV series).

Disney's All-American Sports Nuts (TV) Special on NBC; aired Oct. 16, 1988. Clips from Disney films are combined with real sports footage. Directed by Chep Dobrin. Stars David Leisure, John Matuszak, Susan Ruttan, Martin Mull, Brian Boitano, Bruce Jenner.

Disney's All-Star 4th of July Spectacular See Celebrate the Spirit!

Disney's All-Star Mother's Day Album (TV) Special on CBS; aired May 9, 1984. Includes clips of cartoons about mothers.

Disney's All-Star Valentine Party (TV) Special on CBS; aired Feb. 14, 1984. Includes Disney cartoons on the subject of love.

Disney's America History-themed park announced in 1993, to be built in Prince William County near Haymarket, Virginia. Guests would be able to experience distinct periods in American history. The park would bring history to life, examining the conflicts and successes that have marked the nation's passage from colony to world power. While state officials and local residents were generally in favor of the project, there was intense opposition from a group of historians and environmentalists who complained about its proximity to the Manassas Civil War battlefield. On Sep. 28, 1994, Disney announced that a different site would be sought, but no further work was done on the project.

Disney's Animal Kingdom See Animal Kingdom, Disney's.

Disney's Animal Kingdom: The First Adventure (TV) One-hour special on *The Wonderful World of Disney*; first aired Apr. 26, 1998, giving viewers a first look at the new animal park, which officially opened 4 days earlier. Directed by David Straiton and Joan Tosoni. Stars Tia, Tamara, Tahj, and Tavior Mowry; Will Friedle; Danielle Fishel; Paul Rodriguez; Dr. Jane Goodall. There's music by George Clinton, Lebo M, and Ladysmith Black Mambazo.

Disney's Animals, Science and Environment Team of education, scientific, nutrition, veterinary, and behavioral professionals who lead programs at Disney parks and resorts to care for animals, connect people to nature, and conserve natural resources.

Disney's Animated Alphabet (film) Educational film; released in Aug. 1988. 13 min. Letters of the alphabet come to life to teach the ABCs to young children.

Disney's Blast Online Introduced in 1997 as Disney's Daily Blast, this club by Disney Online offered interactive and educational games for kids and families. In 2007, it became Disney Game Kingdom Online. Memberships ended Aug. 25, 2011.

Disney's California Adventure See California Adventure, Disney.

Disney's Captain EO Grand Opening (TV) Hourlong special on NBC; aired Sep. 20, 1986. Directed by Marty Pasetta. Patrick Duffy hosts a look at the new 3-D film at Disneyland. Stars Justine Bateman, Belinda Carlisle, The Moody Blues.

Disney's Champions on Ice (TV) Special on ABC; aired Mar. 9, 1996. Videotaped on location at Sun Valley, Idaho. Directed by Paul Miller. Features Scott Hamilton, Nicole Bobek, Surya Bonaly, Ekaterina Gordeeva, Sergei Grinkov, Elvis Stojko.

Disney's Christmas Fantasy on Ice (TV) Special (60 min.) on CBS; first aired Dec. 19, 1992. Directed by Paul Miller.

Disney's Christmas on Ice (TV) Special on CBS; aired Dec. 21, 1990. 60 min. Directed by Don Ohlmeyer. In Squaw Valley (now known as Olympic Valley), California, Disney characters perform with ice-skating stars. Stars Peggy Fleming, Tai Babilonia, Randy Gardner, Gary Beacom, Judy Blumberg, Scott Hamilton, The Party, Katarina Witt.

Disney's Countdown (film) Educational film about having fun counting numbers forward and backward; released in Nov. 1988. 12 min.

Disney's Countdown to Kid's Day (TV) Special on NBC; aired Nov. 21, 1993. A lineup of singers, comedians, and TV performers—including Gloria Estefan, Celine Dion, Joey Lawrence, and Sinbad—gather at the 4 worldwide Disney parks to salute children with special entertainment and focus on real-life issues facing the world's youth. 60 min.

Disney's Days of Christmas Holiday shop in the Marketplace at Disney Springs (previously Downtown Disney Marketplace); opened Nov. 1997 in the space previously used by Team Mickey's Athletic Club. The previous holiday shop in the village was the Christmas Chalet, which opened Sep. 1980, taking the place of Buena Vista Interiors. It later expanded into the Pottery Chalet, then relocated in 1996, succeeding the Discover shop, and closed Jan. 5, 1997, replaced by Disney at Home.

Disney's Doug SEE BRAND SPANKING NEW DOUG AND DOUG'S 1ST MOVIE.

Disney's Doug Live Musical stage show in the ABC TV Theater at Disney-MGM Studios; ran Mar. 15, 1999–May 12, 2001, replacing *SuperStar Television*. The 12-year-old Doug Funnie wins tickets to see his favorite band, The Beets, and tries to muster enough courage to ask his secret crush, Patti, to go with him. Based on the popular animated TV series, it premiered in conjunction with *Doug's 1st Movie*.

Disney's DTV Doggone Valentine (TV) Special on NBC; aired Feb. 13, 1987. 60 min. Directed by Andrew Solt. Ludwig Von Drake, Jiminy Cricket, and Mickey Mouse host a show featuring popular songs showcased with Disney animation in MTV style.

Disney's DTV Monster Hits (TV) Hour-long special on NBC; aired Nov. 27, 1987. Directed by Andrew Solt. More popular songs, with a Halloween twist, set to Disney animation, hosted by the Magic Mirror (played by Jeffrey Jones).

Disney's DTV Romancin' (TV) New title for *Disney's DTV Valentine*; aired on NBC Sep. 7, 1986. 60 min.

Disney's DTV Valentine (TV) One-hour special on NBC; aired Feb. 14, 1986. Directed by Andrew Solt. Romantic songs set to Disney animation. A Sep. 7 rerun was titled *Disney's DTV Romancin'*.

Disney's Fairy Tale Weddings (TV) Special on Freeform; first aired May 7, 2017. Hosts Ben Higgins and Lauren Bushnell go behind the scenes of 3 Disney weddings (at Disneyland, Castaway Cay, and EPCOT) and one special marriage proposal at Disney's Animal Kingdom. 90 min. A later special, *Disney's Fairy Tale Weddings: Holiday Magic*, hosted by Allison Holker and Stephen "tWitch" Boss, aired Dec. 11, 2017. Holker and Boss returned to host 6 hour-long documentaries, which aired Jun. 11–Jul. 16, 2018. A new series premiered digitally Feb. 14, 2020, on Disney+, with new couples, musical performances, and celebrations at Disney destinations around the globe. Produced by T Group, Roberts Media, and Legacy Productions for Freeform.

Disney's Fillmore (TV) SEE FILLMORE, DISNEY'S.

Disney's Fluppy Dogs (TV) Animated special on ABC; aired Nov. 27, 1986. Five magical, talking Fluppy dogs from another dimension—Stanley, Tippi, Bink, Ozzie, and Dink—wind up on Earth and enter the lives of 10-year-old Jamie and his snobbish teenage neighbor, Claire, who help them search for their way back home. 60 min. Directed by Fred Wolf. Voices include Marshall Efron (Stanley), Carl Stevens (Jamie Bingham), Cloyce Morrow (Mrs. Bingham), Hal Smith (Dink/Haimish), Lorenzo Music (Ozzie), Jessica Pennington (Claire), Susan Blu (Bink/Tippi). From Disney Television Animation.

Disney's Friends for Change Multi-platform program that encourages kids, friends, and families to join together and create lasting positive changes in the world; began in 2009. Participants create an online account where they pledge to make changes in everyday life and report on their progress. Disney Channel stars serve as ambassadors, and grants are offered to youth-led projects. A 5-week competition, Disney's Friends for Change Games, premiered on Disney Channel Jun. 24, 2011, with Disney Channel and Disney XD stars competing in physical challenges on behalf of charities, ending with a special on Jul. 31.

Disney's Golden Anniversary of Snow White and the Seven Dwarfs (TV) Special; aired on NBC May 22, 1987. Directed by Louis J. Horvitz. A look at the history of the landmark animated film, with Dick Van Dyke, Jane Curtin, Sherman Hemsley, Linda Ronstadt.

Disney's Great American Celebration (TV) Special on CBS; aired Jul. 4, 1991. Directed by Michael Dimich. Entertainers at Disneyland and Walt Disney World celebrate the holiday. Stars Robert Guillaume, Barbara Mandrell, Sheena Easton, Tim Allen, The Party, Steven Banks. 120 min.

Disney's Great Ice Odyssey Title of the 2nd Disney ice show, which premiered Jul. 20, 1982. The original show was Disney's World on Ice. Mickey, Donald, and Prince Charming battle the Evil Queen, who has captured Minnie, Daisy, Cinderella, and Goofy.

Disney's Greatest Dog Stars (TV) Show aired Nov. 28, 1976. Dean Jones hosts a look at famous Disney dog stars, leading up to a preview of *The Shaggy D.A.* A 1980 rerun substituted a segment on *The Fox and the Hound* for the segment on *The Shaggy D.A.*

Disney's Greatest Hits on Ice (TV) Special on CBS; aired Nov. 25, 1994. The world's most celebrated skaters, including Ekaterina Gordeeva, Sergei Grinkov, Scott Hamilton, and Nancy Kerrigan, perform to the best-loved Disney songs and melodies. The show was taped on a soundstage at Paramount Studios, where an ice rink was built specially for the production. The set included a reproduction of the Team Disney Building and the fan-shaped gate at the Disney Studios. Directed by Steve Binder.

Disney's Greatest Villains (TV) Show aired May 15, 1977. The Magic Mirror is used to point out that every hero needs a villain, using clips from Disney cartoons and animated features.

Disney's Halloween Treat (TV) Show aired Oct. 30, 1982. Cartoons cover the Halloween theme.

Disney's Haunted Halloween (film) Educational film with Goofy about the origins of Halloween traditions; released in Sep. 1983.

Disney's Hercules SEE HERCULES (TV SERIES).

Disney's Hollywood Studios The third theme park to debut at Walt Disney World; opened May 1, 1989, as Disney-MGM Studios Theme Park. The name was later shortened to Disney-MGM Studios, and on Jan. 7, 2008, the park was renamed Disney's Hollywood Studios. Originally, the park was an operating movie and TV studio; the first filming was done there Feb. 2, 1988 (the TV movie *Splash, Too*). Walt Disney had originally envisioned a studio tour as part of the Disney Studio in California, but little land was available, and disruptions would interrupt filming. The idea was revived in the 1980s when Disney executives decided that a 3rd gated attraction on the Walt Disney World property would enhance the guests' vacation experience. Visitors enter on Hollywood Boulevard, where there are shops and restaurants designed after actual architecture of buildings from Hollywood's golden age. The park's centerpiece is a detailed reproduction of Grauman's Chinese Theatre, which has housed The Great Movie Ride (1989–2017) and Mickey & Minnie's Runaway Railway (beginning in 2020). From there, the park was originally divided into 2 parts: a theme park area, with attractions and live shows, and the Backstage Studio Tour, a 2-hour guided experience showcasing how movies and TV shows were produced. The park expanded in 1994 with the opening of Sunset Boulevard and its focal point, The Twilight Zone Tower of Terror. Over the years, other attractions and shows have been added and replaced, and the park has been organized into different areas, including Lakeside Circle (later Echo Lake), Mickey Avenue (later Pixar Place), New York Street (later Streets of America), and Animation Courtyard. Eventually, all of the working studio facilities closed, and the park evolved from a behind-the-scenes demonstration of how show business was done to one that takes visitors into the worlds of popular movies and TV shows. The transformation continued with the opening of Toy Story Land in 2018 (replacing much of the former production area) and Star Wars: Galaxy's Edge in 2019 (replacing Streets of America). Dining options range from the quick-service ABC Commissary to the elaborate Sci-Fi Dine-In Theater Restaurant and Hollywood Brown Derby.

Disney's Living Seas (TV) One-hour special on NBC; aired Jan. 24, 1986, showing the opening of The Living Seas in EPCOT Center. Directed by Ken Ehrlich. Stars John Ritter, Laura Branigan, Simon Le Bon, Olivia Newton-John.

Disney's Magic in the Magic Kingdom (TV)

Special on NBC; aired Feb. 12, 1988, featuring magic tricks and illusions in Disneyland, including the disappearance of Sleeping Beauty Castle. 60 min. Directed by Gary Halvorson. Stars George Burns, Harry Anderson, Gloria Estefan, Morgan Fairchild, Siegfried & Roy.

Disney's Mickey MouseWorks (TV) SEE MICKEY MOUSEWORKS.

Disney's Most Unlikely Heroes (TV) Half-hour special on ABC; aired Jun. 18, 1996. Directed by Dan Boothe. Movie and TV stars select their favorite Disney heroes, with a behind-the-scenes look at the making of *The Hunchback of Notre Dame*.

Disney's Nancy Kerrigan Special: Dreams on Ice (TV) One-hour special on CBS; aired Feb. 15, 1995. Nancy Kerrigan performs different roles in this show taped at Lake Placid, New York, and in Disney-MGM Studios at Walt Disney World. Also stars Scott Hamilton, Paul Wylie, Ekaterina Gordeeva and Sergei Grinkov, Paul Martini. Directed by Paul Miller.

Disney's One Too (TV) Two-hour block of cartoons; debuted on UPN Sep. 6, 1999, airing Sunday through Friday, and in syn. until Sep. 1, 2002. The series included *Sabrina, the Animated Series*; *Disney's Doug*; *Disney's Recess*; and *Disney's Hercules*.

Disney's Oscar Winners (TV) Show aired Apr. 13, 1980. Directed by William Reid. Covers some of the Disney Academy Award–winning films. Narrated by John Forsythe.

Disney's PB&J Otter (TV) SEE PB&J OTTER.

Disney's Phineas and Ferb: The Best LIVE Tour Ever! Premiered in Lakeland, Florida, on Aug. 21, 2011; featuring the characters from the Disney Channel series.

Disney's Pirates of the Caribbean Online Virtual multiplayer game; launched in 2007 and ended Sep. 19, 2013. Users could create their own pirate character, set sail on their own pirate ship, build a notorious crew, and master their pirate skills, exploring new myths and untold stories based on the Pirates of the Caribbean films.

Disney's Pocahontas: The Musical Tradition Continues (TV) Half-hour special on ABC; aired Jun. 20, 1995. Directed by John Jopson. Alan Menken

takes the viewer on a musical history tour of his contributions to recent Disney animated films. Features Regina Belle, Peabo Bryson, Celine Dion, Jon Secada, Shanice, Vanessa Williams.

Disney's Sing Along Songs SEE SING ALONG SONGS, DISNEY'S.

Disney's Sing Me a Story: with Belle (TV) Syn. series Sep. 9, 1995–Dec. 11, 1999. Belle invites a group of small children into her enchanting Book and Music Shop for a half hour of stories and songs promoting a special theme, utilizing Disney's classic cartoons. Stars Lynsey McLeod (Belle) and Tim Goodwin (Brioche).

Disney's Soda Fountain and Studio Store An old-fashioned soda fountain; opened next to the El Capitan Theatre in Hollywood Jun. 22, 2005, taking some of the space occupied by a Disney Store since 1998. It became a Ghirardelli Soda Fountain and Chocolate Shop Nov. 15, 2013, with a redesigned Disney Studio Store.

Disney's Sports Special (TV) Syn. look at Disney animated sport segments from 1986.

Disney's TaleSpin: Plunder & Lightning (TV) Syn. special; aired on Sep. 7, 1990, to introduce the new series.

Disney's The Kid (film) Russ Duritz finds his life as a successful "image consultant" turned upside down when he magically meets Rusty, himself as an 8-year-old child. Rusty is a sweet but slightly geeky kid who is not at all happy with who he turns out to be: a 40-year-old guy without a wife or a dog. Ironically, the kid helps Russ learn about himself and remember his dreams in order to become the grown-up he wants to be. Released Jul. 7, 2000. Directed by Jon Turteltaub. Stars Bruce Willis (Russ), Emily Mortimer (Amy), Spencer Breslin (Rusty), Lily Tomlin (Janet), Chi McBride (Kenny), Jean Smart (Deirdre). 104 min. Official title is *Disney's The Kid* because of title rights held by the Charlie Chaplin estate and to emphasize that this is a family film.

Disney's The Little Mermaid (TV) Animated series on CBS; aired Sep. 12, 1992–Sep. 2, 1995. A prequel to the 1989 animated film.

Disney's Timon & Pumbaa in Stand By Me (film) Cartoon released Dec. 22, 1995, with *Tom and Huck*. A frantic music video based on the popular song. Directed by Steve Moore. 3 min. Voices by Kevin Schoen (Timon) and Ernie Sabella (Pumbaa). 3 min.

Disney's Toontown Online Online virtual community, launched officially on Jun. 2, 2003, and ended Sep. 19, 2013. Users participated in a multiplayer quest in which they could create more than 50 million fun-craving Toons that helped defeat the "business robot" nemeses, named Cogs. A social networking component was also included.

Disney's Totally Minnie (TV) Special on NBC; aired Mar. 25, 1988. A clumsy nerd learns to be cool with help from Minnie, animation clips, and an all-new music video with Minnie and Elton John. 60 min. Directed by Scot Garen. Stars Suzanne Somers, Robert Carradine.

Disney's Wide World of Sports SEE ESPN WIDE WORLD OF SPORTS.

Disney's Wonderful World (TV) Title of Disney's long-running series on NBC; aired Sep. 9, 1979–Sep. 13, 1981.

Disney's Wonderful World of Memories Shop in the Marketplace at Disney Springs (previously Downtown Disney Marketplace); opened in 2002, replacing 2Rs Reading and Riting. Scrapbooking products, personalized hats, and seasonal merchandise have been sold.

Disney's Wonderful World of Winter (film) Educational film with Goofy and Stanley the Snowman teaching students about the holidays and customs of winter; released in Sep. 1983.

Disney's World on Ice SEE WORLD ON ICE.

Disney's Wuzzles (TV) Animated series; aired on CBS Sep. 14, 1985–Sep. 6, 1986, and on ABC Sep. 13, 1986–May 16, 1987. Narrated by Stan Freberg, the series explored the adventures of an odd group of characters on the Isle of Wuz. Each creature is a combination of 2 animals; for example, Bumblelion is a lion mixed with a bumblebee, Hoppopotamus is a hippo with rabbit ears and a cotton tail, and Eleroo is an elephant crossed with a kangaroo. Voices include Brian Cummings (Bumblelion), Jo Anne Worley (Hoppopotamus), Henry Gibson (Eleroo), Bill Scott (Moosel), Alan Oppenheimer (Rhinokey). Along with *Disney's Adventures of the Gummi Bears*,

the show marked Disney's entry into Saturday morning cartoons. 13 episodes. SEE ALSO WUZZLES, THE.

DisneySea Proposed ocean-themed park planned by Disney designers for Long Beach, California, for the Queensway Bay area around the *Queen Mary*. It was announced in 1990 as the 225-acre centerpiece of the proposed Port Disney, which would have also consisted of hotels, cruise ship docks, a marina, and other facilities. Disney eventually dropped its plans due to the numerous coastal regulatory agency standards and the expected cost of the project. SEE ALSO QUEEN MARY AND TOKYO DISNEYSEA.

DisneySea AquaSphere The icon of DisneySea Plaza at the front of Tokyo DisneySea. The AquaSphere symbolizes Earth, the "water planet," and sets the stage for the ocean-themed adventures awaiting beyond the main entrance.

DisneySea Electric Railway Elevated electric trolley system which shuttles passengers between American Waterfront and Port Discovery in Tokyo DisneySea; opened Sep. 4, 2001.

DisneySea Transit Steamer Line Attraction in Tokyo DisneySea; opened Sep. 4, 2001. Guests are ferried from Mediterranean Harbor to Lost River Delta or around American Waterfront.

DisneyStyle Shop in Disney Springs West Side at Walt Disney World; opened May 12, 2018. Stylish apparel and accessories are inspired by Disney characters and park attractions.

DisneyToon Studios Division of Walt Disney Feature Animation that produced video/DVD and theatrical sequels to animated features, as well as new stories featuring characters such as Mickey Mouse, Winnie the Pooh, and Tinker Bell. It was part of Walt Disney Television Animation until 2003, when it received the DisneyToon Studios name. The first film was *DuckTales: the Movie, Treasure of the Lost Lamp*, released as a Disney MovieToon. In Australia, DisneyToon Studios Australia operated 1988–2006. In 2013, DisneyToon was changed to Disneytoon. The division ceased production and closed in 2018.

Disneytown Shopping, dining, and entertainment district at Shanghai Disney Resort; opened Jun. 16, 2016. On the shore of Wishing Star Lake, guests find a timeless village inspired by both Disney themes and Chinese culture. The 5 districts include: Marketplace, a bustling central plaza with international shopping; Lakeshore, with waterfront dining; Spice Alley, an eclectic food street; Broadway Boulevard, with elegant shops and galleries; and Broadway Plaza, a theater district with restaurants and the Walt Disney Grand Theatre, which premiered with a Mandarin-language production of *The Lion King*.

Disorganized Crime (film) In a small town in Montana, cunning criminal Frank Salazar has planned the perfect bank robbery and sent invitations to 4 heist experts for help, only to be arrested by 2 New Jersey cops who had been following him. The 4 strangers soon arrive and find themselves in a quandary—what were they gathered to do? How are they to do it? The 4 dislike each other, but strive to work together, even without a leader, for what they hope will be a major payoff. Meanwhile Salazar escapes, and the cops are confounded by his actions as well as those of the bank robbers. There are miscues by both sides as they bungle their operations. Released Apr. 14, 1989. Directed by Jim Kouf. A Touchstone film. 101 min. Stars Hoyt Axton (Sheriff Henault), Corbin Bernsen (Frank Salazar), Rubén Blades (Carlos Barrios), Fred Gwynne (Max Green), Ed O'Neill (George Denver), Lou Diamond Phillips (Ray Forgy), Daniel Roebuck (Bill Lonigan), William Russ (Nick Bartowski). Filmed on location around Hamilton, Montana.

Distinguished Gentleman, The (film) When Florida congressman Jeff Johnson dies, small-time con artist Thomas Jefferson Johnson scams his own name onto the ballot. Launching a campaign based on pure name recognition, he pulls off his biggest hustle yet when he manages to get elected. He quickly finds to his delight that he is raking in sums he never dreamed of without doing anything illegal. But when Thomas becomes aware of the effect of Congress's greed and chicanery on the general public, and the plight of a little girl in particular, he decides to turn the tables on Washington's business as usual and shakes the establishment to its foundations. Released Dec. 4, 1992. Directed by Jonathan Lynn. A Hollywood Pictures film. 112 min. Stars Eddie Murphy (Thomas Jefferson Johnson), Lane Smith (Dick Dodge), Sheryl Lee Ralph (Miss Loretta), Joe Don Baker (Olaf Andersen), Victoria Rowell (Celia Kirby), Grant Shaud (Arthur Reinhardt), Kevin McCarthy (Terry Corrigan). While much of the filming took place in Washington, D.C.,

restrictions on filming around the Capitol necessitated a search for a substitute, and it was the State Capitol building in Harrisburg, Pennsylvania, that doubled for the U.S. Capitol. Additional filming took place in Baltimore.

Diving with Dolphins (film) Documentary chronicling the making of Disneynature's *Dolphin Reef*; digitally released Apr. 3, 2020, on Disney+. From wave surfing with dolphins in South Africa to dancing with humpback whales in Hawai'i, filmmakers go to great lengths to shed new light on the ocean's mysteries. Narrated by Céline Cousteau. Directed and produced by Keith Scholey. 78 min. From Silverback Films and Disneynature.

Dixie Landings Resort A 2,048-room resort hotel at Walt Disney World; opened Feb. 2, 1992. Moderate-priced hotel, themed after the Old South. The registration desk, restaurants, and souvenir shop were in Colonel's Cotton Mill, a building that resembles a steamship. The swimming pool was located on Ol' Man Island among the guest room buildings. One could dine at Boatwright's Dining Hall or in a food court, or buy souvenirs at Fulton's General Store. It was combined with Disney's Port Orleans Resort Apr. 1, 2001, under the name Port Orleans Resort—Riverside.

Dixieland at Disneyland Popular annual event; first held Oct. 1, 1960, and continued for several years. Big-name entertainers, such as Louis Armstrong, performed on rafts on the Rivers of America and at other locations around the park.

D-Luxe Burger Restaurant serving gourmet burgers and gelato shakes in the Disney Springs Town Center at Walt Disney World; opened May 15, 2016. Recalling Florida's cattle ranching heritage, the story goes that early Disney Springs settler Martin Sinclair converted his family's house at the Glowing Oak Ranch into a popular restaurant.

Do Dooni Chaar (*Two Times Two Equals Four*) (film) The first live-action Hindi feature released by The Walt Disney Company in India, on Oct. 8, 2010. The Duggal family struggles as they attempt to buy into the big middle-class dream and get a car—and the resultant journey of chaos, revelations, confrontation, and discovery helps bring them together as a family. Directed by Habib Faisal. Stars Rishi Kapoor, Neetu Kapoor, Aditi Vasudev, Archit Krishna. From Planman Motion Pictures.

Do Dragons Dream? (film) Educational film in which Figment introduces children to their imaginations; part of the EPCOT Educational Media Collection: Language Arts Through Imagination series; released in Sep. 1988. 15 min.

Do You Want to Build a Snowman? Song from *Frozen*; written by Kristen Anderson-Lopez and Robert Lopez.

D.O.A. (film) College professor Dexter Cornell discovers he has been poisoned by a fatal, slow-acting toxin, and he has only 24 hours to unravel the mystery of his imminent demise. Enlisting the aid of Sydney Fuller, a naïve student who has a crush on him, he soon becomes enmeshed in a series of murders as he attempts to find out who killed him—and why. Released Mar. 18, 1988. Directed by Rocky Morton and Annabel Jankel. A Touchstone film. 100 min. Stars Dennis Quaid (Dexter Cornell), Meg Ryan (Sydney Fuller), Daniel Stern (Hal Petersham), Charlotte Rampling (Mrs. Fitzwaring). Filmed on location in and around Austin, Texas.

Doc Self-appointed leader of the Seven Dwarfs; voiced by Roy Atwell.

Doc McStuffins (TV) Animated series for preschoolers on Disney Junior; premiered with the cable network Mar. 23, 2012, and ended Apr. 18, 2020. Doc McStuffins is a 6-year-old girl who has the ability to communicate with toys when she puts on her stethoscope and goes to work in her backyard playhouse. She works with her own stuffed animals to treat and help broken toys in her neighborhood. Voices include Kiara Muhammad (Doc McStuffins), Jaden Betts (Donny McStuffins), Robbie Rist (Stuffy). Produced by Brown Bag Films for Disney Junior.

Docking Bay 7 Food and Cargo Eatery in Star Wars: Galaxy's Edge; opened May 31, 2019, in Disneyland and Aug. 29, 2019, in Disney's Hollywood Studios at Walt Disney World. Inside a hangar bar, visitors select from a variety of intergalactic dishes whose ingredients, according to the story, were sourced by the planet-hopping Chef Strono "Cookie" Tuggs.

Dockside Diner American Waterfront counter-service restaurant in Tokyo DisneySea; opened Aug. 20, 2018, replacing Sailing Day Buffet. Sandwiches, fried chicken, and seasonal items are served in a cargo warehouse near the SS *Columbia*

dock. SEE ALSO MIN AND BILL'S DOCKSIDE DINER (DISNEY'S HOLLYWOOD STUDIOS).

Docter, Pete Academy Award–winning director/writer; he started at Pixar in 1990 as the studio's third animator, helping to develop the story and characters for *Toy Story*, a film for which he also served as supervising animator. He was a storyboard artist for *A Bug's Life* and wrote story treatments for *Toy Story 2* and *WALL•E*. As director, he helmed *Monsters, Inc.*; *Up*; *Inside Out*; and *Soul*. In Jun. 2018, he was named chief creative officer of Pixar Animation Studios. Early in his career, he animated on Cranium Command for EPCOT Center.

Doctor, The (film) A successful surgeon, Dr. Jack MacKee, lacks 1 vital trait: true compassion for the patients under his care. Suddenly faced with throat cancer, he becomes an ordinary patient in his own hospital and finds he has to deal with the red tape and dehumanizing conditions experienced by everyone else. Unable to relate to his wife and young son, he meets June, a fellow patient with extraordinary strength and spirit, who is the catalyst for his own recovery, as well as the realization that a healer must be able to attend to the spirit as well as the body. Initial release on Jul. 24, 1991, in 4 cities; general release on Aug. 2, 1991. Directed by Randa Haines. A Touchstone film. 123 min. Stars William Hurt (Jack), Christine Lahti (Anne), Elizabeth Perkins (June), Mandy Patinkin (Murray). Based on the book *A Taste of My Own Medicine*, by Dr. Ed Rosenbaum.

Dr. Dawson Basil's sensible cohort in *The Great Mouse Detective*, with the full name of Dr. David Q. Dawson; voiced by Val Bettin.

Dr. Facilier Smooth and scheming shadowman in *The Princess and the Frog*; voiced by Keith David.

Dr. Ken (TV) Series on ABC; aired Oct. 2, 2015–Mar. 31, 2017. As general practitioners go, Dr. Ken Park is a good one, but with a lousy bedside manner. He wants the best for his patients but would prefer that they take their whining and complaining elsewhere. Dr. Ken has a smart and beautiful wife, 2 decent kids, and a job in which he gets to help people on a daily basis. If he could only relax, get out of his own way, and stop second-guessing everyone and everything around him, he would be just fine. Stars Ken Jeong (Ken Park), Suzy Nakamura (Allison Park), Tisha Campbell-Martin (Damona Jenkins), Dave Foley (Pat Hein), Jonathan Slavin

(Clark Beavers), Albert Tsai (Dave Park), Krista Marie Yu (Molly Park). From Sony Pictures Television and ABC Studios.

Doctor Strange (film) After a tragic car accident leaves his hands permanently impaired, thus destroying his career, famed neurosurgeon Stephen Strange travels to the farthest corners of the world to find a cure. He crosses paths with The Ancient One, who opens up worlds to the doctor he had only dreamed of, teaching him the secrets of a hidden world of mysticism and alternate dimensions. Based in New York City's Greenwich Village, Doctor Strange must act as an intermediary between the real world and what lies beyond, utilizing a vast array of metaphysical abilities and artifacts to protect the universe. Released in the U.S. Nov. 4, 2016, also in 3-D and IMAX, after an Oct. 25 release in Britain and Ireland. Directed by Scott Derrickson. Stars Benedict Cumberbatch (Doctor Stephen Strange), Tilda Swinton (The Ancient One), Rachel McAdams (Christine Palmer), Mads Mikkelsen (Kaecilius), Benedict Wong (Wong), Chiwetel Ejiofor (Baron Karl Mordo). 115 min. Based on the character created by Steve Ditko for the Marvel comic book series. Filmed in widescreen format in Nepal, Britain, and New York. Nominated for an Academy Award for Visual Effects.

Doctor Strange in the Multiverse of Madness (film) After meeting America Chavez, a teenager with the ability to open doorways from one universe to the other, Doctor Strange soon discovers that she is being pursued by a demon who takes different forms to steal her powers and use it for its own gains. Having sworn an oath to protect the barriers between the universes, the care of America now falls to Doctor Strange and Supreme Sorcerer Wong, as well as Avenger Wanda Maximoff. A wild, mind-blowing adventure ensues that sends Doctor Strange and his allies on a dangerous journey to alternate universes in the Multiverse, where he meets versions of his friends, his enemies, and even himself, and comes face-to-face with a foe whose powers have never been encountered. Directed by Sam Raimi. Released May 6, 2022 (also in 3-D, IMAX, and IMAX 3-D), after international releases beginning May 4. Stars Benedict Cumberbatch (Doctor Stephen Strange), Chiwetel Ejiofor (Baron Mordo), Elizabeth Olsen (Wanda Maximoff/The Scarlet Witch), Benedict Wong (Wong), Xochitl Gomez (America Chavez), Michael Stühlbarg (Dr. Nic West), Rachel McAdams (Dr. Christine Palmer).

126 min. Filmed in wide-screen format at Longcross Studios in London. From Marvel Studios.

Dr. Syn, Alias the Scarecrow (film) Theatrical version of *The Scarecrow of Romney Marsh* TV episodes. Released first in England in Dec. 1963; U.S. theatrical release Nov. 21, 1975. 98 min./75 min. Stars Patrick McGoohan.

Dodd, Dickie (1945–2013) Mouseketeer from the 1950s *Mickey Mouse Club* TV show.

Dodd, Jimmie (1910–1964) The adult Mouseketeer from the 1950s *Mickey Mouse Club* TV show. He was highly admired by all of the Mouseketeers, not to mention the viewers of the show, and his Doddisms gave instruction on the principles of good living. A prolific songwriter, he wrote more than 30 of the *show's* songs—including the "Mickey Mouse Club March"—of which he performed many with his Mousegetar. He was named a Disney Legend in 1992.

Dodger Streetwise dog leader in *Oliver & Company*; voiced by Billy Joel.

Dodo Lively master of ceremonies of the great Caucus Race in *Alice in Wonderland*; voiced by Bill Thompson.

Doerges, Norm He began with Disney in 1967 as pool manager at the Celebrity Sports Center in Denver, then moved to Walt Disney World, where he worked up to vice president in charge of EPCOT Center. He moved to Disneyland in 1990, becoming executive vice president in 1994. He left the company in 1997.

Dog of Destiny (TV) Show; part 2 of *Atta Girl, Kelly!*

Dog Watch (film) Pluto cartoon released Mar. 16, 1945. Directed by Charles Nichols. Pluto is a Navy dog guarding a ship. He ends up in the brig after being blamed when a wharf rat steals the captain's food. He gets some revenge when he shakes the rope the rat is on, causing the rat and food to fall into the water.

Dog with a Blog (TV) Series on Disney Channel; premiered Nov. 4, 2012, after an Oct. 12 preview. A family adopts a dog, Stan, who turns out to be able to talk and blog. Stars G Hannelius (Avery), Blake Michael (Tyler), Francesca Capaldi (Chloe), Beth

Littleford (Ellen), Regan Burns (Bennett). Stan was voiced by Stephen Full and played by 2 talented canine performers, Kuma and Mick. From It's a Laugh Productions and Walt Disney Television.

Dognapper, The (film) Mickey Mouse cartoon released Nov. 17, 1934. Directed by Dave Hand. Minnie's Pekinese is captured by Pete, and Mickey and Donald come to the rescue, discovering Pete's lair in a deserted sawmill.

Dok-Ondar's Den of Antiquities Shop in Star Wars: Galaxy's Edge; opened May 31, 2019, in Disneyland and Aug. 29, 2019, in Disney's Hollywood Studios at Walt Disney World. Visitors browse an eclectic assortment of galactic artifacts which, according to the story, were collected by legendary antiques dealer Dok-Ondar.

Dole Whip First tested at Walt Disney World in 1983, this pineapple soft-serve dessert became a popular treat at Aloha Isle Refreshments in the Magic Kingdom and was later offered at the Tiki Juice Bar in Disneyland. Dole Whip has also been served at Disney's Polynesian Village Resort at Walt Disney World, on Disney Cruise Line ships, and at Aulani, a Disney Resort and Spa and other resorts.

Doli Hot-tempered member of the Fair Folk in The Black Cauldron; voiced by John Byner.

Dollface (TV) Comedy series on Hulu; seasons digitally released Nov. 15, 2019, and Feb. 11, 2022. After being dumped by her longtime boyfriend, Jules must deal with her own imagination when she literally and metaphorically reenters the world of women in order to rekindle the female friendships she left behind. Stars Kat Dennings (Jules), Brenda Song (Madison Maxwell), Shay Mitchell (Stella Cole), Esther Povitsky (Izzy). From Clubhouse Pictures, LuckyChap Entertainment, and ABC Signature Studios.

Dolores Elephant needing a bath by Goofy in The Big Wash; also appeared in Working for Peanuts. The elephant character originally appeared, without a name, in Tiger Trouble.

Dolphin Hotel SEE WALT DISNEY WORLD DOLPHIN.

Dolphin Reef (film) A Disneynature feature. Echo, a young Pacific bottlenose dolphin, seems far more interested in exploring his spectacular coral reef home and its intriguing inhabitants than learning to survive in it. But lessons from his mother, Kumu, and a few close encounters with some of the ocean's greatest predators may encourage Echo to master his vital role in the marine community after all. Directed by Keith Scholey. Digitally released Apr. 3, 2020, on Disney+, after a Mar. 28, 2018, theatrical release in France, as Blue. Narrated by Natalie Portman. 77 min.

Dominguez, Ron (1935–2021) He joined Disneyland in 1955, working his way up from an opening-day ticket taker to a ride operator, supervisor, and manager. By 1970 he was director of operations and in 1974 was named vice president of Disneyland and chairman of the Park Operating Committee. In 1990, he became executive vice president, Walt Disney Attractions, West Coast, and helped pave the way toward the creation of a 2nd theme park at the Disneyland Resort. He retired in 1994 and was named a Disney Legend in 2000. Ron had the distinction of having been born on the Disneyland property; his family was 1 of the 17 families that sold their land to Walt Disney in 1954, and their 2-story, Spanish-style house was relocated behind Main Street, U.S.A. for use as administrative offices.

Dominick, Peter H., Jr. (1941–2009) Architect; designed Disney's Wilderness Lodge, Animal Kingdom Lodge, and Grand Californian Hotel.

Don Defore's Silver Banjo Barbecue food facility in Frontierland at Disneyland; opened Jun. 15, 1957, replacing the original Casa de Fritos. Closed Mar. 4, 1962, and absorbed into an expanded Aunt Jemima Pancake House. Don Defore (1913–1993), an actor who was perhaps best known for his TV portrayal of the neighbor Thorny on The Ozzie and Harriet Show, was a friend of Walt Disney.

Don Donald (film) Mickey Mouse cartoon released Jan. 9, 1937. While released as a Mickey cartoon, Mickey does not appear; Donald Duck is the star, joined by Donna Duck (who later became known as Daisy). Directed by Ben Sharpsteen. In this south-of-the-border adventure, Donald, the troubadour, will go to any lengths, including trading his burro for a car, to please the tempestuous Donna.

Don Karnage Dashing air pirate fox on TaleSpin; voiced by Jim Cummings.

Donald and Jose, Olé! (TV) Show aired Jan. 23,

1982. 90 min. A compilation of cartoons about Latin America, including segments from *The Three Caballeros* and *Saludos Amigos*.

Donald and Pluto (film) Mickey Mouse cartoon released Sep. 12, 1936. Directed by Ben Sharpsteen. While released as a Mickey cartoon, Mickey does not appear; Donald Duck is actually the star. Donald attempts to do his own home plumbing until Pluto swallows a magnet and threatens to destroy all of his work.

Donald and the Wheel (film) Donald Duck cartoon featurette released Jun. 21, 1961. Directed by Hamilton S. Luske. Two "Spirits of Progress" go back in time to discover the inventor of the wheel. Caveduck Donald is selected as the inventor and is shown the evolution and usefulness of the wheel over the centuries. The first stone wheel develops for use on everything from chariots to sports cars. But Donald decides he wants nothing to do with the hassles of modern life, so he returns to pulling his cart without wheels. The spirits decide they picked the wrong person. 18 min. An updated version was released as an educational film in Sep. 1990.

Donald Applecore (film) Donald Duck cartoon released Jan. 18, 1952. Directed by Jack Hannah. Donald's battle with Chip and Dale over their eating his apples escalates until Donald bombs them with atomic pellets. One of his hens eats a pellet, laying an egg bomb. It explodes while Donald is holding it, creating a hole that sends him all the way to the other side of the world.

Donald Duck One of the most popular of the Disney characters, he made his debut in the Silly Symphony *The Wise Little Hen* on Jun. 9, 1934. His fiery temper endeared him to audiences, and in the 1940s he took over for Mickey Mouse in the number of cartoons reaching the theaters. Eventually, there were 128 Donald Duck theatrical cartoons, but he also appeared in a number of others with Mickey Mouse, Goofy, and Pluto. His middle name, shown in a wartime cartoon, was Fauntleroy. The original voice of Donald was Clarence "Ducky" Nash, who was succeeded after 50 years by Disney animator Tony Anselmo. A daily Donald Duck newspaper comic strip began Feb. 7, 1938. The Donald Duck cartoons are:

*Originally released as Mickey Mouse cartoons, but Mickey does not appear.

1. *Donald and Pluto*, 1936*
2. *Don Donald*, 1937*
3. *Modern Inventions*, 1937*
4. *Donald's Ostrich*, 1937
5. *Self Control*, 1938
6. *Donald's Better Self*, 1938
7. *Donald's Nephews*, 1938
8. *Polar Trappers*, 1938
9. *Good Scouts*, 1938
10. *The Fox Hunt*, 1938
11. *Donald's Golf Game*, 1938
12. *Donald's Lucky Day*, 1939
13. *The Hockey Champ*, 1939
14. *Donald's Cousin Gus*, 1939
15. *Beach Picnic*, 1939
16. *Sea Scouts*, 1939
17. *Donald's Penguin*, 1939
18. *The Autograph Hound*, 1939
19. *Officer Duck*, 1939
20. *The Riveter*, 1940
21. *Donald's Dog Laundry*, 1940
22. *Billposters*, 1940
23. *Mr. Duck Steps Out*, 1940
24. *Put-Put Troubles*, 1940
25. *Donald's Vacation*, 1940
26. *Window Cleaners*, 1940
27. *Fire Chief*, 1940
28. *Timber*, 1941
29. *Golden Eggs*, 1941
30. *A Good Time for a Dime*, 1941
31. *Early to Bed*, 1941
32. *Truant Officer Donald*, 1941
33. *Old MacDonald Duck*, 1941
34. *Donald's Camera*, 1941
35. *Chef Donald*, 1941
36. *The Village Smithy*, 1942
37. *Donald's Snow Fight*, 1942
38. *Donald Gets Drafted*, 1942
39. *Donald's Garden*, 1942
40. *Donald's Gold Mine*, 1942
41. *The Vanishing Private*, 1942
42. *Sky Trooper*, 1942
43. *Bellboy Donald*, 1942
44. *Der Fuehrer's Face*, 1943
45. *Donald's Tire Trouble*, 1943
46. *Flying Jalopy*, 1943
47. *Fall Out—Fall In*, 1943
48. *The Old Army Game*, 1943
49. *Home Defense*, 1943
50. *Trombone Trouble*, 1944
51. *Donald Duck and the Gorilla*, 1944
52. *Contrary Condor*, 1944
53. *Commando Duck*, 1944
54. *The Plastics Inventor*, 1944

55. *Donald's Off Day*, 1944
56. *The Clock Watcher*, 1945
57. *The Eyes Have It*, 1945
58. *Donald's Crime*, 1945
59. *Duck Pimples*, 1945
60. *No Sail*, 1945
61. *Cured Duck*, 1945
62. *Old Sequoia*, 1945
63. *Donald's Double Trouble*, 1946
64. *Wet Paint*, 1946
65. *Dumb Bell of the Yukon*, 1946
66. *Lighthouse Keeping*, 1946
67. *Frank Duck Brings 'em Back Alive*, 1946
68. *Straight Shooters*, 1947
69. *Sleepy Time Donald*, 1947
70. *Clown of the Jungle*, 1947
71. *Donald's Dilemma*, 1947
72. *Crazy with the Heat*, 1947
73. *Bootle Beetle*, 1947
74. *Wide Open Spaces*, 1947
75. *Chip an' Dale*, 1947
76. *Drip Dippy Donald*, 1948
77. *Daddy*, 1948
78. *Donald's Dream Voice*, 1948
79. *The Trial of Donald Duck*, 1948
80. *Inferior Decorator*, 1948
81. *Soup's On*, 1948
82. *Three for Breakfast*, 1948
83. *Tea for Two Hundred*, 1948
84. *Donald's Happy Birthday*, 1949
85. *Sea Salts*, 1949
86. *Winter Storage*, 1949
87. *Honey Harvester*, 1949
88. *All in a Nutshell*, 1949
89. *The Greener Yard*, 1949
90. *Slide, Donald, Slide*, 1949
91. *Toy Tinkers*, 1949
92. *Lion Around*, 1950
93. *Crazy Over Daisy*, 1950
94. *Trailer Horn*, 1950
95. *Hook, Lion and Sinker*, 1950
96. *Bee at the Beach*, 1950
97. *Out on a Limb*, 1950
98. *Dude Duck*, 1951
99. *Corn Chips*, 1951
100. *Test Pilot Donald*, 1951
101. *Lucky Number*, 1951
102. *Out of Scale*, 1951
103. *Bee on Guard*, 1951
104. *Donald Applecore*, 1952
105. *Let's Stick Together*, 1952
106. *Uncle Donald's Ants*, 1952
107. *Trick or Treat*, 1952
108. *Don's Fountain of Youth*, 1953

109. *The New Neighbor*, 1953
110. *Rugged Bear*, 1953
111. *Working for Peanuts*, 1953
112. *Canvas Back Duck*, 1953
113. *Spare the Rod*, 1954
114. *Donald's Diary*, 1954
115. *Dragon Around*, 1954
116. *Grin and Bear It*, 1954
117. *Grand Canyonscope*, 1954
118. *Flying Squirrel*, 1954
119. *No Hunting*, 1955
120. *Bearly Asleep*, 1955
121. *Beezy Bear*, 1955
122. *Up a Tree*, 1955
123. *Chips Ahoy*, 1956
124. *How to Have an Accident in the Home*, 1956
125. *Donald in Mathmagic Land*, 1959
126. *How to Have an Accident at Work*, 1959
127. *Donald and the Wheel*, 1961
128. *The Litterbug*, 1961

Donald Duck and the Gorilla (film) Donald Duck cartoon released Mar. 31, 1944. Directed by Jack King. Donald and his nephews try to scare each other when they hear on the radio that a gorilla has escaped from the zoo, but when the gorilla, Ajax, shows up, they unite to defeat the creature with a tear gas bomb.

Donald Duck Cola SEE GENERAL BEVERAGES, INC.

Donald Duck Presents (TV) Series on The Disney Channel featuring Disney cartoons. 125 episodes were produced. Began on Sep. 1, 1983.

Donald Duck Quacks Up (TV) SEE KIDS IS KIDS.

Donald Duck Story, The (TV) Show aired Nov. 17, 1954. Directed by Jack Hannah and Robert Florey. Walt tells a fictional story about Donald's career, encompassing a number of Donald Duck cartoons.

Donald Duck's 50th Birthday (TV) Special; aired on CBS Nov. 13, 1984. Directed by Andrew Solt. Host Dick Van Dyke takes a look at the famous duck, with many of his celebrity friends helping out.

Donald Gets Drafted (film) Donald Duck cartoon released May 1, 1942. The first Disney war-themed cartoon released during World War II. Directed by Jack King. Donald learns to rue his army induction order when his sadistic sergeant, Pete, drills him and teaches him discipline.

Donald in Mathmagic Land (film) Donald Duck featurette released Jun. 26, 1959. Directed by Hamilton S. Luske. Donald Duck explores Mathmagic Land—a fantasy land composed of such things as square root trees and a stream running with numbers. The Spirit of Adventure teaches him the many uses of mathematics in art, architecture, and nature, as well as chess and sports such as football. Donald is introduced to the circle and the triangle, which have been the basis for many great inventions such as the telescope and airplane, and he is shown that mathematical thinking opens the doors to the future. This thoughtful, Academy Award–nominated short ends with a quote from Galileo: "Mathematics is the alphabet with which God has written the universe." 28 min. Made with the collaboration of such people as Disney artists John Hench and Art Riley, voice talent of Paul Frees, and scientific expert Heinz Haber, who had worked on the Disney space shows. Originally released on a bill with *Darby O'Gill and the Little People*. Two years later it had the honor of being introduced by Ludwig Von Drake and shown on the first program of *Walt Disney's Wonderful World of Color*. The featurette was made available to schools and became one of the most popular educational films ever made by Disney. As Walt Disney explained, "The cartoon is a good medium to stimulate interest. We have recently explained mathematics in a film and in that way excited public interest in this very important subject."

Donald Loves Daisy (TV) Syn. show about romance, featuring clips from Disney cartoons.

Donald Takes a Holiday (TV) Syn. show from 1987, incorporating a number of cartoons about vacationing.

Donald's Award (TV) Show aired Mar. 27, 1957. Directed by Jack Hannah. Walt offers Donald a reward if he can remain on his best behavior for a week, and he sends Jiminy Cricket to check up on him. Segments from Donald Duck cartoons emphasize his temper.

Donald's Better Self (film) Donald Duck cartoon released Mar. 11, 1938. Directed by Jack King. Donald is reluctant to go to school but is persuaded to do so by his angelic Better Self, who has to defeat his devilish Evil Self. The latter is continually leading Donald astray.

Donald's Boat Guests can explore Donald Duck's home (a boat named the *Miss Daisy*) in Mickey's Toontown at Disneyland; opened Jan. 24, 1993. Enhancements debuted in 2023, including new water features, balance beams, and rocking toys around Donald's Duck Pond. Similar attractions opened in Toontown at Tokyo Disneyland Apr. 15, 1996, and in Mickey's Toontown Fair at the Magic Kingdom at Walt Disney World Jun. 29, 1996–Feb. 11, 2011.

Donald's Camera (film) Donald Duck cartoon released Oct. 24, 1941. Directed by Dick Lundy. Donald considers hunting with a gun is wrong and hunts wildlife only with a camera. But when a woodpecker becomes a pest and smashes Donald's camera, he goes after it with an arsenal of weapons.

Donald's Cousin Gus (film) Donald Duck cartoon released May 19, 1939. Directed by Jack King. Donald's goose cousin, Gus, comes to visit and practically eats him out of house and home. When Donald's attempts to get rid of Gus are unsuccessful, he gives up in disgust.

Donald's Crime (film) Donald Duck cartoon released Jun. 29, 1945. Directed by Jack King. Donald, broke, steals from his nephews' piggy bank for a date with Daisy, but his conscience gets the best of him, and he gets a job to pay them back. Nominated for an Academy Award.

Donald's Dairy Dip See Village Pavilion.

Donald's Decision (film) Shows the advisability and necessity of purchasing Canadian war bonds. Made for the National Film Board of Canada. Delivered Jan. 11, 1942. Donald wrestles with his good self and bad self to make up his mind about buying war bonds. The film reused animation from *Donald's Better Self* and *Self Control*.

Donald's Diary (film) Donald Duck cartoon released Mar. 5, 1954. Directed by Jack Kinney. The narrator tells of Donald's romance with Daisy through use of Donald's diary. Daisy has almost wooed him into marriage when he has a nightmarish vision of what their married life would be like. He decides to run away, and we see him writing in his diary in the French Foreign Legion.

Donald's Dilemma (film) Donald Duck cartoon released Jul. 11, 1947. Directed by Jack King. Daisy panics when a flowerpot that's fallen on Donald's head leaves him with a magnificent singing voice but has also wiped away his memory of her. A helpful psychiatrist tells her to drop another flowerpot on him to "cure" this condition, and it works.

Donald's Dine 'n Delights Art nouveau–inspired bistro in Disneytown at Shanghai Disney Resort; opened Jan. 17, 2023, succeeding KOKIO Gastrobar. Specialty pizzas, milkshakes, and sundaes are served in a Parisian-style garden setting.

Donald's Dog Laundry (film) Donald Duck cartoon released Apr. 5, 1940. Directed by Jack King. With his squeaker toy cat, Donald attempts to entice Pluto to try his mechanical dog washer but is unexpectedly caught himself, scrubbed, and hung on the line to dry.

Donald's Double Feature Shop in Disney's All-Star Movies Resort at Walt Disney World; opened Jan. 15, 1999, selling apparel, housewares, books, and sundries.

Donald's Double Trouble (film) Donald Duck cartoon released Jun. 28, 1946. Directed by Jack King. Donald meets his double and decides to use him to try to win back Daisy's love. But the trick backfires when the double, with a Ronald Colman voice, falls in love with Daisy himself.

Donald's Dream Voice (film) Donald Duck cartoon released May 21, 1948. Directed by Jack King. Donald, discouraged as a salesman because of his voice, buys miraculous voice pills that improve his vocal range. But he quickly loses the pills and, despite a long search, accidentally drops the last in the mouth of a cow.

Donald's Dynamite: Opera Box (film) Cartoon from the *Mickey MouseWorks* TV series; released Mar. 26, 1999, with *Doug's 1st Movie*. When Donald attends the opera with Daisy, he finds a bomb in her purse and tries, unsuccessfully, to defuse it. Directed by William Speers. 2 min.

Donald's Fire Drill (film) Educational release in 16 mm in Aug. 1991. 15 min. Two kids are contestants on a game show, co-hosted by Trevor Townsend and Donald Duck, and they try to beat the clock by answering questions on fire safety information.

Donald's Fire Survival Plan (film) Educational film showing how the loss of homes and lives by fire may be prevented with a bit of thought beforehand. Released on 16 mm in May 1966. An updated

version, containing new footage and prevention tactics, was released in Aug. 1984.

Donald's Garden (film) Donald Duck cartoon released Jun. 12, 1942. Directed by Dick Lundy. Donald has all sorts of troubles in his garden with the watering can and pump—and a gopher that eats his prize watermelons.

Donald's Gold Mine (film) Donald Duck cartoon released Jul. 24, 1942. Directed by Dick Lundy. Gold miner Donald's conflicts with his donkey result in a gold strike, but Donald gets tangled in his own gold-mining equipment and ends up looking like one of the bars of gold.

Donald's Golf Game (film) Donald Duck cartoon released Nov. 4, 1938. Directed by Jack King. Donald's golfing prowess display to his nephews is undermined by their constant tricks—sudden sneezes, substituting of trick clubs, and their placing of a trapped grasshopper inside a golf ball.

Donald's Happy Birthday (film) Donald Duck cartoon released Feb. 11, 1949. Directed by Jack Hannah. The nephews earn money to buy cigars for Donald's birthday, but Donald thinks they bought the cigars for themselves and forces them to smoke them all. He then discovers the birthday card at the bottom of the box.

Donald's Lucky Day (film) Donald Duck cartoon released Jan. 13, 1939. Directed by Jack King. Bicycle-messenger boy Donald has a series of mishaps on Friday the 13th. He continually tries to avoid an "unlucky" black cat. The cat turns lucky when it knocks a bomb, which Donald is unknowingly delivering, off a pier and into the water as it explodes, showering Donald and the cat with fish.

Donald's Nephews (film) Donald Duck cartoon released Apr. 15, 1938. Directed by Jack King. First film appearance of Huey, Dewey, and Louie, who are sent to visit their uncle by his sister, Dumbella. Donald attempts to practice child psychology, but it is all for naught as the nephews ruin his house and play all manner of tricks on him.

Donald's Off Day (film) Donald Duck cartoon released Dec. 8, 1944. The first cartoon directed by Jack Hannah. Donald is not able to go out for Sunday golf when his nephews and a book he has been reading convince him that he is not well. When he realizes the joke, he attempts to go out again, but a steady downpour sends him back inside.

Donald's Ostrich (film) Donald Duck cartoon released Dec. 10, 1937. Directed by Jack King. When an ostrich named Hortense gets free of her shipping crate and swallows everything in sight, including a radio, train station agent Donald is in for a hilarious day.

Donald's Penguin (film) Donald Duck cartoon released Aug. 11, 1939. Directed by Jack King. Donald gets a baby penguin as a gift, and it causes so much trouble he nearly shoots it, causing it to disappear. Remorseful, Donald is overjoyed to see the penguin return, and they hug affectionately.

Donald's Silver Anniversary (TV) Show aired Nov. 13, 1960. Directed by Hamilton S. Luske. Walt uses various cartoons to reminisce about Donald's career, and he places a special silver version of the Duckster among Donald's other awards to commemorate it.

Donald's Snow Fight (film) Donald Duck cartoon released Apr. 10, 1942. Directed by Jack King. When Donald destroys his nephews' snowman, the snow fight escalates with Donald's snow ship attacking the nephews' snow fort. The nephews win the fight and do a victory dance above a frozen geyser holding Donald after they've melted his ship with hot coals shot by arrows.

Donald's Tire Trouble (film) Donald Duck cartoon released Jan. 29, 1943. Directed by Dick Lundy. Donald, driving in the country, is frustrated in his attempts to fix a flat tire. The jack breaks, the radiator explodes, then the remaining 3 tires go flat. Donald gives up in disgust and drives on with the flats. The film features references to the rubber shortage during World War II.

Donald's Vacation (film) Donald Duck cartoon released Aug. 9, 1940. Directed by Jack King. Donald sets up camp in the great outdoors to find peace and relaxation, only to tangle with his folding equipment, chipmunks who steal his food, and a hungry bear.

Donald's Valentine Day Salute (TV) Show aired Feb. 10, 1980. Cartoons and clips about romance.

Donald's Weekend (TV) Show aired Jan. 15, 1958. Directed by Jack Hannah. Cartoons tied around the theme of a typical weekend with Donald Duck.

Donnelly, Meg Actress; appeared on Disney Channel in the ZOMBIES movies (Addison) and *Bunk'd* (Priscilla); on ABC in *American Housewife* (Taylor), *The Disney Family Singalong*, and the *Disney Parks Magical Christmas Day Parade*; and on Disney+ in *High School Musical: The Musical: The Series* (Val).

Donovan, Tate Actor; appeared in *Holy Matrimony* (Peter) and *The Pacifier* (Howard Plummer); on TV in *No Ordinary Family* (Mitch McCutcheon); and voiced the title character in *Hercules* and Gobu in *Disney's The Legend of Tarzan*.

Donovan's Kid (TV) Two-part show; aired Jan. 7 and 14, 1979. Directed by Bernard McEveety. At the turn of the century, a con man, Timothy Donovan, returns to San Francisco to see his wife and daughter (whom he had thought was a son). He tries to free them from the domination of his wife's uncle. Stars Darren McGavin, Mickey Rooney, Shelley Fabares, Katy Kurtzman, Murray Hamilton, Michael Conrad, Ross Martin.

Don's Fountain of Youth (film) Donald Duck cartoon released May 30, 1953. Directed by Jack Hannah. On his travels through Florida with his nephews, Donald tricks them into believing he has been transformed into a baby and then an egg by a "Fountain of Youth" until an encounter with a mother alligator and her babies spoils Donald's fun.

Don't Look Under the Bed (film) A Disney Channel Original Movie; first aired Oct. 9, 1999. Fourteen-year-old Frances McCausland has always approached life with logic and reason, but that changes when someone starts playing destructive pranks in her community, and all evidence points to Frances as the culprit. Frances discovers she is being framed by a mischievous boogeyman who lives under her bed. With the help of Larry Houdini, her brother's imaginary friend, she learns to rely on her imagination to defeat the Boogeyman. Directed by Kenneth Johnson. Stars Erin Chambers (Frances McCausland), Eric Hodges II (Larry Houdini), Jake Sakson (Darwin McCausland), Robin Riker (Karen McCausland), Steve Valentine (the Boogeyman).

Doodles Pleasure Island shop at Walt Disney World; opened May 1, 1989, offering graphic T-shirts and 1950s-style accessories. Closed Jul. 31,

1996; replaced by a Tabasco shop and in 1997 by Island Depot.

Doogie Kamealoha, M.D. (TV) Original Disney+ drama/comedy series from 20th Television; digitally released beginning Sep. 8, 2021. In modern-day Hawai'i, 16-year-old prodigy Lahela "Doogie" Kamealoha balances a budding medical career and life as a teenager. With the support of her 'ohana and friends, she is determined to make the most of her teenage years and forge her own path. Stars Peyton Elizabeth Lee (Lahela "Doogie" Kamealoha), Kathleen Rose Perkins (Dr. Clara Hannon), Jason Scott Lee (Benny), Mapuana Makia, (Noelani), Jeffrey Bowyer-Chapman (Charles), Matthew Sato (Kai Kamealoha), Wes Tian (Brian), Emma Meisel (Steph), Ronny Chieng (Dr. Lee), Alex Aiono (Walter).

Door Knob One of the stranger characters in *Alice in Wonderland* (1951); voiced by Joseph Kearns. He is the only major Wonderland character not derived from Lewis Carroll's books.

Dopey Youngest of the Seven Dwarfs, who does not speak; as Happy explains, "He never tried."

Dorsey, Don Audio engineer, synthesist, and designer of shows and parades at Disneyland who, after part-time work as synthesist/arranger on *America on Parade* in 1975, arranged and performed the music for the updated *Main Street Electrical Parade* in 1977 and guided the development of the park's parade-control audio computer system in 1980. Beginning in 1983, he created and directed nighttime fireworks spectaculars for Walt Disney World, including *Laserphonic Fantasy*, *Illumi-Nations*, and *Sorcery in the Sky*. He also designed the sound effects for *Fantasmic!* at Disneyland.

Dorsey, Jack Member of the Disney Board of Directors 2014–2018.

Dory Regal blue tang who suffers from short-term memory loss in *Finding Nemo* and *Finding Dory*; voiced by Ellen DeGeneres.

Dos Oruguitas Song from *Encanto*; written by Lin-Manuel Miranda. Nominated for an Academy Award. The title is Spanish for "two little caterpillars."

Dotrice, Karen Child actress; appeared in *The Three Lives of Thomasina* (Mary MacDhui), *Mary Poppins* (Jane Banks), and *The Gnome-Mobile* (Elizabeth). She later made a cameo appearance in *Mary Poppins Returns* (Elegant Woman) and appeared in *Prop Culture* on Disney+. She was named a Disney Legend in 2004.

Double Agent (TV) Two-hour movie; aired Mar. 29, 1987. Directed by Mike Vejar. A veterinarian reluctantly takes his brother's place as a secret agent to complete a mission. He is assigned a bumbling helper and surprisingly manages to outwit the mysterious Scorpion. Stars Michael McKean, John Putch, Susan Walden, Christopher Burton, Lloyd Bochner, Alexa Hamilton.

Double Dribble (film) Goofy cartoon released Dec. 20, 1946. Directed by Jack Hannah. A basketball game of Goofy look-alikes (P.U. vs. U.U.) in which the players play furiously, often breaking the rules of the game. All of the players are named after Disney artists.

Double Switch (TV) Two-hour movie; aired Jan. 24, 1987. Directed by David Greenwalt. A shy teen, who is the exact double of a rock star, switches places with him so the rock star can spend some time with a "real family." Each has problems trying to adapt to his new life, so they decide to switch back again and begin to appreciate their own families. Stars George Newbern, Elisabeth Shue, Michael Des Barres, Peter Van Norden.

Double Take (film) Successful New York City investment banker Daryl Chase is framed for laundering money for a Mexican drug cartel. Wanted by the FBI, he makes a run for the border to find the one man who can clear his name, followed all along the way by Freddy Tiffany, an untrustworthy low-life petty thief. Taking Freddy's identity in order to make his way in the underworld, Daryl, to his horror, discovers that Freddy is even more wanted than he is. Directed by George Gallo. A Touchstone film. Released Jan. 12, 2001. Stars Orlando Jones (Daryl Chase), Eddie Griffin (Freddy Tiffany), Edward Herrmann (Charles Allsworth), Gary Grubbs (T. J. McCready), Daniel Roebuck (Norville). 88 min. Loosely based on the 1957 feature *Across the Bridge*, which in turn was based on a Graham Greene novel. Filmed in Cinema-Scope.

Double Teamed (TV) A Disney Channel Original Movie; first aired Jan. 18, 2002. Inspired by the true story of WNBA players Heidi and Heather Burge, also known as the world's "tallest twins." From their humble high school beginnings to the spotlight of professional women's basketball, the lives and differing goals of the 2 girls are profiled. Directed by Duwayne Dunham. Stars Poppi Monroe (Heather Burge), Annie McElwain (Heidi Burge), Mackenzie Phillips (Mary Burge), Nicky Searcy (Larry Burge), Teal Redmann (Nicky Williams), Chris Olivero (Galen Alderman).

Doubletree Guest Suite Resort Hotel at Lake Buena Vista at Walt Disney World; opened Feb. 23, 1995, taking the place of the Guest Quarters Suite Hotel, which was remodeled and renamed. It became Doubletree Suites by Hilton after Hilton acquired the previous owner, Promus Hotel Corporation, in 1999.

Doubloon Market Treasure Cove shop in Shanghai Disneyland; opened Jun. 16, 2016. Behind the aged walls of Fort Snobbish, guests can purchase pirate costumes, hats, and other souvenirs.

Doug, Doug E. Actor; appeared in *Cool Runnings* (Sanka Coffee), *Operation Dumbo Drop* (H. A.), and *That Darn Cat* (Zeke Kelso, 1997), and on the TV series *Where I Live* (Douglas St. Martin).

Douglas, Kirk (1916–2020) Actor; appeared in *20,000 Leagues Under the Sea* (Ned Land), *Tough Guys* (Archie Long), and *It Runs in the Family* (Mitchell Gromberg). He had an uncredited cameo role in *Oscar* (Papa Provolone).

Douglas, Michael Actor; appeared in *Napoleon and Samantha* (Danny), *It Runs in the Family* (Alex Gromberg), and as Dr. Hank Pim in *Ant-Man* and later Marvel Studios productions. He voiced Waylon in *Phineas and Ferb*.

Douglas, Mike (1925–2006) Entertainer; provided the uncredited singing voice for Prince Charming in *Cinderella*. On TV, he hosted the 1983 *Walt Disney World Very Merry Christmas Parade*. An episode of *The Mike Douglas Show* was shot at Walt Disney World in 1976.

Doug's 1st Movie (film) Doug Funnie, an imaginative and quirky 12½-year-old, finds himself caught between saving an endangered "monster" of Lucky Duck Lake and a burning desire to take his secret crush, Patti Mayonnaise, to the school dance. Not only does he discover the mythical monster is real, and subject to an elaborate cover-up by one of Bluffington's leading citizens, but a slick upperclassman is trying to woe Patti. Directed by Maurice Joyce. From Jumbo Pictures, in association with Walt Disney Pictures. Released Mar. 26, 1999, after a Mar. 16 premiere at Walt Disney World in conjunction with a new stage show at Disney-MGM Studios, *Disney's Doug Live*. Voices include Tom McHugh (Doug Funnie, Lincoln), Fred Newman (Skeeter Valentine, Mr. Dink, Porkchop, Herman Melville, Ned), Constance Shulman (Patti Mayonnaise). 77 min. Doug was originally created by Jim Jinkins for a Nickelodeon cable series. SEE ALSO BRAND SPANKING NEW DOUG (TV SERIES).

Dow Jones Industrial Average The Walt Disney Company joined the prestigious list on May 6, 1991.

Down and Out in Beverly Hills (film) When Jerry, a down-and-out bum, tries to drown himself in a family's Beverly Hills swimming pool, the wealthy homeowner, Dave Whiteman, rescues him and invites him into the house to live. Jerry turns the lives of the Whiteman family completely upside down, and in doing so changes their perception of the world around them. They find they need Jerry and his unconventional attitudes as much as he needs them. Released Jan. 31, 1986. Directed by Paul Mazursky. A Touchstone film. 103 min. The first R-rated film from the Disney Studios. Stars Nick Nolte (Jerry Baskin), Bette Midler (Barbara Whiteman), Richard Dreyfuss (Dave Whiteman), Little Richard (Orvis Goodnight), Tracy Nelson (Jenny Whiteman), Elizabeth Peña (Carmen), Evan Richards (Max Whiteman), Donald F. Muhich (Dr. Von Zimmer). For the role of the lovable Matisse, the Whiteman family's emotionally disturbed dog, a pair of look-alike Scottish border collies were used: Davey did all the action, while Mike did the interrelational scenes. In the brief role as Sadie Whiteman, the mother to Dreyfuss's character, Dreyfuss's own mother, Geraldine Dreyfuss, was tapped. The majority of the film was shot on studio soundstages. The back of the Whiteman house, as well as the swimming pool and a fully landscaped yard, were constructed on the Disney backlot. Daytime shots involving the front of the house were shot at an actual location in Beverly Hills, and because of various permit restrictions, night work in front of the house had to be shot at the Columbia Ranch where a duplicate facade of the Beverly Hills house was built. There was location work at the Rodeo Collection on Rodeo Drive, the Union Rescue Mission in downtown Los Angeles, the Los Angeles International Airport, Venice Beach, the old Cyrano's restaurant on the Sunset Strip, and numerous locations in and around Beverly Hills.

Down and Out in Beverly Hills (TV) Series on the new Fox network; aired Jul. 25–Sep. 12, 1987, after an Apr. 26 preview. The further adventures of the Whiteman family and their domestic upheaval when a vagrant becomes a boarder were the premise of the show. Stars Hector Elizondo (Dave Whiteman), Tim Thomerson (Jerry Baskin), Anita Morris (Barbara Whiteman), Evan Richards (Max Whiteman), April Ovitz (Carmen). Only Evan Richards and Mike the dog (Matisse) repeated from the feature film. From Touchstone Television.

Down and Out with Donald Duck (TV) Show aired Mar. 25, 1987. Directed by Scot Garen. Donald's life traced in *60 Minutes* style, utilizing footage from a number of cartoons.

Down in New Orleans Song from *The Princess and the Frog*; written by Randy Newman. Nominated for an Academy Award.

Down the Long Hills (TV) A Disney Channel Premiere Film; first aired Nov. 15, 1986. A young boy and girl, survivors of an Indian raid, struggle to meet their rescuers, as the boy's father carries out a desperate search for them. Directed by Burt Kennedy. Based on the story by Louis L'Amour. 89 min. Stars Bruce Boxleitner (Scott Collins), Thomas Wilson Brown (Hardy Collins), Lisa MacFarlane (Betty Sue Powell), Jack Elam (Squires).

Down to Earth Song from *WALL•E*; written by Peter Gabriel and Thomas Newman. Nominated for an Academy Award.

Downey, Robert, Jr. Actor; appeared as Dr. Kozak in 2006's *The Shaggy Dog* and as Tony Stark/Iron Man in the Marvel Studios films. He was named a Disney Legend in 2019.

Downtown (film) Animated short; digitally released Jan. 24, 2020, on Disney+. A commuter's disappointment in missing the bus turns into a colorful and unexpected joyride when the surrounding street art bursts to life, revealing the heart of the city from a new perspective. Directed by Kendra Vander Vliet. 2 min. From the Walt Disney Animation Studios Short Circuit program.

Downtown Disney Name given in 1996 to the entertainment-shopping-dining district at Walt Disney World encompassing Disney Village Marketplace (later renamed Downtown Disney Marketplace and now the Marketplace at Disney Springs), Pleasure Island (now The Landing at Disney Springs), and a 66-acre area called Downtown Disney West Side (now the West Side at Disney Springs) that opened Sep. 15, 1997, with Cirque du Soleil, Bongos Cuban Cafe, Wolfgang Puck Cafe, House of Blues, DisneyQuest, and a number of other businesses. On Sep. 29, 2015, the area was renamed Disney Springs as part of a multi-year transformation. A California version called Downtown Disney District (situated between Disneyland, Disney California Adventure, and the Disneyland Hotel) opened Jan. 12, 2001; a multi-year project to reimagine the district, with additional shopping, dining, and green spaces, was announced in 2021.

Downtown Disney Marketplace In 1997, this became the name of Disney Village Marketplace, which had opened Mar. 1975 as Lake Buena Vista Shopping Village. That became Walt Disney World Village in 1977, and then Disney Village Marketplace in 1989. A variety of shops are clustered along the shore of the Buena Vista Lagoon next to the formerly named Pleasure Island, about 5 miles from the Magic Kingdom. The centerpiece was the Captain's Tower, under which seasonal merchandise displays were featured. On Sep. 7, 1997, the Village Marketplace became part of the Downtown Disney complex and was renamed Downtown Disney Marketplace. Over the years, dining included Portobello Yacht Club, Fulton's Crab House (formerly the *Empress Lilly*), and Rainforest Cafe, with shopping at World of Disney, the LEGO Imagination Center, and Once Upon a Toy. With the area's transformation into Disney Springs, the name changed to the Marketplace Sep. 29. 2015.

Downtown Restaurant Buffet-service diner in Disney Hotel New York – The Art of Marvel at Disneyland Paris; opened Jun. 21, 2021, replacing Parkside Diner. International specialties are prepared by chefs in a cosmopolitan New York City atmosphere.

Downward Dog (TV) Half-hour series on ABC; aired May 17–Jun. 27, 2017. Nan attempts to juggle her tumultuous personal life (and stressful career), with her day-to-day story that's told by her increasingly lonely and philosophical dog, Martin. Stars Allison Tolman (Nan), Lucas Neff (Jason),

Kirby Howell-Baptiste (Jenn), Barry Rothbart (Kevin). Martin is voiced by writer/producer Samm Hodges. Based on a web series. From Legendary Television and ABC Studios.

Dragon Around (film) Donald Duck cartoon released Jul. 16, 1954. Directed by Jack Hannah. As a steam shovel operator, Donald is clearing an excavation site when he runs into Chip and Dale, who imagine the machine is a dragon threatening their home. By getting into the tool chest, they unbolt the steam shovel, which falls apart, thus enabling them to vanquish the dragon.

Dragon Wind Restaurant in Disney Explorers Lodge at Hong Kong Disneyland Resort; opened Apr. 30, 2017, with dishes from rural and classical provincial China.

Dragonfly Playground Playground in Wishing Star Park at Shanghai Disney Resort; opened Jun. 16, 2016, with activities designed for children.

Dragonslayer (film) A joint Disney/Paramount production. Directed by Matthew Robbins. After his master's untimely demise, a sorcerer's apprentice takes up his teacher's final duty: the destruction of the world's last dragon. Disney's share of the production was the creation of some of the special effects, including the ferocious dragon, Vermithrax Pejorative. Stars Peter MacNicol (Galen), Caitlin Clarke (Valerian), Ralph Richardson (Ulrich). 110 min. Filmed at Pinewood Studios, London, and on location on the Isle of Skye, Scotland, and in Snowdonia National Park, in England's North Wales. Paramount released the film in the U.S. in Jun. 1981, and Disney released it abroad.

Drake, Lynne She helped oversee the Walt Disney Archives' historical collections as senior manager until leaving the company in 2023. She joined the Archives staff in 2019 after Disney's acquisition of 21st Century Fox, where she had served as associate director of the 20th Century Fox Archives.

Drake Mallard Alter ego of Darkwing Duck.

Drawing Conclusions (film) Educational release in 16 mm in Aug. 1991. 19 min. A high school girl's mother and friends discourage her artistic talent, but she wants to enter a drawing contest at school.

Drawn to Animation Film and live show; premiered Feb. 8, 2001, in Disney Animation at Disney's California Adventure. A live host explained the character development process to Mushu from *Mulan*. The show ended Aug. 16, 2005, to become Animation Academy. On Oct. 18, 2004, it became the preshow for The Magic of Disney Animation in Disney-MGM Studios, closing Jul. 12, 2015. Also presented in L'Art de l'Animation Disney in Walt Disney Studios Park at Disneyland Paris, Mar. 16, 2002–Jan. 2019.

Drawn to Life SEE CIRQUE DU SOLEIL.

Dream Boutique Shop in the Downtown Disney District at Disneyland Resort; opened Oct. 7, 2017, taking the place of Anna & Elsa's Boutique. Character apparel, costumes, accessories, and headwear were sold. Closed Mar. 18, 2018, and superseded by The Disney Dress Shop.

Dream Called EPCOT, The (film) Promo film presented in the EPCOT Preview Center at Walt Disney World; first shown on Jun. 1, 1981. Concept art and detailed models provide a glimpse into the park under construction. 15 min.

Dream Called Walt Disney World, A (film) Video souvenir of a visit to Walt Disney World; released in Jun. 1981 and later shown on TV. 25 min.

Dream Is a Wish Your Heart Makes, A Song from *Cinderella*; written by Mack David, Al Hoffman, and Jerry Livingston.

Dream Is a Wish Your Heart Makes, A: The Annette Funicello Story (TV) Two-hour movie on CBS; aired Oct. 22, 1995. Annette narrates the film about her life, which was not made by Disney. Stars Eva Larue (Annette, from 1958 on), Linda Lavin (Virginia Funicello), Frank Crudelle (Joe Funicello), Len Cariou (Walt Disney).

Dream Is Alive, The: 20th Anniversary Celebration at Walt Disney World (TV) Special on CBS; aired Oct. 25, 1991. Directed by Dwight Hemion. Michael Eisner is searching for the perfect host, but no one will agree to take the job. A look at new company projects, such as *Beauty and the Beast* and *Home Improvement*, is followed by anniversary celebrations at Walt Disney World, as well as President George H. W. Bush's address at the Daily Points of Light Award ceremony. Celebrity appearances include Carol Burnett, Garth Brooks, Angela Lansbury, Tim Allen, Whoopi Goldberg,

Steve Martin, Goldie Hawn, Robin Williams. 60 min.

Dream on Silly Dreamer (film) Non-Disney documentary made by 2 ex-Disney animators, Tony West and Dan Lund, chronicling the shift from 2-D to computer-generated films and the closing of Disney's Feature Animation studio in Florida, including original animation and interviews with dozens of artists. Debuted Jan. 31, 2005, at the Animex International Festival in England. The film is not associated with The Walt Disney Company.

Dream Quest Images Visual-effects company acquired by Disney in May 1996. The company used live-action photography, models, and motion-control cameras, as well as the latest in digital-effects technology, to enhance motion pictures. Prior to the purchase, Dream Quest had won Academy Awards for special effects in *The Abyss* and *Total Recall*. Dream Quest took over the visual effects chores formerly performed by a department at Disney Studios. It was merged with Disney's in-house feature animation computer graphics unit in Oct. 1999 and renamed the Secret Lab. In 2001, the Secret Lab name was retired and the personnel were reassigned.

Dreamer's Lookout Chocolate boutique in Disney Explorers Lodge at Hong Kong Disneyland Resort; opened Nov. 18, 2019. As the story goes, guests continue the tradition of explorers who once gathered in this spot to trade tales about their adventures and the rare ingredients used in the treats they would share.

Dreamers Lounge Elegant lobby lounge in the Tokyo Disneyland Hotel; opened Jul. 8, 2008, serving light meals and afternoon tea.

Dreamers Point Area in World Celebration at EPCOT featuring a statue of Walt Disney, titled *Walt the Dreamer*; planned to debut in 2023.

Dreamfinder Jolly redhead who, along with his purple dragon friend, Figment, hosted the Journey Into Imagination pavilion in EPCOT Center, 1982–1998. Chuck McCann and Ron Schneider provided his voice.

Dreamfinder's School of Drama Image Works exhibit in Journey Into Imagination at EPCOT Center; ran Oct. 1, 1982–Oct. 1998. Guests could

interact in Chroma-key video playlets, appearing live in 1 of 3 films: a western (*Daring Deputies and the Return of Sagebrush Sam*), fantasy (*Enchanted Travelers—Wily Wizard and the Cranky King*), or sci-fi (*Acrobatic Astronauts in Galactic Getaway*).

Dreamflight SEE DELTA DREAMFLIGHT.

Dreams Come True: A Celebration of Disney Animation (TV) A 60-min. special on ABC; aired Dec. 4, 2009. Host Vanessa Williams presents 75 years of Disney animation with a preview of *The Princess and the Frog*. Celebrity appearances include Whoopi Goldberg, Jamie Lee Curtis, Selena Gomez, Miley Cyrus, Kristin Chenoweth, Elton John, Magic Johnson, Ty Pennington, Dick Van Dyke, Sigourney Weaver, Betty White, Serena Williams, Angelica Huston. From Met/Hodder.

DreamWorks On Feb. 9, 2009, Disney announced an exclusive long-term distribution and marketing deal with Steven Spielberg's production company, DreamWorks Studios. The first DreamWorks motion picture released under the Touchstone banner was *I Am Number Four* (Feb. 18, 2011), with the last being *The Light Between Oceans* (Sep. 2, 2016). DreamWorks Animation, a separate company, was not included in the deal.

Dreyer, John Vice president and later senior vice president of corporate communications for The Walt Disney Company, 1992–2001. He had begun his Disney career as a publicist at Walt Disney World in 1977, moving up to press and publicity manager in 1988.

Dreyfuss, Richard Actor; appeared in *Down and Out in Beverly Hills* (Dave Whiteman), *Tin Men* (Bill Babowsky), *Stakeout* (Chris Lecce), *What About Bob?* (Dr. Leo Marvin), *Another Stakeout* (Lecce), *Mr. Holland's Opus* (Glenn Holland), *Krippendorf's Tribe* (James Krippendorf), and *The Crew* (Bobby Bartellemeo). He voiced the Centipede in *James and the Giant Peach*. On TV, he appeared in *Oliver Twist* (Fagin); *Madoff* (Bernie Madoff); *Funny, You Don't Look 200*; and *The Walt Disney Company and McDonald's Present the American Teacher Awards*.

Drinkwallah Asia refreshment kiosk in Disney's Animal Kingdom; opened Mar. 1, 1999, presented by Coca-Cola. The name translates to "drink master" or "drink expert."

Drip Dippy Donald (film) Donald Duck cartoon released Mar. 5, 1948. Directed by Jack King. In his effort to sleep, Donald is disturbed first by a window shade and then by a dripping faucet. After fighting all night with the leak, Donald goes cuckoo when the water company calls saying they are shutting off his water because he hasn't paid his water bill.

Driscoll, Bobby (1937–1968) Child actor; appeared in *Song of the South* (Johnny), *Melody Time, So Dear to My Heart* (Jeremiah Kincaid), and *Treasure Island* (Jim Hawkins); on TV in the specials *One Hour in Wonderland* and *The Walt Disney Christmas Show*; and voiced Peter Pan and Goofy Jr. in the 1950s. He received a special juvenile Academy Award in the year he made *So Dear to My Heart* and the non-Disney *The Window*.

Driver, Minnie Actress; appeared in *Grosse Pointe Blank* (Debi Newberry), *High Heels and Low Lifes* (Shannon), and *Hope Springs* (Vera), and on TV in *Speechless* (Maya DiMeo). She voiced Jane in *Tarzan*.

Drizella One of Cinderella's evil stepsisters in the 1951 animated film; voiced by Rhoda Williams.

Droid Depot Shop in Star Wars: Galaxy's Edge; opened May 31, 2019, in Disneyland and Aug. 29, 2019, in Disney's Hollywood Studios at Walt Disney World. Guests select from a variety of components to build their own BB-series or R-series Custom Astromech Droid Unit.

Drop (film) Animated short; digitally released Jan. 24, 2020, on Disney+. A newly formed raindrop falls to Earth and has an unlikely and heartfelt encounter with a young girl that proves to be uplifting for both. Directed by Trent Correy. 3 min. From the Walt Disney Animation Studios Short Circuit program.

Dru, Joanne (1923–1996) Actress; appeared in *The Light in the Forest* (Milly Elder).

Drury, James (1934–2020) Actor; appeared in *Toby Tyler* (Jim Weaver), *Pollyanna* (George Dodds), and *Ten Who Dared* (Walter Powell), and on TV in *Elfego Baca*.

Drury Plaza Hotel Orlando Opened on Hotel Plaza Blvd. at Walt Disney World Dec. 8, 2022; formerly the Best Western Lake Buena Vista Resort Hotel.

DTV (TV) Series of music videos on The Disney Channel, where segments of Disney cartoons served as backup for popular songs. Premiered May 5, 1984. Also released on several video collections in 1984–1985.

DTV Disney apparel and character merchandise shop in Pleasure Island at Walt Disney World; opened Sep. 1993, taking the place of YesterEars. Closed Mar. 19, 2006.

Dubin, Gary (1959–2016) Actor; provided the voice of Toulouse in *The Aristocats* and appeared on Disney Channel as a pilot in *Sonny with a Chance*.

Duchess Regal mother cat in *The Aristocats*; voiced by Eva Gabor.

Duchovny, David Actor; appeared in *Playing God* (Dr. Eugene Sands).

Duck Flies Coop (TV) Show aired Feb. 13, 1959. Directed by Jack Hannah. The temperamental Donald Duck vows not to return to the Studio and leaves on a vacation. But all does not go well, so he is ready to return when Walt Disney calls. The show uses clips from a number of Donald cartoons.

Duck for Hire (TV) Show aired Oct. 23, 1957. Directed by Jack Hannah. Donald decides to quit show business, but a number of disasters (clips from several Donald Duck cartoons) persuade him to return.

Duck Hunt, The (film) Mickey Mouse cartoon released Jan. 28, 1932. Directed by Burt Gillett. Mickey and Pluto find duck hunting not all they expected it to be when they are turned upon by a group of angry ducks and end up being dropped by them into suits of underwear on the line.

Duck One Name given to a special PSA charter airplane used for a cross-country celebration for Donald Duck's 50th birthday in 1984. Traveling with Donald Duck was Clarence Nash, who provided his famous voice.

Duck Pimples (film) Donald Duck cartoon released Aug. 10, 1945. Directed by Jack Kinney. The character of the murder mystery Donald is reading comes to life, and it is only with the intervention of the author, who proves the cop is the thief, that Donald's life is saved, and the character can return to the book.

Ducking Disaster with Donald and His Friends (TV) SEE MAN IS HIS OWN WORST ENEMY.

Duckster Award consisting of a bronze-colored figure of Donald Duck, used to honor those who have been of service to The Walt Disney Company. It was created in 1952; the Mickey Mouse equivalent is known as the Mousecar.

DuckTales (TV) Animated syn. series; aired Sep. 21, 1987–Sep. 5, 1992. It was introduced with a 2-hour syn. special (*Treasure of the Golden Sun*) Sep. 18, 1987. It returned to the air on ABC Apr. 19, 1997–Aug. 30, 1997. On Sep. 1, 1997, it began a new syn. run. The show featured Scrooge McDuck and the nephews, Huey, Dewey, and Louie. Scrooge's innate sense for making or finding money leads him to outrageous adventures, accompanied by his grandnephews. Helping, though sometimes hindering, are Webbigail Vanderquack ("Webby"), Gyro Gearloose, Mrs. Beakley, Doofus, and Gladstone Gander. The Beagle Boys, Magica de Spell, and Flintheart Glomgold, on the other hand, are out to destroy the McDuck empire. For the series, the nephews were given unique colors to wear for the first time: red for Huey, blue for Dewey, and green for Louie. Voices include Alan Young (Scrooge), Russi Taylor (nephews, Webby), and Terence McGovern (Launchpad). 100 episodes. The theme song was written by Mark Mueller.

DuckTales (TV) A new *DuckTales* series debuted on Disney XD Sep. 23, 2017, preceded by a TV movie, *Woo-oo!*, on Aug. 12. Scrooge McDuck, his curious and mischief-making grandnephews, and the optimistic yet temperamental Donald Duck embark on high-flying adventures worldwide filled with comedy, mystery, and adventure. The animation style is inspired by the classic Carl Barks comic designs. Voices include David Tennant (Uncle Scrooge), Danny Pudi (Huey), Ben Schwartz (Dewey), Bobby Moynihan (Louie), Kate Micucci (Webby Vanderquack), Beck Bennett (Launchpad McQuack), Toks Olagundoye (Mrs. Beakley), Tony Anselmo (Donald Duck). From Disney Television Animation.

DuckTales Movie Special (TV) Syn. special, previewing *DuckTales: the Movie, Treasure of the Lost Lamp*; first aired Aug. 1, 1990. 30 min. Hosted by Tracey Gold and Kadeem Hardison. Directed by Adam Small and Barbara Williams.

DuckTales: the Movie, Treasure of the Lost Lamp (film) Scrooge McDuck travels to the far ends of the Earth in search of the elusive buried treasure of legendary thief Collie Baba. With his companions Huey, Dewey, and Louie, plus Webby and Launchpad McQuack, Scrooge discovers not only the treasure but also that there's a mysterious madman named Merlock who is out to stop him. The travelers have to return home empty-handed except for an old lamp. The kids find it is a magic lamp and discover a genie inside, who grants their wishes. When Merlock and his henchman, Dijon, return, it takes all of Scrooge's ingenuity to thwart them. Released Aug. 3, 1990, as a Disney Movietoon. Directed by Bob Hathcock. 74 min. Voices include Alan Young (Scrooge), Terence McGovern (Launchpad), Russi Taylor (nephews, Webby). A true international production, with the story work and planning done in the U.S., the animation done in England and France, and the cels painted in China. Released on video in 1991.

DuckTales: Time Is Money (TV) Syn. special; aired Nov. 25, 1988. Directed by Bob Hathcock, James T. Walker, Terrence Harrison, James Mitchell.

DuckTales: Treasure of the Golden Suns (TV) Two-hour movie special, which introduced the DuckTales series on Sep. 18, 1987. Donald joins the Navy and leaves Huey, Dewey, and Louie in Duckburg with Uncle Scrooge. The nephews have to prove themselves innocent of stealing an expensive ship model and then help Scrooge find a lost treasure ship.

DuckTales Valentine!, A (TV) Show aired Feb. 11, 1990. Directed by Mircea Manita. Scrooge McDuck goes searching for the lost temple of Aphroducky, the ancient goddess of love. Also includes a lecture by Ludwig Von Drake on love, utilizing 3 cartoons.

DuckTales World Showcase Adventure Interactive scavenger hunt in EPCOT; debuted Dec. 16, 2022. Guests join Scrooge McDuck, the nephews, Webby, and friends in search of priceless treasure around World Showcase. Using the Play Disney Parks mobile app, players discover far-flung destinations and maybe even a few villains. It replaced Phineas and Ferb: Agent P's World Showcase Adventure.

Ducky and Bunny Pair of wisecracking plush carnival prizes in *Toy Story 4*; voiced by Keegan-Michael Key and Jordan Peele.

Dude Duck (film) Donald Duck cartoon released Mar. 2, 1951. Directed by Jack Hannah. Donald, on vacation at a dude ranch, cannot wait to ride a horse. Unfortunately, the only horse available is completely unwilling to cooperate. Donald ends up on a bull's back riding out into the desert with the horse laughing wildly.

Duets (film) Six strangers from all walks of life have one thing in common: a passion for karaoke. In this road-trip comedy, 3 pairs of people converge on the $5,000 Grand Prize Karaoke Contest in Omaha, Nebraska, searching to find something they don't have in their lives. Released Sep. 15, 2000. A Hollywood Pictures film, in association with Seven Arts Pictures and Beacon Pictures. Directed by Bruce Paltrow. Stars Maria Bello (Suzi Loomis), André Braugher (Reggie Kane), Paul Giamatti (Todd Woods), Huey Lewis (Ricky Dean), Gwyneth Paltrow (Liv), Scott Speedman (Billy Hannon), Angie Dickinson (Blair). 112 min. Gwyneth Paltrow is the daughter of the director. Filmed in the Las Vegas area and around Vancouver.

Duff, Hilary Actress; appeared on Disney Channel in the title roles in *Lizzie McGuire* and *Cadet Kelly*, on ABC Family in *Beauty & the Briefcase* (Lane Daniels), and on ABC in the *Walt Disney World Christmas Day Parade* and *Disneyland 60: The Wonderful World of Disney*. In theaters, she starred in *The Lizzie McGuire Movie*. She also became a best-selling recording artist for Hollywood Records.

Duffy, Patrick Actor; appeared in *Perfect Game* (Bobby Geiser) and *You Again* (Richie), on TV in *14 Going on 30*, and made guest appearances in *The Fosters* (Robert Quinn, Sr.), *American Housewife* (Marty), and *Station 19* (Terry). He also hosted *Disney's Captain EO Grand Opening* and voiced Harold Hatchback on *Goof Troop*.

Duffy and Friends Duffy, the Disney Bear, a nautical teddy bear with Mickey Mouse-shaped markings, was introduced in winter 2005 in the American Waterfront at Tokyo DisneySea. As the story goes, Minnie made the bear for Mickey to keep him company on a long ocean voyage, gifting it to him in a duffel bag (hence the name Duffy). Duffy originated as the Disney Bear, which debuted at the Jul. 2002 opening of Once Upon a Toy in the Downtown Disney Marketplace at Walt Disney World. He was later adapted for Japanese audiences with the new name, story, and themed clothing. Duffy also greeted visitors in EPCOT and Disney California Adventure for a number of years beginning Oct. 14, 2010. Over the years, new characters have been added as Duffy's friends across the international Disney parks: ShellieMay (another teddy bear made by Minnie; debuted in Tokyo DisneySea, 2010), Gelatoni (artistic cat who uses his tail as a paintbrush; Tokyo DisneySea, 2014), StellaLou (bunny who dreams of becoming a dancer; Tokyo DisneySea, 2017), Cookie (curious puppy who likes to bake; Hong Kong Disneyland, 2018, and renamed CookieAnn in 2019), 'Olu ('ukulele-playing turtle; Aulani, A Disney Resort & Spa, 2018, and renamed 'Olu Mel in 2020), and LinaBell (mystery-solving fox; Shanghai Disney Resort, 2021). Duffy and his friends, including a mailman seagull named Tippy Blue, have been immensely popular on merchandise and have also made appearances on stage at the Cape Cod Cook-Off in Tokyo DisneySea and online in a series of stop-motion animated shorts. A 6-episode stop-motion animated series starring Duffy and Friends is scheduled to debut on Disney+ in 2023.

Dug Golden retriever, whose collar translates his thoughts into speech, in *Up*; voiced by Bob Peterson.

Dug Days (TV) Animated short series on Disney+; digitally premiered Sep. 1, 2021. Follows the humorous everyday events that take place in and around Dug's backyard, all through the eyes of the dog from Disney • Pixar's *Up*. Written/directed by Bob Peterson. From Pixar Animation Studios.

Dugan, Dennis Actor; appeared in *Unidentified Flying Oddball* (Tom Trimble) and *Can't Buy Me Love* (David Miller), and years later directed the TV remake of *The Shaggy Dog*.

Duggan, Andrew (1923–1988) Actor; appeared in *The Bears and I* (Commissioner Gaines), and on TV in *Fire on Kelly Mountain* (Ed Jorgenson) and *The Saga of Andy Burnett* (Jack Kelly). He voiced the father in the Carousel of Progress in the Magic Kingdom at Walt Disney World 1975–1993.

Dugout The official mascot of Little League baseball was created by artists at Disney Consumer Products, who considered him a cross between a gopher and a beaver. Dugout was introduced by Disney's Sport Goofy at the Little League World Series in Williamsport, Pennsylvania, in 1985.

Dug's Special Mission (film) Special cartoon included as a bonus on the DVD release of *Up* on Nov. 10, 2009. The good-hearted dog, Dug, is sent on a series of quests by his mean canine bosses, but their plans always backfire. Directed by Ronnie Del Carmen. 5 min.

Dukakis, Olympia (1931–2021) Actress; appeared in *The Cemetery Club* (Doris Silverman), *I Love Trouble* (Jeannie), *Mr. Holland's Opus* (Principal Jacobs), and *Jane Austen's Mafia!* (Sophia), and on TV in *Ladies and the Champ* (Sarah Stevenson).

Duke, The (film) Direct-to-video release Apr. 18, 2000, by Buena Vista Home Entertainment, of a Keystone Pictures film (originally released in Iceland Oct. 30, 1999). Hubert, a bloodhound, inherits the estate of the Duke of Dingwall, including royal jewels and the title of Duke, but a disinherited nephew comes up with a plot to seize control. Directed by Philip Spink. Stars Courtnee Draper (Charlotte), James Doohan (Clive Chives), Oliver Muirhead (Cecil Cavendish). 88 min.

Duke Igthorn The menace of the Gummi Bears; voiced by Michael Rye.

Dumb Bell of the Yukon (film) Donald Duck cartoon released Aug. 30, 1946. Directed by Jack King. Arctic trapper Donald kidnaps a cub from a sleeping mother bear to get a fur coat for Daisy. Just as the mother bear is about to attack Donald, a jar of honey falls on his head. Both bears end up licking the honey off Donald.

Dumbella Sister of Donald Duck and mother of Huey, Dewey, and Louie, according to the cartoon *Donald's Nephews* (1938).

Dumbo (film) A baby circus elephant is born with huge ears and named Dumbo. He and his mother suffer humiliation from the other elephants and from the kids visiting the circus. But humiliation turns to triumph as Dumbo is surprised to discover through the help of his faithful mouse friend, Timothy, that he can use the oversized ears to fly. Released Oct. 23, 1941. Directed by Ben Sharpsteen. From a story by Helen Aberson and Harold Pearl. 64 min. Voices include Edward Brophy (Timothy), Sterling Holloway (stork), Cliff Edwards (Dandy Crow). Among the songs are "Baby Mine," "Pink Elephants on Parade," and "When I See an Elephant Fly." The film won an Academy Award for Scoring of a Motion Picture (Frank Churchill and Oliver Wallace) and was nominated for Best Song ("Baby Mine," by Ned Washington and Frank Churchill). From the time that Walt first read the galleys for the story, he knew it would make a fine film. Coming after 2 expensive movies (*Fantasia* and *Pinocchio*) the previous year, *Dumbo* was made for only $812,000, partly because it was able to move very quickly through the animation department due to its succinct story and clear-cut characters. And it made a welcome profit for the Studio. *Dumbo* had been scheduled for the cover of *Time* magazine at the time of its general release in Dec. 1941, but a much more momentous event occurred—Pearl Harbor—and poor Dumbo was supplanted by Japan's General Yamamoto. The movie was rereleased in theaters in 1949, 1959, 1972, and 1976. It was shown on the Disney TV series in 1955.

Dumbo (film) A live-action telling of the classic story. Circus owner Max Medici enlists former circus star Holt Farrier and his children, Milly and Joe, to care for a newborn elephant whose oversized ears make him a laughingstock in an already struggling circus. But when they discover that Dumbo can fly, the circus makes an incredible comeback, attracting persuasive entrepreneur V. A. Vandevere, who recruits the unusual pachyderm for his new larger-than-life entertainment venture, Dreamland. Dumbo soars to new heights alongside a charming and spectacular aerial artist, Colette Marchant, until Holt learns that, beneath its shiny veneer, Dreamland is full of dark secrets. Directed by Tim Burton. Released Mar. 29, 2019 (also in 3-D and IMAX), after a Mar. 27 international release. Stars Colin Farrell (Holt Farrier), Michael Keaton (V. A. Vandevere), Danny DeVito (Max Medici), Eva Green (Colette Marchant), Nico Parker (Milly Farrier), Finley Hobbins (Joe Farrier). For authenticity, filmmakers recruited 4th-generation Hungarian performer Kristian Kristof to share his extensive circus knowledge and connections, resulting in a multicultural array of jugglers, clowns, knife throwers, and contortionists. For Dreamland's parade sequence, costume designer Colleen Atwood oversaw the creation of more than 200 costumes for the performers, plus an additional 500 for the crowd characters. Sharon Rooney (Miss Atlantis) sings the iconic ballad "Baby Mine," written originally for the 1941 animated film. 112 min. Filmed in wide-screen format at Pinewood Studios outside London. The Dreamland sequences were filmed in a massive hangar at Cardington Studios in Bedfordshire, England.

Dumbo: A Lesson in Being Prepared (film) Educational film; released in Sep. 1981. One should not be overeager and try things before one is prepared.

Dumbo the Flying Elephant Fantasyland attraction in Disneyland; opened Aug. 16, 1955. Known as Dumbo the Flying Elephant (1955–1959, and since 1984, Dumbo Flying Elephants (1959–1983), and Dumbo's Flying Elephants (1983–1984). Riders fly in Dumbo-shaped vehicles and are able to control the up-and-down movement with a lever. It was completely remodeled in 1990 when new Dumbo vehicles and a new ride mechanism, which had been prepared for shipment to Euro Disneyland, were found not to be needed in France as early as expected. The attraction was installed at Disneyland instead, and another new one was built for France. Also a Fantasyland attraction in the Magic Kingdom at Walt Disney World; opened Oct. 1, 1971, and remodeled in 1993 and in 2012 (increased to 2 carousels with an added interactive queue, in a new location in Storybook Circus). A version opened in Fantasyland in Tokyo Disneyland Apr. 15, 1983; in Disneyland Paris Apr. 12, 1992; in Hong Kong Disneyland Sep. 12, 2005; and in Gardens of Imagination at Shanghai Disneyland Jun. 16, 2016, marking the first time the attraction appeared in an area other than Fantasyland. For many guests, a ride on Dumbo the Flying Elephant is a rite of passage at the Disney parks. Considered a symbol of American pop culture, a Dumbo vehicle, along with a teacup from the Mad Tea Party, was presented to the Smithsonian's National Museum of American History Jun. 8, 2005.

Dumbo's Circus (TV) Series on The Disney Channel; premiered May 6, 1985. The show follows the adventures of Dumbo and his fellow performers in a traveling circus. Voices include Katie Leigh (Dumbo), Jim Cummings (Lionel, the lion), Hal Smith (Fair Dinkum, the ringmaster koala), Patricia Parris (Lilli, the trapeze artist cat), Ron Gans (Q. T., the calliope-playing orangutan), Will Ryan (Barnaby, the shaggy dog clown), Walker Edmiston (Sebastian, the alley cat janitor). 120 episodes. Longtime Disney Studio artists Ken Anderson and Bob Moore designed the circus animals, which were realized using "puppetronics," a new technique that enabled the characters to perform synchronized facial expressions and lip movements with recorded dialogue. Lionel was the first voice acting role for Jim Cummings, who would go on to voice dozens of Disney characters; the character was puppeteered by 1950s Mouseketeer Sharon Baird.

Dumbo's Circus Parade Ran in the Magic Kingdom at Walt Disney World Jan. 2–Dec. 21, 1979, with a Casey Jr. train and floats with Disney characters as the circus performers. A similar parade ran in Disneyland the same year, Feb. 17–Dec. 16. In 1986, another circus parade debuted in Disneyland for the Circus Fantasy extravaganza.

Duncan, Michael Clarke (1957–2012) Actor; voice of Tug in *Brother Bear* and *Brother Bear 2*. He also provided voices in *The Proud Family*, *Air Buddies*, *Kim Possible: A Sitch in Time*, and *George of the Jungle II*. He appeared in *Breakfast of Champions* (Eli) and *Armageddon* (Bear), and on TV in *The Suite Life of Zack & Cody* (Coach Little).

Duncan, Sandy Actress; appeared in *The Million Dollar Duck* (Katie Dooley)—her movie debut— and *The Cat from Outer Space* (Liz), and voiced Vixey in *The Fox and the Hound*. She headlined the TV special *Sandy in Disneyland* and later appeared in *Christmas in Disneyland with Art Carney* (tour guide) and *The Best of Disney: 50 Years of Magic*. Duncan came to Disney's notice while appearing in an inventive TV commercial for a Los Angeles bank.

Dundy's Sundries Shop in Disney's BoardWalk Inn at Walt Disney World; opened in 1996, offering snacks, cameras, and accessories. Closed Oct. 3, 2022, to become Carousel Coffee.

Durning, Charles (1923–2012) Actor; appeared in *Tough Guys* (Deke Yablonski), *Dick Tracy* (Chief Brandon), *V. I. Warshawski* (Lt. Mallory), *O Brother, Where Art Thou?* (Pappy O'Daniel), *Mr. St. Nick* (Nicholas XX), and *Stephen King's Desperation* (Tom Billingsley).

Duvall, Robert Actor; appeared in *Newsies* (Joseph Pulitzer), *The Scarlet Letter* (Roger Chillingworth), *Phenomenon* (Doc), *Gone in 60 Seconds* (Otto Halliwell), and *A Civil Action* (Jerome Facher).

DVD The first Disney films were released on DVD (Digital Versatile Disc) Dec. 2, 1997. By the early 2000s, the process was rapidly gaining on and eventually surpassing VHS in popularity. One highlight of the DVDs has been the wealth of bonus material that has been added to enhance the enjoyment of the movie. Beginning in Sep. 2006, Disney movies were also released on a new optical disc format, Blu-ray, which offered greater quality and storage capacity. Combo DVD/Blu-ray packs were soon made available, some including a digital HD copy of the title, as well. Select Disney titles have also been released in Blu-ray 3-D (beginning in 2010) and Ultra HD Blu-ray (beginning in 2017) formats.

D-Zertz Pleasure Island coffee and sweets shop at Walt Disney World; open May 1, 1989–Jan. 1, 2005.

Dzundza, George Actor; appeared in *Dangerous Minds* (Hal Griffith), *Crimson Tide* (Cob), *That Darn Cat* (Boetticher, 1997), and *Instinct* (John Murray), and on TV in *2 1/2 Dads* (Pete Selzer) and *Grey's Anatomy* (Harold O'Malley).

1. Enchanted Tiki Room, Walt Disney's 2. Enchanted Tale of Beauty and the Beast 3. *Eureka!* (TV) 4. EPCOT
5. Elliott 6. *Encanto* (film) 7. *Elemental* (film) 8. Evinrude 9. *Enchanted* (film) 10. *Empress Lilly*

E! Entertainment In Jan. 1997, Disney and Comcast Corporation joined together to purchase the majority of the stock of the entertainment industry–themed cable channel, E! Disney sold its 39.5% stake to Comcast in Nov. 2006 for $1.23 billion.

E ticket The coveted coupon for the most exciting attractions in the Disneyland ticket book; first offered in 1959, with the debut of Matterhorn Bobsleds, Submarine Voyage, and the Disneyland-Alweg Monorail System. The term "an E ticket ride" entered the American lexicon meaning the ultimate in thrills. On Jun. 18, 1983, astronaut Sally Ride described her first excursion into space as "definitely an E ticket." SEE ALSO TICKET BOOKS.

Eagle Pines Golf course at Bonnet Creek Golf Club at Walt Disney World; open 1992–2007. Designed by Pete Dye.

Eagle Pines & Osprey Ridge Golf Club Originally opened at Walt Disney World Jan. 23, 1992, as the Bonnet Creek Golf Club; the name changed Feb. 1, 2005. The club closed Aug. 1, 2007. Osprey Ridge closed in 2013 for incorporation into the Four Seasons Orlando resort development, reopening in Nov. 2014 as Tranquilo Golf Club.

Ear Force One A 96-ft.-tall hot-air balloon designed in the shape of Mickey Mouse; debuted in 1986, for the 15th anniversary of Walt Disney World.

Earffel Tower Water tower icon of Disney-MGM Studios (now Disney's Hollywood Studios). Topped by a 10,000-lb. pair of mouse ears, the 130-ft.-tall structure was located in the park's backstage production area. It was removed Apr. 28, 2016, to make way for Toy Story Land. A similar tower, Château d'Eaureilles, is the icon of Walt Disney Studios Park in Disneyland Paris.

Earl of Sandwich Counter-service eatery specializing in hot sandwiches. Now a national franchise, the first restaurant opened in Downtown Disney Marketplace (now the Marketplace at Disney Springs) in Walt Disney World Mar. 19, 2004, taking the place of the Gourmet Pantry. Also in Disney Village at Disneyland Paris (opened Jun. 1, 2011) and in the Downtown Disney District at Disneyland Resort, taking the place of Compass Books (from Nov. 2, 2012–Jan. 27, 2022), then reopening Feb. 1, 2023, in a temporary spot replacing La Brea Bakery, also adding the table-service Earl of Sandwich Tavern on Feb. 27.

Earle, Eyvind (1916–2000) Background artist/color stylist; joined Disney in 1951, working on *For Whom the Bulls Toil*; *Toot, Whistle, Plunk and Boom*; *Pigs Is Pigs*; *Working for Peanuts*; *Peter Pan*; and *Lady and the Tramp*. But it is his distinctive styling for *Sleeping Beauty* that has brought him fame. He appeared on TV in *4 Artists Paint 1 Tree*. He was named a Disney Legend posthumously in 2015.

Early to Bed (film) Donald Duck cartoon released Jul. 11, 1941. Directed by Jack King. Donald spends the night unable to sleep because of a ticking alarm clock and a foldaway bed that keeps trapping him when it constantly folds up—on its own.

EarPort, Disney's SEE ORLANDO INTERNATIONAL AIRPORT.

Earth (film) Documentary telling the story of animal families—emphasizing the polar bear, humpback whale, and elephant—and their amazing journeys across the planet. Directed by Alastair Fothergill and Mark Linfield. Released in the U.S. on Earth Day, Apr. 22, 2009; original release at the Vaduz Film Festival Jul. 14, 2007. Narrated by James Earl Jones (narrator for the earlier version had been Patrick Stewart). From BBC Worldwide and Greenlight Media for Disneynature. 90 min. The first film in the Disneynature series. Filming from a great height from helicopters using the gyro-stabilized Cineflex aerial camera system allowed the filmmakers to track their wild and elusive animal characters from great distances and place them into the context of their environment while not disturbing them. The film broke records for a nature documentary at its opening.

Earth*Star Voyager (TV) Four-hour movie; aired in 2 parts, Jan. 17 and 24, 1988. Directed by James Goldstone. A select group of young cadets in the 21st century is sent off on a spaceship to find a new home for humanity when Earth is deteriorating. Along the way, they happen on an old, failed world's fair, Expo Tomorrow, where they learn that their foe is the Outlaw Technology Zone, or OTZ, a band of criminals. Stars Duncan Regehr, Brian McNamara, Julia Montgomery, Jason Michas. Some of the filming took place at the closed site of Expo '86 in Vancouver.

Earth Station Information and guest services area under Spaceship Earth in EPCOT Center; open Oct. 1, 1982–1994. After exiting the Spaceship Earth attraction, guests could interact with WorldKey Information System monitors to make reservations for park restaurants. Overhead, imagery of the major EPCOT pavilions was projected onto large screens. The space was remodeled into Global Neighborhood, an interactive area presented by AT&T.

Earth to Ned (TV) Original series on Disney+; digitally premiered Sep. 4, 2020. Calling off an invasion of Earth, alien commander Ned and his lieutenant, Cornelius, host a late-night talk show from the bridge of their spaceship, beaming in human celebrities to learn about interesting topics, such as comedy, sports, and fashion. Performers include Paul Rugg (Ned), Michael Oosterom (Cornelius), Colleen Smith (BETI). From The Jim Henson Company and Marwar Junction Productions, in association with Disney+.

Earthquakes (film) Educational film; released in Sep. 1986. 15 min. The hows and whys of natural earth movements, including earthquake safety tips.

Easier Said (film) Direct-to-video release Jan. 16, 2001, by Touchstone Home Video, of a Twenty-Three Frames film from 1999. Things aren't working out for Jack, so he decides to leave the big city and pursue his life's ambition to write the "great American novel." He moves to a small Colorado town, only to find romantic chaos following him. Directed by H. Todd Von Mende. Stars Bo Clancey (Jack), Tricia Gregory (Eldora), Alex McLeod (Anna Sophia), Albie Parisella (Ciro), Walter Rheinfrank (Addison).

East, Jeff Actor; appeared on TV in *The Flight of the Grey Wolf* (Russ Hanson), *Return of the Big Cat* (Josh McClaren), and *The Ghost of Cypress Swamp* (Lonny Bascombe).

Eastside Cafe Elegant Victorian-themed restaurant in World Bazaar at Tokyo Disneyland; opened Apr. 15, 1983.

Eastwood, Jennifer Senior editor for Disney Editions who has helped produce numerous coffee table books, cookbooks, and more for Disney fans. She began her Disney Publishing career in 2003 as part of the editorial staffs of *FamilyFun*, *Disney Magazine*, and *Disney Adventures*. She coauthored *Disney in Details* and *Let the Memories Begin!*

Ebert & Roeper and the Movies (TV) After the death of Gene Siskel, Roger Ebert continued the *Siskel & Ebert* show, using guest critics, with a title of *Roger Ebert & the Movies* during the 1999–2000 season. Starting Aug. 28, 2000, Richard Roeper, a *Chicago Sun-Times* syn. columnist, joined the show, which was then renamed, as a regular. In 2001, the title of the show was shortened to *Ebert & Roeper*, and in 2007 it became *At the Movies with Ebert & Roeper*. In Aug. 2006 Ebert left the show after complications due to surgery, and Roeper continued with guest hosts. Ebert decided in Apr. 2008 that he would be unable to return. SEE ALSO AT THE MOVIES.

Ebsen, Buddy (1908–2003) Actor/dancer; appeared in *Davy Crockett* (George Russel) and *The One and Only, Genuine, Original Family Band* (Calvin

Bower), and on TV in *Dateline Disneyland*, *Corky and White Shadow* on the *Mickey Mouse Club* (Sheriff Matt Brady), *Walt Disney—A Golden Anniversary Salute*, *NBC Salutes the 25th Anniversary of the Wonderful World of Disney*, and *Kraft Salutes Disneyland's 25th Anniversary*. He also narrated *Disney Family Album* on The Disney Channel. In 1951, he danced on film for Walt and his technicians to study for the original Project Little Man, which would lead to the development of Audio-Animatronics technology. He was named a Disney Legend in 1993.

Echo Lake Lake in Disney-MGM Studios (now Disney's Hollywood Studios) at Walt Disney World. Surrounding the lake are Dockside Diner and Dinosaur Gertie's Ice Cream of Extinction, representing 1950s-era California Crazy architecture. Later became the name of the area encompassing Hyperion Theater, Mickey Shorts Theater, *Indiana Jones Epic Stunt Spectacular!*, and Star Tours, as well as the 50's Prime Time Café, Hollywood & Vine, and Backlot Express restaurants.

Economics by Choice (film) Educational film; released in Sep. 1985. The film illustrates basic economic concepts for children through situations that relate to their own lives.

Ed Wood (film) Edward D. Wood Jr., an eccentric actor/writer/director, has only one thing going for him—an optimistic spirit that remains indomitable despite his obviously misguided career choices. Wood tries to make it in Hollywood but earns the reputation of being the "worst director of all time." He has a fetish for wearing women's clothes, and he gathers around him a bizarre band of characters, including the down-and-out screen legend Bela Lugosi, TV horror queen Vampira, hulking Swedish wrestler Tor Johnson, psychic Criswell, and highbrow Bunny Breckinridge. Wood creates ineptly made, offbeat, low-budget independent films that somehow turn out to be cultish classics and turn their director into a legend. Limited release in Los Angeles and New York City on Sep. 28, 1994; general release on Oct. 7, 1994. Directed by Tim Burton. A Touchstone film. Stars Johnny Depp (Ed Wood), Martin Landau (Bela Lugosi), Sarah Jessica Parker (Dolores Fuller), Patricia Arquette (Kathy O'Hara), Jeffrey Jones (Criswell), Bill Murray (Bunny Breckinridge). Based on a true story. Filmed in Los Angeles and its environs in black and white. 127 min. Martin Landau received an Academy Award for Supporting Actor for his portrayal of Lugosi, and the film also won one for Makeup.

Eddie (film) Wild Bill Burgess, a promotion-minded eccentric, takes over a losing NBA franchise, the New York Knicks, and happens to overhear the advice of die-hard fan Edwina "Eddie" Franklin, who yells her opinions from the stands. When Coach Bailey is canned, Eddie, as part of a publicity stunt, becomes the new coach whom no one takes seriously. Standing on the sidelines watching her team lose one game after another, Eddie begins to show herself as a real motivator, with her infectious spirit pushing the team to win and helping to convince Wild Bill to keep them in New York City. A Hollywood Pictures film. Directed by Steve Rash. Released May 31, 1996. Stars Whoopi Goldberg (Eddie), Frank Langella (Wild Bill Burgess), Dennis Farina (Coach John Bailey), Richard Jenkins (Zimmer), and Lisa Ann Walter (Claudine), who are joined by many professional basketball stars. 100 min. While the character of Eddie was originally written as a male bank teller, and the team was originally the Los Angeles Clippers, Goldberg's interest in the project changed everything. The motion picture was filmed in North Carolina, utilizing facilities at the Charlotte Coliseum and Winston-Salem's Lawrence Joel Veteran's Memorial Coliseum.

Eddie's Million Dollar Cook-Off (TV) A Disney Channel Original Movie; first aired Jul. 18, 2003. Fourteen-year-old baseball prodigy Eddie Ogden finds cooking fascinating, to the consternation of his friends and his father, who happens to be the baseball coach. He enters a major cooking contest, which turns out to be on the same day as the baseball playoffs. Eddie has to decide if he can fulfill his obligation to his team, and still be true to himself. Directed by Paul Hoen. Stars Taylor Ball (Eddie Ogden), Orlando Brown (Frankie), Reiley McClendon (DB), Rose McIver (Hannah), Mark L. Taylor (Hank Ogden), Susan Brady (Sarah). Celebrity chef Bobby Flay makes his film debut playing himself. From Solo Productions in association with Disney Channel.

Edelweiss Snacks Alpine chalet in Fantasyland at Disneyland, serving frozen beverages, turkey legs, and snacks; opened Sep. 2009.

Eden, Barbara Actress; appeared on TV in *Brand New Life* (Barbara McCray Gibbons), with guest appearances in *Army Wives* (Victoria Grayson) and the *Walt Disney World Very Merry Christmas Parade*. She voiced Evelyn in *Teamo Supremo*.

Edgar Supercilious butler in *The Aristocats*; voiced by Roddy Maude-Roxby.

Edgar, Cyril (1907–1987) He was in charge of the distribution of Disney films in the United Kingdom for more than 20 years. He was presented posthumously with a European Disney Legends Award in 1997.

Edgren, Don (1923–2006) After serving as chief engineer during the construction of Disneyland, working for Wheeler & Gray, he joined WED Enterprises in 1961. Over the next 2 decades, he supervised engineering on the Disney pavilions for the 1964–1965 New York World's Fair, New Orleans Square at Disneyland, Walt Disney World, and Tokyo Disneyland. He retired in 1987 and was named a Disney Legend in 2006.

Edison, The Lavish 1920s-themed restaurant in the Landing at Disney Springs at Walt Disney World; opened Jan. 4, 2018, after soft openings beginning Dec. 31, 2017. It took the place of the Adventurers Club. Guests enjoy American cuisine, cocktails, and entertainment in a variety of lounges and parlors. The industrial Gothic design tells the restaurant's backstory as a former power plant. Managed by Patina Restaurant Group.

Edison Square Proposed in the late 1950s as a new location behind Main Street, U.S.A. in Disneyland, this unrealized turn-of-the-century area was to celebrate how one invention by Thomas Edison influenced the growth and development of America. It was considered an early inspiration for the Carousel of Progress.

Edison Twins, The (TV) Series on The Disney Channel; premiered Mar. 3, 1984, and continued, with repeats, until Dec. 31, 1989. The 16-year-old twins use science to help them solve mysteries. Each episode ended with an animated explanation for the scientific principles used in that particular show. Stars Andrew Sabiston (Tom Edison), Marnie McPhail (Ann Edison), Sunny Besen Thrasher (Paul). 78 episodes. From Nelvana. Originally aired in Canada beginning in 1982.

Edna "E" Mode Petite and powerful fashionista in *The Incredibles*; voiced by Brad Bird.

Edouarde, Carl (1875–1932) Orchestra conductor; retained by Walt Disney in New York City to record the music for *Steamboat Willie*, which became the first synchronized soundtrack for a cartoon.

Education for Death (film) Special cartoon released Jan. 15, 1943. Directed by Clyde Geronimi. Offscreen narration tells the story of little Hans, a German child being taught Nazi principles of hate and cruelty in school, who grows up to become a soldier. The picture fades out with soldiers' swords and helmets resembling grave markers, showing their education for death is complete. A World War II-era short.

Educational films The first Disney educational film was *Tommy Tucker's Tooth,* which Walt Disney prepared for a local dentist in Kansas City in 1922. When World War II arrived, he realized that animation could help in training, by showing things that could not be shown in live action. The Disney Studio made *Four Methods of Flush Riveting* as a sample (for Lockheed Aircraft Company) and soon was making dozens of films for the U.S. government. With few exceptions, the films did not feature the Disney characters, but instead utilized graphics, stop-motion, limited animation, and diagrams to get across a point. After the war, the techniques he learned on the war films came in handy as he continued to produce films, such as *The ABC of Hand Tools* and *Bathing Time for Baby*, under contract for various companies. *How to Catch a Cold* and *The Story of Menstruation*, produced during this period, became widely used in schools. Soon thereafter, however, Walt decided to get out of the educational film business. He reasoned that his business was entertainment, not education. With the advent of TV and changes in education in the 1950s, however, he saw that there were ways in which he could teach, but still entertain. One of the finest examples was *Donald in Mathmagic Land*. After Walt's death, the company moved even deeper into educational productions, incorporating a subsidiary, the Walt Disney Educational Materials Company (later Walt Disney Educational Media Company), in 1969 and embarking on a prolific program of film strips, films, study prints, and other materials for schools. Many of these materials would win awards from educational organizations. In the 1990s, the education arm was renamed Disney Educational Productions.

Edwards, Cliff (1895–1971) Performer; provided the voice of Jiminy Cricket in *Pinocchio* and *Fun and Fancy Free* and in later TV cartoons. He also voiced crows in *Dumbo*. Also known as Ukulele Ike, he appeared on the *Mickey Mouse Club* and had a solo album released by Disneyland Records in 1956. In the 1942 wartime cartoon *The New Spirit*, he is heard singing "Yankee Doodle Spirit," a song which he co-wrote with Oliver Wallace. He was named a Disney Legend in 2000.

Eega Beeva Character that made his first appearance in the daily *Mickey Mouse* comic strip of Sep. 26, 1947. He looked somewhat beetle-like and was considered a "little man of the future."

Eeyore Gloomy donkey friend of Winnie the Pooh; voiced by Ralph Wright in the original films.

Efron, Zac Actor; appeared in the *High School Musical* films (Troy Bolton), and on TV in *The Disney Family Singalong*. It was announced that he will star in *Three Men and a Baby* on Disney+.

Egan, Richard (1923–1987) Actor; appeared in *Pollyanna* (Dr. Edmund Chilton).

Egan, Susan Actress; starred as Belle on Broadway in *Beauty and the Beast*. She voiced Megara in *Hercules*, Lin in *Spirited Away*, and Renee Frodgers in *Amphibia*, and provided the singing voice of Angel in *Lady and the Tramp II: Scamp's Adventure*. Appeared on Disney Channel in *Gotta Kick It Up!* (Heather Bartlett) and on Disney+ in *Encore!*

Egyptian Melodies (film) Silly Symphony cartoon released Aug. 27, 1931. Directed by Wilfred Jackson. In a spider's misadventures with the Sphynx and the pyramids, hieroglyphics entertain until mummies are disturbed and frighten him away.

Ehrbar, Greg He joined Walt Disney World Marketing Creative Services (later known as Yellow Shoes) in 1990, contributing to advertising and radio, ABC specials, animation, publishing, and other experiences for Disney parks and resorts. He retired in 2016 but continues to consult on company projects. Also coauthor, with Tim Hollis, of *Mouse Tracks: The Story of Walt Disney Records*.

Eight Below (film) Three members of a scientific expedition in Antarctica—Jerry Shepard; his best friend, Cooper; and a rugged American geologist—are forced to leave behind their team of beloved sled dogs due to a sudden accident and perilous weather conditions. During the harsh Antarctic winter, the dogs must struggle for survival alone in the intense frozen wilderness for over 6 months until the adventurers can mount a rescue mission. Directed by Frank Marshall. Released Feb. 17, 2006. Stars Paul Walker (Jerry Shepard), Bruce Greenwood

(Davis McClaren), Moon Bloodgood (Katie), Jason Biggs (Charlie Cooper), Gerald Plunkett (Dr. Andy Harrison), August Schellenberg (Mindo). 120 min. Filmed in Super 35-Scope with Canada's British Columbia and Greenland standing in for Antarctica. Suggested by the film *Nankyoku Monogatari* (1983).

8 mm A number of segments from Disney animated classics, short cartoons, live-action/animal adventures, and Disneyland and Walt Disney World films were released on 8 mm and Super 8 mm film for home use. There were also some sound Super 8 mm versions. Earlier, 8 mm shortened versions of Disney theatrical cartoons were released by Hollywood Film Enterprises.

8 Simple Rules for Dating My Teenage Daughter (TV) Half-hour series on ABC, Sep. 17, 2002–Aug. 19, 2005. Family comedy about a loving, rational dad who suddenly discovers that his 2 darling daughters have unexpectedly become hormonally charged, incomprehensible teenagers. Stars John Ritter (Paul Hennessy), Katey Sagal (Cate Hennessy), Kaley Cuoco (Bridget), Amy Davidson (Kerry), Martin Spanjers (Rory). From Touchstone Television. Based on the book by W. Bruce Cameron. After Ritter's unexpected death during production of the 4th episode of the 2003–2004 season, James Garner joined the cast as Cate's father, Jim (Suzanne Pleshette played her mother, Laura, briefly) and the series title was shortened to *8 Simple Rules* with the 7th episode. David Spade also joined the cast as C. J., Cate's wayward nephew.

8TRAX A 1970s to 1980s–themed dance club in Pleasure Island at Walt Disney World; open Dec. 31, 1992–Sep. 27, 2008. Formerly Cage.

Eiler, Barbara (1922–2006) Actress; appeared on TV in *Bristle Face* (Poor Woman), *For the Love of Willadean* (Mrs. Mason), and *The Swamp Fox* (Mary Videaux).

Eilonwy Young princess heroine in *The Black Cauldron*; voiced by Susan Sheridan.

Einstein Slow-moving Great Dane in *Oliver & Company*; voiced by Richard Mulligan.

Eisenhower, Dwight D. (1890–1969) Former president Eisenhower and his wife visited Disneyland in Dec. 1961. In Feb. 1963, he presented Walt Disney with the George Washington Honor Medal of the

Freedoms Foundation at Valley Forge, Pennsylvania; the 2 men admired each other's accomplishments and regularly exchanged correspondence. A decade earlier, Walt and Roy had authorized studio volunteers to make an animated television ad supporting Eisenhower's presidential campaign; *We'll Take Ike* debuted during the fall 1952 election season and featured a catchy theme song of the same name written by Hazel "Gil" George and Paul Smith.

Eisenmann, Ike Actor; appeared as Tony in *Escape to Witch Mountain* and *Return from Witch Mountain*, and on TV in *Kit Carson and the Mountain Men*, *Shadow of Fear*, *The Sky's the Limit*, and *The Secret of the Pond*. For a time, he spelled his name Iake Eissinmann. He had cameo roles in *Tom and Huck* (Taverner) and *Race to Witch Mountain* (Sheriff Antony).

Eisner, Michael D. He served as chairman of the board and chief executive officer of The Walt Disney Company beginning Sep. 22, 1984. Additionally, he assumed the presidency on Apr. 4, 1994, for a year and a half, after the death of Frank Wells. He was born Mar. 7, 1942, in Mount Kisco, New York, and attended the Lawrenceville School and Denison University, where he received a B.A. in English literature and theater. He was a senior vice president at ABC Entertainment and president and chief operating officer of Paramount Pictures Corp. before coming to Disney. He is married to the former Jane Breckenridge, and they have 3 sons. He stepped down from the chairman post Mar. 3, 2004, and retired from the company Sep. 30, 2005.

Ejiofor, Chiwetel Actor; appeared in *Maleficent: Mistress of Evil* (Conall) and as Baron Karl Mordo in the Doctor Strange films. He voiced Scar in *The Lion King* (2019).

El Bandido (TV) Show about Zorro. SEE ALSO ZORRO.

El Capitan Theatre Historic movie palace on Hollywood Boulevard; remodeled by Disney in 1989 in conjunction with its then-owner, Pacific Theaters. In 1991, the restored theater debuted with the world premiere of *The Rocketeer*. Many Disney films have since premiered at the El Capitan, and regular movie screenings occasionally include a special stage show. A highlight is the Mighty Wurlitzer, which had originally performed at the Fox Theatre in San Francisco beginning in 1929. The original street-level offices for the El Capitan

Theatre became Disney's Soda Fountain and Studio Store; the Soda Fountain was replaced by the Ghirardelli Soda Fountain and Chocolate Shop in 2013. Originally developed by Charles Toberman and built by Sid Grauman for stage productions, the theater debuted May 3, 1926, as a 1,550-seat playhouse. Architect Stiles O. Clements designed the Spanish Colonial–style exterior, with G. Albert Lansburgh contributing the original East Indian–inspired interior. It was converted to a movie palace in 1941 and redesigned into the Hollywood Paramount in Mar. 1942.

El Gaucho Goofy (film) Segment of *Saludos Amigos*, with Goofy as an American cowboy becoming an Argentinian gaucho. Released as a short Jun. 10, 1955.

El Mercado de Coronado Food court in Disney's Coronado Springs Resort at Walt Disney World; opened Sep. 2018, taking the place of the Pepper Market.

El Pirata y el Perico Restaurante SEE TORTUGA TAVERN.

El Ranchito del Norte Shop outside the Mexico pavilion in EPCOT; opened in 1986, offering traditional apparel and souvenirs.

El Río del Tiempo Attraction in Mexico at EPCOT; opened Oct. 1, 1982. Translated as The River of Time, guests took a leisurely 8-min. boat ride through Mexican history and culture—from symbolic dances by Mayan, Toltec, and Aztec civilizations to a stylized festival of the children and a trip through modern resorts and destinations. The catchy theme song, "Fiesta in Mexico," by X Atencio and Armando Corral, played throughout. The attraction was revised in 2007 to become Gran Fiesta Tour Starring The Three Caballeros.

El Teatro Fandango Theater in Treasure Cove at Shanghai Disneyland; opened Jun. 16, 2016, with *Eye of the Storm: Captain Jack's Stunt Spectacular*. When Jack Sparrow sees an actor portraying him onstage, he vows to show the imposter what a real pirate can do. Mayhem ensues when British naval forces and pirates arrive, with stunts and duels continuing despite a raging storm that slams through the theater.

El Terrible Toreador (film) The 2nd Silly Symphony cartoon; released in 1929. Directed by Walt

Disney. This cartoon features a burlesque of bull-fight drama.

Elaborate Lives: The Legend of Aida SEE AIDA.

Elam, Jack (1920–2003) Actor; appeared in *Never a Dull Moment* (Ace Williams), *The Wild Country* (Thompson), *Hot Lead and Cold Feet* (Rattlesnake), and *The Apple Dumpling Gang Rides Again* (Big Mac), and on TV in *Zorro* (Gomez), *Ride a Northbound Horse* (Sheriff), and *Home Improvement* (Hick Peterson). He also appeared on The Disney Channel in *Down the Long Hills* (Squires).

Elastigirl Super-stretching superhero in *The Incredibles*; known as Helen Parr in her civilian life; voiced by Holly Hunter.

Elba, Idris Actor; appeared as Heimdall in the Thor films and *Avengers: Infinity War*, and on TV in *Guerrilla* (Kent). He voiced Shere Khan in *The Jungle Book* (2016), Chief Bogo in *Zootopia*, and Fluke in *Finding Dory*.

Elcar, Dana (1927–2005) Actor; appeared in *The Last Flight of Noah's Ark* (Benchley) and *Condorman* (Russ), and on TV in *Herbie, the Love Bug* (Warden) and *Small and Frye* (Problems).

Electric Holiday Special animated short produced in conjunction with a holiday display in the store windows of Barneys New York on Madison Avenue. Minnie Mouse daydreams of modeling in Paris and meeting fashion industry celebrities. Released Nov. 14, 2012, in New York, and later online. 5 min. Music by Michael Giacchino.

Electric Umbrella Quick-service food facility in Innoventions East at EPCOT; opened Jun. 24, 1994, taking the place of Stargate. Closed Feb. 15, 2020, succeeded by Connections Café and Eatery.

Electrical Parade SEE MAIN STREET ELECTRICAL PARADE.

Electrical Water Pageant Nightly on Bay Lake and the Seven Seas Lagoon at Walt Disney World; premiered Oct. 24, 1971, during the opening ceremonies for the Polynesian Village Hotel. The pageant consists of a string of floating structures, 1,000 feet long, covered with tiny lights that blink on and off to represent creatures of the deep, including a fanciful sea serpent, turtle, and octopus. With a synthesizer soundtrack, the pageant is pulled through the waterways each evening around 9 o'clock. This pageant was the forerunner of the *Main Street Electrical Parade*, which began at Disneyland in 1972.

Electronic Forum (EPCOT Poll) Attraction in Communicore East at EPCOT Center; open Dec. 23, 1982–Mar. 16, 1991. The preshow area then became the World News Center. The poll was taken when guests were ushered into a theater and shown short films, usually on current affairs. Then opinions were solicited, with the guests pressing buttons on the armrests of their seats, and the results being tabulated instantaneously. For several years, compiled results of the EPCOT Poll were distributed to newspapers throughout the country.

Elemental (film) Animated feature from Pixar Animation Studios; scheduled for release Jun. 16, 2023, also in 3-D, following international releases beginning Jun. 14. In a city where fire, water, land, and air residents live together, a fiery young woman, Ember, and a go-with-the-flow guy, Wade, are about to discover something elemental: how much they actually have in common. Directed by Peter Sohn. 90 min. The film is inspired by Sohn's childhood in New York, where immigrants have pursued dreams in beautiful neighborhoods where language and cultures come together. Voices include Leah Lewis (Ember), Mamoudou Athie (Wade).

Elena of Avalor (TV) Animated series on Disney Channel; premiered Jul. 22, 2016. In the enchanted fairy-tale land of Avalor, Elena is a brave and adventurous 16-year-old who has saved her kingdom from an evil sorceress and must now learn to rule as crown princess until she is old enough to be queen. In the meantime, she is advised by a Grand Council, comprised of her Grandfather Francisco, Grandmother Luisa, and Royal Advisor, Duke Esteban. With her sister and some magical friends by her side, Princess Elena learns that her new role requires thoughtfulness, resilience, and compassion, the traits of all truly great leaders. Voices include Aimee Carrero (Princess Elena), Jenna Ortega (Princess Isabel), Christian Lanz (Esteban), Emiliano Díez (Francisco), Julia Vera (Luisa). The stories incorporate influences from diverse Latin and Hispanic cultures through architecture, traditions, food, and customs.

Elephanchine Elephant dancer in "The Dance of the Hours" segment of *Fantasia*.

Elephant (film) A Disneynature feature. African elephant Shani and her spirited son Jomo set out on an epic journey with their herd, traveling hundreds of miles across the vast Kalahari Desert to the Zambezi River. Led by their grand matriarch, Gaia, the family faces brutal heat, dwindling resources, and persistent predators as they follow in the footsteps of their ancestors on a quest to reach paradise. Directed by Mark Linfield. Digitally released Apr. 3, 2020, on Disney+. Narrated by Meghan, Duchess of Sussex. 89 min.

Elephant in the Room (film) Animated short; digitally released Jan. 24, 2020, on Disney+. A lost baby elephant is taken in by a boy and his father to work on their banana plantation. As the 2 bond, the boy discovers that his new best friend yearns for its family and home in the wild. Directed by Brian Scott. 3 min. From the Walt Disney Animation Studios Short Circuit program.

Elephant Journey (TV) A herd of elephants is followed on their epic annual migration through northwestern Namibia, traversing routes that the enormous pachyderms have followed instinctively for centuries. Produced by Adrian Warren. Aired in syn. beginning May 8, 2000, as a New True-Life Adventure film. 45 min.

Elephant Tales Safari-themed shop in the Adventureland Bazaar in the Magic Kingdom at Walt Disney World; opened Apr. 1987, initially as The Elephant's Trunk. It replaced Oriental Imports, Ltd. and The Magic Carpet. Closed ca. 2000.

Elephants and Hippos in Africa (film) Portion of *The African Lion*; released on 16 mm for schools in May 1969. Shows the daily life of elephants and hippos.

Elephant's Trunk, The SEE ELEPHANT TALES.

Elfego Baca (Episode 1): The Nine Lives of Elfego Baca (TV) Show aired Oct. 3, 1958. Directed by Norman Foster. Tales of a gunman who became a lawyer in the Old West. In this first episode, Elfego is deputized to catch a rampaging cowboy, but this leads to problems with other cowboys in the area. Finally Elfego is named sheriff of Socorro. Stars Robert Loggia, Robert F. Simon, Lisa Montell, Nestor Paiva.

Elfego Baca (Episode 2): Four Down and Five Lives to Go (TV) Show aired Oct. 17, 1958. Directed by Norman Foster. Elfego is so feared by the bad guys that when he becomes sheriff and asks them all to turn themselves in, they almost all do so. Later he is badly injured trying to catch a murderer, and he realizes that being sheriff is not what he is cut out to do; instead he decides to study law. Stars Robert Loggia, Robert F. Simon, Lisa Montell, Nestor Paiva.

Elfego Baca (Episode 3): Lawman or Gunman (TV) Show aired Nov. 28, 1958. Directed by Christian Nyby. Elfego tries to defend a rancher friend whose land is in danger of being stolen by a crooked judge. He is able to overcome numerous roadblocks, including capture by the crooks, and escapes just in time to reach the trial and prove his friend the rightful owner of the land. Stars Robert Loggia, James Dunn, Ramon Novarro, Skip Homeier, Valerie Allen, Carl Benton Reid.

Elfego Baca (Episode 4): Law and Order, Incorporated (TV) Show aired Dec. 12, 1958. Directed by Christian Nyby. As a new partner in his law firm, Elfego must try to save the land of a friend whose deeds have been stolen from the archives in Santa Fe, New Mexico. The local banker seems to be one of the crooks. Stars Robert Loggia, James Dunn, Ramon Novarro, Skip Homeier, Raymond Bailey, Valerie Allen.

Elfego Baca (Episode 5): Attorney at Law (TV) Show aired Feb. 6, 1959. Directed by Christian Nyby. Elfego becomes a lawyer, and with his first case, he is to defend an accused thief. He discovers the man is being framed, eventually discovering that the real thief is the local deputy. Stars Robert Loggia, James Dunn, Lynn Bari, Kenneth Tobey, James Drury, Annette Funicello.

Elfego Baca (Episode 6): The Griswold Murder (TV) Show aired Feb. 20, 1959. Directed by Christian Nyby. Elfego defends a rancher who has been unjustly accused of murder. It is up to Elfego to track down the real murderer, and in doing so, he wins his first case in Santa Fe, New Mexico. Stars Robert Loggia, James Dunn, Jay C. Flippen, Patrick Knowles, Audrey Dalton, Annette Funicello.

Elfego Baca (Episode 7): Move Along Mustangers (TV) Show aired Nov. 13, 1959. Directed by George Sherman. Elfego is asked to help a religious sect, the Mustangers, that wants to settle in the area but is being harassed by the local ranchers. When the son of a rancher is captured, the sheriff resigns rather than jail him, and Elfego has to become the law in the town. Stars Robert Loggia, Brian Keith, Arthur Hunnicutt, Beverly Garland, Barry Kelley, Roger Perry, William Schallert, James Coburn.

Elfego Baca (Episode 8): Mustang Man, Mustang Maid (TV) Show aired Nov. 20, 1959. Directed by George Sherman. Elfego continues to help the Mustangers who are being persecuted by the townsfolk who arrange a boycott against them. After the cattlemen cause a stampede through the Mustangers' crops, Elfego captures one of the raiders and again discovers it is the son of the rancher. Eventually Elfego manages to capture the ringleaders and peace comes to the area. Stars Robert Loggia, Brian Keith, Arthur Hunnicutt, Beverly Garland, Barry Kelley, Roger Perry, James Coburn, William Schallert.

Elfego Baca (Episode 9): Friendly Enemies at Law (TV) Show aired Mar. 18, 1960. Directed by William Beaudine. Lawyer Elfego is called upon to accuse a powerful rancher who is suspected of receiving stolen cattle. Elfego finds roadblocks every way he turns, but finally he discovers that the rancher's foreman is the culprit. Stars Robert Loggia, John Kerr, Patricia Crowley, Barton MacLane, Robert Lowery.

Elfego Baca (Episode 10): Gus Tomlin Is Dead (TV) Show aired Mar. 25, 1960. Directed by William Beaudine. Elfego travels to Granite searching for Gus Tomlin, a murderer thought long dead. He discovers that Tomlin is still living but is being protected by the town because he saved it from a typhoid epidemic. Elfego decides to help the town protect the now honest man. Stars Robert Loggia, Alan Hale Jr., Coleen Gray, Brian Corcoran.

Elfman, Danny Composer; wrote the score for many Disney films, including *Dick Tracy, Tim Burton's The Nightmare Before Christmas* (for which he also provided the singing voice of Jack Skellington), *Flubber, A Civil Action, Meet the Robinsons, Alice in Wonderland* (2010), *Real Steel, Frankenweenie* (2012), *Oz The Great and Powerful, Avengers: Age of Ultron, Alice Through the Looking Glass, Dumbo* (2019), and *Doctor Strange in the Multiverse of Madness*. For TV, he wrote the score for *When We Rise* and won an Emmy for the main title theme for *Desperate Housewives*. He also scored the Mystic Manor attraction in Hong Kong Disneyland. On Disney+, he appeared in *Prop Culture*. He was named a Disney Legend in 2015.

Elfman, Jenna Actress; appeared in *Krippendorf's Tribe* (Veronica Micelli), *Grosse Pointe Blank* (Tanya), and *Keeping the Faith* (Anna Reilly), and on TV in *Everything I Know About Men* (Bex Atwell), *Brothers & Sisters* (Lizzie Jones-Baker), and *Imaginary Mary* (Alice). She is best known for her role as Dharma in the ABC comedy series *Dharma and Greg*.

Elgin National Industries, Inc. SEE BRADLEY TIME.

Eli Stone (TV) Drama series on ABC; aired Jan. 31, 2008–Jul. 11, 2009. A thirtysomething San Francisco attorney with an inoperable brain aneurysm begins to have larger-than-life visions that compel him to do unusual things. Stars Jonny Lee Miller (Eli Stone), Victor Garber (Jordan Wethersby), Nathasha Henstridge (Taylor Wethersby), Loretta Devine (Patti), Sam Jaeger (Matt Dowd), James Saito (Dr. Chen), Matt Letscher (Nathan Stone), Julie Gonzalo (Maggie). From ABC Studios.

Elias & Co. Largest shopping location on Buena Vista Street in Disney California Adventure; opened Jun. 15, 2012. The shop is inspired by the opulent art deco–style department stores of yesteryear, selling apparel, watches, handbags, and accessories. Named after Walt Disney's father.

Elizondo, Hector Actor; appeared in *Pretty Woman* (hotel manager), *Taking Care of Business* (warden), *The Other Sister* (Ernie), *Runaway Bride* (Fisher), *The Princess Diaries* and *The Princess Diaries 2* (Joe), and *Raising Helen* (Mickey Massey), and on TV in *Down and Out in Beverly Hills* (Dave Whiteman), *Miracles* (Father Bellamy), *Cane* (Pancho Duque), *Monk* (Dr. Neven Bell), and *Grey's Anatomy* (Carlos Torres). He also had an uncredited role in *Beaches* (judge). He voiced Malcho in the *Aladdin* TV series, Zafiro in *Gargoyles*, Fiero in *Elena of Avalor*, and Grandpa Beagle in *Mickey and the Roadster Racers*.

Ellen (TV) Sitcom on ABC; debuted Mar. 9, 1994, as *These Friends of Mine*, but changed its title in summer 1994. It ended Jul. 29, 1998. A single woman living in Los Angeles is kindhearted but clumsy when it comes to the handling of people and matters that come careening into her life. Stars Ellen DeGeneres (Ellen Morgan), Joely Fisher (Paige Clark), David Anthony Higgins (Joe Farrell), Arye Gross (Adam Green). Joining the regular cast in fall 1995 were Clea Lewis (Audrey) and Jeremy Piven (Spence). The show made headlines when the lead character, Ellen Morgan, came out as a lesbian on Apr. 30, 1997, after actress Ellen DeGeneres had earlier done the same. From The Black/Marlens Company and Touchstone Television.

Ellen Burstyn Show, The (TV) Sitcom on ABC; aired Sep. 20–Nov. 15, 1986, and Aug. 8–Sep. 12, 1987. Professor Ellen Brewer teaches literature at a college in Baltimore. She is divorced and trying to live in a house with her mother, her opinionated daughter, and her daughter's young son. Stars Ellen Burstyn (Ellen Brewer), Elaine Stritch (Sydney), Megan Mullally (Molly), Barry Sobel (Tom Hines), Jesse Tendler (Nick), Winifred Freedman (Carrie). From Touchstone Television.

Ellen's Energy Adventure Attraction starring Ellen DeGeneres in the Universe of Energy at EPCOT; open Sep. 15, 1996–Aug. 13, 2017. Presented by ExxonMobil until 2004. Ellen dreams she is a contestant on *Jeopardy!* and that all the questions are about a topic she knows nothing about: energy. Boarding a traveling theater system, audiences join Ellen and Bill Nye the Science Guy on an adventure through time to learn about energy resources. The highlight was a journey back to the age of the dinosaurs. Armed with her new knowledge, Ellen returns to the present day just in time to unseat her old college roommate as *Jeopardy!* champion. Also starred Alex Trebek (as himself), Jamie Lee Curtis (Dr. Judy Peterson), Benny Wasserman (Dr. Albert Einstein). Michael Richards made a cameo as a caveman discovering fire. Replaced in 2022 by Guardians of the Galaxy: Cosmic Rewind.

Ellenshaw, Harrison Son of Peter Ellenshaw, he came to Disney in 1970 as an apprentice matte artist on *Bedknobs and Broomsticks*. After several years at other studios, he returned in 1990 as vice president of visual effects. He left the company in 1996 and later became a painter of fine art. He appeared in *Prop Culture* on Disney+.

Ellenshaw, Peter (1913–2007) Selected by Walt Disney in England to paint the mattes for *Treasure Island* and the other Disney films made there in the early 1950s. He later came to the states to work on *20,000 Leagues Under the Sea*, *Darby O'Gill and the Little People*, and other films. He painted one of the original layouts for Disneyland on a 4-by-8-ft. storyboard, which was later displayed in Disney exhibitions. He received an Oscar for Special Visual Effects in *Mary Poppins*. Later, he served as

production designer on *The Island at the Top of the World* and *The Black Hole*. He was named a Disney Legend in 1993.

Elliott Green dragon in *Pete's Dragon*; voiced by Charlie Callas. He has the head of a camel, the neck of a crocodile, and the ears of a cow.

Elliott, Chris Actor; appeared in *Cabin Boy* (Nathanial Mayweather) and on TV in *The Barefoot Executive* (Jase Wallenberg) and *According to Jim* (Reverend Pierson). He voiced Triton in the *Hercules* animated series.

Elmer Elephant (film) Silly Symphony cartoon released Mar. 28, 1936. Directed by Wilfred Jackson. Poor Elmer is teased for having a trunk until a fire threatens Tillie Tiger and only he can rescue her. Elmer was one of the first Disney characters since the Three Little Pigs to appear on some merchandise items.

Eloise at Christmastime (TV) A 2-hour movie on *The Wonderful World of Disney*; first aired Nov. 22, 2003. New York's Plaza Hotel is deep in preparations for a Christmas Eve wedding of the owner's daughter, and Eloise decides to "help" with the arrangements. She goes head-to-head with event coordinator Prunella Stickler and even plays matchmaker when she has suspicions about the groom. The wedding isn't the only thing in which Eloise gets involved—as usual she interferes with the lives of all her friends at the hotel and tries to deliver each the best Christmas present imaginable. Directed by Kevin Lima. Stars Julie Andrews (Nanny), Sofia Vassilieva (Eloise), Jeffrey Tambor (Mr. Salomone), Christine Baranski (Prunella Stickler), Debra Monk (Maggie), Gavin Creel (Bill). From Hand Made Films in association with Di Novi Pictures. This movie was filmed at the same time as *Eloise at the Plaza*, which aired 7 months earlier.

Eloise at the Plaza (TV) A 2-hour movie on *The Wonderful World of Disney*; first aired Apr. 27, 2003. Eloise is a precocious but lovable 6-year-old resident of New York's Plaza Hotel, who roams the landmark in search of adventure. Along with her pug dog and turtle, Eloise is always causing mischief and mayhem, often dragging along her beleaguered Nanny. As the Plaza prepares for a debutante ball and the stately visit of a prince, Eloise is determined to get an invitation to the ball with the royal prince as her escort. She befriends a sad boy, Leon, whisking him away for a day of sightseeing, unaware that he is actually the prince. Directed by Kevin Lima. Stars Julie Andrews (Nanny), Sofia Vassilieva (Eloise), Jeffrey Tambor (Mr. Salomone), Christine Baranski (Prunella Stickler), Debra Monk (Maggie), Kintaro Akiyama (Leon). Based on the popular Eloise books by Kay Thompson and illustrated by Hilary Knight (who makes a cameo appearance as himself). From Hand Made Films, in association with Di Novi Pictures.

Elrod, Tom He joined Walt Disney World in the Marketing division in 1973 and served as president of Marketing and Entertainment for Walt Disney Attractions from 1992 until he left the company in 1997.

Elsa SEE QUEEN ELSA.

Elton John Live: Farewell From Dodger Stadium (TV) SEE GOODBYE YELLOW BRICK ROAD: THE FINAL ELTON JOHN PERFORMANCES.

Embarcadero Gifts Shop in Paradise Gardens Park at Disney California Adventure; opened Jun. 2, 2011, selling *Little Mermaid* merchandise.

Embrace the Panda: Making Turning Red (TV) A Disney+ original documentary; digitally released Mar. 11, 2022. A behind-the-scenes look at the powerful, professional, and personal journeys of the all-women team at the helm of Disney • Pixar's *Turning Red*. 47 min.

Embry, Ethan SEE RANDALL, ETHAN.

Emerald Cove (TV) Serial on the *Mickey Mouse Club* on The Disney Channel, first airing Jun. 26, 1993. Kids at the beach for the summer, dealing with teen issues of the day. Stars Tony Lucca (Jeff Chambers), Marc Worden (Will Jenkins), Ricky Luna (Ricky), Matt Morris (Matt), Rhona Bennett (Nicole), J. C. Chasez (Wipeout), Jennifer McGill (Melody). Compiled episodes were shown as a stand-alone series beginning Sep. 8, 1993.

Emergence (TV) Hour-long drama series on ABC; aired Sep. 24, 2019–Jan. 28, 2020. Jo, a police chief, takes in a young child she finds near the site of a mysterious accident who has no memory of what has happened. The investigation draws her into a conspiracy larger than she ever imagined, and the child's identity is at the center of it all. Stars Allison Tolman (Jo Evans), Alexa Swinton (Piper), Owain Yeoman (Benny Gallagher), Ashley Aufderheide (Mia Evans), Robert Bailey Jr. (Officer Chris Minetto), Zabryna Guevara (Abby Frasier). From ABC Studios.

Emerson, Douglas Actor; appeared on TV in *The Leftovers* and the *Herbie, the Love Bug* limited series, and on The Disney Channel in *Good Old Boy*.

Emhardt, Robert (1914–1994) Character actor; appeared in *Rascal* (constable), and on TV in *Kilroy* and *The Mooncussers*.

Emil and the Detectives (film) Emil, on his first trip to Berlin, carries money to his grandmother, a mission of great responsibility. But during it, a pickpocket cannot resist robbing the boy while he is napping on the bus. Awakening in time, Emil follows the crook, and with the aid of a group of resourceful boys his age (the Detectives) comes upon a rendezvous with 2 master thieves who are engaged in a plan to rob the Bank of Berlin. Because of the pickpocket's inability to resist petty theft, the big job falls apart. They might have gotten away with had it not been for Emil and the Detectives watching them. Released Dec. 18, 1964. Directed by Peter Tewksbury. 99 min. Stars Walter Slezak (Baron), Bryan Russell (Emil), Roger Mobley (Gustav), Heinz Schubert (Grundeis), Peter Erlich (Muller), Cindy Cassell (Pony), Elsa Wagner (Nana), Wolfgang Volz (Stucke). The film was made on location in Germany and was based on a book by Erich Kastner. Serialized on the new *Mickey Mouse Club* as *The Three Skrinks*.

Emmy Awards Disney individuals and TV programs have been honored by the Academy of Television Arts and Sciences with many Emmy Awards over the years. The list of awards is:

1. 1955: *Disneyland*, 1954 (Best Variety Series)
2. 1955: *Operation Undersea on Disneyland*, 1954 (Best Individual Show)
3. 1955: *Operation Undersea on Disneyland*, 1954 (Best Television Film Editing: Grant Smith and Lynn Harrison)
4. 1956: *Disneyland*, 1955 (Best Producer of Filmed Series: Walt Disney)
5. 1956: *Davy Crockett series on Disneyland*, 1955 (Best Action or Adventure Series)
6. 1964: *Walt Disney's Wonderful World of Color* (Children's Programming)
7. 1964: *Walt Disney's Wonderful World of*

Color (Art Direction and Scenic Design: Carroll Clark and Marvin Aubrey Davis)

8. 1986: *The Golden Girls*, 9/21/86 (Comedy Series)

9. 1986: *The Golden Girls*, 9/21/86 (Lead Actress in a Comedy Series: Betty White)

10. 1986: *The Golden Girls*, 9/21/86 (Writing in a Comedy Series: Barry Fanaro and Mort Nathan)

11. 1986: *The Golden Girls*, 9/21/86 (Technical Direction/Electronic Camerawork/Video Control: Gerry Bucci, Randy Baer, Dale Carlson, Steve Jones, Donna J. Quante, and Victor Bagdadi)

12. 1986: *Kids Incorporated*, The Disney Channel (Lighting Direction: Carl Gibson [lighting director])

13. 1987: *The Golden Girls*, 9/20/87 (Comedy Series)

14. 1987: *The Golden Girls*, 9/20/87 (Lead Actress in a Comedy Series: Rue McClanahan)

15. 1987: *The Golden Girls*, 9/20/87 (Directing in a Comedy Series: Terry Hughes)

16. 1988: *The Golden Girls*, 8/28/88 (Lead Actress in a Comedy Series: Beatrice Arthur)

17. 1988: *The Golden Girls*, 8/28/88 (Supporting Actress in a Comedy Series: Estelle Getty)

18. 1988: "Old Friends," *The Golden Girls*, 8/28/88 (Technical Direction/Electronic Camerawork/Video Control for Series: O. Tamburri, Jack Chisholm, Stephen A. Jones, Ritch Kenney, Ken Tamburri, and Robert G. Kaufmann)

19. 1989: *The New Adventures of Winnie the Pooh*, Walt Disney Television Animation, 6/29/89 (Best Animated Program, Daytime: Karl Geurs [producer/director] and Mark Zaslove [story editor/writer])

20. 1989: *Empty Nest*, 9/17/89 (Lead Actor in a Comedy Series: Richard Mulligan)

21. 1989: *The Disney-MGM Studios Theme Park Grand Opening*, 9/17/89 (Choreography: Walter Painter)

22. 1989: *Kids Incorporated*, The Disney Channel (Lighting Direction: Carl Gibson [lighting director])

23. 1990: *The New Adventures of Winnie the Pooh*, Walt Disney Television Animation, 6/23/90 (Best Animated Program, Daytime)

24. 1990: *Looking for Miracles*, 6/23/90 (Performer in a Children's Special: Greg Spottiswood)

25. 1990: *DuckTales*, Walt Disney Television Animation, 6/23/90 (Film Sound Editing:

Charles King, Rick Hinson, and Richard Harrison)

26. 1990: *A Conversation with George Burns*, The Disney Channel, 9/15/90 (Individual Achievement—Informational Programming/Performance: George Burns)

27. 1990: *Carol & Co.*, 9/15/90 (Guest Actress in a Comedy Series: Swoosie Kurtz)

28. 1990: *Mother Goose Rock 'n' Rhyme*, The Disney Channel, 9/15/90 (Costume Design—Variety or Music Program: Pat Field)

29. 1990: "A Mother's Courage: The Mary Thomas Story," *The Magical World of Disney*, NBC, 9/15/90 (Children's Program: Ted Field, Robert W. Cort, Patricia Clifford, Kate Wright, Richard L. O'Connor, and Chet Walker [producers])

30. 1991: *Jim Henson's Mother Goose Stories*, The Disney Channel, 6/22/91 (Directing in a Children's Series: Brian Henson and Michael Kerrigan)

31. 1991: *Jim Henson's Mother Goose Stories*, The Disney Channel, 6/22/91 (Achievement in Costume Design: Jacqueline Mills and Jill Thraves)

32. 1991: *Lost in the Barrens*, The Disney Channel, 6/27/91 (Best Children's Special, Daytime: Michael Scott, Michael MacMillan [exec. producers]; Seaton McLean, Joan Scott [producers])

33. 1991: "The Mating Dance," *Dinosaurs*, ABC, 8/25/91 (Art Direction, Series: John C. Mula [production designer], Kevin Pfeiffer [art director], and Brian Savegar [set decorator])

34. 1991: "That Little Extra Something," *Carol & Co.*, NBC, 8/25/91 (Costume Design, Variety or Music Program: Ret Turner [costume designer] and Bob Mackie [costume designer for Carol Burnett])

35. 1991: *The Muppets Celebrate Jim Henson*, CBS, 8/25/91 (Editing, Miniseries or Special [multi-camera production]: David Gumpel and Girish Bhargava)

36. 1991: *The Walt Disney Company Presents the American Teacher Awards*, The Disney Channel, 8/25/91 (Music Direction: Ian Fraser, Bill Byers, Chris Boardman, and J. Hill)

37. 1992: *Spaceship Earth: Our Global Environment*, The Disney Channel, 6/20/92 (Special Class Program: Kirk Bergstrom [exec. producer], Kit Thomas [producer], and Krystyne Haje [host])

38. 1992: *Spaceship Earth: Our Global Environ-*

ment, The Disney Channel, 6/20/92 (Writing, Special Class: Kerry Millerick, Julie Engleman, and Neal Rogin)

39. 1992: *Woof!*, The Disney Channel, 6/20/92 (Directing a Children's Special: David Cobham)

40. 1992: *Disney's Adventures in Wonderland*, The Disney Channel, 6/20/92 (Hairstyling: Richard Sabre [hair designer] and Tish Simpson [hairstylist])

41. 1992: *Scenic Wonders of America*, The Disney Channel, 6/20/92 (Cinematography: Eli Adler, Lex Fletcher [directors of photography])

42. 1992: *Kids Incorporated*, The Disney Channel, 6/20/92 (Lighting Direction: Carl Gibson)

43. 1992: *Vincent and Me*, The Disney Channel, 6/23/92 (Children's Special: Rock Demers [producer], Daniel Louis [line producer], and Claude Nedjar [co-producer])

44. 1992: *Avonlea*, The Disney Channel, 8/30/92 (Lead Actor in a Drama Series: Christopher Lloyd [guest actor])

45. 1992: *Mark Twain and Me*, The Disney Channel, 8/30/92 (Children's Program: Geoffrey Cowan, Julian Fowles [exec. producers], and Daniel Petrie [producer])

46. 1992: "One Flew Out of the Cuckoo's Nest" (parts 1–2), *The Golden Girls*, NBC, 8/30/92 (Technical Direction/Camera/Video for Series: Kenneth Tamburri [technical director], Ritch Kenney, Stephen A. Jones, Dave Heckman, Chester Jackson [camera operators], Randy Johnson, Richard Steiner, and John O'Brien [video control])

47. 1992: "Luck Be a Taylor Tonight," *Home Improvement*, ABC, 8/30/92 (Lighting Direction [Electronic], Comedy Series: Donald Morgan [director of photography])

48. 1992: *Mark Twain and Me*, The Disney Channel, 8/30/92 (Makeup for Miniseries or a Special: Kevin Haney [makeup for Jason Robards] and Donald Mowat [makeup])

49. 1993: *Avonlea*, The Disney Channel, 9/19/93 (Children's Program [tie])

50. 1993: *Harry Connick Jr.: The New York Big Band Concert*, The Disney Channel, 9/19/93 (Sound Mixing, Variety or Music Series or Special: Gregg Rubin, Randy Ezratty, and John Alberts)

51. 1993: *Home Improvement*, ABC, 9/19/93 (Lighting Direction [Electronic], Comedy Series: Donald A. Morgan)

52. 1993: *Great Wonders of the World: Wonders of Nature*, The Disney Channel (Special Class Program: Kim Thomas, James R. Conner, Edward J. Murphy [exec. producers], and Chris Valentini [producer])

53. 1993: *Journey to Spirit Island*, The Disney Channel (Directing in a Children's Special: Laszlo Pal [director])

54. 1993: *This Island Earth*, The Disney Channel (Writing—Special Class: Victoria Costello [writer])

55. 1993: *Great Wonders of the World: Wonders of Nature*, The Disney Channel (Single Camera Photography: Eli Adler, David Breashears, Don Briggs, Tony Clark, Lex Fletcher [directors of photography])

56. 1993: *This Island Earth*, The Disney Channel (Original Song: "This Island Earth"; music and lyrics by Kenny Loggins)

57. 1993: *Walt Disney World Very Merry Christmas Parade*, ABC (Costume Design: Bill Campbell and Doug Enderle [costume designers])

58. 1994: *Disney's Adventures in Wonderland*, The Disney Channel, 5/21/94 (Writing in a Children's Series: Daryl Busby and Tom J. Astle [head writers])

59. 1994: *Disney's Adventures in Wonderland*, The Disney Channel, 5/21/94 (Makeup: Ron Wild and Karen Stephens [makeup artists])

60. 1995: *Dinosaurs: Myths & Reality*, The Disney Channel, 5/13/95 (Special Class Writing: Bob Carruthers)

61. 1995: *Disney's Aladdin*, CBS/syn., 5/13/95 (Music Direction and Composition: Mark Watters [supervising composer], John Given, Harvey Cohen, Carl Johnson, and Thom Sharp [composers])

62. 1995: *Disney's Aladdin*, CBS/syn., 5/13/95 (Film Sound Editing: John O. Robinson III, Michael Geisler [supervising sound editors], Marc S. Perlman, William Griggs [supervising music editors], Melissa Gentry-Ellis, Ray Leonard, Phyllis Ginter, Michael Gollom, Timothy J. Borquez, Thomas Jaeger, Charles Rychwalski, Gregory A. Laplante, Kenneth D. Young, Jenifer Mertins [sound editors], Robert Duran, William Koepnick, and James C. Hodson [sound effects editors])

63. 1995: *Disney's Aladdin*, CBS/syn., 5/13/95 (Film Sound Mixing: Timothy J. Borquez, James C. Hodson [supervising re-recording mixers], Timothy Garrity, William Koepnick, Melissa Gentry-Ellis [re-recording mixers], and Deborah Adair [production mixer])

64. 1995: *Disney's Adventures in Wonderland*,

The Disney Channel, 5/13/95 (Costume Design: Lois de Armond)

65. 1995: "Strictly Melodrama," *Avonlea*, The Disney Channel, 9/10/95 (Costume Design for a Series: Madeleine Stewart [costume designer])

66. 1995: "My Dinner with Wilson," *Home Improvement*, ABC, 9/10/95 (Lighting Direction [Electronic], Comedy Series: Donald A. Morgan [lighting director])

67. 1996: *The Lion King's Timon & Pumbaa*, CBS/syn., 5/22/96 (Performer in an Animated Program: Nathan Lane)

68. 1996: *Disney's Adventures in Wonderland*, The Disney Channel, 5/22/96 (Directing in a Children's Series: David Grossman, Gary Halvorson, and Shelley R. Jensen [directors]

69. 1996: *Bill Nye, the Science Guy*, PBS/syn., 5/22/96 (Writing in a Children's Series: Erren Gottlieb, Bill Nye, James McKenna, Scott Schaefer, Adam Gross, and Seth Gross [writers])

70. 1996: *Disney's Adventures in Wonderland*, The Disney Channel, 5/22/96 (Makeup: Ron Wild [makeup designer] and Karen Stephens [key makeup])

71. 1996: *Bill Nye, the Science Guy*, PBS/syn., 5/22/96 (Sound Editing: Jim Wilson, Tom McGurk, Mike McAuliff [sound designer/editors]; Dave Howe, and Ella Bracket [sound editors])

72. 1996: *Disney's Aladdin*, CBS/syn., 5/22/96 (Sound Mixing—Special Class: Michael E. Jiron and Allen L. Stone [re-recording mixers])

73. 1996: *Home Improvement*, ABC, 9/8/96 (Lighting Direction [Electronic], Comedy Series: Donald A. Morgan [lighting director])

74. 1997: *Bill Nye, the Science Guy*, PBS/syn., 5/17/97 (Directing in a Children's Program,: Darrell Suto, Michael Gross, Erren Gottlieb, and James McKenna [directors])

75. 1997: *Bill Nye, the Science Guy*, PBS/syn., 5/17/97 (Writing in a Children's Series,: Kit Boss, Erren Gottlieb, Michael Gross, James McKenna, Bill Nye, Ias Saunders, Scott Schaefer, Darrell Suto, and William Sleeth [writers])

76. 1997: "Beethoven's Whiff," *The Lion King's Timon & Pumbaa*, CBS/syn., 5/17/97 (Individual Achievement in Animation: Kexx Singleton [color director])

77. 1997: *Bill Nye, the Science Guy*, PBS/syn., 5/17/97 (Single Camera Editing: Darrell Suto, Michael Gross [senior editors]; Felicity Oram, and John Reul [editors])

78. 1997: *Bill Nye, the Science Guy*, PBS/syn., 5/17/97 (Sound Editing: Thomas McGurk, Michael McAuliffe, and Dave Howe [sound editors])

79. 1997: *Mighty Ducks*, ABC, 5/17/97 (Sound Editing—Special Class: Paca Thomas [supervising sound effects editor]; Melissa Gentry-Ellis [sound editor]; Marc Perlman [supervising music editor]; Kris Daly, Phyllis Ginter, Paul Holzborn [sound editors]; William B. Griggs [supervising sound editor]; Nicholas Carr [supervising music editor]; Jeff Hutchins, Ken D. Young, Bill Kean, David Lynch, Otis Van Osten [sound effects editors]; Jennifer E. Mertens, Eric Hertsgaard [sound editors])

80. 1997: *The Lion King's Timon & Pumbaa*, CBS/syn., 5/17/97 (Sound Mixing—Special Class: James C. Hodson, Melissa Gentry-Ellis, Michael Beiriger, Daniel Hiland, Joseph Citarella, Allen L. Stone, Michael Jiron [re-recording mixers]; and Deb Adair [production mixer])

81. 1998: *Bill Nye, the Science Guy*, syn., 5/15/98 (Performer in a Children's Series: Bill Nye)

82. 1998: *Win Ben Stein's Money*, Comedy Central, 5/15/98 (Directing in a Game/Audience Participation Show: Dennis Rosenblatt [director])

83. 1998: *Letters from Africa*, Disney Channel, 5/15/98 (Directing in a Children's Special: Carlyle Kyzer, Greg Poschman, and Krysia Carter-Giez [directors])

84. 1998: *A Magical Walt Disney World Christmas*, ABC, 5/15/98 (Special Class Directing: Gary Halvorson and Alan Carter [directors])

85. 1998: *Bill Nye, the Science Guy*, syn., 5/15/98 (Writing in a Children's Series: Erren Gottlieb, James McKenna, Bill Nye, Michael Gross, Darrell Suto, Scott Schaefer, Kit Boss, Lynne Brunell, Michael Pelleschi, Ian Saunders, Simon Griffith [writers])

86. 1998: *Win Ben Stein's Money*, Comedy Central, 5/15/98 (Special Class Writing: Doug Armstrong, Jonathan Barry, Lou Dimaggio, and Carla Kaufman [writers])

87. 1998: *Bill Nye, the Science Guy*, syn., 5/15/98 (Single Camera Editing: Felicity Oram, John Ruel, Darrell Suto, Michael Gross [editors])

88. 1998: *Bill Nye, the Science Guy*, syn., 5/15/98 (Sound Editing: Dave Howe, Thomas McGurk, and Mike McAuliffe [sound editors])

89. 1998: *Bill Nye, the Science Guy*, syn., 5/15/98

(Sound Mixing: Dave Howe, Thomas McGurk, Mike McAuliffe [re-recording mixers]; Bob O'Hern, Resti Bagcal, and Marion Smith [production mixers])

90. 1998: *101 Dalmatians: The Series*, ABC, 5/15/98 (Individual Achievement in Animation: Craig Kemplin [storyboard artist])

91. 1998: *Ellen*, ABC, 8/29/98 (Guest Actress in a Comedy Series: Emma Thompson)

92. 1998: *Muppets Tonight*, Disney Channel, 8/29/98 (Children's Program: The Jim Henson Company)

93. 1998: *Rodgers & Hammerstein's Cinderella, The Wonderful World of Disney*, ABC, 8/29/98: Art Direction for a Variety or Music Program: Randy Ser [production designer], Edward L. Rubin [art director], and Julie Kaye Fanton [set decorator])

94. 1998: "A Night to Dismember," *Home Improvement*, ABC, 8/29/98 (Lighting Direction (Electronic) for a Comedy Series: Donald A. Morgan [director of photography])

95. 1998: *The Wonderful World of Disney*, ABC, 8/29/98 (Main Title Design: Kasumi Mihori, Billy Pittard, and Ed Sullivan [title designers])

96. 1999: *Bill Nye, the Science Guy*, syn., 5/15/99 (Directing in a Children's Series: Michael Gross and Darrell Suto)

97. 1999: *Win Ben Stein's Money*, Comedy Central, 5/15/99 (Special Class Writing: Doug Armstrong, Jonathan Barry, Jonathan Bourne, and Henriette Mantel [writers])

98. 1999: *Bill Nye, the Science Guy*, syn., 5/15/99 (Single Camera Editing: Felicity Oram, John Reul, Michael Gross, and Darrell Duto [editors])

99. 1999: *Bill Nye, the Science Guy*, syn., 5/15/99 (Sound Editing: Dave Howe, Thomas McGurk, and Michael McAuliffe [sound editors])

100. 1999: *Bill Nye, the Science Guy*, syn., 5/21/99 (Children's Series: Erren Gottlieb, James McKenna, Elizabeth Brock [exec. producers]; Jamie Hammond, Hamilton Mcculloch [coordinating producers]; and Bill Nye [producer])

101. 1999: *Win Ben Stein's Money*, Comedy Central, 5/21/99 (Game/Audience Participation Show: Andrew J. Golder, Al Burton, Byron Glore [exec. producers]; and Terrence McDonnell [producer])

102. 1999: *Win Ben Stein's Money*, Comedy Central, 5/21/99 (Game Show Host: Ben Stein and Jimmy Kimmel [co-hosts])

103. 1999: *The PJs*, Fox, 8/4/99 (Voice-over Performance in Animation: Ja'Net DuBois)

104. 1999: "Todd Mulcahy, Pt. II," *Felicity*, WB, 8/28/99 (Cinematography for a Series: Robert Primes [director of photography])

105. 1999: "Small Town," *Sports Night*, ABC, 8/28/99 (Multicamera Picture Editing for a Series: Janet Ashikaga [editor])

106. 1999: "Mark's Big Break," *Home Improvement*, ABC, 8/28/99 (Lighting Direction [Electronic] for a Comedy Series: Donald A. Morgan [director of photography])

107. 1999: *Rolie Polie Olie*, Disney Channel, 5/15/99 (Animation: William Joyce [production designer])

108. 2000: *Bill Nye, the Science Guy*, syn., 5/13/00 (Children's Series: James McKenna, Erren Gottlieb, Elizabeth Brock [exec. producers]; Jamie Hammond [coordinating producer]; and Bill Nye [science producer])

109. 2000: *Rolie Polie Olie*, Disney Channel, 5/13/00 (Special Class Animated Program: William Joyce, Michael Hirsh, Patrick Loubert, Clive Smith, Fabrice Giger [exec. producers]; Stephen Hodgins [supervising producer]; Scott Dyer, Guillaume Hellouin, Pam Lehn, Corrine Kouper, Eric Flaherty, Christophe Archimbault [producers]; Mike Fallows [supervising director]; Ron Pitts [director]; Nadine Van Der Velde, Ben Joseph, Scott Kraft, Pete Sauder, and Nicola Barton [writers])

110. 2000: *Bill Nye, the Science Guy*, syn., 5/13/00 (Writing in a Children's Series: Bill Nye, Michael Gross, Darrell Suto, Ian G. Saunders, Michael Palleschi, Lynn Brunelle, and Mike Greene)

111. 2000: *Win Ben Stein's Money*, Comedy Central, 5/13/00 (Special Class Writing: Teresa Strasser, Jonathan Barry, Bob Stone, Gary Stuart Kaplan, and Susan Flanagan)

112. 2000: *Who Wants to Be a Millionaire*, ABC, 5/13/00 (Directing in a Game/Audience Participation Show: Mark Gentile)

113. 2000: *Disney's Hercules*, ABC, 5/13/00 (Performer in an Animated Program: James Woods)

114. 2000: *Bill Nye, the Science Guy*, syn., 5/13/00 (Sound Editing: Dave Howe, Mike McAuliffe, and Tom McGurk)

115. 2000: *Bear in the Big Blue House*, Disney Channel, 5/13/00 (Sound Mixing [tie]: Peter

Hefter [production mixer] and John Alberts [re-recording mixer])

116. 2000: *Bill Nye, the Science Guy*, syn., 5/13/00 (Sound Mixing [tie]: Dave Howe, Mike McAuliffe, Tom McGurk [re-recording mixers]; Myron Partman and Resti Bagcal [production mixers])

117. 2000: *Honey, I Shrunk the Kids*, syn., 5/13/00 (Sound Mixing [tie]: R. William A. Thiederman, Dean Okrand, Michael Brooks [re-recording mixers]; and Clancy Livingston [production mixer])

118. 2000: *Disney's Mickey MouseWorks*, ABC, 5/13/00 (Individual Achievement in Animation: Mike Moon [art director] and Chris Roszak [key background painter])

119. 2000: *Who Wants to Be a Millionaire*, ABC, 5/19/00 (Game/Audience Participation Show: Michael Davies, Paul Smith [exec. producers]; Vincent Rubino [producer]; Ann Miller [supervising producer]; Terrence McDonnell [senior producer]; and Nikki Webber [coordinating producer])

120. 2000: *The Color of Friendship*, Disney Channel, 8/26/00 (Children's Program: Alan Sacks [exec. producer]; Christopher Morgan and Kevin Hooks [producers])

121. 2000: *Annie*, ABC, 8/26/00 (Choreography: Rob Marshall [choreographer])

122. 2000: "Cut Man," *Sports Night*, ABC, 8/26/00 (Cinematography for a Multicamera Series: Peter Smokler [director of photography])

123. 2000: *Annie*, ABC, 8/26/00 (Music Direction: Paul Bogaev [music director])

124. 2000: "How the Super Stoled Christmas," *The PJs*, WB, 8/26/00 (Individual Achievement in Animation: Nelson Lowry [art director])

125. 2001: *Disney's Teacher's Pet*, ABC, 5/18/01 (Performer in an Animated Program: Nathan Lane)

126. 2001: *Who Wants to Be a Millionaire*, ABC, 5/18/01 (Game/Audience Participation Show: Michael Davies, Paul Smith [exec. producers]; Leslie Fuller [producer]; Ann Miller, Wendy Roth, Tiffany Trigg [supervising producers]; Leigh Hampton [senior producer]; and Nikki Webber [coordinating producer])

127. 2001: *Who Wants to Be a Millionaire*, ABC, 5/18/01 (Game Show Host: Regis Philbin)

128. 2001: *Live with Regis*, syn., 5/18/01 (Talk Show Host: Regis Philbin)

129. 2001: *Alaska: Dances of the Caribou*, syn., 5/18/01 (Music [News & Documentary]: Mark Watters)

130. 2001: *The PJs*, Fox, 9/8/01 (Voice-over Performance in Animation: Ja'Net DuBois)

131. 2001: *Gideon's Crossing*, ABC, 9/8/01 (Main Title Theme Music: James Newton Howard [composer])

132. 2002: *Disney's Stanley*, Disney Channel, 5/11/02 (Performer in an Animated Program: Charles Shaughnessy)

133. 2002: *Disney's Teacher's Pet*, ABC, 5/11/02 (Special Class Animated Program: Gary Baseman, Bill and Cheri Steinkellner [exec. producers]; Jess Winfield [co-exec. producer]; Nancy Lee Myatt [producer]; Timothy Björklund, Don MacKinnon, Alfred Gimeno, Jamie Thomason, Julie Morgavi [directors]; David Maples and Billiam Coronel [writers])

134. 2002: *Win Ben Stein's Money*, Comedy Central, 5/11/02 (Directing in a Game/Audience Participation Show: Dennis Rosenblatt [director])

135. 2002: *The Book of Pooh*, Disney Channel, 5/11/02 (Directing in a Children's Series: Mitchell Kriegman and Dean Gordon [directors])

136. 2002: *Madeline*, Disney Channel, 5/17/02 (Children's Animated Program: Andy Heyward, Michael Maliani, Robby London, Saul Cooper, Pancho Kohner [exec. producers]; Judy Rothman Rofe [supervising producer]; Judy Reilly, Stephanie Louise Vallance, Marsha Goodman Einstein, and Paul F. Quinn [directors])

137. 2002: "Truth Be Told," *Alias*, ABC, 9/14/02 (Art Direction, Single-Camera Series: Scott Chambliss [production designer], Cece Destefano [art director], Karen Manthey [set decorator])

138. 2002: "Truth Be Told," *Alias*, ABC, 9/14/02 (Cinematography, Single-Camera Series: Michael Bonvillain [director of photography])

139. 2003: *Disney's Teacher's Pet*, ABC, 5/10/03 (Special Class Animated Program: Gary Baseman, Bill Steinkellner, Cheri Steinkellner [exec. producers]; Jess Winfield [coexec. Producer]; Don Mackinnon, Ennio Torresan Jr., Alfred Gimeno, Julie Morgavi [directors]; David Maples and Billiam Coronel [writers])

140. 2003: *Disney's Teacher's Pet*, ABC, 5/10/03 (Individual Achievement in Animation: Gary Baseman [production designer])

141. 2003: *Live with Regis and Kelly*, syn., 5/10/03 (Directing in a Talk Show [tie]: Brian Chapman)

142. 2003: *The Wayne Brady Show*, syn., 5/10/03 (Directing in a Talk Show [tie]: Liz Plonka)

143. 2003: *Bear in the Big Blue House*, Disney Channel, 5/10/03 (Directing in a Children's Series: Mitchell Kriegman and Dean Gordon)

144. 2003: *The Wayne Brady Show*, syn., 5/10/03 (Live & Direct to Tape Sound Mixing: Peter Baird [production mixer])

145. 2003: *Even Stevens*, Disney Channel, 5/16/03 (Performer in a Children's Series: Shia LaBeouf)

146. 2003: *The Wayne Brady Show*, syn., 5/16/03 (Talk Show Host: Wayne Brady)

147. 2003: *The Wayne Brady Show*, syn., 5/16/03 (Talk Show: Bernie Brillstein, Robert Morton [exec. producers]; Krysia Plonka, John Redmann [supervising producers]; K. P. Anderson [coordinating producer]; Danny Breen, Wendy Miller, Lee Farber, Erin Irwin, Maria Notaras, Shane Farley, Josh Gilbert, and Michael Carnes [producers])

148. 2003: "The Counteragent," *Alias*, ABC, 9/13/03 (Makeup for a Series, Non-Prosthetic: Angela Nogaro, Kaori Turner [makeup artists]; and Diana Brown [key makeup])

149. 2003: "Eloise at the Plaza," *The Wonderful World of Disney*, ABC, 9/13/03 (Music Composition for a Miniseries, Movie, or a Special—Dramatic Underscore: Bruce Broughton)

150. 2003: *Monk*, USA, 9/13/03 (Main Title Theme Music: Jeff Beal)

151. 2003: "The Telling" *Alias*, ABC, 9/13/03 (Stunt Coordination: Jeff Habberstad [stunt coordinator])

152. 2003: *Monk*, USA, 9/21/03 (Actor in a Comedy Series: Tony Shalhoub)

153. 2003: *The Amazing Race*, CBS, 9/21/03 (Reality-Competition Program)

154. 2004: *Who Wants to Be a Millionaire*, syn., 5/15/04 (Directing in a Game/Audience Participation Show: Matthew Cohen)

155. 2004: *Live with Regis and Kelly*, syn., 5/15/04 (Hairstyling: Diane D'Agostino)

156. 2004: *Live with Regis and Kelly*, syn., 5/15/04 (Makeup: Michelle Champagne)

157. 2004: *Win Ben Stein's Money*, Comedy Central, 5/15/04 (Special Class Writing: Bob Stone, Phil Andres, Patricia Cotter, Gary Stuart Kaplan Gary Lucy, and Vince Waldron)

158. 2004: *The Wayne Brady Show*, syn., 5/21/04: Talk Show Host: Wayne Brady)

159. 2004: *Monk*, USA, 9/12/04: Guest Actor in a Comedy Series: John Turturro)

160. 2004: "Goodbye," *8 Simple Rules*, ABC, 9/12/04 (Cinematography for a Multicamera Series: Bruce Finn)

161. 2004: *Eloise at Christmastime*, ABC, 9/12/04 (Music Composition for a Miniseries, Movie, or Special: Bruce Broughton)

162. 2004: *Eloise at Christmastime*, ABC, 9/12/04 (Dramatic Underscore)

163. 2004: Main Title Theme, *Monk*, USA, 9/12/04 (Music: Randy Newman)

164. 2004: *The Amazing Race*, CBS, 9/19/04 (Reality-Competition Program)

165. 2005: *Brandy & Mr. Whiskers*, Disney Channel, 5/14/05 (Individual Achievement in Animation: Rossen Varbanov)

166. 2005: *Rolie Polie Olie*, Disney Channel, 5/14/05 (Special Class Animated Program: William Joyce, Michael Hirsh, Scott Dyer, Corinne Kouper [exec. producers]; Guillaume Hellouin, Pamela Lehn [supervising producers]; Susie Grondin, Eric Flaherty, Christophe Archambault [producers]; Mike Fallows [supervising director]; Ron Pitts, Bill Giggie [directors]; Nadine Van Der Velde, Steve Sullivan, Alice Prodanau, and Robin Stein [writers])

167. 2005: *Who Wants to Be a Millionaire*, syn., 5/14/05 (Directing in a Game/Audience Participation Show: Matthew Cohen)

168. 2005: *Live with Regis & Kelly*, syn., 5/14/05 (Hairstyling: Diane D'Agostino)

169. 2005: *Live with Regis & Kelly*, syn., 5/14/05 (Makeup: Michelle Champagne)

170. 2005: *Kim Possible*, Disney Channel, 5/14/05 (Sound Mixing, Live Action and Animation: Melissa Ellis and Fil Brown [re-recording mixers])

171. 2005: *Who Wants to Be a Millionaire*, syn., 5/20/05 (Game Show Host: Meredith Vieira)

172. 2005: *Desperate Housewives*, ABC, 9/18/05 (Lead Actress in a Comedy Series: Felicity Huffman)

173. 2005: "Pilot," *Desperate Housewives*, ABC, 9/18/05 (Directing for a Comedy Series: Charles McDougall)

174. 2005: *Desperate Housewives*, ABC, 9/18/05 (Casting for a Comedy Series: Scott Genkinger and Junie Lowry-Johnson)

175. 2005: "Pilot," *Desperate Housewives*, ABC, 9/18/05 (Single-Camera Picture Editing for a Comedy Series: Michael Berenbaum)

176. 2005: *Desperate Housewives*, ABC, 9/11/05 (Main Title Theme Music: Danny Elfman)

177. 2005: *Desperate Housewives*, ABC, 9/11/05 (Guest Actress in a Comedy Series: Kathryn Joosten)

178. 2005: *Lost*, ABC, 9/18/05 (Drama Series: J. J. Abrams, Damon Lindelof, Bryan Burk, Carlton Cuse, Jack Bender, David Fury, Jesse Alexander, Javier Grillo-Marxuah, Jean Higgins, Sarah Caplan, and Leonard Dick)

179. 2005: "Pilot," *Lost*, ABC, 9/18/05 (Directing for a Drama Series: J. J. Abrams)

180. 2005: *Lost*, ABC, 9/18/05 (Casting for a Drama Series: April Webster, Mandy Sherman, Alyssa Weisberg, and Veronica Collins Rooney)

181. 2005: *Lost*, ABC, 9/11/05 (Single-Camera Picture Editing for a Drama Series: Mary Jo Markey)

182. 2005: "Pilot," *Lost*, ABC, 9/11/05 (Music Composition for a Series (Dramatic Underscore): Michael Giacchino [composer])

183. 2005: *Lost*, ABC, 9/11/05 (Special Visual Effects for a Series: Kevin Blank, Mitch Suskin [visual effects supervisors]; Archie Ahuna [special effects supervisor]; Jonathan Spencer Levy, Benoit "Ben" Girard, Laurent M. Abecassis [CGI supervisors]; Kevin Kutchaver, Bob Lloyd [visual effects compositors])

184. 2005: *The Amazing Race*, CBS, 9/18/05 (Reality-Competition Program)

185. 2005: *Monk*, USA, 9/18/05 (Actor in a Comedy Series: Tony Shalhoub)

186. 2005: "My Life in Four Cameras," *Scrubs*, NBC, 9/11/05 (Multicamera Picture Editing for a Series: John F. Michel)

187. 2005: "We're Moving Up the Food Chain," *The Amazing Race*, CBS, 9/11/05 (Picture Editing for Nonfiction Programming: Matt Deitrich, Mike Bolanowski, Heeyeon Chang, Chris Dalzell, Evan Finn, Danny Flynn, Michael "Mighty" Friedman, Eric Goldfarb, Julian Gomez, Andy Kozar, Paul Neilsen, Jacob Parsons, Jeff Runyan, and Eric Wilson)

188. 2006: *Walt Disney World Christmas Day Parade, 2005*, ABC, 4/28/06 (Special Class Program: Andrew Perrott [exec. producer]; Jeff Palmer [supervising producer]; John Best [coordinating producer]; Philip Hack [line producer]; Darlene Papalini, Kevin Young, Gina D. Jones, Rhonda Parker [producers]; Regis Philbin, Kelly Ripa, Ryan Seacrest [co-hosts])

189. 2006: *High School Musical*, Disney Channel, 8/19/06 (Children's Program)

190. 2006: *Grey's Anatomy*, ABC, 8/19/06 (Casting for a Drama: Linda Lowy and John Brace)

191. 2006: *High School Musical*, Disney Channel, 8/19/06 (Choreography: Kenny Ortega, Charles Klapow, and Bonnie Story)

192. 2006: *The Amazing Race*, CBS, 8/19/06 (Cinematography for Nonfiction Programming [Multicamera]: Per A. C. Larsson [director of photography]; Sylvester Campe, Tom Cunningham, Chip Goebert, Uri Sharon, and Scott Shelley [camera])

193. 2006: *The Amazing Race*, CBS, 8/19/06 (Picture Editing for Nonfiction Programming (Multicamera): Matt Deitrich [supervising editor]; Mike Bolanowski, Evan Finn, Eric Goldfarb, Julian Gomez, Andy Kozar, and Paul Nielsen [editors])

194. 2006: *Monk*, USA, 8/27/06 (Actor in a Comedy Series: Tony Shalhoub)

195. 2006: *The Amazing Race*, CBS, 8/27/06 (Reality/Competition Program)

196. 2007: *Monk*, USA, 9/8/07 (Guest Actor in a Comedy Series: Stanley Tucci)

197. 2007: *Ugly Betty*, ABC, 9/8/07 (Casting for a Comedy Series: Libby Goldstein, Junie Lowry-Johnson)

198. 2007: *The Amazing Race*, CBS, 9/8/07 (Cinematography for Reality Programming: Per A. C. Larsson [director of photography]; John Armstrong, Sylvester Campe, Petr Cikhart, Tom Cunningham, Chip Goebert, Bob Good, Peter Rieveschi, Dave Ross, Uri Sharon, and Alan Weeks [camera])

199. 2007: *The Amazing Race*, CBS, 9/8/07 (Picture Editing for Reality Programming: Jon Bachmann, Steven Escobar, Eric Goldfarb, Julian Gomez, Andy Kozar, Paul Nielsen, and Jacob Parsons [editors])

200. 2007: *Scrubs*, NBC, 9/8/07 (Sound Mixing for a Comedy or Drama Series [Half-Hour and Animation]: Joe Foglia [production mixer]; John W. Cook II and Peter J. Nusbaum [re-recording mixers])

201. 2007: *Brothers & Sisters*, ABC, 9/16/07 (Lead Actress in a Drama Series: Sally Field)

202. 2007: *Ugly Betty*, ABC, 9/16/07 (Lead Actress in a Comedy Series: America Ferrera)

203. 2007: *Lost*, ABC, 9/16/07 (Supporting Actor in a Drama Series: Terry O'Quinn)

204. 2007: *Grey's Anatomy*, ABC, 9/16/07 (Supporting Actress in a Drama Series: Katherine Heigl)

205. 2007: *The Amazing Race*, CBS, 9/16/07 (Reality/Competition Program)

206. 2007: *Ugly Betty*, ABC, 9/16/07 (Directing for a Comedy Series: Richard Shepard)
207. 2008: *Desperate Housewives*, ABC, 9/13/08 (Guest Actress in a Comedy Series: Kathryn Joosten)
208. 2008: "Fifth Year Anniversary Show" and "I'm F*****g Matt Damon," *Jimmy Kimmel Live!*, ABC, 9/13/08 (Picture Editing of Clip Packages for Talk, Performance, Award or Reality-Competition Program [tie]: James Crowe [editor])
209. 2008: "I'm F*****g Matt Damon," *Jimmy Kimmel Live!*, ABC, 9/13/08 (Original Music and Lyrics: Sarah Silverman, Tony Barbieri, Wayne McClammy, Sal Iacono, and Dan Warner [writers/composers])
210. 2008: *Lost*, ABC, 9/13/08 (Sound Mixing for a Comedy or Drama Series [One Hour]: Robert Anderson [production mixer]; Frank Morrone and Scott Weber [re-recording mixers])
211. 2008: *Samantha Who?*, ABC, 9/21/08 (Supporting Actress in a Comedy Series: Jean Smart)
212. 2008: *The Amazing Race*, CBS, 9/21/08 (Reality/Competition Program)
213. 2009: *Wizards of Waverly Place*, Disney Channel, 9/20/09 (Children's Program)
214. 2009: *Legend of the Seeker*, syn., 9/20/09 (Music Composition for a Series [Original Dramatic Score])
215. 2009: *The Amazing Race*, CBS, 9/20/09 (Reality/Competition Program)
216. 2009: *Lost*, ABC, 9/20/09 (Supporting Actor in a Drama Series: Michael Emerson)
217. 2010: *Lanny and Wayne the Christmas Elves in Prep & Landing*, ABC, 8/21/10 (Animated Program)
218. 2010: *Lanny and Wayne the Christmas Elves in Prep & Landing*, ABC, 8/21/10 (Individual Achievement in Animation: Andy Harkness [art director], William M. George III [background key design], and Joe Mateo [storyboard artist])
219. 2010: Episode 09-1266, *Jimmy Kimmel Live!*, ABC, 8/21/10 (Costumes for a Variety/Music Program or a Special: Rodney Munoz [costume designer])
220. 2010: "The End," *Lost*, ABC, 8/21/10 (Single-Camera Picture Editing for a Drama Series: Stephen Semel, Mark J. Goldman, Christopher Nelson, and Henk Van Eeghen [editors])
221. 2010: "Suicide Is Painless," *Grey's Anatomy*, ABC, 8/21/10 (Makeup for a Single-Camera Series [Non-Prosthetic]: Norman Leavitt, Brigitte Bugayong, and Michele Teleis [makeup artists])
222. 2010: "When I'm Gone" (song), "Mr. Monk and the End Part II," *Monk*, ABC, 8/21/10 (Original Music and Lyrics: Randy Newman)
223. 2010: *Wizards of Waverly Place: The Movie*, Disney Channel, 8/21/10 (Children's Program)
224. 2010: "No More Good Days," *FlashForward*, ABC, 8/21/10 (Stunt Coordination, Danny Weselis [stunt coordinator])
225. 2011: *Grey's Anatomy*, ABC, 9/10/11 (Guest Actress in a Drama Series: Loretta Devine)
226. 2011: *Prep & Landing: Operation Secret Santa*, ABC, 9/10/11 (Short-Format Animated Program)
227. 2011: *Phineas and Ferb*, Disney Channel, 9/10/11 (Individual Achievement in Animation [Background Painter]: Jill Daniels)
228. 2011: *Phineas and Ferb*, Disney Channel, 9/10/11 (Individual Achievement in Animation [Background Design]: Brian Woods)
229. 2011: *Disney • ABC Television Group & Academy of Motion Picture Arts and Sciences, Oscar Digital Experience*, ABC.com (Creative Achievement in Interactive Media)
230. 2011: *The Amazing Race*, CBS, 9/18/11 (Reality/Competition Program)
231. 2012: *Phineas and Ferb*, Disney Channel, 9/15/12 (Individual Achievement in Animation [Background Painter]: Jill Daniels)
232. 2012: *Prep & Landing: Naughty vs. Nice*, ABC, 9/15/12 (Character Designer: Bill Schwab)
233. 2012: *Wizards of Waverly Place*, Disney Channel, 9/15/12 (Children's Program)
234. 2012: *The Amazing Race*, CBS, 9/23/12 (Reality/Competition Program)
235. 2013: *Mickey Mouse Croissant de Triomphe*, Disney.com, 9/15/13 (Short-format Animated Program)
236. 2013: *Mickey Mouse Croissant de Triomphe*, Disney.com, 9/15/13 (Individual Achievement in Animation [Background Painter]: Jenny Gase-Baker)
237. 2013: *Mickey Mouse Croissant de Triomphe*, Disney.com, 9/15/13 (Individual Achievement in Animation [Art Direction]: Joseph Holt)
238. 2013: *Tron: Uprising*, Disney XD, 9/15/13 (Art Direction: Alberto Mielgo)
239. 2013: *Scandal*, ABC, 9/15/13 (Guest Actor in a Drama Series: Dan Bucatinsky)

240. 2014: *Scandal*, ABC, 8/16/14 (Guest Actor in a Drama Series: Joe Morton)

241. 2014: *The Amazing Race*, CBS, 8/25/14 (Reality-Competition Program)

242. 2014: *Disney Mickey Mouse*, Disney Channel, 8/16/14 (Short-format Animated Program)

243. 2014: "O Sole Minnie," *Disney Mickey Mouse*, Disney Channel, 8/16/14 (Individual Achievement in Animation: Narina Sokolova [background painter])

244. 2014: "The Adorable Couple," *Disney Mickey Mouse*, Disney Channel, 8/16/14 (Individual Achievement in Animation: Valerio Ventura [background designer])

245. 2014: "Dreamscaperers," *Gravity Falls*, Disney Channel, 8/16/14 (Individual Achievement in Animation: Ian Worrel [art director])

246. 2015: "Not What He Seems," *Gravity Falls*, Disney XD, 9/12/15 (Individual Achievement in Animation: Alonso Ramirez Ramos [storyboard artist])

247. 2015: *American Crime*, ABC, 9/20/15 (Supporting Actress in a Limited Series or Movie: Regina King)

248. 2015: *How to Get Away with Murder*, ABC, 9/20/15 (Lead Actress in a Drama Series: Viola Davis)

249. 2016: *Marvel's Jessica Jones*, Netflix, 9/10/16 (Original Main Title Theme Music: Sean Callery)

250. 2016: *American Crime*, ABC, 9/18/16 (Supporting Actress in a Limited Series or Movie: Regina King)

251. 2017: *David Blaine: Beyond Magic*, ABC, 9/9/17 (Motion Design [Juried]: Orion Tait, Thomas Schmid, Daniel Oeffinger [creative directors]; William Trebutien [lead animator])

252. 2017: "The End of the Galaxy," *Wander Over Yonder*, Disney XD, 9/9/17 (Individual Achievement in Animation [Juried]: Justin Nichols [character animation])

253. 2017: *O.J.: Made in America* "Part 3", ESPN, 9/9/17 (Directing for a Nonfiction Program: Ezra Edelman [director])

254. 2017: *O.J.: Made in America* "Part 4", ESPN, 9/9/17 (Picture Editing for a Nonfiction Program: Bret Granato, Maya Mumma, Ben Sozanski [editors])

255. 2017: *Marvel's Luke Cage*, Netflix, 9/10/17 (Stunt Coordination for a Drama Series, Limited Series, or Movie: James Lew)

256. 2018: *The Scariest Story Ever: A Mickey Mouse Halloween Spooktacular*, Disney Channel, 9/8/18 (Individual Achievement in Animation [Juried]: Justin Martin [background designer])

257. 2020: "Hair Day," *black-ish*, ABC, 9/16/20 (Contemporary Hairstyling: Araxi Lindsey, Robert C. Mathews III, Enoch Williams)

258. 2020: "Chapter 7: The Reckoning," *The Mandalorian*, Disney+, 9/16/20 (Cinematography for a Single Camera Series [Half-Hour]: Greig Fraser, Baz Idoine)

259. 2020: "Chapter 1: The Mandalorian," *The Mandalorian*, Disney+, 9/16/20 (Production Design for a Narrative Program [Half-Hour]: Andrew L. Jones [production designer], Jeff Wisniewski [art director], Amanda Serino [set decorator])

260. 2020: "Chapter 1: The Mandalorian," *The Mandalorian*, Disney+, 9/16/20 (Sound Editing for a Comedy or Drama Series [Half-Hour] and Animation: David Acord, Matthew Wood, Bonnie Wild, James Spencer, Richard Quinn, Richard Gould, Stephanie McNally, Ryan Rubin, Ronni Brown, Jana Vance)

261. 2020: "Chapter 2: The Child," *The Mandalorian*, Disney+, 9/16/20 (Sound Mixing for a Comedy or Drama Series [Half-Hour] and Animation: Shawn Holden [production mixer], Bonnie Wild [re-recording mixer], Chris Fogel [scoring mixer])

262. 2020: "Chapter 2: The Child," *The Mandalorian*, Disney+, 9/16/20 (Special Visual Effects: Richard Bluff, Jason Porter, Hayden Jones, Abbigail Keller, Hal Hickel, Roy Cancino, John Rosengrant, Enrico Damm, Landis Fields)

263. 2020: *Forky Asks a Question: What Is Love?*, Disney+, 9/17/20 (Short Form Animated Program: Bob Peterson [director/writer], Mark Nielsen [producer])

264. 2020: *Godfather of Harlem*, EPIX, 9/19/20 (Outstanding Main Title Design: Mason Nicoll, Peter Pak, Giovana Pham, Cisco Torres)

265. 2020: *The Mandalorian*, Disney+, 9/19/20 (Stunt Coordination for a Drama Series, Limited Series or Movie: Ryan Watson)

266. 2020: "Chapter 8: Redemption," *The Mandalorian*, Disney+, 9/19/20 (Music Composition for a Series [Original Dramatic Score]: Ludwig Göransson)

267. 2021: "Chapter 13: The Jedi," *The Mandalorian*, Disney+, 9/11/21 (Prosthetic Makeup:

Brian Sipe, Alexei Dmitriew, Samantha Ward, Scott Stoddard, Pepe Mora, Cale Thomas, Carlton Coleman, Scott Patton)

268. 2021: "Chapter 13: The Jedi," *The Mandalorian*, Disney+, 9/11/21 (Sound Mixing for a Comedy or Drama Series: Bonnie Wild, Stephen Urata, Shawn Holden, Christopher Fogel)

269. 2021: "Chapter 15: The Believer," *The Mandalorian*, Disney+, 9/11/21 (Cinematography for a Single-Camera Series [Half-Hour]: Matthew Jensen)

270. 2021: *WandaVision*, Disney+, 9/11/21 (Production Design for a Narrative Program [Half-Hour]: Mark Worthington, Sharon Davis, Kathy Orlando)

271. 2021: "Filmed Before a Live Studio Audience," *WandaVision*, Disney+, 9/11/21 (Fantasy/Sci-Fi Costumes: Mayes C. Rubeo, Joseph Feltus, Daniel Selon, Virginia Burton)

272. 2021: *Black Is King*, Disney+, 9/12/21 (Costumes for a Variety, Nonfiction, or Reality Program: Zerina Akers, Timothy White)

273. 2021: "Breaking the Fourth Wall," *WandaVision*, Disney+, 9/12/21 (Original Music and Lyrics: "Agatha All Along," by Kristen Anderson-Lopez, Robert Lopez)

274. 2021: "Chapter 16: The Rescue," *The Mandalorian*, Disney+, 9/12/21 (Music Composition for a Series [Original Dramatic Score]: Ludwig Göransson)

275. 2021: "Chapter 16: The Rescue," *The Mandalorian*, Disney+, 9/12/21 (Stunt Performance: Lateef Crowder)

276. 2021: *The Mandalorian*, Disney+, 9/12/21 (Special Visual Effects in a Season or a Movie: Joe Bauer, Richard Bluff, Abbigail Keller, Hal Hickel, Roy K. Cancino, John Knoll, Enrico Damm, John Rosengrant, Joseph Kasparian)

277. 2021: *The Mandalorian*, Disney+, 9/12/21 (Stunt Coordination: Ryan Watson)

278. 2021: *Hamilton*, Disney+, 9/19/21 (Technical Direction, Camerawork, Video Control for a Special: Pat Capone, Jack Donnelly, Dave Knox, Bruce MacCallum, Bill Winters, Maceo Bishop, Abby Levine, Joe Belack)

279. 2021: *Hamilton*, Disney+, 9/19/21 (Variety Special [pre-recorded])

280. 2022: *The Beatles: Get Back*, Disney+, 9/3/22 (Outstanding Documentary or Nonfiction Series: Paul McCartney, Ringo Starr, Yoko Ono Lennon, Olivia Harrison, Peter Jackson, Clare Olssen, Jonathan Clyde)

281. 2022: "Part 3: Days 17-22," *The Beatles: Get Back*, Disney+, 9/3/22 (Outstanding Direct-ing for a Documentary/Nonfiction Program: Peter Jackson)

282. 2022: "Part 3: Days 17-22," *The Beatles: Get Back*, Disney+, 9/3/22 (Outstanding Sound Editing for a Nonfiction or Reality Program [Single or Multi-Camera]: Martin Kwok, Emile de la Rey, Matt Stutter, Michael Donaldson, Stephen Gallagher, Tane Upjohn-Beatson, Simon Riley)

283. 2022: "Part 3: Days 17-22," *The Beatles: Get Back*, Disney+, 9/3/22 (Outstanding Picture Editing for a Nonfiction Program: Jabez Olssen)

284. 2022: "Part 3: Days 17-22," *The Beatles: Get Back*, Disney+, 9/3/22 (Outstanding Sound Mixing for a Nonfiction or Reality Program [Single or Multi-Camera]: Michael Hedges, Brent Burge, Alexis Feodoroff, Giles Martin)

285. 2022: *What If . . . ?*, Disney+, 9/3/22 (Outstanding Character Voice-Over Performance: Chadwick Boseman)

286. *The Book of Boba Fett*, Disney+, 9/4/22 (Outstanding Special Visual Effects in a Season or a Movie: Richard Bluff, Abbigail Keller, Paul Kavanagh, Cameron Neilson, Scott Fisher, John Rosengrant, Enrico Damm, Robin Hackl, Landis Fields)

287. *Chip 'n Dale: Rescue Rangers*, Disney+, 9/4/22 (Outstanding Television Movie: Alexander Young, Tom Peitzman, Todd Lieberman, David Hoberman)

288. "Gods and Monsters," *Moon Knight*, Disney+, 9/4/22 (Outstanding Sound Editing for a Limited or Anthology Series, Movie, or Special: Bonnie Wild, Mac Smith, Kimberly Patrick, Vanessa Lapato, Matt Hartman, Teresa Eckton, Tim Farrell, Leo Marcil, Joel Raabe, Ian Chase, Anele Onyekwere, Stephanie Lowry, Carl Sealove, Dan O'Connell, John Cucci)

Emperor Penguins, The (film) Live-action short; released Oct. 13, 1955. Directed by Maris Marret. Documents the life and habits of the largest of all penguins; filmed during a French Antarctic expedition led by Paul Emile Victor. 11 min.

Emperor Zurg Sworn enemy of Buzz Lightyear and the Galactic Alliance in the Toy Story films; voiced by Andrew Stanton.

Emperor's New Groove, The (film) In a mythical mountain kingdom, arrogant young Emperor Kuzco is transformed into a llama by his power-hungry adviser—the devious diva Yzma. Stranded in the jungle, Kuzco's only chance to get back home and reclaim the highlife rests with a good-hearted peasant named Pacha. Kuzco's "perfect world" becomes a perfect mess as this most unlikely duo must deal with hair-raising dangers, wild comic predicaments, and, most horrifying of all, each other as they race to return Kuzco to the throne before Yzma (aided by her muscle-bound manservant, Kronk) tracks them down and finishes them off. Ultimately, Kuzco's budding friendship with Pacha teaches this royal pain to see his world in a different way. Released Dec. 15, 2000. Directed by Mark Dindal. Voices include David Spade (Kuzco), John Goodman (Pacha), Eartha Kitt (Yzma), Patrick Warburton (Kronk), Wendie Malick (Chicha). 78 min. With a score by John Debney and songs by Sting and David Hartley. Work started on a project with a very different version of the story, and the title *Kingdom of the Sun*, in 1994. In 1998, the story was completely revamped, maintaining only 2 of the main comedic characters and a few elements from the original treatment. The song "My Funny Friend and Me" was nominated for an Academy Award. A documentary about problems encountered during the making of the film, *The Sweatbox*, was made by Sting's wife, Trudie Styler. There was a direct-to-video sequel, *Kronk's New Groove*, in 2005.

Emperor's New School, The (TV) Animated series; premiered on Disney Channel Jan. 27, 2006, and on ABC Kids beginning Jan. 28. The teenage Kuzco, a self-centered but lovable wise guy, is first in line to be emperor. But before he can officially claim the throne, he must graduate from school. Kuzco's biggest obstacle is the evil Yzma and her dim-witted yet good-natured sidekick, Kronk, who are determined to make Kuzco fail. While pursuing his diploma, Kuzco is banished from the royal palace and forced to live with commoner Pacha and his family. Despite their sometimes turbulent relationship, Pacha is like a father to him, while Kuzco relies on his friend (and biggest crush), Malina, to help him navigate schoolwork. Voices include J. P. Manoux (Kuzco), Patrick Warburton (Kronk), Eartha Kitt (Yzma), Jessica DiCicco (Malina), Wendie Malick (Chicha), Fred Tatasciore (Pacha), Rip Taylor (Royal Records Keeper). From Walt Disney Television Animation.

Empire (TV) A 6-hour miniseries on ABC; aired Jun. 28–Jul. 26, 2005. In 44 BC, Julius Caesar returns from triumphs in Spain to a neglected republic and a corrupt senate drunk with power.

Though he's hailed as a hero by the masses, the senate is wary of Caesar's plans that might place him in a position of ultimate power. Brutus and Cassius plot against Caesar, who is protected by Tyrannus, Rome's finest warrior. The senate manages to separate Tyrannus from Caesar by kidnapping his son—a diversion to get Tyrannus out of the way while Brutus assassinates the great conqueror. As he is drawing his last breath, Caesar swears Tyrannus to protect his successor, Octavius, his 18-year-old nephew. Tyrannus and Octavius are forced into exile, where they are joined by Agrippa, a young soldier, and Camane, a vestal virgin. Together they strive to help Octavius fulfill his destiny and become emperor. Directed by John Gray and Greg Yaitanes. Stars include Jonathan Cake (Tyrannus), Santiago Cabrera (Octavius), Emily Brunt (Camane), Chris Egan (Agrippa), Vincent Regan (Mark Antony), Colm Feore (Julius Caesar), Trudie Styler (Servilia), James Frain (Brutus). Filmed on location in south-central Italy and at Cinecittà Studios. From Storyline Entertainment and Touchstone Television.

Empire Grill Art deco–style restaurant in the Disney Ambassador Hotel at Tokyo Disney Resort; opened Jul. 7, 2000, serving California-inspired international cuisine.

Emporio Largest shop in Tokyo DisneySea, in Mediterranean Harbor; opened Sep. 4, 2001. "Emporio" is Italian for "department store." The painted night sky on the ceiling is a special feature.

Emporium The largest store on Main Street, U.S.A. in Disneyland; opened Jul. 17, 1955. It serves as the primary place for Disneyland to showcase its souvenir merchandise, and, located right at the end the street as one is leaving the park, it is ideal for those last-minute purchases. A highlight at the Emporium are its windows. Facing Main Street, they are usually filled with elaborate dioramas telling the story of the latest Disney animated film release. Also in the Magic Kingdom at Walt Disney World; opened Oct. 1, 1971. There, the proprietor is identified as Osh Popham, based on the character in *Summer Magic*. The Walt Disney World store expanded in 2001, with the new Main Street Gallery taking over west Center Street. Also opened in World Bazaar at Tokyo Disneyland Apr. 15, 1983 (expanding in 2003 as the Grand Emporium, taking over Towne Clothiers and the Main Street Cinema); in Disneyland Paris Apr. 12, 1992; and in Hong Kong Disneyland Sep. 12, 2005.

Empress Lilly A 19th-century-style riverboat moored along the Lake Buena Vista Shopping Village at Walt Disney World; opened May 1, 1977. Dining was offered in 3 restaurants—the Fisherman's Deck, the Steerman's Quarters, and the Empress Room—with lively entertainment performed in the Baton Rouge Lounge. Named after Walt Disney's wife, Lilly Disney, who christened the 217-ft.-long paddle wheeler. Until the opening of Victoria & Albert's at Disney's Grand Floridian Resort & Spa, the Empress Room provided the most elegant dining experience on the Walt Disney World property, with culinary delights prepared by top chefs. The *Empress Lilly* became part of Pleasure Island when the entertainment district was built immediately adjacent to the ship in 1989. It closed as a Disney operation Apr. 22, 1995. Became Fulton's Crab House Mar. 10, 1996, then Paddlefish Feb. 4, 2017.

Empty Nest (TV) Series on NBC; aired Oct. 8, 1988–Jul. 8, 1995. Spin-off of *The Golden Girls*. The contemporary problems and joys in the relationship between a widowed pediatrician father and his daughter living under the same roof with a huge dog. Stars Richard Mulligan (Dr. Harry Weston), Dinah Manoff (Carol Weston), David Leisure (Charley Dietz), Park Overall (Laverne Todd), Estelle Getty (Sophia Petrillo), Marsha Warfield (Dr. Maxine Douglas). Kristy McNichol played a 2nd daughter, Barbara, a policewoman, in the first 5 seasons. Dreyfuss the dog is played by Bear, a combination Saint Bernard/golden retriever. From Witt/Thomas/Harris Productions and Touchstone Television. Mulligan won the Emmy Award for Lead Actor in a Comedy Series in 1989.

Empty Socks (film) Oswald the Lucky Rabbit cartoon; released Dec. 12, 1927. Climbing down the chimney as Santa Claus, Oswald tries to make Christmas special for the children of an orphanage. But his toys fail to work, and 1 kid accidentally starts a fire, resulting in a less-than-merry holiday.

Encanto (film) Animated feature. The Madrigal family lives hidden in the mountains of Colombia, in a magical house, in a vibrant town, in a wondrous, charmed place called an Encanto. The magic of the Encanto has blessed every child in the family with a unique gift, from superstrength to the power to heal—except one, Mirabel. But when she discovers that the magic surrounding the Encanto is in danger, Mirabel decides that she might just be her exceptional family's last hope. Released Nov. 24, 2021, also in 3-D. Directed by Jared Bush and Byron Howard. Voices include Stephanie Beatriz (Mirabel), María Cecilia Botero (Abuela Alma), John Leguizamo (Bruno), Mauro Castillo (Félix), Jessica Darrow (Luisa), Angie Cepeda (Julieta), Carolina Gaitán (Pepa), Diane Guerrero (Isabela), Wilmer Valderrama (Agustín), Rhenzy Feliz (Camilo), Ravi Cabot-Conyers (Antonio), Adassa (Dolores). 102 min. Score by Germaine Franco, with 8 original songs by Lin-Manuel Miranda. For authenticity, a trust of experts advised on Colombian anthropology, dress, botany, music, language, and other subjects. Filmmakers ultimately selected the country's Coffee Region (Eje Cafetero) for the village where the Madrigals would reside. A special feat was bringing the casita to life—to emote, react to the Madrigal family, and misbehave. Released in wide-screen format. *Encanto* continued to gain popularity after its digital release on Disney+ Dec. 24, 2021, and the film returned to participating theaters Feb. 18, 2022. The soundtrack reached No. 1 on the Billboard 200 albums chart dated Jan. 15, 2022, and would spend several nonconsecutive weeks on top. "We Don't Talk About Bruno" held the No. 1 spot on the Billboard Hot 100 for 5 weeks—a record for any song from a Disney film. Nominated for 3 Academy Awards, winning for Best Animated Feature.

Encanto at the Hollywood Bowl (TV) Live-to-film concert special; digitally released Dec. 28, 2022, on Disney+. Stars the original voice cast of *Encanto*, plus an 80-person orchestra, 50 dancers, and special guests. The live event, *Encanto Live-to-Film Concert Experience*, was performed Nov. 11–12, 2022 at the Hollywood Bowl.

Enchanted (film) In this fairy-tale spoof beginning in the colorful, musical, animated world of Andalasia, the beautiful Giselle's wish to meet the handsome prince of her dreams and share "true love's kiss" comes true when Prince Edward hears her lilting soprano raised in song and rushes to her side. The very next day, on her way to marry Edward, Giselle is tricked by the evil Queen Narissa and banished from her fairy-tale kingdom to modern-day New York City, where the film turns to live action as Giselle, a very real woman, experiences the cruelty of the big city. Giselle soon meets a handsome, no-nonsense, divorce lawyer, Robert, and his young daughter, Morgan, and begins to change her views on life and love. Robert also eventually changes, accepting that innocence and joy can exist in our jaded world. Prince Edward and the two-faced lackey Nathaniel, along with an eager chipmunk named Pip, are also transported to Manhattan, with Edward searching for his princess, and Nathaniel, acting under orders from the Queen, trying to keep them apart. With this collision of 2 worlds, Giselle finds herself wondering whether her storybook view of romance, complete with "happily ever after," can survive in our world. Directed by Kevin Lima. Released Nov. 21, 2007. Stars Amy Adams (Giselle), Patrick Dempsey (Robert Philip), James Marsden (Prince Edward), Timothy Spall (Nathaniel), Idina Menzel (Nancy), Rachel Covey (Morgan), Susan Sarandon (Queen Narissa), Julie Andrews (narrator). 107 min. Former Disney princess voice actresses Jodi Benson, Paige O'Hara, and Judy Kuhn have cameo roles. Filmed in Super 35. Music, including 5 original songs, is by Alan Menken and Stephen Schwartz. Three of their songs ("Happy Working Song," "So Close," and "That's How You Know") received Academy Award nominations. Animation supervisor was James Baxter. Location filming took place in New York City. A sequel, *Disenchanted*, was digitally released on Disney+ in 2022.

Enchanted Book Shoppe, The *Beauty and the Beast* show in Plaza Gardens at Disneyland; ran Nov. 28, 1991–Apr. 26, 1992. It was superseded by the more sophisticated *Beauty and the Beast* stage show presented at Videopolis.

Enchanted Chamber Shop inside Sleeping Beauty Castle at Disneyland; opened in 2008, taking the place of Tinker Bell & Friends.

Enchanted Cottage Sweets & Treats, The See Troubadour Tavern.

Enchanted Garden Buffet-service restaurant with Victorian décor in the Hong Kong Disneyland Hotel; opened Sep. 12, 2005. Also a restaurant on the *Disney Dream* and *Disney Fantasy*, inspired by the gardens of Versailles.

Enchanted Grove Fruit refreshments were offered at this Fantasyland juice bar in the Magic Kingdom at Walt Disney World; open Mar. 1983–Nov. 19, 2011. Presented by Minute Maid. Formerly the Fantasyland Art Festival, which offered souvenir portraits of guests. It became Cheshire Café.

Enchanted Rose Lounge in Disney's Grand Floridian Resort & Spa at Walt Disney World; opened Oct. 4, 2019, replacing Mizner's Lounge and Commander Porter's. Cocktails and shareable dishes are served in 4 gathering spaces inspired by the live-action *Beauty and the Beast*.

Enchanted Storybook Castle Central attraction, and Fantasyland landmark, in Shanghai Disneyland; opened Jun. 16, 2016, with the Royal Banquet Hall restaurant, Voyage to the Crystal Grotto, "Once Upon a Time" Adventure, and the Bibbidi Bobbidi Boutique. The structure is the tallest and most complex of all the Disney park castles and the first to represent all the Disney princesses. Chinese elements that signify harmony, prosperity, and purity of heart and mind are integrated into the castle's design. Storybook Court inside the castle offers character-greeting opportunities with Disney princesses and other royal friends. Outside the castle is Storybook Castle Stage, featuring musical performances during the day and a nighttime spectacular with lasers, projections, and fireworks.

Enchanted Tale of Beauty and the Beast Fantasyland ride-through attraction inside the Beast's castle in Tokyo Disneyland; opened Sep. 28, 2020, following a soft-opening period that began Sep. 21. Guests board magical cups that "dance" in rhythm to music from the animated film, brought to life with elaborate scenes and Audio-Animatronics characters.

Enchanted Tales with Belle Fantasyland attraction in the Magic Kingdom at Walt Disney World; opened Dec. 6, 2012. Guests are magically transported from Maurice's cottage to the Beast's library for a delightful storytelling experience. They meet with Belle, Madame Wardrobe, and Lumiere and may even play a part in the story.

Enchanted Tiki Room, Walt Disney's Adventureland show in Disneyland; debuted Jun. 23, 1963. The first attraction to feature sophisticated Audio-Animatronics figures. Four international macaws—named José, Michael, Pierre, and Fritz—host a lively 17-min. musical production, performed by more than 200 singing birds, flowers, and tikis. While waiting to enter the Tiki Room, guests can purchase refreshments and watch an outdoor presentation by the gods and goddesses of the Enchanted Tiki Garden. Songs include "Let's All Sing Like the Birdies Sing" and "Hawaiian War Chant." While the project was nearing completion, Walt Disney brought in Richard M. and Robert B. Sherman to write an opening song that would tie the show together; they ended up with the calypso tune, "The Tiki, Tiki, Tiki Room." Disneyland entertainer Wally Boag was enlisted to write much of the script and also provided the voice of José; his *Golden Horseshoe Revue* counterpart, Fulton Burley, provided the voice of Michael. The term *Audio-Animatronics* had been utilized earlier in describing the movable figures populating Nature's Wonderland, but the process was greatly changed, enabling press releases to call the Enchanted Tiki Room the first to use the technology. The Tiki Room was originally planned as a restaurant, but that would have greatly limited capacity. Sponsored by United Airlines 1964–1973, and from Jan. 1976 on by Dole Pineapple. Also opened in Adventureland in Tokyo Disneyland Apr. 15, 1983. The similar attraction in the Magic Kingdom at Walt Disney World was originally named Tropical Serenade, and located in the Sunshine Pavilion. The Florida show was extensively renovated, reopening spring 1998 as The Enchanted Tiki Room—Under New Management, starring Zazu from *The Lion King*, Iago from *Aladdin*, and Uh-Oa, the Tiki goddess of disaster. After another remodeling in 2011, a shortened version of the original show was restored in Florida, reopening with the name Walt Disney's Enchanted Tiki Room. The Tokyo Disneyland version introduced a revised, nightclub-style show called The Enchanted Tiki Room: Now Playing Get the Fever! in 1999, followed by The Enchanted Tiki Room: Stitch Presents "Aloha E Komo Mai!," featuring an Audio-Animatronics Stitch, in 2008.

Enchanted Treasures Jewelry shop inside the Castle of Magical Dreams in Hong Kong Disneyland; opened Nov. 20, 2020. Presented by Chow Tai Fook.

Encino Man (film) Two high school outcasts, Dave Morgan and his best friend, Stoney, uncover a frozen caveman while excavating a backyard swimming pool. They hope their accidental discovery will bring them fame and fortune, not to mention a newfound social status on campus. When the caveman accidentally thaws out and comes to life, they quickly concoct a scheme to disguise him as a foreign exchange student so no suspicions will be aroused. Link, as he is called, soon learns to speak, dress, and act like a typical "Valley boy," becoming the most popular kid in school, frustrating Dave and Stoney's goals. As Link learns more about the 20th century, he begins to realize that he does not fit in. But an earthquake suddenly hits, unearthing a frozen cavewoman, Link's link to his own past. Released May 22, 1992. Directed by Les Mayfield. A Hollywood Pictures film. 88 min. Stars Sean Astin (Dave Morgan), Brendan Fraser (Link), Pauly Shore (Stoney Brown), Megan Ward (Robyn Sweeney), Mariette Hartley (Mrs. Morgan), Richard Masur (Mr. Morgan). Filmed in California's San Fernando Valley.

Encino Woman (TV) Two-hour movie; aired on ABC Apr. 20, 1996. A beautiful prehistoric woman, to be known as Lucy, awakens from her million-year slumber to encounter an advertising executive, David Horsenfelt, who promotes her to his agency as the "primal" woman they have been searching for to advertise a new perfume; meanwhile, he's also falling in love with her. Stars Katherine Kousi (Lucy), Corey Parker (David), Jay Thomas (Marvin Beckler), John Kassir (Jean Michel). A TV sequel to the theatrical film *Encino Man*. Directed and co-written by Shawn Schepps, who had written the script for the theatrical film.

Encore! (TV) Unscripted series; digitally premiered Nov. 12, 2019, on Disney+. The pilot aired Dec. 10, 2017, on ABC. Exec. producer Kristen Bell brings together former castmates of a high school musical, tasking them with re-creating their original performance in a reunion like no other. Through it all, these unlikely groups of friends—with the help of Broadway's best—just might pull off a standing-ovation–worthy performance of beloved musicals. From Olive Bridge Entertainment, Jason Cohen Productions, and ABC.

End of the Trail (TV) Episode 13 of *Texas John Slaughter*.

End Zone Food Court Dining hall in Disney's All-Star Sports Resort at Walt Disney World; opened Apr. 29, 1994.

Endor Vendors SEE TATOOINE TRADERS.

Endurance (film) The story of distance runner Haile Gebrselassie from Ethiopia and how he eventually won the 10,000-meter race at the Atlanta Olympics in 1996. A Walt Disney Pictures presentation of a La Junta Production in association with Film Four and Helkon Media Film Vertrieb. Directed by Leslie Woodhead. (The race sequence at the Atlanta Olympics is directed by Bud Greenspan.) Limited release in Los Angeles and New York City on May 14, 1999. CinemaScope. 83 min. The film combines elements of cinema vérité, traditional documentary filmmaking, sports coverage, docudrama, and feature-film devices, backed by a score drawn from East African musical traditions.

Enemy of the State (film) A chance encounter with an old friend destroys Robert Dean's fast-track career and happy homelife when he is framed for a murder by a corrupt intelligence official. As an administrator within the National Security Agency, Thomas Brian Reynolds sees his role as being the ultimate guardian of the U.S., and when stakes are high, he believes he must bend the rules to protect its secrets. He thus appropriates the vast resources of his department to commit the perfect crime and conceal a political cover-up of the murder of a congressman by government agents. Dean's only hope to reclaim his life and prove his innocence is a man he's never met, a mysterious underground information broker and ex-intelligence operative known only as Brill. A Don Simpson/Jerry Bruckheimer Production in association with Touchstone Pictures. Directed by Tony Scott. Released Nov. 20, 1998. Stars Will Smith (Robert Dean), Jon Voight (Thomas Brian Reynolds), Gene Hackman (Brill), Regina King (Carla Dean), Loren Dean (Hicks), Jake Busey (Krug), Barry Pepper (David Platt), Jason Lee (Daniel Zavitz), Gabriel Byrne (NSA agent), Lisa Bonet (Rachel Banks). 132 min. CinemaScope. Filming took place around Baltimore and Washington, D.C., and in Los Angeles. For a tunnel sequence, several cars had to be cut in pieces, lowered through a manhole, then rebuilt 20 feet underground.

Energy Creation Story (film) A 70-mm animated story of the creation of fossil fuels for Theater I of the Universe of Energy in EPCOT Center; ran Oct. 1, 1982–1996.

Energy Exchange Display in Communicore East in EPCOT Center; ran Oct. 1, 1982–Jan. 31, 1994. Presented by Exxon. Computers helped tell about elements of the energy story.

Energy in Physics (film) Educational film; released in Aug. 1984. The fundamental law of physics, the Law of Conservation of Energy, is introduced to students.

Energy Savers, The (film) Educational film with Donald Duck, Mickey Mouse, and Goofy helping teach good energy conservation habits; released in Sep. 1982.

Energy, You Make the World Go 'Round (film) Kinetic, multi-image preshow for the Universe of Energy in EPCOT Center; ran Oct. 1, 1982–1996. 8 min. Rapidly changing images, showing our understanding of energy, were presented on a long "moving mosaic" screen, achieved by one hundred 3-ft.-sq. sections that rotated in sync with the imagery; designed by film director/artist Emil Radok. The song of the same name was written by Bob Moline.

Engine Co. 71 SEE FIRE STATION.

EngineEar Souvenirs Shop at the exit of Mickey & Minnie's Runaway Railway at Disneyland; opened Mar. 10, 2023.

Engine-Ears Toys Sunshine Plaza toy shop themed to an oversized model train in Disney's California Adventure; opened Feb. 8, 2001. Closed Jul. 31, 2011, as part of the area's transformation into Buena Vista Street.

Englander, Otto (1906–1969) Story man on animated films for 22 years; he served as story director on *Dumbo*.

English, Liz Actress; provided the voice of Marie in *The Aristocats*.

Enjoy It! Song from *In Search of the Castaways*; written by Richard M. and Robert B. Sherman and sung by Maurice Chevalier.

Entrelazados (TV) SEE INTERTWINED, DISNEY.

Entropy (film) Jake, a young filmmaker, begins to direct his first film, a documentary about the rock band U2, but runs up against cast, budget, and production problems with it, and at the same time sees his personal life unraveling. A Touchstone release on video Feb. 15, 2000, of an independent film from Tribeca Productions, originally shown Apr. 15, 1999, at the Los Angeles Independent Film Festival. Directed by Phil Joanou. Stars Stephen Dorff (Jake Walsh), Judith Godrèche (Stella), Kelly MacDonald (Pia), Hector Elizondo (the chairman). 104 min.

Environmental Sanitation (film) Educational film produced under the auspices of the Coordinator of Inter-American Affairs; shows the growth of a city and the need to build proper water and sanitation systems for a growing populace. Delivered Apr. 3, 1946.

Enzo's Hideaway SEE MARIA & ENZO'S RISTORANTE.

EPCOT Acronym coined by Walt Disney in 1966 meaning Experimental Prototype Community of Tomorrow. The park was called EPCOT Center when it opened Oct. 1, 1982. It was a major undertaking for the Disney company, costing in the neighborhood of $1 billion. Toward the end of his life, Walt became interested in solving the problems of cities; he had read books on the subject and thought he could do something to help. With the vast acreage he was accumulating in Florida, an ideal place was available. In a film shot in Oct. 1966, meant for the people of Florida and leaders of American industry, he explained some of his concepts and called for cooperation in creating a new kind of community—one that would introduce and demonstrate new ideas and systems. The central core would be the commercial center, a completely enclosed district topped by a cosmopolitan hotel. Radiating out from it would be clusters of residences, with a vast greenbelt in between for recreation, schools, and similar facilities. The all-electric PeopleMover and Monorail systems would safely transport residents aboveground, while supply trucks and other traffic would flow on dedicated levels underground. Unfortunately, Walt died before he could refine his ideas. Nothing definite had been planned for Walt Disney World, and Roy O. Disney, taking over for his brother, rationalized that since the company knew how to build a Magic Kingdom, they should start with the theme park to get some cash flow started, and then they could consider Walt's final dream of an experimental community. The Magic Kingdom at Walt Disney World did open successfully in Oct. 1971, and the Disney executives never forgot Walt's ideas for EPCOT, even though Roy Disney passed away later that year. In 1975, Card Walker, president of Walt Disney Productions, announced that the company would proceed with EPCOT. But Walker and his advisers determined that Walt's ideas for an idealistic city were unrealistic; one could not expect people to live under a microscope, as it were. It could not be both a showplace and a place to live. Instead, the Disney Imagineers got busy and soon had their proposals ready for a park consisting of 2 areas—Future World and World Showcase. When it was ready to open in 1982, they decided to call the park EPCOT Center, reasoning that the whole Walt Disney World property was part of Walt's grand idea, and this was only the *center* of it. It was a little difficult marketing a name like EPCOT, but over the first decade of the park's history, guests forgot that it was an acronym, and it became its own word. Thus *Center* was dropped from the

name in Dec. 1993, the letters were lowercased, and *Epcot* came into its own. In 2016, the company announced a multi-year transformation of the park, with new experiences intended to make the park more relevant and family-oriented. The name reverted to the uppercase EPCOT, and the park was reorganized into 4 neighborhoods—World Celebration, World Discovery, and World Nature (all formerly part of Future World), along with the existing World Showcase. The name changes were effective as of Oct. 1, 2021. SEE FUTURE WORLD AND WORLD SHOWCASE.

EPCOT (film) SEE FLORIDA FILM.

EPCOT Advanced Information System (film) Educational film about the development of the WorldKey Information System from concept to completion; released in Aug. 1984.

EPCOT America! America! (TV) Show on The Disney Channel; aired Apr. 21–Aug. 16, 1983, originating from EPCOT Center and featuring filmed segments of all that is best in America.

EPCOT Building Code Embodying Walt Disney's philosophy for the "Florida Project," it was passed by the Reedy Creek Improvement District in 1970 to enable the construction of Walt Disney World. The code was written in such a way that it required strict compliance with current building regulations included in building codes from other governmental bodies, but it also enabled new and innovative construction methods, systems, and structures that were not addressed in most building codes.

EPCOT Center SEE EPCOT.

EPCOT Center: A Souvenir Program (film) Video souvenir; released in Jan. 1984.

EPCOT Center: The Opening Celebration (TV) Show aired Oct. 23, 1982. Directed by Dwight Hemion. Rainy weather fails to dampen the enthusiasm as EPCOT Center is opened. Danny Kaye is the host, looking at the history of the project from Walt's first announcement through construction. Celebrity guests help Kaye look around the park, visit several of the attractions, and join in musical numbers. Also stars Drew Barrymore, Roy Clark, Marie Osmond, Eric Severeid, the West Point Glee Club. For the opening, Disney assembled the All-American Marching Band, consisting of top school musicians from all over the country.

EPCOT Computer Central Display of the actual computers which ran EPCOT Center; opened Oct. 1, 1982, in Communicore East. Presented by Sperry. It featured the Astuter Computer Revue show (later Backstage Magic), interactive computer terminals, and SMRT-1, a robot that demonstrated voice recognition technology in a variety of question-and-answer games. Closed Jan. 30, 1994.

Epcot Daredevil Circus Spectacular Future World thrill show in and above the Communicore Stage; ran Oct. 1, 1987–Mar. 19, 1988. Space-age dancers and Cristiani elephants were accompanied by daredevil acts, such as the Flying Trapeze, the high-wire Skywalker Jay Cochrane, and daring Skycyclist ascents to Spaceship Earth.

Epcot Discovery Center Information area in Epcot; open Jul. 1, 1994–Oct. 3, 1998. Formerly Epcot Outreach and Epcot Teacher's Center. Guests could ask their questions about any of the subjects covered in the park or throughout Walt Disney World. The staff could access their detailed computer programs or consult their library for the answers. In addition, a variety of take-home informational resources were available.

EPCOT Earth Station Film, The (film) An educational look at the wonders of EPCOT Center at Walt Disney World. This film was created for presenting on giant screens within Earth Station, the information center neighboring Spaceship Earth.

EPCOT Forever Nighttime spectacular around World Showcase Lagoon in EPCOT; premiered Oct. 1, 2019, replacing *IllumiNations: Reflections of Earth*. Fireworks, laser effects, music, and choreographed kites paid tribute to the park's past, present, and future. The final performance was held Sep. 28, 2021, and the show was succeeded by *Harmonious*. It was announced *EPCOT Forever* will return Apr. 3, 2023.

EPCOT International Festivals Beginning with the Apr. 29, 1994, debut of the Epcot International Flower and Garden Festival, the park has hosted annual events with themed marketplaces, displays, and entertainment. Holidays Around the World debuted Nov. 25, 1994 (renamed Epcot International Festival of the Holidays in 2017), followed by the Epcot International Food & Wine Festival (Sep. 28, 1996) and the Epcot International Festival of the Arts (Jan. 13, 2017).

EPCOT Magazine (TV) Series on The Disney Channel; debuted Apr. 18, 1983, and ran for 3 seasons. Hosted by Michael Young. Each show included several different segments on topical news and entertainment, ranging from food and fashion to travel and family relationships. A 2-part episode in 1984 visited the Walt Disney Archives.

EPCOT Outreach Information area in Communicore West; open May 26, 1983–Jul. 1, 1994, including the EPCOT Teacher's Center. It moved its location and became Epcot Discovery Center.

EPCOT Poll SEE ELECTRONIC FORUM.

EPCOT Resort Area At Walt Disney World; consists of Disney's Caribbean Beach, Riviera, Yacht Club, Beach Club, and BoardWalk, as well as the Walt Disney World Swan, Dolphin, and Swan Reserve Hotels.

EPCOT 77 (film) A 16-mm promotional film describing World Showcase and Future World, being built in EPCOT Center.

Epic Mickey An action-adventure video game developed by Junction Point Studios and designed by Warren Spector for Disney Interactive Studios. Released Nov. 30, 2010. Mickey Mouse is rebranded to be more of an epic hero, mischievous and adventurous. Included in the game is Oswald the Lucky Rabbit. A sequel, *Epic Mickey 2: The Power of Two*, was released Nov. 18, 2012. Junction Point Studios was purchased by Disney in Jul. 2007 and closed Jan. 2013.

Epstein, Jeffrey R. He joined Disney in 2008, leading marketing for D23: The Official Disney Fan Club. In 2016, he was named director, Corporate Communications and became vice president in 2021. He has written for Disney publications, spoken to fan groups, and created the *D23 Inside Disney* podcast, which he also co-hosted.

Ernest Goes to Camp (film) Ernest P. Worrell, working as a handyman at a boys' summer camp, aspires to be a counselor and is "rewarded" by being put in charge of a group of juvenile delinquents. After initial problems, highlighted by slapstick humor, Ernest and the boys gain some mutual respect and help save the camp from developers. Released May 22, 1987. Directed by John R. Cherry III. A Touchstone film. 92 min. Stars Jim Varney (Ernest P. Worrell), Victoria

Racimo (Nurse St. Cloud), John Vernon (Sherman Krader), Iron Eyes Cody (Old Indian Chief). Filmed in Nashville, Tennessee.

Ernest Goes to Jail (film) When lovable but inept Ernest P. Worrell becomes a juror on a murder trial, the scheming defendant notices that Ernest is a dead ringer for jailed crime boss Felix Nash. A plot is quickly hatched to switch the 2 look-alikes, and soon Ernest finds himself in jail while his notorious double sneaks away to freedom, taking over Ernest's job as a night janitor in a bank. Released Apr. 6, 1990. Directed by John Cherry III. A Touchstone film. 82 min. Stars Jim Varney (Ernest P. Worrell/Felix Nash/Auntie Nelda) and Gailard Sartain (Chuck). Filmed in Nashville, Tennessee.

Ernest Goes to Splash Mountain (TV) Special; first aired on The Disney Channel Jul. 7, 1989, then in syn. beginning Aug. 19, 1989. 30 min. Ernest P. Worrell goes to Disneyland to experience the new attraction before it opens to the public. Stars Jim Varney (Ernest P. Worrell), Danny Breen, Sheryl Bernstein.

Ernest Green Story, The (TV) A Disney Channel Premiere Film; first aired Jan. 17, 1993. Directed by Eric Laneuville. The story of one of the 9 students who, in 1957, were the first African Americans to attend the previously all-white Central High School in Little Rock, Arkansas. Ernest Green overcomes prejudice and threats of violence to pursue his dreams of education. Stars Morris Chestnut (Ernest Green), Ossie Davis (Grandfather), CCH Pounder (Daisy Bates). President-elect Bill Clinton and his longtime friend, Ernest Green, attended a special showing of the film at Little Rock's Central High School before its premiere on The Disney Channel.

Ernest Saves Christmas (film) Santa Claus travels to Orlando to find a successor, a sometime actor, and puppeteer: Joe. On the way to find Joe, Santa meets bumbling cabdriver, Ernest, and by mistake leaves his sack in the cab. Ernest and a runaway girl, Pamela, try to help Santa. Pamela, who had attempted to steal the sack, returns it, and Ernest, after many mishaps, manages to deliver Santa's sleigh and reindeer from the airport, just in time for Joe to take over on Christmas Eve. Released Nov. 11, 1988. Directed by John Cherry III. A Touchstone film. 90 min. Stars Jim Varney (Ernest P. Worrell), Douglas Seale (Santa), Oliver Clark (Joe Carruthers), Noëlle Parker (Pamela Trenton/Harmony Star). Filmed in Disney-MGM Studios at Walt Disney World and on location in Orlando and Nashville, Tennessee.

Ernest Scared Stupid (film) After accidentally using a magic spell to revive a slimy troll, Trantor, who was condemned centuries before by a Worrell ancestor, bumbling Ernest P. Worrell enlists the aid of Old Lady Hackmore, the town eccentric, to dispose of the creature, break the curse, and make the town safe for children once again. Released Oct. 11, 1991. Directed by John Cherry III. A Touchstone film. 92 min. Stars Jim Varney (Ernest P. Worrell), Eartha Kitt (Old Lady Hackmore), and Jonas Moscartolo (Trantor). Filmed in Nashville, Tennessee, and its vicinity. Two later Ernest video releases were from Monarch, not Disney: *Ernest Rides Again* (1993) and *Ernest Goes to School* (1994), the former having had a limited theatrical run. SEE ALSO SLAM DUNK ERNEST (A LATER DIRECT-TO-VIDEO ERNEST MOVIE).

Ernesto de la Cruz Legendary Mexican singer in *Coco*; voiced by Benjamin Bratt.

Erwin, Stuart (1903–1967) Actor; appeared in *Son of Flubber* (Coach Wilson) and *The Misadventures of Merlin Jones* (Capt. Loomis), and on TV in *Moochie of the Little League*.

Escapade in Florence (TV) Two-part show; aired Sep. 30 and Oct. 7, 1962. Directed by Steve Previn. Two teens get involved in intrigue in Florence, Italy, when Tommy Carpenter is given the wrong painting in an art store. A group of criminals try to get it back, causing Tommy to wonder what is so valuable about it. It turns out an art forger is copying valuable paintings and substituting the copy for the original. Tommy and his friend, Annette Aliotto, manage to solve the plot and turn the art thieves into the police. Stars Tommy Kirk, Annette Funicello, Nino Castelnuovo, Ivan Desny.

Escape from the Dark (film) International theatrical title of *The Littlest Horse Thieves*.

Escape from Tomorrow (film) An independent surrealistic cult film surreptitiously filmed at Walt Disney World and Disneyland. A father visiting the Disney parks with his family is haunted by disturbing imagery. Directed by Randy Moore. Premiered Jan. 18, 2013, at the Sundance Film Festival. Stars Roy Abramsohn and Elena Schuber. 103 min. This film is not associated with The Walt Disney Company.

Escape to Nowhere (TV) Part 2 of *Andrews' Raiders*.

Escape to Paradise/Water Birds (TV) Show aired Dec. 18, 1960. A behind-the-scenes show on the filming of *Swiss Family Robinson* on the West Indian island of Tobago, followed by the True-Life Adventure film *Water Birds*. Stars John Mills, Dorothy McGuire, James MacArthur, Janet Munro, Sessue Hayakawa, Tommy Kirk, Kevin Corcoran.

Escape to Witch Mountain (film) Tony Malone, 13, and his sister, Tia, 11, orphaned by the loss of their foster parents, live in a children's home. But their incredible psychic powers attract the rich and powerful Aristotle Bolt, who has his assistant, Lucas Deranian, adopt them as wards to exploit them. Terrified, they escape with the aid of a new friend, Jason O'Day, in his camper. Jason agrees to help them find Stony Creek, a town on a cryptic map in Tia's possession. Pursued by Bolt, Deranian, and the police, the youngsters are jailed but once again escape. As time runs out, the children remember they are castaways from another planet and are soon led by one of their own kind, Uncle Bene, to a flying saucer, which blasts off for the sanctuary of Witch Mountain, leaving their captors below far behind. Released Mar. 21, 1975. Directed by John Hough. 97 min. Stars Eddie Albert (Jason), Ray Milland (Bolt), Donald Pleasence (Deranian), Ike Eisenmann (Tony), Kim Richards (Tia), Walter Barnes (Sheriff Purdy), Reta Shaw (Mrs. Grindley), Denver Pyle (Uncle Bene). Based on the book by Alexander Key. Musical score by Johnny Mandel. The film was shot around Monterey and Palo Alto, in California, including at a Victorian mansion in Menlo Park, California, for the Pine Woods orphanage. Bolt's kingly abode, Xanthus, was filmed in a $3 million replica of a Byzantine castle built by Templeton Crocker between 1926–1934 from lava rock from Mount Vesuvius and materials gathered all over Europe. The castle overlooks the beach at Pebble Beach, California. Other California location scenes were shot at Carmel Valley, Big Sur, and the town of Felton in the Santa Cruz Mountains. The many special effects in the film were created by Art Cruickshank. SEE ALSO RETURN FROM WITCH MOUNTAIN AND RACE TO WITCH MOUNTAIN.

Escape to Witch Mountain (TV) Two-hour movie based on the 1975 feature film; aired on ABC Apr. 29, 1995. A compelling mystery about 2 twins with supernatural powers who are separated as babies and find their way back to each other and to their "real home." Directed by Peter Rader. Stars Robert Vaughn (Edward Bolt), Elisabeth Moss (Anna), Erik von Detten (Danny), Lynne Moody (Lindsay Brown), Perrey Reeves (Zoe Moon), Lauren Tom (Claudia Ford), Henry Gibson (Prof. Ravetch), Kevin Tighe (Sheriff), Brad Dourif (Luther/Bruno).

Escen, Don (1919–2006) Longtime Disney company financial leader, hired in 1949 in the accounting department. He became assistant treasurer and controller in 1960 and was instrumental in helping Roy O. Disney navigate the company through difficult times after Walt Disney's death in 1966. In 1975, he was given the additional titles of financial administrator and treasurer of Buena Vista International. He retired in 1984 and was named a Disney Legend in 1998.

Esmeralda Gypsy character in *The Hunchback of Notre Dame*; singing voice by Heidi Mollenhauer and speaking voice by Demi Moore.

Espace Euro Disney Preview center for Euro Disney; open Dec. 5, 1990–Mar. 22, 1992. The primary feature was a 35-mm film showcasing plans for the resort.

Espinosa, Mary Mouseketeer from the 1950s *Mickey Mouse Club* TV show.

ESPN With the purchase of Capital Cities/ABC, Disney acquired 80% ownership of the ESPN and ESPN2 cable networks. ESPN, the worldwide leader in sports, was launched in 1979, and its sister network, ESPN2, came along in 1993. A 24-hour college sports network, ESPNU, was launched Mar. 4, 2005. ESPN360, a customizable Internet-based service, was unveiled Apr. 27, 2005; it was renamed ESPN3 in 2010. Between 1997–1999, a new division of The Disney Store, named ESPN—The Store, offered sports merchandise in 3 malls, beginning with the Glendale Galleria in California. There was also an *ESPN Magazine*, in publication Mar. 23, 1998–Sep. 2019. ESPN+, a streaming service, premiered Apr. 12, 2018.

ESPN Club SEE ESPN ZONE.

ESPN Clubhouse Shop Sports apparel shop in ESPN Wide World of Sports at Walt Disney World; replaced the D Sports Merchandise Shop. There is also the ESPN Stadium Clubhouse Shop, which replaced Disney's Clubhouse Merchandise Shop. Both shops opened in 2010.

ESPN+ Streaming service offering live sporting events, on-demand content, and programming not available on ESPN's linear TV networks; launched Apr. 12, 2018, as Disney's first domestic subscription-based streaming service.

ESPN—The Store Sports merchandise, clothing, and collectibles shop; the first store opened Sep. 16, 1997, in the Glendale Galleria in California. Two other stores—in Santa Ana and Torrance (both in California)—opened Nov. 1998. All 3 locations closed Oct. 1, 1999, with the merchandise later sold at ESPN Zone and online.

ESPN Wide World of Sports Opening in 1997 as Disney's Wide World of Sports, this complex accommodates professional-caliber training and competition, festival and tournament-type events, and vacation-fitness activities and serves as headquarters for sporting events taking place elsewhere throughout Walt Disney World. Facilities include a 7,000-seat baseball stadium, a 5,000-seat field house, Major League Baseball practice fields, Little League fields, tennis courts, volleyball courts, a track-and-field complex, and a golf driving range. More than 60 sports have been played at the complex, which also includes classrooms, office space, and media facilities. In Feb. 1996, the Atlanta Braves signed an agreement to use the complex as their spring training base, and the Harlem Globetrotters selected it as their headquarters. The complex had its grand opening Mar. 28, 1997, with an exhibition baseball game between the Atlanta Braves and Cincinnati Reds. The complex was rebranded ESPN Wide World of Sports Feb. 25, 2010. The Atlanta Braves held their 22nd, and final, season at the complex in 2019. Sporting venues include The Arena, Baseball Quadraplex, Champion Stadium, HP Field House (originally the Disney Fieldhouse, then The Milk House), Marathon Sports Fields, Softball Diamondplex, Track & Field Complex, and VISA Athletic Center (formerly Jostens Center). Dining is available at the ESPN Wide World of Sports Grill (originally All Star Cafe, then What's Next Café), with shopping at the ESPN Clubhouse Shop. See also Visa Athletic Center; Arena at ESPN Wide World of Sports, The; and National Basketball Association ("NBA bubble").

ESPN Zone Sports-themed dining and entertainment complex; opened in Baltimore Jul. 12, 1998, the first of a number that were later opened in cities around the country such as Chicago, New York City, Atlanta, Washington, Las Vegas, and Denver. An ESPN Zone opened in the Downtown Disney District in Anaheim Jan. 12, 2001. On Dec. 1, 2008, the first ESPN Zone owned by another company (AEG) opened in LA Live adjacent to the Staples Center in Los Angeles. All other ESPN Zone facilities were owned by Disney Regional Entertainment. The Atlanta and Denver locations closed in 2009, followed by the Los Angeles location in 2013 and Anaheim Jun. 2, 2018 (succeeded by Pop-Up Disney! A Mickey Celebration). The remaining ESPN Zones had closed Jun. 2010. A similar facility, ESPN Club, opened on Disney's BoardWalk at Walt Disney World Jul. 1, 1996, and closed Mar. 2020, to later become The Cake Bake Shop by Gwendolyn Rogers.

ESPN's Ultimate X (film) The highlights and dramatic stories behind the 2001 Summer X Games, covering skateboarding, biking, moto X, and street luge competitions and the athletes who compete. Directed by Bruce Hendricks. A Touchstone film. Released May 10, 2002. A documentary released in 70 mm for exclusive showing in IMAX and large-format theaters worldwide. 39 min.

Estevez, Emilio Actor; appeared in *Tex* (Johnny Collins); *Stakeout* and *Another Stakeout* (Bill Reimers); *The Mighty Ducks*, *D2: The Mighty Ducks*, *D3: The Mighty Ducks*, and *The Mighty Ducks: Game Changers* (Gordon Bombay); and *The War at Home* (Jeremy Collier).

Esther Emu star of *Mickey Down Under* (1948).

Estrin, Judith Member of the Disney Board of Directors Jun. 24, 1998–Mar. 18, 2014.

Eternal Sea, The 200° film attraction in Tomorrowland at Tokyo Disneyland; ran Apr. 15, 1983–Sep. 16, 1984. A journey into the world's aquatic frontiers. Superseded by *Magic Journeys* and then *Captain EO*.

Eternals (film) Third film released in "Phase 4" of the Marvel Cinematic Universe. The Eternals are a race of immortal aliens from the distant planet Olympia who arrived on Earth thousands of years ago to protect humanity from a race of alien predators called the Deviants. The group fractured and split apart, content to live among humans, but the prevailing threat of the monstrous Deviants—creatures which once again threaten the existence of mankind—means the Eternals need to put their differences aside and reunite in order to defend humanity once again. Released Nov. 5, 2021 (also in 3-D, IMAX, and IMAX 3-D), after an Oct. 18 premiere in Los Angeles and a Nov. 3 international release. Directed by Chloé Zhao. Stars Gemma Chan (Sersi), Richard Madden (Ikaris), Kumail Nanjiani (Kingo), Lia McHugh (Sprite), Brian Tyree Henry (Phastos), Lauren Ridloff (Makkari), Barry Keoghan (Druig), Don Lee (Gilgamesh), Kit Harington (Dane Whitman), Salma Hayek (Ajak), Angelina Jolie (Thena). 157 min. Inspired by Jack Kirby's *Eternals* comic books, first published by Marvel in 1976. Filmed in wide-screen format in London, Pinewood Studios, the U.K. countryside, and the Canary Islands.

Ethics in the Computer Age (film) Educational film presenting 2 mini-dramas about software piracy and computer hacking; released in Aug. 1984.

Eudora's Chic Boutique Featuring Tiana's Gourmet Secrets New Orleans Square shop in Disneyland; opened Sep. 20, 2022, replacing Le Bat en Rouge. As the story goes, Tiana has collaborated with her dressmaker mother, Eudora, to open this little shop, offering accessories to create and serve Orleans-style cuisine and more.

Eureka! (TV) Animated series on Disney Junior; debuted Jun. 22, 2022. Eureka is a talented young inventor living in the prehistoric world of Rocky Falls. Utilizing creative out-of-the-box thinking, she designs inventions and contraptions in the hopes of making the world a better place and moving her community into a more modern era. With the help of her supportive parents, teacher, best friends—Pepper and Barry—and beloved pet mammoth, Murphy, Eureka is learning to embrace that she is not ordinary . . . she's extraordinary. Voices include Ruth Righi (Eureka), Renée Elise Goldsberry (Roxy), Lil Rel Howery (Rollo), Javier Muñoz (Ohm), Kai Zen (Pepper), Devin Trey Campbell (Barry), Fred Tatasciore (Murphy). From Brown Bag Films, in association with Disney Junior.

Euro Disney SEE DISNEYLAND PARIS.

Euro Disney: When the Dream Becomes Reality (Euro Disney: Quand l'imaginaire devient réalité) (film) Preview film shown at Espace Euro Disney in France; premiered Dec. 5, 1990. 13 min.

Euro Disneyland SEE DISNEYLAND PARIS.

Euro Disneyland Railroad A 20-min. grand circle tour of the park; opened Apr. 12, 1992. Main Street, U.S.A., Frontierland, and Fantasyland stations opened Apr. 12, 1992, followed by the Discoveryland station Jun. 24, 1993. The narrow-gage steam trains are the *W. F. Cody*, the *C. K. Holliday*, the *G. Washington*, and the *Eureka*. It was renamed Disneyland Railroad in 1994.

Eurospain Shop presented by Arribas Brothers in the Disney Village Marketplace at Walt Disney World; open Sep. 15, 1988–Sep. 15, 1995, offering handcrafted gifts and decorative articles from European artists. It was previously named Artespana; opened Mar. 8, 1986, succeeding Toledo Arts, and closed 1988.

Evans, Chris Actor; appeared as the first Captain America in the Marvel Studios films, and voiced the title character in *Lightyear*.

Evans, Monica She provided the voice of Abigail Gabble (*The Aristocats*) and Maid Marian (*Robin Hood*).

Evans, Morgan ("Bill") (1910–2002) With his brother, Jack, he designed the landscaping for Walt Disney's home in Los Angeles's Holmby Hills neighborhood, including the gardens around his backyard railroad, in the early 1950s. Walt then called upon him to continue the same work for Disneyland. He became director of landscape design for WED Enterprises and worked on almost all of the Disney parks, even consulting after his retirement. He was known not only for using unusual plants, but for using plants in unusual ways. He was named a Disney Legend in 1992.

EVE Sleek probe-droid (Extra-Terrestrial Vegetation Evaluator) in *WALL•E*; voiced by Elissa Knight.

Even Stevens (TV) Comedy series on Disney Channel; premiered Jun. 17, 2000, featuring the misadventures of Louis Stevens, a typical 13-year-old middle school kid, and his overachieving sister, Ren. There is constant sibling rivalry as Ren tries to live down the embarrassment of being related to the class clown, while Louis strives to live outside the shadow of his super-successful sister. Stars Shia LaBeouf (Louis), Christy Carlson Romano (Ren), Nick Spano (Donnie), Donna Pescow (Eileen), Tom Virtue (Steve).

Even Stevens Movie, The (TV) A Disney Channel

Original Movie; first aired Jun. 13, 2003. The Stevens family wins an all-expense-paid trip to an exclusive island hideaway. What the family doesn't know is that their week in paradise has been set up by a new "extreme reality" TV series, and the producer's quest for blockbuster ratings threatens to turn their dream vacation into a nightmare. Eventually the Stevens discover that they have been had and set out to even the score. Directed by Sean McNamara. Stars Shia LaBeouf (Louis Stevens), Christy Carlson Romano (Ren Stevens), Nick Spano (Donnie Stevens), Tom Virtue (Steve Stevens), Donna Pescow (Eileen Stevens), Steven Anthony Lawrence ("Beans" Aranguren), A. J. Trauth (Alan Twitty). The first original movie on Disney Channel inspired by an original comedy series.

Everglades, The: Home of the Living Dinosaurs (TV) A look at the animal characters found in Florida's Everglades, with an intimate look at the fascinating life stories of its mysterious native crocodiles and alligators. Produced by Pete Zuccarini. Aired in syn. beginning Nov. 20, 2000, as a New True-Life Adventure film.

Evergreen Playhouse Theater in Fantasyland at Shanghai Disneyland; opened Jun. 16, 2016, with *Frozen: A Sing-Along Celebration*, an interactive musical performance.

Everhart, Rex (1920–2000) Actor; he provided the voice of Maurice in *Beauty and the Beast*.

Evermoor (TV) Four-episode special on Disney Channel; premiered in Britain Oct. 10, 2014, and in the U.S. on Oct. 17. The Crossley family travels to the U.K. from America after inheriting the spooky Evermoor Manor from their Aunt Bridget. There, teenage Tara, an aspiring mystery writer, struggles to get along with her newly blended family while finding a mysterious tapestry that predicts the future and having to deal with a group of strange locals known as the Circle of Everines, led by Esmerelda Dwyer, who wants the Crossley family to leave. Directed by Chris Cottam. Stars Clive Rowe (mayor), Naomi Sequeira (Tara Crossley), Finney Cassidy (Cameron), George Sear (Seb), Georgia Lock (Bella), Georgie Farmer (Jake), Jordon Loughran (Sorsha), Sharon Morgan (Esmerelda Dwyer). Filmed at Arley Hall in Arley, Knutsford, Cheshire. Commissioned by Disney and produced by Lime Pictures. This is the first live-action special to be produced in the U.K. for broadcast on Disney Channel U.S.

Everson, Carolyn Member of the Disney Board of Directors beginning Nov. 21, 2022.

Everything POP Shopping & Dining Shopping location and food court with 7 stations at Disney's Pop Century Resort; opened Dec. 14, 2003.

Everything You Wanted to Know About Puberty . . . for Boys (film) Educational release in 16 mm in Aug. 1991. 16 min. Two boys have questions about recent physical changes but are too embarrassed to ask an older brother to borrow a book on the subject.

Everything You Wanted to Know About Puberty . . . for Girls (film) Educational release in 16 mm in Aug. 1991. 13 min. While staying at a friend's house, a girl has her first period, and the friend's older sister shares her knowledge and experience with the girls.

Everything's Trash (TV) Half-hour comedy series on Freeform; debuted Jul. 13, 2022, and ended Sep. 7. Phoebe is a thirtysomething podcast star navigating through her messy life. Forced to grow up when her older brother Jayden emerges as a leading political candidate, she relies on her friends and close-knit family to help her figure out adulthood. Stars Phoebe Robinson (Phoebe), who also serves as exec. producer and writer, based on her book *Everything's Trash, But It's Okay*. Also stars Jordan Carlos (Jayden), Toccarra Cash (Malika), Nneka Okafor (Jessie), Moses Strom (Michael). From ABC Signature and Tiny Reparations.

Evinrude Dragonfly character in *The Rescuers*; his sounds were provided by Studio sound effects wizard Jim Macdonald.

Evita (film) The musical story of Argentina's controversial and charismatic Eva Perón, a girl who rose from poverty to become one of the most powerful women in the world as the wife of Juan Perón, changing her country's history through sheer determination and a conviction that all Argentinians should prosper. Attracting attention like no other woman before or since, she hypnotized a nation of 18 million people for 7 years before her untimely death at the age of 33 in 1952. Directed by Alan Parker. A Cinergi production released by Hollywood Pictures Dec. 25, 1996, in Los Angeles and New York City; wider release Jan. 1, with a general release Jan. 10, 1997. (The film had an earlier opening Dec. 20 in London.) Stars Madonna (Eva Perón), Antonio

Banderas (Ché), Jonathan Pryce (Juan Perón). 135 min. Filmed in CinemaScope in Argentina; Budapest, Hungary (which more accurately replicated Buenos Aires of the 1930s and 1940s); and the U.K. It took much backstage persuasion, including entreaties by Madonna herself, to the president of Argentina, to obtain last-minute permission to shoot on the balcony of the Casa Rosada, the official government house. Madonna was fitted for over 80 costumes for the production. The film was based on a stage musical by Andrew Lloyd Webber and Tim Rice, which originated in a concept album released in 1976 while still unproduced on the stage; it opened on the stage in London in 1978 to great acclaim. The song "You Must Love Me," written specifically for the film by Webber and Rice, won the Academy Award for Best Song for 1996.

Ev'rybody Wants to Be a Cat Song from *The Aristocats*; written by Floyd Huddleston and Al Rinker.

Ewok Village Entrance to Star Tours in Disney's Hollywood Studios at Walt Disney World; opened Aug. 24, 1989.

Exchange Student (film) Animated short; digitally released Jan. 24, 2020, on Disney+, following a Jun. 14, 2019, premiere at the Annecy International Animation Film Festival. The only Earthling at a school for aliens is the ultimate outsider and must prove her worth to be accepted by her unusual new classmates. Directed by Natalie Nourigat. 2 min. From the Walt Disney Animation Studios Short Circuit program.

Exile (TV) Two-hour movie; aired Jan. 14, 1990. Directed by David Greenwalt. A group of students becomes marooned on an island when their plane is forced to land. The pilot takes the plane to get help, but he crashes. With no adults around, the kids have to manage by themselves. The pilot turns up alive, but he desperately steals their supplies and terrorizes the girls. Stars Christopher David Barnes, Corey Feldman, Mike Preston, Michael Stoyanov, Chris Furrh, Kate Benton, Alice Carter, Gino DeMauro, Stacy Galina, Christian Jacobs, Kiersten Warren.

Expectations: A Story About Stress (film) Educational film; released in Sep. 1985. Helps preadolescents recognize and deal with stress.

Expedition China (film) Documentary chronicling the making of Disneynature's *Born in China*. Filmmakers travel great distances, climb to extreme altitudes, and endure brutal conditions to capture tender moments in the families of pandas, red-crowned cranes, golden monkeys, and chiru. Digitally released on Netflix and other platforms beginning Dec. 27, 2017. Narrated by Maggie Q. Directed by Ben Wallis. 78 min. SEE ALSO GHOST OF THE MOUNTAINS.

Expedition Everest—Legend of the Forbidden Mountain Thrill attraction in Asia at Disney's Animal Kingdom; opened Apr. 7, 2006. As the story goes, Himalayan Escapes invites visitors to board a train to base camp at Mount Everest, but while traveling through the Forbidden Mountain pass, riders discover the havoc created by a legendary beast, the Yeti. The train careens backward and forward through the darkness, sending passengers within toward the clutches of the giant creature. While waiting to board, guests tour The Yeti Museum, which details the creature in legend, lore, and science. For authenticity, extensive research was involved in the attraction's design, from the look of the buildings and temples to the language and layout of signs. Over 2,000 handcrafted items were supplied by artisans in Asia. At just under 200 ft., the mountain is the tallest in Florida.

Experiment 626 SEE STITCH.

Explorer Canoes Treasure Cove attraction in Shanghai Disneyland; opened Jun. 16, 2016. Guests embark on a paddling expedition, enjoying scenic views of Skull Island, shipwrecks, treasure caves, and jungles. SEE ALSO DAVY CROCKETT'S EXPLORER CANOES (DISNEYLAND AND WALT DISNEY WORLD).

Explorer: The Last Tepui (TV) Hour-long documentary from National Geographic and ABC News Studios; digitally released Apr. 22, 2022, on Disney+. Elite climber Alex Honnold and a world-class climbing team led by National Geographic Explorer Mark Synnott take a grueling mission deep in the Amazon jungle as they attempt a first-ascent climb up a 1,000-ft. sheer cliff. Their goal is to deliver legendary biologist and National Geographic Explorer Bruce Means to the top of a massive "island in the sky" known as a *tepui*. The team must first trek miles of treacherous jungle terrain to help Dr. Means complete his life's work, searching the cliff wall for undiscovered animal species. This is an installment of National

Geographic's long-running *Explorer* series. Directed by Taylor Rees and Renan Ozturk.

Explorer's Club Adventureland restaurant in Disneyland Paris; opened Apr. 12, 1992. Closed Mar. 1994, reopening a month later as Colonel Hathi's Pizza Outpost. Also a quick-service eatery in Mystic Point at Hong Kong Disneyland, named The Explorer's Club Restaurant; opened May 17, 2013. Semi-buffet dining here began Dec. 22, 2021. According to the story, diners explore the globe-trotting exploits of Lord Henry Mystic in 5 dining rooms themed to countries he admired: Egypt, Russia, Morocco, India, and China.

Explorers' Landing Area at the base of Mount Prometheus in Mediterranean Harbor at Tokyo DisneySea; opened Sep. 4, 2001. Home to Fortress Explorations.

Expo Robotics Robot demonstration in Communicore West at EPCOT Center; ran Feb. 13, 1988–Oct. 3, 1993. The intricate movements of the robotic arms amazingly performed various programmed tricks. Some robots were set up to draw a picture of a guest's face, taken from a video monitor. This was an expansion of the popular Bird and the Robot presentation in Transcenter in the World of Motion.

Expo Shop Tomorrowland shop in Hong Kong Disneyland; opened Oct. 23, 2016, with Marvel-themed merchandise. Fans can try on Iron Man's armor suit in the interactive game *Become Iron Man*.

ExtraTERRORestrial Alien Encounter, The Sensory thriller attraction in Tomorrowland in the Magic Kingdom at Walt Disney World; open Jun. 20, 1995–Oct. 11, 2003. Inside the Tomorrowland Interplanetary Convention Center, X-S Tech, a corporation from a distant planet, is intent on showcasing its interplanetary teleportation apparatus, the X-S Series 1000. But the demonstration is marred by difficulties, and a horrible alien creature is accidentally teleported into the chamber, breaking loose into the audience. The cast included Jeffrey Jones (Chairman Clench), Kathy Najimy (Dr. Femus), Kevin Pollak (Spinlok), with the voice of Tim Curry (S.I.R.). George Lucas consulted on the attraction. Took the place of Mis-sion to Mars. Replaced in 2004 by Stitch's Great Escape!

Extremely Goofy Movie, An (film) Direct-to-video release Feb. 29, 2000. Goofy enrolls in college with his son, Max, but brings his 1970s ideas on college with him. When he teams up with a like-minded school librarian, the disco lights and mood rings swing back to action on campus. At the College X Games competition, Max is the hot new talent until Goofy joins in and shows the kids a whole new way to skateboard. Directed by Douglas McCarthy. Voices include Bill Farmer (Goofy), Jason Marsden (Max), Pauly Shore (Bobby), Vicki Lewis (Beret Girl), Bebe Neuwirth (Sylvia).

Eye of the Storm: Captain Jack's Stunt Spectacular SEE EL TEATRO FANDANGO.

Eyes & Ears Internal news publication for Walt Disney World Cast Members, 1971–2020. Originally titled *Eyes & Ears of Walt Disney World*.

Eyes Have It, The (film) Donald Duck cartoon released Mar. 30, 1945. Directed by Jack Hannah. Donald experiments with his power of hypnotism to change Pluto into a mouse, turtle, chicken, and finally a lion, which chases Donald about until a fall helps Pluto regain his senses.

Eyes in Outer Space (film) Featurette released Jun. 18, 1959. Directed by Ward Kimball. Winner of the 1960 Thomas Edison Foundation Award, this featurette explores the future of satellites and their ability to forecast and potentially even modify the weather. 26 min. Later shown on *Walt Disney's Wonderful World of Color* in 1962 as part of the episode *Spy in the Sky*.

Eyewitness to History: The Events (film) Educational film; released in Sep. 1978. Famous events from history are shown through newsreel footage.

Eyewitness to History: The Life Styles (film) Educational film; released in Sep. 1978. A glimpse at life in our century from newsreel accounts.

Eyewitness to History: The People (film) Educational film; released in Sep. 1978. Newsreel cameramen capture mini-portraits of famous people from history.

1. *Fantasia* (film) 2. *Frozen 2* (film) 3. *First Aiders* (film) 4. Fantasyland 5. *Flowers and Trees* (film)
6. *Fantasy in the Sky* 7. *Forky Asks a Question* (TV) 8. Flame Tree Barbecue 9. Firehouse Five Plus Two

Fa Zhou Mulan's father in *Mulan*; voiced by Soon-Tek Oh.

FABLife (TV) Nationally syn. daily lifestyle show with tips on beauty, fashion, food, and home design; aired Sep. 14, 2015–Jul. 27, 2016. Stars Tyra Banks, Chrissy Teigen, Joe Zee, Lauren Makk, Leah Ashley. From Disney/ABC's Summerdale Productions.

Fabray, Nanette (1920–2018) Actress; appeared in *Amy* (Malvina). Fabray found it easy to relate to the young boys and girls recruited from the California School for the Deaf in Riverside to act in the film; she herself suffered from a hearing loss that stemmed from a hereditary disease. She underwent several operations spanning 2 decades to have her hearing restored.

Facts of Life Reunion, The (TV) Aired on *The Wonderful World of Disney* Nov. 18, 2001. A reunion of the stars from the 1979–1988 sitcom finds Natalie's 2 boyfriends arriving for Thanksgiving dinner, so Blair, Tootie, and Mrs. Garrett have to attempt to keep the peace. Stars Lisa Whelchel (Blair), Kim Fields (Tootie), Mindy Cohn (Natalie), Charlotte Rae (Mrs. Garrett). From Berger Queen Productions, in association with Laurence Mark Productions, Columbia TriStar, Walt Disney Television, and Buena Vista Television.

Fagin Master of the gang of dog thieves in *Oliver & Company*; voiced by Dom DeLuise.

Fain, Sammy (1902–1989) Composer; wrote songs for *Alice in Wonderland*, *Peter Pan*, and *Sleeping Beauty*. Nominated for an Academy Award with Carol Connors and Ayn Robbins for "Someone's Waiting for You" from *The Rescuers*.

Fair Folk Fairylike characters who help Taran find the cauldron in *The Black Cauldron*.

Fairest of Them All, The (TV) Syn. special for the rerelease of *Snow White and the Seven Dwarfs*; aired May 23, 1983. Directed by Cardon Walker. Dick Van Patten hosts and introduces many of the artists who worked on the film; and Adriana Caselotti and Harry Stockwell, the voices of Snow White and the Prince, are reunited. The director, Cardon Walker, is the son of Disney executive E. Cardon Walker.

Fairfax Market Market stand in Hollywood Land at Disney California Adventure; opened Feb. 8, 2001.

Fairway Villas Two-bedroom accommodations in Lake Buena Vista at Walt Disney World; open 1978–2002. Arranged along the Lake Buena Vista Golf Course, the 64 tri-level villas sported innovative, energy-saving features. Became part of The Disney Institute in 1996.

Fairy Godmother She enables Cinderella to attend the ball; voiced by Verna Felton in the 1950 animated film.

Fairy Godmother's Cupboard Quick-service kiosk in Fantasyland at Shanghai Disneyland;

opened Jun. 16, 2016, with braised minced pork, pizza, and other fare.

Fairy Tale Forest Garden area in Fantasyland at Hong Kong Disneyland; opened Dec. 2015 as part of the park's "Happily Ever After" 10th anniversary celebration. Along a winding path, guests discover fairy tales as "living storybooks" in miniature scale, including *Snow White and the Seven Dwarfs*, *Cinderella*, *The Little Mermaid*, *Beauty and the Beast*, and *Tangled*. Visitors can also meet Tinker Bell in Pixie Hollow. Presented by Pandora.

Fairy Tale Treasures Old-world European shop in Fantasy Faire at Disneyland; opened Mar. 12, 2013, offering princess costumes, toys, and accessories.

Fairy Tale Wedding Pavilion SEE WEDDING PAVILION, DISNEY'S.

Falcon and The Winter Soldier, The (TV) Live-action series on Disney+; digitally released Mar. 19–Apr. 23, 2021. Sam Wilson (aka The Falcon) and Bucky Barnes (aka The Winter Soldier)—2 strong-willed individuals who don't always see eye to eye—team up on a global adventure that tests their abilities and their patience. Stars Anthony Mackie (Falcon), Sebastian Stan (Winter Soldier), Daniel Brühl (Zemo), Emily VanCamp (Sharon Carter), Wyatt Russell (John Walker). From Marvel Studios.

Faline Bambi's girlfriend; voiced by Cammie King and Ann Gillis.

Falk, Peter (1927–2011) Actor; starred in *Roommates* (Rocky Holeczek) and *Corky Romano* (Pops).

Fall Out—Fall In (film) Donald Duck cartoon released Apr. 23, 1943. Directed by Jack King. Donald experiences the trials and tribulations of army life: marching through summer sun and rain day after day and setting up camp in the evening, which takes Donald so long it is sunrise before he is finished.

Fall Varieties (film) Cartoon compilation; released by RKO in 1953.

Fallberg, Becky (1923–2007) Longtime head of the Ink & Paint Department at the Disney Studio. She began at Disney in 1942 as a telephone operator and was soon promoted to a painter on the World War II–era films. She later had roles in the Animation and Layout and Background departments before returning to Ink & Paint in 1950 to serve as a paint matcher and final checker. She was named manager of the department in 1975. She retired in 1986 and was named a Disney Legend in 2000.

Fallberg, Carl (1915–1996) He began at Disney in 1935 as an assistant director on animated shorts, and later became a story man on features and writer of comic book stories. He was given the assignment of scouting out Hollywood costume shops to find a pointed sorcerer's hat for the live-action model to wear for *Fantasia*.

Family, The (TV) Reality series on ABC; aired Mar. 4–Sep. 10, 2003. Ten members of an extended blue-collar, Italian American family are moved to a luxurious Palm Beach mansion where they compete for $1 million, with the mansion's staff doubling as a board of trustees to vote 1 person off at every episode's end. Hosted by George Hamilton. From Buena Vista Productions. 9 episodes.

Family, The (TV) Hour-long drama series on ABC; aired Mar. 3–May 15, 2016. A family is shaken to the core when a politician's presumed dead son suddenly returns. After a disappearance a decade earlier, Adam Warren's homecoming to Red Pines, Maine is initially met with astonishment and joy. But suspicions soon begin to emerge, and there are major repercussions for the family as well as others in the community. Is he really who he says he is? Stars Joan Allen (Claire Warren), Liam James (Adam), Alison Pill (Willa), Zach Gilford (Danny), Rupert Graves (John), Andrew McCarthy (Hank Asher), Margot Bingham (Nina Meyer), Floriana Lima (Bridey Cruz). From ABC Studios.

Family Band, The (TV) SEE ONE AND ONLY, GENUINE, ORIGINAL FAMILY BAND, THE (TITLE OF FEATURE).

FamilyFun Magazine for parents with young children, purchased by Disney in 1992 and sold in 2012. Articles focused on crafts, education, holidays, parties, vacations, and food preparation.

Family PC Magazine published by Disney Aug. 15, 1994; it ended with the Jan. 1998 issue. Appealed to families with children, with articles focused on computers and emerging technologies.

Family Planning (film) Educational film produced in association with the Population Council; released in Dec. 1967. The film explains that the ultimate goal of family life is the enrichment, not the restriction, of life.

Family Reboot (TV) A Disney+ original series; digitally released Jun. 15, 2022. In each episode, a family takes a week away from their busy schedules to go on a journey to rebuild their family bonds the "old-fashioned way"—with just a paper map in hand. Once the families have arrived in their house for the week, a number of activities, games, and conversations remind them to put aside their distractions and make new memories together. From Milojo Productions and Talos Films.

Family Tools (TV) Series on ABC; aired May 1–Jul. 10, 2013. When Jack Shea's father has a heart attack and is forced to hand over his beloved handyman business to his son, Jack is eager to finally step up and make his father proud. Unfortunately Jack's past career efforts have been less than stellar, so everyone seems to be waiting for him to fail. It is up to Jack to show that he has what it takes to find his true calling. Stars Kyle Bornheimer (Jack Shea), J. K. Simmons (Tony Shea), Edi Gathegi (Darren Poynton), Johnny Pemberton (Mason Baumgardner), Danielle Nicolet (Lisa Poynton), Leah Remini (Terry Baumgardner). Based on the U.K. series *White Van Man*. From ABC Studios.

Famous Jett Jackson, The (TV) Half-hour series on Disney Channel; debuted Oct. 25, 1998, and aired through 2001. Jett Jackson, a 13-year-old TV star, longs to have a normal life, so he leaves Hollywood and his TV-star mother behind to go live with his father, the town sheriff in Wilsted, North Carolina, where he was born. But Jett's friends and fans will not let him live the simple life, for they expect him to live up to the image of Silverstone, the heroic private investigator he plays on TV. Stars Lee Thompson Young (Jett), Ryan Sommers Baum (J. B. Halliburton), Kerry Duff (Kayla West), Gordon Greene (Wood Jackson), Montrose Hagins (Coretta Jackson). From Alliance Atlantis and JP Kids, in association with Disney Channel.

Fancy Nancy (TV) Animated series on Disney Junior; premiered Jul. 13, 2018. Six-year-old Nancy likes to be fancy in everything from her advanced vocabulary to her creative attire. Excited to experience what the magnificent world has to offer, she uses ingenuity and imagination to fancify her life and make the most of each day, while encouraging everyone around her to do the same. Directed and exec. produced by Jamie Mitchell. Voices include Mia Sinclair Jenness (Nancy Clancy), Alyson Hannigan (Claire Clancy), Rob Riggle (Doug Clancy), Spencer Moss (JoJo Clancy), Christine Baranski (Mrs. Devine), George Wendt (Grandpa Clancy), Tatyana Ali (Mrs. James), Chi McBride (Gus), Kal Penn (Mr. Singh), Madison Pettis (Brigitte). Based on the best-selling book series by Jane O'Connor. From Disney Television Animation.

Fanelli Boys, The (TV) Series on NBC; aired Sep. 8, 1990–Feb. 16, 1991. Four grown brothers from a boisterous Italian family in Brooklyn move back in with their strong-willed, widowed mother when their lives go awry. Stars Joe Pantoliano (Dominic), Ann Guilbert (Theresa), Christopher Meloni (Frank), Ned Eisenberg (Anthony), Andy Hirsch (Ronnie), Richard Libertini (Father Angelo). From KTMB Productions and Touchstone Television.

Fanning, Jim Author/editor; he has written extensively for the company, including for Disney Publishing, Walt Disney Records, Disney Store, The Walt Disney Collectors Society, Walt Disney Imagineering, the Walt Disney Archives, and D23. In addition to writing episodes of *Disney Family Album* on Disney Channel and bonus material for home entertainment releases, he has authored books, overseen Disney publications released in Japan, and contributed to The Walt Disney Family Museum.

Fantasia (film) One of the most highly regarded of the Disney classics, a symphonic concert with Leopold Stokowski and the Philadelphia Orchestra, embellished by Disney animation. Directed by Samuel Armstrong, James Algar, Bill Roberts, Paul Satterfield, Hamilton S. Luske, Jim Handley, Ford Beebe, T. Hee, Norm Ferguson, and Wilfred Jackson. Narrated by Deems Taylor. Includes 8 sequences: "Toccata and Fugue in D Minor" (Bach), "The Nutcracker Suite" (Tchaikovsky), "The Sorcerer's Apprentice" (Dukas), "Rite of Spring" (Stravinsky), "The Pastoral Symphony" (Beethoven), "The Dance of the Hours" (Ponchielli), "Night on Bald Mountain" (Mussorgsky), and "Ave Maria" (Schubert). Premiered Nov. 13, 1940, at the Broadway Theater in New York City. The film was presented in Fantasound, an early stereo system, devised at the Disney Studio, but one which required theaters to be specially equipped. Because of the expense, the film originally opened in only 14 theaters. The stereo sound enhanced the effect of the movie and won special certificates for

Walt Disney, technicians William Garity and John N. A. Hawkins and RCA, and for Stokowski and his associates (for unique achievement in the creation of a new form of visualized music) at the 1941 Academy Awards. 125 min. New interest in the film in the 1970s led to a new soundtrack in 1982, with the orchestra conducted by Irwin Kostal, narration by Hugh Douglas, and a recording in digital stereo, but its full-length restoration in 1990 brought back the original soundtrack, while trying to duplicate some of the effects of the Fantasound presentation. The film was rereleased theatrically in 1946, 1956, 1963, 1969, 1977, 1982, 1985, and 1990. First released on video in 1991. Corey Burton replaced Deems Taylor on the DVD. *Fantasia* has taken its place as one of the great cinematic classics of all time. It took 60 years, but in line with Walt Disney's plan to add new segments regularly to the film, *Fantasia/2000* retained "The Sorcerer's Apprentice" but added 8 new sequences.

Fantasia Carousel Gardens of Imagination attraction in Shanghai Disneyland; opened Jun. 16, 2016. The 62 multicolor, Pegasus-like horses, along with fairies and chariots, carry guests around memorable scenes from *Fantasia*.

Fantasia Gardens Topiary water garden in Disneyland replacing the Motor Boat Cruise in Jan. 1993.

Fantasia Gardens Miniature Golf and Garden Pavilion Two 18-hole miniature golf courses, a putting course, and a covered 22,000-sq.-ft. outdoor meeting facility; opened May 20, 1996, adjacent to the Swan and Dolphin hotels at Walt Disney World. With 5 whimsical scenes from the 1940 animated film, the Fantasia Gardens course is for families and beginners, while the more challenging Fantasia Fairways resembles a traditional golf course on a miniature scale. The Garden Pavilions (closed in 2018) were designed by Michael Graves.

Fantasia Gelati Ice cream restaurant in the Italian quarter of Fantasyland in Disneyland Paris; open Apr. 12, 1992–Sep. 4, 2022, and replaced by an expansion of Pizzeria Bella Notte.

Fantasia Shop Shop in Disney's Contemporary Resort at Walt Disney World; opened in 1971 and moved to the center of the concourse Feb. 26, 2008. A sundries shop, Fantasia Market, opened nearby Apr. 17, 2009. Also a shop in the Disneyland Hotel; opened Oct. 1998.

Fantasia/2000 (film) A new generation of Disney animators showcase their talents as they visually interpret classical compositions. *Symphony No. 5* by Ludwig van Beethoven features abstract visions of color, shape, and light; Dmitri Shostakovich's "Piano Concerto No. 2, Allegro, Opus 102" tells the Hans Christian Andersen fable of *The Steadfast Tin Soldier*; Ottorino Respighi's "Pines of Rome" tells the story of a pod of whales who can fly; Camille Saint-Saëns's "Carnival of the Animals, Finale" shows what can happen when you give a yo-yo to a flock of flamingos; Sir Edward Elgar's "Pomp and Circumstance, Marches 1, 2, 3, and 4" stars Donald Duck as an assistant on Noah's ark; George Gershwin's "Rhapsody in Blue" presents a stylized look at life in Manhattan during the Jazz Age; and Igor Stravinsky's "Firebird Suite (1919 version)" tells a tale of death and rebirth as a young sprite triumphantly awakens a ravaged forest. These new pieces are combined with one selection ("The Sorcerer's Apprentice") from the 1940 classic. Premiered at Carnegie Hall in New York City Dec. 17, 1999; had a New Year's Eve gala at the Pasadena (California) Civic Auditorium; and then opened Jan. 1, 2000, in IMAX theaters worldwide for 4 months, with a general release Jun. 16. Supervising director was Hendel Butoy, with segment directors Hendel Butoy, Francis Glebás, Eric Goldberg, Paul and Gaëtan Brizzi, Pixote Hunt, and James Algar and host sequences director Don Hahn. The Chicago Symphony Orchestra, conducted by James Levine, provides the soundtrack. This film was a longtime pet project of Roy E. Disney's, receiving his personal supervision. 74 min.

Fantasmic! Evening water show presented on the south end of Tom Sawyer Island in Disneyland; began May 13, 1992. Mickey Mouse appears and uses his magical powers to bring beloved characters to life in his imagination—until such classic Disney villains as Ursula and Maleficent threaten Mickey's fantasy world. To prepare for *Fantasmic!*, the Rivers of America had to be drained to enable the installation of various mechanisms, and the mill and part of the south end of Tom Sawyer Island were removed so the rustic stage setting for the show could be built. (The mill was rebuilt in a new location.) Utilizing projections of film clips on 3 giant screens of mist, music, the *Mark Twain* and the *Columbia*, various rafts, mechanical figures, fire effects, and 50 Disneyland Cast Members in costume, the elaborate show was immediately more popular than had been expected. The audience, which has to line the shores of the Rivers of

America, created initial traffic jams on that side of Disneyland each evening; guests would often stake out their places hours ahead of the show. To help solve some of the challenges, the shore area was terraced to give more guests an unimpeded view. The show was enhanced in 2009 with the addition of Flotsam and Jetsam from *The Little Mermaid*, a new Captain Hook's crocodile, and a more elaborate fire-breathing dragon. An updated version debuted Jul. 17, 2017, with new characters and segments based on *Aladdin*, *Pirates of the Caribbean*, and other more recent films. A 2nd *Fantasmic!* opened in a new Hollywood Hills Amphitheater in Disney-MGM Studios (now Disney's Hollywood Studios) at Walt Disney World Oct. 15, 1998; an updated version of the show debuted Nov. 3, 2022, with a new scene featuring heroes Pocahontas, Mulan, Elsa, Aladdin, and Moana. A 3rd version opened in Mediterranean Harbor in Tokyo DisneySea in 2011, replacing *BraviSEAmo!*

Fantasound Innovative stereophonic sound system created for *Fantasia*.

Fantasy Faire Covered pavilion in Fantasyland in the Magic Kingdom at Walt Disney World. Originally used for outdoor stage shows, it later served as an extended seating area for Pinocchio Village Haus. Also known as the Fantasyland Pavilion after Jan. 1995. Closed in 1996 to make way for Ariel's Grotto.

Fantasy Faire Shop in Fantasyland in the Magic Kingdom at Walt Disney World; opened May 19, 1995, succeeding The Mad Hatter. A *Mickey's PhilharMagic* theme was added when that attraction opened next door in 2003. Also a shop inside Enchanted Storybook Castle in Shanghai Disneyland; opened Jun. 16, 2016.

Fantasy Faire Tudor-style village area in Disneyland; opened Mar. 12, 2013, encompassing the former Carnation Plaza Gardens. Around a medieval courtyard are the Royal Theater, home to fast-paced shows presented in a "renaissance vaudeville" style, and the Royal Hall, where guests can meet Disney princesses. There are snacks at Maurice's Treats and souvenirs at Fairy Tale Treasures.

Fantasy Gardens Area in Hong Kong Disneyland; opened Sep. 12, 2005. Guests can meet and greet Disney characters in 5 themed garden pavilions in a parklike setting.

Fantasy Gifts Fantasyland hat and souvenir shop

in Tokyo Disneyland; open Apr. 15, 1983–Feb. 24, 2018, and succeeded by Magical Market.

Fantasy in the Sky The first Disneyland fireworks began during summer nights in 1956 and were given the title *Fantasy in the Sky* in 1957. The fireworks are timed to coincide with the musical soundtrack being played throughout the park. Tinker Bell began her nightly flights from the top of the Matterhorn and above Sleeping Beauty Castle in 1961 as part of the show. The Disneyland show was changed to *Believe . . . There's Magic in the Stars* for the park's 45th anniversary in Feb. 2000. The Magic Kingdom at Walt Disney World premiered a *Fantasy in the Sky* fireworks show in 1971; it was changed to *Wishes: A Magical Gathering of Disney Dreams* in Oct. 2003.

Fantasy on Parade Long-running Christmas parade in Disneyland with over 350 performers; ran 1965–1976 (succeeded by the *Very Merry Christmas Parade*) and again from 1980–1985 (then renamed *The Christmas Parade* in 1986).

Fantasy on Skis (TV) Show aired Feb. 4, 1962. Directed by Fred Iselin. A 9-year-old girl in Aspen, Colorado, dreams of winning a ski race and works hard to earn the money for new skis. She is almost killed in an avalanche but is saved by her Saint Bernard, Bruno, and recovers in time for the race. A shortened, 28 min. version of the show was released theatrically on Dec. 20, 1975, with *Snowball Express*.

Fantasy Springs In 2018, Tokyo DisneySea announced its 8th themed port—a magical spring that leads to a world of Disney fantasy. With 3 areas, based on *Frozen*, *Tangled*, and *Peter Pan*, it will be comprised of 4 new attractions, 3 new restaurants, and a new Disney-themed hotel situated inside the park that will overlook the area. Fantasy Springs is scheduled to open in 2024.

Fantasyland One of the original lands of Disneyland, called by Walt Disney "the happiest kingdom of them all." The attractions are based on the classic Disney animated tales, so they evoke pleasant memories in the minds of many guests. Fantasyland was originally built to look somewhat like a medieval fair in a castle courtyard, with banners and flags decorating the entrances to the attractions. Snow White's Adventures, Peter Pan's Flight, and Mr. Toad's Wild Ride were the park's original "dark rides," in which participants were transported through black light illuminated scenes telling the stories of the films. One enters Fantasyland over a drawbridge and through Sleeping Beauty Castle. In the center is the majestic King Arthur Carrousel. The land expanded with the opening of It's a Small World in 1966. A totally new Fantasyland opened at Disneyland on May 25, 1983. The dark ride attractions were all completely remodeled, with façades now themed to the locale and era of the films. Thus, the Mr. Toad attraction is now in Toad Hall, as opposed to a medieval circus tent. There are Fantasyland areas in all 6 of the Disney "Magic Kingdom"–style parks. The Fantasyland in the Magic Kingdom at Walt Disney World was expanded 2012–2014, to incorporate an Enchanted Forest with Belle's Village, Be Our Guest Restaurant, Seven Dwarfs Mine Train, and Under the Sea ~ Journey of the Little Mermaid. The Fantasyland in Tokyo Disneyland was expanded in 2020, introducing an elaborate area and ride-through attraction based on *Beauty and the Beast*.

Fantasyland Autopia Attraction in Disneyland from Jan. 1, 1959–Sep. 7, 1999. Became Rescue Rangers Raceway from Mar.–Nov. 1991. This attraction was added to take some of the pressure off the Tomorrowland Autopia, which usually experienced a long wait time. Its main difference was different scenery along the ride. In 2000, Fantasyland Autopia was incorporated into the Tomorrowland Autopia.

Fantasyland Forest Theatre A 1,500-seat indoor venue in Tokyo Disneyland; opened Apr. 1, 2021. The inaugural show, *Mickey's Magical Music World*, finds Mickey and his friends setting off on a journey to find the missing song of a giant music box and encountering Disney characters along the way.

Fantasyland, New Term often used for the extensive remodeling of Fantasyland in Disneyland in 1983, as well as for the expanded area of Fantasyland in the Magic Kingdom at Walt Disney World, which premiered in 2012 and was completed in 2014. See also Believe You Can . . . and You Can!

Fantasyland Theater Theater in Disneyland that showed Disney cartoons. Formerly Mickey Mouse Club Theater (1955–1964); closed Dec. 20, 1981, so that Pinocchio's Daring Journey could be built in its place. During the opening-day TV show, *Dateline Disneyland*, the Mouseketeers streamed out of the theater at one point and were introduced to the TV audience for the first time. This was several months before the *Mickey Mouse Club* TV show went on the air. One fondly remembered highlight at the theater was the *3-D Jamboree*, which played beginning in Jun. 1956 for several years. Besides two 3-D cartoons, the film included specially filmed 3-D footage of the Mouseketeers. The name Fantasyland Theater was reused beginning Jun. 23, 1995, for the former Videopolis. After several shows played in this new theater, it was converted into a character-greeting venue, Princess Fantasy Faire (Oct. 6, 2006–Aug. 12, 2012) and resumed as a theater with the opening of *Mickey and the Magical Map* (May 25, 2013). Performances ended Mar. 2020 due to the COVID-19 pandemic, and a new show, *Tale of the Lion King*, debuted May 28, 2022.

Fantillusion, Disney's Nighttime illuminated parade which succeeded the *Main Street Electrical Parade* in Tokyo Disneyland Jul. 21, 1995–May 15, 2001. It was also presented in Disneyland Paris, Jul. 5, 2003–Oct. 31, 2012.

Fantini, T. J. Actor; appeared in the *Mickey Mouse Club* on The Disney Channel, beginning in 1993.

Far From the Tree (film) Animated short; premiered Jun. 15, 2021, at the Annecy International Animation Film Festival, and in theaters Nov. 24, with *Encanto*. Curiosity gets the best of a young raccoon whose frustrated parent attempts to keep them both safe. Directed by Natalie Nourigat. 7 min. From Walt Disney Animation Studios.

Far Off Place, A (film) When an attack by an elephant poacher on her African home leaves a teenage girl, Nonnie Parker, and her visiting friend, Harry Winslow, orphaned, the 2 teenagers set off to find the 1 man who can help them—Colonel Mopani Theron, who leads an anti-poaching squad. With the help of a Native Bushman, Xhabbo, they set out on a 1,000-mile trek across the Kalahari desert. Many dangers await them there, not the least being the hostile climate, but by sheer determination and courage they reach safety and are able to get their revenge on the poachers. Released Mar. 12, 1993. Directed by Mikael Salomon. 107 min. Stars Reese Witherspoon (Nonnie Parker), Ethan Randall (Harry Winslow), Jack Thompson (John Ricketts), Maximilian Schell (Col. Mopani Theron), Sarel Bok (Xhabbo). Filmed in Zimbabwe and the Namib desert.

Faraway Places—High, Hot and Wet (TV) Show

aired Jan. 1, 1958. Herbert and Trudie Knapp take photo assignments in the Andes mountain range in Peru, on the Fiji Islands, and in Siam (Thailand). The People and Places featurette *Siam* is shown. Narrated by Winston Hibler.

Fariss, Peggie Imagineer; she began her 50-year Disney career at Disneyland as a ride operator and, after serving as a press event hostess to help announce "Phase One" of Walt Disney World, transferred to Florida in 1971. Five years later, she joined WED Enterprises, where she contributed to the planning for EPCOT Center. She became director of Participant Services in 1992 and, beginning in 2010, headed the Imagineering offices at Disneyland Paris. She retired in 2016 as executive, Creative Development.

Farmer, Bill Voice actor; he became the official voice of Goofy and Pluto in 1986, performing the characters for hundreds of film, TV animation, theme park, and other projects. His other voice roles have included Horace Horsecollar, Sleepy, and the Practical Pig, as well as Janitor Jay (*Higglytown Heroes*), Doc (*The 7D*), Ghostly Bob (*Jake and the Never Land Pirates*), and Hop Pop Plantar (*Amphibia*). On Disney+, he hosted and exec. produced *It's a Dog's Life with Bill Farmer*. He was named a Disney Legend in 2009.

Farmers Market Food court area in The Land at EPCOT Center; open Oct. 1, 1982–Oct. 25, 1993. Became Sunshine Season Food Fair in 1993.

Farmyard Symphony (film) Silly Symphony cartoon released Oct. 14, 1938. The first cartoon directed by Jack Cutting. A farmyard musical, set to familiar classical themes, including Franz Liszt's *Hungarian Rhapsody*, is led by a rooster and pullet with all the other animals participating.

Farnsworth, Richard (1920–2000) Actor; appeared in *The Straight Story* (Alvin Straight), for which he received an Academy Award nomination for Best Actor, as well as on TV in *The Cherokee Trail* (Ridge Fenton) and *The High Flying Spy* (Farmer). Also on The Disney Channel in *Good Old Boy* (Grandpa Percy).

Farrell, Colin Actor; appeared in *The Recruit* (James Clayton), *Fright Night* (Jerry), *Saving Mr. Banks* (Travers Goff), *Dumbo* (Holt Farrier, 2019), and *Artemis Fowl* (Artemis Fowl Sr.), and on TV in *Scrubs* (Billy).

Farrow, Mia Actress; appeared in *New York Stories* (Lisa) and *Miami Rhapsody* (Nina), and on TV in *Miracle at Midnight* (Doris Koster). She provided the voice of Doris in *Redux Riding Hood*.

Fast Layne (TV) An 8-episode miniseries on Disney Channel; premiered Feb. 15, 2019. Overachiever Layne, 12, finds a sophisticated talking car named "VIN" hidden in an abandoned shed. With her neighbor, Zora, Layne embarks on a high-speed adventure filled with secret agents and other surprises in order to discover the mystery behind VIN's creation. Stars Sophie Pollono (Layne Reed), Sofia Rosinsky (Zora Morris), Brandon Rossel (Cody Castillo), Winslow Fegley (Mel), Nate Torrence (voice of VIN). From Lakeshore Productions and Omnifilm Entertainment.

FastPass An innovation at the Disney parks whereby guests can retrieve a pass that designates a specific time for them to return and board an attraction with a reduced wait. After initial tests, the pass was first introduced for the most popular Animal Kingdom attractions in Jul. 1999, and soon was used at major attractions and entertainment in the other Walt Disney World parks. It was first offered in Disneyland Paris at Indiana Jones et le Temple de Péril on Oct. 2, 1999, and in Disneyland at It's a Small World on Nov. 19, 1999. Walt Disney World introduced FastPass+ as part of their MyMagic+ program in 2014 to enable guests to reserve access to resort experiences before leaving home. Versions of FastPass were also introduced at Tokyo Disney Resort, Hong Kong Disneyland Resort, and Shanghai Disney Resort. In 2018, a Disney "Priority Special" Attraction Admission Pass was additionally made available at Hong Kong Disneyland, offering paid priority access to a limited number of selected attractions. At Shanghai Disneyland, a similar service, Disney Premier Access, was added in 2017. At Disneyland Paris, the Disney Premier Access paid service replaced FastPass in Aug. 2021; a similar Disney Premier Access service launched at Tokyo Disney Resort May 19, 2022. At Disneyland and Walt Disney World, FastPass was replaced in 2021 by the Disney Genie digital service, which offers paid access to Lightning Lane entrances at popular attractions and entertainment venues. See Disney Genie, Disney MaxPass, and Lightning Lane.

Fat Cat Sadistic crime boss in *Chip 'n' Dale Rescue Rangers*; voiced by Jim Cummings.

Father Hood (film) Jack Charles is a small-time

hood who plans to travel cross-country to New Orleans to participate in a criminal heist that will set him up for life. But his daughter, Kelly, shows up and his plans are endangered. Kelly and her little brother, Eddie, had long ago been abandoned to foster care, and the abuse they received there warranted Kelly's escape. Jack reluctantly rescues Eddie, too, and plans to leave them with their grandmother, Rita. But Rita has her own life of gambling to live and tells Jack to own up to his responsibilities as a father. As the trio makes its way across the country, pursued by the police and the FBI, Jack learns what it takes to raise children. By the time they reach New Orleans, he is ready to sacrifice his criminal activity for his children's welfare. Released Aug. 27, 1993. Directed by Darrell James Roodt. A Hollywood Pictures film. 95 min. Stars Patrick Swayze (Jack Charles), Halle Berry (Kathleen Mercer), Diane Ladd (Rita), Sabrina Lloyd (Kelly Charles), Brian Bonsall (Eddie Charles). Filmed in Texas, Louisiana, Arizona, and California.

Father Noah's Ark (film) Silly Symphony cartoon released Apr. 8, 1933. Directed by Wilfred Jackson. The first Disney version of the biblical tale of Noah, his ark, and its inhabitants, along with their efforts to weather the great flood. There is also a 1959 stop-motion version (*Noah's Ark*).

Father of the Bride (film) After 22 years of being a father to his little girl, Annie, George Banks finds it hard to cope with the fact that she is grown up and ready to marry. He is unable to warm up to his future son-in-law, Bryan MacKenzie, and grumbles every step of the way as their wedding is planned. An eccentric wedding adviser named Franck only makes matters worse. Eventually the wedding is held, and George accepts the new couple. Released Dec. 20, 1991. Directed by Charles Shyer. A Touchstone film. 105 min. Stars Steve Martin (George Banks), Diane Keaton (Nina Banks), Kimberly Williams (Annie Banks), Martin Short (Franck Eggelhoffer), George Newbern (Bryan MacKenzie). Based on the novel by Edward Streeter; a remake of an MGM motion picture from 1950 that had starred Spencer Tracy, Elizabeth Taylor, and Joan Bennett. The house's exterior was filmed in Pasadena, California, with the wedding scene filmed in the Trinity Baptist Church in Santa Monica. The character name of George Banks is coincidentally the same as that of the father in *Mary Poppins*.

Father of the Bride, Part II (film) After George Banks has finally recovered from his daughter's wedding, he receives a double shock. First his daughter announces that he is going to be a grandfather, and then his own wife announces that she also is pregnant. George feels that he is much too young to be a grandfather, and way too old to be a father again. Coming along to coordinate a double baby shower is Franck Eggelhoffer, who had arranged the daughter's wedding. Directed by Charles Shyer. A Touchstone film. Released Dec. 8, 1995. Stars Steve Martin (George), Diane Keaton (Nina), Kimberly Williams (Annie), George Newbern (Bryan), Kieran Culkin (Matty), Martin Short (Franck). 106 min. Sequel to the 1991 film *Father of the Bride*. The production was filmed at an Eastern colonial–style house in Pasadena, California.

Fathers Are People (film) Goofy cartoon released Oct. 21, 1951. Directed by Jack Kinney. Goofy experiences the trials and tribulations of fatherhood with Junior always coming out ahead in each situation.

Father's Day Off (film) Goofy cartoon released Mar. 28, 1953. Directed by Jack Kinney. Goofy takes over the household chores when his wife goes out, but he gets so completely confused that the house is a shambles and on fire when she returns.

Father's Lion (film) Goofy cartoon released Jan. 4, 1952. Directed by Jack Kinney. Goofy and his son go on a camping trip, and in the midst of Goofy's tall tales about himself as a great adventurer, they encounter a mountain lion.

Father's Week End (film) Goofy cartoon released Jun. 20, 1953. Directed by Jack Kinney. Goofy runs his life by the clock all week and relaxes on Sunday. But he has such a frantic day with his son at the beach that he is delighted to go back to work to rest up from his day of rest.

Fauna Peacekeeper good fairy in *Sleeping Beauty* who wore green; voiced by Barbara Jo Allen.

Favreau, Jon Actor/producer/director; he directed/produced *The Jungle Book* (2016) and *The Lion King* (2019), and exec. produced *Marvel's The Avengers*, *Iron Man 3*, *Avengers: Age of Ultron*, and *Avengers: Infinity War*. For Disney+, he has exec. produced *The Mandalorian*, *The Book of Boba Fett*, *Ahsoka*, *Rangers of the New Republic*, *Lion*, and *Star Wars: Skeleton Crew*. He voiced Hurley in *G-Force*, Thark Bookie in *John Carter*, Pygmy Hog in *The Jungle Book* (2016), and Rio

Durant in *Solo: A Star Wars Story*, plus provided voices for TV, including Jealousy in the *Hercules* animated series, Crumford Lorak in *Buzz Lightyear of Star Command*, and Pre Vizsla in the *Star Wars* animated series. He has appeared as Happy Hogan in several of the Marvel Studios films and made a TV appearance as Dr. Oliver Bloom in *Monk*. He was named a Disney Legend in 2019.

Fawcett, Farrah (1947–2009) Actress; appeared in *Man of the House* (Sandra Archer) and voiced Faucet in *The Brave Little Toaster Goes to Mars*.

Faylen, Frank (1907–1985) Actor; appeared in *The Reluctant Dragon* (orchestra leader) and *The Monkey's Uncle* (Mr. Dearborne).

Fear Riley's apprehensive emotion in *Inside Out*; voiced by Bill Hader.

Feast (film) Short cartoon; released with *Big Hero 6* Nov. 7, 2014, after premiering Jun. 10, 2014, at the Annecy International Animation Film Festival. The story of a man's romantic life as seen through the eyes of his best friend and dog, Winston. Directed by Patrick Osborne. 6 min. It won the Academy Award for Best Animated Short.

Feast of July (film) Bella Ford is a young woman setting forth in winter on an arduous journey to locate Arch Wilson, the lover who abandoned her. Suffering a grave personal misfortune along the way, she finds shelter in the home of the Wainwright family, whose 3 sons, Jedd, Con, and Matty, eventually battle among each other for the affections of their enchanting and mysterious guest. After much courtship, Bella agrees to marry the middle son, Con, but tragedy strikes again when the man for whom she has been searching reappears, triggering a series of dramatic events which will forever change the lives of all concerned. Directed by Christopher Menaul. From Touchstone Pictures and Merchant Ivory Productions, in association with Peregrine Productions. Limited release in New York City, Los Angeles, and Montreal on Oct. 13, 1995; wider release on Oct. 20. Stars Embeth Davidtz (Bella Ford), Greg Wise (Arch Wilson), James Purefoy (Jedd Wainwright), Kenneth Anderson (Matty Wainwright), Ben Chaplin (Con Wainwright), Tom Bell (Ben Wainwright), Gemma Jones (Mrs. Wainwright). Filmed in CinemaScope. 118 min. With the story set in Victorian England, the producers had to search throughout the country for appropriate settings before settling on Brecon in Wales, Ironbridge and Dudley's Black Country Museum in the Midlands, and Porlock Weir in Devon.

Feather Farm, The (TV) Show aired Oct. 26, 1969. Ostrich raising in 1915 is not as easy as it seems, as a Boston matron and her niece sadly discover. They almost lose their investment as the ostriches run away, but the hired men finally find them. Stars Nick Nolte, Mel Weiser, Christine Coates, Shirley Fabricant. Narrated by Rex Allen.

Feather in His Collar, A (film) Commercial starring Pluto made for the Community Chests of America; delivered Aug. 7, 1946. Pluto is awarded a Red Feather for giving his life savings of bones to a Community Chest campaign.

Feathered Friends in Flight See FLIGHTS OF WONDER.

Feature Animation The new name given to the Disney animation department in the 1980s to differentiate it from TV animation. Headquartered at the Disney Studio in Burbank, Walt Disney Feature Animation creates the Disney animated feature films and is based in a building occupied in late 1994. A division of Feature Animation operated at Disney-MGM Studios in Walt Disney World 1989–2004. A Feature Animation Studio opened in France in 1994, taking over Brizzi Films, which had worked on Disney TV projects since 1989; it closed in 2003. There was also a Disney animation studio in Tokyo, working primarily on TV and video productions, 1989–2004. Feature Animation changed its name to Walt Disney Animation Studios in 2007. In Aug. 2021, Walt Disney Animation Studios announced it would be increasing production with a new Vancouver studio focused on long-form series for Disney+, with the Burbank studio leading feature-film projects.

Feature film A full-length film, live action or animated, normally over 60 min. in length. *Snow White and the Seven Dwarfs* was the first Disney feature, in 1937. One exception to the general rule of length is *Saludos Amigos*, which at 42 min. is still considered one of the Disney Animated Classic Features. The complete list of feature films (released theatrically, unless otherwise noted) is:

1. 1937: *Snow White and the Seven Dwarfs* (G)
2. 1940: *Pinocchio* (G)

3. 1940: *Fantasia* (G)
4. 1941: *The Reluctant Dragon*
5. 1941: *Dumbo* (G)
6. 1942: *Bambi* (G)
7. 1943: *Saludos Amigos*
8. 1943: *Victory Through Air Power*
9. 1945: *The Three Caballeros* (G)
10. 1946: *Make Mine Music*
11. 1946: *Song of the South* (G)
12. 1947: *Fun and Fancy Free*
13. 1948: *Melody Time*
14. 1949: *So Dear to My Heart* (G)
15. 1949: *The Adventures of Ichabod and Mr. Toad* (G)
16. 1950: *Cinderella* (G)
17. 1950: *Treasure Island* (PG)
18. 1951: *Alice in Wonderland* (G)
19. 1952: *The Story of Robin Hood and His Merrie Men* (PG)
20. 1953: *Peter Pan* (G)
21. 1953: *The Sword and the Rose* (PG)
22. 1953: *The Living Desert* (G)
23. 1954: *Rob Roy, the Highland Rogue*
24. 1954: *The Vanishing Prairie* (G)
25. 1954: *20,000 Leagues Under the Sea* (G)
26. 1955: *Davy Crockett, King of the Wild Frontier* (PG)
27. 1955: *Lady and the Tramp* (G)
28. 1955: *The African Lion*
29. 1955: *The Littlest Outlaw*
30. 1956: *The Great Locomotive Chase*
31. 1956: *Davy Crockett and the River Pirates* (G)
32. 1956: *Secrets of Life*
33. 1956: *Westward Ho the Wagons!*
34. 1957: *Johnny Tremain*
35. 1957: *Perri* (G)
36. 1957: *Old Yeller* (G)
37. 1958: *The Light in the Forest*
38. 1958: *White Wilderness* (G)
39. 1958: *Tonka*
40. 1959: *Sleeping Beauty* (G)
41. 1959: *The Shaggy Dog* (G)
42. 1959: *Darby O'Gill and the Little People* (G)
43. 1959: *Third Man on the Mountain* (G)
44. 1960: *Toby Tyler, or Ten Weeks with a Circus* (G)
45. 1960: *Kidnapped* (PG)
46. 1960: *Pollyanna* (G)
47. 1960: *The Sign of Zorro* (G)
48. 1960: *Jungle Cat*
49. 1960: *Ten Who Dared*
50. 1960: *Swiss Family Robinson* (G)
51. 1961: *One Hundred and One Dalmatians* (G)
52. 1961: *The Absent-Minded Professor* (G)
53. 1961: *The Parent Trap* (G)
54. 1961: *Nikki, Wild Dog of the North* (G)
55. 1961: *Greyfriars Bobby*
56. 1961: *Babes in Toyland*
57. 1962: *Moon Pilot*
58. 1962: *Bon Voyage*
59. 1962: *Big Red*
60. 1962: *Almost Angels*
61. 1962: *The Legend of Lobo* (G)
62. 1962: *In Search of the Castaways* (G)
63. 1963: *Son of Flubber* (G)
64. 1963: *Miracle of the White Stallions* (G)
65. 1963: *Savage Sam*
66. 1963: *Summer Magic* (G)
67. 1963: *The Incredible Journey* (G)
68. 1963: *The Sword in the Stone* (G)
69. 1963: *The Three Lives of Thomasina* (PG)
70. 1964: *The Misadventures of Merlin Jones* (G)
71. 1964: *A Tiger Walks*
72. 1964: *The Moon-Spinners* (PG)
73. 1964: *Mary Poppins* (G)
74. 1964: *Emil and the Detectives*
75. 1965: *Those Calloways* (PG)
76. 1965: *The Monkey's Uncle*
77. 1965: *That Darn Cat!* (G)
78. 1966: *The Ugly Dachshund*
79. 1966: *Lt. Robin Crusoe U.S.N.* (G)
80. 1966: *The Fighting Prince of Donegal*
81. 1966: *Follow Me, Boys!* (G)
82. 1967: *Monkeys, Go Home!* (G)
83. 1967: *The Adventures of Bullwhip Griffin*
84. 1967: *The Happiest Millionaire* (G)
85. 1967: *The Gnome-Mobile* (G)
86. 1967: *The Jungle Book* (G)
87. 1967: *Charlie, The Lonesome Cougar* (G)
88. 1968: *Blackbeard's Ghost* (G)
89. 1968: *The One and Only, Genuine, Original Family Band* (G)
90. 1968: *Never a Dull Moment* (G)
91. 1968: *The Horse in the Gray Flannel Suit* (G)
92. 1969: *The Love Bug* (G)
93. 1969: *Smith!* (G)
94. 1969: *Rascal* (G)
95. 1969: *The Computer Wore Tennis Shoes* (G)
96. 1970: *King of the Grizzlies* (G)
97. 1970: *The Boatniks* (G)
98. 1970: *The Aristocats* (G)
99. 1971: *The Wild Country* (G)
100. 1971: *The Barefoot Executive* (G)
101. 1971: *Scandalous John* (G)
102. 1971: *The $1,000,000 Duck* (G)
103. 1971: *Bedknobs and Broomsticks* (G)
104. 1972: *The Biscuit Eater* (G)
105. 1972: *Napoleon and Samantha* (G)

106. 1972: *Now You See Him, Now You Don't* (G)
107. 1972: *Run, Cougar, Run* (G)
108. 1972: *Snowball Express* (G)
109. 1973: *The World's Greatest Athlete* (G)
110. 1973: *Charley and the Angel* (G)
111. 1973: *One Little Indian* (G)
112. 1973: *Robin Hood* (G)
113. 1973: *Superdad* (G)
114. 1974: *Herbie Rides Again* (G)
115. 1974: *The Bears and I* (G)
116. 1974: *The Castaway Cowboy* (G)
117. 1974: *The Island at the Top of the World* (G)
118. 1975: *The Strongest Man in the World* (G)
119. 1975: *Escape to Witch Mountain* (G)
120. 1975: *The Apple Dumpling Gang* (G)
121. 1975: *One of Our Dinosaurs is Missing* (G)
122. 1975: *The Best of Walt Disney's True-Life Adventures* (G)
123. 1976: *Ride a Wild Pony* (G)
124. 1976: *No Deposit, No Return* (G)
125. 1976: *Gus* (G)
126. 1976: *Treasure of Matecumbe* (G)
127. 1976: *The Shaggy D.A.* (G)
128. 1977: *Freaky Friday* (G)
129. 1977: *The Littlest Horse Thieves* (G)
130. 1977: *The Many Adventures of Winnie the Pooh* (G)
131. 1977: *The Rescuers* (G)
132. 1977: *Herbie Goes to Monte Carlo* (G)
133. 1977: *Pete's Dragon* (G)
134. 1978: *Candleshoe* (G)
135. 1978: *Return from Witch Mountain* (G)
136. 1978: *The Cat from Outer Space* (G)
137. 1978: *Hot Lead and Cold Feet* (G)
138. 1979: *The North Avenue Irregulars* (G)
139. 1979: *The Apple Dumpling Gang Rides Again* (G)
140. 1979: *Unidentified Flying Oddball* (G)
141. 1979: *The Black Hole* (PG)
142. 1980: *Midnight Madness* (PG)
143. 1980: *The Last Flight of Noah's Ark* (G)
144. 1980: *Herbie Goes Bananas* (G)
145. 1981: *The Devil and Max Devlin* (PG)
146. 1981: *Amy* (G)
147. 1981: *The Fox and the Hound* (G)
148. 1981: *Condorman* (PG)
149. 1981: *The Watcher in the Woods* (PG)
150. 1982: *Night Crossing* (PG)
151. 1982: *Tron* (PG)
152. 1982: *Tex* (PG)
153. 1983: *Trenchcoat* (PG)
154. 1983: *Something Wicked This Way Comes* (PG)
155. 1983: *Never Cry Wolf* (PG)
156. 1984: *Splash* (Touchstone) (PG)

157. 1984: *Tiger Town* (G)
158. 1984: *Country* (Touchstone) (PG)
159. 1985: *Baby . . . Secret of the Lost Legend* (Touchstone) (PG)
160. 1985: *Return to Oz* (PG)
161. 1985: *The Black Cauldron* (PG)
162. 1985: *My Science Project* (Touchstone) (PG)
163. 1985: *The Journey of Natty Gann* (PG)
164. 1985: *One Magic Christmas* (G)
165. 1986: *Down and Out in Beverly Hills* (Touchstone) (R)
166. 1986: *Off Beat* (Touchstone) (R)
167. 1986: *Ruthless People* (Touchstone) (R)
168. 1986: *The Great Mouse Detective* (G)
169. 1986: *Flight of the Navigator* (PG)
170. 1986: *Tough Guys* (Touchstone) (PG)
171. 1986: *The Color of Money* (Touchstone) (R)
172. 1987: *Outrageous Fortune* (Touchstone) (R)
173. 1987: *Tin Men* (Touchstone) (R)
174. 1987: *Ernest Goes to Camp* (Touchstone) (PG)
175. 1987: *Benji the Hunted* (G)
176. 1987: *Adventures in Babysitting* (Touchstone) (PG-13)
177. 1987: *Stakeout* (Touchstone) (R)
178. 1987: *Can't Buy Me Love* (Touchstone) (PG-13)
179. 1987: *Hello Again* (Touchstone) (PG)
180. 1987: *Three Men and a Baby* (Touchstone) (PG)
181. 1987: *Good Morning, Vietnam* (Touchstone) (R)
182. 1988: *Shoot to Kill* (Touchstone) (R)
183. 1988: *D.O.A.* (Touchstone) (R)
184. 1988: *Return to Snowy River* (PG)
185. 1988: *Big Business* (Touchstone) (PG)
186. 1988: *Who Framed Roger Rabbit* (Touchstone) (PG)
187. 1988: *Cocktail* (Touchstone) (R)
188. 1988: *The Rescue* (Touchstone) (PG)
189. 1988: *Heartbreak Hotel* (Touchstone) (PG-13)
190. 1988: *The Good Mother* (Touchstone) (R)
191. 1988: *Ernest Saves Christmas* (Touchstone) (PG)
192. 1988: *Oliver & Company* (G)
193. 1988: *Beaches* (Touchstone) (PG-13)
194. 1989: *Three Fugitives* (Touchstone) (PG-13)
195. 1989: *New York Stories* (Touchstone) (PG)
196. 1989: *Disorganized Crime* (Touchstone) (R)
197. 1989: *Dead Poets Society* (Touchstone) (PG)
198. 1989: *Honey, I Shrunk the Kids* (PG)
199. 1989: *Turner & Hooch* (Touchstone) (PG)
200. 1989: *Cheetah* (G)
201. 1989: *An Innocent Man* (Touchstone) (R)
202. 1989: *Gross Anatomy* (Touchstone) (PG-13)
203. 1989: *The Little Mermaid* (G)
204. 1989: *Blaze* (Touchstone) (R)
205. 1990: *Stella* (Touchstone) (PG-13)
206. 1990: *Where the Heart Is* (Touchstone) (R)

207. 1990: *Pretty Woman* (Touchstone) (R)
208. 1990: *Ernest Goes to Jail* (Touchstone) (PG)
209. 1990: *Spaced Invaders* (Touchstone) (PG)
210. 1990: *Fire Birds* (Touchstone) (PG-13)
211. 1990: *Dick Tracy* (Touchstone) (PG)
212. 1990: *Betsy's Wedding* (Touchstone) (R)
213. 1990: *Arachnophobia* (Hollywood Pictures) (PG-13)
214. 1990: *DuckTales: the Movie, Treasure of the Lost Lamp* (Disney MovieToons) (G)
215. 1990: *Taking Care of Business* (Hollywood Pictures) (R)
216. 1990: *Mr. Destiny* (Touchstone) (PG-13)
217. 1990: *The Rescuers Down Under* (G)
218. 1990: *Three Men and a Little Lady* (Touchstone) (PG)
219. 1990: *Green Card* (Touchstone) (PG-13)
220. 1991: *White Fang* (PG)
221. 1991: *Run* (Hollywood Pictures) (R)
222. 1991: *Scenes from a Mall* (Touchstone) (R)
223. 1991: *Shipwrecked* (PG)
224. 1991: *The Marrying Man* (Hollywood Pictures) (R)
225. 1991: *Oscar* (Touchstone) (PG)
226. 1991: *One Good Cop* (Hollywood Pictures) (R)
227. 1991: *What About Bob?* (Touchstone) (PG)
228. 1991: *Wild Hearts Can't Be Broken* (G)
229. 1991: *The Rocketeer* (PG)
230. 1991: *The Doctor* (Touchstone) (PG-13)
231. 1991: *V. I. Warshawski* (Hollywood Pictures) (R)
232. 1991: *True Identity* (Touchstone) (R)
233. 1991: *Paradise* (Touchstone) (PG-13)
234. 1991: *Deceived* (Touchstone) (PG-13)
235. 1991: *Ernest Scared Stupid* (Touchstone) (PG)
236. 1991: *Billy Bathgate* (Touchstone) (R)
237. 1991: *Beauty and the Beast* (G)
238. 1991: *Father of the Bride* (Touchstone) (PG)
239. 1992: *The Hand That Rocks the Cradle* (Hollywood Pictures) (R)
240. 1992: *Medicine Man* (Hollywood Pictures) (PG-13)
241. 1992: *Blame It on The Bellboy* (Hollywood Pictures) (PG-13)
242. 1992: *Noises Off* (Touchstone) (PG-13)
243. 1992: *Straight Talk* (Hollywood Pictures) (PG)
244. 1992: *Newsies* (PG)
245. 1992: *Passed Away* (Hollywood Pictures) (PG-13)
246. 1992: *Encino Man* (Hollywood Pictures) (PG)
247. 1992: *Sister Act* (Touchstone) (PG)
248. 1992: *Honey, I Blew Up the Kid* (PG)
249. 1992: *A Stranger Among Us* (Hollywood Pictures) (PG-13)
250. 1992: *3 Ninjas* (Touchstone) (PG)
251. 1992: *The Gun in Betty Lou's Handbag* (Touchstone) (PG-13)
252. 1992: *Crossing the Bridge* (Touchstone) (R)
253. 1992: *Sarafina!* (Hollywood Pictures) (PG-13)
254. 1992: *Captain Ron* (Touchstone) (PG-13)
255. 1992: *The Mighty Ducks* (PG)
256. 1992: *Consenting Adults* (Hollywood Pictures) (R)
257. 1992: *Aladdin* (G)
258. 1992: *The Distinguished Gentleman* (Hollywood Pictures) (R)
259. 1992: *The Muppet Christmas Carol* (G)
260. 1993: *Alive* (Touchstone) (R)
261. 1993: *Aspen Extreme* (Hollywood Pictures) (PG-13)
262. 1993: *The Cemetery Club* (Touchstone) (PG-13)
263. 1993: *Homeward Bound: The Incredible Journey* (G)
264. 1993: *Swing Kids* (Hollywood Pictures) (PG-13)
265. 1993: *A Far Off Place* (PG)
266. 1993: *Born Yesterday* (Hollywood Pictures) (PG)
267. 1993: *Adventures of Huck Finn* (PG)
268. 1993: *Indian Summer* (Touchstone) (PG-13)
269. 1993: *Bound by Honor* (Hollywood Pictures) (R)
270. 1993: *Super Mario Bros.* (Hollywood Pictures) (PG)
271. 1993: *Guilty as Sin* (Hollywood Pictures) (R)
272. 1993: *Life with Mikey* (Touchstone) (PG)
273. 1993: *What's Love Got to Do with It* (Touchstone) (R)
274. 1993: *Son-In-Law* (Hollywood Pictures) (PG-13)
275. 1993: *Hocus Pocus* (PG)
276. 1993: *Another Stakeout* (Touchstone) (PG-13)
277. 1993: *My Boyfriend's Back* (Touchstone) (PG-13)
278. 1993: *Father Hood* (Hollywood Pictures) (PG-13)
279. 1993: *The Joy Luck Club* (Hollywood Pictures) (R)
280. 1993: *Money for Nothing* (Hollywood Pictures) (R)
281. 1993: *The Program* (Touchstone) (R)
282. 1993: *Cool Runnings* (PG)
283. 1993: *Tim Burton's The Nightmare Before Christmas* (Touchstone) (PG)
284. 1993: *The Three Musketeers* (PG)
285. 1993: *Sister Act 2: Back in the Habit* (Touchstone) (PG)
286. 1993: *Tombstone* (Hollywood Pictures) (R)

287. 1994: *Cabin Boy* (Touchstone) (PG-13)
288. 1994: *The Air Up There* (Hollywood Pictures) (PG)
289. 1994: *Iron Will* (PG)
290. 1994: *My Father the Hero* (Touchstone) (PG)
291. 1994: *Blank Check* (PG)
292. 1994: *Angie* (Hollywood Pictures) (R)
293. 1994: *The Ref* (Touchstone) (R)
294. 1994: *D2: The Mighty Ducks* (PG)
295. 1994: *Holy Matrimony* (Hollywood Pictures) (PG-13)
296. 1994: *White Fang 2: Myth of the White Wolf* (PG)
297. 1994: *The Inkwell* (Touchstone) (R)
298. 1994: *When a Man Loves a Woman* (Touchstone) (R)
299. 1994: *Renaissance Man* (Touchstone) (PG-13)
300. 1994: *The Lion King* (G)
301. 1994: *I Love Trouble* (Touchstone) (PG)
302. 1994: *Angels in the Outfield* (PG)
303. 1994: *In the Army Now* (Hollywood Pictures) (PG)
304. 1994: *Color of Night* (Hollywood Pictures) (R)
305. 1994: *It's Pat* (Touchstone) (PG-13)
306. 1994: *Camp Nowhere* (Hollywood Pictures) (PG)
307. 1994: *A Simple Twist of Fate* (Touchstone) (PG-13)
308. 1994: *Quiz Show* (Hollywood) (PG-13)
309. 1994: *Terminal Velocity* (Hollywood Pictures) (PG-13)
310. 1994: *Ed Wood* (Touchstone) (R)
311. 1994: *Robert A. Heinlein's The Puppet Masters* (Hollywood Pictures) (R)
312. 1994: *Squanto: A Warrior's Tale* (PG)
313. 1994: *The Santa Clause* (PG)
314. 1994: *A Low Down Dirty Shame* (Hollywood Pictures) (R)
315. 1994: *Rudyard Kipling's The Jungle Book* (PG)
316. 1995: *Houseguest* (Hollywood Pictures) (PG)
317. 1995: *Bad Company* (Touchstone) (R)
318. 1995: *Miami Rhapsody* (Hollywood Pictures) (PG-13)
319. 1995: *The Jerky Boys* (Touchstone) (R)
320. 1995: *Heavyweights* (PG)
321. 1995: *Man of the House* (PG)
322. 1995: *Roommates* (Hollywood Pictures) (PG)
323. 1995: *Tall Tale* (PG)
324. 1995: *Funny Bones* (Hollywood Pictures) (R)
325. 1995: *Jefferson in Paris* (Touchstone) (PG-13)
326. 1995: *A Goofy Movie* (G)
327. 1995: *While You Were Sleeping* (Hollywood Pictures) (PG)
328. 1995: *A Pyromaniac's Love Story* (Hollywood Pictures) (PG)
329. 1995: *Crimson Tide* (Hollywood Pictures) (R)
330. 1995: *Mad Love* (Touchstone) (PG-13)
331. 1995: *Pocahontas* (G)
332. 1995: *Judge Dredd* (Hollywood Pictures) (R)
333. 1995: *Operation Dumbo Drop* (PG)
334. 1995: *Dangerous Minds* (Hollywood Pictures) (R)
335. 1995: *A Kid in King Arthur's Court* (PG)
336. 1995: *The Tie That Binds* (Hollywood Pictures) (R)
337. 1995: *Unstrung Heroes* (Hollywood Pictures) (PG)
338. 1995: *The Big Green* (PG)
339. 1995: *Dead Presidents* (Hollywood Pictures) (R)
340. 1995: *Feast of July* (Touchstone) (R)
341. 1995: *The Scarlet Letter* (Hollywood Pictures) (R)
342. 1995: *Frank and Ollie* (PG)
343. 1995: *Powder* (Hollywood Pictures) (PG-13)
344. 1995: *Toy Story* (Pixar) (G)
345. 1995: *Father of the Bride, Part II* (Touchstone) (PG)
346. 1995: *Nixon* (Hollywood Pictures) (R)
347. 1995: *Tom and Huck* (PG)
348. 1996: *Mr. Holland's Opus* (Hollywood Pictures) (PG)
349. 1996: *White Squall* (Hollywood Pictures) (PG-13)
350. 1996: *Mr. Wrong* (Touchstone) (PG-13)
351. 1996: *Muppet Treasure Island* (G)
352. 1996: *Before and After* (Hollywood Pictures) (PG-13)
353. 1996: *Up Close & Personal* (Touchstone) (PG-13)
354. 1996: *Homeward Bound II: Lost in San Francisco* (G)
355. 1996: *Two Much* (Touchstone) (PG-13)
356. 1996: *Little Indian, Big City* (Touchstone) (PG)
357. 1996: *James and the Giant Peach* (PG)
358. 1996: *Celtic Pride* (Hollywood Pictures) (PG-13)
359. 1996: *Last Dance* (Touchstone) (R)
360. 1996: *Boys* (Touchstone) (PG-13)
361. 1996: *Spy Hard* (Hollywood Pictures) (PG-13)
362. 1996: *Eddie* (Hollywood Pictures) (PG-13)
363. 1996: *The Rock* (Hollywood Pictures) (R)
364. 1996: *The Hunchback of Notre Dame* (G)
365. 1996: *Phenomenon* (Touchstone) (PG)
366. 1996: *Kazaam* (Touchstone) (PG)
367. 1996: *Jack* (Hollywood Pictures) (PG-13)
368. 1996: *First Kid* (PG)

369. 1996: *The Rich Man's Wife* (Hollywood Pictures) (R)
370. 1996: *D3: The Mighty Ducks* (PG)
371. 1996: *The Associate* (Hollywood Pictures) (PG-13)
372. 1996: *Ransom* (Touchstone) (R)
373. 1996: *The War at Home* (Touchstone) (R)
374. 1996: *101 Dalmatians* [live action](G)
375. 1996: *The Preacher's Wife* (Touchstone) (PG)
376. 1997: *Evita* (Hollywood Pictures) (PG)
377. 1997: *Metro* (Touchstone) (R)
378. 1997: *Prefontaine* (Hollywood Pictures) (PG-13)
379. 1997: *Shadow Conspiracy* (Hollywood Pictures) (R)
380. 1997: *That Darn Cat* [remake](PG)
381. 1997: *Jungle 2 Jungle* (PG)
382. 1997: *The Sixth Man* (Touchstone) (PG-13)
383. 1997: *Grosse Pointe Blank* (Hollywood Pictures) (R)
384. 1997: *Romy and Michele's High School Reunion* (Touchstone) (R)
385. 1997: *Gone Fishin'* (Hollywood Pictures) (PG)
386. 1997: *Con Air* (Touchstone) (R)
387. 1997: *Hercules* (G)
388. 1997: *George of the Jungle* (PG)
389. 1997: *Nothing to Lose* (Touchstone) (R)
390. 1997: *Air Bud* (PG)
391. 1997: *G. I. Jane* (Hollywood Pictures) (R)
392. 1997: *A Thousand Acres* (Touchstone) (R)
393. 1997: *Washington Square* (Hollywood Pictures) (PG)
394. 1997: *RocketMan* (PG)
395. 1997: *Playing God* (Touchstone) (R)
396. 1997: *Flubber* (PG)
397. 1997: *An American Werewolf in Paris* (Hollywood Pictures) (R)
398. 1997: *Mr. Magoo* (PG)
399. 1998: *Kundun* (Touchstone) (PG-13)
400. 1998: *Deep Rising* (Hollywood Pictures) (R)
401. 1998: *Krippendorf's Tribe* (Touchstone) (PG-13)
402. 1998: *An Alan Smithee Film: Burn, Hollywood, Burn* (Hollywood Pictures) (R)
403. 1998: *Meet the Deedles* (PG)
404. 1998: *He Got Game* (Touchstone) (R)
405. 1998: *The Horse Whisperer* (Touchstone) (PG-13)
406. 1998: *Six Days, Seven Nights* (Touchstone) (PG-13)
407. 1998: *Mulan* (G)
408. 1998: *Armageddon* (Touchstone) (PG-13)
409. 1998: *Jane Austen's Mafia!* (Touchstone) (PG-13)
410. 1998: *The Parent Trap* (PG)
411. 1998: *Firelight* (Hollywood Pictures) (R)
412. 1998: *Simon Birch* (Hollywood Pictures) (PG)
413. 1998: *Holy Man* (Touchstone) (PG)
414. 1998: *Beloved* (Touchstone) (R)
415. 1998: *The Waterboy* (Touchstone) (PG-13)
416. 1998: *I'll Be Home for Christmas* (PG)
417. 1998: *Enemy of the State* (Touchstone) (R)
418. 1998: *A Bug's Life* (Pixar) (G)
419. 1998: *Mighty Joe Young* (PG)
420. 1999: *A Civil Action* (Touchstone) (PG-13)
421. 1999: *Rushmore* (Touchstone) (R)
422. 1999: *My Favorite Martian* (PG)
423. 1999: *The Other Sister* (Touchstone) (PG-13)
424. 1999: *Doug's 1st Movie* (G)
425. 1999: *10 Things I Hate About You* (Touchstone) (PG-13)
426. 1999: *Endurance* (G)
427. 1999: *Instinct* (Touchstone) (R)
428. 1999: *Tarzan* (G)
429. 1999: *Summer of Sam* (Touchstone) (R)
430. 1999: *Inspector Gadget* (PG)
431. 1999: *The Sixth Sense* (Hollywood) (PG-13)
432. 1999: *The 13th Warrior* (Touchstone) (R)
433. 1999: *Breakfast of Champions* (Hollywood) (R)
434. 1999: *Mumford* (Touchstonc) (R)
435. 1999: *Mystery Alaska* (Hollywood) (R)
436. 1999: *The Hand Behind the Mouse: The Ub Iwerks Story* (G)
437. 1999: *The Straight Story* (G)
438. 1999: *The Insider* (Touchstone) (R)
439. 1999: *Toy Story 2* (Pixar) (G)
440. 1999: *Deuce Bigalow: Male Gigolo* (Touchstone) (R)
441. 1999: *Cradle Will Rock* (Touchstone) (R)
442. 1999: *Bicentennial Man* (Touchstone) (PG)
443. 2000: *Fantasia/2000* (G)
444. 2000: *Play It to the Bone* (Touchstone) (R)
445. 2000: *Gun Shy* (Hollywood) (R)
446. 2000: *The Tigger Movie* (G)
447. 2000: *Mission to Mars* (Touchstone) (PG)
448. 2000: *Whispers* (G)
449. 2000: *High Fidelity* (Touchstone) (R)
450. 2000: *Keeping the Faith* (Touchstone) (PG-13)
451. 2000: *Dinosaur* (PG)
452. 2000: *Shanghai Noon* (Touchstone) (PG-13)
453. 2000: *Gone in 60 Seconds* (Touchstone) (PG-13)
454. 2000: *Disney's The Kid* (PG)
455. 2000: *Coyote Ugly* (Touchstone) (PG-13)
456. 2000: *The Crew* (Touchstone) (PG-13)
457. 2000: *Duets* (Hollywood) (R)
458. 2000: *Remember the Titans* (PG)
459. 2000: *Playing Mona Lisa* (no label) (R)
460. 2000: *Unbreakable* (Touchstone) (PG-13)
461. 2000: *102 Dalmatians* (G)
462. 2000: *The Emperor's New Groove* (G)

463. 2000: *O Brother, Where Art Thou?* (Touchstone) (PG-13)
464. 2001: *Double Take* (Touchstone) (PG-13)
465. 2001: *Recess: School's Out* (G)
466. 2001: *Just Visiting* (Hollywood) (PG-13)
467. 2001: *Pearl Harbor* (Touchstone) (PG-13)
468. 2001: *Atlantis: The Lost Empire* (PG)
469. 2001: *Crazy/Beautiful* (Touchstone) (PG-13)
470. 2001: *The Princess Diaries* (G)
471. 2001: *Bubble Boy* (Touchstone) (PG-13)
472. 2001: *New Port South* (Touchstone) (PG-13)
473. 2001: *Max Keeble's Big Move* (PG)
474. 2001: *Corky Romano* (Touchstone) (PG-13)
475. 2001: *High Heels and Low Lifes* (Touchstone) (R)
476. 2001: *Monsters, Inc.* (Pixar) (G)
477. 2001: *Out Cold* (Touchstone) (PG-13)
478. 2001: *The Royal Tenenbaums* (Touchstone) (R)
479. 2002: *Snow Dogs* (PG)
480. 2002: *The Count of Monte Cristo* (Touchstone) (PG-13)
481. 2002: *Return to Never Land* (G)
482. 2002: *Sorority Boys* (Touchstone) (R)
483. 2002: *The Rookie* (G)
484. 2002: *Big Trouble* (Touchstone) (PG-13)
485. 2002: *Frank McKlusky, C.I.* (Touchstone) (PG-13)
486. 2002: *ESPN's Ultimate X* (Touchstone) (PG)
487. 2002: *Bad Company* (Touchstone) (PG-13)
488. 2002: *Lilo & Stitch* (PG)
489. 2002: *Reign of Fire* (Touchstone) (PG-13)
490. 2002: *The Country Bears* (G)
491. 2002: *Signs* (Touchstone) (PG-13)
492. 2002: *Spirited Away* (PG)
493. 2002: *Moonlight Mile* (Touchstone) (PG-13)
494. 2002: *Sweet Home Alabama* (Touchstone) (PG-13)
495. 2002: *Tuck Everlasting* (PG)
496. 2002: *The Santa Clause 2* (G)
497. 2002: *Treasure Planet* (PG)
498. 2002: *The Hot Chick* (Touchstone) (PG-13)
499. 2002: *25th Hour* (Touchstone) (R)
500. 2003: *The Recruit* (Touchstone) (PG-13)
501. 2003: *Shanghai Knights* (Touchstone) (PG-13)
502. 2003: *The Jungle Book 2* (G)
503. 2003: *Bringing Down the House* (Touchstone) (PG-13)
504. 2003: *Piglet's Big Movie* (G)
505. 2003: *Ghosts of the Abyss* (G)
506. 2003: *Holes* (PG)
507. 2003: *The Lizzie McGuire Movie* (PG)
508. 2003: *Finding Nemo* (Pixar) (G)
509. 2003: *Pirates of the Caribbean: The Curse of the Black Pearl* (PG-13)
510. 2003: *Freaky Friday* (PG)
511. 2003: *Open Range* (Touchstone) (R)
512. 2003: *Hope Springs* (Touchstone) (PG-13)
513. 2003: *Cold Creek Manor* (Touchstone) (R)
514. 2003: *Under the Tuscan Sun* (Touchstone) (PG-13)
515. 2003: *Veronica Guerin* (Touchstone) (R)
516. 2003: *Brother Bear* (G)
517. 2003: *The Haunted Mansion* (PG)
518. 2003: *Calendar Girls* (Touchstone) (PG-13)
519. 2003: *The Young Black Stallion* (G)
520. 2004: *Teacher's Pet* (PG)
521. 2004: *Miracle* (PG)
522. 2004: *Confessions of a Teenage Drama Queen* (PG)
523. 2004: *Hidalgo* (Touchstone) (PG-13)
524. 2004: *The Ladykillers* (Touchstone) (R)
525. 2004: *Home on the Range* (PG)
526. 2004: *The Alamo* (Touchstone) (PG-13)
527. 2004: *Sacred Planet* (G)
528. 2004: *Raising Helen* (Touchstone) (PG-13)
529. 2004: *Around the World in 80 Days* (PG)
530. 2004: *America's Heart & Soul* (PG)
531. 2004: *King Arthur* (Touchstone) (PG-13)
532. 2004: *The Village* (Touchstone) (PG-13)
533. 2004: *The Princess Diaries 2: Royal Engagement* (G)
534. 2004: *Mr. 3000* (Touchstone) (PG-13)
535. 2004: *The Last Shot* (Touchstone) (R)
536. 2004: *Ladder 49* (Touchstone) (PG-13)
537. 2004: *The Incredibles* (Pixar) (PG)
538. 2004: *National Treasure* (PG)
539. 2004: *The Life Aquatic with Steve Zissou* (Touchstone) (R)
540. 2005: *Aliens of the Deep* (G)
541. 2005: *Pooh's Heffalump Movie* (G)
542. 2005: *The Pacifier* (PG)
543. 2005: *Ice Princess* (G)
544. 2005: *A Lot Like Love* (Touchstone) (PG-13)
545. 2005: *The Hitchhiker's Guide to the Galaxy* (Touchstone) (PG)
546. 2005: *Howl's Moving Castle* (PG)
547. 2005: *Herbie: Fully Loaded* (G)
548. 2005: *Dark Water* (Touchstone) (PG-13)
549. 2005: *Sky High* (PG)
550. 2005: *Valiant* (G)
551. 2005: *Flightplan* (Touchstone)
552. 2005: *The Greatest Game Ever Played* (PG)
553. 2005: *Shopgirl* (Touchstone) (R)
554. 2005: *Chicken Little* (G)
555. 2005: *The Chronicles of Narnia: The Lion, the Witch and the Wardrobe* (PG)
556. 2005: *Casanova* (Touchstone)
557. 2006: *Glory Road* (PG)

558. 2006: *Annapolis* (Touchstone) (PG-13)
559. 2006: *Roving Mars* (G)
560. 2006: *Eight Below* (PG)
561. 2006: *The Shaggy Dog* (PG)
562. 2006: *Stay Alive* (Hollywood Pictures) (PG-13)
563. 2006: *The Wild* (G)
564. 2006: *Stick It* (Touchstone) (PG-13)
565. 2006: *Goal! The Dream Begins* (Touchstone) (PG)
566. 2006: *Cars* (Pixar) (G)
567. 2006: *Pirates of the Caribbean: Dead Man's Chest* (PG-13)
568. 2006: *Step Up* (Touchstone) (PG-13)
569. 2006: *Invincible* (PG)
570. 2006: *The Guardian* (Touchstone) (PG-13)
571. 2006: *The Prestige* (Touchstone) (PG-13)
572. 2006: *The Santa Clause 3: The Escape Clause* (G)
573. 2006: *Déjà Vu* (Touchstone) (PG-13)
574. 2006: *Apocalypto* (Touchstone) (R)
575. 2007: *Primeval* (Hollywood Pictures) (R)
576. 2007: *Bridge to Terabithia* (PG)
577. 2007: *Wild Hogs* (Touchstone) (PG-13)
578. 2007: *Meet the Robinsons* (G)
579. 2007: *The Invisible* (Hollywood Pictures) (PG-13)
580. 2007: *Pirates of the Caribbean: At World's End* (PG-13)
581. 2007: *Ratatouille* (Pixar) (G)
582. 2007: *The Secret of the Magic Gourd* (NR)
583. 2007: *Underdog* (PG)
584. 2007: *The Game Plan* (PG)
585. 2007: *Dan in Real Life* (PG-13)
586. 2007: *Le Premier Cri* (*The First Cry*) (NR)
587. 2007: *Enchanted* (PG)
588. 2007: *National Treasure: Book of Secrets* (PG)
589. 2008: *Hannah Montana & Miley Cyrus: Best of Both Worlds Concert* (G)
590. 2008: *Step Up 2 the Streets* (Touchstone) (PG-13)
591. 2008: *College Road Trip* (G)
592. 2008: *The Chronicles of Narnia: Prince Caspian* (PG)
593. 2008: *WALL•E* (Pixar) (G)
594. 2008: *Swing Vote* (Touchstone) (PG-13)
595. 2008: *Tinker Bell* (G)
596. 2008: *Miracle at St. Anna* (Touchstone) (R)
597. 2008: *Beverly Hills Chihuahua* (PG)
598. 2008: *Morning Light* (PG)
599. 2008: *High School Musical 3: Senior Year* (G)
600. 2008: *Roadside Romeo* (Disney India) (NR)
601. 2008: *Bolt* (PG)
602. 2008: *Bedtime Stories* (PG)
603. 2009: *Confessions of a Shopaholic* (Touchstone) (PG)
604. 2009: *Hexe Lilli: Der Drache und das Magische Buch* (*Lilly the Witch: The Dragon and the Magic Book*) (NR)
605. 2009: *Jonas Brothers: The 3-D Concert Experience* (G)
606. 2009: *Race to Witch Mountain* (PG)
607. 2009: *Hannah Montana the Movie* (G)
608. 2009: *Earth* (Disneynature) (G)
609. 2009: *Trail of the Panda* (NR)
610. 2009: *The Boys: The Sherman Brothers' Story* (PG)
611. 2009: *Up* (Pixar) (PG)
612. 2009: *The Proposal* (Touchstone) (PG-13)
613. 2009: *G-Force* (PG)
614. 2009: *Ponyo* (G)
615. 2009: *X Games 3-D: The Movie* (PG)
616. 2009: *Walt & El Grupo* (PG)
617. 2009: *Surrogates* (Touchstone) (PG-13)
618. 2009: *Tinker Bell and the Lost Treasure* (G)
619. 2009: *Kniga Masterov* (*The Book of Masters*) (NR)
620. 2009: *Disney's A Christmas Carol* (PG)
621. 2009: *Old Dogs* (PG)
622. 2009: *The Princess and the Frog* (G)
623. 2010: *When in Rome* (Touchstone) (PG-13)
624. 2010: *Alice in Wonderland* (PG)
625. 2010: *Waking Sleeping Beauty* (PG)
626. 2010: *The Last Song* (Touchstone) (PG)
627. 2010: *Oceans* (Disneynature) (G)
628. 2010: *Prince of Persia: The Sands of Time* (PG-13)
629. 2010: *Toy Story 3* (Pixar) (G)
630. 2010: *The Sorcerer's Apprentice* (PG)
631. 2010: *Step Up 3-D* (Touchstone) (PG-13)
632. 2010: *Tales from Earthsea* (PG-13)
633. 2010: *The Switch* (Miramax) (PG-13)
634. 2010: *Tinker Bell and the Great Fairy Rescue* (G)
635. 2010: *You Again* (Touchstone) (PG)
636. 2010: *Secretariat* (PG)
637. 2010: *Do Dooni Chaar* (*Two Times Two Equals Four*) (Disney India) (NR)
638. 2010: *Tangled* (PG)
639. 2010: *The Tempest* (Touchstone/Miramax) (PG-13)
640. 2010: *Tron: Legacy* (PG)
641. 2011: *Anaganaga O Dheerudu* (*Once Upon a Warrior*) (Disney India) (NR)
642. 2011: *Gnomeo & Juliet* (Touchstone) (G)
643. 2011: *Hexe Lilli: Die Reise nach Mandolan* (*Lilly the Witch: The Journey to Mandolan*) (NR)
644. 2011: *I Am Number Four* (Touchstone/DreamWorks) (PG-13)

645. 2011: *Mars Needs Moms* (PG)
646. 2011: *African Cats* (Disneynature) (G)
647. 2011: *Zokkomon* (Disney India) (NR)
648. 2011: *Prom* (PG)
649. 2011: *Pirates of the Caribbean: On Stranger Tides* (PG-13)
650. 2011: *Cars 2* (Pixar) (G)
651. 2011: *Winnie the Pooh* (G)
652. 2011: *The Help* (Touchstone/DreamWorks) (PG-13)
653. 2011: *Fright Night* (Touchstone/DreamWorks) (R)
654. 2011: *Real Steel* (Touchstone/DreamWorks) (PG-13)
655. 2011: *The Muppets* (PG)
656. 2011: *War Horse* (Touchstone/DreamWorks) (PG-13)
657. 2012: *The Secret World of Arrietty* (G)
658. 2012: *John Carter* (PG-13)
659. 2012: *Arjun: The Warrior Prince* (Disney India) (NR)
660. 2012: *Chimpanzee* (Disneynature) (G)
661. 2012: *Marvel's The Avengers* (Marvel) (PG-13)
662. 2012: *Brave* (Pixar) (PG)
663. 2012: *Mad Buddies* (Touchstone) (NR)
664. 2012: *People Like Us* (Touchstone/DreamWorks) (PG-13)
665. 2012: *The Odd Life of Timothy Green* (PG)
666. 2012: *Secret of the Wings* (G)
667. 2012: *Barfi!* (Disney UTV) (NR)
668. 2012: *Frankenweenie* (PG)
669. 2012: *Wreck-It Ralph* (PG)
670. 2012: *Lincoln* (Touchstone/DreamWorks) (PG-13)
671. 2013: *Oz The Great and Powerful* (PG)
672. 2013: *Wings of Life* (Disneynature) (G)
673. 2013: *Iron Man 3* (Marvel) (PG-13)
674. 2013: *Monsters University* (Pixar) (G)
675. 2013: *The Lone Ranger* (PG-13)
676. 2013: *Planes* (PG)
677. 2013: *The Fifth Estate* (Touchstone/DreamWorks) (R)
678. 2013: *The Wind Rises* (Touchstone) (PG-13)
679. 2013: *Thor: The Dark World* (Marvel) (PG-13)
680. 2013: *Delivery Man* (Touchstone/DreamWorks) (PG-13)
681. 2013: *Frozen* (PG)
682. 2013: *Saving Mr. Banks* (PG-13)
683. 2013: *Schuks! Your Country Needs You* (Touchstone) (NR)
684. 2014: *The Pirate Fairy* (G)
685. 2014: *Need for Speed* (Touchstone/DreamWorks) (PG-13)
686. 2014: *Muppets Most Wanted* (PG)
687. 2014: *Captain America: The Winter Soldier* (Marvel) (PG-13)
688. 2014: *Bears* (Disneynature) (G)
689. 2014: *Million Dollar Arm* (PG)
690. 2014: *Maleficent* (PG)
691. 2014: *Planes: Fire & Rescue* (PG)
692. 2014: *Guardians of the Galaxy* (Marvel) (PG-13)
693. 2014: *The Hundred-Foot Journey* (Touchstone/DreamWorks) (PG)
694. 2014: *Khoobsurat* (Disney India) (NR)
695. 2014: *Alexander and the Terrible, Horrible, No Good, Very Bad Day* (PG)
696. 2014: *Big Hero 6* (PG)
697. 2014: *Into the Woods* (PG)
698. 2015: *Strange Magic* (Touchstone/Lucasfilm) (PG)
699. 2015: *Tinker Bell and the Legend of the Never-Beast* (G)
700. 2015: *McFarland USA* (PG)
701. 2015: *Cinderella* (PG)
702. 2015: *Monkey Kingdom* (Disneynature) (G)
703. 2015: *Tini: El gran cambio de Violetta* (*Tini: The New Life of Violetta*) (NR)
704. 2015: *Avengers: Age of Ultron* (Marvel) (PG-13)
705. 2015: *Tomorrowland* (PG)
706. 2015: *Inside Out* (Pixar) (PG)
707. 2015. *ABCD 2* (Disney India) (NR)
708. 2015: *Ant-Man* (Marvel) (PG-13)
709. 2015: *Schuks! Pay Back the Money!* (Touchstone) (NR)
710. 2015: *Bridge of Spies* (Touchstone/DreamWorks) (PG-13)
711. 2015: *The Good Dinosaur* (Pixar) (PG)
712. 2015: *Star Wars: The Force Awakens* (Lucasfilm) (PG-13)
713. 2016: *The Finest Hours* (PG-13)
714. 2016: *Zootopia* (PG)
715. 2016: *The Jungle Book* (PG)
716. 2016: *Captain America: Civil War* (Marvel) (PG-13)
717. 2016: *Alice Through the Looking Glass* (PG)
718. 2016: *Finding Dory* (Pixar) (PG)
719. 2016: *The BFG* (PG)
720. 2016: *Pete's Dragon* (PG)
721. 2016: *The Light Between Oceans* (Touchstone/DreamWorks) (PG-13)
722. 2016: *Queen of Katwe* (PG)
723. 2016: *Doctor Strange* (Marvel) (PG-13)
724. 2016: *Moana* (PG)
725. 2016: *Rogue One: A Star Wars Story* (Lucasfilm) (PG-13)
726. 2016: *Dangal* (Disney India) (NR)
727. 2017: *Beauty and the Beast* (PG)

728. 2017: *Born in China* (Disneynature) (G)

729. 2017: *Guardians of the Galaxy Vol. 2* (Marvel) (PG-13)

730. 2017: *Pirates of the Caribbean: Dead Men Tell No Tales* (PG-13)

731. 2017: *Cars 3* (Pixar) (G)

732. 2017: *Jagga Jasoos* (Disney India) (NR)

733. 2017: *Posledny bogatyr* (*The Last Warrior*) (NR)

734. 2017: *Thor: Ragnarok* (Marvel) (PG-13)

735. 2017: *Coco* (Pixar) (PG)

736. 2017: *Star Wars: The Last Jedi* (Lucasfilm) (PG-13)

737. 2018: *Black Panther* (Marvel) (PG-13)

738. 2018: *A Wrinkle in Time* (PG)

739. 2018: *Avengers: Infinity War* (Marvel) (PG-13)

740. 2018: *Solo: A Star Wars Story* (Lucasfilm) (PG-13)

741. 2018: *Incredibles 2* (Pixar) (PG)

742. 2018: *Ant-Man and the Wasp* (Marvel) (PG-13)

743. 2018: *Christopher Robin* (PG)

744. 2018: *The Nutcracker and the Four Realms* (PG)

745. 2018: *Ralph Breaks the Internet* (PG)

746. 2018: *Mary Poppins Returns* (PG)

747. 2019: *Captain Marvel* (Marvel) (PG-13)

748. 2019: *Dumbo* (PG)

749. 2019: *Penguins* (Disneynature) (G)

750. 2019: *Avengers: Endgame* (Marvel) (PG-13)

751. 2019: *Aladdin* (PG)

752. 2019: *Toy Story 4* (Pixar) (G)

753. 2019: *The Lion King* (PG)

754. 2019: *Maleficent: Mistress of Evil* (PG)

755. 2019: *Lady and the Tramp* (PG) [Disney+]

756. 2019: *Noelle* (G) [Disney+]

757. 2019: *Frozen 2* (PG)

758. 2019: *Star Wars: The Rise of Skywalker* (Lucasfilm) (PG-13)

759. 2019: *Togo* (PG) [Disney+]

760. 2020: *Timmy Failure: Mistakes Were Made* (PG) [Disney+]

761. 2020: *Onward* (Pixar) (PG)

762. 2020: *Stargirl* (PG) [Disney+]

763. 2020: *Dolphin Reef* (Disneynature) (G) [Disney+]

764. 2020: *Elephant* (Disneynature) (G) [Disney+]

765. 2020: *Artemis Fowl* (PG) [Disney+]

766. 2020: *Hamilton* (PG-13) [Disney+]

767. 2020: *Magic Camp* (PG) [Disney+]

768. 2020: *The One and Only Ivan* (PG) [Disney+]

769. 2020: *Mulan* (PG-13) [Disney+]

770. 2020: *Godmothered* (PG) [Disney+]

771. 2020: *Safety* (PG) [Disney+]

772. 2020: *Soul* (Pixar) (PG) [Disney+]

773. 2021: *Posledny bogatyr: Koren' zla* (*The Last Warrior: Root of Evil*) (NR)

774. 2021: *Flora & Ulysses* (PG) [Disney+]

775. 2021: *Raya and the Last Dragon* (PG)

776. 2021: *Cruella* (PG-13)

777. 2021: *Luca* (Pixar) (PG) [Limited Theatrical & Disney+]

778. 2021: *Black Widow* (Marvel) (PG-13)

779. 2021: *Jungle Cruise* (PG-13)

780. 2021: *Shang-Chi and the Legend of the Ten Rings* (Marvel) (PG-13)

781. 2021: *Eternals* (Marvel) (PG-13)

782. 2021: *Encanto* (PG)

783. 2021: *Diary of a Wimpy Kid* (PG) [Disney+]

784. 2021: *Posledny bogatyr: Poslannik t'my* (*The Last Warrior: A Messenger of Darkness*) (NR)

785. 2022: *The Ice Age Adventures of Buck Wild* (PG) [Disney+]

786. 2022: *The Beatles: Get Back – The Rooftop Concert* (PG-13)

787. 2022: *Turning Red* (Pixar) (PG) [Limited Theatrical & Disney+]

788. 2022: *Cheaper by the Dozen* (PG) [Disney+]

789. 2022: *Better Nate Than Ever* (PG) [Disney+]

790. 2022: *Polar Bear* (Disneynature) (PG) [Disney+]

791. 2022: *Doctor Strange in the Multiverse of Madness* (Marvel) (PG-13)

792. 2022: *Chip 'n Dale: Rescue Rangers* (PG) [Disney+]

793. 2022: *Hollywood Stargirl* (PG) [Disney+]

794. 2022: *Lightyear* (Pixar) (PG)

795. 2022: *Rise* (PG) [Disney+]

796. 2022: *Thor: Love and Thunder* (Marvel) (PG-13)

797. 2022: *Mija* (PG-13)

798. 2022: *Pinocchio* (PG) [Disney+]

799. 2022: *Hocus Pocus 2* (PG) [Disney+]

800. 2022: *Black Panther: Wakanda Forever* (Marvel) (PG-13)

801. 2022: *Strange World* (PG)

802. 2022: *Disenchanted* (PG) [Disney+]

803. 2022: *Diary of a Wimpy Kid: Rodrick Rules* (PG) [Disney+]

804. 2022: *Night at the Museum: Kahmunrah Rises Again* (PG) [Disney+]

805. 2023: *Ant-Man and the Wasp: Quantumania* (Marvel) (PG-13)

806. 2023: *Chang Can Dunk* (PG) [Disney+]

807. 2023: *Peter Pan & Wendy* (PG) [Disney+]

808. 2023: *Guardians of the Galaxy Vol. 3* (Marvel)
809. 2023: *The Little Mermaid* (PG)
810. 2023: *Elemental* (Pixar*)*
811. 2023: *Indiana Jones and the Dial of Destiny* (Lucasfilm)
812. 2023: *Haunted Mansion*

For a list of feature films released by 20th Century Studios, 20th Century Animation, and Searchlight Pictures outside the Disney banner, see 21st Century Fox.

Featurette Term used at Disney to refer to a film that is longer than a short (10 min.) but shorter than a feature (60 min.).

Feed the Birds Song from *Mary Poppins*; written by Richard M. and Robert B. Sherman.

Feige, Kevin Film producer; in 2007, he was named president of Marvel Studios, which was acquired by Disney in 2009. Overseeing the Marvel Cinematic Universe franchise, he has produced some of the highest-grossing films of all time. In 2019, he was named chief creative officer of Marvel, additionally overseeing Marvel Television and Marvel Family Entertainment.

Feignoux, Wally (1906–1981) He was instrumental in handling Disney film releases in Europe 1936–1971 and was presented posthumously with a European Disney Legends Award in 1997.

Feldman, Corey Actor; voiced the young Copper in *The Fox and the Hound* and appeared on TV in *Exile.* Provided the voice of SPRX-77 in *Super Robot Monkey Team Hyperforce Go!*

Feldman, Mindy Mouseketeer on the new *Mickey Mouse Club.*

Felicia Feline friend of Ratigan's in *The Great Mouse Detective.*

Felicity (TV) One-hour coming-of-age dramatic series on The WB Network; aired Sep. 29, 1998–May 22, 2002. The life of recent high school graduate Felicity Porter is turned upside down when she suddenly changes her very well-laid-out college plans and moves instead to New York City to attend school. Her defied parents refuse to support her, but she feels she must take charge of her life's plan by striking out on her own for the first time. Stars Keri Russell (Felicity Porter), Scott Speedman (Ben Covington), Amy Jo Johnson (Julie Emrick), Tangi Miller (Elena Tyler), Scott Foley (Noel Crane). In the 1999 season, Felicity becomes a resident adviser, with added regular cast members Greg Grunberg (Sean Blumberg) and Amanda Foreman (Meghan Rotundi). The complete first season was released on DVD in 2002.

Feliz Navidad (film) Segment from *The Three Caballeros*; released on 16 mm in Oct. 1974. Panchito, Donald Duck, and José Carioca explore Christmas traditions in Mexico, including Las Posadas.

Felton, Verna (1890–1966) Popular Disney voice actress; she provided the voice of elephants (*Dumbo* and *The Jungle Book*), the Fairy Godmother (*Cinderella*), the Queen of Hearts (*Alice in Wonderland*), Aunt Sarah (*Lady and the Tramp*), and Flora (*Sleeping Beauty*).

Ferdinand the Bull (film) Special cartoon released Nov. 25, 1938. The first cartoon directed by Dick Rickard. Based on the story by Munro Leaf and the illustrations by Robert Lawson. It centers on a ferocious-looking, but quiet, bull who wants only to sit and smell the flowers. He is mistaken for a feisty animal by a matador when he snorts and charges after being stung by a bee. The matador takes him to the arena in the city, only to see him revert to his peaceful demeanor and refuse to fight. Ferdinand is happily sent back to his flowers. Academy Award winner for Best Cartoon. Several of the characters at the bullfight are caricatures of Disney personnel, including Walt Disney himself as the matador. Animator Milt Kahl took on a slight extra chore by providing the voice of Ferdinand's mother, while Walt Disney added Ferdinand's few words.

Ferdinand the Bull and Mickey (TV) Show aired Jan. 18, 1983. Reluctant and actual heroes are spotlighted in various animation clips.

Ferdy Sometimes spelled Ferdie; a nephew of Mickey Mouse. He appeared only in one cartoon, *Mickey's Steam-Roller* (1934), with his brother, Morty. Morty and Ferdy first appeared in the *Mickey Mouse* comic strip on Sep. 18, 1932.

Fergi Diversifies (film) Educational film about a corporation's growth, stock sales, mergers, and acquisitions. Produced by Dave Bell; released in Sep. 1977.

Fergi Goes Inc. (film) Educational film about

the growth of a small business and its eventual incorporation. Produced by Dave Bell; released in Sep. 1977. SEE ALSO IF THE FERGI FITS, WEAR IT.

Fergi Meets the Challenge (film) Educational film about how to cope with successes and failures in an expanding company. Produced by Dave Bell; released in Sep. 1978.

Ferguson, Norm (1902–1957) Animator and director; started at Disney in 1929 and remained until 1953. He animated on dozens of short cartoons and served as a directing animator on most Disney features from *Snow White and the Seven Dwarfs* to *Peter Pan*. He was responsible for the witch in *Snow White* and J. Worthington Foulfellow and Gideon in *Pinocchio*. He was also known for his animation of Pluto. ASIFA, the animated film society, presented him posthumously the Winsor McCay Award, their highest honor, in 1987. He was named a Disney Legend in 1999.

Ferrante, Orlando Imagineer; he joined the Disney staff in 1962. Beginning with Walt Disney's Enchanted Tiki Room, he was involved with the installation of many Disneyland and Walt Disney World attractions. In 1966, he established a department named PICO (Project Installation and Coordinating Office) and 6 years later moved into Imagineering administration. He retired in 2002 after helping with engineering, production, and installation in Disneyland Paris, Disney Cruise Line, and Tokyo DisneySea. He was named a Disney Legend in 2003.

Ferrera, America Actress; appeared on Disney Channel in *Gotta Kick It Up!* (Yolanda Vargas) and on ABC as the title character, Betty Suarez, in *Ugly Betty*. She provided the voice of Fawn in *Tinker Bell*. She won an Emmy Award for Best Actress in a Comedy, *Ugly Betty*, in 2007.

Festival Disney Area outside the gates of Disneyland Paris consisting of restaurants, shops, and nightclubs, primarily for evening entertainment. A longtime highlight was *Buffalo Bill's Wild West Show*. Designed by architect Frank Gehry. The area name was changed to Disney Village in 1996. Also the name of a shop in the Disney Ambassador Hotel at Tokyo Disney Resort; opened Jul. 7, 2000.

Festival Disney Music festival for middle and high school ensembles at Walt Disney World; established in 2005.

Festival of Fantasy Parade SEE DISNEY FESTIVAL OF FANTASY PARADE.

Festival of Folk Heroes (film) A 16-mm release of *Pecos Bill, Johnny Appleseed, Paul Bunyan, The Saga of Windwagon Smith*, and *Casey at the Bat*; released Apr. 1971.

Festival of Foods The Big Thunder Barbecue at Disneyland was re-themed Jun. 21, 1996–May 29, 1997, to tie in with *The Hunchback of Notre Dame Festival of Fools* outdoor show. FOR THE RESTAURANT AT HONG KONG DISNEYLAND, SEE CLOPIN'S FESTIVAL OF FOODS.

Festival of the Lion King Musical show in Disney's Animal Kingdom; opened Apr. 22, 1998, in the Lion King Theater in Camp Minnie-Mickey. Four singers—Kiume, Zawadi, Kibibi, and Nakawa—host a high-energy extravaganza of dance, puppetry, and acrobatics celebrating the legend of Simba. The formerly roofed, but otherwise open-air, theater was enclosed in 2003. The show used float units from *The Lion King Celebration* parade from Disneyland. Closed Jan. 5, 2014, to move to the Africa section of the park, premiering Jun. 1 in the new Harambe Theater. It is one of the most popular shows at Walt Disney World. Also opened in Hong Kong Disneyland Sep. 12, 2005. A modified show, *A Celebration of Festival of the Lion King*, debuted in Walt Disney World May 15, 2021, during the COVID-19 pandemic.

Fetch (film) Animated short; digitally released Jan. 24, 2020, on Disney+. A child wants to play fetch with her pet, but unfortunately he's wandered deep into an imposing forest. Directed by Mitch Counsell. 3 min. From the Walt Disney Animation Studios Short Circuit program.

Fethry Duck Beatnik-type duck who reads too many "how-to-do-it" books and then gets Donald involved in his harebrained schemes. He was created around 1963 by Dick Kinney for international comic books.

Fey, Tina Actress/comedian; appeared in *Muppets Most Wanted* (Nadya). She narrated *Monkey Kingdom* and voiced 22 in *Soul*, Lisa in *Ponyo*, and Annabelle in *Phineas and Ferb*.

Fflewddur Fflam Wandering minstrel in *The Black Cauldron*; voiced by Nigel Hawthorne.

Fiddler, Fifer & Practical Cafe Quick-service café and bakery on Buena Vista Street in Disney California Adventure; opened Jun. 15, 2012, offering Starbucks coffee, sandwiches, soups, and pastries. The name is inspired by the Three Little Pigs, with décor themed to a 1920s-inspired musical trio, the Silver Lake Sisters.

Fiddling Around (film) Mickey Mouse cartoon released Apr. 21, 1930. Also known as *Just Mickey* (the short's working title). Directed by Walt Disney. One of Mickey's musical adventures in which he is an eager violinist with a full head of unruly hair who stops his playing only to talk to the movie audience.

Fidget Ratigan's peg-legged bat henchman in *The Great Mouse Detective*; voiced by Candy Candido.

Fiedler, John (1925–2005) Character actor; appeared in *Rascal* (Cy Jenkins), *The Shaggy D.A.* (Howie Clemmings), and *Midnight Madness* (Mr. Thorpe), and on TV in *The Mystery in Dracula's Castle* and *The Whiz Kid and the Mystery at Riverton*. He voiced Piglet in the Winnie the Pooh films, the owl in *The Rescuers*, the church mouse in *Robin Hood*, the porcupine in *The Fox and the Hound*, and the Old Man in *The Emperor's New Groove*.

Field, Sally Actress; she was nominated for an Academy Award (Best Actress in a Supporting Role) for her portrayal of Mary Todd Lincoln in *Lincoln*. On TV, she appeared in *Mickey's 50*, as Justice Kate Nolan in *The Court*, and as Nora Walker in *Brothers & Sisters*, receiving the 2007 Emmy for Best Actress in a Drama. She voiced Sassy in the *Homeward Bound* films and Marina Del Ray in *The Little Mermaid: Ariel's Beginning*. Field made her film debut in an uncredited role in *Moon Pilot* and made her directorial debut with *The Christmas Tree* for ABC.

Field Trips Education resource shop for teachers at Innoventions West in EPCOT; opened in 1994 and succeeded by The Art of Disney in 1999.

Fields, Albert Actor; appeared on the *Mickey Mouse Club* on The Disney Channel beginning in 1989, and was a member of the pop band The Party.

Fields, Bonnie Lynn (1944–2012) Mouseketeer from the 1950s *Mickey Mouse Club* TV show.

Fiesta Fun Center Large game and activity area in the Contemporary Resort at Walt Disney World; opened in 1973. It was originally built as a convention exhibit space, the Sunshine State Exhibitorium, but the demand for more evening entertainment facilities necessitated the building of the Fiesta Fun Center. Its video games, air hockey, snack bar, and other amusements seemed to be always popular. A theater in one corner of the room featured screenings of Disney films. Later known as the Food and Fun Center. It closed in 2007 to make room for The Wave.

Fife and Drum Refreshments Liberty Square snack bar in the Magic Kingdom at Walt Disney World; open ca. 1972–ca. 1985. Also known as The Fife and Drum. On Nov. 12, 2007, an outdoor snack kiosk, Fife & Drum Tavern, opened at The American Adventure in EPCOT.

Fifi Mischievous little brown dog with black ears who often played Pluto's girlfriend; appeared in 5 cartoons, beginning with *Puppy Love* (1933).

Fifth Estate, The (film) Based on real events, the film depicts the explosive news leaks and trafficking of classified information that turned an Internet upstart into the 21st century's most fiercely debated organization. WikiLeaks founder Julian Assange and his colleague Daniel Domscheit-Berg team up to create a platform that allows whistle-blowers to anonymously leak covert data, which leads to this question: What are the costs of keeping secrets in a free society—and what are the costs of exposing them? Directed by Bill Condon. Released Oct. 18, 2013, after an Oct. 11 release in the United Kingdom. Stars Benedict Cumberbatch (Julian Assange), Daniel Brühl (Daniel Domscheit-Berg), Anthony Mackie (Sam Colson), David Thewlis (Nick Davies), Stanley Tucci (James Boswell), Laura Linney (Sarah Shaw). 128 min. A DreamWorks film, released by Touchstone.

Fifth Freedom Mural Artwork at the exit of Great Moments with Mr. Lincoln in Disneyland. At 53 feet long, it attempts to depict some of the people who rose to greatness through the 5th freedom, that of free enterprise, including Walt Disney himself.

50's Prime Time Café Restaurant in Disney's Hollywood Studios; opened May 1, 1989. Guests sit around breakfast room Formica-topped tables, with a TV set playing clips from 1950s situation comedies, as "Mom" and the extended family serve wholesome American fare. Memorabilia from the 1950s fills the shelves.

50 Happy Years Yearlong salute to the 50th anniversary of Walt Disney Productions. Began Jan. 1, 1973, with a Disney parade float in the Pasadena Tournament of Roses, and concluded Jan. 1, 1974, with an homage to Disney at the Orange Bowl in Miami. There were parades and entertainment events at Disneyland and Walt Disney World; a tie-in at the *Disney on Parade* traveling arena show; a Walt Disney 50th Anniversary Film Retrospective at the Lincoln Center for the Performing Arts (Jun. 9–Aug. 4, 1973) in New York; commemorative merchandise sold, including a *50 Happy Years of Disney Favorites* album; and a Disney preshow and float in the Macy's Thanksgiving Day Parade (in New York). In addition, a show aired on *The Wonderful World of Disney* Jan. 21, 1973, paying a 50th-anniversary tribute to the Disney company, featuring a history of the Disney Studio and film clips from the 1920s up to its then latest release, *Robin Hood*. Narrated by Danny Dark.

Fifty Happy Years (TV) SEE PRECEDING ENTRY.

Figaro Endearing kitten co-star of *Pinocchio*, who went on to have his own short series of cartoons, making a total of 7 additional appearances.

Figaro and Cleo (film) Figaro cartoon released Oct. 15, 1943. Directed by Jack Kinney. Figaro tries various methods to catch Cleo, the goldfish, but is scolded for his efforts. When Cleo's bowl accidentally falls on Figaro's head, his owner momentarily thinks he has drowned and pampers him. Figaro and Cleo eventually become friends.

Figaro and Frankie (film) Figaro cartoon released May 30, 1947. Directed by Charles Nichols. Though Frankie, the canary, becomes quite an annoyance with his singing and birdseed shooting, Figaro must save him from the jaws of Butch, the bulldog.

Figaro's Clothiers Elegant apparel shop in Mediterranean Harbor at Tokyo DisneySea; opened Sep. 4, 2001. Named after the protagonist of the opera *The Barber of Seville*. Disney characters dressed as famous icons from the opera to welcome guests.

Fight, The (film) Educational film about how to solve problems peaceably, from the What Should I Do? series; released in Aug. 1969.

Fighting Choice, A (TV) A 2-hour movie that aired Apr. 13, 1986. Directed by Ferdinand Fairfax. A teenager, Kellin Taylor, suffering from epilepsy, which seems to be getting worse, wants a serious brain operation, but his parents are afraid of the possible consequences. Kellin has to go to court to get his parents to agree. Stars Beau Bridges, Karen Valentine, Patrick Dempsey, Lawrence Pressman, Frances Lee McCain, Danielle Von Zerneck.

Fighting Prince of Donegal, The (film) In the time of Queen Elizabeth I, the English fear that Spain will attack through Ireland, so English troops occupy the Irish countryside. It is a gallant young man, Hugh O'Donnell, the prince of Donegal, who leads resistance against them. Hugh has many exciting adventures while he is uniting the clans of Ireland. He is captured and imprisoned—twice. But he escapes again to lead and win the final battle against the English, and to rescue Kathleen, his ladylove. Released Oct. 1, 1966. Directed by Michael O'Herlihy. 110 min. Stars Peter McEnery (Hugh O'Donnell), Susan Hampshire (Kathleen MacSweeney), Tom Adams (Henry O'Neill), Gordon Jackson (Capt. Leeds), Andrew Keir (Lord MacSweeney), Donal McCann (Sean O'Toole), Maurice Roeves (Martin), Richard Leech (O'Neill). This was the first live-action theatrical swashbuckler Disney had made since *Kidnapped,* in 1960, and it sparkles with the exuberant talents of its 2 leads and the guidance of first-time theatrical director O'Herlihy. A fictional story—but based on the authentic exploits of the real Prince of Donegal, Red Hugh, as told in a book by Robert T. Reilly.

Figment Curious small purple dragon who, along with the Dreamfinder, hosted the Journey Into Imagination pavilion in EPCOT Center, 1982–1998. Originally voiced by Billy Barty. He returned in 2002 with a new attraction, Journey Into Imagination With Figment.

Fillmore, Disney's (TV) Animated series; premiered Sep. 14, 2002, as part of ABC Kids. Middle school safety patrol officer Cornelius Fillmore is a former delinquent who has turned his life around, and he is making up for his shady past by helping others. Voices include Orlando Brown (Cornelius Fillmore), Tara Strong (Ingrid Third), Horatio Sanz (Commissioner Vallejo), Kyle Sullivan (Danny O'Farrell). 26 episodes.

Filming Nature's Mysteries (film) Educational film taken primarily from the TV show *Searching* *for Nature's Mysteries*; released in Jul. 1976. Shows how filmmakers capture the miracles of nature, with microphotography, time-lapse, stop-action, and underwater photography.

Finch, Peter (1916–1977) Actor; appeared in *The Story of Robin Hood* (Sheriff of Nottingham) and *Kidnapped* (Alan Breck Stewart).

Finding Dory (film) Animated feature from Pixar Animation Studios. Living happily in the reef with Marlin and Nemo, forgetful blue tang Dory suddenly remembers that she has a family out there that may be looking for her. The trio takes off on a life-changing adventure across the ocean to California's prestigious Marine Life Institute, a sea life rehabilitation center and aquarium. In an effort to find her parents, Dory enlists the help of three of the institute's most intriguing residents: Hank, a cantankerous octopus; Bailey, a beluga whale; and Destiny, a nearsighted whale shark. Deftly navigating the complex inner workings of the institute, they discover the magic within their flaws, friendships, and family. Directed by Andrew Stanton. Released Jun. 17, 2016, also in 3-D and IMAX. Voices include Ellen DeGeneres (Dory), Albert Brooks (Marlin), Ed O'Neill (Hank), Kaitlin Olson (Destiny), Ty Burrell (Bailey), Eugene Levy (Charlie), Diane Keaton (Jenny), Hayden Rolence (Nemo). 97 min. The story takes place a year after the events of *Finding Nemo*.

Finding Nemo (film) Animated feature from Pixar Animation Studios. Nemo, a 6-year-old clownfish, is tragically stolen away from the safety of his undersea home at the Great Barrier Reef, ending up in a dentist's office fish tank overlooking Sydney harbor. His timid father, Marlin, launches a search to find and rescue him, accompanied by a forgetful Good Samaritan, a regal blue tang fish named Dory. Meanwhile, Nemo is hatching a few daring plans of his own to return safely home. Directed by Andrew Stanton. Released May 30, 2003. Voices include Alexander Gould (Nemo), Albert Brooks (Marlin), Ellen DeGeneres (Dory), Willem Dafoe (Gill), Brad Garrett (Bloat), Austin Pendleton (Gurgle), Vicki Lewis (Deb/Flo), Geoffrey Rush (Nigel), Allison Janney (Peach), John Ratzenberger (Moonfish), Barry Humphries (Bruce). 100 min. All the animation was done at the Pixar Animation Studios in Emeryville, California. Released with Pixar's 4-min. short *Knick Knack*. The film set a Disney record for an opening weekend, with a gross of $70.2 million, eventually becoming the highest-grossing animated film of all time during its release, with over $339 million, and the box office champ for 2003. It won the Academy Award for Best Animated Feature, as well as 3 other nominations (Original Screenplay, Original Score, and Sound Editing). A 3-D version of the film was released on Sep. 14, 2012.

Finding Nemo Submarine Voyage Tomorrowland attraction in Disneyland; opened Jun. 11, 2007. It replaced the original Submarine Voyage (1959–1998). Guests board a yellow research submarine operated by the Nautical Exploration and Marine Observation Institute (N.E.M.O.) and follow Dory, Marlin, and the rest of the gang from *Finding Nemo* in an undersea adventure, thanks to a new generation of imaging technology.

Finding Nemo: The Big Blue . . . and Beyond! SEE NEXT ENTRY.

Finding Nemo—The Musical Broadway-style stage show in the newly enclosed Theater in the Wild at Disney's Animal Kingdom, with spectacular scenery and elaborate puppetry. The overly cautious father clownfish, Marlin, along with his absent-minded friend, Dory, swim with the sharks and take on the jellyfish as they make a heroic effort to rescue Nemo. Previews began Nov. 5, 2006, with a grand opening Jan. 2007. The first collaboration between Walt Disney Imagineering and Pixar to create an original musical based on a Pixar animated feature. Songs by Robert Lopez and Kristen Anderson-Lopez, who went on to write songs for *Winnie the Pooh* (2011), *Frozen*, and *Coco*. Performances ended Mar. 15, 2020, and a revised production, *Finding Nemo: The Big Blue . . . and Beyond!*, debuted Jun. 13, 2022. In the new show, the fish from Dr. P. Sherman's office tell the story of Nemo with many of the songs from the original production, plus a new custom LED video wall and set pieces inspired by 3-D cut paper art.

Finest Hours, The (film) In Feb. of 1952, one of the worst storms to ever hit the East Coast struck New England, damaging ships off the coast of Cape Cod and literally ripping the SS *Pendleton*, an oil tanker bound for Boston, in half. On a small wooden lifeboat faced with frigid temperatures and 70-ft.-high waves, 4 members of the Coast Guard led by Captain Bernie Webber bravely set out to rescue the more than 30 stranded sailors trapped aboard the rapidly sinking vessel. Directed by Craig Gillespie. Released Jan. 29, 2016, and also in 3-D and IMAX, after a Jan. 21 release in Israel. Stars Chris Pine (Bernie Webber), Holliday Grainger (Miriam), Eric Bana (Daniel Cluff), Ben Foster (Richard Livesey), Casey Affleck (Ray Sybert), John Ortiz (Wallace Quirey). Based on a true story, as published in a 2009 book of the same title by Casey Sherman and Michael J. Tougias, and on interviews conducted by the screenwriters of survivors. 117 min. Filmed in wide-screen.

Fire Birds (film) Jake Preston and Billie Lee Guthrie are pilots in an elite army helicopter task force, flying the high-tech Apache helicopter, the army's most advanced flying fighting machine. Just how far the choppers and their crew can go is put to the test when the Apache task force is assigned to complete a secret mission in Latin America. Infiltrating hostile territory to do combat with an international enemy, the seemingly fearless flyers soon discover they are fighting a desperate war both on the ground and in the sky. Released May 25, 1990. Directed by David Green. A Touchstone film. 86 min. Stars Nicolas Cage (Jake Preston), Tommy Lee Jones (Brad Little), Sean Young (Billie Lee Guthrie), Bryan Kestner (Breaker). Featured the Apache helicopter, also known as the AH-64A, a $10 million high-tech attack helicopter with a 1700-horsepower engine. Filmed on location in Texas and Arizona.

Fire Called Jeremiah, A (TV) Show aired Dec. 3, 1961. Produced by James Algar. This is the story of the "smoke jumpers," specially trained by the Forest Service to reach forest fires when they are in the inaccessible areas of our national forests. Scanning their assigned areas from patrolling planes and lookout towers, they are able to set in motion the operation that converges on the hot spots before they grow into disastrous firestorms that destroy vital watersheds. In one such incident, a small blaze spotted from a fire lookout tower grows ominously and soon turns into a conflagration. The fire changes course and threatens the fire tower itself, and a lookout has to be rescued by helicopter. Stars (all playing themselves) Cliff Blake, Carole Stockner, Roy Carpenter. Released theatrically abroad.

Fire Chief (film) Donald Duck cartoon released Dec. 13, 1940. Directed by Jack King. Fire Chief Donald accidentally sets fire to his own station house. By not listening to his nephews, he attaches the water hose to the gasoline supply and totally incinerates the firehouse, fire truck, and even his fire helmet.

Fire Fighters, The (film) Mickey Mouse cartoon released Jun. 25, 1930. Directed by Burt Gillett. Fire Chief Mickey saves Minnie from her burning house after a series of episodes involving the firehouse and answering the alarm.

Fire on Kelly Mountain (TV) Show aired Sep. 30, 1973. Directed by Robert Clouse. A Forest Service fire lookout gets his wish when he wants to fight fires, for he is sent to check out a blaze, but the fire he finds almost gets the best of him. He also has problems with an enraged bear that has been spooked by the fire. Stars Andrew Duggan, Larry Wilcox, Anne Lockhart, Noam Pitlik, Ted Hartley.

Fire Station Site on Town Square in Disneyland from opening day, where a fire wagon and other firefighting memorabilia are on display. Walt Disney had a small apartment upstairs where he could relax and entertain friends and family members while on visits to the park. It consisted of a large sitting room, with built-in sofas that could be pulled out as beds, a small dressing room, and a bathroom. Many of the furnishings were antiques that had been personally selected by Mrs. Disney. An alcove contained a small sink and a refrigerator. At one time the fire pole from the fire station extended up into the apartment, but it was blocked off after someone climbed up the pole into the apartment. The apartment has been maintained and is still occasionally used by Disney executives. In 1971, a fire station (also known as Engine Co. 71) opened in the Magic Kingdom at Walt Disney World; a highlight is the display of fire department patches contributed by firefighters from across the country. Similar stations are also in Disneyland Paris and Hong Kong Disneyland.

Fire Station, The (film) Educational film in which Mickey tours a fire station. From the Mickey's Field Trips series; released in Sep. 1987. 12 min.

Fire Truck Main Street, U.S.A. vehicle in Disneyland; began operating Aug. 16, 1958. Also in the Magic Kingdom at Walt Disney World, Oct. 1, 1971; in World Bazaar in Tokyo Disneyland, Apr. 15, 1983; and in Disneyland Paris, Apr. 12, 1992.

Fire Wagon Horse-drawn Main Street, U.S.A. vehicle at Disneyland; began Jul. 17, 1955, and operated until 1960. It is now on display in the fire station on Town Square.

Firebuds (TV) Animated comedy-adventure series

on Disney Junior; premiered Sep. 21, 2022, on Disney Junior, Disney Channel, and Disney+. In a fantastical world where talking vehicles live, work, and play with the humans who drive them, a boy and his fire truck team up with their first responder friends to help others in their community with problems, both big and small. Voices include Declan Whaley (Bo), Terrence Little Gardenhigh (Flash), Vivian Vencer (Violet), Lily Sanfelippo (Axl), JeCobi Swain (Jayden), Caleb Paddock (Piston). From Disney Television Animation and Electric Emu.

Firehouse Five Plus Two Dixieland jazz group composed of Disney Studio personnel; evolved from bands created to play in camp shows during World War II. Led by Ward Kimball, the group appeared on TV in *At Home with Donald Duck*, *The Disneyland Tenth Anniversary Show*, and the *Mickey Mouse Club (Fun with Music Day)*, and sometimes performed at Disneyland. Other members included George Probert, Frank Thomas, Harper Goff, and Eddie Forrest. The group was caricatured in the Goofy cartoon *How to Dance*. They had a catalog of a number of phonograph records on the Good Time Jazz label. The group was disbanded in 1971. There was a tribute to it in *The Princess and the Frog*, with Louis the alligator playing in a band named the "Firefly Five Plus Lou."

Firelight (film) Beautiful but poor Swiss governess Elisabeth meets secretly in 1837 with an English landowner, Charles Godwin, to conceive a child in exchange for money. Seven years later, the 2 are drawn together again when Elisabeth joins Charles's forlorn household, Selcombe Place in the Sussex countryside, as governess to Louisa. Sworn to secrecy, Elisabeth must now hide her passionate feelings for the man she loves and the child she brought into the world. A Hollywood Pictures film. Released on a limited basis on Sep. 4, 1998. Directed by William Nicholson. Stars Sophie Marceau (Elisabeth), Stephen Dillane (Charles Godwin), Dominique Belcourt (Louisa), Kevin Anderson (John Taylor), Lia Williams (Constance), Joss Ackland (Lord Clare). CinemaScope. 104 min. Firle Place in the south of England became Selcombe Place, and the surrounding farmlands and village church became primary locations for the film.

Fireworks Factory, The American barbecue restaurant in Pleasure Island at Walt Disney World; opened May 1, 1989. Operated by Levy Restaurants. According to the story, fireworks were once manufactured in the facility. Closed Sep. 7, 1997, and succeeded by Wildhorse Saloon.

First Aiders (film) Pluto cartoon released Sep. 22, 1944. Directed by Charles Nichols. Minnie practices first aid on Pluto, but, being heckled by Figaro, he gives chase which results in both falling downstairs. Minnie rushes to their aid and encourages Pluto and Figaro to make up.

First Americans, The (TV) Serial on the *Mickey Mouse Club* during the 1956–1957 season, hosted by Tony Nakina and Iron Eyes Cody. Tells stories about Indigenous peoples of America. 4 episodes.

First Kid (film) Sam Simms is a Secret Service agent whose sense of style keeps him off the elite force assigned to protect "The Eagle," the president of the U.S. When the president's teenage son, Luke, makes the nightly news mooning a mall opening crowd, Simms is assigned to look after "The Prince." Going through adolescence in the White House is not easy, but Simms helps Luke through many of his youthful skirmishes and together they even foil a threat to the first family's security. A Hollywood Pictures film in association with Caravan Pictures. Released Aug. 30, 1996. Directed by David Mickey Evans. Stars Sinbad (Simms), Robert Guillaume (Wilkes), Timothy Busfield (Woods), Brock Pierce (Luke), James Naughton (President Davenport), Art LaFleur (Morton), Linda Eichhorn (Linda Davenport), Bill Cobbs (Speed), Zachery Ty Bryan (Rob). 101 min. Most of the film was shot in and around Richmond, Virginia, including St. Catherine's School, though exteriors of the landmarks such as the Washington Monument, the Mall, and the Treasury Building were shot in Washington, D.C. Special sets had to be constructed of the Executive Residence and the Oval Office, since filming at the White House was not possible. Retired assistant director of the Secret Service, Bob Snow, served as technical adviser.

First Order Cargo Shop in Star Wars: Galaxy's Edge; opened May 31, 2019, in Disneyland and Aug. 29, 2019, in Disney's Hollywood Studios at Walt Disney World. Inside Docking Bay 9, visitors can browse gear and other products to show their support for the First Order.

Firth, Peter Actor; appeared in *Mighty Joe Young*

(Garth), *Pearl Harbor* (Captain of *West Virginia*), and *The Greatest Game Ever Played* (Lord Northcliffe), and on TV in *Diamonds on Wheels*. He voiced Red in *The Rescuers Down Under*. Known for playing the lead in *Equus*.

Fischinger, Oskar (1900–1967) Experimental animator at the Disney Studio in 1938–1939, during which time he contributed to the "Toccata and Fugue in D Minor" segment of *Fantasia*.

Fish Hooks (TV) Animated series on Disney Channel; premiered Sep. 24, 2010. Created by children's book author and illustrator Noah Z. Jones, the series revolves around 3 tweens, Bea, Milo, and Oscar, as they navigate the choppy waters of high school . . . and they just happen to be fish. Voices include Chelsea Kane (Bea), Kyle Massey (Milo), Justin Roiland (Oscar). From Disney Television Animation.

Fishburne, Laurence Actor; appeared in *What's Love Got to Do with It* (Ike Turner), *Bad Company* (Nelson Crowe), and *Ant-Man and the Wasp* (Dr. Bill Foster), and on TV in *black-ish* and *grown-ish* (Pops). He exec. produced and voiced The Beyonder/Backstory Man in *Marvel's Moon Girl and Devil Dinosaur*.

Fisher, Carrie (1956–2016) Actress; appeared as Leia Organa in the *Star Wars* films and on TV as Franny Jessup in *Sunday Drive*. She was named a Disney Legend in 2017.

Fisher, Isla Actress; appeared in *Confessions of a Shopaholic* (Rebecca Bloomwood) and on Disney+ in *Godmothered* (Mackenzie). She voiced Button in *Sofia the First*.

Fisher, Jordan Actor/singer; appeared on TV in *The Secret Life of the American Teenager* (Jacob), on Disney Channel in *Liv and Maddie* (Holden Dippledorf) and as Seacat in *Teen Beach Movie* and *Teen Beach 2*, and on Disney+ in *High School Musical: The Musical: The Series* (Jamie). He voiced Robaire (4*Town) in *Turning Red* and Dan G'vash in *Star Wars: Visions*. He performed on TV in *The Wonderful World of Disney: Magical Holiday Celebration*, the *Radio Disney Music Awards*, and *The Disney Family Singalong*, hosted *Decorating Disney: Holiday Magic* and the *Disney Parks Magical Christmas Day Parade*, and performed the end-credits song in *Moana* ("You're Welcome") and the title song for the *Happily Ever After* fire-

works show in the Magic Kingdom at Walt Disney World.

Fishin' Around (film) Mickey Mouse cartoon released Sep. 25, 1931. Directed by Burt Gillett. In one of his most mischievous adventures, Mickey, along with Pluto, fishes in a forbidden area and becomes frustrated with the taunting fish until the sheriff chases them away.

Fit to Be You: Flexibility and Body Composition (film) Educational film; released in Sep. 1980. The film explains the relationship of body mass to body fat and stresses the importance of exercise.

Fit to Be You: Heart-Lungs (film) Educational film; released in Sep. 1980. Shows the function of the heart and lungs, and how they perform more effectively if one follows planned, continuous exercise programs.

Fit to Be You: Muscles (film) Educational film; released in Sep. 1980. Shows students the importance of developing the strength and endurance of their muscles.

Fitness and Me (film) Series of 3 educational films; released in Mar. 1984: *How to Exercise, What Is Fitness Exercise, Why Exercise?*

Fitness for Living (film) Series of 3 educational films; released in Sep. 1982: *What Is Physical Fitness?, How to Get Fit, Measuring Up*.

Fitness Fun with Goofy (film) Educational film release in 16 mm in Mar. 1991. 19 min. Sport Goofy takes the class through a complete workout that includes both warm-up and cool-down exercises, illustrating them with clips from Disney films.

Fittings & Fairings, Clothes & Notions Nautical-themed shop in Disney's Yacht Club Resort at Walt Disney World; open Nov. 5, 1990–Apr. 16, 2017. It became The Market at Ale & Compass.

Fitzgerald, Tom Imagineer; he joined WED Enterprises in 1979, and supervised story development and production of many of Disney's most popular park attractions and shows. In 1989, he was made exec. producer of Theme Park Productions, which provides conceptual development, production, and postproduction of film and video presentations for the Disney parks. In 2001 he was given the added responsibility of exec. vice president and senior creative executive for Walt Disney Imagineering, being responsible for the creative direction of the Disneyland Resort and Disneyland Paris. In 2014, he began leading the creative direction for EPCOT and Disneyland Paris.

Fitzpatrick, Robert President of Euro Disney 1987–1993. Formerly president of the California Institute of the Arts.

Five Days at Memorial (TV) Limited drama series; digitally released Aug. 12–Sep. 16, 2022, on Apple TV+. Chronicles the first 5 days in a New Orleans hospital after Hurricane Katrina made landfall. When the floodwaters rose, the power failed, the heat climbed, and exhausted caregivers were forced to make life-and-death decisions that haunted them for years to come. Based on the book by Sheri Fink. From ABC Signature.

5 Keys, The Set of service standards established at Disneyland ca. 1962, originally as the Four Keys to Guest Happiness, as operational criteria for Cast Members to ensure consistent quality service. The Four Keys were originally Safety, Courtesy, Show, and Capacity (later became Efficiency) and were extended to the other Disney parks as they opened. In 2020, a fifth key, Inclusion, was added.

Five Mile Creek (TV) Series on The Disney Channel, based on a book by Louis L'Amour. An isolated coach stop run by 2 women on a stage line between the harbor town of Port Nelson and the mining camp of Wilga in Australia at the time of the 1860s gold rush is the setting for this adventure series. Debuted on Nov. 4, 1983, and continued, with repeats, until Jun. 14, 1987. Stars Louise Caire Clark, Rod Mullinar, Jay Kerr, Liz Burch, Michael Caton, Priscilla Weems. Filmed on location 40 miles north of Sydney. 39 episodes. The pilot for *Five Mile Creek* aired on the Disney CBS series Nov. 28, 1981, as *The Cherokee Trail*. That film was set at Cherokee Station, in the heart of the Colorado wilderness. When producer Doug Netter got the go-ahead for a series, he transplanted the locale to Australia. Over 500 hours of in-depth research ensured accuracy in all phases of the production, from the choice of locations to the construction of the stagecoaches and sets, to the dialogue spoken by the characters.

Fix, The (TV) Legal drama on ABC; aired Mar. 18–May 20, 2019. Maya Travis, an L.A. district attorney, suffers a devastating defeat when prosecuting an A-list actor for double murder. With her high-profile career derailed, she flees for a quieter life in Washington State. Eight years later, when this same celebrity is under suspicion for another murder, Maya is lured back to the DA's office for another chance at justice. Stars Robin Tunney (Maya Travis), Adam Rayner (Matthew Collier), Merrin Dungey (CJ), Breckin Meyer (Alan Wiest), Marc Blucas (Riv), Mouzam Makkar (Loni Kampoor), Alex Saxon (Gabriel Johnson), Scott Cohen (Ezra Wolf), Adewale Akinnuoye-Agbaje (Sevvy Johnson). From Mandeville TV and ABC Studios.

Fix-It Felix Jr. The 8-bit video game "good guy" in *Wreck-It Ralph*; voiced by Jack McBrayer.

Fjording, The Shop in Norway in EPCOT; opened May 6, 1988. The ambience is of the old wharf-side area of Bergen, with the name inspired by the Fjord horse.

Flagler's Restaurant on the 2nd floor in Disney's Grand Floridian Resort & Spa at Walt Disney World; opened Jun. 28, 1988. Featured Italian and continental cuisine. It closed Jul. 6, 1997, and became Cítricos on Nov. 8.

Flame Tree Barbecue Counter-service restaurant on Discovery Island in Disney's Animal Kingdom; opened Apr. 22, 1998. Each dining pavilion depicts a predator hunting its prey.

Flamingo Crossings A 450-acre lodging and shopping district on Walt Disney World property near State Road 429 and Western Way. Parcels of land are offered for sale to developers, though remaining within the Reedy Creek Improvement District, to build value-oriented hotels and motels, along with shops and casual restaurants. Announced in 2007 but delayed, with the groundbreaking held in 2014 for the first 2 hotels (TownePlace Suites and SpringHill Suites), which would open Feb. 12, 2016. Additional hotels opened Dec. 2020 (Home2 Suites by Hilton) and in 2021 (Homewood Suites by Hilton, Residence Inn by Marriott, and Fairfield Inn by Marriott). Flamingo Crossings Village, an apartment community designed for Walt Disney World College Program students, began leasing to Disney Cast Members and operating participants Dec. 21, 2020, and the first College Program participants were welcomed Jun. 15, 2021. A freestanding emergency room was also announced.

Flannery Stationmaster in *Pigs Is Pigs* (1954).

Flash (TV) A 2-hour movie on *The Wonderful World of Disney*; first aired Dec. 21, 1997. The prized possession of the teenaged Connor is his 2-year-old horse, Flash. When hard times force his father to join the merchant marine and go off to sea, and Connor's grandmother dies, Flash must be sold. Working as a stableboy, Connor sees firsthand how the new owner abuses and mistreats his beloved horse. Connor decides to rescue Flash, and together they begin a perilous ride across the country in search of Connor's father. Directed by Simon Wincer. Stars Lucas Black (Connor), Brian Kerwin (David Strong), Shawn Toovey (Tad Rutherford), Tom Nowicki (Alfred Rutherford), Ellen Burstyn (Laura Strong).

Flash Impossibly slow sloth working at the Department of Mammal Vehicles in *Zootopia*; voiced by Raymond Persi.

Flash Forward (TV) Series on The Disney Channel, beginning Jan. 5, 1997, after a 10-episode marathon on New Year's Day. Becca Fisher and Tucker James are lifelong friends. They have the same birthday, they were raised next door to one another, and they shared many of the same experiences. But when they hit the teen years, they find themselves coping with a landslide of changes that occur within and around them. Stars Jewel Staite (Becca), Ben Foster (Tucker), Theodore Borders (Miles Vaughn), Asia Vieira (Chris).

Flash, the Teen-age Otter (TV) Show aired Apr. 30, 1961. Directed by Hank Schloss. An otter battles nature and humans, trying to live in a safe environment. Narrated by Winston Hibler.

FlashForward (TV) Series on ABC; aired Sep. 24, 2009–May 27, 2010. A mysterious event causes the entire world to black out for 137 sec., causing mayhem but also giving everybody an unnerving glimpse of the future exactly 6 months ahead. FBI agent Mark Benford leads an investigation as to what might have caused this. Stars Joseph Fiennes (Mark Benford), John Cho (Demitri Noh), Jack Davenport (Lloyd Simcoe), Sonya Walger (Olivia Benford), Courtney B. Vance (Stanford Wedeck), Brian O'Byrne (Aaron Stark), Christine Woods (Janis Hawk), Zachary Knighton (Bryce Varley), Peyton List (Nicole Kirby), Dominic Monaghan (Simon). From HBO Entertainment and ABC Studios.

Fleischer, Charles Actor/comedian; voiced Roger Rabbit (as well as Benny the Cab, Greasy, and Psycho) in *Who Framed Roger Rabbit* and other appearances of the character. He had roles in *Gross Anatomy* (lecturing professor), *Dick Tracy* (reporter), and *Straight Talk* (Tony). Also appeared on TV in *Disneyland's 35th Anniversary Celebration* and *Mickey's 60th Birthday*, on Disney Channel in *Genius* (Dr. Krickstein), and on Disney+ in *Prop Culture*.

Fleischer, Richard (1916–2006) Son of animation pioneer Max Fleischer, he was selected by Walt Disney to direct *20,000 Leagues Under the Sea*. He was named a Disney Legend in 2003.

Fleishman Is In Trouble (TV) Divorce saga miniseries on Hulu; digitally released Nov. 17–Dec. 29, 2022. The recently divorced, 41-year-old Toby Fleishman dives into the brave new world of app-based dating with the kind of success he never had dating in his youth, before he got married at the tail end of medical school. But when his ex-wife, Rachel, disappears, he is left with 11-year-old Hannah and 9-year-old Solly . . . and no hint of where Rachel is or whether she plans to return. As he balances parenting, he realizes that he'll never be able to figure out what happened to Rachel until he can finally face what happened to their marriage in the first place. Stars Jesse Eisenberg (Toby), Lizzy Caplan (Libby), Adam Brody (Seth), Claire Danes (Rachel), Meara Mahoney Gross (Hannah), Maxim Swinton (Solly). Based on the novel by Taffy Brodesser-Akner. From ABC Signature and FX Productions.

Flight! (film) Educational film; released in Sep. 1985. An innovative discussion of the principles of aerodynamics.

Flight Circle Tomorrowland area in Disneyland; open 1955–1966. Also known as Thimble Drome Flight Circle. Model airplanes were demonstrated here to the enjoyment of kids, but the noise was awesome. At one time, a spaceman in an experimental rocket pack would take off from here and fly around Tomorrowland.

Flight of the Grey Wolf, The (TV) Two-part show; aired Mar. 14 and 21, 1976. Directed by Frank Zuniga. A pet wolf leads to problems for a teenager, Russ Hanson, when the local populace fears it has attacked a girl. Russ realizes the wolf must be returned to the wild, and he tries to teach it how to survive on its own, but only after it meets a female wolf does it start acting like a wolf. Stars Jeff East, Bill Williams, Barbara Hale, William Bryant, Eric Server, Judson Pratt.

Flight of the Navigator (film) A boy goes out into the woods one evening, has a fall, and when he gets up and returns to his house, he discovers his family no longer lives there. It is 8 years later, and everyone has aged except the boy. Eventually it turns out that he had been on a spaceship, helping an alien to navigate it. Released Jul. 30, 1986. Directed by Randal Kleiser. 89 min. Stars Joey Cramer (David Freeman), Cliff De Young (Bill Freeman), Sarah Jessica Parker (Carolyn McAdams). Paul Reubens (credited as Paul Mall) voiced MAX, the ship's computer. Advanced special effects included the first use of image-based lighting. Filmed on location in Broward County, Florida, with some filming also taking place in Norway.

Flight of the White Stallions (TV) Title of *The Miracle of the White Stallions.*

Flight to the Moon Tomorrowland attraction in Disneyland, sponsored by McDonnell Douglas; open Aug. 12, 1967–Jan. 5, 1975, replacing Rocket to the Moon. Also in the Magic Kingdom at Walt Disney World; open Dec. 24, 1971–Apr. 15, 1975. Visitors first entered Mission Control, where director Tom Morrow described the spaceport operations, and then proceeded into a "lunar transport" where they were seated for a simulated trip to the Moon. The attraction was replaced by Mission to Mars in both parks.

Flightplan (film) Flying at 40,000 feet in a cavernous aircraft, Kyle Pratt faces every mother's worst nightmare when her 6-year-old daughter, Julia, vanishes without a trace mid-flight from Berlin to New York City. Already emotionally devastated by the unexpected death of her husband, Kyle desperately struggles to prove her sanity to the disbelieving flight crew and passengers while facing the very real possibility that she may be losing her mind. While neither Captain Rich nor Air Marshal Gene Carson want to doubt the bereaved widow, all evidence indicates that her daughter was never on board, resulting in paranoia and doubt among the passengers and crew of the plane. Finding herself desperately alone, Kyle can only rely on her own wits to solve the mystery and save her daughter. A Touchstone film, with Imagine Entertainment. Directed by Robert Schwentke. Released Sep. 23, 2005. Stars Jodie Foster (Kyle Pratt), Peter Sarsgaard

(Gene Carson), Sean Bean (Captain Rich), Erika Christensen (Fiona), Marlene Lawston (Julia), Kate Beahan (Stephanie), Michael Irby (Obaid), Brent Sexton (Elias), Judith Scott (Estella). 98 min. Filmed in Super 35-Scope. The fictional plane, Alto Air's E-474 Jumbo Jet, seating more than 700 passengers, was conceived by Brian Grazer and Robert Schwentke. Released on DVD in 2006.

Flights of Fantasy Parade At Disneyland Jun. 18– Sep. 10, 1983, commemorating the opening of the New Fantasyland. Featured enormous inflatable characters.

Flights of Wonder Educational show featuring colorful birds in Asia at Disney's Animal Kingdom; opened Apr. 22, 1998, on the Caravan Stage. It closed Dec. 31, 2017, and was succeeded by *UP! A Great Bird Adventure* in 2018. A new show, *Feathered Friends in Flight*, debuted Jul. 7, 2020.

Flik Lead character, a worker ant, in *A Bug's Life*; voiced by Dave Foley.

Flik's Fun Fair Area in A Bug's Land in Disney California Adventure; open Oct. 7, 2002–Sep. 4, 2018. Guests entered through a fallen cereal box for a closer look into the world of bugs as seen from an insect's perspective. The attractions were Flik's Flyers, Tuck & Roll's Drive 'em Buggies, Heimlich's Chew Chew Train, Francis's Ladybug Boogie, and Princess Dot Puddle Park. The area was replaced by Avengers Campus.

Flintheart Glomgold Second-richest duck in the world, after Uncle Scrooge, and thus his longtime rival, in the comics and *DuckTales*. He was created by Carl Barks and made his debut in *Uncle Scrooge* No. 15 in 1956.

Float (film) Animated short; digitally released Nov. 12, 2019, on Disney+. A father discovers that his son is different from other kids in the most unusual way. Dad keeps his son out of sight, but when his son's ability becomes public, he must decide whether to run and hide or to accept his son as he is. Directed by Bobby Rubio. 7 min. From the Pixar Animation Studios SparkShorts program.

Flora Good fairy leader in *Sleeping Beauty* who wore reds; voiced by Verna Felton.

Flora & Ulysses (film) Comedy adventure about 10-year-old Flora, an avid comic book fan and self-avowed cynic whose parents have recently separated. After rescuing a squirrel she names Ulysses, Flora is amazed to discover he possesses unique superhero powers which take them on an adventure of humorous complications that ultimately change Flora's life—and her outlook—forever. Digitally released Feb. 19, 2021, on Disney+. Directed by Lena Khan. Stars Matilda Lawler (Flora), Alyson Hannigan (Phyllis), Ben Schwartz (George), Anna Deavere Smith (Dr. Meescham), Danny Pudi (Miller), Benjamin Evans Ainsworth (William), Janeane Garofalo (Marissa), Kate Micucci (Rita). 91 min. Based on the novel by Kate DiCamillo. After evaluating 200+ species of squirrels, filmmakers decided to fashion Ulysses after the Eurasian red squirrel but scaled him up so he would be comparable in size to an Eastern gray squirrel, common to North America. Filmed in wide-screen format in Vancouver.

Florez, Angel (1963–2006) Mouseketeer on the new *Mickey Mouse Club*. He also appeared in later years as a parade performer at Disneyland.

Florida Film (film) Informal title for the film in which Walt Disney details preliminary plans for the "Florida Project," later known as Walt Disney World. Includes an animated presentation of EPCOT, the city. Walt filmed 2 endings—one for the people of Florida and the other for leaders of American industry. Walt's on-screen segments were shot on Stage 1 at the Disney Studio Oct. 27, 1966, marking his final film. First screened Feb. 2, 1967, for Florida legislators and civic/industrial leaders in Winter Park, Florida, airing later that day on statewide TV. Written by Marty Sklar. Sometimes called the "EPCOT Film." 24 min.

Florida's Disney Decade (TV) Special shown in Florida about the 10-year history of Walt Disney World; aired on Oct. 1, 1981, and simultaneously on all 3 Orlando TV stations. Many Disney executives and Florida businessmen and politicians are interviewed about their roles in bringing Walt Disney World to Florida. Narrated by Gene Burne.

Flo's V8 Cafe Counter-service restaurant seating 300, inspired by vintage roadside eateries along historic Route 66, in Cars Land at Disney California Adventure; opened Jun. 15, 2012.

Flotsam and Jetsam Two slithery eels who act as Ursula's henchmen in *The Little Mermaid*; voiced by Paddi Edwards.

Flounder Fish friend of Ariel in *The Little Mermaid*; voiced by Jason Marin. Edan Gross provided the voice in the TV series.

Flounder's Flying Fish Coaster Attraction in Mermaid Lagoon at Tokyo DisneySea; opened Sep. 4, 2001. Guests ride flying fish, linking the undersea world of *The Little Mermaid* and the human world above the waves.

Flower Skunk friend of Bambi's; voiced by Stanley Alexander (young Flower) and Sterling Holloway (adult Flower).

Flowers and Trees (film) Silly Symphony cartoon released Jul. 30, 1932. Directed by Burt Gillett. The 29th Silly Symphony is indeed a landmark in Disney animation. Originally begun as a black-and-white cartoon, the work was scrapped at great cost, and the cartoon was made in color at Walt Disney's insistence, for he believed color could greatly enhance animation. He signed a 2-year agreement with Technicolor giving him sole rights to the process for animated shorts—and a great head start over all of the other cartoon producers in Hollywood. Very soon all the Disney cartoons would be in color. Disney's faith in the process not only enhanced the quality of his films, but it also helped make Technicolor a respected standard in the film industry. The story of the cartoon concerns 2 trees in love who are threatened by a jealous old stump that attempts to burn the forest down in order to destroy them. But he only succeeds in reducing himself to ash. The forest revives and celebrates the wedding. Academy Award winner for Best Cartoon. The film was rereleased in 2 Academy Award specials in 1937 and 1967, and as part of *Milestones in Animation* (1973).

Flubber Magical substance invented by Professor Ned Brainard in *The Absent-Minded Professor*. Disney gave away its formula for making Flubber in the film's publicity: "To one pound of saltwater taffy add one heaping tablespoon polyurethane foam, one cake crumbled yeast. Mix until smooth, allow to rise. Then pour into saucepan over one cup cracked rice mixed with one cup of water. Add topping of molasses. Boil until it lifts lid and says 'Qurlp.'" At the time of the film's release in 1961, Hassenfeld Brothers (Hasbro) made a pliable plastic-like material that they merchandised as "Flubber." It sold for $1 and was advertised as "Every bubble a bounce."

Flubber (film) Professor Phillip Brainard is a man so lost in thought that he appears, at times, not to pay attention. He's even forgotten 2 dates to marry his sweetheart, Sara. But the guy has a lot on his mind. He is working with his high-voltage, over-amorous flying robot assistant, Weebo, on an idea for a substance that is not only a revolutionary source of energy but may well be the salvation of his financially troubled Medfield College, where his beloved Sara is the president. But it all comes together late on the afternoon of his 3rd attempt at a wedding when the professor creates a miraculous goo that when applied to any object—cars, bowling balls . . . even people—it enables them to fly through the air at miraculous speeds. The stuff, called Flubber, defies gravity and looks like rubber. Chester Hoenicker, a corrupt businessman who at first wants only to punish Brainard for giving his son a failing grade, learns about the existence of the substance, and sends goons to steal it from the professor's lab. Released Nov. 26, 1997. Directed by Les Mayfield. Stars Robin Williams (Phillip Brainard), Marcia Gay Harden (Sara), Christopher McDonald (Wilson Croft), Raymond Barry (Chester Hoenicker), Wil Wheaton (Bennett Hoenicker). The voice of Weebo is provided by Jodi Benson. 94 min. An updated version of the 1961 Disney feature *The Absent-Minded Professor*. Many of the special effects were produced in the huge Building Three at the Treasure Island Naval Base off San Francisco. With 90,000 square feet of space, the producers were able to create the professor's basement laboratory, the interior of the team's locker room, and a 2,500-seat basketball stadium, all under one roof, at one time. Differing from the original film, the substance Flubber is given a personality of its own. Mischievous and uncontrollable, it creates havoc everywhere.

Fluppy Dogs (TV) See Disney's Fluppy Dogs.

Fly 'n' Buy Aviation-themed souvenir shop in Condor Flats at Disney California Adventure; opened Feb. 8, 2001. Closed Jan. 6, 2015, to become Humphrey's Service & Supply.

Fly with Von Drake (TV) Show aired Oct. 13, 1963. Directed by Hamilton S. Luske. The professor, Ludwig Von Drake, describes the history of flight, with segments from previous animated TV shows and *Victory Through Air Power*.

Flying Carpets Over Agrabah (Les Tapis Volants) Toon Studio attraction in Walt Disney Studios Park at Disneyland Paris; opened Mar. 16, 2002. The Genie, as a movie director, invites guests to ride in flying carpets against a large backdrop of Agrabah. See also Magic Carpets of Aladdin, The (Walt Disney World).

Flying Fish Café Elegant seafood restaurant at Disney's BoardWalk at Walt Disney World; opened Oct. 3, 1996. In summer 2016, the restaurant was remodeled, and "Café" was removed from the name.

Flying Gauchito, The (film) Segment of *The Three Caballeros* in which a little boy trains a flying donkey for racing. Released as a short Jul. 15, 1955.

Flying Jalopy (film) Donald Duck cartoon released Mar. 12, 1943. Directed by Dick Lundy. Donald buys a rattletrap plane from Ben Buzzard, who makes Donald's insurance out to himself and then proceeds to try to wreck the plane.

Flying Mouse, The (film) Silly Symphony cartoon released Jul. 14, 1934. Directed by Dave Hand. A mouse is granted his wish to fly by a butterfly fairy he saved from a spider's web. He soon regrets his decision when everyone takes him for a bat. Luckily, the fairy appears to change him back and he returns happily home. Features the popular song "You're Nothin' but a Nothin'," which was released on sheet music.

Flying Saucers A 16,000-sq.-foot Tomorrowland attraction in Disneyland; open Aug. 6, 1961–Sep. 5, 1966. Individually controlled vehicles floated on a cushion of air, but the technology was not perfected, and the attraction closed frequently for maintenance. It later inspired the Luigi's Flying Tires attraction in Disney California Adventure.

Flying Squirrel, The (film) Donald Duck cartoon released Nov. 12, 1954. Directed by Jack Hannah. Donald promises a peanut to a flying squirrel if it will hang his peanut sign in a nearby tree. But when the peanut turns out to be rotten, the squirrel gets his just revenge.

Flynn, Joe (1924–1974) Actor and Disney regular; appeared in *Son of Flubber* (announcer in TV commercial), *The Love Bug* (Havershaw), *The Barefoot Executive* (Francis X. Wilbanks), *The Million Dollar Duck* (Finley Hooper), *Superdad* (Cyrus Hershberger), and as Dean Higgins in *The Computer Wore Tennis Shoes*, *Now You See Him,*

Now You Don't, and *The Strongest Man in the World*. On TV, he appeared in *My Dog, the Thief* (P .J. Applegate), *The Wacky Zoo of Morgan City* (Mayor Philbrick), and as a host on *The Mouse Factory*. He voiced Mr. Snoops in *The Rescuers*.

Flynn Rider Gallant bandit in *Tangled* who convinces Rapunzel to leave her tower; voiced by Zachary Levi. His real name is Eugene Fitzherbert.

Foley, Dave Actor; appeared in *Three Men and a Baby* (Grocery Store Clerk), *It's Pat* (Chris), and *Sky High* (Mr. Boy), and on TV in *Dr. Ken* (Pat Hein), with guest appearances in *Scrubs* (Dr. Hedrick), *Brothers & Sisters* (Paul), *Desperate Housewives* (Monroe Carter), and *Call Your Mother* (Steve). He voiced Flik in *A Bug's Life*, Terry in *Monsters University*, the Rogue Waiter in *Onward*, and Wayne in *Prep & Landing*.

folklore: the long pond studio sessions (TV) Disney+ original concert special; digitally released Nov. 25, 2020. Taylor Swift performs the songs from her best-selling album, *folklore*. In between live performances, she and her collaborators discuss the creation and meaning behind each song. Directed by Taylor Swift. Also stars Aaron Dessner, Jack Antonoff, Justin Vernon. 106 min. From Taylor Swift Productions and Big Branch Productions. Filmed at Long Pond Studios in upstate New York.

Follow Me, Boys! (film) Dissatisfied with his life as a saxophonist in a traveling jazz band, Lemuel Siddons impulsively settles down in the small Illinois town of Hickory (population 4,951), not realizing that he will remain there the rest of his days. This heartwarming and humorous story tells how Lem becomes the local scoutmaster, and how he courts and marries the lovely Vida. But mostly, it is the story of a man who sacrifices his own personal goals to devote himself to several generations of boys, teaching them enduring values through scouting. And, for Lem, this brings the love, respect, and recognition he so richly deserves. Released Dec. 1, 1966. Directed by Norman Tokar. 131 min. Stars Fred MacMurray (Lemuel Siddons), Vera Miles (Vida Downey), Kurt Russell (Whitey), Lillian Gish (Hetty Seibert), Charlie Ruggles (John Everett Hughes), Elliott Reid (Ralph Hastings), Ken Murray (Melody Murphy), Sean McClory (Edward White, Sr.). This was the first big film role for Kurt Russell. The film was a popular Christmastime hit, playing Radio City Music Hall. Based on the book *God and My Country* by Mackinlay

Kantor, the movie also featured onetime Disney starlet Luana Patten in a key role, as Nora White. A tremendous assemblage of vintage cars added to the nostalgic feel of the film; included were a 1915 Baker Electric, a 1927 Lincoln touring car, a fleet of 1929 Fords and Chevrolets, and 3 plush Cadillacs (of 1940, 1946, and 1950 vintage). The title song was written by Richard M. and Robert B. Sherman. The last Disney film released before Walt Disney passed away just 14 days later. The film was rereleased in 1976, but was edited from the original 131-min. version to 107 min.

Follow Us . . . to Walt Disney World (film) Documentary featurette; released first in England on Jul. 11, 1985. 16 min.

Follow Your Heart (TV) Part 1 of *The Horsemasters*.

Fondacaro, Phil Actor and stuntman; he provided the voice of Creeper in *The Black Cauldron* and appeared on TV in the title role in *Fuzzbucket*. He also had an uncredited role in *Something Wicked This Way Comes* (clown).

Fonte, Allison Mouseketeer on the new *Mickey Mouse Club*.

Food and Fun Center SEE FIESTA FUN CENTER.

Food for Feudin' (film) Pluto cartoon released Aug. 11, 1950. Directed by Charles Nichols. The chipmunks and Pluto battle over possession of a supply of nuts.

Food Rocks Audio-Animatronics concert show in The Land at EPCOT; opened Mar. 26, 1994, replacing the Kitchen Kabaret. The theme was "an all-star benefit for good nutrition," inspired by fundraiser rock concerts such as World Aid and Farm Aid. Popular musical artists voiced the oversized food characters, such as Tone Lōc (Fūd Wrapper), Chubby Checker (Chubby Cheddar), Cher (The Sole of Rock & Roll), and Neil Sedaka (Neil Moussaka). The only figure remaining from the previous show was the milk carton. Closed Jan. 3, 2004, to make way for Soarin'.

Food Will Win the War (film) Educational film made for the U.S. Department of Agriculture. Delivered Jul. 21, 1942. Amazing and interesting comparisons regarding the vast food resources of the U.S. are detailed in animation.

Foods and Fun: A Nutrition Adventure (film) Educational film starring the Orange Bird; released in Sep. 1980. The importance of good nutrition and proper exercise, told through animation. Narrated by Rex Allen.

Foodtastic (TV) Competition series on Disney+; digitally premiered Dec. 15, 2021. Artists create Disney-inspired scene work and sculptures entirely out of food. Hosted by Keke Palmer, with Amirah Kassem and Chef Benny as food-art experts. From Endemol Shine.

Football Now and Then (film) Special cartoon released Oct. 2, 1953. Directed by Jack Kinney. A boy and his grandfather argue the merits of football's past and present while watching 2 teams, Bygone U and Present State, on TV. Though the game ends in a tie, Grandfather is more impressed with a commercial and goes out to buy the advertised dishwasher.

Footloose Fox (film) Featurette released Jun. 7, 1979. A young fox and an apartment-hunting badger become roommates and fast friends while sharing a den. One day, the fox, leading a wolf pack away from the badger, ends up far from home. After a winter storm, the fox finds a female counterpart and they return to the fox's den. Knowing that three's company, the badger goes apartment-hunting once again. 30 min. Directed by Jack Speirs.

Footloose Goose, The (TV) Show aired Mar. 9, 1975. Directed by James Algar. A gander in Minnesota is injured and blown far away from his home by a tornado, so after he recovers in a bird sanctuary in Canada, he returns to Minnesota and searches for his mate. Stars Brett Hadley, Paul Preston, Judy Bement.

For Life (TV) Hour-long drama series on ABC; aired Feb. 11, 2020–Feb. 24, 2021. Prisoner Aaron Wallace becomes a lawyer, litigating cases for other inmates while fighting to overturn his own life sentence for a crime he didn't commit. His quest for freedom is driven by his desperate desire to get back to the family he loves and reclaim the life that was stolen from him. Inspired by the life of Isaac Wright Jr. Stars Nicholas Pinnock (Aaron), Indira Varma (Safiya), Joy Bryant (Marie), Glenn Fleshler (Frank), Dorian Missick (Jamal), Tyla Harris (Jasmine). From Sony Pictures Television and ABC Studios.

For the Birds (film) Short cartoon from Pixar; premiered at the Annecy International Animation Film Festival in France, Jun. 5, 2000. It was later released theatrically with *Monsters, Inc.*, on Nov. 2, 2001, and in 3-D as part of the *Monsters, Inc.* 3-D release in 2012. A flock of small birds on a telephone wire make fun of a large, awkward one, with unexpected results. Directed by Ralph Eggleston. 4 min. Academy Award winner for Best Animated Short Film.

For the First Time in Forever: A Frozen Sing-Along Celebration Interactive live show in Disney's Hollywood Studios; opened Jul. 5, 2014, in the Premiere Theater in Streets of America. Two royal historians host a comedic retelling of the *Frozen* story with the help of Anna, Elsa, and Kristoff. In Jun. 2015, it moved to the Hyperion Theater (formerly SuperStar Television Theater) in the Echo Lake area. Also in the Crown Jewel Theater in Disney California Adventure; opened Dec. 23, 2014, replacing *Muppet*Vision 3D*, and closed Apr. 17, 2016. It was succeeded by the Sunset Showcase Theater. There were also versions in Disneyland Paris (*Chantons La Reine des Neiges* played seasonally May 31, 2015–Jan. 7, 2018, in the Chaparral Theater) and Hong Kong Disneyland (*Frozen Festival Show*, which played in the temporary Frozen Village in summer 2015).

For the Love of Willadean (TV) Two-part show; aired Mar. 8 and 15, 1964. Directed by Byron Paul. The 2 parts were titled *A Taste of Melon* and *Treasure in the Haunted House*. A new boy, Harley, joins a club but shows an interest in the leader's girlfriend. The 2 club members trick Harley into stealing a prize watermelon to the dismay of the furious farmer, and later dare him to enter a supposedly haunted house. In the house, they uncover a bag of money stolen in a bank robbery. Stars Ed Wynn, Michael McGreevey, Billy Mumy, Roger Mobley, Terry Burnham, John Anderson, Barbara Eiler.

For the People (TV) Hour-long drama on ABC; aired Mar. 13, 2018–May 16, 2019. At the United States District Court for the Southern District of New York, 6 talented young lawyers work on opposite sides of the law and handle the most high-profile and high-stakes federal cases in the country. Best friends Sandra Bell and Allison Adams serve as public defenders alongside Jay Simmons and their boss, Jill Carlan, as they face off against prosecutors. Stars Britt Robertson (Sandra Bell),

Jasmin Savoy Brown (Allison Adams), Ben Rappaport (Seth Oliver), Susannah Flood (Kate Littlejohn), Wesam Keesh (Jay Simmons), Regé-Jean Page (Leonard Knox), Ben Shenkman (Roger Gunn), Hope Davis (Jill Carlan). From ABC Studios.

For Whom the Bulls Toil (film) Goofy cartoon released May 9, 1953. Directed by Jack Kinney. Goofy, on a tour of Mexico, is mistaken for a great matador and is rushed into the bullring, where a mad, crazy chase ensues.

Foray, June (1917–2017) Voice actress; she voiced dozens of animated characters, including Lucifer in *Cinderella*, Witch Hazel in *Trick or Treat*, Magica de Spell on *DuckTales*, Wheezy and Lena Hyena in *Who Framed Roger Rabbit*, Grammi Gummi on *Disney's Adventures of the Gummi Bears*, Grandma in *Redux Riding Hood*, and Grandmother Fa in *Mulan*. She is known for doing the voices of Natasha and Rocky on *The Bullwinkle Show*.

Forberg, Tom The first captain to join Disney Cruise Line; he was named commodore in 2013, overseeing the fleet of 4 ships. He retired in 2021.

Ford, Glenn (1916–2006) Actor; appeared in *Smith* and on TV in *My Town*.

Ford, Harrison Actor; appeared in *Six Days, Seven Nights* (Quinn Harris), as Han Solo in the *Star Wars* films, and as the title character in the *Indiana Jones* films.

Forky Bonnie's spork-turned-craft-project in *Toy Story 4*; voiced by Tony Hale.

Forky Asks a Question (TV) Animated short-form series; premiered Nov. 12, 2019, on Disney+. Forky, from *Toy Story 4*, asks questions about how the world works, such as "What is time?" and "What is cheese?" Directed by Bob Peterson. Voices include Tony Hale (Forky), John Ratzenberger (Hamm), Robin Atkin Downes (Mr. Pricklepants). From Pixar Animation Studios. The episode *What Is Love?* won the 2020 Emmy for Short Form Animated Program.

Forrest, Steve (1925–2013) Actor; appeared in *Rascal* (Willard North) and *The Wild Country* (Jim Tanner), and narrated *Wild Geese Calling* and *The Owl That Didn't Give a Hoot* on TV.

Fort Langhorne See Fort Sam Clemens.

Fort Sam Clemens Located on Tom Sawyer Island in the Magic Kingdom at Walt Disney World; named after Samuel Clemens (the real name of *Tom Sawyer* author Mark Twain). The name changed to Fort Langhorne (Clemens's middle name) in 1996.

Fort Wilderness Located on Tom Sawyer Island in Disneyland. It was removed because of aging in May 2007.

Fort Wilderness Railway A train trip that operated 1973–1980 at the Fort Wilderness Resort at Walt Disney World.

Fort Wilderness Resort & Campground, Disney's Campground, with cabins, campsites, and trailers, in a 640-acre forest setting of pines and cypress at Walt Disney World; opened Nov. 19, 1971. It has been expanded through the years, with additional facilities in the Settlement area, including Pioneer Hall, Trail's End Restaurant, and Crockett's Tavern. Recreation includes canoeing, jogging, bicycling, and fishing on Bay Lake, with horseback riding at the Tri-Circle-D Ranch. A popular campfire sing-along and outdoor movie screenings are presented in the Meadow recreation area.

Fortress Explorations Attraction in Mediterranean Harbor at Tokyo DisneySea; opened Sep. 4, 2001. Guests step back in time to the 16th-century age of exploration, where a Renaissance fortress and galleon provide the setting for hands-on exhibits presented by the Society of Explorers and Adventurers (S.E.A.).

Fortuosity Song from *The Happiest Millionaire*; sung by Tommy Steele and written by Richard M. and Robert B. Sherman.

Fortuosity Shop Main Street, U.S.A. boutique in Disneyland; opened Oct. 3, 2008, selling jewelry, watches, and accessories. It replaced New Century Timepieces. The eclectic décor is inspired by the former One-of-a-Kind shop in New Orleans Square.

40 Pounds of Trouble (film) Motion picture made by Universal in 1962, starring Tony Curtis and Suzanne Pleshette, notable for a lengthy chase scene that takes place inside Disneyland. This was the first non-Disney motion picture to use Disneyland as a setting.

40 Years of Adventure (TV) Syn. 1-hour special hosted by Wil Shriner, commemorating the 40th anniversary of Disneyland and the opening of the Indiana Jones Adventure; aired on KCAL-TV Mar. 4, 1995. Included are interviews with celebrities on hand for the opening. Directed by Melanie Steensland.

Foster, Ben Actor; appeared in *Big Trouble* (Matt Arnold) and as a co-star of *Flash Forward* on Disney Channel.

Foster, Jodie Actress; appeared in *Napoleon and Samantha* (Samantha), *One Little Indian* (Martha Melver), *Freaky Friday* (Annabel Andrews), *Candleshoe* (Casey), *Flightplan* (Kyle Pratt), and on TV in *Menace on the Mountain* and *Mickey's 50*.

Foster, Lewis R. (1899–1974) Director of *Swamp Fox* and *Zorro* shows/films.

Foster, Norman (1900–1976) Director of *Davy Crockett* and *Zorro* shows/films.

Foster, Robert Price ("Bob") (1924–2022) He began at Walt Disney Productions in 1956, working in real estate law and as a legal counsel for Disneyland. In the 1960s, he headed the property search and land acquisition for Walt Disney World, which totaled more than 27,000 acres, and later managed the legislative package that would establish the Reedy Creek Improvement District. In 1970, he was named president of the Buena Vista Land Company, which developed the 4,000-acre community of Lake Buena Vista. He left the company in 1974 and was named a Disney Legend in 2021.

Fosters, The (TV) Series on Freeform (formerly ABC Family); aired Jun. 3, 2013–Jun. 6, 2018. Two moms raise a multiethnic family, mixed with both foster and biological kids. Stef Foster, a dedicated police officer, and her partner, Lena Adams, a school vice principal, have built a close-knit, loving family with Stef's biological son from a previous marriage, Brandon, and their adopted twins, Mariana and Jesus. Their lives are disrupted in unexpected ways when Lena meets Callie, a hardened teen with an abusive past who has spent her life in and out of foster homes. Lena and Stef welcome Callie and her brother, Jude, into their home thinking it's just for a few weeks, until a more permanent placement can be found. But life has something else in store for the Fosters. Stars Teri Polo (Stef Foster), Sherri Saum (Lena Adams), Jake T. Austin (Jesus), Hayden Byerly (Jude), David Lambert (Brandon), Maia Mitchell (Callie), Danny Nucci (Mike Foster), Cierra Ramirez (Mariana).

Foul Hunting (film) Goofy cartoon released Oct. 31, 1947. Directed by Jack Hannah. Goofy's duck hunting is not going well when he encounters a duck that imitates the decoy and gets his gun soaked. He ends up eating the decoy.

Fountainview Espresso & Bakery Dessert and espresso area, formerly part of Sunrise Terrace, in Innoventions West at EPCOT; opened Nov. 9, 1993. Bakery items were removed in Aug. 2007, and it became an ice cream shop, sponsored by Edy's. In Sep. 2013, it became a Starbucks location with the Fountain View name, closing permanently Sep. 7, 2019.

4 Artists Paint 1 Tree (film) A 16-mm release title of a part of the TV show *An Adventure in Art*; released in May 1964. Four Disney artists were asked to paint the same tree, and their differing styles created widely varying results. They explain their approach and interpretation. SEE ALSO ADVENTURE IN ART, AN.

Four Corners Food Faire Fantasyland restaurant in Tokyo Disneyland; opened Apr. 15, 1983. Name changed to Small World Restaurant in Mar. 1987 and Queen of Hearts Banquet Hall in 1998.

Four Diamonds, The (TV) A Disney Channel Premiere Film; first aired Aug. 12, 1995. Young cancer patient Chris Millard escaped into his imagination by writing *The Four Diamonds*. In the tale, the cast members of his family in various roles, including himself as Sir Millard, and his doctor, Dr. Burke, as Raptenahad, the evil sorceress. Taken prisoner by Raptenahad, Sir Millard must win his freedom by carrying out a quest demanded by the sorceress: he must obtain for her the 4 diamonds of courage, honesty, wisdom, and strength. Directed by Peter Werner. Stars Thomas Guiry (Chris), Christine Lahti (Dr. Burke), Kevin Dunn (Charles Millard), Jayne Brook (Irma Millard), Sarah Rose Karr (Stacie), Michael Bacall (Tony Falco).

Four Down and Five Lives to Go (TV) Episode 2 of *Elfego Baca*.

Four Fabulous Characters (TV) Show aired Sep. 18, 1957. Directed by Hamilton S. Luske. Walt introduces the folk stories *Casey Jones, The Martins and the Coys, Casey at the Bat*, and *Johnny Appleseed*.

Four Keys to Guest Happiness SEE 5 KEYS, THE (DISNEY PARKS).

Four Methods of Flush Riveting (film) Training film produced for Lockheed Aircraft Corp. and then distributed by the National Film Board of Canada. Delivered Jul. 14, 1942. This was Walt's "pilot" film to show how animation could be used effectively in training films.

Four Musicians of Bremen, The (film) Laugh-O-gram film made by Walt in Kansas City in 1922. A cat, dog, donkey, and rooster try to catch some fish by serenading them with music. Later they have a run-in with a house full of robbers and exchange cannon fire.

Four Seasons On Aug. 25, 2008, Walt Disney World Co. finalized the sale of 298 acres on the northeast border of the property to Four Seasons Hotels and Resorts for the building of a 444-room Four Seasons Resort Orlando hotel, Residence Club (fractional ownership vacation homes), and an 18-hole championship golf course, as well as custom single- and multifamily vacation homes. The hotel was designed by Wimberly Allison Tong & Goo and opened Aug. 2014 as part of the Golden Oak residential community, including restaurants Capa, Ravello, PB&G, and Plancha. SEE ALSO TRANQUILO GOLF CLUB.

Four Tales on a Mouse (TV) Show aired Apr. 16, 1958. Directed by Hamilton S. Luske. Tells how Mickey helped other Disney performers with their careers by using a series of cartoons.

Fouret, Didier (1927–1989) He handled Disney publications at the Hachette publishing company in France beginning in 1950 and was presented posthumously with a European Disney Legends Award in 1997.

14 Going on 30 (TV) A 2-part show that aired Mar. 6 and 13, 1988. Directed by Paul Schneider. A young teenage student, Danny, has a crush on a teacher, and, unlike most of his peers, is able to do something about it when he tests a machine, invented by his cousin, that greatly accelerates growth. But, after the test, the machine is destroyed, and Danny has to remain an adult. He masquerades as the new principal in the school, changing rules to

the delight of the kids. Finally the machine is fixed, leading to a surprise ending. Stars Steve Eckholdt, Adam Carl, Gabey Olds, Daphne Ashbrook, Irene Tedrow, Patrick Duffy, Harry Morgan, Loretta Swit, Alan Thicke, Dick Van Patten.

Fourth Anniversary Show, The (TV) Show aired Sep. 11, 1957. Directed by Sidney Miller. Celebrating 4 years on TV, Walt Disney first describes his 1938 meeting with Serge Prokofieff and shows the resulting film, *Peter and the Wolf*. Then he joins the Mouseketeers to tell about plans for future shows, introducing Jerome Courtland (Andy Burnett) and Guy Williams (Zorro). The Mouseketeers then surprise Walt with 2 musical sequences from a movie they hope he will let them star in, *The Rainbow Road to Oz*. He agrees, and they celebrate. Stars Fess Parker and the Mouseketeers. *The Rainbow Road to Oz* was never made, so these are the only 2 sequences that were ever filmed. Instead, in 1985 Disney made *Return to Oz*, with a totally different plotline and no longer a musical.

4th of July Firecrackers (film) Shorts program; released by RKO in 1953.

Fowler, Joseph W. ("Joe") (1894–1993) Retired U.S. Navy rear admiral, chosen in 1954 by Walt Disney to oversee the construction of Disneyland and manage the park's operations. He remained to be in charge of construction of Walt Disney World also. He retired in 1972 and received the Disney Legends Award in 1990. He is fondly remembered for his motto, "Can do." On May 28, 1997, the *Magic Kingdom I* ferryboat at Walt Disney World was relaunched as the *Admiral Joe Fowler*. SEE ALSO ADMIRAL JOE FOWLER RIVERBOAT, FOWLER'S HARBOR, AND SUBMARINE VOYAGE.

FOWLER'S HARBOR Dry dock area of Frontierland in Disneyland where the *Columbia* is usually moored. It was named in honor of retired U.S. Navy rear admiral Joseph Fowler.

Fox, Michael J. Actor; appeared in his film debut in *Midnight Madness* (Scott) and later in *Life with Mikey* (Michael Chapman), and *on TV in Scrubs (Kevin) and Walt Disney World's 25th Anniversary Party*. He voiced Chance in *Homeward Bound: The Incredible Journey* and *Homeward Bound: Lost in San Francisco*, and Milo Thatch in *Atlantis: The Lost Empire*.

Fox and the Hound, The (film) The animated

story of 2 friends who didn't know they were supposed to be enemies. Tod, an orphaned baby fox, raised by Widow Tweed, is best friends with Copper, a young hunting dog. When they grow up, Copper learns to hunt and discovers he must pursue his friend. Tod is taken to a game preserve for safety, and there he falls in love with Vixey, a beautiful female fox. Copper and his master hunt Tod in the preserve, but when the chips are down, Tod and Copper realize that their friendship overcomes all. Released Jul. 10, 1981. Directed by Art Stevens, Ted Berman, and Richard Rich. 83 min. Featuring the voices of Mickey Rooney (older Tod), Keith Mitchell (young Tod), Kurt Russell (older Copper), Corey Feldman (young Copper), Pearl Bailey (Big Mama), Pat Buttram (Chief), Sandy Duncan (Vixey), Dick Bakalyan (Dinky), Paul Winchell (Boomer), Jack Albertson (Amos Slade), Jeanette Nolan (Widow Tweed). Based on a story by Daniel P. Mannix. The feature film marked the premier effort of a new generation of Disney animators who would, in a few years, create *The Little Mermaid* and *Beauty and the Beast*. With the exception of some early scenes and character development done by veteran animators Frank Thomas, Ollie Johnston, and Cliff Nordberg, this film represented the combined talent and imagination of a new team. Production on *The Fox and the Hound* began in spring 1977, but it was delayed by the defection from the animation department of Don Bluth, Gary Goldman, John Pomeroy, and an additional group of animators who were unhappy at the Disney Studio and eager to set up their own studio and produce movies that they felt were more in line with the style and quality of movies that Disney used to make in its golden years. By the time *The Fox and the Hound* was finished, 4 years later, it would require approximately 360,000 drawings, 110,000 painted cels, 1,100 painted backgrounds, and a total of 180 people, including 24 animators. As in all Disney animated features, music served to accentuate the action, highlight the humor, and, in general, enhance the story. The movie features the songs "Best of Friends," by Richard O. Johnston, son of animator Ollie Johnston, and Stan Fidel; "Lack of Education," "A Huntin' Man," and "Appreciate the Lady" by Jim Stafford; and "Goodbye May Seem Forever" by Richard Rich and Jeffrey Patch. The film was an enormous box office success and was rereleased theatrically in 1988. First released on video in 1994.

Fox and the Hound, The: A Lesson in Being Careful (film) Educational film; released in Sep.

1981. The important lesson that warnings should not be ignored is stressed in this film.

Fox and the Hound 2, The (film) Direct-to-DVD release, Dec. 12, 2006. Young pals Tod and Copper head off to a crazy adventure at the County Fair, with Copper trying to discover his greatest talent. Directed by Jim Kammerud. Voices include Reba McEntire (Dixie), Patrick Swayze (Cash), Jonah Bobo (Tod), Harrison Fahn (Copper), Jeff Foxworthy (Lyle), Vicki Lawrence (Granny Rose), Stephen Root (Talent Scout). Trisha Yearwood adds some vocals, along with Little Big Town, Josh Gracin, and Lucas Grabeel. 69 min. From Disney-Toon Studios.

Fox Chase, The (film) Oswald the Lucky Rabbit cartoon; released Jun. 25, 1928. After having several mishaps while on a fox hunt, Oswald and his friends attempt to dislodge their target from a log. But when a skunk appears, the group races away over the hill, and the fox takes off his disguise.

Fox Family Worldwide Disney completed the acquisition on Oct. 24, 2001, of Fox Family Worldwide, including the Fox Family Channel in the U.S. and Fox Kids channels worldwide, for $5.2 billion. The channel was renamed the ABC Family Channel. Fox Kids was rebranded as Jetix in 2004 and later became Disney XD. SEE ALSO ABC FAMILY, JETIX, AND FREEFORM.

Fox Hunt, The (film) Silly Symphony cartoon released Oct. 20, 1931. Directed by Wilfred Jackson. As a gag-filled fox hunt winds down, which includes misadventures with a porcupine, the hunters unfortunately catch a skunk instead of a fox—and flee. The skunk and the fox shake hands. The film was remade in color as a Donald Duck and Goofy cartoon, released on Jul. 29, 1938. Directed by Ben Sharpsteen. In this later film, Donald is the Master of the Hounds and Goofy is one of the riders. Just when it looks as if Donald will capture the fox, a skunk turns up to chase them all away.

Foxx, Jamie Actor; voiced Joe Gardner in *Soul*.

France, Van (1912–1999) Starting work with Disneyland in Mar. 1955, he created the University of Disneyland (later Disney University), where he taught new concepts in guest service. Years later, after his retirement in 1978, he headed the Disneyland Alumni Club. He wrote his reminiscences in

Window on Main Street. He was named a Disney Legend in 1994.

France World Showcase pavilion in EPCOT; opened Oct. 1, 1982. The architecture is modeled after Paris, evoking the belle époque era. The focal point at the rear of the pavilion is a 74-ft. scaled-down replica of the Eiffel Tower. The featured attraction is the presentation in the Palais du Cinema of *Impressions de France*, an enchanting film enhanced by stereophonic recordings of music by the great French classical composers. Repeat visitors to EPCOT often count this film as one must-see return engagement. In 2020, the *Beauty and the Beast Sing-Along* premiered in the cinema, playing in rotation with *Impressions*. Dining options include Les Chefs de France, Monsieur Paul, and Les Halles Boulangerie & Patisserie. An expansion in 2021 introduced the Remy's Ratatouille Adventure ride-through attraction and La Crêperie de Paris.

Francis The oh-so-proper bulldog in *Oliver & Company*; voiced by Roscoe Lee Browne.

Francis, Edna Maiden name of Roy O. Disney's wife. They were married in Hollywood at the home of Robert S. Disney, Roy's uncle, on Apr. 11, 1925. Edna died on Dec. 18, 1984. She was named a Disney Legend in 2003.

Francisco's Lounge in Disney's Coronado Springs Resort at Walt Disney World; open Aug. 1, 1997–Sep. 2007, and succeeded by Rix Lounge.

Franco, James Actor; appeared in *Annapolis* (Jake Huard) and in the title role in *Oz The Great and Powerful*.

Frank Dim-witted frill-necked lizard in *The Rescuers Down Under*; voiced by Wayne Robson.

Frank, Richard Formerly with Paramount Pictures, he joined Disney as president of the Walt Disney Studios in 1985. In 1994, on the resignation of Jeffrey Katzenberg, he was named chairman of Walt Disney Television and Telecommunications. He has also served as president of the Academy of Television Arts and Sciences. He resigned from the company in 1995.

Frank and Ollie (film) Documentary feature film about the lives and careers of legendary Disney animators Frank Thomas and Ollie Johnston, made by Thomas's son, Ted Thomas. Premiered as a Disney film at the Cleveland Film Festival on Apr. 7, 1995, after a Jan. 22, 1995, preview at the Sundance Festival. First theatrical release was Oct. 20, 1995, in Los Angeles for Academy Award consideration. 89 min.

Frank Clell's in Town (TV) Episode 16 of *Texas John Slaughter*.

Frank Duck Brings 'em Back Alive (film) Donald Duck and Goofy cartoon released Nov. 1, 1946. Directed by Jack Hannah. Donald loses his sanity in trying to capture Goofy, who is portraying a Tarzan-like inhabitant of the jungle.

Frank McKlusky, C.I. (film) An insurance claims investigator, Frank McKlusky, traumatized by his father having been left in a coma because of a horribly conceived motorcycle stunt, has developed an unhealthy aversion to any kind of risk—he lives with his parents, wears a helmet everywhere he goes, and lives his life strictly by the rules. He lets his partner do all the dirty work, but when his partner is killed in the line of duty, Frank is forced to come out from under his helmet to crack the case. Directed by Arlene Sanford. A Touchstone film. Limited theatrical release on Apr. 26, 2002, only in 10 Florida cities. Stars Dave Sheridan (Frank McKlusky), Randy Quaid (Madman McKlusky), Enrico Colantoni (Scout Bayou), Kevin Pollak (Ronnie Rosengold), Orson Bean (Gafty), Andy Richter (Herb), Cameron Richardson (Sharon), Dolly Parton (Edith McKlusky). 83 min.

Frankenweenie (film) Featurette released in Los Angeles Dec. 14, 1984, and again Mar. 6, 1992 (with *Blame It on the Bellboy*). An homage to the great horror films of the 1930s. After young Victor Frankenstein's dog, Sparky, is killed by a car, his parents become concerned when their son accumulates a collection of electrical junk in their attic. Using the techniques of his legendary namesake, Victor's secret purpose is to bring his beloved pet back to life. The result of the experiment causes panic in the neighborhood. 30 min. Directed by Tim Burton. Stars Barret Oliver (Victor Frankenstein), Shelley Duvall (Susan Frankenstein), Daniel Stern (Ben Frankenstein), Paul Bartel (Mr. Walsh). The filmmakers managed to find and use some of the same laboratory equipment that had been used in the original *Frankenstein* film many years earlier. Shown on The Disney Channel in 1992.

Frankenweenie (film) Stop-motion animated film, in black and white. After unexpectedly losing his beloved dog, Sparky, young Victor harnesses the power of science to bring his best friend back to life—with just a few minor adjustments. He tries to hide his home-sewn creation, but when Sparky gets out, Victor's fellow students, teachers, and the entire town of New Holland all learn that being brought back to life can have unexpected consequences. Directed by Tim Burton. Released Oct. 5, 2012, in Disney Digital 3-D, after a premiere on Sep. 20 at Fantastic Fest in Austin, Texas. Voices include Charlie Tahan (Victor Frankenstein), Catherine O'Hara (Susan Frankenstein), Martin Landau (Mr. Rzykruski), Christopher Lee (Movie Dracula), Martin Short (Mr. Walsh), Robert Capron (Bob), Conchata Ferrell (Bob's mom), Winona Ryder (Elsa Van Helsing), Atticus Shaffer (Edgar). 87 min. Feature-length version of the 1984 short film from Tim Burton. Nominated for an Academy Award for Best Animated Feature.

Frankie Canary who appeared with Figaro in *Figaro and Frankie* (1947).

Fraser, Brendan Actor; appeared in *Encino Man* and *In the Army Now* (Link), and in the title role in *George of the Jungle*.

Freaky Friday (film) A harried mother thinks her 13-year-old daughter's life is a bed of roses. The daughter is similarly envious of her mother. Each wishes she could trade places with the other, and miraculously, one freaky Friday they exchange bodies. While Mom is experiencing the hilarious horrors of junior high school, the teenager is finding out what it's like to be an overburdened wife and mother. Both are glad to see the end of *that* day. Released Dec. 17, 1976, in Los Angeles; general release Jan. 21, 1977. Directed by Gary Nelson. 98 min. Stars Jodie Foster (Annabel), Barbara Harris (Ellen), John Astin (Bill), Patsy Kelly (Mrs. Schmauss), Dick Van Patten (Harold), Vicki Schreck (Virginia), Sorrell Booke (Mr. Dilk), Ruth Buzzi (opposing coach), Kaye Ballard (Coach Betsy). Based on the book by Mary Rodgers. The song "I'd Like to Be You for a Day" was written by Al Kasha and Joel Hirschhorn. Los Angeles locations were used for the major part of the film, though the dedication at the marina was shot at San Diego's beautiful Mission Bay.

Freaky Friday (film) Dr. Tess Coleman and her 15-year-old daughter, Anna, are not getting along.

They don't see eye to eye on clothes, hair, music, and certainly not in each other's taste in men. One Thursday evening, their disagreements reach a fever pitch. Anna is incensed that her mother doesn't support her musical aspirations, and Tess, a widow about to remarry, cannot see why Anna won't give her fiancé a break. Everything soon changes when 2 identical Chinese fortune cookies cause a little mystic mayhem. Next morning, their Friday gets freaky when Tess and Anna find themselves inside each other's body, eventually gaining a little newfound respect for the other's point of view. But with Tess's wedding coming up on Saturday, the 2 have to find a way to switch back (and fast). Released Aug. 6, 2003. This movie is a remake of the 1977 film and a 1995 TV movie, based on the book by Mary Rodgers. Directed by Mark Waters. Stars Jamie Lee Curtis (Tess Coleman), Lindsay Lohan (Anna), Harold Gould (Grandpa), Chad Michael Murray (Jake), Christina Vidal (Maddie), Mark Harmon (Ryan), Stephen Tobolowsky (Mr. Bates), Haley Hudson (Peg). Marc McClure, who played Boris in the original film, returns in a cameo. 97 min. The film made use of Southern California locations, including Palisades High School, which is in the Brentwood neighborhood of Los Angeles.

Freaky Friday (TV) Two-hour movie, a remake of the 1977 theatrical feature; aired on ABC May 6, 1995. Thirteen-year-old Annabelle Andrews and her mother, Ellen, magically trade places on a fateful Friday the 13th, and each then experiences firsthand the day-to-day difficulties that the other goes through, creating a new sense of empathy in each case. However, because of their different perspectives, they are sometimes able to handle the other's problems and decisions more forthrightly. Directed by Melanie Mayron. Stars Shelley Long (Ellen Andrews), Gaby Hoffman (Annabelle Andrews), Catlin Adams (Mrs. Barab), Sandra Bernhard (Frieda Debny), Eileen Brennan (Principal Handel), Alan Rosenberg (Bill Davidson). Most of the location filming took place in Pasadena, California, doubling for Short Hills, New Jersey, where the story is set.

Freaky Friday (TV) A Disney Channel Original Movie; first aired Aug. 10, 2018. A contemporary musical update of the classic comedy story. Sixteen-year-old Ellie Blake and her uber-organized mom, Katherine, are constantly at odds about Ellie's messy room, sloppy clothes, and seemingly careless attitude. Ellie really misses her dad (who passed away a few years ago), bickers with her younger brother, and argues with Katherine (who's getting ready to marry her fiancé, Mike). As mother and daughter quarrel, they accidentally break the treasured hourglass given to Ellie by her father, and then, suddenly, they magically switch bodies. Ellie and Katherine must now trade places at work and at school, and, during one crazy day, they'll learn to understand and appreciate each other. Directed by Steve Carr. Stars Cozi Zuehlsdorff (Ellie), Heidi Blickenstaff (Katherine), Ricky He (Adam), Jason Maybaum (Fletcher), Alex Désert (Mike). Based on Disney Theatrical Productions' stage adaptation of Mary Rodgers's book. From Bad Angels Productions, Ltd.

Freaky Friday A stage musical version of *Freaky Friday*, with a book by Bridget Carpenter and a score by Tom Kitt and Brian Yorkey, opened in a limited engagement Oct. 4, 2016, at the Signature Theatre in Arlington, Virginia, prior to being made available for licensing to theaters.

Freberg, Stan (1926–2015) Actor; the voice of the Beaver in *Lady and the Tramp* and narrator of *The Wuzzles* and *An All New Adventure of Disney's Sport Goofy*.

Freeform New name, as of Jan. 12, 2016, for the ABC Family network in attempts to edge away from the family market and aim for the 14- to 34-year-olds market. Original series have included *grown-ish*, *Good Trouble*, *Siren*, and *Motherland: Fort Salem*. The network also programs tentpole events such as "31 Nights of Halloween," "Kick Off to Christmas," and "25 Days of Christmas."

Freeman, Jonathan Actor; he provided the voice of Jafar in *Aladdin* and other appearances of the character. On Broadway, he reprised the role in the stage musical of *Aladdin* (ending his run Jan. 23, 2022, after more than 2,000 performances) and played Cogsworth in *Beauty and the Beast*, Admiral Boom in *Mary Poppins*, and originated the role of Grimsby in *The Little Mermaid*. He appeared in *The Associate* (Hockey Game Executive) and voiced Eli Excelsior Pandarus and Jack Frost in *American Dragon: Jake Long*.

Freeman, Morgan Actor; appeared in *The Nutcracker and the Four Realms* (Drosselmeyer). He was the narrator for The Hall of Presidents at Walt Disney World from 2009–2017.

Frees, Paul (1920–1986) Voice actor; he voiced the title character in *Noah's Ark*, Ludwig Von Drake in *Walt Disney's Wonderful World of Color*, and narrated for many TV shows and films. He also provided voices for Disneyland and Walt Disney World, including Great Moments with Mr. Lincoln and Adventure Thru Inner Space (narrator), the Haunted Mansion (Ghost Host), Pirates of the Caribbean (several pirates), and The Hall of Presidents (George Washington, 1971). He made an uncredited appearance as the psychiatrist in *The Shaggy Dog*. He was named a Disney Legend in 2006.

Freewayphobia No. 1 (film) Goofy cartoon released Feb. 13, 1965. Directed by Les Clark. Goofy, essaying the roles of Driverius Timidicus, Motoramus Fidgitus, and Mr. Neglecterus Maximus, graphically enacts the perils timid and neglectful motorists can and do encounter on the nation's freeways. Pointing out that lane changes can often be a direct route to peril, Goofy reminds his audience to maintain a proper distance from vehicles in front of them. 16 min. For No. 2 see *Goofy's Freeway Trouble*.

Freight Train Debuted on the Disneyland Railroad on opening day. Guests rode in closed cattle cars, looking out through the slats. The train later had its cars converted into open viewing cars and still operates today, though now known as "Holiday Red."

French Market Buffeteria restaurant serving Creole cuisine in New Orleans Square in Disneyland; opened in 1966. The seating on the open-air terrace is perfect for watching the passersby and even glimpsing *Fantasmic!* in the evening. A small stage occasionally features jazz performers. On the garden patio, the walk-up Mint Julep Bar serves the beverage (nonalcoholic) and beignets. Closed Feb. 16, 2023, to become Tiana's Palace.

Frenemies (TV) A Disney Channel Original Movie; first aired Jan. 13, 2012. Friendship is a difficult thing, as 3 very different sets of friends discover. There are best friends Halley and Avalon, whose fashion blog is to be turned into a magazine, but only one of them is needed to stay on as senior editor; science-whiz Jake and his dog, Murray (who doesn't like Jake's girlfriend, Julianne); and Savannah and Emma, who look alike but come from very different social classes and realize that life on the other side isn't all it is cracked up to be when they decide to trade places for a while. Directed by Daisy von Scherler Mayer. Stars Bella Thorne (Avalon Greene), Zendaya Coleman (Halley), Stefanie Scott (Julianne), Nick Robinson (Josh Logan), Mary Mouser (Emma/Savannah), Jascha Washington (Kendall Coleman), Connor Price (Walker), Dylan Everett (Lance Lancaster). Based on the novel by Alexa Young.

Friar Tuck Badger holy man in *Robin Hood*; voiced by Andy Devine.

Friar's Nook, The Fantasyland counter-service restaurant in the Magic Kingdom at Walt Disney World; opened Mar. 26, 2009, taking the place of the Village Fry Shoppe. The menu has included macaroni and cheese, hot dogs, and beverages.

Friday Talent Roundup Day on the 1950s *Mickey Mouse Club*. Showtime Day on the 1970s new *Mickey Mouse Club*. Hall of Fame Day on the 1990s *Mickey Mouse Club*.

Friedle, Will Actor; appeared on TV in *Boy Meets World* and *Girl Meets World* (Eric Matthews), *Go Fish* (Pete Troutner), *My Date with the President's Daughter* (Duncan Fletcher), *Walt Disney World's 25th Anniversary Party*, *Disney's Animal Kingdom: The First Adventure*, and *H-E-Double Hockey Sticks* (Griffelkin). He voiced Ron Stoppable on *Kim Possible* and Hardlight on *Big Hero 6 The Series*.

Friend Like Me Song from *Aladdin*; sung by Robin Williams and written by Howard Ashman and Alan Menken. Nominated for an Academy Award.

Friendly Enemies at Law (TV) Episode 9 of *Elfego Baca*.

Friendship in Vienna, A (film) A Disney Channel Premiere Film, first aired Aug. 27, 1988. Two girls—one Jewish, one with Nazi-sympathizer parents—test their friendship in prewar Austria. 99 min. Directed by Arthur Allan Seidelman. Stars Ed Asner (Opah Oskar), Jane Alexander (Hannah Dornenwald), Stephen Macht (Franz Dornenwald), Jenny Lewis (Inge Dornenwald), Kamie Harper (Lise Mueller). Filmed entirely on location in Budapest, Hungary, marking the first time The Disney Channel went behind the Iron Curtain to produce a film.

FriendShips Ferries that ply the World Showcase Lagoon in EPCOT, transporting guests from one side to the other; began operating Oct. 1, 1982. They later began providing service to nearby resort hotels and Disney's Hollywood Studios.

Fright Night (film) High school senior Charley Brewster thinks all is going well for him; he is running with the popular crowd. But trouble arrives when an intriguing stranger, Jerry, moves in next door, and Charley soon discovers that his neighbor is a vampire. Unable to convince anyone to believe him about the vampire, Charley has to find a way to get rid of the monster himself. A Touchstone/DreamWorks film. Directed by Craig Gillespie. Released Aug. 19, 2011. Stars Anton Yelchin (Charley Brewster), Christopher Mintz-Plasse (Ed), Colin Farrell (Jerry), David Tennant (Peter Vincent), Imogen Poots (Amy), Toni Collette (Mom). 106 min. Released also in 3-D. A remake of a 1985 film from Columbia Pictures.

Frolicking Fish (film) Silly Symphony cartoon released Jun. 21, 1930. Directed by Burt Gillett. In an underwater musical, fish ride seahorses, lobsters and starfish play the harp and dance, and a villainous octopus has an anchor dropped on its head for trying to capture a bubble-dancing fish.

From Aesop to Hans Christian Andersen (TV) Show aired Mar. 2, 1955. Directed by Clyde Geronimi. Walt Disney describes the age-old art of storytelling by offering cartoon versions of 2 of Aesop's fables, then de la Fontaine's classic story of the Country Mouse and his cousin the City Mouse, followed by tales from the Brothers Grimm, and finally Andersen's *The Ugly Duckling*.

From All of Us to All of You (TV) Show debuted on the weekly Disney TV series on Dec. 19, 1958, and then later aired during 8 additional Christmas seasons. Directed by Jack Hannah. Hosted by Jiminy Cricket, who sings the title song, this holiday episode, featuring Christmas-themed cartoons and "Memorable Moments" (clips from Disney classics such as *Cinderella* and *Peter Pan*), was changed for later runs, often by adding a segment on the latest animated feature.

From Our Family To Yours Holiday campaign and series of animated ads supporting Make-A-Wish International. In the first 3-min. short (digitally released online Nov. 8, 2020, and later renamed *Lola*), young Nicole and her grandmother, Lola, discover how their bond deepens through traditions passed down through the generations. The second short, *The Stepdad* (Nov. 2, 2021), follows a grown-up Nicole and her own children, Max and Ella, who welcome stepdad Mike into their home. In the third installment, *The Gift* (Nov. 2, 2022), Max gives Ella a Mickey Mouse doll to comfort her as she adjusts to the changing family dynamic; Ella then gifts the toy to her newborn sibling. From Disney Consumer Products, Games and Publishing EMEA, in partnership with Flux Animation Studios.

From Ticonderoga to Disneyland (TV) Part 2 of *Moochie of Pop Warner Football.*

From Time to Time (film) Circle-Vision 360 film, created for Visionarium in Disneyland Paris; played Apr. 12, 1992–Sep. 6, 2004. Audio-Animatronics characters Nine-Eye and Timekeeper interacted with the film, which presented a time-travel journey through Europe, including scenes of 8 countries. Presented by Renault. Open in revised form (American scenes were added) in the Transportarium (The Timekeeper, an Outrageous Blast Through Time) in the Magic Kingdom at Walt Disney World; played Nov. 21, 1994–Feb. 26, 2006. The film was also adapted for Visionarium in Tokyo Disneyland; played 1993–2002. See Timekeeper, The and Le Visionarium.

Froman, Michael B. G. Member of the Disney Board of Directors beginning in 2018.

Front Page Pleasure Island shop at Walt Disney World; open May 1, 1989–Apr. 9, 1995. Guests could appear on the cover of popular magazines.

Frontera Cocina Restaurant serving Mexican cuisine by Chef Rick Bayless in the Disney Springs Town Center at Walt Disney World; opened Jun. 27, 2016.

Frontier Shooting Gallery Frontierland attraction in the Magic Kingdom at Walt Disney World; opened Oct. 1, 1971. Became Frontierland Shootin' Arcade Sep. 26, 1984, after a Sep. 24 preview. It is one of the more elaborate shooting galleries in the world. See also Frontierland Shootin' Arcade (Disneyland), Westernland Shootin' Gallery (Tokyo Disneyland), and Rustler Roundup Shootin' Gallery (Disneyland Paris).

Frontier Trading Post Frontierland shop at Disneyland; opened Jul. 17, 1955. Became Westward Ho Trading Co. in 1987. Also at Walt Disney World, beginning in 1971. Sells Western-themed gifts and souvenirs.

Frontier Woodcraft Shop in Westernland in Tokyo Disneyland; opened Jun. 1986. Guests can have personal messages and names engraved on many of the shop's leather items.

Frontierland One of the original lands of Disneyland. Walt Disney was always interested in the country's Western and Mexican heritages, and he was determined to give his Disneyland guests a feel for the West. That meant mules and horses to add to the ambience, but that also meant trouble. Mules were ornery and occasionally refused to move. Horses pulling the stagecoaches and wagons would get spooked by the whistles of the trains as they passed nearby. Finally, with great regret, Walt agreed that the live animals had to go from Frontierland. Over the years, other attractions have included The Golden Horseshoe, the *Mark Twain* Riverboat, Sailing Ship *Columbia*, Mine Train Through Nature's Wonderland, Tom Sawyer Island, and Big Thunder Mountain Railroad. Versions of Frontierland are also in the Magic Kingdom at Walt Disney World and in Disneyland Paris. In Tokyo Disneyland, the area is known as Westernland.

Frontierland Playground See Pocahontas Indian Village.

Frontierland Shootin' Arcade Frontierland gallery at Disneyland; opened Mar. 29, 1985, taking the place of the former Shooting Gallery. The attraction was completely rebuilt, becoming entirely electronic. The rifles fire infrared beams which, if on target, trigger humorous reactions. This is one of the few attractions in the park that is not included in the price of admission; others are the Main Street Penny Arcade and the Starcade. It was later known as Frontierland Shootin' Exposition. Also an attraction in the Magic Kingdom at Walt Disney World; opened Sep. 26, 1984 (after a Sep. 24 preview), taking the place of the former Frontier Shooting Gallery. See also Westernland Shootin' Gallery (Tokyo Disneyland) and Rustler Roundup Shootin' Gallery (Disneyland Paris).

Frontierland Theater See Chaparral Theater, The.

Frou-Frou Friendly horse in *The Aristocats*; voiced by Nancy Kulp.

Frozen (film) Animated feature. Fearless optimist, the princess Anna, sets off on an epic journey—teaming up with a rugged mountain man, Kristoff, and his loyal reindeer, Sven—to find her sister, Elsa, whose icy powers have trapped the kingdom of Arendelle in eternal winter. Encountering Mt. Everest-like conditions, mystical trolls, and a hilarious snowman named Olaf, Anna and Kristoff battle the elements in a race to save the kingdom. Directed by Chris Buck and Jennifer Lee. Released in 3-D on Nov. 27, 2013, after a Nov. 20 release in Paris and at the El Capitan Theatre in Hollywood. Voices include Kristen Bell (Anna), Jonathan Groff (Kristoff), Idina Menzel (Elsa), Josh Gad (Olaf), Santino Fontana (Hans), Alan Tudyk (Duke of Weselton). 102 min. From Walt Disney Animation Studios. Score by Christophe Beck, with songs by Kristen Anderson-Lopez and Robert Lopez, including "Let It Go," "For the First Time in Forever," and "Do You Want to Build a Snowman?" The production team's visits to Canadian ice hotels influenced the look of Elsa's Ice Palace, though the majority of visual and cultural influences came from Norway, including its fjords, castles, and rosemaling. During the initial release, on Jan. 31, 2014, a special sing-along engagement began in more than 2,000 theaters. It received Academy Awards for Best Animated Feature and Best Song ("Let It Go"). In Mar. 2014, *Frozen* became the highest-grossing animated feature to date, passing $1 billion internationally. The soundtrack became the No. 1 best-selling album for 2014 on the Billboard 200 chart, the first time a Disney soundtrack album headed the list since *Mary Poppins*.

Frozen A stage musical version of the animated film began a tryout at the Buell Theatre in the Denver Center for the Performing Arts Aug. 17, 2017. Opened at the St. James Theatre on Broadway Mar. 22, 2018, after previews starting Feb. 22. In addition to 7 songs they wrote for the film, Kristen Anderson-Lopez and Robert Lopez contributed 12 new ones, including "Dangerous to Dream," "True Love," and "A Little Bit of You." *Frozen* director and screenwriter Jennifer Lee returned to pen the book. The original Broadway cast included Caissie Levy (Elsa), Patti Murin (Anna), Jelani Alladin (Kristoff), Greg Hildreth (Olaf), John Riddle (Hans), Robert Creighton (Duke of Weselton), Kevin Del Aguila (Oaken). Nominated for 3 Tony Awards. Performances ended Mar. 11, 2020, amid the COVID-19 pandemic; it was announced in May 2020 that the show would not reopen on Broadway. A national tour began Nov. 10, 2019, in Schenectady, New York.

Frozen Ever After Attraction in Norway at EPCOT; opened Jun. 21, 2016. Guests take a boat tour through the kingdom of Arendelle on a "Summer Snow Day," traveling up to the icy world of the North Mountain, where Queen Elsa's enchanting Ice Palace awaits. It took the place of Maelstrom. A second version of the attraction is planned for World of Frozen in Hong Kong Disneyland.

Frozen Festival Show SEE FOR THE FIRST TIME IN FOREVER: A FROZEN SING-ALONG CELEBRATION.

Frozen Fever (film) Short cartoon released with the live action *Cinderella*, Mar. 13, 2015. It's Anna's birthday, and Elsa and Kristoff are determined to give her the best celebration ever, though Elsa's icy powers might get in the way. Directed by Chris Buck and Jennifer Lee.

Frozen Fractal Gifts Echo Lake shop in Disney's Hollywood Studios; opened in 2015, in the former Golden Age Souvenirs. *Frozen* apparel, costumes, and toys are sold.

Frozen Kingdom Area announced for Fantasy Springs at Tokyo DisneySea. Included is a boat ride attraction featuring the story of Elsa and Anna, plus a restaurant inside Arendelle Castle.

Frozen – Live at the Hyperion Musical stage adaptation of the animated film; opened May 27, 2016, in the Hyperion Theater at Disney California Adventure. The stage production remains true to the emotional journey of Anna and Elsa, with elaborate costumes and sets, special effects, and production numbers. Performances ended in Mar. 2020.

Frozen Royal Reception SEE ROYAL RECEPTION.

Frozen Sing-Along SEE FOR THE FIRST TIME IN FOREVER: A FROZEN SING-ALONG CELEBRATION.

Frozen 2 (film) Animated feature. Why was Elsa born with magical powers? What truths about the past await Elsa as she ventures into the unknown, to the enchanted forests and dark seas beyond Arendelle? The answers are calling her, but they're also threatening her kingdom. Together with Anna, Kristoff, Olaf, and Sven, she faces a dangerous but remarkable journey. In *Frozen*, Elsa feared her powers were too much for the world. In *Frozen 2*, she must hope they are enough. Released Nov. 22, 2019 (also in 2-D IMAX and 3-D), after Nov. 20–21 international releases. Directed by Chris Buck and Jennifer Lee. Voices include Kristen Bell (Anna), Idina Menzel (Elsa), Josh Gad (Olaf), Jonathan Groff (Kristoff), Sterling K. Brown (Mattias), Alfred Molina (Agnarr), Evan Rachel Wood (Iduna), Martha Plimpton (Yelena), Jason Ritter (Ryder), Rachel Matthews (Honeymaren), Jeremy Sisto (King Runeard), Ciarán Hinds (Pabbie), Alan Tudyk (Guard/Northuldra Leader/Arendellian Soldier/Duke of Weselton). 104 min. Christophe Beck returned to write the score, with songs by Kristen Anderson-Lopez and Robert Lopez, including "Into the Unknown," "Lost in the Woods," and "Show Yourself." Swoop, a new technology from Walt Disney Animation Studios, helped create Gale, the wind spirit. The water spirit, known as the Nokk, was inspired by Nordic folklore, taking the form of a horse with the power of the ocean. Earning $1.45 billion at the global box office, it became the highest-grossing animated feature to date, breaking the record set previously by *Frozen* (2013). Nominated for an Academy Award (Best Original Song, "Into the Unknown").

Fuente del Oro Restaurante Frontierland cantina with Tex-Mex specialties in Disneyland Paris; opened Apr. 12, 1992.

Full-Court Miracle (TV) A Disney Channel Original Movie; first aired Nov. 21, 2003. Alex Schlotsky, team captain for the Philadelphia Hebrew Academy Lions basketball team, dreams of a pro basketball career. When he meets Lamont Carr, who is pursuing a pickup by the NBA, Alex persuades him to coach some seemingly hapless kids into champions. Although their minds are often on basketball, the boys are also studying the miraculous Hanukkah story of Judah and the Maccabees. They soon find similarities between Lamont and Judah and become convinced that Lamont is an incarnation of the Jewish hero. Directed by Stuart Gillard. Stars Alex D. Linz (Alex Schlotsky), Richard T. Jones (Lamont Carr), R. H. Thomson (Rabbi Lewis), Linda Kash (Cynthia Schlotsky), Jason Blicker (Marshall Schlotsky), Sheila McCarthy (Mrs. Klein), Cassie Steele (Julie), Jase Blankfort (Stick Goldstein), David Sazant (Joker Levy), Eric Knudsen (T J Murphy), Sean

Marquette (Big Ben Schwartz). Working title was *Lamont's Maccabees*. Based on a true story. The real Lamont Carr served as consultant and coached the young actors in the basketball scenes.

Fulton's Crab House Restaurant on the former *Empress Lilly* riverboat in Pleasure Island (later The Landing in Disney Springs) at Walt Disney World; operated by Chicago-based Levy Restaurants. The 700-seat crab house opened Mar. 10, 1996, and closed Apr. 4, 2016, to be replaced by Paddlefish.

Fulton's General Store Shop in Disney's Port Orleans Resort – Riverside at Walt Disney World; opened Feb. 1992.

Fun and Fancy Free (film) Jiminy Cricket begins the film by playing a Dinah Shore record that tells the tale of *Bongo* to cheer up a desolate-looking doll and bear. Bongo, a circus bear, meets and falls in love with a girl bear named Lulubelle. But first he must confront a bear rival, Lumpjaw, whose looks match his name, before the 2 become a pair. When the story is completed, Jiminy finds he has been invited to ventriloquist Edgar Bergen's house, where he is entertaining Luana Patten, Charlie McCarthy, and Mortimer Snerd. Bergen tells the story of *Mickey and the Beanstalk*, in which Mickey and his friends, Donald and Goofy, climb a beanstalk to rescue the lovely singing harp from a giant to restore happiness to their Happy Valley. As Bergen finishes the story, the giant appears, lifting the roof, in search of Mickey Mouse, then goes on down the hill toward Hollywood. Released Sep. 27, 1947. Directed by William Morgan, with animation sequences directed by Jack Kinney, Bill Roberts, and Hamilton Luske. 73 min. Songs include "Fun and Fancy Free," "My, What a Happy Day," "Fe-Fi-Fo-Fum," and "My Favorite Dream." The opening song by Jiminy, "I'm a Happy Go Lucky Fellow," was originally written and recorded for *Pinocchio*. Billy Gilbert voiced the giant. Jim Macdonald began providing the voice of Mickey Mouse in this film when Walt Disney became too busy. When the *Beanstalk* segment was to run on the Disney TV series in the 1960s, the Disney Studio animated new introductory material of Ludwig Von Drake and his pet, Herman, to replace Edgar Bergen. First released on video in 1982.

Fun to Be Fit (film) Series of 3 educational films: *Why Be Physically Fit*, *Getting Physically Fit*, *Physical Fitness*; released in Mar. 1983.

Fun with Mr. Future (film) Special cartoon; released only in Los Angeles on Oct. 27, 1982, for Academy Award consideration. Mr. Future, an Audio-Animatronics "talking head," gives us a glimpse of what life will be like tomorrow—and what we thought it would be like today. A new animated sequence depicting a typical day in the life of a "future" family is used along with live-action footage taken from previously released films.

Fun with Music Day Monday on the 1950s *Mickey Mouse Club*.

Funicello, Annette (1942–2013) Actress; besides her *Mickey Mouse Club* work as a Mouseketeer—and on the *Adventure in Dairyland, Annette*, and *Spin and Marty* serials—she appeared in *The Shaggy Dog* (Allison D'Allessio), *Babes in Toyland* (Mary Contrary), and as Jennifer in *The Misadventures of Merlin Jones* and *The Monkey's Uncle*. She appeared on TV in *Backstage Party, Disneyland After Dark, Elfego Baca, Escapade in Florence, The Horsemasters, The Golden Horseshoe Revue, Zorro, The Mouse Factory, The Best of Disney: 50 Years of Magic*, and on The Disney Channel in *Lots of Luck*. Annette also became a recording star, performing a number of popular songs on the Disney record labels. Walt Disney discovered Annette when he saw her while attending an amateur program at the Starlight Bowl in Burbank where she was performing a number entitled "Ballet vs. Jive." She was named a Disney Legend in 1992. A non-Disney film about her life, *A Dream Is a Wish Your Heart Makes*, based on Annette's autobiography of the same title, aired on CBS in 1995. Annette passed away in 2013 after a 25-year fight against multiple sclerosis.

Funny Bones (film) A young comedian, Tommy Fawkes, trying to succeed but living in the shadow of his famous father, George, flees to Blackpool, England, where he spent the first 6 years of his life and where he hopes to find the perfect physical comedy act. While auditioning acts there, he discovers dark secrets about his father's past, but perhaps most importantly that he has a half brother. Directed by Peter Chelsom. A Hollywood Pictures film. Released Mar. 24, 1995, exclusively in New York City. 128 min. Stars Oliver Platt (Tommy Fawkes), Lee Evans (Jack), Richard Griffiths (Jim Minty), Oliver Reed (Dolly Hopkins), George Carl (Thomas Parker), Leslie Caron (Katie), Jerry Lewis (George Fawkes). The film was shot on location in Blackpool, in Las Vegas, and at Ealing Studios in West London.

Funny Little Bunnies (film) Silly Symphony cartoon released Mar. 24, 1934. Directed by Wilfred Jackson. At rainbow's end lies the magic land of the Easter bunnies, preparing Easter eggs and candies. Birds and animals help in the creation of painted eggs, using such oddities as plaid and polka-dot paint, and chocolate bunnies. The only Easter-themed Disney cartoon, this was the first film on which later director Wolfgang Reitherman animated.

Funny, You Don't Look 200 (TV) Special on ABC celebrating the bicentennial of the U.S. Constitution, including new animation done by Disney; aired Oct. 12, 1987. Hosted by Richard Dreyfuss, with a cast of dozens of celebrities. Directed by Jim Yukich.

Further Adventures of Gallegher, The: A Case of Murder (TV) Episode 1 aired on Sep. 26, 1965. Directed by Jeffrey Hayden. The aspiring newspaper reporter, Gallegher, gets involved in the murder of a traveling actor, and must help his reporter friend, Brownie, who is being blamed. Stars Roger Mobley, Edmond O'Brien, Harvey Korman, Victoria Shaw, Peter Wyngarde.

Further Adventures of Gallegher, The: The Big Swindle (TV) Episode 2 aired on Oct. 3, 1965. Directed by Jeffrey Hayden. The young copyboy helps the town's first female newspaper reporter, who is writing a series on confidence men. The swindlers are caught up in a sting, but they catch on and the reporter and Gallegher have to subdue them in order to escape and write their article. Stars Roger Mobley, Edmond O'Brien, Anne Francis, Harvey Korman.

Further Adventures of Gallegher, The: The Daily Press vs. City Hall (TV) Episode 3 aired on Oct. 10, 1965. Directed by Jeffrey Hayden. Gallegher teams with reporter Adeline Jones for an exposé on graft and corruption in city government after a gas explosion implicates the mayor, who awarded a contract that resulted in faulty pipes. The mayor's friend, whose company installed the pipes, is naturally enraged, and he tries to put the paper out of business. Stars Edmond O'Brien, Anne Francis, Roger Mobley, Harvey Korman, Parley Baer, James Westerfield, Edward Platt.

Further Adventures of Spin and Marty, The (TV) Serial on the *Mickey Mouse Club* during the

1956–1957 season. Directed by William Beaudine, Sr. The boys return to camp and Marty now is friendly with the others. The boys plan for a big dance, with girls from a neighboring camp, and a swimming meet. Stars Tim Considine, David Stollery, Annette Funicello, B. G. Norman, Brand Stirling, Roger Broaddus, Kevin Corcoran, Melinda Plowman, Roy Barcroft, Harry Carey, Jr., Lennie Geer, J. Pat O'Malley, Sammee Tong, Sammy Ogg. 23 episodes.

Further Adventures of Thunderbolt, The (film) Short from Walt Disney Animation Studios Special Projects; released on the *One Hundred and One Dalmatians* DVD/Blu-ray Feb. 10, 2015. After escaping a precarious situation, Thunderbolt brings Dirty Dawson to justice. Story direction by Floyd Norman. Voices include Dave Wittenberg (Sheriff), Jim Cummings (Dirty Dawson), Corey Burton (announcer). 2 min.

Further Report on Disneyland, A/Tribute to Mickey Mouse (TV) Show aired Jul. 13, 1955. Cartoon sequences directed by Wilfred Jackson. A preview of Disneyland, just 4 days before its opening, with Winston Hibler hosting a look at how the attractions were designed and built. Time-lapse photography is used to show a speeded-up version of the construction as the deadline approaches. The Mickey Mouse segment was originally shown with *The Disneyland Story*. The show is also known as *A Pre-Opening Report from Disneyland*.

Fusion On Feb. 11, 2013, ABC and Univision announced a joint-venture news and lifestyle network named Fusion for English-speaking U.S. young adult Hispanics; it launched Oct. 28, 2013. Univision purchased Disney's stake in Fusion in 2016.

Future Work (film) Educational film about new careers available in the high-tech workplace; released in Sep. 1983.

Future World Section of EPCOT first visited by guests as they entered through the main entrance. Extensive pavilions, sponsored by major corporations, celebrated human achievement with glimpses at the past and what we might find in the future. Opened Oct. 1, 1982, with Spaceship Earth, Communicore (later Innoventions, which itself closed in 2019), Universe of Energy (later Guardians of the Galaxy: Cosmic Rewind), World of Motion (later Test Track), Journey Into Imagination (later IMAGINATION!), and The Land. Horizons was added in 1983 (later Mission: SPACE), followed by The Living Seas in 1986 (now The Seas with Nemo & Friends) and Wonders of Life in 1989 (closed in 2007). Guests passed through Future World on the way to World Showcase. As part of a multi-year transformation of EPCOT, Future World was divided into 3 distinct areas on Oct. 1, 2021 — World Celebration, World Discovery, and World Nature. SEE EPCOT.

Future-Worm! (TV) Animated comedy-adventure series on Disney XD; debuted Aug. 1, 2016. Danny Douglas, an optimistic 12-year-old, creates a time machine lunch box through which he meets and befriends Future-Worm, a fearless worm from the future. Together, the duo embarks on adventures through space and time. Voices include Andy Milonakis (Danny Douglas), James Adomian (Future-Worm), Jessica DiCicco (Bug), Melanie Lynskey (Megan Douglas), Ryan Quincy (Doug Douglas). From Disney Television Animation.

FutureCom Display in Communicore West sponsored by Bell; open Oct. 1, 1982–Jan. 31, 1994. The exhibit demonstrated how people gather information, including some of the latest technological advances.

Fuzzbucket (TV) Show aired May 18, 1986. An invisible, furry creature befriends a boy who is insecure about the start of junior high school and his parents' arguing. Causing trouble and havoc everywhere he goes, Fuzzbucket helps the boy overcome both school worries and family problems. Directed by Mick Garris. Stars Chris Hebert, Phil Fondacaro, Joe Regalbuto, Wendy Phillips, Robin Lively, John Vernon. This was the first half of a program with *The Deacon Street Deer*.

FX Networks General entertainment television networks, including FX, FXM, and FXX, which air original, library, and licensed TV series and films. Also includes the video-on-demand app FXNOW and the commercial-free on-demand service FX+. Acquired by Disney in 2019 as part of its purchase of 21st Century Fox. FX, the flagship basic cable channel, launched Jun. 1994.

1. *Golden Mickeys, The* 2. Golden Oak 3. Grizzly Peak 4. Gyro Gearloose 5. Gerald 6. Gremlins, The
7. *Goofy and Wilbur* (film) 8. Great Moments with Mr. Lincoln 9. *Gus* (film) 10. *Ghost and Molly McGee, The* (TV)

Gabble Sisters, The Amelia and Abigail are the 2 English spinster geese in *The Aristocats*; voiced by Carole Shelley and Monica Evans.

Gabby Duran & the Unsittables (TV) Series on Disney Channel; debuted Oct. 11, 2019. Courageous and resourceful Gabby Duran constantly feels like she's living in the shadows of her uberpolished mother, Dina, and whip-smart younger sister, Olivia. She finds her moment to shine when she inadvertently lands a job to babysit an unruly group of extraterrestrial children who are hiding out on Earth, disguised as everyday kids. Gabby steps up to the challenge to protect these youngsters and their secret identities—and prove she's the best babysitter in the galaxy. Stars Kylie Cantrall (Gabby Duran), Nathan Lovejoy (Principal Swift), Coco Christo (Olivia), Maxwell Acee Donovan (Wesley), Callan Farris (Jeremy), Valery Ortiz (Dina). From Gabby Productions, a subsidiary of Omnifilm Entertainment.

Gabor, Eva (1921–1995) Actress; she provided the voice of Duchess in *The Aristocats* and Bianca in *The Rescuers* and *The Rescuers Down Under*.

Gad, Josh Actor; he voiced Olaf in *Frozen* and other appearances of the character. He appeared in *Beauty and the Beast* (LeFou, 2017), and on TV in *Mickey's 90th Spectacular* and *The Disney Family Singalong*. On Disney+, he appeared in *Artemis Fowl* (Mulch Diggums) and narrated *Magic of Disney's Animal Kingdom*. He was named a Disney Legend in 2022.

Gadget Inventive mouse in *Chip 'n' Dale Rescue Rangers*; voiced by Tress MacNeille.

Gadget's Go Coaster Attraction in Mickey's Toontown at Disneyland; opened Jan. 24, 1993. A short but fun roller coaster ride themed around the inventive mouse character in *Chip 'n' Dale Rescue Rangers*. Closed Mar. 8, 2022, and scheduled to reopen Mar. 19, 2023, as Chip 'n' Dale's GADGETcoaster. Also opened in Tokyo Disneyland Apr. 15, 1996.

Gadot, Gal Actress; voiced Shank in *Ralph Breaks the Internet*. It was announced she will play the Queen in *Snow White* (2024).

Gag Factory/Five and Dime Wacky shop in Mickey's Toontown in Disneyland; opened Jan. 24, 1993, and closed Mar. 2020 to make way for Mickey & Minnie's Runaway Railway. Also opened in Tokyo Disneyland Apr. 15, 1996.

Gala Day at Disneyland (film) Documentary featurette released Jan. 21, 1960. Produced by Hamilton Luske. The gala dedication ceremonies at the opening of 3 new major "E ticket" attractions at Disneyland—Matterhorn Bobsleds, Submarine Voyage, and the Monorail—include a parade down Main Street, U.S.A. with appearances by Walt and Roy O. Disney and members of their families, along with Vice President Richard Nixon and family, and numerous film stars. The celebrations end at night with fireworks. 27 min.

Galactic Grill See Tomorrowland Terrace.

Galavant (TV) Limited TV series on ABC; aired Jan. 4, 2015–Jan. 31, 2016. Once upon a time, a dashing hero, Galavant, lost the love of his life, Madalena, to the evil King Richard. Now our fallen hero is ready to take revenge and restore his "happily ever after." Stars Joshua Sasse (Galavant), Mallory Jansen (Madalena), Timothy Omundson (King Richard), Vinnie Jones (Gareth), Karen David (Isabella), Luke Youngblood (Sid). 8 episodes. The music is by Alan Menken and Glenn Slater. Produced by Abbey C Studios Ltd. for ABC Studios. Supervising producer was Scott Weinger, who, years earlier, had voiced Aladdin in the animated feature.

Galaxy Palace Theater Performance venue in Tomorrowland in the Magic Kingdom at Walt Disney World; open Dec. 15, 1994–Jan. 4, 2009. For many years, the theater featured "Galaxy Search," an inter-constellational talent competition featuring aliens and inspired by Ed McMahon's *Star Search*. It was formerly the Tomorrowland Stage, 1980–Dec. 1994.

Galifianakis, Zach Actor; appeared in *Bubble Boy* (Bus Stop Man), *Corky Romano* (Dexter), *Out Cold* (Luke), *G-Force* (Ben), *The Muppets* and *Muppets Most Wanted* (Hobo Joe), and *A Wrinkle in Time* (Happy Medium).

Gallagher, Neil (1931–1995) He joined the Studio Machine Shop in 1957 and was soon working on Disneyland projects for WED Enterprises (later known as Walt Disney Imagineering). He helped create the Enchanted Tiki Room and the Mr. Lincoln figure, and spent 18 months in New York City leading show and animation maintenance for the Disney shows at the 1964–1965 New York World's Fair. In 1971 he relocated to Florida, and in 1972 became director of Maintenance for Walt Disney World. He worked with the Buena Vista Construction Company on EPCOT Center and went to Japan to work on Tokyo Disneyland. From 1983–1994, he served as vice president of engineering and construction at Walt Disney World, with 3 years off to help with the planning of Euro Disney in France. He was named a Disney Legend posthumously in 2008.

Gallegher (TV) Three-part show aired Jan. 24, Jan. 31, and Feb. 7, 1965. Directed by Byron Paul. An energetic newspaper copyboy in 1889 wants to become a reporter, and he is soon more deeply involved in his stories than he had expected. When he discovers a bank robbery, he helps the reporter, Brownie, to apprehend the 4-fingered culprit. Later he helps the police chief who has been framed and tries to convince the authorities that he has discovered a wanted felon in town. Stars Roger Mobley (Gallegher), Edmond O'Brien (Jefferson Crowley), Jack Warden (Lt. Fergus), Ray Teal (Snead), Robert Middleton (Dutch Mac), Harvey Korman (Brownie), Philip Ober (Hade), Bryan Russell (Jimmy). Based on a book by Richard Harding Davis. See also Further Adventures of Gallegher, The; Gallegher Goes West; and Mystery of Edward Sims, The.

Gallegher Goes West: Crusading Reporter (TV) Episode 2 aired Oct. 30, 1966. Directed by Joseph Sargent. Gallegher and his colleagues work for the recall of the corrupt mayor of Brimstone, even though the mayor tries to stop them by force. Stars Dennis Weaver, John McIntire, Roger Mobley, Ray Teal, Jeanette Nolan, Larry D. Mann, Peter Graves.

Gallegher Goes West: Showdown with the Sundown Kid (TV) Episode 1 aired Oct. 23, 1966. Directed by Joseph Sargent. Gallegher befriends a man on the stagecoach while heading west, only to discover he is a famous outlaw, the Sundown Kid. The sheriff is crooked, too, so it is difficult for Gallegher and his friend, Detective Snead, to capture the Sundown Kid. Stars Dennis Weaver, John McIntire, Roger Mobley, James Gregory, Ray Teal, Jeanette Nolan, Peter Graves.

Gallegher Goes West: Tragedy on the Trail (TV) Episode 3 aired Jan. 29, 1967. Directed by James Sheldon. Gallegher buys and trains a horse, then is surprised when a local rancher is accused of murder. The boy is sure it is a frame-up, and he tries to help out. Stars Roger Mobley, John McIntire, Beverly Garland, Harry Townes, Ron Hayes, Jeanette Nolan, Bill Williams.

Gallegher Goes West: Trial by Terror (TV) Episode 4 aired Feb. 5, 1967. Directed by James Sheldon. Gallegher continues to help the rancher who has been framed for murder, and after he finds an incriminating watch, he is able to reach the trial just in time to save the day. Stars John McIntire, Roger Mobley, Beverly Garland, Harry Townes, Ron Hayes, Jeanette Nolan, Bill Williams, Ray Teal, Darlene Carr.

Galleria Disney Shop in Mediterranean Harbor at

Tokyo DisneySea; opened Sep. 4, 2001. It features a modern Italian interior design and re-creations of famous paintings featuring Disney characters.

Gallopin' Gaucho, The (film) The 2nd Mickey Mouse cartoon produced. Made as a silent cartoon, but released in 1928 after sound was added. Done as a parody of Douglas Fairbanks's swashbuckler films, Mickey falls in love with Minnie in a South American cantina and then rescues her from unwanted suitor, Pete, after a sword fight. Directed by Walt Disney.

Game, The (film) Educational film about how to follow rules and not demand special treatment. From the What Should I Do? series; released in Dec. 1969.

Game Plan, The (film) A famous Boston football quarterback, Joe Kingman, is shocked one day to find an 8-year-old girl, Peyton, at the door of his elegant bachelor pad, claiming she is his daughter and left there by her mother who is in Africa for a month. Now, just as his career is soaring, Joe must learn to juggle his old lifestyle of parties, practices, and dates with supermodels while tackling the new challenges of ballet, bedtime stories, and baby dolls—all without fumbling. Equally perplexed is his hard-edged mega-agent, Stella Peck. But, as the championship draws nearer, Joe is about to realize that the game that truly matters has nothing to do with money, endorsements, or even touchdowns—it is all about the *really tough* stuff: patience, teamwork, selflessness . . . and winning the heart of the one little fan who turns out to count the most. From Walt Disney Pictures in association with Mayhem Pictures. Directed by Andy Fickman. Released Sep. 28, 2007. Stars Dwayne "The Rock" Johnson (Joe Kingman), Brian White (Jamal Weber), Kyra Sedgwick (Stella Peck), Madison Pettis (Peyton Kelly), Roselyn Sanchez (Monique Vasquez), Morris Chestnut (Travis Sanders), Gordon Clapp (Coach Mark Maddox), Hayes MacArthur (Kyle Cooper), Jamal Duff (Monroe), Paige Turco (Karen Kelly). 110 min. Filmed in Boston in Super 35.

Games of the Boardwalk Games of skill in Paradise Pier at Disney California Adventure; opened Feb. 8, 2001, with Boardwalk Bowl, Shore Shot, San Joaquin Volley, Dolphin Derby, Angels in the Outfield, New Haul Fishery, and Cowhuenga Pass. As part of a re-theming to Paradise Pier, new games with classic Disney characters debuted Apr. 2009: Goofy About Fishin', Bullseye Stallion

Stampede, Casey at the Bat, and Dumbo Bucket Brigade. Became Games of Pixar Pier in 2018, with La Luna Star Catcher, Heimlich's Candy Corn Toss, WALL•E Space Race, and Bullseye Stallion Stampede.

Ganachery, The Chocolate shop in The Landing at Disney Springs at Walt Disney World; opened Dec. 15, 2015. Fresh batches of handcrafted ganache chocolate, a luxurious, proprietary mixture of melted chocolate and cream, are prepared daily.

Gandolfini, James (1961–2013) Actor; appeared in *A Stranger Among Us* (Tony Baldessari), *Money for Nothing* (Billy Coyle), *Angie* (Vinnie), *Terminal Velocity* (Ben Pinkwater), *Crimson Tide* (Lt. Bobby Dougherty), and *A Civil Action* (Al Love). He was best known for portraying Tony Soprano in the HBO series *The Sopranos*.

Gans, Ronald (1931–2010) Actor; provided voices for various Disney TV series, including *Dumbo's Circus* (Sebastian) and *Welcome to Pooh Corner* (Kanga and Roo).

Garay, Joaquin (1911–1990) He voiced Panchito, the charro rooster in *The Three Caballeros*. Thirty-five years later, his son Joaquin Garay III carried on a family tradition by appearing as Paco in *Herbie Goes Bananas*.

Garbage Picking Field Goal Kicking Philadelphia Phenomenon, The (TV) Two-hour movie on *The Wonderful World of Disney*; first aired Feb. 15, 1998. Barney Gorman, a Philadelphia garbageman, finds that his kicking abilities get him a once-in-a-lifetime opportunity to be a placekicker for the Philadelphia Eagles. After a grueling training period, he wins a game for the Eagles with his first professional kick. But, eventually, he finds that happiness can still come from his old garbage route. Directed by Tim Kelleher. Stars Tony Danza (Barney Gorman), Jessica Tuck (Marie Gorman), Art LaFleur (Gus Rogenheimer), Jaime Cardriche (Bubba), Julie Stewart (Wendy Fox), Gil Filar (Danny Gorman), Al Ruscio (Pop Gorman), Ray Wise (Randolph Pratt). The producers used locations in Toronto to double for Philadelphia. The real-life owner of the Eagles, Jeff Lurie, has a small role as a friend of Barney's.

Garber, Matthew (1956–1977) Child actor; appeared in *The Three Lives of Thomasina* (Geordie), *Mary Poppins* (Michael Banks), and *The*

Gnome-Mobile (Rodney). He was named a Disney Legend posthumously in 2004.

Garber, Victor Actor; appeared in *Life with Mikey* (Brian Spiro), *Tuck Everlasting* (Father Foster), and *You Again* (Mark), and on TV in *Rodgers and Hammerstein's Cinderella* (king), *Annie* (Daddy Oliver Warbucks), *Meredith Willson's The Music Man* (Mayor Shinn), *Alias* (Jack Bristow), *Ugly Betty* (Professor Barrett), and *Eli Stone* (Jordan Wethersby).

Garcia, Andy Actor; appeared in *When a Man Loves a Woman* (Michael Green), and on TV in *Rebel* (Cruz). He has provided voices for films and TV shows, including Delgado in *Beverly Hills Chihuahua* and Hetz in *Elena of Avalor*.

Garden Gallery Restaurant in the former Disney Inn, and in its replacement, Shades of Green, the military's R & R establishment, at Walt Disney World. It took the place of the Trophy Room.

Garden Gate Gifts Camera center offering various souvenirs at the entrance to The Oasis in Disney's Animal Kingdom; opened Apr. 22, 1998.

Garden Grill Restaurant Restaurant in The Land at EPCOT; opened Nov. 15, 1993. Originally named The Good Turn Restaurant (Oct. 1, 1982–May 1986), then The Land Grille Room (May 14, 1986–Oct. 4, 1993). The restaurant slowly rotates while one eats, providing views of the Living with the Land (formerly Listen to the Land) boat ride down below. The Good Turn served some of the best breakfasts at Walt Disney World. Later, the restaurant offered family-style dining with greetings by Disney characters dressed in their farming apparel.

Garden of the Twelve Friends Gardens of Imagination attraction in Shanghai Disneyland; opened Jun. 16, 2016. Guests walk through a colorful garden with vignettes of Disney and Disney • Pixar characters chosen to represent the 12 signs of the Chinese zodiac: Remy (rat); Babe, the Blue Ox (ox); Tigger (tiger); Thumper (rabbit, replaced by Judy Hopps in Jan. 2023); Mushu (dragon); Kaa (snake); Maximus (horse); "Jolly Holiday" lambs (sheep); Abu (monkey); Allan-a-Dale (rooster); Pluto (dog); and Hamm (pig). Chinese artisans created the mosaic wall.

Garden of Wonders Attraction in Mystic Point

at Hong Kong Disneyland; opened May 17, 2013. Ancient sculptures and paintings create 3-D illusions.

Gardens of Imagination Area serving as the central hub of Shanghai Disneyland; opened Jun. 16, 2016, with Dumbo the Flying Elephant, Fantasia Carousel, Meet Mickey, Marvel Universe, and *Mickey's Storybook Express Parade*. Celebrating the wonders of nature and joy of imagination, the 6.9-acre area features the longest parade route in a Disney park, along with prime views of the castle entertainment and *ILLUMINATE! A Nighttime Celebration* (formerly *Ignite the Dream—A Nighttime Spectacular of Magic and Light*). The area also contains 7 themed garden areas with displays and activities: Garden of the Twelve Friends, Melody Garden, Romance Garden, Woodland Garden, Garden of the Magic Feather, Fantasia Garden, and Storybook Castle Garden.

Gargoyles (TV) Animated series; premiered in syn. Oct. 24, 1994, and ended Aug. 29, 1997. A mysterious medieval race, stone by day and alive by night, turn up in New York City where they emerge from their stone slumber to protect Manhattan from modern-day barbarians. The voice cast includes Keith David (Goliath), Edward Asner (Hudson), Salli Richardson (Elisa Maza), Jonathan Frakes (David Xanatos), Marina Sirtis (Demona), Bill Fagerbakke (Broadway). 65 episodes. A more mature show on The Disney Afternoon programming block, it quickly garnered a devout fan following.

Gargoyles: The Goliath Chronicles (TV) Animated series on ABC, aired Sep. 7, 1996–Apr. 12, 1997. In this spin-off from the *Gargoyles* series, Goliath and his small clan of Gargoyle warriors must now contend with a growing anti-Gargoyle faction called the Quarrymen. Organized and bitterly hostile, the Quarrymen will stop at nothing until the Gargoyles are captured. Voices include Keith David (Goliath), Edward Asner (Hudson), Bill Fagerbakke (Broadway), Marina Sirtis (Demona), Jonathan Frakes (David Xanatos), Salli Richardson (Elisa Maza). 13 episodes.

Gargoyles the Movie: The Heroes Awaken (film) Video release in Feb. 1995, revealing the mythical origins of the Gargoyles. 80 min.

Garity, William (1899–1971) After helping record the sound for *Steamboat Willie*, sound engineer Bill

Garity joined the Disney Studio, where he helped Walt Disney make his cartoons the most technically advanced in the industry. Bill's team created the multiplane camera and invented Fantasound for *Fantasia*, while supervising the construction of the new Disney Studio in Burbank. He left Disney in 1942. He was named a Disney Legend posthumously in 1999.

Garland, Beverly (1926–2008) Actress; appeared on TV in *Elfego Baca*, *Texas John Slaughter*, and *Gallegher Goes West*.

Garner, James (1928–2014) Actor; appeared in *One Little Indian* (Clint Keyes), *The Castaway Cowboy* (Costain), and *The Distinguished Gentleman* (Jeff Johnson), and on TV in *8 Simple Rules* (Jim Hennessy). He voiced Commander Rourke in *Atlantis: The Lost Empire*.

Garner, Jennifer Actress; appeared in *Washington Square* (Marian Almond), *Mr. Magoo* (Stacey Sampanahoditra), *Pearl Harbor* (Sandra), *The Odd Life of Timothy Green* (Cindy Green), *Alexander and the Terrible, Horrible, No Good, Very Bad Day* (Kelly), and on TV in *Alias* (Sydney Bristow).

Garner (Wall), Marcellite (1910–1993) Member of the Ink & Paint Department at the Disney Studio, and the voice of Minnie Mouse, in the 1930s.

Garofalo, Janeane Actress; appeared in *Romy and Michele's High School Reunion* (Heather) and *Big Trouble* (Monica Romero), and on Disney+ in *Flora & Ulysses* (Marissa). She provided the voice of Bridget in *The Wild* and Colette in *Ratatouille*. On TV, she appeared in an episode of *Stumptown* (Janet Withers).

Garrett, Brad Actor; appeared in *The Pacifier* (Vice Principal Murney), on TV in *Single Parents* (Douglas), and guest starred in *Monk*. For Disney+, he created and exec. produced *Big Shot*. He has voiced numerous characters in films, including Dim in *A Bug's Life*, Bloat in *Finding Nemo* and *Finding Dory*, Auguste Gusteau in *Ratatouille*, Hook Hand Thug in *Tangled*, Eeyore in *Christopher Robin* and *Ralph Breaks the Internet*, Chug in the Planes films, Fred in *The Country Bears*, Riff Raff in *Underdog*, Uttamatomakkin in *Pocahontas II: Journey to a New World*, Tank in *An Extremely Goofy Movie*, and Uto in *Tarzan II*. TV voices include Eduardo in *Marsupilami*, Commissioner Stress/Wrongo in *The Shnookums & Meat Funny*

Cartoon Show, Grin in the *Mighty Ducks* animated series, Boss Beaver in *The Lion King's Timon & Pumbaa*, Dad in *Nightmare Ned*, Torque in *Buzz Lightyear of Star Command*, Big Mike in *Kim Possible*, Hook Hand Thug in *Tangled: The Series*, Professor Buffo in *Special Agent Oso*, and Robert Otto in *Amphibia*.

Garson, Greer (1904–1996) Actress; appeared in *The Happiest Millionaire* (Mrs. Drexel Biddle).

Gary Unmarried (TV) Comedy series on CBS; aired Sep. 24, 2008–Mar. 17, 2010. A recently divorced father of 2, Gary, is looking to start dating again, especially when his ex of 15 years announces that she is engaged to their marriage counselor. Stars Jay Mohr (Gary Brooks), Paula Marshall (Allison Brooks), Ed Begley, Jr. (Dr. Walter Krandall), Jaime King (Vanessa Flood), Al Madrigal (Dennis Lopez), Ryan Malgarini (Tom Brooks), Kathryn Newton (Louise Brooks). From ABC Studios.

Gaskill, Andy Artist; joined Disney first in 1973, hired into the Studio's animation training program. He animated on films, including *Winnie the Pooh and Tigger Too*, *The Rescuers*, and *The Fox and the Hound*. He later served as a storyboard artist on *Tron* and as a visual development artist on *The Little Mermaid*, plus contributed designs for Disney park attractions. He is credited with the art direction for *The Lion King*, *Hercules*, and *Treasure Planet*.

Gasparilla Grill & Games Quick-service restaurant and game arcade at Disney's Grand Floridian Resort & Spa at Walt Disney World; opened in 1988. Known as Gasparilla Island Grill after a makeover in 2013 that removed the arcade games.

Gaston Egotistical hunter who courts Belle in *Beauty and the Beast*; voiced by Richard White and animated by Andreas Deja.

Gaston's Tavern Fantasyland counter-service restaurant in the Magic Kingdom at Walt Disney World; opened Dec. 6, 2012. With a rustic atmosphere and antler décor, a large portrait of Gaston from *Beauty and the Beast*, and a massive fireplace, guests can dine on roasted pork shank or a warm cinnamon roll. LeFou's Brew, made with apple juice, toasted marshmallows, and a fruit-mango foam, is similar to Red's Apple Freeze, available at the Cozy Cone Motel in Disney California Adventure.

Gateway Gifts Souvenir shop underneath Spaceship Earth in EPCOT; opened Oct. 1, 1982.

Gay, Margie (1919–2003) Child actress who starred as Alice in the largest number of Alice Comedies. Her real name was Marjorie Teresa Gossett.

Gaynor's Nightmare Cartoon sequence animated at Disney that was inserted into the 20th Century Fox film *Servant's Entrance* (1934).

Gazebo, The Adventureland refreshment counter in Tokyo Disneyland; opened Apr. 15, 1983.

Gazelle Pop star in *Zootopia*; voiced by Shakira.

Gazzara, Ben (1930–2012) Actor; appeared in *Shadow Conspiracy* (Vice President Saxon).

GCB (TV) Drama series on ABC; aired Mar. 4–May 6, 2012. Amanda Vaughn, once the ultimate high school "mean girl," is forced to return home to Dallas in disgrace after her marriage ends in scandal. Her mother is delighted to have her back and wants to give her 2 teenage kids a good Southern upbringing. But Amanda is hesitant about reentering the world of opulence, status, and salacious rumor mills. She is hopeful for a new start but soon finds it's not that easy to escape her past in this tight-knit community. Stars Leslie Bibb (Amanda Vaughn), Kristin Chenoweth (Carlene Cockburn), Annie Potts (Gigi Stopper), Jennifer Aspen (Sharon Peacham), Miriam Shor (Cricket Caruth-Reilly), Marisol Nichols (Heather Cruz), Brad Beyer (Zack Peacham), Mark Deklin (Blake Reilly), David James Elliott (Ripp Cockburn). The series defines GCB as Good Christian Belles, though it is based on Kim Gatlin's book of a different title.

GCH Craftsman Grill Quick-service restaurant in Disney's Grand Californian Hotel & Spa at Disneyland Resort; opened Jul. 11, 2019, replacing White Water Snacks. A nearby pool bar, GCH Craftsman Bar, opened Jul. 3, 2019, offering artisanal pizzas, chicken skewers, and cocktails.

Geek Charming (TV) A Disney Channel Original Movie; first aired Nov. 11, 2011. When "it" girl Dylan Schoenfield teams up with film geek Josh Rosen to be the star of his documentary exposé about popularity at the upscale Woodlands Academy they become unlikely friends. She can't help making him over, and ultimately, he can't help falling for her as she strives to become the school's Blossom Queen while showing that she has a serious side and isn't really as much of a diva as he thought. Directed by Jeffrey Hornaday. Stars Sarah Hyland (Dylan Schoenfield), Matt Prokop (Josh Rosen), Jordan Nichols (Asher), Sasha Pieterse (Amy), Jimmy Bellinger (Steven), Lili Simmons (Lola). Filmed in Vancouver.

Geena Davis Show, The (TV) Half-hour series on ABC; aired Oct. 10, 2000–Jul. 12, 2001. Teddie Cochran is a successful New York City career woman who meets the man of her dreams, Max Ryan, only to learn he comes with an instant family and a home in the suburbs. Stars Geena Davis (Teddie), Peter Horton (Max), Mimi Rogers (Hillary), Kim Coles (Judy), Harland Williams (Alan), John Francis Daley (Carter), Makenzie Vega (Eliza), Esther Scott (Gladys).

Geer, Will (1902–1978) Actor; appeared in *Napoleon and Samantha* (grandfather).

Gehry, Frank Architect; designed Festival Disney (later Disney Village) at Disneyland Paris, the Team Disney Anaheim building at Disneyland Resort, and the Walt Disney Concert Hall for downtown Los Angeles.

Gelatoni SEE DUFFY AND FRIENDS.

General Beverages, Inc. Chattanooga, Tennessee-based soft drink manufacturer that produced Donald Duck beverages 1952–1955 and sold them throughout the country. The Donald Duck cola bottles often turn up at flea markets and are popular with bottle collectors as well as Disney collectors.

General Electric Carousel of Progress SEE CAROUSEL OF PROGRESS.

General Store Westernland shop in Tokyo Disneyland offering nuts and sweets; opened Apr. 1984. Formerly Rawhide Corral.

Genest, Emile (1921–2003) Actor; appeared in *Nikki, Wild Dog of the North* (Jacques LeBeau), *Big Red* (Emile Fornet), and *The Incredible Journey* (John Longridge), and on TV in *Kit Carson and the Mountain Men*.

Genie Wisecracking, all-powerful force in *Aladdin*; voiced by Robin Williams. In the TV series and in *Return of Jafar*, he was voiced by Dan Castellaneta.

Genius (TV) A Disney Channel Original Movie; first aired Aug. 21, 1999. Charlie, a supersmart 13-year-old, ends up feeling a little out of place when he chooses to attend Northern University to study physics under his favorite professor, Dr. Krickstein. Charlie finds it difficult to fit in until he creates an alter ego, "Chaz," a "cool kid," and simultaneously attends a local junior high so he can be near the girl of his dreams. At first he is able to juggle his double life, but it isn't long before both worlds collide. Directed by Rod Daniel. Stars Trevor Morgan (Charlie Boyle), Emmy Rossum (Claire Addison), Charles Fleischer (Dr. Krickstein), Peter Keleghan (Dean Wallace).

Gentilini, Mario (1909–1988) He was in charge of *Topolino* magazine at the Mondadori publishing company in Italy for many years; presented posthumously with a European Disney Legends Award in 1997.

Gentleman's Gentleman, A (film) Pluto cartoon released Mar. 28, 1941. Directed by Clyde Geronimi. Pluto, sent for the Sunday paper by Mickey, loses the dime in a grate but recovers it with gum on his tail and despite other tribulations finally presents the paper to Mickey all covered with mud.

George, Chief Dan (1899–1981) Native American actor; appeared in *Smith* (Ol' Antoine) and *The Bears and I* (Chief Peter A-Tas-Ka-Nay).

George, Gil [Hazel] (1904–1996) Lyricist on a number of Disney songs in the 1950s, including the title songs for *Old Yeller*, *Tonka*, and *The Light in the Forest*. Gil George was the pseudonym of Hazel George, the Disney Studio nurse.

George of the Jungle (film) Based on the well-known animated 1960s TV series, this live-action film features the klutzy George, who grows up as a Tarzan-like character after surviving a jungle plane crash and being raised by gorillas. He rescues a wayward traveler named Ursula when a lion attacks her while she is on safari. While Ursula warms to George and his fantasy jungle world—complete with a talking ape named Ape and an elephant who thinks it is a dog—Ursula's irksome fiancé, Lyle, plots to regain his ladylove and destroy the balance of nature in George's rain forest kingdom. When George is injured, Ursula brings him back to her world, specifically San Francisco, where he naturally has a difficult time adjusting and longs to return to his jungle home. Directed by Sam Weisman. Released Jul. 16, 1997. Stars Brendan Fraser (George), Leslie Mann (Ursula Stanhope), Thomas Haden Church (Lyle Van de Groot). 92 min. The elephant, Shep, is played by Tai, the 28-year-old veteran of such films as *Rudyard Kipling's The Jungle Book* and *Operation Dumbo Drop*, with his doglike movements added by Dream Quest Images through CG enhancements. Ape and the other gorillas were the result of teaming live actors with a sophisticated radio telemetry system devised by the Jim Henson Creature Shop. Inspired by the wit, style, and humor of Jay Ward, who produced the animated series for 4 years, the film's producers even retained the series' catchy and now-classic theme song. While San Francisco and Hawai'i provided outdoor locations, parts of the jungle were also built indoors, utilizing the former Hughes Aircraft hangar in Playa del Rey, California, the same place where Howard Hughes built his flying boat, the *Spruce Goose*.

George of the Jungle 2 (film) Direct-to-video release Oct. 21, 2003; a sequel to the 1997 film. George's scheming mother-in-law, Beatrice Stanhope, with Ursula's ex-fiancé, Lyle, to hypnotize Ursula into leaving George, so they can turn the jungle to mulch. George and his animal pals must travel to Las Vegas to rescue Ursula before returning to the jungle to stop the bulldozers. Directed by David Grossman. Stars Christopher Showerman (George), Thomas Haden Church (Lyle Van de Groot), Julie Benz (Ursula), Christina Pickles (Beatrice Stanhope), Kelly Miller (Betsy), Angus T. Jones (George Jr.), John Cleese (Ape). Based on characters created by Jay Ward. Filmed on location in Queensland, Australia.

George Wendt Show, The (TV) Half-hour series on CBS; aired Mar. 8–Apr. 12, 1995. Focused on the relationship between 2 brothers, George and Dan Coleman, who own a garage in Madison, Wisconsin, and who also produce a local call-in radio show, dispensing their sage wisdom to the mechanically challenged. Stars George Wendt (George), Pat Finn (Dan), Mark Christopher Lawrence (Fletcher), Kate Hodge (Libby), Brian Doyle-Murray (Finnie).

Georgette Prissy poodle in *Oliver & Company*; voiced by Bette Midler.

Geppetto Kindly wood-carver who made Pinocchio; voiced by Christian Rub in the 1940 animated film.

Geppetto (TV) Two-hour musical on *The Wonderful World of Disney*; first aired May 7, 2000. In Villagio, the lonely toy maker Geppetto yearns for a son. The Blue Fairy grants him his wish by bringing Pinocchio to life, but Geppetto's unrealistic expectations for his son cause the boy to run away and join Stromboli's traveling puppet show. The Blue Fairy helps Geppetto in his search for Pinocchio. Geppetto is horrified to visit Idyllia—where Prof. Buonragazzo has a machine that can create the perfect child—and Pleasure Island. Eventually, Pinocchio and Geppetto are reunited. Stars Drew Carey (Geppetto), Julia Louis-Dreyfus (Blue Fairy), Brent Spiner (Stromboli), Rene Auberjonois (Buonragazzo), Seth Adkins (Pinocchio), Usher Raymond (Ring Leader). There is new music by Stephen Schwartz and 1 reused song ("I've Got No Strings") from the 1940 animated feature.

Geppetto & Son See My Son Pinocchio: Geppetto's Musical Tale.

Geppetto's Arts & Crafts Fantasyland shop in Disneyland; opened in 1983, selling marionettes, cuckoo clocks, and other wood-carved items. Later became Geppetto's Toys & Gifts. In 2004, it became Names Unraveled, which relocated from Sleeping Beauty Castle. On May 12, 2006, it was replaced by Geppetto's Holiday Workshop. Renamed Wishing Star Magic Crystals in Aug. 2008, with product from the former Three Fairies Magic Crystals shop. On May 26, 2010, it became Geppetto's Sweet Shop, superseded Oct. 15 by a *Tangled* character-greeting cottage. Became Frozen Royal Reception in 2013. See also La Bottega di Geppetto (Disneyland Paris).

Gerald Hapless sea lion in *Finding Dory*; voiced by Torbin Xan Bullock.

Gere, Richard Actor; appeared in *Pretty Woman* (Edward Lewis) and *Runaway Bride* (Ike Graham).

Geri's Game (film) Animated short from Pixar Animation Studios as an independent company (not by Disney). Released Nov. 25, 1997. Academy Award winner for Best Cartoon. It was later released with *A Bug's Life* Nov. 25, 1998. An elderly man plays chess with himself, taking on multiple personalities as his opponent. Directed by Jan Pinkava. 5 min.

Germany World Showcase pavilion in EPCOT; opened Oct. 1, 1982, patterned after towns such as the picturesque, walled Rothenburg. A statue honoring St. George, the patron saint of soldiers, is in the center of the square, and a glockenspiel chimes tunes themed to the pavilion. Dining is available in Biergarten Restaurant and Sommerfest, with shopping at Der Teddybär, Volkskunst, Das Kaufhaus, Stein Haus, Karamell-Küche, and Die Weihnachts Ecke.

Geronimi, Clyde ("Gerry") (1901–1989) He was hired at Disney in 1931 as an animator on the short cartoons, promoted to director in 1939, and directed the Academy Award winners *The Ugly Duckling* and *Lend a Paw*. He was a sequence director on features from *Victory Through Air Power* to *One Hundred and One Dalmatians*, and supervising director on *Sleeping Beauty*. He also directed many of the early TV shows. He retired in 1959 and was named a Disney Legend posthumously in 2017.

Geronimo's Revenge (film) John Slaughter has been desperately trying to stop Geronimo from violating the rather delicate and nervous peace that has been established with Natchez, the chief of the Apache tribe, who desires a continued peace rather than fruitless bloodshed. Geronimo stages increasingly damaging and ferocious raids, then escapes below the border. Knowing that he will return, Gen. Nelson A. Miles has sought out Slaughter as the only one who would know how to deal with this dangerous threat. Because of what has happened, Slaughter leaves his ranch and family and plans the strategy that eventually lures Geronimo into a trap that brings to an end his days as a raider. International theatrical compilation of *Texas John Slaughter* TV episodes. First released in England in May 1964. Directed by James Neilson and Harry Keller. 77 min. Stars Tom Tryon, Darryl Hickman. Also the title of Episode 12 of the *Texas John Slaughter* TV series.

Gerson, Betty Lou (1914–1999) She provided the voice of Cruella De Vil in *One Hundred and One Dalmatians*, narrated *Cinderella*, and appeared as the old crone in *Mary Poppins*. She was named a Disney Legend in 1996.

Get a Clue (TV) A Disney Channel Original Movie;

first aired Jun. 28, 2002. Lexy is a 13-year-old fashion queen and budding journalist for the newspaper at Millington, the prep school she attends in Manhattan. After the disappearance of her English teacher, Mr. Walker, she; her street-smart editor, Jack; and her pals find themselves embroiled in a scheme bigger than they ever could have imagined. But they use their investigative skills to rescue Mr. Walker from Meaney's malicious mischief. Directed by Maggie Greenwald. Stars Lindsay Lohan (Alexandra "Lexy" Gold), Bug Hall (Jack Downey), Brenda Song (Jennifer Hervey), Ali Mukaddam (Gabe Nelson), Ian Gomez (Mr. Walker), Amanda Plummer (Miss Dawson), Charles Shaughnessy (Meaney). 83 min.

Get a Horse! (film) Mickey Mouse cartoon. Mickey and Minnie, with their friends Horace Horsecollar and Clarabelle Cow, delight in a musical wagon ride until Peg-Leg Pete shows up and tries to run them off the road. Bursting through the film screen, the group finds themselves mixed up between the black-and-white cartoon world and a colorful, modern-day movie theater. Released initially at the Annecy International Animation Film Festival Jun. 11, 2013. Theatrical release on Nov. 27, 2013, with *Frozen*. Directed by Lauren MacMullan. Created in the 1920s animation style using archival sound recordings, with voices including Walt Disney (Mickey), Billy Bletcher (Pete), Marcellite Garner (Minnie). Russi Taylor and Will Ryan added some new lines for Minnie and Pete, respectively. 6 min. From Walt Disney Animation Studios.

Get it Right: Following Directions with Goofy (film) Educational film; released in Sep. 1982. Goofy helps illustrate why directions—visual, spoken, and written—are so important.

Get Rich Quick (film) Goofy cartoon released Aug. 31, 1951. Directed by Jack Kinney. Again playing Everyman, Goofy wins money at poker and though his wife is initially angry with his gambling, she forgives him when she sees the amount of cash he has won, causing Goofy to say, "Easy come, easy go!"

Get the Message (film) Educational film explaining the importance of communication to mankind and tracing the development of communication techniques; released in Dec. 1971.

Getting Physically Fit (film) Educational film, from the Fun to Be Fit series; released in Mar. 1983.

Students learn how to achieve fitness through a carefully planned program.

Getty, Balthazar Actor; appeared in *Judge Dredd* (Olmeyer), *White Squall* (Tod Johnston), and *Ladder 49* (Ray Gauquin), and on TV in *Brothers & Sisters* (Thomas Walker) and *When We Rise* (David).

Getty, Estelle (1923–2008) Actress; appeared on TV in *The Golden Girls* and *The Golden Palace*, and eventually on *Empty Nest*, all as Sophia Petrillo. She won the Emmy Award as Outstanding Supporting Actress in a Comedy Series in 1988. She was named a Disney Legend posthumously in 2009.

Geyser Point Bar & Grill Fast-casual restaurant and pool bar at Disney's Wilderness Lodge at Walt Disney World; opened Feb. 13, 2017.

G-Force (film) A covert government program trains animals to work in espionage. Armed with the latest high-tech spy equipment, these highly trained guinea pigs discover that the fate of the world is in their paws. Tapped for the G-Force are guinea pigs Darwin, the squad leader determined to succeed at all costs; Blaster, an outrageous weapons expert with tons of attitude and a love for all things extreme; and Juarez, a martial arts pro, plus the literal fly-on-the-wall reconnaissance expert, Mooch, and a star-nosed mole, Speckles, the computer and information specialist. These ultra-intelligent animal commandos try to prevent an evil billionaire from taking over the world. Released Jul. 24, 2009, in the U.S. after a Jul. 23 international release. From Disney and Jerry Bruckheimer Films. Directed by Hoyt Yeatman, Jr. Stars Nicolas Cage (voice of Speckles), Sam Rockwell (voice of Darwin), Steve Buscemi (voice of Bucky), Tracy Morgan (voice of Blaster), Bill Nighy (Saber), Will Arnett (Kip Killian), Zach Galifianakis (Ben), Kelli Garner (Marci), Gabriel Casseus (Agent Carter), Jack Conley (Agent Trigstad), Penélope Cruz (voice of Juarez), Dee Bradley Baker (voice of Mooch). 88 min. In CinemaScope. Filmed in Disney Digital 3-D. A blend of live-action and computer-animated characters. Filmed around Los Angeles.

Ghirardelli Soda Fountain and Chocolate Shop Opened in Downtown Disney Marketplace (now the Marketplace at Disney Springs) at Walt Disney World Dec. 15, 1997, taking the place of Goofy's Grill. Also opened in Disney California Adventure

Jun. 7, 2012, replacing the Mission Tortilla Factory, and next to the El Capitan Theatre in Hollywood Nov. 13, 2013, replacing Disney's Soda Fountain.

Ghost and Molly McGee, The (TV) Animated buddy-comedy series on Disney Channel; premiered Oct. 1, 2021. When one of his curses backfires, a grumpy ghost named Scratch finds himself forever bound to tween optimist Molly. Their unlikely friendship leads to misadventures as they navigate Molly's new school and town. Voices include Ashly Burch (Molly McGee), Dana Snyder (Scratch), Jordan Klepper (Pete McGee), Sumalee Montano (Sharon McGee/Grandma Nin), Michaela Dietz (Darryl McGee). From Disney Television Animation.

Ghost of Cypress Swamp, The (TV) Two-hour movie; aired Mar. 13, 1977. Directed by Vincent McEveety. A teen, Lonny Bascombe, and his dad hunt a black panther that has been terrorizing local farms, but it eludes them. Lonny is captured by and then befriends an escaped fugitive living in the swamp, as both help each other survive. The boy promises to keep the hermit's secret, and finally is able to kill the marauding panther. Stars Vic Morrow, Jeff East, Tom Simcox, Jacqueline Scott, Noah Beery, Louise Latham, Shug Fisher, Cindy Eilbacher.

Ghost of the Mountains (film) Documentary chronicling the making of Disneynature's *Born in China*. An international group of filmmakers sets out on a mission to get up close and personal with a family of elusive snow leopards. Digitally released Jun. 30, 2017, on Disney Movies Anywhere. Narrated by Antoine Fuqua. Directed by Ben Wallis. 78 min. From Disneynature. SEE ALSO EXPEDITION CHINA.

Ghost Whisperer (TV) One-hour series on CBS; aired Sep. 23, 2005–May 21, 2010. Melinda Gordon has a gift of being able to see, and talk to, spirits. These are earthbound ghosts who have yet to cross over to the other side, who seek Melinda's help in communicating with the living. Although Melinda sometimes embraces her abilities as a blessing and other times sees them as a curse, she always helps her clients—alive or dead—find emotional closure. Stars Jennifer Love Hewitt (Melinda Gordon), David Conrad (Jim Clancy), Aisha Tyler (Andrea Moreno). From Sander/Moses Prods., in association with Touchstone Television and Paramount Television. Sets used for the show were dam-

aged in a backlot fire at Universal Studios on Jun. 1, 2008.

Ghosts of Buxley Hall, The (TV) Two-part show; aired Dec. 21, 1980, and Jan. 4, 1981. Directed by Bruce Bilson. Girls come to a private boys' military academy to the horror of the boys and the ghosts of the academy's founders, who come out to help rid the academy of the young women. There is a plot afoot to tear down the school, unless the guardian of one of the cadets comes through with a promised donation. Stars Victor French, Louise Latham, Rad Daly, Monte Markham, Ruta Lee, Vito Scotti, Don Porter, Christian Juttner, Tricia Cast, John Myhers.

Ghosts of the Abyss (film) Cameras make an expedition below the surface of the ocean to the final resting place of the *Titanic*. Using state-of-the-art technology developed expressly for this expedition, the filmmakers are able to explore virtually all of the wreckage, inside and out, as never before. Directed by James Cameron. Produced in association with Walden Media. Released Apr. 11, 2003. With Bill Paxton. 60 min. Simultaneous release in 3-D in regular and large-format/IMAX theaters. James Cameron is known for directing the award-winning *Titanic* (1997), in which Bill Paxton was one of the actors. Released on DVD in 2004.

G.I. Jane (film) Navy intelligence officer Lt. Jordan O'Neil sets a historic precedent when she is recruited as a test case to be the first woman allowed to train for the highly covert operations unit known as the Navy SEALs. Selected for her courage, skills, and levelheadedness, O'Neil is determined to succeed in the most demanding, most merciless, and most honored fighting force in the world, in which 60% of her male counterparts will fail. Under the relentless command of Master Chief John Urgayle, O'Neil is put through weeks of physical and emotional misery and is not expected to succeed. Indeed, military and high-ranking government officials—including her sponsor, Sen. Lillian DeHaven—are *counting* on her to fail. However, to their dismay and perplexity, O'Neil perseveres. When the recruits' final training exercise is diverted to aid in extricating American troops in Libya, Urgayle is critically wounded, and O'Neil must gather all her leadership experience and courage to save him and the mission—even at the risk of her own life. A Hollywood Pictures film, in association with Scott Free Productions and Largo Entertainment. Directed by Ridley Scott. Released Aug. 22, 1997. 125 min. Filmed in CinemaScope. Stars Demi

Moore (Jordan O'Neil), Viggo Mortensen (John Urgayle), Anne Bancroft (Lillian DeHaven), Jason Beghe (Royce). Casting directors began a search for actors and extras who were in perfect physical shape and were lucky in finding many who had military backgrounds. For the training base, the filmmakers selected Camp Blanding, a 30,000-acre National Guard training site in northern Florida. Other filming took place in Jacksonville's Huguenot Park; at Hunting Island State Park near Beaufort, South Carolina; and in Washington, D.C., and neighboring Virginia and Maryland.

Giacchino, Michael Composer; he has scored feature films, including *The Incredibles*, *Sky High*, *Ratatouille* (Academy Award nominee), *Up* (Academy Award winner), *Cars 2*, *John Carter*, *Tomorrowland*, *Inside Out*, *Zootopia*, *Doctor Strange*, *Rogue One: A Star Wars Story*, *Coco*, *Incredibles 2*, *Lightyear*, and *Thor: Love and Thunder*, plus several animated shorts, such as *Day & Night*, *One Man Band*, *Partly Cloudy*, *How to Hook Up Your Home Theater*, *The Ballad of Nessie*, *Electric Holiday*, and *Riley's First Date?* For TV, he wrote the score for *Alias*, *Lost*, *The Muppets' Wizard of Oz*, *Toy Story of Terror!*, and the Prep & Landing specials. For Disney+, he directed and scored *Werewolf by Night*. Also scored music for the Disney parks, including Space Mountain (Disneyland), Star Tours — The Adventures Continue, Ratatouille: L'Aventure Totalement Toquée de Rémy, and the Incredicoaster.

Giamatti, Paul Actor; appeared in *Cradle Will Rock* (Carlo), *Duets* (Todd Woods), *Saving Mr. Banks* (Ralph), and *Jungle Cruise* (Nilo), and on TV in *Tourist Trap* (Jeremiah Piper).

Giantland (film) Mickey Mouse cartoon released Nov. 25, 1933. Directed by Burt Gillett. Mickey tells his nephews a loose version of "Jack and the Beanstalk," in which he climbs the beanstalk and meets a formidable giant. Mickey only manages to escape with the aid of pepper and by burning the beanstalk, which sends the giant hurtling toward the ground and on through to China. A forerunner to the *Mickey and the Beanstalk* segment of *Fun and Fancy Free*.

Gibson SEE CARD CORNER.

Gibson, Blaine (1918–2015) Artist/sculptor; joined Disney in 1939 as an inbetweener and assistant animator, working on features through *One Hundred and One Dalmatians*. In 1954 he began working on projects at WED Enterprises in his spare time and transferred there permanently in 1961. He headed the sculpture department, responsible for most of the heads of the Audio-Animatronics characters, from pirates to the presidents. His statue of Walt and Mickey, called *Partners*, graces the Central Plaza in Disneyland and other Disney locations. He retired in 1983 and was made a Disney Legend in 1993.

Gibson, Charles Anchor of ABC's *World News* May 2006–Dec. 31, 2009. He served 34 years with ABC News, including co-anchoring *Good Morning, America* (1987–1998) and *Primetime Thursday* (1998–2004).

Gibson, Mel Actor; voiced Capt. John Smith in *Pocahontas*, appeared in *Ransom* (Tom Mullen) and *Signs* (Graham Hess), and directed *Apocalypto*. He appeared in the Backstage Studio Tour at Disney-MGM Studios.

Gibson Girl Ice Cream Parlour, The Located on Main Street, U.S.A. in Disneyland Paris; opened Apr. 12, 1992. Also opened on Main Street, U.S.A. in Disneyland in 1997 (using the American spelling of Parlor), taking the place of the former Carnation Ice Cream Parlor, but one door down the street in space formerly occupied by Blue Ribbon Bakery.

Gideon's Crossing (TV) One-hour drama on ABC; aired Oct. 18, 2000–Apr. 9, 2001. As chief of experimental medicine at a prestigious Boston teaching hospital, Benjamin Gideon, an unorthodox doctor who explores the brave new world of cutting-edge medicine, ventures into the even-trickier terrain of his patients' lives. Stars Andre Braugher (Ben Gideon), Rubén Blades (Max Cabranes), Russell Hornsby (Aaron Boies), Hamish Linklater (Bruce Cherry), Eric Lane (Wyatt Cooper), Rhona Mitra (Ollie Klein).

Gifford, Frank (1930–2015) A former NFL football player, Frank joined ABC as a commentator on *ABC's Monday Night Football* in 1971. He received an Emmy Award in 1971 as Outstanding Sports Personality. He received the Pete Rozelle Award from the Pro Football Hall of Fame in 1995 and was named a Disney Legend in 2008.

Gift Card On Nov. 8, 2004, Disneyland began selling a gift card at merchandise locations throughout the resort. The cards can be purchased in any amount from $5–$1,500. This was the first gift card offered in a Disney park. It was later sold at Disney Store locations in the U.S., at Walt Disney World and other Disney destinations, and online, where personalization options are offered.

Gift of Time, A: Pediatric AIDS (film) Educational film discussing drug treatments and other aspects, in the EPCOT Educational Media Collection; released in Oct. 1989. 18 min.

Gift Planet Shop in the Tokyo Disney Resort Toy Story Hotel; opened Apr. 5, 2022.

Gifted, The (TV) Hour-long series on Fox; aired Oct. 2, 2017–Feb. 26, 2019. A suburban couple has their ordinary lives rocked by the sudden discovery that their teenage children possess mutant powers. Forced to go on the run from a hostile government, the family seeks help from an underground network of mutants and must fight to survive. Stars Stephen Moyer (Reed Strucker), Amy Acker (Caitlin Strucker), Natalie Alyn Lind (Lauren Strucker), Percy Hynes White (Andy Strucker), Sean Teale (Eclipse/Marcos Diaz), Jamie Chung (Blink/Clarice Fong), Emma Dumont (Polaris/Lorna Dane). From 20th Century Fox Television in association with Marvel Television.

Gift-Giver Extraordinaire Machine Promotion at Disneyland for its 30th anniversary in 1985. During that year, every 30th guest coming to the park received a prize upon entering the front gate; for the more elaborate prizes, up to and including a new car, selected winners would get to spin the Gift-Giver Machine located in the Central Plaza.

Gilbert, Billy (1893–1971) He voiced Sneezy in *Snow White and the Seven Dwarfs* and Willie the Giant in *Mickey and the Beanstalk*.

Gilbert, Ray (1912–1976) Lyricist; wrote the words for a number of Disney songs in the 1940s, including "Zip-A-Dee-Doo-Dah," "You Belong to My Heart," and "Baia."

Gilkyson, Terry (1916–1999) Composer who contributed memorable songs to *Swiss Family Robinson* ("My Heart Was an Island"), *The Three Lives of Thomasina* ("Thomasina"), *Savage Sam* (title song), *The Moon-Spinners* (title song), *The Scarecrow of Romney Marsh* (title song), *The Jungle Book* ("The Bare Necessities"), *My Dog, the Thief* (title song), and *The Aristocats* ("Thomas O'Malley").

Gill, Florence (1877–1965) She provided the voice of Clara Cluck and the Wise Little Hen.

Gillespie, Darlene Mouseketeer from the 1950s *Mickey Mouse Club* TV show.

Gillett, Burton (1891–1971) Director; he started at Disney in 1929 and remained until 1934, returning for a year in 1936. He directed 48 Disney cartoons, including *The Chain Gang*, *The Picnic*, *The Birthday Party*, *The Moose Hunt*, *Blue Rhythm*, *Flowers and Trees*, *King Neptune*, *Mickey's Good Deed*, *Three Little Pigs*, *Mickey's Gala Premiere*, *Orphans' Benefit*, and *Lonesome Ghosts*.

Gipson, Fred (1908–1973) Author of the book *Old Yeller* on which the Disney movie was based.

Girl Meets World (TV) Comedy series on Disney Channel; premiered Jun. 27, 2014, and ended Jan. 20, 2017, after 69 episodes. Continuing the story line of *Boy Meets World*, Cory and Topanga are married and have 2 children. Daughter Riley and her best friend, Maya, are learning to traverse the twists and turns of middle school while under the watchful eye of their history teacher, who just so happens to be Riley's dad. Stars Rowan Blanchard (Riley Matthews), Sabrina Carpenter (Maya Hart), Danielle Fishel (Topanga Matthews), Ben Savage (Cory Matthews), Corey Fogelmanis (Shamus Farkle), August Maturo (Auggie Matthews), Peyton Meyer (Lucas Friar). Other actors from the original show who make occasional appearances include Rider Strong, Lee Norris, Will Friedle, Betsy Randle, William Russ, and William Daniels. From It's a Laugh Productions and Michael Jacobs Productions.

Girl vs. Monster (TV) A Disney Channel Original Movie; first aired Oct. 12, 2012. Teenaged Skylar inadvertently unleashes an immortal monster, Deimata, while defying her parents' wishes that she stay home on Halloween—discovering the family secret that she is a 5th-generation monster hunter. Skylar and her friends must come together to defeat the monster menace. Directed by Stuart `Gillard. Stars Olivia Holt (Skylar), Brendan Meyer (Henry), Kerris Dorsey (Sadie), Katherine McNamara (Myra), Luke Benward (Ryan Dean), Tracy Dawson (Deimata).

Girl Who Spelled Freedom, The (TV) Two-hour movie; aired Feb. 23, 1986. Directed by Simon

Wincer. A Cambodian refugee living with an American family has problems adjusting to her new life, but she excels at school and within a few years is accomplished enough to enter and win a spelling bee. Stars Wayne Rogers, Mary Kay Place, Jade Chinn.

Giselle Romantic princess-to-be in *Enchanted*; played by Amy Adams.

Give a Little Whistle Song from *Pinocchio*; written by Ned Washington and Leigh Harline.

Givot, George (1903–1984) He voiced Tony, the proprietor of the spaghetti restaurant in *Lady and the Tramp*.

Gladstone Gander Comic book character with an abrasive personality; never appeared in films. Created by Carl Barks, he debuted in *Walt Disney's Comics and Stories* no. 88 in Jan. 1948. He was a cousin of Donald Duck and extremely lucky. He was also a loafer and a chiseler. Gladstone has appeared on TV, in *DuckTales*.

Glago's Guest (film) Computer-animated short; premiered Jun. 10, 2008, at the Annecy International Animation Film Festival. A lonely Russian guard at a Siberian outpost in the 1920s is visited by an alien spaceship during his shift. Directed by Chris Williams. 7 min.

Glas und Porzellan Shop selling Hummel and Goebel collectibles in Germany in EPCOT, presented by W. Goebel Porzellanfabrik; open Oct. 1, 1982–Jul. 12, 2010, replaced by Karamelle-Küche.

Glass (film) David Dunn pursues Kevin Wendell Crumb's superhuman figure of The Beast in a series of escalating encounters, while the shadowy presence of Elijah Price emerges as an orchestrator who holds secrets critical to both men. Released Jan. 18, 2019, in the U.S., after Jan. 16–17 international releases. Directed by M. Night Shyamalan. Stars James McAvoy (Kevin Wendell Crumb/Dennis/The Beast/Hedwig/other roles), Bruce Willis (David Dunn), Samuel L. Jackson (Elijah Price), Anya Taylor-Joy (Casey Cooke), Sarah Paulson (Dr. Ellie Staple). 129 min. A sequel to *Unbreakable* (2000), from Touchstone Pictures, and *Split* (2006), from Universal Pictures, it was distributed domestically by Universal and internationally by Buena Vista International. Shot on location in and around Philadelphia. From Blinding Edge Pictures and Blumhouse with participation from The Walt Disney Studios.

Glass Fantasies Shop on Main Street, U.S.A. in Disneyland Paris; opened Apr. 12, 1992.

Glass Slipper, The Glassware shop in Fantasyland in Tokyo Disneyland; opened Apr. 15, 1983. Skilled artisans demonstrate glass cutting.

Gloaming, The (TV) Eight-part limited drama series; aired Mar. 21–May 9, 2021, on Starz, after a Jan. 1, 2020, digital release on Stan, an Australian streaming service. When an unidentified woman is found brutally murdered, detective Molly McGee must team up with Alex O'Connell, a fellow cop with whom she shares a tragic past. To solve the crime, they have to face the ghosts of their past, the unsettled dead that linger in the liminal space between life and death—The Gloaming. Stars Ewen Leslie (Alex O'Connell), Emma Booth (Molly McGee), Aaron Pedersen (Lewis), Rena Owen (Grace), Anthony Phelan (William), Nicole Chamoun (Jacinta). A Two Jons production for Stan and ABC Studios International.

Global Van Lines Company which operated a locker area on Town Square in Disneyland May 1963–1979. The area was formerly sponsored by Bekins and later by National Car Rentals.

Glory and Pageantry of Christmas, The 38 performers presented the Nativity story in an elaborate musical production held annually on the Village Dock Stage in the Lake Buena Vista Shopping Village (later Disney Village Marketplace), 1975–1994.

Glory Road (film) The inspiring true story of the college underdog Texas Western Miners basketball team. Passionately dedicated coach Don Haskins's decision to play his all-African American starting team helped break down barriers of segregation that affected every segment of society and set a new course for the future as the team did the one thing they could to prove themselves to a watching world—they played their hearts out. The Miners took the country by storm and, in a surprise turn of events, won the 1966 NCAA tournament title against the all-white juggernaut University of Kentucky Wildcats. From Walt Disney Pictures in association with Jerry Bruckheimer Films. Released Jan. 13, 2006. Directed by James Gartner. Stars Josh Lucas (Don Haskins), Derek Luke (Bobby Joe Hill), Austin Nichols (Jerry Armstrong), Jon Voight

(Adolph Rupp), Evan Jones (Moe Iba), Mehcad Brooks (Harry Flournoy), Emily Deschanel (Mary Haskins), Sam Jones III (Willie Worsley), Schin A. S. Kerr (David Lattin), Alphonso McAuley (Orsten Artis), Damaine Radcliff (Willie Cager), Al Shearer (Nevil Shed). 118 min. In order to help duplicate the NCAA championship game, the filmmakers were able to track down rare home movie footage, photos from Texas Western yearbooks, and over 30 priceless rolls of photographic film shot by *Sports Illustrated*. Filmed in New Orleans and El Paso in Super 35-Scope.

Glover, Crispin Actor; appeared in *Where the Heart Is* (Lionel) and *Alice in Wonderland* (Knave of Hearts, 2010).

Glover, Danny Actor; appeared in *Angels in the Outfield* (George Knox), *Operation Dumbo Drop* (Sam Cahill), *Gone Fishin'* (Gus Green), *Beloved* (Paul D), *The Royal Tenenbaums* (Henry Sherman), and *The Shaggy Dog* (Ken Hollister). On TV, he made guest appearances in *Criminal Minds* (Hank Morgan) and *black-ish* (Uncle Norman).

Glover, Donald Actor; appeared in *The Muppets* (Junior CDE Executive); *Alexander and the Terrible, Horrible, No Good, Very Bad Day* (Greg); and *Solo: A Star Wars Story* (Lando Calrissian). He provided the voice of Simba in *The Lion King* (2019).

Glover, William Actor; provided the voice of Winston in *Oliver & Company* and appeared on TV in *Meet the Munceys* (Edmund Haddy).

Gnome-Mobile, The (film) In the redwood forests of California, a multimillionaire lumberman and his 2 young grandchildren encounter 2 gnomes, old Knobby and young Jasper. Supposedly, they're the last of their kind, but everyone sets off on a trip in a Gnome-Mobile (an old Rolls-Royce) to find the rest of the gnomes. After a series of adventures and mishaps, they do, and the lumberman deeds the forest to the gnomes for eternity. Released Jul. 12, 1967. Directed by Robert Stevenson. 85 min. Stars Walter Brennan (Knobby/D. J. Mulrooney), Matthew Garber (Rodney) and Karen Dotrice (Elizabeth) (both billed as "the *Mary Poppins* kids" in the credits), Richard Deacon (Ralph Yarby), Tom Lowell (Jasper), Sean McClory (Horatio Quaxton), Ed Wynn (Rufus), Jerome Cowan (Dr. Ramsey). Based on the book *The Gnomobile* by Upton Sinclair, who was inspired to write the story while on his first car trip visiting the redwood

forests along the Pacific coast. The title song was written by Richard M. Sherman and Robert B. Sherman. Walter Brennan was used to dual advantage as crotchety old Knobby and the wealthy grandfather, D. J. Mulrooney. The wondrous special effects were accomplished by Eustace Lycett and Robert A. Mattey.

Gnomeo & Juliet (film) Two neighbors try to outdo each other with backyards decorated with an array of tacky garden gnomes. What they do not know is that the gnomes come to life when they aren't being seen by humans. The gnomes in one yard, the Reds, are sworn enemies of the gnomes in the other yard, the Blues, with each group constantly trying to outdo the other. When a red gnome, Juliet, falls in love with a blue gnome, Gnomeo, they are caught up in the feud between neighbors, which soon becomes a war. Released Feb. 11, 2011, as a Touchstone film. Directed by Kelly Asbury. Voices include Emily Blunt (Juliet), James McAvoy (Gnomeo), Jason Statham (Tybalt), Michael Caine (Lord Redbrick), Maggie Smith (Lady Bluebury), Patrick Stewart (William Shakespeare), Julie Walters (Lady Montague). 84 min. The computer-animated film had originally been pitched to Walt Disney Feature Animation by Rocket Pictures in 2000 but was taken over by Miramax in 2006. With the sale of Miramax in 2010, distribution rights were retained by Disney. Elton John served as exec. producer, and the film utilized many of his songs.

Go Figure (TV) A Disney Channel Original Movie; first aired Jun. 10, 2005. Fourteen-year-old Katelin Kingsford dreams of being an Olympic figure skating champion. In order to train with a renowned coach, she is forced to join the Buckston Academy girls hockey team. To her surprise, she discovers true friendship and teamwork for the first time and gains a new appreciation of the meaning of family. Directed by Francine McDougall. Stars Jordan Hinson (Katelin), Whitney Sloan (Hollywood Henderson), Amy Halloran (Ronnie), Tania Gunadi (Mojo), Jake Abel (Spencer), Cristine Rose (Natasha Goberman), Ryan Malgarini (Bradley Kingsford), Sabrina Speer (Shelby), Paul Kiernan (Coach Reynolds). Skating star Kristi Yamaguchi appears as herself. Filmed in Salt Lake City.

Go Fish (TV) Half-hour series on NBC; aired Jun. 19–Jul. 3, 2001. High school freshman Andy Troutner plots to become popular and win the affections of the beautiful Jess Riley, while his older brother, Pete, joins the teaching staff, hoping to inspire students with his boundless enthusiasm. Stars Kieran Culkin (Andy), Will Friedle (Pete), Katherine Ellis (Jess), Kyle Sabihy (Henry Krakowski), Taylor Handley (Hazard). From Touchstone Television.

GO Network Internet portal site created by Disney and Infoseek; launched Jan. 12, 1999. The network offered such services as news, stock quotes, chat rooms, search engines, e-mail, and weather, with the ability to personalize certain areas. On Nov. 17, 1999, Disney stockholders approved a spin-off of GO.com and the purchase of Infoseek with that company merging with Disney's Buena Vista Internet Group as a separate Disney entity. The new GO.com's shares began trading on the New York Stock Exchange the next day. This tracking stock in 2000 changed its name to Disney Internet Group. On Mar. 1, 2001, the company converted the stock to Disney Common Stock and closed the GO.com portal business.

Go the Distance Song from *Hercules*; written by Alan Menken and David Zippel. Nominated for an Academy Award.

Go West, Young Dog (TV) Show aired Feb. 20, 1977. Directed by William Stierwalt. Dorsey is a dog in the 1880s who carries the mail and gets mixed up with crooked gold miners. Stars Frank Keith, Charles Granata, Dennis Dillon.

Goal! The Dream Begins (film) A poor Mexican American immigrant from Los Angeles, Santiago Munez, seems destined to follow in his father's path in life—laboring at menial jobs to earn just enough money to support his family—but he has an amazing gift on the soccer field. Discovered by a British scout, he is given a chance with one of England's premier soccer clubs, Newcastle United. Santiago, alone in a world where soccer is a religion and players are gods, must prove that he has the talent and determination to make it among the best in the world. Produced by Milkshake Films and Epsilon Motion Pictures in association with Touchstone Pictures. Released May 12, 2006, after a premiere at the Deauville Film Festival on Sep. 8, 2005, and a first theatrical release in Israel on Sep. 29, 2005. Directed by Danny Cannon. Stars Kuno Becker (Santiago Munez), Stephen Dillane (Glen Foy), Anna Friel (Roz Harmison), Marcel Iures (Erik Dornhelm), Sean Pertwee (Barry Rankin),

Alessandro Nivola (Gavin Harris), Tony Plana (Hernan Munez). 118 min. Filmed in CinemaScope in Newcastle, London, and Los Angeles.

Godboldo, Dale Actor; appeared on the *Mickey Mouse Club* on The Disney Channel, beginning in 1991.

Goddess of Spring, The (film) Silly Symphony cartoon released Nov. 3, 1934. Directed by Wilfred Jackson. One of Disney's early attempts at animating a human female figure. The goddess Persephone is captured by the devil as his bride and sent to the underworld, with an agreement to return to Earth 6 months each year. While the animation of the goddess was unrealistic, it did give the animators some early practice for eventually animating Snow White in the 1937 animated feature.

Godfather of Harlem (TV) Hour-long drama series on MGM+ (previously EPIX); premiered Sep. 29, 2019. Infamous crime boss Bumpy Johnson returns from ten years in prison to find the neighborhood he once ruled in shambles. With the streets controlled by the Italian mob, Bumpy must take on the Genovese crime family to regain control. Inspired by real people and events. Stars Forest Whitaker (Bumpy Johnson), Vincent D'Onofrio (Vincent Gigante), Ilfenesh Hadera (Mayme Johnson), Antoinette Crowe-Legacy (Elise), Nigél Thatch (Malcolm X), Paul Sorvino (Frank Costello), Giancarlo Esposito (Adam Clayton Powell Jr.), Lucy Fry (Stella), Kelvin Harrison Jr. (Teddy Greene). From Chris Brancato and ABC Signature Studios. Emmy Award winner for Outstanding Main Title Design (2020).

Godmothered (film) At Christmastime, upon hearing that her chosen profession is facing extinction, young fairy godmother-in-training Eleanor decides to show the world the importance of her job. She finds a mislaid letter from Mackenzie, a 10-year-old girl in distress whom Eleanor discovers is now a 40-year-old single mom working at a news station in Boston. Having lost her husband several years earlier, Mackenzie has all but given up on the idea of "happily ever after," but Eleanor is determined to give Mackenzie a happiness makeover, whether she likes it or not. Premiered digitally Dec. 4, 2020, on Disney+. Directed by Sharon Maguire. Stars Jillian Bell (Eleanor), Isla Fisher (Mackenzie), Santiago Cabrera (Hugh), Mary Elizabeth Ellis (Paula), Jane Curtin (Moira), June Squibb (Agnes),

Jillian Shea Spaeder (Jane), Willa Skye (Mia), Artemis Pebdani (Duff), Utkarsh Ambudkar (Grant), Stephnie Weir (Barb). 110 min. From Walt Disney Studios. Filmed in wide-screen format on location throughout Massachusetts in Boston, Ipswich, Westford, and Lowell.

Goff, Harper (1912–1993) Artist/production designer; he met Walt Disney in the Bassett-Lowke Ltd. shop in London in 1951, as the two men were both interested in the same model train set. Walt bought the train, but Harper was later offered work at the Disney Studio. He began as a story man for *20,000 Leagues Under the Sea*, for which he designed the *Nautilus*. He later worked as one of the first Imagineers at WED Enterprises, providing initial concepts for Disneyland and designs for Main Street, U.S.A. (which he modeled after his hometown of Fort Collins, Colorado) and the Jungle Cruise. He later proposed the layout for World Showcase at EPCOT Center and contributed to some of the pavilion designs. He was a member of the Firehouse Five Plus Two, playing the banjo. He died in 1993, the same year he was named a Disney Legend.

Going Bonkers (TV) Syn. 2-hour special; aired Sep. 3, 1993. Directed by Robert Taylor. Introducing the *Bonkers* TV series, this special presents an introduction to the character of Bonkers D. Bobcat, showing his transition from Toon TV star to Toon cop. The 2nd half of the show turns to Donald Duck with the show *Down and Out with Donald Duck*.

Going Home (film) Animated short; digitally released Aug. 4, 2021, on Disney+. A young adult repeatedly visits his hometown, but with every new arrival, he starts to face the inevitable: change. Directed by Jacob Frey. 4 min. From the Walt Disney Animation Studios Short Circuit program.

Going to the Mat (TV) A Disney Channel Original Movie; first aired Mar. 19, 2004. When Jace Newfield's family moves from New York City to the Midwest, the accomplished, blind drummer looks for a way—besides music—to fit in at his new school. In addition to experiencing the cultural differences, Jace must learn his way around a new house and school while struggling to maintain his independence. Soon, he takes up wrestling, the only sport in which the blind seem to compete on an equal footing with those who can see. With the help of his wrestling coach, Mr. Rice, and his music teacher, Mr. Wyatt, who is also blind, Jace strives to master his wrestling skills and follow his instincts to bring his team to the championships, as he discovers the importance of self-acceptance. Directed by Stuart Gillard. Stars Andrew Lawrence (Jace Newfield), Khleo Thomas (Vince Shu), Billy Aaron Brown (John Lambrix), Brenda Strong (Patty Newfield), D. B. Sweeney (Coach Rice), Brett Yoder (Mike Mallon), T. J. Lowther (Luke Nolan), Alessandra Toreson (Mary Beth Rice), Tim Whitaker (Boomer Cleason), Brian Wimmer (Tom Newfield), Danny Henze (T-Rex Turner), Wayne Brady (Mr. Wyatt).

Gold, Stanley P. Member of the Disney Board of Directors in 1984 and again 1987–2003. He was CEO of Roy E. Disney's company, Shamrock Holdings.

Goldberg, Eric Animator/director; he directed *Pocahontas* and segments in *Fantasia/2000*, was a supervising animator on *Aladdin* (Genie), *Hercules* (Phil), *The Princess and the Frog* (Louis/Tiana's fantasy sequence), and *Winnie the Pooh* (Rabbit/ "Backson" song); supervised hand-drawn animation in *Moana* and contributed to additional films, including *Wreck-It Ralph*; plus was head of animation in *Get a Horse!* On Disney+, he directed *Goofy in How to Stay at Home* and appeared in *One Day at Disney*, *Sketchbook*, and *Mickey: The Story of a Mouse*.

Goldberg, Whoopi Actress; appeared in *Sarafina* (Mary Masembuko), *The Associate* (Laurel Ayres), *Eddie* (title role), *Sister Act* and *Sister Act 2: Back in the Habit* (Deloris), and as herself in *An Alan Smithee Film: Burn Hollywood Burn* and *The Muppets*. On TV, she appeared in *Rodgers & Hammerstein's Cinderella* (Queen Constantina), *A Knight in Camelot* (Vivien Morgan), *Once Upon a Time in Wonderland* (Mrs. Rabbit), *When We Rise* (Pat Norman), *Godfather of Harlem* (Miss Willa), *Dreams Come True: A Celebration of Disney Animation*, and hosted *Decorating Disney: Holiday Magic* and *The Most Magical Story on Earth: 50 Years of Walt Disney World*. She provided the voice of Shenzi the hyena in *The Lion King* and *The Lion King 1½*, Miss Mittens in *Snow Buddies*, Stretch in *Toy Story 3*, the Magic Mirror in *The 7D*, The GameMaster in *Miles from Tomorrowland*, Lama in *Elena of Avalor*, Ursula in *Descendants 2*, Mother Olm in *Amphibia*, and Marian Pouncy/ Poundcakes in *Marvel's M.O.D.O.K.* She also narrated *Captain EO Backstage* and played Calafia in *Golden Dreams* at Disney's California Adventure. She was named a Disney Legend in 2017.

Goldblum, Jeff Actor; appeared in *Powder* (Donald Ripley), *Holy Man* (Ricky Hayman), *The Life Aquatic with Steve Zissou* (Alistair Hennessey), and as Grandmaster in *Guardians of the Galaxy Vol. 2* and *Thor: Ragnarok*. On Disney+, he hosted *The World According to Jeff Goldblum*.

Golden Age Souvenirs SuperStar Television shop in Lakeside Circle at Disney-MGM Studios (later Echo Lake at Disney's Hollywood Studios); opened May 1, 1989, with gifts inspired by the golden age of radio and TV. In 2009, it became a shop for The American Idol Experience and was later renamed Frozen Fractal Gifts.

Golden Anniversary of Snow White and the Seven Dwarfs SEE DISNEY'S GOLDEN ANNIVERSARY OF SNOW WHITE AND THE SEVEN DWARFS.

Golden Bear Lodge SEE HUNGRY BEAR RESTAURANT.

Golden Crocus Inn Quick-service restaurant in Arendelle Village; planned for World of Frozen in Hong Kong Disneyland in 2023.

Golden Dog, The (TV) Show aired Jan. 2, 1977. Directed by William Stierwalt and Fred R. Krug. A ghost tries to help his 2 former gold-mining partners get along with each other. His first plot backfires as the 2 practically tear the town apart looking for suspected gold, but later he strands them in the desert, and they have to help each other, deciding that friendship is more important than gold. Stars Paul Brinegar, Alan Napier.

Golden Dream Song from The American Adventure at EPCOT; written by Randy Bright and Robert Moline.

Golden Dreams (film) Film attraction in the Golden State area in Disney's California Adventure; open Feb. 8, 2001–Sep. 7, 2008, succeeded by The Little Mermaid ~ Ariel's Undersea Adventure. The film chronicled the hopes, dreams, and hard work of the pioneers who shaped what is California today, covering the Gold Rush, the immigrant experience, and the glittering beginnings of Hollywood. Hosted by Queen Calafia, the spirit of California (played by Whoopi Goldberg). Directed by Agnieszka Holland. 21 min.

Golden Eggs (film) Donald Duck cartoon released Mar. 7, 1941. Directed by Wilfred Jackson. Donald Duck unsuccessfully disguises himself as a chicken to recover a basket of eggs protected by a rooster.

Golden Galleon, The Caribbean Plaza shop in the Magic Kingdom at Walt Disney World; opened Apr. 1974, offering brass, gold, and jeweled fixtures. Closed Aug. 14, 1992, replaced by an expansion of El Pirata y el Perico. Also a pirate-themed shop in Tokyo Disneyland; opened Apr. 15, 1983.

Golden Gateway Main entrance to Disney's California Adventure; opened Feb. 11, 2001. Visitors entered the park through what appeared to be an enormous postcard of the Golden State, comprised of 11-ft.-tall letters that spelled out C-A-L-I-F-O-R-N-I-A, tile murals depicting state landmarks, and a small version of the Golden Gate Bridge. The gateway was replaced by Buena Vista Street Jun. 15, 2012. The huge letters were donated to the California State Fair in Sacramento, the state's capital, in May 2012.

Golden Girls, The (TV) Series on NBC; aired Sep. 14, 1985–Sep. 12, 1992. Three aging, active, and independent women share a house in Miami with the feisty mother of one of them, supporting each other but also occasionally getting on each other's nerves. Stars Rue McClanahan (Blanche Devereaux), Betty White (Rose Nylund), Bea Arthur (Dorothy Zbornak), and Estelle Getty (Sophia Petrillo). The cast and crew won 11 Emmy Awards 1986–1992. *Empty Nest* and *The Golden Palace* were spin-off shows. From Touchstone Television.

Golden Horseshoe Revue Frontierland show in Disneyland; opened Jul. 17, 1955. It was the longest-running show in history when it ended Oct. 12, 1986. It was sponsored by Pepsi-Cola 1955–Sep. 30, 1982, and by Eastman Kodak Oct. 1, 1982–Apr. 30, 1984. The first stars were "silver-toned tenor" Donald Novis, Judy Marsh as saloon owner Slue Foot Sue, and traveling salesman Wally Boag. Betty Taylor joined in 1956 and had a 31-year run as Slue Foot Sue, and Fulton Burley took the tenor role in 1962. A new show, the *Golden Horseshoe Jamboree*, played Nov. 1, 1986–Dec. 18, 1994. Wonder Bread took over sponsorship, 1990–1994. The new show featured talented singers and dancers, including those portraying Lily Langtree and Sam, the owner of the saloon. A mainstay since the beginning was the cancan number. Walt used to enjoy the show, and he had his favorite box right next to the stage. The corny jokes and enduring songs continued to endear the show to guests throughout its long run. Billy Hill and the Hillbillies, a group that first performed in Critter Country in 1989, played in the Golden Horseshoe for most years between 1994–2012. (A *Woody's Roundup* show was performed 1999–2000.) Billy Hill and the Hillbillies relocated to Big Thunder Ranch until the group ended performances at Disneyland in Jan. 2014. FOR THE WALT DISNEY WORLD SHOW, SEE DIAMOND HORSESHOE REVUE.

Golden Horseshoe Revue, The (TV) Show aired Sep. 23, 1962. Directed by Ron Miller. Walt celebrates the 10,000th performance of the Disneyland show with its stars Betty Taylor and Wally Boag, augmented by Annette Funicello, Gene Sheldon, and Ed Wynn.

Golden Mickeys, The Show premiered Aug. 28, 2003, on the Disney Cruise Line ship *Disney Wonder*, and later on *Disney Magic* (Dec. 6, 2003–2010) and *Disney Dream* (beginning in 2011). It is a musical live awards show in which Disney characters are nominated in several categories, including heroism and romance. When the master of ceremonies fails to appear, the stage manager takes over and learns the valuable lesson that anything is possible. A version played in the Storybook Theater in Hong Kong Disneyland, Sep. 12, 2005–Jul. 26, 2015.

Golden Oak Luxury residential resort community at Walt Disney World, encompassing 980 acres (half of which is conservation area) and offering a limited collection of single-family custom homes priced between $1.5 million and $8 million. Designed by Disney Imagineers, the gated community announced in Jun. 2010 features intimate neighborhoods and amenities created with all family members in mind. Homes are designed in traditional European, Caribbean, and Old Florida styles. The first residents moved in Sep. 2011. Concierge services are offered, and there is Summerhouse, a private clubhouse, which opened Jul. 2013. Inside, the dining facilities have names inspired by films shot at the Golden Oak Ranch in California; Markham's, an upscale restaurant, is named after Marty Markham (*The Adventures of Spin and Marty*), and Tyler's, a cocktail and tapas lounge, is named after *Toby Tyler*. Bolton's was added Aug. 22, 2018, as the elegant dining centerpiece of Summerhouse; it is named after Frederick Bolton (*The Horse in the Gray Flannel Suit*). Neighborhoods include Carolwood, Kimball Trace, Kingswell, Marceline, Silverbrook, and Symphony Grove, which also includes a hamlet of custom-designed cottages. The Four Seasons Resort Orlando, which opened in Aug. 2014, is part of the development. In Aug. 2015, sales began for three collections of Four Seasons Private Residences—Starview, Gardenside, and Edgewood. At build-out, Golden Oak is anticipated to include approximately 300 homes.

Golden Oak Ranch Located in Placerita Canyon, about 25 miles north of the Disney Studio in Burbank, this 708-acre ranch was purchased by Disney on Mar. 11, 1959, to serve as a filming location. Walt had become familiar with the area while using it as a location for the *Spin and Marty* serials. Over the years, parts of films such as *Toby Tyler; Follow Me, Boys!; The Parent Trap; The Apple Dumpling Gang; The Horse in the Gray Flannel Suit; Pearl Harbor; The Princess Diaries 2: Royal Engagement;* and *Pirates of the Caribbean: Dead Man's Chest* were filmed there. A meandering stream with a covered bridge has been featured in many films. Other studios use the ranch also, and it has been featured in *Mame, Roots, The Waltons, Back to the Future, Dynasty,* and *Little House on the Prairie*. A western street was constructed in the late 1970s and remained active until its removal in 2008. A massive wooden building, Golden Oak Hall, was created for *The Country Bears* film (as Country Bear Hall). With 20th Century Fox and Paramount selling their large ranches, the Golden Oak Ranch has become practically the sole surviving movie ranch. In 2009, Disney announced plans to transform a 58-acre section of the ranch into Disney/ABC Studios at The Ranch, with 6 pairs of soundstages, production offices, production shops and storage (sets, props, drapery, costumes, etc.), administration offices, and a commissary.

Golden Opportunity (film) Promotional film, introduced by Walt Disney and prepared for Californians for Beaches and Parks to aid in their campaign for a ballot proposition in a state vote in 1964. Walt explains that, with increasing population in California, more state beaches and parks are needed. 13 min.

Golden Palace, The (TV) Series on CBS; aired Sep. 18, 1992–Aug. 6, 1993. Spin-off of *The Golden Girls*. Rose, Blanche, and Sophia from the previous show run a Miami hotel. Stars Rue McClanahan, Betty White, Estelle Getty, Cheech Marin, Don Cheadle.

Golden Press Division of Western Publishing Co.; began publishing Little Golden Books and Big Golden Books featuring the Disney characters in 1948 and later added many other series. Some of the Golden Book titles went through dozens of printings, with millions of copies in circulation. Golden Books are still published today, with new and classic editions, by Penguin Random House.

Golden State SEE CALIFORNIA ADVENTURE, DISNEY.

Golden Touch, The (film) Silly Symphony cartoon released Mar. 22, 1935. Directed by Walt Disney himself, a task he thought would be easy but which he never repeated. Greedy King Midas wants to amass more treasure, so a magical gnome, named Goldie, grants him the power to turn anything he touches to gold. To his horror, he can no longer eat, for even his food turns to gold. Finally, in exchange for a hamburger, the king gives up the golden touch and all his worldly possessions.

Golden Vine Winery Area in Pacific Wharf (formerly in Golden State) at Disney California Adventure; opened Feb. 8, 2001. Originally presented by the Robert Mondavi Family; Disney took over the operation Oct. 1, 2001. The Vineyard Room and Golden Vine Terrace opened Feb. 8, 2001. The Wine Country Trattoria, taking the place of the Wine Country Market, opened Dec. 14, 2001. Sonoma Terrace took over the trattoria's east side patio in Jun. 2010, serving California wines, craft brews, and small bites.

Golden Zephyr Attraction in Paradise Gardens Park (formerly Paradise Pier) in Disney California Adventure; opened Feb. 8, 2001. This swing ride brings back visions of a retro future with zeppelin-shaped 12-passenger stainless steel spaceships suspended by cable from a rotating 85-foot-tall tower.

Goldenson, Leonard H. (1905–1999) Founder and former chairman of the board of ABC, Inc.; Goldenson started with the organization in 1953 when he helped arrange the merger of United Paramount Theaters with the fledgling ABC (a failing collection of 5 TV stations). He took a chance in 1954 by contracting for the first Disney TV series, *Disneyland*, and investing in the park Walt was building in Anaheim. In 1985, he merged ABC with Cap Cities. He was named a Disney Legend posthumously in 2004.

Goldie & Bear (TV) Animated series; premiered Nov. 11, 2015, on Disney Junior and Disney Channel, following a Sep. 12, 2015, release on Watch Disney Junior digital platforms. In the wondrous Fairytale Forest, Goldie and her best friend, Bear, laugh, play, and learn important life lessons as they encounter well-known characters from fairy tales and nursery rhymes. Voices include Natalie Lander (Goldie), Georgie Kidder (Bear), Lesley Nicol (Fairy Godmother), Justine Huxley (Little Red Riding Hood), David Lodge (Magic Gnome), Debby Ryan (Thumbelina), Miles Brown (Jack), Marsai Martin (Jill).

Goldie Locks and the Three Bears (film) Laugh-O-gram film made by Walt in Kansas City in 1922.

Goldrush: A Real Life Alaskan Adventure (TV) Two-hour movie on *The Wonderful World of Disney*; first aired Mar. 8, 1998. A spirited young woman known as Fizzy challenges both the social conventions of her time and nature's harshest elements when she seeks her fortune in the turn-of-the-century Alaskan gold rush. Directed by John Power. Stars Alyssa Milano (Frances Ella Fitz), W. Morgan Sheppard (Whiskers), Stan Cahill (Ed Hawkins), Peter Fleming (Barry Keown), Tom Scholte (Monty Marks), Bruce Campbell (Pierce Thomas Madison).

Goldwyn, Tony Actor; appeared in *Nixon* (Harold Nixon), and on TV in *Scandal* (Fitzgerald Grant). He voiced the title character in *Tarzan*.

Golf Disneyland A 225-acre country club course at Disneyland Paris; opened Oct. 1992, with 18 holes, expanding to 27 in Aug. 1993. Designed by Ronald Fream. Three 9-hole courses (Hundred Acre Wood, Wonderland, and Never Land) can be combined to create a unique 18-hole round, and a Mickey Mouse-shaped area is available for young golfers. The Club House includes Goofy's Pro Shop, a conference room, and changing rooms, with dining at the Club House Grill.

Golf Resort, The A 153-room hotel at Walt Disney World; opened Dec. 15, 1973, as an expansion of the Palm and Magnolia golf course clubhouse. Included a Pro Shop, with dining in the Magnolia Room (later the Trophy Room) and Palm Lounge (later the Player's Gallery). The resort became The Disney Inn in 1986.

Goliath II (film) Special cartoon released Jan. 21, 1960. Directed by Wolfgang Reitherman. Goliath II, at 8, is still only 5 inches tall—to the shame of his father, Goliath I, giant of the jungle and king of the elephants. Little Goliath runs away and though he is rescued by his mother from Raja, the tiger, he is now marked a rogue. But when a mouse attacks the herd, frightening them all away, Goliath II redeems himself by battling and defeating the mouse. Written by Disney story man Bill Peet, with Kevin Corcoran voicing Goliath II, the film also boasts the distinction of being the first Disney film to be fully animated using the new Xerox process for transferring the pencil drawings to cels. (A few scenes of *Sleeping Beauty* had previously used the technique.) It is also notable for being one of the few Disney films in which a mouse is the villain!

Gómez, Carlos A. He was named senior vice president and treasurer of The Walt Disney Company in 2020. He began at Disney as an analyst in the Financial Risk Management group 1995–1999, rejoining the company in 2002. Later served as director, Corporate Finance 2006–2011, and as vice president, Investor Relations 2011–2020.

Gomez, Selena Actress/singer; appeared on Disney Channel in *Hannah Montana* (Mikayla); *Wizards of Waverly Place*, *Wizards of Waverly Place: The Movie*, and *The Wizards Return: Alex vs. Alex* (Alex Russo); and *Princess Protection Program* (Carter Mason). She recorded for Hollywood Records 2008–2014 and had a cameo in *The Muppets* (2011).

Gondolier Snacks Mediterranean Harbor gelato/coffee stand in Tokyo DisneySea; opened Sep. 4, 2001.

Gone Are the Dayes (TV) The second Disney Channel Premiere Film; first aired May 6, 1984. A family witnesses a gangland shooting and has a hard time staying hidden before the trial. A veteran government relocation agent, Charlie Mitchell, is determined to hide and protect them, while the mobsters are just as determined to get them. Directed by Gabrielle Beaumont. Stars Harvey Korman (Charlie Mitchell), Robert Hogan, Susan Anspach, David Glasser, Sharee Gregory.

Gone Fishin' (film) It's the weekend and best friends Gus and Joe have decided to leave their wives and problems at home and go fishing, having won a grand prize vacation to the Florida Everglades from *Bait & Tackle* magazine by writing an essay on "How Come We Fish." But the duo never gets close enough to the water to bait their hooks because they stumble into a wild adventure. They run into a con artist, Dekker Massey, who speeds off in their '68 Plymouth Barracuda, leaving them with their fishing boat and trailer. When two women, Rita and Angie, arrive in hot pursuit of Dekker, Gus and Joe hitch a ride, becoming entangled in the chase and, despite constantly leaving disaster in their wake, proving they are ingenious and daring while on the trail of a dangerous criminal. They return home heroes. A Hollywood Pictures film in association with Caravan Pictures. Directed by Christopher Cain. Released May 30, 1997. Stars Joe Pesci (Joe Waters), Danny Glover (Gus Green), Rosanna Arquette (Rita), Lynn Whitfield (Angie), Nick Brimble (Dekker Massey). 94 min. Location filming took place in the Everglades and nearby Florida towns, including the charming, weathered atmosphere of Everglades City, a sleepy community of 700.

Gone Fishing (film) Animated short; released Mar. 7, 2017, on the *Moana* Blu-ray. On Motunui, Maui tries to catch a fish with his magical fishhook, only to be comically foiled by the ocean. Directed by John Musker and Ron Clements. Voices include Dwayne Johnson (Maui), Auli'i Cravalho (Moana). 2 min.

Gone Hollywood Shop in Hollywood Land at Disney California Adventure; opened Feb. 8, 2001.

Gone in 60 Seconds (film) Automobile aficionado Randall "Memphis" Raines is a car thief of legendary proportions. No fancy lock or alarm can stop him; your car is there, and then suddenly gone in 60 sec. For years Memphis eludes the law while boosting every make and model imaginable. But when the heat becomes too intense, he abandons his life of crime and everything and everyone he loves to find a different life. Now, when his kid brother tries to follow in his footsteps, only to become dangerously embroiled in a high-stakes caper, Memphis is sucked back into his old ways in order to save his brother's life. Released Jun. 9, 2000. A Touchstone/Jerry Bruckheimer film. Directed by Dominic Sena. Stars Nicolas Cage (Memphis Raines), Angelina Jolie (Sway Wayland), Giovanni Ribisi

(Kip Raines), Delroy Lindo (Roland Castelbeck), Will Patton (Atley Jackson), Christopher Eccleston (Raymond Calitri), Chi McBride (Kenny), Robert Duvall (Otto Halliwell). 118 min. Based on a 1974 film of the same title from writer/producer/director H. B. ("Toby") Halicki. Filmed in CinemaScope.

Gonzales, Manuel (1913–1993) Comic strip artist; began with Disney in 1936 as an artist in the publicity and comic strip departments. From 1938 until his retirement in 1981, he penciled and inked the Mickey Mouse Sunday page for newspapers. He was named a Disney Legend posthumously in 2017.

Good & Evil (TV) Series on ABC; aired Sep. 25–Oct. 31, 1991. The lives of 2 sisters: one, Genny, is good, a doctor in microbiology, and the other, Denise, is evil, a vice president of marketing for their mother's cosmetic company. Stars Seth Green (David), Teri Garr (Denise), Margaret Whitton (Genny), Mark Blankfield (George), Lane Davies (Dr. Eric Haan), Mary Gillis (Mary). From Touchstone Television and Witt/Thomas/Harris Productions.

Good Dinosaur, The (film) Animated feature from Pixar Animation Studios. In this story, the giant dinosaurs never became extinct. Arlo is a lively Apatosaurus with a big heart who sets out on a remarkable journey, gaining an unlikely friend along the way—a human boy. While traveling through a harsh and mysterious landscape, Arlo learns the power of confronting his fears and discovers what he is truly capable of. Released Nov. 25, 2015, also in 3-D. Directed by Peter Sohn. Voices include Jeffrey Wright (Poppa), Frances McDormand (Momma), Raymond Ochoa (Arlo), Steve Zahn (Thunderclap), A. J. Buckley (Nash), Anna Paquin (Ramsey), Sam Elliott (Butch), Marcus Scribner (Buck), Jack Bright (Spot). 96 min. To inspire the environments of Arlo's journey, filmmakers studied a diversity of landscapes across the American West, including the Teton mountains, the geysers of Yellowstone National Park, the grasslands of Montana, and the mesas of Wyoming's Red Desert. Filmed in wide-screen format. Released with the short *Sanjay's Super Team.*

Good Doctor, The (TV) Series on ABC; debuted Sep. 25, 2017. Dr. Shaun Murphy, a young surgeon with autism and savant syndrome, joins the staff at St. Bonaventure Hospital. Alone in the world and unable to personally connect with those around him, his only advocate, Dr. Aaron Glassman, challenges the skepticism and prejudices of the hospital's board and staff when he brings him to join the team. Shaun has to work hard to navigate his new environment and relationships to prove to his colleagues that his extraordinary medical skills and insights will save lives. Stars Freddie Highmore (Dr. Shaun Murphy), Richard Schiff (Dr. Aaron Glassman), Antonia Thomas (Dr. Claire Browne), Nicholas Gonzalez (Dr. Neil Melendez), Chuku Modu (Dr. Jared Kalu). From Sony Pictures Television and ABC Studios.

Good Fortune Gifts SEE HOUSE OF GOOD FORTUNE.

Good Housekeeping In the 1930s and early 1940s, *Good Housekeeping* magazine had a monthly page of Disney illustrations, usually tied to a recent cartoon or animated feature release.

Good Life, The (TV) Series on NBC; aired Jan. 3–Apr. 12, 1994. A hardworking, middle-class family man, trying to strike a balance between work and domestic life, discovers that it is harder than it seems to snare a slice of "the good life." Stars John Caponera (John Bowman), Eve Gordon (Maureen Bowman), Drew Carey (Drew Clark), Jake Patellis (Paul Bowman), Shay Astar (Melissa Bowman), Justin Berfield (Bob Bowman), Monty Hoffman (Tommy Bartlett).

Good Luck Charlie (TV) Comedy series on Disney Channel; premiered Apr. 4, 2010. Two teenagers, Teddy and P. J. Duncan, and their 10-year-old brother, Gabe, are enlisted by their parents to help when they return to work after the birth of their 4th child, Charlotte (aka Charlie). With their parents juggling full-time careers, the older Duncan siblings pitch in, getting very familiar with baby formulas, burp clothes, and babysitting while navigating typical teenage life. Each episode features Teddy's video diary, which she creates for Charlie to use for advice after Teddy has grown up and moved out. Stars Bridgit Mendler (Teddy), Jason Dolley (P. J.), Bradley Steven Perry (Gabe), Eric Allan Kramer (Bob Duncan), Leigh-Allyn Baker (Amy Duncan), Mia Talerico (Charlotte "Charlie" Duncan). The 3rd season introduced a new story line as the Duncans prepared for the arrival of another baby. He arrived during a Jun. 24, 2012, special episode and was named Toby as a result of a "name the baby" poll on the Disney Channel website; 25 million votes were tallied. From It's a Laugh Productions, Inc.

Good Luck Charlie, It's Christmas (TV) A Disney Channel Original Movie; first aired Dec. 2, 2011. The Duncans get separated en route to Palm Springs, and with just days before the holiday, everyone scrambles to reunite the family. In true Duncan fashion, and not without facing some hiccups, hurdles, and even a happy surprise, they discover a whole new meaning of family.

Good Morning, Mickey (TV) Original program on The Disney Channel; debuted Apr. 18, 1983, highlighting classic cartoons of the entire Disney gang.

Good Morning, Miss Bliss (TV) Series on The Disney Channel; debuted Nov. 30, 1988. An 8th grade teacher tries to make her class appreciate her lessons. Stars Hayley Mills, Dennis Haskins, Joan Ryan, Max Battimo, Dustin Diamond, Mark-Paul Gosselaar, Heather Hopper, Lark Voorhies. After only 5 episodes, The Disney Channel canceled the series, and it then continued on NBC with a change of title as the long-running *Saved by the Bell*, though without Hayley Mills.

Good Morning, Vietnam (film) When airman disc jockey Adrian Cronauer takes up his post on Armed Forces Radio in Saigon in 1965, he abandons the approved playlist for rock 'n' roll and adds irreverent remarks. His superiors are horrified, but the men love him as he accomplishes his mission of boosting morale. As he gets to know the people of Saigon—Americans and Vietnamese alike—he becomes increasingly frustrated by the military's censorship of the news. After he broadcasts an "unofficial" report and is cut off the air, his commander deliberately sends him into danger, but a young Vietnamese boy helps rescue him. The boy turns out to be a Vietcong rebel, and Cronauer is sent home for having unwittingly fraternized with the "enemy." Still, his broadcasts paved the way for changes on Armed Forces Radio. Premiered Dec. 23, 1987; general release Jan. 15, 1988. Directed by Barry Levinson. A Touchstone film. 121 min. Stars Robin Williams (Adrian Cronauer), Forest Whitaker (Edward Garlick), Tung Thanh Tran (Tuan), Chintara Sukapatana (Trinh), Bruno Kirby (Lt. Steven Hauk), Robert Wuhl (Marty Lee Dreiwitz), J. T. Walsh (Sgt. Major Dickerson). The film is loosely based on the real-life experiences of a disc jockey who had a popular rock 'n' roll show on Armed Forces Radio. It was shot primarily in Bangkok, where many local citizens were introduced to the rigors of moviemaking for the first time. For the final week, the unit moved to Phuket, a lush tropical island located at the southern tip of Thailand, where a Vietnamese village was constructed.

Good Mother, The (film) After weathering a lifeless marriage, single parent Anna Dunlap is totally wrapped up in her daughter, Molly. When an unconventional Irish sculptor, Leo Cutter, enters Anna's life, she falls passionately in love. However, their openness and permissiveness cause her ex-husband to turn against her, and he files a custody suit for Molly. In trying to retain custody, on her lawyer's recommendation, Anna reluctantly sacrifices Leo, to no avail. Eventually she must pick up her life and begin anew with only weekend and vacation visits from Molly. Released Nov. 4, 1988. Directed by Leonard Nimoy. A Touchstone film. 104 min. Stars Diane Keaton (Anna Dunlap), Liam Neeson (Leo Cutter), Jason Robards (Muth), Ralph Bellamy (Grandfather). Based on the novel by Sue Miller. Filmed in Boston and Toronto, and at Whitefish Lake in southern Ontario, Canada.

Good Old Boy (TV) A Disney Channel Premiere Film; first aired Nov. 11, 1988. A 12-year-old boy discovers racial injustice and learns some hard lessons in a small Mississippi town during World War II. Directed by Tom G. Robertson. Based on the novel by Willie Morris. Stars Ryan Francis (Willie), Douglas Emerson (Spit), Kevin Josephs (Henjie), Gennie James (Rivers Applewhite), Ben Wylie (Billy), Richard Farnsworth (Grandpa Percy), Maureen O'Sullivan (Aunt Sue). 101 min. Filmed in and around Natchez, Mississippi.

Good Scouts (film) Donald Duck cartoon released Jul. 8, 1938. Directed by Jack King. Scoutmaster Donald takes his nephews on a scouting expedition filled with many outdoor adventures, including a disagreeable bear and the geyser Old Reliable. Nominated for an Academy Award

Good Time for a Dime, A (film) Donald Duck cartoon released May 9, 1941. Directed by Dick Lundy. Donald has problems in a penny arcade, being frustrated in his efforts to win money from a claw machine and in his encounter with a wild mechanical airplane.

Good Trouble (TV) Series on Freeform; debuted Jan. 8, 2019, as a spin-off of *The Fosters*. After moving to The Coterie in downtown Los Angeles,

Callie and Mariana realize that living on their own is not all that it's cracked up to be. Faced with new neighbors, new challenges, and new romances, the sisters must depend on one another to navigate the City of Angels. Stars Maia Mitchell (Callie), Cierra Ramirez (Mariana), Tommy Martinez (Gael), Sherry Cola (Alice), Zuri Adele (Malika), Roger Bart (Judge Wilson). From Nuyorican Productions, Inc., in association with Freeform.

Good Turn Restaurant, The SEE GARDEN GRILL RESTAURANT.

Goodbye, Miss 4th of July (TV) A Disney Channel Premiere Film; first aired Dec. 3, 1988. In 1917 West Virginia, a Greek girl battles the forces of racism, and her family is able to overcome prejudice and change the town in the process. Directed by George Miller. Stars Roxana Zal (Niki Janus), Chris Sarandon (George Janus), Chantal Contouri (mother), Louis Gossett, Jr. (Big John). 89 min.

Goodbye Yellow Brick Road: The Final Elton John Performances and the Years That Made His Legend (film) Feature documentary announced for a festival run, limited theatrical release, and digital release on Disney+. The definitive portrait of one of the world's most successful musical artists, comprised of unseen concert footage from the past 50 years. The production captured Elton John's final months on the road in his Farewell Yellow Brick Road tour, and his final American stop at Dodger Stadium in Los Angeles Nov. 20, 2022. The concert was livestreamed on Disney+ as the 3-hour event *Elton John Live: Farewell from Dodger Stadium*, which was produced by Fulwell 73 Productions and Rocket Entertainment. Directed by R.J. Cutler and David Furnish. From This Machine Filmworks (part of Sony Pictures Television) and Rocket Entertainment.

Gooding, Cuba, Jr. Actor; appeared in *Instinct* (Theo Calder), *Pearl Harbor* (Doris "Dorrie" Miller), and *Snow Dogs* (Ted), and on TV in *The Oldest Rookie* (street kid leader). He voiced Buck in *Home on the Range*.

Goodman, Benny (1909–1986) Bandleader who was the first big-name star to appear at Disneyland for more than one performance when he headlined a 3-night engagement during Date Nite in May 1961. He and his orchestra had also performed in the "All the Cats Join In" and "After You've Gone" segments of *Make Mine Music*.

Goodman, John Actor; appeared in *Stella* (Ed Munn), *Arachnophobia* (Delbert McClintock), *Born Yesterday* (Harry Brock), *Bringing Out the Dead* (Larry), *Coyote Ugly* (Bill), *O Brother, Where Art Thou?* (Big Dan Teague), and *Confessions of a Shopaholic* (Graham Bloomwood). He voiced Pacha in *The Emperor's New Groove*; James P. Sullivan in *Monsters, Inc.*, *Monsters University*, and *Monsters at Work*; Baloo in *The Jungle Book 2*; and "Big Daddy" La Bouff in *The Princess and the Frog*. He was named a Disney Legend in 2013.

Good's Food to Go Counter-service restaurant at Disney's Old Key West Resort at Walt Disney World; opened Dec. 20, 1991, serving burgers, salads, and desserts.

Goodwin, Ginnifer Actress; appeared on TV in *Once Upon a Time* (Snow White/Mary Margaret) and on Disney+ in *Earth to Ned*. She voiced Judy Hopps in *Zootopia*, Fawn in *Tinker Bell and the Legend of the NeverBeast*, and Gwen in *Sofia the First*. She narrated *Behind the Magic: Snow White and the Seven Dwarfs*.

Goof Troop (TV) Animated series on The Disney Channel; premiered Apr. 20, 1992. Syn. began Sep. 7, 1992, and ended Aug. 30, 1996; aired on ABC Sep. 12, 1992–Sep. 11, 1993. There was a 2-hour syn. TV special that aired Sep. 6, 1992, previewing the series with an episode entitled "Forever Goof," and including a *Goof Troop* music video and an edited version of *The Goofy Success Story*. The Goof, a single-parent family man, struggles to raise his son in suburbia. His son, Max, however, wants to be different from his old man—in other words, cool. The results are misunderstandings and misadventures, complicated by their next-door neighbor Pete, a snarling used car salesman with a big ego and a temper to match. Voices include Bill Farmer (Goofy), Dana Hill (Max), Jim Cummings (Pete), April Winchell (Peg), Nancy Cartwright (Pistol), Rob Paulsen (P. J.), Frank Welker (Waffles/Chainsaw). 78 episodes. Inspired the 1995 film *A Goofy Movie*.

Goof Troop Christmas, A (TV) Syn. special; first aired in Dec. 1992, and repeated the following Christmas season (each having a different group of cartoons for the 2nd half of the show). Pete takes his family to Colorado to avoid the hectic season, but he cannot escape Goofy, a hungry bear, or the destruction of their cabin.

Goofing Around with Donald Duck (TV) See Square Peg in a Round Hole, A.

Goofy Good-natured but clumsy everyman who manages to do everything exactly the wrong way. He made his first appearance, somewhat disguised, as a member of the audience in *Mickey's Revue* (1932). What distinguished Goofy from those sitting around him was not so much his appearance but his raucous laugh. That laugh, supplied by Disney story man, musician, and former circus clown Pinto Colvig, created such an impression on Walt Disney and his staff that the character soon began to be featured in other cartoons. Before long, Goofy was part of the gang that included Mickey, Minnie, Pluto, Clarabelle Cow, and Horace Horsecollar. This new character was first given a name, Dippy Dawg, in the newspaper comic strips. A 1938 book, *The Story of Dippy the Goof*, indicated the first change to Dippy's name. He began being known as Goofy in the comic strip and subsequent animated shorts, and the name was cemented in 1939 with the release of the cartoon *Goofy and Wilbur*. Goofy was created as a human character, as opposed to Pluto, so he walked upright and had a speaking voice (first supplied by Colvig, and later by George Johnson, Bob Jackman, and Bill Farmer). There have been 49 theatrically released Goofy cartoons (primarily in the 1940s and 1950s), but he also appeared in many animated shorts with Mickey Mouse and Donald Duck. He was best known for his series of "How-to" cartoons, in which he bumbled through the explanations. In the 1950s, he appeared in several cartoons as Mr. Geef, with a wife and son. The 1990s TV series *Goof Troop* reintroduced Goofy and son, but by that time the son was Max, who was quite different from his earlier incarnation, and the wife was no longer on the scene. After a gap of many years, a new Goofy cartoon, *How to Hook Up Your Home Theater*, was released theatrically in 2007 during his 75th anniversary. The Goofy cartoons are:

1. *Goofy and Wilbur*, 1939
2. *Goofy's Glider*, 1940
3. *Baggage Buster*, 1941
4. *The Art of Skiing*, 1941
5. *The Art of Self Defense*, 1941
6. *How to Play Baseball*, 1942
7. *The Olympic Champ*, 1942
8. *How to Swim*, 1942
9. *How to Fish*, 1942
10. *Victory Vehicles*, 1943
11. *How to Be a Sailor*, 1944
12. *How to Play Golf*, 1944
13. *How to Play Football*, 1944
14. *Tiger Trouble*, 1945
15. *African Diary*, 1945
16. *Californy 'er Bust*, 1945
17. *Hockey Homicide*, 1945
18. *Knight for a Day*, 1946
19. *Double Dribble*, 1946
20. *Foul Hunting*, 1947
21. *They're Off*, 1948
22. *The Big Wash*, 1948
23. *Tennis Racquet*, 1949
24. *Goofy Gymnastics*, 1949
25. *Motor Mania*, 1950
26. *Hold That Pose*, 1950
27. *Lion Down*, 1951
28. *Home Made Home*, 1951
29. *Cold War*, 1951
30. *Tomorrow We Diet*, 1951
31. *Get Rich Quick*, 1951
32. *Fathers Are People*, 1951
33. *No Smoking*, 1951
34. *Father's Lion*, 1952
35. *Hello, Aloha*, 1952
36. *Man's Best Friend*, 1952
37. *Two Gun Goofy*, 1952
38. *Teachers Are People*, 1952
39. *Two Weeks Vacation*, 1952
40. *How to Be a Detective*, 1952
41. *Father's Day Off*, 1953
42. *For Whom the Bulls Toil*, 1953
43. *Father's Week End*, 1953
44. *How to Dance*, 1953
45. *How to Sleep*, 1953
46. *Aquamania*, 1961
47. *Freewayphobia No. 1*, 1965
48. *Goofy's Freeway Troubles*, 1965
49. *How to Hook Up Your Home Theater*, 2007

Goofy Adventure Story, The (TV) See Adventure Story, The.

Goofy and Wilbur (film) Goofy cartoon released Mar. 17, 1939. Directed by Dick Huemer. Goofy and his pet grasshopper, Wilbur, are fishing partners, with Wilbur attracting fish for Goofy to catch. In trying to avoid being eaten by a fish, Wilbur is swallowed by a frog. Goofy gives chase, but the frog is swallowed by a stork. Goofy is sad when the stork gets away from him at the nest, but he finds Wilbur in the stork's egg.

Goofy Gymnastics (film) Goofy cartoon released

Sep. 23, 1949. Directed by Jack Kinney. Goofy gives a muscle-building course a try but is soon entangled with the various apparatus, which results in his crashing through a window and having the body of a strong man from a chart superimposed over his. The deadpan narration was by John McLeish.

Goofy in How to Stay at Home (TV) Trio of hand-drawn animated shorts on Disney+; digitally released Aug. 11, 2021. Goofy demonstrates how to make the best of challenging situations in *Learning to Cook*, *Binge Watching*, and *How to Wear a Mask*. Voices include Bill Farmer (Goofy), Corey Burton (narrator). 1-2 min. each.

Goofy Look at Valentine's Day, A (film) Educational film; released in Sep. 1983. Goofy learns the significance of Valentine's Day and how people have expressed their love through the years on the holiday.

Goofy Movie, A (film) Goofy takes his son, Max, on a fishing trip in an effort to bridge the generation gap and spend some quality time bonding, even though Max would rather be spending time with his girlfriend, Roxanne. Rather than explaining to Roxanne the real reason for his trip, Max uses a little deception, which results in all sorts of complications. Goofy and Max head for Lake Destiny, and along the way have an encounter with Bigfoot and visit the dilapidated Lester's Possum Park. Will Max learn there's nothing wrong with taking after dear old dad, even if he is a little goofy? Released Apr. 7, 1995. Directed by Kevin Lima. 77 min. Voices include Bill Farmer (Goofy), Jason Marsden (Max), Aaron Lohr (Max, singing), Kellie Martin (Roxanne), Jenna Von Oy (Stacey), Jim Cummings (Pete), Rob Paulsen (P. J.), Wallace Shawn (Principal Mazur), Joey Lawrence (Chad), Julie Brown (Lisa), Frank Welker (Bigfoot), Tevin Campbell (Powerline). From Disney Television Animation. Songs include "After Today," "On the Open Road," "I 2 I," "Stand Out," and "Nobody Else But You." The film was animated primarily at the new Walt Disney Animation studio in France, after character design, art direction, and storyboarding had been completed in Burbank. Inspired by the animated TV series *Goof Troop*. The film was not a box office success, but it gained popularity in home video releases.

Goofy Over Dental Health (film) Educational film in 16 mm, released in Jan. 1991. 13 min. A laser disc version at 22 min. was released in Feb. 1993. A kid neglects brushing his teeth, so that night Goofy leaves a magical toothbrush under his pillow, and he is transported to a dental office where he learns how to have healthy teeth.

Goofy Over Health (film) Educational film in 16 mm, released in Jan. 1991. 11 min. A video version at 19 min. was released in Mar. 1993. By reading Goofy's health journal, an 8-year-old learns that she has been suffering from fatigue caused by poor health habits; Goofy teaches her the keys to good health and fitness.

Goofy Sports Story, The (TV) Show aired Mar. 21, 1956. Directed by Wolfgang Reitherman. Walt introduces a history of the Olympic Games followed by a series of Goofy sports cartoons.

Goofy Success Story, The (TV) Show aired Dec. 7, 1955. Directed by Jack Kinney. A look at Goofy's rise to stardom, leading into several of his cartoons—*Moving Day*, *Moose Hunters*, *How to Ride a Horse*, and *Motor Mania*. Released theatrically abroad.

Goofy Takes a Holiday (TV) SEE HOLIDAY FOR HENPECKED HUSBANDS.

Goofy's Bounce House Attraction in Mickey's Toontown at Disneyland; opened Jan. 24, 1993. This was one attraction where the kids could lord it over the adults; if you were above a certain height, you could not enter. Kids removed their shoes and leaped into the house with its almost balloon-like furniture, walls, and floor. Closed in 2006 to become a walk-through attraction, Goofy's Playhouse. The attraction closed again Mar. 8, 2022, reopening in 2023 with new interiors, plus the addition of Goofy's How-to-Play Yard, where kids can explore a sound garden and an elevated clubhouse. Also opened in Tokyo Disneyland Apr. 13, 1996; it changed to Goofy's Paint 'n' Play House in 2012.

Goofy's Candy Co. Candy shop in the Marketplace at Disney Springs (formerly Downtown Disney Marketplace); opened in 2003, replacing the kitchenware shop in the Gourmet Pantry. Expanded into a new location in 2005, taking the place of Disney at Home; the original location then became Mickey's Pantry. Goofy's Candy Co. became a popular brand of packaged treats sold across the Disney parks.

Goofy's Cavalcade of Sports (TV) Show aired Oct. 17, 1956. Directed by Wolfgang Reitherman. Goofy attempts to participate in a number of sports, as seen in several of his cartoons.

Goofy's Extreme Sports: Paracycling (film) Goofy defies the laws of physics and common sense when he bicycles off a cliff, engages in aerial acrobatics, and ungracefully parachutes to the ground. Directed by Tony Craig. 2 min. From the *Mickey MouseWorks* TV series. Released with *Mighty Joe Young* on Dec. 25, 1998.

Goofy's Extreme Sports: Skating the Half Pipe (film) Goofy demonstrates the beautiful, yet dangerous, sport of stunt skating—complete with all safety precautions. But once he gets rolling, he has trouble putting on the brakes. Directed by Bob Zamboni. 2 min. From the *Mickey MouseWorks* TV series. Released with *I'll Be Home for Christmas* on Nov. 13, 1998.

Goofy's Field Trips (film) Series of 3 educational films: *Ships, Trains, Planes*; released in Aug. 1989.

Goofy's Freeway Troubles (film) Goofy cartoon released Sep. 22, 1965. Directed by Les Clark. Goofy, appearing as Stupidus Ultimas, illustrates what can happen when a careless motorist ignores the state of his tires and the mechanical condition of his vehicle. Showing his audience tires blowing out and wheels coming free, Goofy clearly warns of alcohol and driving being a dangerous combination. Dangerous, too, Goofy concludes, is staying at the wheel while fatigued. 13 min.

Goofy's Glider (film) Goofy cartoon released Nov. 22, 1940. Directed by Jack Kinney. Goofy tries to demonstrate glider flying but is unsuccessful in trying to launch himself—whether it's using foot power, a bicycle, a slingshot, or skates. Finally, a cannon does the job, shooting him into orbit.

Goofy's Grill SEE LITE BITE.

Goofy's How-to-Play Yard SEE GOOFY'S BOUNCE HOUSE.

Goofy's Hygiene Game (film) Educational film; released in Aug. 1987. It presents lessons on cleanliness habits such as bathing, grooming, dental care, and other concerns.

Goofy's Kitchen Buffet and character dining in the Disneyland Hotel at the Disneyland Resort; opened in the West Street complex in 1992, taking the place of the Chef's Kitchen, then relocated Jul. 26, 1999, replacing Stromboli's. Diners are greeted by Chef Goofy and other Disney characters.

Goofy's Office Safety Championship (film) Educational film released Apr. 30, 1990. 12 min. Office workplace hazards turn into an athletic competition.

Goofy's Paint 'n' Play House Attraction in Mickey's Toontown at Tokyo Disneyland; opened Aug. 24, 2012, taking the place of Goofy's Bounce House. Using Toontone Splat Master paint applicators, guests can help Goofy redecorate his room.

Goofy's Plant Safety Championship (film) Educational film released Apr. 30, 1990. 13 min. Plant workplace hazards become an athletic competition.

Goofy's Playhouse SEE GOOFY'S BOUNCE HOUSE.

Goofy's Salute to Father (TV) SEE SALUTE TO FATHER, A.

Goofy's Sky School Roller coaster–style attraction in Paradise Gardens Park at Disney California Adventure; opened Jul. 1, 2011, taking the place of Mulholland Madness. Inspired by the classic Goofy "How-to" shorts of the 1940s and 1950s, as well as the short *Goofy's Glider*, this attraction takes novice pilots on a flying lesson through the wild blue yonder.

Goosebumps HorrorLand Fright Show and Funhouse Live show, walk-through maze, and character-greeting spot in Disney-MGM Studios; ran Oct. 8, 1997–Nov. 1, 1998, in New York Street area. Guests stepped into their own scary adventure based on the book series by R. L. Stine.

Gopher Character Walt Disney created to add to the *Winnie the Pooh* stories; voiced by Howard Morris.

Gordon, Bruce (1951–2007) Imagineer; he joined WED Enterprises in 1979 as a production designer and worked on the Journey Into Imagination attraction for EPCOT Center and the New Fantasyland for Disneyland. He served as show producer for a variety of Disneyland attractions, including Splash Mountain, the 1998 renovation of Tomorrowland, and Finding Nemo Submarine Voyage. As an unofficial historian at Walt Disney Imagineering, he, along with David Mumford, made many appearances as a popular speaker at Disneyana Conventions and wrote several Disney books. He left Disney in 2005 and became show producer for The Walt Disney Family Museum.

Gordon-Levitt, Joseph Actor; appeared in *Plymouth* (Simon), *Angels in the Outfield* (Roger), *Holy Matrimony* (Zeke), *10 Things I Hate About You* (Cameron James), *Miracle at St. Anna* (Tim Boyle), and *Lincoln* (Robert Todd Lincoln), and on TV in *Lady Gaga & The Muppets' Holiday Spectacular* and *The Muppets*. He provided the voice of Jim Hawkins in *Treasure Planet*, Jiro Horikoshi in *The Wind Rises*, Slowen Lo in *Star Wars: The Last Jedi*, and Jiminy Cricket in *Pinocchio* (2022).

Gordy (film) In a world where pigs can talk and be heard by 2 children who are "pure of heart," Gordy sets off to find his family. Gordy and the children try to teach the adult world the meaning of friendship and the value of family. Directed by Mark Lewis. Stars Doug Stone, Tom Lester. 90 min. Originally released theatrically in May 1995 as a Miramax film. Released in 1995 on video by Walt Disney Home Video under the label "Disney Presents."

Gorilla Falls Exploration Trail Africa attraction in Disney's Animal Kingdom; opened Apr. 22, 1998. The name changed to Pangani Forest Exploration Trail Jul. 1998–May 2016, then reverted back to the original name. In the Harambe Wildlife Reserve, guests encounter gorillas in a lush forest, along with hippos, meerkats, and other native African wildlife.

Gorilla Mystery, The (film) Mickey Mouse cartoon released Oct. 10, 1930. Directed by Burt Gillett. When a gorilla escapes from the zoo and threatens Minnie, Mickey races over to save his sweetheart.

Gosalyn Mallard Drake Mallard's daughter on *Darkwing Duck*; voiced by Christine Cavanaugh.

Gosling, Ryan Actor; appeared in *Remember the Titans* (Alan Bosley) and on The Disney Channel in the *Mickey Mouse Club* (beginning in 1993) and *Flash Forward* (Scott Stuckey).

Gotta Kick It Up! (TV) A Disney Channel Original Movie; first aired Jul. 26, 2002. An ex–dot-com executive takes a handful of Latina schoolgirls and motivates them to find their potential and overcome societal obstacles. With her guidance the girls work hard to beat the odds, becoming a championship dance team. Directed by Ramon Menendez. Stars Susan Egan (Heather), Camille Guaty (Daisy), America Ferrera (Yolanda), Sabrina Wiener (Esmeralda), Jhoanna Flores (Alyssa), Suilma Rodriguez (Marisol), Miguel Sandoval (Zavala).

Gottfredson, Floyd (1905–1986) Comic strip artist; hired by Disney in 1929 as an animation inbetweener, but Walt Disney asked him if he would take over the *Mickey Mouse* comic strip for a couple of weeks when the previous artist, Win Smith, left the Studio. Floyd's first strip was for May 5, 1930, and he stayed more than a couple of weeks—actually continuing to do the strip until his retirement in 1975. Besides drawing the Mickey daily strip, he also wrote it (1930–1932), drew the Sunday page (1932–1938), and served as head of the Comic Strip Department (1930–1946). He was named a Disney Legend posthumously in 2003.

Gottfried, Gilbert (1955–2022) Actor/comedian; he provided the voice of Iago in *Aladdin* and other appearances of the character, Two-Bits in *Bonkers*, Woodpecker in *The Lion King's Timon & Pumbaa*, and Clion in *Disney's Hercules*. On Disney Channel, he guest starred in *Adventures in Wonderland* (Mike McNasty) and *Hannah Montana* (Barney Bittman).

Gould, Elliott Actor; appeared in *The Last Flight of Noah's Ark* (Noah Dugan), *The Devil and Max Devlin* (Max Devlin), and *Playing Mona Lisa* (Bernie Goldstein). He voiced Mr. Stoppable in *Kim Possible*.

Gould, Harold (1923–2010) Actor; appeared in *The Strongest Man in the World* (Dietz), *Gus* (Charles Gwynn), and *Freaky Friday* (Grandpa, 2003), and on TV in *Tickets Please* (Jack), *Singer & Sons* (Nathan Singer), *Felicity* (Dr. William Garibay), *The Love Bug* (Dr. Gustav Stumpfel, 1997), and as Miles Webber in 13 episodes of *The Golden Girls* over a 4-year period. He voiced Old Denahi in *Brother Bear*.

Goulet, Robert (1933–2007) Actor; appeared in *Mr. Wrong* (Dick Braxton), and on TV in *Acting Sheriff*. He provided the singing voice of Wheezy in *Toy Story 2* and of Mikey Blumberg in *Recess*.

Gourmet Pantry Deli, grocery, and kitchenware shop in the Lake Buena Vista Shopping Village at Walt Disney World; opened Mar. 1975. It expanded into the former Village Character Shop Nov. 8, 1985. Closed Jun. 22, 2003, to be replaced by Goofy's Candy Co. and Earl of Sandwich.

Governor Ratcliffe Greedy leader of the English settlers in *Pocahontas*; voiced by David Ogden Stiers.

Grabeel, Lucas Actor; appeared in *College Road Trip* (Scooter); on Disney Channel in *High School Musical* (Ryan Evans) and as Ethan Dalloway in *Return to Halloweentown* and *Halloweentown High*; on ABC Family in *Switched at Birth* (Toby Kennish); on Disney+ in *High School Musical: The Musical: The Series* (as himself); and on ABC in *The Disney Family Singalong*. He voiced Peck in *Sheriff Callie's Wild West*.

Grabowski, Norman (1933–2012) Actor; appeared in *Son of Flubber* (football player), *The Misadventures of Merlin Jones* and *The Monkey's Uncle* (Norman), *The Gnome-Mobile* (nurse), *The Happiest Millionaire* (Joe Turner), *Blackbeard's Ghost* (Virgil), *The Horse in the Gray Flannel Suit* (truck driver), and *Herbie Rides Again* (security guard).

Grace Happy-go-lucky cow in *Home on the Range*; voiced by Jennifer Tilly.

Gracey, Yale (1910–1983) Special effects "illusioneer"; joined Disney in 1939 as a layout artist on *Pinocchio* and *Fantasia*. He contributed layouts and backgrounds for dozens of animated films, then moved to WED Enterprises in 1961, where he created special effects and lighting for the Carousel of Progress, Haunted Mansion, and Pirates of the Caribbean among other attractions. He retired in 1975 but continued to consult on EPCOT Center. He was named a Disney Legend posthumously in 1999.

Grad Nites Annual all-night parties for high school graduates, first held at Disneyland on Jun. 15, 1961. The first Grad Nite drew 8,500 students, the largest high school graduation party ever held in the U.S. Within the first decade that number would approach 100,000, and, by the end of the second decade, 135,000. Grad Nite has since stretched over a number of nights, with schools coming from near and far. In 2005, Honda signed a 10-year sponsorship deal for the Grad Nites at Disneyland. Grad Nites were also held at Walt Disney World 1972–2011, in the Magic Kingdom (with one in Disney's Hollywood Studios in 2009). In Apr. 2017, a reimagined Grad Nite H2O was held in Typhoon Lagoon at Walt Disney World. Samuel Jacobo, a graduate from Summit High School in Fontana, California, was named the 5 millionth Grad Nite guest at Disneyland on May 28, 2009. There were no Grad Nites held in 2020–2021 due to the coronavirus pandemic. Grad Nite resumed at Disneyland in 2022.

Grady, Don See Agrati, Don.

Graham, Don (1903–1976) Art instructor at the Chouinard Art Institute in the 1930s; helped organize art classes for Disney Studio artists in 1932.

Grain That Built a Hemisphere, The (film) Educational film produced under the auspices of the Coordinator of Inter-American Affairs; tells the story of corn, including its genealogy and discovery by Native Americans, how it has been developed in modern usage, and how its culture has spread over the Earth and influenced the economic structure of the world. Delivered Jan. 4, 1943. Directed by Bill Roberts. Nominated for an Academy Award for Best Documentary.

Gramatky, Hardie (1907–1979) Artist and story man; he joined Disney in 1930 and worked in animation for 6 years. He wrote the story "Little Toot," which was made into a Disney cartoon.

Grammer, Kelsey Actor; provided voices in *Runaway Brain* (Dr. Frankenollie), *Toy Story 2* (Prospector), *The Hand Behind the Mouse* (narrator), *Teacher's Pet* (Dr. Krank), and *Mickey's Once Upon a Christmas* (narrator). He appeared in *Swing Vote* (President Andrew Boone), and on TV as Nick St. Nicholas in *Mr. St. Nick* and as Dr. Frasier Crane in *Disneyland's 35th Anniversary Celebration* and *Mickey's 60th Birthday*.

Gran Destino Tower The 15-story hotel tower at Disney's Coronado Springs Resort at Walt Disney World; opened Jul. 9, 2019, with 545 guest rooms. The design and amenities are based on the influences of Spanish artists and architects. Visitors enjoy rooftop dining at Toledo – Tapas, Steak & Seafood, while Dahlia Lounge and Chronos Club, a concierge space, are inspired by the heroes of the animated film *Destino*. Barcelona Lounge offers

European coffee by day and cocktails in the evening. See Coronado Springs Resort, Disney's.

Gran Fiesta Tour Starring The Three Caballeros Boat ride attraction in Mexico at EPCOT, replacing El Río del Tiempo in 2007. The Caballeros are reunited for a performance in Mexico City; along the way Donald Duck disappears to take in the sights of the country, leaving José Carioca and Panchito to search for their missing friend. In 2015, Audio-Animatronics characters of the trio, originally from the Mickey Mouse Revue attraction, were added to the finale.

Grand Avenue Area in Disney's Hollywood Studios at Walt Disney World; opened Sep. 29, 2017, in a section of the park formerly known as Streets of America. Inspired by the cultural revitalization of Downtown Los Angeles, with *Muppet*Vision 3D* in the Grand Arts Theatre and dining at Pizze-Rizzo, Mama Melrose's Ristorante Italiano, and BaseLine Tap House.

Grand Californian Hotel & Spa, Disney's The first Disney resort to be located inside a theme park, Disney California Adventure, the Grand Californian celebrates the turn-of-the-century romantic Craftsman movement of California. The design captures the artistic exploration of California's coastline, with its Monterey pines and redwood forests, layered with the memories of the Arroyo craftsmen, the mission pioneers, the Plein Air school of painters, and daring architecture. Debuted with 712 standard rooms, 34 Artisan suites, 2 vice presidential suites, and 2 presidential suites, along with a convention center featuring a large ballroom. Dining options include Napa Rose, Storytellers Cafe, GCH Craftsman Bar & Grill (formerly White Water Snacks), and Hearthstone Lounge, with shopping at Acorns Gifts & Goods. The hotel welcomed its first paying guests Jan. 2, 2001, with the first event held in the hotel's ballroom earlier, on Dec. 1, 2000. Grand opening was Feb. 8, 2001. On Sep. 23, 2009, a vacation club addition—The Villas at Disney's Grand Californian Hotel & Spa—opened with 50 2-bedroom villas and 203 traditional hotel rooms, plus a new swimming pool and additional valet parking spaces. On Sep. 16, 2021, the Mandara Spa was replaced by the Tenaya Stone Spa, with a design inspired by nature, the indigenous cultures of California, and the hotel's Craftsman style.

Grand Canyon (film) CinemaScope featurette; released initially Dec. 17, 1958, with a general release Jan. 29, 1959, with *Sleeping Beauty*. Directed by James Algar. The ever-changing moods of the canyon and its wildlife are portrayed with the background music of the "Grand Canyon Suite" by Ferde Grofé. Academy Award winner for Best Live Action Short Subject. 29 min. The production of this popular film inspired the diorama simulation of the canyon on the Disneyland Railroad route.

Grand Canyon Diorama Dimensional views of the Grand Canyon, added to the Santa Fe and Disneyland Railroad Mar. 31, 1958. To the sounds of Ferde Grofé's "Grand Canyon Suite," guests view scenery from the South Rim of the Grand Canyon in a realistic diorama as they slowly ride by in the train. The diorama is 306 feet in length and features many varieties of animals among the quaking aspens and pine trees. It was billed as the "Longest Diorama in the World." Also on the Disneyland Paris Railroad.

Grand Canyonscope (film) Donald Duck cartoon released Dec. 23, 1954. Directed by Charles Nichols. Filmed in CinemaScope. Donald proves to be a meddlesome tourist to Ranger J. Audubon Woodlore, getting the two of them involved with an angry mountain lion who chases them all about the canyon, ultimately destroying the national monument.

Grand Circuit Raceway Tomorrowland attraction in Tokyo Disneyland; opened Apr. 15, 1983. Similar to Grand Prix Raceway in Magic Kingdom at Walt Disney World. Closed Jan. 11, 2017, to make way for an expansion of Fantasyland.

Grand Floridian Cafe Victorian-style restaurant in Disney's Grand Floridian Resort & Spa at Walt Disney World; opened Jun. 28, 1988. Guests enjoy casual American dining with views of the resort's rose gardens and courtyard pool.

Grand Floridian Resort & Spa, Disney's Resort hotel at Walt Disney World; opened Jun. 28, 1988. This is one of the more elegant hostelries in Florida with its 800 plus rooms, each with ceiling fans and Victorian decor. The 5-story lobby is a wonder to behold, with its stained glass domes and shimmering chandeliers. In the center, a musician may be playing at a grand piano, or a small orchestra may be entertaining from the balcony. A choice of a grand staircase or an open-cage elevator leads upward to shops and restaurants. Dining options include Narcoossee's, Grand Floridian Cafe, Gasparilla Island Grill, 1900 Park Fare, Cítricos, the Enchanted Rose lounge, and the most exclusive of the Walt Disney World dining rooms, Victoria & Albert's. Shops include Basin White, Curiouser Clothiers, M. Mouse Mercantile, Sandy Cove Gifts and Sundries, and the Bibbidi Bobbidi Boutique. An adjacent 27,037-sq.-ft. convention center opened in 1992. In 1997, the name was changed from the original Grand Floridian Beach Resort. A Disney Vacation Club addition, The Villas at Disney's Grand Floridian Resort & Spa, with 106 units ranging from studios to grand villas, opened Oct. 23, 2013. Opening Jun. 23, 2022, approximately 200 hotel rooms were converted into Disney Vacation Club resort studios, with enhancements also made to the existing Disney Vacation Club accommodations.

Grand Hotel (TV) Hour-long drama series on ABC; aired Jun. 17–Sep. 9, 2019. Charismatic Santiago Mendoza owns the last family-owned hotel in Miami Beach, while his glamorous second wife, Gigi, and their adult children enjoy the spoils of success. The hotel's loyal staff round out a contemporary fresh take on an upstairs/downstairs story. Wealthy and beautiful guests bask in luxury, but scandals, escalating debt, and explosive secrets hide beneath the picture-perfect exterior. Based on the Spanish TV series. Stars Demián Bichir (Santiago Mendoza), Roselyn Sánchez (Gigi Mendoza), Denyse Tontz (Alicia Mendoza), Bryan Craig (Javi Mendoza), Wendy Raquel Robinson (Mrs. P), Lincoln Younes (Danny), Shalim Ortiz (Mateo), Anne Winters (Ingrid), Chris Warren (Jason), Feliz Ramirez (Carolina), Justina Adorno (Yoli). From ABC Studios.

Grand Opening of Euro Disney, The (TV) Special on CBS; aired Apr. 11, 1992. Simulcast across Europe in 5 languages, the show was broadcast later the same day in the U.S. Top entertainers from around the world were featured along with the opening ceremonies, information on the building of Euro Disney, and an inside glimpse of some of its attractions. The shows were personalized for each country; for the U.S. the hosts were Melanie Griffith and Don Johnson. Directed by Don Mischer. 120 min.

Grand Opening of Walt Disney World, The (TV) Special on NBC; aired Oct. 29, 1971. A showcase of the new Magic Kingdom and its surrounding hotels, with coverage of the resort's Opening Spectacular and Grand Dedication Ceremony, held Oct. 23–25. Includes the grand opening parade in which "music man" Meredith Willson leads a marching band of 1,076 musicians. Stars Julie Andrews, Glen Campbell, Buddy Hackett, Jonathan Winters, Bob Hope. Directed by Robert Scheerer.

Grand Prix Raceway Tomorrowland attraction in the Magic Kingdom at Walt Disney World; opened Oct. 1, 1971. Similar to Autopia in Disneyland, it enables passengers young and old to drive along a 2,260-foot-long track. The ride path was moved slightly and shortened somewhat to accommodate construction of Mickey's Birthdayland (now Storybook Circus). Originally presented by Goodyear. In Sep. 1996, the name was changed to Tomorrowland Speedway, and in 1999 to Tomorrowland Indy Speedway, before reverting to Tomorrowland Speedway in 2008.

Grandfathered (TV) Half-hour series on CBS; aired Sep. 29, 2015–May 10, 2016. An ultimate bachelor, Jimmy Martino, discovers he is not only a father, but a grandfather. He is suave, handsome, and the most single person in the room, until his adult son, Gerald, makes an appearance, with *his* baby daughter, Edie. Now Jimmy has to unlearn a lifetime of blissful selfishness and grapple with the fact that he went straight from single to grandfather in 6 sec. flat. Stars John Stamos (Jimmy), Josh Peck (Gerald), Paget Brewster (Sara), Christina Milian (Vanessa), Kelly Jenrette (Annelise), Ravi Patel (Ravi). From ABC Studios and 20th Century Fox Television.

Grandma Duck Comic book character; Donald Duck's feisty grandmother (inspired by creator Al Taliaferro's real-life mother-on-law). She first appeared in the *Donald Duck* comic strip in 1943 (though her portrait was seen in 1940). She was given her own comic book series, *Grandma Duck's Farm Friends*, in 1957 and made her first animated appearance on TV in *This is Your Life, Donald Duck*.

Grandma Duck's Farm Petting farm originally featuring Minnie Moo, a cow with Mickey Mouse–shaped markings, in Mickey's Birthdayland (later Mickey's Starland) in the Magic Kingdom at Walt Disney World; open Jun. 18, 1988–Mar. 11, 1996. Presented by Friskies.

Grandma Sara's Kitchen Cozy counter-service

restaurant in Critter Country at Tokyo Disneyland; opened Oct. 1, 1992. Named after the sweet old muskrat, who, according to the story, makes the best comfort food in the area.

Grandpa Duck Donald's grandfather, who appeared in *No Hunting* (1955).

Granny's Cabin SEE MINIATURES.

Grant, Joe (1908–2005) Character designer and story man at the Disney Studio 1933–1949. He headed the character model department in the 1940s and was responsible for approving all model sheets. He worked on such classics as *Snow White and the Seven Dwarfs*, *Fantasia*, *Saludos Amigos*, *Make Mine Music*, and *Alice in Wonderland*. He returned decades later to receive credit for visual development on *Beauty and the Beast* and was a story adviser on *Pocahontas*, *The Hunchback of Notre Dame*, *Hercules*, *Mulan*, *Tarzan*, *Fantasia/2000*, *Treasure Planet*, and *Home on the Range*. He was named a Disney Legend in 1992.

Grasshopper and the Ants (film) Silly Symphony cartoon released Feb. 10, 1934. Directed by Wilfred Jackson. When a lazy grasshopper prefers to sing and dance rather than forage like his friends the ants, he learns to regret it when winter approaches. The ants save his life, and in return he entertains them with his music. Introduced the song "The World Owes Me a Living," sung by Pinto Colvig, who voiced the grasshopper (and also Goofy). The song was published on sheet music.

Graves, Michael (1934–2015) Architect; designed the Team Disney Building at the Disney Studio in Burbank, a building noted for its giant statues of the Seven Dwarfs holding up the roof. He also designed the Swan and Dolphin Hotels at Walt Disney World and the Hotel New York at Disneyland Paris, as well as some merchandise items.

Graves, Peter (1926–2010) Actor; appeared on TV in *Gallegher Goes West* and narrated *Race for Survival*.

Graveyard of Ships (TV) Part 1 of *The Mooncussers*.

Gravity Falls (TV) Animated series on Disney Channel; premiered Jun. 15, 2012. Twin brother and sister Dipper and Mabel Pines are in for an unexpected adventure when they spend the summer with their great-uncle Stan in the weird town of Gravity Falls, Oregon. Upon their arrival, Dipper and Mabel's huckster great-uncle, also known as Grunkle Stan, enlists the siblings' help in running The Mystery Shack, a fun tourist trap he owns that overcharges unsuspecting customers. Although the kids quickly discover The Mystery Shack itself is a hoax, they sense there is something strange about their new town and attempt to unlock the secrets. Voices include Jason Ritter (Dipper Pines), Kristen Schaal (Mabel Pines), Alex Hirsch (Stan/Soos), Linda Cardellini (Wendy). Created by Alex Hirsch; from Disney Television Animation.

Great American Buffalo Hat Company, The Frontierland shop in Disneyland; opened Jun. 29, 1990. Part of Bonanza Outfitters, which took the place of the Pendleton Woolen Mills Dry Goods Store. It became Crockett & Russel Hat Co. Dec. 15, 2004.

Great American Cowboy, The (film) Documentary film, directed and produced by Kieth Merrill in 1973, for which Disney later acquired distribution rights. Disney produced an educational film version in 1980 and released the entire film on video in 1986. The documentary details the yearlong quest of veteran rodeo cowboy Larry Mahan and his new superstar competitor, Phil Lyne, focusing on the explosive, sometimes bone-shattering action of the arena. Mahan and Lyne starred as themselves; the narrator was Joel McCrea. 89 min. Academy Award winner for Best Documentary Feature.

Great American Pastimes Sports collector's shop on Main Street, U.S.A. in Disneyland; open Mar. 22, 1991–Jun. 13, 1999, and succeeded by the 20th Century Music Company. It was previously Patented Pastimes, which sold vintage collectibles and toys, Jun. 15, 1990–Mar. 1991, taking the place of the Tobacconist.

Great American Waffle Co. World Bazaar counter-service restaurant in Tokyo Disneyland; opened Jul. 17, 1998, taking the place of The Rainbow Fruit Market. Mickey Mouse-shaped waffles are prepared in a show kitchen.

Great Cat Family, The (TV) Show aired Sep. 19, 1956. Directed by Clyde Geronimi. Tells the history of cats, from the days of the Egyptians to the present, and shows how they have been used in Disney films.

Great Expectations (TV) Adaptation of Charles Dickens's classic, airing in 3 parts as a Disney Channel Premiere Film. Set in the Victorian era, the story follows the fortunes of Pip from his meeting with a convict, Magwitch, to his early adulthood. Thanks to a mysterious benefactor, Pip becomes a young man with "great expectations"—a gentleman who will one day inherit a fortune. In his rise in society, Pip must constantly confront hard lessons about himself, his values, and his own expectations. First aired beginning Jul. 9, 1989. Directed by Kevin Connor. Stars John Rhys-Davies (Joe Gargery), Jean Simmons (Miss Havisham), Anthony Hopkins (Abel Magwitch), Martin Harvey (young Pip), Anthony Calf (older Pip), Kim Thomson (Estella), Ray McAnally (Mr. Jaggers). 308 min.

Great Guns (film) Oswald the Lucky Rabbit cartoon; released Oct. 17, 1927. After war is declared, Oswald takes to the air to bring down a villain within the enemy's limits. Oswald is shot to pieces, but a large cocktail shaker is used to put him back together.

Great Ice Odyssey SEE WORLD ON ICE.

Great Locomotive Chase, The (film) On Apr. 22, 1862, a party of 22 Union spies stole a train from right under the noses of 4,000 Confederate troops near Atlanta and began a race that might have brought an early end to the Civil War had it succeeded. Intrepid Confederates, led by the train's conductor, William A. Fuller, commandeered rolling stock for the chase and persevered long enough to recapture the train. Union leader James J. Andrews and many of his men were hanged in the South, but those who survived and made their way home were given Congressional Medals of Honor by the secretary of war. Released Jun. 8, 1956. Directed by Francis D. Lyon. 87 min. Stars Fess Parker (James J. Andrews), Jeffrey Hunter (William A. Fuller), Jeff York (William Campbell), Kenneth Tobey (Anthony Murphy). Because of Walt Disney's love of trains, he was especially enthused about this film, and he managed to secure aid from the B&O Railroad Museum to obtain an authentic locomotive. From the B&O (Baltimore and Ohio), he borrowed the *William Mason*, which doubled for the *General*. The *Inyo*, playing the *Texas*, was borrowed from Paramount Pictures. While the 2 original locomotives were still in existence, they were museum objects and not available for filming. (Both can be visited in Atlanta-area museums today.) A section of track near Clayton, Georgia, was utilized for the production. The technical adviser, Wilbur Kurtz, who had performed similar chores on *Gone with the Wind*, happened to be a descendant of one of the Confederates who participated in the chase. The film aired on TV in 2 parts in 1961 as *Andrews' Raiders*. SEE ALSO BEHIND THE SCENES WITH FESS PARKER.

Great Moments in Disney Animation (TV) Show aired Jan. 18, 1987. Directed by Andrew Solt. Carol Burnett hosts this look at some of the finer moments of Disney animation.

Great Moments with Mr. Lincoln Audio-Animatronics attraction featuring Abraham Lincoln reciting excerpts from several of his most famous speeches. Debuted in the State of Illinois pavilion at the 1964–1965 New York World's Fair. The illusion was so convincing that some guests recounted, incorrectly, how the president walked forward and shook hands with them. A duplicate attraction opened in the Main Street, U.S.A. Opera House in Disneyland Jul. 18, 1965, during the second year of the fair. The Disneyland attraction closed Jan. 1, 1973, so The Walt Disney Story could take its place. Due to popular demand, the show returned as The Walt Disney Story Featuring Great Moments with Mr. Lincoln on Jun. 12, 1975. In 1984, the Lincoln figure was reprogrammed utilizing new technology used for artificial human limbs pioneered at the University of Utah. Actor Royal Dano was the voice of Lincoln; he occasionally portrayed Lincoln in films, since he happened to bear an uncanny resemblance to the 16th president. The show went through a major rehab in 2001, adding a story line about a visit to Mathew Brady's photography studio and changing Lincoln's speech to the Gettysburg Address. For that version of the show, a special audio effect used binaural sound delivered through headphones, and Warren Burton provided Mr. Lincoln's voice. In 2005, the show closed so the venue could become a Disneyland 50th anniversary exhibit. It reopened as The Disneyland Story Presenting Great Moments with Mr. Lincoln on Dec. 18, 2009. An updated Abraham Lincoln is based on an all-new sculpture and represents the first Audio-Animatronics human figure to have a fully electric head. With an expanded range of facial movements, the figure can now purse his lips, form an "O" with his lips, smile, grimace, and use his eyebrows to enhance his emotions. For this version of the attraction, Royal Dano's recordings, along with much of the original narration, music, and other elements from the World's Fair show, were restored.

Great Mouse Detective, The (film) Animated adventures of a mouse, Basil of Baker Street, who is called upon to search for a toy maker, Flaversham, who has been kidnapped to make a robot replica of the queen for the evil Ratigan. Basil, aided by the intrepid Dr. Dawson, helps the toy maker's daughter, Olivia, search for her father. They foil Ratigan's plot and eventually save the queen. Released Jul. 2, 1986. Directed by John Musker, Ron Clements, Dave Michener, Burny Mattinson. 74 min. Featured voice actors were Vincent Price (Ratigan), Barrie Ingham (Basil), Val Bettin (Dr. Dawson), Candy Candido (Fidget), Diana Chesney (Mrs. Judson), Alan Young (Hiram Flaversham). The score was written by composer Henry Mancini, who also collaborated on 2 of the 3 featured songs with lyricists Larry Grossman and Ellen Fitzhugh; the 3rd song, "Let Me Be Good to You," was written and performed by Melissa Manchester. Based on Eve Titus's book *Basil of Baker Street*. After a 4-year period of story development, animation took just over 1 year to complete. This remarkably short production span was possible due to new efficiencies in the production process (such as video tests and computer-assisted layouts and graphics) and an increased emphasis on story development prior to the start of production. A total of 125 artists were involved in making the film. An innovative application of computer technology can be seen in the climactic scene where Basil faces Ratigan in a final confrontation inside the turning and thrashing gear works of Big Ben. The 54 moving gears, winches, ratchets, beams, and pulleys were literally drawn by the computer, and created a unique background for the characters that had been animated in the usual way. The film was rereleased in theaters in 1992 under the title *The Adventures of the Great Mouse Detective*. First released on video in 1992.

Great Movie Ride, The Ride-through attraction inside the Chinese Theatre at Disney's Hollywood Studios; open May 1, 1989–Aug. 13, 2017. The tour took guests into the midst of some of the greatest movies ever made, including *Casablanca*, *The Wizard of Oz*, *Alien*, *Mary Poppins*, *Singin' in the Rain*, *Fantasia*, and *Tarzan*, brought to life through an elaborate combination of sets, Audio-Animatronics characters, and live performances by Cast Members. In 2014, Disney announced a sponsorship by Turner Classic Movies; a new preshow film hosted by Robert Osborne, revised narration, and an updated finale montage were unveiled in May 2015. It was replaced by Mickey & Minnie's Runaway Railway. Originally developed as "Great Moments at the Movies," part of a proposed entertainment pavilion for EPCOT Center.

Great Quake Hazard Hunt, The (film) Educational video with Chip and Dale showing children how earthquakes happen and how to prepare for them at home and at school. Produced by KCAL-TV and KFWB News Radio. Released Oct. 18, 1990.

Great Search, The (film) Educational film about humankind's search for power and energy, stressing their responsibility to develop new power potentials that will not upset the ecological balance. Released in Jul. 1972.

Great Southern Craft Co. Country and folk craft boutique in the Lake Buena Vista Shopping Village at Walt Disney World; opened Nov. 19, 1977, taking the place of Von Otto's Antiques. Relocated May 4, 1988, replacing the original 2R's – Read'n & Rite'n. Included Lillie Langtry's old-fashioned photo studio. Replaced by Studio M in 1995. Also known as the Great Southern Craft Store.

Greatest Game Ever Played, The (film) The year is 1913, and golf is a rich man's sport dominated by English and Scottish athletes. Yet a 20-year-old amateur player and former caddy, Francis Ouimet, against all odds, becomes the first American, and amateur, to win the U.S. Open. Caught between a world of hardship and a beckoning life of privilege, Francis needs to prove his unfailing will and ability to make it to the tournament. There, flanked by his 10-year-old caddy, Eddie, he defeats his idol, the defending British champion Harry Vardon. A Touchstone film. Directed by Bill Paxton. Released Sep. 30, 2005. Stars Shia LaBeouf (Francis Ouimet), Stephen Dillane (Henry Vardon), Elias Koteas (Arthur Ouimet), Peter Firth (Lord Northcliffe), Stephen Marcus (Ted Ray), Peyton List (Sarah Wallis), Josh Flitter (Eddie Lowery), Luke Askew (Alec Campbell), Michael Weaver (John McDermott), Marnie McPhail (Mary Ouimet), George Asprey (Wilfred Reid), Max Kasch (Freddie Wallis), Matthew Knight (Young Francis Ouimet), Luke Kirby (Frank Hoyt). 120 min. Filming took place in Montreal. Based on the book of the same title by Mark Frost.

Green, Howard E. He joined Disney as an animation publicist in 1976 and became a key player in the company's motion picture publicity and marketing efforts, including as vice president of communications for The Walt Disney Studios, and later for Walt Disney Animation Studios. He has consulted on many Disney historical projects, conducted interviews with company personnel, and authored books, including *Remembering Walt: Favorite Memories of Walt Disney*.

Green, Judson (1952–2020) He joined Walt Disney World in 1981 as management audit manager. In 1987 he was named senior vice president and CFO for Euro Disneyland and in 1989 became senior vice president and CFO for The Walt Disney Company. He was named president of Walt Disney Attractions in 1991 and chairman in 1998. He served until Apr. 2000.

Green, Seth Actor; appeared in *Can't Buy Me Love* (Chuckie Miller), *Big Business* (Jason), *Enemy of the State* (Selby, uncredited), and *Old Dogs* (Craig), and on TV on *Our Shining Moment* (Wheels), *Good and Evil* (David), and *The Rookie* (Jordan Neil). He performed motion capture for Milo in *Mars Needs Moms*, and voiced Monty Monogram in *Phineas and Ferb*, Howard the Duck in the *Guardians of the Galaxy* films, and Todo 360 in *Star Wars: The Bad Batch*.

Green Card (film) A mutual friend arranges a marriage of convenience for Frenchman George Faure and Brontë Parrish, a native New Yorker. George needs a green card in order to remain in the U.S., while Brontë, a horticulturist, has found the perfect apartment with a greenhouse, but it is only available to a married couple. After a swift legal ceremony, each getting what they want, they part with the intention of never seeing each other again. However, a government investigation brings them back together, and despite initial irritation and incompatibility, the two begin to make some interesting discoveries about themselves and the nature of romance. Initial release in Los Angeles Dec. 23, 1990; general release Jan. 11, 1991. Directed by Peter Weir. A Touchstone film. 107 min. Stars Gérard Depardieu (George), Andie MacDowell (Brontë), Bebe Neuwirth (Lauren). Filmed in New York City as an Australian-French co-production.

Green Thumb Emporium, The Shop in The Land in EPCOT; open Nov. 10, 1993–Apr. 25, 2004, offering gardening supplies and souvenirs. Formerly Broccoli & Co.

Greener Yard, The (film) Donald Duck cartoon released Oct. 14, 1949. Directed by Jack Hannah. When his son is unhappy with only beans to eat,

Bootle Beetle tells him a story about the trouble he had with next-door neighbor Donald Duck in trying to get better food. When his son agrees that beans aren't so bad after all, Bootle Beetle risks going next door to bring back some watermelon for dessert.

Greenhouse Flower Shop Center Street shop on Main Street, U.S.A. in the Magic Kingdom at Walt Disney World; opened Oct. 1, 1971, selling silk flowers, green plants, and decorative pottery. Replaced in 1984 by an expansion of the Emporium. Also known as The Greenhouse.

Greenhouse Tours Guided walking tour in The Land at EPCOT; began Dec. 10, 1993. Superseded Tomorrow's Harvest tours. Guides who are often agricultural graduate students take small groups behind the scenes in the Living with the Land attraction, explaining hydroponics, aquaculture, drip irrigation, and other agricultural concepts, and are available to answer questions one might have posed while riding. The name changed to Behind the Seeds Tour in Sep. 1996.

Greetings from California: Everything Under the Sun Expansive shop in Golden Gateway at California Adventure; open Feb. 8, 2001–Aug. 28, 2011, themed to California icons and postcards.

Gregory, Natalie She appeared as Annie in Cranium Command at EPCOT, Kathy in *Spot Marks the X*, and voiced Jenny Foxworth in *Oliver & Company*.

Gremlins, The Small, mischievous characters in stories told by Royal Air Force Lt. Roald Dahl. Walt Disney planned to make a movie about them, but it was never produced. The only outcome of the project was a book published by Random House in 1943, several limited-edition dolls, and a few insignias created for military units. In the 2000s, the characters reappeared in comic books, merchandise, and the *Epic Mickey* video games.

Greta, the Misfit Greyhound (TV) Show aired Feb. 3, 1963. Directed by Larry Lansburgh. A racing greyhound is deserted and has to learn to live on her own. Finally she is taken in by a shepherd, and she helps him by using her speed to chase away coyotes threatening the flock and to track down a prowling bear. Stars Tacolo Chacartegui. Narrated by Rex Allen.

Greyfriars Bobby (film) When old Jock, a shepherd, is dismissed from service because of age, the little Skye terrier, Bobby, his constant companion, goes with him. And when old Jock dies of exposure a few days later, it is Bobby who travels unseen under the coffin as his friend is taken to be buried in Greyfriars Kirkyard and keeps vigil over the grave. Nothing the caretaker, James Brown, can do prevents the little dog from getting back into the kirkyard, and eventually he stops trying as Bobby wins his heart, as well as the hearts of the poor children in the tenements nearby. The day comes when Bobby is picked up for not having a dog license. Mr. and Mrs. Brown and a band of children come to pay the fine, telling the Lord Provost Bobby's story. He not only gives Bobby a license with his own hands, but he also grants him the Freedom of the City, an honor bestowed only on the brave and faithful. Released Jul. 17, 1961. Directed by Don Chaffey. Based on a true story, as told by Eleanor Atkinson. 91 min. Stars Donald Crisp (James Brown), Laurence Naismith (Mr. Traill), Alex MacKenzie (Old Jock), Kay Walsh (Mrs. Brown). Filmed on location in Scotland. The film received favorable reviews, but the Scottish accents were hard on Americans' ears, so the film very soon appeared on *Walt Disney's Wonderful World of Color* for a TV airing in 1964. Today a visitor to Edinburgh is often surprised to see a statue near the entrance to Greyfriars Kirkyard honoring the devoted Greyfriars Bobby.

Grey's Anatomy (TV) Hour-long medical drama on ABC; premiered Mar. 27, 2005. Grace Hospital has the toughest surgical residency program west of Harvard, a brutal training ground for the newest medical recruits. Meredith, Izzie, Christina, and George are the latest aspiring surgeons, trying to make it through 7 years of the finest hell Grace has to offer. Along the way, they have to deal with impossible bosses, lack of sleep, sick parents, one-night stands, and housing crises, with only each other to rely upon. Stars Ellen Pompeo (Meredith Grey), Patrick Dempsey (Derek Shepherd), James Pickens, Jr. (Richard Webber), T. R. Knight (George O'Malley), Sandra Oh (Christina Yang), Katherine Heigl (Isobel "Izzie" Stevens), Chandra Wilson (Miranda Bailey), Isaiah Washington (Preston Burke). Other actors came in later seasons, including Kate Walsh (Addison Montgomery), Eric Dane (Mark Sloan), Sara Ramirez (Callie Torres), Chyler Leigh (Lexie Grey), Kevin McKidd (Owen Hunt), Jessica Capshaw (Arizona Robbins), Jesse Williams (Jackson Avery), Sarah Drew (April Kepner). Patrick Dempsey left the series in 2015 after 11 seasons, and Ellen Pompeo exited in 2023 during the 19th season. From ABC Signature (previously Touchstone

Television, then ABC Studios). A Spanish-language version entitled *A Corazón Abierto* was produced for the Latin American market. *Private Practice* and *Station 19* are spin-offs. Winner of multiple Emmys, including Casting for a Drama Series (John Brace and Linda Lowy, 2006) and Supporting Actress in a Drama Series (Katherine Heigl, 2007).

Grier, Ed Joining Walt Disney World in 1981, he served as general manager of EPCOT Center and Disney-MGM Studios, did a stint at Disneyland Paris, and later served as exec. managing director of Walt Disney Attractions Japan. In Jul. 2006 he was named president of Disneyland Resort. He retired in 2009.

Griffith, Andy (1926–2012) Actor; appeared in *Spy Hard* (General Rancor).

Griffith, Don (1918–1987) Artist; worked on layouts for animated features from *Victory Through Air Power* through *The Black Cauldron*. He retired in 1984.

Griffith, Melanie Actress; appeared in *Paradise* (Lily Reed), *A Stranger Among Us* (Emily Eden), *Born Yesterday* (Billie Dawn), and *Two Much* (Betty), and on TV in *SMILF* (Enid) and as a host of *The Grand Opening of Euro Disney*.

Griffiths, Richard (1947–2013) Actor; appeared in *Blame It on the Bellboy* (Maurice Horton), *Funny Bones* (Jim Minty), *Bedtime Stories* (Barry), and *Pirates of the Caribbean: On Stranger Tides* (King George), and on TV in *A Muppets Christmas: Letters to Santa* (Santa Claus). He voiced Jeltz in *The Hitchhiker's Guide to the Galaxy*.

Grim Grinning Ghosts Song from the Haunted Mansion at the Disney parks; written by X Atencio and Buddy Baker.

Grimes, Gary Actor; appeared in *Gus* (Andy Petrovic).

Grimm Brothers Authors of the original *Snow White and the Seven Dwarfs* story.

Grimsby Prince Eric's retainer in *The Little Mermaid*; voiced by Ben Wright, who died just before the film was released.

Grin and Bear It (film) Donald Duck cartoon released Aug. 13, 1954. Directed by Jack Hannah. Ranger J. Audubon Woodlore, in his first appearance, tries to get the bears to behave during tourist season at Brownstone National Park. Each of the other bears selects their own tourists, from which they get plenty of food, but Humphrey, with stingy Donald Duck as his tourist, gets nothing to eat. Humphrey tries to trick Donald out of his ham and picnic basket by making Donald think he has run over the bear with his car. In the resulting melee, food gets scattered all over the highway, and the ranger gives both Donald and Humphrey pointed sticks to use to pick it up. He tries surreptitiously to keep the ham for himself, but Donald and Humphrey foil his plan.

Griswold Murder, The (TV) Episode 6 of *Elfego Baca*.

Grizzly Gulch Area in Hong Kong Disneyland; opened Jul. 14, 2012, as part of a major expansion of the park. Guests enter the era of the California Gold Rush, visiting the boomtown of Grizzly Gulch, founded on Aug. 8, 1888, the luckiest day of the luckiest month of the luckiest year. Towering over the town is Big Grizzly Mountain, standing over 88 feet tall. Rocketing through the mountain and around the entire land is a multidirectional coaster, Big Grizzly Mountain Runaway Mine Cars (similar to the Expedition Everest ride system at Disney's Animal Kingdom). There is also Geyser Gulch, a water-based play area, and dining at the Lucky Nugget Saloon.

Grizzly Peak Area in Disney California Adventure; opened Feb. 8, 2001, originally as the Grizzly Peak Recreation Area. A celebration of California's natural beauty, inspired by the national parks of the Sierra Nevada mountain range. Named after the 110-foot-tall mountain shaped like a grizzly bear and home to Grizzly River Run. The neighboring Condor Flats area was renamed Grizzly Peak Airfield in 2015.

Grizzly River Run Whitewater raft attraction, appropriately nicknamed "Grr," in Grizzly Peak at Disney California Adventure; opened Feb. 8, 2001. Up a clattering, 300-foot-long gold ore conveyor, 8-passenger rafts are lifted into swirling rapids 45 feet above the valley along one side of the 110-foot-high Grizzly Peak, the icon for the park. More than 130,000 gallons of water a minute roar down the river flume, carrying riders on a wild and thrilling, and, yes, wet journey.

Grocery Boy, The (film) Mickey Mouse cartoon released Feb. 11, 1932. Directed by Wilfred Jackson.

Mickey is overjoyed to deliver Minnie's groceries to her and help prepare dinner. But the mood is spoiled when Pluto takes off with the turkey and in the resulting chase Mickey gets covered with chocolate cake.

Grodin, Charles (1935–2021) Actor; appeared in *Taking Care of Business* (Spencer), and on TV in *The Muppets at Walt Disney World* (security guard) and *Madoff* (Carl Shapiro). At EPCOT, he appeared as Left Brain in Cranium Command.

Groff, Jonathan Actor; voiced Kristoff in *Frozen*, *Frozen 2*, and other appearances of the character. He received an individual Emmy nomination for his performance as King George III in the filmed production of *Hamilton* on Disney+, a role he originated on Broadway. He was named a Disney Legend in 2022.

Grogu Small and mysterious alien pursued by bounty hunters in *The Mandalorian*; also known as the Child. Upon his debut in Dec. 2019, he became a pop-culture sensation, affectionately, though incorrectly, named "Baby Yoda" by fans.

Gross, Edan Actor; appeared on TV in *We'll Take Manhattan* (Rocky) and the series *Walter and Emily* (Hartley). He provided the voices of Flounder and Christopher Robin on TV.

Gross Anatomy (film) First-year med student Joe Slovak approaches the usually dreaded gross anatomy class—the systematic dissection of the human body—with his usual cocky manner. But he meets his match in Dr. Rachel Woodruff, the uncompromising instructor, who recognizes Joe's natural gift for medicine under his outspoken rebelliousness. She begins a tough campaign to discover whether her class clown really has what it takes to become a doctor. The test of wills ultimately becomes a touching and revealing experience for both student and teacher. Released Oct. 20, 1989. Directed by Thom Eberhardt. A Touchstone film. 107 min. Stars Matthew Modine (Joe Slovak), Daphne Zuniga (Lori Rohrbach), Christine Lahti (Rachel Woodruff). Filmed at various Southern California locations, including the defunct Queen of the Angels Hospital and the University of Southern California. For the anatomy lab scenes shot on a Disney Studio soundstage, 16 realistic-looking cadavers had to be created.

Grosse Pointe Blank (film) A hit man, Martin, specializes in assassinations in this comedy, but he has begun to have an identity crisis, realizing that his life lacks meaning. Therefore, in his twisted search to find "fulfillment and truth," he decides to return home to Grosse Pointe, Michigan, for his 10-year high school reunion, where he plans to reunite with Debi, the girl he left behind, as well as doing "one last hit." However, his archrival, Grocer, shows up with plans to hit Martin instead. Directed by George Armitage. A Hollywood Pictures film in association with Caravan Pictures. Released Apr. 11, 1997. Stars John Cusack (Martin), Minnie Driver (Debi), Dan Aykroyd (Grocer), Alan Arkin (Dr. Oatman). 107 min. Filming took place around Los Angeles, with the communities of Monrovia, Duarte, and Pasadena substituting for Grosse Pointe.

Grosvenor Resort Hotel in Lake Buena Vista at Walt Disney World; opened Jan. 1, 1987. Formerly Americana's Dutch Resort, it changed to the Regal Sun Resort in 2007, and to the Wyndham Lake Buena Vista in 2010.

Growing Up (TV) Experimental docuseries on Disney+; digitally released Sep. 8, 2022. The challenges, triumphs, and complexities of adolescence are explored through 10 coming-of-age stories, with narratives that explore teenage-hood and the diverse social, familial, and internal obstacles they face on their path to self-discovery and acceptance. Created by Brie Larson and Culture House.

Growing Up Animal (TV) A Disney+ original series from National Geographic; digitally premiered Aug. 18, 2021. The intimate and extraordinary adventure of baby animals, from the safety of the womb to the uncertainty of birth and their tentative first steps. Narrated by Tracee Ellis Ross.

Growing Up Wild (film) 5 baby animals—cheetah, chimpanzee, lion, bear, and monkey—from different parts of the world grow up learning to survive in the wild, nurtured by the love and guidance of their families. Released Dec. 6, 2016, on Disney Movies Anywhere, Netflix, and other digital platforms. Directed by Mark Linfield and Keith Scholey. 77 min. From Disneynature, the documentary combines footage from *African Cats*, *Chimpanzee*, *Bears*, and *Monkey Kingdom* with new narration by Daveed Diggs.

Growing up with Winnie the Pooh (film) A series of DVDs and videos from Walt Disney Home

Entertainment giving preschoolers the social skills they need to get a head start to successful learning. The first 2 films in the series, released Feb. 8, 2005, were *A Great Day of Discovery* and *Friends Forever*.

grown-ish (TV) Sitcom on Freeform; premiered Jan. 3, 2018. Zoey Johnson, a popular, entitled, stylish, and socially active 17-year-old, heads off to college and quickly discovers that not everything goes her way once she leaves the nest. A spin-off of ABC's *black-ish*, taking on current issues facing students and administrators in the world of higher education. Stars Yara Shahidi (Zoey), Trevor Jackson (Aaron Jackson), Jordan Buhat (Vivek Shah), Emily Arlook (Nomi Segal), Francia Raisa (Ana Torres), Chris Parnell (Dean Parker), Deon Cole (Professor Charlie Telphy). From ABC Signature Studios.

Grumpy One of the Seven Dwarfs; voiced by Pinto Colvig.

Guardian, The (film) Legendary Coast Guard Rescue Swimmer Ben Randall becomes the sole survivor of a deadly crash at the height of a massive storm. In the wake of the accident, he is sent against his will to teach at "A" School—the elite training program that turns young recruits into the best and bravest of Rescue Swimmers. Reeling with grief and regret, Ben throws himself into teaching the only way he knows how, turning the entire program upside down with his unconventional training methods. But Ben understands exactly what's at stake—his students will one day have to make tough decisions between who dies and who lives. When he knocks heads with cocky swimming champ Jake Fischer, Ben sees someone with what it takes to be the best of the best—if only he can combine his raw talent with the heart and dedication necessary to avoid the mistakes that Ben himself has made. Heading out on his first treacherous mission to the fierce, turbulent waters of Alaska's Bering Sea, Jake will have to put all that he's learned into action as he discovers just what it means to truly risk everything. Directed by Andrew Davis. A Touchstone film. Released Sep. 29, 2006. Stars Kevin Costner (Ben Randall), Ashton Kutcher (Jake Fischer), Sela Ward (Helen Randall), Melissa Sagemiller (Emily Thomas), Bonnie Bramlett (Maggie McGlone), Clancy Brown (Capt. Bill Hadley), Neal McDonough (Jack Skinner), John Heard (Frank Larson), Brian Geraghty (Hodge), Dulé Hill (Ken Weatherly), Shelby Fenner (Cate). Created with the full cooperation of the Coast

Guard. The film was originally slated to shoot in New Orleans in 2005, but the crew was forced to move to Shreveport, Louisiana, after Hurricane Katrina struck, shattering much of the city.

Guardians of the Galaxy (film) Brash adventurer Peter Quill finds himself the object of an unrelenting bounty hunt after stealing a mysterious orb coveted by Ronan, a powerful villain with ambitions that threaten the entire universe. To evade the ever-persistent Ronan, Quill is forced into an uneasy truce with a quartet of disparate misfits—Rocket, a gun-toting raccoon; Groot, a treelike humanoid; the deadly and enigmatic Gamora; and the revenge-driven Drax the Destroyer. But when Peter discovers the true power of the orb and the menace it poses to the cosmos, he must do his best to rally his ragtag rivals for a last desperate stand, with the galaxy's fate in the balance. Directed by James Gunn. Released Aug. 1, 2014. Stars Chris Pratt (Peter Quill), Lee Pace (Ronan), Zoe Saldana (Gamora), Dave Bautista (Drax the Destroyer), Karen Gillan (Nebula), John C. Reilly (Corpsman Dey), Glenn Close (Nova Prime), Benicio del Toro (The Collector), Djimon Hounsou (Korath the Pursuer), and the voices of Vin Diesel (Groot) and Bradley Cooper (voice of Rocket). 121 min. From Marvel Studios. The soundtrack features a mix of '70s pop hits which are juxtaposed with strange planets and settings. Filmed in wide-screen format. Nominated for 2 Academy Awards (Best Visual Effects and Best Makeup and Hairstyling).

Guardians of the Galaxy: Cosmic Rewind Thrill attraction in World Discovery at EPCOT; opened May 27, 2022, replacing the Universe of Energy. Inside the Wonders of Xandar pavilion, special exhibits showcase the culture and technologies of the planet Xandar. Before visitors know it, the Guardians of the Galaxy arrive and recruit them for a thrilling adventure across the cosmos. Along Disney's first reverse-launch roller coaster, the new Omnicoaster ride system allows each cab to rotate 360 degrees, directing riders to the story taking place around them.

Guardians of the Galaxy Holiday Special, The (TV) Original special on Disney+; digitally released Nov. 25, 2022. On a mission to make Christmas unforgettable for Quill, the Guardians head to Earth in search of the perfect present. Stars Chris Pratt (Peter Quill/Star-Lord), Dave Bautista (Drax), Karen Gillan (Nebula), Pom Klementieff (Mantis), Sean Gunn (Kraglin), Kevin Bacon (self), with the voices of Vin Diesel (Groot), Bradley Cooper (Rocket). Written/directed by James Gunn. 42 min. From Marvel Studios.

Guardians of the Galaxy – Mission: BREAK-OUT! Attraction in Avengers Campus (formerly in Hollywood Land) at Disney California Adventure; opened on May 27, 2017, replacing The Twilight Zone Tower of Terror. The Guardians of the Galaxy have been captured by Taneleer Tivan, the Collector, in his fortress, so guests join the intrepid Rocket, who has escaped, in an attempt to save his fellow Guardians. Passengers experience a random free fall sensation with new visual and audio effects. For the 2017 Halloween season, the attraction was transformed into Guardians of the Galaxy – Monsters After Dark.

Guardians of the Galaxy Vol. 2 (film) After the Guardians—Peter Quill, Gamora, Drax, Rocket, and Baby Groot—help Ayesha, who heads the Sovereign race, protect some valuable batteries, Rocket steals some, and the Sovereign drones attack their ship. The Guardians are saved by a man who identifies himself as Ego, Quill's father, a Celestial. Ayesha hires Ravager Yondu and his crew to find and capture the Guardians. But old foes become new allies, and characters from the classic comics come to our heroes' aid as Quill tries to learn the truth about his parentage. Released May 5, 2017, in the U.S. after earlier releases internationally beginning with Italy on Apr. 25. Directed by James Gunn. Stars Chris Pratt (Peter Quill/Star-Lord), Karen Gillan (Nebula), Kurt Russell (Ego), Michael Rooker (Yondu), Zoe Saldana (Gamora), Dave Bautista (Drax), Pom Klementieff (Mantis), Sylvester Stallone (Stakar Ogord), Elizabeth Debicki (Ayesha), and the voices of Bradley Cooper (Rocket) and Vin Diesel (Baby Groot). 136 min. From Marvel Studios. As with the first film, classic songs play a major role, with an "Awesome Mix Volume 2" tape given to Peter Quill by his mother. Filmed in wide-screen format. Nominated for an Academy Award for Best Visual Effects.

Guardians of the Galaxy Vol. 3 (film) The beloved band of misfits is looking a bit different these days. Peter Quill, still reeling from the loss of Gamora, must rally his team around him to defend the universe along with protecting one of their own—a mission that, if not completed successfully, could quite possibly lead to the end of the Guardians as we know them. Planned for theatrical release May 5, 2023, also in 3-D, IMAX, and IMAX 3-D, after international releases beginning May 3. Directed by James Gunn. Stars Chris Pratt, Zoe Saldana, Dave Bautista, Karen Gillan, Pom Klementieff, Sean Gunn, Chukwudi Iwuji, Will Poulter, Maria Bakalova; with the voices of Vin Diesel (Groot), Bradley Cooper (Rocket). From Marvel Studios.

Guatemalan Weavers Adventureland shop in Disneyland; open 1956–Feb. 23, 1986. Became Safari Outpost.

Guerrilla (TV) Six-episode miniseries; released Apr. 13, 2017, on Sky Atlantic in the U.K., and Apr. 16 on Showtime in the U.S. The final episode aired May 14, 2017. During one of the most explosive times in U.K. history, a politically active couple find their relationship and values tested when they liberate a political prisoner and form a radical underground cell in 1970s London. Stars Idris Elba (Kent), Freida Pinto (Jay Mitra), Babou Ceesay (Marcus), Denise Gough (Fallon). From ABC Signature Studios.

Guest Disney term for visitor at the Disney parks.

Guest Quarters Suite Resort Hotel in Lake Buena Vista at Walt Disney World; opened Mar. 29, 1990, taking the place of the Pickett Suite Resort Hotel. It became the Doubletree Guest Suite Resort in 1995.

Guest Star Day Tuesdays on the 1950s TV show *Mickey Mouse Club*.

Gugino, Carla Actress; appeared in *Son-in-Law* (Rebecca), *Miami Rhapsody* (Leslie), *The War at Home* (Leslie), and *Race to Witch Mountain* (Dr. Alex Friedman). She provided the voice of Delilah in *Homeward Bound II: Lost in San Francisco*.

Guillaume, Robert (1927–2017) Actor; appeared in *First Kid* (Wilkes) and *Spy Hard* (Steve Bishop), and on TV in *Pacific Station* (Det. Bob Ballard), *Sports Night* (Isaac Jaffe), and guest starred in *8 Simple Rules* (Cody Grant). Also appeared in *Disney's Great American Celebration* and *Young Musicians Symphony Orchestra*. He voiced Rafiki in *The Lion King* and other appearances of the character, and Dr. Parker in *The Proud Family*.

Guilt (TV) One-hour drama series on Freeform; aired Jun. 13–Aug. 22, 2016. When Natalie Atwood's sister Grace becomes the prime suspect in her roommate Molly's murder, Natalie leaves her life in Boston and heads to London to defend her. With the help of an ethically questionable ex-pat lawyer, Stan Gutterie, Natalie starts to question how innocent her sister may really be as more ugly truths start to emerge. Stars Billy Zane (Stan Gutterie), Emily Tremaine (Natalie Atwood), Cristian Solimeno (Det. Sgt. Bruno), Naomi Ryan (Gwendolyn Hall), Kevin Ryan (Patrick Ryan), Sam Cassidy (Prince Theo). From Lionsgate, with Freeform.

Guilty as Sin (film) Jennifer Haines is a hotshot criminal defense attorney renowned for her ability to get anybody acquitted. She is challenged to defend a playboy, David Greenhill, charged with murdering his wife, but finds him more complex and dangerous than she ever imagined. To her horror, she discovers that he is twisting the law and using his own disarming charm to continue his deadly schemes—with Jennifer as an accomplice. After he is successfully acquitted, Jennifer must decide whether to put her life and career on the line and destroy him. Released Jun. 4, 1993. Directed by Sidney Lumet. A Hollywood Pictures film. 107 min. Stars Rebecca DeMornay (Jennifer Haines), Don Johnson (David Greenhill), Stephen Lang (Phil Garson), Jack Warden (Moe). Filmed on location in Toronto.

Gulager, Clu Actor; appeared on TV in *The Mystery in Dracula's Castle*.

Gulf Coast Room Small fine-dining restaurant with atmosphere entertainment in the Contemporary Resort at Walt Disney World; open 1972–May 28, 1988.

Gulliver Mickey (film) Mickey Mouse cartoon released May 19, 1934. Directed by Burt Gillett. In telling the story to his nephews, Mickey is Gulliver, who is bound on shore by the Lilliputians. He escapes out to sea only to be attacked by the Lilliputians' small navy. But when he saves the town from a huge spider, Mickey becomes the hero of the day.

Gullywhumper Mike Fink's keelboat in *Davy Crockett's Keelboat Race*; also one of the Mike Fink Keel Boats at Disneyland and in the Magic Kingdom at Walt Disney World.

Gummi Bears SEE ADVENTURES OF THE GUMMI BEARS, DISNEY'S.

Gummi Bears: A New Beginning, The (film) International theatrical release of the TV cartoon, first in England on Jul. 18, 1986. A young page,

Cavin, discovers the existence of supposedly mythical Gummi Bears, and with the aid of their magic Gummiberry juice, they help him foil the evil Duke Igthorn's plan to destroy Dunwyn Castle.

Gummi Bears: Faster Than a Speeding Tummi, The (film) International theatrical release of the TV cartoon, debuted in England Apr. 10, 1987. When Tummi is too slow cleaning up a mess of purple bubbles he caused, he tricks Zummi into zapping him with a "speed spell" that goes awry. However, he is able to use the speed to rescue his friends from Igthorn.

Gun in Betty Lou's Handbag, The (film) A shy librarian, Betty Lou Perkins, is bored with her small-town life. Alex, her police detective husband, ignores her, and her job has become routine and uninteresting. The town is stirred awake by the discovery of a murder victim. When Betty Lou stumbles upon the murder weapon, she decides to confess to the crime hoping her bold action will grab everyone's attention. Along comes mobster Billy Beaudeen, who is both intrigued and threatened by the sudden appearance of the new "hit woman" on the scene. Betty Lou uses her newly gained self-confidence and notoriety to uncover the truth about the murder and, at the same time, show her husband that she refuses to be taken for granted. Released Aug. 21, 1992. Directed by Allan Moyle. A Touchstone film. 90 min. Stars Penelope Ann Miller (Betty Lou Perkins), Eric Thal (Alex), Alfre Woodard (Ann), William Forsythe (Beaudeen), Cathy Moriarty (Reba). Filmed in Oxford, Mississippi.

Gun Shy (film) Charlie Cutter is a legendary DEA undercover agent who has a traumatic memory of his latest bust. Even though he loathes his job and wants out, he has carefully planned an operation for the arrest of Cheemo, a drug lord. The bust goes bad and Charlie is forced to watch helplessly as the resulting bloody carnage rips everything apart. He lives to tell the tale, but the memory will not leave him alone. Fear has now taken over his life. He seeks psychiatric help and finds himself relying on the support of an unstable therapy group and nurse, Judy, just to get through his work. A Hollywood Pictures film. Directed by Eric Blakeney. Limited release Feb. 4, 2000. Stars Liam Neeson (Charlie Cutter), Oliver Platt (Fulvio Nesstra), Sandra Bullock (Judy Tipp), Jose Zuniga (Fidel Vaillar), Richard Schiff (Elliott), Andy Lauer (Jason Kent), Taylor Negron (Cheemo).

102 min. Sandra Bullock also served as producer. Filmed on location in New York City (and at Los Angeles locations doubling as areas of New York City).

Gun Shy (TV) Limited 6-episode series on CBS; aired Mar. 25–Apr. 19, 1983. Based on *The Apple Dumpling Gang*, about 2 orphans in Quake City who have become wards of a professional gambler. Stars Barry Van Dyke, Tim Thomerson, Keith Mitchell, Adam Rich, Bridgette Andersen, Henry Jones, Geoffrey Lewis, Janis Paige, Pat McCormick.

Gund Manufacturing Co. Licensee for Disney plush characters, 1947–1971. Many of their dolls are recognizable by their molded plastic faces. For the first 2 Disneyana Conventions, in 1992 and 1993, Gund manufactured reproductions of their earliest Mickey Mouse and Minnie Mouse dolls.

Gunfight at Sandoval (film) International theatrical compilation of *Texas John Slaughter* episodes. First released in Germany in Dec. 1961. 92 min. Stars Tom Tryon.

Gunpowder Brom Bones's scary horse in *The Adventures of Ichabod and Mr. Toad*.

Guns in the Heather (film) International theatrical compilation of TV episodes of *The Secret of Boyne Castle*. Also known as *Spy-Busters*. First released in England in Jul. 1969. 89 min.

Gurgi Nondescript furry creature who joins Taran on his quest in *The Black Cauldron*; voiced by John Byner.

Gurgi's Munchies and Crunchies Fantasyland counter-service restaurant in the Magic Kingdom at Walt Disney World; opened Oct. 26, 1986, taking the place of Lancer's Inn. Closed Feb. 13, 1993, to become Lumiere's Kitchen.

Gurira, Danai Actress; appeared as Okoye in *Black Panther* and later Marvel Studios productions, and voiced Fury in *Tinker Bell and the Legend of the NeverBeast*.

Gurr, Bob Imagineer; he specialized in vehicle design, first being retained by Disney in 1954 to consult on the design of the Autopia cars. At WED Enterprises, he worked on designs for such attractions as the Monorail, Matterhorn Bobsleds, Great Moments with Mr. Lincoln, Flying Saucers, the Haunted Mansion, and the antique cars and double-decker buses utilized on Main Street, U.S.A. He retired in 1981 and was named a Disney Legend in 2004.

Gus (film) The inept California Atoms, floundering in the cellar of the National Football League, welcome the team's newest member—a mule capable of placekicking a football 100 yards with deadly accuracy. The endearing animal turns the league upside down, eludes kidnappers, masterminds the romance of the shy young man who owns him, and single-handedly (single-hoofedly?) turns the hapless Atoms into a championship team. Released Jul. 7, 1976. Directed by Vincent McEveety. 97 min. Stars Ed Asner (Hank Cooper), Don Knotts (Coach), Gary Grimes (Andy), Tim Conway (Crankcase), Liberty Williams (Debbie), Dick Van Patten (Cal), Ronnie Schell (Joe Barnsdale), Bob Crane (Pepper), Tom Bosley (Spinner), Dick Butkus (Rob Cargil), and special guest stars Johnny Unitas, Dick Enberg, George Putnam, Stu Nahan. The film was based on the book by Ted Key. Football scenes were filmed at the Los Angeles Coliseum, the Sports Arena, and on a portable field of sod covering a parking lot at the Disney Studio in Burbank. Backgrounds were filmed at many professional games. The fabled Animation Building on the Burbank lot was even used—as a hospital. Exec. producer Ron Miller had personal background experience for this film; he used to play professionally and spent a year as a tight end with the Los Angeles Rams. A special acknowledgment is made in the credits to the National Football League for its assistance in the football sequences.

Gus Tubby mouse friend of Cinderella; voiced by Jim Macdonald.

Gus Goose Gluttonous title star of *Donald's Cousin Gus* (1939). He became a supporting character in the Disney comic books as Grandma Duck's lazy farmhand.

Gus Tomlin is Dead (TV) Episode 10 of *Elfego Baca.*

Gutierrez, Horacio He joined The Walt Disney Company Feb. 1, 2022, as senior exec. vice president, general counsel, and secretary.

Guttenberg, Steve Actor; appeared as Michael in *Three Men and a Baby* and *Three Men and a Little Lady,* and as Tom Palmer in *The Big Green.* On TV, he appeared in *Tower of Terror* (Buzzy Crocker) and guest starred in *Schooled* (Dr. Katman).

Gwynne, Fred (1926–1993) Actor; appeared in *Off Beat* (commissioner) and *Disorganized Crime* (Max Green), and on TV in *The Christmas Star.*

Gyllenhaal, Jake Actor; starred in *Bubble Boy* (Jimmy Livingston), *Moonlight Mile* (Joe Nast), and *Prince of Persia: The Sands of Time* (Dastan), and voiced Searcher Clade in *Strange World.*

Gyro Gearloose Cartoon character created by artist Carl Barks; debuted in *Walt Disney's Comics and Stories* no. 140 in May 1952. His assistant, a lightbulb called Helper, made his debut in 1956. A fabulous inventor of weird and wonderful things, he also appeared on TV in *DuckTales.*

1. Hatbox Ghost 2. Horizons 3. Happy 4. *Hercules* (film) 5. Hyperion Studio 6. *Happiest Millionaire, The* (film)
7. Hidden Mickeys 8. Horace Horsecollar 9. *Hocus Pocus* (film) 10. Heffalumps and Woozles

Haber, Heinz (1913–1990) Scientist; acted as adviser on Disney space-themed TV shows in the 1950s, personally appearing occasionally on-screen. He collaborated on *Donald in Mathmagic Land* and wrote the book *Our Friend the Atom*.

Hackett, Buddy (1924–2003) Actor; appeared in *The Love Bug* (Tennessee Steinmetz), reprising the role on TV in *The Grand Opening of Walt Disney World* with his *Love Bug* co-star, Herbie. He voiced Louie in *Dinosaurs* and Scuttle in *The Little Mermaid* and other appearances of the character. He was named a Disney Legend posthumously in 2003.

Hackman, Gene Actor; appeared in *Crimson Tide* (Ramsey), *Enemy of the State* (Brill), and *The Royal Tenenbaums* (Royal Tenenbaum).

Hacksaw (TV) Two-part show; aired Sep. 26 and Oct. 3, 1971. Directed by Larry Lansburgh. A girl, on vacation in the Canadian Rockies, tries to capture a wild stallion whose great strength leads to a pulling contest at the Calgary Stampede. Stars Tab Hunter, Susan Bracken, Victor Millan, Ray Teal, Russ McCubbin, George Barrows.

Hader, Bill Actor; appeared on Disney+ in *Noelle* (Nick Kringle) and provided voices in *Monsters University* (Referee/Slug), *Inside Out* and *Riley's First Date?* (Fear), *The BFG* (Bloodbottler), *Finding Dory* (Stan, the husband fish), *Ralph Breaks the Internet* (J.P. Spamley), *Toy Story 4* (Axel the Carnie), and *Marvel's M.O.D.O.K.* (Angar the Screamer/The Leader).

Hades The scheming god of the Underworld in *Hercules*; voiced by James Woods.

Hagen-Renaker Potteries Licensee of Disney ceramic figurines 1955–1961. Their figurines, primarily small in size, were popular souvenirs in Disneyland but today command high prices. The intricate craftsmanship on the small figurines is remarkable. Some of their more popular sets are of characters from *Lady and the Tramp*, *Snow White and the Seven Dwarfs*, and *Sleeping Beauty*. They also had *Fantasia* figurines for sale in the Disney parks in the 1980s.

Hahn, Don Producer/director; he began working for Disney in 1976, first on *Pete's Dragon*. He later served as associate producer on the animated sequences in *Who Framed Roger Rabbit*; produced *Beauty and the Beast*, *The Lion King*, *The Hunchback of Notre Dame*, *Atlantis: The Lost Empire*, and *The Haunted Mansion*, as well as the animated shorts *Lorenzo*, *One by One*, and *The Little Matchgirl*; and was exec. producer on *The Emperor's New Groove*, *Earth*, *Oceans*, *African Cats*, *Chimpanzee* (also co-writer), *Frankenweenie* (2012), *Maleficent*, and *Beauty and the Beast* (2017). He has directed and produced several documentaries, including *Waking Sleeping Beauty*, *Christmas with Walt Disney* for The Walt Disney Family Museum, *Richard M. Sherman: Songs of a Lifetime*, and *Howard* (also writer). He directed/produced the *Beauty and the Beast Sing-Along* for EPCOT and hosted *Adventure Thru the Walt Disney Archives* on Disney+. He was named a Disney Legend in 2022.

Hahn, Kathryn Actress; appeared in *A Lot Like Love* (Michelle) and *Tomorrowland* (Ursula), and on Disney+ in *WandaVision* (Agnes/Agatha). For Hulu, it was announced she will exec. produce and star as Clare in *Tiny Beautiful Things*.

Hailey's On It! (TV) Animated comedy-adventure series on Disney Channel; planned for a 2023 debut. Hailey Banks, a risk-averse but resourceful teenager, is on a mission to complete every item on her long list of challenging (and sometimes impractical) tasks in order to save the world. She will be pushed outside her comfort zone to discover the greatness within as she systematically conquers her fears—whether she is winning a sand-building competition, wrestling a honey badger, eating a raw onion, or facing her ever-growing and complicated feelings toward her best friend, Scott. Voices include Auli'i Cravalho (Hailey), Manny Jacinto (Scott), Gary Anthony Williams (Beta). From Disney Television Animation.

Hair-Jitsu (film) Animated short; digitally released Jan. 24, 2020, on Disney+. A young girl faces off against an evil hairdresser as she goes through imaginative lengths to avoid her first haircut. Directed by Brian Estrada. 2 min. From the Walt Disney Animation Studios Short Circuit program.

Hakuna Matata Song performed by Timon and Pumbaa in *The Lion King*; written by Elton John and Tim Rice. Nominated for an Academy Award. The words mean "no worries" in Swahili. Also an Adventureland restaurant in Disneyland Paris, which took the place of Aux Epices Enchantées in May 1995.

Hale, Barbara (1922–2017) Actress; appeared on TV in *Chester, Yesterday's Horse*; *The Young Runaways*; and *The Flight of the Grey Wolf*.

Hale, Tiffini (1975–2021) Actress; appeared on the *Mickey Mouse Club* on The Disney Channel beginning in 1989, was a member of the pop band The Party, and made a guest appearance in *Blossom*.

Hale, Tony Actor; appeared on Disney+ in *The Mysterious Benedict Society* (Mr. Benedict/L. D. Curtain) and *Hocus Pocus 2* (Mayor/Reverend Traske), and on TV in *Mickey's 90th Spectacular*. He has provided several voices, including Forky in *Toy Story 4*, Vaneé in *LEGO Star Wars Terrifying Tales*, Frazz in *The Chicken Squad*, Apothecary Gary in *Amphibia*, Pie King in *Star vs. The Forces of Evil*,

Tobias in *Doc McStuffins*, Doctor Undergear in *Jake and the Never Land Pirates*, and Butter in *Woke*.

Hale Manu Boutique at Aulani, A Disney Resort & Spa; opened Apr. 29, 2013, offering authentic Hawaiian merchandise, handbags, and luxury items. The name means "house of birds," which are depicted in the décor.

Hall, Bug Actor; appeared in *The Big Green* (Newt Shaw), on video in *Honey, We Shrunk Ourselves* (Adam), and on TV in *Safety Patrol* (Scout Bozell), *Get a Clue* (Jack Downey), and *Castle* (Jesse Jones). He voiced a little boy in *Hercules*.

Hall, David (1905–1964) Story man; worked at Disney 1939–1940, and during that time produced hundreds of detailed story sketches and paintings for *Alice in Wonderland* (with a few also for *Peter Pan*). The concepts for these films changed during the many years before they were made, but Hall's sketches stand out as wonderful works of art. A book containing his *Alice* sketches, *Alice's Adventures in Wonderland*, was published in 1986.

Hall, Huntz (1919–1999) Actor; appeared in *Herbie Rides Again* (judge), and on TV in *The Sky's the Limit*.

Hall Brothers Company later known as Hallmark Cards, Inc. Joyce Hall of Kansas City was a friend of Walt Disney's, and he received the license to produce greeting cards featuring the Disney characters beginning in 1931. Gibson took over the national license after Disneyland opened, but Hallmark was back as a licensee beginning in the 1970s.

Hall of Aluminum Fame Sponsored by Kaiser Aluminum in Tomorrowland in Disneyland from 1955 until Jul. 1960. Told the history of the metal and those who developed the processes for its mass production, and described the methods used. A major icon was KAP, the Kaiser Aluminum pig.

Hall of Champions SEE MAIN STREET ATHLETIC CLUB.

Hall of Presidents, The Liberty Square attraction in the Magic Kingdom at Walt Disney World; opened Oct. 1, 1971. At one time this show had been proposed for Disneyland and later for the 1964–1965 New York World's Fair, under the title One Nation Under God. The presentation begins with a preshow film, which originally explored how the Constitution was drafted and how it has had increased significance at various periods of American history, from the 18th century to the present. The motion picture was shot on 70-mm film, using a special system invented by Ub Iwerks to scan the specially produced paintings (some of which are on display in the attraction), and it is projected on five large screens. Then the screens part, a curtain opens, and all the U.S. presidents appear onstage, represented by realistic Audio-Animatronics figures. They are each introduced by the narrator. George Washington would sit and Abraham Lincoln would rise and speak. Royal Dano provided the original voice of Lincoln. The presidents elected after 1971 were added within a year or so of their elections. When Bill Clinton was added in 1993, the preshow film and Lincoln speech were shortened, and Clinton made a few remarks. The Clinton speech was actually recorded by the president in the White House. The same was done when George W. Bush, Barack Obama, and Donald Trump became president. For the presidents, detailed research was performed by the Disney designers to provide not only images that the sculptors could follow in creating the figures themselves, but garner information on hairstyles, costumes, fabrics, and jewelry. Everything was then reproduced as authentically as possible. In 2009, the film was extensively changed, shifting its focus from a story about the Constitution to one about the individuals who held the office; for this version, both Lincoln and Washington spoke, along with the current president. The film was extensively changed again in 2017, removing the musical finale. Narrators have been Lawrence Dobkin, Maya Angelou, J. D. Hall, Morgan Freeman, and Joy Vandervort-Cobb.

Hallmark Card shop on Main Street, U.S.A. in Disneyland; operated Jun. 15, 1960–1985. The shop was previously sponsored by Gibson Cards. A Hallmark Card Shop was also in the Magic Kingdom at Walt Disney World, 1974–1985. Hallmark was a longtime Disney merchandise licensee. SEE ALSO HALL BROTHERS.

Halloween Hall O' Fame (TV) Show aired Oct. 30, 1977. Directed by Arthur J. Vitarelli. A Disney Studio watchman finds a room of props, including a jack-o'-lantern that comes to life. Several cartoons are used to tell "the real story of Halloween." Stars Jonathan Winters. Director Art Vitarelli was primarily a 2nd unit director at the Disney Studio, unsung for directing many fantastic special effects

scenes in films of the period, at a time when Disney was famed for its effects.

Halloween Hilarities (film) Shorts program; released by RKO in 1953.

Halloween Surprises (film) Educational film with Mickey's clubhouse members learning about Halloween safety rules, in the Mickey's Safety Club series; released in Sep. 1989. 13 min.

Halloweentown (TV) A Disney Channel Original Movie, first aired Oct. 17, 1998. Aggie Cromwell, an eccentric and high-spirited witch, travels from her spooky and wonderful hometown, Halloweentown, to the mortal world to enlist the help of her daughter, Gwen, and her grandchildren in her mission to save Halloweentown from the sinister forces of evil which threaten to take it over. Directed by Duwayne Dunham. Stars Debbie Reynolds (Aggie Cromwell), Judith Hoag (Gwen Piper), Robin Thomas (Kalabar), Kimberly J. Brown (Marnie Piper), Joey Zimmerman (Dylan Piper), Emily Roeske (Sophie Piper), Phillip Van Dyke (Luke). It was followed by *Halloweentown II: Kalabar's Revenge*, *Halloweentown High*, and *Return to Halloweentown*.

Halloweentown High (TV) A Disney Channel Original Movie; first aired Oct. 8, 2004. With the portal opened, much to the chagrin of some in Halloweentown, Marnie sets up an exchange program bringing a group of Halloweentown students to attend her human high school. She inadvertently bets the Cromwell family magic that no harm will come to them. When strange things start happening, Marnie and her family must protect the students from the legendary Knights of the Iron Dagger, and at the same time save their own powers. Directed by Mark A. Z. Dippé. Stars Debbie Reynolds (Aggie Cromwell), Kimberly J. Brown (Marnie), Judith Hoag (Gwen), Joey Zimmerman (Dylan), Clifton Davis (Principal Flannigan), Finn Wittrock (Cody), Michael Flynn (Dalloway), Emily Roeske (Sophie).

Halloweentown II: Kalabar's Revenge (TV) A Disney Channel Original Movie; first aired Oct. 12, 2001. The place where witches, ghosts, and goblins live for 365 days a year is threatened by warlock Kal, who has cast a spell. Halloweentown turns gray and its inhabitants become human caricatures. Kal also has plans for everyone in the mortal world to become the costume they are wearing at midnight on Halloween. Aggie and her granddaughter,

Marnie, must use their skills to vanquish the young and charismatic villain. Directed by Mary Lambert. Stars Debbie Reynolds (Aggie Cromwell), Kimberly J. Brown (Marnie), Judith Hoag (Gwen), Daniel Kountz (Kal), Peter Wingfield (Alex), Joey Zimmerman (Dylan), Emily Roeske (Sophie), Phillip Van Dyke (Luke).

Halyx Sci-fi rock band; performed on the Tomorrowland Space Stage in Disneyland Jun.–Sep. 1981. Developed by the Disney Records division.

Hamad and the Pirates (TV) Two-part show; aired Mar. 7 and 14, 1971. An orphaned pearl diver, Hamad, who lives in the Persian Gulf, is captured by pirates who have been stealing artifacts. When the Royal Navy approaches, the pirates throw their treasure overboard, and Hamad, who escapes, tries to find it while diving with a friend. The pirates return too soon, but Hamad helps foil them and save the treasure for the Bahrain museum. Narrated by Michael Ansara. Stars Khalik Marshad, Abdullah Masoud, Khalifah Shaheen.

Hamill, Mark Actor; appeared as Luke Skywalker in the *Star Wars* films and on Disney+ in *The Mandalorian*. He has provided several voices, including Ian Crookshank in *Bonkers*, Birthday Bandit in *Teamo Supremo*, Skeleton King in *Super Robot Monkey Team Hyperforce Go!*, Turtle in *My Friends Tigger and Pooh*, ShiverJack in *Jake and the Never Land Pirates*, Gadfly Garnett in *Miles from Tomorrowland*, Mr. Block in *Milo Murphy's Law*, and Vuli in *Elena of Avalor*. He was named a Disney Legend in 2017.

Hamilton (film/TV) On Feb. 3, 2020, The Walt Disney Company announced its acquisition of the worldwide distribution rights that would bring the hit musical to cinemas in 2021. Due to the COVID-19 pandemic, the release was instead fast-tracked to premiere digitally on Disney+ Jul. 3, 2020. The musical was filmed at the Richard Rodgers Theatre in Jun. 2016 with the original Broadway cast. Directed by Thomas Kail, with book, music, and lyrics by Lin-Manuel Miranda. The filming was produced by RadicalMedia and distributed by Walt Disney Studios Motion Pictures. Winner of 2 Emmy Awards: Outstanding Variety Special (Pre-Recorded) and Outstanding Technical Direction, Camerawork, Video Control for a Special.

Hamm Know-it-all piggy bank in the Toy Story films; voiced by John Ratzenberger.

Hammer and Fire Pleasure Island shop at Walt Disney World; opened May 1, 1989, selling unusual gifts, jewelry, and accessories. Live models posed as mannequins among the displays. Later replaced by Reel Finds.

Hampshire, Susan Actress; appeared in *The Three Lives of Thomasina* (Lori MacGregor) and *The Fighting Prince of Donegal* (Kathleen MacSweeney).

Hampton, Chase Actor; appeared on the *Mickey Mouse Club* on The Disney Channel, beginning in 1989, and was a member of the pop band The Party.

Hamster & Gretel (TV) Animated superhero comedy series; premiered Aug. 12, 2022, on Disney Channel. Kevin and younger sister Gretel are about to be bestowed superpowers by space aliens. But something goes awry, and it's Gretel and her pet hamster (named Hamster) who suddenly have new abilities. Now, protective older brother Kevin must figure out how to work with both Gretel and her pet Hamster to protect their city from mysterious dangers. Voices include Meli Povenmire (Gretel), Michael Cimino (Kevin), Beck Bennett (Hamster), Joey King (Fred), Matt Jones (Dave), Carolina Ravassa (Carolina). From Disney Television Animation.

Hand, Dave (1900–1986) Animator/director; he joined Disney in 1930 as an animator for 3 years before becoming a director. He is credited with directing 70 shorts and 3 features, including *Building a Building*, *The Mad Doctor*, *Old King Cole*, *Flowers and Trees*, *The Flying Mouse*, *Who Killed Cock Robin?*, *Three Orphan Kittens*, *Thru the Mirror*, *Alpine Climbers*, *Little Hiawatha*, *Snow White and the Seven Dwarfs*, *Bambi*, and *Victory Through Air Power*. Left Disney in 1944 to set up an animation studio in England. He was named a Disney Legend posthumously in 1994.

Hand Behind the Mouse, The: The Ub Iwerks Story (film) Documentary film about animation pioneer and early Walt Disney collaborator Ub Iwerks. Written, produced, and directed by his granddaughter, Leslie Iwerks. Released in Los Angeles for one week for Academy Award qualification on Oct. 8, 1999. 92 min.

Hand That Rocks the Cradle, The (film) A seemingly sweet woman named Peyton becomes a live-in nanny for warmhearted Claire, but the nanny has actually ingratiated herself into the family in order to plot vengeance for her husband's suicide, which she blames on Claire. Released Jan. 10, 1992. Directed by Curtis Hanson. A Hollywood Pictures film. 110 min. Stars Rebecca DeMornay (Peyton), Annabella Sciorra (Claire), Matt McCoy (Michael), Ernie Hudson (Solomon). The home used for the filming was found in Tacoma, Washington; other scenes were shot in the Seattle area.

Handley, Taylor Actor; appeared in *Phantom of the Megaplex* (Pete Riley) on Disney Channel and as a regular on the TV series *Go Fish* (Hazard).

Handy Manny (TV) A Playhouse Disney series on Disney Channel; premiered Sep. 16, 2006. Set in the multicultural community of Sheetrock Hills, the stories follow Manny Garcia, a friendly handyman who has a feisty and sometimes bickering set of tools that band together to eagerly assist neighbors by taking on their fix-it projects, no matter how big or small. Along the way, Manny and his friends model conflict resolution and problem-solving skills, while teaching kids basic Spanish words and phrases and exposing them to aspects of Latin culture. Voices include Wilmer Valderrama (Manny), Carlos Alazraqui (Felipe), Dee Bradley Baker (Turner), Nike Futterman (Stretch and Squeeze), Tom Kenny (Mr. Lopart and Pat), Kath Soucie (Dusty), Fred Stoller (Rusty), Nancy Truman (Kelly), Grey DeLisle (Flicker). From Nelvana Limited in association with Disney Channel.

Hang Your Hat on the Wind (film) Featurette; directed by Larry Lansburgh. A handsome thoroughbred yearling accidentally escapes from a cross-country van in the desert and is found and loved by a young Mexican boy. He hides the horse from searchers but eventually mends his ways and tries to return the animal. However, 2 hoodlums steal the horse. The boy leads a sheriff to the rescue and receives an apt reward. Released Jun. 11, 1969, on a bill with *Rascal*. 48 min. Stars Ric Natoli, Judson Platt, Angel Tompkins, Edward Faulkner.

Hangar Stage Entertainment stage in Lost River Delta at Tokyo DisneySea; opened Sep. 4, 2001, with *Mystic Rhythms*. Later shows included *Out of Shadowland* and *Song of Mirage*.

Hank Escape-artist octopus—though he lost a tentacle along the way—in *Finding Dory*; voiced by Ed O'Neill.

Hanks, Tom Actor; provided the voice of Woody in the Toy Story films. Appeared in *Splash* (Allen Bauer), *Turner & Hooch* (Scott Turner), *The Ladykillers* (Prof. Goldthwait Higginson Dorr), *Saving Mr. Banks* (Walt Disney), and *Bridge of Spies* (James Donovan), on Disney+ in *Pinocchio* (Geppetto), and on TV in *The Wonderful World of Disney: 40 Years of Television Magic* and *The Best of Disney: 50 Years of Magic*.

Hannah, Daryl Actress; appeared in *Splash* (Madison), *The Tie That Binds* (Leann Netherwood), *Two Much* (Liz), and *My Favorite Martian* (Lizzie).

Hannah, Jack (1913–1994) Animator/director; joined Disney's animation staff in 1933 working as an inbetweener and cleanup artist on many early Mickey, Donald, and Silly Symphony cartoons. He was a key animator on the Academy Award–winning film *The Old Mill*. After serving as a story artist, he became the primary Donald Duck director, starting with *Donald's Off Day* in 1944. He directed over 75 shorts, 8 of which were nominated for Academy Awards. After he retired in 1959, he spent a number of years creating and then heading the character animation program at the California Institute of the Arts. He was honored with the Disney Legends Award in 1992.

Hannah Montana (TV) Series on Disney Channel; debuted Mar. 24, 2006, and ended Jan. 16, 2011. Miley Stewart, a 14-year-old living in Malibu, California, leads a double life. She wants to be treated like any other teenager at school and maintain the typical life led by kids her age—from getting good grades to impressing her crush to being accepted by the various social cliques—but unbeknownst to the other students she is famous pop singer Hannah Montana, traveling the world and entertaining fans, with perks like limousines, cool clothes, and hanging out with celebrities. Stars Miley Cyrus (Miley Stewart), Emily Osment (Lilly), Mitchel Musso (Oliver), Jason Earles (Jackson), Billy Ray Cyrus (father). From It's a Laugh Productions and Michael Poryes Productions, in association with Disney Channel.

Hannah Montana & Miley Cyrus: Best of Both Worlds Concert (film) During a hugely successful, sold-out concert tour to 69 cities (which began in St. Louis Oct. 16, 2007, and ended Jan. 31, 2008), a filmed version of the tour was shot in Disney Digital 3-D. Miley Cyrus performs both as herself and in the role of her popular TV character, Hannah Montana. The film includes footage of pre-tour rehearsals, a jam session with Billy Ray Cyrus, and fan testimonials. It was announced that the film would play exclusively in movie theaters in the U.S. and Canada for one week only, Feb. 1–7, 2008, though that week was extended due to overwhelming response. Directed by Bruce Hendricks. Also stars the Jonas Brothers, Kenny Ortega. 75 min.

Hannah Montana the Movie (film) Miley Stewart struggles to juggle school, friends, and her secret pop-star persona. When Hannah Montana's soaring popularity threatens to take over her life, she just might let it. So her father takes the teen home to Crowley Corners, Tennessee, for a dose of reality, kicking off a fun-filled adventure. Directed by Peter Chelsom. Released Apr. 10, 2009, in the U.S., after an Apr. 8 release in Egypt. Stars Miley Cyrus (Miley Stewart/Hannah Montana), Billy Ray Cyrus (Robby Ray), Vanessa Williams (Vita), Emily Osment (Lilly), Margo Martindale (Ruby), Jason Earles (Jackson), Peter Gunn (Oswald Granger), Melora Hardin (Lorelai), Mitchel Musso (Oliver), Lucas Till (Travis Brody), Barry Bostwick (Mr. Bradley), Moises Arias (Rico), Jared Carter (Derek), Rascal Flatts (themselves), Taylor Swift (as herself). 102 min. Based on the Disney Channel TV series. Filmed on location in Los Angeles and around Nashville, Tennessee. The fictional town of Crowley Corners was re-created on the historic town square of Columbia, Tennessee.

Hannigan, Alyson Actress; appeared on Disney Channel in *Kim Possible* (Dr. Ann Possible, 2019) and on Disney+ in *Flora & Ulysses* (Phyllis) and *Earth to Ned*. She voiced Claire in *Fancy Nancy* and Winter in *Sofia the First*.

Hans The example of a brainwashed German youth during World War II in *Education for Death* (1943).

Hans Brinker or the Silver Skates (TV) Two-part show; aired Jan. 7 and 14, 1962. Directed by Norman Foster. Hans's father is injured, and all the family's money saved for Hans's education must go for medical bills. Hans dabbles in art, and hopes to sell some of his paintings, but then there are more problems with his father. Hans hears of an annual skating race, and he is determined to win it for the prize money to help his family. Hans aborts the race to save a fellow racer, who happens to be the mayor's son, and the mayor agrees to pay for the needed surgery. Stars Rony Zeander (Hans),

Carin Rossby, Gunilla Jelf, Erik Strandmark, Inga Landgre.

Hans Christian Andersen's The Ugly Duckling (film) Educational film; released in Sep. 1986, 13 min. Walt Disney introduces an animated biography of Andersen, followed by the Silly Symphony. Re-titled in 1987 as *An Introduction to Hans Christian Andersen.*

Hansel and Gretel (film) Directed by Tim Burton on 16 mm, this live-action film tells the Grimm fairy tale through Japanese actors, kung fu fights, and Japanese toys. It had its premiere with *Vincent*, and was introduced by Vincent Price, on *Disney Studio Showcase* on Disney Channel on Oct. 29, 1983. Stars Michael Yama (Mother/Witch), Jim Ishida (Father). 36 min. The Grimm fairy tale was earlier adapted in the Silly Symphony cartoon *Babes in the Woods.*

Happier than Ever: A Love Letter to Los Angeles (TV) A Disney+ original cinematic concert; digitally released Sep. 3, 2021. Grammy Award winner Billie Eilish performs the songs from her sophomore album, *Happier than Ever*, at the Hollywood Bowl, with animated elements that take viewers on a dreamlike journey through her hometown. Directed by Robert Rodriguez and Patrick Osborne. Guest appearances by FINNEAS, the Los Angeles Children's Chorus, Dudamel, Romero Lubambo, and other artists. 65 min. From Interscope Films and Darkroom Productions, in association with Nexus Studios and ALPWW. A 30-min. behind-the-scenes special, *The Making of Happier than Ever: A Love Letter to Los Angeles*, was digitally released Nov. 12, 2021.

Happiest Celebration on Earth In salute to the 50th anniversary of Disneyland, Disney theme parks around the world united in 2005 to bring guests new attractions, entertainment, and activities. At Disneyland, where the celebration was known as The Happiest Homecoming on Earth, additions included a new parade (*Walt Disney's Parade of Dreams*) and fireworks extravaganza (*Remember . . . Dreams Come True*); a new attraction, Buzz Lightyear Astro Blasters; the relaunch of Space Mountain; and a royal makeover for Sleeping Beauty Castle. In the Opera House was Disneyland: The First 50 Magical Years, an exhibit and film tracing the history of the park. Disney California Adventure received *Block Party Bash*, a street celebration featuring Disney • Pixar's most memorable characters. At Walt Disney World, Soarin', a popular attraction in Disney California Adventure, debuted in EPCOT; Tokyo Disneyland's *Cinderellabration!* premiered in the Magic Kingdom at Walt Disney World; *Lights, Motors, Action! Extreme Stunt Show*, a popular attraction in Walt Disney Studios Park at Disneyland Paris, opened in Disney-MGM Studios; and Expedition Everest – Legend of the Forbidden Mountain opened in Disney's Animal Kingdom. Special events also took place at Tokyo Disney Resort and Disneyland Paris.

Happiest Millionaire, The (film) In words and music, this is the story of "the happiest millionaire," nonconformist Anthony J. Drexel Biddle, and his unusual Philadelphia family, seen through the eyes of their new-to-the-U.S. Irish butler. The year is 1916, and in the busy household on Rittenhouse Square, each of the family members has hopes and dreams. For Mr. Biddle, it is strengthening the "Biddle Bible Class," campaigning for military preparedness, and caring for his prized alligators. For daughter Cordelia Biddle, it is first love with the wealthy Angie Duke, who is infatuated with the automobile. For Mrs. Biddle, it is keeping order in the family despite frozen alligators, a wedding, confrontations with the Duke family, World War I, and comforting her husband when the children have left home. Premiered in Hollywood Jun. 23, 1967. Directed by Norman Tokar. 159 min. (164 min. with overtures) for the original road show version; 144 min. for the stereo general release; 141 min. for the mono general release. Stars Fred MacMurray (Anthony J. Drexel Biddle), Tommy Steele (John Lawless), Lesley Ann Warren (Cordelia Drexel Biddle), John Davidson (Angie Duke), Greer Garson (as Mrs. Biddle in her last feature-film role), Geraldine Page (Mrs. Duke), Gladys Cooper (Aunt Mary), Hermione Baddeley (Mrs. Worth), Paul Petersen (Tony), Eddie Hodges (Liv), and Joyce Bulifant (Rosemary). This was the Disney Studio's most lavish and starry musical production since *Mary Poppins*. The Sherman brothers, Richard and Robert, wrote 12 songs, including "I'll Always Be Irish," "Detroit," "Fortuosity," "Watch Your Footwork," "Valentine Candy," "There Are Those," "Let's Have a Drink On It," and "Strengthen the Dwelling." The film was heavily edited during its release due to the Studio's disappointment that it did not equal *Mary Poppins*'s success. Cut footage from the original 159 min. road show version and the stereophonic soundtrack were restored and a theretofore unseen

musical number, "It Won't Be Long 'Til Christmas," sung by Greer Garson and Fred MacMurray, was added for a Disney Channel airing in Nov. 1984, though some dialogue preceding the song was still missing. The film has many highlights, from Tommy Steele's, Fred MacMurray's, and Greer Garson's portrayals to an alligator who dances with Steele. Some exhilarating dance numbers, including a riotous barroom sequence, were staged by Marc Breaux and Dee Dee Wood. The film's origins date back to the published true story of the Biddles, written by Cordelia Drexel Biddle and Kyle Crichton, which was subsequently made into a successful Broadway comedy. A J Carothers adapted the screenplay when Walt Disney enlisted the Sherman brothers to make it into a musical event. There were other contenders for the role of Mr. Biddle, including Rex Harrison, who was favored by the Sherman brothers, Burt Lancaster, and Brian Keith, but Walt Disney chose his favorite, Fred MacMurray, whom he had wanted from the beginning.

Happiest Turkeys on Earth Each year from 2005–2009, after being pardoned at the White House, the national Thanksgiving turkeys traveled to Disneyland, where they appeared at Big Thunder Ranch and as parade grand marshals. The one exception was in 2007, when the turkeys instead visited the Magic Kingdom at Walt Disney World.

Happily Ever After Nighttime spectacular in the Magic Kingdom at Walt Disney World; debuted May 12, 2017, replacing *Wishes*. The 18-min. production included more projections, lights, and lasers than previous fireworks shows. The score was recorded by a symphony orchestra in London, with the title theme song performed by Angie Keilhauer and Jordan Fisher. The final performance was held Sep. 29, 2021. Succeeded by *Disney Enchantment*. It was announced the show will return Apr. 3, 2023.

Happy The most cheerful of the Seven Dwarfs; voiced by Otis Harlan.

Happy Birthday Donald Duck (TV) See At Home with Donald Duck.

Happy Endings (TV) ABC comedy series; aired Apr. 13, 2011–May 3, 2013. When a couple gets divorced, who gets to keep the friends? Dave and Alex's breakup complicates matters for a long-term, close-knit group of friends. Stars Elisha Cuthbert (Alex), Eliza Coupe (Jane), Zachary

Knighton (Dave), Adam Pally (Max), Damon Wayans, Jr. (Brad), Casey Wilson (Penny). From Sony Pictures TV and ABC Studios. A spin-off web series, *Happy Endings: Happy Rides*, was digitally released Feb. 29–Apr. 4, 2012, with six 2-min. episodes; presented by Subaru.

Happy Ride with Baymax, The *Big Hero 6* attraction in Tomorrowland at Tokyo Disneyland; opened Sep. 28, 2020. Guests board vehicles that are pulled by Nursebots and whirl around for an up-tempo musical ride.

Happy Town (TV) Drama series on ABC; aired Apr. 28–Jun. 16, 2010. Dark truths are revealed about residents of small Haplin, Minnesota, a town called "Happy Town," despite being riddled for years by unsolved kidnappings. Haplin now faces a new crime that brings all of its unresolved fears to the surface. Many residents wonder if the elusive "Magic Man"—who may have been responsible for the bizarre abductions—has returned to claim another innocent victim. The town's most powerful family, the Haplins, run the local bread factory and try to wield control while dealing with the fact that a family member was one of the Magic Man's many victims. Stars Geoff Stults (Tommy Conroy), Lauren German (Henley Boone), Steven Weber (John Haplin), Amy Acker (Rachel Conroy), Sarah Gadon (Georgia Bravin), Jay Paulson (Eli Rogers), Robert Wisdom (Roger Hobbs), Sam Neill (Merritt Grieves), Frances Conroy (Peggy Haplin). From ABC Studios.

Happy Working Song Song from *Enchanted*; written by Alan Menken and Stephen Schwartz. Nominated for an Academy Award.

Harambe Disney designers and Native craftspeople created the fictional port town of Harambe, which features the 800-acre Harambe Wildlife Reserve (Kilimanjaro Safaris), shops, and restaurants in Africa at Disney's Animal Kingdom. The village tells a present-day story through its realistic detail and architecture, inspired by coastal towns in Kenya. Harambe means "come together" in Swahili. SEE AFRICA.

Harambe Market Open-air plaza in Africa at Disney's Animal Kingdom; opened May 23, 2015. Patterned after an African street market with a colonial-era train depot design, shaded tables, and shops. Initially opened with 4 walk-up food windows: Famous Sausages (corn dogs with an Afri-

can curry flavor), Wanjohi's Refreshments (wine, beer, and other beverages), Kitamu Grill (skewered chicken and kebab flatbread sandwiches), and Chef Mwanga's (spice-rubbed ribs with slaw). Zuri's Sweets Shop (candy, flavored popcorn, candy apples) was added Jun. 17, 2015.

Harbor Boulevard Anaheim street on which Disneyland is located. It is a major thoroughfare, beginning at the Pacific Ocean, 15 miles from Disneyland.

Harbour Galley Counter-service restaurant in Critter Country at Disneyland; opened Jul. 1989, serving a healthy seafood menu. From 2001–2008, McDonald's sponsored the facility and offered its own french fries and beverages. When the sponsorship ended in 2009, soups, loaded baked potatoes, salads, and sandwiches were served.

Hard Time on Planet Earth (TV) Series on CBS; aired Mar. 1–Jul. 5, 1989. An alien warrior from the planet Andarius is sent to Earth, transformed into human form, kept under surveillance by a "correctional unit" named Control, and forced to perform a series of good deeds before he can return home. Stars Martin Kove (Jesse), Danny Mann (voice of Control).

Hardball (TV) Series on Fox; aired Sep. 4–Oct. 23, 1994. About the trials and triumphs of the Pioneers, a fictitious American League baseball team. Stars Bruce Greenwood (Dave Logan), Mike Starr (Mike Widmer), Dann Florek (Ernest "Happy" Talbot), Alexandra Wentworth (Lee Emory), Rose Marie (Mitzi Balzer).

Hardoon, Doris Imagineer; she joined WED Enterprises in 1979 as a junior designer, with later roles including lead designer, art director, and producer on projects including EPCOT Center, Tokyo Disneyland, Disneyland Paris, Disney's Animal Kingdom, and Disney Cruise Line. She served as exec. art director, producer, and creative portfolio lead for Hong Kong Disneyland, as well as for the proposed WESTCOT Center for Anaheim and DisneySea for Long Beach. She left Walt Disney Imagineering in 2000 but returned in 2009 to help design and build Shanghai Disney Resort as exec. director and producer. She retired from the Company in 2019 and was named a Disney Legend in 2022.

Hardy Boys, The: The Mystery of Ghost Farm (TV) Serial on the *Mickey Mouse Club* during the

1957–1958 season. Directed by Robert Springsteen. Joe discovers a haunted farm, and Frank helps him investigate. Stars Tim Considine (Frank), Tommy Kirk (Joe), Carole Ann Campbell, Sarah Selby, Russ Conway, John Baer, Hugh Sanders, Bob Amsberry, Andy Clyde. 15 episodes. SEE NEXT ENTRY.

Hardy Boys, The: The Mystery of the Applegate Treasure (TV) Serial on the *Mickey Mouse Club* during the 1956–1957 season. Directed by Charles Haas. Frank and Joe Hardy, sons of a famous detective, try to solve a mystery about a lost treasure themselves. Based on the books by Franklin W. Dixon. Stars Tim Considine, Tommy Kirk, Carole Ann Campbell, Donald MacDonald, Florenz Ames, Russ Conway, Sarah Selby. 20 episodes.

Harem Scarem (film) Oswald the Lucky Rabbit cartoon; released Jan. 9, 1928. In the desert, a dancer is kidnapped at an oasis bar, prompting Oswald and his worse-for-wear camel to try to save her.

Harlan, Otis (1865–1940) Actor; provided the voice of Happy in *Snow White and the Seven Dwarfs*.

Harline, Leigh (1907–1969) Composer/songwriter; at Disney 1932–1941, he wrote songs for short subjects and features, including the underscoring on *Snow White and the Seven Dwarfs* and *Pinocchio* with Paul Smith, and the music for several *Pinocchio* songs. He was named a Disney Legend posthumously in 2001. His name is pronounced Lee Har-LEEN.

Harman, Hugh (1903–1982) One of Walt Disney's first employees, originally at Laugh-O-gram Films in Kansas City, and then in Hollywood. He worked on the Alice Comedies and left in 1928 to partner with another early Disney employee, Rudolf Ising.

Harman-Ising Cartoon production organization headed by Hugh Harman and Rudy Ising, who had worked for Walt Disney in Kansas City. Disney hired them to produce the cartoon *Merbabies* (1938) for him.

Harmonious Nighttime spectacular on World Showcase Lagoon in EPCOT; premiered Sep. 29, 2021, succeeding *Epcot Forever*. Internationally inspired Disney songs were reinterpreted in more than a dozen languages by 240 musical artists from around the world, accompanied with giant floating screens, fireworks, moving fountains, lighting effects, and lasers. It was announced the final performance will be held Apr. 2, 2023, with *Epcot Forever* set to return.

Harmony Barber Shop Located in Main Street, U.S.A. in the Magic Kingdom at Walt Disney World; opened on Center Street in 1971. In a nostalgic setting, many guests decide to have a quick trim. It was relocated to Town Square in 2001 when an expansion of the Emporium took over Center Street. Also in Disneyland Paris; opened Apr. 12, 1992, and renamed Dapper Dan's Hair Cuts Sep. 21, 1993.

Harmony Faire *Mickey's PhilharMagic* shop in Tokyo Disneyland; opened in 2011, selling hats and accessories.

Harnois, Elisabeth Actress; appeared in *One Magic Christmas* (Abbie Grainger) and *Mars Needs Moms* (Ki), and on TV as Alice in *Disney's Adventures in Wonderland* and Hallie Richmond in *My Date with the President's Daughter*.

Harold and His Amazing Green Plants (film) Educational film; released in Aug. 1984. A basic botany lesson for the youngest audience about Harold and his unusual "pet" plant.

Harriet, Judy Mouseketeer from the 1950s *Mickey Mouse Club* TV show.

Harriet the Spy: Blog Wars (TV) Movie; premiered on Disney Channel Mar. 26, 2010. Harriet "The Spy" Welsch vies to become the official blogger of her high school class. Stars Jennifer Stone (Harriet), Kristin Booth (Golly), Wesley Morgan (Skander), Doug Murray (Roger). From 9 Story Entertainment and Disney Channel.

Harrington Bay Clothiers Men's fashions at the Downtown Disney Marketplace at Walt Disney World; opened Mar. 23, 1992, succeeding Sir Edward's Haberdasher. It closed Jul. 15, 2001, and was superseded by Once Upon a Toy.

Harrington's Fine China & Porcelains Main Street, U.S.A. collectibles shop in Disneyland Paris; opened Apr. 12, 1992.

Harrington's Jewelry & Watches SEE NEW CENTURY CLOCK SHOP.

Harris, Barbara (1935–2018) Actress; appeared in 1977's *Freaky Friday* (Ellen Andrews), *The North Avenue Irregulars* (Vickie), and *Grosse Pointe Blank* (Mary Blank).

Harris, Phil (1906–1995) Actor/musician; voiced Baloo (*The Jungle Book*), Thomas O'Malley (*The Aristocats*), and Little John (*Robin Hood*).

Harrison Hightower III The builder of Hotel Hightower and an antiquities collector at the Tower of Terror in Tokyo DisneySea. He mysteriously disappeared Dec. 31, 1899, after acquiring the idol Shiriki Utundu. The character bears a resemblance to Imagineer Joe Rohde.

Harriss, Cynthia After starting with Disney in the Disney Stores in 1992, Harriss moved to Disneyland in 1997 as head of park operations and merchandise. She was promoted to exec. vice president of Disneyland Resort in Dec. 1998, and to president in Dec. 1999. She served until Oct. 2003.

Harrow (TV) One-hour drama series; premiered Mar. 9, 2018, on ABC Australia, followed by a Sep. 7 digital release on Hulu. Daniel Harrow is a brilliant forensic pathologist who solves the cases others can't. When a secret from his past threatens his career and family, he'll need all his wit and forensic genius to keep a crime buried forever. Stars Ioan Gruffudd (Dr. Daniel Harrow), Mirrah Foulkes (Sgt. Soraya Dass), Remi Hii (Simon Van Reyk), Anna Lise Phillips (Stephanie Tolson), Darren Gilshenan (Lyle Fairley). From Hoodlum Entertainment and ABC Studios International.

Harry (TV) Series; aired Mar. 4–25, 1987. Harry Porschak runs the supply room at County General Hospital, and he is not above making questionable deals to keep his operation running smoothly. This alienates some of his superiors, but it endears him to many of his fellow workers. Stars Alan Arkin (Harry), Thom Bray (Lawrence), Matt Craven (Bobby), Barbara Dana (Sandy), Kurt Knudson (Richard).

Hartman, David Actor; appeared as Professor Ivarsson in *The Island at the Top of the World.*

Harvest Theater Attraction in The Land at EPCOT showing films about humanity's relationship with nature. The first film, *Symbiosis*, debuted in 70-mm Oct. 1, 1982, exploring how technology could exist without destroying the environment. A new film, *Circle of Life: An Environmental Fable*, premiered in 1995, followed by *Awesome Planet* in 2020.

Haskin, Byron (1899–1984) Director; he helmed *Treasure Island* for Disney.

Hatbox Ghost Fabled haunt in the attic of the Haunted Mansion at Disneyland. Originally designed by Imagineer Yale Gracey, the ghost's grimacing head would vanish from his body and reappear in the hat box he was holding. The illusion did not work as planned, and the character was removed shortly after the attraction's initial opening in 1969, leading to decades of speculation about its existence. With the help of new technology, a new Hatbox Ghost materialized in the Haunted Mansion in May 2015, and it was announced he would be added to the Walt Disney World attraction in 2023.

Hatcher, Teri Actress; appeared in *Straight Talk* (Janice), and on TV in *Desperate Housewives* (Susan Mayer). She voiced Dottie in *Planes* and Beatrice Le Beak in *Jake and the Never Land Pirates.*

Hatching Pete (TV) A Disney Channel Original Movie; first aired Apr. 24, 2009. Pete, a shy 16-year-old high school student, is struggling to be noticed, especially by a long-admired special girl. Then his best friend, Cleatus Poole, must quietly take a break from performing as the school's chicken mascot, and unbeknownst to fans, he convinces Pete to stand in for him. Once Pete dons the chicken suit, a whole new outgoing personality emerges, and it not only captivates the school but the whole town. No one knows it is not Cleatus in the suit. Meanwhile Cleatus reaps the benefits of Pete's dynamic performances, including a new girlfriend. Now unassuming Pete must decide if he wants everyone to know who the funny guy is. Directed by Stuart Gillard. Stars Jason Dolley (Pete Ivey), Mitchel Musso (Cleatus Poole), Tiffany Thornton (Angela Morissey), Josie Loren (Jamie Wynn), Brian Stepanek (Coach Madden).

Hathaway, Anne Actress; appeared as Mia Thermopolis in *The Princess Diaries* and *The Princess Diaries 2: Royal Engagement,* and as the White Queen in *Alice in Wonderland* (2010) and *Alice Through the Looking Glass.*

Hatmosphere See Mad Hatter Shop.

Haunted House, The (film) Mickey Mouse cartoon; released in 1929. Directed by Walt Disney. When Mickey retreats from a storm into a haunted house, the skeleton inhabitants, including a Grim Reaper skeleton, force him to play the organ for them. Finally, he escapes through a window.

Haunted Mansion New Orleans Square attraction in Disneyland, supposedly the retirement home of 999 happy haunts ("but there's room for a thousand"); opened Aug. 9, 1969. The mansion had actually been built in 1962–1963, but work on the interior was first halted due to Disney's involvement in the 1964–1965 New York World's Fair. Then the designers could not decide on what to put inside, so guests were simply tantalized by a promise of an attraction to come. At one time, it was thought that there would be a walk-through attraction, but it was realized that there would be traffic-flow problems. The advent of the Omnimover—here "Doom Buggies"—provided the solution. From the outside the mansion looks elegant; some designers wanted it to look ominous and scary, in a state of disrepair, but Walt Disney said that he'd keep up the outside and let the ghosts take care of the interior. Within the house, guests hear narration by the Ghost Host (voiced by Paul Frees) as they ride past a number of spooky scenes and special effects that defy explanation. The memorable song, by X Atencio and Buddy Baker, is "Grim Grinning Ghosts." Also opened in Liberty Square in the Magic Kingdom at Walt Disney World Oct. 1, 1971, and in Fantasyland in Tokyo Disneyland Apr. 15, 1983. The Haunted Mansion in Disneyland was temporarily changed to the Haunted Mansion Holiday with a holiday theme of *Tim Burton's The Nightmare Before Christmas*, beginning Oct. 5, 2001, and repeated in later holiday seasons. A Japanese version, the Haunted Mansion Holiday Nightmare, began in Tokyo Disneyland Sep. 15, 2004. SEE ALSO PHANTOM MANOR (DISNEYLAND PARIS) AND MYSTIC MANOR (HONG KONG DISNEYLAND).

Haunted Mansion (film) Film inspired by the Disney theme park attraction; scheduled for theatrical release Jul. 28, 2023. Looking to start a new life, a doctor and her 9-year-old son move into a strangely affordable mansion in New Orleans, only to discover that the place is much more than they bargained for. Desperate to rid their home of supernatural squatters, they enlist a motley crew of so-called spiritual experts, including a priest who, in turn, enlists the aid of a failed paranormal expert, a French Quarter psychic, and a crotchety historian. Directed by Justin Simien. Stars LaKeith Stanfield, Tiffany Haddish, Owen Wilson, Danny DeVito, Rosario Dawson, Chase W. Dillon, Dan Levy, Jamie Lee Curtis (Madame Leota), Jared Leto (The Hatbox Ghost).

Haunted Mansion, The (film) Workaholic real estate agent Jim Evers and his wife and business partner, Sara, drag their family up to the big, creepy Gracey mansion, located on a remote Louisiana bayou, when Jim gets a call that owner Edward Gracey wants to sell. Jim senses the biggest deal of his career, hoping to rebuild the mansion into a lavish new condo development. When the Evers family gets there, however, they are stranded by a torrential thunderstorm and quickly find that they are not alone—not when 999 grim, grinning ghosts come out to socialize. With all these happy haunts that won't leave until their unfinished business has been completed, Jim must figure out how to break the curse, while discovering that his family needs him. Directed by Rob Minkoff. Released Nov. 26, 2003. Stars Eddie Murphy (Jim Evers), Terence Stamp (Ramsley), Nathaniel Parker (Master Gracey), Marsha Thomason (Sara Evers), Jennifer Tilly (Madame Leota), Wallace Shawn (Ezra), Dina Waters (Emma), Marc John Jefferies (Michael), Aree Davis (Megan). 88 min. Filmed in Super 35-Scope. The film features special effects and makeup design by Academy Award winner Rick Baker.

Havoc, June (1912–2010) Actress; appeared on TV in *The Boy Who Stole the Elephant*.

Hawaiian Holiday (film) Mickey Mouse cartoon released Sep. 24, 1937. Directed by Ben Sharpsteen. On a sunny beach, Minnie does the hula, accompanied by Mickey, Donald, and Goofy. Pluto makes an enemy out of a starfish while Goofy attempts to surf despite some troubles with the waves.

Hawaiian Vacation (film) Animated short from Pixar Animation Studios. Released with *Cars 2* on Jun. 24, 2011. When Bonnie leaves on a Hawaiian vacation with her family, she wants to take her Ken and Barbie dolls along, but she forgets her backpack. Ken and Barbie emerge from it expecting a romantic getaway and soon realize they are not in Hawai'i. The rest of the toys then go to work trying to fashion a Hawaiian holiday for the pair in Bonnie's room. Directed by Gary Rydstrom. Voices include Tim Allen (Buzz Lightyear), Jodi

Benson (Barbie), Michael Keaton (Ken), Tom Hanks (Woody). 6 min. Filmed in CinemaScope; also released in 3-D and IMAX versions.

Hawke, Ethan Actor; appeared in *Dead Poets Society* (Todd Anderson), *White Fang* and *White Fang 2: Myth of the White Wolf* (Jack), *Quiz Show* (Don Quixote student, uncredited), and *Alive* (Nando Parrado), on TV in *Alias* (James Lennox), and on Disney+ in *Moon Knight* (Arthur Harrow).

Hawkeye (TV) Series on Disney+; digitally premiered Nov. 24, 2021. In post-blip New York City, former Avenger Clint Barton (aka Hawkeye) has a seemingly simple mission: get back to his family for Christmas. But when a threat from his past shows up, he reluctantly teams up with Kate Bishop, a 22-year-old skilled archer and his biggest fan, to unravel a criminal conspiracy. Stars Jeremy Renner (Hawkeye), Hailee Steinfeld (Kate Bishop), Vera Farmiga (Eleanor), Fra Fee (Kazi), Tony Dalton (Jack), Zahn McClarnon (William), Brian d'Arcy James (Derek Bishop), Alaqua Cox (Maya Lopez). From Marvel Studios. SEE ALSO ROGERS: THE MUSICAL.

Hawley, Philip M. Member of the Disney Board of Directors 1975–1985.

Hawn, Goldie Actress; appeared in *The One and Only, Genuine, Original Family Band* (giggly girl) and *Deceived* (Adrienne), and on TV in *Mickey's 50* and *The Dream Is Alive*. She voiced Peggy McGee in *Phineas and Ferb*.

Hawthorne, Nigel (1929–2001) Voiced Fflewddur Fflam in *The Black Cauldron* and Prof. Porter in *Tarzan*.

Hayakawa, Sessue (1889–1973) Actor; appeared in *Swiss Family Robinson* (pirate chief).

Haydn, Richard (1905–1985) Actor; appeared in *The Adventures of Bullwhip Griffin* (Quentin Bartlett) and voiced the Caterpillar in *Alice in Wonderland*.

Hayes, Helen (1900–1993) Actress; appeared in a cameo as a tourist in *Third Man on the Mountain* (starring her son, James MacArthur) and starred in *Herbie Rides Again* (Mrs. Steinmetz), *One of Our Dinosaurs Is Missing* (Hettie), and *Candleshoe* (Lady St. Edmund).

Hays, Robert Actor; appeared in *Trenchcoat* (Terry Leonard) and as Bob in *Homeward Bound: The Incredible Journey* and *Homeward Bound II: Lost in San Francisco*.

Haysbert, Dennis Actor; provided voices in *Wreck-It Ralph* (General Hologram), *Chip 'n Dale: Rescue Rangers* (Zipper, 2022), and *Puppy Dog Pals* (Crash). On TV, he made a guest appearance in *Trophy Wife* (Russ Bradley Morrison).

Hayward, Lillie (1891–1977) Screenwriter; wrote scripts for *Tonka*, *The Shaggy Dog*, and *Toby Tyler*; the latter two with Bill Walsh. Also worked on the *Mickey Mouse Club*.

He Got Game (film) The Governor, a big supporter of his alma mater, Big State, temporarily paroles Jake Shuttlesworth from prison after over 6 years behind bars and gives him a chance of a commuted sentence, if he can accomplish one task. Jake's estranged son, Jesus, is the No. 1 basketball player in America, and the Governor wants him to turn down the large number of offers he has received and play for Big State. With a deadline only a week away, Jesus's father unexpectedly returns home and must somehow reconcile with his son and induce him to accept Big State's offer. During the often explosive ensuing days, father and son reach a surprising turning point in their lives as they grow to understand and find respect for each other. Directed by Spike Lee. A Touchstone film. Released May 1, 1998. Stars Denzel Washington (Jake Shuttlesworth), Ray Allen (Jesus), Milla Jovovich (Dakota Burns), Hill Harper (Coleman "Booger" Sykes), Bill Nunn (Uncle Bubba), Jim Brown (Spivey). 136 min. Having never acted before, then Milwaukee Bucks star player Ray Allen, chosen for the role of Jesus, took 8 weeks of acting lessons before the start of production. Filmed on location primarily in and around Coney Island, New York.

Headless Horseman Apparition that chases Ichabod Crane in *The Adventures of Ichabod and Mr. Toad*.

Headly, Glenne (1955–2017) Actress; appeared in *Dick Tracy* (Tess Truehart), *Mr. Holland's Opus* (Iris Holland), *Breakfast of Champions* (Francine Petko), and *Confessions of a Teenage Drama Queen* (Karen), and on TV in *Monk* (Karen Stottlemeyer) and *Grey's Anatomy* (Elizabeth Archer). She provided the voice of Miss Sansome in *Recess* and Beckie Little in *Pepper Ann*.

Health for the Americas Series of educational films produced under the auspices of the Coordinator of Inter-American Affairs, made for the South American market 1943–1946. SEE SOUTH AMERICA.

Heard, John (1945–2017) Actor; appeared in *Beaches* (John Pierce), *Deceived* (Jack), and *Before and After* (Wendell Bye), and made guest appearances on TV in *Perception* (Evan Rickford) and *Mistresses* (Bruce).

Heart and Lungs Play Ball, The (film) Educational film in the Wonders of Life series released Jan. 26, 1990. 11 min. The film shows how the heart and lungs work together delivering oxygen and blood to the body parts of a football player.

Heartbreak Hotel (film) Aspiring rock 'n' roller Johnny Wolfe loves his mother but realizes the only person who can bring her out of the doldrums is her idol, Elvis Presley. Johnny arranges to kidnap Elvis after a nearby concert and accuses him of abandoning rock 'n' roll. The idealistic youth's questioning of the celebrity's values causes Elvis to remain in the small town for a few days, and not only help Johnny's mother, but reassess his own place in the music world and the type of person he has become in recent years. Released Sep. 30, 1988. Directed by Chris Columbus. A Touchstone film. 101 min. Stars David Keith (Elvis Presley), Tuesday Weld (Marie Wolfe), Charlie Schlatter (Johnny Wolfe). Filmed entirely on location in Austin and Taylor, Texas. When the call went out for 3,000 extras for a concert scene, the filmmakers were amazed that they all were able to come in 1970s outfits. Producer Lynda Obst remarked, "I could never have gotten these costumes in Los Angeles. What was most amazing is that people didn't rent these outfits; they simply went into their closets and pulled out what they still had on the shelf."

Heath, D. C., and Co. Publisher of a series of popular school readers featuring the Disney characters, beginning in 1939. For collectors, the scarcest title is *Dumbo*, as a much smaller number of that title was published.

Heavyweights (film) An overweight teen, Gerry, and his friends at Camp Hope are forced to spend their vacation with an out-of-control fitness freak and prepare for the end-of-summer Apache Games with their muscle-bound rivals from Camp MVP. Eventually the overweight campers oust their leader, implement sensible diet and training programs of their own, and use their smarts to outwit the Camp MVPers. Released Feb. 17, 1995. 98 min. Directed by Steven Brill. In association with Caravan Pictures. Stars Tom McGowan (Pat), Aaron Schwartz (Gerry), Shaun Weiss (Josh), Tom Hodges (Lars), Leah Lail (Julie), Paul Feig (Tim), Jeffrey Tambor (Maury Garner), Jerry Stiller (Harvey Bushkin), Anne Meara (Alice Bushkin).

Heche, Anne Actress; appeared in *The Adventures of Huck Finn* (Mary Jane Wilks) and *Six Days, Seven Nights* (Robin Monroe), and made guest appearances on TV in *Ellen* (Karen) and *Quantico* (Dr. Susan Langdon). She voiced Gloria the Waitress on *Higglytown Heroes*.

Héctor Charming trickster in the Land of the Dead in *Coco*; voiced by Gael García Bernal.

Hector the Stowaway Dog (TV) SEE BALLAD OF HECTOR THE STOWAWAY DOG, THE.

H-E-Double Hockey Sticks (TV) Two-hour movie on *The Wonderful World of Disney*; first aired Oct. 3, 1999. An underachieving devil-in-training, Griffelkin, is sent to the surface to earn his horns by stealing the soul of Dave Heinrich, a hotshot hockey player with his eye on the Stanley Cup. Griffelkin eventually questions his mission's objective and angers Ms. B, head of the Beelzebub Vocational Institute where he has been studying. Directed by Randall Miller. Stars Will Friedle (Griffelkin), Matthew Lawrence (Dave Heinrich), Gabrielle Union (Gabby), Shawn Pyfrom (Louis), Tara Spencer-Nairn (Anne), Rhea Perlman (Ms. B). Based on the opera *Griffelkin*, by Lucas Foss and Alastair Reid.

Hee, T. (1911–1988) Yes, this was a real person. People for years have chuckled over his name in the credits for many Disney productions. T(hornton) Hee worked at the Disney Studio on and off for 3 decades, beginning in 1938, as director, caricaturist, stylist, and story man. He co-directed "The Dance of the Hours" segment of *Fantasia*, directed the Honest John and Gideon sequence in *Pinocchio*, worked on story on *Victory Through Air Power* and *Make Mine Music*, and created the titles for *The Reluctant Dragon* and *The Shaggy Dog*. He left Disney in 1946 but returned 1958–1961. He later worked for WED Enterprises on the 1964–1965 New York World's Fair projects and developed concepts for Walt Disney World. He also served as an animation instructor and was a renowned caricaturist.

Heffalump Character who appears in *Pooh's Heffalump Movie*; voiced by Kyle Stanger. His full name is Heffridge Trumpler Brompet Heffalump IV, nicknamed Lumpy.

Heffalumps and Woozles Pooh's nightmare characters in *Winnie the Pooh and the Blustery Day* (1968). SEE ALSO POOH'S HEFFALUMP MOVIE.

Heidelberger's Deli Eatery in the Lake Buena Vista Shopping Village at Walt Disney World; opened Mar. 1975. It became the All American Sandwich Shop in the 1980s, then Minnie Mia's Italian Eatery in 1990, and Wolfgang Puck Express in 1997.

Heidi (TV) A Disney Channel Premiere Film; first aired Jul. 18, 1993. The story of a young orphan who struggles to win her stern grandfather's love and who then must struggle to stay with him in their beloved mountains. Stars Jason Robards (grandfather), Noley Thornton (Heidi), Jane Seymour (Fraulein Rottenmeier), Patricia Neal (grandmother), Lexi Randall (Klara). Filmed on location near Salzburg and in the Austrian Alps. 193 min. Directed by Michael Rhodes.

Heigh-Ho Song from *Snow White and the Seven Dwarfs*; written by Larry Morey and Frank Churchill.

Heigl, Katherine Actress; appeared in *My Father the Hero* (Nicole), and on TV in *Romy and Michele: In the Beginning* (Romy White) and *Grey's Anatomy* (Isobel "Izzie" Stevens). She received an Emmy Award as Best Supporting Actress in a Drama for *Grey's Anatomy* in 2007.

Heihei Clueless rooster in *Moana*; voiced by Alan Tudyk.

Hello Again (film) Lucy Chadman is a klutz. She has a hard time fitting in with her doctor-husband's social circle. One day she chokes to death on a Korean chicken ball. Her sister Zelda, who runs a shop devoted to mysticism and the occult, manages 1 year later to work a spell that brings Lucy back to life. Lucy finds her husband has married her former best friend, and she must make a new life for herself. An instant celebrity for "coming back from the dead," Lucy finds true love with the emergency room doctor who tried to save her life. Released Nov. 6, 1987. Directed by Frank Perry. A Touchstone film. 96 min. Stars Shelley Long (Lucy Chadman),

Judith Ivey (Zelda), Gabriel Byrne (Kevin Scanlon), Corbin Bernsen (Jason Chadman), Sela Ward (Kim Lacey). Filmed at various New York City locations, including Mount Sinai Hospital.

Hello Aloha (film) Goofy cartoon released Feb. 29, 1952. Directed by Jack Kinney. Goofy, as Mr. Geef, decides to move to the islands and enjoy the carefree life there. As the guest of honor at a luau, he is suddenly thrown into a nearby volcano to appease the fire goddess, but he manages to save himself.

Hello Ladies (TV) Half-hour comedy series on HBO; aired Sep. 29–Nov. 17, 2013, with an added feature-length special on Nov. 22, 2014. A bumbling English Web designer relocates from England to Los Angeles in hopes of finding excitement, romance, and maybe even a soul mate. Stars Stephen Merchant (Stuart Pritchard), Christine Woods (Jessica), Nate Torrence (Wade), Kevin Weisman (Kives), Kyle Mooney (Rory). From ABC Studios.

Hell's Bells (film) Silly Symphony cartoon released Oct. 30, 1929. The first cartoon directed by Ub Iwerks. In this underworld burlesque, the devil and his creatures cavort.

Help, The (film) Three very different, extraordinary women in Mississippi during the 1960s build an unlikely friendship around a secret writing project that breaks societal rules and puts them all at risk. From their improbable alliance, a remarkable sisterhood emerges, instilling all of them with the courage to transcend the lines that define them, and the realization that sometimes those lines are made to be crossed—even if it means bringing everyone in town face-to-face with the changing times. A Touchstone/DreamWorks film. Directed by Tate Taylor. Released Aug. 10, 2011. Stars Emma Stone (Eugenia "Skeeter" Phelan), Viola Davis (Aibileen Clark), Bryce Dallas Howard (Hilly Holbrook), Octavia Spencer (Minny Jackson), Jessica Chastain (Celia Foote), Ahna O'Reilly (Elizabeth Leefolt), Allison Janney (Charlotte Phelan), Anna Camp (Jolene French), Chris Lowell (Stuart Whitworth), Cicely Tyson (Constantine Jefferson), Mike Vogel (Johnny Foote), Sissy Spacek (Missus Walters), Mary Steenburgen (Elaine Stein). 146 min. Nominated for 3 Academy Awards, with Octavia Spencer winning the Oscar for Best Supporting Actress.

Help Wanted: Kids (TV) Two-hour movie; aired

Feb. 2, 1986. Directed by David Greenwalt. A couple moves from New York City to Arizona for a new job only to discover the husband's boss wants his employees to all have children, so the couple decides to rent some. Two neighborhood youngsters fit the bill, but they see that they can succeed with a little blackmail. Meanwhile, the couple is busy trying to keep their deception secret from nosy neighbors. It turns out the kids are orphans, and soon the 4 start acting like a real family. Stars Cindy Williams, Bill Hudson, Chad Allen, Hillary Wolf, John Dehner, Joel Brooks. Led to a Disney Channel series, *Just Like Family*.

Helstrom (TV) Ten-part drama series on Hulu; digitally premiered Oct. 16, 2020. As the son and daughter of a mysterious and powerful serial killer, Daimon and Ana Helstrom track down the worst of humanity, each with their own skills and attitudes. Stars Tom Austen (Daimon), Sydney Lemmon (Ana), Elizabeth Marvel (Victoria), Ariana Guerra (Gabriella), June Carryl (Dr. Louise Hastings). From Marvel Television and ABC Signature Studios.

Hemsworth, Chris Actor; appeared as Thor in the Marvel Studios films, and on Disney+ in *Limitless with Chris Hemsworth*.

Hen Wen Oracular pig seized by The Horned King in *The Black Cauldron*.

Hench, John (1908–2004) Artist/designer; started as a sketch artist in the Disney Story Department in 1939, later painting backgrounds for "The Nutcracker Suite" segment of *Fantasia*. He worked on *Cinderella* and *Alice in Wonderland*, and aided Salvador Dalí in the shelved *Destino* project. He worked on the special effects in *20,000 Leagues Under the Sea*, helping earn the Studio an Academy Award. In 1955, he transferred to WED Enterprises, where his first assignment was to design attractions for Tomorrowland at Disneyland. He would help master plan Walt Disney World and in 1972 was named exec. vice president of WED. He was a key figure in the conceptualization and creation of EPCOT Center and other Disney parks around the world. John was known for painting the company's official portraits of Mickey Mouse for his 25th, 50th, 60th, 70th, and 75th birthdays. In 1999, at the age of 90, he passed his 60th year with the company, which, at the time, was longer than any other person; he passed away in 2004, just 3 months shy of completing his 65th year of continuous service. He was named a Disney Legend in 1990 and considered one of Walt Disney's greatest Renaissance artists, as an animator, designer, Imagineer, philosopher, storyteller, and voracious reader (devouring 52 magazines a month).

Henn, Mark Animator; he joined the Animation Department in 1980, contributing to *The Fox and the Hound*, *Mickey's Christmas Carol* (Mickey Mouse), and *The Black Cauldron*. In 1989, he moved to Florida to help establish the Feature Animation studio there. He was supervising animator on *The Great Mouse Detective*, *Oliver & Company* (Oliver, Dodger), *The Little Mermaid* (Ariel), *The Rescuers Down Under* (Bernard, Bianca), *Beauty and the Beast* (Belle), *Aladdin* (Jasmine), *The Lion King* (young Simba), *Mulan* (Mulan, Fa Zhou), *Lilo & Stitch* (hula dancers), *Home on the Range* (Grace, other characters), *The Princess and the Frog* (Tiana), *Winnie the Pooh* (Winnie the Pooh, Christopher Robin), and *The Ballad of Nessie*. He also contributed to *Pocahontas*, *The Emperor's New Groove*, *Enchanted*, *Get a Horse!*, *Frozen*, *Saving Mr. Banks*, *Big Hero 6*, *Moana*, *Ralph Breaks the Internet*, *Frozen 2*, and *Encanto*. He directed the 2000 animated short *John Henry*. In 2018, he painted the company's official 90th anniversary portrait of Mickey Mouse, titled *Spreading Happiness Around the World*. On Disney+, he appeared in *Sketchbook* and *Mickey: The Story of a Mouse*, and on ABC, he appeared in *Beauty and the Beast: A 30th Celebration*.

Henry Hugglemonster (TV) Animated series; premiered Apr. 15, 2013, on Disney Junior in the U.S., after a Feb. 8 debut on the channel in the U.K. Henry is a typical 5-year-old middle kid, but he is a member of a loving, bustling, adorable monster family. Voices include Lara Jill Miller (Henry), Tom Kenny (Daddo, Grando), Lori Alan (Momma), and guest stars Brian Blessed (Eduardo Enormomonster), Brenda Blethyn (Ernestine), Geri Halliwell (Isabella Roarsome). Based on the book *I'm a Happy Hugglewug* by Niamh Sharkey. From Brown Bag Films.

Henry O. Tanner: Pioneer Black American Artist (film) Educational film produced by Anthony Corso; released in Sep. 1973. This is the story of the first African American artist to earn worldwide acclaim.

Henson, Jim (1936–1990) Puppeteer and creator of the Muppets; two of Henson's last projects were *Muppet*Vision 3D* for the Disney parks and the NBC TV special *The Muppets at Walt Disney World*. Jim had decided to entrust the Muppet properties to The Walt Disney Company in 1989, although the acquisition would not be completed until 2004. He was named a Disney Legend in 2011. SEE MUPPETS.

Hep Cat Corner, The Front Lot snack stand in Disney Studio 1 at Walt Disney Studios Park in Disneyland Paris; opened Jun. 2013.

Herbie Day at Disneyland (TV) Syn. Special, aired Jul. 11, 1974. A contest for decorated Volkswagens (VWs) at Disneyland was a promotion for the opening of *Herbie Rides Again*. Stars Bob McAllister, Bob Crane, Helen Hayes. An earlier Herbie Day had been held at Disneyland on Mar. 23, 1969, to promote the original *The Love Bug*.

Herbie: Fully Loaded (film) The famous VW enters the world of NASCAR racing with his new owner, Maggie Peyton, a 3rd-generation member of a legendary NASCAR family. Racing is in Maggie's blood, but she has been forbidden from pursuing her dreams by her overprotective father, Ray. Ray offers to buy Maggie a car for her college graduation but takes her to a junkyard where a 1960s-era Volkswagen Beetle catches her eye. She leaves in the rusty, banged-up car, soon discovering it is no ordinary auto, but a charmed car that will literally help change the course of her life. With a little help, Herbie becomes stronger and faster than ever, and he and Maggie get the chance to realize their dreams on the NASCAR track. Released Jun. 22, 2005. Directed by Angela Robinson. Stars Lindsay Lohan (Maggie Peyton), Michael Keaton (Ray Peyton, Sr.), Matt Dillon (Trip Murphy), Justin Long (Kevin), Breckin Meyer (Ray Peyton, Jr.), Cheryl Hines (Sally), Jimmi Simpson (Crash), Jill Ritchie (Charisma). 101 min. Herbie's NASCAR appearance took place at the NASCAR Nextel Cup Series' Pop Secret 500, held on Sep. 4, 2004, at the California Speedway, in Fontana.

Herbie Goes Bananas (film) While Pete Stanchek and his friend, Davie Johns, are transporting a VW (Herbie) via ocean liner from Puerto Vallarta to Brazil for an auto race, their lives are complicated by a stowaway in Herbie's trunk—a lovable Mexican orphan, Paco, who's made the mistake of stealing a map of golden Incan ruins from a criminal now hot in pursuit. The ensuing chase (which grows to include the ship's captain and an unsus-

pecting man-hungry passenger and her niece) stretches across Central and South America—from Panama to Peru to Brazil. Eventually, the gold is saved. Herbie emerges a hero and Paco prepares to be Herbie's driver in the Grande Premio do Brasil auto race. Released Jun. 25, 1980. Directed by Vincent McEveety. 92 min. Stars Cloris Leachman (Aunt Louise), Charlie Martin Smith (D. J.), John Vernon (Prindle), Stephen W. Burns (Pete), Elyssa Davalos (Melissa), Joaquin Garay III (Paco), Harvey Korman (Capt. Blythe), Richard Jaeckel (Shepard), Alex Rocco (Quinn). The songs "Look at Me" and "I Found a Friend" were written by Frank De Vol. Much of the action of the movie was shot on location in the Mexican cities of Puerto Vallarta, Guadalajara, and Tijuana, as well as in the Panama Canal Zone. The enormous amount of special effects in the film required meticulous storyboards, the mechanical techniques department headed by Danny Lee, 26 VW Bugs, and 3 Cessna Centurion airplanes. The film was reissued in 1981.

Herbie Goes to Monte Carlo (film) Driver Jim Douglas, mechanic Wheely Applegate, and Herbie, the magical little VW, enter a spectacular road race from Paris to Monte Carlo, Monaco. One of the competing cars is a beautiful powder blue Lancia named Giselle. For Herbie it is love at first sight. Jim falls for the Lancia's pretty driver, Diane. Meanwhile, a fabulous diamond is stolen from a museum by 2 thieves and hidden in Herbie's gas tank. Throughout the race the thieves try to recover the gem. With Herbie's help, the thieves are caught, Herbie wins the race, and he and Jim both get their girls. Released Jun. 24, 1977. Directed by Vincent McEveety. 113 min. Stars Dean Jones (Jim Douglas), Don Knotts (Wheely Applegate), Julie Sommars (Diane), Jacques Marin (Inspector Bouchet), Roy Kinnear (Quincey), Bernard Fox (Max), Eric Braeden (Bruno). Shot on location in France en route to Monte Carlo and in Paris at the Esplanade du Trocadéro, Eiffel Tower, Place de la Concorde, Place Vendôme, Place d'Iéna, Arc de Triomphe, and down the Champs-Elysées at 80 mph.

Herbie Rides Again (film) In San Francisco, the dreams of Alonzo Hawk to build a skyscraper in his name are thwarted by Grandma Steinmetz who sits stubbornly in her firehouse home on the property he needs. Hawk sends his nephew, Willoughby, to charm Mrs. Steinmetz who, along with a beautiful airline hostess boarder and the magical Volkswagen Herbie, convinces him he should stay out of the whole mess. After many chases and confrontations, Herbie emerges victorious and both Mrs. Steinmetz and Willoughby find romance. Released first in England Feb. 15, 1974; U.S. release Jun. 6, 1974. 88 min. Stars Helen Hayes (Mrs. Steinmetz), Ken Berry (Willoughby), Stefanie Powers (Nicole), John McIntire (Mr. Judson), Keenan Wynn (Alonzo Hawk), Huntz Hall (judge), Raymond Bailey (lawyer), Liam Dunn (doctor). This was the first sequel to the Disney favorite *The Love Bug* and was one of the biggest hits of 1974. It was filmed on location in San Francisco in an obsolete cable car, at the Garden Court of the Sheraton Palace Hotel, and on the Golden Gate Bridge. While the cast was quite different from the first film, the car, Herbie, remained. The car was a 1963 Sunroof model 1200 Volkswagen. Bill Walsh, the producer and writer, explained that he got the decal number 53 for Herbie from TV. In a Disney press release he noted: "I was seeing lots of 53 on TV while I was developing Herbie as a character. It was [Los Angeles Dodgers] pitcher Don Drysdale's number among other things."

Herbie, the Love Bug (TV) Limited series of 5 episodes; aired Mar. 17–Apr. 14, 1982, on CBS. Directed by Charles S. Dubin, Bill Bixby, Vincent McEveety. Jim Douglas is now running a driving school. Stars Dean Jones, Patricia Hardy, Richard Paul, Claudia Wells, Nicky Katt, Douglas Emerson, Larry Linville.

Hercules (film) Hercules, the mighty son of Zeus and Hera, is taken from his Mount Olympus home and raised on Earth. The fiery figure behind Hercules's disappearance is Hades, the hotheaded god of the Underworld who has grown tired of looking after a "bunch of deadbeats" and sees Zeus's son as an obstacle to his plans to take over Olympus. Hades sends his two dim-witted sidekicks, Pain and Panic, to abduct Hercules, though they bungle their mission by not administering the final drop of a potent potion, which leaves the infant with godlike strength but human mortality. As Hercules grows up, he discovers the truth about his origins and sets out to prove himself a true hero (with the help of a veteran hero-training satyr named Philoctetes) so he can return to Olympus. Hades has other plans and tries to kill him by arranging a catalog of calamities (a multiheaded Hydra, a Minotaur, a Cyclops, an army of Titans, and the traitorous damsel in distress, Megara). Along the way, Hercules discovers that a true hero is not measured by the size of his strength but the strength of his heart. Directed by John Musker and Ron Clements. General release on Jun. 27, 1997, after a Jun. 14 premiere at the New Amsterdam Theatre in New York City and a limited release beginning there the next day. Stars the voices of Danny DeVito (Phil), Tate Donovan (adult Hercules), Susan Egan (Megara), James Woods (Hades), Charlton Heston (opening narrator), Matt Frewer (Panic), Bobcat Goldthwait (Pain), Paul Shaffer (Hermes), Rip Torn (Zeus), Samantha Eggar (Hera), Joshua Keaton (teen Hercules speaking), Roger Bart (teen Hercules singing), Hal Holbrook (Amphitryon), Barbara Barrie (Alcmene). 93 min. Music, with 6 songs in a pastiche of styles, including gospel, is by Alan Menken with lyrics by David Zippel. Musker and Clements were attracted by the mythological aspects of the Hercules story and decided to produce the film, along with Alice Dewey, in the fall of 1993. Over the next 9 months, the 2 collaborated on an outline, several treatments, and eventually an initial script, aided by art director Andy Gaskill, who oversaw the visual development on the film. British artist/political cartoonist Gerald Scarfe, with a bold, expressive linear style, was brought in to assist with character design, and he remained involved as an ongoing artistic adviser to the animators. A field trip to Greece and Turkey in the summer of 1994 gave artists a firsthand look at landscapes and ancient sites, plus an opportunity to hear expert accounts of classic Greek mythology. Animation began in early 1995, and eventually a team of nearly 700 artists was involved with the project. The film features the first use in animation of the process of morphing, wherein an object is made to smoothly transform into another, utilizing computer technology.

Hercules (TV) Half-hour animated series; debuted in syn. Aug. 31, 1998, expanding upon the Greek demigod's feats during his formative, adolescent hero-in-training years. Many of the actors reprised their voices from the feature, including Tate Donovan (Hercules) and James Woods (Hades), but added are new friends of Hercules—French Stewart (Icarus) and Sandra Bernhard (Cassandra)—and numerous guest stars. 65 episodes.

Hercules Stage adaptation of the animated musical; ran at the Delacorte Theater in New York City's Central Park Aug. 31–Sep. 8, 2019. Presented by the Public Theater's Public Works program. Professional actors joined 200 community performers onstage. Alan Menken and David Zippel returned to contribute several new songs, including "A Cool Day in Hell," "Forget About It," and "To Be

Human." A second staging is scheduled to run Feb. 16–Mar. 19, 2023, at the Paper Mill Playhouse in Millburn, New Jersey.

Hercules: Zero to Hero (film) Three classic stories from the TV series; released on video as a feature on Aug. 17, 1999. A more vulnerable and mortal Hercules toils to get through his school years without his mythological powers. Directed by Bob Kline. 70 min.

Hercules "Zero to Hero" Victory Parade Ran in Disney-MGM Studios at Walt Disney World Jun. 27, 1997–Apr. 18, 1998, saluting "the greatest hero of all time," and featuring parade commentators Ridges Philbinylus and Appollonia Airheadenese. A *Hercules Victory Parade* also began at Disneyland on the same day.

Here Come the Muppets Live show in Disney-MGM Studios at Walt Disney World; ran May 25, 1990–Sep. 2, 1991. Replaced by *Voyage of the Little Mermaid*.

Heritage House Shop in Liberty Square in the Magic Kingdom at Walt Disney World; opened in 1971, with memorabilia themed to American history. It became a MyMagic+ Service Center in 2014 and the Liberty Square Ticket Office in 2019.

Heritage Manor Gifts Shop in The American Adventure in EPCOT; opened in 1985, selling nostalgic American gifts. It became an Art of Disney shop Dec. 16, 2019.

Herman's Head (TV) Series on Fox; aired Sep. 8, 1991–Jun. 16, 1994. Herman is a young writer who has a group of emotions—Angel, Wimp, Genius, and Animal—who battle in his brain to gain control of him. Stars William Ragsdale (Herman Brooks), Hank Azaria (Jay Nichols), Jane Sibbett (Heddy Newman), Yeardley Smith (Louise Fitzer), Molly Hagan (Angel), Rick Lawless (Wimp), Ken Hudson Campbell (Animal), Peter MacKenzie (Genius). From Witt/Thomas Productions and Touchstone Television.

Hero in the Family (TV) Two-hour show; aired on Sep. 28, 1986. Directed by Eric Fraser. A boy's astronaut father accidentally has his brain switched with that of a chimp, but when he goes home, the boy cannot find anyone to believe the story. If they cannot get the transfer reversed in a short time, it will become permanent. After some exciting escapades, the father is returned to normal, and he has a new respect for his son. Stars Christopher Collet, Cliff De Young, Annabeth Gish, Darleen Carr, Keith Dorman, M. Emmet Walsh.

Hero Training Center Super Hero greeting spot in Avengers Campus in Walt Disney Studios Park at Disneyland Paris; opened Jul. 20, 2022.

Herring, Roqué Actress; appeared on the *Mickey Mouse Club* on The Disney Channel 1989–1990.

Herrmann, Edward (1943–2014) Actor; appeared in *The North Avenue Irregulars* (Michael Hill), *Big Business* (Graham Sherbourne), *Born Yesterday* (Ed Devery), *My Boyfriend's Back* (Mr. Dingle), and *Double Take* (Charles Allsworth); on TV in *MDs* (Jeremiah Orbach); and made guest appearances in *Grey's Anatomy* (Dr. Norman Shales), and *Perception* (Jack Pierce).

Hershey, Barbara Actress; appeared in *Tin Men* (Nora Tilley), *Beaches* (Hillary Whitney Essex), *Swing Kids* (Frau Muller), and *Breakfast of Champions* (Celia Hoover), and on TV in *Once Upon a Time* (Cora/Queen of Hearts).

Hervey, Jason Actor; appeared in *Frankenweenie* (Frank Dale, 1984), and on TV in *Little Spies* (Clint Westwood), *Wildside* (Zeke), and *The Last Electric Knight* (Bobby).

Heston, Charlton (1923–2008) Actor; appeared in *Tombstone* (Henry Hooker), on TV in *Walt Disney World's 15th Birthday Celebration*, and on The Disney Channel in *The Little Kidnappers* (James MacKenzie). He provided the narration for *Hercules* and *Armageddon*.

Hewitt, Alan (1915–1986) Actor; appeared in *The Absent-Minded Professor* (Gen. Hotchkiss), *Son of Flubber* (prosecutor), *The Misadventures of Merlin Jones* and *The Monkey's Uncle* (Prof. Shattuck), *The Horse in the Gray Flannel Suit* (Harry Tomes), *The Computer Wore Tennis Shoes* and *Now You See Him, Now You Don't* (Dean Collingsgood), and *The Barefoot Executive* (Farnsworth).

Hexe Lilli: Der Drache und das Magische Buch (Lilly the Witch: The Dragon and the Magic Book) (film) Fairy tale combining live action and CGI; released by Walt Disney Studios Motion Pictures Germany. With the help of a magical book and a clumsy dragon named Hector, young

Lilly must prove herself to become the successor of Surulunda the witch. Released Feb. 19, 2009, in Germany, Switzerland, and Austria. Directed by Stefan Ruzowitzky. Stars Alina Freund (Lilly), Anja Kling (Mother), Ingo Naujoks (Hieronymus), Pilar Bardem (Surulunda), with the voice of Michael Mittermeier (Hector). 89 min. From Dor Film, Blue Eyes Fiction, Classic Srl, and Buena Vista International Film Production Germany. Based on the book series *Hexe Lilli* by Knister.

Hexe Lilli: Die Reise nach Mandolan (Lilly the Witch: The Journey to Mandolan) (film) Fairy tale combining live action and CGI; released by Walt Disney Studios Motion Pictures Germany. The throne of Mandolan is bewitched—a big problem for grand vizier Guliman, who wants to be king. His evil sorcerer, Abrash, tries to deceive Lilly into helping them, but there's no fooling a super-witch. With the help of the dragon Hector and a crafty rickshaw driver named Musa, Lilly frees the noble King of Mandolan and his people from the tyranny of Guliman. Released Feb. 17, 2011, in Germany, Switzerland, and Austria. Directed by Harald Sicheritz. Stars Alina Freund (Lilly), Tanay Chheda (Musa), Pilar Bardem (Surulunda), Anja Kling (Mother), Michael Mendl (Nandi), Pegah Ferydoni (Leila), Jürgen Tarrach (Guliman), with the voice of Cosma Shiva Hagen (Suki). 91 min. From Dor Film, Blue Eyes Fiction, Trixter Productions, Steinweg Emotion Pictures, and Studio Babelsberg, with Buena Vista International Film Production Germany. A sequel to the 2009 film *Hexe Lilli: Der Drache und das Magische Buch* (*Lilly the Witch: The Dragon and the Magic Book*).

"Hey Disney!" Interactive voice assistant that works with Amazon Alexa; announced in 2021. Features over 1,000 interactions, including Disney storytelling, jokes, and fun facts hosted by the Disney Magical Companion and popular characters. First introduced at Walt Disney World Resort hotels beginning Nov. 2022.

Heymann, Tom Joined Disney in 1991 and was named president of The Disney Store in 1996. He left the company in 1999.

Hi Diddle Dee Dee Song from *Pinocchio*; written by Ned Washington and Leigh Harline.

Hibler, Winston (1911–1976) Longtime Disney producer, associated with the nature films as a writer, and who was perhaps best known as the narrator of the True-Life Adventure films. He joined Disney in 1942, scripting and directing armed services training films during World War II. He went on to be a story man and dialogue director on several animated features, including *Alice in Wonderland, Cinderella*, and *Peter Pan*, and wrote early material for Disneyland, including the park's dedication plaque. Affectionately known as Hib around the Disney lot, he produced such films as *Perri, The Bears and I, The Island at the Top of the World*, and *One Little Indian*. Hib received the Disney Legends Award posthumously in 1992.

Hickman, Darryl Actor; appeared on TV in *Johnny Shiloh* and *Texas John Slaughter*.

Hickman, Dwayne (1934–2022) Actor; appeared on TV in *My Dog, the Thief*.

Hidalgo (film) The film is based on the true story of the greatest long-distance horse race ever run. Held yearly for centuries, the Ocean of Fire, a 3,000-mile survival race across the Arabian Desert, was a challenge restricted to the finest Arabian horses ever bred, the purest and noblest lines, owned by the greatest royal families. In 1890, the wealthy Sheikh Riyadh invited an American and his horse to enter the race for the first time. Frank T. Hopkins was a cowboy and dispatch rider for the U.S. Cavalry who had once been billed as the greatest rider the West had ever known. The sheik would put this claim to the test, pitting the American cowboy and his mustang, Hidalgo, against the world's greatest Arabian horses and Bedouin riders, some of whom were determined to prevent the foreigner from finishing the race. For Frank, the Ocean of Fire becomes not only a matter of pride and honor, but a race for his very survival. Released Mar. 5, 2004. A Touchstone film. Directed by Joe Johnston. Stars Viggo Mortensen (Frank T. Hopkins), Omar Sharif (Sheikh Riyadh), Zuleikha Robinson (Jazira), Peter Mensah (Jaffa), Louise Lombard (Lady Anne Davenport), Said Taghmaoui (Prince Bin Al Reeh), J. K. Simmons (Buffalo Bill Cody), Adam Alexi-Malle (Aziz). 136 min. Filmed in Cinema-Scope. An unbilled Malcolm McDowell appears briefly as Lord Davenport. Filming took place in Morocco, Montana, South Dakota, and California.

Hidden Mickeys Starting out as inside jokes by the Disney Imagineers in the 1980s, the subtly visible silhouette of Mickey Mouse began appearing in a few attractions in the Disney parks. Soon, park guests were having a great time trying to discover these "hidden" Mickeys to such an extent that they were finding the common 3-circle form in areas where it was simply a design fluke and never meant to be a Mickey shape. The position of Walt Disney Imagineering is: "We cannot confirm nor deny the presence of Hidden Mickeys in Disney parks."

Hiddleston, Tom Actor; appeared in *War Horse* (Capt. Nichols), *Muppets Most Wanted* (The Great Escapo), and as Loki in the Marvel Studios films, and on Disney+ in *Loki*. He voiced Capt. James Hook in *The Pirate Fairy*.

Higglytown Heroes (TV) Animated series for preschoolers on Disney Channel; premiered Sep. 12, 2004. Four adventurous kids encounter the diverse residents of colorful Higglytown, who resemble traditional Russian nesting dolls, and learn that there are everyday heroes in the world around them. Among them are a grocer, a librarian, a truck driver, a mail carrier, and a crossing guard. Voices include Rory Thost (Kip), Frankie Ryan Manriquez (Wayne), Taylor Masamitsu (Eubie), Edie McClurg (Fran), Liliana Mumy (Twinkle), Dee Bradley Baker (Pizza Guy). The heroes are voiced by special celebrity guest stars such as Sean Astin, Lance Bass, Tim Curry, Anne Heche, Cyndi Lauper, Susan Lucci, Katey Sagal, Sharon Stone, and Betty White. From Happy Nest and Wild Brain Productions for Playhouse Disney.

High Fidelity (film) Rob Gordon is the owner of a semi-failing record store in Chicago where he sells old-fashioned vinyl records. He is a self-professed music junkie who spends his days at Championship Vinyl with his 2 employees, Dick and Barry. Although they have an encyclopedic knowledge of pop music and are consumed with the music scene, it is of no help to Rob when his longtime girlfriend, Laura, walks out on him. Rob struggles through a sometimes comic, sometimes painful self-examination. Directed by Stephen Frears. Released Mar. 31, 2000. Stars John Cusack (Rob Gordon), Jack Black (Barry), Lisa Bonet (Marie DeSalle), Joelle Carter (Penny), Joan Cusack (Liz), Sara Gilbert (Anna), Iben Hjejle (Laura), Todd Louiso (Dick), Catherine Zeta-Jones (Charlie). 114 min. Based on the novel by Nick Hornby, with the setting changed from London to Chicago. A stage version of the show, based more on the novel than on the film, opened on Broadway in previews at the Imperial Theater on Nov. 20, 2006, and closed Dec. 17.

High Fidelity (TV) Ten-episode romantic comedy-drama series on Hulu; digitally released Feb. 14, 2020. Rob Brooks, a record store owner in the rapidly gentrifying neighborhood of Crown Heights, Brooklyn, revisits past relationships through music and pop culture while trying to get over her one true love. An adaptation of the novel by Nick Hornby. Stars Zoë Kravitz (Rob Brooks), David H. Holmes (Simon), Jake Lacy (Clyde), Da'Vine Joy Randolph (Cherise), Kingsley Ben-Adir (Russell "Mac" McCormack). From ABC Signature Studios.

High Flying Spy, The (TV) Three-part show; aired on Oct. 22, 29, and Nov. 5, 1972. Directed by Vincent McEveety. During the Civil War, Prof. Thaddeus Lowe uses a balloon to spy for the Union forces and hires a young telegrapher to join him and send messages to the ground. His work impresses President Lincoln who sets up the Aeronautic Corps, the country's first air force. Eventually, they are captured by the Confederates and try to get away by stealing hydrogen from a Southern gas factory to fill their balloon. Stars Stuart Whitman, Vincent Van Patten, Darren McGavin, Andrew Prine, Shug Fisher, Jim Davis, Jeff Corey, Robert Pine. The working title was *High Flying Lowe*.

High Heels and Low Lifes (film) London nurse Shannon and her best friend, an American actress named Frances, overhear a mobile phone conversation between gang members involved in a bank robbery, but are unable to convince the police. So they decide, as a dare, to try to extort a little money from the gang in return for not revealing their identities. Of course, the criminals would rather kill than give up their money, so the stakes are raised as the women get further drawn into their scheme. A Touchstone film. Released Oct. 26, 2001. 86 min. Directed by Mel Smith. Stars Minnie Driver (Shannon), Mary McCormack (Frances), Kevin McNally (Mason), Mark Williams (Tremaine), Danny Dyer (Danny), Michael Gambon (Kerrigan).

High School Musical (TV) A Disney Channel Original Movie; first aired Jan. 20, 2006. In this contemporary musical comedy, Troy Bolton, a popular basketball star, and Gabriella Montez, a shy, academically gifted newcomer, discover that they share a secret passion for singing. When they sign up for the lead roles in the school musical, it threatens East High's rigid social order and sends their peers into an uproar. Soon the jocks, the brainiacs, and even the drama club regulars are hatching convoluted plots to separate the pair and keep them offstage. By defying expectations and taking a chance on their dreams, the couple inspires other students to go public with some surprising hidden talents of their own. Directed by Kenny Ortega. Stars Zac Efron (Troy Bolton), Vanessa Anne Hudgens (Gabriella Montez), Ashley Tisdale (Sharpay Evans), Lucas Grabeel (Ryan Evans), Corbin Bleu (Chad Danforth), Monique Coleman (Taylor McKessie), Chris Warren, Jr. (Zeke Baylor). Filming took place in Salt Lake City. The film was very well received, debuting as the No. 1 cable TV program for the week with 7,732,000 viewers, a record high for the network; its soundtrack also reached No. 1 on the *Billboard* Top 200 chart and quickly went platinum. It was the first full-length movie to be made available via digital download on Apple's iTunes Music Store. Released on DVD in 2006. *High School Musical: The Concert* began a 40-city tour on Nov. 29, 2006, in San Diego, featuring members of the original cast, culminating in a 1-hour special on Disney Channel on May 4, 2007.

High School Musical Stage version of the Disney Channel movie; premiered in a professional version Jan. 5, 2007, at the Children's Theater Company's Cargill Stage in Minneapolis. Two new songs were added for the stage version, which was made available for student and amateur groups beginning in Aug. 2006.

High School Musical: China (film) Chinese version of *High School Musical*, in Chinese. Directed by Shi Zhengchen. Released Aug. 10, 2010. 93 min. Co-production of Disney with Shanghai Media Group and Huayi Bros.

High School Musical Summer Celebration Touring stage production featuring musical moments based on the 3 movies; debuted in 2009. Produced by Feld Entertainment, Inc. Feld had also produced High School Musical: The Ice Tour.

High School Musical: The Challenge (*High School Musical: El Desafío*) (film) Argentinean version of *High School Musical*, in Spanish, released Jul. 14, 2008. Fer, captain of the rugby team, is attracted to Agus. The students are invited to participate in a Challenge of the Bands, a musical contest where the kids will have the chance to appear as true music stars. The rugby players form one band, while the conceited Delfi forms an all-girls band. Only 1 band will be the winner, the band capable of

understanding teamwork, personal improvement, and that studying with the best not only makes them better artists, but better people. Directed by Jorge Nisco. Stars Fernando Dente, Agustina Vera, Delfina Peña, Walter Bruno.

High School Musical: The Challenge (*High School Musical: El Desafío*) (film) Mexican version of *High School Musical*, in Spanish, released Sep. 5, 2008. Cristóbal, captain of the soccer team, is attracted to Mariana. The students are invited to participate in a Challenge of the Bands, a musical contest where the kids will have the chance to appear as true music stars. The soccer players form one band, while the conceited Luli forms an all-girls band. Only one band will be the winner, the band capable of understanding teamwork, personal improvement, and that studying with the best not only makes them better artists, but also better people. Directed by Eduardo Ripari. Musical director is Peter McFarlane. Stars Cristóbal Orellana, Mariana Magaña, Maricela Contreras, Fernando Soberanes.

High School Musical: The Challenge (*High School Musical: O Desafío*) (film) Brazilian version of *High School Musical*, in Portuguese, released Feb. 5, 2010. Directed by César Rodrigues. Stars Paula Barbosa, Gisele Batista, Michelle Batista, Wanessa Camargo, Karol Candido, Olavo Cavalheiro, Moroni Cruz. Produced by Buena Vista International.

High School Musical: The Musical: The Series (TV) Scripted series. The first episode aired on ABC, Disney Channel, and Freeform Nov. 8, 2019, followed by a series launch on Disney+ Nov. 15. At the real-life East High, where the original *High School Musical* was filmed, a group of students count down to opening night of their school's first-ever production of *High School Musical*. Friendships are made and tested, rivalries flare, and lives are changed forever as these young people discover the transformative power that only high school theater can provide. Stars Joshua Bassett (Ricky), Olivia Rodrigo (Nini), Matt Cornett (E.J.), Kate Reinders (Miss Jenn), Julia Lester (Ashlyn), Larry Saperstein (Big Red), Sofia Wylie (Gina), Dara Reneé (Kourtney), Frankie A. Rodriguez (Carlos), Mark St. Cyr (Mr. Mazzara). From Salty Pictures, Inc. and Disney Channel.

High School Musical: The Musical: The Series: The Special (TV) Behind-the-scenes documentary;

aired on select ABC-owned stations Dec. 14, 2019, followed by a digital release on Disney+ the next day. 23 min.

High School Musical 2 (TV) A Disney Channel Original Movie; first aired Aug. 17, 2007. School's out for the summer, and the East High Wildcats are looking for summer jobs. Troy Bolton can hardly believe his luck when he's offered a job at Albuquerque's posh country club, Lava Springs. What he doesn't know is that his newfound employment is part of club queen Sharpay's plot to lure him away from Gabriella. But that plan begins to unravel when Troy, unbeknownst to Sharpay, lands a lifeguard position at the club for Gabriella and the rest of his Wildcat pals. The club's annual Midsummer Night's Talent Show provides an opportunity for Troy and Gabriella to sing a duet, while the determined Sharpay plots to ensure they will not upstage her. Directed by Kenny Ortega. Stars Zac Efron (Troy Bolton), Vanessa Hudgens (Gabriella Montez), Ashley Tisdale (Sharpay Evans), Lucas Grabeel (Ryan Evans), Corbin Bleu (Chad Danforth), Monique Coleman (Taylor McKessie), Mark Taylor (Mr. Fulton). Filmed on location in Salt Lake City and St. George, Utah. The movie set records with 17.24 million viewers tuned in for its premiere.

High School Musical 3: Senior Year (film) East High School seniors Troy and Gabriella face the prospect of being separated from one another as they head off in different directions to college. Joined by the rest of the Wildcats, they stage an elaborate spring musical reflecting on their experiences, hopes, and fears about the future. Directed by Kenny Ortega. Released in the U.S. Oct. 24, 2008, after Oct. 22 releases in Denmark, France, Sweden, and the U.K. Stars Zac Efron (Troy Bolton), Vanessa Hudgens (Gabriella Montez), Ashley Tisdale (Sharpay Evans), Lucas Grabeel (Ryan Evans), Corbin Bleu (Chad Danforth), Monique Coleman (Taylor McKessie), Olesya Rulin (Kelsi Nielsen), Matt Prokop (Jimmie Zara), Justin Martin (Donny Dion), Jemma McKenzie-Brown (Tiara Gold). 112 min. Features 10 new songs. Filmed at East High School in Salt Lake City, even though the story is set in Albuquerque. It opened at No. 1 with $42 million in theaters, the biggest opening for a musical ever. Released in an extended 117 min. edition on DVD in 2009.

Highway to Trouble (TV) Show aired Mar. 13, 1959. Directed by Jack Hannah. Donald tries to awaken his nephews' interest in geography through the use of several cartoons and by finally taking them to Disneyland.

Higitus Figitus Song from *The Sword in the Stone*; written by Richard M. and Robert B. Sherman.

Hill, Arthur (1922–2006) Actor; appeared on TV in *Atta Girl, Kelly*, and years later on The Disney Channel in *Love Leads the Way*. Coincidentally, both films were about guide dogs for the blind. He appeared in *One Magic Christmas* (Caleb Grainger) and narrated *Something Wicked This Way Comes*.

Hill, Dana (1964–1996) Actress; she provided the voice of Buddy in *Disney's Adventures of the Gummi Bears*, Max in *Goof Troop*, Tank Muddlefoot in *Darkwing Duck*, Timmy in *Bonkers*, Nefu in *The Lion King's Timon & Pumbaa*, and had an uncredited voice part in *The Hunchback of Notre Dame*. She also played Foxy Cooper in the TV movie *The Kids Who Knew Too Much*.

Hill Street Diner San Francisco-style alfresco dining in Pleasure Island at Walt Disney World; originally named Maxwell's Diner.

Hiller and Diller (TV) Series on ABC; aired Sep. 23, 1997–Mar. 13, 1998. Ted Hiller and Neil Diller are comedy writers who have been best friends and partners for years. In fact, Ted feels he owes his career (and his comfortable lifestyle) to Neil, so he is always there for his partner, no questions asked — a situation his family has learned to accept. Unlike his happily married friend, Neil has neurotic tendencies that drove his wife away, but not before she asked him to care for their 2 children, a proposition he finds frightening. Stars Kevin Nealon (Ted Hiller), Richard Lewis (Neil Diller), Jordan Baker (Jeanne Hiller), Allison Mack (Brooke Diller). From Imagine Television and Touchstone Television.

Hills Brothers Coffee House Opened on Town Square in Disneyland 1958, and closed winter 1976. The restaurant was originally Maxwell House Coffee House and later became the American Egg House and Town Square Cafe.

Hilton Hotel in Lake Buena Vista at Walt Disney World; opened Nov. 18, 1983.

Hilton Head Island Resort, South Carolina See

DISNEY VACATION CLUB AND VACATION CLUB RESORT, HILTON HEAD ISLAND, SOUTH CAROLINA.

Hilton Inn South Hotel on International Drive in Orlando; opened May 26, 1970, originally under Disney management. To help the Disney staff gain experience in hotel operations during the construction of Walt Disney World, it served as a practical training facility, plus a temporary residence for visiting personnel.

Hingle, Pat (1924–2009) Actor; appeared in *One Little Indian* (Captain Stewart) and *Running Brave*, *A Thousand Acres* (Harold Clark), and on TV in *Casebusters* (Sam Donahue) and *The Court* (Chief Justice Amos Townsend).

Hinton, Darby Actor; appeared in *Son of Flubber* (2nd hobgoblin), and on TV in *Boomerang, Dog of Many Talents* (Simon Graham).

Hip Hop Nutcracker, The (TV) A hip-hop reimagining of *The Nutcracker* ballet; digitally released Nov. 25, 2022, on Disney+. On the night of the annual New Year's Eve block party, Maria-Clara embarks on a holiday adventure to bring her parents back together, finding help along the way from the magical toymaker, Drosselmeyer, and the Nutcracker she brings to life. Her journey takes her from the streets of New York to fantasy worlds, where she battles with mice and toy soldiers, and back in time to the Land of Sweets to find the key to unlock her holiday wish before the clock strikes midnight. Directed by Nikki Parsons. 44 min. Stars Run-D.M.C.'s Rev Run (Narrator), Caché Melvin (Maria-Clara), Allison Holker Boss (Mom), Stephen "tWitch" Boss (Dad), Comfort Fedoke (Drosselmeyer), DuShaunt "Fik-shun" Stegall (Nutcracker), with dancers Mikhail Baryshnikov, Tiler Peck, Kida the Great AKA Kida Burns, and the Jabbawockeez. Inspired by the touring stage production. From Done+Dusted.

Hiram Flaversham Toymaker kidnapped by Ratigan in *The Great Mouse Detective*; voiced by Alan Young.

Hiro Hamada 14-year-old robotics prodigy in *Big Hero 6*; voiced by Ryan Potter.

Hirohito, Emperor of Japan (1901–1989) He visited Disneyland in Oct. 1975, and was presented with a Mickey Mouse watch, which he proudly wore.

Hirsch, Lou Actor; provided the adult voice of Baby Herman in *Who Framed Roger Rabbit* and other appearances of the character.

Hirschhorn, Joel (1937–2005) He wrote songs, with Al Kasha, for *Freaky Friday*, *Pete's Dragon*, *Hot Lead and Cold Feet*, and the Universe of Energy at EPCOT Center.

His Lordship Shop in the United Kingdom at EPCOT Center; opened Oct. 1, 1982. It adjoined The Toy Soldier, selling English cottage replicas and similar items. Became Lords & Ladies, and later The Crown & Crest.

His Majesty King of the Beasts (TV) Show aired Nov. 7, 1958. Directed by Jim Algar. Edited version of the True-Life Adventure film *The African Lion*. Narrated by Winston Hibler.

Historia de José, A (film) Portuguese Reading Film #1. Produced under the auspices of the Coordinator of Inter-American Affairs. Delivered Mar. 14, 1945. SEE SOUTH AMERICA.

History Alive! (film) Series of 5 educational films that teach American history through specific historical events, produced by Turnley Walker and released in 1972: *Democracy—Equality or Privilege*, *The Right of Dissent*, *States' Rights*, *The Right of Petition*, *Impeachment of a President*.

History Channel, The With the purchase of Capital Cities/ABC in 1996, Disney obtained a 37.5% ownership of The History Channel, which specializes in historical documentaries.

History of Aviation (film) Humorous history of aviation from the Wright Brothers to World War II, originally part of *Victory Through Air Power*; released as a 16-mm educational film in Dec. 1952.

Hitchhiker's Guide to the Galaxy, The (film) Earthman Arthur Dent is having a very bad day. His house is about to be bulldozed, he discovers that his best friend is an alien, and to top things off, Planet Earth is about to be demolished to make way for a hyperspace freeway. Arthur's only chance for survival is to hitch a ride on a passing spacecraft with the help of his best friend, Ford Prefect. Arthur sets out on a journey in which he finds that nothing is as it seems—for example, a towel is the most important thing in the universe. He finds the meaning of life and discovers that everything anyone ever wanted to know can be found in one fantastically entertaining electronic book, *The Hitchhiker's Guide to the Universe*. A Touchstone film/Spyglass Entertainment film. Released Apr. 29, 2005. World premiere was in London on Apr. 20. Directed by Garth Jennings. Stars Mos Def (Ford Prefect), Zooey Deschanel (Trillian), Martin Freeman (Arthur Dent), Sam Rockwell (Zaphod Beeblebrox), Bill Nighy (Slartibartfast), Warwick Davis (Marvin), Anna Chancellor (Questular), John Malkovich (Humma Kavula). The film is narrated by Stephen Fry and includes the voices of Alan Rickman (Marvin) and Helen Mirren (Deep Thought). 109 min. Based on the novel by Douglas Adams, which was created after a 1978 BBC Radio 4 play. Over the years, the book and 5 more in the series have become more than mere best sellers; they are a cultural phenomenon in their own right with fans the world over discussing and debating them. Adams passed away shortly after finishing the 2nd draft of the screenplay. Filmed in Super 35-Scope at Elstree Studios in England.

Hobbyland Area for hobbyists in Tomorrowland at Disneyland; opened Sep. 4, 1955, with model-building and related activities. Closed ca. 1966 to prepare for the new Tomorrowland of 1967.

Hoberman, David He came to Disney from ICM in 1985, working up to president of Touchstone and Walt Disney Pictures in 1988 and president of motion pictures for Walt Disney Studios in 1994. He resigned in early 1995 to become an independent producer.

Hockey Champ, The (film) Donald Duck cartoon released Apr. 28, 1939. Directed by Jack King. Donald attempts to show off his professional hockey ability to his nephews, but their skills finally get the best of him.

Hockey Homicide (film) Goofy cartoon released Sep. 21, 1945. Directed by Jack Kinney. Goofy plays all the parts in a hockey game until the crowd, in their excitement, comes out on the ice and the players can relax in the bleachers.

Hocus Pocus (film) Accidentally brought back to life in Salem on Halloween night, 3 witches, known as the Sanderson sisters, attempt to steal the life essence from the town's children so they can have eternal life. They are outwitted by a boy, Max Dennison; his young sister, Dani; and his girlfriend, Allison, and aided by a boy, Thackery Binx, who had been changed into a cat for trying to interfere with the witches centuries earlier. Released Jul. 16, 1993. Directed by Kenny Ortega. 96 min. Stars Bette Midler (Winifred), Sarah Jessica Parker (Sarah), Kathy Najimy (Mary), Omri Katz (Max), Thora Birch (Dani), Vinessa Shaw (Allison). The use of computer graphics technology enabled the cat to talk. The flying scenes were accomplished using wires on a soundstage at the Disney Studio. Besides the Studio work, there was 1 week of location filming in Salem, Massachusetts.

Hocus Pocus 2 (film) A Disney+ original film; digitally released Sep. 30, 2022. It's been 29 years since someone lit the Black Flame Candle and resurrected the 17th-century sisters who were executed for practicing witchcraft, and they are looking for revenge. Now it is up to 3 high school students to figure out how to stop the ravenous witches from wreaking a new kind of havoc on Salem before midnight on All Hallows' Eve. Directed by Anne Fletcher. Stars Bette Midler (Winifred), Sarah Jessica Parker (Sarah), Kathy Najimy (Mary), Doug Jones (Billy Butcherson), Whitney Peak (Becca), Lilia Buckingham (Cassie), Belissa Escobedo (Izzy), Sam Richardson (Gilbert), Hannah Waddingham (The Witch Mother), Froy Gutierrez (Mike), Tony Hale (Mayor/Reverend Traske). 104 min. Filmed in Rhode Island. A sequel to the 1993 film. It became the No. 1 film premiere on Disney+, setting a record for streaming minutes on Nielsen's weekly chart.

Hodges, Eddie Actor; appeared in *Summer Magic* (Gilly Carey) and *The Happiest Millionaire* (Livingston Drexel Biddle), though his role in the latter was edited out of shortened versions of the film.

Hoff, Christian Actor; appeared in *Encino Man* (Boog) and was the first actor ever to appear in a Disney film as Walt Disney (as a child)—in the TV movie *Walt Disney—One Man's Dream*. He also appeared on TV in *Ugly Betty* (D.A. Richard Blackman).

Hoffman, Dustin Actor; appeared in *Dick Tracy* (Mumbles), *Billy Bathgate* (Dutch Schultz), and *Moonlight Mile* (Ben Floss).

Hoffman, Gaby Actress; she starred in the TV series *Someone Like Me*, and in the TV remake of *Freaky Friday* (Annabelle Andrews).

Hoffman, Philip Seymour (1967–2014) Actor; appeared in *My Boyfriend's Back* (Chuck Bronski), *Money for Nothing* (Cochran), *When a Man Loves a Woman* (Gary), and *25th Hour* (Jacob Elinsky).

Hog Wild (TV) Two-part show; aired Jan. 20 and 27, 1974. Directed by Jerome Courtland. A man moves his family in the 1880s to Idaho and starts a pig ranch; an accident causes him to rely on his son to take the pigs to market. It is a race against a neighboring pig rancher, since the first one to arrive gets the best prices. While the boy loses the race, he wins a wager large enough to pay for an operation for his father. Stars John Ericson, Diana Muldaur, Clay O'Brien, Nicholas Beauvy, Kim Richards, Shug Fisher, Walter Barnes, Denver Pyle.

Hold that Pose (film) Goofy cartoon released Nov. 3, 1950. Directed by Jack Kinney. Goofy buys photographic equipment for his new hobby and eagerly goes out to find a subject that turns out to be a bear. He so angers the bear with the flash apparatus that it chases him back to his apartment.

Hold Your Horsepower (film) Educational film showing the development of farm machinery, illustrating farmers' ability to produce more crops, lighten their labor, and care for the machinery; made for the Texas Company. Delivered Aug. 8, 1945.

Holdridge, Cheryl (1944–2009) Mouseketeer from the 1950s *Mickey Mouse Club* TV show.

Holes (film) Stanley Yelnats is a young man coming of age, dogged by bad luck stemming from an ancient family curse. Perpetually in the wrong place at the wrong time, Stanley is unfairly sentenced to months of detention at Camp Green Lake for a crime he did not commit. There, he and his camp mates are forced by the menacing warden and her right-hand men to dig holes in order to build character. Nobody knows the real reason they are digging all these holes, but Stanley soon begins to question why the warden is so interested in anything "special" the boys find. Stanley and his camp mates must stick together and keep one step ahead of the warden and her henchmen as they plot a daring escape from the camp to solve the mystery and break the Yelnats family curse. From Walt Disney Pictures in association with Walden Media. Released Apr. 18, 2003. Directed by Andrew Davis. Stars Shia LaBeouf (Stanley), Sigourney Weaver (Warden), John Voight (Mr. Sir), Tim Blake Nelson (Dr. Pendanski), Henry Winkler (Stanley's father), Eartha Kitt (Madame Zeroni), Dulé Hill (Sam), Patricia Arquette (Kissin' Kate Barlow). 117 min. Based on the award-winning book by Louis Sachar. Location filming was primarily on the Cuddeback Dry Lake and in Red Rock Canyon in the desert west of California's Death Valley.

Holiday Corner Main Street, U.S.A. shop in the Magic Kingdom at Walt Disney World; opened in 1981, taking the place of the Wonderland of Wax Candle Shop. It closed in 1986. Christmas accessories, candle making products, and wax creations were sold.

Holiday for Henpecked Husbands (TV) Show aired Nov. 26, 1961. Directed by Wolfgang Reitherman. A series of Goofy cartoons cover the theme. Reruns aired as *Goofy Takes a Holiday*.

Holiday Inn Hotel at Lake Buena Vista at Walt Disney World, taking the place of Courtyard by Marriott on Dec. 30, 2003.

Holiday Time at Disneyland (TV) Show aired Dec. 23, 1962. Directed by Hamilton S. Luske. Festivities at Christmastime at Disneyland with Walt Disney showing viewers around the park (including the since-removed Flying Saucers attraction in Tomorrowland). Past parades for Easter and special events are highlighted before the Candlelight Procession and the Christmas parade make their way down Main Street.

Holidayland Picnic area outside the Disneyland berm; operated Jun. 16, 1957–1961. Holidayland utilized the circus tent that Walt had purchased for his short-lived Mickey Mouse Club Circus. It was used for corporate picnics and other events; the guests could then enter Disneyland through a special gate.

Holland, Tom Actor; appeared as Peter Parker/Spider-Man in the Marvel Studios films and voiced Ian Lightfoot in *Onward*.

Holliman, Earl Actor; appeared in *The Biscuit Eater* (Harve McNeil), and on TV in *The Boy and the Bronc Buster* (Cal Winslow) and *Smoke* (Cal Finch).

Holloway, Sterling (1905–1992) Popular Disney voice actor; first used in *Dumbo* as the stork. He also narrated *Peter and the Wolf*; *The Pelican and the Snipe*; *Susie, the Little Blue Coupe*; *The Little House*; *Goliath II*; and *The Cold-Blooded Penguin*; and voiced the adult Flower (*Bambi*); the Cheshire Cat (*Alice in Wonderland*); Amos (*Ben and Me*); Kaa (*The Jungle Book*); Roquefort (*The Aristocats*); and Winnie the Pooh. Probably no other actor in Hollywood was as well known by his distinctive voice alone. He was named a Disney Legend in 1991.

Hollywood & Dine Fast-casual restaurant in Disney's Hollywood Hotel at Hong Kong Disneyland Resort; opened Sep. 12, 2005, themed as the lobby of a classic movie palace. Also a former soundstage restaurant in Hollywood Pictures Backlot in Disney's California Adventure; opened Feb. 8, 2001. Guests ordered from food counters inspired by famous Hollywood restaurants, including Don the Beachcomber, the Wilshire Bowl, Villa Capri, and Schwab's Pharmacy. It closed after only a few months of operation, and the venue has since been used for private events.

Hollywood & Vine Character dining restaurant in Disney's Hollywood Studios at Walt Disney World; opened May 1, 1989. Also known as Cafeteria of the Stars.

Hollywood Boulevard 1920s/1930s-themed shopping street in Disney's Hollywood Studios at Walt Disney World. Most of the buildings are inspired by originals in Hollywood. Special actors, known as Streetmosphere, portray cops, cabbies, movie starlets, talent agents, and excited autograph seekers. The shops sell movie memorabilia, both old and new, along with Disney souvenirs and clothing. Over the years, the shops have included Movieland Memorabilia, Crossroads of the World, Sights and Sounds, Oscar's Classic Car Souvenirs and Super Service Station, Mickey's of Hollywood, Sid Cahuenga's One-of-a-Kind, Pluto's Toy Palace, Disney & Co., Lakeside News, Cover Story, Celebrity 5 & 10, The Darkroom, Sweet Success, and L.A. Cinema Storage.

Hollywood Brown Derby, The The most elegant restaurant in Disney's Hollywood Studios at Walt Disney World; opened May 1, 1989. Replica of one of the most famous early restaurants of Hollywood (the former location on Vine Street), where the Cobb salad and a delicious grapefruit cake were invented. Both are served here, along with many other tasty meals, in a teak and mahogany setting. The waiters and waitresses are all dressed in tuxedos, a sharp contrast to the attire of the normal theme park guest. On the wall are reproductions of the famous caricatures of Hollywood personalities that graced the wall of the original Brown Derby.

Hollywood Film Enterprises From 1932–1950, Hollywood Film Enterprises was licensed to sell shortened versions of Disney cartoons in 16-mm and 8-mm home movie versions. Most were silent and, since each cartoon was cut into several parts, the segments were given new titles. Some of the films were also in Carmel Hollywood Films and Castle Films boxes. These films turn up quite frequently today, though have little collector value.

Hollywood Hotel, Disney's Hotel at Hong Kong Disneyland Resort with 600 rooms; opened Sep. 12, 2005, inspired by the grandeur of classic Hollywood. There is a buffet restaurant, Chef Mickey, with fast-casual dining at Hollywood & Dine. Guests can relax in the art deco–style Studio Lounge and shop in Celebrity Gifts.

Hollywood Land Name, as of 2012, for the Hollywood Pictures Backlot, the area in Disney California Adventure based on the motion picture and TV industry (opened Feb. 8, 2001).

Hollywood Party, The (film) Black-and-white MGM movie from 1934 that includes a segment with Mickey Mouse and Jimmy Durante leading into a color Silly Symphony–type sequence entitled *The Hot Choc-late Soldiers*.

Hollywood Pictures Division of The Walt Disney Company that produced fare that was of more adult interest than the usual Disney film. It began operations Feb. 1, 1989; its first release was *Arachnophobia* (1990). The division was originally headed by Ricardo Mestres, and he was succeeded by Michael Lynton. In 1996, Hollywood Pictures' role as a producing entity ended, but its label was still used for a while as the distribution designation of certain films. David Vogel became president in 1997. SEE ALSO FEATURE FILM FOR A LISTING OF FILMS MADE BY HOLLYWOOD PICTURES.

Hollywood Pictures Disney movie merchandise shop in Disney Village at Disneyland Paris; open Apr. 12, 1992–Jun. 30, 2013. Succeeded by The LEGO Store.

Hollywood Pictures Backlot SEE HOLLYWOOD LAND.

Hollywood Records Disney label; began operations Jan. 1, 1990. Hollywood Records develops and produces recorded mainstream music from the entire spectrum of popular styles. Its first release was the soundtrack from *Arachnophobia*. Recording artists have included The Party, Queen, and others.

Hollywood Stargirl (film) Stargirl Caraway, a silver-voiced teenager whose simple acts of kindness work magic in the lives of others, journeys from Mica, Arizona into a bigger world of music, dreams, and possibilities. When her mother, Ana, is hired as the costume designer on a movie, they relocate to L.A., where Stargirl quickly becomes involved with an eclectic assortment of characters. Released digitally Jun. 3, 2022, on Disney+, following a May 23 premiere at the El Capitan Theatre in Hollywood. Directed by Julia Hart. Stars Grace VanderWaal (Stargirl), Judy Greer (Ana), Elijah Richardson (Evan), Tyrel Jackson Williams (Terrell), Nija Okoro (Daphne), Al Madrigal (Iggy), Judd Hirsch (Mr. Mitchell), Uma Thurman (Roxanne Martel). 103 min. A sequel to the 2020 film *Stargirl*, based on the characters from the novel by Jerry Spinelli. Filmed in wide-screen format in and around Southern California.

Hollywood Walk of Fame Tile stars along the famous Hollywood sidewalk have honored Walt Disney (added in 1960), Mickey Mouse (1978), Snow White (1987), Roy O. Disney (1998), Donald Duck (2004), Disneyland (special award of excellence, 2005), Winnie the Pooh (2006), Tinker Bell (2010), The Muppets (2012), and Minnie Mouse (2018).

Hollywood's Pretty Woman Stage show in the Theater of the Stars at Disney-MGM Studios; played Sep. 24–Nov. 3, 1991, replacing *Dick Tracy Starring in Diamond Double-Cross*. Roger Rabbit, Mickey Mouse, Minnie Mouse, and Goofy starred in a musical tribute to the women of Hollywood. It was succeeded by *Beauty and the Beast—Live on Stage*.

Holm, Celeste (1917–2012) Actress; appeared in *Three Men and a Baby* (Jack's mother), and on TV in *Kilroy* (Mrs. Fuller) and as Miss Snow in *The Bluegrass Special*, *Polly*, and *Polly—Comin' Home*.

Holmes, Taylor (1878–1959) Provided the voice of King Stefan in *Sleeping Beauty*.

Holster Full of Law, A (film) International theatrical compilation of *Texas John Slaughter* TV episodes: *A Holster Full of Law*, *Frank Clell's in Town*, and *Trip to Tucson*. First released in Italy in Jul. 1966. 90 min. Stars Tom Tryon. Also the title of Episode 14 of *Texas John Slaughter*.

Holt, Harry (1911–2004) Animator; he joined Disney in 1936 and remained until 1956. A few years later he returned as a sculptor and art director for WED Enterprises. He retired in 1982, but beginning in mid-1987, he staffed an animator's desk, doing drawings for park guests for several years in The Walt Disney Story attraction's exit lobby in the Magic Kingdom at Walt Disney World.

Holt, Olivia Actress/singer; appeared on Disney Channel in *Girl vs. Monster* (Skylar), *Shake It Up* (young Georgia), *Dog with a Blog* (Wacky Jackie), *I Didn't Do It* (Lindy Watson), *Evermoor* (Valentina), and the *Radio Disney Music Awards*; on Disney XD in *Kickin' It* (Kim); as Tandy Bowen/Dagger in *Marvel's Cloak & Dagger* and *Runaways*; and on ABC in the *Disney Parks Magical Christmas Day Parade*. She voiced Morgan in *Tinker Bell and the Legend of the NeverBeast* and Amber in *Penn Zero: Part-Time Hero*. She signed with Hollywood Records in 2014.

Holy Man (film) When Ricky Hayman, a top executive at the Good Buy Shopping Network, finds his job on the line, he desperately searches for an innovative idea to boost his network's sales. A chance encounter with "G," an itinerant street guru, gives him an idea—give the charismatic holy man his own TV show and make shopping via the tube a truly religious experience. A Touchstone film in association with Caravan Pictures. Released Oct. 9, 1998. Directed by Stephen Herek. Stars Jeff Goldblum (Ricky Hayman), Eddie Murphy (G), Robert Loggia (McBainbridge), Kelly Preston (Kate Newell), Jon Cryer (Barry). 114 min. CinemaScope. Filming took place in Miami.

Holy Matrimony (film) When sassy and streetwise Havana loses her criminal husband and is forced to hide out with his relatives, a wholesome, strict colony of religious disciples known as Hutterites, she finds that their archaic commandments on chastity and hard work clash with her modern morality. The Hutterites have never met anyone remotely like Havana, and she has never spent time with people who are so uncorrupted by the influences of society. While she goes along with their rules and regulations in order to buy time to find stolen money hidden on their property, she is aghast to discover that—because of a part of their religious law—to remain in the colony she must marry the 12-year-old brother of her former husband. Temporarily stuck with each other, the 2 square off for a comic battle of wills. Released in a limited number of cities Apr. 8, 1994. Directed by Leonard Nimoy. A Hollywood Pictures film. 93 min. Stars Patricia Arquette (Havana), Joseph Gordon-Levitt (Zeke), Tate Donovan (Peter), Armin Mueller-Stahl (Uncle Wilhelm), John Schuck (Markowski). Filmed in Great Falls, Montana.

Holz, Karl He joined Walt Disney World in 1996 as vice president of Downtown Disney, moving to vice president of EPCOT in 2000. In 2001 he was named senior vice president of Walt Disney World operations. He was promoted to president of Disney Cruise Line Services in 2003. He became president of Disneyland Paris in 2004, and chairman in 2005. In Aug. 2008 he began as president, Disney Cruise Line and New Vacation Operations for Walt Disney Parks and Resorts. He retired in 2018.

Home Alone 4 (TV) Two-hour movie from 20th Century Fox Television on *The Wonderful World of Disney*; first aired Nov. 3, 2002. While young Kevin McCallister's parents are divorcing, Kevin is invited to spend Christmas with his dad at the mansion of his girlfriend, Natalie. The mansion is a "smart house" with everything remote-controlled. While there, Kevin meets up with a robber and his girlfriend, and resorts to his usual pranks to get rid of them. Directed by Rod Daniel. Stars Mike Weinberg (Kevin McCallister), Jason Beghe (Peter McCallister), Clare Carey (Kate McCallister), Erick Avari (Prescott), Joanna Going (Natalie), French Stewart (Marv), Missi Pyle (Vera). Based on the previous Home Alone movies produced by Fox. Filmed in Cape Town, South Africa.

Home Defense (film) Donald Duck cartoon released Nov. 26, 1943. Directed by Jack King. Donald falls asleep at his wartime post as aircraft spotter, and his nephews take advantage by frightening him with their toy plane and parachutists.

Home Economics (TV) Half-hour comedy series on ABC; premiered Apr. 7, 2021, exploring the heartwarming, yet uncomfortable and sometimes frustrating, relationship between 3 adult siblings: one in the 1%, one who's middle class, and one barely holding on. Inspired by the life of writer/exec. producer Michael Colton. Stars Topher Grace (Tom), Caitlin McGee (Sarah), Jimmy Tatro (Connor), Karla Souza (Marina), Sasheer Zamata (Denise). From Lionsgate and ABC Signature.

Home Improvement (TV) Series on ABC; aired Sep. 17, 1991–Sep. 17, 1999. The star of TV's *Tool Time* show is often a bungler when he tries his home-improvement skills around the house. He is also not always terribly adept in his relationships with his wife and 3 boys. Stars Tim Allen (Tim Taylor), Patricia Richardson (Jill Taylor), Zachery Ty Bryan (Brad Taylor), Jonathan Taylor Thomas (Randy Taylor), Taran Noah Smith (Mark Taylor), Earl Hindman (Wilson), Richard Karn (Al Borland). The popular show frequently resided at the top of the weekly ratings, and it won Emmy Awards for Electronic Lighting Direction in 1992 and 1993. A special, *Tim Allen Presents: A User's Guide to Home Improvement*, aired May 4, 2003.

Home Made Home (film) Goofy cartoon released Mar. 23, 1951. Directed by Jack Kinney. Goofy encounters many problems building his own house but is relieved when the work is done and he has company in—until the house collapses.

Home of the Future SEE MONSANTO HOUSE OF THE FUTURE.

Home on the Range (film) A greedy outlaw named Alameda Slim schemes to take possession of the Patch of Heaven dairy farm from its kindly owner, Pearl. Unwilling to stand by and see their idyllic way of life threatened, 3 determined cows—Mrs. Caloway, Maggie, and Grace—a karate-kicking stallion named Buck, and a colorful corral of critters join forces to save the farm. This unlikely assortment of animals braves bad guys and the rugged Western landscape as they match wits with a mysterious bounty hunter named Rico in a high-stakes race to capture Slim and collect the reward money. Directed by Will Finn and John Sanford. Released Apr. 2, 2004. Voices include Roseanne Barr (Maggie), Judi Dench (Mrs. Caloway), Jennifer Tilly (Grace), Cuba Gooding, Jr. (Buck), Randy Quaid (Slim), Charles Dennis (Rico), Steve Buscemi (Wesley), Carole Cook (Pearl), Ann Richards (Annie). 76 min. An early title was *Sweating Bullets*. Ann Richards was formerly the governor of Texas. Songs by Alan Menken and Glenn Slater.

Home Store, The World Bazaar tableware and interior goods shop in Tokyo Disneyland; opened Jul. 17, 1998, taking the place of the Signature Shop and China Cabinet.

Home Sweet Home Alone (film) A Disney+ original film from 20th Century Studios. Max Mercer, a mischievous and resourceful young boy, has been left behind while his family is in Japan for the holidays. So when a married couple attempting to retrieve a priceless heirloom sets their sights on the Mercer family's home, it is up to Max to protect it from the trespassers, and he will do whatever it takes to keep them out. Premiered digitally Nov. 12, 2021. 93 min. Directed by Dan Mazer. Stars Ellie Kemper (Pam McKenzie), Rob Delaney (Jeff McKenzie), Archie Yates (Max Mercer), Aisling Bea (Carol Mercer), Kenan Thompson (Gavin Washington), Tim Simons (Hunter), Pete Holmes (Uncle Blake), Devin Ratray (Buzz McCallister), Ally Maki (Mei), Chris Parnell (Uncle Stu). Principal photography took place in and around Montreal.

Homeboys in Outer Space (TV) Half-hour series on UPN; aired Aug. 27, 1996–May 13, 1997. In the 23rd century, spacemen Tyberious Walker and Morris Clay, 2 "brothers" from Earth, scour the galaxies looking for the ultimate mission that will make them their fortunes. The 2 purchased a used space vehicle, the *Hoopty*, that came with a special commuter, the Loquatron 2000, known affectionately as Loquatia. Stars Flex (Tyberious), Darryl M. Bell (Morris), Kevin Michael Richardson (Vashti), Rhona L. Bennett (Loquatia), Paulette Braxton (Amma), James Doohan (Pippen). From Sweet Lorraine Productions and Touchstone Television.

Homeier, Skip (1930–2017) Actor; appeared on TV in *The Strange Monster of Strawberry Cove* (Harry), *Johnny Shiloh* (Captain MacPherson), and *Elfego Baca* (Ross Mantee).

Homeward Bound: The Incredible Journey (film) When a young family decides to make a temporary move from the country to San Francisco, they must leave their beloved pets behind until they can return. Left in the care of a family friend, the 3 forlorn animals—Shadow, an aged golden retriever; Chance, an American bulldog puppy; and Sassy, a Himalayan cat—set off through the wilds of the Sierras to find their owners. Conversing among themselves in human voices, the animals swim deep rivers, outwit a deadly mountain lion, and keep ahead of pursuing humans. Their camaraderie and courage manage to see them through and discover the path that leads to home. Initial release Feb. 3, 1993; general release Feb. 12, 1993. Directed by Duwayne Dunham. 84 min. Stars Robert Hays (Bob), Kim Greist (Laura), Veronica Lauren (Hope), Kevin Chevalia (Jamie), Benj Thall (Peter). Voices of the animals by Michael J. Fox (Chance), Sally Field (Sassy), Don Ameche (Shadow). A remake of the 1963 Disney film *The Incredible Journey*. Filmed in eastern Oregon.

Homeward Bound II: Lost in San Francisco (film) The Seaver family has decided to take Chance, an American bulldog; Sassy, a Himalayan cat; and Shadow, a golden retriever, with them on a trip to the Canadian Rockies. When Chance escapes from his kennel at San Francisco's airport, his friends Shadow and Sassy are forced to rescue him. Being from suburbia, they find themselves unprepared for the dangers that lurk in the perilous streets of San Francisco. Eluding determined dogcatchers and outsmarting alleyway mutts Ashcan and Pete, the 3 friends are aided in their journey by a gang of tough-talking strays led by the charismatic Riley. It is among this pack that Chance encounters the beautiful, streetwise Delilah, with whom he falls hopelessly in love. In their struggles to return home, the 3 pets learn some tough lessons about life, friendship, loyalty, and love. Directed by David R. Ellis. Released Mar. 8, 1996. Stars Robert Hays (Bob Seaver), Kim Greist (Laura Seaver), Veronica Lauren (Hope), Kevin Chevalia (Jamie), Benj Thall (Peter). The lead animals' voices are provided by Michael J. Fox (Chance), Sally Field (Sassy), and Ralph Waite (Shadow). 89 min. A sequel to *Homeward Bound: The Incredible Journey*. Filmed entirely on location in and around Vancouver and San Francisco, and featuring an animal cast of 40 canine and 10 feline performers. Four dogs were used to portray Chance and Shadow, though the lead roles went to dogs named Petey and Clovis; 6 different cats portrayed Sassy.

Honest John See J. Worthington Foulfellow.

Honey Harvester (film) Donald Duck cartoon released Aug. 5, 1949. Directed by Jack Hannah. A bee, taking honey from flowers in Donald's greenhouse and depositing it in the duck's car radiator, attempts to stop Donald from stealing the honey by attacking with the addition of a cactus spine to his stinger.

Honey, I Blew Up the Kid (film) Sequel to *Honey,*

I Shrunk the Kids. Wayne Szalinski's new invention is a ray that expands molecules when they come into contact with electricity, with the unexpected experiment being his own young son, Adam. The toddler wanders in front of the ray, and before long is 112 feet tall, getting even bigger each time he encounters electricity, and heading straight for the bright lights of Las Vegas. Released Jul. 17, 1992. Directed by Randal Kleiser. 89 min. Stars Rick Moranis (Wayne Szalinski), Marcia Strassman (Diane Szalinski), Lloyd Bridges (Clifford Sterling), Robert Oliveri (Nick), John Shea (Charles Henderickson). For the production, the filmmakers were given permission to block off Fremont Street in Las Vegas. Also filmed in Simi Valley, California. Special effects wizards relied on both miniature sets and huge props.

Honey, I Shrunk the Audience (film) 3-D film at Journey Into Imagination in EPCOT; shown Nov. 21, 1994–May 10, 2010, in the Magic Eye Theater. Guests enter the Imagination Institute, where Professor Wayne Szalinski is being honored as Inventor of the Year. When the audience becomes accidental victims of the professor's famed, but flawed, shrinking machine, they must face such terrors as a giant python, a huge sneezing dog, and a humongous 5-year-old child. In Tokyo Disneyland, the film, with new sequences shot specifically for the Japanese audience, debuted Apr. 15, 1997, as *MicroAdventure!* Also open in Disneyland May 22, 1998–Jan. 4, 2010, and opened in Disneyland Paris, as *Chérie, J'ai Rétréci le Public*, Mar. 28, 1999. The attractions closed in 2010 to bring back *Captain EO*.

Honey, I Shrunk the Kids (film) Professor Wayne Szalinski is trying to perfect an electromagnetic shrinking machine, but everyone thinks he is a crackpot. When Szalinski's 2 kids, Amy and Nick, along with neighborhood kids Ron and Little Russ Thompson, are accidentally zapped by the machine, they find themselves a quarter-inch high. The professor unknowingly sweeps them up and throws them out with the trash, and they find it necessary to complete a major trek across the backyard, now a teeming jungle to them. As their parents search for them, the tiny kids face seemingly insurmountable obstacles and unexpected terrors as they make their way toward the house and hope for restoration by the machine. Released Jun. 23, 1989. Directed by Joe Johnston. 93 min. Stars Rick Moranis (Wayne Szalinski), Matt Frewer (Big Russ Thompson), Marcia Strassman (Diane Szalinski),

Kristine Sutherland (Mae Thompson), Amy O'Neill (Amy), Robert Oliveri (Nick), Thomas Brown (Little Russ), Jared Rushton (Ron). Filmed at Churubusco Studio in Mexico City.

Honey, I Shrunk the Kids (TV) One-hour syn. series; premiered the week of Sep. 22, 1997, with zany scientist Wayne Szalinski coming up with inventions from time machines to shrink rays to spaceships and constantly involving his family in a series of misadventures. Wife Diane, a working mother, balances marriage, family, and her career as a top-notch lawyer, acting as the voice of reason in the midst of the outrageousness. Stars Peter Scolari (Wayne Szalinski), Barbara Alyn Woods (Diane), Hillary Tuck (Amy), Thomas Dekker (Nick). While the series was filmed in an old army barracks in Calgary, Alberta, Canada, it is set in the fictional small town of Matheson, Colorado.

Honey, I Shrunk the Kids Adventure Zone Attraction in Disney's Hollywood Studios at Walt Disney World; open Dec. 17, 1990–Apr. 2, 2016. Also known as Honey, I Shrunk the Kids Movie Set Adventure. Guests could discover what it is like to be miniaturized as they wandered in a gigantic world.

Honey, We Shrunk Ourselves (film) Direct-to-video release Mar. 18, 1997. Wayne Szalinski is back, and this time, when his notorious shrink machine misfires, it is the adults who are shrunk. Believing their parents have left them home alone for the weekend, the kids take advantage of their newfound unsupervised freedom by filling up on junk food, Roller-blading in the house, playing loud music, and throwing a party for their friends. While desperately trying to get the kids to notice them, since they are only 3/4th of an inch tall, the adults are able to learn a few things about their kids. Directed by Dean Cundey, making his directorial debut (though previously a renowned cinematographer on such films as *Who Framed Roger Rabbit*, *Hook*, and *Jurassic Park*). Stars Rick Moranis (Wayne), Eve Gordon (Diane), Bug Hall (Adam), Robin Bartlett (Patty), Stuart Pankin (Gordon), Allison Mack (Jenny), Jake Richardson (Mitch). 76 min. Rated PG. The film was extremely complicated to produce, with almost 400 composite shots totaling approximately 40 min. of screen time. Dream Quest Images, which produced the visual effects, had the advantage of new technologies that were not available when the first film in the series was made.

Hong Kong Disneyland The 11th Disney park opened in Hong Kong Sep. 12, 2005. Phase I of the resort development, located on 310 acres of land on Lantau Island, is on land reclaimed from Penny's Bay. In 1999, Disney and the government of the Hong Kong Special Administrative Region (HKSAR) signed a master project agreement for the development and operation of Hong Kong Disneyland; Disney owns a 48% interest in Hong Kong Disneyland Resort, and HKSAR owns a 52% interest. The site is 30 min. from downtown Hong Kong. After initial reclamation work on the land, a groundbreaking ceremony was held Jan. 12, 2003, and after over a year of construction, a castle-topping ceremony was held Sep. 23, 2004. The park debuted with 4 themed lands—Main Street, U.S.A.; Adventureland; Fantasyland (with Sleeping Beauty Castle, a replica of the original in Disneyland); and Tomorrowland (themed as an intergalactic space-port). Major expansions later added Grizzly Gulch (2012) and Toy Story Land and Mystic Point (both in 2013). In 2016, new themed lands were announced, including World of Frozen (scheduled to open in 2023) and a Marvel-themed area. In 2020, coinciding with the park's 15th anniversary cel-ebration, Sleeping Beauty Castle was transformed into the 167-foot-tall Castle of Magical Dreams. In addition to the park, the Hong Kong Disneyland Resort premiered with the Inspiration Lake Rec-reation Centre and 2 resort hotels—Hong Kong Disneyland Hotel and Disney's Hollywood Hotel, totaling 1,000 rooms. The addition of the 750-room Disney Explorers Lodge in 2017 increased the number of hotel rooms at the resort by 75%.

Hong Kong Disneyland Hotel Resort hotel in the grand Victorian style along the shores of the South China Sea; opened Sep. 12, 2005, with 400 rooms. There are restaurants (Crystal Lotus, Enchanted Garden, and Walt's Cafe) and shopping at King-dom Gifts, as well as lounges, a spa, tennis court, conference center, Bibbidi Bobbidi Boutique, and an English garden maze fashioned after Mickey Mouse.

Hong Kong Disneyland Railroad Opened Sep. 12, 2005, with stations in Fantasyland and Main Street, U.S.A. The locomotives are the *Roy O. Dis-ney*, *Walter E. Disney*, and *Frank G. Wells*. The individual train cars are named the Anaheim, Bur-bank, California, Chicago, Glendale, Hollywood, Kansas City, Los Angeles, Marceline, and Orlando.

Honker Muddlefoot Little boy duck and best friend of Gosalyn Mallard in *Darkwing Duck*; voiced by Katie Leigh.

Hook, Lion and Sinker (film) Donald Duck car-toon released Sep. 1, 1950. Directed by Jack Hannah. A mountain lion and cub try various ways to steal fish from Donald, always with the same result—the cub picking Donald's buckshot out of his father's bottom.

Hooked Bear (film) Special cartoon released Apr. 27, 1956. Directed by Jack Hannah. Ranger J. Audubon Woodlore attempts to keep Humphrey the Bear from fishing with the human fisher-men, telling him, "Now go fish like a bear!" But Humphrey keeps looking for an easier way until, before he knows it, fishing season is over and bear-hunting season is on. Filmed in Cinema-Scope.

Hook's Pointe & Wine Cellar Casual table-service restaurant at the Disneyland Hotel; opened Apr. 8, 1999, taking the place of the Shipyard Inn. Closed Jul. 25, 2010, to make way for Tangaroa Terrace and Trader Sam's Enchanted Tiki Bar. Grilled meat and seafood were specialties. SEE ALSO NEVER LAND POOL.

Hook's Tavern Fantasyland snack counter in the Magic Kingdom at Walt Disney World; opened Oct. 21, 1993, replacing Troubadour Tavern. Later replaced by FastPass distribution for Peter Pan's Flight.

Hookworm (film) Educational film produced under the auspices of the Coordinator of Inter-American Affairs tells about the dangers of hook-worm. Careless Charlie and his family are infected with hookworm, and they learn about the proper medications and safe living conditions from a local clinic. Delivered Jun. 30, 1945.

Hoop-Dee-Doo Musical Revue In Pioneer Hall at Fort Wilderness at Walt Disney World, debuted Sep. 5, 1974. The audience joins in a rousing musi-cal celebration of country-and-western entertain-ment by the Pioneer Hall Players: Claire de Lune, Johnny Ringo, Dolly Drew, Six Bits Slocum, Flora Long, and Jim Handy. Fried chicken, barbecued ribs, and corn on the cob are served family-style. Only one significant change to the menu has been made since the show's debut: the apple pie dessert switched to strawberry shortcake in 1979. It is one of the longest-running dinner shows in American history. From 1983–1995, a version played in the Diamond Horseshoe in Tokyo Disneyland.

Hoopz Stage musical in development, about the rise of the Harlem Globetrotters basketball team in the mid-20th century. Announced ca. 1997.

Hoot & Holler Hideout Critter-themed shop in Critter Country in Tokyo Disneyland; opened Mar. 1994.

Hope & Faith (TV) Half-hour comedy series on ABC; aired Sep. 26, 2003–Jun. 23, 2006. Stay-at-home mom Hope leads a busy, family-centered life with her husband, children, and live-in father. But when her Hollywood celebrity sister, Faith, is written out of the soap opera in which she stars and comes to stay with her sister's family in suburbia, Hope's sensible, down-to-earth world changes drastically. Raising 3 kids has never been easy for Hope, but the appearance of trendy, theatrical Faith turns parenting into crisis management. Stars Faith Ford (Hope), Kelly Ripa (Faith), Josh Stamberg (Charley), Harve Presnell (Jack), Maccy Cruthird (Hayley), Brie Larson (Sydney), Slade Pearce (Justin). From Touchstone Television.

Hope Springs (film) British artist Colin Ware discovers that his fiancée, Vera, the love of his life, is going to marry another man. Distraught and despondent, he gets on a plane for America and ends up in the tiny town of Hope, somewhere in New England. At first, Colin is depressed, but he soon finds more than a shoulder to cry on when his innkeepers introduce him to Mandy, a beautiful nurse. All's going well and Colin has almost forgotten his old flame until Vera suddenly shows up with a surprise of her own. A Touchstone film. Directed by Mark Herman. Originally released in England May 9, 2003. Test screened in certain Florida cities Sep. 5, 2003, before a direct-to-video release on Apr. 6, 2004. Stars Colin Firth (Colin Ware), Heather Graham (Mandy), Minnie Driver (Vera), Oliver Platt (Doug Reed), Mary Steenburgen (Joanie Fisher). 92 min. Filmed in CinemaScope. Based on the novel *New Cardiff*, by Charles Webb; working title of the film was *New Cardiff*. Filmed in Vancouver.

Hopkins, Anthony Actor; appeared in *Nixon* (Richard Nixon), *Instinct* (Ethan Powell), *Bad Company* (Gaylord Oakes), *Thor* and *Thor: The Dark World* (Odin), and on The Disney Channel in *Great Expectations* (Abel Magwitch).

Hopper, Dennis (1936–2010) Actor; appeared in *My Science Project* (Bob Roberts), *Super Mario Bros.* (King Koopa), *Meet the Deedles* (Frank Slater), and *Swing Vote* (Donald Greenleaf).

Horace Horsecollar Known for the oversize collar around his neck, this horse character was a bit player primarily in the Mickey Mouse cartoons of the 1930s. He has made a number of appearances, beginning with *The Plowboy* (1929), and is often paired with Clarabelle Cow.

Hordern, Michael (1911–1995) Actor; appeared in *The Story of Robin Hood* (Scathelock), and on TV in *The Scarecrow of Romney Marsh* (Squire).

Horizon Bay Restaurant Buffeteria in Port Discovery in Tokyo DisneySea; opened Sep. 4, 2001. The story goes that a yacht club had been converted into this futuristic marina restaurant to entertain scientists visiting the Center for Weather Control's festival. Character dining is offered.

Horizons Future World pavilion in EPCOT Center; opened Oct. 1, 1983, sponsored by General Electric until Sep. 30, 1993. Closed Jan. 9, 1999, later replaced by Mission: SPACE. Passengers began their ride by "looking back at tomorrow," a sequence showing how the future was once imagined by such visionaries as Jules Verne. Then an Omnimax theater presented new technological breakthroughs on a massive scale. Next, they witnessed how an average family could live in different futuristic environments, such as a desert farm, an undersea floating city, and a space colony. Finally, they could select how they wanted their experience to end by pressing appropriate buttons in their ride vehicle, the first time this was done in a Disney attraction. The theme song, "New Horizons," written by George Wilkins, featured the pavilion's motto: "If we can dream it, we can do it." "There's a Great Big Beautiful Tomorrow," a song originally written for the Carousel of Progress, could be heard by savvy guests here on a TV in an art deco–style scene. The attraction had several proposed names, including Century 3 and Futureprobe. Horizons is one of the more fondly remembered attractions from EPCOT's past.

Horn, Alan He became chairman of The Walt Disney Studios Jun. 11, 2012, succeeding Rich Ross, and then served as cochairman and chief creative officer beginning in 2019. In 2021, he was named chief creative officer, Disney Studios Content. He oversaw the integrations of Lucasfilm and the Fox film studios, as well as the Studios' expansion into content production for Disney's streaming services. During his tenure, The Walt Disney Studios set numerous box office records, surpassing $7 billion globally in 2016 and 2018 and $11 billion in 2019. Horn came from leadership roles at Warner Bros., Castle Rock Entertainment (which he cofounded), 20th Century Fox, and Embassy. He retired Dec. 31, 2021.

Horned King, The Evil villain in *The Black Cauldron* who wants to unleash the Cauldron-Born (undead warriors) as his soldiers; voiced by John Hurt.

Horner, James (1953–2015) Composer; he wrote the scores for *Something Wicked This Way Comes*; *The Journey of Natty Gann*; *Captain EO*; *Tummy Trouble*; *Honey, I Shrunk the Kids*; *The Rocketeer*; *Swing Kids*; *A Far Off Place*; *Mighty Joe Young*; and *Bicentennial Man*.

Horse Called Comanche, A Serialized version of *Tonka* on the new *Mickey Mouse Club*.

Horse in the Gray Flannel Suit, The (film) An executive in an ad agency comes up with a great idea; he gets his firm to buy a horse and gives it to his teenaged daughter. She'll ride it to victory in some horse shows, and the animal, named for the Allied Drug Company product, an indigestion remedy called Aspercel, will get lots of publicity. But it doesn't quite work out that way. His daughter, Helen, is only an amateur, and it is only with the love and support of her father, trainer Suzie Clemens, and her new boyfriend, Ronnie, that she can win the title of Grand Champion Open Jumper in the prestigious Washington International Horse Show. Released Dec. 20, 1968. Directed by Norman Tokar. 113 min. Stars Dean Jones (Frederick Bolton), Diane Baker (Suzie Clemens), Ellen Janov (Helen Bolton), Lloyd Bochner (Archer Madison), Morey Amsterdam (Charlie Blake), Kurt Russell (Ronnie Gardner), Lurene Tuttle (Aunt Martha). Based on the book *The Year of the Horse*, by Eric Hatch. The movie was shot mostly at Disney's Golden Oak Ranch, near Newhall, California. Student riders from the Flintridge Riding Academy were used in the film.

Horse of the West, The (TV) Show aired Dec. 11, 1957. Directed by Larry Lansburgh. The story of the life of a quarter horse through her various own-

ers. Narrated by Rex Allen. Stars Sammy Fancher, George Masek, Jimmy Williams.

Horse Sense (TV) A Disney Channel Original Movie; first aired Nov. 20, 1999. 11-year-old Tommy visits his wealthy cousin, Michael, in Beverly Hills, but Michael ignores the kid. Michael is punished for his behavior by being sent to Tommy's ranch in Montana for the summer, and he has a miserable time trying to acclimate himself to ranch life. However, when Michael discovers that Tommy and his mother are in jeopardy of losing their property due to foreclosure, he and Tommy unite to save the ranch, and in the process he learns an important lesson about hard work, family, and love. Directed by Greg Beeman. Stars Andy Lawrence (Tommy Biggs), Joey Lawrence (Michael Woods), Susan Walters (Jules Biggs), M. C. Gainey (Twister), Leann Hunley (Jacy Woods), Robin Thomas (Glenn Woods). A sequel, *Jumping Ship*, followed in 2001.

Horse Whisperer, The (film) 14-year-old Grace Maclean is physically and emotionally scarred after a terrible riding accident while astride her prized horse, Pilgrim. Her mother, Annie, a high-powered magazine editor, realizes that the fates of her daughter and the horse are inextricably linked, so she searches for a "horse whisperer," someone with a unique gift for curing troubled horses. She finds Tom Booker, a legend for this type of work, and takes both Grace and Pilgrim to Montana to seek his help. There, love blossoms between the gentle horseman and the uprooted sophisticate. Directed by Robert Redford. A Touchstone film. Released May 15, 1998. Stars Robert Redford (Tom Booker), Kristin Scott Thomas (Annie), Sam Neill (Robert Maclean), Dianne Wiest (Diane Booker), Scarlett Johansson (Grace), Chris Cooper (Frank Booker), Cherry Jones (Liz Hammond). 169 min. This is the first time that Redford starred in a film he also produced and directed. Based upon the best-selling first novel by British author Nicholas Evans. Filmed in CinemaScope. After filming at various locations in New York State, the production moved to Montana where a working cattle ranch of the Engle family, located about an hour from Livingston, became the fictitious Double Divide Ranch, though a new ranch house was built.

Horse with the Flying Tail, The (film) Featurette released Dec. 21, 1960, on a bill with *Swiss Family Robinson*. Directed by Larry Lansburgh. The true story of Nautical, star jumper of the U.S. Equestrian

Team. As a cow pony, this palomino is noticed by an ex-cavalry man who trains him. Near disaster overtakes the jumper when he is sold to an unscrupulous trainer. However, Bertalan de Nemethy, coach of the U.S. team, spots Nautical, buys and rejuvenates him, and ships him to Europe where he finally wins the world-famous King George V cup. Made to run 47 min. (for the TV show), the film was instead deemed worthy to receive a theatrical release, and it won the Academy Award for Best Documentary Feature of 1960. It was later telecast on *Walt Disney's Wonderful World of Color* in 1963.

Horse Without a Head, The (TV) Two-part show; aired Sep. 29 and Oct. 6, 1963. Directed by Don Chaffey. The 2 episodes were titled *The 100,000,000 Franc Train Robbery* and *The Key to the Cache*. In France, a daring mail train robbery goes awry, and a group of kids thwart the robbers by finding a key to the hiding place of the loot that the crooks have hidden in a headless horse cart in which the kids enjoy riding. Stars Jean-Pierre Aumont, Herbert Lom, Leo McKern, Pamela Franklin, Vincent Winter, Lee Montague, Denis Gilmore.

Horse-Drawn Streetcars Main Street, U.S.A. vehicles at Disneyland; began on Jul. 17, 1955. The tracks part halfway down the street to form double tracks so that two streetcars can pass each other. The majestic Belgian horses pulling the streetcars are the last remaining horses utilized daily in the park, and they greatly add to the atmosphere of a turn-of-the-century street. Also in the Magic Kingdom at Walt Disney World beginning Oct. 1, 1971, and in Disneyland Paris beginning Apr. 12, 1992.

Horseless Carriages Main Street, U.S.A. vehicles at Disneyland; began in 1956. Designed and built by Disney Imagineers based on cars of the period. Also in the Magic Kingdom at Walt Disney World, opening Oct. 1, 1971, and in World Bazaar in Tokyo Disneyland, opening Apr. 15, 1983.

Horsemasters, The (TV) Two-part show; aired on Oct. 1 and 8, 1961. Directed by William Fairchild. The 2 episodes were titled *Follow Your Heart* and *Tally Ho*. American students are having a difficult time at a prestigious English riding school. Dinah Wilcox is overly cautious because of memories of an accident, but Danny Grant gives her confidence. The strict, but admired, instructor fears she must sell her favorite horse because of school tradition, but the students end up taking up a collec-

tion to buy it back for her. Stars Annette Funicello, Tommy Kirk, Janet Munro, Donald Pleasence, Tony Britton, John Fraser, Jean Marsh, Millicent Martin. The Sherman brothers, Robert and Richard, wrote "The Strummin' Song," their first song for Disney, for this show.

Horses for Greene (TV) Episode 8 of *The Swamp Fox*.

Hortense Title star of *Donald's Ostrich* (1937).

Horvath, Ferdinand Huszti (1891–1973) Story sketch artist; at Disney 1934–1937, Horvath was a very meticulous person who specialized in fine, detailed pencil sketches. Born in Budapest, he brought a European style to the Disney films. He worked on many of the Disney shorts and did preliminary work on *Snow White and the Seven Dwarfs*.

Hoskins, Bob (1942–2014) Actor; appeared in *Who Framed Roger Rabbit* (Eddie Valiant), *Passed Away* (Johnny Scanlan), *Super Mario Bros.* (Mario Mario), *Nixon* (J. Edgar Hoover), and *Disney's A Christmas Carol* (Fezziwig/Old Joe).

Hospital, The (film) Educational film in which Mickey learns about the various parts of a hospital and the work that goes on there. Part of the Mickey's Field Trips series; released in Sep. 1987. 10 min.

Hospitality House Town Square meeting facility on Main Street, U.S.A. in the Magic Kingdom at Walt Disney World; opened Oct. 1, 1971, presented by Gulf. Closed in 1990, succeeded by the Disneyana Shop and, later, Town Square Theater. Attendants provided information on local Central Florida accommodations. The building was inspired by the Grand Union Hotel in Saratoga Springs, New York, and would also host The Walt Disney Story for many years.

Hot Chick, The (film) Jessica Spencer, the hottest, most popular girl in high school, captain of the cheerleading squad, and dating the dreamy quarterback, gets a big dose of reality when she wakes up in the body of a 30-year-old man. Until she can figure out how to change herself back, she must find a way to win the Cheer Competition, go to the prom, and win her boyfriend back—all as a guy. A Touchstone film. Released Dec. 13, 2002. Directed by Tom Brady. Stars Rob Schneider (Clive), Anna Faris (April), Matthew Lawrence (Billy), Eric

Christian Olsen (Jake), Robert Davi (Stan), Melora Hardin (Carol), Rachel McAdams (Jessica Spencer), Michael O'Keefe (Richie). 101 min.

Hot Choc-late Soldiers, The (film) Color Silly Symphony–type sequence produced for the MGM film *Hollywood Party* (1934). The Hot Chocolate Soldiers leave home to battle the Gingerbread Men of Pastry Land, using all sorts of candies and pastries as weapons. The soldiers capture the Gingerbread Men with a "Trojan Horse" trick—a giant candy dish of a dove holding an olive branch. The soldiers return home triumphant with their prisoners, only to melt in the hot sun. Directed by Ben Sharpsteen.

Hot Dog (film) Oswald the Lucky Rabbit cartoon; released Aug. 20, 1928. Attempting to sneak into the circus, Oswald is chased by a cop and soon finds himself in a lion's cage. He then gets a hitch on a passing wagon, which turns out to be the patrol wagon.

Hot Dog! Song from *Mickey Mouse Clubhouse*; written by John Flansburgh and John Linnell, and performed by They Might Be Giants.

Hot Lead and Cold Feet (film) This rip-roaring comedy saga of the Old West involves twin brothers who compete for possession of a rickety cow town founded by their father. The look-alike siblings (one a rough-and-rowdy cowboy, the other a mild-mannered easterner) take part in a winner takes all, no-holds-barred endurance contest, complete with train racing, wagon hauling, river-rapid running, and mountain climbing. All this takes place while a crooked mayor tries to put an end to the competitors so he can inherit the town himself. Eventually, the brothers join forces to save the town from the mayor and his minions. Released Jul. 5, 1978. Directed by Robert Butler. 90 min. Stars Jim Dale (Jasper, Eli, Wild Billy), Karen Valentine (Jenny), Don Knotts (Denver Kid), Jack Elam (Rattlesnake), Darren McGavin (Mayor Ragsdale), John Williams (Mansfield), Warren Vanders (Boss Snead), Debbie Lytton (Roxanne), Michael Sharrett (Marcus). Two songs are featured in the film: "May the Best Man Win," by Al Kasha and Joel Hirschhorn, and "Something Good Is Bound to Happen," by Buddy Baker, Arthur Alsberg, and Don Nelson. Portions of the film were shot on location in Deschutes National Forest in Oregon, from snowy Mt. Bachelor, along the Cascade Range, across the Deschutes River gorge to the black rocks of Lava Butte.

Hotel Cheyenne Hotel at Disneyland Paris; opened Apr. 12, 1992. Designed by architect Robert A.M. Stern. It is themed to an Old West settlement, with the Red Garter Saloon, a General Store, an all-you-can-eat buffet at Chuck Wagon Café, and old-fashioned pony rides. In 2017, guest rooms and public spaces were given a Sheriff Woody/*Toy Story 2* theme.

Hotel MiraCosta SEE TOKYO DISNEYSEA HOTEL MIRACOSTA.

Hotel New York, Disney's Hotel at Disneyland Paris; opened Apr. 12, 1992. Designed by architect Michael Graves. It debuted with dining at the Parkside Diner, 57th Street Bar (became the New York City Bar in 1995), Rainbow Room (later Manhattan Jazz Club and, in 1995, Manhattan Restaurant), and shopping at the Stock Exchange (later New York Boutique). Also featured the Athletic Club, New York Coliseum Convention Center, and Rockefeller Plaza—an outdoor reflecting pool that is turned into a skating rink during the winter. The resort closed Jan. 7, 2019, reopening Jun. 21, 2021, as Disney Hotel New York – The Art of Marvel. The reimagined hotel is styled as a New York art gallery with more than 350 Marvel-inspired works by 110 international artists. New are the Downtown Restaurant, a reimagined Manhattan Restaurant, Skyline Bar, Bleecker Street Lounge, Marvel character greetings at the Super Hero Station, drawing tutorials in the Marvel Design Studio, sports activities in the Hero Training Zone, and guest rooms with Marvel Super Hero artwork.

Hotel Santa Fe Hotel at Disneyland Paris; opened Apr. 12, 1992, with an American Southwest theme, inspired by Native American pueblos and Route 66 motifs. Designed by architect Antoine Predock. Dining options include La Cantina and Rio Grande Bar, with shopping at the Trading Post. In 2013, the resort was redesigned with guest rooms and other features themed to Disney • Pixar's *Cars*.

Hound That Thought He Was a Raccoon, The (film) Featurette released Aug. 10, 1960. Directed by Tom McGowan. A hound puppy, Nubbin, lost in the woods, is nursed by a female raccoon who has lost all her babies, except Weecha. Normally natural enemies, the baby hound and raccoon grow up together, first in the den, later at the farm of Nubbin's master. Weecha wants to escape the farm, and with Nubbin's intervention, is allowed to leave. Based on the story *Weecha the Raccoon* by Rutherford

Montgomery. 48 min. Originally planned to fit an hour-long TV slot, it finally reached TV in 1964. It was cut to 28 min. for a 1975 reissue.

Hounded (TV) A Disney Channel Original Movie; first aired Apr. 13, 2001. Thirteen-year-old Jay Martin is committed to winning a scholarship competition, so he won't be sent to military school, but his rival, Ronny Van Dusen, the principal's son, spoils his plans by stealing Jay's speech. Jay's plans are thwarted again when he accidentally kidnaps his principal's obnoxious dog, Camille. Directed by Neal Israel. Stars Tahj Mowry (Jay Martin), Craig Kirkwood (Mike Martin), Shia LaBeouf (Ronny Van Dusen), Ed Begley, Jr. (Ward Van Dusen), Stephen Bendik (Bill Lipka), Sara Paxton (Tracy Richburg).

House Calls (TV) Syn. half-hour series; aired Sep. 11, 2000–2001. In this reality series, cameras followed psychiatrist Dr. Irvin Wolkoff into the homes of real people as he counseled them about real problems. 88 episodes. From Buena Vista Television.

House of Blues Music-themed restaurant and bar; opened at Downtown Disney West Side (now the West Side at Disney Springs) at Walt Disney World Sep. 15, 1997, as the 6th and largest in the chain. American cuisine with a New Orleans twist is served in dining spaces featuring displays of folk art. The Front Porch Bar offers cold drinks and live entertainment. In 1995, Disney had purchased a 12% interest in the company in anticipation of the Florida location's construction. A version at Downtown Disney District at the Disneyland Resort operated Jan. 12, 2001–May 31, 2016.

House of Good Fortune Shop offering authentic merchandise in China at EPCOT; opened Apr. 4, 2011, replacing Yong Feng Shangdian. A nearby merchandise kiosk, Good Fortune Gifts, had opened previously, in spring 2010.

House of Greetings World Bazaar greeting card and stationery shop in Tokyo Disneyland; opened Apr. 15, 1983.

House of Magic Shop on Main Street, U.S.A. in the Magic Kingdom at Walt Disney World; opened Oct. 1, 1971, and closed Mar. 19, 1995, to become part of the Main Street Athletic Club.

House of Mouse (TV) Animated characters gather each Saturday at this "nightclub" to enjoy musi-cal guests, cartoon shorts, and Mickey Mouse's comical introductions from the stage. There is constant backstage pandemonium as Mickey, Donald Duck, Goofy, Minnie Mouse, Daisy Duck, and Pluto attempt to ensure that "the show goes on." Premiered on ABC Jan. 13, 2001. The last new episodes were produced in 2003; the series ended Feb. 2009. 52 episodes.

House of the Future SEE MONSANTO HOUSE OF THE FUTURE.

House of Treasure Caribbean Plaza shop in the Magic Kingdom at Walt Disney World; open Feb. 1974–2001. It was later succeeded by The Pirates League.

Houseguest (film) Enterprising Kevin Franklin's wishes and dreams turn out to be short-lived when his latest get-rich scheme fails, and he is forced to leave town in a hurry. With loan sharks and hit men after him, he heads to the airport where he meets lawyer Gary Young and convinces him that he is the childhood chum who was due in for a family visit. Masquerading as a houseguest is tricky enough, but soon Franklin is expected to be a world-famous oral surgeon, causing many complications. Released Jan. 6, 1995. Directed by Randy Miller. A Hollywood Pictures film in association with Caravan Pictures. 109 min. Stars Sinbad (Kevin Franklin), Phil Hartman (Gary Young), Kim Greist (Emily Ford), Jeffrey Jones (Ron Timmerman).

Houston, Whitney (1963–2012) Actress; starred in *The Preacher's Wife* (Julia), and on TV in *Cinderella* (Fairy Godmother).

Houston Disney constructed a WEDway People-Mover system in the Houston Intercontinental Airport (later the George Bush Intercontinental Airport). It opened Aug. 17, 1981, and was the only transportation system actually sold by Disney's Community Transportation Services division. The technology for the PeopleMover and monorails was later sold to a Canadian company, Bombardier, Inc. The visitor center at the Johnson Space Center, which opened in 1972, was designed by Walt Disney Imagineering.

How Alaska Joined the World (film) A 16-mm release in Jun. 1973 of a TV film. It traces Alaska's history, in animation, from its discovery to its purchase by the U.S.

How Disease Travels (film) Educational film produced under the auspices of the Coordinator of Inter-American Affairs shows how latrines can be built to prevent the spread of disease. Delivered Aug. 13, 1945.

How Do I Live Song from *Con Air*; written by Diane Warren. Nominated for an Academy Award.

How Does It Feel to Be an Elephant (film) Educational film with Figment in the EPCOT Educational Media Collection: Language Arts Through Imagination series; released in Sep. 1988. Learning skills of comparing and contrasting, observing and interpreting.

How Does It Feel to Fly? (film) Educational film with Figment describing the world through classifying and sequencing, in the EPCOT Educational Media Collection: Language Arts Through Imagination series; released in Sep. 1988. 14 min.

How Does Sound Sound? (film) Educational film with Figment about language and the sound around us, in the EPCOT Educational Media Collection: Language Arts Through Imagination series; released in Sep. 1988. 13 min.

How Far I'll Go Song from *Moana*; written by Lin-Manuel Miranda. Nominated for an Academy Award.

How the West Was Lost (TV) Show aired Sep. 24, 1967. Directed by Hamilton S. Luske. Cartoons about the Old West, introduced by one of Donald Duck's ancestors, known as the Oldtimer, whose voice was provided by Bill Thompson.

How to Be a Detective (film) Goofy cartoon released Dec. 12, 1952. Directed by Jack Kinney. Goofy is "Johnny Eyeball, Private Eye," who gets mixed up in a surreal whodunit involving a classy dame, a cop, weasels, and the mysterious missing Al.

How to Be a Sailor (film) Goofy cartoon released Jan. 28, 1944. Directed by Jack Kinney. Goofy demonstrates methods of navigation of the sea from early vessels to modern ships and engages in a victorious battle. A World War II-era short.

How to Build a Better Boy (TV) A Disney Channel Original Movie; first aired Aug. 15, 2014. Two tech-savvy best friends, high school sophomores Mae Hartley and Gabby Harrison, devise a plan to create the perfect boyfriend with just a few strokes of the keyboard and a wireless connection. What Gabby and Mae don't realize is that the computer they use is set up to generate a robotic super soldier, which they have inadvertently activated in the form of Albert, a macho yet sensitive supercute boy. Directed by Paul Hoen. Stars Kelli Berglund (Mae Hartley), China Anne McClain (Gabby Harrison), Marshall Williams (Albert Banks), Roger Bart (James Hartley).

How to Catch a Cold (film) Educational film, made for International Cellucotton Co. Delivered Aug. 1, 1951. About the myths and facts of the cold virus. Shows the manner in which a cold is caught and spread throughout a community, and how it should be treated. A revised version was released in Sep. 1986.

How to Dance (film) Goofy cartoon released Jul. 11, 1953. Directed by Jack Kinney. A short history of the dance, followed by Goofy trying to learn with the aid of a dummy and dancing school.

How to Exercise (film) Educational film in the Fitness and Me series; released in Mar. 1984. Two weaklings, a knight and a dragon, are used as examples in showing the value of a shape-up plan.

How to Fish (film) Goofy cartoon released Dec. 4, 1942. Directed by Jack Kinney. Goofy's demonstration of fishing is fouled up by his clumsy casting and fly-fishing, and problems with his boat.

How to Get Away with Murder (TV) Hour-long drama series on ABC; aired Sep. 25, 2014–May 14, 2020. Criminal Law professor Annalise Keating is brilliant, passionate, creative, and charismatic, but also glamorous, unpredictable, and dangerous. When not in the classroom, she is a defense attorney who represents those deemed the most hardened, violent criminals, and she will do almost anything to win their freedom. Each year Annalise selects a group of the smartest, most promising students to come work at her law firm under associates Frank Delfino and Bonnie Winterbottom. Stars Viola Davis (Annalise Keating), Billy Brown (Nate), Alfred Enoch (Wes Gibbins), Jack Falahee (Connor Walsh), Katie Findlay (Rebecca), Aja Naomi King (Michaela Pratt), Matt McGorry (Asher Millstone), Karla Souza (Laurel Castillo), Charlie Weber (Frank), and Lisa Weil (Bonnie). From ABC Studios. Viola Davis received an Emmy Award for Lead Actress in a Drama Series in 2015.

How to Get Fit (film) Educational film in the Fitness for Living series; released in Sep. 1982. The film provides a practical guide for students in developing their own fitness plan.

How to Have an Accident at Work (film) Donald Duck cartoon released Sep. 2, 1959. Directed by Charles Nichols. The bearded duck named J. J. Fate, who previously appeared in *How to Have an Accident in the Home*, warns of the dangers of being careless in the workplace, with Donald Duck as the example. Throwing all caution aside, Donald forgets his safety helmet, ignores signs, gets mixed up in the machinery, daydreams, and even gets in an accident in his rush to clock out.

How to Have an Accident in the Home (film) Donald Duck cartoon released Jun. 8, 1956. Directed by Charles Nichols. Filmed in CinemaScope. Donald demonstrates, to his own detriment, how dangerous many household activities can be, such as lighting pipes in gas-filled rooms, climbing a littered stairway, and standing on a rocking chair. The film's narrator is J. J. Fate, voiced by Bill Thompson.

How to Hook Up Your Home Theater (film) Goofy cartoon. Enthusiastic but clueless, Goofy is confronted by a huge instruction "manual" and has to deal with a gargantuan universal remote and a jumble of multicolored cables. Directed by Kevin Deters and Stevie Wermers. Released Dec. 21, 2007, with *National Treasure: Book of Secrets*. 6 min. Filmed in CinemaScope. It was the first theatrical Goofy cartoon released since 1965.

How to Play Baseball (film) Goofy cartoon released Sep. 4, 1942. Directed by Jack Kinney. Goofy demonstrates the game by playing all the positions on both teams and displaying the different types of pitches one can throw, with an offscreen narrator. The film was rushed into production, and made in just 12 weeks, so as to be released to accompany Samuel Goldwyn's *The Pride of the Yankees*.

How to Play Football (film) Goofy cartoon released Sep. 15, 1944. Directed by Jack Kinney. Taking all the places on both teams, Goofy demonstrates the game of football with varying results, having problems with the coach and the goalpost.

How to Play Golf (film) Goofy cartoon released Mar. 10, 1944. Directed by Jack Kinney. Aided by a diagrammatical figure, Goofy demonstrates golf techniques until an angry bull chases them and wrecks the course.

How to Relax (TV) Show aired Nov. 27, 1957. Directed by Wolfgang Reitherman. A series of Goofy cartoons that demonstrate his desire to relax.

How to Ride a Horse (film) Goofy cartoon released Feb. 24, 1950. It was earlier released as part of the feature *The Reluctant Dragon* (1941). Goofy is not very adept at horseback riding, and the horse constantly gets the best of him.

How to Sleep (film) Goofy cartoon released Dec. 25, 1953. Directed by Jack Kinney. Goofy shows the various ways humans sleep and has no trouble falling asleep throughout the day, including at his desk at work, but when he goes home to bed at night, he cannot sleep. He tries various gadgets, but finally a scientist has to hit him over the head.

How to Swim (film) Goofy cartoon released Oct. 23, 1942. Directed by Jack Kinney. In his attempt to demonstrate swimming, Goofy first has trouble undressing in the small locker room but then manages to showcase diving and swimming techniques.

How Walt Disney Cartoons Are Made (film) Black-and-white promotional film released by RKO in 1938 describing the processes used in making cartoons at the Walt Disney Studio on Hyperion Avenue in order to publicize *Snow White and the Seven Dwarfs*. 9 min. A revised version of the film was released around 1942 after the move from L.A.'s Hyperion to Burbank and the substitution of exterior scenes of the new Studio for ones of Hyperion.

Howard, Byron After working as an attractions host at Disney-MGM Studios, including as a tour guide at The Magic of Disney Animation, he joined the Florida animation studio as an inbetweener and cleanup artist on *Pocahontas*. He was an animator on *Mulan* (Yao/the Ancestors) and supervising animator on *Lilo & Stitch* (Cobra Bubbles) and *Brother Bear* (Kenai). He was co-director of *Bolt*, *Tangled*, *Zootopia*, and *Encanto*, and exec. producer of *Frozen 2*.

Howard (film) Documentary about the life of song lyricist Howard Ashman, whose career and vibrant life were cut short by AIDS. Directed by Don Hahn. Premiered Apr. 22, 2018, at the Tribeca Film Festival, before an Aug. 7, 2020, digital release on Disney+. From Stone Circle Pictures. 94 min. Score by Alan Menken, Ashman's songwriting partner.

Howard, Clint Actor; appeared in *The Wild Country* (Andrew), *Splash* (wedding guest), *The Rocketeer* (Monk), *The Waterboy* (Paco), and *Solo: A Star Wars Story* (Ralakili). On Disney Channel, he made a guest appearance on *Just Roll With It* (Adrian Rose). He voiced Roo in *Winnie the Pooh and the Honey Tree* and *Winnie the Pooh and the Blustery Day*, and Baby Elephant in *The Jungle Book*.

Howard, Ron Actor; appeared in *The Wild Country* (Virgil), and on TV in *Smoke* (Chris) and in the title role in *A Boy Called Nuthin'*, returning years later to direct the first Touchstone film, *Splash*. He later directed *Solo: A Star Wars Story* and exec. produced *Willow* for Disney+. Also provided the voice of Mike in the 1969 Disneyland Records album *The Story and Song from The Haunted Mansion*.

Howard Johnson's Hotel in Lake Buena Vista at Walt Disney World; opened in Feb. 1973. Became Courtyard by Marriott in 1995.

Howl's Moving Castle Animated film directed by Hayao Miyazaki and distributed in the U.S. by Disney. Sophie Hatter, an 18-year-old girl, seems doomed to the life of a hatmaker, but when she is cursed by the Witch of the Waste with the body of a 90-year-old woman, she goes to the moving castle of the wizard Howl, who is supposed to have eaten the souls of young girls. But Howl himself has been cursed by the Witch and is looking for the love of a young girl to help him break the curse. Sophie befriends Calcifer, the fire demon, who is under contract to Howl, and she helps him break the contract so Calcifer can help her return to her original shape. Limited release on Jun. 10, 2005, in New York City, Los Angeles, San Francisco, and other selected cities; general release on Jun. 17, 2005. Original release in Japan on Nov. 20, 2004, after a showing in Sep. at the Venice Film Festival. U.S. production directed by Pete Docter and Rick Dempsey. Voices include Jean Simmons (Grandma Sophie), Christian Bale (Howl), Lauren Bacall (Witch of the Waste), Blythe Danner (Madame Suliman), Emily Mortimer (Young Sophie), Josh Hutcherson (Markl), Billy Crystal (Calcifer). 119 min. Based on the book by Diana Wynne Jones. Released on DVD in 2006.

Hudgens, Vanessa Actress; appeared on Disney Channel in the *High School Musical* films (Gabriella Montez) and *The Suite Life of Zack & Cody* (Corrie).

Hudson, Ernie Actor; appeared in *The Hand That Rocks the Cradle* (Solomon) and *Mr. Magoo* (Agent Gus Anders), and on TV in *10–8* (John Henry Barnes) and *Desperate Housewives* (Detective Ridley), with guest appearances in *Criminal Minds* (Lt. Al Garner), *Grey's Anatomy* (Dr. Brad McDougall), *Scandal* (Commander Randolph Boles), and *Once Upon a Time* (King Poseidon). He voiced Pedro in the Beverly Hills Chihuahua films and Buddy in *Puppy Dog Pals*.

Hudson, Jennifer Discovered singing on the Disney Cruise Line, she later starred on *American Idol* and launched a recording and film career. She was named the godmother of the *Disney Dream*, christening the ship at Florida's Port Canaveral. Later appeared on ABC in *The Disney Family Singalong: Volume II*. She voiced Mane in *Marvel's Moon Girl and Devil Dinosaur*.

Hudson River Harvest New York-style food counter in American Waterfront at Tokyo DisneySea; opened Apr. 15, 2016.

Huemer, Dick (1898–1979) Animation story director and comic strip artist; he joined Disney in 1933 as an animator. In 1938–1939, he directed *The Whalers* and *Goofy and Wilbur*. He was story director on *Fantasia* and worked on story on *Dumbo*, *Saludos Amigos*, *Make Mine Music*, *Alice in Wonderland*, and a variety of other projects. He left in 1948 but returned in 1951 to work in story and TV. From 1955 until his retirement in 1973, he wrote the True-Life Adventure newspaper panel for the comic strip department. He was named a Disney Legend in 2007.

Huey One of Donald Duck's 3 nephews; originally voiced by Clarence Nash. Beginning with the *DuckTales* TV series, the nephews were voiced by Russi Taylor and given unique colors to wear (red for Huey). Voiced by Danny Pudi for the new *DuckTales* (2017).

Huey, Dewey, and Louie Donald's three mischievous nephews first appeared in the Donald Duck Sunday comic page Oct. 17, 1937, later making their film debut in *Donald's Nephews*. Originally there was no way to tell the nephews apart, because the colors on their costumes were used interchangeably. Because the stories for the *DuckTales* TV series were more complicated than they were for the short Donald Duck cartoons, it was deemed necessary to distinguish between the 3 nephews. So, Huey was dressed in red, Dewey in blue, and Louie in green. You can remember this by noting that the brightest *hue* of the 3 is red (Huey), the color of water, *dew*, is blue (Dewey), and that *leaves* Louie, and leaves are green.

Huey, Dewey and Louie's Good Time Café Sandwich and snack counter in Toontown at Tokyo Disneyland; opened Apr. 15, 1996.

Huffman, Felicity Actress; appeared in *Raising Helen* (Lindsay Davis), and on TV in *Sports Night* (Dana Whitaker), *Desperate Housewives* (Lynette Scavo), and *American Crime* (Barbara Hanlon). She voiced Dr. Betty Director in *Kim Possible*. Received an Emmy Award for Lead Actress in a Comedy Series (*Desperate Housewives*) in 2005.

Huge (TV) Drama series on ABC Family; debuted Jun. 28, 2010, and ended Aug. 30, 2010. A group of teens from different backgrounds attend Camp Victory, a weight-loss camp, as they embark on their individual journeys of self-discovery. The campers, who include opinionated nonconformist Willamina, deal with issues such as self-esteem, friendship, rivalry, romance, and body image. Stars Nikki Blonsky (Willamina), Hayley Hasselhoff (Amber), Ashley Holiday (Chloe), Harvey Guillen (Alistair), Ari Stidham (Ian), Raven Goodwin (Becca), Gina Torres (Dr. Dorothy Rand), Zander Eckhouse (George). From Alloy Entertainment.

Hughes, Barnard (1915–2006) Actor; appeared in *Tron* (Dr. Walter Gibbs, Dumont) and *Sister Act 2: Back in the Habit* (Father Maurice), and on TV in *Blossom* (Buzz Richman).

Hughes, Linda Mouseketeer from the 1950s *Mickey Mouse Club* TV show.

Hulce, Tom Actor; provided the acting and singing voice of Quasimodo in *The Hunchback of Notre Dame* and other appearances of the character.

Hull High (TV) Musical comedy/drama TV series on NBC; aired Sep. 23–Dec. 30, 1990. There were previews on Aug. 20 and Sep. 15, 1990. The series took an irreverent look at the daily lives of students and teachers at a Southern California high school as they dealt with themselves and each other. Musi-

cal production numbers served to underscore the conflicts and emotions of each show. Stars Will Lyman (John Deerborn), Nancy Valen (Donna Breedlove), George Martin (Mr. Dobosh), Harold Pruett (Cody Rome), Mark Ballou (Mark), Marty Belafsky (Louis Plumb), Marshall Bell (Jim Fancher), Kristin Dattilo (D. J.), Cheryl Pollack (Camilla). The musical numbers were choreographed by Kenny Ortega.

Hulu On Apr. 30, 2009, Disney announced that it was becoming an equity partner (with NBC Universal, News Corp., and Providence Equity Partners) in Hulu, a purveyor of online streaming video, with Disney making a cash investment and providing films and TV programs to the service. ABC series were made available on Hulu beginning Jul. 6, 2009, as the deal was completed. With the acquisition of 21st Century Fox in 2019, Disney's ownership increased to a majority 60% stake; in May 2019, Disney increased its ownership interest to 67%. Through a deal with Comcast, announced May 14, 2019, Disney gained full operational control of Hulu; in exchange, Comcast agreed to sell its stake to Disney within 5 years. Hulu programming is oriented toward general entertainment with more mature themes.

Human Body, The (film) Educational film produced under the auspices of the Coordinator of Inter-American Affairs tells the function of body muscles, bones, food digestion, blood vessels, the heart, and brain and how they react properly to make healthy bodies with proper food and fresh air. Delivered Aug. 13, 1945.

Humphrey Hapless grizzly bear who appeared in 7 theatrical cartoons, beginning with *Hold That Pose* (1950).

Humphrey's Service & Supply Shop in Grizzly Peak Airfield at Disney California Adventure; opened May 15, 2015, taking the place of Fly 'n' Buy. Themed to a small-town gas station, it is named for Humphrey the Bear.

Humunga Kowabunga Three side-by-side, enclosed waterslides in Typhoon Lagoon at Walt Disney World; opened Jun. 1, 1989. At 214 feet, they debuted as the park's fastest and longest waterslides, plummeting riders down Mount Mayday at a 60-degree angle.

Hunchback of Notre Dame, The (film) The tale

of Quasimodo, the lonely outsider who longs to be out in the world beyond his bell tower in the Cathedral of Notre Dame in Paris. Defying the orders of his evil surrogate father, Minister of Justice Frollo, the frightened hunchback journeys into the streets of medieval Paris, where he meets and falls in love with a beautiful gypsy girl named Esmeralda. He also befriends Phoebus, Captain of the Guard. Although heartbroken when he discovers Phoebus and Esmeralda's love for each other, Quasimodo ultimately risks everything to bring them together. Quasimodo's selfless love overcomes both his heartache and Frollo's obsessive hatred of Esmeralda. Along the way, Quasimodo finds support and friendship from the cathedral's trio of comic gargoyles: Victor, Hugo, and Laverne. Directed by Kirk Wise and Gary Trousdale. Released Jun. 21, 1996. With the voices of Tom Hulce (Quasimodo), Demi Moore (Esmeralda), Kevin Kline (Phoebus), Tony Jay (Frollo), Paul Kandel (Clopin), Charles Kimbrough (Victor), Jason Alexander (Hugo), Mary Wickes (Laverne), David Ogden Stiers (Archdeacon). After the passing of Mary Wickes, Jane Withers completed the role of Laverne. 91 min. Based on the epic Victor Hugo novel, first published in 1831. Songs by Alan Menken and Stephen Schwartz, including "The Bells of Notre Dame," "Out There," and "God Help the Outcasts." Nominated for an Academy Award for Original Musical Score. The film had a premiere on Jun. 19 at the Superdome in New Orleans, utilizing 6 enormous screens and preceded by a parade through the French Quarter. The song "Someday" was sung over the credits by the group All-4-One, but the European version replaced them with the British band Eternal.

Hunchback of Notre Dame, The This stage musical version of the story had its world premiere as *Der Glöckner Von Notre Dame* on Jun. 5, 1999, at the Stella Musical Theater at Potsdamer Platz in Berlin and closed Jun. 16, 2002. Composers Alan Menken and Stephen Schwartz wrote 9 new songs for this version and adapted their music from the film as well. A new U.S. version played at the La Jolla Playhouse in California from Nov. 9–Dec. 14, 2014 (after previews beginning Oct. 26), and later played at the Paper Mill Playhouse in Millburn, New Jersey (Mar. 15–Apr. 5, 2015), but it did not transfer to Broadway.

Hunchback of Notre Dame—A Musical Adventure Live Backstage Theater stage show in Disney-MGM Studios at Walt Disney World, replacing

The Spirit of Pocahontas; ran Jun. 21, 1996–Sep. 28, 2002.

Hunchback of Notre Dame Festival of Fools, The A 25-min. French comedic troupe theater-in-the-round experience in Disneyland, in the area formerly known as Big Thunder Ranch; ran Jun. 21, 1996–Apr. 19, 1998.

Hunchback of Notre Dame II, The (film) Direct-to-video release Mar. 19, 2002. Directed by Bradley Raymond. 7 years have passed, and Quasimodo is now accepted by his fellow Parisians, especially his friends, Esmeralda and Phoebus, who have married and have a son, Zephyr. A greedy circus master, Sarousch, plots to steal a treasured bell from the bell tower, and coerces his beautiful assistant, Madellaine, to lure Quasimodo away. However, Madellaine finds she cares for Quasimodo and tries to foil the plot. When the bell is stolen anyway, Quasi blames Madellaine, but eventually realizes she can be trusted to help catch the evil Sarousch. The voice cast includes the stars from the original film, along with Jennifer Love Hewitt (Madellaine), Michael McKean (Sarousch), and Haley Joel Osment (Zephyr). Jane Withers, who finished the role of Laverne after the passing of Mary Wickes, returns.

Hundred Acre Goods Fantasyland shop in the Magic Kingdom at Walt Disney World; opened Nov. 15, 2010, replacing Pooh's Thotful Shop [sic], selling Winnie the Pooh merchandise. Also opened in Fantasyland in Shanghai Disneyland Jun. 16, 2016.

Hundred and One Dalmatians SEE ONE HUNDRED AND ONE DALMATIANS.

Hundred-Foot Journey, The (film) Displaced from their native India, the Kadam family settles in the quaint village of Saint-Antonin-Noble-Val in the south of France. Son Hassan, an excellent chef, decides to open an Indian restaurant, the Maison Mumbai, only to run afoul of Madame Mallory, chef proprietress of the nearby Le Saule Pleurer, a highly rated, classical French restaurant. Her initial protests turn into an all-out war between the 2 establishments, but Hassan's passion for French haute cuisine and for Mme Mallory's enchanting sous chef, Marguerite, wins out and the two cultures come together as Madame Mallory recognizes her rival's undeniable brilliance for preparing masterful meals. Directed by Lasse Hallström. A

DreamWorks film, released by Touchstone Aug. 8, 2014. Stars Helen Mirren (Madame Mallory), Manish Dayal (Hassan Kadam), Om Puri (Papa), Charlotte Le Bon (Marguerite). 122 min. Filmed in wide-screen. Based on the novel by Richard C. Morais.

Hungry Bear Restaurant Opened in Bear Country at Disneyland in 1972. Originally known as Golden Bear Lodge. Set among the forest trees on the shore of the Rivers of America, the restaurant's terrace offers picturesque views of the rivercraft sailing by. Also in Westernland in Tokyo Disneyland; opened Apr. 15, 1983.

Hungry Hoboes (film) Oswald the Lucky Rabbit cartoon; released May 14, 1928. Oswald and a fellow hobo hitch a ride on a freight train loaded with livestock. To serve as a cooking surface, Oswald is dragged along the track until his pants catch fire. Later, the pair escapes a policeman by jumping another freight.

Hunnicutt, Arthur (1911–1979) Actor; appeared in *A Tiger Walks* (Lewis), *The Adventures of Bullwhip Griffin* (referee), and *The Million Dollar Duck* (Mr. Purdham), and on TV in *Elfego Baca*, *The Swamp Fox*, and *Kilroy*.

Hunny Pot Spin Fantasyland attraction in Shanghai Disneyland; opened Jun. 16, 2016. Similar to the Mad Tea Party in Disneyland, guests control the direction and speed of 1 of 18 giant spinning honey jar vehicles.

Hunt, Bonnie Actress; provided the voice of Rosie in *A Bug's Life*, Flint in *Monsters, Inc.* and *Monsters at Work*, Sally in the Cars films, Dolly in the Toy Story films, Mrs. Graves in *Monsters University*, Aunt Tilly in *Sofia the First*, and Mrs. Bonnie Hopps in *Zootopia*. She directed and starred in her own TV series, *Life with Bonnie* (Bonnie Molloy).

Hunt, Linda Actress; she voiced Grandmother Willow in *Pocahontas* and Lady Proxima in *Solo: A Star Wars Story*.

Hunter, Holly Actress; appeared in *Woman Wanted* (Emma), *O Brother, Where Art Thou?* (Penny), and *Moonlight Mile* (Mona Camp), and provided the voice of Helen Parr/Elastigirl in *The Incredibles* and *Incredibles 2*.

Hunter, Jeffrey (1926–1969) Actor; appeared in

The Great Locomotive Chase (William A. Fuller), and on TV in *Behind the Scenes with Fess Parker*.

Hunter, Tab (1931–2018) Actor; appeared on TV in *Hacksaw* (Tim Andrews).

Hunter and the Rock Star, The Alternate title of *Sultan and the Rock Star*.

Hunter's Grill Hunting lodge–style buffet dining in Disney Sequoia Lodge at Disneyland Paris; opened May 27, 1992. International fare is served.

Hunting Instinct, The (TV) Show aired Oct. 22, 1961. Directed by Wolfgang Reitherman. Prof. Von Drake, with his assistant, Herman (Bootle Beetle), teaches about hunting utilizing a series of cartoons.

Huntington, Sam Actor; appeared in *Jungle 2 Jungle* (Mimi-Siku), and on TV in *Cavemen* (Andy) and *A Million Little Things* (Tom).

Hurricane, The (film) Co-production between Buena Vista International and Beacon Pictures. A true story of an innocent man's 20-year fight for justice. Originally shown Sep. 17, 1999, at the Toronto Film Festival. General U.S. release Jan. 14, 2000. Directed by Norman Jewison. Stars Denzel Washington (Rubin "Hurricane" Carter), Vicellous Reon Shannon (Lesra), Deborah Kara Unger (Lisa), Liev Schreiber (Sam), John Hannah (Terry). 145 min. Universal distributed in the U.S., with Buena Vista International handling international distribution.

Hurricane Hannah (TV) Show aired Dec. 16, 1962. The story of a hurricane from its birth, told with the cooperation of the U.S. Weather Bureau National Hurricane Center in Miami. It is spotted first as an unusual cloud formation by a weather satellite, then the meteorologists follow its progress as it grows to a full-blown hurricane and threatens Galveston, Texas. Stars (as themselves) Gordon E. Dunn, Cmdr. Joshua Langfur, Lt. John Lincoln. Narrated by Robert P. Anderson.

Hurricanes A disc jockey spun Top 40 hits in this club at Disney Village at Disneyland Paris; open Apr. 12, 1992–Mar. 14, 2010.

Hurt, John (1940–2017) Actor; appeared in *Night Crossing* (Peter Strelzyk) and provided the voices of The Horned King in *The Black Cauldron* and

Felix in *Valiant*. He narrated *The Tigger Movie*.

Hurt, William (1950–2022) Actor; appeared in *The Doctor* (Jack), *Tuck Everlasting* (Angus Tuck), *The Village* (Edward Walker), and as Thaddeus Ross in *Captain America: Civil War* and later Marvel Studios productions.

Hurter, Albert (1883–1942) Sketch artist; joined Disney in 1931. He was given the freedom to come up with ideas, and he made distinctive contributions to many Disney films from *Three Little Pigs* to *Snow White and the Seven Dwarfs*. In 1953, Walt Disney wrote about him, "That impenetrable mind of his was never easily figured out, but he was a most lovable character when you got to know him. His imagination was rare and unique." *He Drew as He Pleased*, a book featuring a selection of his drawings, was published in 1948.

Hussein, King of Jordan (1935–1999) He visited Disneyland with Walt Disney in Apr. 1959 and again with his wife in Nov. 1981.

Huston, Anjelica Actress; appeared in *The Royal Tenenbaums* (Etheline Tenenbaum), *When in Rome* (Celeste), and *The Life Aquatic with Steve Zissou* (Eleanor Zissou), and in the Disney parks as the Supreme Leader in *Captain EO*. She provided the voice of Queen Clarion in the Tinker Bell films.

Hutton, Timothy Actor; appeared in *Playing God* (Raymond Blossom), and on TV in *Sultan and the Rock Star* (Paul Winters), *American Crime* (Russ Skokie), and *How to Get Away with Murder* (Emmett Crawford).

Huxley, Aldous (1894–1963) Prominent author; he was retained by Walt in 1945 to write a film treatment of *Alice in Wonderland*.

Hyacinth Hippo Hippo dancer in "The Dance of the Hours" segment of *Fantasia*.

Hyperion Disney publishing company; its first book, *Amazing Grace*, was published Sep. 26, 1991. Hyperion's catalog has been quite varied, with adult fiction, biographies, cookbooks, travel guides, and sports titles, as well as a number of Disney-themed publications. In 1999, Disney Editions took over as the imprint of the Disney-themed adult books. Hyperion's adult trade list was purchased by Hachette Book Group in Jul. 2013. Titles tied to Disney/ABC and ABC Family (now Freeform) were retained by Disney and published under Disney Book Group's Kingswell and Kingswell Teen imprints.

Hyperion Lounge Tea, cocktails, and a breakfast buffet served in the Disney Ambassador Hotel at Tokyo Disney Resort; opened Jul. 7, 2000.

Hyperion Studio The Disney brothers moved their Studio from the original Kingswell Avenue location to 2719 Hyperion in Los Angeles in Jan. 1926 and named it The Walt Disney Studio. Over the years, a number of buildings were constructed to house Walt Disney's growing staff. It was at the Hyperion Studio that Mickey Mouse was born and *Snow White and the Seven Dwarfs* was produced. But, with the success of *Snow White*, the Disneys needed more space to increase production, and none was available at that location. So they searched for a new site, which they found in Burbank. They moved from Hyperion to Burbank beginning in Dec. 1939; the move was completed on May 6, 1940. A few of the Hyperion buildings had been moved to Burbank, but the remainder were sold, and 26 years later they were razed for a supermarket.

Hyperion Theater A 2,000-seat theater in Hollywood Land in Disney California Adventure. Inspired by the great movie palaces of the past, the theater features the latest in sound, lighting, and staging technology. Opened Feb. 8, 2001, with the park, with its first show being a Broadway-style compilation of Disney songs entitled *Steps in Time*. This show was followed on Nov. 22, 2001, by *The Power of Blast!*; on Dec. 9, 2002, by *Aladdin: A Musical Spectacular*; and on May 27, 2016, by *Frozen—Live at the Hyperion*. A new one-act production, *Rogers: The Musical*, is scheduled to begin a limited run summer 2023. There is also a Hyperion Theater at Disney's Hollywood Studios (a new name for the SuperStar Television Theater in Echo Lake as of 2015).

1. *Inside Out* (film) 2. It's a Small World 3. *I See the Light* 4. Incredicoaster 5. *It's Tough to Be a Bird* (film)
6. *Imagineering Story, The* (TV) 7. Iwerks, Ub 8. *In the Bag* (film) 9. *Island at the Top of the World, The* (film)
10. *Incredible Journey, The* (film) 11. If You Had Wings

I Am Groot (TV) Original short-form series on Disney+; digitally released Aug. 10, 2022. After the events of *Guardians of the Galaxy* (2014), Baby Groot is finally ready to try taking his first steps out of his pot—only to learn you have to walk before you can run. Voices include Vin Diesel (Baby Groot), Bradley Cooper (Rocket). From Marvel Studios.

I Am Number Four (film) Extraordinary teen John Smith is a fugitive on the run from ruthless and powerful otherworldly enemies sent to destroy him. Changing his identity, moving from town to town with his guardian, Henri, John is always the new kid with no ties to his past. In the small Ohio town he now calls home, John encounters unexpected, life-changing events—his first love, powerful new abilities, and a connection to the others who share his incredible destiny. This is the first DreamWorks motion picture distributed by Disney under a deal announced in 2009. Released in the U.S. Feb. 18, 2011, after an initial release the previous day in Argentina, Hungary, and Israel. Directed by D. J. Caruso. Stars Alex Pettyfer (John), Timothy Olyphant (Henri), Teresa Palmer (Number 6), Dianna Agron (Sarah), Callan McAuliffe (Sam). 110 min. Released also in an IMAX version. Based on the science fiction novel for young adults by Jobie Hughes and James Frey writing as Pittacus Lore.

I Can't Let You Throw Yourself Away Song from *Toy Story 4*; written/performed by Randy Newman. Nominated for an Academy Award.

I Captured the King of the Leprechauns (TV) Show aired May 29, 1959. Directed by Robert Stevenson, Harry Keller. A behind-the-scenes look at the filming of *Darby O'Gill and the Little People*, starring Pat O'Brien and Walt Disney, who really proves himself an actor in this show. He learns about Irish traditions and customs from O'Brien, then heads to Ireland where he meets King Brian of the Leprechauns and Darby O'Gill. He loves their stories so much he invites them back to California to star in his movie.

I Didn't Do It (TV) Comedy series on Disney Channel; premiered Jan. 17, 2014. Fraternal twin sister and brother Lindy and Logan, along with their 3 best friends—Jasmine, Garrett, and Delia—take on their freshman year of high school, with one outrageous adventure after another. Stars Olivia Holt (Lindy Watson), Austin North (Logan Watson), Piper Curda (Jasmine), Peyton Clark (Garrett), Sarah Gilman (Delia Delfino). From It's a Laugh Productions.

I Don't Want to Miss a Thing Song from *Armageddon*; written by Diane Warren and performed by Aerosmith. Nominated for an Academy Award.

I Just Can't Wait to Be King Song from *The Lion King*; written by Elton John and Tim Rice.

I Love Trouble (film) Sabrina Peterson, a cub reporter on a Chicago newspaper, has a resourcefulness and quick wit matched only by her competitive spirit, which spells trouble for seasoned columnist-turned-novelist Peter Brackett, who works for a rival paper. They try to outwit and outscoop each other when they are both sent to cover a train wreck, where they unearth evidence of corruption and murder. Running into each other everywhere they turn, they nearly get themselves killed scrambling for the ultimate front-page story. Along the way, they gain new respect, and love, for each other. Released Jun. 29, 1994. Directed by Charles Shyer. A Touchstone film, in association with Caravan Pictures. 123 min. Stars Julia Roberts (Sabrina Peterson), Nick Nolte (Peter Brackett), Saul Rubinek (Sam Smotherman), Robert Loggia (Matt Greenfield), James Rebhorn (The Thin Man), Olympia Dukakis (Jeannie), Marsha Mason (Sen. Gayle Robbins), Charles Martin Smith (Rick Medwick). Filmed in Wisconsin, Chicago, Las Vegas, and Los Angeles.

i Santi Fine leather goods in Italy at EPCOT Center; open Oct. 1, 1982–ca. 1985. It was replaced by La Bottega Italiana.

I See the Light Song from *Tangled*; written by Glenn Slater and Alan Menken. Nominated for an Academy Award.

I 2 I Song from *A Goofy Movie*; written by Patrick DeRemer and Roy Freeland, and performed by Tevin Campbell.

I Wan'na Be Like You Song from *The Jungle Book*; written by Richard M. and Robert B. Sherman, and performed by Louis Prima and his band, Sam Butera and The Witnesses.

Iago Jafar's loudmouthed parrot henchman in *Aladdin*; voiced by Gilbert Gottfried.

Ian Lightfoot Introverted teenage elf in *Onward*; voiced by Tom Holland.

Ice Age Adventures of Buck Wild, The (film) A Disney+ original animated film from Bardel Entertainment; digitally released Jan. 28, 2022. The thrill-seeking possum brothers Crash and Eddie are desperate for some distance from their older sister, Ellie, and set out to find a place of their own, but quickly find themselves trapped in the Lost World, a massive underground cave. They are rescued by their one-eyed pal, the adventure-loving, dinosaur-hunting weasel Buck Wild, and together, with the help of some new friends, embark on a mission to save the Lost World from dinosaur domination. Directed by John C. Donkin. Voices include Simon Pegg (Buck), Utkarsh Ambudkar (Orson), Justina Machado (Zee), Vincent Tong (Crash), Aaron Harris (Eddie). 80 min. Disney acquired the Ice Age movie franchise, which began in 2002, as part of its purchase of 21st Century Fox in 2019.

Ice Age: Scrat Tales (TV) Animated short-form series on Disney+; digitally released Apr. 13, 2022. Scrat, the hapless saber-toothed squirrel of the Ice Age adventures, experiences the ups and downs of fatherhood, as he and the adorable, mischievous Baby Scrat alternately bond with each other and battle for ownership of the highly treasured Acorn. Voices include Chris Wedges (Scrat), Karl Wahlgren (Baby Scrat). From Blue Sky Studios.

Ice Capades SEE WORLD ON ICE.

Ice Cream Company, The Kiosk on Main Street, U.S.A. in Disneyland Paris; opened Apr. 12, 1992. SEE ALSO GIBSON GIRL ICE CREAM PARLOUR, THE.

Ice Cream Fantasy Fantasyland treat stand in Tokyo Disneyland; open Apr. 15, 1983–Mar. 1984. It became Alpine Haus.

Ice Princess (film) Casey Carlyle, a brainy bookworm, gives up a life devoted to schoolwork for a thrilling new world of ice-skating. After deciding to do a report on the physics of figure skating, she gets to meet the elite skaters at her local rink. It turns out that Casey's smarts have helped her become a skating prodigy. She gets a chance to train with champion-in-the-making Gen Harwood and her famously tough coach and mother, Tina, and soon sets off on a fun, comedic, and life-changing adventure as she prepares for the big championship. At the same time, she gets her first taste of romance as she falls for Gen's teenage brother, Teddy, the rink's Zamboni driver. Released Mar. 18, 2005. Directed by Tim Fywell. Stars Michelle Trachtenberg (Casey Carlyle), Hayden Panettiere (Gen Harwood), Trevor Blumas (Teddy Harwood), Joan Cusack (Joan Carlyle), Kim Cattrall (Tina Harwood). Michelle Kwan and Brian Boitano have cameo roles. 98 min.

Ice shows SEE WORLD ON ICE.

Ice Station Cool SEE CLUB COOL.

Ichabod Crane Gangly schoolmaster hero in *The Adventures of Ichabod and Mr. Toad.*

Ida, the Offbeat Eagle (TV) Show aired Jan. 10, 1965. In Idaho's Snake River Valley, a hermit nurses an injured eagle back to life, and the grateful eagle does not forget this. Eventually she is called upon to save the hermit. Stars Clifton E. Carver.

Idina Menzel: Which Way to the Stage? (TV) Original documentary film on Disney+; digitally released Dec. 9, 2022. An in-depth look at the Tony Award–winning actress and singer as she juggles the challenges of being a working mom with a grueling travel schedule, all while preparing to realize her dream: to perform a concert at Madison Square Garden in her hometown of New York City. Directed by Anne McCabe. 94 min. From Ideal Partners.

If I Didn't Have You Song from *Monsters, Inc.*; written by Randy Newman and performed by Billy Crystal and John Goodman. It won the Oscar as Best Original Song for 2001.

If I'm Lyin' . . . I'm Dyin' (A Program About Smoking) (film) Educational film; released in Nov. 1990. 17 min. Teens learn myths about smoking, develop resistance skills, and discover the effects of smoking on the body.

If Not for You (TV) Half-hour series on CBS; aired Sep. 18–Oct. 9, 1995. Jessie Kent and Craig Schaeffer fall in love, but they happen to be engaged to other people. The series follows the trials and tribulations of their attempts to extricate themselves from their present relationships. Stars Elizabeth McGovern (Jessie), Hank Azaria (Craig), Debra Jo Rupp (Eileen), Jim Turner (Cal), Reno Wilson (Bobby).

If the Fergi Fits, Wear It (film) Educational film teaching free-enterprise principles, produced by Dave Bell; released in Sep. 1975. Young people attempt to run a T-shirt business. SEE ALSO FERGI GOES INC., FERGI DIVERSIFIES, AND FERGI MEETS THE CHALLENGE.

If These Walls Could Sing (TV) A Disney original documentary; digitally released Dec. 16, 2022, on Disney+. Intimate interviews reveal how leading artists, producers, composers, engineers, and staff of Abbey Road Studios all found their musical language and community. Directed by Mary McCartney. 86 min. Features Paul McCartney, Ringo Starr, Elton John, Roger Waters, Liam Gallagher, John Williams, Celeste, Sheku Kanneh-Mason. From Mercury Studios and Ventureland.

If You Could Fly Tomorrowland attraction in the Magic Kingdom at Walt Disney World, from Jun. 6, 1987, until Jan. 3, 1989; sponsored by Delta Air Lines. When Delta replaced Eastern as sponsor of this attraction, they temporarily changed If You Had Wings by giving it this new name, changing the theme song, and dropping references to Eastern. As soon as they could, Disney Imagineers working with Delta came up with the totally new attraction Delta Dreamflight, which opened in 1989.

If You Had Wings Tomorrowland attraction in the Magic Kingdom at Walt Disney World; open Jun. 5, 1972–Jun. 1, 1987. Presented by Eastern Airlines. Guests were transported past travel vignettes, many of them utilizing film projection, showing areas serviced by Eastern, including Mexico City, San Juan, The Bahamas, and New Orleans. A highlight was the speed tunnel simulating the sensation of flight. The title theme song was written by Buddy Baker and X Atencio. Replaced by If You Could Fly when Delta became the sponsor, and later Delta Dreamflight.

Iger, Robert A. (Bob) He served as CEO of The Walt Disney Company from Oct. 1, 2005, to Feb. 25, 2020, and then as executive chairman until his retirement on Dec. 31, 2021. He returned to the company as CEO Nov. 20, 2022. He previously served as chairman of the board from Mar. 2012 until Dec. 2021. From 2000 to 2005, he served as president and chief operating officer of the company, following his roles as chairman of the ABC Group, president of Walt Disney International, and president of ABC.

Iglehart, James Monroe Actor; he originated the role of the Genie in the Broadway production of *Aladdin*, winning the 2014 Tony for Best Featured Actor in a Musical. Later appeared as Philoctetes in the 2019 stage version of *Hercules* and as host/Oogie Boogie in *Tim Burton's The Nightmare Before Christmas* benefit concert (2020). On TV, he appeared in *The Disney Family Singalong* and has provided several voices, including Lance Strongbow in *Tangled: The Series*, Bronzino in *Elena of Avalor*, Taurus Bulba in *DuckTales*, Oliver in *Alice's Wonderland Bakery*, Mr. Puppypaws in *SuperKitties*, and Martin in *Kiff*.

Ikspiari Shopping, dining, and entertainment area adjacent to Tokyo Disneyland; opened Jul. 7, 2000.

Il Bel Cristallo Shop in Italy at EPCOT; opened Oct. 1, 1982. Exquisite Italian wares are sold, such as Murano glass, porcelain, crystal, handbags, and clothing.

Il Paperino Ice cream shop on Mickey Avenue in Shanghai Disneyland; opened Jun. 16, 2016. The shop features Donald Duck and uses the name by which he is known in Italy.

Il Postino Stationery Greeting card and CD shop in Mediterranean Harbor at Tokyo DisneySea; opened Sep. 4, 2001.

I'll Be Home for Christmas (film) Jake Wilkinson, a self-absorbed prep school student, finds himself, just days before Christmas, stranded in the middle of the California desert, wearing a Santa suit and a white beard glued to his face. Put there by the football team who thinks he double-crossed them by not providing the correct answers on a finals test, Jake has to find a way to get to New York City by 6:00 p.m. on Christmas Eve, or risk forfeiting the vintage Porsche his father promised if his son comes home for the holidays. Hitchhiking his way east, Jake finds people looking to Santa for help and advice. Directed by Arlene Sanford. Released Nov. 13, 1998. Stars Jonathan Taylor Thomas (Jake Wilkinson), Jessica Biel (Allie), Adam La Vorgna (Eddie), Gary Cole (Harry Wilkinson), Sean O'Bryan (Max), Eve Gordon (Carolyn), Andy Lauer (Nolan Briggs). 86 min. Principal photography took place in Canmore, Alberta, Canada, and at locations around Vancouver, which doubled for several American towns Jake visits on his cross-country trek. Artificial snow had to be utilized to create a winter landscape in the spring. Additional photography took place at various locations in California, including Red Rock Canyon State Park, the desert east of Lancaster, and the campus of Mount St. Mary's College in Brentwood.

IllumiNations Fireworks, lasers, fountains, and music created a nighttime spectacular around World Showcase Lagoon in EPCOT Center, beginning Jan. 30, 1988. Superseded *Laserphonic Fantasy*. Originally, General Electric sponsored this nightly show, during which different pavilions of World Showcase were individually spotlighted, accompanied by music associated with that particular country. Lasers synchronized to music blasted from the tops of many of the buildings across the lagoon. The climactic fireworks and triumphant symphonic music provided a thrilling end to a day in EPCOT. A special new version of the show, called *IllumiNations 25*, was created for the 25th anniversary of Walt Disney World, 1996–1997. Another version, *IllumiNations 2000: Reflections of Earth*, was introduced Oct. 1, 1999, for the Walt Disney World Millennium Celebration, and it continued thereafter, dropping the "2000" from its title. General Electric ended sponsorship Dec. 31, 2002, and Siemens took over as sponsor 2005–2017. The final performance was held Sep. 30, 2019. The show was succeeded by *Epcot Forever*.

I'm Going to Disney World In 1987, following up on a suggestion by Michael Eisner's wife, Jane, Tom Elrod and his Walt Disney World marketing staff came up with the idea of asking Giants quarterback Phil Simms on camera as he ran off the field, "You've just won the Super Bowl. What are you doing next?" "I'm gonna go to Disney World!" was the reply. Thus began a popular series of TV commercials that has continued. Besides the stars of each ensuing Super Bowl, subjects have included champions from other sports such as baseball, basketball, and the Olympics, and even included Miss America in 1988 and a group of college graduates in 1990. Almost every commercial has been filmed twice: once for Walt Disney World and once for Disneyland.

I'm in the Band (TV) Original comedy series for Disney XD; previewed on Nov. 27, 2009. Teenager Tripp Campbell wins a radio contest to have dinner with his favorite rock band, Iron Weasel, and soon the rock star misfits are bunking out at Tripp's house, and he is trying to help them make an epic comeback. Stars Logan Miller (Tripp Campbell), Steve Valentine (Derek Jupiter), Greg Baker (Burger Pitt), Stephen Full (Ash), Caitlyn Taylor Love (Izzy Fuentes). From It's a Laugh Productions.

I'm Late Song from *Alice in Wonderland*; written by Bob Hilliard and Sammy Fain, and performed by Bill Thompson.

I'm No Fool as a Pedestrian (film) Cartoon made for the *Mickey Mouse Club* and later released, in Oct. 1956, in 16 mm for schools. Jiminy Cricket relates the history of reckless driving from 3000 B.C. to the present, then explains how to walk properly and with safety, showing the problems faced by the pedestrian. He also presents safety rules. An updated version was released in Sep. 1988.

I'm No Fool Having Fun (film) Cartoon made for the *Mickey Mouse Club* and later released, in Apr. 1957, in 16 mm for schools. Jiminy Cricket stresses the importance of recreation and points out safety rules to be observed when having fun.

I'm No Fool in a Car (film) Educational video released in Apr. 1992. 15 min. An alien falls to Earth when he unfastens the safety belt in his spaceship; on Earth he learns the importance of car safety.

I'm No Fool in an Emergency (film) Educational video release in Apr. 1992. 13 min. A patrol officer trying to capture an alien sustains an injury, and 2 kids calmly handle the situation by calling the paramedics.

I'm No Fool in Unsafe Places (film) Educational release in 16 mm in Jan. 1991. 14 min.; videodisc version (28 min.) released in Mar. 1993. Pinocchio becomes a real boy, but he must learn how to be safe in the real world, and not to play in refrigerators or at construction sites.

I'm No Fool in Unsafe Places II (film) Educational release on video in Apr. 1992. 15 min. Two kids try to keep an alien safe and away from hazardous sites.

I'm No Fool in Water (film) Cartoon made for the *Mickey Mouse Club* and later released, in Apr. 1957, in 16 mm for schools. Jiminy Cricket summarizes the rules for water safety and shows how one should behave while swimming. Updated version released in Sep. 1987.

I'm No Fool on Wheels (film) Educational release in 16 mm in Jan. 1991. 13 min.; videodisc version (25 min.) released in Mar. 1993. Pinocchio's friends teach him the vital procedures and equipment that need to be used for roller-skating, bicycling, and skateboarding.

I'm No Fool With a Bicycle (film) Cartoon made for the *Mickey Mouse Club* and later released, in Apr. 1956, in 16 mm for schools. A novel contest between Y-O-U and a Common Ordinary Fool serves to point out basic bicycle safety rules. Jiminy Cricket gives a brief history of this unique transportation vehicle. An updated version was released in Sep. 1988.

I'm No Fool With Electricity (film) Educational film; released in Oct. 1973. Jiminy Cricket explains the basic rules of electrical safety, with information about its discovery and the uses to which man has put it. An updated version was released in Sep. 1988.

I'm No Fool With Fire (film) Cartoon made for the *Mickey Mouse Club* and later released, in Apr. 1956, in 16 mm for schools. Jiminy Cricket shows humankind's reliance on fire through the ages and the necessity of understanding the rules pertaining to fire safety because of its potentially destructive nature. An updated version was released in Sep. 1986.

I'm No Fool With Safety at School (film) Educational release in 16 mm in Jan. 1991. 12 min.; videodisc version (28 min.) released in Mar. 1993. Jiminy Cricket and Pinocchio join elementary school students to learn about safety at school.

Image Works Hands-on area of Journey Into Imagination in EPCOT Center; opened Oct. 1, 1982, on the upstairs level of the pavilion. Guests could experience a multitude of activities in this "creative playground of the future," including the Rainbow Corridor (where neon tubes of all the colors of the rainbow surrounded you), the Stepping Tones (where you composed your own symphony by stepping on lighted spots on the floor causing various tones to sound), and Dreamfinder's School of Drama (where you starred in a movie via Chroma-key video playlets). The Image Works closed Oct. 1998 to reopen on the downstairs level of the newly renamed IMAGINATION! pavilion Oct. 1, 1999, as ImageWorks—The Kodak "What If?" Labs. Kodak ended its sponsorship in 2010. ImageWorks was also the name of a photo studio in Tomorrowland at Tokyo Disneyland; open Apr. 1997–Sep. 2014, and succeeded by Treasure Comet.

ImageMovers Digital A studio specializing in performance-capture CGI, with its first film being *Disney's A Christmas Carol* (2009). Formed in 2007 by Robert Zemeckis in conjunction with Disney. The studio closed Jan. 2011 after producing *Mars Needs Moms*.

Imaginary Mary (TV) Half-hour series on ABC; aired Mar. 29–May 30, 2017. Alice is a fiercely independent career woman whose life is turned upside down when she meets the love of her life—a divorced father with 3 kids. This triggers even more upheaval when the slightly unhinged imaginary friend she created as a child suddenly reappears to help her navigate the transition from single girl to a woman ready for a family. Stars Jenna Elfman (Alice), Stephen Schneider (Ben), Nicholas Coombe (Andy), Matreya Scarrwener (Doris), Erica Tremblay (Bunny), with Rachel Dratch as the voice of Mary. From Sony Pictures Television, Happy Madison, and ABC Studios.

IMAGINATION! SEE JOURNEY INTO IMAGINATION.

Imagination Movers (TV) Half-hour series on Playhouse Disney on Disney Channel; premiered Sep. 6, 2008. The Imagination Movers, a popular New Orleans band, introduces preschoolers to their energetic rock and roll style of music while emphasizing creative problem-solving skills. The series features the band members, Rich, Scott, Dave, and Smitty, as "everyday guy" brainstormers working hard to solve "idea emergencies" in their Idea Warehouse, a place of infinite inspiration. Stars Rich Collins, Scott Durbin, Dave Poche, and Scott "Smitty" Smith. From Zydeco Productions in association with Disney Channel.

ImagiNations Annual design competition presented by Walt Disney Imagineering; launched in 1991 to seek out the next generation of Imagineers. The top teams win a trip to Imagineering headquarters, where the students present their projects and compete for awards. The program has grown to include separate versions sponsored by Hong Kong Disneyland Resort and Shanghai Disney Resort.

Imagine at Home (TV) Streaming video series for ABC Owned Television Stations; digitally released Feb. 12, 2021. Using materials found around the house, Disney Imagineers teach viewers how to draw or craft an item inspired by a Disney park attraction.

Imagine That (TV) Half-hour comedy series on NBC about the life of a sketch comedy writer; aired Jan. 8–15, 2002. Stars Hank Azaria (Josh Miller), Jayne Brook (Wendy), Joshua Malina (Kenny), Katey Sagal (Barb). Produced by Columbia TriStar Television, Seth Kurland Productions, and Touchstone Television.

Imagineering Story, The (TV) Documentary series on Disney+; premiered digitally Nov. 12, 2019. A behind-the-scenes chronicle of the 65-year history of Walt Disney Imagineering—a place equal parts artistic studio, design center, think tank, and innovation laboratory—and the eclectic group of Imagineers who bring to life the Happiest Places on Earth. Narrated by Angela Bassett. Directed/exec. produced by Leslie Iwerks. From Iwerks & Co.

Imagineers Term used by Disney to refer to the designers, engineers, architects, technicians, and others involved in creating the Disney theme parks, resorts, cruise ships, and other entertainment experiences. It is taken from the words *imagination* and *engineers*. At first their company was known as WED Enterprises (Walt Disney's initials), but it was changed to Walt Disney Imagineering in 1986. It was Harrison "Buzz" Price who brought the word "Imagineering" to Walt Disney's attention in the 1950s. SEE WALT DISNEY IMAGINEERING.

I-Man (TV) Two-hour show, meant as a pilot for a possible series; aired Apr. 6, 1986. Directed by Corey Allen. A cab driver, Jeffrey Wilder, is exposed to a mysterious gas that makes him invincible; the government realizes they can use him, and he reluctantly agrees. Jeffrey needs to use his powers to battle an eccentric billionaire, who has stolen a group of experimental military lasers that the government realizes are defective and could cause an atomic explosion. Stars Scott Bakula, Ellen Bry, Joey Cramer, John Bloom, Herschel Bernardi, John Anderson.

Impeachment of a President (film) Educational film in the History Alive! series, produced by Turnley Walker; released in 1972. Thaddeus Stevens leads the attempt to impeach President Andrew Johnson in 1868.

Imperial Trading Station *Star Wars*–themed shop in Tomorrowland in Shanghai Disneyland; opened Jun. 16, 2016, offering collectibles, costumes, and other souvenirs.

Impressions de France (film) Film played in the France pavilion at EPCOT; opened Oct. 1, 1982, in the Palais du Cinema. A tour of the country's scenery is presented against a background of music by French classical composers. About 140 locations were filmed using a 200° 5-camera system, with almost 50 represented in the final presentation. In 2011 a new digital projection system enhanced the look of the original film, which was upgraded to 4K in 2020. That year, the film began playing in rotation with the new *Beauty and the Beast Sing-Along*. In 2017, Guinness World Records identified *Impressions de France* as the longest-running daily screening of a film in the same theater.

In a Clock Store Copyright title of *The Clock Store*.

In a Heartbeat (TV) Original half-hour series on Disney Channel; premiered with a 1-hour episode Aug. 26, 2000, and ended Mar. 25, 2001. Follows the adventures of a volunteer EMT squad staffed by high school students. Stars Shawn Ashmore (Tyler Connell), Reagan Pasternak (Val Lanier), Danso Gordon (Hank Beecham), Christopher Ralph (Jamie Waite), Jackie Rosenbaum (Caitie Roth),

Lauren Collins (Brooke Lanier). 21 episodes. From AAC Kids, in association with Disney Channel.

In Beaver Valley (film) SEE BEAVER VALLEY.

In Case of Emergency (TV) Half-hour comedy series on ABC; aired Jan. 3–Feb. 28, 2007. Harry, Jason, Sherman, and Kelly all went to the same high school. Several years after graduation, their lives haven't exactly turned out the way they'd planned. A series of emergencies reunite this hapless brood and they find, at the end of the day, they've got each other in case of emergency. Stars Jonathan Silverman (Harry Kennison), David Arquette (Jason Ventress), Greg Germann (Sherman Yablonsky), Kelly Hu (Kelly Lee), Lori Loughlin (Dr. Joanna Lupone), Nicholas Roget-King (Dylan). From Touchstone Television.

In Character Costume and accessory shop in Animation Courtyard at Disney's Hollywood Studios; formerly The Princess Shoppe (beginning Jun. 1996) and Under the Sea (Dec. 21, 1991–Jun. 1996).

In Dutch (film) Pluto cartoon released May 10, 1946. Directed by Charles Nichols. Pluto and Dinah fool the villagers with a false flood alarm in Holland, but when the dike does begin to leak, it is up to Pluto to get help while Dinah plugs the leak with her paw. Because of "crying wolf" before, he has a difficult time.

In Justice (TV) One-hour drama series on ABC; aired Jan. 1–Mar. 31, 2006. Every year, hundreds of innocent men and women are convicted of crimes they did not commit. The innocent have finally found a champion in a blustery but legendary litigator named David Swayne. Swayne is head of the Justice Project, a high-profile, nonprofit organization of hungry young associates who fight to liberate the falsely accused and discover the identity of those really to blame. Swayne is ego driven, but he has a partner, crackerjack investigator and ex-cop Charles Conti, to keep him honest. Stars Kyle MacLachlan (David Swayne), Jason O'Mara (Charles Conti), Constance Zimmer (Brianna), Daniel Cosgrove (Jon), Larissa Gomes (Tina). From Touchstone Television.

In Search of the Castaways (film) With good reason to believe that Captain Grant, skipper of the *Britannia*, is still alive, Lord Glenarvan, owner of the Steam Navigation Company, sets out to rescue him. Aboard his ship are Grant's daughter and son,

as well as their companion, a Frenchman named Jacques Paganel. A series of hair-raising incidents as they travel the 37th parallel, including surviving an earthquake, a flood, and an attack by a giant condor, add up to exciting adventure. In Australia, they team up with a former member of Grant's crew, Thomas Ayerton, who turns out to be a gunrunner who set Grant adrift. Eventually, in New Zealand, the children manage to outwit him and rescue Grant. From the Jules Verne story. World premiere in London on Nov. 14, 1962; U.S. release on Dec. 19, 1962. Directed by Robert Stevenson. 98 min. Stars Hayley Mills (Mary Grant), Maurice Chevalier (Prof. Paganel), George Sanders (Thomas Ayerton), Wilfred Hyde-White (Lord Glenarvan), Michael Anderson, Jr. (John Glenarvan). Young Keith Hamshere, who plays Hayley Mills's younger brother Robert, was discovered by Disney talent agents while playing the title role in the original London production of the well-known musical *Oliver!* The film contained some of the most elaborate special effects of any Disney film to that time, with the set designers building a live volcano, part of the Andes Mountains, and reproductions of the ports of Glasgow and Melbourne from the 1870s, along with a complete New Zealand Maori village. All of this was accomplished at Pinewood Studios in England. The special effects team was headed by Syd Pearson and Peter Ellenshaw. The songs, "Merci Beaucoup," "Grimpons," "Enjoy It," and "The Castaways Theme," were written by Richard M. and Robert B. Sherman. The film was rereleased theatrically in 1970 and in 1978.

In Shape with Von Drake (TV) Show aired Mar. 22, 1964. Directed by Hamilton S. Luske. Prof. Von Drake emotes about sports, utilizing a series of cartoons.

In the Army Now (film) Bones Conway is not ideal army material, but that doesn't stop him from joining up for a hitch in the reserves in order to cash in on all the great perks, including free room and board and a steady salary for doing minimal work. He manages to bluff his way through basic training but is then shocked to find his unit called up for service in the African desert. He ends up not only battling the rules and regulations, but also power-hungry authority figures and would-be world dictators. Released Aug. 12, 1994. Directed by Daniel Petrie, Jr. A Hollywood Pictures film. 92 min. Stars Pauly Shore (Bones Conway), Lori Petty (Christine Jones), David Alan Grier (Fred Ostroff), Andy Dick (Jack Kaufman), Esai Morales

(Sgt. Stern). Filmed in California and Arizona, and at Fort Sill, Oklahoma.

In the Bag (film) Special cartoon released Jul. 27, 1956. Directed by Jack Hannah. Filmed in Cinema-Scope. The Ranger enlists the park's bears to help clean up, under threat of starvation, and in desperation all the bears shove the trash in Humphrey's sector. Humphrey stuffs it down a geyser hole, and just as he is about to be rewarded with a meal, the geyser erupts, sending garbage everywhere. Features "Humphrey Hop," originally composed by George Bruns (music) and Daws Butler (lyrics) for the 1950s *Mickey Mouse Club*.

In the Footsteps of Elephant (film) Documentary chronicling the making of Disneynature's *Elephant*; digitally released Apr. 3, 2020, on Disney+. Filmmakers face extreme weather, inaccessible terrain, and close encounters with predators to shine a light on elephants and their ancient migrations. Narrated by Jeremy Sisto. Directed by Vanessa Berlowitz. 88 min. From Wildstar Films, Silverback Films, and Disneynature.

In the Land of the Desert Whales (TV) Part 2 of *Three Without Fear*.

In the Motherhood (TV) Half-hour comedy series on ABC; aired Mar. 26–Jul. 9, 2009. Three mothers try to juggle motherhood, work, and their love lives. Rosemary is a freewheeling mom who plays it fast and loose when it comes to parenting her teenaged son, Luke. Married numerous times, but currently single, Rosemary lives by her own rules. Rosemary's best friend, Jane—a recently divorced working mother of a preteen, Annie, and a baby girl, Sophie—is just trying to keep her career and home afloat. Jane's younger sister, Emily, is married to Jason and sees herself as the model stay-at-home mom for her 2 young children, Esther and Bill. Stars Cheryl Hines (Jane), Jessica St. Clair (Emily), Horatio Sanz (Horatio), RonReaco Lee (Jason), Megan Mullally (Rosemary). Based on a popular Web series of the same name. From ABC Studios.

In the Nick of Time (TV) Movie aired on NBC Dec. 16, 1991. Directed by George Miller. 2 hours. Santa Claus has only 7 days to find his replacement, or Christmas will end forever. He roams the icy streets of New York City in search of the one generous soul destined to be the next Kris Kringle. Stars Lloyd Bridges (Nick), Michael Tucker (Ben Talbot), Alison LaPlaca (Susan Roswell), Jessica

DiCicco (Aimee Misch), A Martinez (Charlie Misch), Cleavon Little (Freddy).

Inbetweener Animation term for the artist who creates the drawings in between the extremes of an action drawn by the animator, assistant animator, and breakdown artist.

Incident at Hawk's Hill (film) Educational film version of part of *The Boy Who Talked to Badgers*; released in Sep. 1979.

Inconceivable (TV) One-hour drama series on NBC; aired Sep. 23–Sep. 30, 2005. Doctors at the Family Options Fertility Clinic follow a noble quest as they help desperate couples give birth, but clinic cofounders Dr. Malcolm Bower and Rachel Lew and their staff are not above their own adventures involving deception and secrets, while they cope with superegos, missing frozen embryos, and impending malpractice suits. Stars Jonathan Cake (Dr. Malcolm Bower), Ming-Na (Rachel Lew), Joelle Carter (Nurse Patrice), Mary Catherine Garrison (Marissa), David Norona (Scott), Davin Alejandro (Angel). From Touchstone Television.

Incredible Journey, The (film) Story of the 200-mile trek across the wilds of Canada by 3 inseparable animal friends in search of their beloved owners, a family that has gone to Europe, leaving the animals with a friend. After hardship, danger, and near-fatal accidents, together with some moving encounters with friendly humans, the 2 dogs, Bodger and Luath, and the cat, Tao, complete their incredible journey, and have a joyful reunion with their owners, who have returned from their own journey and have come to believe their beloved pets to be dead. Released Oct. 30, 1963. Directed by Fletcher Markle. 80 min. Stars Emile Genest (John Longridge), John Drainie (Prof. Jim Hunter), Tommy Tweed (Hermit), Sandra Scott (Mrs. Hunter), with narration provided by Rex Allen. Based on the best seller by Sheila Burnford, the film was reissued in 1969 and remade in 1993 as *Homeward Bound: The Incredible Journey*.

Incredibles, The (film) Animated feature from Pixar Animation Studios. Bob Parr used to be one of the world's greatest superheroes, known to all as "Mr. Incredible," saving lives and fighting evil on a daily basis. But now, 15 years later, he and his wife, Helen, a former superhero in her own right, have been forced, because of a series of unfortunate accidents and frivolous lawsuits, to take on civilian identities and retreat to the suburbs to live normal lives with their 3 kids. As a clock-punching insurance claims adjuster, the only things Bob fights these days are boredom and a bulging waistline. Itching to get back into action, the side-lined superhero gets his chance when a mysterious communication summons him to the remote island of Nomanisan for a top secret assignment. When things go seriously awry, and Bob is taken prisoner by an evil genius named Syndrome, Helen and the kids fly to the rescue to help straighten things out. The whole family has to battle Syndrome and his seemingly unstoppable ominous Omnidroids. Directed by Brad Bird. Released Nov. 5, 2004. Voices include Craig T. Nelson (Bob Parr/Mr. Incredible), Holly Hunter (Helen Parr/Elastigirl), Samuel L. Jackson (Frozone), Wallace Shawn (Gilbert Huph), Jason Lee (Buddy Pine/Syndrome), Sarah Vowell (Violet), John Ratzenberger (The Underminer), Spencer Fox (Dash), Elizabeth Peña (Mirage), Brad Bird (Edna Mode). 115 min. Filmed in CinemaScope. Released with a Disney • Pixar short, *Boundin'*. *The Incredibles* won Academy Awards for Best Animated Feature and for Best Sound Editing (Randy Thom, Michael Silvers). It was also nominated for Best Original Screenplay (Brad Bird) and Best Sound Mixing (Randy Thom, Gary A. Rizzo, Doc Kane).

Incredibles 2 (film) Animated feature from Pixar Animation Studios. The Incredibles, a family of superheroes, is back. Helen leaves Bob at home with Violet and Dash to navigate the day-to-day heroics of "normal" life while she is out saving the world. It is a tough transition for everyone, made tougher by the fact that the family is still unaware of baby Jack-Jack's emerging superpowers. When a new villain hatches a brilliant and dangerous plot, the family and Frozone must find a way to work together again—which is easier said than done. Directed by Brad Bird. Released Jun. 15, 2018, also in 3-D and IMAX, after a Jun. 13 international release. Voices include Holly Hunter (Helen Parr/Elastigirl), Craig T. Nelson (Bob Parr/Mr. Incredible), Sarah Vowell (Violet Parr), Brad Bird (Edna Mode), Samuel L. Jackson (Lucius Best/Frozone), Huck Milner (Dash), John Ratzenberger (The Underminer). 118 min. More urban than the world of *The Incredibles*, *Incredibles 2* features the city of Municiberg, which provided a working-world backdrop for the Incredibles to battle crime—and increased the need for graphics and set design. In Sep. 2018, it became the first animated feature to surpass the $600 million mark at the domestic box office. Nominated for an Academy Award for Best Animated Feature (Brad Bird, John Walker, Nicole Paradis Grindle).

Incredicoaster High-speed roller coaster attraction in Pixar Pier at Disney California Adventure; opened Jun. 23, 2018, replacing California Screamin'. Guests are launched alongside the Incredibles on a mission to chase the elusive baby Jack-Jack. Character figures, lighting, music, and special effects add to the story and thrill.

Independence Lake In the 1970s, after the loss of the Mineral King project, Disney proposed another ski resort in the Sierra Nevada mountain range near Truckee, California. The land around the lake was jointly owned by the Southern Pacific Railroad and the U.S. government. Disney tried to arrange a land swap to put together a workable parcel of land, but nothing came of the project and Disney gave up thoughts of developing a ski resort.

Indian Canoes Frontierland attraction in Disneyland Paris; opened Apr. 12, 1992, and closed Oct. 1994. See Davy Crockett's Explorer Canoes (Disneyland).

Indian Summer (film) A group of adults hoping to relive childhood memories gather for a reunion at their former childhood summer camp, Tamakwa, but each comes with his own problems. Despite the group's efforts to simply relax, the rigorous camp activities, plus 2 decades of memories, trigger each of them to examine where their life choices have taken them, and to wonder if, perhaps, it is possible to come of age more than once. Released Apr. 23, 1993. Directed by Mike Bender. A Touchstone film. 98 min. Stars Alan Arkin (Unca Lou), Matt Craven (Jamie Ross), Diane Lane (Beth Warden), Bill Paxton (Jack Belston), Elizabeth Perkins (Jennifer Morton), Kevin Pollak (Brad Berman), Vincent Spano (Matthew Berman), Julie Warner (Kathy Berman), Kimberly Williams (Gwen Dougherty). Filmed at the actual Camp Tamakwa in Algonquin Provincial Park, Ontario, Canada.

Indian Trading Post Shop in Disneyland; opened in Frontierland Jul. 4, 1962, later in Bear Country (1972), and changed to The Briar Patch in 1988 with the change of the area to Critter Country.

Indian Village Frontierland attraction in Disneyland; open 1955–1971. It moved locations in 1956 and had additions in 1962. Native American dancers would put on regular shows, encouraging audience participation.

Indian War Canoes Frontierland attraction in Disneyland; ran Jul. 4, 1956–1971. Moved to Bear Country and became Davy Crockett's Explorer Canoes.

Indiana Jones and the Dial of Destiny (film) Harrison Ford returns to the role of the legendary hero archaeologist for this 5th installment of the action-adventure film series. Planned for theatrical release Jun. 30, 2023. Directed by James Mangold. Stars Harrison Ford, Phoebe Waller-Bridge, Antonio Banderas, John Rhys-Davies, Shaunette Renee Wilson, Thomas Kretschmann, Toby Jones, Boyd Holbrook, Oliver Richters, Ethann Isidore, Mads Mikkelsen. Music composed by John Williams. From Lucasfilm.

Indiana Jones Adventure Adventureland attraction in Disneyland; opened Mar. 3, 1995. Entering the mysterious Temple of the Forbidden Eye, guests queue past carvings and frescoes that tell the story of Mara, a powerful deity who promises great treasures—and vengeance to those foolish enough to gaze into its all-seeing eyes. Boarding a well-worn troop transport, they embark on what appears to be a standard archaeological tour through the temple. But there are surprises around every bend in this subterranean world—bubbling lava pits, crumbling ceilings, screaming mummies, an avalanche of creepy crawlies, and a massive rolling boulder. The attraction is a collaboration between George Lucas and Disney. For the first years of operation, visitors received a decoder card for the "Maraglyphics" found throughout the temple. The 12-passenger vehicles were a technological feat by the Imagineers, realistically simulating quick driving over rough terrain. SEE ALSO INDIANA JONES ADVENTURE: TEMPLE OF THE CRYSTAL SKULL (TOKYO DISNEYSEA).

Indiana Jones Adventure Outpost Echo Lake shop in Disney's Hollywood Studios; opened Dec. 18, 1990, along Lakeside Circle. Also opened in Adventureland in Disneyland Paris Jul. 1993, and in Disneyland Dec. 16, 1994, replacing Safari Outpost. The Disneyland shop closed in 2017 to make room for indoor seating for Bengal Barbecue.

Indiana Jones Adventure: Temple of the Crystal Skull Attraction, sponsored by Matsushita, in the Lost River Delta in Tokyo DisneySea; opened Sep. 4, 2001. Guests board well-worn jungle transports to search for the Fountain of Youth in an ancient Central American temple guarded by a supernatural and vengeful Crystal Skull, and then can view on-ride photos at Expedition Photo Archives. Similar to the original Indiana Jones Adventure in Disneyland.

Indiana Jones and the Temple of Peril Roller coaster attraction in Adventureland in Disneyland Paris; opened Jul. 30, 1993. In order to quickly add needed capacity at the park, designers selected a roller coaster attraction, then incorporated theming to make it an exciting Disney experience. From Apr. 1, 2000–Dec. 3, 2004, the direction of the roller coaster cars was reversed, so the guests rode backward.

Indiana Jones Epic Stunt Spectacular! Grand opening in Disney-MGM Studios (now Disney's Hollywood Studios) at Walt Disney World Aug. 25, 1989. Thrilling stunts and special effects are presented by a trained cast, aided by a few volunteers from the audience, on a gigantic movie set.

Infant Care (film) Educational film produced under the auspices of the Coordinator of Inter-American Affairs stresses the importance of proper prenatal care, nursing, and weaning. Delivered Jul. 31, 1945.

Inferior Decorator (film) Donald Duck cartoon released Aug. 27, 1948. Directed by Jack Hannah. Donald hangs flowered wallpaper, which fools a bee. The bee gets so irritated with Donald and the fake flowers that he calls in his swarm of bees to attack.

Infoseek Corp. On Nov. 18, 1998, Disney announced the completion of the acquisition of approximately 43% of the outstanding common stock of Infoseek Corp. Combining with a previous Disney acquisition of Starwave Corp., the new Internet entity developed, launched, and promoted a new portal service named GO Network (www.go.com). On Nov. 17, 1999, stockholders approved the acquisition of the remainder of Infoseek, which became a wholly owned subsidiary of the company. The Infoseek brand was phased out in favor of the GO Network.

Ingersoll-Waterbury Co. First licensee of Disney watches, beginning in 1933. SEE ALSO WATCHES.

Ingham, Barrie Actor; he provided the voice of Basil in *The Great Mouse Detective*.

Ink & Paint Shop Shop in Disney's Art of Animation Resort at Walt Disney World themed to the inking and painting process; opened May 31, 2012. Wall spaces resemble oversized paint jars.

Inkwell, The (film) The ritzy resort island of Martha's Vineyard is a vacation haven where the rich relax at the famous Inkwell Beach and where, in 1976, 16-year-old African American Drew Tate is about to spend a summer holiday with wealthy relatives. There he learns to combat his shyness, meet members of the opposite sex, and come of age. Released Apr. 22, 1994. Directed by Matty Rich. A Touchstone film. 112 min. Stars Larenz Tate (Drew Tate), Joe Morton (Kenny Tate), Suzzanne Douglas (Brenda Tate), Glynn Turman (Spencer Phillips). To represent the resort of Martha's Vineyard in 1976, the producers went to North Carolina, using sites in Wilmington, Fort Fisher, Rocky Point, Surf City, Southport, and Swansboro.

Inky, the Crow (TV) Show aired Dec. 7, 1969. A girl, Carol Lee, adopts a mischievous crow but has to work hard to keep it from being shot by a farmer who hates crows. Stars Deborah Bainbridge, Margo Lungreen, Willard Granger, Rowan Pease.

Inner Workings (film) Short cartoon debuted at the Annecy International Animation Film Festival Jun. 17, 2016, then released with *Moana* Nov. 23, 2016. The story of the internal struggle between a man's brain and his heart. Directed by Leo Matsuda.

Innocent Man, An (film) When 2 ruthless, on-the-take narcotics cops mistake Jimmie Rainwood's home for that of a local drug dealer, they break in and shoot him before they realize they've busted the wrong man. Jimmie is convicted of a crime he did not commit and is sent to prison where he learns to survive with the help of veteran con Virgil Cane. He is paroled, a changed man no longer trusting the system, and he vows to set the record straight and settle the score with the sleazy detectives whose lies put an innocent man behind bars for 3 years. Released Oct. 6, 1989. Directed by Peter Yates. A Touchstone film. 113 min. Stars Tom Selleck (Jimmie Rainwood), F. Murray Abraham (Virgil Cane), Laila Robins (Kate Rainwood). The filmmakers selected the Cincinnati "Old Workhouse" for the interior prison scenes, and the Nevada State Penitentiary in Carson City for the exteriors. Several hundred inmates at the latter institution were utilized as extras, though the decision was made to exclude those on death row or in solitary confinement. While they were working in the prison, all of the cast and crew were required to wear oversized fluorescent orange vests to distinguish them from the prisoners.

Innoventions Pair of technology display pavilions in the center of Future World at EPCOT; opened Jul. 1, 1994, taking the place of Communicore. A selection of America's top companies was invited to display some of their latest gizmos and emerging technologies with interactive participation by guests. The exhibits continually changed to keep the area new and cutting edge. For several years, Walt Disney Imagineering presented its own display of virtual reality prototypes. From Sep. 1999–ca. 2007, it was named Innoventions: The Road to Tomorrow. Closed Sep. 7, 2019, as part of a multi-year transformation of EPCOT. An Innoventions attraction opened in Disneyland, in the former Carousel of Progress building, Jul. 3, 1998, with grand opening ceremonies on Nov. 10. It closed Mar. 31, 2015, and was replaced by the Tomorrowland Expo Center.

Insects as Carriers of Disease (film) Educational film produced under the auspices of the Coordinator of Inter-American Affairs. Careless Charlie learns to his horror how household pests such as flies, mosquitoes, and lice carry dangerous diseases, and that cleanliness of food, body, and living conditions can prevent them. Delivered Jun. 30, 1945.

Inside Donald Duck (TV) Show aired Nov. 5, 1961. Directed by Hamilton S. Luske. Professor Von Drake tries to diagnose Donald's problems, deciding that the cause is the opposite sex. The show includes clips from a series of Donald Duck cartoons.

Inside Out (film) Animated feature from Pixar Animation Studios. Growing up can be a bumpy road, and it is no exception for Riley, who is uprooted from her Midwest life when her father gets a new job in San Francisco. Riley is guided by her emotions—Joy, Fear, Anger, Disgust, and Sadness. The emotions live in Headquarters, the control center inside Riley's mind, where they help advise her through everyday life. As Riley and her emotions struggle to adjust to a new life in San Francisco, turmoil ensues in Headquarters. Although Joy, Riley's main and most important emotion, tries to keep things positive, the emotions conflict on how best to navigate a new city, house, and school. Directed by Pete Docter and Ronnie Del Carmen. Released Jun. 19, 2015, after a May 18 showing at the Cannes Film Festival and a Jun. 17 release in Egypt, France, Morocco, and Tunisia. Voices include Diane Lane (Mom), Kyle MacLachlan (Dad), Kaitlyn Dias (Riley), Amy Poehler (Joy), Bill Hader (Fear), Lewis Black (Anger), Mindy Kaling (Disgust), Phyllis Smith (Sadness). 95 min. To understand the science behind emotions, filmmakers consulted with experts and psychologists, while imagining what our thought processes, memories, and feelings might look, act, and sound like. Simple drawings by character art director Albert Lozano inspired the design of the emotions: Joy in the shape of a star, Sadness as a teardrop, Fear as a raw nerve, Anger as a brick, and Disgust as a stalk of broccoli. The film won the Oscar for Best Animated Feature and was also nominated for Best Original Screenplay. FOR THE TV SHOW, SEE WALT DISNEY WORLD INSIDE OUT.

Inside Out Emotional Whirlwind Whimsical spinning attraction in Pixar Pier at Disney California Adventure; opened Jun. 28, 2019, on the site of the former Maliboomer. Guests board one of eight Memory Movers, which help Riley's Emotions sort through memories being collected.

Inside Outer Space (TV) Show aired Feb. 10, 1963. Directed by Hamilton S. Luske. Ludwig Von Drake takes a look at outer space, using footage from the Disney space shows of the 1950s such as *Man in Space* and *Mars and Beyond*.

Inside Pixar (TV) Documentary series on Disney+; digitally premiered Nov. 13, 2020. Personal and cinematic stories give an inside look into the people, artistry, and culture of Pixar Animation Studios.

Inside the Magic — Special Effects and Production Tour SEE BACKSTAGE STUDIO TOUR.

Insider, The (film) Jeffrey Wigand was a central witness in the lawsuits filed by Mississippi and all 49 other states against the tobacco industry, which eventually were settled for $246 billion. Wigand, former head of research and development and a corporate officer at Brown & Williamson, was a top scientist, the ultimate insider. No one like him had ever gone public before. Meanwhile, Lowell Bergman, an investigative reporter and *60 Minutes* producer, arranged a legal defense team for Wigand and taped a famous Mike Wallace interview that contained devastating testimony. However, before the most newsworthy *60 Minutes* segment in years could air, Bergman would lose to a CBS corporate

decision to kill it and experience breakdown and bitter divisions within the staff of *60 Minutes*. Wigand would find himself sued, targeted in a national smear campaign, get divorced, and facing possible incarceration. Wigand, having wagered so much and now unable to deliver his testimony to the American people, and Bergman, who was trying to defeat the smear campaign and force CBS to air the interview, were 2 ordinary people in extraordinary circumstances. Released Nov. 5, 1999. A Touchstone film. Directed by Michael Mann. Stars Al Pacino (Lowell Bergman), Russell Crowe (Jeffrey Wigand), Christopher Plummer (Mike Wallace), Diane Venora (Liane Vigand), Philip Baker Hall (Don Hewitt), Lindsay Crouse (Sharon Tiller), Debi Mazar (Debbie De Luca). Based on the *Vanity Fair* article "The Man Who Knew Too Much," by Marie Brenner. 158 min. Filmed in CinemaScope. While *The Insider* is not a documentary, Mississippi's aggressive attorney general, Michael Moore, and investigator Jack Palladino do play themselves, lending a sense of reality to the drama. Filming locations ranged from Louisville to San Francisco, to Pascagoula, Mississippi, to New York City, and to The Bahamas. The film received 7 Academy Award nominations, including Best Picture and Best Actor (Russell Crowe).

Insignias During World War II, Walt Disney was asked by various military units to design insignias that they could put on their planes, jackets, and ships. Over 1,200 of these insignias were produced, many containing Disney characters, but occasionally, as with the Flying Tigers, the units already had a character in mind. Donald Duck was perhaps the most-requested character, appearing on several hundred insignias. Mickey Mouse, being deemed a less warlike figure, was used only rarely, and then for such units as signal corps and chaplains corps. The drawings were prepared by several Disney artists, led by Hank Porter and Roy Williams. Walt provided these insignias to the units without charge as part of his donation to the war effort. Other animation studios in Hollywood were also called upon for insignias, and during the war, many of the Disney and non-Disney insignias were published on poster stamps for affixing in albums supplied by local newspapers.

Inspector Gadget (film) A mild-mannered security officer, John Brown, is blown to pieces by a nefarious villain, but is then rebuilt as a resourceful detective by the beautiful scientist Brenda Bradford. Fourteen thousand handy devices are stored all over his body, making Inspector Gadget a virtual human Swiss Army knife, and helping inspire him to become the world's top detective. When confronting the insanely wealthy and evil Sanford Scolex, the often clueless Gadget must use all his common sense and robotic parts to save not only his good name but the world as well. A Walt Disney Picture in association with Caravan Pictures. Directed by David Kellogg. Released Jul. 23, 1999. Stars Matthew Broderick (John Brown/Inspector Gadget), Rupert Everett (Sanford Scolex), Joely Fisher (Brenda Bradford), Michelle Trachtenberg (Penny). 78 min. Based on the animated series produced by DIC Entertainment.

Inspector Gadget 2 (film) Direct-to-video release Mar. 11, 2003; sequel to the 1999 film. In idyllic Riverton, the evildoer Dr. Claw escapes from jail and plots to steal trillions of dollars-worth of gold. After half-human, half-robot Inspector Gadget is taken off the case because of glitches in his machinery, he is replaced by the gorgeous and superior G2. Directed by Alex Zamm. Stars French Stewart (Inspector Gadget), Elaine Hendrix (G2), Tony Martin (Dr. Claw), Bruce Spence (Baxter), Caitlin Wachs (Penny), Mark Mitchell (Chief Quimby), Sigrid Thornton (Mayor Wilson), John Batchelor (McKible), James Wardlaw (Brick). Filmed in Brisbane, Australia.

Instinct (film) A brilliant young psychiatrist, Theo Caulder, must unlock the secrets within the mind of Dr. Ethan Powell, an anthropologist who lived in the wilds for 3 years with a family of mountain gorillas. Dr. Powell, who has not spoken in years, has discovered a secret that could alter the future of mankind, but before his knowledge can be revealed, the psychiatrist must learn the truth behind a homicidal attack in the jungles of Rwanda of which the doctor stands accused, and for which he is now held captive in a brutal prison for the criminally insane. Directed by Jon Turtletaub. A Touchstone film from Spyglass Entertainment. Inspired by the novel *Ishmael*, by Daniel Quinn. Released Jun. 4, 1999. Stars Anthony Hopkins (Ethan Powell), Cuba Gooding, Jr. (Theo Caulder), Donald Sutherland (Ben Hillard), Maura Tierney (Lyn Powell), George Dzundza (John Murray). 126 min. CinemaScope. Jamaica substituted for Rwanda in the filming; other filming took place in Wisconsin, Orlando, and Los Angeles.

Intelligence (TV) Hour-long dramatic thriller on CBS; aired Jan. 7–Mar. 31, 2014. Gabriel is a high-tech intelligence operative enhanced with a supercomputer microchip in his brain. With this implant,

Gabriel is the first human ever to be connected directly into the worldwide information grid and have complete access to Internet, Wi-Fi, telephone, and satellite data. He can hack into any data center and access key intel in the fight to protect the U.S. from its enemies. Stars Josh Holloway (Gabriel), Marg Helgenberger (Lillian Strand), Meghan Ory (Riley Neal), Michael Rady (Chris Jameson), James Martinez (Gonzalo Rodriguez) John Billingsley (Dr. Cassidy), P. J. Byrne (Nelson Cassidy). From ABC Television Studios in association with CBS Television Studios.

Intergalactic Imports Tomorrowland shop in Shanghai Disneyland; opened Jun. 16, 2016, offering apparel, toys, headwear, and other souvenirs.

Inter-Governmental Philatelic Corp. Producer of postage stamps for small countries all over the world; received the license to use Disney characters on stamps beginning in 1979. See also Stamps.

Intermission Food Court Dining hall in Disney's All-Star Music Resort at Walt Disney World; opened Nov. 22, 1994.

International Gateway Entrance to EPCOT from the park's resort area; opened Jan. 12, 1990. With the building of the Yacht and Beach Club Resorts, as well as the Swan and Dolphin and eventually the BoardWalk Inn, an entrance was opened into World Showcase so that hotel guests could easily approach the park by foot, FriendShip boat, or tram without having to go all the way around to the other side of the park.

Intertwined, Disney (TV) A Disney+ original series; digitally released Nov. 12, 2021. The first original Disney+ series produced in Latin America, as *Entrelazados*. Allegra dreams of joining the Eleven O' Clock music hall company, but her mother, Caterina, won't accept that. Allegra's life changes drastically when she finds a mysterious bracelet that takes her to 1994—the year Caterina was her age and was starting her career in Eleven O' Clock while she lived in the shadow of her own mother, Cocó. Will Allegra be able to change the past? Stars Carolina Domenech (Allegra), Elena (Cocó), Manuela Menéndez (young Caterina), Clara Alonso (Caterina). From Pampa Films and Gloriamundi Producciones.

Into the Unknown Song from *Frozen 2*; written by Kristen Anderson-Lopez and Robert Lopez. Nominated for an Academy Award.

Into the Unknown: Making Frozen 2 (TV) Six-part documentary series on Disney+; digitally released Jun. 26, 2020. With less than a year until the world premiere of *Frozen 2*, the filmmakers, songwriters, and cast reveal the breakthroughs, artistry, and complexity behind one of the most anticipated films in animation history. Directed by Megan Harding. Exec. produced by Jeanmarie Condon and Amy Astley. From Lincoln Square Productions and Walt Disney Animation Studios.

Into the Woods (film) A modern twist on the beloved Brothers Grimm fairy tales, intertwining the plots of a few choice stories and exploring the consequences of the characters' wishes and quests. This heartfelt musical follows the classic tales of "Cinderella," "Little Red Riding Hood," "Jack and the Beanstalk,"and "Rapunzel"—all tied together by an original story involving a baker and his wife, their wish to begin a family, and their interaction with the witch who has put a curse on them. Directed by Rob Marshall. Released Dec. 25, 2014. Stars Johnny Depp (the wolf), Meryl Streep (witch), James Corden (baker), Emily Blunt (baker's wife), Anna Kendrick (Cinderella), Lilla Crawford (Little Red Riding Hood), Daniel Huttlestone (Jack), MacKenzie Mauzy (Rapunzel), Tracey Ullman (Jack's mother). 125 min. Based on the Broadway musical by James Lapine and Stephen Sondheim. Filmed in wide-screen format. Nominated for 3 Academy Awards (Production Design, Costume Design, and Actress in a Supporting Role [Meryl Streep]).

Intrada American record company specializing in movie and TV soundtracks; founded in 1985. Early Disney soundtrack releases included *Night Crossing* in 1987 and *Honey, I Blew Up the Kid* in 1992. Special Collection and Signature Edition CD sets have since been released, and beginning with the 2011 score release for *Up*, soundtracks have been co-branded with Walt Disney Records, including vintage titles.

Introduction to Aesop, An (film) Re-titled educational film, originally released as *Aesop's Hare and the Tortoise*.

Introduction to Hans Christian Andersen, An (film) Re-titled educational film, originally released as *Hans Christian Andersen's The Ugly Duckling*.

Inventions Buffet and character dining in the Disneyland Hotel at Disneyland Paris; opened Apr. 12, 1992. Décor is inspired by inventions of the Victorian age.

Invincible (film) When Dick Vermeil, the coach of Vince Papale's beloved hometown football team, the Philadelphia Eagles, hosted an unprecedented open tryout in 1976, the public consensus was that it was a waste of time—no one good enough to play professional football was going to be found that way. Certainly no one like Papale, a down-on-his-luck, 30-year-old substitute teacher and part-time bartender, who never even played college football. But against those odds, Papale made the team and soon found himself living every fan's fantasy—to be standing on the field as a professional player—while at the same time inspiring his teammates to break their 11-season losing streak and rediscover their winning spirit. Directed by Ericson Core. From Walt Disney Pictures/Mayhem Pictures. Stars Mark Wahlberg (Vince Papale), Greg Kinnear (Dick Vermeil), Elizabeth Banks (Janet), Kevin Conway (Frank Papale), Michael Rispoli (Max), Kirk Acevedo (Tommy). Released Aug. 25, 2006. 104 min. Filmed in CinemaScope. Based on the life story of Vincent Papale; he and Vermeil acted as consultants on the production. Filmed in Philadelphia, with Franklin Field at the University of Pennsylvania doubling for the now-demolished Veterans Stadium.

Invisible, The (film) By mistake, a high school senior is attacked and left for dead in a forest, but his ghost appears and starts shadowing the people who attacked him, led by a feisty and angry girl who is an outcast in the school. He also visits his family and best friend, trying to clue them in as to where to find his body and save him, though of course he is invisible to them, and they cannot hear him. He comes to realize that his widowed mother really loved him, even though they constantly fought, and she did not accept his desire to go to London to study writing. A Hollywood Pictures/Spyglass Entertainment production. Released Apr. 27, 2007. Directed by David S. Goyer. Stars Justin Chatwin (Nick Powell), Margarita Levieva (Annie Newton), Marcia Gay Harden (Diane Powell), Chris Marquette (Pete Egan), Callum Keith Rennie (Det. Brian Larson), Alex O'Loughlin (Marcus Bohem), Michelle Harrison (Kate Tunney). 102 min. Filming took place in Vancouver. Based on the novel *Den Osynlige*, by Mats Wahl, and the Swedish film of the same title.

Invisible Sister (TV) A Disney Channel Original

Movie; first aired Oct. 9, 2015. Cleo, an introverted young science prodigy in New Orleans, accidentally turns her popular older sister, Molly, invisible while working on a class project. Cleo, who has always lived in Molly's shadow, is forced to step outside her comfort zone and take the place of her older sister on the day of an important lacrosse game. The two sisters gain a better understanding of one another and themselves while relying on each other as never before. They rush to find an antidote for Cleo's experiment before Molly's invisibility becomes permanent. Directed by Paul Hoen. Stars Rowan Blanchard (Cleo), Paris Berelc (Molly), Karan Brar (George), Rachel Crow (Nikki), Will Meyers (Carter), Austin Fryberger (The Coug), Alex Désert (Mr. Perkins). Inspired by the book *My Invisible Sister* by Beatrice Colin and Sara Pinto.

Irish in America, The: Long Journey Home (TV) Six-hour miniseries produced and directed by Thomas Lennon in collaboration with the Walt Disney Studios and WGBH Boston for PBS; aired Jan. 26–28, 1998. Released concurrently on video. The series chronicles the triumphant role that the Irish have played in shaping America, beginning with the potato famine back in Ireland and continuing to the White House. This project was close to the heart of Roy E. Disney, whose great-grandfather was one of the Irish immigrants.

Iron Man Experience The first Marvel-themed attraction at a Disney park; opened Jan. 11, 2017, in Tomorrowland at Hong Kong Disneyland. Guests explore inventor Tony Stark's latest innovations up close and fly in a gravity-defying Iron Wing flight vehicle. At the Iron Man Tech Showcase, visitors can meet Iron Man and participate in the interactive game, Become Iron Man. Iron Man–themed food, beverages, and merchandise are also available.

Iron Man 3 (film) When Tony Stark finds his personal world destroyed at his enemy's hands, he embarks on a harrowing quest to find those responsible. With his back against the wall, Stark is left to survive by his own devices, relying on his ingenuity and instincts to protect those closest to him. As he fights his way back, he discovers the answer to the question that has secretly haunted him: Does the man make the suit or does the suit make the man? Released May 3, 2013, by Walt Disney Studios Motion Pictures in the U.S., after an Apr. 18 premiere in London and international releases beginning Apr. 24. Directed by Shane Black. Stars Robert Downey Jr. (Tony Stark/Iron Man), Gwyneth Paltrow (Pepper Potts), Rebecca Hall (Maya Hansen), Guy Pearce (Aldrich Killian), Ben Kingsley (The Mandarin), Jon Favreau (Happy Hogan), Don Cheadle (James Rhodes). 130 min. Filmed in CinemaScope. Produced by Marvel Studios in association with Paramount Pictures, which produced and distributed *Iron Man* (2008) and *Iron Man 2* (2010). Marvel's iconic Super Hero Iron Man first appeared in the comic book *Tales of Suspense*, No. 39, in 1963, with his solo comic book debut 5 years later.

Iron Will (film) In 1917, young Will Stoneman's life is turned upside down when his father is killed. Jack Stoneman had planned a bright future for his son, including sending him to college. In order to win a $10,000 prize needed to save the family from financial ruin, the courageous young man and his loyal team of sled dogs embark on a treacherous cross-country race, on a 522-mile course from Winnipeg to St. Paul. Nothing in his imagination could prepare him for the perilous trek, however, and his survival depends on the strength and courage of his faithful team of dogs, led by the stalwart Gus. Exhausted and numb from the arduous journey, Will must find the tenacity to persevere against impossible odds, while it seems the whole world is cheering him on through newspaper bulletins sent in by an enterprising reporter, Harry Kingsley, keeping up with the racers by train. Despite the harsh weather and terrain, and the threat of a dangerous opponent, Borg Guillarson, Will wins the race. Released Jan. 14, 1994. Directed by Charles Haid. 109 min. Stars Mackenzie Astin (Will Stoneman), Kevin Spacey (Harry Kingsley), David Ogden Stiers (J. P. Harper), George Gerdes (Borg Guillarson), John Terry (Jack Stoneman). Based on a true story. Principal photography took place in Duluth and the surrounding area in Minnesota, and the neighboring state of Wisconsin. The vintage 1913 steam engine that figures so prominently in the film was borrowed from the Lake Superior Museum of Transportation.

Irons, Jeremy Actor; provided the voice of Scar in *The Lion King*. He appeared in *Casanova* (Bishop Pucci), and on The Disney Channel in *Danny, the Champion of the World* (William Smith). For the Disney parks, he voiced H. G. Wells in The Timekeeper at Walt Disney World and narrated Spaceship Earth (1994–2007) in EPCOT, the Studio Tram Tour: Behind the Magic at Walt Disney Studios Park in Disneyland Paris, and *Seasons of the Vine* in Disney California Adventure.

Irvine, Kim Imagineer; she joined the WED Enterprises Model Shop in 1970, contributing to early projects for Walt Disney World. She later helped establish the first Imagineering offices in Anaheim and served as art director, and later exec. creative director, of Disneyland, stewarding the park as it has been enhanced and expanded over the years. The daughter of Disney Legend Leota Toombs, she appears as Madame Leota in Haunted Mansion Holiday and had a cameo role in *Muppets Haunted Mansion* (Maid) on Disney+.

Irvine, Richard F. ("Dick") (1910–1976) He worked as an art director at the Disney Studio in the 1940s, then returned in 1953 to head the team of designers, artists, architects, and engineers in planning and developing Disneyland. He guided the Disney attractions for the 1964–1965 New York World's Fair and went on to help shape the master plan and attractions for Walt Disney World. In 1967, he was appointed exec. vice president and chief operations officer of WED Enterprises. He retired in 1973 and was honored with a Disney Legends Award posthumously in 1990. SEE ALSO RICHARD F. IRVINE RIVERBOAT.

Ising, Rudolf (1903–1992) Friend of Walt Disney's in Kansas City who joined him in the Laugh-O-gram Films studio. At Disney's request, he left Kansas City to come to California and work at the new Walt Disney Studio on the Alice Comedies and Oswald the Lucky Rabbit cartoons. Later he joined up with Hugh Harman to produce the Harman-Ising cartoons at MGM.

Island at the Top of the World, The (film) In 1907, a wealthy Englishman, Sir Anthony, commands a giant airship as it searches the Arctic for his missing son. The only clues they have are a page from an old Hudson's Bay Company journal mentioning a hidden island "far beyond land's end where the whales go to die" and a curious map of carved whalebone. The crew discovers a volcanic Nordic island, a fabled whales' graveyard, and encounter Viking warriors who are far from friendly. Sir Anthony is reunited with his son, Donald, whose sweetheart, Freyja, helps them escape a death decree. Recaptured after a battle with killer whales, the fugitives are finally given their freedom in exchange for an American professor remaining behind as hostage. Premiered Dec. 16, 1974, in England; U.S. release Dec. 20, 1974. Directed by Robert Stevenson. 94 min. Stars David Hartman (Prof. Ivarsson), Donald Sinden (Sir Anthony Ross), Jacques Marin (Capt. Brieux), Mako (Oomiak), David Gwillim (Donald Ross), Agneta Eckemyr (Freyja), Gunnar Ohlund (The Godi), Lasse Kolstad (Erik), Niels Hinrichsen (Sigurd), Brendan Dillon (The Factor). Based on *The Lost Ones*, by Ian Cameron. With music composed by Maurice Jarre and spectacular special effects by Peter Ellenshaw, Art Cruickshank, and Danny Lee, this lavish film utilized footage captured in locations spanning the Arctic Circle from Alaska to Greenland to Norway. The large budget allowed creation of the airship *Hyperion*, a 220-foot motor-driven tapered dirigible; a complete Viking village with a temple of lava rock; 850 feet of coconut-fiber rope, handmade in Egypt, to hold up a suspension bridge; and a Viking longship to be used on location in Balestrand, Norway. The film was not a box office success but was nominated for an Academy Award for art direction/set direction by Peter Ellenshaw, John B. Mansbridge, Walter Tyler, Al Roelofs, and Hal Gausman.

Island Depot, The Shop in Pleasure Island at Walt Disney World; opened May 1, 1989, selling T-shirts, sundries, and logo merchandise. Closed Jun. 1990, to become a Dick Tracy shop, then Jessica's. It returned briefly, then was replaced by Music Legends in 1993. A new Island Depot opened inside the Rock N Roll Beach Club in 1997, in the site of the former Doodles.

Island Grove Packing Co. Merchandise and sundry shop at Disney's Vero Beach Resort; opened Oct. 1, 1995.

Island Mercantile Shop on Discovery Island in Disney's Animal Kingdom; opened Apr. 22, 1998. The interior décor is themed to animals that migrate.

Island Supply Company Adventureland shop in the Magic Kingdom at Walt Disney World; opened Jan. 7, 1991, taking the place of Colonel Hathi's Safari Club.

Islands of the Sea (film) Documentary featurette released Mar. 16, 1960. Produced by Ben Sharpsteen. Concentrates on the strange and wonderful birds, beasts, and fish found in and around the least-known islands of the world. Included are the Galapagos, the Guadalupes, the Falklands, and the tiny islands and atolls of the Midway group. 28 min. Nominated for an Academy Award.

Isozaki, Arata (1931–2022) Architect; designed the

abstract Team Disney Building at Walt Disney World.

It Runs in the Family (film) Buena Vista International handled the international distribution and MGM the domestic of this film from Further Films. Three generations of an American family, living separate lives, each in its own dysfunctional way, come together every once in a while to laugh, to fight, to cry, and to care for each other. Directed by Frank Schepisi. U.S. release Apr. 25, 2003. Stars Michael Douglas (Alex Gromberg), Kirk Douglas (Mitchell Gromberg), Bernadette Peters (Rebecca), Diana Douglas (Evelyn), Cameron Douglas (Asher), Rory Culkin (Eli). Kirk Douglas is Michael's father, Diana Douglas his mother, and Cameron Douglas his son. Michael produced the film with his brother Joel as co-producer.

Italia '61 (film) Circarama (360°) film prepared in 1961 for the Italia '61 Exposition in Turin, under sponsorship by Fiat; features a tour of Italy with spectacular views of the harbor at Genoa, and Mount Vesuvius. The Italian film crew was taught use of the cameras by Don Iwerks, son of Disney animator and special effects magician Ub Iwerks.

Italy World Showcase pavilion in EPCOT; opened Oct. 1, 1982. Disney designers carefully studied Italian architecture and determined that their pavilion should have the look of Venice. A small island gives the impression of the canals. One can sometimes even get the feeling that they are actually in St. Mark's Square, with the Doge's Palace, statues of Neptune and St. Mark the Evangelist, and the Campanile being smaller versions of their originals. In the square, *Il Commedia di Bologna*, a troupe of actors renowned for their broad comedy, once inveigled passersby to put aside their fears of embarrassment and join in the hilarious 15-min. pageants. The pavilion debuted with several shops selling Italian arts and crafts, along with fine dining at L'Originale Alfredo di Roma Ristorante. Alfredo's was succeeded by Tutto Italia Ristorante in 2007. Other dining options have been added over the years: Via Napoli Ristorante e Pizzeria (Aug. 2, 2010); Tutto Gusto, a wine bar (May 1, 2012); and Gelateria Toscana (May 6, 2021).

It's a Dog's Life with Bill Farmer (TV) Original series on Disney+; digitally premiered May 15, 2020. Disney Legend Bill Farmer, the longtime voice of Goofy and Pluto, travels the country to meet real-life dogs who do all kinds of incredible jobs that make our lives better. From Dog Tale Productions, Inc. and GRB Entertainment, Inc.

It's a Small World Fantasyland attraction, typically presented as "it's a small world," in Disneyland; opened May 28, 1966. Presented by the Bank of America 1966–1992, Mattel 1992–1999, Sylvania 2009–2014, and Siemens (Sylvania's parent company) 2014–2017. The attraction moved to Disneyland from the 1964–1965 New York World's Fair, where it had premiered Apr. 22, 1964, presented by Pepsi-Cola in a salute to UNICEF. Guests board "The Happiest Cruise That Ever Sailed 'Round the World," in which 297 children and 256 toys, brought to life through Audio-Animatronics technology, are presented in colorfully stylized settings representing over 100 regions. As in most of the Disney attractions, there is much to see; each time you experience it, you will likely catch something new and different. Songwriters Richard M. and Robert B. Sherman were asked by Walt to come up with a simple piece that could be repeated over and over, sung in different languages. The resulting song became one of the best-known Disney tunes of all time. In Disneyland, the facade is almost as impressive as the interior attraction; a large ticking clock tower is the centerpiece, and every 15 min. brings a parade of characters marching around it. Also opened in Fantasyland in the Magic Kingdom at Walt Disney World Oct. 1, 1971; in Fantasyland in Tokyo Disneyland Apr. 15, 1983; in Disneyland Paris Apr. 12, 1992; and in Hong Kong Disneyland Apr. 28, 2008. Walt Disney World lacks the elaborate facade, but it was brought back for Tokyo and Paris. Because skies are often overcast in northern France, designers felt that the facade needed a colorful pastel paint job rather than the classical white-and-gold look of the previous incarnations. After the opening of Disneyland Paris, and the general satisfaction with the new look, the facade in Disneyland was repainted to use the new color scheme. For the 1997 Christmas season, and each succeeding year, the Disneyland attraction is redressed for the holidays with colored lights and decorations, both inside and out, with the children singing "Jingle Bells" and "Deck the Halls" interwoven in counterpoint with the original song. The white-and-gold facade returned to the Disneyland attraction as the park prepared for its 50th-anniversary celebration. Stylized versions of several Disney characters were introduced in the Hong Kong Disneyland version of the attraction, and similar characters were incorporated into the Disneyland version in 2009 and the Tokyo Disneyland version in 2018.

It's a Small World After All Children's apparel shop in the Lake Buena Vista Shopping Village at Walt Disney World; open Mar. 1975–May 3, 1988. Replaced by Board Stiff.

It's a Small World: the animated series (TV) Children from different countries circle the globe to explore new lands and learn unique words and customs, with animation inspired by Mary Blair's original designs for the theme park attraction. Includes original music by Richard M. Sherman. Launched online on Disney.com and other platforms on Dec. 3, 2013. 8 episodes.

It's a Small World Toy Shop Fantasyland shop in Disneyland originally sponsored by Mattel; opened Dec. 18, 1992. The shop was built at the end of the exit path from the It's a Small World attraction after Mattel became the sponsor. Also known as It's a Small World Toy Shoppe.

It's A Wonderful Shop Store dressed for Christmas year-round in Disney's Hollywood Studios at Walt Disney World; opened Jun. 1992, on New York Street (later part of Streets of America, then Grand Avenue).

It's All Relative (TV) Half-hour comedy series on ABC; aired Oct. 1, 2003–Apr. 6, 2004. Bobby and Liz get engaged but find that their 2 families clash. Bobby's father owns and operates a Boston pub and heads a close-knit Irish Catholic family. Liz attends Harvard, is Protestant, and has 2 dads, a gay gallery owner and his life partner, a schoolteacher. Stars Lenny Clarke (Mace O'Neil), Harriet Sansom Harris (Audrey), Reid Scott (Bobby), Maggie Lawson (Liz), Christopher Sieber (Simon), Paige Moss (Maddy), John Benjamin Hickey (Philip). From Paramount Television and Touchstone Television.

It's Not My Fault (film) Educational release in 16 mm in Aug. 1991. 18 min. An 11-year-old boy seems to be disagreeing with everyone, but he learns to communicate his feelings and listen to those of others.

It's Pat (film) The obnoxious Pat from *Saturday Night Live* baffles friends and neighbors alike, who cannot decide if Pat is male or female. Pat has a relationship with Chris, a kindly and ambiguous bartender with hippie clothing and hair. Meantime, handsome neighbor Kyle, a married but uptight young man, becomes inexplicably obsessed with Pat. But, basically, it's Pat who is Pat's most devoted admirer. Limited release on Aug. 26, 1994. Directed by Adam Bernstein. A Touchstone film. 78 min. Stars Julia Sweeney (Pat), David Foley (Chris), Charles Rocket (Kyle). Julia Sweeney developed the Pat character at the Los Angeles comedy troupe The Groundlings. Filmed in and around Los Angeles.

It's Tough to Be a Bird (film) Special live-action and cartoon featurette released Dec. 10, 1969. Directed by Ward Kimball. The story is told of the bird's contribution to mankind and his never-ending fight for survival from prehistoric times to the present. There are humorous moments throughout, and even the buzzard is honored in the epic struggle that still continues between humans and birds. This popular short received the Academy Award as Best Cartoon Short Subject of 1969. The film is hosted by M. C. Bird (voiced by Richard Bakalyan) and features many highlights, including a hilarious musical number by Ruth Buzzi entitled "When the Buzzards Return to Hinckley Ridge." 22 min. An extended version aired on TV Dec. 13, 1970.

It's Tough to Be a Bug! (film) Multimedia production inside a 450-seat theater underneath the Tree of Life in Disney's Animal Kingdom; opened Apr. 22, 1998. With a 3-D film, Audio-Animatronics figures, and special effects, the show provides an amusing look at a bug's world, hosted by Flik from *A Bug's Life*. The attraction, minus the tree, was presented in A Bug's Land at Disney California Adventure, Feb. 8, 2001–Mar. 18, 2018.

Ivan Cat friend of Peter in *Peter and the Wolf*, represented by a clarinet.

I've Got No Strings Song from *Pinocchio*; written by Ned Washington and Leigh Harline.

Ives, Burl (1909–1995) Actor/singer; appeared in *So Dear to My Heart* (Uncle Hiram) and *Summer Magic* (Osh Popham). He voiced the host, Eagle Sam, in America Sings at Disneyland and recorded several albums for Disneyland Records.

Iwájú (TV) Animated long-form series planned for digital release on Disney+ in 2023. Inspired by the spirit of Lagos, Nigeria—which is physically divided into an island and a mainland separated by both water and socioeconomic status—this coming-of-age story follows Tola, a young heiress from the wealthy island, and her best friend, Kole, a self-taught tech expert and loving son from the mainland. From Walt Disney Animation Studios in collaboration with Kugali, the Pan-African comic book entertainment company. Iwájú roughly translates to "The Future" in the Yoruba language.

Iwan, Bret Voice actor/artist; he became the official voice of Mickey Mouse in 2009, succeeding Wayne Allwine. His first projects included the Adventurers Celebration in Disney's Animal Kingdom and Disney on Ice: Celebrations, and he has gone on to provide Mickey's voice for TV and theme park shows, video games, and other media and products. An accomplished artist, he has created portraits of Mickey for Disney Fine Art.

Iwerks, Don The son of Ub Iwerks, Don started with Disney in 1950 as a lab technician, eventually heading both the Studio Machine Shop and Studio Camera Service Department. He supervised the camera and projection systems for EPCOT Center before leaving to form his own company in 1986. He was named a Disney Legend in 2009.

Iwerks, Leslie Director/producer; she has created several documentaries, including *The Pixar Story*, *The Hand Behind the Mouse: The Ub Iwerks Story*, and *The Imagineering Story*, and has hosted programs for Disney events, including the D23 Expo. She is the granddaughter of Ub Iwerks and the daughter of Don Iwerks.

Iwerks, Ub (1901–1971) Animator and special effects wizard. A quiet, unassuming man, Ub made his mark not only in animation, but also in the field of motion picture technology. He was an animation genius, perhaps the greatest of all time, whose contributions to the art in the 1920s and 1930s helped make animation much more appealing to a wider audience. Born in Kansas City, Missouri, in 1901, of Dutch extraction, he had his first major job with the Pesmen-Rubin Commercial Art Studio, where he did lettering and airbrush work. It was there that Ub met Walt Disney, another aspiring artist. Both boys were 19 and, when they were laid off, decided to set up their own company to do commercial artwork. The company, established in 1920, was called the Iwerks-Disney Studio. Originally they had thought to call it Disney-Iwerks, but that sounded too much like a place that manufactured eyeglasses. The studio only lasted a month, but then both Ub and Walt were able to get more secure jobs with the Kansas City Slide Company, later known as the Kansas City Film Ad Company. When Walt set up Laugh-O-gram Films in 1922, Ub joined him as chief animator. This

company also lasted only a short time. Walt went to Hollywood to begin producing the Alice Comedies and Ub joined him there in 1924. Ub's starting salary was $40 a week, higher even than Walt's, attesting to his importance. Several years later, when Walt lost the rights to Oswald the Lucky Rabbit, it was Ub who came to his salvation by helping him design a new character—Mickey Mouse. Ub animated the entire cartoon *Plane Crazy* all by himself, working at a tremendous speed. Ub was renowned for doing 700 drawings in a day; today a proficient traditional animator turns out 80–100 drawings a week. *The Gallopin' Gaucho* followed, then *Steamboat Willie*, the first Mickey Mouse cartoon released. Ub continued animating on the Mickeys and also painted the backgrounds and drew the posters. When the Silly Symphonies started, he took over direction of them. Because of disagreements over production techniques and a desire to set up his own studio, Ub left Disney in 1930 for 10 years. By the time he returned in 1940, he had decided to leave animation altogether and turn to his first love, cameras and special effects. One of his first inventions at Disney was the multi-head optical printer, used so successfully in the combination of live action and animation in *Melody Time* and *Song of the South*. Of tremendous importance to animation was Ub's design of the modified Xerox process, whereby pencil animation drawings could be transferred directly to cels without the more expensive hand inking. Over the years, Ub won 2 Academy Awards, for designing an improved optical printer for special effects and for collaborating on the perfection of color traveling matte photography. Ub's inventions helped make the impossible possible, and Disney screenwriters and art directors kept that in mind. It was primarily due to Ub that the Disney Studio moved to the forefront in special photographic effects. Disneyland and Walt Disney World occupied much of Ub's technical attention in the 1960s, including such attractions as It's a Small World and Great Moments with Mr. Lincoln, as well as the Circle-Vision 360 film process used in *America the Beautiful*. The design of the film process for The Hall of Presidents at Walt Disney World was Ub's last project. He was honored posthumously with the Disney Legends award in 1989. Ub's sons Don and Dave were longtime Disney employees. A documentary on his life, *The Hand Behind the Mouse: The Ub Iwerks Story*, was produced by his granddaughter, Leslie Iwerks, in 1999.

Iyanla (TV) One-hour talk show featuring Iyanla Vanzant; aired in syn. Aug. 13, 2001–Mar. 1, 2002.

1. Junior Woodchucks 2. Journey Into Imagination 3. José Carioca 4. *Jungle Book, The* (film) 5. Jungle Cruise
6. Joe Gardner 7. *Johnny Appleseed* (film) 8. Jessie's Critter Carousel 9. Journey to the Center of the Earth

J. Audubon Woodlore SEE RANGER.

J. Worthington Foulfellow Fox character in *Pinocchio*, also known as Honest John; voiced by Walter Catlett.

Jacchus Donkey ridden by Bacchus in "The Pastoral Symphony" segment of *Fantasia*.

Jack (film) Jack Powell appears to be an average 40-year-old man—who plays with toys and wears kids pajamas. But Jack is only 10 years old. He suffers from a rare genetic disorder that causes him to physically age 4 times faster than a normal person. Fearing ridicule from the outside world, Jack's parents have kept him secluded in their home, which they have stocked with every toy a young boy could want, and have had him taught by a kindly tutor, Mr. Woodruff. Toys, however, cannot take the place of the real friends that Jack craves. At the urging of his tutor, his parents finally allow Jack to embark on the greatest adventure of his unusual life—entering the 5th grade. Slowly he gains acceptance from his much smaller classmates, especially after showing his prowess with basketball. Years later, as they graduate from high school, Jack is still a beloved part of the gang, but he is now an elderly man. A Hollywood Pictures film. Directed by Francis Ford Coppola. Released Aug. 9, 1996. Stars Robin Williams (Jack Powell), Diane Lane (Karen Powell), Jennifer Lopez (Ms. Marquez), Brian Kerwin (Brian Powell), Fran Drescher (Dolores Durante), Bill Cosby (Lawrence Woodruff). 113 min. The picturesque town of Ross, California, provided some of the town sets; additional filming was done in San Francisco. Many of the interiors used in the production were built at the Mare Island Naval Base in Vallejo, California.

Jack and Old Mac (film) Special cartoon released Jul. 18, 1956. Directed by Bill Justice. A combination of 2 stories: the nursery rhyme "This Is the House that Jack Built" and a variation on the children's song "Old MacDonald Had a Farm," with "Farm" paraphrased as "Band."

Jack and the Beanstalk (film) Laugh-O-gram film made by Walt Disney in Kansas City in 1922. A later version starring Mickey Mouse, "Mickey and the Beanstalk," appeared in the feature *Fun and Fancy Free*.

Jack Skellington The Pumpkin King of Halloween Town in *Tim Burton's The Nightmare Before Christmas*; voiced by Chris Sarandon (speaking) and Danny Elfman (singing).

Jack the Giant Killer (film) Short cartoon; a modernized version of the story, made by Laugh-O-gram Films in 1922. A boy, Jack, with his girlfriend and cat, travels to a land of giants, where he destroys 4 of them. This is a separate film from *Jack and the Beanstalk*, also made by Laugh-O-gram.

Jack-Jack Attack (film) Animated short from Pixar Animation Studios that appeared first on the DVD for *The Incredibles*, released Mar. 15, 2005. Jack-Jack, the baby of the superhero family, is at home with babysitter Kari while the family is away, and the toddler reveals his latent powers.

Jackman, Bob (1915–1996) He joined Disney in

1942, working in accounting. He moved to the music department in 1955 and became its manager that same year. He voiced Goofy in a number of cartoons in the 1950s.

Jackman, Hugh Actor; appeared in *The Prestige* (Robert Angier) and *Real Steel* (Charlie Kenton). In 1995, he played Gaston in the original Australian stage run of *Beauty and the Beast*.

Jackson, Michael (1958–2009) He wrote the songs for and starred in the 3-D film *Captain EO* at the Disney parks and appeared on TV in *Kraft Salutes Disneyland's 25th Anniversary*. Jackson was an avid Disney fan, making many trips to the parks, occasionally in disguise.

Jackson, Samuel L. Actor; appeared in *Betsy's Wedding* (Taxi Dispatcher), *Unbreakable* (Elijah Price), and as Nick Fury in *Marvel's The Avengers* and later Marvel Studios productions, including *Marvel's Agents of S.H.I.E.L.D.* on ABC. He provided the voice of Frozone in *The Incredibles* and *Incredibles 2*, Mace Windu in *Star Wars: The Rise of Skywalker*, and narrated *African Cats*.

Jackson, Wayne Imagineer; beginning his career at WED Enterprises in 1965, he was instrumental in the development and installation of Disney attractions around the world, and he subsequently oversaw Show Quality Standards at Tokyo Disneyland and Disneyland Paris. After directing show systems for the construction of Tokyo DisneySea, he retired in 2002. He was named a Disney Legend in 2017.

Jackson, Wilfred "Jaxon" (1906–1988) He joined Disney in 1928 and worked on *Steamboat Willie*. He served as an animator, director, and producer-director on the *Disneyland* TV show. He pioneered a method of pre-timing animation with sound and invented the bar sheet to coordinate the animation action with the soundtrack. Several of the cartoons he directed were honored with Academy Awards. He also worked as a sequence director on 11 features, from *Snow White and the Seven Dwarfs* to *Lady and the Tramp*. Jackson retired in 1961 and was honored posthumously as a Disney Legend in 1998.

Jackson Square Gifts and Desires Souvenir shop in Disney's Port Orleans Resort – French Quarter at Walt Disney World; opened May 17, 1991. Mardi Gras mementos and resort logo items are sold.

Jacobson, Eric Imagineer; he joined the Disneyland

Entertainment division in 1971 and transferred to the WED Model Shop in 1978. He served as an art director for Audio-Animatronics figures and soon joined the creative team for Disney-MGM Studios. Over the years, he directed such projects as The Great Movie Ride, The Twilight Zone Tower of Terror, Blizzard Beach, *Mickey's PhilharMagic*, Disney's Art of Animation Resort, and New Fantasyland at Walt Disney World. He retired in 2017 as senior vice president, Creative Development.

Jaeckel, Richard (1926–1997) Actor; appeared in *Herbie Goes Bananas* (Shepard), on TV in *Kit Carson and the Mountain Men* (Ed Kern), and narrated *Adventure in Satan's Canyon*.

Jafar Evil vizier in the Sultan's palace in *Aladdin*; voiced by Jonathan Freeman.

Jagga Jasoos (film) Jagga, a curious-yet-clueless teenage detective, with his companion Shruti, embarks on a mission to locate Jagga's missing father, and they find themselves involved in adventures that take them around the world. Directed by Anurag Basu. Released Jul. 14, 2017, in Hindi, in the U.S. and India. Stars Ranbir Kapoor (Jagga), Katrina Kaif (Shruti), Saswata Chatterjee (Jagga's father). 180 min. From Disney India. Produced by Picture Shuru Entertainment and Walt Disney Pictures.

Jake Australian kangaroo rat in *The Rescuers Down Under*; voiced by Tristan Rogers.

Jake and the Never Land Pirates (TV) Animated series for preschoolers and parents on Disney Junior; premiered Feb. 14, 2011. Jake and his kid pirate fans sail aboard their amazing ship *Bucky* from their Pirate Island hideout on a treasure hunt throughout Never Land. There the team learns that they must work together to try to outsmart Captain Hook and Smee, earning doubloons as they conquer tasks. Voices include Colin Ford (Jake), Madison Pettis (Izzy), Jonathan Morgan Heit (Cubby). Jake was later voiced by Cameron Boyce, Sean Ryan Fox, and Riley Thomas Stewart. There are 2 segments to each episode. From Disney Television Animation.

James, Cyril (1910–1975) He worked with merchandising and film distribution for Disney in London for his entire career (1938–1972). He was presented posthumously with a European Disney Legends Award in 1997.

James and the Giant Peach (film) A 9-year-old orphan, James Henry Trotter, has been sent to live with his wicked, miserly aunts Spiker and Sponge. Life is the pits for the lonely boy, who dreams of going to New York City. He finally gets his chance when he meets a mysterious hobo who presents him with a bag of magical "crocodile tongues." Accidentally spilling his precious treasure at the base of a peach tree, James is astonished to see a peach on the tree grow to an enormous size. Finding a secret entryway into the peach, he crawls inside where he meets a wondrous group of human-sized insects—including a brash centipede, a grandfatherly grasshopper, a motherly ladybug, and a dotty glowworm. When the peach breaks loose from the tree, James and his insect pals find themselves on a roll, headed for the adventure of a lifetime. Directed by Henry Selick. Released Apr. 12, 1996. Stars Miriam Margolyes (Sponge, Glowworm), Joanna Lumley (Spiker), Paul Terry (James), Pete Postlethwaite (old man), and the voices of Richard Dreyfuss (Centipede), Susan Sarandon (Miss Spider), Jane Leeves (Lady Bug), David Thewlis (Earthworm), Simon Callow (Grasshopper). 79 min. Based on the 1961 book by Roald Dahl. Five songs were written by Randy Newman: "My Name Is James," "That's the Life," "Eating the Peach," "We're Family," and "Good News." Newman himself is the vocalist on the last song. The fantasy scenes were filmed using stop-motion animation enhanced by computer-generated imagery and digital effects. Live-action photography took place in a large hangar at a decommissioned naval base on Treasure Island in San Francisco Bay and at nearby Hunter's Point. The animation was done at Skellington Productions in San Francisco, the same studio where *Tim Burton's The Nightmare Before Christmas* was produced, and it utilized some of the same crew. In the underwater sequence, one can even find a cameo by Jack Skellington from the earlier film. More than 50 peaches were constructed for the film, ranging in size from 3-inch miniatures up to 20-foot-diameter jumbos. Two granddaughters of Roald Dahl, children of his daughter, Lucy, appear briefly as extras in the film. Lucy wrote the movie scrapbook, published by Disney Press and illustrated with her own photographs.

James P. ("Sulley") Sullivan Softhearted Scarer in *Monsters, Inc.*; voiced by John Goodman.

Jamie Fort Story, The (A Story About Self-Esteem) (film) Educational film about a fire victim who discovers the power of determination and a positive attitude; released in Sep. 1988. 30 min.

Jamil, Jameela Actress; appeared on Disney+ in *She-Hulk: Attorney at Law* (Titania) and provided the voice of Phoenix in *Big City Greens*, Gandra Dee in *DuckTales* (2017), and Pushpa in *Mira, Royal Detective*.

Jane Researcher in *Tarzan*, the daughter of Professor Porter; voiced by Minnie Driver.

Jane Austen's Mafia! (film) This parody of films about organized crime begins with young Vincenzo Cortino being forced to leave Sicily and swim to America, where he becomes the infamous, though klutzy, patriarch of a powerful crime family. As he ages, he realizes that he will have to hand the reins of power to one of his sons—either the psychotic Joey or the war hero Anthony. In the background are the themes of strong family loyalty, the struggle for power, and relentless treachery. Directed by Jim Abrahams. A Touchstone film. Released Jul. 24, 1998. Stars Lloyd Bridges (Vincenzo Cortino), Jay Mohr (Anthony), Olympia Dukakis (Sophia), Christina Applegate (Diane), Billy Burke (Joey). 87 min. The movie covers the years from 1912 to the present, and was filmed in and around Los Angeles, and in Reno, Nevada. Advertised as *Mafia*, after initial research showed most theatergoers had never heard of Jane Austen.

Jane By Design (TV) Comedy-drama series on ABC Family; debuted Jan. 3, 2012, and ended Jul. 31, 2012. Jane Quimby, a quirky teen with an eclectic and chic fashion sense, lands a job at a hip fashion house when they mistake her for an adult. Jane is soon torn between her love of fashion and the need to finish high school. Stars Erica Dasher (Jane Quimby), Andie MacDowell (Gray Chandler Murray), India De Beaufort (India Jourdain), Rowly Dennis (Jeremy Jones), Matthew Atkinson (Nick Fadden), Nicholas Roux (Billy Nutter).

Jani, Bob (1934–1989) He joined Disneyland in 1955 as head of the Guest Relations department and, after serving as an entertainment director for the U.S. Army, returned to Disney in 1967 as director of entertainment. He was later named vice president, then creative director, of entertainment for Walt Disney Productions. Among his productions were the grand opening dedication events for Walt Disney World in 1971, as well as *America on Parade, Disney on Parade*, and the *Main Street*

Electrical Parade. He left Disney in 1978 but continued to work as a consultant, contributing to Disney-MGM Studios and Disneyland Paris. He was named a Disney Legend posthumously, in 2005.

Japan World Showcase pavilion in EPCOT; opened Oct. 1, 1982. Rather than reproduce a single Japanese region, Imagineers, with consultants from Mitsukoshi, designed the pavilion to represent a sampling of traditional structures. The landscaping is one of the pavilion's highlights. Guests can wander through pathways in Japanese gardens before shopping in the expansive, by EPCOT standards, Mitsukoshi Department Store. Upstairs, visitors can dine in Japanese fashion, watching the cook prepare their food right at their own table. Japan is one of only a few World Showcase pavilions to have a museum area, the Bijutsu-kan Gallery, where rotating displays of rare items, such as costumes, clocks, or kites from Japan are displayed. An upscale restaurant, Takumi-Tei, was added in 2019. SEE ALSO MEET THE WORLD, MITSUKOSHI RESTAURANT, AND YAKITORI HOUSE.

Japan (film) People and Places featurette; released Apr. 6, 1960. Produced by Ben Sharpsteen. This is the story of colorful Japanese customs and manners of the past, and their contrast with present-day Japan. We see ancient farming customs, agricultural ceremonies, ancestor worship, schoolteaching, marriage customs, sports, all against the background of beautiful Japan. Filmed in CinemaScope. 28 min.

Japan Harvests the Sea (film) 16-mm release title of *Ama Girls*; released in Sep. 1961.

Jaq Cunning mouse friend of Cinderella's; voiced by Jim Macdonald.

Jarre, Maurice (1924–2009) Composer; wrote the musical scores for *The Island at the Top of the World*, *The Last Flight of Noah's Ark*, and *Dead Poets Society*.

Jasmine Princess who longs to experience life outside the palace in *Aladdin*; speaking voice by Linda Larkin and singing voice by Lea Salonga.

Jasmine's Flying Carpets Arabian Coast attraction in Tokyo DisneySea; opened Jul. 18, 2011. Riders soar over Jasmine's garden on a flying carpet. SEE ALSO MAGIC CARPETS OF ALADDIN, THE (WALT DISNEY WORLD).

Jay, Tony (1933–2006) Actor; provided several voices, including Monsieur D'Arque in *Beauty and the Beast*, Frollo in *The Hunchback of Notre Dame*, Shere Khan on TV in *TaleSpin* and on film in *The Jungle Book 2*, Wraith in *The Mighty Ducks* TV series, and the narrator in *Treasure Planet*.

Jazz Fool, The (film) Mickey Mouse cartoon; released in 1929. Directed by Walt Disney. Mickey appears to be the toast of this musical cartoon, playing a calliope and a piano to which other animals can dance, until the piano begins to chase him.

Jedi Training Academy Interactive show; Jedi hopefuls train in the ways of the Force and put their skills to the test against *Star Wars* villains. Debuted in 2000, as Jedi Training Camp, during Star Wars Weekends at Disney-MGM Studios (now Disney's Hollywood Studios), prior to being offered year-round beginning in 2007. Renamed Jedi Training: Trials of the Temple in 2015. Also in Disneyland (2006–2018 at Tomorrowland Terrace), Disneyland Paris (2015–2017 at Videopolis), and Hong Kong Disneyland (2016–2021, replacing UFO Zone).

Jefferson in Paris (film) Historical drama about Thomas Jefferson's 5 years, 1784–1789, in romantic, politically charged, prerevolutionary Paris, where he was originally appointed by the Continental Congress to assist Benjamin Franklin as minister to the court of King Louis XVI, though he later took over the post when Franklin returned to America. While in Paris, Jefferson, who had recently lost his wife, entered into a love affair with a beautiful Anglo-Italian painter and musician, Maria Cosway, giving him the experience of an attachment, in the European manner, to a highly sophisticated woman with advanced ideas about love and marriage. When Jefferson's daughter, Polly, arrives in Paris, accompanied by her nurse, Sally Hemings, he finds himself attracted to the enslaved girl. When Jefferson decides to return home, he offers Sally and her brother their freedom if they will join him—Sally is already pregnant with his child—and they consent. Released Mar. 31, 1995, in Los Angeles and New York City; general release Apr. 7, 1995. Directed by James Ivory. 142 min. A Touchstone film. Stars Nick Nolte (Thomas Jefferson), Greta Scacchi (Maria Cosway), Lambert Wilson (Lafayette), Simon Callow (Richard Cosway), Seth Gilliam (James Hemings), James Earl Jones (Madison Hemings), Thandie Newton (Sally Hemings), Estelle Eonnet (Polly). The movie was produced by the prestigious Merchant-Ivory film-making team and was filmed on location in France, garnering special permission to shoot at Versailles, the Chateau of Chantilly, and many other historic sites in the country.

Jennie Project, The (TV) A Disney Channel Original Movie; first aired Jul. 13, 2001. Dr. Hugo Archibald has brought home from Africa a chimpanzee named Jennie. Originally mischievous and destructive, but eventually accepted as a member of the family, Jennie, who is learning sign language, develops a close relationship with 11-year-old Andrew. But there are problems in having even a domesticated wild animal in a home situation, and the family has to figure out what to do with Jennie. Directed by Gary Nadeau. Stars Alex D. Linz (Andrew Archibald), Lance Guest (Hugo Archibald), Sheila Kelley (Lea Archibald), Sheryl Lee Ralph (Dr. Pamela Prentiss), Abigail Mavity (Sarah Archibald).

Jennings, Peter (1938–2005) One of America's most distinguished journalists, he joined ABC News in 1964. For more than 20 years, beginning in 1983, he served as anchor and senior editor of *World News Tonight*. He was named a Disney Legend in 2006.

Jenny Foxworth Rich girl who finds Oliver in *Oliver & Company*; voiced by Natalie Gregory.

Jerky Boys, The (film) A pair of young men from Queens, New York, create outrageous characters with their voices when they make phone calls to the unwary, but they get in trouble both with the law and the mob. Released Feb. 3, 1995. Directed by James Melkonian. A Touchstone film in association with Caravan Pictures. 82 min. Stars John G. Brennan (Johnny B.), Kamal Ahmed (Kamal), Alan Arkin (Lazarro), Brad Sullivan (Worzic), William Hickey (Uncle Freddy). Filmed in New York City.

Jersey, The (TV) Half-hour original series on Disney Channel; premiered Sep. 24, 1999. Two teens' love of sports takes on a life of its own through the fantastic powers of an old football jersey. Each time the 13-year-old cousins don the jersey, they enter a magical portal that transports them into the world of professional athletics, placing them directly into the shoes of major sports celebrities. Stars Michael Galeota (Nick Lighter), Courtnee Draper (Morgan Hudson), Jermaine Williams (Coleman Galloway), Theo Greenly (Elliot Rifkin). Sports superstars guest on each

episode. Based on a Jan. 30, 1999, Disney Channel half-hour special entitled *The Magic Jersey*.

Jessica Rabbit Roger Rabbit's (cartoon) human wife in *Who Framed Roger Rabbit*, with an uncredited speaking voice provided by Kathleen Turner (though she was credited in later Roger Rabbit shorts). Her singing voice was provided by Amy Irving. A Jessica's shop in Pleasure Island at Walt Disney World, featuring lingerie and other items, opened Dec. 15, 1990, replacing the Dick Tracy shop. It closed Feb. 1993 and was superseded by Music Legends.

Jessie Yodeling cowgirl in the *Woody's Roundup* gang, introduced in *Toy Story 2*; voiced by Joan Cusack.

Jessie (TV) Half-hour live-action comedy series on Disney Channel; premiered Sep. 30, 2011. Jessie Prescott, a small-town girl, leaves behind her Texas roots and finds a job in New York City as a nanny to a high-flying couple's 4 precocious kids—Emma, Ravi, Luke, and Zuri. While Jessie's new big-city life is full of opportunity and excitement, she quickly discovers how much she relies on the support and advice of the kids in her care, along with Bertram, the family's butler, and Tony, the building's doorman. Stars Debby Ryan (Jessie), Kevin Chamberlain (Bertram), Peyton List (Emma), Karan Brar (Ravi), Cameron Boyce (Luke), Skai Jackson (Zuri), Chris Galya (Tony). From It's a Laugh Productions for Disney Channel.

Jessie's Critter Carousel Toy Story Boardwalk attraction at Pixar Pier in Disney California Adventure; opened Apr. 5, 2019, replacing King Triton's Carousel. Guests ride on whimsical critters based on the 1950s *Woody's Roundup* show from *Toy Story 2*.

Jessie's Trading Post Shop at the exit of Toy Story Mania! in Toy Story Land at Disney's Hollywood Studios; opened Jul. 22, 2022.

Jet Packs Tomorrowland attraction in Shanghai Disneyland; opened Jun. 16, 2016. Guests sail through the air with jet packs connected to a large, spinning orb by 16 mechanical arms. Handheld controls help guests regulate their elevation.

Jet Propulsion Educational film showing the development of airplanes, from early models to the planes of today, demonstrating the aerodynamics of jet propulsion and breaking down the various parts of a jet. A jet plane's characteristics are compared with those of conventional aircraft. Made for General Electric; delivered Apr. 9, 1946.

Jetix Rebranding in Feb. 2004 of the Fox Kids channels for action-adventure programming worldwide. It aired as a programming block on ABC Family and Toon Disney in the U.S., with other Jetix channels introduced throughout Europe and Latin America. Disney obtained 100% ownership of Jetix Europe in 2008–2009. Jetix was replaced by Disney XD (Disney Channel in some countries).

Jett Jackson: The Movie (TV) A Disney Channel Original Movie; first aired Jun. 8, 2001. Jett trades places with his on-screen alter ego, Silverstone, after Jett has an accident on the set of his popular TV series (*The Famous Jett Jackson*). Now Jett, rather than Silverstone must defeat the evil Dr. Kragg, who is using a dimensional field device to steal the major cities of the world, while Silverstone must navigate Jett's tumultuous teen world. Directed by Shawn Levy. Stars Lee Thompson Young (Jett Jackson), Lindy Booth (Hawk/Riley), Nigel Shawn Williams (Artemus), Ryan Sommers Baum (J. B. Halliburton), Kerry Duff (Kayla West), Michael Ironside (Dr. Kragg).

Jewel of Orleans Jewelry shop in New Orleans Square at Disneyland; opened Jul. 5, 1997, replacing Mlle. Antoinette's Parfumerie. Operated by Dianne's Estate Jewellery [sic] until Apr. 11, 2010, then reopened May 28, offering accessories and designer handbags. Closed Apr. 2011 to prepare for the return of the perfume shop.

Jewelry Shop Fine jewelry establishment along Main Street, U.S.A. at Disneyland; presented by Random Parts, Inc. Jul. 17, 1955–1956, then by Long's Jul. 7, 1956–1966. Later named Rings 'n Things. Closed May 26, 1986, switching locations with the Disneyana Shop, and reopened May 31 as New Century Jewelry.

Jiko – The Cooking Place Signature restaurant in Jambo House at Disney's Animal Kingdom Lodge at Walt Disney World; opened Apr. 16, 2001. A blend of traditional African, Indian, and Mediterranean cuisine is served in an elegant dining room evoking the play of light from dusk into nightfall.

Jim Dear and Darling Human owners of Lady in *Lady and the Tramp*; voiced by Lee Millar and Peggy Lee.

Jim Henson's Muppet*Vision 3-D See Muppet*Vision 3D.

Jiminy Cricket Pinocchio's conscience, who was later used to introduce educational cartoons on the *Mickey Mouse Club* TV show; voiced by Cliff Edwards. Before Walt Disney selected Jiminy Cricket as the character's name, the phrase was used as an exclamation denoting surprise or bewilderment. According to the *Oxford English Dictionary*, the phrase has been around since 1848. In *Snow White and the Seven Dwarfs*, produced over 2 years before *Pinocchio*, the Dwarfs exclaim, "Jiminy Crickets!" when they return to their cottage and find the lights on.

Jiminy Cricket Presents Bongo (TV) Show aired Sep. 28, 1955. Directed by Hamilton S. Luske. Walt discusses the creation of "When You Wish Upon a Star," sung in *Pinocchio* by Jiminy Cricket; then Jiminy introduces *Bongo* along with *Chicken Little* and *Figaro and Cleo*.

Jiminy Cricket, P.S. (Problem Solver) (film) Educational film; released in Sep. 1983. The film uses clips from Disney cartoons to introduce children to logic and critical thinking.

Jimirro, James P. He joined Disney in 1973 in the Walt Disney Educational Media Company, becoming its exec. vice president in 1974. In 1982 he was made exec. vice president—telecommunications for Walt Disney Productions, and he spearheaded the establishment of The Disney Channel, serving as its first president. He left Disney in 1985.

Jimmy Kimmel Live! (TV) Hour-long, late-night talk show starring Jimmy Kimmel; premiered on ABC Jan. 26, 2003. The show features celebrity guests and live comedy segments, and is taped each weeknight on Hollywood Blvd. next door to the El Capitan Theatre in Hollywood. Produced by Jackhole Industries in association with Touchstone Television.

Jimmy Starr's Show Business Main Street, U.S.A. shop in Disneyland; open Mar. 23, 1956–1959, selling movie photos, autographs, and collectibles. It was superseded by Wonderland Music.

Jing Hua (film) Animated short; digitally released Jan. 24, 2020, on Disney+, following a Jun. 14, 2019, debut at the Annecy International Animation Film Festival. A grieving martial artist pays tribute to her recently departed teacher by creating a painted world using a magical form of kung fu. Directed by Jerry Huynh. 2 min. From the Walt Disney Animation Studios Short Circuit program.

Jitney Main Street, U.S.A. vehicle in the Magic Kingdom at Walt Disney World; debuted Oct. 1, 1971.

Jittlov, Mike Filmmaker; created the inventive stop-motion films *The Collector, The Rat Race,* and *Mouse Mania* for the *Mickey's 50* TV special in 1978 and appeared in *Major Effects* along with 2 additional films he made.

J. J. Fate Bearded duck "fall guy" in *How to Have an Accident in the Home* and *How to Have an Accident at Work*; voiced by Bill Thompson. His full name is Jinx Jonah Fate.

Joanna Goanna lizard working with Percival McLeach in *The Rescuers Down Under*; voiced by Frank Welker.

Job, The (TV) Half-hour comedy series on ABC; aired Mar. 14, 2001–Apr. 24, 2002. The lives and high jinks of a group of opportunistic New York City police detectives. From DreamWorks Television and Touchstone Television. Stars Denis Leary (Mike McNeil), Adam Ferrara (Tommy Manetti), Lenny Clarke (Frank Harrigan), Bill Nunn (Pip Phillips), Diane Farr (Jan Fendrich), John Ortiz (Ruben Sommariba), Julian Acosta (Al Rodriguez), Keith David (Lt. Williams). From Apostle, The Cloudland Company, DreamWorks Television, and Touchstone Television.

Jobs, Steven (1955–2011) He is best known for cofounding the Apple Computer Company in 1976. He began a Disney association in 1995 when his Pixar Animation Studios produced *Toy Story*. After selling Pixar to Disney in 2006, he became a member of the Disney Board of Directors. He was named a Disney Legend in 2013.

Jock Plucky terrier friend of Lady's in *Lady and the Tramp*; voiced by Bill Thompson. Jock's real name is Heather Lad o' Glencairn.

Jock Lindsey's Hangar Bar Aviation-themed bar in The Landing at Disney Springs at Walt Disney World; opened Sep. 22, 2015. Named after Jock, Indiana Jones's frequent pilot, the waterfront location offers food, drink, and décor inspired by the aviator's globe-trotting across the continents.

Joe Carioca SEE JOSÉ CARIOCA.

Joe Gardner Middle school band teacher in *Soul* with a passion for jazz; voiced by Jamie Foxx.

Joel, Billy Singer/songwriter; provided the voice of Dodger in *Oliver & Company*. He appeared on TV in *The Dream Is Alive* and *The Wonderful World of Disney: 40 Years of Television Magic*, and on video in *Simply Mad About the Mouse*.

Joerger, Fred (1913–2005) Imagineer; from 1953 until his retirement in 1979, Fred crafted dimensional models for park attractions, as well as for motion pictures, including *20,000 Leagues Under the Sea* and *Mary Poppins*. He had a special knack for creating decorative rockwork out of plaster, including the huge stones featured in the Jungle Cruise and Big Thunder Mountain Railroad. He also established the standards for Imagineering field art direction, assuring that attractions like Submarine Voyage and Pirates of the Caribbean achieved the right look. After his retirement, he returned to Disney as field art director for the building of EPCOT Center. He was named a Disney Legend in 2001.

Joey Baby kangaroo star of *Daddy Duck* (1948).

Johann, Dallas He was hired as a Mouseketeer for the original *Mickey Mouse Club* but was replaced by his brother, John Lee Johann, shortly afterward.

Johann, John Lee Mouseketeer from the 1950s *Mickey Mouse Club* TV show.

Johansson, Scarlett Actress; appeared in *The Horse Whisperer* (Grace), *The Prestige* (Olivia), and as Black Widow in the Marvel Studios films. She voiced Kaa in *The Jungle Book* (2016).

Johari Treasures Meaning "gem" in Swahili, a shop in Disney's Animal Kingdom Villas—Kidani Village at Walt Disney World; opened May 1, 2009, selling African crafts, clothing, and Disney souvenirs.

John, Elton Singer/songwriter; he wrote the music for the songs in *The Lion King*, with Tim Rice writing the lyrics. They won an Academy Award for "Can You Feel the Love Tonight." Returned to provide additional material for the Broadway adaptation and the 2019 film, for which he performed "Never Too Late" for the end credits. John and Rice had previously collaborated on *Elaborate Lives: The Legend* *of Aida* (later *Aida*) for the stage. He made a cameo in *The Country Bears*; appeared on TV in *Mickey's 50, Totally Minnie, The Wonderful World of Disney: 40 Years of Television Magic, Lady Gaga & The Muppets' Holiday Spectacular*, and *Disneyland 60: The Wonderful World of Disney*. He exec. produced and contributed original songs for *Gnomeo & Juliet*. He was named a Disney Legend in 2006. SEE ALSO GOODBYE YELLOW BRICK ROAD: THE FINAL ELTON JOHN PERFORMANCES AND THE YEARS THAT MADE HIS LEGEND (TV).

John The older of Wendy's 2 brothers in *Peter Pan*, wearing a top hat and glasses; voiced by Paul Collins.

John Carter (film) A war-weary, former Civil War captain, John Carter, is accidentally transported to the planet of Barsoom (Mars) where he is befriended by Tars Tarkas, the leader of the Tharks, tall, green, 4-armed creatures. He soon becomes reluctantly embroiled in a conflict among other inhabitants of the planet, with Zodanga fighter, Sab Than, aided by shape-shifting Therns, battling the peaceful community of Helium and attempting to marry their princess, Dejah Thoris, against her wishes. On the mysterious planet, Carter soon finds his strength and jumping abilities greatly amplified. In a world on the brink of collapse, he rediscovers his humanity when he realizes that the survival of Barsoom and its people rests in his hands. Directed by Andrew Stanton. Stars Taylor Kitsch (John Carter), Lynn Collins (Dejah Thoris), Willem Dafoe (Tars Tarkas), Samantha Morton (Sola), Dominic West (Sab Than), Polly Walker (Sarkoja), Ciaran Hinds (Tardos Mors). Based on the Edgar Rice Burroughs novel *A Princess of Mars*. Released Mar. 9, 2012, in Disney Digital 3-D and IMAX. This is the first live-action film directed by Pixar director Andrew Stanton. Filmed in Cinema-Scope. The film was a disappointment at the box office, leading to a significant write-off.

John Henry (film) A short cartoon telling the story of the legendary African American folk hero, who pitted his strength against that of a machine and won the contest. The story is told from the point of view of John's wife, Polly. Directed by Mark Henn. Released in Los Angeles for Academy Award consideration on Oct. 30, 2000. Voices include Geoffrey Jones (John Henry), Alfre Woodard (Polly speaking), Carrie Harrington (Polly singing), Tim Hodge (MacTavish), David Murray (Thomas). 9 min. The cartoon was completely made by Disney's Feature Animation Studio in Florida. The Grammy Award–winning ensemble, Sounds of Blackness, provided the music.

John Muir: Father of Our National Parks (film) Educational film produced by Anthony Corso; released in Sep. 1973. Dramatization of Muir's struggle to preserve our scenic wonders.

Johnny and the Sprites (TV) Half-hour series on Disney Channel; premiered Jan. 13, 2007. Johnny, a singer/songwriter, moves out to the country after inheriting a family home. He soon discovers a portal in his backyard leading to the enchanted world of the Sprites: Ginger, Basil, Lily, Root, and Sage. Together, Johnny and the Sprites share valuable lessons about getting along with others and respecting the world around them. Stars John Tartaglia (Johnny/Sage), Heather Asch (Root), Leslie Carrara-Rudolph (Ginger), Tim Lagasse (Basil), Carmen Osbahr (Lily), Natalie Venetia Belcon (Gwen). A Happy Puppet/Homegirl Production in association with Disney Channel. The show used unique hand and rod puppets.

Johnny Appleseed (film) Segment of *Melody Time*, with Dennis Day telling the story of the young man who planted apple trees throughout the West. Released as a short Dec. 25, 1955. 19 min. Released for schools as *Legend of Johnny Appleseed*.

Johnny Fedora and Alice Bluebonnet (film) Segment of *Make Mine Music*, sung by the Andrews Sisters, about the romance between a boy and girl hat. Released as a short May 21, 1954. The title card on the film uses a variant spelling—*Johnnie*—though *Johnny* is more commonly used, including on the one-sheet poster and sheet music. *Blue Bonnet* has occasionally been spelled as 2 words.

Johnny Kapahala: Back on Board (TV) A Disney Channel Original Movie; first aired Jun. 8, 2007. When avid snowboarder and surfer Johnny Kapahala returns to his hometown in Hawai'i to attend the wedding of his grandfather, a surf legend, he discovers he has a new step-uncle, a 12-year-old boy named Chris who is a mountain boarder with a rebellious attitude. The wedding and the grand opening of the family's new surf shop are soon put in jeopardy by the turmoil Chris and Johnny create as they attempt to come to terms with each other and their newly blended family. Directed by Eric Bross. Stars Brandon Baker (Johnny), Cary-Hiroyuki Tagawa (Grandpa), Jake T. Austin

(Chris), Rose McIver (Val), Lil' J (Sam), Mary Page Keller (Melanie), Yuji Okumoto (Pete), Robyn Lively (Carla), Andrew Allen (Jared). A sequel to *Johnny Tsunami*.

Johnny Shiloh (TV) Two-part show; aired Jan. 20 and 27, 1963. Directed by James Neilson. Johnny Clem becomes a drummer boy in the Civil War at age 10. Though he is too young to join the soldiers as they march off to battle, he sneaks after them. At Shiloh, with the Union soldiers losing, Johnny begins drumming to encourage them, and his courage under battle conditions leads to instant fame. He gets a promotion and becomes a messenger for the general. Stars Kevin Corcoran, Brian Keith, Darryl Hickman, Skip Homeier, Edward Platt, Regis Toomey, Rickie Sorensen, Eddie Hodges. Based on a true story, as told in the book by James A. Rhodes and Dean Jauchius; the real Johnny Clem remained in the army and retired as a brigadier general in 1916.

Johnny Tremain (film) Johnny, through an injury to his hand in a silversmith's shop, gains new insight into himself and those around him as he is plunged into exciting events leading up to the Boston Tea Party at the outbreak of the American Revolution. Released Jun. 19, 1957. The first Disney feature directed by Robert Stevenson, who would go on to be one of the major Disney directors in the 1960s and 1970s. 80 min. Stars Hal Stalmaster (Johnny Tremain), Luana Patten (Cilla Lapham), Dick Beymer (Rab Silsbee), Jeff York (James Otis), Sebastian Cabot (Jonathan Lyte). Sharon Disney has a small part in the film. Features the song "The Liberty Tree" by George Bruns and Tom Blackburn. The film was originally meant as programming for the Disney TV series, but when production costs mounted, Walt decided to release it as a feature film. It aired on TV the following year in 2 parts entitled *The Boston Tea Party* and *The Shot Heard 'Round the World*. The film helped inspire a proposed area for Disneyland called Liberty Street; while the land was never built, the concept would evolve into Liberty Square, which opened in the Magic Kingdom at Walt Disney World in 1971, complete with the Liberty Tree.

Johnny Tsunami (TV) A Disney Channel Original Movie; first aired Jul. 24, 1999. Johnny Kapahala, a teen surfing sensation, is uprooted from his Hawai'i home and forced to move to a tiny ski resort town in Vermont. After getting caught in the middle of a long-standing rivalry between the local prep school

skiers and the public school snowboarders, Johnny Tsunami, with help from his legendary grandfather, learns to use his competitive spirit and athletic abilities to unite the 2 foes. Directed by Steve Boyum. Stars Brandon Baker (Johnny Kapahala), Cary-Hiroyuki Tagawa (Johnny Tsunami), Kirsten Storms (Emily Pritchard), Lee Thompson Young (Sam Sterling).

Johns, Glynis Actress; appeared in *The Sword and the Rose* (Mary Tudor), *Rob Roy* (Helen Mary MacGregor), *Mary Poppins* (Winifred Banks), *The Ref* (Rose), and *While You Were Sleeping* (Elsie). She was honored as a Disney Legend in 1998.

Johnson, Ben (1919–1996) Actor; appeared in *Ten Who Dared* (George Bradley), *Tex* (Cole Collins), and *Angels in the Outfield* (Hank Murphy), and on TV in *Ride a Northbound Horse*.

Johnson, Don Actor; appeared in *Paradise* (Ben Reed), *Born Yesterday* (Paul Verrall), *Guilty as Sin* (David Greenhill), and *When in Rome* (Beth's dad, uncredited), and on TV in *Blood & Oil* (Hap Briggs) and as a host of *The Grand Opening of Euro Disney*.

Johnson, Dwayne Actor; appeared in *The Game Plan* (Joe Kingman), *Race to Witch Mountain* (Jack Bruno), and *Jungle Cruise* (Frank Wolff); on TV in the *Disney Parks Unforgettable Christmas Celebration* and *Mickey's 90th Spectacular*; and had cameo roles on Disney Channel in *Hannah Montana*, *Wizards of Waverly Place*, and *Cory in the House*. He voiced Maui in *Moana*. Also a producer for *Jungle Cruise* and exec. producer for *Behind the Attraction* on Disney+.

Johnson, George A. He voiced Goofy in several cartoons in the 1940s.

Johnson, James A. (1917–1976) He joined Disney in 1938, became assistant secretary of the corporation in 1947, and was named secretary in 1950. He worked with Disney publications 1950–1962 and became general manager (and later president) of the Walt Disney Music Company in 1958. He retired in 1975 and was named a Disney Legend in 2006.

Johnson Space Center (film) Educational film in the EPCOT Educational Media Collection: Minnie's Science Field Trips series; released in Sep. 1988. 18 min. A guided tour through the astronaut training center explaining principles of space science. (Walt Disney Imagineering designed the new visitor center at the Space Center in Houston, which opened in 1992.)

Johnston, O. B. (1901–1992) He joined Disney in 1934 in merchandising and eventually headed the character merchandise division, operating first out of New York City and then Burbank, until his retirement in 1972.

Johnston, Ollie (1912–2008) Animator; known as one of Walt's "Nine Old Men," he joined the Studio in 1935 as an inbetweener on Mickey Mouse cartoons. His work can be seen in 24 animated features beginning with *Snow White and the Seven Dwarfs*, with many as directing animator. He retired in 1978. With his lifelong friend Frank Thomas, he authored *Disney Animation: The Illusion of Life* and several other books on the subject. He was honored with the Disney Legends Award in 1989. He was profiled with Frank Thomas in the documentary *Frank and Ollie*, produced by Thomas's son. Ollie was the last living member of Walt's "Nine Old Men."

JoJo's Circus (TV) Stop-motion animated series on Playhouse Disney on Disney Channel; debuted on Sep. 28, 2003. JoJo Tickle is a curious 6-year-old circus clown who invites preschoolers to join her in lively, imaginative movement with games and songs. Created by Jim Jinkins and David Campbell. Voices include Madeleine Martin (JoJo), Robert Smith (Goliath), Cole Caplan (Tater).

Joker, the Amiable Ocelot (TV) Show aired Dec. 11, 1966. A desert loner adopts an ocelot he finds in an old car, but later realizes that it must be set free. The ocelot finds a mate, and so does the loner, falling for a young nurse who moves to the area. Stars Robert Becker, Jan McNabb. Narrated by Winston Hibler.

Jolie, Angelina Actress; appeared in *Playing God* (Claire), *Gone in 60 Seconds* (Sway Wayland), *Eternals* (Thena), and in the title role in *Maleficent* and *Maleficent: Mistress of Evil*. She voiced Stella in *The One and Only Ivan*.

Jolly Holiday Bakery Café Quick-service restaurant with a *Mary Poppins* theme in the Plaza Pavilion in the Disneyland Central Plaza; opened Jan. 7, 2012, after a soft opening Jan. 5. Sandwiches and pastries are served.

Jolly Trolley Attraction in Mickey's Toontown at Disneyland; opened Jan. 24, 1993. To achieve the cartoon look of the trolley, Imagineers arranged its wheel sizes so it did not just glide down the tracks of Toontown, but it jiggled, lurched, and weaved. The popularity of Toontown meant that it was sometimes difficult for the trolley to get through the masses of people. It was later retired from service but was parked in the land as a photo spot. Also in Tokyo Disneyland, Apr. 15, 1996–2009.

JONAS (TV) Series on Disney Channel; aired May 2, 2009–Oct. 3, 2010. The Lucas brothers try to balance school (Horace Mantis Academy) and family while becoming teenage superstar musicians in a band called JONAS, named after the street on which they live. Stars Kevin Jonas (Kevin Lucas), Joe Jonas (Joe Lucas), Nick Jonas (Nick Lucas), Chelsea Staub (Stella Malone), Nicole Anderson (Macy Misa), John Ducey (Tom Lucas), Frankie Jonas (Frankie Lucas), Rebecca Creskoff (Sandy Lucas), Big Rob Feggans (The Big Man). For the show's 2nd season, beginning Jun. 20, 2010, the title was changed to *JONAS L.A.* to reflect a move to Los Angeles.

Jonas Brothers Kevin, Joe, and Nick Jonas became instant rock star successes in 2007, with their self-titled album from Hollywood Records selling over a million copies. They toured with Miley Cyrus on her concert tour, and then starred in the Disney Channel Original Movie *Camp Rock* and their own TV series, *JONAS*. In a deal with Live Nation, they set out on a 2-year, 140-city tour of their own.

Jonas Brothers: The 3-D Concert Experience (film) A documentary blending excerpts from the brothers' 2008 "Burning Up" concert tour with guest performances, exclusive behind-the-scenes footage, new songs, and swarming fans. Directed by Bruce Hendricks in Disney Digital 3-D. Released Feb. 27, 2009. Stars Kevin Jonas, Joe Jonas, Nick Jonas, with guest performances by Demi Lovato and Taylor Swift. 76 min. The main concert was filmed at the Honda Center in Anaheim, with additional filming at Madison Square Garden and other sites in New York City.

Jones, Dean (1931–2015) Actor; appeared in *That Darn Cat!* (Zeke Kelso), *The Ugly Dachshund* (Mark Garrison), *Monkeys, Go Home!* (Hank Dussard), *Blackbeard's Ghost* (Steve Walker), *The Horse in the Gray Flannel Suit* (Frederick Bolton), *The Love Bug* (Jim Douglas), *The Million Dollar Duck* (Prof. Albert Dooley), *Snowball Express* (Johnny Baxter), *The Shaggy D.A.* (Wilby Daniels),

Herbie Goes to Monte Carlo (Jim Douglas), and *That Darn Cat* (remake, Mr. Flint); and on TV in *Disney's Greatest Dog Stars, Kraft Salutes Walt Disney World's 10th Anniversary*, the 1995 remake of *The Computer Wore Tennis Shoes* (Dean Carlson), and the *Herbie, the Love Bug* limited series and the 1997 TV movie of *The Love Bug*, reprising the role of Jim Douglas. He was named a Disney Legend in 1995.

Jones, Dickie (1927–2014) He voiced Pinocchio and was named a Disney Legend in 2000.

Jones, Freddie (1927–2019) He voiced Dallben in *The Black Cauldron* and appeared in *The Count of Monte Cristo* (Col. Villefort).

Jones, James Earl Actor; appeared in *Three Fugitives* (Dugan), *True Identity* (as himself), *Jefferson in Paris* (Madison Hemings), and *Fantasia/2000* (as himself). He voiced Mufasa in *The Lion King* (1994 and 2019); Santa Claus in *Recess*; Darth Vader in *Rogue One: A Star Wars Story, Star Wars: The Rise of Skywalker*, and the Star Tours – The Adventures Continue attraction; and narrated Disneynature's *Earth*. He was named a Disney Legend in 2019.

Jones, Mary (1915–2008) She began working in Disneyland in 1962 and was soon asked to head Community Relations. She administered the Community Service Awards and other programs, and coordinated visits by heads of state, royalty, and other important dignitaries. She retired in 1986 and was named a Disney Legend in 2005.

Jones, Shirley Actress; appeared on TV in *The Adventures of Pollyanna* (Aunt Polly), and made guest appearances in *Mickey's 50, Ruby & the Rockits* (Shirley Gallagher), *Good Luck Charlie* (Grandma Linda Duncan), and *Cougar Town* (Anne).

Jones, Tommy Lee Actor; appeared in *Fire Birds* (Brad Little) and *Lincoln* (Thaddeus Stevens).

Jordan, Jim (1896–1988) Actor; provided the voice of Orville in *The Rescuers*.

Jordan, Michael B. Actor; appeared in the Black Panther films (Erik Killmonger), and narrated *America the Beautiful* on Disney+.

José Carioca Also known as Joe Carioca, Donald Duck's Brazilian parrot friend first appeared in *Saludos Amigos* (1943); voiced by José Oliveira. The name came from the Portuguese word that is used to refer to a native of Rio de Janeiro, "carioca." The character was so popular he was brought back in *The Three Caballeros* in 1945. He also starred in a newspaper comic strip for 2 years.

José Come Bien (film) Portuguese Reading Film #2. Produced under the auspices of the Coordinator of Inter-American Affairs. Delivered Mar. 14, 1945. SEE SOUTH AMERICA.

Jostens Center SEE VISA ATHLETIC CENTER.

Journey Into Imagination Future World pavilion in EPCOT; opened Oct. 1, 1982, featuring a ride of the same title, which opened Mar. 5, 1983, sponsored by Eastman Kodak (1982–2010). The pavilion itself consists of pyramids of glass at odd angles, which, when lit from within at night, present a unique view. Outside, children and parents are often transfixed by the leapfrog fountains, with plumes of water shooting over their heads that disappear into nearby planters. Some of the kids find themselves getting an unexpected soaking when they leap up to try to impede the path of the water spout. Inside, Disney Imagineers given the near-impossible task of trying to portray imagination nevertheless engineered a fascinating look at the creative process. The jolly, redheaded Dreamfinder, with his small purple dragon creation, Figment, were hosts on a marvelous journey into the realms of art, literature, and science, with the memorable theme song "One Little Spark" by Richard M. and Robert B. Sherman. Also in the pavilion were the hands-on Image Works and the Magic Eye Theater. Originally, *Magic Journeys* was the featured 3-D film; it was followed in 1986 by *Captain EO*, and in 1994 by *Honey, I Shrunk the Audience. Captain EO* returned 2010–2015, and the Disney & Pixar Short Film Festival followed. The ride-through attraction closed Oct. 10, 1998, for a major refurbishment. The pavilion reopened with a new title, IMAGINATION!, Oct. 1, 1999, with a totally revised ride called Journey Into Your Imagination and a new Image Works, called Image Works—The Kodak "What If?" Labs. Dr. Nigel Channing, played by Eric Idle, hosted the ride, which sent passengers through the labs of the Imagination Institute, but missing were the popular Dreamfinder and Figment characters. Based on guest demand, the ride closed Oct. 8, 2001, and reopened Jun. 1, 2002, as

Journey Into Imagination With Figment. In this version of the ride, Figment interrupts Dr. Channing's tour through the Institute's Sensory Labs to prove how "imagination works best when it's set free."

Journey into Jungle Book Live stage musical based on *The Jungle Book*; opened in 1998 as the first show in Theater in the Wild at Disney's Animal Kingdom. Closed Apr. 8, 1999, to be succeeded by *Tarzan Rocks!*

Journey Into Narnia: Creating the Lion, the Witch and the Wardrobe Walk-through experience into Narnia in Soundstage 4 on Mickey Avenue in Disney-MGM Studios; open Dec. 9, 2005–Jan. 1, 2008. Became Journey Into Narnia: Prince Caspian Jun. 26, 2008–Sep. 10, 2011.

Journey of Natty Gann, The (film) During the mid-1930s, the father of 14-year-old Natty has to leave Chicago suddenly to find lumbering work in Washington State. Natty sets off alone to follow him across the country. She hops trains, befriends a wolf and a teenage drifter, and after a series of adventures is reunited with her father. Released Sep. 27, 1985. Directed by Jeremy Kagan. 101 min. Stars Meredith Salenger (Natty Gann), John Cusack (Harry), Ray Wise (Sol Gann), Barry Miller (Parker), Scatman Crothers (Sherman), Lainie Kazan (Connie), Verna Bloom (farm woman), Bruce M. Fischer (Charlie Linfield). Production designer Paul Sylbert was called upon to create a vintage Chicago street scene complete with pushcart vendors, a Hooverville consisting of 60 shacks, and an authentic period logging camp. The film's emphasis on authenticity extended to the activities of the lumber camp. Ray Wise, playing Natty's father, learned how to top trees with a big ax as it was actually done 50 years ago. For some scenes he had to climb 40-foot-high trees. The local experts recognized his talents and at the completion of shooting awarded him a handmade throwing ax and target. Salenger performed most of her own stunts. The "wolf" Natty encounters in the film was a wolf/malamute mix named Jed, who, with the application of some water-based makeup, looked the part. Costume designer Albert Wolsky also relied heavily on photographic research in creating the wardrobe. In all, Wolsky came up with nearly 2,000 costumes for the film, including some scenes with more than 250 extras. Hats were frequently used to disguise the 1980s-style coiffures. The film was nominated for an Academy Award for Best Costume Design.

Journey of Water, Inspired by Moana World Nature attraction planned for EPCOT. Along a self-guided, interactive exploration trail, guests discover the importance of water and its journey from the sky to the seas and back.

Journey to the Center of the Earth Mysterious Island attraction, sponsored by Dai-Ichi Mutual Life Insurance Co., inside Mount Prometheus in Tokyo DisneySea; opened Sep. 4, 2001. Boarding fantastic subterranean vehicles developed by Captain Nemo, guests explore vast underground realms of never-before-seen beauty, mystery, and wonder, along the way encountering unexpected peril—including an encounter with a ferocious lava monster. It is one of the most popular attractions in the park.

Journey to the Valley of the Emu, The (TV) Show aired Jan. 22, 1978. Directed by Roy E. Disney. An aborigine boy in the Australian outback adopts an injured dingo. The 2 of them set off to find an emu so he can bring back a feather and signify that he is a man. A snakebite necessitates an emergency airlift to a hospital, but eventually the boy is able to return to his quest. Stars Victor Palmer. Narrated by Paul Ricketts.

Joy Riley's exuberant emotion in *Inside Out*; voiced by Amy Poehler.

Joy Luck Club, The (film) The lives of 3 generations of Chinese women are interwoven in this story of mothers and daughters attempting to break through the barriers that often stand in the way of understanding each other. Four mothers, born in China, now Americans, have met weekly for 30 years to pay mah-jongg and have named themselves the Joy Luck Club. At the most recent meeting, June, the daughter of Suyuan, who has died, is inducted into the group. Playing with her "aunties," June learns much about them, her culture, and herself. The lives of each of the mothers in China are chronicled as well as the lives of their American daughters. June discovers her mother's secret of having abandoned twin daughters in wartime China, and she is able to realize her mother's greatest dream by going to China herself and reuniting the family. Released Sep. 8, 1993. Directed by Wayne Wang. A Hollywood Pictures release. Based on the best-selling book by Amy Tan. 139 min. Stars Kieu Chinh (Suyuan), Tsai Chin (Lindo), Lisa Lu (An Mei), France Nuyen (Ying Ying), Rosalind Chao (Rose), Lauren Tom (Lena), Tamlyn Tomita

(Waverly), Ming-Na Wen (June). Filmed on location in the San Francisco area, with interiors in a former chocolate factory in Richmond, Virginia, as well as a 6-week location shoot in China.

Joyce, William Author/illustrator; his books inspired *Rolie Polie Olie* on Disney Channel and *Meet the Robinsons*, both of which he exec. produced. He also contributed character concepts for *Toy Story* and visual development for *A Bug's Life*.

Judels, Charles (1881–1969) Actor; provided the voice of Stromboli and the Coachman in *Pinocchio*.

Judge Dredd (film) In the 22nd century, Mega-City One has become a haven for millions of people from the surrounding towns and rural areas destroyed by war and ecological disaster. Thrown together and confined in cramped, overcrowded monolithic apartment buildings, with no hope of employment or a better future, they strike out at each other, rocking the city with rioting and unrest. Since regular law enforcement cannot maintain order amidst such monumental chaos, Judge Dredd is created as part of a top secret DNA experiment, the Janus Project. In his mind are all the great minds of jurisprudence, and he is a one-man police force, judge, jury, and executioner. But part of the project went askew, creating a master criminal, Rico, as evil as Judge Dredd is just. Judge Dredd has to battle the powers of evil for his own soul. A Hollywood Pictures film, in association with Cinergi Productions. Directed by Danny Cannon. Released Jun. 30, 1995. Stars Sylvester Stallone (Judge Dredd), Armand Assante (Rico), Diane Lane (Judge Hershey), Rob Schneider (Fergie), Joan Chen (Ilsa), Jürgen Prochnow (Judge Griffin), Max Von Sydow (Judge Fargo), Balthazar Getty (Olmeyer). 96 min. Filmed in CinemaScope in Iceland and at England's Shepperton Studios. Based on the English science fiction comic hero created by writer John Wagner and artist Carlos Ezquerra.

Judge for Yourself (TV) One-hour syn. series; aired Sep. 12, 1994–Apr. 7, 1995. A talk show/courtroom combination, with the in-studio jury witnessing a discussion of a particular topic among the show's guests, then deliberating and handing down a verdict. Hosted by Bill Handel. From Buena Vista Television and Faded Denim Productions.

Judge Steve Harvey (TV) Hour-long unscripted comedy series on ABC; premiered Jan. 4, 2022. Real-life people with real-life conflicts present their case in Steve Harvey's courtroom. With the help of Nancy Price, his trusted bailiff by trade, Steve plays by his own rules, basing his courtroom on his own life experiences and some good old common sense. From East 112 and Den of Thieves, in association with Walt Disney Television's alternative unit.

Judy Hopps Courageous bunny on Zootopia's police force; voiced by Ginnifer Goodwin.

Jue, Daniel Imagineer; he began at Disney in 1988, designing displays for The Disney Store, and transferred to Walt Disney Imagineering in 1990 as a show set designer. He contributed to The Twilight Zone Tower of Terror at Walt Disney World and Indiana Jones Adventure at Disneyland, and was later production designer and field art director for Test Track, Pooh's Hunny Hunt, and Expedition Everest. He was named portfolio creative executive for Tokyo Disney Resort in 2010, overseeing new attractions and park expansions, and additionally served as vice president of Menu and Master Planning 2011–2013.

Juliet's Collections & Treasures Mediterranean Harbor cosmetics shop in Tokyo DisneySea; open Sep. 4, 2001–Nov. 2012. Décor was inspired by the Capulet family in *Romeo and Juliet*. Replaced by Villa Donaldo Home Shop. SEE ALSO ROMEO'S WATCHES & JEWELRY.

Julius Walt Disney's first named animated cartoon character, a cat who appeared in the Alice Comedies 1924–1927.

Julius Katz & Sons Home décor shop on Buena Vista Street in Disney California Adventure; opened Jun. 15, 2012. "Julius Katz" was inspired by Julius the cat from the Alice Comedies.

Jumba Alien outlaw and mad scientist behind Experiment 626 in *Lilo & Stitch*; voiced by David Ogden Stiers.

Jumbo Pictures Animation company founded by Jim Jinkins and David Campbell in 1991 and acquired by Disney in Feb. 1996. The company produced *Brand Spanking New Doug*, later renamed *Disney's Doug*, after a series that had begun on Nickelodeon, and in 1999 produced *Doug's 1st Movie* for theaters. They also produced *101 Dalmatians: The Series* for ABC and *PB&J Otter* for Disney Channel. The studio closed in 2000.

Jump In! (TV) A Disney Channel Original Movie;

first aired Jan. 12, 2007. A teen, Izzy, is known around his Brooklyn neighborhood as a promising natural-born boxer whose father is a local gym owner. Izzy's neighbor, Mary, is the leader of the Joy Jumpers, a 4-girl double Dutch team trying to make its mark in the tournament world. Double Dutch is a combination of lightning-fast dance steps, gymnastics, and martial arts moves—all executed with pinpoint precision while leaping through 2 ropes twirling at blinding speeds. When one of the Joy Jumpers defects to a rival crew, Mary and her team beg Izzy to substitute for her at the upcoming citywide finals. Izzy is as surprised as anyone to discover he has a penchant for double Dutch, but he's terrified of being ridiculed by his peers and of dashing his father's hopes of raising a boxing champion. When word gets out, Izzy finally learns to follow his heart rather than let others determine his destiny. Directed by Paul Hoen. Stars Corbin Bleu (Izzy Daniels), Keke Palmer (Mary Thomas), David Reivers (Kenneth Daniels), Kylee Russell (Karin Daniels), Shanica Knowles (Shauna Keaton), Laivan Greene (Keisha Ray), Patrick Johnson (Rodney Tyler), Micah Williams (L'il Earl Jackson). David Reivers is Corbin Bleu's real-life father.

Jumpin' Jellyfish Attraction in Paradise Gardens Park (formerly Paradise Pier) in Disney California Adventure; opened Feb. 8, 2001. Young guests bounce up and down in a total of 12 jellyfish-shaped vessels which lurch up two 50-foot towers. Also at Triton's Kingdom in Mermaid Lagoon at Tokyo DisneySea; opened Sep. 4, 2001.

Jumping Ship (TV) A Disney Channel Original Movie; first aired Aug. 17, 2001. Michael has big plans to show his country cousin, Tommy, a good time aboard a luxury yacht, only to discover the yacht he's chartered is actually a dilapidated fishing boat. When modern-day pirates give chase, the boys are forced to jump ship, leaving them stranded on a desert island with the boat's captain, Jake Hunter. Directed by Michael Lange. Stars Andy Lawrence (Tommy Biggs), Joey Lawrence (Michael Woods), Matt Lawrence (Jake Hunter), Susan Walters (Jules Biggs), Stephen Burleigh (Glenn Woods). A sequel to *Horse Sense*, this film was shot on the Gold Coast of Australia.

Jungle Book, The (film) A human boy, Mowgli, is raised in the jungle by wolves until it is deemed unsafe for him to stay because of Shere Khan, the tiger, who has vowed to kill the Man-cub. Bagheera, the panther, is selected to accompany Mowgli on his journey back to civilization but has a difficult time because the boy does not want to leave. Meeting Baloo the bear, a lovable "jungle bum," Mowgli is even more certain he wants to stay with his friends. But after an encounter with the mad ape King Louie, and being pressed to return to the Man-village by Baloo and Bagheera, Mowgli runs away. Alone in the jungle, he meets Shere Khan; but after the last-minute intervention of his friends, he manages to defeat the tiger. Soon after, he meets a young girl from the Man-village and willingly returns to civilization. Released Oct. 18, 1967. Directed by Wolfgang Reitherman. Rudyard Kipling's classic tale of the jungle was the last animated feature Walt Disney supervised. 78 min. Voices include Phil Harris (Baloo), Sebastian Cabot (Bagheera), Louis Prima (King Louie), George Sanders (Shere Khan), Sterling Holloway (Kaa), J. Pat O'Malley (Buzzie), and Bruce Reitherman (Mowgli). The film became one of Disney's top all-time box office winners. Richard M. and Robert B. Sherman wrote the songs, which include "I Wan'na Be Like You," "Trust in Me," "My Own Home," "That's What Friends Are For," and "Colonel Hathi's March," aside from the Terry Gilkyson-provided and Oscar-nominated "The Bare Necessities." It was rereleased in theaters in 1978, 1984, and 1990. First released on video in 1991. A live-action version of the story was released in 1994.

Jungle Book, The (film) Live-action and CG film, based on the Rudyard Kipling stories, and inspired by the 1967 animated feature. Mowgli, a man-cub, has been raised by a family of wolves, but he finds he is no longer welcome in the jungle when fearsome tiger Shere Khan, who bears the scars of Man, promises to eliminate what he sees as a threat. Urged to abandon the only home he has ever known, Mowgli embarks on a journey of self-discovery, guided by panther-turned-stern mentor Bagheera and the free-spirited bear Baloo. Along the way, Mowgli encounters jungle creatures who do not exactly have his best interests at heart, including Kaa, a python, and the smooth-talking King Louie. Directed by Jon Favreau. Released Apr. 15, 2016, also in 3-D and 3-D IMAX. 106 min. Stars Neel Sethi (Mowgli). Voices include Idris Elba (Shere Khan), Ben Kingsley (Bagheera), Bill Murray (Baloo), Scarlett Johansson (Kaa), Christopher Walken (King Louie), Lupita Nyong'o (Raksha), Giancarlo Esposito (Akela). Live action is blended with photorealistic computer-animated animals and environments using up-to-the-minute technology to immerse audiences in an enchanting and lush world. Won an Academy Award for Best Visual

Effects (Robert Legato, Adam Valdez, Andrew R. Jones, Dan Lemmon).

Jungle Book, The Stage musical version of the 1967 Disney film and the stories of Rudyard Kipling; opened Jun. 21, 2013, and ran until Aug. 18 at the Goodman Theatre in Chicago. The show then moved to Boston's Huntington Theatre Company on Sep. 7, and ran until Oct. 13. It chronicles young Mowgli's adventures growing up with the animals in the Indian jungle. Songs by Richard M. and Robert B. Sherman were given new Indian–inspired orchestrations.

Jungle Book, Rudyard Kipling's The (film) Mowgli, a young man raised since childhood by wild animals in the jungles of India, is eventually drawn from the jungle by his attraction to the beautiful Kitty, daughter of Major Brydon, an important English military official. Mowgli's life changes as he reenters civilization. When an avaricious military officer, Capt. Boone, forces Mowgli to reveal the jungle's hidden treasures, Mowgli has to rely on his loyal animal friends—Grey Brother (a wolf), Baloo, and Bagheera—to survive the perilous ordeal and reunite with Kitty. Released Dec. 25, 1994. Directed by Stephen Sommers. Filmed in CinemaScope. 111 min. Stars Jason Scott Lee (Mowgli), Cary Elwes (Boone), Lena Headey (Kitty), Sam Neill (Col. Brydon), John Cleese (Dr. Plumford). The Kipling story had been filmed as a live-action motion picture by Alexander Korda in 1942 with Sabu as Mowgli, and as an animated film by Disney in 1967. For this production, interiors were filmed at the Mehboob Studios in Mumbai (then called Bombay), India, with jungle locations shot in Jodhpur. Because of the problems of shipping trained animals to India, additional "jungle" sets were created in Tennessee and on Fripp Island, South Carolina. The production had the largest group of trained animals—52 tigers, leopards, wolves, bears, elephants, horses, Brahma bulls, and monkeys—that had been assembled for any film since *Doctor Doolittle*.

Jungle Book, The: A Lesson in Accepting Change (film) Educational film; released in Sep. 1981. How change, in friends and environment, can be faced.

Jungle Book, The: Mowgli's Story (film) Direct-to-video live-action sequel to the 1967 animated feature; released Sep. 29, 1998. The narrator, the adult Mowgli, reflects on his childhood jungle adventures, from being raised by wolves to his friendship with Baloo to learning to be cunning and brave against the jungle's most fearsome animal, the menacing and venge-ful tiger Shere Khan. Directed by Nick Marck. Stars Brandon Baker (Mowgli), and the voices of Fred Savage (narrator), Eartha Kitt (Bagheera), Bryan Doyle-Murray (Baloo). 93 min.

Jungle Book Reunion, The (TV) Syn. special aired Jul. 19, 1990. Directed by Eric Schotz. Downtown Julie Brown hosts a look at *The Jungle Book* on the occasion of its reissue. Taped in Disney-MGM Studios at Walt Disney World. 30 min.

Jungle Book 2, The (film) Mowgli now lives in the Man-village, and he loves his new family and friends, especially his feisty little stepbrother Ranjan and his best pal, Shanti, the girl who initially wooed Mowgli from the jungle. But Mowgli misses his buddy Baloo, who likewise pines for his little Man-cub. Baloo isn't the only one hoping to see Mowgli again soon—Shere Khan impatiently awaits his revenge. When Mowgli sneaks away to the jungle, the chase is on to see who will find Mowgli first—his old pals, his new family, or the man-eating tiger. Released Feb. 14, 2003, after earlier releases on Feb. 5 in France and Feb. 7 in Sweden. From DisneyToon Studios. Directed by Steve Trenbirth. Voices include John Goodman (Baloo), Haley Joel Osment (Mowgli), Mae Whitman (Shanti), Tony Jay (Shere Khan), Bob Joles (Bagheera), John Rhys-Davies (Ranjan's father), Phil Collins (Lucky), Connor Funk (Ranjan), Jim Cummings (Kaa/Colonel Hathi/M. C. Monkey). 72 min.

Jungle Carnival Indoor game facility in Adventureland at Tokyo Disneyland; opened in 2015, taking the place of the Safari Trading Company, Pacific Export, and the Tiki Tropic Shop. Players compete in activities themed to *The Jungle Book* and win prizes.

Jungle Cat (film) True-Life Adventure feature; initial release on Dec. 16, 1959; general release on Aug. 10, 1960. Directed by James Algar. In this last of the True-Life Adventure series, Winston Hibler narrates the story of the South American jaguar. After the cat's history is given, the daily life of the jaguar is shown. Two jaguars mate, teach their kittens, hunt, and fight their worst enemies—the crocodile and huge boa constrictor, who are after their kittens. The setting of the film is the vivid jungle, with a striking finale of a sunset on the Amazon River. Animals depicted include giant anteaters, jungle otters, iguana, tapirs, sloths, and monkeys. Three top naturalist-photographers spent over 2 years in the Amazon basin of Brazil filming this superbly photographed documentary. 70 min.

Jungle Cat of the Amazon (film) Segment from *Jungle Cat*; released on 16 mm for schools in Dec. 1974. Shows the jaguar hunting and teaching its cubs the laws of survival.

Jungle Cruise Adventureland attraction in Disneyland; opened Jul. 17, 1955. Passengers board a jungle launch piloted by a witty skipper for an excursion along remote rivers of the world, glimpsing lifelike animals along the way. One of the most eagerly awaited attractions because of extensive publicity given by Walt Disney on pre-opening TV shows. Very little else was far enough along for him to show, but the channel was dug for the Jungle Cruise, trees were being planted, and Walt was able to talk his viewers through a typical ride, and eventually drive them through in his Nash Rambler (one of the TV show's sponsors). The attraction was expanded in 1962 (bathing pool of the Indian elephants), with more additions in 1964 (trapped safari, African veldt region) and 1976 (with 7 new scenes and 31 figures). A new 2-story queue building was added in Jun. 1994, and the channel was moved slightly to allow space for the queue area for the new Indiana Jones Adventure attraction, which opened in 1995. Additional enhancements were made in 2005, including an attack by piranhas. Also opened in Adventureland in the Magic Kingdom at Walt Disney World Oct. 1, 1971; in Tokyo Disneyland Apr. 15, 1983; and in Hong Kong Disneyland (as Jungle River Cruise) Sep. 12, 2005. In Hong Kong, there is a separate line for each language—Cantonese, Putonghua, and English. A Jungle Cruise was not built in Disneyland Paris because after the popularity of the Disneyland attraction, a number of European parks had already built their own jungle cruise based on the concept, so it was thought that to build one in Disneyland Paris would not have provided anything especially exciting to locals. Beginning in 2013, an annual holiday makeover, the "Jingle Cruise," was introduced at Disneyland and the Magic Kingdom at Walt Disney World, with renamed boats, holiday decorations, and spiel changes. The name of the Tokyo Disneyland attraction was changed to Jungle Cruise: Wildlife Expeditions Sep. 8, 2014, with new lighting, special effects, and music. In 2021, the Disneyland and Walt Disney World attractions received new scenes, including a sunken boat, a new trapped safari, and Trader Sam's Gift Shop. The new story line centers on Alberta Falls, proprietor of the Jungle Navigation Company (JNC), who inherited the business from her lost grandfather, and JNC founder, Dr. Albert Falls.

Jungle Cruise (film) Intrepid researcher Dr. Lily Houghton travels from London to the Amazon jungle and enlists wisecracking skipper Frank Wolff's questionable services to guide her downriver on *La Quila*, his ramshackle, but charming, boat. Lily is determined to uncover an ancient tree with unparalleled healing abilities—possessing the power to change the future of medicine. Thrust on this epic quest together, the unlikely duo encounters innumerable dangers and supernatural forces, all lurking in the deceptive beauty of the lush rain forest. But as the secrets of the lost tree unfold, the stakes reach even higher for Lily and Frank, and their fate, and mankind's, hangs in the balance. Inspired by the Disney parks attraction. Directed by Jaume Collet-Serra. Released Jul. 30, 2021, in theaters (also in 3-D and IMAX) and on Disney+, following a Jul. 24 premiere at Disneyland and Jul. 28–29 international releases. Stars Dwayne Johnson (Frank), Emily Blunt (Lily), Edgar Ramírez (Aguirre), Jack Whitehall (McGregor Houghton), Jesse Plemons (Prince Joachim), Paul Giamatti (Nilo). 127 min. Score by James Newton Howard, with a reimagined version of "Nothing Else Matters" by Metallica. A hundred crew members constructed the expansive port town of Porto Velho in and around a hilltop reservoir in Kauai, with fully realized interior sets used for filming. Makeup designer Joel Harlow had his work cut out for him with 400 background characters needing everything from sunburns to insect bites, and 65 tribespeople who needed simulated piercings, body paint, and tattoos. Frank's pet jaguar, Proxima, was completely CG and created by the Weta Workshop in New Zealand, while the filmmakers turned to Industrial Light & Magic (ILM) for the look of the conquistadors. Filmed in wide-screen format in Kauai, Hawai'i, and at Blackhall Studios and Oxford College of Emory University in Atlanta.

Jungle Cubs (TV) Animated series; aired on ABC Oct. 5, 1996–Sep. 5, 1998. The characters from the 1967 feature *The Jungle Book* are back—Baloo, Bagheera, Louie, Shere Khan, Kaa, and Hathi—but this time as youthful "jungle cubs." They are joined by a couple of misguided, laughable buzzards, Cecil and Arthur. The cubs find the jungle an unknown place where they experience the fun—and sometimes, sadness—of growing up. Voices include Jim Cummings (Kaa), E. G. Daily (Bagheera), Jason Marsden (Shere Khan and Prince Louie), Rob Paulsen (Hathi), Pam Segall (Baloo), Michael McKean (Cecil), David Lander (Arthur). 21 episodes. From Walt Disney Television Animation.

Jungle Junction (TV) Computer-animated series on Playhouse Disney on Disney Channel; premiered Oct. 5, 2009, moving to Disney Junior Feb. 14, 2011. A group of fun-loving animals on wheels explores a unique jungle filled with a network of floating roads that twist and loop high off the ground in harmony with the trees. The show emphasizes an appreciation of the environment while highlighting preliteracy skills through the use of road signs and symbols. Voices include Janet James (Zooter), Billy West (Ellyvan), Keith Wickham (Bungo), Jess Harnell (Taxicrab), Jimmy Hibbert (Bobby). From Spider Eye Productions (United Kingdom).

Jungle Navigation Co. Ltd. Skipper Canteen Adventureland table-service dining facility in the Magic Kingdom at Walt Disney World; opened Dec. 16, 2015. The crew of the Jungle Cruise add their signature jungle-skipper humor with every meal in one of three curiously quirky dining rooms. Menu items include LOST AND FOUND SOUP and 'TASTES LIKE CHICKEN' BECAUSE IT IS! Took the place of the former Adventureland Veranda.

Jungle Rhythm (film) Mickey Mouse cartoon; released in 1929. Directed by Walt Disney. With his natural musical flair, Mickey soon has some fierce animals dancing and cavorting through the jungle.

Jungle 2 Jungle (film) Successful commodities trader Michael Cromwell is engaged to marry Charlotte, but first he must finalize his divorce from his estranged wife, Dr. Patricia Cromwell. Leaving everything behind, including his hyperactive business partner, Richard, Michael travels deep into the Amazon jungle, where Patricia has been living since she left him, and gets the surprise of his life when he discovers that he has a 13-year-old son, Mimi-Siku, who has been raised among tribesmen. Michael inadvertently agrees to take Mimi to visit his own jungle—New York City. Cultures collide when the boy, who has more skill with blow darts than with social graces, comes to the most sophisticated city on the planet and wreaks havoc on his father's life. Meanwhile, Richard has bungled a coffee trade on the commodities market, and soon a group of sinister Russians is coming after Richard and Michael. Eventually, the Russians are outsmarted, and Michael and Mimi learn some unexpected lessons from each other about the important things in life. Directed by John Pasquin. Released Mar. 7, 1997. Stars Tim Allen (Michael Cromwell), JoBeth Williams (Dr. Patricia Cromwell), Martin Short (Richard), Sam Huntington

(Mimi-Siku), Lolita Davidovich (Charlotte), David Ogden Stiers (Jovanovic). 105 min. A remake of the French film *Un indien dans la ville*; released by Buena Vista in 1996 in a dubbed version as *Little Indian, Big City*. For the jungle setting, the film's producers selected a remote area near Canaima, Venezuela, experiencing all sorts of problems trying to make a film in a rain forest. In New York, sequences were filmed throughout the city, and in the state's suburban Pound Ridge and at the Playland amusement park in Rye.

Junior Autopia Fantasyland attraction in Disneyland; opened Jul. 23, 1956, and closed Dec. 1958. A block of wood was added to the gas pedal to enable "juniors" to drive.

Junior Woodchucks A pseudo-scout organization to which Donald's nephews belonged, created by artist Carl Barks. It first appeared in *Walt Disney's Comics and Stories* No. 125 in 1951. There were Junior Woodchucks comic books (1966–1984 and in 1991), and even a Junior Woodchucks manual. In 2016, Camp Woodchuck, an area inspired by the organization, debuted in Westernland at Tokyo Disneyland.

Jurgens, Curt (1915–1982) Actor; appeared in *Miracle of the White Stallions* (Gen. Tellheim).

Just a Thought (film) Animated short; digitally released Jan. 24, 2020, on Disney+, after a Jun. 14, 2019, debut at the Annecy International Animation Film Festival. Ollie, an awkward 12-year-old boy, experiences "bubble trouble" when his true feelings for a girl are embarrassingly revealed in the form of a physical thought bubble. Directed by Brian Menz. 3 min. From the Walt Disney Animation Studios Short Circuit program.

Just Beyond (TV) A Disney+ original series from 20th Century Television; digitally premiered Oct. 13, 2021. Astonishing stories inspired by the writings of R.L. Stine follow characters who must go on surprising journeys of self-discovery in a supernatural world of witches, aliens, ghosts, and parallel universes.

Just Dogs (film) Silly Symphony cartoon released Jul. 30, 1932. Directed by Burt Gillett. In an effort to befriend a large mongrel, a little puppy releases all of the dogs in the pound. When the pup finds a bone to share with his unfriendly companion, a free-for-all ensues in which the pup outwits the entire troupe of hungry dogs and finally earns the large dog's friendship.

Just Like Family (TV) Series on The Disney Channel; aired Apr. 30–Jun. 28, 1989. Based on the Disney TV movie *Help Wanted: Kids*, about a couple who have to hire a couple of children to impress the man's boss. Stars Cindy Williams (Lisa Burke), Bill Hudson (Tom Burke), Gabriel Damon (Coop), Grace Johnston (Emily).

Just Mickey (film) SEE FIDDLING AROUND.

Just Perfect (TV) Serial on The Disney Channel's *Mickey Mouse Club*; aired Apr. 9–May 4, 1990. Stars Christopher Daniel Barnes as Trent Beckerman, a model teenager who happens to be left in charge of a big, slobbering 120-lb. Saint Bernard when his parents and grandmother go on vacation. Also stars Jennie Garth (Crystal) and Sean Patrick Flanery (Dion).

Just Roll With It (TV) Series on Disney Channel; premiered Jun. 14, 2019. Combining improvisational comedy with a traditional sitcom, it follows the newly blended Bennett-Blatt family as they navigate everyday life while balancing a household of contrasting personalities. A live studio audience votes on the direction of key scenes while the actors are backstage. Stars Tobie Windham (Byron Blatt), Suzi Barrett (Rachel Bennett-Blatt), Ramon Reed (Owen Blatt), Kaylin Hayman (Blair Bennett). From Kenwood TV Productions, Inc.

Just Visiting (film) French nobleman Count Thibault of Malfete, with his servant André, is transported from the 12th century to modern-day Chicago, due to a wizard's flawed time-travel potion. After meeting the count's descendant, Julia Malfete, they realize that they must quickly find a way back to their own time, or Julia and all of Thibault's lineage will never exist. Thibault and André wreak havoc as they foil diabolical plots in both the 12th and 21st centuries. A Hollywood Pictures release. Directed by Jean-Marie Gaubert. Released Apr. 6, 2001. Stars Jean Reno (Thibault), Christian Clavier (André), Christina Applegate (Julia Malfete/Rosalinda), Matt Ross (Hunter), Tara Reid (Angelique), Bridgette Wilson (Amber), Malcolm McDowell (Wizard). 88 min. Location filming, in CinemaScope, was done in Chicago and England. Based on the 1993 French comedy *Les Visiteurs*. The director, along with stars Reno and Clavier, reprised their roles from that film.

Justice, Bill (1914–2011) Animator; began his Disney career in 1937 and received film credit as an animator on *Fantasia, Bambi, Alice in Wonderland, Peter Pan*, and others. He developed such memorable characters as Thumper and Chip and Dale, and directed acclaimed experimental shorts such as *Jack and Old Mac, Noah's Ark*, and *A Symposium on Popular Songs*. In 1965, Walt Disney moved him to WED Enterprises where he programmed Audio-Animatronics figures for Great Moments with Mr. Lincoln, Pirates of the Caribbean, the Haunted Mansion, Country Bear Jamboree, The Hall of Presidents, and other attractions. He designed many of the character costumes for the parks, as well as floats and costumes for many Disneyland parades, including the *Main Street Electrical Parade*. He retired in 1979, and wrote an autobiography entitled *Justice for Disney*. He was named a Disney Legend in 1996.

Justice, James Robertson (1905–1975) Actor; appeared in *The Story of Robin Hood* (Little John), *The Sword and the Rose* (Henry VIII), and *Rob Roy* (Duke of Argyll).

Justin Case (TV) A pilot for a series aired May 15, 1988 (with *Captain EO Backstage*). Directed by Blake Edwards. A ghost of a private detective helps a young lady find his murderer. After another murder, they are able to prevent a 3rd one and catch the culprit. They are so pleased with their success that they decide to stay in the detective business together. 90 min. Stars George Carlin, Molly Hagan, Timothy Stack, Kevin McClarnon, Douglas Sills, Gordon Jump, Valerie Wildman.

Justin Morgan Had a Horse (TV) Two-part show; aired Feb. 6 and 13, 1972. Directed by Hollingsworth Morse. Justin Morgan develops a new, versatile breed of horse, eventually known as the Morgan Horse, in the years shortly after the Revolutionary War. The horse's value is proven in a thrilling race finale. Stars Don Murray, Lana Wood, Gary Crosby, R. G. Armstrong, Whit Bissell.

Juttner, Christian Actor; appeared in *Return from Witch Mountain* (Dazzler), and on TV in *The Boy Who Talked to Badgers* (Ben), *The Million Dollar Dixie Deliverance, The Mystery of Rustler's Cave, Return of the Big Cat*, and *The Ghosts of Buxley Hall*.

1. Kitchen Kabaret 2. *Kingdom Hearts* 3. Kilimanjaro Safaris 4. *Kim Possible* (TV)
5. Kit Cloudkicker 6. KnowsMore 7. Koda 8. Kansas City 9. King Arthur Carrousel

K for Kelly (TV) Episode 1 of *Atta Girl, Kelly!*

KA WAʻA, a Luʻau at Aulani, A Disney Resort & Spa Debuted on the Hālāwai Lawn Nov. 2016, succeeding Starlit Hui. After guests dine on braised pork, island fish, and teriyaki chicken, a local storyteller presents a journey through Hawaiʻi's history and cultural roots with the ka waʻa (canoe). Tales of Oahu and the legends of Maui are presented through live music and traditional dance.

Kaa Hypnotic slithering snake character in *The Jungle Book*; voiced by Sterling Holloway.

Kagami, Toshio As an executive with the Real Estate Division of the Oriental Land Company (OLC) in the 1970s, Kagami was instrumental in convincing Disney to bring Disneyland to Tokyo. He continued to serve OLC in a variety of roles, and in 2008 was named a Disney Legend.

Kahl, Milt (1909–1987) Animator; one of Walt's "Nine Old Men," he started at Disney in 1934, and worked on many Disney classics, usually as directing animator, including *Snow White and the Seven Dwarfs*, *Sleeping Beauty*, *The Jungle Book*, and *The Rescuers*. He retired in 1976 and was honored with the Disney Legends Award posthumously in 1989. He was often assigned the challenging task of animating realistic human characters, such as Alice, Peter Pan, and Prince Phillip, and has been called one of the finest animators ever to work at the Disney Studio.

Kahn, Madeline (1942–1999) Actress; appeared in *Betsy's Wedding* (Lola Hopper) and *Nixon*

(Margaret Mitchell), and on TV in *Avonlea* (Pidgeon Plumtree). She voiced Gypsy in *A Bug's Life*.

Kakamora Ruthless, coconut-armored pirates in *Moana*.

Kal Penn Approves This Message (TV) Six-episode miniseries on Freeform; aired Sep. 22–Oct. 27, 2020. Actor Kal Penn hosts irreverent comedic field pieces and sit-down interviews covering political topics for young voters. From Embassy Row.

Kala Gorilla who adopts and mothers Tarzan in the 1999 animated film; voiced by Glenn Close.

Kālepa's Store Gift and sundry shop at Aulani, A Disney Resort & Spa; opened Aug. 29, 2011, selling T-shirts, retro art, and artisanal items. Kālepa is the Hawaiian word for "merchant" or "peddler."

Kali River Rapids Whitewater rafting adventure in Asia at Disney's Animal Kingdom; opened Mar. 1, 1999. Guests board 12-person rafts on the Chakranadi River (meaning: river that runs in a circle) and experience heavy runoff and dramatic plunges caused by local deforestation.

Kaling, Mindy Actress; appeared in *A Wrinkle in Time* (Mrs. Who), and on TV guest starred in *The Muppets*. She voiced Taffyta Muttonfudge in *Wreck-It Ralph*, Disgust in *Inside Out*, and Val in *Monsters at Work*.

Kalogridis, George A. He began at Walt Disney World in 1971 as a busser at the Contemporary

Resort and would go on to hold a variety of leadership roles, primarily in resort hotels and human resources. He worked with the development team for Disneyland Paris and later served as vice president of EPCOT 1995–2000, as senior vice president of operations for Disneyland Resort 2000–2002, and as vice president of Travel Operations for Walt Disney World 2002–2006. He then became chief operating officer for Disneyland Paris. He returned to Disneyland Resort in Oct. 2009 to serve as its president. In 2013, he became president of Walt Disney World, and in 2019 was named president, Segment Development and Enrichment for Disney Parks, Experiences and Products, and the global ambassador for the Walt Disney World 50th anniversary celebration. He retired in 2022.

Kamen, Kay (1892–1949) Creative salesman from Kansas City who, in 1932, became the exclusive representative of the Disney character merchandising division in New York City. He was honored posthumously as a Disney Legend in 1998. SEE ALSO MERCHANDISE.

Kane, Brad Actor; provided the singing voice of Aladdin in the 1992 animated film.

Kanga Kangaroo character in the Winnie the Pooh films; voiced by Barbara Luddy and Julie McWhirter Dees.

Kansas City, Missouri When Elias Disney became ill in 1909 and was unable to continue operation of his Marceline, Missouri, farm, he decided to move his family to Kansas City. He purchased a newspaper distributorship (SEE NEXT ENTRY), and soon his sons Walt and Roy were helping out. Walt attended Benton School and graduated from the 7th grade in 1917. At that time, the family was living at 3028 Bellefontaine. With a neighbor kid, Walt Pfeiffer, Walt got interested in the theater, and they occasionally put on shows as "The Two Walts" at local vaudeville theaters. When Elias decided to move again, this time back to Chicago, Walt stayed the summer and got a job as a news butcher on the railroad. It was an exciting job for a teenager. After the summer season, he joined his family in Chicago. Walt returned to Kansas City after his service in the Red Cross at the end of World War I. After a few minor jobs, he managed to land a position at the Kansas City Slide Company (later Kansas City Film Ad Company), a firm that made advertising slides for movie theaters. On the side, Walt borrowed one of the company's cameras and tried some simple animation, selling a few short pieces to the Newman Theater, where they were called Newman Laugh-O-grams. To earn some needed money, Walt made a dental training film, *Tommy Tucker's Tooth*, for a local dentist, Dr. Thomas B. McCrum. In 1922, Walt left Film Ad to set up his own company, which he called Laugh-O-gram Films. He managed to raise the needed capital by selling stock, with the buyers including his sister, parents, and friends. When Laugh-O-gram Films folded in 1923, Walt scraped together enough money, by taking the camera into the neighborhood to photograph babies for their parents, to buy a train ticket to Hollywood. That summer he cut his ties with Missouri to head west.

Kansas City Star, The In 1911, Elias Disney purchased a distributorship for the Missouri newspaper; his son Walt would soon join his brother Roy O. as a delivery boy. Elias sold the paper route in 1917. Walt would later apply to work for *The Kansas City Star* but was turned down. Incidentally, The Walt Disney Company would briefly own the *Star* decades later; in 1977, the paper was purchased by Capital Cities Communications, which would merge with ABC in 1986 and then with Disney in 1996. The *Star* was sold to the Knight Ridder media company in 1997.

Karamell-Küche Shop in Germany at EPCOT; opened Sep. 27, 2010, and presented by Werther's Original. A show kitchen features Cast Members making fresh caramel treats. It opened as the only freestanding retail location in the world for Storck, a German candy producer. It took the place of Glas und Porzellan.

Karnival Kid, The (film) Mickey Mouse cartoon released in 1929. Directed by Walt Disney. While enjoying his day selling hot dogs in an amusement park, Mickey, along with his friends, serenades Minnie, who is working as a "shimmy dancer." It was the first cartoon in which Mickey speaks; his first words are "Hot dogs!"

Kasha, Al (1937–2020) He wrote songs, with Joel Hirschhorn, for *Freaky Friday*, *Pete's Dragon*, *Hot Lead and Cold Feet*, and the Universe of Energy at EPCOT Center.

Kat Saka's Kettle Snack shop in Star Wars: Galaxy's Edge; opened May 31, 2019, in Disneyland and Aug. 29, 2019, in Disney's Hollywood Studios at Walt Disney World. In this market run by grain merchant Kat Saka, visitors can try Outpost Mix, a sweet, savory snack made with popcorn.

Kater, David Actor; appeared on the *Mickey Mouse Club* on The Disney Channel in 1989. He later appeared in *Sister Act 2: Back in the Habit*.

Katie (TV) One-hour syn. daytime talk show with Katie Couric; aired Sep. 10, 2012–Jul. 30, 2014. Distributed by Disney/ABC Domestic Television.

Katrina Song from *The Adventures of Ichabod and Mr. Toad*; written by Don Raye and Gene De Paul. A rendition by Bing Crosby became a hit, and there were other recordings by Lawrence Welk, Tex Beneke, and Kay Kyser.

Katrina Van Tassel Ichabod Crane's love interest in *The Adventures of Ichabod and Mr. Toad*.

Katsura Grill SEE YAKITORI HOUSE.

Katt, William Actor; appeared in *Baby* (George Loomis).

Katz, Omri Actor; appeared in *Hocus Pocus* (Max). Also starred in the non-Disney series *Eerie, Indiana*, which was shown on The Disney Channel.

Katzenberg, Jeffrey Chairman of the Walt Disney Studios 1984–1994. He was credited with helping to bring Disney to the top of the motion picture industry, supervising such box office hits as *Down and Out in Beverly Hills, Pretty Woman, Dead Poets Society, Who Framed Roger Rabbit*, and *Good Morning, Vietnam*. He worked closely with animation, bringing his talents to such films as *The Little Mermaid, Beauty and the Beast, Aladdin*, and *The Lion King*. He left the company to partner with Steven Spielberg and David Geffen in a new studio enterprise, DreamWorks SKG.

Kaufman, J.B. Film historian; he has authored many books on early Disney animation, including *The Fairest One of All: The Making of Walt Disney's Snow White and the Seven Dwarfs, Pinocchio: The Making of the Disney Epic*, and *South of the Border with Disney*. He regularly lectures on the subject and has appeared in Disney documentaries.

Kaye, Stubby (1918–1997) Actor; appeared in *Who Framed Roger Rabbit* (Marvin Acme).

Kazaam (film) Life in the city can be pretty tough,

especially for 12-year-old Max Connor, whose mother has raised him alone since her husband left when Max was 2. To make things worse, Max's mother has found love again with Travis, a kindly firefighter who cannot seem to make friends with Max. Distraught by his mother's impending marriage, Max demands to meet his real father. To add to Max's complicated life, he is the object of torture by a local group of bullies and one day, while hiding in an abandoned building, he accidentally opens the door on a battered boom box, freeing a 7-foot, 3,000-year-old genie, Kazaam. While Max initially does not believe in magic, Kazaam, in trying to give the kid his 3 wishes, soon makes him a believer. Released Jul. 17, 1996. A Touchstone film. Directed by Paul Michael Glaser. Stars Shaquille O'Neal (Kazaam), Francis Capra (Max), Ally Walker (Alice), James Acheson (Nick). 93 min. Filmed in Los Angeles.

Kazan, Lainie Actress; appeared in *The Journey of Natty Gann* (Connie), *Beaches* (Leona Bloom), and *The Cemetery Club* (Selma); on TV in *Safety Patrol* (Mrs. Day) and *The Crew* (Pepper Lowenstein); and made guest appearances on *Ugly Betty* (Dina Talercio), *Desperate Housewives* (Maxine Rosen), *Jessie* (Wanda Winkle), *Grey's Anatomy* (C. J.), and *Young & Hungry* (Susie).

K. C. Undercover (TV) Live-action comedy series on Disney Channel; premiered Jan. 18, 2015. K. C. Cooper, a high school math whiz and karate black belt, learns that her parents are spies when they recruit her to join them in the secret government agency known as The Organization. While she has spy gadgets at her disposal, K. C. has a lot to learn about being a spy. She has to balance everyday family life while on undercover missions, near and far, to save the world. Stars Zendaya (K. C. Cooper), Kadeem Hardison (Craig Cooper), Tammy Townsend (Kira Cooper), Kamil McFadden (Ernie), Trinitee Stokes (Judy), Veronica Dunne (Marisa). From Rob Lotterstein Productions and It's a Laugh Productions.

KCAL TV station in Los Angeles, Channel 9, acquired by Disney on Dec. 2, 1988. Earlier known as KHJ. The TV station was sold to Young Broadcasting in 1996 per the divestiture order received when Disney purchased Cap Cities/ABC. Young formally took over operation of the station on Nov. 23, 1996.

Keane, Glen Animator; began his career at Disney

in 1974, serving as an animator on *The Rescuers* and *Pete's Dragon*. He animated the fierce fight with the bear in *The Fox and the Hound* and later brought to life, as a directing animator, such memorable characters as Ariel in *The Little Mermaid*, Beast in *Beauty and the Beast*, and Aladdin. He worked on story and as a supervising animator on *Pocahontas*, *Tarzan*, and *Treasure Planet*, and served as exec. producer, animation supervisor, and directing animator on *Tangled* before retiring in 2012. He was named a Disney Legend in 2013.

Kearns, Joseph (1907–1962) Actor; provided the voice of the Door Knob in *Alice in Wonderland*.

Keaton, Diane Actress/director; appeared in *The Good Mother* (Anna), *Father of the Bride* and *Father of the Bride, Part II* (Nina Banks), and *The Other Sister* (Elizabeth Tate), and on The Disney Channel in *Northern Lights* (Roberta Blumstein). She voiced Jenny in *Finding Dory* and directed *Unstrung Heroes*.

Keegan, Andrew Actor; appeared in *Camp Nowhere* (Zack Dell) and *10 Things I Hate About You* (Joey Donner), and on TV in *Thunder Alley* (Jack Kelly) and *Freaky Friday* (Luke, 1995).

Keenen Ivory Wayans Show, The (TV) Syn. late-night talk show hosted by Wayans, featuring a mixture of celebrity interviews, comedy sketches, live musical performances, and game elements. Began Aug. 4, 1997, and ended Apr. 24, 1998.

Keeping the Faith (film) Best friends since they were kids, Rabbi Jacob Schram and Father Brian Finn are dynamic and popular young men living and working on New York's Upper West Side. When Anna Reilly, once their childhood friend and now a corporate executive, suddenly returns to the city, she reenters Jake's and Brian's lives with a vengeance. Sparks fly and an unusual and complicated love triangle ensues. A Touchstone Pictures/Spyglass Entertainment production. Released Apr. 14, 2000. Directed by Edward Norton. Stars Edward Norton (Brian Finn), Jenna Elfman (Anna Reilly), Ben Stiller (Jacob Schram), Anne Bancroft (Ruth Schram), Eli Wallach (Rabbi Lewis), Milos Forman (Father Havel), Holland Taylor (Bonnie Rose), Ron Rifkin (Larry Friedman). 129 min. Filming in New York City, the producers selected the locations where the 2 lead actors worked: B'nai Jeshurun on West 88th and the Church of the Ascension on West 107th.

Keith, Brian (1921–1997) Actor; appeared in *Ten Who Dared* (Bill Dunn), *The Parent Trap* (Mitch Evers), *Moon Pilot* (Maj. Gen. John Vanneman), *Savage Sam* (Uncle Beck), *A Tiger Walks* (Pete Williams), *Those Calloways* (Cam Calloway), and *Scandalous John* (John McCanless), and on TV in *The B.R.A.T. Patrol* (Gen. Newmeyer), *Elfego Baca* (Shadrach O'Reilly), *Johnny Shiloh* (Sergeant Gabe Trotter), *The Tenderfoot* (Mose Carson), *Bristle Face* (Lue Swank), and the series *Walter and Emily* (Walter Collins).

Kellaway, Cecil (1891–1973) Actor; appeared in *The Shaggy Dog* (Prof. Plumcutt), *The Adventures of Bullwhip Griffin* (Mr. Pemberton), and on TV in *The Wacky Zoo of Morgan City*.

Keller's Jungle Killers After the closure of the Mickey Mouse Club Circus in Disneyland, animal trainer George Keller remained for several months (Feb. 19–Sep. 7, 1956) with a show featuring his wild animals.

Kelly, Moira Actress; appeared in *Billy Bathgate* (Rebecca) and *The Tie That Binds* (Dana Clifton), and provided the voice for the adult Nala in *The Lion King* and other appearances of the character.

Kelly, Patsy (1910–1981) Actress; appeared in *Freaky Friday* (Mrs. Schmauss) and *The North Avenue Irregulars* (Patsy).

Kelly, Walt (1913–1973) He started at Disney in 1936 and remained until 1941. He specialized in animation of Mickey Mouse, notably on *The Nifty Nineties*. He started as a story man and did some animation on "The Pastoral Symphony" segment of *Fantasia*, working usually with Ward Kimball. He animated on *The Reluctant Dragon* and *Dumbo*, then left to go into comic book work on his own, where he created the character of Pogo.

Kenai Originally human, then a bear character in *Brother Bear*; voiced by Joaquin Phoenix.

Kendrick, Anna Actress; appeared in *Into the Woods* (Cinderella), on Disney+ in the title role in *Noelle*, and on ABC in the *Disney Parks Frozen Christmas Celebration*.

Ken-L-Land Pet boarding facility outside the Disneyland main gate; opened Jan. 18, 1958. Walt felt that it was important that travelers visiting Disneyland have a place where they could board their pets for the day. Hosted by Ken-L-Ration (Quaker Oats Co.) until 1967. Later called Kennel Club and Pet Care Kennel.

Kennedy, Kathleen Film producer; she was named president of Lucasfilm in 2012, also overseeing Industrial Light & Magic and Skywalker Sound, and produced the company's live-action films beginning with *Star Wars: The Force Awakens*. She also served as exec. producer of *Who Framed Roger Rabbit*, *The BFG*, and *The Mandalorian*, and as producer of *Arachnophobia*, *Noises Off*, *A Far Off Place*, *The Sixth Sense*, *The Young Black Stallion*, *Ponyo*, *The Secret World of Arrietty*, *War Horse*, and *Lincoln*.

Kennel Club Pet boarding facility at Disneyland Resort, renamed from Ken-L-Land in 1968 when Kal Kan took over as sponsor. They remained until 1977. Gaines was the sponsor 1986–1991, when it was known as Pet Care Kennel. Friskies took over in 1993, returning to the Kennel Club name. At Walt Disney World, kennels were added to the Transportation and Ticket Center, EPCOT, Disney-MGM Studios, Disney's Animal Kingdom, and Disney's Fort Wilderness Resort and Campground. Beginning in 2010, all of the Walt Disney World kennel locations closed, with the services provided at a new luxury pet resort from Best Friends Pet Care on Bonnet Creek Parkway beginning Sep. 1.

Kent, Ralph (1939–2007) Artist; joined Disneyland as a production artist in 1963, working on projects not only for the park but also for the 1964–1965 New York World's Fair and Celebrity Sports Center. He moved to Walt Disney World in 1971, working in the Merchandise Art department and later as a director of Walt Disney Imagineering East. In 1990, he joined the Disney Design Group as a corporate trainer, passing on his valuable knowledge to newly hired artists, before retiring in 2004—the same year he was named a Disney Legend.

Kentucky Gunslick (TV) Episode 11 of *Texas John Slaughter*.

Kenworthy, Paul (1925–2010) Nature photographer whose work helped ensure the success of *The Living Desert*, *The Vanishing Prairie*, and *Perri*. He was named a Disney Legend in 1998.

Kern, Bonnie Lee (1941–2020) Mouseketeer from the 1950s *Mickey Mouse Club* TV show.

Kern, Kevin M. He joined the Walt Disney Archives staff in 2011, later promoted to manager, Research, then Archives regional manager. He has facilitated numerous Disney legacy and outreach projects, including oral histories and special exhibitions; authored Disney books and articles; hosted tours, special events, presentations, and film festival programming; and has appeared in several Disney documentary and streaming programs.

Kerpoof Studios Disney announced Feb. 19, 2009, that it had bought Kerpoof Studios, a creator of online tools that allow kids to use computers to make artwork, create short films, and write stories. The studio, based in Colorado, closed in 2014.

Kerrigan, Nancy SEE DISNEY'S NANCY KERRIGAN SPECIAL: DREAMS ON ICE.

Kerry, Margaret Actress who was a model for Tinker Bell.

Ketchakiddie Creek Water-play area for youngsters at Typhoon Lagoon at Walt Disney World.

Kevin Elusive,13-foot-tall South American bird character in *Up*.

Kevin from Work (TV) Half-hour comedy series on ABC Family; debuted Aug. 12, 2015, and ended Oct. 7, 2015. Kevin declares his unrequited love for his coworker Audrey in a letter, believing he'll never see her again after he accepts a job overseas. But when the opportunity falls through and Kevin is forced to return to his old job, how will he and Audrey continue to work together now that his feelings are no longer secret? Stars Noah Reid (Kevin), Paige Spara (Audrey), Matt Murray (Brian), Jordan Hinson (Roxie), Punam Patel (Patti). From Hop, Skip and Jump Productions.

Kevin Hill (TV) Hour-long drama on UPN; aired Sep. 29, 2004–Jun. 8, 2005. Kevin Hill, a 28-year-old self-made hotshot attorney in New York City, has the ultimate bachelor life—a high-powered job, plenty of pretty ladies, and enough money to buy whatever he wants. But his whole life turns upside down when he's left to raise the 10-month-old daughter of his cousin, who unexpectedly died. After figuring out how to deal with bottles, diapers, and his new no-nonsense gay nanny, Kevin quits his workaholic law firm for a flex-time, boutique law office, Grey & Associates, owned and completely staffed by women. Stars Taye Diggs (Kevin Hill),

Jon Seda (Dame Butler), Patrick Breen (George Weiss), Christina Hendricks (Nicolette Raye), Kate Levering (Veronica Carter), Michael Michele (Jessie Grey). From Touchstone Television.

Kevin (Probably) Saves the World (TV) Hour-long drama series on ABC; aired Oct. 3, 2017–Mar. 6, 2018. Kevin Finn is not a good person. He's not terrible, but he's selfish, clueless, and values material wealth and status over all else. And he is beginning to realize that those things aren't making him happy—in fact, he is fairly miserable. Just when things seem at their worst, he finds himself tasked with an unbelievable mission: saving the world. Stars Jason Ritter (Kevin Finn), JoAnna Garcia Swisher (Amy Cabrera), Kimberly Hébert Gregory (Yvette), Chloe East (Reese Cabrera), J. August Richards (Deputy Nate Purcell), Dustin Ybarra (Tyler Medina), India de Beaufort (Kristin Allen). From ABC Studios.

Key, Keegan-Michael Actor; appeared in *Tomorrowland* (Hugo) and *Mr. 3000* (Reporter), on TV in *Gary Unmarried* (Curtis), and made guest appearances on *The Muppets*, *Star Wars: Galaxy's Edge—Adventure Awaits*, and the *Disney Parks Magical Christmas Day Celebration*. He voiced Kamari in *The Lion King* (2019), Ducky in *Toy Story 4*, Frog Co-Worker and Bjornson the Cheesemonger in *Chip 'n Dale: Rescue Rangers* (2022), and Honest John in *Pinocchio* (2022).

Key to the Cache, The (TV) Show; part 2 of *The Horse Without a Head*.

Key West Seafood Nautical restaurant in Disney Village at Disneyland Paris; open Apr. 12, 1992–Oct. 13, 1998. Replaced by Rainforest Cafe.

Keystone Clothiers Hollywood Boulevard shop offering adult Disney fashions, accessories, and jewelry in Disney's Hollywood Studios; opened May 1, 1989.

KHJ Los Angeles TV station, Channel 9, acquired by Disney on Dec. 2, 1988; call letters changed to KCAL a year later.

Khoobsurat (film) A film in Hindi produced by Disney in India. A hopelessly romantic physiotherapist meets a handsome young prince, who happens to be engaged to someone else. It leads to a battle of values between two unique families—one encouraging discipline and the other spontaneity. Released in India Sep. 19, 2014. Directed by Shashanka Ghosh. Stars Sonam Kapoor (Dr. Milli Chakravarty), Fawad Afzal Khan (Vikram Rathore). A remake of a 1980 film of the same name. Produced for Disney by the Anil Kapoor Film Company.

Khrushchev, Nikita (1894–1971) Soviet chairman the State Department did not visit Disneyland in Sep. 1959 during a U.S. visit. Walt was all ready to receive him, and in fact Mrs. Disney, who was not impressed by many of the celebrities who visited Disneyland, really wanted to meet Khrushchev.

Kick Buttowski—Suburban Daredevil (TV) Animated series on Disney XD; premiered Feb. 13, 2010. A boy, Clarence "Kick" Buttowski—short in stature but big in heart—overcomes incredible obstacles in his quest to become the world's greatest and most extreme daredevil. Aided by his best friend, Gunther, Kick devises stunts out of his mundane suburban surroundings, and takes on each stunt with unwavering enthusiasm. Voices include Charlie Schlatter (Kick), Matt L. Jones (Gunther), Danny Cooksey (Brad), John DiMaggio (Mr. Vickle), Eric Christian Olsen (Wade). From Disney Television Animation.

Kickin' It (TV) Disney XD comedy series; premiered Jun. 13, 2011. At the underperforming Bobby Wasabi Martial Arts Academy, in a strip mall, a group of lovable misfits from Seaford High School learn about karate. To help save the troubled Academy and vanquish their bitter rivals, The Black Dragon, sensei Rudy recruits a new kid, Jack, a hotshot skateboarder, who helps teach them all about life and friendship and how to just plain "kick it." Stars Dylan Riley Snyder (Milton), Leo Howard (Jack), Jason Earles (Rudy), Mateo Arias (Jerry), Alex Jones (Eddie), Olivia Holt (Kim). The working title was *Wasabi Warriors*. From Disney XD, It's a Laugh Productions, and Poor Soul Productions.

Kid, The SEE DISNEY'S THE KID.

Kid in King Arthur's Court, A (film) An earthquake occurs during a Little League game in Southern California, and 14-year-old Calvin Fuller, playing for a team known as the Knights, falls through a crack in the earth and is inexplicably thrust back in time to the mythical medieval kingdom of Camelot and the court of the legendary King Arthur. Calvin discovers that he has been summoned to the 12th century by Merlin to help restore Arthur's fading glory, and to prevent the realm from falling into the clutches of the sinister Lord Belasco. Calvin must find the courage to face Belasco and prove to himself that he has what it takes to be a worthy knight. Directed by Michael Gottlieb. A Walt Disney Picture in association with Tapestry Films and Trimark Pictures. Released Aug. 11, 1995. 90 min. Stars Thomas Ian Nicholas (Calvin Fuller), Joss Ackland (King Arthur), Ron Moody (Merlin), Art Malik (Lord Belasco). Kate Winslet, before becoming famous for her role in *Titanic*, played the role of Princess Sarah. To gain an authentic look, the producers decided to film in and around Budapest. There they found a medieval castle and village set being used by a BBC TV series that was on hiatus for the season. With a little redressing and redesigning, the set was just right. The production was truly international, as a final scene was filmed in England, the music was scored in Prague, and the final sound mix was done in Australia. An interesting bit of trivia—Ron Moody, who plays Merlin, played the same role for Disney 16 years earlier in *Unidentified Flying Oddball*. A sequel, *A Kid in Aladdin's Palace* (1997), with Thomas Ian Nicholas reprising his role as Calvin Fuller, was made as a direct-to-video film by Trimark and had its world TV premiere on Disney Channel in Mar. 1999.

Kidani Village Part of Disney's Animal Kingdom Villas; opened May 1, 2009. Kidani means "necklace" in Swahili, and the building is shaped like a piece of African jewelry with vacation villas forming the beads, walkways creating the knots in between, and the lobby representing the ornament or jewel at its center. The Disney Vacation Club resort includes a restaurant, Sanaa, and shop, Johari Treasures. SEE ALSO ANIMAL KINGDOM LODGE, DISNEY'S.

Kidder, Margot (1948–2018) Actress; appeared in *Trenchcoat* (Mickey Raymond), and on TV in *Brothers & Sisters* (Emily Craft).

Kidnapped (film) Young David Balfour attempts to regain his rightful inheritance, the house and lands of Shaws in Scotland, and in doing so is nearly killed and then kidnapped due to his treacherous Uncle Ebenezer. But the doughty Scottish laird Alan Breck Stewart intervenes, and after a shipwreck, hairbreadth escapes, and a chase along the length of the Highlands, David, with Alan's help, confronts his uncle and recovers his estate. Released Feb. 24, 1960. Directed by Robert Stevenson.

Although publicists tried to prove otherwise, the director insisted there was no relation between him and the Robert Louis Stevenson who wrote this classic adventure story. 94 min. Stars James MacArthur (David Balfour), Peter Finch (Alan Breck Stewart), Bernard Lee (Capt. Hoseason), Niall MacGinnis (Shaun), John Laurie (Uncle Ebenezer), Finlay Currie (Cluny MacPherson), and the then unknown Peter O'Toole (Robin Og MacGregor).

Kidney, Kevin, and Daily, Jody Best known to Disney fans simply as Kevin and Jody, they began working together as designers in the Disneyland Entertainment Art department in 1990 and went on to design and produce collectibles, artwork, and books. Kevin has contributed concepts for live entertainment (including as an original designer of *Fantasmic!*) and has handcrafted items for films (including the snow globe for *Mary Poppins Returns*). Jody has designed several Disney park parades, including *Disney Stars on Parade* for Disneyland Paris, and the two collaborated on several others, including the *Pixar Play Parade* and *Mickey's Soundsational Parade* at Disneyland Resort.

Kids Are Alright, The (TV) Half-hour series on ABC; aired Oct. 16, 2018–May 21, 2019. A traditional Irish Catholic family in the 1970s, the Clearys, navigate big and small changes during one of America's most turbulent decades in a working-class neighborhood outside Los Angeles. Mike and Peggy raise 8 boisterous boys who live out their days with little supervision. There are 10 people, 3 bedrooms, 1 bathroom, and everyone's in it for themselves. Stars Michael Cudlitz (Mike Cleary), Mary McCormack (Peggy), Sam Straley (Lawrence), Caleb Foote (Eddie), Sawyer Barth (Frank), Christopher Paul Richards (Joey), Jack Gore (Timmy), Andy Walken (William), Santino Barnard (Pat). From ABC Studios.

Kids Is Kids (TV) Show aired Dec. 10, 1961. Directed by Hamilton S. Luske. Reruns were titled *Donald Duck Quacks Up*, and an edited version was shown as *Mickey and Donald Kidding Around*. Prof. Von Drake covers child psychology with a series of cartoons, trying to give Donald some advice on raising his nephews.

Kids of the Kingdom Group of talented and energetic young singers and dancers who perform at the Disney parks; began in Disneyland in 1968.

Kids Who Knew Too Much, The (TV) Two-hour movie aired Mar. 9, 1980. Directed by Robert Clouse. A dying man leaves a note in a kid's toy speedboat; the boy and his friends help a lady reporter solve the case and save the life of a visiting Russian premier. Stars Sharon Gless, Larry Cedar, Rad Daly, Dana Hill, Christopher Holloway, Lloyd Haynes, Jared Martin, Kevin King Cooper, Jackie Coogan. Roger Mobley, who starred as Gallegher 15 years earlier, returned to play a small role as a policeman.

Kiff (TV) Animated buddy-comedy series scheduled to premiere Mar. 10, 2023, on Disney Channel. In a world where animals and magical oddballs tackle day-to-day life alongside one another, Kiff (an optimistic squirrel whose best intentions often lead to complete chaos) and her best friend, Barry (a sweet, mellow bunny), navigate school, relationships, and their often eccentric community. Voices include Kimiko Glenn (Kiff), H Michael Croner (Barry), James Monroe Iglehart (Martin), Lauren Ash (Beryl), Deedee Magno Hall (Miss Deer Teacher), Eugene Cordero (The Pone/Secretary Prince), Josh Johnson (Harry Buns), Eric Bauza (Roy Fox/Reggie). From Titmouse, in association with Disney Channel.

Kilimanjaro Safaris Attraction in Africa at Disney's Animal Kingdom; opened Apr. 22, 1998. At the Harambe Wildlife Reserve, guests board open-sided safari vehicles in the modern-day town of Harambe for an exciting, guided exploration of 110 acres of savanna, forest, rivers, and rocky hills. There are up close encounters with great herds of animals roaming the land. Since animals have minds of their own, every expedition is unique. The attraction premiered with ride vehicles seating 32 guests (although the capacity increased in later years). As the finale, the safari trucks surprised a band of poachers and embarked on a chase to save a baby elephant, named Little Red; this story line was removed in 2012 as part of an extensive refurbishment. A nighttime safari debuted May 27, 2016, providing a look at nocturnal animal behaviors.

Killer Mountain, The (TV) Show; part 2 of *Banner in the Sky*.

Killer Women (TV) Hour-long series on ABC; aired Jan. 7–Feb. 18, 2014. Molly Parker is one of the first women to join the elite Texas Rangers, and she is committed to finding the truth and seeing justice served, even if she has to break some rules to get it done. While she is surrounded by law enforcement colleagues who want to see her fail, there are those within the Rangers who have her back, including her boss, Company Commander Luis Zea. Stars Tricia Helfer (Molly Parker), Marc Blucas (Dan Winston), Marta Milans (Becca Parker), Michael Trucco (Billy Parker), Alex Fernandez (Luis Zea). From ABC Studios. Two unaired episodes, including the finale, were made available to watch on abc.com.

Killers from Kansas (TV) Episode 3 of *Texas John Slaughter*.

Killers of the High Country (TV) Show aired Oct. 16, 1959. Mountain lions and their struggle to live alongside humans in the Rocky Mountains. Directed by Tom McGowan.

Kilmer, Val Actor; appeared in *Tombstone* (Doc Holliday) and *Déjà Vu* (Agent Pryzwarra), and voiced Bravo in *Planes*.

Kilroy (TV) Four-part show aired Mar. 14, 21, 28, and Apr. 4, 1965. Directed by Robert Butler. Oscar Kilroy, discharged from the Marines, visits a small town and decides to stay; his ability to involve himself in other people's problems leads to some unusual results. Stars Warren Berlinger, Celeste Holm, Allyn Joslyn, Bryan Russell, Robert Emhardt, Philip Abbott, Arthur Hunnicutt.

Kim Possible (TV) Animated series on Disney Channel; debuted Jun. 7, 2002. Teenager Kim Possible balances her personal life (including school, boys, and shopping) with her duties, going on missions to save the world from evil villains. Voices include Christy Carlson Romano (Kim), Will Friedle (Ron Stoppable), Nancy Cartwright (Rufus), Kirsten Storms (Bon-Bon Rockwaller), Rider Strong (Brick). 65 episodes.

Kim Possible (TV) A Disney Channel Original Movie; first aired Feb. 15, 2019. In this live-action version of the earlier animated series, Kim Possible and Ron Stoppable are entering high school, where they befriend Athena, who is having even a worse time than they are adapting to the new school. Athena becomes a member of Team Possible, and soon they have to try to stop Drakken and Shego when they resurface in Middleton. Directed by Zach Lipovsky and Adam B. Stein. Stars Sadie Stanley (Kim), Sean Giambrone (Ron), Clara Wilson (Athena), Issac Ryan Brown (Wade).

Christy Carlson Romano, voice of the animated Kim Possible, appears as Poppy Blu.

Kim Possible: A Sitch in Time (TV) Animated special on Disney Channel; first aired Nov. 28, 2003. The fate of the future, humanity, and planet Earth rests in Kim's hands when notorious supervillains exploit time travel to tamper with the past and the future. Kim goes back in time to thwart them, only to have her opponents strike when she is most vulnerable. When she traverses to the future, Kim must team with her now-grown friends to restore the time-space continuum. Directed by Steve Loter. Voices include Christy Carlson Romano (Kim), Will Friedle (Ron), Nancy Cartwright (Rufus), Tahj Mowry (Wade). 65 min.

Kim Possible Movie, Disney's: So the Drama (TV) A Disney Channel Original Movie; first aired Apr. 8, 2005. Kim is swept off her feet by the new guy at school, Erik, who asks her to go to the junior prom, an invitation that makes Kim's best friend, Ron Stoppable, jealous. The omnipresent evil villain, Dr. Drakken, kidnaps Kim's rocket scientist dad, and now it's up to Ron to put his jealousy aside, track down a lovestruck Kim, and together rescue her dad—all before the big school dance. Directed by Steve Loter. Voices include Christy Carlson Romano (Kim Possible), Will Friedle (Ron Stoppable), Ricky Ullman (Erik), John DiMaggio (Drakken), Nancy Cartwright (Rufus), Tahj Mowry (Wade), Kirsten Storms (Bonnie Rockwaller), Raven (Monique), Gary Cole (Dad), Jean Smart (Mom), Rider Strong (Brick). 66 min.

Kim Possible: The Secret Files (film) Direct-to-video release Sep. 2, 2003, consisting of episodes from the TV series (including one never-aired episode). A computer-generated Rufus (the naked mole rat) serves as host. Directed by Chris Bailey and David Block. Voices include Christy Carlson Romano (Kim), Will Friedle (Ron), Nancy Cartwright (Rufus), Tahj Mowry (Wade). 71 min.

Kim Possible World Showcase Adventure Interactive scavenger hunt in EPCOT; offered Jan. 28, 2009–May 17, 2012. Guests transformed into secret agents, joined Team Possible, and helped save the world from supervillains with the help of a high-tech "Kimmunicator." Seven pavilions were utilized, and each hosted a different mission, which could take 45–60 min. Replaced by Disney Phineas and Ferb: Agent P's World Showcase Adventure in Jun. 2012.

Kimball, Ward (1914–2002) Animator and one of Walt's "Nine Old Men"; Kimball joined the Disney Studio in 1934. He animated on such Disney classics as *Pinocchio* (on which he was noted for his creation of Jiminy Cricket), *Dumbo*, *The Three Caballeros*, and *Alice in Wonderland*, and directed the Academy Award–winning films *Toot, Whistle, Plunk and Boom* and *It's Tough to Be a Bird*. He also produced episodes for the TV series *Disneyland*, most notably the shows on the subject of man in space, and later produced/directed *The Mouse Factory*. He also contributed to live-action features, including *Babes in Toyland*, for which he helped write the story and directed stop-motion animation. A jazz trombonist, he led the Firehouse Five Plus Two band. He retired in 1972 but continued to consult on Disney projects, including the World of Motion attraction for EPCOT Center. He was honored with the Disney Legends Award in 1989. His handprints on his Disney Legends plaque feature extra fingers, illustrating his sense of humor. Ward was a train enthusiast whose love of the hobby helped get Walt himself interested; hence, in 2005, a 5th steam engine introduced on the Disneyland Railroad was named the *Ward Kimball* in his honor.

Kind, Richard Actor; appeared on TV in *Carol & Co.*, with guest appearances in *Empty Nest* (Elton Sexton), *Scrubs* (Mr. Korman), the *Walt Disney World Very Merry Christmas Parade* (host, 1998), and on Disney Channel in *Even Stevens* (Uncle Chuck) and the opening special for Disney's California Adventure. He provided voices in films, including *Inside Out* (Bing Bong), *A Bug's Life* (Molt), the Cars films (Van), *Toy Story 3* (Bookworm), *The Wild* (Larry), *The Jungle Book: Mowgli's Story* (Chimp 1), *Roadside Romeo* (Guru), and the Santa Buddies movies (Eddie the Elf Dog). On TV, he provided voices in *Mickey Mouse Funhouse* (Cheezel), *Tangled: The Series* (Monty), *Elena of Avalor* (Cacahuate), *Kim Possible* (Frugal Lucre), *Randy Cunningham: 9th Grade Ninja* (Mort Weinerman), and *Disney's Doug* (Bobby). At Walt Disney World, he voiced Sarge in Stitch's Great Escape!

Kindercare Center Childcare facility at Walt Disney World; opened May 25, 1981. A 2nd center opened Aug. 27, 1984. Kindercare's contract ended in 2004, and Central Florida YMCA took over the operation of childcare centers on resort property.

Kindergarten: The Musical (TV) Animated musical

series announced for Disney Junior. 5-year-old Birdy, with the help of her amazing teacher and new friends, uses her imagination to express her fears, excitement, and joy through big Broadway-style song and dance numbers, proving that kindergarten is just like a big stage and there is nothing a good song can't fix. From Oddbot Entertainment in association with Disney Junior.

King, Jack (1895–1958) Animator/director; worked at Disney 1929–1933 and 1936–1946. He directed the early Donald Duck cartoons before Jack Hannah took over. He was a sequence director on such features as *Pinocchio, Saludos Amigos, Dumbo, The Three Caballeros, Make Mine Music, Melody Time*, and *The Adventures of Ichabod and Mr. Toad*.

King Arthur (film) A reluctant leader, Arthur wishes only to leave Britain and return to the peace and stability of Rome. Before he can, one final mission leads him and his Knights of the Round Table—Lancelot, Galahad, Bors, Tristan, and Gawain—to the conclusion that when Rome is gone, Britain will need a leader to fill the vacuum. Under the guidance of Merlin, a former enemy, and with the beautiful Guinevere by his side, Arthur will have to find the strength within himself to change the course of history and lead Britain into a new age. A story of chivalry, bravery, and one man's destiny, this is a fresh look at the origins of the legendary hero. A Jerry Bruckheimer Films/Touchstone Pictures movie. Released Jul. 7, 2004, after a Jun. 28 world premiere at the Ziegfeld Theater in New York City. Directed by Antoine Fuqua. Stars Clive Owen (Arthur), Keira Knightley (Guinevere), Ioan Gruffudd (Lancelot), Steven Dillane (Merlin), Ray Winstone (Bors), Til Schweiger (Cynric), Stellan Skarsgård (Cerdic), Hugh Dancy (Galahad), Mads Mikkelsen (Tristan), Ray Stevenson (Dagonet), Ken Stott (Marius Honorius). 126 min. Filmed in Ireland in Cinema-Scope.

King Arthur Carrousel Fantasyland attraction in Disneyland; opened Jul. 17, 1955. Walt Disney bought a Dentzel carousel from a Toronto amusement park, where it had operated since 1922, supplementing it with Murphy horses from another at Coney Island. He wanted all horses, so assorted other animals on the purchased carousels were put into storage. He also wanted all of his horses to be leaping, so legs of standing horses were reset into the proper configurations. Each horse is different,

both in carving and in paint configuration. There is a total of 68 horses, 17 rows of 4 abreast, and one bench for guests using a wheelchair. Hand-painted scenes from *Sleeping Beauty* grace the interior. During the reconstruction of Fantasyland in 1982–1983, the carousel was moved back several feet to open up the castle courtyard somewhat and give guests a better view of the impressive ride as they cross the drawbridge and enter the castle. On Apr. 8, 2008, Jingles, the lead horse, was rededicated to honor Julie Andrews.

King David World premiere concert event; opened May 18, 1997, after 3 previews, for 6 performances as the inaugural production at the restored New Amsterdam Theatre in New York City. The musical by Alan Menken and Tim Rice retells the Old Testament story of the shepherd boy, David, who rises from his humble roots to become King of Israel. Directed by Mike Ockrent. Stars Marcus Lovett (David), Roger Bart (Jonathan), Stephen Bogardus (Joab), Judy Kuhn (Michal), Alice Ripley (Bathsheba), Peter Samuel (Samuel), Martin Vidnovic (Saul).

King Eidilleg King of the Fair Folk in *The Black Cauldron*; voiced by Arthur Malet.

King Hubert Father of Prince Phillip in *Sleeping Beauty*; voiced by Bill Thompson.

King Leonidas Ruler of Naboombu in *Bedknobs and Broomsticks*; voiced by Lennie Weinrib.

King Louie Scatting king of the monkey characters in *The Jungle Book*; voiced by Louis Prima.

King Ludwig's Castle Bavarian-style dining hall in Disney Village at Disneyland Paris; opened Jun. 3, 2003, taking the place of Rock 'n' Roll America. Burgers, German sausages, and desserts were served. Inspired by King Ludwig II and his castle, Neuschwanstein. Closed Jan. 7, 2023, to become The Royal Pub.

King Neptune (film) Silly Symphony cartoon released Sep. 10, 1932. Directed by Burt Gillett. When pirates cruelly capture a mermaid, the underwater denizens come to the rescue, alerting King Neptune who stirs up a storm at sea, sinking the pirates and rescuing the mermaid who has discovered the pirates' treasure.

King of the Grizzlies (film) Ernest Thompson

Seton, the well-known American artist and author, tells the story of Wahb, a mighty grizzly who roamed the Greybull country of the old West. Moki, a Cree foreman of a cattle ranch, befriends Wahb as a cub, and, in later years, the two have many strange encounters, but always recognize each other as "brothers." Released Feb. 11, 1970. Directed by Ron Kelly. 93 min. Stars John Yesno (Moki), Chris Wiggins (Colonel), Hugh Webster (Shorty), Jan Van Evera (Slim). Based on *The Biography of a Grizzly*, by Ernest Thompson Seton, the film is narrated by Winston Hibler, who also produced. Lloyd Beebe, long involved with many of Disney's nature films, supervised the film as field producer. The star of the film, Big Ted, the grizzly, was a 7-year-old, 10-foot-tall, 1,300-lb. bear who completed many of his scenes for the reward of his favorite food, marshmallows. Much of the filming was done over a 2-year period on location in the Canadian Rockies of Alberta and British Columbia, including Moraine Lake within Banff National Park, Yoho National Park, and the Kananaskis River and forest.

King Stefan Father of Sleeping Beauty; voiced by Taylor Holmes.

King Stefan's Banquet Hall Restaurant upstairs in Cinderella Castle in the Magic Kingdom at Walt Disney World; opened Oct. 1, 1971. Disney designers were unable to explain why Cinderella Castle held a King Stefan's Banquet Hall, since King Stefan is one of the kings in *Sleeping Beauty*. Controversy aside, the restaurant is one of the park's most charming. Originally, there were 13th-century costumes of brown-and-orange tights and tunics for the hosts, and medieval headdresses and gowns with overskirts for the hostesses. When the park first opened, diners were frequently serenaded by madrigal singers. Renamed Cinderella's Royal Table, beginning Apr. 28, 1997.

King Triton Father of Ariel and ruler of the seas in *The Little Mermaid*; voiced by Kenneth Mars.

King Triton's Carousel Attraction in Paradise Pier at Disney California Adventure; opened Feb. 8, 2001. Guests could ride on 56 California sea critters—dolphins, sea lions, whales, seahorses, otters, and flying fish. Closed Mar. 4, 2018, to be replaced by Jessie's Critter Carousel.

Kingdom Films Partnership formed in 2005 to raise financing for Disney films, with *Flightplan*

being the first film released. Kingdom Films raised $135 million in equity and $370 million in debt, and it was to provide 40% of production and distribution costs and receive 40% of the profit from box office and video sales for about 32 films over the following 4 years. It followed a previous film-financing venture, Mariner Film Partners, which raised $200 million in 1996.

Kingdom Gifts Victorian-style shop in the Hong Kong Disneyland Hotel; opened Sep. 12, 2005.

Kingdom Hearts Action and role-playing video game series for PlayStation, including Disney characters and situations developed by Square Enix and Disney Interactive Studios, debuting in the U.S. Sep. 17, 2002, after a Mar. 28 release in Japan. A sequel, *Kingdom Hearts II*, was released in Japan Dec. 22, 2005, followed by a U.S. release Mar. 28, 2006. *Kingdom Hearts III* debuted in Japan Jan. 25, 2019, followed by a U.S. release 4 days later. The game follows Sora, a Keyblade wielder, as he travels to many Disney worlds with Donald and Goofy to stop the Heartless invasion by sealing each world's keyhole and restore peace to the realms. Additional games have been released for PlayStation Portable, Nintendo Game Boy and DS, and other consoles.

Kingdom Keepers Series of best-selling children's novels by Ridley Pearson that take place in the Disney parks. Five teenage heroes—Finn, Philby, Willa, Charlene, and Maybeck—serve as holographic theme park guides by day, and at night are pitted against an ominous group of Disney villains known as The Overtakers. The first book, *Kingdom Keepers: Disney After Dark*, was released in 2005, and was followed by 6 additional installments. Updated editions were released beginning in 2020. A follow-up trilogy, titled *The Return*, began release in 2015, and a third trilogy began in 2022. *The Syndrome* and *Unforeseen* were additional spin-off books.

Kingdom of Arendelle *Frozen*-themed area announced for Walt Disney Studios Park in Disneyland Paris. Included in the plans are Elsa's Ice Palace, which will stand atop a 131-foot-high mountain, a new attraction, and a village home to a shop, restaurant, and character greetings. SEE ALSO WORLD OF FROZEN (HONG KONG DISNEYLAND) AND FROZEN KINGDOM (TOKYO DISNEYSEA).

Kingdom of Dreams and Magic—Tokyo Disneyland (film) Documentary featurette; released in

Japan on Jul. 23, 1983. 24 min. After the opening of Tokyo Disneyland in 1983, and due to the success of previous short films relating the pleasures of earlier Disney parks, this promotional film was created to document the new facility.

Kingdom Treasures Fantasyland shop in Tokyo Disneyland; opened in 2011, taking the place of The AristoCats shop. Merchandise is themed to Disney heroes.

King's Gallery, The Shop inside Cinderella Castle in the Magic Kingdom at Walt Disney World; opened Dec. 12, 1972, offering handcrafted jewelry, imported European gifts, and Arribas Brothers glasswork. It became an Art of Disney shop Apr. 20, 2004, which itself closed Jul. 5, 2007, to make way for the first Bibbidi Bobbidi Boutique.

Kingsley, Ben Actor; appeared in *Anne Frank* (Otto Frank), *Tuck Everlasting* (Man in the Yellow Suit), *Prince of Persia: The Sands of Time* (Nizam), *Iron Man 3* (The Mandarin), and *Shang-Chi and the Legend of the Ten Rings* (Trevor Slattery). He voiced Bagheera in *The Jungle Book* (2016).

Kingswell Avenue Site of the first Disney Studio in Hollywood. When Walt received a contract to produce a series of Alice Comedies, he was living with his Uncle Robert on Kingswell, near Commonwealth, in Hollywood. A couple of blocks down the same street, he found a real estate firm at 4651 Kingswell that was not using the back half of its office, so he made arrangements to rent it and moved in during Oct. 1923. Soon, however, after a little money had come in, he was able to rent the next-door store at 4649 Kingswell, and the Disney Brothers Cartoon Studio had its own first real location. The Disneys moved to a new studio on Hyperion Avenue in 1926.

Kingswell Camera Shop Photo supply shop on Buena Vista Street in Disney California Adventure; opened Jun. 15, 2012. It became the Kingswell Shop Nov. 2021, offering hats, holiday merchandise, and accessories.

Kinnear, Roy (1934–1988) Actor; appeared in *One of Our Dinosaurs Is Missing* (Supt. Grubbs) and *Herbie Goes to Monte Carlo* (Quincey).

Kinney, Jack (1909–1992) Animator/director; joined Disney in 1931, working first as an animator on the shorts. He was a sequence director on such films as *Pinocchio* and *Dumbo* and directed *Der Fuehrer's Face*. He first directed Goofy in *Goofy's Glider* and soon became established as the director of the Goofy cartoons. He left Disney in 1959 to form his own animation company and in 1988 wrote the book *Walt Disney and Assorted Other Characters*.

Kirby, Bruno (1949–2006) Actor; appeared in *Superdad* (Stanley Schlimmer), *Tin Men* (Mouse), and *Good Morning, Vietnam* (Lt. Steven Hauk).

Kirby, Jack (1917–1994) As a prolific creator of comic books, he helped begin the Marvel Universe with the character of Captain America in 1941. Later, working with co-creator Stan Lee, he introduced the Avengers, Hulk, Thor, Iron Man, Silver Surfer, Ant-Man, X-Men, and many others. He was named a Disney Legend posthumously in 2017.

Kirby Buckets (TV) Comedy series on Disney XD; debuted Oct. 20, 2014. Kirby Buckets, age 13, dreams of becoming a famous animator. With his best friends, Fish and Eli, by his side, Kirby navigates his eccentric town of Forest Hills where the trio usually find themselves trying to get out of a predicament before Kirby's sister, Dawn, and her best friend, Belinda, catch them. Along the way, Kirby is joined by his animated characters that only he (and the show's viewers) can see. Stars Jacob Bertrand (Kirby), Mekai Curtis (Fish), Cade Sutton (Eli), Olivia Stuck (Dawn), Tiffany Espensen (Belinda). From It's a Laugh Productions.

Kirk, Steve Imagineer; he joined WED Enterprises in 1976, developing attractions for the never-built Discovery Bay concept for Disneyland, the Journey Into Imagination and Wonders of Life pavilions for EPCOT Center, and Disney-MGM Studios. He helped create, with his brother and fellow Imagineer, Tim Kirk, The Great Movie Ride and The Twilight Zone Tower of Terror. As senior vice president, Walt Disney Imagineering, he oversaw the Tokyo DisneySea project as creative lead. He left the company in 2001.

Kirk, Tommy (1941–2021) Actor; appeared in *Swiss Family Robinson* (Ernst), *Old Yeller* (Travis Coates), *The Shaggy Dog* (Wilby Daniels), *The Absent-Minded Professor* (Biff Hawk), *Babes in Toyland* (Grumio), *Moon Pilot* (Walter Talbot), *Bon Voyage* (Elliott Willard), *Son of Flubber* (Biff Hawk), *Savage Sam* (Travis Coates), and *The Misadventures of Merlin Jones* and *The Monkey's*

Uncle (Merlin Jones), and on TV on *The Hardy Boys* (Joe) on the *Mickey Mouse Club*, for which he also provided a voice for *Boys of the Western Sea*. Appeared also on TV in *Escapade in Florence* (Tommy Carpenter) and *The Horsemasters* (Danny Grant). He was named a Disney Legend in 2006.

Kiss de Girl Fashions Clothing shop for babies and children in Mermaid Lagoon at Tokyo DisneySea; opened Sep. 4, 2001.

Kiss the Girl Song from *The Little Mermaid*; written by Howard Ashman and Alan Menken. Nominated for an Academy Award.

Kissimmee, Florida Neighboring town to Walt Disney World, in Osceola County.

Kit Carson and the Mountain Men (TV) Two-part show; aired Jan. 9 and 16, 1977. Directed by Vincent McEveety. Kit Carson joins John C. Frémont's survey party, where he is idolized by the general's young brother-in-law; both get caught up in intrigue by those trying to sabotage the expedition. Stars Christopher Connelly, Robert Reed, Ike Eisenmann, Gary Lockwood, Emile Genest, Richard Jaeckel, Val de Vargas.

Kit Cloudkicker Spunky bear cub star of *TaleSpin*; voiced by R. J. Williams.

Kitbull (film) Animated short; premiered Jan. 18, 2019, at the El Capitan Theatre in Hollywood, followed by digital releases. An unlikely connection sparks between 2 creatures: a fiercely independent stray kitten and a pit bull. Together, they experience friendship for the first time. Directed by Rosana Sullivan. 8 min. From the Pixar Animation Studios SparkShorts program. Nominated for an Academy Award for Animated Short Film.

Kitchen Kabaret Audio-Animatronics show in The Land at EPCOT Center; played Oct. 1, 1982–Jan. 3, 1994, originally sponsored by Kraft. Set in host Bonnie Appetit's kitchen, the musical revue taught nutrition in an entertaining way by having representatives of all the food groups sing about their value. The oversized foodstuff performers included Mr. Dairy Goods and the Stars of the Milky Way, the Cereal Sisters, Hamm and Eggz, and the Colander Combo and Fiesta Fruit. Memorable songs included "Boogie Woogie Bakery Boy" and "Veggie Veggie Fruit Fruit." The show was superseded by Food Rocks.

kite's tale, a (film) Experimental short film combining hand-drawn animation and virtual reality technology; premiered at the SIGGRAPH conference Jul. 28, 2019. Two clashing kites—a playful puppy and a pompous dragon—must learn to live with one another, subject to the winds of fate. Directed by Bruce Wright. Part of Walt Disney Animation Studios' experimental program, Short Circuit. 3 min.

Kitsch, Taylor Actor; he starred as the title character in *John Carter*, after a role as a camper in the pilot of *Kyle XY*.

Kitt, Eartha (1927–2008) Actress; appeared in *Ernest Scared Stupid* (Old Lady Hackmore) and *Holes* (Madame Zeroni), and guest starred on Disney Channel in *The Famous Jett Jackson* (Albertine Whethers). She provided the voice of Yzma in *The Emperor's New Groove* and *Kronk's New Groove*, and Bagheera in *The Jungle Book: Mowgli's Story*.

Kiya & the Kimoja Heroes (TV) Animated series announced for digital release on Disney+. With their crystal-charged powers, the martial arts–loving Kiya and her best friends, Jay and Motsie, are superheroes in the Southern African–inspired Kimoja City, shining bright to make things right until harmony and unity are restored in their community.

Kizazi Moto: Generation Fire (TV) Animated anthology series planned for digital release on Disney+. Inspired by Africa's diverse histories and cultures, 10 action-packed sci-fi and fantasy stories present bold visions of advanced technology, aliens, spirits, and monsters imagined from uniquely African perspectives.

Kline, Kevin Actor; appeared in *Consenting Adults* (Richard Parker) and *Beauty and the Beast* (Maurice, 2017). He voiced Phoebus in *The Hunchback of Notre Dame* and *The Hunchback of Notre Dame II*.

Klondike Kid, The (film) Mickey Mouse cartoon released Nov. 12, 1932. Directed by Wilfred Jackson. Mickey, a piano player in a Klondike saloon, finds Minnie outside cold and starving. Peg Leg Pierre takes off with her and Mickey goes after him, saving her just as Pierre is run over a cliff by his own runaway log cabin.

Knell, David Actor; appeared in *The Devil and*

Max Devlin (Nerve Nordlinger), *Splash* (Claude), and *Turner & Hooch* (Ernie).

Knick's Knacks Shop in Pixar Pier at Disney California Adventure offering Pixar art and accessories; opened Apr. 12, 2018, taking the place of Treasures in Paradise. Named after the 1989 short film from Pixar Animation Studios, *Knick Knack*.

Knife & Gun Club, The (TV) Unsold pilot for a series; aired on ABC Jul. 30, 1990. A story of life and death in an emergency room at an inner-city hospital. 60 min. Directed by Eric Laneuville. Stars Dorian Harewood, Perry King, Daniel Jenkins, Cynthia Bain.

Kniga Masterov (The Book of Masters) (film) Disney's first locally produced film in Russia, a children's adventure based on well-known Russian fairy tales and characters. An ancient prophecy is about to come true, putting the world in danger: the Stone Princess will break free from the tower to conquer the world with her evil magic. By coincidence the fate of the world is in the hands of Ivan who will have to face many challenges. Ivan can give the Princess magic powers that can help her rule the world, but he can also defeat her to save his sweetheart, Katya. Many dangers await Ivan in his adventure as he gets to meet the traditional characters of Russian fairy tales—Baba Yaga, Mermaid, Koschey Bessmertny, and many others. Directed by Vadim Sokolovsky. Released Oct. 29, 2009, with the highest-grossing opening for a family film ever in Russia. Cast includes Maksim Loktionov (Ivan), Liya Azhedzhakova (Baba Yaga), Mariya Andreeva (Katya), Irina Apeksimova (Kamennaya Knyazhna), Olga Aroseva (Rasskazchitsa), Mikhail Efremov (Bogatyr).

Knight for a Day, A (film) Goofy cartoon released Mar. 8, 1946. Directed by Jack Hannah. In a jousting tournament, a squire is accidentally put in a knight's place and beats all the contestants, winning the hand of Princess Esmerelda. Goofy plays all the parts.

Knight in Camelot, A (TV) Two-hour movie on *The Wonderful World of Disney*; first aired Nov. 8, 1998. Computer researcher Vivien Morgan finds herself transported back in time to AD 589 to the court of King Arthur. Convincing everyone she has magical powers, she sets about introducing 20th-century "improvements" at Camelot with the aid of Clarence, a quick-witted young page of the court. But perhaps Camelot is not ready for Vivien's "progress." She soon has rivals, including the crafty Merlin. Directed by Roger Young. Stars Whoopi Goldberg (Vivien), Michael York (King Arthur), Simon Fenton (Clarence), Paloma Baeza (Sandy), James Coombes (Sir Lancelot), Robert Addie (Sir Sagramour), Ian Richardson (Merlin), Amanda Donohoe (Queen Guinevere). Filming took place in England and at MaFilm Studios near Budapest.

Knightley, Keira Actress; starred in the Pirates of the Caribbean films (Elizabeth Swann), *King Arthur* (Guinevere), and *The Nutcracker and the Four Realms* (Sugar Plum Fairy), and on TV in *Princess of Thieves* (Gwyn).

Knights of Prosperity, The (TV) Half-hour comedy series on ABC; aired Jan. 3–Aug. 8, 2007. (Two unaired episodes were made available on abc.com.) Janitor Eugene Gurkin has dreamed of opening a bar, but he has no money. Soon he gets the idea to recruit a group of misfits into his "gang" for a heist to finance their dreams. The target: rock icon Mick Jagger's super-luxe Central Park West apartment. Working together, this band of affable, new-age Robin Hoods, who have never even shoplifted a candy bar, is soon casing the joint and prepping for its crime. What they don't know is that there is a much richer target for them, the chance to find hope, self-esteem, and confidence within themselves. Stars Donal Logue (Eugene Gurkin), Maz Jobrani (Gary), Sofia Vergara (Esperanza Villalobos), Kevin Michael Richardson (Rockefeller Butts), Lenny Venito (Francis "Squatch" Scuacieri), Josh Grisetti (Louis Plunk). 13 episodes. From Touchstone Television.

Knotts, Don (1924–2006) Actor; appeared in *The Apple Dumpling Gang* (Theodore Ogelvie), *No Deposit, No Return* (Bert), *Gus* (Coach Venner), *Herbie Goes to Monte Carlo* (Wheely Applegate), *Hot Lead and Cold Feet* (Denver Kid), and *The Apple Dumpling Gang Rides Again* (Theodore). On TV, he hosted an episode of *The Mouse Factory* and appeared on Disney Channel in *Quints* (Governor Healy). He voiced Mayor Turkey Lurkey in *Chicken Little*, Sniffer in *Air Buddies*, and various characters in *101 Dalmatians: The Series*.

Knowles-Carter, Beyoncé Singer/songwriter/producer; she provided the voice of Nala in *The Lion King* (2019); directed, produced, and starred in *Black Is King* for Disney+; and appeared on TV in *The Disney Family Singalong*. In 2019, she produced the album *The Lion King: The Gift*.

KnowsMore Know-it-all search engine character in *Ralph Breaks the Internet*; voiced by Alan Tudyk.

Koblischek, Horst (1926–2002) He led Disney merchandising in Germany from 1958 until his retirement in 1993 and was presented a European Disney Legends Award in 1997.

Koda Playful bear cub character in *Brother Bear*; voiced by Jeremy Suarez.

Kodak Presents Disneyland '59 (TV) SEE DISNEYLAND '59.

Kona Café Table-service restaurant in Disney's Polynesian Village Resort at Walt Disney World; opened Nov. 23, 1998, taking the place of the Coral Isle Café. Traditional American meals are infused with Asian flavors.

Konetzni, Al (1915–2016) He joined Disney's Consumer Products Division in New York City in 1953 as an artist and idea man and for 3 decades was responsible for developing and designing hundreds of different products featuring Disney characters. Among his best-known products are a Disney character lunch box in the shape of a school bus made by Aladdin, and the Mickey and Donald Pez candy dispensers. He retired in 1981 and was named a Disney Legend in 1999.

Korman, Harvey (1927–2008) Actor; appeared in *Son of Flubber* (husband in TV commercial) and *Herbie Goes Bananas* (Capt. Blythe); on TV in the *Gallegher* series (Brownie), *The Nutt House* (Reginald Tarkington), and *The Golden Palace* (Bill); and on The Disney Channel in *Gone Are the Dayes* (Charlie Mitchell). He voiced Baron Efrem von Schnickerdoodle in *101 Dalmatians: The Series*, Arismap in the *Hercules* TV series, and Gularis in *Buzz Lightyear of Star Command*.

Korsmo, Charlie Child actor; appeared in *Dick Tracy* (Kid), *What About Bob?* (Siggy Marvin), and *The Doctor* (Nicky).

Kostal, Irwin (1911–1994) Musical director; worked on the score and background music for *Mary Poppins*, *Bedknobs and Broomsticks*, and *Pete's Dragon*, and for all 3 received Academy Award nominations. He was also called upon to create a new digitally recorded soundtrack for *Fantasia* in 1982, an assignment that he felt was the most challenging of his career. He was named a Disney Legend in 2004.

Kouzzina by Cat Cora Restaurant with Mediterranean-style cuisine operated by Disney in collaboration with chef Cat Cora at the BoardWalk at Walt Disney World, taking the place of Spoodles. Open Aug. 15, 2009–Sep. 30, 2014, and replaced by Trattoria al Forno. *Kouzzina* means *kitchen* in Greek.

Kraft Salutes Disneyland's 25th Anniversary (TV) Special hosted by Danny Kaye, along with many other celebrities in cameo appearances; aired Mar. 6, 1980. Michael Jackson and the Osmonds performed. Directed by Dwight Hemion.

Kraft Salutes Walt Disney World's 10th Anniversary (TV) Special on CBS; aired Jan. 21, 1982. Directed by Dwight Hemion. The Lane family, played by Dean Jones, Michele Lee, Eileen Brennan, Dana Plato, and Ricky Schroder, visit Walt Disney World.

Krag, the Kootenay Ram (TV) A bighorn ram struggles to survive in the wilderness of the Rocky Mountains. Prepared for the weekly anthology TV series but did not air. First aired in Canada on Nov. 27, 1983. Later shown on The Disney Channel. Directed by Frank Zuniga.

Krasinski, John Actor; appeared in *The Muppets* (2011). He voiced Frank McCay in *Monsters University* and Honjô in *The Wind Rises*, and narrated *Born in China*.

Kringla Bakeri og Kafe Quick-service restaurant in Norway at EPCOT; opened May 6, 1988, serving traditional specialties, like kringla sweet pretzels and skolebrød (school bread). The café resembles the mountain hamlets of Setesdal.

Krippendorf's Tribe (film) Anthropologist James Krippendorf, a single father trying to raise 3 kids, has for 2 years been living off a Proxmire Foundation grant to study an "undiscovered" tribe in New Guinea. Unfortunately, there is no tribe and all the grant money he has been collecting has been spent on his kids. When he is told that he must prove the tribe exists by documenting it on film, he begs his dysfunctional family to help him concoct a scheme involving them as the fictional "Krippendorf's

Tribe." He names the tribe the Shelmikedmu after his kids—Shelly, Mickey, and Edmund—and turns his backyard into a jungle for the filming, hoping to match up that film with film he had shot of a New Guinea tribe, the Nishalayku. However, doubts are raised about the "discovery" by anthropologist Veronica Micelli and anthropology department head Ruth Allen. A Touchstone film. Released Feb. 27, 1998. 94 min. Directed by Todd Holland. Stars Richard Dreyfuss (James Krippendorf), Jenna Elfman (Veronica Micelli), Natasha Lyonne (Shelly), Gregory Smith (Mickey), Carl Michael Lindner (Edmund), Stephen Root (Gerald Adams), Elaine Stritch (Irene Harding), Tom Poston (Gordon Harding), Lily Tomlin (Ruth Allen), David Ogden Stiers (Henry Spivey). Based on the novel of the same title by Larry Parkin. The tribal villages of the Nishalayku and the fictitious Shelmikedmu were created at the Kualoa Ranch on the island of Oahu in Hawai'i. Additional filming took place at various Los Angeles locations, including the campuses of USC and UCLA, and the Wilshire Ebell Theatre. For the Krippendorf home, an American Craftsman–style house in San Gabriel was selected.

Krisel, Gary Head of Walt Disney Television Animation 1984–1995 (vice president 1984–1990, president thereafter), he had originally started with the company in marketing in Disneyland in 1972. Later he joined the Walt Disney Music Company and served as its president 1981–1986. He resigned in 1995.

Kristoff Arendelle's Ice Master and Deliverer in *Frozen*; voiced by Jonathan Groff.

Kronk Yzma's oblivious henchman in *The Emperor's New Groove*; voiced by Patrick Warburton.

Kronk's New Groove (film) Direct-to-video release Dec. 13, 2005. Yzma's former henchman, Kronk, has started a new life as the head chef in his very own diner. But when he hears his father is coming to visit, he plots to make himself look like a success in life. Directed by Elliot M. Bour and Saul Blinkoff. Voices include Patrick Warburton (Kronk), Tracey Ullman (Ms. Birdwell), Eartha Kitt (Yzma), David Spade (Kuzco), John Goodman (Pacha). 72 min.

Krumholtz, David Actor; appeared in *Life with Mikey* (Barry Corman), *The Santa Clause* and *The Santa Clause 2* (Bernard), and *10 Things I Hate About You* (Michael Eckman), and on the TV series

Monty (David Richardson). He voiced Cobalt Ferrero in *Star vs. The Forces of Evil*.

Kudrow, Lisa Actress; appeared in *Romy and Michele's High School Reunion* (Michele), on Disney+ in *Better Nate Than Ever* (Aunt Heidi), and on TV in *Scandal* (Congresswoman Josephine Marcus), with a guest appearance on *Cougar Town*. She voiced Aphrodite in the *Hercules* animated series.

Kuhn, Judy Actress; provided the singing voice of the title character in *Pocahontas* and *Pocahontas II: Journey to a New World*, and of Princess Ting Ting in *Mulan II*. She had a cameo as a pregnant woman in *Enchanted* and made a TV guest appearance in *Hope & Faith* (Colleen).

Kulp, Nancy (1921–1991) Actress; appeared in *The Parent Trap* (Mrs. Grunecker) and *Moon Pilot* (nutritionist), and provided the voice of Frou-Frou in *The Aristocats*.

Kundun (film) In 1937, a 2½-year-old boy, Tenzin Gyatso, from a simple family in rural Tibet, was recognized as the 14th reincarnation of the Buddha of love and compassion, and destined to become the spiritual and political leader of his country. Told through the eyes of the Dalai Lama, the movie chronicles his early life, from childhood through the Chinese invasion in 1950, and his journey into exile in 1959. A Touchstone film. Released Dec. 25, 1997, exclusively in Los Angeles and New York City and expanded to more theaters Jan. 16, 1998. Directed by Martin Scorsese. Stars Tenzin Thuthob Tsarong (Dalai Lama as an adult), Gyurme Tethong (Dalai Lama age 12), Tenzin Chodon Gyalpo (mother). 135 min. Filmed in CinemaScope. Screenwriter Melissa Mathison based her script on research, plus 15 interviews with the Dalai Lama himself. The title of the film means "great compassionate teacher." Actors for the film were found among Tibetans living in India, the U.S., and Canada; while none were professional actors, several were members of the Tibetan Institute of Performing Arts. Since it was not possible to film in Tibet or India, the home of the exiled Tibetan government, the company decided to film in Morocco, which has a high desert and mountains as needed to approximate Tibet. The production base was at Atlas Studios outside of Ouarzazate.

Kunis, Mila Actress; appeared in *Krippendorf's Tribe* (Abbey) and *Oz The Great and Power-*

ful (Theodora), and on home video in *Honey, We Shrunk Ourselves* (Jill).

Kunstarbeit in Kristall Crystal and collectibles shop in Germany at EPCOT; opened ca. 1991, presented by Arribas Brothers.

Kuri, Emile (1907–2000) He joined the Disney Studio in 1952 as head decorator. He won an Oscar for his work on *20,000 Leagues Under the Sea*, also supervising set decoration on such films as *The Absent-Minded Professor, Mary Poppins, Bedknobs and Broomsticks*, and *The Million Dollar Duck*. He helped decorate company executive offices and interior and exterior settings at Disneyland Resort and Walt Disney World, including New Orleans Square and Club 33.

Kurtti, Jeff A Disney historian and author of more than 30 books on various Disney subjects; he was employed by Disney in various capacities 1987–1995 and later produced documentaries and other bonus materials for DVDs, as well as producing many in the Walt Disney Treasures DVD series and the 2009 documentary *The Boys: The Sherman Brothers' Story*. He has continued to serve as a Disney consultant and was creative director of The Walt Disney Family Museum.

Kurtz, Swoosie Actress; appeared in *Bubble Boy* (Mrs. Livingston), and guest starred on TV in *Lost* (Emily Locke) and *Desperate Housewives* (Jessie). She won an Emmy Award for a guest appearance on *Carol & Co.* in 1990.

Kurtzman, Katy Actress; appeared on TV in *Child of Glass* (Blossom Culp), *Donovan's Kid* (Jamie Carpenter), and made a guest appearance on *Grey's Anatomy* (Deedee Keller).

Kusafiri Coffee Shop and Bakery Quick-service counter in Africa at Disney's Animal Kingdom; opened Apr. 22, 1998. "Kusafiri" means "to travel" in Swahili.

Kutcher, Ashton Actor; appeared in *A Lot Like Love* (Oliver Martin) and *The Guardian* (Jake Fischer).

Kuzco Arrogant emperor-turned-llama in *The Emperor's New Groove*; voiced by David Spade.

Kyle XY (TV) Hour-long drama series on ABC Family; aired Jun. 26, 2006–Mar. 16, 2009. Kyle is a 16-year-old savant found wandering in the woods. Psychologist Nicole Trager takes him from a youth detention center into her home, realizing that he needs special attention. While the rest of the Trager family is not as welcoming of Kyle, they come to see that he has some unique abilities and a thirst for knowledge. But still, there are questions about his past and, above all, why he does not have a belly button. Stars Matt Dallas (Kyle), Marguerite MacIntyre (Nicole Trager), Bruce Thomas (Stephen Trager), April Matson (Lori Trager), Jean-Luc Bilodeau (Josh Trager). From Touchstone Television.

1. *Lady and the Tramp* (film) 2. Lumiere 3. Le Château de la Belle au Bois Dormant 4. Ludwig Von Drake 5. *Lion King, The* (film)
6. *Luca* (film) 7. Liberty Square 8. Little Mermaid, The ~ Ariel's Undersea Adventure 9. *Lilo & Stitch* (film) 10. Lee, Jennifer

L.A. Bar and Grill Restaurant serving American fare in Disney Village at Disneyland Paris; opened Apr. 12, 1992. Closed Dec. 2001, to become Café Mickey.

L.A. Cinema Storage Shop, also known as L.A. Prop & Cinema Storage, on Hollywood Boulevard at Disney's Hollywood Studios; opened May 1, 1991. Closed Jun. 15, 2014, to become The Trolley Car Café.

La Belle Librairie SEE VILLAGE SHOPPES.

La Bottega di Geppetto Fantasyland toy and stuffed animal shop in Disneyland Paris; opened Apr. 12, 1992. Themed to the wood-carver's home from *Pinocchio*.

La Bottega Italiana Shop in Italy at EPCOT; opened ca. 1989, taking the place of i Santi. Cookware, Venetian masks, decorative items, and Italian foodstuffs are sold.

La Boutique Shop at Disney's Riviera Resort at Walt Disney World; opened Dec. 16, 2019, with merchandise inspired by the European Riviera.

La Boutique de Noel Christmas ornament and holiday decoration shop in New Orleans Square at Disneyland; opened May 17, 1996, replacing the original Le Gourmet. Closed in 2006, to become Le Bat en Rouge.

La Boutique des Provinces Shop in Canada at EPCOT; opened Sep. 24, 1986. Decorative gifts, jewelry, and fashion accessories were offered from French Canada. Closed in 2005.

La Boutique d'Or Shop offering fine gold accessories in New Orleans Square at Disneyland; opened spring 1974, taking the place of Le Forgeron. Closed Mar. 23, 1982, to become The Brass Boutique.

La Boutique du Château Medieval-style Christmas boutique inside Le Château de la Belle au Bois Dormant in Disneyland Paris; opened Apr. 12, 1992.

La Cabane des Robinson The Swiss Family Treehouse in Adventureland at Disneyland Paris; opened Apr. 12, 1992.

La Cantina Buffet-style market with a Route 66 theme in Disney Hotel Santa Fe at Disneyland Paris; opened Apr. 12, 1992. Tex-Mex–inspired cuisine is served.

La Cantina de San Angel Outdoor counter-service eatery facing Mexico in EPCOT; opened Oct. 1, 1982, offering burritos, tacos, and beer. It was remodeled in 2010, reopening Sep. 15 adjacent to a new restaurant, La Hacienda de San Angel.

La Cava del Tequila Bar offering over 200 tequilas and other cocktails, along with light snacks, tucked away in Mexico at EPCOT; opened Aug. 31, 2009. It took the place of La Familia Fashions.

La Chaumière des Sept Nains Fantasyland costume, clothing, and accessory shop in Disneyland

Paris; opened Apr. 12, 1992, with a forest setting inspired by *Snow White and the Seven Dwarfs*.

La Confiserie des Trois Fées Fantasyland sweets boutique in Disneyland Paris; opened Apr. 12, 1992. Candies and housewares are sold in the cottage of the good fairies from *Sleeping Beauty*.

La Crêperie de Paris Crepe and galette restaurant in France at EPCOT; opened Oct. 1, 2021, as part of an expansion of the pavilion.

La Familia Fashions Clothing and accessory shop in Mexico at EPCOT; opened in 1985. La Cava del Tequila took its place in 2009.

La Gemma Elegante Shop in Italy at EPCOT; opened Oct. 1, 1982. In 2001, Venetian mask artisan Giorgio Iurcotta relocated to Florida to introduce his craft at the shop.

La Girafe Curieuse Safari-themed shop in Adventureland at Disneyland Paris; opened Apr. 12, 1992.

La Hacienda de San Angel Indoor table-service restaurant in Mexico at EPCOT; opened adjacent to La Cantina de San Angel Sep. 15, 2010. Authentic Mexican cuisine and premium margaritas are served.

La Luna (film) Animated short from Pixar Animation Studios, directed by Enrico Casarosa. Originally shown at the Annecy International Animation Film Festival on Jun. 6, 2011; U.S. theatrical release with *Brave* Jun. 22, 2012. A fable of a young boy who is coming of age in the most peculiar of circumstances. Tonight is the very first time his Papa and Grandpa are taking him to work. In an old wooden boat they row far out to sea, and with no land in sight, they stop and wait. A big surprise awaits the little boy as he discovers his family's most unusual line of work. Voices include Krista Sheffler (Bambino), Tony Fucile (Papa), Phil Sheridan (Grandpa). 7 min. Nominated for an Academy Award (Animated Short Film).

La Maison du Vin Shop in France at EPCOT; opened Oct. 1, 1982. Visitors can sample a few wines as they visit France. Originally presented by Barton & Guestier. Also known as Les Vins de France and Aux Vins de France.

La Mascarade d'Orleans Merchandise shop offering masks and Mardi Gras–themed items in New Orleans Square at Disneyland; opened Dec. 22, 1994, replacing Marche Aux Fleurs, Sacs et Modes. In Feb. 2015, the location began offering Pandora jewelry items.

La Nouba SEE CIRQUE DU SOLEIL.

La Petite Parfumerie Adventureland shop in Tokyo Disneyland; opened Apr. 15, 1983. Perfumes and soaps from around the world are sold.

La Petite Patisserie Counter-service restaurant offering cinnamon rolls, croissants, and pastries in New Orleans Square at Disneyland; opened next to Café Orléans in Apr. 1988. Closed in 2006 to make way for an expansion of Café Orléans.

La Piñata (film) Segment of *The Three Caballeros* in which Donald Duck learns of "Las Posadas."

La Place de Rémy *Ratatouille*-themed area in Worlds of Pixar (formerly part of Toon Studio) in Walt Disney Studios Park at Disneyland Paris; opened Jul. 10, 2014. There is a ride-through attraction, Ratatouille: L'Aventure Totalement Toquée de Rémy, along with table-service dining at Bistrot Chez Rémy and shopping at Chez Marianne (Souvenirs de Paris).

La Plage des Pirates Playground for young children in Adventureland in Disneyland Paris; opened Dec. 19, 1999. In English, it is known as Pirates' Beach.

La Princesa de Cristal Caribbean Plaza shop in the Magic Kingdom at Walt Disney World; opened in 1974, with glass cutting, blowing, and engraving. Replaced in 1992 by an expansion of El Pirata y el Perico. Also in Mexico at EPCOT; opened in 2009, taking the place of Artesanías Mexicanas. Presented by Arribas Brothers.

La Signature Perfume and cosmetics shop in France at EPCOT; opened Oct. 1, 1982, presented by Guy Laroche.

La Taverne de Gaston Fantasyland counter-service restaurant in Tokyo Disneyland; opened Sep. 28, 2020. Hearty fare is served in a tavern adorned with trophies honoring the huntsman from *Beauty and the Beast*.

La Tienda Encantada Fine jewelry, leather goods, and accessory shop in Mexico at EPCOT.

Lab Rats (TV) Comedy series on Disney XD; premiered Feb. 27, 2012. A billionaire inventor, Donald Davenport, genetically engineers 3 superhuman kids to save the world. Teenager Leo Dooley discovers he has newfound "siblings": one is smart, another has superspeed and stealth reflexes, and another is strong but dumb. They try to navigate a typical high school while dealing with bionic glitches and attempting to keep their extraordinary abilities a secret. Stars Spencer Boldman (Adam), Billy Unger (Chase), Kelli Berglund (Bree), Tyrel Jackson Williams (Leo), Hal Sparks (Davenport). From It's a Laugh Productions.

LaBeouf, Shia Actor; appeared in *Holes* (Stanley Yelnats) and *The Greatest Game Ever Played* (Francis Ouimet), and on Disney Channel in *Even Stevens* (Louis Stevens), *Tru Confessions* (Eddie Walker), *Hounded* (Ronny Van Dusen), and *The Even Stevens Movie*. He voiced Johnny McBride in *The Proud Family*. Winner of a Daytime Emmy in 2003 for Performer in a Children's Series.

Lacroix, André Joined the company as chairman of Euro Disney on Jul. 1, 2003. He was formerly head of the international arm of Burger King Corp. He left the company in May 2005.

Ladd, Alan (1913–1964) Actor; appeared in *The Reluctant Dragon* telling the *Baby Weems* story.

Ladd, Diane Actress; appeared in *Something Wicked This Way Comes* (Mrs. Nightshade), *The Cemetery Club* (Lucille Rubin), and *Father Hood* (Rita).

Ladder 49 (film) A devoted firefighter, Jack Morrison, is trapped in a major warehouse blaze, and while wondering if he will be rescued, he reflects back on his life. He remembers back to his first day with the Baltimore Fire Department and recalls his initiation into the close-knit, prank-filled, courage-fed band of brothers at the firehouse, and the discovery of his own deeply held compulsion to save lives. Pushed to the limits of loyalty and courage, Jack holds tight to indelible memories as he waits for his own rescue. Outside, his best friend, Capt. Mike Kennedy, risks his life to save him. A Touchstone film/Beacon Pictures production. Released Oct. 1, 2004. Directed by Jay Russell. Stars John Travolta (Capt. Mike Kennedy), Joaquin Phoenix (Jack Morrison), Balthazar Getty (Ray Gauquin), Robert Patrick (Lenny Richter), Jacinda Barrett (Linda Morrison), Morris Chestnut (Tommy Drake), Jay Hernandez (Keith Perez), Billy Burke (Dennis Gauquin), Tim Guinee (Tony Corrigan), Kevin Chapman (Frank McKinney), Kevin Daniels (Don Miller). 115 min.

Ladies and the Champ (TV) Two-hour movie on *The Wonderful World of Disney*; first aired Apr. 22, 2001. Two elderly women in Younger, Illinois, a retirement town, break all the rules to become boxing managers to a young homeless man, a small-time crook whom the old ladies mistake for a prizefighter. Directed by Jeff Barry. Stars Olympia Dukakis (Sarah Stevenson), Marion Ross (Margaret Smith), David DeLuise (Darold Boyarsky), Sarah Strange (Jenny), Garwin Sanford (Vossbinder), Blu Mankuma (Royal Reynolds), Paul Michael (Hamp Gilliam). Filmed on location in Vancouver.

Lady Cocker spaniel heroine of *Lady and the Tramp*; voiced by Barbara Luddy. The character was voiced by Jodi Benson for *Lady and the Tramp II: Scamp's Adventure*.

Lady and the Tramp (film) Lady, a young cocker spaniel from a respectable home, falls in love with Tramp, a mutt who lives in the railroad yards. They enjoy several outings together, including a memorable spaghetti dinner by moonlight at Tony's, but their relationship is strained not only by Lady's loyalty to her human family and their newborn baby, but also by Tramp's devil-may-care attitude that at one point gets Lady thrown in the dog pound. Tramp redeems himself by saving the baby from a rat and thereby wins Lady's love and the affection of her human family. The first Disney animated feature filmed in CinemaScope, which necessitated extra work in planning scenes and action to fill the entire screen. World premiere in Chicago on Jun. 16, 1955; general release on Jun. 22, 1955. Directed by Hamilton Luske, Clyde Geronimi, Wilfred Jackson. 76 min. The idea for the film came from a short story by Ward Greene entitled, "Happy Dan, the Whistling Dog." A 1940 script introduced the twin Siamese cats. The film was enlivened by such songs as "He's a Tramp," by Sonny Burke and Peggy Lee. In early script versions, Tramp was first called Homer, then Rags, then Bozo. The film stars such voice talents as Barbara Luddy as Lady; Larry Roberts as Tramp; and Peggy Lee as Darling, the Siamese cats, and Peg, the show dog. Peggy Lee helped promote the film on the Disney TV series, explaining her work with the score and singing a few numbers. *Lady and the Tramp* was rereleased in theaters in 1962, 1971, 1980, and 1986. First released on video in 1987.

Lady and the Tramp (film) A live-action retelling of the 1955 animated film. Life is good for Lady, an overachieving American cocker spaniel who resides in an upscale suburban neighborhood. Her owners, Jim Dear and Darling, spoil her daily, and her neighbors, Jock and Trusty, are always within barking distance. But when a baby enters the picture, Lady is no longer the center of attention, and the arrival of cat-loving Aunt Sarah only complicates matters. Lady soon finds herself alone on the streets in an un-welcoming part of town. Fortunately, Tramp, a streetwise mongrel, is quick to teach her the ways of the world. Before long, the prim and proper purebred and the fast-talking mutt are partaking in moonlight strolls in the park and a romantic spaghetti dinner. Tramp savors the independence of a world without leashes or fences, but Lady misses the comfort and safety of a family, and soon both must decide where—and with whom—they belong. Released digitally Nov. 12, 2019, on Disney+. Directed by Charlie Bean. Stars Kiersey Clemons (Darling), Thomas Mann (Jim Dear), Yvette Nicole Brown (Aunt Sarah), with the voices of Tessa Thompson (Lady), Justin Theroux (Tramp), Janelle Monáe (Peg), Sam Elliott (Trusty). 103 min. Monte, a rescue dog from New Mexico, plays Tramp, while Lady is played by Rose, a prized hunting dog. The famous spaghetti scene took 3 days to film and was achieved using sugarless, undyed licorice soaked in chicken broth—a taste both dogs liked. Filmed in wide-screen format in Savannah, Georgia.

Lady and the Tramp: A Lesson in Sharing Attention Educational film; released in Sep. 1978. The film stresses the importance of sharing attention when a new baby joins a family.

Lady and the Tramp II: Scamp's Adventure (film) Direct-to-video release Feb. 27, 2001. Lady and Tramp are now parents of Scamp, a mischievous pup who longs for the freedom and excitement of a junkyard dog, but soon discovers that life on the streets is not what he expected and that the love of his family is more valuable than he knew. Scamp has 3 sisters—Annette, Colette, and Danielle—and while on his jaunt "to see the world" rescues from the dogcatcher and falls in love with an orphan mutt, Angel. Directed by Darrell Rooney. Voices include Scott Wolf (Scamp), Alyssa Milano (Angel), Jodi Benson (Lady), Jeff Bennett (Tramp,

Jock, Trusty, Dogcatcher), Chazz Palminteri (Buster), Bill Fagerbakke (Mooch), Bronson Pinchot (Francois), Mickey Rooney (Sparky). 70 min.

Lady Gaga & The Muppets' Holiday Spectacular (TV) Special, airing on Nov. 28, 2013, with Lady Gaga going backstage with The Muppets as they combine forces to sing holiday favorites and Lady Gaga hits, with a sneak peek at the upcoming movie, *Muppets Most Wanted*. 90 min. Guest stars include Sir Elton John, Joseph Gordon-Levitt, RuPaul, and Kristen Bell. From Sunset Lane Entertainment and ABC's Lincoln Square Productions.

Lady Kluck Maid Marian's lady-in-waiting, a chicken, in *Robin Hood*; voiced by Carole Shelley.

Lady Tremaine Cinderella's evil stepmother; voiced by Eleanor Audley.

Ladykillers, The (film) An eccentric Southern professor assembles a band of less-than-competent thieves to rob a Mississippi riverboat casino. When the gang rents a room from unsuspecting, straitlaced, churchgoing little old Mrs. Munson, they get more than they bargained for, along with a strong reminder that crime does not pay. Directed by Joel Coen and Ethan Coen. A Touchstone film. Released Mar. 26, 2004. Stars Tom Hanks (Prof. G. H. Dorr), Irma P. Hall (Marva Munson), Marlon Wayans (Gawain MacSam), J. K. Simmons (Garth Pancake), Tzi Ma (The General), Ryan Hurst (Lump), George Wallace (Sheriff Wyner), Jason Weaver (Weemack Funthes). 104 min. Inspired by the 1955 film featuring Alec Guinness. It received a screening at the Cannes Film Festival May 18, 2004.

Lafayette Eager farm dog character in *The Aristocats*; voiced by George Lindsey.

Laffite's Portrait Deck Caribbean Plaza photo shop in the Magic Kingdom at Walt Disney World; opened Aug. 1, 1980, replacing the Caribbean Arcade. It then became a shop, called simply Laffite's, ca. 1994–1997.

Laffite's Silver Shop New Orleans Square jewelry and silver shop in Disneyland; opened in 1966 and relocated in 1987 to prepare for remodeling of Café Orléans. Closed Jan. 10, 1988.

Lafitte's Treasure Chest Former shop in Adventureland at Tokyo Disneyland; opened Apr. 15, 1983, selling gold and silver jewelry and decorative gifts.

Lagomasino, Maria Elena Member of the Disney Board of Directors beginning Dec. 1, 2015.

Lahti, Christine Actress; appeared in *Gross Anatomy* (Rachel Woodruff) and *The Doctor* (Anne), and on Disney Channel in *The Four Diamonds* (Dr. Burke/Raptenahad).

Lake Buena Vista Club SEE BUENA VISTA CLUB.

Lake Buena Vista, Florida One of 2 cities home to Walt Disney World (the other is Bay Lake). Named after Buena Vista St., on which the Disney Studio is located in Burbank. Includes a shopping and entertainment village (now known as Disney Springs), hotels, an office complex, and golf course. A community of recreation-oriented homesites represented Disney's first major venture into a total concept of real estate planning, development, and management. The homes later became part of the Disney Institute, which was then replaced by Disney's Saratoga Springs Resort & Spa.

Lake Buena Vista Golf Course An 18-hole country club course that winds through villas and pine forests at Walt Disney World; opened in 1972. Designed by Joe Lee, the course has hosted the PGA Tour, the LPGA Tour, and USGA events. The Pro Shop sells merchandise and rentals, with snacks offered at Chip 'n' Dale's Café. SEE ALSO BUENA VISTA CLUB AND FAIRWAY VILLAS.

Lake Buena Vista Office Plaza Bank and administration building at Walt Disney World; opened Jul. 18, 1978. Originally known as the Sun Bank Building. The bank later became SunTrust (until 2016), then Partners FCU.

Lake Buena Vista Shopping Village Opened at Walt Disney World Mar. 22, 1975; the name later changed to Walt Disney World Village, Disney Village Marketplace, Downtown Disney Marketplace, and the Marketplace at Disney Springs. Opened with more than 30 shops and restaurants clustered in a delightful setting along the shores of Buena Vista Lagoon. Over the years, the list of shops and eateries has changed many times. The environment was partially inspired by Southern California coastal villages, including Laguna Beach. SEE ALSO DOWNTOWN DISNEY MARKETPLACE.

Lake Disney Man-made body of water at Disneyland Paris surrounded by Disney Village, Disney Newport Bay Club, Disney Sequoia Lodge, and Disney Hotel New York – The Art of Marvel.

Lake Titicaca (film) Segment of *Saludos Amigos*, starring Donald Duck high in the Andes. Released as a short Feb. 18, 1955.

Lakeside Circle Area surrounding Echo Lake in Disney-MGM Studios (now Disney's Hollywood Studios); opened May 1, 1989. The area was later simply known as Echo Lake.

Lakeside Terrace Restaurant SEE LITE BITE.

Lambert, David Actor; appeared on Disney XD in *Aaron Stone* (Jason Landers) and on Freeform as Brandon in *The Fosters* and *Good Trouble*.

Lambert, the Sheepish Lion (film) Special cartoon released Feb. 8, 1952. Directed by Jack Hannah. A stork delivers a lion cub to a flock of sheep by mistake, which eventually proves fortuitous for the sheep when Lambert grows up to realize his power and uses it to protect the sheep from a wolf. Nominated for an Academy Award.

Lamp Life (film) Animated short; digitally released Jan. 31, 2020, on Disney+. Woody and Giggle McDimples recount Bo Peep's wild adventures, revealing what happened to her after the events of *Toy Story 2*. Directed by Valerie LaPointe. 7 min. From Pixar Animation Studios.

Lamplight Lounge Restaurant in Pixar Pier at Disney California Adventure; opened Jun. 23, 2018, taking the place of Cove Bar and Ariel's Grotto. Gastropub cuisine and cocktails are served. The décor reflects the creativity and personalities of the artists and storytellers behind Pixar films.

Lampwick Boy who tempts Pinocchio in Pleasure Island; voiced by Frankie Darro.

Lancaster, Burt (1913–1994) Actor; appeared in *Tough Guys* (Harry Doyle).

Lancer's Inn Fantasyland pizza counter in the Magic Kingdom at Walt Disney World; open Oct. 1, 1971–1986, and succeeded by Gurgi's Munchies & Crunchies.

Lanchester, Elsa (1902–1986) Actress; appeared in *Mary Poppins* (Katie Nanna), *That Darn Cat!* (Mrs. MacDougal), *Blackbeard's Ghost* (Emily

Stowecroft), and *Rascal* (Mrs. Satterfield), and on TV in *My Dog, the Thief*.

Land, The Pavilion in World Nature (formerly Future World) at EPCOT; opened Oct. 1, 1982, with exhibits and shows about agricultural techniques, the importance of good nutrition, and how humans can effectively manage the land while still maintaining its ecology. Sponsored by Kraft (1982–1992) and Nestlé (1992–2009). Covering 6 acres, it opened as the largest pavilion in Future World. Besides the areas that can be seen by guests, there are working greenhouses and laboratories where graduate students in agriculture and other disciplines come together to research the latest processes and ideas. The Land underwent its first major refurbishment beginning in 1993; the atrium was redesigned with a new motif reflecting the sun and moon; the Listen to the Land boat ride became Living with the Land; Food Rocks replaced Kitchen Kabaret; The Land Grille Room became the Garden Grill Restaurant; Farmers Market became Sunshine Season Food Fair; and the *Symbiosis* film became *Circle of Life: An Environmental Fable* in the Harvest Theater. When Food Rocks was replaced by Soarin' in 2005, the pavilion underwent another refurbishment, with the atrium becoming themed around the 4 seasons and Sunshine Season Food Fair becoming Sunshine Seasons. In 2020, a new film, *Awesome Planet*, debuted in the Harvest Theater.

Land Grille Room, The SEE GARDEN GRILL RESTAURANT.

Land of Enemies, The (TV) Episode 4 of *Andy Burnett*.

Landau, Martin (1928–2017) Actor; appeared in *Ed Wood* (Bela Lugosi), winning an Academy Award for Best Supporting Actor for the role. He voiced Mr. Rzykruski in *Frankenweenie* (2012).

Landrum, Gary Imagineer; he joined Disney in 1977 as a Cast Member in the Magic Kingdom at Walt Disney World and supported WED Enterprises in 1981 during construction of EPCOT Center. He was later named curator, exhibit producer of art collections for Walt Disney Imagineering and in 1997 started the Show Awareness program, for which he has documented and archived the design intent and stories of Walt Disney World. He is a regular guest speaker at company events and has appeared in Disney documentaries and TV specials.

Land's End (TV) Hour-long syn. series; aired Sep. 22, 1995–Sep. 15, 1996. Mike Land, a disillusioned former LAPD detective, joins longtime friend Willis P. Dunleevy in opening a private detective agency in Cabo San Lucas, Mexico. When they are invited to provide security for the Westin Regina, a 5-star resort, the cases come rolling in. Stars Fred Dryer (Mike Land), Geoffrey Lewis (Willis P. Dunleevy).

Landscape of Flavors Food court in Disney's Art of Animation Resort at Walt Disney World; opened May 31, 2012. The restaurant is decorated with colorful background paintings from Disney animated films in a gallerylike setting.

Lane, Diane Actress; appeared in *Indian Summer* (Beth Warden), *Judge Dredd* (Judge Hershey), *Jack* (Karen Powell), *Under the Tuscan Sun* (Frances Mayes), and *Secretariat* (Penny Chenery), and voiced Mom in *Inside Out*.

Lane, Nathan Actor; appeared in *Life with Mikey* (Ed Chapman) and *Swing Vote* (Art Crumb), and on TV in *A Muppets Christmas: Letters to Santa* (Officer Meany). He provided the voice of the meerkat Timon in *The Lion King* and other appearances of the character, and voiced Spot/Scott in *Teacher's Pet* (for which he won an Emmy Award) and Tom Morrow in Innoventions at Disneyland.

Laney, Charley (1943–1997) Mouseketeer from the 1950s *Mickey Mouse Club* TV show.

Lange, Jessica Actress; appeared in and co-produced *Country* (Jewell Ivy), and appeared in *A Thousand Acres* (Ginny).

Langhammer, Fred H. Member of the Disney Board of Directors Jan. 2005–2019.

Laniwai – A Disney Spa Spa, salon, fitness center, and hydrotherapy garden at Aulani, A Disney Resort & Spa; opened Aug. 29, 2011. Laniwai means "freshwater heaven."

Lanny and Wayne the Christmas Elves in Prep & Landing SEE PREP & LANDING.

Lansburgh, Larry (1911–2001) Director and producer of animal-themed films for 3 decades, best known for his horse pictures, including the Academy Award–winning *The Horse with the Flying Tail*. He was named a Disney Legend in 1998.

Lansbury, Angela (1925–2022) Actress; appeared in *Bedknobs and Broomsticks* (Eglantine Price), *Mickey's Audition* (Sylvia), *Fantasia/2000* (as herself), and *Mary Poppins Returns* (Balloon Lady), and on TV in *The Dream Is Alive*, *The Grand Opening of Euro Disney*, and *The Best of Disney Music: A Legacy in Song*. She voiced Mrs. Potts in *Beauty and the Beast* (1991), *Beauty and the Beast: The Enchanted Christmas*, and the *Beauty and the Beast Sing-Along* in EPCOT, and narrated *The Age of Believing: The Disney Live Action Classics*. She was named a Disney Legend in 1995.

Lantern Hill (TV) A Disney Channel Premiere Film; premiered Jan. 27, 1990. A girl plans to reunite her parents after discovering her father, long thought to be dead, is alive. Directed by Kevin Sullivan. Stars Sam Waterston (Andrew Stuart), Mairon Bennett (Jane), Colleen Dewhurst, Sarah Polley. 112 min.

Lapland (film) People and Places featurette; released Jul. 3, 1957. Directed by Ben Sharpsteen. Filmed in CinemaScope. 29 min. High in the frigid zone of the continent of Europe, where the Arctic Circle cuts through the upper tips of Norway, Sweden, Finland, and Russia, is the land of the Lapps—a people privileged to cross these frontiers unrestricted because of their nomadic traditions and their owing allegiance to no one nation. Their economy, dependent on migrating livestock, is explained, as well as their customs and gypsylike existence.

L'Arbre Enchanté Quick-service ice cream and refreshment cottage in Fantasyland at Disneyland Paris; opened in 1996.

Large Animals of the Arctic (film) Part of *White Wilderness*; released on 16 mm for schools in Sep. 1964. The musk ox, caribou, and reindeer grazing on the tundra face constant danger from wolf packs and ferocious wolverines.

Large Animals that Once Roamed the Plains (film) Part of *The Vanishing Prairie*; released on 16 mm for schools in Sep. 1962. Few are left of the pronghorn antelope, bighorn sheep, cougar, and coyote, which once roamed the prairie in great numbers.

Larkin, Linda Actress; provided the speaking voice of Jasmine in *Aladdin* and other appearances of the character. She was named a Disney Legend in 2011.

Larsen, Larry (1939–2018) Mouseketeer from the 1950s *Mickey Mouse Club* TV show.

Larson, Brie Actress; appeared in *Hope & Faith* (Sydney Shanowski), *Right on Track* (Courtney Enders), and as the title character in *Captain Marvel* and later Marvel Studios productions. For Disney+, she directed/exec. produced *Growing Up* and starred in *Remembering*.

Larson, Eric (1905–1988) Animator; one of Walt's "Nine Old Men," he began at the Studio in 1933 and worked on such classics as *Snow White and the Seven Dwarfs*, *Bambi*, *Cinderella*, *The Jungle Book*, and *The Great Mouse Detective* as animator and directing animator. His patience and skill in explaining animation techniques made him the obvious choice to work with the training program for new animators in the 1970s, and many of the current animators look to Eric as their mentor. He was honored posthumously with the Disney Legends Award in 1989.

L'Art de l'Animation Disney/Art of Disney Animation Attraction in Toon Studio in Walt Disney Studios Park at Disneyland Paris; opened Mar. 16, 2002. Guests could experience the Disney Classics Theatre, learn how characters are brought to life in the Drawn to Animation show, and then have the chance to learn more about the animation process in exhibits at the Animation Station. The exhibits were remodeled in 2019, with the attraction reopening Nov. 17 as Animation Celebration. Included in the refreshed attraction is a new live show, *La Reine des Neiges: Une Invitation Musicale* (*Frozen: A Musical Invitation*). SEE ALSO MAGIC OF DISNEY ANIMATION, THE (DISNEY'S HOLLYWOOD STUDIOS) AND DISNEY ANIMATION (DISNEY CALIFORNIA ADVENTURE).

L'Artisan des Glaces Artisanal ice cream and sorbet shop in France at EPCOT; opened May 30, 2013, replacing the pavilion's original bakery. They make all their own ice cream.

Laserdisc The first Disney films were released on disc on Dec. 16, 1978.

Laserphonic Fantasy Fireworks and laser show set to classical music in World Showcase Lagoon at EPCOT Center; debuted Jun. 9, 1984, and superseded by *IllumiNations* in 1988. Operated by 12 computers, the show was one of the most complex at Walt Disney World at the time of its premiere, though it was essentially a less sophisticated version of *IllumiNations*, without the spotlighting of the individual countries.

Lasseter, John After a stint in the Disney animation department in the late 1970s and early 1980s, he returned in 1995 as the director of *Toy Story* for Pixar Animation Studios and either directed or produced all of the remaining Disney • Pixar releases. In 2006, with Disney's purchase of Pixar, he was named chief creative officer of both Pixar and Walt Disney Animation Studios, as well as principal creative adviser at Walt Disney Imagineering. He left the company in 2018.

Last Chance Café Frontierland quick-service restaurant in Disneyland Paris; opened Apr. 12, 1992. Barbecue and Tex-Mex favorites are served in an Old West outpost.

Last Dance (film) Rick Hayes is a cocky young lawyer from a wealthy family who is assigned the clemency case of Cindy Liggett, a woman on death row. After years of appeals, Cindy no longer wants to fight to save her life. But during the course of Rick's visits and research to prepare a clemency plea, he comes to know a Cindy very different from the teenager who committed murder so many years ago. As they learn to trust each other, they cannot help but acknowledge the love that has grown between them. No matter what the clemency board decides, Rick and Cindy discover and embrace love for the first time in their lives. Released May 3, 1996. A Touchstone film. Directed by Bruce Beresford. Stars Sharon Stone (Cindy), Rob Morrow (Rick), Randy Quaid (Sam Burns), Peter Gallagher (John Hayes), Jack Thompson (Governor), Don Harvey (Doug), Jayne Brook (Jane). 103 min. Set in an unspecified Southern state, the movie was filmed in Nashville; Eddyville, Kentucky; Ridgeland, South Carolina; and briefly at the Taj Mahal in India. At Ridgeland, a brand-new, not-yet-occupied prison was turned into Bridgeland for the film crew.

Last Electric Knight, The (TV) Show aired Feb. 16, 1986. Directed by James Fargo. A young martial arts expert searches for a pretend guardian when a social worker tries to take him away from his elderly grandfather. The person he picks happens to be a detective. Pilot for the *Sidekicks* series. Stars Ernie Reyes, Gil Gerard, Keye Luke, Nancy Stafford, Jason Hervey.

Last Flight of Noah's Ark, The (film) An unemployed pilot, fleeing debt collectors, accepts the risky mission of flying an old converted B-29, loaded with farm animals, an attractive young missionary, and 2 young orphan stowaways, to an island in the Pacific. The plane crash-lands on a small island inhabited by 2 World War II Japanese naval officers who don't know the war is over. After some confusion, they all end up friends and are rescued by the Coast Guard. Released Jun. 25, 1980. Directed by Charles Jarrott. 98 min. Stars Elliott Gould (Noah Dugan), Geneviève Bujold (Bernadette), Ricky Schroder (Bobby), Tammy Lauren (Julie), Vincent Gardenia (Stoney), John Fujioka (Cleveland), Yuki Shimoda (Hiro), John P. Ryan (Coslough), Dana Elcar (Benchley). The film was based on a story by Ernest K. Gann. The movie's song, "Half of Me," was written by Hal David and Maurice Jarre and performed by Alexandra Brown. Location shooting took place at a dilapidated airfield in the desert near Victorville, California, and on the island of Kauai in Hawai'i. The interior of the plane and many night scenes were filmed on Disney soundstages; for the underwater scenes, the soundstage tank built for *20,000 Leagues Under the Sea* was utilized.

Last Resort, The (TV) Reality series on ABC Family; debuted Jan. 20, 2003, and ended Mar. 31. Couples are taken to a Hawaiian island to work out their relationships. From Buena Vista Prods. and Fisher Entertainment, in association with Wheeler/Sussman Prods.

Last Shot, The (film) Hollywood screenwriter Steven Schats has long held the great ambition of selling his morbid screenplay, but he has had no success. Then he meets Joe Devine, who represents himself as the man who can green-light Schats's low-budget movie. But Devine is not who he claims to be. In truth, he is not an agent—not of the movie industry variety at least—but rather with the FBI, and he is on a covert mission to ferret out mobsters with criminal ties to Hollywood. Devine is as determined to be a star at the Bureau as Schats is to be one in his industry, and Devine is just clever enough to make the trusting screenwriter believe that he is at last on the fast track to filmmaking success. A Touchstone film in association with Mandeville Films. Directed by Jeff Nathanson. Limited release on Sep. 24, 2004. Stars Matthew Broderick (Steven Schats), Alec Baldwin (Joe Devine), Toni Collette (Emily French), Calista Flockhart (Valerie Weston), Ray Liotta (Jack Devine), Tim Blake Nelson (Marshal Paris), Tony

Shalhoub (Tommy Sanz), Buck Henry (Lonnie). Joan Cusack has an uncredited role as Fanny Nash; Pat Morita and Russell Means also have cameo roles playing themselves. 93 min. Based on a true story about aspiring filmmakers, Gary Levy and Dan Lewk, who became unwitting pawns in a covert government operation, as related in the article, "What's Wrong with This Picture?" by Steve Fishman. The working title was *Providence*.

Last Song, The (film) An estranged father in a small Southern beach town gets a chance to spend the summer with his young son, Jonah, and reluctant teenage daughter, Ronnie, who'd rather be home in New York City. He tries to reconnect with Ronnie through the only thing they have in common—music—in a story of family, friendship, secrets, and salvation, as she finds solace in the love of a charming local volleyball player, Will, and eventually gets over her anger toward her father. Directed by Julie Anne Robinson. A Touchstone film. Released Mar. 31, 2010. Stars Miley Cyrus (Ronnie Miller), Liam Hemsworth (Will Blakelee), Greg Kinnear (Steve Miller), Kelly Preston (Kim), Bobby Coleman (Jonah Miller), Hallock Beals (Scott), Nick Lashaway (Marcus), Carly Chaikin (Blaze), Nick Searcy (Tom Blakelee), Kate Vernon (Susan Blakelee). 107 min. Adapted from the novel by Nicholas Sparks. Filming took place on Tybee Island, off the coast of Georgia, with the wedding scene at the Wormsloe State Historic Site near Savannah.

Last Warrior, The (film) SEE POSLEDNY BOGATYR.

Laughing Monkey Traders Adventure Isle general store in Shanghai Disneyland; opened Jun. 16, 2016, selling apparel, toys, and souvenirs. According to the story, it was once a textile dye workshop. Closed Jan. 24, 2020, and superseded by Chip & Dale's Trading Post.

Laugh-O-gram Films Walt Disney's Kansas City company, which made a series of 7 modernized versions of fairy tales: *The Four Musicians of Bremen*, *Little Red Riding Hood*, *Puss in Boots*, *Jack and the Beanstalk*, *Goldie Locks and the Three Bears*, *Jack the Giant Killer*, and *Cinderella*, in 1922. The company had to file for bankruptcy when the distributor defaulted on his payments.

Launch Pad Seasonal water-play area in the Woody Courtyard at the Toy Story Hotel at Shanghai Disney Resort; opened Jun. 16, 2016.

Launchpad McQuack Scrooge's pilot in *DuckTales*, and later in *Darkwing Duck*; voiced by Terence McGovern.

Laurie, Piper Actress; appeared in *Return to Oz* (Aunt Em).

Laurie Hill (TV) Series on ABC; aired Sep. 30–Oct. 28, 1992. A family practitioner seesaws between the needs of her writer-husband and her 5-year-old son, and the demands of her work as a physician and partner in a successful medical practice. Stars DeLane Matthews (Laurie Hill), Robert Clohessy (Jeff Hill), Eric Lloyd (Leo Hill), Ellen DeGeneres (Nancy MacIntire). From Touchstone Television.

Lava (film) Animated short from Pixar. Released Jun. 19, 2015, with *Inside Out*. Inspired by the isolated beauty of tropical islands and the allure of ocean volcanoes, the cartoon is a musical love story that takes place over millions of years. Directed by James Ford Murphy. Voices are Napua Greig (Lele), Kuana Torres Kahele (Uku). 7 min.

Lava Shack Poolside shop at Aulani, A Disney Resort & Spa; opened Aug. 29, 2011, selling snacks and beach essentials.

Lavender Blue (Dilly Dilly) Song from *So Dear to My Heart*; written by Larry Morey and Eliot Daniel. Nominated for an Academy Award.

LaVerne, Lucille (1872–1945) Actress; provided the voice of the Queen/Witch in *Snow White and the Seven Dwarfs*.

Law, Jude Actor; appeared as Yon-Rogg in the Marvel Studios films. On Disney+, he starred in *Peter Pan & Wendy* (Captain Hook) and *Star Wars: Skeleton Crew*.

Law and Order, Incorporated (TV) Episode 4 of *Elfego Baca*.

Lawman or Gunman (TV) Episode 3 of *Elfego Baca*.

Lawrence, Andrew Actor; appeared on TV in *Blossom* (Little Joey), *Walter and Emily* (Andrew), *Brotherly Love* (Andy Roman), and *Castle* (Tommy Marcone); on Disney Channel in *Horse Sense* and *Jumping Ship* (both as Tommy Biggs), *The Famous Jett Jackson*, *The Other Me* (Will Browning/

Twoie), and *Going to the Mat* (Jace Newfield); and on ABC Family in *Melissa & Joey* (Evan McKay). He voiced T. J. Detweiler on *Recess*.

Lawrence, Joey Actor; provided the voice of Oliver in *Oliver & Company*. He appeared in the pilot for an *Adventures in Babysitting* TV series and as Joey Russo in the long-running series *Blossom*. In 1995, he starred in *Brotherly Love* with his real-life brothers, Matthew and Andrew. He appeared on Disney Channel in *Horse Sense* and *Jumping Ship* (both as Michael Woods), on ABC Family in *Melissa & Joey* (Joe Longo), and guest starred in *Dollface* on Hulu. He voiced Chad in *A Goofy Movie*, Franklin Dudikoff in *Recess*, and Dirk Brock in *The Emperor's New School*.

Lawrence, Martin Actor; appeared in *Nothing to Lose* (T. Paul), *Wild Hogs* (Bobby Davis), *College Road Trip* (James Porter).

Lawrence, Matthew Actor; appeared in *The Hot Chick* (Billy), on TV in *Walter and Emily* (Zack Collins), *Blossom* (Young Joey), *Brotherly Love* (Matt Roman), *Boy Meets World* (Jack), *Angels in the Endzone* (Jesse Harper), and the *Walt Disney World Happy Easter Parade* (1996), on ABC Family in *Melissa & Joey* (Tony Longo), and on Disney Channel in *H-E-Double Hockey Sticks* (Dave Heinrich), *Jumping Ship* (Jake Hunter), and *Girl Meets World* (Jack Hunter).

Laybourne, Geraldine Hired by Disney in 1996 to be president of Disney/ABC Cable Networks. She had formerly headed Nickelodeon. She left in 1998 to start Oxygen Media.

Le Bat en Rouge New Orleans Square shop in Disneyland; opened Mar. 1, 1995, replacing Mascarades d'Arlequin, and closed Oct. 1, 1995. Reopened in a new location, taking the place of Port d'Orléans, Oct. 3, 2002, and closed Mar. 13, 2020, to later become Eudora's Chic Boutique Featuring Tiana's Gourmet Secrets. For many years, *Nightmare Before Christmas* merchandise was sold.

Le Carrousel de Lancelot Carousel attraction in Fantasyland at Disneyland Paris; opened Apr. 12, 1992.

Le Cellier Restaurant in Canada at EPCOT; opened Oct. 1, 1982. Guests descend into the cozy cellar of a Canadian château for exquisite steaks and seafood. Originally, salmon, maple-syrup pie, strawberry-rhubarb cobbler, and other delicacies from north of the border were served buffeteria style. After a 9-month refurbishment, the restaurant reopened Jun. 25, 1995, with a new menu featuring deli-style sandwiches and salads. Another change was made as of Jul. 20, 1997, with the restaurant becoming a full-service steak house. The restaurant has become famous for its cheddar cheese soup.

Le Chapeau New Orleans Square hat shop in Disneyland; open 1967–1973, and superseded by Marche Aux Fleurs, Sacs et Modes.

Le Château de la Belle au Bois Dormant Sleeping Beauty Castle in Fantasyland in Disneyland Paris; opened Apr. 12, 1992. Its tallest tower reaches 149.2 ft. above the moat, and, underneath the castle, in La Tanière du Dragon, guests find a sleeping dragon that slowly awakens. Also inside, Le Galerie de la Belle au Bois Dormant tells the story of *Sleeping Beauty* through stained glass windows, tapestries, and lavishly illustrated books. The castle is quite different in its design from those in the other Disney parks; the Imagineers realized they could not rely on a look composed of familiar French architecture to impress a European audience. So rather than compete with the thousands of age-old castles found throughout France, they created an original, more fanciful, castle inspired by Eyvind Earle's artwork for *Sleeping Beauty* as well as Gothic illustrations from the 15th-century manuscript *Les Très Riches Heures du Duc de Berry*.

Le Forgeron New Orleans Square shop in Disneyland; opened in 1966, selling leaded glass, wrought iron, and metal accessories. Succeeded by La Boutique d'Or in 1974.

Le Fou Gaston's clueless sidekick in *Beauty and the Beast*; voiced by Jesse Corti. Also spelled Lefou.

Le Gourmet New Orleans Square shop offering cooking and serving accessories in Disneyland; opened in 1966, and relocated May 16, 1996, taking the place of the One-of-a-Kind shop. Its original location became La Boutique de Noel. The shop closed Sep. 9, 1999, becoming Port d'Orléans.

Le Passage Enchanté d'Aladdin Adventureland attraction in Disneyland Paris; opened Dec. 9, 1993. Explorers can visit the enchanted city of Agrabah and marvel at miniature scenes depicting Disney's story of Aladdin.

Le Pays des Contes de Fées Storybook Land attraction in Fantasyland at Disneyland Paris; opened Apr. 1994. A gentle cruise past miniature scenes, including the Dwarfs' mine, the gingerbread house from *Babes in the Woods*, Rapunzel's tower from *Tangled*, the Beast's castle from *Beauty and the Beast*, and the Emerald City and castle from *Return to Oz*. SEE ALSO STORYBOOK LAND CANAL BOATS (DISNEYLAND).

Le Petit Café Stylish French patisserie in Disney's Riviera Resort at Walt Disney World; opened Dec. 16, 2019, serving coffee in the morning and cocktails and wine later in the day. Named after the café in *The Aristocats*.

Le Petit Chalet Fantasyland souvenir kiosk in Disneyland; opened Mar. 1997. Formerly Small World Gifts, which debuted in 1969.

Le Petit Train du Cirque Casey Jr. circus train attraction through Storybook Land in Fantasyland at Disneyland Paris; opened Apr. 1994. Unlike the original at Disneyland, this version is a graceful family roller coaster.

Le Premier Cri (*The First Cry*) (film) Documentary released by Buena Vista International (France). A story of the very first cry in life, exploring the universal moment of birth through the experiences of 10 women from different cultures around the world. Released Oct. 31, 2007, in France, before releases in Belgium, Japan, and other countries. Directed by Gilles de Maistre. 100 min. From Mai Juin Productions, M6 Films, and Wild Bunch, with participation from Disneynature Productions. The births took place Mar. 29, 2006, in France, Tanzania, Vietnam, Siberia, Mexico, Brazil, Nigeria, Japan, India, and the United States.

Le Pupille (film/TV) Italian live-action short; digitally released on Disney+ Dec. 16, 2022, after a festival run that began at the Cannes Film Festival May 27. A coming-of-age tale about the desires, freedom and devotion, and anarchy capable of flowering in the minds of girls within the confines of a strict boarding school at Christmas. Directed by Alice Rohrwacher. 39 min. Based on an idea for a holiday film series by producer Alfonso Cuarón. From tempesta and Esperanto Filmoj. Shot in Super 16 and in 35-mm format. Nominated for an Academy Award (Best Live Action Short).

Le Visionarium Circle-Vision 360 attraction, with added Audio-Animatronics figures of Timekeeper and Nine-Eye, who interact with the film *From Time to Time* featuring Jules Verne; played in Discoveryland in Disneyland Paris Apr. 12, 1992–Sep. 6, 2004. Also in Tokyo Disneyland, as Visionarium Featuring "From Time to Time," 1993–2002. SEE ALSO TIMEKEEPER, THE (WALT DISNEY WORLD).

Leachman, Cloris (1926–2021) Actress; appeared in *Charley and the Angel* (Nettie Appleby), *The North Avenue Irregulars* (Claire), *Herbie Goes Bananas* (Aunt Louise), *My Boyfriend's Back* (Maggie), *Sky High* (Nurse Spex), and *You Again* (Helen, uncredited); on Disney Channel in *Spies* (Pamela Beale) and *Girl Meets World* (Mrs. Svorski); on TV in *Miracle Child* (Doc Betty) and *Donald Duck's 50th Birthday*; and on the series *The Nutt House* (Edwina Nutt), *Walter and Emily* (Emily Collins), *Maybe This Time* (Beasy), and *Thanks* (Grammy). In 2008, she competed on *Dancing with the Stars* on ABC and served as grand marshal of the 2009 Tournament of Roses Parade in Pasadena, California. She provided the voice of Noriko in *Ponyo*, Dr. Doofenshmirtz's mother in *Phineas and Ferb*, and Hool in *Elena of Avalor*.

Learning with Film and Video (film) Educational film; released in Sep. 1986. 15 min. Demonstration of the important role of film and video in the learning experience.

Leave a Legacy Program began Oct. 1, 1999, in the entrance plaza at EPCOT, whereby guests could have 1-inch-square digital photos of themselves etched on a commemorative metallic tile on large granite monoliths. There were 35 sculptured stones in the plaza, ranging from 3 to 19 ft. high, with space for 750,000 portraits. Sales were discontinued Jun. 16, 2007, and the stones were removed in 2019. On Feb. 9, 2021, the guest photos were reintroduced on an installation of panels outside the park entrance.

Ledger, Heath (1979–2008) Actor; appeared in *10 Things I Hate About You* (Patrick Verona) and *Casanova* (Giacomo Casanova).

LeDoux, Leone She provided the voice of Minnie Mouse in cartoons of the 1930s and 1940s.

Lee, Bill (1916–1980) Member of the Mello Men with singing roles in *Alice in Wonderland*, *One Hundred and One Dalmatians* (Roger Radcliff),

Mary Poppins (ram), *The Jungle Book* (Shere Khan), and other films. He also provided voices for the Disney parks, including Melvin, the moose in Country Bear Jamboree.

Lee, Brittney Visual development artist; she joined Walt Disney Animation Studios in 2010 and contributed to *Wreck-It Ralph*, *Frozen*, *Zootopia*, *Moana*, *Frozen 2*, and *Raya and the Last Dragon*. She has also illustrated Disney children's books. On Disney+, she appeared in *Into the Unknown: Making Frozen 2*.

Lee, Christopher (1922–2015) Actor; appeared in *Return from Witch Mountain* (Victor) and *Frankenweenie* (footage of the 1958 film *Horror of Dracula*). He voiced the Jabberwocky in *Alice in Wonderland* (2010) and Ansem the Wise/DiZ in the *Kingdom Hearts* video games.

Lee, Jason Actor; appeared in *Enemy of the State* (Zavitz), *Mumford* (Skip Skipperton), and *Big Trouble* (Puggy). He voiced Syndrome in *The Incredibles* and the title character in *Underdog*.

Lee, Jason Scott Actor; appeared in *Rudyard Kipling's The Jungle Book* (Mowgli) and *Mulan* (Böri Khan, 2020). He voiced David Kawena in *Lilo & Stitch* and other appearances of the character.

Lee, Jennifer She was named chief creative officer of Walt Disney Animation Studios in 2018. After joining Disney in 2011 as co-writer of *Wreck-It Ralph*, she served as director (with Chris Buck) and writer of *Frozen*, also voicing the Queen of Arendelle and later writing the book for the Broadway musical. She was exec. producer of *Ralph Breaks the Internet*, *Raya and the Last Dragon*, *Encanto*, and *Strange World*, and co-director of *Frozen 2*. She wrote the screenplay for *A Wrinkle in Time* and contributed to the story of *Zootopia*.

Lee, Johnny (1898–1965) He voiced Brer Rabbit in *Song of the South*.

Lee, Peggy (1920–2002) She co-wrote songs and voiced Si, Am, Peg, and Darling in *Lady and the Tramp*. Successfully sued Disney almost 4 decades later for video royalties in a highly publicized case.

Lee, Peyton Elizabeth Actress; appeared on Disney Channel in the title role in *Andi Mack* and in the *Radio Disney Music Awards*, on Disney+ in *Secret Society of Second-Born Royals* (Sam), *Prom Pact* (Mandy Coleman), and in the title role in *Doogie Kamealoha, M.D.*, and guest starred in *Scandal* (Violet) and *Stumptown* (Alyssa Frank). She voiced Rani in *The Lion Guard*.

Lee, Stan (1922–2018) Chairman emeritus of Marvel; he was the creator of superhero comic books, partnering with Jack Kirby to start the Marvel Universe with such characters as Captain America, Doctor Strange, Iron Man, Hulk, Thor, and Spider-Man. He was more recently known for his cameo appearances in the films from Marvel Studios. He was named a Disney Legend in 2017.

Leeds China Co. Chicago manufacturer of ceramic items that was licensed to produce Disney merchandise 1944–1954. Some of their more popular items were various types of vases and planters, and a series of Turnabout cookie jars, each of which consisted of 2 Disney characters, each facing the opposite way.

Leetch, Tom (1933–1993) Producer/director; he began at Disney in 1955 serving as assistant director on such films as *Mary Poppins*, *Son of Flubber*, and *The Happiest Millionaire*. He produced or directed numerous TV shows and films, such as *The Sky's the Limit*, *The Whiz Kid and the Carnival Caper*, *The Adventures of Pollyanna*, *Gun Shy*, *The Watcher in the Woods*, and *Night Crossing*.

Lefkon, Wendy Editorial director of Disney Editions since 1994; she has published hundreds of Disney books, including the *Peter and the Starcatchers* and *Kingdom Keepers* series; *Life, Animated* (later adapted into an Academy Award-nominated documentary); *One Day at Disney*; and all editions of *Disney A to Z: The Official Encyclopedia* (including this one).

LeFou See Le Fou.

LeFou's Fantasyland snack counter in Tokyo Disneyland; opened Sep. 28, 2020, serving churros.

Leftovers, The (TV) Two-hour movie; aired on Nov. 16, 1986. Directed by Paul Schneider. The unorthodox director of an orphanage, who doesn't believe in strict rules, battles to save the home. The owner wants to develop the land, and the director has to use all his wits to foil him. Stars John Denver, Cindy Williams, George Wyner, Pamela

Segall, Andrea Barber, Matthew Brooks, Douglas Emerson, Jason Presson, Jaleel White, Henry Jones, Anne Seymour.

Lefty (TV) Special; aired on Oct. 22, 1980, on NBC. Directed by James E. Thompson. A gymnast with one arm yearns to compete despite her disability. Stars Carol Johnston. Enlarged from an educational film made for the Walt Disney Educational Media Company entitled *The Truly Exceptional: Carol Johnston*.

Lefty, the Dingaling Lynx (TV) Show aired Nov. 28, 1971. Directed by Winston Hibler. A forest ranger befriends a young lynx, who in turn befriends the ranger's Irish setter as its substitute mother. Eventually he has to return the lynx to the wild, but the lynx never forgets his dog friend and later helps him when he is lost. Stars Ron Brown, Harrison Tout, Brooks Woolley. Narrated by Mayf Nutter.

Legacy of Walt Disney SEE WALT DISNEY—A LEGACY FOR THE FUTURE (DISNEYLAND).

Legend of Captain Jack Sparrow, The Attraction in Soundstage 4 on Mickey Avenue in Disney's Hollywood Studios; opened Dec. 6, 2012, replacing Journey Into Narnia: Prince Caspian. Closed Nov. 6, 2014. Guests journeyed deep into a lost grotto to see if they had what it took to set sail with Captain Jack Sparrow.

Legend of Coyote Rock, The (film) Pluto cartoon released Aug. 24, 1945. Directed by Charles Nichols. Pluto is charged with guarding lambs, but a coyote lures him far away in the desert. While Pluto is gone, the coyote captures all of the lambs in a cave, except for a little black lamb who manages to escape. Pluto returns to the scene and chases the coyote, who falls off a cliff, knocking over rock formations, and the tumbling rocks settle in his likeness to become Coyote Rock.

Legend of El Blanco, The (TV) Show aired Sep. 25, 1966. Directed by Arthur J. Vitarelli. The show is based on an old Aztec legend about a white horse owned by Hernando Cortez, with the narration sung rather than spoken, by the group Los Tres Con Ella. The area has been having a drought, and the Native people believe only the return of the white horse can end it. A colt, thought to be the offspring of the legendary horse, is discovered and hidden from an evil horse trader by a peasant. The colt grows up to lead the wild herds. Stars Alfonso Romero, Jose F. Perez.

Legend of Johnny Appleseed (film) Release title of *Johnny Appleseed* for schools.

Legend of Lobo, The (film) With both parents having been killed by man, Lobo has learned the ways of the hunter and becomes the most hated and sought-after wolf in the West. By the time he becomes leader of the pack, he has mated and become a father. Man's relentless determination to eliminate the wolves raiding their cattle leads to the capture of Lobo's mate. In the end, Lobo cleverly leads a raid that frees his loved one and then takes his pack into a land so wild man has not yet invaded it. Released Nov. 7, 1962. Co-produced by James Algar. 67 min. Rex Allen is featured as narrator, with music by Allen and the Sons of the Pioneers; the title song was written by Richard M. and Robert B. Sherman. The film was based on Ernest Thompson Seton's story and was produced in the field by Jack Couffer.

Legend of Mor'du, The (film) Animated short from Pixar; released on the *Brave* DVD/Blu-ray Nov. 13, 2012. The story of the monstrous bear Mor'du is revealed by the eccentric witch who transformed him. Directed by Brian Larsen. Voices include Julie Walters (Witch), Steve Purcell (Crow), Callum O'Neill (Wee Dingwall). 7 min.

Legend of Sleepy Hollow, The (film) Theatrical release of the segment from *The Adventures of Ichabod and Mr. Toad* on Nov. 26, 1958. 33 min. Also shown under this title on TV, airing on Oct. 26, 1955.

Legend of Tarzan, Disney's The (TV) Half-hour animated series; premiered Sep. 3, 2001, on UPN and in syn. Tarzan returns to the jungle, to succeed Kerchak as Lord of the Jungle. He tests his wits, prowess, and ability as the new leader of the gorilla family alongside his ladylove, Jane. Voices include Michael T. Weiss (Tarzan), Olivia d'Abo (Jane), Jeff Glen Bennett (Archimedes Q. Porter), April Winchell (Terk), Jim Cummings (Tantor). 39 episodes.

Legend of the Boy and the Eagle, The (film) In Arizona, while boys of the Hopi tribe perform a traditional eagle dance, an old man tells how the ritual dance began 500 years ago. He relates the story of Tutuvina, a 10-year-old boy who defied the gods and brought shame to his people by saving the life of his pet, an eagle marked for sacrifice. Today, however, Hopis honor his memory. Featurette released on Jun. 21, 1967. Directed by Norman Tokar. 48 min.

Legend of the Lion King Fantasyland attraction in the Magic Kingdom at Walt Disney World; opened Jul. 8, 1994. After a preshow featuring Rafiki and "Circle of Life," costumed characters and puppets combined to present the story of *The Lion King* in the theater that originally housed the Mickey Mouse Revue. Sponsored by Kodak. Closed Feb. 23, 2002, to make way for *Mickey's PhilharMagic*. A different *Legend of the Lion King* show opened at Videopolis in Discoveryland in Disneyland Paris; played Jun. 26, 2004–2009.

Legend of the Seeker (TV) One-hour syn. series; aired Nov. 1, 2008–May 22, 2010. Woodsman Richard Cypher is extraordinarily transformed into a magical leader who joins up with a mysterious woman named Kahlan Amnell and a wise old wizard named Zedd Zu'l Zorander to stop a ruthless tyrant from unleashing an ancient evil and enslaving the world. Stars Craig Horner (Richard Cypher), Bridget Regan (Kahlan), Bruce Spence (Zedd). Based on Terry Goodkind's best-selling epic fantasy series *The Sword of Truth*. Its first announced title was *Wizard's First Rule*. Filmed in New Zealand. From ABC Studios.

Legend of the Three Caballeros (TV) Animated series; digitally released Nov. 12, 2019, on Disney+, after a Jun. 2018 release on DisneyLife in the Philippines. On his most disastrous birthday ever, Donald Duck inherits his great-grandfather's mysterious explorer's cabana, which he must share with José Carioca and Panchito. Inside, the 3 open a magical book, which unleashes the powerful goddess of adventure, Xandra. The trio discovers they are direct descendants of the legendary Three Caballeros and are sent to mystical realms where they must battle the monstrous forces of evil. Voices include Tony Anselmo (Donald Duck), Eric Bauza (José Carioca), Jaime Camil (Panchito), Grey Griffin (Xandra), Dee Bradley Baker (Ari, the Aracuan Bird). From Disney Digital Network, Six Point Harness, Mercury Filmworks, and Atomic Cartoons.

Legend of Two Gypsy Dogs, The (TV) Show aired Mar. 1, 1964. Directed by Dr. Istvan Homoki-Nagy. Two carefree dogs in Hungary come to the attention of an old fisherman. Later they free a hawk from a cage, and he joins them. They have adventures with a flood, a wild boar, and a cheetah.

Legend of Young Dick Turpin, The (TV) Two-part show; aired Feb. 13 and 20, 1966. Directed by James Neilson. The life of an English highwayman from the 18th century is chronicled. When he loses his possessions as the result of a fine for poaching, he steals back his horse, only to become sought as a horse thief. Turpin befriends a boy who eventually helps him escape from prison in London, and he is able to clear his name. Stars David Weston, Bernard Lee, George Cole, Maurice Denham, Leonard Whiting. Four years later, Whiting played Romeo in Franco Zeffirelli's acclaimed version of *Romeo and Juliet*. Newcomer David Weston was advised by Richard Burton to try a film career.

Legends of Frontierland: Gold Rush! Interactive Frontierland experience in Disneyland; ran Jul. 9–Sep. 27, 2014. Guests created, named, and developed their own characters and influenced the direction and action of the story's first chapter, as they entered a feud over gold between Frontierland and its neighbor Rainbow Ridge.

Legends of Hollywood Sunset Boulevard shop resembling a classic movie house in Disney's Hollywood Studios; opened Jun. 12, 1994. Expanded Aug. 23, 2019, overtaking the former Planet Hollywood Superstore and adding a new façade, the Majestic Theater. Also the name of a short-lived shop on Hollywood Boulevard; open Jan. 19–Mar. 9, 1991, later becoming L.A. Cinema Storage.

Legends of the Wild West Frontierland walk-through attraction in Fort Comstock at Disneyland Paris; opened May 30, 1993. Guests can see displays and characters from the Wild West.

Legion (TV) Sci-fi drama series on FX; aired Feb. 8, 2017–Aug. 12, 2019. David Haller is a troubled young man who may be more than human. Diagnosed as schizophrenic, he has been in and out of psychiatric hospitals for years. But after a strange encounter with a fellow patient, he's confronted with the possibility that the voices he hears and visions might be real. Stars Dan Stevens (David Haller), Aubrey Plaza (Lenny Busker), Rachel Keller (Syd Barrett), Jeremie Harris (Ptonomy Wallace), Amber Midthunder (Kerry Loudermilk). From FX Productions in association with Marvel Television.

Leguizamo, John Actor; appeared in *Super Mario Bros.* (Luigi Mario), *A Pyromaniac's Love Story* (Sergio), *Summer of Sam* (Vinny), and *Miracle at St. Anna* (Enrico), and on Disney+ in *The Mandalorian* (Gor Koresh). He voiced Bruno in *Encanto* and Tziloco in *Elena of Avalor*.

Lemmings and Arctic Bird Life, The (film) Part of *White Wilderness*; released on 16 mm for schools in Sep. 1964. The film tells the living legend of the strange migration of the lemmings, along with stories of interesting bird life.

Lemonade Mouth (TV) A Disney Channel Original Movie; first aired Apr. 15, 2011. Five disparate high school students meet in detention and realize they are destined to rock. They ultimately form a band that becomes a champion for students sidelined by the high school elite. Directed by Patricia Riggen. Stars Bridgit Mendler (Olivia White), Hayley Kiyoko (Stella Yamada), Naomi Scott (Mohini "Mo" Banjaree), Blake Michael (Charlie Delgado), Nick Roux (Scott Picket), Chris Brochu (Ray Beech), Tisha Campbell-Martin (Miss Reznick), Christopher McDonald (Principal Brenigan), Adam Hicks (Wen Gifford). Based on the novel by Mark Peter Hughes. Filmed in Albuquerque, New Mexico, by GWAVE Productions.

Lend a Paw (film) Pluto cartoon released Oct. 3, 1941. Academy Award winner for Best Cartoon. Remake of *Mickey's Pal Pluto* (1933). Directed by Clyde Geronimi. Pluto's jealousy over a new kitten almost causes it to be drowned, but Pluto's angelself wins out and the kitten is rescued. Dedicated to "The Tailwagger Foundation."

Lenny (TV) Series on CBS; aired Sep. 19, 1990–Mar. 9, 1991. There was a preview on Sep. 10, 1990. A hardworking, blue-collar man whose everyday life presents him with a series of ups and downs on which he bases his nonstop, commonsense commentary on such topics as making ends meet and his responsibilities to his wife, kids, parents, and brother. Stars Lenny Clarke (Lenny Callahan), Lee Garlington (Shelly Callahan), Peter Dobson (Eddie Callahan), Eugene Roche (Pat Callahan), Jenna Von Oy (Kelly Callahan), Alexis Caldwell (Tracy). From Touchstone Television.

Leonard, Robert Sean Actor; appeared in *Dead Poets Society* (Neil Perry) and *Swing Kids* (Peter), and made a TV guest appearance in *The Good Doctor* (Shamus O'Malley).

Leonardo da Vinci—First Man of the Renaissance (film) 16-mm educational film produced by Anthony Corso; released in 1972. The history of the 15th-century genius and his contributions.

Leroy & Stitch (TV) Direct-to-video release Jun. 27, 2006, after a world premiere on Disney Channel Jun. 23. With the mission to capture all 625 experiments completed, Lilo must say goodbye to her outer space family, including Stitch, not knowing they will reunite for another adventure as their nemesis, Dr. Hämsterviel, has broken out of prison and has forced Jumba to create "Leroy," Stitch's evil twin. To make things worse, Hämsterviel clones Leroy, so it is up to Lilo and the gang to stop the Leroy army. Voices include Daveigh Chase (Lilo), Tia Carrere (Nani), Kevin McDonald (Pleakley), Kevin Michael Richardson (Capt. Gantu), David Ogden Stiers (Dr. Jumba), Jillian Henry (Elena), Chris Sanders (Stitch). 73 min.

Les Chefs de France Restaurant in France at EPCOT; opened Oct. 1, 1982. It was founded by a trio of the most acclaimed French chefs—Paul Bocuse (1926–2018), Roger Vergé (1930–2015), and Gaston LeNôtre (1920–2009)—and has the reputation of serving some of the finest food in EPCOT, such as escargots and soufflés. Expanded in 1997 to incorporate and enclose the former Au Petit Café. For several years, Chef Remy from *Ratatouille*, the smallest Audio-Animatronics figure created by Walt Disney Imagineering, greeted diners at their tables from a rolling food cart.

Les Halles Boulangerie & Patisserie New name and location for the bakery in France at EPCOT as of Jan. 10, 2014, featuring not only baked delicacies, but also soups, salads, and fresh baguette sandwiches. Formerly known as Boulangerie Pâtisserie.

Les Légendes d'Hollywood Movie studio–inspired shop inside Disney Studio 1 in Walt Disney Studios Park at Disneyland Paris; opened Mar. 16, 2002.

Les Mystères du Nautilus *Nautilus* walk-through attraction in Discoveryland at Disneyland Paris; opened Jul. 4, 1994.

Les Trésors de Schéhérazade Adventureland bazaar in Disneyland Paris; opened Apr. 12, 1992, inspired by the tales of the Arabian Nights. Children's products, costumes, and toys are sold.

Les Vins de France SEE LA MAISON DU VIN.

L'Esprit de la Provence Apparel and home goods shop in France at EPCOT.

Less Than Perfect (TV) Half-hour series on ABC; aired Oct. 1, 2002–Jun. 6, 2006. Claudia ("Claude") Casey, a temp who worked at the GBN Television Network for 2 years, unexpectedly lands a job on the coveted desk of handsome news anchor, Will Butler, where she quickly realizes she may be in over her head. But Claude stands up to her coworkers and battles her own insecurities while refusing to compromise her values. Stars Sara Rue (Claude Casey), Eric Roberts (Will Butler), Zachary Levi (Kipp Romano), Sherri Shepherd (Ramona Platt), Andrea Parker (Lydia West), Andy Dick (Owen Kronsky). From Touchstone Television.

Lessing, Gunther (1886–1965) Lawyer, hired by Walt Disney in 1930 to help protect the copyrights of Mickey Mouse. He eventually became a company vice president and general counsel, and was a member of the Board of Directors 1938–1964. One of his pre-Disney claims to fame was as an adviser to Mexican revolutionary Pancho Villa.

Lester, Mark Actor; appeared on TV in *The Boy Who Stole the Elephant*. Best known for starring in the title role in the motion picture *Oliver!*

Lester, Robie (1925–2005) Singer/voice actress; she can be heard on dozens of Disney records, including storyteller albums and read-along sets. She provided the singing voice of Duchess in *The Aristocats* and Bianca in *The Rescuers*.

Let It Go Popular song from *Frozen*; music and lyrics by Kristen Anderson-Lopez and Robert Lopez. Academy Award winner for Best Original Song.

Let It Shine (TV) A Disney Channel Original Movie; premiered Jun. 15, 2012. Cyrus DeBarge, musical director of his father's Atlanta church, has a hard time convincing his father that hip-hop is not the devil's music. At a freestyle rap competition at a local teen club, Cyrus tells his childhood friend and longtime crush, Roxanne Andrews, how he really feels about her. But his best friend, Kris McDuffy, is mistakenly named author of the rap song and winner of the contest, and Roxanne begins to fall for Kris. Cyrus has to overcome self-doubt and seize the opportunity to reveal both his talent and his feelings and pursue his dreams. Directed by Paul Hoen. Stars Tyler James Williams (Cyrus DeBarge), Coco Jones (Roxanne Andrews),

Trevor Jackson (Kris McDuffy), Brandon Mychal Smith (Lord of Da Bling), Nicole Sullivan (Lyla), Courtney B. Vance (Jacob DeBarge), Dawnn Lewis (Gail).

Let the Memories Begin Campaign at the Disney parks, beginning Sep. 23, 2010, and continuing through 2011. Guests were encouraged to share their experiences at the Disney parks, to be used in TV spots, online and in print ads, in broadcast specials, for promotions, and on a website.

Let's Get Together Song from *The Parent Trap*; written by Richard M. and Robert B. Sherman.

Let's Go Day Tuesday on the new *Mickey Mouse Club* (1977–1978).

Let's Go Fly a Kite Song from *Mary Poppins*; written by Richard M. and Robert B. Sherman.

Let's Stick Together (film) Donald Duck cartoon released Apr. 25, 1952. Directed by Jack Hannah. Donald and the bee, Spike, reminisce about their early days together and the scrapes they got into.

Let's Talk Puberty for Boys (film) Animated educational film released in 2006. Describes what happens to a boy's body during puberty. From Disney Educational Productions. 10 min.

Let's Talk Puberty for Girls (film) Animated educational film released in 2006. Girls are given answers to questions about puberty and reproduction. From Disney Educational Productions. 10 min.

Levi, Zachary Actor; provided the voice of Flynn Rider in *Tangled* and other appearances of the character. He appeared in *Thor: The Dark World* and *Thor: Ragnarok* (Fandral), and on TV in *Less Than Perfect* (Kipp). For Disney+, he voiced Larry and Laaa in *Night at the Museum: Kahmunrah Rises Again*.

Levis, Patrick Actor; appeared on Disney Channel in *Brink!* (Peter), *Miracle in Lane 2* (Seth Yoder), and as a regular on *So Weird* (Jack Phillips).

Levy, Eugene Actor; appeared in *Splash* (Walter Kornbluth), *Father of the Bride* (singer), *Father of the Bride, Part II* (Mr. Habib), and *Bringing Down the House* (Howie Rottman), and on TV in *Bride of Boogedy* (Tom Lynch). He voiced Charlie in *Finding Dory*, King Midas in the *Hercules* TV series, and is a narrator of *Canada Far and Wide in Circle-Vision 360* at EPCOT.

Lewis, Aylwin Member of the Disney Board of Directors Jan. 1, 2004–2019.

Lewis, Bert (1879–1948) Composer, joined Disney in Dec. 1929 and became music director when Carl Stalling left in 1930. He scored many of the Mickey Mouse short cartoons 1930–1935.

Lewis, Jenifer Actress; provided the voice of Mama Odie in *The Princess and the Frog* and Flo in the Cars films. She appeared in *Beaches* (Diva), the Sister Act films (Michelle), *What's Love Got to Do with It* (Zelma Bullock), *Renaissance Man* (Mrs. Coleman), *Dead Presidents* (Mrs. Curtis), and *The Preacher's Wife* (Marguerite Coleman), and on TV in *black-ish* (Ruby), with guest appearances in *State of Georgia* (Patrice) and *That's So Raven* (Vivian). Also voiced Aunt Spice in *The Proud Family*, Tornado in *Elena of Avalor*, Professor Granville in *Big Hero 6 The Series*, Mama Hasselback in *Amphibia*, Patty in *The Ghost and Molly McGee*, Wheezelene in *Mickey Mouse Funhouse*, and Bebe Ho in *The PJs*.

Lewis, Nat (1911–1977) He began selling Mickey Mouse-shaped balloons at Disneyland in 1956 and continued providing all balloons for both Disneyland and Walt Disney World until his death in 1977.

Lewis Robinson 12-year-old inventor in *Meet the Robinsons*; voiced by Daniel Hansen and Jordan Fry.

Liberators, The (TV) Two-hour movie; aired Feb. 8, 1987. Directed by Kenneth Johnson. In the years prior to the Civil War, Bill Jackson, an enslaved young man, convinces John Fairchild, the nephew of a plantation owner, to help him escape to Canada, so he poses as the boy's slave to do so. They meet other escaping slaves and help them get to the Underground Railway in Ohio, where they are helped by a Quaker. Their success convinces them to continue helping others escape from bondage. Stars Robert Carradine, Larry B. Scott, Cynthia Dale, Bumper Robinson.

Liberty Arcade Ornate arcade behind the Main Street shops in Disneyland Paris, on the Frontierland side of the street. Guests discover the story of the Statue of Liberty.

Liberty Belle Liberty Square Riverboat in the Magic Kingdom at Walt Disney World, providing a half-mile tour around the Rivers of America. Formerly the *Richard F. Irvine*, it was renamed the *Liberty Belle* after an extensive rehab in 1996.

Liberty Inn Counter-service eatery in The American Adventure at EPCOT Center; opened Oct. 1, 1982. Since each World Showcase country features its own cuisine, hot dogs, hamburgers, french fries, chili, apple pies, and chocolate chip cookies were standard fare. Closed Jul. 7, 2019, to become Regal Eagle Smokehouse: Craft Drafts & Barbecue.

Liberty Landing Diner American Waterfront counter-service restaurant in Tokyo DisneySea; opened Mar. 2003. Pork-rice rolls and snacks are served in what appears to be a converted marine engine repair shop.

Liberty Square Land unique to the Magic Kingdom at Walt Disney World, home to The Hall of Presidents and the Haunted Mansion; opened Oct. 1, 1971. At its debut, Liberty Square was one of the most popular areas in the park, considering the American Bicentennial was just a few years away. Shops, restaurants, and architecture re-create the spirit of America during its founding, including the Dutch New Amsterdam designs of New York, the Georgian style of Virginia, Federal influences of Philadelphia, and the New England character of Massachusetts. As in Disney's movie *Johnny Tremain*, there is a Liberty Tree, with 13 lanterns hanging from its branches. The patriots did the same after they dumped the tea in Boston Harbor. The majestic 135-year-old live oak was actually transplanted from another area of the Walt Disney World property, a major feat when you consider that the full-grown tree weighed about 35 tons. But, the Disney designers knew that a sapling simply would not do, so they posed to the landscaping engineers, headed by Bill Evans, the most difficult task they were ever asked to accomplish. SEE ALSO LIBERTY STREET (CONCEPT FOR DISNEYLAND).

Liberty Story, The (TV) Show aired May 29, 1957. Directed by Hamilton S. Luske, Robert Stevenson. A segment from *Johnny Tremain*, depicting the Boston Tea Party and the battle at Concord, is followed by *Ben and Me*.

Liberty Street In 1956, Walt Disney announced plans for a Liberty Street at Disneyland to be located behind the east side of Main Street. Included would be a Hall of Presidents. But this was long before Audio-Animatronics figures were invented, so the presidential figures would have been mere mannequins. Other projects occupied Disney's time, while eventually the Audio-Animatronics process was perfected and deemed ideal for the planned Hall of Presidents. However, Liberty Street was never built at Disneyland; instead it debuted as Liberty Square in the Magic Kingdom at Walt Disney World in 1971.

Liberty Tree Tavern Restaurant in Liberty Square in the Magic Kingdom at Walt Disney World; opened Oct. 1, 1971. An 18th-century feel is given to the restaurant through the use of antique furniture, oak plank floors, and pewter ware. Each of the 6 rooms commemorates a pivotal figure in U.S. history—Benjamin Franklin, Thomas Jefferson, John Paul Jones, Paul Revere, Betsy Ross, and George Washington.

Lt. Robin Crusoe, U.S.N. (film) This 1960s-era Robinson Crusoe is a pilot for the U.S. Navy who is forced to ditch his plane in the Pacific. Rescued from a tropical island a year later, he writes to his fiancée, explaining why he never showed up for their wedding. His story is a humorous one, involving Floyd, a chimpanzee who is an astro-chimp; Wednesday, a local woman; some warriors; and a harrowing escape from the island by helicopter. Released Jul. 29, 1966. Directed by Byron Paul. The only film on which Walt Disney received a story credit (as Retlaw Yensid). 114 min. Stars Dick Van Dyke (Lt. Robin Crusoe), Nancy Kwan (Wednesday), Akim Tamiroff (Tanamashu), Arthur Malet (Umbrella man), Tyler McVey (Captain). This popular film was reissued theatrically in 1974.

Life, Animated (film) Documentary from A&E IndieFilms, Motto Pictures, and Roger Ross Williams Productions, based on Ron Suskind's 2014 book from Disney Publishing. The story of how Owen Suskind, a once-chatty boy who disappeared into autism at age 3, found a remarkable pathway to language and a framework for making sense of the world through Disney animated films. Premiered Jan. 23, 2016, at the Sundance Film Festival. Directed by Roger Ross Williams. 92 min. Nominated for an Academy Award.

Life Aquatic with Steve Zissou, The (film) Eccentric, down-but-not-out oceanographer Steve Zissou and his motley crew—Team Zissou—find themselves in troubled waters when they attempt to track down the mysterious "jaguar shark" that

ate Zissou's partner while filming a documentary of their latest adventure. Adding to his troubles, Zissou must contend with a beautiful journalist assigned to write a profile and a new member of the team who might possibly be his long-lost son. Zissou faces hilarious complications trying to keep his expedition afloat while contending with budgetary woes and a host of other challenges, including a close encounter with marauding pirates. A Touchstone film. Directed by Wes Anderson. Released Dec. 10, 2004, in Los Angeles and New York City, and on Dec. 25, 2004, nationwide. Stars Bill Murray (Steve Zissou), Owen Wilson (Ned Plimpton), Cate Blanchett (Jane Winslett-Richardson), Anjelica Huston (Eleanor Zissou), Willem Dafoe (Klaus Daimler), Jeff Goldblum (Alistair Hennessey), Michael Gambon (Oseary Drakoulias), Seu Jorge (Pele dos Santos), Bud Cort (Bill Ubell), Seymour Cassel (Esteban du Plantier). 118 min. Filmed in Rome and other Italian locations in Super 35-Scope. For the boat, the *Belafonte*, the filmmakers found a 50-year-old minesweeper in South Africa and then reoutfitted it to become an oceanographic research ship.

life as we know it (TV) Hour-long adult drama series on ABC; aired Oct. 7, 2004–Jan. 20, 2005. Three teenage boys experience the joys and pains of growing up. There's Dino, the handsome jock with the secret sensitive side; Jonathan, the artist who sees life through a camera lens; and Ben, the straight-A student who still can't make his parents happy. Stars Sean Faris (Dino Whitman), Jon Foster (Ben Connor), Chris Lowell (Jonathan Fields), Missy Peregym (Jackie), Kelly Osbourne (Deborah), D. B. Sweeney (Michael Whitman), Lesa Darr (Annie Whitman), Marguerite Moreau (Monica Young), Jessica Lucas (Sue). Adapted from Melvin Burgess's novel. From Touchstone Television. For legal reasons, the show could not use capital letters in the title. Filmed in Vancouver. The entire series, including 2 episodes unaired in the U.S., was released on DVD in 2005.

Life Is Ruff (TV) A Disney Channel Original Movie; first aired Jul. 15, 2005. Calvin Wheeler, a popular yet unmotivated 13-year-old, has a passion for rare comic books and desires to buy a rare, $3,000 first edition. When he learns of a prestigious dog show with a $5,000 first prize, he enters it. His friend Emily, who volunteers at the local animal shelter, helps him adopt Tyco, a slobbering, lovable stray Labrador retriever/Saint Bernard mix. Tyco wreaks havoc at home, but Calvin cleans up after the playful pup and tries to teach him some new tricks so he can win Best in Show. After enduring various trials and tribulations, Calvin learns to appreciate the values of true friendship, responsibility, and hard work. Directed by Charles Haid. Stars Kyle Massey (Calvin Wheeler), Kay Panabaker (Emily Watson), Mitchel Musso (Raymond Figg), Carter Jenkins (Preston Price), Mark Christopher Lawrence (Mr. Wheeler), Judith Moreland (Mrs. Wheeler), Ibrahim Abdel-Baaith (Rondel). Filmed in Salt Lake City by Davis Entertainment and Salty Pictures.

Life on Mars (TV) Hour-long series on ABC; aired Oct. 9, 2008–Apr. 1, 2009. After a car crash, Sam Tyler, a modern-day police detective, finds himself transported back to 1973 and still working as a detective. Based on the BBC series created by Matthew Graham, Tony Jordan, and Ashley Pharoah. Stars Jason O'Mara (Sam Tyler), Gretchen Mol (Annie Norris), Michael Imperioli (Det. Ray Carling), Harvey Keitel (Gene Hunt), Jonathan Murphy (Chris Skelton). From 20th Century Fox Television and ABC Studios.

Life with Bonnie (TV) Half-hour series on ABC; aired Sep. 17, 2002–Jul. 30, 2004. Bonnie Molloy is a woman who creatively balances the roles of wife, mother, and host of the local morning talk show, *Morning Chicago*, with sincerity and humor. Stars Bonnie Hunt (Bonnie Molloy), Mark Derwin (Dr. John Molloy), Marianne Muellerleile (Gloria), Charlie Stewart (Charlie Molloy), Holly Wortell (Holly), Chris Barnes (Marv), Anthony Russell (Tony Russo), David Alan Grier (David Bellows). From Touchstone Television.

Life with Mikey (film) Agent and former TV child star, Michael Chapman, who is co-running a third-rate talent agency with his brother, finds his big chance with the discovery of a young, streetwise urchin, Angie Vega. She has a fresh, unaffected personality and an ability to act her way out of any situation—including illegal ones. Michael comes to learn that his concern for Angie and her future welfare is more important than his own dreams of success. Released Jun. 4, 1993. Directed by James Lapine. A Touchstone film. 91 min. Stars Michael J. Fox (Michael Chapman), Christina Vidal (Angie Vega), Nathan Lane (Ed Chapman), Cyndi Lauper (Geena Briganti). The "Life with Mikey Theme" was written by Alan Menken, with lyrics by Jack Feldman. Filmed on location in Toronto and New York City.

Life's Work (TV) Half-hour series on ABC; aired Sep. 17, 1996–Sep. 29, 1997. When Lisa Hunter becomes an assistant state's attorney, in addition to her already hectic roles as wife and mother, she learns that being a full-time attorney and a full-time mother entails more than she had bargained for. Stars Lisa Ann Walter (Lisa Hunter), Michael O'Keefe (Kevin Hunter), Molly Hagan (DeeDee Lucas), Lightfield Lewis (Matt Youngster), Alexa Vega (Tess Hunter), Andrew Lowery (Lyndon Knox), Larry Miller (Jerome Nash). From Touchstone Television and Weest, Inc.

Life-Size (TV) Two-hour movie on *The Wonderful World of Disney*; first aired Mar. 5, 2000. In trying a magic spell to bring back her deceased mother, lonely 12-year-old Casey accidentally brings to life a beautiful fashion doll, Eve, instead. The doll creates havoc as she tries to fit into the real world. Directed by Mark Rosman. Stars Lindsay Lohan (Casey Mitchell), Tyra Banks (Eve), Jere Burns (Ben Mitchell), Ann Marie Loder (Drew), Garwin Sanford (Richie), Tom Butler (Phil).

Life-Size 2: A Christmas Eve (TV) Movie on Freeform; first aired Dec. 2, 2018. Grace, the young CEO of Marathon Toys, is in the middle of a quarter-life crisis as she struggles with her job. With the help of her young neighbor, Grace's old doll magically awakens to help get her back on track. Directed by Steven Tsuchida. Stars Tyra Banks (Eve), Francia Raisa (Grace Martin), Gavin Stenhouse (Calum), Hank Chen (Brendan Butler), Alison Fernandez (Lex Roberts). 81 min. From Bankable Productions and Homegrown Pictures, with the ABC Television Group. A sequel to *Life-Size*.

Lifestyles of the Rich and Animated (TV) Show aired Aug. 18, 1991. 90 min. Ludwig Von Drake takes a look at famous cartoon stars, with new dialogue written for Von Drake animation from previous shows.

Lifetime Television With the purchase of Capital Cities/ABC in 1996, Disney obtained a 50% ownership of Lifetime Television, which emphasizes original movies, specials, prime-time signature shows, and unique daytime blocks for women.

Lifted (film) An inept young alien student from a distant planet tests the patience of his increasingly weary instructor as he attempts a first-time abduction of a slumbering farmer. Directed by Gary Rydstrom. Initial release at the Laemmle One Colorado Theater in Pasadena, California on Sep. 11, 2006, and later at the Chicago International Film Festival on Oct. 14. General release with *Ratatouille* on Jun. 29, 2007. Received an Academy Award nomination for Animated Short Film. 5 min.

Light & Magic (TV) A Disney+ original documentary series; digitally released Jul. 27, 2022. Filmmaker Lawrence Kasdan takes viewers behind the curtain of Industrial Light & Magic, the special visual effects, animation, and virtual production division of Lucasfilm. From Imagine Documentaries and Lucasfilm.

Light Between Oceans, The (film) Tom and Isabel are a lighthouse-tending couple who stumble upon a boat carrying a dead man and a baby. Tom and Isabel decide to raise the child as their own, with emotionally tortuous consequences. Directed by Derek Cianfrance. A Touchstone/DreamWorks film. Released Sep. 2, 2016. Stars Alicia Vikander (Isabel Sherbourne), Michael Fassbender (Tom Sherbourne), Rachel Weisz (Hannah Roennfeldt). Filmed in wide-screen format in Australia and New Zealand. 133 min. Based on the book by M. L. Stedman. The film's lighthouse location was on Cape Campbell, near Seddon, Marlborough, New Zealand.

Light in the Forest, The (film) In 1764, Col. Henry Bouquet parleys with the Delaware Indians and persuades them to give up their white captives in exchange for peace. Among those freed is Johnny Butler, who despises whites as his enemy and only reaches Fort Pitt, Pennsylvania, after much struggle. He finds the townspeople wary and prejudiced, too, and only after a reckoning with his Uncle Wilse, who, with his gang, has senselessly killed Native peoples for years, and falling in love with a young, indentured girl named Shenandoe, can he settle down to a peaceful life. Released Jul. 8, 1958. Directed by Herschel Daugherty. 93 min. Stars James MacArthur (Johnny Butler/True Son), Carol Lynley (making her movie debut as Shenandoe), Fess Parker (Del Hardy), Wendell Corey (Wilse Owens). This was TV director Daugherty's first feature film after directing such hits as *Alfred Hitchcock Presents* and *Wagon Train*. He shot on location in Tennessee, outside Chattanooga, but the Native American settlement was built in California on the Rowland V. Lee Ranch. A song, "The Light In The Forest," was written for the film by Paul J. Smith and Gil George.

Light Is What You Make It (film) Educational film comparing the human eye to a camera, showing the effect of poor lighting and how eyes can be helped by correcting lighting faults, made for the National Better Light Better Sight Bureau. Delivered Dec. 3, 1945.

Light Magic Show at Disneyland that replaced the *Main Street Electrical Parade*; ran May 23, 1997–Sep. 1, 1997. It featured lights, fiber-optic effects, special effects, music, step-dancing pixies, and Disney characters, encouraging everyone "to dream and to believe that those dreams can come true." Deemed a spectacular, or "streetacular," rather than a parade, the show was presented on 4 moving floats or stages (each 80 feet long and 11 feet wide) that were set up in between the It's a Small World and the Matterhorn attractions, and again on Main Street, U.S.A.

Lighthouse Keeping (film) Donald Duck cartoon released Sep. 20, 1946. Directed by Jack Hannah. Donald is the keeper of a lighthouse who must deal with Marblehead, the pelican who tries to douse the lighthouse lamp over and over again.

Lighthouse Point In 2019, Disney Cruise Line announced plans to create and manage a 550-acre destination at Lighthouse Point on the island of Eleuthera, planned to open in 2024. The design will be rooted in the stories, culture, and nature of The Bahamas, with beach areas, a marina, an art and culture center, and walking paths. Disney is working closely with Bahamian artists and advisors and is also involved in conservation efforts to preserve and protect the local environment.

Lightning in a Bottle (film) Animated short; digitally released Jan. 24, 2020, on Disney+. A boy's effort to capture lightning in a bottle as part of a science fair project succeeds beyond his wildest expectations, but he is shocked to discover the consequences of the unnatural feat. Directed by John Aquino. 3 min. From the Walt Disney Animation Studios Short Circuit program.

Lightning Lane Queue offering a reduced wait time at select attractions; introduced Oct. 19, 2021, at Walt Disney World and Dec. 8 at Disneyland Resort, replacing the FASTPASS, FastPass+, and Disney MaxPass return lanes. Access is available for purchase via the Disney Genie and Disney Genie+ services.

Lightning McQueen Hotshot race car, #95, in the Cars films; voiced by Owen Wilson.

Lightning McQueen's Racing Academy SEE SUNSET SHOWCASE.

Lights! Camera! Fractions! (film) Educational film; released in Aug. 1984. A blend of live action, stop-motion, and clay animation is used to introduce young math students to the basics of fractions.

Lights, Motors, Action! Extreme Stunt Show Action show featuring high-flying, gravity-defying automobile, motorcycle, and high-speed watercraft stunts, and centering on the filming of a spy thriller, with production crew members, stunt managers, and a director and assistant director on the "live" set. Opened in Streets of America at Disney's Hollywood Studios May 5, 2005. Closed Apr. 2, 2016, to make way for Star Wars: Galaxy's Edge. The show was inspired by a similar show at Disneyland Paris. SEE MOTEURS . . . ACTION! STUNT SHOW SPECTACULAR.

Lightyear (film) Animated sci-fi action adventure from Pixar Animation Studios. The origin story of Buzz Lightyear, following the legendary Space Ranger after he is marooned on a hostile planet 4.2 million light-years from Earth alongside his commander and their crew. As Buzz tries to find a way back home through space and time, he's joined by a group of ambitious recruits and his charming robot companion cat, Sox. Complicating matters and threatening the mission is the arrival of Zurg, an imposing presence with an army of ruthless robots and a mysterious agenda. Released Jun. 17, 2022, also in 3-D, and 2-D and 3-D IMAX, after international releases beginning Jun. 15. Directed by Angus MacLane. Voices include Chris Evans (Buzz Lightyear), Uzo Aduba (Alisha Hawthorne), James Brolin (Zurg), Mary McDonald-Lewis (I.V.A.N.), Keke Palmer (Izzy Hawthorne), Efren Ramirez (Airman Díaz), Peter Sohn (Sox), Dale Soules (Darby Steel), Taika Waititi (Mo Morrison), Isiah Whitlock Jr. (Commander Burnside). 105 min. Inspired by sci-fi classics of the late 1970s and early 1980s. According to filmmakers, Buzz Lightyear, from the Toy Story films, had always been thought of as a character that would have originated in an epic blockbuster film; it just wasn't until much later that Pixar decided to bring that story to the big screen. It was the first Pixar film created specifically for IMAX screens; 30 min. of footage were made in the larger IMAX aspect ratios of 1.43 and 1.90.

A 34-min. making-of documentary, *Beyond Infinity: Buzz and the Journey to Lightyear*, was digitally released on Disney+ Jun. 10, 2022; directed by Tony Kaplan.

Like Father, Like Son (TV) Syn. show from 1986; a compilation of animated films.

Like Jake and Me (film) Educational film about how mutual support and understanding turn strangers into a family. Released May 9, 1989. 15 min.

Lilly, Evangeline Actress; appeared in *Real Steel* (Bailey), *Ant-Man* and later Marvel Studios productions (Hope van Dyne/The Wasp), *The Lizzie McGuire Movie* (police officer, uncredited), and on TV in *Lost* (Kate).

Lilly Belle Name of Walt Disney's locomotive for his backyard railroad, the Carolwood Pacific, built by Disney with the help of Studio technician Roger Broggie and his staff, and named after his wife, Lillian. Also the name of a special, elegantly furnished parlor car on the Disneyland Railroad — formerly used for transporting VIPs — and of a locomotive on the Walt Disney World Railroad.

Lilly's Boutique Main Street, U.S.A. gift and housewares shop in Disneyland Paris; opened Jun. 26, 1999, taking the place of first-floor dining areas of Walt's — an American Restaurant. Named after Walt Disney's wife, Lillian.

Lilo & Stitch (film) On the Hawaiian Islands, a lonely little girl, Lilo, adopts what she thinks is a dog. She names her pet Stitch, completely unaware that he is a dangerous genetic experiment gone awry who has escaped from an alien planet. Stitch's only interest in Lilo is using her as a human shield to evade the alien bounty hunters who are bent on recapturing him. In the end, Lilo's unwavering faith in 'ohana, the Hawaiian tradition of family, unlocks Stitch's heart and gives him the one thing he was never designed to have — the ability to care for someone else. Released Jun. 21, 2002. Directed by Chris Sanders and Dean DeBlois. Voices include Daveigh Chase (Lilo), Tia Carrere (Nani), Ving Rhames (Cobra Bubbles), David Ogden Stiers (Jumba), Kevin McDonald (Pleakley), Jason Scott Lee (David Kawena), Zoe Caldwell (Grand Councilwoman), Kevin Michael Richardson (Captain Gantu). 85 min. Music by Alan Silvestri. Co-director Chris Sanders also provides the voice of Stitch.

Produced primarily at Disney's Feature Animation facility at Walt Disney World in Florida. Nominated for an Academy Award for Best Animated Feature. There was a direct-to-video sequel, *Stitch! The Movie* in 2003; and another, *Lilo & Stitch 2: Stitch Has a Glitch*, in 2005; and also *Leroy & Stitch*, a Disney Channel movie/direct-to-video release.

Lilo & Stitch, the Series (TV) Half-hour animated series on ABC; debuted Sep. 20, 2003. Stitch, Dr. Jumba Jookiba's Experiment 626, finds there are 625 other experiments. They land in Hawai'i and, one by one, are activated. Each experiment has its own unique set of extreme capabilities, including Stitch's initial penchant for destruction. Lilo and Stitch search out these experiments and help to turn their nature from bad to good, finding places where each can belong and contribute to the community. Voices include Daveigh Chase (Lilo), Chris Sanders (Stitch), Tia Carrere (Nani), David Ogden Stiers (Jumba), Ving Rhames (Cobra Bubbles), Kevin McDonald (Pleakley), Kevin Michael Richardson (Capt. Gantu), Zoe Caldwell (Grand Councilwoman). 65 episodes.

Lilo & Stitch 2: Stitch Has a Glitch (film) Direct-to-video release Aug. 30, 2005. Stitch, Jumba, and Pleakley have settled into life with their human family, and Stitch blissfully enjoys his new 'ohana with Lilo and Nani. It seems like paradise, but it appears Stitch's molecular makeup is out of whack, which brings out his worst behavior, and his friendship with Lilo is threatened by misunderstanding. Pleakley, Jumba, and Lilo must find a way to restore his goodness level before he ruins everything, including Lilo's big hula competition—the same competition her mother won years before. Lilo must search within her heart to find the key to help her friend and restore their family. Directed by Tony Leondis and Michael LaBash. Voices include Dakota Fanning (Lilo), Chris Sanders (Stitch), Tia Carrere (Nani), David Ogden Stiers (Jumba), Kevin McDonald (Pleakley), Jason Scott Lee (David). 68 min.

Limited Time Magic Promotional campaign at Disneyland and Walt Disney World, running for 52 weeks from Jan. 2013. Guests were offered a variety of short-time surprises, some for 1 day, 1 week, or longer.

LiMOUSEine 40-ft.-long custom limousine that debuted in Orlando Mar. 1989, before launching a 4-month national tour promoting the May 1 opening of Disney-MGM Studios. Special features included a 24-carat-gold grille in Mickey's silhouette, a radio broadcast booth, a satellite tracking system, and closed-circuit TV, plus Disney furnishings, a cheese bar, and soda fountain. Later used at special events and auto shows.

LinaBell See Duffy and Friends.

Lincoln (film) In a nation divided by war and the strong winds of change, President Abraham Lincoln in his tumultuous final months in office pursues a course of action designed to end the war, unite the country, and abolish slavery. A DreamWorks/20th Century Fox/Reliance Entertainment film, distributed by Touchstone in the U.S. Limited release on Nov. 9, expanded on Nov. 16, 2012. Directed by Steven Spielberg. Stars Daniel Day-Lewis (Abraham Lincoln), Sally Field (Mary Todd Lincoln), David Strathairn (William Seward), Joseph Gordon-Levitt (Robert Todd Lincoln), James Spader (W. N. Bilbo), Hal Holbrook (Francis Preston Blair), Tommy Lee Jones (Thaddeus Stevens), John Hawkes (Robert Latham), Jackie Earle Haley (Alexander Stephens), Bruce McGill (Edwin Stanton), Tim Blake Nelson (Richard Schell), Joseph Cross (John Hay), Jared Harris (Ulysses S. Grant), Lee Pace (Fernando Wood). Filmed in CinemaScope. Nominated for 12 Academy Awards, winning 2, for Daniel Day-Lewis (Actor) and Rick Carter and Jim Erickson (Production Design).

Lindo, Delroy Actor; appeared in *Bound by Honor* (Bonafide), *Ransom* (Lonnie Hawkins), and *Gone in 60 Seconds* (Roland Castlebeck), and on TV in *Blood & Oil* (Sheriff Tip Hamilton). He voiced Beta in *Up*.

Lindquist, Jack (1927–2016) He began at Disneyland in 1955 as the park's first advertising manager. He later took other marketing positions and was named marketing director of both Disneyland and Walt Disney World in 1971. He established the marketing division for Tokyo Disneyland and, as exec. vice president of creative marketing concepts for Walt Disney Attractions, developed promotional and entertainment ideas, including Grad Nite, the Ambassador program, Magic Kingdom Club, the Disneyland Pigskin Classic, and Disney Dollars. In Oct. 1990, he was named president of Disneyland. He retired Nov. 18, 1993, and was named a Disney Legend in 1994.

Lindsey, George (1928–2012) Actor; appeared in *Snowball Express* (Double L. Dingman), *Charley and the Angel* (Pete), and *Treasure of Matecumbe* (sheriff), and on TV in *Bristle Face* (Hermie Chadron) and *Herbie, the Love Bug* (Wally). He voiced Trigger (*Robin Hood*), Lafayette (*The Aristocats*), and Deadeye, the rabbit (*The Rescuers*).

Line of Fire (TV) One-hour drama series on ABC; aired Dec. 2, 2003–Feb. 3, 2004, with the final 2 episodes shown May 30. On one side of the FBI's fight against organized crime is the Richmond, Virginia-based Malloy Crime Syndicate headed by Jonah Malloy, a charismatic but dangerous father figure. On the other side is the Richmond FBI branch, led by dynamic Special Agent-in-Charge Lisa Cohen, and aided by a new recruit, Paige Van Doren. Stars Leslie Bibb (Paige Van Doren), David Paymer (Jonah Malloy), Leslie Hope (Lisa Cohen), Anson Mount (Roy Ravelle), Jeffrey Sams (Todd Stevens), Brian Goodman (Donovan Stubbin). Produced by DreamWorks Television in association with Touchstone Television. 9 episodes.

Linguini Timid garbage boy at Gusteau's in *Ratatouille*; voiced by Lou Romano.

Linkletter, Art (1912–2010) TV personality who served, with Ronald Reagan and Bob Cummings, as one of the hosts of *Dateline Disneyland*, the TV show for the opening of Disneyland, Jul. 17, 1955. He returned 4 years later to host another live show, *Disneyland '59*. Also appeared on TV in *Twister, Bull from the Sky*; *Walt Disney World's 15th Birthday Celebration*; and *The Wonderful World of Disney: 40 Years of Television Magic*. He was honored with the Disney Legends Award in 2005, after participating in events for the Disneyland 50th anniversary.

Linz, Alex D. Actor; appeared in the title role in *Max Keeble's Big Move*, on Disney Channel in *The Jennie Project* (Andrew Archibald) and *Full-Court Miracle* (Alex Schlotsky), and on CBS in *The Amazing Race*. He voiced the young Tarzan in the 1999 animated feature.

Lion Around (film) Donald Duck cartoon released Jan. 20, 1950. Directed by Jack Hannah. The nephews disguise themselves as a lion to get a pie from Donald, who, when he discovers the trick, chases them and gets mixed up with a real lion to whom he must keep serving pies in order to stay alive.

Lion Down (film) Goofy cartoon released Jan. 5, 1951. Directed by Jack Kinney. In his attempt to hang a hammock, Goofy searches for a 2nd tree to secure it, but the one he finds dislodges a lion, who returns home with Goofy. Soon the lion wants the hammock, too, and a battle begins with Goofy emerging the victor.

Lion Guard, The (TV) Animated series on Disney Junior, with a Jan. 15, 2016, premiere on Disney Channel. A continuation of *The Lion King* (1994) story, it follows the adventures of Kion, the second-born cub of Simba and Nala, and his diverse group of friends, each with a unique skill, as they unite to protect the Pride Lands. The animal, science, and environment experts at Disney's Animal Kingdom advised on the characteristics, behaviors, and habitats of various animal species. The story was introduced in the Disney Channel movie *The Lion Guard: Return of the Roar*, and a preview episode ("The Rise of Makuu") was available online beginning Dec. 14, 2015. An interactive "appisode," "Bunga the Wise," was made available Jul. 7, 2016, on the Disney Junior Appisodes app. Voices include Max Charles (Kion), Joshua Rush (Bunga), Atticus Shaffer (Ono), Diamond White (Fuli), Dusan Brown (Beshte), Rob Lowe (Simba), Gabrielle Union (Nala), Eden Riegel (Kiara), Jeff Bennett (Zazu), Andrew Kishino (Janja), Vargus Mason (Cheezi), Jonny Rees (Mzingo), Khary Payton (Rafiki), Kevin Schon (Chungu/Timon), Gary Anthony Williams (Mufasa), Ernie Sabella (Pumbaa). From Disney Television Animation.

Lion Guard, The: Return of the Roar (TV) Animated movie; first aired on Disney Channel Nov. 22, 2015. Kion, Simba and Nala's second-born cub, discovers his destiny: to lead the Lion Guard, a team of the Pride Lands' fiercest, bravest, fastest, strongest, and keenest of sight, charged with protecting the savanna. Kion comes up with a very diverse group: Bunga, the honey badger, is the bravest; Fuli, the cheetah, is the fastest; Beshte, the hippo, is the strongest; and Ono, the egret, is the keenest of sight. Directed by Howy Parkins. Voices include Max Charles (Kion), Joshua Rush (Bunga), Atticus Shaffer (Ono), Diamond White (Fuli), Dusan Brown (Beshte), James Earl Jones (Mufasa), Ernie Sabella (Pumbaa), Rob Lowe (Simba), Gabrielle Union (Nala). From Disney Television Animation.

Lion King, The (film) A young lion cub, Simba, struggles to find his place in nature's "circle of life" and follow in the regal paw prints of his father, the great King Mufasa, after his father is killed by his treacherous uncle, Scar. Scar convinces Simba that he is responsible for his father's death and urges him to run far away from the Pride Lands and never return. A frightened and guilt-stricken Simba flees into exile where he is befriended by a wacky but warmhearted warthog, Pumbaa, and his freewheeling meerkat companion, Timon. Simba adopts their "hakuna matata" (no worries) attitude toward life, living on a diet of bugs and taking things one day at a time as he matures into a young adult. When his childhood friend, Nala, arrives on the scene, he is persuaded to return to the Pride Lands, which have fallen into hard times under Scar's reign, and take his rightful place as king. The wise shaman baboon, Rafiki, convinces Simba that his father's spirit lives on in him and that he must accept his responsibility, and when he returns, he manages to defeat Scar and an army of hyenas. Limited release in Los Angeles and New York City on Jun. 15, 1994; general release on Jun. 24, 1994. Directed by Roger Allers and Rob Minkoff. 88 min. Voices include Jonathan Taylor Thomas (young Simba), Matthew Broderick (adult Simba), James Earl Jones (Mufasa), Jeremy Irons (Scar), Nikcta Calame (young Nala), Moira Kelly (adult Nala), Ernie Sabella (Pumbaa), Nathan Lane (Timon), Robert Guillaume (Rafiki), Whoopi Goldberg (Shenzi), Cheech Marin (Banzai), Jim Cummings (Ed). The project originated a number of years earlier under the title *King of the Jungle*. When production began, an artistic team traveled to Africa to search for ways to best present the African settings in the film, and the animators studied actual live lions and other animals that were brought to the Studio. Songs were by Elton John and Tim Rice, with a background score by Hans Zimmer. Computer-generated imagery was used to create the dramatic wildebeest stampede, a visual highlight in the film and a new level of sophistication for the art form. The original release was interrupted when kids went back to school in Sep., to return on Nov. 18, 1994, this time paired with a 3-min. preview of *Pocahontas*. *The Lion King* became one of the highest-grossing films of all time. The song "Can You Feel the Love Tonight" won a Best Song Oscar for Elton John and Tim Rice, and a 2nd Oscar was awarded to Hans Zimmer for Best Original Score. A stage show, based on the film, opened at the New Amsterdam Theatre in New York City in 1997. The film was rereleased in IMAX and large-format theaters on Dec. 25, 2002. For the Special Edition Platinum DVD release in 2003, a song written for the stage play, "The Morning Report," by Elton John and Tim Rice, was adapted, animated, and inserted into the body of the original

film. A 3-D version of the film was released Sep. 16, 2011.

Lion King, The (film) Photo-real animated adaptation of the 1994 Disney feature that journeys to the African savanna where a future king is born. Simba idolizes his father, King Mufasa, and takes to heart his own royal destiny, but Scar, Mufasa's brother and former heir to the throne, has plans of his own. The battle for Pride Rock is ravaged with betrayal, tragedy, and drama, ultimately resulting in Simba's exile. With help from a curious pair of new-found friends, Simba will have to figure out how to grow up and take back what is rightfully his. Directed by Jon Favreau. Released Jul. 19, 2019, also in 3-D, and 2-D and 3-D IMAX, after international releases beginning Jul. 12. Stars Donald Glover (Simba), Beyoncé Knowles-Carter (Nala), James Earl Jones (Mufasa), Seth Rogen (Pumbaa), Chiwetel Ejiofor (Scar), Alfre Woodard (Sarabi), Billy Eichner (Timon), John Kani (Rafiki), John Oliver (Zazu), Florence Kasumba (Shenzi), Eric André (Azizi), Keegan-Michael Key (Kamari), JD McCrary (Young Simba), Shahadi Wright Joseph (Young Nala). 118 min. To help create the photorealistic characters, filmmakers studied live animals in Africa and in Disney's Animal Kingdom at Walt Disney World. The CG environments were uniquely designed within a virtual reality game engine that allowed filmmakers to walk into a virtual set, where they established camera shots, choreographed movements, and adjusted lighting and set pieces in real time before sending the scenes to animators to create. Returning to contribute music were original *Lion King* songwriters Elton John and Tim Rice, composers Hans Zimmer and Lebo M, arranger Mark Mancina, orchestrator Bruce Fowler, and conductor Nick Glennie-Smith. All of the songs were retained from the 1994 animated feature, with 3 more added: "Spirit," by Timothy McKenzie, Ilya Salmanzadeh, and Beyoncé; "Never Too Late," by Elton John and Tim Rice; and "He Lives in You," from the Broadway production, by Mark Mancina, Jay Rifkin, and Lebo M. Pharrell Williams additionally produced 5 songs for the soundtrack. The film earned over $1.6 billion at the global box office, making it the highest-grossing Disney-branded release to date. Nominated for an Academy Award for Visual Effects (Robert Legato, Adam Valdez, Andrew R. Jones, and Elliot Newman).

Lion King, The The stage version of the animated film had a pre-Broadway tryout at the Orpheum

Theater in Minneapolis beginning Jul. 8, 1997, before opening in previews at the New Amsterdam Theatre on Broadway on Oct. 10 (official opening was Nov. 13). The show earned rave reviews and smashed box office records. Directed by Julie Taymor. The performers utilize a wide array of masks and puppetry techniques to portray the story's 13 characters, as well as dozens of other animals. With a wholly original design, there was no attempt to re-create the animated look of the feature film. Eight songs were added to the 5 in the movie. The production was awarded 6 Tony Awards—for Best Choreography (Garth Fagan), Best Costume Design (Julie Taymor), Best Lighting Design (Donald Holder), Best Scenic Design (Richard Hudson), Best Direction of a Musical (Julie Taymor), and Best Musical. The show closed at the New Amsterdam Theatre on Jun. 4, 2006, and moved to the Minskoff Theater on Jun. 13 to make room for *Mary Poppins* at the New Amsterdam. In Apr. 2012, it became the highest-grossing show on Broadway, passing *Phantom of the Opera*. In 2013, it hit $1 billion in grosses from North American touring companies, and in 2014 it became the highest grossing of any production in any entertainment medium, with worldwide grosses of more than $6.2 billion. The show welcomed its 100,000,000th guest worldwide in May 2019. On Jun. 14, 2016, a Mandarin-language version premiered in the Walt Disney Grand Theatre in Disneytown at Shanghai Disney Resort; it closed Oct. 8, 2017, to make way for a Mandarin-language version of Broadway's *Beauty and the Beast*.

Lion King, The: A Musical Journey (TV) Half-hour special about the creation of the music in *The Lion King*, including interviews with Elton John and Tim Rice; aired on ABC Jun. 14, 1994. Directed by John Jopson.

Lion King Celebration, The Parade at Disneyland; ran Jul. 1, 1994–Jun. 1, 1997. For the first time, Audio-Animatronics–like figures were used on the floats, and remote-controlled crocodiles and large African bugs followed them down the street. There was even a waterfall on a float and rain coming down from the jungle canopy. At intervals, the parade would stop, and the performers would put on a brief street show for the guests featuring "Circle of Life."

Lion King Celebration: A Roaring Good Time (TV) Half-hour special on KCAL (Los Angeles); aired Jul. 24, 1994. A behind-the-scenes look at the making of the movie. Included are highlights of the Hollywood premiere with Whoopi Goldberg, Matthew Broderick, and James Earl Jones, along with a look at the new Disneyland parade, *The Lion King Celebration*.

Lion King 1½, The (film) Direct-to-video sequel release Feb. 10, 2004. The story running parallel to *The Lion King*, yet completely original, depicts the history of Timon and Pumbaa—how they met and became friends, and their behind-the-scenes influence on Simba's rise to the throne. The duo discovers their perfect oasis, but after becoming friends with Simba, they learn the limits of the easy life, and they finally find that the real "hakuna matata" happens only when they leave the oasis and reunite with the ones they love. Directed by Brad Raymond. The voice cast from the original film returns, supplemented by Julie Kavner (Timon's mom), Jerry Stiller (Timon's Uncle Max), and Matt Weinberg (Young Simba).

Lion King, The: Rhythms of the Pride Lands Stage show in the Frontierland Theater (formerly The Chaparral Theater) in Disneyland Paris; premiered Jun. 30, 2019, replacing *The Forest of Enchantment: A Disney Musical Adventure*. Dancers, acrobats, and singers bring iconic moments from *The Lion King* to life in a musical production. Approximately 400 costumes were made for the cast of 70 performers.

Lion King II, The: Simba's Pride (film) Direct-to-video release Oct. 27, 1998, sequel to the 1994 feature. An epic story of Simba's infant daughter, Kiara, who is destined to grow into a heroic young lioness and heal the rift in the Pride Lands caused by the banishment of Scar's followers. Meeting Kovu, Scar's handpicked successor and son of Zira, new leader of the Outlanders, Kiara forges a forbidden bond of friendship, which blossoms into love, honor, and trust. Kiara and Kovu eventually reunite the 2 prides, bringing peace to Pride Rock. Directed by Darrell Rooney. Added voices for this video are Suzanne Pleshette (Zira), Neve Campbell (adult Kiara), Jason Marsden (adult Kovu), Michelle Horn (young Kiara), Ryan O'Donahue (young Kovu), Andy Dick (Nuka). 75 min. Included are 5 new songs, as well as "He Lives in You," from the *Rhythm of the Pridelands* CD.

Lion King's Timon & Pumbaa, The (TV) Animated series began Sep. 8, 1995, as part of *The Disney Afternoon*, with different episodes airing

Saturdays on CBS beginning Sep. 16, 1995. The CBS run ended Mar. 29, 1997, and the syn. Aug. 25, 1997. Wacky adventures of the wisecracking meerkat and his good-natured warthog pal. Stars the voices of Nathan Lane and Quinton Flynn (Timon), Ernie Sabella (Pumbaa). 85 episodes.

Lion, the Witch and the Wardrobe, The SEE CHRONICLES OF NARNIA, THE.

Lionel Corp, The Disney licensee in the 1930s of toy railroad handcars and train sets. When they filed for bankruptcy in the mid-1930s, the judge in the court allowed them to produce a Mickey/Minnie handcar for that Christmas season, and the resulting sales pulled them out of bankruptcy. Disney received lots of publicity for having Mickey Mouse save Lionel from bankruptcy. One of their more valuable items is a Mickey Mouse circus train set. Lionel returned as a licensee beginning in the 1960s.

Liotta, Ray (1954–2022) Actor; appeared in *Operation Dumbo Drop* (Captain Doyle), *The Last Shot* (Jack Devine), *Wild Hogs* (Jack), and *Muppets Most Wanted* (Big Papa), and on TV as Principal Luger in *Hannah Montana*.

Listen to the Land SEE LIVING WITH THE LAND.

Lite Bite Sandwich and burger shop in the Lake Buena Vista Shopping Village at Walt Disney World; opened Mar. 1975. It became Lakeside Terrace Restaurant in 1988, then Goofy's Grill Sep. 19, 1993, and Ghirardelli Soda Fountain and Chocolate Shop in 1997. Also a Tomorrowland food stand in Tokyo Disneyland, as Lite Bite Satellite; open until Nov. 2017.

Lithgow, John Actor; appeared in *A Civil Action* (Judge Skinner) and *Confessions of a Shopaholic* (Edgar West), on TV in *Once Upon a Time in Wonderland* (White Rabbit), and narrated on Disney Channel *The Art of Disney Animation* and *Walt Disney World: Past, Present and Future*.

Litterbug, The (film) Donald Duck cartoon released Jun. 21, 1961. Directed by Hamilton Luske. Donald Duck gives us a graphic demonstration of various types of litterbugs: the unconscious carrier, the sports bug, the sneak bug, the highway bug, the beach bug, and the mountain bug. Perhaps, Donald suggests at the end of his demonstration, if we start at home, we can stamp out the pest—the litterbug. This was the last Donald Duck cartoon made.

Little April Shower Song from *Bambi*; written by Larry Morey and Frank Churchill.

Little Big Top, The Fantasyland pavilion serving beverages and shakes in the Magic Kingdom at Walt Disney World; replaced the Tournament Tent in 1994 and became Scuttle's Landing in 1998.

Little Dog Lost (TV) Show aired Jan. 13, 1963. Directed by Walter Perkins. From the well-known book by Newbery Award–winning author Meindert de Jong. Candy, a Welsh corgi, who is terrified of brooms because of an incident in puppyhood, is separated from his family during a storm, and faces all sorts of dangers. Candy is befriended by an old woman whom he helps save when her cart turns over and traps her, and later by a kindly farmer who helps him get over his fear. Narrated by Winston Hibler. Stars Hollis Black, Margaret Gerrity, Grace Bauer, Priscilla Overton.

Little Einsteins (TV) A Disney Channel series; premiered Oct. 9, 2005. Group of 4 children who, with their musical flying ship, *Rocket*, help preschoolers solve an important mission and learn along the way. Spectacular live-action images of nature, art, and landmarks are combined with character animation. A DVD series launched Aug. 23, 2005.

Little Fires Everywhere (TV) Drama miniseries; digitally premiered Mar. 18, 2020, on Hulu. The story explores the intertwined fates of the picture-perfect Richardson family and an enigmatic mother and daughter who upend their lives. Based on the book by Celeste Ng. Stars Reese Witherspoon (Elena Richardson), Kerry Washington (Mia Warren), Joshua Jackson (Bill Richardson), Rosemarie DeWitt (Linda McCullough), Jade Pettyjohn (Lexie Richardson), Jordan Elsass (Trip Richardson), Gavin Lewis (Moody Richardson), Megan Stott (Izzy Richardson), Lexi Underwood (Pearl Warren), Huang Lu (Bebe). From Hello Sunshine, Simpson Street, and ABC Signature Studios.

Little Green Men Store Command Tomorrowland shop in Disneyland offering Buzz Lightyear toys, pins, and souvenirs; opened Mar. 2005. It took the place of the Premiere Pin Store (open Aug. 2, 2002–Mar. 2005), which was formerly Premiere Shop (Dec. 18, 1985–Jul. 2002).

Little Hiawatha (film) Silly Symphony cartoon released May 15, 1937. Directed by Dave Hand.

A little Native boy desires to be a mighty hunter and goes out in the forest to prove it. But he cannot kill a bunny that crosses his path, an act that endears him to the woodland creatures who later rescue him from a grizzly bear. At one time Walt considered making a Hiawatha feature film, but the story never satisfied him, so the idea was shelved.

Little House, The (film) Special cartoon released Aug. 8, 1952. Directed by Wilfred Jackson. The little house begins life happily in the country but with "progress" it is soon completely overtaken and surrounded by the encroaching big city. Fortunately, a caring family has her moved back to the country onto a small hill and there the little house is happy once more. From the popular children's book by Virginia Lee Burton.

Little House on the Prairie (TV) Five-part, 6-hour series on *The Wonderful World of Disney*; aired Mar. 26 and Apr. 2, 9, 16, and 23, 2005. A pioneer family travels across the Kansas Territory late in the 19th century. Directed by David L. Cunningham. Stars Cameron Bancroft (Charles Ingalls), Erin Cottrell (Caroline Ingalls), Danielle Ryan Churchran (Mary), Kyle Chavarria (Laura). From the book by Laura Ingalls Wilder. Filmed near Calgary by Voice Pictures, Inc.

Little Indian, Big City (film) A successful Parisian businessman, Stephan Marchado, travels deep into a South American rain forest to obtain a divorce agreement from his wife, Patricia, only to find that he has a young son who has been raised among the Native community and given the name Mimi-Siku. Stephan is coerced into taking the mischievous lad back to Paris, creating a major culture clash that turns Stephan's well-ordered life upside down. But soon the father begins thinking less about maintaining the status quo of his affluent life in Paris and more about nurturing the friendship and love that have grown between him and his son. Released Mar. 22, 1996. Directed by Hervé Palud. 90 min. U.S. release by Touchstone Pictures of a dubbed version of the French hit comedy, *Un indien dans la ville*, starring Thierry Lhermitte (Stephan Marchado), Miou Miou (Patricia), Ludwig Briand (Mimi-Siku). The U.S. release of this film was a condition for actor/producer Lhermitte selling Touchstone Pictures the remake rights. The remake, which was titled *Jungle 2 Jungle* and starred Tim Allen, was released in 1997.

Little John Robin Hood's lumbering bear pal; voiced by Phil Harris.

Little Kidnappers, The (TV) A Disney Channel Premiere Film, first aired Aug. 17, 1990. Two mischievous boys "borrow" an abandoned infant, keeping their discovery secret, and set their gruff grandfather's temper aflame in turn-of-the-century Nova Scotia. Directed by Donald Shebib. Stars Charlton Heston (James MacKenzie), Patricia Gage (Ruth MacKenzie), Leah Pinsett (Kirsten), Charles Miller (Davy), Leo Wheatley (Harry). 93 min.

Little Lake Bryan Thirty-acre lake on the Walt Disney World property on which Disney built a recreation center for its Cast Members. The area was extensively remodeled and renamed Mickey's Retreat in 1998. In Aug. 1996, an apartment community opened at the same location. The first development was dubbed Plantation Park, and other apartment communities, retail, and commercial centers followed.

Little League Moochie (film) 16-mm release title of *Moochie of the Little League*.

Little Matchgirl, The (film) An animated short, without spoken dialogue, directed by Roger Allers and set to the music of Alexander Borodin's String Quartet No. 2 in D Major: Third Movement: Noturno (Andante). A poor young girl finds visions of happiness in the fiery flames of the matches that she lights to keep warm. 7 min. The music was recorded by the Emerson String Quartet. From a story by Hans Christian Andersen. Released on the *Little Mermaid* DVD on Oct. 3, 2006, after a May 13 screening at the Eugene [Oregon] Film Festival and an Aug. 23 run in Los Angeles for Academy Award consideration. Received an Academy Award nomination for Animated Short Film.

Little Mermaid, The (film) Animated tale of a young mermaid, Ariel, who is fascinated by the human world, to the dismay of her father, King Triton. She spies Prince Eric and falls hopelessly in love. Sebastian the crab is sent by the king to keep an eye on Ariel, though he cannot stop her from rescuing the prince during a storm. Ursula, the sea witch, plots to grant Ariel's wish to be human in exchange for her beautiful voice—and as part of a larger scheme to gain control of Triton's realm. Eric finds himself falling for the now-human mermaid, but Ursula tricks him, and Ariel, who's now mute, cannot warn him. Finally, Ariel and Eric together foil Ursula's evil plans, save the undersea kingdom, and receive Triton's blessing. Initial release on Nov. 15, 1989, in Los Angeles and New York City; general release on Nov. 17, 1989.

Directed by John Musker and Ron Clements. 82 min. Voices include Jodi Benson (Ariel), Pat Carroll (Ursula), Christopher Daniel Barnes (Eric), Buddy Hackett (Scuttle), Kenneth Mars (Triton), Samuel E. Wright (Sebastian), Ben Wright (Grimsby), René Auberjonois (Louis). Songs by Howard Ashman and Alan Menken. The first Disney animated feature based on a classic fairy tale in 3 decades (since *Sleeping Beauty*), this film turned to the famous story by Hans Christian Andersen. Disney artists had considered an animated film of *The Little Mermaid* in the late 1930s, and illustrator Kay Nielsen prepared a number of striking story sketches in pastels and watercolors. For this film, the artists received inspiration from the Nielsen story sketches that were brought out of the Archives for them to study, and they gave Kay Nielsen a "visual development" credit on the film. Actress Sherri Stoner was the live-action model for Ariel. The film had more effects than probably any animated film since *Fantasia*; nearly 80% of the film required some kind of effects work—storms at sea, billowing sails, schools of fish, shadows, raging fire, explosions, magic pixie dust, surface reflections, underwater distortions, ripples, and bubbles. Academy Award winner for best song ("Under the Sea") and best original score. Rereleased in theaters in 1997. A 3-D version of the film played for a month at the El Capitan Theatre in Hollywood beginning Sep. 13, 2013, prior to a Blu-ray release.

Little Mermaid, The (film) A live-action reimagining of the 1989 animated feature, based on the short story by Hans Christian Andersen. The youngest of King Triton's daughters, and the most defiant, Ariel longs to find out more about the world beyond the sea and, while visiting the surface, falls for the dashing Prince Eric. While mermaids are forbidden to interact with humans, Ariel must follow her heart. She makes a deal with the evil sea witch, Ursula, which gives her a chance to experience life on land, but ultimately places her life—and her father's crown—in jeopardy. Planned for theatrical release May 26, 2023, also in 3-D, after international releases beginning May 24. Directed by Rob Marshall. Stars Halle Bailey (Ariel), Daveed Diggs (Sebastian), Jonah Hauer-King (Prince Eric), Javier Bardem (King Triton), Melissa McCarthy (Ursula), Art Malik (Sir Grimsby), Noma Dumezweni (Queen Selina), with the voices of Jacob Tremblay (Flounder), Awkwafina (Scuttle). 110 min. Features songs from the original animated film by Alan Menken and Howard Ashman, with new songs by Menken and Lin-Manuel Miranda.

Little Mermaid, The (TV) Animated series on CBS; aired Sep. 12, 1992–Sep. 2, 1995, utilizing the voices of Jodi Benson, Pat Carroll, Kenneth Mars, and Samuel E. Wright from the original film, and adding others, such as Danny Cooksey (Urchin), Edan Gross (Flounder), and Maurice La Marche (Scuttle). The series continues the stories of Ariel and her rebelling against the rules of her father, though the stories take place prior to the happenings in the motion picture. Urchin is an orphan merboy, full of boyish enthusiasm, who is befriended by Ariel. 31 episodes.

Little Mermaid, The Stage version of the 1989 animated film; opened Jan. 10, 2008, at the Lunt-Fontanne Theatre on Broadway, after previews beginning Nov. 3, 2007. It had a pre-Broadway run at the Ellie Caulkins Opera House of the Denver Center for the Performing Arts that ran Jul. 26–Sep. 9, 2007. Lyricist Glenn Slater worked with Alan Menken on 9 new songs for the production. The original cast included Sierra Boggess (Ariel), Norm Lewis (Triton), Tituss Burgess (Sebastian), Sherie Rene Scott (Ursula), Eddie Korbich (Scuttle). The originally announced opening date of Dec. 6, 2007, was postponed a month due to the 2007 stagehands strike. The show closed Aug. 30, 2009, leading up to a national tour launching in fall 2010. A new version of the show opened at the Paper Mill Playhouse in Millburn, New Jersey, in Jun. 2013.

Little Mermaid, The: Ariel's Beginning (film) Direct-to-video release Aug. 26, 2008, by Walt Disney Studios Home Entertainment. A year before Ariel meets Prince Eric, she and her sisters share a love for music with their mother, Queen Athena. But when the queen is captured by pirates, King Triton is heartbroken and bans music from Atlantica forever. Directed by Peggy Holmes. Voices include Jodi Benson (Ariel), Samuel E. Wright (Sebastian). From DisneyToon Studios.

Little Mermaid, The ~ Ariel's Undersea Adventure Dark ride attraction in Disney California Adventure; opened Jun. 3, 2011, taking the place of *Golden Dreams*. Guests embark in a clamshell Omnimover for a visit to scenes from *The Little Mermaid* film. The attraction opened in a new, elegant Victorian Exposition–style building, featuring an ornate 86-ft.-long hand-painted mural. SEE ALSO UNDER THE SEA ~ JOURNEY OF THE LITTLE MERMAID (WALT DISNEY WORLD).

Little Mermaid II, The: Return to the Sea (film)

Direct-to-video release Sep. 19, 2000. Ariel and Prince Eric, living happily married on land, have a feisty daughter, Melody, who is curious about her roots. Melody, venturing into the sea against her parents' wishes, makes new friends of Tip the penguin and Dash the walrus, but then becomes a pawn in a plot by Morgana, Ursula's sinister sibling, against Ariel's father, King Triton. Ariel must come to the rescue. Directed by Jim Kammerud. Voices include Jodi Benson (Ariel), Tara Charendoff (Melody), Pat Carroll (Morgana), Max Casella (Tip), Stephen Furst (Dash), Samuel E. Wright (Sebastian). 75 min.

Little Red Riding Hood (film) Laugh-O-gram film made by Walt Disney in Kansas City in 1922.

Little Riders, The (TV) A Disney Channel Premiere Film; first aired Mar. 24, 1996. Trapped in Holland during World War II, a young American girl, Joanne Hunter, lives with her Dutch grandparents. Together they must endure—and resist—the Nazi occupation of their village. When Joanne boldly tries to protect the Little Riders, the much beloved symbol of the town, she suddenly finds herself face-to-face with the enemy. Directed by Kevin Connor. Stars Noley Thornton (Joanne Hunter), Rosemary Harris (Juliana Roden), Paul Scofield (Pieter Roden), Malcolm McDowell (Captain Kessel), Benedict Blythe (Lt. Braun). Based on the book by Margaretha Shemin. The film was shot entirely on location in the Netherlands.

Little Shepherd Dog of Catalina, The (TV) Show aired Mar. 11, 1973. Directed by Harry Tytle. A champion Shetland sheepdog is lost on Catalina Island, where he swims after being swept off a boat. He is befriended by a farmer, whose stallion he eventually saves. Stars Clint Rowe, William Maxwell, Joe Dawkins.

Little Spies (TV) Two-hour movie; aired Oct. 5, 1986. Directed by Greg Beeman. A dog gets loose from the pound, but the neighborhood kids save it, and then find a rough nearby gang is involved in a sinister plot to capture dogs and sell them for use in medical experiments. With the help of an old war hero, they plan to save all the dogs. Stars Mickey Rooney, Peter Smith, Robert Costanzo, Candace Cameron, Adam Carl, Sean Hall, Jason Hervey, Scott Nemes, Kevin King Cooper.

Little Toot (film) Segment of *Melody Time* about a little tugboat who is constantly getting into trouble, but who redeems himself by saving a ship from sinking during a big storm. Released as a short Aug. 13, 1954. From a story by Hardie Gramatky. The title song is sung by the Andrews Sisters.

Little Town Traders SEE VILLAGE SHOPPES.

Little Whirlwind, The (film) Mickey Mouse cartoon released Feb. 14, 1941. Directed by Riley Thomson. Mickey gives chase to a baby whirlwind when it frustrates him as he tries to clean up Minnie's yard. Mama Whirlwind shows up to save her youngster and proceeds to destroy the yard and the countryside. Minnie is not at all pleased with Mickey's work.

Littlest Horse Thieves, The (film) When, in 1909, the manager of a Yorkshire coal mine decides to replace the pit ponies who pull the ore carts with machinery and have the ponies destroyed, 3 youngsters (Dave, Tommy, and Alice) get together and daringly kidnap the ponies from the mine. The kids get caught, however, and the ponies seem doomed. An explosion in the mine traps some of the men and they are saved only with the help of one of the ponies, which dies in the attempt. In his honor all the ponies are put out to pasture for life. Released May 26, 1976, in England as *Escape from the Dark*; U.S. release Mar. 11, 1977. Directed by Charles Jarrott. 104 min. Stars Alastair Sim (Lord Harrogate), Peter Barkworth (Richard Sandman), Maurice Colbourne (Luke), Susan Tebbs (Violet), Andrew Harrison (Dave), Chloe Franks (Alice), Benjie Bolgar (Tommy), Prunella Scales (Mrs. Sandman). The Grimethorpe Colliery Band provided the music, composed and conducted by Ron Goodwin. The film was shot on location in and around Yorkshire, England, including at Langthwaite Village, on the moors, at historic Ripley Castle, the Oakworth Railway Station, and the Thorpe-Hesley colliery, and at Pinewood Studios in London. The actual underground mine workings, including the stables housing the pit ponies, were built by studio craftsmen at Pinewood. The working title of the film had been *Pit Ponies*.

Littlest Outlaw, The (film) Story of a young boy, Pablito, in Mexico who has a great love for a horse named Conquistador, owned by a general, and manages to save its life, but only by running away with it. When Pablito loses the horse himself, a friendly priest and some gypsies help him find the horse as it's about to be killed in a bullring. He rescues the horse by leaping onto its back and making it jump a high gate. The general has seen this, and acknowledging Pablito's affection for the horse, presents Conquistador as a gift. Released Dec. 22, 1955. Directed by Roberto Galvadon. 73 min. Stars Andrew Velasquez (Pablito), Pedro Armendariz (Gen. Torres), Enriqueta Zazueta (Señora Garcia), Laila Maley (Celita), Margarito Luna (Silvertre), Ricardo Gonzales (Marcos), Rodolfo Acosta (Chato). From a story by Disney animal film expert Larry Lansburgh, who also produced the movie. Filmed on location in Mexico, once in English and once in Spanish, enabling a quick release in Spanish-speaking countries.

Litvack, Sandy Litvack joined Disney in 1991 as senior vice president and general counsel. He was promoted to exec. vice president the same year, and in 1994 he was named senior exec. vice president—taking over many of Frank Wells's duties after Wells's death—and later vice chairman of the board. He resigned in Dec. 2000.

Liu, Lucy Actress; appeared in *Play It to the Bone* (Lia) and *Shanghai Noon* (Princess Pei Pei), and on TV in *Ugly Betty* (Grace Chin) and *Dirty Sexy Money* (Nola Lyons). She provided the voice of Mei in *Mulan II*, Silvermist in the Tinker Bell films, and Callisto Mal in *Strange World*.

Liv and Maddie (TV) Series on Disney Channel; premiered Sep. 15, 2013, after a Jul. 19 preview. Identical twins Liv and Maddie Rooney have always shared a special bond and cannot wait to reunite with each other when Liv returns home to Wisconsin after starring in a hit Hollywood TV show for the past 4 years. Liv is a cool, confident social butterfly who loves to sing, while Maddie is a smart, athletic high school basketball phenomenon. Though Liv and Maddie have wildly different personalities, dreams, and aspirations, their bond is unbreakable, and—with the help of their family—they can accomplish almost anything. The show was re-titled *Liv and Maddie: Cali Style* for its 4th (and final) season. Stars Dove Cameron (Liv/Maddie), Joey Bragg (Joey), Tanzing Norgay Trainor (Parker), Benjamin King (Pete Rooney), Kali Rocha (Karen Rooney). From It's a Laugh Productions.

Live action Walt Disney experimented with live action along with animation in *The Reluctant Dragon*, *Song of the South*, and *So Dear to My Heart*, but his first completely live-action film was *Treasure Island* (1950). He realized that the financial health of the company would be aided by a program that included live-action features, since animated features took so long to make, thus tying up funds for years.

Live with Kelly and Michael (TV) Talk show series evolving from *Live with Regis and Kathie Lee*, beginning Sep. 2012 in syn. Stars Kelly Ripa and Michael Strahan. It was renamed *Live with Kelly* after Strahan left the show in 2016, and, in 2017, it became *Live with Kelly and Ryan*.

Live with Kelly and Ryan (TV) Talk show series evolving from *Live with Regis and Kathie Lee*, beginning in 2017 in syn., as the longest-running talk show in daytime. Stars Kelly Ripa and Ryan Seacrest. In Feb. 2023, it was announced actor Mark Consuelos, Ripa's husband, would succeed Seacrest as co-host that spring, with the show re-branded *Live with Kelly and Mark*.

Live with Regis and Kathie Lee (TV) Talk show series began Sep. 5, 1988, in syn. Starred Regis Philbin and Kathie Lee Gifford. The series ended Jul. 28, 2000, when Kathie Lee left the show; it started as *Live with Regis* Jul. 31, 2000. On Feb. 12, 2001, Kelly Ripa joined the show, with a new title of *Live with Regis and Kelly*. Regis left the show in Nov. 2011, and Kelly Ripa got a new co-host in Michael Strahan in Sep. 2012. In 2017, Ryan Seacrest became co-host, followed by Mark Consuelos in 2023.

Living Desert, The (film) True-Life Adventure feature released Nov. 10, 1953. Directed by James Algar. Though the desert to most people represents an area of arid desolation, it is really a place teeming with life, including extraordinary plants, desert tortoises, rattlesnakes, scorpions, kangaroo rats, and roadrunners. A flash flood hits the desert, causing much of the plant life to blossom anew. The film stands as a landmark of factual filmmaking. 69 min. Academy Award winner. As Walt Disney had had a difficult time convincing his distributor, RKO, of the value of the True-Life Adventure featurettes, he had renewed problems when he produced his first feature-length True-Life Adventure film. Again they argued audiences would not pay to see a 1-hour-plus film about desert creatures. But again, Disney knew they were wrong. This time he went to Roy O. Disney, and together they decided that it was time to part company with RKO and handle the releases of the Disney product themselves. With some trepidation they made the break and set up the Buena Vista Distribution Company, with its first release being *The Living Desert*. This film, made for only about $500,000, made $5 million during its original release, and Walt and Roy knew they had made the right decision.

Living Seas, The Future World pavilion in EPCOT Center; opened Jan. 15, 1986, originally sponsored by United Technologies. Initially, exhibits on humanity's search to learn the mysteries of the sea (including an actual 11-ft.-long model of the *Nautilus* from *20,000 Leagues Under the Sea*) gave way to a short film on the origins and importance of the ocean. To the accompaniment of a memorable musical backdrop composed by Russell Brower, based on a theme by George Wilkins, guests descended by means of hydrolators to Seabase Alpha. The pavilion became The Seas with Nemo & Friends Jan. 24, 2007, after a soft-opening period that began Oct. 2006. Guests climb aboard clam-mobiles to search for the playful clown-fish before exploring various educational marine displays and looking into the pavilion's 5.7-million-gallon saltwater tank, where fish, dolphins, sea turtles, Florida manatees, and other sea creatures swim by. Divers demonstrate their equipment after completing their dives in the tank. There is also the Coral Reef Restaurant, offering views of the living coral reef and its more than 2,000 inhabitants.

Living Seas, The (film) Educational film in the EPCOT Educational Media Collection: Minnie's Science Field Trips series; released in Sep. 1988. 17 min. Students explore The Living Seas in EPCOT Center.

Living with Change (film) Educational film in the Skills for the New Technology: What a Kid Needs to Know Today series; released in Sep. 1983. A custodian learns that change can mean advances and benefits for society and that he should not fear the future.

Living with Computers (film) Educational film in the Skills for the New Technology: What a Kid Needs to Know Today series; released in Sep. 1983. Elmer the custodian is led on a cross-country tour introducing him to the computer's many applications.

Living with the Land Boat ride in The Land at EPCOT; opened Dec. 10, 1993. Passengers travel through scenes representing diverse ecological areas—including the rain forest, the desert, and the American prairie—before touring an expansive greenhouse of the future, where innovative growing and crossbreeding techniques demonstrate how one might approach feeding a growing

planet. Many of the harvested plants are served in restaurants across Walt Disney World. There is an Aquacel environment for the raising of fish and freshwater shrimp. The attraction was originally named Listen to the Land; open Oct. 1, 1982–Sep. 27, 1993. It featured a theme song of the same name, written/performed by Bob Moline, and began with an imaginative sequence called "Symphony of the Seed." Sponsored by Kraft (1982–1992), Nestlé (1992–2009), and Chiquita (2011–2020).

Livingston, Jerry (1909–1987) Composer; he wrote the songs for *Cinderella*.

Lizzie McGuire (TV) Half-hour series mixing live action and animation on Disney Channel; premiered Jan. 19, 2001. The series covers the life of 13-year-old Lizzie McGuire as she stumbles into her adolescence with all its attendant crises and joys. Stars Hilary Duff (Lizzie McGuire), Hallie Todd (Jo McGuire), Robert Carradine (Sam McGuire), Jake Thomas (Matt McGuire). Working title was *What's Lizzie Thinking?* The series began airing as part of ABC's *ABC Kids* Saturday morning lineup on Sep. 20, 2003.

Lizzie McGuire Movie, The (film) Lizzie McGuire and her pals Gordo, Kate, and Ethan go on a class trip to Italy, where Lizzie is mistaken for Isabella (who is part of an Italian pop duo) and begins to fall for Paolo (Isabella's handsome Italian pop-star former boyfriend). When Lizzie's mom, dad, and annoying brother, Matt, get wind of this, they all jet their way to Italy. In the meantime, Lizzie is transformed from a gawky teen to a beautiful pop star. Gordo struggles to understand his true feelings for her, and a whirlwind of surprising events force Lizzie to find the true meaning of friendship. Released May 2, 2003. Directed by Jim Fall. Stars Hilary Duff (Lizzie), Adam Lamberg (Gordo), Robert Carradine (Sam McGuire), Hallie Todd (Jo McGuire), Jake Thomas (Matt), Yani Gellman (Paolo), Alex Borstein (Miss Ungermeyer), Clayton Snyder (Ethan), Ashlie Brillault (Kate), Brendan Kelly (Sergei), Carly Schroeder (Melina). 94 min. Filmed on location in Rome, in Super 35-Scope.

Lloyd, Christopher Actor; appeared in *Who Framed Roger Rabbit* (Judge Doom), *Angels in the Outfield* (Al), *Camp Nowhere* (Dennis Van Welker), *My Favorite Martian* (the Martian/Uncle Martin), and *Santa Buddies* (Stan Cruge); on TV in *Angels in the Endzone* (Al); and on Disney+ in

Prop Culture. He voiced Merlock in *DuckTales the Movie* and Santa Claus in *Big City Greens.* He received an Emmy Award for Lead Actor in a Drama Series for a guest appearance on *Avonlea* on The Disney Channel.

Lloyd in Space (TV) Half-hour animated series; premiered Feb. 3, 2001. Follows the humorous day-to-day dilemmas of Lloyd, a space station–bound alien teenager who must endure the often confusing transition toward adulthood. Voices include Courtland Mead (Lloyd), Bill Fagerbakke (Kurt), Brian George (Station), April Winchell (Nora), Pam Hayden (Douglas). Created by Paul Germain and Joe Ansolabehere, who also created Disney's *Recess.* 39 episodes.

Loaded Weapon (film) Educational 16-mm release in Feb. 1992. 22 min. Illustrates the lethal combination of drinking and driving when a high school girl is killed.

Lockhart, Anne Actress; appeared on TV in *Fire on Kelly Mountain* and voiced Mission Control Elf in *Prep & Landing* (uncredited) and additional voices in films, including *The Little Mermaid, Chicken Little, Bolt,* and *Tangled.*

Lodge, The (TV) Musical mystery series on Disney Channel; premiered Oct. 17. 2016, after a Sep. 23 release in the U.K. and Canada. After losing her mother, 15-year-old Skye returns with her father to North Star Lodge, the family-owned country hotel where her mother was raised years earlier. Eager to make a fresh start, Skye forges friendships with the locals who live and work at the lodge, but when she learns her father is planning to sell the lodge that holds so many treasured memories, she is determined, with help from her newfound friends, to find a way to change his mind. Stars Sophie Simnett (Skye), Jade Alleyne (Kaylee), Thomas Doherty (Sean), Luke Newton (Ben), Jayden Revri (Noah), Bethan Wright (Danielle), Joshua Sinclair-Evans (Josh). Filmed on location in Ballynahinch, Northern Ireland. From Zodiak Kids Studios. Inspired by the Disney Channel Israel series, *North Star.*

Logan, Ron (1938–2022) After starting his Disney career as a trumpet player in Disneyland, then directing the band at Long Beach City College for over a decade, he returned to Disney as Walt Disney World's music director in 1978. He then held increasingly important positions—director of entertainment at Disneyland in 1980, vice president of entertainment at Walt Disney World in 1982, vice president of creative show development for Walt Disney Attractions in 1987, and finally, exec. vice president, exec. producer for Walt Disney Entertainment. He also served as exec. vice president of the Walt Disney Special Events Group and Disney Special Programs. He was responsible for producing dozens of live shows for the Disney parks worldwide and other Disney enterprises during his lengthy career, including 5 Super Bowl halftime shows. He retired in 2001 and was named a Disney Legend in 2007.

Loggia, Robert (1930–2015) Actor; appeared in *The Marrying Man* (Lew Horner), *I Love Trouble* (Matt Greenfield), and *Holy Man* (McBainbridge), and on TV in *Disneyland '59* and as the title character in *Elfego Baca.* He voiced Sykes in *Oliver & Company.*

Lohan, Lindsay Actress; appeared in *The Parent Trap* (Hallie Parker/Annie James, 1998), *Freaky Friday* (Anna, 2003), *Confessions of a Teenage Drama Queen* (Lola), *Herbie: Fully Loaded* (Maggie Peyton), and on TV in *Life-Size* (Casey Mitchell) and *Get a Clue* (Lexy Gold).

Loki (TV) A Disney+ original series; digitally premiered Jun. 9, 2021. After the events of *Avengers: Endgame,* the God of Mischief finds himself a fish out of water on a cross-timeline journey as he tries to navigate—and manipulate—his way through the bureaucratic nightmare that is the Time Variance Authority. Stars Tom Hiddleston (Loki), Owen Wilson (Mobius), Gugu Mbatha-Raw (Ravonna Renslayer), Sophia Di Martino (Sylvie), Wunmi Mosaku (Hunter B-15), Richard E. Grant (Classic Loki). From Marvel Studios.

Lomboy, Jeanette Imagineer; she began at Disneyland in 1995 as an attractions operator and later joined Walt Disney Imagineering, where, as portfolio executive, she has overseen the creative development, master planning, and delivery for projects at Disneyland Resort and Aulani, A Disney Resort & Spa. She also served as portfolio exec. producer for Disney Cruise Line and Disney's Animal Kingdom, including as exec. producer for Pandora – The World of Avatar.

Lomond, Britt (1925–2006) Actor; appeared in *Tonka* (Gen. Custer), and on TV as Monastario in *Zorro.*

London Connection, The (film) International theatrical version of *The Omega Connection*. Released first in England on Dec. 21, 1979. 84 min.

Lone Chipmunks, The (film) Chip and Dale cartoon released Apr. 7, 1954. Directed by Jack Kinney. Chip and Dale's game of robber and sheriff turns real when they successfully capture Pete, the infamous bank robber.

Lone Ranger, The (film) Motion picture from Jerry Bruckheimer; released Jul. 3, 2013. The origin story of The Lone Ranger. Tonto, a Comanche warrior on a personal quest to find the 2 men responsible for the ruin of his village unintentionally joins forces in a fight for justice with John Reid, a lawman who has been transformed into a masked avenger. Tonto recounts the story of how he and John Reid are brought together by fate and must join forces to battle greed and corruption, personified by Latham Cole, a railroad man who believes that a country's greatness lies in its ability to expand its borders to the furthest reaches—no matter what the cost. Directed by Gore Verbinski. Stars Armie Hammer (John Reid), Johnny Depp (Tonto), Helena Bonham Carter (Red Harrington), Ruth Wilson (Rebecca Reid), William Fichtner (Butch Cavendish), Tom Wilkinson (Latham Cole), James Badge Dale (Dan Reid). 149 min. The film features some of the most exciting railroad footage ever shot. Filmed in Arizona (Monument Valley), New Mexico, Colorado, and Utah. Wide-screen format. Received Academy Award nominations for Makeup and Hairstyling and for Visual Effects.

Lone Survivor of Custer's Last Stand (TV) Show; part 2 of *Comanche*.

Lonesome Ghosts (film) Mickey Mouse cartoon released Dec. 24, 1937. Directed by Burt Gillett. Some overconfident spirits hire professional, but inept, ghost-exterminators Mickey, Donald, and Goofy to try and get rid of them, hoping to have some fun in the process. The exterminators succeed in ridding the house of the ghosts accidentally, after many misadventures in which they crash into molasses and flour and appear more hideous than the ghosts, which scares the ethereal inhabitants into racing out of the house. One of the more interesting inventions of the Disney animation department was transparent paint, used effectively for the ghosts in this film.

Long, Shelley Actress; appeared in *Outrageous For-*

tune (Lauren) and *Hello Again* (Lucy Chadman), on TV in the remake of *Freaky Friday* (Ellen Andrews), and made guest appearances in *The Best of Disney: 50 Years of Magic* (Mary Ellen Doyle), *8 Simple Rules* (Mary Ellen Doyle), *Switched at Birth* (Rya Bellows), and *A.N.T. Farm* (Grandma Mrs. Busby). She voiced Grandma Murphy in *Milo Murphy's Law*.

Long Live the Rightful King (TV) Show; part 3 of *The Prince and the Pauper*.

Longoria, Eva Actress; appeared on TV in *Desperate Housewives* (Gabrielle Solis), *Devious Maids* (as herself), *Grand Hotel* (Beatriz Mendoza), and the *Walt Disney World Christmas Day Parade* (2004), and on Disney+ in *A Celebration of the Music from Coco*.

Looking for Miracles (TV) A Disney Channel Premiere Film; first aired Jun. 3, 1989. A teenager's summer as a camp counselor in 1935 is complicated by his stowaway little brother. Based on the novel by A. E. Hotchner. Directed by Kevin Sullivan. Stars Patricia Phillips (mother), Zachery Bennett (Sullivan), Greg Spottiswood (Ryan), Joe Flaherty (Arnold Berman). 103 min. Greg Spottiswood won the Emmy Award for Outstanding Performer in a Children's Special.

Looking Glass Gifts Convenience shop in the Disneyland Hotel at Tokyo Disney Resort; opened Jul. 8, 2008.

Loony Bin, The Backstage Studio Tour shop in Disney-MGM Studios; opened May 1, 1989, with gag gifts, plush toys, and film souvenirs. Closed ca. Sep. 1997, and superseded by Goosebumps Horrorland.

Loop (film) Animated short; digitally released Jan. 10, 2020, on Disney+. Two kids at canoe camp find themselves adrift on a lake, unable to move forward until they find a new way to connect and see the world through each other's eyes. Directed by Erica Milsom. 8 min. From the Pixar Animation Studios SparkShorts program.

Lopez, Mario Actor; appeared on TV in *The Deacon Street Deer* (Hector), *The Golden Girls* (Mario), *Circus of the Stars Goes to Disneyland*, and as a host of the *Disney Parks Christmas Day Parade*, with guest appearances on *Nashville*, *The Rookie*, and *The Baker and the Beauty*. He voiced Cruz in *Elena of Avalor* and made a cameo in a

Space Mountain queue video (Mission Control) at the Disney parks.

Lopez, Robert SEE ANDERSON-LOPEZ, KRISTEN, AND LOPEZ, ROBERT.

Lord Henry Mystic Adventurer, explorer, collector, and founder of Mystic Manor in Hong Kong Disneyland. The character is a member of the Society of Explorers and Adventurers (S.E.A.).

Lord Is Good to Me, The Song from *Johnny Appleseed*; written by Kim Gannon and Walter Kent, and performed by Dennis Day.

Lords & Ladies Current name for His Lordship shop in the United Kingdom in EPCOT. Perfumes, handbags, and apparel are sold.

Lorentz, Rick He joined the Disney Photo Library staff in 2008, later serving as manager, Acquisitions for the Walt Disney Archives. He has designed and installed worldwide exhibitions, conducted historical tours, and showcased items from the Archives' prop and costume collections for videos and documentary series.

Lorenzo (film) Animated short about a fat and sassy cat terrorized by its own tail into a fit of ballroom dancing. Directed by Mike Gabriel. Premiered at Florida Film Festival 2004 in Orlando Mar. 6, 2004. Released with *Raising Helen* May 28. Based on an original idea by Joe Grant. 5 min. Academy Award nominee for Animated Short Film.

Loretta Claiborne Story, The (TV) Two-hour movie on *The Wonderful World of Disney*; first aired Jan. 16, 2000. The story of a poor, mentally disabled African American girl who goes on to become a champion athlete, teacher, and passionate advocate for those with mental and physical disabilities. Directed by Lee Grant. Stars Kimberly Elise (Loretta), Tina Lifford (Rita), Nicole Ari Parker (Christine), Damon Gupton (Sam), Camryn Manheim (Janet).

L'Originale Alfredo di Roma Ristorante Restaurant in Italy at EPCOT Center; opened Oct. 1, 1982. Guests partake of fettuccine Alfredo or any number of Italian pastas and other delicacies in this full-service restaurant, surrounded by intriguing trompe l'oeil paintings of Italian scenes. Occasionally, a waiter or two might step aside and belt out an operatic aria in between courses to the delight of guests. The restaurant closed Aug. 31, 2007, with the Patina Restaurant Group taking over operation on Sep. 1 with a name change to Tutto Italia Ristorante.

L'Ornament Magique New Orleans Square ornament shop in Disneyland; opened Oct. 10, 1998, taking the place of the original Le Bat en Rouge. It temporarily hosted The Pirates League, Sep.–Nov. 2012. Closed Sep. 2013, to serve as a new entrance to Club 33.

Lorre, Peter (1904–1964) Actor; appeared in *20,000 Leagues Under the Sea* (Conseil), and on TV in *Monsters of the Deep*.

Los Angeles International Airport Designers from Walt Disney Imagineering helped in a redesign of the theme restaurant at LAX, which reopened Dec. 1996. The Encounter Restaurant, originally known as the Theme Building Restaurant, was built in 1961 with a then futuristic look resembling a flying saucer on parabolic stilts.

Lost (TV) One-hour drama series on ABC; aired Sep. 22, 2004–May 23, 2010. A plane crashes on a Pacific island, and the 48 survivors, stripped of everything, scavenge what they can from the plane for their survival. Some panic; some pin their hopes on rescue. The band of friends, family, enemies, and strangers must work together against the cruel weather and harsh terrain. Stars Matthew Fox (Jack), Evangeline Lilly (Kate), Dominic Monaghan (Charlie), Ian Somerhalder (Boone), Jorge Garcia (Hurley), Maggie Grace (Shannon), Malcolm David Kelley (Walt), Naveen Andrews (Sayid), Harold Perrineau (Michael), Josh Holloway (Sawyer), Terry O'Quinn (Locke), Daniel Dae Kim (Jin), Yunjin Kim (Sun). From Touchstone Television. Filmed entirely on location in Hawai'i. The show won an Emmy for Best Drama Series in 2005.

Lost at Home (TV) Half-hour comedy series on ABC; aired Apr. 1–22, 2003. Ad agency superstar Michael Davis is full of ambition, but he is losing touch with his family. The winning strategies that have made him a success at work are surprisingly useless at home. His wife, Rachel, gives him an ultimatum, and he tries to win back his family. Stars Mitch Rouse (Michael), Connie Britton (Rachel), Gregory Hines (Jordan King), Stark Sands (Will), Leah Pipes (Sara), Gavin Fink (Joshua), Aaron Hill (Tucker). From Touchstone Television in association with NBC Studios.

Lost Bar, The SEE NEVER LAND POOL.

Lost Boys, The Peter Pan's youthful pals in Never Land.

Lost on the Baja Peninsula (TV) Show; part 1 of *Three Without Fear*.

Lost River Cookhouse Counter-service eatery in Lost River Delta at Tokyo DisneySea; opened Jul. 21, 2005, in conjunction with Raging Spirits.

Lost River Delta Port of call in Tokyo DisneySea depicting a 1930s explorers' settlement in Central America; opened Sep. 4, 2001. Jungles and ruins of an ancient civilization are home to mysterious attractions, such as Indiana Jones Adventure: Temple of the Crystal Skull.

Lost River Outfitters Shop for explorers in Lost River Delta at Tokyo DisneySea; opened Sep. 4, 2001. Central American–style apparel, sundries, and leather items are sold.

Lot Like Love, A (film) A pair of dynamic, diametrically opposed twentysomethings—Oliver and Emily—have an initial fateful meeting that sets off sparks, but then seems to go nowhere. Over the next 7 years, they continue to meet through changing careers and different relationships. There always seems to be plenty keeping them apart, and yet there is also something utterly inexplicable pulling them together. Released Apr. 22, 2005. A Touchstone/Beacon Pictures film. Directed by Nigel Cole. Stars Ashton Kutcher (Oliver Martin), Amanda Peet (Emily Friehl), Ty Giordano (Graham Martin), Melissa van der Schyff (Carol Martin), Taryn Manning (Ellen Martin), Kathryn Hahn (Michelle). 107 min. The film uses more than 55 locations, from New York City's Chinatown to Los Angeles's El Matador Beach.

Lots of Luck (TV) A housewife's winning lottery ticket starts a lucky streak in the family as everyone starts bringing home prizes, but there are problems that go with this Midas touch. A TV movie for The Disney Channel, first aired Feb. 3, 1985. Directed by Peter Baldwin. Stars Annette Funicello (Julie Maris), Martin Mull (Frank Maris), Fred Willard, Polly Holliday.

Lotso Jumbo strawberry-scented teddy bear character in *Toy Story 3*; voiced by Ned Beatty. His name is short for Lots-o'-Huggin' Bear.

Lotso Garden Cafe Buffet dining in the Tokyo Disney Resort Toy Story Hotel; opened Apr. 5, 2022.

Lotso Shop Shop at the Toy Story Hotel at Shanghai Disney Resort; opened Jun. 16, 2016. *Toy Story*-themed apparel, toys, and sundries are sold.

Lottery, The (film) Short film about a music teacher who finds and loses a winning lottery ticket, illustrating various special effects techniques for guests at the Backstage Studio Tour in Disney-MGM Studios; debuted May 1, 1989, and ended Jun. 29, 1996. 4 min. Stars Bette Midler.

Lotus Blossom Café Counter-service restaurant in China at EPCOT; opened Sep. 24, 1985. It underwent a renovation in 2007, providing a more modern look.

Lou (film) Short cartoon from Pixar; released with *Cars 3* Jun. 16, 2017. When a toy-stealing bully ruins recess for a playground of kids, only one thing stands in his way: the "Lost and Found" box. Directed by Dave Mullins. 7 min. Received an Academy Award nomination for Animated Short Film.

Louie One of Donald Duck's 3 nephews; originally voiced by Clarence Nash. Beginning with the *DuckTales* TV series, the nephews were voiced by Russi Taylor and given unique colors to wear (green for Louie). Voiced by Bobby Moynihan for the new *DuckTales* (2017).

Louis Frantic cook in *The Little Mermaid*; voiced by René Auberjonois.

Louis Trumpet-playing alligator character in *The Princess and the Frog*; voiced by Michael-Leon Wooley.

Louis-Dreyfus, Julia Actress; appeared as Valentina Allegra de Fontaine in *The Falcon and The Winter Soldier* and *Black Widow*, and on TV in *Geppetto* (Blue Fairy). She voiced Princess Atta in *A Bug's Life*, Laurel Lightfoot in *Onward*, Rochelle in *Planes*, and Heather Worthington in *Dinosaurs*. It was announced she will appear in *Thunderbolts* from Marvel Studios.

Louis L'Amour's The Cherokee Trail SEE CHEROKEE TRAIL, THE.

Lounsbery, John (1911–1976) Animator; one of

Walt's "Nine Old Men," he started his career with Disney in 1935 as an animator on *Snow White and the Seven Dwarfs* and later specialized in the Pluto shorts. He worked on most of the classic features, as an animator or directing animator, including *Alice in Wonderland, Peter Pan, Sleeping Beauty, The Jungle Book,* and *The Rescuers.* He recalled that one of his favorite characters to animate was Ben Ali Gator in *Fantasia*; other memorable characters included Honest John in *Pinocchio*, Timothy Mouse in *Dumbo*, and Tony in *Lady and the Tramp.* He was directing animator on some of the Winnie the Pooh featurettes, including *Winnie the Pooh and the Blustery Day*, which won an Academy Award for Best Cartoon Short Subject. He was honored posthumously in 1989 with the Disney Legends Award.

Lovato, Demi Appeared in *Jonas Brothers: The 3-D Concert Experience*, on Disney Channel in *Camp Rock* and *Camp Rock 2: The Final Jam* (Mitchie Torres), *Sonny with a Chance* (Sonny Munroe), and *Princess Protection Program* (Rosalinda Marie Montoya Flore), and on ABC in *The Disney Family Singalong.* Also recorded for Hollywood Records, sang the pop version of "Let It Go" for the end credits of *Frozen*, and co-wrote and performed "I Believe" for *A Wrinkle in Time.*

Love Song from *Robin Hood*; written by Floyd Huddleston and George Bruns. Nominated for an Academy Award.

Love and Duty: Which Comes First? (film) Educational film; using sequences from *Old Yeller.* In the Questions!/Answers? series; released in Oct. 1975. Helps students understand the relationship of duty to feelings of love and loyalty.

Love Bug, The (film) A down-and-out racetrack driver, Jim Douglas, acquires a little Volkswagen, but doesn't realize that the "bug" is almost human. The car helps Jim win many races but runs away when it feels it is not appreciated into the clutches of a villainous rival, Peter Thorndyke. With the help of his friends Tennessee and Carole, Jim changes his attitude, finds the "bug," and apologizes. They win another race—and then Jim falls in love with Carole. Released Mar. 13, 1969. Directed by Robert Stevenson. Stars Dean Jones (Jim Douglas), Michele Lee (Carole), David Tomlinson (Thorndyke), Buddy Hackett (Tennessee), Joe Flynn (Havershaw), Benson Fong (Mr. Wu), Andy Granatelli. The movie was based on the story "Car-Boy-Girl" by Gordon Buford. On-location shooting was done in California in San Francisco, as well as Willow Springs, the Riverside Raceway, and on the Monterey Peninsula. 108 min. The highest-grossing film in the U.S. during 1969; the film was so successful that it led to the sequels, *Herbie Rides Again, Herbie Goes to Monte Carlo, Herbie Goes Bananas, Herbie: Fully Loaded*, a limited TV series, *Herbie, the Love Bug*, and a 1997 TV-movie sequel. Reissued in 1979.

Love Bug, The (TV) Two-hour movie on *The Wonderful World of Disney*; first aired Nov. 30, 1997. Now owned by egotistical Englishman Simon Moore III, Herbie is junked when he places last in a big race. The little car is saved from demolition by Hank Cooper, a washed-up racer-turned-mechanic. Hank discovers Herbie's special personality, and Herbie tries to help out Hank in his romance with Alex Davis, while defending himself against Moore's newly created car-with-a-personality—Horace, the Hate Bug. Directed by Peyton Reed. Stars Bruce Campbell (Hank Cooper), John Hannah (Simon Moore), Alexandra Wentworth (Alex Davis), Kevin J. O'Connor (Roddy Martel). Dean Jones returns to play Jim Douglas, Herbie's first owner, 3 decades after he made the original film.

Love in the Time of Corona (TV) Four-part limited series on Freeform; aired Aug. 22–23, 2020. Four interwoven stories explore the hopeful search for love and connection during the 2020 coronavirus pandemic. Filmed using remote technologies and shot in the cast's actual homes. Stars Leslie Odom Jr. (James), Nicolette Robinson (Sade), Tommy Dorfman (Oscar), Rainey Qualley (Elle), Gil Bellows (Paul), Rya Kihlstedt (Sarah), Ava Bellows (Sophie), L. Scott Caldwell (Nanda). From Anonymous Content.

Love Is a Song Song from *Bambi*; written by Larry Morey and Frank Churchill. Nominated for an Academy Award.

Love Leads the Way (TV) Movie for The Disney Channel; first aired Oct. 7, 1984. A blind man, Morris Frank, fights prejudice and skepticism to prove the worth of guide dogs in America in the 1930s. Directed by Delbert Mann. Stars Timothy Bottoms (Morris Frank), Eva Marie Saint (Dorothy Eustis), Ralph Bellamy (Senator), Ernest Borgnine (Senator), Arthur Hill (father), Patricia Neal (mother), Glynnis O'Connor (Lois), Susan Dey

(Beth). Filmed on location in Nashville, Tennessee, and in Washington State.

Lovestruck: The Musical (TV) Original movie musical; premiered on ABC Family Apr. 21, 2013. Harper, a choreographer and former Broadway dancer, is dismayed when her daughter, Mirabella, quits Harper's next big production in order to get married to an Italian playboy. Harper, determined not to let her daughter give up her career for love, travels to Italy, but in drinking a strange elixir becomes 30 years younger. Teaming with her ex-husband, who also drinks the elixir, she infiltrates the wedding, but eventually realizes she is wrong and tries to reverse the damage she has caused. Directed by Sanaa Hamri. Stars Jane Seymour (Harper), Sara Paxton (Mirabella), Alexander DiPersia (Marco), Tom Wopat (Ryan). The younger Harper and Ryan are played by Chelsea Kane and Drew Seeley, respectively. Working title was *Elixir*. Produced by Boss Productions for ABC Family.

Low Down Dirty Shame, A (film) Andre Shame has been fired from the police force because of a botched drug bust, so he is now down on his luck, working as a private investigator, taking big risks for small rewards. He is tough talking and knows the ways of the streets, and he has a trusty secretary, Peaches, whose resourcefulness and feistiness are often necessary to get him out of a jam. When he is retained by DEA agent Rothmiller to track down $20 million in missing drug money, he finds himself facing the notorious Ernesto Mendoza, the man he thought he killed in the failed drug raid. Now he has a chance to clear his name as well as shut down Mendoza's illegal operations. Released Nov. 23, 1994. Directed by Keenen Ivory Wayans. A Hollywood Pictures film release, in association with Caravan Pictures. 100 min. Stars Keenen Ivory Wayans (Shame), Charles S. Dutton (Rothmiller), Jada Pinkett (Peaches), Salli Richardson (Angela), Andrew Divoff (Mendoza). The final scenes were shot in a closed 5-level shopping mall in Scottsdale, Arizona. Wayans did most of his own stunts for the film.

Lowell, Tom Actor; appeared in *That Darn Cat!* (Canoe), *The Gnome-Mobile* (Jasper), and *The Boatniks* (Wagner).

Lozano, Ignacio E., Jr. Member of the Disney Board of Directors 1981–Mar. 6, 2001.

Lozano, Monica C. Member of the Disney Board of Directors Sep. 19, 2000–2016.

Luau Cove SEE POLYNESIAN REVUE (WALT DISNEY WORLD).

Luca (film) Animated feature from Pixar Animation Studios. Luca Paguro is a young boy experiencing an unforgettable summer filled with gelato, pasta, and endless scooter rides in the beautiful seaside town of Portorosso on the Italian Riviera. He shares these adventures with his newfound best friend, Alberto Scorfano, but all the fun is threatened by a deeply held secret: they are sea monsters from another world just below the water's surface. Digitally released Jun. 18, 2021, on Disney+, in conjunction with a limited run at the El Capitan Theatre in Hollywood through Jun. 24. This followed a Jun. 17 international release and screening at the Annecy International Animation Film Festival. Directed by Enrico Casarosa. Voices include Jacob Tremblay (Luca), Jack Dylan Grazer (Alberto), Emma Berman (Giulia), Saverio Raimondo (Ercole), Maya Rudolph (Daniela), Marco Barricelli (Massimo), Jim Gaffigan (Lorenzo), Sandy Martin (Grandma Paguro). 95 min. Music by Dan Romer. The filmmakers took inspiration from Italian myths and 1950s–1960s pop culture, especially classic films like *La Strada* and *Roman Holiday*, with additional influences from Japanese animation and woodblock prints. Alberto was based on Casarosa's own childhood best friend of the same name; actor Jack Dylan Grazer did not have to travel far to perform his dialogue for the character—he recorded every line inside his mother's closet. Meanwhile, all of the background kid voices were recorded by local children in Italy. Received an Academy Award nomination for Animated Feature.

Lucas, George Noted producer/director and founder of Lucasfilm; collaborated with Walt Disney Imagineering on 6 theme park attractions. The first was *Captain EO*, which opened in Disneyland in 1986 and later in EPCOT Center and other Disney parks. He also co-created Star Tours for Disneyland, Disney's Hollywood Studios, Tokyo Disneyland, and Disneyland Paris; The ExtraTERRORestrial Alien Encounter in the Magic Kingdom at Walt Disney World; Indiana Jones and the Temple of Peril in Disneyland Paris; *Indiana Jones Epic Stunt Spectacular!* in Disney's Hollywood Studios; Indiana Jones Adventure: Temple of the Crystal Skull in Tokyo Disneyland; and the Indiana Jones Adventure in Disneyland. Lucas would remain as creative consultant after Disney's acquisition of Lucasfilm in 2012. He was named a Disney Legend in 2015.

Lucasfilm On Oct. 30, 2012, Disney announced it had agreed to purchase Lucasfilm Ltd. from George Lucas; Lucas would remain as creative consultant. Included in the deal were the special effects house Industrial Light & Magic and Skywalker Sound, along with the rights to the *Star Wars* and Indiana Jones franchises. The acquisition was completed Dec. 21, 2012, for a value of approximately $4.06 billion in cash and stock. Disney has released the following theatrical motion pictures from Lucasfilm:

1. *Strange Magic* (2015) (Touchstone)
2. *Star Wars: The Force Awakens* (2015)
3. *Rogue One: A Star Wars Story* (2016)
4. *Star Wars: The Last Jedi* (2017)
5. *Solo: A Star Wars Story* (2018)
6. *Star Wars: The Rise of Skywalker* (2019)
7. *Indiana Jones and the Dial of Destiny* (2023)

Lucca, Tony Actor; appeared on the *Mickey Mouse Club* on The Disney Channel, beginning in 1991.

Lucci, Susan Actress; she portrayed Erica Kane for 4 decades on the ABC daytime drama *All My Children*, also appearing on Lifetime in *Devious Maids* (Genevieve Delatour) and *Army Wives* (Audrey Whitaker). She made guest appearances in *Hope & Faith* (Jacqueline Karr) and on Disney Channel in *That's So Raven* (Miss Charlotte Romano), and voiced Weather Person Hero in *Higglytown Heroes*. She was named a Disney Legend in 2015.

Lucifer Tough alley cat character in *Pluto's Kid Brother* (1946).

Lucifer The cat menace in Cinderella's household.

Luck of the Irish (TV) A Disney Channel Original Movie; premiered Mar. 9, 2001. When junior high basketball star Kyle Johnson questions his heritage, he discovers that his mother is actually a leprechaun, and he is starting to change into one too, all because someone stole his gold Celtic good luck coin. To get it back, and keep him and his family human, Kyle has to ward off an evil, step-dancing leprechaun, Seamus McTiernan, and challenge him to a contest. Directed by Paul Hoen. Stars Ryan Merriman (Kyle Johnson), Alexis Lopez (Bonnie Lopez), Glenndon Chatman (Russell Holloway), Marita Geraghty (Kate Johnson), Paul Kiernan (Bob Johnson), Henry Gibson (Reilly O'Reilly), Timothy Omundson (Seamus McTiernan). Filmed in Salt Lake City.

Luckey, Bud (1934–2018) Pixar animator, the 5th hired by the company; he worked as an animator, character artist, or story artist on films beginning with *Toy Story* (1995). Also provided voices in *The Incredibles* (Rick Dicker), *Toy Story 3* (Chuckles), *Winnie the Pooh* (Eeyore, 2011), and *Boundin'* (narrator and all characters), a short film he also directed and composed.

Lucky Fortune Cookery Counter-service Chinese food eatery in Pacific Wharf at Disney California Adventure; opened Feb. 8, 2001. The restaurant was removed Jan. 12, 2009, to allow for an enhanced and expanded Cocina Cucamonga, then reopened in the former Cocina Cucamonga location Sep. 4, 2009.

Lucky Nugget Cafe Restaurant in Westernland at Tokyo Disneyland; open Apr. 15, 1983–Aug. 31, 2015. It became Camp Woodchuck Kitchen.

Lucky Nugget Saloon, The Frontierland restaurant in Disneyland Paris; opened Apr. 12, 1992. The extravagantly decorated saloon features a menu typical of the American West. Also an outdoor counter-service eatery in Grizzly Gulch at Hong Kong Disneyland; opened Jul. 14, 2012, serving hearty fare, such as crispy battered fish filets and shrimp and chips.

Lucky Number (film) Donald Duck cartoon released Jul. 20, 1951. Directed by Jack Hannah. Donald, unbeknownst to him, has won a new car, and his nephews go to pick it up as a surprise. But when the car arrives, Donald wrecks it thinking his nephews played a trick.

Lucky 7 (TV) One-hour series on ABC; aired Sep. 24–Oct. 1, 2013. A group of 7 gas station employees in Queens, New York, have been chipping in to a lottery pool for years, never thinking they'd actually win. Suddenly their lives are transformed by an unexpected lottery win. Aside from the money, relationships change as the trust between 2 brothers is uprooted, budding romances develop, and secrets come to the surface. Stars Summer Bishil (Samira Lashari), Lorraine Bruce (Denise Dibinsky), Alex Castillo (Bianca Clemente) Christine Evangelista (Mary Lavecchia), Louis Grush (Nicky Korzak), Matt Long (Matt Korzak), Anastasia Phillips (Leanne Maxwell), Luis Antonio Ramos (Antonio Clemente), Isiah Whitlock, Jr. (Bob Harris). From ABC Studios and Amblin Television, based on the British hit *The Syndicate*.

Lucky the Dinosaur The first Audio-Animatronics figure to roam freely and personally interact with park guests. Created by Walt Disney Imagineering after 5 years of effort, Lucky the Dinosaur was introduced in Disney California Adventure as a test Aug. 28, 2003. Lucky walks on 2 legs, stands approximately 9 ft. tall and 12 ft. long, and pulls a cart of flowers. Lucky next appeared in Disney's Animal Kingdom at Walt Disney World in 2005 and later in Hong Kong Disneyland.

Lucky Toupée (film) Animated short; digitally released Jan. 24, 2020, on Disney+. An original tale about a hijacked hairpiece, a gang of larcenous leprechauns, and a budding romance. Directed by Nikki Mull. 2 min. From the Walt Disney Animation Studios Short Circuit program.

Luddy, Barbara (1907–1979) Actress; provided the voice of Lady in *Lady and the Tramp*, Merryweather in *Sleeping Beauty*, Rover in *One Hundred and One Dalmatians*, Kanga in the Winnie the Pooh films, Mother Church Mouse and Mother Rabbit in *Robin Hood*, and Grandma in the original Carousel of Progress. She appeared on TV in *A Story of Dogs*.

Ludwig, Irving (1910–2005) He joined Disney in 1940 to manage the road show engagements of *Fantasia* and later became part of the sales administration staff of Walt Disney Productions. He was first vice president and domestic sales manager for the newly formed Buena Vista Distribution Company in 1953. In 1959, he became its president, a post he held until his retirement in 1980. He was honored with the Disney Legends Award in 1993.

Ludwig Von Drake Donald Duck's erudite, though eccentric, uncle who emceed several TV shows, debuting in the first show of *Walt Disney's Wonderful World of Color* in 1961: *An Adventure in Color*. The following year, he starred in his own theatrical featurette, *A Symposium on Popular Songs*. Professor Von Drake appeared in a total of 18 TV shows and later appeared in animated series such as *House of Mouse*, *Mickey Mouse Clubhouse*, and *DuckTales*. Described by Walt Disney as a "self-appointed expert on everything." His voice was originally supplied by Paul Frees.

Luigi's Flying Tires Cars Land attraction in Disney California Adventure; opened Jun. 15, 2012, and closed Feb. 15, 2015, to make way for Luigi's Rol-

lickin' Roadsters. At Luigi's Casa Della Tires, *Cars* characters Luigi and Guido hosted guests in a "Festival of Flying Tires." The tires floated and glided, and guests could shift their body weight to guide their tire. For many, the ride brought back memories of the former Flying Saucers attraction in Disneyland.

Luigi's Rollickin' Roadsters Cars Land attraction in Disney California Adventure; opened Mar. 7, 2016, taking the place of Luigi's Flying Tires. Guests ride along with Luigi's cousins from Carsoli, Italy, as they move and spin to upbeat Italian music, performing the traditional dances of their hometown village. Each dancing car has its own signature moves, making each ride different.

Lukas, Paul (1887–1971) Actor; appeared in *20,000 Leagues Under the Sea* (Prof. Aronnax).

Lullaby Land (film) Silly Symphony cartoon released Aug. 19, 1933. Directed by Wilfred Jackson. A little baby and a toy dog have an adventure in a land of patchwork quilt fields, trees laden with rattles, and magic nursery crockery, safety pins, and bottles of castor oil. Frightened by a Forbidden Garden of penknives, scissors, and matches, the pair are rescued by the sandman and sent back to the cradle on a blanket of flowers. The title song was published on sheet music.

Lulubelle Bongo's love interest, a bear, in *Fun and Fancy Free*.

Lumiere Enchanted candlestick/butler in *Beauty and the Beast*; voiced by Jerry Orbach.

Lumiere's Kitchen Fantasyland counter-service restaurant in the Magic Kingdom at Walt Disney World; open Feb. 13, 1993–Apr. 30, 2006. Formerly Gurgi's Munchies and Crunchies. It became the Village Fry Shoppe and, later, The Friar's Nook. Also opened Jun. 16, 2016, as a buffet-style restaurant at the Shanghai Disneyland Hotel, where décor is inspired by the "Be Our Guest" segment from *Beauty and the Beast*.

Luminaria Holiday-themed nighttime show, with fireworks, on the lagoon in Disney California Adventure; began Nov. 9, 2001, for that one Christmas season.

Lumpjaw Bongo's rival in *Fun and Fancy Free*.

Luna, Ricky Actor; appeared on The Disney

Channel in the *Mickey Mouse Club* beginning in 1990, and later as a cashier in *Lizzie McGuire*. He composed music for *Step Up Revolution* and *Shake It Up*.

Luna, La (film) SEE LA LUNA.

Lunch Money (film) Educational film about the necessity of honesty and integrity in dealing with others, from the What Should I Do? series; released in Jul. 1970.

Lunching Pad, The Tomorrowland counter-service restaurant in the Magic Kingdom at Walt Disney World; open 1971–Jan. 9, 1994, and succeeded by Auntie Gravity's Galactic Goodies. Reopened as a snack bar underneath the Tomorrowland Transit Authority station Jun. 1994, succeeding the Space Bar. Another Lunching Pad opened in Disneyland in 1977, replacing the Space Bar, and closed ca. 1998, to become a Radio Disney broadcast station. Also open in Tokyo Disneyland Apr. 15, 1983–Jan. 6, 1988, replaced by Pan Galactic Pizza Port.

Lund, Sharon Disney SEE DISNEY, SHARON.

Lundy, Dick (1907–1990) Animator; began at Disney in 1929. He worked on *Snow White and the Seven Dwarfs* and various shorts. He first directed on *Sea Scouts* and continued directing Donald cartoons in the 1939–1943 period. He left Disney in 1943.

Lupton, John (1928–1993) Actor; appeared in *The Great Locomotive Chase* (William Pittenger), *Napoleon and Samantha* (Pete), and *The World's Greatest Athlete* (race starter), and on TV in *The Secret of Lost Valley*.

Luske, Hamilton "Ham" (1903–1968) He began at Disney in 1931 and animated on cartoons until 1943, when he became a director for training films; later he directed *Ben and Me*, *Donald in Mathmagic Land*, *Donald and the Wheel*, and *Scrooge McDuck and Money*. He was supervising director on *Pinocchio*; sequence director on *Fantasia*, *Saludos Amigos*, *Make Mine Music*, *Cinderella*, *Alice in Wonderland*, *Peter Pan*, *Lady and the Tramp*, and

One Hundred and One Dalmatians; cartoon director on *The Reluctant Dragon*, *Fun and Fancy Free*, *Melody Time*, *So Dear to My Heart*, and *Mary Poppins*. He was noted for his animation of Max Hare in *The Tortoise and the Hare*, of Jenny Wren in *Who Killed Cock Robin?*, Elmer in *Elmer Elephant*, and Snow White herself in *Snow White and the Seven Dwarfs*. He shared a Visual Effects Oscar in 1965 for *Mary Poppins* with Peter Ellenshaw and Eustace Lycett, and was named a Disney Legend posthumously in 1999.

Luske, Tommy (1947–1990) He voiced Michael in *Peter Pan*. The son of Disney animator and director Ham Luske.

Lynch, Jane Actress; appeared on TV in *MDs* (Nurse "Doctor" Poole) and *Criminal Minds* (Diana Reid), with guest appearances in *Empty Nest*, *Felicity*, *According to Jim*, *Monk*, *Desperate Housewives*, *Girl Meets World*, and *The Real O'Neals*. She has provided several voices, including Sgt. Calhoun in *Wreck-It Ralph* and *Ralph Breaks the Internet*, Neptuna in *Small Fry*, Mrs. Johnson in *Phineas and Ferb*, Jackie Greenway in *Handy Manny*, Mrs. Locks in *Goldie and Bear*, Dr. Dirt in *The Chicken Squad*, Supersonic Sue in *Big Hero 6 The Series*, and Ms. Roop in *The Ghost and Molly McGee*. On Disney+, she narrated *Meet the Chimps*.

Lynche, Tate (1981–2015) Actress; appeared on the *Mickey Mouse Club* on The Disney Channel, beginning in 1993.

Lynton, Michael He joined Disney in 1987 as manager of business development for Consumer Products, moving into the publishing area in 1989. In 1994, he was named president of Hollywood Pictures. He left the company in 1996.

Lyric Street Records Disney announced in 1997 the founding of this new country music label, named after the street on which Walt and Roy Disney used to live. Their first album, *Stepping Stone*, with Lari White, debuted in 1998. Lyric Street Records closed in Apr. 2010.

1. *Mary Poppins* (film) 2. Mystic Manor 3. Merchandise 4. *Main Street Electrical Parade* 5. Mickey Mouse
6. *Mira, Royal Detective* (TV) 7. *Monsters at Work* (TV) 8. *Moana* (film) 9. Monorail 10. *Man in Space* (TV)
11. Mickey & Minnie's Runaway Railway 12. *Mickey Mouse Funhouse* (TV)

M, Lebo SEE MORAKE, LEBOHANG.

M. Mouse Mercantile Souvenir shop on the mezzanine level in Disney's Grand Floridian Resort & Spa at Walt Disney World; opened Jun. 28, 1988.

Mac, Bernie (1957–2008) Actor; appeared in *Mr. 3000* (Stan Ross) and *Old Dogs* (Jimmy Lunchbox).

McAdams, Rachel Actress; appeared in *The Hot Chick* (Jessica Spencer) and as Christine Palmer in the Doctor Strange films, and on Disney Channel in *The Famous Jett Jackson* (Hannah Grant).

MacArthur, James (1937–2010) Actor; appeared in *Swiss Family Robinson* (Fritz), *The Light in the Forest* (Johnny Butler/True Son), *Third Man on the Mountain* (Rudi Matt), and *Kidnapped* (David Balfour), and on TV in *Willie and the Yank*, *Wonderful World of Disney: 40 Years of Television Magic*, and *The Age of Believing: The Disney Live Action Classics*. His mother, Helen Hayes, had a cameo role in *Third Man on the Mountain* with him.

McBrayer, Jack Actor; he has provided several voices, including Felix in *Wreck-It Ralph* and *Ralph Breaks the Internet*, the title character in *Wander Over Yonder*, Irving in *Phineas and Ferb*, Hedgie in *Puppy Dog Pals*, Toadie in *Amphibia*, Badili in *The Lion Guard*, Pirate Mummy in *Jake and the Never Land Pirates*, and Sad Face in *Woke*. On Disney+, he appeared in *Marvel's 616* and *Earth to Ned*.

McCallum, David Actor; appeared in *The Watcher in the Woods* (Paul Curtis) and voiced C.A.R. in *The Replacements*.

McCarthy, Christine She was named chief financial officer for The Walt Disney Company in Jun. 2015. She had joined Disney in 2000 as senior vice president and treasurer, continuing as treasurer until becoming CFO. Other titles have included exec. vice president, Corporate Finance, and real estate and exec. vice president, Corporate Real Estate and Alliances.

McCarthy, Melissa Actress; appeared in *Disney's The Kid* (Sky King Waitress) and *Thor: Love and Thunder* (Actor Hela, uncredited); on TV in *Samantha Who?* (Dena) and made a guest appearance in *Private Practice*. She voiced DNAmy in *Kim Possible*. It was announced she will play Ursula in the live-action version of *The Little Mermaid* (2023).

McCartney, Jesse Actor/singer; voiced Terence in the Tinker Bell films and Ventus/Roxas in *Kingdom Hearts*. He made TV appearances on Lifetime in *Army Wives* (Tim Truman), on ABC Family in *Young & Hungry* (Cooper), on ABC in the *Walt Disney World Christmas Day Parade* (2004), and on Disney Channel in *The Suite Life of Zack & Cody* and *Hannah Montana*.

McClanahan, Rue (1934–2010) Actress; appeared as Blanche in *The Golden Girls* (for which she won the Emmy Award as Outstanding Lead Actress in a Comedy Series in 1987) and *The Golden Palace*, with additional TV appearances in *Boy Meets World* (Bernice Matthews), *A Saintly Switch* (Aunt

Fanny Moye), *Disneyland's All Star Comedy Circus*, and *The Disney-MGM Studios Theme Park Grand Opening*. She was named a Disney Legend in 2009.

McClure, Marc Actor; appeared in *Freaky Friday* (Boris Harris), and on TV in *The Sky Trap*. He made a cameo appearance in the 2003 remake of *Freaky Friday* as Boris.

McCrum, Thomas B. (1877–1948) Dentist in Kansas City who hired the young Walt Disney to produce a dental training film for him in 1922, *Tommy Tucker's Tooth*. Several years later, after Walt was in California, McCrum commissioned another film, *Clara Cleans Her Teeth*.

McDaniel, Hattie (1895–1952) Actress; portrayed Tempy in *Song of the South*.

McDonald, Calvin R. Member of the Disney Board of Directors beginning in 2021.

Macdonald, Jim ("Jimmy") (1906–1991) Longtime Disney sound effects wizard; he created sound effects for many of the Disney films beginning in 1934. Rarely was there a sound Jimmy could not make with one of more than 500 contraptions that he built from scratch. In 1946, he was asked by Walt to take over the voice of Mickey Mouse, a role he handled until his retirement 3 decades later. He appeared as the silhouetted figure of a timpani player in *Fantasia*, made TV appearances playing the drums as a member of the Firehouse Five Plus Two jazz band, and came out of retirement to provide sounds for Evinrude in *The Rescuers* in 1977. He was named a Disney Legend in 1993.

Macdonald, Kelly Actress; provided the voice of Princess Merida in *Brave* and other appearances of the character. She appeared in *The Hitchhiker's Guide to the Galaxy* (Reporter) and made a TV guest appearance on *Alias* (Kiera MacLaine).

McDonald's For many years, Disney has partnered with McDonald's restaurants in marketing its movies and theme park attractions. On Jan. 8, 1998, after the signing of a 10-year agreement in 1996, the first McDonald's restaurant opened at a Disney resort, in the Downtown Disney Marketplace at Walt Disney World, following the 1997 introduction of kiosks selling McDonald's french fries in the Magic Kingdom and at Disneyland. At Walt Disney World, McDonald's also sponsored

DinoLand U.S.A. in Disney's Animal Kingdom (until 2008) and opened a standalone restaurant near the park Mar. 14, 1998 (remodeled in 2009 and 2019). The Downtown Disney location closed in 2010. At Disneyland Paris, a McDonald's restaurant opened in Disney Village Jan. 25, 1999, and another opened in Ikspiari at the Tokyo Disney Resort Dec. 21, 2021. Starting in 2006, Disney films were no longer promoted on McDonald's Happy Meals, until the companies signed a new multi-year agreement in 2018.

McDowall, Roddy (1928–1998) Actor; appeared in *That Darn Cat!* (Gregory Benson), *The Adventures of Bullwhip Griffin* (Bullwhip Griffin), *Bedknobs and Broomsticks* (Mr. Jelk), *The Cat from Outer Space* (Mr. Stallwood), and *The Black Hole* (voice of V.I.N.Cent). He appeared in the pilot of *Small and Frye* (Prof. Vermeer) and voiced Mr. Soil in *A Bug's Life* and Proteus in *Gargoyles*.

McDuck's Department Store Grand department store in American Waterfront at Tokyo DisneySea; opened Sep. 4, 2001. The shop is set in New York City and owned by Scrooge McDuck.

McEnery, Peter Actor; appeared in *The Moon-Spinners* (Mark Camford) and *The Fighting Prince of Donegal* (Hugh O'Donnell).

McEveety, Bernard (1924–2004) Director of *The Bears and I*, *Napoleon and Samantha*, *One Little Indian*, and *The Boy and the Bronc Buster*. One of 3 brothers who had extensive directing careers at Disney.

McEveety, Joe (1926–1976) Assistant director, director, and writer at Disney beginning in 1957. He wrote scripts for *Now You See Him, Now You Don't*; *Michael O'Hara the Fourth*; *The Wacky Zoo of Morgan City*; *The Computer Wore Tennis Shoes*; *The Barefoot Executive*; *The Apple Dumpling Gang*; and *The Strongest Man in the World*.

McEveety, Vince (1929–2018) Director; he began at Disney as an assistant director on the *Mickey Mouse Club*, and later directed such films as *The Ballad of Hector the Stowaway Dog*, *Gus*, *Treasure of Matecumbe*, *The Strongest Man in the World*, *The Million Dollar Duck*, *The Biscuit Eater*, *Charley and the Angel*, *Superdad*, *The Castaway Cowboy*, and *The High Flying Spy*.

McFarland USA (film) High school coach Jim

White's job-hopping leads him to predominantly Latino McFarland High School, located in an agricultural community in California's farm-rich Central Valley. Jim knows he has to make this school his last stop—he's out of options, with both his career and his family—and finds himself in a diverse, economically challenged community that feels worlds apart from his previous hometowns. Admittedly, the White family and the students have a lot to learn about each other, but when Coach White notices the boys' exceptional running ability, things begin to change. Soon something beyond their physical gifts impresses White—the power of family relationships, their unwavering commitment to one another, and their incredible work ethic. With grit and determination, Coach White's unlikely band of runners eventually overcomes the odds to become not only a championship cross-country team but an enduring legacy as well. Along the way, Jim and his family realize that they've finally found a place to call home, and both he and his team achieve their own kind of American dream. Directed by Niki Caro. Released Feb. 20, 2015. Stars Kevin Costner (Jim White), Maria Bello (Cheryl), Morgan Saylor (Julie), Elsie Fisher (Jamie), Vincent Martella (Brandon), Daniel Moncada (Eddie), Martha Higareda (Lupe), Vanessa Martinez (Maria Marisol), Carlos Pratts (Thomas). 129 min. Inspired by a 1987 true story. Filmed in California's San Joaquin Valley in wide-screen format.

McGavin, Darren (1922–2006) Actor; appeared in *No Deposit, No Return* (Duke) and *Hot Lead and Cold Feet* (Mayor Ragsdale); on TV in *Disneyland '59*, *Small and Frye* (Nick Small), *Boomerang, Dog of Many Talents* (Barney), *The High Flying Spy* (John Jay Forrest), and *Donovan's Kid* (Timothy Donovan); and on The Disney Channel in *Perfect Harmony* (Mr. Hobbs).

McGill, Jennifer Actress; appeared on the *Mickey Mouse Club* on The Disney Channel, beginning in 1989.

McGinnis, George (1929–2017) Imagineer; hired at WED Enterprises in 1966 after Walt Disney saw a demonstration of his model of a high-speed transportation system. For 30 years, he served as an industrial and show designer for Disney park attractions and ride systems, including the Progress City model, Adventure Thru Inner Space, the Walt Disney World Monorail System, Space Mountain, Horizons, and Indiana Jones Adventure. He also designed the robots Maximillian and V.I.N.Cent

for *The Black Hole* and SMRT-1 for EPCOT Center.

McGoohan, Patrick (1928–2009) Actor; appeared in *The Three Lives of Thomasina* (Andrew MacDhui), *Baby* (Dr. Eric Kiviat), and on TV in the title role of *The Scarecrow of Romney Marsh*. He later went on to fame on *The Secret Agent* and *The Prisoner* TV series. He voiced Billy Bones in *Treasure Planet*.

McGreevey, Michael Actor; appeared in *The Computer Wore Tennis Shoes*; *The Strongest Man in the World*; *Now You See Him, Now You Don't* (Richard Schuyler); *Snowball Express* (Wally Perkins); and *The Shaggy D.A.* (Sheldon), and on TV in *For the Love of Willadean*; *Texas John Slaughter*; *Sammy, the Way-out Seal*; *The Wacky Zoo of Morgan City*; and *Michael O'Hara the Fourth*.

McGregor, Ewan Actor; appeared in the title roles in *Christopher Robin* and *Obi-Wan Kenobi*. He voiced the title character in *Valiant*, Obi-Wan Kenobi in *Star Wars: The Force Awakens* and *The Rise of Skywalker*, and Lumière in *Beauty and the Beast* (2017).

McGuire, Dorothy (1916–2001) Actress; appeared in *Swiss Family Robinson* (mother), *Old Yeller* (Katie Coates), and *Summer Magic* (Margaret Carey). On TV she narrated part of *The Best Dog-goned Dog in the World*.

Machiavelli Suspicious pet cat in *Luca*.

McIntire, John (1907–1991) Actor; appeared in *The Light in the Forest* (John Elder) and *Herbie Rides Again* (Mr. Judson), and on TV in *Bayou Boy*, *Gallegher Goes West*, and *The Mystery of Edward Sims*. He voiced Rufus in *The Rescuers* and Badger in *The Fox and the Hound*.

McKennon, Dallas (1919–2009) Perennial voice actor for Disney projects for records, movies, and the parks. He appeared in *Son of Flubber* (First Juror), *The Misadventures of Merlin Jones* (Detective Hutchins), *The Cat from Outer Space* (Farmer), and *Hot Lead and Cold Feet* (Saloon Man), and lent his voice to such characters as the Fisherman Bear in *Bedknobs and Broomsticks*, Toughy and Professor in *Lady and the Tramp*, Owl in *Sleeping Beauty*, and several animated characters in *Mary Poppins*. He voiced the narrator for Mine Train Through Nature's Wonderland, Zeke in Country Bear Jamboree, the prospector on Big Thunder Mountain Railroad, and Ben Franklin in The American Adventure at EPCOT.

Mackie, Anthony Actor; appeared in *Real Steel* (Finn), *The Fifth Estate* (Sam Colson), and as Sam Wilson/The Falcon/Captain America in the Marvel Studios films and streaming series.

McKim, Sam (1924–2004) Imagineer; McKim started at Disney in 1955 as a conceptual artist for Disneyland. He sketched attractions for Main Street, U.S.A. and Frontierland, as well as worked on Disney films such as *Nikki, Wild Dog of the North*, and *The Gnome-Mobile*. He contributed sketches for such Disneyland favorites as Great Moments with Mr. Lincoln, It's a Small World, the Haunted Mansion, the Monorail, and the Carousel of Progress. For Walt Disney World, he worked on The Hall of Presidents, Universe of Energy, and Disney-MGM Studios. He retired in 1987. McKim had been charged with creating many of the Disneyland maps that were sold to guests through the years, and they were so highly regarded that he was persuaded to come out of retirement to design a map for Disneyland Paris. He was named a Disney Legend in 1996.

McKinley High School Chicago school where Walt attended his freshman year and served as an artist on the school magazine, *The Voice*. When World War I intervened, Walt left to serve in the Red Cross, and he never returned to school. Some art classes at night school prepared him for his future profession, and an inquiring mind and retentive memory contributed to his lifelong quest for knowledge.

MacLachlan, Kyle Actor; appeared on TV in *In Justice* (David Swayne), *Desperate Housewives* (Orson Hodge), and *Marvel's Agents of S.H.I.E.L.D.* (Calvin Zabo). He voiced Dad in *Inside Out* and a bus driver in *Gravity Falls*.

McLeish, John (1916–1968) Narrator of the Goofy "how to" cartoons, as well as *Dumbo*; also known as John Ployardt. According to the story, McLeish was a very serious and dignified person. When the staff realized that his educated voice would be perfect for narrating the Goofy cartoons, they asked him to do it, but did not bother to explain that the erudite narration was really tongue in cheek, and that Goofy would be doing almost exactly the opposite of what was being described. He also provided the voice for the prosecuting attorney in *The Adventures of Ichabod and Mr. Toad* and a barker in *Pinocchio*. McLeish worked at Disney in animation and story 1939–1941.

McLiam, John (1918–1994) Actor; appeared on TV in *The Secret of the Pond*, *Shadow of Fear*, and *The Mystery of Edward Sims*.

MacManus, Dan (1900–1990) Effects animator; began at the Disney Studio in 1935, and remained until his retirement in 1973, working on most of the Disney features during that period.

McMorehouse Customer in *Pigs Is Pigs* (1954).

MacMurray, Fred (1908–1991) Actor; appeared in *The Shaggy Dog* (Wilson Daniels), *The Absent-Minded Professor* and *Son of Flubber* (Prof. Ned Brainard), *Bon Voyage* (Harry Willard), *Follow Me, Boys!* (Lemuel Siddons), *The Happiest Millionaire* (Anthony J. Drexel Biddle), and *Charley and the Angel* (Charley Appleby). His TV appearances included *Gala Day at Disneyland*, *Holiday Time at Disneyland*, *Herbie Day at Disneyland*, *Walt Disney—A Golden Anniversary Salute*, and *NBC Salutes the 25th Anniversary of the Wonderful World of Disney*. He was the first to be named a Disney Legend, in 1987.

McNair, Terra Actress; appeared on the *Mickey Mouse Club* on The Disney Channel 1991–1993.

McNamara, William Actor; appeared in *Stella* (Pat Robbins) and *Aspen Extreme* (Todd Pounds).

MacNeille, Tress Voice actress; she became the official voice of Chip (the chipmunk) in the late 1980s and of Daisy Duck in the late 1990s. Other roles have included Lady Bane in *Disney's Adventures of the Gummi Bears*, Gadget in *Chip 'n' Dale Rescue Rangers*, Cornelia in *101 Dalmatians: The Series*, Mrs. Bolt in *Lloyd in Space*, Fang in *Dave the Barbarian*, Anastasia in the Cinderella video sequels, Bassy in *Fish Hooks*, and Merryweather in *Sofia the First*.

McPherson, Stephen He served as president of Touchstone Television from 2001 until he was named president of ABC Primetime Entertainment in 2004. He left Disney in 2010.

Macy, William H. Actor; appeared in *A Civil Action* (James Gordon), *Wild Hogs* (Dudley

Frank), and *Mr. Holland's Opus* (Vice Principal Wolters). He had an uncredited role as a railroad magnate in *Tall Tale* and voiced Satomi in *The Wind Rises*.

Macy's Thanksgiving Day Parade An oversize Mickey Mouse balloon first made its appearance in the 1934 Macy's Thanksgiving Day Parade in New York City, and Disney characters and icons have been popular subjects ever since. Also in 1934, a small book was published as a promotion, *Mickey Mouse and Minnie at Macy's*, followed the next year by *Mickey and Minnie's March to Macy's*.

Mad Buddies (film) Comedy film produced in South Africa by Keynote Films. Boetie de Wett was a champion rugby player until Beast shot off his toe in a freak accident and ruined his life. Five years later, when the sworn enemies run into each other at the wedding of Minister Mda's daughter, another altercation leads them on an adventure they never dreamed they would share with each other, a trip on foot from Durban to Johannesburg, as they become unwitting subjects of a new reality TV show. Directed by Gray Hofmeyr. Released Jun. 22, 2012, in South Africa. Stars Leon Schuster (Boetie de Wett), Kenneth Nkosi (Beast), Tanit Phoenix (Kelsey), Alfred Ntombela (Mr. Mda). 96 min. Distributed worldwide by Touchstone Pictures.

Mad Doctor, The (film) Mickey Mouse cartoon released Jan. 21, 1933. Directed by Dave Hand. Pluto is captured by an evil scientist and taken to an old castle. Mickey attempts to rescue him, in spite of bats, skeletons, and a giant skeletal spider. Just as a buzz saw is about to cut Mickey in two, he awakens to a mosquito biting him; it was all a nightmare and Pluto is safe. The British film censor at the time thought the film too frightening for some audiences.

Mad Dog, The (film) Mickey Mouse cartoon released Mar. 5, 1932. Directed by Burt Gillett. Pluto learns a lesson in submission when he refuses to be bathed by Mickey. In the resulting tug-of-war, Pluto swallows the soap, is taken by everyone to be a mad dog, and is forced to flee the dog-catcher, Pete. Now humbled, Pluto meekly allows himself to be bathed.

Mad Hatter Character who puts on a tea party in *Alice in Wonderland*; voiced by Ed Wynn. Being somewhat befuddled, he has left the price tag on his hat; the 10/6 is the price, 10 shillings sixpence.

Mad Hatter Shop Fantasyland shop in Disneyland beginning in 1956. Also on Main Street, U.S.A., where it opened in the Penny Arcade building Jun. 1958 and then moved to the Opera House in 1963. Guests can buy hats and have their names embroidered on them. In Tomorrowland, there was a Mad Hatter kiosk named The Mod Hatter; it was renamed Hatmosphere Apr. 1987–2006 and was then succeeded by Autopia Winner's Circle. Also a Fantasyland shop in the Magic Kingdom at Walt Disney World (open 1971–1994, succeeded by Fantasy Faire) and in Tokyo Disneyland (opened Apr. 15, 1983, replaced by Harmony Faire in 2011).

Mad Hatter's Tea Cups Fantasyland attraction in Disneyland Paris; opened Apr. 12, 1992. Guests board colorful teacups for a spin around a giant teapot. Also opened in Hong Kong Disneyland Sep. 12, 2005, as Mad Hatter Tea Cups. SEE ALSO MAD TEA PARTY (DISNEYLAND AND WALT DISNEY WORLD) AND ALICE'S TEA PARTY (TOKYO DISNEYLAND).

Mad Hermit of Chimney Butte, The (TV) Show aired Apr. 1, 1960. Directed by Jack Hannah. Donald Duck is the hermit; what led him to that fate is revealed through a series of cartoons.

Mad Love (film) Two teenagers, Matt Leland and Casey Roberts, are involved in a passionate affair, during which Matt abandons everything he has worked for to follow Casey on a cross-country trip. Eventually, he discovers an irrational and dangerous side to Casey, and must find a way to release her from his life. Directed by Antonia Bird. A Touchstone film. Released May 26, 1995. Stars Chris O'Donnell (Matt), Drew Barrymore (Casey), Joan Allen (Margaret), T. J. Lowther (Adam), Amy Sakasitz (Joanna), Jude Ciccolella (Richard), Kevin Dunn (Clifford). 96 min.

Mad Tea Party Fantasyland attraction in Disneyland; opened Jul. 17, 1955. It closed 1982–1983 and moved to a new location as part of the New Fantasyland. Based on the sequence from the 1951 film *Alice in Wonderland*. Guests spin, and can control their speed, in giant, colorful teacups in a ride best not taken just after having eaten. Also a Fantasyland attraction in the Magic Kingdom at Walt Disney World; opened Oct. 1, 1971. SEE ALSO MAD HATTER'S TEA CUPS (DISNEYLAND PARIS AND HONG KONG DISNEYLAND) AND ALICE'S TEA PARTY (TOKYO DISNEYLAND).

Madam Mim Mad witch who battles Merlin in *The Sword in the Stone*; voiced by Martha Wentworth.

Madame Adelaide Bonfamille Aristocratic owner of the cats in *The Aristocats*; voiced by Hermione Baddeley.

Madame Leota "Head spiritualist" in the crystal ball in the Haunted Mansion; played by Imagineer Leota Toombs and voiced by Eleanor Audley.

Madame Medusa Evil pawnshop owner in *The Rescuers*; voiced by Geraldine Page.

Madcap Adventures of Mr. Toad, The (film) Theatrical reissue of the *Wind in the Willows* segment from *The Adventures of Ichabod and Mr. Toad* on Dec. 25, 1975. 32 min.

Mlle. Antoinette's Parfumerie Perfume shop in New Orleans Square at Disneyland; opened in 1966. Closed Oct. 1, 1995, to become Jewel of Orleans. Mlle. Antoinette's Parfumerie returned May 28, 2011.

Mlle. Lafayette's Parfumerie Liberty Square shop in the Magic Kingdom at Walt Disney World; opened Oct. 1, 1971, offering custom-blend perfumes that guests could order again on later visits. Closed in 1986, to be incorporated into Olde World Antiques.

Mademoiselle Upanova Ostrich dancer in "The Dance of the Hours" segment of *Fantasia*.

Madigan Men (TV) Half-hour series on ABC; aired Oct. 6–Dec. 12, 2000. Benjamin, Seamus, and Luke Madigan are 3 generations of Irishmen trying to make their way in the dating world of New York City. Together, they might be able to teach each other something about what it means to be a man in the 21st century. Stars Gabriel Byrne (Benjamin), Roy Dotrice (Seamus), John C. Hensley (Luke), Grant Shaud (Alex Rossetti), Sabrina Lloyd (Wendy Lipton). From Touchstone Television in association with Artists Television Group.

Madoff (TV) Four-hour miniseries on ABC; aired Feb. 3–4, 2016. Former investment adviser Bernie Madoff's Ponzi scheme is considered to be the largest financial scam in U.S. history, but the impact was global, leading to the loss of billions of dollars for clients worldwide. Madoff, 3-time NASDAQ chair, dominated headlines in 2008–2009, and the miniseries explores the complicated family dynamics within the Madoff clan and exposes the motivations and mechanics behind the monumental fraud. Directed by Raymond De Felitta. Stars Richard Dreyfuss (Bernie Madoff), Blythe Danner (Ruth), Tom Lipinski (Mark Madoff), Danny Defarrari (Andrew Madoff), Peter Scolari (Peter Madoff), Erin Cummings (Eleanor Squillari). Based on the book *The Madoff Chronicles* by Brian Ross, and additional reporting on the topic. From Lincoln Square Productions, in association with ABC Entertainment.

Madonna Actress/singer; appeared as Breathless Mahoney in *Dick Tracy* and as Eva Perón in *Evita*.

Maelstrom Boat ride attraction in Norway at EPCOT; open Jul. 5, 1988–Oct. 5, 2014. Guests boarded a Viking ship for a short ride through scenes from Norwegian history while being menaced by trolls. A unique part of the journey was a backward plummet down some rapids, narrowly missing a waterfall, before plunging into the North Sea. The journey ended at a theater where guests watched a short film about Norwegian scenery and culture. Replaced by Frozen Ever After.

Maestro Mickey's Souvenir and sundry shop in Disney's All-Star Music Resort at Walt Disney World; opened Nov. 22, 1994.

Mafia! SEE JANE AUSTEN'S MAFIA!

Magellan's Fine-dining restaurant inside the Fortress at Explorers' Landing in Tokyo DisneySea; opened Sep. 4, 2001, serving international cuisine. The exquisite décor celebrates the exploration of the sea and the discovery of astronomy in the 16th century.

Maggie Headstrong show cow in *Home on the Range*; voiced by Roseanne Barr.

Magic and Music (TV) Show aired Mar. 19, 1958. Directed by Hamilton S. Luske. The Magic Mirror emcees a show on the magic of music, using footage of visual fantasies from *Melody Time* and *Fantasia*. Stars Hans Conried.

Magic Camp (film) As a young boy, Andy Duckerman was a camp legend at the Institute of Magic, a mountain retreat that hosts aspiring young magicians each summer. Now, at 35, he's struggling to make ends meet as a professional illusionist. But when the institute invites him to return as a counselor, Andy finds himself in charge of the greenest and most awkward wannabe magicians—and having to deal with his former partner (now fellow counselor), Kristina Darkwood. As

Andy prepares the ragtag artists to compete in the annual Top Hat magic contest, they in turn inspire him to nurture their unique talents and rediscover his own love of magic. Digitally released Aug. 14, 2020, on Disney+. Directed by Mark Waters. Stars Adam Devine (Andy), Gillian Jacobs (Darkwood), Nathaniel McIntyre (Theo), Jeffrey Tambor (Roy Preston), Cole Sand (Nathan), Isabella Crovetti (Ruth). 100 min. During auditions, the young actors were tasked to perform real magic tricks. Magician Justin Willman served as a coach during production. Filmed in wide-screen format in Southern California. From Walt Disney Studios.

Magic Carpet, The Adventureland Bazaar shop in the Magic Kingdom at Walt Disney World; opened Oct. 1, 1971, selling brass and inlaid pearl gifts. Closed Apr. 1987, to be incorporated into Elephant Tales.

Magic Carpet 'Round the World (film) Tour of landmarks and scenery around the world in Circle-Vision 360, prepared for the Monsanto-sponsored attraction at Walt Disney World; ran Mar. 16, 1974–Mar. 14, 1975. Later shown in Tokyo Disneyland Apr. 15, 1983–May 16, 1986 (including new footage of Europe and the U.S.).

Magic Carpets of Aladdin, The Adventureland attraction in the Magic Kingdom at Walt Disney World; opened May 23, 2001. Guests take flight aboard a magic carpet, spinning around a giant genie bottle while dodging expectorating golden camels. Front-row passengers press a lever that controls the height of the carpet, while those in the back row press a magic scarab to tip the carpet forward or backward. SEE ALSO FLYING CARPETS OVER AGRABAH (WALT DISNEY STUDIOS PARK) AND JASMINE'S FLYING CARPETS (TOKYO DISNEYSEA).

Magic Eye Theater Indoor 3-D movie venue; opened at the Journey Into Imagination pavilion in EPCOT Oct. 1, 1982, and in Tomorrowland at Disneyland in 1986, taking the place of the Space Stage. Films have included *Magic Journeys, Captain EO,* and *Honey, I Shrunk the Audience.* At EPCOT, the theater debuted the Disney & Pixar Short Film Festival Dec. 23, 2015, while at Disneyland sneak previews for upcoming films were shown beginning in 2014. The Disneyland theater was renamed Tomorrowland Theater Mar. 2015.

Magic Gourd, The SEE SECRET OF THE MAGIC GOURD, THE.

Magic Happens Parade at Disneyland; premiered Feb. 28, 2020, with floats depicting magical moments from *Frozen 2, Moana, Coco, Sleeping Beauty, The Sword in the Stone,* and other Disney stories. Features 2 original songs co-composed by Todrick Hall. Also the name of a corporate Disney brand campaign launched Feb. 2001.

Magic Highway U.S.A. (TV) Show aired May 14, 1958. Directed by Ward Kimball. The importance of America's highways is depicted, from the earliest days to the highways (and vehicles) of the future. Narrated by Marvin Miller. Segments of the show were later presented in a scene of Horizons in EPCOT Center and at Autopia in Disneyland.

Magic in the Magic Kingdom SEE DISNEY'S MAGIC IN THE MAGIC KINGDOM.

Magic in the Mountains (film) An independent film about how Squaw Valley (now known as Olympic Valley, California) became the site of the 1960 Winter Olympics and, with the help of Walt Disney, forever changed how the games were presented. Premiered Nov. 14, 2021, at the St. Louis International Film Festival. 79 min. This film is not associated with The Walt Disney Company.

Magic is Endless, The 2016–2017 Disney Parks campaign focused on making memories at both popular and lesser-known park experiences.

Magic Jersey, The SEE JERSEY, THE.

Magic Journeys (film) A 3-D impressionistic view of a child's imagination, created for Journey Into Imagination in EPCOT Center; opened Oct. 1, 1982. Shot in 70 mm using an innovative camera rig. Directed by Murray Lerner. 18 min. Moved to the Fantasyland Theater in the Magic Kingdom at Walt Disney World, Dec. 15, 1987–Dec. 1, 1993. Presented by Kodak. Also played in Disneyland 1984–1986, and in Tokyo Disneyland 1985–1987. The title theme song was written by Richard M. and Robert B. Sherman.

Magic Key Reservation-based park admission program for the Disneyland Resort replacing the Annual Pass program. The passes first went on sale Aug. 25, 2021, with 4 admission types based on guest preferences—the Dream Key, Believe Key, Enchant Key, and Imagine Key.

Magic Kingdom Club Created in 1958 under the

direction of Milt Albright. Companies and organizations primarily near Disneyland, and later Walt Disney World, could offer memberships to employees, which gave them discounts at the parks. The club published *Disney News*, later *The Disney Magazine*, before that magazine went national. The club ceased operation in 2000, to be superseded by The Disney Club, a consumer-affinity membership program, which ended in Dec. 2003. Also the name of the club-level floors of the Shanghai Disneyland Hotel; opened Jun. 16, 2016.

Magic Kingdom on Ice SEE WORLD ON ICE.

Magic Kingdom Park The first theme park at Walt Disney World; opened with a preview period beginning Oct. 1, 1971, with a grand dedication weekend held Oct. 23–25. Guests enter a world of "yesterday, tomorrow, and fantasy," originally with 6 themed lands: Main Street, U.S.A.; Adventureland; Frontierland; Liberty Square; Fantasyland; and Tomorrowland. Mickey's Birthdayland was added in 1988; it later became Mickey's Starland, then Mickey's Toontown Fair, and, finally, Storybook Circus. The name has also been used generally to refer to Disneyland ever since its opening in 1955 as the Magic Kingdom. The name takes on added importance in Florida, because it refers to only a part of Walt Disney World.

Magic Kingdom Resort Area Group of resort hotels at Walt Disney World surrounding the Seven Seas Lagoon and Bay Lake; includes the Contemporary Resort, Polynesian Village Resort, Wilderness Lodge, Grand Floridian Resort & Spa, and Fort Wilderness Resort & Campground.

Magic Lamp Theater, The Attraction, sponsored by Fuji, in Tokyo DisneySea; opened Sep. 4, 2001. A magic show featuring Shaban, the "greatest magician in the world." But the real star of the show is the hilarious and unpredictable Genie from Disney's *Aladdin*, brought to life with the latest in 3-D magic.

Magic Mirror Character voiced by Moroni Olsen in *Snow White and the Seven Dwarfs*; later used by Walt as a co-host on his TV show with Hans Conried usually playing the part.

Magic Music Days Program begun at Walt Disney World in 1985, followed by Disneyland in Sep. 1987, which gave school choral, band, and other music groups the unique opportunity to perform at a Disney park as well as learn about musical perfor-

mance from Disney professionals. Prior to Magic Music Days, the program for guest performing groups had various names, including Disneyland Music Festival Program beginning in the late 1970s. Walt Disney World had its Disney Band Festival Program beginning in 1972. A Guest Band Program, where Disney first solicited nationwide for high school bands to perform, was begun for *America on Parade* in 1975. Magic Music Days was renamed Disney Performing Arts in 2011, which became part of Disney Imagination Campus in 2021.

Magic of Disney, The SEE ORLANDO INTERNATIONAL AIRPORT (SHOP).

Magic of Disney Animation, The Tour attraction and gallery at Disney-MGM Studios (later Disney's Hollywood Studios); open May 1, 1989–Jul. 12, 2015. It featured the film *Back to Neverland* [sic], followed by a walking tour through a working animation studio where the processes were explained on video monitors. The tour ended with a film in the Disney Classics Theater. Elements of the tour changed over the years, especially after the animation studio closed in 2003, including the addition of the Drawn to Animation show, Animation Academy, and other interactive areas. It became Star Wars Launch Bay Dec. 1, 2015.

Magic of Disneyland, The (film) A 16-mm film; released in Oct. 1969. A guided tour of Disneyland, exploring many of the attractions, including Pirates of the Caribbean, the PeopleMover, Walt Disney's Enchanted Tiki Room, the Carousel of Progress, and It's a Small World.

Magic of Disney's Animal Kingdom (TV) An 8-episode docuseries on Disney+; digitally released Sep. 25, 2020. Josh Gad narrates a behind-the-scenes look at the animal care and conservation efforts that take place across Walt Disney World. Filmed at Disney's Animal Kingdom, Animal Kingdom Lodge, and The Seas with Nemo & Friends in EPCOT. From National Geographic.

Magic of Healthy Living, Disney Company-wide consumer initiative partnering with parents to inspire children to live healthier lifestyles; launched in 2010. In 2006, Disney became the first major media company to establish nutrition guidelines, which associate its brands and characters with more nutritionally balanced foods. In 2007, the parks and resorts phased out all added trans fats in foods. In 2011, the TRYit campaign was launched, encouraging kids to try new foods and exercise. In 2012, a "Mickey Check" was introduced on food products and menus, making it easier to identify nutritious choices in stores, online, and in theme parks.

Magic of the Rails (film) Circle-Vision 360 film prepared for the Swiss Federal Railways and shown at an exposition in Lucerne, Switzerland, and later in Germany. The film focuses on a train tour around Europe. Released in 1965.

Magic of Walt Disney World, The (film) Documentary featurette released Dec. 20, 1972, with *Snowball Express*. Directed by Tom Leetch. A look at the pleasures of the Disney resort, in the year after its opening. 29 min. An expanded version aired on TV Mar. 31, 1974.

Magic Shop SEE MAIN STREET MAGIC SHOP.

Magic, The Memories, and You!, The Special nighttime spectacular in the Magic Kingdom at Walt Disney World in which projections transform Cinderella Castle into a kaleidoscope of Disney characters and stories. Premiered Jan. 19, 2011. A 2nd version was introduced in Disneyland beginning Jan. 27, 2011, featuring projections on the It's a Small World attraction. Special versions celebrating holidays and new Disney films have been done. The Magic Kingdom show was replaced by *Celebrate the Magic* Nov. 2012, followed by *Once Upon a Time* beginning Nov. 4, 2016.

Magic Whistle, The (film) Educational film about a small boy whose wonderful imagination gives magic to an old broken whistle, produced by Dave Bell; released in 1972.

Magica de Spell Evil sorceress, created by Carl Barks for the comic books, who debuted in *Uncle Scrooge* No. 36 in 1961 and later appeared in *Duck-Tales*.

Magical Disney Christmas, A (TV) Show aired Dec. 5, 1981. A grouping of holiday cartoons and segments.

Magical Express, Disney's Special service began May 5, 2005, whereby guests staying at Walt Disney World hotels received complimentary round-trip transfers and baggage transportation from Orlando International Airport. Disney representatives claimed the previously tagged baggage, which was delivered directly to the guests' rooms. On departure, guests could complete airport check-in and receive boarding passes at the resort. The service welcomed its 10 millionth guest, Lori Ogurkis, from Hazelton, Pennsylvania, on May 3, 2010. The service ended Jan. 2022.

Magical Gatherings 2003–2004 Walt Disney World campaign and group travel program, introducing new planning tools and services for parties of 8 or more guests.

Magical Market Fantasyland sandwich counter in Tokyo Disneyland; opened Apr. 27, 2018, taking the place of Fantasy Gifts.

Magical Walt Disney World Christmas, A (TV) SEE WALT DISNEY WORLD VERY MERRY CHRISTMAS PARADE.

Magical World of Barbie, The Stage show at the America Gardens Theatre in Epcot; ran Nov. 17, 1993–May 11, 1995. Barbie, Ken, and their friends take a musical adventure around the world.

Magical World of Disney, The (TV) Series on NBC; aired Oct. 9, 1988–Sep. 9, 1990. The show then moved to The Disney Channel, where it began Sep. 23, 1990. Michael Eisner hosted.

Magical World of Disney, The (TV) Show aired Oct. 9, 1988. The first show of the series with this title, introducing the season's programs. Michael Eisner talks about the return to NBC 27 years after *Walt Disney's Wonderful World of Color* began on the network. Stars Betty White, Dawnn Lewis, Harry Anderson, Countess Vaughn, Johnny Cash, Charles Fleischer, Kate Jackson. Directed by Max Fader.

MagicBand A technological innovation as part of MyMagic+, introduced at Walt Disney World in 2013, which guests wear on their wrist. It serves as their all-in-one room key, theme park ticket, access to FastPass+ selections, PhotoPass card, and optional payment account. By Jan. 30, 2015, more than 10 million MagicBands had been used to enter Walt Disney World parks. A next-generation MagicBand+ debuted Jul. 27, 2022, enabling guests to experience the parks in a new way, with smart features including color-changing LED lights, haptic vibrations, and gesture recognition. A version of MagicBand+ debuted at Disneyland Resort Oct. 26, 2022.

Magician Mickey (film) Mickey Mouse cartoon released Feb. 6, 1937. Directed by Dave Hand. Donald continually heckles Mickey's magic act, but Mickey bests him at every turn. Donald shoots off a magic pistol that causes all the stage props to fall down on them at the end of the act.

Magnificent Rebel, The (TV) Two-part show; aired Nov. 18 and 25, 1962. Directed by Georg Tressler. The life of musical genius and nonconformist composer Ludwig van Beethoven, from his arrival in Vienna in 1792 through the writing of the famous Ninth Symphony, who along the way fought those who opposed something new in music. Rejected by the family of the only woman he truly loved, he devoted himself to music, rising to the height of his career only to be shattered by the loss of hearing. After a period of seclusion, he began anew with a new flood of inspiration that carried him on to even greater acclaim. Stars Karl Boehm, Giulia Rubini, Peter Arens. Boehm was an accomplished pianist and was able to perform his own musical sequences in the film. Filmed in the sumptuous concert halls of Vienna. This was Walt Disney's first filmmaking venture in Austria, and he chose actual locales—many of them unchanged over the centuries—where Beethoven lived, found inspiration, and worked. Released theatrically abroad.

Magno Hall, Deedee Actress; appeared on the *Mickey Mouse Club* on The Disney Channel beginning in 1989 and was a member of the pop band The Party. She later appeared in *Sister Act 2: Back in the Habit* (classroom kid), on TV in the *Walt Disney World Very Merry Christmas Parade* and *Blossom*, and made a guest appearance in *Grey's Anatomy* (Katrina Scott). She voiced Snuggs in *Doc McStuffins* and Miss Deer Teacher in *Kiff*. Beginning in 2002, she played Jasmine in *Aladdin: A Musical Spectacular* in the Hyperion Theater at Disney California Adventure.

Magnolia Golf Course, Disney's Located across from the Polynesian Village Resort at Walt Disney World. Formerly served by The Disney Inn. Designed by Joe Lee, it is the longest of the Walt Disney World golf courses. Provided the setting each year for the final round of the Walt Disney World/Oldsmobile Golf Classic. Substantial changes were made to the course in 2015, followed by more improvements in 2022.

Magnolia Room SEE TROPHY ROOM.

Magnolia Tree Terrace When Quaker Oats ceased their sponsorship of Aunt Jemima's Kitchen in Frontierland in 1970, Disneyland changed the name to Magnolia Tree Terrace. The following year, the name was changed again to River Belle Terrace, when Oscar Mayer became the sponsor.

Maharajah Jungle Trek Attraction in Asia at Disney's Animal Kingdom; opened Mar. 1, 1999. Guests enter the Anandapur Royal Forest and explore an animal sanctuary (a former hunting palace, as the story goes), where Komodo dragons, bats, Eld's deer, and tigers roam.

Maid Marian Robin Hood's love interest, a vixen; voiced by Monica Evans.

Mail Dog (film) Pluto cartoon released Nov. 14, 1947. Directed by Charles Nichols. When a pilot has to turn back due to a severe storm, he drops the mail at a remote outpost where it can be delivered by dogsled. The falling mail pouch lands on Pluto, and he sets out to deliver it. He is continually delayed by a rabbit along the way, but, in the end, the rabbit helps Pluto deliver the mail pouch.

Mail Pilot, The (film) Mickey Mouse cartoon released May 13, 1933. Directed by Dave Hand. In Mickey's devotion to getting the mail through in his battered little plane, he must fight the elements and Pete, engaging in an aerial battle in which he captures Pete.

Mail to the Chief (TV) Two-hour movie on *The Wonderful World of Disney*; first aired Apr. 2, 2000. A struggling president begins an anonymous e-mail correspondence with a middle schooler, Kenny, who is having trouble in his civics class, but provides savvy political advice to the chief executive. Directed by Eric Champnella. Stars Randy Quaid (President Osgood), Bill Switzer (Kenny Witowski), Holland Taylor (Katherine Horner), Dave Nichols (Senator Harris), Ashley Gorrell (Heather). Filmed on location in Toronto.

Main Street Arcade SEE PENNY ARCADE.

Main Street Athletic Club Sports clothing shop on Main Street, U.S.A. in the Magic Kingdom at Walt Disney World; opened Jun. 28, 1995, taking the place of the Penny Arcade, House of Magic, and Main Street Book Store. It became the Hall of Champions in 2006 and Main Street Fashion and Apparel, ca. 2011.

Main Street Bake Shop Bakery on Main Street, U.S.A. in the Magic Kingdom at Walt Disney World; opened in 1971. A tearoom that offered pastries, cinnamon rolls, and cookies. Formerly hosted by Nestlé Toll House. The name was changed to Main Street Bakery Aug. 2001. Expanded into the former Crystal Arts shop in spring 2007 and began serving Starbucks products Jun. 2013. There is also a Main Street Bakery in Hong Kong Disneyland, originally known as the Market House Bakery.

Main Street Bakery SEE PRECEDING ENTRY.

Main Street Book Store Shop on Main Street, U.S.A. in the Magic Kingdom at Walt Disney World; opened in 1989, presented by Western Publishing Co. Closed Mar. 19, 1995, to become the Main Street Athletic Club.

Main Street Cinema Attraction in Disneyland; opened Jul. 17, 1955. Inside, 6 screens continuously play a showcase of early cartoons, including *Steamboat Willie*. Also opened in the Magic Kingdom at Walt Disney World Oct. 1, 1971, becoming a shop Jun. 1998; in World Bazaar in Tokyo Disneyland Apr. 15, 1983, replaced in 2002 by an expansion of the Grand Emporium; and in Hong Kong Disneyland Sep. 12, 2005, as a shop (Midtown Jewelry, presented by Chow Sang Sang). In Jul. 2016, the Hong Kong Disneyland shop became a character-greeting spot, Main Street Cinema: My Journeys with Duffy – Presented by Fujifilm.

Main Street Confectionery Shop on Main Street, U.S.A. in the Magic Kingdom at Walt Disney World; opened Oct. 1, 1971. Many varieties of candy are sold, some of it prepared fresh in the shop. Expanded into the former Camera Center Nov. 26, 1998. With another refurbishment, the Confectionery expanded again, this time transforming the Chapeau into the Kernel Kitchen, and reopened Sep. 29, 2021; hosted by Mars Wrigley. SEE ALSO CANDY PALACE (DISNEYLAND), WORLD BAZAAR CONFECTIONERY (TOKYO DISNEYLAND), BOARDWALK CANDY PALACE (DISNEYLAND PARIS), MAIN STREET SWEETS (HONG KONG DISNEYLAND), AND SWEETHEARTS CONFECTIONERY (SHANGHAI DISNEYLAND).

Main Street Corner Café Victorian table-service restaurant serving American and Chinese comfort food, along with afternoon tea, in Hong Kong Disneyland; opened Sep. 12, 2005. Presented by Coca-Cola.

Main Street Electrical Parade Began as a summertime parade in Disneyland Jun. 17, 1972, ending its original run Nov. 25, 1996. Featuring half a million tiny lights on floats themed primarily to Disney movies, it became one of the most beloved traditions at the park. The lights were dimmed, and the illuminated parade snaked from a gate next to It's a Small World past the Matterhorn, skirted the Central Plaza, and then continued down Main Street, U.S.A. to conclude in Town Square. The parade's synthesizer music was based on a piece titled "Baroque Hoedown," with themes from Disney songs worked in. The parade did not run 1975–1976 because of *America on Parade* for the Bicentennial, but it returned in 1977 with a whole new edition. A 108-ft.-long "To Honor America" finale unit was added in 1979. During 1980, there was a special unit reproducing Sleeping Beauty Castle in honor of the park's 25th anniversary. The parade did not run during the summers of 1983 or 1984. A duplicate version of the *Main Street Electrical Parade* ran in the Magic Kingdom at Walt Disney World Jun. 11, 1977–Sep. 14, 1991, when it was replaced by *SpectroMagic*. The Walt Disney World parade was moved to Disneyland Paris in Apr. 1992. Another version of the parade, called the *Tokyo Disneyland Electrical Parade*, ran Mar. 9, 1985–Jun. 21, 1995, replaced by *Disney's Fantillusion*. The Disneyland parade floats were completely refurbished for a limited run in the Magic Kingdom at Walt Disney World, May 28, 1999–Apr. 1, 2001. They returned to Disneyland Resort Jul. 4, 2001, this time as *Disney's Electrical Parade* in Disney's California Adventure. The *Tokyo Disneyland Electrical Parade Dreamlights* returned Jun. 1, 2001. The Disneyland Paris parade ended Mar. 23, 2003. Beginning Jun. 12, 2009, a new Tinker Bell float was created to lead the parade in Disney California Adventure, along with other updates. The parade concluded Aug. 23, 2009, to henceforth operate seasonally until Apr. 18, 2010. It then returned to the Magic Kingdom at Walt Disney World, Jun. 5, 2010–Oct. 9, 2016. Limited engagements resumed in Disneyland Jan. 20–Aug. 20, 2017, and Aug. 2–Sep. 30, 2019. For the parade's 50th anniversary, it returned to Disneyland Apr. 22–Sep. 1, 2022, this time replacing the "To Honor America" finale with 7 floats representing more than a dozen Disney and Pixar stories.

Main Street Gallery Art and collectibles shop in the Magic Kingdom at Walt Disney World; opened Sep. 6, 1997, in the former Sun Bank. Closed Apr. 17, 2004, to become the Main Street Chamber of Commerce, a package pickup spot. SEE ALSO ART OF DISNEY, THE.

Main Street Hat Market World Bazaar shop in Tokyo Disneyland; open Apr. 15–Jul. 1983, and succeeded by Disney & Co.

Main Street Jewelers Shop in Hong Kong Disneyland; opened in 2016, succeeding Crystal Arts.

Main Street Magic Shop Opened at Disneyland in 1957, taking the place of the original Wonderland Music Store. Magic tricks, disguises, and makeup are available, and the shop hosts will often offer a demonstration. At one time, before his career took off, actor Steve Martin worked in this shop. A similar Magic Shop opened in World Bazaar at Tokyo Disneyland Apr. 15, 1983. SEE ALSO MERLIN'S MAGIC SHOP AND HOUSE OF MAGIC (WALT DISNEY WORLD).

Main Street Motors Shop/display, originally sponsored by Esso, on Main Street, U.S.A. in Disneyland Paris; opened Apr. 12, 1992.

Main Street Photo Supply Co. SEE CAMERA CENTER.

Main Street Stationers Card and stationery shop in the Magic Kingdom at Walt Disney World; opened in 1985, taking the place of the Tobacconist. Presented by Gibson Greeting Cards, Inc. Closed in 1989 to become the Main Street Book Store.

Main Street Sweets Candy shop in Hong Kong Disneyland; opened Sep. 12, 2005.

Main Street, U.S.A. One of the original lands of Disneyland; opened Jul. 17, 1955, with its interconnected shops making it one of the world's first "shopping malls." Walt's plan was to present a nostalgic American hometown at the turn of the century, with period shops, restaurants, and a penny arcade. Set in the timeframe of roughly 1890–1910, it represents the optimistic crossroads of an idealized era, when small towns were turning fast into cities, gas lamps were giving way to the electric lamp, and the horse-drawn car coexisted with the automobile. Various towns from Walt Disney's past have claimed that he got the idea from them, but the most likely candidate for this honor would be Marceline, Missouri, the town in which Walt spent the formative years of his childhood. Designer Harper Goff based the design of several buildings on ones from his hometown of Fort Collins, Colorado. Using forced perspective, the Disney designers gave a fantasy look to the street,

making a small place seem large. The ground floors were built at about 7/8th size, with the succeeding floors proportionately smaller. This fudging on the size gives the whole area a fantasy, not-quite-real feeling, which increases one's appreciation of it. Main Street, U.S.A. runs from the railroad station and Town Square for 2 blocks to the Central Plaza. Looking straight down Main Street, U.S.A., guests can catch a glimpse of the castle leading to Fantasyland. On the windows above the ground floor, Disney started a tradition of honoring the people who were instrumental in the design, construction, and operation of the park. One of the few exceptions is a window honoring Walt's father, Elias, above the Emporium. To accommodate a larger planned capacity for the Magic Kingdom at Walt Disney World, the designers found inspiration in the lofty Victorian architecture of popular resort towns and upscale neighborhoods of the eastern U.S., including Saratoga Springs, New York. Disneyland Paris and Hong Kong Disneyland also have their own versions of Main Street, but Tokyo Disneyland opted instead for World Bazaar, which looks very similar except for a roof covering the entire area. At Shanghai Disneyland, guests enter the park through Mickey Avenue.

Majestic Theater SEE LEGENDS OF HOLLYWOOD.

Major Effects (TV) Show aired Dec. 16, 1979. Directed by Nicholas Harvey Bennion. Joseph Bottoms as Major Effects explains some of the secrets of special effects in the movies. Mike Jittlov appears with 2 stop-motion animated films he has made. With Hans Conried.

Makahiki – The Bounty of the Islands Casual buffet dining at Aulani, A Disney Resort & Spa; opened Aug. 29, 2011, serving international cuisine. Glass designs and murals depict the story of the Makahiki season, a traditional celebration of the harvest.

Make It or Break It (TV) Series on ABC Family; debuted Jun. 22, 2009, and ended May 14, 2012. Teen gymnasts from the Rocky Mountain Gymnastics Training Center (The Rock) hope to make it to the Olympic Games, while antagonizing the head of the National Gymnastics Committee who chafes at their independence. Stars Chelsea Hobbs (Emily Kmetko), Ayla Kell (Payson Keeler), Josie Loren (Kaylie Cruz), Cassie Scerbo (Lauren Tanner), Candace Cameron Bure (Summer), Zachary

Burr Abel (Carter Anderson). Produced by ABC Family.

Make Me Laugh (TV) Half-hour game show on Comedy Central; aired Jun. 2, 1997–Jun. 2000, with contestants able to win cash prizes if they can resist the impulse to laugh at the stand-up acts of a series of wisecracking comedians. Hosted by Ken Ober.

Make Mine Music (film) Ten shorts are combined in a tuneful compilation. Disney's first postwar-"package" picture, produced because financial problems prevented Walt Disney from finding enough money to create a full animated feature. By tying a group of shorts together, he was able to get the production into theaters sooner. Premiered in New York City Apr. 20, 1946, followed by a general release Aug. 15. Production supervisor was Joe Grant; directors were Jack Kinney, Clyde Geronimi, Hamilton Luske, Robert Cormack, and Joshua Meador. 75 min. Theater program titles are animated to announce the title of the subject that follows. The segments are: (1) *The Martins and the Coys*, which deals with 2 feuding families who shoot and kill each other off except for Henry Coy and Grace Martin, who fall in love, but continue fighting after marriage (sung by The King's Men); (2) *Blue Bayou*—originally created for *Fantasia* to accompany "Clair de Lune" and sung by the Ken Darby Chorus—which follows a majestic crane that lands in a bayou, then rises again to join another in the moonlit sky; (3) *All the Cats Join In*, with Benny Goodman and His Orchestra playing while animated teenagers go out and dance at a malt shop; (4) *Without You*, in which Andy Russell sings a "Ballad in Blue" as a petal falls, changing to a tear; light reveals a love letter containing lyrics of the song, and rain washes paintings onto a window illustrating the lyrics; (5) *Casey at the Bat*, with Jerry Colonna reciting the sad story of Mighty Casey, a baseball player who loses his touch and can no longer hit the ball; (6) *Two Silhouettes*, with Dinah Shore singing as 2 figures dance in ballet, the boy meeting, losing, and finding the girl theme (live-action dancing was performed by Tania Riabouchinska and David Lichine); (7) *Peter and the Wolf*, told by Sterling Holloway, with Peter going with a duck, cat, and bird to catch a wolf; (8) *After You've Gone*, with the Benny Goodman Quartet and a musical cartoon fantasy of personalized instruments; (9) *Johnny Fedora and Alice Bluebonnet*, with singing by the Andrews Sisters, illustrating the romance between boy and girl hats; and (10) *The Whale Who Wanted to Sing at the Met*, in which Nelson Eddy tells the story and sings the songs about a whale found singing grand opera with a beautiful voice; a dream sequence shows the whale at the Met as a sensation, but the return to reality shows him being harpooned because it is believed he swallowed an opera singer. The film was never theatrically reissued. Many of the individual segments would later be used on TV or released theatrically as shorts. Released on video in 2000 minus *The Martins and the Coys*.

Maker Studios SEE DISNEY DIGITAL NETWORK.

Making Friends (film) Educational film in the Songs for Us series; released in Sep. 1989. 8 min. Songs teach the value of friendship and other relationship skills.

Making of Arachnophobia, The SEE THRILLS, CHILLS & SPIDERS: THE MAKING OF ARACHNOPHOBIA.

Making of Me, The (film) Film that answers the question "Where did I come from?" in Wonders of Life at EPCOT; opened Oct. 30, 1989, and closed Jan. 1, 2007. 15 min. Starred Martin Short. Directed by Glen Gordon Caron.

Making of the NHL's Mighty Ducks, The (TV) Special on KCAL, Los Angeles; airing Oct. 10, 1993.

Making the Wish: Disney's Newest Cruise Ship (TV) Documentary special on the *Disney Wish*; first aired Dec. 24, 2022, on National Geographic. At a shipyard on Germany's North Sea, a marvel of modern engineering is taking shape; hundreds of construction workers, engineers, architects, designers, storytellers, and crew are transforming 144,000 tons of steel into perhaps the most enchanting vessel ever to take to sea. Directed by Chad Cohen. 90 min.

Mako (1933–2006) Actor; appeared in *The Ugly Dachshund* (Kenji), *The Island at the Top of the World* (Oomiak), *Taking Care of Business* (Sakamoto), and *Pearl Harbor* (Admiral Yamamoto), and made a TV guest appearance in *Monk* (Master Zi).

Malden, Karl (1912–2009) Actor; appeared in *Pollyanna* (Rev. Paul Ford) and *The Adventures of Bullwhip Griffin* (Judge Higgins).

Maleficent Evil fairy who transforms into a dragon in *Sleeping Beauty*; voiced by Eleanor Audley.

Maleficent (film) The untold story of Disney's iconic villain from the 1959 classic *Sleeping Beauty* and the elements of her betrayal that ultimately turn her pure heart to stone. Driven by revenge and a fierce desire to protect the moors over which she presides, Maleficent cruelly places an irrevocable curse upon the human king's newborn infant, Aurora. As the child grows, Aurora is caught in the middle of the seething conflict between the forest kingdom she has grown to love and the human kingdom that holds her legacy. Maleficent realizes that Aurora may hold the key to peace and is forced to take drastic actions that will change both worlds forever. Directed by Robert Stromberg. Released May 30, 2014, also in 3-D and 3-D IMAX, after May 28 releases in Belgium, France, the U.K., and Italy. Stars Angelina Jolie (Maleficent), Elle Fanning (Aurora), Lesley Manville (Flittle), Imelda Staunton (Knotgrass), Sharlto Copley (King Stefan), Brenton Thwaites (Prince Philip), Juno Temple (Thistlewit), Sam Riley (Diaval). 98 min. Approx. 40 sets were constructed for filming, from a 12-sq.-ft. room to the 5,000-sq.-ft. Great Hall. To create the more than 2,000 handmade costumes, costume designer Anna B. Sheppard researched French and Italian paintings, sketches, and sculptures from the 15th century to the Renaissance period; her work earned an Academy Award nomination. Filmed in wide-screen format, primarily at Pinewood Studios in England. In *Sleeping Beauty* (1959), the prince's name is spelled Phillip.

Maleficent: Mistress of Evil (film) Aurora's impending marriage to Prince Philip is cause for celebration in the kingdom of Ulstead and the neighboring Moors. But when an unexpected encounter introduces a powerful new alliance, Maleficent and Aurora are pulled apart to opposing sides in a Great War, testing their loyalties and causing them to question whether they can truly be family. Directed by Joachim Rønning. Released Oct. 18, 2019, also in 2-D IMAX and 3-D, after Oct. 16–17 international releases. 119 min. Stars Angelina Jolie (Maleficent), Elle Fanning (Aurora), Chiwetel Ejiofor (Conall), Sam Riley (Diaval), Harris Dickinson (Prince Philip), Ed Skrein (Borra), Imelda Staunton (Knotgrass), Juno Temple (Thistlewit), Lesley Manville (Flittle), Michelle Pfeiffer (Queen Ingrith). A sequel to the 2014 film. Sets for Castle Ulstead (1 of 3 castles in the film) were spread out over 5 different soundstages due to its massive size. Received an Academy Award nomination for Makeup and Hairstyling (Paul Gooch, Arjen Tuiten, and David White). Filmed in wide-screen format at England's Pinewood Studios and in and around the U.K., including Syon House Lake, Burnham Beeches, and Windsor Great Park.

Malet, Arthur (1927–2013) Actor; appeared in *Mary Poppins* (Mr. Dawes, Jr.), *Lt. Robin Crusoe, U.S.N.* (Umbrella man), and *Dick Tracy* (diner patron), and on TV in *The Further Adventures of Gallegher* (Sir James), *The Nutt House* (Raymond), and *The Fanelli Boys* (Arthur). He voiced King Eidilleg in *The Black Cauldron*.

Maliboomer Paradise Pier attraction in Disney California Adventure; open Feb. 8, 2001–Sep. 6, 2010. Seated guests catapulted 180 feet straight up steel-girder towers in just 2 sec., then came down bungee-style in a series of thrilling ups and downs.

Malibu Country (TV) Series on ABC; aired Nov. 2, 2012–Mar. 22, 2013. With a divorce pending, a Nashville woman, who put her career as a country music star on hold to raise a family, packs up her sharp-tongued Southern mother and her 2 kids and moves to Malibu, where all view the Malibu lifestyle as a chance to begin anew. Stars Reba (Reba), Lily Tomlin (Lillie Mae), Sara Rue (Kim), Justin Prentice (Cash). From ABC Studios.

Malibu-Ritos Paradise Pier burrito counter in Disney's California Adventure; debuted Feb. 8, 2001, though it was rarely open. Removed in 2006 to make way for Toy Story Midway Mania!

Malone, Charles A. ("Chuck"), Jr. (1921–1988) Chief pilot at Walt Disney Productions; as chief pilot of Sky Roamers Air Travel in Burbank, he flew Walt Disney in chartered airplanes beginning in 1962. Walt soon hired Chuck as his personal pilot and to establish the company's aviation department. Chuck was joined by his son, Mark Malone, in 1979 to pilot the company plane and retired in 1982. SEE ALSO AIRCRAFT, WALT DISNEY'S.

Malotte, Albert Hay (1895–1964) Composer; at Disney 1935–1938, he wrote the scores for such award-winning cartoons as *Ferdinand the Bull* and *The Ugly Duckling*. He is probably best known for writing "The Lord's Prayer."

Maltin, Leonard Film historian/commentator; wrote *The Disney Films* (first edition Crown, 1973), the first filmography to annotate the Disney output of shorts and features. He has appeared in documentaries, including *Walt: The Man Behind the Myth* and *The Age of Believing: The Disney*

Live Action Classics; as a speaker at Disney conventions; and has hosted the popular series of Walt Disney Treasures DVDs.

Mama Melrose's Ristorante Italiano Table-service pizza and pasta restaurant in Grand Avenue (previously Streets of America) in Disney's Hollywood Studios; opened Sep. 26, 1991. Checked curtains and walls crowded with mementos create a cozy dining space. Formerly The Studio Pizzeria.

Mama Odie The 197-year-old magic queen of the bayou in *The Princess and the Frog*; voiced by Jenifer Lewis.

Mamma Biscotti's Bakery Mediterranean Harbor coffee counter at Tokyo DisneySea; opened Sep. 4, 2001.

Mammoth Records In Jul. 1997, Disney announced the purchase of Mammoth Records, a top independent label in the music industry, based in Carrboro, North Carolina. President/founder Jay Faires entered into a long-term employment contract. Became part of Hollywood Records in the mid-2000s.

Man and the Moon (TV) Show aired Dec. 28, 1955. Directed by Ward Kimball. Rerun in 1959 as *Tomorrow the Moon*. The show looks at how scientists are preparing for a flight to the moon, beginning with a live-action segment and then animation as the rocket ship takes off to film the back side of the moon. Dr. Wernher von Braun worked as a technical adviser and appeared in the film.

Man from Bitter Creek, The (TV) Episode 5 of *Texas John Slaughter*.

Man Hat 'n' Beach Paradise Pier shop in Disney's California Adventure; opened Feb. 8, 2001. Closed in 2012, to become Boardwalk Bazaar.

Man in Flight (TV) Show aired Mar. 6, 1957. Directed by Hamilton S. Luske. The history of flight, told in a humorous animated sequence using parts of *Victory Through Air Power* with new narration. Walt Disney also takes viewers to Disneyland by helicopter and shows some of the flying attractions. A rerun in 1961 incorporated a preview of *The Absent-Minded Professor*.

Man in Space (TV) Show aired Mar. 9, 1955. Directed by Ward Kimball. Space scientists Willy

Ley, Heinz Haber, and Wernher von Braun help explain the challenges of space exploration, including a discussion of some of the perceived problems of weightlessness. The history of rockets is shown in animation, beginning with 13th-century Chinese experiments. Von Braun unveils a 4-stage, passenger-carrying rocket ship that could break free of the Earth's gravitational pull, leading to an animated depiction of man's first trip into space. An abridged version (33 min.) was released theatrically as a featurette on Jul. 18, 1956. This was the first of several Disney shows on space exploration. President Eisenhower requested a print of this film to show the brass at the Pentagon, and it was evidently instrumental in pushing them into the space program. The doughnut-shaped space station model has been on long-term loan to the National Air and Space Museum in Washington, D.C. Received an Academy Award nomination for Best Short Subject (Documentary). The educational film *All About Weightlessness* was excerpted from this TV show.

Man Is His Own Worst Enemy (TV) Show aired Oct. 21, 1962. Directed by Hamilton S. Luske. Ludwig Von Drake tells how people cause most problems, and without them, there wouldn't be problems. He uses cartoons such as *Reason and Emotion*, *Chicken Little*, and *How to Have an Accident in the Home* to prove his point. Some later reruns aired as *Ducking Disaster with Donald and His Friends*.

Man, Monsters and Mysteries (film) International-release featurette, first on Dec. 6, 1974, in South Africa. 26 min. A film about Nessie, the Loch Ness monster, revealing the existence of ancient legends previously known only to the Scottish Highlanders. In addition to reproduced photos, there are interviews with citizens, scientists, and even a hypothetical one with Nessie. Directed by Les Clark.

Man of the House (film) A resourceful 11-year-old boy, Ben, tries to scare off his mother's suitor, Jack, a beleaguered federal prosecutor unprepared for step-fatherhood, by forcing him to join the YMCA's Indian Guides program and participate in Native American–inspired rituals and games. The boy's scheme seems to be working until a vengeful indicted mob boss enters the picture and decides to have Jack eliminated. Ultimately, the guides take on the mob and use their superior wilderness warfare tactics to capture Jack's pursuers. In the process,

Jack and the boy forge a bond of friendship, respect, and love. Released Mar. 3, 1995. Directed by James Orr. 98 min. Stars Chevy Chase (Jack), Jonathan Taylor Thomas (Ben), Farrah Fawcett (Sandy), George Wendt (Chet), Nicholas Garrett (Monroe). Farrah Fawcett's former real-life husband, Ryan O'Neal, has a brief uncredited cameo at the beginning of the movie.

Man on Wheels (TV) Show aired Mar. 26, 1967. Directed by Hamilton S. Luske. The effect of the invention of the wheel on society, featuring 2 featurettes: *Donald and the Wheel* and *Freewayphobia*.

Man or Muppet Song from *The Muppets*; written by Bret McKenzie. Academy Award winner.

Man Up! (TV) Comedy series on ABC; aired Oct. 18–Dec. 6, 2011. Three modern men try to get in touch with their inner tough guys and redefine what it means to be a "real man." Will and his friends, Craig and Kenny, start to wonder: what does it really mean to be a guy anymore. Stars Mather Zickel (Will Keen), Christopher Moynihan (Craig Griffith), Dan Fogler (Kenny Hayden), Teri Polo (Theresa Hayden Keen), Amanda Detmer (Brenda Hayden), Henry Simmons (Grant Sweet), Jake Johnson (Nathan Keen), Charlotte Labadie (Lucy Keen). From ABC Studios.

Mandalorian, The (TV) *Star Wars* series on Disney+; premiered digitally Nov. 12, 2019. After the fall of the Empire and before the emergence of the First Order, a lone gunfighter emerges in the outer reaches of the galaxy, far from the authority of the New Republic. Stars Pedro Pascal (The Mandalorian), Gina Carano (Cara Dune), Carl Weathers (Greef Carga), Werner Herzog (The Client), Nick Nolte (Kuiil), Emily Swallow (Armorer), Taika Waititi (IG-11), Giancarlo Esposito (Moff Gideon), Omid Abtahi (Dr. Pershing). From Lucasfilm. Winner of 7 Emmy Awards in 2020 and another 7 in 2021. Spin-off series include *The Book of Boba Fett*, *Ahsoka*, and *Rangers of the New Republic*. SEE ALSO GROGU.

Mang, Mary Anne Beginning in convention and tour sales at Disneyland in 1961, she moved into public and community relations, retiring in 1994 after being instrumental in consolidating the company-wide VoluntEars program. She was named a Disney Legend in 2005.

Manhattan Jazz Club Live entertainment venue in Disney's Hotel New York at Disneyland Paris; succeeded the Rainbow Room. It became the Manhattan Restaurant in 1995.

Manhattan Love Story (TV) Half-hour romantic comedy series on ABC; aired Sep. 30–Oct. 21, 2014. Dana and Peter, a couple, navigate the complicated terrain of modern-day relationships. But the audience will hear Dana's and Peter's inner thoughts, highlighting the differences of men and women as this couple traverses the highs and lows of dating. Also featured are dilettante Amy (Peter's wealthy sister-in-law and Dana's college roommate); her husband, David (who is perfectly happy letting his wife run their lives); Chloe (Peter's intelligent and perceptive half sister); and William (the kids' father and authority figure). Stars Analeigh Tipton (Dana), Jake McDorman (Peter), Nicolas Wright (David), Chloe Wepper (Chloe), and Kurt Fuller (William). Filmed in New York City by ABC Studios. The final 7 episodes produced were released on Hulu and WATCH ABC in Dec. 2014.

Manhattan Restaurant Jazz-inspired table-service restaurant in Disney's Hotel New York at Disneyland Paris; opened Sep. 1, 1995, succeeding Manhattan Jazz Club. Reopened with a contemporary look Jun. 21, 2021, when the resort became Disney Hotel New York – The Art of Marvel.

Manheim, Milo Actor; appeared on Disney Channel in the ZOMBIES movies (Zed), *Prom Pact* (Ben), and *Disney QUIZney*, on ABC in *American Housewife* (Pierce), *The Disney Family Singalong*, and *The Wonderful World of Disney: Magical Holiday Celebration*, and on Disney+ in *Doogie Kamealoha, M.D.* (Nico).

Mannequins Nightclub in Pleasure Island at Walt Disney World; open May 1, 1989–Sep. 27, 2008. Featured dressed mannequins around a turntable dance floor with a sophisticated lighting system.

Man's Best Friend (film) Goofy cartoon released Apr. 4, 1952. Directed by Jack Kinney. Goofy acquires a puppy and has difficulties with the neighbors as well as with his attempts to train the puppy to be a watchdog.

Man's Hunting Instinct (TV) Show aired Jan. 2, 1982. Used footage from *The Hunting Instinct*.

Mansson, Gunnar (1927–2007) He led Disney merchandising in Scandinavia for 26 years, beginning in 1963, and was presented a European Disney Legends Award in 1997.

Manticore Legendary warrior-turned-tavern proprietor in *Onward*; voiced by Octavia Spencer. She is part lion, part bat, part scorpion.

Many Adventures of Winnie the Pooh, The (film) In the Hundred Acre Wood, Winnie the Pooh, the roly-poly little bear, and his animal friends (plus Christopher Robin) find themselves in one ticklish situation after another. These adventures included a compilation of *Winnie The Pooh and the Honey Tree*, *Winnie The Pooh and the Blustery Day*, and *Winnie the Pooh and Tigger Too*, with newly animated linking material from the original books by A. A. Milne. Released Mar. 11, 1977. Directed by Wolfgang Reitherman and John Lounsbery. 74 min. Features the voices of Sebastian Cabot (narrator), Sterling Holloway (Winnie the Pooh), Junius Matthews (Rabbit), Barbara Luddy (Kanga), Howard Morris (Gopher), John Fiedler (Piglet), Ralph Wright (Eeyore), Hal Smith (Owl), Clint Howard (Roo), Paul Winchell (Tigger), and Bruce Reitherman, Jon Walmsley, Timothy Turner (Christopher Robin). Music and lyrics were provided by Richard M. and Robert B. Sherman, who wrote 10 songs for the entire series of Pooh films: "Winnie The Pooh," "Up, Down, and Touch the Ground," "Rumbly In My Tumbly," "Little Black Rain Cloud," "Mind Over Matter," "A Rather Blustery Day," "The Wonderful Thing About Tiggers," "The Rain, Rain, Rain Came Down, Down, Down," "Heffalumps and Woozles," and "Hip Hip Pooh-Ray."

Many Adventures of Winnie the Pooh, The Fantasyland attraction in the Magic Kingdom at Walt Disney World; opened Jun. 5, 1999, taking the place of Mr. Toad's Wild Ride. Guests board giant honey pots for their journey through famous spots from the Hundred Acre Wood. They then exit through Hundred Acre Goods (it was Pooh's Thotful Shop [sic] until 2010), featuring Pooh-themed merchandise. Retired Disney Studio composer Buddy Baker, who scored the original Winnie the Pooh featurettes in the 1960s, returned to score the attraction, enlisting several original orchestra members, as well. An attraction with the same name opened in Critter Country at Disneyland (replacing the Country Bear Playhouse, with beehive vehicles rather than honey pots) Apr. 11, 2003. Also a Fantasyland attraction in Hong Kong Disneyland (opened Sep. 12, 2005), and in Shanghai Disneyland (opened Jun.

16, 2016). SEE ALSO POOH'S HUNNY HUNT (TOKYO DISNEYLAND).

MAPO Incorporated in 1965 as the manufacturing area of WED Enterprises. Named after MAry POppins (a film successfully released the year before, which helped fund the facility), it is short for Manufacturing and Production Organization.

Mara, The Quick-service restaurant in Jambo House at Disney's Animal Kingdom Lodge at Walt Disney World; opened Apr. 16, 2001. The aesthetic is inspired by an oasis, with West African artist Baba Wagué Diakité's animals painted on the walls.

Marahute Majestic eagle in *The Rescuers Down Under*.

Marano, Laura Actress/singer; appeared on Disney Channel in *Austin & Ally* (Ally Dawson), *Bad Hair Day* (Monica), and the *Radio Disney Music Awards*, with TV guest appearances in *Liv and Maddie*, *Girl Meets World*, *Jessie*, *Kirby Buckets*, *FlashForward*, *Gary Unmarried*, and the *Disney Parks Frozen Christmas Celebration*. She voiced Rachel in *Randy Cunningham: 9th Grade Ninja* and Veronica in *Pickle and Peanut*.

Marblehead Pelican character in *Lighthouse Keeping* (1946).

Marceline Missouri town where Walt Disney lived during his early childhood. Fearing that crime was becoming rampant in his area of Chicago, Elias Disney decided to move his family to the country. His brother, Robert, owned a farm in Marceline, a small town northeast of Kansas City, so Elias decided to move there, too, and he bought a small farm just north of town. He moved his family there in 1906, and the young Walt thrived. He loved the farmyard animals and the rural atmosphere, both of which would figure prominently in his early cartoons. Walt began school in Marceline and adoringly tagged around after his big brother, Roy. The two brothers found their workload around the farm increased when older brothers, Herb and Ray, tiring of Elias's domination, ran away from home. Walt, punished for drawing on the side of the farmhouse with tar, was given drawing materials by his aunt Margaret, and he began some of his earliest artwork. He even received a small payment for drawing a horse belonging to a neighbor. Eventually, Elias became ill and had to sell the farm. In 1911, he moved the family to Kansas City to begin a new life. In Jul. 1956, Walt and Roy made a visit to Marceline, where they presented *The Great Locomotive Chase* at the Uptown Theatre and attended the dedication of the Walt Disney Municipal Park and swimming pool. Walt made another visit in Oct. 1960, this time to attend the dedication of the new Walt Disney Elementary School, for which he had Disney Studio publicity artist Bob Moore contribute a series of Disney character murals. In 1966, Walt donated the former Midget Autopia attraction from Disneyland to the Walt Disney Municipal Park. The U.S. issued a 6¢ Walt Disney commemorative postage stamp in Marceline on Sep. 11, 1968. In 2001, the Walt Disney Hometown Museum was established on E. Santa Fe Ave., in commemoration of the 100th anniversary of the birth of Walt Disney; its director is Kaye Malins.

Marceline's Confectionery Old-fashioned candy shop in the Downtown Disney District at Disneyland Resort; opened Jan. 12, 2001.

March, Ryan After participating in the Walt Disney World College Program, he joined the company full time in 2000, later serving as editor of the *Eyes & Ears* Cast Member news publication. Moving in 2004 to Disney Vacation Club (DVC), he became editor of *Disney Files Magazine*, the quarterly publication for DVC Members, before expanding his role to serve as creative director of annual DVC Member Cruise voyages and as a producer and host of live fan events and video series.

March Hare The Mad Hatter's zany friend at the unbirthday party in *Alice in Wonderland*; voiced by Jerry Colonna.

March Hare Refreshments Quick-service coffee and ice cream cottage in Fantasyland at Disneyland Paris; opened Apr. 12, 1992.

March of the Penguins 2: The Next Step (film) A Hulu Original film, initially released as a Disneynature feature in France. A young penguin, driven by his instinct, prepares for his first trip across the Antarctic on a journey of survival. Narrated by Morgan Freeman. Directed by Luc Jacquet. Digitally released Mar. 23, 2018, following a Feb. 15, 2017, theatrical release as *L'empereur* in France. From Bonne Pioche Cinéma and Paprika Films, in association with Wild-Touch and The Walt Disney Company France. 76 min. A sequel to Jacquet's 2005 film *March of the Penguins* (*La Marche de l'empereur*), which was released in France by Buena

Vista International and in the U.S. by Warner Independent Pictures.

Marche Aux Fleurs, Sacs et Modes Shop offering handbags and fashion items in New Orleans Square at Disneyland; opened in 1974 and closed Dec. 1994, to become La Mascarade d'Orleans.

Maria & Enzo's Ristorante Italian trattoria in The Landing at Disney Springs at Walt Disney World; opened Jan. 4, 2018. Themed as a 1930s airline terminal, the restaurant serves traditional Sicilian dishes. Next door is Pizza Ponte for counter-service pizza, and downstairs is Enzo's Hideaway, a tunnel bar with a 1920s speakeasy vibe (opened Jan. 12). Managed by Patina Restaurant Group. Replaced the former BET Soundstage.

Mariachi Cobre Traditional mariachi band at Walt Disney World; played in the Magic Kingdom and in the Contemporary Resort 1973–1974, then at EPCOT beginning Oct. 1, 1982. They began as a youth mariachi group in Tucson, Arizona, playing occasionally at Disneyland beginning in 1967.

Marie Small white kitten in *The Aristocats*; voiced by Liz English.

Marin, Cheech Actor; appeared in *Race to Witch Mountain* (Eddie); on TV in *The Golden Palace* (Chuy Castillos), *Mickey's 60th Birthday* (janitor), *Wonderful World of Disney: 40 Years of Television Magic*, the *Walt Disney World Very Merry Christmas Parade* (1992), and *Home Economics* (Roberto); and on The Disney Channel in *Mother Goose Rock 'n' Rhyme* (Carnival Barker). He voiced Banzai in *The Lion King*, Tito in *Oliver & Company*, Ramone in the Cars films, Manuel in *Beverly Hills Chihuahua*, Hare in *Tales from Earthsea*, the Corrections Officer in *Coco*, and Quita Moz in *Elena of Avalor*.

Marin, Jacques (1919–2001) Actor; appeared in *The Island at the Top of the World* (Capt. Brieux) and *Herbie Goes to Monte Carlo* (Inspector Bouchet). He had an uncredited voice role as the French TV news reporter in *Monsters, Inc.*

Marin, Jason Actor; provided the voice of Flounder in *The Little Mermaid*.

Marine Life Interviews (film) Animated short from Pixar; debuted with the *Finding Dory* digital release Oct. 25, 2016, and on Blu-ray Nov.

15. Inhabitants of the Marine Life Institute comment on their favorite blue tang. Directed by Ross Haldane Stevenson. Voices include Ellen DeGeneres (Dory), Ed O'Neill (Hank), Kaitlin Olson (Destiny). 2 min.

Mark Twain and Me (TV) A Disney Channel Premiere Film; first aired Nov. 22, 1991. An 11-year-old girl happens upon her favorite author, Mark Twain, on board the SS *Minnetonka*, sailing from England to America, and they strike up a friendship that will endure until the last days of Twain's life. Directed by Daniel Petrie. Stars Jason Robards (Mark Twain), Amy Stewart (Dorothy Quick), Talia Shire. The show won 2 Emmy Awards for Best Children's Program and Best Makeup in 1992.

Mark Twain Riverboat Frontierland attraction in Disneyland; opened Jul. 17, 1955. The Disneyland Publicity Department originally trumpeted the fact that this was the first paddle wheeler built in the U.S. in 50 years. Its 105-ft.-long hull was built at the Todd Shipyards in San Pedro, California, but the superstructure was constructed in a soundstage at the Disney Studio in Burbank, and then trucked down the Santa Ana Freeway to Disneyland. The *Mark Twain* travels around Tom Sawyer Island, providing views of a Native American village and assorted wildlife, brought to life by the Disney Imagineers. The riverboat weighs 150 tons and is designed to carry 300 passengers. Also a Frontierland riverboat in Disneyland Paris; opened Apr. 12, 1992, where it shares the Rivers of the Far West with the *Molly Brown*. Also in Westernland in Tokyo Disneyland; opened Apr. 15, 1983. The Walt Disney World riverboats were the *Admiral Joe Fowler* (retired in 1980) and the *Richard F. Irvine* (later named the *Liberty Belle*).

Market at Ale & Compass, The Quick-service food and merchandise shop in Disney's Yacht Club Resort at Walt Disney World; opened May 15, 2017, replacing Fittings & Fairings.

Market Clearing Price (film) Educational film; from The People on Market Street series, produced by Terry Kahn; released in Sep. 1977. A butcher shop serves as an example for students to learn economic concepts of inventory and the prevention of shortages and surpluses by pricing.

Market House Store on Main Street, U.S.A. in Disneyland; originally sponsored by Swift. It is patterned after an old-fashioned general store.

Enlarged and remodeled in 2013, with new sponsorship by Starbucks. A Market House opened in the Magic Kingdom at Walt Disney World Oct. 1, 1971; it was replaced in 2007 by a relocated Crystal Arts shop. Also in Hong Kong Disneyland; opened Aug. 24, 2018, offering Starbucks products.

Market House Bakery Counter-service bake shop on Main Street, U.S.A. in Hong Kong Disneyland; opened Sep. 12, 2005, and originally hosted by Maxim's. On Aug. 24, 2018, it became the Market House, a Victorian-themed Starbucks shop, with a separate Main Street Bakery.

Market House Deli Turn-of-the-century New York–style deli on Main Street, U.S.A. in Disneyland Paris; opened Apr. 12, 1992.

Marketplace Co-Op Flexible emporium that serves as a testing space for new Disney retail concepts, shops, and products; opened Jun. 6, 2014, taking the place of Team Mickey Athletic Club in Downtown Disney Marketplace (now the Marketplace at Disney Springs) at Walt Disney World. Originally offered 6 different boutiques: Beautifully Disney, Cherry Tree Lane, D-Tech on Demand, The Trophy Room, Disney Centerpiece, and Zoey & Pickles. An online version of the Marketplace Co-Op was also launched Jun. 6, offering select items from Cherry Tree Lane, Disney Centerpiece, and Beautifully Disney. The shops are refreshed with new concepts from time to time: WonderGround Gallery was added Jul. 2014 (expanding and replacing Beautifully Disney in Mar. 2015); Twenty Eight & Main replaced The Trophy Room Nov. 6, 2015; Disney TAG (Travel–Accessories–Gear) replaced Zoey & Pickles Mar. 11, 2016; The Dress Shop opened in Cherry Tree Lane Apr. 2017 (switching locations with WonderGround Gallery in 2019); and Disney Tails replaced Disney TAG Oct. 12, 2018. In 2022, WonderGround Gallery became Super Hero Showcase (Marvel products), and The Dress Shop on Cherry Tree Lane temporarily became the National Geographic Lifestyle Collection.

Markham, Monte Actor; appeared on TV in *The Ghosts of Buxley Hall* (Col. Joe Buxley), *Honey, I Shrunk the Kids* (William Jennings, 1997), and made guest appearances on *The Golden Girls* (Clayton Hollingsworth).

Marks, Franklyn (1911–1976) Composer; joined Disney in 1955 and, as a staff composer, wrote music for many Disney projects, including *Charlie the Lonesome Cougar*; *Sancho, the Homing Steer*; and *The Legend of the Boy and the Eagle*. He retired in 1976.

Marlin Nemo's overprotective father, a clownfish, in *Finding Nemo* and *Finding Dory*; voiced by Albert Brooks.

Maroon Cartoon Studio Movie studio in *Who Framed Roger Rabbit*.

Marrakesh SEE RESTAURANT EL MARRAKESH.

Marrying Man, The (film) During his bachelor party, Charley Pearl meets and falls for sultry lounge singer Vicki Anderson, girlfriend of mobster Bugsy Siegel. When the gangster catches the new lovebirds together, he forces them to marry at gunpoint, spoiling Charley's wedding plans with his real fiancée, Adele. His life then becomes a series of ups and downs as he and Vicki separate and remarry several times over the next 8 tumultuous years, wondering if they will ever get it right. Released Apr. 5, 1991. Directed by Jerry Rees. A Hollywood Pictures film. 116 min. Stars Kim Basinger (Vicki Anderson), Alec Baldwin (Charley Pearl), Robert Loggia (Lew Homer), Elisabeth Shue (Adele Homer), Paul Reiser (Phil), Fisher Stevens (Sammy), Peter Dobson (Tony), Armand Assante (Bugsy Siegel).

Mars, Kenneth (1935–2011) Actor; appeared in *The Apple Dumpling Gang Rides Again* (Marshal Woolly Bill Hitchcock), and guest starred on Disney Channel in *Hannah Montana* (Gunther). He voiced King Triton in *The Little Mermaid* and other appearances of the character, Vulcan in *DuckTales*, Buzz in *TaleSpin*, and Tuskernini in *Darkwing Duck*.

Mars and Beyond (TV) Show aired Dec. 4, 1957. Directed by Ward Kimball. With the help of technical advisers Dr. Wernher von Braun, Dr. Ernst Stuhlinger, and Dr. E. C. Slipher. Walt presents a humorous look at what man might find on Mars, coupled with predictions for the exploration of the planet with an atomic-powered spaceship. Humankind's place in the universe is explored, from early cavemen's awareness of the stars through 20th-century writers and scientists who see Mars as a new frontier for future plans to solve the overpopulation and depletion of resources on Earth. The film was released theatrically as a 49-min. featurette on Dec. 26, 1957. Portions of the film were reedited into a short, *Cosmic Capers*, in 1979.

Mars Needs Moms (film) Nine-year-old Milo finds out just how much he needs his mom when she's nabbed by Martians who plan to steal her "mom-ness" for their own young. Milo goes on a quest to save his mom, stowing away on a spaceship, navigating an elaborate, multi-level planet, and taking on the alien nation and their leader. With the help of a tech-savvy, underground earthman named Gribble and a rebel Martian girl called Ki, Milo just might find his way back to his mom—in more ways than one. Released in the U.S. Mar. 11, 2011, after an original release in Greece Mar. 3. Directed by Simon Wells. Stars Seth Green (Milo), Joan Cusack (Mom), Mindy Sterling (The Supervisor), Dan Fogler (Gribble), Elisabeth Harnois (Ki), Kevin Cahoon (Wingnut), Tom Everett Scott (Dad). Seth Dusky voiced Milo. 88 min. Released also in 3-D and IMAX versions. Filmed in CinemaScope. Created using performance capture by ImageMovers Digital (that studio's final product before it closed).

Marsden, Jason Actor; appeared in *White Squall* (Shay Jennings), and on TV in *Almost Home* (Gregory Morgan) and *Blossom* (Jimmy). He voiced Max in *A Goofy Movie* and other appearances of the character, Thackery Binx in *Hocus Pocus*, Haku in *Spirited Away*, Cavin in *Disney's Adventures of the Gummi Bears*, Shnookums in *The Shnookums & Meat Funny Cartoon Show*, young Shere Khan in *Jungle Cubs*, Tino in *The Weekenders*, adult Kovu in *The Lion King II: Simba's Pride*, and Kovu in *The Lion Guard*.

Marsh, Jean Actress; appeared in *Return to Oz* (Nurse Wilson/Mombi), on TV in *The Horsemasters* (Andrienne), and on Disney Channel in *Bejewelled* (Barbara Donaldson) and *Danny, the Champion of the World* (Miss Hunter). Much of her fame has come from her starring in the public TV miniseries *Upstairs, Downstairs*.

Marshall, Garry (1934–2016) Creator/producer of many memorable series for ABC; he went on to direct *Beaches*, *Pretty Woman*, *The Princess Diaries*, and *The Princess Diaries 2: Royal Engagement*, as well as *The Lottery* for the Disney-MGM Studios Theme Park. Appeared in *Race to Witch Mountain* (Dr. Donald Harlan) and *Hocus Pocus* (Devil [husband]), and made guest appearances on TV in *Monk* (Warren Beach), *Brothers & Sisters* (Major Jack Wiener), *According to Jim* (doctor), and *Liv and Maddie* (Vic Defazerelli). He voiced Buck Cluck in *Chicken Little* and Soda Jerk in *Penn Zero: Part-Time Hero*. He was named a Disney Legend posthumously in 2017. A documentary about his career, *The Happy Days of Garry Marshall*, from Crew Neck Productions, aired May 12, 2020, on ABC.

Marshall, Sean Child actor; starred as Pete in *Pete's Dragon* and voiced the boy in *The Small One*.

Marsupilami (TV) Animated series on CBS; aired Sep. 18, 1993–Aug. 27, 1994. Based on a popular European comic book character from the mid-1960s. Marsupilami, called Marsu, and his ape pal, Maurice, don't go looking for trouble, but it usually finds them. *Marsupilami* segments debuted earlier on *Raw Toonage*. Voices are Steve Mackall (Marsu), Dan Castellaneta (Stuie), Steve Landesberg (Edúardo), Jim Cummings (Norman, Maurice). In 1999, Disney was successfully sued by the European owners of Marsupilami, claiming that Disney failed to adequately promote and merchandise the character. There were 13 episodes. From Walt Disney Television Animation.

Martha (film) "Song-o-reel" film made by Walt Disney for his Laugh-O-gram Films company in Kansas City in 1923. A filmed rendition of the song "Martha; Just a Plain Old-Fashioned Name" by Joe L. Sanders.

Martin, Bill (1917–2010) He joined Disney in 1953 to aid in the design effort for Disneyland. He was associated with such attractions as Snow White's Adventures, Peter Pan's Flight, Mine Train Through Nature's Wonderland, the Monorail, the Submarine Voyage, Pirates of the Caribbean, and the Haunted Mansion. He was named vice president of design at WED Enterprises in 1971 and assumed responsibility for the master layout of Magic Kingdom at Walt Disney World. He helped design Cinderella Castle, the riverboats, and the Utilidors beneath the Magic Kingdom. Bill retired in 1977 but returned to WED Enterprises as a consultant on EPCOT Center and Tokyo Disneyland. He was named a Disney Legend in 1994.

Martin, Dewey (1923–2018) Actor; appeared in *Savage Sam* (Lester White), and on TV as Daniel Boone.

Martin, Lucille (1922–2012) She began at Disney in the steno pool in 1964 and has the distinction of serving with Disney chief executives over 4 decades. She became one of Walt Disney's two

executive assistants shortly before his death. Later she served as Ron Miller's executive secretary and Michael Eisner's administrative assistant. In 1995, she was named vice president and special assistant to the Board of Directors. She retired in Jan. 2006 and was named a Disney Legend in 2007.

Martin, Pete (1902–1980) He ghostwrote Diane Disney Miller's biography of her father.

Martin, Ross (1920–1981) Actor; appeared on TV in *Donovan's Kid* (Mayor Stokes), *Zorro* (Marcos Estrada), and *Texas John Slaughter* (Cesario Lucero).

Martin, Stacia Disney artist/historian; she joined Disneyland in 1978, finding her niche in the Disneyana Shop and, later, The Disney Gallery. Her projects have included audio art direction for the New Fantasyland at Disneyland, the 1984 restoration of *The Happiest Millionaire*, and books and liner notes accompanying soundtrack releases. She illustrates and writes for company publications and makes regular appearances in documentaries, conventions, and press events.

Martin, Steve Actor; appeared in *Father of the Bride* and *Father of the Bride Part II* (George Banks), *A Simple Twist of Fate* (Michael McCann), and *Bringing Down the House* (Peter Sanderson). In *Father of the Bride*, Martin's character name was coincidentally the same as that of the father in *Mary Poppins*. Martin had as a young man worked in the Magic Shop at Disneyland. Also appeared on TV in *The Dream Is Alive* and was one of the hosts of *Fantasia/2000*. He appeared with Donald Duck in a film for the Disneyland: The First 50 Magical Years attraction and was named a Disney Legend in 2005.

Martin, Strother (1919–1980) Actor; appeared in *The Shaggy Dog* (Thurm), and on TV in *The Boy and the Bronc Buster* (Buckshot).

Martinez, Oscar SEE CARNATION CAFÉ.

Martins and the Coys, The (film) Segment of *Make Mine Music* about 2 feuding families. Sung by the King's Men. Released as a short Jun. 18, 1954.

Marty's General Store Main Street, U.S.A. shop in Hong Kong Disneyland; opened Feb. 1, 2018, taking the place of Town Square Photo. Named after late Walt Disney Imagineering vice chairman Marty Sklar.

Marvel Entertainment On Aug. 31, 2009, Disney announced a reported $4 billion agreement to acquire Marvel Entertainment, Inc., including its library of 5,000 characters such as Iron Man, Spider-Man, X-Men, Captain America, Fantastic Four, and Thor. The acquisition was completed on Dec. 31, 2009, after acceptance by Marvel stockholders. Disney took over Paramount Pictures' entire marketing and distribution deal with Marvel on Jun. 30, 2013, including rights to *Iron Man*, *Iron Man 2*, *Thor*, and *Captain America: The First Avenger*. Disney has released the following theatrical films from Marvel Studios, which—in addition to 5 titles previously produced and distributed outside Disney, plus 3 Spider-Man films financed and distributed by Sony—comprise the Marvel Cinematic Universe:

1. *Marvel's The Avengers* (2012)
2. *Iron Man 3* (2013)
3. *Thor: The Dark World* (2013)
4. *Captain America: The Winter Soldier* (2014)
5. *Guardians of the Galaxy* (2014)
6. *Avengers: Age of Ultron* (2015)
7. *Ant-Man* (2015)
8. *Captain America: Civil War* (2016)
9. *Doctor Strange* (2016)
10. *Guardians of the Galaxy Vol. 2* (2017)
11. *Thor: Ragnarok* (2017)
12. *Black Panther* (2018)
13. *Avengers: Infinity War* (2018)
14. *Ant-Man and the Wasp* (2018)
15. *Captain Marvel* (2019)
16. *Avengers: Endgame* (2019)
17. *Black Widow* (2021)
18. *Shang-Chi and the Legend of the Ten Rings* (2021)
19. *Eternals* (2021)
20. *Doctor Strange in the Multiverse of Madness* (2022)
21. *Thor: Love and Thunder* (2022)
22. *Black Panther: Wakanda Forever* (2022)
23. *Ant-Man and the Wasp: Quantumania* (2023)
24. *Guardians of the Galaxy Vol. 3* (2023)

Marvel Experience, The Marvel Entertainment and Hero Ventures joined forces with a touring themed attraction, which previewed in Phoenix Dec. 19, 2014–Jan. 3, 2015, and then had its world premiere Jan. 9 in Dallas. The Marvel Experience is a first-of-its-kind, hyperreality attraction that covers over 2 acres and encompasses 7 domes, a life-size Quinjet from *The Avengers*, the world's only 360-degree, 3-D stereoscopic full-dome attraction, and a state-of-the-art 4-D motion ride.

Marvel: L'Alliance des Super Héros / Marvel: Super Heroes United Studio Theater stage show in Production Courtyard in Walt Disney Studios Park at Disneyland Paris; premiered Jun. 9, 2018, replacing *CinéMagique*, for the Marvel Summer of Super Heroes event. Thanos finds a way to manipulate the Avengers, turning them against each other, but the Heroes unite to thwart his evil plans. The 20-min. production featured enhanced special effects, including one of the biggest LED screens in Europe and the first indoor use of drones at a Disney park. The show returned in 2019, and the theater later offered character greetings. A new show for the Studio Theater, *Pixar: We Belong Together*, was announced in 2022.

Marvel Mementos Marvel-themed shop in Tomorrowland in Shanghai Disneyland; opened Jun. 16, 2016. Toys, apparel, headwear, and other souvenirs are sold.

Marvel One-Shots A series of short films, beginning with the 4-min. *The Consultant*, in 2011, which premiered first at the San Diego Comic-Con and then on the *Thor* Blu-ray. Other Marvel One-Shots have included *A Funny Thing Happened on the Way to Thor's Hammer* (2011), *Item 47* (2012), *Agent Carter* (2013), and *All Hail the King* (2014). Three shorts previously included on home releases—*Team Thor* (2016), *Team Thor: Part 2* (2017), and *Team Darryl* (2018)—were each classified as a Marvel One-Shot when they were added to Disney+ in 2022.

Marvel Studios Assembled (TV) Series of hour-long, documentary-style specials; digitally premiered on Disney+ Mar. 12, 2021, with *The Making of WandaVision*. Examines the creation of Marvel Studios' new shows and theatrical releases.

Marvel Studios: Assembling a Universe (TV) Hour-long documentary special on ABC; premiered Mar. 18, 2014. Audiences are taken further into the Marvel Cinematic Universe than ever before, with a front-row seat to the inception of Marvel Studios, the record-breaking films, the cultural phenomenon, and further expansion of the universe by Marvel Television. Featured are exclusive interviews, behind-the-scenes footage from all of the Marvel films, and footage from upcoming TV and theatrical releases.

Marvel Studios: Legends (TV) A Disney+ original series; digitally premiered Jan. 8, 2021. Each

6- to 12-min. episode explores heroes, villains, and moments from across the Marvel Cinematic Universe in preparation for the stories still to come. From Marvel Studios.

Marvel Studios What If…? (TV) SEE WHAT IF…?

Marvel Universe Gardens of Imagination attraction in Shanghai Disneyland; opened Jun. 16, 2016. Guests explore the Marvel Cinematic Universe, including the "Marvel Now" gallery of movie props and costumes, Marvel Comics Academy drawing class, and access to Tony Stark's Hall of Armor to try on a virtual Iron Man suit.

Marvels, The (film) A sequel to *Captain Marvel* planned for theatrical release in 2023, also in 3-D, IMAX, and IMAX 3-D. Directed by Nia DaCosta. Stars Brie Larson (Carol Danvers), Iman Vellani (Ms. Marvel), Teyonah Parris (Monica Rambeau). From Marvel Studios.

Marvel's Agent Carter (TV) Hour-long series on ABC; aired Jan. 6, 2015–Mar. 1, 2016. In 1946, Peggy Carter works for the covert SSR (Strategic Scientific Reserve) doing administrative work when she would rather be out in the field, putting her vast skills into play and taking down the bad guys. Women are not recognized as being as smart or as tough as their male counterparts, so Peggy has work to do to prove herself. When an old acquaintance, Howard Stark, finds himself being framed in a plot regarding deadly weapons, he contacts Peggy, the only person he can trust, to track down those responsible, dispose of the weapons, and clear his name. She is assisted by Edwin Jarvis, Stark's butler, who is a creature of habit and sticks to a rigid daily routine, but who has to make some major life changes if he is going to be able to keep up with Peggy. Stars Hayley Atwell (Peggy Carter), James D'Arcy (Edwin Jarvis), Chad Michael Murray (Agent Jack Thompson), Enver Gjokaj (Agent Daniel Sousa), Shea Whigham (Chief Roger Dooley), Dominic Cooper (Howard Stark). From ABC Studios and Marvel Television.

Marvel's Agents of S.H.I.E.L.D. (TV) Hour-long series on ABC; aired Sep. 24, 2013–Aug. 12, 2020. The existence of superheroes and aliens has become public knowledge, with the world trying to come to grips with this new reality. Agent Phil Coulson has his eye on a mysterious group called The Rising Tide. In order to track this unseen, unknown enemy, he has assembled a small, highly select group of agents from the worldwide law enforcement organization known as S.H.I.E.L.D. (Strategic Homeland Intervention, Enforcement, and Logistics Division). Stars Clark Gregg (Phil Coulson), Brett Dalton (Grant Ward), Ming-Na Wen (Melinda May—expert pilot and martial artist), Iain De Caestecker (Leo Fitz—brilliant engineer), Elizabeth Henstridge (Jemma Simmons—genius biochemist), Chloe Bennet (Skye—computer hacker). From ABC Studios and Marvel Television. This was the first TV series tied to the Marvel Cinematic Universe.

Marvel's Behind the Mask (TV) Documentary on Disney+; digitally released Feb. 12, 2021. Explores the inspirations behind Marvel's greatest heroes. Directed by Michael Jacobs. 62 min.

Marvel's Captain America: 75 Heroic Years (TV) Hour-long special on ABC; aired Jan. 19, 2016. The history of the superhero is covered from his creation in 1941 to recent big-screen adventures. Directed by Zak Knutson. Interviewees include Stan Lee, Joe Quesada, Clark Gregg, Chris Evans, Hayley Atwell, and family members of creators Jack Kirby and Joe Simon.

Marvel's Cloak & Dagger (TV) Series on Freeform; aired Jun. 7, 2018–May 30, 2019. Tandy Bowen and Tyrone Johnson, two teenagers from very different backgrounds, find themselves burdened and awakened to newly acquired superpowers, which are mysteriously linked to one another: Tandy can emit light daggers, and Tyrone has the ability to control the power of darkness. The only constant in their lives is danger and each other. They quickly learn they are better together than apart. Stars Olivia Holt (Tandy/Dagger), Aubrey Joseph (Tyrone/Cloak), Emma Lahana (Brigid O'Reilly/Mayhem), Jaime Zevallos (Delgado), Andrea Roth (Melissa Bowen), Gloria Reuben (Adina Johnson), Miles Mussenden (Otis Johnson), Carl Lundstedt (Liam Walsh), J. D. Evermore (James Connors). From Marvel Television and ABC Signature Studios.

Marvel's Daredevil (TV) Series on Netflix; digitally released Apr. 10, 2015–Oct. 19, 2018. Matt Murdock, blinded as a young boy, is imbued with extraordinary senses, and he fights against injustice by day as a lawyer and by night as the superhero Daredevil in modern-day Hell's Kitchen, a part of New York City. Stars Charlie Cox (Daredevil),

Deborah Ann Woll (Karen Page), Elden Henson (Foggy Nelson), Rosario Dawson (Claire Temple), Vincent D'Onofrio (Kingpin), Ayelet Zurer (Vanessa Marianna), Bob Gunton (Leland Owlsley), Toby Leonard Moore (Wesley), Vondie Curtis-Hall (Ben Urich). Filmed in New York City. From Marvel Television and ABC Studios.

Marvel's Hero Project (TV) Unscripted series on Disney+; digitally released Nov. 12, 2019–Mar. 20, 2020. Each week, Marvel celebrates kids from across the U.S. who have made remarkable, positive changes in their communities. From Marvel New Media in partnership with MaggieVision Productions.

Marvel's Hit-Monkey (TV) Animated adult series on Hulu; digitally released Nov. 17, 2021. A Japanese snow monkey, aided by the ghost of an American assassin, goes on a revenge quest through the Tokyo underworld and becomes the famous "killer of killers." Voices include Jason Sudeikis (Bryce), George Takei (Shinji Yokohama), Olivia Munn (Akiko), Ally Maki (Haruka), Nobi Nakanishi (Ito), Fred Tatasciore (Hit-Monkey). From Floyd County Productions and Marvel Television.

Marvel's Inhumans (TV) Series on ABC; aired Sep. 29–Nov. 10, 2017. A version of the first 2 episodes was shown globally in IMAX theaters for a 2-week period beginning Sep. 1. The Royal Family—including Black Bolt, the enigmatic, commanding King of the Inhumans whose voice is so powerful that the slightest whisper can destroy a city—is splintered by a military coup. They barely escape to Hawai'i, where they are greeted with surprising interactions with the lush world and humanity around them. They must find a way to reunite with each other and return to their home before their way of life is destroyed forever. Stars Anson Mount (Black Bolt), Iwan Rheon (Maximus), Serinda Swan (Medusa), Eme Ikwuakor (Gorgon), Isabelle Cornish (Crystal), Ken Leung (Karnak), Sonya Balmores (Aaron), Mike Moh (Triton). From Marvel Television and ABC Studios.

Marvel's Iron Fist (TV) Series on Netflix; digitally released Mar. 17, 2017–Sep. 7, 2018. Danny Rand, a martial arts expert, resurfaces 15 years after being presumed dead. Now, with the power of the Iron Fist, he seeks to reclaim his past and fulfill his destiny. Stars Finn J ones (Danny Rand), Jessica Henwick (Colleen Wing), Jessica Stroup (Joy Meachum), Tom Pelphrey (Ward Meachum),

David Wenham (Harold Meachum). From Marvel Television and ABC Studios.

Marvel's Jessica Jones (TV) Series on Netflix; digitally released Nov. 20. 2015–Jun. 14, 2019. After a tragic ending to her short-lived superhero stint, Jessica Jones is rebuilding her personal life and career as a detective who gets pulled into cases involving people with extraordinary abilities in New York City. Stars Krysten Ritter (Jessica Jones), David Tennant (Kilgrave), Mike Colter (Luke Cage), Rachael Taylor (Patricia Walker). From Marvel Television in association with ABC Studios for Netflix.

Marvel's Luke Cage (TV) Series on Netflix; digitally released Sep. 30, 2016–Jun. 22, 2018. After a sabotaged experiment leaves him with superstrength and unbreakable skin, Luke Cage becomes a fugitive trying to rebuild his life in modern-day Harlem, New York City. But he is soon pulled out of the shadows and must fight a battle for the heart of his city—forcing him to confront a past he had tried to bury. Stars Mike Colter (Luke Cage), Mahershala Ali (Cornell Stokes), Erik LaRay Harvey (Diamondback), Darius Kaleb (Lonnie), Frank Whaley (Rafael Scarfe), Alfre Woodard (Mariah Dillard). From Marvel Television and ABC Studios. It won the 2017 Emmy Award for stunt coordination for a drama series, limited series, or movie.

Marvel's M.O.D.O.K. (TV) Stop-motion-animated adult comedy series on Hulu; digitally released May 21, 2021. The megalomaniacal supervillain M.O.D.O.K. (Mental Organism Designed Only for Killing) has long pursued his dream of one day conquering the world. But after years of failure fighting the Earth's mightiest heroes, M.O.D.O.K. has run his evil organization, A.I.M., into the ground. Ousted as A.I.M.'s leader, while also dealing with his crumbling marriage and family life, he is set to confront his greatest challenge yet. Voices include Patton Oswalt (M.O.D.O.K.), Melissa Fumero (Melissa Tarleton), Aimee Garcia (Jodie Tarleton), Wendi McLendon-Covey (Monica Rappaccini), Ben Schwartz (Lou Tarleton), Beck Bennett (Austin Van Der Sleet), Jon Daly (Iron Man), Sam Richardson (Gary). From Marvel Television, 10k, Multiverse Cowboy, and Stoopid Buddy Stoodios.

Marvel's Moon Girl and Devil Dinosaur (TV) Animated series; premiered on Disney Channel

Feb. 10, 2023. After 13-year-old super-genius Lunella accidentally brings Devil Dinosaur, a 10-ton T. rex, into present-day New York City, the duo works together to protect the city's Lower East Side from danger. Voices include Diamond White (Lunella/Moon Girl), Fred Tatasciore (Devil Dinosaur), Libe Barer (Casey), Alfre Woodard (Mimi), Sasheer Zamata (Adria), Jermaine Fowler (James Jr.), Gary Anthony Williams (Pops), Laurence Fishburne (The Beyonder). Based on the Marvel comic books. From Disney Television Animation.

Marvel's Runaways (TV) Series on Hulu; digitally released Nov. 21, 2017–Dec. 13, 2019. Many teenagers think their parents are evil. What if they actually were? When 6 teenagers in Los Angeles stumble onto a terrible secret, they realize their parents have been lying to them all their lives. While the kids investigate their parents, the adults start to wonder if their kids are hiding secrets of their own. The parents close in on the truth just as the kids uncover a plan with devastating consequences. Now, this unlikely crew must band together to stop their parents before it is too late. Stars Rhenzy Feliz (Alex Wilder), Ariela Barer (Gert Yorkes), Lyrica Okano (Nico Minoru), Gregg Sulkin (Chase Stein), Virginia Gardner (Karolina Dean), Allegra Acosta (Molly Hernandez). From Marvel Television and ABC Signature.

Marvel's 616 (TV) An 8-episode docuseries on Disney+; digitally premiered Nov. 20, 2020. Explores the cultural, societal, and historical impacts of the Marvel Universe and its intersection with the everyday world. From Marvel New Media and Supper Club.

Marvel's Spidey and his Amazing Friends (TV) Animated series on Disney Channel and Disney Junior; premiered Aug. 6, 2021, as the first full-length Marvel series for preschoolers. Young heroes Peter Parker, Gwen Stacy, and Miles Morales team up with Hulk, Ms. Marvel, and Black Panther to defeat foes and learn that teamwork is the best way to save the day. Voices include Benjamin Valic (Peter Parker), Lily Sanfelippo (Gwen Stacy), Jakari Fraser (Miles Morales), Tru Valentino (Black Panther), Sandra Saad (Ms. Marvel). From Disney Junior and Marvel Entertainment, with Atomic Cartoons.

Marvel's The Avengers (film) SEE AVENGERS, MARVEL'S THE.

Marvel's The Defenders (TV) An 8-episode limited series on Netflix; digitally released Aug. 18, 2017. Daredevil, Jessica Jones, Luke Cage, and Iron Fist join forces to take on common enemies as a sinister conspiracy threatens New York City. Stars Finn Jones (Danny Rand), Mike Colter (Luke Cage), Charlie Cox (Daredevil), Jessica Henwick (Colleen Wing), Krysten Ritter (Jessica Jones), Sigourney Weaver (Alexandra). From ABC Studios and Marvel Television.

Marvel's The Punisher (TV) Series on Netflix; digitally released Nov. 17, 2017–Jan. 18, 2019. After exacting revenge on those responsible for the death of his wife and children, Frank Castle uncovers a conspiracy that runs far deeper than New York's criminal underworld. Now known throughout the city as The Punisher, Castle must discover the truth about injustices that affect more than his family alone. Stars Jon Bernthal (Frank Castle/Punisher), Ben Barnes (Billy Russo), Ebon Moss-Bachrach (David Lieberman/Micro), Amber Rose Revah (Dinah Madani), Deborah Ann Woll (Karen Page). A spin-off of *Marvel's Daredevil*. From Marvel Television in association with ABC Studios.

Marx, Louis, and Co. Licensee manufacturing Disney toys 1936–1961, and then again beginning in 1968. Some of the more valuable Marx items are the windup or mechanical tin toys, usually sold under the LineMar trademark. The Disneykins, a series of over 100 tiny Disney character figures, were manufactured by Marx; they have become popular with collectors.

Mary Poppins (film) A magical English nanny, Mary Poppins, arrives at the home of George and Winifred Banks, facing the park at No. 17, Cherry Tree Lane in London, to the delight of their young children, Jane and Michael. The proper English father is too preoccupied with his responsibilities at the bank; the mother, an ardent suffragette, is not really aware that their 2 children, left in the care of one nanny after another, are unhappy and unable to communicate with the parents they truly love. Mary Poppins has come to change all this. She settles into the house and soon has everyone wrapped around her little finger. Mary, along with her friend Bert and a host of chimney sweeps, teaches the children how to have fun, and in so doing makes the Banks household a happier place. By the time she opens her umbrella and flies off on a beautiful spring evening, the family is united together in the park, flying a kite. General release on Aug. 29, 1964. Directed by Robert Stevenson. 139 min. This famed Disney masterwork is indeed "practically perfect" in every way from its cast—Julie Andrews (Mary Poppins), Dick Van Dyke (Bert), David Tomlinson (Mr. Banks), Glynis Johns (Mrs. Banks), Ed Wynn (Uncle Albert), Hermione Baddeley (Ellen), Karen Dotrice (Jane), Matthew Garber (Michael), Elsa Lanchester (Katie Nanna), Arthur Treacher (Constable Jones), Reginald Owen (Admiral Boom), Reta Shaw (Mrs. Brill), Jane Darwell (bird woman)—to its lavish musical score and delightful songs provided by Richard M. and Robert B. Sherman, which includes such favorites as "A Spoonful of Sugar," "Feed the Birds," "Jolly Holiday," "Sister Suffragette," "The Life I Lead," "Step in Time," "Supercalifragilisticexpialidocious," and "Let's Go Fly a Kite." The Academy of Motion Picture Arts and Sciences agreed, too, giving it 13 nominations, from which it won 5 Oscars, for Best Actress (Julie Andrews), Best Song ("Chim Chim Cher-ee"), Best Music Score (the Sherman brothers), Best Film Editing (Cotton Warburton), and Best Special Visual Effects (Peter Ellenshaw, Eustace Lycett, and Hamilton Luske). There was also a special Technical Award to Petro Vlahos, Wadsworth E. Pohl, and Ub Iwerks for the creation and application to use of Color Traveling Matte Composite Cinematography, which helped make possible the combination of live action with animated characters in the film. The special effects work on *Mary Poppins* was the most challenging the Studio had ever undertaken. Everything from the 2-strip sodium process and newly developed Audio-Animatronics figures to piano wire and bungee cords were used to create the magical sequences. The work of the special effects crew, as well as all the production staff, was the culmination of years of Disney innovation. In fact, only Marc Breaux and Dee Dee Wood, the choreographers, and Irwin Kostal, musical arranger, had to be brought in from the outside; Disney staff members could be called upon for all of the other tasks. The entire film was shot on soundstages at the Disney Studio in Burbank. A lavish premiere at Grauman's Chinese Theatre in Hollywood Aug. 27, 1964, began its fabulous box office run that made it Disney's most successful feature to that point. P. L. Travers, author of the popular books on which the film is based, continued writing new adventures for Mary Poppins long after the film, and in the late 1980s worked with a Disney screenwriter on a film sequel that never materialized. Reissued theatrically in 1973 and in 1980; first released on video in 1980. In 2004, a stage adaptation of *Mary Poppins* opened in England. *Saving Mr. Banks* later told a dramatization of the film's inception.

Mary Poppins Stage musical produced by Disney and theatrical producer Cameron Macintosh; opened for previews in England at the Bristol Hippodrome on Sep. 15, 2004, with regular performances beginning Sep. 28. After the Bristol run ended Nov. 6, the show moved to London for an opening at the Prince Edward Theatre on Dec. 15. Laura Michelle Kelly originated the role of Mary Poppins with Gavin Lee as Bert. George Stiles and Anthony Drewe wrote 6 new songs to be included with the original songs by Richard M. and Robert B. Sherman. The book was by Julian Fellowes, with direction by Richard Eyre and Matthew Bourne. The show premiered at the New Amsterdam Theatre on Broadway Nov. 16, 2006, with Ashley Brown starring as Mary and Gavin Lee as Bert, after previews beginning Oct. 14. Among the show's 7 nominations, Bob Crowley won the 2007 Tony Award for Scenic Design of a Musical. The show closed on Broadway Mar. 3, 2013, after 2,619 performances.

Mary Poppins Returns (film) In Depression-era London, this sequel to the 1964 film finds Jane and Michael Banks now grown. Michael and his three children have lost wife and mother, so the enigmatic Mary Poppins returns to the household. With her magical skills, and aided by her friend, Jack, a street lamplighter, Mary helps the family discover the joy and wonder missing in their lives. Directed by Rob Marshall. Released Dec. 19, 2018, also in IMAX. Stars Emily Blunt (Mary Poppins), Lin-Manuel Miranda (Jack), Ben Whishaw (Michael Banks), Meryl Streep (Topsy), Colin Firth (William Weatherall Watkins), Emily Mortimer (Jane Banks), Dick Van Dyke (Mr. Dawes, Jr.), Angela Lansbury (Balloon Lady), Julie Walters (Ellen). Songs by Marc Shaiman and Scott Wittman include "Can You Imagine That?," "A Cover Is Not the Book," "Trip a Little Light Fantastic," and "Nowhere to Go But Up." 130 min. Based on the Mary Poppins stories by P. L. Travers. The Walt Disney Archives provided artist Peter Ellenshaw's original *Mary Poppins* concept artwork for use in the opening and closing credits. To create the animated sequences, more than 70 animators, including several coming out of retirement, worked out of Duncan Studio in Pasadena, California, for 16 months. Filmed in wide-screen format on location in London, and at Pinewood Studios and Shepperton Studios. Received 4 Academy Award nominations, for Costume Design (Sandy Powell), Original Score (Marc Shaiman), Original Song ("The Place Where Lost Things Go"), and Production Design (John Myhre, Gordon Sim).

Mascarades d'Arlequin Shop selling Mardi Gras–themed merchandise in New Orleans Square at Disneyland; opened Mar. 11, 1988, replacing Chocolat Rue Royal. Closed Nov. 28, 1994, to become Le Bat en Rouge. SEE ALSO LA MASCARADE D'ORLEANS.

Mason, James (1909–1984) Actor; appeared in *20,000 Leagues Under the Sea* (Captain Nemo).

Mason, Marsha Actress; appeared in *Stella* (Janice Morrison) and *I Love Trouble* (Senator Gayle Robbins), and on TV in *Army Wives* (Charlotte Meade).

Mastrantonio, Mary Elizabeth Actress; appeared in *The Color of Money* (Carmen) and *Consenting Adults* (Priscilla Parker).

Masur, Richard Actor; appeared in *My Science Project* (Detective Isadore Nulty), *Shoot to Kill* (Norman), *Encino Man* (Mr. Morgan), and *Play It to the Bone* (Artie), and on TV in *Mr. Boogedy* and *Bride of Boogedy* (Carleton Davis), with guest appearances on *Blossom* (Terry Russo) and *Felicity* (Dr. Auerbach).

Match Point (TV) Serial on the *Mickey Mouse Club* on The Disney Channel; aired May 22–Jun. 23, 1989. Archrivals Bart and Jason tangle at the Match Point tennis camp. Stars Brian Krause (Bart), Renee O'Connor (Robin), Anthony Palermo (Jason), Zero Hubbard (Joel), Evan Richards (Runkle), Crystal Justine (Francie).

Matchmaker, The (TV) Episode 3 of *Willie and the Yank*.

Mater Rusty, but loyal, tow truck in the Cars films; voiced by Larry the Cable Guy.

Mater and the Ghostlight (film) Mater, from *Cars*, is haunted by a mysterious blue light that teaches him not to play pranks on the other cars in Radiator Springs. Directed by John Lasseter and Dan Scanlon. Voices include Larry the Cable Guy (Mater), Owen Wilson (Lightning McQueen). 7 min. Created for the DVD release of *Cars*, pre-miered first in Australia Oct. 25, 2006, and in the U.S. Nov. 7. SEE ALSO CARS TOONS.

Mater's Junkyard Jamboree Cars Land attraction in Disney California Adventure; opened Jun. 15, 2012. In a toe-tapping hoedown hosted by Mater, riders spin around in trailers hitched to small tractors (new characters inspired by the movie *Cars*).

Mater's Tall Tales (film) SEE CARS TOONS.

Matheison, Bob (1934–2020) Beginning at Disneyland as a sound coordinator in 1960, he was later selected by Walt Disney to manage Disney's 4 shows at the 1964–1965 New York World's Fair. Involved in the early planning of Walt Disney World, he moved to Florida in 1970 as director of operations. He became vice president of operations in 1972, vice president of the Magic Kingdom and EPCOT Center in 1984, and executive vice president of Walt Disney World in 1987. He retired in 1994 and was named a Disney Legend in 1996.

Matheson, Tim Actor; appeared in *The Apple Dumpling Gang Rides Again* (Private Jeff Reid). At EPCOT, he appeared as Captain Braddock in Body Wars in Wonders of Life. He provided uncredited narration (replacing Deems Taylor) for the 1982 reissue of *Fantasia*.

Matschullat, Robert W. Member of the Disney Board of Directors Dec. 3, 2002–Mar. 8, 2018.

Matterhorn Bobsleds Fantasyland attraction with dual bobsled runs at Disneyland; opened Jun. 14, 1959. The first thrill attraction to be added to Disneyland, based on the Disney film *Third Man on the Mountain*. The Matterhorn at Disneyland is 147 feet high, about 1/100th the size of its Swiss counterpart, but to make it look larger, forced perspective was used. The mountain was built of wood and steel, with a plaster coating over a layer of metal mesh. Trees growing on the side of the mountain get progressively smaller as they get higher. The ride was innovative at the time it opened, because it utilized cylindrical rails and urethane wheels for the first time, which have since become standard for roller coasters. An ice cavern, glowing ice crystals, and the Abominable Snowman were added in 1978, along with a new ride system, featuring tandem bobsleds, greatly increasing capacity. Until it was removed in 1994, the Skyway's cable passed directly through the mountain, providing more leisurely views of the Abominable Snowman. In 2012, new bobsled ride vehicles were introduced, and 3 years later, the show scenes were enhanced, including a more menacing Abominable Snowman. Since 1959, mountain climbers have occasionally scaled the Matterhorn.

Matthews, Junius C. (1890–1978) Actor; provided the voice of Archimedes in *The Sword in the Stone* and Rabbit in *Winnie the Pooh*.

Mattinson, Burny (1935–2023) Animator; starting at the Disney Studio mail room in 1953, he soon moved up to become an inbetweener on *Lady and the Tramp*. He was promoted to assistant animator on *Sleeping Beauty* and *One Hundred and One Dalmatians*. After working under Eric Larson on films from *The Sword in the Stone* to *The Aristocats*, he became a key animator on *Winnie the Pooh and Tigger Too* and worked on storyboards for *The Rescuers*. It was Burny's recollection of a Disneyland Records Christmas LP that led him to suggest, and eventually produce and direct, the featurette *Mickey's Christmas Carol*, a role he continued with *The Great Mouse Detective*. He contributed to development and story on films from *Beauty and the Beast* to *Mulan* and *Winnie the Pooh*, and provided additional story for *How to Hook Up Your Home Theater*. He was named a Disney Legend in 2008. In 2013, he celebrated his 60th anniversary with Disney as the last full-time employee at the Disney Studio who worked there during Walt Disney's time. He passed away Feb. 27, 2023, as Disney's longest-serving employee—approx. 3 months shy of his 70th year of continuous service.

Mattraw, Scotty (1880–1946) Actor; provided the voice of Bashful in *Snow White and the Seven Dwarfs*.

Maude-Roxby, Roddy Actor; provided the voice of Edgar in *The Aristocats*.

Maui Boastful demigod in *Moana*; voiced by Dwayne Johnson.

Maurice Belle's befuddled father in *Beauty and the Beast*; voiced by Rex Everhart. Tom Bosley originated the role on Broadway.

Max Prince Eric's big shaggy dog in *The Little Mermaid*.

Max Goofy's rebellious teenage son in *A Goofy Movie*; voiced by Jason Marsden. In *Goof Troop*, Max is younger and voiced by Dana Hill.

Max Hare Cocky star of *The Tortoise and the Hare* (1935) and its sequel, *Toby Tortoise Returns* (1936). The character was said to have been the inspiration for Bugs Bunny.

Max Keeble's Big Move (film) After a depressing first day at school, much-bullied 7th grader Max Keeble finds out he's moving to a new city in a week. Rather than put up with the normal routine of school, he starts getting revenge on all the people who have picked on him. After creating all kinds of mayhem, Max finds out he's not moving after all, and he must face up to the consequences of his actions. Directed by Tim Hill. Released Oct. 5, 2001. Stars Alex D. Linz (Max Keeble), Larry Miller (Jindraike), Jamie Kennedy (Evil Ice Cream Man), Zena Grey (Megan), Josh Peck (Robe), Nora Dunn (Lily), Robert Carradine (Don), Justin Berfield (Caption Writer). 86 min.

Max Q: Emergency Landing (TV) Two-hour movie from Jerry Bruckheimer Films, Inc., in association with Touchstone Television; aired on ABC Nov. 19, 1998. A routine space shuttle mission is struck by a disastrous explosion, forcing NASA into fast crisis management to rescue the disabled crew floating perilously in space. ("Max Q" refers to the period of maximum aerodynamic stress during launch.) Directed by Michael Shapiro. Stars Bill Campbell (Clay Jarvis), Paget Brewster (Rena Wynter), Ned Vaughn (Scott Hines), Geoffrey Blake (Jonah Randall), Tasha Smith (Karen Daniels).

Maximus The Captain of the Guard's fearless horse in *Tangled*.

Maxwell House Coffee House Restaurant in Town Square at Disneyland; open Dec. 1, 1955–Oct. 8, 1957. It later became Hills Brothers Coffee House.

Maya Grill Elegant table-service restaurant serving Yucatan specialties in Disney's Coronado Springs Resort at Walt Disney World; opened Aug. 1, 1997. Depicts the inside of a Maya temple, with dining areas themed to the elements of fire, sun, and water.

Maybe It's Me (TV) Half-hour series on The WB Network; aired Oct. 5, 2001–Jul. 19, 2002. Molly Stage, 15, like most girls her age, feels that she is surrounded by a family of freaks. Stars Reagan Dale Neis (Molly Stage), Julia Sweeney (Mary Stage), Fred Willard (Jerry Stage), Patrick Levis (Grant Stage), Andrew Walker (Rick Stage), Daniella &

Deanna Canterman (Mindy & Cindy Stage), Vicki Davis (Mia), Ellen Albertini Dow (Grandma), Dabbs Greer (Grandpa), Shaun Sipos (Nick). From Warner Bros. Television and Touchstone Television.

Maybe This Time (TV) Series on ABC; premiered Sep. 16, 1995, after a preview on Sep. 15, and ended Feb. 17, 1996. Comedy ensues when 3 generations of women find themselves working together in their family-owned coffee shop. Stars Marie Osmond (Julia), Betty White (Shirley), Ashley Johnson (Gracie), Craig Ferguson (Logan), Amy Hill (Kay). 18 episodes. From Michael Jacobs Productions and Touchstone Television.

Mayer, Kevin He joined the Disney Strategic Planning group in 1993 and was later named executive vice president of the Buena Vista Internet Group. He left the company in 2000, returning 5 years later as exec. vice president, Corporate Strategy, Business Development, and Technology. In 2015, he was promoted to senior exec. vice president and chief strategy officer, and in 2018 was named chairman of the Direct-to-Consumer and International segment, overseeing the launch of Disney+. He left the company in 2020.

Mayor, The (TV) Half-hour series on ABC; aired Oct. 3–Dec. 12, 2017. The last 4 episodes were released digitally on Hulu, ending Jan. 25, 2018. Young rapper Courtney Rose needs a big break to get his music career on track. Tired of waiting for opportunity to knock, he cooks up the publicity stunt of the century: running for mayor of his California hometown, Fort Grey, to generate buzz for his music. But his master plan goes wildly awry when he is surprisingly elected. He soon discovers that he is good at politics. Stars Brandon Micheal Hall (Courtney Rose), Lea Michele (Valentina Barella), Bernard David Jones (Jermaine Leforge), Marcel Spears (T.K. Clifton), Yvette Nicole Brown (Dina Rose). From ABC Studios.

Mazloum, Thomas He was named president of Disney Signature Experiences in May 2020, expanding his role in May 2022 to additionally oversee the New Experiences Portfolio. He joined Walt Disney Parks and Resorts in 1998 as hotel director for Disney Cruise Line, later leading restaurant operations and events at EPCOT. He left Walt Disney World in 2002, returning in 2017 to lead the resort hotel and transportation businesses.

Mazurki, Mike (1907–1990) Actor; appeared in

Davy Crockett (Bigfoot Mason), *The Adventures of Bullwhip Griffin* (Mountain Ox), and *Dick Tracy* (old man at hotel).

MDs (TV) Hour-long drama series on ABC; aired Sep. 25–Dec. 11, 2002. Two San Francisco superdoctors pay little heed to the rules while saving lives and having fun. Stars William Fichtner (Dr. Bruce Kellerman), John Hannah (Dr. Robert Dalgety), Leslie Stefanson (Shelly Pangborn), Aunjanue Ellis (Dr. Quinn Joyner), Jane Lynch (Nurse "Doctor" Poole), Robert Joy (Frank Coones), Michaela Conlin (Dr. Maggie Yang). From Touchstone Television and Marc Platt Productions.

Meador, Josh (1911–1965) Longtime Disney special effects animator and painter, loaned out to create the animation effects for *Forbidden Planet* (1956). He worked at Disney from 1936 until his death in 1965.

Meadow Trading Post Shop offering camping supplies, sundries, and groceries at Disney's Fort Wilderness Resort & Campground at Walt Disney World; opened in 1973. SEE ALSO SETTLEMENT TRADING POST.

Measuring Up (film) Educational film in the Fitness for Living series; released in Sep. 1982. The film explains the reasons behind fitness measurements.

Mechanical Cow, The (film) Oswald the Lucky Rabbit cartoon; released Oct. 3, 1927. Oswald is kidnapped by a bandit, but his mechanical cow and a young maiden save the day.

Meck, Ed (1898–1973) Veteran entertainment publicist who became the head of publicity for Disneyland in 1955 and helped make the world aware of the new park. He retired in 1972, after helping with the opening of Walt Disney World, and passed away a year later. He was named a Disney Legend posthumously in 1995.

Medicine Man (film) In the Amazon rain forest, a brilliant but eccentric research scientist, Dr. Robert Campbell, is on the verge of a medical breakthrough, a cure for cancer, but he has lost the formula and must now rediscover the elusive serum. The pharmaceutical corporation sponsoring the research has sent another biochemist, Dr. Rae Crane, to investigate the reclusive genius. A hardheaded female scientist is the last thing Campbell wants around his camp, but Crane refuses to leave and is soon caught up in the quest to find the rare antidote. In a race against time and the coming physical destruction of the jungle, the pair climbs to the tops of the tallest trees in what becomes the most exciting adventure of their lives. Released Feb. 7, 1992. Directed by John McTiernan. A Hollywood Pictures film; the first film produced by Cinergi Productions. Filmed in CinemaScope. 104 min. Stars Sean Connery (Dr. Robert Campbell), Lorraine Bracco (Dr. Rae Crane), and 57 representatives from 9 Brazilian tribes. The jungle scenes were shot in Catemaco, Mexico.

Mediterranean Cruise (TV) Show aired Jan. 19, 1964. Directed by Hamilton S. Luske. Ludwig Von Drake explores the countries around the Mediterranean Sea. In Portugal, we see the Corrida festival. Village singers are featured in Italy; then we go to Africa to learn about the tribes of nomads. Finally, Von Drake leads viewers to Sardinia and a fishing fleet, and to Sicily, where he witnesses a festive parade and dance.

Mediterranean Harbor Seaport gateway to Tokyo DisneySea; opened Sep. 4, 2001. The area is comprised of Porto Paradiso, Explorers' Landing, and Palazzo Canals.

Meeko Pocahontas's mischievous raccoon sidekick; voiced by John Kassir.

Meeko's Fantasyland fast-food counter near The Spirit of Pocahontas in Disneyland. Formerly called Yumz, it operated Jun. 23, 1995–Sep. 5, 1997, later renamed Fantasyland Theater Snacks.

Meet Me at Disneyland (TV) A summer series of TV shows on Los Angeles's independent station KTTV airing live from Disneyland weekly Jun. 9–Sep. 8, 1962. The Osmond brothers made one of their early TV appearances on the show.

Meet the Chimps (TV) A Disney+ original series from National Geographic; digitally released Oct. 16, 2020. A real-life drama that tracks the ups and downs of an extraordinary group of chimpanzees that are given a second chance in one of the largest and most unique wildlife sanctuaries in the world—Chimp Haven, a 200-acre refuge in Louisiana home to more than 300 chimps. Narrated by Jane Lynch. Produced in collaboration with Blink Films. 6 episodes.

Meet the Deedles (film) Two surfer-dude brothers from Hawai'i, Phil and Stew Deedle, have to prove to their millionaire father that they have matured, or risk being disinherited. The guys wind up training as rookie rangers in Yellowstone National Park and soon find themselves in hot water when they uncover a plot by a deranged ranger who plans to steal Old Faithful geyser. Released Mar. 27, 1998. Directed by Steve Boyum. Stars Dennis Hopper (Frank Slater), Paul Walker IV (Phil), Steve Van Wormer (Stew), John Ashton (Capt. Douglas Pine), A. J. Langer (Jesse Ryan). 94 min. Filmed on location in the Wasatch National Forest near Park City, Utah, since the filmmakers could not utilize Yellowstone National Park itself in the heart of the tourist season. A replica of Old Faithful geyser was created utilizing a jet engine on loan from Utah State University to spew water to the requisite height.

Meet the Munceys (TV) Show aired May 22, 1988. Directed by Noel Black. A lower-class family moves into a mansion when a maid is left in charge of an elderly woman's fortune. Naturally, the woman's relatives are not at all pleased, and they plot to get rid of the Munceys. It was a pilot for a series. Stars Nana Visitor, Peggy Pope, Carmine Caridi, Dan Gauthier, Mark Neely, Lee Weaver. Vanna White makes a cameo appearance.

Meet the Robinsons (film) Computer-animated feature. Lewis is a brilliant 12-year-old with a surprising number of clever inventions to his credit. His latest and most ambitious project is the Memory Scanner, which he hopes will retrieve early memories of his mother and maybe even reveal why she put him up for adoption. But before he can get his answer, his invention is stolen by the dastardly Bowler Hat Guy and Doris, his diabolical hat and constant companion. Lewis has all but given up hope in his future when a mysterious boy named Wilbur Robinson whisks him away in a time machine and the two travel forward in time to spend a day with Wilbur's eccentric family. In a world filled with flying cars and floating cities, they hunt down Bowler Hat Guy, save the future, and uncover the amazing secret of Lewis's future family. Released Mar. 30, 2007, in a regular version, and in Disney Digital 3-D on more than 600 screens. Directed by Stephen Anderson. Voices include Angela Bassett (Mildred), Daniel Hansen (Lewis), Jordan Fry (Lewis), Tom Kenny (Mr. Willerstein), Harland Williams (Carl), Adam West (Uncle Art), Laurie

Metcalf (Lucille Krunklehorn), Wesley Singerman (Wilbur), Stephen John Anderson (Bowler Hat Guy), Ethan Sandler (Doris/CEO/Spike/Dimitri), Tom Selleck (Cornelius), Nicole Sullivan (Franny). Anderson, the director, voiced not only Bowler Hat Guy, but also Grandpa Bud and Tallulah. Two actors were needed to voice Lewis—Daniel Hansen began recording the voice in 2003, but as he grew and his voice changed, the producers had to find another kid, and they were lucky to find Jordan Fry, a young actor who sounded much like Daniel. 94 min. Based on the book *A Day with Wilbur Robinson* by William Joyce; Disney had originally acquired the book in order to make a live-action feature, but the animation staff saw great possibilities in it for animation. Danny Elfman provided the score. The songs "Another Believer" and "The Motion Waltz (Emotional Commotion)" were performed by Rufus Wainright, with "Little Wonders" performed by Rob Thomas and "The Future Has Arrived" by The All-American Rejects.

Meet the World Audio-Animatronics and multimedia attraction in Tomorrowland at Tokyo Disneyland in a Carousel of Progress–type theater; opened Apr. 15, 1983, and closed Jun. 30, 2002. A crane, a traditional symbol of historic knowledge, leads a Japanese boy and girl on a journey through Japan's past. The title theme song was written by Richard M. and Robert B. Sherman. Superseded by Monsters, Inc. Ride & Go Seek! Meet the World was also planned for, but never built in, Japan at EPCOT.

Megara Smart and sassy femme fatale in *Hercules*; voiced by Susan Egan.

Meilin Lee Exuberant Chinese Canadian middle schooler who poofs into a giant red panda in *Turning Red*; voiced by Rosalie Chiang.

Melissa & Joey (TV) Comedy series on ABC Family; debuted Aug. 17, 2010, and ended Aug. 5, 2015. Mel Burke, the grown-up former wild child of a political family, is now a politician herself. When her sister ends up in prison and brother-in-law flees after a scandal hits, Mel must take responsibility for her teenaged niece, Lennox, and adolescent nephew, Ryder. Spread too thin to manage by herself, Mel finds help in the unlikely form of Joe Longo, who, desperate for a job, moves in and becomes the family's "manny." Stars Melissa Joan Hart (Mel), Joey Lawrence (Joe), Taylor Spreitler

(Lennox Scanlon), Nick Robinson (Ryder). From Hartbreak Films.

Mello Men Singing group that provided vocals in many Disney films and theme park attractions. Consisted of Bill Lee, Max Smith, Bob Stevens, and Thurl Ravenscroft. They are shown recording the voices of the dogs in the dog pound for *Lady and the Tramp* in the TV show *Cavalcade of Songs*. Sometimes spelled The Mellomen or MelloMen.

Melody SEE ADVENTURES IN MUSIC: MELODY.

Melody Time (film) An animation/live-action feature consisting of 7 sequences: (1) *Once Upon a Wintertime*, sung by Frances Langford, tells of a winter romance by both human and bunny couples sleighing and skating in the 1800s; (2) *Bumble Boogie*, played by Freddy Martin and His Orchestra, is a fantasy of a bee's nightmare; (3) *Johnny Appleseed*, in which Dennis Day portrays the characters of the old settler, Johnny Appleseed, and Johnny's angel, telling the story of the pioneer who heads out west planting apple trees as he goes; (4) *Little Toot*, sung by the Andrews Sisters, tells of a little tugboat who wants to be like his father, but keeps getting into trouble; (5) *Trees*, with Fred Waring and his Pennsylvanians interpreting Joyce Kilmer's poem; (6) *Blame It on the Samba*, sung by the Dinning Sisters, in which Donald is taught to samba by José Carioca, and interacts with Ethel Smith at the organ; and (7) *Pecos Bill*, told and sung by Roy Rogers and the Sons of the Pioneers to Luana Patten and Bobby Driscoll; after singing "Blue Shadows on the Trail," Roy recounts how the legendary Pecos Bill was born, raised, and fell in love with Slue Foot Sue. Released May 27, 1948. Directed by Clyde Geronimi, Hamilton Luske, Jack Kinney, Wilfred Jackson. 75 min. Songs include "Melody Time," "The Apple Song," "Little Toot," and "Pecos Bill." Many of the segments were later released separately as shorts. First released on video in 1998.

Memento Mori Liberty Square shop in the Magic Kingdom at Walt Disney World; opened Oct. 15, 2014, replacing The Yankee Trader. Haunted Mansion collectibles are sold.

Men Against the Arctic (film) People and Places featurette released Dec. 21, 1955. Directed by Winston Hibler. Academy Award winner. 30 min. The film shows how icebreakers, specially constructed ships built by the U.S. Coast Guard, make their way through heavy Arctic ice packs. They maneuver with the aid of helicopters in their effort to reach the weather station at Alert, only 400 miles from the Arctic Circle, in Operation Alert, an annual task.

Menace on the Mountain (TV) Two-part show; aired Mar. 1 and 8, 1970. Directed by Vincent McEveety. A boy struggles to take care of his family during the Civil War, after his father joins the Confederate army. To help pay the taxes, he captures a mountain lion for the bounty, angering another man who also wanted the money. When the war ends, outlaws take over the family's ranch and the army has to come to save the day. Stars Mitch Vogel, Charles Aidman, Patricia Crowley, Albert Salmi, Richard Anderson, Dub Taylor, Eric Shea, Jodie Foster.

Menehune Shy, mischievous craftspeople of the Hawaiian Islands, represented in hidden carvings throughout Aulani, A Disney Resort & Spa.

Menjou, Adolphe (1890–1963) Actor; appeared in *Pollyanna* (Mr. Pendergast).

Menken, Alan Composer; joined Disney in 1987 to work on *The Little Mermaid*, later composing the music for such Disney animated classics as *Beauty and the Beast* and *Aladdin*. His early Disney songs included "Under the Sea," "Beauty and the Beast," and "A Whole New World," all of which won him Academy Awards. Partnering first with lyricist Howard Ashman, he helped engineer the rebirth and popularity of Disney animation that reignited in the 1980s. After Ashman's death, he worked with Tim Rice to finish the songs for *Aladdin*; Rice also worked with Menken on new songs for Disney's first major Broadway musical, *Beauty and the Beast*, as well as for the musical *King David*. Menken also wrote the music for the songs in *Newsies* and *Polly*. In 1995, he joined with lyricist Stephen Schwartz to write the songs for *Pocahontas*, winning the Academy Award for the score and "Colors of the Wind." The following year, he partnered with Schwartz again for *The Hunchback of Notre Dame* and in 1997 with David Zippel for *Hercules*. Menken wrote the score and worked with Glenn Slater on the songs for *Home on the Range* and, in 2007, wrote songs for *Enchanted* with Schwartz once again (returning 15 years later to write songs for *Disenchanted*). In 2010, he partnered with Slater yet again to write the songs for *Tangled* and later earned his first Grammy Award

for the song "I See the Light." He also earned an Emmy nomination for his song "More or Less the Kind of Thing You May or May Not Possibly See on Broadway" for the ABC series *The Neighbors*. He contributed new songs to later Disney shows on Broadway, including *The Little Mermaid*, *Sister Act*, *Newsies* (earning him a Tony Award for Best Original Score), and *Aladdin*. He returned to contribute music to *Beauty and the Beast* (2017), *Ralph Breaks the Internet*, *Aladdin* (2019), and the documentary *Howard*, and, for TV, *Galavant*, *Tangled: Before Ever After*, and *Tangled: The Series*. He appeared in *Disney's Broadway Hits at Royal Albert Hall* and on TV in *The Disney Family Singalong*. On ABC, he appeared in *Beauty and the Beast: A 30th Celebration*. He has earned 8 Oscars for his Disney work and was named a Disney Legend in 2001.

Menzel, Idina Actress; provided the voice of Elsa in *Frozen* and other appearances of the character. She appeared in *Enchanted* and *Disenchanted* (Nancy Tremaine), also on Disney+ in *Idina Menzel: Which Way to the Stage*, and on TV in *Disneyland 60: The Wonderful World of Disney*, *Mickey's 90th Spectacular*, and *The Disney Family Singalong: Volume II*. Her 1998 debut album, *Still I Can't Be Still*, was released by Hollywood Records. She was named a Disney Legend in 2022.

Merbabies (film) Silly Symphony cartoon released Dec. 9, 1938. Actually produced for Disney by Harman-Ising Studios, directed by Rudolf Ising and supervised for the Walt Disney Studio by Ben Sharpsteen, Dave Hand, Otto Englander, and Walt Disney. The workload at the Disney Studio was getting out of hand, so Walt decided to help his former colleagues (from Laugh-O-grams) by passing some work their way. A sequel to *Water Babies*, in which ocean waves change to form merbabies who are summoned to a playground on the floor of the ocean for an underwater circus. When a whale blows them all to the surface, they disappear into the waves from which they came.

Merchandise Shoppers are so accustomed to seeing the wide variety of Disney merchandise on store shelves today that it is hard to imagine a time before you could buy a Mickey Mouse doll, book, toothbrush, or pair of bedroom slippers. Actually, it all started by chance back in 1929. Walt Disney was walking through a hotel lobby in New York City, and a man came up to him asking if he could put Mickey Mouse on a children's pencil tablet he was manufacturing. He offered $300, and as Walt needed the money, he agreed. That tablet began Disney licensing. Within a year, the first Mickey Mouse book and comic strip had been licensed, and other items soon followed. In 1932, a major change in Disney licensing occurred with the appearance of Kay Kamen. Kamen, a born entrepreneur, convinced Walt that licensing could open up whole new vistas for the company. For the next 17 years, until he died in a plane crash, Kamen handled the licensing of Disney merchandise. Insisting on quality control, Kamen set the standard for character licensing that would later be copied by many others. Shortly after the opening of Walt Disney World in 1971, Disney founded the Walt Disney Distributing Company (WDDC) to actually produce merchandise, for sale primarily in the parks. Up until then, Disney had simply licensed the Disney characters to other manufacturers. The WDDC experiment was not successful, but a decade later, the Disney company would try again. This time, the manufacturing was being done for The Disney Store, a chain of outlets for Disney merchandise opening up in malls throughout the country. The Disney Store concept was tremendously successful, and other areas of the company, such as Walt Disney Attractions, the Walt Disney Classics Collection, and Disney Art Editions, were soon following suit and getting into the manufacturing business. While the company is ever wary of oversaturation of the market, that point has evidently not been reached, and the various divisions of Disney Consumer Products, Games, and Publishing continue to grow each year. Over 9 decades after that first pencil tablet, Disney merchandising is still going strong.

Merchant of Venice Confections Chocolate and sweets store in Mediterranean Harbor at Tokyo DisneySea; opened Sep. 4, 2001. The shop is themed to Venice, the city of water.

Merchant of Venus Tomorrowland shop in the Magic Kingdom at Walt Disney World; opened Jun. 1994, replacing The Space Port. The shop became themed to Stitch with the opening of Stitch's Great Escape! in 2004 and was converted into a seating area in Aug. 2022.

Merciful Law of the King, The (TV) Episode 2 of *The Prince and the Pauper*.

Meredith, Burgess (1908–1997) Actor; appeared

on TV in *The Strange Monster of Strawberry Cove* (Henry Meade) and had an uncredited role as an old man in *Tall Tale*.

Merida Headstrong princess in *Brave*; voiced by Kelly Macdonald.

Merkel, Una (1903–1986) Actress; appeared in *The Parent Trap* (Verbena), *Summer Magic* (Maria Popham), and *A Tiger Walks* (Mrs. Watkins).

Merlin Wart's magical, but absent-minded, mentor in *The Sword in the Stone*; voiced by Karl Swenson.

Merlin l'Enchanteur Fantasyland shop in Disneyland Paris; opened Apr. 12, 1992. Curiosities, etched crystals, and medieval gifts are sold inside the sorcerer's cave.

Merlin's Magic Recipe Fantasyland food kiosk in Shanghai Disneyland; opened Jun. 16, 2016, serving sandwiches and snacks.

Merlin's Magic Shop Fantasyland shop in Disneyland; opened Jul. 17, 1955. Closed Jan. 16, 1983, to become Mickey's Christmas Chalet. Also a Fantasyland shop in the Magic Kingdom at Walt Disney World, Mar. 1972–May 1986; succeeded by Mickey's Christmas Carol shop. SEE ALSO MAIN STREET MAGIC SHOP.

Merlin's Marvelous Miscellany Fantasyland merchandise shop in Disneyland; opened Mar. 11, 2022, succeeding the Castle Holiday Shoppe in the site of the original Merlin's Magic Shop.

Merlin's Treasures Fantasyland shop in Hong Kong Disneyland; opened Sep. 12, 2005. Souvenirs are sold in a quaint cottage.

Merlock Villainous sorcerer in *DuckTales: the Movie*; voiced by Christopher Lloyd.

Mermaid Lagoon Fully enclosed port of call in Tokyo DisneySea; opened Sep. 4, 2001. The cartoonlike undersea home of Ariel's, offering family attractions, a live musical production, a supper club, and shopping.

Mermaid Lagoon Theater Mermaid Lagoon attraction in Tokyo DisneySea; opened Sep. 4, 2001. Guests enter through the wooden hull of a sunken ship to experience the *Under the Sea* show, featuring puppetry, colorful costumes, special effects, and suspended actors who "swim" above the audience. A new live show, *King Triton's Concert*, debuted in 2015.

Mermaid Treasures Mermaid Lagoon shop, themed to Ariel and her sisters' dressing room, in Tokyo DisneySea; opened Sep. 4, 2001.

Merrily Song, The Song from the *Wind in the Willows* segment of *The Adventures of Ichabod and Mr. Toad*; written by Frank Churchill, Ray Gilbert, Larry Morey, and Charles Wolcott.

Merriman, Ryan Actor; appeared on TV in *Smart House* (Ben Cooper), *The Luck of the Irish* (Kyle Johnson), *A Ring of Endless Light* (Adam Eddington), and *Veritas* (Nikko).

Merriweather's Market Pleasure Island food court at Walt Disney World; opened May 1, 1989, named for the island's fictional founder, Merriweather Adam Pleasure. Closed Feb. 3, 1991, and succeeded by Pleasure Island Jazz Company.

Merry Dwarfs, The (film) Silly Symphony cartoon released Dec. 16, 1929. Directed by Walt Disney. Small, bearded dwarfs perform musical numbers in their woodland village.

Merry Mickey Celebration, A (TV) Hour-long special on ABC; aired Dec. 20, 2003. Celebrities salute Mickey Mouse on the occasion of his 75th anniversary through music and song, and *Mickey's Christmas Carol* is shown. Stars Jim Belushi, Wayne Brady, George Lopez, Masiela Lusha, Sara Rue, Katey Sagal.

Merryweather Pugnacious good fairy in *Sleeping Beauty* who wore blue; voiced by Barbara Luddy.

Mestres, Ricardo Joined Disney in 1984, first as vice president of production, and then headed over to Hollywood Pictures when it was formed in 1988, where he was made president. He resigned in 1994.

Metro (film) Scott Roper is a fast-talking, wise-cracking hostage negotiator whose unorthodox but winning ways make him the San Francisco Police Department's top arbitrator. But even his silver tongue cannot change his fortune when he and rookie SWAT team sharpshooter Kevin McCall come face-to-face with a psychotic killer in a lethal game of cat and mouse. A Touchstone film, in association with Caravan Pictures. Directed by Thomas Carter. Released Jan. 17, 1997. Stars Eddie Murphy (Scott Roper), Michael Rapaport (Kevin McCall), Michael Wincott (Korda), Carmen Ejogo (Ronnie Tate), Denis Arndt (Capt. Frank Solis), Art Evans (Lt. Sam Baffert), Donal Logue (Earl). Filmed in Cinema-Scope. 117 min. This is the American film debut for British actress Ejogo. Filming took place over 15 weeks in and around San Francisco, including Chinatown, the Tenderloin, the Financial District, Treasure Island, Pier 50, Half Moon Bay, and the former Naval Shipyard at Mare Island, in Vallejo, where the film's action-packed finale utilized several of the cavernous dry docks.

Metzler, Jim Actor; appeared in *Tex* (Mason McCormick), and on TV in *The Christmas Star* (Stuart Jameson), with a guest appearance on *Grey's Anatomy* (priest).

Mexico World Showcase pavilion in EPCOT; opened Oct. 1, 1982. Guests enter what appears to be an ancient Mesoamerican temple, where just inside can be found a display on Mexican history and culture. Farther on is the Plaza de los Amigos, where colorful stalls are situated under a simulated night-time sky, flanked by other shops and a cozy bar, La Cava del Tequila (added in 2009). The San Angel Inn Restaurante, along the water's edge, offers diners tempting and authentic Mexican fare. To one side, guests can board a boat for the Gran Fiesta Tour Starring The Three Caballeros (formerly El Río del Tiempo, until 2007), a tuneful journey celebrating the vistas and culture of present-day Mexico. Outside, beside World Showcase Lagoon, guests can partake of counter-service fare in La Cantina de San Angel or enjoy table-service dining in La Hacienda de San Angel (added in 2010).

Miami Rhapsody (film) A young woman is forced to confront the true essence of marriage when her boyfriend finally pops the question. To determine if marriage is worth the impact it will have on her carefree life, she tries to discover what relationships and marriage are all about. Along the way, she discovers that the marriages of her brother, sister, and parents are not as happy as she thought, as each one of them is engaging in an extramarital affair. Limited release Jan. 27, 1995, in Los Angeles and New York City; general release Feb. 3, 1995. Directed by David Frankel. A Hollywood Pictures film. 95

min. Stars Sarah Jessica Parker (Gwyn), Antonio Banderas (Antonio), Gil Bellows (Matt), Mia Farrow (Nina), Carla Gugino (Leslie), Paul Mazursky (Vic), Kevin Pollak (Jordan).

Michael Wendy's youngest brother in *Peter Pan*, who clutches his teddy bear; voiced by Tommy Luske.

Michael and Mickey (film) Michael Eisner and Mickey Mouse star in a film introducing a changing array of coming-attraction trailers shown at the end of the Backstage Tour, Disney-MGM Studios; opened May 1, 1989, and ended in 1992. 2 min.

Michael O'Hara the Fourth (TV) Two-part show; aired Mar. 26 and Apr. 2, 1972. A police captain's daughter yearns to be a detective and tries to solve some cases regarding counterfeiters and murderers. Her successes impress her father, who had been longing for a son to carry on the family name. Directed by Robert Totten. Stars Jo Ann Harris, Dan Dailey, Michael McGreevey, Nehemiah Persoff, William Bramley, James Almanzar. Episodes are "To Trap a Thief" and "The Deceptive Detective."

Michelle Kwan: Princess on Ice (TV) One-hour special on ABC; aired Jan. 20, 2001. Features ice-skating to the sounds of hot singing groups along with songs that feature classic Disney princesses. Stars Michelle Kwan, Dorothy Hamill, Katarina Witt, SHeDAISY, O-Town.

Michelle Kwan Skates to Disney's Greatest Hits (TV) One-hour special on ABC; aired Mar. 5, 1999, featuring Olympic medalist Michelle Kwan, along with Oksana Baiul, Ilia Kulik, and Elvis Stojko. Featured is a countdown of the Top Ten Disney songs as voted upon by Internet users on Disney.com.

Mickey & Co. Disney character fashions in Walt Disney World Village; opened Mar. 6, 1985, taking the place of the Plus You boutique. Presented by J. G. Hook. Closed Apr. 19, 1987, later becoming part of Team Mickey's Athletic Club.

Mickey and Donald Kidding Around (TV) Show aired May 3, 1983. It is an edited version of *Kids Is Kids*.

Mickey and Donald Present Sport Goofy (TV) SEE SPORT GOOFY.

Mickey & Minnie's Mercantile Fantasyland shop themed to *Brave Little Tailor* in Shanghai Disneyland; opened Jun. 16, 2016. Disney Princess costumes, apparel, and plush are sold.

Mickey & Minnie's Runaway Railway Attraction inside the Chinese Theatre at Disney's Hollywood Studios; opened Mar. 4, 2020, replacing The Great Movie Ride. During a premiere screening of Mickey and Minnie's latest animated short, *Perfect Picnic*, an unexpected event sends the audience through the movie screen and right into the cartoon. In the animated setting of Runnamuck Park, passengers hop aboard engineer Goofy's train for a whirlwind ride through the wacky and unpredictable cartoon world. Based on the 2013 series of Mickey Mouse shorts on Disney Channel, it is the first ride-through attraction starring Mickey and Minnie. Also a Mickey's Toontown attraction in Disneyland; opened Jan. 27, 2023, inside the new El CapiTOON Theater.

Mickey and Nora (TV) Pilot for a series on CBS; aired Jun. 26, 1987. An ex-CIA agent can't convince anyone (including his new bride) that he is no longer a spy. Directed by Paul Bogart. Stars Ted Wass, Barbara Treutelaar, George Furth, Nancy Lenehan. 30 min.

Mickey & Pals Market Café Counter-service restaurant on Mickey Avenue in Shanghai Disneyland; opened Jun. 16, 2016. At its opening, the market featured 4 unique kitchens and 4 themed dining rooms: Mickey's Galley, Daisy's Café, Tony's (from *Lady and the Tramp*), and The Three Caballeros.

Mickey and the Beanstalk (film) Segment of *Fun and Fancy Free*, with Edgar Bergen telling the story.

Mickey and the Magical Map Musical stage show in the Fantasyland Theater at Disneyland; debuted May 25, 2013. Mickey, as the Sorcerer's Apprentice, stumbles upon a wondrous map capable of taking dreamers to any place imaginable. The show came alive with a company of singing and dancing mapmakers and a variety of Disney characters. The innovative map featured nearly 1 million pixels and more than 35,000 square inches of LED screen surface; sections were moved on wagons that weighed more than 9,000 lbs. each. Ended Mar. 2020, and was succeeded by *Tale of the Lion King* in 2022.

Mickey and the Magician Musical stage show in Toon Studio at Walt Disney Studios Park in Disneyland Paris; debuted Jul. 2, 2016, taking the place of *Animagique*. Disney magicians, like Rafiki, Elsa, and Genie, help Mickey Mouse realize his dream of becoming a great magician.

Mickey and the Roadster Racers (TV) Half-hour computer-animated series on Disney Junior; debuted Jan. 15, 2017. Mickey Mouse and the gang, with their unique transforming vehicles, go on high-spirited races around the globe and engage in hometown capers in Hot Dog Hills. When Minnie and Daisy are not busy racing, they run their own successful business as the Happy Helpers, solving problems for anyone in need of a helping hand. Voices include Bret Iwan (Mickey Mouse), Russi Taylor (Minnie Mouse), Bill Farmer (Goofy, Pluto), Daniel Ross (Donald Duck). Aimed at kids 2–7, each episode features two 11-minute stories. On Apr. 9, 2019, the existing seasons were renamed *Mickey Mouse Roadster Racers*. For the 3rd season, premiering Oct. 14, 2019, the series was given the new title *Mickey Mouse Mixed-Up Adventures*, with an updated version of the popular "Hot Dog!" song. The show inspired the short-form series *Mickey Mouse: Hot Diggity Dog Tales*. From Disney Television Animation.

Mickey and the Seal (film) Mickey Mouse cartoon released Dec. 3, 1948. Directed by Charles Nichols. Pluto finds a baby seal in Mickey's basket when he returns from a visit to the zoo but does not get a chance to tell him until the seal is in the bathtub with Mickey. They return it to the zoo, only to return home and find the bathroom full of seals. Nominated for an Academy Award.

Mickey and the Wondrous Book Musical stage show in Disney's Storybook Theater in Hong Kong Disneyland; debuted Nov. 17, 2015, replacing *The Golden Mickeys*. Live vocalists, Disney characters, and dancers perform numbers from *The Jungle Book*, *Tangled*, *Brave*, *Aladdin*, and other films in the setting of an enchanted storybook. A similar show, *Mickey's Storybook Adventure*, debuted in the Walt Disney Grand Theatre in Disneytown at Shanghai Disney Resort Jun. 16, 2021.

Mickey Avenue Area in Shanghai Disneyland; opened Jun. 16, 2016, as the first Disney park main entry inspired by Mickey Mouse and his friends and settings found in classic Disney ani-mated shorts. This whimsical hometown of shops and restaurants is comprised of 3 areas: Celebration Square, the Market District, and the Theatre District. Imagineers worked closely with local artists to incorporate Chinese culture into the area's design and merchandise areas. The name Mickey Avenue is inspired by a street at the Disney Studio in Burbank. Also the name of a street in Disney-MGM Studios (now Disney's Hollywood Studios), originally part of the backstage production area; the area would later open to the public and feature character-greeting spots and attractions such as Backstage Pass to 101 Dalmatians, Who Wants to Be a Millionaire—Play It!, and Walt Disney: One Man's Dream. A portion of the street became Pixar Place in 2008, with the rest later integrated into the Animation Courtyard area.

Mickey Cuts Up (film) Mickey Mouse cartoon released Nov. 30, 1931. Directed by Burt Gillett. Mickey is mowing Minnie's lawn with Pluto helping to pull the mower. Playing a trick on Minnie, Mickey crawls into her birdhouse, pretending to be a bird, but a cat pounces on him. Pluto causes widespread destruction with the mower attached to him when he chases the cat.

Mickey, Donald and Sport Goofy Show (TV) Limited series of 3 syn. half-hour shows featuring cartoons; first aired Sep. 7, Nov. 17, and Dec. 1, 1984.

Mickey, Donald, Goofy: The Three Musketeers (film) SEE THREE MUSKETEERS, THE.

Mickey Down Under (film) Mickey Mouse cartoon released Mar. 19, 1948. Directed by Charles Nichols. Mickey, in the Australian bush, throws a boomerang that gets caught in Pluto's mouth. Mickey then discovers an egg of an emu. Unfortunately, the parent chases him, but Pluto and the boomerang zoom into his path, leaving the emu all tangled.

Mickey in a Minute (film) Hand-drawn animated short; debuted in the documentary *Mickey: The Story of a Mouse* in 2022. While strolling the hallways of the Disney Animation Building, Mickey is sucked into a whirlwind that sends him through some of his most iconic roles and moments. Animated by Eric Goldberg, Mark Henn, and Randy Haycock. 1 min.

Mickey in Arabia Mickey Mouse cartoon released

Jul. 18, 1932. Directed by Wilfred Jackson. Mickey and Minnie are tourists when an evil sheik, Pete, kidnaps Minnie. Mickey's attempted rescue of Minnie is complicated by a drunken camel. After a furious battle with Pete and his soldiers, a rooftop chase ensues. Mickey and Minnie fall into an awning, but Pete tumbles onto the sand, running off into the desert, after being speared by his own soldiers.

Mickey in Paradise Souvenir and sundry shop in Disney's Paradise Pier Hotel at Disneyland Resort; opened Apr. 13, 2001, taking the place of The Disney Touch.

Mickey Mania Parade in the Magic Kingdom at Walt Disney World; ran Jun. 1, 1994–Sep. 1996 as a zany salute to Mickey Mouse in pop culture. Also ran in Tokyo Disneyland in 1995.

Mickey Mouse Walt Disney's primary cartoon character and international personality who made his debut in *Steamboat Willie* Nov. 18, 1928, at the Colony Theater in New York City. Walt once famously said, "I only hope that we never lose sight of one thing—that it was all started by a mouse." He told the story of coming up with the character in 1928, on a train ride from New York to Los Angeles, after losing control of his previous cartoon star, Oswald the Lucky Rabbit. According to legend, Walt came up with the name Mortimer for his new mouse character, but his wife, Lillian, thought the name was too pretentious and suggested Mickey instead. Walt and Ub Iwerks began work on the first Mickey Mouse cartoons, *Plane Crazy* and *The Gallopin' Gaucho*, but the advent of sound films prompted them to start on a third cartoon, *Steamboat Willie*, which would be released first and make Mickey an overnight sensation. Mickey's heyday was the 1930s; in the 1940s his popularity on the screen was overtaken by Donald Duck and Goofy. In all, there have been 121 Mickey Mouse theatrical cartoons, with a 30-year gap between *The Simple Things* (1953) and *Mickey's Christmas Carol* (1983). He starred in the *Mickey Mouse Club* TV show in the 1950s, appeared on countless merchandise items, and acted as chief greeter at the Disney theme parks. Walt Disney provided Mickey Mouse's voice up to 1946, when Jim Macdonald took over until his retirement 3 decades later. He was followed by Wayne Allwine and Bret Iwan. Chris Diamantopoulos began doing Mickey's voice for a new TV series of Mickey Mouse cartoons, debuting on Disney Channel in 2013. Mickey was

originally drawn using circles; many commentators have noted the character has one of the most powerful graphic designs ever created. In fact, the simplified 3-circle symbol of Mickey's head and ears has become an internationally recognized icon. *The Pointer*, in 1939, was the first cartoon that featured a drastically new design for Mickey. His body became more pear-shaped than round, and pupils were added to his eyes, making them more expressive. In the early 1940s, animators gave him perspective ears—shadowing them to give a 3-D effect—but this change was short-lived. Later changes consisted mainly of costume changes, taking him out of his red shorts, for instance, and putting him in more contemporary clothes. Mickey was the first cartoon character honored with a star on the Hollywood Walk of Fame, with a presentation held Nov. 13, 1978. The Mickey Mouse cartoons are:

1. *Steamboat Willie*, 1928
2. *The Gallopin' Gaucho*, 1928
3. *Plane Crazy*, 1928
4. *The Barn Dance*, 1929
5. *The Opry House*, 1929
6. *When the Cat's Away*, 1929
7. *The Barnyard Battle*, 1929
8. *The Plowboy*, 1929
9. *The Karnival Kid*, 1929
10. *Mickey's Follies*, 1929
11. *Mickey's Choo Choo*, 1929
12. *The Jazz Fool*, 1929
13. *Jungle Rhythm*, 1929
14. *The Haunted House*, 1929
15. *Wild Waves*, 1929
16. *Fiddling Around,* 1930 (working title was *Just Mickey*)
17. *The Barnyard Concert*, 1930
18. *The Cactus Kid*, 1930
19. *The Fire Fighters*, 1930
20. *The Shindig*, 1930
21. *The Chain Gang*, 1930
22. *The Gorilla Mystery*, 1930
23. *The Picnic*, 1930
24. *Pioneer Days*, 1930
25. *The Birthday Party*, 1931
26. *Traffic Troubles*, 1931
27. *The Castaway*, 1931
28. *The Moose Hunt*, 1931
29. *The Delivery Boy*, 1931
30. *Mickey Steps Out*, 1931
31. *Blue Rhythm*, 1931
32. *Fishin' Around*, 1931
33. *The Barnyard Broadcast*, 1931

34. *The Beach Party*, 1931
35. *Mickey Cuts Up*, 1931
36. *Mickey's Orphans*, 1931
37. *The Duck Hunt*, 1932
38. *The Grocery Boy*, 1932
39. *The Mad Dog*, 1932
40. *Barnyard Olympics*, 1932
41. *Mickey's Revue*, 1932
42. *Musical Farmer*, 1932
43. *Mickey in Arabia*, 1932
44. *Mickey's Nightmare*, 1932
45. *Trader Mickey*, 1932
46. *The Whoopee Party*, 1932
47. *Touchdown Mickey*, 1932
48. *The Wayward Canary*, 1932
49. *The Klondike Kid*, 1932
50. *Mickey's Good Deed*, 1932
51. *Building a Building*, 1933
52. *The Mad Doctor*, 1933
53. *Mickey's Pal Pluto*, 1933
54. *Mickey's Mellerdrammer*, 1933
55. *Ye Olden Days*, 1933
56. *The Mail Pilot*, 1933
57. *Mickey's Mechanical Man*, 1933
58. *Mickey's Gala Premiere*, 1933
59. *Puppy Love*, 1933
60. *The Steeple Chase*, 1933
61. *The Pet Store*, 1933
62. *Giantland*, 1933
63. *Shanghaied*, 1934
64. *Camping Out*, 1934
65. *Playful Pluto*, 1934
66. *Gulliver Mickey*, 1934
67. *Mickey's Steam-Roller*, 1934
68. *Orphans' Benefit*, 1934
69. *Mickey Plays Papa*, 1934
70. *The Dognapper*, 1934
71. *Two-Gun Mickey*, 1934
72. *Mickey's Man Friday*, 1935
73. *The Band Concert*, 1935 (first color)
74. *Mickey's Service Station*, 1935 (black-and-white)
75. *Mickey's Kangaroo*, 1935 (black-and-white)
76. *Mickey's Garden*, 1935
77. *Mickey's Fire Brigade*, 1935
78. *Pluto's Judgement Day*, 1935
79. *On Ice*, 1935
80. *Mickey's Polo Team*, 1936
81. *Orphan's Picnic*, 1936
82. *Mickey's Grand Opera*, 1936
83. *Thru the Mirror*, 1936
84. *Mickey's Rival*, 1936
85. *Moving Day*, 1936
86. *Alpine Climbers*, 1936
87. *Mickey's Circus*, 1936
88. *Mickey's Elephant*, 1936
89. *The Worm Turns*, 1937
90. *Magician Mickey*, 1937
91. *Moose Hunters*, 1937
92. *Mickey's Amateurs*, 1937
93. *Hawaiian Holiday*, 1937
94. *Clock Cleaners*, 1937
95. *Lonesome Ghosts*, 1937
96. *Boat Builders*, 1938
97. *Mickey's Trailer*, 1938
98. *The Whalers*, 1938
99. *Mickey's Parrot*, 1938
100. *Brave Little Tailor*, 1938
101. *Society Dog Show*, 1939
102. *The Pointer*, 1939
103. *Tugboat Mickey*, 1940
104. *Pluto's Dream House*, 1940
105. *Mr. Mouse Takes a Trip*, 1940
106. *The Little Whirlwind*, 1941
107. *The Nifty Nineties*, 1941
108. *Orphans' Benefit*, 1941 (remake)
109. *Mickey's Birthday Party*, 1942
110. *Symphony Hour*, 1942
111. *Mickey's Delayed Date*, 1947
112. *Mickey Down Under*, 1948
113. *Mickey and the Seal*, 1948
114. *Plutopia*, 1951
115. *R'coon Dawg*, 1951
116. *Pluto's Party*, 1952
117. *Pluto's Christmas Tree*, 1952
118. *The Simple Things*, 1953
119. *Mickey's Christmas Carol*, 1983
120. *Runaway Brain*, 1995
121. *Get a Horse!*, 2013

Mickey Mouse (TV) Series of Mickey Mouse cartoons released on Disney Channel, online, and on additional platforms. The shorts have a slapstick feel of classic Mickey Mouse combined with contemporary direction and pacing. Each cartoon finds Mickey in a different modern setting. The first 6 shorts were *Croissant de Triomphe* (Mar. 8, 2013), *New York Weenie* (Jun. 24, 2013), *No Service* (Jun. 28, 2013), *Yodelberg* (Jun. 29, 2013), *Tokyo Go* (Jul. 12, 2013), and *Stayin' Cool* (Jul. 19, 2013). Exec. producer and director is Paul Rudish. Mickey Mouse is voiced by Chris Diamantopoulos. Winner of 3 Emmy Awards in 2013 and 3 more in 2014. The series later inspired the ride-through attraction Mickey & Minnie's Runaway Railway for Disney's Hollywood Studios and Disneyland. SEE ALSO WONDERFUL WORLD OF MICKEY MOUSE, THE (DISNEY+).

Mickey Mouse Anniversary Show, The (TV) Show aired Dec. 22, 1968. Directed by Robert Stevenson. Dean Jones hosts a look at Mickey Mouse's 40 years, through film clips and the return of a group of Mouseketeers.

Mickey Mouse Book The first Disney book; published by Bibo-Lang in 1930.

Mickey Mouse Club In 1929, the Fox Dome Theater in Ocean Park (Santa Monica, California) began a Mickey Mouse Club. Soon there were hundreds of other Mickey Mouse Clubs associated with theaters all over the country. These were real clubs that kids joined. The children attended Saturday meetings where Mickey Mouse cartoons were shown, a Chief Mickey Mouse and a Chief Minnie Mouse were elected, Mickey Mouse credos were recited, and Mickey Mouse Club bands entertained. At the height of their popularity in 1932, these clubs had more than a million members. The TV version of the Mickey Mouse Club would not come along until 23 years later.

Mickey Mouse Club (TV) One of the most popular children's series of all time; aired on ABC Oct. 3, 1955–Sep. 25, 1959. The show began as an hour-long show Monday through Friday and introduced 24 talented kids, known as Mouseketeers, who performed skits, musical numbers, and introduced special guest stars, serials, and Disney cartoons. Adult leaders were Jimmie Dodd and Roy Williams. Many of the Mouseketeers—including Annette, Tommy, Darlene, Lonnie, Sharon, Sherry, Doreen, Bobby, Cubby, Karen, Dennis, and Cheryl—became instantaneous celebrities. Over the next 2 seasons, 15 additional kids would become Mouseketeers, for a total of 39. Monday was Fun with Music Day, Tuesday was Guest Star Day, Wednesday was Anything Can Happen Day, Thursday was Circus Day, and Friday was Talent Roundup Day. Serials included *The Adventures of Spin and Marty*, *Border Collie*, *The Hardy Boys*, *Clint and Mac*, *San Juan River Expedition*, *Adventure in Dairyland*, *The Boys of the Western Sea*, *The Secret of Mystery Lake*, *Corky and White Shadow*, and *Annette*. *Mickey Mouse Club Newsreels* featured footage sent in by camera crews roaming the world looking for interesting stories featuring kids. Each show began with an animated segment culminating with Donald Duck striking a gong (with a variety of unexpected consequences) and ended with Mousekartoon Time. The show began as part of Walt Disney's original contract with ABC, which

gave him needed money to build Disneyland, a year after the debut of the nighttime *Disneyland* show. In all, 260 hour-long and 130 half-hour shows were produced. *Mickey Mouse Club* returned in syn. 1962–1965 (with some new footage produced) and again in 1975. Because of the popularity of that 1975 syn., a new version of the club, known as the "new" *Mickey Mouse Club*, ran in syn. Jan. 17, 1977–Dec. 1, 1978. Twelve children were selected to be Mouseketeers, and the show was updated to appeal more to contemporary kids. The primary change was that the show was videotaped in color. Also, the days were changed—Monday was Who, What, Why, Where, When and How Day; Tuesday was Let's Go Day; Wednesday was Surprise Day; Thursday was Discovery Day; and Friday was Showtime Day. There was only one original serial produced—*The Mystery of Rustler's Cave*—though a number of Disney films were shown in serialized form. Because of high production costs and so-so ratings, the show only ran for 2 years. When The Disney Channel launched Apr. 18, 1983, the original *Mickey Mouse Club* episodes were featured daily. The Disney Channel produced its own updated version of the *Mickey Mouse Club* Apr. 24, 1989, though by then the Mickey Mouse element was no longer emphasized, the kids in the cast no longer wore the distinctive mouse-ear hats, and the show was aimed at a slightly older age group. There were a number of new serials produced: *Teen Angel*, *Match Point*, *Teen Angel Returns*, *Just Perfect*, *The Secret of Lost Creek*, *My Life as a Babysitter*, and *Emerald Cove*. The last new episodes of the *Mickey Mouse Club* were taped in the fall of 1994. Responding to the now older ages of the cast, and thus the target audience, the show had a new title, *MMC*, and any references to Mickey Mouse were dropped. SEE ALSO MOUSEKETEERS.

Mickey Mouse Club Circus Special circus under a tent at Disneyland; open Nov. 24, 1955–Jan. 8, 1956, starring some of the Mouseketeers who were thrilled to be able to ride horses and work the trapezes. This circus was one of Walt Disney's few failures. He was fascinated by circuses, but guests visiting Disneyland had too many other fun things to see and do to spend their time sitting under the big top. After all, they could see a circus anywhere; there was only one Disneyland. Mickey Mouse Club Circus only lasted over 1 Christmas season. The tent, which Disney had bought, saw later usage in Holidayland for corporate picnics and other events.

Mickey Mouse Club Headquarters Located in the

Opera House at Disneyland 1963–1964. During a period of the TV series' syn., Walt Disney opened up an area where children could sign up and get their own membership cards in the Mickey Mouse Club. At the time of the original run of the show in the 1950s, everyone who watched the show was automatically a member of the club.

Mickey Mouse Club Magazine Quarterly magazine beginning publication at the height of the popularity of the *Mickey Mouse Club* with the winter 1956 issue. In Jun. 1957, it went bimonthly and changed its name to *Walt Disney's Magazine*. It ceased publication with the Oct. 1959 issue. Included were stories on the *Mickey Mouse Club*, its stars, and various Disney TV and theatrical films of the period.

Mickey Mouse Club March Theme song for the *Mickey Mouse Club*; written by Jimmie Dodd.

Mickey Mouse Club Theater Fantasyland theater in Disneyland that showed Disney cartoons; opened Aug. 27, 1955, but changed its name to Fantasyland Theater in 1964, and closed Dec. 20, 1981. At one time, the *3-D Jamboree* was featured, and guests donned polarized glasses to watch Mouseketeers and Disney cartoons in 3-D. The cartoon fare in the theater changed from time to time, and the theater itself was only open during busy periods. Before the theater was built in the Opera House as the home to Great Moments with Mr. Lincoln, this was the only auditorium in the park, so it was also used for press conferences and Cast Member events. It made way for Pinocchio's Daring Journey as part of the New Fantasyland in 1983.

Mickey Mouse Clubhouse (TV) Half-hour computer-animated series on Disney Channel; premiered May 5, 2006. The "Sensational Six"— Mickey Mouse, Minnie Mouse, Donald Duck, Daisy Duck, Goofy, and Pluto—star in a music-filled series for preschoolers designed to encourage problem-solving and promote early math skills. The show combines the timeless characters with modern 21st-century devices that help solve the day's challenge. Voices include Wayne Allwine (Mickey), Russi Taylor (Minnie), Bill Farmer (Goofy, Pluto), Tony Anselmo (Donald), Tress MacNeille (Daisy, Chip, Dale). The popular closing song, "Hot Dog!," is performed by They Might Be Giants. Bret Iwan took over voicing Mickey in 2010. The show inspired the short-form series *Mickey Mousekersize* and *Minnie's Bow-Toons*, as

well as the spin-off series *Mickey and the Roadster Racers* (later *Mickey Mouse Mixed-Up Adventures*) and *Mickey Mouse Funhouse*.

Mickey Mouse Disco (film) Cartoon compilation featuring footage from a number of cartoons starring Mickey, Donald, and Goofy, reedited, with a new soundtrack from the best-selling 1979 record album, which earned gold, platinum, and double platinum certifications. The project was the birthplace of The Disney Channel's DTV music videos, which also marry classic Disney animation with contemporary songs and artists. Released Jun. 25, 1980. 7 min.

Mickey Mouse Funhouse (TV) Animated series for preschoolers; debuted Aug. 20, 2021, on Disney Junior and Disney Channel. An enchanted fun house named Funny takes Mickey and the gang on adventures to unique worlds that inspire the imagination. Premiered with a prime-time special, *Mickey the Brave!*, Jul. 16, in which Mickey and pals meet Funny and are transported to the Kingdom of Majestica, where they encounter a troublemaking dragon named Farfus. Voices include Bret Iwan (Mickey Mouse), Kaitlyn Robrock (Minnie Mouse), Bill Farmer (Goofy/Pluto), Tress MacNeille (Daisy Duck), Tony Anselmo (Donald Duck), Harvey Guillén (Funny). From Disney Television Animation.

Mickey Mouse Happy Birthday Show (film) Half-hour compilation of Disney cartoons in commemoration of Mickey's 40th anniversary. Released with *Never a Dull Moment* in 1968.

Mickey Mouse Magazine In Jan. 1933, Kay Kamen created *Mickey Mouse Magazine*, which was a small publication containing short stories, articles, gags, games, and poems. There were 9 monthly issues of the magazine, distributed through movie theaters and department stores. In Nov. 1933, a 2nd version of the magazine, in the same format but distributed through dairies, debuted and continued until Oct. 1935. The dairies would print their name on the cover of the magazine above the title. This dairy magazine was superseded by a 3rd, and much more elaborate, magazine, which began publication with a large issue in the summer of 1935. In Oct. 1935, it turned into a monthly magazine. Over the years, several different sizes were experimented with, until finally in 1940 the magazine reached the size we know today as the normal comic book size. The last issue of *Mickey Mouse Magazine* was for

Sep. 1940. In Oct. 1940, *Walt Disney's Comics and Stories* took over.

Mickey Mouse Mixed-Up Adventures (TV) SEE MICKEY AND THE ROADSTER RACERS.

Mickey Mouse Playhouse Family activity center at the Shanghai Disneyland Hotel; opened Jun. 16, 2016, with games, puzzles, and arts and crafts.

Mickey Mouse Revue Fantasyland musical attraction in the Magic Kingdom at Walt Disney World; open Oct. 1, 1971–Sep. 14, 1980, when it was removed and the venue was used seasonally as the Fantasyland Theater. The revue featured a large cast of Audio-Animatronics Disney characters—more than 80 in total, from a 12-inch Dormouse to the 6-ft.-tall Baloo—performing selections of the most memorable of the Disney songs. A 23-piece orchestra played under the baton of maestro Mickey Mouse himself. At opening, the revue was one of the few attractions totally unique to the Magic Kingdom, though Walt had conceived such a show a decade earlier, before the technology was available to pull it off. After the show closed, *Magic Journeys* was shown for a time in 3-D, and in 1994, *Legend of the Lion King* opened in the theater. It is the current home of *Mickey's PhilharMagic*. The Mickey Mouse Revue was moved to Tokyo Disneyland, where it played Apr. 15, 1983–May 25, 2009, also replaced by *Mickey's PhilharMagic*.

Mickey Mouse: Safety Belt Expert (TV) Educational film; a musical courtroom drama encouraging students to buckle up; released in Sep. 1988. 16 min.

Mickey Mouse Theater of the Air Short-lived radio program on NBC in 1938. Walt Disney provided Mickey's voice.

Mickey Mousekersize (TV) Series of 10 short-form cartoons encouraging kids to get up and move with Mickey and his friends; debuted Feb. 14, 2011, on the Disney Junior programming block on Disney Channel. A spin-off from *Mickey Mouse Clubhouse* featuring the same voice actors as in the series.

Mickey MouseWorks (TV) Animated series on ABC; premiered May 1, 1999, and ended Jan. 6, 2001, with new cartoons starring Mickey, Donald Duck, Goofy, Pluto, and Minnie Mouse of vary-ing lengths (12, 7½, and 6 min., and 90 sec.). Exec. produced by Roberts Gannaway and Tony Craig.

Mickey Plays Papa (film) Mickey Mouse cartoon released Sep. 29, 1934. Directed by Burt Gillett. Mickey discovers a baby on his doorstep and, with Pluto's help, tries to find different ways to stop its crying by imitating screen greats Charlie Chaplin and Jimmy Durante. An edited version, without Mickey, titled *Pluto and the Baby*, aired on the 1950s *Mickey Mouse Club*.

Mickey Saves Christmas (TV) Half-hour stop-motion-animated holiday special; first aired Nov. 27, 2022, on ABC, Disney Channel, Disney Junior, and Disney XD, followed by a digital release the following day on Disney+ and Hulu. Mickey, Minnie, and pals attempt to celebrate the perfect Christmas at their snowy cabin, but when Pluto causes Santa to lose all the presents on his sleigh, the friends travel to the North Pole on a quest to save the holiday. Directed by David Brooks. Voices include Bret Iwan (Mickey Mouse), Kaitlyn Robrock (Minnie Mouse), Bill Farmer (Goofy/Pluto), Tony Anselmo (Donald Duck), Debra Wilson (Daisy Duck), Brock Powell (Santa Claus/Prancer). Animation by Stoopid Buddy Stoodios.

Mickey Shorts Theater Echo Lake attraction in Disney's Hollywood Studios; opened Mar. 4, 2020, replacing the ABC Sound Studio. An original cartoon, *Vacation Fun*, shows Mickey and Minnie's favorite vacation memories accompanied with segments from Disney Channel's 2013 series of *Mickey Mouse* shorts. After the show, guests can pose for their own vacation photos in displays of Mickey's world.

Mickey Steps Out (film) Mickey Mouse cartoon released Jul. 7, 1931. Directed by Burt Gillett. Dressed up and on his way to see Minnie, Mickey falls in some mud but makes up for his disheveled appearance with some entertaining dance and juggling routines. When Pluto chases a cat into the house, the resulting chaos wrecks the house and covers the inhabitants with soot from the stove.

Mickey the Brave! (TV) SEE MICKEY MOUSE FUNHOUSE.

Mickey: The Story of a Mouse (film) A Disney+ original documentary; digitally released Nov. 18, 2022, following a Mar. 19 premiere at the South by Southwest (SXSW) film festival in Austin. Mickey Mouse is one of the most enduring symbols in history. This film explores Mickey's significance, getting to the core of what the character's cultural impact says about each of us and about our world. Directed by Jeff Malmberg. Appearances include Eric Goldberg, Mark Henn, Randy Haycock, Floyd Norman, Carmenita Higginbotham, Rebecca Cline, Kevin M. Kern, Bob Iger. 93 min. From Tremolo Productions. SEE ALSO MICKEY IN A MINUTE (FILM).

Mickey: The True Original Exhibition A 16,000-sq.-ft. interactive exhibit celebrating 90 years of Mickey Mouse in pop culture, featuring historic and contemporary works by renowned artists. Opened Nov. 8, 2018, in a pop-up site on 10th Avenue in New York City. Closed Feb. 10, 2019.

MickeyAngelo Gifts Shop in the Tokyo DisneySea Hotel MiraCosta at Tokyo Disney Resort; opened Sep. 4, 2001.

Mickey's Amateurs (film) Mickey Mouse cartoon released Apr. 17, 1937. Walt decided to try using some fresh directors, with story men Pinto Colvig, Walt Pfeiffer, and Ed Penner handling the chores for this cartoon. When Donald's recitation is booed off Mickey's radio broadcast, Clara Cluck sings, Clarabelle plays the piano, and Goofy performs as a one-man band. Despite these diversions (and the audience's earlier response), Donald is back at the end with his recitation.

Mickey's Audition (film) SEE MICKEY'S BIG BREAK.

Mickey's Big Break (film) Short film being a humorous portrayal of Mickey Mouse's interview for a job with Disney, featuring Roy E. Disney portraying Walt Disney. Directed by Rob Minkoff. Cameo roles by Mel Brooks, Angela Lansbury, Ed Begley Jr., Dom DeLuise. The film was originally known as *Mickey's Audition* and used during summer 1991 in Disney-MGM Studios at Walt Disney World for a temporary attraction on one of the soundstages. Beginning in 1994, it was shown at the Main Street Cinema in the Magic Kingdom, and in 1998 in the Town Square Exhibition Hall.

Mickey's Birthday Party (film) Mickey Mouse cartoon released Feb. 7, 1942. Directed by Riley Thomson. The gang gives Mickey a surprise party that turns into a jam session with everyone play-ing instruments while Goofy has problems baking the cake.

Mickey's Birthdayland Area near Fantasyland in the Magic Kingdom at Walt Disney World, created to honor Mickey's 60th birthday; open Jun. 18, 1988–Apr. 22, 1990. At short notice, Disney executives decided that there should be a special area to honor the landmark birthday. A town, known as Duckburg, was quickly designed, and Disney artists helped the architects make it look like a dimensional cartoon. In order to build Mickey's Birthdayland, the Grand Prix Raceway had to be moved slightly. When it was suggested that there should be a statue to honor Duckburg's founder, the designers started coming up with ideas as to whom it should be, but one of the artists, Russell Schroeder, reminded them that there already was a founder of Duckburg, Cornelius Coot, in a comic book story, and he already had a statue in that comic book. Thus, the designers unexpectedly had something on which to base their statue. A train station was added along the route of the Walt Disney World Railroad, and special signs and displays lined the tracks leading from the Main Street, U.S.A. station to Mickey's Birthdayland. There was Grandma Duck's Farm (a petting farm), a live show featuring Disney characters, Mickey's house, and guests could even visit Mickey himself in his dressing room. After the birthday celebration was over, the area became Mickey's Starland and was remodeled in 1996 as Mickey's Toontown Fair. Today, the site is home to Storybook Circus.

Mickey's Character Shop Large store featuring Disney character merchandise in the Disney Village Marketplace at Walt Disney World; opened Oct. 25, 1985, on the site of the former Port of Entry, with a grand opening held Nov. 16. With the opening of the nearby World of Disney Oct. 3, 1996, the Character Shop closed Oct. 2, and was replaced by Toys Fantastic, Studio M, and a new location for Team Mickey's Athletic Club. SEE ALSO VILLAGE CHARACTER SHOP.

Mickey's Choo Choo (film) Mickey Mouse cartoon; released in 1929. Directed by Walt Disney. Engineer Mickey and his anthropomorphic train share some harrowing adventures with Minnie when one of the cars breaks away from the train with Mickey and Minnie on top.

Mickey's Christmas Carol (film) Mickey Mouse

cartoon featurette. Charles Dickens's well-known Christmas story is retold with Uncle Scrooge taking the role of Ebenezer Scrooge and many other Disney favorites who were returning to the silver screen after quite an absence. Mickey, for instance, had not been seen in a theatrical cartoon since *The Simple Things* in 1953. Premiered in England Oct. 20, 1983, followed by a U.S. release Dec. 16, 1983. Directed by Burny Mattinson. Voices include Alan Young (Scrooge), Wayne Allwine (Bob Cratchit/Mickey Mouse), Hal Smith (Jacob Marley's ghost/Goofy), Will Ryan (Ghost of Christmas Present/Willie the Giant, Ghost of Christmas Future/Pete), Eddy Carroll (Ghost of Christmas Past/Jiminy Cricket), Patricia Parris (Isabelle/Daisy Duck), Dick Billingsley (Tiny Tim), Clarence Nash (Fred/Donald Duck). 25 min. The song "Oh, What a Merry Christmas Day" was written by Frederick Searles and Irwin Kostal. The idea for the film was inspired by a 1974 Disney record album of the same name. Director Mattinson was inspired to begin the project, with the okay from Disney president and chief executive officer Ron Miller in May 1981. One of the difficult tasks in bringing back such favorite characters as Mickey and Donald was finding the right voices. Clarence "Ducky" Nash was still available to voice Donald, as he had since Donald's debut, but Mickey's voice would introduce a new talent—Wayne Allwine. Received an Academy Award nomination for Short Film. Began an annual TV airing in 1984 on NBC.

Mickey's Christmas Carol Fantasyland shop in the Magic Kingdom at Walt Disney World; opened in 1986, taking the place of Merlin's Magic Shop. Closed Feb. 4, 1996, to become Sir Mickey's.

Mickey's Christmas Chalet Fantasyland shop in Disneyland featuring Christmas holiday merchandise; opened May 25, 1983, taking the place of Merlin's Magic Shop. Closed May 17, 1987, to become Briar Rose Cottage.

Mickey's Circus (film) Mickey Mouse cartoon released Aug. 1, 1936. Directed by Ben Sharpsteen. At a circus benefit, orphans continually give Mickey and Donald trouble. When Donald chases seals who steal fish, orphans shoot him from a cannon onto Mickey's high-wire act. The orphans try to get Mickey and Donald to fall, and when they do, into the pool below, all the seals jump in to get a fish that a young seal throws into Donald's mouth.

Mickey's Delayed Date (film) Mickey Mouse

cartoon released Oct. 3, 1947. Directed by Charles Nichols. Minnie phones Mickey from a party to hurry up, and, with the aid of Pluto, he gets all dressed up in his tux. But on the way to the party, he and Pluto tangle with a trash can. Minnie sees Mickey with his torn clothes, and, to Mickey's amazement, is not mad, for the party is a hard times party. She compliments him on his costume.

Mickey's Elephant (film) Mickey Mouse cartoon released Oct. 10, 1936. Directed by Dave Hand. Happy with his gift, Mickey makes a home for Bobo, his new elephant, incurring Pluto's jealousy. Putting pepper in Bobo's trunk, Pluto succeeds in not only getting Bobo's new home blown to bits, but his own doghouse as well.

Mickey's Field Trips Series of 4 educational films; released Sep. 1987–Jul. 1989: *The Police Station, The Fire Station, The Hospital,* and *The United Nations.*

Mickey's 50 (TV) A 90-min. special; aired Nov. 19, 1978. Dozens of celebrities, many of them in very short cameo appearances, stop by to help wish Mickey a happy birthday. Included among them are Gerald Ford, Billy Graham, Lawrence Welk, Jodie Foster, Goldie Hawn, Willie Nelson, Gene Kelly, Roy Rogers and Dale Evans, Edgar Bergen, O. J. Simpson, Eva Gabor, Anne Bancroft, Jo Anne Worley, Burt Reynolds. Filmmaker Mike Jittlov provides a trio of stop-motion sequences on Mickey Mouse merchandise through the years—titled *The Collector, The Rat Race,* and *Mouse Mania*—using new items from Disneyland shops and vintage merchandise from the Walt Disney Archives.

Mickey's Fire Brigade (film) Mickey Mouse cartoon released Aug. 3, 1935. Directed by Ben Sharpsteen. Mickey, Donald, and Goofy come to put out a fire in Clarabelle Cow's house. She's unaware, taking a bath when the trio comes crashing in to the rescue and into her bathtub.

Mickey's Follies (film) Mickey Mouse cartoon; featuring Mickey's theme song "Minnie's Yoo Hoo." Released in 1929. The first cartoon directed by Wilfred Jackson. In the midst of a musical revue, 2 chickens do an Apache dance, a pig sings opera, and Mickey brings it to a successful finale by singing and dancing on a piano.

Mickey's Fun Wheel Ferris wheel attraction in

Disney California Adventure; replaced the Sun Wheel May 4, 2009. A large image of Mickey Mouse took the place of the sun image on the side of the wheel. Closed Jan. 7, 2018, to become the Pixar Pal-A-Round.

Mickey's Gala Premiere (film) Mickey Mouse cartoon released Jul. 1, 1933. Directed by Burt Gillett. Mickey and the gang are treated to a lavish premiere of their new picture (*Galloping Romance*) at Grauman's Chinese Theatre, at which many screen stars—including Greta Garbo, Clark Gable, Charlie Chaplin, Mae West, Laurel and Hardy, Harold Lloyd, and Marlene Dietrich, plus Sid Grauman himself—praise Mickey. But Mickey awakens to find it is only a dream. Spelled *Mickey's Gala Premier* on the film's title card.

Mickey's Garden (film) Mickey Mouse cartoon released Jul. 13, 1935. Directed by Wilfred Jackson. Mickey and Pluto as pest exterminators sniffing around when Mickey gets a whiff of his own potent insecticide and dreams of battles with gigantic insects.

Mickey's Good Deed (film) Mickey Mouse cartoon released Dec. 17, 1932. Directed by Burt Gillett. Mickey is a street singer who selflessly sells Pluto to a rich family to raise money for a poor family at Christmas. But Pluto is mistreated and flees, returning to his beloved master.

Mickey's Grand Opera (film) Mickey Mouse cartoon released Mar. 7, 1936. Directed by Wilfred Jackson. Mickey conducts the orchestra as Donald Duck and Clara Cluck sing a duet, which is marred by Pluto's antics with a magician's hat and its magical inhabitants.

Mickey's Groove Disney merchandise shop in Downtown Disney West Side at Walt Disney World; open Oct. 21, 1999. Closed Apr. 2, 2011, to become Orlando Harley-Davidson.

Mickey's Happy Valentine Special (TV) Show aired Feb. 12, 1989. Directed by Scot Garen. Ludwig Von Drake looks at love in this reedited show told in an MTV style.

Mickey's Hollywood Theater Area at Mickey's Starland in the Magic Kingdom at Walt Disney World; open Jun. 18, 1988–Mar. 11, 1996. Guests could go backstage and meet Mickey in his dressing room.

Mickey's House Attraction in Mickey's Toontown at Disneyland; opened Jan. 24, 1993. Guests can walk through the house, seeing Mickey's living quarters along with memorabilia from his long career. Farther on, they can see a short film and then meet Mickey on the set from one of his famous cartoons. There was also a Mickey's House in Mickey's Birthdayland (later named Mickey's Country House when the area became Mickey's Toontown Fair) in the Magic Kingdom at Walt Disney World, as well as one in Toontown at Tokyo Disneyland.

Mickey's House of Villains (film) Direct-to-video release Sep. 3, 2002; film pits Mickey Mouse and his friends versus Disney's greatest villains as they try to turn the House of Mouse into the House of Villains. 70 min.

Mickey's Kangaroo (film) Mickey Mouse cartoon released Apr. 13, 1935. The last black-and-white Disney cartoon. Directed by Dave Hand. Mickey receives a kangaroo from Australia that delights in boxing with him. They make Pluto's life miserable with their antics, but by the end all are good friends.

Mickey's Kitchen The Walt Disney Company's first restaurant venture outside of its theme parks, begun in 1990 with one facility next door to The Disney Store in Montclair, California. A 2nd location later opened in Schaumburg, Illinois. The fast-food restaurants, which emphasized healthier fare, did not catch on and the two were eventually removed.

Mickey's Magic Show SEE DISNEY LIVE! MICKEY'S MAGIC SHOW.

Mickey's Magical TV World Show at Mickey's Starland; opened Apr. 26, 1990, and closed Mar. 11, 1996. Upon exiting Mickey's House, guests entered the theater where they could watch a live show featuring Disney TV characters from shows, including *Disney's Adventures of the Gummi Bears*, *DuckTales*, and *TaleSpin*. It was formerly *Minnie's Surprise Birthday Party*.

Mickey's Man Friday (film) Mickey Mouse cartoon released Jan. 19, 1935. Directed by Dave Hand. Loosely based on the story of Robinson Crusoe, and one of Mickey's last black-and-white cartoons. Mickey, shipwrecked, lands on an island inhabited by cannibals. He befriends a local who helps him escape.

Mickey's Mart Souvenir store in Tomorrowland in the Magic Kingdom at Walt Disney World; open Oct. 1, 1971–Jun. 27, 1991. Became Mickey's Star Traders. Also a shop selling low-priced souvenirs in the Downtown Disney Marketplace at Walt Disney World; open Nov. 11, 2004–Jan. 15, 2011, replaced by LittleMissMatched.

Mickey's Mechanical Man (film) Mickey Mouse cartoon released Jun. 17, 1933. Directed by Wilfred Jackson. Inventor Mickey creates a robot that fights the hairy star of *The Gorilla Mystery* and overpowers him with the help of Minnie, who revives the robot at one point with a horn.

Mickey's Mellerdrammer (film) Mickey Mouse cartoon released Mar. 18, 1933. Directed by Wilfred Jackson. Mickey and the gang put on a production of *Uncle Tom's Cabin* with Horace Horsecollar as Simon Legree and Mickey as Uncle Tom. The bloodhounds in the play become unruly and bring down the curtain early.

Mickey's Moderne Memories World Bazaar shop selling Disney and special event items in Tokyo Disneyland; open Apr. 15, 1993. Closed May 2007, to become the Toy Station.

Mickey's Nightmare (film) Mickey Mouse cartoon released Aug. 13, 1932. Directed by Burt Gillett. Mickey dreams he is married to Minnie, but the dream turns into a nightmare when he is overwhelmed by their children. He happily wakes up to repeated lickings from Pluto.

Mickey's 90th Spectacular (TV) In celebration of the 90th anniversary of the creation of Mickey Mouse in 1928, ABC aired this 2-hour special Nov. 4, 2018. Special appearances by Kristen Bell, Josh Groban, the K-Pop group NCT 127, Leslie Odom Jr., Meghan Trainor, Zac Brown Band, Skylar Astin, Kelsea Ballerini, Miles Brown, Anna Camp, Josh Gad, Wendi McLendon-Covey, Sage Steele. Produced at the Shrine Auditorium in Los Angeles.

Mickey's Not-So-Scary Halloween Party Annual after-hours ticketed event in the Magic Kingdom at Walt Disney World; began as a 1-night-only party Oct. 31, 1995, and then later expanded to multiple evenings over subsequent years. Guests can go trick-or-treating in the park and enjoy special entertainment. Over the years, themed fireworks and shows, including *Mickey's Boo-to-You Halloween Parade*, have been added. A similar event at

Disneyland, Mickey's Halloween Treat, was held 1995–1996, returning in 2005 as an annual, special-admission event in Disney's California Adventure. The event was renamed Mickey's Trick-or-Treat Party in 2008 and moved back to Disneyland in 2010 as Mickey's Halloween Party. In 2019, the party returned to Disney California Adventure as Oogie Boogie Bash – A Disney Halloween Party, including a new *World of Color* show titled *Villainous!* General Halloween festivities first began at Disneyland in 1959, with a Parade of the Pumpkins. Thereafter, little was done until 1967, when a Halloween Festival Parade that featured the Disney characters started. Walt Disney World began annual Halloween celebrations in 1972.

Mickey's Nutcracker Christmas musical show at Videopolis in Disneyland during the 1991–1992 holiday seasons.

Mickey's of Hollywood Clothing and memento shop on Hollywood Boulevard in Disney's Hollywood Studios; opened May 1, 1989. The name was inspired by Frederick's of Hollywood.

Mickey's Once Upon a Christmas (film) Released on videocassette on Nov. 9, 1999; segments include *Donald Duck: Stuck on Christmas*, *A Very Goofy Christmas*, and *Mickey and Minnie's Gift of the Magi*, tied together with narration by Kelsey Grammer and concluding with a rendition of "Deck the Halls" by the country trio SHeDAISY. 70 min.

Mickey's Orphans (film) Mickey Mouse cartoon released Dec. 9, 1931. Directed by Burt Gillett. Nominated for an Academy Award. A basket of kittens is left on Minnie's doorstep at Christmas, and Mickey and Minnie charitably bring it inside. But they soon regret their action as the cats wreck the house, strip the tree, and take the gifts and candy.

Mickey's Pal Pluto (film) Mickey Mouse cartoon released Feb. 18, 1933. Directed by Burt Gillett. When Mickey and Minnie find some kittens, Pluto is jealous, torn between his angel good and devil bad consciences. When the cats fall into a well, Pluto and his angel-self rescue them. It was remade as *Lend a Paw* (1941), which won an Academy Award.

Mickey's Pantry Kitchenware shop in Downtown Disney Marketplace (later the Marketplace at Disney Springs) at Walt Disney World; opened

Apr. 15, 2005, in the former Goofy's Candy Co. Closed Nov. 15, 2019, to become The Spice & Tea Exchange.

Mickey's Parrot (film) Mickey Mouse cartoon released Sep. 9, 1938. The first cartoon directed by Bill Roberts. Overhearing a radio broadcast about an escaped killer, Mickey and Pluto hear a voice they assume to be the felon. After a scary few minutes, they discover it is only Mickey's pet parrot and all are relieved, including the parrot.

Mickey's PhilharMagic Fantasyland 3-D film attraction in the Magic Kingdom at Walt Disney World; opened Sep. 30, 2003, before a grand opening ceremony Oct. 8, replacing *Legend of the Lion King*. Donald Duck swipes Mickey's sorcerer's hat, then tries to conduct a symphony, but ends up stumbling into musical scenes from classic Disney animated features, including *Beauty and the Beast, Fantasia, The Little Mermaid, The Lion King, Peter Pan*, and *Aladdin*. 12 min. The 150-ft.-wide wraparound screen was the largest ever created for a 3-D attraction. The show also marked the first time the classic Disney characters were completely modeled and animated by a computer. Donald's dialogue was created using archival recordings of the late Clarence Nash, with a few new lines provided by the current voice of Donald, Tony Anselmo. Also opened in Hong Kong Disneyland Sep. 12, 2005; Tokyo Disneyland Jan. 24, 2011 (replacing the Mickey Mouse Revue); the Discoveryland Theatre in Disneyland Paris Sep. 29, 2018, as *Mickey et son Orchestre PhilharMagique*; and the Sunset Showcase Theater at Disney California Adventure Apr. 26, 2019 (replacing *For the First Time in Forever: A Frozen Sing-Along Celebration*). In 2021, a new musical segment from Disney • Pixar's *Coco* was added at Disney California Adventure, Disneyland Paris, and the Magic Kingdom at Walt Disney World; the scene was later added to the Tokyo Disneyland show Sep. 15, 2022.

Mickey's Polo Team (film) Mickey Mouse cartoon released Jan. 4, 1936. Directed by Dave Hand. Walt's interest in this sport found its way into a cartoon that features many Hollywood celebrities versus Disney characters, such as the Big Bad Wolf and Mickey. The horses all seem to resemble their riders. By the time the dust settles, the horses are riding the players.

Mickey's Retreat SEE LITTLE LAKE BRYAN.

Mickey's Revue (film) Mickey Mouse cartoon released May 25, 1932. Directed by Wilfred Jackson. First appearance of the character who would become Goofy; here he is a member of the audience cheering on Mickey's musical comedy. The show is brought to an abrupt end when Pluto creates havoc by chasing cats onstage.

Mickey's Rival (film) Mickey Mouse cartoon released Jun. 20, 1936. Directed by Wilfred Jackson. Mickey's rival, Mortimer, strives for Minnie's affections on an afternoon outing. As he woos Minnie, he plays practical jokes on Mickey and even his car threatens Mickey's car. But, when Mortimer is responsible for a bull attacking, it is Mickey who finally rescues Minnie, while Mortimer runs away.

Mickey's Safety Club Series of 4 educational films released in Sep. 1989: *Halloween Surprises, Playground Fun, What to Do at Home*, and *Street Safe, Street Smart*.

Mickey's Service Station (film) Mickey Mouse cartoon released Mar. 16, 1935. Directed by Ben Sharpsteen. Mickey, Donald, and Goofy are service station attendants who attempt to fix Pete's car but eventually find the problem is the squeak of a cricket. They do such a poor job putting the car back together again that the furious Pete ends up being chased by the motor.

Mickey's 60th Birthday (TV) Show aired Nov. 13, 1988. Directed by Scot Garen. Mickey disappears and everyone is searching for him. The cause? A wizard has punished Mickey for using his magic hat by making everyone forget what he looks like. But, finally, all is forgiven, and there is a big celebration at Disneyland. Stars John Ritter, Jill Eikenberry, Carl Reiner, Cheech Marin, Phylicia Rashad, Charles Fleischer, and a host of other celebrities.

Mickey's Soundsational Parade Musical extravaganza in Disneyland; ran May 27, 2011–Jul. 17, 2019, with 9 whimsical floats, live musicians and percussionists, and characters from films, including *The Little Mermaid, The Lion King, The Three Caballeros, The Princess and the Frog*, and *Mary Poppins*.

Mickey's Star Traders Tomorrowland souvenir and sun-care-product shop in the Magic Kingdom at Walt Disney World; opened Jun. 28, 1991. Presented by Coppertone. Formerly Mickey's Mart. Renamed Star Traders Nov. 8, 2019.

Mickey's Starland Area near Fantasyland in the Magic Kingdom at Walt Disney World; opened May 26, 1990, taking the place of Mickey's Birthdayland after the conclusion of the 60th-birthday celebrations. Became Mickey's Toontown Fair in 1996.

Mickey's Steam-Roller Mickey Mouse cartoon released Jun. 16, 1934. Directed by Dave Hand. When Mickey's nephews crawl into his steamroller while he is romancing Minnie, a chase ensues as the machine goes out of control and causes massive destruction until it stops after smashing a hotel.

Mickey's Storybook Adventure SEE MICKEY AND THE WONDROUS BOOK.

Mickey's Storybook Express Train-themed daytime parade throughout Gardens of Imagination in Shanghai Disneyland; premiered Jun. 16, 2016, along the longest parade route in a Disney park. Each train car in the procession features Disney characters with music from classic films.

Mickey's Surprise Party (film) Cartoon commercial starring Minnie and Fifi, made for the National Biscuit Co. for showing at the 1939–1940 New York World's Fair. Delivered Feb. 18, 1939. Fifi interferes with Minnie's cooking, but Mickey saves the day by his purchase of Nabisco cookies. He uses the opportunity to show Minnie the company's various products.

Mickey's Toontown Area in Disneyland; opened Jan. 24, 1993. Disney designers Dave Burkhart and Joe Lanzisero looked to the Toon world and created it as the place where Mickey, Minnie, Donald, and the other Disney characters live. There is a downtown section, where guests can have fun pushing buttons, twisting knobs, and opening boxes, all leading to a comic happening—the fireworks factory explodes, the mailbox talks back, weasels make snide comments under the manhole. The Jolly Trolley originally transported one to the residential area, where guests can visit the characters at their houses. Goofy's Bounce House was limited to children only; it was changed to Goofy's Playhouse in 2006. In back of Mickey's House, one can meet the mouse himself on the set from one of his classic cartoons. Other attractions include Minnie's House, Donald's Boat (the *Miss Daisy*), Gadget's Go Coaster, Chip 'n Dale Treehouse, and Roger Rabbit's Car Toon Spin, a zany ride through the Toon world. The area closed Mar. 8, 2022, for an elaborate reimagining, including the addition of Mickey & Minnie's Runaway Railway, changes to many of the existing attractions, and new grassy play areas for young children in the form of CenTOONial Park. It was announced the land will reopen Mar. 19, 2023. A Toontown opened in Tokyo Disneyland Apr. 15, 1996, sponsored by Kodansha, with its downtown and residential districts reversed from the ones at Disneyland.

Mickey's Toontown Fair Character-greeting area in the Magic Kingdom at Walt Disney World; opened Jun. 29, 1996. A remodeling of Mickey's Starland (originally known as Mickey's Birthdayland). A complement to Mickey's Toontown in Disneyland, the refreshed land represented the country home for the Disney characters, with Mickey's Country House, Minnie's Country House, Donald's Boat, the Toontown Hall of Fame, and a roller coaster, The Barnstormer at Goofy's Wise Acres Farm. Shopping was offered at Cornelius Coot's County Bounty and the Toontown Farmer's Market. Closed Feb. 11, 2011, to become Storybook Circus.

Mickey's Trailer (film) Mickey Mouse cartoon released May 6, 1938. Directed by Ben Sharpsteen. On their trip out of the city for a vacation, Mickey, Donald, and Goofy plan on having lots of fun and relaxation with their trailer, but all does not go as they plan, and they soon have their hands full when the trailer gets away from them. Despite a steep mountain road and a speedy express train, the car and trailer eventually meet once again. Includes some fun gags about marvelous contraptions built into the trailer.

Mickey's Twice Upon a Christmas (film) Direct-to-video release Nov. 9, 2004. The Disney gang is presented in computer-generated animation in 5 segments about the holiday. Directed by Matt O'Callaghan. Voices include Wayne Allwine (Mickey), Tony Anselmo (Donald), Bill Farmer (Goofy), Tress MacNeille (Daisy), Jason Marsden (Max), Chuck McCann (Santa), Russi Taylor (Minnie Mouse), Alan Young (Scrooge McDuck), Clive Revill (Narrator). 68 min.

Mickey's Very Merry Christmas Party After-hours ticketed event in the Magic Kingdom at Walt Disney World; began as a 1-night-only celebration Dec. 16, 1983, then later expanding to multiple evenings. Guests enjoy the park with special holiday decorations, entertainment, and treats.

MicroAdventure! Revised version of *Honey, I Shrunk the Audience*; opened in Tokyo Disneyland Apr. 15, 1997. Closed May 10, 2010, and succeeded by a return engagement of *Captain EO* in summer 2011.

Middleton, Robert (1911–1977) Actor; appeared on TV in *Gallegher* (Dutch Mac) and *Texas John Slaughter* (Frank Davis).

Midget Autopia Fantasyland attraction in Disneyland; open Apr. 23, 1957–Apr. 3, 1966. Walt supposedly did not like the attraction because only children could ride it. When he had it removed from Disneyland, he donated it to his boyhood hometown of Marceline, Missouri, where it was installed in the Walt Disney Municipal Park (though it has not operated for many years).

Midler, Bette Actress; appeared in *Down and Out in Beverly Hills* (Barbara Whiteman), *Ruthless People* (Barbara Stone), *Outrageous Fortune* (Sandy), *Big Business* (Sadie Shelton/Sadie Ratliff), *Beaches* (C. C. Bloom), *Stella* (Stella Claire), *Scenes from a Mall* (Deborah), *Hocus Pocus* and *Hocus Pocus 2* (Winifred), and *Fantasia/2000* (as herself), and on TV in *Mickey's 60th Birthday* and *The Dream Is Alive*. She voiced Georgette in *Oliver & Company* and starred in the short demonstration film *The Lottery* in Disney-MGM Studios. She was named a Disney Legend in 2019.

Midnight in a Toy Shop (film) Silly Symphony cartoon released Aug. 16, 1930. Directed by Wilfred Jackson. In its exploration of a toy shop, a spider has unnerving experiences with various activated toys, a lighted candle, and firecrackers.

Midnight Madness (film) A genius grad student organizes an all-night treasure hunt in which 5 rival teams composed of colorful oddballs furiously match wits with one another while trying to locate and decipher various cryptic clues planted ingeniously around Los Angeles. Released Feb. 8, 1980. Directed by David Wechter and Michael Nankin. 112 min. Stars David Naughton (Adam), Debra Clinger (Laura), Eddie Deezen (Wesley), Brad Wilkin (Lavitas), Maggie Roswell (Donna), Stephen Furst (Harold), Irene Tedrow (Mrs. Grimhaus), Michael J. Fox (in his Disney and film debut as Scott), Dirk Blocker (Blaylak). The film underwent 4 title changes during production: *The All-Night Treasure Hunt*, *The Ultimate Game*, *The Great All-Nighter*, and finally the final title, which proved most popular in audience research tests. The movie was shot at 25 locations around Los Angeles, from the Griffith Park Observatory to the Hollywood Wax Museum, Osko's Disco, Occidental College, Sherman Clay Piano Museum, and the Bonaventure Hotel. Three songs, "Midnight Madness," "Don't Know Why I Came," and "Someone New," were written for the movie by David and Julius Wechter. The film was released without the Disney name on it, with the hope that it would reach teenagers and young adults who often shied away from "Disney" films. To build a cast of fresh, new faces, more than 2,000 actors and actresses were interviewed by the directors. Of the 25 feature roles, 7 were cast from the open call, and 4 others were cast for supporting parts.

Midtown Delights Main Street, U.S.A. ice cream shop in Hong Kong Disneyland; opened Dec. 18, 2019.

Midtown Jewelry SEE MAIN STREET CINEMA.

Mighty Ducks, The (film) A competitive, aggressive trial lawyer, Gordon Bombay, is sentenced to community service—coaching a peewee hockey team full of clumsy misfits. Bombay, who formerly played hockey himself, finds his work cut out for him, as he has to teach the team to skate, score, and win. The reluctant coach becomes committed, names his team "The Ducks," and slowly molds his group of losers into a championship team while he himself realizes that the sport may be even more satisfying to him than his chosen profession. Released Oct. 2, 1992. Directed by Stephen Herek. 103 min. Stars Emilio Estevez (Gordon Bombay), Joss Ackland (Hans), Lane Smith (Coach Reilly). Filmed on location in Minneapolis, the heart of peewee hockey country. Two sequels were released: *D2: The Mighty Ducks* in 1994 and *D3: The Mighty Ducks* in 1996.

Mighty Ducks (TV) Animated series; premiered Sep. 6, 1996, in syn. and on ABC the following day. The ABC run ended Aug. 30, 1997. A combination hockey team and band of superheroes, part-duck and part-human, show off their hockey prowess at the Anaheim Pond rink. Elsewhere, they use their high-tech tools and teamwork to save the world from the evil Lord Dragaunus and his henchmen, whom they've followed from the planet Puckworld. The Mighty Ducks team includes the role-model captain Wildwing, his renegade brother Nosedive, martial arts expert Mallory, stylish ex-criminal Duke L'Orange, science-whiz Tanya, and huge Zen master Grin. The only human who knows the Ducks' true identities is Phil, the team's manager. Voices include Ian Ziering (Wildwing), Steve Mackall (Nosedive), April Winchell (Mallory), Jeff Bennett (Duke L'Orange), Jennifer Hale (Tanya), Brad Garrett (Grin), Jim Belushi (Phil), Tim Curry (Lord Dragaunus). 26 episodes. From Buena Vista Television, Walt Disney Television Animation, and Helium Productions.

Mighty Ducks Disney's first entry into the realm of professional sports. In 1992, the company founded the Mighty Ducks hockey team, named for the team in Walt Disney Pictures' *The Mighty Ducks*, as an expansion team in the National Hockey League. They were ready for league play in the 1993–1994 season, and their first exhibition game was held on Sep. 18, 1993. They played at the Arrowhead Pond (later known as the Honda Center) in Anaheim. Henry and Susan Samueli agreed to purchase the Mighty Ducks from Disney on Feb. 25, 2005, taking Disney out of the professional sports business 2 years after selling Major League Baseball's Anaheim Angels. The sale was completed Jun. 20, 2005, and the team's name was changed to the Anaheim Ducks.

Mighty Ducks, The: Game Changers (TV) Original series on Disney+; digitally premiered Mar. 26, 2021, with the last episode released Nov. 30, 2022. The Mighty Ducks have evolved from scrappy underdogs to an ultracompetitive youth hockey team. After 12-year-old Evan is unceremoniously cut from the Ducks, he and his mom, Alex, set out to build their own team of misfits to challenge the cutthroat, win-at-all-costs culture of youth sports today. With the help of Gordon Bombay, they rediscover the joys of playing just for the love of the game. Stars Lauren Graham (Alex Morrow), Emilio Estevez (Gordon Bombay), Brady Noon (Evan Morrow), Maxwell Simkins (Nick), Swayam Bhatia (Sofi Hudson-Batra), Luke Islam (Koob), Kiefer O'Reilly (Logan), Taegen Burns (Maya), Bella Higginbotham (Lauren), DJ Watts (Sam). From ABC Signature.

Mighty Ducks the Movie: The First Face-Off (video) Animated movie, tying together TV episodes; released on video Apr. 8, 1997. The evil Lord Dragaunus returns to Puckworld, a peaceful planet of hockey-loving ducks, from a distant galaxy to take revenge against the inhabitants who once banished him. A special strike team of 6 young

courageous superheroes—The Mighty Ducks—is formed to face off against Lord Dragaunus's dark forces. After a fierce battle, Dragaunus manages to escape, and the Ducks must follow him and find themselves transported to the weird, alien metropolis of Anaheim. Trapped there, the Ducks build a supersecret headquarters under the Anaheim Pond to thwart Dragaunus's plans to take over the world. Directed by Joe Barruso. 66 min. Stars Ian Ziering (Wildwing), Jim Belushi (Phil), Tim Curry (Lord Dragaunus). From Walt Disney Television Animation.

Mighty Joe Young (film) Zoologist Gregg O'Hara is exploring the remote Pangani Mountains in Central Africa when he comes upon an incredible discovery: an awesome 15-ft.-tall gorilla. Fearsome and dangerous when provoked, he is tame in the hands of Jill, the 21-year-old orphan who raised the gorilla and named him Joe. When Joe's life is threatened by poachers, Gregg and Jill rescue him by moving him to a California animal preserve. However, Joe is not safe for long. His newfound notoriety makes him a target for an enemy from his past, a ruthless poacher who is eager to steal Joe for his unique value in the endangered species black market. Feeling threatened and confused in his man-made confines, Joe finally escapes from captivity. With only Los Angeles and its terrified residents in his way, this powerful force of nature attempts to traverse a modern metropolis, leaving a trail of destruction and chaos in his wake. Jill and Gregg race to save Joe's life before he is destroyed by the encircling authorities, and the chase culminates in an incredible and selfless display of courage by the mighty Joe, proving that within his fearsome frame beats a noble and heroic heart. Released Dec. 25, 1998. Directed by Ron Underwood. Stars Bill Paxton (Gregg O'Hara), Charlize Theron (Jill), Rade Sherbedgia (Strasser), Regina King (Cecily Banks), Peter Firth (Garth), David Paymer (Dr. Harry Ruben), Naveen Andrews (Pindi). 115 min. Based on the classic RKO motion picture from 1949. Locations in Hawai'i, such as the jungles and mountains of Oahu's Kualoa Valley, doubled for the Pangani Mountains in Tanzania. Animatronics and computer graphics, as well as forced perspective and blue-screen camerawork with actor John Alexander in a 40% scale "Joe" costume, all contributed to the character of the gorilla. Three different hydraulic versions of Joe, as well as the 40% scale suits, were created by Academy Award–winning designer Rick Baker. In scenes where the suits were used, the sets and props also had to be created at 40% size.

Miguel The 12-year-old aspiring musician who travels to the Land of the Dead in *Coco*; voiced by Anthony Gonzalez.

Miguel's El Dorado Cantina Counter-service Mexican restaurant in Lost River Delta at Tokyo DisneySea; opened Sep. 4, 2001. The story goes that the owner, Miguel, dreamed of hitting it rich but found success when he established this relaxing gathering place for friends.

Mija (film) A Disney original documentary; began a festival run Jan. 21, 2022, starting at the Sundance Film Festival, and a limited theatrical run starting Aug. 5. Doris Muñoz and Jacks Haupt, two American-born daughters of immigrants from Mexico, are navigating their careers in the music industry while seeking to provide for their families. The pressure of success is heightened as it is their family's hope for green cards and family reunification. Directed by Isabel Castro. 88 min. From Impact Partners, in association with Cinereach.

Mike & Maty (TV) Hour-long daytime talk show on ABC; aired Apr. 11, 1994–Jun. 7, 1996. The show featured upbeat funny events and stories. Stars Michael Burger and Maty Monfort. From Buena Vista Television and Valleycrest Productions.

Mike Fink Keel Boats Frontierland attraction in Disneyland; opened Dec. 25, 1955. Based on the TV episode *Davy Crockett's Keelboat Race*. The boats are the *Gullywhumper*, named for Mike Fink's boat, and the *Bertha Mae*, named for Davy's boat. Fink was the legendary King of the River to go along with his opponent's title of King of the Wild Frontier. The Keel Boats attraction closed in 1994 but reopened Mar. 30, 1996. They closed again May 17, 1997. Also Frontierland attraction in the Magic Kingdom at Walt Disney World, open Oct. 1, 1971–Apr. 29, 2001 (though it continued for a while to operate seasonally). SEE ALSO RIVER ROGUE KEELBOATS (DISNEYLAND PARIS).

Mike Wazowski James P. Sullivan's 1-eyed monster friend and scare assistant in *Monsters, Inc.*; voiced by Billy Crystal.

Mike's New Car (film) Animated short from Pixar Animation Studios, featuring the stars of *Monsters,*

Inc.; created as bonus material for the Sep. 17, 2002, DVD release of the feature. Mike Wazowski shows off his new car to his friend James P. "Sulley" Sullivan, but neither knows how to operate it. 4 min. Released initially at the El Capitan Theatre in Hollywood May 17, 2002, for Academy Award consideration; it received a nomination for Best Animated Short Film.

Mile Long Bar Frontierland counter-service restaurant in the Magic Kingdom at Walt Disney World; opened Oct. 1, 1971, serving light fare and cool drinks. An ingenious use of mirrors made the bar seem like it was a mile long. Melvin, Buff, and Max, the mounted animals from Country Bear Jamboree, welcomed guests entering from the adjacent show. Closed Jan. 5, 1998, for an expansion of the Pecos Bill Tall Tale Inn and Cafe. Also open in Bear Country at Disneyland 1972–1988 (later named Brer Bar, 1989–2002) and in Westernland at Tokyo Disneyland Apr. 15, 1983–2010 (replaced by an expansion of Hungry Bear Restaurant).

Miles, Vera Actress; appeared in *A Tiger Walks* (Dorothy Williams), *Those Calloways* (Liddy Calloway), *Follow Me, Boys!* (Vida Downey), *The Wild Country* (Kate), *One Little Indian* (Doris Melver), and *The Castaway Cowboy* (Henrietta MacAvoy). On TV, she played the Coca-Cola girl on *One Hour in Wonderland*.

Miles from Tomorrowland (TV) Animated series from Disney Junior in partnership with Wild Canary; debuted Feb. 6, 2015, on Disney Channel. The Callisto family lives on board a space station, carrying out a key mission on behalf of the Tomorrowland Transit Authority: connecting the universe. Son Miles, age 7, is a space adventurer, always ready for action. He blasts through the universe with his best friend and robo-ostrich, Merc. Voices include Olivia Munn (Phoebe Callisto), Cullen McCarthy (Miles), Tom Kenny (Leo), Fiona Bishop (Loretta), Dee Bradley Baker (Merc). For its 3rd season, beginning Oct. 16, 2017, the series was renamed *Mission Force One*.

Milestones for Mickey (film) A 16-mm compilation of *Plane Crazy*, *Mickey's Service Station*, *The Band Concert*, *Thru the Mirror*, "The Sorcerer's Apprentice" segment of *Fantasia*, and the *Mickey Mouse Club*'s "Mickey Mouse Club March." Released in May 1974.

Milestones in Animation (film) A 16-mm compilation of *Steamboat Willie*, *The Skeleton Dance*, *Flowers and Trees*, *Three Little Pigs*, and *The Old Mill*. Released in Mar. 1973.

Miley Cyrus – Endless Summer Vacation (Backyard Sessions) (TV) Music-focused performance special on Disney+; scheduled to digitally premiere Mar. 10, 2023, in conjunction with her album release (*Endless Summer Vacation*). Produced by RadicalMedia, Miley Cyrus, HopeTown Entertainment, Crush Management, and Columbia Records. From Disney Branded Television.

Milk Stand Drink stall in Star Wars: Galaxy's Edge; opened May 31, 2019, in Disneyland and Aug. 29, 2019, in Disney's Hollywood Studios at Walt Disney World. Guests enjoy a cup of Batuu's legendary blue or green milk, served frozen.

Milland, Ray (1905–1986) Actor; appeared in *Escape to Witch Mountain* (Aristotle Bolt).

Millar, Lee (1924–1980) Actor; provided the voice of Jim Dear and the dogcatcher in *Lady and the Tramp*. Incidentally, he was the son of voice actors Verna Felton, who voiced Aunt Sarah in the same film, and Lee Millar Sr. (1888–1941), who voiced Pluto in the 1930s.

Millennium Celebration With the theme of "Celebrate the Future Hand in Hand," Walt Disney World celebrated the new millennium concentrating its efforts on EPCOT. There, an enormous Mickey Mouse hand held a 116-ft.-tall, star-topped magic wand that trailed a giant "2000" over Spaceship Earth for 15 months beginning in Oct. 1999. The "2000" was replaced with the word "Epcot," until the icon was removed in 2007. In World Showcase, the 65,000-sq.-ft. Millennium Village presented exhibits, attractions, and cuisine from countries around the world. Additionally, there was a new program of Pin Trading, an updated Innoventions, and special entertainment, including the *Tapestry of Nations* parade (later *Tapestry of Dreams*) and *IllumiNations 2000: Reflections of Earth*. Guests had the opportunity to have their photos etched into steel tiles on 35 granite slabs at Leave a Legacy at the park's main entrance. Disney also commissioned 2 Millennium Symphonies: *Four Seasons* by Michael Torke, and *Garden of Light* by Aaron Jay Kernis, which premiered at New York City's Avery Fisher Hall on Oct. 8, 1999. After the close of the celebration, Millennium Village was remodeled and opened in 2001

as World ShowPlace, an event/convention meeting facility.

Millennium Falcon: Smugglers Run Attraction in Star Wars: Galaxy's Edge; opened May 31, 2019, in Disneyland and Aug. 29, 2019, in Disney's Hollywood Studios at Walt Disney World. At Ohnaka Transport Solutions, guests board the cockpit of the *Millennium Falcon* for a thrilling, interactive smuggling mission, playing the role of pilot, engineer, or gunner.

Miller, Bob Vice president and publisher of Hyperion Books beginning with its creation in 1990. He left the company in 2008.

Miller, Diane Disney SEE DISNEY, DIANE.

Miller, Ilana Actress; appeared on the *Mickey Mouse Club* on The Disney Channel beginning in 1990.

Miller, Julius Sumner (1909–1987) College professor who, as Professor Wonderful, hosted the Fun with Science segment on the syn. version of the *Mickey Mouse Club* in the 1964–1965 season.

Miller, Roger (1936–1992) Singer; he provided the voice of Allan-a-Dale in *Robin Hood* and appeared on TV in *Mickey's 50*. He narrated on TV *Deacon, the High Noon Dog* and *Go West, Young Dog*.

Miller, Ronald W. (1933–2019) Walt Disney's son-in-law and the husband of Diane Disney; he joined Disney in 1957 and served as associate producer on films, including *Bon Voyage*, *Summer Magic*, *Moon Pilot*, and *A Tiger Walks*. He became co-producer with Walt Disney on such films as *The Monkey's Uncle*; *That Darn Cat!*; *Lt. Robin Crusoe, U.S.N.*; and *Monkeys, Go Home!* His first full producer credit was on *Never a Dull Moment*. Beginning in 1968, he served 12 years as exec. producer of motion pictures and TV for the company. He served as president of Walt Disney Productions from 1980–1984 and was a member of the Board of Directors 1966–1984.

Million Dollar Arm (film) In a last-ditch effort to save his career as a sports agent, J. B. Bernstein concocts a scheme to find baseball's next great pitching ace. Hoping to find a young cricket pitcher he can turn into a Major League Baseball star, J. B. travels to India to produce a reality show competition called "Million Dollar Arm." With the help of a cantankerous but eagle-eyed retired baseball scout, he discovers Dinesh and Rinku, two 18-year-old boys who have no concept what playing baseball is yet have a knack for throwing a fastball. Hoping to sign them to major-league contracts and make a quick buck, J. B. brings the boys home to America to train. While the Americans are definitely out of their element in India, the boys, who have never left their rural villages back in India, are equally challenged when they come to the states. As the boys learn the finer points of baseball, J. B., with the help of his charming friend Brenda, learns valuable lessons about teamwork, commitment, and what it means to be a family. Directed by Craig Gillespie. Released May 16, 2014, after a May 15 release in Greece. Stars Jon Hamm (J. B. Bernstein), Alan Arkin (Ray Poitevint), Madhur Mittal (Dinesh), Suraj Sharma (Rinku), Lake Bell (Brenda), Bill Paxton (Tom House). 124 min. Filmed in Atlanta and Kennesaw, Georgia, and in India, in widescreen format.

Million Dollar Collar, The (film) International theatrical title of the 2-part *Ballad of Hector the Stowaway Dog*. Released in 1967.

Million Dollar Dixie Deliverance, The (TV) Two-hour movie; aired Feb. 5, 1978. Directed by Russ Mayberry. A Confederate officer kidnaps for a $1 million ransom 5 well-to-do children from a Yankee boarding school; a wounded Black Union soldier helps them escape after they perform the necessary surgery to remove the bullet from his leg. But they are captured again, and it takes a lucky Union army attack to save them. Stars Brock Peters, Christian Juttner, Chip Courtland, Kyle Richards, Alicia Fleer, Christian Berrigan, Joe Dorsey, Kip Niven.

Million Dollar Duck, The (film) By chance, a white duck in a science lab eats some terrible tasting applesauce and is exposed to a radiation beam. The result: the duck lays golden eggs! This upsets the life—and moral values—of a university professor, Albert Dooley, who soon has troubles with his wife, son, and even government T-men. But, after a wild chase and zany court battle, Professor Dooley reforms, and all his problems are solved. Released Jun. 30, 1971. Directed by Vincent McEveety. 92 min. Stars Dean Jones (Albert Dooley), Sandy Duncan (Katie), Joe Flynn (Finley Hooper), Tony Roberts (Fred), James Gregory (Rutledge), Lee Harcourt Montgomery (Jimmy), Jack Kruschen (Dr. Gottlieb). From the story by Ted Key. The

Studio held open auditions for the duck role, with Webfoot Waddle winning the part. The 2nd- and 3rd-place winners, Carlos and Jennifer, got to be stand-ins. The ducks were given the full Hollywood treatment: their own drinking water pails, lettuce, and chicken scratch, plus evenings and weekends free to rest floating around the Disney Studio pond. Also known as *The $1,000,000 Duck*.

Million Little Things, A (TV) Hour-long series on ABC; premiered Sep. 26, 2018, with the 5th and final season premiering Feb. 8, 2023. Friendship is not one big thing; it is a million little things, and that is true for a group of friends from Boston who bonded under unexpected circumstances. Some have achieved success, others are struggling in their careers and relationships, but all of them feel stuck in life. After one of them dies unexpectedly, it is just the wake-up call the others need to finally start living. And along the way, they discover that friends may be the one thing to save them from themselves. Stars David Giuntoli (Eddie Savile), Ron Livingston (Jon Dixon), Romany Malco (Rome Howard), Allison Miller (Maggie Bloom), Christina Moses (Regina Howard), Christina Ochoa (Ashley Morales), Grace Park (Katherine Kim), James Roday (Gary Mendez), Stephanie Szostak (Delilah Dixon), Lizzy Greene (Sophie Dixon). From ABC Studios and Kapital Entertainment.

Mills, Hayley Actress; appeared in *Pollyanna* (Pollyanna), *The Parent Trap* (Sharon McKendrick/Susan Evers), *In Search of the Castaways* (Mary Grant), *Summer Magic* (Nancy Carey), *The Moon-Spinners* (Nikky Ferris), *That Darn Cat!* (Patti Randall), and *The Boys: The Sherman Brothers' Story* documentary (as herself). On TV, she appeared in *The Disneyland Tenth Anniversary Show*, *Parent Trap III*, *Parent Trap Hawaiian Honeymoon*, *Disney Animation: The Illusion of Life*, *The Disney-MGM Studios Theme Park Grand Opening*, *Wonderful World of Disney: 40 Years of Television Magic*, and *The Age of Believing: The Disney Live Action Classics*; and on The Disney Channel in *Back Home*, *Parent Trap II*, and the series *Good Morning, Miss Bliss*. She is the daughter of actor John Mills. Hayley received a special Academy Award for *Pollyanna* and was named a Disney Legend in 1998.

Mills, John (1908–2005) Actor; appeared in *Swiss Family Robinson* (Father), *The Disneyland Tenth Anniversary Show*, and *Escape to Paradise*. He was named a Disney Legend in 2002.

Milo Murphy's Law (TV) Animated adventure series on Disney XD; debuted Oct. 3, 2016. The 13-year-old Milo Murphy is a direct descendant of the Murphy's Law namesake. He is the personification of Murphy's Law, where anything that can go wrong will go wrong, but he is prepared for every possibility, armed with knowledge, a backpack full of supplies, and his fearless friends Melissa and Zack. Together, with an endless sense of optimism and enthusiasm, the trio turns any catastrophe into an adventure. Voices include Al Yankovic (Milo Murphy), Sabrina Carpenter (Melissa Chase), Mekai Curtis (Zack Underwood). From Disney Television Animation.

Milotte, Alfred and Elma (1904–1989, 1907–1989) Husband and wife team of cinematographers responsible for creating the True-Life Adventure series of nature films. Walt Disney hired them to film on location in the wilderness of Alaska, and the result was *Seal Island*, the first True-Life Adventure film, and *The Alaskan Eskimo*, both of which won Academy Awards. Other award-winning films they helped photograph were *Beaver Valley*, *Bear Country*, *Nature's Half Acre*, *Prowlers of the Everglades*, *Nature's Strangest Creatures*, *Water Birds*, and *The African Lion*. For the latter film, the couple spent 33 months in Africa. They were named Disney Legends in 1998.

Milton Cat nemesis of Pluto, in 3 cartoons beginning with *Puss-Cafe* (1950).

Mimieux, Yvette (1942–2022) Actress; appeared in *Monkeys, Go Home!* (Maria Riserau) and *The Black Hole* (Dr. Kate McCrea).

Min and Bill's Dockside Diner A tramp steamer docked at Echo Lake in Disney's Hollywood Studios; opened May 1, 1989, serving quick-service seafood. Based on the 1930 film starring Marie Dressler and Wallace Beery. The name was shortened to Dockside Diner in 2017.

Minado, the Wolverine (TV) Show aired Nov. 7, 1965. A young wolverine torments a trapper who has killed the wolverine's mother, by stealing his food, tools, and other supplies, and eventually driving him away. Narrated by Sebastian Cabot.

Mine Train Through Nature's Wonderland Frontierland attraction in Disneyland; open May 28, 1960–Jan. 2, 1977. Formerly Rainbow Caverns Mine Train (1956–1959). Guests rode a train through a new wilderness area populated by 204 lifelike bears, beavers, and other critters, then continued through the area of the former attraction—the painted desert and Rainbow Caverns, where the coolness of colored waterfalls and pools were a refreshing respite on a hot day. When Walt was planning this attraction, he was not satisfied with his designers' creations, so he took drawing materials home and drew up the entire ride himself. Today, this drawing is one of the treasures of the Walt Disney Archives. The attraction was removed for construction of Big Thunder Mountain Railroad.

Mineo, Sal (1939–1976) Actor; appeared in *Tonka* (White Bull).

Mineral Hall Shop and display of minerals in Frontierland at Disneyland; open Jul. 30, 1956–1963. The front part of the shop offered minerals for sale; in back, guests could see displays of minerals alternately under regular light and black light. It was fun to see how clothing would also glow under the black light.

Mineral King Area in the Sierra Nevada mountain range of California that the U.S. government opened to private development in the 1960s. Walt Disney put in a bid, which was accepted by the government. However, a groundswell of criticism arose over what environmentalists felt would be the desecration of a major untouched wilderness area. While Disney tried to show that their development would enhance the area and enable more people to see its beauty, the critics prevailed. Congress voted to make the Mineral King area part of Sequoia National Park, and no private development was allowed. A proposed show for the resort featuring musical bears would eventually open as Country Bear Jamboree in the Magic Kingdom at Walt Disney World.

Ming-Na SEE WEN, MING-NA.

Miniatures One of Walt Disney's hobbies was the collecting of miniatures, and this hobby actually helped bring about Disneyland. For years Walt had been collecting tiny furniture and household items and displaying them in little room settings. Out of this collection came an idea for a miniature Americana display with dioramas that would travel the country by truck and teach people about how life in the U.S. developed to the present. His first completed model was Granny's Cabin, which he exhibited at a Festival of California Living at the Pan Pacific Auditorium in Los Angeles in 1952. Because of the obvious problem of not being able to show dioramas to large numbers of people, Disney put aside his idea of a miniature display and expanded his sights to what eventually became Disneyland.

Minion, The (film) Touchstone Home Video release on Jul. 11, 2000, of a Mahogany Pictures film. A mysterious key is unearthed beneath the streets of New York City and the Minion, a domestic servant of the Antichrist, will do everything in its power to possess the key and see that his master is freed to wreak havoc on the world. Only Lucas, a modern-day warrior trained in the ancient arts, can defeat the ultimate evil. Directed by Jean-Marc Piché. Stars Dolph Lundgren (Lukas), Françoise Robertson (Karen Goodleaf), Roc LaFortune (David Schulman), David Newman (Lt. Roseberry). 96 min.

Minkoff, Rob Animator/director; joined Disney in 1983 and worked as an inbetweener on *The Black Cauldron*. He helped design the characters of Basil in *The Great Mouse Detective* and Ursula in *The Little Mermaid* before becoming associated with the character Roger Rabbit as the director of *Tummy Trouble* and *Roller Coaster Rabbit* and co-producer of *Trail Mix-Up*. He directed *The Lion King* with Roger Allers, was exec. producer of *The Haunted Mansion*, and directed *Mickey's Audition*.

Minnie Mia's Pizzeria Restaurant in Walt Disney World Village; opened Aug. 23, 1986, replacing the Verandah Restaurant. Relocated in 1990, taking the place of the All American Sandwich Shop, as Minnie Mia's Italian Eatery. In 1997, it became Wolfgang Puck Express.

Minnie Mouse Like her sweetheart, Mickey Mouse, this popular cartoon character debuted in *Steamboat Willie* Nov. 18, 1928. She did not have her own theatrical cartoon series but appeared in 74 shorts with Mickey and Pluto. She has been a popular character at the Disney parks, where 1986 was declared Minnie's year at Disneyland, with much deserved recognition. Walt Disney and other staff members provided the voice for Minnie in the earliest cartoons; then in the early 1930s, Marcellite Garner from the Ink & Paint Department took over. She was succeeded by several others from that department, until Russi Taylor supplied her voice from 1986 until her passing in 2019; Kaitlyn

Robrock then began voicing the character. Minnie Mouse has 2 nieces, Millie and Melody, who were introduced in a 1962 comic book story. In 2016, Minnie stepped into the world of high fashion as the inspiration for the "Rock the Dots" art and fashion campaign, with annual exhibits and shows celebrating her signature style. In honor of her 90th anniversary, she received a star on the Hollywood Walk of Fame Jan. 22, 2018, in a ceremony with pop superstar Katy Perry, where then-Disney CEO Bob Iger introduced Minnie as "a true legend, a real character, and the first lady of The Walt Disney Company."

Minnie Van Personal ride service at Walt Disney World; debuted Jul. 2017 for guests staying at Disney's BoardWalk Inn and Yacht & Beach Club Resorts, and later offered to all guests on property. From their smartphone, users could order their own private Disney vehicle, wrapped in a polka-dot style inspired by Minnie Mouse. By Jun. 2019, the service had carried 1 million passengers.

Minnie's Bow-Toons (TV) Animated short-form series on Disney Junior; debuted Nov. 14, 2011. A spin-off from a *Mickey Mouse Clubhouse* episode entitled "Minnie's Bow-tique," in which Minnie opens a store that sells bow and bow ties. The Bow-tique was managed by Minnie Mouse and her best friend, Daisy Duck, in the first 2 seasons, but in the 3rd season, Daisy and their assistant, Cuckoo Loca, start a pet grooming salon next door to the Bow-tique. Voices include Russi Taylor (Minnie Mouse), Tress MacNeille (Daisy Duck), Nika Futterman (Cuckoo Loca). From Disney Television Animation.

Minnie's House Attraction in Mickey's Toontown at Disneyland; opened Jan. 24, 1993. Visitors take a self-guided tour of Minnie's home, presented in an ultra-cartoony style with surprises around every turn. Also in Toontown at Tokyo Disneyland (opened Apr. 15, 1996) and in Mickey's Toontown Fair in the Magic Kingdom at Walt Disney World (as Minnie's Country House, Jun. 29, 1996–Feb. 11, 2011).

Minnie's Style Studio Character-greeting attraction in Toontown at Tokyo Disneyland; opened Sep. 28, 2020. Fashion designer Minnie Mouse greets visitors in her studio, wearing her latest creation.

Minnie's Surprise Birthday Party Show in

Mickey's Birthdayland from Jun. 18, 1988, until Apr. 22, 1990. It reopened as *Mickey's Magical TV World*.

Minnie's Yoo Hoo The Mickey Mouse Club theme song from the original club; it was the first Disney song to be released on sheet music, in 1930, and a filmed version, using animation from *Mickey's Follies*, was prepared for showing at Mickey Mouse Club events. Written by Walt Disney and Carl Stalling.

Minor, Jason Actor; appeared on the *Mickey Mouse Club* on The Disney Channel 1990–1993.

Mint Julep Bar SEE FRENCH MARKET.

Mintz, Margaret Winkler (1895–1990) Film distributor in New York City who signed a contract with Walt Disney on Oct. 16, 1923, to distribute the Alice Comedies. She later married Charles Mintz and let him take over the business.

Minutemen (TV) A Disney Channel Original Movie; first aired Jan. 25, 2008. Three high school outcasts—Virgil, Charlie, and Zeke—shake their school's social structure by inventing a time machine that allows them to go back in time and prevent other misfits from enduring humiliating situations. Soon, the 3 kids, calling themselves the Minutemen, learn there are unexpected consequences of changing the course of time. Government officials suspect them of hacking into top secret files, and their plans go further awry when covert agents arrive in hot pursuit of their time machine. Directed by Lev L. Spiro. Stars Jason Dolley (Virgil Fox), Luke Benward (Charlie Tuttle), Nicholas Braun (Zeke Thompson), Chelsea Staub (Stephanie Jameson), Steven R. McQueen (Derek Beaugard).

Mira, Royal Detective (TV) Animated mystery-adventure series on Disney Junior; premiered Mar. 20, 2020. In the magical, India-inspired land of Jalpur, the brave and resourceful commoner Mira is appointed to the role of royal detective by the Queen. Along with her friend Prince Neel, creative cousin Priya, and comical mongoose sidekicks Mikku and Chikku, Mira will stop at nothing to solve a case. Voices include Leela Ladnier (Mira), Freida Pinto (Queen Shanti), Kal Penn (Mikku), Utkarsh Ambudkar (Chikku), Hannah Simone (Pinky), Jameela Jamil (Auntie Pushpa). From Wild Canary, in association with Disney Junior.

Mirabel The only "ordinary" child in the magical Madrigal family in *Encanto*; voiced by Stephanie Beatriz.

Miracle (film) In 1980, the U.S. Olympic ice hockey team needed a miracle. Coach Herb Brooks was charged with taking his ragtag squad to the Winter Olympic Games at Lake Placid, New York, but even the encouraging coach was not sure what his boys could do against the storied teams from the Eastern bloc countries and especially the juggernaut Soviet Union squad. Despite long odds, Team U.S.A. rose to the occasion in one of the most thrilling moments in the country's sports history. Released Feb. 6, 2004. Directed by Gavin O'Connor. Stars Kurt Russell (Herb Brooks), Eddie Cahill (Jim Craig), Patricia Clarkson (Patty Brooks), Noah Emmerich (Craig Patrick), Sean McCann (Walter Bush), Kenneth Welsh (Doc Nagobads), Patrick O'Brien Demsey (Mike Eruzione), Michael Mantenuto (Jack O'Callahan), Nathan West (Rob McClanahan), Kenneth Mitchell (Ralph Cox). 136 min.

Miracle at Midnight (TV) Two-hour movie on *The Wonderful World of Disney*; first aired May 17, 1998. During World War II, the members of the Koster family in Denmark risk their lives to help their Jewish countrymen who are about to be arrested by the Nazis occupying their country. Directed by Ken Cameron. Stars Sam Waterston (Dr. Karl Koster), Mia Farrow (Doris Koster), Justin Whalin (Hendrik Koster), Patrick Malahide (Duckwitz), Benedick Blythe (General Best). Since progress has changed Copenhagen, the country's capital, and Danish fishing villages so much in recent years, the filmmakers turned instead to Ireland for their locations.

Miracle at St. Anna (film) This is the story of 4 Black American soldiers who are members of the U.S. Army's all-Black 92nd "Buffalo Soldier" Division, stationed in Tuscany, Italy, during World War II. They experience the tragedy and triumph of the war as they find themselves trapped behind enemy lines in a Tuscan village, separated from their unit after one of them risks his life to save a traumatized young Italian boy. As the Nazis approach, the American soldiers rely on help from the villagers and a small group of partisan fighters. Released Sep. 26, 2008, after a world premiere on Sep. 7 at the Toronto Film Festival. Directed by Spike Lee. A Touchstone film in association with On My Own Produzioni Cinematografiche and RAI Cinema. Stars Derek Luke (Aubrey Stamps), Michael Ealy (Bishop Cummings), Laz Alonso (Hector Negron), Omar Benson Miller (Sam Train), Pierfrancesco Favino (Peppi Grotta), Valentina Cervi (Renata), Matteo Sciabordi (Angelo Torancelli), John Turturro (Antonio Ricci), John Leguizamo (Enrico), Joseph Gordon-Levitt (Tim Boyle). Based on the novel by James McBride. 160 min. Filmed in CinemaScope on location in Italy, with additional scenes in New York City, Louisiana, and The Bahamas.

Miracle Child (TV) Two-hour movie on NBC; aired Apr. 6, 1993. Lisa Porter is a young mother whose infant daughter miraculously changes her life and the life of a small town. Directed by Michael Pressman. Stars Crystal Bernard (Lisa), Cloris Leachman (Doc Betty), John Terry (Buck Sanders), Graham Sack (Lyle Sanders). Based on the novel *Miracle at Clement's Pond* by Patricia Pendergraft.

Miracle Down Under (film) Video release title of *The Christmas Visitor*.

Miracle in Lane 2 (TV) Two-hour Disney Channel Original Movie, first aired May 13, 2000. A heartwarming tale about Justin Yoder, a courageous 12-year-old kid who has a real zest for life and a wonderful sense of humor. Despite his physical challenges, he strives to compete in a Soap Box Derby, and, against all odds, his talent, perseverance, and enthusiasm take him to the national championships. Directed by Greg Beeman. Stars Frankie Muniz (Justin Yoder), Rick Rossovich (Myron Yoder), Molly Hagan (Sheila Stopher Yoder), Patrick Levis (Seth Yoder), Roger Aaron Brown (Vic Sauder).

Miracle of the White Stallions (film) True story of how Colonel Alois Podhajsky, director of Vienna's world-famous Spanish Riding School, saves the school and its beautiful Lipizzan white horses during World War II. When the bombs start falling on Vienna near the end of the war, Podhajsky secretly defies the Nazis and smuggles the marvelous performing white stallions into rural St. Martin. Meanwhile, the Lipizzan mares, on which the future of the breed depend, are in Czechoslovakia in the path of the advancing Russians, who are slaughtering all livestock coming into their hands. Under the direct order of General George Patton, an expert horseman, the mares are rescued, reunited with the stallions, and both the Lipizzans and the Spanish Riding

School are saved for posterity. Released Mar. 29, 1963. Directed by Arthur Hiller. 118 min. Stars Robert Taylor (Col. Podhajsky), Lilli Palmer (Vedena Podhajsky), Curt Jurgens (Gen. Tellheim), Eddie Albert (Rider Otto), James Franciscus (Maj. Hoffman), John Larch (Gen. Patton). Based on the book *The Dancing White Horses of Vienna*, by Colonel Podhajsky. Features the song "Just Say Auf Wiedersehen," by Richard M. and Robert B. Sherman.

Miracle Worker, The (TV) Two-hour movie on *The Wonderful World of Disney*; first aired Nov. 12, 2000. The story of 8-year-old Helen Keller, blind, deaf, and mute, who in 1887 blossoms under the care and teaching of Annie Sullivan, whose groundbreaking techniques for teaching deaf and blind people are still being used today. Directed by Nadia Tass. Stars Hallie Kate Eisenberg (Helen Keller), Alison Elliott (Annie Sullivan), David Strathairn (Capt. Keller), Lucas Black (James Keller), Kate Greenhouse (Kate Keller). Based on the Tony Award–winning play by William Gibson.

Miracles (TV) Hour-long drama series on ABC; aired Jan. 27–Mar. 3, 2003. A former Vatican miracle investigator joins forces with Sodalitas Quaerito, a shadowy organization interested in studying good vs. evil. Stars Skeet Ulrich (Paul Callan), Angus Macfadyen (Alva Keel), Marisa Ramirez (Evelyn Santos). From Touchstone Television in association with Spyglass Entertainment.

Miracles from Molecules Song from Adventure Thru Inner Space in Disneyland; written by Richard M. and Robert B. Sherman.

Miramax Films Disney bought Miramax Films, founded by Harvey and Bob Weinstein, on Jun. 30, 1993, gaining the rights to its library of more than 200 films. As part of the deal, Disney financed future Miramax productions. Under Disney, Miramax released such hits as *The Piano*, *The Crow*, *Little Buddha*, *Pulp Fiction*, *Trainspotting*, *Sling Blade*, *Life Is Beautiful*, *The English Patient* (Best Picture Oscar), *Shakespeare in Love* (Best Picture Oscar), *Good Will Hunting*, *Chicago* (Best Picture Oscar), *Gangs of New York*, and *No Country for Old Men* (Best Picture Oscar). After winning its Academy Award for Best Picture, *Chicago* became Miramax's highest-grossing release ever. Miramax also released under its Dimension Films label. On Sep. 30, 2005, the Weinsteins left Miramax to form their own new company, The Weinstein Company. Disney continued to run Miramax and own its film library. In Oct. 2009, Disney greatly cut back Miramax's staff and film output, and on Jan. 29, 2010, closed Miramax's offices, moving the operations to Disney's Burbank headquarters. Arrangements were announced in Jul. 2010 to sell Miramax to an investor group led by Ron Tutor for more than $660 million, though Disney continued with plans to release 2 films under the Miramax label—*The Switch* and *The Tempest*. The sale was completed in December.

Miranda, Lin-Manuel Composer/lyricist/actor; he wrote songs for *Moana* and *Encanto*, and collaborated with Alan Menken on songs for *The Little Mermaid* (2023). Also provided music for *Star Wars: The Force Awakens* and *The Rise of Skywalker* (in which he had an uncredited role as a Resistance pilot). He appeared in *The Odd Life of Timothy Green* (Reggie) and *Mary Poppins Returns* (Jack); on TV in *Disney's Fairy Tale Weddings: Holiday Magic*, *The Wonderful World of Disney: Magical Holiday Celebration*, and the *Disney Parks Magical Christmas Day Parade*; and voiced Fenton Crackshell Cabrera/Gizmoduck in *DuckTales* (2017). He is perhaps best known for creating, writing the songs for, and starring in the Broadway hit *Hamilton*.

Mirren, Helen Actress; appeared in *Raising Helen* (Dominique), *National Treasure: Book of Secrets* (Emily Appleton), *The Tempest* (Prospera), *The Hundred-Foot Journey* (Madame Mallory), and *The Nutcracker and the Four Realms* (Mother Ginger), and on TV in *Disneyland 60: The Wonderful World of Disney*. She voiced Deep Thought in *The Hitchhiker's Guide to the Galaxy*, Dean Hardscrabble in *Monsters University*, and Snickers in *The One and Only Ivan*.

Misadventures of Chip 'n' Dale, The (TV) Rerun title of *The Adventures of Chip 'n' Dale*.

Misadventures of Merlin Jones, The (film) Merlin Jones is the brightest young student at a small midwestern college. Possessing an extremely high IQ, he is head and shoulders above his fellow classmates, particularly in the field of scientific endeavor. Although admonished by his professor to proceed slowly, he is already applying the results of his research not only to the problems confronting the college, but also to assist some of his fellow students. His efforts as a do-gooder boomerang on all concerned, but eventually everything works out. The application of Merlin's meager knowledge of extrasensory perception and hypnotism results in some way-out hilarious involvements. Released Jan. 22, 1964. Directed by Robert Stevenson. 91 min. Stars Tommy Kirk (Merlin Jones), Annette Funicello (Jennifer), Leon Ames (Judge Holmby), Stuart Erwin (Capt. Loomis), Alan Hewitt (Prof. Shattuck), Connie Gilchrist (Mrs. Gossett). Features a musical hit for Annette in the form of the title song written by Richard M. and Robert B. Sherman. This teenage comedy was originally made as a 2-parter for the Disney TV show, but it turned out so well that Walt decided it deserved a theatrical release, and it was in fact so popular that it led to a sequel—*The Monkey's Uncle*. The film was reissued in 1972.

Misery Loves Company (TV) Half-hour series on Fox premiered Oct.1,1995 and ended Oct. 23, 1995. Four men, whose dreams of youth have not survived to adulthood, still have their friendship despite divorces and failing marriages. Stars Dennis Boutsikaris (Joe), Christopher Meloni (Mitch), Julius Carry (Perry), Stephen Furst (Lewis), Wesley Jonathan (Connor), Nikki DeLoach (Tracy).

Misner, Terri One of the adult hosts on the *Mickey Mouse Club* on The Disney Channel 1991–1994.

Miss Daisy Attraction in Mickey's Toontown at Disneyland; opened Jan. 24, 1993. Donald's house is actually a boat, named the *Miss Daisy*, which fits the nautical theme of a duck who wears a sailor suit. *Miss Daisy* is also the name of Donald's Boat in Toontown at Tokyo Disneyland and in the former Mickey's Toontown Fair in the Magic Kingdom at Walt Disney World.

Miss Disneyland Beginning with Valerie Watson in 1962, a knowledgeable and enthusiastic tour guide was selected to host celebrities and dignitaries, and to represent the park at special events across America. The program soon evolved into the Disneyland Ambassador program. SEE AMBASSADOR.

Miss Fritter's Racing Skoool (film) Animated short from Pixar; debuted on the *Cars 3* digital release Oct. 24, 2017, and on Blu-ray Nov. 7. Blindsided testimonials from the Crazy 8s tout the transformative impact Miss Fritter's Racing School has had in reshaping the direction of their lives. Directed by James Ford Murphy. Voices include Lea DeLaria (Miss Fritter), Jeremy Maxwell (Arvy), Cristela Alonzo (Cruz Ramirez). 3 min.

Miss Guided (TV) Half-hour comedy series on ABC; premiered with a special on Mar. 18, then moved to its regular night Mar. 20, 2008, ending Apr. 3. A former high school ugly duckling, Becky Freeley, comes back to her alma mater as a guidance counselor, after having finally conquered the awkward, traumatic world of high school, only to see an ex-cheerleader and former nemesis return as an English teacher, forcing Becky to relive her past and to find she has a competitor for the affections of a Spanish teacher. Stars Judy Greer (Becky), Brooke Burns (Lisa Germain), Earl Billings (Principal Huffy), Kristoffer Polaha (Tim O'Malley), Chris Parnell (Bruce Terry). From 20th Century Fox Television and ABC Studios.

Ms. Marvel (TV) A Disney+ original series; digitally premiered Jun. 8, 2022. Kamala Khan, a Pakistani American teenager, is a stellar student and avid gamer who writes super hero fan fiction in her spare time, with a special affinity for Captain Marvel. But Kamala struggles to fit in at home and at school—that is, until she gets super powers like the heroes she's always admired. Stars Iman Vellani (Kamala Khan/Ms. Marvel), Saagar Shaikh (Aamir), Rish Shah (Kamran), Zenobia Shroff (Muneeba), Mohan Kapur (Yusuf), Matt Lintz (Bruno), Yasmeen Fletcher (Nakia), Azhar Usman (Najaf), Nimra Bucha (Najma). From Marvel Studios.

Miss Merrily's Madness Women's apparel, from country and western to high fashion, in the Lake Buena Vista Shopping Village at Walt Disney World; opened Mar. 1975, and expanded Dec. 1976. Also known as Miss Merrily's Fashions. Closed Mar. 28, 1986, to become the new site of Country Address.

Miss Tilly Shrimp boat perched atop Mount Mayday in Disney's Typhoon Lagoon at Walt Disney World.

Missing (TV) Drama series on ABC; aired Mar. 15–May 17, 2012. Becca Winstone's son is kidnapped while studying abroad, and it is a race against time when she travels to Rome to track him down. She begins piecing together the clues left behind, and it isn't long before the kidnappers realize they have picked a fight with the wrong woman, because Becca has a secret of her own—before her husband's death, she was also a lethal CIA operative. If she wants to find her son alive, she will have to rely on old friends and reopen old wounds, putting her resourcefulness, skill, and determination to the test. Stars Ashley Judd (Becca Winstone), Sean Bean (Paul Winstone), Cliff Curtis (Dax Miller), Adriano Giannini (Giancarlo Rossi), Nick Eversman (Michael Winstone), Tereza Voriskova (Oksana). Produced by Stillking Films with ABC Studios.

Mission Equipment Shop in Avengers Campus in Walt Disney Studios Park at Disneyland Paris; opened Jul. 20, 2022, offering hero souvenirs and accessories. As the story goes, the building was once owned by Howard Stark.

Mission Force One SEE MILES FROM TOMORROWLAND.

Mission: SPACE Pavilion in World Discovery (formerly Future World) in EPCOT; opened Aug. 15, 2003, on the site of the former Horizons. Originally sponsored by Compaq (later Hewlett-Packard). Guests find themselves 40 years in the future, where spaceflight is routine for ordinary citizens. After a quick orientation inside the ISTC (International Space Training Center), the trainees have a briefing on their training mission and board an X-2 Deep Space Shuttle simulator for a thrilling mission to Mars. They experience the sensations and sounds of a shuttle launch, including high g-forces (using centrifuge technology). During the mission, the team encounters challenges, and each member has a task to perform. When they return to Earth, guests move on to interactive experiences in the Advanced Training Lab. To create a realistic simulation, the Imagineers worked with more than 25 space experts from NASA and the Jet Propulsion Laboratory, including 5 astronauts. The innovative ride system, with 5 massive "arms" holding 2 capsules each, has more computing power than a space shuttle. In 2006, a less intense Green Team option was introduced (without g-forces), with the more intense training participants designated as the Orange Team. On Aug. 13, 2017, the Green mission changed to an orbit around Earth, emphasizing the idea of space tourism. In 2021, Space 220, a restaurant set 220 miles above Earth, opened next door.

Mission: SPACE Cargo Bay Shop in EPCOT; opened Aug. 15, 2003, offering space-themed souvenirs.

Mission to Mars Tomorrowland attraction in Disneyland; open Mar. 21, 1975–Nov. 2, 1992, as an update to the former Flight to the Moon. Also in Tomorrowland in the Magic Kingdom at Walt Disney World, Jun. 7, 1975–Oct. 4, 1993. After astronauts set foot on the moon, the Flight to the Moon attraction was passé. Disney designers changed the destination to Mars several years later, and for a few months even utilized some film clips from the Disney TV show *Mars and Beyond*, showing fantastic creatures that one might encounter on the Red Planet. In the preflight show, a Mr. Johnson briefed guests from Mission Control, which featured Audio-Animatronics technicians.

Mission to Mars (film) In the year 2020, Luke Graham leads the first manned mission to Mars, but his crew is decimated by a catastrophic and mysterious disaster. A rescue mission, copiloted by Commander Woody Blake and Jim McConnell, is hurriedly launched to investigate the tragedy and bring back any survivors. The astronauts face almost insurmountable dangers on their journey through space, and they make an amazing discovery when they finally reach the Red Planet. A Touchstone film. Directed by Brian De Palma. Released Mar. 10, 2000. Stars Gary Sinise (Jim McConnell), Don Cheadle (Luke Graham), Connie Nielsen (Terri Fisher), Jerry O'Connell (Phil Ohlmyer), Tim Robbins (Woody Blake), Armin Mueller-Stahl (Ray Beck). 113 min. Filmed in CinemaScope. Photography took place in and around Vancouver, with the Mars surface, at 55 acres, one of the largest sets ever built for a movie, constructed at the Fraser Sand Dunes. Some landscape elements were also filmed in Jordan and the Canary Islands.

Mission Tortilla Factory Attraction in Pacific Wharf at Disney California Adventure; opened Feb. 8, 2001. After watching a short film about the origins of the tortilla, visitors could watch machines turning them out and taste a sample. Sponsored by Mission Foods. Closed May 31, 2011, to become the Ghirardelli Soda Fountain and Chocolate Shop.

Mrs. Beakley The nephews' governess in *Duck-Tales*; voiced by Joan Gerber.

Mrs. Caloway Regal, hat-wearing cow in *Home on the Range*; voiced by Judi Dench.

Mrs. Judson Basil's housekeeper in *The Great Mouse Detective*; voiced by Diana Chesney.

Mrs. Jumbo Dumbo's mother in the 1941 animated feature.

Mrs. Peabody's Beach (film) Educational film teaching basic economics, produced by Dave Bell; released in 1972. A teenager uses his interest in surf-ing to create a profitable business, learning valuable lessons in economics.

Mrs. Potts Kindly enchanted teapot/housekeeper in *Beauty and the Beast*; voiced by Angela Lansbury.

Mrs. Potts' Cupboard Fantasyland counter-service restaurant in the Magic Kingdom at Walt Disney World; open Mar. 1994–Dec. 13, 2010, serving ice cream treats and beverages. It took the place of The Round Table and was superseded by Storybook Treats.

Mr. Boogedy (TV) One-hour movie aired Apr. 20, 1986. Directed by Oz Scott. A family finds their new house is haunted by the ghost of a man who loved to leap out and yell "boogedy" at the local children. The family eventually manages to stop him by stealing his magic cloak. Stars Richard Masur, Mimi Kennedy, David Faustino, John Astin, Benjamin Gregory, Kristy Swanson, Howard Witt. SEE ALSO BRIDE OF BOOGEDY.

Mr. Destiny (film) Larry Burrows is certain that his ultra-ordinary life is the direct result of losing his high school championship baseball game. Twenty years later, a mysterious stranger, Mr. Destiny, comes along with the power to alter Larry's past. Now, instead of being married to his high school sweetheart, he is the rich husband of prom queen Cindy Jo, father of 2 spoiled brats, president of the company, and owner of the biggest house in town. And everybody hates him. Realizing that toying with destiny can lead to grave complications, Larry strives to extricate himself from the predicament. Released Oct. 12, 1990. Directed by James Orr. A Touchstone film. 110 min. Stars James Belushi (Larry Burrows), Linda Hamilton (Ellen Burrows), Michael Caine (Mike), Jon Lovitz (Chip Metzler), Hart Bochner (Niles Pender). Filmed at the Biltmore Estate in Asheville, North Carolina.

Mr. Duck Steps Out (film) Donald Duck cartoon released Jun. 7, 1940. Directed by Jack King. Donald's frustration level is stretched to the limit when he attempts to court Daisy without the interference of his nephews.

Mr. Headmistress (TV) Two-hour movie on *The Wonderful World of Disney*; first aired Mar. 15, 1998. A notorious con man dresses up as the headmistress of an all-girls boarding school in order to escape 2 dangerous thugs who are intent on collecting on a bad debt, and in the interim changes the lives of everyone he meets. Directed by James Frawley. Stars Harland Williams (Tucker), Shawna Waldron (Beryl), Duane Martin (Jim), Joel Brooks (Ferguson), Lori Hallier (Sally), Lawrence Dane (Rawlings), Conrad Dunn (Farley), Katey Sagal (Harriet Magnum). The 120-year-old Alma College in St. Thomas, Ontario, Canada, subbed for the fictional Rawlings School for Girls.

Mr. Holland's Opus (film) Glenn Holland is a music teacher who had dreams of composing a great symphony, but life got in the way. His dream was deferred, and he came to regard himself as a failure. But, on his last day at Kennedy High School, after 30 years of instilling his vision and imagination into his students, Holland comes to realize that the true measure of a man's success can best be seen through the eyes of those he has aided and inspired. Each student thus became a note in a lasting composition—Mr. Holland's Opus—and they have come to honor their precious and underappreciated teacher. A Hollywood Pictures film from Interscope Communications/PolyGram Filmed Entertainment, in association with the Charlie Mopic Company. Released Jan. 19, 1996, after a Dec. 29, 1995, release in Los Angeles for Academy Award consideration. Directed by Stephen Herek. Stars Richard Dreyfuss (Glenn Holland), Glenne Headly (Iris Holland), Jay Thomas (Bill Meister), Olympia Dukakis (Principal Jacobs), Alicia Witt (Gertrude Lang). The film was shot on location in and around Portland, Oregon, with Grant High School serving as the school. Grant High's drama director brought in many current and former students, who won roles as dancers, musicians, and actors in the film. 145 min.

Mr. Incredible Crime-fighting superhero with mega-strength in *The Incredibles*, known as Bob Parr in his civilian life; voiced by Craig T. Nelson.

Mr. Magoo (film) When a stolen and priceless ruby, the Star of Kuristan, lands in the possession of nearsighted millionaire Quincy Magoo, a sinister plot is hatched to steal it back. Perpetually the target of evil culprits, the elderly and bumbling curmudgeon Magoo manages to consistently escape unharmed, totally oblivious to the dangers that surround him. Hunted by robbers and set up by a conniving thief, Luanne Leseur, Magoo ultimately nabs the villains with the help of his nephew, Waldo, and his trusty bulldog, Angus, and is hailed a hero. Released Dec. 25, 1997. Directed by Stanley Tong. Stars Leslie Nielsen (Mr. Magoo), Kelly Lynch (Luanne Leseur), Ernie Hudson (Gus Anders), Stephen Tobolowsky (Chuck Stupak), Nick Chinlund (Bob Morgan), Matt Keeslar (Waldo), Malcolm McDowell (Austin Cloquet). 87 min. Angus, Magoo's trusty companion, is an English bulldog, actually played by 4 different bulldogs, 3 female and 1 male, dyed with hair coloring to match each other. Based on the Mr. Magoo cartoons, which were released by UPA Productions beginning in 1949, first in theaters, then in a long-running TV series. Filming took place on location in Vancouver.

Mr. Mittens Therapy cat enlisted to assist Joe Gardner in *Soul*.

Mr. Mouse Takes a Trip (film) Mickey Mouse cartoon released Nov. 1, 1940. Directed by Clyde Geronimi. Mickey must do some quick thinking and don a few disguises to foil Pete, the train conductor, who wants him off the train for concealing Pluto.

Mr. Potato Head Wisecracking spud toy in *Toy Story*; voiced by Don Rickles.

Mr. St. Nick (TV) Two-hour movie on *The Wonderful World of Disney*; first aired Nov. 17, 2002. Nick St. Nicholas, a philanthropist from Florida has a secret—he is the son of Santa Claus. Santa wants to retire and have his son take over, but Nick is too busy being scammed by a holiday charity with the help of a shady weathercaster, Heidi. Meanwhile, he has a growing affection for his outspoken Venezuelan cook, Lorena, who recognizes Heidi as a phony. Directed by Craig Zisk. Stars Kelsey Grammer (Nick), Charles Durning (Santa), Elaine Hendrix (Heidi Gardelle), Ana Ortiz (Lorena Braga), Brian Bedford (Jasper), Brian Miranda (Danny). Produced by Hallmark Entertainment.

Mr. Smee Captain Hook's faithful first mate in *Peter Pan*; voiced by Bill Thompson.

Mr. Snoops Madame Medusa's bumbling assistant in *The Rescuers*; voiced by Joe Flynn. The character was patterned by animator Milt Kahl after author John Culhane.

Mr. 3000 (film) A middle-aged, retired baseball star's 3,000 career-base-hits achievement is in jeopardy when 3 of those hits are now being disqualified. Reluctantly getting back into a Milwaukee Brewers uniform to pursue his goal, the onetime great rediscovers his love of the game, realizes the importance of teamwork and ethics, and, in the process, falls for a tough-minded sports reporter. A Touchstone film/Spyglass Entertainment production. Released Sep. 17, 2004. Directed by Charles Stone III. Stars Bernie Mac (Stan Ross), Angela Bassett (Mo Simmons), Dondré T. Whitfield (Skillet), Evan Jones (Fryman), Michael Rispoli (Boca), Amaury Nolasco (Minadeo), Paul Sorvino (Gus Panas), Brian White (T-Rex Pennebaker), Ian Anthony Dale (Fukuda), Earl Billings (Lenny Koron), Chris Noth (Schembri). 103 min. The 3,000-career-hits achievement is so rare in the Majors that only 33 players (as of 2022) have ever achieved it.

Mr. Toad's Wild Ride Fantasyland attraction in Disneyland; debuted Jul. 17, 1955. Riders zig and zag in a motorcar on a manic drive through J. Thaddeus Toad's Toad Hall and venture out to the English countryside. An encounter with an oncoming train leads to a devilish finale. One of the park's original dark rides, it was completely remodeled with the New Fantasyland in 1983, with the most obvious change being the exterior. It became Toad Hall itself, rather than a pavilion from a medieval fair. Based on the *Wind in the Willows* segment from *The Adventures of Ichabod and Mr. Toad* (1949). Also a Fantasyland attraction in the Magic Kingdom at Walt Disney World; open Oct. 1, 1971–Sep. 7, 1998, and replaced by The Many Adventures of Winnie the Pooh. The Florida attraction featured 2 different ride paths, each with unique scenes.

Mr. Toad's Wild Ride (film) Video release on Dec. 8, 1998, of an Allied Filmmakers 1996 live-action film originally entitled *The Wind in the Willows*. Mr. Toad has a passion for motorcars but crashes every car he buys. In order to finance his mania, Toad has been selling land to the nefarious weasels. Mole, Rat, and Badger try to save their homes and Toad Hall from them. Stars Eric Idle (Rat), Steve Coogan (Mole), Terry Jones (Mr. Toad), Nicol Williamson (Badger). 87 min.

Mr. Wrong (film) Bright and sassy Martha Alston, a 1990s woman, has an age-old problem—how to recognize Mr. Right when he comes along. A radio talk show producer, Martha definitely gets her signals crossed when she suddenly meets Whitman Crawford, a handsome stranger with whom she instantly falls head over heels in love. However, she soon realizes she is dating a guy who is as right on the outside as he is wrong on the inside, and the ratings on this romance quickly plummet. Calamity prevails as she tries to pull the plug on her love life altogether. But Whitman proceeds to prove that too often dream dates become nightmares. A Touchstone film. Directed by Nick Castle. Released Feb. 16, 1996. Stars Ellen DeGeneres (Martha), Bill Pullman (Whitman), Joan Cusack (Inga), Dean Stockwell (Jack Tramonte), Joan Plowright (Mrs. Crawford), Peter White and Polly Holliday (Mr. and Mrs. Alston), Robert Goulet (Dick Braxton). 97 min. Principal photography took place in and around San Diego, where the story is set.

Mistle-Tones, The (TV) An ABC Family original holiday musical; premiered Dec. 9, 2012. Holly, blessed with an amazing singing voice, is all set to audition for the newly vacated spot in a legendary local Christmas group, which was founded by her late mother years ago. Shocked and upset when the slot goes to the barely talented best friend of the group's leader, Marci, Holly sets out to create her own musical group, The Mistle-Tones. After challenging their rivals to a sing-off on Christmas Eve, Holly finds the real meaning of Christmas with some new friends and a new love thrown in for good measure. Directed by Paul Hoen. Stars Tori Spelling (Marci), Tia Mowry-Hardrict (Holly), Jonathan Patrick Moore (Nick), Reginald VelJohnson (Holly's dad).

Mistresses (TV) One-hour series on ABC; aired Jun. 3, 2013–Sep. 6, 2016. Based on a hit U.K. series of the same name, it covers the scandalous lives of a sassy group of 4 girlfriends, each on her own path to self-discovery. They find support and guidance with each other as they brave their turbulent journeys and life's storms of excitement, secrecy, and betrayal, all the while bound by the complex relationships they've created. Stars Alyssa Milano (Savannah "Savi" Davis), Yunjin Kim (Karen Kim), Rochelle Aytes (April Malloy), Jes Macallan (Josslyn Carver), Brett Tucker (Harry Davis), Jason George (Dominic Taylor), Erik Stocklin (Sam Grey). From ABC Studios.

Mitchell, George J. Former U.S. Senate majority leader, he was elected to the board of The Walt Disney Company in 1995, becoming presiding director Dec. 3, 2002, and later elected chairman Mar. 3, 2004. He left the board Dec. 31, 2007.

Mitchell, Keith SEE COOGAN, KEITH.

Mitsukoshi Department Store Merchandise store

in Japan at EPCOT; opened Oct. 1, 1982, offering Japanese apparel, crafts, toys, and souvenirs. An area is devoted to snacks and candies, and a sake bar is also available.

Mitsukoshi Restaurant Establishment in Japan at EPCOT Center; opened Oct. 1, 1982. It featured 2 dining areas: Tempura Kiku, where items were deep-fried in the tempura style, and Teppanyaki Dining Room, where the chef chops and stir-frys food at the table, usually seating several parties. In 2007, Teppanyaki Dining Room became Teppan Edo and Tempura Kiku became Tokyo Dining.

Mittens Jaded and abandoned house cat in *Bolt*; voiced by Susie Essman.

Mixed Nuts (TV) Rerun title of *The Adventures of Chip 'n' Dale*.

mixed-ish (TV) Half-hour sitcom on ABC; aired Sep. 24, 2019–May 18, 2021. Rainbow Johnson recounts her experience growing up in a mixed-race family in the 1980s and the dilemmas faced to acclimate in the suburbs while staying true to themselves. This family's experiences illuminate the challenges of finding one's own identity. A spin-off from ABC's *black-ish*. Stars Mark-Paul Gosselaar (Paul Johnson), Tika Sumpter (Alicia Johnson), Christina Anthony (Denise), Arica Himmel (Bow Johnson), Ethan William Childress (Johan Johnson), Mykal-Michelle Harris (Santamonica Johnson), Gary Cole (Harrison Johnson). From ABC Studios.

Mixology (TV) Half-hour comedy on ABC; aired Feb. 26–May 21, 2014. Taking place in one bar on one night, the show chronicles the misadventures of 10 people in search of love. As the night unfolds and closing time approaches, some people may get lucky while others are destined to spend the night alone. Stars Adam Campbell (Ron), Adan Canto (Dominic), Alexis Carra (Jessica), Craig Frank (Cal), Ginger Gonzaga (Maya), Blake Lee (Tom), Vanessa Lengies (Kacey), Andrew Santino (Bruce), Frankie Shaw (Fabienne), Kate Simses (Liv). From ABC Studios and Ryan Seacrest Productions.

Miyazaki, Hayao As part of a distribution deal with the master Japanese animator, Buena Vista Home Video began distributing his films on video in the U.S. with *Kiki's Delivery Service* in 1998. Miramax released in theaters Miyazaki's *The Princess Mononoke* in 1999, and Disney released *Spirited Away* in 2002 (winning the Oscar for Animated Feature),

Howl's Moving Castle in 2005, *Ponyo* in 2009, *Tales from Earthsea* in 2010, *The Secret World of Arrietty* in 2012, and *The Wind Rises* in 2013.

Miziker, Ron Entertainment producer and director at Disney during the 1970s and 1980s. Reporting to Bob Jani, he was responsible for numerous opening ceremonies, parades, and special events. He produced network specials from the parks, and in 1983 moved to the Disney Channel as vice president of original programming.

Mizner's Lounge Library lounge and bar in Disney's Grand Floridian Resort & Spa at Walt Disney World; opened Jun. 28, 1988. Named after the famous South Florida architect. Closed Apr. 5, 2019, to become the Enchanted Rose lounge.

MMC See Mickey Mouse Club.

Moana (film) Animated feature. An adventurous teenager, Moana, sails out on a daring mission to save her people. During her journey, she meets the once-mighty demigod Maui, who guides her in her quest to become a master wayfinder. Together they sail across the open ocean, encountering enormous monsters and impossible odds. Along the way, Moana fulfills the ancient quest of her ancestors and discovers the 1 thing she has always sought: her own identity. Released Nov. 23, 2016, after a Nov. 14 premiere at the AFI Fest in Los Angeles and international releases beginning Nov. 16. Directed by Ron Clements and John Musker. Voices include Auli'i Cravalho (Moana), Dwayne Johnson (Maui), Rachel House (Gramma Tala), Temuera Morrison (Chief Tui), Jemaine Clement (Tamatoa), Nicole Scherzinger (Sina), Alan Tudyk (Heihei). From Walt Disney Animation Studios. 107 min. Music by Opetaia Foa'i, Mark Mancina, and Lin-Manuel Miranda. The story was inspired in part by oral histories of the people and cultures of the Pacific Islands. A group of advisers, known as the Oceanic Story Trust, included anthropologists, linguists, choreographers, haka specialists, master navigators, and tattooists. Because the ocean plays a central role in the story, 80% of the film includes effects shots, thus requiring the development of a proprietary software called Splash to create a softer, believable look to water. Eric Goldberg supervised the hand-drawn animation of Maui's tattoos, which were inspired by Marquesan tattoos from French Polynesia. Received Academy Award nominations for Original Song ("How Far I'll Go") and Animated Feature. Released in wide-screen format.

Moana: A Homecoming Celebration Adventureland stage show in Hong Kong Disneyland; debuted at the new Jungle Junction May 25, 2018, following a May 24 preview. Audiences interact with performers and drummers who recount Moana's travels with Maui to restore the heart of Te Fiti.

Moana Mercantile Apparel, snack, and sundry shop in Disney's Polynesian Village Resort at Walt Disney World; opened Aug. 2014, taking the place of Trader Jack's and Samoa Snacks.

Mobley, Mary Ann (1937–2014) Actress; appeared on TV in *The Secret of Lost Valley* (Susan Harkness) and *My Dog, the Thief* (Kim Lawrence).

Mobley, Roger Actor; appeared in *Emil and the Detectives* (Gustav) and *The Apple Dumpling Gang Rides Again* (Sentry #1), and on TV in *For the Love of Willadean*, *The Treasure of San Bosco Reef*, and in the title role on the *Gallegher* series. After playing Gallegher, Mobley served as a paratrooper and worked in a Texas hospital before returning years later to the Disney Studio to play a bit part of a policeman in *The Kids Who Knew Too Much*. Mobley had actually made his very first Disney appearance Jan. 10, 1958, on Talent Roundup Day on the *Mickey Mouse Club*, as part of the Mobley Trio.

Moby Duck One of the many distant relatives of Donald Duck, used only once on film, in the TV show *Pacifically Peeking*. A seafarer, he was introduced in a *Donald Duck* comic book, No. 112, in Mar. 1967, and later had his own comic book series, starting Oct. 1967.

Mod Hatter, The SEE MAD HATTER SHOP.

Model Behavior (TV) Two-hour movie on *The Wonderful World of Disney*; first aired Mar. 12, 2000. Directed by Mark Rosman. Two teen girls with strikingly similar looks—one a glasses-wearing, self-described geek and the other a successful fashion model—trade places and turn their mutual lives topsy-turvy. Stars Maggie Lawson (Alex, Janine), Kathie Lee Gifford (Deirdre), Justin Timberlake (Jason). Kathie Lee's son, Cody, appears in the cameo role of Janine's precocious brother, Max. Based on the book *Janine and Alex, Alex and Janine* by Michael Levin.

Modern Inventions (film) Mickey Mouse cartoon released May 29, 1937. The first cartoon directed by Jack King. While released as a Mickey cartoon, Mickey does not appear; Donald Duck is the star. A robotic butler continually takes Donald's hat when he doesn't want the butler to have it; Donald keeps pulling new hats out of thin air.

Modine, Matthew Actor; appeared in *Gross Anatomy* (Joe Slovak).

Molina, Alfred Actor; appeared in *Cabin Boy* (Professor), *White Fang 2: Myth of the White Wolf* (Rev. Leland Drury), *Before and After* (Panos Demeris), *Prince of Persia: The Sands of Time* (Sheikh Amar), *The Sorcerer's Apprentice* (Maxim Horvath), and *The Tempest* (Stephano), and guest starred on TV in *Monk* (Peter Magneri). He has provided several voices, including King Agnarr in *Frozen 2*, Double Dan in *Ralph Breaks the Internet*, Professor Knight in *Monsters University* and *Monsters at Work*, the Fairy King in *Strange Magic*, Multi-Bear in *Gravity Falls*, Rippen in *Penn Zero: Part-Time Hero*, and Cogburn in *Big City Greens*.

Moline, Bob (1935–2011) Composer for many Disney projects, especially known for his songs for EPCOT—"Listen to the Land," "Golden Dream," "Canada (You're a Lifetime Journey)," and "Energy (You Make the World Go 'Round)." He also co-wrote the songs for Delta Dreamflight in the Magic Kingdom. His first song for Disney was the jingle "It Could Only Happen at Disneyland."

Molly Brown One of 2 steamboats in Frontierland in Disneyland Paris.

Molony, Alexander Actor; he starred as Peter Pan in *Peter Pan & Wendy* on Disney+.

Mom for Christmas, A (TV) Movie on NBC; aired Dec. 17, 1990. A young girl's Christmas wish magically comes true with the help of a department store mannequin. Directed by George Miller. 120 min. Stars Olivia Newton-John, Juliet Sorcey, Doug Sheehan, Carmen Argenziano.

Mombasa Marketplace SEE ZIWANI TRADERS.

Mom's Got a Date with a Vampire (TV) A Disney Channel Original Movie; first aired Oct. 13, 2000. To get their divorced mother out of the house, Adam and Chelsea Hansen hatch a plot, setting her up on a date with Dimitri Dentatos, who just happens to be a vampire. When the kids learn the truth, they try to save their mother from becoming Dimitri's everlasting soul mate. Directed by Steve Boyum. Stars Caroline Rhea (Lynette Hansen), Charles Shaughnessy (Dimitri Dentatos), Matthew O'Leary (Adam), Laura Vandervoort (Chelsea), Myles Jeffrey (Taylor), Robert Carradine (Malachi Van Helsing).

Mondadori, Arnoldo (1889–1971) He secured the license for the Italian *Topolino* magazine in 1935 and continued to publish it throughout his career. He was presented a European Disney Legends Award in 1997.

Monday Fun with Music Day on the 1950s *Mickey Mouse Club*. Who, What, Why, Where, When, and How Day on the 1970s new *Mickey Mouse Club*. Music Day on the 1990s *Mickey Mouse Club*.

Money for Nothing (film) When an unemployed longshoreman, Joey Coyle, finds a bag containing $1.2 million in unmarked, untraceable currency that has fallen off an armored truck, he attempts to keep it, only to find that the cash brings myriad unwanted problems. When a dedicated detective, Pat Laurenzi, begins to close in, Joey and his girlfriend attempt to launder the money through an underworld leader, but even that goes awry, and Joey is soon forced to own up to his mistake. Released Sep. 10, 1993. Directed by Ramon Menendez. A Hollywood Pictures film. Filmed in Cinema-Scope. 100 min. Stars John Cusack (Joey Coyle), Debi Mazar (Monica Russo), Michael Madsen (Det. Laurenzi). Filmed on location in Pittsburgh and Philadelphia. Joey Coyle, upon whose true-life exploits of finding a fortune on Feb. 26, 1981, this film was based, died shortly before its release.

Monk (TV) One-hour series about a brilliant but obsessive-compulsive private detective; premiered Jul. 12, 2002, as a 2-hour movie on USA Network. In an unusual move, it was then picked up by ABC for airing on the network after its cable airing (the first 13 episodes), beginning Aug. 13, 2002. Due to the tragic unsolved murder of his wife, Adrian Monk has developed an abnormal fear of germs, heights, crowds, and virtually everything else, which cost him his position as a legendary homicide detective on the San Francisco police force, and provides an unusual challenge to solving crimes, not to mention his day-to-day existence. Stars Tony Shalhoub (Adrian Monk), Bitty Schram (Sharona), Ted Levine (Capt. Stottlemeyer), Jason Gray-Stanford (Randall Disher), Traylor Howard (Natalie Teeger). Produced by Mandeville Films in association with Touchstone Television. Shalhoub won an Emmy for Best Actor in a Comedy Series in 2003 and in 2005. Repeats of full seasons of *Monk* began on NBC Mar. 2, 2008; the series ended Dec. 4, 2009.

Monkey Kingdom (film) Disneynature documentary; released Apr. 17, 2015, after an Apr. 16 release in Argentina. The story of a newborn macaque monkey, Kip, and its mother, Maya, and their struggle for survival, set among ancient ruins in the storied jungles of South Asia. Directed by Mark Linfield and Alastair Fothergill. Narrated by Tina Fey. 81 min. Filmed in Sri Lanka.

Monkey Melodies (film) Silly Symphony cartoon released Sep. 26, 1930. Directed by Burt Gillett. Monkeys and other jungle animals sing and dance. A boy and girl monkey continue their romance despite being threatened by an alligator, hippo, snake, and leopard.

Monkeys Monkeys and apes, primarily chimpanzees, were popular for a number of years in Disney features, including *The Barefoot Executive*; *The Misadventures of Merlin Jones*; *The Monkey's Uncle*; *Monkeys, Go Home!*; *Moon Pilot*; *Swiss Family Robinson*; *Toby Tyler*; and *Lt. Robin Crusoe, U.S.N.* They were later featured in films like *George of the Jungle* and the Pirates of the Caribbean series. Primates have also been the subject of a number of Disneynature films, such as *Chimpanzee*, *Monkey Kingdom*, and *Born in China*.

Monkeys, Go Home! (film) A young American, Hank Dussard, inherits a large olive farm in Provence, France. Labor is too costly to harvest the olives, so Hank trains 4 chimpanzees to do the job, and thus incurs the wrath of the villagers. Eventually, the American foils a local labor leader, wins the girl he loves, and the olives are harvested. Released Feb. 2, 1967. Directed by Andrew V. McLaglen. Based on the book *The Monkeys* by G. K. Wilkinson. 101 min. Stars Dean Jones (Hank Dussard), Maurice Chevalier (Father Sylvain), Yvette Mimieux (Maria Riserau), Bernard Woringer (Marcel Cartucci), Clement Harari (Emile Paraulis), Yvonne Constant (Yolande Angelli). For the filming at the Disney Studio, a grove of olive trees was planted near the Studio's Animation Building. It remained for years until the space was needed for the Studio's expansion. The film featured the song "Joie de Vivre" by Richard

M. and Robert B. Sherman, which was sung by Chevalier and Darleen Carr.

Monkey's Uncle, The (film) Young Merlin Jones, the legal uncle of his chimpanzee, Stanley, devises a "sleep learning" machine to sharpen his "nephew's" intellect. And when 2 Midvale College football players, Norm and Leon, are in danger of being scrubbed from the team due to poor grades, Merlin produces his sleep-learning machine, and the 2 muscle-bound students soon stun all on campus by walking off with straight As. After drinking a strength potion and using it to prove man-powered flight in his bicycle-driven contraption is possible in order to gain an endowment for the school from the slightly mad Darius Green, Merlin settles down knowing that football is forever secure at Midvale. Released Jun. 23, 1965. Directed by Robert Stevenson. 90 min. Stars Tommy Kirk (Merlin Jones), Annette Funicello (Jennifer), Leon Ames (Judge Holmby), Frank Faylen (Mr. Dearborne), Arthur O'Connell (Darius Green III), Leon Tyler (Leon), Norman Grabowski (Norman). The film featured the popular title tune sung by Annette and the Beach Boys, written by Richard M. and Robert B. Sherman.

Monorail Tomorrowland attraction in Disneyland; opened Jun. 14, 1959. It was the first daily operating monorail in the country. Originally known as the Disneyland-Alweg Monorail System, with Alweg being the German company that aided in its design. At first, there were two 85-ft.-long trains, 1 red and 1 blue, which glided on their beam around Tomorrowland. In 1961, the system was extended, with new, 112-ft.-long Mark II trains (red, blue, and gold) providing service to the Disneyland Hotel. At this time, it was the first monorail in the country to actually cross a public street, and it became more of a transportation system than a theme park ride, delivering hotel guests directly into the park and vice versa. In 1969, four 137-ft.-long Mark III trains (adding green) replaced the Mark II, followed by four 150-ft.-long Mark V trains (purple, orange, blue, red) debuting between 1986–1988. The Mark VII trains were introduced in 2008–2009 (red, blue, orange), with seating facing toward the windows. At Walt Disney World, an elaborate Monorail transportation system debuted Oct. 1, 1971, originally with 4 Mark IV trains (green, gold, orange, blue), and with 6 more added between Nov. 1971–Dec. 1972 (red, yellow, pink, silver, purple, black). The system is larger in scale, connecting the main Transportation and Ticket Center at the parking

lot with several of the resort hotels and the Magic Kingdom. The fleet was manufactured in Orlando by the Martin Marietta Corporation, with more than three hundred 50-ton beams hauled in from Tacoma, Washington. The system introduced an elevated double-loop configuration in which trains pass side by side in opposite directions, unlike the original single, continuous loop at Disneyland. A separate line was built all the way from the Transportation and Ticket Center to EPCOT Center on Jun. 1, 1982, expanding the system to 13.7 miles. A lime-colored train was added in 1984, followed by the coral train in 1985. Mark VI trains began replacing the Mark IV in 1989, and the changeover was completed in 1991, with a total of 12 trains. After 2 Mark IV trains (coral and lime) were retired in the early 1990s, they found a new home on the Las Vegas Strip, where they were operated 1995–2003. In more recent years, themed wraps have been added to the trains at Walt Disney World and Disneyland to promote films, park attractions, and campaigns. In the 1970s, Disney started a Community Transportation division to market the clean-running and dependable monorails and PeopleMovers to cities, but the only installation of such systems was a WEDway PeopleMover at the Houston Intercontinental Airport. Later, the technology was licensed to Bombardier, Inc. There is also a monorail system at Tokyo Disney Resort called the Disney Resort Line, linking all the major destinations. It is managed by the Maihama Resort Line Co., Ltd. (a subsidiary of the Oriental Land Company) and debuted Jul. 27, 2001.

Monorail Cafe Restaurant in the Disneyland Hotel at the Disneyland Resort; opened in 1986, succeeding the Coffee Shop. Comfort food, burgers, and milkshakes were served. Closed Aug. 6, 1999, to make way for the Downtown Disney District.

Monorail Lounge A favorite stop at the Disneyland Hotel, ca. 1961–1981. Adjacent to the hotel's Monorail station, cocktails were served in a transportation-themed lounge. Also known as the Monorail Bar.

Monsanto Hall of Chemistry Tomorrowland display in Disneyland; open Jul. 17, 1955–Sep. 19, 1966. Visitors glimpsed products made through chemistry. The centerpiece was the CHEMA-TRON, featuring tubes of the 8 basic materials found in nature from which chemicals and plastics can be made. Replaced by Adventure Thru Inner Space, also presented by Monsanto.

Monsanto House of the Future Modernistic house on display in Tomorrowland in Disneyland; open Jun. 12, 1957–Dec. 1967. Built of plastics, the 4-winged, cantilevered house featured the latest in furniture and appliances, along with intercoms and other gadgets that were uncommon in the homes of the time. By 1967, the future had caught up with the house, so preparations were made to tear it down. But it was so well built that when the wrecker's ball struck the house, it merely bounced off. Eventually, the demolition experts had to take their saws and crowbars and pry the place apart piece by piece.

Monsieur D'Arque Fawning head of the lunatic asylum in *Beauty and the Beast*; voiced by Tony Jay.

Monsieur Paul Upscale restaurant in France at EPCOT; opened Dec. 11, 2012, taking the place of Bistro de Paris, but somewhat less formal. The restaurant features gourmet French cuisine, open for dinner only. Named after the acclaimed chef Paul Bocuse, who was one of the 3 chefs who opened Les Chefs de France in 1982. His son, Jerome Bocuse, owns the company behind Monsieur Paul.

Monster Sound Show Attraction in Disney-MGM Studios at Walt Disney World; opened May 1, 1989. Four audience members were selected to act as Foley artists and add eerie sounds to a creepy comedy film starring Martin Short as a deranged butler who tries to do in insurance salesman Chevy Chase. In the postshow area, called Soundworks, guests could create their own sound effects, add their voices to classic movies, and enter the 3-D world of Soundsations. Presented by Sony. Adjacent were 2 state-of-the-art radio broadcast studios, from which stations could air their shows. In Jul. 1997, the attraction became One Saturday Morning, with the film changed to animated offerings from ABC. SEE ALSO ABC SOUND STUDIO.

Monsters at Work (TV) Original animated series on Disney+; digitally premiered Jul. 7, 2021. Tylor Tuskmon, an eager young monster, always dreamed of becoming a Scarer until he lands a job at Monsters, Incorporated, and discovers that scaring is out—and laughter is in. After Tylor is temporarily reassigned to the Monsters, Inc. Facilities Team (MIFT), he must work alongside a misfit bunch of mechanics while setting his sights on becoming a Jokester. Voices include Billy Crystal (Mike), John Goodman (Sulley), Ben Feldman (Tylor), Mindy Kaling (Val), Henry Winkler (Fritz), Lucas Neff (Duncan), Alanna Ubach (Cutter). From Disney Television Animation.

Monsters, Inc. (film) Animated feature from Pixar Animation Studios. There's a reason why there are monsters in children's closets—it's their job. Monsters, Incorporated is the largest and most successful scream-processing factory in the monster world, and there is no better Scarer than James P. ("Sulley") Sullivan. But when he accidentally lets Boo, a little human girl, into Monstropolis, life turns upside down for him and his Scare Assistant, best friend, and roommate Mike Wazowski. Directed by Pete Docter. Released Nov. 2, 2001. Voices include John Goodman (James P. "Sulley" Sullivan), Billy Crystal (Mike Wazowski), James Coburn (Henry J. Waternoose), Jennifer Tilly (Celia), Steve Buscemi (Randall Boggs), Mary Gibbs (Boo), John Ratzenberger (Yeti), Bonnie Hunt (Ms. Flint). 92 min. A computer-animated production with a breakthrough achievement being the depiction of hair and fur, which has the shadowing, density, lighting, and movement consistent with the real thing. Music is by Randy Newman. Released with the Disney • Pixar animated short *For the Birds* (2000), which won an Oscar for Best Animated Short. *Monsters, Inc.* won the Oscar for Best Song ("If I Didn't Have You," written by Newman) and was nominated for Original Score, Sound Effects Editing, and Animated Feature Film. Released on video in 2002, it became the top-selling title of the year. A 3-D version was released Dec. 19, 2012.

Monsters, Inc. Company Store Tomorrowland shop in Tokyo Disneyland; opened in 2009 with Monsters, Inc. Ride & Go Seek!

Monsters, Inc. Laugh Floor Tomorrowland attraction in the Magic Kingdom at Walt Disney World; opened Apr. 2, 2007, replacing The Timekeeper. Monster of Ceremonies Mike Wazowski, who has opened a comedy club, collects laughs that will generate electricity for Monstropolis. Scareacters, like Buddy Boil, the 2-headed Sam and Ella, and Mike's nephew, Marty, engage the audience who become part of the show.

Monsters, Inc. Mike & Sulley to the Rescue! Hollywood Land attraction in Disney California Adventure; opened to guests in Dec. 2005, with a grand opening Jan. 23, 2006. Guests boarding a Monstropolis taxicab discover that something is wreaking havoc on the city—the presence of a little girl named Boo. She's escaped into Monstropolis and, without knowing it, is terrorizing the monsters. Friendly monsters Mike and Sulley are determined to get Boo home before any harm comes to her. The attraction took the place of the short-lived Superstar Limo.

Monsters, Inc. Ride & Go Seek! Tomorrowland attraction in Tokyo Disneyland; opened Apr. 15, 2009. Guests board a security tram through the Monsters, Inc. factory and Monstropolis, looking for hiding monsters and using flashlights to activate special effects and Audio-Animatronics figures. Rocky, a small orange monster, was created especially for the attraction and is popular among guests. Presented by Panasonic.

Monsters of the Deep (TV) Show aired Jan. 19, 1955. Directed by Hamilton S. Luske, Peter Godfrey. Walt discusses historical and mythical monsters, including a look at *20,000 Leagues Under the Sea* and its squid. He also covers dinosaurs, sea serpents, and whales.

Monsters University (film) Animated feature from Pixar Animation Studios. Released Jun. 21, 2013. A prequel to *Monsters, Inc.* (2001). Ever since college-bound Mike Wazowski was a little monster, he dreamed of becoming a Scarer—and he knew better than anyone that the best Scarers come from Monsters University (MU). But during his first semester at MU, Mike finds his plans derailed when he crosses paths with hotshot James P. Sullivan, "Sulley," a natural-born Scarer. The pair's out-of-control competitive spirit gets them both kicked out of the university's elite Scare Program. To make matters worse, they realize they will have to work together, along with an odd bunch of misfit monsters, if they ever hope to make things right. Directed by Dan Scanlon. Voices include Steve Buscemi (Randy Boggs), John Goodman (Sulley), Billy Crystal (Mike Wazowski), Helen Mirren (Dean Hardscrabble). 103 min. Filmmakers made special effort to "monsterize" the university setting, like adding scales to the trees and designing horns and teeth above doors and windows.

Monstro The gigantic whale in *Pinocchio*.

Montalban, Ricardo (1920–2009) Actor; appeared on TV in *Zorro* (Ramon Castillo), with guest appearances in *The Golden Palace* (Lawrence Gentry) and *NBC Salutes the 25th Anniversary of the Wonderful World of Disney*. He narrated *Mustang* and *Chango, Guardian of the Mayan Treasure* and voiced Vartkes in *Buzz Lightyear of Star Command* and Señor Senior, Sr. in *Kim Possible.*

Montan, Chris Music producer/executive; he joined Disney in 1984, creating scores for animated TV series. By 1987, he was vice president, later senior vice president, of music for film and television, contributing to projects including *The Little Mermaid* and *The Lion King*. In 1995, he began producing music-driven films for TV, including *Rodgers and Hammerstein's Cinderella* and *Annie*. In 1999, he was named president of Walt Disney Music, additionally overseeing music for Disney Theatrical and Disney Parks and Resorts. His work has been nominated for 45 Academy Awards, with 16 wins. He retired in 2017 but continued to consult on projects, including *Frozen* on Broadway. He was named a Disney Legend in 2022.

Monte Sleepwalking pelican in *The Pelican and the Snipe* (1944).

Monterey Jack Australian sidekick of Chip and Dale in *Chip 'n' Dale Rescue Rangers*; voiced by Jim Cummings.

Monty (TV) Sitcom on Fox; aired Jan. 11–Feb. 15, 1994. A conservative talk show host, Monty Richardson, is a politically incorrect man of the 1990s whose opinions are constantly challenged by his liberal-minded wife and children. Stars Henry Winkler (Monty Richardson), Kate Burton (Fran Richardson), David Schwimmer (Greg Richardson), China Kantner (Geena Campbell), David Krumholtz (David Richardson), Tom McGowan (Clifford Walker), Joyce Guy (Rita Simon). From Touchstone Television.

Monty City mouse in *The Country Cousin* (1936).

Moochie of Pop Warner Football (TV) Two-part show; aired Nov. 20 and 27, 1960. Directed by William Beaudine. Episode titles are *Pee Wees Versus City Hall* and *From Ticonderoga to Disneyland*. Moochie joins a Pop Warner Football team but has his troubles with the mayor's son. When the 2 make amends, they help the team win and go to the Disneyland Bowl and get to enjoy a visit to the park. Stars Kevin Corcoran, Dennis Joel, Reginald Owen, John Howard, Alan Hale, Jr., Frances Rafferty. Walt Disney appears in a cameo role in the Disneyland segment.

Moochie of the Little League (TV) Two-part show; aired Oct. 2 and 9, 1959. Directed by William Beaudine. A young newspaper boy who is on a Little League team works hard to persuade an elderly Englishman, with whom he had a previous run-in, to donate land for a baseball diamond. Stars Kevin Corcoran, Reginald Owen, Alan Hale, Jr., Stuart Erwin, Frances Rafferty, Lee Aaker, Annette Gorman. The 16-mm release is known as *Little League Moochie*.

Moody, Ron (1924–2015) Actor; appeared in *Unidentified Flying Oddball* (Merlin) and played the same role in *A Kid in King Arthur's Court* years later.

Moon Knight (TV) A Disney+ original series; digitally premiered Mar. 30, 2022. Steven Grant is a mild-mannered gift shop employee who becomes plagued with blackouts and memories of another life. He discovers he has dissociative identity disorder and shares a body with mercenary Marc Spector. As Steven/Marc's enemies converge upon them, they must navigate their complex identities while thrust into a deadly mystery among the powerful gods of Egypt. Stars Oscar Isaac (Marc Spector/Steven Grant, Moon Knight/Mr. Knight), Ethan Hawke (Arthur Harrow), May Calamawy (Layla El-Faouly). From Marvel Studios.

Moon Pilot (film) Richmond Talbot, a young space scientist, is tricked into volunteering for a space trip to the moon. On a last visit to see his mother, he is contacted by Lyrae, a messenger from a planet off in space. They know everything and want to help America get there before the Russians. The FBI moves in when Lyrae makes contact, but she slips through their hands. After a series of comical experiences that confound and confuse the Air Force and the FBI, Lyrae winds up in the space capsule in the arms of Richmond, culminating the romance that was gathering impetus as the story unfolded. Instead of going to the moon, they detour to her planet, Beta Lyrae, to meet her folks. Released Feb. 9, 1962. Directed by James Neilson. 98 min. Stars Tom Tryon (Capt. Richmond Talbot), Brian Keith (Gen. Vanneman), Dany Saval (Lyrae), Tommy Kirk (Walter Talbot), Edmond O'Brien (McClosky), Bob Sweeney (Sen. McGuire), and a mischievous chimp named Cheeta (Charlie). This was the Studio's first feature film about outer space. The songs, written by the Richard M. and Robert B. Sherman, were "Seven Moons of Beta Lyrae," "True Love's an Apricot," and "The Void." This was Tom Tryon's only Disney feature film, after a long run as Texas John Slaughter on the Disney TV series, as well as director Neilson's first of several directing efforts for the Disney Studio.

Mooncussers, The (TV) Two-part show; aired Dec. 2 and 9, 1962. Directed by James Neilson. Based on Iris Vinton's book *Flying Ebony*. Episode titles are *Graveyard of Ships* and *Wake of Disaster*. Pirates prey on unsuspecting ships in the 1840s off New York's Long Island, luring them to run aground, but the son of a shipowner and the locals try to outwit them. Stars Oscar Homolka, Kevin Corcoran, Robert Emhardt, Joan Freeman, Erin O'Brien-Moore, Dub Taylor. It won an Emmy for art direction.

Mooney, Andy Joined Disney as president of Consumer Products (coming from Nike) in Dec. 1999; promoted to chairman in May 2003. He resigned in Sep. 2011.

Moonlight Mile (film) Joe Nast, recovering from the death of his fiancée, tries to be the perfect would-be son-in-law to Ben and Jojo, while falling in love with another woman. Joe learns to let go and discovers that love comes in the most unexpected circumstances. Directed by Brad Silberling. Limited release on Sep. 27, 2002, with an expanded release on Oct. 4. Stars Jake Gyllenhaal (Joe Nast), Dustin Hoffman (Ben Floss), Susan Sarandon (Jojo Floss), Holly Hunter (Mona Camp), Ellen Pompeo (Bertie Knox), Richard T. Jones (Ty), Allan Corduner (Stan Michaels), Dabney Coleman (Mike Mulcahey). 117 min. Filmed in CinemaScope. Massachusetts towns, such as Gloucester and Marblehead, filled in for the fictional Cape Anne in the movie. Working title was *Goodbye Hello*.

Moonliner SEE ROCKET TO THE MOON.

Moon-Spinners, The (film) On vacation in Greece, an English woman and her young niece, Nikky, stumble into the midst of intrigue involving a young Englishman and jewel thieves who have hidden their loot in the vicinity of the tourist hotel. The young people survive a series of dangerous escapades with desperately serious criminals who try twice to kill. Determination and ingenuity eventually save the day, and the youth not only clears his name but also wins the affection of a much-in-love young English lady. Released Jul. 2, 1964. Directed by James Neilson. 119 min. Based on Mary Stewart's best-selling novel. Stars Hayley

Mills (Nikky Ferris), Eli Wallach (Stratos), Pola Negri (Madame Habib), Peter McEnery (Mark Camford), Joan Greenwood (Aunt Frances), Irene Papas (Sophia). Pola Negri, the famous silent film star who had not made a film in over 20 years, was personally coaxed out of retirement by Walt Disney to appear as the treacherous Madame Habib. This was Peter McEnery's Disney film debut, the success of which landed him the title role in *The Fighting Prince of Donegal*. The film features gorgeous on-location photography in Crete by Paul Beeson, and a memorable musical score by Ron Grainer. "The Moon-Spinners Song" was written by Terry Gilkyson.

Moore, Bob (1920–2001) Publicity artist; joined the Disney Studio as an apprentice animator in 1940, contributing to *Dumbo*, *The Reluctant Dragon*, *The Three Caballeros*, and wartime training films. After serving in the U.S. Navy, he returned to Disney as a story man. In 1951, he was asked to run the 1-man art department for Publicity, which he did for 3 decades. Bob developed promotional art concepts for Disney films and, later, theme parks, as creative director of marketing, designing movie posters, Christmas cards, letterheads, logos, and characters. He is noted for designing the 1968 U.S. Disney postage stamp of Walt Disney (with Paul Wenzel) and the Sam the Olympic Eagle character for the 1984 Los Angeles Summer Olympics, as well as murals for a number of Walt Disney schools. Moore was one of the artists whom Walt Disney authorized to sign his name, and, being an artist, he could copy it quite well. He was named a Disney Legend in 1996.

Moore, Demi Actress; appeared in *The Scarlet Letter* (Hester Prynne) and *G.I. Jane* (Jordan O'Neil), and provided the speaking voice of Esmeralda in *The Hunchback of Notre Dame*.

Moore, Dudley (1935–2002) Actor; appeared in *Blame It on the Bellboy* (Melvyn Orton).

Moore, Fred (1911–1952) Animator; he joined Disney in 1930 and soon became known for adding emotion and appeal to the animated characters while making their actions more convincing. His work on the pigs in *Three Little Pigs*, for instance, is considered a landmark in personality animation. He is credited with work on *Snow White and the Seven Dwarfs* and with updating Mickey Mouse's appearance in the late 1930s. He served as animator or directing animator for most of the animated features from *Snow White* to *Peter Pan*, and is noted for his work on such characters as the Dwarfs, Lampwick, Timothy, Katrina, and Mr. Smee. He was named a Disney Legend posthumously in 1995.

Moore, Mandy Actress; provided the voice of Rapunzel in *Tangled* and other appearances of the character. She appeared in *The Princess Diaries* (Lana Thomas) and *Bubble Boy* (Lorraine), and on TV in *Scrubs* (Julie) and the *Walt Disney World Christmas Day Parade*. Also voiced Mara in *Tron: Uprising*, Nita in *Brother Bear 2*, and the title character in *Sheriff Callie's Wild West*.

Moore, Rich Animation director; directed *Wreck-It Ralph* and *Ralph Breaks the Internet* (also voicing Sour Bill and Zangief), and co-directed *Zootopia* (also voicing Doug and Larry).

Moorehead, Agnes (1906–1974) Actress; appeared in *Pollyanna* (Mrs. Snow), and on TV in *The Strange Monster of Strawberry Cove* (Mrs. Pringle).

Moose Hunt, The (film) Mickey Mouse cartoon released May 3, 1931. The first cartoon where Pluto is known by that name. In their misadventures on a moose hunt, Mickey accidentally shoots Pluto, who only pretends to be harmed, and when the pair are later chased by a moose over a cliff, Pluto saves the day by flying with his ears. Directed by Burt Gillett.

Moose Hunters (film) Mickey Mouse cartoon released Feb. 20, 1937. Directed by Ben Sharpsteen. In their search for a moose, Goofy and Donald dress up as a female moose to lure a stag. But their plans go too far, and they soon are running for their lives with Mickey not far behind.

Morake, Lebohang [Lebo M] Composer; collaborated with Hans Zimmer on, and provided vocals for, the soundtrack for *The Lion King*, also contributing to the animated sequels, the 1997 stage musical (also performing in the original Broadway cast), and the 2019 film adaptation. He composed and performed in the short film *One by One* and arranged music for *Dinosaur* and *Tarzan II*. He made a TV appearance in *Disney's Animal Kingdom: The First Adventure*.

Moranis, Rick Actor; appeared as Wayne Szalinski in *Honey, I Shrunk the Kids* and *Honey, I Blew Up the Kid*, on video in *Honey, We Shrunk Ourselves*, and at EPCOT in *Honey, I Shrunk the Audience*.

He voiced Rutt in *Brother Bear* and *Brother Bear 2*, and appeared on Disney+ in *Prop Culture*.

More, Kenneth (1914–1982) Actor; appeared in *Unidentified Flying Oddball* (King Arthur).

More About the Silly Symphonies (TV) Show aired Apr. 17, 1957. Directed by Clyde Geronimi. Walt presents a series of Silly Symphonies, explaining how many of them are based on early folktales and stories.

More Kittens (film) Silly Symphony cartoon released Dec. 19, 1936. Directed by Dave Hand. In this sequel to *Three Orphan Kittens*, the turned-out kittens seek shelter with a Saint Bernard and have more misadventures with a turtle, a bird, and some milk.

More Than Robots (TV) A Disney+ original documentary; digitally premiered Mar. 18, 2022. Four teams of teenagers from 3 locales (Los Angeles, Mexico City, and Chiba, Japan) prepare for the 2020 FIRST Robotics Competition. Although they face challenges along the way—such as having limited resources within their community or putting everything on hold because of a worldwide pandemic—the kids persevere and learn that there is a lot more to the competition than just robots. Directed by Gillian Jacobs. From Supper Club and Disney+.

Moreno, Rita Actress; appeared on TV in *Zorro* (Chulita), *Cane* (Amalia Duque), and *Beauty and the Beast: A 30th Celebration* (narrator), with guest appearances on *The Golden Girls* (Renee Corliss), *Ugly Betty* (Aunt Mirta), *Grey's Anatomy* (Gayle McColl), *Bless This Mess* (Theresa), and the *Walt Disney World 4th of July Spectacular*. She voiced Tanya Trunk in *Bonkers*, Abuela in *Special Agent Oso*, and Queen Camila in *Elena of Avalor*.

Morgan, Harry (1915–2011) Actor; appeared in *The Barefoot Executive* (E. J. Crampton), *Scandalous John* (Hector Pippin), *Snowball Express* (Jesse McCord), *Charley and the Angel* (angel), *The Apple Dumpling Gang* (Homer McCoy), *The Cat from Outer Space* (General Stilton), and *The Apple Dumpling Gang Rides Again* (Major Gaskill), and on TV in *14 Going on 30* (Uncle Herb) and *The Mouse Factory*.

Morimoto Asia Upscale Pan-Asian restaurant in The Landing at Disney Springs at Walt Disney World; opened Sep. 30, 2015, with an open kitchen, outdoor terrace, lounges, and one of the largest sculptural bars in the world, at more than 207 feet long. A collaboration between Chef Masaharu Morimoto and the Patina Restaurant Group. It was built on the site of the former Mannequins dance club in Pleasure Island.

Morning Light (film) A true-story documentary about a group of 11 (selected from an initial 15) intrepid and daring young men and women, on the cusp of adulthood, who embark on the TRANSPAC, the most revered of open-ocean sailing competitions, in a high-performance 52-foot sloop, the *Morning Light*. The crew matches wits and skill in a dramatic 2,300-mile showdown against top professionals. From their earliest training sessions in Hawai'i, conducted by world-class teachers, through their test of endurance on the high seas, they form an unbreakable bond in the process of becoming a singular team that is greater than the sum of its parts. Released Oct. 17, 2008. Directed by Mark Monroe. Roy E. Disney and Leslie DeMeuse were exec. producers. 98 min.

Morocco World Showcase pavilion in EPCOT; opened Sep. 7, 1984. The first country to be added to the park after its opening. It was also the first to have direct participation of a foreign government, opening with an information center for the Moroccan National Tourist Office. Although the pavilion was designed by WED Imagineers, King Hassan II of Morocco sent 23 of his artisans to create the intricate tile work, mosaics, and carved plaster throughout the pavilion, making it arguably the most authentic in all of World Showcase. Like most Moroccan cities, the pavilion is divided into two sections: the ville nouvelle ("new city") and the Medina ("old city"), where guests will find Restaurant Marrakesh and bazaars and shops offering Moroccan crafts, jewelry, clothing, baskets, and brass work. A counter-service restaurant, Tangierine Café, was added in 1999, and a waterside restaurant, Spice Road Table, followed in 2014.

Morpheus God of night in "The Pastoral Symphony" segment of *Fantasia*.

Morris, Matt Actor; appeared on the *Mickey Mouse Club* on The Disney Channel, beginning in 1991.

Morris, Tom Imagineer; he joined WED Enterprises in 1979 as a show set designer for EPCOT Center and would help create attractions, including Journey Into Imagination, Star Tours, and Cars Land. He designed Le Château de la Belle au Bois Dormant for Disneyland Paris, developed concepts for DisneyQuest and Rock 'n' Roller Coaster Starring Aerosmith, and served as executive producer for Hong Kong Disneyland. He left the company in 2016.

Morris, the Midget Moose (film) Special cartoon released Nov. 24, 1950. Directed by Jack Hannah. Morris is the laughingstock of the whole moose herd because he is so small but has a full set of antlers. Everything changes, however, when he meets another outcast moose, Balsam, who is huge but has only puny antlers. The 2 become a great pair, and by getting up on Balsam's back and using his antlers, Morris and Balsam are able to defeat the leader of the herd.

Morrow, Richard T. ("Dick") (1926–2017) Attorney; he joined the legal staff of Walt Disney Productions in 1953 and was promoted in 1964 to vice president. In this role, he was instrumental in the early planning for the "Florida Project," later known as Walt Disney World. He served as the company's general counsel Nov. 1968–Feb. 1985 and was a member of the Board of Directors 1971–1984.

Morrow, Rob Actor; appeared in *Last Dance* (Rick Hayes) and *Quiz Show* (Dick Goodwin), and on TV in *The Fosters* (Will) and *Designated Survivor* (Abe Leonard). He voiced Bernie in *Phineas and Ferb* and Mr. Brulee in *Milo Murphy's Law*.

Morrow, Vic (1932–1982) Actor; appeared in *Treasure of Matecumbe* (Spangler), and on TV in *The Ghost of Cypress Swamp*.

Morse, Robert (1931–2022) Actor; appeared in *The Boatniks* (Ensign Garland), and voiced Gnuckles and Marshak in *Sofia the First*.

Mortensen, Viggo Actor; appeared in *Crimson Tide* (Weps), *G.I. Jane* (Master Chief), and *Hidalgo* (Frank T. Hopkins).

Mortimer Mouse According to legend, Walt Disney had originally wanted to name his mouse star Mortimer, but Mrs. Disney objected and suggested Mickey instead. Disney later used a character named Mortimer Mouse in *Mickey's Rival* (1936).

Morty and Ferdy Mickey Mouse's nephews, first appeared in the Mickey Mouse comic strip on Sep. 18, 1932 (where Ferdie had this different spelling). Their only film appearance was in *Mickey's Steamroller* in 1934.

Mosby Raiders, The (TV) Show; part 2 of *Willie and the Yank*.

Mosby's Marauders (film) International theatrical release of *Willie and the Yank* TV episodes. First released in England in May 1967. 80 min.

Most Magical Story on Earth, The: 50 Years of Walt Disney World (TV) Two-hour special; aired on ABC Oct. 1, 2021, and digitally released on Hulu the next day. Whoopi Goldberg hosts a look back at the evolution of Walt Disney World as a cultural phenomenon. Celebrity appearances include Anthony Anderson, Christina Aguilera, Halle Bailey, John Stamos, Marsai Martin, Gary Sinise. From ABC News, with ABC Entertainment and Disney Parks Global Content.

Moteurs . . . Action! Stunt Show Spectacular Live stunt show featuring cars and motorbikes in Walt Disney Studios Park at Disneyland Paris; open Mar. 16, 2002–Mar. 13, 2020. The action took place in a 3,000-seat theater facing a Mediterranean-style village complete with shops, street stalls, and cafés bordering a market square. A similar production, *Lights, Motors, Action! Extreme Stunt Show*, opened in Disney's Hollywood Studios at Walt Disney World May 5, 2005, and closed Apr. 2, 2016, to make way for Star Wars: Galaxy's Edge.

Moth and the Flame (film) Silly Symphony cartoon released Apr. 1, 1938. Directed by Burt Gillett. A boy and girl moth run away to live in an old costume shop where the girl is caught by a cruel flame. Only by calling on the aid of his friends can the boy moth save her.

Mother Goose Goes Hollywood (film) Silly Symphony cartoon released Dec. 23, 1938. Directed by Wilfred Jackson. Pages from "Mother Goose" come alive with famous motion picture stars, including W. C. Fields, Katharine Hepburn, Spencer Tracy, and Eddie Cantor, caricatured as nursery rhyme characters.

Mother Goose Melodies (film) Silly Symphony cartoon released Apr. 16, 1931. Directed by Burt

Gillett. The Mother Goose characters come to life to entertain Old King Cole with their nursery rhymes.

Mother Goose Rock 'n' Rhyme (TV) A Disney Channel Premiere Film; first aired May 19, 1990. A hip musical-comedy retelling of familiar nursery rhymes, with Little Bo Peep leading the search for Mother Goose, who has disappeared from her home of Rhymeland. Stars Jean Stapleton (Mother Goose), Shelley Duvall (Little Bo Peep), Paul Simon (Simple Simon), Harry Anderson (Peter Piper), Art Garfunkel (Georgie Porgie), Pia Zadora (Little Miss Muffet), Woody Harrelson (Lou, the lamb), Cyndi Lauper (Mary), Little Richard (Old King Cole). 77 min. Pat Field won an Emmy Award for costume design.

Mother Gothel Manipulative old woman posing as Rapunzel's mother in *Tangled*; voiced by Donna Murphy.

Mother Pluto (film) Silly Symphony cartoon released Nov. 14, 1936. Directed by Wilfred Jackson. When a family of baby chicks hatches in his doghouse, Pluto feels duty-bound to protect them, despite the many hazards that continue to appear.

Motherland: Fort Salem (TV) Series on Freeform; debuted Mar. 18, 2020, and ended Aug. 23, 2022. In an alternate, present-day America, 3 young women go from basic training in combat magic to terrifying and thrilling early deployment. In this world, the traditional roles of gender and power are flipped, with women on the front lines fighting looming terrorist threats that are strikingly familiar to our world, but with supernatural tactics and weapons. Stars Taylor Hickson (Raelle), Jessica Sutton (Tally), Ashley Nicole Williams (Abigail), Amalia Holm (Scylla), Demetria McKinney (Anacostia), Lyne Renée (General Sarah Alder). From Freeform Studios, Gary Sanchez Productions, and Hyperobject Industries.

Mother's Courage, A: The Mary Thomas Story (TV) Two-part show; aired Dec. 3 and 10, 1989. Directed by John Patterson. The story of Detroit Pistons basketball star Isiah Thomas and the struggles of Isiah's mother in raising him. It takes all her power, and the death of a buddy, to convince him that he should get out of the local street gang. She works hard to put him through school, bullying him not to quit like his older brother did. When he becomes athlete of the year, he publicly thanks his mother for her never-ending confidence in him. Emmy Award winner for Individual Achievement for a Children's Program. Stars Alfre Woodard, A. J. Johnson, Leon, Garland Spencer, Chick Vennera, Larry O. Williams, Jr.

Motion Dance club which had the latest music videos shown on a massive screen; open at Downtown Disney Pleasure Island at Walt Disney World May 12, 2001–Sep. 27, 2008.

Motocrossed (TV) A Disney Channel Original Movie; first aired Feb. 2, 2001. Motocross is a hot topic for 15-year-old twins Andrew and Andrea Carson, but their father wants Andrea to stick with more feminine pursuits. When Andrew is injured, Andrea sets up a scheme to pose as her brother in an all-important race that's just days away, and into which her father has sunk the family's finances. But she did not reckon with her father finding out or her falling for a fellow competitor. Directed by Steve Boyum. Stars Alana Austin (Andrea Carson), Mary-Margaret Humes (Geneva Carson), Trever O'Brien (Andrew Carson), Timothy Carhart (Edward Carson), Scott Terra (Jason Carson), Michael Cunio (Rene Cartier), Riley Smith (Dean Talon). The motocross track used in the film was Barona Oaks, located on the Barona Indian Reservation in eastern San Diego County in Southern California.

Motor Boat Cruise Fantasyland attraction in Disneyland; opened in Jun. 1957, and closed Jan. 11, 1993, with the area becoming Fantasia Gardens. In 1991 (Mar. 15–Nov. 10), it was redecorated to become a special Motor Boat Cruise to Gummi Glen. This attraction was popular with children, who enjoyed piloting their crafts around the waterways under the Autopia bridges and Monorail beams, but adults tended to find it pretty tame.

Motor Mania (film) Goofy cartoon released Jun. 30, 1950. Directed by Jack Kinney. Goofy portrays both the roles of a normal family man, Mr. Walker, who becomes a monster, Mr. Wheeler, behind the wheel of his car. He changes back to a mild pedestrian attempting to cross the street, only to revert back once again behind the wheel. This cartoon has long been a favorite one in driver's training classes.

Mount Disney In 1938, after Walt Disney helped finance skiing champion Hannes Schroll's Sugar Bowl resort in the Sierra Nevada mountain range, Schroll rechristened Hemlock Peak, an approx. 7,950-ft. skiing mountain, as Mount Disney. There,

California's first chairlift, known as the Disney Express, would be installed. Incidentally, the Sugar Bowl Lodge is the setting for the Goofy "How-to" cartoon *The Art of Skiing*, in which Schroll, also a yodeler, originated the "Goofy holler."

Mount Prometheus The 189-ft.-tall volcano icon of Tokyo DisneySea; debuted Sep. 4, 2001. Towering over Mysterious Island, it was constructed using 750,000 sq. feet of rock. The volcano erupts with lava and flames that shoot up to 50 feet. Inside are 2 attractions inspired by the works of Jules Verne—Journey to the Center of the Earth and 20,000 Leagues Under the Sea.

Mountain Born (TV) Show aired Jan. 9, 1972. Directed by James Algar. A boy learns the duties of a shepherd from his idol, the ranch foreman, high in the Colorado mountains. When the foreman becomes ill, the boy has to take the sheep into the mountains where they will graze for the summer season. A fierce storm almost causes tragedy as the boy leads the sheep back home. Stars Sam Austin, Walter Stroud, Jolene Terry.

Mountainside Treasures Fantasyland shop in Shanghai Disneyland; opened Jun. 16, 2016. Apparel, toys, and other items inspired by *Snow White and the Seven Dwarfs* are sold.

Mouse About Town Sunset Boulevard apparel and souvenir shop in Disney's Hollywood Studios; opened Oct. 23, 1995.

Mouse Club, The With the growth in interest in the collecting of Disneyana, collectors enjoyed getting together to share stories and buy and sell items for their collections. The Mouse Club was the first major club to begin, in 1980; originally run by Ed and Elaine Levin. The primary activity was an annual convention held at a hotel in Anaheim in the summer. In 1985, Kim and Julie McEuen led the club to ever-larger convention events, until its final one was held in 1993. The Mouse Club, along with other Disneyana groups, was not sponsored by Disney; their logo was a certain mouse unrecognizable because it had a paper bag over its head. The Mouse Club is no longer in operation.

Mouse Factory, The (TV) Syn. series produced and directed by Ward Kimball; aired for 2 seasons beginning Jan. 26, 1972. There were 43 shows, each featuring classic Disney animated cartoons tied to the appearance of a guest star host or hostess in a specially produced live-action sequence. For example, Jo Anne Worley hosted a show about horses, Jonathan Winters did one about space travel, and Bill Dana starred in one about bullfighting. The other hosts were Wally Cox, Pat Buttram, Pat Paulsen, Dom DeLuise, Charles Nelson Reilly, Skiles & Henderson, Johnny Brown, Don Knotts, Phyllis Diller, John Byner, Jim Backus, Joe Flynn, Harry Morgan, Dave Madden, Henry Gibson, Kurt Russell, John Astin, Nipsey Russell, Shari Lewis, Ken Berry, Annette Funicello. Shows were 30 min.

Mouse House, The Disney gift shop in Pleasure Island at Walt Disney World; opened May 1, 1989. Closed Feb. 3, 1991, to become the Pleasure Island Jazz Company. Another location opened Feb. 9, 2000, taking the place of Avigators, and closed Feb. 15, 2005.

Mouse Mania (film) SEE MICKEY'S 50.

Mousecar Award created in the 1940s, consisting of a bronze-colored figure of Mickey Mouse; used by the Disney company to honor its employees and those who have done a notable service to the company. The name is a reference to the motion picture academy's Oscar. In 1973, at the time of the Disney Studio's 50th anniversary, special Mousecars were given to every employee who had worked at the former Disney Studio on Hyperion Avenue—naming them members of the exclusive Hyperion Club. The Donald Duck equivalent to the Mousecar is known as the Duckster.

MouseGear Shop in Innoventions East in EPCOT; opened Sep. 20, 1999, after a Sep. 19 soft opening, taking the place of Centorium. Apparel, souvenirs, housewares, and toys were sold in a colorful factory where, as the story went, Disney characters created the merchandise. Covering 25,500 sq. feet, it was the largest character shop inside a Disney park. Closed Jan. 2020 to become Creations Shop. During construction of the new shop, the merchandise was moved to a temporary MouseGear, which closed Sep. 14, 2021.

Mousegetar The original Mousegetar was built specially for Jimmie Dodd to use on the *Mickey Mouse Club* show. It was a 4-string instrument, which Jimmie called a tenor guitar. Mattel produced and sold toy versions of the Mousegetar in the late 1950s. The original Mousegetar was donated to the Walt Disney Archives by Jimmie's widow, Ruth Dodd Braun, in the 1980s.

Mousekartoon The final segment of each 1950s *Mickey Mouse Club* show. The Mouseketeers would open the treasure mine and introduce the showing of a Disney cartoon.

Mouseketeer Reunion, The (TV) Show aired Nov. 23, 1980. Directed by Tom Trbovich. The original Mouseketeers return for the 25th anniversary, hosted by Paul Williams. When it was announced to the wire services that the company had found all except 4 of the original 39 Mouseketeers, the story went out and in less than 24 hours the missing "mice" had been found—one in Winnipeg, and the other 3 nearby in Southern California.

Mouseketeers A total of 39 talented kids originally performed on the 1950s *Mickey Mouse Club*; there were 24 regulars the first season. The 39 Mouseketeers were Nancy Abbate, Don Agrati, Sherry Alberoni, Sharon Baird, Billie Jean Beanblossom, Bobby Burgess, Lonnie Burr, Tommy Cole, Johnny Crawford, Dennis Day, Eileen Diamond, Dickie Dodd, Mary Espinosa, Bonnie Lynn Fields, Annette Funicello, Darlene Gillespie, Judy Harriet, Cheryl Holdridge, Linda Hughes, Dallas Johann, John Lee Johann, Bonni Lou Kern, Charley Laney, Larry Larsen, Cubby O'Brien, Karen Pendleton, Paul Petersen, Lynn Ready, Mickey Rooney, Jr., Tim Rooney, Mary Lynn Sartori, Bronson Scott, Michael Smith, Jay-Jay Solari, Ronald Steiner, Margene Storey, Mark Sutherland, Doreen Tracey, Don Underhill. The adult leaders were Jimmie Dodd and Roy Williams, aided occasionally by Bob Amsberry. There were 12 Mouseketeers on the new *Mickey Mouse Club* (1977–1978): Billy "Pop" Attmore, Scott Craig, Nita Dee, Mindy Feldman, Angel Florez, Allison Fonte, Shawnte Northcutte, Kelly Parsons, Julie Piekarski, Todd Turquand, Lisa Whelchel, Curtis Wong. The latest version of the *Mickey Mouse Club* on Disney Channel (1989–1994) added 35 additional kids to the Mouseketeer list, though they were not actually called Mouseketeers: Josh Ackerman, Christina Aguilera, Lindsey Alley, Rhona Bennett, Nita Booth, Mylin Brooks, Brandy Brown, Blain Carson, J. C. Chasez, Braden Danner, Tasha Danner, Nikki DeLoach, T. J. Fantini, Albert Fields, Dale Godboldo, Ryan Gosling, Tiffini Hale, Chase Hampton, Roqué Herring, David Kater, Tony Lucca, Ricky Luna, Tate Lynche, Deedee Magno, Jennifer McGill, Terra McNair, Ilana Miller, Jason Minor, Matt Morris, Kevin Osgood, Damon Pampolina, Keri Russell, Britney Spears, Justin Timberlake, Marc Worden. Adult leaders were Fred Newman and Mowava Pryor, with the latter succeeded by Terri Misner in 1991.

Mouseketeers at Walt Disney World, The (TV) Show aired Nov. 20, 1977. Directed by John Tracy. The kids from the new *Mickey Mouse Club* head for Florida to do a show. They set up camp at Fort Wilderness and visit the new River Country. Because of several misadventures, their chaperone has a difficult time keeping them all friends. Stars Jo Anne Worley, Ronnie Schell, Dennis Underwood, the Mouseketeers.

Mouseorail, Mickey's For Disneyland's 35th anniversary in 1990, the front car of the red Mark III Monorail train was transformed into the 40-ft.-long Mouseorail, which embarked on a 35-city tour, beginning in Palm Desert, California. The vehicle was later displayed in the Rocket Rods queue, from 1998–2000, before it was dismantled.

Mousercise (TV) Aerobics show on The Disney Channel; first aired Apr. 18, 1983. Stars Kellyn Plasschaert, Steve Stark, Garett Pearson. 60 episodes. Inspired by the 1982 Disneyland Records exercise album of the same title that achieved platinum certification.

Mouseterpiece Theater (TV) Series of Disney cartoon shows on The Disney Channel; hosted by George Plimpton (à la Alistair Cooke on PBS's *Masterpiece Theatre*). Began Apr. 18, 1983. There were 60 episodes prepared.

Move Along Mustangers (TV) Episode 7 of *Elfego Baca*.

Movie Premiere Showcase World Bazaar shop in Tokyo Disneyland; opened Jul. 21, 1994, selling character merchandise. Closed Aug. 2005, to be taken over by World Bazaar Confectionery.

Movieland Memorabilia Main entrance souvenir and sundry shop at Disney-MGM Studios (now Disney's Hollywood Studios); opened May 1, 1989.

Movies Anywhere SEE DISNEY MOVIES ANYWHERE.

Moving Day (film) Mickey Mouse cartoon released Jun. 20, 1936. Directed by Ben Sharpsteen. When the sheriff, Pete, evicts them from their home due to overdue rent, Mickey and Donald get Goofy, an iceman, to help them move out. Soon all is pandemonium with Goofy's struggles with a piano that will not stay in the moving truck and Donald wrestling with various household items. The house is utterly destroyed when Pete strikes a match near a gas leak, resulting in all the belongings being blown into the truck as they drive away.

Mowgli Boy raised by wolves in *The Jungle Book*; voiced by Bruce Reitherman.

Moynihan, Bobby Actor; appeared in *When in Rome* (Puck) and *Delivery Man* (Aleksy), and on Disney+ in *Flora & Ulysses* (Stanlee). He has provided several voices, including Chet (*Monsters University*), Forgetter Bobby (*Inside Out*), Louie (*DuckTales*, 2017), Dude (*Descendants 2* and *3*), Blizzy Stormfront (*Vampirina*), Geezer (*Star Wars: Visions*), Orka (*Star Wars Resistance*), Tweedle Don't (*Alice's Wonderland Bakery*), and Bobby Boots (*Pupstruction*).

Mucha, Zenia She became senior vice president of Corporate Communications for The Walt Disney Company in May 2002 and was promoted to executive vice president in 2005. During her tenure, she led the communications and positioning strategy for all of the company's business initiatives, including international expansion and the acquisitions of Pixar, Marvel, Lucasfilm, and 21st Century Fox. She had originally joined ABC as senior vice president of communications in Feb. 2001. She retired in Dec. 2021.

Mufasa Lion ruler, and father of Simba, in *The Lion King*; voiced by James Earl Jones.

Mulan (film) Based on a 2,000-year-old Chinese folktale, this animated feature is the story of a high-spirited girl who tries hard to please her parents and be the perfect daughter, but who feels that she is always disappointing them. When Mulan's aged father is called to serve (and certain death) in war, bold compassion compels her to save his life by disguising herself as a man and joining the Chinese army in his place. Brought to life by Mulan's extraordinary actions, a feisty, flimflam "guardian" dragon, Mushu, joins the heroine's quest and leads her into a series of comic misadventures. At the height of their success, their masquerade is revealed, and both are abandoned in disgrace. When all seems lost, Mulan's irrepressible will spurs her once again to courageously fight against all odds, defeat the terrible Hun invaders, and save the Emperor, bringing honor to her beloved parents. Released Jun. 19, 1998. There was a world premiere at the Hollywood Bowl on Jun. 5. Directed by Barry Cook and Tony Bancroft. Voices include Ming-Na Wen (Mulan speaking), Lea Salonga (Mulan singing), B. D. Wong (Shang speaking), Donny Osmond (Shang singing), Eddie Murphy (Mushu), Miguel Ferrer (Shan-Yu), Harvey Fierstein (Yao), Gedde Watanabe (Ling), Jerry Tondo (Chien-Po), June Foray (Grandmother Fa). 88 min. Five new songs by Matthew Wilder and David Zippel—"Honor to Us All," "Reflection," "I'll Make a Man Out of You," "A Girl Worth Fighting For," and "True to Your Heart." Jerry Goldsmith provided the underscore. *Mulan* was the first feature to be primarily produced at the Disney Feature Animation studio at Walt Disney World in Florida. In order to prepare the filmmakers for the task, a select group of the film's artistic supervisors made a 3-week trip to China to sketch and photograph the intriguing sites and soak up the culture. Then, under the direction of production designer Hans Bacher, they found a unique look for the film, inspired by the simple graphic style of traditional Chinese art.

Mulan (film) Live-action retelling of the story of China's legendary warrior who risks everything out of love for her family and country. When the Emperor issues a decree that 1 man per family must serve in the Imperial Army to defend the country from northern invaders, Hua Mulan, the eldest daughter of an honored warrior, steps in to take the place of her ailing father. Masquerading as a man, Hua Jun, she is tested every step of the way. She must harness her inner strength in an epic journey that will transform her into an honored warrior and earn her the respect of a grateful nation and a proud father. Originally planned for theatrical release in the U.S., but instead released digitally Sep. 4, 2020, on Disney+, following a Mar. 9 Hollywood premiere at the Dolby Theatre and international releases beginning Sep. 3. Directed by Niki Caro. Stars Yifei Liu (Mulan), Donnie Yen (Commander Tung), Tzi Ma (Zhou), Jason Scott Lee (Böri Khan), Yoson An (Honghui), Ron Yuan (Sergeant Qiang), Gong Li (Xianniang), Jet Li (the Emperor). 115 min. In addition to adapting elements from the 1998 animated feature, filmmakers took inspiration from the original Chinese "Ballad of Mulan." Filmed in wide-screen format in China, with additional filming in New Zealand. Received Academy Award nominations for Costume Design and Visual Effects.

Mulan II (film) Direct-to-video release Feb. 1,

2005. Mulan receives a marriage proposal from General Shang, making everyone happy except Mushu who tries to keep Mulan single on learning he'll lose his guardian job if she marries. With China threatened by a Mongol invasion, the Emperor calls upon Mulan, Shang, and their lovable "gang of three" friends, Yao, Ling, and Chien-Po, to escort his daughters to arranged marriages with vital allies in the northern provinces. When the 3 princesses unexpectedly fall in love with the gang of 3, Mulan decides to help them, even though this contradicts the emperor's orders and calls Mulan's relationship with Shang into question. Mulan remains true to her heart, however, by solving the problem in her own unique way, saving both the princesses and China. Directed by Darrell Rooney and Lynne Southerland. Voices include Ming-Na (Mulan), Pat Morita (Emperor), B. D. Wong (Shang), Mark Moseley (Mushu), Lucy Liu (Mei), Harvey Fierstein (Yao), Sandra Oh (Ting Ting), Gedde Watanabe (Ling), Lauren Tom (Su), Jerry Tondo (Chien-Po), George Takei (First Ancestor), Michelle Kwan (Shopkeeper), Lea Salonga (Mulan, singing).

Mule Pack Frontierland attraction in Disneyland; operated Jul. 17, 1955–Feb. 1, 1956. Became Rainbow Ridge Pack Mules (1956–1959) and Pack Mules Through Nature's Wonderland (1960–1973). Walt Disney insisted that mules be a part of his Frontierland, even though they were ornery animals that would often nip the guests or refuse to move. Disney felt that they helped give the necessary ambience to the western theme. As new attractions were added to Frontierland, there was more to view while riding the mules.

Mulholland Madness Paradise Pier attraction in Disney's California Adventure; open Feb. 8, 2001–Oct. 11, 2010. A mini-roller coaster ride as vehicles careen across a crazy map of the Hollywood Hills and Santa Monica Mountains. It became Goofy's Sky School Jul. 1, 2011.

Mulligan, Richard (1932–2000) Actor; appeared on TV in *The Deacon Street Deer* (Shorty) and the *Walt Disney World Happy Easter Parade* (1992). He appeared as Dr. Harry Weston in *The Golden Girls* and its spin-off *Empty Nest*, for which he won the Emmy Award for Best Lead Actor in a Comedy Series in 1989. He voiced Einstein in *Oliver & Company*.

Multiplane camera Camera that gave depth to an animated film by use of layers of backgrounds painted on glass; first used in *The Old Mill* (1937) but used most effectively in the features of the 1940s, such as *Pinocchio*, *Fantasia*, and *Bambi*. It was the invention of Disney staff members under William Garity, and its creators received a special Scientific and Technical–category Academy Award. The vertical camera stand could hold up to 6 background layers. Ub Iwerks, who had left the Disney Studio several years earlier, created his own version of a multiplane camera at his studio about the same time, but it was a horizontal arrangement. The last film to shoot multiplane scenes on the camera was *Oliver & Company*.

Mumford, David (1956–2003) Imagineer; joined WED Enterprises in 1979 as a show set draftsman working on The Land for EPCOT Center. He later worked on show set design for several attractions before becoming show producer for Star Tours in Tokyo Disneyland and Aladdin's Oasis at Disneyland. As a Disney aficionado, he became an unofficial historian at Walt Disney Imagineering, writing a number of articles and speaking at Disneyana Conventions with his colleague Bruce Gordon. Together Mumford and Gordon wrote the book *Disneyland: The Nickel Tour*.

Mumford (film) A psychologist named Dr. Mumford hangs out his shingle in a small town that also happens to be named Mumford and begins dispensing no-nonsense advice to an array of quirky locals. Included are a shop-by-mail-addicted housewife, an eccentric young billionaire, and a mild-mannered pharmacist with delusions of lascivious grandeur. Dr. Mumford's unique style of therapy has a surprising effect on the community, sparking romance in some of the most unlikely places. A Touchstone film. Directed by Lawrence Kasdan. Released Sep. 24, 1999. Stars Loren Dean (Mumford), Hope Davis (Sofie Crisp), Mary McDonnell (Althea Brockett), Ted Danson (Jeremy Brockett), Martin Short (Lionel Dillard), David Paymer (Dr. Ernest Delbanco), Alfre Woodard (Lily), Pruitt Taylor Vince (Henry Follett), Jane Adams (Dr. Phyllis Sheeler), Jason Lee (Skip Skipperton). 112 min. Since no one town had all the elements required by the producers to pass for the town of Mumford, they filmed in a total of 11 California locations—St. Helena, Healdsburg, Santa Rosa, Petaluma, Sebastopol, Calistoga, Napa, Guerneville, Sonoma, Kenwood, and Tomales. Filmed in CinemaScope.

Mumy, Bill Actor; appeared in *Rascal* (Sterling), and on TV in *For the Love of Willadean* (Freddy) and *Sammy, the Way-out Seal* (Petey). He voiced Eon in *Buzz Lightyear of Star Command*.

Muncey English sheepdog who appears in *The New Neighbor* (1953).

Munro, Janet (1934–1972) Actress; appeared in *Swiss Family Robinson* (Roberta), *Darby O'Gill and the Little People* (Katie O'Gill), and *Third Man on the Mountain* (Lizbeth Hempel), and on TV in *The Horsemasters* (Janet).

Muppet Babies (TV) Animated series on Disney Junior; debuted Mar. 23, 2018, on Disney Channel. Almost 30 years after the original *Muppet Babies*, this reimagined CG series chronicles the playroom antics of a young Kermit the Frog, Piggy, Fozzie Bear, Gonzo, and Animal—plus a brand-new Muppet Baby, Summer Penguin. Under the watchful eye of Miss Nanny, the Muppet Babies use their imaginations to embark on countless adventures that take them to the farthest corners of the universe and demonstrate to young viewers the power and potential of imaginative play. Voices include Jenny Slate (Miss Nanny), Matt Danner (Kermit), Melanie Harrison (Piggy), Dee Bradley Baker (Animal), Ben Diskin (Gonzo), Eric Bauza (Fozzie), Jessica DiCicco (Summer). A co-production between Disney Junior, Disney Consumer Products and Interactive Media's Publishing and Digital Media group, and The Muppets Studio.

Muppet Christmas Carol, The (film) Musical version of the Dickens tale about a miserly, unsympathetic old man who learns the true meaning of Christmas with the visitation of 3 spirits—of Christmases past, present, and future. Enacted by Jim Henson's Muppets, with Kermit the Frog as Bob Cratchit and Miss Piggy as his faithful wife. The Great Gonzo narrates the tale as Charles Dickens himself, with the aid of a hungry rat named Rizzo. Released Dec. 11, 1992. From Jim Henson Productions. Directed by Brian Henson. 86 min. Stars the Muppets, along with Michael Caine as Ebenezer Scrooge. Made at Shepperton Studios, London. The first Muppet feature produced after Jim Henson's death, with longtime performer Steve Whitmire performing the role of Kermit/Bob Cratchit. Songs by Paul Williams include "It Feels Like Christmas," "One More Sleep 'til Christmas," and "Thankful Heart." A song cut from the original theatrical release, "When Love Is Gone," was restored for select home entertainment releases and for digital release on Disney+.

Muppet Mobile Lab Audio-Animatronics Muppet characters Dr. Bunsen Honeydew and Beaker roam the park and interact with each other and with guests. First tested for the public in Disney's California Adventure Feb. 27, 2007, and later appeared in other Disney parks, including EPCOT and Hong Kong Disneyland.

Muppet Moments (TV) Short-form series starring the Muppets on Disney Junior, meant for children ages 2–7; debuted Apr. 3, 2015. The Muppets have amusing conversations with young kids on a variety of topics, including apologies, food, and manners. Produced by The Muppets Studios in association with Disney Junior.

Muppet Treasure Island (film) Young Jim Hawkins is given a treasure map by a mysterious sailor, and he sets sail with his pals, Gonzo and Rizzo, on a high-seas adventure. Joining them on the expedition is the Squire Trelawney (Fozzie Bear), the dashing Captain Smollett (Kermit), and the mutinous Long John Silver. When Silver and his crew seize the map and take Jim hostage, it is up to Captain Smollett and his men to come to the rescue. But, first, who will rescue *them* from a tribe of native warthogs, ruled by their queen, Benjamina Gunn (Miss Piggy)? Directed by Brian Henson. Released Feb. 16, 1996. Stars Tim Curry (Long John Silver), Kevin Bishop (Jim Hawkins), Billy Connolly (Billy Bones), Jennifer Saunders (Mrs. Bluveridge). 99 min. The film was shot over 14 weeks on 7 stages at Shepperton Studios outside London. More than 400 Muppets were used in the production. Score by Hans Zimmer. Songs by Barry Mann and Cynthia Weil include "Love Led Us Here," "Sailing For Adventure," "Cabin Fever," and "Professional Pirate."

Muppets While working with Jim Henson on the production *Jim Henson's Muppet*Vision 3D*, Disney announced an agreement with Henson to acquire the merchandise, licensing, and publishing rights to the Muppets on Aug. 29, 1989. However, estate tax problems encountered by Henson's heirs after his unexpected passing in May 1990 caused them to end the deal in December of that year. Finally, 14 years later, in Apr. 2004, Disney was able to complete an acquisition of the Muppet properties and *Bear in the Big Blue House*.

Muppets, The (film) In Smalltown, U.S.A., Kermit-obsessed Walter (a brand-new Muppet) travels to Hollywood with his brother Gary and Gary's girlfriend, Amy. When they go to tour Muppet Studios, they find out it is falling into ruin and the Muppets are no longer there. In order to save the Muppet Theater from being razed so a dishonest businessman can tear it down to drill for oil, Gary, Amy, and Walter search out Kermit at his home. They all work to get the Muppets together again for a telethon to raise the $10 million necessary to save the theater. This is easier said than done, as the Muppets have for years all gone their separate ways: Miss Piggy, for example, is a plus-size fashion editor in Paris, Gonzo runs a high-class plumbing business, and Fozzie plays with a tribute band called The Moopets in Reno, Nevada. Released Nov. 23, 2011. Directed by James Bobin. Stars Jason Segel (Gary), Amy Adams (Mary), Chris Cooper (Tex Richman), Rashida Jones (Veronica), cameos by a couple dozen celebrities, and more than 100 Muppets. Walter is voiced by Peter Linz. 103 min. The song, "Man or Muppet," by Bret McKenzie, won the Oscar for Original Song in 2012.

Muppets, The (TV) The Muppets returned on ABC with a documentary-style show, which aired Sep. 22, 2015–Mar. 1, 2016. It explored the Muppets' personal lives and relationships, both at home and at work, as well as romances, breakups, achievements, disappointments, wants, and desires. Kermit the Frog and the rest of the Muppet gang are producing a late-night talk show, *Up Late with Miss Piggy*. Although Kermit and Miss Piggy are officially broken up and dating other people, Kermit still serves as exec. producer of her talk show, which proves to be a very challenging task. From ABC Studios and The Muppets Studio.

Muppets at Walt Disney World, The (TV) Show aired May 6, 1990. Directed by Peter Harris. Kermit and his friends go to Paradise Swamp in Florida and then decide to visit the nearby Walt Disney World. They visit many of the attractions, and Mickey Mouse welcomes Kermit as an old friend. Stars Charles Grodin, Raven-Symoné, and the Muppets.

Muppets Celebrate Jim Henson, The (TV) Special on CBS; aired Nov. 21, 1990. A tribute to the Muppet creator. Directed by Don Mischer. 60 min. Stars Harry Belafonte, Carol Burnett, Ray Charles, John Denver, Steven Spielberg, Frank Oz. The special won an Emmy for Editing of a Miniseries or Special (Multicamera Production).

Muppets Christmas, A: Letters to Santa (TV) Musical special on NBC; first aired Dec. 17, 2008. When Kermit and the gang cause 3 letters on their way to Santa Claus to go missing, the troupe sets off to save Christmas for the letter writers. Directed by Kirk R. Thatcher. The Muppets are joined by Nathan Lane (Officer Meany), Whoopi Goldberg (cabdriver), Richard Griffiths (Santa Claus), Jane Krakowski (Claire's mom), Jesse L. Martin (postal worker), Petra Nemcova (Beaker's girlfriend), Uma Thurman (Joy), Tony Sirico (Mafia guy), Steve Schirripa (Mafia guy), Michael Bloomberg (as himself), Madison Pettis (Claire), Paul Williams (Elf). 60 min. A production of The Muppet Studios.

Muppets Haunted Mansion (TV) Special on Disney+; digitally released Oct. 8, 2021. Teamed with his friend Pepé the Prawn, The Great Gonzo takes the greatest challenge of his life by spending the night in the scariest place on Earth—the Haunted Mansion. Celebrity appearances include Will Arnett (The Host), Yvette Nicole Brown (The Driver), Darren Criss (The Caretaker), Taraji P. Henson (The Bride), Ed Asner (Ghost of Claude), Alfonso Ribeiro (Ghost of Fred), Pat Sajak (Singing Bust), John Stamos (Famous Person). Songs by Ed Mitchell and Steve Morrell. Inspired by the Disney parks attraction. From The Muppets Studio and Soapbox Films.

Muppets Mayhem, The (TV) Comedy series planned for digital release on Disney+. After 45 years of rockin' out, The Electric Mayhem goes on an epic musical journey to finally record their first studio album. With the help of a driven young music executive, Nora, the old-school Muppet band comes face-to-face with the current-day music scene as they try to finally go platinum. Based on characters created by Jim Henson. Stars Lilly Singh (Nora), Tahj Mowry (Moog), Saara Chaudry (Hannah), Anders Holm (JJ). From ABC Signature and The Muppets Studio.

Muppets Most Wanted (film) The entire Muppets gang goes on a global tour, selling out grand theaters in some of Europe's most exciting destinations: Berlin, Madrid, London, and Dublin. But mayhem follows the Muppets overseas, as they find themselves unwittingly entangled in an international jewel-heist caper headed by Constantine—the World's Number One Criminal and a dead ringer for Kermit—and his dastardly sidekick Dominic Badguy, aka Number Two. Constantine has escaped from a Gulag in Siberia, but it is Kermit who is arrested and incarcerated, believed to be Constantine. Directed by James Bobin. Released Mar. 21, 2014, after a Mar. 20 release in Chile and Hong Kong. Stars Ricky Gervais (Dominic), Tina Fey (Nadya), Ty Burrell (Jean Pierre Napoleon). Numerous actors and singers make cameo appearances, including Lady Gaga, Tony Bennett, Celine Dion, Frank Langella, Christoph Waltz, Josh Groban, Ray Liotta, and Ross Lynch. Muppet voices are provided by Steve Whitmire, Peter Linz, Dave Goelz, Eric Jacobson, Bill Barretta, and others. 108 min. Songs by Bret McKenzie include "We're Doing a Sequel," "I'll Get You What You Want (Cockatoo in Malibu)," and "Something So Right."

Muppets Now (TV) The Muppets Studio's first unscripted series; digitally released on Disney+ beginning Jul. 31, 2020. Rushing to upload a brand-new Muppet series for streaming, Scooter will need to navigate whatever obstacles, distractions, and complications the rest of the Muppet gang throws at him. 6 episodes. From The Muppets Studio and Soapbox Films.

Muppets on Location—The Days of Swine and Roses Live show in Disney-MGM Studios at Walt Disney World; ran Sep. 16, 1991–Jan. 23, 1994.

Muppets' Wizard of Oz, The (TV) Movie on ABC; aired May 20, 2005. In this fun, contemporary take on the classic story, featuring the Muppets, Dorothy Gale is a teenager with dreams of showbiz that seem far from coming true in the Kansas trailer park where she lives. When she's transported to the magical land of Oz, she and her sidekick Toto, join the Scarecrow, the Tin Thing, and the Lion to fight the Wicked Witch of the West and find the Wizard who might make her a star. From Touchstone Television. Directed by Kirk R. Thatcher. Stars Ashanti (Dorothy), Queen Latifah (Auntie Em), David Alan Grier (Uncle Henry), Jeffrey Tambor (Wizard). Miss Piggy plays the 4 witches (2 good and 2 bad), Kermit is the Scarecrow, The Great Gonzo is the Tin Thing, and Fozzie Bear is the Lion. Based on the novel *The Wonderful Wizard of Oz* by L. Frank Baum.

Muppet*Vision 3D Attraction in Disney's Hollywood Studios at Walt Disney World; opened May 16, 1991. Kermit the Frog gives audiences a tour of Muppet Labs and their new film process,

Muppet*Vision 3D, but in classic Muppets fashion, things go awry when Waldo, the spirit of 3-D, is unleashed and wreaks havoc. Sensational in-theater effects and Audio-Animatronics Muppets add to the impact. Highlights include a song by Miss Piggy and a musical finale by Sam Eagle, called "A Salute to All Nations, but Mostly America." Originally sponsored by Kodak. Waldo was performed live through a groundbreaking motion-capture apparatus—the Henson Digital Puppetry System—allowing for the real-time performance of a digital character to be recorded live. The attraction was originally part of New York Street (renamed Streets of America in 2004); it became part of Grand Avenue in 2017, with the theater renamed Grand Arts Theatre. Also played in Disney California Adventure, Feb. 8, 2001–2014, where it was replaced by *For the First Time in Forever: A Frozen Sing-Along Celebration*. Originally known as *Jim Henson's Muppet*Vision 3-D*.

Murder She Purred: A Mrs. Murphy Mystery (TV) A 2-hour movie on *The Wonderful World of Disney*; first aired Dec. 13, 1998. Mystery-solving postmistress Mary Minor Haristeen, known to her friends as Harry, has 2 remarkable pets: a cat named Mrs. Murphy and a Welsh corgi named Tucker, whose detective skills are every bit as keen as her own. When Harry gets mixed up with a man who may be involved in a murder, Mrs. Murphy and Tucker do some snooping on their own. Directed by Simon Wincer. Stars Ricki Lake (Harry), Blythe Danner (Mrs. Murphy), Anthony Clark (Tucker), Linden Ashby (Blair Bainbridge). Based on a novel by Rita Mae Brown.

Murphy, Eddie Actor; provided the voice of Mushu in *Mulan* and Thurgood Stubbs in *The PJs*. He appeared in *The Distinguished Gentleman* (Thomas Jefferson Johnson), *Metro* (Scott Roper), *Holy Man* (G), and *The Haunted Mansion* (Jim Evers), and on TV in *The Dream Is Alive*.

Murphy, Thomas S. (1925–2022) Member of the Disney Board of Directors Feb. 9, 1996–Mar. 3, 2004. His company, Capital Cities, merged with ABC in 1985, and he headed the combined companies until Capital Cities/ABC merged with Disney. He was named a Disney Legend in 2007.

Murray, Bill Actor; appeared in *What About Bob?* (Bob Wiley), *Ed Wood* (Bunny Breckinridge), *Rushmore* (Mr. Blume), *Cradle Will Rock* (Tommy Crickshaw), *The Royal Tenenbaums* (Raleigh

St. Clair), *The Life Aquatic with Steve Zissou* (Steve Zissou), and *Ant-Man and the Wasp: Quantumania* (Lord Krylar). He voiced Baloo in *The Jungle Book* (2016).

Murray, Don Actor; appeared on TV in *Brand New Life* (Roger), *Justin Morgan Had a Horse* (Justin), and *Mr. Headmistress* (Reporter).

Murray, Ken (1903–1988) Actor; appeared in *Son of Flubber* (Mr. Hurley) and *Follow Me, Boys!* (Melody Murphy), and on TV in *Dateline Disneyland*.

Murry, Paul (1911–1989) Comic strip artist; known primarily for his work on the Mickey Mouse comic books.

Mushu Feisty dragon character in *Mulan*; voiced by Eddie Murphy.

Music Music has been an important part of Disney films ever since *Steamboat Willie*. The Silly Symphony series was built around musical themes, and the animated features, beginning with *Snow White and the Seven Dwarfs*, carefully integrated music into the plots. Disney songs were released on sheet music beginning in 1930 with "Minnie's Yoo Hoo." "Who's Afraid of the Big Bad Wolf?" in 1933, from *Three Little Pigs*, was the most popular song to come out of a short cartoon. Practically all of the songs from *Snow White* made it onto the hit parade, and with "When You Wish Upon a Star," Disney songs began receiving Oscar honors. *Snow White* was the first feature film to have a soundtrack album. In recent years, the music from *Frozen* was especially popular, with the soundtrack surpassing *The Lion King* with the longest run at the top of the Billboard 200 chart. Then, in 2020, the *Frozen 2* soundtrack broke records when it reached its 45th nonconsecutive week at No. 1 on Billboard's soundtracks chart. Also popular was the *Encanto* soundtrack, with the song "We Don't Talk About Bruno" holding the No. 1 spot on the Billboard Hot 100 for 5 weeks—a record for any song from a Disney film. TV contributed to the Disney song catalog, with "The Ballad of Davy Crockett" and the "Mickey Mouse Club March" perhaps the most popular. In 1949, Disney established its own Walt Disney Music Company, and soon began releasing its own records. Storyteller albums were introduced, and eventually cassettes and CDs. The establishment of Hollywood Records in 1990 represented a move into the field of contemporary music, primarily unrelated to Disney films. Mammoth Records and Lyric Street Records were added as new labels in 1997 but have since shut down. SEE ALSO DISNEY MUSIC GROUP.

Music for Everybody (TV) Show aired Jan. 30, 1966. Directed by Hamilton S. Luske. Ludwig Von Drake studies the importance of music in people's lives, utilizing sequences from *Melody Time*, *Make Mine Music*, and the "Clair de Lune" sequence originally planned for *Fantasia*. For a 1970 rerun, the latter sequence was deleted to include footage from *Sleeping Beauty*, then having a theatrical reissue.

Music Land (film) Silly Symphony cartoon released Oct. 5, 1935. Directed by Wilfred Jackson. In this innovative cartoon, a war between the Land of Symphony and the Isle of Jazz is the background for this musical tale in which Romeo and Juliet–type characters finally help bring about peace and the Bridge of Harmony is established. All the characters are musical instruments, with the "dialogue" furnished in musical sounds.

Music Land (film) A grouping of selected shorts from *Make Mine Music* and *Melody Time*; released by RKO on Oct. 5, 1955.

Music Legends Music memorabilia shop in Pleasure Island at Walt Disney World; opened in 1993, taking the place of The Island Depot. Closed in 1999, to become Fuego by Sosa Cigars.

Music Man, Meredith Willson's The (TV) A 3-hour presentation of the classic musical on *The Wonderful World of Disney*; first aired Feb. 16, 2003. Matthew Broderick stars as Professor Harold Hill, the charming, fast-talking con man who stops off in River City, Iowa, hoping to make a killing selling band instruments and uniforms for the local kids. The town librarian sees through his scam but falls in love with him. Directed by Jeff Bleckner. Also stars Kristin Chenoweth (Marian Paroo), Victor Garber (Mayor Shinn), Debra Monk (Mrs. Paroo), Molly Shannon (Eulalie MacKechnie Shinn), David Aaron Baker (Marcellus Washburn), Cameron Monaghan (Winthrop). *The Music Man*, starring Robert Preston as Harold Hill, was a huge hit when it opened on Broadway in 1957, winning 6 Tony Awards. Preston reprised his role in the 1962 film version, which starred Shirley Jones as Marian.

Musical Christmas at Walt Disney World, A (TV) A 60-min. special on ABC; premiered Dec. 18,

1993. Directed by Jeff Margolis. Performances by Natalie Cole, Andy Williams, Kathie Lee Gifford, Trisha Yearwood, Peabo Bryson, Lorrie Morgan, Steven Curtis Chapman.

Musical Farmer (film) Mickey Mouse cartoon released Jul. 9, 1932. Directed by Wilfred Jackson. Mickey and Pluto chase away crows eating their seeds and then don the scarecrow to tease Minnie. This leads to a musical extravaganza with all the farmyard animals taking part. One of the hens, who has been unable to lay eggs, lays an enormous egg. Mickey takes a picture but uses too much powder, exploding all the feathers off the hens.

Musker, John Animator/director; he joined the Disney Studio in 1977 where he animated on *The Small One*, *The Fox and the Hound*, and *The Black Cauldron*, also working on the story of the latter film. He co-directed, with Ron Clements, *The Great Mouse Detective*, *The Little Mermaid*, *Aladdin*, *Hercules*, *Treasure Planet*, *The Princess and the Frog*, and *Moana*. He retired in 2018.

Musse Pigg Swedish name for Mickey Mouse.

Mustang! (TV) Two-part show; aired Oct. 7 and 21, 1973. Directed by Roy Edward Disney. A Mexican boy saves an injured wild mustang and attempts to train him, but the spirited horse resists. Stars Charles Baca, Flavio Martinez, Ignacio Ramirez.

Mustang Man, Mustang Maid (TV) Episode 8 of *Elfego Baca*.

My Adventures in Television SEE WEDNESDAY 9:30 (8:30 CENTRAL).

My Babysitter's a Vampire (TV) Canadian-produced TV movie, and 13-episode series; premiered Jun. 10, 2011, with the movie on Disney Channel. The comedic spin on pop-culture vampires and scary movies in general features 3 teens who believe their new babysitter is a real bloodsucking vampire, and it is now up to them to rid Whitechapel, their sleepy little town, of the menace. Stars Matthew Knight (Ethan), Ella Jonas Farlinger (Jane), Atticus Mitchell (Benny), Vanessa Morgan (Sarah). Produced by Fresh TV and distributed by Fremantle-Media Enterprises.

My Boyfriend's Back (film) A teen, Johnny Dingle, plots a fake robbery so he can "rescue" a pretty girl, Missy, and get a chance to take her out on a date. When the staged robbery turns out to be a real one, Johnny only manages to protect Missy by getting himself shot. But, before he dies, she promises him that elusive date. Now, even death cannot stop Johnny. He comes back as a zombie, and with the help of his parents, who are willing to adapt to his new flesh-eating ways, and a mad doctor, who attempts to find other ways to keep him alive, Johnny does at last manage to go out with Missy. Despite the help he receives, however, he decomposes, and dies once again. But due to a heavenly error, it is found he should not have died at all, so he is brought back to life and to Missy, who has fallen in love with him. Released Aug. 6, 1993. Directed by Bob Balaban. A Touchstone film. 85 min. Stars Andrew Lowery (Johnny), Traci Lind (Missy), Bob Dishy (Murray), Paul Dooley (Big Chuck), Danny Zorn (Eddie), Edward Herrmann (Mr. Dingle), Cloris Leachman (Maggie), Austin Pendleton (Dr. Bronson), Jay O. Sanders (Sheriff McCloud), Paxton Whitehead (Judge in heaven), Mary Beth Hurt (Mrs. Dingle). Much of the film was shot in and around Austin, Texas.

My Date with the President's Daughter (TV) A 2-hour movie on *The Wonderful World of Disney*; first aired Apr. 19, 1998. Duncan Fletcher, a somewhat shy high school junior, meets a girl at the mall and asks her to the school's spring dance. She agrees, but what he does not know is that she is Hallie Richmond, the daughter of the president of the U.S. After picking her up at 1600 Pennsylvania Avenue and the requisite meeting of parents, Duncan is really flustered, and becomes even more so when Hallie tells him the only way they will have fun is to ditch the Secret Service agents. Directed by Alex Zamm. Stars Dabney Coleman (President Richmond), Will Friedle (Duncan Fletcher), Elisabeth Harnois (Hallie Richmond), Mimi Kuzyk (Caroline Richmond), Wanda Cannon (Rita Fletcher), Jay Thomas (Charles Fletcher). Ron Reagan, Jr., plays a cameo role as the White House security guard.

My Disney Experience SEE MYMAGIC+.

My Dog, the Thief (TV) Two-part show; aired Sep. 21 and 28, 1969. Directed by Robert Stevenson. A helicopter traffic reporter, Jack Crandall, finds a stowaway Saint Bernard, and while he is horrified, the station director and the listening audience are delighted. After he sneaks the dog, which he names Barabbas, into his rooming house, he discovers the dog is a kleptomaniac. One of the items he steals is a valuable necklace, and the jewel thieves are now after Jack. He eventually manages to capture them and save the day. Stars Dwayne Hickman, Mary Ann Mobley, Elsa Lanchester, Joe Flynn, Roger C. Carmel, Mickey Shaughnessy.

My Family Is a Menagerie (TV) Show aired Feb. 11, 1968. A young widow who has a way with animals moves to Northern California and is asked to care for the local strays. A wreck of a circus truck sets a menagerie of circus animals free, and she has to use all her wits to catch them. Only a leopard eludes her, and he is befriended by a local renegade dog. Eventually she is able to trap them, and she trains them to be in her animal act. Stars Ann Harrell, Jack Garrity, Kathy Thorn. Narrated by Rex Allen.

My Father the Hero (film) A 14-year-old girl, Nicole, is not happy to be going on a vacation on a tropical island with her dad, André; she is angry at him for being away for so long and mortified at the thought of spending 2 weeks with him amongst her peers. But then along comes Ben, a sexy young man whose good looks and charm spin Nicole into impetuous, adolescent love. Determined to impress her boyfriend, Nicole gets carried away with a scheme to attract his attention by appearing sophisticated and alluring. She fabricates an elaborate tale about her life, including the idea that André is really her lover and an international spy, masquerading as her father. Nicole sets in motion a comedy of errors and confusion that wreaks havoc on her budding romance as well as her father's reputation. But Ben eventually does indeed find her more attractive than the indifferent, fickle girls he is used to. Released Feb. 4, 1994. Directed by Steve Miner. A Touchstone film, produced by Cité Films/Film par Film/D.D. Productions, in association with the Edward S. Feldman Company. 90 min. Stars Gérard Depardieu (André), Katherine Heigl (Nicole), Dalton James (Ben), Lauren Hutton (Megan), Faith Prince (Diana). Filmed at Ocean Club, Paradise Island Resort, Nassau, Bahamas.

My Favorite Martian (film) When a Martian's spacecraft accidentally crash-lands on Earth, ambitious TV reporter Tim O'Hara visualizes his upcoming fame at breaking what he sees as the story of the century. The Martian takes human form and poses as Tim's Uncle Martin. Hoping to repair his ship for a return to Mars, he system-atically thwarts all of Tim's attempts to divulge the truth. Eventually the 2 become friends and decide to work together to outwit scientists who have discovered the Martian's existence. Released Feb. 12, 1999. Directed by Donald Petrie. Stars Jeff Daniels (Tim O'Hara), Christopher Lloyd (the Martian/Uncle Martin), Elizabeth Hurley (Brace Channing), Daryl Hannah (Lizzie), Wallace Shawn (Coleye Epstein). 93 min. Based on the 1963–1966 TV series that starred Ray Walston and Bill Bixby. Walston returned for a role (Armitan) in the new movie. Filming took place in Santa Barbara and other areas of Southern California.

My Friends Tigger and Pooh (TV) Computer-animated series on Disney Channel; premiered May 12, 2007. The Pooh characters are joined by Lumpy, the Heffalump, and a 6-year-old girl, Darby, and her puppy, Buster. Darby, who has her own pink scooter, loves to solve mysteries with her friends, the Super Sleuths, in the Hundred Acre Wood. Voices include Jim Cummings (Tigger/Pooh), Chloe Moretz (Darby), Kath Soucie (Kanga), Max Burkholder (Roo), Peter Cullen (Eeyore), Travis Oates (Piglet), Dee Baker (Buster/Woodpecker), Ken Sansom (Rabbit), Oliver Dillon (Lumpy), Struan Erlenborn (Christopher Robin). From Walt Disney Television Animation.

My Funny Friend and Me Song from *The Emperor's New Groove*; written by Sting and David Hartley. Nominated for an Academy Award.

My Generation (TV) Drama series on ABC; aired Sep. 23–Sep. 30, 2010. In 2000, a documentary crew follows a disparate group of 9 students from Greenbelt High School in Austin, Texas, who cannot wait to graduate and head out into the real world, then revisits these former classmates 10 years later as they return home, revisiting their old hopes for the future and discovering that just because they're not where they planned doesn't mean they're not right where they need to be. Stars Michael Stahl-David (Steven), Kelli Garner (Dawn), Jaime King (Jacqueline), Keir O'Donnell (Kenneth), Sebastian Sozzi (the Falcon), Mehcad Brooks (Rolly), Anne Son (Caroline), Daniella Alonso (Brenda), Julian Morris (Anders). From ABC Studios.

My Life as a Babysitter (TV) Serial on the *Mickey Mouse Club* on The Disney Channel; aired Oct. 15–Nov. 9, 1990. A young man is saddled with babysitting a bratty kid. Stars Jim Calvert (Nick Cramer), Kelli Williams (Kelly), Shane Meier

(Ben), Michele Abrams (Jennifer Edwards), Sean Patrick Flannery (Mitch Buckley).

My Science Project (film) High school senior Michael Harlan and his best friend, Vince, must put together a passing science project in 2 weeks in order to graduate. With the deadline rapidly approaching, Michael risks the wrath of armed military guards and stages a midnight raid on a nearby U.S. Air Force supply dump. They discover a mysterious instrument that can cause a space-time warp. Michael's teacher is sucked into a cosmic whirlpool, and the device madly drains power from the school and then the surrounding city. Michael and his friends try to stop the device, while fighting everything from a Neanderthal man, mutants, gladiators, and Egyptian queens to Vietcong soldiers. Finally, the kids are able to shut off the device and return it to the supply dump. Released Aug. 9, 1985. Directed by Jonathan Betuel. A Touchstone film. 95 min. Stars John Stockwell (Michael Harlan), Danielle Von Zerneck (Ellie Sawyer), Fisher Stevens (Vince Latello), Raphael Sbarge (Sherman), Dennis Hopper (Bob Roberts), Richard Masur (Det. Isadore Nulty), Barry Corbin (Lew Harlan), Ann Wedgeworth (Dolores). The film was shot at the Walt Disney Studio in Burbank and at local Southern California locations, including Van Nuys High School, Alhambra High School, and Portola Highly Gifted Magnet School. The final 2 weeks of production consisted of night shooting in Tucson, Arizona, where key sequences were filmed amid a thousand acres of decommissioned military aircraft. The elaborate special effects included a T. rex, which was a complex puppet built and animated by Doug Beswick Productions, Inc. Matte paintings, special lighting effects, miniature photography, and effects animation were also used. The title song "My Science Project" was written by Bob Held, Michael Colina, and Bill Heller, and performed by The Tubes.

My Son Pinocchio: Geppetto's Musical Tale Stage version of the *Geppetto* TV production; premiered under a former title of *Disney's Geppetto & Son* at the Coterie Theatre in Kansas City, Missouri, Jun. 27–Aug. 6, 2006. The Pinocchio story, told from the perspective of Geppetto, features a score of original songs by Stephen Schwartz and a book by David Stern. Licensing to schools and community theaters is by Music Theatre International.

My Town (TV) Show aired May 25, 1986. Development threatens a small town. Stars Glenn Ford, Meredith Salenger. Directed by Gwen Arner.

My Wife and Kids (TV) Half-hour series on ABC; aired Mar. 28, 2001–Aug. 9, 2005. Michael Kyle, a modern-day man, loving husband, and traditional father, is at the center of his household, ruling with his own distinctive parenting style. Stars Damon Wayans (Michael Kyle), Tisha Campbell-Martin (Janet Kyle), George O. Gore II (Jr. Kyle), Jazz Raycole (Claire Kyle), Parker McKenna Posey (Kady Kyle). From Touchstone Television, Impact Zone Productions, and Wayans Bros. Entertainment.

My Yard Goes Disney (TV) Half-hour series on HGTV; aired Jun. 6, 2011–Aug. 12, 2012. Disney Imagineers help transform the backyard of a selected family into a Disney-themed playground. Stars R. Brandon Johnson. Produced by JayTV in cooperation with Walt Disney Parks and Resorts.

Myhers, John (1921–1992) Actor; appeared in *Now You See Him, Now You Don't* (golfer), *Snowball Express* (Mr. Manescue), *Treasure of Matecumbe* (Captain Boomer), and *The Shaggy D.A.* (Admiral Brenner), and on TV in *The Ghosts of Buxley Hall* (E.L. Hart).

MyMagic+ A collection of tools at Walt Disney World giving guests more opportunities to customize and personalize their entire visit. A major component is the My Disney Experience mobile app and website where guests can access their room reservations, book dining and other experiences, and reserve times for their favorite attractions and shows (originally through an advanced FastPass system called FastPass+). To link the entire MyMagic+ experience together is the MagicBand, an innovative piece of technology that is worn on the wrist and serves as the guest's room key, theme park ticket, access to FastPass+ (later Lighting Lane) queues, PhotoPass card, and optional payment account all rolled into one. After months of testing, on Mar. 31, 2014, MyMagic+ was made available to all guests to use before their visit as part of the test and adjust process. SEE ALSO DISNEY GENIE AND LIGHTNING LANE.

Mystères du Nautilus, Les SEE LES MYSTÈRES DU NAUTILUS.

Mysteries of the Deep (film) Documentary featurette released Dec. 16, 1959. Production associate Ben Sharpsteen. In this Oscar-nominated short, a submerged reef is the home of many strange creatures of the sea. We see mating, birth, and development of the young into adults, with the laws of nature being fulfilled as the battle for survival goes continually on. One of the shorts in which Walt Disney's nephew Roy E. Disney wrote the narration, photographed by, among others, H. Pederson. 24 min.

Mysterious Benedict Society, The (TV) Disney+ original series from 20th Television and Sonar Entertainment; digitally premiered Jun. 25, 2021. After winning a scholarship competition, 4 gifted orphans are recruited by the peculiar Mr. Benedict for a dangerous mission to save the world from a global crisis. When the headmaster, Dr. Curtain, appears to be behind this worldwide panic, the kids of The Mysterious Benedict Society must devise a plan to defeat him. Stars Tony Hale (Mr. Benedict/L.D. Curtain), Kristen Schaal (Number Two), MaameYaa Boafo (Rhonda Kazembe), Ryan Hurst (Milligan), Gia Sandhu (Ms. Perumal), Mystic Inscho (Reynie Muldoon), Seth B. Carr (George "Sticky" Washington), Emmy DeOliveira (Kate Wetherall), Marta Kessler (Constance Contriare).

Mysterious Island Port of call in Tokyo DisneySea; opened Sep. 4, 2001. As the story goes, Captain Nemo established this hidden scientific base inside the caldera of Mount Prometheus, inviting visitors to explore secrets in 20,000 Leagues Under the Sea and Journey to the Center of the Earth.

Mystery, Alaska (film) Completely isolated by glaciers and vast snowy mountains, the residents of the little town of Mystery are experts at one sport—hockey played on the glacier. The weekly hockey game has become a ritual celebration attended with religious devotion. However, an article in a sports magazine prompts the NHL to send the New York Rangers to challenge these local heroes, and the publicity stunt threatens to change the way of life in Mystery forever. Directed by Jay Roach. Released Oct. 1, 1999. Stars Russell Crowe (John Biebe), Hank Azaria (Charles Danner), Mary McCormack (Donna Biebe), Lolita Davidovich (Mary Jane Pitcher), Ron Eldard (Skank Marden), Colm Meaney (Scott Pitcher), Maury Chaykin (Bailey Pruitt), Michael McKean (Walsh), Judith Ivey (Joanne Burns), Burt Reynolds (Walter Burns). 119 min. The town of Mystery was built from scratch for the production at the site of a former strip coal mine near Canmore, Alberta. Filmed in CinemaScope.

Mystery Girls (TV) Series on ABC Family; premiered Jun. 25, 2014, and ended Aug. 27. Two former detective TV show starlets are brought back together by a real-life mystery when a major fan of their show witnesses a crime and will only speak to the infamous duo. The girls reunite and put their TV crime-solving skills to the test. Stars Tori Spelling (Holly Hamilton), Jennie Garth (Charlie Contour), Miguel Pinzon (Nick).

Mystery in Dracula's Castle, The (TV) Two-part show; aired Jan. 7 and 14, 1973. Directed by Robert Totten. Two bored kids in a vacation town get involved with thieves when they try to make their own horror movie. They find a stray dog, who brings them a stolen necklace, which they use in their movie. The thieves are then after the kids, but after a series of misadventures, they are captured, and the kids finish their movie. Stars Clu Gulager, Mariette Hartley, Johnny Whitaker, Scott Kolden, Mills Watson, John Fiedler, James Callahan, Gerald Michenaud.

Mystery of Edward Sims, The (TV) Two-part show; aired Mar. 31 and Apr. 7, 1968. Directed by Seymour Robbie. The cub reporter, Gallegher, becomes involved in land fraud, when some valueless land is sold to a group of Cornish immigrants. A murder implicates 1 of the immigrants, and it is up to Gallegher to prove that a local resident is actually the murderer, and the swindler is a local banker. Stars Roger Mobley, John McIntire, John Dehner, Warren Oates, John McLiam, Jeanette Nolan, Ray Teal. SEE ALSO GALLEGHER FOR OTHER TV SHOWS ABOUT THE CUB REPORTER.

Mystery of Rustler's Cave, The (TV) Serial on the new *Mickey Mouse Club*, starring Kim Richards, Robbie Rist, Christian Juttner, Bobby Rolofson, Tony Becker, Ted Gehring, Lou Frizzell, Bing Russell, Dennis Fimple. Directed by Tom Leetch. A motorcycle enthusiast and his sister join with 3 visiting city kids to chase cattle rustlers. Aired Feb. 1–Mar. 1, 1977.

Mystery of the Applegate Treasure, The (TV) Hardy Boys serial on the *Mickey Mouse Club*. 20 episodes.

Mystic Manor Mystic Point dark ride attraction in Hong Kong Disneyland; opened May 17, 2013. Boarding the Mystic Magneto-Electric Carriage, visitors begin their tour of the manor house and private museum of Lord Henry Mystic—eccentric adventurer, explorer, and collector of art—and his monkey friend, Albert. The curious Albert opens a newly acquired Balinese music box, which causes intriguing artifacts from around the globe to mysteriously come to life and wreak havoc in the manor. Partially inspired by the Haunted Mansion attraction at other Disney parks, but with a totally new spin and using a trackless ride system. Music by Danny Elfman.

Mystic Point Area in Hong Kong Disneyland; opened May 17, 2013. Mystic Manor is the main attraction, along with Garden of Wonders, dining at the Explorer's Club Restaurant, and shopping at The Archive Shop.

Myth: A Frozen Tale (film) Virtual reality short; debuted Nov. 7, 2019, at the premiere of *Frozen 2* in Hollywood's Dolby Theatre. As a mother reads her children a bedtime story, the audience is transported to an enchanted forest outside Arendelle where elemental spirits come to life and myths of the past and future are revealed. Directed by Jeff Gipson. 8 min.

1. Nine Old Men 2. Norman, Floyd 3. New Orleans Square 4. New York World's Fair 5. Nash, Clarence
6. Nemo & Friends SeaRider 7. *Night Before Christmas, The* (film) 8. Nana 9. *National Treasure* (film) 10. nuiMOs 11. Napa Rose

Nabbe, Tom As Disneyland's youngest Cast Member, he began work at the park in Jul. 1955 as a "newsie" on Main Street, U.S.A. before being selected by Walt Disney to portray Tom Sawyer on Tom Sawyer Island in 1956. He later worked on other attractions, transferring to Walt Disney World in 1971 as an opening-day manager for the Monorail system. He retired in 2003 as manager of distribution services for the Florida resort. He was named a Disney Legend in 2005.

Naboombu Mythical island kingdom ruled by King Leonidas in *Bedknobs and Broomsticks*.

Naismith, Laurence (1908–1992) Actor; appeared in *Third Man on the Mountain* (Teo Zurbriggen), *Greyfriars Bobby* (Mr. Traill), and *The Three Lives of Thomasina* (Rev. Angus Peddie), and on TV in *The Prince and the Pauper* (Earl of Hertford).

Najimy, Kathy Actress; appeared in *Sister Act* and *Sister Act 2: Back in the Habit* (Sister Mary Patrick), *Hocus Pocus* and *Hocus Pocus 2* (Mary), *It's Pat* (Tippy), and *Step Up 3-D* (Moose's mom), and on Disney Channel in *Scream Team* (Mariah) and *Descendants* (Evil Queen). She voiced Chil in *The Jungle Book: Mowgli's Story*, Aunt Taggig in *Brother Bear 2*, Mary in *WALL•E*, Minister of Summer in *Tinker Bell* and *Secret of the Wings*, Sareena Secord in *The Rocketeer* animated series, and Peaches in *Elena of Avalor*. At Walt Disney World, she appeared as Dr. Femus in The Extra-TERRORestrial Alien Encounter.

Nala Spunky lioness friend of Simba's in *The Lion King*; voiced by Niketa Calame (young) and Moira Kelly (adult).

Nana Dog nursemaid in the Darling house in *Peter Pan*.

Nani Lilo's older sister and guardian in *Lilo & Stitch*; voiced by Tia Carrere.

Nanula, Richard He went to work at Disney in 1986 as a senior planning analyst. He was named vice president and treasurer in 1989, senior vice president and chief financial officer in 1991, and executive vice president in 1994. In Nov. 1994, he was named worldwide president of The Disney Store. In Feb. 1996, he was promoted to senior executive vice president as chief financial officer of The Walt Disney Company. He left the company on May 31, 1998.

Napa Rose Fine-dining restaurant at Disney's Grand Californian Hotel & Spa; opened Feb. 8, 2001, serving upscale Californian fare and regional wines. Craftsman décor is inspired by the natural beauty of the Golden State. Nearby, the Napa Rose Lounge offers casual dining and cocktails.

Napier, Alan (1903–1988) Actor; provided the voice of Sir Pelinore in *The Sword in the Stone* and appeared on TV in *The Golden Dog* (Archie).

Naples Ristorante e Bar Neapolitan eatery in the Downtown Disney District at Disneyland Resort; opened Jan. 26, 2001. A quick-service counterpart, Napolini Pizzeria, opened next door Aug. 22, 2003, taking the place of the Tin Pan Alley shop. Managed by Patina Restaurant Group.

Napoleon Militaristic dog in *The Aristocats*; voiced by Pat Buttram.

Napoleon and Samantha (film) Upon the death of his grandfather, a young boy inherits a full-grown African lion, who is really a gentle pet. It is impossible to keep the lion in a small town, so the boy and his young girlfriend head for the mountains with the lion to find him a safe home. The trek leads to excitement and danger before all ends happily. Released Jul. 5, 1972. Directed by Bernard McEveety. 91 min. Stars Johnny Whitaker (Napoleon), Jodie Foster (Samantha), Michael Douglas (Danny), Will Geer (Grandpa), Arch Johnson (Chief of Police), Henry Jones (Mr. Gutteridge). This was Jodie Foster's movie debut. Producer Winston Hibler discovered the beautiful scenery utilized in this film in the Strawberry Mountains wilderness area of eastern Oregon. The rugged 33,000 acres of unspoiled terrain contains the largest stand of Ponderosa pines in the world. Filming also took place in the adjoining picturesque historic gold country towns of John Day and Canyon City. The lion, Major, a 500-lb. 16-year-old, was a film veteran, having appeared in Tarzan movies with Mike Henry, and in a TV series with Ron Ely. Academy Award nomination for Original Score by Buddy Baker.

Napolini Pizzeria SEE NAPLES RISTORANTE E BAR.

Narcoossee's Signature restaurant at Disney's Grand Floridian Resort & Spa at Walt Disney World; opened Jun. 28, 1988. Octagon-shaped, it sits near the boat dock and from its open kitchen serves a variety of grilled fare.

Nash, Clarence "Ducky" (1904–1985) Voice of Donald Duck from the character's beginning with *The Wise Little Hen* in 1934 until 1985. Nash performed Donald's voice for more than 150 shorts and TV shows, including dubbing the voice in other languages. He made extensive promotional appearances, including a cross-country trip in 1984 for Donald's 50th anniversary. He also provided the original voices of Huey, Dewey, and Louie, and of Daisy Duck, as well as the bullfrog in *Bambi*, dogs in *One Hundred and One Dalmatians*, and birds in Walt Disney's Enchanted Tiki Room. He was named a Disney Legend posthumously in 1993.

Nashville (TV) Series on ABC; aired Oct. 10, 2012–May 25, 2016. The series moved to CMT in 2016. Music legend Rayna Jaymes has been one of the industry's top female vocalists for 2 decades, but she discovers that her passion for the business is not enough to compete with the new generation of talent lighting up the charts. She is going to have to start over and reinvent herself if she plans on being relevant. Things are not made easier by Rayna's father, Lamar Wyatt, Nashville's most powerful businessman, with whom she has had a distant relationship strained by years of resentment and powerful secrets that begin to boil over as Rayna's husband, Teddy Conrad, aligns himself with her father to run for office. There is also Juliette Barnes, a sassy singer who is not about to let anyone stand in the way of her success, much less Rayna Jaymes. Stars Connie Britton (Rayna Jaymes), Hayden Panettiere (Juliette Barnes), Powers Boothe (Lamar Wyatt), Charles Esten (Deacon Claybourne), Eric Close (Teddy Conrad), Clare Bowen (Scarlett O'Connor), Jonathan Jackson (Avery Barkley), Sam Palladio (Gunnar Scott), Robert Wisdom (Coleman Carlisle). From Lionsgate, ABC Studios, and Gaylord Entertainment.

Nashville Coyote, The (TV) Show aired Oct. 1, 1972. Directed by Winston Hibler. A surprised coyote stowaway on a freight train ends up in Nashville where he meets a friendly beagle and an aspiring songwriter. The songwriter is unable to sell his songs, so he returns to California, taking the coyote back to his desert home. Stars Walter Forbes, William Garton, Eugene Scott, Michael Edwards. Narrated by Mayf Nutter.

National Basketball Association After its 2019–2020 season had been interrupted by the COVID-19 pandemic, the National Basketball Association (NBA) announced it would finish the season at ESPN Wide World of Sports. Walt Disney World developed a new concept to host professional sports teams inside a "bubble," becoming the center of pro basketball in summer 2020. It took 30 days to assemble the game and practice courts, and 3 resort hotels housed the players, coaches, team staffs, media, and broadcasters. For each NBA Finals game in the AdventHealth Arena, 320 fans watching from home were displayed on courtside screens. Throughout the 94-day season, 22 teams played 172 games, which ended Oct. 11 when the Los Angeles Lakers defeated the Miami Heat in 6 games. The sports complex also hosted Major League Soccer, which finished its 25th season Jul. 8–Aug. 11, 2020.

National Car Rental Operated a locker area in Town Square at Disneyland, 1980–1990. The locker area was formerly operated by Bekins and, later, Global Van Lines.

National Fantasy Fan Club (NFFC) A group of Disney collectors and enthusiasts broke away from the Mouse Club in 1984 and began their own club, called the National Fantasy Fan Club, later shortened to the NFFC. It has operated as a nonprofit organization, not sponsored by Disney, with regular conventions held in Anaheim around the birthday of Disneyland each July, since 1985. In recent years, a mini-convention was added in January. The NFFC publishes a regular newsletter and has chapters all over the country. The club voted to change its name to Disneyana Fan Club in 2009.

National Film Registry Each year since 1989, the U.S. government, through the Library of Congress, names 25 films it deems as "culturally, historically, or aesthetically important." As of Jan. 2023, a total of 24 Disney films have been added to the Registry: *Snow White and the Seven Dwarfs* in 1989; *Fantasia* in 1990; *Pinocchio* in 1994; *Steamboat Willie* in 1998; *The Living Desert* in 2000; *Beauty and the Beast* in 2002; *Toy Story* in 2005; *Three Little Pigs* in 2007; *Disneyland Dream* in 2009; *Bambi* in 2011; *Mary Poppins* in 2013; *The Old Mill* and *The Story of Menstruation* in 2015; *The Lion King, Rushmore,* and *Who Framed Roger Rabbit* in 2016; *Dumbo* in 2017; *Cinderella* in 2018; *Old Yeller* and *Sleeping Beauty* in 2019; *The Joy Luck Club* in 2020; *Flowers and Trees* and *WALL•E* in 2021; and *The Little Mermaid* in 2022.

National Geographic With Disney's acquisition of 21st Century Fox on Mar. 20, 2019, National Geographic Partners became a joint venture between The Walt Disney Company and the National Geographic Society, an independent nonprofit organization. National Geographic Partners combines the global National Geographic television channels (National Geographic Channel, Nat Geo WILD, Nat Geo MUNDO, and Nat Geo PEOPLE) with magazines, studios, digital and social media platforms, books, maps, children's media, and ancillary activities that include travel, global experiences and events, archival sales, licensing, and e-commerce businesses. Every year, a portion of profits is distributed to the nonprofit Society to fund work in the areas of science, exploration, conservation, and education. National Geographic Expeditions offers guided tour packages as part of Disney Signature Experiences. The National Geographic Society was founded Jan. 13, 1888, when a group of scholars, explorers, and scientists met to discuss the organization of a society for the increase and diffusion of geographic knowledge. On Jan. 27, a certificate of incorporation was formally signed. The first issue of *National Geographic* magazine was published later that year, and the publication would eventually become famous for its stunning color photography of the natural world.

National Student Fire Safety Test, The (film) Educational film; released in Sep. 1979. The film covers the basics of fire prevention in humorous fashion.

National Student First Aid Test, The (film) Educational film; released in Sep. 1979. The film provides reinforcement of basic first aid procedures.

National Student Recreational Safety Test, The (film) Educational film; released in Sep. 1979. Young people should be aware of their environment while they play.

National Student School Safety Test, The (film) Educational film; released in Sep. 1979. Some school safety precautions are not always considered by youngsters.

National Student Traffic Safety Test, The (film) Educational film; released in Sep. 1979. The film instructs young people on safety habits out on the street.

National Treasure (film) A patriotic 3rd-generation treasure hunter, Benjamin Franklin Gates, has spent his life searching for a great treasure that no one believed existed. Hidden by our Founding Fathers, they left clues to the treasure's location right before our eyes—from our nation's birthplace to the nation's Capitol to clues buried within the symbols on the dollar bill. Gates's journey takes him to the last place anyone thought to look, on the back of the Declaration of Independence. But what he thought was the final clue is only the beginning. Joining with 2 friends, he realizes that in order to protect the legendary treasure, he must now do the unthinkable: steal the most revered, best-guarded document in American history before it falls into the wrong hands. In a race against time, Gates must elude the FBI, stay one step ahead of a ruthless adversary, decipher the remaining clues, and unlock the mystery behind our greatest national treasure. A Jerry Bruckheimer Films production. Released Nov. 19, 2004. Directed by Jon Turteltaub. Stars Nicolas Cage (Benjamin Franklin Gates), Jon Voight (Patrick Gates), Justin Bartha (Riley Poole), Diane Kruger (Abigail Chase), Sean Bean (Ian Howe), Harvey Keitel (Sadusky), Christopher Plummer (John Adams Gates). 131 min. Filmed in Super 35-Scope by award-winning cinematographer Caleb Deschanel. Filming took place at many of the country's most hallowed historical sites, including the Library of Congress, Lincoln Memorial, and DAR Building in Washington, and Independence Hall, The Franklin Institute, the Reading Terminal Market, City Hall, and Pine Street Church Cemetery in Philadelphia. Because of ongoing renovations at the National Archives, the filmmakers had to build extensive sets based on reality.

National Treasure: Book of Secrets (film) When a missing page from the diary of assassin John Wilkes Booth surfaces, treasure hunter Ben Gates discovers that his great-great grandfather, Thomas Gates, is implicated as a key conspirator in Abraham Lincoln's death. Determined to prove his ancestor's innocence, Ben uses portions of a cipher on the page fragment to follow an international chain of clues, searching for the true story. The search for truth turns into a race to discover the whereabouts of a mythological treasure, taking Ben on a chase from Paris to London to Washington to South Dakota's Black Hills. Doggedly pursuing Ben is Mitch Wilkinson, a descendant of Confederate general Albert Pike, who seems to have a fiendish and less noble desire to uncover his own family history and find the treasure for himself. Along the way, and while keeping the FBI at bay, Ben enlists the help of his ex-girlfriend, his technology-whiz partner, his long-separated university professor parents, and even the president of the U.S., who is purported to have a highly guarded, enigmatic book of secrets, kept by presidents and known only to them, which holds the final clue. Released Dec. 21, 2007. From Walt Disney Pictures/Jerry Bruckheimer Films/Sparkler Entertainment. Directed by Jon Turteltaub. Stars Nicolas Cage (Ben Gates), Jon Voight (Patrick Gates), Helen Mirren (Emily Appleton), Ed Harris (Mitch Wilkinson), Diane Kruger (Abigail Chase), Justin Bartha (Riley Poole), Harvey Keitel (Sadusky), Bruce Greenwood (President). 125 min. Filmed in Super 35. For scenes in the Library of Congress, the filmmakers were allowed to build a special set, the President's Library, on the balcony above the Main Reading Room in the historic

Jefferson Building. Special permission was also given to film, for 2 full nights, a birthday party sequence just off the front portico of Mt. Vernon in nearby Virginia. In London, the interior of Lancaster House doubled for Buckingham Palace.

National Treasure: Edge of History (TV) A Disney+ original series; digitally premiered Dec. 14, 2022. Jess has a natural talent for solving puzzles and a proclivity for unraveling good mysteries. In search of answers about her own family, she embarks on the adventure of a lifetime and recruits a few treasure-hunting friends—Tasha, Ethan, Oren, and Liam—and an FBI agent to help uncover the truth about her parents and their connection to a long-lost Pan-American treasure. Stars Lisette Olivera (Jess), Catherine Zeta-Jones (Billie), Zuri Reed (Tasha), Jordan Rodrigues (Ethan), Antonio Cipriano (Oren), Jake Austin Walker (Liam), Lyndon Smith (Agent Ross). An expansion of the National Treasure film series. From ABC Signature.

Nature of Things, The—The Camel (film) Jiminy Cricket tells the story of the camel for the *Mickey Mouse Club*; later released in 16 mm for schools (Jun. 1956).

Nature of Things, The—The Elephant (film) Jiminy Cricket uses animation and live action to tell the story of the elephant on the *Mickey Mouse Club*; later released in 16 mm for schools (Jun. 1956).

Nature's Better Built Homes (TV) Show aired Mar. 2, 1969. Directed by Ward Kimball, Hamilton S. Luske. Ranger J. Audubon Woodlore hosts a look at beavers, birds, squirrels, bees, and other creatures, with cartoon and live-action film clips. Narrated by Olan Soulé.

Nature's Charter Tours (TV) Show aired Apr. 28, 1968. Directed by Hamilton S. Luske. Ranger J. Audubon Woodlore looks at migration, using footage from *White Wilderness* and *Seal Island*.

Nature's Half Acre (film) True-Life Adventure featurette released Jul. 28, 1951. Directed by James Algar; photographed by Murl Deusing and 8 other photographers; music by Paul Smith; narrated by Winston Hibler. Academy Award winner for Best Two-Reel Short Subject. 33 min. The film tells the story of the amazing amount of life to be found each season in almost any small plot of ground and the way nature maintains her balance in the "grass-roots" world of insects and their ever-present fight for survival. The time-lapse photography by John Nash Ott is particularly notable. Originally released in the U.S. with *Alice in Wonderland*.

Nature's Strangest Creatures (film) Featurette released Mar. 19, 1959. Produced by Ben Sharpsteen. Filmed in Australia by Alfred and Elma Milotte. Since Australia broke from the Asian mainland many eons ago, it has developed a unique population of wildlife, free from outside influences. Such creatures as the giant bat, the duck-billed platypus, kangaroos, wallabies, and the bush-tailed opossum pursue their business of survival in this isolated land where nature has preserved a sanctuary for the strangest of its creatures. 16 min.

Nature's Strangest Oddballs (TV) Show aired Mar. 29, 1970. Directed by Les Clark, Hamilton S. Luske. Professor Ludwig Von Drake looks at animals that have not changed greatly over the years, such as the platypus, iguana, koala, and anteater. The story of *The Cold-Blooded Penguin* from *The Three Caballeros* and *Goliath II* are also shown.

Nature's Wild Heart (film) Educational film; two city children spend a summer in the Canadian wilderness and learn about some of the wonders of the natural world. Released in Nov. 1973. The film is from the TV program *Wild Heart*.

Nature's Wonderland SEE MINE TRAIN THROUGH NATURE'S WONDERLAND.

Natwick, Grim (1890–1990) Animator; known for designing Betty Boop before coming to Disney in 1934. He specialized in the development of female characters, including animating Snow White in *Snow White and the Seven Dwarfs*. He left the Studio in 1938.

Naughty or Nice (TV) Two-hour holiday movie on *The Wonderful World of Disney*; first aired Dec. 11, 2004. A rude sports-radio disc jockey, Henry Ramiro, gets a lesson on the importance of family and the values of life when a young listener, Michael, with a life-threatening illness, forces him into a deal to be nicer on the air for just 1 day. The episode has a positive effect on Henry's life and those around him. Directed by Eric Laneuville. A von Zerneck-Sertner Films production. Stars George Lopez (Henry Ramiro), James Kirk (Michael), Roger Lodge (The Hitman), Lisa Vidal (Diana), Bianca Collins (Olivia), Chris Collins (Bobby), Dan McLean (Kevin Giles), John Salley (Dion Bailey).

Nautilus Galley Counter-service restaurant built across from Captain Nemo's submarine in Mysterious Island at Tokyo DisneySea; opened Dec. 12, 2003.

Nautilus Gifts Shop in Mysterious Island at Tokyo DisneySea; opened Sep. 4, 2001. Designed as the place where the *Nautilus* submarine came for repairs; ship parts, diving suits, and Captain Nemo's inventions are found throughout.

Navajo Adventure (film) International theatrical featurette; released first in France in Dec. 1957. Produced by Ben Sharpsteen. The story of the Navajo, at work and play, in the southwestern U.S., and in particular, in scenic Monument Valley. The film focuses on a typical Native American family, its daily life, struggles, and folkways, as every aspect of living is governed by Navajo gods and legends. SEE ALSO NEXT ENTRY.

Navajos, The: Children of the Gods (film) 16-mm release title of *Navajo Adventure* (international release featurette from 1957); released in Sep. 1967.

Na'vi River Journey Attraction in Pandora – The World of Avatar at Disney's Animal Kingdom; opened May 27, 2017. Passengers board a reed boat and glide down the Kapsavan River to witness unique life-forms and bioluminescent rain forests. In the finale, the Na'vi Shaman of Songs demonstrates her deep connection to the life force of Pandora through music.

Navidad Mágica Disney (TV) Hour-long Spanish-language holiday special on Univision; aired Dec. 24, 2001. Entertainers appear at the 4 Walt Disney World parks to help celebrate Christmas. Stars include Bobby Pulido, Jaime Camil, Daniela Aedo, Myra, Pablo Montero, and José Feliciano. A 2nd special aired Dec. 24, 2002, with host Karla Martinez and entertainers, including Olga Tañon, Juanes, Jennifer Peña, Odalys, Control, and Mariachi Cobre. Directed by Emilio Pimentel. A joint production of Univision and Walt Disney World.

NBA Experience Interactive basketball venue in Disney Springs West Side at Walt Disney World; open Aug. 12, 2019–Mar. 16, 2020, on the site of the former DisneyQuest. Inside this 44,000-sq.-foot world of professional basketball, visitors put their skills to the test in a variety of activities, including Dribble!; Dunk!; Slingshot; Shoot!; Combine; Draft; Replay; Players; Champions; Arcade; and Trivia. Two original short films played on-site as well: *Game Time* and *Together*.

NBA Store Specialty shop adjacent to the NBA Experience in Disney Springs West Side at Walt Disney World; open Jul. 8, 2019–Mar. 16, 2020, offering basketball merchandise and apparel.

NBC Salutes the 25th Anniversary of the Wonderful World of Disney (TV) Special aired Sep. 13, 1978. Directed by Art Fisher. Stars Ron Howard, Suzanne Somers, Fess Parker, Buddy Ebsen, Crystal Gayle, Melissa Gilbert, Gavin MacLeod, Ed Asner, Fred MacMurray, Bob Hope.

Neary, Kevin Former Disney Cast Member and coauthor with Dave Smith of *The Ultimate Disney Trivia Book* (1992), *The Ultimate Disney Trivia Book 2* (1994), *The Ultimate Disney Trivia Book 3* (1997), and *The Ultimate Disney Trivia Book 4* (2000). He also coauthored, with Susan Neary, the 2016 books *Maps of the Disney Parks* and *The Hidden Mickeys of Walt Disney World*.

Neck 'n' Neck (film) Oswald the Lucky Rabbit cartoon; released Jan. 23, 1928. Oswald takes a rabbit for a ride in his new car. He is so charmed by her singing that he forgets everything else—including his speedometer—which leads to a wild chase with a motor cop.

Need for Speed (film) In a last attempt to save his struggling garage, blue-collar mechanic Tobey Marshall—who, with his team, skillfully builds and races muscle cars on the side—reluctantly partners with wealthy, arrogant ex-NASCAR driver Dino Brewster. Just as a major sale to a car broker, Julia Maddon, looks like it will save the business, a disastrous, unsanctioned race results in Dino framing Tobey for manslaughter. Two years later and fresh out of prison, Tobey is set on revenge with plans to take down Dino in the high-stakes De Leon race, the Super Bowl of underground racing. To get there in time, Tobey must run a gauntlet, dodging cops coast-to-coast while dealing with fallout from a dangerous bounty Dino has put on his car. With his loyal crew and the resourceful Julia as allies, Tobey defies odds at every turn and proves that, even in the flashy world of super cars,

the underdog can still finish first. Directed by Scott Waugh. From DreamWorks/Touchstone Pictures. Released Mar. 14, 2014, after a Mar. 12 release in the U.K. Stars Aaron Paul (Tobey Marshall), Dominic Cooper (Dino Brewster), Imogen Poot (Julia Maddon), Scott Mescudi (Benny), Ramon Rodriguez (Joe Peck). Rami Malek (Finn), Dakota Johnson (Anita), Harrison Gilbertson (Little Pete), Michael Keaton (Monarch). 131 min. Filmed in widescreen. Based on the video game series created by Electronic Arts.

Neeson, Liam Actor; appeared in *The Good Mother* (Leo), *Before and After* (Ben Ryan), and *Gun Shy* (Charlie Cutter). He voiced Aslan in the Chronicles of Narnia films, Fujimoto in *Ponyo*, and Qui-Gon Jinn in *Star Wars: The Rise of Skywalker*.

Negri, Pola (1895–1987) Actress; appeared in *The Moon-Spinners* (Madame Habib).

Neighbors, The (TV) Half-hour show on ABC; aired Sep. 26, 2012–Apr. 11, 2014. Wanting the best for his wife and 3 kids, Marty Weaver moves his family to Hidden Hills, New Jersey, a gated community complete with its own golf course. But then they meet the neighbors—aliens from the planet Zabvron—and the Weavers are the first humans they have ever met. Stars Lenny Venito (Marty Weaver), Jami Gertz (Debbie), Simon Templeman (Larry Bird), Toks Olagundoye (Jackie Joyner-Kersee), Clara Mamet (Amber Weaver), Tim Jo (Reggie Jackson), Ian Patrick (Dick Butkus), Max Charles (Max Weaver), Isabella Cramp (Abby Weaver). From ABC Studios.

Neilson, James (1909–1979) Director of such films as *Moon Pilot*, *Bon Voyage*, *Summer Magic*, *The Scarecrow of Romney Marsh*, *The Moon-Spinners*, and *The Adventures of Bullwhip Griffin*. He retired in 1975.

Nelson, Craig T. Actor; appeared in *Turner & Hooch* (Chief Hyde) and *The Proposal* (Joe Paxton), and made TV guest appearances in *Monk* (Judge Ethan Rickover). He voiced Bob Parr/Mr. Incredible in *The Incredibles* and *Incredibles 2*.

Nelson, Gary (1934–2022) Director of such films as *Freaky Friday*, *The Black Hole*, *Bayou Boy*, *The Secrets of the Pirate's Inn*, and *The Boy Who Talked to Badgers*.

Nelson, Tim Blake Actor; appeared in *Heavy-*

weights (Camp Hope salesman), *O Brother, Where Art Thou?* (Delmar), *Holes* (Dr. "Mom" Pendanski), *The Last Shot* (Marshal Paris), and *Lincoln* (Richard Schell). He voiced "Grampa" Green in *Big City Greens*.

Nemo Impressionable young clownfish; voiced by Alexander Gould in *Finding Nemo* and by Hayden Rolence in *Finding Dory*.

Nemo & Friends SeaRider Port Discovery attraction in Tokyo DisneySea; opened May 12, 2017. Guests board a submersible that "shrinks" to the size of a fish to explore the wondrous world of marine life from the same point of view as Nemo and Dory from the Disney • Pixar films. Replaced StormRider.

Neon Armadillo Music Saloon Nightclub in Pleasure Island at Walt Disney World; open May 1, 1989–Jan. 1998. Country-and-western music was performed in a southwestern saloon. It became the BET Soundstage Club, with country moving to a new venue, the Wildhorse Saloon.

Neon Cactus Country-and-western bar and grill at the Disneyland Hotel at Disneyland Resort; open May 25, 1992–Aug. 6, 1999, hosting live entertainment and dancing. It took the place of Sgt. Preston's Yukon Saloon.

Nero and Brutus Madame Medusa's pet crocodiles in *The Rescuers*.

Netflix In 2013, Disney announced a deal with Netflix for the production of live-action adventures featuring Marvel characters Daredevil, Jessica Jones, Iron Fist, and Luke Cage.

Never a Dull Moment (film) Mistaken for a hired killer, TV actor Jack Albany impersonates the man to save his own life. However, he is forced to join a gang of hoodlums attempting to heist an enormous 42-foot-long painting, *A Field of Sunflowers*, from the Manhattan Museum of Art. Then the real killer shows up. But Jack outwits him, thwarts the robbery, and also finds time to fall in love. Released Jun. 26, 1968. Directed by Jerry Paris. 100 min. Stars Edward G. Robinson (Smooth), Dick Van Dyke (Jack Albany), Dorothy Provine (Sally), Jack Elam (Ace Williams). The film was based on the book by John Godey.

Never Cry Wolf (film) A young biologist, Tyler, is sent by the Canadian government into the Arctic wilderness to study the wolves, which have been accused of killing off the caribou herds. He suffers hardships in the wild but gains a respect for the wolves. He adopts some of their lifestyle and discovers that hunters and not the wolves are the main enemy of the caribou. Premiere in Toronto on Oct. 6, 1983; general release on Oct. 7, 1983. Directed by Carroll Ballard. 105 min. Stars Charles Martin Smith (Tyler), Brian Dennehy (Rosie), Zachary Ittimangnaq (Ootek), Samson Jorah (Mike), Hugh Webster (Drunk), Martha Ittimangnaq (Woman). The film is based on the best-selling book by Farley Mowat, published in 1963 and since translated into more than 20 languages. Exec. producer Ron Miller had sought the rights to the book for 10 years. The movie was shot in the awesome wilderness of Canada's Yukon territory and in Nome, Alaska, and was more than 2 years in production. Alan Splet, an Oscar-winning sound effects editor fashioned a uniquely aural experience for the Arctic wilderness.

Never Land Island home of Peter Pan (not Never-Never Land, which was used in non-Disney versions, or Neverland).

Never Land Pool *Peter Pan*–themed pool at the Disneyland Hotel at Disneyland Resort; opened Jul. 2, 1999, on the site of the hotel's former marina. Featured were a pirate galleon and Skull Rock, with nearby cove pools, a beach, and playground. Dining, snacks, and libations were available at Hook's Pointe & Wine Cellar (opened Apr. 8, 1999, replacing Shipyard Inn), Croc's Bits 'n Bites (Aug. 14, 1999, replacing Wharf Ice Cream Galley), Captain's Galley (Aug. 14, 1999, replacing the Bottle Shop and Maisie's Kitchen), and The Lost Bar (Dec. 3, 1999, succeeding the Wharf Bar). The dining facilities closed Aug. 2010 to make way for Tangaroa Terrace and Trader Sam's Enchanted Tiki Bar. The main pool closed in 2011 and was succeeded by the E-Ticket Pool. SEE ALSO DISNEYLAND HOTEL.

Neverland Club [sic] Supervised children's activities were offered in this *Peter Pan*–themed facility at Disney's Polynesian Resort at Walt Disney World; opened Sep. 12, 1988, replacing the Mouseketeer Clubhouse (aka Mouseketeer's Village Clubhouse, which opened in 1971). It closed Apr. 2014 for refurbishment, reopening Jun. 16, 2014, as Club Disney. The updated facility was inspired by the classic Disney Little Golden Books and featured dress-up, crafts, and storytelling in a supervised atmosphere. In Nov. 2014, the location was renamed Lilo's Playhouse, which closed Jul. 31, 2018.

New Adventures of Spin and Marty, The (TV) Serial on the *Mickey Mouse Club* during the 1957–1958 season. Directed by Charles Barton. Spin and Marty have an old jalopy, which crashes into the kitchen, and the boys volunteer to raise the money to pay for the damages. Marty tries to tame a wild stallion, and then the guys get the girls to help put on a talent show. Stars Tim Considine (Spin), David Stollery (Marty), Kevin Corcoran, Annette Funicello, Darlene Gillespie, J. Pat O'Malley, Harry Carey, Jr., Roy Barcroft, B. G. Norman, Sammy Ogg, Tim Hartnagel, Don Agrati. 30 episodes.

New Adventures of Spin and Marty, The: Suspect Behavior (TV) Two-hour movie on *The Wonderful World of Disney*; first aired Aug. 13, 2000. Snooty Marty must make a friend while his parents are away, or he'll be sent to a dude ranch for the summer. Enter Spin, the mischievous son of his building superintendent, and the 2 boys try to crack the case of their creepy neighbors. Directed by Rusty Cundieff. Stars David Gallagher (Marty), Jeremy Foley (Spin), Charles Shaughnessy (Jordon), Judd Nelson (Hulka). This update of the 1950s *Mickey Mouse Club* serial features cameos by the original Spin and Marty as Mayor [Tim] Considine and Commissioner [David] Stollery. Based on the novel *The Undertaker's Gone Bananas* by Paul Zindel.

New Adventures of Winnie the Pooh, The (TV) Series on The Disney Channel; premiered Jan. 10, 1988, and ran on ABC Sep. 10, 1988–Sep. 4, 1992. It returned to ABC Jan. 4, 1997. It won the Emmy Award for Best Animated Program, Daytime, in both 1989 and 1990. Voices are Jim Cummings (Winnie the Pooh, Tigger), Paul Winchell (Tigger), John Fiedler (Piglet), Ken Sansom (Rabbit), Hal Smith (Owl), Peter Cullen (Eeyore), Michael Hough (Gopher), Tim Hoskins (Christopher Robin), Nicholas Melody (Roo), Patty Parris (Kanga). 50 episodes.

New Amsterdam Theatre In 1995, Disney signed a 99-year lease on this historic theater on West 42nd Street and began a 2-year restoration in partnership with the City of New York, to help with the company's expanding commitment to live entertainment. The theater opened May 18, 1997,

with a world premiere concert performance of Alan Menken and Tim Rice's *King David*, following several previews.

New! Animal World (TV) Series on The Disney Channel; beginning Apr. 18, 1983, featuring Bill Burrud traveling the world to search out interesting stories about animals.

New Century Clock Shop Main Street, U.S.A. shop in Disneyland; opened Jan. 1972. It replaced the Upjohn Pharmacy when Elgin (Bradley) became the licensee for Disney watches and clocks. Sponsored by Lorus and renamed New Century Timepieces in 1986. It closed Jul. 2008, to reopen as the Fortuosity Shop Oct. 3, 2008. Also in the Magic Kingdom at Walt Disney World (open Oct. 1971–Apr. 1986, later becoming part of Uptown Jewelers) and in World Bazaar at Tokyo Disneyland (open Apr. 15, 1983–Mar. 2007; succeeded by Harrington's Jewelry & Watches).

New Century Jewelry SEE JEWELRY SHOP.

New Century Notions—Flora's Unique Boutique Collectibles shop on Main Street, U.S.A. in Disneyland Paris; opened Jul. 29, 2014, taking the place of Town Square Photography.

New Girl, The (film) Educational film about acceptance of differences, from the What Should I Do? series; released in Mar. 1970.

New Kids on the Block at Walt Disney World—Wildest Dreams (TV) Special aired on ABC Jan. 21, 1991. Directed by Jim Yukich. 60 min. Stars the New Kids on the Block, who share their fantasies about being movie stars and in concert in Disney-MGM Studios at Walt Disney World.

New Mickey Mouse Club, The SEE MICKEY MOUSE CLUB.

New Neighbor, The (film) Donald Duck cartoon released Aug. 1, 1953. Directed by Jack Hannah. Donald tries hard to get along with his new neighbor, Pete, and Pete's terrible dog, but when Pete borrows all of Donald's food and throws stuff in his backyard, the fight is on.

New Orleans Square Land dedicated at Disneyland Jul. 24, 1966, by Walt Disney and the mayor of New Orleans. Disney had always enjoyed New Orleans; in fact, it was in an antique shop there that he found an old windup mechanical bird that would give him the idea for Audio-Animatronics figures. He felt the unique New Orleans architecture would add an ideal touch along the banks of the Rivers of America, so he set his designers to coming up with a plan. The space they had to work with was not large, and they were ingenious in fitting in everything that they wanted to include. It not only houses the major attractions of Pirates of the Caribbean and the Haunted Mansion, but also features a variety of shops and restaurants, including Café Orléans, Blue Bayou Restaurant, and the private Club 33. It was also here that Walt wanted his own apartment built (SEE DISNEY GALLERY AND DISNEYLAND DREAM SUITE). Tucked in, around, underneath, and out of view of the daily guests, are offices, kitchens, and a Cast Member cafeteria.

New Port South (film) Four high school students, sick of being censored by their teachers, attempt to change things by uncovering a scandal involving an ex-student, resulting in their plotting a revolution at the school. A Touchstone film. Very limited theatrical release on Sep. 7, 2001. Directed by Kyle Cooper. Stars Todd Field (Walsh), Chad Christ (Moorehouse), Kevin Christy (Clip), Will Estes (Chris), Melissa George (Amanda), Blake Shields (Maddox), Nick Sandow (Armstrong), Mike Shannon (Stanton), Gabriel Mann (Wilson), Raymond Barry (Principal Edwards). 97 min.

New Spirit, The (film) Donald Duck is persuaded to willingly and promptly pay his income tax in order to help the war effort in this cartoon made for the Treasury Department and distributed by the War Activities Committee of the Motion Picture Industry. Delivered Jan. 23, 1942. Directed by Wilfred Jackson and Ben Sharpsteen. Nominated for an Academy Award as Best Documentary. Cliff Edwards sings "Yankee Doodle Spirit." The secretary of the Treasury originally questioned using Donald Duck in this film, but Disney assured him that Donald was the equivalent of MGM offering him Clark Gable. The film caused a commotion in Congress, which balked at paying the high costs, most of which were necessitated by the Treasury Department's insistence on a speedy production period and enough prints to blanket the country. Surveys showed that the film succeeded in convincing Americans to pay their taxes promptly.

New Swiss Family Robinson, The (TV) Two-hour movie on *The Wonderful World of Disney*; first aired Jan. 10, 1999. A contemporary version of the classic family adventure, with the Robinson family sailing from Singapore to Sydney, being attacked by pirates, and shipwrecked on a deserted tropical island. Directed by Stewart Raffill. Stars Jane Seymour (Anna), James Keach (Jack), David Carradine (Sheldon Blake), Jamie Renee Smith (Elizabeth), Blake Bashoff (Todd), John Mallory Asher (Shane).

New True-Life Adventures (TV) A new True-Life Adventure series; premiered Feb. 14, 2000, in syn. Titles were *Disney Presents Alaska: Dances of the Caribou*, *Disney Presents Elephant Journey*, *Disney Presents Sea of Sharks*, and *Disney Presents The Everglades: Home of the Living Dinosaurs*.

New Year's Eve A popular party begun at Disneyland in 1957 and continued in the Magic Kingdom at Walt Disney World starting in 1971. Until 2005, Pleasure Island celebrated New Year's Eve festivities every night of the year. There have also been elaborate New Year's celebrations at other parks, including EPCOT and Disney's Hollywood Studios, over the years.

New Year's Jamboree (film) Shorts program released by RKO in 1953.

New York Boutique Shop in Disney Hotel New York – The Art of Marvel at Disneyland Paris; succeeded the Stock Exchange. Superhero artwork and souvenirs are sold.

New York Deli Counter-service restaurant in American Waterfront at Tokyo DisneySea; opened Sep. 4, 2001. The story goes that the big-city deli was so popular that nearby shops were converted into dining areas.

New York Stock Exchange Disney stock was first listed on Nov. 12, 1957.

New York Stories (film) Combination of 3 short stories—*Life Lessons*, *Life Without Zoe*, and *Oedipus Wrecks*—each about life with intriguing characters in New York City. In *Life Lessons*, contemporary New York City artist Lionel Dobie is suffering from "painter's block" when his lover-assistant Paulette announces that she is leaving him. He convinces her to stay, and while her coolness to him infuriates him, it at the same time inspires him. The more their relationship deteriorates, the more compelled and creative he becomes, while Paulette doubts her own talents as an artist. Ultimately Paulette leaves, and the successful artist finds a new student to whom he can give "life lessons." In *Life Without Zoe*, 12-year-old Zoe lives on her own at the Sherry Netherland Hotel with her butler, Hector, while her famous parents follow their own separate careers all over the world. Zoe becomes friends with a lonely rich boy, upon hearing him play the flute. She gets involved in a plot between a princess and her jealous husband that might cause Zoe's father harm. Her worldly wisdom and affection for her parents save the day and brings mother and father back together again. In *Oedipus Wrecks*, Sheldon is embarrassed by his mother, who doesn't seem to approve of anything about him—especially his shiksa fiancée, Lisa. Sheldon's wish that his mother just "disappear" comes true during a magic show. He is first distraught but then increasingly content with life without Mother. Suddenly, Mother reappears—personality intact, but in a rather different "form"—creating havoc for Sheldon and all the people of New York City. On the advice of his psychiatrist, Sheldon turns to psychic Treva, who tries to return Mother to her original state. The strain is too much for Lisa, and she leaves Sheldon. Treva fears she is a failure at everything, since she hasn't been able to bring Mother back, but Sheldon finds consolation in her, making everyone happy: Sheldon, Treva, and Mother. Premiered in New York City Mar. 1, 1989; general release Mar. 10, 1989. The 3 segments were each directed by a different director— Martin Scorsese, Francis Ford Coppola, and Woody Allen, respectively. A Touchstone film. 124 min. Stars Nick Nolte (Lionel Dobie), Rosanna Arquette (Paulette), Patrick O'Neal (Phillip Fowler)/Heather McComb (Zoe), Talia Shire (Charlotte)/Woody Allen (Sheldon), Mae Questel (Mother), Mia Farrow (Lisa), Julie Kavner (Treva). Filmed in New York City.

New York Street Backlot area in Disney-MGM Studios at Walt Disney World; opened May 1, 1989. Miniature skyscrapers provided an illustration of forced perspective at the end of the street. At first the street was only accessible to guests riding the tram tours, but later it was opened to pedestrians as new attractions were built around it. With the incorporation of San Francisco elements, the area was renamed Streets of America in 2004. Closed in 2016, to become Grand Avenue and Star Wars: Galaxy's Edge.

New York Style Sandwiches Manhattan-style deli in Disney Village at Disneyland Paris; opened Apr. 12, 1992, originally as Carnegie's – New York Style Sandwiches.

New York World's Fair Two-year exhibition, 1964–1965, which included 4 Disney shows: Ford's Magic Skyway, It's a Small World presented by Pepsi-Cola (to honor UNICEF), General Electric's Progressland, featuring the Carousel of Progress, and the State of Illinois' Great Moments with Mr. Lincoln. The fair premiered Apr. 22, 1964. After the opening and success of Disneyland, more and more cities had asked Walt Disney to build a Disneyland in their neighborhoods. He resisted at first, making sure that Disneyland was operating smoothly, but when he began listening to the entreaties from the East Coast, he wondered if Disneyland-style attractions would be popular among the easterners. The fair provided an opportunity for him to test that popularity. If Disney attractions were popular at the fair, then they should be popular anywhere on the Eastern Seaboard—and they were. The Disney attractions had some of the longest lines at the fair. After the fair closed in Oct. 1965, Disney was able to remove his attractions and reinstall them at Disneyland (though a second Great Moments with Mr. Lincoln had already premiered in the park Jul. 18). The organizations that sponsored the fair attractions helped fund Disney's research and development of the 4 pavilions, which featured extensive use of Audio-Animatronics figures, including human characters for the first time, and innovative, high-capacity ride systems.

Newbern, George Actor; appeared in *Adventures in Babysitting* (Dan) and as Bryan MacKenzie in *Father of the Bride* and *Father of the Bride Part II*; on TV in *Double Switch* (Bartholomew Holton/ Matt Bundy) and *Scandal* (Charlie), with guest appearances in *Grey's Anatomy*, *Criminal Minds*, and *Castle*; on Disney Channel in *Buffalo Dreams* (Dr. Nick Townsend) and *Dadnapped* (Neal); and on Blu-ray in *Santa Paws 2: The Santa Pups* (Thomas Reynolds).

Newhart, Bob Actor; provided the voice of Bernard in *The Rescuers* and *The Rescuers Down Under*, and appeared on TV in *Desperate Housewives* (Morty Flickman).

Newman, Fred Actor/composer; adult leader on the *Mickey Mouse Club* on The Disney Channel 1989–1994. For *Brand Spanking New Doug* and *Doug's 1st Movie*, he composed music and did voice work for several characters, including Porkchop and Skeeter, and voiced Stupid (a weasel) in *Who Framed Roger Rabbit*.

Newman, Paul (1925–2008) Actor; appeared in *The Color of Money* (Eddie), for which he won an Academy Award as Best Actor, and *Blaze* (Earl Long). He voiced Doc Hudson in *Cars*.

Newman, Randy Composer; he wrote scores and songs for *Toy Story*, *James and the Giant Peach*, *A Bug's Life*, *Toy Story 2*, *Monsters, Inc.*, *Cars*, *The Princess and the Frog*, *Toy Story 3*, *Monsters University*, and *Toy Story 4*, as well as *Monk* (TV series). He won Oscars for "If I Didn't Have You" in *Monsters, Inc.* and for "We Belong Together" in *Toy Story 3*. He was named a Disney Legend in 2007.

Newman Laugh-O-grams (film) Short untitled cartoons made for the Newman Theater in Kansas City, Missouri, by Walt Disney in 1920. Typical local problems, such as Kansas City's road conditions and corruption in the police force, were the subjects of the approximately 1-min. shorts. These were the first films Disney made.

Newport Bay Club Hotel at Disneyland Paris; opened Apr. 12, 1992. Similar to Disney's Yacht Club Resort at Walt Disney World in feel, it is themed as a charming 1900s coastal mansion and located next to Lake Disney, a 15-minute walk to the theme parks. The hotel was designed by Robert A.M. Stern. A convention center was added in 1997. It was completely renovated in 2016. Dining includes Cape Cod (a buffet), Yacht Club (table-service), and Captain's Quarters (lounge), with shopping at Bay Boutique.

Newsies (film) The young newsboys of New York City are dismayed when, in an attempt to squeeze out more profits for his newspaper, publisher Joseph Pulitzer increases the price they pay for their papers. Led by the spirited Jack Kelly, the newsies set out to challenge the power of the press bosses and go on strike. With the help of reporter Bryan Denton, the newsies get word of the strike out to the whole city, and other child laborers rally to the cause. Jack himself confronts Pulitzer in a battle of wills. The strike is eventually successful, thanks in part to the intervention of Teddy Roosevelt. Released Apr. 10, 1992. Directed by Kenny Ortega. Filmed in CinemaScope. 121 min.

Stars Christian Bale (Jack Kelly), David Moscow (David Jacobs), Max Casella (Racetrack), Marty Belafsky (Crutchy), Bill Pullman (Bryan Denton), Ann-Margret (Medda Larkson), Robert Duvall (Joseph Pulitzer). The first live-action film musical from The Walt Disney Studios in over a decade. Songs by Alan Menken and Jack Feldman include "Carrying the Banner," "Once and for All," "The World Will Know," "Santa Fe," "Seize the Day," and "King of New York." Filmed primarily on the Universal Studios backlot, the first movie shot on their New York Street set that had just been rebuilt after a disastrous fire in 1990. (Another Disney film, *Oscar*, was the last film shot on the set before the fire.)

Newsies A stage musical version of the motion picture opened at New Jersey's Paper Mill Playhouse in Millburn Sep. 15, 2011. Additional songs were written by Alan Menken and Jack Feldman, with the book by Harvey Fierstein. Previews at the Nederlander Theatre on Broadway began Mar. 15, 2012, with opening night on Mar. 29. A limited 101-performance run was planned, but it was extended due to the show's success. It received 8 Tony Award nominations in 2012, including Best Musical, and won for music (composer Menken and lyricist Feldman) and choreography (Christopher Gattelli). The Broadway production closed Aug. 24, 2014, to give way to a national tour. A production was filmed live on stage at the Hollywood Pantages Theater in Sep. 2016 and was made available to theaters Feb. 16, 18, and 22, 2017. Distributed by Fathom Events, this production was directed by Brett Sullivan and starred Jeremy Jordan (Jack Kelly), Kara Lindsay (Katherine), Ben Fankhauser (Davey), Andrew Keenan-Bolger (Crutchie).

Newsies! Newsies! See All About It (TV) Syn. special aired Mar. 28, 1992. About the making of the movie *Newsies*. Directed by Gayle Hollenbaugh.

Newton, Robert (1905–1956) Actor; appeared in *Treasure Island* (Long John Silver), one of the classic performances of his career that would influence how pirates would be portrayed in film and on TV for decades to come. He was named a Disney Legend posthumously in 2002.

NFFC See National Fantasy Fan Club.

Nichols, Charles ("Nick") (1910–1992) Longtime animation director of shorts and TV shows at the Disney Studio beginning there in 1935. He began at the Studio as an animator on the shorts, then moved up to director beginning with *First Aiders* in 1944. He had responsibility for most of the Pluto cartoons, and he animated the coachman in *Pinocchio*. He left the Studio in 1962. Also known as C. August Nichols.

Nick & Jessica Variety Hour (TV) Hour-long special on ABC; aired Apr. 11, 2004. Nick Lachey and Jessica Simpson, multiplatinum artists from their hit MTV series, *Newlyweds*, showcase their singing and comedic talents in a series of sketches and musical performances with such guests as Jewel, Kenny Rogers, Johnny Bench, and Muppets stars Kermit and Miss Piggy. From Tenth Planet Productions & JT Television, in association with Touchstone Television.

Nick & Jessica's Family Christmas (TV) Hour-long special on ABC; aired Dec. 1, 2004. Nick Lachey and Jessica Simpson star in a fun-filled family variety hour of comedy and music celebrating the holidays. From Bob Bain Productions & JT Television, in association with Touchstone Television.

Nick & Jessica's Tour of Duty (TV) Two-hour special on ABC; aired May 23, 2005. Nick Lachey and Jessica Simpson perform for more than 6,000 servicemen and servicewomen at the Ramstein Air Base in Germany, with an added special trip to give much needed love and support to those serving our country in Tikrit, Iraq. From Bob Bain Productions & JT Television, in association with Touchstone Television.

Nick Price Story of Non-Manipulative Selling, The Series of educational films from 1981: *The Danbury Secret of Flexible Behavior*, *A Better Way to Go*, and *The Voice*.

Nick Wilde Con artist fox character in *Zootopia*; voiced by Jason Bateman.

Nicky and Rock—Working Sheep Dogs (film) 16-mm release title of *Arizona Sheepdog*; released in Nov. 1966.

Nicolo's Workshop Mediterranean Harbor shop in Tokyo DisneySea; opened Sep. 4, 2001, offering pottery and glass crafts. Closed Jun. 2012 to become Bella Minni Collections.

Nielsen, Kay (1886–1957) Sketch artist/story man/designer; joined the Disney Studio in 1939 and worked on concepts for films, including *The Little Mermaid* and *Ride of the Valkyries*. He created designs for the "Night on Bald Mountain" segment of *Fantasia*. Nielsen's *Little Mermaid* designs were brought out of the Archives in the 1980s to inspire the artists who were again working on that story, and they thought enough of Nielsen's sketches to give him a film credit. Nielsen left Disney in 1941 and returned briefly in 1952–1953. He is known for his non-Disney work as a book illustrator of such classics as *East of the Sun and West of the Moon*.

Nielsen, Leslie (1926–2010) Actor; appeared in *Spy Hard* (Dick Steele) and *Mr. Magoo* (title role), on TV as *The Swamp Fox*, and narrated *Wild Heart*. He also appeared on TV in *Safety Patrol* (Mr. Penn) and *Santa Who?* (Santa Claus), and made guest appearances in *The Golden Girls* (Lucas) and *Circus of the Stars Goes to Disneyland*.

Nifty Nineties, The (film) Mickey Mouse cartoon released Jun. 20, 1941. Directed by Riley Thomson. Turn-of-the-century Mickey and Minnie attend a vaudeville show and later ride in a new "horsecar" that ends in a wreck when a cow interferes. The 2 vaudeville performers are caricatures of Disney animators Ward Kimball and Fred Moore.

Night (film) Silly Symphony cartoon released Apr. 28, 1930. Directed by Walt Disney. This early version of *The Old Mill* depicts the musical nighttime frolics of owls, fireflies, frogs, and other inhabitants of an old mill pond.

Night at the Museum: Kahmunrah Rises Again (film) A Disney+ original animated film from 20th Century Studios, Atomic Cartoons, and 21 Laps Entertainment, released under the Disney banner. Nick Daley's summer gig as night watchman at the American Museum of Natural History is a challenging job for a high schooler following in his father's footsteps. Luckily, he is familiar with the museum's ancient tablet that brings everything to life when the sun goes down and is happy to see old friends when he arrives. But when the maniacal ruler Kahmunrah escapes with plans to unlock the Egyptian underworld and free its Army of the Dead, it is up to Nick to stop the demented overlord and save the museum once and for all. Digitally premiered Dec.

9, 2022, on Disney+. Directed by Matt Danner. 78 min. Voices include Joshua Bassett (Nick), Jamie Demetriou (Dr. McPhee), Alice Isaaz (Joan of Arc), Gillian Jacobs (Erica), Joseph Kamal (Kahmunrah), Thomas Lennon (Teddy Roosevelt), Zachary Levi (Larry/Laaa), Akmal Saleh (Seth), Kieran Sequoia (Sacajawea), Jack Whitehall (Octavius), Bowen Yang (Ronnie), Steve Zahn (Jedediah). Music by John Paesano. Based on the popular film franchise acquired by Disney in 2019 as part of its purchase of 21st Century Fox.

Night Before Christmas, The (film) Silly Symphony cartoon released Dec. 9, 1933. Color. Directed by Wilfred Jackson. In a sequel to *Santa's Workshop*, Santa arrives at a house, setting up the tree, its trimmings, and toys. The noise awakens the children, who are in time only to see Santa driving away on his sleigh. The 16-mm release title was *Santa's Toys*.

Night Crossing (film) Peter Strelzyk and Günter Wetzel hope to escape with their families from East Germany to the freedom of the West. Realizing that a balloon might be the answer, Peter and Günter buy materials and begin building one in secret. The first flight, with just Peter's family—Günter's wife had convinced him to abandon the project—crashes just short of the border. Later, with the police closing in rapidly, the Strelzyks, once more joined by the Wetzels, make a final attempt to fly to freedom and this time succeed. Released Feb. 5, 1982. Directed by Delbert Mann. 107 min. Stars John Hurt (Peter Strelzyk), Jane Alexander (Doris), Glynnis O'Connor (Petra), Doug McKeon (Frank), Beau Bridges (Günter Wetzel), Ian Bannen (Josef), Klaus Löwitsch (Schmalk), Anne Stallybrass (Magda Keller), Kay Walsh (Doris's mother). Moved by newspaper accounts of the daring escape, Disney executive Ron Miller and producer Tom Leetch contacted European story editor Eva Redfern with instructions to pursue the film rights. Impressed by the Disney TV shows that were beamed from West to East Germany, the 2 couples accepted Disney's offer. The families flew to California to provide background material with the added inducement of a grand tour of Disneyland. To assure authenticity, the producers decided to film the entire production in West Germany in Landsberg, Muhltal, Harthausen, and Munich. Near the town of Eulenschwang, production designer Rolf Zehetbauer and art director Herbert Strabel spent $300,000 to re-create a half-mile section of the border that separated then East and West Germany, authentic

down to the wire-mesh fencing, concrete posts, automated shrapnel guns, leashed guard dogs, and impregnable cast-iron barricades. One of the large exhibition halls at the I.B.O. fairgrounds, in Friedrichshafen on Lake Constance, was turned into the world's largest "green set" for filming scenes under controlled conditions. Within the 5,000-sq.-yard area, 300 pine trees were transplanted for the forest, and to shut out the light from the glass-walled structure, 6,000 sq. yards of black plastic covered the walls. The final cost for the set was $150,000. At the Bavaria Film Studio, interior filming was done on 4 soundstages. Gary Cerveny of Balloon Ventures, Inc. of Glendale, California, made and flew a total of 7 hot-air balloons for the production. The balloons were re-created as closely as possible to the original. The only changes were in the material used and adherence to certain technical improvements to comply with FAA standards. What made the real-life flight all the more miraculous was that the experts say their balloon shouldn't have flown at all. With all the proper equipment, sophisticated electronic devices and human expertise, Cerveny had extreme difficulty getting the exact reproductions airborne.

Night on Bald Mountain (film) Music by Modest Mussorgsky, a segment of *Fantasia*.

Night Stalker, The (TV) One-hour drama series on ABC; aired Sep. 29–Nov. 10, 2005. When a pregnant woman is snatched from her home, crime reporter Carl Kolchak suspects all is not as it seems. That is because 18 months ago, his wife was killed in a bizarre fashion, and he has been the FBI's number one suspect ever since. Kolchak's determination to find the truth leads him to investigate other crimes that seem to have a supernatural component. But he's trying to piece together a puzzle that keeps changing shape. Who or what is committing these crimes? How are they all related? With sidekick Perri Reed, a skeptical fellow reporter in tow, Kolchak will go to any lengths to answer these questions. But when he does discover the truth—will anyone believe him? Stars Stuart Townsend (Carl Kolchak), Gabrielle Union (Perri Reed), Eric Jungmann (Jain McManus), Cotter Smith (Tony Vincenzo). From Touchstone Television. Three unaired episodes debuted on iTunes Feb. 7, 2006, joining 7 previously released episodes, and all 10 episodes aired on the Sci-Fi Channel in summer 2006.

Night Train to Kathmandu (TV) A Disney Channel Premiere Film; first aired Jun. 5, 1988. An adventure of an American girl on vacation in Nepal and a prince who has left his secret city to explore the real world. Directed by Robert Wiemer. 102 min. Stars Pernell Roberts (Professor Hadley-Smythe), Milla Jovovich (Lily), Eddie Castrodad (Prince Johar).

Nightjohn (TV) A Disney Channel Premiere Film; first aired Jun. 1, 1996. In the 1830s, Sarny, a young, Black enslaved girl, meets the mysterious Nightjohn, who freely risks his life to give the girl a gift that white law forbids: the gift of teaching reading and writing. Directed by Charles Burnett. Stars Beau Bridges (Clel Waller), Carl Lumbly (Nightjohn), Allison Jones (Sarny), Lorraine Toussaint (Delie). Based on the novel by Gary Paulsen. 103 min. Filmed entirely on the Rip Raps Plantation in Sumter, South Carolina.

Nightmare Before Christmas, Tim Burton's The (film) Jack Skellington is the Pumpkin King of Halloween Town who, though busy, feels a void in his life. Upon discovering Christmas Town, he rejoices with a fervor to take over a new holiday. With the help of 3 mischievous trick-or-treaters, Lock, Shock, and Barrel, he manages to capture Santa Claus, whom he calls Sandy Claws, and proceeds to turn Halloweentown into a Christmas manufacturing plant. Sally, a lonely ragdoll who loves Jack, fears his new obsession will bring him trouble. Despite her efforts, Jack and his reindeer, created by the local evil scientist, set off on Christmas Eve with a lot of ghoulish presents. When the world responds with horror to Jack's earnest efforts and cries for the real Santa Claus, Jack realizes his mistake. He manages to save Sally and Santa Claus from the dangerous Oogie Boogie and restore the Christmas holiday. With his newfound love for Sally, he can happily return to being himself. This film is Tim Burton's tour de force using stop-motion animation. Initial release in New York City on Oct. 13, 1993; expanded release on Oct. 22, 1993, and general release on Oct. 29, 1993. Directed by Henry Selick. A Touchstone film. 76 min. Voices include Chris Sarandon (Jack Skellington), Catherine O'Hara (Sally), Glenn Shadix (Mayor), William Hickey (evil scientist), Ken Page (Oogie Boogie). Tim Burton created the story and characters for the film. The original score was by Danny Elfman, who also provided the singing voice of Jack Skellington. Produced in a studio in San Francisco, utilizing more than 227 animated characters. It has had a limited reissue at Halloween beginning in 2000, and the film has become a cult classic. For the holiday season in 2001, the Disneyland Haunted Mansion was outfitted with *Tim Burton's The Nightmare Before Christmas* elements, characters, and scenes, and its popularity ensured its return in ensuing years. A holiday version premiered in Tokyo Disneyland in 2004. In Disneyland, the attraction is the Haunted Mansion Holiday; in Tokyo Disneyland, it is the Haunted Mansion Holiday Nightmare. The film was rereleased in Disney Digital 3-D on Oct. 20, 2006, marking the first time that a once-analog 2-D film had been turned into a wholly digital 3-D film. The 3-D version was produced by Don Hahn with 3-D visual effects by ILM under Colum Slevin. It was brought back to theaters at Halloween time thereafter.

Nightmare Ned (TV) Animated series on ABC; aired Apr. 19–Aug. 30, 1997. Ned Needlemeyer is a misunderstood, solitary, bespectacled 8-year-old boy, who happens to have wild nightmares. Voices include Courtland Mead (Ned), Brad Garrett (Dad), Victoria Jackson (Mom). 12 episodes.

Nighy, Bill Actor; appeared in *The Hitchhiker's Guide to the Galaxy* (Slartibartfast), *G-Force* (Saber), and as Davy Jones in *Pirates of the Caribbean: Dead Man's Chest* and *Pirates of the Caribbean: At World's End*.

Nikki, Wild Dog of the North (film) Andre Dupas, a French Canadian hunter, finds a dead mother bear, and deciding to save her cub from sure death by raising it himself, ties the cub, Neewa, to his malamute pup, Nikki, and continues paddling down the river. At the rapids, the canoe overturns, and the animals are washed away, still tied together. They discover they have to cooperate to survive, and even though they eventually break loose from each other, they become friends until a winter hibernation leaves Nikki on his own. Nikki grows into a powerful dog but is captured by a cruel hunter, LeBeau, who makes him into a savage fighter and takes him to the trading post run by Dupas, who has banned the customary dogfighting. LeBeau ignores the ruling, fights Nikki, and is thrown out by Dupas whom he then shoves into the dog pit, expecting the savage Nikki to tear him to bits. Nikki recognizes his old master, and the enraged LeBeau springs into the pit to kill Dupas himself. When he finds he is losing the battle he treacherously pulls a knife, but Nikki springs on him. LeBeau falls on his own knife, killing himself. Nikki and Dupas are reunited. Released Jul. 12, 1961. Directed by Jack Couffer and Dan Haldane. The screenplay was based on James Oliver Curwood's book *Nomads of* *the North.* 73 min. Stars Jean Coutu (Andre Dupas), Emile Genest (Jacques LeBeau), with narration by Jacques Fauteux. Filmed on location in Canada by 2 separate film units. The film helped prove that Disney had perfected the method of blending a True-Life Adventure nature film style with a dramatic story.

Nine Dragons Restaurant Table-service restaurant in China at EPCOT; opened Oct. 23, 1985. It seemed a little odd that World Showcase opened with China, but with no Chinese restaurant, because of the popularity of Chinese cuisine. That omission was remedied 3 years later, and the resulting restaurant has been honored with awards for its blend of Chinese cuisine from many of the provinces.

Nine Lives of Elfego Baca, The (TV) Episode 1 of *Elfego Baca.* Also an international and video release title for an *Elfego Baca* feature. SEE ALSO ELFEGO BACA.

Nine Old Men Walt called his key animators in the 1950s his "Nine Old Men," after Franklin D. Roosevelt's "Nine Old Men" on the Supreme Court. They were Frank Thomas, Ollie Johnston, John Lounsbery, Marc Davis, Ward Kimball, Wolfgang ("Woolie") Reitherman, Les Clark, Eric Larson, Milt Kahl.

1900 Park Fare Restaurant in Disney's Grand Floridian Resort & Spa at Walt Disney World; opened Jun. 28, 1988. Food is served buffet style, and there are frequent appearances by Disney characters, as well as entertainment from a huge band organ named Big Bertha.

1901 SEE CARTHAY CIRCLE RESTAURANT AND LOUNGE.

Niok (film) Featurette released Aug. 28, 1957. Directed by Edmond Sechan. Near Angkor Wat in northern Cambodia, a group of children capture a baby elephant and are just growing attached to it when it is sold to a traveling safari. Pursuing the new owner, a boy manages to steal it back, and the children free it to return to its mother. 29 min.

Niven, David (1910–1983) Actor; appeared in *No Deposit, No Return* (J. W. Osborne) and *Candleshoe* (Priory).

Nixon (film) The political life of Richard Nixon is covered, with flashbacks showing his Quaker upbringing, from his congressional days to Water-

gate and his resignation, presenting a psychological portrait of the complex public figure and a look at the people who surrounded him. Released on a limited basis Dec. 20, 1995; expanded release Jan. 5, 1996. A Hollywood Pictures release of an Andrew G. Vajna presentation of an Illusion Entertainment Group/Cinergi production. Directed by Oliver Stone. Stars Anthony Hopkins (Richard Nixon), Joan Allen (Pat Nixon), Powers Boothe (Alexander Haig), Ed Harris (E. Howard Hunt), Bob Hoskins (J. Edgar Hoover), E. G. Marshall (John Mitchell), David Paymer (Ron Ziegler), David Hyde Pierce (John Dean), Paul Sorvino (Henry Kissinger), Mary Steenburgen (Hannah Nixon), J. T. Walsh (John Ehrlichman), James Woods (H. R. Haldeman), Brian Bedford (Clyde Tolson), Ed Herrmann (Nelson Rockefeller), Madeleine Kahn (Margaret Mitchell). 191 min. Filmed in CinemaScope. The production was filmed almost exclusively in Southern California and utilized White House sets that had been built at Sony Studios in Culver City for the movie *The American President.* The wedding scene was shot at the Mission Inn in Riverside, where Richard and Pat Nixon had said their vows. The Nixon family's East Whittier white-frame house and grocery store/filling station were re-created on a road running between citrus groves in Redlands. Released on video in 1996, with additional footage included.

Nixon, Richard M. (1913–1994) Vice President Nixon first visited Disneyland shortly after its opening in Jul. 1955. He returned with his family on Jun. 14, 1959, to help dedicate the Monorail. As president, he famously answered questions at the 1973 Annual Convention of the Associated Press Managing Editors Association, held at the Contemporary Resort at Walt Disney World on Nov. 17. He visited Disneyland and Walt Disney World several times from the 1960s to the 1980s.

No Big Deal (film) Educational release on video in Jun. 1992. 20 min. A story of the dangers of inhalants and how they can cause paranoia and increased aggression.

No Deposit, No Return (film) Tracy, 11, and Jay, 8, who would like to be with their mother in Hong Kong, are stuck spending their Easter holiday with their wealthy grandfather in California. When the kids fall in with 2 bumbling safecrackers, they pretend to be kidnapped to con their grandfather into paying ransom money, which they can use as airfare to Hong Kong. Their ploy backfires with hilarious results as everyone from the police to the kids' mother tries to rescue them from their "kidnappers." Released Feb. 11, 1976. Directed by Norman Tokar. 111 min. Stars David Niven (J. S. Osborne), Darren McGavin (Duke), Don Knotts (Bert), Herschel Bernardi (Sgt. Turner), Barbara Feldon (Carolyn), Kim Richards (Tracy), Brad Savage (Jay), John Williams (Jameson), Vic Tayback (Big Joe), Charlie Martin Smith (Longnecker), Bob Hastings (Peter). The story was written by Disney veteran Joe McEveety.

No Hunting (film) Donald Duck cartoon released Jan. 14, 1955. Directed by Jack Hannah. Donald is inspired by his grandpappy's hunting skills to go out with him on a modern-day hunt where the pair spend most of their time avoiding the bullets of the other hunters and never have a chance to bag any game. Filmed in CinemaScope. Nominated for an Academy Award.

No Ordinary Family (TV) Drama series on ABC; aired Sep. 28, 2010–Apr. 5, 2011. During a plane trip on a family vacation, Jim and Stephanie and their 2 children crash-land into the Amazon River. They soon discover that something is not quite right. Each of them now possesses unique and distinct superpowers. They try to find purpose for their new powers, as they try to save and savor their family life. Stars Michael Chiklis (Jim Powell), Julie Benz (Stephanie Powell), Romany Malco (George St. Cloud), Tate Donovan (Mitch McCutcheon), Autumn Reeser (Katie Andrews), Christina Chang (Yvonne Cho), Kay Panabaker (Daphne Powell), Jimmy Bennett (JJ Powell). From ABC Studios.

No Sail (film) Donald Duck and Goofy cartoon released Sep. 7, 1945. Directed by Jack Hannah. Donald and Goofy are sailing in a rented boat that runs on nickels. When they run out of coins, they are marooned for days until Donald's beak gets caught in the coin slot, starting the boat, and they sail off toward the horizon.

No Smoking (film) Goofy cartoon released Nov. 23, 1951. Directed by Jack Kinney. Goofy decides to give up smoking but experiences so many temptations that he grows desperate and gets into various situations trying to get a cigarette.

Noah (TV) Two-hour movie on *The Wonderful World of Disney*; first aired Oct. 11, 1998. Set in modern times, a building contractor, Norman Waters, is asked to build an ark and fill it with animals, 2 by 2. Despite his skepticism, and problems with his 3 boys, Norman begins the ark and befriends a pet store owner who agrees to supply the animals. Directed by Ken Kwapis. Stars Tony Danza (Norman Waters), Wallace Shawn (Zack), Jane Sibbett (Angela), John Marshall Jones (Ernie), Don McManus (Gavin), Jesse Moss (Levon), Christopher Marquette (Daniel), Michal Suchanek (Benny). For the production, the ark was built in Hoodoo Provincial Park near Drumheller, Alberta, Canada.

Noah's Ark (film) Special featurette released Nov. 10, 1959. Directed by Bill Justice. Using the magic of stop-motion animation, X Atencio and a team of artists brought to life a variety of objects normally found in a hardware store as characters in the biblical story of Noah and his ark. With his sons Ham, Shem, and Japheth, Noah managed to cut enough gopher wood to fabricate the ark, preparing to set sail with his family, and inviting various animals to join them and wait out the Great Flood safe in the hold. Music by George Bruns, with songs by Mel Leven. Nominated for an Academy Award. 21 min. There was also a Silly Symphony cartoon from 1933 entitled *Father Noah's Ark*.

Nobody Like U Song from *Turning Red*; written by Billie Eilish and Finneas O'Connell.

Noelle (film) Kris Kringle's daughter is full of Christmas spirit and holiday fun but wishes she could do something "important" like her beloved brother Nick does, like taking over for their father this Christmas. When Nick is about to crumble from all the pressure, Noelle suggests he take a break and get away. But when he doesn't return, Noelle must find her brother and bring him back in time to save Christmas. Released digitally Nov. 12, 2019, on Disney+. Directed by Marc Lawrence. Stars Anna Kendrick (Noelle Kringle), Bill Hader (Nick Kringle), Kingsley Ben-Adir, (Jake Hapman), Billy Eichner (Gabe Kringle), Julie Hagerty (Mrs. Claus), Shirley MacLaine (Elf Polly). 100 min. From Walt Disney Studios. Filmed in wide-screen format in Vancouver and Woodstock, Georgia.

Noises Off (film) A less-than-stellar American acting troupe attempts to put on a wacky British farce entitled *Nothing On*. The cast lumbers through a last-minute run-through under the direction of the exasperated Lloyd Fellowes; then the camera swings backstage for a behind-the-scenes view of the chaos going on there, as the actors vent their frustrations and jealousies. The play is shown to an unenthusiastic preview audience that barely sits through a disastrous full production complete with missed cues, misplaced props, and missing actors. Thinking that his career will be ruined after the Broadway opening, the director has hidden in a bar until the final curtain when he hears the cheers of approval from the audience. His motley acting crew has somehow turned out a hit after all. Released Mar. 20, 1992. Directed by Peter Bogdanovich. A Touchstone film, with Amblin Entertainment. 104 min. Stars Carol Burnett (Dotty Otley/Mrs. Clackett), Michael Caine (Lloyd Fellowes), Denholm Elliott (Selsdon Mowbray/The Burglar), Julie Hagerty (Poppy Taylor), Marilu Henner (Belinda Blair/Flavia Brent), Mark Linn-Baker (Tim Allgood), Christopher Reeve (Frederick Dallas/Philip Brent), John Ritter (Gary Lejuene/Roger Tramplemain), Nicollette Sheridan (Brooke Aston/Vicki). This was Denholm Elliott's last film; he died shortly after its release. From the Tony Award–nominated play by Michael Frayn.

Nolan, Jeanette (1911–1998) Actress; appeared in *The Horse Whisperer* (Ellen Booker), and on TV in *Bayou Boy* (Tanta Louise), *Gallegher Goes West* and *The Mystery of Edward Sims* (Erm White), and The *Sky's the Limit* (Gertie), with guest appearances in *The Golden Girls* and *The Nutt House* (uncredited). She voiced Ellie Mae in *The Rescuers* and Widow Tweed in *The Fox and the Hound*.

Nolan, Lloyd (1902–1985) Actor; appeared on TV in *The Sky's the Limit* (Cornwall).

Nolte, Nick Actor; appeared in *Down and Out in Beverly Hills* (Jerry Baskin), *Three Fugitives* (Lucas), *New York Stories* (Lionel Dobie), *I Love Trouble* (Peter Brackett), *Jefferson in Paris* (Thomas Jefferson), and *Breakfast of Champions* (Harry Le Sabre), and on TV in *The Feather Farm* (Les). He voiced Kuiil in *The Mandalorian*.

Nomad Lounge Cocktail lounge in Discovery Island at Disney's Animal Kingdom; opened May 27, 2016. Decorative banners, featuring journal entries from Imagineers who worked on the park, pose a series of questions about travel. Guests are invited to jot down their answers on tags and have them displayed above the bar.

Nona (film) Animated short; digitally released Sep. 17, 2021, on Disney+. A grandmother's plan for a special day alone is upended by an unexpected visit from her granddaughter. Directed by Louis Gonzales. From the Pixar Animation Studios SparkShorts program. 7 min.

Norman, Floyd Artist/animator; he started as an inbetweener and animator on *Sleeping Beauty*, *The Sword in the Stone*, and *The Jungle Book*, and later worked on *Robin Hood*, *The Hunchback of Notre Dame*, and *Mulan*, and for Disney • Pixar on *Toy Story 2* and *Monsters, Inc.* He was named a Disney Legend in 2007 and later appeared in *Mickey: The Story of a Mouse*.

North Avenue Irregulars, The (film) When organized crime hits their town, a reverend and a group of unusual ladies from his church decide to hit back. By posing as knockout performers, masters of disguise, and cunning mistresses of pursuit, they bring the underworld to its knees in a wild and crazy car chase and roundup finale. Released Feb. 9, 1979. Directed by Bruce Bilson. 100 min. Stars Edward Herrmann (Michael Hill), Barbara Harris (Vickie), Susan Clark (Anne), Karen Valentine (Jane), Michael Constantine (Marv), Patsy Kelly (Rose), Ivor Francis (Rev. Wainwright), Douglas V. Fowley (Delaney), Virginia Capers (Cleo), Steve Franken (Tom), Dena Dietrich (Mrs. Carlisle), Dick Fuchs (Howard), Herb Voland (Dr. Fulton), Alan Hale (Harry the Hat), Ruth Buzzi (Dr. Rheems), Cloris Leachman (Claire). The film is based on the book by Rev. Albert Fay Hill. Though many of the incidents in the film are fictional, the story is based on the factual account of Reverend Hill. The group's name comes from the Baker Street Irregulars, a reference to the youth of Victorian London who gathered information for Sherlock Holmes for a pittance. Scenes were filmed on the backlot of the Disney Studio and at 42 separate locations in and around the Los Angeles area from florist shops in Burbank to alleys in Pasadena to desert roads near Newhall (in Santa Clarita) and to streets in Long Beach. More than $155,000 was paid for cars involved in the filming. Fourteen autos and 1 motorcycle were destroyed in the final scenes. The film was released in other countries under the title *Hill's Angels*.

Northcutte, Shawnte Mouseketeer on the new *Mickey Mouse Club*.

Northern Delights Sweets shop inspired by the Northern Lights planned for World of Frozen in Hong Kong Disneyland.

Northern Lights (TV) A Disney Channel Original Movie; first aired Aug. 23, 1997. A New York City woman goes to her brother's funeral in a small town in New England, along with his onetime buddy, Ben, and gets the shock of her life. They are inheriting a young nephew she never knew about. Directed by Linda Yellen. Stars Diane Keaton (Roberta Blumstein), Joseph Cross (Jack), Maury Chaykin (Ben). 95 min.

Northwest Mercantile and Trading Post Shop in Canada at EPCOT; opened Oct. 1, 1982. The merchandise originally fell into the categories of Indian, Eskimo, and Hudson Bay trappers. Maple syrup, soapstone carvings, lumberjack shirts, and other Canadian wares have been sold.

Northwest Passage Apparel and gift boutique in Disney Sequoia Lodge at Disneyland Paris; opened May 27, 1992. The atmosphere is inspired by the American West of yesteryear.

Norton, Edward Actor; appeared in *Keeping the Faith* (Brian) and *25th Hour* (Monty Brogan).

Norway World Showcase pavilion in EPCOT; opened May 6, 1988. The most recent country to be added to World Showcase. The architecture reminds the visitor of cities and towns such as Oslo and Bergen, with a castle patterned after Oslo's Akershus from the 14th century. The focal point is a large stave church in which one can explore displays of Norwegian cultural objects; the structure is inspired by the Gol Stave Church of Hallingdal. A boat ride attraction (initially Maelstrom), Akershus Royal Banquet Hall, and Kringla Bakeri og Kafé are the main features here. The shops—The Fjording and The Puffin's Roost—are based on Norwegian animals. The pavilion was significantly expanded in 2016, with the new Royal Sommerhus (a character-greeting cabin), The Wandering Reindeer shop, and with Frozen Ever After replacing Maelstrom.

Norway—the Film (film) A 70-mm film on the people and culture of Norway at the conclusion of the Maelstrom attraction in Norway at EPCOT; ran Jul. 5, 1988–Oct. 5, 2014. 5 min. Also known as *The Spirit of Norway*.

Norwood, Brandy SEE BRANDY.

Nosey, the Sweetest Skunk in the West (TV) Show aired Nov. 19, 1972. An orphaned skunk comes into the lives of an artist and his daughter in a desolate area of Arizona, and he tangles with an owl and a pair of poodles. Stars Jane Biddle, James Chandler, Walter Carlson, Lois Binford. Narrated by Rex Allen.

Not Quite Human (TV) A Disney Channel Premiere Film; first aired Jun. 19, 1987. An android goes to high school with the daughter of his inventor. Directed by Steven H. Stern. 91 min. With Jay Underwood (Chip Carson), Alan Thicke (Dr. Carson), Joe Bologna (Vogel), Robyn Lively (Becky). There were 2 sequels, *Not Quite Human II* and *Still Not Quite Human*.

Not Quite Human II (TV) A Disney Channel Premiere Film; first aired Sep. 23, 1989. Chip the android goes to college to learn more about human emotions in this sequel, and he meets and falls for an android created by a rival scientist. Directed by Eric Luke. 92 min. Stars Jay Underwood, Alan Thicke, Robyn Lively, Katie Barberi (Roberta).

Not So Lonely Lighthouse Keeper, The (TV) Show aired Sep. 17, 1967. This is the story of a lighthouse keeper on Anacapa Island and his pet goat. Progress decrees that the lighthouse give way to an automated beacon, but the keeper is unhappy on the mainland, and he is able to return to the island as a game warden. Stars Clarence Hastings, Ingrid Niemela. Narrated by Roy Barcroft.

Nothing to Lose (film) Things couldn't get any worse for advertising executive Nick Beam, whose life has just completely unraveled when he thinks he has caught his wife being unfaithful to him with his boss. But while he is sitting at a traffic light in a state of shock and unable to get a grip on reality, a fast-talking carjacker named T. Paul leaps into his car, attempting to rob him. With nothing to lose and on the verge of a nervous breakdown, Nick turns the tables on his mugger, taking him hostage while he decides what to do. An unlikely friendship gradually unfolds between this offbeat pair in a madcap comedy of holdups, high-speed chases, mistaken identities, and revenge. A Touchstone film. Directed by Steve Oedekerk. Released Jul. 18, 1997. Stars Martin Lawrence (T. Paul), Tim Robbins (Nick Beam), John C. McGinley (Rig), Giancarlo Esposito (Charlie), Michael McKean (Philip Barrows), Kelly Preston (Ann Beam). 98 min. Filming began in the desert near Lancaster, California, then continued at locations around Los Angeles.

Notorious (TV) Hour-long drama series on ABC;

aired Sep. 22–Dec. 8, 2016. There is a symbiotic relationship between charismatic defense attorney Jake Gregorian and powerhouse TV producer Julia George. When Jake's clients find themselves in the nation's spotlight, he uses the media to sway public opinion. Meanwhile, Julia, the exec. producer of *Louise Herrick Live*, the No. 1 TV news program in the country, capitalizes on the notoriety of Jake's clients. Everyone's motives are suspect, and morality is subjective, but together they make great TV and determine the nation's headlines. Stars Kate Jennings Grant (Louise Herrick), Daniel Sunjata (Jake Gregorian), Piper Perabo (Julia George), Sepideh Moafi (Megan Byrd), Ryan Guzman (Ryan Mills), J. August Richards (Bradley Gregorian), Aimee Teegarden (Ella Benjamin), Kevin Zegers (Oscar Keaton). From Sony Pictures Television and ABC Studios.

Nouba, La SEE CIRQUE DU SOLEIL.

Novarro, Ramon (1899–1968) Actor; appeared on TV in *Elfego Baca* (Don Esteban Miranda).

Novis, Donald (1906–1966) Actor/singer; an English-born tenor, he performed "Love Is a Song" in *Bambi*, "'Twas the Night Before Christmas" in *The Night Before Christmas*, and "Peace on Earth" in *Lady and the Tramp*. He was the original silver-toned tenor in the *Golden Horseshoe Revue* at Disneyland.

Novis, Julietta (1909–1994) Singer; performed "Ave Maria" in *Fantasia*.

Now I Can Tell You My Secret (film) Educational film; released in Aug. 1984. Shows how children can protect themselves from dangerous advances by saying "no," getting away, and telling an adult.

Now More Than Ever The 2019 Disney Parks campaign highlighting new park experiences and live entertainment.

Now You See Him, Now You Don't (film) At Medfield College, Dexter Riley comes up with a lab experiment that produces fantastic results—invisibility! But the magic potion is stolen and put to use by a bank robber. Nevertheless, Dexter and his pals foil the robbers and recover the potion, which wins an award and saves Medfield from financial ruin and being transformed into a gambling mecca. Premiere in Edmonton, Alberta, Canada on Jul. 7, 1972; general release on Jul. 12, 1972. Directed by Robert Butler. 88 min. Stars Kurt Russell (Dexter), Joyce Menges (Debbie Dawson), Joe Flynn (Dean Higgins), Cesar Romero (A. J. Arno), William Windom (Lufkin), Jim Backus (Forsythe).

Now You See It (TV) A Disney Channel Original Movie; premiered Jan. 14, 2005. Aspiring student producer Allyson Miller is producing a new reality show that will search for the world's greatest kid magician. She stumbles upon Danny Sinclair, who becomes 1 of 3 finalists. While the other 2 contestants are good magicians, Danny appears to have something more. When Allyson finally learns that Danny's powers are real, she must protect him from those who want to destroy him. Directed by Duwayne Dunham. Stars Alyson Michalka (Allyson Miller), Johnny Pacar (Danny Sinclair), Frank Langella (Max), Chris Olivero (Hunter), Gabriel Sunday (Brandon), Deneen Tyler (Ms. McAllister), Amanda Shaw (Zoe), Patty French (Madam Susette).

Nowhere Man (TV) One-hour psychological suspense TV series on UPN; premiered Sep. 4, 1995, after a preview Aug. 28, and ended Aug. 19, 1996. In the course of one evening, a man seemingly has his entire identity erased. Now he is engaged in a life-consuming quest for the truth. Stars Bruce Greenwood (Thomas Veil), and in the premiere episode Megan Gallagher (Alyson Veil), Ted Levine (Dave Powers), Murray Rubenstein (Larry Levy). Michael Tucker (Dr. Bellamy). From Lawrence Hertzog Productions and Touchstone Television.

N.T.S.B.: The Crash of Flight 323 (TV) Two-hour movie on ABC; aired Mar. 22, 2004. The National Transportation Safety Board investigates the fictional crash of a commuter plane in the Colorado mountains, trying to find out what went wrong, and decide whether it was mechanical failure, pilot error, or an act of terrorism. Produced by Omnibus, Inc. and Touchstone Television. Directed by Jeff Bleckner. Stars Mandy Patinkin (Al Cummings), Ted McGinley (Reese Faulkner), Eric Close (N'Tom), Kevin Dunn (Dr. Cyrus Lebow), Tyra Ferrell (Jessamyn). Originally scheduled to air in 2001 but postponed due to the World Trade Center attacks; then a later airdate in Feb. 2003 was postponed due to the crash of the space shuttle *Columbia*.

Nucci, Danny Actor; appeared in *Alive* (Hugo Diaz), *Crimson Tide* (Danny Rivetti), and *The Rock* (Spec. Agent Shepard), and on TV in *Brand*

New Life (D. J.), *10–8* (Rico Amonte), and *The Fosters* (Mike Foster), with guest roles in *Blossom* (Lou), *Castle* (Gilbert), and *The Rookie* (Detective Sanford Motta).

nuiMOs Pocket-sized plush characters with an assortment of fashionable outfits and accessories; first introduced in China and Japan in 2018, then in North America and Europe Jan. 19, 2021. The name is a combination of the Japanese words "nuigurumi" (plush) and "moderu" (model).

No. 2 to Kettering (film) Animated short; digitally released Aug. 4, 2021, on Disney+. On a dreary, ordinary morning, a girl learns how the power of laughter can lift even the most sullen among her fellow bus riders along their journey to Kettering, the U.K. town that is the bus's destination. Directed by Liza Rhea. 4 min. From the Walt Disney Animation Studios Short Circuit program.

Nunis, Dick He began his Disney career in summer 1955 at Disneyland as an assistant to Van France in orientation training. He worked up through the ranks as area supervisor, supervisor of the mail room and steno pool, director of Disneyland operations (1961), and vice president of Disneyland operations (1968). In 1972, he became executive vice president of both Disneyland and Walt Disney World, and president in 1980. He was a member of the Disney Board of Directors 1981–1999 and was named chairman of Walt Disney Attractions in 1991. He retired in 1999 and was named a Disney Legend the same year. His book, *Walt's Apprentice: Keeping the Disney Dream Alive*, was published in 2022.

Nurses (TV) Series on NBC; aired Sep. 14, 1991–Jun. 18, 1994. A dedicated team of health care professionals uses humor to handle the daily pressures of demanding work and complex personal lives. Stars Stephanie Hodge (Sandy), Arnetia Walker (Anne), Mary Jo Keenen (Julie), Ada Maris (Gina), Kenneth David Gilman (Dr. Kaplan), Carlos LaCamara (Paco). The 2nd season added David Rasche (Jack Trenton) and Markus Flanagan (Luke Fitzgerald); during the 3rd season, Loni Anderson (Casey MacAfee) joined as a new, ruthlessly ambitious hospital administrator. From Witt/Thomas/Harris Productions and Touchstone Television.

Nutcracker and the Four Realms, The (film) All Clara wants is a one-of-a-kind key that will unlock a box that holds a priceless gift. A golden thread, presented to her at Godfather Drosselmeyer's annual holiday party, leads her to the coveted key, which promptly disappears into a strange and mysterious parallel world. It is there that Clara encounters a soldier named Phillip, a gang of mice, and the regents who preside over 3 Realms: the Land of Snowflakes, Land of Flowers, and Land of Sweets. Clara and Phillip must brave the ominous Fourth Realm, home to the tyrant Mother Ginger, to retrieve Clara's key and hopefully return harmony to the unstable world. Directed by Lasse Hallström and Joe Johnston. Released Nov. 2, 2018, also in 3-D, after an Oct. 24 international release. Stars Mackenzie Foy (Clara), Keira Knightley (Sugar Plum Fairy), Morgan Freeman (Drosselmeyer), Matthew Macfadyen (Mr. Stahlbaum), Helen Mirren (Mother Ginger), Eugenio Derbez (Hawthorn), Jayden Fowora-Knight (Phillip), Misty Copeland (Ballerina). 99 min. Inspired by E. T. A. Hoffmann's classic tale. James Newton Howard composed the score, which added a modern twist to themes from Tchaikovsky's 1892 ballet. Conductor Gustavo Dudamel makes a cameo in a moment referencing Leopold Stokowski's appearances in *Fantasia*. Filmed at Minley Manor in Hampshire, England, and at Pinewood Studios. From The Mark Gordon Company and Walt Pictures.

Nutcracker Suite, The (film) Music by Tchaikovsky, a segment of *Fantasia*.

Nutt House, The (TV) Series on NBC; aired Sep. 20–Oct. 25, 1989. The adventures of a zany hotel staff at the Nutt House, a New York City hotel owned by elderly Edwina Nutt. Stars Cloris Leachman (Mrs. Frick/Edwina Nutt), Harvey Korman (Reginald J. Tarkington), Brian McNamara (Charles Nutt III), Molly Hagan (Sally Lonnaneck). The TV show utilized the expensive replica of the Plaza Hotel lobby that had been built as a set for the Disney feature, *Big Business*. The series was created by Mel Brooks and Alan Spencer.

Nye, Bill SEE BILL NYE, THE SCIENCE GUY.

Nyong'o, Lupita Actress; appeared in *Queen of Katwe* (Nakku Harriet), the Black Panther films (Nakia), and as Maz Kanata in *Star Wars: The Force Awakens* and later films in the saga, and on Disney+ in *Black Is King* (as herself). She voiced Raksha in *The Jungle Book* (2016) and appeared on TV in *Disneyland 60: The Wonderful World of Disney*.

1. Offices, Walt Disney's 2. Orange Bird 3. Oswald the Lucky Rabbit 4. *Old Mill, The* (film)
5. *Onward* (film) 6. Oo-De-Lally 7. Orbitron 8. *Olaf Presents* (TV)

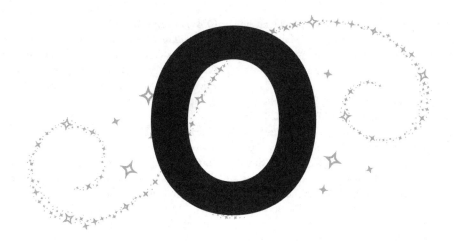

O Brother, Where Art Thou? (film) In the Depression-era Deep South, 3 escapees from a Mississippi prison chain gang—Everett Ulysses McGill, sweet-and-simple Delmar, and the perpetually angry Pete—embark on the adventure of a lifetime as they set out to pursue their freedom and return to their homes. With nothing to lose and still in shackles, they make a hasty run for their lives and end up on an incredible journey filled with challenging experiences and colorful characters. However, they must also match wits with the cunning and mysterious lawman Cooley, who tracks the men, bent on bringing the trio back to the prison farm. Released Dec. 22, 2000, in Los Angeles and New York City, and elsewhere Dec. 29 and Jan. 12, 2001. It had earlier been released abroad, first by Bac Films in France Aug. 30, 2000, after a preview at the Cannes Film Festival on May 13. Directed by Joel Coen. A Touchstone/Universal co-production. Stars George Clooney (McGill), John Turturro (Pete), Tim Blake Nelson (Delmar), Daniel Van Bargen (Cooley), Charles Durning (Pappy O'Daniel), John Goodman (Big Dan Teague), Holly Hunter (Penny Wharvey). 103 min. Filmed in CinemaScope on location in a 75-mile radius from Jackson, Mississippi, and at Disney's Golden Oak Ranch. Based on Homer's *The Odyssey*. The film was nominated for Academy Awards for Best Screenplay Adaptation and Cinematography. The multiplatinum soundtrack earned 5 Grammys, including the Album of the Year award, renewing interest in traditional bluegrass and folk music.

O Canada! (film) Glimpses of the beauty of Canada caught by the Circle-Vision 360 film cameras for Canada in EPCOT Center; opened Oct. 1, 1982. It took director Bill Bosché and his crew of 7 over 2 years to research and produce the film. It was updated Sep. 2007, with Martin Short as host. Bob Moline wrote the song "Canada (You're a Lifetime Journey)" for the original film; for the updated version, the song was re-recorded by *Canadian Idol* winner Eva Avila. The updated film closed Jul. 31, 2019, to be replaced the following year by *Canada Far and Wide in Circle-Vision 360*.

Oak Trail Golf Course, Disney's Family golf course at Walt Disney World; opened in 1990, replacing Wee Links. 9 holes.

Oaks Tavern Frontierland counter-service facility next to The Golden Horseshoe in Disneyland; open 1956–Sep. 1978. It later became Stage Door Cafe.

Oasis, The Area in Disney's Animal Kingdom at Walt Disney World; opened Apr. 22, 1998. Guests can roam lush, tropical garden pathways, just inside the park entrance, to view small animals in natural habitats.

Oasis, The Snack stand near the Jungle Cruise in the Magic Kingdom at Walt Disney World; open Jun. 1972–ca. 1998.

Oasis Bar & Grill Poolside quick-service restaurant at Disney's Polynesian Village Resort at Walt Disney World, offering Polynesian-themed food and cocktails; opened Mar. 17, 2016.

Obama, Barack On Jan. 19, 2012, as president, he delivered remarks on U.S. tourism on Main Street, U.S.A. in the Magic Kingdom at Walt Disney World.

Obi-Wan Kenobi (TV) A limited *Star Wars* series on Disney+; digitally premiered May 27, 2022. Set 10 years after the events of *Star Wars: Revenge of the Sith*, the atmospheric series explores how Obi-Wan went from warrior hero to Jedi Master. Stars Ewan McGregor (Obi-Wan Kenobi), Hayden Christensen (Darth Vader), Moses Ingram (Reva), Joel Edgerton (Owen Lars), Bonnie Piesse (Beru Lars), Kumail Nanjiani (Haja Estree), Rupert Friend (Grand Inquisitor), Sung Kang (Fifth Brother). From Lucasfilm. A making-of documentary, *Obi-Wan Kenobi: A Jedi's Return*, from Lucasfilm and Supper Club, was released Sep. 8, 2022, on Disney+.

O'Brien, Clay Child actor; appeared in *One Little Indian* (Mark) and *The Apple Dumpling Gang* (Bobby Bradley), and on TV in *Hog Wild* (Sterling) and as Shoie in *The Whiz Kid and the Carnival Caper* and *The Whiz Kid and the Mystery at Riverton*.

O'Brien, Cubby (Carl) Child actor/drummer; Mouseketeer from the 1950s *Mickey Mouse Club* TV show.

O'Brien, Edmond (1915–1985) Actor; appeared in *Moon Pilot* (McClosky), and on TV in the *Gallegher* series.

O'Brien, Ken (1915–1990) He joined the Disney Studio as an animator in 1937, working on the animated features from *Snow White and the Seven Dwarfs* to *Sleeping Beauty*. In 1962, he transferred to WED Enterprises, to help program Audio-Animatronics figures for the 1964–1965 New York World's Fair. He continued at WED working on such attractions as Pirates of the Caribbean, The Hall of Presidents, Country Bear Jamboree, and World of Motion. He retired in 1982.

O'Brien, Pat (1899–1983) Actor; appeared on TV in *I Captured the King of the Leprechauns* and *The Sky's the Limit* (Abner Therman).

Observatron Sculptural clock in Tomorrowland at Disneyland; debuted in 1998 on the site of the former Rocket Jets. According to the story, it is made up of satellite dishes and disks that broadcast musical messages into the universe every 15 min.

O'Byrne, Bryan (1931–2009) Actor; appeared in *The Million Dollar Duck* (Bank Teller), *The Apple Dumpling Gang Rides Again* (Photographer), and *Gus* (Grocery Store Manager), and on TV in *The High Flying Spy* (Telegraph Operator) and *Return of the Big Cat* (Perc).

Ocean Hop, The (film) Oswald the Lucky Rabbit cartoon; released Nov. 14, 1927. During a transatlantic hop, a rival wrecks Oswald's flying machine. Oswald solicits the help of an accommodating dachshund, who collapses just as they near their goal. Oswald finishes the journey in a parachute, earning the prize money.

Oceano Mediterranean restaurant in the Tokyo DisneySea Hotel MiraCosta at Tokyo Disney Resort; opened Sep. 4, 2001. Three dining areas feature ocean-inspired motifs.

Oceans (film) Disneynature documentary. Nearly 3/4 of the Earth's surface is covered by water, and the film chronicles the mysteries that lie beneath. Filmmakers armed with specially designed camera units spent 4 years filming sea life in 54 different locations, coming up with extraordinary images of 80 different species of fish, crabs, turtles, iguanas, whales, penguins, polar bears, and seals. Directed by Jacques Perrin and Jacques Cluzaud. Narrated by Pierce Brosnan. Released on Earth Day, Apr. 22, 2010, in the U.S., after a Jan. 22, 2010, release in Japan, and an Oct. 17, 2009, screening at the Tokyo International Film Festival. Disney handled the U.S. release. 84 min.

OceanWorld 3-D (film) Through the viewpoint of a sea turtle, viewers voyage to kelp forests off California, Australia's Great Barrier Reef, Mexico's Roca Partida Island, and Argentina's Peninsula Valdez encountering intriguing sea life—such as sharks, dolphins, lionfish, manta rays. Directed by Jean-Jacques Mantello. Produced by London's 3-D Entertainment and originally released in France on Aug. 26, 2009; Disneynature handled the U.S. and Mexican release. It took 7 years, and 200 hours of footage, to produce this first feature-length nature documentary filmed and released entirely in 3-D.

O'Connor, Carroll (1924–2001) Actor; appeared on TV in *Ride a Northbound Horse* (Mr. Davis).

O'Connor, Ken (1908–1998) Layout artist; started working at Disney in 1935 and served as art director or layout man on 13 features and nearly 100 shorts, including *Snow White and the Seven Dwarfs*, *Fantasia*, *Lady and the Tramp*, and the Academy Award–winning *Toot, Whistle, Plunk and Boom*. He retired in 1978 but returned to work on the development of park shows such as World of Motion and Universe of Energy at EPCOT Center and the film *Back to Neverland* [sic] in The Magic of Disney Animation tour at Disney-MGM Studios. He was honored with the Disney Legends Award in 1992.

October Road (TV) One-hour drama series on ABC; aired Mar. 15, 2007–Mar. 10, 2008. Nick Garrett, a young, acclaimed novelist at a crossroads in life returns to his hometown of Knights Ridge, Massachusetts, hoping to get over his writer's block. Back home on October Road, he must face the family and friends, including his widowed father and jilted girlfriend, 2 of those he wrote about unfavorably in his successful novel and whom he has avoided for the past 10 years. Stars Tom Berenger (The Commander), Geoff Stults (Eddie Latekka), Brad William Henke (Owen Rowan), Evan Jones (Ikey), Jay Paulson (Physical Phil), Warren Christie (Ray "Big Cat" Cataldo), Odette Yustman (Aubrey), Slade Pearce (Sam Daniels), Laura Prepon (Hannah Daniels), Bryan Greenberg (Nick Garrett). From GroupM and ABC TV Studio.

O'Day, Tim After several years in the Disneyland Entertainment division, he would hold roles in marketing, public relations, and communications, including executive marketing consultant for Buena Vista Publishing Group, director of communications for Disney Consumer Products, and director of publicity for Disneyland Resort. Among his contributions were the creation of an Olympic-size lap pool at Disneyland for U.S. gold medalists, procuring a Disneyland star on the Hollywood Walk of Fame, and putting Dumbo in the Smithsonian. He left the company in 2006 but continues to consult, produce events, and author Disney books.

Odd Life of Timothy Green, The (film) A happily married couple, Cindy and Jim Green, cannot wait to start a family, but when circumstances interfere, they bury notes in the garden about what their dream child would be like. When young Timothy, covered in mud, shows up on their doorstep one stormy night, Cindy and Jim—and their small town of Stanleyville—are in for a surprise. And from it they all learn that sometimes the unexpected can bring some of life's greatest gifts. Released Aug.

15, 2012. Directed by Peter Hedges. Stars Jennifer Garner (Cindy Green), Joel Edgerton (Jim Green), Cameron "CJ" Adams (Timothy Green), Ron Livingston (Franklin Crudstaff), Dianne Wiest Ms. Crudstaff), David Morse (James Green, Sr.), M. Emmet Walsh (Uncle Bub). 104 min. Set in Stanleyville, a fictitious small town in Anywhere, U.S.A., the film's color palette was influenced by the classic American paintings of Norman Rockwell and Edward Hopper. Filmed across Georgia, including Atlanta, Newnan, Monroe, Decatur, Tucker, Rex, and Canton.

O'Donnell, Chris Actor; appeared in *The Three Musketeers* (D'Artagnan) and *Mad Love* (Matt Leland), and on TV in *Grey's Anatomy* (Dr. Finn Dandridge).

O'Donnell, Rosie Actress; provided the voice of Terk in *Tarzan* and appeared in *Another Stakeout* (Gina Garrett). On TV, she voiced Bouncing Bumble Queen in *Jake and the Never Land Pirates* and appeared in *The Fosters* (Rita Hendricks), *When We Rise* (Del Martin), *SMILF* (Tutu), *Walt Disney World's 25th Anniversary Party*, and the *Disney Parks Frozen Christmas Celebration* (2014). At Disney California Adventure, she was co-host of The Bakery Tour, hosted by Boudin Bakery.

O'Donovan, Leo J., SJ Member of the Disney Board of Directors Sep. 30, 1996–Mar. 8, 2007.

Odyssey Originally a counter-service restaurant between Future World and World Showcase in EPCOT; opened Oct. 1, 1982. The hexagonal facility is located on a pool of water, reachable by several bridges/walkways. Closed Jul. 30, 1994, to be used for special events, banquets, and EPCOT festivals. From Oct. 1, 2019–Mar. 13, 2022, the pavilion hosted Walt Disney Imagineering presents the EPCOT Experience, a preview of upcoming attractions.

Of Cats and Men (film) A 16-mm release of footage from a TV show; released in Apr. 1968. Traces the history of the cat—a god in Egyptian days, an evil spirit in the Dark Ages, and a pet today.

Of Horses and Men (film) Educational film; released in Aug. 1968. The film tells the story of the horse and how humans have depended upon it.

Of Kings and Prophets (TV) Series on ABC; aired Mar. 8–15, 2016. An epic biblical saga of faith, ambition, and betrayal as told through the eyes of the battle-weary King Saul, the resentful prophet Samuel, and the resourceful young shepherd David, all on a collision course with destiny that will change the world. One thousand years before Christ, the first King of the Israelites, Saul, struggles to unify the Twelve Tribes of Israel and defend his fledgling nation against savage enemy attacks. But he comes to realize that his greatest threat emerges not from his known enemies but from a simple shepherd, David. Stars Ray Winstone (Saul), Olly Rix (David), Mohammad Bakri (Samuel), Simone Kessell (Queen Ahinoam), Nathaniel Parker (King Achish). From ABC Studios.

Off Beat (film) As a favor, library clerk Joe Gower takes the place of his friend, police officer Abe Washington, at a dance audition for cops. He is supposed to fail, and get his friend out of the show, but he falls in love with his dance partner, hostage negotiator Rachel, who thinks he is really a cop, and passes the audition. Joe continues the impersonation in order to win Rachel, but finally decides to confess. But before he can do so, he is taken hostage—still in uniform—by bank robbers. He foils the robbers, and Rachel learns the truth. They realize their love makes up for his masquerade, and dance together at the policeman's show. Released Apr. 11, 1986. Directed by Michael Dinner. A Touchstone film. 92 min. Stars Judge Reinhold (Joe Gower), Meg Tilly (Rachel Wareham), Cleavant Derricks (Abe Washington), Joe Mantegna (Pete Peterson), Jacques D'Amboise (August), Amy Wright (Mary Ellen Grunewald), John Turturro (Neil Pepper). This was Judge Reinhold's first starring picture. The film was made entirely in New York City at locations ranging from the bustling sections of Midtown Manhattan and SoHo to a tree-lined residential section of Brooklyn. Among the key shooting sites were Central Park, the Times Square subway station, the Vivian Beaumont Theater in Lincoln Center, the New York School of Ballet on the Upper West Side, and the New York Public Library.

Off His Rockers (film) The magical tale of a young boy who has abandoned his faithful rocking horse playmate in favor of the latest video games. Unwilling to be "put out to pasture," the wooden horse uses some inventive and hilarious means to remind his fickle friend of the great times they used to have when his imagination was free to roam. Soon the boy is back in the saddle again as he gallops off into the sunset in search of exciting new adventures.

Special experimental cartoon, making some use of computer animation released Jul. 17, 1992. Directed by Barry Cook. Animated in Disney-MGM Studios at Walt Disney World. 5 min.

Off the Hook Pool lounge at Aulani, A Disney Resort & Spa; opened Aug. 29, 2011. Designed to resemble a fisherman's seaside shack.

Off the Map (TV) Drama series on ABC; aired Jan. 12–Apr. 6, 2011. A tiny town in the South American jungle has one understaffed, understocked medical clinic, founded by a legendary and enigmatic young chief of surgery from UCLA, Dr. Ben Keeton, and his right-hand man, Dr. Otis Cole. Idealistic Dr. Lily Brenner arrives, with fellow doctors Mina Minard and Tommy Fuller. All 5 doctors have had problems with their lives and try to remember why they wanted to become doctors in the first place. In the jungle, the doctors learn how to save lives in the most challenging environment they have ever worked in. Stars Martin Henderson (Ben Keeton), Caroline Dhavernas (Lily Brenner), Zach Gilford (Tommy Fuller), Mamie Gummer (Mina Minard), Jason George (Otis Cole), Valerie Cruz (Zitajalehrena "Zee" Alvarez), Jonathan Castellanos (Charlie), Rachelle Lefevre (Ryan Clark). Filmed in Hawai'i. From ABC Studios.

Off the Page Gallery/shop in Hollywood Land in Disney California Adventure; opened Feb. 8, 2001. Features animation-related merchandise, books, and artwork.

Officer Duck (film) Donald Duck cartoon released Oct. 10, 1939. Directed by Clyde Geronimi. Donald is a cop who has to serve eviction papers on Pete. He finally manages to arrest him by posing as a doorstep baby to get access to the house.

Offices, Walt Disney's Walt Disney had 2 offices in the 3H wing of the Animation Building at the Disney Studio in Burbank. He met with visitors in his formal office, which was adjoined to a working office where he conducted his day-to-day business. After his death in 1966, the offices were locked, and the furnishings were left intact. In 1970, the suite became the first home of the Walt Disney Archives, and the offices were photographed and inventoried by Archives founder Dave Smith. This documentation, as well as original blueprints, proved especially useful when the offices were reconstructed and displayed at the Disneyland Opera House from 1973–2005. The scene outside the window was a photographic backdrop which had been used at the Studio when a version of Walt's office was built on a soundstage for several of his TV lead-ins. In 2001, the working office was moved to the Walt Disney: One Man's Dream gallery at Disney-MGM Studios (now Disney's Hollywood Studios). The formal office was later displayed in the "Treasures of the Walt Disney Archives" exhibit at the Ronald Reagan Presidential Library and Museum, Jul. 5, 2012–Apr. 30, 2013. In 2015, the Archives staff restored both offices to their original home in the Animation Building, with a dedication ceremony held Dec. 15. In addition to original furnishings, awards, and some of Walt's personal items, the permanent display for Disney employees includes rotating exhibits on various Disney subjects.

Oga's Cantina Watering hole in Star Wars: Galaxy's Edge; opened May 31, 2019, in Disneyland and Aug. 29, 2019, in Disney's Hollywood Studios at Walt Disney World. Intergalactic concoctions are served while musical entertainment is provided by droid DJ R-3X, the former pilot from Star Tours. In the story, bounty hunters, smugglers, and travelers visit to refuel and conduct meetings—no questions asked.

Ogg, Sammy Actor; appeared in *Adventure in Dairyland* and as Joe Simpson in *Spin and Marty* on the *Mickey Mouse Club*.

Oh, Teacher (film) Oswald the Lucky Rabbit cartoon; released Sep. 19, 1927. Oswald takes his girlfriend out on a bicycle ride, but a rival cat takes possession of the vehicle. After they all fall in a lake, Oswald sets matters right.

Oh, What a Knight (film) Oswald the Lucky Rabbit cartoon; released in 1928. With his lariat and mule, Oswald approaches a castle and joins his ladylove on her balcony, in spite of her warnings about an irate parent. The two manage to escape the castle and end up in outer space, heading earthward blissfully unaware of everything but each other.

'Ohana Restaurant in the Great Ceremonial House in Disney's Polynesian Village Resort at Walt Disney World; opened Apr. 12, 1995, taking the place of the Papeete Bay Verandah. Guests enjoy live entertainment as Hawaiian-flavored specialties are grilled in an 18-foot semicircular fire pit, on skewers up to 3 feet long, and then served family style.

O'Hara, Catherine Actress; appeared in *Dick Tracy* (Texie Garcia), *Betsy's Wedding* (Gloria Henner), *A Simple Twist of Fate* (Mrs. Simon), and *Tall Tale* (Calamity Jane). She voiced Sally and Shock in *Tim Burton's The Nightmare Before Christmas*; Tina – Alien Mom in *Chicken Little*; Kata in *Brother Bear 2*; Susan Frankenstein, Weird Girl, and Gym Teacher in *Frankenweenie* (2012); and Morgana in *Sofia the First*. At Walt Disney World, she is a narrator of *Canada Far and Wide in Circle-Vision 360* at EPCOT.

O'Hara, Paige Actress; voiced Belle in *Beauty and the Beast*, *Ralph Breaks the Internet*, and other appearances of the character. She appeared in *Enchanted* (Angela), and on TV in *A Magical Walt Disney World Christmas* and *Beauty and the Beast: A 30th Celebration*. She was named a Disney Legend in 2011.

Oilspot and Lipstick (film) Special computer-animated cartoon; released at the SIGGRAPH convention in Anaheim on Jul. 28, 1987. Computer animation is utilized to bring to life objects in a junkyard. The junk monster threatens 2 small "junk" dogs, but the boy dog (Oilspot) manages to defeat the monster and rescue his girlfriend (Lipstick).

O. J.: Made in America (film/TV) Exploring the themes of race and celebrity, this documentary traces the story of Orenthal James Simpson from his fame as a football star, to his being arrested on charges of murdering his ex-wife, Nicole, and Ron Goldman; his trial and acquittal; and the Las Vegas crime that eventually put him in jail. Directed by Ezra Edelman. Opened in theaters in New York and Los Angeles May 20, 2016, after a Jan. 22 premiere at the Sundance Film Festival. Shown on ESPN in four 2-hour episodes beginning Jun. 11, 2016. From ESPN Films. It won the Academy Award for documentary feature and Emmy Awards for outstanding directing for a nonfiction program and outstanding picture editing for a nonfiction program.

Okun, Erwin (1934–1992) He joined Disney in 1981 to handle corporate communications, became a corporate officer in 1984, and by 1992 was senior vice president. He prepared corporate press releases, dealt with press inquiries, and helped write the company's annual report.

Ol' Swimmin' 'ole, The (film) Oswald the Lucky Rabbit cartoon; released Feb. 6, 1928. Oswald and friends enjoy the frivolity of the local swimming hole. They use a mule as a springboard and, unwisely, the town marshal's suspenders as a swing.

Olaf Friendly snowman character created by Elsa's powers in *Frozen*; voiced by Josh Gad.

Olaf Presents (TV) Animated short-form series; released digitally Nov. 12, 2021, on Disney+. Olaf is producer, actor, and set builder for his unique "retelling" of favorite Disney animated tales, taking on such roles as a mermaid, a genie, and a lion king for his Arendelle audience. Directed by Hyrum Osmond. Voiced by Josh Gad.

Olaf's Frozen Adventure (film) Animated featurette. Olaf enlists Sven to help him create some Christmas family traditions for Anna and Elsa. Directed by Kevin Deters and Stevie Wermers. Released theatrically Nov. 22, 2017, with *Coco* for 2 weeks; then aired as a TV special on ABC Dec. 14. Voices include Josh Gad (Olaf), Kristen Bell (Anna), Idina Menzel (Elsa), Jonathan Groff (Kristoff). 22 min. From Walt Disney Animation Studios.

Old Army Game, The (film) Donald Duck cartoon released Nov. 5, 1943. Directed by Jack King. Though Donald is in the army, he enjoys his evenings out by fooling Sgt. Pete, leaving a snoring record in the barracks. But one evening he is caught, escaping in 1 of 3 boxes, which turns into the famous shell game. A chase ensues.

Old Curiosity Shop, The (TV) Four-hour Disney Channel Premiere Film; aired Mar. 19–20, 1995. In 19th-century England, Nell's secure and innocent childhood is threatened when the family's curio shop, owned by her compulsive gambling grandfather, is repossessed by the evil moneylender Daniel Quilp. Nell and her grandfather must take to the road in search of safety and happiness. On their travels, they encounter bizarre and fascinating characters who make the world itself seem like a curiosity shop. Directed by Kevin Connor. Stars Peter Ustinov (Grandfather), Tom Courtenay (Quilp), Sally Walsh (Nell), James Fox (Single Gentleman), William Mannering (Kit). Filming took place at various locales throughout Ireland, with the majority of the film being shot at Ardmore Studios in Dublin. The streets of Dickensian London, as well as Quilp's wharf and dockland, were built entirely for the production and then burned to the ground as part of the film's dramatic conclusion.

Old Dogs (film) Two best friends—one unlucky-in-love divorcée and the other a fun-loving bachelor—have their lives turned upside down when they are unexpectedly charged with the care of 6-year-old twins while on the verge of the biggest business deal of their lives. The not-so-kid-savvy bachelors stumble in their efforts to take care of the twins, leading to one debacle after another, and perhaps to a newfound understanding of what's really important in life. A Touchstone film. Released Nov. 25, 2009. Directed by Walt Becker. Stars John Travolta (Charlie), Robin Williams (Dan), Kelly Preston (Vicki), Ella Bleu Travolta (Emily), Conner Rayburn (Zach), Seth Green (Craig), Lori Loughlin (Amanda), Matt Dillon (Barry), Ann-Margret (Martha). 88 min. Kelly Preston is John Travolta's wife; this marks the first time the couple has appeared in the same film in more than 20 years. Ella Bleu is their daughter. In addition, John Travolta's brother, Sam, and sister, Margaret, had small roles as a singing waiter and hostess. Filmed on location in New York City and Miami, with the zoo scene at the Santa Ana (California) Zoo.

Old Key West Resort, Disney's New name, in Jan. 1996, for the Disney Vacation Club Resort at Walt Disney World. Disney Vacation Club Members enjoy the romance of the Florida Keys in the fictional community of Conch Flats, with dining at Olivia's Cafe, Good's Food to Go, Turtle Shack Poolside Snacks, and the Gurgling Suitcase Libations & Spirits, and with shopping at the Conch Flats General Store. A recreational highlight is the 149,000-gallon Sandcastle Pool. The resort initially sold out its membership inventory at 25,000 member families in 1998. New accommodations were added in Nov.–Dec. 1999.

Old King Cole (film) Silly Symphony cartoon released Jul. 29, 1933. Directed by Dave Hand. King Cole's ball at the castle is attended by the many characters of Mother Goose, emerging from the pages of a large book. Later, problems occur in trying to get all the characters back into the book.

Old MacDonald Duck (film) Donald Duck cartoon released Sep. 12, 1941. Directed by Jack King. Donald, to the accompaniment of "Old MacDonald Had a Farm," does chores, and feeds the chickens and pigs. When he attempts to milk a cow, a fly bothers him, and his attempts to combat it causes the pail to be upset and Donald to be kicked by the cow.

Old Mill, The (film) Silly Symphony cartoon released Nov. 5, 1937. Directed by Wilfred Jackson. The first film to use the multiplane camera. Night in an old mill is dramatically depicted in this Oscar-winning short in which the frightened occupants, including birds, timid mice, owls, and other creatures, try to stay safe and dry as a storm approaches. As the thunderstorm worsens, the mill wheel begins to turn and the whole mill threatens to blow apart until at last, the storm subsides. Besides the award for Best Cartoon, Walt Disney received a 2nd Academy Award, a Scientific and Technical Class II plaque, for the design and application of the multiplane camera.

Old Mill, The Fantasyland quick-service restaurant in Disneyland Paris; opened Apr. 12, 1992. A Ferris wheel–style attraction, Les Pirouettes du Vieux Moulin, was added to the mill Jun. 5, 1993, but only operated through the rest of the decade.

Old Port Royale Central shopping and food-service area for Disney's Caribbean Beach Resort at Walt Disney World; opened Oct. 1, 1988. Features Centertown Market (quick-service dining) and Calypso Trading Post. It also became the front desk and concierge area in 2018, after the resort's Customs House was removed to make way for Disney's Riviera Resort.

Old Sequoia (film) Donald Duck cartoon released Dec. 21, 1945. Directed by Jack King. Forest ranger Don is charged with guarding a sequoia tree, but he must deal with some troublesome beavers who, despite Donald's pleading and promises, manage to fell the tree. Donald is fired.

Old Yeller (film) In the late 1860s on a ranch in Texas, a big, mongrel yellow dog befriends the Coates family, and in particular the 2 boys, Travis and Arliss. He proves his loyalty by saving Arliss from a huge bear, Travis from wild pigs, and Mrs. Coates from a wolf infected with hydrophobia. Though Travis shoots the wolf, he must soon after shoot the dog, Old Yeller, who has contracted the dreaded disease. Travis is inconsolable until he accepts one of Old Yeller's puppies as his own for its uncanny resemblance to Old Yeller. Released Dec. 25, 1957. Directed by Robert Stevenson. 84 min. Based on the well-known book by Fred Gipson, the film grossed over $8 million in its initial release and has proved a perennial Disney favorite. Stars Dorothy McGuire (Katie Coates), Fess Parker (Jim Coates), Tommy Kirk (Travis), Kevin Corcoran (Arliss). The dog who played Old Yeller was named Spike. Gil George and Oliver Wallace wrote the title song. Two educational films were made from the film, *Love and Duty: Which Comes First?* (1975) and an episode in the Films as Literature series. A program on the *Disneyland* TV series, *The Best Doggoned Dog in the World*, aired shortly before the film's release to promote the film. *Old Yeller* was reissued in 1965 and in 1974.

Olde World Antiques Liberty Square shop in the Magic Kingdom at Walt Disney World; open Mar. 1972–Jan. 30, 1996. European furniture, perfumes, toys, paintings, tools, and other miscellaneous items represented the international influence prevalent in the U.S. since before its birth. The antiques buyer, Otto Rabby, spent several weeks in Europe each year searching for unusual items to bring back to Walt Disney World. SEE ALSO ONE-OF-A-KIND (DISNEYLAND) AND VON OTTO'S ANTIQUES.

Oldest Rookie, The (TV) Series on CBS; aired Sep. 16, 1987–Jan. 6, 1988. After 25 years on the police force as a senior-ranking public relations officer, Ike Porter decides to hit the streets and is paired with a freewheeling partner, Tony Jonas, who is half his age. Through a growing mutual respect for each other, their own brand of charm, and unorthodox methods, the 2 solve more than their share of cases, while driving their superiors crazy. Stars Paul Sorvino (Ike), D. W. Moffett (Tony), Raymond J. Barry (Zaga), Marshall Bell (Lane).

ʻŌlelo Room, The Upscale lounge at Aulani, A Disney Resort & Spa; opened Aug. 29, 2011. ʻŌlelo is Hawaiian for "word," so the décor consists of carvings of common objects labeled with their Hawaiian names.

Oliveira, José (1914–1995) Voice actor/musician; he provided the voice of José Carioca.

Oliver Lead character, a kitten, in *Oliver & Company*; voiced by Joey Lawrence.

Oliver, Barret Actor; appeared in *Frankenweenie* (1984), and on TV in *Spot Marks the X*.

Oliver & Company (film) The Oliver Twist story animated with a twist. The setting is New York City, and Oliver is a kitten and Fagin the human master of a pack of pickpocket dogs. When a wealthy little girl from Fifth Avenue finds Oliver and takes him uptown to live in her mansion, Fagin's evil boss, Sykes, steps in and kidnaps the pair. His nasty plan is foiled, however, when Oliver's motley crew of dog buddies, aided by Jenny's prissy poodle, Georgette, decide to use their street *savoir faire* in order to rescue their feline friend. Released Nov. 18, 1988. Directed by George Scribner. 72 min. With the voices of Joey Lawrence (Oliver), Billy Joel (Dodger), Cheech Marin (Tito), Richard Mulligan (Einstein), Roscoe Lee Browne (Francis), Sheryl Lee Ralph (Rita), Dom DeLuise (Fagin), Robert Loggia (Sykes), Bette Midler (Georgette). Then 12-year-old Joey Lawrence would later go on to become a teenage heartthrob on *Blossom*. Six supervising animators and a team of over 300 artists and technicians worked for over 2½ years to create this hand-drawn feature film in the time-honored Disney tradition. More than a million story sketches and drawings were required to produce the 119,275 hand-painted cels that comprise the finished film. Designers went to New York City and photographed street scenes from a dog's perspective—18 inches off the ground—getting stares from passersby but providing excellent reference material for the layout artists. To give the backgrounds a contemporary and hard-edged look, Xerox overlays were used, the first time for this approach since *One Hundred and One Dalmatians*. Many of the inanimate objects in the film were created and animated on the computer—cars, cabs, buses, Sykes's limousine, Fagin's trike (part scooter and part shopping cart), a cement mixer, a sewer pipe, a spiral staircase, a piano, subway tunnels and trains, cityscapes, and even the Brooklyn Bridge. This was the first film to have its own department set up expressly for the purpose of generating computer animation. Many different songwriters contributed to the production, including Howard Ashman and Barry Mann ("Once Upon a Time in New York City"), Dan Hartman and Charlie Midnight ("Why Should I Worry?"), Barry Manilow, Jack Feldman, and Bruce Sussman ("Perfect Isn't Easy"), and Dean Pitchford and Tom Snow ("Streets of Gold"). Rereleased in 1996.

Oliver Twist (TV) Movie on *The Wonderful World of Disney*; first aired Nov. 16, 1997. An orphaned boy in 19th-century England is given shelter and clothed by an old criminal who provides a family-type setting for many orphan boys, while preying on their naiveté and teaching them to steal. Directed by Tony Bill. Stars Richard Dreyfuss (Fagin), Elijah Wood (The Artful Dodger), David O'Hara (Bill Sykes), Alex Trench (Oliver), Antoine Byrne (Nancy). This represents 10-year-old Alex Trench's acting debut. Dreyfuss's young son, Harry, played one of the street urchins. Filming took place at Ardmore Studios in Dublin, and at local locations.

Olivia Flaversham Cute child mouse whose father is kidnapped in *The Great Mouse Detective*; voiced by Susanne Pollatschek.

Olivia Rodrigo: driving home 2 u (a SOUR film) (TV) A Disney+ original documentary; digitally released Mar. 25, 2022. Singer-songwriter Olivia Rodrigo takes a familiar road trip from Salt Lake City, where she began writing her debut album *SOUR*, to Los Angeles. Along the way, she recounts memories of writing and creating it. Directed by Stacey Lee. From Disney Branded Television, Interscope Films, and Supper Club.

Olivia's Cafe Restaurant at Disney's Old Key West Resort at Walt Disney World; opened Dec. 20, 1991. The backstory goes that Olivia Farnsworth, longtime resident of Conch Flats, would invite curious passersby to pull up a chair at her cottage along Turtle Krawl. Her cooking became so popular that she created this haven for guests to enjoy her island-inspired dishes.

Ollie Hopnoodle's Haven of Bliss (TV) A Disney Channel Premiere Film; first aired Aug. 6, 1988. The trials of a family in the 1950s as they prepare for 2 weeks of vacation. Directed by Dick Bartlett. 90 min. Stars James B. Sikking ("the Old Man"), Dorothy Lyman (Mom), Jerry O'Connell (Ralph), Jason Clarke Adams (Randy).

Olmos, Edward James Actor; appeared on TV in *Marvel's Agents of S.H.I.E.L.D.* (Roberto Gonzales) and *Bless This Mess* (Randy), and voiced El Diablo in *Beverly Hills Chihuahua*, Chicharrón in *Coco*, and King Pescoro in *Elena of Avalor*. Also narrated *D.A.R.E. to Care: A Program for Parents*.

Olsen, Jack (1923–1980) He joined Disney in 1955 to handle merchandising at Disneyland, serving as director of merchandise at the park until 1970, when he moved to Florida to begin the merchandise operation at Walt Disney World. He retired in 1977 and was named a Disney Legend in 2005.

Olsen, Moroni (1889–1954) Actor; provided the voice of the Magic Mirror in *Snow White and the Seven Dwarfs*.

Olson, Nancy Actress; appeared in *Pollyanna* (Nancy Furman), *The Absent-Minded Professor* (Betsy Carlisle), *Son of Flubber* (Betsy Brainard), *Smith* (Norah), *Snowball Express* (Sue Baxter), and *Flubber* (cameo as secretary), and on TV in *The Age of Believing: The Disney Live Action Classics*.

'Olu Mel SEE DUFFY AND FRIENDS.

Olympic Champ, The (film) Goofy cartoon released Oct. 9, 1942. Directed by Jack Kinney. Goofy traces the history of the Olympic Games by demonstrating various events—walking, running, hurdles, pole-vaulting, discus, and javelin throwing.

Olympic Elk, The (film) True-Life Adventure featurette released Feb. 13, 1952. Directed by James Algar. Depicts the lives of elk living on the Olympia Peninsula in Washington State, including their feeding habits, breeding, and battles for supremacy of the herd.

Olympic Games Walt Disney helped produce the pageantry for the Olympic Winter Games in Squaw Valley (now known as Olympic Valley), California, beginning Feb. 18, 1960, with Disney artist John Hench in charge of décor, designing the towering sculptures and the Olympic torch. In 1932, *Barnyard Olympics,* a cartoon starring Mickey Mouse, was released to coincide with the Summer Olympics in Los Angeles. For the 1984 Los Angeles Summer Olympics, Disney Studio publicity artist Bob Moore designed the Sam the Olympic Eagle mascot.

O'Malley, J. Pat (1901–1985) Actor; appeared in *Son of Flubber* (sign painter), and on TV in *The Adventures of Spin and Marty* (Perkins) and *The Swamp Fox* (Sgt. O'Reilly). He voiced many characters, including Cyril in *The Adventures of Ichabod and Mr. Toad*; the Walrus, Carpenter, Tweedledee, and Tweedledum in *Alice in Wonderland*; Jasper Badun and The Colonel in *One Hundred and One Dalmatians*; Colonel Hathi and Buzzie in *The Jungle Book*; and Otto in *Robin Hood*.

Omega Connection, The (TV) Two-hour movie aired Mar. 18, 1979. Directed by Robert Clouse. Young American government agent, Luther Starling, arrives in London to vacation with a friend, Roger Pike, but immediately gets involved unintentionally with intrigue surrounding a defecting Eastern European scientist. Through the use of James Bond-like inventions, Luther and Roger are able to outwit the international crime organization which is trying to abduct the scientist. Stars Jeffrey Byron, Larry Cedar, Roy Kinnear, Lee Montague, Mona Washbourne, David Kossoff, Frank Windsor. Filmed on location in London. Released theatrically abroad as *The London Connection*.

Omnibus Main Street, U.S.A. vehicles in Disneyland, beginning in 1956. Also in the Magic Kingdom at Walt Disney World, beginning Oct. 1, 1971. The double-decker buses were urgently needed to transport guests around the World Showcase Lagoon in EPCOT Center, so those from California and the Magic Kingdom were moved to EPCOT in the 1980s, where they operated for many years. Also began at World Bazaar in Tokyo Disneyland Apr. 15, 1983, in Disneyland Paris Apr. 12, 1992, and in Hong Kong Disneyland Sep. 12, 2005.

Omnisphere (film) Projected in Omnimax 70 mm on hemispherical screens, this film was produced as part of Horizons in EPCOT Center and included footage of a space shuttle blastoff, a flight over Manhattan, and a computerized journey across the Earth's surface. Horizons closed Jan. 9, 1999.

On Ice (film) Mickey Mouse cartoon released Sep. 28, 1935. Directed by Ben Sharpsteen. Mickey and friends have various levels of enjoyment skating on a frozen river. As Mickey and Minnie glide romantically, Donald plays tricks on Pluto and ends up in trouble himself with a kite, from which Mickey must save him.

On Pointe (TV) A 6-part docuseries on Disney+; digitally premiered Dec. 18, 2020. Follows the lives of students pursuing their dreams to become ballet dancers at the School of American Ballet in New York City. While older students rigorously train for professional careers, younger ones are put through their paces as they rehearse and perform in *George Balanchine's The Nutcracker* onstage at Lincoln Center. Directed/produced by Larissa Bills. From Imagine Documentaries and DCTV.

On Promised Land (TV) A Disney Channel Premiere Film; first aired Apr. 17, 1994. A poignant drama set in the American South of the 1950s about 2 families, 1 black and 1 white, and the dreams and broken promises that bind them together. Directed by Joan Tewkesbury. Stars Joan Plowright (Mrs. Appletree), Norman D. Golden II, Judith Ivey. 99 min.

On Seal Island SEE SEAL ISLAND.

On the Record Stage presentation set in a recording studio, consisting of over 50 classic Disney songs performed by a cast of singers, dancers, and musicians. Directed by Robert Longbottom. It premiered at the Palace Theater in Cleveland on Nov. 9, 2004, with an official opening of Nov. 19, prior to setting out on a national tour until Jul. 31, 2005. The original cast was headed by Emily Skinner and Brian Sutherland.

On Vacation (TV) Show aired Mar. 7, 1956. Directed by Jack Hannah. Some later reruns as *On Vacation with Mickey Mouse and Friends*. Jiminy Cricket hosts and tries to find the other Disney characters, but they are all on vacation.

On Your Own (film) Educational film; released in Sep. 1985. The film outlines safety measures and self-care skills for children who are home alone, and methods for confronting their fears.

Once and Again (TV) One-hour series on ABC; aired Sep. 21, 1999–May 2, 2001. Two divorced parents meet by chance and start a romance but are caught in a cross fire of conflicting opinions about their relationship from children, ex-spouses, and society at large. Stars Bill Campbell (Rick Sammler), Sela Ward (Lily Manning), Shane West (Eli), Julia Whelan (Grace), Susanna Thompson (Karen), Jeffrey Nordling (Jake). From Touchstone Television and the Bedford Falls Company.

Once Upon a Dream Song from *Sleeping Beauty*; written by Sammy Fain and Jack Lawrence. Adapted from a theme by Tchaikovsky.

Once Upon a Mattress (TV) A 2-hour movie on *The Wonderful World of Disney*; first aired Dec. 18, 2005. A made-for-TV version of the 1959 Broadway musical comedy based on *The Princess and the Pea*. Directed by Kathleen Marshall. Stars Carol Burnett (Queen Aggravain), Tracey Ullman (Princess Winnifred), Denis O'Hare (Prince Dauntless), Zooey Deschanel (Lady Larken), Michael Boatman (Jester), Edward Hibbert (Wizard), Matthew Morrison (Sir Harry), Tom Smothers (King Sextimus). Burnett originated the role of Princess Winnifred in 1959, when the play debuted off-Broadway and later moved to the Great White Way. It eventually became one of her signature roles, not only onstage but also in 2 TV productions, in 1964 and in 1972. Produced by Mattress Productions, Ltd. in association with Touchstone Television.

Once Upon a Mouse (film) Kaleidoscopic magic carpet ride through the world of Disney animation, including segments from hundreds of films shown through the use of montages, collages, computerized optical effects, behind-the-scenes footage, and special tributes to Walt Disney and Mickey. Released Jul. 10, 1981. Produced by Kramer/Rocklin Studios in association with Walt Disney Productions. 28 min.

Once Upon a Snowman (TV) Animated *Frozen* short; digitally released Oct. 23, 2020, on Disney+. The previously untold origins of Olaf are revealed as the snowman first comes to life and searches for his identity in the mountains outside Arendelle. Directed by Dan Abraham and Trent Correy. 8 min. Voices include Josh Gad (Olaf), Idina Menzel (Elsa), Kristen Bell (Anna), Jonathan Groff (Kristoff), Chris Williams (Oaken).

Once Upon a Time (film) A 1944 Columbia film; starring Janet Blair and Cary Grant as a freewheeling promoter who finds a caterpillar who can dance. The caterpillar, Curly, is a child's pet, and the kid does not want to give Curly up when the promoter wants him to go to work for Walt Disney and become famous. An actor (Walter Fenner) portrays Walt Disney in the film.

Once Upon a Time (TV) Drama series on ABC; aired Oct. 23, 2011–May 18, 2018. Emma Swan, a 28-year-old bail bonds collector, has been on her own ever since she was abandoned as a baby. But when Henry, the son she gave up years ago, finds her, everything starts to change. He believes that Emma actually comes from an alternate world and is Snow White and Prince Charming's missing daughter. According to his book of fairy tales, they sent her away to protect her from the Evil Queen's curse, which trapped the fairytale world forever, frozen in time, and brought them into our modern world. Emma doesn't believe a word, but when she brings Henry back to Storybrooke, she finds herself drawn to this unusual boy and his strange New England town. Stars Jennifer Morrison (Emma Swan), Jared Gilmore (Henry), Ginnifer Goodwin (Snow White/Mary Margaret), Robert Carlyle (Rumpelstiltskin/Mr. Gold), Lana Parrilla (Evil Queen/Regina), Jamie Dornan (Sheriff Graham), Josh Dallas (Prince Charming/John Doe), Raphael Sbarge (Jiminy Cricket/Archie).

Once Upon a Time Sunset Boulevard shop in

Disney's Hollywood Studios; opened Jun. 12, 1994. Apparel, jewelry, and headwear are sold in a movie palace that resembles the Carthay Circle Theatre.

Once Upon a Time SEE MAGIC, THE MEMORIES, AND YOU!, THE (WALT DISNEY WORLD SHOW).

"Once Upon a Time" Adventure Fantasyland attraction inside Enchanted Storybook Castle at Shanghai Disneyland; opened Jun. 16, 2016. Summoned by the Enchanted Storybook to be part of Snow White's adventure, guests follow a trail of pixie dust to the Magic Mirror, which serves as a portal to the princess's world. During the interactive adventure, guests meet the creatures who befriended Snow White in the forest, confront the Evil Queen, and even help to tidy the Seven Dwarfs' cottage.

Once Upon a Time in New York City Song from *Oliver & Company*; written by Howard Ashman and Barry Mann.

Once Upon a Time in Wonderland (TV) One-hour series on ABC; aired Oct. 10, 2013–Apr. 3, 2014. In a new twist on the *Alice in Wonderland* story, Alice cannot get anyone to believe her stories about a strange new land on the other side of a rabbit hole. Thinking her insane, doctors intend to cure her with a treatment that will make her forget everything. But in her heart Alice knows this world is real, and just in the nick of time, the sardonic Knave of Hearts and the irrepressible White Rabbit arrive to save her from her fate and return with her to Wonderland. Stars Sophie Lowe (Alice), Michael Socha (Knave of Hearts), Peter Gadiot (Cyrus), Emma Rigby (Red Queen), Naveen Andrews (Jafar), John Lithgow (voice of White Rabbit). From ABC Studios.

Once Upon a Time . . . The Disney Princess Shoppe SEE TINKER BELL TOY SHOPPE (DISNEY-LAND).

Once Upon a Toy A 16,000-sq.-ft. toy store at Downtown Disney Marketplace (now the Market-place at Disney Springs) at Walt Disney World; opened Jul. 19, 2002, taking the place of Harrington Bay Clothiers, with several themed areas offering toys, games, and Disney collectibles. The Disney Bear, who later evolved into Duffy, originated at the shop's opening. In 2017, much of the store was replaced by The VOID.

Once Upon a Warrior (film) In the land called Sangarashtra, a 9-year-old girl, Moksha, using her special healing powers (and helped by a blind swordsman named Yodha), attempts to save her country from the tyranny of an evil sorceress, Irendri. Directed by Prakash Kovelamudi. Released in India Jan. 14, 2011, and in the U.S. Jan. 21, 2011. Stars Ali (Kufli), Ravi Babu (Sudigundam), Tanikella Bharani (Kaksheera), Brahmanandam (Jaffa), Shruti K. Haasan (Priya), Harshitha (Moksha), Lakshmi Manchu (Irendri), Vallabhaneni Ramji (Druki), Siddharth (Yodha). The first Disney film in the Telugu language; the original title was *Anaganaga O Dheerudu*. Filmed in wide-screen format.

Once Upon a Wintertime (film) Frances Langford sings about a boy and girl's outing on the ice in the 1800s in this segment from *Melody Time*. Released as a short Sep. 17, 1954. The song is by Bobby Worth and Ray Gilbert.

One and Only, Genuine, Original Family Band, The (film) In the year 1888, the 11 members of the Bower family comprise "The One and Only, Genuine, Original Family Band," which is practicing its performance for the Democratic National Convention for nominee Grover Cleveland. But their plans go askew when a young Republican newspaperman, who supports Cleveland's rival, Benjamin Harrison, falls in love with Alice Bower and convinces even Grandpa that they should move to the Dakota Territory. The family inescapably becomes involved in personal and political problems once they arrive. Difficulties end on Election Day, however, and the family band harmonizes once more. World premiere in New York City on Mar. 21, 1968. Directed by Michael O'Herlihy. 110 min. Stars Walter Brennan (Grandpa Bower), Buddy Ebsen (Calvin), Lesley Ann Warren (Alice), John Davidson (Joe Carder), Kurt Russell (Sidney), Janet Blair (Katie), Wally Cox (Mr. Wampler). Goldie Jean Hawn plays a bit part as a giggly girl and later shortened her name as she moved into stardom in a host of films. The film is based on the autobiographical novel by Laura Bower Van Nuys. The musical numbers were choreographed by Hugh Lambert and written by Richard M. and Robert B. Sherman. The songs include: "Dakota," "The One and Only, Genuine, Original Family Band," "Let's Put it Over with Grover," "Ten Feet Off the Ground," "'Bout Time," "The Happiest Girl Alive," and "West o' the Wide Missouri."

One and Only Ivan, The (film) Live-action/CGI

film adaptation of the children's book by Katherine Applegate. Ivan is a 400-pound silverback gorilla who shares a communal habitat in a suburban shopping mall with Stella the elephant, Bob the dog, and various other animals. He has few memories of the jungle where he was captured, but the arrival of a baby elephant named Ruby touches something deep within him. Ivan begins to question his life, where he comes from, and where he ultimately wants to be. Originally planned for theatrical release, but instead premiered digitally Aug. 21, 2020, on Disney+. Directed by Thea Sharrock. 94 min. Stars Bryan Cranston (Mack), Ramon Rodriguez (George), Ariana Greenblatt (Julia), with the voices of Sam Rockwell (Ivan), Angelina Jolie (Stella), Danny DeVito (Bob the dog), Helen Mirren (Snickers the poodle), Brooklynn Prince (Ruby). The original song "Free" was written by Diane Warren and performed by Charlie Puth. Filmed in wide-screen format at London's Pinewood Studios and in Lakeland, Florida. Received an Academy Award nomination for Visual Effects.

One and Only You (film) Educational film about positive self-image and getting along with others, in the Think It Through with Winnie the Pooh series; released in Sep. 1989. 14 min.

One by One (film) Animated short; released Aug. 31, 2004, on *The Lion King II: Simba's Pride* special edition DVD. On a rainy day, a group of children in a South African township decide to build their own kites. As they complete these kites, the sky starts to clear. The children run out into a field that is now golden with sunshine and proceed to fly their homemade kites. In the end, they release the kites, a metaphor for freedom. Directed by Pixote Hunt and David A. Bossert. Music by Lebo M, being a song from the stage production of *The Lion King*. 6 min.

One Day at Disney (TV) Documentary series on Disney+ spotlighting many of the talented Cast Members who drive creativity, innovation, and storytelling across The Walt Disney Company. A 59-min. film digitally premiered Dec. 3, 2019, with narrator Sterling K. Brown introducing the inspiring personal stories of 10 Disney employees through the lens of Disney CEO Bob Iger. The feature was followed by a series of 52 short films that celebrate the journeys of Cast Members around the world. From Endeavor Content. Released in conjunction with a collectible book of the same title from Disney Publishing.

One Day at Teton Marsh (TV) Show aired on Nov. 8, 1964. Depicts the animal life, including ospreys, otters, beavers, and others, in a small area near the Teton Range. Based on the book by Sally Carrighar. Narrated by Sebastian Cabot.

One Day on Beetle Rock (TV) Show aired on Nov. 19, 1967. A small area of Sequoia National Park is teeming with wildlife. Narrated by Sebastian Cabot.

One Good Cop (film) New York City police lieutenant Artie Lewis faces a major dilemma in his life when his longtime partner, Stevie Diroma, is killed in the line of duty. Artie and his wife, Rita, take in Stevie's 3 orphaned daughters but cannot make ends meet on a cop's salary. He soon finds himself straddling the fine line between his ethical code as a "good cop" or the temptation of the corrupt ways of the street in order to keep his suddenly enlarged family together. Released May 3, 1991. Directed by Heywood Gould. A Hollywood Pictures film. 105 min. Stars Michael Keaton (Artie Lewis), Rene Russo (Rita Lewis), Anthony LaPaglia (Stevie Diroma). Filmed in New York City and Los Angeles.

One Hour in Wonderland (TV) The first Disney TV show; aired Dec. 25, 1950. Sponsored by Coca-Cola. Directed by Richard Wallace. The show serves as a promo for the upcoming *Alice in Wonderland*. Joining Walt Disney are Edgar Bergen with Charlie McCarthy and Mortimer Snerd, Kathy Beaumont, Bobby Driscoll, and Diane and Sharon Disney. Hans Conried portrays the Magic Mirror.

One Hundred and One Dalmatians (film) Animated feature about Pongo, a clever Dalmatian who arranges to get married to the female of his choice, Perdita, and to round things out, gets his master, Roger Radcliff, wed to Perdita's pretty mistress, Anita. Soon Perdita produces 15 puppies, which the evil Cruella De Vil arranges to have kidnapped in her quest to make a fabulous Dalmatian-fur coat, also gathering many other puppies in order to accomplish her aim. Helped by the Twilight Bark, whereby dogs throughout the city and the countryside pass along the word of the missing puppies by barking, Pongo and Perdita go into action and locate 99 stolen puppies in Cruella's sinister-looking home, Hell Hall. Pongo, Perdita, and the puppies manage to escape and through various ruses elude the pursuing Cruella. Cruella and her henchmen, Horace and Jasper Badun, get their just desserts. Roger and Anita adopt the puppies, and with their new family of 101 Dalmatians and Nanny to look after them, plan to build a "Dalmatian Plantation" and live happily ever after. Released Jan. 25, 1961. Directed by Wolfgang Reitherman, Hamilton Luske, Clyde Geronimi. Based on the book by Dodie Smith. The songs "Cruella De Ville (*sic*)," "Dalmatian Plantation," and "Kanine Krunchies Commercial" were written by Mel Leven. Costing $4 million, the film did phenomenal business on its original release, and in its subsequent reissues in 1969, 1979, 1985, and 1991. First released on video in 1992. It was the first feature to solely use the Xerox process for transferring the animators' drawings to cels. Prior to this, each one of the animators' drawings had to be hand-traced in ink onto a cel. The new process sped up production greatly, especially in a film that had so many dogs—and not just dogs, but spotted dogs. It would have been horribly time-consuming to hand-ink each of the cels. Voice actors include Rod Taylor (Pongo), Betty Lou Gerson (Cruella De Vil), Lisa Davis (Anita), Ben Wright (Roger), and Cate Bauer (Perdita). 79 min. The famous Twilight Bark, used to rescue the puppies, was later adopted as the name for the newsletter for Disney Feature Animation. Note the spelling of *Dalmatians*. This word is probably the most-misspelled Disney word, with most people spelling it "Dalmations." Dalmatia, however, is a place, so people, and dogs, from there are Dalmatians.

101 Dalmatians (film) Live-action version of the Dodie Smith book and Disney's 1961 animated feature. Anita, who works as a designer for Cruella De Vil, is fired when she will not sell her boss the 15 Dalmatian puppies that have been born to Pongo and Perdy. Not willing to take no for an answer, Cruella arranges to have the puppies stolen by her hapless henchmen, Jasper and Horace, setting in motion a countrywide search. Directed by Stephen Herek. A Walt Disney Picture in association with Great Oaks Entertainment. Released Nov. 27, 1996. Stars Glenn Close (Cruella), Jeff Daniels (Roger), Joely Richardson (Anita), Hugh Laurie and Mark Williams (Jasper and Horace), Joan Plowright (Nanny). 103 min. Filmed on 7 soundstages at Shepperton Studios in England, as well as at selected locations in and around London. A major task was the finding and training of over 200 Dalmatian puppies whose welfare was of top concern to the filmmakers.

One Hundred and One Dalmatians: A Lesson in Self-Assertion (film) Educational film; released in Sep. 1981. The film teaches how to stand up to a bully through self-assertion.

101 Dalmatians Musical, The Non-Disney stage musical began a national tour in Minneapolis on Oct. 13, 2009, and closed prematurely after playing Madison Square Garden in New York City on Apr. 18, 2010. Taken from Dodie Smith's book, with a score by Dennis DeYoung. It was not based on any of the Disney films. Presented by Purina Dog Chow.

101 Dalmatians: The Series (TV) Animated series, in syn. beginning Sep. 1, 1997, and on ABC beginning Sep. 13, 1997. The spotted puppies go on wild adventures that are both entertaining and educational. In a playful, fun, and subtle way, each episode explores an important issue for kids—the perils of exaggerating, the responsibility of babysitting, the true meaning of winning, dealing with a bully, etc. Voices include Pam Segall and Debi Mae West (Lucky), Kath Soucie (Anita, Rolly, and Cadpig), Jeff Bennett (Roger), Tara Charendoff (Spot), April Winchell (Cruella De Vil), David Lander (Horace), Michael McKean (Jasper), Charlotte Rae (Nanny), Kevin Schon (Pongo), Pam Dawber (Perdita). From Walt Disney Television Animation and Jumbo Pictures, Inc. 65 episodes.

101 Dalmatians II: Patch's London Adventure (film) Direct-to-video release Jan. 21, 2003; sequel to *One Hundred and One Dalmatians*. Patch is accidentally left behind when his family moves to their new farm, and he sets out to meet his hero, canine star Thunderbolt. Thunderbolt uses Patch to help him execute real-life heroics, while Cruella De Vil seeks the puppies—dead or live—as models for a spot-fixated artist, Lars. Directed by Jim Kammerud and Brian Smith. Voices include Barry Bostwick (Thunderbolt), Jason Alexander (Lightning), Martin Short (Lars), Susanne Blakeslee (Cruella), Bobby Lockwood (Patch), Samuel West (Pongo), Maurice LaMarche (Horace), Jeff Bennett (Jasper), Jodi Benson (Anita), Tim Bentinck (Roger), Kath Soucie (Perdita), Mary Macleod (Nanny), Michael Lerner (Producer). Original songs by Randy Rogel.

101 Problems of Hercules, The (film) Television show; aired on Oct. 16, 1966. Three mismatched dogs must care for the sheep when the shepherd in charge is injured by raiders, guarding them against the elements, man, and various predators. Stars Harold Reynolds, David Farrow, Elliott Lindsey, Kathe McDowell.

102 Dalmatians (film) Cruella De Vil is released from prison on good behavior swearing that she will have nothing to do with fur ever again. Everyone marvels at her miraculous transformation, but she, however, cannot keep her promise and soon is plotting another scheme with French fashion designer Jean Pierre Le Pelt to get her ultimate Dalmatian coat as she and the dogs romp through Paris. Released Nov. 22, 2000. Directed by Kevin Lima. Stars Glenn Close (Cruella De Vil), Ioan Gruffudd (Kevin Shepherd), Alice Evans (Chloe Simon), Tim McInnerny (Alonso), Gérard Depardieu (Jean Pierre Le Pelt). 100 min. Filmed in England and France. Nominated for an Academy Award for Costume Design.

100 Lives of Black Jack Savage, The (TV) Series on NBC; debuted with a 2-hour pilot Mar. 31, 1991, and then aired Apr. 5–May 26, 1991. Set on the Caribbean island of San Pietro, the story concerns the ghost of a 17th-century pirate who teams up with an exiled billionaire to save 100 lives as atonement for their wrongdoings. In the pilot episode, the unlikely crime fighters set out to solve the mysterious disappearance of the island's fishermen from a remote reef on which Black Jack's treasure is buried. Stars Daniel Hugh Kelly (Barry Tarberry), Steven Williams (Black Jack Savage), Steve Hytner (Logan Murphy), Roma Downey (Danielle St. Claire), Bert Rosario (Abel Vasquez).

100,000,000 Franc Train Robbery (TV) Show; part 1 of *The Horse Without a Head.*

100 Years of Magic Special celebration at Walt Disney World for the 100th anniversary of the birth of Walt Disney, started in 2001 and extended into 2003. For the first time, 4 special parades were created, 1 at each park. The Magic Kingdom had *Share a Dream Come True Parade*, EPCOT had *Tapestry of Dreams*, Disney's Animal Kingdom had *Mickey's Jammin' Jungle Parade*, and Disney-MGM Studios had *Disney Stars and Motor Cars Parade*. Disney-MGM Studios also featured the celebration icon (a 122-ft.-tall "Sorcerer's Apprentice" Mickey hat) and a special exhibit on Walt's life and career, Walt Disney: One Man's Dream. Originally planned as an 18-month exhibition, One Man's Dream operated 16 years and became Walt

Disney Presents in 2017. The "Sorcerer's Apprentice" hat icon was removed in 2015.

One Little Indian (film) A story of the army in the Old West. Clint Keys has deserted because soldiers have killed his Indigenous wife. While fleeing to Mexico with 2 camels stolen from the army, he becomes friends with Mark, a 10-year-old boy raised by a Native community, who is also a fugitive. During Mark's capture, Clint is almost hanged, but is finally set free. The pair then head for Colorado to find the widow and her daughter they met during their flight from the army. Released Jun. 20, 1973. Directed by Bernard McEveety. 91 min. Stars James Garner (Clint), Vera Miles (Doris), Clay O'Brien (Mark), Jodie Foster (Martha), Pat Hingle (Capt. Stewart), Morgan Woodward (Sgt. Raines), John Doucette (Sgt. Waller), Jim Davis (trail boss), Jay Silverheels (Jimmy Wolf). Eleven-year-old O'Brien wanted the part so badly that he showed up for auditions in full costume and black wig; only later did the director discover that Clay had blond hair. The film was shot near Kanab, Utah, which is surrounded by the Grand Canyon, Kaibab National Forest, Bryce and Zion National Parks, and Lake Powell. Cooperation was gained with the U.S. Department of the Interior's Bureau of Land Management. The production was constantly delayed by accidents and freak mishaps, such as flooding, lightning striking the plane flying the cast and crew into Kanab, and the truck containing all the props catching fire, destroying both.

One Little Spark Song from Journey Into Imagination at EPCOT; written by Richard M. and Robert B. Sherman.

One Magic Christmas (film) Though her husband and kids try to cheer up, a young mother, Ginny Grainger, has lost the spirit of Christmas. Gideon, a Christmas angel, appears to help, but instead causes a number of seeming tragedies in the family's life. He then takes the daughter on a visit to Santa Claus to retrieve a letter the mother had written ten years before. The letter helps the mother regain her Christmas spirit, and Gideon turns back the clock to negate the tragic events. Released Nov. 22, 1985. Directed by Phillip Borsos. 89 min. Stars Mary Steenburgen (Ginny Grainger), Harry Dean Stanton (Gideon), Arthur Hill (Caleb Grainger), Elizabeth Harnois (Abbie), Gary Basaraba (Jack), Robbie Magwood (Cal). Walt Disney Pictures agreed to co-finance this film with the participation of Silver Screen Partners II and Telefilm Canada.

Filming took place in Toronto. The Christmas spirit prevailed during the early stages of principal photography at a Toronto shopping center when more than 300 extras turned out for a Sunday shoot. At the location, 50 shopkeepers took down their current Valentine's Day decorations and replaced them with Christmas décor. The shopping center also offered a Santa Claus Village complete with Santa, a 20-piece brass band and an all-girl choir singing Christmas carols. In the Toronto suburb of Scarborough, all the residents in a 3-block radius also joined in the true spirit of Christmas and happily bedecked their houses with seasonal decorations for the 6 days of filming in their area. Throughout the filming, as the production moved to the towns of Owen Sound and Meaford, the constantly changing weather nearly made filming impossible, as the crew faced rain, fog, sleet, blizzard, winds gusting up to 50 mph, mud, 15-ft.-high snowdrifts denying access to country locations and, often, zero visibility. Production designer Bill Brodie constructed 3 major sets: the Grainger house, the grandfather's home, and Santa's workshop and cottage, which was filled with real rare toys, insured for $1 million prior to filming, and 20,000 actual letters to Santa from the Toronto main post office.

One Man Band (film) Animated short from Pixar Animation Studios. A little peasant girl has 1 coin with which to make a wish in a fountain, but she encounters 2 competing street performers who would like the coin in their tip jars. The 2 overly eager musicians battle to win the girl's attention. Directed by Mark Andrews and Andrew Jimenez. Distributed by Buena Vista Pictures Distribution. Released Jun. 9, 2006, with *Cars*, after an Aug. 6, 2005, release at the Melbourne International Film Festival. 4 min. Nominated for an Academy Award.

One Man's Dream Show at Videopolis in Disneyland; ran Dec. 16, 1989–Apr. 29, 1990. Originally produced in Tokyo Disneyland, where it ran Apr. 15, 1988–Sep. 3, 1995, in Showbase 2000. Tells Walt Disney's story through his animated triumphs. One unique element of the show was that the beginning was all in black and white; the characters and sets then almost magically changed to full color. The show returned to Tokyo Disneyland Jul. 3, 2004, as One Man's Dream II—The Magic Lives On, and ended Dec. 13, 2019, to be succeeded in 2020 by It's Very Minnie.

One Man's Dream: 100 Years of Magic (film) Film created in 2001 by Walt Disney Imagineering for an exhibit in Disney-MGM Studios for the 100 Years of Magic celebration of the 100th anniversary of the birth of Walt Disney. Michael Eisner introduced and Walt Disney himself, through rare, digitally enhanced audio commentary, narrated the film, which documented Walt's life. Later, after Michael Eisner resigned, Julie Andrews narrated the film. It also screened in the Disney Animation attraction at Disney California Adventure, Dec. 5, 2001–Apr. 6, 2005. 16 min.

$1,000,000 Duck See Million Dollar Duck, The.

One More Disney Day Advertised as an extra day of magic, this event kept both Disneyland and the Magic Kingdom open for 24 hours straight: 6 a.m. on Feb. 29–6 a.m. on Mar. 1, 2012. In 2013, the "Monstrous Summer All-Nighter" kept both parks, along with Disney California Adventure, open 6 a.m. on May 24–6 a.m. on May 25. A "Rock Your Disney Side Party" kept all 3 parks open 6 a.m. on May 23–6 a.m. on May 24, 2014. In 2015, all 3 parks stayed open 6 a.m. on May 22–6 a.m. on May 23 for "Coolest Summer Ever!" at Walt Disney World and as a kickoff to the Diamond Celebration at Disneyland Resort. Disneyland had been open for 24 hours or more on earlier occasions, including a celebration for the park's 30th birthday on Jul. 17, 1985, and for 60-hour parties welcoming *Captain EO* in 1986 and Star Tours in 1987.

One More Mountain (TV) Two-hour movie on ABC; first aired Mar. 6, 1994. Margaret Reed, a fragile pioneer woman, struggles to overcome hardships, and keep her family alive, while traveling to California over the Sierra Nevada range during the mid-1800s. Directed by Dick Lowry. Stars Meredith Baxter (Margaret), Chris Cooper (James Reed), Larry Drake (Patrick Breen), Jean Simmons (Sarah Keyes).

One-of-a-Kind Antique shop in New Orleans Square in Disneyland; opened in 1967. Lillian Disney was very fond of antiques and was supposedly Walt Disney's inspiration for opening this shop. In 1995, the shop began carrying antique reproductions and gifts rather than true antiques. Closed May 13, 1996, and changed to a Gourmet Shop. The antique shop at Walt Disney World was called Olde World Antiques.

One of Our Dinosaurs Is Missing (film) Lord

Southmere, a British intelligence agent, steals a piece of top secret microfilm, the Lotus X, from a Chinese warlord, and hides it in the skeleton of a dinosaur in a London museum after escaping from a Chinese agent, Hnup Wan, who soon recaptures him. Southmere has told his childhood nanny Hettie what has happened, and she, aided by a small army of fellow nannies, helps foil the machinations of Hnup and his gang. Released Jul. 9, 1975. Directed by Robert Stevenson. 94 min. Stars Peter Ustinov (Hnup Wan), Helen Hayes (Hettie), Clive Revill (Quon), Derek Nimmo (Lord Southmere), Joan Sims (Emily), Bernard Bresslaw (Fan Choy), Natasha Pyne (Susan). The film was shot on location in London, including the London Zoo in Regent's Park, the Natural History Museum in Kensington, Hyde Park, and parts of Soho. Based on the book *The Great Dinosaur Robbery* by "David Forrest" who was, in actuality, 2 authors: David Eliades and Bob Forrest Webb. Art director Michael Stringer engaged a team of 6 modelers who worked for 2 months replicating two 75-foot-long dinosaur skeletons weighing several tons, which had necks that could bob up and down during the chase sequence. Adding to the 1920s look of the film is a collection of vintage vehicles ranging from a Daimler for Hnup Wan's limousine to Nanny Emily's 1920 Godfrey and Nash cyclecar.

One Paddle, Two Paddle Poolside sandwich counter at Aulani, A Disney Resort & Spa; open Aug. 29, 2011–ca. 2014.

One Saturday Morning (TV) Two-hour Saturday morning cartoon block on ABC; debuted Sep. 13, 1997, and included *Brand Spanking New Doug*, *Pepper Ann*, and *Recess*, along with segments featuring the Genie from *Aladdin*, a roving reporter named Manny the Uncanny, *the Monkey Boys*, *Mrs. Munger's Class*, and an educational segment. A series of short segments (90 sec. apiece), entitled *Great Minds Think 4 Themselves*, aired during the show, featuring Robin Williams as the voice of Genie, taking viewers through a mixed-media overview of the life of great Americans who "thought for themselves"—such as John Muir, Jackie Robinson, Clara Barton, Ben Franklin, and Cesar Chavez. These segments received 2 Emmy nominations in 1998. A variety of other shows and segments aired in succeeding years. The programming block ended Sep. 7, 2002.

O'Neal, Shaquille Athlete/actor; appeared in *Kazaam* (title role).

Onward (film) Animated feature from Pixar Animation Studios. Ian Lightfoot, an introverted teenage elf, lost his father before he was born and, on his 16th birthday, finds himself wanting to become better and bolder—more like his dad had been. His mother, Laurel, surprises him and his older brother, Barley, with a magical gift from their late father that, if conjured properly, will give the brothers 1 more day with their dad. The spell goes awry, so the Lightfoot brothers embark on an extraordinary quest aboard Barley's van, *Guinevere*, to discover if there might be a little magic left in the world. When Laurel realizes her sons are missing, she teams up with The Manticore—a former warrior—to find them. Perilous curses aside, this one day could mean more than any of them ever dreamed. Directed by Dan Scanlon. Released Mar. 6, 2020, also in 3-D and IMAX, after a Feb. 18 world premiere at the El Capitan Theatre in Hollywood, a festival run beginning Feb. 21, and international releases beginning Mar. 4. Voices include Tom Holland (Ian), Chris Pratt (Barley), Julia Louis-Dreyfus (Laurel Lightfoot), Octavia Spencer (The Manticore), Mel Rodriguez (Colt Bronco), Kyle Bornheimer (Wilden Lightfoot), Lena Waithe (Officer Specter), Ali Wong (Officer Gore), Grey Griffin (Dewdrop), Tracey Ullman (Grecklin), Wilmer Valderrama (Gaxton), George Psarras (Officer Avel), John Ratzenberger (Construction Worker Fennwick). 102 min. Inspired by director Dan Scanlon's own family experiences. The end-credits song, "Carried Me With You," is written/produced/performed by Brandi Carlile, in collaboration with Phil Hanseroth and Tim Hanseroth. To create the unique suburban-fantasy world, filmmakers mixed approximately 70% familiar elements with 30% fantasy elements. Released on digital platforms early, for purchase beginning Mar. 20, 2020, followed by an Apr. 3 streaming release on Disney+, during the COVID-19 pandemic. Nominated for an Academy Award for Animated Feature.

Onyx Collective Content brand which curates premium entertainment programming by creators of color and underrepresented voices, primarily for Hulu. Announced by Disney General Entertainment Content in May 2021. The debut project, Questlove's award-winning documentary *Summer of Soul (. . . or, When the Revolution Could Not Be Televised)*, premiered in 2021.

Oo-De-Lally Song from *Robin Hood* (1973); written and performed by Roger Miller.

Open Range (film) In 1882, Charley Waite, Boss

Spearman, and Mose Harrison are all men trying to escape their pasts by driving cattle on the open range. They try to avoid violence, but one frontier town that is ruled through fear and tyranny changes their lives and forces them into action. Amidst this turmoil, Charley meets the spirited Sue Barlow, who embraces both his heart and his soul. A Touchstone film, in association with Cobalt Media Group. Directed by Kevin Costner. Released Aug. 15, 2003. Stars Robert Duvall (Boss Spearman), Kevin Costner (Charley Waite), Annette Bening (Sue Barlow), Michael Gambon (Denton Baxter), Michael Jeter (Percy), Diego Luna (Button), James Russo (Sheriff Poole), Abraham Benrubi (Mose Harrison). 138 min. Based on the novel, *The Open Range Men*, by Lauran Paine. Filmed in Cinema-Scope on location at the Stoney Indian Reservation and other locations in Alberta, Canada.

Operation Dumbo Drop (film) A U.S. Army captain, Sam Cahill, wrapping up his final tour of duty in Vietnam, finds himself trying to replace a village's prized elephant, which had been caught in cross fire between American troops and the North Vietnamese. The task of moving a grown elephant across 300 miles of mine-laden, enemy-infested jungle is more than Cahill had counted on. When travel by road and river does not work, the intrepid crew decides to parachute the elephant in using a very big parachute. Released Jul. 28, 1995. Directed by Simon Wincer. Stars Danny Glover (Sam Cahill), Ray Liotta (Capt. Doyle), Denis Leary (David Poole), Doug E. Doug (Harvey Ashford), Corin Nemec (Lawrence Farley). Filmed in Cinema-Scope. 108 min. The 26-year-old elephant star, Tai, weighed 8,000 lbs., was 8½ feet tall, and had to be transported from the U.S. to the filming location in Thailand by means of a custom-made steel crate carried in a Korean Air Lines 747 jumbo jet.

Operation Undersea (TV) Show aired Dec. 8, 1954. Directed by Winston Hibler, Hamilton S. Luske. Walt Disney tells the history of the exploration of the sea, then takes viewers behind the scenes of the making of *20,000 Leagues Under the Sea*, describing new techniques that had to be invented for underwater filming. While this show was essentially an hour-long commercial for the new Disney movie, it was of such excellent quality that it won the Emmy Award for Best Individual Show of the year.

Oprah Winfrey Presents: Their Eyes Were Watching God (TV) ABC Premiere Event; aired Mar. 6, 2005. The story of a beautiful and resil-

ient woman's quest for love, sensual excitement, and spiritual fulfillment, despite society's expectations of a woman of color in 1920s America. Janie Crawford's journey takes her through 3 marriages with very different men, during which she experiences everything from tremendous success to unspeakable heartbreak. Directed by Darnell Martin. Stars Halle Berry (Janie Crawford), Ruben Santiago-Hudson (Joe Starks), Michael Ealy (Tea Cake), Terrence Howard (Amos Hicks), Lorraine Toussaint (Pearl Stone), Nicki Micheaux (Pheoby Watson), Mel Winkler (Logan Killicks), Ruby Dee (Nanny). Based on the novel by Zora Neale Hurston. Produced by Harpo Films/Touchstone Television.

Opry House, The (film) Mickey Mouse cartoon; released in 1929. Directed by Walt Disney. In the first real Disney musical, Mickey is the proprietor of and pianist for a small-town vaudeville show. For his piano performance, Mickey wears a pair of white gloves, but the garments would not become part of his standard look until his next cartoon, *When the Cat's Away*.

Optimist/Pessimist: Which Are You? (film) Educational film; using sequences from *Pollyanna*. In the Questions!/Answers? series; released in Oct. 1975. The film shows that negativism is wrong and that one should form healthy attitudes.

O'Quinn, Terry Actor; appeared in *The Rocketeer* (Howard Hughes), *Tombstone* (Mayor Clum), and *Shadow Conspiracy* (Frank Ridell), and on TV in *Phenomenon II* (Jack Hatch), *Alias* (Kendall), *Secrets and Lies* (John Warner), *Emergence* (Richard Kindred), and *Lost* (John Locke), for which he received the 2007 Emmy Award for Best Supporting Actor in a Drama. For Disney Channel, he voiced Professor Mystery in *Phineas and Ferb*.

Orange Bird Character with the head of an orange and leafy wings created for Walt Disney World when the Florida Citrus Growers signed on to sponsor the Sunshine Pavilion in the Magic Kingdom. Orange Bird merchandise could be found at welcome centers and citrus stands across Florida, and his story was told on an album with songs written by Richard M. and Robert B. Sherman. The character also appeared in the educational film *Foods and Fun: A Nutrition Adventure*. A roaming Orange Bird character greeted visitors in Adventureland until the mid-1980s. After a quarter century away from the park, a figure of the character returned to Sunshine Tree Terrace in 2012. The Orange Bird was designed by Disney Studio publicity artist Bob Moore. SEE ALSO SUNSHINE TREE TERRACE.

Orange Stinger Paradise Pier attraction in Disney's California Adventure; open Feb. 8, 2001–Jul. 13, 2009. Guests whirled on "buzzing bumblebees" inside a giant peeling orange. Reimagined as Silly Symphony Swings on Jun. 11, 2010.

Orbach, Jerry (1935–2004) Actor; appeared in *Straight Talk* (Milo Jacoby), and voiced Lumiere in *Beauty and the Beast*, Sa'luk in *Aladdin and the King of Thieves*, and Pierre in The Enchanted Tiki Room—Under New Management at Walt Disney World.

Orbitron—Machines Volantes Attraction, similar to Rocket Jets and Star Jets, in Discoveryland at Disneyland Paris; opened Apr. 12, 1992. Inspired by Leonardo da Vinci's visionary drawings of the solar system. Also opened in Hong Kong Disneyland (with a different design and without the French subtitle) Sep. 12, 2005.

Orddu, Orgoch, and Orwen The Witches of Morva in *The Black Cauldron*; voiced respectively by Eda Reiss Merin, Billie Hayes, and Adele Malis-Morey.

Oriental Imports, Ltd. Adventureland Bazaar shop in the Magic Kingdom at Walt Disney World; opened Oct. 1, 1971. Purses, silks, inlaid woods, and jewelry were sold. Closed in 1987 to become part of The Elephant's Trunk.

Origin of Stitch, The (film) Animated short from Toonacious Family Entertainment; released Aug. 30, 2005, on the *Lilo & Stitch 2: Stitch Has a Glitch* DVD. The secret of Experiment 626's origins are revealed. Directed by Mike Disa and Tony Bancroft. Voices include Chris Sanders (Stitch), David Ogden Stiers (Jumba). 5 min.

Originale Alfredo di Roma Ristorante, L' SEE L'ORIGINALE ALFREDO DI ROMA RISTORANTE.

Orlando, Florida City near which Walt Disney decided to build his "Florida Project." After the success of his California park, Walt realized that an East Coast enterprise would likely attract many visitors who would be unable to travel all the way to California. Thus, he searched for the ideal location, eventually deciding on the Orlando area of Central Florida. He was able to amass more than 27,000 acres southwest of the city, and there planned a destination that would ultimately open as Walt Disney World. Its announcement, the construction, and the subsequent 1971 opening forever changed the face of Orlando, which quickly grew from a sleepy town into a major metropolis.

Orlando International Airport On their way to Walt Disney World or a Disney Cruise, many visitors to Central Florida have their first interactions with Disney at the Orlando International Airport. Disney shops have included Greetings from Walt Disney World in Terminal B (open Nov. 1992–1997, becoming The Magic of Disney Aug. 13, 1997) and Disney's EarPort in Terminal A (open Dec. 10, 2002–Jul. 28, 2019, and reopening Nov. 22 as a second Magic of Disney). Another shop, Flights Fantastic, operated in the Delta Airside terminal Apr. 1997–Apr. 30, 2003. With the opening of the new South Terminal C in Sep. 2022, the Walt Disney World Store debuted, with a ribbon cutting ceremony held Sep. 21. The airport was previously the site of McCoy Air Force Base (hence the airport code MCO). SEE ALSO MAGICAL EXPRESS, DISNEY'S.

Orphans' Benefit (film) Mickey Mouse cartoon released Aug. 11, 1934. Directed by Burt Gillett. Donald and Goofy were featured together for the first time as they, Mickey, Horace Horsecollar, and Clarabelle Cow try to put on a show for orphans. But the mischievous children take delight in taunting the performers, including eggs that fall on Donald as he tries to recite "Mary Had a Little Lamb." A remake, in color with updated animation, was released Aug. 22, 1941, and directed by Riley Thomson.

Orphan's Picnic (film) Mickey Mouse cartoon released Feb. 15, 1936. Directed by Ben Sharpsteen. Donald has problems with rambunctious orphans, as in *Orphans' Benefit*, who tease and torment the poor duck into getting in trouble with a beehive and swallowing a bee.

Ortega, Kenny Director/choreographer; he worked on *Newsies* and *Hocus Pocus* and, for TV, *Hull High*, the High School Musical films, *The Cheetah Girls 2*, the Descendants films, *Mickey's 60th Birthday*, and *Totally Minnie*. He produced and appeared in *Hannah Montana & Miley Cyrus: Best of Both Worlds Concert* and later made a TV appearance on *The Disney Family Singalong*. He was named a Disney Legend in 2019.

Orville Baby bird character in *Pluto's Fledgling* (1948).

Orville Inept albatross, proprietor of Albatross Air Charter Service, in *The Rescuers*; voiced by Jim Jordan.

Osberg, Anne She joined Disney in 1988 and served in various positions in Disney Consumer Products, until being named president of U.S. and Canada operations in 1994. She was named president of the division in 1997 and left the company in 1999.

Osborne Family Spectacle of Lights Jennings Osborne, an Arkansas businessman, designed a major holiday light show at his home. In 1995, his show, with millions of bulbs, was moved to Disney-MGM Studios (later Disney's Hollywood Studios), where it dazzled guests each holiday season until 2015 (except for 2003, when a move from the park's Residential Street to the Streets of America prevented their installation). In 2006, it became the Osborne Family Spectacle of Dancing Lights, newly programmed to "dance" to a musical score. Back in 1995, while unloading the trucks of lights from Arkansas, the staff found they had accidentally transported a purple cat rope light that the Osborne family used for their Halloween display. So each year, the cat was placed in a different location in the display, and finding it was a fun annual activity for insiders.

Oscar (film) At his father's deathbed in 1931, notorious bootlegger Angelo "Snaps" Provolone, in a moment of remorse, agrees to his father's plea that he give up his shameful life, become an honest man, and restore his family's name to honor. The bewildered Snaps tries to go straight, but his new image is far too fantastic for either the cops or new, easily bribed banker friends. Things are not helped by Snaps's surroundings—a madhouse of peculiar characters and relatives. Mistaken identities and misplaced suitcases all help add up to a day full of surprises for the former gangster. Released Apr. 26, 1991. Directed by John Landis. A Touchstone film. 109 min. During production, the film crew lost many of their sets, props, and 21 period cars leased for the production in a disastrous fire on the Universal Studios backlot, where the movie was being shot. This necessitated an unexpected move to Orlando, Florida, for filming at both Disney-MGM Studios and Universal/Florida, the first movie shot at the latter studio. Stars Sylvester Stallone (Angelo "Snaps" Provolone), Yvonne DeCarlo (Aunt Rosa), Don Ameche (Father Clemente), Tim Curry (Dr. Poole). Kirk Douglas had an uncredited cameo role as Snaps's dying father.

Oscar's Classic Car Souvenirs Gas station–themed shop on Hollywood Boulevard in Disney's Hollywood Studios; opened May 1, 1989. There is also Oscar's Super Service, which offers locker, stroller, and wheelchair rentals.

Osgood, Kevin Actor/dancer; appeared on the *Mickey Mouse Club* on The Disney Channel 1989–1993.

Osment, Emily Actress; appeared on TV in *Hannah Montana* (Lilly Truscott), *Cyberbully* (Taylor Hillridge), *Dadnapped* (Melissa Morris), *Young & Hungry* (Gabi), and the *Radio Disney Music Awards*. She voiced Kendall Perkins in *Kick Buttowski: Suburban Daredevil* and Pep in *Beverly Hills Chihuahua 2*.

Osment, Haley Joel Actor; appeared in *The Sixth Sense* (Cole Sear), for which he received an Oscar nomination for Best Supporting Actor; and on TV in *Thunder Alley* (Harry Turner). He voiced Chip in *Beauty and the Beast: The Enchanted Christmas*, Zephyr in *The Hunchback of Notre Dame II*, Beary Barrington in *The Country Bears*, Sora in the *Kingdom Hearts* interactive game, and Mowgli in *The Jungle Book 2*.

Osmond, Donny Actor; appeared in *College Road Trip* (Doug Greenhut), and on TV in *The Disney Family Singalong*. He provided the singing voice of Shang in *Mulan*. SEE ALSO NEXT ENTRY.

Osmond Brothers, The Singing group; in 1961, the boys, dressed alike, were noticed by the barbershop quartet on Main Street, U.S.A. in Disneyland. When asked if they sang, they agreed to do a number. Each group sang a song, and the concert went on for almost an hour, attracting and delighting a large crowd. The Osmonds were then brought to the Disneyland entertainment office where their talents were recognized, and they were signed to their first professional contract. Later on they appeared on TV in *Meet Me at Disneyland*, *Disneyland After Dark*, *Disneyland Showtime*, and *Kraft Salutes Disneyland's 25th Anniversary*.

Osprey Ridge Golf course at Bonnet Creek Golf Club at Walt Disney World; opened in 1992, nestled in some of the outer reaches of the resort. Designed by Tom Fazio. Casual dining was offered at the Sand Trap Bar & Grill. The course closed in 2013 for incorporation into the Four Seasons Orlando resort development, reopening in Nov. 2014 as Tranquilo Golf Club.

Oswald the Lucky Rabbit Series of 26 silent cartoons made by Walt Disney between 1927–1928 for Charles Mintz, who contracted with Universal for their distribution. When Walt lost the rights to Oswald, he came up with the character of Mickey Mouse. The Oswald character was later continued by Walter Lantz. Sound was added by Universal, the copyright holder, to some of the Disney Oswalds in the early days of TV. Oswald was the first Disney character to generate merchandise—there was a candy bar, a stencil set, and a pinback button. Disney acquired the rights to Oswald from Universal in 2006. The Oswald cartoons are:

1. *Trolley Troubles*, 1927
2. *Oh, Teacher*, 1927
3. *Great Guns*, 1927
4. *The Mechanical Cow*, 1927
5. *All Wet*, 1927
6. *The Ocean Hop*, 1927
7. *The Banker's Daughter*, 1927
8. *Empty Socks*, 1927
9. *Rickety Gin*, 1927
10. *Harem Scarem*, 1928
11. *Neck 'n' Neck*, 1928
12. *The Ol' Swimmin' 'ole*, 1928
13. *Africa Before Dark*, 1928
14. *Rival Romeos*, 1928
15. *Bright Lights*, 1928
16. *Sagebrush Sadie*, 1928
17. *Ride 'em Plowboy*, 1928
18. *Ozzie of the Mounted*, 1928
19. *Hungry Hoboes*, 1928
20. *Oh, What a Knight*, 1928
21. *Poor Papa*, 1928
22. *Sky Scrappers*, 1928
23. *The Fox Chase*, 1928
24. *Tall Timber*, 1928
25. *Sleigh Bells*, 1928
26. *Hot Dog*, 1928

On Dec. 1, 2022, Walt Disney Animation Studios digitally released a short cartoon titled *Oswald the Lucky Rabbit*, which marked the character's first animated appearance from the Studio in nearly 95 years. Directed by Eric Goldberg, the 1-min. short follows Oswald as he attempts to enter a movie screen and reunite with his love.

Oswald's Sundries shop on Buena Vista Street in Disney California Adventure; opened Jun. 15, 2012. Themed as a gas station selling Oswald the Lucky Rabbit merchandise.

Oswalt, Patton Actor; provided the voice of Remy in *Ratatouille*. He appeared in *Eternals* (Pip the Troll), on TV in *Marvel's Agents of S.H.I.E.L.D.* (Billy/Sam), and in the Disney Channel Original Movie *Kim Possible* (Professor Dementor). Also voiced Professor Dementor in the *Kim Possible* animated series, Hubie in *Miles from Tomorrowland*, Papa in *Pickle and Peanut*, Mr. Sparkles in *Big Hero 6 The Series*, Mr. McSnorter in *Mickey and the Roadster Racers*, the Mayor in *The Ghost and Molly McGee*, Mr. Fluffenfold in *Big City Greens*, the title character in *Marvel's M.O.D.O.K.*, and Duke the Duckbus in *Firebuds*.

Other Me, The (TV) A Disney Channel Original Movie; first aired Sep. 8, 2000. A 13-year-old, Will Browning, accidentally clones himself, calling the clone Twoie. Will gets Twoie to go to school in his place, but soon gets bored with the routine and becomes jealous of his "twin." The pair may have the same genetic makeup, but Twoie is everything Will is not: popular at school and at home, and a whiz to boot. Directed by Manny Coto. Stars Andrew Lawrence (Will/Twoie), Brenden Jefferson (Chuckie), Lori Hallier (Mom), Mark Taylor (Dad), Alison Pill (Alanna Browning). Based on the book *Me Two* by Mary C. Ryan.

Other Side of Heaven, The (film) John Groberg, 19, is sent on a 3-year Mormon mission to Tonga, where he finds himself in the midst of a culture as remote to him as the island is to his Idaho Falls home. Not understanding the language, and longing for the girl he left behind John faces suspicion, distrust, typhoons, mosquitoes, and other perils of man and nature as he reaches out to the people of Tonga. Released on video Apr. 1, 2003, by Walt Disney Home Entertainment after a limited theatrical release by Excel Entertainment beginning Dec. 14, 2001. Directed by Mitch Davis. Stars Christopher Gorham (John Groberg), Anne Hathaway (Jean Sabin), Joe Folau (Feki), Miriama Smith (Lavania). 113 min.

Other Sister, The (film) Carla Tate, while mentally

challenged, has matured into a young woman with dreams and ambitions, searching for her independence. But she has a handicap—her mother—who refuses to accept her daughter's personal needs. Carla falls in love for the first time with a young man who is also mentally challenged, and defies her family in order to prove that, despite all appearances, she has the capacity to be a responsible adult, worthy of being loved. Released Feb. 26, 1999. Directed by Garry Marshall. A Touchstone film. Stars Juliette Lewis (Carla Tate), Diane Keaton (Elizabeth Tate), Tom Skerritt (Radley Tate), Giovanni Ribisi (Danny McMahon). 131 min. Filmed in CinemaScope.

O'Toole, Peter (1932–2013) Actor; appeared in *Kidnapped* (Robin MacGregor) and voiced Anton Ego in *Ratatouille*.

Otter in the Family, An (TV) Show aired Feb. 21, 1965. A boy in Wisconsin cares for an injured otter, who is then suspected of stealing eggs. The boy eventually discovers that the real culprits are skunks. Stars Tom Beecham, Mable Beecham, Gary Beecham, Donald Cyr. Narrated by Rex Allen.

Ouimet, Matt He joined Disney in 1989, holding several leadership titles, including senior vice president and chief financial officer of the Disney Development Company, senior vice president of Finance and Business Development for Walt Disney World, and executive general manager of Disney Vacation Club and Disney's Wide World of Sports. He was named president of Disney Cruise Line in 1999 and became president of the Disneyland Resort Oct. 2003, overseeing its 50th anniversary celebration. He resigned Jul. 2006.

Our Friend the Atom (TV) Show aired Jan. 23, 1957. Directed by Hamilton S. Luske. Dr. Heinz Haber looks at the atom as a potential power source, stressing that strict controls are necessary. He traces the history of the atom from the tale of "The Fisherman and the Genie" through the days of the ancient Greek philosophers to the discoveries of modern scientists. The film uses excerpts from *20,000 Leagues Under the Sea* as well as new animation sequences. A popular book version of this show by Dr. Haber was published by Golden Press. In 1980, an updated version was produced as an educational film entitled *The Atom: A Closer Look*.

Our Planet Tonight (TV) Unsold pilot for a comedy series on NBC; aired Apr. 22, 1987, spoofing TV newsmagazine shows. Directed by Louis J. Horvitz. Stars John Houseman, Morgan Fairchild.

Our Shining Moment (TV) Pilot on NBC (60 min.); aired Jun. 2, 1991. Directed by Mark Tinker. Michael McGuire looks back on his childhood in the 1960s. Stars Cindy Pickett, Max Gail, Jonathan Brandis, Seth Green, Don Ameche.

Our Town Song from *Cars*; written by Randy Newman. Nominated for an Academy Award.

Our Unsung Villains (TV) Show aired Feb. 15, 1956. Directed by Hamilton S. Luske. The Magic Mirror hosts a look at the Disney villains from several different Disney films. Hans Conried played the Magic Mirror.

Out (film) Animated short; digitally released May 22, 2020, on Disney+. On an average day, Greg's life is filled with family, love, and a rambunctious little dog. But despite all of this, he has a secret. With some help from his precocious pup and a little bit of magic, Greg might learn he has nothing to hide. Directed by Steven Clay Hunter. 9 min. From the Pixar Animation Studios SparkShorts program.

Out Cold (film) Good-hearted but single-minded teen snowboarding dudes Rick, Luke, Anthony, and Pig Pen are into extreme boarding, as well as extreme partying in the winter wonderland around their tiny hamlet of Bull Mountain, Alaska. John Majors, a slick Colorado ski mogul, plans to buy Bull Mountain to turn it into a ski resort, and joining him is his beautiful Swiss stepdaughter, Inga. The competitive foursome antagonize each other into a frenzy. A Touchstone film in association with Spyglass Entertainment. Directed by Brendan Malloy and Emmett Malloy. Released Nov. 21, 2001. Stars Flex Alexander (Anthony), A. J. Cook (Jenny), David Denman (Lance), Caroline Dhavernas (Anna), Zach Galifianakis (Luke), Willie Garson (Ted Muntz), Derek Hamilton (Pig Pen), David Koechner (Stumpy), Jason London (Rick Rambis), Thomas Lennon (Eric), Lee Majors (John Majors), Victoria Silvstedt (Inga). 90 min. Filming took place in British Columbia, Canada (especially in Vancouver and Salmo).

Out of Control (film) Educational video release in Nov. 1992. 17 min. A boy has a problem with his temper, but after he vandalizes the campsite of a homeless man, he wrestles with his conscience and finds more creative and humorous ways to deal with his anger.

Out of Scale (film) Donald Duck cartoon released Nov. 2, 1951. Directed by Jack Hannah. Donald, as engineer of a miniature train in his backyard, runs into difficulties with Chip and Dale when he replaces their oak tree with a miniature one. The only way the clever animals can save their home is by putting a GIANT REDWOOD sign on it and letting the train pass through a tunnel in its trunk.

Out of the Frying Pan into the Firing Line (film) Made during World War II, the film, starring Minnie Mouse and Pluto, shows the importance of housewives saving waste fats for the purpose of making shells and explosives. Made for the U.S. government; delivered Jul. 30, 1942. Directed by Ben Sharpsteen.

Out of the Wild Gift and sundry shop at Rafiki's Planet Watch in Disney's Animal Kingdom; open Apr. 22, 1998–Jan 2022.

Out on a Limb (film) Donald Duck cartoon released Dec. 15, 1950. Directed by Jack Hannah. In his work as a tree surgeon, Donald discovers the tree home of Chip and Dale and harasses them with a tree pruner they believe to be a monster. They soon realize their error and have the frustrated Donald venting his temper.

Out There Song from *The Hunchback of Notre Dame*; written by Stephen Schwartz and Alan Menken.

Outlaw Cats of Colossal Cave, The (TV) Show aired Sep. 28, 1975. Directed by Hank Schloss. A cave guide befriends bobcats he finds living inside the Arizona cave, and eventually transports them to a national park where they will be safe from hunters. Stars Gilbert de la Peña, José Maierhauser.

Outpost Shop, The Main entrance souvenir and sundry shop at Disney's Animal Kingdom; opened Apr. 22, 1998.

Outrageous Fortune (film) Two aspiring actresses, rivals in drama class, discover they are also rivals for the affections of the same man. When he disappears, they team up to find him so he can choose between them. When they finally catch him, they discover he is a renegade CIA agent, escaping to the Russian KGB with a dangerous toxin. They team up, as friends now, to thwart their former lover and save the U.S. Released Jan. 30, 1987. Directed by Arthur Hiller. 100 min. Stars Bette Midler (Sandy), Shelley Long (Lauren), Peter Coyote (Michael), Robert Prosky (Stanislav Korzenowski), John Schuck (Atkins), George Carlin (Frank). Filmed in Los Angeles and New York City and in the area around Santa Fe, New Mexico.

Ovalle, Edward He joined Disney in 2001 as a senior clerk in the Corporate Legal Main Files department and transferred to the Walt Disney Archives in 2006. He has consulted on a variety of Disney projects, written for company publications, and has supported events, tours, and Archives exhibitions around the world. In 2015, he served as lead archivist on the restoration of Walt Disney's offices at The Walt Disney Studios in Burbank.

Ovitz, Michael In Aug. 1995, he was named the president of The Walt Disney Company, to take office in October. Ovitz had been chairman of the Creative Artists Agency. He left the company on Dec. 27, 1996.

Owen, Reginald (1887–1972) Actor; appeared in *Mary Poppins* (Admiral Boom) and *Bedknobs and Broomsticks* (Gen. Teagler), and on TV as J. Cecil Bennett in *Moochie of the Little League* and *Moochie of Pop Warner Football*.

Owens, Gary (1936–2015) Actor/radio announcer; he made his on-screen film debut in *The Love Bug* as a race announcer and also appeared in *Spy Hard* (MC). He narrated *The Wonderful World of Disney* for 5 years, provided the narration for World of Motion in EPCOT Center, and provided voices for numerous cartoon shorts and TV programs, including *Dinosaurs*, *Buzz Lightyear of Star Command*, and *Wizards of Waverly Place*.

Owl Pseudo-intellectual character in the Winnie the Pooh films; originally voiced by Hal Smith.

Owl House, The (TV) Animated fantasy-comedy series on Disney Channel; premiered Jan. 10, 2020. Luz, a self-assured teenage girl, accidentally stumbles upon a portal to a magical world where she befriends a rebellious witch, Eda, and a tiny warrior, King. Despite not having magical abilities, Luz pursues her dream of becoming a witch by serving as Eda's apprentice at the Owl House and ultimately finds a new family in an unlikely setting.

Voices include Sarah-Nicole Robles (Luz), Wendie Malick (Eda), Alex Hirsch (King), Tati Gabrielle (Willow), Issac Ryan Brown (Gus), Mae Whitman (Amity), Parvesh Cheena (Tibbles), Eden Riegel (Boscha), Bumper Robinson (Principal Bump). From Disney Television Animation.

Owl That Didn't Give a Hoot, The (TV) Show aired Dec. 15, 1968. A boy cares for an abandoned owl and prepares her for life in the wild. Stars David Potter, Marian Fletcher, John Fetzer. Narrated by Steve Forrest.

Own the Room (TV) A Disney+ original documentary from National Geographic; digitally released Mar. 12, 2021. Five students from disparate corners of the planet take their big ideas to the Global Student Entrepreneur Awards in Macau, China. They've each overcome immense obstacles in pursuit of their dreams, from hurricanes to poverty to civil unrest. Their ideas have already changed their own lives, but are they ready to change the world? Directed by Cristina Costantini and Darren Foster. From Saville Productions and Shopify Studios.

Oz SEE STORYBOOK LAND CANAL BOATS; RAINBOW ROAD TO OZ, THE; RETURN TO OZ; AND OZ THE GREAT AND POWERFUL.

Oz The Great and Powerful (film) A prequel to L. Frank Baum's original Oz story, *The Wonderful Wizard of Oz*, and the 1939 MGM film, *The Wizard of Oz*, showing how the Wizard arrived in Oz and became its ruler. Oscar Diggs, a small-time circus magician with dubious ethics, is hurled away from dusty Kansas to the vibrant Land of Oz, where he thinks he has hit the jackpot—fame and fortune are his for the taking—that is, until he meets 3 witches, Theodora, Evanora, and Glinda, who are not convinced he is the great wizard everyone has been expecting. Reluctantly drawn into the epic problems facing the Land of Oz and its inhabitants, Oscar must find out who is good and who is evil before it is too late. Putting his magical arts to use through illusion, ingenuity, and even a bit of wizardry, Oscar, aided by a flying monkey, Finley, and China Girl, transforms himself not only into the great wizard but into a better man as well. Released in the U.S. Mar. 8, 2013, in Disney Digital 3-D, after a Mar. 7 international release. Directed by Sam Raimi. Stars James Franco (Oz), Mila Kunis (Theodora), Rachel Weisz (Evanora), Zach Braff (Frank/voice of Finley), Michelle Williams (Annie/Glinda), Joey King (girl in wheelchair/voice of China Girl), Tony Cox (Knuck). 131 min. Produced by Walt Disney Pictures and Roth Films. Music by Danny Elfman. Nearly 2,000 costumes were created for the inhabitants of Oz, with 100 characters requiring prosthetic enhancements. Filmed in CinemaScope in Los Angeles and at Raleigh Michigan Studios in Pontiac, Michigan.

Ozzie of the Mounted (film) Oswald the Lucky Rabbit cartoon; released Apr. 30, 1928. Oswald, the Mountie, is sent into a snowstorm to catch a villainous wolf. His mechanical mount suffers from static but finally bounces him right onto the outlaw's trail.

1. PeopleMover 2. Polynesian Village Resort, Disney's 3. *Phineas and Ferb The Movie: Candace Against the Universe* (TV)
4. *Princess and the Frog, The* (film) 5. *Pluto's Party* (film) 6. Peter Pan's Flight 7. *Pinocchio* (film) 8. *Parent Trap, The* (film)
9. *Pigs Is Pigs* (film) 10. PizzeRizzo 11. Pirates of the Caribbean—Battle for the Sunken Treasure

Pablo Cold-blooded penguin who appeared in *The Three Caballeros*.

Pablo and the Dancing Chihuahua (TV) Two-part show; aired Jan. 28 and Feb. 4, 1968. Directed by Walter Perkins. A Mexican boy, Pablo, searches for his missing uncle and is joined by a Chihuahua, lost by an American tourist. They have to battle wild pigs, a mountain lion, and a rattlesnake, but finally find the dog's owner, who offers Pablo a place to live. Stars Armando Islas, Francesca Jarvis, Walker Tilley, Manuel Rivera.

Pacheco, David He began as an animator at Disney in 1980, contributing to *Who Framed Roger Rabbit* and *The Little Mermaid*, later contributing to such live-action films as *Three Men and a Baby* and *The Hand Behind the Mouse: The Ub Iwerks Story*. In 1989, he joined Disney Publishing Group, eventually becoming creative director. He helped establish the Disney Collectible Division and was later named creative director for Walt Disney Art Classics and, later, Disney Consumer Products. After more than 40 years with the Company, he retired in 2021 but has continued to consult on special projects.

Pacific Electric Pictures Shop on Hollywood Boulevard in Disney-MGM Studios at Walt Disney World; opened May 1, 1989. Guests could star in their own home video version of a Hollywood film. It closed in 1990 to become Calling Dick Tracy, tying in with the feature film released that year.

Pacific Export Adventureland shop in Tokyo Disneyland; opened in 2013, replacing Chiba Traders – Arts & Crafts. Closed Jun. 21, 2015, to become Jungle Carnival.

Pacific Station (TV) Series on NBC; aired Sep. 15, 1991–Jan. 3, 1992. Stationed in the quirky beach community of Venice, California, by-the-book detective Bob Ballard finds his life is disrupted when he is partnered with Richard Capparelli, an officer full of New Age insights and unorthodox techniques. Stars Robert Guillaume (Bob Ballard), Richard Libertini (Richard Capparelli), Joel Murray (Kenny Epstein), John Hancock (Hal Bishop), Ron Leibman (Al Burkhardt). From Touchstone Television and KTMB Productions.

Pacific Wharf Area in Disney California Adventure; opened Feb. 8, 2001, originally as a district within the former Golden State area. Diverse cultures, products, and industries of California are represented in a waterfront inspired by Monterey's Cannery Row. In 2023, the area became San Fransokyo Square.

Pacific Wharf Café Counter-service restaurant at Pacific Wharf in Disney California Adventure; opened Feb. 8, 2001. It is known for its soups served in Boudin sourdough bowls.

Pacifically Peeking (TV) Show aired Oct. 6, 1968. Directed by Ward Kimball. Moby Duck leads a study of life on several Pacific islands—including Pitcairn, Fiji, and Hawai'i. Paul Frees provided the voice of Moby Duck.

Pacifier, The (film) Assigned to protect the endangered children of an assassinated scientist working on a secret invention, Navy SEAL Shane Wolf is suddenly faced with juggling 2 incompatible jobs—fighting evil while keeping house. Shane must not only defeat a world-threatening enemy but also wrangle teen rebel Zoe, uplift sullen 14-year-old Seth, and outwit 8-year-old Ninja-wannabe Lulu, simultaneously keeping toddler Peter and baby Tyler out of mischief, not to mention harm's way. Being used to drop zones, demolitions, and destroying enemy targets, he has no idea what tough really is until he pits his courage against diapering, den-mothering, and driver's education. He is truly out of his element, but this tough-guy loner soon realizes that he is facing the most important mission of his life: becoming part of a family and bringing them all closer together. Directed by Adam Shankman. From Walt Disney Pictures/Spyglass Entertainment. Released Mar. 4, 2005. Stars Vin Diesel (Shane Wolf), Lauren Graham (Principal Claire Fletcher), Carol Kane (Helga), Faith Ford (Julie Plummer), Brittany Snow (Zoe), Max Thieriot (Seth), Brad Garrett (Vice Principal Murney), Morgan York (Lulu), Chris Potter (Capt. Bill Fawcett), Tate Donovan (Howard Plummer). 95 min. Filmed in CinemaScope.

Pacino, Al Actor; appeared in *Dick Tracy* (Big Boy Caprice), *The Insider* (Lowell Bergman), and *The Recruit* (Walter Burke).

Pack Mules Through Nature's Wonderland Frontierland attraction in Disneyland; operated Jun. 10, 1960, until 1973. Formerly Mule Pack (1955–1956) and Rainbow Ridge Pack Mules (1956–1959).

Paddlefish Modern seafood restaurant at The Landing in Disney Springs; opened Feb. 4, 2017, replacing Fulton's Crab House in the riverboat once known as the *Empress Lilly*. The menu includes a daily catch, seafood boils, and steaks. There are also 3 lounges which provide views of Lake Buena Vista.

Page, Geraldine (1924–1987) Actress; appeared in *The Happiest Millionaire* (Mrs. Duke) and voiced Madame Medusa in *The Rescuers*.

Paint the Night Parade in Hong Kong Disneyland; debuted Sep. 11, 2014, before an official opening Oct. 1. Also ran in Disneyland May 22, 2015–Sep. 5, 2016, for the park's 60th anniversary celebration. The first fully LED nighttime parade,

it featured floats with advanced technologies and Disney and Pixar characters.

Pair of Kings, A (TV) Comedy-adventure series on Disney XD; aired Sep. 22, 2010–Feb. 18, 2013. Fraternal twins Brady and Boomer must relocate from their Chicago home to the island of Kinkow after they learn they are the rightful heirs to the throne of this odd kingdom, one that's filled with peculiar superstitions and customs—and one that may not be ready for 2 teenage kings. Stars Mitchel Musso (Brady), Doc Shaw (Boomer), Kelsey Chow (Mikayla), Ryan Ochoa (Lanny), Geno Segers (Mason). In the 3rd season, Adam Hicks joined the show as a long-lost brother, Boz, while Mitchel Musso left. From It's A Laugh Productions, Inc.

Pal Mickey Interactive Mickey Mouse doll that acts as a tour guide, sharing park tips, fun facts, and jokes, and playing 3 different games; available for rental or purchase at Walt Disney World beginning in Apr. 2003. A Spanish-language version was introduced on Oct. 5, 2003. Due to guest preference, while the Mickeys continued to be sold, the rental program ended Dec. 1, 2004. A new enhanced version of Pal Mickey was released in May 2005 for the Happiest Celebration on Earth. Sales ended in 2008 as existing stock ran out, but the interactive plush continued to operate in the 4 parks.

Palace Pets SEE WHISKER HAVEN TALES WITH THE PALACE PETS.

Palazzo Canals Area in Mediterranean Harbor at Tokyo DisneySea; opened Sep. 4, 2001. Visitors can enjoy fine dining, a romantic stroll, and even an authentic gondola ride in an old-world Italian ambience.

Palivoda, Armand (1906–1960) He handled the distribution of Disney films in Switzerland from 1937 until his death in 1960. He was presented posthumously with a European Disney Legends Award in 1997.

Palm Golf Course, Disney's An 18-hole championship course located across from Disney's Polynesian Village Resort at Walt Disney World, along with Disney's Magnolia Golf Course. Formerly served by The Disney Inn. Designed by Joe Lee. It has been rated by *Golf Digest* as one of the top 25 resort courses. Completely redesigned in summer 2013 by the Arnold Palmer Design Company.

Palmer, Lilli (1914–1986) Actress; appeared in *Miracle of the White Stallions* (Vedena Podhajsky).

Palmer, Norman "Stormy" (1918–2013) Film editor; he joined the Disney Studio as a projectionist in 1938 and soon transferred to the Editorial department, where he contributed to such films as *Pinocchio* and *Fantasia*. He left the company during World War II, later returning as editor on features, shorts, and TV shows. He is best known for his work on the True-Life Adventure series. He retired in 1983 and was named a Disney Legend in 1998.

Paltrow, Gwyneth Actress; appeared in *Jefferson in Paris* (Patsy Jefferson), *Duets* (Liv), *The Royal Tenenbaums* (Margot Tenenbaum), and as Pepper Potts in *Marvel's The Avengers* and later Marvel Studios films.

Pampolina, Damon Actor; appeared on the *Mickey Mouse Club* on The Disney Channel, beginning in 1989, with other TV appearances in *Blossom*, the *Walt Disney World Happy Easter Parade* (1990), the *Walt Disney World Very Merry Christmas Parade* (1991), and *Nashville* (programmer). Also a member of the pop band The Party.

Pan Galactic Pizza Port Tomorrowland restaurant in Tokyo Disneyland; opened Jul. 1989. The fictional Italian-Alien owner, Tony Solaroni, entertains guests as he prepares pizza on the fully automated pizza-making machine, the PZ-5000.

Pancake Races Held at Disneyland for several years beginning in Mar. 1957. The winners qualified for national races.

Panchito Mexican charro rooster, one of The Three Caballeros; voiced by Joaquin Garay.

Panchito's Gifts and Sundries Shop in Disney's Coronado Springs Resort at Walt Disney World; opened Aug. 1, 1997. The name was shortened to Panchito's in 2018.

Pancho, the Fastest Paw in the West (TV) Show aired Feb. 2, 1969. A runaway orphan and his Chesapeake Bay retriever in 1880 are helped by an itinerant peddler, and they help him when his horses are stolen. Stars Armando Islas, Frank Keith, Albert Hachmeister. Based on the book by Bruce Grant. Narrated by Rex Allen.

Pandora – The World of Avatar Area in Disney's Animal Kingdom; opened May 27, 2017, taking the place of Camp Minnie-Mickey. According to the story, guests explore the Valley of Mo'ara on Pandora, a moon 4.4 light-years from Earth. There are 2 main attractions—Na'vi River Journey and Avatar Flight of Passage—with dining at Satu'li Canteen and shopping at Windtraders. Views of flora and fauna, the impressive floating mountains, and special entertainment all help connect visitors to the natural world. At nightfall, the area illuminates with bioluminescence. *Time* magazine ranked the area as one of the 100 top destinations on its 2018 list of the "World's Greatest Places."

Pangani Forest Exploration Trail SEE GORILLA FALLS EXPLORATION TRAIL (DISNEY'S ANIMAL KINGDOM).

PanoraMagique SEE CHARACTERS IN FLIGHT.

Pantry Pirate (film) Pluto cartoon released Dec. 27, 1940. Directed by Clyde Geronimi. Pluto has conflicts with the cook when he tries to steal a roast, encountering a troublesome ironing board and soap flakes.

Pants on Fire (TV) An original movie for Disney XD; premiered Nov. 9, 2014. A 15-year-old Jack Parker has always gotten by on his lies—a seemingly great plan until one day his lies, including that on a boy he claims to be tutoring, a possessive girlfriend, and a duo of alien body-snatchers, start showing up in his life for real. Directed by Jon Rosenbaum. Stars Bradley Steven Perry (Jack Parker), Joshua Ballard (Ryan), Tyrel Jackson Williams (Mikey). Produced for Disney XD by MarVista Entertainment and Two 4 the Money Media.

Papeete Bay Verandah Restaurant in the Polynesian Village Resort at Walt Disney World; open Oct. 1, 1971–Sep. 1994 (to reopen the following year as 'Ohana). An elegant restaurant serving Polynesian cuisine with dancers and singers providing entertainment.

Paperino Italian name for Donald Duck.

Paperman (film) Minimalist black-and-white animated short with innovative hybrid use of computer animation and hand-drawn techniques; released with *Wreck-It Ralph* on Nov. 2, 2012, after a Jun. 6, 2012, premiere at the Annecy International Animation Film Festival. A lonely young man in mid-century New York City has a chance meeting with a beautiful woman on his morning commute. After figuring he will never see her again, destiny gives him a second chance when he spots her in a skyscraper window across from his office. He uses a stack of papers to try to get her attention. Directed by John Kahrs. Voices by John Kahrs, Jeff Turley, Kari Wahlgren. It won the Academy Award for Best Animated Short.

Parade of the Award Nominees (film) Short animated film produced in color for the Nov. 18, 1932, Academy Awards ceremony held at the Ambassador Hotel in Los Angeles, in which Mickey leads a parade of the nominees, including Fredric March turning from Dr. Jekyll to Mr. Hyde. This marked the first animation of Mickey Mouse in color. Released on the laser disc set *Mickey Mouse: The Black and White Years* in 1993.

Parade of Toys SEE CHRISTMAS IN MANY LANDS (DISNEYLAND).

Paradise (film) A troubled 10-year-old boy, Willard Young, who wonders why his father hasn't come home for about 3 months, is packed off by his mother to stay with friends in the rural town of Paradise. Painfully shy, Willard discovers that his new guardians, Ben and Lily Reed, are having deep problems, too. The couple is still grieving over the accidental death of their son, and it is tearing them apart. Willard's presence eventually becomes a healing catalyst for the troubled pair, and they, in turn, along with a sensitive little girl, Billie, help Willard prevail over his greatest fears. Initial release in New York City on Sep. 18, 1991; general release on Oct. 4, 1991. Directed by Mary Agnes Donoghue. A Touchstone film. 111 min. Stars Melanie Griffith (Lily Reed), Don Johnson (Ben Reed), Elijah Wood (Willard Young), Thora Birch (Billie Pike). Filmmakers used the town of McClellanville, South Carolina, to double for Paradise. Additional filming was done in other areas around Charleston.

Paradise Garden Grill Counter-service restaurant in Paradise Gardens Park at Disney California Adventure; opened Jul. 1, 2011. Mediterranean skewers and Middle Eastern–inspired meals are offered.

Paradise Gardens Park Area in Disney California Adventure; new name for a section of the former Paradise Pier as of Jun. 23, 2018. Inspired by classic Pacific Coast amusement parks, with seaside restaurants and attractions, including The Little Mermaid ~ Ariel's Undersea Adventure, the Golden Zephyr, Goofy's Sky School, and Jumpin' Jellyfish. SEE ALSO PIXAR PIER.

Paradise Pier Former area in Disney California Adventure themed to California beach culture; opened Feb. 8, 2001, with a variety of amusements, including California Screamin', the Sun Wheel, Games of the Boardwalk, Golden Zephyr, Jumpin' Jellyfish, King Triton's Carousel, the Maliboomer, Mulholland Madness, Orange Stinger, and the S.S. *rustworthy*. The Disney Imagineers got creative when naming the original shops (including Man Hat 'n' Beach, Point Mugu Tattoo, Reboundo Beach) and food locations (including Catch a Flave, Malibu-Ritos, Pizza Oom Mow Mow). Toy Story Midway Mania! opened in 2008, and starting in 2009 a major transformation began to re-theme the area to a seaside amusement park from back in the 1930s. In 2009, the Sun Wheel was re-themed to Mickey's Fun Wheel and the Games of the Boardwalk were changed to feature classic Disney characters. In 2010, the nighttime spectacular *World of Color* was added, the Maliboomer was removed, and the Orange Stinger became Silly Symphony Swings. In 2011, The Little Mermaid ~ Ariel's Undersea Adventure opened, Mulholland Madness became Goofy's Sky School, and Pizza Oom Mow Mow became Boardwalk Pizza & Pasta. In 2018, Paradise Pier was divided into two areas: Pixar Pier and Paradise Gardens Park.

Paradise Pier Hotel, Disney's New name for the Disneyland Pacific Hotel as of Oct. 2000. It was re-themed to tie in with Paradise Pier in Disney California Adventure across the street. Sand-and-surf-themed décor adds to the modern, seaside-inspired guest rooms. Dining includes Disney's PCH Grill and Surfside Lounge, with shopping at Mickey in Paradise. On the rooftop Paradise Pool area, swimmers can plunge down the California Streamin' waterslide and dine at The Sand Bar. In 2022, it was announced that the hotel would be transformed into the Pixar Place Hotel.

Paradiso 37 Tapas-oriented restaurant at The Landing at Disney Springs at Walt Disney World; opened Jun. 5, 2009, featuring menu items from some of the 37 countries of the Americas. It took the site of the former Rock N Roll Beach Club in Pleasure Island. An expansion in 2015 provided an outdoor stage and additional seating. Managed by E-Brands.

Parallels (TV) Science fiction mystery series from France; digitally released Mar. 23, 2022, on Disney+. Follows 4 teenage friends on the French-Swiss border whose lives are turned upside down when a mysterious event scatters the group across time and into separate universes. With 2 friends in the present, and the other 2 in a completely separate time line, they race to find each other, hoping to unravel the mystery of the event and return home before forever alerting their futures. Stars Thomas Chomel (Samuel), Omar Mebrouk (Bilal), Maxime Bergeron (Victor), Victoria Eber (Romane). From Daïmôn Films and Empreinte Digitale. 6 episodes.

Parent Trap, The (film) After an imaginative title sequence using stop-motion animation (by experts T. Hee, Bill Justice, and X Atencio) and the song "The Parent Trap," sung by Annette Funicello and Tommy Sands, the film introduces twins Sharon and Susan, who were separated as children by their divorced parents, and then accidentally meet during the summer at Camp Inch. Determined never to be separated again, the sisters decide to bring their parents, Mitch and Maggie, back together again. In this they have a rival, the devious Vicky, who wants to marry Mitch for his money. But after a fateful camping trip, Vicky finds living with the twins is not worth it and flees, leaving Mitch and Maggie to reunite happily. Released Jun. 21, 1961. Directed by David Swift. 129 min. Starring Hayley Mills in the dual role of both sisters. The careful use of double-exposure and split screen shots, as well as a double for Hayley Mills, Susan Henning, provided the illusion of there being twins. Stars Hayley Mills (Susan/Sharon), Maureen O'Hara (Maggie McKendrick), Brian Keith (Mitch Evers), Charlie Ruggles (Charles McKendrick), Joanna Barnes (Vicky Robinson), Una Merkel (Verbena), Leo G. Carroll (Rev. Mosby). Oscar nominations were awarded for Sound by Robert O. Cook and for Film Editing by Philip W. Anderson. Richard M. and Robert B. Sherman provided the songs, which, besides the title song, included "For Now, For Always" and "Let's Get Together" and added to the film's enormous popularity. The film was shot mostly in California at various locales, including millionaire Stuyvesant Fish's 5,200-acre ranch in Carmel, Monterey's Pebble Beach golf course, and the Studio's Golden Oak Ranch in Placerita Canyon, where Mitch's ranch was built. It was the design of this set that proved the most popular, and to this day the Walt Disney Archives receives requests for plans of the home's interior design. But there, of course, never was such a house; the set was simply various rooms built on a soundstage. The film was rereleased theatrically in 1968. The Studio later produced 3 TV sequels starring Hayley Mills.

Parent Trap, The (film) A remake of the 1961 Hayley Mills film. This time the identical twins are Hallie and Annie, and when they meet for the first time at Camp Walden for Girls in Maine, they conspire to reunite their mom (a wedding gown designer in London) and dad (a vineyard owner in the Napa Valley), who never should have been apart. Directed by Nancy Meyers. Released Jul. 29, 1998. Stars Lindsay Lohan (Hallie/Annie), Dennis Quaid (Nick Parker), Natasha Richardson (Elizabeth James), Lisa Ann Walter (Chessy), Elaine Hendrix (Meredith Blake). 128 min. Joanna Barnes, who plays Mrs. Vicki Blake, played the role of Vicki in the original film. Eleven-year-old newcomer Lohan hailed from Long Island. After filming in London, the production moved to the Staglin Family vineyard near Rutherford in California's Napa Valley. Camp Seely in Crestline, California, doubled for Camp Walden. Special effects technology had progressed tremendously in the 37 years since the original film, so it was much easier for the cinematographer, Dean Cundey, to accomplish the more than 100 shots combining both girls.

Parent Trap Hawaiian Honeymoon (TV) Two-part, made-for-TV movie; aired Nov. 19 and 26, 1989. Directed by Mollie Miller. The family has inherited a dilapidated hotel in Hawai'i, which they visit and decide to clean up. The triplets practice deception by impersonating each other and try to help their father save the hotel from being sold to a developer. Stars Hayley Mills, Barry Bostwick, John M. Jackson, the Creel triplets, Sasha Mitchell, Jayne Meadows.

Parent Trap II, The (TV) A Disney Channel Premiere Film; first aired Jul. 26, 1986. Mistaken identities once again disrupt the twins' lives 25 years later, as Sharon's daughter, Nikki, turns mischief-making matchmaker for her divorced mother. 81 min. Stars Hayley Mills, Tom Skerritt, Carrie Kei Heim, Bridgette Andersen, Alex Harvey, Gloria Cromwell. Directed by Ronald F. Maxwell.

Parent Trap III (TV) Two-part, made-for-TV movie; aired Apr. 9 and 16, 1989. Directed by Mollie Miller. The fiancée of a man with triplet daughters hires one of the twins as an interior decorator. Before long, the decorator steals the man's heart, encouraged by the daughters who don't like the fiancée. Stars Hayley Mills, Barry Bostwick, Patricia Richardson, the Creel triplets, Ray Baker, Christopher Gartin.

Park, Tom He joined Walt Disney Imagineering as director of finance in 1991, headed Walt Disney Art Classics and Disney Direct Marketing 1996–1999, and was then named head of The Disney Store worldwide. He left the company in Jul. 2001.

Parker, Fess (1924–2010) Actor; best known for his role as Davy Crockett on TV. Also appeared in *The Great Locomotive Chase* (James J. Andrews), *Westward Ho the Wagons!* (John Doc Grayson), *Old Yeller* (Jim Coates), and *The Light in the Forest* (Del Hardy), and on TV in *Along the Oregon Trail* (John "Doc" Grayson), *The Disneyland Story*, *Dateline Disneyland*, *Behind the Scenes with Fess Parker*, and *The Fourth Anniversary Show*. Parker had not been the first one considered for Davy Crockett; James Arness had been recommended to Walt Disney, but when he screened the science fiction film *Them*, Walt was attracted not to Arness but to another actor in the thriller: Parker. Parker was hired and proved to be perfect as Davy Crockett. He was named a Disney Legend in 1991.

Parker, Jayne She joined Disney in 1988 developing training and leadership programs, with later titles including director of the Disney University, director and vice president of Organization Improvement, and vice president of Organization and Professional Development. She was later named senior vice president of Human Resources, Diversity and Inclusion for Walt Disney Parks and Resorts, and in 2009 became senior executive vice president and chief human resources officer for The Walt Disney Company. She retired in 2021.

Parker, Mark G. Member of the Disney Board of Directors beginning in 2016. It was announced he will succeed Susan E. Arnold as chairman of the board in 2023.

Parker, Sarah Jessica Actress; appeared in *Flight of the Navigator* (Carolyn McAdams), *Hocus Pocus* and *Hocus Pocus 2* (Sarah), *Ed Wood* (Dolores), and *Miami Rhapsody* (Gwyn).

Parker Bros. Game manufacturer that has had one of the longest-running Disney merchandise licenses, beginning in 1933. Their popular games

and puzzles have featured Disneyland attractions and the standard Disney characters, as well as those from the feature films.

Parkside Diner Buffet dining in Disney's Hotel New York at Disneyland Paris; opened Apr. 12, 1992, serving international fare in a 1930s Manhattan atmosphere. Closed Jan. 7, 2019, to become the Downtown Restaurant.

Parkway Gifts North and South Pair of merchandise shops at Tokyo DisneySea; opened Sep. 4, 2001, just outside the park's main entrance.

Parsons, Kelly Mouseketeer on the new *Mickey Mouse Club*.

Part of Your World Song from *The Little Mermaid*; written by Howard Ashman and Alan Menken.

Partly Cloudy (film) Up in the stratosphere, cloud people sculpt babies from clouds and bring them to life, to then be delivered by storks. Gus, a lonely and insecure gray cloud, is a master at creating "dangerous" babies such as crocodiles, porcupines, and rams, but these cause no end of trouble for his loyal delivery stork partner, Peck. As Gus's creations become more and more rambunctious, Peck's job gets harder and harder. Directed by Peter Sohn. Animated short from Pixar; released with *Up* May 29, 2009. 6 min.

Partners Bronze statue of Walt Disney and Mickey Mouse installed in the Central Plaza in Disneyland Nov. 18, 1993, to commemorate the 65th birthday of Mickey Mouse. Master Disney sculptor Blaine Gibson came out of retirement to create the sculpture. Identical statues were installed in the Magic Kingdom at Walt Disney World Jun. 19, 1995, in Tokyo Disneyland Apr. 15, 1998, in Walt Disney Studios Park at Disneyland Paris Jul. 19, 2002, and at the Disney Studio in Burbank Feb. 10, 2003. Blaine chose to depict Walt in what he considered to be the showman's prime—the mid-1950s, when he became a familiar face through the weekly Disney TV show. He shared a few explanations of what Walt is saying to Mickey; one is, "Look, Mickey, see all the happy people? That's what it's all about." The other version is, "Mickey, look what we've done." Walt is presented as slightly larger than life; he actually stood at 5'10" tall, and the *Partners* statue sets him at 6'5". To make Mickey fit in comparative scale, Blaine consulted the only film he could find of Mickey holding a human hand—

"The Sorcerer's Apprentice" scene from *Fantasia*, in which Mickey shakes hands with conductor Leopold Stokowski. Many guests wonder about the STR symbol on Walt Disney's tie; it refers to Smoke Tree Ranch, a development in Palm Springs, California, where he had a vacation home. Blaine also sculpted a statue of Walt Disney's brother, Roy O. Disney, on a bench with Minnie Mouse, which was installed on Town Square in the Magic Kingdom at Walt Disney World Oct. 1, 1999, and dedicated Oct. 25. It is known as the *Sharing the Magic* statue. A copy of that statue was installed at the Disney Studio in Burbank Feb. 10, 2003. There is also a Roy and Minnie statue in World Bazaar in Tokyo Disneyland. SEE ALSO STORYTELLERS AND WALT THE DREAMER.

Partners Federal Credit Union Created on Nov. 5, 2007, with the merger of Vista Federal Credit Union (started at the Studio Apr. 26, 1960, and expanded to Walt Disney World in 1970) and Partners Federal Credit Union (started at Disneyland Mar. 18, 1968). Disneyland's credit union actually began life with different names, first as the DRC (Disneyland Recreation Club) Federal Credit Union and later the Disneyland Employees Federal Credit Union. But Disney credit unions go back even further—for unions at the Disney Studio spurred the creation of a short-lived Walt Disney Employees Federal Credit Union as early as 1945.

Party, The Singing group composed of cast members of The Disney Channel's *Mickey Mouse Club*—Tiffini Hale, Albert Fields, Deedee Magno, Chase Hampton, and Damon Pampolina. Their first single was "Summer Vacation," which broke into the *Billboard* charts in 1990.

Party Central (film) Animated short from Pixar Animation Studios. Released with *Muppets Most Wanted* on Mar. 21, 2014, after a preview at the 2013 D23 Expo. Mike, Sulley, and their Oozma Kappa frat brothers throw a monster blowout party but are dismayed when no one shows up. But, with the help of some extra inter-dimensional doors, the party soon gets rocking. Directed by Kelsey Mann. 6 min.

Party Gras Gifts New Orleans–themed shop in Adventureland at Tokyo Disneyland; opened Jul. 20, 2007, replacing Le Gourmet. Colorful fashion accessories and glassware are sold.

Party Gras Parade Parade at Disneyland, Jan. 11–Nov. 18, 1990. Disney's version of Mardi Gras in New Orleans, this parade featured large floats, stilt-walkers, dancers, and performers, who would toss special Party Gras coins and strings of beads out to the guests. The parade would stop at intervals and a special performance would be given. Also in Tokyo Disneyland Apr. 1991–Apr. 1993.

Party Tilyadrop Tour, The (film) Video release; behind the scenes on tour with this musical group from the *Mickey Mouse Club*; released Apr. 19, 1991. 25 min.

Partysaurus Rex (film) Animated short from Pixar Animation Studios, with the dinosaur Rex meeting some new toys during Bonnie's bath time and transforming himself into a self-proclaimed "Partysaurus." Directed by Mark Walsh, working with Pixar Canada. Released with *Finding Nemo 3-D* Sep. 14, 2012. 6 min.

Pascal Rapunzel's feisty chameleon confidant in *Tangled*.

Passed Away (film) During one long weekend, 4 grown children come together under the family roof for their 70-year-old father's funeral. Each tries to cope with his or her personal failures and the family's expectations. They find themselves confronting each other, past scandals, current secrets, a failing business, an unwed mother, and an illegal alien. Family friction and turmoil rule as the family prepares for the burial. Released Apr. 24, 1992. Directed by Charlie Peters. A Hollywood Pictures film. 96 min. Stars Bob Hoskins (Johnny Scanlan), Blair Brown (Amy Scanlan), Tim Curry (Boyd Pinter), Frances McDormand (Nora Scanlan), William Petersen (Frank Scanlan), Pamela Reed (Terry Scanlan), Peter Riegert (Peter Scanlan), Maureen Stapleton (Mary Scanlan), Nancy Travis (Cassie Slocombe), Jack Warden (Jack Scanlan). Filmed at various locations around Pittsburgh.

Pasta Piazza Ristorante Restaurant in Innoventions West at EPCOT; opened May 1994, replacing Sunrise Terrace Restaurant. Closed in 2001 and became a character photo spot in 2005.

Pastoral Symphony, The Music composed by Ludwig van Beethoven, a segment of *Fantasia*.

Pastry Palace World Bazaar baked goods and packaged treat shop in Tokyo Disneyland; opened Apr. 15, 1983. Hosted by Juchheim's Co., Ltd.

Patented Pastimes SEE GREAT AMERICAN PASTIMES.

Path to 9/11, The (TV) A 5-hour dramatization of the events leading up to the attack on the World Trade Center, beginning with the bombing of the Center in 1993. Directed by David L. Cunningham. Aired, without commercials, on ABC on Sep. 10–11, 2006. Stars Harvey Keitel (John O'Neill), Stephen Root (Richard Clarke), Donnie Wahlberg (Kirk), Barclay Hope (John Miller), Patricia Heaton (Amb. Bodine), Shaun Toub (Emad Salem), Amy Madigan (Patricia Carver), Nabil Elouahabi (Ramzi Yousef), Mido Hamada (Massoud), Dan Lauria (George Tenet). From Touchstone Television. Before airing, controversy was raised regarding alleged historical inaccuracies. Eventually, ABC made some slight cuts and ran a disclaimer reminding viewers that the film was fiction. In 2008, a documentary, *Blocking the Path to 9/11*, was produced by John Ziegler and Citizens United, claiming former President and Mrs. Clinton pressured TV and studio executives into quashing a DVD release of the miniseries.

Patinkin, Mandy Actor; appeared in *Dick Tracy* (88 Keys), *The Doctor* (Murray), *Life with Mikey* (irate man), and *Squanto: A Warrior's Tale* (friar), and on TV in *Criminal Minds* (Jason Gideon). He voiced Hattori in *The Wind Rises*.

Patrick, Butch Actor; appeared in *The One and Only, Genuine, Original Family Band* (Johnny, uncredited), and on TV in *The Young Loner* (Bumper) and *Way Down Cellar* (Frank Wilson).

Patriot, The (film) Non-Disney film from Interlight Pictures and Baldwin/Cohen Productions; released on video by Touchstone Home Video on Jun. 15, 1999. An immunologist, retired to a small Montana town, finds the town infected by a rare virus, and he rushes to discover a cure while fending off the paramilitary group that released it. Directed by Dean Semler. Stars Steven Seagal (Wesley McClaren), Gailard Sartain (Floyd Chisolm), L. Q. Jones (Frank), Silas Weir Mitchell (Pogue), Camilla Belle (Holly), Dan Beene (Richard Bach). Originally released theatrically in Spain on Jul. 10, 1998.

Patten, Luana (1938–1996) Actress; appeared in *Song of the South* (Ginny), *Fun and Fancy Free*, *Melody Time*, *So Dear to My Heart* (Tildy), *Johnny Tremain* (Cilla Lapham), and *Follow Me, Boys!* (Nora White).

Paul Bunyan (film) Special cartoon featurette released Aug. 1, 1958. Directed by Les Clark. One day, after a great storm on the coast of Maine, the townspeople found baby Paul Bunyan on the beach where the heavy seas had left him. Paul grows to a great size and becomes a legend with his double-bladed ax and friend, Babe, the Blue Ox. But the prosperity Paul brought to his land ultimately defeats him when steam saws are produced that can do the job easier and faster than Paul and his ox. 17 min.

Paull, Michael He joined The Walt Disney Company in 2017 with the acquisition of BAMTech Media, where he served as CEO. As president of Disney Streaming Services, he oversaw the launch of ESPN+ in 2018, Disney+ in 2019, and Star+ in Latin America in 2021. In Jan. 2022, he was named president, Disney Streaming, additionally overseeing Hulu.

Paulsen, Rob Voice actor; he has voiced numerous characters, including P. J. in *Goof Troop* and *A Goofy Movie*, the Troubadour in *The Three Musketeers*, Detective Donald Drake in *Chip 'n' Dale Rescue Rangers*, Gusto Gummi in *Disney's Adventures of the Gummi Bears*, Steelbeak in *Darkwing Duck*, Dr. Debolt in *TaleSpin*, Gladstone Gander in the original *DuckTales* and Gibbous in the 2017 version, Vernon in *Nightmare Ned*, Ian in *Teacher's Pet*, Mr. Vanderbosh in *The Replacements*, Hathi in *Jungle Cubs*, Raccoon in *My Friends Tigger & Pooh*, Toodles in *Mickey Mouse Clubhouse*, Denzel Dugglemonster in *Henry Hugglemonster*, Sir Kirby in *Doc McStuffins*, Commander Rax in *Mission Force One*, Rustler Leader in *Sheriff Callie's Wild West*, Grandpa Bones in *Jake and the Never Land Pirates*, and Bubba in *Firebuds*. Voices in animated sequels include Experiment 625 in *Stitch! The Movie* and *Leroy & Stitch*, Jukes in *Return to Never Land*, Otis in *Lady and the Tramp II: Scamp's Adventure*, Prince Eric in the *Little Mermaid* sequels, and Jaq, the Grand Duke, Sir Hugh, and the Baker in the *Cinderella* sequels.

Pauper King, The (TV) Show; part 1 of *The Prince and the Pauper*.

Pavilion Gifts Tomorrowland shop in Hong Kong Disneyland; opened Dec. 14, 2018, replacing Star Command Suppliers. S.H.I.E.L.D. and Marvel merchandise is sold.

Paxton, Bill (1955–2017) Actor; appeared in *Indian*

Summer (Jack Belston), *Tombstone* (Morgan Earp), *Mighty Joe Young* (Gregg O'Hara), *Million Dollar Arm* (Tom House), and *Ghosts of the Abyss* (host), and on TV in *Marvel's Agents of S.H.I.E.L.D.* (John Garrett). He directed *The Greatest Game Ever Played*.

Pay-TV The first Disney films were shown on pay-TV on Apr. 1, 1978. On Apr. 18, 1983, The Disney Channel began operation.

Payant, Gilles (1947–2012) Actor; appeared in *Big Red* (Rene Dumont).

Paying the Price (film) Educational release in Mar. 1991. 17 min. A new teen in town is coerced to shoplift by friends, only to be arrested and forced to face the consequences.

Paymer, David Actor; appeared in *Quiz Show* (Dan Enright), *Nixon* (Ron Ziegler), *The Sixth Man* (Coach Pederson), *Mighty Joe Young* (Harry Ruben), and *Mumford* (Dr. Ernest Delbanco), and on TV in *Sky High* (Vic), *The Absent-Minded Professor* (Oliphant), *Rock 'n' Roll Mom* (Boris), and *Line of Fire* (Jonah Malloy), with guest appearances in *Brothers & Sisters* (Donald Dudley) and *Perception* (Rueben Bauer).

Pays des Contes de Fées, Le SEE LE PAYS DES CONTES DE FÉES.

PB&J Otter (TV) Half-hour animated series on Disney Channel; premiered Mar. 15, 1998. The show features the adventures of 3 young river otters named Peanut, Jelly, and Baby Butter, and their friends, the Raccoon, Duck, and Beaver families who live in the close-knit community of Lake Hoohaw. Voices include Adam Rose (Peanut), Jenell Slack (Jelly), Gina Marie Tortorici (Baby Butter), Chris Phillips (Ernest), Gwendolyn S. Shepherd (Opal). 65 episodes. From Jumbo Pictures.

PCH Grill, Disney's Casual buffet dining in Disney's Paradise Pier Hotel (formerly the Disneyland Pacific Hotel) at Disneyland Resort; opened May 23, 1997, taking the place of Summertree. In a colorful, surfing-inspired atmosphere, diners greeted characters at breakfast and enjoyed Italian fare at dinner. Closed in Mar. 2020.

Pearl Harbor (film) On Dec. 7, 1941, squadrons of Japanese warplanes launched a surprise attack on the U.S. armed forces at Pearl Harbor in Hawai'i. This infamous day jolted America from peaceful isolationism to total war and altered the course of history. It has an especially devastating impact on 2 daring young American pilots and a dedicated nurse. Directed by Michael Bay. A Touchstone/Jerry Bruckheimer film. Released May 25, 2001, after a May 21 premiere aboard the USS *John C. Stennis*, a nuclear aircraft carrier, at Pearl Harbor. Stars Ben Affleck (Rafe McCawley), Josh Hartnett (Danny Walker), Kate Beckinsale (Evelyn Stewart), Cuba Gooding, Jr. (Dorie Miller), Tom Sizemore (Earl), Jon Voight (President Roosevelt), Colm Feore (Admiral Kimmel), Dan Aykroyd (Capt. Thurman), Mako (Admiral Yamamoto), Alec Baldwin (Jimmy Doolittle), William Lee Scott (Billy), Mike Shannon (Gooz), Peter Firth (Captain of the *West Virginia*), Scott Wilson (General George Marshall). 183 min. Filmed in Cinema-Scope on location on Oahu, and in California and Texas. It won the Oscar for Sound Editing for 2001 for George Watters II and Christopher Boyes, as well as nominations for Sound, Original Song ("There You'll Be"), and Visual Effects.

Pearson, Ridley Best-selling author of suspense and young adult adventure books, including the *Kingdom Keepers* and *Peter and the Starcatchers* (with Dave Barry) series, published by Disney.

Pecos Bill (film) Segment of *Melody Time*, featuring "Blue Shadows on the Trail," sung by Roy Rogers and the Sons of the Pioneers. Released as a short in 1955. 23 min.

Pecos Bill Cafe Frontierland counter-service restaurant in the Magic Kingdom at Walt Disney World; opened Oct. 1, 1971. Served Mexican fare along with hamburgers and grilled chicken breast sandwiches. It closed Jan. 5, 1998, and was then remodeled and enlarged to become Pecos Bill Tall Tale Inn & Cafe, opening May 1998. Also in Westernland in Tokyo Disneyland; opened Apr. 15, 1983.

Peculiar Penguins (film) Silly Symphony cartoon released Sep. 1, 1934. Directed by Wilfred Jackson. Peter and Polly Penguin are sweethearts. Their wintry antics include catching fish and escaping the jaws of a hungry shark.

Pedro (film) Segment of *Saludos Amigos*, about a baby airplane carrying the mail. Released as a short May 13, 1955.

Pee Wees vs. City Hall, The (TV) Show; part 1 of *Moochie of Pop Warner Football.*

Peet, Bill (1915–2002) He worked in story at the Disney Studio 1938–1964, with credits on films from *Fantasia* to *The Sword in the Stone.* Peet made a name for himself in later years by writing and illustrating children's books. He wrote his autobiography for Houghton Mifflin in 1989. He was named a Disney Legend in 1996.

Peg Vampish dog in the dog pound in *Lady and the Tramp*; voiced by Peggy Lee.

Pelican and the Snipe, The (film) Special cartoon released Jan. 7, 1944. Directed by Hamilton Luske. Vidi, the snipe, tries to stop his pelican friend, Monte, from sleepwalking, which puts him in danger of being killed. But Monte ends up rescuing Vidi in a bombing raid. The film was originally meant to be part of *The Three Caballeros.*

Pélisson, Gilles He was named chairman of Euro Disney in Feb. 1997; he had joined the company as executive vice president in Jul. 1995, and was elevated to president in Feb. 1996, serving in that post until leaving the company in Apr. 2000.

Pendleton, Karen (1946–2019) Mouseketeer from the 1950s *Mickey Mouse Club* TV show. Also appeared in *Westward Ho the Wagons!* (Myra Thompson), and on TV in *Along the Oregon Trail.*

Pendleton Woolen Mills Dry Goods Store Frontierland shop in Disneyland; open Jul. 18, 1955–Apr. 29, 1990. It was one of the longest-running original participants of Disneyland, popular for its heavy woolen and leather goods. It later became Bonanza Outfitters.

Penguins (film) A Disneynature feature released Apr. 17, 2019, also in IMAX. In this coming-of-age story, an Adélie penguin named Steve joins millions of fellow males in the icy Antarctic spring on a quest to build a suitable nest, find a life partner, and start a family. None of it comes easy for him, especially considering he's targeted by everything from killer whales to leopard seals. Directed by Alastair Fothergill and Jeff Wilson. Narrated by Ed Helms. 76 min. It was the first Disneynature film to be released in IMAX.

Penguins: Life on the Edge (film) Documentary chronicling the making of Disneynature's *Pen-guins*; digitally released Apr. 3, 2020, on Disney+. Cinematographers brave the brutal Antarctic, pushing through frigid temperatures, hurricane-force winds, and the overwhelming aroma of 1 million penguins. Narrated by Blair Underwood. Directed by Alastair Fothergill and Jeff Wilson. 78 min. From Silverback Films and Disneynature.

Penn, Kal Actor; appeared on TV in *Designated Survivor* (Seth Wright), on Disney+ in *The Santa Clauses* (Simon Choksi), and starred in/exec. produced *Kal Penn Approves This Message* on Freeform. He voiced Mr. Singh in *Fancy Nancy* and Mikku in *Mira, Royal Detective.*

Penn Zero: Part-Time Hero (TV) Animated comedy-adventure series on Disney XD; debuted Feb. 13, 2015. Penn Zero is a regular boy who inherits the not-so-regular job of part-time hero. Every day after school, Penn leads his team of best friends as they zap to other dimensions to fill in for heroes in need and battle the evil part-time villain Rippen. Penn uses his unconventional heroic skills to save the day—his own way. Voices include Thomas Middleditch (Penn Zero), Adam DeVine (Boone), Tania Gunadi (Sashi), Alfred Molina (Rippen), Larry Wilmore (Larry). From Disney Television Animation.

Pennsylvania Miners' Story, The (TV) Two-hour movie on ABC; aired Nov. 24, 2002. Based on the summer 2002 rescue of 9 coal miners at Quecreek mine, after they had been trapped for 77 hours underground. Directed by David Frankel. Stars Graham Beckel (Randy Fogle), Michael Bowen (Robert Pugh), Tom Bower (John Unger), Dylan Bruno (Blaine Mayhugh), Brad Greenquist (Ronald Hileman), Robert Knepper (Moe Popernack), William Mapother (John Phillippi), John Ratzenberger (Tom Foy), John David Souther (Dennis Hall). From Touchstone Television in association with The Sanitsky Company. Filmed in Valencia, California, and on location in Somerset County, Pennsylvania. From Sanitsky and Touchstone Television.

Penny Girl kidnapped by Madame Medusa in *The Rescuers*; voiced by Michelle Stacy.

Penny Arcade Attraction on Main Street, U.S.A. in Disneyland; opened Jul. 17, 1955. Themed to Main Street's turn-of-the-century era, the arcade features antique Mutoscopes and Cail-o-Scopes, along with more modern video games. Also on Main Street, U.S.A. in the Magic Kingdom at Walt Disney

World (open Oct. 1, 1971–Mar. 19, 1995, later becoming part of the Main Street Athletic Club) and in World Bazaar at Tokyo Disneyland.

Pentatonix: Around the World for the Holidays (TV) Holiday special on Disney+; digitally premiered Dec. 2, 2022. Superstar a cappella group Pentatonix is struggling to find inspiration for their annual holiday album, and to make matters worse, their manager mistakenly locks them in a magic mailroom. But with the help of some Disney magic, viewers are sent on a whirlwind tour to discover holiday traditions and inspiration from Pentatonix fans all around the globe: from Tokyo to Grenada, Ghana to Mexico and Iceland. Stars Pentatonix (Mitch Grassi, Scott Hoying, Kirstin Maldonado, Kevin Olusola, Matt Sallee), Nico Santos (manager). From Done+Dusted.

People and Places Series of 17 travelogue featurettes released 1953–1960 (*The Alaskan Eskimo*; *Siam*; *Switzerland*; *Men Against the Arctic*; *Sardinia*; *Disneyland, U.S.A.*; *Samoa*; *The Blue Men of Morocco*; *Lapland*; *Portugal*; *Wales*; *Scotland*; *Ama Girls*; *Seven Cities of Antarctica*; *Cruise of the Eagle*; *Japan*; *The Danube*). Three of the films (*The Alaskan Eskimo*, *Men Against the Arctic*, and *Ama Girls*) won Academy Awards. A 2010 documentary, *Archiving the Archives*, was an unofficial People and Places film.

People and Places—Tiburon, Sardinia, Morocco, Icebreakers (TV) Show aired Oct. 5, 1955. Directed by Winston Hibler. Segments featuring 3 People and Places films and 1 that was never completed—*Tiburon*, an island in the Gulf of California inhabited by a Native tribe.

People Like Us (film) A DreamWorks film distributed by Disney. A fast-talking salesman, Sam, has his latest deal collapse on the day he learns that his father has suddenly died. Against his wishes, Sam is called home, where he must put his father's estate in order and reconnect with his estranged family. In the course of fulfilling his father's last wishes for him to deliver $150,000 from the estate to a young lady, money he could desperately use himself, Sam uncovers a startling secret that turns his entire world upside down: he has a sister he never knew about. As their relationship develops, Sam is forced to rethink everything he thought he knew about his family—and re-examine his own life choices in the process. Directed by Alex Kurtzman. Released Jun. 29, 2012. Stars Elizabeth

Banks (Frankie), Olivia Wilde (Hannah), Michelle Pfeiffer (Lillian), Chris Pine (Sam). 115 min. Filmed in CinemaScope.

People of the Desert (TV) Show aired Apr. 10, 1957. Includes *Navajo Adventure* and *The Blue Men of Morocco*.

People on Market Street, The (film) Educational film series of 7 films released in Sep. 1977: *Wages and Production*, *Scarcity and Planning*, *Market Clearing Price*, *Demand*, *Cost*, *Supply*, *Property Rights and Pollution*.

PeopleMover Tomorrowland attraction in Disneyland; opened Jul. 2, 1967, with major improvements in 1968. The Superspeed Tunnel was added in 1977, with *Tron* footage added in 1982. Closed Aug. 21, 1995, to become Rocket Rods. By riding the PeopleMover, guests traveled inside several of the Tomorrowland attractions and were thus able to get a preview. The technology, innovative in 1967, featured electric motors in the track itself which propelled the vehicles. SEE ALSO WEDway PeopleMover.

Pepper, John E., Jr. Became a member of the Disney Board of Directors Jan. 1, 2006. He became chairman of the board Jan. 1, 2007, and retired in Mar. 2012.

Pepper Ann (TV) Animated series on *One Saturday Morning* on ABC; debuted Sep. 13, 1997. A spunky, quirky 12-year-old girl is on an eternal quest for coolness, but she's caught between childhood and adulthood. Voices include Kathleen Wilhoite (Pepper Ann), April Winchell (Lydia), Pam Segall (Moose), Clea Lewis (Nicky), Danny Cooksey (Milo), Jenna Von Oy (Trinket). From Walt Disney Television Animation. 65 episodes.

Pepper Market Food court in Disney's Coronado Springs Resort at Walt Disney World; opened Aug. 1, 1997. It became El Mercado de Coronado Sep. 2018.

Pepsi E-Stage Tomorrowland theater in Shanghai Disneyland; opened Jun. 16, 2016. It originally presented a daytime workout show called *Baymax Super Exercise Expo* and transformed at night into Club Destin-E at Tomorrowland, a high-energy, interactive musical revue featuring a disc jockey, an anime pop star, and androids.

Perception (TV) Hour-long drama series on TNT; aired Jul. 9, 2012–Mar. 17, 2015. An eccentric neuroscientist with a unique view of the world, Dr. Daniel Pierce, teams up with the FBI to crack difficult cases. He has an intimate knowledge of human behavior and a masterful understanding of the mind, but limited social skills. Stars Eric McCormack (Daniel Pierce), Rachael Leigh Cook (Agent Kate Moretti), Arjay Smith (Max Lewicki), Kelly Rowan (Natalie Vincent). From ABC Studios.

Percival McLeach Poacher villain in *The Rescuers Down Under*; voiced by George C. Scott.

Percy Governor Ratcliffe's pampered dog in *Pocahontas*.

Perdita Female lead Dalmatian in *One Hundred and One Dalmatians*; voiced by Cate Bauer and Lisa Daniels. Perdita had a litter of 15 puppies.

Peregoy, Walt (1925–2015) After a few years as an inbetweener in the late 1930s, Walt left the Studio for over a decade, returning in 1951 to work as a designer and animator on *Peter Pan* and *Lady and the Tramp*. He became lead background painter on *Sleeping Beauty* and did color styling on *One Hundred and One Dalmatians*. He left Disney after working on features from *The Sword in the Stone* to *The Jungle Book*, but returned in 1977 as an Imagineer working on architectural facades, sculptures, and murals for The Land and Journey Into Imagination in EPCOT Center. He was named a Disney Legend in 2008.

Perfect American, The Unauthorized opera by Philip Glass, which paints an unappealing look at the last years of Walt Disney's life, portraying him as a megalomaniac. The company denied use of the Disney characters. The opera, based on a novel by Peter Stephan Jungk, opened Jan. 22, 2013, at the Teatro Real in Madrid, Spain.

Perfect Game (film) Direct-to-video release Apr. 18, 2000, by Buena Vista Home Entertainment, of a film by Up to Bat Productions. When 11-year-old Kanin gets a new coach for his Little League baseball team, he discovers that the coach thinks he's a terrible player and spends all his time coaching the good players. Kanin and some other "Little League losers" fire their coach and set their sights on the championship with the aid of Kanin's mom and a retired high school coach. Directed by Dan Guntzelman. Stars Ed Asner (Billy Hicks), Patrick Duffy (Bobby Geiser), Cameron Finley (Kanin), Tracy Nelson (Diane), Drake Bell (Bobby Jr.). 99 min.

Perfect Harmony (TV) A Disney Channel Premiere Film; first aired Mar. 31, 1991. Directed by Will MacKenzie. Two young men at a Southern prep school overcome the boundaries of racism to pursue a friendship based on their love of music. Stars Justin Whalin (Taylor Bradshaw), Eugene Byrd (Landy Allen), David Faustino (Paul Bain), Cleavon Little (Rev. Clarence Branch), Peter Scolari (Derek Sanders), Darren McGavin (Roland Hobbs). 93 min. Filmed at Berry College in Rome, Georgia.

Perfect Isn't Easy Song from *Oliver & Company*, sung by the pampered poodle, Georgette; written by Jack Feldman, Bruce Sussman, and Barry Manilow.

Perilous Assignment (TV) Show aired Nov. 6, 1959. Directed by Hamilton S. Luske. Behind the scenes of the filming of *Third Man on the Mountain* on location in Zermatt, Switzerland, where the cast and crew endure many hardships.

Perils of a Homesick Steer, The (TV) Show; part 2 of *Sancho, the Homing Steer*.

Perkins, Anthony (1932–1992) Actor; appeared in *The Black Hole* (Dr. Alex Durant).

Perkins, Elizabeth Actress; appeared in *The Doctor* (June) and *Indian Summer* (Jennifer Morton), and made TV guest appearances in *Monk* (Christine Rapp) and *How to Get Away with Murder* (Marren Trudeau). She voiced Coral in *Finding Nemo*.

Perkins, Les He originated the Disney Character Voices department in 1988 to standardize the character voices, also voicing Mickey Mouse on 2 TV specials and Toad in *Who Framed Roger Rabbit*. He has produced documentaries and bonus features for home entertainment releases and written extensively on Disney history.

Perlman, Rhea Actress; appeared on TV in *H-E-Double Hockey Sticks* (Ms. B), as Carla Tortelli in *Mickey's 60th Birthday* and *Disneyland's 35th Anniversary Celebration*, and made a cameo in *Blossom* (godmother). She voiced Cid in *Star Wars: The Bad Batch* and Nine-Eye in The Timekeeper at Walt Disney World.

Perrault, Charles (1628–1703) Author of the stories upon which *Cinderella* and *Sleeping Beauty* were based.

Perri (film) The first, and only, True-Life Fantasy. Directed by N. Paul Kenworthy Jr. and Ralph Wright. Released Aug. 28, 1957. The story of a little pine squirrel named Perri and her life from childhood to maturity. When Perri's life is threatened by a marten, her father sacrifices his life to lure it away from Perri's nest. Now alone with her brothers, she seeks a new nest of her own, and even falls in love with Porro, all the while dodging marten and wildcat. Based on a story by Felix Salten, who had written *Bambi*, the film was shot in Jackson Hole, Wyoming, and the Uintah National Forest in Utah. 74 min. Nominated for an Academy Award. Animated effects were credited to Joshua Meador, Ub Iwerks, and Peter Ellenshaw; and Paul Smith wrote the musical score. Roy E. Disney, Walt's nephew, contributed some of the footage.

Perry the Platypus Crime-fighting pet platypus, aka Agent P, in *Phineas and Ferb*; voiced by Dee Bradley Baker.

Persephone Female lead character in *The Goddess of Spring* (1934), which may have been an attempt by the Disney animators to practice animating a human character before *Snow White and the Seven Dwarfs*.

Persoff, Nehemiah (1919–2022) Actor; appeared on TV in *Michael O'Hara the Fourth* (Artie Moreno) and *The Treasure of San Bosco Reef* (Captain Malcione).

Pesci, Joe Actor; appeared in *Betsy's Wedding* (Oscar Henner) and *Gone Fishin'* (Joe Waters).

Pests of the West (film) Pluto cartoon released Jul. 21, 1950. Directed by Charles Nichols. Bent-Tail, the coyote, and his son, Junior, try again to steal what Pluto guards, this time chickens in a henhouse, but this proves as unsuccessful as their previous outing in *Sheep Dog* (1949).

Pet Store, The (film) Mickey Mouse cartoon released Oct. 28, 1933. Directed by Wilfred Jackson. Working in a pet store, Mickey, with the help of the store animals, saves Minnie from a gorilla that escapes from its cage. In the fight, the store is trashed. Mickey quits and he and Minnie leave just before Tony, the owner, returns.

Petal to the Metal (film) Special cartoon, starring Bonkers, released Aug. 7, 1992. Directed by David Block. In delivering a bouquet of flowers across town to a stunning starlet named Fawn Deer, a delirious delivery-cat named Bonkers D. Bobcat turns a relatively easy assignment into a catalog of catastrophes. Racing against the clock to meet his 5-min. delivery deadline and keep his job, Bonkers encounters a wide array of ridiculous roadblocks, ranging from banana peels to the world's slowest taxi driver. Released with *3 Ninjas*. While the original pre-production work took place in California, the animation was done in France. From Walt Disney Television Animation. 8 min.

Pete Also known as Peg Leg Pete and Black Pete, this gruff, catlike character appeared first in the Alice Comedies in 1925 (making him the longest recurring Disney character), but soon became better known as Mickey Mouse's, and later Donald Duck's and Goofy's, primary nemesis. In the earliest cartoons he had a peg leg, but that was dispensed with in his later appearances.

Peter and the Starcatchers A prequel to *Peter Pan*, telling the backstory of the characters; a novel by Dave Barry and Ridley Pearson and released by Disney Publishing in 2004. The initial book eventually became a series of books. A stage version of the novel, entitled *Peter and the Starcatcher*, prepared in conjunction with Disney Theatrical Productions had its premiere performance in a tryout engagement at California's La Jolla Playhouse for 3 weeks beginning Feb. 13, 2009. An off-Broadway production opened Mar. 9, 2011. It opened on Broadway at the Brooks Atkinson Theatre Apr. 15, 2012, after previews began Mar. 28. The play won 5 Tony Awards: Christian Borle (Actor in a Featured Role), Donyale Werle (Scenic Design), Paloma Young (Costume Design), Jeff Croiter (Lighting Design), and Darron L. West (Sound Design). The Broadway show closed Jan. 20, 2013.

Peter and the Wolf (film) Segment of *Make Mine Music*, told by Sterling Holloway, about the brave young boy who goes with a duck, cat, and bird to catch the wolf, with each character represented by a musical instrument in the orchestra. Peter is represented by a string quartet; Sasha the bird is by a flute, Sonia the duck is by an oboe, Ivan the cat is by a clarinet, Grandpa is by a bassoon, and the hunters are by kettledrums. The music is by Prokofiev. Released as a short Sep. 14, 1955. 16 min.

Peter Pan (film) Story of the magical boy who wouldn't grow up who teaches the 3 Darling children—Wendy, John, and Michael—to fly to Never Land with him where they embark on adventures with the chief inhabitants, Captain Hook and his crew of pirates. The fairy, Tinker Bell, is jealous of Peter's attentions to Wendy, and duped into helping Captain Hook. After rescuing the princess, Tiger Lily, Peter must save his band, the Lost Boys, and the Darlings from Hook. Released Feb. 5, 1953. Directed by Hamilton Luske, Clyde Geronimi, Wilfred Jackson. Features the voices of Bobby Driscoll (Peter Pan), Kathryn Beaumont (Wendy), Hans Conried (Captain Hook/Mr. Darling), Bill Thompson (Mr. Smee). 77 min. Songs include "You Can Fly! You Can Fly! You Can Fly!" "The Second Star to the Right," and "Your Mother and Mine" by Sammy Cahn and Sammy Fain. Walt Disney planned as early as 1935 to make this film, arranging in 1939 with the Great Ormond Street Hospital in London (who had the rights to the play bequeathed by author James M. Barrie) for permission, but it was not until 1949 that production actually began. Captain Hook introduced a new kind of Disney villain—one who could be ruthless, but that audiences could also laugh at. It was rereleased in theaters in 1958, 1969, 1976, 1982, and 1989. First released on video in 1990.

Peter Pan & Wendy (film) Live-action adventure/fantasy scheduled for digital release on Disney+ Apr. 28, 2023. The timeless tale of a young girl who, defying her parents' wishes to attend boarding school, travels with her 2 younger brothers to the magical Neverland [sic]. There, she meets a boy who refuses to grow up, a tiny fairy, and an evil pirate captain, and they soon find themselves on a thrilling and dangerous adventure far, far away from their family and the comforts of home. Directed by David Lowery. Stars Alexander Molony (Peter Pan), Ever Anderson (Wendy), Jude Law (Captain Hook), Yara Shahidi (Tinker Bell), Molly Parker (Mrs. Darling), Alan Tudyk (Mr. Darling), Joshua Pickering (John), Jacobi Jupe (Michael), Alyssa Wapanatâhk (Tiger Lily), Jim Gaffigan (Smee). Based on J. M. Barrie's novel *Peter and Wendy* and inspired by the 1953 animated film. Filming locations include Canada's Vancouver and its province of Newfoundland. From Walt Disney Studios.

Peter Pan Story, The (film) Made in the early days of TV, this promotional film for *Peter Pan* took audiences behind the scenes; released in 1952. 12 min.

Peter Pan's Flight Fantasyland attraction in Disneyland; opened Jul. 17, 1955, and redesigned in 1983. Also opened in Fantasyland in the Magic Kingdom at Walt Disney World Oct. 3, 1971; Tokyo Disneyland Apr. 15, 1983; Disneyland Paris Apr. 12, 1992; and Shanghai Disneyland Jun. 16, 2016, with a unique ride system. Based on Disney's 1953 film. The attraction is different because the vehicles are suspended from an overhead rail, giving guests the feeling of flying through the evening skies over London and Never Land. Makes use of black light and fiber optics. A new interactive queue was added to the Walt Disney World attraction in Jan. 2015, with new special effect enhancements added to the Disneyland version in Jul. 2015.

Peter Pan's Never Land Area announced for Fantasy Springs in Tokyo DisneySea with two main attractions—a flight over Never Land to rescue John Darling in a battle with Captain Hook and a visit to Pixie Hollow, where Tinker Bell and her fairy friends live. Guests will also explore a pirate ship and dine in a secret hideaway.

Peter Penguin Star of *Peculiar Penguins* (1934).

Peter Tchaikovsky Story, The (TV) Show aired Jan. 30, 1959. Directed by Charles Barton. Background information on Tchaikovsky gathered during the making of *Sleeping Beauty* led to this biographical show, telling stories of the life of the great Russian composer from a child, born in 1840, to adulthood. The film covers his education and early displays of musical genius. Later, after a number of rebuffs by the public and a great disappointment in love, young Tchaikovsky has a stunning success with his "Sleeping Beauty Ballet," whose premiere he directs himself. Stars Grant Williams, Rex Hill, Lilyan Chauvin, Leon Askin. This was the first TV show ever to be simulcast in stereo. An FM radio had to be placed near the TV set to get the full effect. The film was released theatrically abroad.

Peters, Brock (1927–2005) Actor; appeared on TV in *The Million Dollar Dixie Deliverance* (Zechariah) and *Polly* (Mr. Pendergast), and voiced Druid Chief in *DuckTales* and Usula in *The Legend of Tarzan*.

Petersen, Paul Actor; he was hired as a Mouseketeer for the *Mickey Mouse Club* in 1955 but let go shortly afterward. He wrote the book *Walt, Mickey and Me* (Dell, 1977) about the show and his experiences with it. He also appeared in *The Happiest Millionaire* (Tony).

Pete's Dragon (film) Lively musical comedy in which a magical and sometimes mischievous dragon, Elliott, inadvertently causes chaos and confusion in Passamaquoddy, a Maine fishing village. To help a young orphan, Pete, break away from his evil foster parents, the Gogans, and find a happy home with Nora and her father, Lampie, in their lighthouse, Elliott must avoid the clutches of the greedy Dr. Terminus, who wants to exploit him. Premiered Nov. 3, 1977; general release Dec. 16, 1977. Directed by Don Chaffey. 135 min. Stars Helen Reddy (Nora), Mickey Rooney (Lampie), Jim Dale (Dr. Terminus), Red Buttons (Hoagy), Shelley Winters (Lena Gogan), Sean Marshall (Pete), Jane Kean (Miss Taylor), Jim Backus (Mayor), Charles Tyner (Merle), Gary Morgan (Grover), Jeff Conaway (Willie), Cal Bartlett (Paul), and featuring the voice of Charlie Callas as Elliott the dragon. This was internationally known vocalist Helen Reddy's first starring role, and the film debut of Sean Marshall, as Pete, who went on to provide the voice for the boy in *The Small One*. The musical score was written by Al Kasha and Joel Hirschhorn and included "Candle on the Water," "It's Not Easy," "There's Room for Everyone," "Brazzle Dazzle Day," "In These Hills," "Every Little Piece," and "Passamaschloddy." Animation art director Ken Anderson, animation director Don Bluth, and effects animator Dorse A. Lanpher were responsible for the ebullient animated dragon and his memorable interactions with the live actors. The story originated from writers Seton I. Miller and S. S. Field, who brought the property to Disney, where it was purchased years earlier. However, it was not until 1975 that producer Jerome Courtland asked screenwriter Malcolm Marmorstein to adapt a screenplay. The Passamaquoddy town square and wharf area were constructed on the Disney Studio lot partly from the old Western set. Jack Martin Smith, the art director, face-lifted 30 existing buildings and constructed 8 more, with interiors designed on the Disney soundstages. The lighthouse for the film was built on a point above Morro Bay, California, substituting for Maine. It was equipped with a large Fresnel-type lighthouse lens, with a wick stand inside that created a beacon visible from 18–24 miles. In fact, it worked so well that Disney had to get special permission from the Coast Guard to operate it, since its operation would have confused passing ships. The domestic gross on the film's initial release was $18 million, a disappointment to the Disney Studio, which had hoped for another *Mary Poppins* success. The movie was nominated for Best Original Song ("Candle on the Water") and Best Original Song Score, by Al Kasha, Joel Hirschhorn, and Irwin Kostal. Because of the disappointing box office, the film was cut from its original 135 min. to 129 min. during its initial run. A reissue appeared in 1984 that was edited further to 106 min.

Pete's Dragon (film) For years, old wood-carver Mr. Meacham has delighted local children with stories of the fierce dragon that resides deep in the woods of the Pacific Northwest. To his daughter, Grace, who works as a forest ranger, these stories are little more than tall tales, until she meets Pete. Pete is a mysterious 10-year-old with no home or family who claims to live in the woods with a giant green dragon named Elliot, who seems remarkably similar to the dragon from Mr. Meacham's stories. With the help of Natalie, an 11-year-old girl whose father, Jack, owns the local lumber mill, Grace sets out to determine where Pete came from, where he belongs, and the truth about this dragon. Directed by David Lowery. Released Aug. 12, 2016, in the U.S., after an Aug. 10 release in Italy. Stars Bryce Dallas Howard (Grace), Karl Urban (Gavin), Robert Redford (Mr. Meacham), Wes Bentley (Jack), Oona Laurence (Natalie), Oakes Fegley (Pete). 102 min. Filmed in wide-screen format in New Zealand. A reimagining of the 1977 Disney film of the same title (for which the dragon's name is spelled Elliott).

Pete's Silly Sideshow Character meeting location in Storybook Circus in the Magic Kingdom at Walt Disney World; opened Oct. 4, 2012. Inside the circus tent, Pete shines the spotlight on Minnie Magnifique (Minnie as a circus star), Madame Daisy Fortuna (Daisy as a fortune teller), The Great Goofini (Goofy as a stunt pilot), and The Astounding Donaldo (Donald as a snake charmer). It replaced the Judge's Tent in Mickey's Toontown Fair. Beginning in 2019, Pluto, the Wonder Pup, appeared in Minnie's place.

Petit Café, Le See Le Petit Café.

Petit Train du Cirque, Le See Le Petit Train du Cirque.

Pfeiffer, Michelle Actress; appeared in *Dangerous Minds* (LouAnne Johnson), *Up Close & Personal* (Tally Atwater), *A Thousand Acres* (Rose Cook Lewis), *People Like Us* (Lillian), *Maleficent: Mistress of Evil* (Queen Ingrith), and as Janet van Dyne in *Ant-Man and the Wasp* and later Marvel Studios films.

Pfeiffer, Walt (1901–1976) Childhood friend of Walt Disney's from Kansas City; Walt considered the Pfeiffer home as his "laughing place." The 2 boys would put on acts in vaudeville theaters as "The Two Walts." Pfeiffer was employed by Walt Disney Productions in various capacities from 1935 until his retirement in 1972.

Phantom Boats Tomorrowland attraction in Disneyland until Sep. 1956. The boats sported large fins. Replaced Tomorrowland Boats. The site was later used for the Submarine Voyage.

Phantom Manor A version of the Haunted Mansion in Frontierland at Disneyland Paris; opened Apr. 12, 1992. As the story goes, the dilapidated manor was once home to one of Thunder Mesa's founding families that struck it rich during the Gold Rush. Today, the house is a ghostly shadow of its former opulence, and visitors are invited inside to discover its discomforting secrets. The story centers on the manor's owner, Henry Ravenswood, his daughter, Melanie, and the restless spirits that haunt the manor. The attraction underwent an extensive refurbishment in 2018, reopening with new illusions, along with upgraded audio and Audio-Animatronics figures. Visitors may recognize the voice of Vincent Price as the narrator; the Imagineers resurfaced the actor's dialogue, originally recorded for the attraction in 1992, but not used until this point.

Phantom of the Megaplex (TV) A Disney Channel Original Movie; first aired Nov. 10, 2000. A teenage boy, Pete Riley, is proud of his responsibilities as assistant manager at a megaplex, until a special premiere night is sabotaged by a mysterious figure. Directed by Blair Treu. Stars Taylor Handley (Pete Riley), Jacob Smith (Brian Riley), Caitlin Wachs (Karen Riley), Corinne Bohrer (Julie Riley), Richard Hutchman (Shawn MacGibbon), Mickey Rooney (Movie Mason). Filmed at the 10-screen Eaton Center in Toronto.

Phenomenon (film) George Malley, a regular guy, finds his life turned upside down when he is struck by a blinding white light on his 37th birthday. Suddenly George has a newfound intelligence, and an insatiable appetite for learning, and rapidly becomes a genius. Through a series of unusual situations, he gains widespread attention. Renowned scientists want to meet him, the military wants to control him, and people all over the country seek his counsel. The townspeople, on the other hand, afraid and in awe of George's genius, turn their back on him. But, as his intellectual powers grow, so does his understanding of humanity. A Touchstone film. Directed by Jon Turteltaub. Released Jul. 3, 1996. Stars John Travolta (George), Kyra Sedgwick (Lace), Robert Duvall (Doc), Forest Whitaker (Nate Pope), Richard Kiley (Dr. Wellin). Filmed in CinemaScope. 123 min. The town of Auburn, California, doubled for the fictional town of Harmon, but it was extensively redesigned, with practically every facade altered. Farmhouses were utilized in California's Petaluma and Bodega Bay.

Phenomenon II (TV) A 2-hour movie on *The Wonderful World of Disney*; first aired Nov. 1, 2003. Based on the 1996 motion picture, the story continues with George Malley, who miraculously gained increased mental and physical powers, escaping to San Francisco and beginning a new life under an assumed identity. As he adjusts to life in the big city, he senses other people may share his newfound abilities. Directed by Ken Olin. Stars Christopher Shyer (George Malley), Jill Clayburgh (Nora Malley), Peter Coyote (Dr. John Ringold), Terry O'Quinn (Jack Hatch), Gina Tognoni (Claire), Stoney Westmoreland (Nate Pope). From Touchstone Television.

Phil of the Future (TV) A Disney Channel original series; debuted Jun. 18, 2004, also airing as part of *ABC Kids* beginning in fall 2004. Phil Diffy, a teen from the year 2121, gets stranded in the present day when his family's time machine malfunctions during a vacation. Phil has to handle universal issues like being the new kid in school and making friends, while also needing to learn how to get along in a new century and keep his family's future origins a secret. Stars Ricky Ullman (Phil Diffy), Alyson Michalka (Keely Teslow), Craig Anton (Lloyd), Lise Simms (Barbara), Amy Bruckner (Pim), JP Manoux (Curtis).

Philbin, Regis (1931–2020) ABC Television personality who, for more than 50 years, entertained millions of people through talk and game shows. He starred in the nationally syn. *Live with Regis and Kelly* and served as emcee of the popular *Who*

Wants to Be a Millionaire. For many years, he was a host of the *Walt Disney World Christmas Day Parade* (later the *Disney Parks Christmas Day Parade*) and the *Walt Disney World Happy Easter Parade.* Also appeared on TV in *Walt Disney World's 20th Anniversary Celebration.* He was named a Disney Legend in 2011.

Philippe Maurice's horse in *Beauty and the Beast.*

Phillips, Frank (1912–1994) Director of cinematography on dozens of Disney TV shows and features during the 1960s and 1970s, including *The Apple Dumpling Gang, Bedknobs and Broomsticks, Escape to Witch Mountain, Herbie Rides Again, Pete's Dragon, The Mouse Factory,* and *The High Flying Spy.*

Philoctetes Hero-training satyr in *Hercules,* known as Phil; voiced by Danny DeVito.

Phineas and Ferb (TV) Animated series on Disney Channel; previewed Aug. 17, 2007, then debuted Feb. 1, 2008. Two stepbrothers attempt to make every day of their summer vacation count by building innovative creations, including the world's largest Popsicle and a backyard roller coaster, much to the exasperation of their tween sister, Candace. Meanwhile, the family's simpleminded pet platypus, Perry, leads a double life as a secret agent and faces off with the evil Dr. Doofenshmirtz in each episode. Voices include Vincent Martella (Phineas Flynn), Thomas Sangster (Ferb Fletcher), Dee Bradley Baker (Perry the Platypus), Mitchel Musso (Jeremy), Caroline Rhea (Mom), Richard O'Brian (Dad), Alyson Stoner (Isabella), Ashley Tisdale (Candace). Created by Dan Povenmire and Jeff "Swampy" Marsh. Five-time Emmy Award winner. From Walt Disney Television Animation. In Jan. 2023, it was announced the series will return with 40 new episodes.

Phineas and Ferb: Agent P's World Showcase Adventure Interactive scavenger hunt in EPCOT; available Jun. 2012–Feb. 16, 2020, replacing Kim Possible World Showcase Adventure. Guests joined Agent P and solved clues to thwart some of Dr. Doofenshmirtz's most daringly evil plots. It was replaced by DuckTales World Showcase Adventure in 2022.

Phineas and Ferb: Mission Marvel (TV) A Disney Channel special; first aired Aug. 16, 2013. Two iconic universes collide when Marvel Super Heroes and Phineas and Ferb defeat Marvel Super Villains and Dr. Doofenshmirtz in an epic battle of good versus evil. Directed by Robert Hughes and Sue Perrotto. Voices include Vincent Martella (Phineas Flynn), Ashley Tisdale (Candace Flynn), Thomas Brodie-Sangster (Ferb Fletcher), Caroline Rhea (Linda Flynn-Fletcher), Richard O'Brien (Lawrence Fletcher), Dee Bradley Baker (Perry the Platypus), Alyson Stoner (Isabella), Jeff "Swampy" Marsh (Major Monogram), Dan Povenmire (Dr. Doofenshmirtz), Tyler Mann (Carl), John Viener (Norm), Jack McBrayer (Irving), Drake Bell (Spider-Man), Adrian Pasdar (Iron Man), Travis Willingham (Thor), Fred Tatasciore (Hulk), Liam O'Brien (Red Skull), Charlie Adler (M.O.D.O.K.), Peter Stormare (Whiplash), Danny Trejo (Venom), Chi McBride (Nick Fury). From Disney Television Animation.

Phineas and Ferb: Star Wars (TV) Special on Disney Channel; debuted Jul. 26, 2014. Phineas and Ferb are living just one moisture farm over from Luke Skywalker on the planet of Tatooine when R2-D2 and the Death Star plans inadvertently fall into their speeder. With the fate of the galaxy thrust upon their shoulders, they hire Isabella, Han Solo's rival, as their pilot to help them return the plans to the Rebel Alliance. Voices include Vincent Martella (Phineas), Ashley Tisdale (Candace), Thomas Brodie-Sangster (Ferb), Caroline Rhee (Linda Flynn-Fletcher), Richard O'Brien (Lawrence Fletcher), Dee Bradley Baker (Perry the Rebelpus), Alyson Stoner (Isabella). From Disney Television Animation.

Phineas and Ferb the Movie: Across the 2nd Dimension (TV) An animated Disney Channel Original Movie; first aired Aug. 5, 2011. Phineas and Ferb discover that their pet platypus, Perry, is a secret agent, and they join him on a grand adventure that blasts them to another dimension where a truly evil Dr. Doofenshmirtz has taken over an alternate Tri-State Area. When they uncover his plot to travel back to their dimension to take over their Tri-State Area, the gang and their alter egos must band together to stop him. Voices include Dee Bradley Baker (Perry the Platypus), Thomas Sangster (Ferb Fletcher), Vincent Martella (Phineas Flynn), Bobby Gaylor (Buford Van Stomm), Kelly Hu (Stacy Hirano), Mitchel Musso (Jeremy Johnson), Dan Povenmire (Dr. Heinz Doofenshmirtz).

Phineas and Ferb The Movie: Candace Against the Universe (TV) Animated film; released digitally

Aug. 28, 2020, on Disney+. Phineas and Ferb set out across the galaxy to rescue Candace, who, after being abducted by aliens, finds utopia in a far-off planet, free of pesky little brothers. Voices include Ashley Tisdale (Candace Flynn), Vincent Martella (Phineas Flynn), David Errigo Jr. (Ferb Fletcher), Caroline Rhea (Mom), Dee Bradley Baker (Perry the Platypus), Alyson Stoner (Isabella), Maulik Pancholy (Baljeet). From Disney Television Animation.

Phipps, William (1922–2018) He voiced Prince Charming in *Cinderella* and appeared in a *Texas John Slaughter* episode ("Wild Horse Revenge") and *Homeward Bound: The Incredible Journey* (Quentin).

Phoebus Dashing Captain of the Guard in *The Hunchback of Notre Dame*; voiced by Kevin Kline.

Phoenix, Joaquin Actor; appeared in *Signs* (Merrill Hess), *The Village* (Lucius Hunt), and *Ladder 49* (Jack Morrison), and voiced Kenai in *Brother Bear*.

Physical Fitness (film) Educational film from the Fun to Be Fit series; released in Mar. 1983. The film defines fitness and shows the need for developing it to improve the quality of studying, working, and playing.

Physical Fitness and Good Health (film) Educational film made for Upjohn's Triangle of Health series; released in Aug. 1969. Exercise, rest, and proper diet are essential for physical fitness.

Pick of the Litter (TV) Unscripted docuseries; digitally released Dec. 20, 2019–Jan. 24, 2020, on Disney+. Six lovable dogs—Paco, Pacino, Tulane, Raffi, Amara, and Tartan—embark on a fascinating and suspenseful quest to become Guide Dogs for the Blind, the ultimate canine career. Based on the film of the same name. From ABC Studios. 6 episodes.

Pickens, Slim (1919–1983) Character actor; appeared in *The Great Locomotive Chase* (Pete Bracken), *Tonka* (Ace), *Savage Sam* (Wily Crup), *Never a Dull Moment* (Cowboy Schaeffer), and *The Apple Dumpling Gang* (Frank Stillwell), and on TV in *Bristle Face* (Newt Pribble); *The Saga of Andy Burnett* (Old Bill Williams); *Texas John Slaughter* (Buck); *Stub, The Best Cow Dog in the West* (Bill); *The Swamp Fox* (Plunkett); and *Runaway on the Rogue River* (Bucky Steele).

Pickett, Cindy Actress; appeared in *Son-in-Law* (Connie), and on TV in *Plymouth* (Addy Mathewson), *The Cherokee Trail* (Mary Breydon), and *Our Shining Moment* (Betty).

Pickett Suite Resort Hotel in Lake Buena Vista at Walt Disney World; opened Mar. 15, 1987. The name later changed to Guest Quarters Suite Resort. It later became DoubleTree Suites by Hilton.

Pickle and Peanut (TV) Animated buddy-comedy series on Disney XD; premiered Sep. 7, 2015. Small-town teens Pickle and Peanut embark upon their last year of high school. Determined to cram in as much fun as possible before taking on the inevitable adulthood responsibilities, the 2 underdogs dream up plans to be anything but ordinary in their slightly bizarre fictional suburb of Reno, Nevada. Voices include Jon Heder (Pickle), Johnny Pemberton (Peanut). From Disney Television Animation.

Picnic, The (film) Mickey Mouse cartoon released Oct. 23, 1930. Directed by Burt Gillett. Mickey and Minnie are having a troubled picnic with Minnie's big dog, Rover, the biggest nuisance. But the loyal animal proves his worth in a thunderstorm by providing his tail as a windshield wiper.

Picnic Basket Food kiosk in Gardens of Imagination at Shanghai Disneyland; opened Jun. 16, 2016, originally serving tea-smoked duck legs and pineapple puffs.

Pidgeon, Walter (1897–1984) Actor; appeared in *Big Red* (James Haggin) and as the voice of Sterling North in *Rascal*.

Pieces of Eight Pirate souvenir shop in New Orleans Square at Disneyland; opened in 1980, taking the place of the Pirates Arcade.

Pied Piper, The (film) Silly Symphony cartoon released Sep. 16, 1933. Directed by Wilfred Jackson. When the Pied Piper lures the rats from Hamelin Town but is not paid in gold by the mayor as promised, he lures all the children of the town to the magical Garden of Happiness in a mountain to punish the parents.

Piekarski, Julie Mouseketeer on the new *Mickey Mouse Club*.

Pierce, Bradley Michael Actor; voiced Chip in

Beauty and the Beast, Nibs in *Return to Never Land*, and Flounder in *The Little Mermaid* TV series.

Pierce, David Hyde Actor; appeared in *Nixon* (John Dean), and on TV in *When We Rise* (Dr. Jones). He provided the voice of Slim in *A Bug's Life*, Dr. Doppler in *Treasure Planet*, and Daedalus in the TV series *Hercules*.

Pigeon that Worked a Miracle, The (TV) Show aired Oct. 10, 1958. Directed by Walter Perkins. Chad, a boy who uses a wheelchair, raises pigeons, and they are the therapy that he needs to walk again, when he forgets his own troubles to try to save his favorite pigeon. Stars Bradley Payne, Winifred Davenport.

Piglet Timid pig character in the Winnie the Pooh films; originally voiced by John Fiedler.

Piglet's Big Movie (film) Piglet gets an inferior feeling when his friends begin a "honey harvest" and he is told that he is too small to help. When Piglet disappears, the others use his scrapbook as a map to find him, and in the process discover that this "very small animal" has been a big hero in a lot of ways. After an eventful search and a dramatic climax, Piglet once again demonstrates how large an influence he has been on his pals. Released Mar. 21, 2003. Directed by Francis Glebas. Voices include Jim Cummings (Winnie the Pooh and Tigger), John Fiedler (Piglet), Ken Sansom (Rabbit), Nikita Hopkins (Roo), Kath Soucie (Kanga), Peter Cullen (Eeyore), André Stojka (Owl), Tom Wheatley (Christopher Robin). 75 min. The film features several new songs written and performed by Carly Simon, including "If I Wasn't So Small (The Piglet Song)," "Mother's Intuition," and "With a Few Good Friends." A production of DisneyToon Studios, a former division of Walt Disney Feature Animation. Preproduction work was done in Burbank, but the film was animated primarily by Walt Disney Animation Japan.

Pigs Is Pigs (film) Special cartoon released May 21, 1954. Directed by Jack Kinney. Backgrounds by Eyvind Earle. McMorehouse goes to collect his 2 guinea pigs from station master Flannery and argues the animals are pets and not pigs, and therefore the shipping charges should be cheaper. While the dispute goes on, the pigs multiply, McMorehouse leaves, and Flannery sends all the pigs to the main office. Produced in the popular UPA style of limited animation. Nominated for an Academy Award.

Pin trading Program began at Walt Disney World in Oct. 1999, at Disneyland Resort in Apr. 2000, at Tokyo Disney Resort in Nov. 2000, and at Disneyland Paris in Oct. 2001, whereby guests and Cast Members exchange Disney pins among each other at special pin stations and throughout the parks. Pin trading ended at Tokyo Disney Resort in 2002. Disney pin trading was sparked by interest created by pin trading at the 1984 Summer Olympics in Los Angeles. Some pins were given free at the Disneyland main entrance to guests in 1985 during the Gift-Giver Extraordinaire Machine promotion.

Pinchot, Bronson Actor; appeared in *Blame It on the Bellboy* (bellboy), on TV in *A Million Little Things* (Berge), and on Disney Channel in *Shake It Up* (Kashlack Hessenheffer). He voiced Francois in *Lady and the Tramp II: Scamp's Adventure* and Shakey in *Buzz Lightyear of Star Command*.

Pine, Chris Actor; appeared in *The Princess Diaries 2: Royal Engagement* (Nicholas Devereaux), *People Like Us* (Sam), *The Finest Hours* (Bernie Webber), *Into the Woods* (Cinderella's Prince), and *A Wrinkle in Time* (Mr. Murry).

Pinocchio (film) A wooden puppet is brought to life by the Blue Fairy, with the promise he can become a real boy if he earns it. He is led astray by the wicked Honest John and his companion, Gideon, who turn him over to an evil puppeteer, Stromboli. Pinocchio is sent to Pleasure Island, where the wicked boys are turned into donkeys, but he escapes with the aid of his friend and conscience, Jiminy Cricket, and eventually redeems himself by saving his father, Geppetto, who had been swallowed by Monstro, the whale. The Blue Fairy rewards Pinocchio by turning him into a real boy. From an original serialized story written for a children's magazine by Collodi (the pen name of Carlo Lorenzini) in 1881. Premiered in New York City Feb. 7, 1940. Directed by Ben Sharpsteen and Hamilton Luske. Voices include Dickie Jones (Pinocchio), Cliff Edwards (Jiminy Cricket), Christian Rub (Geppetto), Evelyn Venable (Blue Fairy). 87 min. The film required the talents of 750 artists, including animators, assistants, inbetweeners, layout artists, background painters, special effects animators, and inkers and painters, who produced more than 2 million drawings and used some 1,500 shades of paint for the Technicolor production. Jiminy Cricket became the film's most popular and enduring character, appearing in subsequent Disney films and TV shows, including *Fun and Fancy Free* and the *Mickey Mouse Club*. The character, brought to life by animator Ward Kimball, was only a minor one in Collodi's tale, in which he was eventually squashed by Pinocchio. The Disney film gave him a much more important role. Gustaf Tenggren, an award-winning illustrator, was assigned to the production to give the film the kind of lavish European storybook flavor that Walt Disney envisioned. Academy Award winner for Best Score and Best Song ("When You Wish Upon a Star"). Other songs include "Hi Diddle Dee Dee" and "I've Got No Strings." Many film historians describe the film as the most beautifully realized and technically perfect of all the Disney animated features. The film cost $2.6 million in 1940, but using the same techniques and processes, it would cost well over $100 million today. *Pinocchio* was rereleased theatrically in 1945, 1954, 1962, 1971, 1978, and 1984. In 1992, it again returned to theaters in a new, painstakingly restored print by Buena Vista Worldwide Services and YCM Labs of Burbank. It was first released on video in 1985.

Pinocchio (film) Live-action and CGI musical remake of the 1940 animated feature; digitally released Sep. 8, 2022, on Disney+. A living puppet, with the help of a cricket as his conscience, must prove himself worthy to become a real boy. Directed by Robert Zemeckis. Stars Tom Hanks (Geppetto), Cynthia Erivo (Blue Fairy), Luke Evans (Coachman), Kyanne Lamaya (Fabiana), Giuseppe Battiston (Stromboli), Lewin Lloyd (Lampwick), with the voices of Benjamin Evan Ainsworth (Pinocchio), Joseph Gordon-Levitt (Jiminy Cricket), Keegan-Michael Key (Honest John), Lorraine Bracco (Sofia the Seagull), Jaquita Ta'le (Sabina). 105 min. The film retains many of Leigh Harline and Ned Washington's songs from the original animated film, with Alan Silvestri (who composed the new background score) and Glen Ballard contributing new ones, including "When He Was Here with Me," "Pinocchio Pinocchio," and "I Will Always Dance." Filmed in wide-screen format at Cardington Studios in Bedford, England, in a converted hanger where giant zeppelin airships were once built.

Pinocchio Stage musical version of the 1940 Disney film; ran in the Lyttelton Theatre at the Royal National Theatre in London Dec. 1, 2017–Apr. 10, 2018. Songs and score from the animated film adapted by Martin Lowe.

Pinocchio: A Lesson in Honesty (film) Educational film; released in Sep. 1978. A boy who plays hooky from school learns that lies only exacerbate a problem.

Pinocchio Village Haus Fantasyland counter-service restaurant in the Magic Kingdom at Walt Disney World; opened Oct. 1, 1971. Murals and furnishings are modeled after the *Pinocchio* film. SEE ALSO VILLAGE HAUS RESTAURANT (DISNEYLAND), AU CHALET DE LA MARIONNETTE (DISNEYLAND PARIS), AND PINOCCHIO VILLAGE KITCHEN (SHANGHAI DISNEYLAND).

Pinocchio Village Kitchen Fantasyland quick-service restaurant in Shanghai Disneyland; opened Jun. 16, 2016. Rice bowls, noodles, and pizza are served in an eatery decorated with murals of Pinocchio's adventures.

Pinocchio's Daring Journey Fantasyland dark-ride attraction; opened in Tokyo Disneyland Apr. 15, 1983, and in Disneyland May 25, 1983. Riders board a wood-carver's cart and follow the boy puppet as he ventures to the ominous Pleasure Island. This attraction had been in design at WED Enterprises for many years, with a plan of putting it in Disneyland. But the schedules for the New Fantasyland there and Tokyo Disneyland resulted in the attraction premiering in Tokyo a month before it opened at Disneyland. Makes ample use of special effects, including holograms and fiber optics. SEE ALSO LES VOYAGES DE PINOCCHIO (DISNEYLAND PARIS).

Pintel & Ragetti's Grub to Grab Treasure Cove quick-service counter in Shanghai Disneyland; opened Jun. 16, 2016, with barbecue meats and grilled squid skewers among the pirate-themed grub.

Pioneer Days (film) Mickey Mouse cartoon released Dec. 5, 1930. Directed by Burt Gillett. As Mickey and Minnie head west in a covered wagon, they are set upon by indigenous peoples who capture Minnie. Mickey rescues her, and when they return, they frighten off the indigenous peoples from the pioneer encampment by pretending to be an army of soldiers.

Pioneer Hall Fort Wilderness entertainment hall at Walt Disney World; opened Apr. 1, 1974. Features the *Hoop-Dee-Doo Musical Revue* and dining facilities.

Pioneer Mercantile See Davy Crockett's Pioneer Mercantile (Disneyland).

Pioneer Trails, Indian Lore and Bird Life of the Plains (film) Includes part of *Vanishing Prairie*; released on 16 mm for schools in Sep. 1962. Shows the wagon trails made by the pioneers, explains the origins of Native dance forms, and describes the types of birdlife of the prairie.

Pipe Dream Tobacconist in the Lake Buena Vista Shopping Village at Walt Disney World; open Mar. 1975–Sep. 23, 1977. Replaced by Sachet In.

Piper (film) Short cartoon from Disney • Pixar, released with *Finding Dory* Jun. 17, 2016. A hungry baby sandpiper, Piper, has to learn from a parent and a small hermit crab to overcome hydrophobia in order to eat. Directed by Alan Barillaro. 6 min. Academy Award winner. Piranha Bites Adventure Isle snack shop in Shanghai Disneyland; opened Jun. 16, 2016. As the story goes, it is run by Gar, a cook known for his tasty concoctions.

Piranha Bites Adventure Isle snack shop in Shanghai Disneyland; opened Jun. 16, 2016. As the story goes, it is run by Gar, a cook known for his tasty concoctions.

Pirate Fairy, The (film) When a misunderstood dust-keeper fairy named Zarina steals Pixie Hollow's all-important Blue Pixie Dust and flies away to join forces with the pirates of Skull Rock, Tinker Bell and her fairy friends must embark on an adventure to return it to its rightful place. However, in the midst of their pursuit of Zarina, Tink's world is turned upside down. She finds that their respective talents have been switched as they race against time to retrieve the Blue Pixie Dust and return home to save Pixie Hollow. Directed by Peggy Holmes. Voices include Lucy Hale (Periwinkle), Christina Hendricks (Zarina), Tom Hiddleston (Capt. James Hook), Matt Lanter (Sled), Lucy Liu (Silvermist), Debby Ryan (Spike), Mae Whitman (Tinker Bell). Theatrical release only at the El Capitan Theatre in Hollywood beginning Feb. 28, 2014, followed by a DVD and Blu-ray release on Apr. 1. Working title was *Tinker Bell and the Pirate Fairy*. From Disneytoon Studios.

Pirate Galleon Adventureland attraction in Disney-

land Paris; opened Mar. 2012, replacing Captain Hook's Galley. Guests can explore the *Jolly Roger*.

Pirate Treasure Adventureland shop in Tokyo Disneyland; opened Jul. 20, 2007, replacing Blackbeard's Portrait Deck.

Pirate's Adventure, A: Treasures of the Seven Seas Interactive adventure in the Magic Kingdom at Walt Disney World; debuted May 31, 2013. Guests join an interactive hunt for secret treasures hidden throughout Adventureland.

Pirates Arcade Open Feb. 14, 1967–c.1979, in New Orleans Square at Disneyland. Visitors could play a variety of pirate-themed electromechanical games. Originally known as Pirates Arcade Museum. It became the Pieces of Eight shop. See also Caribbean Arcade (Walt Disney World).

Pirates' Beach See La Plage des Pirates.

Pirates League, The Along the lines of the Bibbidi Bobbidi Boutique, The Pirates League opened in Caribbean Plaza in the Magic Kingdom at Walt Disney World on Jun. 29, 2009, and closed Mar. 15, 2020. Young guests could get a pirate makeover with beards and bandanas, swords and scars, earrings and eye patches. Also open in the Court des Anges in New Orleans Square at Disneyland Sep.–Nov. 2012, returning for the 2013 Halloween season at the Festival Arena at the Big Thunder Ranch Jamboree. On Pirate Party Nights on the Disney Cruise Line ships, The Pirates League has also taken over Bibbidi Bobbidi Boutique.

Pirates of the Caribbean New Orleans Square attraction in Disneyland; opened Mar. 18, 1967. One of the most elaborate uses of Audio-Animatronics figures ever attempted by Disney and still considered the favorite attraction by many guests. Walt Disney worked extensively on this attraction but passed away before it was finished. Guests travel by boat through scenes of pirate treasure, ghost ships, and a Caribbean town being plundered by an inept bunch of brigands, to the sounds of the attraction's theme song, "Yo Ho (A Pirate's Life for Me)." Also opened in Adventureland in the Magic Kingdom at Walt Disney World Dec. 15, 1973; in Tokyo Disneyland Apr. 15, 1983; and in Disneyland Paris Apr. 12, 1992. Revisions were made to the Disneyland and the Magic Kingdom attractions in 2006, to Tokyo Disneyland in 2007, and to Disneyland Paris in 2017, adding the Captain Jack Sparrow and Barbossa characters. An entirely new version, based on the Pirates of the Caribbean films, opened as Pirates of the Caribbean—Battle for the Sunken Treasure in Shanghai Disneyland Jun. 16, 2016.

Pirates of the Caribbean: At World's End (film) Lord Cutler Beckett of the East India Company has gained control of the terrifying ghost ship, the *Flying Dutchman*, and its malevolent, vengeful captain, Davy Jones. The *Dutchman* now roams the 7 seas and is unstoppable, destroying pirate ships without mercy under the command of Admiral Norrington. Will Turner, Elizabeth Swann, and Captain Barbossa embark on a desperate quest to gather the Nine Lords of the Brethren Court, their only hope to defeat Beckett, the *Flying Dutchman*, and his armada. But one of the Lords is missing—Captain Jack Sparrow—now trapped in Davy Jones' Locker, thanks to his encounter with the mysterious Kraken. Our heroes travel to Singapore to confront Chinese pirate Captain Sao Feng to gain charts, and a ship, that will take them off to world's end to rescue Jack. But, even if Jack is successfully rescued, the Lords may not be able to hold back the fearsome tide of Beckett and his cohorts, unless the capricious sea goddess, Calypso, imprisoned in human form, can be freed and convinced to come to their aid. As betrayal piles upon betrayal, with no one to be trusted, each must make their final alliances for one last battle, in a titanic showdown that could eliminate the freedom-loving pirates from the 7 seas forever. Directed by Gore Verbinski. Released May 25, 2007, after numerous special screenings the night before, and a May 23 release in France and Belgium. Stars Johnny Depp (Captain Jack Sparrow), Orlando Bloom (Will Turner), Keira Knightley (Elizabeth Swann), Stellan Skarsgård (Bootstrap Bill), Tom Hollander (Cutler Beckett), Chow Yun-Fat (Captain Sao Feng), Geoffrey Rush (Barbossa), Bill Nighy (Davy Jones), Jack Davenport (Norrington), Kevin McNally (Gibbs), Jonathan Pryce (Gov. Weatherby Swann), Naomie Harris (Tia Dalma), Lee Arenberg (Pintel), Mackenzie Crook (Ragetti), David Bailie (Cotton), Keith Richards (Captain Teague). 168 min. Filmed in Super 35. Second sequel to *Pirates of the Caribbean: The Curse of the Black Pearl*, with much of it filmed concurrently with *Pirates of the Caribbean: Dead Man's Chest*. Nominated for Academy Awards for Visual Effects and Makeup.

Pirates of the Caribbean—Battle for the Sunken Treasure Treasure Cove attraction in Shanghai Disneyland; opened Jun. 16, 2016. A new take on the classic Disneyland attraction, celebrating the popular characters and creativity of the Pirates of the Caribbean films. Guests embark on a journey through the Caves of Misfortune, plummet to the Graveyard of the Lost Ships, explore the undersea world of Davy Jones, and become caught in the cross fires of an epic battle. Along the way, they encounter Captain Jack Sparrow, mermaids, and the savage Kraken. The attraction features Audio-Animatronics figures and large-scale media projection, as well· as a new ride system in which boats can spin, travel sideways, and move backward.

Pirates of the Caribbean: Dead Man's Chest (film) First sequel to *Pirates of the Caribbean: The Curse of the Black Pearl*. The decidedly eccentric Capt. Jack Sparrow is caught up in another tangled web of supernatural intrigue when he is reminded of a blood debt he owes to the Ruler of the Ocean Depths, the legendary captain Davy Jones. Unless the ever-crafty Jack figures a cunning way out of this Faustian pact, he will be cursed to an afterlife of eternal servitude and damnation in the service of Jones aboard the ghostly *Flying Dutchman*. This startling development interrupts the wedding plans of Will Turner and Elizabeth Swann, who are once again thrust into Jack's misadventures, leading to escalating confrontations with Jones's destructive sea monster (the Kraken), cannibalistic islanders, flamboyant soothsayer Tia Dalma, and the mysterious appearance of Will's long-lost father, Bootstrap Bill. Meanwhile, ruthless pirate hunter Lord Cutler Beckett of the East India Trading Company sets his eye on retrieving the fabled Dead Man's Chest. According to legend, whoever possesses the Dead Man's Chest gains control of Davy Jones, and Beckett intends to use this awesome power to destroy every last pirate of the Caribbean. A Walt Disney Pictures film in association with Jerry Bruckheimer Films. Directed by Gore Verbinski. Released Jul. 7, 2006, after a premiere at Disneyland on Jun. 24. Stars Johnny Depp (Jack Sparrow), Orlando Bloom (Will Turner), Keira Knightley (Elizabeth Swann), Stellan Skarsgård (Bootstrap Bill), Bill Nighy (Davy Jones), Jack Davenport (Norrington), Jonathan Pryce (Gov. Weatherby Swann), Kevin R. McNally (Gibbs), Naomie Harris (Tia Dalma), Tom Hollander (Cutler Beckett), Lee Arenberg (Pintel), Mackenzie Crook (Ragetti), David Bailie (Cotton). 151 min. Filmed in Super 35-Scope in Burbank and at several locations in the Caribbean. The film broke all box office records on its release, including taking in $135.6 million on its first weekend, and soon became the company's highest-grossing release with over $1 billion internationally, passing *Finding Nemo*. Nominated for 4 Academy Awards, winning for Best Visual Effects (John Knoll, Hal Hickel, Charles Gibson, Allen Hall). Released on DVD in 2006.

Pirates of the Caribbean: Dead Men Tell No Tales (film) Down-on-his-luck Captain Jack Sparrow feels the winds of ill fortune blowing strongly his way when deadly ghost sailors, led by the terrifying Captain Salazar, escape from the Devil's Triangle bent on killing every pirate at sea—including Jack. Jack's only hope of survival lies in the legendary Trident of Poseidon, but to find it, he must forge an uneasy alliance with Carina Smyth, a brilliant astronomer, and Henry Turner, a headstrong young sailor in the Royal Navy. At the helm of the *Dying Gull*, his pitifully small and shabby ship, Captain Jack seeks not only to reverse his recent spate of ill fortune, but to save his very life from the most formidable and malicious foe he has ever faced. Directed by Joachim Rønning and Espen Sandberg. Released May 26, 2017, also in 3-D and IMAX, after a May 24 international release. A world premiere was held May 11, 2017, in the Walt Disney Grand Theatre at Shanghai Disney Resort. Stars Johnny Depp (Captain Jack Sparrow), Javier Bardem (Captain Salazar), Kaya Scodelario (Carina Smyth), Brenton Thwaites (Henry Turner), Kevin R. McNally (Joshamee Gibbs), Golshifteh Farahani (Shansa), David Wenham (Scarfield), Geoffrey Rush (Captain Hector Barbossa), Stephen Graham (Scrum), Orlando Bloom (Will Turner). Paul McCartney makes a cameo as a jail guard. 129 min. The 5th film in the *Pirates of the Caribbean* series. Filmed in wide-screen format at Village Roadshow Studios and other locations in Australia.

Pirates of the Caribbean: On Stranger Tides (film) Angelica, a ravishing pirate with whom Captain Jack Sparrow shares a dubious past, forces him aboard the *Queen Anne's Revenge*, the ship of the legendary pirate Blackbeard. Jack finds himself on an unexpected journey to find the fabled Fountain of Youth. Along the way, Jack must use all his wiles to deal with the barbarous Blackbeard and his crew of zombies, Angelica, the beautiful, enchanting mermaids whose masterful cunning can lure even the most seasoned sailor to his doom, and crews of Spaniards also searching for the fountain. Released May 20, 2011, after a premiere at Disneyland on May 7, and many earlier international releases, beginning with May 15 in Belgium. Directed by

Rob Marshall. Stars Johnny Depp (Captain Jack Sparrow), Penélope Cruz (Angelica), Geoffrey Rush (Captain Barbossa), Ian McShane (Blackbeard), Kevin R. McNally (Joshamee Gibbs), Sam Claflin (Philip), Astrid Bergès-Frisbey (Syrena), Keith Richards (Captain Teague), Richard Griffiths (King George). 136 min. Third sequel to *Pirates of the Caribbean: The Curse of the Black Pearl*. Released also in 3-D and IMAX versions. Filmed in CinemaScope partially in England and Hawai'i.

Pirates of the Caribbean: Tales of the Code: Wedlocked (film) Live-action short released Oct. 18, 2011, as part of a Blu-ray collection of 4 *Pirates* movies. Serves as a prequel to *The Curse of the Black Pearl*, inspired by the auction scene in the Disneyland attraction. Two wenches believe they are both betrothed to Jack Sparrow, but he has secretly traded them to the auctioneer for a fancy hat. They think the auctioneer is raising money for them, when in actuality, they are being sold as brides to the highest bidder. Directed by James Ward Byrkit. Stars John Vickery (auctioneer), Vanessa Branch (Giselle), Lauren Maher (Scarlett). 10 min. Three pirates—Marquis D'avis, Atencio, and Slurry Gibson—are named after Imagineers who worked on the original attraction.

Pirates of the Caribbean: The Curse of the Black Pearl (film) In the 18th century, Captain Jack Sparrow is roguish, yet charming, as he sails the Caribbean. But Jack's idyllic life capsizes after his nemesis, the wily Captain Barbossa, steals his ship, the *Black Pearl*, and later attacks the town of Port Royal, kidnapping the governor's daughter, Elizabeth Swann. Elizabeth's childhood friend, Will Turner, joins forces with Jack to commandeer the fastest ship in the British fleet, the HMS *Interceptor*, in a gallant attempt to rescue her and recapture the *Black Pearl*. The duo and their motley crew are pursued by Elizabeth's betrothed, the debonair, ambitious Commodore Norrington, aboard the HMS *Dauntless*. Unbeknownst to Will, whose father once served with the crew, there is a curse that has doomed Barbossa and his men to live forever as the undead, where each moonlight, they are transformed into living skeletons. The curse they carry can only be broken if a once-plundered treasure is restored and blood is spilt. Released Jul. 9, 2003. A Walt Disney Pictures film in association with Jerry Bruckheimer Films. Directed by Gore Verbinski. Stars Johnny Depp (Captain Jack Sparrow), Keira Knightley (Elizabeth Swann), Geoffrey Rush (Captain Barbossa), Orlando

Bloom (Will Turner), Jonathan Pryce (Governor Swann), Jack Davenport (Commodore Norrington). 143 min. Filmed in Super 35-Scope. The set for Port Royal's Fort Charles was built on a bluff at Palos Verdes, California; Caribbean filming took place in St. Vincent and the Grenadines. Since the film is an homage to the popular Disneyland attraction, the film's premiere was held at Disneyland on Jun. 28, 2003. The film eventually grossed over $300 million, placing it right behind *Finding Nemo* as the No. 3 film of the year. It received 5 Academy Award nominations (Best Actor [Johnny Depp], Sound Mixing, Sound Editing, Visual Effects, and Makeup).

Pirouettes de Vieux Moulin, Les Ferris wheel attached to an old mill in Fantasyland in Disneyland Paris; opened Jun. 6, 1993, closing after several years of operation. SEE ALSO OLD MILL, THE (DISNEYLAND PARIS).

Pixar Animation Studios American computer animation film studio based in Emeryville, California; founded Feb. 3, 1986. It produced *Toy Story* (the first full-length animated feature produced entirely by computer) for Disney, and in Feb. 1997, signed a 5-picture deal, with Disney agreeing to purchase up to 5% of Pixar stock. Additional productions have included *A Bug's Life, Toy Story 2, Monsters, Inc., Finding Nemo,* and *The Incredibles*. On Jan. 24, 2006, Disney announced an agreement to purchase Pixar, and the purchase was completed May 5, 2006. After the acquisition by Disney, Pixar continued its string of hits with *Cars, Ratatouille, WALL•E, Up, Toy Story 3, Cars 2, Brave, Monsters University, Inside Out, The Good Dinosaur, Finding Dory, Cars 3, Coco, Incredibles 2, Toy Story 4, Onward, Soul, Luca, Turning Red, Lightyear,* and *Elemental*. Pixar opened a Canadian subsidiary, Pixar Canada, Apr. 20, 2010, where 100 artists worked on animating short films based on characters from the Pixar feature films. Pixar Canada closed in 2013. Original series on Disney+ include *Forky Asks a Question, Dug Days, Cars on the Road,* and *Win or Lose*. SEE ALSO SPARKSHORTS.

Pixar Animation Studios: Celebrating 20 Years (TV) Special on *The Wonderful World of Disney* on ABC; aired Jun. 3, 2006, with *Toy Story*. Directed by Leslie Iwerks. John Ratzenberger hosts a comedic journey through 20 years of Pixar animation.

Pixar in Real Life (TV) Live-action short-form series on Disney+; premiered Nov. 12, 2019.

Iconic characters and moments from Pixar films are brought into the real world, surprising people when they least expect it. Filmed in and around New York City. From Improv Everywhere.

Pixar Pal-A-Round Ferris wheel attraction in Pixar Pier at Disney California Adventure; opened Jun. 23, 2018, replacing Mickey's Fun Wheel. It celebrates the stories and friendships from Disney • Pixar films, with each of the 24 gondolas featuring a different character.

Pixar Pier Boardwalk area in Disney California Adventure, based on Disney • Pixar films; opened Jun. 23, 2018, replacing a section of Paradise Pier. Pixar stories are represented in themed neighborhoods, including Incredibles Park (featuring the Incredicoaster), the Toy Story Boardwalk (with Toy Story Midway Mania! and Jessie's Critter Carousel), and Pixar Promenade (including the land's focal point, the Pixar Pal-A-Round). Dining locations include the Lamplight Lounge, Poultry Palace, Señor Buzz Churros, Angry Dogs, Jack-Jack Cookie Num Nums, and Adorable Snowman Frosted Treats. SEE ALSO GAMES OF THE BOARDWALK.

Pixar Place Area in Disney's Hollywood Studios; opened May 31, 2008, replacing Mickey Avenue. Featured Toy Story Midway Mania!, Hey Howdy Hey Take Away, and the Toy Story Dept. shop. Closed after Toy Story Mania! became part of the new Toy Story Land Jun. 30, 2018, though the area is sometimes used for special entertainment.

Pixar Place Hotel New name, announced in 2022, for Disney's Paradise Pier Hotel at Disneyland Resort. The hotel is planned to weave the artistry of Pixar into a contemporary setting, with features including a *Finding Nemo*–themed splash pad area. Great Maple, an upscale comfort food eatery, is planning to open a flagship restaurant on the first floor and operate additional food and beverage spots throughout the hotel.

Pixar Popcorn (TV) Animated series on Disney+; digitally released Jan. 22, 2021. Each "mini short" features Disney • Pixar characters in bite-size stories. From Pixar Animation Studios.

Pixar Putt Pop-up mini-golf course with 18 holes inspired by Disney • Pixar films. Debuted Aug. 1, 2021, in New York City, before traveling on to other destinations. Co-presented by Rockefeller Productions and TEG Life Like Touring.

Pixar Short Films Collection (film) Video released of animated shorts from Pixar Animation Studios Nov. 6, 2007; some were made before Pixar's contract with Disney. The shorts are: *The Adventures of Andre & Wally B*, *Luxo Jr.*, *Red's Dream*, *Tin Toy*, *Knick Knack*, *Geri's Game*, *For the Birds*, *Mike's New Car*, *Boundin'*, *Jack-Jack Attack*, *One Man Band*, *Mater and the Ghostlight*, and *Lifted*. A second volume was released on DVD and Blu-ray Nov. 13, 2012, containing *Presto*, *Day & Night*, *La Luna*, *Your Friend the Rat*, *BURN•E*, *Partly Cloudy*, *Dug's Special Mission*, *George & A. J.*, *Hawaiian Vacation*, *Air Mater*, *Time Travel Mater*, and *Small Fry*, along with student films by John Lasseter, Andrew Stanton, and Pete Docter.

Pixar Shorts Film Festival SEE DISNEY & PIXAR SHORT FILM FESTIVAL.

Pixar Story, The (film) Documentary produced, written, and directed by Leslie Iwerks about the history of Pixar Animation Studios. Through interviews with the original 3 Pixar principals (John Lasseter, Ed Catmull, Steve Jobs) and others, the story is told of the development of computer-generated animation and how Pixar helped bring audiences back to the animated film. Premiered in San Rafael, California, at the Mill Valley Film Festival Oct. 6, 2007, and released on the *WALL•E* DVD Nov. 18, 2008. 88 min. Narrated by Stacy Keach.

Pixar: We Belong Together Stage show announced in 2022 for the Studio Theater in Production Courtyard at Walt Disney Studios Park in Disneyland Paris. An emotional journey with Pixar characters highlighting the importance of friendship and family, combining stage technology, state-of-the-art video and lighting design, and a large cast of characters from many beloved Pixar films.

Pixel Perfect (TV) A Disney Channel Original Movie; first aired Jan. 16, 2004. Techno-wiz Roscoe sees his friend Samantha's band, the Zettabytes, floundering because they don't have the right image, so he uses computer technology designed by his dad to craft singer Loretta Modern—a perfect rockin' hologram who fronts the band and makes it an overnight success. But Roscoe's good deed backfires when Samantha starts to feel like an outsider in the group. Meanwhile Loretta has the world at her feet but knows it doesn't compare to being "real." At the height of the Zettabytes' success, Roscoe struggles with newfound feelings for

Samantha, a lack of nurturing from his father, and Loretta's quest to become an individual. Directed by Mark A. Z. Dippé. Stars Ricky Ullman (Roscoe), Leah Pipes (Samantha), Spencer Redford (Loretta Modern), Chris Williams (Daryl Fibbs), Brett Cullen (Xander), Tania Gunadi (Cindy), Porscha Coleman (Rachel).

Pixie Hollow Secret hideaway in Never Land, the home of Tinker Bell and her fairy friends, introduced in 2008 as part of the Disney Fairies franchise. A Pixie Hollow area opened in Disneyland in Oct. 2008, replacing Ariel's Grotto. SEE ALSO DISNEY FAIRIES PIXIE HOLLOW (ONLINE), FAIRY TALE FOREST (HONG KONG DISNEYLAND), PETER PAN'S NEVER LAND (TOKYO DISNEYSEA), AND TINKER BELL (FILM).

Pizza Oom Mow Mow Counter-service pizza restaurant in Paradise Pier at Disney California Adventure; open Feb. 8, 2001–Sep. 6, 2010. Became Boardwalk Pizza & Pasta.

Pizza Planet Arcade Counter-service restaurant in Streets of America at Disney's Hollywood Studios; opened Dec. 15, 1995, serving personal pizzas, meatball subs, and antipasto salads. Named after the arcade in *Toy Story*. Closed Jan. 18, 2016, to become PizzeRizzo when the area was transformed into Grand Avenue.

Pizza Ponte SEE MARIA & ENZO'S RISTORANTE.

Pizzafari Discovery Island counter-service restaurant in Disney's Animal Kingdom; opened Apr. 22, 1998. The colorful animal murals, together spanning more than 5,500 sq. ft. across 5 dining rooms, were painted by Imagineers Frank Armitage and his daughter, Nicole Armitage Doolittle.

Pizzeria Bella Notte Fantasyland counter-service bistro in Disneyland Paris; opened Apr. 12, 1992. Italian fare is served in a romantic setting inspired by Tony's Restaurant in *Lady and the Tramp*. An expansion of the restaurant began in 2022, taking over the former Fantasia Gelati, to add a new dining area themed to *Luca*.

PizzeRizzo Grand Avenue counter-service restaurant in Disney's Hollywood Studios; opened Nov. 18, 2016, replacing Pizza Planet Arcade. Italian favorites are served in a 2-story eatery where Rizzo the Rat from The Muppets is the proprietor. A neon billboard advertises THE CITY'S BEST RATED

PIZZA, but a handful of letters occasionally flicker off to reveal, IT'S RAT PIZZA.

PJs, The (TV) Half-hour comedy series on Fox; premiered Jan. 12, 1999, after a Jan. 10 preview, and ended Jun. 17, 2001. Produced in a stop-motion animation technique called "foamation," the series is set in a big-city housing project and takes a satirical look at urban family values through the eyes of Thurgood Stubbs, the cantankerous superintendent of the Hilton-Jacobs Projects, his wife, relatives, and friends. Voices include Eddie Murphy (Thurgood Stubbs), Loretta Devine (Muriel Stubbs), James Black (Tarnell), Michael Paul Chan (Jimmy), Ja'net DuBois (Mrs. Avery). Animation by Will Vinton Studios.

Place, Mary Kay Actress; appeared in *Captain Ron* (Katherine Harvey) and *Sweet Home Alabama* (Pearl), and on TV in *The Girl Who Spelled Freedom* (Prissy Thrash), with guest appearances in *black-ish* (Dr. Barris) and *Grey's Anatomy* (Olive Warner).

Place Where the Lost Things Go, The Song from *Mary Poppins Returns*; written by Marc Shaiman and Scott Wittman. Nominated for an Academy Award.

Plane Crazy (film) The first Mickey Mouse cartoon made, but the 3rd one released, after sound was added, in 1929. Directed by Walt Disney. Inspired by Charles Lindbergh's exploits. With the help of his farmyard friends, Mickey builds a plane and goes on an adventurous flight with Minnie until an unwilling cow passenger and an unwanted kiss ends the trip. Also later released as part of *Milestones for Mickey* (1974).

Plane Crazy Musical show at Videopolis in Disneyland; ran Mar. 15–Oct. 31, 1991. Fat Cat and Don Karnage battle it out with Baloo, Chip and Dale, and Launchpad McQuack in this comedy/mystery musical adventure. It was the first Disneyland show to feature primarily original music.

Planes (film) Computer-animated feature from Disneytoon Studios. Dusty, a bighearted, fast-flying crop duster plane from Propwash Junction, is encouraged by his mentor, a naval aviator named Skipper, to follow his dreams of competing in the most notoriously grueling air race in history, alongside the fastest air racers from around the world. There are only a couple of not-so-small problems—Dusty is not exactly built for racing, and he also happens to be afraid of heights. Dusty narrowly qualifies for the big competition, and his sportsmanship and speed begin to rattle the defending champ of the race circuit, Ripslinger, who will stop at nothing to see Dusty fail. When disaster strikes during the climax of the final race, Dusty's courage is put to the ultimate test. Released in 3-D on Aug. 9, 2013. Directed by Klay Hall. Voices include Dane Cook (Dusty), Carlos Alazraqui (El Chupacabra), Julia Louis-Dreyfus (Rochelle), Roger Craig Smith (Ripslinger), Stacy Keach (Skipper), Teri Hatcher (Dottie), Brad Garrett (Chug), Cedric the Entertainer (Leadbottom), John Cleese (Bulldog). 92 min. From Disneytoon Studios and Prana Studios in India.

Planes (film) Educational film in the Goofy's Field Trips series released Aug. 18, 1989. 15 min. Goofy shows 2 children what goes on behind the scenes at an airport.

Planes: Fire & Rescue (film) Animated comedy-adventure about second chances, featuring a dynamic crew of elite firefighting aircraft devoted to protecting historic Piston Peak National Park from raging wildfires. When world-famous air racer Dusty learns that his engine is damaged and he may never race again, he must shift gears and is launched into the world of aerial firefighting. Dusty joins forces with veteran fire and rescue helicopter Blade Ranger and his courageous team, including spirited super-scooper Dipper, heavy-lift helicopter Windlifter, ex-military transport Cabbie, and a lively bunch of all-terrain vehicles known as The Smokejumpers. Together the fearless team battles a massive wildfire and Dusty learns what it takes to become a true hero. Directed by Bobs Gannaway. Released Jul. 18, 2014. Voices include Dane Cook (Dusty), Julie Bowen (Dipper), Ed Harris (Blade Ranger), Wes Studi (Windlifter). From Disneytoon Studios and Prana Studios in India. 84 min. Filmed in wide-screen format.

Planet Hollywood A 400-seat spherical entertainment restaurant featuring displays of movie memorabilia; opened Dec. 18, 1994, in Pleasure Island at Walt Disney World. It later became part of the Town Center at Disney Springs, reopening Jan. 27, 2017, as the Planet Hollywood Observatory. Another Planet Hollywood opened in Disney Village at Disneyland Paris in summer 1996 and closed Jan. 7, 2023. A Planet Hollywood Superstore operated on Sunset Boulevard in Disney's

Hollywood Studios Jun. 26, 1997–Feb. 2, 2019, prior to it being superseded by an expansion of the Legends of Hollywood shop.

Planet M Tomorrowland toy shop in Tokyo Disneyland; opened Dec. 13, 1996. The story goes that when Mickey discovered the small "Planet M," he found the raw material toys are made from and began overseeing the production of toys at this shop.

Planning for Good Eating (film) Educational film produced under the auspices of the Coordinator of Inter-American Affairs. Careless Charlie is utilized to teach a family all about good dietary habits. Delivered Apr. 3, 1946.

Plantation Park SEE LITTLE LAKE BRYAN.

Plastics Inventor, The (film) Donald Duck cartoon released Sep. 1, 1944. Directed by Jack King. Donald bakes a plastic airplane from radio instructions and proudly goes to try it out. But it melts in a storm, coming down on a flock of blackbirds like a pie.

Platt, Oliver Actor; appeared in *The Three Musketeers* (Porthos), *Tall Tale* (Paul Bunyan), *Funny Bones* (Tommy Fawkes), *Simon Birch* (Ben Goodrich), *Bicentennial Man* (Rupert Burns), *Gun Shy* (Fulvio Nesstra), *Hope Springs* (Doug Reed), and *Casanova* (Papprizzio). For TV, he narrated *Walt Disney* (American Experience series) and voiced Everburn in *Sofia the First*.

Plausible Impossible, The (TV) Show aired Oct. 31, 1956. Directed by Wilfred Jackson, William Beaudine. Walt Disney explains some of the techniques of animation and includes, for the first time the pencil test footage of the "Soup Eating Sequence" from *Snow White and the Seven Dwarfs*. Disney used a prop book in the show called *The Art of Animation*, and many people expected to be able to find it in their bookstores, but the book was never completed quite in the manner he foresaw; instead, Bob Thomas used that title 2 years later on a book to tie in with the upcoming release of *Sleeping Beauty*.

Play It to the Bone (film) Best friends and professional boxing rivals Vince Boudreau and Caesar Dominguez have not worked in years. Finally, from out of the blue, they get the chance of a lifetime: an assignment to work together in Las Vegas. The job promises big money, but there's a hitch: they have to be there immediately. They quickly hit the road with Grace Pasic at the wheel, embarking on a circuitous route through the sizzling desert. Sparks fly as the competitive Vince and Caesar antagonize each other to a frenzy matched only by Grace's own combative temper. The going gets rougher when they pick up a sultry hitchhiker, Lia, whose presence throws the trio into further upheaval. A riotous race ensues as Vince and Caesar scramble to make it to Vegas for their big showdown. A Touchstone film. Released Dec. 25, 1999, in Los Angeles, and elsewhere Jan. 21, 2000. Directed by Ron Shelton. Stars Woody Harrelson (Vince Boudreau), Antonio Banderas (Caesar Dominguez), Lolita Davidovich (Grace Pasic), Lucy Liu (Lia). 125 min. Filmed in CinemaScope.

Playdom Disney announced in Jul. 2010 its purchase of Playdom, a leader in the business of social games—casual games that consumers played on Facebook and MySpace. The deal was completed Aug. 27, 2010. A variety of games and apps were published, including *Gardens of Time, Animal Kingdom Explorers, Marvel: Avengers Alliance*, and *Pirates of the Caribbean: Isles of War*. The final games were discontinued Sep. 2016.

Playful Pan (film) Silly Symphony cartoon released Dec. 27, 1930. Directed by Burt Gillett. Pan's musical pipe causes flowers and trees to come to life, and also saves the woodland creatures by extinguishing a fire that threatens to destroy the forest by luring the flames into the water as the animals take refuge on an island.

Playful Pluto (film) Mickey Mouse cartoon released Mar. 3, 1934. Directed by Burt Gillett. Pluto tries to help Mickey with his spring cleaning but instead becomes a nuisance and ends up caught in flypaper. The flypaper-gag sequence, animated by Norm Ferguson, has been praised as a masterful piece of animation.

Playground Fun (film) Educational film with safety experts Huey, Dewey, and Louie introducing safe ways to have fun, in the Mickey's Safety Club series; released in Sep. 1989. 20 min.

Playhouse Disney—Live on Stage! Show in Animation Courtyard at Disney's Hollywood Studios; opened Oct. 1, 2001, succeeding *Bear in the Big Blue House—Live on Stage*. Segments from *Rolie Polie Olie, Stanley, The Book of Pooh*, and *Bear in the Big Blue House* helped provide life lessons to kids.

Over the years, the show was refreshed to incorporate the newest Playhouse Disney characters. A similar show opened in Hollywood Pictures Backlot (now Hollywood Land) in Disney California Adventure Apr. 11, 2003, replacing the ABC Soap Opera Bistro. Also opened in Production Courtyard at Walt Disney Studios Park in Disneyland Paris Apr. 4, 2009, replacing Disney Channel CyberSpace Mountain at Walt Disney Television Studios. The Disney's Hollywood Studios show changed to *Disney Junior—Live on Stage!* Mar. 4, 2011, starring *Jake and the Never Land Pirates, Mickey Mouse Clubhouse, Handy Manny*, and *Little Einsteins*, followed by similar changes in Disney California Adventure Mar. 25, 2011, and later in Walt Disney Studios Park. The Disney California Adventure and Disney's Hollywood Studios attractions became *Disney Junior Dance Party!* May 26, 2017, and Dec. 22, 2018, respectively, with a new interactive concert format; performances ended in Mar. 2020 amid the global outbreak of COVID-19, with the Walt Disney World version reopening Jul. 28 as the modified *Disney Junior Play and Dance!* The Disney California Adventure show resumed Oct. 15, 2021. At Walt Disney Studios Park, it became the *Disney Junior Dream Factory* musical show Jul. 1, 2021.

Playhouse Disney Live! on Tour A stage musical celebration featuring characters from Playhouse Disney shows—*Mickey Mouse Clubhouse, Little Einsteins, My Friends Tigger & Pooh, Handy Manny*. Premiered Aug. 25, 2007, in Lakeland, Florida.

Playhouse in the Woods Venue in Arendelle Forest planned for World of Frozen in Hong Kong Disneyland. Guests will meet Anna and Elsa and participate in other activities.

Playing God (film) Stripped of his medical license after performing an operation while high on amphetamines, famed Los Angeles surgeon Dr. Eugene Sands abandons his former life only to find himself crossing paths with Raymond Blossom, a ruthless criminal. Raymond hires Eugene as his "gunshot doctor," treating associates who cannot risk visiting a hospital. Lured deeper and deeper into the dangerous underworld and growing treacherously close to Claire, Raymond's seductive girlfriend, Eugene is faced with his most challenging decision—to continue a life on the run or to face his demons and regain control of his destiny. A Touchstone film. Directed by Andy Wilson.

Released Oct. 17, 1997. Stars David Duchovny (Eugene Sands), Timothy Hutton (Raymond Blossom), Angelina Jolie (Claire). 93 min. Set in Los Angeles in the 1990s, the film used local locations all around the city.

Playing Mona Lisa (film) A brilliant 23-year-old pianist, Claire Goldstein, living in San Francisco, suddenly finds her life in a downward spiral. Her own misfortunes are the catalyst for introspection in those around her and, as she picks up the pieces of her own life, she finds that no one has a perfect life—they are just hiding behind contrived smiles, playing Mona Lisa. Directed by Matthew Huffman. Very limited theatrical release; opened Oct. 27, 2000, in San Francisco. Released without a label. Stars Alicia Witt (Claire), Harvey Fierstein (Bennett), Brooke Langton (Sabrina Pagniatti), Johnny Galecki (Arthur Kapp), Elliott Gould (Bernie Goldstein), Marlo Thomas (Sheila Goldstein), Ivan Sergei (Eddie). Based on the play *Two Goldsteins on Acid*, by Marni Freedman. 93 min.

Playing with Sharks (TV) A Disney+ feature documentary from National Geographic; digitally released Jul. 23, 2021. The daring trajectory of ocean explorer Valerie Taylor from champion spear-fisher to passionate shark protector. From the birth of cage diving to *Jaws* hysteria to the dawn of cageless shark diving, Valerie became a trailblazing advocate for the ocean's most maligned and misunderstood creatures. Directed/written by Sally Aitken. From Wildbear Entertainment, in association with Screen Australia and Screen NSW.

Plaza de los Amigos Marketplace inside Mexico at EPCOT; opened Oct. 1, 1982, selling piñatas, sombreros, ceramics, baskets, leather goods, and Mexican foodstuffs. The plaza is one of the more unique areas in World Showcase, providing a continual dusk atmosphere.

Plaza del Sol Caribe Bazaar Caribbean Plaza shop in the Magic Kingdom at Walt Disney World; opened in 1973, selling pirate merchandise.

Plaza East and Plaza West Boutiques Pair of turn-of-the-century-style shops in Disneyland Paris; opened Apr. 12, 1992, at the park main entrance. The Plaza East Boutique is themed to Main Street, U.S.A., while the Plaza West features artwork of the Wild West.

Plaza Gardens Restaurant Victorian pavilion on

Main Street, U.S.A. in Disneyland Paris; opened Apr. 12, 1992.

Plaza Ice Cream Parlor A mainstay on Main Street, U.S.A. in the Magic Kingdom at Walt Disney World; opened Oct. 1, 1971. Presented originally by Borden, later by Sealtest, Kraft, Nestlé, and Edy's.

Plaza Inn Restaurant in the Central Plaza at Disneyland; opened Jul. 18, 1965. It was formerly called the Red Wagon Inn. One of the most attractively decorated restaurants in the park, the buffeteria is furnished with authentic antiques, stained glass, crystal chandeliers and sconces, and tufted velvet upholstery. Lillian Disney handpicked many of the restaurant's 19th-century furnishings. The fried chicken is a longtime specialty. Also a Victorian-themed restaurant in Hong Kong Disneyland; opened Sep. 12, 2005, hosted by Maxim's and serving Chinese cuisine.

Plaza Pavilion Buffeteria restaurant in the Central Plaza at Disneyland; opened Jul. 17, 1955. Before the Tahitian Terrace Restaurant was built on the backside of its building, guests could take their meals from the Plaza Pavilion to tables on a terrace overlooking the Jungle Cruise. An early specialty was a French dip beef sandwich. Open only during summer and holiday seasons. It closed Jul. 1998 and became an annual passport processing center Nov. 2000–Jun. 6, 2004. Starting May 5, 2005, the patio was themed to a Main Street Fair, with pin trading, a pianist, lemonade stand, etc., and a Jr. Chef Baking Experience, hosted by Nestlé. It became Jolly Holiday Bakery Café Jan. 7, 2012. A Plaza Pavilion, with a Tomorrowland theme, opened in the Magic Kingdom at Walt Disney World in 1973; it was later renamed Tomorrowland Terrace Noodle Station and Tomorrowland Terrace Restaurant. Also a Westernland buffeteria in Tokyo Disneyland; opened Apr. 15, 1983. Hosted by Prima Meat Packers, Ltd. and set in a frontier-era mansion.

Plaza Point Main Street, U.S.A. holiday shop in Disneyland; opened Oct. 21, 2021, taking the place of the Main Street Photo Supply Co. As the story goes, the proprietor, Miss Evelyn Toro, displays holiday items found during her world travels.

Plaza Restaurant, The Table-service restaurant on Main Street, U.S.A. in the Magic Kingdom at Walt Disney World; opened in 1974. Guests enjoy casual dining in art nouveau elegance. Also in Tokyo Disneyland; opened Apr. 15, 1983, and closed Jan. 4, 2017, to make way for Plazma Ray's Diner.

Plaza Swan Boats Leisurely cruise around the Central Plaza in the Magic Kingdom at Walt Disney World; opened May 20, 1973, and operated occasionally during peak periods until Aug. 1983. The Swan Boats, each ornamented with a giant swan figurehead and seating 30 passengers, used an automatic electronic guidance system that directed their path down the waterways, but which ultimately led to operational challenges. The Swan Boat landing was not removed until 2014. Swan boats trace their history to Europe's royal gardens of long ago but gained some recognition in the U.S. after they appeared at the World's Columbian Exposition of 1893 in Chicago, where Walt's father, Elias Disney, worked as a carpenter.

Plazma Ray's Diner Tomorrowland counterservice restaurant in Tokyo Disneyland; opened Mar. 25, 2017, replacing the Plaza Restaurant. Themed to an intergalactic restaurant chain named after its owner, an alien.

Pleakley One-eyed alien, and Earth "expert" of the Galactic Federation, in *Lilo & Stitch*; voiced by Kevin McDonald.

Pleasence, Donald (1919–1995) Actor; appeared in *Escape to Witch Mountain* (Deranian), on TV in *The Horsemasters* (Captain Pinski), and on The Disney Channel in *Black Arrow*.

Pleasure Island Evening entertainment district at Walt Disney World; opened May 1, 1989. Disney Imagineers felt that there should be a place where guests staying on the property could find nighttime entertainment, without having to travel into Orlando. This was one of the first Disney attractions that came with a mythology all its own, about the recent discovery of an abandoned shipbuilding operation of one Merriweather Adam Pleasure that the Disney designers decided to restore. It became the location of a group of nightclubs, restaurants, a multiplex movie theater, and shops, with entertainment culminating in a New Year's Eve celebration every night. Popular spots included the Adventurers Club, Comedy Warehouse, and Mannequins. The mascot, a lively moon character, was named the Funmeister. The *Empress Lilly* became part of Pleasure Island. Originally, there was an entrance fee to the island only in the evenings; during the day guests could wander around the shops at leisure. In 1996, Pleasure Island became part of the Downtown Disney complex. In 2004, entrance to the island became complimentary in the evenings; payment was only required to enter the clubs. The Pleasure Island clubs closed Sep. 27, 2008, although many of the shops and restaurants remained open. It was eventually replaced by The Landing at Disney Springs.

Pleasure Island Candies Fantasyland candy shop in Tokyo Disneyland; opened Apr. 15, 1983.

Pleasure Island Jazz Company A 1930s-style nightspot in Pleasure Island at Walt Disney World; opened Aug. 27, 1993, taking the place of Merriweather's Market. Closed Jan. 5, 2005, replaced by Raglan Road Irish Pub and Restaurant.

Pleshette, Suzanne (1937–2008) Actress; appeared in *The Ugly Dachshund* (Fran Garrison), *The Adventures of Bullwhip Griffin* (Arabella Flagg), *Blackbeard's Ghost* (Jo Anne Baker), and *The Shaggy D.A.* (Betty Daniels), and guest starred on TV in *8 Simple Rules for Dating My Teenage Daughter* (Laura Hennessy). She voiced Zira in *The Lion King II: Simba's Pride* and Yubaba and Zeniba in *Spirited Away*.

Plight of the Bumble Bee (film) Mickey Mouse cartoon planned in 1951 but never completed. Mickey grooms a talented bee to be an opera star, but the bee gets drunk on pollen from the flowers onstage and ruins the show. Directed by Jack Kinney.

Plowboy, The (film) Mickey Mouse cartoon; released in 1929. Directed by Walt Disney. When Mickey and Minnie attempt to milk a cow, they meet Clarabelle Cow and Horace Horsecollar (in their first cartoon), and the 2 couples play tricks on each other.

Plowright, Joan Actress; appeared in *A Pyromaniac's Love Story* (Mrs. Linzer), *The Scarlet Letter* (Harriet Hibbons), *Mr. Wrong* (Mrs. Crawford), *101 Dalmatians* (live action; Nanny), and *Bringing Down the House* (Mrs. Arness), and on TV in *On Promised Land* (Mrs. Appletree) and *Bailey's Mistake* (Aunt Angie). She voiced Baylene in *Dinosaur*.

Ployardt, John SEE MCLEISH, JOHN.

Plumb, Ed (1907–1958) He joined Disney in 1938 and served as musical director on *Fantasia*. He later served as co-musical director on such films as *Bambi*, *Saludos Amigos*, and *The Three Caballeros*, and worked on orchestration on such films as *Song of the South*, *Peter Pan*, *The Living Desert*, *Lady and the Tramp*, *Davy Crockett*, *Secrets of Life*, and *Johnny Tremain*.

Plume et Palette Shop in France at EPCOT; opened Oct. 1, 1982, offering art, Limoges porcelain, and crystal. The shop is designed with beautiful wood paneling and cabinets, and wrought iron balustrades. Fine paintings by French artists were shown on the mezzanine. More recently, designer French bags and fragrances have been sold.

Plummer, Christopher (1929–2021) Actor; appeared in *Where the Heart Is* (The !#&@), *Cold Creek Manor* (Mr. Massie), *The Insider* (Mike Wallace), *National Treasure* (John Adams Gates), and *The Tempest* (Prospero). He voiced Charles Muntz in *Up*.

Plus You Fashion and novelty boutique in the Lake Buena Vista Shopping Village at Walt Disney World; open Mar. 1975–Mar. 4, 1985. It became Mickey & Co.

Plush Corner Shop on Main Street, U.S.A. in Disneyland; opened Jan. 28, 1986, replacing the Book and Candle Shop. It later became Main Street Menagerie.

Pluto Mickey's faithful pet dog starred in 48 of his own theatrical shorts, but he also appeared along with Mickey Mouse and Donald Duck in many of their cartoons. The dog who would eventually evolve into Pluto made his debut as an unnamed bloodhound in the Mickey Mouse cartoon, *The Chain Gang*, in 1930. Later that year, he appeared as Minnie Mouse's dog, Rover, in *The Picnic*, and the following year finally became Mickey's dog, Pluto, in *The Moose Hunt*. Pluto was created as an actual dog character, with no speaking voice, as opposed to Goofy, who was created as a human character. The Pluto cartoons are:

1. *Pluto's Quin-Puplets*, 1937
2. *Bone Trouble*, 1940
3. *Pantry Pirate*, 1940
4. *Pluto's Playmate*, 1941
5. *A Gentlemen's Gentleman*, 1941
6. *Canine Caddy*, 1941
7. *Lend a Paw*, 1941
8. *Pluto, Junior*, 1942

9. *The Army Mascot*, 1942
10. *The Sleepwalker*, 1942
11. *T-Bone for Two*, 1942
12. *Pluto at the Zoo*, 1942
13. *Pluto and the Armadillo*, 1943
14. *Private Pluto*, 1943
15. *Springtime for Pluto*, 1944
16. *First Aiders*, 1944
17. *Dog Watch*, 1945
18. *Canine Casanova*, 1945
19. *The Legend of Coyote Rock*, 1945
20. *Canine Patrol*, 1945
21. *Pluto's Kid Brother*, 1946
22. *In Dutch*, 1946
23. *Squatter's Rights*, 1946
24. *The Purloined Pup*, 1946
25. *Pluto's Housewarming*, 1947
26. *Rescue Dog*, 1947
27. *Mail Dog*, 1947
28. *Pluto's Blue Note*, 1947
29. *Bone Bandit*, 1948
30. *Pluto's Purchase*, 1948
31. *Cat Nap Pluto*, 1948
32. *Pluto's Fledgling*, 1948
33. *Pueblo Pluto*, 1949
34. *Pluto's Surprise Package*, 1949
35. *Pluto's Sweater*, 1949
36. *Bubble Bee*, 1949
37. *Sheep Dog*, 1949
38. *Pluto's Heart Throb*, 1950
39. *Pluto and the Gopher*, 1950
40. *Wonder Dog*, 1950
41. *Primitive Pluto*, 1950
42. *Puss-Cafe*, 1950
43. *Pests of the West*, 1950
44. *Food for Feudin'*, 1950
45. *Camp Dog*, 1950
46. *Cold Storage*, 1951
47. *Plutopia*, 1951
48. *Cold Turkey*, 1951

Pluto (devil) The king of the underworld who menaced Persephone in *The Goddess of Spring* (1934).

Pluto and His Friends (TV) Show aired Jul. 31, 1982. 30 min. A salute to Pluto, with 4 cartoons. Narrated by Gary Owens.

Pluto and the Armadillo (film) Pluto cartoon released Feb. 19, 1943. Directed by Clyde Geronimi. Mickey and Pluto are in South America, where they meet a playful friend for Pluto—an armadillo. When Pluto plays too rough, it hides, but finally

returns to join Pluto and Mickey on the plane back home.

Pluto and the Baby (film) Title of an edited version of *Mickey Plays Papa*, which aired on the *Mickey Mouse Club* in the 1950s; all scenes of Mickey are edited out.

Pluto and the Gopher (film) Pluto cartoon released Feb. 10, 1950. Directed by Charles Nichols. Pluto digs up Minnie's garden and destroys her house in order to catch a pesky gopher—in spite of Minnie's scoldings.

Pluto at the Zoo (film) Pluto cartoon released Nov. 20, 1942. Directed by Clyde Geronimi. Pluto is disgusted with his small bone when he sees a huge one in a lion's cage. He manages to get away with it but has conflicts with other zoo animals in an exhausting attempt to keep the bone. Finally, he props the lion's jaw open with the bone and leaves the zoo happy with his small bone.

Pluto Gets the Paper: Spaceship (film) While fetching the newspaper for Mickey, Pluto is abducted by an alien spaceship and subjected to a number of humorous experiments. Directed by William Speers. Released Feb. 12, 1999. 2 min. From the *MouseWorks* TV series. Released with *My Favorite Martian*.

Pluto, Junior (film) Pluto cartoon released Feb. 28, 1942. Directed by Clyde Geronimi. Pluto's rest is continually disturbed by scrapes an energetic puppy gets into, including the puppy's troubles with a worm and a goofy bird.

Plutopia (film) Mickey Mouse and Pluto cartoon released May 18, 1951. Directed by Charles Nichols. While on vacation at a mountain resort with Mickey, Pluto dreams he is in Utopia with an overly obsequious cat acting as his butler. The butler will perform anything Pluto's heart desires when the dog bites his tail. Awakening, Pluto bites the cat's tail, and a furious battle ensues.

Pluto's Blue Note (film) Pluto cartoon released Dec. 26, 1947. Directed by Charles Nichols. When Pluto's singing annoys everyone, he entices female dogs by miming to a record (the song is "You Belong to My Heart," from *The Three Caballeros*). Nominated for an Academy Award.

Pluto's Christmas Tree (film) Mickey Mouse

cartoon released Nov. 21, 1952. Directed by Jack Hannah. The tree that Mickey chops down to bring home for Christmas turns out to be the home of Chip and Dale. In discovering the chipmunks' presence and trying to get them out of the trimmed tree, Pluto destroys it.

Pluto's Day (TV) Show aired Dec. 12, 1956. Directed by Wolfgang Reitherman. Walt Disney presents a typical day in Pluto's life through several cartoons.

Pluto's Dog House Hot dog counter in Mickey's Toontown at Disneyland; opened Jan. 24, 1993. Closed in 2020, with the facility later used for Café Daisy. SEE ALSO VILLAGE PAVILION (WALT DISNEY WORLD).

Pluto's Dream House (film) Mickey Mouse cartoon released Aug. 30, 1940. Directed by Clyde Geronimi. Mickey wishes on a magic lamp to build an ideal doghouse and to bathe Pluto, but his plans go awry when garbled radio announcements interfere with the lamp's instructions.

Pluto's Fledgling (film) Pluto cartoon released Sep. 10, 1948. Directed by Charles Nichols. Pluto tries to teach Orville, a baby bird, how to fly with some tricks of his own.

Pluto's Heart Throb (film) Pluto cartoon released Jan. 6, 1950. Directed by Charles Nichols. When Butch and Pluto vie for Dinah's attention, it appears the brute strength of the bulldog will vanquish Pluto until Dinah must be rescued from a swimming pool. Only Pluto manages to rescue her and, in doing so, win her.

Pluto's Housewarming (film) Pluto cartoon released Feb. 21, 1947. Directed by Charles Nichols. Pluto moves into his new house, only to find Butch the bulldog and a turtle have also taken up residence there. With the help of the turtle, they get rid of Butch and live happily together.

Pluto's Judgement Day (film) Mickey Mouse cartoon released Aug. 31, 1935. Directed by Dave Hand. Mickey chastises Pluto for chasing a kitten, which causes Pluto to have a nightmare in which cats try him in court for his crimes against the feline world. As he is sentenced to a grisly end, he awakens to make amends with the kitten.

Pluto's Kid Brother (film) Pluto cartoon released Apr. 12, 1946. Directed by Charles Nichols. Pluto and his kid brother have many adventures together trying to keep some stolen wieners, including eluding a bulldog and the dogcatcher.

Pluto's Party (film) Mickey Mouse cartoon released Sep. 19, 1952. Directed by Milt Schaffer. At his own birthday party, Pluto gets pushed around by the nephews and cannot get any of his own cake until after the party when Mickey presents him with a piece. The short marked Mickey's first animated appearance with eyebrows.

Pluto's Playmate (film) Pluto cartoon released Jan. 24, 1941. Directed by Norm Ferguson. Pluto thinks he has an enemy when a baby seal steals his ball on the beach, but when the seal rescues him from a squid, they soon become fast friends.

Pluto's Purchase (film) Pluto cartoon released Jul. 9, 1948. Directed by Charles Nichols. Pluto is in for a surprise when Mickey sends him to buy a salami at the butcher shop, and he has to fight to keep Butch, the bulldog, from stealing it. When Pluto gets home with the salami, Mickey presents it to Butch as a birthday gift.

Pluto's Quin-Puplets (film) Pluto cartoon released Nov. 26, 1937. Directed by Ben Sharpsteen. Left in charge of 5 pups when Fifi goes out, Pluto has his paws full when he gets drunk and the puppies get mixed up in paint spray. Disgusted, Fifi shoves them all out of the doghouse to sleep in a barrel.

Pluto's Surprise Package (film) Pluto cartoon released Mar. 4, 1949. Directed by Charles Nichols. Pluto has quite a time getting Mickey's mail into the house, what with the wind blowing the letters about and a turtle emerging from one package.

Pluto's Sweater (film) Pluto cartoon released Apr. 29, 1949. Directed by Charles Nichols. Minnie knits Pluto a sweater that he hates and tries everything in his power to remove. When it gets wet and shrinks to a tiny size, Minnie gives it to a disgusted Figaro instead.

Pluto's Toy Palace Part of the Mickey's of Hollywood shop in Disney's Hollywood Studios; opened May 1, 1989. Inspired by the Moxley's Dog & Cat Hospital in Hollywood.

Plymouth (TV) Two-hour movie on ABC; aired May 26, 1991. Directed by Lee David Zlotoff. A

Pacific Northwest town resettles on the moon but finds living conditions there difficult. Stars Cindy Pickett (Addy Mathewson), Richard Hamilton (Mayor Wendell Mackenzies), Matthew Brown (Jed Mathewson). From Touchstone Television and Zlotoff, in association with Rai 1.

Pocahontas (film) The first Disney animated feature based on historical fact, *Pocahontas* tells the story of the meeting of the English settlers in Jamestown with the local Powhatan tribe. The adventurous young Native American woman, Pocahontas, along with her constant companions, Meeko, a raccoon, and Flit, a hummingbird, visit Grandmother Willow, a counseling tree spirit, because she is uncertain about the path her life should take. She soon meets the brave English captain John Smith, and while opening his eyes to an understanding and respect for the world around him, the two fall in love. The other English settlers, led by Governor Ratcliffe, are intent on finding gold in the New World and become convinced the Native Americans are hiding the precious substance from them. Thomas, an inexperienced settler, kills the warrior, Kocoum, but Smith lets the Native Americans think he is responsible, so he is condemned to death. In begging her father, Chief Powhatan, to spare Smith's life, Pocahontas finds that her path in life is to be instrumental in establishing the early peace between the Jamestown settlers and her tribe. Smith, however, is severely wounded by an enraged Ratcliffe and must return to England. Pocahontas and he part, each knowing their lives are richer for the love they share. Directed by Mike Gabriel and Eric Goldberg. Limited release on Jun. 16; general release on Jun. 23, 1995. Voices include Irene Bedard (Pocahontas, speaking), Judy Kuhn (Pocahontas, singing), Mel Gibson (Capt. John Smith), David Ogden Stiers (Ratcliffe/ Wiggins), Linda Hunt (Grandmother Willow), Christian Bale (Thomas), Russell Means (Chief Powhatan). 81 min. Music is by Alan Menken, with lyrics by Stephen Schwartz. Songs include "Just Around the Riverbend," "Steady as the Beating Drum," and "Colors of the Wind." The look and style of the film were inspired by the filmmakers' numerous visits to Jamestown, Virginia, as well as by extensive research into the colonial period. The use of strong vertical and horizontal imagery in the design springs from the tall, vertical shapes of the Virginia pine forests and the vast horizontal landscapes. At various stages of the production, the creative team consulted with Native American scholars and storytellers to incorporate authentic aspects of the Powhatan culture into the film. The film had an outdoor premiere in New York City's Central Park on Jun. 10, 1995. Alan Menken and Stephen Schwartz were presented Oscars for Best Song ("Colors of the Wind"), and Menken also won for Best Score.

Pocahontas II: Journey to a New World (film) Direct-to-video release Sep. 5, 1998; sequel to *Pocahontas*. Pocahontas sets sail for England on an important mission of peace, escorted by a dashing English diplomat, John Rolfe, her bodyguard, Uti, and stowaways Meeko, Percy, and Flit. She is awed by London, as are the Londoners by her. Ratcliffe plots against Pocahontas, and she is eventually saved by Rolfe and John Smith. Directed by Bradley Raymond and Tom Ellery. Voices include actors from the original film, along with Billy Zane (John Rolfe), Jean Stapleton (Mrs. Jenkins), Donal Gibson (John Smith), Finola Hughes (Queen Anne). 72 min. Donal Gibson is the brother of Mel Gibson, who voiced John Smith in the original film.

Pocahontas Indian Village Children's play area themed to Pocahontas's village; opened Jun. 14, 1996, at the former Indian Canoes dock in Frontierland at Disneyland Paris. It became the Frontierland Playground in 2019.

Poehler, Amy Actress; provided the voice of Joy in *Inside Out* and Homily in *The Secret World of Arrietty*. She appeared in *Deuce Bigalow: Male Gigolo* (Ruth).

Point Mugu Tattoo Paradise Pier shop in Disney California Adventure; opened Feb. 8, 2001, offering fashion jewelry, cosmetics, and accessories.

Point of Honor (TV) Pilot film for a proposed, but never made, TV series; digitally released Jan. 15, 2016, on Amazon. At the start of the Civil War, a prominent Virginia family makes the controversial decision to defend the South while freeing all of their slaves, pitting the family against one another and testing their strength, courage, and love. Directed by Randall Wallace. Stars Luke Benward (Garland Rhodes), Patrick Heusinger (Col. Palmer Kane), Lucien Laviscount (Elijah), Hanna Mangan Lawrence (Estella Rhodes), Christopher O'Shea (Robert Summer). 56 min. From ABC Signature Studios, ABC Studios, and Amazon Studios.

Pointer, The (film) Mickey Mouse cartoon released

Jul. 21, 1939. Directed by Clyde Geronimi. Mickey tries to teach Pluto to be a pointer in their hunt for quail. But they have a harrowing encounter with a huge bear and Pluto points instead to a can of beans—their dinner. Nominated for an Academy Award. It was in this cartoon that the public saw for the first time a redesigned Mickey Mouse, supervised by animator Fred Moore. Most noticeable were his eyes; now they had pupils in a white eye, where before they were simple black ovals.

Poitier, Sidney (1927–2022) Actor; appeared in *Shoot to Kill* (Warren Stantin). He was named to the Disney Board of Directors Nov. 22, 1994, to fill the vacancy caused by the death of Frank Wells, serving until Mar. 19, 2003.

Polar Bear (film) A Disneynature feature. The story of a new mother whose memories of her own youth prepare her to navigate motherhood in the increasingly challenging world that polar bears face today. Directed by Alastair Fothergill and Jeff Wilson. Digitally released Apr. 22, 2022, on Disney+. Narrated by Catherine Keener. 83 min.

Polar Trappers (film) Donald Duck cartoon released Jun. 17, 1938. Directed by Ben Sharpsteen. Goofy tries to trap a walrus but echoes and icicles in a cave are his downfall. Donald uses Pied Piper tactics to try to trap a colony of penguins but ends up destroying the trappers' camp.

Police Station, The (film) Educational film in which Mickey meets and learns from a police officer, in the Mickey's Field Trips series; released in Sep. 1987. 11 min.

Pollard, Michael J. (1939–2019) Actor; appeared in *Summer Magic* (Digby Popham) and *Dick Tracy* (Bug Bailey), and guest starred on TV in *Blossom* (Randy).

Pollatschek, Susanne Actress; provided the voice of Olivia Flaversham in *The Great Mouse Detective*.

Polley, Sarah Actress; on The Disney Channel, she appeared in *Lantern Hill* (Jody Turner) and *Avonlea* (Sara Stanley).

Polly (TV) Two-hour movie; aired Nov. 12, 1989. Directed by Debbie Allen. An adaptation of the *Pollyanna* story as a musical with an African American cast. Stars Keshia Knight Pulliam (Polly), Phylicia Rashad (Aunt Polly), Dorian Harewood (Dr. Shannon), Barbara Montgomery (Mrs. Conley), T. K. Carter (George), Brandon Adams (Jimmy Bean), Butterfly McQueen (Miss Priss), Brock Peters (Eban Pendergast), Celeste Holm (Miss Snow). The repeat airing of *Polly* on Sep. 9, 1990, marked the final episode of *The Magical World of Disney*.

Polly—Comin' Home (TV) Movie on NBC; aired Nov. 18, 1990. Polly restores racial and political harmony in a town split in two in this musical sequel. 120 min. Directed by Debbie Allen. Stars Keshia Knight Pulliam (Polly), Phylicia Rashad (Aunt Polly), Dorian Harewood (Dr. Shannon), Barbara Montgomery (Mrs. Conley), Brandon Adams (Jimmy Bean), Celeste Holm (Miss Snow), Anthony Newley (Dabney Mayhew).

Polly Penguin Co-star of *Peculiar Penguins* (1934).

Pollyanna (film) Orphaned Pollyanna, coming to live with Aunt Polly Harrington, who sternly runs her small New England town, brings her cheerful philosophy to the grim household and eventually to the whole town. With her "Glad Game" she intrigues Mr. Pendergast, an old hermit, who shows the kids his glass prisms and eventually decides to adopt orphan Jimmy Bean; coaxes Mrs. Snow, a crotchety hypochondriac, from her sickbed; teaches the Reverend Ford to stand up for himself; and re-instills a romance between Aunt Polly and Dr. Edmund Chilton. Under the girl's influence, the town resists Aunt Polly and stages its own benefit for building a new orphanage. Pollyanna is severely injured in trying to join the festivities, with the accident giving Aunt Polly a whole new outlook. It wins her the goodwill of the town and the love of the doctor who will restore Pollyanna's health. Directed by David Swift. Released May 19, 1960. 134 min. Stars Hayley Mills (Pollyanna), Jane Wyman (Aunt Polly), Richard Egan (Dr. Edmund Chilton), Karl Malden (Rev. Paul Ford), Agnes Moorehead (Mrs. Snow), Nancy Olson (Nancy Furman), Adolphe Menjou (Mr. Pendergast), Donald Crisp (Mayor Karl Warren), Kevin Corcoran (Jimmy Bean). This was Hayley Mills's first film for Disney, and she immediately became the Studio's newest star. She won an Academy Award for the most outstanding juvenile performance of 1960. Wyman and Moorehead had earlier appeared together in *Johnny Belinda*, a film for which each was nominated for an Academy Award. Wyman won the Oscar. Based on the book by Eleanor H. Porter, published in 1913, which became perhaps the best-known American novel since *Uncle Tom's Cabin*. It was so popular that the word *Pollyanna* even got into everyday usage, and eventually the dictionary, meaning someone who looks for the best in things. The film was director Swift's first Disney feature, and in fact he appears briefly as the fireman scolding Jimmy Bean. With a then lavish $2.5 million budget, Swift gathered a crew and cast unlike any other Disney live-action feature. Disney set decorator Emile Kuri was on hand, but outsiders Walter Plunkett (costumes), Russell Harlan (cinematographer), and art directors Carroll Clark and Robert Clatworthy came from established careers at other studios. To find a house to use as the residence of Aunt Polly, Walt Disney had to go far afield from his Studio in Burbank. An ideal house was found in Santa Rosa, near the famed Napa Valley. It occupied a full block in the center of the town and was surrounded by spacious lawns and gardens. It was built in 1877 as a replica of an old Natchez, Mississippi, antebellum house. The vintage train station and water hole were also filmed in Santa Rosa, but the interiors were completed at the Disney Studio. See ADVENTURES OF POLLYANNA, THE; POLLY; AND POLLY—COMIN' HOME (TV PRODUCTIONS).

Polo Walt Disney became interested in polo in 1932 and enlisted several Disney staff members and his brother Roy to join in. Walt eventually had a stable of 7 polo ponies, named June, Slim, Nava, Arrow, Pardner, Tacky, and Tommy. The Disney team competed in matches at the Riviera Country Club against such luminaries as Spencer Tracy, Darryl F. Zanuck, and Will Rogers. The film *Mickey's Polo Team* reflected the Disney staff's interest in the sport.

Polynesian Revue Luau at the Polynesian Village Resort at Walt Disney World; debuted Oct. 1971. Also known as *Kaui-Pono Polynesian Revue* and *Polynesian Luau*. Performed originally along the shores of Seven Seas Lagoon, the revue was moved to a new, dedicated venue, Luau Cove, in 1973, to accommodate high demand. The luau had its final performance Jan. 4, 2003, to make way for *Disney's Spirit of Aloha Dinner Show*, which ran Feb. 25, 2003–Mar. 2020. In 2022, plans were announced for a new Disney Vacation Club addition to replace Luau Cove.

Polynesian Terrace Restaurant Adventureland restaurant in Tokyo Disneyland; opened Apr. 15, 1983, hosted by Kikkoman Corporation. Hawaiian pancakes are served in a tropical atmosphere.

Polynesian Village Resort, Disney's Resort hotel at Walt Disney World; opened Oct. 1, 1971. The resort is 1 of the 2 original Disney hotels on the property and originally featured lush vegetation filling much of the lobby in the Great Ceremonial House. The hotel rooms are in several longhouses, originally named for Pacific islands both real (such as Samoa, Oahu, and Tonga) and mythical (Bali Hai). The Monorail stops at the hotel, making it convenient to get around the Magic Kingdom Resort Area. In 1984–1985, the resort was expanded with 2 new longhouses, a second pool, the opening of the Tangaroa Terrace restaurant (which closed permanently in 1996), and the King Kamehameha rooms. The resort, which opened as the Polynesian Village in 1971, was renamed Disney's Polynesian Resort in the late 1980s. It became Disney's Polynesian Village Resort as part of a major refurbishment that began in 2014. A Disney Vacation Club area, called Disney's Polynesian Villas & Bungalows, opened Apr. 1, 2015. There are 20 waterside bungalows, each sleeping up to 8 guests, and 360 Deluxe Studios. Dining is available at 'Ohana (formerly Papeete Bay Verandah), Kona Café (formerly Coral Isle Café), Capt. Cook's, Pineapple Lanai, Tambu Lounge, and Trader Sam's Grog Grotto (formerly Moana Mickey's Arcade), with *Disney's Spirit of Aloha Dinner Show* at Luau Cove. Shops include Bou-Tiki and Moana Mercantile. Guest rooms themed to the animated feature *Moana* were introduced in 2021. In 2022, a proposed multistory Disney Vacation Club property was announced for the resort; it is planned to debut in 2024, on the site of Luau Cove.

Pompano Grill Restaurant in the Buena Vista Club; previously and later known as the Lake Buena Vista Club Restaurant.

Pompeo, Ellen Actress; appeared on TV as Dr. Meredith Grey in *Grey's Anatomy* and *Station 19*, and voiced Willow in *Doc McStuffins*. She was named a Disney Legend in 2022.

Pongo Male lead Dalmatian in *One Hundred and One Dalmatians*; voiced by Rod Taylor.

Pony Farm Home of the stables for Disneyland, originally behind Frontierland and Fantasyland, established by Dolly and Owen Pope before the park opened in 1955. Name changed to Circle D Corral in 1980, and the stables were relocated in 2016 to make way for Star Wars: Galaxy's Edge. At Walt Disney World, the stables at Fort Wilderness are known as the Tri-Circle-D Ranch.

Ponyo (film) An animated feature about Sosuke, a 5-year-old boy who meets a goldfish girl who desires to become human and be his friend. When Sosuke, who lives on a cliff by the sea, finds her, he names her Ponyo. Her father, Fujimoto, an undersea god, sends his wave demons to look for his daughter and bring her back to him. Ponyo uses her father's magic to become human, but this causes imbalance in the world, which in turn results in a gigantic storm submerging much of the land. Ponyo rides the waves of the storm back to Sosuke, uses her magic to enlarge Sosuke's toy boat, and they set out to find his mother who went to check on the residents of the nursing home where she worked. Gran Mamare, Ponyo's mother, has rescued Lisa and the old ladies at the home, and she asks Sosuke if he can love Ponyo even if she is a fish; when he agrees, she restores the balance to the world. Released in the U.S. by Disney on Aug. 14, 2009; original release in Japan Jul. 19, 2008. Directed by Hirao Miyazaki. Voices include Cate Blanchett (Gran Mamare), Matt Damon (Koichi), Tina Fey (Lisa), Liam Neeson (Fujimoto), Frankie Jonas (Sosuke), Noah Cyrus (Ponyo), Cloris Leachman (Noriko), Lily Tomlin (Toki), Betty White (Yoshie). Frankie Jonas is the younger brother of the members of the Jonas Brothers singing group, and Noah Cyrus is the younger sister of Miley Cyrus. Inspired by Hans Christian Andersen's *The Little Mermaid*. From Studio Ghibli; the Japanese title is *Gake no ue no Ponyo*.

Pooch and the Pauper, The (TV) Movie on *The Wonderful World of Disney*; first aired Jul. 16, 2000. The president's pampered pet bulldog, Liberty, accidentally swaps places with a scrappy look-alike, Moocher, from the wrong side of the tracks. Stars Richard Karn (Drainville), Fred Willard (President Caldwell), George Wendt (Sparks), Cody Jones (Nate).

Poof Point, The (TV) A Disney Channel Original Movie; first aired Sep. 14, 2001. Two teenage siblings must save the lives of their inventor parents after mom and dad's time machine experiment goes awry, and they become younger versions of themselves. Directed by Neal Israel. Stars Taj Mowry (Eddie Ballard), Dawnn Lewis (Marigold Ballard),

Raquel Lee (Marie Ballard), Mark Curry (Norton Ballard).

Pooh Corner Critter Country shop in Disneyland; opened 1995, taking the place of Crocodile Mercantile. Versions also opened in Fantasyland at Tokyo Disneyland Jul. 14, 2000, and in Hong Kong Disneyland Sep. 12, 2005. Also a shop in Downtown Disney Marketplace (now the Marketplace at Disney Springs) at Walt Disney World; opened Nov. 24, 1997, replacing Authentic All Star, and closed Jan. 15, 2011, to become Marketplace Fun Finds. FOR THE DISNEY CHANNEL SHOW, SEE WELCOME TO POOH CORNER.

Pooh for President SEE WINNIE THE POOH FOR PRESIDENT DAYS.

Pooh's Grand Adventure: The Search for Christopher Robin (film) Direct-to-video release Aug. 5, 1997. The group of animals in the Hundred Acre Wood misunderstand that Christopher Robin has gone away to school, and they head off on a grand journey to find their childhood friend. Directed by Karl Geurs. Voices include Jim Cummings (Pooh), Paul Winchell (Tigger), John Fiedler (Piglet), Brady Bluhm (Christopher Robin), Ken Sansom (Rabbit), Andre Stojka (Owl), David Warner (narrator). 70 min.

Pooh's Great School Bus Adventure (film) Educational film; released in Sep. 1986. Hundred Acre Wood characters illustrate rules for bus safety.

Pooh's Heffalump Halloween Movie (film) Direct-to-video release Sep. 13, 2005. At Halloween, Roo's best pal, Lumpy, is excited to trick-or-treat for the first time. That is, until Tigger warns them about the dreaded Gobloon, who will turn you into a jaggedy lantern if he catches you. But if they catch the Gobloon before it catches them, they get to make a wish. When Pooh eats all the Halloween candy, Lumpy and Roo decide to be brave and catch the Gobloon. Directed by Saul Blinkoff and Elliot Bour. Voices include Kyle Stanger (Lumpy), Jimmy Bennett/Nikita Hopkins (Roo), Jim Cummings (Pooh/Tigger), John Fiedler (Piglet). 66 min.

Pooh's Heffalump Movie (film) An animated feature from DisneyToon Studios. Roo, the half-pint kangaroo, sets off on a solo journey to face and capture the dreaded Heffalump. While the older characters head off to save Roo from certain peril by setting makeshift traps to thwart the Heffalumps, Roo comes upon a young, playful Heffa-lump and makes friends with him. The Heffalump's name is Heffridge Trumpler Brompet Heffalump IV, known as Lumpy. Roo discovers that Heffalumps are nothing like the creatures of the ominous stories he has been told, and that the creature is equally afraid of his silly pals. Roo and Lumpy work together to dispel the unfounded fears of their respective friends and families. Directed by Frank Nissen. Released in the U.S. Feb. 11, 2005, after initial releases on Feb. 4 in Iceland and Poland. 68 min. Voices include Jim Cummings (Winnie the Pooh/Tigger), Nikita Hopkins (Roo), Kath Soucie (Kanga), Ken Sansom (Rabbit), Peter Cullen (Eeyore), Brenda Blethyn (Mama Heffalump), Kyle Stanger (Lumpy). Heffalumps and Woozles made their first Disney appearance in *Winnie the Pooh and the Blustery Day*. Carly Simon composed 6 new songs for the film.

Pooh's Hunny Hunt Fantasyland attraction in Tokyo Disneyland; opened Sep. 1, 2000. Guests enter the world of Winnie the Pooh in large "hunny" pot vehicles through the pages of a giant storybook, experiencing scenes from the animated featurettes. The elaborate attraction uses a trackless ride system and is considered a guest favorite. SEE ALSO MANY ADVENTURES OF WINNIE THE POOH, THE (ATTRACTION).

Pooh's Hunny Spot Critter Country candy shop in Disneyland; opened Apr. 7, 2003, taking the place of Brer Bar as an expansion of Pooh Corner.

Pooh's Place Character shop in the Lake Buena Vista Shopping Village at Walt Disney World; opened Dec. 16, 1978. It became the Village Character Shop, ca. 1982.

Pooh's Thotful Shop SEE HUNDRED ACRE GOODS (WALT DISNEY WORLD).

Poor Papa (film) Oswald the Lucky Rabbit cartoon; the first made, though not the first released. Released Jun. 11, 1928. Oswald is surprised when not one stork, but a squadron of them dumps young rabbits by the score down his chimney. The Oswald home becomes a bedlam of vivacious bunnies who run the place ragged. He is unsuccessful in preventing more storks from dropping off a stream of more young rabbits—and even more of them than what was in the earlier brood.

Poor Unfortunate Souls Song from *The Little Mermaid*; written by Howard Ashman and Alan Menken.

Pop Century Resort, Disney's Value resort adjacent to ESPN Wide World of Sports at Walt Disney World; opened Dec. 14, 2003. The theme highlights the toys, fads, technology breakthroughs, dance crazes, and catchphrases that defined 20th-century pop culture through the decades. Larger-than-life icons include Play-Doh, Duncan Yo-Yo, bowling pins, a laptop computer, and cellular phones. Inside the colorful check-in facility, Classic Hall, guests can dine at Everything Pop, which doubles as a merchandise shop. There were 2 phases planned, each with 2,880 rooms: the "Legendary Years" (1900s to 1940s) and the "Classic Years" (1950s to 1990s). The first phase, the Classic Years, was originally planned to debut in 2002, but was postponed due to a slowdown in Florida tourism after the 9/11 attacks; it eventually opened in late 2003. The Legendary Years never opened, even though extensive work had been done; the site was eventually used for Disney's Art of Animation Resort, which opened in 2012.

Pop-Up Disney! A Mickey Celebration Interactive exhibit celebrating 90 years of Mickey Mouse; opened in the Downtown Disney District at Disneyland Resort Apr. 26, 2019, replacing ESPN Zone, and closed Sep. 2, 2019. Guests could explore whimsical galleries and themed rooms, with photo opportunities and a merchandise shop.

Pop Warner Football SEE MOOCHIE OF POP WARNER FOOTBALL.

Pope, Owen and Dolly (1910–2000, 1914–2003) The Popes, Owen and Dolly, were hired by Walt Disney in Nov. 1951 to start putting together some livestock for his future park. They first lived in a trailer at the Studio, where they raised and trained the first horses and helped build wagons and coaches. During the construction of Disneyland, Disney gave them their choice of the houses being moved on the property, and they staked out a 10-acre site for the Pony Farm. Three days before the park opened, they moved to Disneyland but had to live in their trailer for a while until their house was ready. They were the park's only residents. The Popes continued with the company, running the Disneyland Pony Farm and then moving to Florida in 1971 to start the Tri-Circle-D Ranch there. They retired in 1975.

Popeye (film) The cartoon character comes to life in this joint Disney/Paramount musical fantasy. Popeye blows into Sweethaven on the heels of a story. He is looking for his long-lost dad but ends up mopping up various town bullies, falling for Olive Oyl, adopting an abandoned baby, and fighting an undersea battle with Bluto and a giant octopus. Original theatrical release by Paramount in Dec. 1980. Directed by Robert Altman. Music by Harry Nilsson. Stars Robin Williams (Popeye), Shelley Duvall (Olive Oyl), Ray Walston (Pappy), Paul Dooley (Wimpy). Filmed on location in Malta, where the coast of Anchor Bay was transformed into the make-believe harbor town of Sweethaven. A 16-mm release by Disney on Sep. 15, 1981.

Popular (TV) One-hour series on The WB Network; aired Sep. 29, 1999–May 18, 2001. A series about popularity in high school and the students' constant struggle to define themselves. Stars Leslie Bibb (Brooke McQueen), Carly Pope (Sam McPherson), Tamara Mello (Lily Esposito), Christopher Gorham (Harrison John), Bryce Johnson (Josh Ford), Tammy Lynn Michaels (Nicole Julian), Ron Lester (Mike Bernadino), Sara Rue (Carmen Ferrara), Lisa Darr (Jane McPherson), Scott Bryce (Mike McQueen), Leslie Grossman (Mary Cherry). In the 2nd season, Diane Delano (Bobbi Glass) joined the cast as a regular. From Touchstone Television.

Port Discovery Port of call in Tokyo DisneySea; opened Sep. 4, 2001. The area presents a fantasy future where science and nature are in balance. Visitors can ride aboard water vehicles in Aquatopia or board a submersible to probe new frontiers in Nemo & Friends SeaRider (formerly StormRider).

Port Disney SEE DISNEYSEA.

Port d'Orléans Shop in New Orleans Square at Disneyland; opened Sep. 10, 1999, replacing Le Gourmet. Closed Sep. 19, 2002, to become the second location for Le Bat en Rouge.

Port of Entry Shop in World Showcase Plaza at EPCOT; opened Mar. 28, 1987, offering merchandise from many countries, including some not featured in World Showcase. Later became a Disney apparel and souvenir shop. Also an international goods and curiosities shop in the Lake Buena Vista Shopping Village at Walt Disney World; open Mar. 1975–Sep. 21, 1985, and superseded by Mickey's Character Shop.

Port Orleans Resort, Disney's Resort hotel at Walt Disney World; opened May 17, 1991, themed after the French Quarter in New Orleans, with 1,008 rooms. One could dine at Bonfamille's Cafe (closed Aug. 5, 2000), select from the fare at the Sassagoula Floatworks and Food Factory, enjoy libations at Scat Cat's Club or Mardi Grogs, and shop at Jackson Square Gifts & Desires. The swimming pool is called Doubloon Lagoon and is built around a Mardi Gras sea serpent. Disney's Dixie Landings Resort was combined with the Port Orleans Resort Apr. 1, 2001, with Dixie Landings becoming Disney's Port Orleans Resort – Riverside (with Magnolia Bend mansions and Alligator Bayou cottages), and the original resort becoming Disney's Port Orleans Resort – French Quarter. At Riverside, dining is offered at Boatwright's Dining Hall and Riverside Mill Food Court, with bar service at River Roost and Muddy Rivers, and shopping at Fulton's General Store. Ol' Man Island is a 3.5-acre swimming and fishing hole area, fashioned after an abandoned sawmill. In 2011, many of the rooms in the Riverside area became Royal Guest Rooms, themed to the Disney princesses.

Porter, Hank (1900–1951) Artist; came to Disney in 1936 as a publicity artist. He designed posters, penciled and inked several Sunday comic pages, and, during World War II, designed many insignias for military units. He was one of the first to be authorized to sign Walt Disney's name for him, and his stylized signature was found for years on fan cards and other items. He left Disney in 1950.

Portman, Natalie Actress; appeared as Jane Foster in the Thor and Avengers films, and narrated *Dolphin Reef*.

Porto Paradiso Turn-of-the-century port city in Mediterranean Harbor at Tokyo DisneySea; debuted Sep. 4, 2001.

Portobello Disney Springs restaurant at Walt Disney World, operated by Levy Restaurants; originally opened as Portobello Yacht Club May 1, 1989, becoming Portobello Country Italian Trattoria Oct. 12, 2008. Guests could enjoy the flavors of Italy in an airy dining room or waterfront patio. Closed Apr. 24, 2017, to become Terralina Crafted Italian.

Portobello Road Song in *Bedknobs and Broom-*

sticks; written by Richard M. and Robert B. Sherman. It is where Eglantine Price and the children go searching for a rare book. Portobello Road is an actual street in London, site of a famous antiques market.

Portraits of Canada (film) Circle-Vision 360 film tour of Canada prepared for Expo '86 in Vancouver, in conjunction with Telecom Canada; released May 2, 1986.

Portugal (film) People and Places featurette released Dec. 25, 1957. Directed by Ben Sharpsteen. Filmed in CinemaScope. 30 min. Opening with animation showing the adventurous and courageous Portuguese explorers and the routes they traveled, this film then looks at some of the main elements of the Portuguese people's economy—shipping, harvesting grapes for wine, marketing of cork, as well as the country's bullfighting traditions.

Portuguese Reading Film SEE HISTORIA DE JOSÉ, A, AND JOSÉ COME BIEN.

Porzellanhaus Porcelain figure and dinnerware shop in Germany at EPCOT; opened Oct. 1, 1982. It later became a Christmas shop, selling nutcrackers and holiday items, and was renamed Die Weihnachts Ecke in 1989. The traditional tree with pickle ornaments is a guest favorite.

Posh Pets Pet store in the Lake Buena Vista Shopping Village at Walt Disney World; open Mar. 22, 1975–Oct. 9, 1976, and succeeded by Toys Fantastique. Guests could bring home fish, hamsters, parrots, and even less common animals, like an albino skunk.

Positively Minnie Digital short-form video series (approx. 1 min. each) featuring Minnie Mouse as a modern lifestyle icon. Debuted Jan. 22, 2020, on Instagram and other platforms.

Posledny bogatyr (The Last Warrior) (film) A Disney feature produced in Russia; released Oct. 19, 2017. Ivan, a young con artist and orphan, is transported from modern Moscow to a fantastic world where the heroes of Russian fairy tales live. There, magic is part of everyday life, and conflicts are solved by the clash of heroic swords. Unexpectedly, Ivan finds himself at the very center of the struggle between light and dark forces—but why? Directed by Dmitriy Dyachenko. Stars Wolfgang Cerny (Alyosha Popovich), Mila Sivatskaya (Vasilisa), Viktor Khorinyak (Ivan). Produced in

collaboration with Yellow, Black and White. It became the highest-grossing local-language release of all time in Russia.

Posledny bogatyr: Koren' zla (The Last Warrior: Root of Evil) (film) A Disney feature produced in Russia; released Jan. 1, 2021, as the 2nd in the Last Warrior fantasy/comedy series. When an ancient evil rises, Ivan sets out on a long journey beyond the known world to defeat the enemies and return peace to Belogorie. Directed by Dmitriy Dyachenko. Stars Viktor Khorinyak (Ivan), Mila Sivatskaya (Vasilisa), Elena Yakovleva (Baby Yaga), Ekaterina Vilkova (Varvara). Produced in collaboration with Yellow, Black and White.

Posledny bogatyr: Poslannik t'my (The Last Warrior: A Messenger of Darkness) (film) A Disney feature produced in Russia; released Dec. 23, 2021, as the 3rd in the Last Warrior fantasy/comedy series. Ivan has finally gained superhero strength, the evil sorcerer has been defeated, and he and Vasilisa are about to celebrate their wedding. In the midst of preparations, Vasilisa is kidnapped, and Ivan and his friends find themselves in modern Moscow, where he will have a chance to finally defeat an ancient darkness. Directed by Dmitriy Dyachenko. Stars Viktor Khorinyak (Ivan), Mila Sivatskaya (Vasilisa). Produced in collaboration with Yellow, Black and White.

Postlethwaite, Pete (1946–2011) Actor; appeared in *James and the Giant Peach* (Old Man) and *Dark Water* (Veeck).

Potrock, Ken He joined Disney in 1995 as vice president of marketing for Disney Cruise Line and later headed the rebranding of Disney's Wide World of Sports (to ESPN Wide World of Sports) and of Downtown Disney (to Disney Springs) at Walt Disney World. In 2013, he was named senior vice president and general manager of Disney Vacation Club and Adventures by Disney and in 2018 became president of Consumer Products Commercialization. On May 18, 2020, he was named president of the Disneyland Resort.

Potter, William E. ("Joe") (1905–1988) Retired army major general and Panama Canal Zone governor who was hired by Walt Disney in 1965 to direct construction of the infrastructure for Walt Disney World, utilizing techniques that were considered revolutionary at the time. He oversaw an innovative network of utility systems, water treatment plants, and the carving of 43 miles of winding canals across the property. After the opening of Walt Disney World, he became its senior vice president. He retired in 1974 and was named a Disney Legend posthumously in 1996. On Jun. 18, 1997, a Walt Disney World ferryboat, the *Kingdom Queen*, was renamed the *General Joe Potter* in his honor.

Pottery Chalet Pottery, ceramics, and glassware shop in the Lake Buena Vista Shopping Village at Walt Disney World; open Mar. 22, 1975–May 3, 1988, and succeeded by Guest Services & Photo Express. Craftspeople practiced the art in old-world style. The patio was taken by the Christmas Chalet Oct. 1986. For several years, visitors could have custom candles made in the nearby Chalet Candle Shop.

Poultry Palace Pixar Pier food counter in Disney California Adventure; opened Jun. 23, 2018. Based on the restaurant in *Small Fry*.

Powder (film) An enigmatic young man with startlingly white skin and extraordinary abilities is discovered living in the cellar of a remote farmhouse and brought to live in a community that does not quite know what to make of him. Befriended by the head of a school for troubled youths and an enthusiastic science teacher, the young man, known as Powder, demonstrates an astoundingly high IQ and a tremendous compassion to persist regardless of the distrust, hatred, and fear that his presence seems to generate. Ultimately, Powder has a profound effect on all who come in contact with him but learns that he is the only one who can help himself. A Hollywood Pictures film in association with Caravan Pictures. Directed by Victor Salva. Released Oct. 27, 1995. Stars Sean Patrick Flanery (Powder), Mary Steenburgen (Jessie), Jeff Goldblum (Donald Ripley), Lance Henriksen (Sheriff Barnum). 111 min. Filmed in and around Houston. Special makeup for Powder was created by the Burman Studio and was applied with an airbrush. It took from 2–3½ hours to apply each day, and another hour to remove.

Power Rangers (TV) Disney acquired *Power Rangers*, and the brand's merchandising rights, when the company purchased Fox Family Channel in 2001. *Power Rangers Ninja Storm*, which debuted in 2003, was the first production solely managed by Disney. Production moved to New Zealand and included a new producer, cast, and crew. Power Rangers first appeared on American TV in 1993. Production on new episodes ceased in 2009, and the franchise was sold to Saban Brands, the original owner, on May 12, 2010. Power Rangers made live appearances in Disney's Hollywood Studios at Walt Disney World for a few years.

Power Supplies *Tron*-themed shop in Tomorrowland at Shanghai Disneyland; opened Jun. 16, 2016. Glow toys, apparel, and other souvenirs are sold.

Powerline Pop music star in *A Goofy Movie*; voiced by Tevin Campbell.

Powers, Mala (1931–2007) Actress; appeared on TV in *Daniel Boone* (Rebecca).

Powers, Stefanie Actress; appeared in *The Boatniks* (Kate) and *Herbie Rides Again* (Nicole).

Practical Pig, The (film) Silly Symphony cartoon released Feb. 24, 1939. Directed by Dick Rickard. The 2 foolish pigs are captured by the Big Bad Wolf and almost made into pork pies by the 3 little wolves when Practical Pig comes to save them with the use of an inventive lie detector machine.

Prairie Outpost & Supply Frontierland shop in the Magic Kingdom at Walt Disney World; opened Feb. 26, 1991. Formerly Bearly Country. Once offering decorative gifts and clothing themed to the Southwest, it now sells confections and baked treats.

Prairie/Seal Island (TV) Show aired Nov. 10, 1954. Directed by James Algar, Richard Bare. Walt Disney introduces Jim Algar who hosts behind-the-scenes footage of *The Vanishing Prairie* and *Seal Island*. Winston Hibler also appears on the show.

Pratt, Chris Actor; appeared in *The X-Team* (Keenan Kranjac), *Delivery Man* (Brett), and as Peter Quill in the Guardians of the Galaxy and Avengers films. He voiced Barley Lightfoot in *Onward*.

Pratt, Joanna She began in the Disney Corporate Communications department in 2006 and transferred to the Walt Disney Archives in 2010. As director, Operations and Business Strategy, she oversees all operations and programs of the Archives, including the Disney Photo Library and digitization departments, the Archives' exhibitions programs, and the Disney Legends program.

Pratt, Judson (1916–2002) Actor; appeared in *The Barefoot Executive* (policeman) and *The Computer Wore Tennis Shoes* (detective, uncredited), and on TV in *The Flight of the Grey Wolf* (Mr. Pomeroy), *Texas John Slaughter* (Capt. Cooper), *The Whiz Kid and the Mystery at Riverton* (Sergeant O'Halloran), *Michael O'Hara the Fourth* (Andy), *Hang Your Hat on the Wind* (Father O'Flaherty), *The Wacky Zoo of Morgan City* (Scott Shellog), and *The Tenderfoot* (sergeant).

Preacher's Wife, The (film) A preacher, Henry Biggs, is having problems with his church, seeing its congregation declining while its debts are mounting, along with a general feeling of inadequacy that causes problems in his personal life. When he asks for divine intervention, he and his gospel-singing wife, Julia, are visited by an angel, Dudley, and Dudley soon becomes both the source of and solution to their problems. Directed by Penny Marshall. A Touchstone film. Released Dec. 13, 1996. Stars Whitney Houston (Julia), Courtney B. Vance (Henry Biggs), Denzel Washington (Dudley), Gregory Hines (Joe Hamilton), Jenifer Lewis (Marguerite Coleman), Loretta Devine (Beverly), Lionel Richie (Britsloe). 124 min. Whitney Houston's mother, famed gospel singer Cissy Houston, appeared as choir member Mrs. Havergal. Doubling as the exterior of Rev. Biggs's church, St. Matthew's, was the Good Shepherd Presbyterian Church in the Nodine Hill District of Yonkers, New York. The interiors were filmed at the Trinity United Methodist Church in Newark, New Jersey. The church's choir was made up of members of the Georgia Mass Choir, founded by Rev. Milton Biggham. Other filming took place in Jersey City and Paterson, New Jersey; Portland, Maine (where the ice-skating sequence was filmed on a local pond); and New York City (with an abandoned jazz club in Greenwich Village providing the setting for Jazzie's). Based on *The Bishop's Wife* (RKO, 1947). When Walt Disney and his wife saw that film shortly after its opening, he wrote a warm letter of praise to the producer, Samuel Goldwyn, noting that the movie was in "excellent taste and interspersed with superb light, humorous touches" leaving you with "a very good feeling."

Predators of the Desert (film) Segment from *The Living Desert*; released on 16 mm for schools in Nov. 1974. Shows nature's impartiality as predator and prey combat each other in a struggle for survival.

Prefontaine (film) The inspiring true-life story of an incomparable athlete who attained greatness, challenged defeat, and transformed adversity into personal triumph. From early childhood, the handsome, charismatic, brash, "Pre"—as he was affectionately known throughout his life—was filled with determination to succeed at the highest level no matter the odds. He began distance running in his home state in high school and at the University of Oregon and gained worldwide popularity with his participation in the 1972 Munich Olympics. Losing a race there, he became an activist, championing rights for sports figures. And though his life was tragically cut short, at age 24, in a car accident in 1975, Steve Prefontaine not only became a sports legend but also changed the sport of distance running forever. A Hollywood Pictures film. Directed by Steve James. Limited release Jan. 24, 1997. Stars Jared Leto (Steve Prefontaine), R. Lee Ermey (Coach Bill Bowerman), Ed O'Neill (Bill Dellinger), Breckin Meyer (Pat Tyson), Lindsay Crouse (Elfriede Prefontaine), Amy Locane (Nancy Alleman). 106 min. Some of the members of the production company had worked on an award-winning Steve Prefontaine documentary, *Fire on the Track*, which aired on CBS in 1995. For the feature film, the producers decided to photograph it in Super 16 mm film stock, designed to be enlarged to 35 mm for theatrical exhibition, in order to give it a documentary feel, and to employ intercut interviews. The locale selected for the filming was Seattle and its environs.

Prejudice: Hatred or Ignorance (film) Educational film; using sequences from *Light in the Forest*. In the Questions!/Answers? series; released in 1976. A young man tries to overcome prejudice—is it hatred, misunderstanding, or ignorance?

Premiere Shop SEE LITTLE GREEN MEN STORE COMMAND (DISNEYLAND).

Pre-Opening Report from Disneyland, A Alternate title of *A Further Report on Disneyland*.

Prep & Landing, Lanny and Wayne the Christmas Elves in (TV) Half-hour special for ABC; first aired Dec. 8, 2009. An elite elf unit, the high-tech North Pole Christmas Eve Command Center, makes sure that homes are ready for Santa's visit at Christmas. Two elves, rookie Lanny and veteran Wayne, go on their first Christmas Eve mission, encountering a raging snowstorm and a number of other near disasters that threaten to undo Santa's yearly visit to one deserving child. Directed by Kevin Deters and Stevie Wermers-Skelton. Voices include Dave Foley (Wayne), Derek Richardson (Lanny), Sarah Chalke (Magee). From Walt Disney Animation Studios.

Prep & Landing: Naughty vs. Nice (TV) Half-hour animated special on ABC; first aired Dec. 5, 2011, after a preview showing at the D23 Expo in Anaheim Aug. 19, 2011. Santa's dauntless elves, Wayne and Lanny, find themselves up to their pointy ears in trouble, as they race to recover classified North Pole technology, which has fallen into the hands of a computer-hacking Naughty Kid, and which could cause Christmas to descend into chaos. Directed by Kevin Deters and Stevie Wermers-Skelton. Voices include Dave Foley (Wayne), Derek Richardson (Lanny), Sarah Chalke (Magee). From Walt Disney Animation Studios.

Prep & Landing: Operation Secret Santa (TV) Animated short on ABC; premiered Dec. 7, 2010, during the airing of *A Charlie Brown Christmas*. With Christmas only days away, Mrs. Claus and Magee enlist Wayne and Lanny on a secret mission to retrieve a mysterious item hidden deep with Santa Claus's office. Directed by Kevin Deters and Stevie Wermers-Skelton. Voices include Dave Foley (Wayne), Derek Richardson (Lanny), Sarah Chalke (Magee), Betty White (Mrs. Claus). 7 min. From Walt Disney Animation Studios. It won the Emmy in 2011 for Outstanding Short-Format Animated Program.

Prescot Press (TV) Serialized sitcom on the *Mickey Mouse Club*, beginning Sep. 19, 1992, running for 14 episodes that homed in on the humorous happenings on the school newspaper. Stars Terra McNair (Katie), Keri Russell (Heather), Jennifer McGill (Tracy), Tony Lucca (Tommy), Dale Godboldo (Brian), Marc Worden (Arthur), Lindsey Alley (Kelly), Kevin Osgood (Dennis).

Present for Donald, A (TV) Show aired Dec. 22, 1954. Walt Disney presents a Christmas show, with footage primarily from *The Three Caballeros*.

Presidential Medal of Freedom Presented to Walt Disney by President Lyndon B. Johnson at the White House on Sep. 14, 1964.

Pressler, Paul He began at Disney in 1987 in the Consumer Products Division with general responsibilities for merchandise licensing; he was pro-moted to head of The Disney Stores beginning in 1992. He was named president of the Disneyland Resort on Nov. 7, 1994. In 1998, he was named president of Walt Disney Attractions, and in 2000 he became chairman. He left Disney in Sep. 2002.

Prestige, The (film) Two young Victorian-era magicians in London, where magicians are idols and celebrities of the highest order, set out to carve their own paths to fame. The flashy, sophisticated Robert Angier is a consummate entertainer, while the rough-edged purist Alfred Borden is a creative genius who lacks the panache to showcase his magical ideas. They start out as admiring friends and partners. But when their biggest trick goes terribly awry, it sparks a powerful rivalry that builds into an escalating battle of tricks and an unquenchable thirst to uncover the other's trade secrets. Trick by trick, show by show, and now enemies for life, their ferocious competition builds until it knows no bounds, even utilizing the fantastical new powers of electricity and the scientific brilliance of Nikola Tesla, while the lives of everyone around them hang in the balance. A Touchstone/Warner Bros./Newmarket Films production. Released Oct. 20, 2006. Directed by Christopher Nolan. Stars Hugh Jackman (Robert Angier), Christian Bale (Alfred Borden), Michael Caine (Cutter), Scarlett Johansson (Olivia Wenscombe), David Bowie (Tesla), Piper Perabo (Julia McCullough), Rebecca Hall (Sarah), Samantha Mahurin (Jess), Andy Serkis (Alley). 130 min. Filmed in CinemaScope. Based on the novel by Christopher Priest. Released on DVD in 2007. Nominated for Academy Awards for Art Direction and Cinematography.

Presto (film) Short cartoon from Pixar; released with *WALL•E* on Jun. 27, 2008. Presto DiGiotagione, a turn-of-the-century magician, is famous for an astounding hat trick. Presto's apprentice rabbit, Alec, however, is dissatisfied as he shares in none of Presto's wild success. While Presto is out eating lavish dinners, Alec is left behind, locked in a birdcage with a carrot torturously out of reach. Directed by Doug Sweetland. Sweetland also voices Presto and Alec. Filmed in CinemaScope. 5 min. Academy Award nominee for Animated Short Film.

Pretty Irish Girl Song from *Darby O'Gill and the Little People*; written by Lawrence Edward Watkin and Oliver Wallace.

Pretty Woman (film) Corporate mogul Edward

Lewis finds himself in Los Angeles and needing a female companion for some business get-togethers. When a chance encounter with a prostitute, Vivian, brings them together, Edward offers her the job for a week, promising a $3,000 fee. His friendly takeover of her life introduces Vivian to a fantasy world of power and privilege, and thanks to Edward's extravagance, her natural charm and grace emerge. Edward is soon captivated by his prize Cinderella, and romance comes out of what was a purely business arrangement. Released Mar. 23, 1990. Directed by Garry Marshall. A Touchstone film. 119 min. Stars Richard Gere (Edward Lewis), Julia Roberts (Vivian Ward), Ralph Bellamy (James Morse), Jason Alexander (Philip Stuckey), Hector Elizondo (hotel manager). Filmed at various locations around Los Angeles.

Prevention and Control of Distortion in Arc Welding (film) Training film made for the Lincoln Electric Co. delivered Apr. 12, 1945. Using educational film techniques perfected during World War II, Disney animators show the methods of proper welding.

Preview Center Walt Disney World preview exhibit facility; open Jan. 10, 1970–Sep. 30, 1971, in Lake Buena Vista. Because of the interest in the project that was under construction in Florida, Disney opened a preview center where guests could learn about the project firsthand. Besides the displays and drawings, there was a 12-min. filmed presentation, along with a snack bar and merchandise shop. The highlight was a 625-sq.-ft. model of the resort's first phase. Receiving more than 1 million visitors, the Preview Center had a higher attendance during the short time it was open than many major attractions in Florida. The building was later used as an office facility, including for the Buena Vista Land Co., and in 1996 became the headquarters for the Amateur Athletic Union.

Price, Harrison "Buzz" (1921–2010) A research economist, he was given the task, while working for Stanford Research Institute, of determining the economic feasibility and surveying the ideal location for Walt Disney's Disneyland park. In 1958, Walt Disney encouraged him to form his own company, which became Economics Research Associates (ERA). ERA was involved in numerous studies leading to the building and expansion of Walt Disney World, and for other projects including CalArts, Mineral King, and Tokyo Disneyland. He was named a Disney Legend in 2003.

Price, Vincent (1911–1993) He voiced Ratigan in *The Great Mouse Detective* and inspired Tim Burton to produce *Vincent*, which he narrated. He also hosted short segments for The Disney Channel's *Read, Write, and Draw* in 1987–1988. As of 2018, he can be heard as the narrator of Phantom Manor in Disneyland Paris.

Pride & Joy (TV) Series on NBC; aired Mar. 21–Jul. 11, 1995. A young New York City couple, Amy and Greg Sherman, with a 6-month-old son, experience the humorous side of the anguish, tumult, and guilt that accompanies the love and joy of starting a new family. Stars Julie Warner (Amy Sherman), Craig Bierko (Greg Sherman), Jeremy Piven (Nathan Green), Caroline Rhea (Carol Green), Natasha Pavlovic (Katya).

Priestley, Jason Actor; appeared in *Tombstone* (Billy Breckenridge), and on The Disney Channel's *Mickey Mouse Club* serial as Teen Angel, with a TV guest appearance in *8 Simple Rules* (Carter).

Prima, Louis (1910–1978) He voiced King Louie in *The Jungle Book*.

Primeval (film) In Africa, a legendary and bloodthirsty 25-foot crocodile known as Gustave has claimed over 300 victims. A news producer, cameraman, and reporter are dispatched to track him down and bring him back alive. However, they find their work much more difficult and deadly than they expected, especially after a feared warlord targets them for death. A Hollywood Pictures film in association with Pariah. Released Jan. 12, 2007. Directed by Michael Katleman. Stars Dominic Purcell (Tim Manfrey), Orlando Jones (Steven Johnson), Brooke Langton (Aviva Masters), Jürgen Prochnow (Jacob Krieg), Gideon Emery (Mathew Collins). 94 min. Inspired by a true story. Filmed in South Africa in Super 35.

Primeval Whirl Carnival-style roller coaster attraction in Chester & Hester's Dino-Rama! at Disney's Animal Kingdom; opened Apr. 18, 2002. Guests boarded "time machine" vehicles and whirled past flying asteroids and dinosaur cutouts, with a final descent into a giant fossil. It began seasonal operation in 2019 and closed the following year.

Primeval World Diorama on the Santa Fe and Disneyland Railroad; opened Jul. 1, 1966. The display used elements from the Ford Magic Skyway at the 1964–1965 New York World's Fair. Several varieties of prehistoric creatures are represented by Audio-Animatronics figures, set in a misty swamp. The brontosaurus snacks on greenery from the swamp while nearby a stegosaurus and Tyrannosaurus rex ready themselves for battle. The Ford pavilion at the fair also included cavemen, but the humans did not make it to the Disneyland attraction. Also on the Western River Railroad in Tokyo Disneyland.

Primitive Pluto (film) Pluto cartoon released May 19, 1950. Directed by Charles Nichols. Pluto's Primitive Instinct, in the form of a little wolf, Primo, convinces Pluto to hunt for food like a wild dog. When Pluto is unable to catch anything, he returns to his food, only to find Primo has eaten it.

Primo Pluto's Primitive Instinct, in the form of a little wolf, in *Primitive Pluto* (1950).

Primo Piatto Counter-service restaurant in Disney's Riviera Resort at Walt Disney World; opened Dec. 16, 2019. The name is Italian for "first course."

Prince Character in *Snow White and the Seven Dwarfs* who did not have a name; voiced by Harry Stockwell.

Prince Ali Song from *Aladdin*; written by Howard Ashman and Alan Menken.

Prince and the Pauper, The (film) Animated featurette released Nov. 16, 1990. Directed by George Scribner. Mickey Mouse plays the classic dual roles of the impoverished youth and the prince who discover they look exactly alike. When the prince suggests they change places for a day, the evil captain of the guards, Pete, plots to take over the country after the king's death. But the prince, aided by Donald Duck, and Mickey and his pals Goofy and Pluto, manages to save the day. 25 min. Voices include Wayne Allwine (Mickey/Prince), Bill Farmer (Goofy), Arthur Burghardt (Captain Pete), Tony Anselmo (Donald), Roy Dotrice (narrator). Released with *The Rescuers Down Under* and included an additional 10 min. of intermission animation, tying the 2 films together.

Prince and the Pauper, The (TV) Three-part show; aired Mar. 11, 18, and 25, 1962. Directed by Don Chaffey. The 3 episodes were titled "The Pauper King," "The Merciful Law of the King," and "Long Live the Rightful King." The classic Mark Twain story of the poor boy who trades places with the prince, filmed on location in England. Stars Guy Williams, Sean Scully (who plays both title roles), Laurence Naismith, Donald Houston, Niall MacGinnis.

Prince Charming The handsome prince in *Cinderella* (1950); speaking voice by William Phipps and singing voice by Mike Douglas.

Prince Charming Regal Carrousel SEE CINDERELLA'S GOLDEN CARROUSEL.

Prince Eric Prince who falls for Ariel in *The Little Mermaid*; voiced by Christopher Daniel Barnes.

Prince John Spineless ruler of England, portrayed as a scrawny lion, in *Robin Hood*; voiced by Peter Ustinov.

Prince Naveen Ne'er-do-well prince of Maldonia in *The Princess and the Frog*; voiced by Bruno Campos.

Prince of Persia: The Sands of Time (film) In the 6th century, a Persian street urchin named Dastan, after defending a boy caught stealing an apple, is spared, and then adopted by the noble King Sharaman. He is raised alongside Sharaman's sons Tus and Garsiv, and grows into a strong young warrior. Later, Dastan, driven to prove his worth, leads an attack on Alamut, a peaceful holy city which is reported by spies to be supplying weapons to Persia's enemies. When the king is assassinated and Dastan is accused of the crime, he must join forces with a feisty princess, Tamina, to prevent a villainous nobleman from possessing an ancient dagger capable of releasing the Sands of Time, a gift from the gods that can reverse time and allow its possessor to rule the world. Directed by Mike Newell. Released May 28, 2010, after a May 9 world premiere in London. Stars Jake Gyllenhaal (Prince Dastan), Gemma Arterton (Tamina), Ben Kingsley (Nizam), Alfred Molina (Sheikh Amar), Steve Toussaint (Seso), Toby Kebbell (Garsiv), Richard Coyle (Tus), Ronald Pickup (King Sharaman). 116 min. An adaptation of Ubisoft's hit fantasy game, created by Jordan Mechner. A Jerry Bruckheimer production. Filmed in CinemaScope on location in Morocco and on 9 sound stages at Pinewood Studios in Britain.

Prince Phillip Courageous prince in *Sleeping Beauty*; voiced by Bill Shirley.

Princess and the Frog, The (film) Animated feature. Tiana, a young African American woman, is living amid the charming elegance and grandeur of the French Quarter of New Orleans in this musical set in the legendary birthplace of jazz. Her lifelong goal is to own her own restaurant. But when she meets ne'er-do-well Prince Naveen, who has been turned into a frog, she falls for the "kiss the frog" line and becomes a frog herself with the fateful kiss instead of transforming the handsome prince. This leads to an adventure through the mystical bayous of Louisiana. Directed by Ron Clements and John Musker. Released Nov. 25, 2009, in New York City and Burbank (exclusive 2 1/2-week engagement at the Disney Studio theater) and nationwide on Dec. 11. Voices include Anika Noni Rose (Tiana), Bruno Campos (Prince Naveen), John Goodman ("Big Daddy" La Bouff), Keith David (Dr. Facilier), Michael-Leon Wooley (Louis), Jennifer Cody (Charlotte), Jim Cummings (Ray), Peter Bartlett (Lawrence), Jenifer Lewis (Mama Odie), Oprah Winfrey (Eudora). 97 min. Songs and score by Randy Newman, who also provides the voice of Cousin Randy. Celebrity chef Emeril Lagasse, known for his Creole and Cajun cuisine, voices Marlon the Gator. Based on an original story by Ron Clements and John Musker, and inspired in part by *The Frog Princess* by E. D. Baker. The film marked Walt Disney Animation Studios' return to hand-drawn animation, after 5 years of only CG releases, and a return to a fairy-tale musical. For authenticity, the filmmakers made several trips to New Orleans, taking more than 50,000 reference photos as inspiration. Nominated for 3 Academy Awards: Animated Feature and 2 for Original Song ("Almost There" and "Down in New Orleans").

Princess Anna Princess of Arendelle in *Frozen*; voiced by Kristen Bell. She becomes queen in *Frozen 2*.

Princess Aurora Lead character in *Sleeping Beauty*; voiced by Mary Costa. When she was disguised by the fairies, she was known as Briar Rose.

Princess Boutique, The Costume jewelry and accessory shop inside Sleeping Beauty Castle at Disneyland; opened Dec. 16, 1996, taking the place of Hugo's Secret Chamber. Became the Disneyland 50th Anniversary Shop in 2005 and Tinker Bell & Friends in 2006.

Princess Diaries, The (film) Shy San Francisco teenager Mia Thermopolis receives the astonishing news that she is a real-life princess, the heir apparent to the crown of Genovia, a small European principality. Her strict and formidable grandmother, Queen Clarisse Renaldi, arrives to give her "princess lessons," but the two clash because Mia has no intention of leaving her normal life, and a budding romance, to become the ruler of a far-off country. Directed by Garry Marshall. Released Aug. 3, 2001. Stars Anne Hathaway (Mia Thermopolis), Caroline Goodall (Helen), Hector Elizondo (Joseph), Robert Schwartzman (Michael), Heather Matarazzo (Lilly), Mandy Moore (Lana), Sean O'Bryan (O'Connell), Sandra Oh (Vice Principal Gupta), Eric Von Detten (Josh), Julie Andrews (Queen Clarisse Renaldi). 115 min. Based on the novel by Meg Cabot. During her audition for the lead role, actress Anne Hathaway accidentally fell out of her chair, which was reportedly one of the reasons Garry Marshall selected her to play the clumsy Mia. Production began at The Walt Disney Studios in 2000 on Stage 2. Because the stage had also been used decades earlier for *Mary Poppins*, it was dedicated as the Julie Andrews Stage in 2001.

Princess Diaries 2, The: Royal Engagement (film) Mia is ready to assume her role as princess of Genovia, but no sooner has she moved into the royal palace with her beautiful, wise grandmother, Queen Clarisse, than she learns her days as a princess are numbered—Mia has to take the crown herself. And, according to Genovian law, princesses must be married before being crowned, so Mia faces a parade of suitors who would all like to be her king. Released Aug. 11, 2004. Directed by Garry Marshall. Stars Anne Hathaway (Mia Thermopolis), Julie Andrews (Queen Clarisse), Hector Elizondo (Joseph), Heather Matarazzo (Lilly), John Rhys-Davies (Viscount Mabrey), Chris Pine (Nicholas Devereaux), Callum Blue (Andrew Jacoby), Kathleen Marshall (Charlotte Kutaway), Tom Poston (Lord Palimore), Raven (Asana). 113 min. According to Garry Marshall, the mythical Genovia "is probably somewhere between Spain and Italy." The film was shot in Southern California; the enormous palace set was built at the Disney Golden Oak Ranch.

Princess Elsa SEE QUEEN ELSA.

Princess Fairytale Hall Fantasyland character-greeting attraction in the Magic Kingdom at Walt Disney World; opened Sep. 12, 2013. Behind the castle-like entrance are stained glass windows with images from *Cinderella*, and then the Royal Gallery. Guests meet the princesses in elegant royal chambers, richly paneled in wood. The attraction took the space of Snow White's Scary Adventures. SEE ALSO FANTASY FAIRE (DISNEYLAND).

Princess Fantasy Faire Attraction replacing the Fantasyland Theater in Disneyland; open Oct. 6, 2006–Aug. 12, 2012. Area for guests to meet Disney princesses, originally featuring a coronation show. Beginning Mar. 12, 2013, guests could meet the Disney princesses at the Royal Hall in the new Fantasy Faire area.

Princess of Thieves (TV) 2-hour movie on *The Wonderful World of Disney*; first aired Mar. 11, 2001. Robin Hood's daughter, Gwyn, against her father's wishes, goes to battle against the evil Sheriff of Nottingham in order to bring the crown to Prince Philip, heir of King Richard. Directed by Peter Hewitt. Stars Malcolm McDowell (Sheriff of Nottingham), Stuart Wilson (Robin Hood), Jonathan Hyde (Prince John), Keira Knightley (Gwyn), Stephen Moyer (Prince Philip), Del Synnott (Froderick). Filmed in Romania. From Granada Entertainment U.S.A.

Princess Protection Program (TV) A Disney Channel Original Movie; first aired Jun. 26, 2009. A teenage princess must escape her country, Costa Luna, and be placed into a top secret protection program. Hidden in the home of its lead agent in the small town of Lake Monroe, she now must learn to fit in as an average teenager and, ultimately, show the agent's insecure daughter that she too has all the qualities of a true "princess." Directed by Allison Liddi-Brown. Stars Demi Lovato (Rosalinda Marie Montoya Flore), Selena Gomez (Carter Mason), Nicholas Braun (Ed), Jamie Chung (Chelsea), Tom Verica (Joe Mason).

Principal Takes a Holiday (TV) 2-hour movie on *The Wonderful World of Disney*; first aired Jan. 4, 1998. A notorious high school prankster, John Scaduto, has to make it through his senior year without any demerits in order to claim a $10,000 inheritance. So he engineers his first prank of the year and recruits a scruffy, unconventional drifter, Franklin Fitz, to pose as a substitute principal of the conservative private school in order to obtain access to the school's computer records and remove the demerits. Directed by Robert King. Stars Kevin Nealon (Franklin Fitz), Zachery Ty Bryan (John Scaduto), Jessica Steen (Celia Shine), Rashaan H. Nall (Peter Heath), Kurt Fuller (Principal Hockenberry). Point Grey High School in Van-

couver, British Columbia, Canada, doubled for the film's fictitious Patton High.

Pringle of Scotland United Kingdom shop in EPCOT; opened Oct. 1, 1982. Scottish woolens and cashmere were the highlight here, and guests could purchase something with their family tartan. Closed ca. 2001, superseded by the relocated Toy Soldier shop.

Private Pluto (film) Pluto cartoon released Apr. 2, 1943. Directed by Clyde Geronimi. Pluto gets mixed up in his drilling by Sergeant Pete and is ordered to guard a pillbox that 2 pesky chipmunks are using for acorn storage. First appearance of the as yet unnamed Chip and Dale.

Private Practice (TV) Medical drama series on ABC; aired Sep. 26, 2007–Jan. 22, 2013. This spin-off from *Grey's Anatomy* sees Addison Forbes Montgomery, the renowned neonatal surgeon, moving to Los Angeles and reuniting with recently divorced friends from medical school at their chic, co-op Oceanside Wellness Center in Santa Monica. There, the doctors are dedicated pros; it's their private lives that need a little practice. Stars Kate Walsh (Addison Forbes Montgomery), Amy Brenneman (Dr. Violet Turner), Tim Daly (Dr. Peter Wilder), Taye Diggs (Dr. Sam Bennett), Audra McDonald (Dr. Naomi Bennett), Paul Adelstein (Dr. Cooper Freedman), KaDee Strickland (Dr. Charlotte King), Chris Lowell (William "Dell" Parker). From ABC Studios and the Mark Gordon Co.

Professor Barnaby Owl's Photographic Art Studio Photo facility at the exit of Splash Mountain in Disneyland; opened Jan. 31, 1992. A camera was added in the attraction, so that each log full of guests is photographed as it plummets down the long drop. The photos are then ready for viewing when guests exit. Closed Mar. 1, 2020.

Professor Owl Zany music teacher in *Adventures in Music: Melody* and *Toot, Whistle, Plunk and Boom* (both 1953); voiced by Bill Thompson.

Professor Porter's Trading Post Adventureland shop in Hong Kong Disneyland; opened Sep. 12, 2005. Named for the character from *Tarzan*.

Program, The (film) Darnell Jefferson has just been inducted into the football program at Eastern State University. With his great skills on the field, and a lovely girl, Autumn Haley, to show him around the college, Darnell intends to enjoy himself. But his severe academic problems, and a heated rivalry with Ray Griffen for the starting tailback position and for Autumn's affection, makes him realize that things will not be so easy. Darnell and his teammates discover the intense pressures, both on and off the field, of being on the football team. Released Sep. 24, 1993. Directed by David S. Ward. A Touchstone film. 112 min. Edited from a 115-min. version a month after its release after several people had imitated a dangerous stunt of lying down in the middle of a busy highway that was depicted in the film. Stars James Caan (Coach Winters), Halle Berry (Autumn), Omar Epps (Darnell Jefferson), Craig Sheffer (Joe Kane), Kristy Swanson (Camille). Duke University in Durham, North Carolina, doubled for the fictional Eastern State University, and locations were also used at the University of South Carolina in Columbia. The crew was allowed exactly 14 min. to film during halftime at an actual South Carolina/ Tennessee game in the University of South Carolina's 78,000-seat William Brice Stadium, and 9 plays had to be worked out with precision to fit within the allotted time.

Progress City 6,900-sq.-ft. animated model on the second level of the Carousel of Progress in Disneyland; displayed 1967–1973. It depicted an all-electric city of tomorrow based on Walt Disney's vision for EPCOT. A portion of the model was moved to the Magic Kingdom at Walt Disney World in 1975, where it has since been displayed along the PeopleMover route in Tomorrowland.

Progress Report, A/Nature's Half Acre (TV) Show aired Feb. 9, 1955. Directed by Winston Hibler, Al Teeter. Walt Disney takes his viewers by helicopter to Anaheim and shows them some previews of Disneyland, including stop-motion photography of construction, a model of Main Street, U.S.A., and a drive by car through the yet-to-be-filled Jungle Cruise riverbed, followed by the True-Life Adventure film *Nature's Half Acre*.

Progressland SEE CAROUSEL OF PROGRESS.

Project, The (film) Educational film to help develop attitudes about the need for involvement and cooperation, from the What Should I Do? series; released in Dec. 1970.

Project Florida (film) Marketing film for Walt Disney World showing the creation of the new theme park, with footage of WED designers at work, actual construction, scale models, the Preview Center, and Walt Disney discussing his hopes for the project from an earlier film, shot in 1966. 16-mm release in 1971. Directed by James Algar.

Project Tomorrow: Inventing the Wonders of the Future Postshow exhibit area at Spaceship Earth in EPCOT; opened Apr. 25, 2007, replacing the AT&T Global Neighborhood. Presented by Siemens until 2017. Guests explore a series of exhibits that explore advances in medicine, technology, and energy management, including Body Builder, Super Driver, Innervision, and Power City. A smaller version of Project Tomorrow opened in Innoventions at Disneyland in 2008 and closed in 2015.

Prom (film) Several intersecting stories unfold at Brookside High School as the big dance approaches and excitement mounts for the big night. Boys are figuring out who to ask to the prom and girls are shopping for dresses. Senior class president, Nova Prescott, a real go-getter and the prom organizer, plans the perfect prom, only to have her plans ruined a few weeks before the big event by a fire that burns up all the decorations, requiring her to reconstruct the entire event. The principal orders school bad boy Jesse to help Nova remake the prom decorations if he wants to graduate. But even though Nova is upset by this development, she has to do as the principal requests. During their work together, Nova begins to realize that Jesse is not as bad as he seems. Released Apr. 29, 2011. Directed by Joe Nussbaum. Stars Aimee Teegarden (Nova Prescott), Danielle Campbell (Simone Daniels), Yin Chang (Mei Kwan), Jared Kusnitz (Justin Wexler), Nicholas Braun (Lloyd Taylor), Thomas McDonell (Jesse Richter), DeVaughn Nixon (Tyler Barso), Nolan Sotillo (Lucas Arnaz), Cameron Monaghan (Corey Doyle). 103 min. While the movie is set in Michigan, it was shot in and around Los Angeles, with that city's John Burroughs Middle School becoming Brookside High.

Prom Pact (TV) An original movie scheduled to premiere Mar. 30, 2023, on Disney Channel, followed by a digital release on Disney+ the next day. It's the height of prom season, and high school senior Mandy Coleman and her best friend and fellow outsider, Ben, are surrounded by over-the-top '80s-themed Promposals. However, Mandy keeps her eyes focused on a different goal: her lifelong dream of attending

Harvard. When she finds out her acceptance has been deferred, she is determined to do whatever she can do to get herself off the waitlist, even if that means asking for help from the one person she abhors—popular all-star jock Graham Lansing, whose father is a powerful senator and Harvard alum. Once Mandy becomes Graham's tutor, she begins to realize there's more to him than she thought and perhaps something more to life than Harvard. Stars Peyton Elizabeth Lee (Mandy Coleman), Milo Manheim (Ben), Monique Green (LaToya), Arica Himmel (Zenobia), Jason Sakaki (Charles), Margaret Cho (Ms. Chen), Wendi McLendon-Covey (Alyssa), David S. Jung (Tom). From Bowen & Sons, The Detective Agency, and Disney Branded Television.

Promised Land, The (TV) Episode 4 of *Daniel Boone*.

Promised Land (TV) Hour-long drama series on ABC; aired Jan. 24–Feb. 21, 2022. The final 5 episodes were digitally released on Hulu, Mar. 1–29. Two families vie for wealth and power in California's Sonoma Valley. Stars John Ortiz (Joe Sandoval), Cecilia Suárez (Lettie Sandoval), Augusto Aguilera (Mateo), Christina Ochoa (Veronica Sandoval), Mariel Molino (Camila Sandoval), Tonatiuh (Antonio Sandoval), Andres Velez (Carlos Rincón), Katya Martín (Juana Sánchez), Rolando Chusan (Billy Rincón), Bellamy Young (Margaret Honeycroft). From ABC Signature.

Prop Culture (TV) A Disney+ original series; digitally premiered May 1, 2020. Collector Dan Lanigan reunites famous Disney movie props with the filmmakers, actors, and crew who created and used them in such films as *Mary Poppins*, *Pirates of the Caribbean: The Curse of the Black Pearl*, *Tron*, and *Who Framed Roger Rabbit*. From ABC Studios. The series was produced in collaboration with the Walt Disney Archives. 8 episodes.

Property Rights and Pollution (film) Educational film; from The People on Market Street series, produced by Terry Kahn; released in Sep. 1977. The economic concepts of property rights and pollution are discussed, focusing on the theft of a bicycle.

Proposal, The (film) When high-powered book editor Margaret Tate faces deportation to her native Canada, the quick-thinking executive declares that she is actually engaged to her unsuspecting put-upon assistant Andrew, whom she has tormented for years. He agrees to participate in the charade, but with a few conditions of his own. The unlikely couple heads to Alaska to meet his quirky family and the always-in-control city girl finds herself in one fish-out-of-water comedic situation after another. With an impromptu wedding in the works and an immigration official on their tails, Margaret and Andrew reluctantly vow to stick to the plan despite the precarious consequences. A Touchstone film. Released Jun. 19, 2009, in the U.S., after a Jun. 17 release in Belgium. Directed by Anne Fletcher. Stars Sandra Bullock (Margaret), Ryan Reynolds (Andrew Paxton), Malin Akerman (Gertrude), Mary Steenburgen (Grace Paxton), Craig T. Nelson (Joe Paxton), Betty White (Grandma Annie), Denis O'Hare (Mr. Gilbertson), Aasif Mandvi (Bob Spaulding), Oscar Nuñez (Ramone), Michael Nouri (chairman Bergen). 108 min. Filmed in Massachusetts, in CinemaScope. Some minor adjustments turned the Massachusetts towns of Rockport, Manchester-by-the-Sea, and Gloucester into Sitka, Alaska.

Prosky, Robert (1930–2008) Actor; appeared in *Outrageous Fortune* (Stanislav Korzenowski), *Green Card* (Bronte's lawyer), and *The Scarlet Letter* (Horace Stonehall).

Prospect Studios Built in 1919 as the Vitagraph Studios, the complex is the longest-operating studio in Hollywood, and eventually became a home to ABC. The news broadcasts originated there for many years, and the soundstages housed the series *Grey's Anatomy* and soaps such as *General Hospital* and *Port Charles*. The Studios experienced a major renovation in 2002. Located in Los Angeles's Silver Lake neighborhood, just a few blocks from the home of Walt Disney's uncle Robert.

Protector, The (TV) Hour-long series on Lifetime; aired Jun. 12–Sep. 19, 2011. Divorced mother Gloria Sheppard juggles her demanding personal and professional life as an intuitive LAPD homicide detective while raising 2 boys, with the live-in help of her troubled younger brother Davey. Stars Ally Walker (Gloria Sheppard), Tisha Campbell-Martin (Michelle Dulcett), Miguel Ferrer (Felix Valdez), Chris Payne Gilbert (Davey Sheppard), Terrell Tilford (Ramon Rush), Thomas Robinson (Leo Sheppard), Sage Ryan (Nick Sheppard). From ABC Studios.

Proud Bird from Shanghai, The (TV) Show aired Dec. 16, 1973. Directed by Harry Tytle. Chinese pheasants set loose in Oregon in 1881 find it difficult to survive in their new home, where there are different kinds of predators, but eventually they multiply and create a breed of ring-necked pheasants that can be found throughout the country.

Proud Family, The (TV) Animated sitcom on Disney Channel that follows the adventures and misadventures of Penny, a 14-year-old African American girl, along with her best friend, the sassy and scheming Dijonay. Premiered Sep. 21, 2001. Voices include Kyla Pratt (Penny Proud), Tommy Davidson (Oscar Proud), Paula Jai Parker (Trudy Proud), Jo Marie Payton (Suga Mama), Karen Malina White (Dijonay), Orlando Brown (Sticky), Alisa Reyes (LaCienega Boulevardez), Soleil Moon Frye (Zoey). The opening theme, "Here Comes Penny Proud," was performed by Destiny's Child.

Proud Family, The: Louder and Prouder (TV) A Disney+ original animated series; digitally premiered Feb. 23, 2022. A continuation of the 2000s Disney Channel series that follows the misadventures of newly 14-year-old Penny Proud and her Proud Family as they navigate modern life. The 2020s brings new career highs for mom Trudy, wilder dreams for dad Oscar, and new challenges for Penny. Suga Mama also returns, ready to dispense tough love or a gentle hand whenever Penny needs it. Voices include Kyla Pratt (Penny), Tommy Davidson (Oscar), Paula Jai Parker (Trudy), JoMarie Payton (Suga Mama), Cedric the Entertainer (Uncle Bobby), Karen Malina White (Dijonay), Alisa Reyes (LaCienega Boulevardez), Soleil Moon Frye (Zoey Howzer). From Disney Television Animation.

Proud Family Movie, The (TV) A Disney Channel Original Movie; first aired Aug. 19, 2005. Penny and her family are held captive by Dr. Carver, a mad scientist, who tries to get his hands on Oscar Proud's Instant Everlasting Multiplying Formula, which would allow Dr. Carver to create an army of G-nomes to take over the world. Produced by Jambalaya Studio and Disney Channel. Directed by Bruce W. Smith. Voices include Kyla Pratt (Penny Proud), Tommy Davidson (Oscar Proud), Paula Jai Parker (Trudy Proud), Jo Marie Payton (Suga Mama), Orlando Brown (Sticky Webb), Soleil Moon Frye (Zoey), Arsenio Hall (Dr. Carver/Bobby Proud). 91 min.

Provine, Dorothy (1935–2010) Actress; appeared in *That Darn Cat!* (Ingrid Randall) and *Never a Dull Moment* (Sally Inwood).

Provost, Jon Actor; appeared in *The Computer Wore Tennis Shoes* (Bradley), and on TV in *Disneyland '59*. He was perhaps best known for appearing as a child in the *Lassie* TV series.

Prowlers of the Everglades (film) True-Life Adventure featurette released Jul. 23, 1953. Directed by James Algar. Story of the vast and primeval Everglades in Florida, told through the lives of its animal inhabitants, including alligators, raccoons, skunks, otters, and birds. 32 min.

Pryce, Jonathan Actor; appeared in *Something Wicked This Way Comes* (Mr. Dark), *Evita* (Juan Perón), *Confessions of an Ugly Stepsister* (The Master), the *Pirates of the Caribbean* films (Governor Swann), and *Bedtime Stories* (Marty Bronson).

Pryor, Mowava Actress; adult leader on the *Mickey Mouse Club* on The Disney Channel 1989–1991, and later appeared in *Halloweentown High* (vampire council member).

PSP Disney released 2 films, *Pirates of the Caribbean: The Curse of the Black Pearl* and *Kill Bill: Vol. 1* (from Miramax), as its first on Sony's PSP (PlayStation Portable) video game format Apr. 19, 2005. PSP uses a Universal Media Disc, which is about 2 inches in diameter.

P.T. Flea Market Shop in A Bug's Land at Disney California Adventure; opened Sep. 2002, taking the place of Santa Rosa Seed and Supply. Closed Sep. 2010 to make way for Cars Land.

Puddles (film) Animated short; digitally released Jan. 24, 2020, on Disney+. An adventurous young boy discovers that puddles can be portals to a fantastical world but struggles to get his sister's attention away from her phone to see the magic in the world around her. Directed by Zach Parrish. 2 min. From the Walt Disney Animation Studios Short Circuit program.

Pueblo Pluto (film) Pluto cartoon released Jan. 14, 1949. Directed by Charles Nichols. Pluto and Ronnie the pup fight and chase each other for possession of a bone until they end up in a cactus bed and Ronnie must lead Pluto out, ending the argument and restoring peace.

Pueblo Trading Post Frontierland shop in Disneyland Paris; opened Apr. 12, 1992. Later used for special events and Pin Trading.

Puffin Bakery Shop on Main Street, U.S.A. in Disneyland; open Jul. 18, 1955–Jun. 3, 1960. It later became Sunkist Citrus House.

Puffin's Roost, The Shop in Norway at EPCOT; opened May 6, 1988. Offering Norwegian curios and collectibles, it is designed as a charming stabbur cottage.

Pullman, Bill Actor; appeared in *Ruthless People* (Earl), *Newsies* (Bryan Denton), *While You Were Sleeping* (Jack), and *Mr. Wrong* (Whitman Crawford), and on Disney Channel in *Tiger Cruise* (Cmdr. Gary Dolan).

Pumbaa Good-natured warthog in *The Lion King*; voiced by Ernie Sabella.

P.U.N.K.S. (TV) A Disney Channel Original Movie; first aired Sep. 4, 1999. Five 13-year-old underdogs band together in a club whose name is an acronym formed from the initials of their last names. Their mission is to protect others and maintain peace. When they discover that Edward Crow, the evil head of Crow, Inc., plans to test a new invention called the Augmentor on one of the kids' engineer father, they realize the invention is not perfected and could cause death. They try to overcome their fears to steal the device and stop the potentially deadly experiment. Directed by Sean McNamara. Stars Randy Quaid (Pat Utley), Tim Redwine (Drew Utley), Henry Winkler (Edward Crow), Kenneth Brown IV (Miles Kitchen), Patrick Renna (Lanny Nygren), Brandon Baker (Jonny Pasiotopolis), Jessica Alba (Samantha Swaboda).

Puppet Masters, Robert A. Heinlein's The (film) When a local TV station reports that something strange has landed in the small town of Ambrose, Iowa, the government's covert Office of Scientific Intelligence is called upon to investigate. Andrew Nivens, his son Sam, and NASA scientist Mary Sefton are the team who make the frightening discovery: alien creatures have taken over and are rapidly multiplying and spreading beyond the borders of cities and states. Against impossible odds, Nivens, Sam, and Mary must find a way to eliminate the aliens who seem unstoppable—without killing the innocent human hosts. Released Oct. 21, 1994. Directed by Stuart Orme. A Hollywood Pictures film. Filmed in CinemaScope. 109 min. Stars Donald Sutherland (Andrew Nivens), Eric Thal (Sam Nivens), Julie Warner (Mary Sefton), Yaphet Kotto (Ressler). Based on the novel by Robert A. Heinlein. Filmed primarily in Los Angeles and Fresno, California.

Puppy Dog Pals (TV) Animated series on Disney Junior; debuted Apr. 14, 2017, on Disney Channel. The show follows 2 fun-loving pug brothers, Bingo and Rolly, whose thrill-seeking appetites take them on exhilarating adventures throughout their neighborhood and around the globe. Voices include Issac Ryan Brown (Bingo), Sam Lavagnino (Rolly), Harland Williams (Bob), Tom Kenny (A.R.F. the robot dog), Jessica DiCicco (Hissy the cat), Huey Lewis (Bulworth), Patrick Warburton (Captain Dog), Jack McBrayer (Hedgie the hedgehog), Yvette Nicole Brown (Daisy). From Wild Canary in association with Disney Junior.

Puppy Love (film) Mickey Mouse cartoon released Sep. 2, 1933. Directed by Wilfred Jackson. When Mickey and Pluto mix up their gifts to their sweethearts, Minnie and Fifi, all sorts of romantic complications ensue over Fifi receiving a box of candy and Minnie a bone. Minnie is enraged until she sees the mistake, and there is a happy reunion for both couples.

Pupstruction (TV) Series planned for Disney Junior and for digital release on Disney+ in 2023. Phinny is an innovative young corgi who might be the smallest pup at the world's first all-dog construction company, Pupstruction, but proves that you don't need big paws to have big dreams or big ideas. Voices include Yonas Kibreab (Phinny), Carson Minniear (Tank), Scarlett Kate Ferguson (Roxy), Mica Zeltzer (Luna), Justina Machado (Maya), Bobby Moynihan (Bobby Boots), Kari Wahlgren (Scratch), Eric Bauza (Harry/Sniff/Lloyd), Alessandra Perez (Bailey). From Titmouse, in association with Disney Junior.

Purl (film) Animated short; premiered Jan. 18, 2019, at the El Capitan Theatre in Hollywood, following an Aug. 14, 2018, screening at the SIGGRAPH conference. Later digitally released online and on Disney+. An earnest ball of yarn named Purl gets a job at a fast-paced, high-energy, male-centric start-up. Things start to unravel as she tries to fit in with this close-knit group. Purl must ask herself how far she is willing to go to get the acceptance she yearns for. Directed by Kristen Lester. 8 min. From the Pixar Animation Studios SparkShorts program.

Purloined Pup, The (film) Pluto cartoon released Jul. 19, 1946. Directed by Charles Nichols. Pluto is a rookie policeman who saves a cuddly pup named Ronnie from Butch, a kidnapper. Together the pair send Butch to jail.

Push, Nevada (TV) One-hour series on ABC; premiered Sep. 19, 2002, after a preview on Sep. 17, and ended Oct. 24. Mild-mannered IRS agent Jim Prufrock travels to a remote desert town in search of missing money, and stumbles upon a place where mystery, danger, and peculiar characters lurk around every corner. Everyone has a secret in Push, Nevada, but no one is talking. Stars Derek Cecil (Jim Prufrock), Scarlett Chorvat (Mary), Liz Vassey (Dawn), Eric Allan Kramer (Sheriff Gaines), Melora Walters (Grace), Raymond J. Barry (Sloman). Exec. producers include Matt Damon and Ben Affleck. From Touchstone Television. The show featured a contest, where a viewer could win a $1 million prize.

Puss in Boots (film) Laugh-O-gram film made by Walt in Kansas City, Missouri, in 1922. A young man is kicked out of the palace when he tries to see the princess. His cat, in exchange for his buying her a pair of boots, comes up with a plan for him to win a bullfight and thus the princess.

Puss-Cafe (film) Pluto cartoon released Jun. 9, 1950. Directed by Charles Nichols. Two cats disturb Pluto's napping by trying to help themselves to the milk on the back step, and to birds and fish in his yard. Pluto continually chases them away, finally chasing them all the way back to their alley, where a huge 3rd cat chases Pluto away.

Put-Put Troubles (film) Donald Duck cartoon released Jul. 19, 1940. Directed by Riley Thomson. Pluto tangles with a spring coil on land while Donald has trouble starting the outboard motor on his boat. In the finale, the motor clamps on to Donald's tail and drags Pluto surfboard fashion.

Pyle, Denver (1920–1997) Actor; appeared in *Escape to Witch Mountain* (Uncle Bene), and on TV in *The Boy Who Talked to Badgers* (adult Ben), *Three on the Run* (Clay Tanner), *Hog Wild* (Dr. Larson), and with uncredited roles in *The Swamp Fox* (Amos) and *Texas John Slaughter* (Mr. Royal).

Pym Test Kitchen Science lab–themed quick-service restaurant in Avengers Campus at Disney California Adventure; opened Jun. 4, 2021, serving inventive food and drink, both small and large. Nearby, the Pym Tasting Lab serves craft beer and cocktail "experiments." Also a buffet-service restaurant in Walt Disney Studios Park at Disneyland Paris, as PYM Kitchen; opened Jul. 20, 2022, taking the place of Restaurant des Stars.

Pyromaniac's Love Story, A (film) After being dumped by his girlfriend, arsonist Garet Lumpke burns down a pastry shop. Garet's wealthy father tries to get the shop's employee, Sergio, to take the blame, but he refuses until the owner himself is accused and he decides to be gallant. But this makes Garet mad, because he wants the blame so he can show his ex-girlfriend he can be passionate about something. The police do not believe the owner, so then his wife steps forward to confess. The resulting clash of confessed arsonists and hopelessly devoted lovers confounds everyone. Directed by Joshua Brand. A Hollywood Pictures film. Released Apr. 28, 1995. 96 min. Stars William Baldwin (Garet), John Leguizamo (Sergio), Erika Eleniak (Stephanie), Sadie Frost (Haltie), Armin Mueller-Stahl (Mr. Linzer), Joan Plowright (Mrs. Linzer). Though filmed in many locations around Toronto, the filmmakers tried to ensure the neighborhood looked anonymous.

1. *Quack Pack* (TV) 2. Queen Elinor 3. Queen of Hearts Banquet Hall 4. Queen Moustoria
5. Quasimodo 6. Queen Elsa 7. Q'aráq 8. Quark 9. Quizmaster

Q'aráq Mythic roaring creature, the Guardian of the Water, at Roaring Rapids in Shanghai Disneyland.

Quack Pack (TV) Animated series; premiered Sep. 3, 1996, as part of *The Disney Afternoon*. Donald Duck is a cameraman chasing after compelling stories for a TV entertainment/news show, *What in the World*. Daisy Duck is a field reporter, and they work with an insufferably pompous anchorman, Kent Powers. Operating from their Duckburg home base, the crew is constantly on the move in a Mobile Video Van, visiting far-flung locales. Don also has the responsibility of riding herd on his 3 rebellious teenage nephews: Huey, Dewey, and Louie. Voices include Tony Anselmo (Donald), Kath Soucie (Daisy), Roger Rose (Kent Powers), Jeanne Elias (Huey), E. G. Daily (Louie), Pam Segall (Dewey). 39 episodes.

Quaid, Dennis Actor; appeared in *D.O.A.* (Dexter Cornell), *The Parent Trap* (Nick Parker, 1998), *The Rookie* (Jim Morris), *Cold Creek Manor* (Cooper Tilson), and *The Alamo* (Sam Houston). He also provided the voice of Jaeger Clade in *Strange World*.

Quaid, Randy Actor; appeared in *Last Dance* (Sam Burns) and *Frank McKlusky, C.I.* (Madman McKlusky), and on TV in *P.U.N.K.S.* (Pat Utley) and *Mail to the Chief* (President Osgood). He voiced Alameda Slim in *Home on the Range*.

Quantico (TV) Hour-long drama series on ABC; aired Sep. 27, 2015–Aug. 3, 2018. A diverse group of recruits has arrived at the FBI Quantico base for training. They are the best, the brightest, and the most vetted, so it seems impossible that 1 of them is suspected of masterminding the biggest attack on New York City since 9/11. Stars Yasmine Al Massri (Nimah Amin), Johanna Braddy (Shelby Wyatt), Priyanka Chopra (Alex Parrish), Jake McLaughlin (Ryan Booth), Aunjanue Ellis (Miranda Shaw), Tate Ellington (Simon Asher), Graham Rogers (Caleb Haas). From ABC Studios.

Quark The Szalinski family dog in the Honey, I Shrunk the Kids films.

Quasimodo Lead character in *The Hunchback of Notre Dame*; voiced by Tom Hulce.

Queen Snow White's jealous stepmother who transforms into an old peddler in *Snow White and the Seven Dwarfs*; voiced by Lucille LaVerne.

Queen Elinor Merida's mother dedicated to her kingdom in *Brave*; voiced by Emma Thompson.

Queen Elsa Queen of Arendelle, with icy powers, in *Frozen*; voiced by Idina Menzel. She becomes the Snow Queen in *Frozen 2*.

Queen Mary When Disney purchased the Wrather Corporation to acquire the Disneyland Hotel in 1988, it also obtained Wrather's lease to operate the *Queen Mary* in Long Beach, California, along with the adjacent Spruce Goose dome and a small village of shops. For several years, Disney tried to enhance the guests' experience at the monumental ocean liner, offering special entertainment, such as a lengthy and elaborate "Voyage to 1939" celebration, and upgrading the restaurants and shops. The Spruce Goose dome, where Howard Hughes's gigantic wooden airplane was displayed, also hosted exhibits and a stage, which was built for regular shows. But Disney was never able to help the *Queen Mary* turn a profit, so when the proposed DisneySea project in Long Beach fell through, the lease was not renewed. The city of Long Beach took over the lease for the ship, and the *Spruce Goose* was moved to an aviation museum in Oregon.

Queen Moustoria Ruler of the country whom Ratigan wants to get out of the way in *The Great Mouse Detective*; voiced by Eve Brenner.

Queen of Hearts Pompous character, known for yelling, "Off with her head," in *Alice in Wonderland*; voiced by Verna Felton.

Queen of Hearts Banquet Hall Fantasyland buffeteria in Tokyo Disneyland; opened Nov. 13, 1998. Themed to Wonderland, with a varied menu. Previously the Small World Restaurant.

Queen of Katwe (film) "Can you do big things from such a small place?" This is the question that Phiona Mutesi asks her mother, Harriet, in this film inspired by the true story of a young girl from the streets of Kampala, Uganda, whose world opens up and changes rapidly through the game of chess. Katwe is a small and difficult place—one of Kampala's most poverty-stricken slums—where Phiona and her family spend their days selling vegetables, struggling to get by. Robert Katende runs a chess program for Katwe children, whom he counsels, "Use your minds and you will all find safety." Phiona quickly takes to the game that makes it possible for the smallest of pawns to become the most formidable of queens, but while she can see 8 moves ahead in a chess match, she finds it more challenging to figure out where she actually belongs in the world. Directed by Mira Nair. Limited release on Sep. 23, 2016; expanded release on Sep. 30. Stars Lupita Nyong'o (Harriet Mutesi), David Oyelowo (Robert Katende), Ntare Guma Mbaho Mwine (Tendo), Madina Nalwanga (Phiona Mutesi). 124 min. The film was shot with the widest lenses possible to create larger-than-life images, a task that proved to be challenging but produced the desired end result. The film's Afrobeat soundtrack was curated by Ugandan rapper Young Cardamom (aka Zohran Kwame Mamdani), who served as music co-supervisor and appeared in the film as Bookie Student. Filmed in Uganda and South Africa. Produced by Walt Disney Pictures and ESPN Films.

Queen: The Days of Our Lives (TV) Syn. special; aired Aug. 11, 1991. Axl Rose, of the rock band Guns N' Roses, hosts a show about the musical group Queen, with interviews and concert footage. Directed by Rudi Dolezal and Hannes Rossacher.

Queens (TV) Musical drama series on ABC; aired Oct. 19, 2021–Feb. 15, 2022. Four women in their 40s reunite for a chance to recapture their fame and regain the swagger they had in the '90s when they were legends in the hip-hop world. Stars Eve (Brianna), Naturi Naughton (Jill), Nadine Velazquez (Valeria), Taylor Selé (Eric Jones), Pepi Sonuga (Lil Muffin), Brandy (Naomi). From ABC Signature.

Queen's Table, The Shop in the United Kingdom at EPCOT; opened Oct. 1, 1982. Figurines, fragrances, and fine china are sold.

Quest, The (TV) Unscripted competition series; digitally premiered May 11, 2022, on Disney+. For thousands of years, the fantastic world of Everealm has been a land of powerful magic. Now, it is threatened by a powerful evil Sorceress. As a last hope, the noble Fates summon 8 teenagers, known as Paladins, from a world beyond to work together to fulfill an ancient prophecy and vanquish the Sorceress. From Court Five, The New Media Collective, and Scout Productions.

Questions!/Answers? Series of 10 educational films, utilizing segments from earlier Disney films; released in Oct. 1975: *Alcoholism, Stepparents, Responsibility, Love and Duty, Optimist/Pessimist, Death, Prejudice, Your Career, Being Right, Ambition.*

Quints (TV) A Disney Channel Original Movie; first aired Aug. 18, 2000. Jamie Glover, 13, was the center of her parents' world until suddenly her mother gave birth to quintuplets. At first Jamie is thrilled to escape her parents' constant doting, but soon Jamie feels neglected and unappreciated as the quints take up all of her parents' time. Directed by Bill Corcoran. Stars Kimberly J. Brown (Jamie Grover), Daniel Roebuck (Jim Grover), Elizabeth Morehead (Nancy Grover), Shadia Simmons (Zoe), Jake Epstein (Brad), Don Knotts (Governor Healy).

Quiz Show (film) Contestant Herb Stempel on the popular TV quiz show *Twenty-One* in 1958 is persuaded to lose to Columbia University English instructor Charles Van Doren, who becomes the nation's darling as he continues week after week answering difficult questions. Disgruntled, Stempel blows the whistle—he reveals that the quiz show is rigged. The contestants are given the answers in advance. Congressional investigator Richard Goodwin likes Van Doren and his Pulitzer Prize–winning father, Mark, but he still doggedly pursues the investigation, and when the deception is exposed, shock waves are sent reverberating across America. Limited release in New York City on Sep. 14, 1994; general release on Sep. 16, 1994. Directed by Robert Redford. A Hollywood Pictures film. 133 min. Stars John Turturro (Herbie Stempel), Rob Morrow (Dick Goodwin), Ralph Fiennes (Charles Van Doren), David Paymer (Dan Enright), Paul Scofield (Mark Van Doren). Based on the book *Remembering America: A Voice from the Sixties* by Richard N. Goodwin. Filmed on location in New York City. Received an Academy Award nomination for Best Picture, as well as for Best Supporting Actor (Paul Scofield), Best Director, and Best Screenplay Adaptation.

Quizmaster TV host of *What's My Crime?* in *One Hundred and One Dalmatians*; voiced by Tom Conway.

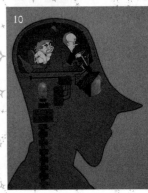

1. *Raya and the Last Dragon* (film) 2. *Rocketeer, The* (film) 3. *Reluctant Dragon, The* (film)
4. *Ralph Breaks the Internet* (film) 5. *Remy's Ratatouille Adventure* 6. *Rescuers, The* (film)
7. Radiator Springs Racers 8. Red Cross 9. Riviera Resort, Disney's 10. *Reason and Emotion* (film)

R'coon Dawg (film) Mickey Mouse cartoon released Aug. 10, 1951. Directed by Charles Nichols. Mickey is raccoon hunting with Pluto, tracking the animal that tricks the pair into believing Mickey's raccoon hat is its baby. Mickey and Pluto apologize and leave quietly as the "baby" waves goodbye.

Race, The (film) Animated short; digitally released Jan. 24, 2020, on Disney+. Grim desperately needs 1 more soul to win his work competition, but his last scheduled collection at a rigorous bike race turns his world upside down. At the finish line, he learns that life is not always about the trophy at the end of the race. Directed by Terry Moews. 2 min. From the Walt Disney Animation Studios Short Circuit program.

Race for Survival (TV) Show aired Mar. 5, 1978. When a game warden crashes in East Africa, his greyhound goes for help, only to find unexpected assistance from an aging lion. Directed by Jack Couffer. Stars Bosco Hogan, Peter Lukoye, Saeed Jaffrey, Dick Thomsett. Narrated by Peter Graves.

Race to Witch Mountain (film) For years, stories have circulated about Witch Mountain, a secret place in the middle of the Nevada desert, known for unexplained phenomena and strange sightings. When a Las Vegas cab driver, Jack Bruno, finds 2 teens with supernatural powers in his cab, he suddenly finds himself in the middle of an adventure he cannot explain. When they discover that the only chance to save the world lies in unraveling the secrets of Witch Mountain, the race begins, as the government, mobsters, and even extraterrestri-

als try to stop them. Directed by Andy Fickman. Released Mar. 13, 2009, after a Mar. 11 release in Egypt. Stars Dwayne Johnson (Jack Bruno), Carla Gugino (Dr. Alex Friedman), AnnaSophia Robb (Sara), Ciaran Hinds (Burke), Alexander Ludwig (Seth), Tom Everett Scott (Matheson), Chris Marquette (Pope), Cheech Marin (Eddie), Garry Marshall (Dr. Donald Harlan). Kim Richards and Iake Eissinmann, who starred in the original 1975 classic *Escape to Witch Mountain*, have cameo roles as Tina and Sheriff Antony. 99 min. Based on characters created by Alexander Key. Filmed in Super 35, on location in Las Vegas, and in Pomona and Santa Clarita (Saugus neighborhood), California.

Rachel and Marla (film) Educational film that explores physical and emotional abuse in this story of friendship between 2 girls released Jul. 5, 1990. 24 min.

Rackety's Raccoon Saloon Critter Country refreshment counter in Tokyo Disneyland; opened Oct. 1, 1992. The story goes that Rackety the raccoon, once a moonshine maker, had a brewing accident when his "still" exploded, causing the dam to break and flood the area, thus leading to the naming of Splash Mountain at that park.

Radiator Springs Curios Cars Land collectibles shop in Disney California Adventure; opened Jun. 15, 2012, offering *Cars* and Route 66–themed souvenirs.

Radiator Springs 500½, The (film) Animated

short from Pixar; released May 20, 2014, on Disney Movies Anywhere, followed by an Aug. 1, 2014, airing on Disney Channel. The *Cars* characters are enjoying a Founders Day celebration at Radiator Springs to honor the late Stanley when a group of Baja racers descend on the town and challenge Lightning McQueen to a race. Directed by Rob Gibbs and Scott Morse. 6 min. Part of the *Tales from Radiator Springs* series, utilizing the same voice actors as in the Cars feature films. SEE ALSO CARS TOONS.

Radiator Springs Racers Attraction based on the movie *Cars* in Cars Land at Disney California Adventure; opened Jun. 15, 2012. A leisurely, scenic tour of Ornament Valley turns into an all-out race for the Piston Cup as guests race through the mountain range, around Willys Butte, and past Radiator Falls. Along the way, there is a stop at either Luigi's Casa Della Tires or Ramone's House of Body Art. The 6-passenger ride vehicles come in 8 colors, each with its own personality. At almost 6 acres, the attraction is the largest by acreage at Disneyland Resort. The ride system is similar to that of Test Track in EPCOT.

Radio SEE MICKEY MOUSE THEATER OF THE AIR.

Radio Disney A live 24-hour music-intensive radio network, produced and distributed by ABC Radio Networks; debuted Nov. 18, 1996. Targeting children under 12 and their families, the network featured an educational and entertaining Top 40–style music format from a variety of genres—pop, oldies, soundtracks, and kid songs—as well as contests and short-form features such as ABC News for Kids and ESPN Sports for Kids. Programming highlights have included the *Radio Disney Music Awards, NBT (Next Big Thing), Radio Disney Insider, Radio Disney's Top 10 Countdown, The Freshest, In Case You Missed It, Fearless Everyday with Alexa Curtis,* and *Really Good Time with Lela B.* During its peak, Radio Disney owned 23 over-the-air stations. In 2014, 22 of the stations were sold and moved to digital and satellite distribution. The remaining station was KRDC-AM in Los Angeles. On Nov. 4, 2015, Radio Disney Country launched, featuring some of country music's biggest entertainers. On Dec. 3, 2020, it was announced that Radio Disney and Radio Disney Country would end in early 2021; KRDC-AM ceased operations Apr. 14. Radio Disney in Latin America, a separate operation, was not impacted.

Radio Disney Music Awards Awards show for kids and families allowing viewers to determine the winners through multiple weeks of submitting votes via text message, Radio Disney's social media profiles, and RadioDisney.com. The first ceremony was held Apr. 27, 2013, at the Nokia Theatre (as the Radio Disney Music Awards) in Los Angeles, featuring such young artists as Selena Gomez, Bridgit Mendler, and Coco Jones. The 2nd ceremony was held Apr. 26, 2014, and continued annually on Apr. 25, 2015, Apr. 30, 2016, Apr. 29, 2017, and up to Jun. 22, 2018; all later shows aired as TV specials titled *Disney Channel Presents the Radio Disney Music Awards.* In 2019, it was re-titled *ARDYs: A Radio Disney Music Celebration,* televised live on Jun. 16. In 2020, during the coronavirus pandemic, the *Radio Disney Presents ARDYs Summer Playlist* aired on Disney Channel Jul. 10, hosted by Laura Marano and featuring performances from the first 7 years of the event. The winners received a special award named the ARDY, which was designed by Disney Design Group artist Lin Shih and incorporates a blank, 9-inch Vinylmation figure. Radio Disney ended in early 2021.

Radio Rebel (TV) A Disney Channel Original Movie; first aired Feb. 17, 2012. Tara is a shy 17-year-old whose secret life begins with podcasts from her bedroom as the smooth-talking, edgy on-air personality Radio Rebel. When her alter ego becomes all the rage, Tara is given a shot at hosting her own show on her stepfather's radio station. Tara must choose between keeping her on-air identity secret and continuing the status quo or owning her voice and risk losing everything. Directed by Peter Howitt. Stars Debby Ryan (Tara Adams), Sarena Parmar (Audrey), Adam DiMarco (Gavin), Merritt Patterson (Stacy), Atticus Mitchell (Gabe). Based on the book *Shrinking Violet,* by Danielle Joseph. Filmed in Vancouver.

Rafferty, Kevin Imagineer; he started at Disneyland as a dish room operator in 1974 and later transferred to WED Enterprises, where he would rise through the ranks to show writer and up to executive creative director. Some of his projects included Comedy Warehouse, Typhoon Lagoon, The Twilight Zone Tower of Terror, Test Track, *It's Tough to Be a Bug!,* Rock 'n' Roller Coaster, *Mickey's PhilharMagic,* Toy Story Midway Mania!, Cars Land, and Mickey & Minnie's Runaway Railway. His book, *Magic Journey: My Fantastical Walt Disney Imagineering Career,* was released by Disney Editions in 2019. He retired in 2021.

Rafiki Shaman baboon in *The Lion King*; voiced by Robert Guillaume.

Rafiki's Planet Watch SEE CONSERVATION STATION.

Rafts to Tom Sawyer Island Frontierland attraction in Disneyland; opened Jun. 16, 1956. The dock where the guests board the rafts has moved several times over the years as construction has changed the face of Frontierland. SEE ALSO TOM SAWYER ISLAND RAFTS (WALT DISNEY WORLD, TOKYO DISNEYLAND).

Rag, a Bone, a Box of Junk, A (TV) Show aired Oct. 11, 1964. Directed by Bill Justice. A lesson on stop-motion animation, as used in the titles for *The Parent Trap*, the cartoon *Noah's Ark*, and the Ludwig Von Drake–hosted featurette *A Symposium on Popular Songs*.

Raging Spirits Roller coaster attraction in Lost River Delta at Tokyo DisneySea; opened Jul. 21, 2005. Guests take a high-speed ride through the ruins of an ancient ceremonial site, passing by vengeful statues and bursts of water and flame before experiencing a 360° loop followed by a hair-raising plunge into a steam-filled sinkhole.

Raglan Road Irish Pub and Restaurant Restaurant with an Irish theme; opened Oct. 21, 2005, in Pleasure Island (now The Landing at Disney Springs) at Walt Disney World. There is nightly entertainment, with Irish musicians and dancers. It replaced Pleasure Island Jazz Company. Next door, Cookes of Dublin, a counter-service eatery, serves fish-and-chips, Dublin-style pies, salads, and desserts.

Rainbow Caverns Mine Train Frontierland attraction in Disneyland; operated Jul. 2, 1956–Oct. 11, 1959. Later became Mine Train Through Nature's Wonderland (1960–1977). The caverns held beautiful colored pools and small waterfalls set among stalagmites and stalactites. As the story goes, German physicist Heinz Haber, who was working on the space TV shows at the Disney Studio, suggested to attraction designer Claude Coats that incorporating different colored waterfalls in one room would be impossible. After hearing of Haber's comment, Walt responded with the now oft-quoted line, "It's kind of fun to do the impossible."

Rainbow Fruit Market, The World Bazaar juice and sandwich shop in Tokyo Disneyland; opened Nov. 1992, taking the place of the Citrus House. Closed Jun. 1998, to become the Great American Waffle Co.

Rainbow Mountain Stage Coaches Frontierland attraction in Disneyland; operated Jun. 26, 1956–Sep. 13, 1959. It was formerly the Stage Coach (1955–1956). The stagecoaches were removed after the horses became spooked by the Disneyland Railroad trains that traveled nearby around the park.

Rainbow Reef Man-made reef in the Waikolohe Valley pool area at Aulani, A Disney Resort & Spa; opened Aug. 29, 2011. Visitors encounter tropical fish as they snorkel in the saltwater lagoon.

Rainbow Ridge Pack Mules Frontierland attraction in Disneyland; operated Jun. 26, 1956–Oct. 2, 1959. Earlier Mule Pack (1955–1956) and later Pack Mules Through Nature's Wonderland (1960–1973).

Rainbow Road to Oz, The Proposed film project. On Nov. 16, 1954, Disney purchased the rights to 11 of L. Frank Baum's Oz books from the author's son, Robert S. Baum. Originally, the Oz stories were considered as the basis for a 2-part TV show in the *Disneyland* series, and in Apr. 1957 the Studio hired Dorothy Cooper to write a preliminary outline. Her original story line was called *Dorothy Returns To Oz*. The title changed in August to *The Rainbow Road to Oz*, and it was largely based on *The Patchwork Girl of Oz*. Walt realized that his Oz film had become too ambitious a project for TV. He announced in November of the same year that a multimillion-dollar live-action musical feature was to start production. Bill Walsh was named as producer and Sid Miller its director. Miller wrote songs and musical numbers with Tom Adair and Buddy Baker. To arouse public interest in the project, Walt featured a short *Rainbow Road to Oz* segment on one of his TV shows (*The Fourth Anniversary Show*, which aired Sep. 11, 1957). It featured 2 production numbers on 3 sets, including 120 feet of Yellow Brick Road. The Mouseketeers played all the roles. Fearing that another studio might rush out an Oz film, Disney bought a 12th title from Lippert Pictures, paying almost as much for it as he had for the 11 he already owned. By Feb. 1958, however, the project had folded because of Walt's frustrations with the script and designs—and perhaps fear of competing with the 1939 MGM musical, which was gaining renewed popularity via

TV exposure at that time. Many years would pass before the Disney Studio would produce *Return to Oz*, finally fulfilling that early dream of Walt Disney's. SEE ALSO RETURN TO OZ AND OZ THE GREAT AND POWERFUL.

Rainforest Cafe A 450-seat themed restaurant and retail emporium; opened Aug. 6, 1996, in the Downtown Disney Marketplace (now the Marketplace at Disney Springs) at Walt Disney World. Taking the place of Chef Mickey's, the restaurant features cascading waterfalls, tropical showers, an erupting volcano, trumpeting elephants, and chest-pounding gorillas. Other Rainforest Cafe locations opened next to Disney's Animal Kingdom in 1998, Disney Village at Disneyland Paris in 1999, Downtown Disney at Disneyland in 2001 (closed Jun. 2018, to later become Star Wars Trading Post), and Ikspiari at Tokyo Disney Resort in 2002.

Raising Helen (film) A career-minded head of a top Manhattan modeling agency and party girl, Helen Harris, finds herself plunged into motherhood when her sister's 3 children come to live with her, bringing her carefree lifestyle to a screeching halt. She learns that dancing at 3:00 a.m. doesn't mix with getting the kids ready for school on time. Along the way, Helen finds support from Dan Parker, the handsome young pastor and principal of the kids' new school. Directed by Garry Marshall. A Touchstone film. Released May 28, 2004. Stars Kate Hudson (Helen Harris), John Corbett (Dan Parker), Joan Cusack (Jenny Portman), Hayden Panettiere (Audrey Davis), Spencer Breslin (Henry Davis), Abigail Breslin (Sarah Davis), Hector Elizondo (Mickey Massey), Helen Mirren (Dominique). 119 min. Filmed at locations in New York City and Los Angeles.

Raising the Bar (TV) Series on TNT; aired Sep. 1, 2008–Dec. 24, 2009. The story follows the lives and cases of young lawyers who have been friends since law school but who now work on opposing sides. Stars Mark-Paul Gosselaar (Jerry Kellerman), Gloria Reuben (Rosalind Whitman), Jane Kaczmarek (Judge Trudy Kessler), Teddy Sears (Richard Patrick Woolsley), Melissa Sagemiller (Michelle Ernhardt), Currie Graham (Nick Balco), J. August Richards (Marcus McGrath), Jonathan Scarfe (Charlie Sagansky). From ABC Studios.

Raize, Jason (1975–2004) Actor; portrayed Simba in the original cast of *The Lion King* on Broadway and voiced Denahi in *Brother Bear*.

Rajah Jasmine's tiger bodyguard and companion in *Aladdin*.

Ralph, Sheryl Lee Actress; appeared in *The Distinguished Gentleman* (Miss Loretta) and *Sister Act 2: Back in the Habit* (Florence Watson); on TV in *Criminal Minds* (Hayden Montgomery) and *Motherland: Fort Salem* (President Kelly Wade); and on Disney Channel in *The Jennie Project* (Dr. Pamela Prentiss) and *Hannah Montana* (Clarice Johnson). She voiced Rita in *Oliver & Company*, Mrs. Lasalle in *Disney's Recess*, and Diana and Aunt Dee in *The Proud Family*.

Ralph Breaks the Internet (film) Ralph and fellow misfit Vanellope risk it all by traveling to the World Wide Web in search of a part to save her game, *Sugar Rush*. They're in way over their heads, so they must rely on the citizens of the Internet—including Yesss, the head algorithm and heart and soul of the trend-making site BuzzzTube, and Shank, a tough-as-nails driver from the gritty online auto-racing game *Slaughter Race*—to help them navigate their way. Directed by Phil Johnston and Rich Moore. Released Nov. 21, 2018, also in 3-D. Voices include John C. Reilly (Ralph), Sarah Silverman (Vanellope), Taraji P. Henson (Yesss), Alan Tudyk (KnowsMore), Gal Gadot (Shank), Alfred Molina (Double Dan), Ed O'Neill (Mr. Litwak), Jane Lynch (Calhoun), Jack McBrayer (Felix). 112 min. To create the vast and bustling world of the Internet, artists took inspiration from big cities like New York, Shanghai, and Dubai, with each building representing a website—and the bigger the building, the bigger the site. In one scene, Vanellope goes backstage at the Oh My Disney website to meet a group of Disney princesses; much of the original voice talent returned to reprise their roles, including Jodi Benson (Ariel), Paige O'Hara (Belle), Linda Larkin (Jasmine), Irene Bedard (Pocahontas), Ming-Na Wen (Mulan), Anika Noni Rose (Tiana), Mandy Moore (Rapunzel), Kelly Macdonald (Merida), Idina Menzel (Elsa), Kristen Bell (Anna), and Auli'i Cravalho (Moana). Alan Menken composed the song "A Place Called Slaughter Race" for Vanellope in the vein of classic "I want" songs in the Disney canon, such as "Part of Your World." Released in wide-screen format. A sequel to *Wreck-It Ralph* (2012). Received an Academy Award nomination for Best Animated Feature.

Ralph Breaks VR Hyperreality experience from ILMxLAB and The VOID; opened Nov. 21, 2018, in Disney Springs at Walt Disney World and in

Downtown Disney at the Disneyland Resort. In groups of 4, guests join Wreck-It Ralph and Vanellope von Schweetz to break into the Internet and play video games while facing the antagonist B.E.V. ("Built to Eradicate Viruses"). SEE ALSO VOID, THE.

Ralph Brennan's Jazz Kitchen Two-story, New Orleans–themed jazz restaurant in the Downtown Disney District at Disneyland Resort; opened Jan. 12, 2001, serving traditional Creole and Cajun dishes. Food can be ordered to go at Jazz Kitchen Express. Managed by the Ralph Brennan Restaurant Group.

Ramone's House of Body Art Cars Land shop in Disney California Adventure; opened Jun. 15, 2012, with apparel and souvenirs inspired by California car culture.

Rancho del Zocalo Frontierland restaurant in Disneyland, built on the site of the former Casa Mexicana; opened Feb. 6, 2001, originally serving Mexican and barbecue dishes. In Nov. 2004, the restaurant switched to an all-Mexican menu.

Randall, Ethan Actor; appeared in *A Far Off Place* (Harry Winslow). He changed his name to Ethan Embry and appeared in *White Squall* (Tracy Lapchick) and *Sweet Home Alabama* (Bobby Ray), and on TV in *Celeste in the City* (Kyle) and *Once Upon a Time* (Greg Mendell), with a guest role in *Grey's Anatomy*.

Randall, Tony (1920–2004) Actor; appeared on TV in *Sunday Drive* (Uncle Bill), *Walt Disney World Celebrity Circus* (host), *The Disney-MGM Studios Theme Park Grand Opening*, and on The Disney Channel in *Save the Dog*.

Randall Boggs Sneaky Scarer with chameleon abilities in *Monsters, Inc.*; voiced by Steve Buscemi. Also appears in *Monsters University*.

Randy Cunningham: 9th Grade Ninja (TV) Animated buddy-comedy series on Disney XD; premiered Sep. 17, 2012, after an Aug. 11 online preview, and ended Jul. 27, 2015. Unlikely hero Randy Cunningham is an average freshman with a secret identity as a ninja taking on monsters, madmen, and an evil 800-year-old Sorcerer. As the sole protector of Norrisville High, Randy must continue to believe in himself, even if he is sometimes misguided, and to quickly learn the teachings of the "NinjaNomicon" to prevent utter chaos from happening at school. Voices include Ben Schwartz (Randy), Andrew Caldwell (Howard), Kevin Michael Richardson (Willem Viceroy III), John DiMaggio (Hannibal McFist), Dave Wittenberg (Bash Johnson), Jim Rash (Principal Slimovitz), Tim Curry (The Sorcerer), Megan Mullally (Mrs. Driscoll), John Oliver (Coach Green). From Boulder Media and Titmouse.

Ranft, Joe (1960–2005) Story artist; joined Disney in 1980 working on such films as *Oliver & Company*, *Who Framed Roger Rabbit*, *Beauty and the Beast*, and *The Lion King*. In 1992, he joined his schoolmate John Lasseter at Pixar, where he made significant contributions to their features between *Toy Story* and *Cars*—not only in story development, but also by providing such voices as Heimlich in *A Bug's Life* and Jacques in *Finding Nemo*. Ranft was considered by many to be one of the best story men in the business. He was named a Disney Legend in 2006.

Range War at Tombstone (TV) Episode 8 of *Texas John Slaughter*.

Ranger Fussy character named J. Audubon Woodlore; appeared in 5 shorts with Donald Duck and Humphrey, beginning with *Grin and Bear It* (1954).

Ranger of Brownstone, The (TV) Show aired Mar. 17, 1968. Directed by Hamilton S. Luske. A selection of cartoons with Ranger J. Audubon Woodlore and Humphrey the Bear.

Ranger's Guide to Nature, The (TV) Show aired Nov. 13, 1966. Directed by Hamilton S. Luske. Walt introduces the Ranger's new "book" about nature, which acts as the theme for a series of cartoons and live-action nature footage.

Ransom (film) Maverick New York City tycoon Tom Mullen is used to mediating tough business deals for his high-tech corporation, and he seems to have it made with a position in New York City society, a Fifth Avenue penthouse, and a beautiful wife and son. But when his son, Sean, is kidnapped, and an FBI ransom drop goes awry, Tom must mastermind a daring countermeasure to get his son back. With time running out, and his wife horrified by her husband's shocking plans, Tom faces the most difficult negotiation of his life and the possibility that his strategy, of turning the ransom into a bounty on the kidnappers, may have already backfired. A Touchstone film. Directed by Ron Howard. Released Nov. 8, 1996. Stars Mel Gibson (Tom), Rene Russo (Kate Mullen), Gary Sinise (Jimmy Shaker), Delroy Lindo (Lonnie Hawkins), Lili Taylor (Maris), Evan Handler (Miles), Liev Schreiber (Clark), Donnie Wahlberg (Cubby), Brawley Nolte (Sean). Brawley Nolte is the son of actor Nick Nolte; Donnie Wahlberg is the former member of the musical group New Kids on the Block. 121 min. Filming took place on soundstages in the borough of Queens and other locations around New York City.

Rapids Ahead/Bear Country (TV) Show aired Oct. 16, 1960. Directed by William Beaudine. Walt presents a behind-the-scenes look at the filming of *Ten Who Dared* on the Colorado River, along with the True-Life Adventure film *Bear Country*.

Rapp, Anthony Actor; appeared in *Adventures in Babysitting* (Daryl), and on TV in *Sky High*.

Rapunzel Princess, with long, magical hair, who leaves her tower in *Tangled*; voiced by Mandy Moore.

Rapunzel's Forest *Tangled*-themed area announced for Fantasy Springs in Tokyo DisneySea. Guests will board gondolas for a romantic journey to the lantern festival and dine at a restaurant inspired by the hideout of a band of thugs.

Rapunzel's Tangled Adventure (TV) SEE TANGLED: THE SERIES.

Rascal (film) The voice of 60-year-old Sterling North recalls his youth in the Wisconsin heartland when he found a raccoon kit, named it Rascal, and took it home. During a summer in central Wisconsin, the boy and raccoon have many adventures; and Rascal even helps a friend—a horse—win a race against a Stanley Steamer. But eventually, young Sterling lets Rascal seek his natural freedom. Released Jun. 11, 1969. Directed by Norman Tokar. 85 min. Stars Steve Forrest (Willard North), Bill Mumy (Sterling), Pamela Toll (Theo), Elsa Lanchester (Mrs. Satterfield), Henry Jones (Garth), Bettye Ackerman (Miss Whalen), Jonathan Daly (Rev. Thurman), and narrated by Walter Pidgeon. The story was based on the book by Sterling North and features the song "Summer Sweet," by Bobby Russell.

Rashad, Phylicia Actress; appeared on TV in *When We Rise* (Yvette Flunder) and as the title character in *Polly* and *Polly—Comin' Home*, with guest appearances in *Mickey's 60th Birthday*, *Blossom* (dream mom), *Grey's Anatomy* (Nell Timms), and *Station 19* (Pilar). She voiced Libba Gardner in *Soul* and Glacia in *Sofia the First*.

Rasulo, Jay He joined Disney in 1986 and worked in Corporate Alliances and Strategic Planning before moving in 1995 to Disney Regional Entertainment, where he was responsible for helping to develop and launch Club Disney. He was named exec. vice president of Disneyland Paris in 1998, president in 1999, and chairman in 2000. He was promoted to president of Walt Disney Parks and Resorts in 2002 and became the company's chief financial officer in 2010. He was also exec. vice president of The Walt Disney Company. He resigned in 2015.

Rat Race, The (film) SEE MICKEY'S 50.

Ratatouille (film) Animated feature from Pixar Animation Studios. A rat named Remy dreams of becoming a great chef despite his family's wishes and the obvious problem of being a rat in a decidedly rodent-phobic profession. When fate places Remy in the city of Paris, he finds himself ideally situated beneath a restaurant made famous by his culinary hero, Auguste Gusteau. Despite the apparent dangers of being an unwanted visitor in the kitchen at one of Paris's most exclusive restaurants, Remy forms an unlikely partnership with Linguini, the garbage boy, who inadvertently discovers Remy's amazing talents. They strike a deal, ultimately setting into motion an exciting chain of extraordinary events that turns the culinary world of Paris upside down. Remy finds himself torn between following his dreams or returning forever to his previous existence as a rat. He learns the truth about friendship, family, and having no choice but to be who he really is: a rat who wants to be a chef. Released Jun. 29, 2007. Directed by Brad Bird. Voices include Brad Garrett (Gusteau), Patton Oswalt (Remy), Lou Romano (Linguini), Brian Dennehy (Django), Peter Sohn (Emile), Peter O'Toole (Anton Ego), Janeane Garofalo (Colette), Ian Holm (Skinner), John Ratzenberger (Mustafa). Director Brad Bird voiced Ambrister Minion. 111 min. Filmed in CinemaScope. The film is the first animated feature produced by Pixar after Disney's purchase of the company. Its premise was invented by Jan Pinkava, who received a co-director credit.

The film received 5 Oscar nominations (Animated Feature, Sound Editing, Sound Mixing, Screenplay, Original Score), winning for Best Animated Feature. It also won the Golden Tomato Award as the best-reviewed film of the year. Having broken new ground with their elaborate computer-generated renderings, the Pixar artists decided to give the film a classic finale; the end titles utilize hand-drawn animation, which filled the halls of Pixar with the unfamiliar sound of rustling paper.

Ratatouille: L'Aventure Totalement Toquée de Rémy / Ratatouille the Adventure Ride-through attraction in Walt Disney Studios Park at Disneyland Paris; opened Jul. 10, 2014. Riders are shrunk down to Remy's size and chased through Gusteau's famous Parisian restaurant. The attraction is the centerpiece of La Place de Rémy, a *Ratatouille*-themed district in Worlds of Pixar (previously in Toon Studio). Also opened in EPCOT, as Remy's Ratatouille Adventure, Oct. 1, 2021, as part of an expansion of the France pavilion.

Ratatouille: The TikTok Musical Crowd-sourced virtual musical not associated with The Walt Disney Company; digitally premiered online Jan. 1, 2021. In fall 2020, during the COVID-19 pandemic, users on the TikTok video app began posting songs for a hypothetical stage musical version of the 2007 Disney • Pixar film. Within weeks, Broadway actors and creatives joined the project, which culminated in a filmed concert presented by Seaview Productions, as a benefit for The Actors Fund and partially funded by Lowe's. Stars Andrew Barth Feldman (Linguini), Tituss Burgess (Remy), Wayne Brady (Django), Kevin Chamberlin (Gusteau), André De Shields (Ego), Adam Lambert (Emile), Priscilla Lopez (Mabel), Ashley Park (Colette), Owen Tabaka (Young Ego), Mary Testa (Skinner).

Rathbone, Basil (1892–1976) Narrator of the Mr. Toad segment of *The Adventures of Ichabod and Mr. Toad*.

Ratigan Evil denizen of the sewers who aspires to rule in *The Great Mouse Detective*; voiced by Vincent Price.

Ratings After the Motion Picture Association of America created its rating system in 1968, Disney, with its long tradition of "family entertainment," attempted to maintain a G rating for all of its releases. In a few cases when earlier films, such as *Treasure Island*, were reissued, they had to be slightly edited to qualify for the G rating. However, as the motion picture business and tastes of the public changed in the 1970s, Disney released its first PG-rated film, *The Black Hole*, in 1979. *The Black Cauldron*, in 1985, was the first animated feature to receive a PG rating. After the management change that brought in Michael Eisner to head the company, and the move into more adult-themed motion pictures being released under the Touchstone label, the first R-rated film, *Down and Out in Beverly Hills*, came along in 1986. *Adventures in Babysitting*, in 1987, was Touchstone's first to receive a PG-13 rating. The first PG-13 film under the Disney banner did not come until 2003, with *Pirates of the Caribbean: The Curse of the Black Pearl*. No Disney film has ever received an NC-17 or X rating. Some earlier films, in being rated for video release, have been rated PG. SEE ALSO FEATURES FOR RATINGS OF INDIVIDUAL FILMS.

Ratzenberger, John Actor; provided voices in the Toy Story films (Hamm); *A Bug's Life* (P. T. Flea); *Monsters, Inc.* and *Monsters University* (Yeti); *Finding Nemo* (Moonfish); *The Incredibles* and *Incredibles 2* (The Underminer); *Spirited Away* (Assistant Manager); the Cars films (Mack); *Ratatouille* (Mustafa); *WALL•E* (John); *Up* (Tom); *Brave* (Gordon); *Planes* (Harland); *Planes: Fire and Rescue* (Brodi); *Inside Out* (Fritz); *The Good Dinosaur* (Earl); *Finding Dory* (Bill the husband crab); *Coco* (Juan Ortodoncia); and *Onward* (Fenwick, the construction worker). He appeared in *That Darn Cat* (Dusty, 1997), on TV in *Disneyland's 35th Anniversary Celebration*, *Mickey's 60th Birthday* (Cliff Clavin), *Disney's Magic in Magic Kingdom Park*, *The Pennsylvania Miners' Story* (Tom Foy), and on Disney Channel in *Just Roll with It* (George Bennett).

Raven-Symoné Actress; appeared in *The Princess Diaries 2: Royal Engagement* (Asana) and *College Road Trip* (Melanie Porter), and on TV in *My Wife and Kids* (Charmaine), *State of Georgia* (Georgia), *black-ish* (Rhonda), *Nashville* (as herself), *The Disney Family Singalong*, *The Muppets at Walt Disney World*, and the *Walt Disney World Christmas Day Parade*. On Disney Channel, she has appeared as Raven Baxter in *That's So Raven*, *Raven's Home*, *The Suite Life of Zack & Cody*, *Cory in the House*, and *Bunk'd*, and in *Zenon* and *Zenon: Z3* (Nebula Wade), *The Cheetah Girls* and *The Cheetah Girls 2* (Galleria Garibaldi), *K. C. Undercover* (Simone Deveraux), *Just Roll* with It (Betsy Hagg), and the *Radio Disney Music Awards*. On Disney+, she appeared in *Earth to Ned*. She voiced Monique in *Kim Possible* and *Kim Possible: So the Drama*, Iridessa in the Tinker Bell films, Stephanie in *The Proud Family*, Alexandria Quarry/Maryanne Greene in *Fillmore*, Playground Monitor Hero in *Higglytown Heroes*, and Maria Media in *Big City Greens*.

Raven's Home (TV) Series on Disney Channel; premiered Jul. 21, 2017. A spin-off of *That's So Raven*. Best friends Raven and Chelsea are divorced and raising their children—Raven's twins, Booker and Nia, and Chelsea's son, Levi—in one chaotic but fun household. While Raven still catches glimpses of the future, so does Booker, who uses his newly found power to try and make sense of middle school and his new family life. Stars Raven-Symoné (Raven), Anneliese van der Pol (Chelsea), Ryan Brown (Booker), Navia Robinson (Nia), Jason Maybaum (Levi). From It's a Laugh Productions, with Rough Draft Productions and Entertainment Force.

Ravenscroft, Thurl (1914–2005) Bass singer with the Mello Men, whose deep voice was utilized in many Disney films and park projects. His bust in the graveyard scene in the Haunted Mansion at Disneyland is often mistakenly identified as a bust of Walt Disney. Along with various pirates and the lead singing bust in the Haunted Mansion, he provided the voice for Fritz and Tangaroa at Walt Disney's Enchanted Tiki Room and Buff, the buffalo, in Country Bear Jamboree. He was named a Disney Legend in 1995. He was perhaps best known as the voice of Tony the Tiger for Kellogg's.

Raw Toonage (TV) Animated series on CBS; aired Sep. 19, 1992–Sep. 11, 1993. A Disney cartoon star is guest host for each show, which contains animated parodies, kid-oriented music videos, and original cartoon shorts of *Bonkers* and *Marsupilami*. Voices for *Bonkers* include Jeff Bennett (Jitters), Rodger Bumpass (Grumbles), Nancy Cartwright (Fawn Deer), Jim Cummings (Bonkers); for *Marsupilami*: Jim Cummings (Norman, Maurice), Steve Mackall (Marsupilami). From Walt Disney Television Animation. 12 episodes.

Rawhide Corral Westernland shop in Tokyo Disneyland; open Apr. 15, 1983–1984, and succeeded by the General Store.

Ray Lovestruck Cajun firefly in *The Princess and the Frog*; voiced by Jim Cummings.

Raya and the Last Dragon (film) Animated journey to the fantasy world of Kumandra, where humans and dragons lived together long ago in harmony. But when an evil force (the Druun) threatened the land, the dragons sacrificed themselves to save humanity. Now, 500 years later, that same evil has returned, and it's up to a lone warrior, Raya, to track down the legendary last dragon to restore the fractured land and its divided people. Along her journey, she'll learn that it will take more than a dragon to save the world—it's going to take trust and teamwork, as well. Directed by Don Hall and Carlos López Estrada. Released Mar. 5, 2021, in select U.S. theaters and digitally on Disney+, following a Mar. 3–4 international release. Voices include Kelly Marie Tran (Raya), Awkwafina (Sisu), Izaac Wang (Boun), Gemma Chan (Namaari), Daniel Dae Kim (Benja), Benedict Wong (Tong), Jona Xiao (Young Namaari), Sandra Oh (Virana), Thalia Tran (Little Noi), Lucille Soong (Dang Hu), Alan Tudyk (Tuk Tuk). 107 min. The 5 lands of Kumandra form the shape of a dragon: Heart, a land of peace and magic; Fang, a thriving land surrounded by water; Spine, an insular land whose people distrust outsiders; Talon, a bustling crossroads; and Tail, a desert. The lands were animated with more than 72,000 individual elements, including 18,987 human and 35,749 nonhuman characters. For authenticity, combat sequences were inspired by martial arts specific to the cultures of Southeast Asia, such as Pencak Silat and Muay Thai. The end-credits song, "Lead the Way," was written/performed by Jhené Aiko. Nearly all shot production took place in the homes of more than 450 artists and crew members during the COVID-19 pandemic. Received an Academy Award nomination for Best Animated Feature.

RC Racer Attraction opened Aug. 17, 2010, in Toy Story Playland in Walt Disney Studios Park at Disneyland Paris and Nov. 17, 2013, in Toy Story Land in Hong Kong Disneyland. Riders zip back and forth aboard RC on a U-shaped track. In Shanghai Disneyland, a similar attraction is named Rex's Racer; opened Apr. 26, 2018.

Rea, Stephen Actor; appeared in *Angie* (Noel).

Reaching Out: A Story About Mainstreaming (film) Educational film produced by Dave Bell; released in Sep. 1981. With multiple disabilities, Mary faces much curiosity and uneasiness as she enters a regular classroom, but her determination wins the support and friendship of her classmates.

Read It and Weep (TV) A Disney Channel Original Movie; first aired Jul. 21, 2006. Teenager Jamie accidentally turns her personal, private journal in as her homework. The teacher loves what she's written—a story chronicling the adventures of a confident and cool teenager named Isabella ("Is")—and it ends up getting published as a novel. When the book turns into an overnight success, Jamie cannot help but get caught up in her newfound celebrity status. Between book signings, interviews, and her new boyfriend, Jamie struggles to find a balance between her old life and her new life. She doesn't want to lose her friends or change who she is, but she is haunted by Is, the star of her novel and her alter ego, who is pushing her to embrace her life as a celebrity. Directed by Paul Hoen. Stars Kay Panabaker (Jamie), Danielle Panabaker (Is), Alexandra Krosney (Harmony), Marquise C. Brown (Lindsay), Jason Dolley (Connor), Nick Whitaker (Lenny), Tom Virtue (Ralph), Chad Broskey (Marco), Allison Scagliotti (Sawyer). Based on the book, *How My Private, Personal Journal Became a Bestseller*, by Julia DeVillers. Filmed in Salt Lake City.

Read, Write, and Draw (TV) Beginning in Jan. 1987, Disney Channel asked kids 12 and under to send in endings to short stories that were published in the *Disney Channel Magazine*. Within a few months, short videos were made of Vincent Price reading the children's submissions, and these aired at various times during the week until fall 1988.

Reading Magic with Figment and Peter Pan (film) Educational film in the EPCOT Educational Media Collection; released in Aug. 1989. 16 min. Figment and Wendy show Peter Pan the value and fun of learning to read.

Ready, Lynn (1944–2018) Mouseketeer from the 1950s *Mickey Mouse Club* TV show.

Ready to Run (TV) A Disney Channel Original Movie; first aired Jul. 14, 2000. A 14-year-old, Corrie Ortiz, discovers she has an ability to talk to horses, and Thunderjam, her thoroughbred racehorse, becomes her best buddy. With a dream of standing proudly in the winner's circle, she and Thunderjam team up. Directed by Duwayne Dunham. Stars Krissy Perez (Corrie), Nestor Serrano (Machado), Theresa Saldana (Sonja), Lillian Hurst (Lourdes), Cristian Guerrero (Gabby).

Reagan, Ronald (1911–2004) Long before he became president of the U.S., Reagan, a friend of Walt Disney's, served as one of the emcees for *Dateline Disneyland*, the TV show on the opening day of Disneyland, Jul. 17, 1955. As president, he visited EPCOT Center Mar. 8, 1983, where he addressed students of the World Showcase Fellowship Program. He returned to EPCOT May 27, 1985, to attend his 2nd Inaugural Celebration, which included a parade along World Showcase and an address at the America Gardens amphitheater. This was due to extremely cold weather having canceled many of the originally planned events in Washington, D.C., in January. In 1990, he returned to Disneyland, with his co-emcees Art Linkletter and Bob Cummings, for the park's 35th anniversary. Disney exhibits were mounted at the Ronald Reagan Presidential Library in Simi Valley, California, in 2001 and 2012.

Real O'Neals, The (TV) Series on ABC; aired Mar. 2, 2016–Mar. 14, 2017. In Chicago, the O'Neals appear to be the all-American perfect family, but mom, Eileen, is forced to admit that her marriage is on the rocks. Her soon-to-be ex-husband, a police officer, is the emotional center of the family, and he and Eileen try to parent the best they can through all of this upheaval. When teenage son, Kenny, decides to come out as gay, it proves to be a good thing, but he never would have imagined his admission would result in also outing his entire family's secrets. The O'Neals stop pretending to be perfect and actually start being real, which actually brings them closer together. Stars Martha Plimpton (Eileen), Jay R. Ferguson (Pat), Noah Galvin (Kenny), Matt Shively (Jimmy), Bebe Wood (Shannon), Mary Hollis Inboden (Jodi). From Windsor & Johnson, Di Bonaventura Pictures, and ABC Studios.

Real Right Stuff, The (TV) A Disney+ original documentary from National Geographic; digitally released Nov. 20, 2020. A gripping account of NASA's Project Mercury program, which revolutionized America's role in space exploration and inspired future generations of space enthusiasts. Free of modern-day narration and interviews, it is told through archival film and radio broadcasts, interviews, and home movies. Directed/produced by Tom Jennings. SEE ALSO RIGHT STUFF, THE (DRAMA SERIES).

Real Steel (film) In the near future, the sport of boxing has gone high-tech. Charlie Kenton, a washed-up fighter, lost his chance at a title when

2,000-lb., 8-foot-tall steel robots took over the ring. Now a small-time promoter, Charlie earns just enough money piecing together low-end bots from scrap metal to get from one underground boxing venue to the next. When Charlie hits rock bottom, he reluctantly teams up with his estranged son Max to build and train a championship contender. As the stakes in the brutal, no-holds-barred arena are raised, Charlie and Max, against all odds, get one last shot at a comeback at the robot Real Steel World Championship. From DreamWorks, distributed by Touchstone. Released on Oct. 7, 2011. Directed by Shawn Levy. Stars Hugh Jackman (Charlie Kenton), Dakota Goyo (Max), Evangeline Lilly (Bailey), Anthony Mackie (Finn), Kevin Durand (Ricky), Hope Davis (Deborah Barnes). 127 min. Based on a short story by Richard Matheson. Nominated for an Academy Award for Visual Effects.

Reaper (TV) Series on The CW; aired Sep. 25, 2007–May 26, 2009. Sam, having skipped college, works in a dead-end job at the local Work Bench home-improvement store and wastes endless hours playing video games. His parents never challenged him as they did his younger brother, Kyle. Now, turning 21, he finds out the reason—his parents sold his soul to the devil before he was born. Satan himself drops by to explain that Sam must now serve as his bounty hunter, tracking down evil souls that have escaped and returning them to Hell. While he initially rejects his fate, Sam soon realizes that breaking a deal with the devil has dire consequences. So, with the aid of friends from work, Sam is surprised to find that he somehow feels good about his newfound mission—removing evildoers from the world as the Reaper. Stars Bret Harrison (Sam Oliver), Tyler Labine (Bert "Sock" Wysocki), Ray Wise (Devil), Missy Peregrym (Andi), Rick Gonzalez (Ben), Valerie Rae Miller (Josie), Kyle Switzer (Kyle), Donavon Stinson (Ted), Allison Hossack (Mrs. Oliver), Andrew Airlie (Mr. Oliver). From ABC Studios.

Reason and Emotion (film) Special cartoon released Aug. 27, 1943. Directed by Bill Roberts. A morale-building wartime film, presenting an explanation and demonstration of how reason combats emotion within our minds. Illustrations show how the 2 could work together in winning the war against the Axis. Nominated for an Academy Award. A World War II-era short.

Reasonable Doubt (TV) Drama series on Hulu; digitally premiered Sep. 27, 2022. Jax Stewart has questionable ethics and wild interpretations of the law—until you're the one in trouble. Then you'll see her for what she is: the most brilliant and fearless defense attorney in Los Angeles who bucks the justice system at every chance she gets. Stars Emayatzy Corinealdi (Jax Stewart), Christopher Cassarino (Rich Reed), Michael Ealy (Damon Cooke), Brooke Lyons (Sarah Miller), Sean Patrick Thomas (Brayden Miller). The first scripted series from the Onyx Collective. From ABC Signature.

Rebel (TV) Hour-long drama series on ABC; aired Apr. 8–Jun. 10, 2021. Annie "Rebel" Bello is a funny, messy, brilliant, and fearless blue-collar legal advocate without a law degree. When she applies herself to a fight she believes in, she will win at almost any cost. Inspired by the life of Erin Brockovich. Stars Katey Sagal (Annie "Rebel" Bello), John Corbett (Grady Bello), James Lesure (Benji), Lex Scott Davis (Cassidy), Tamala Jones (Lana), Ariela Barer (Ziggy), Kevin Zegers (Nate), Sam Palladio (Luke), Andy Garcia (Cruz). From ABC Signature and Sony Pictures Television.

Rebhorn, James (1948–2014) Actor; appeared in *Plymouth* (Ezra), *Blank Check* (Fred Waters), *I Love Trouble* (the thin man), *White Squall* (Tyler), *Up Close & Personal* (John Merino), *The Last Shot* (Abe White), *Real Steel* (Marvin), and *The Odd Life of Timothy Green* (Joseph Crudstaff).

Recess, Disney's (TV) Animated series; debuted on *One Saturday Morning* on ABC Sep. 13, 1997. A quirky group of 4th graders make friends, learn how to get along with each other, and discover that cool things happen at recess. From the team who helped produce the award-winning *Rugrats*, Paul Germain and Joe Ansolabehere. Voices include Andy Lawrence (T. J.), Rickey D'Shon Collins (Vince), Pamela Segall (Spinelli), Jason Davis (Mikey), Ashley Johnson (Gretchen), Courtland Mead (Gus), April Winchell (Miss Finster), Dabney Coleman (Principal Prickly), Allyce Beasley (Miss Grotke), Glenne Headley (Miss Salamone). From Walt Disney Television Animation and Paul & Joe Productions. 65 episodes.

Recess: School's Out (film) T. J. Detweiler, whose friends are all at summer camp, is bored until he uncovers a plot by the school's former principal to do away with summer vacation, by using a laser beam to alter the weather and create permanent winter. T. J. calls in his friends to help, and eventually the faculty joins in to help save summer vacation. Released Feb. 16, 2001. Directed by Chuck Sheetz. Voices include Andy Lawrence (T. J.), Rickey D'Shon Collins (Vince), Pamela Segall (Spinelli), Jason Davis (Mikey), Ashley Johnson (Gretchen), Courtland Mead (Gus), James Woods (Dr. Benedict), Melissa Joan Hart (Becky), Peter MacNicol (Fenwick), Dabney Coleman (Principal Prickly), April Winchell (Miss Finster). 83 min. Based on the animated TV show.

Recovery Road (TV) Hour-long series on Freeform; aired Jan. 26–Mar. 28, 2016. Maddie, a teenage girl dealing with addiction, has a reputation as a party girl who doesn't think she has a problem, until she is confronted one day by her school counselor and is forced to choose between expulsion and rehab. Maddie makes the difficult decision to live with other recovering addicts at a sober living facility while facing the daily pressures of teenage life. Stars Jessica Sula (Maddie), Sebastian De Souza (Wes Stewart), Sharon Leal (Charlotte Graham), Alexis Carra (Cynthia Molina), Kyla Pratt (Trish Tomlinson), Daniel Franzese (Vern Testaverde), David Witts (Craig Weiner). Based on the popular young adult novel by Blake Nelson. From Pilgrim Studios.

Recruit, The (film) James Clayton joins the CIA and is sent to their ultrasecret training facility, known as The Farm. There the recruit comes under the supervision of instructor Walter Burke, who tries to mold him into a seasoned veteran. When Clayton starts to question his role and his cat-and-mouse relationship with his mentor, Burke taps him for a special assignment to root out a mole. Released Jan. 31, 2003. From Touchstone Pictures and Spyglass Entertainment. Directed by Roger Donaldson. Stars Al Pacino (Walter Burke), Colin Farrell (James Clayton), Bridget Moynahan (Layla), Gabriel Macht (Zack), Mike Realba (Ronnie). 115 min. Filmed in Super 35 wide-screen.

Recycle Rex (film) Educational film release Feb. 5, 1993 (California version), 12 min.; Feb. 26, 1993 (generic version), 11 min. An animated program about a group of dinosaur friends who learn about recycling.

Red Band Society (TV) One-hour series on Fox; aired Sep. 17, 2014–Feb. 7, 2015. Story of a group of friends in the pediatric ward of Los Angeles's Ocean Park Hospital and the adults who mentor them. The kids form a life-changing bond and singular kinship, represented by their red hospital wristbands. They face shared experiences, both uplifting and challenging, and tragic and comedic. Stars Octavia Spencer (Nurse Jackson), Griffin Gluck (Charlie), Nolan Sotillo (Jordi Palacios), Charlie Rowe (Leo Roth), Clara Bravo (Emma Chota), Zoe Levin (Kara Souders), Dave Annable (Dr. Jack McAndrew), Rebecca Rittenhouse (Brittany Dobler). From ABC Studios in association with Amblin Television.

Red Car Trolley Attraction in Disney California Adventure; opened Jun. 15, 2012. Guests ride down Buena Vista Street and into Hollywood Land in one of 2 trolleys modeled after those of the historic Pacific Electric Railway system, which operated in Southern California 1901–1961. Each seats 20 and is battery-powered (the catenary lines—above-vehicle electric cabling—are only for show).

Red Cross During World War I, Walt Disney's brothers were in the Army and the Navy, and he wanted to do his part for his country, too. He was too young, at 16, to get into the military, but a Red Cross unit that would take 17-year-olds seemed ideal. Walt felt he could pass for 17. After falsifying his age on his passport application, Walt became a 17-year-old, and he was accepted by the Red Cross on Sep. 16, 1918. After training in Sound Beach, Connecticut, he was sent over to France 1 week after the Armistice was signed. Landing in Le Havre, Walt took the train to Paris and was then stationed at St. Cyr, near Versailles. Two weeks later he had his 17th birthday. Walt was first assigned to driving ambulances for Evacuation Hospital No. 5 in Paris and later to a motor pool. In his spare time, he drew. A local canteen had him make up some posters. An enterprising friend thought up a racket of searching dumps for discarded German army helmets, then having Walt paint on camouflage to make them into snipers' helmets. These would then be sold to raw recruits coming in on the troop trains. While Walt enjoyed his time in France, the American troops were quickly being sent home, and by Sep. 1919, there were few American faces to be seen in Paris. Walt put in for a discharge and was sent home late that month.

Red Garter Saloon Old West bar in Disney Hotel Cheyenne at Disneyland Paris; opened Apr. 12, 1992.

Red Rose Taverne SEE VILLAGE HAUS RESTAURANT (DISNEYLAND).

Red Wagon Inn Elegant restaurant in the Central Plaza at Disneyland; opened Jul. 17, 1955. It became the Plaza Inn in 1965. Sponsored by Swift and named after their logo—a red delivery wagon.

Red Widow (TV) One-hour drama on ABC; aired Mar. 3–May 5, 2013. Marta Walraven is a stay-at-home mom in Marin County, California, but the brutal murder of her husband opens up a complicated story of organized crime and Bratva, Russian gangsters in San Francisco. Hounded by the FBI on one hand and an international crime boss on the other, Marta hunts for the truth about her husband's death while struggling to keep her 3 children safe. In doing so, she discovers a tenacity she never knew she had. Stars Radha Mitchell (Marta Walraven), Sterling Beaumon (Gabriel Walraven), Clifton Collins (James Ramos), Luke Goss (Luther), Suleka Mathew (Dina Tomlin), Erin Moriarty (Natalie Walraven), Jaime Ray Newman (Kat Castillo), Jakob Salvati (Boris Walraven). Based on a Dutch series, *Penoza*. From ABC Studios in association with Endemol Studios.

Redcoat Strategy (TV) Episode 5 of *The Swamp Fox*.

Redd Rockett's Pizza Port Restaurant in the new Tomorrowland at Disneyland; opened May 22, 1998, in the former Mission to Mars attraction. In front is a 50-ft. replica of the original red-and-white *Moonliner* rocket ship that was an icon at Disneyland 1955–1966. Its name changed to Alien Pizza Planet Apr. 13, 2018.

Reddy, Helen (1941–2020) Actress/singer; appeared in *Pete's Dragon* (Nora).

Redford, Robert Actor; appeared in *Up Close & Personal* (Warren Justice), *The Horse Whisperer* (Tom Booker), *Captain America: The Winter Soldier* and *Avengers: Endgame* (Alexander Pierce), and *Pete's Dragon* (Mr. Meacham, 2016), and narrated *Sacred Planet*.

Redmond, Dorothea (1910–2009) Painter/illustrator; after a prolific Hollywood career, she joined WED Enterprises in 1964. One of her first projects was redesigning Disneyland's Red Wagon Inn into the Plaza Inn. She later designed interior settings for New Orleans Square and worked on designs for Walt Disney World, with one of her most famous contributions being the 5 elaborate tile murals in the passage through Cinderella Castle. She retired in 1974 and was named a Disney Legend in 2008.

Redux Riding Hood (film) In this quirky 1997 short cartoon sequel to the classic fairy tale, the wolf is obsessed with his failure to catch Red Riding Hood. He can't sleep, he is mocked by his coworkers, and he's driving his wife crazy. He ultimately devises an outrageous plan to rectify the situation—including the use of a time machine. Directed by Steve Moore. It was released theatrically only for Academy Award consideration in Encino, California, on Aug. 5, 1997. Voices include Garrison Keillor (narrator), Michael Richards (wolf), Mia Farrow (Doris), Don Rickles (wolf's boss), Lacey Chabert (Red Riding Hood), Adam West (Leonard Fox), Fabio (woodsman), June Foray (grandma), Jim Cummings (Thompkins). From Walt Disney Television Animation. Nominated for an Academy Award.

Redwood Creek Challenge Trail Grizzly Peak attraction in Disney California Adventure; opened Feb. 8, 2001. Families can explore tree-lined paths, climb towers, and zip down slides. Over the years, the trail has added tie-ins to *Brother Bear* and the Wilderness Explorers program from *Up*.

Reedy Creek Improvement District In 1967, the Florida Legislature created this district, having most of the powers of a county to provide municipal services and build infrastructure, which would encompass the Walt Disney World property, including its two municipalities—Bay Lake and Lake Buena Vista. In early 2023, the Florida Legislature approved a bill that would give the district a new name: the Central Florida Tourism Oversight District.

Reef Break (TV) Hour-long drama series on ABC; aired Jun. 20–Sep. 13, 2019. Impulsive Cat Chambers is a thief-turned-fixer for the governor of a stunning Pacific Island paradise. Cat's less-than-perfect past gives her an instinctive gift for understanding criminals as she becomes enmeshed in fast-paced, high-octane adventures and island intrigue. Stars Poppy Montgomery (Cat Chambers), Ray Stevenson (Jake Elliot), Desmond Chiam (Wyatt Cole), Melissa Bonne (Ana Dumont), Tamala Shelton (Petra). From ABC Studios, ABC Studios International, and M6.

Reel Finds Hollywood collectibles shop in Pleasure Island at Walt Disney World; opened ca. 1994, taking the place of Hammer and Fire. Closed Apr. 1, 2006.

Reel Vogue Sunset Boulevard apparel and souvenir shop inside the Beverly Sunset Theater at Disney's Hollywood Studios; opened Jul. 2015, taking the place of Villains in Vogue.

Reeves, Keanu Actor; appeared on TV in *Young Again* (Michael Riley), and voiced Duke Caboom in *Toy Story 4*.

Ref, The (film) An inept cat burglar, Gus, sets off a booby-trapped alarm system and, in his haste to escape, grabs 2 obnoxious hostages, Caroline and Lloyd Chasseur, both of whom argue incessantly, playing one-upmanship to see who can be the most abusive. His hoped-for heist turns into a visit with the family from hell for Gus. There is a rebel son, Jesse, along with an abominable, money-pinching matriarch, Rose, and a coterie of contemptuous relatives coming over for a Christmas Eve dinner. Soon Gus finds that his survival necessitates that he become a referee for the domestic disputes. Limited release in Los Angeles and New York City Mar. 9, 1994; general release Mar. 11, 1994. Directed by Ted Demme. A Touchstone film. 97 min. Stars Denis Leary (Gus), Judy Davis (Caroline), Kevin Spacey (Lloyd), Glynis Johns (Rose), Raymond J. Barry (Huff), Robert J. Steinmiller, Jr. (Jesse). Glynis Johns had made her first film for Disney, *The Sword and the Rose*, 4 decades earlier. Even though the film was set on Christmas Eve, it was filmed in and around Toronto in Jul., so the filmmakers had to create over 400 feet of snowbanks, using chicken wire and burlap sprayed with insulation foam. They also used 3,200 lbs. of dry, bleached wood pulp for flocking. The snowbanks were then moved from location to location.

Reflect (film) Animated short; digitally released Sep. 14, 2022, on Disney+. Bianca, a young ballet student, overcomes her doubt and fear by channeling her inner strength. Directed by Hillary Bradfield. 3 min. From the Walt Disney Animation Studios Short Circuit program.

Reflection Song from *Mulan*; written by Matthew Wilder and David Zippel.

Reflections of China (film) Circle-Vision 360 film in China at EPCOT; opened May 2003, as an update to *Wonders of China*. There is updated footage of many of the cities and landmarks shown in the original film, as well as some additions, including Hong Kong and Macau, which are now part of China. Shanghai, especially, had dramati-cally changed over 20 years, with its now stunning, ultramodern skyline. Directed by Jeff Blyth. 13 min. Guests enter the attraction through a ½-scale reproduction of Beijing's Hall of Prayer for Good Harvests.

Reflections on Ice: Michelle Kwan Skates to the Music of Disney's Mulan (TV) Special on ABC; aired Jun. 16, 1998, with skaters Michelle Kwan and Michael Weiss spotlighting music from the animated feature. Directed by Steve Binder.

Refreshment Corner SEE COCA-COLA REFRESHMENT CORNER.

Refreshment Outpost Snack and drink bar in an area originally planned to be an Equatorial Africa pavilion in World Showcase at EPCOT; opened Jun. 11, 1983.

Regal Eagle Smokehouse: Craft Drafts & Barbecue Counter-service eatery in The American Adventure at EPCOT; opened Feb. 19, 2020, replacing the Liberty Inn. Presented by Coca-Cola. As the story goes, Sam Eagle, from The Muppets, has hosted a competition that brings together several barbecue selections from across the country.

Regal Sun Resort Hotel in Lake Buena Vista at Walt Disney World; opened Sep. 1, 2007, taking the place of the Grosvenor Resort. It became the Wyndham Lake Buena Vista Resort in 2010.

Regular Joe (TV) Half-hour comedy series on ABC; aired Mar. 28–Apr. 18, 2003. Recent widower Joe Binder has his hands full as he tries to run a household composed of a teenage son, Grant, and a college freshman daughter, Joanie, who is a single mother. Complicating his life further are his well-meaning but intrusive father, Baxter, and a high-strung employee at his hardware store. Stars Daniel Stern (Joe Binder), John Francis Daley (Grant), Kelly Karbacz (Joanie), Judd Hirsch (Baxter), Brian George (Sitvar). From Touchstone Television.

Reid, Elliott (1920–2013) Actor; appeared in *The Absent-Minded Professor* and *Son of Flubber* (Shelby Ashton), *Follow Me, Boys!* (Ralph Hastings), and *Blackbeard's Ghost* (TV commentator).

Reign of Fire (film) In present-day London, 12-year-old Quinn watches as his mother, a construction engineer, inadvertently awakens an enormous fire-breathing beast from its centuries-long slumber. Twenty years later, much of the world has been scarred by the beast and its offspring. As a fire chief, Quinn is responsible for warding off the beasts and keeping a small community alive as they eke out a meager existence. Into their midst comes a hotshot American, Denton Van Zan, who says he has a way to kill the beasts and save mankind. Directed by Rob Bowman. A Touchstone film from Spyglass Entertainment. Released Jul. 12, 2002. Stars Matthew McConaughey (Van Zan), Christian Bale (Quinn), Izabella Scorupco (Alex), Gerard Butler (Creedy), Scott James Moutter (Jared Wilke), David Kennedy (Eddie Stax). 102 min. Filmed in CinemaScope on location in Ireland.

Reihm Casaletto, Julie She was selected by Walt Disney to be the first Disneyland Ambassador in 1965, starting a long-standing tradition. Appeared on TV with Walt on *The Disneyland Tenth Anniversary Show*. She was named a Disney Legend during the 60th anniversary of Disneyland in 2015. SEE ALSO TENCENNIAL.

Reilly, John C. Actor; appeared in *Boys* (Kellogg Curry), *Dark Water* (Mr. Murray), and *Guardians of the Galaxy* (Corpsman Dey). He voiced Ralph in *Wreck-It Ralph* and *Ralph Breaks the Internet*, and narrated Disneynature's *Bears*.

Reimagine Tomorrow Initiative from The Walt Disney Company announced in 2020 to advance opportunities for diverse communities, amplify underrepresented voices, and champion the importance of representation in media and entertainment. A Reimagine Tomorrow website was launched Sep. 1, 2021.

Reiner, Carl (1922–2020) Actor/comedian; appeared on TV in *Life with Bonnie* (Mr. Portinbody), *Walt Disney—One Man's Dream*, and *Mickey's 60th Birthday*. He voiced Carl Reineroceros in *Toy Story 4*, Prometheus in the *Hercules* TV series, and Captain Treasure Tooth in *Jake and the Never Land Pirates*.

Reinhold, Judge Actor; appeared in *Off Beat* (Joe Gower), *Ruthless People* (Ken Kessler), *Swing Vote* (Walter), and as Dr. Neal (also spelled Neil) Miller in *The Santa Clause* films.

Reitherman, Bruce He voiced Christopher Robin in *Winnie the Pooh and the Honey Tree* and Mowgli in *The Jungle Book*; son of Disney animator/director Wolfgang Reitherman. Much later he produced and filmed *Alaska: Dances of the Caribou* and appeared on The Disney Channel in *Disney Family Album*.

Reitherman, Robert He provided part of the voice of Arthur in *The Sword in the Stone*; son of Disney animator/director Wolfgang Reitherman.

Reitherman, Wolfgang ("Woolie") (1909–1985) Animator/director; began at Disney in 1933. He was one of Walt's "Nine Old Men," known for his dynamic animation style in films like *Fantasia*. He first tried his hand at directing on *Sleeping Beauty*, and he was one of the first of the directing animators to be given the directorial reins of an entire animated feature, with *The Sword in the Stone*. After Walt's passing, he took over the producing and direction of all of the animated features until his retirement in 1980. He was honored posthumously with the Disney Legends Award in 1989.

Reluctant Dragon, The (film) Feature in which actor/humorist Robert Benchley visits the Disney Studio in Burbank to sell Walt Disney on the idea of making a film of Kenneth Grahame's book, *The Reluctant Dragon*. After explorations of an art class, dialogue stage, sound effects stage, multiplane camera department, story, and animation departments, Benchley discovers Walt has already finished the cartoon version of his story. In the story department, actor Alan Ladd, portraying a Disney story man, tells of Baby Weems, a child prodigy whose fame takes him away from his parents until a serious illness makes him a regular baby once more. In the final segment, the audience learns about the poetry-writing dragon who must prove his mettle if he wants to coexist with a neighboring village. He and Sir Giles stage a mock battle in order to show everyone that the dragon really is fierce. Released Jun. 20, 1941. Directed by Alfred Werker. Begins in black and white and then switches to color. For the opening credits, story man T. Hee prepared clever caricatures of Studio staff. 73 min. Cartoon segments include *Casey, Jr.*, *Old MacDonald Duck*, and *How to Ride a Horse*. The animated *Reluctant Dragon* segment by itself was released on 16 mm in Oct. 1975. The full feature was released on video in 1998.

Remember . . . Dreams Come True Fireworks spectacular at Disneyland for the 50th anniversary; debuted May 5, 2005. Narrated by Julie Andrews. A nostalgic journey through the different lands of the park. For the first time, Tinker Bell appeared twice in a fireworks show, with a new flight over Sleeping Beauty Castle. Sponsored by American Honda Motor Co.

Remember Me Song from *Coco*; written by Kristen Anderson-Lopez and Robert Lopez. Academy Award winner.

Remember the Magic Parade in the Magic Kingdom for the 25th anniversary of Walt Disney World; ran Oct. 1, 1996–1998. The title song was written by Ira Antelis, Cheryl Berman, and David Pack. Later ran as *Disney's Magical Moments Parade*, 1998–2001.

Remember the Titans (film) In Alexandria, Virginia, in 1971, high school football was everything to the city. But when the local school board was forced to integrate an all-Black school with an all-white school, the very foundation of football's great tradition was put to the test. Herman Boone, a young Black coach new to the community, was hired as head coach of the T. C. Williams High Titans over Bill Yoast, a white man with several years seniority, a steadfast following, and a tradition of winning. As the pair learned to work together, they found they had much more than football in common. Although from vastly different backgrounds, these 2 coaches not only molded a group of angry, unfocused boys into a dynamic, winning team, but helped guide them into becoming responsible young men, and along the way initiated a lifelong friendship. Released Sep. 29, 2000, after a Sep. 23 world premiere at the Rose Bowl in Pasadena, California. Directed by Boaz Yakin. A Walt Disney Pictures/Jerry Bruckheimer Films production. Stars Denzel Washington (Herman Boone), Will Patton (Bill Yoast), Donald Faison (Petey Jones), Wood Harris (Julius Campbell), Ryan Hurst (Gerry Bertier), Ethan Suplee (Louie Lastik), Hayden Panettiere (Sheryl Yoast), Ryan Gosling (Alan Bosley). 113 min. Filmed in CinemaScope.

Remembering (TV) Original short film on Disney+; digitally released Sep. 8, 2022. A writer loses a very important idea when her phone rings. Personified as golden light, this lost idea is found by the writer's inner child, who embarks on a journey through The World of Imagination. Directed by Elijah Allan-Blitz. Stars Brie Larson. 8 min. The film debuted with a companion augmented reality app, allowing viewers to interact with the story and extend the world into their home by scanning the TV.

Remy Gourmet-cooking rat in *Ratatouille*; voiced by Patton Oswalt. A tiny Chef Remy Audio-Animatronics figure, the smallest ever created by Walt Disney Imagineering, entertained periodically at Restaurant des Stars in Walt Disney Studios Park in Disneyland Paris beginning in 2008, and later at Les Chefs de France in EPCOT.

Remy's Patisserie French–inspired bakery on Mickey Avenue in Shanghai Disneyland; opened Jun. 16, 2016. Based on characters from *Ratatouille*, with baked sweets, sandwiches, and cookies prepared fresh in an open kitchen. Closed Nov. 1, 2021, to become CookieAnn Bakery Café.

Remy's Ratatouille Adventure SEE RATATOUILLE: L'AVENTURE TOTALEMENT TOQUÉE DE RÉMY / RATATOUILLE THE ADVENTURE.

Renaday, Pete Actor; he joined the Disney Studio traffic department in 1959, soon transferring to Art Props and later heading the script morgue, before his retirement in 1995. He performed many acting and voice roles for Disney films in the 1970s and 1980s, including *Lt. Robin Crusoe, U.S.N.*; *The Computer Wore Tennis Shoes*; *The Million Dollar Duck*; and *The Cat from Outer Space*. He also provided the voice of Mickey Mouse for several record albums. For Walt Disney World, he provided the voices of Henry and Max in Country Bear Jamboree; Captain Nemo in 20,000 Leagues Under the Sea; the narrator of *The Walt Disney Story* film; Abraham Lincoln in The Hall of Presidents (1993–2008); the announcer on the Tomorrowland Transit Authority (1994–2009); and additional voices in Flight to the Moon and Mission to Mars. For Disneyland, he has been narrator/announcer for The Many Adventures of Winnie the Pooh, the Sailing Ship *Columbia*, and the Astro Orbitor, among other roles. His real name is Pete Renoudet.

Renaissance Man (film) When a middle-aged advertising executive, Bill Rago, loses his job, he realizes that he is not really qualified to do anything else. Finally, an imperious unemployment office counselor finds Bill a short-term assignment teaching basic comprehension to a group of borderline washouts at a nearby army post. Hesitantly, Bill accepts the job, but then has difficulty adjusting to the regimentation of life on an army base and in communicating with the recruits. When he accidentally brings a copy of *Hamlet* to class, the students get involved and Bill begins to inspire and motivate them with Shakespeare. He eventually proves to them and to himself that they can achieve more than they ever dreamed. Released Jun. 3, 1994. Directed by Penny Marshall. A Touchstone film. 128 min. Stars Danny DeVito (Bill Rago), Gregory Hines (Sgt. Cass), James Remar (Capt. Murdoch), Cliff Robertson (Col. James), Ed Begley, Jr. (Jack Markin). Also in the cast as one of the recruits is Mark Wahlberg in his film debut. Filmed primarily at Fort Jackson, South Carolina, with generous cooperation from military officials. The film received a short test run in Seattle in Sep. 1994, under the title *By the Book*.

Rendez-Vous des Stars Restaurant Production Courtyard buffet-style restaurant, seating 300, in Walt Disney Studios Park at Disneyland Paris; opened Mar. 16, 2002. Art deco décor and framed photos of movie stars added to the classic Hollywood atmosphere. In 2007, it became Restaurant des Stars, with new *Ratatouille* elements and tableside greetings by a small Audio-Animatronics Chef Remy, who greeted diners on a traveling food cart. The restaurant closed Jan. 5, 2020, to become PYM Kitchen.

Renfro, Brad (1982–2008) Actor; appeared in *Tom and Huck* (Huckleberry Finn).

Renner, Jeremy Actor; appeared as Clint Barton/Hawkeye in the Marvel Studios films, and on Disney+ in *Hawkeye* and *Rennervations*.

Rennervations (TV) A Disney+ original series planned for digital release Apr. 12, 2023. Actor and construction aficionado Jeremy Renner reimagines unique, purpose-built vehicles to meet a community's needs. 4 episodes.

Rennie, Michael (1909–1971) Actor; appeared in *Third Man on the Mountain* (Capt. John Winter).

Replacements, The (TV) Animated series on Disney Channel; premiered Sep. 8, 2006. Orphaned tween siblings Riley and Todd come across a comic book ad that promises a new set of parents sent directly from the Fleemco Company in Canton, Ohio. The quirky new family consists of a British international spy mom named Agent K, a renowned stuntman, daredevil dad named Dick Daring, and C.A.R.T.E.R., a cynical talking spy car (and Agent K's former partner). Riley and Todd soon realize that they can replace any adult in their life simply by making a call to Conrad Fleem, owner of the Fleemco

Company. Voices include Nancy Cartwright (Todd), Grey DeLisle (Riley), Kath Soucie (Agent K), Daran Norris (Dick Daring), David McCallum (C.A.R.T.E.R.), Lauren Tom (Tasumi), Jeff Bennett (Shelton). From Walt Disney Television Animation.

Rescue, The (film) When a group of Navy SEAL officers are captured while on a secret mission off North Korea, the U.S. government hesitates to use force to rescue them, despite the threat of their impending execution as spies. So, at the Navy base, the men's children steal a top secret plan and go off to rescue their fathers on their own. Sneaking into North Korea, but spurned by South Korean intelligence operatives because of their ages, the kids manage to break into a high-security prison by themselves and effect the rescue under cover of a barrage of fireworks. Released Aug. 5, 1988. Directed by Ferdinand Fairfax. A Touchstone film. 97 min. Stars Kevin Dillon (J. J. Merrill), Christina Harnos (Adrian Phillips), Marc Price (Max Rothman), Ned Vaughn (Shawn Howard), Ian Giatti (Bobby Howard), Charles Haid (Cmdr. Howard), Edward Albert (Cmdr. Merrill). Filmed entirely on location in Queenstown, New Zealand (and its nearby Whenuapai Air Force Base); Auckland, New Zealand; and in Hong Kong and Macau.

Rescue Dog (film) Pluto cartoon released Mar. 21, 1947. Directed by Charles Nichols. Pluto loses his brandy keg to a baby seal and gives chase. But when Pluto falls through the ice and must be rescued by the seal, they become friends.

Rescue Rangers Fire Safety Adventure (film) Educational release in 16 mm in Aug. 1991. 14 min. Rescue Rangers Chip and Dale, along with their friends, must foil the plans of Fat Cat as he leaves a trail of fire hazards throughout the fire station and neighboring bank.

Rescue Rangers Raceway Overlay to the Fantasyland Autopia in Disneyland for the Disney Afternoon Avenue promotion, Mar. 15–Nov. 10, 1991. Cutouts of the animated TV characters were placed throughout the attraction.

Rescuers, The (film) The Rescue Aid Society, an international organization of mice with headquarters in the basement of the United Nations building, receives a plea for help from a little orphan girl named Penny. Penny has been kidnapped by an evil woman, Madame Medusa, who intends to use her to retrieve a fabulous diamond, the Devil's Eye, from a pirate cave. The case is taken by lovely Bianca and Rescue Aid Society custodian Bernard, who becomes her shy assistant. Together, after avoiding 2 brutish alligators, enlisting the help of the local swamp folk, and turning Medusa and her henchman Snoops against one another, they rescue Penny and the diamond. Released Jun. 22, 1977. Directed by Wolfgang Reitherman, John Lounsbery, Art Stevens. 76 min. Voices include Eva Gabor (Bianca), Bob Newhart (Bernard), Geraldine Page (Madame Medusa), Jim Jordan (Orville), John McIntire (Rufus), James Macdonald (Evinrude), Michelle Stacy (Penny), Bernard Fox (Chairmouse), Larry Clemmons (Gramps), George Lindsey (Deadeye), Dub Taylor (Digger), John Fiedler (Deacon), Pat Buttram (Luke). Based on 2 books by Margery Sharp: *The Rescuers* and *Miss Bianca*. The film was nominated for an Academy Award for "Someone's Waiting for You," as Best Song, written by Sammy Fain, Carol Connors, and Ayn Robbins. The other songs, by Connors and Robbins, were "The Journey," "Rescue Aid Society," and "Tomorrow Is Another Day." The film was 4 years in the making, with the combined talents of 250 people, including 40 animators who produced approximately 330,000 drawings; there were 14 sequences with 1,039 separate scenes and 750 backgrounds. The film was rereleased in theaters in 1983 and in 1989. First released on video in 1992. *The Rescuers Down Under* was the sequel; released in 1990.

Rescuers Down Under, The (film) In Australia, the young Cody discovers that evil Percival McLeach has captured the magnificent eagle, Marahute. He manages to set her free only to be kidnapped himself, and later to see her recaptured. A frantic call for help goes out to the Rescue Aid Society, which sends the intrepid Bernard and Miss Bianca to help. They are aided by Wilbur from Albatross Air Lines, and in Australia are joined by Jake and frill-necked lizard Frank, in trying to outwit McLeach and save Marahute. Released Nov. 16, 1990. Directed by Hendel Butoy and Mike Gabriel. 74 min. Voices include Bob Newhart (Bernard), Eva Gabor (Bianca), John Candy (Wilbur), Tristan Rogers (Jake), Adam Ryen (Cody), Wayne Robson (Frank), George C. Scott (Percival McLeach), Douglas Seale (Krebbs), Frank Welker (Joanna). The first Disney animated classic essentially to be a sequel, to the 1977 hit film, *The Rescuers*. The production required a team of more than 415 artists and technicians. Five key members of the cre-

ative team traveled to the Australian outback to observe for themselves its unique beauty, which they wanted to capture on film. They came home with hundreds of photographs of Ayers Rock, Katherine Gorge, and Kakadu National Park, and countless filled sketchbooks. Since Jim Jordan, who had voiced the albatross Orville in the original *The Rescuers*, had passed away, it was Roy E. Disney who suggested the character of Wilbur, Orville's brother, as a replacement. The names, of course, were a play on the Wright brothers. While the animation itself would be done by hand as it always has been, computer technology took the place of the Xerox process and the hand painting of cels for the first time (and it also enabled the inclusion of several spectacular visuals). The marketing effort for the film did not call attention to the fact that cels were not used, so that the film would be reviewed on its own merits and not in comparison to earlier Disney films.

Residential Street Area in Disney-MGM Studios; opened May 1, 1989. Part of the Backstage Studio Tour, it featured houses from *Splash, Too*; *Empty Nest*; and *The Golden Girls* (a replica), among others. The Osborne Family Spectacle of Lights was presented during the holidays, 1995–2002. It was removed in 2003 to make way for Lights, Motors, Action! Extreme Stunt Show.

Resistance Supply Shop in Star Wars: Galaxy's Edge; opened May 31, 2019, in Disneyland and Aug. 29, 2019, in Disney's Hollywood Studios at Walt Disney World. As the story goes, members of the Resistance have set up this secret makeshift gear and supply post in a forested area near ancient ruins.

Resortwear Unlimited Women's sports- and swimwear shop in Walt Disney World Village; opened Apr. 1986, replacing Country Address. Closed May 2000, to become Disney at Home. Also a former shop in the Disneyland Hotel at Disneyland Resort; opened Jun. 29, 1992, taking the place of California Woman and Riptides.

Responsibility: What Are Its Limits? (film) Educational film; using sequences from *Those Calloways*. In the Questions!/Answers? series; released in Oct. 1975. The film helps present the personal quality of responsibility.

Responsible Persons (film) Educational film in which Pooh and friends demonstrate responsibility and promote interpersonal skills, in the Think It Through with Winnie the Pooh series; released in Sep. 1989. 15 min.

Restaurant Agrabah Café Mediterranean-Asian-style buffet in Adventureland at Disneyland Paris; opened Dec. 23, 1999, taking over part of the Adventureland Bazaar.

Restaurant Akershus Opened in Norway at EPCOT May 6, 1988. Differing from other restaurants at World Showcase, Akershus featured a koldtbord, or buffet, with both hot and cold dishes. Pickled herring, meatballs, cold cuts, and salads were featured. It began offering a Princess Storybook breakfast Jul. 28, 2002, and switched Apr. 10, 2005, to also offer Princess Storybook dining during lunch and dinner. With the character greetings came a name change, to Akershus Royal Banquet Hall. The building is patterned after a medieval fortress in Oslo.

Restaurant des Stars SEE RENDEZ-VOUS DES STARS RESTAURANT.

Restaurant el Marrakesh Morocco restaurant in EPCOT; opened Sep. 16, 1984, serving traditional cuisine, such as couscous, lamb and chicken dishes, and bastila. Often there is a performance by a belly dancer. The dining room is styled after Moroccan palaces. The Imagineers were inspired by the seating arrangement of a traditional Moroccan home, in which the meal would be served on low, tray-like tables, and guests would sit on low couches or cushions. They decided that park guests would be more comfortable dining at tables and chairs; but take a look and you'll see the seating is designed to be closer to the floor for a more traditional ambience. Later known as Restaurant Marrakesh. Originally managed by operating participants Rachid and Rachid; Disney assumed the operation in late 2020.

Restaurant en Coulisse Counter-service restaurant, seating 670, in Disney Studio 1 in the Front Lot at Walt Disney Studios Park at Disneyland Paris; opened Mar. 16, 2002. Sandwiches and salads are served in a Hollywood-inspired atmosphere.

Restaurant Hakuna Matata SEE HAKUNA MATATA.

Restaurant Hokusai World Bazaar restaurant in Tokyo Disneyland; opened Jul. 1984. Tokyo Disneyland had opened without a restaurant serving Japanese cuisine, but there turned out to be a demand by many of the Japanese visitors, especially elderly ones. So this restaurant was added a little over a year later. Named after Hokusai Katsushika, an artist famous for his Japanese ukiyo-e prints.

Restaurant Sakura American Waterfront restaurant in Tokyo DisneySea; opened Sep. 4, 2001, creating the atmosphere of a turn-of-the-century wharf-side fish market. There is traditional Japanese cuisine along with new dishes that combine tastes of Japan with flavors from around the world.

Restaurantosaurus Counter-service restaurant in DinoLand U.S.A. at Disney's Animal Kingdom; opened Apr. 22, 1998. As the story goes, the restaurant is a former fishing lodge, which currently serves as the living/research quarters for the local paleontology students (who have apparently found the addition of "-osaurus" to constitute an improvement to any word). Presented by McDonald's until 2008.

Restless Sea, The (TV) The story of the sea, in live action and animation, prepared for the Bell System Science Series on TV. It depicts the beginnings of the sea and primal life, the sea's chemical composition, continental drift, and the effect of gravitational pull on tides and currents. Aired Jan. 24, 1964. A revised version was released as an educational film in Sep. 1979 and aired on The Disney Channel in 1983.

Resurrection (TV) One-hour drama on ABC; aired Mar. 9, 2014–Jan. 25, 2015. The people of Arcadia, Missouri, are forever changed when their deceased loved ones suddenly start to reappear. J. Martin Bellamy, an immigration agent, and Maggie Langston, a local doctor, join forces to figure out why the unexplainable is happening in Arcadia. Stars Omar Epps (J. Martin Bellamy), Frances Fisher (Lucille Langston), Matt Craven (Fred Langston), Mark Hildreth (Pastor Tom Hale), Devin Kelley (Maggie Langston), Samaire Armstrong (Elaine Richards), Sam Hazeldine (Caleb Richards), Landon Gimenez (Jacob), Kurtwood Smith (Henry Langston). From ABC Studios.

Retlaw Enterprises The Walt Disney family corporation, with the name being *Walter* spelled backward. Retlaw took over the family interests when Walt Disney sold his original WED Enterprises holdings to Walt Disney Productions in 1965.

Return from Witch Mountain (film) Sequel to

Escape to Witch Mountain in which the 2 extraterrestrial youngsters, Tony and Tia, return to Earth for a vacation in Los Angeles. Tony is kidnapped by an evil scientist, Dr. Victor Gannon, who discovers Tony's amazing psychic powers and wishes to control him with his mind-control device. As Tia searches for her brother, with the aid of a group of kids named the Earthquake Gang, Dr. Gannon's greedy partner, Letha, uses Tony to steal gold bars from a museum. Using telepathy, Tia finds Gannon's subterranean lab but is also kidnapped. Gannon's master plan is, with Tony's help, to seize a plutonium processing plant, and vow to destroy it unless $5 million is brought to him. Tia manages to thwart the scheme with the help of the Earthquake Gang, but not before a fantastic contest of psychic strength with the brain-controlled Tony. Once Gannon's mind-control device is destroyed, the villains are vanquished, and Tony and Tia are free to return to Witch Mountain. Released Mar. 10, 1978. Directed by John Hough. 94 min. Stars Bette Davis (in her Disney film debut and 83rd picture, as Letha), Christopher Lee (Victor), Ike Eisenmann (Tony), Kim Richards (Tia), Jack Soo (Yokomoto), Anthony James (Sickle), Dick Bakalyan (Eddie), Christian Juttner (Dazzler), Brad Savage (Muscles), Poindexter (Crusher), Jeffrey Jacquet (Rocky). The film was based on the characters created by Alexander Key. On-location filming was done in downtown Los Angeles; in the Hollywood Hills, at "Wolf House," built in the 1920s (used as Dr. Gannon's mansion); in a dilapidated Victorian mansion near Los Angeles's Union Station that was built in 1887 (used as the Earthquake Gang's hideout); and in the Natural History Museum of Los Angeles County in Exposition Park, where the gold heist took place. Finally, a rocket-missile testing facility in the nearby San Fernando Valley and a steam generating plant in Los Angeles's Wilmington neighborhood were combined to create the nuclear processing plant that's being threatened.

Return of Jafar, The (film) Video release on May 20, 1994. Directed by Toby Shelton, Tad Stones, Alan Zaslove. A made-for-video sequel to *Aladdin* that picks up where the feature left off with the evil Jafar trapped inside a magic lamp. A clumsy thief, Abis Mal, inadvertently unleashes the now ultrapowerful "genie Jafar," who proceeds to plot his revenge against Aladdin. It is up to Aladdin and his friends to foil Jafar and save their home. Scott Weinger, Brad Kane, Linda Larkin, Gilbert Gottfried, and Jonathan Freeman reprise their voice roles

from the feature, with Val Bettin (Sultan), Liz Callaway (Jasmine singing), and Dan Castellaneta (Genie) added to their ranks. It became one of the top-selling videos of all time within weeks of its release.

Return of the Big Cat (TV) Two-part show; aired Oct. 6 and 13, 1974. Directed by Tom Leetch. A boy, Leroy McClaren, trains a wild dog to hunt the cougar that has been threatening the family. Stars Christian Juttner, Jeremy Slate, Patricia Crowley, David Wayne, Kim Richards, Ted Gehring, Jeff East.

Return of the Shaggy Dog, The (TV) Two-hour movie; aired on Nov. 1, 1987. Directed by Stuart Gillard. The magic ring's spell still turns Wilby into a dog much to his consternation. Plus, he has to battle a pair of wicked servants who want to use the ring's power. Stars Gary Kroeger, Todd Waring, Michelle Little, Cindy Morgan, Jane Carr, Gavin Reed. The film inspired The Walt Disney Company to honor original *Shaggy Dog* actor Fred MacMurray, a commemoration which in turn inspired the Disney Legends program.

Return of True Son (TV) Part 1 of the airing of *The Light in the Forest*.

Return to Halloweentown (TV) A Disney Channel Original Movie; first aired Oct. 20, 2006. As Halloweentown nears its 1,000th anniversary, Marnie Piper and younger brother Dylan enroll at the prestigious Witch University. After Marnie's freshman year gets off to a rocky start, she stumbles onto a devious plot to destroy Halloweentown. With the town's destiny in her hands, Marnie must use all her powers, both magical and mortal, to head off disaster. Directed by David Jackson. Stars Sara Paxton (Marnie Piper), Summer Bishil (Aneesa), Lucas Grabeel (Ethan Dalloway), Judith Hoag (Gwen Piper), J. Paul Zimmerman (Dylan Piper), Kristy Wu (Scarlett Sinister), Keone Young (Silas Sinister), Millicent Martin (Prof. Periwinkle), Leslie Wing-Pomeroy (Dr. Goodwyn), Debbie Reynolds (Agatha Cromwell).

Return to Never Land (film) During World War II, Wendy has grown up and has children of her own. Her daughter, Jane, is kidnapped by Captain Hook and taken to Never Land. He thought she was Wendy and hoped to use her as bait to catch Peter Pan. Peter rescues Jane, and they, along with Tinker Bell and the Lost Boys, defeat the old pirate. Jane eventually realizes that with faith, trust, and pixie dust anything is possible. Released Feb. 15, 2002. Directed by Robin Budd; co-director Donovan Cook. Voices include Harriet Kate Owen (Jane), Blayne Weaver (Peter Pan), Corey Burton (Captain Hook), Jeff Bennett (Smee), Kath Soucie (Wendy), Roger Rees (Edward), Spencer Breslin (Cubby). 72 min. From Walt Disney Television Animation.

Return to Oz (film) Dorothy Gale, who's thought to have psychological problems because of her tales of Oz, is sent to an institution and is about to receive shock treatment when a lightning storm enables her to escape down a raging river. She awakens the next day in Oz. But her happiness in returning to Oz soon dissolves into horror as she finds the magical land in ruins, and the Emerald City a wasteland. The kingdom is now ruled by the Nome King and the wicked Princess Mombi, who captures Dorothy. But she escapes with the aid of new friends: Tik-Tok, Billina (a talking hen), Jack Pumpkinhead, and the Gump. They travel to the Nome King's mountain in the Deadly Desert to find the Scarecrow and must play a nightmarish game with the evil monarch to save their friend. Dorothy manages to emerge victorious, save her friends, and rescue the mystical princess Ozma, thereby restoring Oz to its former glory. Released Jun. 21, 1985. Directed by Walter Murch. 109 min. Stars Nicol Williamson (Dr. Worley/Nome King), Fairuza Balk (Dorothy), Jean Marsh (Nurse Wilson/Princess Mombi), Piper Laurie (Aunt Em), Matt Clark (Uncle Henry), Emma Ridley (Ozma), Michael Sundin (Tik-Tok puppeteer), Peter Elliot (Wheeler), Pons Maar (Lead Wheeler), Justin Case (Scarecrow), John Alexander (Cowardly Lion), Deep Roy (Tin Man), and puppet performers Brian Henson and Mac Wilson. The production marked the culmination of 3 years of preparatory work and research in the U.S. and Britain. New systems of remote control, stop-motion photography, and a pioneering clay animation process created a wonderland that blended the realistic with the surreal. Sixteen weeks of shooting included interior work on 5 Elstree stages and filming on the Studio lot. There was an additional location on Salisbury Plain in England, the site of Stonehenge. The production was the realization of Walt Disney's personal interest in the Oz stories by L. Frank Baum (SEE RAINBOW ROAD TO OZ, THE). Unfortunately, it was not a box office success, though it was nominated for an Academy Award for Best Visual Effects to Will Vinton, Ian Wingrove, Zoran Perisic, and Michael Lloyd.

Return to Sender (film) Educational release in 16 mm in Mar. 1991. 13 min. A young girl learns the problems when many people litter.

Return to Snowy River (film) The "Man from Snowy River" Jim Craig returns to his homeland with a herd of wild horses, to claim the woman he loves and set up his stake as a horse breeder. Jessica's father still opposes the match, as does her would-be suitor, Alistair Patton. Jessica defies her father and goes with Jim, but Patton, bitter at his loss, steals Jim's herd. When Jim follows, Patton and his gang shoot his horse, leaving it to die in the wilderness. A mysterious black stallion comes to Jim's aid, along with Jessica and her father and his men, and together they rescue the herd. Jessica is reunited with her father and her lover, and they begin their new life in Snowy River. Released Apr. 15, 1988. Directed by Geoff Burrowes. A sequel to the non-Disney *The Man from Snowy River*. 99 min. Stars Tom Burlinson (Jim), Sigrid Thornton (Jessica), Brian Dennehy (Harrison), Nicholas Eadie (Alistair Patton), Bryan Marshall (Hawker), Mark Hembrow (Seb). Filmed on location in Australia.

Return to Treasure Island (film) Ten-hour miniseries on The Disney Channel; premiered Apr. 5, 1986. Directed by Piers Haggard. The one-legged pirate, Long John Silver, has plans for retrieving the remaining treasure he and his young shipmate, Jim Hawkins, left on Treasure Island 10 years before. They join forces and embark on a voyage filled with danger, romance, excitement, and suspense. Stars Brian Blessed (Long John Silver), Christopher Guard (Jim Hawkins), Kenneth Colley (Ben Gunn), Morgan Sheppard (Boakes). Filmed on location in Spain, Jamaica, and the United Kingdom.

Reubens, Paul Actor; appeared in *Midnight Madness* (pinball proprietor) and provided voices in *Tim Burton's The Nightmare Before Christmas* (Lock), *Beauty and the Beast: The Enchanted Christmas* (Fife), *Teacher's Pet* (Dennis), *Tron: Uprising* (Pavel), *Phineas and Ferb* (Prof. Parenthesis), *Pickle and Peanut* (Couch Dracula), and *Penn Zero: Part-Time Hero* (milkman). At the Disney parks, he has voiced RX-24 ("Rex") in Star Tours and DJ R-3X in Oga's Cantina in Star Wars: Galaxy's Edge.

Reunion, The (film) Educational film on career awareness produced by Glenn Johnson Prods.; released in Sep. 1976. Shows 6th graders and their career choices 10 years later.

Revenge (TV) Drama series on ABC; aired Sep. 21, 2011–May 10, 2015. Emily Thorne has come to the Hamptons, met some of her wealthy neighbors, made a few new friends, and seemingly blended into the town. But she isn't exactly new to the neighborhood. In fact, this was once her own neighborhood, until something bad happened that ruined her family and their reputation. Now Emily has returned to right some wrongs with a vengeance. Stars Emily Van Camp (Emily Thorne), Madeleine Stowe (Victoria Grayson), Gabriel Mann (Nolan Ross), Henry Czerny (Conrad Grayson), Ashley Madekwe (Ashley Davenport), Nick Wechsler (Jack Porter), Connor Paolo (Declan Porter), Josh Bowman (Daniel Grayson), Christa B. Allen (Charlotte Grayson). From ABC Studios.

Rex Apprehensive plastic T. rex in the Toy Story films; voiced by Wallace Shawn.

Rex's Racer SEE RC RACER.

Reyes, Ernie, Jr. Actor; appeared on TV in *Sidekicks* and its pilot movie, *The Last Electric Knight* (Ernie), and on The Disney Channel in the *Secret Bodyguard* serial on the *Mickey Mouse Club*.

Reynolds, Burt (1936–2018) Actor; appeared in *Mystery, Alaska* (Walter Burns) and *The Crew* (Joey Pistella), and guest starred on TV in *The Golden Girls*, *Mickey's 50*, *Walt Disney World 4th of July Spectacular*, and *Mickey's 60th Birthday*. He created/exec. produced *Win, Lose or Draw*.

Reynolds, Debbie (1932–2016) Actress; starred as Aggie Cromwell in *Halloweentown*, *Halloweentown II: Kalabar's Revenge*, *Halloweentown High*, and *Return to Halloweentown* on Disney Channel, and guest starred as Truby in *The Golden Girls*. She voiced Nana Possible in *Kim Possible* and Great-Great-Grandmommers Whimsical in *The 7D*.

Reynolds, Ryan Actor; appeared in *The Proposal* (Andrew Paxton), and on TV in *Tourist Trap* (Wade Early) and *Scrubs* (Spence).

Rhimes, Shonda Lynn Creator, head writer, and exec. producer of the ABC-TV series *Grey's Anatomy*, *Private Practice*, and *Scandal*. Also exec. producer of *How to Get Away with Murder* and *Station 19*.

Rhino TV-obsessed hamster character in *Bolt*; voiced by Mark Walton.

Rhys-Davies, John Actor; appeared in *The Princess Diaries 2* (Viscount Mabrey) and *Indiana Jones and the Dial of Destiny* (Sallah), on TV in *Once Upon a Time* (Grand Pabbie), and on The Disney Channel in *Great Expectations* (Joe Gargery). He voiced Macbeth in *Gargoyles* and King Sokwe in *The Lion Guard*. At Disneyland, he appears as Sallah in the preshow film for the Indiana Jones Adventure.

Ribbons & Bows Hat Shop Shop on Main Street, U.S.A. in Disneyland Paris; opened Apr. 12, 1992. Over the years, hats, plush toys, and Christmas products have been sold here.

Ricci, Barnette She began at Disneyland as a choreographer in the late 1960s and went on to direct popular entertainment, such as the Kids of the Kingdom, the *Main Street Electrical Parade*, *America on Parade*, and *Fantasmic!* She helped coordinate the grand dedication ceremonies for Walt Disney World in 1971 and worked on the openings for other Disney parks around the world. She later transferred to The Walt Disney Studios, where she served as vice president and show director of Special Events. She retired in 2013 and was named a Disney Legend in 2019.

Rice, Derica W. Member of the Disney Board of Directors beginning in 2019.

Rice, Joan (1930–1997) Actress; appeared in *The Story of Robin Hood* (Maid Marian).

Rice, Peter He joined The Walt Disney Company in 2019, during the acquisition of 21st Century Fox, as chairman of Walt Disney Television and co-chair of Disney Media Networks. In 2020, he was named chairman of Disney General Entertainment Content, overseeing original programming for Disney's streaming platforms and cable and broadcast networks. He had previously served as president of 21st Century Fox and chairman and CEO of Fox Networks Group. He left the company in Jun. 2022.

Rice, Tim Lyricist; joined Disney to work on the lyrics for *Aladdin* after the death of Howard Ashman. He wrote songs for *Beauty and the Beast* and *The Lion King* (also contributing to the 2017 and 2019 versions of each), as well as for *Evita* and the stage productions *The Lion King*, *Aida*, and *King David*. He received Oscars for "You Must Love Me," "A Whole New World," and "Can You Feel the Love Tonight." He was named a Disney Legend in 2002.

Rich, Adam Actor; appeared in *The Devil and Max Devlin* (Toby Hart), and on TV in *Gun Shy* (Clovis) and *Kraft Salutes Disneyland's 25th Anniversary.*

Rich Man's Wife, The (film) Josie, who is married to a successful TV producer, Tony, has been unhappy in her marriage. First, she has an affair with a restaurant owner, Jake Golden, and later offhandedly remarks to a sympathetic stranger that she wishes she were "free" of her estranged husband. When her husband is murdered, Josie is the primary suspect and soon the victim of blackmail, with no one to turn to. A Hollywood Pictures presentation in association with Caravan Pictures. Released Sep. 13, 1996. Directed by Amy Holden Jones. Stars Halle Berry (Josie Potenza), Clive Owen (Jake Golden), Peter Greene (Cole Wilson), Christopher McDonald (Tony Potenza). 95 min. For Tony's house, the filmmakers found a modern Spanish mansion in Malibu, California. A mountain cabin was located after a long search at a Seattle Council Boy Scout camp in the Cascade Mountains of Washington.

Richard F. Irvine Riverboat Liberty Square attraction in the Magic Kingdom at Walt Disney World; opened May 20, 1973. Dick Irvine was one of the early Disney designers and one of the first executives of WED Enterprises. The boat is an authentic steamboat, in which the steam helps turn the huge paddle wheel. The riverboat was renamed the *Liberty Belle* after a rehab in 1996. In 1997, the *Magic Kingdom II* ferryboat, transporting guests from the Transportation and Ticket Center to Magic Kingdom, was renamed the *Richard F. Irvine*.

Richard M. Sherman: Songs of a Lifetime (TV) Special produced by Don Hahn; debuted on PBS SoCal Dec. 17, 2015. Richard Sherman sits at a piano to reminisce, playing and singing songs he wrote with his brother, Robert B. Sherman. He is joined by singers Ashley Brown, Juliana Hansen, and others. From Stone Creek Pictures, Inc.

Richards, Beah (1926–2000) Actress; appeared in *The Biscuit Eater* (Charity Tomlin) and *Beloved* (Baby Suggs).

Richards, Evan Actor; appeared in *Down and Out in Beverly Hills* (Max Whiteman) and in the same role in the TV series of the same name; and in *Match Point* on the *Mickey Mouse Club* on The Disney Channel.

Richards, Kim Actress; appeared in *Escape to Witch Mountain* and *Return from Witch Mountain* (Tia) and *No Deposit, No Return* (Tracy), and on TV in *Hog Wild* (Sara), *Return of the Big Cat* (Amy), *The Whiz Kid and the Carnival Caper* and *The Whiz Kid and the Mystery at Riverton* (Daphne), *The Mystery of Rustler's Cave* serial on the new *Mickey Mouse Club*, and *Kraft Salutes Disneyland's 25th Anniversary*. She also appeared in *The Age of Believing: The Disney Live Action Classics* and had a cameo role in *Race to Witch Mountain* (Tina).

Richardson, Lloyd (1915–2002) Film editor; he started at the Disney Studio in 1937 as a traffic boy and before long moved to the Editorial Department, where he worked on *Snow White and the Seven Dwarfs* and other films. Over the years, he worked in foreign editing and directed/edited segments for the *Disneyland* and *Walt Disney's Wonderful World of Color* TV series. Some of his most notable work was on the True-Life Adventure films. He retired in 1980 and was named a Disney Legend in 1998.

Richardson, Patricia Actress; appeared on TV in *Home Improvement* (Jill Taylor) and *Parent Trap III* (Cassie McGuire).

Richardson, Paul In 2021, he was named senior exec. vice president and chief human resources officer of The Walt Disney Company. He previously led human resources at ESPN 2007–2021, also serving as Disney's first chief diversity officer, 2011–2017. He left the company in 2023.

Richest Cat in the World, The (film) Two-hour movie; aired Mar. 9, 1986. Directed by Greg Beeman. A wealthy man leaves his fortune to his cat, but his relatives plot the cat's demise because they are next in line. It turns out the cat can talk, and he befriends the son of one of the servants. Stars Brandon Call, Kellie Martin, Ramon Bieri, Steven Kampmann, Caroline McWilliams.

Rick, You're in: A Story About Mainstreaming (film) Educational film produced by Dave Bell; released in Sep. 1980. A student who uses a wheelchair enters a regular high school, and in trying to be accepted has both triumphs and frustrations.

Rickety Gin (film) Oswald the Lucky Rabbit cartoon; released Dec. 26, 1927. Police officer Oswald invites a nurse to go for a stroll with him, leaving his trusty wooden horse to look after her baby, but an archvillain throws a wrench into their plans.

Riddle of Robin Hood, The (film) Promotional film for *The Story of Robin Hood*, featuring Walt Disney and production personnel; released in 1952. 15 min.

Ride a Northbound Horse (TV) Two-part show; aired Mar. 16 and 23, 1969. Directed by Robert Totten. An orphan boy, Cav Rand, saves to buy a horse, but others plot to get it. Stars Carroll O'Connor; Michael Shea; Ben Johnson; Dub Taylor; Andy Devine; Harry Carey, Jr.; Jack Elam; Edith Atwater. Carroll O'Connor later went on to fame in the role of Archie Bunker on TV's *All in the Family*.

Ride a Wild Pony (film) In Australia, a wild 13-year-old boy, Scott Pirie, who is poor, and a haughty teenage girl named Josie Ellison, who is rich, find themselves at odds over the ownership of a beloved pony. The boy calls the Welsh pony Taff and uses him to get to school, while Josie loves the pony as well for its wild spirit and names it Bo. Since she is a victim of polio, Bo allows her to get around in a pony cart. The children's fight for the animal leads to the courtroom where it is decided that it is up to the pony to decide who its owner should be. The pony hesitantly picks Scott but also comforts Josie. The Ellisons bring feed for Taff to the Pirie ranch, and Josie invites the boy and horse to visit her often in the future. They become friends, and the bond in the relationship is the pony. Initial release in Los Angeles on Dec. 25, 1975; general release Mar. 26, 1976. Directed by Don Chaffey. 91 min. Stars Michael Craig (James), John Meillon (Charles Quayle), Robert Bettles (Scott), Eva Griffith (Josie), Graham Rouse (Bluey), Peter Gwynne (Sgt. Collins), John Meillon Jr. (Kit Quayle), Alfred Bell (Angus Pirie), Melissa Jaffer (Mrs. Pirie). The film was based on the novel *A Sporting Proposition* by James Aldridge. The first Disney feature filmed in Australia; shot on location in Victoria and New South Wales. The ideal location for the derelict Pirie farm was found in the Horton Valley, but the nearest towns were 60 miles away, so the cast and crew were divided between Barraba and Bingara. For the Ellison ranch, the crew used the historic Belltrees, an expansive 20,000-acre country estate, which was available only after His Royal Highness Prince Charles ended his vacation-

ing there. The small Victorian town of Chiltern was also used as the town of Barambogie, after considerable restoration of the storefronts and the pouring of tons of earth over the paved roads. An old K class steam locomotive and coach cars were brought out of mothballs, spruced up, and transported from Melbourne, more than 200 miles away. Most of Chiltern's population signed on as extras.

Ride 'em Plowboy (film) Oswald the Lucky Rabbit cartoon; released Apr. 16, 1928. While Oswald plows the cornfield, the denizens of the barnyard go about their raucous affairs. The show is stopped short by a cyclone, which gobbles up the whole scene.

Ridgway, Charlie (1923–2016) He started in publicity at Disneyland in 1963, 8 years after covering the park's opening as a news reporter. He was promoted to publicity supervisor in 1966, eventually becoming director of press and publicity for the Walt Disney World project 2 years before its opening. Ridgway was instrumental in arranging for so much free publicity for the opening of Walt Disney World that paid advertising was felt unnecessary. He also helped open EPCOT Center and Disneyland Paris, and developed memorable celebrations, such as Donald Duck's 50th birthday campaign. He retired in 1994 but continued to consult on company projects. He was named a Disney Legend in 1999.

Ridley, Daisy Actress; starred as Rey in *Star Wars: The Force Awakens* and later films in the saga.

Rigdon, Cicely (1923–2013) After starting at Disneyland as a ticket seller in 1957, she joined the tour guide department in 1959, being responsible for initiating its growth and development, and later for all of Guest Relations and ticket sales. From 1982 until her retirement in 1994, she headed the Disneyland Ambassador program. She was named a Disney Legend in 2005.

Right of Dissent, The (film) Educational film in the History Alive! series, produced by Turnley Walker; released in 1972. Should a private citizen have the right to criticize the president, as shown in the story of John Adams vs. Matthew Lyon, 1798?

Right of Petition, The (film) Educational film in the History Alive! series, produced by Turnley Walker; released in 1972. John Quincy Adams and Thomas Marshall clash over a gag rule preventing antislavery petitions from being introduced in the House of Representatives.

Right on Track (TV) A Disney Channel Original Movie; first aired Mar. 21, 2003. When Erica Enders enters the male-dominated world of drag racing at the age of 8, she quickly becomes a force to be reckoned with on the drag strip. Her younger sister, Courtney, follows in her footsteps, helping make Enders a household name in the world of drag racing, though not without challenges from their fierce competitors who would rather not have women drivers winning in their sport. Directed by Duwayne Dunham. Stars Beverley Mitchell (Erica Enders), Jon Robert Lindstrom (Gregg Enders), Brie Larson (Courtney Enders), Marcus Toji (Randy Jones), Jodi Russell (Janet Lee Enders). 88 min. Based on a true story. The real Erica and Courtney Enders are featured in cameo roles.

Right Spark Plug in the Right Place, The (film) Training film made for the Electric Auto-Lite Company; delivered Feb. 12, 1945. The film stresses the need to keep spark plugs in good order to keep in harmony with the ignition system.

Right Stuff, The (TV) A Disney+ original series from National Geographic; digitally premiered Oct. 9, 2020. An inspirational look at the early days of the U.S. space program and the story of America's first astronauts, the Mercury Seven. Newly formed NASA has the monumental task of sending a man into space, and its engineers estimate they need decades to accomplish the feat. They are given 2 years. Project Mercury would recruit and train astronauts from a handful of the military's best pilots. Within days of being presented to the world, the Mercury Seven become instant celebrities, forged into heroes before they achieve a single act. Stars Patrick J. Adams (Maj. John Glenn), Jake McDorman (Lcdr. Alan Shepard), Colin O'Donoghue (Cpt. Gordon Cooper), Eloise Mumford (Trudy Cooper), James Lafferty (Cpt. Scott Carpenter), Nora Zehetner (Annie Glenn), Eric Laden (Chris Kraft, Jr.), Patrick Fischler (Bob Gilruth). Based on the book by Tom Wolfe. Produced by Appian Way and Warner Bros. Televison.

Riley's First Date? (film) Animated short from Pixar; released on Disney Movies Anywhere Oct. 13, 2015, and on the *Inside Out* Blu-ray Nov. 3. Riley, the young girl from *Inside Out*, is now 12. Her parents are dismayed when a boy shows up at the door asking for her. The emotions have to deal with Riley going on her first date. Directed by Josh Cooley. Voices include Pete Docter (Dad's Anger), Kyle MacLachlan (Dad), Diane Lane (Mom), Kaitlyn Dias (Riley), Amy Poehler (Joy). 5 min.

Ring of Endless Light, A (TV) A Disney Channel Original Movie; first aired Aug. 23, 2002. When 3 kids go to visit their grandfather for the summer, they meet a boy who is studying dolphins and trying to save them from fishermen using illegal methods. Sixteen-year-old Vicky discovers she has a unique ability to communicate with the dolphins and confronts her growing feelings for Adam while maintaining her friendship with the previous summer's boyfriend, Zachery. Directed by Greg Beeman. Stars Mischa Barton (Vicky Austin), Ryan Merriman (Adam Eddington), Jared Padalecki (Zachery Gray), James Whitmore (Rev. Eaton), Scarlett Pomers (Suzy Austin), Soren Fulton (Rob Austin). Based on the book by Madeleine L'Engle.

Ringer (TV) Drama series on The CW; aired Sep. 13, 2011–Apr. 17, 2012. Bridget Kelly goes on the run after witnessing a murder. She assumes the life of her wealthy identical twin sister, only to learn that her sister's seemingly idyllic life is just as complicated and dangerous as the one she's trying to leave behind. Stars Sarah Michelle Gellar (Bridget), Kristoffer Polaha (Henry), Ioan Gruffudd (Andrew), Nestor Carbonell (Agent Victor Machado), Tara Summers (Gemma). From CBS Television Studios and Warner Bros. Television, in association with ABC Studios and Brillstein Entertainment.

Ringmaster Character in *Dumbo*; voiced by Herman Bing.

Ringo, the Refugee Raccoon (TV) Show aired Mar. 3, 1974. A raccoon's habitat is destroyed by construction of a new shopping center, and he gets into all sorts of trouble trying to find a new place to live. Finally, he is transported to the forest by the Humane Society. Stars William Hochstrasser, the Foutz family. Directed by Roy Edward Disney.

Rings 'n Things SEE JEWELRY SHOP.

Ringwald, Molly Actress; appeared in *Betsy's Wedding* (Betsy Hopper), on TV in *The Secret Life of the American Teenager* (Anne Juergens), and guest starred in *Earth to Ned* on Disney+. She voiced Darla in *Doc McStuffins*. In 1977, she made her TV debut with an appearance on the new *Mickey Mouse Club*.

Rip Girls (TV) A Disney Channel Original Movie; first aired Apr. 22, 2000. Thirteen-year-old Sydney returns to her native Hawai'i to claim an inheritance consisting of a run-down plantation set on several acres of pristine beachfront property. As the sole heir, she has to decide whether to sell the plantation to land developers or keep it. While at the house, she befriends some local kids and comes to fall in love with the island paradise. Directed by Joyce Chopra. Stars Camilla Belle (Sydney), Dwier Brown (Ben), Stacie Hess (Gia), Brian Christopher Mark (Kona), Jeanne Mori (Malia), Lauren Sinclair (Elizabeth), Keone Young (Bo Kauihau), Kanoa Chung (Kai), Meleana White (Mele).

Rise (film) After emigrating from Nigeria to Greece, Charles and Vera Antetokounmpo struggle to survive and provide for their 5 children. When they aren't selling items to tourists on the streets of Athens with the rest of the family, the brothers (Giannis and Thanasis) play basketball with a local youth team and ultimately discover their great abilities. Working hard to become world-class athletes, along with brother Kostas, Giannis enters the NBA Draft in 2013 as a long shot prospect, and he and Thanasis help bring the Milwaukee Bucks their first championship ring in 50 years. Kostas, meanwhile, plays for the previous season champs, the Los Angeles Lakers. Based on a true story. Digitally released Jun. 24, 2022, on Disney+. Directed by Akin Omotoso. Stars Dayo Okeniyi (Charles), Yetide Badaki (Vera), Uche Agada (Giannis), Ral Agada (Thanasis), Jaden Osimuwa (Kostas), Elijah Sholanke (Alex), Manish Dayal (Kevin), Taylor Nichols (John Hammond). 111 min. Antetokounmpo is a Nigerian surname that, according to the Yoruba people of West Africa, means "the crown has returned from overseas." Filmed on location in Athens. From The Walt Disney Studios.

Ristorante di Canaletto Italian restaurant overlooking the Palazzo Canals of Mediterranean Harbor in Tokyo DisneySea; opened Sep. 4, 2001. Décor is based on the Italian artist Giovanni Antonio Canal, nicknamed "Canaletto."

Rita Sensuous Afghan hound in *Oliver & Company*; voiced by Sheryl Lee Ralph.

Rite of Spring (film) Music by Igor Stravinsky; a segment of *Fantasia*.

Ritter, John (1948–2003) Actor; appeared in *The Barefoot Executive* (Roger), *Scandalous John* (Wendell), and *Noises Off* (Garry Lejeune), and on TV in *8 Simple Rules for Dating My Teenage Daughter* (Paul Hennessy), with guest appearances in *Celebrate the Spirit*, *Mickey's 60th Birthday*, *The Disney-MGM Studios Theme Park Grand Opening*, *Scrubs* (Sam Dorian), and *Felicity* (Ben's father). His father, actor and country-and-western singer Tex Ritter, provided the voice of Big Al in the original Country Bear Jamboree.

Rival Romeos (film) Oswald the Lucky Rabbit cartoon; released Mar. 5, 1928. Speeding along on his way to visit his sweetheart, Oswald is overtaken by a rival in a magnificent roadster. Oswald manages to wallow through, but another suitor arrives on a motorcycle, wooing the lady and leaving Oswald and his rival behind.

River, The (TV) Drama series on ABC; aired Feb. 7–Mar. 20, 2012. Famed explorer Dr. Emmet Cole went looking for magic deep in the uncharted Amazon and never returned. When his emergency beacon suddenly goes off, his family and friends set out on a mysterious and deadly journey to find him. Led by his wife, Tess, and estranged son, Lincoln, the rescue mission takes them to unexplored territory, where nothing is what it seems. To fund the rescue, Tess and Lincoln agree to let Dr. Cole's cagey ex-producer, Clark, film the mission documentary style. Stars Bruce Greenwood (Emmet Cole), Joe Anderson (Lincoln), Leslie Hope (Tess), Eloise Mumford (Lena Landry), Paul Blackthorne (Clark Quietly), Thomas Kretschmann (Capt. Kurt Brynildson), Daniel Zacapa (Emilio Valenzuela), Shaun Parkes (Andreus Jude Poulain), Paulina Gaitán (Jahel Valenzuela). From ABC Studios, with Steven Spielberg's Amblin and DreamWorks Television.

River Belle Terrace Frontierland restaurant at Disneyland; opened in 1971 with Oscar Mayer Co. as sponsor. Formerly Aunt Jemima's Pancake House, Aunt Jemima's Kitchen, and Magnolia Tree Terrace. Later sponsored by Hormel and Sunkist. Pancakes have always been the specialty for breakfast here, and kids (and kids at heart) can even get one shaped like Mickey Mouse.

River Country Water park at Walt Disney World; open Jun. 20, 1976–Sep. 1, 2001. The Disney designers longed for an old-fashioned swimming hole, so they created one next to Fort Wilderness campground. It meant building miniature mountains for the waterslides, since Florida has no mountains to offer. Bay Cove, the swimming hole, was actually part of Bay Lake and held 330,000 gallons of water. The popularity of River Country convinced Disney executives to build Typhoon Lagoon some years later, to be followed by Disney's Blizzard Beach. First Daughter Susan Ford helped officiate the grand opening ceremonies.

River Rogue Keelboats Frontierland attraction in Disneyland Paris; opened Apr. 12, 1992. The boats are named *Raccoon* and *Coyote*. Closed ca. 2000, later reopening for seasonal operation. SEE ALSO MIKE FINK KEEL BOATS (DISNEYLAND AND WALT DISNEY WORLD).

River View Café Adventureland restaurant in Hong Kong Disneyland; opened Sep. 12, 2005. Chinese cuisine is served family style.

Rivera, Jonas Producer; he joined Pixar Animation Studios as a production intern on *Toy Story*. He was an art department coordinator on *A Bug's Life*, then art department manager on *Monsters, Inc.*, production manager on *Cars*, and producer on *Up, Inside Out*, and *Toy Story 4*. In 2022, he was named executive vice president of film production at Pixar.

Riverboats SEE MARK TWAIN, ADMIRAL JOE FOWLER, RICHARD F. IRVINE, MOLLY BROWN, LIBERTY BELLE.

Rivers of America Waterways in Frontierland at Disneyland, the Magic Kingdom at Walt Disney World, and Tokyo Disneyland. The waterways flow around Tom Sawyer Island with scenes depicting the early days of the American frontier. At Disneyland, the Rivers of America were rerouted to accommodate the construction of Star Wars: Galaxy's Edge and reopened in 2017 with new enhancements. At Disneyland Paris, the waterways are called Rivers of the Far West and encircle Big Thunder Mountain. At Hong Kong Disneyland, the waterways are located in Adventureland, as Rivers of Adventure, encircling Tarzan's Treehouse and utilized by the Jungle River Cruise.

Rivers of Light Nighttime show in Asia/DinoLand U.S.A. at Disney's Animal Kingdom; premiered in the new Discovery River Amphitheater Feb. 17, 2017, after several previews. With a symbolic lantern ceremony, the show combined 11 floats with fountains, projections, and a musical score celebrating animals and nature. An updated version, *Rivers of Light: We Are One*, premiered May 24, 2019, adding moments from Disneynature and Disney animated films. The final performance was held Mar. 15, 2020, and the amphitheater was later used for a daytime show, *Disney KiteTails*.

Riverside Depot SEE DISNEY OUTFITTERS (DISNEY'S ANIMAL KINGDOM).

Riverside Mill Food Court Dining hall in Disney's Port Orleans Resort – Riverside at Walt Disney World; opened Apr. 1, 2001, succeeding Colonel's Cotton Mill.

Riveter, The (film) Donald Duck cartoon released Mar. 15, 1940. Directed by Dick Lundy. Donald is a riveter who has trouble with the riveting gun, heights, and the foreman, Pete. Pete chases him throughout the construction site, causing the building to collapse. Donald runs away while Pete is trapped in cement, holding a water hose in the pose of a statue.

Riviera Resort, Disney's A deluxe Disney Vacation Club resort at Walt Disney World; opened Dec. 16, 2019. Inspired by the grand hotels and casual elegance of the French and Italian Riviera, the resort features 489 studios and villas, including 12 grand villas, all with modern amenities and Disney touches. European-style dining is offered at Topolino's Terrace – Flavors of the Riviera, Primo Piatto, Le Petit Café, and Bar Riva, with shopping at La Boutique. Outdoor recreation includes the Riviera Pool, Beau Soleil Pool, and S'il Vous Play, a water-play area inspired by "The Dance of the Hours" segment from *Fantasia*. The resort's art collection is comprised of more than 40 original works by Disney and Pixar artists, inspired by the region's great art movements of the late-19th and early-20th century.

Rix Sports Bar & Grill Restaurant in Disney's Coronado Springs Resort at Walt Disney World; opened May 2018. It was previously Rix Lounge, which superseded Francisco's in Oct. 2007. Managed by Palmas Services.

RKO Distributor of the Disney cartoons 1937–1956 and features 1937–1954. In 1953, as they were losing the Disney license, they released 6 shorts programs: *Christmas Jollities, New Year's Jamboree, 4th of July Firecrackers, Halloween Hilarities,*

Fall Varieties, and *Thanksgiving Day Mirthquakes*. In 1955, they released another—*Music Land*.

Roadside Romeo (film) A Disney animated co-production with Yash Raj Films (India). Romeo, a pet dog, is having the time of his life, until his owners move and leave him behind on the streets of Mumbai. After a run-in with 4 strays, he encounters Laila, the most beautiful girl dog he has ever seen, and he loses his heart to her at first sight. But their romance is dogged by a snarling villain, Charlie Anna, and his gang. Directed by Jugal Hansraj. Released in Hindi in India, and with subtitles in selected theaters in the U.S., on Oct. 24, 2008. Voices include Saif Ali Khan (Romeo), Kareena Kapoor (Laila), Jaaved Jaaferi (Charlie Anna). 93 min. Disney's first co-production in India.

Roaring Fork Quick-service eatery in Disney's Wilderness Lodge at Walt Disney World; opened May 28, 1994, as Roaring Fork Snacks and Arcade. Décor is based on fly-fishing and sporting in the Northwest.

Roaring Mountain The 108-ft.-tall icon of Adventure Isle in Shanghai Disneyland; opened Jun. 16, 2016. The mountain contains approx. 24,000 square meters of hand-sculpted and painted rockwork. Its waterfall is 105 feet tall. SEE NEXT ENTRY.

Roaring Rapids Rafting attraction in Adventure Isle at Shanghai Disneyland; opened Jun. 16, 2016. Guests plunge down a mountain and enter a dark cavern, where secrets of an ancient legend and the ferocious reptilian creature, the Q'aráq, are revealed.

Rob Roy, the Highland Rogue (film) Rob Roy, leader of the rebel Highlanders in Scotland, manages to elude the English again and again as he weds his sweetheart, Helen Mary. But he inadvertently causes his mother's death when the English try to capture her instead. In revenge, he captures Inversnaid Fort and plans to continue the fight until Helen Mary pleads for an end to the bloodshed. When he surrenders to George I, the king is so impressed he pardons Rob Roy and his clan. Released Feb. 4, 1954. Directed by Harold French. 83 min. Richard Todd's 3rd Disney movie co-starred Glynis Johns (Helen Mary MacGregor), James Robertson Justice (Duke of Argyll), and Finlay Currie (Hamish MacPherson). It would be Disney's last United Kingdom production until

Kidnapped in 1960. The Argyll and Sutherland Highlanders who simulated the English redcoats and the Blues were loaned to Disney for the occasion by the Scottish Command of the British War Office.

Robards, Jason (1922–2000) Actor; appeared in *Something Wicked This Way Comes* (Charles Halloway), *The Good Mother* (Muth), *The Adventures of Huck Finn* (The King), *Crimson Tide* (unbilled cameo as an admiral), *A Thousand Acres* (Larry Cook), *Beloved* (Mr. Bodwin), and *Enemy of the State* (unbilled cameo as a congressman), and on The Disney Channel in *Mark Twain and Me* (Mark Twain) and *Heidi* (grandfather).

Robb, AnnaSophia Actress; appeared in *Bridge to Terabithia* (Leslie Burke) and *Race to Witch Mountain* (Sara), and on Hulu in *Little Fires Everywhere* (young Elena).

Robber Kitten, The (film) Silly Symphony cartoon released Apr. 20, 1935. Directed by Dave Hand. An adventurous young kitten runs away from home to become a robber and joins up with a notorious badman. When he is robbed and nearly frightened out of his wits, he returns home and even submits to a bath.

Robber Stallion, The (TV) Episode 7 of *Texas John Slaughter*.

Robert A. Heinlein's The Puppet Masters SEE PUPPET MASTERS, THE.

Roberts, Dodie (1919–2008) She spent 45 years in Disney's Ink & Paint Department, the last decade of which she was supervisor of the paint lab. She retired in 1984 and was named a Disney Legend in 2000.

Roberts, Julia Actress; appeared in *Pretty Woman* (Vivian Ward), *I Love Trouble* (Sabrina Peterson), and *Runaway Bride* (Maggie).

Roberts, Larry (1926–1992) He voiced Tramp in *Lady and the Tramp*.

Roberts, Robin Anchor/broadcaster; during her 15 years with ESPN, she contributed to *NFL Primetime* and hosted *SportsCenter* and *In the Game with Robin Roberts*. She made appearances on ABC's *Good Morning America* beginning in 1995, becoming co-anchor in 2005. Other hosting duties have included *In the Spotlight with Robin*

Roberts: All Access Nashville and, on Disney+, *Turning the Tables with Robin Roberts.* In 2007, Hyperion publishing released her first book, *From the Heart: Seven Rules to Live By.* She was named a Disney Legend in 2019.

Robertson, Cliff (1923–2011) Actor; appeared in *Wild Hearts Can't Be Broken* (Dr. Carver) and *Renaissance Man* (Colonel James).

Robertson, Jaquelin T. (1933–2020) Architect/planner; designed the master plan for Val d'Europe near Disneyland Paris and, with Robert A.M. Stern, the community of Celebration in Florida.

Robin Hood (film) Story of England's legendary hero of the common people is told by traveling minstrel Allan-a-Dale, a rooster. The story is enacted by an assortment of animated animal characters (Robin Hood and Maid Marian are foxes, Little John is a bear, King Richard and Prince John are lions, etc.). Robin Hood rebels against the villainy of Prince John and his accomplices, Sir Hiss and the Sheriff of Nottingham. Prince John has usurped the throne of King Richard, his brother, who was captured on the Crusades. With Little John, Friar Tuck, and the townspeople of Nottingham, Robin defeats the runty prince and his minions, and Richard is free to return and reclaim his kingdom. Released Nov. 8, 1973. Directed by Wolfgang Reitherman. 83 min. Features the voices of Phil Harris (Little John), Brian Bedford (Robin Hood), Roger Miller (Allan-a-Dale), Peter Ustinov (Prince John/King Richard), Terry-Thomas (Sir Hiss), Andy Devine (Friar Tuck), Monica Evans (Maid Marian), Pat Buttram (Sheriff of Nottingham), George Lindsey (Trigger), Ken Curtis (Nutsy), Carole Shelley (Lady Kluck). The songs, by Johnny Mercer, George Bruns, Roger Miller, and Floyd Huddleston, include "Whistle-Stop," "The Phony King of England," "Love," "Oo-de-lally," and "Not in Nottingham." The song "Love," by George Bruns and Floyd Huddleston, was nominated for an Academy Award. In several sequences, Bruns sought to capture the flavor of the period by using medieval instruments such as French horns and harpsichords, and occasionally just a mandolin. The Robin Hood legend has long been popular with moviemakers, from the silent version starring Douglas Fairbanks in 1922, the Errol Flynn classic of 1938, Disney's own live-action version *The Story of Robin Hood and His Merrie Men* in 1952, Sean Connery and Audrey Hepburn's *Robin and Marian* in 1976, to Kevin Costner's version in

1991. Some 350,000 drawings were made for the production, with over 100,000 painted cels and 800 painted backgrounds. The film was rereleased in theaters in 1982 and was first released on video in 1984.

Robinson, Edward G. (1893–1973) Actor; appeared in *Never a Dull Moment* (Smooth).

RoboGobo (TV) Animated series announced for Disney Junior. Five adorable pets are without a home, until kid inventor Jax adopts them and gives them super-powered robo-suits. Now Hopper, Boomer, Allie, Shelly, and Winger are a team of superheroes saving other pets in trouble and learning how to become a family in the process. From Brown Bag Films, in association with Disney Junior.

Robrock, Kaitlyn Voice actor; she began providing the voice of Minnie Mouse in Sep. 2019. Also the voice of Felicia Sundew in *Amphibia* and additional characters at the Disney parks.

Robson, Wayne (1946–2011) Actor; appeared in *One Magic Christmas* (Harry Dickens), *In the Nick of Time* (Melvin), *Murder She Purred* (Ben Seifert), and *Cold Creek Manor* (Stan Holland). He voiced Frank in *The Rescuers Down Under.*

Rock, The (film) Brigadier General Francis X. Hummel, a legendary military hero, and his crack team of commandos seize control of Alcatraz, taking a group of tourists hostage, threatening to launch poison gas missiles on San Francisco if their demands of restitution for the families of his men who lost their lives during highly covert military operations are not met. The city's only chance for survival is a young FBI chemical weapons expert, Stanley Goodspeed, and a federal prisoner, John Patrick Mason, who also happens to be the only known convict to have escaped the island prison. With the clock ticking, they embark on a desperate bid to sneak onto the island and detoxify the weapons before disaster strikes. A Hollywood Pictures film. Directed by Michael Bay. Released Jun. 7, 1996. Stars Sean Connery (Mason), Nicolas Cage (Goodspeed), Ed Harris (Hummel), Michael Biehn (Anderson), William Forsythe (Paxton). Filmed in CinemaScope. 136 min. The production company filmed extensively on almost every part of Alcatraz Island, for both interiors and exteriors. In fact, some areas, such as the laundry and industries building, had been closed to public tours for years because they contained hazardous materials. The moviemakers undertook the expense and effort to clean up the hazardous waste and, in so doing, enabled the National Park Service to expand their public tour into areas that were once restricted. The tunnels of Alcatraz were built in the huge, 30-ft.-deep tank under the floor of Stage 30 at Sony Studios; this was the tank, when the studio was the MGM Studios, where Esther Williams did much of her swimming and diving work for the MGM musicals she starred in. Some 500 invited guests attended a world premiere of the film on Alcatraz Island Jun. 3, 1996.

Rock Around the Shop Music items and Aerosmith gear sold at the exit of Rock 'n' Roller Coaster in Disney's Hollywood Studios; opened in 1999. Also in Walt Disney Studios Park at Disneyland Paris; open Mar. 16, 2002–Sep. 1, 2019.

Rock 'n' Roll America Restaurant/nightclub in Disney Village at Disneyland Paris replacing the Streets of America shop. Rock music acts reflecting 1950s–1990s sounds and influences were performed live at the venue. Closed Nov. 3, 2002, to become King Ludwig's Castle.

Rock N Roll Beach Club SEE XZFR ROCK & ROLL BEACH CLUB (WALT DISNEY WORLD).

Rock 'n' Roll Mom (TV) Two-hour movie; aired Feb. 7, 1988. Directed by Michael Schultz. A suburban mother, Annie, who loves rock music, is discovered while singing at a local club and is given a new identity as Mystere. When her secret is discovered, Annie has to be persuaded to come back, agreeing only if her children can join her act. Stars Dyan Cannon, Michael Brandon, Telma Hopkins, Nancy Lenehan, Josh Blake, Amy Lynne, Alex Rocco, Heather Locklear.

Rock 'n' Roller Coaster Starring Aerosmith Sunset Boulevard attraction in Disney's Hollywood Studios; dedicated Jul. 29, 1999, and opened to guests the next day. It is the first roller coaster–style attraction at Walt Disney World to feature a high-speed launch and multiple complete inversions. During a recording session at G-Force Records, Aerosmith invites visitors to tag along as special guests of their concert. Passengers then take a twisting, turning journey through a Hollywood night in a "super-stretch" limo, booming to the driving beat of rock 'n' roll music performed by the band. Also a Backlot attraction in Walt Disney Studios Park at Disneyland Paris, though themed

to a music video; open Mar. 16, 2002–Sep. 1, 2019, as Rock 'n' Roller Coaster avec Aerosmith, and became Avengers Assemble: Flight Force when the area became Avengers Campus in 2022.

Rockefeller, Nelson SEE SOUTH AMERICA.

Rocket Jets Tomorrowland attraction in Disneyland; opened Jul. 2, 1967, replacing the Astro-Jets (Tomorrowland Jets). The attraction afforded a great view over the park, since the guests could adjust the height of their jets as they circled the towering rocket. Rocket Jets closed Jan. 6, 1997, to be replaced by the similar Astro Orbitor in 1998. SEE STAR JETS (WALT DISNEY WORLD, LATER ASTRO ORBITER, AND TOKYO DISNEYLAND).

Rocket Rods High-speed Tomorrowland attraction in Disneyland, built on the site of the former PeopleMover; open May 22, 1998–Sep. 5, 2000. The 5-passenger modernistic vehicles whisked guests at high speeds, the fastest in Disneyland, on nearly a mile of roadway. The preshow, showcasing films about the future of transportation, utilized the former Circle-Vision attraction; this space later became Buzz Lightyear Astro Blasters.

Rocket to the Moon Tomorrowland attraction in Disneyland; open Jul. 22, 1955–Sep. 5, 1966. Sponsored by TWA 1955–1961 and McDonnell Douglas Jun. 8, 1962–1966. Later became Flight to the Moon (1967–1975) and Mission to Mars (1975–1992). Spaceflight was still years away when Disneyland opened in 1955, so the Rocket to the Moon experience was a big thrill to park guests. They would sit in a pseudo-rocket and experience a simulated trip to observe the far side of the moon. Projections above and below enabled guests to see where they were going and where they had been. It was always impressive to see Disneyland and then the Earth getting smaller and smaller as the rocket left for the moon. After American astronauts actually set foot on the moon, the Disneyland attraction became outdated, and by 1975 it was changed to be a trip to Mars instead. The icon for the attraction was the *Moonliner*, a large standing rocket at first labeled TWA and later Douglas. The rocket was destroyed when Tomorrowland was totally remodeled in 1966. In 1998, a smaller version of the rocket was installed outside the new Redd Rockett's Pizza Port (later renamed Alien Pizza Planet).

Rocketeer, The (film) In 1938, a young air racing

pilot, Cliff Secord, and his partner, Peevy, discover a secret rocket pack that enables a man to fly. They quickly become entangled in international intrigue in their attempts to keep the device away from Nazi spies and other villains, including Hollywood matinee idol Neville Sinclair. With the help of his actress girlfriend, Jenny Blake, Cliff, dubbed "The Rocketeer" by the press, embarks on a mission that could alter the course of history and make him a true hero. Released Jun. 21, 1991. Directed by Joe Johnston. 108 min. Stars Bill Campbell (Cliff Secord), Jennifer Connelly (Jenny Blake), Alan Arkin (Peevy), Paul Sorvino (Eddie Valentine), Timothy Dalton (Neville Sinclair). Based on a comic character created by Dave Stevens. The airport scenes were filmed in Santa Maria, California, where an airport was built in an area that could pass for Los Angeles in 1938. The Bulldog Cafe was based on an actual restaurant in Los Angeles built in the 1920s. Nearly 30 years after the film's original release, Campbell returned to voice Cliff Secord's grandson, Dave, in the animated TV series of the same name.

Rocketeer, The (TV) Animated comedy-adventure series on Disney Junior; premiered Nov. 8, 2019, on Disney Channel, Disney Junior, and Disney-NOW. A young girl named Kit receives a surprise package on her birthday revealing she's next in line to become the Rocketeer, a legendary superhero who has the ability to fly with the help of a rocket pack. Armed with her cool new gear and secret identity, Kit is ready to take flight and save the day with her gadget-minded best friend, Tesh, and Butch the bulldog by her side. Inspired by Dave Stevens's comic book series and the 1991 Walt Disney Pictures film. Voices include Kitana Turnbull (Kit), Billy Campbell (Dave Secord), Kathy Najimy (Sareena Secord), Callan Farris (Tesh), Frank Welker (Grandpa Ambrose), Navia Robinson (Valerie Valkyrie), Kari Wahlgren (Harley). From Disney Television Animation.

Rocketeer: Excitement in the Air (TV) Syn. special; aired on Jun. 19, 1991. Directed by Douglas Burnet. Bill Campbell, star of *The Rocketeer*, hosts a look at the movie.

Rocketeer Gallery Display of props and costumes from the film in Disney-MGM Studios at Walt Disney World; open Jul.–Sep. 1991. Replaced by Studio Showcase.

RocketMan (film) When a member of the first manned mission searching for life on Mars is injured during training, NASA turns to a very unlikely replacement—the designer of the ship's operating system, Fred Z. Randall, who, for a rocket scientist, is no rocket scientist. Comic chaos ensues en route to the Red Planet as Fred butts heads with a no-nonsense crew, as captain William Overbeck falls hopelessly in love with humorless officer Julie Ford, and teams up with Ulysses, a trained chimpanzee. Directed by Stuart Gillard. Released Oct. 10, 1997. Stars Harland Williams (Fred Z. Randall), Jessica Lundy (Julie Ford), William Sadler (William Overbeck), Jeffrey DeMunn (Paul Wick), Beau Bridges (Bud Nesbitt). Ulysses is played by Raven, a 3-year-old female chimpanzee, whose principal trainer was David Allsberry. 94 min. Location filming took place in and around Houston, so the filmmakers could utilize NASA's Johnson Space Center and the Sonny Carter Training Facility for authenticity. For the surface of Mars, the filmmakers moved to Moab, Utah, where they found giant cliffs, red rocks, a lack of vegetation, and an overall scale of what could be a distant planet.

Rodgers & Hammerstein's Cinderella SEE CINDERELLA (TV).

Rodney (TV) Half-hour comedy series on ABC; aired Sep. 21, 2004–Jun. 6, 2006. Rodney Hamilton is getting fired from jobs he hates while doing stand-up comedy in dive bars at night. He may not have much money, but he still finds excitement, and hopes to make stand-up his career. Stars Rodney Carrington (Rodney Hamilton), Jennifer Aspen (Trina Hamilton), Amy Pietz (Charlie), Nick Searcy (Barry), Oliver Davis (Jack Hamilton), Matthew Josten (Bo Hamilton). From Touchstone Television.

Rodrigo, Olivia Actress/singer; appeared on Disney Channel in *Bizaardvark* (Paige Olvera); on Disney+ in *High School Musical: The Musical: The Series* (Nini), *Olivia Rodrigo: driving home 2 u (a SOUR film)*, and *Earth to Ned*; and on ABC in *The Disney Family Singalong*.

Rogen, Seth Actor; the voice of Pumbaa in *The Lion King* (2019). He appeared on TV in *The Disney Family Singalong: Volume II*, and had roles on Disney+ in *Muppets Now* and *Chip 'n Dale: Rescue Rangers* (Bob the Warrior Viking/Pumbaa/Mantis/B.O.B., 2022).

Roger and Anita Radcliff Human owners of the

Dalmatians in *One Hundred and One Dalmatians*; voiced by Ben Wright and Lisa Davis.

Roger Rabbit Frantic star of *Who Framed Roger Rabbit*, along with the cartoons *Roller Coaster Rabbit*, *Tummy Trouble*, and *Trail Mix-Up*; voiced by Charles Fleischer.

Roger Rabbit & the Secrets of Toon Town (TV) Special on CBS; aired Sep. 13, 1988. 60 min. Directed by Les Mayfield. Behind the scenes of the filming of *Who Framed Roger Rabbit*, hosted by Joanna Cassidy. Actors and crew members are interviewed.

Roger Rabbit's Car Toon Spin Mickey's Toontown attraction in Disneyland; opened Jan. 26, 1994. The first dark ride built at Disneyland in a decade, it takes guests in Lenny (not Benny) the Cab on a joyride through Roger's wacky milieu, with all sorts of intriguing effects. For the first time in a Disney dark ride, the rider can turn the steering wheel of the cab and change the direction in which the vehicle is pointing. For example, with a little effort, guests can go through much of the attraction backward if they so desire, and because of this, the designers had to create things to see in all directions. This attraction did not open until a year after the rest of Mickey's Toontown. Also opened in Tokyo Disneyland Apr. 15, 1996.

Rogers, Bill Voice actor; in 1991, he succeeded Jack Wagner as the official announcer for Disneyland.

Rogers, Roy (1911–1998) Cowboy actor; appeared in *Melody Time* with the Sons of the Pioneers singing the hauntingly beautiful "Blue Shadows on the Trail" to introduce the story of Pecos Bill.

Rogers, Tristan Actor; provided the voice of Jake in *The Rescuers Down Under*.

Rogers, Wathel (1919–2000) Artist/sculptor; he started at the Disney Studio in 1939 and sculpted on his own time. He animated on the feature films between *Pinocchio* and *Sleeping Beauty* and created props and miniatures for such films as *Darby O'Gill and the Little People* and *The Absent-Minded Professor*, and TV shows such as the *Mickey Mouse Club* and *Zorro*. In 1954, Wathel was one of 3 founding members of the WED Enterprises model shop, where he assisted in the construction of architectural models for Disneyland. He participated in Project Little Man, leading to Audio-Animatronics

technology, which he programmed for many years for Disneyland, Walt Disney World, the 1964–1965 New York World's Fair, and EPCOT Center. He retired in 1987 and was named a Disney Legend in 1995.

Rogers, Wayne (1933–2015) Actor; appeared on TV in *The Girl Who Spelled Freedom* (George Thrash).

Rogers, William, and Son SEE WILLIAM ROGERS & SON.

Rogers: The Musical One-act Marvel production scheduled to begin a limited run summer 2023 in the Hyperion Theater at Disney California Adventure. The spoof Broadway musical featuring Steve Rogers, the first Captain America, was introduced in *Hawkeye* on Disney+, with a song, "Save the City," by Marc Shaiman and Scott Wittman.

Rogue One: A Star Wars Story (film) A standalone film in the *Star Wars* saga. In a time of conflict, a group of unlikely heroes band together on a mission to steal the plans to the Death Star, the Empire's ultimate weapon of destruction. This key event in the *Star Wars* time line brings together ordinary people who choose to do extraordinary things and, in doing so, become part of something greater than themselves. Released on Dec. 16, 2016, also in 3-D and 3-D IMAX, after a Dec. 14 international release. Directed by Gareth Edwards. Stars Felicity Jones (Jyn Erso), Mads Mikkelsen (Galen Erso), Ben Mendelsohn (Director Orson Krennic), Forest Whitaker (Saw Gerrera), Diego Luna (Capt. Cassian Andor), Donnie Yen (Chirrut Imwe), Alan Tudyk (K-2SO), Jiang Wen (Baze Malbus), Genevieve O'Reilly (Mon Mothma). 134 min. Filmed in wide-screen format at Pinewood Studios in England. Nominated for 2 Academy Awards (Sound Mixing and Visual Effects).

Rogue Trip (TV) A Disney+ original series from National Geographic; digitally premiered Jul. 24, 2020. ABC News correspondent Bob Woodruff and his son, Mack Woodruff, travel to all the places the average tourist is least likely to venture: the roguish nations, territories and regions often misunderstood and frequently overlooked, but each possessing a unique power to surprise, amaze, and inspire. 6 episodes.

Rohde, Joe Imagineer; served as exec. designer on Disney's Animal Kingdom, which he would continue to oversee for 23 years, and as creative lead on Aulani, A Disney Resort & Spa. He joined WED Enterprises in 1980, working on such projects as EPCOT's Mexico and Norway pavilions, and Pleasure Island for Walt Disney World; *Captain EO*; Guardians of the Galaxy – Mission: BREAKOUT! for Disney California Adventure; and Lighthouse Point for Disney Cruise Line. He retired in 2021.

Rolie Polie Olie (TV) Animated series on Disney Channel; debuted Oct. 4, 1998. Created by William Joyce. The series takes place in the world of Olie, a simple 6-year-old boy who lives in a magical, all-robot, round world. Voices include Cole Caplan (Olie), Kristen Bone (Zowie), Catherine Disher (Mrs. Polie), Adrian Truss (Mr. Polie), Rob Smith (Spot), Len Carlson (Pappy). From Nelvana Ltd./ Metal Hurlant Productions in association with Disney Channel.

Roller Coaster Rabbit (film) Roger Rabbit cartoon; released Jun. 15, 1990. Directed by Rob Minkoff. Roger is drafted into service as Baby Herman's babysitter during a visit to the county fair. When the infant goes off in search of his airborne balloon, Roger has to follow him on a perilous course that takes them through a volley of darts, a shooting gallery, into a close encounter with a bull, and ultimately onto the wildest roller coaster ride ever captured on film. Charles Fleischer provides the voice of Roger Rabbit. A Touchstone film.

Romano, Christy Carlson Actress; appeared on Disney Channel in *Even Stevens* (Ren Stevens) and *Cadet Kelly* (Jennifer Stone), and on ABC in the *Walt Disney World Christmas Day Parade*. She voiced the title character in *Kim Possible* (also appearing as Poppy Blue in the 2019 Disney Channel Original Movie) and Trina in *Big Hero 6 The Series*. In 2004, she starred as Belle in *Beauty and the Beast* on Broadway.

Romano, Lou Actor/designer; he has served as a production/development artist for several Disney • Pixar films, also providing the voice of Bernie Kropp in *The Incredibles*, Snotrod in *Cars*, and Linguini in *Ratatouille*.

Romeo's Watches & Jewelry Mediterranean Harbor shop in Tokyo DisneySea; opened Sep. 4, 2001. Décor was inspired by the Montague family in *Romeo and Juliet*. Closed Nov. 2012 to become Villa Donaldo Home Shop. SEE ALSO JULIET'S COLLECTIONS & TREASURES.

Romero, Cesar (1907–1994) Actor; appeared in *The Computer Wore Tennis Shoes*; *Now You See Him, Now You Don't*; and *The Strongest Man in the World*, all as A. J. Arno, and later guest starred on TV in *The Golden Girls* (Tony).

Romy and Michele: In the Beginning (TV) Movie on ABC Family; premiered May 30, 2005. Before they rocked their high school reunion, Romy and Michele took a rocking road trip to Hollywood. It's 10 years ago, and all Romy and Michele have is a destination and a dream. Soon they are dipping their toes in the Pacific, but they can't even set foot in Ozone, the coolest club in town. With their future on the line, they are sabotaged by a crazed PR agent and a super-needy supermodel until their California dreaming seems to be coming to a very un-Hollywood ending. Are they destined for drabness or can a little help from some lucky shoes, unlikely friends, and their idol Paula Abdul show them what it really means to be a star? Directed by Robin Schiff. Stars Katherine Heigl (Romy White), Alex Breckinridge (Michele Weinberger), Nat Faxon (Chad), Scott Vickaryous (Taylor), Kelly Brook (Linda), Dania (Elena), Alexandra Billings (Donna), Rhea Seehorn (Ashley Schwartz), Paula Abdul (as herself). A prequel to the 1997 film *Romy and Michele's High School Reunion*. From Touchstone Television.

Romy and Michele's High School Reunion (film) With their 10-year high school reunion fast approaching, best friends and party girls Romy and Michele review their lives since high school and are surprised to find them sorely lacking. They were misfits in high school, so they decide to reinvent themselves, concocting fantasies of wealth and success to impress their former classmates. The scheme unfolds perfectly, until Heather Mooney shows up and knows their real stories. Directed by David Mirkin. A Touchstone film. Released Apr. 25, 1997. Stars Mira Sorvino (Romy), Lisa Kudrow (Michele), Alan Cumming (Sandy Frink), Julia Campbell (Christie), Janeane Garofalo (Heather Mooney). 91 min. The characters of Romy and Michele were created nearly a decade earlier in the play *Ladies Room*, by playwright Robin Schiff, who focuses exclusively on the play's 2 most popular characters in her screenplay for this movie. Lisa Kudrow originated the role of Michele in the play before moving to the film.

Ronnie Saint Bernard puppy, first appearing in *The Purloined Pup* (1946).

Ronto Roasters Meat stall in Star Wars: Galaxy's Edge; opened May 31, 2019, in Disneyland and Aug. 29, 2019, in Disney's Hollywood Studios at Walt Disney World. The grilled items are apparently heated in the engine of a hanging Podracer.

Roo Baby kangaroo character in the Winnie the Pooh films.

Rookie, The (film) A shoulder injury seemingly ended Jim Morris's pitching career in the minor leagues 12 years ago. Now he's a high school chemistry teacher and baseball coach in Big Lake, Texas. It's there Jim's team makes a deal with him—if they win the district championship, he tries out with a major-league organization. The bet is incentive enough for the team, and they go from worst to first. Jim, forced to live up to his end of the deal, is nearly laughed off the field when he shows up for a tryout. But he takes the mound and throws successive 98 mph fastballs. The Tampa Bay Devil Rays (now the Tampa Bay Rays) are impressed—and sign him to a minor-league contract. Directed by John Lee Hancock. Released Mar. 29, 2002, after a special world premiere at the Loews Astor Plaza in New York City attended by a large group of baseball legends, Olympic medalists, and other sports personalities. Stars Dennis Quaid (Jim Morris), Rachel Griffiths (Lorri), Jay Hernandez (Joaquin "Wack" Campos), Beth Grant (Jimmy's mother), Angus T. Jones (Hunter), Brian Cox (Jim, Sr.). Filmed in CinemaScope. 128 min. Filmed on location in and around Austin, Texas, with the nearby town of Thorndale doubling for Big Lake. Based on a true story.

Rookie, The (TV) Hour-long series on ABC; premiered Oct. 16, 2018. John Nolan is a small-town guy who, because of a life-altering incident, has to practically start all over again. To that end, he pursues his dream of being a Los Angeles police officer. But as the force's oldest rookie, he's met with skepticism from some higher-ups. He'll have to prove that he can keep up with the young cops and criminals but at the same time use his life experience, determination, and sense of humor to give him an edge. Stars Nathan Fillion (John Nolan), Alyssa Diaz (Angela Lopez), Richard T. Jones (Sgt. Wade Grey), Titus Makin (Jackson West), Mercedes Mason (Capt. Zoe Anderson). From Entertainment One, co-produced by ABC Studios.

Rookie, The: Feds (TV) One-hour drama series on ABC; premiered Sep. 27, 2022. Fresh out of the FBI Academy, Simone Clark arrives in Los Angeles and has her sights set on joining Matthew Garza's newly formed special unit as they investigate the murder of a federal engineer. Garza's squad includes Carter Hope, a promotion-hungry traditionalist, Laura Stenson, a talented agent in desperate need of a second chance, and Brendon Acres, a former actor who graduated from Quantico with Simone. Stars Niecy Nash-Betts (Simone Clark), Frankie R. Faison (Christopher "Cutty" Clark), James Lesure (Carter Hope), Britt Robertson (Laura Stensen), Felix Solis (Matthew Garza), Kevin Zegers (Brendon Acres). A spin-off from *The Rookie*, introduced as a 2-part event during the show's 4th season. From Entertainment One and ABC Signature.

Room for Heroes (film) Educational film describing the exploits of American heroes and legends such as Johnny Appleseed, Davy Crockett, Pecos Bill, and Casey Jones; released in Aug. 1971.

Roommates (film) An irascible but lovable elderly grandfather, Rocky Holeczek, plays an important role in the life of his grandson, Michael. At 107, Rocky is the oldest employed baker in Pittsburgh, and this saga, covering 30 years of his life, shows how he raises Michael from childhood, and continues to guide him into manhood as he marries, has children, and embarks on a busy career in medicine. The relationship makes for a powerful statement about the value of family, as Rocky is determined to stick around for as long as it takes to teach Michael what he needs to know about living. Released Mar. 3, 1995. Directed by Peter Yates. A Hollywood Pictures film. Stars Peter Falk (Rocky Holeczek), D. B. Sweeney (Michael), Julianne Moore (Beth), Jan Rubes (Bolek Krupa), Ellen Burstyn (Judith). 109 min. The film's inspiration was the real-life, unconventional relationship between the author, Max Apple, and his grandfather. Filmed in Pittsburgh, encompassing the blue-collar world of Polish Hill and the nearby fashionable community of Sewickley Heights, the movie's time span covering 4 decades created many challenges for the production designer, Dan Bishop. Perhaps the most arduous element of the production was the makeup job of aging Peter Falk at various stages from 75 to 107, with the actor having to put up with sitting under layers of latex for hours at a time.

Rooney, Mickey (1920–2014) Actor; appeared in *Pete's Dragon* (Lampie), on TV in *Donovan's Kid* (Old Bailey), *Little Spies* (James Turner), *Mickey's*

50, and *The Disney-MGM Studios Theme Park Grand Opening*, and on Disney Channel in *Phantom of the Megaplex* (Movie Mason). He voiced the adult Tod in *The Fox and the Hound* and Sparky in *Lady and the Tramp II: Scamp's Adventure*. His last Disney role was a cameo in *The Muppets*.

Rooney, Mickey, Jr. (1945–2022) He was hired as a Mouseketeer for the 1950s *Mickey Mouse Club* but was dismissed shortly afterward.

Rooney, Tim (1947–2006) He was hired as a Mouseketeer for the 1950s *Mickey Mouse Club* but was dismissed shortly afterward along with his brother, Mickey.

Roquefort Polite mouse character in *The Aristocats*; voiced by Sterling Holloway.

Rosalie French brasserie in Disney Village at Disneyland Paris; scheduled to open in 2023, taking the place of Café Mickey. The 2-floor contemporary restaurant will celebrate the French "Art de Vivre" with classic cuisine and expanded terraces overlooking Lake Disney. Managed by Groupe Bertrand.

Roscoe and DeSoto Sykes's Doberman henchmen in *Oliver & Company*; voiced by Taurean Blacque and Carl Weintraub, respectively.

Rose, Anika Noni Actress; provided the voice of Tiana in *The Princess and the Frog* and in other appearances of the character. On TV, she appeared in *Private Practice* (Corinne Bennett), *Little Fires Everywhere* (Paula Hawthorne), *The Chew*, *The Disney Family Singalong: Volume II*, and the *Disney Parks Christmas Day Parade*, and she voiced Dr. Jan in *Amphibia*. She was named a Disney Legend in 2011.

Rose & Crown Pub & Dining Room Restaurant in the United Kingdom at EPCOT; opened Oct. 1, 1982, serving traditional fare like fish-and-chips, steak-and-kidney pie, and trifle for dessert. In the pub section, guests can order English ale or stout. The Rose & Crown combines the styles of several kinds of pubs, from the normal street-side ones in the cities and country towns to London's famed Ye Olde Cheshire Cheese. The motto is, "Otium cum Dignitate" ("Leisure with Dignity").

Rose Parade See Tournament of Roses Parade.

Ross, Rich He joined Disney Channel in 1996 as senior vice president and became president of Disney Channel Worldwide in 2004. On Oct. 5, 2009, he was named chairman of Walt Disney Studios, serving until Apr. 2012. He was succeeded by Alan Horn.

Ross, Tracee Ellis Actress; appeared on TV in *black-ish* (Rainbow Johnson), also serving as producer and director. Also created, exec. produced, and narrated *mixed-ish* and made guest appearances in *grown-ish*, *Private Practice*, and *The Disney Family Singalong*. She was named a Disney Legend in 2022.

Roth, Joe He joined Disney in 1992 with a contract to produce films under the Caravan Pictures label. In 1994, he was named chairman of the Walt Disney Motion Pictures Group on the resignation of Jeffrey Katzenberg. In Apr. 1996, he was named chairman, Walt Disney Studios, adding TV and video production responsibilities. He left the company in Jan. 2000.

Round Table, The Fantasyland counter-service restaurant in the Magic Kingdom at Walt Disney World; opened Oct. 1, 1971, presented by Borden. It became Mrs. Potts' Cupboard in 1994.

Roundup Rodeo BBQ Table-service eatery for Toy Story Land in Disney's Hollywood Studios; scheduled to open Mar. 23, 2023. As the story goes, Andy has created a new rodeo arena using some of his favorite toys and games, where guests dine among all the festivities.

Roving Mars (film) Documentary presenting a look at the awe-inspiring and amazing Mars landscape as seen through the eyes of *Spirit* and *Opportunity*, the 2 Mars rovers. Their dogged quest over the rugged terrain enables audiences to explore the surface of Mars as never before. Released Jan. 27, 2006. Directed by George Butler. Filmed in 70 mm large format/IMAX.

Royal Banquet Hall Fantasyland restaurant themed to the Disney princesses in Hong Kong Disneyland; opened Sep. 12, 2005, with a food court and 4 specialized show kitchens. Also a signature restaurant inside Enchanted Storybook Castle at Shanghai Disneyland; opened Jun. 16, 2016, with regal dining halls themed to Cinderella, Mulan, Tiana, Snow White, and Princess Aurora. See also Restaurant Akershus (EPCOT).

Royal Candy Factory, The Fantasyland shop in the Magic Kingdom at Walt Disney World; opened Oct. 1, 1971. Later known as The Royal Candy Shoppe. Closed Oct. 1994 to become Seven Dwarfs' Mine.

Royal Plaza Hotel in Lake Buena Vista at Walt Disney World; opened Jan. 1973 as Royal Inn, with 17 stories and 396 rooms. It became the Royal Plaza in 1975. Closed in 2013 to reopen as B Resort the following year.

Royal Pub, The British-themed restaurant in Disney Village at Disneyland Paris; opened Feb. 17, 2023, succeeding King Ludwig's Castle. Fish-and-chips, authentic pies, and toasted sandwiches are served. Operated by Groupe Bertrand.

Royal Reception Fantasyland boutique in Disneyland; opened Feb. 2017, offering *Beauty and the Beast* gifts and accessories. It was previously Frozen Royal Reception, where guests could meet Queen Elsa and Princess Anna, Nov. 2013–Dec. 19, 2015, and prior to that a *Tangled* character-greeting cottage (opened Oct. 15, 2010, succeeding Geppetto's Sweet Shop).

Royal Reception Hall, The Regal character-greeting venue in the Castle of Magical Dreams at Hong Kong Disneyland; opened Nov. 20, 2020.

Royal Sommerhus Character-greeting venue in Norway at EPCOT; opened Jun. 21, 2016. Elsa and Anna from *Frozen* meet guests and pose for photographs in their charming summer cabin.

Royal Street Veranda Counter-service restaurant in New Orleans Square at Disneyland; opened in 1967, serving gumbo and other soups in sourdough bread bowls. Also an Adventureland counter-service restaurant in Tokyo Disneyland; opened Apr. 15, 1983.

Royal Tenenbaums, The (film) Royal Tenenbaum and his wife, Etheline, had 3 children: Chas, who became a real estate mogul with a deep understanding of international finance; Richie, a champion tennis player; and Margot, a gifted playwright. But the brilliance of the young Tenenbaums is erased over 2 decades of betrayal, failure, and disaster, mostly attributable to their father. One recent winter, the family has a sudden, unexpected reunion. Directed by Wes Anderson. A Touchstone film. Released Dec. 14, 2001, in Los Angeles and New York City, with general release on Dec. 21. Stars Gene Hackman (Royal Tenenbaum), Anjelica Huston (Etheline), Ben Stiller (Chas), Gwyneth Paltrow (Margot), Owen Wilson (Eli Cash), Danny Glover (Henry Sherman), Bill Murray (Raleigh St. Clair), Luke Wilson (Richie Tenenbaum). 110 min. Filmed in CinemaScope on location in New York City. The filmmakers discovered a dilapidated limestone mini-mansion in a historic neighborhood of Harlem called Hamilton Heights to use as the Tenenbaum house. The film received an Academy Award nomination for Best Original Screenplay.

Roz Grouchy dispatch manager, a slug, at Monsters, Inc.; voiced by Bob Peterson.

Rub, Christian (1886–1956) Actor; voiced Geppetto in *Pinocchio*.

Ruby & The Rockits (TV) Series on ABC Family; aired Jul. 21–Sep. 22, 2009. Patrick Gallagher, a former teen idol, has chosen to lead a quiet life with his wife, Audie, and 2 sons, Jordan and Ben. But when his former Rockits bandmate and brother, David, shows up unexpectedly with his newfound teenage daughter, Ruby, in tow, the Gallagher family's life becomes anything but normal. David, who refuses to give up his past glory days, comes to Patrick for help raising Ruby while he continues to perform. Patrick must now put aside the past in order to help raise Ruby and keep order within the rest of the Gallagher clan. Stars Alexa Vega (Ruby), Patrick Cassidy (Patrick Gallagher), David Cassidy (David Gallagher), Katie Amanda Keane (Audie), Austin Butler (Jordan), Kurt Doss (Ben). Third brother, Shaun Cassidy, served as an exec. producer. From ABC Studios.

Ruby Bridges (TV) A 2-hour movie on *The Wonderful World of Disney*; first aired Jan. 18, 1998. The poignant story about a 6-year-old girl's struggle for equality during the tumultuous American civil rights movement of the 1960s who's one of the first African American students to be integrated into the New Orleans public schools. Directed by Euzhan Palcy. Stars Chaz Monét (Ruby), Penelope Ann Miller (Barbara Henry), Kevin Pollak (Dr. Robert Coles), Michael Beach (Abon Bridges), Jean Louisa Kelly (Jane Coles), Peter Francis James (Dr. Broyard), Patrika Darbo (Jill), Diana Scarwid (Miss Woodmore), Lela Rochon (Lucielle Bridges). Shot entirely on location in Wilmington, North Carolina. As a first for Disney, President Bill Clinton joined Michael Eisner in introducing the show; the

2 were taped in the Cabinet Room at the White House.

Rudd, Paul Actor; appeared as Scott Lang/Ant-Man in the Marvel Studios films and as himself in *Chip 'n Dale: Rescue Rangers* (2022).

Rudolph, Maya Actress; appeared in *Duets* (Omaha Karaoke Hostess) and on Disney+ in *Disenchanted* (Malvina Monroe). She voiced Aunt Cass in *Big Hero 6* and *Big Hero 6 The Series*, Griselda in *Strange Magic*, and Daniela in *Luca*.

Rufus Elderly cat in the orphanage in *The Rescuers*; voiced by John McIntire.

Rufus Naked mole rat character in the animated TV series *Kim Possible*; voiced by Nancy Cartwright.

Rugged Bear (film) Donald Duck cartoon released Oct. 23, 1953. Directed by Jack Hannah. When hunting season opens, a terrified bear hides in Donald's cabin and endures the tortures of being a household bear rug until the season closes. Nominated for an Academy Award.

Ruggles, Charlie (1886–1970) Actor; appeared in *The Parent Trap* (Charles McKendrick), *Son of Flubber* (Judge Murdock), *The Ugly Dachshund* (Dr. Pruitt), and *Follow Me, Boys!* (John Everett Hughes). He voiced Ben Franklin in *Ben and Me*.

Ruggles China and Glass House Shop on Main Street, U.S.A. in Disneyland; opened Jul. 17, 1955. Closed Mar. 1964 and succeeded by the China Closet.

Rummell, Peter He joined Disney as president of the Disney Development Company in 1985; he had been an officer with the Arvida Corporation, which Disney had bought. Rummell was later promoted to head Disney Design and Development, which encompassed both Walt Disney Imagineering and the Disney Development Company. When Walt Disney Imagineering and Disney Development Company merged in 1996, Rummell was named chairman of the new organization. He left the company in 1997.

Run (film) A carefree summer road trip turns into a living nightmare for a law school student, Charlie Farrow, when he accidentally kills the son of a notorious mobster. Stranded in a small New England town, Charlie becomes the target both for the cold-blooded mob and a corrupt police force and is on the run. With a single ally, Karen Landers, a pretty casino card dealer, Charlie struggles to stay one step ahead of his pursuers. Released Feb. 1, 1991. Directed by Geoff Burrowes. A Hollywood Pictures film. 91 min. Stars Patrick Dempsey (Charlie Farrow), Kelly Preston (Karen Landers), Ken Pogue (Halloran). Vancouver doubled for the fictitious city of Sawtucket.

Run, Appaloosa, Run (film) Featurette about Mary, a girl of the Nez Perce Tribe in northwest Idaho, who raises a motherless Appaloosa colt, Sky Dancer, one of the unique, spotted horses developed by the tribe. The girl and horse are separated, but after a series of adventures they are reunited at a rodeo, which leads to their entry in the dangerous Hell's Mountain Suicide Relay Race. Released Jul. 29, 1966, on a bill with *Lt. Robin Crusoe, U.S.N.* Directed by Larry Lansburgh. 48 min. Stars Adele Palacios, Wilbur Plaugher, Jerry Gatlin.

Run, Cougar, Run (film) When a professional hunter and 2 sportsmen use a helicopter to scout for big game in the southwestern wilderness of the U.S., Seeta, a tawny, 3-year-old mountain lion, her mate, and their 3 kits are endangered. She'll now have to struggle even more to protect her family from these dangerous intruders. Released Oct. 18, 1972. Directed by Jerome Courtland. 87 min. Stars Stuart Whitman (Hugh McRae), Lonny Chapman (Harry Walker), Douglas V. Fowley (Joe Bickley), Harry Carey, Jr. (Barney), Alfonso Arau (Etie). The film's song, "Let Her Alone," was written by Terry Gilkyson and sung by Ian & Sylvia. The movie was narrated by Ian Tyson and filmed entirely on location in the great Southwest, along the Colorado River in Utah and Arizona.

Run, Light Buck, Run (TV) Show aired Mar. 13, 1966. A grizzled, backwoods prospector in the wild mesa country north of Arizona's Grand Canyon twice helps a young antelope, and the animal becomes a pet. Eventually he meets another antelope and heads back to the wild. Stars Al Niemela.

Runaway Brain (film) Mickey Mouse cartoon. Dr. Frankenollie, a mad scientist, transplants Mickey's brain into a monster's body and vice versa. The monster-ized Mickey, known as Julius, becomes obsessed with pursuing Minnie, and Mickey (whose intentions are misunderstood because he is in the monster's body) tries to save her. Released Aug. 11,

1995, with *A Kid in King Arthur's Court*. Directed by Chris Bailey. Voices are Wayne Allwine, Russi Taylor, Kelsey Grammer, Jim Cummings, Bill Farmer. The name Dr. Frankenollie was inspired by the famed animators Frank Thomas and Ollie Johnston. The cartoon was nominated for an Academy Award. 8 min.

Runaway Bride (film) Touchstone Pictures and Paramount jointly produced for release on Jul. 30, 1999, this story of Maggie Carpenter, a Maryland woman who has a penchant for leaving grooms at the altar. Ike Graham is a reporter who tries to uncover Maggie's story, with the 2 fated to end up together. Directed by Garry Marshall. Stars Julia Roberts (Maggie Carpenter), Richard Gere (Ike Graham), Joan Cusack (Peggy), Hector Elizondo (Fisher). 116 min. This film reunited Roberts, Gere, Elizondo, and director Marshall for the first time since their hit *Pretty Woman*, in 1990. Most of the filming took place in and around Baltimore, with the small Eastern Shore town of Berlin, Maryland, portraying the fictitious town of Hale. Released on video by Paramount in 2000.

Runaway on the Rogue River (TV) Show aired Dec. 1, 1974. Directed by Larry Lansburgh. A boy, Jeff, comes upon a runaway elephant while fishing. He has adventures taking the elephant to show his father, and the elephant ends up helping save the father's life. Stars Slim Pickens, Willie Aames, Denis Arndt.

runDisney Beginning with a Walt Disney World Marathon in 1994, Disney has continued to sponsor a number of race events, both at Walt Disney World and Disneyland. Rebranded in 2010 as *run*Disney races, they are appealing to new runners because there is less pressure, no required qualifying time, and guests can enjoy the sights of a Disney park and characters during their race. Events include marathons, half-marathons, health and fitness expos, kids races, and specially themed races. In 2009, over 200,000 runners participated in a variety of Disney runs. A Castaway Cay Challenge 5K event began in 2014, and a half-marathon at Disneyland Paris was introduced in 2016. In Jan. 2020, a membership program, Club *run*Disney, was announced, offering such perks as early race registration and access to an exclusive lounge. Races were paused beginning in Apr. 2020 due to the COVID-19 pandemic; runners were instead invited to participate in online meetings and take part in "virtual races" in their local communities.

In-person races returned to Walt Disney World Nov. 5–7, 2021, with the Disney Wine & Dine Half Marathon Weekend. *run*Disney events at Disneyland Resort were suspended as of 2018 but are scheduled to return in 2024.

Running Brave (film) Not made by Disney, but distributed by Buena Vista Distribution Co. The true story of Marine Corps Lt. Billy Mills, a half-Sioux rank outsider who won America's first and only top award in the 10,000-meter race during the Summer Olympic Games in Tokyo in 1964. Directed by D. S. Everett. Released in Nov. 1983. 107 min. Stars Robby Benson (Billy Mills), Pat Hingle, Claudia Cron, Jeff McCracken.

Rush, Barbara Actress; appeared in *Superdad* (Sue McCready).

Rush, Geoffrey Actor; appeared as Captain Barbossa in the Pirates of the Caribbean films and provided the voice of Nigel in *Finding Nemo*.

Rushin' River Outfitters Grizzly Peak shop in Disney California Adventure; opened Feb. 8, 2001, selling outdoor-inspired apparel and gifts.

Rushmore (film) A chronicle of a year in the life of 15-year-old student Max Fischer at Rushmore Academy, one of the finest schools in the country. Max loves his prestigious school, is editor of the school paper, and is involved in practically every student organization. Because of all of his extracurricular activities, he is also one of the worst students in the school. Threatened with expulsion, he begins a new interest—pursuing a first-grade teacher. When Max's tycoon mentor starts an affair with the same teacher, it triggers a war between Max and his "friend." Released for one week Dec. 11, 1998, in Los Angeles and New York City for Academy Award consideration; on a limited basis Feb. 5, 1999; and then nationwide Feb. 12, 1999. Directed by Wes Anderson. Stars Jason Schwartzman (Max Fischer), Olivia Williams (Miss Cross), Brian Cox (Dr. Guggenheim), Seymour Cassell (Bert Fischer), Mason Gamble (Dirk Calloway), Bill Murray (Mr. Blume). 93 min. Filmed in CinemaScope. Doubling for the fictional Rushmore was St. John's School in Houston, the alma mater of director/co-writer Wes Anderson. The public school scenes at "Grover Cleveland" were actually filmed at Lamar High School, across the street from St. John's.

Russell, Bryan (1952–2016) Child actor; appeared

in *Babes in Toyland* (boy), *Emil and the Detectives* (Emil), and *The Adventures of Bullwhip Griffin* (Jack Flagg), and on TV in *Gallegher* (Bootblack) and *Kilroy* (Billy Fuller).

Russell, Irwin E. (1926–2013) Member of the Disney Board of Directors 1987–Mar. 6, 2001.

Russell, Keri Actress; appeared in *Honey, I Blew Up the Kid* (Mandy), *Bedtime Stories* (Jill), and *Star Wars: The Rise of Skywalker* (Zorii Bliss), on The Disney Channel in the *Mickey Mouse Club* beginning in 1991, and on TV in the title role in *Felicity*, with guest appearances in *Scrubs* (Melody).

Russell, Kurt Actor; appeared in *Follow Me, Boys!* (Whitey); *The One and Only, Genuine, Original Family Band* (Sidney Bower); *The Horse in the Gray Flannel Suit* (Ronnie Gardner); *The Computer Wore Tennis Shoes / Now You See Him, Now You Don't / The Strongest Man in the World* (Dexter Reilly); *The Barefoot Executive* (Steven Post); *Charley and the Angel* (Ray Ferris); *Superdad* (Bart); *Captain Ron* (Ron); *Tombstone* (Wyatt Earp); *Miracle* (Herb Brooks); *Sky High* (Steve Stronghold/The Commander); and *Guardians of the Galaxy Vol. 2* (Ego). Also on TV in *Disneyland Showtime, Willie and the Yank* (Private Willie Prentiss), *The Secret of Boyne Castle* (Rich Evans), *The Mouse Factory*, and *The Age of Believing: The Disney Live Action Classics*. He voiced the older Copper in *The Fox and the Hound* and narrated *Dad, Can I Borrow the Car?* Russell was one of the few child stars to make a successful transition to adult film roles. He was named a Disney Legend in 1998.

Rustler Roundup Shootin' Gallery Located in Frontierland in Disneyland Paris; opened Apr. 12, 1992.

Rusty and the Falcon (TV) Show aired Oct. 24, 1958. Directed by N. Paul Kenworthy. Jerome Courtland describes falconry and then helps tell the story of a boy who finds an injured falcon and tries to train him. Stars Rudy Lee, Jay W. Lee.

Ruthless People (film) A husband plans to murder his loud, overbearing wife, but before he can carry out his plan, she is kidnapped. The inept kidnappers keep lowering their ransom demands when the husband refuses to pay. The wife takes advantage of her confinement to go on a crash reducing-weight program, and she eventually teams with the kidnappers against her husband. Released Jun. 27, 1986. Directed by Jim Abrahams, David Zucker, Jerry Zucker. A Touchstone film. 94 min. Stars Danny DeVito (Sam Stone), Bette Midler (Barbara Stone), Judge Reinhold (Ken Kessler), Helen Slater (Sandy Kessler). Filmed at various Southern California locations.

Ryan, Meg Actress; appeared in *D.O.A.* (Sydney Fuller) and *When a Man Loves a Woman* (Alice Green), and on TV in *Wildside* (Cally Oaks).

Ryan, Will (1949–2021) Actor; provided the voices of Pete and Willie the Giant in *Mickey's Christmas Carol* and other appearances of the characters, the seahorse in *The Little Mermaid*, and Rabbit in *Winnie the Pooh and a Day for Eeyore*, as well as many voices for Disney records and TV shows, including *Welcome to Pooh Corner* (Barnaby) and *DuckTales*.

Ryen, Adam Actor; provided the voice of Cody in *The Rescuers Down Under*.

Rylance, Mark Actor; appeared in the title role in *The BFG* and won a supporting actor Oscar for his role in *Bridge of Spies* (Rudolf Abel).

Ryman, Herb (1910–1989) Art director/designer; Herbert Dickens Ryman, known as Herbie, joined the Disney Studio in 1938, and served as an art director on such features as *Fantasia* and *Dumbo*. In 1953, Walt Disney asked him to draw the original concept for Disneyland so Roy O. Disney could use it to help sell investors. He designed Sleeping Beauty Castle and worked on various Imagineering projects over the years until he retired in 1971. Ryman still continued on after that as a consultant, illustrating concepts for EPCOT Center and Tokyo Disneyland. He was working on Euro Disneyland plans when he died in 1989. Lithographs of a number of his concept paintings have been sold by The Disney Gallery at Disneyland. He was named a Disney Legend posthumously in 1990.

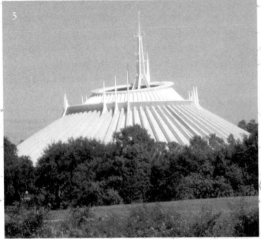

1. Stamps 2. Silly Symphony 3. Scrooge McDuck 4. *Shaggy Dog, The* (film) 5. Space Mountain
6. *So Dear to My Heart* (film) 7. *Sofia the First* (TV) 8. *Scarecrow of Romney Marsh, The* (TV)
9. *Snow White and the Seven Dwarfs* (film) 10. Smith, Dave

Sabella, Ernie Actor; appeared in *Tough Guys* (hotel clerk), *Roommates* (Stash), and *Quiz Show* (car salesman), on ABC in *Annie* (Mr. Bundles), and on Disney Channel in *That's So Raven* (Mr. Petracelli). He voiced Pumbaa in *The Lion King* and other appearances of the character.

Sachet In Soap/sachet shop accompanying the Bath Parlour in the Lake Buena Vista Shopping Village at Walt Disney World; opened Nov. 19, 1977, taking the place of Pipe Dream. Closed Feb. 6, 1987, to become Team Mickey's Athletic Club.

Sacred Planet (film) An inspiring journey around the world viewing the landscape, the people, and the animals indigenous to the land, showcasing the natural beauty of our planet's diverse regions. Released Apr. 22, 2004, in large-format/IMAX theaters. Filmed in 70 mm. Directed by Jon Long. 47 min. Narrated by Robert Redford. A Walt Disney Pictures presentation of a New Street/Allied Films production.

Sadness Riley's glum emotion in *Inside Out*; voiced by Phyllis Smith.

Safari Club Adventureland arcade in the Magic Kingdom at Walt Disney World; opened Oct. 1, 1971. It became Colonel Hathi's Safari Club in 1972.

Safari Outpost Adventureland shop at Disneyland; opened Mar. 1, 1986. It closed Nov. 1994 to reopen Dec. 16, 1994, as Indiana Jones Adventure Outpost.

Safari Shooting Gallery Adventureland attraction in Disneyland; open 1962–1982. Also known as Big Game Safari Shooting Gallery and Big Game Shooting Gallery. The area later was remodeled with several shops.

Safari Trading Company Adventureland shop in Tokyo Disneyland offering accessories and African-inspired craftwork; opened Mar. 1987, replacing Tropic Toppers. Closed Jun. 21, 2015, to become Jungle Carnival.

Safari Village Island in the midst of Disney's Animal Kingdom; opened Apr. 22, 1998, with a name change to Discovery Island in Dec. 2000. This mythical community is dominated by the majestic Tree of Life, from where bridges provide access to The Oasis, Africa, Asia, DinoLand U.S.A., and Pandora – The World of Avatar. Dining and snacking venues include Pizzafari, Flame Tree Barbecue, and Creature Comforts, with shopping at Discovery Trading Company (formerly Disney Outfitters) and Island Mercantile. All throughout, bright animal motifs are designed into the architecture in a folk art style. The Discovery Island Trails offer guests self-guided tours to glimpse nature and wild animals at their own pace.

Safety (film) The story of former Clemson University football safety Ray McElrathbey, a young man facing a series of challenging circumstances whose dedication and persistence help him triumph over repeated adversities. Aided by his teammates and the Clemson community, he succeeds on the field while simultaneously raising and caring for his 11-year-old brother, Fahmarr. Digitally released Dec. 11, 2020, on Disney+. Directed by Reginald Hudlin. Stars Jay Reeves (Ray), Thaddeus J. Mixson (Fahmarr), Corinne Foxx (Kaycee Stone), Matthew Glave (Coach Tommy Bowden), Hunter Sansone (Daniel Morelli), Amanda Warren (Tonya), Miles Burris (Keller), Isaac Bell (Fresh/Eugene), Elijah Bell (Pop/Marcus), James Badge Dale (Coach Simmons). 120 min. Inspired by a true story. From Walt Disney Studios, with Select Films and Mayhem Pictures. The production team planned their shooting schedule around an actual game between Clemson and UNC Charlotte, but it turned out the game was to be televised live, giving the crew less time than originally expected—7 min. and 20 sec.—to shoot 4 scenes during halftime, all in front of 85,000 mostly Clemson fans. Filmed in wide-screen format in Georgia and at Clemson University in South Carolina.

Safety Patrol (TV) A 2-hour movie on *The Wonderful World of Disney*; first aired Mar. 29, 1998. Eleven-year-old Scout Bozell is a safety fanatic, whose lifelong dream is to become a member of his school's Safety Patrol. While clumsy and accident-prone, he still manages to outwit the school bullies, who make up the patrol at Laurelview Middle School, and a couple of evil adults, and become a hero. Directed by Savage Steve Holland. Stars Bug Hall (Scout Bozell), Lainie Kazan (Mrs. Day), Curtis Armstrong (Mr. Miller), Leslie Nielsen (Mr. Penn), Stephanie Faracy (Principal Marlow), Alex McKenna (Hannah), Ed McMahon (Grandpa). Filmed in Los Angeles.

Safety Smart Science with Bill Nye, the Science Guy (film) Series of educational films demonstrating how science knowledge and awareness provide the opportunities to learn and practice safe behaviors. Titles are *Safety Smart Science with Bill Nye, the Science Guy: Fire* (2009), *Electricity* (2009), *Germs & Your Health* (2011), and *Energy* (2012). Released by Disney Educational Productions.

Saga of Andy Burnett, The (Episode 1): Andy's Initiation (TV) Show aired Oct. 2, 1957. Directed by Lewis R. Foster. Set in 1820, Andy, an easterner, is introduced; his ambition is to become a farmer, but a penniless mountain man convinces him that is not the life for him. His band puts Andy through a series of tests to see if he has what it takes to become a mountain man. Stars Jerome Courtland, Jeff York, Andrew Duggan, Slim Pickens.

Saga of Andy Burnett, The (Episode 2): Andy's First Chore (TV) Show aired Oct. 9, 1957. Directed by Lewis R. Foster. Andy is educated by the mountain men, who are asked by Senator Tom Benton to deliver an urgent message to Santa Fe, New Mexico. They are tracked by a rough band of men led by Bill Sublette, whom Andy helps outwit. Stars Jerome Courtland, Jeff York, Andrew Duggan, Slim Pickens.

Saga of Andy Burnett, The (Episode 3): Andy's Love Affair (TV) Show aired Oct. 16, 1957. Directed by Lewis R. Foster. On their way to Santa Fe, New Mexico, the mountain men have problems with the Spanish border patrol, and Andy makes the *capitán* jealous by falling in love with his sweetheart. But she is only using Andy for her own purposes; when he discovers that, he and the other mountain men leave the city to return to the wilds of the mountains. Stars Jerome Courtland, Jeff York, Andrew Duggan, Slim Pickens, Britt Lomond.

Saga of Andy Burnett, The (Episode 4): The Land of Enemies (TV) Show aired Feb. 26, 1958. Directed by Lewis R. Foster. Andy and his friends continue their trip to Taos and are attacked and taken prisoners. But Andy kills a white buffalo, making him almost a god to his captors, and he learns sign language in order to communicate with them. Stars Jerome Courtland, Jeff York, Andrew Duggan, Slim Pickens, Iron Eyes Cody.

Saga of Andy Burnett, The (Episode 5): White Man's Medicine (TV) Show aired Mar. 5, 1958. Directed by Lewis R. Foster. Still held captive, Andy has to use his wiles to keep himself and his companions alive. Stars Jerome Courtland, Jeff York, Andrew Duggan, Slim Pickens, Iron Eyes Cody.

Saga of Andy Burnett, The (Episode 6): The Big Council (TV) Show aired Mar. 12, 1958. Directed by Lewis R. Foster. In this final chapter, Andy and the mountain men remain captives. Andy then saves the chief's son's life, which gives the group a chance to escape. Eventually the captors and the mountain men smoke the peace pipe—and settle matters. Stars Jerome Courtland, Jeff York, Andrew Duggan, Slim Pickens, Iron Eyes Cody.

Saga of Windwagon Smith, The (film) Special cartoon released Mar. 16, 1961. Directed by Charles Nichols. Capt. Windwagon Smith rigs a Conestoga prairie wagon like a schooner with sails and tiller, and sweeps into a Kansas town where he meets the mayor's lovely daughter, Molly, and falls in love. The townspeople are transfixed with Smith's new form of transportation and build a super *wind-wagon* only to have a hurricane literally blow it off, with the Captain and Molly aboard, into the skies never to be seen again—except when the sunset turns to gold; it's only then that they can be seen. Look for Jasper and Horace Badun from *One Hundred and One Dalmatians* who put in an anonymous appearance. 13 min.

Sagal, Katey Actress; appeared in *The Good Mother* (Ursula), and on TV in *Mr. Headmistress* (Harriet Magnum), *Smart House* (PAT), *8 Simple Rules for Dating My Teenage Daughter* (Cate Hennessy), *Imagine That* (Barb), *Lost* (Helen Norwood), *Grand Hotel* (Teresa Williams), *Rebel* (Annie "Rebel" Bello), and *A Merry Mickey Celebration*. She voiced Flo Spinelli in *Disney's Recess* and Policewoman Hero in *Higglytown Heroes*.

Sagebrush Sadie (film) Oswald the Lucky Rabbit cartoon; released Apr. 2, 1928. Sadie is kidnapped at the Sagebrush Saloon, and Oswald mounts his horse in pursuit. He eventually rescues her from the side of a cliff.

Sailing Day Buffet Restaurant in American Waterfront at Tokyo DisneySea; opened Sep. 4, 2001. Closed Mar. 31, 2018, to become Dockside Diner. The establishment celebrated the S.S. *Columbia*'s maiden voyage in rooms throughout the U.S. Steamship Company's main cargo terminal, workshop, and offices.

Sailing Ship Columbia SEE COLUMBIA SAILING SHIP.

Saint X (TV) Eight-episode psychological drama; scheduled for digital release Apr. 26, 2023, on Hulu. A young woman's mysterious death during a Caribbean vacation creates a traumatic ripple effect that pulls her surviving sister into a dangerous pursuit of the truth. Based on the novel of the same title by Alexis Schaitkin. Stars Alycia Debnam-Carey (Emily), Josh Bonzie (Clive Richardson), Jayden Elijah (Edwin Hastings), West Duchovny (Alison). From ABC Signature.

Saintly Switch, A (TV) A 2-hour movie on *The Wonderful World of Disney*; first aired Jan. 24, 1999. A pro quarterback dad and feminist mom literally exchange personalities—but not bodies—thanks

to their meddling children and some good old-fashioned magic. Directed by Peter Bogdanovich. Stars Vivica A. Fox (Sara Anderson), David Alan Grier (Dan Anderson), Al Waxman (Coach Beasily), Scott Owen Cumberbatch (Clarke), Shadia Simmons (Annette), David Keeley (Otis), Rue McClanahan (Aunt Fanny).

Saldana, Zoe Actress; appeared in *Pirates of the Caribbean: The Curse of the Black Pearl* (Anamaria) and as Gamora in the Guardians of the Galaxy and Avengers films.

Salenger, Meredith Actress; appeared in the title role in *The Journey of Natty Gann*, and later made a cameo as Natalie Gann in *Race to Witch Mountain*. On TV, she starred in *My Town* (Amber Wheeler) and made a guest appearance in *Grey's Anatomy*. She provided voices for *Marvel's M.O.D.O.K.* (various) and *Super Robot Monkey Team Hyperforce Go!* (Aurora Six).

Salonga, Lea Actress; Broadway singing star of *Miss Saigon* fame who provided the singing voice of Jasmine in *Aladdin* and the title character in *Mulan*. She was named a Disney Legend in 2011.

Salt & Straw Family-run ice cream shop in the Downtown Disney District at Disneyland Resort; opened Oct. 12, 2018, replacing Häagen-Dazs.

Salten, Felix (1869–1945) Author; born in Budapest and educated in Vienna, he wrote several adult novels and plays, but he is best known for *Bambi*, first published in English in 1928. Disney later also adapted his *Perri* for the screen. Most fans of the classic comedy *The Shaggy Dog* do not realize that it is from a Salten story, *The Hound of Florence*.

Salty Seal who appears with Pluto in *Rescue Dog* (1947).

Salty, the Hijacked Harbor Seal (TV) Show aired Dec. 17, 1972. Directed by Harry Tytle. A biologist helps save a young seal who was caught in a fishing net, but the seal hides in a small boat, not knowing that it is about to be towed far from the bay. The seal causes all sorts of trouble, until the biologist takes him back to the bay. Stars John Waugh, Doug Grey, Lance Rasmussen, Bud Sheble, Hal Stein.

Saludos Amigos (film) Animated feature film about Latin America, made up of 4 animated segments tied together by live-action footage of the activities of Walt Disney and his artists on their trip south of the border—and beyond. The segments are *Lake Titicaca*, chronicling Donald's exploration of the Andes; *Pedro*, the story of a baby airplane who replaces his father in getting the mail through; *Aquarela do Brasil*, with art showing the various landscapes of Brazil and José Carioca, the parrot, teaching Donald to dance the samba; and *El Gaucho Goofy*, in which American cowboy Goofy becomes a gaucho on the Argentine pampas, learning the routines through offstage narration. World premiere in Rio de Janeiro on Aug. 24, 1942; released in the U.S. Feb. 6, 1943. It was rereleased in 1949. Animation directed by Bill Roberts, Jack Kinney, Hamilton Luske, Wilfred Jackson. 42 min. While the film is shorter than a normal feature film, it has always been grouped with the Disney animated classic features. C. O. Slyfield received an Academy Award nomination for Best Sound, and additional nominations went to Charles Wolcott and Ned Washington for Best Song ("Saludos Amigos") and to Edward H. Plumb, Paul J. Smith, and Charles Wolcott for Best Scoring of a Musical Picture. Released on laser disc in 1995. See also THREE CABALLEROS, THE; SOUTH OF THE BORDER WITH DISNEY; AND WALT & EL GRUPO.

Salute to Alaska, A (TV) Show aired Apr. 2, 1967. Directed by Hamilton S. Luske, Ward Kimball. Celebrating Alaska's 100th birthday, Walt Disney looks at Alaska's past.

Salute to Father, A (TV) Show aired Jan. 22, 1961. Directed by Wolfgang Reitherman. Some reruns aired as *Goofy's Salute to Father*. Various Goofy cartoons, showing him as a father, are featured as Walt Disney dedicates the show to all fathers.

Sam Andreas Shakes Milkshake stand in Bountiful Valley Farm at Disney's California Adventure; opened Feb. 8, 2001. Closed Sep. 2010 to make way for Cars Land.

Samantha Who? (TV) Half-hour series on ABC; aired Oct. 15, 2007–Jul. 23, 2009. Following a hit-and-run accident that leaves her with amnesia, Sam Newly learns that she wasn't a particularly honest, good-hearted, or loving person in the past. She thus has a rare opportunity to start anew and rediscover who she really is. Stars Christina Applegate (Sam Newly), Jennifer Esposito (Andrea), Jean Smart (Regina). From Donald Todd Productions, Brillstein Entertainment Partners, and ABC Studios.

Sammy, the Way-Out Seal (TV) Two-part show; aired Oct. 28 and Nov. 4, 1962. Directed by Norman Tokar. Two brothers adopt an injured seal on their vacation and decide to bring it home. The seal wrecks an outdoor party and leaves a supermarket in complete disarray, which makes the boys decide that he has to go back to the ocean. Stars Michael McGreevey, Billy Mumy, Jack Carson, Robert Culp, Patricia Barry, Elisabeth Fraser, Ann Jilliann. Note that Ann Jilliann wears a Camp Inch sweatshirt, left over in the Studio's wardrobe department from *The Parent Trap*.

Samoa (film) People and Places featurette released Dec. 25, 1956. Directed by Ben Sharpsteen. Filmed in CinemaScope. 32 min. The story of a happy people on an island paradise begins with a description of life and cultural events in the communities. There are glimpses of fishing and local foods being prepared, and the building of a guesthouse (*fale tele*) is shown, with the resulting housewarming festivities climaxed by an evening *fia fia*, or happy time, including ritual dances.

Samoa Snacks Shop in Disney's Polynesian Resort at Walt Disney World; took the place of Trader Jack's Grog Hut. Closed Aug. 2014, to become Moana Mercantile.

Samurai Girl (TV) Three-part miniseries on ABC Family; premiered Sep. 5, 2008. A 19-year-old Japanese girl named Heaven discovers that the wealthy businessman who adopted her as an infant is really the head of the Yakuza, the Japanese mafia, and may have had her beloved brother brutally murdered. She breaks from her family and begins training to become a samurai, and with the help of a group of new American friends, sets out to take down her father's evil empire. Directed by Bryan Spicer. Stars Jamie Chung (Heaven Kogo), Brendan Fehr (Jake Stanton), Saige Thompson (Cheryl), Kyle Labine (Otto), Anthony Brandon Wong (Tasuke Kogo), Steven Brand (Severin), Kenneth Choi (Sato), Stacy Keibler (Linda). Filmed in Vancouver. Based on a series of popular young adult novels by Carrie Asai. From Big Light Prods., Space Floor, and Alloy Entertainment in association with ABC Studios.

San Angel Inn Restaurant in Mexico at EPCOT; opened Oct. 1, 1982. With an atmosphere similar to that of the Blue Bayou in Disneyland, set under a simulated evening sky, this attractive restaurant serves authentic Mexican food, much of which is unfamiliar to most Americans who are used to the Tex-Mex style. Over the years, dishes have included mole poblano (chicken covered in a sauce that adds chocolate and chiles) and pollo en pipian (chicken simmered in a pumpkin seed sauce). The restaurant is operated by the company that runs the San Angel Inn in Mexico City.

San Diego Zoo (film) Educational film in the EPCOT Educational Media Collection: Minnie's Science Field Trips series; released in Sep. 1988. 16 min. Behind the scenes at the world-renowned zoo.

San Fransokyo Square In 2022, it was announced Pacific Wharf at Disney California Adventure would be reimagined into San Fransokyo, the fictional setting (a mash-up of San Francisco and Tokyo) of *Big Hero 6*. The area is scheduled to debut summer 2023 with dining, shopping, and a place to meet Baymax. The area's landmark is the San Fransokyo Gate Bridge.

San Juan River Expedition (TV) Serial on the *Mickey Mouse Club* during the 1955–1956 season. Narrated by Alvy Moore. Directed by Al Teeter. Youngsters touring the San Juan River by boat learn about the Native Americans who used to live in the area, and the explorers who came later. 5 episodes.

Sanaa Restaurant at Disney's Animal Kingdom Villas—Kidani Village at Walt Disney World; opened May 1, 2009. The restaurant celebrates the art of African cooking with Indian flavors. From their table, guests are offered views of African wildlife on the Sunset Savanna outside. Inside, traditional artisan and market goods, including "love note" necklaces and beaded geckos, decorate the space. The nearby Sanaa Lounge offers appetizers and cocktails.

Sancho on the Rancho . . . and Elsewhere (TV) Show; part 1 of *Sancho, the Homing Steer*.

Sancho, the Homing Steer (TV) Two-part show; aired Jan. 21 and 28, 1962. Directed by Tom McGowan. The 2 episodes were titled *Sancho on the Rancho . . . and Elsewhere* and *The Perils of a Homesick Steer*. A pet steer, Sancho, is awkward to keep when it is full grown at the rancho, and he almost ruins a cattle drive. Sancho heads off toward home by himself, a journey of 1,200 miles, finding many obstacles along the way. Stars Bill Shurley, Rosita Fernandez, Arthur Curtis.

Sanctuary of Quasimodo, The SEE DISNEY VILLAINS (DISNEYLAND).

Sand Bar, The Rooftop pool bar at Disney's Paradise Pier Hotel at the Disneyland Resort; burgers, salads, and cocktails are served.

Sandberg, Sheryl Member of the Disney Board of Directors 2010–2018.

Sandcastle Club Children's care and activity center in Disney's Beach Club Resort at Walt Disney World; arts and crafts, video and board games, Disney movies, and meals were offered. Closed Jul. 31, 2018, to become a family activity area, the Seaside Retreat.

Sanders, Chris Animator/director; he began at Walt Disney Feature Animation as a story artist, contributing to *The Rescuers Down Under*, *Beauty and the Beast*, *Aladdin*, and *The Lion King*, and later wrote the screenplay for *Mulan*. He created and directed *Lilo & Stitch*, also providing the voice of Stitch. He left the company in 2006. Sanders later directed *The Call of the Wild* for 20th Century Studios.

Sanders, George (1906–1972) Actor; appeared in *In Search of the Castaways* (Thomas Ayerton), and voiced Shere Khan in *The Jungle Book*.

Sanders, Richie He voiced Toby Turtle in *Robin Hood*.

Sanderson, Adam He joined Disney in 1997 with Disney Channel marketing and later worked with franchise management at Disney•ABC Television Group. In Jan. 2014, he was named senior vice president of Corporate Communications, with one of his tasks being the administration of D23: The Official Disney Fan Club. He left the company in Mar. 2016.

Sandler, Adam Actor; appeared in *The Waterboy* (Bobby Boucher), *The Hot Chick* (uncredited bongo player), and *Bedtime Stories* (Skeeter Bronson), and guest starred on Disney Channel in *Jessie*.

Sands, Tommy Actor; appeared in *Babes in Toyland* (Tom Piper) and recorded the title song for *The Parent Trap* with Annette Funicello. TV appearances include *The Title Makers* and *Backstage Party*.

Sandy Cove Gifts and Sundries Shop in Disney's

Grand Floridian Resort & Spa at Walt Disney World; opened Jun. 28, 1988, offering souvenirs, postcards, luggage, and snacks.

Sandy in Disneyland (TV) Special taped in Disneyland aired Apr. 10, 1974. Directed by Marty Pasetta. Sandy Duncan visits Disneyland. Stars also Ernest Borgnine, Ruth Buzzi, Ted Knight, John Davidson, Lorne Greene, The Jackson 5, Kenny Loggins, Doc Severinsen.

Sanjay's Super Team (film) Animated short from Pixar Animation Studios. A young boy in India, bored with his father's meditation, dreams of Hindu gods as superheroes. Directed by Sanjay Patel. Released Nov. 25, 2015, with *The Good Dinosaur*, after premiering at the Annecy International Animation Film Festival in France Jun. 15, 2015. 7 min. Nominated for an Academy Award.

Santa Buddies (film) Direct-to-video release Nov. 24, 2009. When Puppy Paws, the feisty son of Santa Paws, forgets the true meaning of the season, it is up to the Buddies to remind him that the true meaning of Christmas spirit is about things you cannot wrap in a box or tie with a bow. Directed by Robert Vince. Stars Christopher Lloyd (Stan Cruge), Danny Woodburn (Eli), George Wendt (Santa Claus), and the voices of Field Cate (Buddha), Josh Flitter (Budderball), Skyler Gisondo (B-Dawg), Ty Panitz (Mudbud), Liliana Mumy (Rosebud), Tom Bosley (Santa Paws), Zachary Gordon (Puppy Paws), Richard Kind (Eddie the Elf Dog). 88 min. From Keystone Entertainment and Walt Disney Studios Home Entertainment. Continues the Air Bud/Air Buddies franchise. *The Search for Santa Paws* (2010) is a prequel.

Santa Clause, The (film) Scott Calvin is a divorced father whose strained relationship with his 8-year-old son, Charlie, begins to mend only after a bizarre twist of fate transforms him into the new Santa. When the current Santa Claus falls off his roof on Christmas Eve, Scott dons Santa's suit, and soon he and his son are whisked off to the North Pole. The head elf, Bernard, tells Scott about the clause, a contract stating that whoever puts on the Santa suit must also take on all the responsibilities that go with the position. While Scott is not too thrilled, Charlie is overjoyed. Over 12 months, Scott puts on an enormous amount of weight and sprouts a full white beard, and when Christmas arrives, it becomes clear that Scott is the real Santa. Released Nov. 11, 1994. Directed by John Pasquin.

97 min. Stars Tim Allen (Scott Calvin), Judge Reinhold (Dr. Neal Miller), Wendy Crewson (Laura Calvin), David Krumholtz (Bernard), Peter Boyle (Mr. Whittle), Eric Lloyd (Charlie Calvin). For the elves, the filmmakers selected 125 children ranging in age from 2–13 years; but even though they happen to look like children, they are supposed to be hundreds of years old. Through makeup and "fat suits," Tim Allen changes from a 32- to a 53-inch waist during the course of the production. The film was shot on location in Oakville, Ontario, Canada, and at the Raleigh Studios in Hollywood.

Santa Clause 2, The (film) Scott Calvin has been Santa Claus for the past 8 years, and his loyal elves consider him the best Santa ever. Then he gets bad news: not only has his son, Charlie, landed on this year's "naughty" list, but if Scott doesn't marry by Christmas Eve, he'll stop being Santa forever. (It's right in his contract—the "Mrs. Clause.") Desperate, Scott turns to the elves' new invention, a machine that can replicate anything, to create Santa II, a toy version of himself, whom he leaves in charge. Things get worse when Santa II institutes some strange redefinitions of what's naughty and nice; and when Scott finally falls for a potential Mrs. Claus, she threatens to drive a wedge between him and Charlie. In a climactic battle pitting Santa, Charlie, the new Mrs. Claus, and the elves against Santa II and his army of tin soldiers, the future of Scott's family, the North Pole, and Christmas itself hang in the balance. Directed by Michael Lembeck. Released Nov. 1, 2002. Stars Tim Allen (Scott Calvin/Santa), Spencer Breslin (Curtis), Judge Reinhold (Neil Miller), Wendy Crewson (Laura Miller), Elizabeth Mitchell (Carol), David Krumholtz (Bernard), Eric Lloyd (Charlie Calvin), Liliana Mumy (Lucy Miller). 104 min.

Santa Clause 3, The: The Escape Clause (film) Scott Calvin, aka Santa, juggles a full house of family and the mischievous Jack Frost, who is trying to take over Santa's holiday. At the risk of giving away the secret location of the North Pole, Scott invites his in-laws to share in the holiday festivities and upcoming birth of baby Claus with expectant wife, Carol, aka Mrs. Claus. Along for the adventure are Scott's extended family—son Charlie; ex-wife Laura; her husband, Neil; and their daughter, Lucy—who, together with head elf Curtis, foil Jack Frost's crafty scheme to control the North Pole. Released Nov. 3, 2006. Directed by Michael Lembeck.

Stars Tim Allen (Santa/Scott Calvin), Elizabeth Mitchell (Mrs. Claus/Carol), Judge Reinhold (Neil Miller), Wendy Crewson (Laura Miller), Ann-Margret (Sylvia Newman), Alan Arkin (Bud Newman), Eric Lloyd (Charlie), Spencer Breslin (Curtis), Liliana Mumy (Lucy), Martin Short (Jack Frost). 92 min.

Santa Clauses, The (TV) A Disney+ original series from 20th Television; digitally premiered on Nov. 16, 2022. Scott Calvin is on the brink of his 65th birthday and realizing that he can't be Santa forever. He's suddenly starting to lose his Santa magic, and more importantly, he's got a family that could benefit from a life in the normal world, especially his 2 kids who have grown up at the North Pole. With a lot of elves, children, and family to please, Scott sets out to find a suitable replacement Santa while preparing his family for a new adventure in a life south of the Pole. Stars Tim Allen (Scott Calvin/Santa Claus), Elizabeth Mitchell (Carol/Mrs. Claus), Kal Penn (Simon Choksi), Elizabeth Allen-Dick (Sandra), Austin Kane (Cal), Rupali Redd (Grace Choksi), Devin Bright (Noel), Matilda Lawler (Betty).

Santa Fe and Disneyland Railroad Disneyland attraction; opened Jul. 17, 1955, with the name changing to Disneyland Railroad Oct. 1, 1974. SEE ALSO DISNEYLAND RAILROAD.

Santa Paws 2: The Santa Pups (film) Direct-to-Blu-ray release Nov. 20, 2012. When Mrs. Claus travels to Pineville, the playful Santa Pups (Hope, Jingle, Charity, and Noble) stow away on her sled. They begin granting joyful wishes to Pineville's boys and girls, but something goes terribly wrong—the Christmas spirit begins to disappear. The Santa Pups and Mrs. Claus must race to save Christmas around the world. Directed by Robert Vince. Stars Danny Woodburn (Eli), Cheryl Ladd (Mrs. Santa Claus), Kaitlyn Maher (Sarah Reynolds), Josh Feldman (Carter Reynolds), Richard Kind (voice of Eddy the Elf Dog). From Walt Disney Studios Home Entertainment. A sequel to *The Search for Santa Paws*.

Santa Rosa Seed and Supply Gardening shop in Bountiful Valley Farm at Disney's California Adventure; open Feb. 8, 2001–Sep. 2002 and succeeded by P. T. Flea Market.

Santa Who? (TV) A 2-hour movie on *The Wonderful World of Disney*; first aired Nov. 19, 2000. Two days before Christmas, Santa Claus accidentally falls out of his sleigh and develops amnesia. It is up to Santa's head elf, Max, to find the missing man and save Christmas. Directed by William Dear. Produced by Gleneagle Prods., in association with Hearst Entertainment, Inc. Stars Leslie Nielsen (Santa Claus), Steven Eckholdt (Peter Albright), Robyn Lively (Claire Dreyer), Tommy Davidson (Max), Max Morrow (Zack).

Santa's Toys (film) A 16-mm release title of the 1933 Silly Symphony cartoon *The Night Before Christmas*; released in Oct. 1974.

Santa's Workshop (film) Silly Symphony cartoon released Dec. 10, 1932. Directed by Wilfred Jackson. Santa is assisted by his elves in preparing for the famous sleigh ride on Christmas Eve. As the toys are finished, they come to life and march into Santa's big bag. Its sequel is *The Night Before Christmas* (1933).

Sarabi Simba's mother in *The Lion King*; voiced by Madge Sinclair.

Sarafina! (film) Set in turbulent South Africa, the movie tells of a young student in Soweto who is inspired by a teacher, Mary Masembuko, to take pride in herself and her heritage. When Mary is sent to prison for stepping outside the prescribed curriculum, Sarafina and her schoolmates must choose between violence and nonviolent means of protest. A school musical production celebrating the life of Nelson Mandela, with Sarafina in the lead, eventually does take place amid the burnt ruins of the schoolyard. Initial release on Sep. 18, 1992; general release on Sep. 25, 1992. Directed by Darrell James Roodt. A Hollywood Pictures film, in association with Miramax Films, Videovision Enterprises, Les Films Ariane, Vanguard Films, and the BBC. 101 min. Stars Whoopi Goldberg (Mary Masembuko), Miriam Makeba (Angelina), John Kani (school principal), Mbongeni Ngema (Sabela), Leleti Khumalo (Sarafina). Based on the play by Mbongeni Ngema. Filmed on location in Soweto, South Africa. The director's cut was released on laser disc, adding about 20 min. to the length.

Sarandon, Susan Actress; appeared in *Cradle Will Rock* (Margheritta Sarfatti), *Moonlight Mile* (JoJo Ross), and *Enchanted* (Queen Narissa). She voiced Miss Spider in *James and the Giant Peach*.

Saratoga Springs Resort & Spa, Disney's A

Disney Vacation Club resort at Walt Disney World; opened May 17, 2004, on the site of the former Disney Institute, with 184 units in 2004, expanding to 552 in early 2005. The architecture was inspired by the upstate New York country retreats of the late 1800s and designed around the themes of natural springs and Saratoga's tradition of horse racing. An expansion in 2007 resulted in a grand total of 828 vacation home units within 18 villa buildings. In 2009, the Treehouse Villas opened at the resort. Dining is offered at The Turf Club Bar & Grill, The Artist's Palette, and The Paddock Grill, with recreation at the High Rock Spring Pool and The Paddock Pool. Senses – A Disney Spa opened in 2013.

Sardinia (film) People and Places featurette released Feb. 15, 1956. Directed by Ben Sharpsteen. 30 min. A train ride takes the audience through the island's rugged countryside to see the Sardinian people of today. Their independence and self-reliance are emphasized. Sheep are tended and the treatment of their wool is depicted. A wedding and a funeral service are shown, as well as the annual "Ardia" festival with horsemen commemorating historical events.

Sarge's Surplus Hut Cars Land shop in Disney California Adventure; opened Jun. 15, 2012. *Cars* toys, apparel, and hats are sold in a Quonset hut.

Sartori, Mary Lynn Mouseketeer from the 1950s *Mickey Mouse Club* TV show. One of 2 Marys on the show; the other was Mary Espinosa. This was the only name duplication among the Mouseketeers.

Sasha Bird friend of Peter in *Peter and the Wolf*, represented by a flute.

Sassagoula Name of the river connecting Disney's Port Orleans Resort, Disney's Old Key West Resort, Disney's Saratoga Springs Resort & Spa, and Disney Springs at Walt Disney World. Nine 32-passenger and six 37-passenger motor launches make up the Sassagoula River Cruise fleet that transports guests.

Sassagoula Floatworks and Food Factory Food court at Disney's Port Orleans Resort – French Quarter at Walt Disney World; opened May 17, 1991. Giant Mardi Gras parade icons decorate the space.

Sassy's Preteen apparel and gift shop in the Lake Buena Vista Shopping Village at Walt Disney World; opened Dec. 1976, taking the place of the original Toys Fantastique. Closed Nov. 29, 1987, to become Team Mickey's Athletic Club.

Satellite-View of America SEE SPACE STATION X-1.

Satu'li Canteen Fast-casual eatery in Pandora – The World of Avatar at Disney's Animal Kingdom; opened May 27, 2017. Internationally inspired cuisine, vegetarian dishes, and libations are served. The restaurant is set in a Quonset-hut facility, which, as the story goes, was once a mess hall for the Resources Development Administration but is now operated by Alpha Centauri Expeditions.

Saturday Night at the Movies with Disney (TV) Series of 11 programs on NBC 1974–1977.

Saturdays (TV) Coming-of-age comedy series on Disney Channel; scheduled to premiere Mar. 24, 2023. Fourteen-year-old Paris Johnson and her best friends, Simone and Ari, hone their roller-skating skills on the cool parquet floor of Saturdays, a local skating rink in Chicago. Together, they form the We-B-Girlz skate crew and are determined to prove they have the hottest routines on the planet. Stars Danielle Jalade (Paris), Daria Johns (Simone Samson), Golden Brooks (Deb Johnson), Omar Gooding (Cal Johnson), Jermaine Harris (London Johnson), Peyton Basnight (Ari), Tim Johnson Jr. (Derek "D-Rok"). From Genius Entertainment and Disney Branded Television.

Savage, Ben Actor; appeared on TV as Cory Matthews, the title character in *Boy Meets World*, and later reprised the role in *Girl Meets World*. Guest appearances include *Shake It Up* (Andy Burns), *Criminal Minds* (Jason Gideon), and the *Radio Disney Music Awards*.

Savage, Brad Actor; appeared in *The Apple Dumpling Gang* (Clovis Bradley), *No Deposit, No Return* (Jay), and *Return from Witch Mountain* (Muscles), and on TV in *The Secret of Lost Valley* (Adam Harkness).

Savage Sam (film) In this sequel to *Old Yeller*, Travis, now 18, and Arliss, 12, are alone at the homestead while their parents are away. Bud Searcy arrives with Lisbeth, his 16-year-old daughter, to announce the presence of marauders in the vicinity while Arliss and his beloved dog, Savage Sam, a son of the famous hound dog, Old Yeller, are out hunting. Travis and Lisbeth locate him just as the raiders appear. The kids are taken prisoner, and the captors take off on their horses as they trek back to their distant village. Savage Sam, who had been knocked on the head and left for dead, regains consciousness. Though still injured, it is he who leads Beck Coates, the boys' uncle, and a party of men on the search for the kids. After a wild chase of several days' duration, Savage Sam leads the rescue party to where the warriors are camping out. And after a furious battle, Arliss, Travis, and Lisbeth are rescued. Released Jun. 1, 1963. Directed by Norman Tokar. 103 min. Stars Brian Keith (Uncle Beck), Tommy Kirk (Travis), Kevin Corcoran (Arliss), Dewey Martin (Lester White), Jeff York (Bud Searcy), Marta Kristen (Lisbeth Searcy). The film was based on Fred Gipson's book, but it was not as successful at the box office as its predecessor.

Saval, Dany Actress; appeared in *Moon Pilot* (Lyrae).

Save Our Squad with David Beckham (TV) Four-episode U.K. original docuseries; digitally released on Disney+ Nov. 9, 2022. A career that has taken David Beckham to the summit of world football is now heading back to its source: East London. Here, he joins up with the Westward Boys, a young, grassroots team that is at the bottom of its league. However, this isn't just any league; this is the same one that David played in as a young boy. David is going to have to draw on all of his years of experience in the game if he's going to stand a chance of saving them from relegation. From Twenty Twenty and Studio 99.

Save the Dog (TV) A Disney Channel Premiere Film; first aired Mar. 19, 1988. An out-of-work actress comes to her sick dog's rescue and gets her big break at the same time. 87 min. Stars Cindy Williams (Becky Dale), Tony Randall (Oliver Bishop), Katherine Helmond (Maude).

Saved by the Bell SEE GOOD MORNING, MISS BLISS (TV).

Saving Mr. Banks (film) Inspired by the story of how Walt Disney's famous classic motion picture, *Mary Poppins*, made it to the screen. In the film, Walt seeks to obtain the rights to the *Mary Poppins* books and comes upon a curmudgeonly, uncompromising writer, P. L. Travers, who has absolutely no intention of letting her beloved magical nanny get mauled by the Hollywood machine.

In 1961, she reluctantly agrees to go to Los Angeles to hear Disney's plans for the adaptation. Armed with imaginative storyboards and songs from the talented Sherman brothers, Walt launches an all-out onslaught on Mrs. Travers, but finds himself watching helplessly as she becomes increasingly immovable, and the possibility of obtaining the screen rights begins to move further away. When Walt realizes that there are ghosts that haunt her from her childhood in Queensland, Australia, he reaches into his own childhood to find a solution. Directed by John Lee Hancock. Limited release Dec. 13, 2013, with a general release Dec. 20, after a release in the United Kingdom Nov. 29. Stars Tom Hanks (Walt Disney), Emma Thompson (P. L. Travers), Bradley Whitford (Don DaGradi), Jason Schwartzman (Richard Sherman), B. J. Novak (Robert Sherman), Kathy Baker (Tommie), Paul Giamatti (Ralph), Colin Farrell (Travers Goff), Ruth Wilson (Margaret Goff). 125 min. Filming took place in Burbank, Los Angeles, and Disneyland. Filmed in CinemaScope. Nominated for an Academy Award for Music (Original Score). The Walt Disney Archives was consulted throughout the film's development and provided a wealth of reference material, although the film is a dramatization and not a precise historical account.

Saving Mr. Banks: The Untold Story of a Hollywood Classic (TV) Half-hour special on ABC; aired Jan. 11, 2014. Interviews with Richard Sherman, Julie Andrews, cast members, and production staff are included, along with film clips, to tell the story of the motion picture.

Savi's Workshop – Handbuilt Lightsabers Shop in Star Wars: Galaxy's Edge; opened May 31, 2019, in Disneyland and Aug. 29, 2019, in Disney's Hollywood Studios at Walt Disney World. In a covert workshop, guests can customize their own lightsaber and bring it to life through the power of kyber crystals.

Sawyer, Diane Broadcast journalist; joined ABC as co-anchor of *Primetime Live* with Sam Donaldson in 1989 and became co-anchor of *Good Morning America* in 1999. She hosted *World News* Dec. 2009–Aug. 2014 and stayed on with ABC News to provide original reporting. She was named a Disney Legend in 2019.

Sayers, Jack (1914–1986) He joined Disney in 1955 as director of customer relations for Disneyland. He served as chairman of the Park Operating

Committee 1956–1959, and then became director, and later vice president, of Lessee Relations, a group later known as Corporate Alliances. He was instrumental in the development of Walt Disney World. He retired in 1975.

Scamp One of Lady and Tramp's puppies in *Lady and the Tramp*. He first appeared in comic strips in the *Treasury of Classic Tales Lady and the Tramp* strip for Jul. 10, 1955. His own daily strip began Oct. 31, 1955, and the Sunday color page began Jan. 15, 1956. The character is not named in the original film.

Scandal (TV) Drama series on ABC; aired Apr. 5, 2012–Apr. 19, 2018. Olivia Pope, a prominent crisis manager, has dedicated her life to protecting and defending the public images of the nation's elite and keeping their secrets under wraps. A former communications director to the president of the U.S., she has opened her own firm, but while she and her dysfunctional staff can fix other people's lives, they cannot quite fix their own. Stars Kerry Washington (Olivia Pope), Henry Ian Cusick (Stephen Finch), Columbus Short (Harrison Wright), Guillermo Diaz (Huck), Darby Stanchfield (Abby Whelan), Katie Lowes (Quinn Perkins), Tony Goldwyn (Fitzgerald Grant), Jeff Perry (Cyrus Beene). From ABC Studios.

Scandalous John (film) In modern times, a ripsnorting, 79-year-old western rancher, with the loveliest granddaughter, ugliest horse, scrawniest herd, and puniest partner (a handyman named Paco), go on a cattle drive (of one cow) and do battle against a wealthy, land-grabbing industrialist. After an adventurous (and humorous) trek, à la Don Quixote, the rancher confronts the villain in a shoot-out that parallels the classic struggle of good and evil in the Old West. Released Jun. 22, 1971 (a rather limited release; it never played New York City). Directed by Robert Butler. Filmed in CinemaScope. 114 min. Stars Brian Keith (John McCanless), Alfonso Arau (Paco), Michele Carey (Amanda), Rick Lenz (Jimmy), Harry Morgan (Hector Pippin), Simon Oakland (Whitaker), Bill Williams (Sheriff Hart), John Ritter (Wendell). The film was based on the book by Richard Gardner. Rod McKuen composed the musical score and sang the theme song, "Pastures Green," which interprets the hero's love of open land. Location scenes were filmed in Alamogordo, White Sands National Monument, and near Las Cruces (all in New Mexico); at the western town of Old Tucson, Arizona; and along the 10-mile route of an 1880-period train from Hill City to Keystone, South Dakota.

Scar Simba's villainous uncle, a lion, in *The Lion King*; voiced by Jeremy Irons.

Scarcity and Planning (film) Educational film from The People on Market Street series, produced by Terry Kahn; released in Sep. 1977. Economic concepts of scarcity and planning are explored using the visit of a man and his wife to a clinic as an example.

Scarecrow of Romney Marsh, The (TV) Three-part show; aired Feb. 9, 16, and 23, 1964. Directed by James Neilson. Adapted from the book *Christopher Syn* by Russell Thorndike and William Buchanan. The adventures of a disguised vicar who fights for justice in 18th-century England. The people in Kent and Sussex have turned to smuggling to get around unjust and heavy import taxes. The Vicar of Dymchurch disguises himself as a scarecrow to help the people against the king's men, eventually aided by one of the royal officers. Stars Patrick McGoohan, George Cole, Tony Britton, Michael Hordern, Geoffrey Keen, Kay Walsh, Sean Scully. Filmed on location in England, including the actual Romney Marsh. A theatrical version was called *Dr. Syn, Alias the Scarecrow*.

Scariest Story Ever, The: A Mickey Mouse Halloween Spooktacular (TV) Animated special; aired Oct. 8, 2017, on Disney Channel. Mickey is challenged to tell a scary story on Halloween night. His stories are mostly fun and silly, until he is finally pushed to tell a truly terrifying tale. Voices include Chris Diamantopoulos (Mickey), Tony Anselmo (Donald), Tress MacNeille (Daisy), Bill Farmer (Goofy), Russi Taylor (Minnie/Huey/Dewey/Louie). Emmy Award winner for Individual Achievement in Animation.

Scarlet Letter, The (film) A retelling of Nathaniel Hawthorne's timeless classic. Set in puritanical 17th-century Boston, this romantic drama follows the sensational life of a bright and beautiful woman who becomes a social outcast when she bears the child of a respected reverend and refuses to divulge the name of the father. Shunned by the townspeople for her indiscretion and threatened with the loss of her child, she bravely bears the mark of disgrace—a scarlet "A"—until a conflict with Algonquian warriors unites the Puritans and causes them to reevaluate their attitudes and laws. Directed by Roland Joffe. A Hollywood Pictures film. Released Oct. 13, 1995. Stars Demi Moore (Hester Prynne), Gary Oldman (Rev. Arthur Dimmesdale), Robert Duvall

(Roger Prynne). 135 min. The production was filmed on Vancouver Island, British Columbia, and in Shelburne, Nova Scotia (both in Canada), where a small maritime fishing village was turned into a replica of 17th-century New England. Filmed in CinemaScope.

Scat Cat Leader of the jazz band of cats in *The Aristocats*; voiced by Scatman Crothers.

Scat Cat's Club Jazz lounge in Disney's Port Orleans Resort – French Quarter; opened May 17, 1991, offering beignets and Big Easy–inspired cocktails.

Scenes from a Mall (film) A modern couple—she, Deborah, a successful psychologist who has recently written a best-selling book on marriage, and he, Nick, a high-powered sports lawyer—embark on their 16th wedding anniversary by going to the local mall for party supplies. Nick decides to put his wife's modern mating theories to the test by revealing that he has just ended a 6-month affair with a younger woman. Deborah, shocked and hostile, parries with some equally astonishing revelations of her own. The twin true confessions lead to a major verbal battle, until the underlying love the couple has for each other wins out. Released Feb. 22, 1991. Directed by Paul Mazursky. A Touchstone film. 87 min. Stars Bette Midler (Deborah), Woody Allen (Nick), Bill Irwin (Mime). Filmed on location at Stamford Town Center in Stamford, Connecticut, and at the Beverly Center in Los Angeles. A 2-story reproduction of the Stamford mall was also created on a huge soundstage at Kaufman Astoria Studios in New York City, since it was determined that it would be impossible to shoot the entire film in a mall that was open for business.

Schake, Kristina She joined The Walt Disney Company in Apr. 2022 as executive vice president, Global Communications, then was appointed senior executive vice president and chief communications officer in Jun., overseeing worldwide communications strategy and operations, and serving as lead spokesperson for the company.

Schallert, William (1922–2016) Actor; appeared as Professor Quigley in *The Computer Wore Tennis Shoes* and *The Strongest Man in the World*; on TV in *Elfego Baca* (Deputy Sheriff Denbigh) and *The Torkelsons* (Wesley Hodges); and guest starred in *The Suite Life of Zack & Cody*, *Desperate Housewives*, and *According to Jim*.

Scheider, Roy (1932–2008) Actor; appeared in *Tiger Town* (Billy Young).

Schell, Maximilian (1930–2014) Actor; appeared in *The Black Hole* (Dr. Hans Reinhardt) and *A Far Off Place* (Col. Mopani Theron).

Schell, Ronnie Actor; appeared in *The Strongest Man in the World* (referee), *Gus* (Joe Barnsdale), *The Shaggy D.A.* (TV director), *The Cat from Outer Space* (Sgt. Duffy), and *The Devil and Max Devlin* (Greg Weems), and on TV in *The Mouseketeers at Walt Disney World* (Mr. Brown) and *The Whiz Kid and the Carnival Caper* (Deputy Scruff), plus made guest appearances in *Empty Nest*, *The Golden Girls*, *Phil of the Future*, *Jessie*, *Kraft Salutes Disneyland's 25th Anniversary*, and *Mickey's 50*. He also voiced Mayor Fitzhugh in *Disney's Recess*.

Scheme of Things, The (TV) Series on The Disney Channel; debuted Apr. 18, 1983, hosted by James MacArthur and Mark Shaw. Examines the world of science. 65 episodes.

Schiffer, Bob (1916–2005) Makeup artist; joined Disney in 1968 after a successful career at MGM and other studios, and was in charge of makeup for almost every subsequent Disney feature into the 1980s. He retired in 2001 and was named a Disney Legend in 2007.

Schmid Bros., Inc. Licensee of collectible Disney merchandise, often dated or limited-edition items, beginning in 1970. Their series of Christmas plates, first sold in 1973, have become popular, with the first one bringing several hundreds of dollars. Through Hudson Pewter they also distributed a series of popular pewter figures. When the Walt Disney Classics Collection was begun in the 1990s, Schmid was chosen to handle the distribution, a relationship which continued until 1995.

Schmoozies! Hollywood Land counter-service restaurant offering smoothies, juices, coffees, and teas in Disney California Adventure; opened Feb. 8, 2001.

Schneider, Peter He joined Disney in 1985 as vice president of Feature Animation and was promoted to president in 1992, playing a key role in the revitalization of the division. He was named president of The Walt Disney Studios in Jan. 1999 and chairman in Jan. 2000, adding other Disney-branded films, TV, and park entertainment to his responsibilities. He left the company in Jun. 2001.

Schneider, Rob Actor; appeared in *Judge Dredd* (Fergie), *The Waterboy* (Townie), *The Hot Chick* (Clive), *Around the World in 80 Days* (San Francisco hobo), and as the title character in *Deuce Bigalow: Male Gigolo*. He made an uncredited appearance as a robber in *Bedtime Stories*.

School Hero (A Story About Staying in School) (film) Educational film in the EPCOT Educational Media Collection; released in Aug. 1988. 20 min. A custodian impresses upon a student the importance of sticking with school.

Schooled (TV) Comedy series on ABC; aired Jan. 9, 2019–May 13, 2020. At William Penn (WP) Academy, new music teacher and WP graduate Lainey Lewis, Principal Glascott, Coach Mellor, and super-teacher Charlie Brown all have their eccentricities and crazy personal lives, but they are heroes to their students. Set in the 1990s. Stars AJ Michalka (Lainey Lewis), Tim Meadows (Principal Glascott), Bryan Callen (Coach Mellor), Brett Dier (Charlie Brown). From Sony Pictures Television and ABC Studios.

Schroeder, Russell Disney artist; began at Walt Disney World in 1971, eventually moving into Marketing Art as a character artist. Later he joined Disney Publishing in California overseeing character art for Disney books. He has written and illustrated a number of books and comic books, including *Mickey Mouse: My Life in Pictures*, *Walt Disney: His Life in Pictures, Disney: The Ultimate Visual Guide*, and *Disney's Lost Chords*, vol. 1–3.

Schuck, John Actor; appeared in *Outrageous Fortune* (Atkins), *Dick Tracy* (reporter), and *Holy Matrimony* (Markowski), and on TV in *Zeke and Luther* (Carl).

Schuks! Pay Back the Money! (film) Hidden-camera comedy produced in South Africa. Responsible for the loss of rugby's holy grail, the Currie Cup, Schuks sets off on a journey to pay for what he has done. In lieu of an R1 million fine (1 million South African rands), he is offered a lifeline to create a reality film—one that ultimately plays pranks on unsuspecting locals and a host of famous personalities. Directed by Gray Hofmeyr. Released Aug. 28, 2015, in South Africa. Stars Leon Schuster (Schuks), Desmond Dube (Minister), Gerrit Schoonhoven (Savage), Ivan Lucas (Bossie), Lionel Newton (Pawnbroker). 89 min. From Touchstone Pictures. A follow-up to *Schuks! Your Country Needs You.*

Schuks! Your Country Needs You (film) Hidden-camera comedy produced in South Africa. Leon Schuster pranks unsuspecting everyday victims and famous faces using hidden cameras. Directed by Gray Hofmeyr. Released Nov. 29, 2013, in South Africa. Stars Leon Schuster (Schuks), Rob van Vuuren (Wayne), Alfred Ntombela (Shorty), Laré Birk (as herself). 97 min. From Touchstone Pictures.

Schumacher, Thomas He joined Disney in 1988 as producer of *The Rescuers Down Under* and later was exec. producer of *The Lion King*. He played a key role in revitalizing Walt Disney Feature Animation as exec. vice president, while co-leading Walt Disney Theatrical Productions. In Jan. 1999, he was promoted to president of Feature Animation, Walt Disney Television Animation, and Buena Vista Theatrical Group (later Disney Theatrical Group). He left animation in 2003 to concentrate on Disney's live stage entertainment, including Broadway, touring, and licensed productions. Also exec. producer on *Beauty and the Beast* (2017), *The Lion King* (2019), and, for TV, *Freaky Friday* (2018).

Schumann China Corp. One of the earliest of the Disney licensees, the company had a license 1932–1934 to sell Disney chinaware they had manufactured in Germany's Bavaria. These early dishes are quite a collector's item today.

Schwartz, Ben Actor; appeared on Disney+ in *Flora & Ulysses* (George) and *Earth to Ned*. He voiced Dewey in *DuckTales* (2017), Rilo in *Tron: Uprising*, the title character in *Randy Cunningham: 9th Grade Ninja*, TAY-0 in *Star Wars: The Bad Batch*, and Lou Tarleton in *Marvel's M.O.D.O.K.*

Schwartz, Stephen Lyricist; wrote the words for the songs in *Pocahontas*, *The Hunchback of Notre Dame*, *Enchanted*, and *Disenchanted*. For TV, he wrote the songs for *Geppetto* and the theme song for *Johnny and the Sprites*.

Schwartzman, Jason Actor; appeared in *Rushmore* (Max Fischer), *Shopgirl* (Jeremy), and *Saving Mr. Banks* (Richard Sherman), and on Disney+ in *Prop Culture*.

Schwarzenegger, Arnold Actor; appeared in *Around the World in 80 Days* (Prince Hapi).

Science Behind Pixar, The Interactive exhibit which premiered at the Museum of Science in Boston on Jun. 28, 2015. The 10,000-sq.-ft. exhibit showcases the science, engineering, technology, and mathematical concepts used by the artists and computer scientists at Pixar in making their award-winning animated films.

Sci-Fi Dine-In Theater Restaurant Establishment on Commissary Lane in Disney's Hollywood Studios; opened Apr. 20, 1991, re-creating a 1950s drive-in theater. Guests sit in pseudo-convertibles under an evening sky facing a huge drive-in movie screen on which clips of sci-fi trailers and intermission animation are shown.

Scotland (film) People and Places featurette released Jun. 11, 1958. Directed by Geoffrey Foot. Scotland is a country of 3 distinct regions—the Highlands, the Islands, and the Lowlands. These regions are examined, showing how the isolated people contact the outside world with their use of channel boats called "Puffers," how they observe the customs of the seasons, and how the various clans and regiments celebrate their history at the Edinburgh Festival. Filmed in CinemaScope. 25 min.

Scott, Bronson The youngest Mouseketeer from the 1950s *Mickey Mouse Club* TV show.

Scott, George C. (1927–1999) Actor; voiced Percival McLeach in *The Rescuers Down Under* and appeared in *The Whipping Boy* on The Disney Channel.

Scott (Worcester), Retta (1916–1990) The first woman animator at the Disney Studio, first receiving screen credit on *Bambi*. After 6 years at the Studio, she left Disney, but continued to illustrate Disney books as a freelance artist. She was named a Disney Legend posthumously in 2000.

Scoundrels (TV) Hour-long drama series on ABC; aired Jun. 20–Aug. 15, 2010. The West family is forced to change their lifestyle after the man of the house gets sent to jail. Cheryl, the loving mother and devoted wife, will do everything to keep her family together and on the straight and narrow. Stars Virginia Madsen (Cheryl West), David James Elliott (Wolfgang "Wolf" West), Patrick Flueger (Logan West/Calvin West), Leven Rambin (Heather West), Vanessa Marano (Hope West), Carlos Bernard (Sergeant Mack). Based on a New Zealand series entitled *Outrageous Fortune*. From ABC Studios.

Scream Team, The (TV) A Disney Channel Original Movie; first aired Oct. 4, 2002. With Halloween looming, teenagers Ian and Claire Carlyle accompany their father to his childhood home of Steeple Falls for their grandfather's funeral. The kids make a startling discovery that ghosts flock to the town as it is a "soul processing center," and an angry spirit won't allow their late grandfather's soul to rest. Soon, the siblings get some supernatural help from a trio of bumbling, yet well-meaning spirits, The Scream Team, who are assigned to police the district. Directed by Stuart Gillard. Stars Tommy Davidson (Jumper), Kathy Najimy (Mariah), Eric Idle (Coffin Ed), Mark Rendall (Ian), Kat Dennings (Claire), Kim Coates (Zachariah Kull), Robert Bockstael (Richard Carlyle), Nigel Bennett (Warner MacDonald), Gary Reineke (Grandpa Frank).

Screen Door General Store Shop on Disney's BoardWalk at Walt Disney World; opened Jul. 1, 1996, offering snacks and spirits.

Scrooge McDuck Donald Duck's popular rich uncle; created by Carl Barks in a 1947 comic book story, "Christmas on Bear Mountain," and soon starred in his own comic series. He went on to star in the films *Scrooge McDuck and Money* and *Mickey's Christmas Carol*, and the TV series, *DuckTales*.

Scrooge McDuck and Money (film) Special cartoon featurette released Mar. 23, 1967. Directed by Hamilton Luske. Scrooge McDuck is visited by his nephews, who wish to become as wealthy as their uncle. In an illustrated lecture, punctuated by song, Scrooge tells about the history of money, and explains how budgeting works, for both home and country. He says money should be wisely invested and should circulate. And he charges his nephews 3¢ for this good advice, "for nothing good is ever free." This was Scrooge McDuck's theatrical debut. 17 min.

Scrubs (TV) Half-hour series on NBC; premiered Sep. 25, 2001. A new doctor and his fellow first-year medical interns navigate the transition from medical school to practicing in a busy teaching hospital, with the help and sometimes hindrance of 2 seasoned doctors and a sympathetic nurse. Stars Zach Braff (John "J. D." Dorian), Sarah Chalke (Elliot Reid), Donald

Faison (Chris Turk), Ken Jenkins (Dr. Bob Kelso), John C. McGinley (Dr. Perry Cox), Judy Reyes (Carla Espinosa). From Touchstone Television. The show ended on NBC May 8, 2008, and moved to ABC beginning Jan. 6, 2009. In 2010, the locale of the series switched from a hospital to a medical school. The series ended Mar. 17, 2010.

Scully, Sean Actor; appeared in *Almost Angels* (Peter Schaefer), and on TV in *The Prince and the Pauper* (both title roles) and *The Scarecrow of Romney Marsh* (John Banks).

Scuttle Seagull in *The Little Mermaid* who shows off to Ariel his false knowledge of humans; voiced by Buddy Hackett.

Scuttle's Landing Fantasyland pavilion serving shave ice, beverages, and snacks in the Magic Kingdom at Walt Disney World; opened 1998, replacing The Little Big Top. Closed Apr. 11, 2010, to make way for the New Fantasyland.

Scuttle's Scooters Attraction in Mermaid Lagoon at Tokyo DisneySea; opened Sep. 4, 2001. Guests ride in comical hermit crab vehicles.

Sea of Sharks (TV) The mysteries of the volcanic islands of the Pacific, home to a rich panoply of marine life, including the giant manta ray, green turtle, humpback whale, and the shark, are plumbed in this New True-Life Adventure documentary. Produced by Pete Zuccarini. Aired in syn. beginning Jul. 24, 2000.

Sea Salts (film) Donald Duck cartoon released Apr. 8, 1949. Directed by Jack Hannah. Bootle Beetle reminisces about his relationship with Donald through the years, including the time they were shipwrecked and the time the Duck cheated him out of a soda.

Sea Scouts (film) Donald Duck cartoon released Jun. 30, 1939. The first cartoon directed by Dick Lundy. Donald is an admiral on a seagoing voyage with his nephews in which they encounter a ravenous shark.

Seal Island (film) The first True-Life Adventure featurette. The fur seals arrive on the fogbound islands known as the Pribilofs to mate and bear pups. The young "bachelors" challenge the older bulls for their harems of females, which results in a terrific fight. In the fall, the herd sets out on a long migration into the Pacific Ocean to spend the winter. Initial release on Dec. 21, 1948; general release on May 4, 1949. Directed by James Algar. 27 min. Alfred and Elma Milotte shot the fascinating footage that formed the beginning of the True-Life Adventure series. Walt Disney had hired them to do some filming for him in Alaska, but as he studied the footage they sent back to the Studio, he zeroed in on the seal footage as having the most promise. He asked them to emphasize the life cycle of the seals, and not show any indication of human presence. The resulting film did not appeal to RKO, the Disney distributor, who felt that no one would want to sit in a theater for a half hour watching a nature film, so Walt had a friend of his, who ran the Crown Theater in Pasadena, run the film for a week in order to qualify for an Academy Award. Sure enough, it won the award for Best Documentary. According to legend, Walt took the Oscar down to Roy Disney's office and said, "Here, Roy, take this over to RKO and bang them over the head with it." As one could expect, RKO was soon clamoring for more True-Life Adventure films.

Seale, Douglas (1913–1999) He voiced Krebbs in *The Rescuers Down Under* and the Sultan in *Aladdin*, and appeared in *Ernest Saves Christmas* (Santa) and *Mr. Destiny* (Boswell).

Search for Santa Paws, The (film) Direct-to-video release Nov. 23, 2010. When Santa and his new best friend, Paws, discover that the boys and girls of the world have lost the spirit of the season, they take a trip to New York City. But after Santa loses his memory, it is up to Paws, a faithful orphan named Quinn, her new friend Will, and a wonderful group of elves and magical talking dogs to save St. Nick and show the world what Christmas is really about. Directed by Robert Vince. Stars Kaitlyn Maher (Quinn), Richard Riehle (Santa Claus), Patrika Darbo (Mrs. Claus), Madison Pettis (Willamina), Danny Woodburn (Eli), Richard Kind (Eddy); and with the voices of Zachary Gordon (Santa Paws), Josh Flitter (T-Money), Diedrich Bader (Comet). A prequel to 2009's *Santa Buddies*.

Searcher Clade A family man who finds himself on an unpredictable mission in *Strange World*; voiced by Jake Gyllenhaal.

Searching for Nature's Mysteries (TV) Show aired Sep. 26, 1956. Directed by Winston Hibler. Hibler describes the cameras and special techniques developed for nature photography, illustrating his points with segments from the True-Life Adventure series.

Searchlight Pictures Specialty film company founded in 1994 as Fox Searchlight Pictures, which both finances and acquires motion pictures. It became part of The Walt Disney Studios with the 2019 acquisition of 21st Century Fox. FOR A LIST OF FILMS RELEASED SINCE THE DISNEY ACQUISITION, SEE 21ST CENTURY FOX.

Sears, Ted (1900–1958) Starting in animation at the Disney Studio in 1931, he became the first head of the Story Department, working on the features from *Snow White and the Seven Dwarfs* to *Sleeping Beauty*.

Seas, The (film) Preshow in The Living Seas at EPCOT Center; played Jan. 15, 1986–2005. The dramatic story of the ocean's origins and mysterious depths. Directed by Paul Gerber.

Seas with Nemo & Friends, The SEE LIVING SEAS, THE.

Seashore Sweets Old-fashioned, Atlantic shore–style candy shop on Disney's BoardWalk at Walt Disney World; opened Jul. 1, 1996. Closed Jan. 31, 2016, to become AbracadaBar. The fictional proprietors were the Sweet Sisters.

Seaside Souvenirs Shop in Paradise Gardens Park at Disney California Adventure; opened May 2011, taking the place of Souvenir 66. Inspired by classic souvenir stands of the 1930s.

Seasons of the Vine (film) Attraction in the Golden Vine Winery in Disney California Adventure; open Feb. 8, 2001–Mar. 30, 2008. Guests viewed a film about wine making, from spring vine cutting to bountiful harvest. Narrated by Jeremy Irons. The film was later screened occasionally at the EPCOT International Food & Wine Festival.

Sebastian Crab who is court composer and serves at King Triton's bidding in *The Little Mermaid*; voiced by Samuel E. Wright. The crab's full name is Horatio Thelonious Ignacious Crustaceous Sebastian.

Sebastian's Bistro Casual table-service restaurant in Disney's Caribbean Beach Resort at Walt Disney World; opened Oct. 8, 2018, in Old Port Royale. Surf-and-turf meals with Latin and Caribbean flavors are served.

Sebastian's Calypso Kitchen Counter-service restaurant in Mermaid Lagoon at Tokyo DisneySea; opened Sep. 4, 2001. The walls are filled of pictures of Sebastian's ocean friends.

Second Star to the Right, The Song from *Peter Pan*; written by Sammy Cahn and Sammy Fain.

Secret Bodyguard (TV) Serial on the *Mickey Mouse Club* on The Disney Channel beginning on Sep. 9, 1991. A wealthy father is protective of his daughter, who is entering a regular high school for the first time, so he hires a teenage martial arts expert to be her bodyguard (without her being aware of it). Stars Ernie Reyes, Jr. (Ernie), Heather Campbell (Brittany Belmont), Stephen Burton (Rick), Johnny Moran (Kevin), James O'Sullivan (Mr. Belmont).

Secret Invasion (TV) Series planned for digital release on Disney+ in 2023. A faction of shapeshifting Skrulls has infiltrated every level of life on Earth. The series marks the return of Nick Fury and Talos, who first met in *Captain Marvel*. Stars Samuel L. Jackson (Nick Fury), Ben Mendelsohn (Talos). From Marvel Studios.

Secret Lab, The SEE DREAM QUEST IMAGES.

Secret Mission (TV) Show; part 1 of *Andrew's Raiders*.

Secret of Boyne Castle, The (TV) Three-part show; aired Feb. 9, 16, and 23, 1969. A later rerun was under the title *Spy-Busters*. Directed by Robert Butler. A young American studying in Ireland, Rich Evans, becomes involved with Russian agents and a defecting scientist, after he hears a warning from a dying man. It seems that Rich's brother, Tom, is an American agent trying to meet a defecting scientist, and the Russians are trying to stop the meeting before it happens. Stars Glenn Corbett, Kurt Russell, Alfred Burke, Patrick Dawson, Patrick Barr, Hugh McDermott. Released theatrically abroad as *Guns in the Heather*.

Secret of Lost Creek, The (TV) Serial on the *Mickey Mouse Club* on The Disney Channel; aired Oct. 30–Nov. 27, 1989. Two kids, Jeannie Fogle and her brother Robert, reluctantly go to visit their grandparents for the summer in the High Sierra town of Lost Creek. Jeannie digs up a story about a lost treasure and is soon involved in intrigue about an illegal mining operation. Stars Shannen Doherty (Jeannie), Scott Bremner (Robert), Jody Montana (Travis), Dabbs Greer (Grandpa).

Secret of Lost Valley, The (TV) Two-part show; aired Apr. 27 and May 4, 1980. Directed by Vic Morrow. While on a family outing, a boy, Adam, gets lost in the forest and discovers a wild boy there. Communicating by sign language, they become friends. When the wild boy is captured by scientists, Adam helps him escape. Stars Gary Collins, Mary Ann Mobley, Brad Savage, Eddie Marquez, Tom Simcox, Barry Sullivan, Jackson Bostwick, John Lupton.

Secret of Mystery Lake, The (TV) Serial on the *Mickey Mouse Club* during the 1956–1957 season. Directed by Larry Lansburgh. A naturalist finds a mystery when he goes to study a remote swamp area of northeastern Tennessee. Stars George Fenneman, Gloria Marshall, Bogue Bell, R. P. Alexander. 7 episodes.

Secret of Old Glory Mine, The (TV) Show aired Oct. 31, 1976. Directed by Fred R. Krug. An old prospector, Charlie, living alone with his burro in Arizona tries to keep a rich silver vein a secret. He takes out only enough to pay his expenses. When another miner arrives, Charlie tries to dissuade him from finding the vein, but when he saves Charlie's life, the 2 decide to share the secret. Stars Rowan Pease, Barry Dowell.

Secret of the Magic Gourd, The (film) A young boy named Wang Bao finds a gourd with magical powers but discovers that its power to fulfill his wishes comes at a great price—everything the gourd helps him obtain is taken away from its rightful owner. He eventually learns that working hard is the only way to earn the things that truly matter. A joint venture between Buena Vista International, Centro Digital Pictures Ltd. of Hong Kong, and the China Film Group Corporation. The film had its premiere in Beijing on Jun. 29, 2007. Directed by John Chu and Frankie Chung. The first Disney co-production in China, in the Mandarin language. Adapted from a 1958 novel by Zhang Tian Yi. The film was released on DVD in the U.S. in 2009, with an English-language soundtrack featuring the voices of Drake Johnston, Takayo Fischer, Megan Hilty, Aaron Drozin, Grace Fulton, Josh Reames, Jeremy Shada, Corbin Bleu (the Magic Gourd).

Secret of the Pond, The (TV) Two-part show; aired Oct. 5 and 12, 1975. Directed by Robert Day. A spoiled city boy, Joey, doesn't know the ways of the backwaters of Virginia when he goes there on vacation. He makes friends with 2 local boys whose alcohol-addicted father is secretly poaching alligators. Stars Anthony Zerbe, Ike Eisenmann, Eric Shea, John McLiam, Moses Gunn, Rex Corley.

Secret of the Wings (film) In this animated feature, Tinker Bell and her fairy friends journey into the forbidden world of the mysterious Winter Woods, where curiosity and adventure lead Tink to an amazing discovery and reveal a magical secret that could change her world forever. Released Aug. 31, 2012, in an exclusive engagement at the El Capitan Theatre in Hollywood, after earlier international releases beginning Aug. 17, 2012, in Turkey. Released on DVD and Blu-ray on Oct. 23. Directed by Peggy Holmes and Bobs Gannaway. Working title was *Tinker Bell and the Mysterious Winter Woods*. Voices include Mae Whitman (Tinker Bell), Lucy Hale (Periwinkle), Lucy Liu (Silvermist), Megan Hilty (Rosetta), Anjelica Huston (Queen Clarion), Jesse McCartney (Terence), Raven-Simoné (Iridessa), Timothy Dalton (Lord Milori), Matt Lanter (Sled). Produced by DisneyToon Studios.

Secret Society of Second-Born Royals (TV) A Disney+ original film; digitally released Sep. 25, 2020. Sam, a teenage royal rebel, is second in line to the throne of the kingdom of Illyria. Just as her disinterest in the royal way of life is at an all-time high, she discovers she has superhuman abilities and is invited to join a secret society of similar extraordinary second-born royals charged with keeping the world safe. With guidance from their Secret Society instructor, James, Sam, and a new class of royal recruits must first learn to harness their new powers at a top secret training camp before they can save the world. Directed by Anna Mastro. Stars Peyton Elizabeth Lee (Sam), Niles Fitch (Prince Tuma), Isabella Blake Thomas (January), Olivia Deeble (Roxana), Noah Lomax (Mike), Faly Rakotohavana (Matteo), Ashley Liao (Eleanor), Greg Bryk (Inmate 34), Elodie Yung (Queen Catherine), Skylar Astin (James). 97 min. From Gulfstream Pictures, Maple Plus Productions, and Disney Channel.

Secret World of Arrietty, The (film) Residing beneath the floorboards are little people who live undetected in a secret world. Arrietty, a tiny but tenacious 14-year-old, lives with her parents in the recesses of a suburban garden home, unbeknownst to the homeowner and her housekeeper. Like all little people, Arrietty remains hidden from view, except during occasional covert ventures beyond the floorboards to "borrow" scrap supplies like sugar cubes from her human hosts. But when 12-year-old Shawn, a human boy who comes to stay in the home, discovers his mysterious housemate one evening, a secret friendship blossoms. If discovered, their relationship could drive Arrietty's family from the home and straight into danger. Directed by Hiromasa Yonebayashi, with an English-language version directed by Gary Rydstrom. Released Feb. 17, 2012, after an original release in Japan on Jul. 17, 2010. Voices include Bridgit Mendler (Arrietty), Will Arnett (Pod), Amy Poehler (Homily), Carol Burnett (Hara), David Henrie (Shawn), Gracie Poletti (Aunt Jessica), Moises Arias (Spiller). 95 min. Based on Mary Norton's acclaimed children's book series *The Borrowers*. The original version, produced by Hayao Miyazaki and Keiko Niwa at Studio Ghibli, was known in Japan as *Kari-gurashi no Arietti.*

Secretariat (film) The story of the horse that won the 1973 Triple Crown. Housewife and mother Penny Chenery agrees to take over her ailing father's Virginia-based Meadow Stables, despite her lack of horse racing knowledge. Against all odds, Chenery—with the help of veteran trainer Lucien Laurin—manages to navigate the male-dominated business, ultimately fostering the first Triple Crown winner in 25 years and what may be the greatest racehorse of all time. Directed by Randall Wallace. Stars Diane Lane (Penny Chenery), John Malkovich (Lucien Laurin), Dylan Walsh (Jack Tweedy), Scott Glenn (Chris Chenery), Dylan Baker (Hollis Chenery), Nelsan Ellis (Eddie Sweat), Otto Thorwarth (Ronnie Turcotte), Fred Thompson (Bull Hancock), A. J. Michalka (Kate Tweedy), Kevin Connolly (Bill Nack), Margo Martindale (Miss Ham), Eric Lange (Andy Beyer), James Cromwell (Ogden Phipps). 123 min. Filming took place in Louisiana and Kentucky. Released on Oct. 8, 2010. The Triple Crown consists of the 3 top horse races—the Kentucky Derby, the Preakness Stakes, and the Belmont Stakes. Filmed in CinemaScope.

Secrets and Lies (TV) Hour-long drama series on ABC; aired Mar. 1, 2015–Dec. 4, 2016. Ben Crawford, a family man and housepainter, goes from Good Samaritan to murder suspect after he discovers the body of his neighbor's young son, Tom Murphy, in the woods. Detective Andrea Cornell digs for the truth in her investigation, pegging Ben as a person of interest. Ben tries to clear his name, and he peels back the layers of the lives of the suburbanites in their quiet cul-de-sac, revealing dirty little deceptions and all-too-crowded closets overflowing with skeletons. No one is above deception. Stars Ryan Phillippe (Ben Crawford), Juliette Lewis (Detective Cornell), KaDee Strickland (Christy Crawford), Natalie Martinez (Jess Murphy), Dan Fogler (Dave Lindsey), Indiana Evans (Natalie Crawford), Belle Shouse (Abby Crawford). Based on an original Australian series, *Secrets & Lies*. From ABC Studios.

Secrets of Life (film) True-Life Adventure feature released Nov. 6, 1956. Directed by James Algar. A look at nature's endless variety of species and a common concern—that of reproduction and survival. In order to show the vastness and minuteness of nature, the technique of time-lapse photography is utilized. We see plants growing and learn about such creatures as the stickleback fish and the diving spider. The film impressively switches to Cinema-Scope for the final segment on volcanoes. 70 min.

Secrets of Sulphur Springs (TV) Suspense series on Disney Channel; premiered Jan. 15, 2021. The family of 12-year-old Griffin Campbell has just uprooted their lives to move to the small town of Sulphur Springs and take ownership of The Tremont, an abandoned hotel rumored to be haunted by the ghost of a girl who disappeared long ago. Griffin and his mystery-obsessed classmate, Harper, uncover a secret portal that allows them to travel back in time, where they attempt to uncover the key to solving the mystery. Stars Preston Oliver (Griffin Campbell), Kyliegh Curran (Harper), Elle Graham (Savannah), Kelly Frye (Sarah Campbell), Josh Braaten (Ben Campbell), Landon Gordon (Wyatt Campbell), Madeleine McGraw (Zoey Campbell). From Gwave Productions.

Secrets of the Animal Kingdom (TV) Syn. half-hour series; aired Sep. 18, 1998–Sep. 13, 1999, serving as a vehicle to teach kids about the life and habits of animals. Stars Brian Donnelly, Talia Osteen. Taped in Disney's Animal Kingdom at Walt Disney World, it was the first and only series produced by Walt Disney Attractions Television.

Secrets of the Ant and Insect World (film) Educational film comprising part of *Secrets of Life*; released in Sep. 1960. Microphotography reveals that the ant society offers many parallels to human society.

Secrets of the Bee World (film) Educational film comprising part of *Secrets of Life*; released in Sep. 1960. Tells the story of a bee colony with the queen bee reproducing the species and the workers building the honeycombs.

Secrets of the Pirate's Inn, The (TV) Two-part show; aired Nov. 23 and 30, 1969. Directed by Gary Nelson. A man, Dennis McCarthy, in Louisiana befriends 3 kids and enlists them to help search for Jean Lafitte's treasure. An unscrupulous newspaper reporter is also searching, and when the kids and McCarthy find the treasure, he takes it from them by force. Stars Ed Begley, Jimmy Bracken, Annie McEveety, Patrick Creamer, Charles Aidman.

Secrets of the Plant World (film) Educational film comprising part of *Secrets of Life*; released in Sep. 1960. Time-lapse photography shows the germinating of seeds and the growth of plants.

Secrets of the Underwater World (film) Educational film comprising part of *Secrets of Life*; released in Sep. 1960. A study of the intriguing life beneath the water's surface where lives a whole world of bizarre creatures.

Secrets, Stories & Magic of the Happiest Place on Earth (film) Direct-to-video release Dec. 11, 2007; a documentary prepared for the 50th anniversary of Disneyland, featuring interviews with dozens of Imagineers, Cast Members, and Disneyland enthusiasts. Directed by Bob Garner and Pete Schuermann. Executive produced by Jim Garber.

Seeing Eye, The (TV) Show; part 3 of *Atta Girl Kelly*.

Seems There Was This Moose (TV) Show aired Oct. 19, 1975. Directed by Roy Edward Disney. A moose has problems when he stumbles into civilization, including managing the destruction of the local market, so he heads back to the forest. Stars Bob Cox, Ron Brown.

Seiberling Latex Products Co. A Disney licensee 1934–1942, they made rubber figures of various characters. Their Mickey Mouse figures are fairly common, as are those of the Seven Dwarfs. However, Snow White herself from the latter set is almost impossible to find. She was made of hollow rubber; the Dwarfs were solid. While the Dwarfs have survived, it is sad to see the few remaining Snow Whites, which have in most cases collapsed into themselves from age.

Seize the Day Song from *Newsies*; written by Jack Feldman and Alan Menken.

Self Control (film) Donald Duck cartoon released Feb. 11, 1938. Directed by Jack King. Though he tries to take radio philosopher Uncle Smiley's advice about controlling his temper, Donald soon flies into a rage when his rest is upset by various pests, including a woodpecker and an uncooperative hammock.

Selleck, Tom Actor; appeared in *Three Men and a Baby* and *Three Men and a Little Lady* (Peter) and *An Innocent Man* (Jimmie Rainwood). He voiced Cornelius in *Meet the Robinsons*.

Selma, Lord, Selma (TV) A 2-hour movie on *The Wonderful World of Disney*; first aired Jan. 17, 1999. Two little girls remember the infamous and violent Bloody Sunday in Selma, Alabama, during the tumultuous American civil rights movement of the 1960s, when freedom fighters organize a Black registration march amidst Southern violence, hatred, racial prejudice, and the ever-present threat of the Ku Klux Klan. Directed by Charles Burnett. Stars Mackenzie Astin (Jonathan Daniels), Jurnee Smollett (Sheyann Webb), Clifton Powell (Martin Luther King, Jr.), Ella Joyce (Betty Webb), Yolanda King (Miss Bright), Stephanie Peyton (Rachel West). Ms. King is the daughter of Martin Luther King, Jr.

Senses – A Disney Spa Spa fully owned and operated by Disney; opened Dec. 17, 2012, at Disney's Grand Floridian Resort & Spa at Walt Disney World, replacing the Grand Floridian Spa (which had closed Sep. 19, 2011). Holds 15 rooms that offer full-service pampering treatments, including water therapy, sugar exfoliation body treatment, and a citrus facial. Magical Manicures or Princess Pedicures are offered to youngsters. Closed Mar. 2020, and reopened Jan. 26, 2022, again as The Grand Floridian Spa. A second location opened at Disney's Saratoga Springs Resort & Spa Jul. 25, 2013, with a nature-inspired theme, replacing the resort's existing spa. The Senses name was first used on the Disney Cruise Line ships, beginning with the Senses Spa & Salon on the *Disney Dream* in 2011.

Sequels Even though Walt Disney professed that

he did not like to make sequels, he was occasionally persuaded by economic reality to make them against his best judgment. One of the first of his films to lead to sequels was the cartoon *Three Little Pigs*; the pigs were brought back for *The Big Bad Wolf*, *Three Little Wolves*, and *The Practical Pig*. *Three Orphan Kittens* had *More Kittens* as a sequel. Some Disney features also had sequels, such as *Old Yeller* (sequel was *Savage Sam*), *The Misadventures of Merlin Jones* (*The Monkey's Uncle*), and *The Absent-Minded Professor* (*Son of Flubber*). Over the years, sequels became more common, with *The Shaggy Dog* (*The Shaggy D.A.*), *The Love Bug* (*Herbie Rides Again*, *Herbie Goes to Monte Carlo*, *Herbie Goes Bananas*), *Escape to Witch Mountain* (*Return from Witch Mountain*, *Race to Witch Mountain*), *The Apple Dumpling Gang* (*The Apple Dumpling Gang Rides Again*), *Stakeout* (*Another Stakeout*), *Three Men and a Baby* (*Three Men and a Little Lady*), *Honey, I Shrunk the Kids* (*Honey, I Blew Up the Kid*), *White Fang* (*White Fang 2: Myth of the White Wolf*), *The Mighty Ducks* (*D2: The Mighty Ducks* and *D3: The Mighty Ducks*), *Homeward Bound: The Incredible Journey* (*Homeward Bound II: Lost in San Francisco*), *Sister Act* (*Sister Act 2: Back in the Habit*), *101 Dalmatians* (*102 Dalmatians*), *The Santa Clause* (*The Santa Clause 2* and *The Santa Clause 3: The Escape Clause*), *The Princess Diaries* (*The Princess Diaries 2: Royal Engagement*), *National Treasure* (*National Treasure: Book of Secrets*), *Tron* (*Tron: Legacy*), *Alice in Wonderland* (*Alice Through the Looking Glass*), *Mary Poppins* (*Mary Poppins Returns*), *Maleficent* (*Maleficent: Mistress of Evil*), not to mention the Ernest, Air Bud, Pirates of the Caribbean, Chronicles of Narnia, Muppets, *Star Wars*, and Marvel Studios films. Some animated features have had a theatrical sequel, including *The Rescuers* (*The Rescuers Down Under*), *Fantasia* (*Fantasia/2000*), *Peter Pan* (*Return to Never Land*), *The Jungle Book* (*The Jungle Book 2*), *Toy Story* (*Toy Story 2, 3,* and *4*), *Cars* (*Cars 2* and *3*), *Monsters, Inc.* (*Monsters University*), *Planes* (*Planes: Fire & Rescue*), *Finding Nemo* (*Finding Dory*), *The Incredibles* (*Incredibles 2*), *Wreck-It Ralph* (*Ralph Breaks the Internet*), *Frozen* (*Frozen 2*), and *Inside Out* (*Inside Out 2*). There have been a number of TV sequels to theatrical features, such as *The Love Bug* and *The Parent Trap*, and to other TV shows and movies, such as *Davy Crockett*, *Not Quite Human*, *Halloweentown*, *Zenon: Girl of the 21st Century*, *The Cheetah Girls*, *Twitches*, *High School Musical*, *Camp Rock*, *Teen Beach Movie*, *Descendants*, *ZOMBIES*, and *Under Wraps*. In past years there have been a number of direct-to-video sequels to the classic animated features. For Disney+, sequels have been made for films including *Stargirl* (*Hollywood Stargirl*), *Hocus Pocus* (*Hocus Pocus 2*), and *Enchanted* (*Disenchanted*).

Sequoia Lodge, Disney Hotel at Disneyland Paris; opened May 27, 1992, as the only hotel at the resort not to debut with the others on the park's opening day. Reminiscent of some of the National Park hotels in the U.S. Dining options include Hunter's Grill, Beaver Creek Tavern, and the Redwood Bar and Lounge, with shopping at Northwest Passage. Designed by Antoine Grumbach.

Sequoyah (film) Educational film about the Cherokee silversmith who single-handedly created a written Indian language. Produced by Anthony Corso. Released in Sep. 1974.

Sgt. Preston's Yukon Saloon and Dancehall Watering hole in the Disneyland Hotel at Disneyland Resort; debuted Nov. 1981, with an 1890s-style live show and impromptu performances by the Yukon Characters. The dance hall was added in Mar. 1984. It became the Neon Cactus in 1992.

Serka Zong Bazaar Shop at the exit of Expedition Everest – Legend of the Forbidden Mountain in Disney's Animal Kingdom; opened Apr. 7, 2006, offering Yeti-themed merchandise. Serka Zong is the name of the fictional Himalayan village in the park's Asia area.

Servants' Entrance (film) 20th Century Fox film starring Janet Gaynor containing a Disney cartoon insert of a nightmare sequence featuring kitchen utensils; released in 1934.

Sethi, Neel Actor; appeared as Mowgli in *The Jungle Book* (2016).

Settlement Trading Post Grocery and supply store at Disney's Fort Wilderness Resort & Campground at Walt Disney World. SEE ALSO MEADOW TRADING POST.

Seven Cities of Antarctica (film) People and Places featurette released Dec. 25, 1958. Directed by Winston Hibler. The biography of Earth's final frontier, Antarctica, and how this last of our planet's continents was finally opened up by humans after millions of years of seclusion. The picture ends with a summary of Antarctica's future potentials as a source of natural wealth, and as a strategic hub for air travel in the Southern Hemisphere. Filmed in CinemaScope. Footage was obtained when Walt Disney sent cameramen Lloyd Beebe and Elmo Jones with Navy photographers to capture the U.S. expedition Operation Deepfreeze on film. 30 min.

7D, The (TV) Animated series on Disney XD; debuted Jul. 7, 2014. In the whimsical world of Jollywood, Queen Delightful relies on the 7D—Happy, Bashful, Sleepy, Sneezy, Dopey, Grumpy, and Doc—to keep the kingdom in order. Standing in their way are 2 laughably evil villains, Grim and Hildy Gloom, who plot to take over the kingdom by stealing the magical jewels in the 7D's mine. Voices include Jay Leno (Crystal Ball), Whoopi Goldberg (Magic Mirror), Kelly Osbourne (Hildy Gloom), Jess Harnell (Grim Gloom), Leigh-Allyn Baker (Queen Delightful), Maurice LaMarche (Grumpy), Bill Farmer (Doc), Dee Bradley Baker (Dopey), Scott Menville (Sneezy), Kevin Michael Richardson (Happy), Stephen Stanton (Sleepy), Billy West (Bashful). From Disney Television Animation.

Seven Dwarfs Doc, Sleepy, Happy, Grumpy, Sneezy, Bashful, Dopey.

Seven Dwarfs' Mine Fantasyland souvenir shop in the Magic Kingdom at Walt Disney World; opened Nov. 22, 1994, taking the place of The Royal Candy Shoppe. Closed Jan. 5, 2014.

Seven Dwarfs Mine Train Fantasyland roller coaster–style attraction in the Magic Kingdom at Walt Disney World; opened May 28, 2014, after a May 2 dedication. Guests ride in mine carts through the Dwarfs' diamond mine. The innovative ride system features 5-car trains designed to swing independently from side to side as they move along the track. Some of the props and figures from Snow White's Scary Adventures, which closed in 2012, were used, along with new, state-of-the-art Audio-Animatronics characters. Also opened in Fantasyland in Shanghai Disneyland Jun. 16, 2016.

Seven Seas Lagoon A 200-acre man-made body of water between the Transportation and Ticket Center and Magic Kingdom at Walt Disney World. Ferryboats and resort launches cross the lagoon, providing an alternative to the Monorail. Disney's Contemporary Resort, Polynesian Village Resort, and Grand Floridian Resort & Spa are all located around the lagoon, with the latter 2 having boat docks. (The dock for the Contemporary Resort is on Bay Lake.) The lagoon was envisioned by WED designers in 1967 after the site was deemed unsuitable for development. It took 3 years to clear the land, carve three islands, and fill it with water. The excavated land was then used to raise the surface of the Magic Kingdom by some 16 feet, allowing for a network of utility corridors, or Utilidors, to run below the park.

7 Wise Dwarfs (film) Film showing the advisability and necessity of purchasing Canadian war bonds. Made for the National Film Board of Canada. Delivered Dec. 12, 1941. The Dwarfs wisely invest in war bonds with their diamonds, with revamped lyrics to "Heigh-Ho."

Seymour, Anne (1909–1988) Actress; appeared on TV in *The Leftovers* (Aunt Winifred) and *The Wacky Zoo of Morgan City* (Maggie Hargrove).

Shades of Green at Walt Disney World Resort R&R hotel leased Feb. 1, 1994, by the U.S. government for military personnel and purchased by them Jan. 12, 1996. Formerly The Golf Resort and The Disney Inn. It is no longer available to non-military guests, although the golf courses are. The army has a 100-year lease on the land from Disney. Dining includes the Garden Gallery (buffet service), Mangino's (full service), and Evergreen's (sports bar).

Shadix, Glenn (1952–2010) Actor; voiced the Mayor in *Tim Burton's The Nightmare Before Christmas*, with TV credits in *Parent Trap Hawaiian Honeymoon* (Chuck Schtutz) and *Student Exchange* (Mr. Barton). He guest starred on *The Golden Girls* and *Empty Nest* and provided voices for several animated series.

Shadow Conspiracy (film) A trusted presidential adviser, Bobby Bishop, suddenly finds himself a murder suspect and his own life threatened by a ruthless professional killer. He goes underground with a former girlfriend and ace reporter, Amanda Givens, and uncovers a plot to assassinate the president, with conspirators including the vice president and the crafty chief of staff, who feel he has become too liberal. A Hollywood Pictures film from Cinergi Pictures Entertainment. Directed by George P. Cosmatos. Released Jan. 31, 1997, after earlier releases in Europe and Asia (Dec. 20, 1996, in Taiwan). Stars Charlie Sheen (Bobby Bishop), Sam Waterston (President), Linda Hamilton (Amanda Givens), Stephen Lang (the Agent), Donald

Sutherland (Jake Conrad), Theodore Bikel (Yuri Pochenko), Ben Gazzara (Saxon). Gore Vidal has a cameo role as a crooked congressman. 103 min. Filming took place, mostly at night, in Washington, D.C., as well as in Baltimore and Richmond, Virginia. A total of 85 locations were utilized over 12 weeks of filming. Filmed in Cinema-Scope.

Shadow of Fear (TV) Two-part show; aired Jan. 28 and Feb. 4, 1979. Directed by Noel Nosseck. A boy turns to his pets after his father dies, and on a visit to his great-uncle in the Amish country, he learns their legends and superstitions. He soon discovers he has the power to make mind contact with the animals. Stars Ike Eisenmann, John Anderson, Peter Haskell, Joyce Van Patten, Lisa Whelchel, Kip Niven, John McLiam, Charles Tyner.

Shadowhunters (TV) Hour-long series on Freeform; aired Jan. 12, 2016–May 6, 2019. Clary Fray finds out on her birthday that she is not who she thinks she is but rather comes from a long line of Shadowhunters—human-angel hybrids who hunt down demons. Now thrown into the world of demon hunting after her mother is kidnapped, Clary must rely on the mysterious Jace and his fellow Shadowhunters Isabelle and Alec to navigate this dark world. With her best friend, Simon, in tow, Clary must now live among faeries, warlocks, vampires, and werewolves to find answers that could help her find her mother. Stars Katherine McNamara (Clary Fray), Dominic Sherwood (Jace Wayland), Alberto Rosende (Simon), Emeraude Toubia (Isabelle Lightwood), Matthew Daddario (Alec Lightwood), Isaiah Mustafa (Luke Garroway), Harry Shum, Jr. (Magnus Bane). Based on the young adult fantasy book series *The Mortal Instruments* by Cassandra Clare. Produced by Constantin Film.

Shaggy D.A., The (film) In this sequel to the hit film *The Shaggy Dog*, Wilby Daniels, his wife, and their son return from a vacation to find their home stripped bare by housebreakers. Angry, Wilby decides to run against the rascally incumbent district attorney, "Honest John" Slade, and he launches a fumbling campaign. When an ice cream man, who innocently bought a mysterious scarab ring from the thieves, recites the Latin inscription, Wilby once again turns into a shaggy dog. A mad chase ensues as everyone realizes the worth of the ring and searches for it, even through a huge stack of cherry pies. Slade confiscates the ring and sends Wilby to the pound,

where the cunning dog masterminds a breakout. There are still more misadventures, but eventually "Honest John" and his slippery sidekick are brought to heel, and Wilby and his family adopt the gallant dogs from the pound who helped him become district attorney. Released Dec. 18, 1976. Directed by Robert Stevenson. 92 min. Stars Dean Jones (Wilby Daniels), Tim Conway (Tim), Suzanne Pleshette (Betty), Keenan Wynn (John Slade), Jo Anne Worley (in her motion picture debut as Katrinka), Dick Van Patten (Raymond), Shane Sinutko (Brian Daniels), Vic Tayback (Eddie Roschak). The film was suggested by *The Hound of Florence* by Felix Salten, author of *Bambi*. The song "The Shaggy D.A.," written by Shane Tatum and Richard McKinley, was sung by Dean Jones. The amusing special effects were provided by Eustace Lycett, Art Cruickshank, and Danny Lee.

Shaggy Dog, The (film) Young misfit teenager Wilby Daniels accidentally discovers a magic ring in a museum, and, by repeating the Latin inscription, he becomes a large and clumsy Bratislavan sheepdog. This amuses his younger brother, Moochie, but shocks his parents, and endears him to his neighbor Franceska, who thinks he is her dog, Chiffon. But when her father turns out to be a Russian spy, it is up to Wilby to capture the gang, which he manages to do after a hair-raising chase. Unfortunately, it is Franceska's Chiffon who gets all the attention and credit at the end—for who would believe Wilby's story? Released Mar. 19, 1959. Directed by Charles Barton in black and white. One of the biggest and most unexpected film milestones in Disney history, the Studio's first live-action comedy set the formula for many Disney movies to come: youngsters, animals, strange—sometimes magical—events, music, and a catchy main title sequence. 101 min. Stars Fred MacMurray (Wilson Daniels), Jean Hagen (Frieda Daniels), Tommy Kirk (Wilby Daniels), Annette Funicello (Allison D'Allessio), Tim Considine (Buzz Miller), Roberta Shore (Franceska Andrassy), Kevin Corcoran (Moochie). The first Disney film starring Fred MacMurray. The film has grossed over $12 million and spawned 2 sequels—*The Shaggy D.A.* (1976) and *The Return of the Shaggy Dog*, a TV movie in 1987, plus 2 remakes (for TV in 1994 and for theaters in 2005). The film was originally devised for the Disney anthology TV series. First released on video in 1981.

Shaggy Dog, The (film) In this update of the 1959 comedy classic, workaholic Deputy D.A.

Dave Douglas takes on a case involving an animal laboratory—one that will take him away from his wife and kids, who already yearn for his all-too-distracted attention. But when Dave is accidentally infected with a top secret, genetic mutation serum, he's transformed from family dad to family dog. As a dog, Dave is able to gain a whole new perspective into his family's secrets and dreams, learning what it really means to be his family's best friend. He wants nothing more than to become human again, but first he has to stop the evil forces behind the serum. From Walt Disney Pictures, Mandeville Films, and Boxing Cat Films. Released Mar. 10, 2006. Directed by Brian Robbins. Stars Tim Allen (Dave Douglas), Robert Downey Jr. (Dr. Kozak), Danny Glover (Ken Hollister), Kristin Davis (Rebecca Douglas), Spencer Breslin (Josh Douglas), Zena Grey (Carly Douglas), Joshua Leonard (Justin Forrester), Shawn Pyfrom (Trey), Bess Wohl (Dr. Gwen Lichtman), Jane Curtin (Judge Claire Whittaker), Philip Baker Hall (Lance Strickland), Craig Kilborn (Baxter). 99 min. Filmed in Super 35-Scope. The dog was played by Coal, a Bearded Collie, trained by Mark Forbes. Released on DVD in 2006.

Shaggy Dog, The (TV) A remake of the 1959 film, with various changes to the story line; aired as a 2-hour movie on ABC Nov. 12, 1994. Stars Scott Weinger (Wilby), Ed Begley, Jr. (Mr. Daniels), and Jordan Blake Warkol (Moochie). Directed by Dennis Dugan.

Shake It Up (TV) Comedy series on Disney Channel; premiered Nov. 7, 2010, and ended Nov. 10, 2013. High-spirited best friends CeCe Jones and Raquel "Rocky" Blue have their dreams of becoming professional dancers realized when they become background dancers on the most popular teen dance show, *Shake It Up Chicago*, a gig they land thanks to their long-time and well-connected friend, Deuce. Between learning a wide range of new dance styles, navigating the backstage antics at the show (especially with their rivals Tinka and Gunther) and their newfound social status at school, the girls are on their way to new and fun adventures, even some that will test their friendship. Stars Bella Thorne (CeCe Jones), Zendaya (Rocky Blue), Kenton Duty (Gunther), Adam Irigoyen (Deuce), Davis Cleveland (Flynn Jones).

Shakespeare in Love Stage version of the 1998 Miramax film, from Disney Theatrical Produc-

tions and Sonia Friedman Productions. Ran at the Noël Coward Theatre in London's West End Jul. 23, 2014–Apr. 18, 2015, with a U.S. debut at the Angus Bowmer Theatre at the Oregon Shakespeare Festival in Ashland Feb. 18–Oct. 28, 2017. A romantic piece of historical fiction, the story centers around a young Will Shakespeare as he struggles to find his inspiration.

Shakira Singer/songwriter; provided the voice of Gazelle in *Zootopia*. She made guest appearances on TV in *Ugly Betty* and *The Disney Family Singalong: Volume II*, and on Disney Channel in *Wizards of Waverly Place* and the *Radio Disney Music Awards*.

Shan-Yu Ruthless leader of the Huns in *Mulan*; voiced by Miguel Ferrer. The name means "Invader from the North."

Shang Chinese army captain in *Mulan*; voiced by BD Wong (speaking) and Donny Osmond (singing).

Shang-Chi and the Legend of the Ten Rings (film) The 2nd film in "Phase 4" of the Marvel Cinematic Universe. Shang-Chi, having adopted the name Shaun, is living in San Francisco and working as a parking valet when a group of assassins takes a pendant that his mother gave him when he was young. Along with his best friend, Katy, he journeys to Macau to warn his sister Xialing that danger is coming for her, as well. Confronting the past he thought he left behind, Shang-Chi is drawn into the web of the mysterious Ten Rings organization, led by his estranged father, and realizes he must stop him and his cabal. Released Sep. 3, 2021, also in 3-D and IMAX, after a Sep. 1 international release. Directed by Destin Daniel Cretton. Stars Simu Liu (Shaun/Shang-Chi), Tony Leung (Xu Wenwu), Awkwafina (Katy), Fala Chen (Li), Meng'er Zhang (Xialing), Florian Munteanu (Razor Fist), Ronny Chieng (Jon Jon), Michelle Yeoh (Ying Nan). 140 min. Filmed in wide-screen format in San Francisco and Sydney. Shang-Chi was a fairly obscure character created by Marvel Comics in the 1970s. Nominated for an Academy Award (Visual Effects).

Shanghai Disney Resort The 963-acre resort is jointly owned by Disney (43%) and a Shanghai municipal government-owned company, the Shanghai Shendi Group (57%), and is managed by the joint venture's management company, in which Disney has a majority stake (70%). The resort opened Jun. 16, 2016, with a Magic Kingdom-style theme park, Shanghai Disneyland, featuring 6 themed lands. The resort also features 2 themed hotels, Shanghai Disneyland Hotel (420 rooms) and Toy Story Hotel (800 rooms); Disneytown (a shopping, dining, and entertainment district divided into Lakeshore, Marketplace, Spice Alley, and Broadway Boulevard with its Broadway Plaza home to the Walt Disney Grand Theatre); and the Wishing Star Park recreation area.

Shanghai Disneyland The 12th Disney park; opened at Shanghai Disney Resort Jun. 16, 2016. The park features 6 themed lands: Mickey Avenue, Gardens of Imagination, Fantasyland, Treasure Cove, Tomorrowland, and Adventure Isle. At the heart of the park is Enchanted Storybook Castle, the tallest and most interactive Disney castle with attractions, entertainment, and dining. An 11-acre green space welcomes guests to the park and provides viewing for parades and nighttime entertainment. The park welcomed its 10 millionth guest after only 11 months. In 2018, the park had its first major expansion with the opening of Disney-Pixar Toy Story Land, and a *Zootopia*-themed land was announced the following year.

Shanghai Disneyland Band Entertainment ensemble on Mickey Avenue in Shanghai Disneyland; performances began Jun. 16, 2016.

Shanghai Disneyland Hotel The signature hotel of Shanghai Disney Resort, featuring an art nouveau–inspired design; opened Jun. 16, 2016. With 420 guest rooms, the hotel is nestled on the banks of Wishing Star Lake and provides views of Shanghai Disneyland, Disneytown, and the resort's recreation area. Featuring a 3-story lobby; Aurora, Lumiere's Kitchen, and Ballet Café restaurants; the King Triton indoor pool; Hakuna Matata Oasis water-play area; Mickey Mouse Playhouse; a landscaped Rose Garden; and the Cinderella Ballroom, designed specifically for weddings. Premium services are offered on the top 2 levels of the hotel for the Magic Kingdom Club.

Shanghai Knights (film) After taming the Wild West in *Shanghai Noon*, Chon Wang and Roy O'Bannon are out to settle a score in civilized London in this sequel. When Chon's estranged father is mysteriously murdered, Chon and Roy make their way to London to track down the killer. Chon's sister, Lin, has the same idea, and uncovers a worldwide conspiracy to murder the royal family—but almost no one will believe her. With the help of a kindly Scot-land Yard inspector and a 10-year-old street urchin, the acrobatic Chon uses his high-flying martial arts skills in Victorian Britain as he attempts to avenge his father's death—and keep the romance-minded Roy away from his sister. A Touchstone/Spyglass Entertainment film. Directed by David Dobkin. Released Feb. 7, 2003. Stars Jackie Chan (Chon Wang), Owen Wilson (Roy O'Bannon), Aaron Johnson (Charlie), Thomas Fisher (Artie Doyle), Aidan Gillen (Rathbone), Fann Wong (Chon Lin), Donnie Yen (Wu Chan). 114 min. The production utilized locations throughout the Czech Republic. Filmed in CinemaScope.

Shanghai Noon (film) The Wild West meets the Far East in a battle for honor, royalty, and a trunk full of gold when acrobatic Imperial Guard Chon Wang comes to Nevada in the 1890s to rescue a beautiful kidnapped Chinese princess. With the help of a partner he does not trust, a wife he does not want, a horse he cannot ride, and martial arts moves that no one can believe, Wang finds himself facing the meanest gunslingers in the West. Directed by Tom Dey. A Touchstone/Spyglass Entertainment production. Released May 26, 2000. Stars Jackie Chan (Chon Wang), Owen Wilson (Roy O'Bannon), Lucy Liu (Princess Pei Pei), Roger Yuan (Lo Fong), Xander Berkeley (Van Cleef). 110 min. Doubling for Nevada was the Drumheller area, near Calgary. Filmed in Cinema-Scope.

Shanghaied (film) Mickey Mouse cartoon released Jan. 13, 1934. Directed by Burt Gillett. In this pirate adventure, Mickey saves Minnie from Peg Leg Pete and his crew with the aid of a stuffed swordfish, taking over the ship in the process.

Shank Tough street racer in *Ralph Breaks the Internet*; voiced by Gal Gadot.

Share a Dream Come True Parade Ran in the Magic Kingdom at Walt Disney World Oct. 1, 2001–2006, originally for the 100 Years of Magic celebration. Ornate floats featured Disney characters in oversized snow globes, and spectators could interact in the streets during a series of "show stops." Introduced by Julie Andrews. It became the Disney Dreams Come True Parade in 2006, followed by Celebrate a Dream Come True Parade from 2009–2014.

Sharif, Omar (1932–2015) Actor; appeared in *The 13th Warrior* (Melchisidek) and *Hidalgo* (Sheik).

Sharing and Cooperation (film) Educational film in the Songs for Us series; released in Sep. 1989. 8 min. The film shows through songs the importance of sharing and cooperation.

Sharing the Magic SEE PARTNERS (STATUE).

Shark Reef Snorkel pool at Typhoon Lagoon at Walt Disney World. Guests could swim among the fish, and sharks (though they weren't the dangerous type). It closed Oct. 3, 2016.

Sharpay's Fabulous Adventure (TV) Direct-to-video release Apr. 19, 2011, and airing on Disney Channel May 22. Aspiring thespian Sharpay Evans, who is about to head to Broadway to meet her destiny, gets a big break when a talent scout spots her performing with her dog Boi at a charity gala. But life in the big city is a shock, and there's an even bigger bombshell when Sharpay finally realizes that the Broadway role is really for Boi, not her. Putting her disappointment aside, she sets out to make Boi the most fabulous canine star to hit the stage, with the hope that his fame will become her fame. Before long, she makes a new friend in a student filmmaker, Peyton, who finds her to be a fascinating subject. Meanwhile, Boi finds puppy love on a Big Apple adventure of his own. Directed by Michael Lembeck. Stars Ashley Tisdale (Sharpay), Austin Butler (Peyton Leverett), Bradley Steven Perry (Roger Elliston III), Cameron Goodman (Amber Lee Adams), Alec Mapa (Gill Samms), Jack Plotnick (Neal Roberts). Filmed in Toronto.

Sharpe, Albert (1885–1970) Actor; appeared in *Darby O'Gill and the Little People* (Darby).

Sharpsteen, Ben (1895–1980) Animator/director; joined the Disney Studio in 1929 and left in 1959. He animated on shorts until 1934 when he became a director for the next 4 years. He was a sequence director on *Snow White and the Seven Dwarfs*; supervising co-director on *Pinocchio*; supervising director on *Dumbo*; production supervisor on *Fantasia, Fun and Fancy Free, Cinderella, Alice in Wonderland*, and several of the True-Life Adventure films; and was considered one of Walt's right-hand men. He directed *Water Birds* and served as associate producer or producer on several other of the nature and People and Places films, and TV shows. He received an Oscar for *The Ama Girls*. He was named a Disney Legend posthumously in 1998.

Shaughnessy, Mickey (1920–1985) Actor; appeared in *Never a Dull Moment* (Francis) and *The Boatniks* (Charlie), and on TV in *A Boy Called Nuthin'* (Sheriff Hoop) and *My Dog, the Thief* (Foley).

Shaw, Evan K., Ceramics Company also known as American Pottery. They created some of the most handsome and collectible Disney ceramic figurines 1943–1955. The products are highly coveted on the collector's market, especially if the figurines have their original gold label.

Shaw, Mel (1914–2012) Shaw was hired by Disney in 1937, and worked on story for *Fantasia, Bambi*, and *The Adventures of Ichabod and Mr. Toad*. After leaving the Studio for many years, he returned in the mid-1970s to work on story for *The Rescuers, The Fox and the Hound, The Great Mouse Detective, Beauty and the Beast*, and *The Lion King*. He was named a Disney Legend in 2004.

Shaw, Reta (1912–1982) Actress; appeared in *Pollyanna* (Tillie Lagerlof), *Mary Poppins* (Mrs. Brill), and *Escape to Witch Mountain* (Mrs. Grindley).

Shaw, Steve (1965–1990) Child actor; appeared on TV in *Child of Glass* (Alexander).

Shawn, Wallace Actor; appeared in *The Cemetery Club* (Larry), *My Favorite Martian* (Coleye Epstein), and *The Haunted Mansion* (Ezra); on Disney+ in *Timmy Failure: Mistakes Were Made* (Mr. Crocus); and on TV in *Noah* (Zack) and *Mr. St. Nick* (Mimir), with a guest role in *Desperate Housewives*. He has voiced many characters, including Rex in the Toy Story films, Principal Mazur in *A Goofy Movie*, Principal Strickler in *Teacher's Pet*, Gilbert Huph in *The Incredibles*, Principal Fetchit in *Chicken Little*, Humphrey Westwood in *Amphibia*, and Billy in *Air Buddies*.

She-Hulk: Attorney at Law (TV) Comedy series on Disney+; digitally premiered Aug. 17, 2022. Jennifer Walters—an attorney who specializes in superhuman-oriented legal cases—tries to navigate the world and be taken seriously as a working professional, despite the fact she is over 6'7" and green. Stars Tatiana Maslany (Jennifer Walters/She-Hulk), Jameela Jamil (Titania), Josh Segarra (Pug), Ginger Gonzaga (Nikki Ramos), Jon Bass (Todd), Renée Elise Goldsberry (Mallory Book), Mark Ruffalo (Bruce Banner/Hulk), Tim Roth (Emil Blonsky/Abomination). From Marvel Studios.

She Stood Alone (TV) Movie on NBC; aired Apr.

15, 1991. Directed by Jack Gold. One woman's battle in 1832 to establish America's first Black female academy. 120 min. Stars Mare Winningham, Ben Cross, Robert Desiderio.

Shea, Eric Child actor; appeared in *The Castaway Cowboy* (Booten MacAvoy), and on TV in *Menace on the Mountain* (Mark), *The Whiz Kid and the Carnival Caper* and *The Whiz Kid and the Mystery at Riverton* (Alvin Fernald), and *The Secret of the Pond* (Joey).

Sheedy, Ally Actress; appeared in *Betsy's Wedding* (Connie Hopper), and on TV in *Kyle XY* (Sarah), with a guest role in *SMILF*.

Sheen, Charlie Actor; appeared in *The Three Musketeers* (Aramis), *Shadow Conspiracy* (Bobby Bishop), and *Terminal Velocity* (Ditch Brodie).

Sheep Dog (film) Pluto cartoon released Nov. 4, 1949. Directed by Charles Nichols. Bent-Tail, the coyote, tries to teach his son to steal sheep from Pluto's flock, but when the 2 attempt it, Bent-Tail runs away with a sheep, which turns out to be his son in disguise.

Sheldon, Gene (1909–1982) Actor; appeared in *Toby Tyler* (Sam Treat) and *Babes in Toyland* (Roderigo), and on TV in *Zorro* (Bernardo) and *The Golden Horseshoe Revue*.

Shelley, Carole (1939–2018) Actress; appeared in *Quiz Show* (Cornwall aunt) and *Jungle 2 Jungle* (Fiona). She voiced Amelia Gabble (*The Aristocats*), Lady Kluck (*Robin Hood*), a Fate (*Hercules*), and Lachesis in the *Hercules* animated series.

ShellieMay See Duffy and Friends.

Shepard, Sam (1943–2017) Actor; appeared in *Country* (Gil Ivy).

Shere Khan Suave tiger villain in *The Jungle Book*; voiced by George Sanders.

Sheridan, Nicolette Actress; appeared in *Noises Off* (Brooke Ashton/Vickie) and *Spy Hard* (Veronique Ukrinsky), and on TV in *Desperate Housewives* (Edie Britt). She voiced Eleanor in *The Legend of Tarzan*.

Sheridan, Susan (1947–2015) Voice actress; provided the voice of Eilonwy in *The Black Cauldron*.

Sheriff Callie's Wild West (TV) Animated series on Disney Junior; debuted first on the Disney Junior App Nov. 24, 2013, then on Disney Junior Jan. 20, 2014. The very first western for preschoolers, the show follows Callie, a lovable Calico cat, as she keeps the peace in a little town called Nice and Friendly Corners. The show uses folklore of the Old West to impart life's lessons about kindness, friendship, and honesty. Each story is 11 min., with 2 to an episode. Voices include Mandy Moore (Callie), Lucas Grabeel (Peck), Jessica DiCicco (Toby). From Disney•ABC Television Group.

Sheriff of Nottingham Lumbering tax collector, a wolf, in *Robin Hood*; voiced by Pat Buttram.

Sherman, Richard M., and Robert B. Songwriters; known primarily for their Disney work, they first wrote pop songs for Annette Funicello, starting with "Tall Paul." The record sold 700,000 singles. Later they wrote songs for Disney films, such as *The Parent Trap, Summer Magic, Winnie the Pooh and the Honey Tree, That Darn Cat!, The Jungle Book, The Aristocats, Mary Poppins, The Happiest Millionaire, Bedknobs and Broomsticks*, and *The Tigger Movie*, as well as for numerous TV shows. Their songs for *Mary Poppins* earned them 2 Academy Awards, for Best Score and Best Song, "Chim Chim Cher-ee." In all, they wrote over 200 songs featured in 27 films and 2 dozen TV productions and received 9 Academy Award nominations. Some of their most popular songs include "Supercalifragilisticexpialidocious," "A Spoonful of Sugar," "I Wan'na Be Like You," and "Winnie the Pooh." Probably their best-known song was not for a film at all, but for a Disney attraction at the 1964–1965 New York World's Fair: It's a Small World. Also for the fair, they wrote "There's a Great Big Beautiful Tomorrow" for the G.E. Carousel of Progress. They came back to write songs for EPCOT Center in 1982 and Tomorrowland at Disneyland in 1998. They were named Disney Legends in 1990. In 1992, Disney Records released a special retrospective collection on CD entitled *The Sherman Brothers: Walt Disney's Supercalifragilistic Songwriting Team*, followed by *The Sherman Brothers Songbook* in 2009. They received the National Medal of Arts—the highest award bestowed upon artists by the U.S. government—from President George W. Bush in 2008. A documentary, *The Boys: The Sherman Brothers' Story*, was released in 2009. They were portrayed in *Saving Mr. Banks*, for which Richard served as consultant. Robert passed away in 2012. In 2015, a special about Richard's life, *Richard M. Sherman: Songs of a Lifetime*, aired on PBS SoCal. He contributed the song "A Kiss Goodnight" for the Disneyland 60th anniversary celebration, also writing a 2017 book from Disney Editions of the same name. He wrote new lyrics for *The Jungle Book* (2016) and songs for *Christopher Robin*, also making a cameo in the film's end credits. The Sherman brothers' father, Al Sherman, was a Tin Pan Alley songwriter who penned such Depression-era songs as "You Gotta Be a Football Hero" and "Potatoes Are Cheaper, Tomatoes Are Cheaper, Now's the Time to Fall in Love" (a song the brothers later referenced in one of their compositions for the featurette *A Symposium on Popular Songs*).

Sherwood Garden Restaurant Victorian-style buffet dining in the Tokyo Disneyland Hotel; opened Jul. 8, 2008. Large windows provide views out to the resort's formal garden of the same name.

Shindig, The (film) Mickey Mouse cartoon released Jul. 29, 1930. Directed by Burt Gillett. At a barn dance, Mickey, Minnie, and the gang perform and dance. Mickey dances with several partners, including a dachshund and a hippo.

Ships (film) Educational film in the Goofy's Field Trips series released on Aug. 7, 1989. Goofy escorts 2 children on a tour of a passenger ship. 15 min.

Shipwreck Shore Interactive water-play area in Treasure Cove at Shanghai Disneyland; opened Jun. 16, 2016. A variety of activity zones offer hands-on adventures in a long abandoned French galleon.

Shipwrecked (film) A 14-year-old, Hakon Hakonsen, bravely agrees to become a sailor in order to help pay his parents' debts. But danger comes as Hakon's ship is hijacked by a mysterious stranger, Merrick, who charts a course for a South Seas island where he has hidden a fortune in stolen treasure. A fierce hurricane scuttles the ship, and Hakon and a young stowaway girl, Mary, find themselves marooned on a tropical island paradise. The 2 must now face the unknown perils of the jungle, and the eventual return of Merrick, as he comes looking for his treasure, and to take the young adventurers prisoner. Released Mar. 1, 1991. Directed by Nils Gaup. 93 min. Stars Stian Smestad (Hakon Hakonsen), Gabriel Byrne (Merrick). Based on the classic Norwegian novel, *Haakon Haakonsen*, by Oluf Vilhelm Falck-Ytter. The filming took place in Norway, England, Spain, and Fiji.

Shiriki Utundu Mysterious idol that was once the protective spirit of the Mtundu tribe at the Tower of Terror in Tokyo DisneySea. Its name means "believe in mischief."

Shirley, Bill (1921–1989) Actor; voiced Prince Phillip in *Sleeping Beauty*.

Shnookums & Meat Funny Cartoon Show, The (TV) Syn. series, Jan. 2–Aug. 28, 1995. Three different animated comedy shorts mixing nutty gags, bad puns, weird events, surrealistic flavor, and wacky story lines in a fast-paced half hour of humor. The segments are *Shnookums & Meat*, with Shnookums a cat and Meat a dog, who are both friends and enemies; *Pith Possum: Super Dynamic Possum of Tomorrow*, a satire of the superhero genre; and *Tex Tinstar: the Best in the West*, with Tex a frontier sheriff who faces certain destruction in each episode. Voices for *Shnookums & Meat* include Jason Marsden (Shnookums), Frank Welker (Meat), Tress MacNeille (wife), Steve Mackall (husband); for *Pith Possum* they include Jeff Bennett (Pith/Peter Possum), Brad Garrett (Comm. Stress), Jess Harnell (Lt. Tension), April Winchell (Doris Deer), Patric Zimmerman (Obediah); and for *Tex Tinstar* they are Charlie Adler (Chafe), Jeff Bennett (Tex Tinstar), Corey Burton (Ian), Jim Cummings (narrator), Brad Garrett (Wrongo). 13 episodes.

Shoe Time Designer footwear in the Lake Buena Vista Shopping Village at Walt Disney World; opened Nov. 1976, taking the place of Michael's barbershop. It became Team Mickey's Athletic Club in 1987.

Shokee, the Everglades Panther (TV) Show aired Sep. 29, 1974. Directed by Roy Edward Disney. A Native boy spending the summer alone in the Everglades as a rite of passage helps a lost panther cub survive, but the village does not welcome him when he follows the boy home. The boy has to steal an airboat to take the panther deep into the swamp. Stars Curtis Osceola.

Shook (TV) Short-form series; digitally premiered Sep. 28, 2019, on Disney Channel YouTube, followed by a Jan. 20, 2020, debut on Disney Channel. With the support of her extroverted best friend, Fredgy, and a new mentor, Ritz, 15-year-old Mia Brooks begins to express her true self through the art of street dance. Stars Sofia Wylie (Mia), Somali Rose (Skyler), LeShay Tomlinson (Sandra), Wayne Mackins (Ritz), Sydney Sepulveda (Fredgy). From DBP Donut.

Shoot to Kill (film) FBI agent Warren Stantin is in pursuit of a ruthless murderer/extortionist who is fleeing the country by posing as one of a group of fishermen on a trek through the mountains near the Canadian border. In order to track his man in the rugged wilderness, Stantin teams up with Jonathan Knox, the loner partner/boyfriend of the fishermen's guide, Sarah. Knox is angry about being saddled with a tenderfoot whose inexperience in the wild might keep him from reaching Sarah until it is too late, but he and Stantin gradually come to rely on each other. The pursuit continues to Vancouver, where Stantin is on *his* turf and takes the lead in an exciting chase and climax. Released Feb. 12, 1988. Directed by Roger Spottiswoode. A Touchstone film. 106 min. Stars Sidney Poitier (Warren Stantin), Tom Berenger (Jonathan Knox), Kirstie Alley (Sarah). Filmed primarily in Vancouver and its environs.

Shooting Gallery Frontierland gallery at Disneyland; opened Jul. 12, 1957. Remodeled as Frontierland Shootin' Arcade in Mar. 1985. SEE ALSO FRONTIERLAND SHOOTIN' ARCADE (WALT DISNEY WORLD), WESTERNLAND SHOOTIN' GALLERY (TOKYO DISNEYLAND), AND RUSTLER ROUNDUP SHOOTIN' GALLERY (DISNEYLAND PARIS).

Shop Class (TV) Competition series on Disney+; digitally premiered Feb. 28, 2020. Teams of young builders arc tasked with designing, building, and testing unique creations. A panel of experts evaluate and test their work based on creativity and functionality. In the final episode, one team is named Shop Class Champs. Hosted by Justin Long. From Hanger 56 Media.

Shop Together Sundry shop in the Tokyo Disney Resort Toy Story Hotel; opened Apr. 5, 2022.

Shopgirl (film) Mirabelle is a "plain Jane" overseeing the rarely frequented glove counter at Saks Fifth Avenue in Beverly Hills. An artist struggling to keep up with even the minimum payment on her credit card and student loans, she keeps to herself until a rich, handsome fifty-something named Ray Porter sweeps her off her feet. Simultaneously Mirabelle is being pursued by Jeremy, a basic bachelor who is not quite as cultured and

successful as Ray. The film is a glimpse inside the lives of 3 very different people on diverse paths, but all in search of love. A Touchstone film in association with Hyde Park Entertainment. Directed by Anand Tucker. Limited release on Oct. 21, 2005, in Los Angeles, New York City, and Toronto; general release on Oct. 28, 2005. Original release on Nov. 11, 2004, in Russia. Stars Steve Martin (Ray Porter), Claire Danes (Mirabelle Buttersfield), Jason Schwartzman (Jeremy), Bridgette Wilson-Sampras (Lisa Cramer), Frances Conroy (Catherine Buttersfield), Sam Bottoms (Dan Buttersfield), Rebecca Pidgeon (Christie Richards). 106 min. Based on Steve Martin's best-selling novella. Filmed in CinemaScope.

Shore, Dinah (1917–1994) She narrates *Bongo* in *Fun and Fancy Free* and sings *Two Silhouettes* in *Make Mine Music*.

Shore, Pauly Actor; appeared in *Encino Man* (Stoney Brown), *Son-in-Law* (Crawl), and *In the Army Now* (Bones Conway). He voiced Bobby in *A Goofy Movie* and *An Extremely Goofy Movie* and Johnny Blowhole in *Star vs. The Forces of Evil*.

Shore, Roberta Actress; appeared in *The Shaggy Dog* (Franceska Andrassy), and on TV in *Annette* serial on the *Mickey Mouse Club*.

Short, Martin Actor; appeared in *Three Fugitives* (Perry), *Father of the Bride* and *Father of the Bride Part II* (Franck Eggelhoffer), *Jungle 2 Jungle* (Richard), *Mumford* (Lionel Dillard), *Captain Ron* (Martin Harvey), and *The Santa Clause 3: The Escape Clause* (Jack Frost), and on TV in *Beauty and the Beast: A 30th Celebration* (Lumière). He provided voices in *Treasure Planet* (B.E.N.), *101 Dalmatians II: Patch's London Adventure* (Lars), *Frankenweenie* (Mr. Frankenstein/Mr. Burgermeister/Nassor, 2012), and *The Wind Rises* (Kurokawa). At Walt Disney World, he appeared in *The Making of Me* and *O Canada!* (revised version, 2007) in EPCOT and in the Monster Sound Show at Disney-MGM Studios; at Walt Disney Studios Park in Disneyland Paris, he starred in *CinéMagique*.

Short Circuit Experimental shorts program at Walt Disney Animation Studios in which staff can pitch an idea and be selected to create an original, innovative short film. A similar program at Pixar is called SparkShorts.

Shot Heard 'Round the World, The (film) A

16-mm release title of a portion of *Johnny Tremain*; released in May 1966. The Sons of Liberty supply information about British plans, which enables Paul Revere to alert the Minutemen to take up arms. Also the TV title of part 2.

Show Biz Is Show in Tomorrowland in the Magic Kingdom at Walt Disney World; played Jul. 12, 1983–Sep. 27, 1985. The Kids of the Kingdom starred in a revue of Broadway and movie tunes.

Show Me America Entertainment event at Disneyland in summer 1970, helping to celebrate the park's 15th anniversary. The fast-paced show combined favorite tunes, old and new, with plenty of humor, lavish costumes, and spectacular sets.

Show Your Disney Side The 2014 Disney Parks campaign inviting guests to share their own "Disney side" with the world by uploading photos and videos of their theme park experiences.

Showbase 2000 Tomorrowland amphitheater in Tokyo Disneyland; opened with *One Man's Dream*, Apr. 15, 1988–Sep. 3, 1995. Later shows included *Feel the Magic* (Oct. 1995–Jun. 14, 1999), *Once Upon a Mouse* (Jul. 1999–May 23, 2004), *One Man's Dream II—The Magic Lives On* (Jul. 3, 2004–Dec. 13, 2019), *It's Very Minnie* (Jan. 10–Feb. 28, 2020), and *Club Mouse Beat* (opened Jul. 2, 2021). In 2000, the venue name was shortened to Showbase.

Showdown at Sandoval (TV) Episode 4 of *Texas John Slaughter*.

Showdown with the Sundown Kid (TV) Show; part 1 of *Gallegher Goes West*.

Showman of the World Award presented by the National Association of Theater Owners in New York; Walt Disney was the first recipient on Oct. 1, 1966, and would be the only person to receive the honor.

Showtime Day Friday on the new *Mickey Mouse Club* (1977–1978).

Shue, Elisabeth Actress; appeared in *Adventures in Babysitting* (Chris), *Cocktail* (Jordan Mooney), and *The Marrying Man* (Adele Horner), and on TV in *Double Switch* (Kathy Shelton). She narrated *Tuck Everlasting* and appeared at Walt Disney World in Body Wars at EPCOT.

Shutters Old Port Royale table-service restaurant in Disney's Caribbean Beach Resort at Walt Disney World; opened Dec. 21, 2002. Closed Apr. 30, 2017, to become Sebastian's Bistro. Also a restaurant at Disney's Vero Beach Resort; open Oct. 1, 1995–Jun. 17, 2016, and succeeded by the Wind & Waves Grill.

Si and Am Pair of Siamese cats owned by Aunt Sarah in *Lady and the Tramp*; voiced by Peggy Lee.

Siam (film) People and Places featurette released Dec. 24, 1954. Photographed by Herb and Trudy Knapp. Directed by Ralph Wright. 32 min. The featurette shows the everyday lives of the people of Siam (now better known as Thailand), their classic dances, how they avoid the monsoon rains, a visit to a teak camp with elephants at work, as well as a visit to Bangkok, the "Venice of the Orient."

Sid Cahuenga's One-of-a-Kind Shop on Hollywood Boulevard in Disney's Hollywood Studios; opened May 1, 1989. Buyers scoured the memorabilia auctions and sales to find interesting items to sell in the shop, whether it was a movie star's autograph or a costume or a prop from a film. Occasionally, there was an authentic Walt Disney autograph in stock, priced well over $1,000, and there were also stills, posters, and press kits from Disney movies of the past. The shop closed Nov. 16, 2013, to become a MyMagic+ service center, later becoming a Disney PhotoPass shop.

Sidekicks (TV) Series on ABC; aired Sep. 26, 1986–Jun. 27, 1987. The pilot movie was called *The Last Electric Knight*, which first aired Feb. 16, 1986, and was repeated, under the title *Sidekicks*, Sep. 19, 1986. The evolving relationship between Ernie, an 11-year-old mystically gifted martial arts expert, and Jake Rizzo, the hard-nosed but softhearted homicide detective who takes Ernie into his home. Stars Gil Gerard (Jake), Keye Luke (Sabasan), Ernie Reyes, Jr. (Ernie), Nancy Stafford (Patricia Blake). From Motown Productions, in association with Walt Disney Productions.

Sideshow Shirts Beachside fashions sold on Paradise Pier in Disney California Adventure; opened Feb. 8, 2001. Closed Jan. 7, 2018, to become Bing Bong's Sweet Stuff.

Siempre Fui Yo (It Was Always Me) (TV) A Disney+ original series; digitally premiered Jul.

20, 2022, after a Jun. 15 debut in Latin America. Twenty-two-year-old Lupe's life suddenly changes after she learns that her father, a famous Colombian singer-songwriter, has died. Upon arriving in Colombia, Lupe meets Noah, a mysterious character who turns out to be her father's assistant. Suspecting that the musician's death was not an accident, Lupe embarks on a musical adventure full of danger, mystery, and romance in the Caribbean region of Colombia. Stars Karol Sevilla (Lupe), Pipe Bueno (Noah), Christian Tappan (El Faraón). From The Mediapro Studio.

Sights and Sounds Recording studio on Hollywood Boulevard in Disney-MGM Studios; opened May 1, 1989, presented by Selah. Guests could create their own music video. Later became part of Keystone Clothiers.

Sigman Lowery, Paula An archivist at the Walt Disney Archives for 15 years, she later was the founding head of the Walt Disney Collectors Society. She has served as creative manager at Disney Character Voices (1989–1992), creative consultant at The Walt Disney Family Museum (beginning in 2005), curatorial consultant for the Walt Disney 110th Anniversary exhibit (for Walt Disney Consumer Products Japan, 2011–2012) and the traveling "Treasures of the Walt Disney Archives" exhibit (for The Walt Disney Company Japan), and curator for "Disney100: The Exhibition."

Sign of Zorro, The (film) Theatrical compilation of several *Zorro* shows; released first in Japan in Nov. 1958, and in the U.S. on Jun. 11, 1960; an edited version was released on Jun. 9, 1978. Directed by Norman Foster and Lewis R. Foster. Don Diego returns to the pueblo of Los Angeles after completing his schooling in Spain. At home he challenges the cruel tyranny of Monastario, becoming the secret savior of the oppressed, but outwardly playing the fop. When he is captured, he turns the tables on Monastario by revealing his true identity to his friend, the Viceroy from Spain. 90 min. Black and white. Stars Guy Williams (Zorro), Henry Calvin (Sgt. Garcia), Gene Sheldon (Bernardo), Britt Lomond (Monastario). First released on video in 1982.

Signature Shop Personalizing services offered in the Lake Buena Vista Shopping Village at Walt Disney World; opened Dec. 1975. It became part of 2R's – Read'n & Rite'n the following year. Also

a World Bazaar shop in Tokyo Disneyland; open Apr. 15, 1983–1998 and succeeded by The Home Store.

Signs (film) In Bucks County, Pennsylvania, a mysterious, intricate 500-foot design of circles and lines appears carved into a family's field of crops. Graham Hess, the family patriarch, still bereft over the accidental death of his wife, is tested in his journey to find the truth behind the unfolding mystery. Directed by M. Night Shyamalan. A Touchstone film. Released Aug. 2, 2002. Stars Mel Gibson (Graham Hess), Joaquin Phoenix (Merrill Hess), Cherry Jones (Officer Paski), Rory Culkin (Morgan Hess), Abigail Breslin (Bo Hess), Patricia Kalember (Colleen Hess). The director himself plays the role of Ray Reddy. 107 min. Filmed on location in Pennsylvania.

Silent Trigger (film) Direct-to-video release Sep. 16, 1997, by Hollywood Pictures, of a Dolph Lundgren action/adventure feature co-starring Gina Bellman, Conrad Dunn, and Christopher Heyerdahl. A professional government hit man partners with a novice young woman for a final hit from the top of a still unfinished skyscraper, only to discover that there are plans to make them the victims. Directed by Russell Mulcahy. 98 min.

Silhouette Studio Since 1955, guests have had their silhouette made on Main Street, U.S.A. in Disneyland, and similar shops have opened in the Magic Kingdom at Walt Disney World, Tokyo Disneyland, Disneyland Paris, and Hong Kong Disneyland. The artists are famous for working at a rate of 60 seconds per portrait.

Silk Road Garden Restaurant in the Tokyo DisneySea Hotel MiraCosta at Tokyo Disney Resort; opened Sep. 4, 2001. Cantonese dishes are served in an intriguing atmosphere where murals depict Marco Polo's journey.

Silly Symphony A series of 75 cartoons, beginning with *The Skeleton Dance* in 1929. Composer Carl Stalling suggested to Walt Disney that there be a second cartoon series to be different from the Mickey Mouse series, which was based on comedic action centered around one character. The Silly Symphonies would be based on musical themes, and each would feature a different cast of characters. The series served as the training ground for the animators and other Disney artists as they prepared for the feature films. Seven Silly Symphonies won

Academy Awards for best cartoon. The Silly Symphony cartoons are:

1. *The Skeleton Dance*, 1929
2. *El Terrible Toreador*, 1929
3. *Springtime*, 1929
4. *Hell's Bells*, 1929
5. *The Merry Dwarfs*, 1929
6. *Summer*, 1930
7. *Autumn*, 1930
8. *Cannibal Capers*, 1930
9. *Night*, 1930
10. *Frolicking Fish*, 1930
11. *Arctic Antics*, 1930
12. *Midnight in a Toy Shop*, 1930
13. *Monkey Melodies*, 1930
14. *Winter*, 1930
15. *Playful Pan*, 1930
16. *Birds of a Feather*, 1931
17. *Mother Goose Melodies*, 1931
18. *The China Plate*, 1931
19. *The Busy Beavers*, 1931
20. *Egyptian Melodies*, 1931
21. *The Cat's Out*, 1931
22. *The Clock Store*, 1931
23. *The Spider and the Fly*, 1931
24. *The Fox Hunt*, 1931
25. *The Ugly Duckling*, 1931
26. *The Bird Store*, 1932
27. *The Bears and Bees*, 1932
28. *Just Dogs*, 1932
29. *Flowers and Trees*, 1932 (first color)
30. *King Neptune*, 1932
31. *Bugs in Love*, 1932 (black and white)
32. *Babes in the Woods*, 1932
33. *Santa's Workshop*, 1932
34. *Birds in the Spring*, 1933
35. *Father Noah's Ark*, 1933
36. *Three Little Pigs*, 1933
37. *Old King Cole*, 1933
38. *Lullaby Land*, 1933
39. *The Pied Piper*, 1933
40. *The Night Before Christmas*, 1933
41. *The China Shop*, 1934
42. *Grasshopper and the Ants*, 1934
43. *Funny Little Bunnies*, 1934
44. *The Big Bad Wolf*, 1934
45. *The Wise Little Hen*, 1934
46. *The Flying Mouse*, 1934
47. *Peculiar Penguins*, 1934
48. *The Goddess of Spring*, 1934
49. *The Tortoise and the Hare*, 1935
50. *The Golden Touch*, 1935
51. *The Robber Kitten*, 1935
52. *Water Babies*, 1935
53. *The Cookie Carnival*, 1935
54. *Who Killed Cock Robin?*, 1935
55. *Music Land*, 1935
56. *Three Orphan Kittens*, 1935
57. *Cock o' the Walk*, 1935
58. *Broken Toys*, 1935
59. *Elmer Elephant*, 1936
60. *Three Little Wolves*, 1936
61. *Toby Tortoise Returns*, 1936
62. *Three Blind Mouseketeers*, 1936
63. *The Country Cousin*, 1936
64. *Mother Pluto*, 1936
65. *More Kittens*, 1936
66. *Woodland Café*, 1937
67. *Little Hiawatha*, 1937
68. *The Old Mill*, 1937
69. *Moth and the Flame*, 1938
70. *Wynken, Blynken and Nod*, 1938
71. *Farmyard Symphony*, 1938
72. *Merbabies*, 1938
73. *Mother Goose Goes Hollywood*, 1938
74. *The Practical Pig*, 1939
75. *The Ugly Duckling*, 1939 (remake)

Note: *Ferdinand the Bull*, originally planned as a Silly Symphony, was released instead as a special short.

Silly Symphony Swings Classic swing ride attraction in Paradise Gardens Park (formerly Paradise Pier) in Disney California Adventure; opened Jun. 11, 2010, replacing the Orange Stinger. The attraction's opening coincided with the 75th anniversary of its inspiration, *The Band Concert*. As in the short, the soundtrack features excerpts from Rossini's opera *William Tell*, and gilded artwork panels ("cartouches") depict scenes from the film.

Silver Fox and Sam Davenport, The (TV) Show aired Oct. 14, 1962. Field producer was Hank Schloss. A fox stows away in a farmer's wagon and is soon mistakenly accused of being a chicken thief. Stars Gordon Perry (Sam).

Silver Screen Partners A limited partnership formed to put up money for the production costs of films, with the investors recouping their investment from the gross amounts the films earned in all their markets and forms. The partners were guaranteed their principal back 5 years after a film's initial theatrical release. There have been 3 offerings, all with shares priced as $500 per unit: Silver Screen Partners II began in Jan. 1985 and raised $193 million. Its 28,000 investors put money into such films as *The Color of*

Money, Down and Out in Beverly Hills, and *Ruthless People*. Silver Screen Partners III began in Jan. 1987 and raised $300 million through 44,000 investors. Their films included *Good Morning, Vietnam*; *Three Men and a Baby*; *Who Framed Roger Rabbit*; and *Honey, I Shrunk the Kids*. Silver Screen Partners IV began in Jun. 1988 and through 52,000 investors raised $400 million. Their films included *The Good Mother*, *Beaches*, *Dead Poets Society*, *Turner & Hooch*, and *The Little Mermaid*. (There was a Silver Screen Partners I, but it invested in HBO films, not in Disney.) The successor to Silver Screen Partners for Disney films was Touchwood Pacific Partners.

Silver Spur Steakhouse Frontierland restaurant in Disneyland Paris; opened Apr. 12, 1992.

Silver Spur Supplies Frontierland shop in Disneyland; opened Jun. 29, 1990. Part of Bonanza Outfitters, which succeeded the Pendleton Woolen Mills Dry Goods Store.

Silvers, Phil (1912–1985) Actor; appeared in *The Boatniks* (Harry Simmons) and *The Strongest Man in the World* (Krinkle).

Sim, Alastair (1900–1976) Actor; appeared in *The Littlest Horse Thieves* (Lord Harrogate).

Simba Lion hero of *The Lion King*; voiced by Jonathan Taylor Thomas (young) and Matthew Broderick (adult).

Simba's Clubhouse Children's care and play area at Disney's Animal Kingdom Lodge; arts and crafts, video and board games, Disney movies, and meals were offered. In 2018, it became an activity center for families.

Simmons, Jean (1929–2010) Actress; appeared on The Disney Channel in *Great Expectations* (Miss Havisham), and on ABC in *One More Mountain* (Sarah). She voiced Grandma Sophie in *Howl's Moving Castle*.

Simon Birch (film) Simon Birch is the smallest baby ever born at Gravestown Memorial Hospital, and as he gets older, he remains small. Certain he is going to become a hero, he argues about faith with his Sunday school teacher and priest, and pals around with his best friend, Joe. However, when his first hit in a baseball game, a high foul ball, accidentally kills Joe's mother, the destinies of the 2 boys become linked. Simon helps Joe look for his father, while trying to figure out how he is supposed to become a hero. A Hollywood Pictures film in association with Caravan Pictures. Released Sep. 11, 1998. Directed by Mark Steven Johnson. Stars Ian Michael Smith (Simon Birch), Joseph Mazzello (Joe Wenteworth), Ashley Judd (Rebecca Wenteworth), Oliver Platt (Ben Goodrich), David Strathairn (Rev. Russell), Jan Hooks (Miss Leavey). Jim Carrey appears briefly as the adult Joe Wenteworth and narrator. Eleven-year-old Smith is afflicted with Morquio's syndrome, a rare genetic disorder that causes dwarfism. 114 min. Suggested by John Irving's best-selling novel *A Prayer for Owen Meany*. Filmed on location mostly in Canada, ranging from Toronto to Lunenburg, Nova Scotia. The bus accident scene was filmed both in the French River, 250 miles north of Toronto, and, to get underwater close-ups safely, in the USC Olympic Stadium pool in Los Angeles.

Simple Machines: A Moving Experience (film) Educational film; released in Mar. 1986. 15 min. Introduction to basic concepts of mechanical physics using simple machines and mimes performing the same movements.

Simple Things, The (film) Mickey Mouse cartoon released Apr. 18, 1953. Directed by Charles Nichols. While Mickey fishes at the beach, Pluto has bad encounters with a clam and then a seagull that also steals Mickey's bait and fish. The pair is eventually chased away by all the gull's friends. The last Mickey Mouse cartoon for 30 years (until *Mickey's Christmas Carol*).

Simple Twist of Fate, A (film) Cabinetmaker Michael McCann has withdrawn from society to lead a solitary, unencumbered life, but one fateful winter's night, the beguiling baby daughter of a young mother who has died in the snow wanders into Michael's secluded cabin. As a result, his life changes forever. A strong attachment develops between the man and the girl, and he legally adopts her, naming her Mathilda McCann. Together, they begin life anew, thriving on mutual devotion. But, unknown to Michael, his daughter's biological father is a local politician who observes the girl's progress from a distance, while making plans of his own for the child's future. When he eventually comes forth and demands custody, a bitter controversy ensues. Released Sep. 2, 1994. Directed by Gillies MacKinnon. A Touchstone film. 106 min. Stars Steve Martin (Michael McCann), Gabriel Byrne (John Newland), Catherine O'Hara (Mrs.

Simon), Stephen Baldwin (Tanny Newland). Written by Steve Martin, who was inspired by the 19th-century novel *Silas Marner*, by George Eliot. Filmed on location in and around Atlanta.

Simply Mad About the Mouse (video) Classic Disney songs sung to a modern beat, with performers surrounded by animated backgrounds and special effects. Directed by Scot Garen. Features Billy Joel, Ric Ocasek, LL Cool J, the Gipsy Kings, Harry Connick Jr., Bobby McFerrin, Soul II Soul, Michael Bolton. Video release on Sep. 27, 1991. 35 min.

SIMporium SEE AFTER MARKET SHOP.

Simpsons, The (TV) With the purchase of 21st Century Fox in 2019, Disney acquired the long-running animated sitcom created by Matt Groening that first aired on Fox in 1989. Episodes were made available on Disney+ beginning Nov. 12, 2019, and new shorts have also been made, beginning with *Playdate with Destiny* (released in theaters Mar. 6, 2020, with *Onward*). Other shorts have digitally premiered on Disney+, including *The Force Awakens from Its Nap* (May 4, 2021); *The Good, The Bart, and The Loki* (Jul. 7, 2021); *The Simpsons in Plusaversary* (Nov. 12, 2021); *When Billie Met Lisa* (Apr. 22, 2022); *Welcome to the Club* (Sep. 8, 2022); and *The Simpsons Meet the Bocellis in "Feliz Navidad"* (Dec. 15, 2022).

Sinbad Actor; starred in *Houseguest* (Kevin Franklin) and *First Kid* (Sam Simms), and on TV in *The Sinbad Show*. He voiced Roper in *Planes* and Uroho in *The Lion Guard*.

Sinbad Show, The (TV) Series on Fox; aired Sep. 16, 1993–Jul. 28, 1994. When David Bryan, a young and single computer graphics designer with no thoughts beyond next Saturday night's date, takes in 2 foster children, he slowly realizes that he has kissed his carefree bachelor life goodbye. Stars Sinbad (David Bryan), T. K. Carter (Clarence), Willie Norwood (Little John), Erin Davis (Zana), Hal Williams (Rudy Bryan). From Touchstone Television, Michael Jacobs Productions, and David & Goliath Productions.

Sinclair, Madge (1938–1995) Actress; voiced Sarabi in *The Lion King*.

Sindbad's Seven Voyages Arabian Coast attraction in Tokyo DisneySea, sponsored by Nippon Express; opened Sep. 4, 2001. Guests embarked on an enchanting boat ride experiencing fantastic realms, unknown dangers, and unimaginable riches in the fabled lands of the Arabian Nights. After a story revision in 2007, the attraction was renamed Sindbad's Storybook Voyage. In the revised version, Sindbad appears younger and is joined by his loyal tiger cub, Chandu. A new song, "Compass of Your Heart," was written by Alan Menken and Glenn Slater.

Sinden, Donald (1923–2014) Actor; appeared in *The Island at the Top of the World* (Sir Anthony Ross).

Sing Along Songs, Disney's Popular collection from Walt Disney Home Video, first released in 1986. Viewers are invited to sing along to Disney melodies by following the bouncing Mickey Mouse icon. The original releases were hosted by Professor Owl, using footage repurposed from *Melody* and *Toot, Whistle, Plunk and Boom*. Later releases were available on Disney DVD, as *Disney Sing Along Songs*, ending in 2006.

Sing Me a Story: with Belle SEE DISNEY'S SING ME A STORY: WITH BELLE (TV).

Singer & Sons (TV) Series on NBC; aired Jun. 9–27, 1990. A contemporary comedy in the nostalgic setting of a kosher delicatessen on New York's Upper East Side, it chronicles the day-to-day comic crises of an aging Jewish deli owner who hires his black housekeeper's 2 sons as his partners in the family business. Stars Harold Gould (Nathan Singer), Esther Rolle (Mrs. Patterson), Bobby Hosea (Mitchell Patterson), Tommy Ford (Reggie Patterson), Fred Stoller (Sheldon Singer), Arnetia Walker (Claudia James). From Touchstone Television.

Single Parents (TV) Half-hour comedy series on ABC; aired Sep. 26, 2018–May 13, 2020. A group of single parents lean on each other to help raise their 7-year-old kids and maintain some kind of personal lives outside of parenthood. The series begins when the group meets Will, a thirtysomething guy who's been so focused on raising his daughter that he's lost sight of who he is as a man. When the other single parents see just how far down the rabbit hole of PTA, parenting, and princesses Will has gone, they band together to get him out in the world and make him realize that being a great parent doesn't mean sacrificing everything about your own identity. Stars Taran Killam (Will), Leighton Meester

(Angie), Kimrie Lewis (Poppy), Jake Choi (Miggy), Marlow Barkley (Sophie), Tyler Wladis (Graham), Devin Trey Campbell (Rory), Mia Allan (Emma), Ella Allan (Amy), Brad Garrett (Douglas). From 20th Century Fox Television and ABC Studios.

Sinise, Gary Actor; appeared in *Ransom* (Jimmy Shaker), *Snake Eyes* (Kevin Dunne), and *Mission to Mars* (Jim McConnell), and on TV in *Criminal Minds* and *Criminal Minds: Beyond Borders* (Jack Garrett), and *The American Teacher Awards*. He voiced the Smithsonian narrator in *Captain America: The Winter Soldier* and appeared at EPCOT as the Capcom in Mission: SPACE, 2003–2017.

Sir Ector Wart's foster father in *The Sword in the Stone*; voiced by Sebastian Cabot (who also narrated the film).

Sir Edward's Haberdasher Men's designer clothing, shoes, and accessories in the Lake Buena Vista Shopping Village at Walt Disney World; opened Mar. 1975, expanding in 1977. Closed Mar. 22, 1992, and succeeded by Harrington Bay Clothiers. Named after Walt Disney World executive Ed Moriarity.

Sir Giles The "brave" knight in *The Reluctant Dragon*; voiced by Claud Allister.

Sir Hiss Prince John's right-hand snake in *Robin Hood*; voiced by Terry-Thomas.

Sir Kay Sir Ector's oafish son in *The Sword in the Stone*; voiced by Norman Alden.

Sir Mickey's Fantasyland boutique, inspired by *Mickey and the Beanstalk* and *Brave Little Tailor* in Disneyland Paris; opened Apr. 12, 1992. Also in the Magic Kingdom at Walt Disney World, where it replaced both The AristoCats and Mickey's Christmas Carol shops in Mar. 1996. A large beanstalk is found throughout the shop, and Willie the Giant makes an appearance holding the roof. SEE ALSO BRAVE LITTLE TAILOR SHOPPE (TOKYO DISNEYLAND).

Sir Pelinore Scrawny knight in *The Sword in the Stone*; voiced by Alan Napier.

Siren (TV) Hour-long drama series on Freeform; aired Mar. 29, 2018–May 28, 2020. A mysterious and otherworldly girl is wreaking havoc in Bristol Cove, a sleepy coastal town that legends say was once home to mermaids. Marine biologists Ben and Maddie must work together to find out who she is and what she wants. Could she be a mermaid, a primal hunter of the deep sea driven to land? And, if so, are there more out there? Stars Eline Powell (Ryn), Alex Roe (Ben), Fola Evans-Akingbola (Maddie), Ian Verdun (Xander), Rena Owen (Helen).

Siren's Revenge Treasure Cove attraction in Shanghai Disneyland; opened Jun. 16, 2016. Guests discover hands-on activities and pirate-themed experiences as they roam 3 decks of *Siren's Revenge*, a ship once commandeered by Joshamee Gibbs and now moored at Landlubber's Landing.

Siskel & Ebert (TV) Syn. series beginning Sep. 18, 1986. Chicago film critics Gene Siskel and Roger Ebert reviewed current films each week. Originally aired as *Siskel & Ebert and the Movies*. Gene Siskel passed away in Feb. 1999. For the 1999–2000 season, beginning Sep. 4, 1999, the title of the show was changed to *Roger Ebert & the Movies*. In 2000, it became *Ebert & Roeper and the Movies* when Richard Roeper joined the cast. Roger Ebert died in Apr. 2013. SEE ALSO AT THE MOVIES AND EBERT & ROEPER AND THE MOVIES.

Siskel & Ebert, the Future of the Movies with Steven Spielberg, George Lucas and Martin Scorsese (TV) Syn. special aired on CBS May 21, 1990. 60 min.

Sister Act (film) When a second-rate lounge singer in a Reno, Nevada, casino, Deloris Van Cartier, accidentally witnesses a murder at the hands of her mobster boyfriend, Vince LaRocca, she finds herself on the run. A smart cop out to nab LaRocca places Deloris in the witness protection program, hiding her out in a convent of nuns. The Mother Superior insists that Deloris—now Sister Mary Clarence—take a job in the convent, and she becomes the new choir director. In no time at all she has the group singing hymns with a 1960s beat, spurring unheard of attendance at Sunday Masses. When Deloris is kidnapped and taken back to Reno, the nuns effect a rescue in the heart of the gambling city. With LaRocca captured, Deloris is free to go on her way, but she stays with the nuns long enough to appear in a special performance for the pope. Released May 29, 1992. Directed by Emile Ardolino. A Touchstone film. 100 min. Stars Whoopi Goldberg (Deloris), Maggie Smith (Mother Superior), Harvey Keitel (Vince LaRocca), Kathy Najimy (Sister Mary Patrick), Mary Wickes (Sister Mary Lazarus). Filmed in Los Angeles; San Francisco; and Reno.

Sister Act the Musical Stage show licensed by Disney based on the motion picture; opened Oct. 24, 2006, at the Pasadena (California) Playhouse, starring Dawnn Lewis. Directed by Peter Schneider, with music by Alan Menken and Glenn Slater, and co-produced by the Alliance Theatre Company in Atlanta. On Apr. 20, 2011, a new adaptation opened in the Broadway Theater in New York City, after previews began Mar. 24; it closed Aug. 26, 2012. Also known as *Sister Act* and *Sister Act: A Divine Musical Comedy*.

Sister Act 2: Back in the Habit (film) This sequel has Deloris Van Cartier as a successful Las Vegas nightclub singer being asked by the nuns of St. Catherine's Convent to lead a choir in an inner-city school in San Francisco. Having trouble with rowdy teenagers and shrinking budgets, the Sisters enlist Deloris to masquerade as Sister Mary Clarence and help save the school from being closed. She transforms her music class into a first-rate choir and enters them in a Los Angeles choral competition where they go all out to win first prize. Released Dec. 10, 1993. Directed by Bill Duke. A Touchstone film. 107 min. Stars Whoopi Goldberg (Deloris), Kathy Najimy (Sister Mary Patrick), James Coburn (Mr. Crisp), Barnard Hughes (Father Maurice), Mary Wickes (Sister Mary Lazarus), Lauryn Hill (Rita Louise Watson). Two of the kids in the choir are played by David Kater and DeeDee Magno, who had been Mouseketeers on The Disney Channel's *Mickey Mouse Club*.

Sisu Self-deprecating last dragon of Kumandra in *Raya and the Last Dragon*; voiced by Awkwafina. The dragon's name is short for Sisudatu.

Six Days, Seven Nights (film) Quinn Harris is a rough-hewn cargo pilot who makes his living flying freight in his weather-beaten old plane. His life changes when he meets Robin Monroe, a sharp, driven, magazine editor on holiday with her new fiancé, Frank Martin. When an unexpected editorial deadline requires Robin to be in Tahiti, she reluctantly bribes Quinn to fly her there. Forced down in a storm, the 2 suddenly find themselves stranded on a deserted island, where over the next week danger and romance ensue as the two castaways are thrown into a series of adventures conquering the wilds, evading pirates, and trying to find a way to get off the island. A Touchstone film, in association with Caravan Pictures. Directed by Ivan Reitman. Released Jun. 12, 1998. Stars Harrison Ford (Quinn Harris), Anne Heche (Robin Monroe), David Schwimmer (Frank Martin), Jacqueline Obradors (Angelica). 102 min. The production filmed for 2 months on the Hawaiian island of Kauai, with additional filming in Burbank and New York City. As a trained pilot, Ford did some of his own flying in the film. Filmed in CinemaScope.

Six Degrees (TV) One-hour drama series on ABC; aired Sep. 21, 2006–Mar. 30, 3007. Six very different New Yorkers go about their lives without realizing the impact they are having on one another. A mysterious web of coincidences will gradually draw these strangers closer, changing the course of their lives forever. Stars Jay Hernandez (Carlos), Bridget Moynahan (Whitney), Hope Davis (Laura), Campbell Scott (Steven Casemen), Dorian Missick (Damian), Erika Christensen (Mae Anderson). From Touchstone Television.

Six Gun Law (film) International theatrical compilation of *Elfego Baca* episodes. First released in England in Dec. 1962. 78 min. Stars Robert Loggia. Released on video in 1986.

16 Wishes (TV) Movie on Disney Channel; first aired Jun. 25, 2010. Abby Jensen, a girl who has been eager to reach her 16th birthday, has kept a secret wish list since she was a little girl. But when the big day actually arrives, she makes a wish that changes everything. Directed by Peter DeLuise. Stars Debby Ryan (Abby), Jean-Luc Bilodeau (Jay). Filmed in Vancouver. Co-production between Disney Channel and MarVista Entertainment.

Sixth Man, The (film) Just as college basketball star Antoine Tyler is about to realize his dream of making it to the NCAA Championships, he dies, leaving his brother Kenny to lead the Washington Huskies to victory. Heartbroken, scared, and lonely, Kenny loses his drive to win until Antoine's ghost appears, determined to take his team all the way. Kenny finds his self-confidence and comes to realize he must ask "The Sixth Man" to leave the team so he and his teammates can play fair and square. A Mandeville Films Production from Touchstone Pictures. Directed by Randall Miller. Released Mar. 28, 1997. Stars Marlon Wayans (Kenny Tyler), Kadeem Hardison (Antoine Tyler), Kevin Dunn (Mikulski), Michael Michele (R. C. St.

John), David Paymer (Gunnar Peterson). 108 min. Filming took place at the University of Washington, and at other locations in Seattle and Vancouver, British Columbia.

Sixth Sense, The (film) Cole Sear, an 8-year-old boy, is haunted by his ability to "see dead people." A helpless and reluctant channel, Cole is terrified by threatening visitations from those with unresolved problems who appear from the shadows. Confused by his paranormal powers, Cole is too young to understand his purpose, and too terrified to tell anyone, except child psychologist Dr. Malcolm Crowe, about his torment. As Dr. Crowe tries to uncover the ominous truth about Cole's supernatural abilities, they both receive a jolt that awakens them to something harrowing and unexplainable. Directed by M. Night Shyamalan. A Hollywood Pictures/Spyglass Entertainment presentation. Released Aug. 6, 1999. Stars Bruce Willis (Malcolm Crowe), Toni Collette (Lynn Sear), Olivia Williams (Anna Crowe), Haley Joel Osment (Cole Sear), Donnie Wahlberg (Vincent Gray). 107 min. The film was produced at various locations in Shyamalan's hometown, Philadelphia, and it went on to do phenomenal business at the box office, becoming Disney's highest-grossing live-action motion picture. It also received 6 Academy Award nominations, including Best Picture, Best Supporting Actor (Haley Joel Osment), and Best Supporting Actress (Toni Collette).

Skeleton Dance, The (film) The first Silly Symphony cartoon released Aug. 22, 1929. Directed by Walt Disney. At midnight, skeletons in a cemetery perform a macabre, often humorous, dance before scurrying back to their graves when the cock crows the approach of dawn. It was later featured on the 16-mm release *Milestones in Animation* (1973).

Skelton, Red (1913–1997) SEE AMERICA ON PARADE.

Sketchbook (TV) A Disney+ original documentary series; digitally premiered Apr. 27, 2022. Each episode features a Walt Disney Animation Studios artist or animator who teaches viewers how to draw a character from an animated film. Stars Gabby Capili, Hyun-Min Lee, Eric Goldberg, Jin Kim, Samantha Vilfort, Mark Henn. From Walt Disney Animation Studios and Supper Club.

Skills for the New Technology: What a Kid Needs to Know Today (film) Series of 3 educational films; released in Sep. 1983.

Skin Deep (film) Educational film released Oct. 4, 1993. 26 min. The film educates about eating disorders, for teenagers.

Skinner Head chef at Gusteau's in *Ratatouille*; voiced by Ian Holm.

Skipper's Galley, The Adventureland food stand in Tokyo Disneyland; opened in 1997. Teriyaki chicken legs are served from a shack that, as the story goes, was established by a former Jungle Cruise skipper.

Skippy An alien victim experimented upon by S.I.R. in The ExtraTERRORestrial Alien Encounter. The voice was provided by Danny Mann. Skippy made a cameo appearance as a "Level One" prisoner in Stitch's Great Escape!

Skippy Young fan of Robin Hood, a bunny, in the 1973 animated film; voiced by Billy Whitaker.

Sklar, Marty (1934–2017) Former vice chairman of Walt Disney Imagineering, involved with concepts and writing contributions for most Disney theme park shows. He joined Disney in 1956 and helped develop *Vacationland* magazine. He moved over to WED Enterprises in 1961 to develop shows for the 1964–1965 New York World's Fair, also contributing to special assignments for Walt Disney. Sklar became a vice president, concepts/planning of WED in 1974, was made vice president of creative development in 1979, and in 1982 became executive vice president. He was named president in 1987. He was promoted to vice chairman and principal creative executive when Walt Disney Imagineering and Disney Development Company merged in 1996. In 2006, he transitioned to his new role as an international ambassador for Walt Disney Imagineering. He had originally worked at Disneyland in 1955 to create *The Disneyland News* while a UCLA student. Sklar retired on Jul. 17, 2009, the same day a window was dedicated to him on City Hall in Town Square at Disneyland. His 2013 autobiography was *Dream It! Do It!: My Half-Century Creating Disney's Magic Kingdoms*, followed by *One Little Spark! Mickey's Ten Commandments and the Road to Imagineering* in 2015 and *Travels with Figment: On the Road in Search of Disney Dreams* in 2019. He was named a Disney Legend in 2001.

Sky High (TV) Three-hour show aired Mar. 11 (120 min.) and Aug. 26, 1990 (60 min.).

Directed by James Whitmore, Jr., James Fargo. Two teenagers find themselves the owners of a 1917 biplane and they learn to fly it. They get into various adventures as they fly around the country. Stars Damon Martin, Anthony Rapp, James Whitmore, Traci Lind, Page Hannah, Annie Oringer, David Paymer, Barney Martin, Heidi Kozak. These shows were meant to be the start of a series that never happened.

Sky High (film) When you are the son of the world's most legendary superheroes, The Commander and Jetstream, there is only one school for you—Sky High, an elite high school that is entrusted with the responsibility of molding today's power-gifted students into tomorrow's superheroes. The problem is that Will Stronghold is starting with no superpowers of his own and, worst of all, instead of joining the ranks of the "Hero" class, he finds himself relegated to being a "sidekick." Now he must somehow survive his freshman year while dealing with an overbearing gym coach, a bully with superspeed, and a dangerous rebel with a grudge (and the ability to shoot fire from his hands)—not to mention the usual angst, parental expectations, and girl problems that accompany teenage life. But when an evil villain threatens his family, friends, and the very sanctity of Sky High, Will must use his newfound superpowers to save the day and prove himself a "hero" worthy of the family tradition. Directed by Mike Mitchell. A Touchstone/Gunn Films presentation. Released Jul. 29, 2005. Stars Kurt Russell (Steve Stronghold/The Commander), Kelly Preston (Josie Stronghold/Jetstream), Michael Angarano (Will Stronghold), Danielle Panabaker (Layla), Mary Elizabeth Winstead (Gwen Grayson/Royal Pain), Bruce Campbell (Coach Boomer), Lynda Carter (Principal Towers), Dave Foley (Mr. Boy), Steven Strait (Warren Peace), Nicholas Braun (Zach), Kevin McDonald (Mr. Medulla), Cloris Leachman (Nurse Spex). 99 min. Filmed in Super 35-Scope.

Sky Scrappers (film) Oswald the Lucky Rabbit cartoon; released Jun. 11, 1928. While working on a construction site, Oswald notices a charming lass selling box lunches. He attempts to ward off the advances of the surly wolf foreman toward her, but what Oswald lacks in weight and size he makes up in cleverness, eventually precipitating the wolf into outer space.

Sky Trap, The (TV) Two-hour movie aired May 13, 1979. Directed by Jerome Courtland. A young man in Arizona, in trying to save his mother's business, takes off in a sailplane and finds a secret landing strip. He finds that it is being used by drug smugglers, and he works to catch them. Stars Jim Hutton, Marc McClure, Patricia Crowley, Kitty Ruth, John Crawford, Kip Niven.

Sky Trooper (film) Donald Duck cartoon released Nov. 6, 1942. Directed by Jack King. In his desire to be an army pilot, Donald is tricked into training to be a paratrooper by Pete. In Donald's battle with Pete to avoid jumping, they dislodge a bomb from under the plane that destroys the General's headquarters. As a result, both end up doing KP duty.

Skyfest The city of Anaheim saluted Disneyland on Walt Disney's birthday, Dec. 5, in 1985 with a world-record release of 1 million balloons. Seven thousand lbs. of helium were used, enough to lift 190 people.

Skyleidoscope Daytime fireworks spectacular at World Showcase Lagoon at EPCOT Center; ran Aug. 31, 1985–Aug. 8, 1987. Dreamfinder directed over 70 colorful flying and sailing objects, including ultralight airplanes, 4-story kites, hang gliders, and sailboats, which battled fire-breathing dragons. The working name was Magical Rainbows.

Skyliner SEE DISNEY SKYLINER.

Skyrunners (TV) The first original movie produced for Disney XD. Teenage brothers Tyler and Nick commandeer a small UFO that crashes near their town. They soon realize that the spacecraft is "alive," and Tyler begins to develop superhuman abilities. When the brothers uncover an ominous alien plot to take over Earth, Tyler is captured by the extraterrestrials, so now it is up to Nick to rescue his brother. Directed by Ralph Hemecker. Stars Joey Pollari (Tyler Burns), Kelly Blatz (Nick Burns), Linda Kash (Robin Burns), Conrad Coates (Agent Armstrong), Jacqueline MacInnes Wood (Julie Gunn), Nathan Stephenson (Darryl Butler). Produced by Ranger Productions and Shaftesbury Services II, Inc.

Sky's the Limit, The (TV) Two-part show; aired Jan. 19 and 26, 1975. Directed by Tom Leetch. A boy, Abner, at an English boarding school, resists visiting his grandfather's California farm, but when he does, he is intrigued to find the old man's ancient airplane, which they fix up and fly. Stars Pat O'Brien (Abner Therman), Lloyd Nolan (Cornwall), Ike Eisenmann (Abner III), Jeanette Nolan, Ben Blue, Alan Hale, Richard Arlen, Huntz Hall, Robert Sampson.

Skyway Station Shop Tomorrowland souvenir shop in the Magic Kingdom at Walt Disney World; opened Oct. 1971. Closed May 1994, to become Ursa's Major Minor Mart.

Skyway to Fantasyland Tomorrowland attraction in Disneyland; open Jun. 23, 1956–Nov. 10, 1994. Four-passenger buckets were suspended from a 2,400-ft.-long cable, traveling between Tomorrowland and Fantasyland. The Tomorrowland station was very modernistic; the Fantasyland station resembled a mountain chalet. In the early days of Disneyland, guests could purchase either a one-way or round-trip ticket. Later, it was one-way only. Also a Tomorrowland attraction in the Magic Kingdom at Walt Disney World from Oct. 1, 1971–Nov. 9, 1999, and in Tokyo Disneyland from Apr. 15, 1983–Nov. 3, 1998.

Skyway to Tomorrowland Fantasyland attraction in Disneyland; open Jun. 23, 1956–Nov. 10, 1994. There were 44 gondolas on the cable, passing through the Matterhorn on the way to Tomorrowland. It was the first ride of its kind to be built in the U.S. Also a Fantasyland attraction in the Magic Kingdom at Walt Disney World from Oct. 1, 1971–Nov. 9, 1999, and in Tokyo Disneyland from Apr. 15, 1983–Nov. 3, 1998.

Slam Dunk Ernest (film) Direct-to-video release Jun. 20, 1995, from Touchstone Home Video. The lovable Ernest P. Worrell becomes a basketball star. Directed by John Cherry III. Stars Jim Varney (Ernest P. Worrell), Jay Brazeau, Kareem Abdul-Jabbar. 93 min.

Slater, Glenn Lyricist; wrote the words for the songs in *Home on the Range*, *Tangled*, and *Ralph Breaks the Internet*, and for TV in *Galavant* and *American Housewife*. He also contributed lyrics for *The Little Mermaid* and *Sister Act* musicals on Broadway and for Sindbad's Storybook Voyage in Tokyo DisneySea.

Slater, Helen Actress; appeared in *Ruthless People* (Sandy Kessler), and on TV in *Toothless* (Mrs. Lewis), with guest appearances in *Grey's Anatomy* and *Private Practice*.

Slaughter Trail, The (TV) Episode 6 of *Texas John Slaughter*.

Sleeping Beauty (film) In spectacular style, the film recounts the story of Princess Aurora, who is cursed by the evil fairy, Maleficent, to die before the sun sets on her 16th birthday by pricking her finger on the spindle of a spinning wheel. Despite the loving attempts of the 3 good but often bumbling fairies, Flora, Fauna, and Merryweather, the curse is fulfilled. The good fairies put everyone in the castle into a deep sleep until the spell can be broken. It is only with the aid of Prince Phillip that Maleficent, transformed into a towering, fire-breathing dragon, is destroyed, and the Sleeping Beauty is awakened by a kiss. Released Jan. 29, 1959. Supervising director Clyde Geronimi. In Technirama 70. 75 min. The voice talents include Mary Costa (Princess Aurora), Bill Shirley (Prince Phillip), Eleanor Audley (Maleficent), Verna Felton (Flora), Barbara Luddy (Merryweather), Barbara Jo Allen (Fauna), Candy Candido (Goons). George Bruns's orchestral score, which was nominated for an Academy Award, expertly blended famous themes from Tchaikovsky's ballet. Sammy Fain, Jack Lawrence, Tom Adair, Winston Hibler, Erdman Penner, and Ted Sears wrote lyrics to such songs as "I Wonder" and "Once Upon a Dream." Based upon the Charles Perrault version of "Sleeping Beauty," the film had an overall stylistic look conceived by artist Eyvind Earle, today known for his paintings and Christmas card designs. With a budget that exceeded $6 million in 1959, this was Walt Disney's most lavish and expensive animated feature to date. Though not an initial box office success, the film has proven to be a unique asset with popular reissues in 1970, 1979, and 1986. First released on video in 1986.

Sleeping Beauty Castle Fantasyland landmark in Disneyland. On opening day, the drawbridge was lowered for the only time until the New Fantasyland opened in 1983. In order to use vacant space, the interior of the castle was opened as a walk-through attraction featuring dioramas telling the *Sleeping Beauty* story in 1957, with Shirley Temple making the dedication Apr. 28. The interior was expanded in 1968 and redesigned in Nov. 1977. It has been questioned why Walt Disney built the castle relatively small (it only rises 77 feet above the moat), but he actually had a very good reason. He recalled that the tyrants in Europe built huge, imposing castles in order to intimidate the peasants. Walt wanted his castle to be friendly, so it was built on a smaller scale. While it looks in many ways similar to Neuschwanstein Castle in Bavaria, this one is actually modeled after a number of medieval European castles. The faux building stones give a forced perspective, making the castle seem larger than it is, with larger ones at the bottom and smaller ones above. Herb Ryman, the Disneyland designer extraordinaire, was responsible for much of the look of the castle; after Ryman's death in 1989, a tree was planted in front of the castle in his honor. The walk-through attraction closed Oct. 7, 2001, and was later redesigned and upgraded, reopening to guests in Dec. 2008. Hong Kong Disneyland opened with a Sleeping Beauty Castle patterned after the one at Disneyland; the structure closed Jan. 1, 2018, reopening Nov. 2020, as a towering new icon, the Castle of Magical Dreams. SEE ALSO LE CHÂTEAU DE LA BELLE AU BOIS DORMANT (DISNEYLAND PARIS).

Sleepwalker, The (film) Pluto cartoon released Jul. 3, 1942. Directed by Clyde Geronimi. Walking in his sleep, Pluto presents a female dachshund with a bone but wants it back when he awakens, until he realizes the dog and her family of puppies need it more than he does.

Sleepy One of the Seven Dwarfs; voiced by Pinto Colvig.

Sleepy Hollow Refreshments Liberty Square counter-service cottage in the Magic Kingdom at Walt Disney World; opened in 1971. The structure bears a resemblance to the home of *Legend of Sleepy Hollow* author Washington Irving.

Sleepy Time Donald (film) Donald Duck cartoon released May 9, 1947. Directed by Jack King. Donald is a sleepwalker. When he sleepwalks to Daisy's house, she humors him and gets him home only to have him wake up and accuse her of sleepwalking.

Sleepy Whale Shoppe, The Shop in the shape of a lazy, kindhearted whale in Mermaid Lagoon at Tokyo DisneySea; opened Sep. 4, 2001. Nearby, guests can have their portraits drawn as a character from *The Little Mermaid* and have their silhouette made.

Sleigh Bells (film) Oswald the Lucky Rabbit cartoon; released Jul. 23, 1928. After getting into a fast hockey game, Oswald catches sight of a maiden

struggling to stay up on the ice. A balloon attachment proves unreliable, for suddenly the lady is on her way skyward.

Slezak, Walter (1902–1983) Actor; appeared in *Emil and the Detectives* (Baron).

Slide, Donald, Slide (film) Donald Duck cartoon released Nov. 25, 1949. Directed by Jack Hannah. A fight between Donald and a bee over which radio program to listen to (Donald wants a baseball game; the bee wants a classical music concert) ends up with Donald locked in the shower, stung, and the bee happily listening to his favorite program.

Slinky Dog Trusty dachshund toy in the Toy Story films; voiced originally by Jim Varney, then by Blake Clark beginning with *Toy Story 3*.

Slinky Dog Dash Family coaster attraction in Toy Story Land at Disney's Hollywood Studios; opened Jun. 30, 2018. Guests board the coils of Slinky Dog, whom Andy has placed on the track of his Dash & Dodge Mega Coaster Kit, for a rip-roaring ride around the backyard.

Slinky Dog Spin Attraction in Toy Story Land at Hong Kong Disneyland (opened Nov. 17, 2013), Disney-Pixar Toy Story Land in Shanghai Disneyland (Apr. 26, 2018), and Toy Story Playland in Walt Disney Studios Park at Disneyland Paris (Aug. 17, 2010, as Slinky Dog Zigzag Spin). Guests ride atop Slinky Dog as he chases his tail around a giant dog bowl.

Slue Foot Sue Cowgirl in the *Pecos Bill* segment of *Melody Time*.

Slumber Party, The (TV) A Disney original movie announced for future release. Depicts the hilarious aftermath of a sleepover birthday party hypnotism gone wrong as best friends Megan and Paige, along with soon-to-be stepsister Veronica, wake up with absolutely no memory of the night before. Now they must retrace their steps to find missing birthday girl Anna Maria and explain why there's a flock of baby ducks in the bathtub, what happened to Megan's left eyebrow, and why she's wearing dreamboat Jake Ramirez's signature black hoodie. Stars Darby Camp (Megan), Emmy Liu-Wang (Paige), Valentina Herrera (Anna Maria), Dallas Liu (Mikey), Alex Cooper Cohen (Veronica), Ramon Rodriguez (Jake). Based on the teen novel

The Sleepover by Jen Malone. From Imagine Kids+Family.

Small and Frye (TV) Limited series of 6 episodes, airing Mar. 7–Jun. 15, 1983, on CBS. A detective has the ability to shrink to 6 inches in height. Stars Darren McGavin, Jack Blessing, Debbie Zipp, Bill Daily, Warren Berlinger, Kristoffer Tabori.

Small Animals of the Plains (film) Part of *The Vanishing Prairie*; released on 16 mm for schools in Sep. 1962. Tells of prairie dogs, badgers, cottontails, porcupines, and other small animals in their daily struggle against predators.

Small Fry (film) Animated short from Pixar Animation Studios; released with *The Muppets* Nov. 23, 2011. Buzz Lightyear is left behind at a fast-food restaurant when a 3-inch kids' meal toy version of Buzz takes his place. While the toys are stuck with the annoying Buzz impersonator, the real Buzz is trapped in the restaurant at a support group for discarded, unloved fast-food toys. As Woody and the gang devise a way to rescue their friend, Buzz tries to escape the toy psychotherapy session. Directed by Angus MacLane. Voices include Tim Allen (Buzz), Tom Hanks (Woody), Joan Cusack (Jessie), Teddy Newton (Mini Buzz), Jane Lynch (Neptuna). 7 min.

Small Light, A (TV) Limited series planned for digital release on Disney+. The story of 20-something secretary Miep Gies, who didn't hesitate when her boss asked her to hide him and his family from the Nazis during World War II. For the next 2 years, Miep; her husband, Jan; and several other everyday heroes watched over the 8 souls hiding in the secret annex. Stars Bel Powley (Miep Gies), Joe Cole (Jan), Liev Schreiber (Otto Frank), Amira Casar (Edith Frank), Billie Boullet (Anne Frank), Ashley Brooke (Margot Frank). From ABC Signature, with Keshet Studios for National Geographic.

Small One, The (film) Special cartoon featurette telling a Christmas story released Dec. 16, 1978. Directed by Don Bluth. Ordered by his father to sell his old, small donkey, Small One, a Hebrew boy in ancient Israel takes the donkey to the Jerusalem market. Finding no buyers there for Small One, the boy is about to give up when he meets a kind man named Joseph. Joseph buys Small One and uses him to take his pregnant wife, Mary, to Bethlehem. 25 min. Featuring the voices of Sean Marshall (Small One), Olan Soulé (father), Joe

Higgins (Roman guard), William Woodson (tanner), Hal Smith (auctioneer), Gordon Jump (Joseph). Based on a story by Charles Tazewell, published in 1947. In 1960, rights to the book were bought by Walt Disney, but the property was never developed. Then, in 1973, Disney writer/artist Pete Young rediscovered the book in the Studio Library and fell in love with it. When the project was approved by Ron Miller, vice president in charge of productions, Young and writer Vance Gerry further developed the script. After several delays, actual production began in 1977. This was the first Disney production created exclusively by the new generation of animators at the Studio, except for "old timer" directing animator Cliff Nordberg, to prove their ability to create a success. More than 150 artists and technicians were involved in the production. Nearly 100,000 final drawings were used in the finished film, with at least triple that number drawn as sketches, pencil tests, and for rough animation. The 3 songs—"The Small One," "A Friendly Face," and "The Market Song"—were written by Don Bluth and Richard Rich. For the first time since *Sleeping Beauty*, a choral sound was used extensively consisting of a 12-voice choir and a 42-piece orchestra.

Small World Gifts & Sundries Shop in the Disneyland Hotel at Disneyland Resort; hats, apparel, gifts, and snacks are sold.

Small World Restaurant Fantasyland restaurant in Tokyo Disneyland; opened Mar. 1987, taking the place of Four Corners Food Faire. It was succeeded by Queen of Hearts Banquet Hall.

Smart, Jean Actress; appeared in *Homeward Bound: The Incredible Journey* (Kate), *Disney's The Kid* (Deirdre), *Sweet Home Alabama* (Stella Kay), and *Bringing Down the House* (Kate), and on TV in *Style and Substance* (Chelsea Stevens) and *Legion* (Dr. Melanie Bird). She won an Emmy for her role as Regina in *Samantha Who?*, and voiced Dr. Ann Possible in *Kim Possible* and Momalus in the *Hercules* animated series.

Smart Guy (TV) Half-hour series on The WB Network; aired Apr. 2, 1997–Aug. 1, 1999. T. J. Henderson is a 10-year-old genius, who leaps from the 4th grade to high school, while in other respects remaining a typical kid. It is difficult for T. J.'s family, African Americans living in suburban Washington, D.C., to adjust to the need to live with and raise a child prodigy, leading to often unpredictable and hilarious situations. Stars Tahj Mowry (T. J. Henderson), John Marshall Jones (Floyd Henderson), Jason Weaver (Marcus Henderson), Essence Atkins (Yvette Henderson), Anne-Marie Johnson (Denise Williams). Omar Gooding became a regular in the 1997–1998 season as Morris "Mo" L. Tibbs.

Smart House (TV) A Disney Channel Original Movie; first aired Jun. 26, 1999. Ben Cooper, a 13-year-old computer whiz, helps his widowed father win a computerized house named PAT (Personal Applied Technology) to take care of their every need. To prevent his father from dating, Ben tries programming PAT to become a surrogate mom, but things get wildly out of hand and PAT literally takes on a life of her own, becoming a very overbearing mom. As chaos ensues, Ben has to outsmart the house, realizing that a computer cannot take the place of a real person. Directed by LeVar Burton. Stars Katey Sagal (PAT), Ryan Merriman (Ben Cooper), Kevin Kliner (Nick Cooper), Jessica Steen (Sara Barnes), Katie Volding (Angie Cooper).

Smash and Grab (film) Animated short; premiered Jan. 18, 2019, in the El Capitan Theatre in Hollywood, followed by digital releases online and on Disney+. After years of toiling away inside the engine room of a towering locomotive, 2 antiquated robots will risk everything for freedom and for each other. Directed by Brian Larsen. 8 min. From the Pixar Animation Studios SparkShorts program.

Smestad, Stian Actor; appeared in *Shipwrecked* (Hakon Hakonsen).

SMILF (TV) Half-hour series on Showtime; aired Nov. 5, 2017–Mar. 31, 2019. Bridgette Bird is a smart, scrappy, young single mom trying to navigate life in South Boston with an extremely unconventional family. She struggles to make ends meet, which leads her to impulsive and at times immature decisions. Above all, Bridgette wants to make a better life for her 3-year-old son. Stars Frankie Shaw (Bridgette), Miguel Gomez (Rafi), Rosie O'Donnell (Tutu), Samara Weaving (Nelson Rose Taylor), Connie Britton (Ally). From Showtime and ABC Signature Studios.

Smith, Alexis (1921–1993) Actress; appeared in *Tough Guys* (Belle).

Smith, Charles Martin Actor; appeared in *Herbie*

Goes Bananas (D. J.), *No Deposit, No Return* (Longnecker), *I Love Trouble* (Rick Medwick), and *Never Cry Wolf* (Tyler).

Smith, Dave (1940–2019) Established the Walt Disney Archives on Jun. 22, 1970, and served as chief archivist for over 40 years until his retirement in Oct. 2010. He wrote numerous articles on Disney subjects as the company's official historian, a regular column in *The Disney Channel Magazine* and *Disney Magazine*, and, in addition to writing 5 editions of *Disney A to Z: The Official Encyclopedia*, coauthored *The Ultimate Disney Trivia Book* (1992), *The Ultimate Disney Trivia Book 2* (1994), *The Ultimate Disney Trivia Book 3* (1997), and *The Ultimate Disney Trivia Book 4* (2000) with Kevin Neary. He coauthored *Disney: The First 100 Years* (1999) with Steven Clark, compiled *The Quotable Walt Disney* (2001), and wrote *Disney Trivia from the Vault* (2012) and *Disney Facts Revealed* (2016), compiling his "Ask Dave" column answers from over a 33-year period. He was a featured speaker at the Disneyana Conventions and the D23 Expo. He was named a Disney Legend in 2007 and continued to consult for the company as chief archivist emeritus after his retirement.

Smith, Dodie (1896–1990) Playwright/author; wrote *The Hundred and One Dalmatians*, which the Disney animated feature was based on.

Smith, Lane (1936–2005) Actor; appeared in *The Mighty Ducks* (Coach Reilly), *The Distinguished Gentleman* (Dick Dodge), and *Son-in-Law* (Walter), and on TV in *Good & Evil* (Harlan Shell).

Smith, Maggie Actress; appeared as the Mother Superior in *Sister Act* and *Sister Act 2: Back in the Habit*, and in *Washington Square* (Aunt Lavinia Penniman). She voiced Lady Bluebird in *Gnomeo & Juliet*.

Smith, Michael (1945–1983) Mouseketeer from the 1950s *Mickey Mouse Club* TV show.

Smith, Orin Became a member of the Disney Board of Directors Jan. 1, 2006, and was elected independent lead director in 2012. He left the board in 2018.

Smith, Paul (1906–1985) Composer; he joined the Disney Studio in 1934 and won an Academy Award for the score of *Pinocchio*, along with nominations for scores of such films as *Snow*

White and the Seven Dwarfs, Cinderella, Song of the South, Saludos Amigos, and *The Three Caballeros.* He wrote the background music for almost all of the True-Life Adventure films and nearly 70 animated short subjects. He left Disney in 1962 and was named a Disney Legend posthumously in 1994.

Smith, Phil (1932–2016) Lawyer; hired as Walt Disney World's first employee in Nov. 1965. He initially helped put together deals for the purchase of the land and helped establish the Reedy Creek Improvement District. He and his family actually lived in a house on the property during early construction of the resort. As legal counsel, Smith held various positions with Walt Disney World for 27 years until retiring as senior vice president of administration and support in Dec. 1992.

Smith, Webb (1895–ca. 1950) Story man; began at the Disney Studio in 1931. He is credited with coming up with the idea of the storyboards, used for planning an animated film instead of a script. He left the Studio in 1942.

Smith, Will Actor; appeared in *Enemy of the State* (Robert Dean) and *Aladdin* (Genie/Mariner, 2019), on TV in *Disneyland's 35th Anniversary Celebration,* and on Disney+ in *Welcome to Earth.*

Smith! (film) A rancher, Smith, who is trying to make a go of a small spread, sometimes aggravates his family with his lackadaisical ways and his friendship with the local Nez Perce people. When one of the members, Gabriel Jimmyboy, is falsely accused of murder, Smith comes to the rescue at the trial. The accused is freed, and the tribe is grateful, coming to the Smith ranch to help with the cutting of the hay crop, and to train Smith's son's prized Appaloosa. Released Mar. 21, 1969. Directed by Michael O'Herlihy. 102 min. Stars Glenn Ford (Smith), Nancy Olson (Norah), Dean Jagger (Judge), Chief Dan George (Ol' Antoine), Keenan Wynn (Vince Heber), Warren Oates (Walter), Frank Ramirez (Gabriel Jimmyboy), Christopher Shea (Smith's son, Alpie). Based on *Breaking Smith's Quarter Horse* by Paul St. Pierre. The song "The Ballad of Smith and Gabriel Jimmyboy" was written by Bobby Russell.

Smoke (TV) Two-part show; aired Feb. 1 and 8, 1970. Directed by Vincent McEveety. A boy, Chris, mourning the loss of his father, cares for an injured dog named Smoke. When he finds out the dog's real owner may be around, he runs away, only to become a hero by saving an elderly couple from a fire. Stars Earl Holliman, Ronny Howard, Jacqueline Scott, Shug Fisher, Andy Devine, Pamelyn Ferdin, Kelly Thordsen.

Smoke Signals (film) A dramatic educational film for children about cigarette smoking. 18 min. Released in Jan. 1995.

Smoke Tree Ranch Walt Disney agreed to buy a lot at this Palm Springs, California, ranch in 1946, with the deed signed in 1949 and the architect hired in Apr. 1950. In order to help fund Disneyland, Walt Disney sold his vacation home, but after the park proved successful, he moved into his second home on the ranch in 1957. Over the years, the Disney family enjoyed horseback riding on the ranch, and Walt became an avid lawn bowler, sponsoring tournaments and having trophies made for the winners. The ranch was considered Walt's getaway, and he frequented the property for the rest of life. He often wore a necktie emblazoned with the stylized STR emblem; sculptor Blaine Gibson even incorporated the logo onto Walt's tie in the *Partners* statue found in the Disney theme parks.

Smokejumpers Grill Quick-service restaurant in Grizzly Peak Airfield at Disney California Adventure; opened Mar. 20, 2015, replacing Taste Pilots' Grill. Inspired by the brave people who fight wildfires that tend to break out in California's forests.

Smokeless Tobacco: The Sean Marsee Story (film) Educational film, a true story about the dangers of snuff; released in Sep. 1986. 16 min.

Smoking: The Choice Is Yours (film) Educational film, produced by Reynolds Film Export and animation director John Ewing; released in Sep. 1981. The film deals with problems of self-image and peer pressure that influence students to begin smoking.

Snackin' Kraken, The Treasure Cove food counter in Shanghai Disneyland; opened Jun. 16, 2016. As the story goes, the ramshackle of a kiosk is run by Driftwood Derwin and pays homage to the legendary multitentacled sea creature.

Snake Eyes (film) A joint production between Touchstone Pictures and Paramount (with Buena Vista International handling international distribution) of a Brian De Palma–directed film. An Atlantic City police detective, Rick Santoro, joins an old friend, Navy Commander Kevin Dunne, who is working with the Secretary of Defense, at a heavyweight boxing match. Suddenly the secretary is assassinated, and Santoro and Dunne join forces to investigate the murder. Released Aug. 7, 1998. Stars Nicolas Cage (Rick Santoro), Gary Sinise (Kevin Dunne), John Heard (Gilbert Powell), Carla Gugino (Julia Costello), Stan Shaw (Lincoln Tyler). 98 min.

Sneakerella (TV) A Disney+ original film; digitally released May 13, 2022, following a May 11 rooftop premiere at New York City's Pier 17. El is an aspiring sneaker designer from Queens who works as a stock boy in the shoe store that once belonged to his late mother. He hides his artistic talent from his overburdened stepfather and 2 mean-spirited stepbrothers who constantly thwart any opportunity that comes his way. When El meets Kira King, the daughter of legendary basketball star and sneaker tycoon Darius King, sparks fly as the 2 bond over their mutual affinity for sneakers. With a little nudge from his best friend and a sprinkle of Fairy Godfather magic, El finds the courage to use his talent to pursue his dream of becoming a "legit" sneaker designer in the industry. Directed by Elizabeth Allen Rosenbaum. Stars Chosen Jacobs (El), Lexi Underwood (Kira King), Devyn Nekoda (Sami), John Salley (Darius King), Bryan Terrell Clark (Trey), Kolton Stewart (Zelly), Hayward Leach (Stacy), Juan Chioran (Gustavo), Robyn Alomar (Liv King), Yvonne Senat Jones (Denise King). 111 min. From Jane Startz Productions, Maple Plus Productions, and Disney Branded Television.

Sneezy One of the Seven Dwarfs; voiced by Billy Gilbert.

Snow (TV) A 2-hour ABC Family original movie; premiered Dec. 12, 2004. In a reinvention of the Santa Claus myth, Nick Snowden reluctantly takes over the family business. But, with only 3 days before the big night, one of Nick's young reindeer is captured by a hunter and taken to a zoo. Not only must Nick rescue the reindeer in time to complete his Christmas deliveries, but he must also do it before the young buck learns to fly and the zoo realizes what it has. In the course of his adventures, Nick touches the lives of those at a boarding house, including Sandy, who works at the zoo and has lost heart during the holidays since the death of her parents, and 8-year-old Hector, who lives there with his mom. Nick tries to bring back the

spirit of Christmas they lost long ago. Directed by Alex Zamm. Stars Tom Cavanagh (Nick Snowden), Ashley Williams (Sandy), Patrick Fabian (Buck Seger), Bobb'e J. Thompson (Hector).

Snow Bear (TV) Two-part show; aired on Nov. 1 and 8, 1970. Directed by Gunther Von Fritsch. A polar bear cub is befriended by Timko, a teenage Eskimo boy, while he is on a year's self-imposed exile from his community, learning the art of the hunt. The soon-grown bear has to be returned to the wilds after it destroys the village's meager supply of food. Stars Steve Kalcak, Rossman Peetook, Laura Itta. Filmed on location in Point Barrow and other Alaskan sites. Released for schools on 16 mm film as *The Track of the Giant Snow Bear*.

Snow Buddies (film) Direct-to-video release Feb. 5, 2008. An unauthorized detour onto an ice cream truck lands the 5 talking puppies on the next plane to Alaska. Stranded in the small Arctic town of Ferntiuktuk, the pups are befriended by Shasta, a husky pup, and his owner, a boy named Adam. The boy has big dreams of becoming a sled dog racer, and even his dad's fears can't stop him from entering the big race. If the Buddies can get him to the finish line, they will be on their way home; so they turn to the wise old husky hermit Talon for mentorship. Sure they can win with the former champion in their corner, the pups go into intensive training. But on the day of the race, they unexpectedly find themselves on their own. Unfamiliar terrain, harsh weather conditions, and dirty tricks from a rival musher teach the Buddies some valuable lessons about heart, friendship, and following your dreams. Directed by Robert Vince. Stars Dominic Scott Kay (Adam), John Kapelos (Jean George), Lise Simms (Meg), Mike Dopud (Joe), Richard Karn (Patrick), Molly Shannon (Molly); with the voices of Kris Kristofferson (Talon), Josh Flitter (Budderball), Henry Hodges (Mudbud), Liliana Mumy (Rosebud), Jimmy Bennett (Buddha), Skyler Gisondo (B-Dawg), Tom Everett Scott (Buddy), Dylan Sprouse (Shasta), Jim Belushi (Bernie). From Keystone Entertainment and Buena Vista Home Entertainment. Continues the Air Bud/Air Buddies franchise.

Snow Dogs (film) When Miami dentist Ted Brooks finds out that he has been named in a will, he travels to Tolketna, Alaska, to claim his inheritance. However, he discovers that he has been left a mischievous team of sled dogs, who have got it in for him. A crusty mountain man, Thunder Jack, also has it in for the city slicker. Wanting to claim the dogs for himself, he urges Ted to return to warmer climates. Released Jan. 18, 2002. Directed by Brian Levant. Stars Cuba Gooding, Jr. (Ted Brooks), James Coburn (Thunder Jack), Sisqo (Dr. Rupert Brooks), Nichelle Nichols (Amelia), Graham Greene (Peter Yellowbear), Brian Doyle-Murray (Ernie), Joanna Bacalso (Barb), M. Emmet Walsh (George). 99 min. For the filming, the town of Canmore, Alberta, Canada, doubled for the fictitious town of Tolketna.

Snow 2 Brain Freeze (TV) Movie on ABC Family; first aired Dec. 14, 2008. It is 3 days before Christmas—crunch time up at the North Pole. Nick Snowden is so busy with his Santa duties that he forgets all about the early Christmas he promised to celebrate with his wife. They have a tiff, and he goes out for a walk as only Santa can, right through his magic mirror, and ends up with amnesia. His old nemesis Buck Seger is on hand to use Santa's amnesia to his own advantage. Directed by Mark Rosman. Stars Tom Cavanagh (Nick Snowden), Ashley Williams (Sandy), Patrick Fabian (Buck Seger).

Snow White Lead character in *Snow White and the Seven Dwarfs*; voiced by Adriana Caselotti. According to the Magic Mirror, she is "the fairest one of all," with "lips red as the rose, hair black as ebony, skin white as snow."

Snow White (film) Live-action reimagining of the 1937 animated classic scheduled for release in 2024. Directed by Marc Webb. Stars Rachel Zegler (Snow White), Gal Gadot (the Queen). New songs by Benj Pasek and Justin Paul.

Snow White: A Lesson in Cooperation (film) Educational film; released in Sep. 1978. Cooperating, even when doing chores, can be a rewarding experience.

Snow White—An Enchanting New Musical A 28-min. stage adaptation of the film; opened in the Fantasyland Theater in Disneyland Feb. 23, 2004, after a Feb. 21 premiere. At the time, it was the most elaborate stage show to be produced exclusively for that theater. Patrick Stewart voiced the Magic Mirror. The show closed Sep. 4, 2006.

Snow White and the Seven Dwarfs (film) A beautiful girl, Snow White, takes refuge in the forest in the house of the Seven Dwarfs to hide from her stepmother, the wicked Queen. The Queen is jealous because she wants to be known as the fairest in the land, and Snow White's beauty surpasses her own. The Dwarfs grow to love their unexpected visitor, who cleans their house and cooks their meals. But one day when they are at their diamond mine, the Queen arrives at the cottage, disguised as an old peddler woman, and she persuades Snow White to bite into a poisoned apple. The Dwarfs, alerted by the forest animals, rush home to chase the witch away, but they are too late to save Snow White. They place her in a glass coffin in the woods and mourn for her. The Prince, who has fallen for Snow White, happens by and awakens her from the wicked Queen's deathlike spell by "love's first kiss." Supervising director was David Hand. Premiered Dec. 21, 1937, at the Carthay Circle Theatre in Hollywood, as the first animated feature film. The film cost $1.4 million and featured such classic songs as "Some Day My Prince Will Come," "Heigh-Ho," and "Whistle While You Work." More than 750 artists worked on the film, which took 3 years to produce. Of many who auditioned for the voice of Snow White (Walt Disney turned down Deanna Durbin), he chose the young singer Adriana Caselotti. Harry Stockwell, the father of Dean Stockwell, voiced the Prince, and many radio and screen personalities were selected for other roles, such as Lucille LaVerne as the Queen and Billy Gilbert as Sneezy. Pinto Colvig (Goofy) provided the voices of 2 of the Dwarfs. Walt had gotten the idea for the film when he was a newsboy in Kansas City, and he saw a major presentation of a silent film version of the story starring Marguerite Clark. The screening was held at the city's Convention Hall in Feb. 1917, and the film was projected onto a 4-sided screen using 4 separate projectors. The movie made a tremendous impression on the 15-year-old viewer because he was sitting where he could see 2 sides of the screen at once, and they were not quite in sync. The film received a special Academy Award in 1939 consisting of one full-size Oscar and 7 small Oscars, presented to Walt Disney by Shirley Temple. For a while after its release, the film became the highest-grossing motion picture of all time, until finally surpassed by *Gone with the Wind* a couple of years later. This statistic is all the more surprising when one realizes that children were paying a dime to get into the theaters in 1937, and the film, of course, had great appeal to that age group. The original worldwide gross was $8.5 million, a figure that would translate into several hundreds of millions in today's dollars. In England, the film was deemed too scary for children, and those under 16 had to be accompanied by a parent. Because it took several years to make the film, there was time to contract licensees during production, and *Snow White* marked the first time a complete licensed merchandise campaign was in place upon a film's release. In Jan. 1938, RCA Victor released a 3-record set of recordings from *Snow White and the Seven Dwarfs*, WITH, as the sleeve reads, THE SAME CHARACTERS AND SOUND EFFECTS AS IN THE FILM OF THAT TITLE. It was essentially the first feature-film soundtrack release, before the word "soundtrack" was used. 83 min. A stage version of the movie played at Radio City Music Hall in New York in 1979. For its 1993 reissue, the film was completely restored, being the first production ever to be completely digitized by computer, cleaned up, and then printed back to film. The film was reissued 8 times, in 1944, 1952, 1958, 1967, 1975, 1983, 1987, and 1993, and first released on video in 1994. In 1978, a 16-mm release, *Snow White: A Lesson in Cooperation*, was released for schools. SEE ALSO FAIREST OF THEM ALL, THE (1983 TV REISSUE) AND GOLDEN ANNIVERSARY OF SNOW WHITE AND THE SEVEN DWARFS (1987 50TH ANNIVERSARY REISSUE).

Snow White and the Seven Dwarfs (stage show) (TV) Taped version of the production at Radio City Music Hall, which added 4 songs to those in the motion picture score; released in Dec. 1980 on pay-TV and then on video. Aired on The Disney Channel in 1987 as *Snow White Live*.

Snow White Grotto Marble figures of the Snow White characters from Italy displayed just outside Sleeping Beauty Castle at Disneyland; opened Mar. 27, 1961. Disney designer John Hench was dismayed when he was given the figures by Walt Disney to display—Snow White was the same size as the Dwarfs. Hench solved the problem by placing her above the rest of the characters, so her small size is not noticeable. Also in Tokyo Disneyland and Hong Kong Disneyland.

Snow White: The Fairest of Them All (TV) A 2-hour movie on *The Wonderful World of Disney* from Hallmark Entertainment; first aired Mar. 17, 2002. Directed by Caroline Thompson. A Gothic version of the classic tale from the Brothers Grimm. After Snow White's mother's death, her father, John, is granted 3 wishes and becomes king, though he soon finds himself under the spell of Queen Elspeth, who becomes Snow White's stepmother. The queen is obsessed with being the "fairest of

them all," and is reassured by her towering hall of mirrors, until Snow White's growing beauty surpasses her own. Stars Kristin Kreuk (Snow White), Tom Irwin (John), Miranda Richardson (Elspeth), Tyron Leitso (Prince Alfred). The Dwarfs are named after the days of the week. Originally aired on TV in Israel in Oct. 2001.

Snow White's Adventures Fantasyland dark ride in Disneyland; opened Jul. 17, 1955. The original attraction used to have a large sign out front, featuring the Witch, warning guests the attraction was scary. When it was rebuilt for New Fantasyland, the attraction was renamed Snow White's Scary Adventures, opening May 25, 1983. It closed for another refurbishment Jan. 6, 2020, reopening Apr. 30, 2021, as Snow White's Enchanted Wish, with new effects and Audio-Animatronics figures. Also a Fantasyland dark ride in the Magic Kingdom at Walt Disney World; opened Oct. 1, 1971, with extensive renovations made in 1994 to actually put the character of Snow White into the ride for the first time. It reopened Dec. 16 as Snow White's Scary Adventures, and closed May 31, 2012, to become Princess Fairytale Hall. Also in Tokyo Disneyland, where it opened Apr. 15, 1983. SEE ALSO BLANCHE-NEIGE ET LES SEPT NAINS (DISNEYLAND PARIS) AND SEVEN DWARFS MINE TRAIN.

Snow White's Enchanted Wish SEE PRECEDING ENTRY.

Snowball Express (film) A New Yorker unexpectedly inherits the "Grand Imperial Hotel" in Colorado, so he quits his job and takes his family west, only to discover that the hotel does not live up to its name at all and in fact is a dilapidated ruin. But the New Yorker perseveres and turns the hotel into a colorful ski lodge. However, he has to enter a cross-country snowmobile race and thwart the local banker in order to do it. Released Dec. 20, 1972. Directed by Norman Tokar. 93 min. Stars Dean Jones (Johnny Baxter), Nancy Olson (Sue), Harry Morgan (Jesse McCord), Keenan Wynn (Martin Ridgeway). Filmed on location in the Colorado Rockies. A city ordinance banning snowmobiles on the main street of Crested Butte had to be temporarily suspended in order to allow the Disney crew to film the snowmobile race sequence.

Snowdrop (TV) A Disney+ period drama series from Korea; digitally premiered Feb. 9, 2022. When a blood-soaked man bursts into the dormitory of a women's university in Seoul, Korea, Yeong-ro will go against her better judgment and risk being expelled to hide the man from his attackers and tend to his wounds. Unbeknownst to Yeong-ro, the man has a harrowing secret that threatens to put her friends' and family's safety at risk, and the 2 young lovers will have to work together to overcome the obstacles. Stars Jung Hae-in, Jisoo, Yoo In-na, Jang Seung-jo, Yoon Se-ah, Kim Hye-yoon, Jung Yoo-jin. From JTBC Studios.

So Close Song from *Enchanted*; written by Alan Menken and Stephen Schwartz. Nominated for an Academy Award.

So Dear to My Heart (film) Jeremiah Kincaid lives on his grandmother's farm, adopts a baby black lamb, and names him Danny. When Uncle Hiram tells him of the prizes sheep can win at the fair, Jeremiah begins to train Danny to be a champion, although once too often the sheep runs afoul of Granny because of his destructive tendencies. But they do go to the fair where the lamb wins a special award. Contains several animated sequences that teach Jeremiah lessons such as "It's Whatcha Do with Whatcha Got" and "Stick-to-it-ivity." Released Jan. 19, 1949. Directed by Harold Schuster. 82 min. Stars Burl Ives (Uncle Hiram), Beulah Bondi (Granny Kincaid), Bobby Driscoll (Jeremiah Kincaid), Luana Patten (Tildy). Ives sings the famous "Lavender Blue (Dilly Dilly)" by Larry Morey and Eliot Daniel (adapted from a folk song); nominated for an Academy Award for Best Song. Bobby Driscoll, the young lead, received a special outstanding juvenile Oscar for his movies that year (which included the non-Disney film *The Window*). Filmed in Sequoia National Park and the San Joaquin Valley, both in California. The train station used on the set had another life after the film was shot. Disney artist Ward Kimball was given the station by Walt Disney to install at his Southern California home. Kimball was an avid railroad buff who had railroad tracks running down his driveway, and he enjoyed surprising new neighbors by stoking up his full-size locomotive on a Sunday afternoon. The film was reissued in 1964.

So Random! (TV) Comedy series on Disney Channel; premiered Jun. 5, 2011. Original comedic vignettes parodying pop culture and a wide variety of everyday events in life. The series brings viewers into the audience of *So Random!*, the hit comedy TV show for kids first introduced in *Sonny with a Chance*. Each episode showcases a performance by a special guest or recording artist. Stars Tiffany

Thornton (Tawni Hart), Sterling Knight (Chad Dylan Cooper), Brandon Mychal Smith (Nico Harris), Doug Brochu (Grady Mitchell), Allisyn Ashley Arm (Zora Lancaster).

So This Is Love Song from *Cinderella*; written by Mack David, Al Hoffman, and Jerry Livingston.

So Weird (TV) Series on Disney Channel; premiered Jan. 18, 1999, and ended Sep. 2, 2001. Explored various mysteries of the paranormal with musician Molly Phillips, her family, and their friends, the Bells, as they traveled across the country. Stars Cara DeLizia (Fi Phillips), Mackenzie Phillips (Molly Phillips), Patrick Levis (Jack Phillips), Erik von Detten (Clu Bell). In the 3rd season, Alexz Johnson (Annie Thelan) joined the cast in place of Cara DeLizia as Fi went off to school. 65 episodes.

SOAPnet Launched by Disney/ABC Jan. 24, 2000, as the first and only cable channel dedicated to soap operas. The channel featured same-day episodes of daytime dramas, as well as original soap-related programming and acquired dramatic series. In Mar. 2012, Disney Junior began replacing SOAPnet, which ceased operations Dec. 31, 2013.

Soarin' Over California (film) Film attraction in Grizzly Peak Airfield (formerly Condor Flats) in Disney California Adventure; opened Feb. 8, 2001. Guests are lifted up to 40 feet in the air and surrounded by a giant projection dome, providing a bird's-eye view of much of the beauty and wonder of California, with an extraordinary sensation of free flight and a musical score by Jerry Goldsmith. 4 min. Walt Disney Imagineering ride engineer Mark Sumner came up with the idea of the unique ride system one weekend by building a model with an Erector Set he had at home. Actor Patrick Warburton plays the chief flight attendant. A similar attraction, called Soarin', opened as part of The Land in EPCOT May 5, 2005. In 2016, the film at both parks became Soarin' Around the World, taking riders above many of Earth's natural and man-made wonders. Soarin' Over California would return to Disney California Adventure for limited runs. Another version, Soaring Over the Horizon, debuted in Adventure Isle at Shanghai Disneyland Jun. 16, 2016. There, guests walk through an ancient observatory before experiencing an aerial tour of every continent, with special segments overlooking Shanghai and the Great Wall of China. The attraction also inspired Soaring: Fantastic Flight in Mediterranean Harbor at Tokyo DisneySea; opened Jul. 23, 2019. In this version, guests enter the Museum of Fantastic Flight, which is presenting a retrospective on visionary aviation innovator Camellia Falco, whose spirit appears and invites visitors to board her greatest achievement—a vehicle called the *Dream Flyer*—for a journey over famous landmarks of the world.

Soaring: Fantastic Flight SEE SOARIN' OVER CALIFORNIA.

Soccermania SEE ALL NEW ADVENTURE OF DISNEY'S SPORT GOOFY FEATURING SPORT GOOFY IN SOCCERMANIA, AN.

Social Lion (film) Special cartoon released Oct. 15, 1954. Directed by Jack Kinney. A lion, feared by all in the wilds of Africa, learns that no one fears him when he escapes in the big city after being captured. However, when he tries to dress up like a human, everyone then recognizes him as a lion and is terrified. The lion ends up in the zoo, scaring all the visitors.

Social Side of Health, The (film) Educational film made for Upjohn's Triangle of Health series; released in Aug. 1969. The film focuses on learning how to live with others while retaining one's own individuality.

Social Studies (TV) Half-hour series on UPN; aired Mar. 18–Aug. 5, 1997. Manhattan's once-posh Woodridge girls' boarding school has its financial problems and tries to weather them by becoming coeducational and taking in students of greater financial, cultural, and ethnic diversity. Stars Bonnie McFarlane (Katherine "Kit" Weaver), Adam Ferrara (Dan Rossini), Julia Duffy (Frances Harmon), Lisa Wilhoit (Madison Lewis), Vanessa Evigan (Sara Valentine), Corbin Allred (Chip Wigley). From Touchstone Television, Film Fatale Inc., and Sandollar Productions.

Society Dog Show (film) Mickey Mouse cartoon released Feb. 3, 1939. Directed by Bill Roberts. Mickey enters Pluto in a dog show, but they are thrown out when Pluto bites the judge. When a fire starts, Pluto saves a female dog, Fifi, and receives a medal for his heroism.

Society of Explorers and Adventurers Secretive worldwide adventure group, known as the S.E.A., first introduced in the Fortress Explorations

attraction in Tokyo DisneySea in 2001, and later carried over to other Disney parks and beyond. According to the legend, the organization originally was comprised of a distinguished body of mariners, scientists, engineers, and artists dedicated to exploring the unknown and living to tell the tale. In the storytelling, the group has existed since the early 1500s. The ever-growing list of Society members includes Captain Mary Oceaneer (Oceaneer Lab on the *Disney Magic* and Miss Adventure Falls in Typhoon Lagoon), Dr. Albert Falls (Jungle Cruise in Disneyland and Walt Disney World), Harrison Hightower III (Tower of Terror in Tokyo DisneySea), Lord Henry Mystic (Mystic Manor in Hong Kong Disneyland), and Camelia Falco (Soaring: Fantastic Flight in Tokyo DisneySea).

Sofia the First (TV) Series on Disney Junior; premiered Jan. 11, 2013. A commoner, Sofia, has to learn how to adjust to royal life after her mom marries the king, and suddenly she is a princess. Along the way, she discovers that the inner character of kindness, generosity, loyalty, honesty, and grace is what makes a real princess. Voices include Ariel Winter (Sofia), Sara Ramirez (Queen Miranda), Wayne Brady (Clover), Tim Gunn (Baileywick). The series is aimed at kids ages 2–7. From Disney Television Animation.

Sofia the First: Once Upon a Princess (TV) Animated TV movie; premiered Nov. 18, 2012, on Disney Channel, and Nov. 22 on Disney Junior. A seemingly normal little girl in Enchancia, Sofia, has her world changed when her mother marries King Roland II. Moving to a castle, Sofia navigates the extraordinary and sometimes magical life of royalty, learning to be a princess in the Royal Prep Academy with Flora, Fauna, and Merryweather as headmistresses. Directed by Jamie Mitchell. Voices include Ariel Winter (Sofia), Darcy Rose Byrnes (Amber), Sara Ramirez (Queen Miranda), Wayne Brady (Clover), Travis Willingham (King Roland II), Tim Gunn (Baileywick), Russi Taylor (Fauna), Barbara Dirickson (Flora), Tress MacNeille (Merryweather), Jennifer Hale (Cinderella). The pilot for the TV series. From Disney Television Animation.

Sofia the First: The Floating Palace (TV) Special on Disney Junior; aired Nov. 24, 2013. Sofia and her family take to the high seas for a royal vacation. At Merriway Cove, Sofia is magically transformed into a mermaid after meeting a young mermaid, Oona. The mermaids mistrust the humans and are angry that Sofia's family's floating palace is in their cove. Sofia gets help from Princess Ariel from *The Little Mermaid* when Oona is captured by a horrible sea monster. Voices include Ariel Winter (Sofia), Jodi Benson (Ariel), Kiernan Shipka (Oona). From Disney Television Animation.

Soft Landing Counter-service ice cream shop in Tomorrowland at Tokyo Disneyland; opened Jul. 1989. Hosted by Meiji.

Solari, Jay-Jay (John Joseph) Mouseketeer from the 1950s *Mickey Mouse Club* TV show.

Solo: A Star Wars Story (film) Through a series of daring escapades deep within a dark and dangerous criminal underworld, the young Han Solo meets his mighty future copilot Chewbacca and encounters the notorious gambler Lando Calrissian years before joining the Rebellion. Released May 25, 2018, also in 3-D and IMAX. Directed by Ron Howard. Stars Alden Ehrenreich (Han Solo), Emilia Clarke (Qi'Ra), Thandie Newton (Val), Donald Glover (Lando Calrissian), Woody Harrelson (Tobias Beckett), Joonas Suotamo (Chewbacca). 135 min. From Lucasfilm. Filmed in wide-screen format. Nominated for an Academy Award (Visual Effects: Rob Bredow, Patrick Tubach, Neal Scanlan, Dominic Tuohy).

Solomon, the Sea Turtle (TV) Show aired Jan. 5, 1969. Scientists study the migratory habits of the green sea turtles, attaching a transmitter to the shell of Solomon, a 350-lb. example. Solomon has to fight storms and a tiger shark as he migrates from the Virgin Islands to his birthplace far off in the Caribbean. Stars Dr. Archie Carr (as himself), Henry Del Giudice (Dr. Hamilton), Steve Weinstock (Mark).

Some Day My Prince Will Come Song from *Snow White and the Seven Dwarfs*; written by Larry Morey and Frank Churchill.

Someone Like Me (TV) Comedy series on NBC; aired Mar. 14–Apr. 25, 1994. Focuses on an 11-year-old girl's realistic views of today's fast-changing world. Stars Gaby Hoffman (Gaby), Patricia Heaton (Jean), Anthony Tyler Quinn (Steven), Nikki Cox (Sam), Raegan Kotz (Jane), Joseph Tello (Evan), Matthew Thomas Carey (Neal). From Touchstone Television.

Someone's Waiting for You Song from *The Rescu-*

ers; written by Carol Connors, Ayn Robbins, and Sammy Fain. Nominated for an Academy Award.

Something Wicked This Way Comes (film) The ominous arrival of Dark's Pandemonium Carnival in Green Town sparks the curiosity of two boys, Will Halloway and Jim Nightshade. Dark transforms some of the townspeople as the boys try to find out the secret of the carnival. The boys hide from Dark, who threatens Will's father, the town librarian, who in turn finally helps good triumph over evil as he saves the boys and causes the destruction of the ominous carnival. Released Apr. 29, 1983. Directed by Jack Clayton. 95 min. Stars Jason Robards (Charles Halloway), Jonathan Pryce (Mr. Dark), Diane Ladd (Mrs. Nightshade) Pam Grier (Dust Witch), Royal Dano (Tom Fury), Vidal Peterson (Will), Shawn Carson (Jim). The film began life as a short story titled "Black Ferris," written by famed science fiction author Ray Bradbury, in a publication called *Weird Tales* in May 1948. It became his favorite work, and when he saw Gene Kelly's direction of *Invitation to a Dance,* he personally delivered the story to the star's home in order to work for and with Kelly on a film version of his story. Kelly agreed but failed to raise the necessary funding. Over the next several years Bradbury converted his screenplay into the novel that was published in 1962 as *Something Wicked This Way Comes* and was an immediate, and enduring, bestseller. Producers Robert Chartoff and Irwin Winkler, plus directors Sam Peckinpah, Mark Rydell, and Steven Spielberg, are among those who were associated with the property over the years. Producer Peter Vincent Douglas's fascination with Bradbury's works culminated in a chance meeting with the celebrated author in 1976, in a bookstore, where Douglas discovered the rights to the novel were available again. Acquiring them, he met with director Jack Clayton and over the next several years, they worked on a script. In 1980, Disney production vice president Tom Wilhite expressed an interest in the project, and in Sep. 1981 the production went before the cameras. Green Town was created on the Disney Studio backlot, after the long-standing generic town square set was bulldozed. It took nearly 200 construction workers to build the one-acre set featuring the elaborate, Victorian-style town. The carnival, a tent, and caravan-lined midway covering 2 acres were likewise constructed on the Disney lot. Some sequences were shot on location in Vermont to provide the proper atmosphere. Live tarantulas were provided for the movie by Animal Actors of Hollywood, and though they performed dutifully, Studio veterans claim that a few got loose on the lot, causing consternation wherever they turned up.

Something You Didn't Eat (film) Educational film depicting the dangers of an unbalanced diet; made for the Cereal Institute, O.W.I. (Office of War Information), War Food Administration. Delivered Jun. 11, 1945.

Somethin's Cookin' (film) Maroon Cartoon starring Roger Rabbit and Baby Herman that opened the feature film *Who Framed Roger Rabbit* (1988). Roger, left as a babysitter, has to try to save Baby Herman from destroying the kitchen and himself.

Son-in-Law (film) When a college coed, Rebecca Warner, brings home to South Dakota her weird resident adviser, Crawl, for Thanksgiving, the traditional-minded family is horrified. But slowly he is accepted by them as he helps each family member learn the value of their own individuality. Released Jul. 2, 1993. Directed by Steve Rash. A Hollywood Pictures film. 95 min. Stars Pauly Shore (Crawl), Carla Gugino (Rebecca), Lane Smith (Walter). The college scenes were filmed at California State University, Northridge, whose campus would be devastated by an earthquake 6 months after the film's release. A farm in Visalia, California, doubled for the South Dakota farm in the story.

Son of Flubber (film) In this sequel to *The Absent-Minded Professor*, the unpredictable Ned Brainard continues his scientific ventures at Medfield College. The professor's use of a Flubber by-product, which emerged from his efforts in controlling the weather with "dry rain" (and his assistant's discovery of Flubbergas), results in a series of climactic incidents that add up to a hilarious finale. Released Jan. 18, 1963. Directed by Robert Stevenson in black and white. 102 min. Stars Fred MacMurray (Ned Brainard), Nancy Olson (Betsy), Keenan Wynn (Alonzo Hawk), Tommy Kirk (Biff Hawk), Elliott Reid (Shelby Ashton), Ed Wynn (A. J. Allen), and many others from the cast of *The Absent-Minded Professor*. Walt Disney's grandson, Walter Elias Disney Miller, makes a short appearance as a baby in a TV commercial. For the football game in the film, exterior shooting was prohibitive because of the special effects and trick shots involved in the sequence. So, a section of the stadium and a major part of the field were reproduced on one of Disney's largest soundstages. It was exact in every detail, from the transplanted green sod and the goalposts to the cheering spectators and the enthusiastic cheerleaders. Since the team opposing Medfield College was composed of professional football players and not actors, they were surprised to be asked to play indoors.

Song, Brenda Actress; appeared in *College Road Trip* (Nancy); on Disney Channel in *Phil of the Future* (Tia), *The Suite Life of Zack & Cody*, *The Suite Life Movie*, and *The Suite Life on Deck* (London Tipton), *Get a Clue* (Jennifer Hervey), *Stuck in the Suburbs* (Natasha), *The Ultimate Christmas Present* (Samantha Kwan), and as the title character in *Wendy Wu: Homecoming Warrior*; on ABC in *Scandal* (Alissa), *Station 19* (JJ), and the *Walt Disney World Christmas Day Parade*; on Hulu in *Dollface* (Madison Maxwell); and guest starred in *Earth to Ned* on Disney+. She has provided several voices, including Chloe in *Disney Fairies: Pixie Hollow Games*, Frida in *Miles from Tomorrowland*, Anne Boonchuy in *Amphibia*, and Vanessa Vue in *The Proud Family: Louder and Prouder*.

Song of Mirage Stage show in Lost River Delta at Tokyo DisneySea; debuted Jul. 23, 2019, on the Hangar Stage, succeeding *Out of Shadowland*. Mickey Mouse and friends seek out the Rio Dorado and its legendary city of gold.

Song of the South (film) Live-action feature about a boy learning about life through the stories of Uncle Remus, which are shown in animated segments. Little Johnny is taken to his grandmother's plantation where he meets Uncle Remus and is guided by his stories ("Running Away," "The Tar Baby," and "The Laughing Place") about Brer Rabbit, Brer Fox, and Brer Bear. Johnny finds friendship with a local girl, Ginny Favers, but is bullied by her cruel brothers. When he is accidentally gored by a bull, it takes more than Uncle Remus to save him. His parents must reunite, creating a happy family once more. The film was nominated for Best Scoring of a Musical Picture and received an Oscar for Song ("Zip-A-Dee-Doo-Dah") and an honorary Oscar to James Baskett for his portrayal of Uncle Remus. Premiered Nov. 12, 1946, at Loew's Grand in Atlanta. Directed by Harve Foster; cartoon direction by Wilfred Jackson. 94 min. Stars Ruth Warrick (Sally), Bobby Driscoll (Johnny), James Baskett (Uncle Remus), Luana Patten (Ginny), Hattie McDaniel (Tempy). Based on the stories of Joel Chandler Harris.

Other songs included "Uncle Remus Said," "How Do You Do?" and "Ev'rybody's Got a Laughing Place." The film and its songs provided the inspiration for the Splash Mountain attractions in the Disney parks. Bobby Driscoll and Luana Patten were Disney's first contract players, since this was the Studio's first major plunge into live-action filmmaking. But since Walt Disney was considered an animated film producer, it was felt that the film should contain at least some animated sequences. Thus, Uncle Remus's stories are shown in animation, along with some clever combinations of the live-action and animated characters. The film was reissued in 1956, 1972, 1980, and 1986.

Songs for Us (film) Series of 3 educational films: *Appreciating Differences*, *Making Friends*, *Sharing and Cooperation*; released in Sep. 1989.

Songs for Us: Part 2 (film) A 3-part educational music video for young children; covers ethnic songs. 10 min. Released in Jan. 1995.

Songs to Sing in the Dark (film) Animated short; digitally released Aug. 4, 2021, on Disney+. Two creatures living in a dark cave engage in a battle of acoustic one-upmanship. As things escalate, they come to realize they are stronger together. Directed by Riannon Delanoy. From the Walt Disney Animation Studios Short Circuit program. 2 min.

Sonia Duck friend of Peter in *Peter and the Wolf*, represented by an oboe.

Sonny Eclipse Audio-Animatronics alien presenting his act in Cosmic Ray's Starlight Cafe beginning in 1995 in Tomorrowland in the Magic Kingdom at Walt Disney World. Sonny is voiced by Kal David.

Sonny with a Chance (TV) Comedy series on Disney Channel; debuted Feb. 8, 2009. Sonny Munroe, a talented midwestern girl, relocates to Los Angeles to join the cast of the most popular sketch comedy show for teens and tweens, *So Random!* But life behind the scenes on a Hollywood set is not as idyllic as Sonny imagined, especially because of her fellow performers: the self-absorbed Tawni, suave Nico, funnyman Grady, quirky Zora, and dreamy Chad Dylan Cooper, star of *MacKenzie Falls*, the teen drama that films in the adjacent studio, and whose cast has a simmering rivalry with the *So Random!* cast. Stars Demi Lovato (Sonny Munroe), Tiffany Thornton (Tawni Hart), Sterling Knight (Chad Dylan Cooper), Brandon Mychal Smith (Nico Harris), Doug Brochu (Grady Mitchell), Allisyn Ashley Arm (Zora Lancaster), Nancy McKeon (Connie Munroe), Michael Kostroff (Marshall Pike), Vicki Lewis (Ms. Bitterman). From It's a Laugh Productions.

Sonoma Terrace SEE GOLDEN VINE WINERY.

Sons of the Pioneers Singing group; appeared with Roy Rogers in *Melody Time* (introducing the *Pecos Bill* segment) and also recorded songs for such films as *The Saga of Andy Burnett*; *The Swamp Fox*; *Sancho, the Homing Steer*; *The Legend of Lobo*; *Johnny Shiloh*; and *The Saga of Windwagon Smith*.

Sooner or Later (I Always Get My Man) Song from *Dick Tracy*; written by Stephen Sondheim. Academy Award winner.

Sorcerer's Apprentice, The (film) Music by Paul Dukas; a segment of *Fantasia*. The film was originally meant to be released as a short cartoon, but since it turned out to be so elaborate (and expensive), it was combined with other segments into the feature film.

Sorcerer's Apprentice, The (film) Balthazar Blake is a centuries-old master sorcerer, a former student of Merlin, in modern-day Manhattan trying to defend the world from his archnemesis Maxim Horvath and other evildoers who had been imprisoned in a series of nesting dolls. Balthazar cannot do it alone, so he recruits Dave Stutler, a seemingly average guy who demonstrates remarkable hidden potential, as his reluctant protégé. The sorcerer gives his unwilling accomplice a crash course in the art and science of magic, and together, these unlikely partners work to stop the forces of darkness. It takes all the courage Dave can muster to survive his training, save the city, and get the girl as he becomes the sorcerer's apprentice. Directed by Jon Turteltaub. Released Jul. 14, 2010. Stars Nicolas Cage (Balthazar Blake), Jay Baruchel (Dave Stutler), Alfred Molina (Maxim Horvath), Teresa Palmer (Becky Barnes), Monica Bellucci (Veronica), Toby Kebbell (Drake Stone), Alice Krige (Morgana). A Jerry Bruckheimer production. Filmed in CinemaScope.

Sorcerer's Lounge Establishment in the Hong Kong Disneyland Hotel; opened Sep. 12, 2005, and closed Jun. 30, 2011, to become Walt's Cafe.

Sorcerers of the Magic Kingdom Interactive role-playing game in the Magic Kingdom at Walt Disney World; began Feb. 22, 2012, after several weeks of testing, and ended Jan. 24, 2021. Players teamed up with Merlin to defeat Disney villains throughout the park by the use of special "spell cards," after following magic symbols that led them to villain hideouts throughout the park.

Sorcery in the Sky Fireworks show presented in Disney-MGM Studios at Walt Disney World; premiered May 29, 1990. It featured a large inflatable Mickey Mouse with fireworks shooting from his pointing finger. Ended in 1998, with *Fantasmic!* becoming the park's nighttime spectacular. Versions of the show have returned occasionally over the years for special events, including the Fourth of July and New Year's Eve holidays.

Sorensen, Ricky (1946–1994) Actor; provided the voice of Wart (Arthur) in *The Sword in the Stone*. He appeared in *The Cat from Outer Space* (technician), and on TV in *Johnny Shiloh* (Rusty).

Sorority Boys (film) Dave, Adam, and Doofer, 3 college playboy chauvinists, are strapped for cash and find one last, desperate hope for free housing—one of the campus sororities, Delta Omicron Gamma (i.e., DOG). The boys go undercover as Daisy, Adina, and Roberta, and everything goes well until Dave falls for Leah. The boys, with a long history of treating women badly, see firsthand how the other half lives. Dave wants to tell Leah who he is, but without destroying Daisy's relationship with the girl of his dreams. A Touchstone film. Released Mar. 22, 2002. Directed by Wally Wolodarsky. Stars Barry Watson (Dave), Harland Williams (Doofer), Michael Rosenbaum (Adam), Melissa Sagemiller (Leah), Heather Matarazzo (Katie), Brad Beyer (Spence), Tony Denman (Jimmy), Kathryn Stockwood (Patty). 94 min.

Sorvino, Paul (1939–2022) Actor; appeared in *Dick Tracy* (Lips Manlis), *The Rocketeer* (Eddie Valentine), *Nixon* (Henry Kissinger), and *Mr. 3000* (Gus Panas); on TV in *The Oldest Rookie* (Ike Porter) and *Godfather of Harlem* (Frank Costello); and guest starred in *Grandfathered* (Jack Martino) and *Criminal Minds: Beyond Borders* (Dr. Scarpa).

Sotto, Eddie He began at Walt Disney Imagineering in 1986 to lead the design for Main Street, U.S.A. at Disneyland Paris and later helped develop such attractions as Indiana Jones Adventure, Pooh's Hunny Hunt, and Mission: SPACE. As senior vice president of concept design, he ran a think tank behind such projects as ABC Times Square Studios in New York City and the Encounter Restaurant at Los Angeles International Airport. He also provided several voices for the parks, including the railroad boarding calls at Walt Disney World and Disneyland Paris.

Souk-Al-Magreb Morocco goods and apparel shop in EPCOT.

Soul (film) Animated feature from Pixar Animation Studios. Joe Gardner is a middle school band teacher who gets the chance of a lifetime to play at the best jazz club in town. But one small misstep takes him from the streets of New York City to The Great Before—a fantastical place where new souls get their personalities, quirks, and interests before they go to Earth. Determined to return to his life, Joe teams up with a precocious soul, 22, who has never understood the appeal of the human experience. As Joe desperately tries to show 22 what's great about living, he may just discover the answers to some of life's most important questions. Directed by Pete Docter. Originally planned for theatrical release, it was delayed due to the COVID-19 pandemic and was instead released digitally Dec. 25, 2020, on Disney+, following an Oct. 11 premiere at the London Film Festival and other international releases. It later had a run at the El Capitan Theatre in Hollywood, Mar. 29–Apr. 1, 2021. Voices include Jamie Foxx (Joe), Tina Fey (22), Phylicia Rashad (Libba Gardner), Graham Norton (Moonwind), Rachel House (Terry), Alice Braga (Counselor Jerry), Richard Ayoade (Counselor Jerry), Donnell Rawlings (Dez), Angela Bassett (Dorothea Williams), Wes Studi (Counselor), Fortune Feimster (Counselor), Zenobia Shroff (Counselor), June Squibb (Gerol), with talent from the music world, including Ahmir "Questlove" Thompson (Curley), Daveed Diggs (Paul). 100 min. Features original jazz compositions by Jon Batiste, with a score by Trent Reznor and Atticus Ross that drifts between the real and soul worlds. For authentic piano playing, multiple camera setups captured footage of Batiste's fingers on the keys; new technology was used, which lit up piano keys on a rig, allowing animators to accurately place Joe's fingers. Filmmakers took special care to ensure different skin types were authentically depicted, also rendering an array of black hair with a variety of textures and colors. To showcase the vast expanse of The Great Before, the film uses the cinematic 2.39:1 aspect ratio. Pixar technology also had to be modified to give the ethereal realm its soft look, such as giving grass a feather-like quality, versus the highly realistic grass-blades used in other Pixar films. Nominated for 3 Academy Awards, winning for Best Animated Feature and Best Original Score.

Soul Man (TV) Comedy series on ABC; aired Apr. 15, 1997–Aug. 25, 1998. Reverend Mike Weber is a widowed Episcopalian minister who is trying to raise 4 rambunctious children. He is also unorthodox, rides a motorcycle, and is constantly stymied in trying to lead his kids down the straight and narrow path. Stars Dan Aykroyd (Mike Weber), Dakin Matthews (the bishop), Kevin Sheridan (Kenny), Brendon Ryan Barrett (Andy), Courtney Chase (Meredith), Spencer Breslin (Fred). From Hostage Productions, in association with Wind Dancer Production Group and Touchstone Television.

Sounder (TV) A 2-hour movie on *The Wonderful World of Disney*; first aired Jan. 19, 2003. The classic story of an 11-year-old boy who grows into manhood while on a years-long search for his beloved father, who has been sentenced to 5 years of hard labor for stealing a ham to help feed his family. The family includes a young coon dog puppy, Sounder, a loyal friend to the boy and an enthusiastic hunter. Directed by Kevin Hooks. Stars Carl Lumbly (Father), Suzanne Douglass (Mother), Daniel Lee Robertson III (Boy), Paul Winfield (Teacher), Peter MacNeill (Sheriff), Bill Lake (Deputy). Hooks and Winfield starred in the original 1972 Oscar-nominated feature film from 20th Century Fox. From Touchstone Television in association with Jaffe/Braunstein Films.

Sounds Dangerous–Starring Drew Carey See ABC Sound Studio: Sounds Dangerous.

Soundstage Restaurant Establishment in Disney-MGM Studios; open May 1, 1989–Nov. 14, 1998. It was initially set up as the Plaza Hotel set from the movie *Big Business*, as if it was the movie's wrap party. Later on, it was themed to *Beauty and the Beast*, then to Agrabah from *Aladdin*, and finally *Pocahontas*. It became Bear in the Big Blue House—Live on Stage in 1999.

Soundstages See Walt Disney Studio.

Soup's On (film) Donald Duck cartoon released Oct. 15, 1948. Directed by Jack Hannah. Donald is soon chasing after his nephews when they steal his prepared supper. But when he falls over a cliff and is knocked out, the nephews trick him into believing that he is an angel. They soon regret their ruse. Features the song "Zip-A-Dee-Doo-Dah."

South America In the early 1940s, as Europe was moving deeply into World War II, America was not yet involved, but dark clouds were gathering on the horizon. President Franklin D. Roosevelt was worried about the influence of Nazi Germany extending to our neighbors in South America. As part of the government's Good Neighbor Policy, Nelson Rockefeller, then Coordinator of Inter-American Affairs, asked Walt Disney if he would travel to Latin America on a goodwill tour. Walt argued that he did not want to go on a hand-shaking trip—but he was willing to take some of his artists and make some animated films about the area. This was agreeable to Rockefeller, so the Disney contingent set off on Aug. 17, 1941, for Argentina, Brazil, and Chile, bringing back to Hollywood sketches, songs, and impressions of the South American life and culture. Two feature films came out of the trip: *Saludos Amigos* and *The Three Caballeros*. Both proved so successful with theater audiences that Walt did not need the subsidy promised him by the government. In addition to the films for theaters, Disney made a number of educational films for the South American market, in the Health for the Americas series. *Walt & El Grupo*, a documentary about the 1941 trip, premiered Apr. 26, 2008.

South of the Border with Disney (film) Documentary featurette produced under the auspices of the Coordinator of Inter-American Affairs to help promote unity between the U.S. and South America; a 16-mm film about the visit of a group of the Disney artists to Brazil, Argentina, Uruguay, and Chile. The artists react to the beauty of the Latin American countries through their sketches. The film emphasizes local customs and ends with the group returning with souvenirs. Delivered Nov. 23, 1942. Directed by Norm Ferguson. See also South America.

South Pacific (TV) A 3-hour special of the classic Rodgers and Hammerstein musical set against the backdrop of World War II; aired on ABC Mar. 26, 2001. A nurse falls in love with a local planter and is devastated when he is sent on a dangerous mission. A young naval officer falls for a beautiful

Native girl, daughter of the local promoter, Bloody Mary. Directed by Richard Pearce. Stars Glenn Close (Ensign Forbush), Rade Sherbedgia (Emile de Becque), Harry Connick, Jr. (Lt. Cable), Robert Pastorelli (Luther Billis), Lori Tan Chinn (Bloody Mary). Produced for Touchstone Television by John Braunstein Films in association with Trillium Productions and White Cap Productions.

South Seas Traders Adventureland shop in Disneyland; opened Jun. 30, 1984, carrying Pacific-themed apparel. Closed Jun. 11, 2017, reopening later that month as a refreshment and seating area.

Southside Haberdashery World Bazaar apparel in Tokyo Disneyland; opened Apr. 15, 1983. Closed in 1988 to become The Bebop Hop.

Souvenir 66 Paradise Pier tourist shop in Disney's California Adventure; opened Feb. 8, 2001. Closed in 2009, to become Seaside Souvenirs.

Souvenirs de France Cultural items sold at the exit of *Impressions de France* in EPCOT.

Space Bar Tomorrowland counter-service restaurant in Disneyland; opened in 1955, offering a preview of futuristic food-service techniques. Closed Sep. 5, 1966, to make way for the Carousel of Progress. It later reopened as a snack bar below the PeopleMover station and was renamed The Lunching Pad in 1977. Also in the Magic Kingdom at Walt Disney World; opened ca. 1974, serving sandwiches and snacks below the PeopleMover station, and also renamed The Lunching Pad in 1994.

Space Buddies (film) Direct-to-video release Feb. 3, 2009. Golden retriever puppies Rosebud, Buddha, Budderball, B-Dawg, and Mudbud travel to the moon in search of a dream, only to realize that what they want is back on Earth. Moving at warp speed, dodging asteroids and more, the Buddies and their 2 new friends, Spudnick, a sweet bull terrier, and Gravity, a resourceful ferret, must summon their courage and ingenuity to launch plans for a moon landing and a rocket trip back home. Directed by Robert Vince. Stars Bill Fagerbakke (Pi), Kevin Weisman (Dr. Finkel), Lochlyn Munro (Slats), Ali Hillis (Astro), Pat Finn (Bill Wolfson), Nolan Gould (Sam), Wayne Wilderson (Tad Thompson), Diedrich Bader (Yuri); with the voices of Jason Earles (Spudnick), Field Cate (Buddha), Liliana Mumy (Rosebud),

Josh Flitter (Budderball), Skyler Gisondo (B-Dawg), Henry Hodges (Mudbud), Amy Sedaris (Gravity). 84 min. Based on the character Air Bud created by Kevin DiCicco. From Walt Disney Studios Home Entertainment.

Space Mountain Tomorrowland attraction in the Magic Kingdom at Walt Disney World; opened Jan. 15, 1975, with a grand ceremony attended by astronauts Scott Carpenter, James Irwin, and Gordon Cooper. Appealing to younger guests who like thrill rides, Space Mountain debuted as a unique type of roller coaster, designed such that passengers ride inside, in the dark—a concept originally conceived by Walt Disney more than a decade earlier. Since riders are unable to see the direction of the tracks, it is hard to brace for the drops and turns, adding to the thrill. Comets, shooting stars, and other outer space effects add interest. For many years, a moving sidewalk at the exit led one past displays of how electronics might affect future living. The mountain itself is over 180 feet high and 300 feet in diameter. Unlike the other versions of the attraction, the original Walt Disney World attraction features 2 tracks and 2 load areas. It was also the first roller coaster to be controlled completely by computer. Also a Tomorrowland attraction in Disneyland; opened with a May 27, 1977, dedication ceremony, following a soft-opening period that began May 4. First sponsored by RCA at Walt Disney World; Federal Express became the sponsor in both parks 1993–2003. Also opened in Tomorrowland at Tokyo Disneyland Apr. 15, 1983, followed by a version in Hong Kong Disneyland Sep. 12, 2005. The Tokyo Disneyland attraction had a major re-theming with new special effects, reopening Apr. 2007. In Disneyland Paris, Space Mountain: de la Terre à la Lune opened in Discoveryland Jun. 1, 1995. A synchronized onboard soundtrack was added to the Disneyland version in 1996 (after the success of a similar system in the Disneyland Paris version). And on Apr. 10, 2003, that attraction closed for a major rebuild, reopening Jul. 15, 2005, with enhanced elements and a new soundtrack by Michael Giacchino. The Disneyland Paris attraction was redesigned the same year as Space Mountain: Mission 2. In Disneyland, the ride was transformed into Rockin' Space Mountain for spring 2007, featuring new lighting, technology, and music. On Sep. 25, 2009, a Halloween overlay called Space Mountain Ghost Galaxy opened in Disneyland, 2 years after debuting in Hong Kong Disneyland. In Nov. 2009, Space Mountain was refreshed at Walt Disney World with a new theme as Starport Seven-Five, a nod to the opening year of the attraction. The upgraded version featured an interactive queue, enhanced load area, on-ride photography, new lighting projections, and "Starry-o-phonic" sound projected through the attraction. A new postshow showcases various intergalactic travel destinations. Hyperspace Mountain, a new version in which passengers join an X-wing starfighter battle, was introduced in Disneyland Nov. 16, 2015, as part of the *Star Wars* seasonal event, Season of the Force. Hyperspace Mountain also opened in Hong Kong Disneyland Jun. 11, 2016, and in Disneyland Paris (as Star Wars Hyperspace Mountain) May 7, 2017, after special event previews May 5–6. In 2022, Tokyo Disney Resort announced that Space Mountain would be rebuilt by 2027 as part of a major renovation of Tomorrowland beginning in 2024. The new story line will showcase a greater connection between Earth and the universe.

Space Place, The A 670-seat Tomorrowland fast-food facility in the Space Mountain complex at Disneyland; open 1977–1996, replaced by the Toy Story Funhouse Jan. 27, 1996. Toy Story Funhouse closed later that year to prepare for the new Tomorrowland. Space Place was also a Tomorrowland merchandise and snack stand in the Magic Kingdom at Walt Disney World; open 1985–1994 and succeeded by Geiger's Counter. In Tokyo Disneyland, Space Place FoodPort was a counter-service sandwich shop housed below StarJets; open Apr. 15, 1983–Oct. 10, 2017.

Space Port, The Tomorrowland shop in the Magic Kingdom at Walt Disney World; opened Oct. 1971, selling contemporary decorative gifts. Closed Jan. 9, 1994, to become Merchant of Venus.

Space Stage See Tomorrowland Stage.

Space Station X-1 Tomorrowland exhibit in Disneyland; open Jul. 17, 1955–Feb. 17, 1960. Beginning in 1957, it was known as Satellite-View of America. Guests viewed a shaped scenic painting of Earth as if it was being viewed from space. The attraction was created by artist Peter Ellenshaw.

Space Traders Tomorrowland shop in Hong Kong Disneyland; opened Sep. 12, 2005.

Space 220 World Discovery restaurant next to Mission: SPACE in EPCOT; opened Sep. 20, 2021. As the story goes, visitors board a space elevator and ascend to a space station 220 miles above Earth. Managed by Patina Restaurant Group.

Spaced Invaders (film) On Halloween, a group of Martians intercept a 50th anniversary rebroadcast of Orson Welles's dramatic "The War of the Worlds" and misinterpret it as their cue to attack Earth. The small town of Big Bean, Illinois, happens to be their destination. Ten-year-old resident Kathy Hoxly is unfazed by the pint-sized invaders, and with the help of her friend Brian, her father, and Old Man Wrenchmuller, she rescues the Martians from a frenzied posse of townsfolk, saves the Earth from the aliens' blitz, and helps blast the visitors back to their planet. Released Apr. 27, 1990. Directed by Patrick Read Johnson. A Touchstone film. 102 min. Stars Douglas Barr (Sam), Royal Dano (Wrenchmuller), Ariana Richards (Kathy), J. J. Anderson (Brian). The "aliens" had electronically controlled heads made of foam, latex, and fiberglass. Unfortunately, the actors could not see out of the elaborate heads, so they were in constant contact with the director by way of wireless headphones.

Spacek, Sissy Actress; appeared in *The Straight Story* (Rose), *Tuck Everlasting* (Mae Tuck), *The Help* (Missus Walters), and as a guest on *Disney's Captain EO Grand Opening*.

Spaceman and King Arthur, The (film) International theatrical title of *Unidentified Flying Oddball*.

Spaceman in King Arthur's Court, The (TV) Title of *Unidentified Flying Oddball*; shown in 2 parts in 1982.

Spaceship Earth Geodesic sphere attraction, the symbol of EPCOT; opened Oct. 1, 1982, and sponsored by AT&T 1982–2002, and Siemens 2005–2017. The story was written from concepts by Ray Bradbury and a host of advisers to the Disney designers. Futurist R. Buckminster Fuller, who invented the geodesic dome and wrote *Operating Manual for Spaceship Earth*, helped inspire the original look and concept for the attraction. The impressive geosphere is 165 feet in diameter and stands 15 feet above the ground on 6 legs. The outer-sphere façade is made of anodized panels smoother than glass and contains aluminum frames for 954 triangular panels with 11,448 decorative facets. Inside, guests board a slow-moving Time Machine vehicle for a journey past highlights of communication history through the ages, from

Cro-Magnon hunters to the present day and into the future. At the very top of the sphere is a majestic star field, which begins a descent back to Earth. The attraction was originally narrated by Vic Perrin. A new narration script with Walter Cronkite and theme song ("Tomorrow's Child," written by Ron Ovadia and Pete Stougaard) were added as part of a refurbishment, debuting May 29, 1986. The show received major renovations in 1994, reopening Nov. 23, with Jeremy Irons providing the narration and a new score composed by Edo Guidotti. With the new sponsorship by Siemens, the attraction reopened Dec. 2007 after extensive renovations. The story line now follows the history of human innovation from prehistoric times to the 21st century, with new narration by Dame Judi Dench and a musical score by Bruce Broughton. The new finale enables guests to imagine their own future through the use of touch screen technology. Guests originally exited into Earth Station, presented by the Bell System (AT&T) 1982–1994. The area became the Global Neighborhood on Feb. 2, 1995, then AT&T's New Global Neighborhood Dec. 1999–Apr. 2004. A new postshow, Project Tomorrow: Inventing the Wonders of Tomorrow, premiered Apr. 25, 2007. From 1999–2007, a giant "2000," and then "Epcot," trailed over Spaceship Earth, supported by an enormous Mickey Mouse hand and wand icon (SEE MILLENNIUM CELEBRATION). For the Walt Disney World 50th anniversary in 2021, new lighting was introduced across Spaceship Earth to create the effect of twinkling stars in the evening sky.

Spacey, Kevin Actor; appeared in *Consenting Adults* (Eddy Otis), *Iron Will* (Harry Kingsley), and *The Ref* (Lloyd), and voiced Hopper in *A Bug's Life*.

Spade, David Actor; provided the voice of Kuzco in *The Emperor's New Groove* and other appearances of the character. He appeared on TV in *8 Simple Rules* (C. J.) and guest starred in *The Mayor* (Ed Gunt).

Spall, Timothy Actor; played Nathaniel in *Enchanted*, and provided the voice of Bayard in *Alice in Wonderland* (2010) and *Alice Through the Looking Glass*.

Spanjers, Martin Actor; appeared in *Max Keeble's Big Move* (Runty Band Member), on TV in *Daddio* (Max Woods) and *8 Simple Rules for Dating My Teenage Daughter* (Rory), and on Disney Channel

in *Good Luck Charlie* (Justin). He voiced Malcolm in *Kim Possible*.

Spare the Rod (film) Donald Duck cartoon released Jan. 15, 1954. Directed by Jack Hannah. Donald's conscience, in the form of a "guidance counselor duck," advises him to deal with his nephews' misbehavior psychologically, rather than physically. Donald mistakes some pygmy cannibals, who have escaped from the circus, for his nephews playing in disguise.

Spark Story, A (TV) A Disney+ original documentary; digitally released Sep. 24, 2021. An intimate look at the filmmaking process behind Pixar's SparkShorts, including *Twenty Something* and *Nona*. Directed by Louis Gonzales. 87 min. From Pixar and Supper Club.

SparkShorts Experimental film program at Pixar Animation Studios to discover new storytellers and explore storytelling techniques. Filmmakers are given 6 months to assemble a team and create an animated short film, and no major rules apply. The initiative's first 3 shorts—*Purl, Smash and Grab*, and *Kitbull*—premiered Jan. 18, 2019, at the El Capitan Theatre in Hollywood, prior to digital releases online and on Disney+. A similar program at Walt Disney Animation Studios is called Short Circuit.

Speaking of Weather (film) Educational film; released in Sep. 1982. The film shows basic weather.

Spears, Britney Actress; appeared on the *Mickey Mouse Club* on The Disney Channel, beginning in 1993. She later became a top-selling pop vocalist and made TV appearances in the *Radio Disney Music Awards* and *Mickey's 90th Spectacular*.

Special Agent Oso (TV) Animated series on Disney Channel; premiered Apr. 4, 2009. Oso, a stuffed panda bear, works for U.N.I.Q.U.E. (United Network for Investigating Quite Usual Events), an international organization of stuffed animals charged with helping kids accomplish everyday tasks such as mailing a letter, cleaning their room, or learning how to use the library. Throughout each special assignment the accident-prone Oso maintains a sunny outlook on life and an enthusiasm for his job with his catchphrase, "It's all part of the plan." Voices include Sean Astin (Oso), Meghan Strange (Paw Pilot), Gary Anthony Williams (Mr. Dos), Amber Hood (Agent Dotty),

Phill Lewis (Agent Wolfie), Cam Clarke (Whirly Bird/R. R. Rapide). From Walt Disney Television Animation. A short-form series about healthy living, *Special Agent Oso: Three Healthy Steps*, premiered Feb. 14, 2011, on Disney Junior.

SpectroMagic Parade in the Magic Kingdom at Walt Disney World; debuted Oct. 1, 1991, on the park's 20th anniversary. The new parade was designed so the former *Main Street Electrical Parade* could be sent to Disneyland Paris. *Spectro-Magic* differed from the *Electrical Parade* through increased use of fiber optics, appearances by a number of newly created characters, and a symphonic score by John Debney. The floats were themed after Disney animated classics, including *Sleeping Beauty*, *The Little Mermaid*, *Fantasia*, and the Silly Symphony cartoons. The parade ended its run May 22, 1999, to accommodate the return of the *Main Street Electrical Parade* (May 28, 1999–Apr. 1, 2001), and returned Apr. 2, 2001. *SpectroMagic* was officially retired Jun. 5, 2010.

Speechless (TV) Half-hour series on ABC; aired Sep. 21, 2016–Apr. 12, 2019. Maya DiMeo is a mom on a mission who will do anything for her husband, Jimmy, and kids, Ray, Dylan, and J.J., her eldest son with cerebral palsy. As she fights injustices both real and imagined, the family works to make a new home for themselves and searches for just the right person to help give J.J. his "voice." Stars Minnie Driver (Maya DiMeo), John Ross Bowie (Jimmy DiMeo), Mason Cook (Ray), Micah Fowler (J.J.), Kyla Kenedy (Dylan), Cedric Yarbrough (Kenneth). From Twentieth Century Fox Television and ABC Studios.

Spellbinder (TV) Series on Disney Channel; premiered Feb. 5, 1996. A mischievous student, Paul, involved in a prank, interacts with a solar eclipse, a strange electrical storm, and a mysterious magnetic field, and finds himself transported into another dimension. Lost in this parallel world, he discovers people living in a time when the industrial revolution did not occur, exploited by a ruthless elite called Spellbinders. With the help of the resourceful and strong-willed Riana, Paul attempts to outwit the Spellbinders and return to his world. Stars Zbych Trofimiuk (Paul Reynolds), Gosia Piotrowska (Riana), Brian Rooney (Alex), Michela Noonan (Katrina). 26 episodes.

Spell-mageddon (TV) Game show on ABC Family; aired Jul. 23–Sep. 11, 2013. On a fresh spin of a spelling bee, contestants take on hilarious distractions while spelling increasingly challenging words. Hosted by Alfonso Ribeiro.

Spencer, Fred (1904–1938) Animator; helped create the characters of Donald Duck and Dopey. He was known as one of the best animators on Donald Duck. He was hired by Disney in 1931 and worked at the Studio until he was killed in a car accident in 1938.

Spencer, Octavia Actress; won an Oscar for Supporting Actress for her role in *The Help* (Minny Jackson) and appeared on TV in *Ugly Betty* (Constance Grady) and *Red Band Society* (Nurse Jackson), with guest appearances in *Wizards of Waverly Place* and *black-ish*. She voiced Mrs. Otterton in *Zootopia* and The Manticore in *Onward*.

Spice Road Table Restaurant in Morocco at EPCOT; opened Jan. 2014, along World Showcase Lagoon. Inspired by the outdoor cafes along the Mediterranean, serving regional small plates, along with specialty wines, beers, and aperitifs.

Spider and the Fly, The (film) Silly Symphony cartoon released Oct. 23, 1931. Directed by Wilfred Jackson. To defend themselves from a hungry spider, flies enlist all of their kin, including horseflies and dragonflies. In the battle, a boy fly manages to save a captured girl fly and the spider is caught on flypaper.

Spider-Man: Far From Home (film) A collaboration between Marvel Studios and Columbia Pictures. Released Jul. 2, 2019, after international releases beginning Jun. 28. An extended version was released Sep. 2. Directed by Jon Watts. Following the events of *Avengers: Endgame*, Peter Parker decides to join his best friends on a European vacation, but his plans are quickly scrapped when he begrudgingly agrees to help Nick Fury uncover the mystery of several elemental creature attacks. Spider-Man and Mysterio join forces to fight the havoc unleashed across the continent, but all is not as it seems. Stars Tom Holland (Peter Parker/Spider-Man), Samuel L. Jackson (Nick Fury), Zendaya (MJ), Cobie Smulders (Maria Hill), Jon Favreau (Happy Hogan), JB Smoove (Mr. Dell), Jacob Batalon (Ned Leeds), Martin Starr (Mr. Harrington), Marisa Tomei (May Parker), Jake Gyllenhaal (Mysterio). The production was financed and distributed by Sony Pictures, which has franchise rights; Marvel owns merchandising rights.

Spider-Man: Homecoming (film) A collaboration between Marvel Studios and Columbia Pictures. Released Jul. 7, 2017, after international releases Jul. 5-6. Directed by Jon Watts. Young Peter Parker (Spider-Man) begins to navigate his newfound identity as a superhero. Thrilled by his experience with the Avengers (in *Captain America: Civil War*), Peter returns home, where he lives with his Aunt May. Under the watchful eye of new mentor Tony Stark, Peter tries to fall back into his normal daily routine, but the emergence of a villain, the Vulture, threatens everything that Peter holds most important. Stars Tom Holland (Peter Parker/Spider-Man), Robert Downey Jr. (Tony Stark/Iron Man), Marisa Tomei (Aunt May), Michael Keaton (Adrian Toomes/Vulture), Jon Favreau (Happy Hogan), Gwyneth Paltrow (Pepper Potts), Zendaya (Michelle), Donald Glover (Aaron Davis). The production was financed and distributed by Sony Pictures, which has franchise rights; Marvel owns merchandising rights.

Spider-Man: No Way Home (film) A collaboration between Marvel Studios and Columbia Pictures. Released Dec. 17, 2021, after international releases beginning Dec. 15. Directed by Jon Watts. Spider-Man's identity is revealed, bringing his superhero responsibilities into conflict with his normal life and putting those he cares about most at risk. When he enlists Doctor Strange's help to restore his secret, the spell tears a hole in their world, releasing the most powerful villains who've ever fought a Spider-Man in any universe. Now, Peter will have to overcome his greatest challenge yet, which will not only forever alter his own future but the future of the Multiverse. Stars Tom Holland (Peter Parker/Spider-Man), Zendaya (MJ), Benedict Cumberbatch (Doctor Strange), Jacob Batalon (Ned Leeds), Jon Favreau (Happy Hogan), Marisa Tomei (May Parker). The production was financed and distributed by Sony Pictures, which has franchise rights; Marvel owns merchandising rights.

Spider-Man W.E.B. Adventure See WEB SLINGERS: A SPIDER-MAN ADVENTURE.

Spies (TV) A Disney Channel Premiere Film; first aired Mar. 7, 1993. In 1942, 12-year-old Harry Prescott, who has lost his brother in wartime service, and an English refugee pal stumble upon a Nazi plot to assassinate President Franklin D. Roo-

sevelt. But no one will listen to them. Stars Shiloh Strong (Harry Prescott), David Dukes (Robert Prescott), Cloris Leachman (Pamela Beale). 88 min. Filmed aboard the USS *North Carolina*. Directed by Kevin Connor.

Spike See BUZZ-BUZZ. Also the name of a frost-talent fairy in *Secret of the Wings*; voiced by Debby Ryan.

Spin (TV) A Disney Channel Original Movie; first aired Aug. 13, 2021. Rhea, an Indian American teen, discovers her passion for creating DJ mixes that blend her South Asian culture and the world around her. Rhea's life revolves around her eclectic group of friends, her after-school coding club, her family's Indian restaurant, and her tight-knit, multigenerational family. Everything changes when she falls for aspiring DJ Max, and her long-lost fervor for music is reignited. Rhea discovers that she has a natural gift for creating beats and producing music but must find the courage to follow her true inner talent. Directed by Manjari Makijany. Stars Avantika (Rhea), Abhay Deol (Arvind), Meera Syal (Grandmother Asha), Aryan Simhadri (Rohan), Michael Bishop (Max), Anna Cathcart (Molly), Jahbril Cook (Watson), Kerri Medders (Ginger).

Spin and Marty See ADVENTURES OF SPIN AND MARTY, THE AND NEW ADVENTURES OF SPIN AND MARTY, THE: SUSPECT BEHAVIOR.

Spiral Snacks Helix-shaped snack shop in Tomorrowland at Shanghai Disneyland; opened Jun. 16, 2016.

Spirit of Aloha Dinner Show See POLYNESIAN REVUE.

Spirit of '43, The (film) A sequel to *The New Spirit*, made for the U.S. Treasury Department. Delivered Jan. 7, 1943. Directed by Jack King. Donald stars in this cartoon to teach the general public to be careful with their money and save it for increased income taxes needed to fight World War II.

Spirit of Pocahontas, The Stage show at the Fantasyland Theater in Disneyland; ran Jun. 23, 1995–Sep. 4, 1997. Also played in Disney-MGM Studios at Walt Disney World, where it closed Feb. 24, 1996.

Spirit of Pocahontas Shop, The See DAVY CROCKETT'S PIONEER MERCANTILE.

Spirited Away (film) A 10-year-old girl, Chihiro, discovers a secret world when she and her family get lost and venture through a hillside tunnel. When her parents undergo a mysterious transformation, Chihiro must fend for herself as she encounters strange spirits, assorted creatures, and a grumpy sorceress who seeks to prevent her from returning to the human world. Directed by Hayao Miyazaki. Limited North American release on Sep. 20, 2002, with an expanded release on Sep. 27. 125 min. Produced by Studio Ghibli in Japan; John Lasseter supervised the dubbed version for American audiences. Voices include Daveigh Chase (Chihiro), Suzanne Pleshette (Yubaba, Zeniba), Jason Marsden (Haku), Susan Egan (Lin), David Ogden Stiers (Kamaji), Lauren Holly (Chihiro's mother), Michael Chiklin (Chihiro's father), John Ratzenberger (assistant manager), Tara Strong (Boh). Originally released in Japan on Jul. 20, 2001, as *Sen to Chihiro no kamikakushi*. The film was the highest-grossing film in Japan in 2001. It won the Academy Award as Best Animated Feature.

Splash (film) Allen Bauer discovers a mermaid, whom he had originally seen as a child, at Cape Cod in Massachusetts. She goes to New York City to find him, and on land, her tail transforms into legs. Allen and the mermaid, who calls herself Madison, fall in love, and he tries to teach her the ways of human life. Scientists capture Madison, but she is saved by Allen and his philandering brother, Freddie. Allen and Madison finally elude their captors by leaping into the ocean. Released Mar. 9, 1984. The first Touchstone film. Directed by Ron Howard. 110 min. Stars Tom Hanks (Allen Bauer), Daryl Hannah (Madison), Eugene Levy (Walter Kornbluth), John Candy (Freddie Bauer), Dody Goodman (Mrs. Stimler), Shecky Greene (Mr. Buyrite), Richard B. Shull (Dr. Ross), Bobby Di Cicco (Jerry), Howard Morris (Dr. Zidell), Tony Di Benedetto (Tim). The production took 17 days of principal photography on location in New York City, filming at such landmarks as the Statue of Liberty, the American Museum of Natural History and its renowned whale room, Bloomingdale's department store, and Columbus Circle. When Rockefeller Center's ice-skating rink closed prematurely for reconstruction, the production was granted permission to build a special rink and film in Central Park. The production then moved to Los Angeles for additional filming at locations throughout Southern California before traveling to The Bahamas for the underwater sequences. Producer Brian Grazer spent much of 4 years exploring various approaches to the undersea filming that is seen in *Splash*. He opted for the real thing, filming 50 feet down in the Caribbean waters surrounding The Bahamas. The actors received special training in diving and adapting to their confining locations. Each was required to swim from one safety diver to another, through a shot, for their supply of air. Noted underwater cinematographer Jordan Klein storyboarded each frame of film they would be shooting. The director and producer were so pleased with Daryl Hannah's swimming that they allowed her to do all her own stunts. The film was nominated for an Academy Award for Best Screenplay. The TV sequel was *Splash, Too*.

Splash Mountain Critter Country flume attraction in Disneyland; opened Jul. 17, 1989. Based on animated sequences and characters from *Song of the South*. Many of the Audio-Animatronics characters from the closed America Sings attraction were renovated and placed in Splash Mountain. Some new ones were also added, namely Brer Bear, Brer Fox, and Brer Rabbit. A total of 103 figures ended up in the attraction. Guests travel through backwoods swamps and bayous in their hollowed-out log. The culmination is a high-speed, 52-foot flume drop, at a 45-degree angle, which almost assures the guests they'll get splashed. At opening, it was the longest flume chute in the world. Disney designer Tony Baxter came up with the idea for the attraction while stuck in his car during rush hour traffic in 1983. Also opened in Frontierland at the Magic Kingdom at Walt Disney World Jul. 17, 1992, and in Critter Country at Tokyo Disneyland Oct. 1, 1992. The attractions at Disneyland and Walt Disney World are scheduled to be replaced by Tiana's Bayou Adventure in late 2024; the Walt Disney World version closed Jan. 22, 2023.

Splash, Too (TV) Two-part show; aired May 1 and 8, 1988. Directed by Greg Antonacci. Sequel to the 1984 feature, with Allen and the mermaid, Madison, returning to New York City to help Allen's brother, who is in danger of losing the family business. Madison plots to save a dolphin from the aquarium, when she discovers it is going to be used for scientific experiments. Stars Todd Waring (Allen Bauer), Amy Yasbeck (Madison Bauer), Donovan Scott (Freddie Bauer), Rita Taggart (Fern Hooten), Noble Willingham (Karl Hooten), Dody Goodman (Mrs. Stimler), Joey Travolta (Jerry).

This was the first motion picture to film at the new Disney-MGM Studios in Florida.

Splashdown Photos Frontierland photo shop at Splash Mountain in the Magic Kingdom at Walt Disney World; opened Jun. 1, 1993, and closed Jan. 22, 2023. Also in Critter Country at Tokyo Disneyland. The shop is similar to Professor Barnaby Owl's Photography Studio at Disneyland.

Splashtacular Musical fantasy stage show at the newly renovated Fountain of Nations in Future World at Epcot; premiered Nov. 20, 1993, and ended Jun. 11, 1994. Mickey and friends brought elements of water and color to life, battling intergalactic invaders.

Splitsville Luxury Lanes A 50,000-sq.-ft. facility featuring 30 lanes of bowling on 2 floors; opened Dec. 19, 2012, at Downtown Disney West Side (now the West Side at Disney Springs) at Walt Disney World. Guests can dine at a restaurant with a menu guided by celebrity chef Tim Cushman. Billiards and live music are also offered. It replaced Ridemakerz in the former Virgin Megastore building. Also opened Jan. 29, 2018, in the Downtown Disney District at Disneyland Resort, replacing House of Blues.

Spoodles Mediterranean restaurant on Disney's BoardWalk at Walt Disney World; opened Jul. 1, 1996. It closed Aug. 1, 2009, to become the Greek-themed Kouzzina. Trattoria al Forno is the current restaurant in the space.

Spooky Buddies (film) Direct-to-video release Sep. 20, 2011. It is Halloween, and the talking puppies go far across town to a mysterious mansion where something very spooky is going on. In a race against the Howlloween Hound, the Buddies and their new friends Pip, Zelda, Rodney, and Skip must stop Warlock the Magician—and save the world from his dastardly deeds. Directed by Robert Vince. Stars Harland Williams (Warwick), Rance Howard (Mr. Johnson), Pat Finn (Frank Carroll), Jennifer Elise Cox (Mrs. Carroll), Sierra McCormick (Alice), Sage Ryan (Pete), Elisa Donovan (Janice). From Walt Disney Studios Home Entertainment. 88 min.

Spoon, Mickey Mouse SEE WILLIAM ROGERS & SON.

Spooner (TV) A Disney Channel Premiere Film; first aired Dec. 2, 1989. An escaped convict starts a new life as a Texas high school English teacher and wrestling coach, attempting to turn a fledgling team into a championship squad. He tries to make a difference in the life of a tough juvenile delinquent and falls in love with a fellow teacher, all while trying to keep out of sight of pursuing lawmen. Directed by George Miller. Stars Robert Urich (Michael Gillette/Harry Spooner), Jane Kaczmarek (Gail), Brent Fraser (Shane). 98 min.

Spoonful of Sugar, A Song from *Mary Poppins*, sung by Julie Andrews; written by Richard M. and Robert B. Sherman. The song was written later in the development of the film as an anthem for the Mary Poppins character. The Shermans came up with the song's title when Robert's son Jeff came home from school one day and told his father how he received the Salk vaccine to prevent polio via a cube of sugar.

Spoonful of Sugar Confection shop in the Marketplace in Disneytown at Shanghai Disney Resort; open Jun. 16, 2016–2018. Guests could watch sweets being made through a 180-degree observation window. Succeeded by HEYTEA, a tea store.

Sport Goofy (TV) Syn. specials aired May 21, Sep. 16, and Nov. 24, 1983. Also known as *Walt Disney's Mickey and Donald Present Sport Goofy*.

Sport Goofy Gifts and Sundries Souvenir, apparel, and snack shop in Disney's All-Star Sports Resort at Walt Disney World; opened Apr. 29, 1994.

Sport Goofy in Soccermania (TV) SEE ALL NEW ADVENTURE OF DISNEY'S SPORT GOOFY FEATURING SPORT GOOFY IN SOCCERMANIA, AN.

Sports Bar American fare joint in Disney Village at Disneyland Paris; opened Apr. 12, 1992, originally as Champions Sports Bar.

Sports Night (TV) Half-hour series on ABC; aired Sep. 22, 1998–May 16, 2000. Explores the professional and personal lives of the people who produce a live nightly cable sports news show. Stars Josh Charles (Dan Rydell), Peter Krause (Casey McCall), Felicity Huffman (Dana Whitaker), Joshua Malina (Jeremy Goodwin), Sabrina Lloyd (Natalie Rosen), Robert Guillaume (Isaac Jaffee). From Imagine Television and Touchstone Television.

Sportsman's Shoppe United Kingdom team apparel and pop-culture shop in EPCOT; opened ca. 2001, taking the place of the original Toy Soldier. The exterior resembles Scotland's Abbotsford manor. A favorite sight is the diorama just inside the entrance of a medieval banquet hall and its royal court.

Spot Wild human boy in *The Good Dinosaur*; voiced by Jack Bright.

Spot Marks the X (TV) A Disney Channel Premiere Film; first aired Oct. 18, 1986. An adopted dog with a checkered past leads his new young owner on a wild chase after buried loot. Directed by Mark Rosman. 90 min. Stars Barret Oliver (Ken), Geoffrey Lewis (dog pound attendant), Natalie Gregory (Kathy), David Huddleston (Ross), Mike the Dog (Capone).

Spottiswood, Greg Actor; appeared in *Looking for Miracles* (Ryan Delaney) on The Disney Channel, for which he won the Emmy Award in 1990 as Outstanding Performer in a Children's Special.

Spring Fling Entertainment event, first held in Disneyland Apr. 14, 1962, featuring top bands, and continuing for the next decade.

Springtime (film) Silly Symphony cartoon released Oct. 24, 1929. Directed by Walt Disney. In the first of a series of Silly Symphonies based on the seasons, a fantasy of spring is portrayed through the lives of woodland creatures.

Springtime for Pluto (film) Pluto cartoon released Jun. 23, 1944. The first cartoon directed by Charles Nichols. Pluto is awakened by the Spirit of Spring, which causes him to dance about, getting mixed up with angry bees and poison ivy. Out for revenge, he goes after the spirit.

Sprouse, Dylan and Cole Twin actors; appeared in *The Suite Life of Zack & Cody*, *The Suite Life Movie*, *The Suite Life on Deck*, and other programs on Disney Channel. Dylan played Zack Martin, and Cole played Cody Martin. Dylan voiced Shasta in *Snow Buddies*.

Spy Hard (film) Dick Steele, Agent WD-40, is lured back to active service by the Agency's director as the only man who can stop the evil General Rancor. Rancor, a malevolent madman presumed dead after losing 2 limbs in an explosive altercation with Steele 15 years earlier, is alive. He's mad and armless but still dangerous. Steele joins forces with

the mysterious and beautiful Agent 3.14 to thwart the diabolical scheme for global power his old nemesis has come up with. Together they elude Rancor's henchmen, escape speeding vehicles, and evade kidnap attempts as they make their way to General Rancor's lair. A Hollywood Pictures film. Directed by Rick Friedberg. Released May 24, 1996. Stars Leslie Nielsen (Steele), Andy Griffith (Rancor), Nicollette Sheridan (Agent 3.14), Charles Durning (Director), John Ales (Kabul), Barry Bostwick (Coleman). 81 min. Completely filmed in Los Angeles area locations.

Spy in the Sky (TV) Show aired Apr. 1, 1962. Directed by Harmon Jones, Ward Kimball. Walt Disney presents a preview of *Moon Pilot*, with some behind-the-scenes footage, and then shows *Eyes in Outer Space*.

Spy-Busters Alternate title of *The Secret of Boyne Castle*.

Spyglass Entertainment Successor company to Caravan Pictures, with Roger Birnbaum teaming up with Gary Barber. They had a co-financing and distribution deal with Disney, with their first and biggest release being *The Sixth Sense*, with Bruce Willis, in 1999.

Spyglass Grill Quick-service restaurant in the Trinidad area at Disney's Caribbean Beach Resort at Walt Disney World; opened Mar. 19, 2018.

Squanto: A Warrior's Tale (film) Cultures collide when English explorers and traders sail to the New World and encounter the friendly Native peoples of the land. But the wayfarers violate their trust by abducting 2 men—Squanto and Epenow—whom they intend to take back to England to display. Driven by a passion for freedom, Squanto makes a dramatic escape and, against nearly impossible odds, survives a long and perilous journey back to his homeland. Upon his return, however, he discovers that everything has changed during his absence—his noble tribe has been wiped out by disease and the *Mayflower* pilgrims have settled into what little remains of Squanto's village. Squanto must summon all he has learned over the course of his travels about goodwill and understanding if he is to survive. And the colonists, unprepared for the struggle they face, must learn to trust Squanto, the only man who can help them survive and broker a peace that will enable them to coexist with the Native community. Released

Oct. 28, 1994. Directed by Xavier Koller. 102 min. Stars Adam Beach (Squanto), Michael Gambon (Sir George), Nathaniel Parker (Thomas Dormer), Mandy Patinkin (Brother Daniel). Beach is one of the first Native actors to have the lead in a major motion picture. Filmed on location in Canada, primarily at the restored Fortress of Louisbourg and elsewhere in Nova Scotia and in Quebec.

Square Peg in a Round Hole (TV) Show aired Mar. 3, 1963. Directed by Hamilton S. Luske. A later rerun was titled *Goofing Around with Donald Duck*. Ludwig Von Drake studies psychology this time, by looking at several Donald Duck and Goofy cartoons.

Squatter's Rights (film) Pluto cartoon released Jun. 7, 1946. Directed by Jack Hannah. Chip and Dale battle Mickey and Pluto to keep an old stove as their home in a cabin Mickey is using for vacation. The chipmunks trick Mickey and Pluto into thinking Pluto has accidentally been shot. Nominated for an Academy Award.

Squeegees (film) The first example of short-form programming created by Stage 9 Digital Media. Entrepreneurial slackers have a fledgling window-washing business. Debuted on ABC.com and YouTube Feb. 28, 2008. Stars Adam Countee, Brendan Countee, Marc Gilbar, Aaron Greenberg.

Squeezer's Tropical Juice Bar Adventureland refreshment stand in Tokyo Disneyland; opened Jul. 21, 1992. Named for the friendly snake on the marquee.

Squirt Plucky young sea turtle, son of Crush, in *Finding Nemo*; voiced by Nicholas Bird.

S.S. Columbia Dining Room Fine-dining restaurant on the 3rd deck of the ocean liner docked in New York Harbor in American Waterfront in Tokyo DisneySea; opened Sep. 4, 2001. Guests find the service and quality of the dining experience just as it might have been on one of the great luxury liners of yesteryear during a transatlantic crossing.

S.S. rustworthy Interactive fireboat play zone in Paradise Pier at Disney California Adventure; open Feb. 8, 2001–Sep. 2010, originally presented by McDonald's.

Stacy, Michelle Actress; provided the voice of Penny in *The Rescuers*.

Stage Coach Frontierland attraction in Disneyland; operated Jul. 17, 1955–Feb. 1, 1956. It became Rainbow Mountain Stage Coaches, which operated until 1959. The stagecoaches were removed because the horses were spooked by the Disneyland Railroad trains that traveled on nearby tracks.

Stage Door Café Frontierland counter-service restaurant in Disneyland; opened Sep. 1978, taking the place of Oaks Tavern.

Stage 9 Digital Media Part of the Disney•ABC Television Group, formed in Feb. 2007. Stage 9 created original short-form programming, debuting with the comedy series *Squeegees* on ABC.com and YouTube Feb. 28, 2008.

Stage 1 Company Store Grand Avenue (formerly Streets of America) shop in Disney's Hollywood Studios; opened Jun. 1, 1991, offering Muppet character merchandise. Inside, movie sets present scenes from Muppet films.

Staggs, Thomas O. He joined Disney in strategic planning in 1990 and was a key member of the team that put together the acquisition of Capital Cities/ABC. He was named executive vice president and chief financial officer of The Walt Disney Company in May 1998, and chairman of Walt Disney Parks and Resorts in Jan. 2010. In Feb. 2015 he was named chief operating officer of The Walt Disney Company. He resigned in 2016.

Stainton, David President of Walt Disney Animation, beginning in 2003. He had started with Disney in 1989, and in 2002 was named president of Walt Disney Television Animation. He left the company in 2006.

Stakeout (film) Seattle detectives Chris Lecce and Bill Reimers pull an unwanted assignment—the night shift stakeout of the home of an ex-girlfriend of a vicious escaped convict. Lecce becomes smitten by the object of their stakeout, Maria McGuire, and soon is bending rules and having dinner with her. Eventually the convict arrives, kidnaps Lecce and McGuire, and sets off a frantic chase. Released Aug. 5, 1987. Directed by John Badham. A Touchstone film. 117 min. Stars Richard Dreyfuss (Chris Lecce), Emilio Estevez (Bill Reimers), Madeleine Stowe (Maria McGuire), Aidan Quinn (Richard "Stick" Montgomery). Filmed in and around Vancouver, British Columbia. *Another Stakeout* was a sequel.

Stalling, Carl (1891–1972) Musician/composer; Walt Disney knew him in Kansas City in the 1920s when he was a theater organist. When Disney decided to add a soundtrack to *Steamboat Willie*, he turned to Stalling. Stalling came out to the Disney Studio beginning in 1928 and remained for a little over a year before beginning a long career in the animation department at Warner Bros. It was Stalling who gave Walt the idea for the Silly Symphony series.

Stallone, Sylvester Actor; appeared in *Oscar* (Angelo "Snaps" Provolone), *Judge Dredd* (Judge Dredd), *An Alan Smithee Film: Burn Hollywood Burn* (as himself), and *Guardians of the Galaxy Vol. 2* (Stakar Ogord).

Stalmaster, Hal Actor; appeared in *Johnny Tremain* (Johnny), and on TV in *The Swamp Fox* (Gwynn).

Stamos, John Actor; appeared on Disney+ in *Big Shot* (Marvyn Korn) and *Muppets Haunted Mansion* (Famous Person); and on TV in *Grandfathered* (Jimmy) and *The Wonderful World of Disney presents The Little Mermaid Live!* (Chef Louis), with guest appearances in the *Mickey Mouse Club* (1989), *Walt Disney World 4th of July Spectacular*, *Disneyland 60: The Wonderful World of Disney*, *Mickey's 90th Spectacular*, and *The Disney Family Singalong*. He also voiced Captain Salty Bones in *Mickey Mouse Funhouse* and Tony Stark/Iron Man in *Marvel's Spidey and his Amazing Friends*. Stamos is a Disney fan and collector.

Stampede at Bitter Creek (film) International theatrical compilation of *Texas John Slaughter* episodes. First released in Mexico in Nov. 1962. 80 min. Stars Tom Tryon. Released in the U.S. on video in 1986.

Stamps The first Disney postage stamp was a 6¢ commemorative issued by the U.S. to honor Walt Disney on Sep. 11, 1968. The stamp featured children from all over the world streaming from Sleeping Beauty Castle at Disneyland, along with a portrait of Walt Disney. Designers were Bob Moore (castle and children) and Paul Wenzel (portrait). The first-day ceremonies were held in Marceline, Missouri. It was followed in 1971 by a set of 10 stamps from the tiny Republic of San Marino. After some unauthorized Disney stamps from Persian Gulf sheikdoms in the 1970s (legal proceedings eventually stopped their distribution), the Inter-Governmental Philatelic Corp. in New York City was licensed in 1979 to use Disney characters on the stamps that they produced for a number of small countries around the world. This created a whole new stamp-collecting subfield, with special albums, newsletters, and catalogs created for those interested in the Disney stamps. In 2004, the U.S. Postal Service partnered with Disney for a series of "Art of Disney" Disney-themed 37¢ postage stamps. The first set of 4—The Art of Disney: Friendship—accrued sales of more than 250 million stamps. Four other "Art of Disney" sets followed: Celebration (2005), Romance (2006), Magic (2007), and Imagination (2008). Since then, other Disney stamp series have been released, including ones featuring Disney • Pixar characters, the Muppets, and Disney villains.

Stan Lee (TV) An original documentary exploring the life of the creator of the Marvel Universe; planned for digital release on Disney+ in 2023.

Stand by Me SEE DISNEY'S TIMON AND PUMBAA IN STAND BY ME.

Stanley, Helene (1928–1990) Actress; appeared in *Davy Crockett* (Polly Crockett). She was also the live-action model of Cinderella and Aurora in *Sleeping Beauty* for the animators.

Stanley (TV) Playhouse Disney animated series on Disney Channel; premiered Sep. 15, 2001. Follows the adventures of 6-year-old Stanley Griff, an extremely imaginative and creative little boy who is wild about animals. He loves to make simple drawings of his favorite animals and to do research using his *Great Big Book of Everything*. Voices include Jessica D. Stone (Stanley), Charles Shaughnessy (Dennis), Ari Myers (Mom), David Landsberg (Dad), Rene Mujica (Harry), Hynden Walch (Elsie). From Walt Disney Television Animation and Cartoon Pizza.

Stanton, Harry Dean (1926–2017) Actor; appeared in *One Magic Christmas* (Gideon), *The Straight Story* (Lyle Straight), and *Marvel's The Avengers* (security guard).

Stapleton, Maureen (1925–2006) Actress; appeared in *Passed Away* (Mary Scanlan).

Star With the 2019 purchase of 21st Century Fox, Disney acquired Mumbai-based broadcast company Star India Private Limited; the company had originated in Aug. 1991 as STAR TV (Satellite Television Asian Region), as the continent's first satellite network. On Apr. 3, 2020, Star India's Hotstar video streaming service became Disney+ Hotstar. In Aug. 2020, plans were announced to launch an international general entertainment streaming service under the Star brand. On Feb. 23, 2021, Disney+ added Star general entertainment content in Australia, New Zealand, Canada, and Western Europe, and Singapore became the first market to launch with the new general entertainment brand, Disney+ with Star. It was announced that in late 2021, Disney+ with Star would roll out in Eastern Europe, Hong Kong, Japan, and South Korea, and that in Latin America, the general entertainment offering would launch as a standalone streaming service, called Star+.

Star Command Suppliers Tomorrowland shop in Hong Kong Disneyland; opened Sep. 12, 2005, adjacent to Buzz Lightyear Astro Blasters. Closed Aug. 31, 2017, and reopened the following year as Pavilion Gifts.

Star Jets Tomorrowland attraction in the Magic Kingdom at Walt Disney World; opened Nov. 28, 1974. Guests boarded rockets for a spin above Tomorrowland. Closed in 1994 and became Astro Orbiter as part of a general renovation of Tomorrowland. Also in Tomorrowland at Tokyo Disneyland, as StarJets; open Apr. 15, 1983–Oct. 10, 2017. SEE ALSO ROCKET JETS (DISNEYLAND).

Star Today Program in Disney-MGM Studios at Walt Disney World where motion picture and TV stars made personal appearances, participated in interviews, and placed their handprints in the cement in the Chinese Theatre forecourt.

Star Tours Tomorrowland attraction in Disneyland, created in cooperation with George Lucas; opened Jan. 9, 1987, with an "inaugural flight" event for which the park operated for 60 straight hours. Also opened Dec. 15, 1989, in Disney-MGM Studios at Walt Disney World; Jul. 12, 1989, in Tomorrowland at Tokyo Disneyland; and Apr. 12, 1992, in Discoveryland at Disneyland Paris. The premise is that an interstellar tour company, called Star Tours, carries tourists to fascinating locales in the *Star Wars* galaxy. Guests boarded vehicles called *StarSpeeders*, each holding 40 passengers, for a trip to the Moon of Endor, but mistakes by the new pilot droid RX-24 (or "Rex," voiced by Paul Reubens) sent the craft on a thrilling adventure. In the pre-show area, one can watch R2-D2 and C-3PO

from the *Star Wars* films working to service the fleet. In the U.S., the attraction closed in 2010 and was completely revised, reopening May 20, 2011, at Walt Disney World and Jun. 3 at Disneyland as Star Tours – The Adventures Continue. The new version, in 3-D, includes 4 main "acts," each of which has multiple versions. The result is an unpredictable experience in which there are more than 60 possible story and location combinations. The new attraction later opened in Tokyo Disneyland (May 7, 2013) and in Disneyland Paris (soft opening Mar. 18, 2017, followed by the official opening Mar. 26). Star Tours – The Adventures Continue is a prequel to the original Star Tours, with the story line originally set between the first 2 *Star Wars* trilogies; as such, its working name was "Star Tours 3.5." Guests now ride in a *StarSpeeder* 1000 vehicle, with C-3PO "accidentally" as pilot, instead of the original *StarSpeeder* 3000. New sequences inspired by the third *Star Wars* trilogy were added in conjunction with the film releases (in 2015, 2017, and 2019), now offering more than 100 potential storytelling combinations.

Star Traders Large souvenir shop in Tomorrowland at Disneyland; opened Nov. 21, 1986, succeeding The Character Shop. Also in Discoveryland at Disneyland Paris; opened Apr. 12, 1992. It is also the shortened name, as of Nov. 8, 2019, for Mickey's Star Traders in the Magic Kingdom at Walt Disney World.

Star vs. The Forces of Evil (TV) Animated series on Disney XD; debuted Mar. 30, 2015, after a Jan. 18 preview on Disney Channel. Teen princess Star Butterfly, who was given an all-powerful magic wand, is sent by her Royal Parents to live with the Diaz family on Earth, bringing along her own unique inter-dimensional style. Together with the Diaz's teenage son, Marco, they navigate high school and embark on dimension-hopping adventures across the multiverse while keeping her wand out of the clutches of archnemesis Ludo and his monstrous forces of evil. Voices include Eden Sher (Star Butterfly), Adam McArthur (Marco Diaz), Alan Tudyk (Ludo/King Butterfly), Nia Vardalos (Mrs. Diaz). From Disney Television Animation.

Star Wars: A Galactic Spectacular Fireworks show at Disney's Hollywood Studios; began Jun. 17, 2016. State-of-the-art projection effects, lighting, lasers, pyrotechnics, and John Williams's musical themes present memorable moments from the

Star Wars films. An earlier version, *Symphony in the Stars: A Galactic Spectacular*, was presented at select *Star Wars* events before a regular run Dec. 18, 2015–Jun. 2016.

Star Wars: Andor See Andor.

Star Wars Biomes (TV) Series on Disney+; digitally premiered May 4, 2021, with flyover tours of some of the *Star Wars* films' most iconic locations.

Star Wars: Command Post Tomorrowland character-greeting location in Hong Kong Disneyland; opened in 2016, taking the place of Stitch Encounter, and closed ca. 2021. Guests could meet *Star Wars* heroes in a Resistance base. Also a Production Courtyard character spot in Walt Disney Studios Park at Disneyland Paris; opened in 2019.

Star Wars Galactic Outpost Apparel and collectibles shop in Disney Springs West Side; opened Dec. 15, 2015, taking the place of D Street.

Star Wars: Galactic Starcruiser Immersive vacation/resort experience in Walt Disney World; opened Mar. 1, 2022. Guests become heroes of their own *Star Wars* story during a 2-night adventure aboard the *Halcyon* starcruiser. Activities include lightsaber and bridge training, with dining in the Crown of Corellia Dining Room and Sublight Lounge, and shopping in The Chandrila Collection boutique. Guests also have direct access into Star Wars: Galaxy's Edge in Disney's Hollywood Studios, where their missions influence events back on the ship. Cabins include sleeping berths built into the walls and a viewport out to space that continuously changes throughout the journey.

Star Wars: Galaxy of Sounds (TV) Series on Disney+; digitally premiered Sep. 29, 2021. Sound effects and imagery from the *Star Wars* films create the ambience of a galaxy far, far away through such themes as wonder, excitement, and oddities.

Star Wars: Galaxy's Edge Immersive *Star Wars*–themed land at the Disney parks; opened May 31, 2019, in Disneyland, taking the place of Big Thunder Ranch and some backstage facilities, and Aug. 29, 2019, in Disney's Hollywood Studios at Walt Disney World, replacing Streets of America. Guests explore the remote Black Spire Outpost, the largest settlement on the planet Batuu. In this unique village of secrets, visitors encounter scoundrels, rogues, and smugglers, and become participants in their own *Star Wars* adventure—from piloting the *Millennium Falcon* (Millennium Falcon: Smugglers Run) to joining the Resistance in a climactic battle against the First Order (Star Wars: Rise of the Resistance). In a bustling market and merchant row, shopping includes Savi's Workshop – Handbuilt Lightsabers, Droid Depot, Black Spire Outfitters, and Dok-Ondar's Den of Antiquities, with dining at Docking Bay 7 Food and Cargo, Ronto Roasters, Oga's Cantina, and the Milk Stand. Covering more than 14 acres, it is considered the largest and most technologically advanced single-themed expansion in a Disney park. *Star Wars* composer John Williams provided an all-new suite of themes especially for the land, titled "Star Wars: Galaxy's Edge Symphonic Suite," which earned him the 2020 Grammy for Best Instrumental Composition.

Star Wars: Galaxy's Edge—Adventure Awaits (TV) Special on Freeform; first aired Sep. 29, 2019. A behind-the-scenes tour of Star Wars: Galaxy's Edge, revealing how the planet of Batuu came to life at Disneyland and Walt Disney World. Hosted by Neil Patrick Harris. Celebrity guests include Kaley Cuoco, Keegan-Michael Key, Jay Leno, Sarah Hyland, Miles Brown. 120 min. From Brad Lachman Productions.

Star Wars Launch Bay Attraction offering special exhibits and sneak peeks at the third *Star Wars* trilogy, with merchandise, food offerings, and opportunities to meet *Star Wars* characters. Opened in the Tomorrowland Expo Center at Disneyland Nov. 16, 2015, taking the place of Innoventions, followed by versions in Animation Courtyard at Disney's Hollywood Studios Dec. 1, 2015 (replacing The Magic of Disney Animation) and in Tomorrowland at Shanghai Disneyland Jun. 16, 2016–2019 (replaced by Tomorrowland Pavilion).

Star Wars: Path of the Jedi (film) A 10-min. retelling of the epic *Star Wars* saga; premiered Dec. 1, 2015, in the ABC Sound Studio at Disney's Hollywood Studios. Closed in 2018 for seasonal operation and succeeded in 2020 by Mickey Shorts Theater. Also played in the Tomorrowland Theater at Disneyland during *Star Wars* events, 2015–2020; in Star Wars Launch Bay at Shanghai Disneyland beginning Jun. 2016; and in the Discoveryland Theatre at Disneyland Paris, 2017–2018.

Star Wars Rebels (TV) Series on Disney XD; began Oct. 13, 2014. It was preceded by a special one-hour movie, *Star Wars Rebels: Spark of Rebellion*, airing Oct. 3 on Disney Channels worldwide. The story unfolds during a dark time when the evil Galactic Empire is tightening its grip of power on the galaxy. Imperial forces have occupied a remote planet and are ruining the lives of its people. The motley, but clever, crew of the starship *Ghost*—cowboy Jedi Kanan, ace pilot Hera, street-smart teenager Ezra, the "muscle" Zeb, warrior firebrand Sabine, and cantankerous old astromech droid Chopper—is among a select few who are brave enough to stand against the Empire. Together, they face threatening new villains, encounter colorful adversaries, embark on thrilling adventures, and become heroes with the power to ignite a rebellion. Voices include Freddie Prinze Jr. (Kanan), Vanessa Marshall (Hera), Steve Blum (Zeb), Tiya Sircar (Sabine), Taylor Gray (Ezra), David Oyelowo (Agent Kallus), Jason Isaacs (the Inquisitor). From Lucasfilm Animation.

Star Wars Resistance (TV) Animated series; debuted on Disney XD Oct. 8, 2018, after a one-hour premiere on Disney Channel Oct. 7. Kazuda Xiono, a young pilot recruited by the Resistance, is tasked with a top secret mission to spy on the growing threat of the First Order. While undercover aboard the *Colossus*, a massive aircraft refueling platform on an outer rim water planet, Kaz works as a mechanic and lives with Poe's longtime friend Yeager, a veteran pilot who operates a starship repair shop. In his quest to become the best pilot in the galaxy, Kaz's journey with his new friend BB-8 finds him facing off against stormtroopers and pirates, all the while struggling to maintain his secret mission from his newfound family. The series takes place prior to the events of *Star Wars: The Force Awakens*. Created by Dave Filoni. Voices include Christopher Sean (Kaz), Suzie McGrath (Tam Ryvora), Scott Lawrence (Jarek Yeager), Myrna Velasco (Torra Doza), Josh Brener (Neeku Vozo), Donald Faison (Hype Fazon), Bobby Moynihan (Orka), Jim Rash (Flix). From Lucasfilm Animation.

Star Wars: Rise of the Resistance Attraction in Star Wars: Galaxy's Edge; opened Nov. 5, 2019, in Disney's Hollywood Studios and Jan. 17, 2020, in Disneyland. After launching into space aboard a transport shuttle, passengers are captured by a Star Destroyer and pursued by Supreme Leader Kylo Ren. Searching for a way to escape, they become heroes of the Resistance in a climactic battle with the First Order. It is one of the most ambitious and

technologically advanced attractions created for a Disney park.

Star Wars: Secrets of the Empire Hyperreality experience from ILMxLAB and The VOID; opened in Disney Springs at Walt Disney World Dec. 16, 2017, and in Downtown Disney at Disneyland Resort Jan. 5, 2018, and closed Mar. 15, 2020. Participants were transported deep into the *Star Wars* universe in a multisensory experience, with groups of 4 going undercover as stormtroopers to capture Imperial intelligence vital to a budding rebellion's survival. A traveling pop-up version was offered in London Dec. 16, 2017–Jun. 19, 2018. SEE ALSO VOID, THE.

Star Wars: Skeleton Crew (TV) An original series announced for digital release on Disney+, centering around a group of children lost in space, set in the New Republic time frame. Stars Jude Law. From Lucasfilm.

Star Wars: Tales of the Jedi (TV) Six-part animated short series on Disney+; digitally released Oct. 26, 2022. Built around Jedi from the prequel era, parables journey into the lives of Ashoka Tano and Count Dooku who are put to the test as they make choices that will define their destinies. Voices include Ashley Eckstein (Ahsoka Tano), Corey Burton (Qui-Gon Jinn). From Lucasfilm.

Star Wars: The Bad Batch (TV) Animated series on Disney+; digitally premiered May 4, 2021. The elite clones of the Bad Batch—a squad of experimental clones who vary genetically from their brothers in the Clone Army—find their way in a rapidly changing galaxy in the immediate aftermath of the Clone War. Voices include Dee Bradley Baker (The Bad Batch), Archie Panjabi (Depa Billaba), Michelle Ang (Omega), Liam O'Brien (Bolo), Rhea Perlman (Cid), Sam Riegel (Ketch). A spin-off from *Star Wars: The Clone Wars*. From Lucasfilm Ltd.

Star Wars: The Clone Wars (TV) The 7th, and final, season of the animated series—which had debuted in 2008, prior to Disney's acquisition of Lucasfilm—premiered Feb. 21, 2020, on Disney+. It is the end of the historic Clone Wars, as the forces of darkness have amassed great power in their bid to transform the Republic into the Galactic Empire. Clone troopers specialize for the dangerous missions ahead, Ahsoka Tano confronts life outside of the Jedi Order, and a familiar menace returns to wreak havoc. Created by George Lucas and exec. produced by Dave Filoni. Voices include Matt Lanter (Anakin Skywalker), Ashley Eckstein (Ahsoka Tano), Dee Bradley Baker (Clone Troopers), James Arnold Taylor (Obi-Wan Kenobi), Katee Sackhoff (Bo-Katan), Sam Witwer (Darth Maul). From Lucasfilm Animation. *Star Wars: The Bad Batch* is a spin-off.

Star Wars: The Force Awakens (film) The first film in the 3rd *Star Wars* trilogy. Thirty years ago, the Galactic Empire was defeated, but now the galaxy faces a new threat known as the First Order. Led by the mysterious Supreme Leader Snoke, and his ruthless emissaries General Hux, Kylo Ren, and Captain Phasma, they aim to hunt down the last Jedi, Luke Skywalker (who has been missing for some time), and to rule the galaxy by destroying all opposition with the help of their planetary weapon, Starkiller Base. General Leia Organa and ace pilot Poe Dameron of the Resistance are also searching for Luke's whereabouts. Old friends Han Solo and Chewbacca are joined by Finn, a former First Order stormtrooper, and Rey, a scavenger from the planet Jakku, to aid in the search. When Rey finds Dameron's one-of-a-kind astromech droid, BB-8, who holds the key to Luke's location, the unexpected team is thrust into the middle of a battle between the Resistance and the feared First Order, leading our heroes down unexpected paths that will change their lives forever. Directed by J. J. Abrams. Released Dec. 18, 2015, also in 3-D and IMAX, after some international openings Dec. 15–17. Stars Harrison Ford (Han Solo), Mark Hamill (Luke Skywalker), Carrie Fisher (General Leia), Adam Driver (Kylo Ren), Daisy Ridley (Rey), John Boyega (Finn), Oscar Isaac (Poe Dameron), Lupita Nyong'o (Maz Kanata), Andy Serkis (Snoke), Domhnall Gleeson (Gen. Hux), Gwendoline Christie (Capt. Phasma). 136 min. Music by John Williams. Filmed in wide-screen format. From Lucasfilm Ltd. and Bad Robot. A lavish world premiere was held Dec. 14, 2015, along Hollywood Boulevard in Los Angeles (shutting down several city blocks) and took over 3 large movie houses: the El Capitan, Dolby, and the TCL Chinese theatres. With several thousand guests in attendance, the premiere was one of the largest Hollywood had ever seen. The film was a huge hit and set an all-time industry opening weekend record of $248 million domestically, and $281 million internationally, plus record-breaking ticket pre-sales. Nominated for 5 Academy Awards, including Visual Effects and Original Score.

Star Wars: The Last Jedi (film) The 2nd film in the third *Star Wars* trilogy. Luke Skywalker's hermitlike existence on a distant planet is endangered when he encounters Rey, a young woman who just may be the one to continue the Jedi Order. Her desire to learn the ways of the Jedi meets with resistance from Luke. Meanwhile, Kylo Ren and General Hux, under Supreme Leader Snoke, lead the First Order in an all-out assault against General Leia Organa and the Resistance for supremacy of the galaxy. Due to innovations in light speed technology, the Resistance fleet finds they can no longer outrun Snoke's powerful ships, so Poe Dameron, ex-stormtrooper Finn, and a ship maintenance worker, Rose, join forces with DJ, a mercenary, to try to save the Resistance from annihilation. Released Dec. 15, 2017, also in 3-D and IMAX, after a Dec. 13 international release. Directed by Rian Johnson. Stars Daisy Ridley (Rey), John Boyega (Finn), Gwendoline Christie (Capt. Phasma), Domhnall Gleeson (Gen. Hux), Andy Serkis (Supreme Leader Snoke), Laura Dern (Vice Adm. Amilyn Holdo), Oscar Isaac (Poe Dameron), Kelly Marie Tran (Rose Tico), Benicio Del Toro (DJ), Mark Hamill (Luke Skywalker), Carrie Fisher (Leia Organa). 152 min. Filmed in the U.K. From Lucasfilm. Filmed in wide-screen format. Nominated for 4 Academy Awards: Original Score (John Williams), Sound Editing, Sound Mixing, and Visual Effects.

Star Wars: The Rise of Skywalker (film) The final film in the third *Star Wars* trilogy. The fledgling Resistance is outgunned against the overwhelming First Order and a new fleet of Sith warships led by the feared Emperor Palpatine. As a new Jedi, Rey must confront the evil threat, uncovering secrets of her own past and finding the strength to transcend it. Twisted between light and dark, Kylo Ren must choose his own path in the midst of the conflict. Released Dec. 20, 2019, also in 3-D, IMAX, and IMAX 3-D, after a Dec. 18 international release. Directed by J. J. Abrams. Stars Carrie Fisher (Leia Organa), Mark Hamill (Luke Skywalker), Adam Driver (Kylo Ren), Daisy Ridley (Rey), John Boyega (Finn), Oscar Isaac (Poe Dameron), Anthony Daniels (C-3PO), Naomi Ackie (Jannah), Domhnall Gleeson (Gen. Hux), Richard E. Grant (General Pryde), Lupita Nyong'o (Maz Kanata), Keri Russell (Zorii Bliss), Joonas Suotamo (Chewbacca), Kelly Marie Tran (Rose Tico), Billy Dee Williams (Lando Calrissian). 142 min. Filmed in the U.K. From Lucasfilm. Filmed in wide-screen format. The film marked the last time Carrie Fisher appeared on-screen as Leia Organa; although she passed away before filming began, Abrams—with the blessing of Fisher's daughter, Billie Lourd, who plays Lt. Connix—was able to integrate unused footage from *Star Wars: The Force Awakens* into the movie. Received Academy Award nominations for Original Score (John Williams), Sound Editing (Matthew Wood and David Acord), and Visual Effects (Roger Guyett, Neal Scanlan, Patrick Tubach, and Dominic Tuohy).

Star Wars Trading Post Rebel base shop in the Marketplace at Disney Springs; opened Aug. 3, 2017, replacing Marketplace Fun Finds. Also in the Downtown Disney District at Disneyland Resort; temporarily took over the WonderGround Gallery Sep. 2020–Feb. 2021, then took the place of Rainforest Cafe Feb. 19, 2021.

Star Wars Vehicle Flythroughs (TV) Series on Disney+; digitally premiered May 4, 2021, with tours of some of the most iconic ships in the *Star Wars* films.

Star Wars: Visions (TV) Animated short film series on Disney+; digitally released Sep. 22, 2021. Seven Japanese anime studios use their animation and storytelling styles to realize their own visions of the galaxy far, far away. From Lucasfilm.

Star Wars Weekends *Star Wars*–themed event in Disney's Hollywood Studios; held on several weekends each summer in 1997, 2000, and 2001, and then annually from 2003–2015. Guests visited with actors and filmmakers, met *Star Wars* characters, and enjoyed special themed entertainment.

Star Wars: Young Jedi Adventures (TV) Animated series scheduled to premiere on Disney+ and Disney Junior May 4, 2023. Younglings start their journeys on the path to becoming Jedi Knights, learning valuable skills for our galaxy and the galaxy far, far away. The series is part of the era known as the High Republic, set centuries before the events of *Star Wars: The Phantom Menace*. Voices include Jamaal Avery Jr. (Kai Brightstar), Emma Berman (Nash Durango). It is the first full-length animated *Star Wars* series created for preschoolers, early grade schoolers, and their families. From Lucasfilm, ICON Creative Studio, and Disney Junior.

Starabilias Showbiz memorabilia shop in Down-

town Disney West Side at Walt Disney World; open Sep. 15, 1997–Aug. 2009, and succeeded in 2011 by Orlando Harley-Davidson. Also in the Downtown Disney District at Disneyland Resort, Jan. 12, 2001–2009; replaced by Kitson Kids.

Starcade Video arcade in Tomorrowland at Disneyland; opened May 4, 1977. Originally covered 2 floors, with an escalator taking guests to the upper level, but now uses only the lower level for special events, retail, and character greetings. Also in Tomorrowland at Tokyo Disneyland Apr. 15, 1983–Nov. 14, 2007.

Stargate Restaurant Counter-service restaurant in Communicore East at EPCOT Center; open Oct. 1, 1982–Apr. 10, 1994. It later became Electric Umbrella.

Stargazer Grill Quick-service restaurant on the upper concourse of Tomorrowland in Shanghai Disneyland; opened Jun. 16, 2016. Guests dine on burgers, chicken fingers, and salads on an open-air terrace offering a grand view of the park.

Stargirl (film) Leo Borlock, an average student at Mica High School, gets decent grades, is a member of the school's marching band, and has always been content flying under the radar. But all that changes when he meets "Stargirl" Caraway, a confident and colorful new student with a penchant for the 'ukulele. Her eccentricities and infectious personality charm Leo and the student body, and she quickly goes from being ignored and ridiculed to accepted and praised, then back again, sending Leo on a roller-coaster ride of emotions. Released digitally on Disney+ Mar. 13, 2020, after a Mar. 10 premiere at the El Capitan Theatre in Hollywood. Directed by Julia Hart. Stars Grace VanderWaal (Susan "Stargirl" Caraway), Graham Verchere (Leo Bolock), Karan Brar (Kevin Quinlant), Maximiliano Hernandez (Mr. Robineau), Darby Stanchfield (Gloria Borlock), Giancarlo Esposito (Archie Brubaker). 107 min. From Walt Disney Studios. Based on the best-selling young adult novel by Jerry Spinelli. VanderWaal composed and performed the end-credits song, "Today and Tomorrow." Filmed in wide-screen format on location in New Mexico.

Stark Factory Quick-service restaurant in Avengers Campus at Walt Disney Studios Park at Disneyland Paris; opened Jul. 20, 2022, taking the place of Disney Blockbuster Cafe. Pizza, pasta, and salads are served in a high-tech work space where Super Heroes assemble.

Starlight Amphitheater A 900-seat amphitheater for special events in Wishing Star Park at Shanghai Disney Resort; opened Jun. 16, 2016.

Starliner Diner Counter-service restaurant in Tomorrowland at Hong Kong Disneyland; opened Sep. 12, 2005. American-style cuisine is served in a spaceport atmosphere.

Starlit Hui Nighttime show at Aulani, A Disney Resort & Spa; performed 2011–Sep. 26, 2016. Guests participated in cultural activities on the resort's Hālāwai Lawn before watching live performances celebrating Hawaiian traditions. A new show, KA WA'A, a luau, debuted Nov. 2016.

Starring Rolls Café Hollywood Boulevard food facility in Disney's Hollywood Studios; opened May 1, 1989. After several years of seasonal operation, it closed Feb. 5, 2017.

Starship Troopers (film) A handful of dedicated young soldiers must rise to the challenge of intergalactic warfare against a species of terrifying giant alien insects that threaten to eliminate the human race. Johnny Rico, a Mobile Infantry squad leader, who is disillusioned and about to resign, finds his home city attacked and destroyed, so he determines to remain in the Mobile Infantry and fight to destroy the insect threat to human civilization. A co-production of TriStar and Touchstone Pictures, distributed abroad by Buena Vista International. Released in the U.S. on Nov. 7, 1997. Directed by Paul Verhoeven. Stars Casper Van Dien (Johnny Rico), Dina Meyer (Dizzy Flores), Denise Richards (Carmen Ibanez), Jake Busey (Ace Levy), Neil Patrick Harris (Carl Jenkins), Michael Ironside (Jean Rasczak). 129 min. From the novel by Robert A. Heinlein.

StarStruck (TV) A Disney Channel Original Movie; first aired Feb. 14, 2010. Jessica Olson, a down-to-earth girl from the Midwest who is visiting her grandmother in Los Angeles with her family has a chance meeting with Hollywood pop star Christopher Wilde. It seems that Christopher has it all—fame, fortune, and a big-budget Hollywood movie awaiting him—but after spending time with Jessica, he realizes that he has been missing out on something very important—being himself. As he shows her the city sights, the pair develop a friendship, but their bond is tested when he publicly denies knowing her. Now Christopher must decide what is more important—being true to himself or becoming a movie star. Directed by Michael Grossman. Stars Sterling Knight (Christopher Wilde), Danielle Campbell (Jessica Olson), Brandon Mychal Smith (Stubby), Maggie Castle (Sara Olson), Chelsea Staub (Alexis Bender), Dan O'Connor (Dean Olson), Beth Littleford (Barbara Olson). Filmed at landmark locations in Los Angeles.

STAT (TV) Series on ABC; aired Apr. 16–May 21, 1991. Irreverent, frenetic, and wildly comic, the show takes a look at life in a big-city trauma center staffed by highly skilled, fiercely dedicated nurses and doctors whose offbeat senses of humor are often their only weapon against the struggle to save lives. Stars Dennis Boutsikaris (Dr. Tony Menzies), Alison LaPlaca (Dr. Elizabeth Newberry), Casey Biggs (Dr. Lewis Droniger), Alex Elias (Jeanette Lemp). From Touchstone Television.

State Fair Entertainment spectacular at Disneyland in fall 1987 and 1988. Fair-style game and food booths were set up around the Central Plaza, with displays of quilts and other homemade items. There was a "Come to the Fair" parade, along with pig races and thrilling daredevil feats.

State of Georgia (TV) Half-hour comedy series on ABC Family; aired Jun. 29–Aug. 17, 2011. Georgia, an aspiring actress with a larger-than-life personality, and her science geek best friend try to make headway in New York City. Stars Raven-Symoné (Georgia Chamberlin), Majandra Delfino (Jo), Loretta Devine (Aunt Honey), Kevin Covals (Lewis), Jason Rogel (Leo). From ABC Studios.

States' Rights (film) Educational film in the History Alive! series, produced by Turnley Walker; released in 1972. The film documents U.S. president Andrew Jackson's fight with former vice president/senator John C. Calhoun over a tariff law in 1832.

Station Break Refreshments Snack stand beneath the Walt Disney World Railroad Station in the Magic Kingdom at Walt Disney World; opened ca. 1973. Also known as The Station Break.

Station 19 (TV) Drama series spin-off from *Grey's Anatomy* on ABC; premiered Mar. 22, 2018. In Seattle, a group of heroic firefighters at Fire Station 19, from captain to newest recruit, risk their lives and hearts both in the line of duty and off the clock. All firefighters there are also trained EMTs, and the crew of Station 19 is second to none. Stars Jaina Lee Ortiz (Andy Herrera), Miguel Sandoval (Captain Pruitt), Grey Damon (Jack Gibson), Danielle Savre (Maya Bishop), Okieriete Onaodowan (Dean Miller), Jason George (Ben Warren). From ABC Studios.

Stay Alive (film) After the mysterious, brutal death of an old friend, a group of teenagers find themselves in possession of *Stay Alive*, an ultrarealistic 3-D video game based on the spine-chilling story of a 17th-century noblewoman known as "The Blood Countess." The gamers don't know anything about the game other than they are not supposed to have it, and they are dying to play it. Not able to resist temptation, the group begins to play the grisly game and soon a chilling connection is made—they are each being murdered one by one in the same method as the character they played in the game. As the line between the game world and the real world disappears, the teens must find a way to defeat the vicious and merciless Blood Countess, all the while trying to *stay alive*. A Hollywood Pictures/Spyglass Entertainment production. Directed by William Brent Bell. Released Mar. 24, 2006. Stars Jon Foster (Hutch MacNeil), Samaire Armstrong (Abigail), Frankie Muniz (Swink Sylvania), Sophia Bush (October Bantum), Jimmi Simpson (Phineus Bantum), Adam Goldberg (Miller), Milo Ventimiglia (Loomis Crowley). 86 min. Filmed in CinemaScope in New Orleans (just before the devastation of Hurricane Katrina).

Steakhouse, The A 1950s-style jazz restaurant in Disney Village at Disneyland Paris; opened Apr. 12, 1992. It is themed as a former 1800s Chicago meatpacking house turned high-class steak house.

Steakhouse 55 Table-service restaurant in the Disneyland Hotel at the Disneyland Resort; opened Nov. 27, 2006, replacing Granville's Steak House, which had opened Jul. 20, 1983. Guests dine on prime steaks, chops, and seafood in an elegant Old Hollywood atmosphere. The private Oak Room can be reserved for parties. The restaurant was named to highlight the year that Disneyland opened. Closed in 2020 amid the COVID-19 pandemic.

Steakhouse 71 Casual table-service restaurant and lounge in Disney's Contemporary Resort; opened Oct. 1, 2021, succeeding The Wave . . . of American Flavors. Named to pay tribute to the year Walt Disney World opened.

Steamboat Mickey's Shop in American Waterfront at Tokyo DisneySea; opened Sep. 4, 2001. Classic Disney character goods are found alongside decorative boat-related displays. The name is a nod to *Steamboat Willie*.

Steamboat Ventures Venture capital arm of The Walt Disney Company, formed in Sep. 2000, to invest in early- to mid-stage technology-focused companies that are pursuing opportunities in emerging media and entertainment markets.

Steamboat Willie (film) The first Mickey Mouse cartoon released, and the first cartoon with synchronized sound. Directed by Walt Disney. After unsuccessfully trying to make a deal to record through RCA or Western Electric, Disney contracted with the bootleg Powers Cinephone process and, after an initial disastrous recording session, finally record the soundtrack with a 15-piece band and his own squeaks for Mickey. Released at the Colony Theater in New York City on Nov. 18, 1928, the date used for the birth of Mickey Mouse and Minnie Mouse. As a mischievous deckhand on a riverboat, Mickey, to Minnie's delight, plays "Turkey in the Straw" utilizing an animal menagerie as his instruments. The tyrannical Captain Pete is not amused, and Mickey ends up peeling potatoes in the galley. Later released on the 16-mm compilation *Milestones in Animation* (1973).

Steel and America (film) Donald Duck stars in this educational film telling the story of steel from the ore to the finished product, along with its effect on America's growth and economy; produced for the American Iron & Steel Institute. Released on 16 mm in 1965. Revised version released in 1974 as *Steel and America—A New Look*.

Steel Chariots (TV) One-hour pilot on the Fox network; aired Sep. 23, 1997. A high school drama set at a NASCAR stock car racetrack. Directed by Tommy Lee Wallace. Stars John Beck (Dale), Ben Browder (D. J.), Scott Gurney (Brett), Heidi Mark (Amber), Kathleen Nolan (Ethyl), Heather Stephens (Josie), Randy Travis (Jones), Brian Van Holt (Franklin).

Steele, Tommy Actor; appeared in *The Happiest Millionaire* (John Lawless).

Steenburgen, Mary Actress; appeared in *One Magic Christmas* (Ginny Grainger), *Powder* (Jessie), *Nixon* (Hannah Nixon), *Hope Springs* (Joanie

Fisher), *The Proposal* (Grace Paxton), and *The Help* (Elaine Stein).

Steeplechase, The (film) Mickey Mouse cartoon released Sep. 30, 1933. Directed by Burt Gillett. Mickey is a jockey getting ready for the big race when he finds his horse is drunk. Swiftly he has 2 stable boys dress up in a horse costume and manages to win the race with the aid of angry hornets.

Stein Haus SEE SÜSSIGKEITEN (EPCOT).

Steiner, Ronnie Mouseketeer from the 1950s *Mickey Mouse Club* TV show.

Stella (film) Fiercely independent Stella, a wise-cracking bartender, refuses to marry the doctor, Stephen Dallas, who gets her pregnant. Instead she decides to raise their daughter Jenny single-handedly. Through the years, Stella and Jenny share a special bond of friendship, but as Jenny blooms into a precocious young woman, Stella is confronted with the reality of their lower-class existence. Realizing that Jenny's wealthy father could offer Jenny a much better life, Stella decides to make the ultimate sacrifice in order to give her daughter the life she never had. Released Feb. 2, 1990. Directed by John Erman. A Touchstone film, in association with the Samuel Goldwyn Company. 106 min. Stars Bette Midler (Stella Claire), John Goodman (Ed Munn), Trini Alvarado (Jenny Claire), Stephen Collins (Stephen Dallas). Based on the novel *Stella Dallas* by Olive Higgins Prouty. A remake of 2 previous Samuel Goldwyn films (in 1925 and 1937, the latter the classic starring Barbara Stanwyck and Anne Shirley). Filmed on location in Toronto; Boca Raton, Florida; and New York City.

StellaLou SEE DUFFY AND FRIENDS.

Step Up (film) Hip-hop dancing rebel Tyler Gage has grown up all his life on the streets, and he knows he is unlikely to ever make it out of there. But after a brush with the law lands Tyler with a community-service gig at Baltimore's Maryland School of the Arts, everything changes. He meets Nora, the school's prima ballerina, an alluring diva who is desperately searching for someone to replace her injured partner before the school's all-important Senior Showcase. Spying Tyler's moves, Nora can't help but notice he's got a raw but natural gift. She decides to take a chance on Tyler, but as they begin to train, the tension between them, triggered by

their polar-opposite backgrounds, skyrockets. The only thing standing between Tyler and the void are his dreams of making it off the streets—and the only thing standing in the way of Nora's obviously brilliant future is the Senior Showcase. Now, with everything on the line, Tyler will have just one performance to prove to Nora, and to himself, that he can step up to a life far larger than he ever imagined. Released Aug. 11, 2006. A Touchstone/Summit Entertainment film. Directed by Anne Fletcher. Stars Channing Tatum (Tyler Gage), Jenna Dewan (Nora Clark), Damaine Radcliff (Mac Carter), De'Shawn Washington (Skinny Carter), Mario (Miles Darby), Drew Sidora (Lucy Avila), Rachel Griffiths (Director Gordon), Josh Henderson (Brett Dolan). 103 min. Filmed in CinemaScope on location in Baltimore.

Step Up 2: The Streets (film) A sequel to *Step Up*. Andie, a rebellious street dancer, lands at the elite Maryland School of the Arts where she finds herself fighting to fit in while also trying to hold on to her old life. When she joins forces with the school's hottest dancer, Chase, to form a crew of classmate outcasts to compete in Baltimore's underground dance battle—The Streets—she ultimately finds a way to live her dream while building a bridge between her 2 separate worlds. A Touchstone film. Directed by Jon M. Chu. Released Feb. 14, 2008. Stars Briana Evigan (Andie), Robert Hoffman (Chase), Cassie Ventura (Sophie), Will Kemp (Blake), Adam G. Sevani (Moose), Danielle Polanco (Missy), Christopher Scott (Hair), Mari Koda (Jenny Kido), Janelle Cambridge (Fly), Luis Rosado (Monster), Harry Shum, Jr. (Cable), Lajon Dantzler (Smiles), Telisha Shaw (Felicia). 98 min. Filmed in Baltimore.

Step Up 3-D (film) In this third installment of the Step Up franchise, New York City's intense street-dancing underground comes alive as a tight-knit group of street dancers, including Luke and Natalie, team up with New York University freshman Moose and find themselves pitted against the world's best hip-hop dancers in a high-stakes show-down that will change their lives forever. A Touchstone film. Released Aug. 6, 2010. Directed by Jon M. Chu. Stars Rick Malambri (Luke), Sharni Vinson (Natalie), Adam Sevani (Moose), Alyson Stoner (Camille), Keith "Remedy" Stallworth (Jacob), Kendra Andrews (Anala), Stephen "tWitch" Boss (Jason), Joe Slaughter (Julian), Martin and Facundo Lombard (Santiago Twins). 107 min. The first 3-D motion picture to shoot entirely in New York City, and the first-ever 3-D dance drama. The fourth film in the series, *Step Up Revolution* (2012), was not made or distributed by Disney.

Stephanie Miller Show, The (TV) Syn. late-night comedy talk show; aired Sep. 15, 1995–Jan. 20, 1996, with the first in-studio, phone-in audience. From Lipshtick Productions and Buena Vista Television.

Stephen King's Desperation (TV) A 3-hour movie on ABC; first aired May 23, 2006. Visitors to the town of Desperation, Nevada, are jailed by a sinister sheriff, only to find that everyone in the area has suddenly died. A small group has to discover what has been killing them and what can be done to stop it. It is a child, David, who, with the help of some friendly ghosts, discovers how the group can conquer the evil that is bubbling out of the town's recently opened mines. Directed by Mick Garris. Stars Tom Skerritt (Johnny Marinville), Steven Weber (Steve Ames), Annabeth Gish (Mary Jackson), Charles Durning (Tom Billingsley), Matt Frewer (Ralph Carver), Henry Thomas (Peter Jackson), Shane Haboucha (David Carver), Ron Perlman (Collie Entragian). From Sennet/Gernstein Entertainment in association with Touchstone Television.

Stephen King's Kingdom Hospital (TV) Drama series on ABC; aired Mar. 3–Jul. 15, 2004. A hospital built on the exact site of the Gates Falls Mills, where a mysterious fire killed scores of children laboring in the basement in 1869, seems to be haunted. Certain patients hear the tortured sounds of a little girl crying in the elevator shaft. The hospital staff, trained as rational scientists, dismisses the report of ghosts as foolish superstition, but does so at their own peril. Stars Andrew McCarthy (Dr. Hook), Bruce Davison (Dr. Stegman), Ed Begley, Jr. (Dr. Jesse James). Based on the Danish miniseries *Riget*. From Sony Pictures/Touchstone Television.

Stepparents: Where Is the Love? (film) Educational film, using sequences from the TV show *Smoke*. In the Questions!/Answers? series; released in Oct. 1975. The film depicts the adjustments and understanding needed to build a positive stepfamily relationship.

Steps Toward Maturity and Health (film) Educational film, made for Upjohn's Triangle of Health series; released in Jun. 1968. Tracing human life from birth to adolescence, the film shows how a sound mind, a sound body, and social adjustment form the Triangle of Health.

Stepsister from Planet Weird (TV) A Disney Channel Original Movie; first aired Jun. 17, 2000. Fourteen-year-old Megan Larsen is stunned to discover that her mother's exuberant new fiancé and his seemingly perfect daughter are actually aliens who have taken sanctuary on Earth. Directed by Steve Boyum. Stars Courtnee Draper (Megan Larsen), Tamara Hope (Ariel Cola), Khrystyne Haje (Kathy Larson), Lance Guest (Cosmo Cola), Myles Jeffrey (Trevor Larson). Based on the book by Frances Lantz.

Stepsisters Anastasia and Drizella made life difficult for Cinderella; voiced by Lucille Bliss and Rhoda Williams, respectively.

Stern, Daniel Actor; appeared in *Celtic Pride* (Mike O'Hara) and *D.O.A.* (Hal Petersham), and on TV in *Tourist Trap* (George Piper) and *Regular Joe* (Joe Binder).

Stern, Robert A.M. Architect; designed Disney's Yacht and Beach Club Resorts at Walt Disney World and Disney's Hotel Cheyenne and Newport Bay Club at Disneyland Paris. He was named to the Board of Directors of The Walt Disney Company in 1992, serving until 2003. He designed the new Animation Building at the Disney Studio that opened Dec. 1994, as well as the Walt Disney World Casting Center, Disney's BoardWalk Resort, Celebration Health, and the Disney Ambassador Hotel at the Tokyo Disney Resort.

Steven Banks Show, The (TV) Unsold pilot for a cable series; first aired on Showtime Jan. 12, 1991. Reality and fantasy merge in this comedy about a bachelor copywriter's life at work and at home. Directed by Tom McLoughlin. 30 min. Stars Steven Banks, David Byrd, Signy Coleman, Alex Nevil.

Stevens, Art (1915–2007) Co-director, with Woolie Reitherman and John Lounsbery, of *The Rescuers*, and producer and co-director of *The Fox and the Hound*. He had started at the Studio in 1939 and, among other films, received credit as an animator on *Peter Pan*, *One Hundred and One Dalmatians*, *Bedknobs and Broomsticks*, *Robin Hood*, and *The Many Adventures of Winnie the Pooh*. He contributed story concepts and animation to the "man in space" shows for TV in the 1950s. He retired in 1983.

Stevens, Fisher Actor; appeared in *My Science Project* (Vince Latello), *The Marrying Man* (Sammy), and *Super Mario Bros.* (Iggy), and on TV in *Lost* (George Minkowski), with a guest role in *Ugly Betty*.

Stevenson, Robert (1905–1986) Extremely prolific and successful director of Disney live-action films, including some of the most popular box office hits—*Johnny Tremain, Old Yeller, Darby O'Gill and the Little People, Kidnapped, The Absent-Minded Professor, In Search of the Castaways, Son of Flubber, The Misadventures of Merlin Jones, Mary Poppins, The Monkey's Uncle, That Darn Cat!, The Gnome-Mobile, Blackbeard's Ghost, The Love Bug, Bedknobs and Broomsticks, Herbie Rides Again, The Island at the Top of the World, One of Our Dinosaurs Is Missing, The Shaggy D.A.* In 1977, he was labeled "the most commercially successful director in the history of films" by *Variety*. He was named a Disney Legend in 2002.

Stewart, Nicodemus (1910–2000) Actor; provided the voice of Brer Bear in *Song of the South* and returned to voice the character in Splash Mountain 4 decades later.

Stick It (film) Independent 17-year-old Haley Graham defies authority and the laws of gravity with her dirt-biking pals. When a joyride results in a trip to juvenile court, the judge sentences Haley to do time at the elite Vickerman Gymnastics Academy that's run with military regimentation by hard-nosed coach Burt Vickerman. It is a return to a world Haley knows only too well—she was a former Junior Finals gymnastics champion who inexplicably walked out in the middle of the prestigious championships, betraying her teammates, scrapping her own aspirations, and trashing her reputation. There is a battle of wills with Vickerman, who sees Haley's innate talent, and he is committed to helping her come back to a world she could easily rule, whether she wants to or not. Haley's talent and one-of-a-kind personality galvanize the squad, which finds a hero in their new teammate and learn that, along the way, some rules are meant to be broken. A Touchstone film in conjunction with Happy Landing Productions and Spyglass Entertainment. Released Apr. 28, 2006. Directed by Jessica Bendinger. Stars Jeff Bridges (Burt Vickerman),

Missy Peregrym (Haley Graham), Vanessa Lengies (Joanne Charis), Nikki Soohoo (Wei Wei Yong), Maddy Curley (Mina Hoyt), Kellan Lutz (Frank), John Patrick Amedori (Poot), Jon Greis (Brice Graham), Gia Carides (Alice Graham). 103 min. Filming took place in Los Angeles, even though the story is set in Plano, Texas, and Houston. Over a dozen elite international gymnasts were recruited for the competition scenes.

Stiers, David Ogden (1942–2018) Actor; he provided voices in *Beauty and the Beast* (narrator/Cogsworth), *Pocahontas* (Governor Ratcliffe/Wiggins), *The Hunchback of Notre Dame* (Archdeacon), *Teacher's Pet* (Mr. Jolly), *Atlantis: The Lost Empire* (Fenton Q. Harcourt), *Lilo & Stitch* (Jumba), *Spirited Away* (Kamaji), and *The Cat That Looked at a King* (King Cole/Prime Minister). He appeared in *Iron Will* (J. P. Harper), *Bad Company* (Judge Beach), *Jungle 2 Jungle* (Jovanovic), and *Krippendorf's Tribe* (Henry Spivey).

Still Not Quite Human (TV) A Disney Channel Premiere Film; first aired May 31, 1992. Further adventures of the teenage android, who first appeared in *Not Quite Human*. Chip discovers, after Dr. Carson's mysterious disappearance while attending a scientific conference, that something is now "not quite human" about his dad. Directed by Eric Luke. Stars Jay Underwood (Chip), Alan Thicke (Dr. Carson).

Still Star-Crossed (TV) Hour-long period drama on ABC; aired May 29–Jul. 29, 2017. It picks up where the famous story of Romeo and Juliet ends, charting the treachery, fight for power, and ill-fated romances of the Montagues and Capulets in the wake of the young lovers' tragic fate. Stars Grant Bowler (Lord Damiano Montague), Wade Briggs (Benvolio Montague), Torrance Coombs (Count Paris), Dan Hildebrand (Friar Lawrence), Lashana Lynch (Rosaline Capulet), Ebonee Noel (Livia Capulet), Medalion Rahimi (Princess Isabella), Anthony Head (Lord Silvestro Capulet). Based on the book by Melinda Taub. From Shondaland and ABC Studios.

Still the Beaver (TV) Series on The Disney Channel; premiered Nov. 7, 1984, as a continuation of *Leave It to Beaver*. Barbara Billingsley (Mrs. Cleaver), Tony Dow (Wally), Ken Osmond (Eddie Haskell), and Jerry Mathers (the Beaver) all returned, with the addition of Janice Kent (Mary Ellen Rogers Cleaver), Kaleena Kiff (Kelly

Cleaver), John Snee (Oliver Cleaver), Eric Osmond (Freddie Haskell), and Kipp Marcus (Kip Cleaver).

Still Waters (film) Educational film for teenagers about the effect of alcohol on family communication. 26 min. Released in Jan. 1995.

Stiller, Ben Actor; appeared in *Stella* (Jim Uptegrove), *Heavyweights* (Tony Perkis/Tony Perkis Sr.), *Keeping the Faith* (Jacob Schram), and *The Royal Tenenbaums* (Chas). He voiced Khaka Peü Peü in *Phineas and Ferb*.

Stiller, Jerry (1927–2020) Actor; appeared in *Heavyweights* (Harvey Bushkin). He voiced Timon's Uncle Max in *The Lion King 1½* and Harvey in *Planes: Fire & Rescue*, with TV voices, including the Caucasian Eagle in *Hercules*, Pretty Boy in *Teacher's Pet*, and Principal Stickler in *Fish Hooks*.

Stitch Feisty alien (Experiment 626) adopted by Lilo in *Lilo & Stitch*; voiced by Chris Sanders, who co-directed the film.

Stitch Encounter Tomorrowland attraction in Hong Kong Disneyland; opened Jul. 13, 2006, and closed in 2016, to become Star Wars: Command Post. Stitch interacted with guests as he offered a tour of the stars. Also opened in Tokyo Disneyland Jul. 17, 2015, taking the place of *Captain EO*, and in Shanghai Disneyland Jun. 16, 2016. Another version, called *Stitch Live!*, opened in Production Courtyard in Walt Disney Studios Park at Disneyland Paris Mar. 22, 2008. Based on an earlier attraction in Innoventions at Disneyland.

Stitch! The Movie (film) Direct-to-video movie; released Aug. 26, 2003, as a sequel to *Lilo & Stitch*. Stitch was Experiment 626; now the other 625 alien experiments are landing on Earth, and it is up to Lilo and Stitch to rescue these outrageous cousins and change them from bad to good before they are captured by evil captain Gantu. For example, Experiment 221 causes island-wide power surges (while Experiment 625, a lazy, yellow Stitch look-alike, makes great sandwiches). Directed by Tony Craig, Roberts Gannaway. Voices include Daveigh Chase (Lilo), Tia Carrere (Nani), Zoe Caldwell (Grand Councilwoman), Ving Rhames (Cobra Bubbles), David Ogden Stiers (Jumba), Kevin MacDonald (Pleakley), Chris Sanders (Stitch).

Stitchers (TV) Hour-long drama series on Free-

form (formerly ABC Family); aired Jun. 2, 2015– Aug. 14, 2017. A young woman, Kirsten, is recruited into a covert government agency to be "stitched" into the minds of the recently deceased, using their memories to investigate murders and decipher mysteries that otherwise would have gone to the grave. Stars Emma Ishta (Kirsten Clark), Kyle Harris (Cameron Goodkin), Ritesh Rajan (Linus Ahluwalla), Salli Richardson-Whitfield (Maggie Baptiste), Allison Scagliotti (Camille Engelson).

Stitch's Great Escape! Tomorrowland attraction in the Magic Kingdom at Walt Disney World; opened Nov. 16, 2004. Stitch has been captured by the Galactic Federation, and park guests are asked to provide security. They aren't very good security guards, and Stitch escapes. The attraction was similar in format to its predecessor, The ExtraTERRORestrial Alien Encounter, but less thrilling. Began seasonal operation Oct. 2, 2016, and closed Jan. 6, 2018.

STK Orlando Steak house in The Landing at Disney Springs at Walt Disney World; opened May 25, 2016, taking the place of the Comedy Warehouse. The restaurant features a main dining level and a rooftop dining area. Managed by The ONE Group Hospitality, Inc.

Stock, Disney The first prospectus to sell Disney common stock was Apr. 2, 1940. The stock was listed on the New York Stock Exchange on Nov. 12, 1957.

Stock Exchange Shop in Disney's Hotel New York at Disneyland Paris; opened Apr. 12, 1992, and succeeded by New York Boutique.

Stockwell, Guy (1934–2002) Actor; appeared on TV in *The Ballad of Hector the Stowaway Dog*.

Stockwell, Harry (1902–1984) Actor; the voice of the Prince in *Snow White and the Seven Dwarfs*. He was the father of actors Guy and Dean Stockwell.

Stokowski, Leopold (1882–1977) Conductor of the Philadelphia Orchestra, selected by Walt Disney to conduct the music for *Fantasia*. He and his colleagues won a special Academy Award for their work on that film.

Stollery, David Actor; appeared in *Westward Ho*

the Wagons! (Dan Thompson) and *Ten Who Dared* (Andrew Hall). On TV, he appeared in the title role in *A Tribute to Joel Chandler Harris*, and as Marty in the *Spin and Marty* serials and as Mike in the *Annette* serial on the *Mickey Mouse Club*. He provided a voice for *Boys of the Western Sea* and made a cameo as Commissioner Stollery in *The New Adventures of Spin and Marty: Suspect Behavior*. He was named a Disney Legend in 2006.

STOLport, Lake Buena Vista Former airstrip for commuter aircraft near the Magic Kingdom at Walt Disney World; used principally by Shawnee Airlines, fall 1971–late 1972. An abbreviation of Short Take-Off and Landing airport.

Stone, Emma Actress; appeared in *The Help* (Eugenia "Skeeter" Phelan) and in the title role in *Cruella*. She voiced Ivana, the pet dog, in *The Suite Life of Zack & Cody*.

Stone, Sharon Actress; appeared in *Last Dance* (Cindy Liggett) and *Cold Creek Manor* (Leah Tilson), and voiced Nikki in *Higglytown Heroes*.

Stop that Tank (film) Humorous cartoon segment included in a wartime training film on the *Boys Anti-tank Rifle*, made for the National Film Board of Canada in 1942.

Storey, Margene Mouseketeer from the 1950s *Mickey Mouse Club* TV show.

Storm Called Maria, A (TV) Show aired Nov. 27, 1959. Directed by Ken Nelson. Covers the birth and development of a major storm in the Sierra Nevada mountain range, creating increasing danger for the people in the area; based on the book *Storm*, by George R. Stewart.

Stormalong Bay Water recreation area at Disney's Yacht and Beach Club Resorts at Walt Disney World. The 3-acre site features a life-sized shipwreck replica, a sand-bottomed pool, meandering waterways, a 230-ft.-long waterslide, and other activities for the aquatic-minded.

StormRider Port Discovery attraction in Tokyo DisneySea; open Sep. 4, 2001–May 16, 2016, replaced by Nemo & Friends SeaRider. Aboard a new class of flying weather laboratory, guests embarked on a flight right into the middle of the storm of the century, experiencing a harrowing encounter with the forces of nature.

Storms (film) Educational film; released in Mar. 1986. 14 min.

Stormy, the Thoroughbred with an Inferiority Complex (film) Featurette released Mar. 12, 1954. Directed by Larry Lansburgh. 46 min. Stormy, a handsome colt with a famous bloodline, is sold to a cattle ranch when he misses his chance to be a glamorous racehorse, but soon he accepts and enjoys his new life. He proves his thoroughbred training when he is bought by a famous polo player and helps his master win a game. Lansburgh later produced many animal featurettes for the Studio.

Story Book Shop SEE STORYBOOK STORE, THE (DISNEYLAND).

Story of Anyburg, U.S.A., The (film) Special cartoon released Jun. 19, 1957. Directed by Clyde Geronimi. The problems of traffic are examined by the city of Anyburg in judicial court as several automobiles are tried for various crimes and declared "not guilty" since it is the people who drive them who must admit their guilt and promise to drive carefully.

Story of Dogs, A (TV) Show aired Dec. 1, 1954. Directed by Clyde Geronimi, C. August Nichols, Robert Florey. A look behind the scenes at *Lady and the Tramp*, with information on the work of the animators, director, voice artists, background artists, inkers and painters, and camera operators, along with a group of Pluto cartoons.

Story of Donald Duck, The Alternate title of *The Donald Duck Story*.

Story of Frozen, The: Making a Disney Animated Classic (TV) One-hour special on ABC; aired Sep. 2, 2014. Interviews with the stars and filmmakers, along with behind-the-scenes footage.

Story of Menstruation, The (film) Educational film, made for the International Cellucotton Co.; delivered Oct. 18, 1946. Through animation and diagrams, the film discusses the female reproductive organs and functions, and follows development from babyhood to motherhood. A popular Disney film for girls in school for several decades.

Story of Robin Hood and His Merrie Men, The (film) When King Richard the Lionhearted leaves England for the Crusades, his evil brother, Prince John, conspires for the throne with the Sheriff of

Nottingham. But loyal Robin Hood and his followers defy them with the aid of Maid Marian, ward of King Richard, raising the ransom when the King is held prisoner in Germany. When Richard returns, he rewards Robin by making him Earl of Locksley and giving him the hand of Maid Marian in marriage. Released Jun. 26, 1952. Directed by Ken Annakin. 84 min. Stars Richard Todd (Robin), Joan Rice (Maid Marian), Peter Finch (Sheriff), Hubert Gregg (Prince John), Patrick Barr (King Richard). Disney's second fully live-action feature, produced at Denham Studios in England with blocked funds that Walt Disney had been unable to get out of the country. Early plans had called for the film to be cast with actors from *Treasure Island*, including Bobby Driscoll as a member of Robin's band and Robert Newton as Friar Tuck. SEE ALSO ROBIN HOOD (1973 ANIMATED FILM).

Story of the Animated Drawing, The (TV) Show aired Nov. 30, 1955. Directed by Wilfred Jackson, William Beaudine. Walt discusses the history of animation, beginning with J. Stuart Blackton and his *Humorous Phases of Funny Faces* in 1906, and including *Gertie the Dinosaur* (Winsor McCay). Disney composer Oliver Wallace, who at one time accompanied silent films on the organ in movie theaters, re-creates a scene featuring a Koko the Clown cartoon.

Story of the Silly Symphony, The (TV) Show aired Oct. 19, 1955. Directed by Clyde Geronimi. Walt Disney provides a look at some of the Silly Symphony cartoons, while explaining how newly learned techniques were later used by his artists on the animated features.

Storyboards Disney story man Webb Smith is credited with coming up with the idea of storyboards in the early 1930s. These 4-x-8-foot boards had story sketches pinned up on them in order, and the Disney artists found it much easier to visualize a story this way than to read a script. Since the 1930s, storyboards as invented at the Disney Studio have come into general usage throughout the motion picture industry, especially for filmmakers planning commercials and action sequences of live-action films.

Storybook Circus Area in Fantasyland in the Magic Kingdom at Walt Disney World; opened in 2012, taking the place of Mickey's Toontown Fair. It features circus-themed attractions, like The Barnstormer Featuring the Great Goofini, Dumbo

the Flying Elephant, Casey Jr. Splash 'n' Soak Station, Pete's Silly Sideshow, and also a Fantasyland Station for the Walt Disney World Railroad.

Storybook Land Canal Boats Fantasyland attraction in Disneyland; opened Jun. 16, 1956. Formerly Canal Boats of the World (1955). Guests board a 12-passenger boat for a guided tour that begins through the mouth of Monstro, the whale. They then cruise past miniature scenes from Disney animated films, from the homes of the Three Little Pigs to Geppetto's Village. Above on the hill is Cinderella Castle, with the pumpkin coach visible on its way up the winding road. At one time, it was thought that a Big Rock Candy Mountain would be built here, and the boats would enter the mountain and come upon Dorothy having a party with her friends from Oz. In Jul. 1994, the attraction was renovated, adding Agrabah from *Aladdin* and scenes from *The Little Mermaid*, relocating Toad Hall in the process. In 2014, the Kingdom of Arendelle and Elsa's Ice Palace from *Frozen* were added, displacing *The Old Mill* tableau. SEE ALSO LE PAYS DES CONTES DE FÉES (DISNEYLAND PARIS).

Storybook Shoppe Fantasyland shop in Hong Kong Disneyland; opened Sep. 12, 2005. It became the Bibbidi Bobbidi Boutique Jul. 1, 2019.

Storybook Store, The Shop on Main Street, U.S.A. in Disneyland; opened Jul. 17, 1955, as the Book and Candle Shop. It became the Storybook Store 1972–Apr. 1995 (also known as Story Book Shop). Western Publishing Co., the original sponsor, was one of the few companies that invested in what was in 1955 thought to be Walt Disney's risky venture. Also a World Bazaar shop in Tokyo Disneyland (opened Apr. 15, 1983, replaced in 2007 by Town Center Fashions) and a Main Street, U.S.A. shop in Disneyland Paris (opened Apr. 12, 1992).

Storybook Theater Fantasyland theater in Hong Kong Disneyland; opened Sep. 12, 2005, with *The Golden Mickeys*. A new concert-style show, *Mickey and the Wondrous Book*, premiered Nov. 17, 2015, as part of the Happily Ever After celebration commemorating the park's 10th anniversary.

Storybook Treats Fantasyland ice cream counter in the Magic Kingdom at Walt Disney World; opened Nov. 2011, taking the place of Mrs. Potts' Cupboard.

Storyhouse Stage Adventure Isle theater in Shanghai Disneyland; opened Jun. 16, 2016, with *Tarzan: Call of the Jungle*, a live musical and acrobatic performance based on the Disney animated feature. The show ended Aug. 6, 2019. The theater is designed as though it was once a storehouse for expedition supplies.

Storyliving by Disney Business within Disney Signature Experiences announced Feb. 16, 2022, to develop residential communities concepted by Disney Imagineers in conjunction with developers and home builders. Disney will operate the community association and, through a club membership, provide access to entertainment, seminars, and other programs. The first location, the Cotino community, is planned to open in Rancho Mirage, in California's Greater Palm Springs area. Master planned in partnership with DMB Development, the community will be available for homeowners of all ages, with home types including estates, single-family homes, and condominiums. The community is expected to surround an approx. 24-acre oasis and a mixed-use district with shopping, dining, a beachfront hotel, and a beach park with water activities accessible to the public with a day pass. Additional Storyliving by Disney communities are under exploration for future development, with some neighborhoods for residents ages 55+.

Storytellers Bronze statue of Walt Disney with Mickey Mouse outside the Carthay Circle Restaurant in Disney California Adventure; debuted Jun. 15, 2012. The statue depicts Walt as a humble, optimistic, young man arriving in Los Angeles in 1923, dreaming of achievements to come. The sculptor was Rick Terry. A version of the statue was unveiled in Tokyo DisneySea in fall 2013, to commemorate the resort's 30th anniversary, and another debuted in Shanghai Disneyland with the park's opening in 2016. SEE ALSO PARTNERS AND WALT THE DREAMER.

Storytellers Cafe Buffet dining in Disney's Grand Californian Hotel & Spa at the Disneyland Resort; opened Feb. 8, 2001. Roasted chicken, seasonal fish, and carved skirt steak are served in a cozy, Craftsman-style dining room, with visits by Disney characters at breakfast.

Stoyanov, Michael Actor; appeared on TV in *Blossom* (Anthony) and *Exile*, and guest starred in *Monk* (Stephen Dorn).

Straight Shooters (film) Donald Duck cartoon released Apr. 18, 1947. Directed by Jack King. Don is a barker in a shooting gallery, where he has troubles with his nephews, who retaliate for being cheated by him by dressing up first as a female duck and then as a mummy to get the candy prizes.

Straight Story, The (film) Alvin Straight, a 73-year-old man with failing eyesight who uses 2 canes to walk, receives a call that his brother Lyle, several hundred miles away, has suffered a stroke. Without a driver's license, the eccentric Alvin sets out, at 5 mph, to get to his brother aboard his 1966 John Deere ride-on lawn mower. On his difficult odyssey, Alvin encounters a number of strangers with whom he shares his life's earned wisdom with simple stories, and has a profound impact on their lives. Released in New York City, Los Angeles, and Chicago on Oct. 15, 1999. Directed by David Lynch. Stars Richard Farnsworth (Alvin Straight), Sissy Spacek (Rose Straight), Harry Dean Stanton (Lyle Straight). 112 min. Filmed in CinemaScope. Based on the true story of Alvin Straight's 260-mile journey in 1994 from Laurens, Iowa, to Mt. Zion, Wisconsin, which was discovered by the producers in a *New York Times* article. They eventually filmed the story in the actual area where it had happened. The film was a hit at the 1999 Cannes Film Festival, and Richard Farnsworth received an Academy Award nomination as Best Actor.

Straight Talk (film) Shirlee Kenyon, a small-town dance instructor, gets fired because she spends more time counseling her customers than teaching them to dance. She heads to Chicago to make a fresh start and gets a job as the receptionist at WNDY, a radio station. While looking for the coffee room on a break, she is mistakenly identified as the station's new on-air radio psychologist. Her warm heart and common sense make her an instant celebrity, arousing the suspicions of news reporter Jack Russell, whose secret assignment is to woo her in order to discredit her in a newspaper exposé. The more Jack learns about Shirlee, the harder he falls for her charms, and he ultimately yields to his integrity, falls in love, and gives up the story. Released Apr. 3, 1992. Directed by Barnet Kellman. A Hollywood Pictures film. 90 min. Stars Dolly Parton (Shirlee), James Woods (Jack), Griffin Dunne (Alan), Michael Madsen (Steve). Filmed on location in Chicago and its environs.

Strange Companions (TV) A veteran bush pilot and an orphan stowaway crash in a dense Canadian forest, encounter many hardships, and are finally rescued many months later. Prepared for the Disney TV anthology series in America but did not air. First aired in Canada on Dec. 4, 1983. Directed by Frank Zuniga. Later shown on The Disney Channel. Stars Doug McClure (Archie), Michael Sharrett (David), Marj Dusay (Mae).

Strange Magic (film) A fairy-tale musical inspired by *A Midsummer Night's Dream*, with popular songs from the past six decades helping to tell the tale of a colorful cast of goblins, elves, fairies, and imps—and their misadventures sparked by the battle over a powerful potion. Animated film from Lucasfilm, Ltd., released by Touchstone Pictures Jan. 23, 2015. Directed by Gary Rydstrom. Voices include Alan Cumming (Bog King), Evan Rachel Wood (Marianne), Kristin Chenoweth (Sugar Plum Fairy), Maya Rudolph (Griselda), Sam Palladio (Roland), Meredith Anne Bull (Dawn), Alfred Molina (Fairy King), Elijah Kelley (Sunny), Bob Einstein (Stuff), Peter Stormare (Thang). 99 min. From a story by George Lucas.

Strange Monster of Strawberry Cove, The (TV) Two-part show; aired on Oct. 31 and Nov. 7, 1971. Directed by Jack Shea. Three kids building a fake sea monster stumble upon a smuggling operation but cannot get the sheriff to believe them, so they have to try to catch the smugglers themselves. Stars Burgess Meredith, Agnes Moorehead, Annie McEveety, Jimmy Bracken, Patrick Creamer, Larry D. Mann, Parley Baer, Skip Homeier, Bill Zuckert, Kelly Thordsen.

Strange World (film) Action-adventure feature from Walt Disney Animation Studios. A legendary family of explorers, the Clades, attempts to navigate an uncharted, treacherous land alongside a motley crew that includes a mischievous blob, a three-legged dog, and a slew of ravenous creatures. Released Nov. 23, 2022, also in 3-D. Directed by Don Hall and co-directed by Qui Nguyen. Voices include Jake Gyllenhaal (Searcher Clade), Dennis Quaid (Jaeger Clade), Jaboukie Young-White (Ethan Clade), Gabrielle Union (Meridian Clade), Lucy Liu (Callisto Mal). 102 min. Music by Henry Jackman. The film was created in the spirit of pulp novels and the movies inspired by them, with art direction based on pulp magazines from the 1930s–1940s.

Stranger Among Us, A (film) Emily Eden is a New York City police detective absorbed by her career and emotionally detached from the violence she sees in her daily life. Her routine investigation of a missing person report develops into a complex undercover murder case in the Hassidic Jewish community. She meets Ariel, a spiritual young man destined to be the community's next rabbi and learns from him the centuries-old Jewish traditions while the 2 of them struggle with their growing but forbidden feelings for one another. With Ariel's help, Emily eventually solves the case of murder and diamond theft, and the 2 of them part ways—each with a better understanding of life and of their distinct worlds. Released Jul. 17, 1992. Directed by Sidney Lumet. A Hollywood Pictures film. 109 min. Stars Melanie Griffith (Emily Eden), Eric Thal (Ariel). Filmed on location in New York City.

Strassman, Marcia (1948–2014) Actress; appeared in *Honey, I Shrunk the Kids* and *Honey, I Blew Up the Kid* (Diane Szalinski) and *Another Stakeout* (Pam O'Hara).

Streep, Meryl Actress; appeared in *Before and After* (Carolyn Ryan) and *Mary Poppins Returns* (Topsy), and narrated *Wings of Life*. Nominated for an Oscar for her role in *Into the Woods* (Witch).

Street Safe, Street Smart (film) Educational film with Mickey and friends taking a close look at important street safety situations, in the Mickey's Safety Club series; released in Sep. 1989. 13 min.

Streetmosphere Known as the Citizens of Hollywood, these are the actors on Hollywood Boulevard in Disney's Hollywood Studios at Walt Disney World portraying starlets, casting directors, taxicab drivers, policemen, and avid autograph seekers who provide comic entertainment while one strolls down the street.

Streets of America Area in Disney's Hollywood Studios originally known as New York Street. The name changed in 2004. The area included *Muppet*Vision 3D*; Honey, I Shrunk the Kids Movie Set Adventure; *Lights, Motors, Action! Extreme Stunt Show*; Studio Backlot Tour; Mama Melrose's Ristorante Italiano; Pizza Planet Arcade; and Studio Catering Co. It was also the site for the annual Osborne Family Spectacle of Lights, 2004–2015. Closed Apr. 2, 2016, to make way for Star Wars: Galaxy's Edge.

Streets of America Festival Disney shop in Disneyland Paris; opened Apr. 12, 1992, with merchandise representing American cities. Closed in 1994, to become Rock 'n' Roll America.

Stromboli Puppet-show proprietor in *Pinocchio*; voiced by Charles Judels.

Stromboli's Ristorante Italian eatery in the Disneyland Hotel at Disneyland Resort; opened May 12, 1995, taking the place of Caffe Villa Verde. Closed Apr. 10, 1999, to become Goofy's Kitchen.

Strongest Man in the World, The (film) Medfield College science student Dexter Riley eats a bowl of cereal accidentally containing a chemical compound he has been working on. He develops superhuman strength, which he mistakenly attributes to a vitamin formula devised by a fellow student. Two cereal companies compete for ownership of the secret ingredient and back a weight lifting contest between Medfield and rival State College. Medfield is losing badly when Dexter realizes his compound, not the other student's, is the secret of his strength, and he leads his team to victory. Released Feb. 6, 1975. Directed by Vincent McEveety. 92 min. Stars Kurt Russell (Dexter), Joe Flynn (Dean Higgins), Eve Arden (Harriet), Cesar Romero (A. J. Arno), Phil Silvers (Krinkle), Dick Van Patten (Harry), Harold Gould (Dietz). The main building of Medfield College, the setting for numerous Disney movies, including *The Computer Wore Tennis Shoes* and *Now You See Him, Now You Don't*, was, in fact, the Animation Building on the Disney Studio lot in Burbank. Location shooting was done on this film in New Chinatown, Griffith Park, Echo Park, and the federal penitentiary, all in Los Angeles. Robert F. Brunner composed the music score, which included a running theme, called "Instant Muscle," featuring jazz themes, as well as 2 school marching band songs.

Stub, The Best Cow Dog in the West (TV) Show aired Dec. 8, 1974. Directed by Larry Lansburgh. A wild Brahman bull is endangering the herds, so a ranch owner and his daughter track him down. An Australian herding dog helps out, and years later its offspring are still active in the area. Stars Slim Pickens, Jay Sisler, Mike Hebert, Luann Beach. An updated version of the featurette *Cow Dog* (from 1956).

Stuck in the Middle (TV) Comedy series on Disney Channel; debuted Feb. 14, 2016, and ended Jul. 23, 2018. Harley Diaz is an engineering whiz who uses her inventions to navigate through life as the middle child in a large family of 7 kids. Her overlooked status proves to be both a blessing and a curse as she maneuvers her way through the everyday antics that come with being part of a big family. Stars Jenna Ortega (Harley), Ronni Hawk (Rachel), Kayla Maisonet (Georgie), Isaak Presley (Grant), Nicolas Bechtel (Danny), Malachi Barton (Beast), Ariana Greenblatt (Daphne). From Horizon Productions, Inc.

Stuck in the Suburbs (TV) A Disney Channel Original Movie; first aired Jul. 16, 2004. Two tween girls are bored with their suburban lives until a famous pop-singing/dancing sensation arrives in their area and his personal digital assistant (PDA) falls into their hands. As they attempt to return it to him, the girls discover that the singing sensation's entire image is manufactured by his record company, despite his true artistic singer/songwriter style. When they set out to reveal his authentic persona, they discover that it doesn't matter where you live or what you do, as long as you are true to yourself and others. Directed by Savage Steve Holland. Stars Danielle Panabaker (Brittany Aarons), Brenda Song (Natasha), Taran Killam (Jordan Cahill), Ryan Belleville (Eddie), Amanda Shaw (Kaylee), CiCi Hedgpeth (Ashley), Jennie Garland (Olivia), Kirsten Nelson (Susan Aarons), Todd Stashwick (Len), Corri English (Jessie Aarons), Ric Reitz (David Aarons). Filmed in and around New Orleans.

Student Exchange (TV) Two-hour show; aired Nov. 29–Dec. 6, 1987. Directed by Mollie Miller. Carol and Neil are nobodies, whom no one notices in their high school. But when they plot to exchange places with 2 arriving French and Italian exchange students who are suddenly transferred to another school, they take their school by storm and cause no end of trouble for the vice principal. Stars Viveka Davis (Carol/Simone), Todd Field (Neil/Adriano), Mitchell Anderson (Rod), Heather Graham (Dorie), Maura Tierney (Kathy), Gavin MacLeod (Dupiner).

Studio SEE BACKLOT, WALT DISNEY STUDIO.

Studio Backlot Tour SEE BACKSTAGE STUDIO TOUR.

Studio Catering Co. Food facility in Disney's Hollywood Studios; open May 1, 1989–Apr. 2, 2016. Meals and snacks were available here, at the end of the Backstage Studio Tour tram excursion. Hosted by Coca-Cola. Also the name of a backlot catering truck in Hollywood Land at Disney California Adventure.

Studio D Theater in Production Courtyard at Walt Disney Studios Park at Disneyland Paris; opened Jul. 1, 2021, with the Disney Junior Dream Factory show. It replaced Disney Junior Live on Stage!

Studio Disney 365 Children's boutique in the Downtown Disney District at Disneyland Resort offering makeovers inspired by Disney Channel stars; opened Jun. 26, 2009, taking the place of Club Libby Lu. Packages included cosmetic and hair makeovers, wardrobe options, and a photo shoot. Closed Sep. 22, 2014, to become Anna & Elsa's Boutique.

Studio M Included Mickey's Photo Studio and robotic T-shirt painting in Downtown Disney Marketplace at Walt Disney World; opened Oct. 26, 1995, taking the place of the Great Southern Craft Co. Moved to a new location next to Arribas Bros. in 1997, and closed ca. 2003.

Studio Pizzeria, The Restaurant in Disney-MGM Studios; opened Jun. 15, 1991. The name changed in Sep. 1991 to Mama Melrose's Ristorante Italiano.

Studio Showcase Attraction in Disney's Hollywood Studios; opened Sep. 29, 1991. Props, costumes, and other memorabilia from the latest box office hits were exhibited. It replaced the Rocketeer Gallery and later moved to the end of the Backstage Studio Tour. Became the AFI Showcase in Dec. 1995, then closed Aug. 16, 2014.

Studio Store, The Animation Courtyard shop in Disney's Hollywood Studios; opened May 1, 1989, offering Disney clothing and accessories. Also known as The Disney Studio Store. A Studio Store opened inside the Commissary at the Disney Studio in Burbank, California, Feb. 12, 1987, and a Disney Store later opened on the lot Oct. 16, 1995, becoming the Walt Disney Studio Store Jul. 12, 2004. SEE ALSO DISNEY'S SODA FOUNTAIN AND STUDIO STORE (HOLLYWOOD) AND WALT DISNEY STUDIOS STORE (DISNEYLAND PARIS).

Studio Tram Tour: Behind the Magic Behind-the-scenes attraction in Walt Disney Studios Park at Disneyland Paris; ran Mar. 16, 2002–Jan. 5, 2020, replaced by Cars ROAD TRIP. Passengers toured backlot sets, props, and vehicles, with a stop at Catastrophe Canyon. An onboard video showed how film effects were done. SEE ALSO BACKSTAGE STUDIO TOUR (DISNEY'S HOLLYWOOD STUDIOS).

StudioLAB A 3,500-sq.-ft. tech hub at The Walt Disney Studios in Burbank focused on advancing storytelling with cutting-edge technologies, such as virtual reality, artificial intelligence, and mixed reality experiences. Launched in 2018, in the original Animation Building.

Stumptown (TV) Hour-long drama series on ABC; aired Sep. 25, 2019–May 25, 2020. Dex Parios, an assertive, sharp-witted army veteran with a complicated love life, gambling debt, and a brother to take care of, works as a PI in Portland, Oregon. With only herself to rely on, she solves other people's messes with a blind eye toward her own, finding herself at odds with the police and in the firing line of criminals. Based on the graphic novel series of the same name. Stars Cobie Smulders (Dex Parios), Jake Johnson (Grey McConnell), Tantoo Cardinal (Sue Lynn Blackbird), Cole Sibus (Ansel Parios), Adrian Martinez (Tookie). From ABC Studios.

Stuntman (TV) A Disney+ original documentary; digitally released Jul. 23, 2021. A rare look into the entertainment industry's most dangerous and anonymous profession through the eyes of Hollywood stuntman Eddie Braun, who teams up with Scott Truax—son of the NASA rocket scientist who built Evel Knievel's original doomed rocket—to re-create the 1974 infamous Snake River Canyon rocket jump attempt in Idaho. Directed by Kurt Mattila. 95 min. From Seven Bucks Productions and Driven Pictures.

Stuntronics Stunt-double animatronics figures combining advanced robotics with untethered movement to create realistic aerial stunts. The first figure, a swinging Spider-Man in Avengers Campus at Disney California Adventure, debuted Jun. 4, 2021.

Style and Substance (TV) Half-hour series on CBS; aired Jan. 5–Sep. 9, 1998. Chelsea Stevens has written books and produced videotapes on home decorating and entertaining, and even has her own TV show. She lives in an efficiently ordered world, totally oblivious to the chaotic and hysterical reality surrounding her. Jane Sokol comes on board as the new manager of Chelsea's business enterprises, and they collide on an almost daily basis. Stars Jean Smart (Chelsea Stevens), Nancy McKeon (Jane Sokol), Heath Hyche (Terry), Linda Kash (Trudy), Joseph Maher (Mr. John), Alan Autry (Earl). From The Cloudland Company and Touchstone Television.

Sublight Lounge Stylish lounge aboard Star Wars: Galactic Starcruiser Wat Walt Disney World; opened Mar. 1, 2022. Guests can enjoy a beverage or play a game of holo-sabacc.

Submarine Voyage Tomorrowland attraction in Disneyland; opened Jun. 6, 1959, and dedicated Jun. 14, as one of the first "E ticket" attractions. Billed as a voyage through "liquid space" in which passengers looked out of a porthole to view underwater wonders, including marine life, a graveyard of lost ships, a giant squid, and the lost city of Atlantis. Air bubbles gave riders a sensation of diving deep under the ocean. Originally the 8 submarines were painted gray, based on America's newest nuclear submarines, and named after them — *Nautilus, Seawolf, Skate, Skipjack, Triton, George Washington, Patrick Henry,* and *Ethan Allen.* The subs, constructed at Todd Shipyards in Los Angeles's San Pedro neighborhood under the supervision of retired U.S. Navy rear admiral Joseph W. Fowler, were 52 feet long and held a pilot and 38 passengers. New props and animated figures were added in 1961. For several years, live mermaids could be seen swimming in the lagoon's waters. In the 1980s, the subs were repainted bright yellow to resemble scientific research vessels and renamed *Argonaut, Explorer, Nautilus, Neptune, Sea Star, Sea Wolf, Seeker,* and *Triton.* The attraction closed Sep. 7, 1998, although a group of Imagineers, led by Tony Baxter, sought ways to bring it back. The answer ultimately came with the success of Disney • Pixar's *Finding Nemo,* and the attraction reopened in 2007 as the Finding Nemo Submarine Voyage. The Walt Disney World attraction was 20,000 Leagues Under the Sea, with subs patterned after Captain Nemo's *Nautilus;* it closed in 1994.

Substitutiary Locomotion Song from *Bedknobs and Broomsticks;* written by Richard M. and Robert B. Sherman. It is a magic spell that causes inanimate objects to take on a life force of their own; the 5 mystic words are Treguna, Mekoides, Trecorum, Satis, Dee.

Sugar Bowl Lodge SEE MT. DISNEY.

Suite Life Movie, The (TV) A Disney Channel

Original Movie; first aired Mar. 25, 2011. When Cody receives the opportunity to study at the Gemini Institute, a high-tech center which studies dynamics between twins, he and Zack find themselves connected in a way they never have been before. When one twin experiences a sensation, the other twin feels it. While this newfound power helps the boys see eye to eye for the first time in their lives, it ultimately puts them in more danger than they could have ever imagined. Directed by Sean McNamara. Stars: Cole Sprouse (Cody Martin), Dylan Sprouse (Zach Martin), Debby Ryan (Bailey Pickett), Brenda Song (London Tipton), Phill Lewis (Mr. Moseby), Matthew Timmons (Woody Fink), Matthew Glave (Dr. Olsen), Katelyn Pacitto (Nellie), John Ducey (Dr. Spaulding), Kara Pacitto (Kellie). Filmed in Vancouver and other British Columbia, Canada, locations.

Suite Life of Zack & Cody, The (TV) Comedy series on Disney Channel; debuted Mar. 18, 2005. Twin 12-year-old boys, Zack and Cody, have a single mom who is a headlining singer at the Tipton, an upscale hotel in Boston. As part of her contract, she is given an upper-floor suite in the hotel, where the family lives. To the chagrin of the hotel manager, Mr. Moseby, the twins turn the hotel into their playground, and the staff and guests into unwitting participants in the outrageous situations they manage to create. Stars Cole Sprouse (Cody Martin), Dylan Sprouse (Zack Martin), Ashley Tisdale (Maddie Fitzpatrick), Brenda Song (London Tipton), Phill Lewis (Mr. Moseby), Kim Rhodes (Carey Martin), Estelle Harris (Murielle), Adrian R'Mante (Esteban). Also aired on *ABC Kids* beginning Sep. 17, 2005.

Suite Life on Deck, The (TV) A spin-off of *The Suite Life of Zack & Cody;* premiered on Disney Channel Sep. 26, 2008. Zack and Cody are now aboard the SS *Tipton,* a luxury cruise ship owned by London's father. The ship cruises the world with tourists and students who attend classes at Seven Seas High, the one high school that London's dad thinks will make his daughter a better student. While out at sea, Zack and Cody still manage to get into a lot of mischief, and London learns to live a simpler life, including sharing a small room with Bailey, a country girl from Kansas. Stars Dylan Sprouse (Zack Martin), Cole Sprouse (Cody Martin), Brenda Song (London Tipton), Phill Lewis (Mr. Moseby), Debby Ryan (Bailey).

Suited for the Sea (film) The evolution of diving

suit technology, from the early diving bell to the Deep Rover, for The Living Seas in EPCOT Center; opened Jan. 15, 1986. The film, and the rest of the surrounding Undersea Exploration module, closed in 2004, making way for exhibits themed to *Finding Nemo*.

Sullivan, Bill ("Sully") He joined the staff at Disneyland in 1955, progressing from ticket taker to ride operator to operations supervisor. He assisted in the pageantry for the 1960 Olympic Winter Games in what is now known as Olympic Valley, California, the Disney attractions for the 1964–1965 New York World's Fair, and notable Disney film premieres. Sullivan relocated to Florida to help open Walt Disney World. There, he would serve as director of the Project Installation and Coordination Office (PICO), director of EPCOT Center operations, and vice president of the Magic Kingdom. He retired in 1993 and was named a Disney Legend in 2005.

Sultan Ruler of Agrabah, Jasmine's father, in *Aladdin*; voiced by Douglas Seale.

Sultan and the Rock Star (TV) Show aired Apr. 20, 1980. Rerun as *The Hunter and the Rock Star*. Directed by Ed Abroms. A gentle tiger is taken to an island to become the object of a hunting party, but they don't reckon on a popular rock star escaping from his adoring public for a few days and helping the tiger. Stars Timothy Hutton (Paul Winters), Ken Swofford (George McKinzie), Bruce Glover (Alec Frost), Ned Romero (Joe Ironwood).

Sultan's Oasis Counter-service refreshment stand in Arabian Coast at Tokyo DisneySea; opened Sep. 4, 2001. Named after the Sultan in *Aladdin*.

Summer (film) Silly Symphony cartoon released Jan. 16, 1930. Directed by Ub Iwerks. In this summer fantasy, the woodland animals, bugs, and flowers celebrate the season.

Summer House on the Lake Full-service restaurant with a beach house environment at Disney Springs West Side at Walt Disney World; planned to open in 2023, on the site of the former Bongos Cuban Cafe. California-inspired fare is served. Operated by Lettuce Entertain You Restaurants.

Summer Lace Women's designer apparel in Disney's Grand Floridian Resort & Spa at Walt Disney World; open Jun. 28, 1988–2019 and succeeded by Curiouser Clothiers.

Summer Magic (film) Based on the novel *Mother Carey's Chickens* by Kate Douglas Wiggin, which has become an American classic, the film tells the story of how the recently widowed Margaret Carey and her brood of 3 lively children, Nancy, Peter, and Gilly, left almost penniless when her late husband's investments prove worthless, leave their lovely Boston home to make a new life in Beulah, a quaint rural town in Maine. Osh Popham, the local postmaster, sets them up in an empty home owned by the mysterious Mr. Hamilton, who turns up only to fall in love with Nancy. When their snobbish cousin Julia comes to visit, she too soon becomes one of the family and falls in love with the new schoolteacher Charles Bryan. Released Jul. 7, 1963. Directed by James Neilson. 109 min. Stars Hayley Mills (Nancy Carey), Burl Ives (Osh Popham), Dorothy McGuire (Margaret Carey), Deborah Walley (Julia), Eddie Hodges (Gilly), Jimmy Mathers (Peter), Peter Brown (Tom Hamilton). One of the earliest Disney "musicals," the film features songs written by Richard M. and Robert B. Sherman, highlighted by Burl Ives's rendition of "The Ugly Bug Ball." Other songs include "Flitterin'," "Beautiful Beulah," "The Pink of Perfection," "On the Front Porch," and "Femininity." Prior to the film having its final name, the Sherman brothers had written a song titled "City People." Walt Disney asked to have the number re-titled as "Summer Magic," which then became the name for the motion picture. Filmed at the Disney Studio and Columbia Ranch (now the Warner Ranch) in Burbank, California.

Summer of Sam (film) During the summer of 1977, the serial killer dubbed the Son of Sam terrorized New York City. With the media playing an integral role in creating mass fear and paranoia, the whole city becomes a hotbed of trepidation and panic. As the vicious murderer, preying on young women and couples, stalks his way through the Italian American section of the Bronx, a 32-year-old thug, Joey T., and his gang of flunkies begin a witch hunt for the murderer, obsessed with the idea that he is someone from "the neighborhood." Directed by Spike Lee. Released Jul. 2, 1999. Stars John Leguizamo (Vinny), Adrien Brody (Ritchie), Jennifer Esposito (Ruby), Ben Gazzara (Luigi), Bebe Neuwirth (Gloria), Patti LuPone (Helen), Anthony LaPaglia (Petrocelli), Mira Sorvino (Dionna), Michael Rispoli (Joey T.). 142 min.

Summer of the Monkeys (film) Non-Disney film from Edge Productions released on video on Dec. 18, 1998, as *Disney's Summer of the Monkeys* by Walt Disney Home Video. A 12-year-old boy tries to capture 4 runaway circus chimps for the reward money. Directed by Michael Anderson. Stars Michael Ontkean (John Lee), Leslie Hope (Sara Lee), Wilford Brimley (Grandpa), Corey Sevier (Jay Berry Lee). 101 min.

Summer Sands Swimwear and beach accessory shop in Downtown Disney Marketplace at Walt Disney World; opened Nov. 30, 1995, taking the place of the Discover store. In 2001, Pooh Corner expanded into Summer Sands, which moved to a new location Aug. 1, 2002, replacing Toys Fantastic. It became Tren-D in 2009.

Summertree Character dining buffet in the Disneyland Pacific Hotel (later known as Disney's Paradise Pier Hotel) at the Disneyland Resort. It became Disney's PCH Grill May 23, 1997.

Sun Bank A branch operated on Main Street, U.S.A. in the Magic Kingdom at Walt Disney World, Jun. 24, 1977–Jun. 20, 1997, and was succeeded by the Main Street Gallery. FOR THE SUN BANK BUILDING, SEE LAKE BUENA VISTA OFFICE PLAZA.

Sun Wheel Ferris wheel attraction in Paradise Pier at Disney's California Adventure; opened Feb. 8, 2001. Enormous A-frame struts hold a 168-feet-in-diameter wheel that takes passengers for a ride in gondolas, some just swinging but others zigzagging toward the hub in a perpetual state of centrifugal excitement. It closed Oct. 13, 2008, to be remodeled as Mickey's Fun Wheel, opening May 4, 2009, and then became the Pixar Pal-A-Round Jun. 23, 2018.

Sunday Drive (TV) Two-hour movie; aired on Nov. 30, 1986. Two bored children, Christine and John, are mistakenly left behind at a restaurant while on a Sunday drive with their aunt and uncle, due to 2 identical cars. Everyone has a hassle trying to get back together. Stars Tony Randall, Ted Wass, Carrie Fisher, Audra Lindley, Claudia Cron, Norman Alden. Directed by Mark Cullingham.

Sunkist Citrus House Shop on Main Street, U.S.A. in Disneyland; open Jul. 31, 1960–Jan. 3, 1989. Originally took the place of Puffin Bakery. It later became Blue Ribbon Bakery.

Sunkist "I Presume" Adventureland refreshment stand in Disneyland; opened Jun. 1962, taking the place of the Adventureland Cantina. A guest favorite was the Jungle Julep. Closed Jan. 20, 1989, to become Bengal Barbecue. Named after the famous greeting by explorer Henry Morton Stanley upon encountering Dr. David Livingstone in Africa in 1871: "Dr. Livingstone, I presume?"

Sunnyside Café Casual-dining restaurant at Toy Story Hotel at Shanghai Disney Resort; opened Jun. 16, 2016, serving dim sum, noodles, and hot meals. Inspired by the preschool in *Toy Story 3*.

Sunnyside Market Quick-service counter at Toy Story Hotel at Shanghai Disney Resort; opened Jun. 16, 2016, serving salads, sandwiches, and desserts.

Sunrise Terrace Restaurant Quick-service restaurant in Communicore West at EPCOT Center; opened Oct. 23, 1982. It became Pasta Piazza Ristorante in May 1994.

Sunset Boulevard Area in Disney's Hollywood Studios; opened summer 1994 as the park's first major expansion. Like the nearby Hollywood Boulevard, the street honors the golden age of Hollywood, but is set slightly later, in the 1930s–1940s, and presents a glamorous theater district. The area contains boutiques and dining facilities, some with a war-era home front theme, and leads to The Twilight Zone Tower of Terror and Rock 'n' Roller Coaster Starring Aerosmith. There are also venues for live entertainment: the Theater of the Stars (*Beauty and the Beast—Live on Stage*), the Hollywood Hills Amphitheater (*Fantasmic!*), and Sunset Showcase (Lightning McQueen's Racing Academy).

Sunset Club Couture Shop on Sunset Boulevard in Disney's Hollywood Studios; opened Oct. 23, 1995.

Sunset Ranch Market Dining area on Sunset Boulevard in Disney's Hollywood Studios; opened Jun. 1994. Food stands have included Anaheim Produce, Catalina Eddie's, Rosie's Red Hot Dogs (later Rosie's All-American Café), Toluca Legs Turkey Co. (became Sunshine Day Café in 2016, then Sunshine Day Bar in 2018), Fairfax Fries (later Fairfax Fare), and Hollywood Scoops. Inspired by the Los Angeles Farmers Market.

Sunset Showcase Venue hosting various types of

entertainment on Sunset Boulevard in Disney's Hollywood Studios; opened Dec. 4, 2015. It debuted with Club Disney, an electric club environment with a dance floor and DJ host. Lightning McQueen's Racing Academy debuted Mar. 31, 2019, with the *Cars* star demonstrating his skills using a racing simulator.

Sunset Showcase Theater Hollywood Land venue in Disney California Adventure; took the place of the Crown Jewel Theater May 6, 2016. Over the years, previews of feature films, the Pixar Shorts Film Festival, and *Mickey's PhilharMagic* have been presented.

Sunset Sundries Convenience shop in the Disney Ambassador Hotel at Tokyo Disney Resort; opened Jul. 7, 2000.

Sunshine Pavilion Adventureland pavilion in the Magic Kingdom at Walt Disney World; opened Oct. 1, 1971, originally sponsored by the Florida Citrus Growers. It debuted with the Tropical Serenade (also known as The Enchanted Tiki Birds, the Florida equivalent of the Enchanted Tiki Room in Disneyland) and Sunshine Tree Terrace (a refreshment counter featuring the Orange Bird). Tropical Serenade closed Sep. 1, 1997, for extensive renovations, reopening spring 1998 as The Enchanted Tiki Room—Under New Management. In 2011, a shortened version of the original show opened as Walt Disney's Enchanted Tiki Room. Sunshine Tree Terrace switched locations with Aloha Isle Refreshments in Mar. 2015.

Sunshine Plaza Central plaza in Disney's California Adventure; opened Feb. 11, 2001, anchored by a 50-ft.-tall sun icon and wave fountain. Replaced by Buena Vista Street in 2012.

Sunshine Season Food Fair Counter-service food court in The Land at EPCOT; open Nov. 9, 1993–Jan. 2, 2005, and formerly called the Farmers Market. Guests selected their meal in a farmers' market atmosphere and dined in the pavilion atrium, where décor was themed around the sun and moon. It reopened Apr. 2005 as Sunshine Seasons, with the dining area now themed around the four seasons.

Sunshine Tree Terrace Adventureland refreshment counter in the Magic Kingdom at Walt Disney World; opened Oct. 1, 1971. Originally presented by the Florida Citrus Growers, it initially served citrus items, including juices, jellied citrus salad, and soft freezes, and later offered soft-serve ice cream. A guest favorite is the Citrus Swirl, a blend of frozen orange juice and vanilla soft serve. A figure of the Orange Bird mascot, which had been removed in the 1980s, was brought back Apr. 17, 2012. The location switched places with Aloha Isle Refreshments Mar. 12, 2015.

Super Buddies (film) Direct-to-video/Blu-ray release Aug. 27, 2013. An ordinary day at Fernfield Farms turns extraordinary when Budderball, Mudbud, B-Dawg, Buddha, and Rosebud discover mysterious rings that grant them each a unique superpower. The pups unleash their amazing abilities and race to the rescue when a shape-shifting bully from outer space threatens the planet. Directed by Robert Vince. Stars John Ratzenberger (Marvin Livingstone), Michael Teigen (Sheriff Dan), Jason Earles (Jack Schaeffer). Voices include Cooper Roth (B-Dawg), Tenzing Trainor (Buddha), Jeremy Shinder (Budderball), Ty Panitz (Mudbud), G. Hannelius (Rosebud), Tim Conway (Deputy Sniffer).

Super Diner Grab-and-go restaurant in Avengers Campus at Walt Disney Studios Park at Disneyland Paris; opened Jul. 20, 2022, taking the place of Café des Cascadeurs. Reuben sandwiches are served.

Super DuckTales (TV) Two-hour animated show; aired Mar. 26, 1989. Directed by James T. Walker. Scrooge McDuck's new accountant, Fenton Crackshell, becomes a superhero by means of a robotic suit. He fights the Beagle Boys' attempt to steal Scrooge's fortune by building a highway through the site of the money vault. The battle continues at the bottom of the sea and in outer space.

Super Goof He made his debut in *Donald Duck* comic No. 102 in Jul. 1965 and had his own comic series from Nov. of that year until 1972.

Super Hero Headquarters Apparel and toy shop in the Disney Springs West Side at Walt Disney World; opened Apr. 30, 2015, taking the place of United World Soccer. At Disneyland, Super Hero HQ debuted Nov. 16, 2015, in the Tomorrowland Expo Center (formerly Innoventions), offering Marvel hero exhibits, character greetings, and shopping; it closed Apr. 2, 2016.

Super Mario Bros. (film) Brother plumbers Mario

and Luigi enter a subterranean kingdom, a world of men evolved from dinosaurs, where they attempt to rescue a pretty college student with an interesting heritage from King Koopa, the sinister ruler of the underground. Released May 28, 1993. Directed by Rocky Morton and Annabel Jankel. A Hollywood Pictures film. 104 min. Stars Bob Hoskins (Mario Mario), John Leguizamo (Luigi Mario), Dennis Hopper (King Koopa), Samantha Mathis (Daisy), Fisher Stevens (Iggy), Fiona Shaw (Lena), Richard Edson (Spike). Based on the characters from the Nintendo video game. Filming took place in Wilmington, North Carolina.

Super Rhino (film) Special short on the DVD of *Bolt* released Mar. 22, 2009. Super Rhino (the hamster) is called upon to save Penny and Bolt from the nefarious Dr. Calico. Directed by Nathan Greno. Voices include Miley Cyrus (Penny), Mark Walton (Rhino), Malcolm McDowell (Dr. Calico). 4 min.

Super Robot Monkey Team Hyperforce Go! (TV) Science fiction anime adventure series; debuted on ABC Family Sep. 18, 2004, in the Jetix programming block, and on Toon Disney 2 days later. A young teen named Chiro teams up with 5 high-tech cyborg monkeys and becomes the brave fighter, bold leader, and great hero he always wanted to be. Voices include Greg Cipes (Chiro), Kevin Michael Richardson (Antauri), Kari Wahlgren (Nova), Corey Feldman (SPRX-77), Tom Kenny (Gibson), Clancy Brown (Otto), Mark Hamill (Skeleton King). The first original Jetix property from Walt Disney Television Animation. 26 episodes.

Supercalifragilisticexpialidocious Song from *Mary Poppins*; written by Richard M. and Robert B. Sherman.

Superdad (film) Successful lawyer Charlie McCready has big plans for his teenage daughter, Wendy: the right college, the right people, and Mr. Right for her perfect future. These plans do not include her current boyfriend, Bart. But the "generation gap" is happily closed when Charlie realizes his daughter will be happiest going to college with Bart and marrying him rather than going away to fashionable Huntington College with a stuffy law student or becoming engaged to the radical artist Klutch. Released in Los Angeles Dec. 14, 1973; general release Jan. 18, 1974. Directed by Vincent McEveety. 95 min. Stars Bob Crane (Charlie), Barbara Rush (Sue), Kurt Russell (Bart), Kathleen Cody (Wendy), Joe Flynn (Hershberger), B. Kirby,

Jr. (Stanley Schlimmer), Joby Baker (Klutch), Dick Van Patten (Ira Kershaw), Nicholas Hammond (Roger Rhinehurst). Filmed in California, including in the hills of San Francisco, along its famed Fisherman's Wharf, across the bay among the houseboats of Waldo Point Harbor in picturesque Sausalito, and at the Wedge at Newport Beach and the area's Back Bay. The church used for the wedding scene was the First Christian Church in Pasadena. The songs, written by Shane Tatum, are "These Are the Best Times," sung by Bobby Goldsboro, "Los Angeles," and "When I'm Near You." The former has become a perennially popular song for weddings, since it was used in the film's wedding scene.

SuperKitties (TV) Animated series; debuted on Disney Channel and Disney Junior Jan. 11, 2023. Four fierce and furry superhero kittens—Ginny, Sparks, Buddy, and Bitsy—are on a mission to make Kittydale a more caring and "pawesome" place by defeating villains and imparting important messages of kindness, empathy, friendship, resilience, and problem-solving. Voices include Emma Berman (Ginny), Cruz Flateau (Sparks), JeCobi Swain (Buddy), Pyper Braun (Bitsy). From Silvergate Media, in association with Disney Junior.

Superstar Goofy (TV) Show aired Jul. 25, 1976. Features Goofy sports cartoons, and is a tie-in to the 1976 Olympics.

Superstar Limo Dark-ride attraction in Hollywood Pictures Backlot at Disney California Adventure; open Feb. 8, 2001–Jan. 11, 2002. Guests took a wild ride in purple limousines through Tinseltown amid a sea of colorful signs, caricatures of real celebrities, and cartoonish Hollywood landmarks. It was one of the shortest-lived attractions in the park, and was replaced in 2005 by Monsters, Inc. Mike & Sulley to the Rescue!

Superstar Studio Pleasure Island shop at Walt Disney World; open May 1, 1989–Mar. 3, 2006. Guests could create their own music video or audio recording.

SuperStar Television Attraction in Disney-MGM Studios at Walt Disney World; opened May 1, 1989, presented by Sony. Audience members co-starred in memorable scenes from such TV shows as *I Love Lucy*, *Cheers*, *The Tonight Show*, *Gilligan's Island*, and *The Golden Girls*. Closed Sep. 26, 1998, to become *Disney's Doug Live*.

Supply (film) Educational film released Sep. 1977. From The People on Market Street series; produced by Terry Kahn. The factors that influence supply are surveyed, as well as production costs and rate of production, using an ant farm as an example.

Surf Shop Swimwear and beach accessory shop in Festival Disney at Disneyland Paris; open Apr. 12, 1992–1993. Replaced by Mattel's World of Toys.

Surfside Lounge Beach-style eatery in Disney's Paradise Pier Hotel at Disneyland Resort.

Surprise Celebration Parade Ran in the Magic Kingdom at Walt Disney World Sep. 22, 1991–Jun. 4, 1994, succeeded by the *Mickey Mania Parade*. Similar to the *Party Gras* parade at Disneyland and Tokyo Disneyland, with enormous balloons of Disney characters. It was tied to the park's 20th anniversary celebration.

Surprise Day Wednesday on the new *Mickey Mouse Club* (1977–1978).

Surreys Main Street, U.S.A. vehicles at Disneyland in the early years. Eventually motorized vehicles took over everything except the horse-drawn streetcars.

Surrogates (film) Two FBI agents investigate the mysterious murder of a college student linked to the man who helped create a high-tech surrogate phenomenon that allows people to purchase unflawed robotic versions of themselves—fit, good-looking, remote-controlled machines that ultimately assume their life roles—enabling people to experience life vicariously from the comfort and safety of their own homes. After the first murder in this utopia in years, FBI agent Greer discovers a vast conspiracy behind the surrogate phenomenon and must abandon his own surrogate, risking his life to unravel the mystery. A Touchstone film. Directed by Jonathan Mostow. Released Sep. 25, 2009, in the U.S., after a Sep. 24 international release. Stars Bruce Willis (Greer), Radha Mitchell (Peters), Rosamund Pike (Maggie), James Francis Ginty (Canter), Boris Kodjoe (Stone), James Cromwell (Older Canter), Ving Rhames (The Prophet). 89 min. Based on the graphic novel by Robert Venditti and Brett Weldele. From Mandeville Films. Filmed in Super 35 on location in Massachusetts, primarily in Boston and surrounding suburbs.

Survival in Nature (TV) Show aired Feb. 8, 1956.

Directed by Winston Hibler. Teaches about survival of the fittest in nature.

Survival of Sam the Pelican, The (TV) Show aired Feb. 29, 1976. Directed by Roy Edward Disney. A listless teenager in Florida, Rick, gets a job helping conduct a survey of the pelican population; he finds an injured bird and nurses it back to health. Stars Kim Friese, Scott Lee, Bill DeHollander.

Susie Determined mother bird in *Wet Paint* (1946).

Susie, the Little Blue Coupe (film) Special cartoon released Jun. 6, 1952. Directed by Clyde Geronimi. Susie, a vehicle in an auto showroom, is bought by a man who takes good care of her; but as time passes, she of course grows older, and her owner trades her in. She has a succession of neglectful owners who mistreat her, and just as she is about to be abandoned in a junkyard, an eager young man buys her, tinkers with her, and soon has her running again.

Suspended Animation Pleasure Island shop at Walt Disney World; open May 1, 1989–Apr. 2004. Disney animation cels, posters, and lithographs were sold.

Süssigkeiten Shop selling cookies, chocolates, and candies in Germany at EPCOT Center; opened Oct. 1, 1982, presented by Bahlsen of America, Inc. It later became Stein Haus, offering gifts and housewares.

Sutherland, Donald Actor; appeared in *The Puppet Masters* (Andrew Nivens), *Shadow Conspiracy* (Conrad), and *Instinct* (Ben Hillard), and on TV in *Commander-in-Chief* (Nathan Templeton) and *Dirty Sexy Money* (Patrick "Tripp" Darling III).

Sutherland, Kiefer Actor; appeared in *The Three Musketeers* (Athos) and *Woman Wanted* (Wendall Goddard), and on TV in *Designated Survivor* (Tom Kirkman). He voiced Samson in *The Wild*.

Sutherland, Mark Mouseketeer from the 1950s *Mickey Mouse Club* TV show.

Sven Kristoff's reindeer friend and conscience in *Frozen*.

Swamp Fox, The (Episode 1): Birth of the Swamp Fox (TV) Show aired Oct. 23, 1959. Directed by Harry Keller. The first episode tells the story of the patriot, Francis Marion, who fought the British using unusual methods during the Revolutionary War. Marion learns that the British are about to attack Charleston, South Carolina, and he helps by leading the governor and his party safely out of the city. Eluding Tarleton, his British adversary, in the swamps, Marion becomes known as the Swamp Fox, as he works with a band of loyal colonists to free a group of captured patriots. Stars Leslie Nielsen, Joy Page, Tim Considine, John Sutton, Dick Foran, Patrick Macnee, Louise Beavers.

Swamp Fox, The (Episode 2): Brother Against Brother (TV) Show aired Oct. 30, 1959. Directed by Harry Keller. The pro-British Tories stage raids against their patriot neighbors but leave standing the Videaux mansion. Marion is enamored with Mary Videaux, even though her parents are Tory sympathizers, and he stops the patriots from taking revenge and burning her place when she agrees to provide valuable information. On hearing that Tarleton is about to transfer a group of American prisoners, Marion plots to free them. Stars Leslie Nielsen, Joy Page, John Sutton, Dick Foran, Richard Erdman, Tim Considine.

Swamp Fox, The (Episode 3): Tory Vengeance (TV) Show aired Jan. 1, 1960. Directed by Louis King. Marion gathers information from informers, but the British begin to suspect his friend, Mary Videaux. Marion's nephew, Gabe, joins the army, but he is captured, tortured, and eventually killed. Marion vows vengeance. Stars Leslie Nielsen, John Sutton, Henry Daniell, Barbara Eiler, Dick Foran, Tim Considine, Myron Healey.

Swamp Fox, The (Episode 4): Day of Reckoning (TV) Show aired Jan. 8, 1960. Directed by Louis King. Marion vows revenge on the man, Amos Briggs, who killed his nephew, Gabe, and in searching for him, helps the patriots acquire some needed quinine from the British. Later, a boy, Gwynn, attacks Marion, believing he was responsible for killing his family, when it was really Briggs. Gwynn kills Briggs and later saves Marion's life. Stars Leslie Nielsen, John Sutton, Barbara Eiler, Henry Daniell, Rhys Williams, Slim Pickens, Hal Stalmaster. Stalmaster, who plays Gwynn, had starred as Johnny Tremain for Disney.

Swamp Fox, The (Episode 5): Redcoat Strategy (TV) Show aired Jan. 15, 1960. Directed by Louis King. Marion captures a British colonel, and later battles Colonel Tarleton, who has orders to capture the Swamp Fox or else. Tarleton invades the Marion home, but the servants manage to outwit him. Stars Leslie Nielsen, Robert Douglas, John Sutton, Barbara Eiler, Myron Healey, Henry Daniell, Jordan Whitfield, Louise Beavers, Eleanor Audley.

Swamp Fox, The (Episode 6): A Case of Treason (TV) Show aired Jan. 22, 1960. Directed by Louis King. Tarleton discovers Mary Videaux's spying and arrests her, hoping that Marion will try to rescue her. Using various ruses, Marion enters Charleston and shows up at a masked ball where Mary is in attendance, only to be captured himself. His men free him and Mary, and she sails for New Orleans and safety. Stars Leslie Nielsen, Robert Douglas, Barbara Eiler, John Sutton, Myron Healey, J. Pat O'Malley, Hal Stalmaster, Slim Pickens.

Swamp Fox, The (Episode 7): A Woman's Courage (TV) Show aired Jan. 8, 1961. Directed by Lewis R. Foster. Marion and his men outwit the British forces who follow them out of Charleston. Mary Videaux, hiding on a ship in Charleston harbor, discovers a ship full of prisoners and tries to help them, at great peril to herself. Stars Leslie Nielsen, Barbara Eiler, Arthur Hunnicutt, Sean McClory, J. Pat O'Malley, Jordan Whitfield.

Swamp Fox, The (Episode 8): Horses for Greene (TV) Show aired Jan. 15, 1961. Directed by Lewis R. Foster. In the final episode, Marion plots to steal horses from the British, eventually getting them to stampede through the streets of Charleston. Stars Leslie Nielsen, Barbara Eiler, Arthur Hunnicutt, Ralph Clanton, J. Pat O'Malley, Jordan Whitfield, Slim Pickens.

Swampy Disney's first original character for mobile, created for Disney Mobile's puzzle game, *Where's My Water*, in Sep. 2011. Swampy, a mischievous alligator, searches to find clean water for his bathtub in the popular app.

Swan Hotel SEE WALT DISNEY WORLD SWAN.

Swap, The (TV) A Disney Channel Original Movie; first aired Oct. 7, 2016. Ellie O'Brien is trying to juggle rhythmic gymnastics practice and troubles with her best friend. Meanwhile, classmate Jack Malloy is struggling to live up to his brothers' hockey-star legacies and his dad's high expectations. When a text argument about whose life is easier gets out of hand, Ellie and Jack trigger an unexplainable real-life swap. As each tries to navigate the other's life, Ellie (as Jack) tries to learn about brotherly bonding and hockey lingo, while Jack (as Ellie) has to decipher girl-code and experience a spa day. With a rhythmic gymnastics championship and a spot on the varsity hockey team on the line, they must figure out how to get back in their own bodies before the swap becomes permanent. Directed by Jay Karas. Stars Peyton List (Ellie), Jacob Bertrand (Jack), Claire Rankin (Ellie's mom), Darrin Rose (Jack's dad). Based on the book by Megan Shull. Produced by MarVista Entertainment for Disney Channel.

Swayze, Patrick (1952–2009) Actor; appeared in *Father Hood* (Jack Charles) and *Tall Tale* (Pecos Bill), and voiced Cash in *The Fox and the Hound 2*.

Sweatbox, The (film) Documentary about production problems during the making of "Kingdom of the Sun," the film ultimately released as *The Emperor's New Groove*. Directed by John-Paul Davidson and Trudie Styler. Premiered Sep. 13, 2002, at the Toronto Film Festival. 86 min. Rated PG-13. Styler is the wife of musician/singer Sting, who wrote music for the film. Produced by Xingu Films and distributed by Buena Vista Films.

Sweeney, Anne Hired in 1996 to serve as president of The Disney Channel and exec. vice president of Disney/ABC Cable Networks. She was promoted to president, Disney/ABC Cable Networks in 1998 and president, ABC Cable Networks Group/Disney Channel Worldwide in 2000. In 2004, she became co-chairman of Disney Media Networks and president of Disney•ABC Television Group. She retired in Jan. 2015.

Sweeney, Bob (1918–1992) Actor; appeared in *Toby Tyler* (Harry Tupper), *Moon Pilot* (Senator McGuire), and *Son of Flubber* (Mr. Harker).

Sweeney, D. B. Actor; provided the voice of Aladar in *Dinosaur* and Sitka in *Brother Bear*. He appeared in *Roommates* (Michael) and *Miracle at St. Anna* (Col. Driscoll); on Disney Channel in *Going to the Mat* (Coach Rice); and on ABC in *life as we know it* (Michael Whitman) and *Once and Again* (Graham Rympalski), with guest appearances in *Criminal Minds* and *Betrayal*.

Sweet Home Alabama (film) New York City fashion designer Melanie Carmichael suddenly finds herself engaged to the city's most eligible bachelor. But Melanie's past holds many secrets, including Jake, the redneck husband she married in high school, who refuses to divorce her. Bound and determined to end their contentious relationship once and for all, Melanie sneaks back home to Alabama to confront her past. A Touchstone film. Released Sep. 27, 2002. Directed by Andy Tennant. Stars Reese Witherspoon (Melanie Carmichael), Fred Ward (Earl), Mary Kay Place (Pearl), Patrick Dempsey (Andrew), Josh Lucas (Jake), Jean Smart (Stella Kay), Candice Bergen (Kate), Ethan Embry (Bobby Ray). 109 min. Ethan Embry, as Ethan Randall, starred with Reese Witherspoon years earlier in *A Far Off Place*. The film crew was one of the few ever allowed to film in Tiffany & Co. in New York City. Filmed in CinemaScope.

Sweet Spells Candy shop in the Beverly Sunset Theater on Sunset Boulevard at Disney's Hollywood Studios; open Sep. 14, 1998–Apr. 15, 2018, and succeeded by the Beverly Hills Boutique.

Sweet Success Hollywood Boulevard candy shop in Disney-MGM Studios; open May 1, 1989–Sep. 1998, and succeeded by Adrian and Edith's Head to Toe.

Sweet Surrender Song from *The Bears and I*; composed and performed by John Denver. Also a former ice cream and dessert shop in Pleasure Island at Walt Disney World.

Sweetheart Café World Bazaar bakery in Tokyo Disneyland; opened in 1993, taking the place of the original Ice Cream Parlor.

Sweethearts Confectionery Mickey Avenue shop in Shanghai Disneyland; opened Jun. 16, 2016. Guests enter the childhood home of Minnie Mouse, where sweets are prepared fresh.

Swenson, Karl (1908–1978) Actor; provided the voice of Merlin in *The Sword in the Stone* and appeared in *The Wild Country* (Jensen).

Swift, David (1919–2001) He initially worked for the Disney Studio in the 1930s, first as an office boy and then as an animator and assistant to Ward Kimball, but left in the 1940s, establishing himself in TV directing the successful series *Mr. Peepers*. He returned as a director and screenwriter of *Pollyanna* and *The Parent Trap*.

Swift, Taylor Singer/songwriter; appeared in *Jonas Brothers: The 3-D Concert Experience* and *Hannah Montana the Movie*, for which she contributed songs. For Disney+, she directed and starred in *folklore: the long pond studio sessions*. Also appeared on Disney Channel in *Take Two with Phineas and Ferb* and the *Radio Disney Music Awards*.

Swing Kids (film) In 1939, German youths Peter and Thomas enjoy American swing music, despite its illegality under Hitler's regime. Hitler's harsh discipline, which crushes individuality, is sweeping Germany as the country prepares for full-scale war. Yet the 2 friends fight to remain loyal to their music. But soon Thomas is drawn into the Hitler Youth, absorbing Nazi principles and growing antagonistic toward his still independent friend Peter. A Nazi official takes an interest in Peter's family and talks Peter into joining the Hitler Youth also. For a brief time, Peter and Thomas believe they can have it all—Hitler Youth by day and Swing Kids by night. When a mutual friend, Arvid, who has remained a rebel, commits suicide after being badly beaten by Nazis, Peter realizes he cannot live contrary to his conscience. He rebels and is arrested. Released Mar. 5, 1993. Directed by Thomas Carter. A Hollywood Pictures film. 114 min. Stars Christian Bale (Thomas), Robert Sean Leonard (Peter), Frank Whaley (Arvid), Barbara Hershey (Frau Muller). Musical score by James Horner. Kenneth Branagh played an uncredited role as the Nazi official. Since Germany's look has changed drastically over the years, the filmmakers turned instead to the Czech Republic, and filmed in a studio and on location in its capital, Prague.

Swing Vote (film) Bud Johnson, an apathetic, beer-slinging, lovable loser in the small town of Texico, New Mexico, is coasting through a life that has passed him by. The one bright spot is his precocious, overachieving 12-year-old daughter, Molly. She takes care of both of them, until one mischievous moment on Election Day, when she accidentally sets off a chain of events that culminates in the presidential election coming down to a single vote—her dad's. Bud becomes the most famous man in the world for 10 days as both sides campaign to get his vote. A Touchstone film. Released Aug. 1, 2008. Directed by Joshua Michael Stern. Stars Kevin Costner (Bud Johnson), Paula Patton (Kate Madison), Kelsey Grammer (President Andrew Boone), Dennis Hopper (Donald Greenleaf), Nathan Lane (Art Crumb), Stanley Tucci (Martin Fox), George Lopez (John Sweeney), Judge Reinhold (Walter), Willie Nelson (as himself), Mare Winningham (Larissa Johnson), Richard Petty (as himself), Madeline Carroll (Molly Johnson). 120 min. Filmed in CinemaScope in Albuquerque, Belen, and Santa Fe, New Mexico.

Swiss Family Robinson (film) The members of a Swiss family are the sole survivors of a shipwreck on an uncharted tropical island. With great courage and ingenuity, they use the salvage from the wreck to build a home in a huge tree, raise food, and protect themselves from a raiding band of pirates. The rescue of the granddaughter of a sea captain from pirates precipitates the ultimate attack by the buccaneers. The furious battle is almost won by the brigands when her grandfather's ship arrives and routs the attackers. The romance between the eldest Robinson boy and the granddaughter culminates in their marriage. The new couple and much of the family decide to stay on the island paradise, but scholarly brother Ernst decides to go back on the ship to civilization. Released Dec. 21, 1960. Directed by Ken Annakin. 126 min. Stars John Mills (Father), Dorothy McGuire (Mother), James MacArthur (Fritz), Tommy Kirk (Ernst), Kevin Corcoran (Francis), Janet Munro (Roberta), Sessue Hayakawa (Pirate chief). The film was based on the book by Johann Wyss, written to preserve the tales he and his sons made up while imagining themselves in Robinson Crusoe's predicament. Not originally intended for publication, the narrative was later edited and illustrated by Wyss's descendants. Filmed on the Caribbean island of Tobago, the motion picture's lavish pre-production planning and on-location shooting (22 weeks) resulted in a budget that exceeded $4 million. But the extraordinary box office returns; subsequent popular reissues in 1969, 1972, 1975, 1981; and an initial release on home video in 1982 has made it one of Disney's top-grossing films. The creation of an intriguing tree house, matching the one in the movie, through which guests can climb in the Disney parks, has perpetuated the popularity of the film.

Swiss Family Treehouse Adventureland attraction in Disneyland; opened Nov. 18, 1962. John Mills, daughter Hayley, and the rest of the family were there for the dedication with Walt Disney. Mills had starred in the 1960 Disney film *Swiss Family Robinson*. The tree has been called a *Disneyodendron semperflorens grandis* (translated as large ever-blooming Disney tree) and is entirely man-made. The roots are concrete and the limbs are steel, covered in concrete. The 300,000 plastic leaves all had to be attached by hand. The Swiss flag flies from the top of the tree house. This is one of the few Disneyland attractions where guests have to walk (or more appropriately, climb) through to view the rooms that the Robinson family built in the tree. A fascinating pulley system, using bamboo buckets and a waterwheel, provides water high up in the tree. It closed Mar. 8, 1999, to become Tarzan's Treehouse. Also an Adventureland attraction in the Magic Kingdom at Walt Disney World; opened as Swiss Family Island Treehouse Oct. 1, 1971. In Florida, the tree is known as a *Disneyodendron eximus* (or out-of-the-ordinary Disney tree). A Tokyo Disneyland version opened Jul. 21, 1993, and a Disneyland Paris version opened Apr. 12, 1992, as Le Cabane des Robinson. SEE ALSO ADVENTURE-LAND TREEHOUSE (DISNEYLAND).

Swit, Loretta Actress; appeared on TV in *14 Going on 30*.

Switch, The (film) Neurotic Wally Mars is a financial success in New York City with his stock trading partner Leonard. But he still has a gloomy perspective on the world. The one bright spot is his girlfriend, Kassie, who, unfortunately for Wally, just wants to be friends. Even when she decides she wants a child, she searches elsewhere for Mr. Perfect Sperm Donor. Seven years later, Kassie has a precocious son, Sebastian, who hits it off with Wally. They are so much alike that Wally becomes convinced that Sebastian is his son and wonders if he might have hijacked Kassie's pregnancy. A Miramax film released on Aug. 20, 2010. Directed by Josh Gordon and Will Speck. Stars Jason Bateman (Wally Mars), Victor Pagan (Knit Hat Guy), Jennifer Aniston (Kassie Larson), Jeff Goldblum (Leonard), Juliette Lewis (Debbie), Patrick Wilson (Roland), Thomas Robinson (Sebastian). 101 min. Filmed in CinemaScope in New York City.

Switched at Birth (TV) One-hour drama series on Freeform (formerly ABC Family); aired Jun. 6, 2011–Apr. 11, 2017. Two teenage girls discover that they were accidentally switched as newborns in the hospital. Bay Kennish grew up in a wealthy family with 2 parents and a brother, while Daphne Vasquez, who lost her hearing at an early age due to meningitis, grew up with a single mother in a working-class neighborhood. Both families eventually meet and struggle to learn how to live together for the sake of the girls. Stars Katie Leclerc (Daphne Vasquez), Vanessa Marano (Bay Kennish), Constance Marie (Regina Vasquez), D. W. Moffett (John Kennish), Lea Thompson (Kathryn Kennish), Lucas Grabeel (Toby Kennish), Sean Berdy (Emmett), Austin Butler (Wilke). From ABC Studios.

Switching Goals (TV) A 2-hour movie on *The Wonderful World of Disney*; first aired May 26, 2002. Twin sisters switch places on the soccer field to help their father's youth soccer team win the championship. Directed by David Steinberg. Stars Mary-Kate Olsen (Sam), Ashley Olsen (Emma), Eric Lutes (Jerry Stanton), Kathryn Greenwood (Denise), Trevor Blumas (Greg Jeffries). From Dualstar Productions and Warner Bros.

Switzerland (film) People and Places featurette released Jun. 16, 1955. Directed by Ben Sharpsteen. Filmed in CinemaScope. 33 min. The film visits the cities and small towns of Switzerland to explore the local customs and activities during the seasons. The climax is a climb to the top of the Matterhorn with 3 mountaineers. Along with *Third Man on the Mountain*, it was this film that helped inspire Walt to build a Matterhorn at Disneyland.

Sword and the Rose, The (film) An adventure tale set in England during the reign of King Henry VIII. Charles Brandon, a handsome young commoner, becomes attached to the court and falls in love with the king's sister and political pawn, Mary Tudor. When Henry discovers this, Brandon is banished and Mary is sent off to marry the aging Louis of France, but when the French king dies, Mary extracts a promise from Henry to let her choose her second husband and she happily marries Brandon. Released Jul. 23, 1953. Directed by Ken Annakin. 92 min. Despite its historical inaccuracy, the film was a success due to the acting talents of Richard Todd (Charles Brandon), Glynis Johns (Princess Mary Tudor), James Robertson Justice (King Henry VIII), Michael Gough (Duke of Buckingham), Jean Mercure (King Louis XII), and the wizardry of Peter Ellenshaw's more than 60 matte paintings that helped give the film the feel of Tudor England. It was the 3rd and most elaborate of the Disney live-action features made in England to use up blocked funds that Disney could not take out of the country. It aired on TV in 1956 as *When Knighthood Was in Flower*, the title of the book on which the film was based.

Sword in the Stone, The (film) An animated feature, set in the medieval era at a time when the English king dies leaving no heir. In the churchyard of a cathedral in London, a sword appears embedded in a stone, inscribed: WHOSO PULLETH OUT THIS SWORD OF THIS STONE AND ANVIL IS RIGHTWISE KING BORN OF ENGLAND. Although many try, no one can budge the sword from the stone. Deep in the dark woods, kindly, but absent-minded Merlin the wizard begins to teach 11-year-old Arthur (who is called "Wart"), who lives in the castle of Sir Ector where he is an apprentice squire to burly, oafish Sir Kay, whenever he is not washing mounds of pots and pans in the scullery. By being changed by Merlin into various animals, Wart learns the basic truths of life, but he also runs into the evil Madam Mim, who tries to destroy him. Merlin and Mim have a Wizard's Duel during which each changes into various creatures, with Merlin using his wits to win. On New Year's Day, a great tournament is held in London to pick a new king. Wart, attending as Kay's squire, forgets Kay's sword, and runs back to the inn to get it, but the inn is locked. Seeing the sword in the stone, Wart, innocently, and easily, pulls it out. When the knights marvel at the wondrous sword, and question where he got it, Wart has to prove himself all over again, and again he pulls the sword from the stone. Wart is proclaimed king by the marveling warriors. Wart as King Arthur is apprehensive of his ability to govern, but Merlin returns to reassure him. Released Dec. 25, 1963. Directed by Wolfgang Reitherman. Based on the book by T. H. White. 79 min. Features the voices of Ricky Sorensen (Wart), Sebastian Cabot (Narrator), Karl Swenson (Merlin), Junius Matthews (Archimedes), Norman Alden (Sir Kay), Martha Wentworth (Madam Mim, Granny Squirrel, Scullery Maid). The film marked Wolfgang Reitherman's first solo directorial effort for a feature film. The songs, including "A Most Befuddling Thing," "That's What Makes the World Go Round," "Higitus Figitus," and "The Legend of the Sword in the Stone," were written by Richard M. and Robert B. Sherman. The motion picture was rereleased theatrically in 1972 and in 1983 and inspired *The Sword in the Stone Ceremony* at the Disney theme parks. Initial release on video in 1986.

Sword in the Stone Ceremony, The In Fantasyland, Merlin challenges young guests to pull the sword from the stone in regular presentations. Began in Disneyland as part of the New Fantasyland in 1983, in the Magic Kingdom at Walt Disney World in 1994, in Disneyland Paris in 1992, and in Hong Kong Disneyland in 2005. The ceremony ended at Walt Disney World in 2006, but lucky guests can sometimes pull the sword from the stone as a "magical moment."

Sydney to the Max (TV) Comedy series on Disney Channel; debuted Jan. 25, 2019. Good-hearted middle schooler Sydney Reynolds and her protective, doting, and sometimes clueless single dad, Max, navigate the challenges of growing up. Set during 2 time frames, decades apart, flashback scenes to young Max and his best friend, Leo, in the 1990s parallel many of the funny predicaments Sydney and her BFF, Olive, find themselves in. Aided by Sydney's kicky grandmother Judy, Sydney and Max come to realize they have more in common than either one realizes. Created by Mark Reisman. Stars Ruth Righi (Sydney), Ian Reed Kesler (adult Max), Jackson Dollinger (young Max), Caroline Rhea (Judy), Ava Kolker (Olive), Christian J. Simon (Leo). From It's A Laugh Productions, Inc.

Sykes Loan shark villain in *Oliver & Company*; voiced by Robert Loggia.

Symbiosis (film) Film about the delicate balance between technological progress and environmental integrity; played in the Harvest Theater in The Land at EPCOT Center, Oct. 1, 1982–Jan. 1, 1995. 17 min. Replaced by *Circle of Life: An Environmental Fable*.

Symphony Hour (film) Mickey Mouse cartoon released Mar. 20, 1942. Directed by Riley Thomson. Mickey's radio orchestra is to present an interpretation of the "Light Cavalry Overture" when Goofy smashes the instruments in an elevator. Sponsor Pete's fury subsides when the rendition is a success due to Mickey's improvisation.

Symphony in the Stars: A Galactic Spectacular SEE STAR WARS: A GALACTIC SPECTACULAR (DISNEY'S HOLLYWOOD STUDIOS).

Symposium on Popular Songs, A (film) Special cartoon featurette released Dec. 19, 1962. Directed by Bill Justice. Nominated for an Academy Award for Cartoon Short Subject. Ludwig Von Drake invites the audience into his home, where he tells all about popular music, introducing several songs illustrated with stop-motion photography. 20 min. The songs, written by Richard M. and Robert B. Sherman, were released on the 1965 Buena Vista Records album *Tinpanorama*.

Syndrome Villain in search of superhero fame in *The Incredibles*; voiced by Jason Lee.

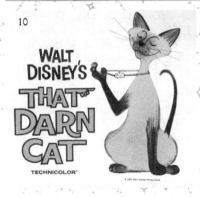

1. Tokyo DisneySea 2. *20,000 Leagues Under the Sea* (film) 3. TRON Lightcycle Power Run
4. True-Life Adventures 5. *Two Chips and a Miss* (film) 6. Ticket books 7. *Three Little Pigs* (film)
8. Tinker Bell 9. Topolino 10. *That Darn Cat!* (film) 11. Tree of Life

Tag Team (TV) Unsold pilot for a series; aired on ABC Jan. 26, 1991. A couple of ex-pro wrestlers become Los Angeles city cops. Directed by Paul Krasny. 60 min. Stars Jesse Ventura, Roddy Piper, Phill Lewis.

Tahitian Terrace Adventureland restaurant in Disneyland; opened Jun. 1962, on the back side of the Plaza Pavilion. A Polynesian-themed show with live performers entertained diners, with a waterfall serving as the stage "curtain." During construction, Walt Disney was a little dismayed by the short height of the man-made tree that formed the backdrop for the small stage. When his designers were baffled as to how to rectify the problem, Walt posed the obvious solution: just slice the tree horizontally in the center, lift up the top, and add some more cement trunk. The designers were thinking of it as a real tree and had been wondering how they could raise the entire thing. The restaurant closed Apr. 17, 1993, and was replaced by Aladdin's Oasis and later, in 2018, The Tropical Hideaway. A Tahitian Terrace counter-service restaurant in Hong Kong Disneyland opened Sep. 12, 2005, serving South Asian and Cantonese cuisine.

Takahashi, Masatomo (1913–2000) As president of the Oriental Land Co., he was instrumental in convincing Disney to build Tokyo Disneyland. He was named a Disney Legend at a special ceremony in Japan in 1998.

Take Down (film) A disillusioned teenager's bitterness and defeatism is turned around by the girl who loves him and the hopelessly overmatched high school wrestling team that only he can lead to victory. Not a Disney film, but a Buena Vista release of an American Film Consortium production in 1979. Directed by Kieth Merrill. Stars Edward Herrmann, Kathleen Lloyd, Lorenzo Lamas, Maureen McCormick, Nick Beauvy, Stephen Furst, Kevin Hooks. 107 min.

Take Flight SEE DELTA DREAMFLIGHT.

Take Two (TV) Hour-long comedy/drama series on ABC; aired Jun. 21–Sep. 13, 2018. Sam Swift, the former star of a hit cop series, is fresh out of rehab following a bender of epic proportions. Desperate to restart her career, she talks her way into shadowing rough-and-tumble private investigator Eddie Valetik as research for a potential comeback role. Stars Rachel Bilson (Sam), Eddie Cibrian (Eddie), Aliyah O'Brien (Christine Rollins), Xavier de Guzman (Berto Vasquez), Alice Lee (Monica). From ABC Studios, Tandem Productions, Studio-Canal, and MilMar Pictures.

Taking Care of Business (film) Petty criminal and Chicago Cubs fan Jimmy Dworski has won tickets to the World Series. The only obstacle standing in his way is that the game is scheduled for the day before he gets released on parole from prison. Scheming his way out early, he finds the lost daily planner of ultra-organized business executive Spencer Barnes, complete with credit cards, keys to a mansion, and everything he needs for an all-expenses-paid weekend of luxury. Spencer, meanwhile, is hopelessly lost without his organizer, not even being able to prove his identity while Jimmy passes himself off as Spencer at important business meetings. After crossing paths and missing signals, the 2 men end up at the ball game together, having made discoveries about themselves. Released Aug. 17, 1990. Directed by Arthur Hiller. A Hollywood Pictures film. 108 min. Stars James Belushi (Jimmy), Charles Grodin (Spencer), Anne DeSalvo (Debbie), Mako (Sakamoto), Veronica Hamel (Elizabeth), Hector Elizondo (Warden). Filmed at various locations around the Los Angeles area.

Takumi-Tei Upscale table-service restaurant in Japan at EPCOT; opened Jul. 5, 2019. Specialties include Wagyu beef, sushi, sashimi, and signature cocktails. Handcrafted artwork tells the story of the natural elements.

Tale of the Lion King Stage show in the Fantasyland Theater at Disneyland; debuted May 28, 2022. The Storytellers of the Pride Lands present the story of Simba's journey with live music and dance. Originally an outdoor production in Disney California Adventure; ran Jun. 7–Sep. 2, 2019.

Tale of Two Critters, A (film) Featurette about a bear cub and a young raccoon accidentally thrown together who become friends. Released Jun. 22, 1977, on a bill with *The Rescuers*. 48 min.

Talent Roundup Day Friday on the 1950s *Mickey Mouse Club*. The Mouseketeers wore Western outfits.

Tales from Earthsea (film) Lord Archmage Sparrowhawk, a master wizard, journeys to search for the force behind a mysterious disturbance that has caused an imbalance in the land of Earthsea—for suddenly crops and livestock are dwindling, dragons have reappeared, and humanity is giving way to chaos. Along the way, he rescues Arren, a troubled young prince who fled his home and is being pursued by an enigmatic shadow. Arren and Sparrowhawk cross paths with Tenar, a former priestess, and her disfigured adopted daughter, Therru. With Sparrowhawk's magical powers dissipating, all of them must band together to defeat the evil Cob and his henchman Hare before Cob's mania to find immortality destroys Earthsea. Directed by Goro Miyazaki. Released in the U.S. on Aug. 13, 2010, after an original Jan. 29, 2006, release in Japan. Voices include Matt Levin (Arren), Willem Dafoe (Cob), Timothy Dalton (Ged/Sparrowhawk), Mariska Hargitay (Tenar), Cheech Marin (Hare), Blaire Restaneo (Therru). 115 min. Produced by Studio Ghibli; Japanese title is *Gedo senki*.

Tales from Radiator Springs (TV) SEE CARS TOONS AND RADIATOR SPRINGS 500½, THE.

Tales of Texas John Slaughter, The SEE TEXAS JOHN SLAUGHTER.

Tales of the Apple Dumpling Gang (TV) Show aired Jan. 16, 1982. Directed by E. W. Swackhamer. Remake of the 1975 feature *The Apple Dumpling Gang*, used as a pilot for a series. The resulting limited series had a different cast and was titled *Gun Shy*. Russell Donavan in Quake City becomes the unwilling guardian of 2 children, Clovis and Celia. Stars John Bennett Perry, Sandra Kearns, Ed Begley Jr., Henry Jones, Arte Johnson, Keith Mitchell, Sara Abeles, William Smith.

TaleSpin (TV) Animated series on The Disney Channel; premiered May 5, 1990, and syn. Sep. 10, 1990–Sep. 2, 1994. Ace cargo pilot Baloo is teamed with feisty Kit Cloudkicker; they're pitted against a band of air pirates led by Don Karnage. Louie the ape is a music-loving owner. They find mystery, intrigue, and humor in the colorful setting of Cape Suzette, a huge, bustling city in a tropic zone. Voices include Ed Gilbert (Baloo), Sally Struthers (Rebecca Cunningham), Jim Cummings (Louie, Don Karnage), Pat Fraley (Wildcat), Tony Jay (Shere Khan), R. J. Williams (Kit). The theme song was written by Michael and Patty Silversher. 65 episodes. A syn. TV special serving as a preview to the series was *Disney's TaleSpin: Plunder and Lightning*, airing on Sep. 7, 1990.

Taliaferro, Al (1905–1969) Comic strip artist; joined Disney in 1931 as an assistant to Floyd Gottfredson on the *Mickey Mouse* comic strip, and then worked on the *Silly Symphonies* Sunday comic page. He originated the *Donald Duck* daily strip in Feb. 1938, and the Sunday page in Dec. 1939, and continued with these 2 for 3 decades. He is credited with the idea of giving Donald 3 nephews, who made their debut in the *Donald Duck* Sunday comic page Oct. 17, 1937. He was named a Disney Legend posthumously in 2003.

Talk to Me (TV) Ensemble comedy series on ABC; aired Apr. 11–Apr. 25, 2000, ending after 3 episodes. About the life of Janey Munro, a successful radio talk show host in New York City. Stars Kyra Sedgwick (Janey Munro), Beverly D'Angelo

(Dr. Debra), David Newsom (Rob), Nicole Sullivan (Kat), Peter Jacobson (Sandy), Max Baker (Marshall), Michael J. Estime (Cam). From Touchstone Television.

Tall Tale (film) A strong-willed boy conjures up a trio of legendary Old West characters—John Henry, Paul Bunyan, and Pecos Bill—to help him save the family farm and their entire way of life on the American frontier. With the help of his larger-than-life pals and a steadfast determination, the boy heroically confronts the archetypal bad guy, J. P. Stiles, to achieve the impossible. Released Mar. 24, 1995. Directed by Jeremiah Chechik. In association with Caravan Pictures. Stars Scott Glenn (J. P. Stiles), Oliver Platt (Paul Bunyan), Stephen Lang (Jonas Hackett), Roger Aaron Brown (John Henry), Nick Stahl (Daniel Hackett), Catherine O'Hara (Calamity Jane), Patrick Swayze (Pecos Bill). Filmed in CinemaScope. 96 min. Locations throughout the West included the Roaring Fork Valley of Colorado, Monument Valley in Utah, Lake Powell and Glen Canyon in Arizona, and Death Valley in California. Advertised with the title *Tall Tale: The Unbelievable Adventures of Pecos Bill.*

Tall Timber (film) Oswald the Lucky Rabbit cartoon; released Jul. 9, 1928. Oswald fancies himself a canoeist until he strikes the rapids. When he finally reaches calm water, he takes aim at the geese, but instead shoots a hole in his canoe and is soon chased by everything in sight.

Tally Ho (TV) Show; part 2 of *The Horsemasters.*

Tamatoa Treasure-hoarding, 50-ft. crab in *Moana*; voiced by Jemaine Clement.

Tamblyn, Russ Actor; appeared in *Cabin Boy* (Chocki).

Tamiroff, Akim (1899–1972) Actor; appeared in *Lt. Robin Crusoe, U.S.N.* (Tanamashu).

Tamron Hall (TV) Syn. daytime talk show broadcast from New York City; debuted Sep. 9, 2019. From the personal to the purely fun, Tamron Hall connects viewers with people shaping lives through meaningful conversations. Distributed in national syn. by Disney Media Networks. From Walt Disney Television. Hall won the 2019 Daytime Emmy Award for Outstanding Informative Talk Show Host.

Tamu Tamu Refreshments Food counter in Africa at Disney's Animal Kingdom; opened Apr. 22, 1998. Guests dine in the shaded courtyard of a fort that, as the story goes, once guarded the town of Harambe's waterfront. "Tamu" is Swahili for "tasty."

Tandy, Jessica (1909–1994) Actress; appeared in *The Light in the Forest* (Myra Butler).

Tangaroa Terrace Casual dining at the Polynesian Village Resort at Walt Disney World; open summer 1978–Jun. 1996. Also a quick-service restaurant at the Disneyland Hotel; opened May 25, 2011, with island-inspired fare offered for breakfast, lunch, and dinner.

Tangier Traders Shop in Morocco at EPCOT; opened Sep. 7, 1984. Clothing, jewelry, ceramics, and housewares have been sold.

Tangierine Café Quick-service restaurant in Morocco at EPCOT; opened Sep. 30, 1999. Famous for its shawarma, wraps, platters, and other Mediterranean cuisine.

Tangled (film) Rapunzel, a princess stolen from her parents' castle as a baby, is locked away for years in a hidden tower. When the kingdom's most wanted—and most charming—bandit, Flynn Rider, hides out in her tower, he's taken hostage by Rapunzel, now a spirited teen with 70 feet of magical golden hair. Flynn's curious captor, who is looking for a way out of the tower, strikes a deal with the handsome thief, and the unlikely duo sets off on an action-packed escapade, complete with a supercop horse named Maximus, an overprotective chameleon named Pascal, and a gruff gang of pub thugs. With the secret of her royal heritage hanging in the balance and her captor in pursuit, Rapunzel and her cohort find adventure, heart, and humor. Released Nov. 24, 2010, also in 3-D. Directed by Byron Howard and Nathan Greno. Stars Mandy Moore (Rapunzel), Zachary Levi (Flynn Rider), Donna Murphy (Mother Gothel), Ron Perlman (Stabbington Brother), M. C. Gainey (Captain of the Guard), Jeffrey Tambor (Big Nose Thug), Brad Garrett (Hook Hand Thug), Paul F. Tompkins (Short Thug), Richard Kiel (Vlad). 100 min. Songs by Alan Menken (music) and Glenn Slater (lyrics) include "When Will My Life Begin?," "Mother Knows Best," and "I've Got a Dream." Nominated for an Academy Award for Original Song ("I See the Light"). The computer-animated feature raised the bar for human animation in its field. A driving force behind the character design and their expressive performances was Glen Keane, who helped imbue the film with classic Disney principles of character and sincerity. A new software, called Dynamic Wires, was developed to animate Rapunzel's long hair in a visually appealing way. The technical team would animate 147 tubes representing the structure of the hair, which would then be rendered into a final image with up to 140,000 individual strands. Adapted from the Grimm Brothers' fairy tale. The working title of the film was *Rapunzel*. Flynn's real name is Eugene Fitzherbert.

Tangled Before Ever After (TV) A Disney Channel Original Movie; first aired Mar. 10, 2017, as a pilot for *Tangled: The Series*. Rapunzel grapples with both the new responsibilities of being princess and the overprotective ways of her father. Even though she loves her boyfriend, Eugene (aka Flynn Rider), she does not share his immediate desire to get married and settle down within the castle walls. Determined to live life on her own terms, she and her friend Cassandra embark on a secret adventure which leads to Rapunzel's long blond hair growing back. She must learn to embrace her hair and all that it represents. Supervising director is Chris Sonnenburg. Besides returning voice cast members from the 2010 feature, new ones include Eden Espinosa (Cassandra), Julie Bowen (Rapunzel's mother), Clancy Brown (King Frederic), James Monroe Iglehart (Lance Strongbow). From Disney Television Animation.

Tangled Ever After (film) Short 3-D cartoon released Jan. 13, 2012, with *Beauty and the Beast 3-D* (and also in 2-D). Directed by Nathan Greno and Byron Howard. As everyone gathers for the royal wedding of Rapunzel and Flynn, Pascal and Maximus, the flower chameleon and ring bearer, respectively, lose the wedding rings. They immediately start a frenzied search, hoping to find them before anyone discovers that they are missing. Voices include Mandy Moore (Rapunzel), Zachary Levi (Flynn).

Tangled: The Series (TV) Animated series on Disney Channel; began Mar. 24, 2017, after a TV movie, *Tangled Before Ever After*, aired 2 weeks earlier. Rapunzel acquaints herself with her parents, her kingdom, and the people of Corona. Her irrepressible spirit and natural curiosity make her realize that there is so much more she needs to learn about the world and herself before she can

assume her role as Princess of Corona. Formerly known as Flynn Rider, Eugene is her partner in life, and Cassandra is her good friend and confidante. Supervising director is Chris Sonnenburg. Besides Mandy Moore (Rapunzel), Zachary Levi (Eugene), and other returning cast members from the 2010 feature, additional voices include Eden Espinosa (Cassandra), Julie Bowen (Rapunzel's mother), Clancy Brown (King Frederic), James Monroe Iglehart (Lance Strongbow). Beginning with its second season Jun. 24, 2018, the series was renamed *Rapunzel's Tangled Adventure*.

Tangled Tree Tavern Fantasyland quick-service restaurant in Shanghai Disneyland; opened Jun. 16, 2016, with roasted chicken, fish-and-chips, and other hot dishes. Inspired by the Snuggly Duckling pub from *Tangled*.

Tapestry of Nations Parade for the Millennium Celebration at EPCOT; began Oct. 1, 1999, following an initial performance Sep. 25. Led by the Sage of Time, more than 120 larger-than-life puppetlike figures—along with percussion units resembling colossal time pieces—processed around the World Showcase Promenade. An elaborate concert version of the parade was performed at the Super Bowl XXXIV halftime show in 2000. The parade ended at EPCOT Sep. 9, 2001, and was modified to become *Tapestry of Dreams*, which ran Oct. 1, 2001–Mar. 1, 2003.

Tapulous Disney announced on Jul. 1, 2010, the purchase of Tapulous, Inc., headquartered in Palo Alto, California, a leading developer of music games for the iPad, iPhone, and iPod Touch. Operations ceased in 2014.

Taran Adventurous young pig keeper in *The Black Cauldron*; voiced by Grant Bardsley.

Tarzan (film) From the classic tale by Edgar Rice Burroughs, this animated feature traces the story of a baby who is orphaned in the African jungle and raised by a family of gorillas, led by Kerchak and his mate, Kala. Tarzan matures into a young man with all the instincts of a jungle animal and the physical prowess of an athletic superstar, befriending a garrulous gorilla named Terk and a neurotic elephant named Tantor. He is even able to use his cunning and strength to defeat the bloodthirsty leopard, Sabor, who had killed his parents. But Tarzan's peaceful and sheltered world is turned upside down by the arrival of a human expedition, led by an arrogant adventurer, Clayton, and including Professor Porter, a noted authority on gorillas, and his dynamic daughter, Jane. Tarzan spies on them, and soon comes to the revelation that he is one of them. As he struggles to decide which "family" he belongs with, his dilemma is further complicated by his feelings for Jane and the discovery that Clayton is plotting to harm the gorillas. Directed by Chris Buck, Kevin Lima. General release on Jun. 18, 1999, after a world premiere at the El Capitan Theatre in Hollywood on Jun. 12 and a limited release in that theater only beginning on Jun. 16. (The film began its run in Malaysia, Singapore, and Israel on Jun. 17.) Voices include Tony Goldwyn (Tarzan), Glenn Close (Kala), Rosie O'Donnell (Terk), Minnie Driver (Jane), Nigel Hawthorne (Prof. Porter), Brian Blessed (Clayton), Wayne Knight (Tantor), Alex D. Linz (young Tarzan), Lance Henriksen (Kerchak). 88 min. Includes 5 songs by Phil Collins (singing 4 of them himself— "Two Worlds," "You'll Be in My Heart," "Son of Man," and "Strangers Like Me") and a score by Mark Mancina. "You'll Be in My Heart" won the Oscar for Best Original Song. Disney also received an Academy Award in 2003 for the Deep Canvas software that enabled dimensional effects. Animator Glen Keane designed the character of Tarzan, drawing inspiration for Tarzan's persona from his teenage son, Max, who loved performing fearless skateboarding stunts and watching extreme sports, such as snowboarding. Thus, Tarzan seems to "surf" through the trees. The directors and artistic supervisors received inspiration by taking an African safari to study the jungles, the animal reserves, and the domain of the mountain gorillas firsthand. There was also a TV series, *The Legend of Tarzan*, and a video sequel, *Tarzan II*.

Tarzan A stage production, *Disney Presents Tarzan*, with the book by David Henry Hwang (and with Bob Crowley as director and set and costume designer), opened in the Richard Rodgers Theatre on Broadway in 2006, with previews beginning Mar. 24 and an official opening May 10. Original cast included Josh Strickland (Tarzan), Jenn Gambatese (Jane), Merle Dandridge (Kala), Shuler Hensley (Kerchak), Chester Gregory II (Terk). Inventive aerial design was by Pichon Baldinu, with music by Phil Collins. Nominated for a Tony Award for Lighting Design of a Musical. A Dutch production opened in The Hague in Apr. 2007. The Broadway show closed Jul. 8, 2007.

Tarzan and Jane (film) Direct-to-video release Jul.

23, 2002. As Tarzan and Jane's one-year marriage anniversary approaches, Jane searches the jungle for the perfect gift for Tarzan, enlisting the help of Terk and Tantor. As they recall the many adventures they have shared so far, Jane realizes what an exciting year it has been in the jungle. But Tarzan also has a surprise for Jane that will show her just how much he understands her world. Supervising director Steve Loter. Voices include Michael T. Weiss (Tarzan), Olivia d'Abo (Jane), Jeff Bennett (Prof. Porter), Jim Cummings (Tantor), April Winchell (Terk). 75 min.

Tarzan: Call of the Jungle SEE STORYHOUSE STAGE.

Tarzan Encounter, The Live show in The Chaparral Theater in Disneyland Paris; played Apr. 1, 2000–2008, returning 2011–2012. The story of the animated feature told through musical, acrobatic, and gymnastic performances.

Tarzan Rocks Show in the Theater in the Wild in DinoLand U.S.A. at Disney's Animal Kingdom; played Jul. 2, 1999–Jan. 21, 2006. In the 30-min. rock concert, singers, dancers, gymnasts, aerialists, and in-line skaters joined Tarzan, Jane, and Terk.

Tarzan II (film) Direct-to-video release Jun. 14, 2005. As a child, Tarzan feels like the worst ape ever. Kala reassures him that his differences will one day be his strengths, but these very differences cause an accident that leaves Kala injured, and Tarzan missing and presumed dead. Convinced that everyone would be better off without him, Tarzan sets off to find his place in the world. A dramatic encounter with an outcast family of gorillas sends Tarzan up to Dark Mountain, where he uncovers the myth of the dreaded Zugor, a legendary monster who turns out to be nothing more than a cranky old hermit ape. With Zugor's help, Tarzan is able to find his own set of remarkable jungle skills. Glenn Close and Lance Henriksen return to provide the voices of Kala and Kerchak; other voices include Harrison Chad (Tarzan), Brenda Grate (Terk), Harrison Fahn (Tantor), Estelle Harris (Mama Gunda), Brad Garrett (Uto), Ron Perlman (Kago), George Carlin (Zugor). Featured are 2 original songs by Phil Collins.

Tarzan's Treehouse Adventureland attraction in Disneyland; opened Jun. 23, 1999, taking the place of the Swiss Family Treehouse. Guests could climb a wooden staircase made from salvaged items from a shipwreck, cross an aged suspension bridge, then in the moss and vine-covered tree find the homes of Tarzan's human parents, of his foster mother, Kala, as well as the main hut where Tarzan lives. An interactive play area was at the base of the tree. The attraction closed Sep. 2021, to be re-themed as the Adventureland Treehouse. A version opened on an island in the Rivers of Adventure in Hong Kong Disneyland Sep. 12, 2005; guests take rafts to the island.

Taste of Melon, A (TV) Show; part 1 of *For the Love of Willadean*.

Taste Pilots' Grill Quick-service restaurant in Condor Flats at Disney California Adventure; open Feb. 8, 2001–Jan. 7, 2015, and replaced by Smoke-jumpers Grill. Themed as an airfield hangar, the facility was a tribute to test pilots. Emerging from the front entrance was a reproduction of the Bell X-1 *Glamorous Glennis*, used by Charles Yeager to break the sound barrier in 1947.

Tatooine Traders Shop in Echo Lake near the exit of Star Tours in Disney's Hollywood Studios; opened Nov. 10, 1999. Themed after *Star Wars: The Phantom Menace*. Guests can build their own droid and purchase Star Tours memorabilia. It was formerly Endor Vendors, themed after *Star Wars: Return of the Jedi*, which operated May 1, 1989–Jun. 6, 1999.

Tattooed Police Horse, The (film) Featurette released Dec. 18, 1964. Directed by Larry Lansburgh. Registered trotting horse Jolly Roger is thrown out of racing for speeding into a gallop (instead of the required trot) whenever he races. Bought by a Boston police captain, the horse manages to redeem himself by winning and becoming a champion racer. 48 min. Stars Sandy Saunders, Charles Steel, Shirley Skiles.

Tatum, Donn B. (1913–1993) He joined Walt Disney Productions as production business manager in 1956 and was later executive vice president of Disneyland, Inc. After 1960, he returned to the Studio, where he was vice president of TV sales and vice president of administration. He served as president of Walt Disney Productions 1968–1971 and succeeded Roy O. Disney as chairman of the board and chief executive officer, serving 1971–1980. He became chairman of the executive committee 1980–1983. He became a member of the Board of Direc-

tors in 1964, until his resignation in 1992, at which time he was named director emeritus. He was well known by stockholders for his adeptness in handling the corporate annual meetings. With Card Walker, he ably led the company after Roy O. Disney's death. He was posthumously named a Disney Legend in 1993.

Tayback, Vic (1929–1990) Actor; appeared in *No Deposit, No Return* (Big Joe) and *The Shaggy D.A.* (Eddie Roschak).

Taylor, Betty (1919–2011) Performer in the *Golden Horseshoe Revue* in Disneyland, from 1956 until the show's final curtain in 1987. As Slue Foot Sue, she personified the spunky leader of a troupe of western dance hall girls and Pecos Bill's sweetheart. She also had a singing role in America Sings at Disneyland. She was named a Disney Legend in 1995, and died Jun. 4, 2011, just one day after her Golden Horseshoe co-star, Wally Boag, passed away.

Taylor, Dub (1907–1994) Actor; appeared in *The Adventures of Bullwhip Griffin* (timekeeper), *The Wild Country* (Phil), and *Treasure of Matecumbe* (Sheriff Forbes), and on TV in *Menace on the Mountain, Ride a Northbound Horse*, and *The Mooncussers*. He voiced Digger in *The Rescuers*.

Taylor, Robert (1911–1969) Actor; appeared in *The Miracle of the White Stallions* (Colonel Podhajsky).

Taylor, Rod (1930–2015) Actor; provided the voice of Pongo in *One Hundred and One Dalmatians*.

Taylor, Russi (1944–2019) Voice actress; she became the official voice of Minnie Mouse in 1986, and could be heard in dozens of films, TV shows, music albums, theme park shows and attractions, and other projects over the years. She also voiced Donald's nephews Huey, Dewey, and Louie, as well as Nurse Mouse in *The Rescuers Down Under*, Webbigail Vanderquack in *DuckTales*, and Fairy Godmother in the *Cinderella* animated sequels. She provided additional TV voices in *TaleSpin, Disney's Adventures of the Gummi Bears, The Little Mermaid, Buzz Lightyear of Star Command, Kim Possible, Jake and the Never Land Pirates, Sofia the First, The Lion Guard*, and *Tangled: The Series*. Russi was named a Disney Legend in 2008. She was married to Wayne Allwine, the longtime voice of Mickey Mouse.

Taymor, Julie Acclaimed for her work with puppetry and mask making, she was chosen to adapt *The Lion King* for Broadway. It opened in 1997, garnering 11 Tony Award nominations, with Taymor receiving awards for Best Director and Costume Designer. The show became the most successful stage musical of all time, and Taymor presided over 24 global productions. She also directed the Touchstone/Miramax film *The Tempest*. She was named a Disney Legend in 2017.

T-Bone for Two (film) Pluto cartoon released Aug. 14, 1942. Directed by Clyde Geronimi. When Pluto steals a bone from Butch, the bulldog, he has a difficult time keeping hold of it.

Te Fiti Life-giving mother island in *Moana*.

Tea Caddy, The Shop offering Twinings tea and tea accessories in the United Kingdom at EPCOT; opened Oct. 1, 1982. With its thatched roof and weathered half-timbers, the cottage is based on that of Anne Hathaway, the wife of William Shakespeare.

Tea for Two Hundred (film) Donald Duck cartoon released Dec. 24, 1948. Directed by Jack Hannah. Donald is at war with an army of ants who are after his picnic food, but it is a losing battle from the start and soon the ants have even taken his clothes. Nominated for an Academy Award.

Teachers Are People (film) Goofy cartoon released Jun. 27, 1952. Directed by Jack Kinney. Goofy is a teacher with a class of children so full of mischief that by the end of the day Goofy is exhausted—and wiser.

Teacher's Pet (TV) Animated series created by Gary Baseman; part of *One Saturday Morning* on ABC; debuted Sep. 9, 2000, and ended Jan. 13, 2001. A tale of a boy and his dog, Spot—a talking canine that yearns for the education afforded his master. Spot disguises himself as a boy in order to attend school and becomes the teacher's pet. Voices include Nathan Lane (Spot/Scott), Debra Jo Rupp (Mrs. Helperman), Wallace Shawn (Principal Strickler), David Ogden Stiers (Mr. Jolly), Shaun Fleming (Leonard), Jerry Stiller (Pretty Boy), Rob Paulsen (Ian). Emmy Award winner. 39 episodes.

Teacher's Pet (film) Spot, a talking canine, has the ultimate wish of becoming a real boy. When the opportunity presents itself, through the DNA manipulations of wacko scientist Dr. Ivan Krank, Spot quickly follows his family to Florida in order to make the evolution to human form. However, Dr. Krank's experiments have had far-from-perfect results and, although Spot's transformation to human is complete, not all the calculations are exactly correct. It will take his best buddy, Leonard, and his quirky pet pals, Mr. Jolly (a cat) and Pretty Boy (a bird), to help him out of his predicament and try to right this genetic wrong. Directed by Timothy Björklund. Released Jan. 16, 2004. Voices include Nathan Lane (Spot/Scott), Kelsey Grammer (Dr. Krank), Shaun Fleming (Leonard), Debra Jo Rupp (Mrs. Helperman), David Ogden Stiers (Jolly), Jerry Stiller (Pretty Boy), Paul Reubens (Dennis), Megan Mullally (Adele), Rob Paulsen (Ian), Wallace Shawn (Principal Strickler), Estelle Harris (Mrs. Boogin), Barry Anger (Jay Thomas). 74 min. Based on the TV series created by Gary Baseman.

Team Disney Building Corporate headquarters for The Walt Disney Company; opened in 1990 at The Walt Disney Studios in Burbank, California. The building was designed by Michael Graves and features enormous statues of the Seven Dwarfs "holding" up the roof; six of the Dwarfs are 19 feet tall, while Dopey is 12 feet tall. In 2006, the building was renamed Team Disney—The Michael D. Eisner Building in honor of the former CEO. There is also a Team Disney administration building at Walt Disney World designed by Arata Isozaki; it opened in 1991, and features an enormous, 120-ft. sundial. A Team Disney Anaheim building, designed by Frank O. Gehry, opened in early 1996 to house all of the Disneyland administrative staff, for the first time in one facility. It features a façade of iridescent green, violet, and blue. There are also Team Disney buildings in Paris, Hong Kong, and Shanghai.

Team Mickey's Athletic Club Sports apparel and merchandise shop in the Disney Village Marketplace (later Downtown Disney Marketplace) at Walt Disney World; opened Apr. 19, 1987, taking the place of Shoe Time, Country Address, and Mickey & Co. It was relocated ca. 1997 into the former Mickey's Character Shop, with the original Team Mickey's location replaced by Disney's Days of Christmas. Closed Jan. 2014 to become the Marketplace Co-Op. Also known as Team Mickey Athletic Club. Team Mickey was also a shop in Festival Disney (later Disney Village) at Disneyland Paris; open Apr. 12, 1992–2007 and succeeded by Disney Fashion. At Disneyland Resort, Team

Mickey's Workout was a gym at the Disneyland Hotel for some years.

Teamo Supremo (TV) Animated series, part of *One Saturday Morning* on ABC; premiered Jan. 19, 2002. A quirky triumvirate of superheroes—Captain Crandall, Rope Girl, and Skate Lad—are sworn to protect their state from the forces of evil . . . and still finish all their homework. Voices include Spencer Breslin (Crandall), Alanna Ubach (Brenda, Hector), Martin Mull (Gov. Kevin), Fred Willard (Paulsen), Brian Doyle-Murray (Chief). From Walt Disney Television. 39 episodes.

Technicolor Walt Disney had the foresight to sign an exclusive 2-year contract for the use of Technicolor's new 3-color process in cartoons, and he first used it in *Flowers and Trees* (1932). For the first time it brought full color to cartoons. The first Mickey Mouse cartoon in color was *The Band Concert* (1935). SEE ALSO COLOR.

Teddi Barra's Swingin' Arcade Critter Country game arcade in Disneyland, featuring games with a distinctive backwoods flavor; open 1972–2002. Replaced by an expansion of Pooh Corner.

Teddy Bear & Doll Convention Annual event at Walt Disney World showcasing collectibles from international doll and toy makers, with limited-edition merchandise, workshops, and an auction. The inaugural event, the Walt Disney World Teddy Bear Convention, took place Dec. 7–11, 1988. Also known as the Doll and Teddy Bear Showcase and, beginning in 2000, the Teddy Bear & Doll Weekend. The final event was held in 2008. A similar event at Disneyland, the Teddy Bear and Doll Classic, was held 1992–1993.

Teddy Roosevelt Lounge, The Cozy bar and restaurant on the "C" deck of the S.S. *Columbia* in Tokyo DisneySea; opened Sep. 4, 2001, serving cocktails, light meals, and desserts. Elaborate décor and displays tell the story of U.S. president Theodore Roosevelt. Hosted by Kirin Brewery.

Teddybär, Der SEE DER TEDDYBÄR.

Tedrow, Irene (1907–1995) Actress; appeared in *Midnight Madness* (Mrs. Grimhaus), and on TV in *14 Going on 30* (Aunt May) and *Child of Glass* (Ms. Merryweather).

Teen Angel (TV) Serial on the *Mickey Mouse Club* on The Disney Channel; aired Apr. 24–May 19, 1989. Guardian angel Buzz Gunderson receives his first assignment: to help a shy misfit named Dennis Mullen gain self-confidence, not to mention the love of the beautiful Nancy Nichols. Only Dennis can see the angel, who has to succeed with his task in order to get into heaven. Stars Jason Priestley (Buzz), Adam Biesk (Dennis), Renee O'Connor (Nancy).

Teen Angel (TV) Half-hour comedy series on ABC; aired Sep. 26, 1997–Sep. 11, 1998. As high school buddies, Marty, who prefers partying over studying, and Steve, a guy who plays by the rules, couldn't be more different. When Marty dies from eating a tainted hamburger, he learns from the Court of Eternal Judgment that he must prove himself worthy of entry into Heaven by serving as his friend's guardian angel. Invisible to everyone but Steve, Marty helps his friend navigate the pitfalls of high school life while getting himself into trouble with his newfound celestial powers. Stars Mike Damus (Marty DePolo), Corbin Allred (Steve Beauchamp), Maureen McCormick (Judy Beauchamp), Katie Volding (Katie Beauchamp), Jordan Brower (Jordan Lubell), Ron Glass (Head), Conchata Ferrell (Pam). At mid-season, Maureen McCormick's character was dropped, and Tommy Hinkley and Jerry Van Dyke were added as Steve's father and grandfather. From Spooky Magic Productions and Touchstone Television.

Teen Angel Returns (TV) Serial on the *Mickey Mouse Club* on The Disney Channel; aired Oct. 2–27, 1989. Guardian angel Buzz decides to help Cindy, the daughter of a friend whose gas station is threatened by a cruel developer. The developer's kids constantly hassle Cindy, who initially refuses to believe in her angel, but eventually he helps her gain the self-confidence she needs to save the gas station and win over her boyfriend. Stars Jason Priestley (Buzz), Robyn Lively (Cindy), Scott Reeves (Brian), Jennie Garth (Karrie).

Teen Beach Movie (TV) A Disney Channel Original Movie; first aired Jul. 19, 2013. Two surfers, Brady and McKenzie, take the last wave of summer and find themselves mysteriously transported into a classic beach party movie, *Wet Side Story* (circa 1962). There it is surfers versus bikers for control of the beach hangout, and everyone spontaneously breaks into song and dance. Brady and McKenzie must try to return to the present day, but they inadvertently change the movie's romantic story line, a mistake that could alter their lives forever. Directed by Jeffrey Hornaday. Stars Ross Lynch (Brady), Mala Mitchell (McKenzie), Grace Phipps (Lela), Garrett Clayton (Tanner), John Deluca (Butchy), Chrissie Fit (Cheechee), Kevin Chamberlin (Dr. Fusion), Steve Valentine (Les Cambert), Barry Bostwick (Big Poppa). Filmed on location in Puerto Rico. It debuted as the 2nd most popular movie in cable TV history.

Teen Beach 2 (TV) A Disney Channel Original Movie; first aired Jun. 26, 2015. This sequel to *Teen Beach Movie* picks up at the close of summer. With surf season over and high school back in session, laid-back Brady and studious Mack's relationship is headed for a wipeout when they receive a surprise real-world visit from their 1960s silver screen friends Lela and Tanner, who have remarkably departed *Wet Side Story*, quickly followed by their 1960s biker rivals and surfer friends. Knowing firsthand that the "real" world and the movie world don't mix, Mack, Brady, and their friends must quickly devise a plan and use the magic of Lela's necklace to get everyone back to their movie world before it is too late. Directed by Jeffrey Hornaday. Stars Ross Lynch (Brady), Maia Mitchell (McKenzie, aka Mack), Grace Phipps (Lela), Garrett Clayton (Tanner), Piper Curda (Alyssa), Raymond Cham, Jr. (Devon), Ross Butler (Spencer).

Teen Win, Lose or Draw (TV) A Disney Channel series; debuted May 6, 1989. Hosted by Marc Price and his Dalmatian pup, Tyler, with teen guest stars competing in drawing clues for contestants to decipher. The show was a spin-off from *Win, Lose, or Draw.*

Teenage Mutant Ninja Turtles They appeared in Disney-MGM Studios at Walt Disney World beginning Jul. 1, 1990, demonstrating some of their karate moves and signing autographs.

Teenage Substance Abuse: An Open Forum with John Callahan (film) Educational film; released in Nov. 1989. 23 min. A man recovering from an alcohol-use disorder tells his story to teenagers.

Teeth Are for Chewing (film) Educational film; released in Sep. 1971. Designed to make children aware of the unique functions human teeth perform and the importance of good dental safety habits.

Television Walt Disney was one of the first of the major movie producers to go into TV. He started with Christmas specials in 1950 (*One Hour in Wonderland*) and 1951 (*The Walt Disney Christmas Show*), and then began his regular series on Oct. 27, 1954. Disney was persuaded to begin the series on ABC because he knew he could use it to help sell his movies and, especially, because ABC offered to advance money to help him build Disneyland park. The evening series remained on the air for 29 seasons, airing on all 3 networks during this period. This made it the longest-running weekly primetime show of all time. While there were a few other series during the first 3 decades, notably the *Mickey Mouse Club* and *Zorro*, Disney, beginning in the 1980s, became a mainstream producer of series for TV. The complete list of Disney TV series follows:

1. *Disneyland* (ABC), 10/27/54–9/3/58
   Walt Disney Presents (ABC), 9/12/58–9/17/61
   Walt Disney's Wonderful World of Color (NBC), 9/24/61–9/7/69
   The Wonderful World of Disney (NBC), 9/14/69–9/2/79
   Disney's Wonderful World (NBC), 9/9/79–9/13/81
   Walt Disney (CBS), 9/26/81–9/24/83
2. *Mickey Mouse Club* (ABC), 10/3/55–9/25/59
3. *Zorro* (78 episodes) (ABC), 10/10/57–9/28/59
4. *The Mouse Factory* (43 episodes, syn.), 1/26/72–1973
5. *Saturday Night at the Movies with Disney* (11 programs, NBC), 2/23/74–1/29/77
6. *[New] Mickey Mouse Club* (syn.), 1/17/77–12/1/78
7. *Herbie, the Love Bug* (5 episodes, CBS), 3/17/82–4/14/82
8. *Small and Frye* (6 episodes, CBS), 3/7/83–6/15/83
9. *Gun Shy* (6 episodes, CBS), 3/25/83–4/19/83
10. *Zorro and Son* (5 episodes, CBS), 4/6/83–6/1/83
11. *Wildside* (6 episodes, ABC), 3/21/85–4/25/85
12. *The Golden Girls* (NBC), 9/14/85–9/12/92
13. *Disney's Adventures of the Gummi Bears* (NBC), 9/14/85–9/2/89
    _____ (ABC), 9/9/89–9/8/90
    _____ (syn.), 9/10/90–9/6/91
14. *Disney's Wuzzles* (CBS), 9/14/85–9/6/86
    _____ (ABC), 9/13/86–5/16/87
15. *The Disney Sunday Movie* (ABC), 2/2/86–9/11/88

16. *The Wonderful World of Disney* (syn.), 9/4/86–ca. 2009
17. *Disney Magic* (syn.), 9/8/86–ca. 1994
18. *Siskel & Ebert at the Movies* (syn.), 9/18/86–8/29/99 (Became *Roger Ebert & the Movies* 9/4/99–8/20/00, and *Ebert & Roeper and the Movies* 8/27/00–ca. 2010.)
19. *The Ellen Burstyn Show* (ABC), 9/20/86–11/15/86, 8/8/87–9/12/87
20. *Sidekicks* (ABC), 9/26/86–6/27/87
21. *Today's Business* (syn.), 9/26/86–4/26/87
22. *Harry* (ABC), 3/4/87–3/25/87
23. *Down and Out in Beverly Hills* (Fox), 7/25/87–9/12/87
24. *Win, Lose or Draw* (NBC), 9/7/87–9/1/89
      _____ (syn.), 9/7/87–8/31/90
25. *The Oldest Rookie* (CBS), 9/16/87–1/6/88
26. *DuckTales* (syn.), 9/21/87–9/5/92, 9/1/97–ca. 1999
      _____ (ABC), 4/19/97–8/30/97
27. *Live with Regis and Kathie Lee* (syn.), 9/5/88–7/28/00 (Became *Live with Regis* 7/31/00–2/9/01, *Live with Regis & Kelly* 2/12/01–11/18/11, *Live with Kelly* 11/21/11–8/31/12, *Live with Kelly and Michael* 9/4/12–2017, and *Live with Kelly and Ryan* 2017–).
28. *The New Adventures of Winnie the Pooh* (ABC), 9/10/88–9/4/92, 1/4/97–2002 (Premiered 1/10/88 on The Disney Channel.)
29. *Empty Nest* (NBC), 10/8/88–7/8/95
30. *The Magical World of Disney* (NBC), 10/9/88–9/9/90
31. *Hard Time on Planet Earth* (CBS), 3/1/89–7/5/89
32. *Chip 'n' Dale Rescue Rangers* (syn.), 9/18/89–9/3/93 (Premiered 3/4/89 on The Disney Channel.)
33. *The Nutt House* (NBC), 9/20/89–10/25/89
34. *Carol & Co.* (NBC), 3/31/90–8/19/91
35. *Singer & Sons* (NBC), 6/9/90–6/27/90
36. *The Challengers* (syn.), 9/3/90–8/30/91
37. *The Fanelli Boys* (NBC), 9/8/90–2/16/91
38. *TaleSpin* (syn.), 9/10/90–9/2/94 (Premiered 5/5/90 on The Disney Channel; *DuckTales*, *Gummi Bears*, *Chip 'n' Dale Rescue Rangers*, and *TaleSpin* made up *The Disney Afternoon* package [syn.], 9/10/90.)
39. *Lenny* (CBS), 9/19/90–3/9/91 (Preview was 9/10/90.)
40. *Hull High* (NBC), 9/23/90–12/30/90 (Preview was 8/20/90 and 9/15/90.)
41. *Blossom* (NBC), 1/3/91–6/5/95
42. *The 100 Lives of Black Jack Savage* (2-hour pilot, NBC), 3/31/91

      _____ (series, NBC), 4/5/91–5/26/91
43. *STAT* (ABC), 4/16/91–5/21/91
44. *Dinosaurs* (ABC), 4/26/91–7/20/94
45. *Darkwing Duck* (ABC), 9/7/91–9/11/93
      _____ (syn.), 9/9/91–9/1/95, 9/2/96–8/29/97 (Premiered 4/6/91 on The Disney Channel; *Darkwing Duck* replaced *Gummi Bears* in *The Disney Afternoon* package [syn.]; the network show ran concurrently with *The Disney Afternoon* version.)
46. *Herman's Head* (Fox), 9/8/91–6/16/94
47. *Nurses* (NBC), 9/14/91–6/18/94
48. *Pacific Station* (NBC), 9/15/91–1/3/92
49. *Home Improvement* (ABC), 9/17/91–9/17/99
50. *The Torkelsons* (NBC), 9/21/91–6/20/92
51. *Good and Evil* (ABC), 9/25/91–10/31/91
52. *The Carol Burnett Show* (CBS), 11/1/91–12/27/91
53. *Walter and Emily* (NBC), 11/16/91–2/22/92
54. *Goof Troop* (syn.), 9/7/92–8/30/96
      _____ (ABC), 9/12/92–9/11/93 (Premiered 4/20/92 on The Disney Channel; *Goof Troop* replaced *DuckTales* in *The Disney Afternoon* package [syn.]; the network show ran concurrently with *The Disney Afternoon* version.)
55. *Disney's The Little Mermaid* (CBS), 9/12/92–9/2/95
56. *The Golden Palace* (CBS), 9/18/92–8/6/93
57. *Raw Toonage* (CBS), 9/19/92–9/11/93
58. *Woops!* (Fox), 9/27/92–12/6/92
59. *Laurie Hill* (ABC), 9/30/92–10/28/92
60. *Almost Home* (NBC), 2/6/93–7/3/93 (Formerly *The Torkelsons*.)
61. *Where I Live* (ABC), 3/5/93–11/20/93
62. *Cutters* (CBS), 6/11/93–7/9/93
63. *Bonkers* (syn.), 9/6/93–8/30/96 (Premiered 2/28/93 on The Disney Channel; *Bonkers* replaced *Chip 'n' Dale Rescue Rangers* in *The Disney Afternoon* package; *Chip 'n' Dale Rescue Rangers* ran on Saturdays.)
64. *Disney's Adventures in Wonderland* (syn.), 9/6/93–9/10/95 (Premiered 3/23/92 on The Disney Channel.)
65. *Bill Nye, the Science Guy* (syn.), 9/10/93–10/3/97
66. *The Crusaders* (syn.), 9/10/93–1/21/95
67. *Bakersfield P.D.* (Fox), 9/14/93–1/4/94
68. *The Sinbad Show* (Fox), 9/16/93–7/28/94
69. *Countdown at the Neon Armadillo* (syn.), 9/17/93–12/12/93
70. *Marsupilami* (CBS), 9/18/93–8/27/94
71. *Boy Meets World* (ABC), 9/24/93–9/8/00
72. *The Good Life* (NBC), 1/3/94–4/12/94
73. *Monty* (Fox), 1/11/94–2/15/94

74. *Thunder Alley* (ABC), 3/9/94–7/25/95
75. *Ellen* (ABC), 3/9/94–7/29/98 (Aired as *These Friends of Mine*, 3/9/94–5/24/94; began airing as *Ellen* 8/2/94.)
76. *Someone Like Me* (NBC), 3/14/94–4/25/94
77. *Mike & Maty* (ABC), 4/11/94–6/7/96
78. *Hardball* (Fox), 9/4/94–10/23/94
79. *Disney's Aladdin* (syn.), 9/5/94–8/29/97
____ (CBS), 9/17/94–8/24/96 (Replaced *TaleSpin* on *The Disney Afternoon*, which then consisted of *Darkwing Duck*, *Goof Troop*, *Bonkers*, and *Disney's Aladdin*.)
80. *Judge for Yourself* (syn.), 9/12/94–4/7/95
81. *All-American Girl* (ABC), 9/14/94–3/22/95
82. *Gargoyles* (syn.), 10/24/94–8/29/97
83. *Shnookums & Meat Funny Cartoon Show* (syn.), 1/2/95–8/28/95
84. *Unhappily Ever After* (The WB), 1/11/95–9/19/99
85. *The George Wendt Show* (CBS), 3/8/95–4/12/95
86. *Pride & Joy* (NBC), 3/21/95–7/11/95
87. *Nowhere Man* (UPN), 9/4/95–8/19/96 (Previewed on 8/28/95.)
88. *The Lion King's Timon & Pumbaa* (syn.), 9/8/95–8/29/97 (Part of *The Disney Afternoon*.)
____ (CBS), 9/16/95–3/29/97
89. *Disney's Sing Me a Story: with Belle* (syn.), 9/9/95–2000
90. *Danny!* (syn.), 9/11/95–2/2/96
91. *The Stephanie Miller Show* (syn.), 9/15/95–1/20/96
92. *Maybe This Time* (ABC), 9/16/95–2/17/96 (Previewed on 9/15/95.)
93. *If Not for You* (CBS), 9/18/95–10/9/95
94. *Land's End* (syn.), 9/22/95–9/15/96
95. *Brotherly Love* (NBC), 9/24/95–4/1/96 (Previewed on 9/16/95.)
____ (The WB), 9/15/96–6/1/97
96. *Misery Loves Company* (Fox), 10/1/95–10/23/95
97. *Buddies* (ABC), 3/5/96–3/27/96
98. *Debt* (Lifetime), 6/3/96–7/3/98
99. *Homeboys in Outer Space* (UPN), 8/27/96–5/13/97
100. *Quack Pack* (syn.), 9/3/96–ca. 1997
101. *The Mighty Ducks* (syn.), 9/6/96–ca. 1997
____ (ABC), 9/7/96–8/30/97 (*The Mighty Ducks* and *Quack Pack* were added to *The Disney Afternoon*.)
102. *Gargoyles: The Goliath Chronicles* (ABC), 9/7/96–4/12/97
103. *Brand Spanking New Doug* (ABC), 9/7/96–

1999 (New title: *Disney's Doug* [syn.], 8/31/98–2004.) SEE ALSO ONE SATURDAY MORNING.
104. *Life's Work* (ABC), 9/17/96–7/29/97
105. *Dangerous Minds* (ABC), 9/30/96–7/12/97
106. *Jungle Cubs* (ABC), 10/5/96–9/5/98
107. *Vital Signs* (ABC), 2/27/97–7/3/97
108. *Social Studies* (UPN), 3/18/97–8/5/97
109. *Smart Guy* (The WB), 4/2/97–8/1/99
110. *Soul Man* (ABC), 4/15/97–8/25/98
111. *Nightmare Ned* (ABC), 4/19/97–8/30/97
112. *Make Me Laugh* (Comedy Central), 6/2/97–6/00
113. *Win Ben Stein's Money* (Comedy Central), 7/28/97–1/31/03
114. *The Keenan Ivory Wayans Show* (syn.), 8/4/97–4/24/98
115. *101 Dalmatians: The Series* (syn.), 9/1/97–8/98
____ (ABC), 9/13/97–1999
116. *One Saturday Morning* (ABC), 9/13/97–9/7/02
117. *Recess* (ABC), 9/13/97–2001 (Part of *One Saturday Morning*.)
118. *Pepper Ann* (ABC, syn.), 9/13/97–11/18/00 (Part of *One Saturday Morning*.)
119. *Honey, I Shrunk the Kids* (syn.), 9/22/97–5/20/00
120. *Hiller and Diller* (ABC), 9/23/97–3/13/98
121. *Teen Angel* (ABC), 9/26/97–9/11/98
122. *You Wish* (ABC), 9/26/97–9/4/98
123. *The Wonderful World of Disney* (ABC), 9/28/97–6/28/08, 12/12/15–11/5/19, 5/20/20–
124. *Style and Substance* (CBS), 1/5/98–9/9/98
125. *Hercules* (syn.), 8/31/98–1999
126. *Costello* (Fox), 9/8/98–10/13/98
127. *Secrets of the Animal Kingdom* (syn.), 9/18/98–9/13/99
128. *Sports Night* (ABC), 9/22/98–5/16/00
129. *Felicity* (The WB), 9/29/98–5/22/02
130. *The PJs* (Fox), 1/12/99–6/17/01
131. *Zoe, Duncan, Jack & Jane* (The WB), 1/17/99–7/18/99
132. *Mickey's MouseWorks* (ABC), 5/1/99–1/6/01
133. *Thanks* (CBS), 8/2/99–9/6/99
134. *Who Wants to Be a Millionaire* (ABC), 8/16/99–6/27/02
135. *Disney's One Two* (UPN, syn.), 9/6/99–9/1/02
136. *Once and Again* (ABC), 9/21/99–5/2/01
137. *Your Big Break* (syn.), 9/23/99–6/16/01
138. *Popular* (The WB), 9/29/99–5/18/01
139. *The Ainsley Harriott Show* (syn.), 1/10/00–9/15/00

140. *Brutally Normal* (The WB), 1/24/00–2/14/00
141. *The Weekenders* (ABC), 2/26/00 (Part of *One Saturday Morning*.)
142. *Daddio* (NBC), 3/23/00–10/13/00
143. *Wonderland* (ABC), 3/30/00–4/6/00
144. *Talk to Me* (ABC), 4/11/00–4/25/00
145. *Clerks* (ABC), 5/31/00–6/7/00
146. *Teacher's Pet* (ABC), 9/9/00–1/13/01 (Part of *One Saturday Morning*.)
147. *House Calls* (syn.), 9/11/00–2001
148. *Buzz Lightyear of Star Command* (ABC), 10/14/00–3/13/01 (Part of *One Saturday Morning*.)
_____ (UPN, syn.), 10/2/00–ca. 2008
149. *Madigan Men* (ABC), 10/6/00–12/12/00
150. *The Geena Davis Show* (ABC), 10/10/00–7/12/01
151. *Gideon's Crossing* (ABC), 10/18/00–4/9/01
152. *Disney's House of Mouse* (ABC), 1/13/01–2/09
153. *Disney's Lloyd in Space* (ABC), 2/3/01–2006 (Part of *One Saturday Morning*.)
154. *The Job* (ABC), 3/14/01–4/24/02
155. *My Wife and Kids* (ABC), 3/28/01–8/9/05
156. *Go Fish* (NBC), 6/19/01–7/3/01
157. *The Beast* (ABC), 6/20/01–7/18/01
158. *The Wayne Brady Show* (ABC), 8/8/01–9/19/01
_____ (syn.), 9/2/02–5/04
159. *Iyanla* (syn.), 8/13/01–3/1/02
160. *The Legend of Tarzan* (UPN, syn.), 9/3/01–9/7/02
161. *The Amazing Race* (CBS), 9/5/01–
162. *Alias* (ABC), 9/30/01–5/22/06
163. *Bob Patterson* (ABC), 10/2/01–10/31/01
164. *Scrubs* (NBC), 10/2/01–5/8/08
_____ (ABC), 1/6/09–3/17/10
165. *According to Jim* (ABC), 10/3/01–6/9/09
166. *Maybe It's Me* (The WB), 10/5/01–7/19/02
167. *Imagine That* (NBC), 1/8/02–1/15/02
168. *Teamo Supremo* (ABC), 1/19/02–2004 (Part of *One Saturday Morning*.)
169. *The Court* (ABC), 3/26/02–4/9/02
170. *Wednesday 9:30 (8:30 Central)* (ABC), 3/27/02–6/12/02
171. *Monk* (USA), 7/12/02–12/4/09
172. *ABC Kids* (ABC), 9/14/02–8/27/11 (Includes *Fillmore*.)
173. *8 Simple Rules for Dating My Teenage Daughter* (ABC), 9/17/02–8/19/05
174. *Life with Bonnie* (ABC), 9/17/02–7/30/04
175. *Push, Nevada* (ABC), 9/17/02–10/24/02
176. *MDs* (ABC), 9/25/02–12/11/02
177. *That Was Then* (ABC), 9/27/02–10/18/02

178. *Less Than Perfect* (ABC), 10/1/02–6/6/06
179. *Dinotopia* (ABC), 11/28/02–12/26/02
180. *The Last Resort* (ABC Family), 1/20/03–3/31/03
181. *Jimmy Kimmel Live!* (ABC), 1/26/03–
182. *Miracles* (ABC), 1/27/03–3/3/03
183. *Veritas: The Quest* (ABC), 1/27/03–3/10/03
184. *The Family* (ABC), 3/4/03–9/10/03
185. *Regular Joe* (ABC), 3/28/03–4/18/03
186. *Lost at Home* (ABC), 4/1/03–4/22/03
187. *Threat Matrix* (ABC), 9/18/03–1/29/04
188. *Lilo & Stitch, The Series* (ABC), 9/20/03–6/23/06
189. *Hope & Faith* (ABC), 9/26/03–6/23/06
190. *10-8* (ABC), 9/28/03–1/25/04
191. *It's All Relative* (ABC), 10/1/03–4/6/04
192. *Line of Fire* (ABC), 12/2/03–2/3/04
193. *Stephen King's Kingdom Hospital* (ABC), 3/3/04–7/15/04
194. *The Tony Danza Show* (syn.), 9/13/04–5/26/06
195. *Rodney* (ABC), 9/21/04–6/6/06
196. *Lost* (ABC), 9/22/04–5/23/10
197. *Kevin Hill* (UPN), 9/29/04–6/8/05
198. *Desperate Housewives* (ABC), 10/3/04–5/13/12
199. *life as we know it* (ABC), 10/7/04–1/20/05
200. *W.I.T.C.H.* (ABC Family), 1/15/05–12/23/06
201. *Grey's Anatomy* (ABC), 3/27/05–
202. *Empire* (ABC), 6/28/05–7/26/05
203. *Criminal Minds* (CBS), 9/22/05–2/19/20
204. *Inconceivable* (NBC), 9/23/05–9/30/05
205. *Ghost Whisperer* (CBS), 9/23/05–5/21/10
206. *Commander-in-Chief* (ABC), 9/27/05–6/14/06
207. *The Night Stalker* (ABC), 9/29/05–11/10/05
208. *In Justice* (ABC), 1/1/06–3/31/06
209. *Crumbs* (ABC), 1/12/06–2/7/06
210. *Courting Alex* (CBS), 1/23/06–3/29/06
211. *What About Brian* (ABC), 4/26/06–3/26/07
212. *Kyle XY* (ABC Family), 6/26/06–3/16/09
213. *Three Moons Over Milford* (ABC Family), 8/6/06–9/24/06
214. *Six Degrees* (ABC), 9/21/06–3/30/07
215. *Brothers & Sisters* (ABC), 9/24/06–5/8/11
216. *Ugly Betty* (ABC), 9/28/06–4/14/10
217. *Day Break* (ABC), 11/15/06–12/13/06
218. *Dirt* (FX), 1/2/07–4/13/08
219. *The Knights of Prosperity* (ABC), 1/3/07–8/8/07
220. *In Case of Emergency* (ABC), 1/3/07–2/28/07
221. *October Road* (ABC), 3/15/07–3/10/08
222. *Army Wives* (Lifetime), 6/3/07–6/9/13
223. *Cane* (CBS), 9/25/07–12/18/07
224. *Reaper* (The CW), 9/25/07–5/26/09

225. *Private Practice* (ABC), 9/26/07–1/22/13
226. *Dirty Sexy Money* (ABC), 9/26/07–8/8/09
227. *Cavemen* (ABC), 10/2/07–11/13/07
228. *Carpoolers* (ABC), 10/2/07–3/4/08
229. *Samantha Who?* (ABC), 10/15/07–7/23/09
230. *Eli Stone* (ABC), 1/31/08–7/11/09
231. *Miss Guided* (ABC), 3/18/08–4/3/08
232. *Raising the Bar* (TNT), 9/1/08–12/24/09
233. *At the Movies* (syn.), 9/6/08–8/15/10
234. *Gary Unmarried* (CBS), 9/24/08–3/17/10
235. *Life on Mars* (ABC), 10/9/08–4/1/09
236. *Legend of the Seeker* (syn.), 11/1/08–5/22/10
237. *Castle* (ABC), 3/9/09–5/16/16
238. *In the Motherhood* (ABC), 3/26/09–7/9/09
239. *Cupid* (ABC), 3/31/09–6/16/09
240. *Make It or Break It* (ABC Family), 6/22/09–5/14/12
241. *10 Things I Hate About You* (ABC Family), 7/7/09–5/24/10
242. *Ruby & The Rockits* (ABC Family), 7/21/09–9/22/09
243. *Cougar Town* (ABC), 9/23/09–5/29/12 _____ (TBS), 1/8/13–3/31/15
244. *FlashForward* (ABC), 9/24/09–5/27/10
245. *Happy Town* (ABC), 4/28/10–6/16/10
246. *Scoundrels* (ABC), 6/20/10–8/15/10
247. *Huge* (ABC Family), 6/28/10–8/30/10
248. *Melissa & Joey* (ABC Family), 8/17/10–8/5/15
249. *Detroit 1-8-7* (ABC), 9/21/10–3/20/11
250. *My Generation* (ABC), 9/23/10–9/30/10
251. *No Ordinary Family* (ABC), 9/28/10–4/5/11
252. *Off the Map* (ABC), 1/12/11–4/6/11
253. *Criminal Minds: Suspect Behavior* (CBS), 2/16/11–5/25/11
254. *Body of Proof* (ABC), 3/29/11–5/28/13
255. *Happy Endings* (ABC), 4/13/11–5/3/13
256. *Switched at Birth* (ABC Family), 6/6/11–4/11/17
257. *The Protector* (Lifetime), 6/12/11–9/19/11
258. *State of Georgia* (ABC Family), 6/29/11–8/17/11
259. *Ringer* (The CW), 9/13/11–4/17/12
260. *Revenge* (ABC), 9/21/11–5/10/15
261. *The Chew* (ABC), 9/26/11–6/15/18
262. *Man Up!* (ABC), 10/18/11–12/6/11
263. *Once Upon a Time* (ABC), 10/23/11–5/18/18
264. *Jane By Design* (ABC Family), 1/3/12–7/31/12
265. *The River* (ABC), 2/7/12–3/20/12
266. *GCB* (ABC), 3/4/12–5/6/12
267. *Missing* (ABC), 3/15/12–5/17/12
268. *Scandal* (ABC), 4/5/12–4/19/18
269. *Bunheads* (ABC Family), 6/11/12–2/25/13
270. *Baby Daddy* (ABC Family), 6/20/12–5/22/17
271. *Perception* (TNT), 7/9/12–3/17/15
272. *Katie* (syn.), 9/10/12–7/30/14
273. *The Neighbors* (ABC), 9/26/12–4/11/14
274. *Nashville* (ABC), 10/10/12–5/25/16
275. *Malibu Country* (ABC), 11/2/12–3/22/13
276. *Zero Hour* (ABC), 2/14/13–8/3/13
277. *Red Widow* (ABC), 3/3/13–5/5/13
278. *Family Tools* (ABC), 5/1/13–7/10/13
279. *Mistresses* (ABC), 6/3/13–9/6/16
280. *The Fosters* (ABC Family), 6/3/13–6/6/18
281. *Twisted* (ABC Family), 6/11/13–4/1/14
282. *Devious Maids* (Lifetime), 6/23/13–8/8/16
283. *The Vineyard* (ABC Family), 7/23/13–9/10/13
284. *Spell-mageddon* (ABC Family), 7/23/13–9/11/13
285. *Lucky 7* (ABC), 9/24/13–10/1/13
286. *Marvel's Agents of S.H.I.E.L.D.* (ABC), 9/24/13–8/12/20
287. *Trophy Wife* (ABC), 9/24/13–5/13/14
288. *Betrayal* (ABC), 9/29/13–1/19/14
289. *Hello Ladies* (HBO), 9/29/13–11/17/13 (Finale special 11/22/14.)
290. *Once Upon a Time in Wonderland* (ABC), 10/10/13–4/3/14
291. *Killer Women* (ABC), 1/7/14–2/18/14
292. *Intelligence* (CBS), 1/7/14–3/31/14
293. *Mixology* (ABC), 2/26/14–5/21/14
294. *Resurrection* (ABC), 3/9/14–1/25/15
295. *Chasing Life* (ABC Family), 6/1/14–9/28/15
296. *Mystery Girls* (ABC Family) 6/25/14–8/27/14
297. *Young & Hungry* (ABC Family), 6/25/14–7/25/18
298. *Red Band Society* (Fox), 9/17/14–2/7/15
299. *black-ish* (ABC), 9/24/14–4/19/22
300. *How to Get Away with Murder* (ABC), 9/25/14–5/14/20
301. *Manhattan Love Story* (ABC), 9/30/14–10/21/14 _____ (Hulu), 12/4/14 (Final 7 episodes.)
302. *Benched* (USA), 10/18/14–12/30/14
303. *Galavant* (ABC), 1/4/15–1/31/16
304. *Marvel's Agent Carter* (ABC), 1/6/15–3/1/16
305. *Secrets and Lies* (ABC), 3/1/15–12/4/16
306. *American Crime* (ABC), 3/5/15–4/30/17
307. *Marvel's Daredevil* (Netflix), 4/10/15–10/19/18
308. *The Whispers* (ABC), 6/1/15–8/31/15
309. *Stitchers* (ABC), 6/2/15–8/14/17
310. *The Astronaut Wives Club* (ABC), 6/18/15–8/20/15
311. *Kevin from Work* (ABC Family), 8/12/15–10/7/15
312. *FABLife* (syn.), 9/14/15–7/27/16
313. *The Muppets* (ABC), 9/22/15–3/1/16
314. *Blood & Oil* (ABC), 9/2/15–12/13/15
315. *Quantico* (ABC), 9/27/15–8/3/18

316. *Grandfathered* (Fox), 9/29/15–5/10/16
317. *Code Black* (CBS), 9/30/15–7/18/18
318. *Dr. Ken* (ABC), 10/2/15–3/31/17
319. *Wicked City* (ABC), 10/27/15–11/10/15
     _____ (Hulu), 12/23/15 (4 episodes), 12/30/15 (final episode)
320. *Marvel's Jessica Jones* (Netflix), 11/20/15–6/14/19
321. *Shadowhunters* (Freeform), 1/12/16–5/6/19
322. *Recovery Road* (Freeform), 1/26/16–3/28/16
323. *The Family* (ABC), 3/3/16–5/15/16
324. *Of Kings and Prophets* (ABC), 3/8/16–3/15/16
325. *The Real O'Neals* (ABC), 3/2/16–3/14/17
326. *Criminal Minds: Beyond Borders* (CBS), 3/16/16–5/17/17
327. *The Catch* (ABC), 3/24/16–5/11/17
328. *Guilt* (Freeform), 6/13/16–8/22/16
329. *Uncle Buck* (ABC), 6/14/16–7/5/16
330. *Dead of Summer* (Freeform), 6/28/16–8/30/16
331. *Designated Survivor* (ABC), 9/21/16–5/16/18
332. *Speechless* (ABC), 9/21/16–4/12/19
333. *Notorious* (ABC), 9/22/16–12/8/16
334. *Marvel's Luke Cage* (Netflix), 9/30/16–6/22/18
335. *Conviction* (ABC), 10/3/16–1/29/17
336. *American Housewife* (ABC), 10/11/16–3/31/21
337. *Beyond* (Freeform), 1/2/17–3/22/18
338. *Legion* (FX), 2/8/17–8/12/19
339. *Marvel's Iron Fist* (Netflix), 3/17/17–9/7/18
340. *Imaginary Mary* (ABC), 3/29/17–5/30/17
341. *Guerrilla* (Showtime), 4/16/17–5/14/17
342. *Downward Dog* (ABC), 5/17/17–6/27/17
343. *Still Star-Crossed* (ABC), 5/29/17–7/29/17
344. *Marvel's The Defenders* (Netflix), 8/18/17 (Full season release.)
345. *The Good Doctor* (ABC), 9/25/17–
346. *Marvel's Inhumans* (ABC), 9/29/17–11/10/17
347. *The Gifted* (Fox), 10/2/17–2/26/19
348. *Kevin (Probably) Saves the World* (ABC), 10/3/17–3/6/18
349. *The Mayor* (ABC), 10/3/17–12/12/17
     _____ (Hulu), 1/9/18–1/25/18
350. *SMILF* (Showtime), 11/5/17–3/31/19
351. *Marvel's The Punisher* (Netflix), 11/17/17–1/18/19
352. *Marvel's Runaways* (Hulu), 11/21/17–12/13/19
353. *Encore!* (pilot, ABC), 12/10/17
     _____ (series, Disney+), 11/12/19–1/24/20
354. *grown-ish* (Freeform), 1/3/18–
355. *Alone Together* (Freeform), 1/10/18–8/29/18
356. *Sundays with Alec Baldwin* (pilot, ABC), 3/4/18 (Aired as *The Alec Baldwin Show*, 10/14/18–12/29/18.)
357. *For the People* (ABC), 3/13/18–5/16/19
358. *Station 19* (ABC), 3/22/18–
359. *Alex, Inc.* (ABC), 3/28/18–5/16/18
360. *Siren* (Freeform), 3/29/18–5/28/20
361. *The Crossing* (ABC), 4/2/18–6/9/18
362. *Marvel's Cloak & Dagger* (Freeform), 6/7/18–5/30/19
363. *Take Two* (ABC), 6/21/18–9/13/18
364. *All About the Washingtons* (Netflix), 8/10/18 (Full season release.)
365. *Harrow* (Hulu), 9/7/18–
366. *Single Parents* (ABC), 9/26/18–5/13/20
367. *A Million Little Things* (ABC), 9/26/18–
368. *The Kids Are Alright* (ABC), 10/16/18–5/21/19
369. *The Rookie* (ABC), 10/16/18–
370. *Good Trouble* (Freeform), 1/8/19–
371. *Schooled* (ABC), 1/9/19–5/13/20
372. *The Fix* (ABC), 3/18/19–5/20/19
373. *Bless This Mess* (ABC), 4/16/19–5/5/20
374. *Grand Hotel* (ABC), 6/17/19–9/9/19
375. *Reef Break* (ABC), 6/20/19–9/13/19
376. *Tamron Hall* (syn.), 9/9/19–
377. *Emergence* (ABC), 9/24/19–1/28/20
378. *mixed-ish* (ABC), 9/24/19–5/18/21
379. *Stumptown* (ABC), 9/25/19–3/25/20
380. *Godfather of Harlem* (EPIX), 9/29/19–
381. *The Mandalorian* (Disney+), 11/12/19–
382. *Dollface* (Hulu), 11/15/19–2/11/22
383. *Pick of the Litter* (Disney+), 12/20/19–1/24/20
384. *For Life* (ABC), 2/11/20–2/24/21
385. *High Fidelity* (Hulu), 2/14/20 (Full season release.)
386. *Little Fires Everywhere* (Hulu), 3/18/20–4/22/20
387. *Motherland: Fort Salem* (Freeform), 3/18/20–8/23/22
388. *The Baker and the Beauty* (ABC), 4/13/20–6/1/20
389. *Prop Culture* (Disney+), 5/1/20 (Full season release.)
390. *United We Fall* (ABC), 7/15/20–8/26/20
391. *Woke* (Hulu), 9/9/20–4/8/22
392. *Helstrom* (Hulu), 10/16/20 (Full season release.)
393. *The Wilds* (Amazon Prime Video), 12/11/20–5/6/22
394. *Call Your Mother* (ABC), 1/13/21–5/19/21
395. *WandaVision* (Disney+), 1/15/21–3/5/21
396. *The Falcon and The Winter Soldier* (Disney+), 3/19/21–4/23/21
397. *The Gloaming* (Starz), 3/21/21–5/9/21
398. *The Mighty Ducks: Game Changers* (Disney+), 3/26/21–11/30/22

399. *Home Economics* (ABC), 4/7/21–
400. *Rebel* (ABC), 4/8/21–6/10/21
401. *Big Shot* (Disney+), 4/16/21–10/12/22
402. *Marvel's M.O.D.O.K.* (Hulu), 5/21/21 (Full season release.)
403. *Loki* (Disney+), 6/9/21–
404. *What If . . . ?* (Disney+), 8/11/21–
405. *Queens* (ABC), 10/19/21–2/15/22
406. *Marvel's Hit-Monkey* (Hulu), 11/17/21 (Full season release.)
407. *Hawkeye* (Disney+), 11/24/21–12/22/21
408. *The Book of Boba Fett* (Disney+), 12/29/21–
409. *Judge Steve Harvey* (ABC), 1/4/22–
410. *Promised Land* (ABC), 1/24/22–2/21/22
_____ (Hulu), 3/1/22–3/29/22 (Final 5 episodes.)
411. *Moon Knight* (Disney+), 3/30/22–
412. *Who Do You Believe?* (ABC), 5/3/22–
413. *Obi-Wan Kenobi* (Disney+), 5/27/22–
414. *Ms. Marvel* (Disney+), 6/8/22–
415. *Everything's Trash* (Freeform), 7/13/22–9/7/22
416. *Five Days at Memorial* (Apple TV+), 8/12/22–9/16/22
417. *This Fool* (Hulu), 8/12/22–
418. *She-Hulk: Attorney at Law* (Disney+), 8/18/22–
419. *Bad Sisters* (Apple TV+), 8/19/22–
420. *Andor* (Disney+), 9/21/22–
421. *Reasonable Doubt* (Hulu), 9/27/22–
422. *The Rookie: Feds* (ABC), 9/27/22–
423. *Fleishman Is In Trouble* (Hulu), 11/17/22–12/29/22
424. *Criminal Minds: Evolution* (Paramount+), 11/24/22–
425. *Willow* (Disney+), 11/30/22–
426. *National Treasure: Edge of History* (Disney+), 12/14/22–
427. *The Watchful Eye* (Freeform), 1/30/23–
428. *UnPrisoned* (Hulu), 3/10/23–
429. *Tiny Beautiful Things* (Hulu), 4/7/23–
430. *Saint X* (Hulu), 4/26/23–

Tempest, The (film) The sorceress Prospera (the unseated Duchess of Milan) has spent 12 years perfecting her magic to avenge the foul play done to her and her young daughter, Miranda. Her journey spirals through vengeance to forgiveness as she reigns over a magical island while caring for her daughter and unleashing her powers against shipwrecked enemies. A Touchstone Picture/Miramax Film, released on Dec. 10, 2010, in New York City and Los Angeles, with a limited expansion on Dec. 17. The premiere had been at the Venice Film Festival on Sep. 11, 2010. Directed by Julie Taymor. Stars Helen Mirren (Prospera), Russell Brand (Trinculo), David Strathairn (King Alonso), Chris Cooper (Antonio), Alan Cumming (Sebastian), Ben Whishaw (Ariel), Reeve Carney (Prince Ferdinand), Felicity Jones (Miranda), Tom Conti (Gonzalo), Djimon Hounsou (Caliban). 110 min. Filmed in CinemaScope. The film is adapted from the William Shakespeare play, though the main character is changed from a man to a woman. It was nominated for an Oscar in Costume Design (Sandy Powell).

Temple, Shirley SEE BLACK, SHIRLEY TEMPLE.

Tempura Kiku Tempura bar in the Mitsukoshi restaurant in Japan at EPCOT Center; opened Oct. 1, 1982, with seafood, vegetables, chicken, and beef battered and deep-fried in the crisp tempura style. It became Tokyo Dining in 2007.

10–8 (TV) Hour-long drama series on ABC; aired Sep. 28, 2003–Jan. 25, 2004. As a graduate of the Los Angeles County Sheriff's academy, Rico Amonte, former Brooklyn bad boy, becomes a deputy sheriff trainee, but he is totally unprepared for the hazing he gets from his own department. And his training officer, John Henry Barnes, is the meanest, toughest veteran on the force, determined to hammer the rookie into a by-the-book officer of the law. Stars Danny Nucci (Rico Amonte), Ernie Hudson (John Henry Barnes), Indigo (Tisha Graves), Scott William Winters (Matt Jablonski), Mercedes Colón (Sheryl Torres), Travis Schuldt (Chase Williams). From Spelling Television and Touchstone Television.

10 Things I Hate About You (film) Bianca and Kat Stratford are sisters, but there the similarity ends. Bianca, a popular and attractive Padua High School sophomore, is unable to date until older sister Kat does so, but Kat is so ill-tempered she alienates any boy who might be remotely interested in her. So, Bianca and her hoped-for boyfriend concoct a scheme to match Kat with someone with whom she might be compatible. Directed by Gil Junger. A Touchstone film. Released Mar. 31, 1999. Stars Larisa Oleynik (Bianca), Julia Stiles (Kat), Joseph Gordon-Levitt (Cameron James), Heath Ledger (Patrick Verona), Andrew Keegan (Joey Donner), David Krumholtz (Michael Eckman), Susan May Pratt (Mandela), Gabrielle Union (Chastity). 97 min. Based on Shakespeare's *The Taming of the Shrew*, which is set in Padua, Italy. Stadium High School in Tacoma, Washington, became Padua

High for the film, and the Stratford family home was found nearby. Additional photography took place in Seattle.

10 Things I Hate About You (TV) ABC Family series inspired by the 1999 motion picture; premiered Jul. 7, 2009 and ended May 24, 2010. Walter Stratford is the overprotective father of Kat, a feminist looking to save the world, and Bianca, a girl planning to climb the social ladder at their new high school. With their contradictory goals, the girls start out on a bumpy year at Padua High. Stars Meaghan Martin (Bianca), Lindsey Shaw (Kat), Ethan Peck (Patrick Verona), Larry Miller (Walter Stratford), Nicholas Braun (Cameron James), Dana Davis (Chastity Church), Kyle Kaplan (Michael Bernstein), Chris Zylka (Joey Donner). Miller played the same role in the movie, whose director, Gil Junger, helmed the series.

Ten Who Dared (film) The film is based on the journal of Maj. John Wesley Powell, who led the expedition that made the journey, hitherto thought impossible, down the Colorado River through the Grand Canyon in 1869. It is both a reenactment of this historical scientific expedition and a dramatic story of the struggles, dangers, and conflicts of the 10 men who made the trip. Released Oct. 18, 1960. Directed by William Beaudine. 92 min. Stars Brian Keith (Bill Dunn), John Beal (Maj. John Wesley Powell), James Drury (Walter Powell), R. G. Armstrong (Oramel Howland), David Stollery (Andy Hall). Beal had years earlier done voice work for the animation in *So Dear to My Heart*. Songs in the film include "Ten Who Dared," "Roll Along," and "Jolly Rovers," by Lawrence E. Watkin and Stan Jones.

Tencennial Yearlong celebration for the 10th anniversary of Disneyland in 1965; included special entertainment, press tours, and the opening of Great Moments with Mr. Lincoln and the Plaza Inn on Jul. 18. A Disneyland Tencennial Ambassador, Julie Reihm, was selected to represent the park; she logged more than 52,000 miles in appearances across the U.S., Europe, and Asia. There was also a Tencennial celebration for Walt Disney World beginning Oct. 1, 1981, including a parade and the *Disney World Is Your World* show. SEE ALSO DISNEYLAND TENTH ANNIVERSARY SHOW, THE AND TENCENNIAL PARADE.

Tencennial Parade Ran in the Magic Kingdom at Walt Disney World Oct. 1, 1981–Sep. 30, 1982, celebrating the resort's 10th anniversary. Performers and themed floats represented each of the park's lands. Bob Hope was grand marshal for the first performance, with an additional 1,000 band members joining the lineup. Disneyland had celebrated its Tencennial in 1965 with yearlong festivities.

Tenderfoot, The (TV) Three-part show; aired Oct. 18, 25, and Nov. 1, 1964. Directed by Byron Paul. Natural dangers and warriors create problems for travelers in the West in the 1850s; a young man almost killed in a raid looks to a frontier scout, Mose Carson, for an education. They get involved in a plan to sell wild mustangs to the army. Stars Brian Keith, Brandon de Wilde, James Whitmore, Richard Long, Rafael Campos, Donald May, Christopher Dark, Judson Pratt.

Tenggren, Gustaf (1896–1970) Swedish sketch artist; he worked at the Disney Studio 1936–1939, illustrating early concept paintings for *Snow White and the Seven Dwarfs* and *Pinocchio*. For the former film, he created the design for the one-sheet promotional poster and illustrated several children's storybooks. His work gave these films a lavish European storybook flavor that Walt Disney had envisioned.

Tennis Racquet (film) Goofy cartoon released Aug. 26, 1949. Directed by Jack Kinney. Goofy's game of tennis confounds the sports announcer and the crowd, but one player does indeed win the gigantic trophy.

Tennisland Racquet Club Tennis courts at Disney's Vacationland Campground, across the street from Disneyland. It closed Nov. 1994.

Teppan Edo SEE MITSUKOSHI RESTAURANT.

Teppanyaki Dining Rooms Restaurant in Japan at EPCOT Center; opened Oct. 1, 1982. A number of guests sat together around a table where a chef prepared the stir-fried meal on a grill in front of them. It became Teppan Edo in 2007.

Terk Gorilla and best friend of Tarzan in the 1999 animated film; voiced by Rosie O'Donnell.

Terminal Velocity (film) A devil-may-care professional skydiving instructor, Richard "Ditch" Brodie, finds himself hurled into a world of international espionage and intrigue when a mysterious woman named Chris signs up for a parachute jump. During her initial free fall, however, the chute fails to open. But Ditch soon learns that nothing is as it seems—least of all Chris, who is revealed to be a former deep-cover KGB espionage agent. A Hollywood Pictures film. Filmed in CinemaScope. Released Sep. 23, 1994. Directed by Deran Sarafian. 102 min. Stars Charlie Sheen (Ditch Brodie), Nastassja Kinski (Chris Morrow), James Gandolfini (Ben Pinkwater), Christopher McDonald (Kerr). Filmed on location in Tucson and Phoenix, Arizona; San Bernardino, California, and the state's Mojave Desert; and in Moscow.

Terralina Crafted Italian Restaurant in The Landing at Disney Springs at Walt Disney World; opened Jun. 28, 2018, taking the place of Portobello Country Italian Trattoria. Authentic Italian dishes are served in an atmosphere inspired by Italy's Lake District.

Terrible Toreador, El (film) See El Terrible Toreador.

Terry-Thomas (1911–1990) Actor; voiced Sir Hiss in *Robin Hood*, a character given the same gap between his front teeth as the actor had.

Test Pilot Donald (film) Donald Duck cartoon released Jun. 8, 1951. Directed by Jack Hannah. Chip and Dale fight Donald over possession of his model airplane.

Test Track Attraction in World Discovery (formerly Future World) at EPCOT; it took the place of World of Motion. Soft openings began Dec. 1998, a year and a half after the original announced debut, with the grand opening Mar. 17, 1999. Guests experienced the exhilarating twists and turns in a General Motors test vehicle as it steered through the attraction in a demonstration of auto safety. At a length of just a fraction less than a mile from start to finish, the test track wound through the pavilion and then on a loop outside reaching speeds of up to 65 mph. Up to 6 guests sit in each vehicle. On Dec. 6, 2012, after an 8-month refurbishment, the attraction reopened as Test Track Presented by Chevrolet with a totally new look and focus on automotive design. In the Chevrolet Design Center, guests design their own virtual concept, then board a SimCar (simulation car) to learn how their choices perform against 4 performance attributes (capability, efficiency, responsiveness, and power) in an electronic world.

Test Track SIMporium See After Market Shop.

Tetti Tatti Impresario who harpoons the whale in *The Whale Who Wanted to Sing at the Met.*

Tex (film) Fifteen-year-old Tex McCormick and his 17-year-old brother, Mason, are trying to make it on their own in the absence of their rodeo-riding father. Mason takes over running the household and, to make ends meet, sells Tex's beloved horse, Rowdy. Tex gets mad at Mason and heedlessly tumbles into scrape after scrape. Released Jul. 30, 1982, briefly, then withdrawn and released again on Sep. 24, 1982. Directed by Tim Hunter. 103 min. Stars Matt Dillon (Tex McCormick), Jim Metzler (Mason), Meg Tilly (Jamie), Bill McKinney (Pop), Frances Lee McCain (Mrs. Johnson), Ben Johnson (Cole), Emilio Estevez (Johnny Collins). *Tex* represented the film debuts of both Meg Tilly and Emilio Estevez. The film is based on the novel by S. E. Hinton. It was an experiment by the Disney Studio to reach a new generation of teenagers who often abandoned Disney films for more "realistic" live-action fare, and this accounts for the PG rating. The movie represents a faithful adaptation of the novel where teen problems are confronted directly and honestly with no easy solutions or false hopes necessarily offered. Aware that Disney was seeking to broaden the content horizon of their films, it was director and screenwriter Tim Hunter who originally recommended *Tex* to the Studio, suggesting Matt Dillon (a fan of Ms. Hinton's books, which included *The Outsiders*) as the lead. Hunter viewed the association between Disney and Hinton as "a lucky convergence that compromises neither the book nor the Studio's high standards for family entertainment." But the experiment was not a box office success, despite the time, care, and talent that went into the production.

Texas John Slaughter (film) Theatrical compilation of several TV episodes. Released first in Malaysia in Apr. 1960. Directed by Harry Keller. In 1870, Slaughter rides into Friotown, kills 2 gunmen, and is asked to join the Texas Rangers. He initially refuses, but when his herd is stolen by the Davis gang, he becomes a Ranger fighting many spectacular battles with the gang. Eventually, Davis overplays his hand and dies by Slaughter's gun in the great climactic battle. 74 min. Stars Tom Tryon (Texas John Slaughter), Robert Middleton (Frank Davis), Norma Moore (Adeline Harris).

Texas John Slaughter (Episode 1) (TV) Show aired Oct. 31, 1958. Directed by Harry Keller. Slaughter is persuaded by circumstances to enlist in the Texas Rangers and to go after a local outlaw. Stars Tom Tryon, Robert Middleton, Norma Moore, Harry Carey Jr., Judson Pratt, Robert J. Wilke, Edward Platt. First episode of the series of 17 shows about a Texas Ranger. This was the longest miniseries to air on the Disney TV anthology show. Tom Tryon later went on to become a best-selling author.

Texas John Slaughter (Episode 2): Ambush at Laredo (TV) Show aired Nov. 14, 1958. Directed by Harry Keller. Gang leader Frank Davis is out on bail and being followed by Slaughter. Davis plans to divide the area into separate spheres of influence, each to be under a different gang leader, but first he yearns to get rid of Slaughter. Slaughter just misses being killed by gunmen and ambushed by Davis, but he manages to vanquish his foes. Episode 1 (titled *Texas John Slaughter*) and this episode of the TV show were edited together to become an international feature entitled *Texas John Slaughter*. Stars Tom Tryon, Robert Middleton, Harry Carey, Jr., Norma Moore, Judson Pratt.

Texas John Slaughter (Episode 3): Killers from Kansas (TV) Show aired Jan. 9, 1959. Directed by Harry Keller. Slaughter is wounded in a bank robbery but still goes after the Barko gang that was responsible. They are finally trapped at Slaughter's fiancée's house, and she barely escapes. Stars Tom Tryon, Lyle Bettger, Beverly Garland, Norma Moore, Harry Carey, Jr., Judson Pratt, Don Haggerty.

Texas John Slaughter (Episode 4): Showdown at Sandoval (TV) Show aired Jan. 23, 1959. Directed by Harry Keller. Slaughter and a group of Rangers pose as the Barko gang to get the confidence of a major outlaw. The deception works, but Slaughter has to duel with the outlaw and then steal their booty out from under their noses. Stars Tom Tryon, Dan Duryea, Beverly Garland, Norma Moore, Harry Carey, Jr., Judson Pratt.

Texas John Slaughter (Episode 5): The Man from Bitter Creek (TV) Show aired Mar. 6, 1959. Directed by Harry Keller. Slaughter has resigned from the Texas Rangers, but he still has to fight to keep his ranch's water supply and to bring a herd of cattle from Mexico. Stars Tom Tryon, Stephen McNally, Sidney Blackmer, Bill Williams, John Larch, Norma Moore.

Texas John Slaughter (Episode 6): The Slaughter Trail (TV) Show aired Mar. 20, 1959. Directed by

Harry Keller. Slaughter and a neighboring rancher agree to combine their herds on a drive to market and head down a new trail. After an attack by Native warriors and Slaughter's false arrest for murder, he hears that his wife is seriously ill, but she dies before he can rush home. Stars Tom Tryon, Sidney Blackmer, Bill Williams, John Larch, Norma Moore, Grant Williams.

Texas John Slaughter (Episode 7): The Robber Stallion (TV) Show aired Dec. 4, 1959. Directed by Harry Keller. Slaughter meets Ashley Carstairs and decides to help him capture some mustangs. But they didn't reckon on Jason Kemp, who tries to get rid of the 2 men. Stars Tom Tryon, Darryl Hickman, Barton MacLane, John Vivyan, Jean Inness.

Texas John Slaughter (Episode 7A): Wild Horse Revenge (TV) Show aired Dec. 11, 1959. Directed by Harry Keller. Slaughter continues trying to capture a wild mustang, while being opposed by a local rancher. Stars Tom Tryon, Darryl Hickman, Barton MacLane, John Vivyan, William Phipps, Bing Russell.

Texas John Slaughter (Episode 8): Range War at Tombstone (TV) Show aired Dec. 18, 1959. Directed by Harry Keller. Slaughter and his friend Ashley are accused of being thieves by a girl, Viola, but eventually they help her and her parents. A local cattleman battles them when they try to settle on land he covets. Viola turns down Ashley's proposal, but Slaughter begins to get interested in her himself. Stars Tom Tryon, Darryl Hickman, Betty Lynn, Regis Toomey, Jan Merlin, James Westerfield.

Texas John Slaughter (Episode 9): Desperado from Tombstone (TV) Show aired Feb. 12, 1960. Directed by Harry Keller. Slaughter is overjoyed that his children are coming to live with him, but neighbor Viola argues that the frontier is no place for a single father to raise children. A local cattle rustler is giving Slaughter trouble at the same time that his children arrive, so he has to juggle caring for them with trying to capture the outlaw. The kids find it hard to adjust, but they are attracted to Viola, and even Slaughter begins to fall in love. Stars Tom Tryon, Gene Evans, Regis Toomey, Betty Lynn, Brian Corcoran, Annette Gorman, Don Haggerty.

Texas John Slaughter (Episode 10): Apache Friendship (TV) Show aired Feb. 19, 1960. Directed by Harry Keller. Slaughter is looking for a mother for his children and woos Viola Howell. She will consider marrying but wants him to give up his guns; when he does that, he is set upon by an escaped outlaw, Crispin, while he is still unarmed. He finally takes up his guns again and manages to capture Crispin; Viola admits her mistake and the wedding is planned. Stars Tom Tryon, Gene Evans, Regis Toomey, Betty Lynn, Brian Corcoran, Jay Silverheels.

Texas John Slaughter (Episode 11): Kentucky Gunslick (TV) Show aired Feb. 26, 1960. Directed by Harry Keller. Slaughter saves a man from gunmen, only to discover that it is the former beau, Ashley Carstairs, of Slaughter's wife. Johnson sets up ranching in the area, but causes no end of trouble, with Slaughter constantly having to save him. Stars Tom Tryon, Darryl Hickman, Betty Lynn, Brian Corcoran, Allan Lane, Don Haggerty, Jay Silverheels.

Texas John Slaughter (Episode 12): Geronimo's Revenge (TV) Show aired Mar. 4, 1960. Directed by Harry Keller. Geronimo is an outcast from his tribe, hating the settlers, and especially Slaughter. He lures him away from his ranch in order to attack, but Slaughter's family manages to hold out until help arrives. Stars Tom Tryon, Darryl Hickman, Betty Lynn, Brian Corcoran, Jay Silverheels, Pat Hogan.

Texas John Slaughter (Episode 13): End of the Trail (TV) Show aired Jan. 29, 1961. Directed by James Neilson. Slaughter agrees to help the army search for the Apache, Geronimo, who has been terrorizing the populace, but he takes refuge in Mexico, where the army cannot follow. Slaughter lures him back across the border and eventually captures him. Stars Tom Tryon, Betty Lynn, Onslow Stevens, Harry Carey, Jr., Pat Hogan, Brian Corcoran.

Texas John Slaughter (Episode 14): A Holster Full of Law (TV) Show aired Feb. 5, 1961. Directed by James Neilson. Slaughter's cattle are rustled, and when the sheriff is powerless to do anything about it, Slaughter is elected sheriff himself. With a band of skilled deputies, he brings law and order to Tombstone, and eventually settles his feud with the cattle rustler. Stars Tom Tryon, Betty Lynn, R. G. Armstrong, Jim Beck, Robert Burton, Brian Corcoran, Ross Martin.

Texas John Slaughter (Episode 15): Trip to Tucson (TV) Show aired Apr. 16, 1961. Directed by James Neilson. The people in Tombstone are not happy with Sheriff Slaughter's harsh ways, but he enjoys the reputation, for it makes the outlaws fear him. He tricks his wife into going on vacation to Tucson, but it is really to catch a wanted killer. Stars Tom Tryon, Betty Lynn, Joe Maross, Jim Beck, Brian Corcoran, Peggy Knudsen, Annette Gorman.

Texas John Slaughter (Episode 16): Frank Clell's in Town (TV) Show aired Apr. 23, 1961. Directed by James Neilson. Some of the businessmen in Tombstone long for the return of the desperadoes Slaughter has run out of town, for they had helped the town's economy. A saloon keeper hires a notorious killer to kill Slaughter, but the sheriff finally wins the battle. Stars Tom Tryon, Betty Lynn, Brian Corcoran, Jim Beck, Robert Burton, Michael McGreevey, Ralph Meeker, Raymond Bailey.

Thanks (TV) Half-hour series on CBS; aired Aug. 2–Sep. 6, 1999. A satirical comedy skewering contemporary life as it looks at the venerable Pilgrims, whose landing at Plymouth Rock in 1620 literally got this country going. Stars Tim Dutton (James Winthrop), Kirsten Nelson (Polly Winthrop), Jim Rash (Cotton), Erika Christensen (Abigail Winthrop), Amy Centner (Elizabeth Winthrop), Andrew Ducote (William Winthrop), Cloris Leachman (Grammy). From Mauretania Productions and Touchstone Television.

Thanksgiving Day Mirthquakes (film) Shorts program; released by RKO in 1953.

Thanksgiving Promise, The (TV) Show aired Nov. 23, 1986. A boy must care for an injured Canada goose until it is ready to grace the table at Thanksgiving. However, he becomes attached to his new companion and must decide whether to break his promise or lose his new friend. Stars Lloyd, Beau, and Jordan Bridges (3 generations of the same family). Directed by Beau Bridges.

That Darn Cat! (film) A Siamese cat named D. C. stumbles upon the hideout where 2 bank robbers are keeping a woman bank teller prisoner. When the woman manages to slip her wristwatch around his neck, D. C. saunters from the hideout to the Randall family with whom he lives. When 19-year-old Patti Randall recognizes the wristwatch as belonging to the woman teller, the FBI is called in to watch D. C.'s every move. The young FBI agent working the case follows D. C., despite his allergic reaction to the animal, and in due time the bank robbers are collared and their prisoner is set free. Released Dec. 2, 1965. Directed by Robert Stevenson. 116 min. Stars Hayley Mills (Patti Randall), Dean Jones (Zeke Kelso), Dorothy Provine (Ingrid Randall), Roddy McDowall (Gregory Benson), Neville Brand (Dan), Elsa Lanchester (Mrs. MacDougall), Ed Wynn (Mr. Hofstedder), William Demarest (Mr. MacDougall). The film was a big Christmas release, grossing more than $9 million at the box office, due in part to a screenplay that was written by the original authors of the story *Undercover Cat*, Millie and Gordon Gordon, along with Bill Walsh, and a popular title tune written by Richard M. and Robert B. Sherman. One of the featured cats was actually Tao from Disney's *The Incredible Journey*.

That Darn Cat (film) Updated remake of the 1965 feature. Sixteen-year-old Patti Randall is totally bored with her sleepy hometown, but she awakens to feverish excitement when her tomcat, D. C. (Darn Cat), delivers an important clue in a mysterious kidnapping of a wealthy family's maid. With inept novice FBI agent Zeke Kelso at her side, she must track D. C. through all his favorite hangouts, hoping to solve the mystery. Directed by Bob Spiers. Released Feb. 14, 1997. 89 min. Stars Christina Ricci (Patti Randall), Doug E. Doug (Kelso), Dean Jones (Mr. Flint), George Dzundza (Boetticher), Peter Boyle (Pa), Michael McKean (Peter Randall), Bess Armstrong (Judy Randall), Dyan Cannon (Mrs. Flint), John Ratzenberger (Dusty), Estelle Parsons (Old Lady McCracken). Based on the novel *Undercover Cat* by the Gordons and the screenplay by the Gordons and Bill Walsh for the 1965 Disney film. Dean Jones, who starred as Kelso in the earlier film, returned for a role in this version. The star cat, Elvis, was discovered by his trainer, Larry Madrid, at the North Hollywood animal shelter. Elvis was actually selected because he was a perfect double for some other cats selected earlier, but Elvis turned out to be the star himself. And he hardly needed any doubles; he did 98% of the work himself. Edgefield, South Carolina, was selected to portray the fictional Massachusetts town in the movie, with the filmmakers even changing the town name to match the filming location.

That Was Then (TV) Hour-long series on ABC; aired Sep. 27–Oct. 18, 2002. Travis Glass, about to turn 30, and unhappy with his life, makes a wish during a lightning storm and is jolted back in time to when he was 16. He has a chance to try again to woo the girl of his dreams. Stars James Bulliard (Travis Glass), Tyler Labine (Donnie Pinkus), Kiele Sanchez (Claudia Wills-Glass), Brad Raider (Gregg Glass), Tricia O'Kelley (Sophie Frisch), Andrea Bowen (Zooey Glass), Bess Armstrong (Mickey Glass), Jeffrey Tambor (Gary Glass). From Touchstone Television.

That's How You Know Song from *Enchanted*; written by Alan Menken and Stephen Schwartz. Nominated for an Academy Award.

That's So Raven (TV) Comedy series on Disney Channel; aired in the U.S. Jan. 17, 2003–Nov. 10, 2007, after a Sep. 2, 2002, debut in Britain. Raven Baxter is a teen whose ability to glimpse flashes of the future often gets her into hot water as she tries to alter the course of future events. She is aided by her loyal best friends, Eddie and Chelsea. Luckily her parents and little brother are always there to set Raven on the right course. Stars Raven (Raven Baxter), Orlando Brown (Eddie Thomas), Kyle Orlando Massey (Cory Baxter), Anneliese van der Pol (Chelsea Daniels), T'Keyah Crystal Keymáh (Tonya Baxter), Rondell Sheridan (Victor Baxter). Raven was formerly known as Raven-Symoné. The show began airing on ABC's *ABC Kids* Saturday morning lineup on Sep. 20, 2003. The 2017 series *Raven's Home* is a spin-off.

Theater in the Wild Theater in DinoLand U.S.A. in Disney's Animal Kingdom; opened in 1998 with *Journey into Jungle Book* and next, in 1999, to *Tarzan Rocks*. The theater temporarily closed Jan. 2006 so it could be enclosed. It reopened with *Finding Nemo—The Musical* with previews in Nov. 2006. Also in Adventureland at Hong Kong Disneyland, featuring *Festival of the Lion King*.

Theater of the Stars Theater on Hollywood Boulevard in Disney-MGM Studios (now Disney's Hollywood Studios); opened May 1, 1989, with the show *Hollywood! Hollywood!* It closed May 2, 1993, and relocated to Sunset Boulevard, opening Jun. 15, 1994. The latest show, *Beauty and the Beast—Live on Stage*, debuted Nov. 22, 1991.

Their Eyes Were Watching God SEE OPRAH WINFREY PRESENTS: THEIR EYES WERE WATCHING GOD.

There You'll Be Song from *Pearl Harbor*; written by Diane Warren. Nominated for an Academy Award.

There's a Great Big Beautiful Tomorrow "Shining at the end of every day," which is how the song, written by Richard M. and Robert B. Sherman, begins. It was written for the General Electric Carousel of Progress built by Disney at the 1964–1965 New York World's Fair, and it followed the attraction when it moved to Disneyland. Due to a change in corporate philosophy at General Electric, however, the song was dropped when the attraction moved to Magic Kingdom at Walt Disney World in 1975. Instead, a new song, "The Best Time of Your Life," was commissioned. But by then, the original song was a favorite among many park goers, and its return in Nov. 1993 marked a historic moment for those who recalled the original show. The song was also heard in Horizons at EPCOT Center, as it had been removed from the Magic Kingdom when that attraction premiered. In 1998, the Sherman brothers returned to write a new version of the song, "There's a Great Big World of Innoventions," for the Innoventions attraction in Disneyland, which was built in the former carousel theater.

These Friends of Mine (TV) Series on ABC; aired Mar. 9–May 24, 1994, and began airing as *Ellen* Aug. 2, 1994. The series features a close-knit group of spirited singles who look out for each other. Stars Ellen DeGeneres (Ellen), Arye Gross (Adam), Holly Fulger (Holly), Maggie Wheeler (Anita). SEE ALSO ELLEN.

They're Off Goofy cartoon released Jan. 23, 1948. Directed by Jack Hannah. At a horse race, the expert bets on the favorite, Snapshot, and the novice bets on the long shot, Old Moe. After a series of racing misadventures, Old Moe wins by a nose when Snapshot turns his head to pose for the camera.

Thicke, Alan (1947–2016) Actor; appeared in *Raising Helen* (Hockey Cantor), on TV in *14 Going on 30* (Harold Forndexter) and the *Walt Disney World Very Merry Christmas Parade*, and on The Disney Channel as the father, Dr. Carson, in the Not Quite Human films.

Thimble Drome Flight Circle SEE FLIGHT CIRCLE.

Thimbles & Threads Apparel and accessory shop on Disney's BoardWalk at Walt Disney World; opened Jul. 1, 1996.

Think It Through with Winnie the Pooh (film)

Series of 2 educational films: *Responsible Persons* and *One and Only You*; released in Sep. 1989.

Third Man on the Mountain, The (film) In 1865, as young kitchen helper Rudi Matt climbs the unconquered Citadel, he rescues Captain John Winter, a famous English climber, and discloses that his father was legendary guide Joseph Matt, who, like many others, had tried to reach the top of the mountain, but was killed in the attempt. Despite his inexperience, he is chosen to scale the mountain with Winter, his Uncle Lerner, and Saxo, a guide from a rival village. Released Nov. 10, 1959. Directed by Ken Annakin. 107 min. Stars James MacArthur (Rudi Matt), Michael Rennie (Capt. John Winter), Janet Munro (Lizbeth Hempel), James Donald (Franz Lerner), Herbert Lom (Emil Saxo). Walt Disney's interest at the time in Switzerland (he took his family there on summer vacation) not only brought about this "Tom Sawyer in the Alps" (*Time* magazine), but later the popular Matterhorn Bobsleds attraction in Disneyland. Aired on TV in 2 parts in 1963 as *Banner in the Sky*, which was the name of the original book by James Ramsey Ullman. (Ullman happened to be vacationing in Zermatt at the foot of the Matterhorn while the film was being made, and the director gave him a cameo role as an American tourist, as he did with revered actress Helen Hayes, MacArthur's mother.)

Thirsty River Bar Opened in Asia at Disney's Animal Kingdom Dec. 22, 2015; themed as a base camp for Mt. Everest trekkers and serving specialty beverages.

13th Warrior, The (film) When an important emissary from Baghdad, Ibn Fahdlan, accompanied by his manservant, Melchisidek, is abducted by a band of Viking warriors, he is forced to join their quest and battle cannibal creatures legendary for consuming every living thing in their path. Ibn realizes he must conquer his fear and go to battle with the warriors or face being devoured as well. A Touchstone film. Directed by John McTiernan. Released Aug. 27, 1999. Stars Antonio Banderas (Ahmed Ibn Fahdlan), Diane Venora (Queen Weilew), Omar Sharif (Melchisidek), Vladimir Kulich (Buliwyf), Dennis Storhoi (Herger the Joyous), Sven Wollter (King Hrothgar). 103 min. Based on the novel *Eaters of the Dead* by Michael Crichton. In searching for the perfect northern setting, the filmmakers traveled extensively before settling on the north-central coast of Vancouver

Island, near Campbell River, British Columbia, Canada, at Elk Bay. Filmed in CinemaScope.

Thirteenth Year, The (TV) A Disney Channel Original Movie; first aired May 15, 1999. A young boy, Cody, begins to experience an unusual phenomenon as he approaches his 13th birthday. He gets scales and fins, begins to breathe underwater, and communicates with fish. Cody soon discovers the real reason for the unusual changes—he is the child of a mermaid and is transforming into a "merboy." Directed by Duwayne Dunham. Stars Chez Starbuck (Cody Griffin), Dave Coulier (Whit Griffin), Lisa Stahl Sullivan (Sharon Griffin), Brent Briscoe (Big John Wheatley).

This Fool (TV) Half-hour comedy series on Hulu; digitally released Aug. 12, 2022. Julio Lopez still lives at home, where he goes out of his way to help everyone but himself. The series explores his work at a gang-rehabilitation nonprofit and his quest to take on his codependency issues with his family as he navigates working-class life in South Central Los Angeles. Inspired by the life and stand-up comedy of co-creator Chris Estrada, who stars as Julio. Also stars Frankie Quinones (Luis), Laura Patalano (Esperanza), Michelle Ortiz (Maggie), Julia Vera (Maria), Michael Imperioli (Minister Payne). From ABC Signature.

This Is You SEE YOU (EDUCATIONAL FILMS).

This Is Your Life, Donald Duck (TV) Show aired Mar. 11, 1960. Directed by Jack Hannah, C. August Nichols. Walt Disney turns the show over to Jiminy Cricket, who presents a tribute to Donald Duck using a number of his cartoons.

Thomas, Bob (1922–2014) Author; wrote several books on Disney: *The Art of Animation*; *Walt Disney: Magician of the Movies*; *Walt Disney: An American Original*; *Building a Company: Roy O. Disney and the Creation of an Entertainment Empire*; and *The Art of Animation, from Mickey Mouse to Beauty and the Beast*, and its revision, *The Art of Animation, from Mickey Mouse to Hercules*. He was issued a special commendation at the Disney Legends ceremony in 2001.

Thomas, Frank (1912–2004) Animator/author; one of Walt's "Nine Old Men" of animation. He joined Disney in 1934 as an assistant animator, contributing to such shorts as *Mickey's Circus* and *Little Hiawatha*. He worked on *Snow White and the Seven Dwarfs* and went on to work on 18 more features, through *The Fox and the Hound*. Some of his most memorable sequences are Bambi and Thumper on the ice and Lady and Tramp eating spaghetti. He retired in 1978 but then embarked upon a writing career with his longtime friend and colleague, Ollie Johnston, turning out *Disney Animation: The Illusion of Life* (the ultimate treatise on Disney-style animation), *Too Funny for Words*, *The Disney Villain*, and *Bambi: The Story and the Film*. He was honored with the Disney Legends Award in 1989. He and Ollie Johnston were profiled in the documentary *Frank and Ollie*, made by his son, Ted Thomas.

Thomas, Jonathan Taylor Child actor; appeared in *Man of the House* (Ben), *Tom and Huck* (Tom Sawyer), and *I'll Be Home for Christmas* (Jake), and on TV in *Home Improvement* (Randy), *8 Simple Rules* (Jeremy), and the *Walt Disney World Very Merry Christmas Parade*. He voiced the young Simba in *The Lion King*.

Thomas O'Malley Alley cat who helps Duchess and her kittens in *The Aristocats*; voiced by Phil Harris. The cat's full name is Abraham de Lacy Giuseppe Casey Thomas O'Malley.

Thompson, Bill (1913–1971) Popular Disney voice actor, with characters such as the White Rabbit and Dodo in *Alice in Wonderland*; Mr. Smee in *Peter Pan*; Joe, Bull, Dachsie, and Jock in *Lady and the Tramp*; King Hubert in *Sleeping Beauty*; Uncle Waldo in *The Aristocats*; Professor Owl; and Ranger J. Audubon Woodlore.

Thompson, Emma Actress; appeared in *My Father the Hero* (uncredited, Andre's girlfriend), *Saving Mr. Banks* (P. L. Travers), and *Cruella* (The Baroness), and won an Emmy for her guest role in *Ellen*. She voiced Captain Amelia in *Treasure Planet*, Queen Elinor in *Brave*, and Mrs. Potts in *Beauty and the Beast* (2017).

Thor: Love and Thunder (film) The God of Thunder embarks on a journey unlike anything he's ever faced—one of self-discovery. But his efforts are interrupted by a galactic killer known as Gorr the God Butcher, who seeks the extinction of the gods. To combat the threat, Thor enlists the help of King Valkyrie, Korg, and ex-girlfriend Jane Foster, who, to Thor's surprise, inexplicably wields his magical hammer, Mjolnir, as the Mighty Thor. Together, they venture out on a harrowing cosmic adventure to uncover the mystery of the God Butcher's vengeance and stop him before it's too late. Directed by Taika Waititi. Released Jul. 8, 2022, also in 3-D and 3-D IMAX, after international releases beginning Jul. 6. Stars Chris Hemsworth (Thor), Natalie Portman (Jane Foster/the Mighty Thor), Christian Bale (Gorr the God Butcher), Tessa Thompson (Valkyrie/King of New Asgard), Russell Crowe (Zeus), Taika Waititi (Korg), Chris Pratt (Peter Quill), Dave Bautista (Dra), Karen Gillan (Nebula), Pom Klementieff (Mantis). 119 min. From Marvel Studios. Filmed in wide-screen format, primarily at Fox Studios in Sydney, Australia.

Thor: Ragnarok (film) Thor's world is about to explode. His devious brother, Loki, has taken over Asgard, the powerful Hela has emerged to steal the throne for herself, and Thor is imprisoned on the planet Sakaar on the other side of the universe. To escape captivity and save his homeworld from Ragnarok (the imminent destruction of Asgardian civilization) by the ruthless Hela, Thor must first win a deadly alien contest by defeating his former ally and fellow Avenger, The Incredible Hulk. Released Nov. 3, 2017, also in 3-D and IMAX, after an Oct. 25 international release. Directed by Taika Waititi. Stars Chris Hemsworth (Thor), Idris Elba (Heimdall), Cate Blanchett (Hela), Tom Hiddleston (Loki), Benedict Cumberbatch (Dr. Stephen Strange), Tessa Thompson (Valkyrie), Anthony Hopkins (Odin), Mark Ruffalo (Bruce Banner/Hulk). 130 min. Filmed in wide-screen format. From Marvel Studios.

Thor: The Dark World (film) Thor, the Mighty Avenger, fights to restore order across the cosmos, but an ancient race led by the vengeful Malekith returns to plunge the universe back into darkness. To defeat the enemy, Thor sets upon his most dangerous and personal journey yet, forced into an alliance with the treacherous Loki to save not only his people and those he loves but also our universe itself. Directed by Alan Taylor. From Marvel Studios. Released Nov. 8, 2013, after an Oct. 30 international release. Stars Chris Hemsworth (Thor), Natalie Portman (Jane Foster), Tom Hiddleston (Loki), Stellan Skarsgård (Dr. Erik Selvig), Idris Elba (Heimdall), Christopher Eccleston (Malekith), Ray Stevenson (Volstagg), Zachary Levi (Fandral), Jaimie Alexander (Sif), Rene Russo (Frigga), Anthony Hopkins (Odin). 112 min. Filmed is CinemaScope.

Thorne, Bella Actress/singer; appeared in *Alexan-*

der and the Terrible, Horrible, No Good, Very Bad Day (Celia), on Disney Channel in *Frenemies* (Avalon Greene) and *Shake It Up* (CeCe Jones), and on ABC in *Dirty Sexy Money* (Margaux Darling), with TV guest appearances in *Good Luck Charlie*, *Wizards of Waverly Place*, *K. C. Undercover*, *October Road*, *In the Motherhood*, *Speechless*, *Red Band Society*, the *Radio Disney Music Awards*, and the *Disney Parks Christmas Day Parade*. She voiced Birgitte in *Phineas and Ferb*.

Thornton, Billy Bob Actor; appeared in *Bound by Honor* (Lightning), *Tombstone* (Johnny Tyler), *An Alan Smithee Film: Burn Hollywood Burn* (as himself), *Armageddon* (Dan Truman), and *The Alamo* (Davy Crockett).

Thornton, Randy Supervising producer and music historian at Walt Disney Records, best known for his work digitally restoring the classic Disney soundtracks. With Walt Disney Records since 1986, he also produces their spoken-word projects and has been honored with many industry awards.

Those Calloways (film) New England trapper Cam Calloway, a poor provider for his wife and son, dreams of the day he can build a sanctuary for migrating geese. Using the money his son earned as a fur trapper, Calloway buys a lake and plants it with corn to attract the migrating birds. Learning that 2 rascally operators want the lake as a resort site, Calloway sets his corn afire, and then is shot by one of the operators. Later, with the area declared a sanctuary by officials, Calloway is able to see his dream realized when the geese come to the lake. Released Jan. 28, 1965. Directed by Norman Tokar. 131 min. Stars Brian Keith (Cam Calloway), Vera Miles (Liddy Calloway), Brandon de Wilde (Bucky Calloway), Walter Brennan (Alf Simes), Ed Wynn (Ed Parker), Philip Abbot (Dell Fraser), Tom Skerritt (Whit Turner), John Larkin (Jim Mellott). The cast includes Linda Evans as Bridie Mellott in one of her first film appearances. Most of the film takes place during the fall foliage season. After beautiful establishing shots were filmed in Vermont, some extra work was needed to turn the Disney Studio backlot, where the lake, Calloway cabin, and village were created, into a similar setting. Since California is not known for its fall colors, 280,000 hand-painted leaves and bushes had to be meticulously prepared to match the Vermont scenes. The film marked the only time the prominent film composer Max Steiner, of *Gone with* the Wind and Casablanca fame, produced a score for Disney. There were also 2 songs, "The Cabin-Raising Song" and "Rhyme-Around," written by Richard M. and Robert B. Sherman.

Thousand Acres, A (film) The saga of the Cook family, headed by the indomitable patriarch, Larry Cook. Cook's kingdom is a fertile farm that spans 1,000 acres, but the seeds of its destruction are sown when he impulsively decides to distribute it among his 3 daughters, Ginny, Rose, and Caroline. The apportioned land soon begins to divide the family. Long-guarded secrets, unspoken rivalries, and denied desires lay buried just beneath the surface and are unwillingly unearthed with profound, catastrophic, and ultimately liberating repercussions. A Touchstone film. Directed by Jocelyn Moorhouse. Released Sep. 19, 1997. Stars Jessica Lange (Ginny), Michelle Pfeiffer (Rose), Jennifer Jason Leigh (Caroline), Jason Robards (Larry Cook), Keith Carradine (Ty Smith), Kevin Anderson (Peter Lewis), Colin Firth (Jess Clark). 105 min. Based on the Pulitzer Prize–winning novel by Jane Smiley, who told the *King Lear* story from the outlook of the daughters. Although the story is set in Iowa, most of the location filming took place on several farms in the area of Rochelle, Illinois.

Threat Matrix (TV) One-hour drama series on ABC; aired Sep. 18, 2003–Jan. 29, 2004. To guard against terrorist threats, the Homeland Security Department has created a highly specialized, elite task force trained and equipped to counter anyone or anything that threatens our nation. The head of this supersecret team is Special Agent John Kilmer, who reports only to the president and has authority to call upon the technical skills, firepower, and specialist agents of the FBI, CIA, and NSA. Stars Jamie Denton (John Kilmer), Kelly Rutherford (Frankie Ellroy Kilmer), Will Lyman (Col. Roger Atkins), Kurt Caceres (Tim Serrano), Mahershalalhashbaz Ali (Jelani), Melora Walters (Anne Larken), Anthony Azizi (Mo), Shoshannah Stern (Holly Brodeen). From Touchstone Television and Industry Television.

Three Blind Mouseketeers (film) Silly Symphony cartoon released Sep. 26, 1936. Directed by Dave Hand. In their quest for survival, 3 mice continually outwit Captain Katt. While he is in pursuit of them, the mice get mixed up in a collection of bottles that serve to increase their number, confusing Captain Katt and causing him to be caught in his own traps.

Three Bridges Bar & Grill Table-service dining and central bar in Villa del Lago at Disney's Coronado Springs Resort at Walt Disney World; opened Jun. 10, 2019. It is a crossroads at the center of the resort lake, Lago Dorado, where guests enjoy drinks and shared plates.

Three Caballeros, The (film) Four short films on Latin America, in a story about Donald Duck receiving birthday gifts from his Latin American amigos: José Carioca, the parrot, and Panchito, the Mexican charro rooster. He unwraps a 16-mm projector and views *The Cold-Blooded Penguin* about Pablo Penguin who flees the cold for a tropical isle and then misses the winter. Then he views *The Flying Gauchito*, about a racing donkey with wings; *Baia*, in which Donald and José go to Baia, meet a cookie girl, and dance; and *La Piñata*, in which Donald learns of Las Posadas, the children's procession before Christmas, and finds friendly shelter and the breaking of the piñata. Interspersed throughout the film is live action of native dancing and Latin American songs being performed. The world premiere was in Mexico City Dec. 21, 1944; released in the U.S. Feb. 3, 1945. Directed by Norm Ferguson. 71 min. It was rereleased in theaters in an abridged version in 1977 at a time when the film had gained increased awareness because of its almost psychedelic sequences. Aurora Miranda, sister of Hollywood star Carmen Miranda, dances with Donald in the *Baia* sequence, showing how far the Studio had advanced the art of combining animation with live actors. This is the first time Walt Disney had attempted incorporating live-action characters in an animated scene since the Alice Comedies in the 1920s. Songs from the film include "You Belong to My Heart," "Baia," and "The Three Caballeros." Parts of the film were released separately as shorts and extracts appeared in the educational film *Creative Film Adventures, No. 1*, in 1976. The motion picture was nominated for 2 Academy Awards—Best Sound (C. O. Slyfield) and Best Scoring of a Musical Picture (Edward H. Plumb, Paul J. Smith, Charles Wolcott). See also Saludos Amigos, South of the Border with Disney, and Walt & El Grupo.

3-D Over the years, Disney has experimented with three-dimensional techniques for its films. The first cartoon made in 3-D was *Adventures in Music: Melody* (1953) followed shortly by *Working for Peanuts*. A *3-D Jamboree*, which was shown at Disneyland beginning in 1956. However, it took a quarter century before the next 3-D film was produced by Disney: *Magic Journeys*, for EPCOT Center, in 1982. It has been followed by other 3-D park films: *Captain EO*; *Jim Henson's Muppet*Vision 3D*; *Honey, I Shrunk the Audience*; *It's Tough to Be a Bug!*; *The Magic Lamp Theater*; and *Mickey's PhilharMagic*. Beginning with *Chicken Little* (2005), Disney perfected a new process called Disney Digital 3-D. It was used in 2006 for the first time to transfer a film originally released in analog 2-D into 3-D—*Tim Burton's The Nightmare Before Christmas*. The 3-D process is also used in the Disney parks in Toy Story Midway Mania!, Star Tours – The Adventures Continue, the Disney & Pixar Short Film Festival, Avatar Flight of Passage, and WEB SLINGERS: A Spider-Man Adventure.

3-D Jamboree (film) Special cartoon shown only in the Fantasyland Theater at Disneyland beginning Jun. 16, 1956, containing color footage of the Mouseketeers along with *Working for Peanuts* and *Adventures in Music: Melody*. Filmed in 3-D. Besides these, there were no other Disney 3-D films until *Magic Journeys* was produced for EPCOT Center over 25 years later.

Three Fairies Magic Crystals, The Shop selling illuminated crystals inside Sleeping Beauty Castle in Disneyland; opened Nov. 2006 in the original Castle Heraldry Shoppe. Relocated in 2008, taking the place of Geppetto's Holiday Workshop, as Wishing Star Magic Crystals.

Three for Breakfast (film) Donald Duck cartoon released Nov. 5, 1948. Directed by Jack Hannah. In their attempt to steal Donald's pancakes, Chip and Dale are fooled into taking rubber ones until they realize their mistake and trick Donald out of his meal.

Three Fugitives (film) Newly released from prison, former bank robber Lucas has decided to go straight. As he is trying to deposit his prison paycheck in a local bank, Ned Perry, an inept but desperate robber, stumbles into the bank and takes him hostage. Because of Lucas's notorious reputation, the police think he masterminded the robbery, and when Perry endangers everyone with a live grenade, Lucas reluctantly takes charge of the situation and engineers their escape. Released Jan. 27, 1989. Directed by Francis Veber. A Touchstone film. 96 min. Stars Nick Nolte (Lucas), Martin Short (Perry), James Earl Jones (Dugan), Sarah Rowland Doroff (Meg). Filmed in Los Angeles and in Tacoma, Washington. The prison scenes were shot at McNeil Island Prison, near Steilacoom, Washington.

Three Investigators and the Secret of Skeleton Island, The (film) A trio of young amateur detectives from Rocky Beach, California, go on vacation to Skeleton Island, off Cape Town, South Africa, where an amusement park is being built. But when the detectives arrive, they find a mysterious beast, known as Tokolosh, is wreaking havoc and causing terror among the construction workers. Directed by Florian Baxmeyer. Released in Germany Feb. 9, 2007. Stars Chancellor Miller (Jupiter Jones), Nick Price (Pete Crenshaw), Cameron Monaghan (Bob Andrews), Naima Sebe (Chris), Nigel Whitmey (Al Crenshaw), James Faulkner (Bill), Fiona Ramsey (Miss Wilbur). A production of Studio Hamburg International Production and Medienfonds in English, in association with Buena Vista International. Released in Germany as *Die Drei Fragezeichen und das Geheimnis der Geisterinsel*. Based on the 6th book in a lengthy series of 187 young peoples' detective novels set in the 1960s. The first of a planned trilogy.

Three Little Pigs (film) Silly Symphony cartoon released May 27, 1933. Directed by Burt Gillett. While 2 happy-go-lucky pigs frolic and build flimsy houses of straw and sticks, the third pig toils at building a secure brick dwelling. The Big Bad Wolf manages to huff and puff and blow down the first 2 houses but meets his match at the third. When he tries to slide down the chimney, he is scalded by landing in a boiling pot. When released in 1933, this cartoon not only strengthened Depression-weary audiences, who made the theme song, "Who's Afraid of the Big Bad Wolf?" their anthem, but it proved to be another milestone of Disney animation in the scope of characterization, as well as in score and song. Walt Disney, who entrusted Frank Churchill with the score for the picture and Fred Moore with animating the pigs, was justifiably proud, saying, "At last we have achieved true personality in a whole picture." The film became so popular that it often ranked higher on the marquee than the accompanying feature and often stayed long after feature films came and went. At one New York City theater, the manager had beards put on the pigs' faces that grew longer as the short's run extended. One of the most famous animated films of all time, it won the Academy Award for Best Cartoon. A major merchandising campaign led to many items featuring the Big Bad Wolf and the Three Little Pigs. The film is included in

Milestones in Animation (1973). The names of the pigs were Fiddler Pig, Fifer Pig, and Practical Pig. The writing of the song was reenacted in the TV show, *Cavalcade of Songs* (1955). The popularity of the film led to 3 sequels: *The Big Bad Wolf, Three Little Wolves,* and *The Practical Pig.*

Three Little Pigs (film) A 26-min. animated film made by Disney Television Animation and released in one theater for Academy Award consideration on Oct. 21, 1997. Directed by Darrell Rooney. When the Three Little Pigs allow Barnabas the Wolf, a professed vegan, to become their roommate, they quickly become paranoid after a series of misunderstandings that could only have one explanation—the Wolf intends to make the Pigs his protein source. Part of a Twisted Tales series, which included *Redux Riding Hood.*

Three Little Wolves (film) Silly Symphony cartoon released Apr. 14, 1936. Directed by Dave Hand. In this 2nd sequel to *Three Little Pigs*, the frivolous pigs blow the Practical Pig's wolf horn one too many times, and he refuses to come when they are actually captured by the Big Bad Wolf and Three Little Wolves. Practical Pig manages to save them in the nick of time with a "Wolf Pacifier."

Three Lives of Thomasina, The (film) Thomasina, a big, 4-year-old ginger cat, comes to live with widowed veterinary surgeon Andrew MacDhui and his 5-year-old daughter, Mary, in a little village in Scotland. When the cat is hurt, Andrew "puts her to sleep." Mary is so heartbroken she accuses her father of killing her beloved pet. So far as Mary is concerned, her father is dead, too. But Thomasina has not died. She has been discovered, still breathing, by Lori MacGregor, a mysterious young woman who loves animals and has an almost supernatural ability to cure their ills. Lori brings Thomasina back to life, eventually brings Andrew and little Mary together again, and becomes Andrew's wife and mother to the little girl. But it is really Thomasina, home again with the MacDhuis, who rules the family. Initial release in New York City on Dec. 11, 1963; general release on Jun. 6, 1964. Directed by Don Chaffey. 97 min. Based on Paul Gallico's story, *Thomasina*. Stars Patrick McGoohan (Andrew MacDhui), Susan Hampshire (Lori MacGregor), Karen Dotrice (Mary MacDhui), Matthew Garber (Geordie), Vincent Winter (Hughie Stirling), Finlay Currie (Grandpa Stirling), Laurence Naismith (Rev. Angus Peddie), and Elspeth March as the voice of Thomasina. Dotrice

and Garber were selected by Walt Disney for the major roles of the children in *Mary Poppins* after he witnessed their performances in this film. Shot at Pinewood Studio, in England, where the entire village of Inveranoch was built, with leftover sets from Disney's *Horse Without a Head.* The song "Thomasina" was written by Terry Gilkyson.

Three Men and a Baby (film) Happy-go-lucky bachelors, Peter, Michael, and Jack, live together in an avant-garde apartment in New York City. When Jack goes off on a trip telling his roommates to expect a package, the 2 are amazed to find a baby on their doorstep. Totally inexperienced at caring for a baby, Peter and Michael learn quickly and soon find themselves becoming very protective of "their" baby, as does Jack when he returns. Meanwhile, drug dealers who are after the real package threaten the baby's safety. The trio foil the dealers and arrange for baby Mary—and her mother—to live with them permanently. Released Nov. 25, 1987. Directed by Leonard Nimoy. A Touchstone film. 102 min. Stars Tom Selleck (Peter), Steve Guttenberg (Michael), Ted Danson (Jack), Nancy Travis (Sylvia). Filmed primarily in Toronto, with some sequences shot in New York City. A wild rumor ran rampant after the film's release and moviegoers caught a glimpse of what was reported to be a ghostly figure in the background of one shot. The rumor was that it was the ghost of a child who had lived in the house where the filming took place. The rumor was false. There was no house; the set was built on a soundstage, and the "ghost" turned out to be a prop left inadvertently where it could be seen in the shot.

Three Men and a Little Lady (film) A sequel to *Three Men and a Baby*, taking up the story 5 years later, with the 3 bachelors—Peter, Michael, and Jack—having settled into a comfortable functioning household with the little girl, Mary, and her single mom, Sylvia. Their 5-part harmony is shaken when Sylvia agrees to appear in a play in London, directed by the man she has decided to marry, and to take Mary with her to live there permanently. The 3 men soon discover how empty their lives are without Mary and go to great lengths to stop the wedding, bring Mary back to New York City, and, coincidentally, find the perfect husband for Sylvia. Released Nov. 21, 1990. Directed by Emile Ardolino. A Touchstone film. 100 min. Stars Tom Selleck (Peter), Steve Guttenberg (Michael), Ted Danson (Jack), Nancy Travis (Sylvia), Christopher

Cazenove (Edward), Fiona Shaw (Miss Lomax), Sheila Hancock (Vera). Filmed in the Los Angeles and New York City areas, and in London and Banbury in Britain's Cotswolds.

Three Moons Over Milford (TV) Hour-long series on ABC Family; premiered Aug. 6, 2006, and ended Sep. 24. After a meteor blasts the moon into 3 pieces, the town of Milford has never been the same with everyone worried that the next day may be their last. The residents begin acting peculiarly, throwing caution to the wind and acting on their wildest whims. Questions are raised as to whether Syndek, the mysterious conglomerate in town, is to blame. What if, with its high-tech telescopes and satellites, it set the meteor on a collision course with the moon. In any case, the Milford residents have decided to live for the moment, seize the day, make the most of every minute. Stars Elizabeth McGovern (Laura Davis), Rob Boltin ("Mack" McIntyre), Nora Dunn (Michelle Graybar), Sam Murphy (Alex Davis), Teresa Calentano (Lydia Davis), Samantha Leigh Quan (Claire Ling). From Three Moons Productions in association with Touchstone Television.

Three Musketeers, The (film) The classic story of the young D'Artagnan journeying to Paris to join the Musketeers, only to find the powerful Cardinal Richelieu plotting against them and attempting to make himself king. Richelieu is thwarted in this action by the 3 remaining Musketeers, Athos, Porthos, and Aramis. The cardinal dispatches the Count De Rochefort, a nefarious former Musketeer, to kill them, and arranges for his cohort, Milady De Winter, to travel to England to make a secret treaty with the Duke of Buckingham, the true ruler of England. On the young king's birthday, Richelieu plans to have him murdered, and rule himself with Queen Anne. The Musketeers and D'Artagnan come through, capturing Milady and then boldly gathering up the old Musketeer regiment to finally conquer Richelieu. Released Nov. 12, 1993. Produced in association with Caravan Pictures. Directed by Stephen Herek. 105 min. Stars Charlie Sheen (Aramis), Kiefer Sutherland (Athos), Chris O'Donnell (D'Artagnan), Oliver Platt (Porthos), Tim Curry (Cardinal Richelieu), Rebecca De Mornay (Milady De Winter), Gabrielle Anwar (Queen Anne). Based on the novel by Alexandre Dumas. Filmed on location in Austria.

Three Musketeers, The (film) Direct-to-video

Aug. 17, 2004, from DisneyToon Studios. Working as janitors at Musketeer headquarters, Mickey, Donald, and Goofy dream of becoming Musketeers. Peg Leg Pete, the Captain of the Musketeers, and his sinister lieutenant Clarabelle, have a dastardly plot to rid the kingdom of the Princess Minnie so Pete can take over the throne. Pete makes the trio official Musketeers and assigns them to "protect" the princess, assuming they will fail to get the job done. But, Mickey, Donald, and Goofy learn an invaluable lesson about friendship, teamwork, and the true meaning of "All for one and one for all!" Directed by Donovan Cook. Voices include Wayne Allwine (Mickey), Tony Anselmo (Donald), Bill Farmer (Goofy), Russi Taylor (Minnie), Tress MacNeille (Daisy), Jim Cummings (Peg Leg Pete), April Winchell (Clarabelle Cow), Jeff Bennett and Maurice LaMarche (the Beagle Boys), Rob Paulsen (Troubadour). 68 min. Later referred to as *Mickey, Donald, Goofy: The Three Musketeers*.

3 Ninjas (film) Three young boys who feel neglected by their FBI-agent father spend their summer learning the ways of the ninja from their grandfather. The old man also teaches them to rely upon themselves and each other. But when an evil arms dealer decides to kidnap the boys to keep their father from thwarting his illegal business deal, the boys dodge their kidnappers and realize that their family ties are just as important as their ninja skills. Released Aug. 7, 1992. Directed by Jon Turteltaub. A Touchstone film. 84 min. Stars Victor Wong (Grandpa), Michael Treanor (Rocky), Max Elliott Slade (Colt), Chad Power (Tum Tum). Filmed on locations in Los Angeles by an American, European, and Far Eastern crew. Two sequels, *3 Ninjas Kick Back* and *3 Ninjas Knuckle Up*, were made in 1994 and 1995 by TriStar.

Three on the Run (TV) Show aired Jan. 8, 1978. Directed by William Beaudine, Jr. Two brothers enter an annual sled dog race to try to match their deceased father's record. They eventually win, thanks to a grumpy bear who gives the inept dogs the incentive to increase their speed. Stars Denver Pyle, Davey Davison, Brett McGuire, Donald Williams, Ron Brown, Peggy Rea.

Three Orphan Kittens (film) Silly Symphony cartoon released Oct. 26, 1935. Directed by Dave Hand. Remarkable animation design and perspective was created by artist Ken Anderson for this cartoon, which tells the story of 3 castaway kittens who find refuge in a warm house and get into trouble with the occupant for their antics with the furniture and a grand piano. Academy Award winner for Best Cartoon. The film led to a sequel, *More Kittens*.

Three Skrinks, The (TV) Serialized version of *Emil and the Detectives* on the new *Mickey Mouse Club*.

Three Tall Tales (TV) Show aired Jan. 6, 1963. Directed by Hamilton S. Luske. Walt Disney explains about Baron Munchausen and his tall tales; then Ludwig Von Drake tells the stories of *Casey at the Bat*, *The Saga of Windwagon Smith*, and *Paul Bunyan*.

Three Without Fear (TV) Two-part show; aired Jan. 3 and 10, 1971. The 2 episodes are titled *Lost on the Baja Peninsula* and *In the Land of the Desert Whales*. Two Mexican orphans help save the life of an American boy, Dave, left stranded after a plane crash, who has also been bitten by a scorpion. The orphans are being tracked by an evil guardian, and Dave volunteers to help them. Narrated by Hugh Cherry. Stars Bart Orlando, Pablo Lopez, Marion Valjalo, Claude Earls.

Thrifty Pig, The (film) Shows the advisability and necessity of purchasing Canadian War Bonds. Footage from *Three Little Pigs* was reanimated, with the wolf as a Nazi and the pigs' house being made of bricks made from Canadian War Savings Certificates. The song "Who's Afraid of the Big Bad Wolf?" is used with new lyrics. Made for the National Film Board of Canada. Delivered Nov. 19, 1941.

Thrills, Chills & Spiders: The Making of Arachnophobia (TV) Syn. special aired Jul. 15, 1990. Directed by John Schultz. A behind-the-scenes look at the making of *Arachnophobia*, hosted by Mark Taylor.

Thru the Mirror (film) Mickey Mouse cartoon released May 30, 1936. Directed by Dave Hand. Mickey dreams he steps through his bedroom mirror into a land where all the furnishings and objects are animated and he can interact with them. But they are not all friendly, and after Mickey dances with the queen in a deck of playing cards, making the king jealous, they attack him and send him back through the mirror as the alarm clock wakes him up. Based on Lewis Carroll's *Through the Looking-Glass*.

Thumper Rabbit friend of Bambi's; voiced by Peter Behn (young) and Tim Davis (adult).

Thunder Alley (TV) Series on ABC; aired Mar. 9, 1994–Jul. 25, 1995. A divorced liberal 1990s mom is raising her 3 children in a household headed by her father, a crusty retired stock car racer. She experiences a clash of child-rearing styles when she and her children move in with her traditionalist father, in his home above the garage where he works—his refuge since his days on the track. Stars Edward Asner (Gil Jones), Diane Venora (Bobbi Turner), Jim Beaver (Leland), Lindsay Felton (Jenny Turner), Haley Joel Osment (Harry Turner), Kelly Vint (Claudine Turner), Andrew Keegan (Jack Kelly). After 8 episodes, Robin Riker took over the role of Bobbi. From Touchstone Television and Wind Dancer Productions.

Thunder Mesa Mercantile Building Frontierland shop in Disneyland Paris; opened Apr. 12, 1992, containing Bonanza Outfitters, Eureka Mining Supplies and Assay Office, and Tobias Norton & Sons–Frontier Traders.

Thunder Mesa Riverboat Landing Located in Frontierland in Disneyland Paris; opened Apr. 12, 1992. It is the port for the *Mark Twain* and the *Molly Brown*.

Thursday Circus Day on the 1950s *Mickey Mouse Club*. Discovery Day on the new *Mickey Mouse Club*. Party Day on the 1990s *Mickey Mouse Club*.

Tiana Restaurant entrepreneur who is turned into a frog in *The Princess and the Frog*; voiced by Anika Noni Rose.

Tiana's Bayou Adventure Flume attraction inspired by *The Princess and the Frog*; planned to open in Disneyland and in the Magic Kingdom at Walt Disney World in late 2024 as a replacement for Splash Mountain. Guests embark on a musical trip through the bayou as they help Tiana and Louis find a missing ingredient for their Mardi Gras party, meeting unexpected new friends who have a special role to play at the celebration.

Tiana's Palace New Orleans Square quick-service restaurant at Disneyland; planned to open in 2023, replacing the French Market. Inspired by Tiana's restaurant in *The Princess and the Frog*.

Tiburon SEE PEOPLE AND PLACES—TIBURON, SARDINIA, MOROCCO, ICEBREAKERS.

Tick Tock Diner A 1950s-style counter-service

restaurant in the Disney Ambassador Hotel at Tokyo Disney Resort; opened Jul. 7, 2000.

Tick Tock Tale (film) In this animated short, a quirky mantle clock is the laughingstock of the antique shop. But when the little clock foils a robbery, the unlikely hero proves that even imperfection can lead to something extraordinary. Directed by Dean Wellins. Premiered at the Annecy Animation Film Festival on Jun. 8, 2010. 6 min. From Walt Disney Animation Studios.

Tick Tock Toys & Collectibles Shop in Arendelle Village planned for World of Frozen in Hong Kong Disneyland.

Ticket books Disneyland began offering ticket books to guests on Oct. 11, 1955. The first books cost $2.50 for adults, $2.00 for juniors, and $1.50 for children for a day at the park and consisted of A, B, and C tickets for the different attractions. A D ticket was added in 1956 for attractions like Storybook Land Canal Boats, Tom Sawyer Island Rafts, and the Rainbow Caverns Mine Train. An E ticket followed in 1959 for more sophisticated attractions like the Disneyland-Alweg Monorail System, Matterhorn Bobsleds, and Submarine Voyage. In Jun. 1982, ticket books were phased out in favor of all-inclusive passports, good for admission and unlimited use of park attractions. Tokyo Disneyland continued to utilize ticket books until Mar. 31, 2001. Annual passports were available at Walt Disney World starting Sep. 28, 1982; at Disneyland they were first offered to Magic Kingdom Club members exclusively in Jun. 1983, but in the following year they were made available to all guests. SEE ALSO E TICKET.

Tickets Please (TV) Unsold pilot; aired on CBS Sep. 6, 1988. Directed by Art Dielhenn. Life of a group of regulars on the commuter trains of New York City. 30 min. Stars Cleavon Little, Marcia Strassman, Joe Guzaldo, David Marciano, Yeardley Smith, Harold Gould, Bill Macy.

Tie That Binds, The (film) A loving couple, the Cliftons, decide to adopt a child, and after visiting an adoption agency, they are immediately bewitched by a shy 6-year-old girl, Janie. But it turns out that Janie already has parents, the Netherwoods, who happen to be drifters and dangerous criminals. The Netherwoods appear to reclaim their child, and they will stop at nothing, including

murder, in their quest. The Cliftons are forced to fight for their very lives to protect their daughter. Released Sep. 8, 1995. A Hollywood Pictures film. Directed by Wesley Strick. Stars Vincent Spano (Russell Clifton), Moira Kelly (Dana Clifton), Julia Devin (Janie), Daryl Hannah (Leann Netherwood), Keith Carradine (John Netherwood). 98 min. Filming took place around the Los Angeles area.

Tieman, Robert Archives manager; joined the Walt Disney Archives in 1990 after several years as a photo librarian with The Disney Channel. He has spoken at Disneyana gatherings and on the Disney Cruise Line about the Archives' collections, and wrote the books *Disney's Photomosaics* (1998), *The Disney Treasures* (2003), *The Disney Keepsakes* (2005), *Quintessential Disney* (2005), and *The Mickey Mouse Treasures* (2007). He retired in 2010.

Tierra Incógnita (TV) Horror/mystery/adventure series developed in Latin America; digitally released Sep. 8, 2022, on Disney+. Raised by his maternal grandparents and his sister, Uma, Eric decides to run away from home and go back to his childhood town, Cabo Qwert, to find answers concerning where his parents were last seen: the Tierra Incognita horror theme park. Together with his friends, his sister, and his aunt, Eric must overcome his fears to solve the mystery in a dark and unfamiliar world. Stars Pedro Maurizi (Eric Dalaras), Mora Fisz (Uma), Tomás Kirzner (Axel), Carla Pandolfi (Carmen), Verónica Intile (Julia), Ezequiel Rodríguez (Roberto), Osmar Núñez (Santiago). From Non Stop and Disney+ Original Productions.

Tiffins Signature restaurant in Discovery Island at Disney's Animal Kingdom; opened May 27, 2016, serving international cuisine. Guests dine among lavish artwork themed to Africa, Asia, and South America, inspired by notes and field sketches produced by Imagineers during the creation and development of the park. "Tiffins" refers to a midday meal prepared for workers in India and the type of container in which their meals are served.

Tiger Cruise (TV) A Disney Channel Original Movie; first aired Aug. 6, 2004. Operation Tiger allows sailors to invite their families to ship out with them for a week to learn what their loved ones do in the military. But in 2001, when teen Maddie Dolan embarks on a weeklong tour with a mission to persuade her father, the ship's executive officer, to give up his military career and come home, she and other families are trapped aboard when the USS

Constellation is mobilized in full combat alert after the terrorist attacks of 9/11. Maddie thus sees first-hand her father's courage, honor, and commitment to those aboard his ship. Directed by Duwayne Dunham. Stars Bill Pullman (Cmdr. Gary Dolan), Hayden Panettiere (Maddie Dolan), Bianca Collins (Tina Torres), Nathaniel Lee, Jr. (Anthony), Mehcad Brooks (Kenny), Mercedes Colon (Grace Torres), Jansen Panettiere (Joey), Lisa Dean Ryan (Diane Coleman), Ty O'Neal (Danny Horner), Troy Evans (Chuck Horner), Gary Weeks (Lt. Tom Hillman). Filmed aboard the USS *John C. Stennis*, which was docked in San Diego, and aboard the USS *Nimitz* at sea.

Tiger Lily Princess in Never Land in *Peter Pan*.

Tiger Town (TV) The first motion picture created exclusively for The Disney Channel, on which it aired Oct. 9, 1983; the film had a brief theatrical release only in Detroit beginning Jun. 8, 1984. Twelve-year-old Alex is a die-hard Tigers fan who is convinced that a true believer can make anything happen. He idolizes aging baseball star Billy Young, who dreams of winning the pennant. When Alex is in the stands, watching and wishing, Billy suddenly begins playing flawlessly, and the Tigers draw closer to winning the pennant. Alex continues to believe in Billy, and the Tigers do indeed win the championship. Directed by Alan Shapiro. 76 min. Stars Justin Henry (Alex), Roy Scheider (Billy Young), Ron McLarty, Bethany Carpenter (Mother). Filmed at Tiger Stadium and at other landmarks in Detroit.

Tiger Trouble (film) Goofy cartoon released Jan. 5, 1945. Directed by Jack Kinney. Goofy and his elephant get into all sorts of trouble when they attempt to catch a tiger while on safari.

Tiger Walks, A (film) By accident, a mistreated tiger escapes from captivity while its circus wagon is undergoing repairs in a small country town. Never out of captivity, the tiger is hungry, frightened, and incapable of coping with this new way of life. Julie, the young daughter of the local sheriff, realizes that the gathering hordes of local hunters, the army, and her father's deputies will kill the tiger, who does not belong in the wilds but back in captivity. She succeeds in winning over her father; the animal is spared and returned to the only life it knows, but now at a local zoo. Released Mar. 12, 1964. Directed by Norman Tokar. 91 min. Stars Brian Keith (Pete Williams), Vera Miles (Dorothy Williams), Pamela Franklin (Julie Williams), Sabu (Ram Singh), Kevin Corcoran (Tom Hadley), Peter Brown (Vern Goodman). One of the highlights of this film is the truly extraordinary supporting cast, which featured such favorites as Una Merkel (Mrs. Watkins), Connie Gilchrist (Lewis's wife), Frank McHugh (Bill Watkins), Edward Andrews (Governor), Doodles Weaver (Bob Evans), Jack Albertson (Sam Grant), Arthur Hunnicutt (Lewis), and Hal Peary (Uncle Harry). This was Sabu's last film role. With sets built at the Disney Studio in Burbank, things got a little exciting during filming when at one point the trained tiger leapt through a sheet of plate glass that had been placed between him and the camera. But the trainers soon had him back under control before anyone was injured. Because of the serious subject matter and the unflattering look at small-town life, the film was only moderately successful.

Tigger Tiger character who first appeared in *Winnie the Pooh and the Blustery Day* (1968); voiced by Paul Winchell. According to Tigger, the most wonderful thing about Tiggers is that he is the only one.

Tigger Movie, The (film) As the gang is busy preparing a suitable winter home for Eeyore, Tigger interrupts their efforts with his boisterous bouncing. Rabbit suggests Tigger find some other tiggers to bounce with. Tigger thinks the suggestion absurd, since he is the only one, but then he decides that being the one and only can be kind of lonely. So he begins thinking that there must be other tiggers out there. This leads him on an amazing journey through the Hundred Acre Wood in search of the "biggest and bestest" family tree around. When his search proves fruitless, Tigger's pals try to cheer him up by masquerading as his family and dressing up in tigger costumes. This only serves to deepen Tigger's longing and he stubbornly bounces off into a cold winter storm to find his reclusive relatives. Pooh, Piglet, Rabbit, Roo, and Eeyore become concerned and form a search party to find him. In the end, Tigger's heart leads him home and he comes to realize that his family has always been with him—those friends who love and care for him. Directed by Jun Falkenstein. Released Feb. 11, 2000. Voices include Jim Cummings (Tigger, Pooh), Nikita Hopkins (Roo), Ken Sansom (Rabbit), John Fiedler (Piglet), Eeyore (Peter Cullen), Andre Stojka (Owl), Kath Soucie (Kanga), Tom Attenborough (Christopher Robin), John Hurt, (narrator). 77

min. Included are 6 new songs by Richard M. and Robert B. Sherman.

Tiki Juice Bar Refreshment stand outside Walt Disney's Enchanted Tiki Room in Disneyland; opened in 1968. Dole began sponsorship in 1976, offering pineapple juice and, beginning in the 1980s, Dole Whip. SEE ALSO ALOHA ISLE REFRESHMENTS (WALT DISNEY WORLD).

Tiki, Tiki, Tiki Room, The Song from Walt Disney's Enchanted Tiki Room at the Disney parks; written by Richard M. and Robert B. Sherman.

Tiki Tropic Shop Adventureland Bazaar shop in the Magic Kingdom at Walt Disney World; open Oct. 1, 1971–ca. 2000, selling casual apparel and swimwear accessories. Also in Tokyo Disneyland; open Apr. 15, 1983–Jun. 21, 2015, and succeeded by Jungle Carnival.

Tillie Tiger Character saved by Elmer Elephant in the 1936 Silly Symphony *Elmer Elephant*; voiced by Alice Ardell.

Tilly, Jennifer Actress; appeared in *The Crew* (Ferris), *The Haunted Mansion* (Madame Leota), and *Play It to the Bone* (Ringside Fan). She voiced Celia in *Monsters, Inc.* and *Monsters at Work*, Grace in *Home on the Range*, and Amanda in *Randy Cunningham: 9th Grade Ninja*.

Tilly, Meg Actress; appeared in *Tex* (Jamie Collins) and *Off Beat* (Rachel Wareham), and on The Disney Channel in *Avonlea* (Evelyn).

Tim Allen Presents: A User's Guide to Home Improvement (TV) Aired on ABC May 4, 2003. Directed by Andy Cadiff. Allen presents his own favorite clips, show bloopers, and personal reflections on the long-running series. Stars Tim Allen, Richard Karn, Debbe Dunning. From Touchstone Television.

Tim Burton's The Nightmare Before Christmas (film) SEE NIGHTMARE BEFORE CHRISTMAS, TIM BURTON'S THE.

Timber (film) Donald Duck cartoon released Jan. 10, 1941. Directed by Jack King. In payment for stealing food, Donald is forced by Pierre, alias Pete, to chop down trees, and he gets involved in close encounters with axes and saws, and a furious chase on railroad handcars.

Timberlake, Justin Actor; appeared in the *Mickey Mouse Club* on The Disney Channel beginning in 1993. He was later a member of the boy band *NSYNC. Other TV appearances include *Model Behavior* (Jason), the *Walt Disney World Very Merry Christmas Parade*, and *Mickey's 90th Spectacular*.

Time Flyer (TV) Title in 1986 of *The Blue Yonder*.

Time for Table Manners (film) Educational film; released in Sep. 1987. 6 min. The film teaches standard etiquette and cleanliness at mealtime.

Time Jumper, Stan Lee's Serialized digital motion comic; released on cell phones and the Internet beginning Jul. 24, 2009. Terry Dixon, a famed agent from HUNT (Heroes United, Noble and True) has a unique cell phone, The Articulus, which doubles as a time machine. Only Terry and his brother Sam can operate Articulus, but Sam is lost in time and Terry is searching for him. Hindering Terry's work is Charity Vyle, head of CULT (Council of Unstoppable, Lethal Terrorists), who wants the Articulus for her own schemes. Each episode is 5 min.

Time to Tell, A: Teen Sexual Abuse (film) Educational film; released in Sep. 1985. Adolescents in a peer support group share their experiences and learn how to protect themselves.

Time Traveler's Guide to Energy, The (film) Educational film; released in Sep. 1983. A boy from the future accidentally erases computer data on 20th-century energy history, so he calls upon a student to help him re-create it.

Timekeeper, The Tomorrowland attraction in the Magic Kingdom at Walt Disney World; opened Nov. 21, 1994. Inside the Metropolis Science Center, Timekeeper demonstrates his latest invention— a time machine—and in the process takes Jules Verne on an outrageous blast through time. Presents the Circle-Vision 360 film *From Time to Time* from Le Visionarium in Disneyland Paris, changing the language to English and adding in some U.S. footage. Voices include Robin Williams (Timekeeper) and Rhea Perlman (Nine-Eye). Closed Apr. 29, 2001, but continued to operate seasonally until it closed for good Feb. 26, 2006 (the last show had been Dec. 31, 2005). Originally known as Transportarium, the show succeeded *American Journeys* and later became Monsters, Inc. Laugh Floor. SEE

ALSO LE VISIONARIUM (DISNEYLAND PARIS AND TOKYO DISNEYLAND).

Times Square Studios Located at 1500 Broadway between 43rd and 44th Streets in New York City, this 46,750-sq.-ft., multiuse production facility opened Sep. 13, 1999. It spans 3 floors, including 2 studios, office space, extensive production support facilities, production control room, radio broadcast studio, green room, and dressing rooms. As the home for ABC News's *Good Morning America*, it features glass walls to utilize Times Square as a live backdrop. Along the exterior, the giant ABC SuperSign presents enormous media screens and curved LED news ticker ribbons, created under the design premise of "media as architecture."

Timmy Failure: Mistakes Were Made (film) Timmy Failure is a quirky, deadpan 5th grader from Portland, Oregon, who, along with a 1,500-lb. polar bear named Total, operates Total Failure Inc., a detective agency. Somewhat of an outsider at his elementary school, Timmy is clueless but confident and wants to see his detective agency become the best in the world. But first he must navigate the world of adults around him and figure out what it means to be normal when you know deep down inside you're different. Digitally released Feb. 7, 2020, on Disney+, after a Jan. 25 premiere at the Sundance Film Festival. Directed by Tom McCarthy. Stars Winslow Fegley (Timmy Failure), Ophelia Lovibond (Patty Failure), Kyle Bornheimer (Crispin), Wallace Shawn (Mr. Crocus), Craig Robinson (Mr. Jenkins). 99 min. Based on the children's book by Stephan Pastis, who cowrote the screenplay. Total is computer-generated, with a physical look based on a polar bear at the Canadian Polar Bear Habitat in Cochrane, Ontario. Filmed in wide-screen format in Vancouver, British Columbia and Portland, Oregon. From Walt Disney Studios.

Timon Carefree and wisecracking meerkat in *The Lion King*; voiced by Nathan Lane.

Timothy Mouse Dumbo's streetwise friend in the 1941 animated film; voiced by Ed Brophy.

Timothy's Treats Circus-car snack bar in Gardens of Imagination at Shanghai Disneyland; opened Jun. 16, 2016, serving hot dogs. According to the story, it is run by Timothy Mouse.

Tin Men (film) In Baltimore in 1963, 2 rival aluminum siding salesmen ("tin men"), Bill (BB) Babowsky and Ernest Tilley, start feuding when Tilley runs into BB's brand-new Cadillac. Their feud escalates until finally BB plays what he thinks is a winning card: he seduces Tilley's wife, Nora. BB's plan backfires because Tilley is glad to be rid of Nora, and BB finds himself falling in love with her. In addition to BB's and Tilley's personal struggles, the IRS is after Tilley, and both men face losing their licenses because of unscrupulous sales practices. But BB and Tilley are survivors, and together they face the future with new dreams. Released Mar. 6, 1987. Directed by Barry Levinson. A Touchstone film. 112 min. Stars Richard Dreyfuss (Bill Babowsky), Danny DeVito (Ernest Tilley), Barbara Hershey (Nora Tilley). Filmed on location in Baltimore, where Levinson had filmed his earlier film *Diner*.

Tin Pan Alley Tin product and magnet shop in the Downtown Disney District at Disneyland Resort; opened Jan. 12, 2001. Closed Jul. 1, 2002, with the product moved to Starabilias.

Tini: El gran cambio de Violetta (Tini: The New Life of Violetta) (film) International feature from Walt Disney Studios Motion Pictures. After returning home from a world tour, teen pop star Violetta finds herself at a crossroads. She accepts a spontaneous invitation to travel to a beautiful Italian coastal town, where she recovers from heartbreak and transforms into Tini, the woman and artist she was destined to become. The film was localized for markets around the world, debuting Apr. 23, 2015, in the Netherlands, followed by releases in France, Spain, Italy, and other countries, then digitally released Dec. 6, 2016, on Disney Movies Anywhere and other platforms. Directed by Juan Pablo Buscarini. Stars Martina "Tini" Stoessel (Tini), Jorge Blanco (León), Mercedes Lambre (Ludmila), Diego Ramos (Germán), Clara Alonso (Angie), Adrián Salzedo (Caio), Sofia Carson (Melanie). 99 min. From Gloriamundi Producciones. Filmed in Spanish, on location in Italy. Based on *Violetta*, the first original live-action series from Disney Channel Latin America and EMEA (Europe, Middle East, and Africa).

Tinker Bell Pixie character who tries to protect Peter Pan, modeled after actress Margaret Kerry (not Marilyn Monroe as frequently written). Tinker Bell began flying above Sleeping Beauty Castle preceding the *Fantasy in the Sky* fireworks at Disneyland in 1961. Contrary to frequent usage,

Tinker Bell is 2 words; in *Peter Pan* she is referred to as Miss Bell.

Tinker Bell (film) Animated feature; released on DVD on Oct. 28, 2008, by Walt Disney Studios Home Entertainment. The film had an initial release in theaters in Argentina on Sep. 11, 2008, and an exclusive theatrical release at the El Capitan Theatre in Hollywood for 2 weeks beginning Sep. 19, 2008. In Pixie Hollow, a secret hideaway deep in the heart of Never Land, Tinker Bell thinks her fairy talent as a "tinker" isn't as special or important as the other fairies' talents. But when Tink tries to change who she is, she creates nothing but disaster. With encouragement from her friends Rosetta (the garden fairy), Silvermist (an upbeat water fairy), Fawn (a rascally animal fairy), and Iridessa (a perfectionist light fairy), Tink learns the key to solving her problems lies in her unique tinker abilities and discovers that, when she's true to herself, magical things can happen. Directed by Bradley Raymond. Voices include Mae Whitman (Tinker Bell), Kristin Chenoweth (Rosetta), America Ferrera (Fawn), Lucy Liu (Silvermist), Raven-Symoné (Iridessa), Jesse McCartney (Terence), Anjelica Huston (Queen Clarion). Produced by DisneyToon Studios. The first of a series of films featuring the Disney Fairies.

Tinker Bell & Friends Fairy costume, jewelry, and souvenir shop inside Sleeping Beauty Castle at Disneyland; opened in 2006, taking the place of the Disneyland 50th Anniversary Shop. It became the Enchanted Chamber in 2008.

Tinker Bell and the Great Fairy Rescue (film) Exclusive engagement at the El Capitan Theatre in Hollywood, beginning Sep. 3, 2010; DVD release on Sep. 21, 2010. There were earlier international theatrical releases, beginning with Hungary on Jul. 29, 2010. Before she was ever introduced to Wendy and the Lost Boys, Tinker Bell met Lizzy, a girl with a steadfast belief in fairies. In the summertime in the beautiful English countryside, Tinker Bell has an enchanting encounter when she is discovered by Lizzy, and as their different worlds unite, Tink develops a special bond with the curious girl in need of a friend. Directed by Bradley Raymond. Voices include Mae Whitman (Tinker Bell), Michael Sheen (Dr. Griffiths), Kristin Chenoweth (Rosetta), Lucy Liu (Silvermist), Raven-Symoné (Iridessa), Jesse McCartney (Terence), Lauren Mote (Lizzy). 76 min. From DisneyToon Studios.

Tinker Bell and the Legend of the NeverBeast (film) Released on Blu-ray Mar. 3, 2015, after a theatrical release in the United Kingdom Dec. 12, 2014, and a run at the El Capitan Theatre in Hollywood beginning Jan. 30, 2015. An ancient myth of a massive creature sparks the curiosity of Tinker Bell and her good friend Fawn, an animal fairy who is not afraid to break the rules to help an animal in need. But this creature is not welcome in Pixie Hollow— and the scout fairies are determined to capture the mysterious beast, who they fear will destroy their home. Fawn must convince her fairy friends to risk everything to rescue the NeverBeast. Voices include Mae Whitman (Tinker Bell), Ginnifer Goodwin (Fawn), Rosario Dawson (Nix), Anjelica Huston (Queen Clarion). Produced by Disney-Toon Studios.

Tinker Bell and the Lost Treasure (film) Direct-to-DVD release Oct. 27, 2009; 2nd film in the series on the Disney Fairies, after a one-week run at the El Capitan Theatre in Hollywood beginning Oct. 16. In autumn, as the fairies on the mainland are changing the colors of the leaves and helping geese fly south for the winter, Tinker Bell accidentally puts all of Pixie Hollow in jeopardy. She must venture out across the sea on a secret quest to set things right. Along her journey Tink meets new friends, including Blaze, a cute and courageous firefly that helps Tinker Bell complete her mission. Directed by Klay Hall. Voices include Mae Whitman (Tinker Bell), Kristin Chenoweth (Rosetta), Lucy Liu (Silvermist), Raven-Symoné (Iridessa), Jesse McCartney (Terence), Anjelica Huston (Queen Clarion), Angela Bartys (Fawn), Eliza Pollack Zebert (Blaze). From DisneyToon Studios.

Tinker Bell and the Mysterious Winter Woods SEE SECRET OF THE WINGS.

Tinker Bell and the Pirate Fairy SEE PIRATE FAIRY, THE.

Tinker Bell Gifts Disney Fairies–themed shop in the Shanghai Disneyland Hotel; opened Jun. 16, 2016, offering collectibles, apparel, and sundries.

Tinker Bell Toy Shoppe Fantasyland shop in Disneyland; opened in 1957, and became Once Upon a Time . . . The Disney Princess Shoppe in Jul. 2002. Once Upon a Time closed Jan. 4, 2009, to become Bibbidi Bobbidi Boutique. Also opened in Fantasyland in the Magic Kingdom at Walt Disney World Nov. 1971 and became Tinker Bell's Treasures Dec. 6, 1992. In Nov. 2008, the Walt Disney World shop was divided into 2 new shops: Tinker Bell's Fairy Treasures and Castle Couture. Tinker Bell's Fairy Treasures closed Feb. 2010 to become part of Castle Couture. Also in Fantasyland at Tokyo Disneyland; open Apr. 15, 1983–2001, and succeeded by Baby Mine.

Tinker Bell's Treasures SEE TINKER BELL TOY SHOPPE.

Tiny Beautiful Things (TV) Half-hour comedy series planned for digital release on Hulu Apr. 7, 2023. When an old writing pal asks Clare, a foundering writer whose own life is falling apart, to take over as the advice columnist Dear Sugar, Clare thinks she has no business giving anyone advice. She reluctantly accepts, and her life unfurls in a complex fabric of memory, excavating the beauty, struggle, and humor in her unhealed wounds. Stars Kathryn Hahn (Clare), Sarah Pidgeon, Quentin Plair, Tanzyn Crawford. Based on the collection of advice columns by Cheryl Strayed. From ABC Signature and Hello Sunshine.

Tisdale, Ashley Actress; appeared as Sharpay Evans in the High School Musical films and *Sharpay's Fabulous Adventure*. Also on Disney Channel in *The Suite Life of Zack & Cody* and *Hannah Montana* (Maddie Fitzpatrick), and on Disney+ in *Becoming*, with additional TV appearances in *Young & Hungry* (Logan Rawlings), *FABLife*, the *Radio Disney Music Awards*, *The Disney Family Singalong*, and *Tamron Hall*. She voiced a Blueberry Troop scout in *A Bug's Life*, Candace Flynn in *Phineas and Ferb*, and Camille Leon in *Kim Possible*.

Title Makers, The/Nature's Half Acre (TV) Show aired Jun. 11, 1961. Directed by Robert Stevenson, James Algar. The show explains how Bill Justice, X Atencio, and T. Hee prepared the titles for *The Parent Trap* by using stop-motion animation, and how Tommy Sands and Annette Funicello recorded the title song. The end of the program shows the True-Life Adventure film *Nature's Half Acre*.

Tito Frenetic little Chihuahua in *Oliver & Company*; voiced by Cheech Marin. His full name is Ignacio Alonzo Julio Federico De Tito.

To Conquer the Mountain (TV) Show; part 1 of *Banner in the Sky*, the airing of *Third Man on the Mountain*.

To My Daughter, with Love (TV) Two-hour movie on NBC; first aired Jan. 24, 1994. A young father's tragic loss of his wife turns to crisis when his in-laws try to take custody of his child. Directed by Kevin Hooks. Stars Rick Schroder (Joey), Lawrence Pressman (Arthur), Khandi Alexander (Harriet), Megan Gallivan (Alice), Keith Amos (Tim), Ashley Malinger (Emily), Linda Gray (Eleanor). From Steve White Productions and Walt Disney Television.

To the South Pole for Science (TV) Show aired Nov. 13, 1957. Directed and narrated by Winston Hibler. The program shows how scientists struggled to construct 5 bases in Antarctica during the International Geophysical Year. The other shows on the subject were *Antarctica: Past and Present* and *Antarctica—Operation Deepfreeze*.

To Trap a Thief (TV) Episode 1 of *Michael O'Hara the Fourth*.

Toad Hall Restaurant Fantasyland counter-service restaurant in Disneyland Paris; opened Apr. 12, 1992, serving traditional British fare.

Tobacconist Main Street, U.S.A. shop in Disneyland; opened Jul. 17, 1955, and closed Jun. 3, 1990, to become Patented Pastimes. Also in the Magic Kingdom at Walt Disney World; opened Oct. 1, 1971, and closed in 1985, to become Main Street Stationers.

Toby Overgrown puppy in *The Great Mouse Detective*.

Toby Tortoise Plodding but persistent star of *The Tortoise and the Hare* (1935) and its sequel, *Toby Tortoise Returns* (1936).

Toby Tortoise Returns (film) Silly Symphony cartoon released Aug. 22, 1936. Directed by Wilfred Jackson. Max Hare and Toby Tortoise are opponents in a boxing match. Max becomes frustrated when Toby retreats into his shell during punches. Max cheats by dumping fireworks into Toby's shell, but the plan backfires when it helps Toby win. A sequel to *The Tortoise and the Hare*.

Toby Turtle Shy friend of Skippy's in *Robin Hood*; voiced by Richie Sanders.

Toby Tyler, or Ten Weeks with a Circus (film) Toby, a 12-year-old orphan, believing his aunt and uncle do not want him, runs away and joins a circus. He is exploited by Harry, the concessionaire, helped by Ben, the strong man, and becomes fast friends with Mr. Stubbs, the chimp. When the boy equestrian is hurt, Toby takes his place, becoming a tremendous success when Mr. Stubbs joins the act. He is reunited with his now understanding guardians. Released Jan. 21, 1960. Directed by Charles Barton. 95 min. Stars Kevin Corcoran (Toby Tyler), Bob Sweeney (Harry Tupper), Henry Calvin (Ben Cotter), Gene Sheldon (Sam Treat), Barbara Beaird (Mademoiselle Jeanette). Note the final credits INTRODUCING OLLIE WALLACE. This referred to the circus bandleader, played by the veteran Disney composer. Based on the novel by James Otis Kaler. Disney donated the authentic, restored circus wagons used in the film to the Circus World Museum in Baraboo, Wisconsin.

Toccata and Fugue in D Minor Music composed by Johann Sebastian Bach; a segment of *Fantasia*. The piece was also played on the organ by Captain Nemo in his parlor in the *Nautilus* in *20,000 Leagues Under the Sea*.

Tod Lead fox character in *The Fox and the Hound*; voiced by Keith Mitchell (young) and Mickey Rooney (adult).

Today's Business (TV) Syn. show; aired Sep. 26, 1986–Apr. 26, 1987. Consuelo Mack anchored this daily early morning business news show.

Todd, Richard (1919–2009) Actor; appeared in the leading roles in *The Story of Robin Hood* (Robin Hood), *The Sword and the Rose* (Charles Brandon), and *Rob Roy* (Rob Roy). He was named a Disney Legend in 2002.

Togetherville Social network for school children up to age 13, acquired by Disney on Feb. 18, 2011, and discontinued the following year. It was founded by Mandeep S. Dhillon.

Togo (film) The untold true story of one of the greatest sled dogs in history. In the winter of 1925, when a deadly epidemic strikes the town of Nome, Alaska, and the only cure is more than 600 miles away, the town looks to champion dogsled trainer Leonhard Seppala to help transport an antitoxin serum. Seppala turns to Togo, an unassuming, undersized, and aging Siberian husky, to be his lead. Undaunted by the massive storm heading their way or his wife's urging him not to go, Seppala and Togo set out on the deadliest leg of what becomes a larger relay involving multiple mushers, gale-force winds, subfreezing temperatures, and little-to-no visibility. Digitally released Dec. 20, 2019, on Disney+. Directed by Ericson Core. 113 min. Stars Willem Dafoe (Leonhard Seppala), Julianne Nicholson (Constance Seppala), Christopher Heyerdahl (George Maynard), Richard Dormer (Dr. Curtis Welch), Michael Greyeyes (Amituck), Michael McElhatton (Jafet Lindberg), Michael Gaston (Joe Dexter). In their search to find a dog to play Togo, an agouti-colored Siberian husky, filmmakers discovered Diesel, a 5-year-old dog with sledding training and a direct descendant of Togo, with paperwork to prove it. Filmed in wide-screen format on location in Alberta, Canada, with temperatures dropping to 50 degrees below zero.

Tokar, Norman (1920–1979) Prolific director of Disney live-action films; signed by the Disney Studio in 1961 to direct *Big Red*, he remained from then until his death in 1979. Among his films were *Savage Sam*; *A Tiger Walks*; *Those Calloways*; *The Ugly Dachshund*; *Follow Me, Boys!*; *The Happiest Millionaire*; *Candleshoe*; *The Cat from Outer Space*; *No Deposit, No Return*; *The Apple Dumpling Gang*; *Snowball Express*; *The Boatniks*; *Rascal*; and *The Horse in the Gray Flannel Suit*, plus the featurette *The Legend of the Boy and the Eagle*.

Tokyo Dining Contemporary table-service restaurant in Japan at EPCOT; opened Oct. 19, 2007, replacing Tempura Kiku and Matsu No Ma Lounge. SEE MITSUKOSHI RESTAURANT.

Tokyo Disney Celebration Hotel Value-level hotel in the Shin-Urayasu area near Tokyo Disney Resort, with 702 guest rooms. There are 2 themed buildings—the Wish (opened Jun. 1, 2016) and the Discover (Sep. 10, 2016)—with lobby furnishings, art displays, and garden features inspired by attractions and entertainment at Tokyo Disneyland and Tokyo DisneySea. Dining is available at the Wish Cafe and Discover Cafe. It replaced the former Palm and Fountain Terrace Hotel (which had opened Feb. 2005), joining 3 other Disney hotels in Japan. Managed and operated by Brighton Corporation Co., Ltd.

Tokyo Disney Resort A 494-acre resort complex 6 miles east of downtown Tokyo, owned and operated by Oriental Land Co., Ltd. (OLC). In Apr. 1979, OLC and Walt Disney Productions concluded an agreement on the licensing, design, construction, and operation of Tokyo Disneyland, which opened Apr. 15, 1983. The resort expanded in 2000, with the opening of the Disney Ambassador Hotel and Ikspiari, a dining and entertainment complex. A second theme park oriented more toward adults, Tokyo DisneySea, debuted in 2001, along with the Tokyo DisneySea Hotel MiraCosta, Disney Resort Line monorail system, and Bon Voyage outlet at Maihama Station. The Tokyo Disneyland Hotel was added in 2008, followed by the Tokyo Disney Celebration Hotel in 2016. Six additional hotels are operated by other third parties. The Tokyo Disney Resort Toy Story Hotel opened Apr. 5, 2022, and the 475-room Tokyo DisneySea Fantasy Springs Hotel is set to follow in 2024, connecting to the new Fantasy Springs area in Tokyo DisneySea. SEE ALSO TOKYO DISNEYLAND.

Tokyo Disney Resort Toy Story Hotel An 11-floor themed hotel near Bayside Station at Tokyo Disney Resort; opened Apr. 5, 2022. With 595 guest rooms, it is the first moderate-level Disney hotel at the resort. Guests can dine at the Lotso Garden Cafe, shop at Gift Planet and Shop Together, and pose with oversized *Toy Story* characters in Slinky Dog Park and Toy Friends Square. The guest rooms are inspired by Andy's bedroom, with toylike furnishings.

Tokyo Disneyland Park opened Apr. 15, 1983, in Urayasu, just outside of Tokyo. In the 1970s, after the success of the then 2 American Disney parks, many different countries made entreaties to Disney about building their own Disneyland. It was only after Disneyland and Walt Disney World were running smoothly that the Disney executives decided to consider some of the requests. Japan's request seemed eminently feasible. The Oriental Land Company had some land, reclaimed from Tokyo Bay, which had to be used for recreational purposes, and there was a huge local population within a 30-mile radius. A Disneyland would be an ideal fit for the site. Japanese audiences had long been enamored with Disneyland, and when contracts were signed, it was determined that they did not want a Japanese version of Disneyland; they wanted a distinctly American park. So, Disney Imagineers worked carefully to design an ideal park for the site, combining some of the best features from both Disneyland and the Magic Kingdom at Walt Disney World, including a replica of Cinderella Castle. Because of the locale's more inclement weather, Main Street, U.S.A. was redesigned as World Bazaar, with a Victorian-style

roof over it. The other themed lands are Adventureland (which includes its own New Orleans Square–themed area), Westernland (an adaptation of Frontierland, with Camp Woodchuck added Nov. 22, 2016), Critter Country (added Oct. 1, 1992), Fantasyland (which expanded with a *Beauty and the Beast* area in 2020), Toontown (added Apr. 15, 1996), and Tomorrowland. There was one Audio-Animatronics attraction that explored Japanese history, Meet the World. The park had a successful opening and ever since has been one of the world's most visited Disney destinations. Over the years, many new attractions, such as Big Thunder Mountain; Star Tours; Splash Mountain; Monsters, Inc. Ride & Go Seek!; and Enchanted Tale of Beauty and the Beast have been added to encourage repeat visitors. In 2022, Tokyo Disney Resort announced a major renovation of Tomorrowland, which will represent a future where humans are in harmony with nature. Tokyo Disneyland welcomed its 250 millionth guest, Mrs. Hisae Do, on Jul. 14, 2000; its 300 millionth guest (combined with Tokyo DisneySea), Mrs. Yoko Kusunoki, entered on Nov. 8, 2002; and its 400 millionth guest, Mrs. Aiko Hironaka, arrived Nov. 1, 2006. A 500 millionth guest, Ms. Megumi Soma, visited Aug. 27, 2010; its 600 millionth guest, Ms. Yumi Sakai, came in Apr. 12, 2014. The 700 millionth guest was Mrs. Sae Tanaka, on Jul. 31, 2017; and the 800 millionth guest was recorded on Feb. 26, 2022. A major earthquake and tsunami hit Japan Mar. 11, 2011, forcing Tokyo Disneyland and Tokyo DisneySea to close for several weeks beginning Mar. 12. The closures were not due to any sustained damage but because of problems getting reliable electrical power to the resort. Tokyo Disneyland reopened on its anniversary, a little over a month later, on Apr. 15.

Tokyo Disneyland Hotel The third official hotel at Tokyo Disney Resort; opened Jul. 8, 2008. The 9-story, Victorian-inspired resort complements the nearby entrance to Tokyo Disneyland. Among the 705 guest rooms are elaborate character rooms based on *Cinderella*, *Peter Pan*, *Alice in Wonderland*, and *Beauty and the Beast*. Dining includes Sherwood Garden Restaurant and Canna, with shopping at Looking Glass Gifts and Disney Mercantile. Also includes Dreamers Lounge in the atrium lobby; Bibbidi Bobbidi Boutique; the Marceline Salon concierge lounge; the Misty Mountains Pool, inspired by *Peter Pan*; the Cinderella Dream ballroom, plus smaller banquet facilities;

and 4 outdoor gardens featuring topiary: Mickey & Friends Square, Sherwood Garden, Fantasia Court, and Alice's Garden.

Tokyo DisneySea A 100-acre, aquatic-themed park opened next to Tokyo Disneyland Sep. 4, 2001. On entering and viewing a unique AquaSphere, guests choose between 7 distinct areas (called ports of call): Mediterranean Harbor, Mysterious Island, Mermaid Lagoon, Arabian Coast, Lost River Delta, Port Discovery, and American Waterfront. Attractions, dining, and shopping experiences immerse guests in ocean life and lore. An 8th port of call, Fantasy Springs, is scheduled to open in 2024; here, magical springs lead to a world of Disney fantasy, with areas and attractions themed to *Tangled*, *Frozen*, and *Peter Pan*. The park welcomed its 10 millionth guest, Tetsuya Goto, on Jul. 7, 2002. Included within the park is the Tokyo DisneySea Hotel MiraCosta, with 502 guest rooms. Tokyo DisneySea had to close for several weeks beginning Mar. 12, 2011, due to the major earthquake and tsunami that hit Japan on Mar. 11. The park reopened Apr. 28, 2011. That was the longest closing of any Disney park until the COVID-19 pandemic of 2020.

Tokyo DisneySea Fantasy Springs Hotel The 6th Disney hotel at Tokyo Disney Resort; scheduled to open in 2024. Situated near Fantasy Springs at Tokyo DisneySea, with designs and paintings based on Disney Princesses and floral motifs. There will be 419 "deluxe-type" rooms and 56 "luxury-type" rooms.

Tokyo DisneySea Hotel MiraCosta Luxury 5-story hotel in Tokyo Disney Resort; opened Sep. 4, 2001. Located physically within Mediterranean Harbor in Tokyo DisneySea, it provides a dedicated entrance to the park. There are 502 guest rooms spread across 3 different sides (Tuscany, Venice, and Porto Paradiso), offering unique one-of-a-kind ambience. The richly detailed atmosphere is of old-world Italy, with dining at Oceano, Silk Road Garden, and BellaVista Lounge, and shopping at MickeyAngelo Gifts. There is also the Salone dell'Amico concierge lounge; Terme Venezia, an indoor pool styled as an ancient Roman bath; the Hippocampi poolside bar; 5 banquet halls; and Chapel MiraCosta, a wedding venue that provides a view of Mount Prometheus.

Tokyo Mater (film) A routine tow lands Mater in Tokyo, where he is challenged to a drift-style race against a gang leader and his posse of ninjas. Larry the Cable Guy voices Mater. A Disney Digital 3-D

short released on Dec. 12, 2008, with *Bolt*. SEE ALSO CARS TOONS.

Toledo Arts Jewelry, art, and artifacts from Spain in the Lake Buena Vista Shopping Village at Walt Disney World; opened Mar. 1975, adjacent to Crystal Arts. Visitors watched demonstrations of gold inlaying. It became Artespana in 1986.

Toledo – Tapas, Steak & Seafood Rooftop restaurant in Gran Destino Tower at Disney's Coronado Springs Resort overlooking Walt Disney World; opened Jul. 9, 2019. Spanish dishes and small plates are served in a dining room inspired by Spain's modernist architecture.

Tom, Lauren Actress; appeared in *The Joy Luck Club* (Lena), on TV in *Escape to Witch Mountain* (Claudia Ford, 1995) and *My Wife and Kids* (Annie Hoo), on Disney Channel in *Andi Mack* (Celia Mac), and guest starred in *Monk* and *Grey's Anatomy*. She has provided voices in *Mulan II* (Su), *Pepper Ann* (Alice Kane), *Fillmore* (Karen Tehama), *Kim Possible* (Yoshiko), *W.I.T.C.H.* (Yan Lin/Susan Vandom), *Handy Manny* (Nelson), *The Replacements* (Tasumi), *American Dragon: Jake Long* (Susan Long), and *Fish Hooks* (Barb).

Tom and Huck (film) Tom Sawyer and Huck Finn team up to steal a pirate's treasure map from Injun Joe in order to save an innocent man from being wrongly convicted in court. Witnessing a heinous crime, they are forced to run away from home. Presumed lost in the Mississippi River, they must decide whether to come forward and save the innocent man or risk retribution from Injun Joe. Released Dec. 22, 1995. Directed by Peter Hewitt. Stars Jonathan Taylor Thomas (Tom), Brad Renfro (Huck), Eric Schweig (Injun Joe), Charles Rocket (Judge Thatcher), Amy Wright (Aunt Polly), Michael McShane (Muff Potter), Marian Seldes (Widow Douglas). Filmed in CinemaScope. 92 min. Based on the Mark Twain book, *The Adventures of Tom Sawyer*. For the movie, the town of Mooresville, Alabama, doubles for Hannibal, Missouri, which today looks too polished as a tourist attraction. Cathedral Caverns served as the location for Injun Joe's cave. Ike Eisenmann, of Disney's *Witch Mountain* fame, has a bit part as a taverner. For its original release, it was combined on a program with *Disney's Timon and Pumbaa in Stand by Me*.

Tom Morrow Character name (a pun on the word

tomorrow) of the operations director in the Flight to the Moon attraction in Disneyland and the Magic Kingdom at Walt Disney World; renamed Mr. Johnson in Mission to Mars. Voiced by George Walsh, whose voice introduced the *Gunsmoke* TV series. (After retiring from broadcasting, Walsh worked in the shops on Main Street, U.S.A. in Disneyland.) Also the name of the robot host of Innoventions in Disneyland; voiced by Nathan Lane. Tom Morrow 2.0, a smaller robot voiced by Max Casella, was introduced at Innoventions at Walt Disney World and hosted the "Imagineer That!" interstitial on Disney Channel.

Tom Sawyer Island Frontierland attraction in Disneyland; opened Jun. 16, 1956, based on *The Adventures of Tom Sawyer* by Mark Twain. Guests can explore at their leisure, after reaching the island by raft. Points of interest have included the Suspension Bridge, Barrel Bridge, Injun Joe's Cave, Castle Rock Ridge with its Teeter-Totter Rock and Merry-Go-Round Rock, and Fort Wilderness. For several years, guests could meet Tom Sawyer himself and fish for river perch and catfish. On opening day, a modern-day Tom Sawyer and Becky Thatcher, played by Missouri youngsters Chris Winkler and Perva Lou Smith, christened the rafts with bottles of Mississippi River water and planted a box of soil from Jackson's Island, which was made famous by Twain in his books. Tom Sawyer Island underwent a major refurbishment in 2007, reopening May 25 as Pirate's Lair on Tom Sawyer Island, to tie in with the release of *Pirates of the Caribbean: At World's End*. Harper's Mill became Lafitte's Tavern, and Injun Joe's Cave became Dead Man's Grotto. At the same time, the aging Fort Wilderness was torn down. A Tom Sawyer Island also opened in the Magic Kingdom at Walt Disney World May 20, 1973. The fort in Florida is Fort Langhorn (formerly Fort Sam Clemens, both named after Samuel Langhorne Clemens, Mark Twain's real name). Aunt Polly's Landing served refreshments on the island; in 1995, it became Aunt Polly's Dockside Inn and is open seasonally. Both islands were in the middle of their respective Rivers of America on opening day, but the attractions were not built until many months later. Also in Westernland at Tokyo Disneyland; it opened Apr. 15, 1983, with Fort Sam Clemens. At Disneyland Paris, Big Thunder Mountain is on an island in the middle of the park's Rivers of the Far West, and at Hong Kong Disneyland, Tarzan's Treehouse is on an island in the Rivers of Adventure.

Tom Sawyer Island Rafts Frontierland attraction in the Magic Kingdom at Walt Disney World; opened May 20, 1973. Also in Westernland in Tokyo Disneyland; opened Apr. 15, 1983. SEE ALSO RAFTS TO TOM SAWYER ISLAND (DISNEYLAND).

Tombstone (film) Wyatt Earp and his wife, Mattie, arrive in the booming silver town of Tombstone intending to settle down with the rest of the Earp clan. Leaving his violent life as a Kansas lawman behind, Wyatt wants nothing more than to run a gambling establishment with his brothers, Virgil and Morgan. But peace for the Earps is not to be. A feud between the Earp brothers and an evil gang, the "Cowboys," culminates with the gunfight at the O.K. Corral. Released Dec. 25, 1993. Directed by George P. Cosmatos. A Hollywood Pictures film. 128 min. Stars Kurt Russell (Wyatt Earp), Val Kilmer (Doc Holliday), Michael Biehn (Ringo), Powers Boothe (Curly Bill), Robert Burke (Frank McLaury), Dana Delany (Josephine), Sam Elliott (Virgil Earp), Stephen Lang (Ike Clanton), Joanna Pacula (Kate), Bill Paxton (Morgan Earp), Jason Priestley (Billy Breckenridge), Michael Rooker (Sherman McMasters), Jon Tenney (Behan), Billy Zane (Mr. Fabian), Charlton Heston (Henry Hooker). Filmed on locations in and around Tucson, Arizona.

Tomei, Marisa Actress; appeared in *Oscar* (Lisa Provolone), *Wild Hogs* (Maggie), and as May Parker in *Captain America: Civil War* and later Marvel Studios films.

Tomlin, Lily Actress; appeared in dual roles in *Big Business* (Rose Shelton/Rose Ratliff), *Krippendorf's Tribe* (Ruth Allen), and *Disney's The Kid* (Janet), and on TV in *Desperate Housewives* (Roberta Simmons). She voiced Toki in *Ponyo*.

Tomlinson, David (1917–2000) Actor; appeared in *Mary Poppins* (George Banks), *The Love Bug* (Thorndyke), and *Bedknobs and Broomsticks* (Emelius Browne). A veteran of over 35 British films, Tomlinson had never sung on-screen before making *Mary Poppins*. A little polishing of his fine baritone voice soon had him singing like a pro. He was named a Disney Legend posthumously in 2002.

Tommy Tucker's Tooth (film) Dental training film made by Walt Disney for Dr. Thomas B. McCrum in Kansas City in 1922. Tommy Tucker takes pride in his appearance and very good care of his teeth, but Jimmie Jones is careless about his appearance and neglects his teeth. The first Disney educational film.

Tomorrow the Moon Alternate title of *Man and the Moon*.

Tomorrow We Diet (film) Goofy cartoon released Jun. 29, 1951. Directed by Jack Kinney. Goofy's willpower to diet is quashed by a voice from the mirror that tells him to eat, drink, and be merry—and tomorrow we'll diet.

Tomorrowland One of the original lands at Disneyland, presenting visions of the future. At first, Tomorrowland depicted what the world might be like in 1986, with attractions including Rocket to the Moon, the Monsanto Hall of Chemistry, and Autopia. A major expansion in 1959 introduced the Disneyland-Alweg Monorail System and Submarine Voyage. Tomorrowland was completely remodeled in 1967 with a new "world on the move" theme, adding the Rocket Jets, PeopleMover, Carousel of Progress, and other attractions. Versions of Tomorrowland opened in the Magic Kingdom at Walt Disney World, Tokyo Disneyland, Hong Kong Disneyland, and Shanghai Disneyland; but the area was re-envisioned as Discoveryland for Disneyland Paris. Over the years, the future always seemed to catch up with Tomorrowland, eventually inspiring the Imagineers to incorporate more timeless sci-fi themes. Tomorrowland in the Magic Kingdom was completely remodeled 1994–1995, giving the land the look of a metropolis like those imagined by science fiction writers and moviemakers of the 1920s–1930s. An extensively remodeled Tomorrowland in Disneyland opened May 1998, inspired by the dreams of futurists.

Tomorrowland (film) An epic science fiction film in which, bound by a shared destiny, a bright, optimistic teen, bursting with scientific curiosity, and a former boy-genius inventor, jaded by disillusionment, embark on a danger-filled mission to unearth the secrets of an enigmatic place somewhere in time and space that exists in their collective memory as Tomorrowland. What they must do there changes the world—and them—forever. Directed by Brad Bird. Released May 22, 2015, also in IMAX. Stars George Clooney (Frank Walker), Hugh Laurie (David Nix), Raffey Cassidy (Athena), Thomas Robinson (young Frank Walker), Britt Robertson (Casey). 130 min. Working title was *1952*. Some filming, for a 1964–1965 New York World's Fair sequence, took place at Disneyland. Tomorrowland scenes were shot in part in the City of Arts & Sciences in Valencia, Spain, and the wheat fields in Alberta, Canada.

Tomorrowland Boats Attraction in Disneyland; operated Jul. 30, 1955–Jan. 15, 1956, between Tomorrowland and Fantasyland. Later became Phantom Boats. The Motor Boat Cruise, Boat Cruise to Gummi Glen, and Fantasia Gardens, located in the same space, were usually considered Fantasyland attractions.

Tomorrowland Expo Center Attraction in Disneyland; opened Nov. 16, 2015, in the former Innoventions building. Debuted with Star Wars Launch Bay on the first floor and Super Hero HQ (Marvel exhibits and character greetings) upstairs. Super Hero HQ closed Apr. 2, 2016. On May 26, 2017, the second-floor balcony became the Tomorrowland Skyline Lounge Experience, providing views of the park.

Tomorrowland Indy Speedway New name, in 1999, for the Tomorrowland Speedway. The name reverted to Tomorrowland Speedway in 2009.

Tomorrowland Jets SEE ASTRO-JETS.

Tomorrowland Light & Power Co. Shop and arcade at the exit to Space Mountain in the Magic Kingdom at Walt Disney World; opened Feb. 1, 1995. The arcade area closed Feb. 9, 2015. It became Tomorrowland Launch Depot in 2023.

Tomorrowland Pavilion Exhibition space in Shanghai Disneyland; opened Sep. 22, 2022, with *Avatar: Explore Pandora*, a 15,000-sq.-ft. exhibition featuring life-sized re-creations of icons and landmarks from the film *Avatar*. Inside is also the Tomorrowland Pavilion Shop. Replaced Star Wars Launch Bay.

Tomorrowland Speedway New name, beginning Sep. 28, 1996, of the Grand Prix Raceway in the Magic Kingdom at Walt Disney World. Riders take the wheel of a gas-powered car and cruise along a scenic miniature motorway. In 1999, it became Tomorrowland Indy Speedway. The name reverted to Tomorrowland Speedway in 2009.

Tomorrowland Stage Outdoor entertainment venue in Disneyland; open 1967–1977, taking the place of the Flying Saucers attraction. Shows included *Show Me America, Country Music Jubilee*, and the *Kids of the Kingdom*, along with performances by visiting artists. In 1969, the Apollo 11 moonwalk was famously presented live on a huge screen at the venue. The stage was rebuilt in 1977 as the 1,100-seat Space Stage, part of the new Space Mountain complex. It was replaced in 1986 by the Magic Eye Theater, with the outdoor shows moved to Videopolis. Also a theater in the Magic Kingdom at Walt Disney World; open 1979–Dec. 1994, and succeeded by the Galaxy Palace Theater. SEE ALSO SHOWBASE 2000 (TOKYO DISNEYLAND) AND PEPSI E-STAGE (SHANGHAI DISNEYLAND).

Tomorrowland Terrace Counter-service restaurant and bandstand in Disneyland; originally open Jul. 2, 1967–Jun. 2001and succeeded by Club Buzz. The Tomorrowland Terrace name returned after a refurbishment in 2006. There is a popular dance floor, and the bandstand is constructed such that performers can arrange themselves in the basement level. Then the stage is raised to the restaurant level. In Nov. 2015, the restaurant was given a *Star Wars* theme and renamed Galactic Grill. Also a quick-service restaurant in the Magic Kingdom at Walt Disney World (opened Oct. 1, 1971) and in Tokyo Disneyland (opened Apr. 15, 1983). The Walt Disney World facility closed Sep. 1994 to become Cosmic Ray's Starlight Cafe. On Mar. 16, 2005, the nearby Plaza Pavilion reopened as Tomorrowland Terrace Noodle Station and was later renamed Tomorrowland Terrace Restaurant.

Tomorrowland Theater New name, beginning Mar. 2015, for the Magic Eye Theater in Disneyland. Screenings have included *Star Wars: Path of the Jedi*, previews of Disney feature films, and the Pixar Shorts Film Festival.

Tomorrowland Transit Authority Magic Kingdom attraction at Walt Disney World; opened Jun. 11, 1994, as an update to the WEDway People-Mover. Passengers take a 10-minute elevated tour of Tomorrowland, previewing attractions in a transit system of the future. It was renamed Tomorrowland Transit Authority PeopleMover Aug. 5, 2010. SEE WEDWAY PEOPLEMOVER.

Tomorrow's Harvest Guided walking tour in The Land greenhouses at EPCOT Center; offered Oct. 1, 1982–Sep. 27, 1993. Became Greenhouse Tours on Dec. 10, 1993, and the Behind the Seeds Tour in Sep. 1996.

Tompson, Ruthie (1910–2021) After appearing as an extra in the Alice Comedies as a child in the 1920s, she joined the Disney Studio's Ink & Paint Department in 1937, helping to put the finishing touches on *Snow White and the Seven Dwarfs*. She was soon promoted to final checker, reviewing the animation cels before they were photographed onto film. She eventually became supervisor of the Scene Planning Department. She retired in 1975 and was named a Disney Legend in 2000.

Tonka (film) In the territory of the Dakotas in the 1870s, a young Native man, White Bull, captures a wild stallion and decides to keep him as his own, naming him Tonka Wakan—The Great One. After White Bull frees the horse once more, Tonka's new master, Capt. Myles Keogh, rides him into the Battle of the Little Big Horn, where Keogh is killed. Tonka survives and is officially retired by the U.S. Seventh Cavalry on Apr. 10, 1878, to be ridden only by his exercise boy, his beloved master, White Bull. Directed by Lewis R. Foster. Based on the novel by David Appel. Released Dec. 25, 1958. 96 min. Stars Sal Mineo (White Bull), Philip Carey (Capt. Myles Keogh), Jerome Courtland (Lt. Henry Nowlan), H. M. Wynant (Yellow Bull). The picture was filmed at the Warm Springs Indian Reservation in Oregon. The title song was written by Gil George and George Bruns. The remarkable photography was by Loyal Griggs, who had filmed such famous westerns as *Shane*. It aired on TV as *Comanche* and was serialized on the new *Mickey Mouse Club* as *A Horse Called Comanche*.

Tony Proprietor of the Italian restaurant where Lady and Tramp share a meal of spaghetti in *Lady and the Tramp*; voiced by George Givot. He is aided by Joe; voiced by Bill Thompson.

Tony Awards With the success of *Beauty and the Beast* on Broadway, Disney began qualifying for Tony Awards. The winners have been:

1. 1994: *Beauty and the Beast* (Ann Hould-Ward, Costume Design)
2. 1998: *The Lion King* (Garth Fagan, Choreography)
3. 1998: *The Lion King* (Julie Taymor, Costume Design)
4. 1998: *The Lion King* (Donald Holder, Lighting Design)
5. 1998: *The Lion King* (Richard Hudson, Scenic Design)

6. 1998: *The Lion King* (Julie Taymor, Director of a Musical)
7. 1998: *The Lion King* (Musical)
8. 2000: *Aida* (Elton John, Tim Rice, Original Score)
9. 2000: *Aida* (Heather Headley, Actress in a Musical)
10. 2000: *Aida* (Bob Crowley, Scenic Design)
11. 2000: *Aida* (Natasha Katz, Lighting Design)
12. 2007: *Mary Poppins* (Bob Crowley, Scenic Design)
13. 2012: *Newsies* (Alan Menken and Jack Feldman, Music)
14. 2012: *Newsies* (Christopher Gattelli, Choreography)
15. 2012: *Peter and the Starcatcher* (Christian Borle, Actor in a Featured Role in a Play)
16. 2012: *Peter and the Starcatcher* (Donyale Werle, Scenic Design)
17. 2012: *Peter and the Starcatcher* (Paloma Young, Costume Design)
18. 2012: *Peter and the Starcatcher* (Jeff Croiter, Lighting Design)
19. 2012: *Peter and the Starcatcher* (Darron L. West, Sound Design)
20. 2014: *Aladdin* (James Monroe Iglehart, Actor in a Featured Role in a Musical)

Tony Danza Show, The (TV) Syn. talk show; aired Sep. 13, 2004–May 26, 2006. From Buena Vista Television.

Tony's Town Square Restaurant Table-service restaurant on Town Square in the Magic Kingdom at Walt Disney World; opened Jul. 24, 1989. Themed to characters from *Lady and the Tramp*, featuring Italian dishes. Formerly Town Square Cafe.

Too Smart for Strangers, with Winnie the Pooh (film) Educational home video release, warning children about strangers; released in Jun. 1985.

Toombs Thomas, Leota (1925–1991) Imagineer; after starting her Disney career as a member of the Ink & Paint Department in 1940, she left to start a family, but returned to WED Enterprises in 1962 where she worked in figure finishing and maintaining attractions. She is best known for the use of her visage as Madame Leota, the medium in the crystal ball at the Haunted Mansion (voiced by Eleanor Audley); meanwhile, Toombs's face and voice are immortalized as the "Ghostess" (unofficially known as "Little Leota") at the end of the attraction. She was named a Disney Legend posthumously in 2009.

Toon Disney A 24-hour cable network that launched Apr. 18, 1998, offering cartoons and animated TV shows from the vast Disney library. It became Disney XD in 2009.

Toon Studio New name, beginning in 2007, for the Animation Courtyard in Walt Disney Studios Park at Disneyland Paris. Toon Studio consisted of 3 sections: the original Animation Courtyard, featuring Mickey and the Magician (formerly *Animagique*) and Animation Celebration (formerly The Art of Disney Animation); an area consisting of Les Tapis Volants – Flying Carpets Over Agrabah, along with Crush's Coaster and Cars Quatre Roues Rallye; Toy Story Playland, featuring Toy Soldiers Parachute Drop, Slinky Dog Zigzag Spin, and RC Racer; and La Place de Rémy, a *Ratatouille*-themed area featuring Ratatouille: L'Aventure Totalement Toquée de Rémy. On Aug. 27, 2021, the Pixar-themed attractions became part of a separate area, Worlds of Pixar.

Toontown Residence of toon characters in *Who Framed Roger Rabbit*. SEE ALSO MICKEY'S TOON-TOWN.

Toontown Hall of Fame Character-greeting attraction in Mickey's Toontown Fair at Walt Disney World; open Jun. 1996–2011.

Toontown Railroad Station Opened Nov. 25, 1992, in Disneyland; formerly the Fantasyland Railroad Station and Videopolis Railroad Station. A railroad station was also part of Mickey's Toontown Fair in the Magic Kingdom at Walt Disney World.

Toot, Whistle, Plunk and Boom (film) Special cartoon released Nov. 10, 1953. Directed by Charles Nichols and Ward Kimball. Academy Award winner for Best Cartoon. Professor Owl explains to his students about musical instruments, illustrating with the song, "Toot, Whistle, Plunk and Boom." From the cave dwellers to modern times, we find that all instruments are based on the toot, the whistle, and so on, and they finally evolve into modern musical instruments. First cartoon filmed in CinemaScope. The unique backgrounds were devised by artist Eyvind Earle who would later give *Sleeping Beauty* its distinctive look. The first short cartoon released by Buena Vista. 10 min.

Toot, Whistle, Plunk and Boom (TV) Show aired Mar. 27, 1959. Directed by Wilfred Jackson. The Academy Award–winning cartoon is shown, along with several others that use music to tell a story.

Toothless (TV) A 2-hour movie on *The Wonderful World of Disney*; first aired Oct. 5, 1997. Dr. Katherine Lewis is an attractive, successful dentist who has fulfilled her career dream but in reality leads a very empty life. While walking down the street one day, she gets hit by a bicycle messenger and is killed. Ending up in a place called Limbo, she finds she must atone for inflicting pain on her patients through the years by becoming the Tooth Fairy. But when she gets involved in the life of a 12-year-old boy, she risks not going to heaven. Directed by Melanie Mayron. Stars Kirstie Alley (Katherine Lewis), Dale Midkiff (Thomas Jameson), Ross Malinger (Bobby Jameson), Daryl Mitchell (Raul), Lynn Redgrave (Mrs. Rogers). Interiors were filmed in the historic former I. Magnin department store building on Wilshire Boulevard in Los Angeles.

Tootsie Title star of *Donald's Penguin* (1939).

Top of the World Nightclub/restaurant on the 15th floor of the Contemporary Resort at Walt Disney World; open Oct. 1, 1971–Sep. 30, 1993, offering a spectacular view over Seven Seas Lagoon toward the Magic Kingdom. Lounge entertainment included visiting celebrity acts, comedy groups, and dancing. The longtime dinner show presented twice nightly was *Broadway at the Top* (1981–1993), with talented performers singing hit numbers from Broadway shows. An all-you-can-eat Sunday brunch was also popular. The restaurant was replaced by the California Grill in May 1995. On Aug. 4, 2009, the Top of the World name was reused for the 77-seat Top of the World Lounge, which opened on the 16th floor of the new Bay Lake Tower, offering dining and an observation deck; it reopened as the re-themed Top of the World Lounge – A Villains Lair on Jul. 11, 2022.

Topolino Italian name for Mickey Mouse, and the title of an Italian comic book that began publication in Dec. 1932, making it the first of the Disney comic books.

Topolino's Terrace – Flavors of the Riviera Rooftop restaurant at Disney's Riviera Resort at Walt Disney World; opened Dec. 16, 2019. Handmade pastas, seafood, and meat dishes are served in the evening, with character dining at breakfast. Inspired by the cliffside restaurants of Europe's Mediterranean coast, it offers views of the EPCOT Resort Area and Disney's Hollywood Studios.

Torkelsons, The (TV) Series on NBC; aired Sep. 21, 1991–Jun. 20, 1992. Continued in 1993 with story changes as *Almost Home*. The show focuses on an eccentric but lovable single mother and her brood of 5, headed by Millicent Torkelson's wistful eldest daughter Dorothy Jane, in Pyramid Corners, Oklahoma. Like most 14-year-olds, she is perpetually embarrassed by her mother. Sharing the Torkelson house is a lodger, the grandfatherly Wesley Hodges. Stars Connie Ray (Millicent Torkelson), Olivia Burnette (Dorothy Jane), Aaron Michael Melchik (Steven Floyd), Lee Norris (Chuckie Lee), Rachel Duncan (Mary Sue), William Shallert (Wesley Hodges). See also Almost Home.

Tornado Name of Zorro's majestic black stallion. (Zorro also had a white horse, named Phantom, in a few episodes.)

Torres, Gina Actress; appeared on TV in *Alias* (Anna Espinosa), *Huge* (Dr. Dorothy Rand), and *The Catch* (Justine Diaz), with guest appearances in *Revenge*, *Castle*, *Dirty Sexy Money*, *Eli Stone*, and *Criminal Minds*. She voiced Chatana in *Elena of Avalor*, Queen of Ingvarr in *Tangled: The Series*, and Ketsu Onyo in *Star Wars Rebels*. At EPCOT, she replaced Gary Sinise as the Capcom in Mission: SPACE in 2017.

Tortilla Jo's Mexican restaurant and tequila bar in the Downtown Disney District at Disneyland Resort; opened Apr. 15, 2004, taking the place of Y Arriba Y Arriba. Food is also ordered to-go at the Taqueria. Managed by Patina Restaurant Group.

Tortoise and the Hare, The (film) Silly Symphony cartoon released Jan. 5, 1935. Directed by Wilfred Jackson. An overconfident Max Hare races against Toby Tortoise. But in his belief that he'll easily win the race no matter what, Max spends his time entertaining the female rabbits along the course. Persistent Toby comes from behind and wins the race. Academy Award winner for Best Cartoon. An educational version was titled *Aesop's Hare and the Tortoise*.

Tortuga Tavern Adventureland counter-service restaurant in the Magic Kingdom at Walt Disney

World; opened Feb. 6, 2011. Themed after the Pirates of the Caribbean films. Opened originally as El Pirata y el Perico Apr. 16, 1974, serving burritos, nachos, and snacks.

Tortuga Treats Treasure Cove snack counter in Shanghai Disneyland; opened Jun. 16, 2016. According to the story, it belongs to Tortuga Tambo, a boat repairman whose wife, Tallulah, prepares the treats.

Tory Vengeance (TV) Episode 3 of *The Swamp Fox*.

Totally Circus (TV) Half-hour documentary/adventure series on Disney Channel; premiered Jun. 16, 2000. Features the 37 kids, ages 9–19, of the Vermont-based traveling Circus Smirkus, learning the circus acts and putting on performances. 15 episodes.

Totally Hoops (TV) Half-hour reality series on Disney Channel; premiered Jan. 7, 2001, following the lives of the Dayton Lady Hoopstars, eleven 13- and 14-year-old girls, as they head for the state championships and a national tournament.

Totally in Tune (TV) Half-hour reality series on Disney Channel; premiered Jun. 17, 2002. Cameras followed kids at Los Angeles's Hamilton High's magnet program for music.

Totally Minnie SEE DISNEY'S TOTALLY MINNIE (TV).

Totally Minnie Parade Event at Disneyland in summer 1986. Minnie Mouse was given her due, updated with 1980s fashions and a rocking theme song, in this parade with over 100 performers. Another event, Totally Minnie Mouse, was held at Tokyo Disney Resort, Jan. 18–Mar. 30, 2022.

T.O.T.S. (TV) Animated comedy series on Disney Junior; premiered Jun. 14, 2019. As the only non-stork delivery-birds-in-training at Tiny Ones Transport Service (T.O.T.S.), best friends Pip and Freddy, a tenacious penguin and a kind-hearted flamingo, must use tender care in taking baby animals from the nursery to their forever families around the globe. Voices include Vanessa Williams (Captain Beakman), Megan Hilty (K. C. the koala), Jet Jurgensmeyer (Pip the penguin), Christian J. Simon (Freddy the flamingo). Created by Travis Braun. From Titmouse in association with Disney Junior.

Touchdown Mickey (film) Mickey Mouse cartoon released Oct. 15, 1932. Directed by Wilfred Jackson. In a spirited game of football between Mickey and the gang and local alley cats, both sides share misadventures with the ball, but Mickey is undeniably the hero by single-handedly winning the game.

Touchstone Pictures New label created at the Disney Studio by Ron Miller for films that had more mature themes than the standard "Disney" film; the first film to be released as a Touchstone Picture was *Splash* in 1984. Eventually Touchstone would have its own production personnel, and when the number of films being released greatly increased, another label, Hollywood Pictures, was established to spread out the work. The Touchstone logo is meant to imply a high standard or quality of film—a hallmark of Disney entertainment—from the very first frame. The famous "streak" was created using a Japanese calligraphy brush, painted across an oval, which represents the physical "touchstone," a tool traditionally used to test the quality of precious metals. Some of the more notable films include *Down and Out in Beverly Hills*; *Ruthless People*; *The Color of Money*; *Three Men and a Baby*; *Good Morning, Vietnam*; *Who Framed Roger Rabbit*; *Beaches*; *Dead Poets Society*; *Turner & Hooch*; *Pretty Woman*; *Father of the Bride*; *Sister Act*; *Tim Burton's The Nightmare Before Christmas*; *Ed Wood*; *Con Air*; *Armageddon*; *Rushmore*; *10 Things I Hate About You*; *Runaway Bride*; *Bicentennial Man*; *High Fidelity*; *O Brother, Where Art Thou?*; *Pearl Harbor*; *The Royal Tenenbaums*; *Sweet Home Alabama*; and *The Prestige*. On Feb. 9, 2009, Disney announced an exclusive distribution and marketing deal with DreamWorks Studios, ultimately releasing 13 DreamWorks motion pictures under the Touchstone label between 2011–2016. The last theatrical film released under the Touchstone banner was *The Light Between Oceans*. SEE ALSO FEATURES FOR A LIST OF FILMS MADE BY TOUCHSTONE PICTURES.

Touchstone Television Production studio for TV series with more mature themes, beginning with programs like *The Golden Girls*, *Wildside*, and *The Ellen Burstyn Show*. Other shows have included *Empty Nest*, *Blossom*, *Home Improvement*, *Boy Meets World*, *Ellen*, *Felicity*, *The Amazing Race*, *Alias*, *Scrubs*, *Monk*, *Lost*, *Desperate Housewives*, *Grey's Anatomy*, and *Criminal Minds*. In 2007, Touchstone Television was renamed ABC Studios, which became ABC Signature in 2020. Separately, it was announced in Aug. 2020 that Fox 21 Television Studios (acquired by Disney with its 2019 purchase of 21st Century Fox) would be renamed Touchstone Television; four months later, the studio was folded into 20th Television.

Touchwood Pacific Partners I Limited partnership formed in Oct. 1990, to finance live-action films at Disney, with the $600 million equity underwritten by Japanese financial institutions. It succeeded Silver Screen Partners IV. Its films included *Billy Bathgate, Captain Ron, Encino Man, Father of the Bride, Homeward Bound: The Incredible Journey, Newsies, Sister Act*, and *What About Bob?*

Tough Guys (film) Two train robbers, Harry Doyle and Archie Long, are released from prison after many years on the inside, but they find it very difficult adjusting to modern society. Aided by their probation officer, who has hero-worshipped them for years, they attempt to pull off one last train robbery—on the final run of the train they had failed to rob 18 years before. Premiere in San Luis Obispo, California, on Sep. 30, 1986; general release on Oct. 3, 1986. Directed by Jeff Kanew. A Touchstone film. 103 min. Stars Burt Lancaster (Harry Doyle), Kirk Douglas (Archie Long), Charles Durning (Deke Yablonski), Alexis Smith (Belle), Dana Carvey (in his motion picture debut as Richie Evans), Eli Wallach (Leon B. Little). The train used in the film is Southern Pacific's steam engine 4449, an oil-burning locomotive constructed in 1940 and designed for passenger trains on the Los Angeles-San Francisco run. The engine had been retired in 1957 and placed on display in Oaks Park in Portland, Oregon. As it traveled south to the Los Angeles area for the filming, thousands of train buffs frequently lined the route to catch a glimpse of the venerable old locomotive. The climactic railroad sequences were filmed south of Palm Springs on the Eagle Mountain line.

Toulouse Aspiring artist kitten in *The Aristocats*; voiced by Gary Dubin.

Tour of the West, A See Circarama, U.S.A.

Tourist Trap (TV) A 2-hour movie on *The Wonderful World of Disney*; first aired Apr. 5, 1998. Bored banker George Piper takes his reluctant family on a motor home vacation to retrace the footsteps of his heroic ancestor and idol, Jeremiah Piper, who fought during the Civil War. Hoping to bond with his family, George instead finds them facing a series of misadventures and unexpected dangers before they realize that they really are a close-knit family. Directed by Richard Benjamin. Stars Daniel Stern (George Piper), Julie Hagerty (Bess), David Rasche (Derek Early), Paul Giamatti (Jeremiah), Margot Finley (Rachel), Blair Slater (Josh), Rodney Eastman (Stork), Ryan Reynolds (Wade Early). Filming took place on location around Vancouver.

Tournament of Roses Parade Disney has long participated in this New Year's Day tradition in Pasadena, California, famous for its procession of elaborate floats made from hundreds of thousands of flowers. In 1938, the Disney Studio presented a *Snow White and the Seven Dwarfs*–themed float featuring Marjorie Belcher, the live-action reference model for the title princess. In 1955, the Helms Bakery float, titled "There's a Good Time Coming," presented a preview of Disneyland, with floral depictions of Mickey Mouse, flying pink Dumbo elephants, and Sleeping Beauty Castle. Walt Disney served as grand marshal of the Jan. 1, 1966, parade, riding in an open car accompanied by Mickey Mouse. The car was followed by the City of Burbank float, titled "Our Small World of Make Believe." Other Disney floats have included "A Dream Come True in Anaheim" (1971, with 2 dozen Disney characters); "50 Happy Years" (1973, with more than 100 characters commemorating the 50th anniversary of Walt Disney Productions); a block-long cavalcade for the Disneyland 25th anniversary (1980), followed by a float with the Firehouse Five Plus Two band; "Happy Birthday, Donald Duck—50 Years of American Spirit" (1985, for the City of Glendale); "Communicating Freedom" (1988, the California Bicentennial Foundation float with Mickey Mouse and Bisontennial Ben); "Salute to Sports" (1995, with floral depictions of Disney characters in sporting gear); a "human theme banner" (2000, as a promotion for *Fantasia/2000*, with Roy E. Disney as grand marshal and Mickey Mouse as the Sorcerer's Apprentice); "A Sudden Drop in Pitch" (2004, depicting the new Twilight Zone Tower of Terror at Disneyland Resort, breaking a float height record at 100 ft.); "The Happiest Celebration on Earth" (2005, celebrating Disneyland's 50th anniversary, with Mickey as grand marshal); "The Most Magical Celebration on Earth" (2006, depicting Disney park castles around the world as one of the longest floats in parade history, at 150 ft.); "Destination: Cars Land" (2013, promoting the new area in Disney California Adventure); and "Disneyland

Diamond Celebration: Awaken Your Adventure" (2016, a 3-unit float for the park's 60th anniversary, depicting Sleeping Beauty Castle, Elsa's Ice Palace, and the future Star Wars: Galaxy's Edge). In 2020, the Rose Parade held its first-ever halftime show, including a live performance from the musical *Frozen*, which was playing at the Pantages Theatre in Hollywood. In 2023, Mickey Mouse and Minnie Mouse joined the parade on the Disneyland Fire Engine and delivered the "football toss" to the Rose Bowl, where it was caught by Chip, Dale, Goofy, Pluto, and Donald Duck with some TV magic. Beginning in 1960, the Rose Queen and Royal Court, along with the competing Rose Bowl college football teams, visited Disneyland each year, sometimes with a Rose Court Jubilee parade held at the park.

Tournament Tent Fantasyland snack pavilion in the Magic Kingdom at Walt Disney World; opened Oct. 1, 1971. Replaced in 1994 by The Little Big Top.

Tower Hotel Gifts Hollywood Tower Hotel shop at The Twilight Zone Tower of Terror; opened in Disney's Hollywood Studios Jul. 22, 1994, and in Walt Disney Studios Park in Disneyland Paris Dec. 22, 2007. Also in Disney California Adventure May 5, 2004–Jan. 2, 2016, succeeded by The Collector's Warehouse. At Tokyo DisneySea, the shop is Tower of Terror Memorabilia; opened Sep. 4, 2006, in what appears to be the Hotel Hightower's former pool and spa.

Tower of Terror SEE TWILIGHT ZONE TOWER OF TERROR, THE.

Tower of Terror (TV) A 2-hour movie on *The Wonderful World of Disney*; first aired Oct. 26, 1997. When lightning strikes the deluxe Hollywood Tower Hotel in 1939, 5 people, including child superstar Sally Shine, suddenly vanish from an elevator en route to a Halloween gala at the Tip Top Club on the top floor. Haunted by the incident, the swank hotel closes overnight and falls into disrepair. Nearly 60 years later, a down-on-his-luck journalist, Buzzy Crocker, with help from his spunky niece, Anna, and former boss/old flame Jill Whitman, is suddenly given reason to believe he can solve the mystery. Directed by D. J. MacHale. Stars Lindsay Ridgeway (Sally Shine), Steve Guttenberg (Buzzy Crocker), Kirsten Dunst (Anna Petterson), Nia Peeples (Jill Whitman). This movie is perhaps the first to be based on a theme park attraction, rather than vice versa. However, since it was not possible to film in The Twilight Zone Tower of Terror at the Disney-MGM Studios (in the film, the lobby had to be shown in its 1939 splendor and then aged to 1997), an accurate replica was built in a warehouse.

Tower of Terror Memorabilia SEE TOWER HOTEL GIFTS.

Tower of the Four Winds Kinetic structure at the entrance to the Pepsi-Cola pavilion at the 1964–1965 New York World's Fair, welcoming guests to the It's a Small World attraction. Designed by Imagineer Rolly Crump, the mobile represented the boundless energy of youth and featured depictions of animals from across the world along with other figures driven by the 4 winds. The 12-story structure required a 60-foot foundation to support it. It was dismantled after the fair closed.

Town Center Fashions World Bazaar boutique in Tokyo Disneyland; opened Sep. 21, 2007, taking the place of The Toy Kingdom, The Storybook Store, and Uptown Boutique. According to the story, Minnie Mouse and Daisy Duck are the owners.

Town Square Cafe Restaurant in Disneyland; open winter 1976–spring 1978. Formerly Maxwell House Coffee House and Hills Brothers Coffee House. It became the American Egg House (1978–1983). On Oct. 1, 1983, the name reverted to Town Square Cafe, and it eventually closed Aug. 23, 1992. Also opened on Town Square in the Magic Kingdom at Walt Disney World Oct. 1, 1971, and later became Tony's Town Square Restaurant.

Town Square Exposition Hall Exhibit venue on Town Square in the Magic Kingdom at Walt Disney World, housing the Camera Center and various photo displays; opened Aug. 27, 1998, in the former Walt Disney Story location. Closed Apr. 2, 2010, to become the Town Square Theater.

Town Square Photography Main Street, U.S.A. shop in Disneyland Paris; opened Apr. 12, 1992. Presented by Kodak. It closed Jan. 18, 2014, to become New Century Notions—Flora's Unique Boutique. A similar shop, Town Square Photo, opened in Hong Kong Disneyland Sep. 12, 2005, and became Marty's General Store Feb. 1, 2018. SEE ALSO CAMERA CENTER.

Town Square Theater Character-greeting venue

on Town Square in the Magic Kingdom at Walt Disney World; opened Mar. 30, 2011, replacing Town Square Exposition Hall. Guests can meet magician Mickey Mouse in his rehearsal room and shop at Box Office Gifts. The area is filled with references to Disney characters, films, and theme park attractions.

Towne Clothiers World Bazaar apparel and luggage shop in Tokyo Disneyland; opened Apr. 15, 1983. It later became part of the Grand Emporium.

Toy Box Café Outdoor food court themed as a café play set in Disney-Pixar Toy Story Land at Shanghai Disneyland; opened Feb. 9, 2018, taking the place of Celebration Café. Menu items resemble the Toy Story characters.

Toy Kingdom, The World Bazaar toy and game shop in Tokyo Disneyland; opened Apr. 15, 1983, and closed in 2007 to make way for Town Center Fashions.

Toy Soldier, The United Kingdom shop in EPCOT; opened Oct. 1, 1982, selling games, dolls, and books. Relocated ca. 2001, taking the place of Pringle of Scotland. The original location became the Sportsman's Shoppe.

Toy Soldiers Parachute Drop Attraction in Toy Story Playland in Walt Disney Studios Park at Disneyand Paris (opened Aug. 17, 2010), and in Toy Story Land at Hong Kong Disneyland (opened Nov. 17, 2013, as Toy Soldier Parachute Drop). Guests board 6-person parachute jump vehicles and drop 82 ft. in a thrilling drill.

Toy Station World Bazaar toy shop, decorated with tin rockets and model airships, in Tokyo Disneyland; opened Sep. 21, 2007, taking the place of Mickey's Modern Memory and The Bebop Hop.

Toy Story (film) Animated feature from Pixar Animation Studios. Andy's toys are fearful of being replaced when the boy's birthday comes along. Woody, his favorite toy, a pull-string cowboy doll, discovers the boy has a new toy, Buzz Lightyear, the latest, greatest action figure, complete with pop-out wings and laser action. Woody's plan to get rid of Buzz backfires, and he finds himself lost in the world outside of Andy's room, with Buzz as his only companion. Together they must try to find their way back to Andy. Directed by John Lasseter. Released Nov. 22, 1995. Voices provided by Tom Hanks (Woody), Tim Allen (Buzz Lightyear), Jim Varney (Slinky Dog), Don Rickles (Mr. Potato Head), John Ratzenberger (Hamm), Annie Potts (Bo Peep), Wallace Shawn (Rex). Songs by Randy Newman include "You've Got a Friend in Me," "Strange Things," and "I Will Go Sailing No More." 81 min. The film is the first animated feature ever generated completely on computers, produced as part of a partnership between Disney and Northern California-based Pixar. John Lasseter was presented a special Academy Award for "the development and inspired application of techniques that have made possible the first feature-length computer-animated film." A Disney Digital 3-D version was released on Oct. 2, 2009, along with one for *Toy Story 2*. During production, early versions of Woody included a ventriloquist's dummy and an ill-tempered cowboy before he became the affable hero seen on-screen. Buzz Lightyear offered a different challenge: inventing a brand-new toy that instantly felt familiar. In an early version of the film, the pizza parlor had a miniature golf theme. When Buzz Lightyear entered the picture, the designers turned it into Pizza Planet, a space-themed restaurant that Buzz could mistake for a spaceport and his ticket home. It also supplied the name and logo for the Pizza Planet delivery truck, which went on to make cameos in subsequent Pixar films.

Toy Story 2 (film) Animated feature from Pixar Animation Studios. Andy goes off to summer cowboy camp, and the toys are left to their own devices. When an obsessive toy collector, Al McWhiggin, kidnaps Woody, who, unbeknownst to him, is a highly valued collectible, it's up to Buzz Lightyear and the gang from Andy's room to spring into action and save their pal from winding up as a museum piece. The toys get into one predicament after another in their daring race to get Woody home before Andy returns. Released Nov. 24, 1999, after a Nov. 19 release at the El Capitan Theatre in Hollywood. Directed by John Lasseter. Voices include Tom Hanks (Woody), Tim Allen (Buzz Lightyear), Don Rickles (Mr. Potato Head), Jim Varney (Slinky Dog), Wallace Shawn (Rex), John Ratzenberger (Hamm), Annie Potts (Bo Peep), Kelsey Grammer (Stinky Pete, the Prospector), Joan Cusack (Jessie), Wayne Knight (Al McWhiggin), Estelle Harris (Mrs. Potato Head). 92 min. Produced as a partnership between Walt Disney Pictures and Pixar Animation Studios. The film was originally planned for direct-to-video release, but an enthused Pixar team got it upgraded to a full theatrical feature. When John

Lasseter decided the sequel wasn't yet up to Pixar standards, the animation studio had 9 months to deliver a finished product—though it's a process that typically takes 2 years. Composer Randy Newman added 2 new songs: "When She Loved Me" and "Woody's Roundup," with the former nominated for an Academy Award for Best Original Song. Improved computer programs and controls gave the animators more flexibility in moving the characters and allowed more subtle articulation than ever before. The film did phenomenal business and became Disney's 3rd highest-grossing film ever (after *The Lion King* and *The Sixth Sense*). It was the first motion picture to be entirely created, mastered, and exhibited digitally. It was also the first animated film sequel to gross more than its original. A Disney Digital 3-D version was released on Oct. 2, 2009, along with one for the original *Toy Story*.

Toy Story 3 (film) Animated feature from Pixar Animation Studios. As Andy prepares to depart for college, Buzz Lightyear, Woody, and the rest of his loyal toys are troubled about their uncertain future. Andy packs Woody, his favorite toy, to take to college with him, but the rest are to be left behind. The toys land at the Sunnyside Daycare center in a room full of untamed tots who cannot wait to get their sticky little fingers on these "new" toys. It's pandemonium as the toys try to stay together, endeavoring to return to Andy's house. Hindering their escape plans is a smooth-talking Ken doll, a Big Baby, and a pink, strawberry-scented teddy bear named Lots-o'-Huggin' Bear (called "Lotso"), who deceptively runs the center as a prison. Unimagined terrors await the toys as they are mistakenly picked up by a garbage truck and delivered to a landfill. Directed by Lee Unkrich. Released Jun. 18, 2010, and in Disney 3-D and IMAX versions after a Jun. 16 release in China and Egypt. Voices include Tom Hanks (Woody), Tim Allen (Buzz Lightyear), Joan Cusack (Jessie), Don Rickles (Mr. Potato Head), Wallace Shawn (Rex), Estelle Harris (Mrs. Potato Head), John Ratzenberger (Hamm), Ned Beatty (Lotso), John Morris (Andy), Laurie Metcalf (Andy's Mom), R. Lee Ermey (Sarge), Jodi Benson (Barbie), Bonnie Hunt (Dolly), Jeff Garlin (Buttercup), Whoopi Goldberg (Stretch), Michael Keaton (Ken), Timothy Dalton (Mr. Pricklepants), Bud Luckey (Chuckles). 103 min. In Aug. 2010, the film became the highest-grossing animated film of all time, passing $1 billion worldwide. (U.S. grosses were over $400 million, making it Disney's 2nd highest grosser after *Pirates of the Carib-*

bean: Dead Man's Chest.) For authenticity, the Pixar filmmakers toured several daycare centers, and soon felt that a daycare facility might feel like prison to a toy. To that end, they also studied and toured the infamous Alcatraz in San Francisco Bay. Nominated for 5 Academy Awards, including Best Picture, winning 2: Best Animated Feature and Best Song ("We Belong Together").

Toy Story 4 (film) Animated feature from Pixar Animation Studios. Woody has always been confident about his place in the world and that his priority is taking care of his kid, whether that's Andy or Bonnie. So when Bonnie's beloved new craft-project-turned-toy Forky declares himself as "trash" and not a toy, Woody takes it upon himself to show him why he should embrace being a toy. But when Bonnie takes the whole gang on her family's road trip excursion, Woody ends up on an unexpected detour that includes a reunion with his long-lost friend Bo Peep. After years of being on her own, Bo's adventurous spirit and life on the road belie her delicate porcelain exterior. As Woody and Bo realize they're worlds apart when it comes to life as a toy, they come to find that's the least of their worries. Directed by Josh Cooley. Released Jun. 21, 2019, also in 3-D and IMAX, after international releases beginning Jun. 19. Voices include Tom Hanks (Woody), Tim Allen (Buzz Lightyear), Annie Potts (Bo Peep), Tony Hale (Forky), Keegan-Michael Key (Ducky), Madeleine McGraw (Bonnie), Christina Hendricks (Gabby Gabby), Jordan Peele (Bunny), Keanu Reeves (Duke Caboom), Ally Maki (Giggle McDimples), Jay Hernandez (Bonnie's Dad), Lori Alan (Bonnie's Mom), Joan Cusack (Jessie), Bonnie Hunt (Dolly), Kristen Schaal (Trixie), Emily Davis (Billy, Goat & Gruff), Wallace Shawn (Rex), John Ratzenberger (Hamm), Blake Clark (Slinky Dog), Carl Weathers (Combat Carl), Don Rickles (Mr. Potato Head), Jeff Garlin (Buttercup). 100 min. Randy Newman reintroduced the song "You've Got a Friend in Me," also composing 2 new songs: "I Can't Let You Throw Yourself Away" (Academy Award nominee) and "The Ballad of the Lonesome Cowboy." Don Rickles passed away before his recording sessions began, so to source the lines for Mr. Potato Head, filmmakers searched through his past dialogue—from films, video games, toys, and theme park attractions. The film won the Academy Award for Best Animated Feature.

Toy Story at 20: To Infinity and Beyond (TV) Hour-long special on ABC; aired Dec. 10, 2015.

For the 20th anniversary of *Toy Story*, viewers take a look at how Pixar's early beginnings making short, digitally animated films led them to take the bold step of creating the first feature-length computer-animated film. Producers, animators, technical artists, designers, and voice talent discuss making the film and the impact it has had over the years. Directed by Brad Lachman. Interviewees include John Lasseter, Ed Catmull, Bob Iger, Andrew Stanton, Tim Allen, Tom Hanks, Pete Docter, George Lucas, Randy Newman.

Toy Story Hotel An 800-room hotel in Shanghai Disney Resort; opened Jun. 16, 2016, with wings themed to Woody and Buzz Lightyear. Featuring the Launch Pad water-play area, Play Room family activity center, and Sunnyside Café and Sunnyside Market restaurants. The hotel has a figure eight "infinity" layout; in China, the number 8 is considered to be very lucky. SEE ALSO TOKYO DISNEY RESORT TOY STORY HOTEL.

Toy Story Land Themed area in Hong Kong Disneyland; opened Nov. 17, 2013. Guests can experience the feeling of being shrunk to the size of a toy in Andy's backyard to play with their favorite Toy Story friends. Attractions include RC Racer, Slinky Dog Spin, and Toy Soldier Parachute Drop. In Shanghai Disneyland, Disney-Pixar Toy Story Land opened Apr. 26, 2018, with 3 attractions (Slinky Dog Spin, Rex's Racer, and Woody's Roundup), a quick-service restaurant (Toy Box Café), and a merchandise shop (Al's Toy Barn). On Jun. 30, 2018, Toy Story Land opened in Disney's Hollywood Studios at Walt Disney World, with 2 new attractions—Slinky Dog Dash and Alien Swirling Saucers—joining the existing Toy Story Mania!, and dining at Woody's Lunch Box. A table-service restaurant, Roundup Rodeo BBQ, was added in 2023. SEE ALSO TOY STORY PLAYLAND (WALT DISNEY STUDIOS PARK IN DISNEYLAND PARIS).

Toy Story Midway Mania! Attraction at the Disney parks; opened at Disney's Hollywood Studios May 31, 2008, in Pixar Place (in the space formerly occupied by Who Wants to Be a Millionaire—Play It!); at Disney California Adventure Jun. 17, 2008, on Paradise Pier (later Pixar Pier); and at Tokyo DisneySea, as Toy Story Mania!, Jul. 9, 2012, in American Waterfront. The attraction was designed and built for the California and Florida parks simultaneously. Guests wearing 3-D glasses ride themed vehicles along a route lined with "classic midway games of skill," shooting toy cannons at animated targets. Various characters from the Toy Story films host the ride. At Walt Disney World, the attraction's name was shortened to Toy Story Mania! Jun. 30, 2018, when the entrance moved to the new Toy Story Land.

Toy Story of Terror! (TV) Half-hour special on ABC; first aired Oct. 16, 2013. What starts out as a fun road trip for the Toy Story gang takes an unexpected turn for the worse when the trip detours to a roadside motel. After one of the toys goes missing, the others find themselves caught up in a mysterious sequence of events that must be solved before they all suffer the same fate. Directed by Angus MacLine. Voices include Tom Hanks (Woody), Michael Keaton (Ken), Kristen Schaal (Trixie), Jodi Benson (Barbie), Tim Allen (Buzz Lightyear). From Disney • Pixar.

Toy Story Playland Area in Walt Disney Studios Park at Disneyland Paris; opened Aug. 17, 2010, as an expansion of Toon Studio. Attractions include Toy Soldiers Parachute Drop (a simulated parachute drop), Slinky Dog Zigzag Spin (Slinky Dog spins as if to catch his own tail), and RC Racer (a half-pipe coaster), with shopping at Toy Story Playland Boutique. It became part of Worlds of Pixar in 2021. SEE ALSO TOY STORY LAND (DISNEY'S HOLLYWOOD STUDIOS, HONG KONG DISNEYLAND, AND SHANGHAI DISNEYLAND).

Toy Story That Time Forgot (TV) Animated short from Pixar Animation Studios. Christmas special on ABC; first aired Dec. 2, 2014. During a post-Christmas playdate, the Toy Story gang finds itself in uncharted territory when the coolest set of action figures ever turn out to be dangerously delusional. Trixie, the triceratops, is the one hope they have to return to Bonnie's room. Directed by Steve Purcell. Voices include Tom Hanks (Woody), Tim Allen (Buzz Lightyear), Kristen Schaal (Trixie), Timothy Dalton (Mr. Pricklepants), Joan Cusack (Jessie), Wallace Shawn (Rex), Don Rickles (Mr. Potato Head).

Toy Tinkers (film) Donald Duck cartoon released Dec. 16, 1949. Directed by Jack Hannah. Chip and Dale invade Donald's home for his Christmas goodies. This turns into an all-out war, with the chipmunks victorious, leaving with a convoy of nuts and candies. Nominated for an Academy Award. A 16-mm release title was *Christmas Capers*.

Toydarian Toymaker Shop in Star Wars: Galaxy's Edge; opened May 31, 2019, in Disneyland and Aug. 29, 2019, in Disney's Hollywood Studios at Walt Disney World. Visitors browse toys and collectibles in the workshop of the busy toy maker, Zabaka the Toydarian.

Toys Fantastique Toy store in Lake Buena Vista Shopping Village (later Downtown Disney Marketplace) at Walt Disney World, presented by Mattel for many years; opened Mar. 1975. It moved to a new location Dec. 1976 (replacing Posh Pets), and closed May 1988, to become Conched Out. In Aug. 1992, Toys Fantastic opened next to the Christmas Chalet, then relocated in 1996 to the former Mickey's Character Shop. It became the new location for Summer Sands in 2002, after a larger toy store, Once Upon a Toy, debuted.

Tracey, Doreen (1943–2018) Mouseketeer from the 1950s *Mickey Mouse Club* TV show.

Track of the African Bongo, The (TV) Show aired Apr. 3, 1977. Directed by Frank Zuniga. A young Kenyan boy, Kamua, spots a rare African antelope, protects the animal from hunters, and helps save the breed. Stars Johnny Ngaya, Oliver Litondo, Tony Parkinson. Narrated by Michael Jackson (not the singer but the Los Angeles talk show host).

Track of the Giant Snow Bear (film) A 16-mm release title of *Snow Bear*; released in Mar. 1972.

Trader Jack's Shop offering character merchandise, snacks, and sundries at Disney's Polynesian Village Resort at Walt Disney World; opened as Village Drugs and Sundries (offering floral arrangements and camera supplies) in Oct. 1971. Closed Jun. 2014 to become Moana Mercantile. Next door, the original Trader Jack's Grog Hut (offering food and beverages) became Samoa Snacks.

Trader Mickey (film) Mickey Mouse cartoon released Aug. 20, 1932. The first cartoon directed by Dave Hand. In the midst of their African safari, Mickey and Pluto are captured by a native tribe. To save themselves from the cannibals, Mickey and Pluto perform an impromptu jam session with musical instruments in their canoe.

Trader Sam's Enchanted Tiki Bar Tiki bar at the Disneyland Hotel; opened May 25, 2011. Named after the original salesman of the Jungle Cruise, the bar recounts Trader Sam's worldly travels with the artifacts and memorabilia he collected. Special interactive effects are triggered when certain signature cocktails are ordered. On Apr. 27, 2015, after a Mar. 28 soft opening, the similarly themed Trader Sam's Grog Grotto, with an adjacent Trader Sam's Tiki Terrace, opened off the lobby at Disney's Polynesian Village Resort at Walt Disney World. Cocktails are served in collectible tiki mugs.

Traders of Timbuktu Adventureland Bazaar shop in the Magic Kingdom at Walt Disney World; open Oct. 1, 1971–ca. 2000, offering African imports and apparel.

Trading Post Westernland store in Tokyo Disneyland; opened Apr. 15, 1983. Western and Native American items and arts and crafts are sold. Also a gift and collectibles shop in Disney Hotel Santa Fe at Disneyland Paris (opened Apr. 12, 1992) and in Disney Explorers Lodge at Hong Kong Disneyland Resort (opened Apr. 30, 2017).

Traffic Troubles (film) Mickey Mouse cartoon released Mar. 17, 1931. Directed by Burt Gillett. Mickey is a reckless taxi driver who has a series of hilarious adventures involving a flat tire, a medicine man, a cow, and a collision with a barn.

Tragedy on the Trail (TV) Episode 3 of *Gallegher Goes West*.

Trail Creek Hat Shop Frontierland shop in the Magic Kingdom at Walt Disney World; opened Jul. 29, 1991, taking the place of the Tricornered Hat Shoppe. It was later named Trail Creek Traders.

Trail Mix-Up (film) Roger Rabbit cartoon released Mar. 12, 1993. Directed by Barry Cook. Roger Rabbit is left to care for Baby Herman in Yellowstone National Park. When Baby Herman's curiosity gets the better of him, Roger is plunged into all sorts of zany adventures. He upsets a beehive, meets a tree-hungry beaver, and has several misadventures with a sawmill that conclude with Roger being sawed into hundreds of tiny Rogers. Roger, Baby Herman, the beaver, and an angry bear are saved from going over a waterfall only to plummet over a cliff. They land on a geyser that shoots them all into the faces carved on Mount Rushmore, ruining the national landmark. Voices by Charles Fleischer, Kathleen Turner, April Winchell. Produced in Disney-MGM Studios at Walt Disney World. Originally released with *A Far Off Place*.

Trail of Danger (TV) Two-part show; aired Mar. 12 and 19, 1978. Directed by Andrew V. McLaglen. Two men taking horses to market run afoul of angry sheepherders and are hampered by a lack of water for the horses. Stars Larry Wilcox, Jim Davis, Robert Donner, David Ireland.

Trail of the Panda (film) The second Disney collaboration with Chinese filmmakers. Lu, an orphan, finds a lost panda cub (Pang Pang), carries his new friend of his back, and begins an exciting trip to return it to its mother. Released in China May 8, 2009, after an Apr. 27 premiere in Chengdu, China. Directed by Xhong Yu. Stars Daichi Harashima (Lu). Chinese title is *Xiong mao hui jia lu*. Filmed at Siguniang Mountain, Balang Mountain, and the Wolong Giant Panda Reserve in Sichuan Province. Six different panda cubs were utilized to play Pang Pang; Mao Mao, who played Pang Pang's mother, perished in the May 12, 2008, Sichuan earthquake which nearly destroyed the Wolong Reserve.

Trailer Horn (film) Donald Duck cartoon released Apr. 28, 1950. Directed by Jack Hannah. Donald and the chipmunks, Chip and Dale, are after each other again, this time when they come upon Donald vacationing in a trailer. When he goes swimming, they fool him by moving the diving board and end up wrecking his car.

Trail's End Restaurant Frontier buffet dining adjacent to Pioneer Hall at Disney's Fort Wilderness Resort & Campground at Walt Disney World; opened in 1974, originally as Trail's End Buffeteria.

Trains (film) Educational film in the Goofy's Field Trips series released Aug. 10, 1989. 14 min. Goofy takes 2 kids on a field trip to learn about trains.

Tramp Happy-go-lucky mutt hero in *Lady and the Tramp*; voiced by Larry Roberts.

Tran, Kelly Marie Actress; appeared as Rose Tico in *Star Wars: The Last Jedi* and *The Rise of Skywalker*, and voiced Raya in *Raya and the Last Dragon*.

Tranquilo Golf Club Part of the Four Seasons Orlando resort development, replacing Osprey Ridge; opened in Nov. 2014. Tom Fazio, who had designed Osprey Ridge, returned to redesign the new 18-hole course. The clubhouse includes Plancha, a Cuban American restaurant.

Transcenter Automotive display at the exit of World of Motion in EPCOT Center; open Oct. 1, 1982–Jan. 2, 1996. The display featured films and shows such as Bird and the Robot and *The Water Engine*, future vehicles, and the latest models from General Motors.

Trattoria al Forno Restaurant on Disney's Board-Walk at Walt Disney World; opened Dec. 18, 2014, taking the place of Kouzzina. Italian meals, including pizzas and pastas, are served. A character breakfast was added in 2017.

Trauth, A. J. Actor; appeared on Disney Channel in *Even Stevens* and *The Even Stevens Movie* (Alan Twitty), *You Wish* (Alex Lansing), and voiced Josh in *Kim Possible.*

TraveLodge Hotel in Lake Buena Vista at Walt Disney World; opened Nov. 1972. From 1984–1989, its name was the Viscount. In 1999, it became the Best Western Lake Buena Vista Resort Hotel.

TravelPort Exhibit in Communicore East in EPCOT Center; open Oct. 1, 1982–Apr. 27, 1992. Sponsored by American Express. Guests could touch a TV screen to preview vacation trips to many areas of the world or ask for help from the American Express personnel.

Travers, P. L. (1899–1996) Australian-born English author of the Mary Poppins books, with the first one published in 1934. While she admired Walt Disney, she never quite approved of the film he made about her fictional nanny. She was portrayed by Emma Thompson in *Saving Mr. Banks.*

Travis, Nancy Actress; appeared in *Three Men and a Baby* and *Three Men and a Little Lady* (Sylvia) and *Passed Away* (Cassie Slocombe). She also made guest appearances on TV in *Desperate Housewives* and *Grey's Anatomy.*

Travolta, John Actor; appeared in *Phenomenon* (George Malley), *A Civil Action* (Jan Schlictmann), *Ladder 49* (Capt. Mike Kennedy), *Wild Hogs* (Woody Stevens), and *Old Dogs* (Charlie). He also voiced the title character in *Bolt.*

Treacher, Arthur (1894–1975) Actor; appeared in *Mary Poppins* (Constable Jones).

Treasure Buddies (film) Direct-to-DVD release

Jan. 31, 2012. The Buddies travel to the ruins of ancient Egypt. In a race against a devious cat, they, and their new friends Cammy (a baby camel) and Babi (a mischievous monkey), must avoid booby traps, solve puzzles, and explore a mysterious tomb, all in search of the greatest treasure known to animal-kind: the legendary lost collar of Cleocatra. Directed by Robert Vince. Stars Richard Riehle (Thomas Howard), Edward Herrmann (Philip Wellington), Mason Cook (Pete Howard). With the voices of G. Hannelius (Rosebud), Skyler Gisondo (B-Dawg), Nico Ghisi (Budderball), Field Cate (Buddha), Ty Panitz (Mudbud), Kaitlyn Maher (Cammy). 93 min.

Treasure Comet Tomorrowland shop in Tokyo Disneyland; opened in 2015, taking the place of ImageWorks. It was later themed to Hiro's lab from *Big Hero 6*.

Treasure Cove Pirate-themed land in Shanghai Disneyland; opened Jun. 16, 2016. Guests explore 5 areas (the entry, Shipwreck Shore, Fort Snobbish, Landlubber Landing, and the Village) and attractions, including Pirates of the Caribbean—Battle for the Sunken Treasure, Siren's Revenge, El Teatro Fandango, and Explorer Canoes.

Treasure from the Sea (film) Educational film demonstrating the benefits of magnesium, which, because of its lightness, can save energy. The film was made for Dow Chemical Co.; delivered Sep. 30, 1946.

Treasure in the Haunted House (TV) Show; part 2 of *For the Love of Willadean*.

Treasure Island (film) Young Jim Hawkins, possessor of a map to buried treasure, and his friends, Squire Trelawney and Dr. Livesey, plan to travel to Treasure Island to hunt for the treasure. Captain Smollett rounds up a crew that includes Long John Silver, who secretly plots a mutiny to secure the map and treasure for himself. When the mutiny fails, Silver escapes, taking Jim with him. When they reach the island, Jim gets away and meets a strange old hermit named Ben Gunn who helps him return to his crewmates, now battling the pirates led by Silver. Finally, the Squire, Smollett, and Gunn disarm Silver, and Gunn leads them to the treasure he had re-hidden years earlier. With their captive and the treasure, the crew rows back to the ship, only to have Silver escape with the rowboat, aided by Jim, who has a grudging affection for the rascally pirate. Released

Jul. 19, 1950. Based on the book published in 1881 by Robert Louis Stevenson. Directed by Byron Haskin. The first Disney live-action film without any animation. Also the first Disney film shot in England, in locations off the Cornish coast and Falmouth Bay. 96 min. Stars Bobby Driscoll as Jim Hawkins and Robert Newton as Long John Silver, with Basil Sydney (Capt. Smollett), Finlay Currie (Capt. Bones), Walter Fitzgerald (Squire Trelawney), Denis O'Dea (Dr. Livesey), Geoffrey Wilkinson (Ben Gunn). The Disney company had "blocked funds" in England after the war, money that Disney films had earned in the country, which could not be exported due to currency regulations. Walt Disney decided that he could use the money to make some films in England, but since he could not find trained animators there to produce his usual fare, he decided to turn to live action instead. Over the next few years, 4 live-action films would be made in England. The film was cut for its 1975 rerelease in order to gain a G rating, but the so-called violent scenes were restored on a later video release.

Treasure Island Nature preserve on Bay Lake at Walt Disney World; opened Apr. 8, 1974. Guests could explore a lush island filled with tropical plants, colorful birds, and areas themed to the *Treasure Island* story. Destinations included Doubloon Lagoon, Mutineer Falls, Dead Man's Island, and Scavenger Beach, where "pieces of eight" could sometimes be found buried in the sand. In 1977, it became Discovery Island, removing the pirate theme. The island itself, formerly known as Riles Island, was purchased by Disney in the mid-1960s from an investment club of 13 couples who used it as a vacation spot. Prior to that, the island was owned by Florida's first radio disc jockey, "Radio Nick" Nicholson, a conservation enthusiast who lived on the island with his wife and sandhill crane.

Treasure of Matecumbe (film) Shortly after the Civil War, two 13-year-old boys set out from Kentucky to seek a treasure buried in a Florida swamp. During the course of their exciting and often hilarious experiences, they acquire 3 colorful traveling companions—a dashing adventurer, a tart-tongued Southern belle, and a jaunty old medicine man. It takes the talents and ingenuity of all 5 to overcome the sinister forces working against them. Released Jul. 9, 1976. Directed by Vincent McEveety. 116 min. Stars Robert Foxworth (Jim), Joan Hackett (Lauriette), Peter Ustinov (Dr. Snodgrass), Vic Morrow (Spangler), Johnny Doran (David), Billy Attmore (Thad), Jane Wyatt (Aunt Effie), Don

Knight (Skaggs), Val De Vargas (Charlie), Dub Taylor (Sheriff Forbes), Dick Van Patten (Gambler). The movie was based on the book *A Journey to Matecumbe* by Robert Lewis Taylor. The song "Matecumbe" was written by Richard McKinley and Shane Tatum. Danville, Kentucky, was chosen for the opening scenes, and an old 217-acre estate, built around 1830, became "Grassy." The Sacramento River above Colusa, California, became the Mississippi, but the actual Everglades of Florida were used as such in the film, with the cast setting up production headquarters in Kissimmee. The man-made hurricane was shot in part of a rain forest inhabited by Seminoles and made by using giant wind machines and tons of water pumped in and blasted at the cast by airplane engines. During the last night of filming the disaster sequence, Ustinov was struck by a wave, fell, and was hospitalized for pulled ligaments in his left ankle. The company then moved to a beach at Walt Disney World, where final scenes in the picture were filmed.

Treasure of San Bosco Reef, The (TV) Two-part show; aired Nov. 24 and Dec. 1, 1968. Directed by Robert L. Friend. A young man, Dave Jones, visiting his uncle in Italy becomes involved with smugglers as they explore a sunken wreck and learn of stolen artifacts. Stars Roger Mobley, James Daly, Nehemiah Persoff, John van Dreelen. The star, Roger Mobley, moved on to this show directly after his work on the *Gallegher* series.

Treasure Planet (film) With a nod to Robert Louis Stevenson's *Treasure Island*, this animated feature follows 15-year-old Jim Hawkins's journey across a fantasy universe as the cabin boy aboard a glittering solar galleon, the RLS *Legacy*. Befriended by the ship's cyborg cook (part man, part machine) John Silver, Jim thrives under his guidance. He and the all-alien crew battle supernovas, black holes, and ferocious space storms. But greater dangers lie ahead when Jim discovers that his trusted mentor Silver is actually a scheming pirate with mutiny in mind. Confronted with a betrayal which cuts deep to his soul, Jim is transformed from boy to man as he finds the strength to face down the mutineers and discovers a "treasure" greater than he had ever imagined. Directed by John Musker and Ron Clements. Released Nov. 27, 2002, simultaneously in regular and large-screen theaters, after a world premiere on Nov. 5 in Paris and a release beginning there Nov. 6. Voices include Joseph Gordon-Levitt (Jim), Brian Murray (John Silver), Martin Short (B.E.N.), David Hyde Pierce (Doctor Doppler), Emma

Thompson (Captain Amelia), Michael Wincott (Scroop), Michael McShane (Hands), Roscoe Lee Browne (Mr. Arrow), Corey Burton (Onus), Tony Jay (Narrator), Austin Majors (young Jim), Patrick McGoohan (Billy Bones). 95 min. This was the first animated feature for which the backgrounds were all painted in the computer. While most of the characters were drawn by hand, John Silver was a complicated blend of hand-drawn and computer animation. Nominated for an Academy Award for Best Animated Feature.

Treasures in Paradise Paradise Pier toy and trinket shop in Disney California Adventure; opened Feb. 8, 2001. Closed Jan. 7, 2018, to become Knick's Knacks.

Treasures of the Walt Disney Archives Series of exhibits curated by the staff of the Walt Disney Archives to showcase prominent historical objects from the Archives' collection. Premiered at the first D23 Expo, Sep. 10–13, 2009, at the Anaheim Convention Center. Iterations have since been featured at subsequent domestic and international D23 Expos, the Ronald Reagan Presidential Library and Museum (Jul. 5, 2012–Apr. 30, 2013), the Chicago Museum of Science and Industry (Oct. 16, 2013–Jan. 4, 2015), and as a touring exhibit throughout Japan.

Treasures of Xandar Shop at the Wonders of Xandar pavilion (Guardians of the Galaxy: Cosmic Rewind) in EPCOT; opened May 27, 2022. As the story goes, it is operated by The Broker, a proud Xandarian offering otherworldly items from throughout the galaxy.

Tree Farm Also known as the Walt Disney World Nursery. Established in 1967 as one of the first sites on the property, sharing 30 acres with a Horticultural Research Center near the future Magic Kingdom. Landscape architect Bill Evans and superintendent Charlie Sepulveda experimented with nonnative plant species—sourced from as far away as Australia, Asia, and Africa—to determine how they would acclimate to Florida. By Oct. 1971, more than 60,000 plants and 800 varieties of trees were acquired, moved, and transplanted across the property. The Tree Farm was later relocated to the property's western end.

Tree of Life Located in the center of Discovery Island in Disney's Animal Kingdom, the tree towers 14 stories above the landscape and is 50 feet wide (and sprawls to 170 feet in diameter at its base). The trunk of the tree is intricately carved with a tapestry of more than 325 intertwining animal forms that symbolize the richness and diversity of animal life on Earth. Inside, guests experience a 3-D show about insects, entitled *It's Tough to Be a Bug! Tree of Life Awakenings*, a nighttime experience in which fireflies seem to bring animal spirits to life, revealing colorful stories on the tree, debuted Mar. 27, 2016.

Treehouse Villas Accommodations at Lake Buena Vista, built on pedestals in forested glens; opened in 1975 and closed in 2002. Became part of The Disney Institute in Feb. 1996. They were used for housing International College Program students Nov. 2005–Jan. 2008. On Jun. 1, 2009, after a major remodeling, they reopened as Treehouse Villas at Disney's Saratoga Springs Resort & Spa.

Trees (film) Segment of *Melody Time*. A 16-mm release in Nov. 1971.

Trek Snacks Quick-service snack bar in Asia at Disney's Animal Kingdom; opened Dec. 22, 2015, offering breakfast pastries, healthful snacks, sandwiches, sushi, and desserts.

Trenchcoat (film) While vacationing in Malta, aspiring mystery writer Mickey Raymond gets mixed up with disappearing corpses, disbelieving police, a federal agent in disguise, kidnappers, terrorists, and stolen plutonium. She and the federal agent—with whom she is becoming romantically involved—narrowly escape an explosion set to kill them, and they capture the terrorists instead. Released Mar. 11, 1983. Directed by Michael Tuchner. 92 min. Stars Margot Kidder (Mickey), Robert Hays (Terry), David Suchet (Inspector Stagnos), Gila Von Weitershausen (Eva Warner), Ronald Lacey (Princess Aida), Donald Faraldo (Nino), John Justin (Marquis de Pena). Before the creation of the Touchstone label, of which this would most likely have been an example, the film was simply not released as a "Disney" film. The film was shot on location on the island of Malta, in the town of Valletta, and at various sites such as Verdala Castle, Hagar Qim Temple, the Grand Master's Palace Armory, the Mosta Dome, St. Paul's Catacombs, and the Dragonara Palace Hotel and Casino.

Tren-D A 2,500-sq.-foot urban clothing and accessories store at the Downtown Disney Marketplace (now the Marketplace at Disney Springs) at Walt Disney World; opened Mar. 19, 2009, taking the place of Summer Sands. Organic loungewear, embroidered handbags, and trendy accessories are sold.

Trevor: The Musical (TV) Filmed version of the off-Broadway stage production following a 13-year-old force of nature with a vivid imagination. As Trevor deals with becoming a teenager in 1981, he struggles to navigate his own identity and determine how he fits in a challenging world. Digitally released Jun. 24, 2022, on Disney+. Directed by Marc Bruni. Stars Holden William Hagelberger, Mark Aguirre, Aaron Alcaraz, Ava Briglia, Sammy Dell, Tyler Joseph Gay, Ellie Kim, Colin Konstanty, Brigg Liberman. Book and lyrics by Dan Collins, with music by Julianne Wick Davis. Based on the 1995 short film *Trevor* that inspired the nonprofit organization The Trevor Project, the suicide prevention and crisis intervention organization for LGBTQ youth. The filming, directed by Robin Mishkin Abrams, took place at Stage 42 in New York City in Jan. 2022. From RadicalMedia.

T-REX Prehistoric-themed restaurant, from Landry's; opened at Downtown Disney Marketplace (now the Marketplace at Disney Springs) at Walt Disney World Oct. 14, 2008.

Tri-Circle-D Ranch Guests can enjoy trail, pony, wagon, and carriage rides in Disney's Fort Wilderness Resort & Campground at Walt Disney World. A variety of horses call the ranch home, including Appaloosas, Arabians, Belgians, Clydesdales, paint horses, Percherons, and quarter horses, plus Shetland ponies. The Tri-Circle-D was established by Owen and Dolly Pope, who had previously started the Pony Farm at Disneyland. Featured is the Dragon Calliope, a horse-drawn musical instrument originally acquired for the Mickey Mouse Club Circus at Disneyland and later used in *Toby Tyler*. The original ranch closed Aug. 19, 2019, reopening in a new and expanded facility Jun. 22, 2020.

Trial by Terror (TV) Episode 4 of *Gallegher Goes West*.

Trial of Donald Duck, The (film) Donald Duck cartoon released Jul. 30, 1948. Directed by Jack King. Donald refuses to pay his $35 lunch bill at a swanky restaurant and is sentenced in court to washing dishes, which he smashes in revenge.

Tribal Table Quick-service restaurant in Adventure Isle at Shanghai Disneyland; opened Jun. 16, 2016. Guests watch the action of live cooking with woks and rotisseries. The restaurant represents a gathering house in the Arbori village, with native artwork and artifacts on display. A Duffy and Friends theme was later added, with merchandise sold.

Triangle of Health (film) Series of 4 educational films made for Upjohn in 1968–1969: *Steps Toward Maturity and Health*, *Understanding Stresses and Strains*, *Physical Fitness and Good Health*, and *The Social Side of Health*.

Triangle of Health: Keeping the Balance (film) Educational release in Nov. 1992. 11 min. A girl at camp puts herself on a rigorous training schedule that excludes all other activities, and she becomes ill. She has to learn how to maintain a balance in all areas of life.

Triangle of Health: Moving On (film) Educational release in Nov. 1992. 11 min. A young boy becomes sullen and depressed when he learns his family is moving.

Triangle of Health: Personal Challenge (film) Educational release in Nov. 1992. 10 min. A boy's best friend at camp helps him with a strict training program so he can compete in a race.

Triangle of Health: True Friends (film) Educational release in Nov. 1992. 10 min. A Hungarian girl feels ostracized because she is unfamiliar with American ways at summer camp, and she loses her only friend who doesn't want to be ostracized either.

Tribute to Joel Chandler Harris, A (TV) Show aired Jan. 18, 1956. Directed by William Beaudine, Clyde Geronimi. The early years of author, journalist, and storyteller Harris (celebrated for his collection of Uncle Remus stories) as apprentice to a printer and budding writer are re-created; then a sequence from *Song of the South* is shown. Stars David Stollery (Joel Chandler Harris), Jonathan Hale (J. A. Turner), Sam McDaniel (Herbert), Harry Shannon (Mr. Wilson), Barbara Woodell (Mrs. Harris).

Tribute to Mickey Mouse (TV) Sequence featuring Mickey Mouse cartoons included in the shows *The Disneyland Story* and *A Further Report on Disneyland*. It is in his introduction that Walt Disney says the famous line, "I only hope that we never lose sight of one thing—that it was all started by a mouse."

TriceraTop Spin Carnival-inspired attraction in Chester & Hester's Dino-Rama! in Disney's Animal Kingdom; opened Nov. 18, 2001. Guests board 4-passenger triceratops gondolas and spin around a tin-toy top.

Trick or Treat (film) Donald Duck cartoon released Oct. 10, 1952. Directed by Jack Hannah. When the nephews come to Donald's house in their Halloween costumes, he plays tricks on them until Witch Hazel joins up with them and with her magical powers teaches Donald a lesson.

Tricks of Our Trade (TV) Show aired Feb. 13, 1957. Directed by Wilfred Jackson. Walt Disney explains some of the techniques of animation, including exaggeration, pantomime, effects animation, caricature, and the multiplane camera.

Tricornered Hat Shoppe Liberty Square shop in the Magic Kingdom at Walt Disney World; open Oct. 1, 1971–Jul. 28, 1991, and succeeded by the Trail Creek Hat Shop.

Trigger and Nutsy Two vulture soldiers of the sheriff in *Robin Hood*; voiced by George Lindsey and Ken Curtis, respectively.

Trip Through Adventureland, A/Water Birds (TV) Show aired Feb. 29, 1956. Directed by Winston Hibler. A visit to the Jungle Cruise and the rest of Adventureland in Disneyland, plus the True-Life Adventure film *Water Birds*.

Trip to Tucson (TV) Episode 15 of *Texas John Slaughter*.

Triton Gardens A King Triton leapfrog fountain was the centerpiece of this garden opened Feb. 1996, on the site of the former Alpine Gardens (where the Monsanto House of the Future once stood) at Disneyland. It closed in 2008, replaced by Pixie Hollow on Oct. 28 of that year.

Triton's Kingdom Attraction in King Triton Castle in Mermaid Lagoon at Tokyo DisneySea; opened Sep. 4, 2001, consisting of The Whirlpool, Blowfish Balloon Race, and Jumpin' Jellyfish.

Triviateers Name by which the finalists of the

Disney Store National Trivia Competition were known. From 1989–1999, the Store held an annual trivia showdown for its Cast Members, with the finalists going to Disneyland in the fall to compete for a trophy. Of the 50 Disney experts who competed for their stores, only 11 became national champs: Tony Anderson, Michael McNiel, Kevin Neary, Tim Huebner, Tommy Byerly, Tony Davis, Yvonne Mercer, John Kurowski, Antonio Ruberto, Carol Dobson, and Kevin Burk. Longtime runner-up Gary Pyle participated in more contests than any other Cast Member. Disney trivia competitions returned 2013–2019; winners of the Disney Store North America Trivia Championship have included Jenny Albers (2013 and 2014), Andrew Herbert (2015), and Mariah Lambes (2018).

Trolley Car Café, The Counter-service restaurant at the corner of Hollywood Boulevard and Sunset Boulevard in Disney's Hollywood Studios, serving Starbucks products; opened Feb. 6, 2015, replacing L.A. Cinema Storage.

Trolley Treats Shop on Buena Vista Street in Disney California Adventure; opened Jun. 15, 2012. Classic candies and freshly made treats are sold.

Trolley Troubles (film) Oswald the Lucky Rabbit cartoon; the first released, on Sep. 5, 1927. Oswald is the conductor on a trolley car and takes passengers on a wild ride.

Trombone Trouble (film) Donald Duck cartoon released Feb. 18, 1944. Directed by Jack King. The gods Vulcan and Jupiter are disturbed by Pete's sour trombone playing, so they give Donald the power to stop him. After Donald wins, he picks up the trombone and starts playing it himself.

Tron (film) Flynn, a young computer genius, breaks into the ENCOM computer looking for evidence that the video game programs he wrote were stolen by Dillinger, an ENCOM executive. Dillinger's Master Control Program (MCP) must stop Flynn, and it blasts him into its own computer dimension. Flynn awakens in an electronic world, where computer programs are the alter egos of the programmers who created them, and he is sentenced to die on the video game grid. Together with Tron, an electronic security program, Flynn escapes, destroys the MCP, and is able to return to the "real" world. Released Jul. 9, 1982. Directed by Steven

Lisberger. 96 min. Photographed in Super Panavision 70 mm, this special effects tour de force stars Jeff Bridges (Kevin Flynn/Clu), Bruce Boxleitner (Alan/Tron), David Warner (Dillinger/Sark), Cindy Morgan (Lora/Yori), Barnard Hughes (Dr. Walter/Gibbs), Dan Shor (Ram), Peter Jurasik (Crom), Tony Stephano (Peter/Sark's Lieutenant). The idea for *Tron* grew out of the director's passion for computer games. Lisberger and producer Donald Kushner spent 2 years researching the technology that plays such a prominent role in the film on which he made his live-action directorial debut. The film was the first motion picture to make extensive use of computer imagery, requiring much expertise and imagination. Though computer imagery had been previously seen as an effect in motion pictures such as in the *Star Wars* films, *Tron* was the first film to use the technique to create a 3-D world. The special effects team was headed by futuristic industrial designer Syd Mead, comic artist Jean "Moebius" Giraud, and high-tech commercial artist Peter Lloyd. Harrison Ellenshaw supervised the effects with Richard Taylor. Computer graphics were first applied to aerospace and scientific research in the mid-1960s, when methods of simulating objects digitally in their dimensions proved to be as effective as building models. The technology was then diverted into the entertainment field. Information International Inc. (Triple-I), Robert Able & Associates of Los Angeles, the Mathematic Applications Group Inc. (MAGI), and Digital Effects of New York City produced the computer imagery for the film. MAGI, the single largest contributor of computer imagery, sped up the process of supplying its work to Disney Studios in Burbank through a transcontinental computer hookup. This link cut by anywhere from 2½–5 days off the processing for each scene in the movie. The electronic world was shot on soundstages at the Disney Studio in Burbank. Photography for the real world took place at locations around Los Angeles, and at the U.S. government's futuristic Lawrence Livermore National Laboratory outside Oakland, California. The film was not the box office bonanza the Studio had hoped for, but it did spawn a number of popular video games. *Tron* was nominated for an Academy Award for Sound, by Michael, Bob, and Lee Minkler and Jim La Rue, and for Costume Design by Elois Jenssen and Rosanna Norton.

Tron: Legacy (film) Sam Flynn, the tech-savvy, rebellious 27-year-old son of Kevin Flynn, is haunted by the mysterious disappearance of his father, a man once known as the world's leading tech visionary. When Sam investigates a strange signal sent from the old Flynn's Arcade—a signal that could only come from his father—he finds himself pulled into the digital world of *Tron*, where his father has been living for 20 years. Along with Kevin's loyal confidant and fearless warrior, Quorra, father and son embark on a life-and-death journey of escape across a visually stunning cyber universe created by Kevin himself that has become far more advanced, with never-before-imagined vehicles, weapons, landscapes, and a ruthless villain who will stop at nothing to prevent their escape. Sequel to Steven Lisberger's 1982 cult classic film. Directed by Joseph Kosinski. Released in Disney Digital 3-D and IMAX 3-D on Dec. 17, 2010. Stars Garrett Hedlund (Sam Flynn), Jeff Bridges (Kevin Flynn/CLU), Olivia Wilde (Quorra), Bruce Boxleitner (Alan Bradley/Tron), James Frain (Jarvis), Beau Garrett (Gem), Michael Sheen (Castor/Zeus). 125 min. Original music by Daft Punk. It was the first 3-D movie to integrate a fully digital head and body (to create the younger version of Kevin Flynn); the first to create molded costumes using digital sculpture exclusively; the first 3-D movie shot with 35-mm lenses and full 35-mm chip cameras; and the first to make extensive use of self-illuminated costumes. Filmmakers challenged themselves to create the lighted suits without the use of CGI, turning to electroluminescent lamps made from a flexible polymer film; the actors had to be significantly compressed within the suits to compensate for the bulk of the electronics. On the back of each suit was a light disc consisting of 134 radio-controlled LED lights, attached with a magnet and housing the batteries and electronics that powered them. Filmed in CinemaScope. Nominated for an Academy Award for Sound Editing.

TRON Lightcycle Power Run Tomorrowland attraction in Shanghai Disneyland; opened Jun. 16, 2016. Guests ride atop two-wheeled Lightcycles into a mysterious computer game world inspired by *Tron: Legacy*. Nearly 10 years in development, the ride system is one of the most advanced ever designed. The attraction is one of the fastest indoor roller coasters in a Disney park and also offers a unique view of the area. A second version of the attraction, named TRON Lightcycle / Run, is slated to open Apr. 4, 2023, as an expansion of Tomorrowland in the Magic Kingdom at Walt Disney World; presented by Enterprise.

Tron: The Next Day (film) Short film released on the *Tron: Legacy* Blu-ray Apr. 5, 2011, chronicles the "Flynn Lives" movement that followed the mysterious disappearance of ENCOM computer programmer Kevin Flynn. Stars Dan Shor (Roy "Ram" Kleinberg), Bruce Boxleitner (Alan Bradley), Jeff Bridges (Kevin Flynn, voice). 10 min.

Tron: Uprising (TV) Animated series on Disney XD; premiered Jun. 7, 2012, with the story taking place between *Tron* and *Tron: Legacy*. Beck, a young program trained by Tron, becomes the unlikely leader of a revolution inside the computer world of The Grid. His mission is to free his home and friends from the reign of the villainous Clu and his henchman, General Tesler. Tron, the greatest warrior The Grid has ever known, not only teaches Beck the fighting skills he needs to challenge the brutal military occupation, but also guides and mentors him as he grows from an impulsive youth to a courageous, powerful leader. Destined to become the new protector of the system, Beck adopts Tron's persona and becomes the archenemy of Tesler and his oppressive forces. Voices include Elijah Wood (Beck), Bruce Boxleitner (Tron), Emmanuelle Chriqui (Paige), Mandy Moore (Mara), Paul Reubens (Pavel), Lance Henriksen (General Tesler). The series was preceded by a 30-min. prelude, *Tron: Uprising—Beck's Beginning*, airing first on Disney Channel May 18, 2012.

Trophy Room Gourmet dining at The Golf Resort at Walt Disney World, taking the place of the Magnolia Room. Succeeded by the Garden Gallery in 1986 when the resort became The Disney Inn. SEE ALSO CLUB 33.

Trophy Wife (TV) Half-hour series on ABC; aired Sep. 24, 2013–May 13, 2014. A reformed party girl, Kate, becomes the third wife of a slightly older man, Pete, and finds herself with an instant family of 3 stepchildren and 2 ex-wives. Kate has no experience with kids but is determined to learn and become part of the new family. Stars Malin Akerman (Kate), Bradley Whitford (Pete) Michaela Watkins (Jackie), Natalie Morales (Meg), Ryan Lee (Warren), Bailee Madison (Hillary), Albert Tsai (Bert), Marcia Gay Harden (Diane). From ABC Studios.

Tropic Toppers Adventureland Bazaar hat shop in the Magic Kingdom at Walt Disney World; opened Oct. 1, 1971. Closed ca. 1988 to become the Zanzibar Shell Company. Also in Tokyo Disneyland

Apr. 15, 1983–1987; succeeded by the Safari Trading Company.

Tropical Hideaway, The Adventureland marketplace in Disneyland; opened Dec. 21, 2018, replacing Aladdin's Oasis. Along the Jungle Cruise waterfront, guests enjoy Dole Whip and global-inspired snacks. Rosita, the cockatoo referenced in Walt Disney's Enchanted Tiki Room, can be found entertaining diners.

Tropical Serenade SEE SUNSHINE PAVILION AND ENCHANTED TIKI ROOM, WALT DISNEY'S.

Troubadour Tavern Fantasyland refreshment counter in the Magic Kingdom at Walt Disney World; opened Oct. 1, 1971, and presented by Welch's. Closed Oct. 20, 1993, to become Hook's Tavern. Also a quick-service counter in Tokyo Disneyland (opened Apr. 15, 1983) and in Disneyland (opened Nov. 20, 2009); the latter was previously named The Enchanted Cottage Sweets & Treats (Feb. 2004–Jul. 2009) and Troubadour Treats (2001–2003). At Shanghai Disneyland, a Troubadour Treats opened in Fantasyland Jun. 16, 2016, outside the Evergreen Playhouse.

Trousdale, Gary Animation director; he started at Disney as an effects artist on *The Black Cauldron*, later transferring to the Story Department, where he contributed to *Oliver & Company*, *The Little Mermaid*, *The Rescuers Down Under*, and *The Lion King*. With Kirk Wise, he co-directed the animated preshow film for Cranium Command at EPCOT, then *Beauty and the Beast*, *The Hunchback of Notre Dame*, and *Atlantis: The Lost Empire*. He left the company in 2003.

Trout, Dink (1898–1950) Actor/radio personality; he voiced Bootle Beetle and the King of Hearts in *Alice in Wonderland*.

Tru Confessions (TV) A Disney Channel Original Movie; first aired Apr. 5, 2002. High school freshman Trudy "Tru" Walker aspires to have her own TV show, and, to enter a cable TV contest that awards a TV hosting job, she produces a documentary about her twin brother, Eddie, a boy with a developmental disability. The filmmaking process becomes a perfect outlet for Tru to express herself and discover a greater appreciation for Eddie. Stars Clara Bryant (Tru Walker), Shia LaBeouf (Eddie Walker), Mare Winningham (Ginny Walker), William Francis McGuire (Bob Walker).

Truant Officer Donald (film) Donald Duck cartoon released Aug. 1, 1941. Directed by Jack King. Donald, as a truant officer, battles with his nephews to force them to go to school. When Donald finally wins and they reach the schoolhouse, he is embarrassed to learn that it is closed for summer vacation. Nominated for an Academy Award.

True Identity (film) After a series of discouraging auditions, an aspiring Black actor, Miles Pope, takes a flight home. When his plane begins to crash, the passenger in the seat next to him confesses that he is the infamous mob boss Frank Luchino, a man the FBI believes to be dead. The airplane eventually lands safely, but now Miles is the only man alive who knows the truth about Luchino. He soon becomes the target of a contract hit man. Forced to hide his true identity under a parade of disguises, including changing his skin color to white, Miles sets out to protect his life, reveal the crime lord's secret, and realize his dream of being a great actor. Released Aug. 23, 1991. Directed by Charles Lane. A Touchstone film. 93 min. Stars Lenny Henry (Miles), Frank Langella (Carver), Charles Lane (Duane). Filmed at locations in Los Angeles and New York City.

True Son's Revenge (TV) Show; part 2 of the airing of *The Light in the Forest*.

True-Life Adventure Festival (film) Reissues of the True-Life Adventure films in 6 packages in summer 1964.

True-Life Adventures (film) Series of 13 nature films between 1948–1960, including 7 featurettes (*Seal Island*, *Beaver Valley*, *Nature's Half Acre*, *The Olympic Elk*, *Water Birds*, *Bear Country*, *Prowlers of the Everglades*) and 6 features (*The Living Desert*, *The Vanishing Prairie*, *The African Lion*, *Secrets of Life*, *White Wilderness*, and *Jungle Cat*). Eight of them won Academy Awards. A new series, called New True-Life Adventures, began airing in syn. Feb. 2000. SEE ALSO SEAL ISLAND AND DISNEYNATURE.

Truly Exceptional, The: Carol Johnston (film) Educational film; released in Sep. 1979. The film depicts the story of a top-ranked gymnast with only one arm and her struggle toward a national championship. Aired as a TV special titled *Lefty*.

Truly Exceptional, The: Dan Haley (film) Educational film; released in Sep. 1979. A blind 16-year-old overcomes seemingly insurmountable obstacles, giving other students a clearer sense of individual human potential.

Truly Exceptional, The: Tom and Virl Osmond (film) Educational film; released in Sep. 1979. Two young men, deaf since birth, have not let their deafness hinder their success in helping to manage the Osmond family entertainment business.

Truman, Harry S. (1884–1972) Former President Truman visited Disneyland in Nov. 1957.

Trust in Me Song from *The Jungle Book*; written by Richard M. and Robert B. Sherman. The melody originated as "The Land of Sand," originally written for an unused sequence in *Mary Poppins*.

Trusty Lady's plodding bloodhound friend in *Lady and the Tramp*; voiced by Bill Baucom.

Truth About Mother Goose, The (film) Special cartoon featurette released Aug. 28, 1957. Directed by Wolfgang Reitherman and Bill Justice. Tells the historical stories behind 3 popular nursery rhymes ("Little Jack Horner"; "Mary, Mary Quite Contrary"; and "London Bridge"). 15 min. Nominated for an Academy Award.

Truth About Mother Goose, The (TV) Show aired Nov. 17, 1963. Directed by Hamilton S. Luske. Prof. Ludwig Von Drake and his co-host, Herman, present the theatrical featurette, plus sequences from other Disney films, including *Mickey and the Beanstalk*.

Truth & Iliza (TV) Late-night talk show on Freeform; aired May 2–Jun. 6, 2017. Using field pieces, audience interaction, and commentary, comedian Iliza Shlesinger explored sociopolitical issues of the day. 6 episodes.

Try Everything Song from *Zootopia*; written by Sia Furler, Tor Erik Hermansen, and Mikkel S. Eriksen, and performed by Shakira (as Gazelle).

Tryon, Tom (1919–1991) Actor; appeared in *Moon Pilot* (Capt. Richmond Talbot), on TV as *Texas John Slaughter*, and later became a best-selling novelist.

Tuberculosis (film) Educational film produced under the auspices of the Coordinator of Inter-American Affairs. The film describes tuberculosis as man's deadliest enemy and tells how it can be cured. It stresses prevention and communication. Delivered Aug. 13, 1945.

Tuck Everlasting (film) Teenager Winnie Foster longs for a life outside the control of her domineering mother, and when lost in the woods, she happens upon Jesse Tuck. He and his family are kind and generous, and they immediately take her in as one of their own. However, the Tucks hold a powerful secret, that of immortality, and with the mysterious Man in the Yellow Suit tracking them down, they fear that their world could end. Released Oct. 11, 2002. Directed by Jay Russell. Stars Alexis Bledel (Winnie Foster), Ben Kingsley (Man in the Yellow Suit), Sissy Spacek (Mae Tuck), Amy Irving (Mother Foster), Victor Garber (Robert Foster), Jonathan Jackson (Jesse Tuck), Scott Bairstow (Miles Tuck), William Hurt (Angus Tuck). Narrated by Elisabeth Shue. 90 min. Based on the book by Natalie Babbitt. Filmed in CinemaScope.

Tucker, Forrest (1919–1986) Actor; appeared on TV in *A Boy Called Nuthin'* (Turkeyneck).

Tudyk, Alan Actor; appeared on Disney+ in *Peter Pan & Wendy* (Mr. Darling) and *Earth to Ned*, and guest starred on ABC in *The Rookie* (Ellroy Basso). He has provided voices for films, including *Wreck-It Ralph* (King Candy), *Frozen* (Duke of Weselton), *Big Hero 6* (Alistair Krei), *Zootopia* (Duke Weaselton), *Moana* (Heihei), *Rogue One: A Star Wars Story* (K-2SO), *Ralph Breaks the Internet* (KnowsMore), *Aladdin* (Iago, 2019), *Frozen 2* (Guard/Northuldra Leader/Arendellian Soldier), *Raya and the Last Dragon* (Tuk Tuk), *Encanto* (Toucan), *Disenchanted* (Scroll), *Strange World* (Narrator/Radio Host 1/Duffle), and *Wish* (Valentino). TV voices include Ludo/King Butterfly in *Star vs. The Forces of Evil*, Alistair Krei in *Big Hero 6 The Series*, and Arcade in *Marvel's M.O.D.O.K.*

Tuesday Guest Star Day on the 1950s *Mickey Mouse Club*. Let's Go Day on the 1970s new *Mickey Mouse Club*. Guest Day on the 1990s *Mickey Mouse Club*.

Tugboat Mickey (film) Mickey Mouse cartoon released Apr. 26, 1940. Directed by Clyde Geronimi. Captain Mickey issues orders to shipmates Donald and Goofy to respond to an SOS. But in getting the ship underway, it explodes. Later, they find out the cry for help was only a radio show broadcast.

Tuk Tuk Raya's best friend and steed—part pill bug, part pug, and part off-road vehicle—in *Raya and the Last Dragon*; voiced by Alan Tudyk.

Tummy Trouble (film) Roger Rabbit cartoon released Jun. 23, 1989. Directed by Rob Minkoff. Roger Rabbit is left to babysit with the mischievous Baby Herman. The infant swallows a toy rattle, which is just the beginning of Roger's troubles. When he rushes the baby to the hospital, the duo gets involved in a multitude of misadventures. Voices by Charles Fleischer (Roger Rabbit), Kathleen Turner (Jessica), April Winchell/Lou Hirsch (Baby Herman). The first short cartoon made by the Disney Studio in 24 years. Released on video in 1990 with *Honey, I Shrunk the Kids*.

Tunes Behind the Toons, The (film) Documentary, released in 2014 at film festivals, which celebrates music in animation, from silent film days with organists and pianists accompanying cartoons to contemporary animated features. Prominent composers offer their insights on how the animation art form developed hand in hand with music. Directed by Dave Bossert. 28 min. Produced by Walt Disney Animation Studios Special Projects.

Turf Club Bar & Grill, The Table-service restaurant in Disney's Saratoga Springs Resort & Spa at Walt Disney World; opened Jul. 2006. Themed to a racetrack clubhouse with views of the Lake Buena Vista Golf Course. It was previously the Turf Club lounge, May 17, 2004–Oct. 31, 2005, though a lounge continues to operate just outside the restaurant.

Turnabout cookie jars SEE LEEDS CHINA CO.

Turner, Kathleen Actress; appeared in *V. I. Warshawski* (Vic) and provided the voice (uncredited) of Jessica Rabbit in *Who Framed Roger Rabbit*. She is credited in later Roger Rabbit shorts. On Disney+, she appeared in *Prop Culture*.

Turner & Hooch (film) Small-town police detective Scott Turner's life is suddenly turned around when an elderly friend is murdered and Turner unwillingly takes in Hooch, the friend's huge, sloppy, ill-mannered dog, who is the only witness to the murder. Soon Hooch has completely wrecked Turner's house and complicated his budding romance with veterinarian Emily Carson. But the mismatched pair eventually form a partnership in outwitting the crooks. Released Jul. 28, 1989.

Directed by Roger Spottiswoode. A Touchstone film. 98 min. Stars Tom Hanks (Scott Turner), Mare Winningham (Emily Carson). Hooch was portrayed by Beasley, a dog of the French breed called the de Bordeaux. Filmed on Terminal Island near Los Angeles, in San Pedro, and on the Monterey Peninsula.

Turner & Hooch (TV) Unsold pilot for a series based on the 1989 Touchstone feature about a detective with an unruly Saint Bernard for a partner. Aired on NBC Jul. 9, 1990. Directed by Donald Petrie. 30 min. Stars Tom Wilson, Wendee Pratt, Bradley Mott, Al Fann, John Anthony.

Turner & Hooch (TV) A Disney+ original series from 20th Television; digitally premiered Jul. 21, 2021. When Scott Turner, an ambitious, buttoned-up U.S. marshal, inherits a big unruly dog, he soon realizes the dog he didn't want may be the partner he needs. Stars Josh Peck (Scott Turner), Carra Patterson (Jessica Baxter), Brandon Jay McLaren (Xavier Wilson), Anthony Ruivivar (Chief James Mendez), Lyndsy Fonseca (Laura Turner), Jeremy Maguire (Matthew Garland), Vanessa Lengies (Erica Mounir). In the story, Turner is the son of detective Scott Turner, who was played by Tom Hanks in the 1989 Touchstone film. 5 French mastiffs play Hooch, the dog.

Turning Red (film) Animated feature from Pixar Animation Studios. Mei Lee, a confident, dorky 13-year-old, is torn between staying her mother's dutiful daughter and the chaos of adolescence. Her protective, if not slightly overbearing, mother, Ming, is never far from her daughter—an unfortunate reality for the teenager. And as if changes to her interests, relationships, and body weren't enough, whenever she gets too excited (which is practically always), she "poofs" into an 8-ft.-tall red panda. Digitally released on Disney+ Mar. 11, 2022, with a limited run at the El Capitan Theatre in Hollywood, after international releases beginning Mar. 10. Directed by Domee Shi. Voices include Rosalie Chiang (Meilin Lee), Sandra Oh (Ming), Ava Morse (Miriam), Hyein Park (Abby), Maitreyi Ramakrishnan (Priya), Orion Lee (Jin), Wai Ching Ho (Grandma), Tristan Allerick Chen (Tyler), Addison Chandler (Devon). 100 min. The film's overall aesthetic is described as "chunky cute," a principle that informed the simpler, rounder look of the characters and settings. Additional design inspiration came from anime, stop-motion animation, and the anatomy of Chinese porcelain sculptures. The story takes place in Toronto in 2002 and features a boy band named 4*Town, for which songwriters Billie Eilish and Finneas O'Connell composed 3 songs: "Nobody Like U," "U Know What's Up," and "1 True Love." Score by Ludwig Göransson. Nominated for an Academy Award for Best Animated Feature Film.

Turning the Tables with Robin Roberts (TV) A 4-episode series on Disney+; digitally premiered Jul. 28, 2021. Host Robin Roberts and some of Hollywood's groundbreaking women bear witness to their incredible journeys on their path to purpose. Also stars Debbie Allen, Sofia Carson, Jamie Lee Curtis, Jenna Dewan, Sheila E., Melissa Etheridge, Mickey Guyton, Betsey Johnson, Billie Jean King, Tig Notaro, Raven-Symoné, Josie Totah. From Rock'n Robin Productions and SpringHill Company.

Turquand, Todd Actor; Mouseketeer on the new *Mickey Mouse Club*.

Turtle Talk with Crush Interactive show within The Seas with Nemo & Friends in EPCOT; opened Nov. 2004. By the use of digital projection and voice-activated animation, Crush, the sea turtle from *Finding Nemo*, has a real-time conversation with guests. Also opened in Disney Animation at Disney California Adventure Jul. 15, 2005, as a temporary attraction in Hong Kong Disneyland in 2008, and in the Undersea Observatory on the S.S. *Columbia* in Tokyo DisneySea (as simply Turtle Talk) Oct. 1, 2009. A similar experience is featured inside the Animator's Palate restaurant on the *Disney Dream* (2011) and *Disney Fantasy* (2012), and another was introduced at the CHOC Children's Hospital in Orange, California, Feb. 2, 2013. On May 6, 2016, characters from *Finding Dory* were incorporated into the show at EPCOT and Disney California Adventure.

Turturro, John Actor; appeared in *Off Beat* (Neil Pepper), *The Color of Money* (Julian), *Quiz Show* (Herbert Stempel), *Unstrung Heroes* (Sid), *He Got Game* (Coach Billy Sunday), *O Brother, Where Art Thou?* (Pete), *Cradle Will Rock* (Aldo Silvano), and *Miracle at St. Anna* (Antonio Ricci). He voiced Francesco Bernoulli in *Cars 2*.

Tusker House Restaurant Marketplace-style eatery in Africa at Disney's Animal Kingdom; opened Apr. 22, 1998, originally as a counter-service restaurant. Meals are ordered in what appears to be an outdoor courtyard, with dining in the Safari Orien-

tation Centre, an information area for Harambe's tourists. The restaurant changed to buffet service Nov. 2007. Adjacent is the Dawa Bar, offering South African wines, African beers, and specialty cocktails.

Tutto Italia Ristorante Restaurant in Italy at EPCOT, sponsored by the Patina Restaurant Group, taking the place of L'Originale Alfredo di Roma Ristorante in Sep. 2007. After later closing for renovations, it reopened May 1, 2012, with an adjacent wine cellar, Tutto Gusto.

TWA Rocket to the Moon SEE ROCKET TO THE MOON.

'Twas the Night (TV) A Disney Channel Original Movie; first aired Dec. 7, 2001. Fourteen-year-old Danny Wrigley and his irresponsible but well-meaning Uncle Nick almost ruin Christmas when they decide to take Santa's new high-tech sleigh for a joyride. When they discover that Santa, on Christmas Eve, has been temporarily knocked out by an accident on the family's roof, they decide to take the holiday into their own hands and even out the inequities of Christmas once and for all. Directed by Nick Castle. Stars Bryan Cranston (Nick Wrigley), Josh Zuckerman (Danny Wrigley), Jefferson Mappin (Santa), Brenda Grate (Kaitlin Wrigley), Rhys Williams (Peter Wrigley), Barclay Hope (John Wrigley), Torri Higginson (Abby Wrigley).

Tweedledum and Tweedledee Obnoxious twins in *Alice in Wonderland*; voiced by J. Pat O'Malley.

Twentieth Century Fox SEE 21ST CENTURY FOX.

20th Century Music Company Shop on Main Street, U.S.A. in Disneyland; opened Jun. 20, 1999, taking the place of Great American Pastimes. Soundtracks and collectibles are sold.

20th Century Studios Production studio for feature films for theatrical and streaming release. Known as 20th Century Fox when it was acquired by Disney as part of the purchase of the parent company, 21st Century Fox, in 2019. It was renamed 20th Century Studios in Jan. 2020. SEE ALSO 21ST CENTURY FOX, INCLUDING FOR A LIST OF FILMS RELEASED SINCE THE DISNEY ACQUISITION.

20th Television Production studio for prime-time television and other entertainment content.

Known as 20th Century Fox Television when it was acquired by Disney as part of the purchase of the parent company, 21st Century Fox, in 2019. In Aug. 2020, it was announced that 20th Century Fox Television would be renamed 20th Television (as part of Disney Television Studios), and that its cable production division, Fox 21 Television Studios, would be renamed Touchstone Television. In Dec. 2020, Touchstone Television was folded into 20th Television. Prior to the Disney acquisition, popular shows included *Daniel Boone*; *Room 222*; *Julia*; *Lost in Space*; *M*A*S*H*; *America's Most Wanted*; *Doogie Howser, M.D.*; *The Simpsons*; *Beverly Hills 90210*; *Melrose Place*; *The X-Files*; *Ally McBeal*; *Malcolm in the Middle*; *The Bernie Mac Show*; *24*; *American Idol*; *Arrested Development*; *The O.C.*; *Boston Legal*; *House*; *Glee*; *Modern Family*; *Bob's Burgers*; *Last Man Standing*; *Brooklyn Nine-Nine*; *Empire*; *This Is Us*; and *9-1-1*. Series debuting since the Disney acquisition have included *Perfect Harmony*; *Bless the Harts*; *Outmatched*; *Central Park*; *Love, Victor*; *Big Sky*; *American Horror Stories*; *Turner & Hooch; Only Murders in the Building*; *Doogie Kamealoha, M.D.*; *The Wonders Years*; *Abbott Elementary*; *Single Drunk Female*; *Alaska Daily*; and *The Santa Clauses*.

20th Television Animation A unit of Disney Television Studios launched in 2021 to develop and produce adult animated series.

25th Anniversary of the Wonderful World of Disney (TV) SEE NBC SALUTES THE 25TH ANNIVERSARY OF THE WONDERFUL WORLD OF DISNEY.

25th Hour (film) In 24 hours, Monty Brogan, New York City highflyer, is off to jail for 7 years. On his last day, he tries to reconnect with his father and gets together with his 2 closest friends, Jacob and Slaughtery. Plus, there is his girlfriend, Naturelle, who might have been the one who tipped off the cops on him. Time is running out, and Monty has some tricks up his sleeve. Limited release Dec. 19, 2002, in Los Angeles and New York City; expanded release Jan. 10, 2003. A Touchstone film. Directed by Spike Lee. Stars Edward Norton (Monty Brogan), Philip Seymour Hoffman (Jacob Elinsky), Barry Pepper (Francis Xavier Slaughtery), Rosario Dawson (Naturelle Riviera), Anna Paquin (Mary D'Annunzio), Brian Cox (James Brogan). 135 min. Filmed in Super 35 wide-screen on location in the 5 boroughs of New York City.

21st Century Fox On Dec. 14, 2017, Disney announced its agreement to purchase a large part of the Murdoch family's 21st Century Fox. Included in the deal were 21st Century Fox's film production businesses, including 20th Century Fox, Fox Searchlight Pictures, Fox 2000 Pictures, Fox Family, and Fox Animation. Fox's television creative units were also acquired, including 20th Century Fox Television, FX Productions, and Fox21, plus FX Networks; National Geographic Partners; Fox Networks Group International; Star India; and Fox's interests in Hulu, Tata Sky, and Endemol Shine Group. The acquisition was completed Mar. 20, 2019, for a total equity and transaction value of approx. $71 billion. In Jan. 2020, the 20th Century Fox film studio was renamed 20th Century Studios and Fox Searchlight Pictures was renamed Searchlight Pictures, with 20th Century Fox Animation later renamed 20th Century Animation; its main animation unit, Blue Sky Studios, would close in Apr. 2021. In Aug. 2020, it was announced that 20th Century Fox Television would be renamed 20th Television and that Fox 21 Television Studios would be renamed Touchstone Television. Then in Dec. 2020, Touchstone Television was folded into 20th Television. The company began in 1915 as the Fox Film Corporation, a motion picture production company created by pioneering film exhibitor William G. Fox. In 1935, it merged with Twentieth Century Pictures — a company that was formed a few years earlier by Joseph Schenck and Darryl F. Zanuck — and became Twentieth Century-Fox. Media tycoon Rupert Murdoch acquired the company in 1985 and merged it with his television companies under Fox, Inc., a unit of Murdoch's News Corp. In 2013, News Corp. split its publishing and entertainment divisions into two groups — News Corp. and 21st Century Fox, the latter of which included Twentieth Century Fox and Twentieth Television.

The film studio has been one of the most successful in Hollywood, with movies and franchises including *The Grapes of Wrath, Miracle on 34th Street, All About Eve, Cleopatra, The Sound of Music, Planet of the Apes, Patton, M*A*S*H, Young Frankenstein, Star Wars, Alien, Die Hard, Home Alone, Mrs. Doubtfire, Independence Day, Titanic, X-Men, Fight Club, Cast Away, Moulin Rouge!, Ice Age, Night at the Museum, Slumdog Millionaire, Avatar, Life of Pi, Deadpool,* and *The Greatest Showman.* Since the acquisition by Disney, the following feature-length films have been released (theatrically, unless otherwise noted):

1. *Breakthrough* (Fox 2000 Pictures), 4/17/19 (PG)
2. *Tolkien* (Fox Searchlight Pictures), 5/10/19 (PG-13)
3. *Dark Phoenix* (20th Century Fox), 6/7/19 (PG-13)
4. *Stuber* (20th Century Fox), 7/12/19 (R)
5. *The Art of Racing in the Rain* (Fox 2000 Pictures), 8/9/19 (PG)
6. *Ready or Not* (Fox Searchlight Pictures), 8/21/19 (R)
7. *Ad Astra* (New Regency), 9/20/19 (PG-13)
8. *Lucy in the Sky* (Fox Searchlight Pictures), 10/4/19 (R)
9. *Jojo Rabbit* (Fox Searchlight Pictures), 10/18/19 (PG-13)
10. *Terminator: Dark Fate* (20th Century Fox), 11/1/19 (R)
11. *Ford v Ferrari* (20th Century Fox), 11/15/19 (PG-13)
12. *A Hidden Life* (Fox Searchlight Pictures), 12/13/19 (PG-13)
13. *Spies in Disguise* (Blue Sky Studios), 12/25/19 (PG)
14. *Underwater* (20th Century Fox), 1/10/20 (PG-13)
15. *Downhill* (Searchlight Pictures), 2/14/20 (R)
16. *The Call of the Wild* (20th Century Studios), 2/21/20 (PG)
17. *Wendy* (Searchlight Pictures), 2/28/20 (PG-13)
18. *The Personal History of David Copperfield* (Searchlight Pictures), 8/28/20 (PG)
19. *The New Mutants* (20th Century Studios), 8/28/20 (PG-13)
20. *The Empty Man* (20th Century Fox), 10/23/20 (R)
21. *Nomadland* (Searchlight Pictures), 2/19/21 (R) [Theatrical & Hulu]
22. *The Woman in the Window* (Fox 2000 Pictures), 5/14/21 (R) [Netflix]
23. *Summer of Soul (. . . Or, When the Revolution Could Not Be Televised)* (Searchlight Pictures), 7/2/21 (PG-13) [Theatrical & Hulu]
24. *Free Guy* (20th Century Studios), 8/13/21 (PG-13)
25. *The Night House* (Searchlight Pictures), 8/20/21 (R)
26. *Vacation Friends* (20th Century Studios), 8/27/21 (R) [Hulu]
27. *Everybody's Talking About Jamie* (New Regency), 9/17/21 (PG-13) [Amazon Prime]
28. *The Eyes of Tammy Faye* (Searchlight Pictures), 9/17/21 (PG-13)
29. *The Last Duel* (20th Century Studios), 10/15/21 (R)
30. *Ron's Gone Wrong* (20th Century Animation), 10/22/21 (PG)
31. *The French Dispatch of the Liberty, Kansas Evening Sun* (Searchlight Pictures), 10/22/21 (R)
32. *Antlers* (Searchlight Pictures), 10/29/21 (R)
33. *Home Sweet Home Alone* (20th Century Studios), 11/12/21 (PG) [Disney+]
34. *West Side Story* (20th Century Studios), 12/10/21 (PG-13)
35. *Nightmare Alley* (Searchlight Pictures), 12/17/21 (R)
36. *The King's Man* (20th Century Studios), 12/22/21 (R)
37. *Death on the Nile* (20th Century Studios), 2/11/22 (PG-13)
38. *No Exit* (20th Century Studios), 2/25/22 (R) [Hulu]
39. *Fresh* (Searchlight Pictures), 3/4/22 (R) [Hulu]
40. *Deep Water* (New Regency), 3/18/22 (R) [Hulu]
41. *The Bob's Burgers Movie* (20th Century Animation), 5/27/22 (PG-13)
42. *Fire Island* (Searchlight Pictures), 6/3/22 (R) [Hulu]
43. *Good Luck to You, Leo Grande* (Searchlight Pictures), 6/17/22 (R) [Hulu]
44. *The Princess* (20th Century Studios), 7/1/22 (R) [Hulu]
45. *Not Okay* (Searchlight Pictures), 7/29/22 (R) [Hulu]
46. *Prey* (20th Century Studios), 8/5/22 (R) [Hulu]
47. *Barbarian* (New Regency), 9/9/22 (R)
48. *Brahmāstra: Part One: Shiva* (Fox Star), 9/9/22 (NR)
49. *See How They Run* (Searchlight Pictures), 9/16/22 (PG-13)
50. *Amsterdam* (New Regency), 10/7/22 (R)
51. *Rosaline* (20th Century Studios), 10/14/22 (PG-13) [Hulu]
52. *The Banshees of Inisherin* (Searchlight Pictures), 10/21/22 (R)
53. *The Menu* (Searchlight Pictures), 11/18/22 (R)
54. *Darby and the Dead* (20th Century Studios), 12/2/22 (PG-13) [Hulu]
55. *Empire of Light* (Searchlight Pictures), 12/9/22 (R)
56. *Avatar: The Way of Water* (20th Century Studios), 12/16/22 (PG-13)

57. *Boston Strangler* (20th Century Studios), 3/17/23 (R) [Hulu]
58. *Rye Lane* (Searchlight Pictures), 3/31/23 (R) [Hulu]

24KT Precious Adornments Jewelry shop in the Lake Buena Vista Shopping Village at Walt Disney World; open Mar. 1975–Oct. 1995 and succeeded by Rainforest Cafe.

21 Royal Formal luxury dining experience in Disneyland; reservations opened Jan. 25, 2017, after testing that began in fall 2015. Parties of up to 12 guests dine in an elaborately designed room connected to the Disneyland Dream Suite in New Orleans Square. Initially Club 33 members could book reservations for a 5-course meal. The name refers to the address on Royal Street. Designed in the Empire style, popular in 19th-century New Orleans, the dining room features murals painted by Disney artist Leslee Turnbull. SEE ALSO DISNEYLAND DREAM SUITE.

Twenty Something (film) Hand-drawn animated short; digitally released Sep. 10, 2021, on Disney+. Adulting can be hard; some days you're nailing it, while other days, you're just a stack of kids hiding in a trench coat hoping no one notices. Gia finds herself in this exact scenario the night of her 21st birthday. Directed by Aphton Corbin. From the Pixar Animation Studios SparkShorts program. 8 min.

20,000 Leagues Under the Sea (film) In 1868, an armed frigate sent to seek out a fabled destroyer of ships is itself sunk, and 3 passengers from the frigate—a harpooner, Ned Land, along with a professor who is an expert on the creatures of the sea and his assistant—are rescued. They discover that the "monster" which they searched for is in reality the first man-made submarine, the *Nautilus*, commanded by Captain Nemo, a madman who is willing to share his secrets of nuclear energy with the world only on his own terms. Land rescues Nemo from the clutches of a giant squid and eventually manages to alert the outside world as to the location of Nemo's secret island base. Nemo and his creations are destroyed. Released Dec. 23, 1954. Stars James Mason (Capt. Nemo), Kirk Douglas (Ned Land), Paul Lukas (Prof. Aronnax), Peter Lorre (Conseil). Based on the classic story by Jules Verne. Academy Award winner for Best Special Effects and Best Art Decoration/Set Decoration (John Meehan and Emile Kuri); nominated also for Best Film Editing. 127 min. The first Disney feature filmed in CinemaScope. Disney special effects wizards constructed the giant squid of rubber, steel spring, flexible tubing, glass cloth, Lucite, and plastic, with tentacles measuring 40 feet with 2 feelers of 50 feet. It could rear up 8 feet out of water, its tentacles and feelers moving with frightening realism. It took a staff of 28 men to operate the intricate remote controls. Using hydraulics, electronics, and compressed air, they succeeded in giving a lifelike appearance to the squid. But there were problems. The squid fight had to be filmed again after Walt Disney and the director, Richard Fleischer, were unhappy with the initial results. It had been filmed in a special tank on brand-new Soundstage 3 at the Disney Studio as if it was sunset on a placid sea; unfortunately this allowed viewers to see too much of the mechanics that enabled the squid to move, and it looked too fake. Instead, the scene was shot a second time, as if it was a stormy night, with 100 backstage workers on hand providing the needed lightning, rain, turbulent seas, and hurricane winds—and everything worked much better. The movie featured the song "A Whale of a Tale" by Al Hoffman and Norman Gimbel. Fleischer was the son of Walt's early animation rival, Max Fleischer, who created the *Out of the Inkwell* and *Betty Boop* cartoons, and Disney made sure that Max did not object before he hired his son. Locations for the film included the Disney and 20th Century Fox lots in California, and various locales in The Bahamas and Jamaica. The *Nautilus* was designed by Harper Goff. Reissued in theaters in 1963 and in 1971. A TV show on the making of the film, *Operation Undersea*, won the Emmy for best TV program of the year. The *Nautilus* set was displayed for a time at Disneyland.

20,000 Leagues Under the Sea Fantasyland submarine attraction in the Magic Kingdom at Walt Disney World; open Oct. 14, 1971–Sep. 5, 1994. While Disneyland had based its submarine attraction on the nuclear submarines that had been so much in the news in the late 1950s, by the time Walt Disney World was planned, the designers decided instead to pattern their fleet after Captain Nemo's *Nautilus* from the 1954 live-action film, with Nemo himself (voiced by Pete Renaday) providing the narration. From Nemo's home port of Vulcania, passengers journeyed through an 11.5-million-gallon lagoon to lost undersea worlds, including a graveyard of ships, the sunken ruins of Atlantis, and a volcano that sent the *Nautilus* into the tentacles of a giant squid. The 12 submarine vehicles, each 61 feet long and weighing 58 tons, were built at Tampa

Shipyards. The attraction quickly became one of the most popular in the park. Also known as 20,000 Leagues Under the Sea Submarine Voyage. Although the attraction closed in 1994, demolition did not occur until summer 2004. The site later became home to Under the Sea ~ Journey of the Little Mermaid.

20,000 Leagues Under the Sea Mysterious Island attraction in Tokyo DisneySea; opened Sep. 4, 2001, sponsored by Coca-Cola. Guests join Captain Nemo's crew and undertake a mysterious deep-sea exploration mission aboard a 6-passenger submarine boat, encountering shipwrecks, sea monsters, and the lost continent of Atlantis.

20,000 Leagues Under the Sea Exhibit Display of sets from the 1954 feature; open in Tomorrowland in Disneyland Aug. 3, 1955–Aug. 28, 1966. When Walt Disney was rushed to finish Disneyland on time, he fell behind on Tomorrowland. So, since the movie *20,000 Leagues Under the Sea* was so successful, he decided to display the original sets there. The stopgap attraction turned out to be one of the more popular ones in Disneyland, so it remained for 11 years. The popularity of movie sets was proven again when Disney-MGM Studios opened in Florida in 1989. In 1994, Disneyland Paris opened a walk-through attraction, Les Mystères du Nautilus, similar to the one that had been in Disneyland, but this time most of the set pieces had to be reconstructed.

22 Cynical soul who refuses to leave The Great Before in *Soul*; voiced by Tina Fey.

22 vs. Earth (film) Animated short from Pixar; digitally released Apr. 30, 2021, on Disney+. Set before the events of *Soul*, 22 defies the rules of The Great Before and refuses to go to Earth, enlisting a gang of 5 other new souls in her attempt at rebellion. Directed by Kevin Nolting. Voices include Tina Fey (22), Richard Ayoade (Jerry), Alice Braga (Jerry). 6 min.

Twilight Bark, The The barking of dogs that sounds the alert about the missing puppies in *One Hundred and One Dalmatians*. The phrase was used years later as the title of Disney Feature Animation's weekly employee newsletter.

Twilight Zone Tower of Terror, The Sunset Boulevard thrill attraction in Disney's Hollywood Studios; opened Jul. 22, 1994. Guests take a strange odyssey through the remains of a decaying Hollywood hotel. As the story goes, the Hollywood Tower Hotel was once a beacon for the show business elite—until the fateful Halloween night of 1939, when it was struck by a lightning bolt that engulfed the building, sending an elevator carrying 5 passengers plummeting 13 floors down the length of the tower. Today, visitors are invited into the hotel, where they walk through the abandoned lobby, library (where *Twilight Zone* host Rod Serling appears on a TV to introduce the story), and boiler room. The adventure culminates in a trip through the fifth dimension and a 13-story drop in a runaway service elevator. The experience was enhanced with the addition of 2 more drops on the elevator over the next 2 years. In 1999, even more drops were added, and on Dec. 31, 2002, the drop sequences became randomized, controlled by the attraction itself. Technically, the ride system is not actually an elevator, but rather a vertical vehicle conveyance. The 199-ft.-tall hotel structure was designed in the Spanish revival style, recalling the opulence of grand hotels from Hollywood's golden age. A similar attraction, 183 feet in height and designed in a pueblo deco style, opened in the Hollywood Pictures Backlot at Disney California Adventure May 5, 2004; it closed Jan. 2, 2016, to become Guardians of the Galaxy – Mission: BREAKOUT! Another Tower of Terror attraction opened in American Waterfront at Tokyo DisneySea Sep. 4, 2006, with a completely new backstory. In this version, adventurer Harrison Hightower III, who founded the Hotel Hightower and filled it with curios gathered on his worldwide treks, mysteriously disappeared in 1899 after unveiling a stolen idol, Shiriki Utundu; and now, 13 years later in 1912, the New York Preservation Society has opened the hotel for tours. A 4th version, The Twilight Zone Tower of Terror: Un Saut dans la Quatrième Dimension, opened in Production Courtyard at Walt Disney Studios Park in Disneyland Paris Dec. 22, 2007, closely resembling the version at Disney California Adventure. Beginning Sep. 28, 2019, 3 new story line scenarios were added to the Paris attraction. They were titled The Malevolent Machine, The Shaft Creatures, and The 5th Dimension; each scenario follows a little girl who was one of the passengers who vanished when the hotel was struck by lightning.

Twisted (TV) One-hour mystery series on ABC Family; aired Jun. 11, 2013–Apr. 1, 2014. Danny Desai, a charismatic 16-year-old with a troubled past, reconnects with his 2 female best friends from childhood, but he becomes the prime suspect when a fellow student is found dead in her home. Stars Avan Jogia (Danny Desai), Maddie Hasson (Jo Masterson), Kylie Bunbury (Lacey Porter), Kimberly Quinn (Tess Masterson), Sam Robards (Kyle Masterson), Ashton Moio (Rico), Denise Richards (Karen Desai), and Greg Damon (Archie). From Prodco, Inc.

Twister, Bull from the Sky (TV) Show aired Jan. 4, 1976. Directed by Larry Lansburgh. A young man raises a cast-off Brahman calf to become a champion bucking bull, but to lighten a disabled in-flight plane's load, the bull has to be pushed out while harnessed into 3 parachutes. The bull lands unscathed in a wildlife safari park, but is endangered because of the wild and predatory animals there. Stars Larry Wilcox, Willie Aames, Keith Andes, Denis Arndt.

Twitches (TV) A Disney Channel Original Movie; first aired Oct. 14, 2005. Twin sisters Alex and Camryn, separated shortly after birth in the otherworldly kingdom of Coventry, are quickly sent to Earth to escape the dangers of an evil force. At birth, their wizard father assigned each twin a protector, Ileana and Karsh, and from there, each girl was adopted and raised in wildly disparate homes. When they finally meet each other on their 21st birthday, they learn they have extraordinary, mysterious powers. Now, Alex and Camryn struggle to accept the truth about their past and must battle the evil forces of Darkness that once threatened to destroy them. Directed by Stuart Gillard. Stars Tia Mowry (Alex), Tamera Mowry (Camryn), Kristen Wilson (Miranda), Patrick Fabian (Thantos), Pat Kelly (Karsh). 86 min.

Twitches Too (TV) A Disney Channel Original Movie; first aired Oct. 12, 2007. After discovering they are both twin sisters and princesses, Alex Fielding and Camryn Barnes begin learning about each other and what it means to have magical powers. As Camryn embraces the royal lifestyle in the magical kingdom of Coventry, Alex is eager to begin her new life as a college student. Directed by Stuart Gillard. Stars Tia Mowry (Alex Fielding), Tamera Mowry (Camryn Barnes), Kristen Wilson (Miranda), Jackie Rosenbaum (Beth Fish), Pat Kelly (Karsh), Leslie Sieler (Ileana), Patrick Fabian (Thantos), Chris Gallinger (Demitri), Jayne Eastwood (Mrs. Norseng), Kevin Jubinville (Aaron). A sequel to *Twitches*.

Two Against the Arctic (TV) Two-part show; aired Oct. 20 and 27, 1974. Directed by Robert Clouse. Two Eskimo children are stranded on an ice cap with little food. They struggle not only with nature but with polar bears and wolves as they head toward home. Stars Susie Silook, Marty Smith, Rossman Peetook.

2½ Dads (TV) Show aired Feb. 16, 1986. Faced with rising housing costs, a widower/father with 2 kids, a divorced dad with 3, and a bachelor friend hit on an ingenious solution: they decide to share a house. As the kids try to adjust to their new "siblings," the 3 men struggle to cope with running the household. Stars George Dzundza, Lenore Kasdorf, Marissa Mendenhall. Directed by Tony Bill.

Two Chips and a Miss (film) Chip and Dale cartoon released Mar. 21, 1952. Directed by Jack Hannah. Chip and Dale attend a nightclub and fall in love with the female entertainer, another chipmunk named Clarice, who divides her attention between the 2.

Two for the Record (film) Special cartoon combining *After You've Gone* and *All the Cats Join In* from *Make Mine Music*; released Apr. 23, 1954.

Two Gun Goofy (film) Goofy cartoon released May 16, 1952. Directed by Jack Kinney. Goofy, by accident, becomes a hero and a sheriff when he interrupts a stagecoach robbery.

Two-Gun Mickey (film) Mickey Mouse cartoon released Dec. 15, 1934. The first cartoon directed by Ben Sharpsteen. In this western adventure, Pete and his bandits rob and fire on Minnie before she is rescued by Mickey, who disposes of the gang.

Two Happy Amigos (TV) Show aired Feb. 5, 1960. Directed by Jack Hannah, C. August Nichols. Walt introduces a visit by José Carioca in a show that combines Donald Duck and other cartoons.

Two More Eggs (TV) Animated short-form series on Disney XD; premiered Jun. 23, 2015, on the network's online platforms. With ultra-wacky humor and a surreal mixture of animation techniques, the series marked Disney XD's first original program created for digital, nonlinear platforms. Produced by The Brothers Chaps' Citywide Hoop Champs, Inc., in association with Disney Television Animation.

Two Much (film) A struggling art gallery owner in

Miami, Art Dodge, works a scam of trying to get widowed spouses of recently deceased men to pay for paintings the men allegedly purchased. But he gets into trouble when one of his patsies turns out to be the widow of a purported mob boss, and Art finds himself in the middle of a bizarre romantic triangle involving the man's son and ex-wife, Betty. Needless to say, this leads to chaos. Released Mar. 15, 1996. Directed by Fernando Trueba. A Touchstone Pictures presentation of an Interscope Communications production, in association with Occidental Media. Stars Antonio Banderas (Art/Bart), Danny Aiello (Gene), Melanie Griffith (Betty), Daryl Hannah (Liz), Eli Wallach (Sheldon Dodge), Joan Cusack (Gloria Fletcher). 118 min. Filmed in CinemaScope. Based on the novel by Donald E. Westlake. The movie was based on a script originally created in Spain by Fernando and David Trueba and filmed on location in Miami.

2R's – Read'n & Rite'n Book and stationery shop in the Lake Buena Vista Shopping Village at Walt Disney World; opened Mar. 22, 1975. It later took the place of Village Spirits, when the original shop became the Great Southern Craft Store in 1988. It became Disney's Wonderful World of Memories in 2002. Also known as 2R's Reading and Riting.

Two Silhouettes (film) Segment of *Make Mine Music*, with "Ballade Ballet," featuring Tania Riabouchinska and David Lichine dancing and Dinah Shore singing. The song is by Charles Wolcott and Ray Gilbert.

Two Weeks Vacation (film) Goofy cartoon released Oct. 31, 1952. Directed by Jack Kinney. Goofy goes on his vacation but gets tangled up with a trailer and has various other mishaps until he ends up peacefully in jail.

Tyler, Ginny (1930–2012) She began with Disney narrating phonograph records for Disneyland Records but moved to TV to serve as head Mouseketeer for the syn. *Mickey Mouse Club* in 1962. For films, she provided voices for 2 amorous female squirrels in *The Sword in the Stone* and sang for several barnyard animals in the "Jolly Holiday" sequence of *Mary Poppins*. She was named a Disney Legend in 2006.

Tyner, Charles (1925–2017) Actor; appeared in *Pete's Dragon* (Merle), and on TV in *Shadow of Fear*.

Typhoon Lagoon A 56-acre water park at Walt Disney World; opened Jun. 1, 1989. After the popularity of River Country, Disney designers decided that another aquatic experience was needed, and they tried to outdo their earlier effort. The mythology of the place is that a typhoon hit the town in the past, marooning a shrimp boat, the *Miss Tilly*, perched precariously atop Mount Mayday and leaving all in ruins. Now, with the water park, guests climb the mountain to slide down into the pools below. Highlights have included Castaway Creek, Shark Reef (closed in 2016), Ketchakiddee Creek, and the waterslides Humunga Kowabunga, Keelhaul Falls, Gangplank Falls, Mayday Falls, Jib Jammer, Stern Burner, and Rudder Buster. The main lagoon features the world's largest artificially created waves. Refreshments are available at Leaning Palms and Typhoon Tilly's Galley & Grog. The Crush 'n' Gusher water coaster attraction was added in 2005, and Miss Adventure Falls, a whitewater attraction with a backstory featuring Captain Mary Oceaneer and her parrot friend, Duncan, opened Mar. 12, 2017.

Tytla, Vladimir ("Bill") (1904–1968) Highly regarded animator; at the Disney Studio 1934–1943, he animated on the shorts, then on *Snow White and the Seven Dwarfs*, *Pinocchio* (Stromboli), *Fantasia* (the demon, Chernabog, on Bald Mountain), and *Dumbo*. He was named a Disney Legend posthumously in 1998.

Tytle, Harry (1909–2004) He joined the Disney Studio in 1936 in the Animation Department, where he served as an assistant director. Tytle moved up through the ranks to production manager in 1944, shorts manager in 1946, cartoon production manager in 1955, and production coordinator in 1963. In the 1970s, he became a producer of such films as *Chandar, the Black Leopard of Ceylon*; *Salty, the Hijacked Harbor Seal*; *The Little Shepherd Dog of Catalina*; *Barry of the Great St. Bernard*; and *The Proud Bird from Shanghai*. For a number of years, he served as the Disney representative in Europe for the projects that were being filmed there. In 1998, he wrote his autobiography entitled *One of Walt's Boys*.

1. *Up* (film) 2. Unbirthday Song, The 3. Universe of Energy 4. Utilidors 5. *Ugly Dachshund, The* (film)
6. *Ugly Duckling, The* (film) 7. Ursula 8. United Kingdom 9. *Us Again* (film)

Ugly Betty (TV) One-hour comedy series on ABC; aired Sep. 28, 2006–Apr. 14, 2010. Even though plain Betty Suarez does not fit in the superficial world of high fashion, when she goes to work for the new, young publisher of the fashion magazine, *Mode*, her indomitable spirit and bright ideas eventually win him over. Neither of them really knows the ins and outs of the fashion world, but the 2 of them are a formidable team against the label-wearing sharks who will do anything to see them fail. Stars America Ferrera (Betty Suarez), Eric Mabius (Daniel Meade), Ana Ortiz (Hilda), Vanessa Williams (Wilhelmina Slater), Tony Plana (Ignacio), Ashley Jensen (Christina), Becki Newton (Amanda), Mark Indelicato (Justin), Alan Dale (Bradford Meade). From Touchstone Television.

Ugly Dachshund, The (film) When a Great Dane puppy is put into a litter of dachshunds, the puppy grows up thinking he's a dachshund, too, thereafter causing no end of humorous complications in the lives of Mark Garrison, a magazine illustrator, and his lovely wife, Fran. The Great Dane finally proves his worth, realizing just what kind of an animal he is, and peace once more descends on the Garrison household. Released Feb. 4, 1966. Directed by Norman Tokar. 93 min. Stars Dean Jones (Mark Garrison), Suzanne Pleshette (Fran Garrison) in her Disney debut, along with Charlie Ruggles (Dr. Pruitt), Kelly Thordsen (Officer Carmody), and Parley Baer (Mel Chadwick). For the title role of Brutus, the animal trainer found a 3-year-old prize-winning Great Dane named Diego of Martincrest. But needing a dog with more experience for some of the more demanding scenes, he found a double

in Duke, whom he had used earlier as one of the Great Danes in *Swiss Family Robinson*.

Ugly Duckling, The (film) Silly Symphony cartoon released Dec. 17, 1931. Directed by Wilfred Jackson. When a mother hen scorns a little duckling, it runs away in dismay. But when a tornado dumps her chicks into the flooded river, the duckling saves them from going over the waterfall. A hero, he is now one of the family. The film is from a story by Hans Christian Andersen. Remade in color as the last Silly Symphony released Apr. 7, 1939. Directed by Jack Cutting. The remake changed the story to have a baby "duckling" shunned by his family because of his ugliness until a mother swan recognizes him as a swan and adopts him as one of her brood. It won an Academy Award as Best Cartoon. An educational version was entitled *Hans Christian Andersen's The Ugly Duckling*.

Ullman, Ricky Actor; on Disney Channel, he appeared in the title role in *Phil of the Future* and as Roscoe in *Pixel Perfect*, plus guest starred in *That's So Raven* (Jake), and voiced Eric in *Kim Possible: So the Drama*. As Raviv Ullman, he appeared on TV in *Criminal Minds: Suspect Behavior* (Ben Armus).

Ultimate Christmas Present, The (TV) A Disney Channel Original Movie; first aired Dec. 1, 2000. In Los Angeles, a 13-year-old, Allie Thompson, and her friend Sam find a discarded contraption that turns out to be Santa Claus's weather-making machine. They decide to use it to make it snow so they can get a school snow day and not have to turn in an assignment. But the machine gets out of hand

and causes no end of problems that threaten to ruin Christmas. Allie and Sam team up with Santa in an attempt to save the day. Directed by Greg Beeman. Stars Hallie Hirsh (Allie Thompson), Brenda Song (Samantha Kwan), Peter Scolari (Edwin Hadley), Hallie Todd (Michelle Thompson), John B. Lowe (Santa Claus), Bill Fagerbakke (Sparky), John Salley (Crumpet), Spencer Breslin (Joey Thompson). Canada's Vancouver substituted for Los Angeles for the filming.

Ultimate X See ESPN's Ultimate X.

Ultra Violet & Black Scorpion (TV) Live-action comedy on Disney Channel; premiered Jun. 3, 2022. Violet Rodriguez, an everyday Mexican American teen, is chosen by a magical luchador mask which transforms her into Ultra Violet, a superhero fighting crime alongside her luchador uncle, Cruz (aka Black Scorpion). Although Cruz takes Violet under his wing to teach her the responsibilities of her special powers, she doesn't always see eye to eye with him when it comes to his methods for capturing crooks. In the meantime, she must keep her superhero identity secret from her parents and older brother, as well as her friends and schoolmates. But she does lean on one close confidante: her best friend, Maya, who documents Ultra Violet's adventures on social media. Stars Scarlett Estevez (Violet/Ultra Violet), J.R. Villarreal (Cruz De la Vega/Black Scorpion), Marianna Burelli (Nina Rodriguez), Juan Alfonso (Juan Carlos Rodriguez), Brandon Rossel (Santiago "Tiago" Rodriguez), Zelia Ankrum (Maya Miller-Martinez), Bryan Blanco (Luis León). From Chu Garcia and GWave Productions.

Ulu Cafe Restaurant at Aulani, A Disney Resort & Spa; opened Oct. 19, 2013. Diners enjoy self-serve and cooked-to-order specialties with an ocean view.

Unbirthday Song, The Song from *Alice in Wonderland*; written by Mack David, Al Hoffman, and Jerry Livingston.

Unbreakable (film) David Dunn is the sole survivor of a devastating train wreck. Elijah Price is a mysterious stranger who offers a bizarre explanation as to why David escaped without a single scratch, an explanation that threatens to change David's family and life forever. Released Nov. 22, 2000. A Touchstone film. Directed by M. Night Shyamalan. Stars Bruce Willis (David Dunn), Samuel L. Jackson (Elijah Price), Robin Wright Penn (Audrey Dunn), Charlayne Woodard (Elijah's mother), Spencer Treat Clark (Joseph Dunn). 107 min. Filmed in CinemaScope. Shot on location in and around Philadelphia.

Uncle Buck (TV) Series on ABC; aired Jun. 14–Jul. 5, 2016. Uncle Buck is a charismatic hustler who has gotten by on his charm for years. But when his brother, Will, and family move to town and need help with the kids, he steps up to become their nanny. Will and wife Alexis are wary of Buck's questionable parenting skills, but his unique perspective and street smarts provide some unconventional solutions to raising 3 rambunctious kids, Tia, Miles, and Maizy, who typically make a hobby out of terrorizing their nannies. Stars Mike Epps (Buck), Nia Long (Alexis), James Lesure (Will), Iman Benson (Tia), Sayeed Shahidi (Miles), Aalyrah Caldwell (Maizy). Based on the 1989 comedy film of the same name starring John Candy. Produced by Universal Television and ABC Studios.

Uncle Donald's Ants (film) Donald Duck cartoon released Jul. 18, 1952. Directed by Jack Hannah. Donald has ant trouble when sugar spills from a bag he is carrying. This leads to a battle with the ants at his home over a jug of maple syrup, eventually resulting in Donald's car exploding and the ants enjoying the syrup.

Uncle Remus Character created by Joel Chandler Harris and played by James Baskett in *Song of the South*.

Uncle Scrooge See Scrooge McDuck.

Under the Gun (film) Dramatic educational film for children about handgun violence, produced in cooperation with the Center to Prevent Handgun Violence and sponsored by MetLife. 26 min. Released in Jan. 1995.

Under the Sea Song from *The Little Mermaid*; written by Howard Ashman and Alan Menken. Academy Award winner.

Under the Sea ~ Journey of the Little Mermaid Dark-ride attraction in Fantasyland in the Magic Kingdom at Walt Disney World; opened Dec. 6, 2012. The same attraction, with a new exterior (Prince Eric's Castle), interactive queue area, and some changes to the attraction itself, as The Little Mermaid ~ Ariel's Undersea Adventure in Disney California Adventure.

Under the Tuscan Sun (film) Freshly divorced San Francisco writer Frances Mayes is depressed, but her best friend, Patti, offers a gift—a 10-day trip to Tuscany, in the heart of Italy. Once there, Frances impulsively buys a run-down villa named Bramasole, literally "something that yearns for the sun." As she embraces the local ways and devotes herself to the restoration of her new home, Frances finds herself forming close bonds with people around her and slowly rediscovers the pleasures of laughter, friendship, and romance. A Touchstone film. Directed by Audrey Wells. Released Sep. 26, 2003. Stars Diane Lane (Frances Mayes), Sandra Oh (Patti), Lindsay Duncan (Katherine), Raoul Bova (Marcello), Vincent Riotta (Martini). 115 min. Based on the book by Frances Mayes. Filmed on location in Cortona, Positano, Rome, and Florence, Italy.

Under Wraps (TV) A Disney Channel Original Movie; first aired Oct. 25, 1997. Three kids discover a 3,000-year-old mummy on Halloween and accidentally set him free. They discover that they must return their new friend to his resting place before midnight, or he will turn to dust and lose his immortal soul. Directed by Greg Beeman. Stars Maria Yedidia (Marshall), Adam Wylie (Gilbert), Clara Bryant (Amy), Bill Fagerbakke (mummy).

Under Wraps (TV) A Disney Channel Original Movie; first aired Oct. 1, 2021. Three 12-year-old friends awaken a mummy, which they name Harold. Together, they must rush to return him to his resting place before midnight on Halloween, narrowly escaping a nefarious group of criminals who are determined to sell the mummy to the highest bidder. Directed by Alex Zamm. Stars Malachi Barton (Marshall), Christian J. Simon (Gilbert), Sophia Hammons (Amy), Phil Wright (Harold), Melanie Brook (Buzzy), Brent Stait (Kubot), Jordana Largy (Diane), Jaime M. Callica (Ted), Karin Konoval (Ravensworth). A contemporary remake of the 1997 Disney Channel Original Movie.

Under Wraps 2 (TV) A Disney Channel Original Movie (DCOM); first aired Sep. 25, 2022, on Disney Channel, followed by a Sep. 30 digital release on Disney+. Amy is preparing for her father's Halloween-themed wedding to his fiancée. However, plans quickly go awry when Amy, Gilbert, and Marshall discover that their mummy friend, Harold, and his beloved Rose may be in danger. Sobek, an evil mummy with a 1,000-year-old grudge against his best friend-turned-bitter rival Harold, is unexpectedly awakened and out for revenge. With help from his hypnotized lackey Larry, Sobek kidnaps Rose; Amy, Gilbert, Marshall, Buzzy, and Harold must use their skills once again to save her and get back in time for the wedding. Stars Malachi Barton (Marshall), Christian J. Simon (Gilbert), Sophia Hammons (Amy), Phil Wright (Harold), Melanie Brook (Buzzy), Ryla McIntosh (Rose), Jordan Conley (Larry), T.J. Storm (Sobek), Claude Knowlton (Pop), Antonio Cayonne (Carl), Adam Wylie (Beuller). A sequel to *Under Wraps*, the 2021 remake of the first DCOM.

Underdog (film) After an accident in the mysterious lab of maniacal scientist Dr. Simon Barsinister, an ordinary beagle, Shoeshine, unexpectedly finds himself with unimaginable powers and the ability to speak. Armed with a fetching superhero costume, Underdog vows to protect the beleaguered citizens of Capitol City and, in particular, one beautiful spaniel named Polly Purebred. From Walt Disney Pictures in association with Spyglass Entertainment. Released Aug. 3, 2007. Directed by Frederik Du Chau. Stars James Belushi (Dan), Alex Neuberger (Jack), Peter Dinklage (Dr. Simon Barsinister), Patrick Warburton (Cad), Jason Lee (voice of Underdog), Amy Adams (voice of Polly Purebred), Brad Garrett (voice of Riff Raff). Shoeshine/Underdog is played by Leo, a lemon beagle, Polly by Ginger, a Cavalier King Charles spaniel, and Riff Raff by Bronco, a rottweiler. 82 min. Filmed in Super 35. Based on the 1960, 121-episode, animated TV series created by W. Watts Biggers. Providence, Rhode Island, portrayed the movie's Capitol City.

Undergrads, The (TV) Pay-TV movie for The Disney Channel; debuted May 5, 1985. A 68-year-old enrolls with his grandson, Jody, at a local university after Jody spirits him away from a rest home to which he has been sent by his son". He finds his study skills have rusted over the years. 101 min. Directed by Steven H. Stern. Stars Art Carney (Mel Adler), Chris Makepeace (Jody), Len Birman (Verne), Lesleh Donaldson (Kim), Jackie Burroughs (Nancy). The film was shot in Canada, with the University of Toronto a major location.

Underhill, Don Mouseketeer from the 1950s *Mickey Mouse Club* TV show.

Understanding Alcohol Use and Abuse (film) Educational film produced by Reynolds Film Export and animation director John Ewing;

released in Sep. 1979. The dangers of alcohol abuse are shown through animation.

Understanding Stresses and Strains (film) Educational film made for Upjohn's Triangle of Health series; released in Jun. 1968. The film suggests the use of common sense to minimize the normal stresses and strains of life.

Underwood, Jay Actor; appeared on The Disney Channel in *Not Quite Human*, *Not Quite Human II*, and *Still Not Quite Human* (Chip Carson).

Unforgettable Happens Here The 2015–16 Disney Parks campaign theme celebrating unforgettable Disney memories.

Unhappily Ever After (TV) Series on The WB Network; aired Jan. 11, 1995–Sep. 19, 1999. Used-car salesman Jack Mulloy is getting a divorce from his wife, Jennie, after 16 years, and their 3 self-centered kids hope they will be spoiled rotten by their competing parents. Jack's only confidant is an old stuffed bunny—a parting gift from his 8-year-old son—that just happens to talk. Stars Geoff Pierson (Jack), Stephanie Hodge (Jennie), Joyce Van Patten (Maureen), Justin Berfield (Ross), Kevin Connolly (Ryan), Nikki Cox (Tiffany). Bobcat Goldthwait provides the voice of Mr. Floppy, the talking bunny. From Touchstone Television.

UFO Zone Water-play area in Tomorrowland at Hong Kong Disneyland; opened Jul. 13, 2006. Guests splashed around a UFO crash site, dodging water ray guns and watching alien plants as they sprang to life. Replaced in 2016 by Jedi Training: Trials of the Temple.

Unidentified Flying Oddball (film) In this updated adaptation of Mark Twain's *A Connecticut Yankee in King Arthur's Court*, an astronaut and his robot companion accidentally fly backward in time and end up as prisoners at the court of King Arthur. A jealous Merlin and Mordred plot to overthrow the king, but thanks to modern technology, the Knights of the Round Table are able to defeat the evil forces in a rousing climactic battle. Released first in England as *The Spaceman and King Arthur* on Jul. 10, 1979; U.S. release on Jul. 26, 1979. Directed by Russ Mayberry. 93 min. The TV title was *The Spaceman in King Arthur's Court*. Stars Dennis Dugan (Tom), Jim Dale (Sir Mordred), Ron Moody (Merlin), Kenneth More (King Arthur), Rodney Bewes (Clarence), John Le Mesurier (Sir Gawain), Sheila

White (Alisande). The film was shot on location at Alnwick Castle and at Pinewood Studios, London. Alnwick Castle, which dates back to the 11th century, doubled for Camelot. A banquet hall within the castle walls was converted into a commissary to provide meals for the more than 150 filmmakers and 1,000 extras. All of the extras were rounded up from within a 50-mile radius, including the people of the historic market town of Alnwick. A large special effects team headed by Cliff Culley and Ron Ballanger created Hermes, the robot; laser guns; a jet-pack that flies; a magnetized sword; and a 25-foot-long space shuttle aircraft with a retractable ramp and compact 4-foot moon rover that expands to 7 feet, with various screens, a solar disc, and a large hydraulic arm that emerges and operates on cue.

United Artists Distributor of the Disney cartoons 1932–1937, along with *Victory Through Air Power* in 1943.

United Kingdom World Showcase pavilion in EPCOT; opened Oct. 1, 1982. A street winding past buildings that evoke the small towns of England leads guests to a series of shops selling typical wares, such as The Toy Soldier, The Crown & Crest, Sportsman's Shoppe, Lords and Ladies, and The Tea Caddy. Concerts are performed in Britannia Square, a formal 1800s-style city park with a traditional gazebo modeled after the one in Hyde Park, London. Dining includes the Rose & Crown Pub and Dining Room and Yorkshire County Fish Shop. For many years in the square, the World Showcase Players, formerly the Old Globe Players, enticed passersby into participating in their little comedies.

United Nations, The (film) Educational film, in Mickey's Field Trips series, released Jul. 27, 1989. 16 min. It provides a guided tour through the United Nations complex.

U.S. Junior Tournament; World Junior Tennis Tournament (TV) Two 2-hour syn. specials commemorating the national and international Sport Goofy Junior Tennis Championships. The first special, aired Sep. 1983, covered the national championship held the preceding month in Coto de Caza, California. The second, aired Dec. 1983, covered the world championship, in which international players had competed at Walt Disney World in Sep. 1983. Directed by Andrew Young. Hosted by Dick and Patti Van Patten.

United We Fall (TV) Half-hour family sitcom on ABC; aired Jul. 15–Aug. 26, 2020. Jo and Bill, the parents of 2 young kids, try to make it day to day as a functioning family, but Bill's judgmental live-in mother and Jo's overzealous extended family will never hesitate to let the couple know they're messing up. United against everyone, Jo and Bill will always have each other's backs, proving that barely anything is possible. Stars Will Sasso (Bill Ryan), Christina Vidal Mitchell (Jo Rodriguez), Jane Curtin (Sandy Ryan), Guillermo Díaz (Chuy Rodriguez), Ella Grace Helton (Emily Ryan). From Sony Pictures Television, Exhibit A Film, Julius Sharpe International Petroleum & Writing Inc., and ABC Studios.

Universe of Energy Future World pavilion in EPCOT Center; opened Oct. 1, 1982. It was sponsored by Exxon (later ExxonMobil) 1982–2004. On the roof of the pavilion were 2 acres of solar panels that generated enough electricity to power much of the attraction. Inside, guests learned about energy in a series of films and a trip into the prehistoric past—a primeval forest diorama showcasing Earth's molten beginnings with 36 lifelike dinosaurs. Guests rode in 30,000-lb. traveling theater cars, which each held 96 passengers and were guided along a very thin wire embedded in the concrete floor. The title song, "Universe of Energy," was written by Al Kasha and Joel Hirschhorn, with "Energy (You Make the World Go 'Round)" by Bob Moline. The pavilion closed Jan. 1996, for a major refurbishment, and a new show, Ellen's Energy Adventure, debuted Sep. 15, starring Ellen DeGeneres and Bill Nye, the Science Guy. The pavilion closed for good Aug. 13, 2017, to become Guardians of the Galaxy: Cosmic Rewind.

UnPrisoned (TV) An 8-episode half-hour dramedy; scheduled for digital release Mar. 10, 2023, on Hulu. The life of a messy, but perfectionist, relationship therapist and single mom is turned right-side-up when her dad gets out of prison and moves in with her and her teenage son. Stars Kerry Washington (Paige Alexander), Delroy Lindo (Edwin). Inspired by the life of creator Tracy McMillan. Part of the Onyx Collective. From ABC Signature.

Unstrung Heroes (film) Steven Lidz is 12 years old, and his world is falling apart. Overwhelmed by his life with an ailing mother and an emotionally disturbed father, Steven runs off to live with his 2 wildly eccentric uncles, Danny and Arthur. Baffled by the tragedies surrounding him, Steven finds solace in the idiosyncrasies of his uncles' strange and wonderful world, and he begins understanding his life. Limited release on Sep. 15, 1995; general release on Sep. 22. A Hollywood Pictures film. Directed by Diane Keaton. Stars Andie MacDowell (Selma Lidz), John Turturro (Sid Lidz), Michael Richards (Danny), Maury Chaykin (Arthur), Nathan Watt (Steven). 93 min. Filmed on location in Los Angeles and Pasadena, California.

Up (film) Animated feature from Pixar Animation Studios. Carl Fredricksen spent his entire life dreaming of exploring the globe and experiencing life to the fullest. But at age 78, life seems to have passed him by, until a twist of fate (and a persistent and overly optimistic 8-year-old Junior Wilderness Explorer named Russell) gives him a new lease on life. Tying thousands of balloons to his house, Carl takes a thrilling journey to find a mountaintop waterfall in Venezuela where his late wife, Ellie, had always dreamed of visiting, only to discover all too late that his biggest nightmare, Russell, has stowed away on the "trip." The unlikely pair encounter wild terrain and unexpected villains as they try to save a rare 13-foot-tall flightless bird they name Kevin. Directed by Pete Docter and Bob Peterson. Released May 29, 2009, in the U.S., after a May 28 release in Russia and a May 13 screening at the Cannes Film Festival. Voices include Ed Asner (Carl), Jordan Nagai (Russell), Christopher Plummer (Charles Muntz), Bob Peterson (Dug/Alpha), John Ratzenberger (Tom), Delroy Lindo (Beta), Jerome Ranft (Gamma). 96 min. Pixar's first title produced in Disney Digital 3-D. A total of 10,297 animated balloons were used to float Carl's house, though 20,622 were used to lift the structure from its foundation. The crew determined that approx. 20 million–30 million balloons would be needed to raise a full-sized house in real life. When director Pete Docter happened on a TV documentary about the Tepuis of South America, he discovered the perfect world to explore; Pixar sent a team of artists to study the mile-high plateaus in Venezuela, one of the most uncharted places on Earth. Nominated for 5 Academy Awards, winning 2: Best Animated Feature (Pete Docter) and Best Original Score (Michael Giacchino). It became the second animated feature, after *Beauty and the Beast*, to be nominated for a Best Picture Academy Award.

UP! A Great Bird Adventure Theater show in Asia at Disney's Animal Kingdom; opened Apr. 22, 2018, succeeding *Flights of Wonder*. Senior Wilderness Explorer Russell and his friend Dug from Disney • Pixar's *Up* discovered and shared up-close encounters with birds from around the world. Replaced by a new show, *Feathered Friends in Flight*, in 2020.

Up a Tree (film) Donald Duck cartoon released Sep. 23, 1955. Directed by Jack Hannah. Donald Duck, a logger in a logging camp, is getting ready to topple a tree that is the home of Chip and Dale, who quickly get revenge that ultimately leads to the destruction of Donald's house.

Up Close & Personal (film) Tally Atwater is determined to capture the coveted news anchor position, a spot many assured her she would never achieve. Blazing a trail from small-town weathergirl to prime-time anchor, she has a meteoric rise to fame that causes her to collide with Warren Justice, a brilliant older newsman who becomes her mentor and lover. A Touchstone film in association with Cinergi Pictures Entertainment. Directed by Jon Avnet. Released Mar. 1, 1996. Stars Robert Redford (Warren Justice), Michelle Pfeiffer (Tally Atwater), Stockard Channing (Marcia McGrath), Joe Mantegna (Bucky Terranova), Kate Nelligan (Joanna Kennelly), Glenn Plummer (Ned), James Rebhorn (John Merino). 124 min. Suggested by the book *Golden Girl: The Story of Jessica Savitch* by Alanna Nash. The movie was filmed in such disparate settings as Miami's Orange Bowl, Holmesburg Prison in Philadelphia, and various soundstages in Hollywood.

Up, Up and Away (TV) A Disney Channel Original Movie; first aired Jan. 22, 2000. Scott Marshall, who's approaching his 14th birthday and the supposed arrival of superpowers that the rest of his superhero family possess, exhibits no signs of extraordinary behavior of any kind. When the family is captured by a criminal mastermind intent on taking over the world, it is up to Scott to use his brains instead of supernatural brawn to stop the evil plan and save humankind. Directed by Robert Townsend. Stars Robert Townsend (Jim), Michael J. Pagan (Scott), Alex Datcher (Judy), Sherman Hemsley (Edward), Kasan Butcher (Adam).

Upjohn SEE TRIANGLE OF HEALTH.

Upjohn Pharmacy Drugstore display on Main Street, U.S.A. in Disneyland; open Jul. 1955–Sep. 1970. Decorated like a turn-of-the-century pharmacy, it was primarily a display, though in the early days guests could pick up tiny free sample bottles of vitamins. Became the New Century Clock Shop.

Upside-Down Magic (TV) A Disney Channel Original Movie; first aired Jul. 31, 2020. The 13-year-old Nory discovers that she can flux into animals and that her best friend, Reina, can manipulate flames. Together, they enter the Sage Academy for Magical Studies. Reina's expert ability lands her at the top of her class, but Nory's wonky magic and proclivity for turning into a Dritten (a half-kitten, half-dragon) lands her in a class for those with upside-down magic. While Headmaster Knightslinger believes these unconventional powers leave the students vulnerable to dangerous shadow magic, Nory and her classmates set out to prove that upside-down magic beats the right-side-up kind. Directed by Joe Nussbaum. Stars Izabela Rose (Nory Boxwood Horace), Siena Agudong (Reina Carvajal), Kyle Howard (Budd Skriff), Max Torina (Andres Padillo), Elie Samouhi (Elliot Cohen), Alison Fernandez (Pepper Paloma), Vicki Lewis (Headmaster Knightslinger). Based on the book series by Sarah Mlynowski, Lauren Myracle, and Emily Jenkins.

Uptown Boutique World Bazaar apparel and accessory shop in Tokyo Disneyland; opened Apr. 15, 1983. Closed in 2007, to become Town Center Fashions.

Uptown Jewelers Jewelry shop on Main Street, U.S.A. in the Magic Kingdom at Walt Disney World; opened Oct. 1971. On May 5, 1986, it took over The Cup'n Saucer and New Century Clock Shop.

Ursula Sea witch villain in *The Little Mermaid*; voiced by Pat Carroll.

Ursus H. Bear's Wilderness Outpost Shop in Bear Country in Disneyland; opened in 1972. Named after the (fictional) founder of the nearby Country Bear Playhouse, and also Grizzly Hall in the Magic Kingdom at Walt Disney World. Became Crocodile Mercantile in 1988.

Us Again (film) Experimental animated short; released in theaters Mar. 5, 2021, with *Raya and the Last Dragon*. In a vibrant city pulsating with rhythm, an elderly man and his young-at-heart wife rekindle their passion for life and revive fond memories across the exciting cityscape of their youth. Directed by Zach Parrish. 7 min. From Walt Disney Animation Studios.

Us Weekly Disney purchased a 50% stake in the

Us Weekly celebrity happenings magazine in 2001 for $40 million from Wenner Media. That stake was sold back to Wenner in 2006 for $300 million.

Using Simple Machines (film) Educational film; released in Sep. 1986. 14 min. The film explains basic concepts of mechanical physics.

Ustinov, Peter (1921–2004) Actor; appeared in the title role in *Blackbeard's Ghost, One of Our Dinosaurs Is Missing* (Hnup Wan), and *Treasure of Matecumbe* (Dr. Snodgrass), and on The Disney Channel in *The Old Curiosity Shop* (Grandfather).

He voiced Prince John and King Richard in *Robin Hood*.

Utilidors Network of tunnels which connect all areas of the Magic Kingdom at Walt Disney World. Actually, because of the high water table in Florida, the Utilidors had to be built on top of the ground. Then the park was added on top of that, essentially putting it on the second floor. Encompassing 392,000 square feet, the Utilidors allow easy maintenance, stocking of shops, and movement of costumed Cast Members from place to place, without disturbing the guests or disrupting the ambience in the park above.

1. *Vampirina* (TV) 2. *Vanishing Prairie, The* (film) 3. Vinylmation 4. Very Merry Christmas Parade
5. Videopolis 6. Video 7. Viewliner 8. V.I.N.Cent 9. Vixey

Vacation Club Resort Time-share hotel facility at Walt Disney World; a Preview Center opened Oct. 7, 1991, with accommodations available to members beginning Dec. 20. Guests can learn about time-share ownership in the Commodore House. The resort includes dining at Olivia's Cafe and shopping at the Conch Flats General Store. In Jan. 1996, it was renamed Disney's Old Key West Resort. It was the first Disney Vacation Club property. SEE ALSO DISNEY VACATION CLUB AND OLD KEY WEST RESORT, DISNEY'S.

Vacation Club Resort, Hilton Head Island, South Carolina A 123-unit resort designed as a 1940s Carolina Lowcountry vacation lodge; opened Mar. 1, 1996, adjacent to Shelter Cove Harbour along the Atlantic Intracoastal Waterway, as Disney's Hilton Head Island Resort. Disney Vacation Club Members and guests check in at The Live Oak Lodge, where Big Murggie's Den provides a cozy gathering space. Dining and snacks are available at Signals and Tide Me Over, with shopping at Broad Creek Mercantile. Guests can zip down the Water Tower Slide at the Big Dipper pool and spa, while younger swimmers can play in the Little Dipper Pool. Separate from the lodge itself, but part of the resort, is Disney's Beach House in Palmetto Dunes, featuring private access to a 12-mile beach. A golden retriever named Shadow has served as the resort's mascot.

Vacation Club Resort, Vero Beach, Florida Ground was broken Jul. 28, 1994, for a new Disney Vacation Club Resort in Vero Beach. Located 100 miles southeast of Walt Disney World, this was the first Disney resort built separately from a Disney park and Disney's first oceanfront resort. Opened Oct. 1, 1995, with an inn and villas, The Green Cabin Room lounge, shopping at Island Grove Packing Company, and dining at Shutters, Sonya's Steak & Chops, and Bleachers Bar & Grill. On Dec. 10, 2016, the latter 3 venues became Wind & Waves Grill, Wind & Waves Market, and Wind & Waves Bar. Disney's Vero Beach Resort was built in the style of grand, turn-of-the-century hotels of the Eastern Seaboard, with details celebrating Florida's Treasure Coast—such as citrus farming, treasure ships, and sea turtle conservation. Each summer, guests can witness some of the 100,000 turtle hatchlings that make their way to the ocean. The resort has also hosted an annual Tour de Turtles, in which adult loggerheads start their 3-month journey to their feeding grounds.

Vacation Villas Opened at Lake Buena Vista at Walt Disney World in Dec. 1971 as town houses primarily for lease to corporations; the original 27 units were eventually expanded to 133. By 1977, the town houses were known as Vacation Villas and were available for overnight guest rentals. They became part of The Disney Institute in 1996 and were removed in 2002, making way for Disney's Saratoga Springs Resort & Spa.

Vacationland Campground A 10-acre campground across West Street from Disneyland; originally with 280 camping sites, plus a recreation hall, swimming pool, picnic area, and playground.

Opened in 1970 by the Wrather Corporation, which also managed the nearby Disneyland Hotel, and acquired by Disney in 1988. It closed at the end of 1996 to make way for construction on the Disneyland Resort, with the site eventually becoming the Mickey & Friends parking structure.

Vagnini, Steven After several years as a Walt Disney World Cast Member and an associate at the Walt Disney Archives, he joined the Archives staff as head of research in 2010. He has authored Disney books and articles, spoken to Disney groups, and produced special events. He later served as manager of content marketing for D23, moved to Walt Disney Imagineering in 2018, and returned to the Archives in 2022 to help produce "Disney100: The Exhibition." He collaborated with Dave Smith on the 4th and 5th editions of *Disney A to Z: The Official Encyclopedia* and was assigned by Dave to update future editions of the book.

Vahle, Jeff He joined Walt Disney World in 1990, and over the years held leadership and executive roles in Operations, Technology, and Engineering Services. In 2018, he became president of Disney Signature Experiences, overseeing Disney Cruise Line; Disney Vacation Club; Adventures by Disney; Golden Oak; and Aulani, A Disney Resort & Spa. On May 18, 2020, he was named president of Walt Disney World, additionally overseeing global facilities and operations services for Disney parks worldwide.

Val de France Lakeside hotel district at Disneyland Paris containing "selected hotels": Hotel Kyriad (opened Mar. 31, 2003; later Campanile Val de France), MyTravel's Explorers Hotel (opened Mar. 31, 2003; later Thomas Cook's Explorers Hotel, and then Explorers Fabulous Hotels Group), Holiday Inn (opened May 28, 2003; later Magic Circus, then Grand Magic Hotel), Mövenpick Dream Castle Hotel (opened Jul. 2004; later Dream Castle Fabulous Hotel Group), and B&B Hotel (opened Jan. 28, 2016). As of Oct. 2022, the Grand Magic and Dream Castle are no longer partner hotels.

Val d'Europe Town and shopping center located next to Disneyland Paris in Marne-la-Vallée, France. The 1-million-sq.-ft. international shopping center, with an adjacent factory outlet mall, opened Oct. 25, 2000, and was expanded in 2017 with an additional 30 shops. The 60-acre site has been leased to SEGECE, a Paris-based company. Like the town of Celebration, Florida, Val d'Europe was designed following New Urbanism principles.

Valentina's Sweets Chocolate and sweets shop in Mediterranean Harbor at Tokyo DisneySea; opened Sep. 4, 2001.

Valentine, Karen Actress; appeared in *Hot Lead and Cold Feet* (Jenny) and *The North Avenue Irregulars* (Jane), and on TV in *A Fighting Choice* (Meg Taylor).

Valentine from Disney, A (TV) Show aired Feb. 8, 1983. A salute to romance, with clips from a number of animated films.

Valiant (film) In England during World War II, a young pigeon, Valiant, inspired by the heroic exploits of squadron leader Gutsy of the Royal Homing Pigeon Service, decides to join up. In Trafalgar Square, Valiant meets up with a Cockney con-bird, Bugsy, who also enlists. After a rigorous training period, they and their Squadron F are sent to France to collect a message from the Resistance despite attacks by a brigade of vicious enemy falcons, led by the ruthless General Von Talon. Computer-animated film produced by Vanguard Animation and Ealing Studios; released in the U.S. by Buena Vista on Aug. 19, 2005. Originally released in the United Kingdom Mar. 25, 2005. Directed by Gary Chapman. Voices include Ewan McGregor (Valiant), Ricky Gervais (Bugsy), Tim Curry (General Von Talon), Jim Broadbent (Sergeant), Hugh Laurie (Gutsy), John Cleese (Mercury), John Hurt (Felix). 76 min.

Vampirina (TV) Animated series on Disney Junior; premiered Oct. 1, 2017. A young vampire girl, Vampirina (aka Vee), is the new kid in town after her family moves from Transylvania to Pennsylvania. In her unfamiliar surroundings, Vee first tries to adapt, change, and blend in with her schoolmates, but ultimately she learns to appreciate her unique individuality and her friends' too. Voices include Isabella Crovetti (Vampirina), James Van Der Beek (Boris), Lauren Graham (Oxana), Wanda Sykes (Gregoria). Patti LuPone voices Nanpire in a recurring guest role. Inspired by Disney Publishing's popular children's book series Vampirina Ballerina by Anne Marie Pace. From Brown Bag Films in association with Disney Junior.

Van de Kamp, Andrea L. Member of the Disney Board of Directors Sep. 29, 1998–Mar. 19, 2003.

Van Dyke, Barry Actor; appeared on TV in *Gun Shy* (Russell Donovan).

Van Dyke, Dick Actor; appeared in *Mary Poppins* (Bert/Mr. Dawes, Sr.), *Lt. Robin Crusoe, U.S.N.* (Lt. Robin Crusoe), *Never a Dull Moment* (Jack Albany), *Dick Tracy* (D. A. Fletcher), *Alexander and the Terrible, Horrible, No Good, Very Bad Day* (as himself), and *Mary Poppins Returns* (Mr. Dawes, Jr.); and on TV in *The Best of Disney: 50 Years of Magic*, *Walt Disney—One Man's Dream*, *Disney's Golden Anniversary of Snow White and the Seven Dwarfs*, *Donald Duck's 50th Birthday*, *The Age of Believing: The Disney Live Action Classics*, and *Disneyland 60: The Wonderful World of Disney*. He narrated *Walt: The Man Behind the Myth*, guest starred in *The Golden Girls* (Ken) and *Scrubs* (Dr. Townshend), and voiced Captain Goof-Beard in *Mickey Mouse Clubhouse*. He was named a Disney Legend in 1998.

Van Osten, Carson (1945–2015) Artist and Disney Consumer Products executive; he started with Disney in 1970 illustrating Mickey Mouse comic books, later serving for many years in Creative Resources for Consumer Products, in both the U.S. and Europe. He was named a Disney Legend in 2015.

Van Patten, Dick (1928–2015) Actor; appeared in *Snowball Express* (Mr. Carruthers), *Superdad* (Ira Kershaw), *The Strongest Man in the World* (Harry), *Gus* (Cal Wilson), *Treasure of Matecumbe* (gambler), *The Shaggy D.A.* (Raymond), and *Freaky Friday* (Harold Jennings), and on TV in *Mickey's 50* and *14 Going on 30* (Principal John Loonies), with a guest role in *Boy Meets World* (farmer).

Van Patten, Jimmy Actor; appeared in *Freaky Friday* (cashier), *Hot Lead and Cold Feet* (Jake), and *The Apple Dumpling Gang Rides Again* (Soldier #1).

Van Patten, Vincent Actor; appeared in *Charley and the Angel* (Willie Appleby), and on TV in *The Boy and the Bronc Buster* and *The High Flying Spy*. The son of actor Dick Van Patten, Vincent went on to become a top-seeded tennis pro.

Vance, Courtney B. Actor; appeared in *The Adventures of Huck Finn* (Jim), *Holy Matrimony* (Cooper), and *The Preacher's Wife* (Henry Biggs), and on TV in *FlashForward* (Stanford Wedeck), *Let It Shine* (Jacob DeBarge), and *Revenge* (Benjamin Brooks), with a guest role in *Scandal* (Clarence Parker).

Vanellope von Schweetz Misfit video game character, a kart racer, in *Wreck-It Ralph* and *Ralph Breaks the Internet*; voiced by Sarah Silverman.

Vanessa Ursula's human guise to get the prince to marry her in *The Little Mermaid*.

Vanishing Prairie, The (film) True-Life Adventure feature released Aug. 16, 1954. Directed by James Algar. Academy Award winner. 71 min. The film relates the story of the American prairie, whose birds and animals were brought to the verge of extinction, and yet managed to continue their fight for survival. Pronghorn antelope, the prairie dog, bighorn sheep, mountain lion, buffalo, and numerous other creatures are shown. A team of 12 photographers, led by Tom McHugh, filmed in the wilderness from the Mississippi to the Rockies and from the Gulf of Mexico to the plains of Canada. They turned to 16-power telephoto lenses, which were often used to get intimate close-ups. It is one of the best known and most highly regarded of the True-Life Adventures.

Vanishing Private, The (film) Donald Duck cartoon released Sep. 25, 1942. Directed by Jack King. After Donald camouflages a cannon with invisible paint, Pete tries to catch him, so he makes himself invisible. The general sees Pete chasing nothing and puts him in a straitjacket, with Donald guarding him.

Vanneste, André (1927–1995) He handled Disney licensing and publications in Belgium for 40 years, beginning in 1953, and was presented a European Disney Legends Award posthumously in 1997.

Varda, the Peregrine Falcon (TV) Show aired Nov. 16, 1969. A Seminole captures a falcon on its yearly migration, but it yearns to be free. Stars Peter de Manio, Noreen Klincko, Denise Grisco. Narrated by Hugh Cherry.

Vargo, Michael He joined Disney in 1992 at Disneyland Entertainment and later worked in special events at the Walt Disney Special Events Group and Disney Live Entertainment. In 2004, he was named director of Corporate Special Events, where he has produced a variety of experiences such as the

Annual Meeting of Shareholders, employee events and conferences, and several D23 Expos. In May 2016, he was named vice president of Corporate Communications, where he oversees D23: The Official Disney Fan Club, Special Events, Disney Corporate Creative Resources, and the Walt Disney Archives.

Varney, Jim (1949–2000) He appeared as Ernest P. Worrell in the Ernest films, also playing the roles of Mr. Nash and Auntie Nelda in *Ernest Goes to Jail*. He appeared on TV in *Disneyland's 35th Anniversary Celebration*, *Walt Disney World Celebrity Circus*, *Ernest Goes to Splash Mountain*, and *The Wonderful World of Disney: 40 Years of Television Magic*. He voiced Slinky Dog in *Toy Story* and *Toy Story 2* and Cookie in *Atlantis*.

Vaughn, Bruce He served as chief creative executive for Walt Disney Imagineering (WDI) 2007–2016, then returned as chief creative officer Mar. 20, 2023. He first joined WDI in 1993 and held several roles over the years, including vice president, Research & Development.

Vault Disney Programming block on Disney Channel airing classic Disney films, TV shows, and specials; aired Sep. 21, 1997–Sep. 8, 2002.

VD Attack Plan Animated educational film; released in Jan. 1973. Directed by Les Clark. The film explores the dangers of venereal disease, where to go for help, how to cure it, and how to prevent it. Narrated by Keenan Wynn.

Venable, Evelyn (1913–1993) Actress; provided the voice of the Blue Fairy in *Pinocchio*.

Venetian Carnival Market Shop offering mugs, glasses, dishes, and cutlery in Mediterranean Harbor at Tokyo DisneySea; opened Sep. 4, 2001.

Venetian Gondolas Attraction in Tokyo DisneySea; opened Sep. 4, 2001. Guests in Palazzo Canals can tour this Mediterranean Harbor neighborhood aboard an Italian gondola.

Veranda Juice Bar Adventureland refreshment counter in the Magic Kingdom at Walt Disney World; opened Oct. 1, 1971, serving tropical punch and snacks. Became Aloha Isle Refreshments in 1982.

Verandah Restaurant SEE VILLAGE PAVILION.

Vergara, Sofia Actress; appeared in *Big Trouble* (Nina), and on TV in *The Knights of Prosperity* (Esperanza Villalobos), *Dirty Sexy Money* (Sofia Montoya), and *My Wife and Kids* (Selma). She is perhaps best known for her role as Gloria Pritchett in the 20th Century Fox series *Modern Family*.

Veritas: The Quest (TV) Hour-long, action-adventure drama series on ABC; aired Jan. 27–Mar. 10, 2003. After being kicked out of an expensive private school, Nikko Zond discovers that his estranged father, Solomon, is not just an archaeology professor but is secretly leading an international search for the truth about a civilization that vanished long before known history began. Stars Ryan Merriman (Nikko Zond), Alex Carter (Solomon Zond), Eric Balfour (Calvin Banks), Cynthia Martells (Maggie). Filmed in Montreal and Toronto. From Touchstone Television, with Storyline Entertainment and Massett/Zinman Productions.

Vernon Kilns Manufacturer of licensed Disney ceramics 1940–1942. They produced figurines from only 3 films: *Fantasia*, *Dumbo*, and the *Baby Weems* segment of *The Reluctant Dragon*. Their set of 36 *Fantasia* figurines, featuring hippos, ostriches, sprites, elephants, and mushrooms, is especially noteworthy. Besides the figurines, they produced dinnerware in 8 different *Fantasia* patterns, as well as a series of vases and bowls.

Vero Beach, Florida SEE DISNEY VACATION CLUB AND VACATION CLUB RESORT, VERO BEACH, FLORIDA.

Veronica Guerin (film) As a journalist covering the crime beat in Dublin in the 1990s, Veronica Guerin starts a crusade to expose local drug dealers, and in doing so she neglects her family and is accused of glory-seeking. Guerin still relentlessly pursues her mission, and her obsession eventually leads to her murder. A Touchstone film with Jerry Bruckheimer Films. Released in the U.S. on Oct. 17, 2003, after a premiere (Jul. 8) and initial release (Jul. 11) in Ireland. Directed by Joel Schumacher. Stars Cate Blanchett (Veronica Guerin), Brenda Fricker (Bernie Guerin), Ciaran Hinds (John Traynor), Gerard McSorley (John Gilligan), Barry Barnes (Graham Turley), Joe Hanley (Eugene "Dutchie" Holland), David Murray (Charles Bowden), David Herlihy (Peter "Fatso" Mitchell). 98 min. Filmed on location in Ireland in Super 35-Scope.

Very Merry Christmas Parade Holiday parade

in Disneyland 1977–1979 and 1987–1994. Beginning in 1995, the parade was A Christmas Fantasy. The Very Merry Christmas Parade was also offered annually in the Magic Kingdom at Walt Disney World 1977–1979; later, Mickey's Very Merry Christmas Parade ran for most years 1989–2007, till it was replaced by Mickey's Once Upon a Christmastime Parade. The first Mickey's Very Merry Christmas Party was held in the Magic Kingdom in 1983. See also Walt Disney World Very Merry Christmas Parade.

V. I. Warshawski (film) A tough-talking, fiercely independent female private investigator (with a weakness for pretty shoes), Warshawski is often forced to play hardball with Chicago's crime element. When her new flame, ex-hockey player Boom-Boom Grafalk turns up murdered, his 13-year-old daughter, Kat, hires V. I. to find her father's killer. She soon uncovers a startling conspiracy for murder and money. Released Jul. 26, 1991. Directed by Jeff Kanew. A Hollywood Pictures film. 89 min. Stars Kathleen Turner (Vic), Jay O. Sanders (Murray), Charles Durning (Lt. Mallory). Based on the novels by Sara Paretsky. Filmed on location in Chicago.

Via Napoli Ristorante e Pizzeria Restaurant in Italy at EPCOT; opened Aug. 2, 2010, operated by Patina Restaurant Group. Features an open kitchen and 3 woodburning pizza ovens that represent Italy's 3 active volcanoes (Etna, Vesuvius, Stromboli). As the story goes, the restaurant once served as the stables for a family who built the adjoining palazzo.

Victoria & Albert's The most elegant restaurant at Walt Disney World, in Disney's Grand Floridian Resort & Spa; opened Jun. 28, 1988. With ingredients sourced from around the world, modern American cuisine is served in the Dining Room, private Queen Victoria Room, and at the Chef's Table in the kitchen. Originally, all the servers introduced themselves as Victoria or Albert. The chef prepares a special selection of gourmet dishes each evening, which are described by the waitstaff and later in the individually inscribed menus that are delivered to each diner. A harpist provides background music. Recipient of AAA's highest achievement, the Five Diamond Award.

Victorian Collection Main Street, U.S.A. apparel and gift shop in Hong Kong Disneyland; opened Aug. 2012, as an expansion onto Center Street.

Victoria's Home-Style Cooking Counter-service restaurant on Main Street, U.S.A. in Disneyland Paris; opened Apr. 12, 1992, as a cozy, 19th-century-style boarding house. Also known as Victoria's Home-Style Restaurant.

Victoria's Jewelry Box World Bazaar jewelry shop in Tokyo Disneyland; opened Apr. 15, 1983. Closed Nov. 2007; absorbed into House of Greetings.

Victory Through Air Power (film) Based on Maj. Alexander P. de Seversky's book of the same title, the film shows how long-range airpower could defeat the Axis during World War II. It opens with an animated history of aviation, followed by scenes of Major de Seversky expressing his theories about airpower and its further development. Filmmakers use animation to produce strikingly vivid graphics of the Allied forces pounding the Axis strongholds. To the strains of a stirring "Song of the Eagle," an animated eagle is dramatically shown attacking the heart of Japan with a dagger. Released Jul. 17, 1943, by United Artists, although all other Disney films at the time were being released by RKO. Sequence directors were Clyde Geronimi, Jack Kinney, James Algar. Animation supervisor was David Hand. 65 min. Nominated for an Academy Award for Best Scoring of a Dramatic or Comedy Picture. The history of aviation sequences were reissued as part of *Man in Flight* and *Fly with Von Drake* on TV, and as an educational film, *History of Aviation*.

Victory Vehicles (film) Goofy cartoon released Jul. 30, 1943. Directed by Jack Kinney. Goofy demonstrates, with offscreen narration, various devices used to replace the automobile during wartime, finally ending up with a pogo stick.

Video After initial reticence to releasing films on videocassette for home usage, Disney finally marketed its first videos, for rental and sale, in both Beta and VHS format, in Oct. 1980. Besides some cartoon compilations, among the 10 features released that month were *The Apple Dumpling Gang, The Black Hole, The Love Bug,* and *Escape to Witch Mountain. Dumbo* was the first of the animated classics to be released, in Jun. 1981, for rental only. *Alice in Wonderland* followed, for rental only, in Oct. 1981. Both films were available for sale in 1982, but it was not until Jul. 1985 that Disney dipped into its library of top-ranked animated features, with the release of *Pinocchio*. Following the success of that film on video, other animated features followed on a regular basis. Each film would be available for a limited time only, then would go into a moratorium period with plans made to rerelease it at a future date. While the earliest video releases were expected to be primarily for rental through video dealers, the desire of consumers to actually own private copies of Disney films moved the company to offer selected videos, and later DVDs, at a sell-through price. With its growing acceptance, some features have been produced directly for video, bypassing a theatrical or TV release. The direct-to-video/DVD/Blu-ray features are:

1. *Breakin' Through*, 1985
2. *The Return of Jafar*, 1994
3. *Aladdin and the King of Thieves*, 1996
4. *Honey, We Shrunk Ourselves*, 1997
5. *Mighty Ducks the Movie: The First Face-Off*, 1997
6. *Pooh's Grand Adventure: The Search for Christopher Robin*, 1997
7. *Beauty and the Beast: The Enchanted Christmas*, 1997
8. *Belle's Magical World*, 1998
9. *Air Bud: Golden Receiver*, 1998
10. *Pocahontas II: Journey to a New World*, 1998
11. *The Jungle Book: Mowgli's Story*, 1998
12. *The Lion King II: Simba's Pride*, 1998
13. *The Wonderful Ice Cream Suit*, 1999 (Touchstone)
14. *Hercules: Zero to Hero*, 1999
15. *Belle's Tales of Friendship*, 1999
16. *Mickey's Once Upon a Christmas*, 1999
17. *Winnie the Pooh: Seasons of Giving*, 1999
18. *An Extremely Goofy Movie*, 2000
19. *Buzz Lightyear of Star Command: The Adventure Begins*, 2000
20. *The Little Mermaid II: Return to the Sea*, 2000
21. *Air Bud: World Pup*, 2000
22. *Lady and the Tramp II: Scamp's Adventure*, 2001
23. *The Book of Pooh: Stories from the Heart*, 2001
24. *Cinderella II: Dreams Come True*, 2002
25. *The Hunchback of Notre Dame II*, 2002
26. *Air Bud: Seventh Inning Fetch*, 2002
27. *Tarzan and Jane*, 2002
28. *Winnie the Pooh: A Very Merry Pooh Year*, 2002
29. *101 Dalmatians II: Patch's London Adventure*, 2003
30. *Inspector Gadget 2*, 2003
31. *Atlantis: Milo's Return*, 2003
32. *Air Bud Spikes Back*, 2003
33. *Stitch! The Movie*, 2003
34. *Kim Possible: The Secret Files*, 2003
35. *George of the Jungle II*, 2003
36. *The Lion King 1½*, 2004
37. *Winnie the Pooh: Springtime with Roo*, 2004
38. *The Three Musketeers*, 2004
39. *Mickey's Twice Upon a Christmas*, 2004
40. *Mulan II*, 2005
41. *Tarzan II*, 2005
42. *Lilo & Stitch 2: Stitch Has a Glitch*, 2005
43. *Pooh's Heffalump Halloween Movie*, 2005
44. *Kronk's New Groove*, 2005
45. *Bambi II*, 2006
46. *Leroy & Stitch*, 2006
47. *Brother Bear 2*, 2006
48. *Air Buddies*, 2006
49. *The Fox and the Hound 2*, 2006
50. *Cinderella III: A Twist in Time*, 2007
51. *Snow Buddies*, 2008
52. *The Little Mermaid: Ariel's Beginning*, 2008
53. *Space Buddies*, 2009
54. *Santa Buddies*, 2009
55. *The Crimson Wing: Mystery of the Flamingos*, 2010
56. *The Search for Santa Paws*, 2010
57. *Beverly Hills Chihuahua 2*, 2011
58. *Sharpay's Fabulous Adventure*, 2011
59. *Spooky Buddies*, 2011
60. *Treasure Buddies*, 2012
61. *Beverly Hills Chihuahua 3: Viva la Fiesta!*, 2012
62. *Santa Paws 2: The Santa Pups*, 2012
63. *Super Buddies*, 2013

SEE ALSO ANIMATED FEATURES, OTHER.

Videopolis Opened next to Fantasyland in Disneyland Jun. 22, 1985, as a high-tech teen dance area, with a 5,000-sq.-foot dance floor and 70 TV monitors offering popular music videos; later seats covered the dance floor and Videopolis was used for outdoor stage shows such as *One Man's Dream, Dick Tracy*, and *Beauty and the Beast*. The name of the amphitheater was changed to Fantasyland Theater Jun. 23, 1995, with the opening of *The Spirit of Pocahontas*. Also opened in Discoveryland in Disneyland Paris Apr. 12, 1992, where the building features a re-creation of the airship *Hyperion* from *The Island at the Top of the World*. Videopolis East was briefly a nightclub in Pleasure Island at Walt Disney World, from May 1, 1989–Mar. 1990; it was replaced by Cage.

Videopolis Railroad Station The renamed Fantasyland Railroad Station in Disneyland; opened Jun. 30, 1988. It became the Toontown Railroad Station in 1992.

Vidi Protective snipe in *The Pelican and the Snipe*.

Vienna Boys Choir They appeared in *Almost Angels*.

Viewliner Tomorrowland train in Disneyland; ran Jun. 26, 1957–Sep. 15, 1958. This modernistic train traveled around Tomorrowland for little more than a year.

Villa del Lago SEE THREE BRIDGES BAR & GRILL (WALT DISNEY WORLD).

Villa Donaldo Home Shop Household goods in Mediterranean Harbor at Tokyo DisneySea; opened Feb. 21, 2013, taking the place of Romeo's Watches & Jewelry and Juliet's Collections & Treasures. Statues and painted ceilings depict the romance between Donald and Daisy.

Village, The (film) In 1897, a close-knit community lives with the frightening knowledge that a mythical race of creatures resides in the woods around them. The evil and foreboding force is so unnerving that none dare venture beyond the borders of the village and into the woods. But when curious, headstrong Lucius Hunt plans to step beyond the boundaries of the town and into the unknown, his bold move threatens to forever change the future of the village. Directed by M. Night Shyamalan. A Touchstone film. Released Jul. 30, 2004. Stars Joaquin Phoenix (Lucius Hunt), Bryce Dallas Howard (Ivy Walker), Adrien Brody (Noah Percy), William Hurt (Edward Walker), Sigourney Weaver (Alice Hunt), Brendan Gleeson (August Nicholson). 108 min. Bryce Dallas Howard is the daughter of director/producer Ron Howard. Filmed in and around Philadelphia. Nominated for an Academy Award for Best Score (James Newton Howard).

Village Character Shop Opened ca. 1982 in Walt Disney World Village, taking the place of Pooh's Place. Closed Oct. 24, 1985, to make way for an expansion of the Gourmet Pantry; a new character merchandise store, Mickey's Character Shop, opened the next day in the former Port of Entry.

Village Fry Shoppe, The Fantasyland counter serving McDonald's french fries in the Magic Kingdom at Walt Disney World; opened May 1, 2006, replacing Lumiere's Kitchen, and closed in 2009, to become The Friar's Nook.

Village Gifts & Sundries Souvenir and convenience shop in the Lake Buena Vista Shopping Village at Walt Disney World; opened ca. 1978, taking the place of the Apothecary. It became a new location for the Country Address shop Mar. 1987.

Village Haus Restaurant Fantasyland counter-service restaurant in Disneyland; opened May 25, 1983, first as the Village Inn Restaurant. Themed after *Pinocchio*, it began serving pizza and pasta along with hamburgers in 1994. It became the Red Rose Taverne Feb. 24, 2017, and was themed after *Beauty and the Beast*. SEE ALSO PINOCCHIO VILLAGE HAUS (WALT DISNEY WORLD).

Village Pastry Fantasyland snack wagon in Tokyo Disneyland; opened in 1997. Tipo Torta pastries (sticks filled with flavored cream) are served.

Village Pavilion Included the Verandah Restaurant, Ice Cream Parlor, and Bake Shop in the Lake Buena Vista Shopping Village at Walt Disney World; opened Jun. 1, 1977. The Victorian-style restaurant, serving sandwiches and crepes, closed in 1985, and was succeeded the following year by Minnie Mia's Pizzeria, and then by Pluto's Dog House (hot dogs) in 1991. The Ice Cream Parlor and Bake Shop became Donald's Dairy Dip, opening Apr. 20, 1991. The LEGO Imagination Center replaced the Village Pavilion Oct. 13, 1997.

Village Resorts Located at Walt Disney World, near what is now Disney Springs, the resort debuted in Dec. 1971 with 27 town houses for lease primarily to corporations. Eventually they became known as Vacation Villas; and Treehouses, Fairway Villas, and Club Lake Villas were added over the next decade. By 1977 the focus had changed to overnight rentals to Walt Disney World guests. In 1996, the Village Resorts became part of The Disney Institute.

Village Restaurant, The Intimate restaurant in the Lake Buena Vista Shopping Village at Walt Disney World; open 1975–Jul. 1990, later becoming Chef Mickey's Village Restaurant. The Village Chummery, later called the Village Lounge, was the restaurant's popular nightspot.

Village Shoppes Trio of shops in Belle's village in Tokyo Disneyland; opened Sep. 28, 2020, as part of an expansion of Fantasyland. *Beauty and the Beast* merchandise is sold in La Belle Librairie (a re-creation of Belle's favorite bookshop), Bonjour

Gifts (a shop belonging to the village's clothier and hatmaker), and Little Town Traders (where, as the story goes, village craftspeople sell their wares).

Village Smithy, The (film) Donald Duck cartoon released Jan. 16, 1942. Directed by Dick Lundy. Donald's pride in his trade is put to the test when he attempts to work with a cartwheel and to shoe Jenny the donkey.

Village Spirits Fine wine, liqueurs, and ales sold in the Lake Buena Vista Shopping Village at Walt Disney World; opened Mar. 1975. Also inside was the Vintage Cellar, a tasting area. Closed Apr. 1994, to become the new location for 2R's – Read'n & Rite'n.

Village Traders Open-air marketplace inspired by Africa in The Outpost at EPCOT; opened Nov. 12, 1993. The area was originally planned to be an Equatorial Africa pavilion, but it was never built; Africa later opened as an area in Disney's Animal Kingdom.

Villages Nature Paris Ecotourism destination in the Bailly-Romainvilliers commune of north-central France, near Disneyland Paris; opened Oct. 10, 2017. On a nearly 300-acre property, nature and architecture combine to offer guests a new type of vacation experience. There are 900 apartment- and cottage-style accommodations and 5 immersive areas: the Aqualagon, a large, covered water park; the BelleVie Farm, with a grocery store and tearoom; the 5-acre Extraordinary Gardens, celebrating the 4 elements of nature; the Lakeside Promenade; and the Forest of Legends. Guests can also partake in recreational activities, hut building, bread making, and wine tastings. With an artistic vision overseen by Disney Imagineers, the property represents a partnership with landscape architect and town developer Thierry Huau and is the result of a multi-year collaboration between Euro Disney S.C.A. and European tourism leader Pierre & Vacances-Center Parcs Group.

Villains in Vogue Disney villains–themed shop in the Beverly Sunset Theater on Sunset Boulevard at Disney's Hollywood Studios; opened Sep. 14, 1998. It became Reel Vogue in Jun. 2015.

Villain's Lair SEE DISNEY VILLAINS (DISNEYLAND).

Villains of Valley View, The (TV) Series on Disney Channel; premiered Jun. 3, 2022. When teenage supervillain Havoc stands up to the head of the League of Villains, her family is forced to change their identities and relocate to a sleepy Texas suburb. With the help of her effervescent new neighbor, Hartley, Havoc—going incognito as Amy—must somehow hide her superpowers and quell her villainous nature in favor of something she and the rest of her family have fought against all their lives: being normal. Stars Isabella Pappas (Havoc/Amy), Lucy Davis (Eva/Surge), James Patrick Stuart (Vic/Kraniac), Malachi Barton (Colby/Flashform), Reed Horstmann (Jake/Chaos), Kayden Muller-Janssen (Hartley), Patricia Belcher (Celia). From Britelite Productions and It's a Laugh Productions.

Vincent, Jan-Michael (1944–2019) Actor; appeared in *The World's Greatest Athlete* (Nanu).

Vincent, Virginia (1918–2013) Actress; appeared in *$1,000,000 Duck* (Eunice Hooper), *Amy* (Edna Hancock), and *Treasure of Matecumbe* (Aunt Lou).

V.I.N.Cent Small multi-purpose robot (Vital Information Necessary Centralized) in *The Black Hole*; voiced by Roddy McDowall. Also known as V.I.N.Cent. L.F. 396.

Vincent (film) Special cartoon about 7-year-old Vincent Malloy, who would rather be Vincent Price than a little boy. His fantasies turn his life into scenes from a horror film—much to the dismay of his mother. Released in New York City on Oct. 1, 1982. Directed by Tim Burton. Narrated by Vincent Price, this black-and-white film uses 3-D models and animation. The animation work was done by Stephen Chiodo. The short was popular enough to Disney for the Studio to back such later Burton creations as *Frankenweenie* and *Tim Burton's The Nightmare Before Christmas*, which use some of the same techniques. A 3-D version was released with a reissue of *Tim Burton's Nightmare Before Christmas* in 2007.

Vineyard, The (TV) Reality series on ABC Family; premiered Jul. 23, 2013, and ended Sep. 10, 2013. A group of 20-somethings are on Martha's Vineyard for the summer, leading to mischief and romance.

Vinylmation A brand of small vinyl collectibles, first sold in 2008 at the Disney parks and the Disney Stores. They are all shaped liked Mickey Mouse, but each has been designed in a vast array of different themes, characters, designs, colors, and patterns. Original sizes were 3 inches and 9 inches, though 1½-inch key chain ones were introduced later. Disney began encouraging trading of the figures at the first D23 Expo in 2009, and they became very popular. The one-millionth Vinylmation figure was sold in 2010.

Violet Insecure teenage superhero who can turn invisible and create force fields in *The Incredibles* and *Incredibles 2*; voiced by Sarah Vowell.

Virtual Magic Kingdom Online multiplayer game in which users create their own characters and visit Disneyland and the Magic Kingdom at Walt Disney World. It was presented by Walt Disney Parks and Resorts Online 2005–May 21, 2008.

Visa Athletic Center A 70,000-sq.-ft. indoor sports facility in ESPN Wide World of Sports at Walt Disney World as of 2018. Included are basketball and volleyball courts, roller hockey rinks, spectator seats, and locker rooms. Opened summer 2008, originally as the Jostens Center, and renamed the J Center Feb. 11, 2017, after the Jostens sponsorship ended.

Viscount SEE TRAVELODGE (WALT DISNEY WORLD).

Visionarium SEE LE VISIONARIUM (DISNEYLAND PARIS AND TOKYO DISNEYLAND).

Visit to EPCOT Center, A (film) A 16-mm film released in Sep. 1983.

Vista Federal Credit Union SEE PARTNERS FEDERAL CREDIT UNION.

Vista-United Telecommunications Partnership between Disney and United Telephone System (originally known as Vista-Florida Telephone System when created in 1971) to handle the telephone needs of Walt Disney World. But after industry deregulation in 1981, it began selling systems to customers around the country, including Disneyland and the Walt Disney Studio. Vista-United was the first phone company to use fiber-optic cable commercially, installed the first computer-controlled telephone operating center, began the first 911 emergency telephone system in Florida, and in 1986 became the first fully digital phone company.

Vital Signs (TV) One-hour dramatic medical reality series on ABC; aired Feb. 27–Jul. 3, 1997. Showcased doctors who race against time to solve baffling medical mysteries. The stories were told in the first person by physicians and were accompanied by reenactments of the events. Hosted by Robert Urich. The reenactments were shot in an actual, though recently closed, hospital—the Tustin Medical Center in California. From Bonnie View Productions, in association with Buena Vista Television.

Vitaminamulch Air Spectacular (film) Animated short; released Nov. 4, 2014, on the *Planes: Fire & Rescue* Blu-ray. When a star stunt duo doesn't show up for an air show promoting Vitaminamulch fertilizer, Dusty and Chug find themselves filling in. Directed by Dan Abraham. Voices include Dane Cook (Dusty), Cedric the Entertainer (Leadbottom), Brad Garrett (Chug), Danny Mann (Sparky). 6 min.

Vixey Tod's love interest, a fox, in *The Fox and the Hound*; voiced by Sandy Duncan.

Vogel, David President of Buena Vista Motion Pictures Group, encompassing the Disney, Touchstone, and Hollywood Pictures labels, in 1998. He had joined Walt Disney Pictures in 1989 where he served in various capacities. He left the company in 1999.

Vogel, Mitch Child actor; appeared on TV in *Bayou Boy* and *Menace on the Mountain*.

Voght (Scott), Dolores (1897–1981) Longtime executive secretary to Walt Disney, from 1930 until her retirement in 1965.

Voice, The: Questions that Help You Sell (film) Educational film from The Nick Price Story of Non-Manipulative Selling series; released in Feb. 1981. Communication with customers is important and keeps them coming back.

Voices of Liberty Group of 8 a cappella singers performing in The American Adventure Rotunda at EPCOT; debuted Oct. 1, 1982, with dynamic renditions of American folk and patriotic songs arranged by founder/producer Derric Johnson. The singers are costumed in the period finery of the 1800s.

Voices on the Road Back: A Program About Drugs (film) Educational film; released in Oct. 1990. 15 min. The film includes interviews with teenagers who began using drugs at an early age.

VOID, The Virtual experience by ILMxLAB; opened Dec. 17, 2017, in Disney Springs at Walt Disney World (replacing a portion of Once Upon a Toy), and Jan. 5, 2018, in the Downtown Disney District at Disneyland Resort (replacing Disney Vault 28, D Street, Fossil, and Something Silver). Virtual reality was paired with walk-through experiences and physical effects like heat and wind. Debuted with *Star Wars: Secrets of the Empire*. Another experience, *Ralph Breaks VR*, inspired by *Ralph Breaks the Internet*, was added Nov. 21, 2018. On Oct. 18, 2019, *Avengers: Damage Control* opened at Disneyland Resort. The locations closed Mar. 16, 2020.

Voight, Jon Actor; appeared in *Enemy of the State* (Reynolds), *Pearl Harbor* (President Roosevelt), *Holes* (Mr. Sir), *National Treasure* and *National Treasure: Book of Secrets* (Patrick Gates), and *Glory Road* (Adolph Rupp).

Volkskunst Shop specializing in cuckoo clocks in Germany at EPCOT; opened Oct. 1, 1982.

Volunteer Worker, The (film) Community Chest trailer starring Donald Duck. Delivered Sep. 1, 1940. Donald has a hard time collecting for charity when he meets a kindly ditchdigger.

von Detten, Erik Actor; voiced Sid in *Toy Story* and *Toy Story 3*, Croney #1 in *Tarzan*, and on TV as Erwin Lawson in *Recess* and Flynt in *Disney's The Legend of Tarzan*. Also appeared in *The Princess Diaries* (Josh Bryant), on TV in *Escape to Witch Mountain* (Danny, 1995), *Dinotopia* (Karl Scott), and the *Walt Disney World Christmas Day Parade*, and on Disney Channel in *So Weird* (Clu Bell) and *Brink* (Andy Brinker).

Von Drake in Spain (TV) Show aired Apr. 8, 1962. Directed by Norman Foster. Ludwig Von Drake looks at the dances and customs of Spain. Guest stars Jose Greco, along with many other Spanish dancers, including Rafael de Cordova, Pedro Azorin, Oscar Herrera, Mariemma, and Lola de Ronda.

Von Otto's Antiques European antiques shop in the Lake Buena Vista Shopping Village at Walt Disney World; opened Mar. 1975. Items ranged from traditional jewelry and furniture to an 1860 Swiss music box and a 4-ft. wooden French artist's model. Closed Sep. 27, 1977, to make way for an expansion of Sir Edward's Haberdasher. SEE ALSO OLDE WORLD ANTIQUES (MAGIC KINGDOM).

von Oy, Jenna Actress; appeared in the TV series *Blossom* (Six LeMeure) and *Lenny* (Kelly Callahan), and voiced Stacey in *A Goofy Movie* and Trinket in *Pepper Ann*.

Voyage of the Little Mermaid Musical show featuring animation, live performers, puppetry, lasers, and special effects, taking audiences under the sea to Ariel's domain. Opened Jan. 7, 1992, on Mickey Avenue (later Animation Courtyard) in the Disney-MGM Studios (now Disney's Hollywood Studios). Replaced *Here Come the Muppets*.

Voyage to the Crystal Grotto Fantasyland boat ride attraction in Shanghai Disneyland; opened Jun. 16, 2016. Passengers glide past sculpture gardens depicting scenes from *Aladdin*, *Beauty and the Beast*, and other Disney animated classics. The journey culminates beneath Enchanted Storybook Castle, revealing a secret underground cavern and the ultimate source of inspiration behind the classic stories: the Crystal Grotto.

Voyages de Pinocchio, Les Fantasyland dark ride attraction in Disneyland Paris; opened Apr. 12, 1992. Guests board a wooden car and follow Pinocchio on his journey to become a real boy. SEE ALSO PINOCCHIO'S DARING JOURNEY (DISNEYLAND AND TOKYO DISNEYLAND).

Voyageurs' Lounge Library-inspired lounge in Disney's Riviera Resort at Walt Disney World; opened Dec. 16, 2019. Displays celebrate Walt Disney's love of European travel.

Vulcania Island home port of Captain Nemo in *20,000 Leagues Under the Sea*.

Vulcania Restaurant Buffeteria in Mysterious Island at Tokyo DisneySea; opened Sep. 4, 2001. Set in the geothermal power station for Captain Nemo's scientific base.

1. Wedding Pavilion, Disney's 2. *Winnie the Pooh and the Honey Tree* (film) 3. *Wonderful World of Color, Walt Disney's* (TV) 4. *WALL•E* (film) 5. *World of Color* 6. Walt Disney World Resort 7. Walt Disney Archives 8. Watches 9. *Wish* (film) 10. *Wise Little Hen, The* (film)

Wacky Zoo of Morgan City, The (TV) Two-part show; aired Oct. 18 and 25, 1970. Directed by Marvin Chomsky. Based on Charles Goodrum's book, *I'll Trade You an Elk*. The mayor wants to close down the run-down city zoo and use the site for a museum, but an accountant and his children fight to save it. Stars Hal Holbrook, Joe Flynn, Cecil Kellaway, Wally Cox, Mary LaRoche, Michael-James Wixted, Anne Seymour, Michael McGreevey, Christina Anderson, Annie McEveety, Judson Pratt. The film was shot on the site of the former Los Angeles Zoo, after the animals had all been moved to a new zoo nearby.

Waco & Rhinehart (TV) An unsold pilot for a proposed series; aired on ABC Mar. 27, 1987. Directed by Christian I. Nyby. Two unorthodox U.S. marshals search for the person who killed a member of their unique agency. 90 min. Stars Charles C. Hill, Justin Deas, Bill Hootkins, Bob Tzudiker, Kathleen Lloyd.

Wages and Production (film) Educational film, from The People on Market Street series, produced by Terry Kahn; released in Sep. 1977. A visit to a furniture company helps students understand the concept of labor as a salable service.

Waging Peace (film) Educational film on The Disney Channel; premiered Nov. 6, 1996. Produced by Disney Educational Productions in association with Jazbo Productions. Based on the Elie Wiesel Foundation for Humanity's Tomorrow's Leaders conference held in Venice, Italy, the film documents the meeting of world leaders, conflict resolution facilitators, and 30 teenagers, repre-senting divergent points of view from some of the world's most serious crisis regions, with a goal of working toward mutual understanding and peace. Follow-up trips to each area provide a series of profiles showing the reality of the lives of a group of young people.

Wagner, Jack (1925–1995) Actor; he began at Disneyland providing narration for Christmas parades and other special programs and, beginning in 1970, served as the official "voice of Disneyland" for 2 decades. Wagner's familiar voice was heard in most recorded announcements at the park, as well as in the narration heard at several of the attractions. He also produced music and sound for live entertainment as well as background music for the themed lands. He later performed similar work for Walt Disney World, Tokyo Disneyland, and Disneyland Paris. His voice could also be heard on the shuttles at the Orlando and Houston airports. Jack prepared most of his recordings in a state-of-the-art studio at his Anaheim home. He was named a Disney Legend in 2005.

Wahlberg, Mark Actor; appeared in *Renaissance Man* (Tommy Lee Haywood) and *Invincible* (Vince Papale).

Wahoo Bobcat, The (TV) Show aired Oct. 20, 1963. An old fisherman in the Okefenokee Swamp befriends an aging bobcat. But the bobcat has no place in civilization, so the fisherman transports him to a deserted island where he can live out his days. Narrated by Rex Allen. Stars Jock MacGregor, Bill Dunnagan, Lloyd Shelton.

Waikolohe Valley Outdoor recreation area at Aulani, A Disney Resort & Spa; opened Aug. 29, 2011, with waterslides, snorkeling, and the Waikolohe Stream (lazy river). Ka Maka Landing was added Oct. 19, 2013, with Ka Maka Grotto (an infinity-edge pool overlooking Ko Olina Beach), the Keiki Cove Splash Zone, and Ulu Cafe. SEE ALSO RAINBOW REEF.

Wake of Disaster (TV) Show; part 2 of *The Mooncussers*.

Waking Sleeping Beauty (film) Documentary about a decade of Disney animation history beginning in 1984. After the poorly received film *The Black Cauldron*, Roy E. Disney, Peter Schneider, and Jeffrey Katzenberg engineered a renaissance in Disney animation from *The Little Mermaid* to *The Lion King*. Directed by Don Hahn. 86 min. Premiered Sep. 5, 2009, at the Telluride Film Festival, and released in theaters Mar. 26, 2010.

Walden, Dana With the acquisition of 21st Century Fox in 2019, she joined Disney as chairman of Disney Television Studios and ABC Entertainment. In Jun. 2022, she was named chairman, Disney General Entertainment Content and in Feb. 2023 was appointed co-chairman of Disney Entertainment, overseeing the company's worldwide portfolio of entertainment media and content businesses.

Wales (film) People and Places featurette released Jun. 10, 1958. Directed by Geoffrey Foot. Wales prides herself in her wealth of natural resources, foundries, mills, and factories. Beyond this modern facade lies another treasure—a rich historical background and ancient lore. The great granite fortresses still remain as reminders that from the struggle and strife was born a pure and distinctive national culture. Filmed in CinemaScope. 25 min.

Walk Around the World, Disney's Pathway around the Magic Kingdom and Transportation and Ticket Center at Walt Disney World. In 1994, it was announced that individuals could sponsor a 10-inch hexagonal brick in the pathway, which would be inscribed with the sponsor's name, for a fee of $96. The project was completed Jul. 2000. The bricks were removed beginning Jul. 2019 to accommodate changes to the park's main entrance.

Walker, E. Cardon ("Card") (1916–2005) He served as president of Walt Disney Productions 1971–1980 and chairman of the board 1980–1983. He originally began at the Disney Studio in 1938 delivering mail and worked his way up in the company in the Camera and Story Departments, finally moving into Advertising. In 1956, he was named vice president of Advertising and Sales, and he joined the Board of Directors in 1960. In 1965, he was appointed vice president of Marketing. He became executive vice president and chief operating officer in 1968. It was Walker who, with Donn Tatum, ably led the company after Roy O. Disney's death and who, in 1975, announced plans to move forward with the EPCOT project. He was elected president in 1971 and became CEO in 1976. In this capacity, he oversaw the design and construction of EPCOT Center. In 1980, he was named chairman of the board. He retired in 1983 after supervising the opening of EPCOT Center, Tokyo Disneyland, and the launch of The Disney Channel. He remained on the company's Board of Directors until 1999, qualifying for his 50-year service award in 1988. He received the Disney Legends Award in 1993.

Walker, Tommy (1922–1986) Showman; served as director of Entertainment for Disneyland 1955–1967. Besides the park's parades and fireworks spectaculars, he was in charge of many special events, including the grand opening ceremonies for Disneyland, and later the pageantry for the 1960 Winter Olympics in Squaw Valley (later known as Olympic Valley), California. He was the son of Vesey Walker.

Walker, Vesey (1893–1977) Original director of the Disneyland Band from 1955. He led the band in thousands of parades and concerts during his years at the park. Vesey was named "founding director" and retired in 1967, but he remained available as a guest conductor and for special appearances. He was named a Disney Legend in 2005.

Walker Ranch SEE DISNEY WILDERNESS PRESERVE, THE.

Wallace, Oliver (1887–1963) Composer; he began at Disney in 1936 and worked on the scores for many Disney films, including *Dumbo* (earning an Academy Award), *Cinderella*, *Peter Pan*, *Alice in Wonderland*, *Lady and the Tramp*, *Darby O'Gill and the Little People*, and *Ten Who Dared*, along with the People and Places and True-Life Adventure films, the *Disneyland* TV series, and dozens of animated shorts. He later estimated he had written more than 30 miles of soundtrack in his years with Disney. He was named a Disney Legend in 2008.

Wallach, Eli (1915–2014) Actor; appeared in *The Moon-Spinners* (Stratos), *Tough Guys* (Leon B. Little), *The Associate* (Frank), *Two Much* (Sheldon), and *Keeping the Faith* (Rabbi Lewis).

WALL•E (film) Animated feature from Pixar Animation Studios. What if mankind had to leave Earth 700 years in the future, and somebody forgot to turn off the last robot? WALL•E (Waste Allocation Load Lifter Earth-Class), a robot, spends every day doing what he was made for, cleaning the trash-covered planet, but he discovers a new purpose in life when he meets a sleek search robot named EVE (Extra-terrestrial Vegetation Evaluator). EVE comes to realize that WALL•E has inadvertently stumbled upon the key to the planet's future, and races back to space to the luxury spaceship *Axiom* to report her findings to the humans, who have been eagerly awaiting word that it is safe to return home. Meanwhile, WALL•E chases EVE across the galaxy and sets into motion an exciting adventure. Released Jun. 27, 2008, after a Jun. 21 invitational premiere at the Greek Theatre in Griffith Park in Los Angeles, and a Jun. 26 release in Bolivia and Chile. Directed by Andrew Stanton. Voices include Fred Willard (Shelby Forthright, who also appears in the film), Jeff Garlin (Captain), Ben Burtt (WALL•E), Elissa Knight (EVE), John Ratzenberger (John), Kathy Najimy (Mary), Sigourney Weaver (Ship's Computer). 98 min. The film features a score by Thomas Newman, with Peter Gabriel collaborating on the song "Down to Earth." The soundtrack includes 2 songs from *Hello, Dolly!* (Fox, 1969), on a videotape that WALL•E repeatedly watches (marking this the first Pixar feature to include scenes with live actors). Filmmakers turned to *Star Wars* veteran Ben Burtt to assist with the sound design for the many robot beeps and clicks. Filmed in CinemaScope. Nominated for 6 Academy Awards, winning Best Animated Feature (Andrew Stanton).

Walley, Deborah (1943–2001) Actress; appeared in *Bon Voyage* (Amy Willard) and *Summer Magic* (Cousin Julia), and provided voices on TV in *Chip 'n' Dale Rescue Rangers*.

Walmsley, Jon Actor; appeared in *The One and Only, Genuine, Original Family Band* (Quinn Bower) and voiced Christopher Robin in *Winnie the Pooh and the Blustery Day*. Walmsley later went on to fame in the role as Jason Walton on *The Waltons*.

Walrus and the Carpenter Characters in the tale of the gullible oysters in *Alice in Wonderland*; voiced by J. Pat O'Malley.

Walsh, Bill (1913–1975) Producer; joined Disney in 1943 as a writer for the *Mickey Mouse* comic strip, later moving into TV and films. In 1950, Walt Disney selected Bill to write and produce the first Disney TV show, *One Hour in Wonderland*. He later produced the spectacularly successful *Davy Crockett* and *Mickey Mouse Club* shows. In 1956, he became a movie producer, soon reaching the ranks of one of the most successful producers of all time with such titles as *Westward Ho the Wagons!*, *The Shaggy Dog*, *Toby Tyler*, *The Absent-Minded Professor*, *That Darn Cat!*, *Blackbeard's Ghost*, *Mary Poppins*, *The Love Bug*, and *Bedknobs and Broomsticks*. He was named a Disney Legend posthumously in 1991.

Walsh, Kay (1914–2005) Actress; appeared in *Greyfriars Bobby* (Mrs. Brown) and *Night Crossing* (Doris's mother), and on TV in *The Scarecrow of Romney Marsh* (Mrs. Waggett).

Walston, Ray (1914–2001) Actor; appeared in *My Favorite Martian* (Martin), and on TV in *Ask Max* (Harmon).

Walt & El Grupo (film) Documentary about Walt Disney's trip to South America in 1941, out of which came *Saludos Amigos* and *The Three Caballeros*, from Walt Disney Family Foundation Films in association with Theodore Thomas Productions. The film draws from personal letters and artwork from the trip, remembrances by descendants and survivors, and archival footage to provide a candid glimpse of Walt Disney and his artists. Directed by Theodore Thomas. 107 min. The film premiered at the San Francisco International Film Festival Apr. 26, 2008. Limited release in Los Angeles, New York City, and Anaheim beginning Sep. 11, 2009. Released on DVD in 2010.

Walt Before Mickey (film) An independent motion picture detailing the early life and career of Walt Disney; released Aug. 14, 2015. Directed by Khoa Le. Stars Thomas Ian Nicholas (Walt Disney), Jon Heder (Roy Disney), David Henrie (Rudy Ising), Kate Katzman (Lillian Disney), Armando Gutierrez (Ub Iwerks), Hunter Gomez (Hugh Harman), Jodie Sweetin (Charlotte Disney). 120 min. Based on the book by Timothy Susanin. Produced by Conglomerate Media and Lensbern Productions.

The film is not associated with The Walt Disney Company.

Walt Disney (TV) Title of the regular Disney series on CBS, following *Disney's Wonderful World* on NBC; aired Sep. 26, 1981–Sep. 24, 1983. The series was not renewed at that time, so it would not conflict with The Disney Channel.

Walt Disney (TV) Four-hour documentary produced for *American Experience*, a production of WGBH Boston. Aired on PBS Sep. 14–15, 2015. A look at the life and legacy of Walt Disney, told with rare film footage and interviews with biographers, animators, artists, and designers. Directed by Sarah Colt. Narrated by Oliver Platt.

Walt Disney—A Golden Anniversary Salute (TV) Tribute to Walt Disney Productions' 50th anniversary on ABC's *Wide World of Entertainment*; aired Oct. 23, 1973. Directed by Lou Tedesco.

Walt Disney—A Legacy for the Future Display of Walt Disney's awards and other memorabilia, along with an exhibit on the California Institute of the Arts, on Main Street, U.S.A. in Disneyland; open Jan. 15, 1970–Feb. 11, 1973. Also known as the Legacy of Walt Disney. It took the space used previously by the Wurlitzer shop, until the major awards were moved to The Walt Disney Story attraction (both in Disneyland and in the Magic Kingdom at Walt Disney World). At that time, the exhibit became Disneyland Presents a Preview of Coming Attractions (1973–1989).

Walt Disney Animation Studios New name, in 2007, for Walt Disney Feature Animation. SEE FEATURE ANIMATION.

Walt Disney Animation Studios Short Films Collection (film) Home entertainment release of shorts from Walt Disney Animation Studios on Aug. 18, 2015: *Frozen Fever, Feast, Get a Horse!, Paperman, Tangled Ever After, The Ballad of Nessie, Prep & Landing: Operation Secret Santa, Tick Tock Tale, How to Hook Up Your Home Theater, The Little Matchgirl, Lorenzo,* and *John Henry.*

Walt Disney Archives Founded on Jun. 22, 1970, with Dave Smith as the archivist, to collect, preserve, and make available for use the various historical materials of The Walt Disney Company. While the Archives works primarily with departments of The Walt Disney Company, it also handles mail, e-mail, and telephone inquiries relating to Disney history. Rebecca Cline became director with Dave Smith's retirement in 2010. Over the years, the Archives has grown in size and responsibilities, including the creation of web content and programming for special events, the administration of the Disney Legends Program, and the curation and touring of domestic and international exhibitions.

Walt Disney Christmas Show, The (TV) Show promo for *Peter Pan*, starring Walt Disney, Kathy Beaumont, Bobby Driscoll, and the Magic Mirror (Hans Conried); sponsored by Johnson & Johnson. Aired on Dec. 25, 1951. Directed by Robert Florey.

Walt Disney Classics Collection, The Premiered in 1992 as the first line of fine animation art sculptures produced directly by the Walt Disney Studios. Licensees took over in 2001. It used authentic Disney animation principles and materials to bring to life memorable moments and characters from Disney animated classics. The meticulously crafted figurines, created from a special low-fire porcelain, could be displayed singly or grouped to re-create entire scenes, and some were plussed with materials such as crystal, blown glass, and precious metals. Each sculpture bore a special symbol connoting the year in which it was made, along with a backstamp featuring Walt Disney's signature. From its introduction, the collection became highly popular because of its attention to quality and because early pieces produced in limited editions increased dramatically in value. Numerous clubs of Classics Collection collectors sprang up around the country, as well as an official one, The Walt Disney Collectors Society.

Walt Disney Collectors Society, The Launched in 1993 to support the Walt Disney Classics Collection, this society was the first official membership organization for Disney fans and enthusiasts sponsored by Disney itself. Headed originally by Paula Sigman, the Society published *Sketches*, a quarterly magazine, and offered members-only exclusive Classics Collection pieces. The Society ceased operations on Dec. 31, 2009, as did *Sketches*.

Walt Disney Company, The Corporate name of the company as of Feb. 6, 1986. It was formerly Walt Disney Productions.

Walt Disney Educational Materials Co. Incorporated on Jun. 25, 1969; later known as Walt Disney Educational Media Co. and Disney Educational Productions.

Walt Disney Enterprises The entity of the Disney company during the 1930s, which handled the licensing of character merchandise. It was consolidated to become a part of Walt Disney Productions on Sep. 30, 1938.

Walt Disney Family Museum, The Diane Disney Miller spearheaded the establishment of a museum in a restored building in the Presidio area of San Francisco to honor her father. It opened in 2009, with the first preview on Sep. 19 and official opening Oct. 1. After closely supervising the operations of the museum for 4 years, Diane passed away in 2013.

Walt Disney Gallery, The A new concept in retail merchandising began on Nov. 4, 1994, with the opening of the first Walt Disney Gallery connected to a Disney Store at Main Place in Santa Ana, California. The Gallery featured collectibles, artwork, and other special items of Disneyana in an attractively designed setting.

Walt Disney Grand Theatre A 1,200-seat theater in Disneytown at the Shanghai Disney Resort; opened Jun. 14, 2016, with a Mandarin-language live production of *The Lion King*. The theater has also hosted movie premieres (including for *Beauty and the Beast* and *Pirates of the Caribbean: Dead Men Tell No Tales* in 2017) and film festivals. A Mandarin-language live production of *Beauty and the Beast* opened Jun. 14, 2018, directed by Rob Roth, who had directed the original Broadway production. The musical show *Mickey's Storybook Adventure* debuted Jun. 16, 2021, along with a new theater entrance from Shanghai Disneyland park.

Walt Disney Imagineering New name, as of Jan. 1986, of WED Enterprises, which was founded in 1952. In 1996, Walt Disney Imagineering merged with the Disney Development Company, the Disney company's real estate development subsidiary. Part design firm, development company, storytelling studio, and innovation lab, Walt Disney Imagineering is the creative force behind Disney parks, resorts, and other experiences around the globe. The word "Imagineering" was suggested to Walt Disney and early WED president Bill Cottrell by Harrison "Buzz" Price, of Economics Research Associates, and the word was later defined as the blending of creative imagination with technical know-how. In 2021, it was announced that Walt Disney Imagineering would move its headquarters from Glendale, California, where the organization had been based since 1961, to a new campus in Central Florida's Lake Nona community. SEE ALSO IMAGINEERS AND WED ENTERPRISES.

Walt Disney Motion Pictures Group Division of The Walt Disney Company established in 1994 with Joe Roth as chairman.

Walt Disney Music Company Formed in Oct. 1949, to publish and license Disney songs. It was affiliated with ASCAP, while its sister music publishing arm at Disney, the Wonderland Music Co., formed in 1952, was affiliated with BMI. The first songs published by the Walt Disney Music Company were those from *Cinderella* (1950).

Walt Disney—One Man's Dream (TV) Two-hour movie; aired on Dec. 12, 1981. Directed by Dwight Hemion. A look at Walt Disney's life and influence leading up to the building of EPCOT Center. The story emphasizes the many times that Walt refused to listen to advisers and critics who tried to tell him that his plans would not work. But he was always an innovator and visionary looking years ahead and continued to dream—and most of his dreams came true. Stars Christian Hoff, Michael Landon, Mac Davis, Dick Van Dyke, Marie Osmond, Carl Reiner, Ben Vereen, Julie Andrews, and many other stars in cameo roles. Hoff was the first actor to portray Walt Disney in a Disney film, albeit as a child.

Walt Disney: One Man's Dream Multimedia gallery exhibit on Mickey Avenue at Disney-MGM Studios (later Animation Courtyard at Disney's Hollywood Studios); opened Oct. 1, 2001, as part of the 100 Years of Magic celebration at Walt Disney World. The story of Walt Disney is told through artifacts and an inspiring 15-min. film, narrated originally by Michael Eisner and later by Julie Andrews. It was initially planned to be an 18-month attraction, but its popularity extended its run by many years. A highlight was a display of Walt Disney's working office, complete with original furnishings. In 2010, the gallery was refreshed with several new displays, and it became Walt Disney Presents Sep. 8, 2017, incorporating previews for upcoming films and park attractions.

Walt Disney Presents (TV) Series on ABC; aired Sep. 12, 1958–Sep. 17, 1961. The series then moved to NBC as *Walt Disney's Wonderful World of*

Color. FOR THE WALT DISNEY WORLD ATTRACTION, SEE PRECEDING ENTRY.

Walt Disney Productions Corporate name of the Disney company until it changed to The Walt Disney Company Feb. 6, 1986. The company began as Disney Brothers Cartoon Studio on Oct. 16, 1923, when Walt Disney signed his first contract to produce the Alice Comedies. On Dec. 16, 1929, the company was incorporated, taking over the assets previously held as a partnership between Walt and Roy O. Disney.

Walt Disney Records After its success in the early 1950s with music publishing, the Walt Disney Music Company entered the phonograph record business in 1956. The "Disneyland" record label was created for the new record line, with the first release in 1956 being *A Child's Garden of Verses*. Walt Disney himself narrated one of the earliest LPs, *Walt Disney Takes You to Disneyland*. There was a WDL series for soundtracks, an ST series for Storytellers, and an MM series for music from the *Mickey Mouse Club* TV show. Non-Disney music was included in the line with adult easy listening and novelty records. In 1959, the Buena Vista label began a more prestigious line and in 1964 had a huge hit with the *Mary Poppins* soundtrack (14 weeks at number one on the Billboard chart, and 2 Grammy Awards). Forty-five rpm singles promoted songs from Disney films and heralded performances by Annette Funicello, Darlene Gillespie, Fess Parker, and other Disney stars. A popular LLP (Little Long Playing) series began in 1967. The Disney records have earned a large number of gold and platinum records, with one of the biggest sellers being the 1979 *Mickey Mouse Disco*. The CD revolution reached Disney in 1988 with the release of its last 12-inch vinyl record—the *Oliver & Company* soundtrack. The following year, Disneyland/Vista Records changed its name to Walt Disney Records, which today continues to represent a broad and diverse selection of audio entertainment for the family. Walt Disney Records is part of Disney Music Group, which is also home to Hollywood Records and Disney Music Publishing.

Walt Disney Story, The Main Street, U.S.A. attraction in the Opera House at Disneyland; opened Apr. 8, 1973, taking the place of Great Moments with Mr. Lincoln. A film, narrated by Walt himself through interview and other historical recordings, told his life story. Many guests missed Lincoln, however, so the movie closed Feb.

12, 1975, enabling Great Moments with Mr. Lincoln to return to the theater. A Lincoln display and a model of the U.S. Capitol replaced some of the Walt Disney display in 1985. Memorabilia related to Walt Disney from the Walt Disney Archives was displayed, including awards, letters written to Walt Disney by famous personalities, and even an exact reproduction of his offices from the Disney Studio in Burbank. The offices were on display until 2005. The *Walt Disney Story* film, which features rare stills and film clips, was eventually released as an educational film and, in 1994, put on videocassette for purchase in the parks. Also an attraction on Main Street, U.S.A. in the Magic Kingdom at Walt Disney World, Apr. 15, 1973–Oct. 5, 1992. A fondly remembered mural, with more than 170 Disney characters, was illustrated by Bill Justice with later additions made by Russell Schroeder at the attraction. The postshow area included an EPCOT Center preview from 1981–1982 and a Disney-MGM Studios preview from 1987–1989. The Walt Disney Story display area temporarily reopened in 1993 to serve as a center for annual passport redemption. New displays debuted Oct. 1, 1996, when the facility was converted into an exhibit for the Walt Disney World 25th anniversary. In 1998, it became the Town Square Exposition Hall. SEE ALSO WALT DISNEY: ONE MAN'S DREAM AND OFFICES, WALT DISNEY'S.

Walt Disney Studios, The The Disney corporate headquarters, located at the corner of Buena Vista Street and Alameda Avenue in Burbank, at 500 South Buena Vista Street. Completed in 1940, the Studio covers 44 acres and was designed originally with the purpose of producing animated films. There are buildings for animation, camera, sound recording, live-action production, editing, costume, music, and so on. In close collaboration with Walt Disney, industrial designer Kem Weber designed the buildings and furniture in the art moderne style, and technical adviser Bill Garity and architect Frank Crowhurst oversaw construction, incorporating a number of unique innovations. The Studio has a pleasant, campus-like feel, with lawns lined with oak trees. The buildings were designed to allow for maximum sunlight to enter the artists' offices. While most studio water towers have 4 legs, Roy O. Disney suggested a 6-legged design, as he found it more aesthetically pleasing. There were also backlot sets, but these have given way to offices (SEE BACKLOT). One soundstage was built in 1940, and 3 more were added over the next 2 decades. (Stage 4 was eventually divided into 2 separate stages.) Two more soundstages were added in 1997. Perhaps the most famous landmark is a signpost at the corner of Mickey Avenue and Dopey Drive. It was placed there for the Studio tour segment of *The Reluctant Dragon* in 1941 and never removed. There were earlier Disney Studios on Kingswell Avenue (1923) and Hyperion Avenue (1926) in Los Angeles.

Walt Disney Studios Park Theme park giving guests an insight into movies, animation, and TV; opened adjacent to Disneyland Paris Mar. 16, 2002. The park was inspired by the classic Hollywood movie studios from the 1920s to today. After passing through the main entrance, with a fountain featuring Mickey as the Sorcerer's Apprentice, guests can choose from several different areas to explore: Front Lot, Toon Studio (new name for Animation Courtyard beginning in 2007), Worlds of Pixar (new name for the Pixar sections of Toon Studio beginning in 2021), Production Courtyard, and Avengers Campus (formerly the Backlot). Kingdom of Arendelle, a new area based on *Frozen*, is planned. In 2022, a new area was announced that will offer guests opportunities to relax and stroll along a new lake and promenade of themed gardens, including the Tangled Garden and Toy Story Garden.

Walt Disney Studios Store Main entrance apparel and collectibles shop in Walt Disney Studios Park at Disneyland Paris; opened Mar. 16, 2002. SEE ALSO STUDIO STORE, THE (DISNEY'S HOLLYWOOD STUDIOS AND WALT DISNEY STUDIOS, BURBANK).

Walt Disney Television Alternative Production unit for non-scripted TV programming; established in 2021 under Disney Television Studios.

Walt Disney Television Animation Department formed in Nov. 1984, with Gary Krisel as president, to produce special animation for TV. Their first series were *Disney's Adventures of the Gummi Bears* and *The Wuzzles*. A decade later, they were producing 150 half-hour episodes of programming a year, plus specials, movies, direct-to-video features, music videos, featurettes, and commercials. A Japanese branch, Walt Disney Animation (Japan), operated 1989–2003. SEE ALSO DISNEYTOON STUDIOS.

Walt Disney Television Studios Production Courtyard attraction in Walt Disney Studios Park at Disneyland Paris; opened Mar. 16, 2002. Guests could take a behind-the-scenes tour of the production facility for Disney Channel France. The tour closed in 2007, with a section replaced by Stitch Live! Mar. 22, 2008. The tour's postshow, which included the Disney Channel CyberSpace Mountain attraction, became *Playhouse Disney—Live on Stage!* Apr. 4, 2009, and then *Disney Junior Dream Factory* Jul. 1, 2021.

Walt Disney Travel Co. Company established in Florida in 1972 to work with travel agents and individuals planning vacations to Walt Disney World, with expansion that same year to California for Disneyland vacations.

Walt Disney Treasures Series of 30 two-disc DVD volumes from Walt Disney Home Entertainment, featuring classic Disney films, specials, and bonus features. Released between 2001–2009. The first volumes were *Mickey Mouse in Living Color, Silly Symphonies, Disneyland USA*, and *Davy Crockett–The Complete Televised Series*. Each volume was presented by Leonard Maltin, individually numbered with a certificate of authenticity, and in an attractive collector's tin case.

Walt Disney World SEE WALT DISNEY WORLD RESORT.

Walt Disney World at Home: Garden Magic (film) Video release of step-by-step gardening tips from the gardens of Walt Disney World. Segments are Telling the Story with Plants, Portable Gardens, Parterre Gardens, Topiary, and Environmental Gardening. 55 min. Released in 1996.

Walt Disney World Boys and Girls Club Located in Orlando's Pine Hills neighborhood, this 25,000-sq.-ft. facility was made possible in part by a $1 million contribution from Walt Disney World and Disney Worldwide Outreach; opened Mar. 19, 2008. The Club offers numerous educational programs for children, including computer training, mentoring programs, a health and life skills center, career center, digital arts program, and instruction in visual and performing arts. Also known as the Walt Disney World Clubhouse.

Walt Disney World Casting Center Building opened Mar. 27, 1989. Designed by Robert A.M. Stern Architects, this 60,000-sq.-ft. facility is themed as a Venetian palace with whimsical touches. Some have likened its diamond-shaped decorations to a giant argyle sock. Inside, a 30-ft.-wide rotunda features gold-colored statues of Disney characters, positioned up on pedestals. It is here that those hopeful of working for Walt Disney World put in their applications. Prior to the opening of this facility, the employment offices were located in back-of-house areas.

Walt Disney World Celebrity Circus (TV) Special on NBC; aired Nov. 27, 1987. Some of the world's greatest circus acts are performed across World Showcase at EPCOT Center. For the finale, Mickey Mouse performs on a trapeze suspended by a helicopter over the park. Directed by Marty Pasetta. Stars Tony Randall as host, with Allyce Beasley, Tim Conway, Kim Fields, Jim Varney, Malcolm-Jamal Warner.

Walt Disney World Christmas Day Parade (TV) SEE WALT DISNEY WORLD VERY MERRY CHRISTMAS PARADE.

Walt Disney World College Program SEE DISNEY COLLEGE PROGRAM.

Walt Disney World Conference Center Facility opened Aug. 1980 in Lake Buena Vista. Surrounded by the Club Lake Suites, it offered meeting facilities. In 1996, it became part of The Disney Institute.

Walt Disney World Dolphin A 1,514-room hotel at Walt Disney World near EPCOT; opened Jun. 4, 1990. Originally operated by Sheraton, which was later acquired by Starwood Lodging and then by Marriott International. Designed by Michael Graves, the architecture is based on Florida's natural landscape, with elements like enormous banana leaf murals, 56-ft.-tall dolphin statues, and a coral and turquoise color palette. SEE ALSO WALT DISNEY WORLD SWAN AND WALT DISNEY WORLD SWAN RESERVE.

Walt Disney World 4th of July Spectacular (TV) Special; aired in syn. Jul. 3, 1988. Directed by Don Ohlmeyer. 120 min. Hosted by Tempestt Bledsoe and Marc Summers, with Burt Reynolds, Carol Burnett, Rita Moreno, Tommy Tune, the Beach Boys, Mark Price, Willard Scott. Includes parade performances, a visit to the new Mickey's Birthdayland, and a fireworks finale. This show marked the first of an annual Jul. 4th holiday special through 1992.

Walt Disney World Golf Classic Beginning in its first year, 1971, Walt Disney World, at the urging of then-Disney president and golf enthusiast Card Walker, sponsored the Walt Disney World Golf Classic. It was arranged by marketing direc-

tor Sandy Quinn with just a few weeks remaining before the resort's opening. There was an individual tourney each year, except for 1974–1981 when it served as the venue for the PGA Tour's 2-man National Team Championship. The winner of the tournament the first 3 years was Jack Nicklaus. Walt Disney World hosted a PGA Tour event every year 1971 through 2012, when the PGA Tour announced an end to its relationship with Walt Disney World.

Walt Disney World Happy Easter Parade (TV) The first of many annual specials; aired on ABC beginning Apr. 7, 1985. Directed by Paul Miller. Hosted by Rick Dees and Joan Lunden. Only in 1986 did the Walt Disney World Easter Parade appear as part of *The CBS Easter Parade* (Mar. 30, 1986), which switched between the Walt Disney World parade and one on Fifth Avenue in New York City. The 1988 parade was hosted by Joan Lunden, Alan Thicke, and Regis Philbin. The telecasts continued until 1999.

Walt Disney World Inside Out (TV) Series on The Disney Channel; premiered Jun. 7, 1994. Stars Scott Herriott in a wacky, witty, offbeat look at life at Walt Disney World. A new version of the show, featuring J. D. Roth and Brianne Leary, with commentary by George Foreman, began Dec. 12, 1995. One show a month originated from Disneyland.

Walt Disney World Marching Band Formed in 1971, the band performed concerts in Town Square and occasionally at Fantasy Faire in Fantasyland, as well as in various parades throughout the Magic Kingdom. The group retired in 2000 and was eventually replaced by the Main Street Philharmonic.

Walt Disney World—Phase I (film) Film prepared for a Florida press event, Apr. 30, 1969. Plans are unveiled for the property's first phase, including an imaginary visit to the Magic Kingdom, resort hotels, and recreation areas through concept art and models. Prepared by Marty Sklar, Randy Bright, and Jim Love.

Walt Disney World Preview Center SEE PREVIEW CENTER.

Walt Disney World Railroad Attraction in the Magic Kingdom; opened Oct. 1, 1971. The 4 locomotives are the *Walter E. Disney*, the *Roy O. Disney*, the *Lilly Belle*, and the *Roger Broggie*, all discovered in Mexico's Yucatan region, where they hauled freight and passengers. (Lilly was Walt Disney's wife, and Broggie was a Disney engineer who ran the Studio Machine Shop and helped Walt with his miniature railroad hobby.) The railroad tracks circle the park and provide a good introduction to a visit, on a 20-min., 1.5-mile scenic journey.

Walt Disney World Resort Opened near Orlando on Oct. 1, 1971, with the Magic Kingdom and 2 resort hotels (Contemporary Resort and Polynesian Village Resort). After the success of Disneyland in California, Walt Disney was besieged by those suggesting and seeking a second park. Everyone wanted this new park to be built in *their* hometown—especially when observing the growth of the economy in Anaheim after Disneyland opened there in 1955. Disney bided his time, however. First, he wanted Disneyland to be running smoothly before he considered another site; and second, he wanted to be sure that he selected the right place. Starting in the early 1960s, Walt and Roy O. Disney began searching for an area on the East Coast where they could build a new Disney enterprise. They knew it should be located east of the Mississippi, where it could draw from a different segment of the population than did Disneyland. Walt Disney also knew he needed a site with a pleasant climate. Many other factors were considered, such as land cost, population density, and accessibility. In Florida, the nation's fastest-growing tourist state, the climate seemed the best for year-round operation. Plus, there was land available, so they secretly began buying up property. Learning their lesson from the urban clutter that had built up around Disneyland in California, the Disneys wanted enough land to insulate their development. After roughly 17,000 acres were acquired, Walt became interested in a huge 10,000-acre tract. Roy balked at first, but when Walt asked him what he would do if he had an extra 10,000 acres around Disneyland, he realized that they should go ahead and purchase. They ended up with 27,443 acres, a parcel twice the size of Manhattan Island. While they were able to buy most of the land they needed before the word leaked out who the mysterious buyer was, eventually *Orlando Sentinel* reporter Emily Bavar dug out the story. A press conference was put together at the Cherry Plaza Hotel in Orlando, where Walt and Roy announced their plans publicly on Nov. 15, 1965. It was a major shock for the Disney company when Walt Disney suddenly died a year later in Dec. 1966. Roy, who was 73 years old,

was ready to retire, but decided to stay on the job long enough to see that Walt's final project was built. Construction on the massive project progressed, and the costs eventually rose to $400 million, but due to Roy's business acumen, the park was able to open in 1971 with the company having no outstanding debt. Roy presided over the Grand Opening Dedication Ceremony on Oct. 25 and passed away in December. In size, the Magic Kingdom was similar to Disneyland, but there was more—2 luxury hotels, golf courses, lakes and lagoons offering fishing and water sports, and a campground, which debuted Nov. 19. The Magic Kingdom opened with several attractions similar to those in Disneyland, but also with its own original shows, such as the Country Bear Jamboree, The Hall of Presidents, and the Mickey Mouse Revue. Since 1971, Walt Disney World has seen steady growth, highlighted by the opening of EPCOT Center (now EPCOT) in 1982, Disney-MGM Studios (now Disney's Hollywood Studios) in 1989, and Disney's Animal Kingdom in 1998. Over the years, numerous resort hotels (more than 25), water parks, sports and entertainment facilities, and shopping areas have made Walt Disney World the premier destination resort in the world.

The special record-setting guests at Walt Disney World have been:

1st guest, Oct. 1, 1971: William Windsor, Jr.
50 millionth guest, Mar. 2, 1976: Susan Brummer
100 millionth guest, Oct. 22, 1979: Kurt Miller
150 millionth guest, Apr. 7, 1983: Carrie Stahl
200 millionth guest, Jul. 20, 1985: Virgil Waytes, Jr.
300 millionth guest, Jun. 21, 1989: Matt Gleason
400 millionth guest, Aug. 5, 1992: Brandon Adams
500 millionth guest, Oct. 13, 1995: Michelle Davi
600 millionth guest, Jun. 24, 1998: Jacqueline D'Ambrosi

In 1994, Walt Disney World welcomed the one billionth guest worldwide to enter a Disney park (Mary Pat Smith of Decatur, Illinois); the 500 millionth guest had been welcomed only 9 years earlier, on Mar. 25, 1986 (Don McGrath of Millis, Massachusetts). By 2021, more than 1.6 billion guests had visited Walt Disney World.

Walt Disney World Speedway Built in a corner of the Transportation and Ticket Center parking lot at Walt Disney World and dedicated Nov. 28, 1995, the one-mile racetrack was used for various speed events, beginning with a Formula Ford

2000 support race Jan. 26, 1996, and the Indy Racing League's Indy 200 Jan. 27 (of the same year). Beginning Feb. 7, 1997, the Richard Petty Driving Experience offered behind-the-wheel and ride-along experiences in stock cars on the speedway. Beginning in Nov. 2008, the Indy Racing Experience was added, allowing guests to drive and ride in open-cockpit cars used in the Indy Racing League. The Exotic Driving Experience was offered beginning Jan. 2012, wherein guests could ride in "supercars" by Ferrari, Lamborghini, Audi, and Porsche; a new one-mile circuit, called the Exotics Course, was custom-built for the experience. The speedway closed Aug. 9, 2015.

Walt Disney World Store Shop on International Drive in Orlando; opened May 31, 2022. Offers merchandise and ticket sales, plus an interactive Disney Vacation Club Virtual Discovery Station. FOR THE AIRPORT STORE, SEE ORLANDO INTERNATIONAL AIRPORT.

Walt Disney World Summer Jam Concert (TV) Three hour-long specials on ABC, each with performances by pop artists. The first aired Jun. 18, 1999 (with *NSYNC, Britney Spears, Tyrese, and 98 Degrees); the second aired Jun. 23, 2000 (with Christina Aguilera, Enrique Iglesias, and Destiny's Child); and the third aired Jun. 10, 2001 (with Shaggy, BBMak, Baha Men, and Sugar Ray). From If Productions and Walt Disney Attractions Television Productions.

Walt Disney World Swan A 756-room hotel at Walt Disney World near EPCOT; opened Nov. 22, 1989. Operated originally by Westin, which was later acquired by Starwood Lodging and then by Marriott International. Designed by Michael Graves, the 12-story structure features 56-ft.-tall swan statues and a motif of curving waves. SEE ALSO WALT DISNEY WORLD DOLPHIN AND WALT DISNEY WORLD SWAN RESERVE.

Walt Disney World Swan Reserve A 349-room boutique addition to the Swan and Dolphin hotels at Walt Disney World; opened Nov. 3, 2021. Operated by Marriott. Designed by the Gensler architecture firm. A large glassy façade is inspired by the idea of a wellspring. SEE ALSO WALT DISNEY WORLD SWAN AND WALT DISNEY WORLD DOLPHIN.

Walt Disney World 'Twas the Night Before Christmas (TV) SEE WALT DISNEY WORLD VERY MERRY CHRISTMAS PARADE.

Walt Disney World—Vacation Kingdom (film) A 16-mm promotional film for the Florida park; released in Sep. 1969.

Walt Disney World Very Merry Christmas Parade (TV) Now a holiday tradition, a special that first aired on Christmas Day in 1983 on ABC, hosted by Joan Lunden and Mike Douglas. In 1984, the hosts were Joan Lunden, Bruce Jenner, and Regis Philbin; with Ben Vereen succeeding Bruce Jenner 1985–1986; Alan Thicke succeeding Ben Vereen from 1987–1990; and co-hosted by Joan Lunden and Regis Philbin from 1991–1996. Other hosts have included Jerry Van Dyke and Suzanne Somers (1996); Melissa Joan Hart and Ben Savage (1997, *A Magical Walt Disney World Christmas*); Caroline Rhea and Richard Kind (1998); and Mitchell Ryan, Susan Sullivan, and Wayne Brady (1999). The 1999 parade was the first to be taped at night. A Christmas Day special was not televised in 2000; instead, there was a Christmas Eve program, *Walt Disney World 'Twas the Night Before Christmas*, hosted by Colin Mochrie, Ryan Stiles, and Wayne Brady. The Christmas Day special returned in 2001 with Regis Philbin and Kelly Ripa as hosts. Also known as the *Walt Disney World Christmas Day Parade* (beginning in 2002); *Disney Parks Christmas Day Parade* (beginning in 2009, with hosts Kelly Ripa, Nick Cannon, Ryan Seacrest); *Disney Parks Frozen Christmas Celebration* (2014, with Robin Roberts, Tim Tebow, Rob Marciano); *Disney Parks Unforgettable Christmas Celebration* (2015, with Robin Roberts, Jesse Palmer, Janel Parrish); *Disney Parks Magical Christmas Celebration* (beginning 2016, with Derek Hough, Julianne Hough, Jesse Palmer); and *Disney Parks Magical Christmas Day Parade* (beginning 2018, with Jordan Fisher, Sarah Hyland, Jesse Palmer). In 2020, a modified special without the parade was titled *Disney Parks Magical Christmas Celebration*, with hosts Tituss Burgess and Julianne Hough. The *Disney Parks Magical Christmas Day Parade* returned in 2021, with hosts Derek and Julianne Hough at Walt Disney World and Trevor Jackson and Sherry Cola at Disneyland. The special won Emmy Awards in 1993 (Costume Design), 1998 (Special Class Directing), 2006 (Special Class Program), 2008 and 2011 (Special Class Directing), 2013 (Special Class Directing, Live and Direct-to-Tape Sound Mixing), and 2014 and 2016 (Technical Team).

Walt Disney World Village New name, beginning Jun. 2, 1977, for the Lake Buena Vista Shopping Village, which had opened Mar. 1975. A large outdoor retail and dining area, with specialty shops all built by Disney designers. SEE ALSO DOWNTOWN DISNEY MARKETPLACE.

Walt Disney World's 15th Birthday Celebration (TV) Betty White and Bea Arthur were the hosts for this 2-hour special on the Disney Sunday Movie, airing on Nov. 9, 1986. Directed by Marty Pasetta. Entertainers include Diahann Carroll, Ray Charles, the Everly Brothers, the Monkees, Emmanuel Lewis, Dolly Parton, Harry Shearer. President Reagan, Senator Edward Kennedy, former Supreme Court chief justice Warren Burger, and Charlton Heston were on hand to pay tribute to the U.S. Constitution.

Walt Disney World's 10th Anniversary (TV) SEE KRAFT SALUTES WALT DISNEY WORLD'S 10TH ANNIVERSARY.

Walt Disney World's 25th Anniversary Party (TV) Special on ABC; aired Feb. 28, 1997, with Melissa Joan Hart and Will Friedle hosting. Drew Carey takes viewers on a behind-the-scenes tour of the parks, and Gloria Estefan performs "Remember the Magic." Also stars Michael J. Fox, Rosie O'Donnell, Donna Summer, the Village People, and Hillary Rodham Clinton.

Walt Disney's Comics and Stories Comic book first published in Oct. 1940; the original price was 10¢. One of the longest-running comic books in history, it was originally released by Western Publishing, variously under the Dell, Gold Key, and Whitman imprints. More recent publishers include Gladstone, Boom! Studios, and IDW Publishing, which shortened the name to *Disney Comics and Stories* in 2018. SEE ALSO COMIC BOOKS.

Walt Disney's Mickey and Donald (TV) Show aired Jan. 1, 1983 (30-min. format) and Sep. 24, 1983 (60-min. format). The show is a grouping of cartoons.

Walt Disney's Parade of Dreams Special parade for the 50th anniversary of Disneyland; ran May 5, 2005–Nov. 11, 2008, featuring a large number of Disney characters along with dancers, rhythmic gymnasts, trampoline performers, and aerial artists. The parade floats, some nearly 20 feet high, acted as rolling stages and featured jumping fountains, confetti blasts, and wafting bubbles. There were 4 performance stops along the parade route, with large musical production numbers being performed at

each one. The main anthem was an updated version of the song "Welcome," from *Brother Bear*.

Walt Disney's Wet and Wild (TV) Hour-long syn. special. This animation compilation features cartoons showing ways of getting wet. First aired on Oct. 1, 1986.

Walt Disney's Wonderful World of Color (TV) Series on NBC; first aired Sep. 24, 1961, presented in color, and replacing the *Walt Disney Presents* series, which had aired on ABC. The theme song was written by Richard M. and Robert B. Sherman. The series ended Sep. 7, 1969, and was re-titled *The Wonderful World of Disney* the following week.

Walt the Dreamer Bronze statue of Walt Disney in Dreamers Point at World Celebration at EPCOT; debuted in 2023. Sculpted by Imagineer Scott Goddard, the statue depicts a more casual Walt later in his life, when he was dreaming up EPCOT. SEE ALSO PARTNERS AND STORYTELLERS.

Walt: The Man Behind the Myth (TV) Two-hour documentary about the life of Walt Disney, told through rare film clips and still photos, and by interviews with coworkers, historians, and celebrities. Dick Van Dyke narrates. Directed by Jean-Pierre Isbouts. Aired on *The Wonderful World of Disney* Sep. 16, 2001, to help celebrate the 100th anniversary of Walt Disney's birth. Exec. produced by Walter Elias Disney Miller. From Pantheon Productions in association with the Walt Disney Family Foundation.

Walter and Emily (TV) Series on NBC; aired Nov. 16, 1991–Feb. 22, 1992. After 40 years of marriage, Walter and Emily Collins still bicker, but this disguises their deep love for each other. Their divorced son moves back in with them, bringing his 11-year-old son, Zack, and hoping that Walter and Emily will help care for him. Stars Cloris Leachman (Emily Collins), Brian Keith (Walter Collins), Christopher McDonald (Matt Collins), Matthew Lawrence (Zack Collins), Edan Gross (Hartley Thompson).

Walters, Barbara (1929–2022) Broadcast journalist; she joined ABC in 1976 as the first woman to co-host the network news and later became noted for her interviews of prominent American and international celebrities and politicians. She created and co-hosted *The View*. She has received numerous honors, including induction into the Academy of Television

Arts & Sciences Hall of Fame and receipt of their Lifetime Achievement Award. Her autobiography, *Audition*, was published in 2008, the same year that she was named a Disney Legend. She retired from regular TV appearances in May 2014.

Walt's—an American Restaurant Elegant, Victorian-style restaurant on Main Street, U.S.A. in Disneyland Paris; opened Apr. 12, 1992. Contemporary American cuisine with European influences is served. Décor pays tribute to the life and works of Walt Disney, with upper-floor dining rooms themed to areas in the park: Fantasyland, Adventureland, Discoveryland, Frontierland, Grand Canyon, and the Disneyland Hotel. Downstairs dining rooms, themed to Main Street, U.S.A. and Walt and Lillian Disney, were replaced by Lilly's Boutique Jun. 26, 1999.

Walt's Cafe Victorian-themed table-service restaurant at the Hong Kong Disneyland Hotel; opened Oct. 24, 2011, replacing Sorcerer's Lounge. Menu items pay tribute to Walt Disney.

Waltz King, The (TV) Two-part show; aired Oct. 27 and Nov. 3, 1963. Directed by Steve Previn. A look at the life of Johann Strauss, Jr., beginning when, as a boy, he earns his famous father's displeasure when he tries his hand at composing. But he eventually proves to his father and the world that he is a fine musician. Stars Kerwin Mathews, Senta Berger, Brian Aherne, Peter Kraus, Fritz Eckhardt. The show was filmed on location in Europe, utilizing some of the continent's most ornate concert halls. It was released as a feature abroad.

WandaVision (TV) A Disney+ original series; digitally premiered Jan. 15, 2021. Wanda Maximoff and Vision—2 super-powered beings living idealized suburban lives—begin to suspect that everything is not as it seems. Presented chiefly in the style of classic sitcoms from the 1950s–2000s. Stars Elizabeth Olsen (Wanda Maximoff), Paul Bettany (Vision), Kathryn Hahn (Agnes), Teyonah Parris (Monica Rambeau), Kat Dennings (Darcy Lewis), Randall Park (Jimmy Woo). From Marvel Studios. The series won Emmy Awards for Outstanding Production Design for a Narrative Program (Half-Hour), Fantasy/Sci-Fi Costumes, and Original Music and Lyrics ("Agatha All Along," by Kristen Anderson-Lopez and Robert Lopez). A spin-off series, *Agatha: Coven of Chaos*, was announced.

Wander Over Yonder (TV) Animated comedy series on Disney XD; premiered Sep. 13, 2013. Wander, an eternally optimistic intergalactic traveler and constant do-gooder, sets out across the galaxies with his quick-tempered but loyal steed and best friend, Sylvia, to spread good cheer and help anyone he can. Voices include Jack McBrayer (Wander), April Winchell (Sylvia), Keith Ferguson (Lord Hater), Tom Kenny (Commander Peepers). From Disney Television Animation.

Wandering Moon Teahouse Counter-service restaurant in Gardens of Imagination at Shanghai Disneyland; opened Jun. 16, 2016, with Wagyu beef noodle soup, Shanghai pork belly rice, and other hot dishes. The teahouse honors the spirit of China's wandering poets and the landscapes that inspired them.

Wandering Oaken's Sliding Sleighs Attraction planned for World of Frozen in Hong Kong Disneyland. Entering through Oaken's store, guests board sleds for a winding roller-coaster journey through Arendelle.

Wandering Reindeer, The Shop in Norway at EPCOT; opened Jun. 17, 2016. *Frozen* merchandise is sold in a split-log structure reminiscent of Norway's rural communities.

War at Home, The (film) A Vietnam veteran, Jeremy Collier, has returned to his Texas hometown, but a year later, at Thanksgiving 1973, he has still been unable to forget his traumatic experiences during the war. His family does not know how to deal with him. During the Thanksgiving weekend, Jeremy's rancor ignites a family confrontation that shakes the Colliers down to their very foundation as a family. A Touchstone film, in association with Avatar Entertainment and the Motion Picture Corporation of America. Directed by Emilio Estevez. Limited release in Los Angeles and New York City on Nov. 22, 1996. Stars Emilio Estevez (Jeremy Collier), Kathy Bates (Maurine Collier), Martin Sheen (Bob Collier), Kimberly Williams (Karen Collier). 124 min. Based on the 1984 Broadway play *Homefront*, by James Duff. Filmed on location in Austin, Texas.

War bond certificate During World War II, to encourage parents to purchase war bonds in the names of their children, the Treasury Department had Disney artists design a colorful certificate, featuring many of the Disney characters around the perimeter, that would be given to each child in whose name a war bond was bought. These certificates are intriguing collectibles today, though some people erroneously think that they are the bonds themselves and can be cashed.

War Horse (film) In rural England, a remarkable friendship occurs between a horse named Joey and a young man called Albert, who tames and trains him. They are forcefully parted when Joey is sold to the cavalry and sent to the trenches during World War I, changing and inspiring the lives of all those he meets—British cavalry, German soldiers, and a French farmer and his granddaughter. Back in England, Albert cannot forget Joey, and even though he is not old enough to enlist in the army, he embarks on a dangerous mission to find his horse and bring him home. A DreamWorks film; released by Touchstone on Dec. 25, 2011. Directed by Steven Spielberg. 146 min. Stars Jeremy Irvine (Albert Narracott), Emily Watson (Rose Narracott), Peter Mullan (Ted Narracott), David Thewlis (Lyons), Benedict Cumberbatch (Major Stewart), Toby Kebbell (Geordie), Tom Hiddleston (Capt. Nicholls). Based on a 1982 children's novel by Michael Morpurgo and a 2007 stage adaptation. Filmed in CinemaScope. Nominated for 6 Academy Awards, including Best Picture.

Warburton, Cotton (1911–1982) Film editor at the Disney Studios for 22 years beginning in 1955; he won an Academy Award for his editing of *Mary Poppins*. He also edited such films as *The Love Bug* and *The Absent-Minded Professor*. Before his Disney years, Warburton had gained fame as an All-American quarterback in the early 1930s, leading the USC Trojans during a 27-game winning streak, which remained a school record until 1980.

Warburton, Patrick Actor; appeared in *Big Trouble* (Walter Kramitz), and on TV in *Ellen* (Jack), *Angels in the Infield* (Eddie "Steady" Everett), *Marvel's Agents of S.H.I.E.L.D.* (General Rick Stoner), and the *Disney Parks Christmas Day Parade*. He has provided several voices, including Kronk in *The Emperor's New Groove* and other appearances of the character, Patrick in *Home on the Range*, Royal Pain in *Sky High*, Alien Cop in *Chicken Little*, Buzz Lightyear in *Buzz Lightyear of Star Command*, Blag in *The Wild*, Cad in *Underdog*, Steve Barkin in *Kim Possible*, Pulaski in *Planes: Fire & Rescue*, Captain Dog in *Puppy Dog Pals*, and Grand Macaw in *Elena of Avalor*. For the Disney parks, he voiced the droid G2-4T in Star Tours – The Adventures Continue and plays the chief flight attendant in *Soarin'*.

Ward, Sela Actress; appeared in *Hello Again* (Kim Lacey), *The Guardian* (Helen Randall), and *Runaway Bride* (Pretty Bar Woman), and on TV in *Cameo by Night* (Jennifer) and *Once and Again* (Lily Manning).

Warden, Jack (1920–2006) Actor; appeared in *Passed Away* (Jack Scanlan), *Guilty as Sin* (Moe), and *While You Were Sleeping* (Saul), and on TV in *Gallegher*.

Wardrobe One of the enchanted objects in *Beauty and the Beast*; voiced by Jo Anne Worley.

Waring, Todd Actor; appeared on TV in *The Return of the Shaggy Dog* (Montgomery "Moochie" Daniels), *Splash, Too* (Allen Bauer), and *Chasing Life* (Bruce Hendrie), with guest appearances in *Ellen* (William), *The George Wendt Show* (Teddy), *Honey, I Shrunk the Kids* (Mr. McGann, 1998), *Monk* (maintenance worker), *Desperate Housewives* (Dr. Martin), *Grey's Anatomy* (Tobin), and *Scandal* (Peter Nystrom).

Warren, Lesley Ann Actress; appeared in *The Happiest Millionaire* (Cordelia Drexel Biddle), *The One and Only, Genuine, Original Family Band* (Alice Bower), and *Color of Night* (Sondra), and on TV in *Desperate Housewives* (Sophie Bremmer), *Marvel's Daredevil* (Esther Falb), and *The Age of Believing: The Disney Live Action Classics*.

Warrick, Ruth (1915–2005) Actress; played Johnny's mother, Sally, in *Song of the South*.

Warrior's Path, The (TV) Show; part 1 of *Daniel Boone*.

Wart Nickname for Arthur in *The Sword in the Stone*.

Washington, Denzel Actor; starred in *Crimson Tide* (Hunter), *The Preacher's Wife* (Dudley), *He Got Game* (Jake Shuttlesworth), *The Hurricane* (Rubin Carter), *Remember the Titans* (Herman Boone), and *Déjà Vu* (Doug Carlin).

Washington, Kerry Actress/producer; appeared in *Bad Company* (Julie), and on TV in *Scandal* and *How to Get Away with Murder* (Olivia Pope), *Little Fires Everywhere* (Mia Warren), *Disneyland 60: The Wonderful World of Disney*, and *The Disney Holiday Singalong*. She voiced Natalie Certain in *Cars 3*. For Hulu, she exec. produced

Reasonable Doubt and *UnPrisoned* (also starring as Paige Alexander).

Washington, Ned (1901–1976) Lyricist; worked at the Disney Studio 1938–1940, during which time he wrote songs for *Pinocchio*, *Dumbo*, and *Saludos Amigos*. "When You Wish Upon a Star" and the score from *Pinocchio* won him 2 Oscars. He was named a Disney Legend in 2001.

Washington Square (film) In 1850s New York City, shy and awkward Catherine Sloper, the daughter of a wealthy physician, and favored by neither beauty nor brilliance, is tottering into spinsterhood when she falls tempestuously in love with the dashing wastrel, Morris Townsend. She is encouraged by her incurably romantic aunt Lavinia. Catherine is heir to an imposing fortune, and her father is highly suspicious of the young man's intentions, feeling that he is only after her money. He does not see how a man of such youthful charm could possibly be in love with his daughter. Thus, Catherine is forced to make a fateful choice that will affect her happiness and the rest of her life. A Hollywood Pictures film in association with Caravan Pictures. Directed by Agnieszka Holland. Released in New York City on Oct. 5, 1997, and in an additional limited number of cities on Oct. 10. Stars Jennifer Jason Leigh (Catherine Sloper), Albert Finney (Dr. Austin Sloper), Ben Chaplin (Morris Townsend), Maggie Smith (Aunt Lavinia Penniman), Judith Ivey (Aunt Elizabeth Almond). 115 min. From Henry James's classic novella, which had previously been adapted for Broadway in 1947 and as William Wyler's 1949 film, *The Heiress*, with Olivia de Havilland winning an Oscar for her portrayal of Catherine Sloper. Since Washington Square in New York City no longer looks anything like it did in the 1850s, the filmmakers turned instead to classic Union Square in Baltimore for their location filming.

Watcher in the Woods, The (film) When an American composer and his family rent a foreboding house in England from an eccentric recluse, Mrs. Aylwood, a series of terrifying events occur, primarily to 17-year-old daughter Jan. It turns out that the eerie experiences are connected to Mrs. Aylwood's teenage daughter's disappearance 30 years earlier. A reenactment of the disappearance unexpectedly reveals the secret of the unknown force. Released Oct. 7, 1981. An earlier version premiered Apr. 16, 1980, in New York City but was withdrawn so a new ending could be filmed. Directed by John Hough. 84 min. Stars Bette Davis (Mrs. Aylwood), Carroll Baker (Helen), David McCallum (Paul), Lynn-Holly Johnson (Jan Curtis), Kyle Richards (Ellie), Ian Bannen (John Keller), Richard Pasco (Tom Colley), Frances Cuka (Mary Fleming), Benedict Taylor (Mike Fleming), Eleanor Summerfield (Mrs. Thayer), Georgina Hale (young Mrs. Aylwood). The film was based on the novel *A Watcher in the Woods* by Florence Engel Randall. St. Hubert's Manor, a huge estate situated near Ivor Heath, Buckinghamshire, was used as the site of the Curtises' vacation dwelling. Ettington Park Manor, a Gothic mansion, and an old stone chapel nearby were also used in the film. Scenes were also filmed at Pinewood Studios, London. Art Cruickshank and Bob Broughton supervised the supernatural effects, utilizing Disney's ACES (Automated Camera Effects System), which culminated in the finale. However, when early audiences in New York City saw its premiere and disliked that special effects–laden ending, the Studio cut it. *Mary Poppins* was rereleased to fill the gap, while a new ending was filmed, and the movie was released again in Oct. 1981. But it was too late, and the film was a box office disappointment despite the wonderfully eerie direction, music, and Bette Davis's performance.

Watches The original Mickey Mouse watch was manufactured by Ingersoll in 1933 and sold for $3.25, and later lowered to $2.95. They also made a pocket watch at the same time, selling it for $1.50. The original wristwatch had a round dial and featured 3 tiny Mickeys on a disk that indicated the seconds. These early watches have become some of the most sought-after types of Disneyana collectibles. The Mickey Mouse watch has been made continuously since 1933, though there was a period in the 1960s when only the words MICKEY MOUSE appeared on the dial. Ingersoll became U.S. Time, which became Timex. One of the more interesting watches was a backward Goofy watch. The numbers were placed in backward order, and Goofy's hands moved backward as well. It took some effort to learn how to tell time backward, but the watches became popular collectibles after their 1972 manufacture by Helbros. It originally cost $19.95 and within 2 decades was up to about $700 on the collector market. In a program focused on reproducing some of the classic Disney watches, The Disney Store selected the backward Goofy watch as the first in their series of reproductions. In 1972, Bradley, a division of Elgin National Industries, Inc., took over the manufacture of Disney watches, and in 1987 the contract went to Lorus. Today a number of different companies make Disney watches.

Watchful Eye, The (TV) Drama series on Free-form; premiered Jan. 30, 2023. Elena Santos, a savvy young woman with a complicated past, maneuvers her way into working as a live-in nanny for an affluent family in Manhattan. She quickly learns that everyone in the mysterious building has deadly secrets and ulterior motives. What they don't know is that Elena has some shocking secrets of her own. Stars Mariel Molino (Elena Santos), Warren Christie (Matthew), Kelly Bishop (Mrs. Ivey), Amy Acker (Tory), Jon Ecker (Scott), Lex Lumpkin (Elliott), Henry Joseph Samiri (Jasper), Aliyah Royale (Ginny). From Ryan Seacrest Productions and ABC Signature.

Water Babies (film) Silly Symphony cartoon released May 11, 1935. Directed by Wilfred Jackson. In this musical water fantasy based on Charles Kingsley's story, myriad tiny fairy folk find fun in riding rodeo style on frogs, flying with birds, and sailing in lily pad boats. *Merbabies*, released in 1938, was a sequel.

Water Birds (film) True-Life Adventure featurette released Jun. 26, 1952. Directed by Ben Sharpsteen. Vignettes depict the lives of waterbirds, showing how nature has forced each one of them to adapt and evolve in order to survive. Their different types of beaks and bodies, as well as their feeding habits and courtships, are thoroughly covered in this film. Film editor Norman "Stormy" Palmer used Liszt's Hungarian Rhapsody No. 2 to great effect in capturing the mood and adding entertainment value to the film. Academy Award winner. 31 min.

Water, Friend or Enemy (film) Educational film produced under the auspices of the Coordinator of Inter-American Affairs shows the benefits derived from water, cautions against polluting drinking water, and teaches how to avoid cholera, typhoid, and dysentery. Delivered May 1, 1943.

Waterboy, The (film) Lowly water boy Bobby Boucher is 31 years old, overly protected by his mother, and socially inept. But he loves his job with the university football team, even though he is constantly the target of gross jokes and public humiliation. When he is unceremoniously fired for his ineptitude, he gets a chance with a team that is as clumsy as he is. Surprisingly, Bobby is discovered to have a dazzling talent for tackling, and is quickly signed to a college athletic scholarship, though inadvertently he wreaks havoc in the classroom and on the gridiron. A Touchstone film. Directed by Frank Coraci. Released Nov. 6, 1998. Stars Adam Sandler (Bobby Boucher), Kathy Bates (Mama Boucher), Fairuza Balk (Vicki Vallencourt), Jerry Reed (Red Beaulieu), Henry Winkler (Coach Klein). 90 min. The 9-week shooting schedule for the film took place in and around Orlando.

Watson, Emma Actress; starred as Belle in *Beauty and the Beast* (2017).

Watson, Raymond L. (1926–2012) Became a member of the Disney Board of Directors in 1974. When Card Walker retired in 1983, Watson was asked to take over as chairman of the board, a post which he held until Michael Eisner arrived in Sep. 1984. He left the board in 2004. He was named a Disney Legend in 2011.

Wave, The Casual first-floor, table-service restaurant and lounge in Disney's Contemporary Resort at Walt Disney World; opened Jun. 7, 2008, taking the place of the Food and Fun Center. Rebranded The Wave . . . of American Flavors in early 2010. Diners entered through a brushed–steel arched tunnel, inspired by an ocean wave pipeline. Closed Jul. 15, 2021, to become Steakhouse 71.

Way Down Cellar (TV) Two-part show; aired Jan. 7 and 14, 1968. Directed by Robert Totten. Three friends find a secret tunnel under a destroyed church that leads them to a supposedly haunted house and, incidentally, a group of counterfeiters. Stars Butch Patrick, Sheldon Collins, Lundy Davis, Frank McHugh, Richard Bakalyan, David McLean, Ben Wright.

Wayans, Damon Actor; appeared in *Celtic Pride* (Lewis Scott), and on TV in *My Wife and Kids* (Michael Kyle), with a guest role in *Happy Endings* (Francis Williams).

Wayans, Damon, Jr. Actor; appeared on TV in *My Wife and Kids* (John) and *Happy Endings* (Brad Williams), and voiced Wasabi in *Big Hero 6*.

Wayans, Keenen Ivory Actor; appeared in *A Low Down Dirty Shame* (Shame), on TV in the syn. *Keenen Ivory Wayans Show*, and made a guest appearance in *My Wife and Kids* (Ken Kyle).

Wayne, David (1914–1995) Actor; appeared in *The Apple Dumpling Gang* (Col. T. R. Clydesdale), and on TV in *The Boy Who Stole the Elephant* (Col.

Rufus Ryder) and *Return of the Big Cat* (Grandpa Jubal).

Wayne, Patrick Actor; appeared in *The Bears and I* (Bob Leslie).

Wayne Brady Show, The (TV) Series on ABC; aired Aug. 8–Sep. 19, 2001, featuring comedy skits and musical numbers and starring Wayne Brady. Included are special guests and improv, with audience participation. Stars Brooke Dillman, Jonathan Mangum, J. P. Manoux, Missi Pyle. From Brad Grey Television, Don Mischer Productions, and Touchstone Television. A new show with the same title (but a 1-hour entertainment talk/variety show) premiered in syn. Sep. 2, 2002, in a limited rollout to about half the country; it launched nationally Sep. 1, 2003, and ended May 21, 2004.

Wayward Canary, The (film) Mickey Mouse cartoon released Nov. 12, 1932. Directed by Burt Gillett. Minnie is thrilled with Mickey's gift, a pet bird. But the mischievous bird escapes, takes a bath in ink, and is only saved from being a cat's lunch by Pluto's quick action.

We Belong Together Song from *Toy Story 3*; written/performed by Randy Newman. It won the Academy Award for Best Song.

We Don't Talk About Bruno Song from *Encanto*; written by Lin-Manuel Miranda. It held the No. 1 spot on the Billboard Hot 100 for 5 weeks—a record for any song from a Disney film.

Weasel Family, The (film) Educational film; released in May 1968. Tells of the habits and traits of the weasel, otter, mink, marten, skunk, and wolverine.

Weaver, Doodles (1911–1983) Actor; appeared in *A Tiger Walks* (Bob Evans).

Weaver, Sigourney Actress; appeared in *Holes* (The Warden), *The Village* (Alice Hunt), and *You Again* (Ramona), and on TV in *Marvel's The Defenders* (Alexandra Reid) and *Little Fires Everywhere* (Mia Warren). She voiced the ship's computer in *WALL•E*, the aquarium announcer in *Finding Dory*, and Lady Starblaster in *Penn Zero: Part-Time Hero*, and narrated *Secrets of the Whales* on Disney+.

WEB SLINGERS: A Spider-Man Adventure Interactive attraction in Avengers Campus at Disney California Adventure; opened Jun. 4, 2021. Riders fire webs to trap rogue Spider-Bots before they wreak havoc. Also in Walt Disney Studios Park at Disneyland Paris, as Spider-Man W.E.B. Adventure; opened Jul. 20, 2022, taking the place of Armageddon: Les Effets Speciaux.

WEB Suppliers Avengers Campus shop in Disney California Adventure; opened Jun. 4, 2021, with inventive items, such as interactive Spider-Bots.

Webbigail Vanderquack Companion of the nephews in *DuckTales*; voiced by Russi Taylor. Voiced by Kate Micucci in the new *DuckTales* (2017).

Weber, Karl Emanuel Martin ("Kem") (1889–1963) Industrial designer of the Disney Studio in Burbank. In the late 1930s, he collaborated with Walt Disney to design the Studio campus's distinctive buildings and furniture to suit the needs of the artists and production staff.

WED Enterprises Design and development organization founded by Walt Disney in Dec. 1952, to help him create Disneyland. With its independent financial resources, Walt could gamble his own money to research, design, and develop his own family recreation concept. Walt sold his interest in WED Enterprises in Feb. 1965. Originally headquartered at the Disney Studio in Burbank, WED moved to facilities in nearby Glendale in 1961. It later became known as Walt Disney Imagineering (1986). See also WALT DISNEY IMAGINEERING.

Wedding Pavilion, Disney's After starting to promote weddings at Walt Disney World with a Fairy Tale Weddings department in 1991, the park opened a special Wedding Pavilion on Jul. 15, 1995, featuring a view of Cinderella Castle and seating for up to 250 guests. The pavilion actually had its first wedding, and a preview, on *Weddings of a Lifetime* on the Lifetime cable network Jun. 18, 1995, when David Cobb and Susanne Mackie were married there. The pavilion is located on an island along Seven Seas Lagoon near Disney's Grand Floridian Resort & Spa, and adjacent to it is Franck's, a wedding salon where couples can make their wedding plans. Franck's is named after the wedding adviser played by Martin Short in *Father of the Bride*.

Wedding Season (TV) Romantic comedy/action thriller series; digitally released Sep. 8, 2022, on

Hulu in the U.S., Disney+ globally, and Star+ in Latin America. Katie and Stefan fall for each other at a wedding, despite Katie already having a fiancé. Two months later, at Katie's wedding, her new husband and his entire family are murdered. The police think Stefan did it, Stefan thinks Katie did it, and no one knows for sure what the truth is. Katie and Stefan go on the run across the U.K. and U.S., all while trying to prove their innocence. Stars Rosa Salazar (Katie McConnell), Gavin Drea (Stefan Bridges), Jamie Michie (DI James Donahue), Jade Harrison (DCI Danielle Metts). From Dancing Ledge Productions and JAX Media.

Wednesday Anything Can Happen Day on the 1950s and 1990s *Mickey Mouse Club* shows. Surprise Day on the 1970s new *Mickey Mouse Club*.

Wednesday 9:30 (8:30 Central) (TV) Half-hour series on ABC; aired Mar. 27–Jun. 12, 2002. IBS, a fledgling TV network, is trying its best to be number one. Behind its walls are some of the craziest, quirkiest, and somewhat damaged personalities that have ever paraded through the executive halls of Hollywood. Stars Ivan Sergei (David Weiss), Ed Begley, Jr. (Paul Weffler), Melinda McGraw (Lindsay Urich), Sherri Shepherd-Tarpley (Joanne Waters), James McCauley (Mike McClarren). From The Cloudland Company and Touchstone Television. Because the title was deemed too quirky, the show returned after a hiatus as *My Adventures in Television*. Working title was *The Web*.

WEDway PeopleMover Tomorrowland attraction in the Magic Kingdom at Walt Disney World; opened Jul. 1, 1975. It became the Tomorrowland Transit Authority in 1994, then Tomorrowland Transit Authority PeopleMover in 2010. In Disneyland, a similar attraction was known simply as the PeopleMover. A journey in the 5-car trains, powered by silent, environmentally friendly linear induction motors, provides a visit inside a number of the Tomorrowland attractions. The innovative transit system was envisioned as part of Walt Disney's concept for a city of tomorrow, EPCOT. The WEDway PeopleMover was later certified by the federal government for city use, and Disney's Community Transportation Services division used the technology to build a similar system at the Houston Intercontinental Airport (now known as the George Bush Intercontinental Airport), with cars that were larger and enclosed. SEE PEOPLE-MOVER, TOMORROWLAND TRANSIT AUTHORITY, AND HOUSTON.

Wee Links A 6-hole family golf course at Walt Disney World; opened Oct. 1980 near Disney's Magnolia Golf Course. Designed to have all the fun of an adult course, but with special features, like shallow water hazards, which made it easy for kids. The mascot was a golfing bird named Birdie. It expanded to 9 holes and became an executive golf course May 1, 1989, reopening the following year as Disney's Oak Trail Golf Course.

Weekend Family (TV) Family comedy series on Disney+; digitally premiered Mar. 9, 2022. The first French original series for Disney+. Every weekend, Fred takes care of his girls, Clara (15), Victoire (12), and Romy (9). Each has a different mother with whom she lives during the week. A new stepmother joins in this happy mix when Fred falls madly in love with Emma, a Canadian doctoral student in child psychology. Stars Eric Judor (Fred), Daphnée Côté-Hallé (Emmanuelle), Liona Bordonaro (Clara), Midie Dreyfus (Victoire), Jeanne Bournaud (Marie-Ange), Anabel Lopez (Helena), Annelise Hesme (Laurence), Séphora Pondi (Cora), Hafid Benamar (Stan). From Elephant International.

Weekenders, The (TV) Animated series on *One Saturday Morning*; debuted Feb. 26, 2000. Four friends, Tino, Carver, Lor, and Tish, spend each weekend discovering and creating new levels of fun, while negotiating the obligatory obstacles of adolescence. Voices include Jason Marsden (Tino Tonitini), Phil LaMarr (Carver Descartes), Kath Soucie (Tish Katsufrakis), Grey Delisle (Lor MacQuarrie), Lisa Kaplan (Tino's Mom). 39 episodes.

Weems Family name in the Baby Weems segment of *The Reluctant Dragon*.

Weinger, Scott Actor; voiced Aladdin in the 1992 animated film and other appearances of the character, and appeared on TV in *The Shaggy Dog* (Wilby, 1994), *Scrubs* (Dr. Kershnar), and *Mistresses* (father). Also for TV, he served as co-exec. producer of *The Muppets* and as a supervising producer for *The Neighbors*, *black-ish*, and *Galavant*.

Weinkeller Shop in Germany at EPCOT; opened Oct. 1, 1982, selling wines, accessories, and cheeses. Originally presented by H. Schmitt Söhne GmbH.

Weinrib, Lennie (1935–2006) Actor; voiced King Leonidas and the Secretary Bird in *Bedknobs and Broomsticks*.

Weis, Bob Imagineer; he was named president of Walt Disney Imagineering (WDI) in Jan. 2016, after leading the creative and design aspects of Shanghai Disney Resort. Starting at WED Enterprises in 1980, he had major creative roles with Disney-MGM Studios and Tokyo DisneySea. After leaving the company in 1994 to found his own design business, he returned to WDI as exec. vice president in 2007 to oversee the transformation of Disney California Adventure. In Mar. 2021, he became president, Creative and New Experience Development for WDI, and in Dec. was named Global Imagineering Ambassador. He retired from WDI in 2023.

Weiss, Al President of Walt Disney World beginning in 1996. He had joined Walt Disney World in 1972 in the accounting department and held various positions over the years in the finance and resort management areas, being elevated to executive vice president in 1994. He was named president of worldwide operations for Walt Disney Parks and Resorts in 2005 and retired in 2011.

Welcome: Portraits of America (film) Presented by Walt Disney Parks and Resorts in partnership with the U.S. Department of Homeland Security and the State Department. This multimedia show was created to welcome international visitors to the U.S. at major airports. It includes a 7-min. film and hundreds of still images, featuring American people from all regions and walks of life. It premiered Oct. 2007. Features the score from *IllumiNations: Reflections of Earth* at EPCOT.

Welcome to Earth (TV) A Disney+ limited series from National Geographic; digitally released Dec. 8, 2021. Host Will Smith is guided by elite explorers on an awe-inspiring journey around the world to explore Earth's greatest wonders — from volcanoes that roar in silence to deserts that move beyond our perception. Produced by Protozoa Pictures, Westbrook Studios, and Nutopia. 6 episodes.

Welcome to Pooh Corner (TV) Show on The Disney Channel; debuted Apr. 18, 1983, featuring life-size puppets of the favorite Pooh characters performing in storybook settings and discovering the values of friendship, honesty, and cooperation. The puppets are what is known as "advanced puppetronics:" live performers in costumes and masks whose facial expressions are controlled by sophisticated electronic circuitry.

Welcome to the "World" (TV) Show aired Mar. 23, 1975. Directed by Marty Pasetta. Entertainers perform at Walt Disney World for the opening of Space Mountain. The attraction is dedicated by former astronauts L. Gordon Cooper, Scott Carpenter, and Jim Irwin, and featured is a band composed of 2,000 instrumentalists along with daytime fireworks. Stars Lucie Arnaz, Lyle Waggoner, Tommy Tune, Scotty Plummer.

Welker, Frank Actor; appeared in *The Computer Wore Tennis Shoes* (Henry) and *Now You See Him, Now You Don't* (Myles). He is one of the world's most prolific voice actors, heard in dozens of Disney projects, often uncredited, including *My Science Project* (alien), *Oliver & Company* (Louie), *The Rescuers Down Under* (Joanna), *Beauty and the Beast* (footstool), *The Gun in Betty Lou's Handbag* (Scarlet's vocals), *Aladdin* (Abu/Cave of Wonders/Rajah), *Homeward Bound: The Incredible Journey*, *Super Mario Bros.*, *A Goofy Movie* (Bigfoot), the Toy Story films (Bullseye), *The Hunchback of Notre Dame* (Djali), *Doug's 1st Movie* (Herman Melville), *Mulan* (Khan), *Return to Never Land*, *Alice in Wonderland* (2010), *Frankenweenie* (Sparky, 2012), and *Aladdin* (Cave of Wonders, 2019). On TV, he provided voices in such shows as *DuckTales*, *Gargoyles*, *Bonkers*, *Goof Troop*, *Buzz Lightyear of Star Command*, *Recess*, *House of Mouse*, *Kim Possible*, *Mickey Mouse Clubhouse*, *Mickey Mouse Mixed-Up Adventures*, and *The Rocketeer*. Also voiced Oswald the Lucky Rabbit in *Epic Mickey* and *Epic Mickey 2: The Power of Two*.

We'll Take Manhattan (TV) Pilot for a series on NBC; aired Jun. 16, 1990. Seeking to make it big-time in New York City, 2 very different women — a street-smart singer and a gullible country girl who wants to become an actress — become roommates. Directed by Andy Cadiff. Stars Jackée Harry, Karin Bohrer, Edan Gross, Joel Brooks. 30 min.

Wells, Frank G. (1932–1994) Formerly at Warner Bros., he served as president of The Walt Disney Company from Sep. 22, 1984, until his death in a helicopter accident on Apr. 3, 1994. He is noted for his attempt to climb the highest peaks on each continent, failing only to conquer Mt. Everest. An extremely adept businessman who aided Michael Eisner in bringing Disney back to its former glory, he focused on all aspects of the company and was a key supporter of Disneyland Paris. He was named a Disney Legend posthumously in 1994. Frank Wells was also honored by having a new office building at the Disney Studio in Burbank named for him. The Frank G. Wells Building opened in 1997, with original tenants, including the Disney University, Walt Disney Archives, and Television Animation.

Wen, Ming-Na Actress; appeared in *The Joy Luck Club* (June) and provided the speaking voice of Mulan in the 1998 film and other appearances of the animated character. She later shortened her name to Ming-Na. Also appeared on TV in *Inconceivable* (Rachel Lew) and *Marvel's Agents of S.H.I.E.L.D.* (Melinda May), and provided several voices, including Dr. Hirano in *Phineas and Ferb*, Savannah in *Milo Murphy's Law*, and Vega in *Sofia the First*. On Disney+, she appeared in *The Mandalorian* and *The Book of Boba Fett* (Fennec Shand) and made a cameo in the live-action *Mulan* (Esteemed Guest). She was named a Disney Legend in 2019.

Wendt, George Actor; appeared in *Man of the House* (Chet) and *Santa Buddies* (Santa Claus), and on TV in *The George Wendt Show*, *The Pooch and the Pauper* (Sparks), *Mickey's 60th Birthday*, and *Disneyland's 35th Anniversary Celebration*, with a guest role in *Kickin' It* (Uncle Blake). He voiced Grandpa Frank in *Fancy Nancy* and played the Stomach in Cranium Command at EPCOT.

Wendy Character visited by Peter Pan and brought to Never Land to tell stories to the Lost Boys; voiced by Kathryn Beaumont.

Wendy Wu: Homecoming Warrior (TV) A Disney Channel Original Movie; first aired Jun. 16, 2006. Wendy Wu, a popular Chinese American teen is asked to choose between thwarting evil as a reincarnated warrior and running for high school Homecoming Queen. Saving the world cannot compete with her lifelong dream of holding court with her "perfect" boyfriend at her side, but her 1,000-year-old destiny proves difficult to resist. Directed by John Laing. Stars Brenda Song (Wendy Wu), Shin Koyamada (Shen), Tsai Chin (Grandma). Produced by Rubicon Films Ltd.

Wentworth, Martha (1889–1974) Actress; voiced Jenny Wren in *Who Killed Cock Robin?*, Nanny in *One Hundred and One Dalmatians*, and Madam Mim in *The Sword in the Stone*, among other Disney voices.

We're All in This Together Song from *High School Musical*; written by Matthew Gerrard and Robbie Nevil.

Werewolf by Night (TV) Horror/action-adventure special on Disney+; digitally released Oct. 7, 2022. On a dark and somber night, a secret cabal of monster hunters emerge from the shadows and gather at the foreboding Bloodstone Temple following the death of their leader. In a strange and macabre memorial to the leader's life, the attendees are thrust into a mysterious and deadly competition for a powerful relic—a hunt that will ultimately bring them face-to-face with a dangerous monster. Directed by Michael Giacchino. Stars Gael Garcia Bernal (Jack Russell), Laura Donnelly (Elsa Bloodstone), Harriet Sansom Harris (Verussa), Kirk R. Thatcher (Jovan), Eugenie Bondurant (Azarel). 53 min. From Marvel Studios.

Wesson, Dick (1919–1979) He served as the program announcer for the weekly Disney TV show from 1954 until his death. His easily recognized voice would introduce the show and Walt Disney at the beginning and give details on the next week's show at the conclusion.

WESTCOT Center Planned as a West Coast version of EPCOT Center, WESTCOT was envisioned as a dramatic showcase of international lands and themed pavilions exploring the natural environment, human body, and new horizons, with the golden Spacestation Earth as the centerpiece. The park was to be organized into the "seven wonders"—including the Wonders of Living, Wonders of Earth, and Wonders of Space pavilions, surrounded by four World Showcase pavilions inspired by the corners of the world (Asia, Europe, The Americas, and Africa), with themed hotel accommodations inside the park. The project was initially announced in Mar. 1991 as part of an expansion of the Disneyland Resort, but the company decided instead to build Disney California Adventure on the proposed site.

Western Publishing Co., Inc. One of the earliest Disney licensees, producing Disney books (primarily under the Whitman and Golden Press imprints) beginning in 1933. Western sponsored the Story Book Shop at Disneyland and was one of the original investors in the park.

Western River Expedition Frontierland attraction planned for the Magic Kingdom at Walt Disney

World, but never built. As the centerpiece of a proposed complex called Thunder Mesa, this musical Audio-Animatronics boat ride through the Old West was designed by Imagineer Marc Davis as an alternative to Pirates of the Caribbean, as it was felt that Florida already offered tourist attractions based on its own pirate history. But when park visitors continued to ask for the Pirates attraction, which was very popular at Disneyland, Pirates of the Caribbean was ultimately built in Adventureland, and the Thunder Mesa concept was shelved. One element from the complex, a runaway mine train ride, would evolve into Big Thunder Mountain Railroad.

Western River Railroad Steam train attraction in Tokyo Disneyland, accessed in Adventureland; opened Apr. 15, 1983. Unlike the railroads at Disneyland and Walt Disney World, it does not encircle the whole park, but instead provides a round-trip tour through Adventureland, Critter Country, and Westernland, including the Primeval World diorama. The locomotives are named after American western rivers: the *Colorado*, *Missouri*, and *Rio Grande*, with the *Mississippi* added Dec. 1991. Presented by Tomy Company, Ltd.

Western Wear Westernland boutique and folk-crafts in Tokyo Disneyland; opened Apr. 15, 1983.

Westernland Frontierland area in Tokyo Disneyland. Designers felt the concept of the frontier had little meaning in Japan, so the name of the land was changed. Attractions include Country Bear Theater, *Mark Twain* Riverboat, Tom Sawyer Island Rafts, and Big Thunder Mountain, with dining at The Diamond Horseshoe, Cowboy Cookhouse, Hungry Bear Restaurant, Pecos Bill Café, and Plaza Pavilion Restaurant. A new area, Camp Woodchuck, opened within Westernland in 2016.

Westernland Shootin' Gallery Located in Westernland at Tokyo Disneyland; opened Apr. 15, 1983. Guests test their skills and might even earn a sheriff badge. SEE ALSO FRONTIERLAND SHOOTIN' ARCADE (DISNEYLAND AND WALT DISNEY WORLD) AND RUSTLER ROUNDUP SHOOTIN' GALLERY (DISNEYLAND PARIS).

Westward Ho the Wagons! (film) A wagon train composed of a number of emigrant families is making the crossing from the Missouri River to the rich farming country of the Pacific Northwest in 1844. Despite raids and misunderstandings with the Paw-

nee tribe, Captain Stephen's leadership of the train with the help of a veteran scout, and especially Dr. John Grayson's medical skills, see them through on their westward trek. Released Dec. 20, 1956. Directed by William Beaudine. Filmed in CinemaScope on location at the Conejo Ranch in Thousand Oaks, California. 86 min. Includes the popular song "Wringle Wrangle," by Stan Jones. Stars Fess Parker (John Grayson), Kathleen Crowley (Laura Thompson), George Reeves (James Stephen), and features several cast members of the *Mickey Mouse Club*, including Tommy Cole (Jim Stephen), Karen Pendleton (Myra Thompson), David Stollery (Dan Thompson), Cubby O'Brien (Jerry Stephen), and Doreen Tracey (Bobo Stephen). The film was promoted on TV by the show *Along the Oregon Trail*.

Westward Ho Trading Co. Frontierland shop in Disneyland; opened Sep. 2, 1987. It was formerly the Frontier Trading Post. A small shop, Westward Ho, operated for a few years in in the Magic Kingdom at Walt Disney World, later serving as queue space for Country Bear Jamboree.

Wet Paint (film) Donald Duck cartoon released Aug. 9, 1946. Directed by Jack King. A bird, Susie, ruins Donald's new paint job on his car, damages his upholstery, and unravels his hat while gathering nest material. He corners her with an ax when he sees Susie's babies and gives up.

Wetback Hound, The (film) Featurette released Jun. 19, 1957. Directed by Larry Lansburgh. Paco is a young hound owned by mountain lion hunters in Sonora, Mexico. When he is mistreated, he runs away, and even swims across a river to enter the U.S. in his search for a kindly master. He finds one and, in saving a little doe from a lion, ensures himself a home. 18 min. An expanded version was shown on TV Apr. 24, 1959. Academy Award winner for Best Live Action Short Subject. Also won numerous other awards, including ones from the Southern California Motion Picture Council and the Berlin International Film Festival.

Whale of a Tale, A Song from *20,000 Leagues Under the Sea*; sung by Kirk Douglas and written by Al Hoffman and Norman Gimbel.

Whale Who Wanted to Sing at the Met, The (film) Segment of *Make Mine Music*, an "Opera Pathetique," sung by Nelson Eddy, about an opera-singing whale. Also known as *Willie the Operatic Whale*.

Whalers, The (film) Mickey Mouse cartoon released Aug. 19, 1938. The first cartoon directed by Dick Huemer. Mickey, Donald, and Goofy are on a tramp steamer when a whale is sighted. Later, Mickey must come to the rescue when Goofy is swallowed by the whale and the boat is destroyed.

Whale's Tooth, The (TV) A South Sea islander boy receives his first outrigger canoe and tries to save a sacred talisman that is stolen by enemy warriors. Prepared for the Disney TV series in America but did not air. First aired in Canada on Oct. 22, 1983. It was later shown on The Disney Channel. Directed by Roy Edward Disney.

What About Bob? (film) Saddled with a multitude of phobias, quirky Bob Wiley enlists the help of sane and sensible psychiatrist Dr. Leo Marvin. But Leo soon discovers that he does not want to be the new "best friend" of his obsessive/compulsive patient. Skipping town for a restful summer holiday with his family, Leo is dismayed when the panicked Bob tracks down the family's private vacation hideaway and insinuates himself into their lives. The family comes to adore the guest who won't leave. Well, all except Leo, who is driven frantic, to the point where one wonders who is really the crazy one. Released May 17, 1991. Directed by Frank Oz. A Touchstone film. 99 min. Stars Bill Murray (Bob Wiley), Richard Dreyfuss (Dr. Leo Marvin), Julie Hagerty (Fay Marvin), Charlie Korsmo (Siggy Marvin). Filmed in New York City, and at Smith Mountain Lake, Virginia, which doubled for the New Hampshire resort depicted in the story.

What About Brian (TV) One-hour drama series on ABC; aired Apr. 16, 2006–Mar. 26, 2007. At 34, Brian is the last single guy in his group of friends, a serial monogamist who still holds out hope that one day he will open the door and be blinded by love. But questions arise in his head: Why does love have to be so complicated? What is his problem with commitment? And the most pressing question of all: Could all his problems stem from the fact that he is harboring a crush on his best friend's girl? Stars Barry Watson (Brian), Matthew Davis (Adam), Sarah Lancaster (Marjorie), Rick Gomez (Dave), Amanda Detmer (Deena), Raoul Bova (Angelo), Rosanna Arquette (Nic). From Touchstone Television and Bad Robot.

What Can You See by Looking? (film) Educational film with Figment about critical thinking and observation skills through rhymes, anagrams, puzzles, and other brainteasers, in the EPCOT Educational Media Collection: Language Arts Through Imagination series; released in Sep. 1988. 15 min.

What I Want to Be (TV) Serial on the *Mickey Mouse Club*, beginning on Oct. 3, 1955, and running for 10 episodes. It was filmed at the TWA headquarters in Kansas City and depicted the special training procedures for becoming an airline pilot and flight attendant.

What If . . . ? (TV) A Disney+ original animated series; digitally premiered Aug. 11, 2021. Famous events from the Marvel Cinematic Universe are reimagined in unexpected ways. Each episode focuses on a different hero. Voices include stars from the Marvel films who reprise their roles. From Marvel Studios. Winner of the 2022 Emmy for Outstanding Character Voice-Over Performance (Chadwick Boseman).

What Is a Desert? (film) Segment from *The Living Desert*; released on 16 mm for schools in Nov. 1974. Explains the geographic features that cause a desert and shows how weather affects it.

What Is Disease? (film) Educational film produced under the auspices of the Coordinator of Inter-American Affairs explaining that disease is caused by microbes, and shows how to take the necessary precautions to keeping one's body free from them. Delivered Aug. 13, 1945.

What Is Disneyland? SEE DISNEYLAND STORY, THE.

What Is Fitness Exercise? (film) Educational film in the Fitness and Me series; released in Mar. 1984. A good sorceress teaches a scrawny knight the value of physical fitness.

What Is Physical Fitness? (film) Educational film in the Fitness for Living series; released in Sep. 1982. The film demonstrates cardiorespiratory endurance, muscle strength, muscle endurance, flexibility, and body composition, the 5 elements of physical fitness.

What Should I Do? (film) Series of 5 educational films released in 1969–1970: *The Fight*, *The Game*, *The New Girl*, *Lunch Money*, *The Project*. The series was revised and updated in 1992. SEE FOLLOWING ENTRIES.

What Should I Do? The Baseball Card (film)

Educational release in Aug. 1992. 8 min. When a boy steals a friend's valuable baseball card, he gets caught in a lie; the action freezes as he considers various decisions and consequences to his actions.

What Should I Do? The Fight (film) Educational release in Aug. 1992. 8 min. Kids get into a fistfight after a water balloon is thrown. This film is different from the previous film entitled *The Fight* in the What Should I Do? series.

What Should I Do? The Game (film) Educational release in Aug. 1992. 8 min. An overweight girl considers the strategies to become accepted by her peers. This film is different from the previous film entitled *The Game* in the What Should I Do? series.

What Should I Do? The Lunch Group (film) Educational release in Aug. 1992. 8 min. Students make fun of a girl from El Salvador because she is different.

What Should I Do? The Mural (film) Educational release in Aug. 1992. 8 min. Three friends painting a school mural shun a boy because they consider him a geek.

What Should I Do? The Play (film) Educational release in Aug. 1992. 9 min. A girl who uses a wheelchair is told she cannot help build a set for the school play because of her physical challenge.

What to Do at Home (film) Educational film in the Mickey's Safety Club series; released in Sep. 1989. 16 min. The film gives home-safety information and tips to children home alone.

What Will You Celebrate? Campaign theme for the Disney parks in 2009, promoting free admission on the guest's birthday. The first person in the country to receive free admission, on Jan. 1, 2009, was Andrew DaCosta from Seattle, who visited the Magic Kingdom at Walt Disney World. The campaign also featured new park entertainment, added celebration experiences, and set up new ways for guests to customize their own celebration vacation. It was followed by a new campaign, Let the Memories Begin, in 2011.

What's an Abra Without a Cadabra? (film) Educational film; Figment presents a magical lesson about antonyms, homonyms, synonyms, and rhymes in the Language Arts Through Imagination series; released in Sep. 1989. 15 min.

What's Love Got to Do with It (film) The story of singer Tina Turner's tumultuous life. She meets Ike Turner in a local nightclub. Ike is attracted to her and impressed with her powerful voice. With his help, the couple shoot straight to the top of the music world. Tina marries Ike and seems to have it all, but Ike becomes a brooding, brutal husband who threatens to destroy both their careers. With great courage, and the help of religious meditation, she leaves Ike and their career behind, and starts over again by herself. As Tina's personal successes mount, Ike realizes that she can indeed do it alone, and reach even greater heights of success and fulfillment. Initial release on Jun. 9, 1993; general release on Jun. 11, 1993. Directed by Brian Gibson. A Touchstone film. 118 min. Stars Angela Bassett (Tina Turner), Laurence Fishburne (Ike Turner). Based on Tina Turner's autobiography, *I, Tina*. Rather than construct a film set, the producers used Ike and Tina Turner's actual California home. Tina Turner recorded the songs for the film herself.

What's Next? Café Fast, casual restaurant at Disney's Wide World of Sports (now ESPN Wide World of Sports) at Walt Disney World; opened Nov. 21, 2007. Took the place of the All Star Cafe. In 2010, it became the ESPN Wide World of Sports Grill.

What's Next? (commercial) SEE I'M GOING TO DISNEY WORLD.

What's This? Song from *Tim Burton's The Nightmare Before Christmas*; written/performed by Danny Elfman.

What's Wrong with This Picture? (film) Educational release in 16 mm in Aug. 1991. 19 min. A teen has behavioral problems because of low self-esteem resulting from a difficult homelife. He improves his self-image through group counseling.

Wheezy Forgotten penguin squeeze toy in *Toy Story 2*; voiced by Joe Ranft.

Whelchel, Lisa Mouseketeer on the new *Mickey Mouse Club*. She later appeared on TV in *Shadow of Fear* (Robin) and starred on the non-Disney series *The Facts of Life*. She appeared in *The Facts of Life Reunion* (Blair) on *The Wonderful World of Disney*.

When a Man Loves a Woman (film) Alice and Michael Green have a marriage filled with genuine passion, caring, and sharing as they are raising 2 young daughters. However, beneath the surface of their loving family relationship simmers a painful personal secret Alice has been keeping, not only from her loved ones, but also from herself. She has an alcohol-use disorder, and when the family realizes this, they must embark on a courageous struggle to pick up the pieces of their lives and deal head-on with Alice's problem. Limited release in Los Angeles and New York City Apr. 29, 1994; general release May 13, 1994. Directed by Luis Mandoki. A Touchstone film. 126 min. Stars Andy Garcia (Michael Green), Meg Ryan (Alice Green), Lauren Tom (Amy), Ellen Burstyn (Emily). Filmed in Los Angeles and San Francisco. The hotel utilized for filming the vacation sequence was La Casa Que Canta Hotel in Zihuatanejo, Mexico.

When in Rome (film) An ambitious young New York City art museum curator, Beth, disillusioned with romance, takes a whirlwind trip to Rome for her sister's wedding. There she defiantly plucks some coins from a fountain of love, which inexplicably and magically ignites passion for her in those who had thrown them in. They are an odd group of suitors who show up in New York City where they aggressively stalk her: a sausage magnate, a street magician, an adoring painter, and a self-admiring model. But, when a charming reporter pursues her with equal zest, how will she know if his love is the real thing? A Touchstone film. Directed by Mark Steven Johnson. Released Jan. 29, 2010. Stars Kristen Bell (Beth), Anjelica Huston (Celeste), Danny DeVito (Al), Dax Shepard (Gale), Josh Duhamel (Nick), Jon Heder (Lance), Will Arnett (Antonio), Alexis Dziena (Joan), Kate Micucci (Stacy), Bobby Moynihan (Puck), Luca Calvani (Umberto), Keir O'Donnell (Father Dino). 91 min. Don Johnson has an uncredited cameo as Beth's father. Filmed in CinemaScope. Filmed around New York City, including at the Guggenheim Museum, and in Rome, where the fictional Venus statue, sculpted by Gianni Gianese, and its Fontana d'Amore were specially constructed in the Piazza Borghese.

When Knighthood Was in Flower (TV) Two-part show; aired Jan. 4 and 11, 1956. The airing of *The Sword and the Rose*.

When She Loved Me Song from *Toy Story 2*; written by Randy Newman. Nominated for an Academy Award.

When the Cat's Away (film) Mickey Mouse cartoon; released in 1929. Directed by Walt Disney. Mickey with Minnie and his band of mice raise havoc in a cat's house, including doing a tap dance on a piano keyboard. The cartoon marked Mickey's first appearance wearing gloves for an entire short.

When We Rise (TV) An 8-part miniseries on ABC; aired Feb. 27–Mar. 3, 2017. Chronicles the real-life personal and political struggles, setbacks, and triumphs of a diverse family of LGBT men and women who helped pioneer one of the last legs of the U.S. Civil Rights Movement, from its turbulent infancy in the 20th century to the once-unfathomable successes of today. Stars Guy Pearce (Cleve Jones), Mary-Louise Parker (Roma Guy), Rachel Griffiths (Diane), Michael K. Williams (Ken Jones), Ivory Aquino (Cecilia Chung). Portraying the 4 leads as their younger selves are Austin McKenzie (Cleve), Emily Skeggs (Roma), Jonathan Majors (Ken), Fiona Dourif (Diane). From ABC Studios.

When You Wish: The Story of Walt Disney Stage musical about the life of Walt Disney; not produced by The Walt Disney Company. It premiered at the Freud Playhouse at UCLA on Oct. 11, 2013. Written by Dean McClure.

When You Wish Upon a Star Song from *Pinocchio*; written by Ned Washington and Leigh Harline. Performed by Cliff Edwards as Jiminy Cricket. It won the Academy Award for Best Song and has become an anthem for The Walt Disney Company. For years it opened the *Disneyland* TV series, is played as guests enter the castle at Disneyland and the Magic Kingdom at Walt Disney World, and is even the melody of the ship horn on the vessels of the Disney Cruise Line fleet.

Where Do the Stories Come From? (TV) Show aired Apr. 4, 1956. Directed by Jack Hannah. Walt Disney explains how the hobbies of his staff provide ideas for cartoons. *Crazy Over Daisy* was born from a song written by composer Oliver Wallace. The True-Life Adventure films led to *R'Coon Dawg*, and wartime experiences of the staff led to a number of cartoons featuring Donald Duck. The scale-model train hobbies of animators Ward Kimball and Ollie Johnston, and of Walt Disney himself, led to *Out of Scale*. Footage is shown of Disney's backyard train, the Carolwood Pacific Railroad.

Where Does Time Fly? (film) Educational film

teaching past, present, and future vocabulary words in a time-travel adventure with Figment, in the Language Arts Through Imagination series; released in Sep. 1989. 17 min.

Where Dreams Come True Marketing and business initiative to unify Disney's global efforts for its worldwide theme parks and resorts under a singular Disney Parks name; announced Jun. 7, 2006.

Where I Live (TV) Series on ABC; aired Mar. 5–Nov. 20, 1993. With the support of his family and friends, offbeat teenager Doug St. Martin learns the fundamental lessons about life as he enters adulthood in his Harlem neighborhood. Stars Doug E. Doug (Douglas St. Martin), Flex (Reggie Coltrane), Shaun Baker (Malcolm), Yunoka Doyle (Sharon St. Martin), Jason Bose Smith (Kwanzie), Sullivan Walker (James St. Martin). From Michael Jacobs Productions, Sweet Lorraine Productions, and Touchstone Television.

Where the Heart Is (film) Demolition contractor Stewart McBain's 3 spoiled children have grown up in the lap of luxury and are none too anxious to leave their extravagant lifestyle. But McBain is determined to teach them a lesson in self-sufficiency, so he turns them out of the family home. Forced to live in a dilapidated Brooklyn tenement, the siblings struggle to survive. When McBain's business goes under, he must move in with his children, and together they learn lessons on where their real family values lie. Released Feb. 23, 1990. Directed by John Boorman. A Touchstone film. 107 min. Stars Dabney Coleman (Stewart McBain), Uma Thurman (Daphne), Joanna Cassidy (Jean), Crispin Glover (Lionel), Suzy Amis (Chloe), Christopher Plummer (the !#&@). Filmed primarily on location in Toronto. The film had only a limited theatrical release.

Where the Heck Is Hector? (TV) Show; part 1 of *The Ballad of Hector the Stowaway Dog*.

Where the Red Fern Grows (film) Video release on Dec. 21, 2004, by Walt Disney Home Entertainment of a film made by Crusader Entertainment, Elixir Films, and Bob Yari Productions. Based on the best-selling novel by Wilson Rawls, the story follows a young boy named Billy Coleman whose hard work and determination help him realize his dream of buying a pair of redbone coonhounds. Billy and his hounds become an inseparable trio, as he trains them to become the best hunting dogs in the state. Directed by Lyman Dayton and Sam Pillsbury. Stars Dave Matthews (Will Coleman), Dabney Coleman (Grandpa), Joseph Ashton (Billy Coleman), Ned Beatty (Sheriff), Renee Faia (Jenny Coleman), Kris Kristofferson (older Billy Coleman). Originally shown at the Tribeca Film Festival May 3, 2003.

Where's My Water See Swampy.

While You Were Sleeping (film) Lucy Moderatz is a subway token-booth worker at the Chicago Transit Authority who falls in love with a stranger from afar. When he (Peter Callaghan) is mugged on Christmas Day, Lucy saves his life and then finds herself mistaken as Peter's fiancée when he is hospitalized in a coma. Welcomed into the close-knit Callaghan family through the holidays, she brings new life to the family's household. But Lucy has misgivings about taking advantage of the misunderstanding and begins to question her infatuation as she learns more about the man in a coma and finds herself falling in love with Peter's brother, Jack. Released Apr. 21, 1995. A Hollywood Pictures film, in association with Caravan Pictures. Directed by Jon Turteltaub. 103 min. Stars Sandra Bullock (Lucy), Peter Gallagher (Peter Callaghan), Glynis Johns (Elsie), Micole Mercurio (Midge), Monica Keena (Mary), Jack Warden (Saul Tuttle), Bill Pullman (Jack).

Whipping Boy, The (TV) A Disney Channel Premiere Film; first aired Jul. 31, 1994. In the mid-18th century, a bratty prince seizes an urchin from the town to be his new whipping boy, but when the prince runs away from home with the whipping boy, they go through many adventures and learn to accept each other as friends. Stars Truan Munro (Jemmy), Nic Knight (Prince Horace), George C. Scott (Blind George), Kevin Conway (Hold Your Nose Billy), Vincent Schiavelli (Cutwater), Karen Salt (Annyrose), Mathilda May (Gypsy). Adaptation of the Newbery Award–winning novel by Sid Fleischman. Directed by Syd MacArtney.

Whisker Haven Tales with the Palace Pets (TV) Animated short-form series; digitally released on the Watch Disney Junior app beginning May 2015, followed by airings on Disney Junior. Deep in a secret realm between the Disney Princess kingdoms is Whisker Haven, the royal animal kingdom of the princesses' Palace Pets. As they fulfill their royal duties, the pets discover the beauty of kindness and the royal heart of friendship. Whisker Haven is also home to horses, birds, ferrets, and other animals, known as Critterzens. Voices include Natalie Coughlin (Petite), Sanai Victoria (Treasure), Bailey Gambertoglio (Pumpkin), Henry Kaufman (Sultan), Myla Beau (Dreamy). From Ghostbot Studios and Disney Publishing. An extension of the Disney Princess franchise, the Palace Pets were first introduced in the *Disney Princess Palace Pets* app in Jun. 2013 and became popular merchandise items.

Whispering Canyon Cafe Western restaurant serving food family style at Disney's Wilderness Lodge at Walt Disney World; opened May 28, 1994. Skillets of food are placed on the table, and diners are welcome to all they can eat. Cast Members have a reputation for sassing their guests.

Whispers, The (TV) Series on ABC; aired Jun. 1– Aug. 31, 2015. In Washington, D.C., several kids have been talking about their imaginary friend, Drill. What their parents don't know is that this friend is not as imaginary as they think. When the mysterious games Drill convinces the kids to play turn dangerous, FBI child specialist Claire Bennigan is called in to investigate. Stars Lily Rabe (Claire Bennigan), Barry Sloane (Wes Lawrence), Milo Ventimiglia (John Doe), Derek Webster (Jessup Rollins), Kristen Connolly (Lena Lawrence), Kylie Rogers (Minx Lawrence), Kyle Harrison Breitkopf (Henry Bennigan). From ABC Studios and Amblin TV.

Whispers: An Elephant's Tale (film) A baby elephant, Whispers, separated from his mother, searches desperately for her, but he finds instead the sassy and fiercely independent Groove, an outcast from her own herd and the last elephant in the world ever to be a substitute mom. The 2 join to make an unlikely family as they brave the hidden dangers of the dark forest and make their way toward The Great River, a rumored paradise for elephants. Very limited release, opening in Denver Mar. 10, 2000, and in New York City on Oct. 13, 2000. Directed by Dereck Joubert. Voices include Angela Bassett (Groove), Debi Derryberry (Whispers), Anne Archer (Gentle Heart), Joanna Lumley (Half Tusk), Kat Cressida (Princess). 72 min. The film takes its plot entirely from real elephant behavior, with 80% being footage of elephants in the wild and 20% being footage of trained elephants. The filmmakers made an effort not to fake anything the elephants did, with the exception of giving them human voices. Filmed entirely in and around Chobe National Park in Botswana by Emmy Award– winning naturalist and cinematographer Dereck

Joubert and his wife, Beverly, who had lived and worked together in the wild for over 20 years.

Whistle-Stop Song from *Robin Hood*; written/ performed by Roger Miller.

Whistle Stop Shop Train station–themed toy and keepsake shop on Mickey Avenue in Shanghai Disneyland; opened Jun. 16, 2016. For the first time, guests can have their Mickey Mouse ear hats embroidered in English or Chinese.

Whistle While You Work Song from *Snow White and the Seven Dwarfs*; written by Larry Morey and Frank Churchill.

Whitaker, Billy Actor; provided the voice of Skippy in *Robin Hood*.

Whitaker, Forest Actor; appeared in *The Color of Money* (Amos), *Good Morning, Vietnam* (Edward Garlick), *Stakeout* (Jack Pismo), *Mr. Holland's Opus* (adult Bobby Tidd, uncredited), *Consenting Adults* (David Duttonville), *Phenomenon* (Nate Pope), *Rogue One: A Star Wars Story* (Saw Gerrera), and *Black Panther* (Zuri). On TV, he played Sam Cooper in *Criminal Minds: Suspect Behavior* and Bumpy Johnson in *Godfather of Harlem*.

Whitaker, Johnny Actor; appeared in *The Biscuit Eater* (Lonnie McNeil), *Napoleon and Samantha* (Napoleon), and *Snowball Express* (Richard Baxter); and on TV in *The Mystery in Dracula's Castle* (Alfie).

White, Betty (1922–2021) Actress; appeared as Rose in *The Golden Girls* (for which she won the Emmy Award as Outstanding Lead Actress in a Comedy Series in 1986), reprising her role in *Empty Nest* and *The Golden Palace*. Also appeared on TV in *Maybe This Time* (Shirley Wallace), *Ugly Betty* (as herself), *My Wife and Kids* (June Hopkins), *Young & Hungry* (Ms. Wilson), and *Walt Disney World's 15th Birthday Celebration*. Film appearances included *Holy Man* (as herself), *Bringing Down the House* (Mrs. Kline), *The Proposal* (Grandma Annie), and *You Again* (Grandma Bunny). She provided several voices, including Round in *Whispers: An Elephant's Tale*, Granny in *Teacher's Pet*, Yoshie in *Ponyo*, Grandma in *Higglytown Heroes*, Mrs. Claus in *Prep & Landing: Operation Secret Santa*, and Bitey White in *Toy Story 4*. She was named a Disney Legend in 2009.

White, Jesse (1918–1997) Actor; appeared in *The Cat from Outer Space* (Earnest Ernie).

White, Richard Broadway actor; voiced Gaston in *Beauty and the Beast* and other appearances of the character. On TV, he made a cameo in *Beauty and the Beast: A 30th Celebration* (Baker).

White Fang (film) A young adventurer, Jack Conroy, in the harsh wilderness of Alaska, along with Klondike prospector Alex Larson, come upon a wolf dog, White Fang, who has been raised by a Native American. White Fang, through deception, becomes the property of the devious Beauty Smith who mistreats him. Jack rescues the animal and patiently begins to rebuild his spirit and trust. Jack learns the ways of the wilderness as he and White Fang risk their lives for each other. Released Jan. 18, 1991. Directed by Randal Kleiser. 109 min. Stars Klaus Maria Brandauer (Alex Larson), Ethan Hawke (Jack Conroy), Seymour Cassel (Skunker), James Remar (Beauty Smith), Susan Hogan (Belinda). Based on the novel by Jack London. Filmed on location in Alaska. A sequel, *White Fang 2: Myth of the White Wolf*, was released in 1994.

White Fang (film) Educational production; released on laser disc in Mar. 1995. A companion to the laser disc of the Disney film, containing an interview with the screenwriter and segments on wolves, Jack London, and the Native people of the Yukon.

White Fang 2: Myth of the White Wolf (film) Young prospector Henry Casey, along with his magnificent half-wolf/half-dog named White Fang, is set to make his fortune during the Alaskan gold rush. After being separated from White Fang during a canoe accident, Henry is found and nursed back to health by a Native American girl named Lily and her uncle Moses. Moses tries to convince Henry that he carries the spirit of the White Wolf and should stay with the starving tribe because he may have the power to bring back the caribou. When White Fang reappears, the Native Americans feel sure that Henry and the wolf dog have been sent to save them. Released Apr. 15, 1994. Directed by Ken Olin. 106 min. Stars Scott Bairstow (Henry Casey), Charmaine Craig (Lily Joseph), Alfred Molina (Rev. Leland Drury), Geoffrey Lewis (Heath). Filmed entirely on location in Aspen, Colorado, and in these British Columbia, Canada, cities: Vancouver, Squamish, Whistler, and Hope. The replica of the Haida village was built on the banks of the Squamish River. Sequel to *White Fang*.

White Man's Medicine (TV) Episode 5 of *Andy Burnett*. Also used as the title of part 2 of the airing of *Westward Ho the Wagons!*

White Rabbit Flighty character chased by Alice in *Alice in Wonderland*; voiced by Bill Thompson.

White Squall (film) A recounting of a 1961 adventure-filled ordeal of a sea captain and a group of teenage boys who set off on a brigantine sailing school called *The Albatross* for an 8-month Caribbean voyage. When a freak storm sinks their ship, the survivors are forced to confront their tragic situation and discover their own inner strengths. A Hollywood Pictures film. Directed by Ridley Scott. Released Feb. 2, 1996. Stars Jeff Bridges (Sheldon), Caroline Goodall (Dr. Alice Sheldon), John Savage (McCrea), Scott Wolf (Chuck Gieg), Balthazar Getty (Tod Johnstone). 128 min. Filmed in CinemaScope. Filming took place in the Caribbean and on the islands of St. Vincent, St. Lucia, and Grenada. Additional filming was done in a water tank on Malta; near Cape Town, South Africa; and in the U.S. The boat used as *The Albatross* was the *Eye of the Wind*, a 110-foot topsail schooner built in Germany.

White Water Snacks Counter-service restaurant in Disney's Grand Californian Hotel & Spa; opened Feb. 8, 2001. It was renamed GCH Craftsman Grill Jul. 11, 2019.

White Wilderness (film) True-Life Adventure feature released Aug. 12, 1958. Directed by James Algar. Academy Award winner. 72 min. A dozen photographers, including Hugh A. Wilmar, Herb and Lois Crisler, and James R. Simon, created this film after spending nearly 3 years in the Arctic, diligently filming animals in their natural habitat. The narrator's foreword describes the nature and origin of some of the largest and most savage beasts on the North American continent. The dramatic setting for the wildlife spectacle is Canada's subarctic and Alaska's arctic wilds. Successive scenes depict the various animals and birds in battle, play, and migration. Included among the larger of the predatory beasts are polar bears, gray wolves, and wolverines; among the migratory animals followed are the musk ox, caribou, and reindeer. Those in the icy seas, like the walrus, ring seal, and white beluga whales, are covered as well. The film was reissued in 1972.

Whitman, Mae Actress; voiced the title character in the Tinker Bell films, Shanti in *The Jungle Book 2*, Amity Blight in *The Owl House*, Leslie Dunkling in *Teacher's Pet*, Robin in *Fillmore*, and Rose in *American Dragon: Jake Long*. She made guest appearances on TV in *Phil of the Future*, *Desperate Housewives*, *Grey's Anatomy*, and *Criminal Minds*.

Whitman, Stuart (1928–2020) Actor; appeared in *Run, Cougar, Run* (Hugh McRae) and on TV in *The High Flying Spy* (Professor Lowe).

Whitman Publishing Co. See Western Publishing Co., Inc.

Whitmore, James (1921–2009) Actor; appeared on TV in *Sky High* (Gus Johnson) and *The Tenderfoot* (Captain Ewell), and on Disney Channel in *A Ring of Endless Light* (Rev. Eaton).

Whiz Kid and the Carnival Caper, The (TV) Two-part show; aired Jan. 11 and 18, 1976. Directed by Tom Leetch. A young inventor, Alvin, and his friends run into bank robbers using a carnival as a front. Alvin volunteers his skills in rebuilding an aging sideshow robot. The kids learn of the plot to rob the bank but cannot get anyone to listen to them, so they try to get more evidence, which puts them in more danger. Stars Jack Kruschen, John Colicos, Jaclyn Smith, Eric Shea, Clay O'Brien, Kim Richards, Dick Bakalyan, Ronnie Schell, Ted Gehring, John Lupton. A sequel to *The Whiz Kid and the Mystery at Riverton*.

Whiz Kid and the Mystery at Riverton, The (TV) Two-part show; aired Jan. 6 and 13, 1974. Directed by Tom Leetch. A young inventor, Alvin Fernald, learns while gathering information for an essay on city government that the city treasurer is a crook. But only in winning the essay contest and becoming mayor for the day does Alvin get access to city files to help prove his case against the treasurer. Stars Edward Andrews, John Fiedler, Eric Shea, Clay O'Brien, Kim Richards, Lonny Chapman, Ted Gehring, Larry J. Blake. Based on books by Clifford B. Hicks.

Who Do You Believe? (TV) Unscripted series on ABC; premiered May 3, 2022. The audience steps into the shoes of 2 contrasting true-crime narratives to hear the recounts directly from the victims and criminals. Then the viewer plays armchair detective to deduce and piece together different versions of the truth. From Lime Pictures in association with Walt Disney Television's alternative production unit.

Who Framed Roger Rabbit (film) Roger Rabbit is a toon, an animated star at Maroon Cartoon Studio. After an opening cartoon, *Somethin' Cookin'*, we discover that Roger is suspected of the murder of Marvin Acme, who owned Toontown and the company that makes all cartoon props, and who had been flirting with Roger's wife, Jessica. Down-on-his-luck private detective Eddie Valiant is asked by Roger to find the real culprit. He reluctantly agrees and soon discovers that there is more to the mysterious Judge Doom than meets the eye. Chased by Doom's weasel henchmen, Eddie visits Toontown, with its many well-known toon inhabitants, before discovering the identity of the murderer. Premiered at Radio City Music Hall in New York City on Jun. 21, 1988; general release on Jun. 22, 1988. Directed by Robert Zemeckis. A Touchstone film in association with Steven Spielberg. 103 min. Stars Bob Hoskins (Eddie Valiant), Christopher Lloyd (Judge Doom), Joanna Cassidy (Dolores), Stubby Kaye (Marvin Acme), with voices including Charles Fleischer (Roger Rabbit/Benny the Cab), Kathleen Turner (Jessica Rabbit, uncredited), Lou Hirsch (Baby Herman). Based on the novel *Who Censored Roger Rabbit?* by Gary K. Wolf. Original work on the film began many years before it was produced. The expected high costs for the necessary special effects made Disney executives move cautiously, and it was only when Spielberg and Zemeckis became interested in the project that the green light was given. They were excited by the prospect of creating a Toon community with a variety of cartoon characters, culled from different studios and presented together on-screen for the first time. It was Spielberg who was able to help along the complicated negotiations necessary to bring the classic animated personalities together. Zemeckis welcomed the chance to create a new cartoon character, Roger Rabbit. He joked that the character was a combination of "a Disney body, a Warner's head, and a Tex Avery attitude." It was filmed in Los Angeles and at Elstree Studios in London. Richard Williams headed the large staff of animators at a new studio set up in London, with some additional animation done in Burbank. The special visual effects were created by Industrial Light & Magic. The film won 4 Academy Awards, the most for a Disney film since *Mary Poppins*. They were for Film Editing

(Arthur Schmidt), Sound Effects Editing (Charles L. Campbell, Louis L. Edemann), Visual Effects (Ken Ralston, Richard Williams, Edward Jones, George Gibbs), and an award for Special Achievement in Animation Direction to Richard Williams.

Who Killed Cock Robin? (film) Silly Symphony cartoon released Jun. 29, 1935. Directed by Dave Hand. Cock Robin is shot while singing to Jenny Wren (a clever caricature of Mae West), and the court is convened to try the suspects. But it is found that it was only Cupid's arrow that pierced Robin, and he is revived by Jenny's kiss.

Who Owns the Sun? (film) Educational film about the son of an enslaved man learning about prejudice, freedom, and self-respect; released Aug. 14, 1990. 18 min.

Who the Heck Is Hector? (TV) Show; part 2 of *The Ballad of Hector the Stowaway Dog.*

Who Wants to Be a Millionaire (TV) Game show on ABC, hosted by Regis Philbin, in which contestants answer multiple-choice questions on the way to a possible $1 million payoff. Aired nightly for 2 weeks Aug. 16–29, 1999, and returned Nov. 7–21; it then continued airing several nights a week. The show ended as a regular prime-time series on Jun. 27, 2002. Based on a hit British series, it became a nationwide phenomenon, pushing ABC to the top of the ratings in 1999–2000. A syn. show, featuring Meredith Vieira as host, premiered Sep. 16, 2002. Cedric the Entertainer, Terry Crews, and Chris Harrison succeeded Meredith Vieira as host before the show ended May 31, 2019. It returned to prime time in 2020, beginning with an Apr. 8 special hosted by Jimmy Kimmel; celebrity contestants now played for charity, and, for the first time, contestants were allowed to invite a guest in the hot seat to help answer questions. A park attraction based on the series, entitled Who Wants to Be a Millionaire—Play It!, operated in Disney-MGM Studios Apr. 7, 2001–Aug. 19, 2006, and in Disney's California Adventure Sep. 14, 2001–Aug. 20, 2004.

Who, What, Why, Where, When and How Day Monday on the new *Mickey Mouse Club* (1977–1978).

Whole New World, A Song from *Aladdin*; written by Alan Menken and Tim Rice. Academy Award

winner. In 1993, it became the first song from a Disney animated film to top the Billboard Hot 100.

Whoop-'n'-Holler Hollow Man-made ridge from which swimmers could ride the flumes in River Country at Walt Disney World; opened Jun. 20, 1976. River Country closed Sep. 1, 2001.

Whoopee Party, The (film) Mickey Mouse cartoon released Sep. 17, 1932. Directed by Wilfred Jackson. After a buffet supper, Mickey and the gang engage in a red-hot treatment of "Running Wild." The rhythm is so catchy that the furniture, household items, and even cops sent to quiet the noise get caught up in the revelry.

Who's Afraid of the Big Bad Wolf? Popular song hit from the 1933 cartoon *Three Little Pigs*, probably the most famous song to come out of an animated short. It was written by Disney composer Frank Churchill. Walt Disney re-created the writing of the song for *Cavalcade of Songs* on his TV series 2 decades later.

Why Be Physically Fit? (film) Educational film from the Fun to Be Fit series; released in Mar. 1983. Shows students how being fit can help them have more energy, look better, and cope with stress.

Why Exercise? (film) Educational film in the Fitness and Me series; released in Mar. 1984. The adventures of 2 knights show students that exercise strengthens the heart, muscles, and other body systems, giving one more energy for work and play.

Why We Fight (film) Frank Capra-made series during World War II, containing animated graphs, arrows, and other effects that were supplied by Disney.

Wicked City (TV) Series on ABC; aired Oct. 27–Nov. 10, 2015. Centered on the rock 'n' roll revelry of Los Angeles's Sunset Strip in 1982, where alliances are formed between detectives, reporters, drug dealers, and club-goers to solve a serial murder case. Stars Ed Westwick (Kent), Erika Christensen (Betty), Taissa Farmiga (Karen), Gabriel Luna (Paco), Karolina Wydra (Dianne), Anne Winters (Vicki). From ABC Studios. The 5 remaining episodes were digitally released on Hulu in Dec. 2015.

Wickes, Mary (1916–1995) Actress; appeared in *Napoleon and Samantha* (clerk), *Snowball Express*

(Miss Wigginton), *Sister Act* and *Sister Act 2: Back in the Habit* (Sister Mary Lazarus), and on TV in the *Annette* serial on the *Mickey Mouse Club*. She provided the voice of Laverne in *The Hunchback of Notre Dame*.

Wide Open Spaces (film) Donald Duck cartoon released Sep. 12, 1947. Directed by Jack King. Donald tries to get accommodations at a motel and is told he can sleep on the porch for $16. When he complains, he is kicked out. He tries an air mattress, which flies through the air and onto the porch, where he again confronts the manager and ends up in a cactus bed.

Wide World of Sports, Disney's SEE ESPN WIDE WORLD OF SPORTS.

Wideload Games Disney announced in Sep. 2009 that it had acquired this Chicago-based producer/developer of original interactive entertainment, with founder Alexander Seropian selected to oversee creative development for Disney Interactive. Wideload was originally founded in 2003 and closed in 2014.

Widow Tweed Kindly farm woman who adopts Tod, the fox, in *The Fox and the Hound*; voiced by Jeanette Nolan.

Widowmaker Pecos Bill's horse in the *Melody Time* segment.

Wiest, Dianne Actress; appeared in *The Associate* (Sally), *The Horse Whisperer* (Diane Booker), *Dan in Real Life* (Nana), and *The Odd Life of Timothy Green* (Bernice Crudstaff).

Wilbur Ebullient albatross, Orville's brother, in *The Rescuers Down Under*; voiced by John Candy.

Wilbur Robinson Time-traveling teenager in *Meet the Robinsons*; voiced by Wesley Singerman.

Wilck, Thelma "Tommie" (1922–2012) Personal secretary to Walt Disney 1958–1966. She remained at Disney until 1968, playing a major role in the development of the California Institute of the Arts.

Wilcox, Larry Actor; appeared on TV in *Fire on Kelly Mountain* (Phil Wilcox), *Twister, the Bull from the Sky*, and *Trail of Danger* (Beech Carter).

Wild, The (film) Animated comedy from C.O.R.E.

Feature Animation & Complete Pandemonium. A group of animals leave their comfy life at the New York City Zoo to head out on a rescue mission to Africa. Led by the lion, Samson; Bridget, a nearsighted, intellectual giraffe; her boyfriend Benny, a cheeky streetwise squirrel; and Larry, a boa constrictor, the group manages to make it through the urban jungle, but when they reach Africa, it is a whole new world. Directed by Steve "Spaz" Williams. Released Apr. 14, 2006, after an Apr. 12 release in Belgium and France. Voices include Kiefer Sutherland (Samson), Jim Belushi (Benny), Eddie Izzard (Nigel), Janeane Garofalo (Bridget), William Shatner (Kazar), Richard Kind (Larry), Greg Cipes (Ryan), Patrick Warburton (Blag). 85 min.

Wild About Safety, Disney's Safety education initiative by Walt Disney Parks and Resorts, in cooperation with Underwriters Laboratories; unveiled in May 2003. Timon and Pumbaa from *The Lion King* are mascots, educating children on how to prevent accidents. Activity books, safety tip cards, park signage, and DVDs—including the Wild About Safety: Timon and Pumbaa, Safety Smart series—are part of the campaign. At the Test the Limits Lab, which opened in 2003 in Innoventions at Epcot, 5 hands-on activities allowed guests to "test" products for safety just as Underwriters Laboratories engineers do.

Wild About Safety: Timon and Pumbaa, Safety Smart at Home (film) Animated educational film released Jan. 27, 2008. Directed by Dave Bossert. When moving to a new house, Timon and Pumbaa, armed with a Safety Smart Checklist, find some serious safety problems which they discuss how to fix. Voices include Bruce Lanoil (Timon), Ernie Sabella (Pumbaa). From Disney Educational Productions. 11 min. Other Wild About Safety: Timon and Pumbaa films are *Safety Smart Healthy & Fit!*, *Safety Smart on the Go!*, *Safety Smart Goes Green!*, *Safety Smart About Fire!*, *Safety Smart Honest & Real!*, *Safety Smart Online!*, and *Safety Smart in the Water!*

Wild Africa Trek Immersive private expedition in Africa at Disney's Animal Kingdom; premiered Jan. 2011. Guests venture off the beaten path in small groups through this personalized, expert-led, add-on excursion. Included are a bushwalk through unexplored areas of the forest and a trip through an animal-filled savanna in safari vehicles. Extended time is spent observing and learning about wildlife.

Wild Burro of the West (TV) Show aired Jan. 29, 1960. Directed by Walter Perkins. A stolen burro in Mexico escapes from her captors and tries to find her way home across the desert, having adventures with an old prospector and a herd of wild burros. Stars Bill Keys, Bill Pace, Jim Burch. Narrated by Winston Hibler.

Wild Cat Family, The—The Cougar (film) Educational film, made up from stock footage from various Disney nature films; released in May 1968. Shows the family life and hunting habits of the cougar and tells how it fits into the world family of cats.

Wild Country, The (film) The Tanner family comes from the East to a broken-down homestead in Wyoming, and, in trying to make a go of it, face hardship and opposition from man and nature as they struggle for their water rights and survive cyclone and fire. In the process, they persevere and mature. And, after "bringing the law to Jackson's Hole," they face a happier future. Released Jan. 20, 1971. Directed by Robert Totten. 100 min. Stars Steve Forrest (Jim), Jack Elam (Thompson), Ron Howard (Virgil), Frank de Kova (Two Dog), Morgan Woodward (Ab), Vera Miles (Kate), Clint Howard (Andrew), Dub Taylor (Phil). This film marked the first time in a theatrical film that 3 members of the Howard family acted together— father, Rance, and sons, Ron and Clint. Based on the book *Little Britches* by Ralph Moody, the movie was filmed almost in its entirety in Jackson Hole, Wyoming, the original locale of the story. The diverse scenery provided all the needed locations for the 7-week exterior shooting schedule. Only one day of inclement weather sent the Disney company to a covered set erected in a barn. The spectacular twister that plagues the pioneer family was manufactured by 7 wind machines from the Disney Studio in Burbank, assisted by 3 snowplanes from Jackson Hole. Together they stirred up dark clouds of dust that could be seen for 30 miles.

Wild Dog Family, The—The Coyote (film) Educational film, made up of stock footage from other Disney nature films; released in Apr. 1968. This is the story of the intelligent wild dog of the West and how it has survived and adjusted to encroaching civilization.

Wild Geese Calling (TV) Show aired Sep. 14, 1969. A boy, Dan Tolliver, discovers an injured Canadian gander shot by a hunter and nurses it back to health. He then sadly bids it goodbye as it flies south with the other geese for the winter. Stars Carl Draper, Persis Overton. Narrated by Steve Forrest.

Wild Heart (TV) Show aired Mar. 10, 1968. Directed by Jack Couffer. Two Canadian children have adventures with an injured sea lion, a red-tailed hawk, and a seagull when they visit their aunt and uncle on Puget Sound. Stars Andrew Penn, Kitty Porteous, Stanley Bowles. Narrated by Leslie Nielsen. Released as an educational film with the title *Nature's Wild Heart*.

Wild Hearts Can't Be Broken (film) During the Depression, Sonora Webster, growing up in rural Georgia, longs for more excitement. With the stubborn confidence of a young woman determined to prove she can do anything she sets her mind to, Sonora answers a newspaper ad for a diving girl, one who leaps, astride a horse, from a 40-foot tower platform into a tank of water. Despite setbacks, including sudden blindness, Sonora's spirit and determination make her a legendary attraction at Atlantic City's Steel Pier. Released May 24, 1991. Directed by Steve Miner. 89 min. Stars Gabrielle Anwar (Sonora Webster), Cliff Robertson (Dr. W. F. Carver), Michael Schoeffling (Al Carver). Based on the life story of Sonora Webster Carver, whose autobiography, *A Girl and Five Brave Horses*, was published in 1961. Filmed at location sites in South Carolina. The Atlantic City set was built in Myrtle Beach.

Wild Hogs (film) Four friends wear suits and work in offices during the week but transform into leather-bound Harley riders on the weekend, hoping to unleash some of that free spirit that dwells within and get out into the great outdoors to ride. Then, one day, they decide to rev up their ho-hum suburban lives with one last-hurrah, cross-country motorcycle trip. But they find themselves in an unwitting rivalry with the real-life biker gang known as the Del Fuegos, for whom biking is not a hobby but a way of life. The foursome's members soon find themselves out of their league with unexpected travails and secrets within their own ranks. From Touchstone Pictures. Directed by Walt Becker. Released Mar. 2, 2007. Stars John Travolta (Woody Stevens), Tim Allen (Doug Madsen), Martin Lawrence (Bobby Davis), William H. Macy (Dudley Frank), Ray Liotta (Jack), Marisa Tomei (Maggie), Kevin Durand (Red), M. C. Gainey (Murdock), Jill Hennessy (Kelly Madsen). Peter

Fonda has a cameo role as Damien Blade. 100 min. Filmed on location in New Mexico.

Wild Horse Revenge (TV) Episode 7A of *Texas John Slaughter*.

Wild Jack (TV) Miniseries aired Jan. 15, Jul. 9, and Jul. 16, 1989. An Alaskan wilderness guide becomes the unwilling trustee of a publishing empire. Stars John Schneider (Jack McCall), Carol Huston (Constance Fielding). Directed by Harry Harris and James Quinn.

Wild Waves (film) Mickey Mouse cartoon released Apr. 25, 1930. The first cartoon directed by Burt Gillett. Mickey and Minnie's fun day at the beach is spoiled when Minnie is swept out to sea and Mickey must save her.

Wilderness Explorers Interactive game in Disney's Animal Kingdom; debuted Jun. 2013 and inspired by the Disney • Pixar film *Up*. Guests become a Wilderness Explorer by completing challenges throughout the park and can earn approximately 30 badges.

Wilderness Lodge, Disney's Resort hotel in the Magic Kingdom Resort Area at Walt Disney World; opened May 28, 1994. The lodge is fashioned after the fine rustic National Park lodges in the West such as the Old Faithful Inn in Yellowstone. Guests can dine at Artist Point, Whispering Canyon Cafe, Roaring Fork, and Territory Lounge, with shopping at Wilderness Lodge Mercantile. Outside, the Fire Rock Geyser erupts high in the air on a regular hourly schedule. The majestic, 6-story timbered lobby rivals that of Disney's Grand Floridian Resort & Spa for its grandeur; its ceiling is supported by 60-ft.-tall pine timbers, and an 82-ft.-tall stone fireplace is based on the rock strata of the Grand Canyon, representing 1.6 billion years of geological history. In 2000, Disney Vacation Club accommodations were added, originally as The Villas at Disney's Wilderness Lodge (and renamed Boulder Ridge Villas in 2016). The Copper Creek Villas & Cabins were added along Bay Lake in 2017, along with the Reunion Station lounge and a new open-air eatery, Geyser Point Bar & Grill.

Wilderness Lodge Mercantile Shop in Disney's Wilderness Lodge at Walt Disney World; opened May 28, 1994. It is themed as a trading post, offering sundries, edibles, apparel, and souvenirs.

Wilderness Road, The (TV) Episode 3 of *Daniel Boone*.

Wildhorse Saloon A 27,000-sq.-ft. entertainment venue in Pleasure Island at Walt Disney World; opened May 31, 1998, replacing The Fireworks Factory. It closed Feb. 25, 2001, to become Magic Masters. Rising country artists performed live music, and dancers taught new steps to patrons.

Wilds, The (TV) Young adult drama series on Amazon Prime Video; seasons digitally released Dec. 11, 2020, and May 6, 2022. A group of teen girls from different backgrounds must fight for survival after a plane crash strands them on a deserted island. The castaways both clash and bond as they learn more about each other, the secrets they keep, and the traumas they've all endured. There's just one twist: these girls did not end up on this island by accident. Stars Rachel Griffiths (Gretchen Klein), Sophia Ali (Fatin Jadmani), Shannon Berry (Dot Campbell), Jenna Clause (Martha Blackburn), Reign Edwards (Rachel Reid), Mia Healey (Shelby Goodkind), Helena Howard (Nora Reid), Erana James (Toni Shalifoe), Sarah Pidgeon (Leah Rilke), David Sullivan (Daniel Faber), Troy Winbush (Dean Young). From Amazon Studios and ABC Signature.

Wildside (TV) Limited hour-long adventure series on ABC; aired Mar. 21–Apr. 25, 1985. A group of 5 men calling themselves the Wildside Chamber of Commerce work to rid the town of the criminal element in order to make it a better place to live. Stars Howard Rollins, William Smith, J. Eddie Peck, John DiAquino, Terry Funk, Sandy McPeak, Meg Ryan, Jason Hervey. From Touchstone Television. 6 episodes.

Wildwing Mascot for the Mighty Ducks (later Anaheim Ducks) hockey team. Also the team captain in the *Mighty Ducks* animated TV series; voiced by Ian Ziering.

Wilhite, Tom He joined Disney in 1977 as director of TV publicity and later of motion pictures as well, and then director of creative affairs. In 1980, he was named vice president of creative development for motion pictures and TV, and in 1982 he became vice president of production. He left the Studio in 1983.

Willard, Fred (1933–2020) Actor; appeared in *WALL•E* (Shelby Forthright), and on TV in *The Pooch and the Pauper* (President), *Lots of Luck*

(A. J. Foley), and *Maybe It's Me* (Jerry Stage), with guest appearances in *The Golden Girls*, *Nurses*, *Wizards of Waverly Place*, *Castle*, *Good Luck Charlie*, and *Kevin from Work*. He provided several voices, including Melvin – Alien Dad in *Chicken Little*, Secretary of the Interior in *Planes: Fire & Rescue*, Pa in *Buzz Lightyear of Star Command*, Baruti in *Disney's The Legend of Tarzan*, Mr. Paulsen in *Teamo Supremo*, Jack Hench in *Kim Possible*, Grandpa Murphy in *Milo Murphy's Law*, and Mr. Doozy in *Mickey and the Roadster Racers*.

William Rogers & Son Company also known as International Silver; produced a number of pieces of Disney silverware, cups, and bowls 1931–1939. A Mickey Mouse spoon, designated Branford Silver Plate on the verso of the handle, is one of the most common items of Disney merchandise from the 1930s. It was sold as a premium by Post Toasties; you sent in 25¢ and a box top and you got a spoon.

Williams, Bill (1915–1992) Actor; appeared in *Scandalous John* (Sheriff Hart), and on TV in *Texas John Slaughter* (Paul Forbes), *Chester, Yesterday's Horse* (Ben Kincaid), *Gallegher Goes West* (Joe Carlson), and *The Flight of the Grey Wolf* (Sheriff).

Williams, Cindy (1947–2023) Actress; appeared on TV in *The Leftovers* (Heather Drew) and *Help Wanted: Kids* (Lisa Burke), and on The Disney Channel in *Save the Dog* (Becky Dale) and *Just Like Family* (Lisa Burke), with guest appearances in *Less Than Perfect* and *8 Simple Rules*.

Williams, Don "Ducky" He began at Walt Disney World in 1980 as a Fantasyland artist in the Magic Kingdom and later transferred to the resort's art department. He contributed designs for the parks and served as a longtime senior character artist for the Yellow Shoes creative services division, drawing characters for books, brochures, magazines, TV, lithographs, and other uses. He retired in 2018.

Williams, Guy (1924–1989) Actor; starred on TV as Zorro and in *The Prince and the Pauper* (Miles Hendon). He later appeared in the non-Disney series *Lost in Space* on TV and retired to Buenos Aires. He was named a Disney Legend in 2011.

Williams, Kimberly Actress; appeared in *Indian Summer* (Gwen Daugherty), *Father of the Bride* and *Father of the Bride Part II* (Annie Banks), and *The War at Home* (Karen Collier); and on TV in *According to Jim* (Dana) and *Nashville* (Peggy Kenter).

Williams, R. J. Child actor; on TV, he voiced Cavin in *Disney's Adventures of the Gummi Bears* and Kit Cloudkicker in *TaleSpin*, and he made a guest appearance in *Empty Nest* (Timmy).

Williams, Rhoda (1930–2006) Actress; provided the voice of the stepsister Drizella in *Cinderella*.

Williams, Robin (1951–2014) Actor; appeared in *Good Morning, Vietnam* (Adrian Cronauer), *Dead Poets Society* (John Keating), *Jack* (Jack Powell), *Flubber* (Phillip Brainard), *Bicentennial Man* (Andrew Martin), and *Old Dogs* (Dan), and voiced the Genie in *Aladdin* and the direct-to-video *Aladdin and the King of Thieves*. On TV, he made guest appearances in *The Dream Is Alive* and *Life with Bonnie* (Kevin Powalski). At Walt Disney World, he appeared in *Back to Neverland* [sic] in The Magic of Disney Animation tour at Disney-MGM Studios and voiced The Timekeeper in the Magic Kingdom. He was named a Disney Legend in 2009.

Williams, Roy (1907–1976) Adult Mouseketeer on the 1950s *Mickey Mouse Club*, known as the Big Mooseketeer because of his size. He joined the Disney Studio as an artist in 1930 and later served as a story man for shorts, comic strips, TV shows, and features, including *Saludos Amigos*, *The Three Caballeros*, and *Make Mine Music*. He was a popular character artist at Disneyland, designed the famous *Mickey Mouse Club* ears worn by the cast, served as a Disney Studio publicity representative, and consulted on the *Disney on Parade* stage show. He was named a Disney Legend posthumously in 1992.

Williams, Samuel L. (1933–1994) Lawyer; named to the Disney Board of Directors in 1983. He served until his death on Jul. 28, 1994.

Williams, Vanessa Actress/singer; appeared in *Hannah Montana the Movie* (Vita), and on TV in *Ugly Betty* (Wilhelmina Slater), *Desperate Housewives* (Renee Perry), and the *Walt Disney World Christmas Day Parade*. She has provided several voices, including Debra in *The Proud Family*, Dr. Eileen Underwood in *Milo Murphy's Law*, Delilah in *Doc McStuffins*, and Captain Beakman in *T.O.T.S.* She performed "Colors of the Wind" for the end credits of *Pocahontas*, later guest-starring in the TV special *Disney's Pocahontas: The Musical Tradition Continues.*

Willie and the Yank (TV) Three-part show aired Jan. 8, 15, and 22, 1967. Directed by Michael O'Herlihy. The 3 episodes are *The Deserter*, *The Mosby Raiders*, and *The Matchmaker*. A lonely Confederate guard, Willie Prentiss, befriends his Union counterpart, Henry Jenkins, across the river, and their friendship lasts through many incidents. Henry helps Willie escape after he accidentally wounds his commanding officer, Lieutenant Mosby, but he is arrested as a spy. When he escapes, he joins Mosby's band in trying to capture a Union general. Jenkins is captured, and falls for Willie's cousin, Oralee. Stars James MacArthur, Nick Adams, Kurt Russell, Jack Ging, Peggy Lipton, Jeanne Cooper. Released theatrically abroad as *Mosby's Marauders.*

Willie the Giant Character in the *Mickey and the Beanstalk* segment of *Fun and Fancy Free*; voiced by Billy Gilbert. Also appeared in *Mickey's Christmas Carol*; voiced by Will Ryan.

Willie the Operatic Whale (film) Rerelease title (on Aug. 17, 1954) of *The Whale Who Wanted to Sing at the Met*. Released on 16 mm for schools in 1959.

Willis, Bruce Actor; appeared in *Billy Bathgate* (Bo Weinberg), *Color of Night* (Capa), *Armageddon* (Harry Stamper), *Breakfast of Champions* (Dwayne Hoover), *The Sixth Sense* (Malcolm Crowe), *Disney's The Kid* (Russ), *Unbreakable* and *Glass* (David Dunn), and *Surrogates* (Greer).

Willow (TV) Live-action fantasy adventure series based on the 1988 feature from Lucasfilm; digitally premiered Nov. 30, 2022, on Disney+. In a magical world where brownies, sorcerers, trolls, and other mystical creatures flourish, an unlikely group of heroes sets off on a dangerous quest to places far beyond their home, where they must face their inner demons and come together to save their world. Stars Warwick Davis (Willow Ufgood), Ruby Cruz (Kit Tanthalos), Erin Kellyman (Jade Claymore), Ellie Bamber (Dove), Tony Revolori (Graydon Hastur), Amar Chadha-Patel (Thraxus Boorman), Dempsey Bryk (Airk Tanthalos), Joanne Whalley (Queen Sorsha). From Lucasfilm and Imagine Entertainment. A 32-min. documentary, *Willow: Behind the Magic*, directed by Adam Countee, was released Jan. 25.

Wilson, Gary He joined Disney in 1985 as chief financial officer and a member of the Board of Directors. He left in 1990 but remained a member of the board until 2006. Oversaw the financial arrangements for Euro Disney.

Wilson, Owen Actor; provided the voice of Lightning McQueen in the Cars films. He appeared in *Armageddon* (Oscar Choi), *Breakfast of Champions* (Monte Rapid), *Shanghai Noon* and *Shanghai Knights* (Roy O'Bannon), *The Royal Tenenbaums* (Eli Cash), *Around the World in 80 Days* (Wilbur Wright), *The Life Aquatic with Steve Zissou* (Ned Plimpton), and *Haunted Mansion* (2023), and on Disney+ in *Loki* (Mobius).

Win Ben Stein's Money (TV) Game show on Comedy Central; aired Jul. 28, 1997–Jan. 31, 2003. Contestants were pitted against host Ben Stein to win $5,000 of his money in a test of knowledge.

Win, Lose or Draw (TV) Game show; aired in syn. Sep. 7, 1987–Aug. 31, 1990 (570 episodes), and on NBC Sep. 7, 1987–Sep. 1, 1989 (505 episodes). Bert Convy hosted the syn. show, while Vicki Lawrence was the host on NBC. The game, based on charades, had contestants and celebrity players sketch clues rather than acting them out. The game was played by separate teams of men and women, with 2 celebrities and a contestant on each. Exec. producers were Bert Convy and Burt Reynolds. The show spawned a Disney Channel spin-off called *Teen Win, Lose or Draw*. A new *Win, Lose or Draw* series premiered on Disney Channel Mar. 3, 2014, hosted by Justin Willman.

Win or Lose (TV) Animated series from Pixar planned for digital release on Disney+ in fall 2023. Follows the Pickles, a coed middle school softball team in the week leading up to their championship game, with the drama of bad calls made on and off the field. Each episode takes place that same week, highlighting the perspective of a different main character—including the players, their parents, and the umpire—each reflected in a unique visual style. Voices include Will Forte (Coach Dan).

Winchell, April Voice actress; she has provided the voice of Clarabelle Cow since the 1990s. Additional voice roles include Mrs. Herman/young Baby Herman in *Who Framed Roger Rabbit*, Peg in *Goof Troop*, Dyl Piquel in *Bonkers*, Doris Deer in *The Shnookums & Meat Funny Cartoon Show*, Lydia in *Pepper Ann*, Miss Finster in *Disney's Recess*, Mallory in the *Mighty Ducks* animated series, Cruella De Vil in *101 Dalmatians: The Series*, Terk in *Disney's The Legend of Tarzan* and *Tarzan and Jane*, Nora in *Lloyd in Space*, Mrs. Edmonds in *Lilo & Stitch: The Series*, the Matchmaker in *Mulan II*, Sylvia in *Wander Over Yonder*, Black Heron/Zenith in *DuckTales* (2017), and Fens in *Amphibia*. She is the daughter of actor Paul Winchell.

Winchell, Paul (1922–2005) Actor/comedian; provided the voice of Tigger in the original Winnie the Pooh films, Boomer in *The Fox and the Hound*, the Chinese Cat in *The Aristocats*, and Zummi Gummi in *Disney's Adventures of the Gummi Bears*. On The Disney Channel, he appeared in *Disney Family Album*.

Wind (film) Animated short; digitally released Dec. 13, 2019, on Disney+. In a world of magical realism, a grandmother and grandson are trapped in an endless chasm, scavenging debris to realize their dream of escaping to a better life. Directed by Edwin Chang. 9 min. From the Pixar Animation Studios SparkShorts program.

Wind in the Willows (film) Segment of *The Adventures of Ichabod and Mr. Toad*. U.S. theatrical release as *The Madcap Adventures of Mr. Toad* (1975). Educational release as *The Adventures of J. Thaddeus Toad*.

Wind in the Willows (TV) Airing Feb. 2, 1955, this show was devoted to the British writer Kenneth Grahame, featuring the Disney versions of his *The Reluctant Dragon* and *Wind in the Willows*.

Wind Rises, The (film) Japanese animated film from Hayao Miyazaki. A fictional look at the life of Jiro Horikoshi, who designed Japanese fighter planes during World War II. Released under the Touchstone Pictures label for Academy Award consideration in Los Angeles and New York City, in Japanese with English subtitles, on Nov. 8, 2013. There was a limited-dubbed release Feb. 21, 2014, with an expanded release Feb. 28. It was originally released in Japan Jul. 20, 2013, under the title *Kaze Tachinu*. 127 min. It was nominated for an Academy Award for Animated Feature.

Windom, William (1923–2012) Actor; appeared in *Now You See Him, Now You Don't* (Lufkin), and on TV in *The Bluegrass Special* (Phil Wainright), with guest roles in *Boy Meets World* (Ned) and *Goof Troop* (voice of Uncle Bob).

Window Cleaners (film) Donald Duck cartoon released Sep. 20, 1940. Directed by Jack King. Donald is having enough trouble with his helper, Pluto, in washing the windows of a tall building when a bee, goaded by Donald, enters the scene and causes total disaster.

Windtraders Shop in Pandora – The World of Avatar in Disney's Animal Kingdom; opened May 27, 2017, with souvenirs based on the area's flora, fauna, and Na'vi culture.

Windwagon Smith Eccentric lunk in *The Saga of Windwagon Smith* (1961).

Wine Country Trattoria SEE GOLDEN VINE WINERY.

Winebaum, Jake He started *Family PC* magazine in a joint venture deal with Disney in 1993. In 1995, he was named president of Disney Online, and in 1997 his duties were expanded as president of Buena Vista Internet Services. In 1999, as chairman of Buena Vista Internet Group, he left to form eCompanies, an Internet start-up and development company in which Disney and EarthLink were founding investors.

Winfrey, Oprah Actress/TV personality; starred in *Beloved* (Sethe) after entering an exclusive overall deal with Walt Disney Studios in 1995, and later appeared in *A Wrinkle in Time* (Mrs. Which). She voiced Eudora in *The Princess and the Frog* and made a guest appearance on TV in *Ellen* (therapist). She was named a Disney Legend in 2017.

Winged Scourge, The (film) Educational film produced under the auspices of the Coordinator of Inter-American Affairs; the first and most elaborate of the health films produced for the CIAA. To protect themselves from the mosquito, a malaria-carrying parasite, the Seven Dwarfs show effective methods of mosquito control. Delivered Jan. 15, 1943. Directed by Bill Roberts.

Wings of Life (film) A Disneynature film providing an intimate look at the lives of pollinators— butterflies, hummingbirds, bees, and bats. Released in the U.S. for one week at the Chinese Theatre in Hollywood Apr. 5, 2013, prior to a Blu-ray and digital release on Apr. 16. Originally released in France Mar. 16, 2011, as *Pollen*, and released in the U.K. as *Hidden Beauty: A Love Story That Feeds* *the Earth*. Directed by Louie Schwartzberg. Narrated by Meryl Streep. Produced by Blacklight Films. 77 min.

Winkie Villain who acquires Toad Hall in *The Adventures of Ichabod and Mr. Toad*; voiced by Alec Harford. Also at times spelled Winkey and Winky.

Winkler, Henry Actor; appeared in *The Waterboy* (Coach Klein) and *Holes* (Stanley's father), on TV in *Mickey's 50* and in the title role in *Monty*, and on Disney Channel in *P.U.N.K.S.* (Edward Crow) and *So Weird* (Fergus McGarrity). He has provided several voices, including Mr. Diller in *Handy Manny*, the Snowman in *Penn Zero: Part-Time Hero*, Santa in *Puppy Dog Pals*, Uncle Dieter in *Vampirina*, Bailiff in *DuckTales* (2017), and Fritz in *Monsters at Work*.

Winkler, Margaret SEE MINTZ, MARGARET WINKLER.

Winkler, Paul (1898–1981) He began promoting Mickey Mouse in France in 1930, and in 1934 began *Le Journal de Mickey*. He was presented posthumously with a European Disney Legends Award in 1997.

Winnie the Pooh A. A. Milne character first animated by Disney artists in *Winnie the Pooh and the Honey Tree* (1966), and later appearing in 3 additional theatrical featurettes, along with educational films, TV series, and other theatrical films. Pooh became one of the more popular Disney characters on merchandise due to an early exclusive marketing agreement with Sears. Voiced by Sterling Holloway and later Hal Smith and Jim Cummings. Three of the featurettes were combined, with connecting animation, and released as a feature—*The Many Adventures of Winnie the Pooh*. Walt Disney had originally sought the screen rights to the Winnie the Pooh stories as early as 1937, but the rights were not secured until Jun. 1961. SEE ALSO NEW ADVENTURES OF WINNIE THE POOH, THE (TV SERIES); TIGGER MOVIE, THE; PIGLET'S BIG MOVIE; POOH'S HEFFALUMP MOVIE; AND WINNIE THE POOH (FILM).

Winnie the Pooh (film) Animated feature film released in the U.S. on Jul. 15, 2011, after an Apr. 6, 2011, release in Belgium. Pooh wakes up absolutely famished, and he happens to have no honey, so he sets out on a journey that is ultimately derailed by a search to replace Eeyore's lost tail. Everything then becomes even more complicated when Christopher Robin goes missing. Pooh finds a note from Christopher Robin that reads, "Gone out. Busy. Back soon." But then Owl misinterprets the note, proclaiming that the boy has been captured by a creature called a "Backson." Soon the whole gang is on a wild quest to save Christopher Robin from the imaginary culprit. Directed by Don Hall and Stephen Anderson. Voices include Jim Cummings (Winnie the Pooh, Tigger), Bud Luckey (Eeyore), Craig Ferguson (Owl), Jack Boulter (Christopher Robin), Travis Oates (Piglet), Kristen Anderson-Lopez (Kanga), Wyatt Dean Hall (Roo), Tom Kenny (Rabbit), Huell Howser (Backson), John Cleese (narrator). Songs by Kristen Anderson-Lopez and Robert Lopez include "A Very Important Thing to Do," "It's Gonna Be Great," and "Everything Is Honey," with "So Long" written and performed by Zooey Deschanel. Done in traditional animation, it is the last hand-drawn theatrical feature from Walt Disney Animation Studios to date. Burny Mattinson, who had been an animator on *Winnie the Pooh and Tigger Too* nearly 4 decades earlier, served as a story supervisor. 63 min.

Winnie the Pooh: A Valentine for You (TV) Half-hour special on ABC; first aired Feb. 13, 1999. Pooh and his friends worry that because Christopher Robin is making a valentine for someone else, he is now lovesick and will no longer have time for them. They search for a Smitten, whose "love bug bite" will cure Christopher Robin of his new affection. But eventually they realize that the heart has room for new friends and old. Voices include Jim Cummings (Winnie the Pooh), Paul Winchell (Tigger), John Fiedler (Piglet), Peter Cullen (Eeyore), Brady Bluhm (Christopher Robin), David Warner (narrator).

Winnie the Pooh: A Very Merry Pooh Year (film) Video release, on Nov. 12, 2002. All of Pooh's friends gather for fond recollections of a Christmas past, and then the New Year's countdown begins. Directed by Gary Katona and Ed Wexler. Voices include Jim Cummings (Winnie the Pooh/Tigger), Paul Winchell (Tigger, in the Christmas portion only), John Fiedler (Piglet), Peter Cullen (Eeyore), Michael Gough (Gopher), Ken Sansom (Rabbit), Nikita Hopkins (Roo), Michael Green (Christopher Robin), Michael York (narrator). 65 min.

Winnie the Pooh and a Day for Eeyore (film) Special cartoon featurette released Mar. 11, 1983.

Directed by Rick Reinert. Winnie the Pooh is teaching his friends how to play "Pooh Sticks" under a bridge when Eeyore floats by. It is his birthday, and no one has remembered. That is soon remedied, and the gang gathers with a party, presents, and a cake. Featuring the voices of Hal Smith (Pooh), Ralph Wright (Eeyore), John Fiedler (Piglet), Will Ryan (Rabbit), Kim Christianson (Christopher Robin), Dick Billingsley (Roo), Julie McWhirter Dees (Kanga), Paul Winchell (Tigger). This 4th installment of the Disney Pooh films was, like the others, based on the stories written by A. A. Milne, specifically "In Which Eeyore Has a Birthday and Gets Two Presents" and "Pooh Invents a New Game and Eeyore Joins In." However, the film lacks some of the major voice talents used in the other featurettes, most notably Sebastian Cabot as narrator and Sterling Holloway as Pooh. 24 min.

Winnie the Pooh and Christmas Too (TV) Special on ABC; first aired Dec. 14, 1991. Supervising director was Ken Kessell. When Winnie the Pooh and Piglet retrieve a letter to Santa, in hopes of adding some forgotten Christmas wishes, their plans go awry. Realizing now that the letter won't find its way to the North Pole on time, Pooh and Piglet decide to play Santa with some decidedly comic results. Voices are Jim Cummings (Winnie the Pooh), Peter Cullen (Eeyore), John Fiedler (Piglet), Michael Gough (Gopher), Ken Sansom (Rabbit), Paul Winchell (Tigger), Edan Gross (Christopher Robin).

Winnie the Pooh and Friends (TV) Show aired Dec. 11, 1982. Directed by John Lounsbery. Pooh footage is combined with segments from other Disney cartoons.

Winnie the Pooh and the Blustery Day (film) Special cartoon featurette released Dec. 20, 1968, with *The Horse in the Gray Flannel Suit*. Directed by Wolfgang Reitherman. A blustery day turns into a storm for Winnie the Pooh and his friends in the Hundred Acre Wood. They seek safety at Christopher Robin's, but Pooh and Piglet are washed away in a flood, and Owl's house is lost. But, before the day is over, Owl finds a new home, and Pooh and Piglet become heroes. Featuring the voices of Sterling Holloway (Pooh), Sebastian Cabot (narrator), Jon Walmsley (Christopher Robin), Ralph Wright (Eeyore), Howard Morris (Gopher), Barbara Luddy (Kanga), Hal Smith (Owl), John Fiedler (Piglet), Junius Matthews (Rabbit), Paul Winchell (Tigger). The film proved

a bigger success than its predecessor, *Winnie the Pooh and the Honey Tree*, by winning an Academy Award as Best Cartoon Short Subject, which was accepted by Woolie Reitherman on behalf of the late Walt Disney. The featurette marked the on-screen debut of Tigger, who was animated almost entirely by Milt Kahl. In its most imaginative sequence, Pooh has a nightmare inhabited by such fantastic creatures as Heffalumps and Woozles. Songs by Richard M. and Robert B. Sherman include "The Wonderful Thing About Tiggers," "The Rain, Rain, Rain Came Down, Down, Down," and "Heffalumps and Woozles." Based on the stories of A. A. Milne. 25 min. SEE ALSO POOH'S HEFFALUMP MOVIE.

Winnie the Pooh and the Honey Tree (film) Special cartoon featurette released Feb. 4, 1966, with *The Ugly Dachshund*. Directed by Wolfgang Reitherman. The Studio's first animated treatment of the famous children's books written by A. A. Milne. Winnie the Pooh and his friends, Christopher Robin, Eeyore the donkey, Owl, Kanga, and baby Roo, as well as Rabbit and Gopher, encounter a swarm of bees and a fabulous honey tree. Voices include Sterling Holloway (Winnie the Pooh), Sebastian Cabot (narrator), Bruce Reitherman (Christopher Robin), Ralph Wright (Eeyore), Howard Morris (Gopher), Barbara Luddy (Kanga), Hal Smith (Owl), Junius Matthews (Rabbit), Clint Howard (Roo). Little modification was done on the original stories of the world's most famous teddy bear. The most noticeable change was the introduction of a new character, Gopher. Songs by Richard M. and Robert B. Sherman include "Winnie the Pooh," "Up, Down, and Touch the Ground," "Rumbly In My Tumbly," and "Little Black Rain Cloud." Sterling Holloway was perfectly cast as the voice of Pooh and added to the popularity of the short, which inspired many sequels. 26 min.

Winnie the Pooh and Tigger Too (film) Special cartoon featurette released Dec. 20, 1974, with *The Island at the Top of the World*. Directed John Lounsbery. Inhabitants of the Hundred Acre Wood have a problem. Ebullient Tigger has been getting on everyone's nerves, introducing himself about the Wood and then turning to mischief. Rabbit calls a protest meeting, and it is decided to lose Tigger in the woods. But they in fact become lost, and it is up to Tigger to rescue them. When Tigger then bounces himself and little Roo onto a high tree limb, he must promise to never bounce again to be rescued. When he is, Rabbit holds him to his promise, and Tigger is heartbroken. Pressure from the others causes Rabbit to relent, admitting that he, too, liked the old bouncy Tigger better. 26 min. Featuring the voices of Sebastian Cabot (narrator), Sterling Holloway (Pooh), Junius Matthews (Rabbit), Paul Winchell (Tigger), John Fiedler (Piglet), Barbara Luddy (Kanga), Dori Whitaker (Roo), Timothy Turner (Christopher Robin). This was the 3rd installment in the Winnie the Pooh animated series, based on A. A. Milne's classic children's tales. Music and lyrics by Richard M. and Robert B. Sherman. The film was nominated for a Best Animated Short Film Oscar by the Academy of Motion Picture Arts and Sciences.

Winnie the Pooh Discovers the Seasons (film) Educational film; released in Sep. 1981. In discussing seasons, the film covers animal behavior, hibernation, temperature, and weather patterns. Voices are Ronald Feinberg (Eeyore), Hal Smith (Tigger, Owl), Kim Christenson (Christopher Robin), John Fiedler (Piglet), Ray Erlenborn (Rabbit).

Winnie the Pooh for President Days Event held at Disneyland in Oct. 1972, and repeated in Oct. 1976, with the national convention held at Walt Disney World each of those years. Winnie the Pooh was touted as a presidential candidate to tie in with the national elections. The campaign included a parade, rallies, and a cross-country whistle-stop tour. Sears offered special merchandise, including a storybook and record, with a song by Stratton & Christopher, who were then entertainers at Walt Disney World. The event actually began in Jul. 1968 as a "Winnie the Pooh for President" segment during Family Night at the Hollywood Bowl, soon moving to the Tomorrowland Stage at Disneyland as part of the *On Stage U.S.A.* show.

Winnie the Pooh: Seasons of Giving (film) Direct-to-video release Nov. 9, 1999. Pooh and friends set out on a quest for winter, leading to a wild search for the perfect ingredients for a festive Thanksgiving feast, and finally to Christmas. 70 min.

Winnie the Pooh: Springtime with Roo (film) Direct-to-video release Mar. 9, 2004. Every year Rabbit plays the Easter bunny, but not this year. Instead Rabbit expects the gang to spring into action: scrubbing, dusting, sweeping, and mopping. But Roo's love and wisdom show Rabbit that special days are to be shared in special ways. Directed by Elliot M. Bour and Saul Andrew Blinkoff.

Voices include Jim Cummings (Winnie the Pooh and Tigger), Ken Sansom (Rabbit), Jimmy Bennett (Roo), David Ogden Stiers (narrator), Kath Soucie (Kanga), John Fiedler (Piglet), Peter Cullen (Eeyore). 65 min.

Winnie the Pooh Thanksgiving, A (TV) A 30-min. animated special on ABC; first aired Nov. 26, 1998. Pooh and the gang go on a wild search for the ingredients for a perfect Thanksgiving feast. When the search goes awry, they frantically assemble a hysterically untraditional dinner and ultimately realize that Thanksgiving isn't about the trimmings but about family, friends, and the blessings you already have. Directed by Jun Falkenstein. Voices include Jim Cummings (Winnie the Pooh), Paul Winchell (Tigger), John Fiedler (Piglet), Peter Cullen (Eeyore), Brady Bluhm (Christopher Robin), David Warner (narrator).

Winnie the Pooh: The New Musical Stage Adaptation Stage version of Disney's Winnie the Pooh stories; opened in Times Square's Theatre Row in New York City Nov. 4, 2021, after previews beginning Oct. 21. Life-size puppetry, music by Richard M. and Robert B. Sherman, and further songs by A. A. Milne help set the scene for an adventure in the Hundred Acre Wood. Developed and presented by Jonathan Rockefeller in association with Disney Theatrical Productions. A 13-week limited run began at Mercury Theater Chicago Mar. 15, 2022, followed by an off-Broadway revival, national tour, and international premiere at London's West End (spring 2023).

Winnie the Pooh's ABC of Me (film) Educational film released Jan. 18, 1990. 12 min. Learn the alphabet by associating each letter with sounds or words.

Winningham, Mare Actress; appeared in *Turner & Hooch* (Emily Carson) and *Swing Vote* (Larissa Johnson); on TV in *She Stood Alone* (Prudence Crandall), *Grey's Anatomy* (Susan Grey), and *Criminal Minds* (Nancy Riverton); and on Disney Channel in *Tru Confessions* (Ginny Walker).

Winslet, Kate Actress; appeared in *A Kid in King Arthur's Court* (Princess Sarah) and voiced the title character in *Black Beauty* on Disney+.

Winston Chauffeur in *Oliver & Company*; voiced by William Glover.

Winter, Vincent (1947–1998) Actor; appeared in

Greyfriars Bobby (Tammy), *Almost Angels* (Toni Fiala), and *The Three Lives of Thomasina* (Hughie Stirling), and on TV in *The Horse Without a Head* (Fernand).

Winter (film) Silly Symphony cartoon released Oct. 30, 1930. Directed by Burt Gillett. Despite the cold wind and snow, woodland animals come out from their shelters to dance and skate until threatening clouds cause them to scamper back to their homes.

Winter Storage (film) Donald Duck cartoon released Jun. 3, 1949. Directed by Jack Hannah. When Chip and Dale can find no more acorns, they go after the supply Donald is using to reseed the area. Though he manages to trap them, they escape and take revenge on Donald.

Winter Summerland Miniature Golf Two 18-hole miniature golf courses at Walt Disney World, purporting to represent a vacation destination Santa created for his off-duty elves; opened Mar. 12, 1999, after the success of Fantasia Gardens Miniature Golf 3 years earlier. The snow course, named Winter, reflects the snow-clad Florida look of nearby Blizzard Beach, while the sand course, named Summer, features a tropical, holiday theme.

Winters, Jonathan (1925–2013) Actor; appeared on TV in *The Grand Opening of Walt Disney World*, *Mickey's 50*, and *Halloween Hall O' Fame*; hosted an episode of *The Mouse Factory*; and made a guest appearance in *Life with Bonnie* (Q. T. Marlens).

Winters, Shelley (1922–2006) Actress; appeared in *Pete's Dragon* (Lena Gogan).

Winwood, Estelle (1883–1984) Actress; appeared in *Darby O'Gill and the Little People* (Sheelah).

Wise, Kirk Animation director; he served as an assistant animator on *The Great Mouse Detective* and later became a storyboard artist. He was co-director, with Gary Trousdale, on the animated preshow film for Cranium Command at EPCOT, then on *Beauty and the Beast*, *The Hunchback of Notre Dame*, and *Atlantis: The Lost Empire*. He also exec. produced *Homeward Bound: The Incredible Journey* and directed the English-language voice cast of *Spirited Away*. He left the company in 2002 but later consulted on

educational and Disneynature films, including *Chimpanzee*.

Wise Little Hen, The (film) Silly Symphony cartoon released Jun. 9, 1934. Directed by Wilfred Jackson. Donald Duck made his debut in this fable about a mother hen who needs help planting corn and harvesting it. When Donald and his friend Peter Pig, sole members of the Idle Hour Club, refuse, she does it herself with the help of her chicks. When all is finished, and various types of corn delicacies are on the table, Donald and Peter, now interested, are not invited.

Wise Old Owl Kindly animated mentor to Danny and Jeremiah in *So Dear to My Heart*; voiced by Ken Carson.

Wise One, The (TV) A Native American chief and his grandson pursue a rare black beaver through the Rocky Mountain wilderness. The show was prepared for the Disney TV anthology series in America but did not air. First aired in Canada on Dec. 31, 1983. Later shown on The Disney Channel. Directed by Frank Zuniga.

Wish (film) Feature from Walt Disney Animation Studios planned for theatrical release fall 2023. The film asks the question, "How did the wishing star, upon which so many characters wished, come to be?" In Rosas, a kingdom where wishes can literally come true, 17-year-old Asha is an optimist with a sharp wit who cares endlessly about her community. In a moment of desperation, she makes an impassioned plea to the stars, which is answered by a cosmic force—a little ball of boundless energy called Star. Together, they face the most formidable of foes to save her community and prove that when the will of one courageous human connects with the magic of the stars, wondrous things can happen. Directed by Chris Buck and Fawn Veerasunthorn. Voices include Ariana DeBose (Asha), Alan Tudyk (Valentino). Songs by Julia Michaels include "More for Us."

Wish Upon a Star (TV) Series on The Disney Channel; debuted Apr. 19, 1983, with Joyce Little and Sharon Brown giving kids a chance to act out their fantasies. 26 episodes.

Wishes: A Magical Gathering of Disney Dreams Fireworks spectacular in the Magic Kingdom at Walt Disney World; premiered Oct. 9, 2003, taking the place of the long-running *Fantasy in the*

Sky. Narrated by Jiminy Cricket. Special holiday shows included *Happy HalloWishes* and *Holiday Wishes: Celebrate the Spirit of the Season*. The final performance was held May 11, 2017, to make way for *Happily Ever After*. A similar *Wishes* fireworks show played in Disneyland Paris Jul. 16, 2005–2007 and was replaced in 2008 by *Les Feux Enchantés* (*The Enchanted Fireworks*).

Wishing Star Magic Crystals See Geppetto's Arts & Crafts.

Wishing Star Park Nearly 90-acre lake recreation area at Shanghai Disney Resort; opened Jun. 16, 2016. Along an almost 1½-mile walking path, visitors explore woodlands, gardens, and a colorful space featuring tile birds and butterflies. The park also features the Dragonfly Playground and Starlight Amphitheater. Wishing Star Ferry provides exclusive transportation across the lake for the guests of the Shanghai Disneyland Hotel.

Witch Character in *Snow White and the Seven Dwarfs*; voiced by Lucille LaVerne.

W.I.T.C.H. (TV) In Candracar, a team of 13- and 14-year-old girls, W.I.T.C.H. (acronym of their names—Will, Irma, Taranee, Cornelia, Hay Lin), has magical powers. The girls, a new generation of an ancient and venerable group, the Guardians of the Veil, stress the positive values of courage, loyalty, togetherness, tolerance, and team spirit as they are charged with protecting their world from the evil warlord, Prince Phobos, in a parallel universe. Back at home and school, the girls don't even get a break as they face very contemporary and universal teen issues. Created by Disney Publishing Worldwide, the series launched in Italy in 2001, appearing first in international magazines; W.I.T.C.H. debuted in the U.S. in a series of 9 paperback books in Apr. 2004, and in an animated TV series airing as part of Jetix on ABC Family beginning Jan. 15, 2005, after a preview on ABC Dec. 18, 2004.

Witch Hazel Witch star of *Trick or Treat* (1952); voiced by June Foray. Her broomstick is named Beelzebub.

Witches of Morva, The Orddu, Orgoch, and Orwen have hidden the cauldron in *The Black Cauldron*; voiced by Eda Reiss Merin, Billie Hayes, and Adele Malis-Morey.

Witherspoon, Reese Actress/producer; appeared in *A Far Off Place* (Nonnie Parker), *Sweet Home Alabama* (Melanie), and *A Wrinkle in Time* (Mrs. Whatsit); on Hulu in *Little Fires Everywhere* (Elena Richardson; also exec. producer); and on ABC in *The Muppets*. For Disney Junior, she was named exec. producer and the voice of Fern in *Tiny Trailblazers*. She exec. produced *Tiny Beautiful Things*.

Without You (film) Segment of *Make Mine Music*, subtitled "A Ballad in Blue." Written by Osvaldo Farres, with English lyrics by Ray Gilbert; sung by Andy Russell.

Witt, Alicia Actress; appeared in *Mr. Holland's Opus* (Gertrude Lang) and *Playing Mona Lisa* (Claire Goldstein); and on TV in *Nashville* (Autumn Chase) and *Betrayal* (Zoe).

Wizards of Waverly Place (TV) Series on Disney Channel; premiered Oct. 12, 2007, and ended Jan. 6, 2012. Alex Russo and her 2 brothers, Justin and Max, engage in typical family squabbles with one significant difference—they are all wizards in training, under the tutelage of their dad, Jerry. Stars Selena Gomez (Alex), David Henrie (Justin), Jake T. Austin (Max), David DeLuise (Jerry), Maria Canals-Barrera (Theresa), Jennifer Stone (Harper). The show won an Emmy Award for Children's Program in 2009, 2010, and 2012.

Wizards of Waverly Place: The Movie (TV) A Disney Channel Original Movie; first aired Aug. 28, 2009. Manhattan's magical wizard siblings Alex, Justin, and Max Russo accompany their parents on a Caribbean vacation where Alex's inadvertent magic spell renders her parents as having never met. When they learn that the only thing that will reverse the spell is the magical Stone of Dreams, they embark on a quest through the jungle to find it. Time is running out to save their family, however. Directed by Lev L. Spiro. Stars Selena Gomez (Alex), David Henrie (Justin), Jake T. Austin (Max), Jennifer Stone (Harper), Maria Canals-Barrera (Theresa), David DeLuise (Jerry). Filmed in San Juan, Puerto Rico. Based on the TV series created by Todd J. Greenwald.

Wizards Return: Alex vs. Alex (TV) A Disney Channel special event; aired Mar. 13, 2013. On the eve of a planned family reunion in Italy, newly crowned Family Wizard Alex Russo is torn between living up to her new responsibilities and totally living it up, thanks to magic. Frustrated, she casts a spell to banish her selfish impulses and accidentally creates an evil doppelganger. Soon the "Good Alex" and "Bad Alex" face off in the ultimate wizard showdown. Stars Selena Gomez (Alex Russo), Jake T. Austin (Max), Jennifer Stone (Harper Finkle), Maria Canals-Barrera (Theresa), David DeLuise (Jerry). 60 min.

Woke (TV) Comedy series on Hulu; seasons digitally released Sep. 9, 2020, and Apr. 8, 2022. Keef, an African American cartoonist, is finally on the verge of mainstream success when an unexpected incident changes everything. With a fresh outlook on the world around him, Keef must now navigate the new voices and ideas that confront and challenge him, all without setting aflame everything he's already built. Inspired by the life and work of artist Keith Knight. Stars Lamorne Morris (Keef Knight), T. Murph (Clovis), Blake Anderson (Gunther), Sasheer Zamata (Ayana). From ABC Studios and Sony Pictures Television, Inc.

Wolcott, Charles (1906–1987) Composer; he joined the Disney Studio in 1938 as an arranger and accompanied Walt and a group of artists to South America in 1941 to study the music of the Latin American countries. He wrote songs, or arranged film scores, for *The Reluctant Dragon, Bambi, Saludos Amigos, The Three Caballeros, Song of the South*, and *Fun and Fancy Free*. He left Disney in 1949.

Wolfgang (film) A Disney+ original documentary; digitally released Jun. 25, 2021. The inspiring true story of Wolfgang Puck, a man who survived a troubled childhood and whose perseverance led him to become one of the world's most prolific chefs. (And that's despite frenetic professional demands disrupting his family life at home.) Directed by David Gelb. 78 min. From Supper Club.

Woman Wanted (film) Direct-to-video release Jan. 25, 2000, by Touchstone Home Video, of a Phoenician Entertainment/Annex Entertainment production. In a house divided by rivalry and burning resentment, a wealthy widower and his son maintain a lonely, uneasy existence. Then, as tensions rise, the mysterious Emma enters their lives and immediately creates a complex romantic triangle. Directed by Kiefer Sutherland. Stars Holly Hunter (Emma), Kiefer Sutherland (Wendell Goddard), Michael Moriarty (Richard Goddard). 110 min.

Woman's Courage, A (TV) Episode 7 of *The Swamp Fox*.

Wonder Dog (film) Pluto cartoon released Apr. 7, 1950. Directed by Charles Nichols. Pluto tries to become girlfriend Dinah's dream of a Wonder Dog, despite Butch's interference. And he succeeds by performing various circus stunts, to his own wonderment as well as Dinah's.

Wonderful Ice Cream Suit, The (film) Direct-to-video release Mar. 16, 1999, by Touchstone Home Video, of a film based on a Ray Bradbury story. The lives of 5 Latino men are changed when they, all being approximately the same size and weight, jointly purchase a gorgeous white suit in a local clothing store and wear it in the barrio. Directed by Stuart Gordon; produced by Gordon and Roy E. Disney. Stars Joe Mantegna (Gomez), Esai Morales (Dominguez), Edward James Olmos (Vamenos), Clifton Gonzalez-Gonzalez (Martinez), Gregory Sierra (Villanazul), Sid Caesar (Leo Zellman). 77 min.

Wonderful Thing About Tiggers, The Song from *Winnie the Pooh and the Blustery Day*; written by Richard M. and Robert B. Sherman.

Wonderful World of Animation Nighttime show at Disney's Hollywood Studios; debuted May 1, 2019, on the occasion of the park's 30th anniversary. Projection mapping on the Chinese Theatre and other effects take guests on a journey through more than 90 years of Disney and Pixar animated films.

Wonderful World of Color (TV) See Walt Disney's Wonderful World of Color.

Wonderful World of Disney, The (TV) Series on NBC; debuted Sep. 14, 1969, succeeding *Walt Disney's Wonderful World of Color*, and ended Sep. 2, 1979, to be followed by *Disney's Wonderful World*. Also the title of a syn. package of TV shows and a Disney Channel series. *The Wonderful World of Disney* returned to the air on ABC Sep. 28, 1997–Jun. 28, 2008, with films and specials airing occasionally beginning Dec. 12, 2015. More regular airings of Disney films resumed May 20, 2020.

Wonderful World of Disney, The: 40 Years of Television Magic (TV) Two-hour special on ABC; aired Dec. 10, 1994. Directed by Frank Martin. Kirstie Alley is the host, with celebrity interviews and reminiscences by such people as Debbie Allen, Bobby Burgess, Margaret Cho, Roy E. Disney, George Foreman, Hugh Hefner, Ward Kimball, James MacArthur, Hayley Mills, Fess Parker, Jim Varney.

Wonderful World of Disney, The: Magical Holiday Celebration (TV) Holiday special on ABC; first aired Nov. 24, 2016. Julianne and Derek Hough host a 2-hour musical special from Walt Disney World. Special guests include Trisha Yearwood, Garth Brooks, Kelly Clarkson. A 2nd show, which added Disneyland Resort and aired Nov. 30, 2017, was hosted by Julianne Hough and Nick Lachey, with co-host Jesse Palmer and guests, including Ciara, Darius Rucker, Fifth Harmony, Hanson. The 3rd special aired Nov. 29, 2018, with hosts Jordan Fisher, Sarah Hyland, and Jesse Palmer and guests, including Gwen Stefani, Meghan Trainor, Brett Eldredge, Andrea Bocelli. The 4th special aired Nov. 28, 2019, with hosts Matthew Morrison, Emma Bunton, and Jesse Palmer and guests, including Sting, Shaggy, Ingrid Michaelson, Andy Grammer, Ally Brooke, Lindsey Stirling. A 5th-anniversary edition aired Nov. 26, 2020, during the COVID-19 pandemic, with hosts Julianne and Derek Hough, and Trevor Jackson, plus flashback performances from past specials. The 6th special aired Nov. 28, 2021, with the original hosts, as well as Ariana DeBose and special guests, including Jimmie Allen, Kristin Chenoweth, Darren Criss, Gwen Stefani. The hosts returned for the 7th special, aired Nov. 27, 2022, with performers including Becky G, the Black Eyed Peas, Jordin Sparks, and Meghan Trainor.

Wonderful World of Disney presents The Little Mermaid Live!, The (TV) Two-hour live musical event on ABC; aired Nov. 5, 2019. Performances of songs from the animated film and Broadway stage adaptation are interwoven into a broadcast of the 1989 feature. Stars Auli'i Cravalho (Ariel), Queen Latifah (Ursula), Shaggy (Sebastian), John Stamos (Chef Louis), Graham Phillips (Prince Eric). Performed before a live audience at The Walt Disney Studios in Burbank.

Wonderful World of Disney, The: 25th Anniversary SEE NBC SALUTES THE 25TH ANNIVERSARY OF THE WONDERFUL WORLD OF DISNEY.

Wonderful World of Mickey Mouse, The (TV) Series of 7-min. animated shorts on Disney+; digitally premiered Nov. 18, 2020. Mickey and the gang navigate the curveballs of a wild and zany world where the magic of Disney makes the impossible possible. Voices include Chris Diamantopoulos (Mickey Mouse), Kaitlyn Robrock (Minnie Mouse), Bill Farmer (Goofy), Tony Anselmo (Donald Duck), Tress MacNeille (Daisy Duck). The 2nd season—consisting of 4 extended-length specials, each themed around a different season of the year—digitally premiered Feb. 18, 2022. From Disney Television Animation.

WonderGround Gallery Gallery in the Downtown Disney District at Disneyland Resort; opened Jun. 9, 2012. Limited-edition collectibles are sold among a distinct and eclectic art display. A WonderGround Gallery was added to the Marketplace Co-Op at Downtown Disney Marketplace (now the Marketplace at Disney Springs) at Walt Disney World in Jul. 2014.

Wonderland (TV) One-hour drama series on ABC; aired Mar. 30–Apr. 6, 2000, ending after 2 episodes had aired. Delved into the lives of the doctors manning Rivervue Hospital's psychiatric and emergency programs. Stars Ted Levine (Dr. Robert Banger), Martin Donovan (Dr. Neil Harrison), Michelle Forbes (Dr. Lyla Garrity), Billy Burke (Dr. Abe Matthews), Michael Jai White (Dr. Derrick Hatcher), Joelle Carter (Dr. Heather Miles). From Touchstone Television and Imagine Television. The entire series, including 6 unaired episodes, was shown on DirecTV beginning Jan. 14, 2009.

Wonderland Music Store Shop on Main Street, U.S.A. in Disneyland; opened Jul. 17, 1955, offering Disney albums and sheet music. It moved to a new location in 1956, replacing Blue Bird Shoes for Children. In 1959, it moved a final time, to Town Square, where it took the place of Jimmy Starr's Show Business. Closed Jan. 1, 1973, to become the Gulf Oil Hospitality Center. SEE ALSO 20TH CENTURY MUSIC COMPANY.

Wonderland of Wax Candle Shop Store on Main Street, U.S.A. in the Magic Kingdom at Walt Disney World; open 1971–1981. It became the Holiday Corner.

Wonders of China (film) Circle-Vision 360 film tour in China at EPCOT Center; opened Oct. 1, 1982. An ancient Chinese poet, Li Bai, appears from the past to guide audiences through the history, culture, and lands of China, including Inner Mongolia, the Great Wall, the Yangtze River, Shanghai, and China's outer provinces. It marked the first time that the country had allowed a Western company to film inside the Forbidden City and other remote areas. The film also played in the Circle-Vision 360 theater in Disneyland 1984–1996, alternating with *American Journeys*. It ended its run at EPCOT Mar. 26, 2003, replaced by *Reflections of China*. Written/produced by Jeff Blyth and directed by Greg MacGillivray.

Wonders of Life Future World pavilion in EPCOT; opened Oct. 19, 1989, sponsored by Metropolitan Life Insurance Co. from 1989–2000. A "life and health" pavilion had been planned to open with EPCOT Center, but it took many years for Imagineers to develop the right concept. Ultimately, this major pavilion provided a fun look at healthy living in the form of a colorful, kinetic fair. Guests could try out various fitness machines and interactive computers, experience the Cranium Command or Body Wars attractions, laugh out loud at the Ana-Comical Players, and explore the Sensory Funhouse. *Goofy About Health* and *The Making of Me* were film shows presented in the pavilion. Guests could shop at Well & Goods Limited or dine at the Pure and Simple counter-service restaurant. The pavilion closed Jan. 4, 2004, to operate seasonally, prior to finally closing for good Jan. 2007. It was later used as an EPCOT Festival Center.

Wonders of Life (film) Series of 3 educational films released in Jan. 1990: *The Bones and Muscles Get Rhythm*, *The Brain and the Nervous System Think Science*, and *The Heart and Lungs Play Ball*.

Wonders of the Water World (TV) Show aired May 21, 1961. Directed and narrated by Winston Hibler. A look at water and its importance to people, as well as fish. From a storm cloud, rain falls and forms streams which become rivers, eventually reaching the sea.

Wonders of Walt Disney World Series of classes on ecology, creative arts, energy, and entertainment offered for children ages 10–15 whose parents had taken them out of school for a trip to Walt Disney World. The classes were prepared by the Walt Disney World staff in cooperation with educators and were so highly regarded that many school districts provided excused absences and credit for participation in the classes. The classes began in fall 1979 and continued until summer 1996. It was absorbed by the Disney Institute and known as Camp Disney until it ended in 2000.

Wonders of Xandar See Guardians of the Galaxy: Cosmic Rewind (EPCOT).

Wondertime Magazine begun by Disney Worldwide Publishing in Feb. 2006; aimed at moms of children from birth to age 6. It was canceled after its Mar. 2009 issue.

Wondrous Journeys Nighttime fireworks spectacular at Disneyland celebrating the 100th anniversary of The Walt Disney Company; debuted Jan. 27, 2023, after a Jan. 26 preview, with projection effects on Main Street, U.S.A., Sleeping Beauty Castle, It's a Small World, and Rivers of America. The production features an original song, "It's Wondrous," as well as nods to all Walt Disney Animation Studios films to date.

Wong, BD Actor; appeared in *Father of the Bride* and *Father of the Bride Part II* (Howard Weinstein), and on TV as Bradd Wong in *Double Switch* (waiter) and *All-American Girl* (Stuart). He provided the speaking voice of Shang in *Mulan* and other appearances of the character, Agent Will Du in *Kim Possible*, and Toad Liu Hai in *DuckTales* (2017).

Wong, Benedict Actor; appeared as Wong in *Doctor Strange* and later Marvel Studios films, and provided the voice of Bull in *Lady and the Tramp* (2019) and Tong in *Raya and the Last Dragon*.

Wong, Curtis Mouseketeer on the new *Mickey Mouse Club*.

Wong, Tyrus (1910–2016) Inspirational artist with Disney 1938–1941, with his concepts primarily responsible for the look of *Bambi*. Animators Frank Thomas and Ollie Johnston later wrote, "He set the color schemes along with the appearance of the forest in painting after painting. Paintings that captured the poetic feeling that had eluded us for so long." He was named a Disney Legend in 2001.

Wood, C. V., Jr. (1921–1992) Walt Disney hired Wood from the Stanford Research Institute in 1954 to be vice president and general manager of Disneyland, Inc., a post he held for 22 months. During this period, Wood supervised the site selection and land purchase, and the first year of operation of the park. He left in 1956 to become a consultant to the leisure industry.

Wood, Elijah Actor; appeared in *Paradise* (Willard Young) and in the title role in *The Adventures of*

Huck Finn, and on TV in *Day-o* (Dayo) and *Oliver Twist* (Artful Dodger). He voiced Beck in *Tron: Uprising*, Sone in *The Wind Rises*, and Jace Rucklin in *Star Wars Resistance*. He appeared, uncredited, as Pinocchio in the 1991 educational film *I'm No Fool on Wheels*.

Woodard, Alfre Actress; appeared in *The Gun in Betty Lou's Handbag* (Ann), *Mumford* (Lily), and *Captain America: Civil War* (Miriam), and on TV in the title role in *A Mother's Courage: The Mary Thomas Story*, *Desperate Housewives* (Betty Applewhite), and *Marvel's Luke Cage* (Mariah Dillard), with guest appearances in *Grey's Anatomy* and *Private Practice*. She voiced Plio in *Dinosaur*, the narrator and Polly in *John Henry*, Sarabi in *The Lion King* (2019), and Mimi in *Marvel's Moon Girl and Devil Dinosaur*.

Woodland Café (film) Silly Symphony cartoon released Mar. 13, 1937. Directed by Wilfred Jackson. At a popular bug nightclub, various caterpillars, fireflies, spiders, and other insects dance the evening away. Some even look like famous Hollywood celebrities, including Lionel Barrymore.

Woods, Ilene (1929–2010) Walt Disney selected Ilene to be the voice of Cinderella. In later years, she appeared at various special events commemorating that film. She was named a Disney Legend in 2003.

Woods, James Actor; appeared in *Straight Talk* (Jack) and *Nixon* (H. R. Haldeman). He voiced Hades in *Hercules* and other appearances of the character, and Dr. Benedict in *Recess: School's Out*.

Woodward, Morgan (1925–2019) Actor; appeared in *The Great Locomotive Chase* (Alex), *Westward Ho the Wagons!* (Obie Foster), *The Wild Country* (Ab Cross), and *One Little Indian* (Sgt. Raines).

Woody Cowboy toy in *Toy Story*, the favorite of the boy Andy, until the coming of Buzz Lightyear threatens his dominance; voiced by Tom Hanks.

Woody's Lunchbox Counter-service eatery in Toy Story Land at Disney's Hollywood Studios; opened Jun. 30, 2018. Guests order meals from a vintage *Woody's Roundup*–themed lunch box.

Woody's Roundup Song from *Toy Story 2*; written by Randy Newman and performed by Riders in the Sky. Also an attraction in Disney-Pixar Toy Story Land in Shanghai Disneyland; opened Apr. 26, 2018. Guests swing around in an Old West cart pulled by a pony.

Woody's Roundup Village Frontierland character-greeting spot in Disneyland Paris; opened in 2007, taking the place of the Cottonwood Creek Ranch Critter Corral. Closed in 2012, although the site has since been used occasionally for character greetings.

Woolverton, Linda Writer; wrote the screenplay for *Beauty and the Beast*, *Homeward Bound: The Incredible Journey*, *Alice in Wonderland* (2010), *Maleficent*, and *Alice Through the Looking Glass*; co-wrote the screenplay for *The Lion King* and *Maleficent: Mistress of Evil* (also exec. producer); and did pre-production story work on *Aladdin*. She also adapted her *Beauty and the Beast* screenplay for the stage and wrote the book for *Aida*.

Woops! (TV) Series on Fox; aired Sep. 27–Dec. 6, 1992. Humankind gets a chance to start over in this comedy about the unlikely survivors of an accidental nuclear war who set about the task of re-creating society. Stars Fred Applegate (Jack Connors), Lane Davies (Curtis Thorpe), Cleavant Derricks (Dr. Frederick Ross), Meagen Fay (Alice McConnell), Evan Handler (Mark Braddock). From Heartfelt Productions, Witt/Thomas Productions, and Touchstone Television.

Worden, Marc Actor; appeared on the *Mickey Mouse Club* on The Disney Channel beginning in 1990, and later made TV appearances in *Felicity* (Jerry), *According to Jim* (maître d'), and *Dirty Sexy Money* (D. J. Pillowhead).

Working for Peanuts (film) Donald Duck cartoon released Nov. 11, 1953. Directed by Jack Hannah. Filmed in 3-D. Chip and Dale are stealing peanuts from an elephant, Dolores, until zookeeper Donald comes to the rescue. Chip and Dale win eventually, getting all the peanuts they can eat by using white paint to pass themselves off as rare albino chipmunks. Shown at Disneyland as part of *3-D Jamboree*, and later in the Magic Kingdom at Walt Disney World with *Magic Journeys*. It was rereleased in theaters in 2007 with the Disney Digital 3-D version of *Meet the Robinsons*. SEE ALSO 3-D.

World According to Goofy Parade Parade in Disneyland; ran Jun. 19–Nov. 15, 1992. Mounted in honor of Goofy's 60th anniversary, this (historically inaccurate) procession showcased the character's evolution from prehistoric roots and ancient Egypt to the Renaissance and then as a modern-day president.

World According to Jeff Goldblum, The (TV) A Disney+ original nonfiction series; digitally premiered Nov. 12, 2019. Through the prism of Jeff Goldblum's inquisitive mind, nothing is as it seems. Pulling the thread on deceptively familiar objects, like sneakers or ice cream, Goldblum unravels a wonderful world of astonishing connections, fascinating science and history, amazing people, and surprising big ideas and insights. From National Geographic and Nutopia.

World Bazaar Turn-of-the-century Victorian America–themed area in Tokyo Disneyland; opened Apr. 15, 1983. Similar to Main Street, U.S.A., but covered.

World Bazaar Confectionery Opened Apr. 15, 1983, in Tokyo Disneyland, offering Disney character sweets and Japanese-style snacks.

World Beneath Us, The (film) Tomorrowland film presentation in Disneyland, sponsored by Richfield Oil; began in 1955 and ran for several years. A professor narrates the story of the forces that have shaped "the world beneath us," as well as the search for oil, by use of Disney animation. Presented in CinemaScope.

World Celebration Area in EPCOT encompassing Spaceship Earth, Dreamers Point, and IMAGINATION!; the new name for Future World Central as of Oct. 1, 2021.

World Discovery Area in EPCOT dedicated to science and technology, including Test Track, Mission: SPACE, and Guardians of the Galaxy: Cosmic Rewind; the new name for Future World East as of Oct. 1, 2021.

World Is Born, A (film) The Stravinsky segment, "Rite of Spring," taken from *Fantasia*, and released in Jul. 1955, on 16 mm for schools.

World Junior Tennis Tournament (TV) See U.S. Junior Tournament; World Junior Tennis Tournament.

World Nature Area in EPCOT dedicated to the natural world, with The Land, The Seas with Nemo & Friends, and Journey of Water, Inspired by Moana; the new name for Future World West as of Oct. 1, 2021.

World News Center TV monitors providing top news stories, formerly the preshow for Electronic Forum in Communicore East at EPCOT Center; open Mar. 17, 1991–spring 1996.

World of Color Nighttime water, fire, music, and projection spectacular in Paradise Bay at Disney California Adventure; opened Jun. 11, 2010. The colorful show features almost 1,200 programmable fountains and 36 fire-emitting cannons, plus 28 high-definition projectors that present scenes from Disney and Pixar films across 19,000 square feet of water. A special holiday version of the show, *World of Color – Winter Dreams*, was introduced Nov. 2013, and was succeeded by *World of Color – Season of Light* beginning Nov. 10, 2016. *World of Color – Celebrate! The Wonderful World of Walt Disney* played May 22, 2015–Sep. 5, 2016, for the Disneyland Resort Diamond Celebration. A Halloween version of the show, *Villainous!*, premiered in 2019 as part of Oogie Boogie Bash – A Disney Halloween Party. For the 100th anniversary of The Walt Disney Company, a new show, *World of Color – ONE*, debuted Jan. 27, 2023, following a Jan. 25 preview, celebrating the storytelling legacy started by Walt Disney and including an original song, "Start a Wave."

World of Color Restaurant Table-service restaurant in Disney Explorers Lodge at Hong Kong Disneyland Resort; opened Apr. 30, 2017. Dishes incorporate flavors from the world's seas, islands, and continents.

World of Disney The largest, at 50,000 square feet, Disney merchandise location in the world opened Oct. 3, 1996, in the Downtown Disney Marketplace (now the Marketplace at Disney Springs) at Walt Disney World, with sections themed to classic Disney films. A second World of Disney opened in the Downtown Disney District at the Disneyland Resort in 2001. In 2018, the 2 locations were given a totally new layout and look based around the idea of a repurposed animation studio. In 2004, with the sale of the Disney Stores, the flagship store on Fifth Avenue in New York City became a World of Disney (later closing Dec. 31, 2009). At the New York City store, young guests could participate in a role-playing romp entitled Cinderella's Princess

Court. On Jul. 12, 2012, a 15,000-sq.-ft. World of Disney opened as the flagship store in Disney Village at Disneyland Paris, as part of the resort's 20th anniversary. The store features a 1920s art deco design, with 8 bas-reliefs showing Disney characters and the Eiffel Tower, along with a rotating domed roof. Inside, a series of murals pay tribute to the 5 continents. On Jun. 16, 2016, a 3,000-sq.-meter World of Disney Store opened in the Marketplace in Disneytown at Shanghai Disney Resort, themed as a vintage railroad roundhouse.

World of Frozen In 2016, it was announced that, as part of a multi-year transformation of Hong Kong Disneyland, the park would debut a new *Frozen*-themed land, with shopping, dining, entertainment, and attractions, including Frozen Ever After (a boat ride based on the attraction in EPCOT) and Wandering Oaken's Sliding Sleighs (a roller coaster–style attraction). SEE ALSO FROZEN KINGDOM (TOKYO DISNEYSEA) AND KINGDOM OF ARENDELLE (DISNEYLAND PARIS).

World of Motion Future World pavilion in EPCOT Center; open Oct. 1, 1982–Jan. 2, 1996, sponsored by General Motors. The attraction, narrated by Gary Owens, offered a tongue-in-cheek, but inspiring, ride through the history and future possibilities of transportation, from foot and animal power to sailing ships, balloons, steam power, railroads, automobiles, planes, and futuristic concepts. A record 139 Audio-Animatronics human and animal figures humorously told the story, bringing to life sequences devised by Imagineer Marc Davis with show design by Ward Kimball. More than 3,375 props, including authentic antique cars and wagons, decorated the sets. X Atencio and Buddy Baker wrote the attraction's theme song, "It's Fun to Be Free." The finale featured Center Core, an impressionistic view of a future city using cables, lasers, liquid neon, and fiber optics. The Transcenter at the conclusion of the ride featured the latest technology for cars of the future. World of Motion was replaced by Test Track in 1999.

World of Toys Shop in Disney Village in Disneyland Paris; opened as Mattel's World of Toys in 1993, taking the place of the Surf Shop. Closed Sep. 2019, to become Disney Fashion Junior.

World on Ice The first edition of Walt Disney's World on Ice premiered in an arena in East Rutherford, New Jersey, on Jul. 14, 1981. The show was produced by Ringling Bros. and Barnum & Bailey Combined Shows, Inc. (Irvin and Kenneth Feld), and combined the Disney characters and stories and the best in musical theater with championship skating, touring 20 major markets in the U.S. Spotlighted in the first show was skater Linda Fratianne. In the years since, new touring live ice shows have been mounted, usually tied to a specific Disney theme or movie, such as *Peter Pan*, *Beauty and the Beast*, *Aladdin*, Mickey Mouse's Diamond Jubilee, and *Snow White and the Seven Dwarfs*. Walt Disney's World on Ice became international in 1986, performing first in Japan. In 1994, there were 7 productions touring on 6 continents simultaneously, including dual companies of both *Beauty and the Beast* and *Aladdin* because of their unprecedented popularity. Annual attendance numbers upward of 10 million people worldwide were the norm. Through 1985, the shows were also called Walt Disney's Magic Kingdom on Ice and Walt Disney's Great Ice Odyssey. In 1996, the show title became Disney on Ice. (In the early 1950s, the Ice Capades had mounted Disney-themed segments in their shows, and it was in fact from the Ice Capades that Walt Disney had borrowed Disney character costumes to use for the opening of Disneyland.)

World Owes Me a Living, The Popular song hit from *Grasshopper and the Ants* (1934) that became Goofy's theme song; composed by Larry Morey and Leigh Harline.

World Premiere Circle-Vision Tomorrowland attraction in Disneyland, sponsored by PSA (Pacific Southwest Airlines) from its opening on Jul. 4, 1984, until Jul. 17, 1989, when Delta took over. The *American Journeys* 360° film played, later alternating with *Wonders of China*, until Jul. 1996, when *America the Beautiful* was brought back. The attraction closed Sep. 7, 1997. Originally *Circarama* and *America the Beautiful*. The words "World Premiere" were later dropped from the name. Delta ended its sponsorship Jan. 1, 1996. The attraction was later used as the queue for Rocket Rods.

World Premiere Food Court Cinema-themed dining facility in Cinema Hall at Disney's All-Star Movies Resort at Walt Disney World; opened Jan. 15, 1999.

World Showcase Area in EPCOT based on cross-cultural understanding; opened Oct. 1, 1982, originally with 9 pavilions celebrating the art, architecture, wares, and cuisines of countries around the world. The first 9 were Canada, United Kingdom,

France, Japan, U.S. (The American Adventure), Italy, Germany, China, and Mexico. The Morocco pavilion was added Sep. 7, 1984, followed by Norway May 6, 1988. The World Showcase Promenade, 1.3 miles in length, links the pavilions. There is an entrance from the EPCOT Resort Area between France and the United Kingdom through the International Gateway. Disney designers had conceived internationally themed areas throughout the years, including a proposed International Street for Disneyland in the 1950s. An enclosed downtown shopping district featuring international shops and restaurants was designed for Walt Disney's original vision for EPCOT, the city. In 1974, the World Showcase was announced for Walt Disney World, first as 2 semicircular structures housing international pavilions, to be located along the Seven Seas Lagoon. Within a few years, the idea moved to a site toward the center of the resort property, to join the Future World portion as one park: EPCOT Center. The design for World Showcase was finalized when Harper Goff envisioned the individual pavilions in their own buildings themed to the architecture of each nation, complementing each other around a central lagoon. The pavilions were designed at varying scales to stand side by side in harmony such that no one country overshadows another. For example, the Campanile Bell Tower is a ¼ scale to the original in Italy, while the Hall of Prayer for Good Harvests in China is set in a ½ scale. Known as an international, people-to-people exchange, World Showcase is staffed by friendly Cast Members recruited from the different nations around the world through the World Showcase Fellowship Program (later known as the Cultural Representative Program).

World Showplace SEE MILLENNIUM CELEBRATION.

World Traveler, The Shop offering Disney souvenirs and cold beverages at International Gateway in EPCOT; opened Dec. 26, 1989.

World War I Toward the end of the war, the young Walt Disney, wanting to do his part for his country, tried to enlist in the military, but he was too young. Instead, he managed to join a Red Cross unit and was sent to France just as the war concluded. For 9 months, he drove an ambulance, chauffeured dignitaries, and did other cleanup chores as the troops were getting ready to come home.

World War II The day after Pearl Harbor, the military moved onto the Disney Studio lot in Burbank, utilizing the soundstage and parking sheds for automotive maintenance and ammunition storage facilities. But they also turned to Disney for the production of training and propaganda films, and for the duration of the war, 93% of the company's output was war-related. The films did not feature the normal Disney characters, but rather used graphics, maps, diagrams, and simple animation to get their points across. To help entertain those on the home front, the Disney characters went to war too, with such cartoons as *Donald Gets Drafted*, *The Old Army Game*, and *Private Pluto*. Films were also produced for other agencies, such as *The New Spirit* for the Treasury Department, and as his contribution to the war effort, Walt had his artists design 1,200 insignias for military units at no charge to the units. Many ships, planes, and the jackets of soldiers featured decals and patches with illustrations of Donald Duck, Pluto, and other characters.

World's Greatest Athlete, The (film) Discovered in Africa by 2 U.S. college sports coaches, Nanu, a blond boy raised by locals after the death of his missionary parents, is an incredible athlete. Entered in a Los Angeles NCAA track-and-field meet, he wins all the events despite voodoo magic being used against him. Released Feb. 1, 1973. Directed by Robert Scheerer. 92 min. Stars Tim Conway (Milo), Jan-Michael Vincent (Nanu), John Amos (Coach Archer), Roscoe Lee Browne (Gazenga), Dayle Haddon (Jane), Billy De Wolfe (Maxwell), Nancy Walker (Mrs. Peterson), Danny Goldman (Leopold Maxwell). Bill Toomey, a world and Olympic decathlon champion, acted as a technical adviser to the film crew. The film also included sportscaster favorites Howard Cosell, Bud Palmer, Frank Gifford, and Jim McKay. For one scene in which a 3-inch-tall Tim Conway, under a spell by Nanu's witch doctor godfather, falls into a lady's handbag, Disney prop-makers fashioned a number of giant props: lipstick, compact, hairpins, needle and thread, safety pins, reading glasses, comb and brush, pills, keys, and matches. Ordinary items, but these particular ones were 24 times normal size, weighed 1 ton, and cost over $15,000. In other scenes, Conway encountered many other giant props; a huge telephone cost the Studio $7,900. A cocktail glass was 7 feet tall and held a 1,245-gallon old-fashioned displaced by ice cubes 2 feet square.

World's Most Magical Celebration, The An 18-month-long event honoring the 50th anniversary of Walt Disney World; began Oct. 1, 2021, after a rededication of the Magic Kingdom on Sep. 30, and scheduled to end Mar. 31, 2023. Included were new attractions, including Remy's Ratatouille Adventure at EPCOT; two nighttime spectaculars (*Disney Enchantment* and *Harmonious*); and the *Disney KiteTails* show at Disney's Animal Kingdom. Each evening, Cinderella Castle, Spaceship Earth, the Hollywood Tower Hotel, and the Tree of Life were transformed into Beacons of Magic, illuminated with special effects. Across the parks, 50 gold-colored statues of Disney characters made up the Disney Fab 50 Character Collection, and special décor and merchandise featured a shimmering "EARidescent" color scheme.

Worlds of Pixar Area in Walt Disney Studios Park at Disneyland Paris, as of Aug. 27, 2021, featuring Pixar attractions, some previously part of Toon Studio, including Toy Story Playland, Crush's Coaster, La Place de Rémy, and Cars ROAD TRIP.

Worley, Jo Anne Actress; appeared in *The Shaggy D.A.* (Katrinka Muggelberg), and on TV in *The Mouseketeers at Walt Disney World* (Miss Osborne), *Mickey's 50*, *Kraft Salutes Disneyland's 25th Anniversary*, and as a host of *The Mouse Factory*, with guest roles in *Boy Meets World* (Mrs. Stevens), *Wizards of Waverly Place* (Maggie), and *Jessie* (Nana Banana). She voiced the wardrobe in *Beauty and the Beast*, Miss Maples in *A Goofy Movie*, Hoppopotamus in *The Wuzzles*, Bouffant Beagle in *DuckTales*, and Mrs. Rockwaller in *Kim Possible*.

Worm Turns, The (film) Mickey Mouse cartoon released Jan. 2, 1937. Directed by Ben Sharpsteen. Mickey mixes together a magic potion that gives both strength and courage. The potion allows a series of "underdogs"—a fly, a mouse, and a cat—to get their revenge on their enemies, and finally it enables Pluto to get the best of dogcatcher Pete.

Would You Eat a Blue Potato? (film) Educational film with Figment about color and its effect on everything we see, in the EPCOT Educational Media Collection: Language Arts Through Imagination series; released in Sep. 1988. 15 min.

Wrather, Bonita (1923–1988) As actress Bonita Granville, she married Jack Wrather and worked with him throughout his career, as he built and ran the Disneyland Hotel. Her first name, Bonita, was given to a tower at the hotel, and her last name, Granville, was used for a restaurant there. She was named a Disney Legend in 2011.

Wrather, Jack (1918–1984) A TV producer (*Lassie*, *The Lone Ranger*), he struck a deal with Walt Disney in 1954 to build and operate the Disneyland Hotel on land owned by Disney. Wrather's company was acquired by The Walt Disney Company in 1988. He was named a Disney Legend in 2011.

Wrather Corporation Company headed by Jack Wrather that built and ran the Disneyland Hotel and operated the docked (in Long Beach, California) *Queen Mary* and *Spruce Goose*; acquired by The Walt Disney Company in 1988.

Wreck-It Ralph (film) Animated feature released on Nov. 2, 2012, in Disney Digital 3-D. Wreck-It Ralph longs to be as beloved as his arcade game's perfect Good Guy, Fix-It Felix. The problem is that nobody loves a Bad Guy. But they do love heroes, so when a modern, first-person shooter game arrives featuring tough-as-nails Sgt. Calhoun, Ralph sees it as his ticket to heroism and happiness. He sneaks into the game with a simple plan to win a medal, but soon wrecks everything, and accidentally unleashes a deadly enemy that threatens every game in the arcade. Ralph's only hope is Vanellope von Schweetz, a young troublemaking "glitch" from a candy-coated cart racing game who might just be the one to teach Ralph what it means to be a Good Guy. But will he realize he is good enough to become a hero before it's "Game Over" for the entire arcade? Directed by Rich Moore. Voices include John C. Reilly (Ralph), Jack McBrayer (Fix-It Felix), Jane Lynch (Sgt. Calhoun), Sarah Silverman (Vanellope), Alan Tudyk (King Candy), Ed O'Neill (Mr. Litwak), Dennis Haysbert (General Hologram). 101 min. Working title was *Reboot Ralph*. The story takes place within 4 distinct worlds: the 8-bit arcade game, *Fix-It Felix Jr.*; the hyperrealistic shooter game, *Hero's Duty*; the candy-themed racing game, *Sugar Rush*; and Game Central Station, a bustling hub for video game characters, inspired by Grand Central Station. Populating these worlds are nearly 190 unique characters, 3 times that of any previous Disney animated film. New technological innovations were employed, including Camera Capture, which allowed designers to quickly visualize numerous takes and explore a wide range of virtual camera moves, as well as Disney's BRDF (bidirectional reflectance distribution function), which improved the way light reflects and rolls over a surface. Filmed in Cinema-Scope. This was the first Disney film released on digital platforms (Feb. 12, 2014, including iTunes, Google Play, and YouTube) before its DVD/Blu-ray release (Mar. 5, 2014). Nominated for an Academy Award for Animated Feature Film.

Wright, Ben (1915–1989) Actor; voiced Roger Radcliff in *One Hundred and One Dalmatians*, a wolf in *The Jungle Book* (1967), and Grimsby in *The Little Mermaid*. He appeared on TV in *Way Down Cellar* (Ethan Marcus) and narrated *Chandar, the Black Leopard of Ceylon*.

Wright, Ralph (1908–1983) Actor; voiced Eeyore in the original Winnie the Pooh films.

Wright, Samuel E. (1946–2021) Actor; voiced Sebastian in *The Little Mermaid* (and other appearances of the character and Kron in *Dinosaur*. He originated the role of Mufasa in *The Lion King* on Broadway, for which he garnered a Tony nomination.

Wrinkle in Time, A (film) Young Meg Murry, a bit of a misfit in a family of brilliant scientists, finds herself journeying through space and time, or "tessering," to save her father, with a little help from 3 truly incredible celestial beings: Mrs. Which, Mrs. Whatsit, and Mrs. Who. The three Mrs.'s impart the knowledge they have gleaned from across the cosmos to guide Meg to strange and sometimes perilous planets and help her discover the warrior that lies within her. Directed by Ava DuVernay. Released Mar. 9, 2018, also in IMAX and 3-D, after international releases beginning Mar. 8. Stars Storm Reid (Meg Murry), Reese Witherspoon (Mrs. Whatsit), Chris Pine (Dr. Alex Murry), Zach Galifianakis (The Happy Medium), Mindy Kaling (Mrs. Who), Oprah Winfrey (Mrs. Which), Michael Peña (Red), Levi Miller (Calvin). 109 min. Based on Madeleine L'Engle's classic novel. Filmed primarily in New Zealand and Southern California.

Wrinkle in Time, A (TV) A 3-hour presentation on *The Wonderful World of Disney*; first aired May 10, 2004. When astrophysicist Dr. Jack Murry disappears without a trace, his children, Meg and Charles Wallace, and neighbor Calvin, take it upon themselves to find him. Guided by Mrs. Whatsit, Mrs. Who, and Mrs. Which, the children embark on a cosmic quest before finally reaching the dark planet Camazotz. Directed by John Kent Harrison. Stars Alfre Woodard (Mrs. Whatsit), Kate Nelligan (Mrs. Which), Alison Elliott (Mrs. Who), Kyle Secor (the Prime Coordinator), Chris Potter (Jack Murry), Sarah-Jane Redmond (Dana Murry), David Dorfman (Charles Wallace), Katie Stuart (Meg), Gregory Smith (Calvin O'Keefe). Based on the Newbery Award–winning book by Madeleine L'Engle. Produced by BLT Productions and Fireworks International, and distributed by Miramax Television in association with Dimension. Originally aired in Canada Apr. 25, 2003.

Writer's Stop, The See Buy the Book.

Writing Magic: With Figment and Alice in Wonderland (film) Educational film, in the EPCOT Educational Media Collection; released in Aug. 1989. 16 min. Brainstorming, writing, and rewriting are the keys to solving Alice's dilemma.

Writing Process, The: A Conversation with Mavis Jukes (film) Educational film released Jul. 3, 1989. 20 min. The award-winning author shares her perspectives on creative writing.

Wrong Way Moochie (TV) Part 2 of *Moochie of the Little League*.

Wrubel, Allie (1905–1973) Songwriter; won an Academy Award for "Zip-A-Dee-Doo-Dah" and wrote songs also for *Make Mine Music* and *Melody Time*.

Wurlitzer Music Hall Shop on Main Street, U.S.A. in Disneyland; open Jul. 1955–Sep. 1968. A fondly remembered store where guests could hear pianos, player pianos, and organs demonstrated, or buy rolls for their own player piano. It was replaced by Walt Disney—A Legacy for the Future.

Wuzzles, The Odd group of characters, each 2 animals in one, living on the Isle of Wuz, created for a 1985 TV series. Voices include Brian Cummings (Bumblelion), Jo Anne Worley (Hoppopotamus), Henry Gibson (Eleroo), Bill Scott (Moosel), Alan Oppenheimer (Rhinokey). See also Disney's Wuzzles (TV).

Wuzzles: Bulls of a Feather, Disney's (film) International theatrical release of the TV cartoon; debuted in England Mar. 21, 1986. Everything's fine with the fanciful Wuzzles in the Land of Wuz until Eleroo accidentally causes a Brahma Bullfinch to hatch prematurely. The villainous Croc tries to steal the baby for its valuable feathers, but the Wuzzles outwit him, and the baby is reunited with its mama.

Wyatt, Jane (1910–2006) Actress; appeared in *Treasure of Matecumbe* (Aunt Effie).

Wyman, Jane (1914–2007) Actress; appeared in *Pollyanna* (Aunt Polly) and *Bon Voyage* (Katie Willard).

Wyndham Lake Buena Vista Resort in Lake Buena Vista at Walt Disney World; opened Nov. 10, 2010, taking the place of the Regal Sun Resort.

Wyndham Palace Resort and Spa Hotel in Lake Buena Vista at Walt Disney World beginning Nov. 1, 1998; formerly known as the Buena Vista Palace (1983–1998). It reverted to the Buena Vista Palace name in Aug. 2005.

Wynken, Blynken and Nod (film) Silly Symphony cartoon released May 27, 1938. Directed by Graham Heid. In this fanciful dream fantasy, 3 babies float among the clouds in the night sky in a wooden ship, fishing for stars and even a comet, which speeds them on. When a storm breaks, they slide down to Earth on moonbeams and into the cradle of one sleepyhead.

Wynn, Ed (1886–1966) Actor; a Disney favorite who appeared in *The Absent-Minded Professor* (fire chief), *Babes in Toyland* (The Toymaker), *Son of Flubber* (A. J. Allen), *Mary Poppins* (Uncle Albert), *Those Calloways* (Ed Parker), *That Darn Cat!* (Mr. Hofstedder), and *The Gnome-Mobile* (Rufus). He voiced the Mad Hatter in *Alice in Wonderland*, and appeared on TV in *Backstage Party*, *The Golden Horseshoe Revue*, and *For the Love of Willadean*. He was named a Disney Legend posthumously in 2013.

Wynn, Keenan (1916–1986) Actor; appeared as Alonzo Hawk in *The Absent-Minded Professor*, *Son of Flubber*, and *Herbie Rides Again*, with additional appearances in *Smith* (Vince Heber), *Snowball Express* (Martin Ridgeway), and *The Shaggy D.A.* (John Slade). He narrated the educational film, *VD Attack Plan*.

1. Xerox process 2. Xerox process 3. XZFR Rock & Roll Beach Club 4. Xerox process
5. *X Games 3-D: The Movie* (film) 6. X-S Tech 7. Xandra 8. Xemnas

X Games 3-D: The Movie (film) Emphasizing 6 of the sports event's biggest stars—Shaun White, Travis Pastrana, Danny Way, Ricky Carmichael, Bob Burnquist, and Kyle Loza—this documentary covers the death-defying extreme action sports of the 2008 X Games. Released Aug. 21, 2009, in Digital 3-D. Directed by Steve Lawrence. Narrated by Emile Hirsch. 92 min.

Xandra Goddess of adventure in *Legend of the Three Caballeros*.

Xemnas An antagonist in the *Kingdom Hearts* video game series.

Xerox process Electrostatic process adapted for transferring animators' pencil drawings to cels. It was tested in *Sleeping Beauty* and used in *Goliath II* and *One Hundred and One Dalmatians*. The process was then used in practically every Disney animated film up through *The Little Mermaid*, after which the computer obviated the need for cels.

X-S Tech Mysterious corporation, the galaxy's authority in technological innovation, in the former ExtraTERRORestrial Alien Encounter at Walt Disney World. Its motto is "Seize the Future."

X-Team, The (TV) Two-hour movie on ABC; first aired Jan. 9, 2003. The X-team is an elite rescue and extraction team made up of world-class athletes whose ability to navigate impossible terrain makes them the final option to free hostages or political prisoners. Team member R. J. is kidnapped along with a trio of businessmen on a ski vacation in New Zealand. One of those in the group, it turns out, has developed a computer program that will revolutionize the Internet. R. J. manages to send out a radio signal seeking help from her colleagues. Directed by Leslie Libman. Stars Bai Ling (R. J. Fillmore), Scott Paulin (Harris Beckett), Paul Francis (Rasputin Wojohovitz), Elizabeth Lackey (Palmer Marix), Eric Mabius (Darby Gibson), Chris Pratt (Keenan Kranjac), Clarence Williams III (Pat Zachary). From Mandalay Television Productions in association with Touchstone Television. Filmed in New Zealand.

XZFR Rock & Roll Beach Club Nightclub in Pleasure Island at Walt Disney World; opened Apr. 7, 1990, originally as the XZFR Rockin' Rollerdrome (which had debuted May 1, 1989). The roller-skating was a novelty, but it was removed in favor of the beach club theme. Later known as Rock N Roll Beach Club, eventually closing Feb. 3, 2008.

1. Yo Ho (A Pirate's Life for Me) 2. Yen Sid 3. *Yellowstone Cubs* (film) 4. *You—The Human Animal* (film)
5. You've Got a Friend in Me 6. *Ye Olden Days* (film) 7. Yzma 8. Yong Feng Shangdian

Y Arriba Y Arriba A 600-seat Latin restaurant and club in the Downtown Disney District at Disneyland Resort; opened Feb. 7, 2001, serving pan-Latin American tapas. Managed by EstrellaMundo. Closed Sep. 19, 2002, to become Tortilla Jo's.

Yacht Bar, The Tomorrowland snack facility in Disneyland, offering views of the Tomorrowland Boats (later Phantom Boats and Motor Boat Cruise) lagoon; opened in summer 1955, originally as The Yacht Club, and relocated in 1957. It closed Sep. 6, 1966.

Yacht Club Restaurant in Disney Newport Bay Club at Disneyland Paris; opened Apr. 12, 1992, serving New England–inspired specialties with Mediterranean influences.

Yacht Club Galley Seafood restaurant in Disney's Yacht Club Resort at Walt Disney World; opened Nov. 5, 1990. It became Captain's Grille Jan. 1, 2008.

Yacht Club Resort, Disney's Resort along Crescent Lake in the EPCOT Resort Area at Walt Disney World; opened Nov. 5, 1990. Designed by Robert A.M. Stern, the hotel is connected to Disney's Beach Club Resort and offers a short walk to EPCOT via the International Gateway. With 635 rooms, it is designed in the nautical style of New England–shore hotels of the 1880s, such as those found in Nantucket and Martha's Vineyard. Dining options include the Ale & Compass Restaurant (formerly Captain's Grille), The Market at Ale & Compass (formerly the Fittings & Fairings shop), and Crew's Cup Lounge, with signature dining at Yachtsman Steakhouse, where diners can select their own cut of meat. An Americana-themed convention center, expanded in 2018, offers nearly 100,000 square feet of meeting space. SEE ALSO BEACH CLUB RESORT, DISNEY'S.

Yachtsman Steakhouse New England–style signature restaurant for dinner in Disney's Yacht Club Resort at Walt Disney World; opened Nov. 5, 1990, serving premium steaks and seafood. Pine, leather, brass, and copper give the feel of a well-trimmed sailing vessel.

Yak & Yeti Restaurant Nepalese-style restaurant in Asia at Disney's Animal Kingdom; opened Nov. 14, 2007, and operated by Landry's. Guests feast on pan-Asian cuisine in what appears to be a former village home. Next door, the Yak & Yeti Local Food Cafe offers counter-service meals.

Yakitori House Counter-service restaurant in Japan at EPCOT; opened Oct. 1, 1982. Located in the midst of a Japanese garden, it was named after the skewered chicken dish served here. The architecture is inspired by Japan's Katsura Imperial Villa in Kyoto. It was renamed Katsura Grill in Dec. 2011.

Yale & Towne Shop on Main Street, U.S.A. in Disneyland; open Jul. 17, 1955–1964, with an exhibit showcasing the evolution of locks. Succeeded by a souvenir store known as Fantasia Shop and, later, Main Street Gifts, which closed in 1966. The space was then integrated into the Jewelry Shop.

Yamabuki Table-service restaurant in the Disneyland Pacific Hotel (later Disney's Paradise Pier Hotel) at the Disneyland Resort; open 1995–Apr. 2009. Traditional Japanese cuisine was served in a dining room adorned with Kabuki masks, brush paintings, and bonsai.

Yankee Trader, The Liberty Square shop in the Magic Kingdom at Walt Disney World selling culinary aids; opened Sep. 1973. Originally known as The Yankee Pedlar. Closed Jul. 27, 2014, to become the Haunted Mansion–themed shop Memento Mori.

Yankovic, Alfred Matthew (Weird Al) Singer/songwriter/actor; appeared on TV in *Safety Patrol* (as himself) and *Galavant* (Confessional Monk). He voiced the title character in *Milo Murphy's Law*, the singing minstrel in *Lilo & Stitch: The Series*, Probabilitor the Annoying in *Gravity Falls*, Dr. Screwball Jones in *Wander Over Yonder*, Preston Change-O in *Star vs. The Forces of Evil*, Shapeshifter in *The 7D*, the Shirt Cannon Guy in *Phineas and Ferb The Movie: Candace Against the Universe*, and Wacko Wally in *Hamster & Gretel.* He wrote/performed the theme song for *Spy Hard*.

Ye Olde Christmas Shoppe Christmas-themed shop in Liberty Square in the Magic Kingdom at Walt Disney World; opened Feb. 5, 1996, replacing Olde World Antiques and the Silversmith.

Ye Olden Days (film) Mickey Mouse cartoon released Apr. 8, 1933. Directed by Burt Gillett. Princess Minnie is locked in a tower when she refuses to marry the prince, Dippy Dawg (later known as Goofy), chosen by her father. Mickey, a wandering minstrel, rescues Minnie and wins a joust with the prince in order to marry her.

Year of a Million Dreams, The Event that began Oct. 1, 2006, celebrating the dreams of Disneyland and Walt Disney World guests. Special Cast Members, known as the Dream Squad, randomly selected guests for special prizes as part of the Disney Dreams Giveaway—including FastPasses, exclusive pins or Mouse ears, and unique experiences such as spending the night in the Dream Suite at Disneyland or Cinderella Castle Suite at Walt Disney World, taking an Adventures by Disney vacation, or going on a Disney Cruise. The celebration was extended to Dec. 31, 2008.

Year of 100 Million Smiles Disneyland anxiously awaited the arrival of its 100 millionth guest in 1971. The day came on Jun. 17, 1971, when, at 11:13 a.m., Valerie Suldo from New Brunswick, New Jersey, walked through the turnstiles. The 200 millionth guest, Gert Schelvis, arrived Jan. 8, 1981.

Yellow Shoes Internal creative agency for Disney Parks, Experiences and Products. It was established in 2000, having evolved from the former Walt Disney World Marketing Creative Services department.

Yellowstone Cubs (film) Tuffy and Tubby, bear cubs of insatiable curiosity, are trapped during their investigation of a tourist's car at Yellowstone Park. In attempting their rescue, their mother is branded a "dangerous bear" and taken to the outskirts of the park. By the time she finds her mischievous progeny, they have just about the whole park in an uproar. Produced by Charles Draper. Released Jun. 13, 1963. 48 min.

Yellowstone Story, The/Bear Country (TV) Show aired May 1, 1957. Directed by James Algar. Walt Disney tells about the search for far-off locations for the True-Life Adventure series, then lets Jim Algar tell about the history and geography of Yellowstone National Park, where *Bear Country* was filmed. He then shows the Academy Award–winning True-Life Adventure film.

Yen Sid Stern sorcerer in "The Sorcerer's Apprentice" segment of *Fantasia*. His name is Disney spelled backward.

Yensid, Retlaw Walt Disney's name spelled backward, used for the story credit for *Lt. Robin Crusoe, U.S.N.* This was the only film on which Walt Disney received a story credit.

Yesss Digital arbiter of all things buzz-worthy in *Ralph Breaks the Internet*; voiced by Taraji P. Henson.

YesterEars Pleasure Island shop at Walt Disney World; opened May 1, 1989, offering nostalgic Disney memorabilia. Closed Sep. 1993, to become DTV.

Yin Yang Yo! (TV) Animated series on Toon Disney and Jetix; premiered Sep. 4, 2006. Tween rabbits, Yin and Yang, must put aside their sibling rivalry to learn the lost martial art form "woo foo" from grumpy panda Master Yo, who was forced out of retirement to train and guide the brother and sister to help them save the world from comical evildoers, such as Carl the Evil Cockroach Wizard. Voices include Stephanie Morgenstern (Yin/Chung Pow Kitties), Scott McCord (Yang/Yuck), Martin Roach (Yo), Jamie Watson (Carl/Zarnot), David Hemblen (Night Master), Tony Daniels (Ultimoose/ Kraggler), Linda Ballantyne (Saranoia), Jonathan Wilson (Dave/Coop). From Walt Disney Television Animation.

Yippies Group of protestors who invaded Disneyland on Aug. 6, 1970, causing the park to close early. Disneyland executive Jack Lindquist chronicles the story in his book, *In Service to the Mouse: My Unexpected Journey to Becoming Disneyland's First President.*

Yo Ho (A Pirate's Life for Me) Song from Pirates of the Caribbean at the Disney parks; written by X Atencio and George Bruns.

Yokoyama, Matsuo Beginning in 1961, Yokoyama helped create the foundation for Disney's merchandise licensing business in Japan. He retired in 1994 as chairman of Walt Disney Enterprises of Japan but continued to work as a consultant for Walt Disney Consumer Products Asia-Pacific Ltd., followed by a position as chairman emeritus of Walt Disney Enterprises of Japan from 1996–1998. He was named a Disney Legend at a special ceremony in Japan in 1998.

Yong Feng Shangdian Shopping gallery in China at EPCOT; open Apr. 3, 1983–Feb. 3, 2011, offering Chinese silk robes, jade jewelry, lacquer chests, rugs, vases, and other authentic items. After an extensive refurbishment, it was renamed House of Good Fortune Apr. 4, 2011.

York, Jeff (1912–1995) Actor; appeared in *The Great Locomotive Chase* (William Campbell), *Davy Crockett and the River Pirates* (Mike Fink), *Westward Ho the Wagons!* (Hank Breckenridge), *Johnny Tremain* (James Otis), and *Old Yeller* and *Savage Sam* (Bud Searcy), and on TV in *Davy Crockett's Keelboat Race* (Mike Fink), *Along the Oregon Trail*, and *The Saga of Andy Burnett* (Joe Crane).

Yorkshire County Fish Shop Fish-and-chips counter-service restaurant in the United Kingdom at EPCOT; opened Oct. 1, 1999. Presented by Harry Ramsden's until Dec. 2010.

You Again (film) Successful PR pro Marni heads home for her older brother's wedding and discovers that he is marrying her high school archnemesis, who seems to have conveniently forgotten all the rotten things she did so many years ago. Then the bride's jet-setting aunt bursts in and Marni's not-so-jet-setting mom comes face-to-face with her own high school rival. The claws come out and old wounds are opened in this crazy comedy about what happens when you are reunited with the one person you would like to forget. Released in the U.S. Sep. 24, 2010, after a Sep. 23 release in Russia. 105 min. Directed by Andy Fickman. Stars Jamie Lee Curtis (Gail), Kristin Chenoweth (Georgia), Odette Yustman (Joanna), Betty White (Grandma Bunny), Victor Garber (Mark), Kristen Bell (Marni), Jimmy Wolk (Will), Sigourney Weaver (Aunt Ramona), Patrick Duffy (Richie). A Touchstone film. Filmed in CinemaScope.

You and Me Kid Shop offering children's games, toys, and apparel in Disney Village Marketplace at Walt Disney World; open May 4, 1988–Oct. 25, 1995, taking over merchandise from Toys Fantastique. Tied to the Disney Channel show (SEE NEXT ENTRY).

You and Me, Kid (TV) Series on The Disney Channel; debuted Apr. 18, 1983, with host Sonny Melendrez. Parents and children participate in games and easy-to-learn activities together, enhancing the youngsters' self-awareness and physical coordination. Features occasional guest appearances by celebrities with their children.

You—and Your Ears (film) Cartoon made for the *Mickey Mouse Club* and later released, in May 1957, in 16 mm for schools. Jiminy Cricket presents the structure of the ear, traces a sound wave through the 3 parts of the ear, and gives care rules. An updated version was released in Mar. 1990.

You—and Your Eyes (film) Cartoon made for the *Mickey Mouse Club* and later released, in May 1957, in 16 mm for schools. Jiminy Cricket explains the structure of the eyes, the mechanics of seeing, and the rules for the proper care and safety of the eyes. An updated version was released in Mar. 1990.

You—and Your Five Senses (film) Cartoon made for the *Mickey Mouse Club* and later released, in May 1956, in 16 mm for schools. Jiminy Cricket explains and compares human responses to stimuli, and how they are highly developed because of reasoning power. This reasoning ability separates humans from other animals that have senses. An updated version was released on Aug. 23, 1990.

You—and Your Food (film) Cartoon made for the *Mickey Mouse Club* and later released, in Dec. 1958, in 16 mm for schools. Jiminy Cricket shows the value of food—the important role of a well-balanced diet in being healthy and active. An updated version was released on Aug. 23, 1990.

You—and Your Sense of Smell and Taste (film) Cartoon prepared for the *Mickey Mouse Club* and later released, in Sep. 1962, on 16 mm for schools. These 2 senses work together, producing the sensation of flavor. An updated version was released in Mar. 1990.

You—and Your Sense of Touch (film) Cartoon prepared for the *Mickey Mouse Club* and later released, in Sep. 1962, on 16 mm for schools. Touch is really 4 sensations, and our skin is the special receptor for all. An updated version was released in Mar. 1990.

You Can Always Be #1 (film) Sport Goofy theme song, featuring Goofy in various sports predicaments; released as a music video in Feb. 1982. Composed by Dale Gonyea.

You Can Fly! You Can Fly! You Can Fly! Song from *Peter Pan*; written by Sammy Cahn and Sammy Fain.

You Lucky Dog (TV) A Disney Channel Original Movie; first aired Jun. 27, 1998. A dog therapist, Jack Morgan, is charged in a rich man's will to care for his dog, Lucky, who has inherited the $64 million estate. The man's relatives are furious and determined to put an end to both Jack and Lucky. Directed by Paul Schneider. Stars Kirk Cameron (Jack Morgan), Chelsea Noble (Alison), James Avery (Calvin), Christine Healey (Margaret), John de Lancie (Lyle), Taylor Negron (Reuben). 90 min.

You Must Love Me Song from *Evita*; written by Andrew Lloyd Webber and Tim Rice. Academy Award winner.

You Ruined My Life (film) Two-hour movie; aired Feb. 1, 1987. Directed by David Ashwell. Minerva, the unruly niece of a casino owner, comes to visit her uncle in Las Vegas. A fired teacher tries to beat the odds at blackjack with a portable computer, but he is caught and is forced to tutor Minerva, since he cannot pay back the money he owes. Stars Soleil Moon Frye (Minerva), Paul Reiser (Dexter Bunche), Mimi Rogers (Charlotte Waring), Allen Garfield (Howie Edwards), Edith Fields (Aunt Hermione), Yoshi Hoover (Yaki), Tony Burton (Moustache), John Putch (Winston), Peter Lind Hayes (Congressman Riley), Mary Healy (Mrs. Riley).

You—the Human Animal (film) Cartoon made for the *Mickey Mouse Club* and later released, in May 1956, in 16 mm for schools. Jiminy Cricket shows people's unique ability to reason and think, which sets humans apart from all other living creatures. He explains humans' adaptability, language skills, and intelligence. An updated version was released on Aug. 23, 1990.

You—the Living Machine (film) Cartoon made for the *Mickey Mouse Club* and later released, in Dec. 1958, in 16 mm for schools. Host Jiminy Cricket discusses the "human machine" and how it converts food into energy to perform properly. An updated version was released on Aug. 23, 1990.

You Wish (TV) Series on ABC; aired Sep. 26, 1997–Sep. 4, 1998. Gillian Apple is trying her best to balance postdivorce parenting and a career when a shopping trip changes her life forever. When she is haggling for a rug in a store stocked with old-world wares, the rug's design of a man magically comes to life in the form of a genie. The genie is anxious for a new master but cannot get Gillian to make a wish binding him to her forever. Stars Harley Jane Kozak (Gillian Apple), John Ales (genie), Nathan Lawrence (Travis), Alex McKenna (Mickey), Jerry Van Dyke (Grandpa Max). From Michael Jacobs Productions and Touchstone Television.

You Wish! (TV) A Disney Channel Original Movie; first aired Jan. 10, 2003. Alex, a 16-year-old, wishes that his tagalong younger brother, Stevie, would disappear, and his wish comes true after he acquires a magical coin. Alex's life is suddenly transformed, with wealthy parents, improved athletic skills, the dog he always wanted, and even a popular girlfriend. But not Stevie, who has been transformed into a child star with his own TV show. Soon, Alex realizes that his new life is not as great as he thought it might be; he misses his brother and searches for a way to bring him back.

Directed by Paul Hoen. Stars A. J. Trauth (Alex Lansing), Spencer Breslin (Stevie Lansing/Terence Russell McCormack), Lalaine (Abby Richardson), Tim Reid (Larry), Peter Feeney (Dave Lansing), Sally Stockwell (Pam Lansing), Ari Boyland (James), Emma Lahana (Fiona), Joshua Leys (Gary), Jay Bunyan (Charles). Based on the novel by Jackie French Koller. Filmed in New Zealand.

You'll Be in My Heart Song from *Tarzan*; words and music by Phil Collins. Academy Award winner.

Young, Alan (1919–2016) Actor; provided the voice of Scrooge McDuck for over 30 years, including in *Mickey's Christmas Carol*, the original *DuckTales* series, *DuckTales the Movie*, and *House of Mouse*. He appeared in *The Cat from Outer Space* (Dr. Wenger), on The Disney Channel in *The Disney Family Album*, voiced Flaversham in *The Great Mouse Detective*, and attended the invitational opening of Disneyland in 1955, appearing on TV in *Dateline Disneyland*.

Young, Sean Actress; appeared in *Baby . . . Secret of the Lost Legend* (Susan Matthews-Loomis) and *Fire Birds* (Billie Lee Guthrie).

Young Again (TV) Two-hour movie aired May 11, 1986. A 40-year-old man wishes he was 17 again. When his wish is granted by an angel, he returns to his hometown to attempt to recapture his long-lost love, but their age difference now makes that impossible. In the end, he learns that happiness is not restricted to any particular age. Directed by Steven H. Stern. Stars Lindsay Wagner, Jack Gilford, Robert Urich, Jessica Steen, Jason Nicoloff, Peter Spence, Jeremy Ratchford, Jonathan Welsh, and introducing Keanu Reeves.

Young & Hungry (TV) Series on Freeform (formerly ABC Family); debuted Jun. 25, 2014, and ended Jul. 25, 2018. Two worlds collide when Josh Kaminski, a wealthy young tech entrepreneur, hires Gabi Diamond, a feisty young food blogger, to be his personal chef. Gabi must prove herself, mostly to Josh's aide, who prepares a famous chef for the job. Stars Emily Osment (Gabi), Jonathan Sadowski (Josh), Rex Lee (Elliot Park).

Young Black Stallion, The (film) This prequel to the 1979 classic film (*The Black Stallion*) presents the horse's adventures with a young girl named Neera, who has been separated from her family in Arabia by World War II. Left alone in the desert, she befriends the wild colt, which she names Shetan ("the devil"). Once reunited with her grandfather, however, Neera remains haunted by images of the "lost horse of the desert," one of a few stallions of legend, rumored to be "born of the sands, sired by the night sky, drinkers of the wind." Neera devises a plan to race the wild Shetan in the annual horse race and help restore her grandfather's reputation. Released Dec. 25, 2003. Directed by Simon Wincer. Stars Richard Romanus (Ben Ishak), Biana G. Tamimi (Neera), Patrick Elyas (Aden), Gerard Rudolf (Rhamon), Ali al Ameri (Mansoor), Andries Rossouw (Kadir). 50 min. Disney's first dramatic feature filmed in 70 mm specifically for IMAX and other large-format theaters. Based on the book by Walter Farley and Steven Farley. Filmed on location in Namibia and South Africa.

Young Harry Houdini (TV) Two-hour show aired Mar. 15, 1987. A young magician and escape artist runs off to join a traveling carnival. Stars Wil Wheaton. Directed by James Orr.

Young Loner, The (TV) Two-part show; aired Feb. 25 and Mar. 3, 1968. Directed by Michael O'Herlihy. A young migrant worker is injured in an accident and ends up at a ranch to recover. He runs away but realizes that his heart is not in traveling and that he needs to settle down, so he returns to a job as a shepherd at the ranch. Stars Kim Hunter, Frank Silvera, Butch Patrick, Edward Andrews, Jane Zachary.

Young Musicians Symphony Orchestra Annual program, begun in 1992, where musicians under the age of 12 gathered at a remarkable music camp. There they rehearsed, listened to guest lecturers, and prepared for a concert that was televised on The Disney Channel. The Disney's Young Musicians Symphony Orchestra program culminated in 1999 after 8 successful years. The annual special inspired the 2002 Disney Channel series *Totally in Tune*.

Young Runaways, The (TV) Two-hour movie aired May 28, 1978. Directed by Russ Mayberry. Uncaring parents leave 2 of their 4 children with foster parents as they depart for Alaska, but the children plot to get back together, even though in the meantime they have the misfortune of running into bank robbers. Stars Gary Collins, Anne Francis, Sharon Farrell, Robert Webber, Alicia Fleer, Chip Courtland, Tommy Crebbs, Pat Delany, Dick Bakalyan, Barbara Hale, Lucille Benson.

Your Big Break (TV) Syn. series in which ordinary people with extraordinary voices fulfill their musical fantasies on an innovative talent show; released Sep. 23, 1999, and ending Jun. 16, 2001. Hosted by Christopher "Kid" Reid. Produced by dick clark productions, inc. and ENDEMOL Entertainment for Buena Vista Television.

Your Career: Your Decision? (film) Educational film, using sequences from *Ballerina*. In the Questions!/Answers? series released in 1976. A girl wants to be a ballerina despite opposition from her mother.

Your Friend the Rat (film) Animated film released on the *Ratatouille* DVD Nov. 6, 2007. Remy and Emile expound on the history and behavior of rats in an effort to persuade human viewers not to kill rats. A combination of CGI, hand-drawn, and stop-motion animation, reminiscent of Ward Kimball's shows for the various Disney anthology TV series. Directed by Jim Capobianco. Voices include Patton Oswalt (Remy), Peter Sohn (Emile). 11 min.

Your Host, Donald Duck (TV) Show aired Jan. 16, 1957. Directed by Jack Hannah. Walt Disney allows Donald to host the show, and he shows several cartoon clips tied in with the Disneyland theme of Fantasyland, Frontierland, Tomorrowland, and Adventureland.

You're Nothin' but a Nothin' Popular song hit from *The Flying Mouse* (1934); composed by Larry Morey and Frank Churchill.

Youse Guys Moychindice Merchandise kiosk on Streets of America (formerly New York Street) at Disney's Hollywood Studios; open ca. 1990–Apr. 2, 2016.

Youth Education Series (Y.E.S.) The Y.E.S. programs for youth groups began in 1990 with one program in Disney-MGM Studios at Walt Disney World: *Lights, Camera, Education*. From there it grew into almost 2 dozen programs in all 4 Walt Disney World parks. Children from kindergarten to 12th grade participate in 2- to 3½-hour programs taught by professional Disney facilitators using the resources of the resort and covering topics in the arts and humanities, life management, and physical and natural sciences, with most programs aligned with state and national educational standards. Participants see how principles that they are learning in their classrooms are making exciting things happen every day in and around Walt Disney World. Y.E.S. programs were introduced at Disneyland Resort in Oct. 2006 and at Hong Kong Disneyland Resort in Jan. 2007. The programs were rolled into Disney Imagination Campus, which was launched in 2022.

You've Got a Friend in Me Song from *Toy Story*; written/performed by Randy Newman. It was nominated for an Academy Award.

Yucatan Base Camp Grill Counter-service restaurant in Lost River Delta at Tokyo DisneySea; opened Sep. 4, 2001. Themed as a base camp for archaeologists.

Yumz Fast-food facility at Videopolis in Disneyland; opened Jun. 19, 1985. On Jun. 23, 1995, the name was changed to Meeko's, with the opening of *The Spirit of Pocahontas*. It later became Fantasyland Theater Snacks, Troubadour Treats, The Enchanted Cottage Sweets & Treats, and Troubadour Tavern.

Yzma Evil, plotting adviser to Kuzco in *The Emperor's New Groove*; voiced by Eartha Kitt.

1. Zazu 2. *Zootopia* (film) 3. Zipper 4. *ZOMBIES* (TV) 5. *Zenith* (film)
6. Zeus 7. Zawadi Marketplace 8. *Zenimation* (TV)

Zambini Brothers' Ristorante Counter-service restaurant in Mediterranean Harbor at Tokyo DisneySea; opened Sep. 4, 2001. As the story goes, an old winery established by the 3 Zambini brothers has been converted into an Italian restaurant.

Zanzibar Shell Company Adventureland shell, hat, and handbag shop in the Magic Kingdom at Walt Disney World; opened in 1988. It became Zanzibar Trading Company in 2000.

Zapped (TV) A Disney Channel Original Movie; first aired Jun. 27, 2014. Sixteen-year-old straight-A student Zoey Stevens, a skilled dancer, is having a difficult time adjusting to her new life when her mom remarries. But then things really change when she gets a dog-training app on her smartphone that enables her to magically control boys. Directed by Peter DeLuise. Stars Zendaya (Zoey Stevens), Chanelle Peloso (Rachel Todds), Spencer Boldman (Jackson Kale), Emilia McCarthy (Taylor Dean), Adam DiMarco (Adam Thompson).

Zawadi Marketplace Shop in Jambo House at Disney's Animal Kingdom Lodge at Walt Disney World; opened Apr. 16, 2001, with African art, handcrafted objects, toys, and sundries.

Zazu Hornbill in *The Lion King*, the Pride Land's chief of protocol; voiced by Rowan Atkinson.

Zegers, Kevin Actor; appeared in *Life with Mikey* (Little Mikey) and the Air Bud films (Josh Framm); on ABC in *Notorious* (Oscar Keaton), *Rebel* (Dr.

Nathaniel Flynn), and *The Rookie: Feds* (Brendon Acres); and on Disney Channel in *So Weird* (Ryan Ollman).

Zegler, Rachel Actress; it was announced she will star as the title character in the live-action *Snow White*. She also starred as María in the 20th Century Studios adaptation of *West Side Story*.

Zeke and Luther (TV) Comedy series on Disney XD; aired Jun. 15, 2009–Apr. 2, 2012. Two teenage best friends in the town of Pacific Terrace are on a quest to become world-famous skateboarders. While they use their skateboards as their principle means of transportation, the boys also strive to master the art of skateboarding while being challenged by neighborhood friend and foe, Kojo. Another thorn in their side is Ginger, Zeke's 12-year-old sister, who finds her brother's skateboarding dreams childish. Stars Hutch Dano (Zeke), Adam Hicks (Luther), Daniel Curtis Lee (Kojo), Ryan Newman (Ginger). Produced on location in and around Torrance, California. From Turtle Rock Productions, Inc. Hutch Dano is the grandson of Royal Dano, who provided the voice for Abraham Lincoln in Great Moments with Mr. Lincoln.

Zemeckis, Robert Director of *Who Framed Roger Rabbit*. Enlisted by Steven Spielberg and Disney, he insisted the illusion of animated characters interacting in a live-action setting be realistic, and the resulting film represented a tremendous leap forward in animation art. He also produced *Mars Needs Moms*, exec. produced *Real Steel*, and produced/directed/wrote *Disney's A Christmas Carol*. For Disney+ he directed and co-wrote *Pinocchio* (2022).

Zen – Grogu and Dust Bunnies (TV) Animated short; digitally premiered Nov. 12, 2022, on Disney+, in honor of the 3rd anniversary of the streaming service and *The Mandalorian*. Directed by Katsuya Kondō. From Studio Ghibli and Lucasfilm. 3 min.

Zendaya SEE COLEMAN, ZENDAYA.

Zenimation (TV) A Disney+ original short-form series; digitally released May 22, 2020. Scenes from Disney animated films create a calming aural and visual experience designed to refresh the senses for a moment of mindfulness. Created by David Bess and exec. produced by Amy Astley. From Walt Disney Animation Studios.

Zenith (film) Animated short; digitally released Jan. 24, 2020, on Disney+. A luminous, ethereal stag bounds through a dark expanse of the universe, leaving a galaxy of stars in its wake. When it accidentally creates a black hole that threatens to devour everything in sight, the stag is forced to make a decision that will leave a lasting impression. Directed by Jennifer Stratton. 2 min. From the Walt Disney Animation Studios Short Circuit program.

Zenon: Girl of the 21st Century (TV) A Disney Channel Original Movie; first aired Jan. 23, 1999. Zenon, a mischievous 13-year-old girl, has lived most of her life in a space station with her family. Her curiosity gets her in trouble once too often and she's grounded, which in her world means she's sent to Earth. The horrified Zenon has to learn how to handle gravity, Earth culture, and being an outsider with Earth-side teens, as well as having to thwart a sinister plot to destroy her space station. Directed by Kenneth Johnson. Stars Kirsten Storms (Zenon Kar), Raven-Symoné (Nebula), Greg Smith (Greg), Holly Fulger (Aunt Judy), Phillip Rhys (Proto Zoa). Filmed in Vancouver.

Zenon: The Zequel (TV) A Disney Channel Original Movie; first aired Jan. 12, 2001. Zenon and Nebula are back to their old tricks, and Zenon soon finds herself on a mission to help out some homeless aliens. Directed by Manny Coto. Stars Kirsten Storms (Zenon), Shadia Simmons (Nebula), Holly Fulger (Aunt Judy), Phillip Rhys (Proto Zoa), Stuart Pankin (Commander Plank). Shadia Simmons

takes the role of Nebula played by Raven-Symoné in the first film. Since sets from the original movie were not saved, new sets had to be constructed for the filming, which took place in Auckland, New Zealand.

Zenon: Z3 (TV) A Disney Channel Original Movie; first aired Jun. 11, 2004. Zenon Kar is competing to win the Galactic Teen Supreme contest and celebrate at the Moonstock Festival in 2054. However, she is torn when her need to beat handsome competitor Bronley Hale runs headlong into moon activist Sage Borealis. Stars Kirsten Storms (Zenon), Alyson Morgan (Dasha), Glenn McMillan (Bronley Hale), Benjamin J. Easter (Sage Borealis), Raven (Nebula Wade), Lauren Maltby (Margie Hammond), Phumi Mthembo (Cassiopeia Wade), Stuart Pankin (Commander Plank), Holly Fulger (Aunt Judy), Nathan Anderson (Proto Zoa), Carol Becker (Selena).

Zero Hour (TV) One-hour drama series on ABC; aired Feb. 14–Aug. 3, 2013. As publisher of *Modern Skeptic Magazine*, Hank Galliston has spent his career following clues, debunking myths, and cracking conspiracies. But when his wife is abducted from her antique clock shop, Hank gets pulled into one of the most compelling mysteries in human history. Stars Anthony Edwards (Hank Galliston), Carmen Ejogo (Rebecca Riley), Scott Michael Foster (Arron Martin), Addison Timlin (Rachel Lewis), Jacinda Barrett (Laila Galliston) Michael Nyqvist (White Vincent). From ABC Studios.

Zeus Mighty ruler of the gods in "The Pastoral Symphony" segment of *Fantasia*. In *Hercules*, the Greek god is voiced by Rip Torn.

Zimmer, Hans Composer; his work on *The Lion King* earned him the 1995 Academy Award for Best Original Score. He also composed music for *White Fang*, *Cool Runnings*, *Crimson Tide*, *White Squall*, *Muppet Treasure Island*, *The Rock*, *Pearl Harbor*, *King Arthur*, *The Prestige*, several Pirates of the Caribbean films, and *The Lion King* (2019). He was named a Disney Legend in 2019.

Zip-A-Dee-Doo-Dah Song from *Song of the South*; written by Ray Gilbert and Allie Wrubel. Sung by James Baskett as Uncle Remus. Academy Award winner.

Zipper Plucky housefly character in *Chip 'n' Dale Rescue Rangers*; voiced by Corey Burton.

Ziwani Traders Rustic supply shop in Africa at Disney's Animal Kingdom; opened Apr. 22, 1998. Safari-themed souvenirs, including authentic African imports, are sold. It shares space with Mombasa Marketplace, a boutique designed as a traditional Swahili home.

Zoe, Duncan, Jack & Jane (TV) Half-hour comedy series on The WB Network; aired Jan. 17–Jul. 18, 1999. Four teenage friends come of age in New York City. Stars Selma Blair (Zoe Bean), Michael Rosenbaum (Jack Cooper), David Moscow (Duncan Milch), Azura Skye (Jane Cooper), Mary Page Keller (Iris Bean). From Michael Jacobs Productions and Touchstone Television. The show was sold to Warner Bros., which continued production.

Zokkomon (film) Motion picture produced by Walt Disney Co. India in Hindi. Released Apr. 22, 2011, after a world premiere at the Indian Film Festival in Los Angeles on Apr. 17. The orphan Kunal, after being abandoned by his uncle, has to fend for himself. He finds the strength to face extraordinary challenges and begins the journey to become the superhero Zokkomon. Directed by Satyajit Bhatkal. Stars Darsheel Safary (Kunal/Zokkomon), Anupam Kher (Deshraj/Dr. Vivek Rai), Akhil Mishra (Security Guard), Manjari Phadnis (Kittu), Giselli Monteiro (Phunsukh). Filmed in widescreen format.

ZOMBIES (TV) A Disney Channel Original Movie; first aired Feb. 16, 2018. When Zombietown transfer students integrate in Seabrook High School, a Zombie football player and a mortal cheerleader challenge tradition, becoming friends and shaking up the populace in a suburban town preoccupied with uniformity, traditions, and pep rallies. Directed by Paul Hoen. Stars Milo Manheim (Zed), Meg Donnelly (Addison), Trevor Tordjman (Bucky), Kylee Russell (Eliza), Carla Jeffery (Bree).

ZOMBIES: Addison's Moonstone Mystery (TV) Animated short-form series on Disney Channel and DisneyNOW; premiered Oct. 16, 2020. Vanna, a new girl at Seabrook High, threatens to shake up the dynamic when it's discovered she is not all that she seems. The second season, *ZOMBIES: Addison's Monster Mystery*, debuted Oct. 1, 2021.

ZOMBIES 2 (TV) A Disney Channel Original Movie; first aired Feb. 14, 2020, on Disney Channel and DisneyNOW. When a group of mysterious teenage werewolves arrives in search of an ancient life source buried somewhere in Seabrook, a fearful city council reenacts the town's anti-monster laws, making it impossible for football player Zed and cheerleader Addison to attend prom together. Zed is determined to keep their plans, and Addison must confront the truth about her identity. Directed by Paul Hoen. Stars Milo Manheim (Zed), Meg Donnelly (Addison), Trevor Tordjman (Bucky), Kylee Russell (Eliza), Carla Jeffery (Bree), James Godfrey (Bonzo), Kingston Foster (Zoey), Chandler Kinney (Willa), Pearce Joza (Wyatt), Ariel Martin (Wynter).

ZOMBIES 3 (TV) A Disney Channel Original Movie; digitally premiered Jul. 15, 2022, on Disney+, followed by an Aug. 12 debut on Disney Channel. Zed and Addison are beginning their final year at Seabrook High in the town that's become a safe haven for monsters and humans alike. Zed is anticipating an athletic scholarship that will make him the first Zombie to attend college, while Addison is gearing up for Seabrook's first international cheer-off competition. Then suddenly, telepathically connected extraterrestrial beings appear around Seabrook, provoking something other than friendly competition. Stars Milo Manheim (Zed), Meg Donnelly (Addison), Matt Cornett (A-Lan), Kyra Tantao (A-Li), Terry Hu (A-Spen), Chandler Kinney (Willa), Pearce Joza (Wyatt) Ariel Martin (Wynter), Trevor Tordjman (Bucky), Carla Jeffery (Bree), Kylee Russell (Eliza), James Godfrey (Bonzo), Kingston Foster (Zoey). From Bloor Street Productions.

Zoog Disney Programming block for tweens on Disney Channel encouraging online interactivity; aired 1998–2002.

Zootopia (film) Animated feature taking place in a modern mammal metropolis built by animals. When Zootopia's top cop, optimistic Officer Judy Hopps, arrives, she discovers that being the first bunny on a police force of big, tough animals isn't so easy. Determined to prove herself, she jumps at the opportunity to crack a case, even if it means partnering with a fast-talking, scam-artist fox, Nick Wilde, to solve the mystery. Released Mar. 4, 2016, also in 3-D, after international releases beginning Feb. 10. Directed by Bryan Howard and Rich Moore. Voices include Jason Bateman (Nick Wilde), Ginnifer Goodwin (Judy Hopps), Idris Elba (Chief Bogo), Alan Tudyk (Duke Weaselton), J. K. Simmons (Mayor Lionheart), Jenny Slate

(Bellwether), Bonnie Hunt (Mrs. Bonnie Hopps), Octavia Spencer (Mrs. Otterton), Tommy Chong (Yax), Katie Lowes (Dr. Madge Honey Badger), Shakira (Gazelle). 108 min. The film was partially inspired by *Robin Hood*, in which animals talk and wear clothes, and asks the question, "What would a mammal metropolis look like if it were designed by animals?" The resulting Zootopia is made up of 6 environmental districts, designed for different types of animals: the ritzy Sahara Square, for desert animals; Tundratown, for the polar bears and moose; the hot and humid Rain Forest District; Little Rodentia, for the tiniest mammals; Bunny-burrow, for the millions of bunnies; and Savanna Central, a downtown melting pot where mammals from every environment come together. To study the personalities and behaviors of real animals, filmmakers traveled to Kenya and also met with animal experts, including those at Disney's Animal Kingdom. In total, Zootopia is populated by 64 different species. The film marked composer Michael Giacchino's first feature collaboration with Walt Disney Animation Studios. The song "Try Everything," performed by Shakira, was written by singer-songwriter Sia and songwriting duo Stargate. In 2017, the film won the Academy Award for Best Animated Feature (Byron Howard, Rich Moore, Clark Spencer).

Zootopia A themed area based on the 2016 animated feature was announced in 2019 for Shanghai Disneyland. Guests are invited to experience the mammalian metropolis with a new attraction, entertainment, shops, and restaurants. The large animal animated figures were developed at Shanghai Disney Resort, marking the first time Imagineering has built complex Audio-Animatronics figures outside of the U.S.

Zootopia+ (TV) Animated short-form series; digitally released on Disney+ Nov. 9, 2022. A closer look at the fast-paced mammal metropolis, diving deeper into the lives of some of the feature film's most intriguing characters, including Fru Fru, the newly married arctic shrew; Gazelle's talented tiger dancers; and the sloth full of surprises, Flash. From Walt Disney Animation Studios.

Zoradi, Mark Joining Disney in 1980, he worked in Home Entertainment marketing and film TV sales before being named president of Buena Vista International in 1992. In 2006, he was promoted to president of Walt Disney Studios Motion Pictures Group. He resigned in Nov. 2009.

Zorro (TV) Series about a masked avenger, the alter ego of the mild-mannered Don Diego de la Vega, defending the poor and acting as the scourge of military tyrants on his black stallion, Tornado, in early California. A total of 78 episodes aired Oct. 10, 1957–Sep. 28, 1959. Zorro's trademark was the ragged "Z" symbol, which he slashed with his sword. Four hour-long episodes were later filmed for airing on the Sunday night show, and episodes of the half-hour show were compiled into theatrical features for domestic (*The Sign of Zorro*) and international (*Zorro the Avenger*) audiences. Stars Guy Williams (Don Diego de la Vega/Zorro), Henry Calvin (Sgt. Garcia), Gene Sheldon (Bernardo), Don Diamond (Corp. Reyes). The popular title song was by director Norman Foster and George Bruns. The cast and crew of the TV series, and subsequent films, had an unusual amount of experience with the Zorro legend: George Lewis, who plays Zorro's father, Don Alejandro de la Vega, starred in the 1944 *Zorro's Black Whip*, and William Lava, who composed the score for the TV series also wrote the music for the Republic Zorro serial. The series began as a side project for Walt Disney, who had licensed the rights to writer Johnston McCulley's character through WED Enterprises, hoping the series could provide the funds needed to expand Disneyland. The outdoor sets were the first permanent sets of their kind built on the Disney Studio backlot; they were eventually removed in 1988. The show was syn. for years and returned to a regular time slot on The Disney Channel beginning Apr. 18, 1983. It was especially popular in Latin America, and the star, Guy Williams, retired to Argentina partly because of his fame there. In the 1990s, The Disney Channel had the black-and-white episodes colorized, and they were able to reach an even wider audience.

Zorro: Adios El Cuchillo (TV) One-hour show; aired Nov. 6, 1960. Directed by William Witney. Zorro battles a bandit named El Cuchillo, played by Gilbert Roland. Also starred Guy Williams, Henry Calvin, Gene Sheldon, Rita Moreno. Continuation of *Zorro: El Bandido*. El Cuchillo manages to discover the identity of Zorro through numerous encounters with him, but "honor among thieves" prevents him from revealing the truth when he is finally captured.

Zorro and Son (TV) Limited series of 5 episodes; aired Apr. 6–Jun. 1, 1983, on CBS. A comedy version of the *Zorro* theme. Stars Henry Darrow,

Paul Regina, Bill Dana, Gregory Sierra, Richard Beauchamp, Barney Martin, John Moschitta, Jr.

Zorro: Auld Acquaintance (TV) One-hour show; aired Apr. 2, 1961. Directed by James Neilson. Two bandits attempt to steal the army's payroll, and Zorro's identity is almost compromised, until he uses his wits to foil the bandits and ruin their credibility. Stars Guy Williams, Henry Calvin, Gene Sheldon, Ricardo Montalban, Ross Martin, Suzanne Lloyd.

Zorro: El Bandido (TV) One-hour show; aired Oct. 30, 1960. Directed by William Witney. A band of Mexican outlaws, led by El Cuchillo, is tempted by riches in Los Angeles, but they did not reckon on Zorro. The story is concluded in *Adios El Cuchillo*.

Zorro the Avenger (film) International theatrical compilation of several *Zorro* episodes. Released first in Japan on Sep. 10, 1959. With the success of *The Sign of Zorro*, director Charles Barton returned to direct this sequel, again pieced together from the popular Disney TV series. Zorro and his sidekick, Bernardo, must defeat the wicked "Eagle," who has taken over the commandant post of Los Angeles, by destroying the conspiracy with swordplay and trickery until the flag of Spain can fly once more over the plaza. 97 min. Stars Guy Williams, Henry Calvin, Gene Sheldon.

Zorro: The Postponed Wedding (TV) One-hour show; aired Jan. 1, 1961. Directed by James Neilson. Constancia de la Torre returns to the pueblo to get married, carrying a bag full of jewels as her dowry. But her intended wants the jewels more than he wants the girl. Zorro discovers the plot and comes to help. Stars Guy Williams, Annette Funicello, Henry Calvin, Gene Sheldon, Mark Damon, Carlos Romero.

Zort Sorts (film) Educational release in 16 mm in May 1991. 16 min. Zort is an alien who comes to Earth to learn how earthlings deal with garbage.

Zuri's Sweets Shop Shop in Harambe Market at Disney's Animal Kingdom; opened Jun. 17, 2015. It offers candy, flavored popcorn, and candy apples and is inspired by the sights and flavors of Africa.

Image Credits

Photographs and artwork courtesy the **Walt Disney Archives** and the **Walt Disney Archives Photo Library**; the **Yellow Shoes Marketing Resource Center**; the **Digital Media Center**; and the **Vagnini Family Collection**. Character artwork on cover and title page courtesy the **Disney Consumer Products Creative Design Team**.

Acknowledgments

We would like to extend special thanks to those who have contributed to *Disney A to Z* over its nearly thirty-year history. For the first editions, Michael Troyan acted as research assistant on the theatrical titles, ferreting out little-known facts and helping draft the original film entries, while Steven Clark and David Mumford helped with the research and entries for the original park-related items.

The staff of the Walt Disney Archives continues to be of inestimable help to this work. We would like to express our deepest appreciation to Archives director Becky Cline and regional manager Kevin M. Kern for their invaluable support, as well as to research team members Nicole Carroll, Matt Moryc, Madlyn Moskowitz, Edward Ovalle, Francesca Scrimgeour, and Julia Vargas, who provided helpful suggestions and fact-finding for this latest edition. Michael Buckhoff at the Walt Disney Archives Photo Library continues to be an instrumental contributor, generously compiling and processing the majority of images found throughout this edition.

For their dedication to collecting and preserving Disney history, we would also like to recognize fellow Archives staff members Matthew Adams, Jennifer Alcoset, Jessica Amezcua, Brian Ball, Lynne Drake, Maggie Evenson, Darlene Fogg, Cesar Gallegos, Jeff Golden, Jarett Hartman, Heather Hoffman, Alex Koch, Rick Lorentz, Amaris Ma, Daniel Marquand, Nikki Nguyen, Amy Opoka, Jesus Padilla, Christina Pappous, Ty Popko, Joanna Pratt, Chris Rexroad, Katie Strobel, Kimi Thompson, and Kelsey Williams.

This book could never have been compiled had it not been for the indexes, lists, bibliographies, and catalogs prepared in the Walt Disney Archives over the past fifty years. For that reason, we are indebted to former manager Robert Tieman and staff members Lizza Andres, Justin Arthur, Holly Brobst, Karen Brower, John Cawley, Brigitte Dubin, Nancy Dunn, Josh Eisenberg, Dennis Emslie, Collette Espino, Shelly Graham, Jennifer Hendrickson, Brian Hoffman, Adina Lerner, Jan Loveton, Grace Loza, Robert McGrath, Rose Motzko, Melissa Pankuch Hernandez, Les Perkins, Nate Rasmussen, Andrea Recendez-Carbone, Alesha Reyes, Steve Rogers, Paula Sigman-Lowery, Ed Squair, Carol Svendsen, Joanne Warren, and Randy Yantek.

We extend special thanks to Disney Corporate Communications and the D23 team, including Kristina Schake, David Jefferson, Michael Vargo, Jeffrey R. Epstein, Mitch Powers, and Nan Song, as well as current and former editorial and web staff, including Carly Bezilla, Carmen Capone, Beth Deitchman, Jim Frye, Zach Johnson, Max Lark, Jonathan McMullen, Sohrab Osati, Courtney Potter, Billy Stanek, and Bruce C. Steele.

From coast to coast and around the globe, we thank many colleagues who have provided helpful updates, information, and fact-checking, especially Stacy Shoff, as well as Margaret Adamic, Amy Astley, Will Baggett, Becky Ballentine, Jayne Bieber, Debby Dane Browne, Fox Carney, Jim Clark, Jody Daily, Alyce Diamandis, Greg Ehrbar, Doug Engalla, David J. Fisher, Lindsay Frick, Rebecca Godsil, Jason Grandt, Howard Green, Doug Griffith, Don Hahn, Grace Han, Jesse Haskell, Garrett Hicks, Karlynn Holbrook, Kevin Kidney, Kelly Kipp, Debra Kohls, Aileen Kutaka, Mark LaVine, Renee Leask, Reva Lee, Kevin Lively, Christopher Merritt, Steven Miller, Tom Morris, Tim O'Day, Chris Ostrander, Scott Otis, Chris Pajonk, Diego Parras, Brandon Peters, Debbie Petersen, Sara Pollock, Paula Potter, Kevin Rafferty, Frank Reifsnyder, Joseph Reyes, Ashley Richards, Estella Rodriguez, Jaime Savasta, Russell Schroeder, Loriann Shank, Josh Shipley, Laurel Slater, Shawn Slater, Lon Smart, Libby Spatz, Sara Spike, Cappy Surette, Jason Surrell, Rose Thomas, Janice Thomson, Alyssa Tryon, Mary Walsh, Lauren Williams, Wyatt Winter, Juleen Woods, Alex Wright, and Cecil Wu.

Advice and encouragement have also come from Bruce Aguilar, Graham Allan, Luis Alonso, Ingrid Angulo, Tony Anselmo, Eli Barbour, Jennifer Barbour, Tony Baxter, Antonio Beach, Matt Bond, Benji Breitbart, Russell Brower, Keith Burrell, Jen Camp, Dawn Carter, Bryan Castleberry, Wing T. Chao, Beka Ciolek, Jonathan Clough, the Collazo Family (Becky, Happy, Enrique, Manny), Bill Cotter, Michael Crawford, Rob and Zinnia Cress, Brian Crosby, Linda Culmone, Robert Culmone, Erica and Zach Dade, Elise Bacon Dailey, the Dale Family (Edwin, Karen, Caroline, Benjamin), Carol Davis-Perkins, Marc Delle, Derek and Melissa Kratish Depot, Jason Dewey, Duncan and Carole Dickson, Penny Diebold, Cathy Eastman, Gil and Val Eastman, Nathan Eick, Tyson Ervin, Bill and Jenn Farmer, Christy Fragetta, Erin Fragetta, Lena Gamble, Bethany Glazewski, John Gleim, Bob Gurr, Kara Hahn, Diane Hancock, Matthew Hanson, Ruston Harker, Drew Hayashida, Alan Helm, Angie and Colin Hennessy, Will Herbig, Justin Higley, Matthew Hughes, Brett Hulverson, Joshua and Rachel Iscovich, John Johnson, Casey Jones, Richard Jordan, Daniel and Marina Joseph, the Kalov Family, Lauren Kern, Marshal Knight, Doug Kokx, Anders Krantz, Ryan Kraska, Maria Laboy, Ryan Letts, Ethan Lewis, Michael Lingley, Erissa MacKaron, Kevin Maker, Michael Maney, Jean Marana, Ryan and Christina March, Stacia Martin, John Mauro, Shannon McCosker, Chris McElroy, Tom McKee, Diane Michioka, Brainard Miller, Yogi Mueller, Tom Nabbe, Trevor Nelson, Russell Newell, Chris Nolte, Beth Nowlin, Allen and Mary McRae Parrott, Hans Perk, Matthew Pilla, Cassie Potter, Steve Probus, Kent Ramsey, Ethan Reed, Alex Reif, Nancy Ricardo, Jason and Laura Rowitt, Laura and Paul Sanchez, Lauren and Benjamin Sanders, Troy Scrimgeour, Clay Shoemaker, Jeanna Sims, Angie Sola, Bret and Laura Staples, Andrew Swailes, Dennis Tanida, Tracy Terhune, Debbee Baxter Thibault, Josh Tidwell, Scott Tobias, Moises Torres, the Trevino Family (Ruben Sr., Aixa, Ruben Jr., Tricia, Gavin), Lindsay Trock, Bonnie and Chris Utley, Mike Vaughn, Dan Warren, Jim and Susie Wilber, Shay Willard, Aaron Willcott, Alex Williams, James Wilson, Craig Wingerson, and Monica Woods.

We are especially grateful to Michael Vagnini and Julian Lowy, whose perspectives and inspirations made an indelible impact on the front matter. And for their unwavering support, we thank Gary Landrum, Ken Ricci, Tom and Iris Vagnini, Marco Vagnini, and Melody Vagnini.

Finally, with immense appreciation, we thank Wendy Lefkon, Jennifer Eastwood, Jim Fanning, and Lindsay Broderick at Disney Editions, whose dedication to *Disney A to Z* made this sixth edition possible, as well as Nancee Adams, Jennifer Black, Arlene Goldberg, Warren Meislin, Rachel Rivera, Megan Speer-Levi, and Monica Vasquez for lending their talents, time, and expertise.

—Steven Vagnini and Dave Smith

For the Selected Bibliography, please visit D23.com/bibliography.